This is

Volume

5

of

WEST'S
NEW YORK PRACTICE
SERIES

West's New York Practice Series

Vol. 1 Walker, et al., New York Limited Liability Companies and Partnerships: A Guide to Law and Practice

Vols. 2–4 Haig, et al., Commercial Litigation in New York State Courts

Vol. 5 Barker and Alexander, Evidence in New York State and Federal Courts

Vol. 6 Greenberg, Marcus, et al., New York Criminal Law

Vol. 7 Marks, et al., New York Pretrial Criminal Procedure

COORDINATED RESEARCH IN NEW YORK FROM WEST

WEST'S McKINNEY'S FORMS

Civil Practice Law and Rules
Uniform Commercial Code
Business Corporation Law
Matrimonial and Family Law
Real Property Practice
Estates and Surrogate Practice

Criminal Procedure Law
Not-For-Profit Corporation Law
Tax Practice and Procedure
Local Government Forms
Selected Consolidated Law Forms

McKinney's Consolidated Laws of New York Annotated

West's New York Legal Update

New York Digest

New York Law Finder

New York Estate Administration
Margaret V. Turano and
C. Raymond Radigan

Handling the DWI Case in New York
Peter Gerstenzang

New York Practice 2d
David D. Siegel

New York State Administrative Procedure and Practice
Patrick J. Borchers and
David J. Markell

PAMPHLETS

New York Civil Practice Law and Rules

New York Sentence Charts

WESTLAW®

WEST*Check*® and WESTMATE®

West CD–ROM Libraries™

To order any of these New York practice tools, call your West Representative or 1–800–328–9352.

NEED RESEARCH HELP?
If you have research questions concerning WESTLAW or West Publications, call West's Reference Attorneys at 1–800–733–2889.

EVIDENCE IN NEW YORK STATE AND FEDERAL COURTS

By

ROBERT A. BARKER

and

VINCENT C. ALEXANDER

ST. PAUL, MINN.
WEST PUBLISHING CO.
1996

LIST OF ABBREVIATIONS FOR FREQUENTLY CITED SOURCES

Abbrevation	*Full Citation*
CPLR	N.Y. Civil Practice Law & Rules, McKinney's Consolidated Laws of New York Annotated.
Graham	M. Graham, Handbook of Federal Evidence (3d ed.1991).
James, Hazard & Leubsdorf	F. James, G. Hazard & J. Leubsdorf, Civil Procedure (4th ed.1992).
Lilly	G. Lilly, An Introduction to the Law of Evidence (2d ed.1987).
McCormick	McCormick on Evidence (J. Strong, ed., 4th ed.1992) (2-volume Practitioner Treatise Series).
Mueller & Kirkpatrick	C. Mueller & L. Kirkpatrick, Evidence (1995).
Proposed New York Evidence Code	Code of Evidence for the State of New York, submitted to the 1991–92 Session of the Legislature by the Governor; prepared by the New York State Law Revision Commission (Not adopted as of December 1995).
Weinstein & Berger	J. Weinstein & M. Berger, Weinstein's Evidence (1995).
Wigmore	J. Wigmore, Evidence in Trials at Common Law (Vols. 1–1A, Tillers rev. 1983; Vols. 2–7, Chadbourne rev.1974–1978; Vol. 8, McNaughton rev.1961; Vol. 9, Chadbourne rev.1981).

COPYRIGHT © 1996 By WEST PUBLISHING CO.
610 Opperman Drive
P.O. Box 64526
St. Paul, MN 55164–0526
1–800–328–9352

All rights reserved
Printed in the United States of America
ISBN 0–314–08636–6

TEXT IS PRINTED ON 10% POST CONSUMER RECYCLED PAPER

Printed with Printwise
Environmentally Advanced Water Washable Ink

TO
Ellen, who has provided great support.
R.A.B.

My Family:
Nancy, Jack, Tom, and Jim
V.C.A.

*

PREFACE

This book presents New York evidence law in a modern analytical framework. It contains a complete exposition of the law of evidence in New York, followed by a summary of the corresponding law under the Federal Rules of Evidence. In the federal sections of the book, special emphasis is given to the rulings of the United States Court of Appeals for the Second Circuit. This parallel arrangement of state and federal law not only facilitates trial practice in both court systems but also provides a quick and ready source of potential guidance for the resolution of unsettled or evolving issues under New York law.

Comparisons are also made to the proposed New York Evidence Code, the current draft of which was submitted to the Legislature during its 1991–1992 session. The code originated in the New York Law Revision Commission over 15 years ago but still has not been acted upon. The Legislature would do well to adopt such a code of evidence.[1]

As it is, the law of evidence in New York consists of a mix of rules derived from caselaw, Article 45 of the Civil Practice Law and Rules (CPLR), Article 60 of the Criminal Procedure Law, and other scattered statutes and rules. The Federal Rules of Evidence, while not perfect in every detail, provide an admirable model. The very fact that so many of today's litigators practice in both the state and federal courts is reason enough to have rules of evidence that are at least roughly comparable to each forum. Although the latest draft of the proposed New York Evidence Code differs in many respects from its Federal Rules counterpart, there is nevertheless a significant movement toward uniformity.

The New York Court of Appeals on more than one occasion has been influenced by one or another of the federal rules, as have other state courts, indicating that a process of integration is already underway. A need was perceived by the authors of this work to bring together the state caselaw and statutory rules, the Federal Rules of Evidence, and the proposed New York Evidence Code. The organization of the book is described in greater detail in § 100.1 *infra*.

The authors wish to acknowledge the important contributions of others. In Albany, Donna Parent was the "right arm" of this operation. She labored long and hard inputting the manuscript to disk and was of great help in many other ways. Students Peter Lauricella and Nicole van Gendt spent many hours with the footnotes and the text. Much appreciation is extended to Robert Begg and Robert Emery, Director and Associate Director of the Albany Law School Schaffer Law Library, and their staff, for their cooperation and help.

---

1. See generally Salken, "To Codify or Not to Codify—That Is the Question: A Study of New York's Efforts to Enact an Evidence Code," 58 Brooklyn L.Rev. 641 (1992). But see Bamberger, "Let's Think Before We Leap: Why Should the Law of Evidence Be Codified?," N.Y.L.J., May 13, 1992, p.1, col.1.

PREFACE

At St. John's, students Douglas Deutsch, Claire Gegan, Scott Kapusta and William Stelwagon ably assisted with the research. The secretarial staff, especially Vivian Parham, Jean Saratella, Rosetta Seijo, Ramona Mahesh and Somna Maraj—under the direction of Denise Enriquez and Yolanda Ocasio—kept the stream of paper flowing. The encouragement and insights of colleagues Dean Rudolph C. Hasl and Professor Thomas F. Shea were of enormous benefit.

ROBERT A. BARKER
VINCENT C. ALEXANDER

December, 1995

ABOUT THE AUTHORS

Robert A. Barker is a Professor of Law at Albany Law School, Union University. He is a former Associate Dean of the Law School and Executive Director of the New York State Law Revision Commission. He coordinated the original study and proposal for the New York Code of Evidence. For fifteen years he has authored the evidence article for the Annual Survey of New York Law, published by the *Syracuse Law Review*. Additionally, for many years he was a lecturer on evidence, with Dean Jerome Prince, at the annual New York State Judicial Seminars. He is co-author, with Oscar Chase, of *Civil Litigation in New York* (2d ed.), and he writes a monthly column on New York Practice for the *New York Law Journal*. Professor Barker received both his undergraduate and law degrees from Syracuse University.

Vincent C. Alexander is a Professor of Law at St. John's University School of Law. He is author of the current Practice Commentaries on CPLR Articles 45 and 78 in *McKinney's Consolidated Laws of New York Annotated* and the annual Supplementary Practice Commentaries (since 1991) in seven other McKinney's CPLR volumes. He is a contributing author of *New York Forms of Jury Instruction* (Vol. 1) and has written various articles on civil procedure and evidence, including a book-length empirical study of the corporate attorney-client privilege in Volume 63 of the *St. John's Law Review*. Since 1985, he has edited the annual *Second Circuit Redbook* of the Federal Bar Council, and he is a frequent lecturer for judges and bar groups in New York. Professor Alexander holds degrees from Yale University (B.A.), St. John's Law School (J.D.) and Columbia University School of Law (LL.M. and J.S.D.).

*

WESTLAW® ELECTRONIC RESEARCH GUIDE

Coordinating Legal Research With WESTLAW

The *New York Practice Series* is an essential aid to legal research. WESTLAW provides a vast, online library of over 6000 collections of documents and services that can supplement research begun in this publication, encompassing:

- Federal and state primary law (statutes, regulations, rules, and case law), including West's editorial enhancements, such as headnotes, Key Number classifications, annotations;

- Secondary law resources (texts and treatises published by West Publishing Company and by other publishers, as well as law reviews);

- Legal news

- Directories of attorneys and experts

- Court records and filings

- Citators

Specialized topical subsets of these resources have been created for more than thirty areas of practice.

In addition to legal information, there are general news and reference databases and a broad array of specialized materials frequently useful in connection with legal matters, covering accounting, business, environment, ethics, finance, medicine, social and physical sciences.

This guide will focus on a few aspects of WESTLAW use to supplement research begun in this publication, and will direct you to additional sources of assistance.

Databases

A database is a collection of documents with some features in common. It may contain statutes, court decisions, administrative materials, commentaries, news or other information. Each database has a unique identifier, used in many WESTLAW commands to select a database of interest. For example, the database containing New York cases has the identifier NY-CS.

The WESTLAW Directory is a comprehensive list of databases with information about each database, including the types of documents each contains. The first page of a standard or customized WESTLAW Directory is displayed upon signing on to WESTLAW, except when prior, saved research is resumed. To access the WESTLAW Directory at any time, enter DB.

Databases of potential interest in connection with your research include:

NY-AG	New York Attorney General Opinions
NY ETH-EO	New York Ethics Opinions
NY-JLR	New York Journals and Law Reviews
NY-JI	New York Jury Instructions
WLD-NY	West's Legal Directory - New York
FEDEVID	Handbook of Federal Evidence
PAPERSNY	New York Newspapers (DIALOG)

For information as to currentness and search tips regarding any WESTLAW database, enter the SCOPE command SC followed by the database identifier (e.g., SC NY-CS). It is not necessary to include the identifier to obtain scope information about the currently selected database.

WESTLAW Highlights

Use of this publication may be supplemented through the WESTLAW Bulletin (WLB), the WESTLAW New York State Bulletin (WSB-NY) and various Topical Highlights. Highlights databases contain summaries of significant judicial, legislative and administrative developments and are updated daily; they are searchable both from an automatic list of recent documents and using general WESTLAW search methods for documents accumulated over time. The full text of any judicial decision may be retrieved by entering FIND.

Consult the WESTLAW Directory (enter DB) for a complete, current listing of highlights databases.

Retrieving a Specific Case

The FIND command can be used to quickly retrieve a case whose citation is known. For example:

FI 616 A.2d 1336

Updating Case Law Research

There are a variety of citator services on WESTLAW for use in updating research.

Insta-Cite® may be used to verify citations, find parallel citations, ascertain the history of a case, and see whether it remains valid law. References are also provided to secondary sources, such as Corpus Juris Secundum®, that cite the case. To view the Insta-Cite history of a displayed case, simply enter the command IC. To view the Insta-Cite history of a selected case, enter a command in this form:

IC 574 A.2d 502

WESTLAW ELECTRONIC RESEARCH GUIDE

Shepard's® Citations provides a comprehensive list of cases and publications that have cited a particular case, with explanatory analysis to indicate how the citing cases have treated the case, e.g., "followed," "explained." To view the Shepard's Citations about a displayed case, enter the command SH. Add a case citation, if necessary, as in the prior Insta-Cite example.

For the latest citing references, not yet incorporated in Shepard's Citations, use Shepard's PreView® (SP command) and QuickCite™ (QC command), in the same way.

To see a complete list of publications covered by any of the citator services, enter its service abbreviation (IC, SH, SP or QC) followed by PUBS. To ascertain the scope of coverage for any of the services, enter the SCOPE command (SC) followed by the appropriate service abbreviation. For the complete list of commands available in a citator service, enter its service abbreviation (IC, SH, SP or QC) followed by CMDS.

Retrieving Statutes, Court Rules and Regulations

Annotated and unannotated versions of the New York statutes are searchable on WESTLAW (identifiers NY-ST-ANN and NY-ST), as are New York court rules (NY-RULES).

The United States Code and United States Code - Annotated are searchable databases on WESTLAW (identifiers USC and USCA, respectively), as are federal court rules (US-RULES) and regulations (CFR).

In addition, the FIND command may be used to retrieve specific provisions by citation, obviating the need for database selection or search. To FIND a desired document, enter FI, followed by the citation of the desired document, using the full name of the publication, or one of the abbreviated styles recognized by WESTLAW.

If WESTLAW does not recognize the style you enter, you may enter one of the following, using US, NY, or any other state code in place of XX:

FI XX-ST	Displays templates for codified statutes
FI XX-LEGIS	Displays templates for legislation
FI XX-RULES	Displays templates for rules
FI XX-ORDERS	Displays templates for court orders

Alternatively, entering FI followed by the publication's full name or an accepted abbreviation will normally display templates, useful jump possibilities, or helpful information necessary to complete the FIND process. For example:

FI USCA	Displays templates for United States Code - Annotated
FI FRAP	Displays templates for Federal Rules of Appellate Procedure
FI FRCP	Displays templates for Federal Rules of Civil Procedure
FI FRCRP	Displays templates for Federal Rules of Criminal Procedure
FI FRE	Displays templates for Federal Rules of Evidence
FI CFR	Displays templates for Code of Federal Regulations
FI FR	Displays templates for Federal Register

To view the complete list of FINDable documents and associated prescribed forms, enter FI PUBS.

Updating Research in re Statutes, Rules and Regulations

When viewing a statute, rule or regulation on WESTLAW after a search or FIND command, it is easy to update your research. A message will appear on the screen if relevant amendments, repeals or other new material are available through the UPDATE feature. Entering the UPDATE command will display such material.

Documents used to update New York statutes are also searchable in New York Legislative Service (NY-LEGIS). Those used to update rules are searchable in New York Orders (NY-ORDERS).

Documents used to update federal statutes, rules, and regulations are searchable in the United States Public Laws (US-PL), Federal Orders (US-ORDERS) and Federal Register (FR) databases, respectively.

When documents citing a statute, rule or regulation are of interest, Shepard's Citations on WESTLAW may be of assistance. That service covers federal constitutional provisions, statutes and administrative provisions, and corresponding materials from many states. The command SH PUBS displays a directory of publications which may be Shepardized on WESTLAW. Consult the WESTLAW manual for more information about citator services.

Using WESTLAW as a Citator

For research beyond the coverage of any citator service, go directly to the databases (cases, for example) containing citing documents and use standard WESTLAW search techniques to retrieve documents citing specific constitutional provisions, statutes, standard jury instructions or other authorities.

Fortunately, the specific portion of a citation is often reasonably distinctive, such as 22:636.1, 301.65, 401(k), 12-21-5, 12052. When it is, a search on that specific portion alone may retrieve applicable documents without any substantial number of inapplicable ones (unless the number happens to be coincidentally popular in another context).

Similarly, if the citation involves more than one number, such as 42 U.S.C.A. § 1201, a search containing both numbers (e.g., 42 +5 1201) is likely to produce mostly desired information, even though the component numbers are common.

If necessary, the search may be limited in several ways:

A. Switch from a general database to one containing mostly cases within the subject area of the cite being researched;

B. Use a connector (&, /S, /P, etc.) to narrow the search to documents including terms which are highly likely to accompany the correct citation in the context of the issue being researched;

WESTLAW ELECTRONIC RESEARCH GUIDE

C. Include other citation information in the query. Because of the variety of citation formats used in documents, this option should be used primarily where other options prove insufficient. Below are illustrative queries for any database containing New York cases:

N.Y.Const.! Const.! Constitution /s 6 VI +3 3

will retrieve cases citing the New York State Constitution, Art. 6, § 3; and

"borrowing statute" ("Civil Practice" CPLR /7 202)

will retrieve cases citing Civil Practice Law § 202.

Alternative Retrieval Methods

WIN® (WESTLAW Is Natural™) allows you to frame your issue in plain English to retrieve documents:

What acts waive the protection of the dead man's statute?

Alternatively, retrieval may be focused by use of the Terms and Connectors method:

DI(WAIVE! /P DEAD-MAN)

In databases with Key Numbers, either of the above examples will identify Witnesses ⬩175, ⬩176, ⬩178, and ⬩181 as Key Numbers collecting headnotes relevant to this issue if there are pertinent cases.

Since the Key Numbers are affixed to points of law by trained specialists based on conceptual understanding of the case, relevant cases that were not retrieved by either of the language-dependent methods will often be found at a Key Number.

Similarly, citations in retrieved documents (to cases, statutes, rules, etc.) may suggest additional, fruitful research using other WESTLAW databases (e.g., annotated statutes, rules) or services (e.g., citator services).

Key Number Search

Frequently, case law research rapidly converges on a few topics, headings and Key Numbers within West's Key Number System that are likely to contain relevant cases. These may be discovered from known, relevant reported cases from any jurisdiction; Library References in West publications; browsing in a digest; or browsing the Key Number System on WESTLAW using the JUMP feature or the KEY command.

Once discovered, topics, subheadings or Key Numbers are useful as search terms (in databases containing reported cases) alone or with other search terms, to focus the search within a narrow range of potentially relevant material.

WESTLAW ELECTRONIC RESEARCH GUIDE

For example, to retrieve cases with at least one headnote classified to Witnesses ⇨181, sign on to a caselaw database and enter

410k181 [use with other search terms, if desired]

The topic name (Witnesses) is replaced by its numerical equivalent (410) and the ⇨ by the letter k. A list of topics and their numerical equivalents is in the WESTLAW Reference Manual and is displayed in WESTLAW when the KEY command is entered.

Other topics of special interest include: Appeal and Error (30), Criminal Law (110), Evidence (157), and New Trial (275).

Using JUMP

WESTLAW's JUMP feature allows you to move from one document to another or from one part of a document to another, then easily return to your original place, without losing your original result. Opportunities to move in this manner are marked in the text with a JUMP symbol (▶). Whenever you see the JUMP symbol, you may move to the place designated by the adjacent reference by using the Tab, arrow keys or mouse click to position the cursor on the JUMP symbol, then pressing Enter or clicking again with the mouse.

Within the text of a court opinion, JUMP arrows are adjacent to case cites and federal statute cites, and adjacent to parenthesized numbers marking discussions corresponding to headnotes.

On a screen containing the text of a headnote, the JUMP arrows allow movement to the corresponding discussion in the text of the opinion,

▶ (3)

and allow browsing West's Key Number System beginning at various heading levels:

- ▶ 410   WITNESSES
- ▶ 410II   Competency
- ▶ 410II(C)   Dead Man's Statutes and Rules
- ▶ 410k181   k. Waiver of objections.

To return from a JUMP, enter GB (except for JUMPs between a headnote and the corresponding discussion in opinion, for which there is a matching number in parenthesis in both headnote and opinion). Returns from successive JUMPs (e.g., from case to cited case to case cited by cited case) without intervening returns may be accomplished by repeated entry of GB or by using the MAP command.

General Information

The information provided above illustrates some of the ways WESTLAW can complement research using this publication. However, this brief overview illustrates only some of the power of WESTLAW. The full

WESTLAW ELECTRONIC RESEARCH GUIDE

range of WESTLAW search techniques is available to support your research.

Please consult the WESTLAW Reference Manual for additional information or assistance or call West's Reference Attorneys at 1–800–REF–ATTY (1–800–733–2889).

For information about subscribing to WESTLAW, please call 1–800–328–0109.

*

SUMMARY OF CONTENTS

Chapter	Page
1. General Principles	1
2. Judicial Notice	34
3. Burden of Proof and Presumptions	54
4. Relevancy	107
5. Privileges	210
6. Witnesses	323
7. Opinions and Expert Testimony	500
8. Hearsay	543
9. Authentication and Identification	767
10. Best Evidence	806
11. Real and Demonstrative Evidence	837
Table of Statutes	887
Table of Rules	899
Table of Cases	905
Index	989

*

TABLE OF CONTENTS

CHAPTER 1. GENERAL PRINCIPLES

100 INTRODUCTION

Sec.
100.1 Overview and Organization of Book.
100.2 Definitions: New York and Federal.

101 [RESERVED]

102 [RESERVED]

103 RULINGS ON EVIDENCE

103.1 New York.
    a. Objections and Motions to Strike.
    b. General vs. Specific Objections.
    c. Offer of Proof and Offer "to Connect Up".
    d. Motions *in Limine*.
    e. Harmless Error.
103.2 Federal.
    a. Objections and Motions to Strike.
    b. General vs. Specific Objections.
    c. Offer of Proof and Offer to "Connect Up".
    d. Motions *in Limine*.
    e. Harmless Error.

104 PRELIMINARY RULINGS

104.1 New York.
    a. Respective Responsibilities of Judge and Jury, In General.
    b. Admissions; Confessions; Illegally Seized Evidence; Privileges.
104.2 Federal.

105 LIMITED ADMISSIBILITY

105.1 New York.
105.2 Federal.

106 RULE OF COMPLETENESS

106.1 New York.
106.2 Federal.

CHAPTER 2. JUDICIAL NOTICE

200 INTRODUCTION

200.1 Judicial Notice, In General.

201 JUDICIAL NOTICE OF ADJUDICATIVE FACTS

201.1 New York.
    a. In General.
    b. Facts Subject to Judicial Notice.

TABLE OF CONTENTS

Sec.
201.1 New York—Continued
    c. Examples.
    d. Procedure.
    e. Effect of Taking Judicial Notice.
    f. Proposed New York Evidence Code.
201.2 Federal.

202 JUDICIAL NOTICE OF LEGISLATIVE FACTS

202.1 New York and Federal.

203 JUDICIAL NOTICE OF LAW

203.1 New York.
203.2 Federal.

CHAPTER 3. BURDEN OF PROOF AND PRESUMPTIONS

300 BURDEN OF PROOF

300.1 Burden of Proof, In General.
300.2 Allocation of Burden of Proof, In General.
300.3 Satisfying the Burden of Production.
    a. New York.
        1. The Test for Sufficiency.
        2. Shifting of the Burden of Production.
    b. Federal.
300.4 Satisfying the Burden of Persuasion.
    a. In General.
    b. Civil Cases: New York.
        1. Preponderance of the Evidence.
        2. Clear and Convincing Evidence.
    c. Civil Cases: Federal.
    d. Criminal Cases: New York.
        1. Reasonable Doubt.
        2. Defenses and Affirmative Defenses.
    e. Criminal Cases: Federal.

301 PRESUMPTIONS IN CIVIL CASES

301.1 New York: Introduction.
301.2 The Meaning of a Presumption.
301.3 Rebuttable Presumptions.
301.4 Reasons for Presumptions; Illustrative Presumptions.
301.5 Effect of Presumptions in New York.
    a. In General.
        1. Thayer (the "Bursting Bubble" Rule).
        2. Morgan.
    b. New York Approach.
301.6 Res Ipsa Loquitur.
301.7 Prima Facie Evidence.
301.8 Effect of Presumptions in Federal Proceedings.
    a. Cases Governed by Federal Law.
    b. Cases Governed by State Law.

TABLE OF CONTENTS

302 PRESUMPTIONS IN CRIMINAL CASES

Sec.
302.1   New York.
    a. Constitutional Restraints.
    b. New York Approach.
302.2   Federal.

CHAPTER 4. RELEVANCY

400 INTRODUCTION

400.1   New York and Federal—Introduction.

401 RELEVANCY

401.1   New York.
    a. Probability.
    b. Factors Precluding Admissibility of Relevant Evidence—Prejudice and Exclusionary Rules.
    c. Proposed New York Evidence Code.
401.2   Federal.

402 CHARACTER EVIDENCE

402.1   New York.
    a. Introduction.
    b. Character in Issue.
    c. Character Evidence as Proof of Conduct in Civil Cases.
    d. Character Evidence as Proof of Conduct in Criminal Cases.
    e. The Effect of Character Evidence—Jury Charge.
    f. Character Trait of the Victim in a Homicide Case.
    g. Character Evidence Used to Impeach, Generally.
    h. Proposed New York Evidence Code.
402.2   Federal.

403 [RESERVED]

404 UNCHARGED CRIMES

404.1   New York.
    a. Generally.
    b. Motive.
    c. Intent.
    d. Absence of Accident or Mistake.
    e. Common Scheme or Plan.
    f. Identity.
    g. Background.
    h. Inextricably Intertwined.
    i. Multiple Counts.
    j. Sex Cases—"Amorous Design."
    k. Rebuttal.
    l. Civil Cases.
404.2   Federal.
    a. Generally.
    b. Procedure.
    c. Civil Cases.

TABLE OF CONTENTS

405 SIMILAR OCCURRENCES

Sec.
405.1 New York.
    a. Generally.
    b. Other Accidents.
    c. Other Business Transactions.
    d. Sales of Property.
405.2 Federal.
    a. Other Accidents.
    b. Other Business Transactions.
    c. Sales of Property.

406 HABIT AND CUSTOM

406.1 New York.
    a. Generally.
    b. Business and Professional Habit.
    c. Habit Evidence in the Workplace.
    d. Habit in Negligence Cases—Non-Workplace Situations.
    e. Eyewitnesses.
    f. Custom and Usage as a Standard of Care.
406.2 Federal.
    a. Business and Professional Habit.
    b. Evidence of Habit in Negligence Cases.
    c. Custom and Usage as a Standard of Care.

407 SUBSEQUENT REMEDIAL MEASURES

407.1 New York.
    a. Generally.
    b. Negligence.
    c. Products Liability.
    d. Feasibility.
    e. Ownership, Control and Impeachment.
    f. Criminal Cases and Proposed New York Code Provision.
407.2 Federal.

408 COMPROMISES AND OFFERS TO COMPROMISE

408.1 New York.
408.2 Federal.

409 PAYMENT OF MEDICAL AND SIMILAR EXPENSES

409.1 New York.
409.2 Federal.

410 PLEAS AND PLEA DISCUSSIONS

410.1 New York.
410.2 Federal.

411 LIABILITY INSURANCE

411.1 New York.
411.2 Federal.

412 SHIELD LAWS

412.1 New York.

TABLE OF CONTENTS

Sec.

412.2   Federal.

413   DEFENDANT'S SEXUAL HISTORY

413.1   Federal.

CHAPTER 5. PRIVILEGES

500   INTRODUCTION

500.1   New York.
500.2   Federal.

501   ATTORNEY–CLIENT PRIVILEGE AND WORK PRODUCT

501.1   New York: Attorney–Client Privilege.
      a. In General.
      b. Attorney–Client Relationship.
      c. Communications.
      d. Legal Advice.
      e. Confidentiality.
      f. Application in the Corporate Context.
      g. Exceptions.
      h. Waiver.
501.2   Federal: Attorney–Client Privilege.
501.3   Work Product Immunities.
      a. In General.
      b. New York.
          1. Civil Cases.
          2. Criminal Cases.
          3. Waiver.
      c. Federal.

502   PHYSICIAN–PATIENT AND RELATED PRIVILEGES

502.1   New York.
      a. In General.
      b. Scope of the Physician–Patient Privilege.
      c. Waiver.
      d. Exceptions.
      e. Psychologists.
502.2   Federal.

503   SPOUSAL PRIVILEGES

503.1   New York: Generally.
503.2   New York: Incompetency in Adultery Cases.
503.3   New York: Privilege for Confidential Communications.
      a. Confidentiality.
      b. Induced by the Marital Relationship.
      c. Communication Made During the Marriage.
      d. Waiver.
      e. Exceptions.
503.4   New York: Parent–Child Privilege.
503.5   Federal.
      a. Testimonial Privilege.
      b. Marital Communications Privilege.

TABLE OF CONTENTS

504 COMMUNICATIONS WITH CLERGY PRIVILEGE

Sec.
504.1 New York.
504.2 Federal.

505 SOCIAL WORKER PRIVILEGE

505.1 New York.
505.2 Federal.

506 RAPE CRISIS COUNSELOR

506.1 New York.
506.2 Federal.

507 LIBRARY RECORDS

507.1 New York.
507.2 Federal.

508 JOURNALIST PRIVILEGE

508.1 New York.
508.2 Federal.

509 SELF–INCRIMINATION

509.1 New York State and Federal.
    a. Civil Cases.
    b. Criminal Proceedings.
       1. *Testimony.*
       2. *Documents.*
    c. Application of the Privilege During the Investigation Stage—Connection to the Trial.

510 THE INFORMER PRIVILEGE

510.1 New York.
510.2 Federal.

511 GOVERNMENT COMMUNICATIONS

511.1 New York.
511.2 Federal.

512 POLITICAL VOTE

512.1 New York.
512.2 Federal.

513 TRADE SECRETS

513.1 New York.
513.2 Federal Rule.

514 COMMENT UPON OR INFERENCE FROM CLAIM OF PRIVILEGE

514.1 New York.
514.2 Federal.

TABLE OF CONTENTS

CHAPTER 6. WITNESSES

600 INTRODUCTION

Sec.
600.1. Overview.

601 GENERAL RULE OF COMPETENCY

601.1 New York.
    a. In General.
    b. Interest.
    c. Spouses of Parties.
    d. Convictions.
    e. Children.
    f. Mental, Sensory or Communicative Infirmities.
    g. Alcohol and Drugs.
    h. Hypnotically–Induced Memory.
601.2 New York Dead Man's Statute.
    a. In General.
    b. Disqualified Witnesses.
    c. Protected Persons.
    d. Prohibited Subject Matter.
    e. Exceptions.
    f. Waiver.
    g. Inapplicability Before Trial.
601.3 Federal.

602 PERSONAL KNOWLEDGE

602.1 New York.
602.2 Federal.

603 OATH OR AFFIRMATION

603.1 New York.
603.2 Federal.

604 INTERPRETERS

604.1 New York.
604.2 Federal.

605 JUDGE'S COMPETENCY AS WITNESS

605.1 New York.
605.2 Federal.

606 JUROR'S COMPETENCY AS WITNESS

606.1 New York.
606.2 Federal.

607 IMPEACHMENT AND REHABILITATION OF WITNESSES

607.1 Credibility: New York and Federal.
607.2 Impeachment, In General: New York and Federal.
607.3 Contradiction; Collateral and Noncollateral Matters.
607.4 Party Impeachment of Her Own Witness.
    a. New York, In General.
    b. New York Exception for Prior Inconsistent Statements.

TABLE OF CONTENTS

Sec.

607.4 Party Impeachment of Her Own Witness—Continued
    c. Federal.
607.5 Support and Rehabilitation of Credibility.
    a. New York.
        1. Advance Accreditation.
        2. Rehabilitation.
            (a) Explanation.
            (b) Good Character for Truthfulness.
            (c) Prior Consistent Statements.
    b. Federal.
607.6 Impeachment by Bias and Similar Forms of Partiality.
    a. New York.
607.7 Impeachment by Mental or Sensory Impairment.
    a. New York.
    b. Federal.
607.8 Impeachment by Prior Inconsistent Statements.
    a. New York.
        1. In General.
        2. Nature of the Inconsistency.
        3. Foundation Requirements; Extrinsic Evidence.
    b. Federal.

608 IMPEACHMENT BY EVIDENCE OF UNTRUTHFUL CHARACTER AND PRIOR MISCONDUCT

608.0 In General.
608.1 Bad Character for Truthfulness.
    a. New York.
    b. Federal.
608.2 Prior Acts of Misconduct.
    a. New York.
    b. Federal.

609 IMPEACHMENT BY EVIDENCE OF CRIMINAL CONVICTIONS

609.1 New York.
    a. In General.
    b. Civil Cases.
    c. Criminal Cases.
609.2 Federal.

610 RELIGIOUS BELIEFS OR OPINIONS

610.1 New York.
610.2 Federal.

611 PRESENTATION OF TESTIMONY

611.1 New York: Order of Trial.
611.2 New York: Form of Questioning.
    a. In General.
    b. Leading Questions.
611.3 New York: Cross–Examination.
    a. In General.
    b. Scope of Cross–Examination.
    c. Judicial Discretion.
    d. Voir Dire of the Witness.

TABLE OF CONTENTS

Sec.
611.4 New York: Redirect and Recross Examination.
611.5 Federal: Mode and Order of Interrogation and Presentation.
    a. Order of Trial.
    b. Form of Questioning.
    c. Cross–Examination, Redirect and Recross.

612 REFRESHING THE WITNESS' RECOLLECTION

612.1 New York.
    a. In General.
    b. Adversary's Right of Inspection.
612.2 Federal.

613 [RESERVED]

614 CALLING AND QUESTIONING OF WITNESSES BY THE COURT OR JURY

614.1 New York.
    a. Calling of Witnesses by the Court.
    b. Judicial Questioning of Witnesses.
    c. Questioning by Jurors.
614.2 Federal.

615 EXCLUSION OF WITNESSES FROM THE COURTROOM

615.1 New York.
615.2 Federal.

CHAPTER 7. OPINIONS AND EXPERT TESTIMONY

700 OPINION TESTIMONY: INTRODUCTION

700.1 New York and Federal.

701 OPINION TESTIMONY BY LAY WITNESSES

701.1 New York.
701.2 Federal.

702 EXPERT TESTIMONY

702.1 New York.
    a. Generally.
    b. Novel Scientific Theories and Methods.
    c. Recurring Problems of Expert Testimony.
    d. The "Interested Observer".
    e. Qualifications.
    f. Impeachment of Experts.
702.2 Federal.
    a. Generally.
    b. Scientific Evidence.

703 BASIS OF EXPERT OPINION TESTIMONY

703.1 New York.
703.2 Federal.

704 OPINION ON ULTIMATE ISSUES

704.1 New York.

TABLE OF CONTENTS

Sec.
704.2   Federal.

705 DISCLOSURE OF FACTS AND DATA UNDERLYING EXPERT OPINION

705.1   New York.
705.2   Federal.

706 COURT–APPOINTED EXPERTS

706.1   New York.
706.2   Federal.

CHAPTER 8. HEARSAY

801 HEARSAY, NEW YORK AND FEDERAL—GENERALLY

801.1   Introduction.
    a. The Nature of Hearsay.
    b. Assertions.
    c. Operative Words (Verbal Acts).
    d. State of Mind.
    e. Indirect Hearsay.

801(1) STATEMENTS NOT HEARSAY

801(1).1   Generally.
801(1).2   Prior Statements—New York.
    a. Inconsistent Statements.
    b. Prior Consistent Statements.
801(1).3   Prior Statements—Federal.
    a. Inconsistent Statements.
    b. Consistent Statements.

801(2) IDENTIFICATION

801(2).1   New York.
801(2).2   Federal.

802 ADMISSIONS

802.1   New York & Federal—Introduction.
802.2   A Party's Statement—New York.
    a. Admission by a Party's Conduct.
    b. Admissions by Silence.
    c. Privity.
    d. Representative Capacity.
    e. Adoptive Admissions.
    f. Statements by the Party's Agent or Servant.
    g. Coconspirator's Statements.
802.3   A Party's Statement—Federal.
    a. Pleadings.
    b. Admissions by a Party, by Statements, Acts, Adoption or in a Representative Capacity.
    c. Statements Made by an Agent or Servant, and Statements Otherwise Authorized.
    d. Coconspirator's Statements.

TABLE OF CONTENTS

803 HEARSAY EXCEPTIONS WHERE AVAILABILITY OF THE DECLARANT IS IMMATERIAL

Sec.
803.1 New York and Federal, In General.

803(1) SPONTANEOUS STATEMENTS, STATEMENTS EVIDENCING A STATE OF MIND OR PHYSICAL CONDITION, AND STATEMENTS MADE FOR PURPOSES OF MEDICAL DIAGNOSIS OR TREATMENT

803(1).1 New York.
    a. Present Sense Impression.
    b. Excited Utterance.
    c. State of Mind or Physical Condition.
    d. Statements Made for Purposes of Medical Diagnosis or Treatment.

803(1).2 Federal.
    a. Present Sense Impression.
    b. Excited Utterance.
    c. State of Mind or Physical Condition.
    d. Statements Made for Purposes of Medical Diagnosis or Treatment.

803(2) RECORDED RECOLLECTION

803(2).1 New York.
803(2).2 Federal.

803(3) REGULARLY KEPT RECORDS

803(3).1 New York.
    a. General Principles, Accident Reports.
    b. Agency Documents Offered by the Prosecution in Criminal Cases.
    c. Records of Hospitals, Libraries, and Other Government Bureaus.
    d. The Proposed New York Evidence Code.

803(3).2 Federal.

803(4) ABSENCE OF RECORD

803(4).1 New York.
    a. Business Records.
    b. Public Records.

803(4).2 Federal.

803(5) PUBLIC RECORDS

803(5).1 New York.
    a. Common Law Exception and Business Entry Exception.
    b. CPLR 4520.
    c. Investigatory Reports Made by Government Agencies.
    d. Ancient Maps and Real Property Records.
    e. Records of Sister State Real Property Conveyances.
    f. Marriage Certificates.
    g. Presumption of Death or of Being Missing.
    h. Birth and Death Certificates.
    i. Weather Records.

TABLE OF CONTENTS

Sec.

803(5).1 New York—Continued
- j. Agriculture Inspection Certificates.
- k. Certificate of Population.
- l. Surveyor's Standard.
- m. Justice of the Peace Proceedings.
- n. Absence of Public Record.
- o. Criminal Judgments of Conviction.
- p. Records of Religious Organizations.

803(5).2 Federal.
- a. Public Records Generally.
- b. Vital Statistics.
- c. Documents Affecting Interests in Real Property.
- d. Judgment of Previous Conviction; Judgment as Proof of Family History and Boundaries.
- e. Absence of Public Record.
- f. Records of Religious Organizations.

803(6) LEARNED TREATISES, MARKET REPORTS AND COMMERCIAL PUBLICATIONS

803(6).1 New York.
803(6).2 Federal.

803(7) ANCIENT DOCUMENTS, AND REPUTATION

803(7).1 New York.
- a. Family Records.
- b. Ancient Documents.
- c. Reputation.

803(7).2 Federal.
- a. Family Records.
- b. Ancient Documents.
- c. Reputation.

804 HEARSAY STATEMENTS ADMISSIBLE IF DECLARANT UNAVAILABLE

804.1 Unavailability—New York and Federal.

804(1) FORMER TESTIMONY

804(1).1 New York.
- a. Civil Cases.
- b. Criminal Cases.

804(1).2 Federal.

804(2) DYING DECLARATIONS

804(2).1 New York.
804(2).2 Federal.

804(3) DECLARATIONS AGAINST INTEREST

804(3).1 New York.
- a. Civil Cases.
- b. Criminal Cases.

804(3).2 Federal.

TABLE OF CONTENTS

Sec.

804(4) PEDIGREE

804(4).1 New York.
804(4).2 Federal.

804(5) RESIDUAL HEARSAY EXCEPTION

804(5).1 New York.
804(5).2 Federal.

805 HEARSAY WITHIN HEARSAY

805.1 New York.
805.2 Federal.

806 ATTACKING AND SUPPORTING DECLARANT'S CREDIBILITY

806.1 New York and Federal.

807 ADMISSIBILITY OF HEARSAY WHERE PARTY CAUSES DECLARANT'S UNAVAILABILITY

807.1 New York and Federal.

CHAPTER 9. AUTHENTICATION AND IDENTIFICATION

900 INTRODUCTION

900.1 Authentication and Identification In General—New York and Federal.

901 COMMON INSTANCES REQUIRING AUTHENTICATION OR IDENTIFICATION

901.1 Testimony of Witness With Knowledge.
    a. New York.
    b. Federal.
901.2 Lay Opinion on Handwriting.
    a. New York.
    b. Federal.
901.3 Comparisons by Trier or Expert Witness.
    a. New York.
    b. Federal.
901.4 Circumstantial Evidence of Authenticity.
    a. New York.
    b. Federal.
901.5 Voice Identification.
    a. New York.
    b. Federal.
901.6 Telephone Conversations.
    a. New York.
    b. Federal.
901.7 Public Records.
    a. New York.
    b. Federal.
901.8 Ancient Documents.
    a. New York.
    b. Federal.
901.9 Process or System.
    a. New York.
    b. Federal.

TABLE OF CONTENTS

Sec.

901.10 Methods Provided by Statute or Rule.
    a. New York.
    b. Federal.

902 SELF-AUTHENTICATION

902.1 Self-Authentication.
    a. New York.
    b. Federal.

903 SUBSCRIBING WITNESSES

903.1 Subscribing Witnesses—New York and Federal.

CHAPTER 10. BEST EVIDENCE

1001 BEST EVIDENCE

1001.1 The Best Evidence Rule—New York and Federal.
    a. Generally.
    b. Federal Rule of Evidence 1001—Definitions.

1002 ORIGINALS

1002.1 Originals—New York and Federal.

1003 DUPLICATES

1003.1 Duplicates—New York and Federal.

1004 SECONDARY EVIDENCE

1004.1 Secondary Evidence—New York and Federal.
    a. Loss or Destruction.
    b. Original Not Obtainable.
    c. Original in Possession of Opponent.
    d. Collateral Matters.

1005 PUBLIC RECORDS

1005.1 New York and Federal.
    a. New York.
    b. Federal.

1006 SUMMARIES

1006.1 Summaries—New York and Federal.
    a. New York.
    b. Federal.

1007 TESTIMONY OR WRITTEN ADMISSION OF PARTY

1007.1 Admission as to Genuineness—New York and Federal.

1008 FUNCTIONS OF COURT AND JURY

1008.1 Functions of Court and Jury.
    a. New York.
    b. Federal.

TABLE OF CONTENTS

CHAPTER 11. REAL AND DEMONSTRATIVE EVIDENCE

1100 INTRODUCTION

Sec.
1100.1 Real and Demonstrative Evidence, In General: New York and Federal.

1101 TANGIBLE OBJECTS

1101.1 New York.
1101.2 Federal.

1102 PERSONS: PHYSICAL FEATURES, INJURIES AND THEIR EFFECTS

1102.1 New York.
1102.2 Federal.

1103 DRAWINGS, DIAGRAMS, AND MODELS

1103.1 New York.
1103.2 Federal.

1104 PHOTOGRAPHIC AND RELATED FORMS OF EVIDENCE

1104.1 New York.
    a. Photographs.
    b. X-rays and Analogous Medical Pictorial Processes.
    c. Sound Recordings.
    d. Motion Pictures and Videotapes.
1104.2 Federal.
    a. Photographs.
    b. X-Rays.
    c. Sound Recordings.
    d. Motion Pictures and Videotapes.

1105 EXPERIMENTS AND DEMONSTRATIONS

1105.1 New York.
1105.2 Federal.

1106 COMPUTER-GENERATED GRAPHICS

1106.1 Computer-Generated Graphics: New York and Federal.

1107 JURY VIEWS

1107.1 New York.
1107.2 Federal.

1108 TAKING EXHIBITS INTO THE JURY ROOM; JURY EXPERIMENTATION

1108.1 New York.
1108.2 Federal.

	Page
Table of Statutes	887
Table of Rules	899
Table of Cases	905
Index	989

*

Chapter 1

GENERAL PRINCIPLES

Table of Sections

100 INTRODUCTION

100.1 Overview and Organization of Book.
100.2 Definitions: New York and Federal.

101 [RESERVED]

102 [RESERVED]

103 RULINGS ON EVIDENCE

103.1 New York.
    a. Objections and Motions to Strike.
    b. General vs. Specific Objections.
    c. Offer of Proof and Offer "to Connect Up."
    d. Motions in Limine.
    e. Harmless Error.
103.2 Federal.
    a. Objections and Motions to Strike.
    b. General vs. Specific Objections.
    c. Offer of Proof and Offer "to Connect Up."
    d. Motions in Limine.
    e. Harmless Error.

104 PRELIMINARY RULINGS

104.1 New York.
    a. Respective Responsibilities of Judge and Jury, In General.
    b. Admissions; Confessions; Illegally Seized Evidence; Privileges.
104.2 Federal.

105 LIMITED ADMISSIBILITY

105.1 New York.
105.2 Federal.

106 RULE OF COMPLETENESS

106.1 New York.
106.2 Federal.

WESTLAW Electronic Research

See WESTLAW Electronic Research Guide preceding the Summary of Contents.

100 Introduction

§ 100.1 Overview and Organization of Book

This book is designed to afford one source for the practitioner, judge or student who is interested in unearthing the rules of evidence as applied in the state courts of New York, or the federal courts in New York, or both. The New York law of evidence is a combination of caselaw and a few statutory rules found chiefly in CPLR Article 45 and Criminal Procedure Law Article 60.[1] The New York State Law Revision Commission has promulgated a proposed codification of the New York law of evidence patterned on the Federal Rules of Evidence, but differing in many respects and as yet unenacted by the Legislature. Without losing sight of our main objective to present New York law as it is, all of these provisions are set forth so that the rules—common law, statutory, codified and proposed—can be compared. Significant distinctions are highlighted, and it will be noted in several contexts how the New York Court of Appeals has infused the law of New York with principles enumerated in various and sundry federal rules.

Each chapter of the book contains a comprehensive discussion of the New York law of evidence, followed by a summary of the corresponding federal law. Because of the legal profession's nearly universal familiarity with the Federal Rules of Evidence, the organization of the material is based on that of the Federal Rules. Section headings track as closely as possible the numbering system of those rules. Topics not addressed by the Federal Rules, such as burden of proof, privileges and demonstrative evidence, are treated under new numbers.

In general, the basic concepts of each topic are presented in the New York sections of the book, thus eliminating the need for repetition in the parallel federal sections. The plan of each federal section is simply to reflect federal authority, with emphasis on Second Circuit caselaw, relating to points already developed in the preceding state section. Of course, if the law on a particular topic has been more fully developed by federal rules or caselaw, lengthier treatment is provided. Where the New York and federal rules are fairly homogeneous, as in the case of the self-incrimination privilege and some aspects of the best evidence rule, both are dealt with in one section.

Consistent with the order of presentation in the Federal Rules of Evidence, we cover the procedural framework of the trial, including the order of trial, order of direct and cross-examination and form of questioning in Chapter 6.[2] Basic rules relating to objections and the allocation of responsibility between judge and jury are described below in §§ 103.1–106.2.

§ 100.1

1. The same rules of evidence that are applicable in civil actions are applicable in criminal cases, "[u]nless otherwise provided by statute or by judicially established rules of evidence applicable to criminal cases." N.Y.Crim.Proc.Law § 60.10.

2. See §§ 611.1–611.5 infra.

§ 100.2 Definitions: New York and Federal

The definition of evidence is self-evident, or as Wigmore put it, "so simple and so exempt from practical controversy,"[1] that little space need be devoted to its exposition.[2] The rules of evidence, whether embodied in judicial decisions, statutes or codified rules, are designed to provide an effective and expeditious means for the determination of disputed facts at trial.[3] Evidence itself is the information that the fact-finder may properly rely upon in deciding a disputed issue of fact.[4] It is customary for the trial judge to instruct the jury that they must decide the facts based solely on the evidence that has been presented in court.[5] Of critical importance is an instruction, when request is timely made, to disregard evidence that has been stricken.[6] In addition, jurors typically

---

§ 100.2

1. 1 Wigmore § 1, at 9.

2. McCormick does not even pause to formally define the subject; but the opening sentence of the treatise succinctly states: "The law of evidence is the system of rules and standards by which the admission of proof at the trial of a lawsuit is regulated." McCormick § 1, at 2.

3. Mueller and Kirkpatrick in their treatise list five purposes served by the rules of evidence: (1) to control the diet of facts that untrained jurors reasonably can be expected to consume; (2) to advance the substantive law through such mechanisms as presumptions and burdens of proof; (3) to further public or social policy, unrelated to the issues in the case, by certain exclusionary rules such as the marital privilege; (4) to insure accuracy of the information upon which the fact-finder acts, through such requirements as authentication and original documentation; and (5) to control the scope and duration of the trial. Mueller and Kirkpatrick § 1.1, at 1–2.

4. See Dibble v. Dimick, 143 N.Y. 549, 554, 38 N.E. 724, 725 (1894)(evidence is the means by which an alleged matter of fact, the truth of which is in issue, is established or disproved). Wigmore collects nine definitions and concludes with these words: "Evidence, then, is any matter of fact that is furnished to a legal tribunal otherwise than by reasoning or a reference to what is noticed without proof—as the basis of inference in ascertaining some other matter of fact." 1 Wigmore § 1, at 11.

Courts often refer to "competent evidence," which means nothing more than admissible evidence. See People v. Swamp, 84 N.Y.2d 725, 730, 622 N.Y.S.2d 472, 474, 646 N.E.2d 774, 776 (1995)(competent evidence is "evidence not subject to an exclusionary rule"). See § 601.1(a), at note 1, infra.

5. See, e.g., 3 E. Devitt, C. Blackmar, and M. Wolf, Federal Jury Practice and Instructions § 70.03 (4th ed.1987); 1 N.Y.Forms of Jury Instruction §§ 1.23 and 1.71 (1992). In evaluating evidence, however, jurors may properly draw upon their general knowledge of the nature of things. See § 201.1, at note 32, infra.

6. See, e.g., Robinson v. City of Albany, 14 A.D.2d 626, 218 N.Y.S.2d 421 (3d Dep't 1961); Tomaschoff v. Stapleton Drug Co., 263 App.Div. 728, 30 N.Y.S.2d 724 (2d Dep't 1941). See United States v. Kellerman, 431 F.2d 319, 324 (2d Cir.), cert. denied, 400 U.S. 957, 91 S.Ct. 356, 27 L.Ed.2d 266 (1970)("The effectiveness of the judge's charge to disregard stricken evidence has been debated and challenged for generations. * * * But the entire jury system is dependent upon the assumption—whether it be fiction or not—that the jury will follow the court's instructions. It is only in extreme cases that this fiction is disregarded."). See also People v. Arce, 42 N.Y.2d 179, 187, 397 N.Y.S.2d 619, 624, 366 N.E.2d 279, 284 (1977); Gall v. Gall, 114 N.Y. 109, 122, 21 N.E. 106, 110 (1889).

§ 100.2 GENERAL PRINCIPLES Ch. 1

are advised that neither the statements[7] nor the questions[8] of counsel are evidence.

Beyond these basic concepts, space will not be expended here intoning the definitions of testimony,[9] documentary evidence,[10] real evidence,[11] and direct and circumstantial evidence,[12] since such definitions are virtually meaningless in a vacuum and will be developed in context in the chapters which follow.

101 [Reserved]

102 [Reserved]

103 Rulings on Evidence

§ 103.1 New York

a. Objections and Motions to Strike

It is a fundamental rule of evidentiary procedure that the parties are responsible for making timely objections to the introduction of inadmissible evidence. As a general matter, the failure to timely object results in a waiver of the issue.[1] The consequence is that inadmissible evidence

---

7. See, e.g., People v. Sullivan, 160 A.D.2d 161, 163–64, 559 N.Y.S.2d 881, 882–83 (1st Dep't), appeal denied, 76 N.Y.2d 987, 563 N.Y.S.2d 775, 565 N.E.2d 524 (1990)(statements of counsel are not evidence); People v. Musmacher, 133 A.D.2d 352, 353, 519 N.Y.S.2d 253, 253 (2d Dep't), appeal denied, 70 N.Y.2d 802, 522 N.Y.S.2d 120, 516 N.E.2d 1233 (1987)(opening statement is not evidence); Mertsaris v. 73rd Corp., 105 A.D.2d 67, 78, 482 N.Y.S.2d 792, 799 (2d Dep't 1984)(summations are not evidence).

8. See, e.g., People v. Grant, 210 A.D.2d 166, 167, 620 N.Y.S.2d 358, 359 (1st Dep't 1994), appeal denied, 85 N.Y.2d 862, 624 N.Y.S.2d 381, 648 N.E.2d 801 (1995); People v. Ortiz, 135 A.D.2d 743, 744, 522 N.Y.S.2d 647, 648 (2d Dep't 1987), appeal denied, 70 N.Y.2d 1009, 526 N.Y.S.2d 944, 521 N.E.2d 1087 (1988).

9. Testimonial evidence can be any statement made orally and under oath in a formal proceeding. It would include a deposition, which even when reduced to writing is the simple recordation of the deponent's testimony.

10. Issues concerning documentary evidence (writings) arise in various contexts, such as the business records hearsay exception dealt with in Chapter 8, the rules of authentication covered in Chapter 9, and the best evidence rule in Chapter 10.

11. Real evidence, consisting of writings and objects, is covered in Chapter 11.

12. Direct and circumstantial evidence are distinguished in § 300.3(a), at notes 1–2, infra. Circumstantial evidence is a concept that permeates Chapter 3 (burden of proof and presumptions) and Chapter 4 (relevancy).

§ 103.1

1. See, e.g., People v. Russell, 71 N.Y.2d 1016, 530 N.Y.S.2d 101, 525 N.E.2d 747 (1988); Horton v. Smith, 51 N.Y.2d 798, 799, 433 N.Y.S.2d 92, 93, 412 N.E.2d 1318, 1319 (1980); People v. Dunn, 204 A.D.2d 919, 612 N.Y.S.2d 266 (3d Dep't), appeal denied, 84 N.Y.2d 907, 621 N.Y.S.2d 524, 645 N.E.2d 1224 (1994).

The proposed New York Evidence Code § 103 states only that "[e]rror may not be predicated upon a ruling admitting or excluding evidence unless a substantial right of a party is affected and the requirements of law regarding a protest or objection have been satisfied." The comment to this section expresses the decision not to replicate Rule 103 of the Federal Rules of Evidence (see § 103.2 infra) because "the Code is primarily directed to the trial process and given the unique appellate questions involved, it seems best to leave all issues involving preservation to existing statutes and the common law process."

may be considered by the fact-finder in its deliberations,[2] and generally no appeal may be predicated on the inadmissibility of the evidence in question.[3] The relevant statutes are CPLR 4017,[4] CPLR 5501(a)(3),[5] and New York Criminal Procedure Law § 470.05(2).[6] The only thing that will save the delinquent objector's potential appeal is a discretionary determination that relief is appropriate in the "interest of justice."[7]

2. See, e.g., In re Estate of Findlay, 253 N.Y. 1, 11, 170 N.E. 471, 474 (1930); Ford v. Snook, 205 App.Div. 194, 198, 199 N.Y.S. 630, 634 (4th Dep't 1923), aff'd, 240 N.Y. 624, 148 N.E. 732 (1925).

3. See, e.g., People v. Bowen, 50 N.Y.2d 915, 431 N.Y.S.2d 449, 409 N.E.2d 924 (1980); Mashley v. Kerr, 47 N.Y.2d 892, 419 N.Y.S.2d 476, 393 N.E.2d 471 (1979).

4. CPLR 4017 states as follows:

Formal exceptions to rulings of the court are unnecessary. At the time a ruling or order of the court is requested or made a party shall make known the action which he requests the court to take or, if he has not already indicated it, his objection to the action of the court. Failure to so make known objections, as prescribed in this section or in section 4110-b, may restrict review upon appeal in accordance with paragraphs three and four of subdivision (a) of section 5501.

The last sentence of the rule contains the critical language on waiver. CPLR 4110–b, to which reference is made, contains an analogous waiver rule that requires the making of objections to a judge's jury instructions before the jury begins its deliberations.

5. CPLR 5501(a)(3) states as follows: "An appeal from a final judgment brings up for review: * * * 3. any ruling to which the appellant objected or had no opportunity to object or which was a refusal or failure to act as requested by the appellant, and any charge to the jury, or failure or refusal to charge as requested by the appellant, to which he objected."

6. N.Y.Crim.Proc.Law § 470.05(2) provides:

2. For purposes of appeal, a question of law with respect to a ruling or instruction of a criminal court during a trial or proceeding is presented when a protest thereto was registered, by the party claiming error, at the time of such ruling or instruction or at any subsequent time when the court had an opportunity of effectively changing the same. Such protest need not be in the form of an "exception" but is sufficient if the party made his position with respect to the ruling or instruction known to the court, or if in reponse [sic] to a protest by a party, the court expressly decided the question raised on appeal. In addition, a party who without success has either expressly or impliedly sought or requested a particular ruling or instruction, is deemed to have thereby protested the court's ultimate disposition of the matter or failure to rule or instruct accordingly sufficiently to raise a question of law with respect to such disposition or failure regardless of whether any actual protest thereto was registered.

Only "jurisdictional" or "fundamental" errors are preserved in the absence of an objection. See, e.g., People v. Banks, 53 N.Y.2d 819, 439 N.Y.S.2d 916, 422 N.E.2d 576 (1981)(deprivation of right to counsel). See generally Preiser, Practice Commentaries, McKinney's N.Y.Crim.Proc.Law § 470.05.

7. In criminal cases, N.Y.Crim.Proc.Law § 470.15(3)(c) provides that the Appellate Division may act "[a]s a matter of discretion in the interest of justice." The statute goes on to state:

6. The kinds of determinations of reversal or modification deemed to be made as a matter of discretion in the interest of justice include, but are not limited to, the following:

(a) That an error or defect occurring at a trial resulting in a judgment, which error or defect was not duly protested at trial as prescribed in subdivision two of section 470.05 so as to present a question of law, deprived the defendant of a fair trial;

In criminal cases, "jurisdictional" or "fundamental" errors may also be considered on appeal. See note 6 supra.

CPLR 5501(a)(see note 5 supra) contains no "interest of justice" language, but the concept may also be applicable (although rarely invoked as to evidentiary issues) in civil actions. Cf. Martin v. City of Cohoes, 37 N.Y.2d 162, 165, 371 N.Y.S.2d 687, 689, 332 N.E.2d 867, 869 (1975), appeal denied, 39 N.Y.2d 705, 384 N.Y.S.2d 1027, 349 N.E.2d 882 (1976)(notice-of-claim defense to municipal liability); Graham v. Murphy, 135 A.D.2d 326, 329–30, 525 N.Y.S.2d 414, 417 (3d Dep't 1988)(excessive damages); Tompkins v. R.B.D. Land Exchange, Inc., 89 A.D.2d 698, 453 N.Y.S.2d 817 (3d Dep't

Although a timely objection is necessary to preserve error for appeal, by statute no "exception" need be taken to a court's unfavorable ruling.[8] The ability to appeal the evidentiary issue will be preserved so long as the aggrieved party's objection to the action of the court has been made clear in a timely manner.

When the objectionable evidence is part of a series of questions and ongoing testimony, a timely objection, once raised, will serve as "a continuing objection * * * [that will make] it unnecessary to challenge other improper evidence of the same sort adduced from that witness."[9] Another protective principle is that no waiver occurs when a party whose timely objection has been overruled thereafter introduces rebuttal evidence to counter the improperly admitted evidence.[10]

With respect to the timeliness issue, to be effective an objection must be made as soon as the opponent either asks a question that apparently calls for improper testimony or introduces an improper exhibit.[11] In fairness, of course, exceptions are recognized where the witness answers before the objection reasonably can be interposed,[12] where the question is proper but the response is objectionable,[13] or where the objectionable nature of the evidence does not become apparent until a later point in the trial.[14] The remedy in these situations is a timely motion to strike, with a request that the court instruct the jury to disregard the offending evidence.[15] If the evidence is only partially improper, the motion to strike, to be effective, should be specifically directed to the improper portion.[16]

1982)("fundamental error" in jury instructions).

8. CPLR 4017 (note 4 supra); N.Y.Crim.Proc.Law § 470.05(2)(note 6 supra).

9. Kulak v. Nationwide Mutual Ins. Co., 40 N.Y.2d 140, 145, 386 N.Y.S.2d 87, 90, 351 N.E.2d 735, 738 (1976)(objection at outset of expert's testimony that the matter was not proper subject for expert opinion).

10. Manse v. Hossington, 205 N.Y. 33, 38, 98 N.E. 203, 205 (1912). But see People v. Workman, 283 App.Div. 1066, 131 N.Y.S.2d 100 (2d Dep't), aff'd, 308 N.Y. 668, 124 N.E.2d 314 (1954)(even if prosecution's use of chart was improper, defendant waived objection by thereafter using same chart in his own case).

11. Quin v. Lloyd, 41 N.Y. 349, 355 (1869)("A party against whom a witness is called and examined cannot lie by and speculate on the chances, first learn what the witness testifies, and then when he finds the testimony unsatisfactory, object either to the competency of the witness or to the form or substance of the testimony.") See also People v. Maschi, 49 N.Y.2d 784, 426 N.Y.S.2d 727, 403 N.E.2d 449 (1980)(objection to 20th question in series of questions on same matter was too late).

12. See Wightman v. Campbell, 217 N.Y. 479, 482, 112 N.E. 184, 185 (1916).

13. Simpson v. Foundation Co., 201 N.Y. 479, 490, 95 N.E. 10, 14–15 (1911); Platner v. Platner, 78 N.Y. 90, 102 (1879); Kramer v. Haeger Storage Warehouse Co., 123 App.Div. 316, 321, 108 N.Y.S. 1, 5 (1st Dep't 1908).

14. See, e.g., Quin v. Lloyd, 41 N.Y. 349, 355 (1869)(motion to strike may lie where impropriety of evidence does not become apparent until cross-examination or at some later stage of trial); Lopato v. Kinney Rent–A–Car, Inc., 73 A.D.2d 565, 423 N.Y.S.2d 42 (1st Dep't 1979) (insufficient basis for expert's opinion did not become apparent until cross-examination). See also text at notes 34–36 infra.

15. See cases cited in notes 12–14 supra. See also Jarvis v. Metropolitan St. Ry. Co., 65 App.Div. 490, 72 N.Y.S. 829 (2d Dep't 1901).

16. See, e.g., Fein v. Weir, 129 App.Div. 299, 310–11, 114 N.Y.S. 426, 434–35 (1st Dep't 1908), aff'd, 199 N.Y. 540, 92 N.E. 1084 (1909).

b. General vs. Specific Objections

Objections may be general, such as "I object: inadmissible" or "Objection: the evidence is incompetent, irrelevant and immaterial."[17] Alternatively, objections may be specific, such as "Objection: hearsay." Counsel must be alert to the effect that the generality or specificity of objections at the trial court level can have on a later appeal.

On appeal, a general objection will stand the objector in good stead only if the trial court sustained the objection. "When evidence is *excluded* upon a mere general objection, the ruling will be upheld, if any ground in fact existed for the exclusion. It will be assumed, in the absence of any request by the opposing party or the court to make the objection definite, that it was understood, and that the ruling was placed upon the right ground."[18]

Conversely, if a general objection is overruled, the objector cannot complain on appeal that the evidence should have been excluded on some specific ground that might be valid.[19] The theory is that the trial judge and adversary were entitled to know what the specific ground of objection was so that steps might have been taken to obviate any defects before it was too late.[20] An exception to this rule might save the objector. Appellate relief with respect to the alleged error may be had if the evidence was not admissible on any ground whatsoever.[21]

If a specific objection is made and sustained, the risk for the objector in the event of an appeal is that the appellate court will adjudge the propriety of the trial court's ruling only in relation to the precise ground for exclusion that was articulated below. If that ground was invalid, the objector will lose on appeal even if some other proper but unarticulated ground for exclusion existed.[22] The rationale is that the proponent of

---

17. Superficially, the objection of "incompetent, irrelevant and immaterial" has an aura of specificity to it. "Incompetent," however, simply means inadmissible (see § 601.1, at note 1, infra), and "irrelevant and immaterial" merely means that the evidence has no bearing on the disputed issues (see Chapter 4 infra). Thus, the "three i's" constitute a general objection except where counsel is in fact challenging the relevancy of the evidence. See, e.g., M. Groh's Sons v. Groh, 177 N.Y. 8, 14, 68 N.E. 992, 994 (1903). See generally McCormick § 52, at 206.

18. Tooley v. Bacon, 70 N.Y. 34, 37 (1877)(emphasis in original). See also Bloodgood v. Lynch, 293 N.Y. 308, 312, 56 N.E.2d 718, 719 (1944).

19. See, e.g., People v. Tevaha, 84 N.Y.2d 879, 620 N.Y.S.2d 786, 644 N.E.2d 1342 (1994); Gonzalez v. New York State Liquor Auth., 30 N.Y.2d 108, 112–13, 331 N.Y.S.2d 6, 8–9, 282 N.E.2d 101, 102–03 (1972); Wightman v. Campbell, 217 N.Y. 479, 482–83, 112 N.E. 184, 185 (1916).

20. See People v. Vidal, 26 N.Y.2d 249, 254, 309 N.Y.S.2d 336, 340, 257 N.E.2d 886, 889–90 (1970). See generally Lilly § 11.3, at 474.

21. People v. Vidal, 26 N.Y.2d 249, 254, 309 N.Y.S.2d 336, 340, 257 N.E.2d 886, 889 (1970)("[I]f the proffered evidence is inherently incompetent, that is, there appears, without more, no purpose whatever for which it could have been admissible, then a general objection, though overruled, will be deemed to be sufficient").

22. Bloodgood v. Lynch, 293 N.Y. 308, 312–13, 56 N.E.2d 718, 719–20 (1944).

§ 103.1　　　GENERAL PRINCIPLES　　　Ch. 1

the evidence might have been able to obviate the defect had she been alerted at trial to the proper ground of objection.[23] Similarly, if a specific objection is overruled, the appellate court will consider only the ground that was articulated in the trial court. There will be an affirmance if the particular ground was invalid even if there might have been some other meritorious basis for exclusion.[24]

The upshot of the foregoing appellate rules is that an objector may be well advised to make a general objection in the first instance. If the objection is overruled, the objector should immediately follow up with a specific objection.[25] If the general objection is sustained, the opponent, for her part, should request that a specific ground be stated.[26] If the excluded evidence is important to the opponent's case, she should also make an offer of proof, which is the subject of the next subdivision.

Library References:

West's Key No. Digests, Criminal Law ⇔695; Trial ⇔80.

c. Offer of Proof and Offer "to Connect Up"

As discussed above, a party aggrieved by the admission of evidence must make a timely objection, or motion to strike, in order to effectively preserve error for appeal. As to a party aggrieved by the exclusion of evidence, the making of an offer of proof is necessary to preserve the point for appeal.[27] An offer of proof is an explanation to the court, outside the presence of the jury,[28] of the substance and relevance of the excluded evidence.[29] From the offer of proof, the appellate court will be able to ascertain the significance of the excluded evidence and whether the exclusion was error.[30] An offer of proof also gives the trial judge an opportunity to reconsider the ruling.[31] Offers of proof, to be effective,

---

23. Id. See also People v. Mullins, 179 A.D.2d 48, 52–53, 582 N.Y.S.2d 810, 813 (3d Dep't 1992)(where prosecutor was able to exclude defendant's evidence at trial on basis of ground A, which was improper, he could not argue on appeal that exclusion was proper on basis of ground B, because B "could have been remedied if timely interposed"). See generally Lilly § 11.3, at 475–76.

24. People v. Regina, 19 N.Y.2d 65, 75, 277 N.Y.S.2d 683, 690, 224 N.E.2d 108, 113 (1966). See also People v. Qualls, 55 N.Y.2d 733, 447 N.Y.S.2d 149, 431 N.E.2d 634 (1981)(objection at trial that testimony constituted improper bolstering was insufficient to preserve appeal on hearsay and confrontation grounds); People v. Woods, 202 A.D.2d 1043, 610 N.Y.S.2d 108 (4th Dep't 1994)(hearsay objection was insufficient to preserve defendant's argument that his sixth amendment right of confrontation was violated).

25. See People v. Vidal, 26 N.Y.2d 249, 254, 309 N.Y.S.2d 336, 340, 257 N.E.2d 886, 889 (1970); Gonzalez v. New York State Liquor Auth., 30 N.Y.2d 108, 112–13, 331 N.Y.S.2d 6, 8, 282 N.E.2d 101, 102–03 (1972).

26. See generally D. Siegel, New York Practice § 396, at 596 (2d ed.1991).

27. People v. Williams, 6 N.Y.2d 18, 23, 187 N.Y.S.2d 750, 754, 159 N.E.2d 549, 552 (1959), cert. denied, 361 U.S. 920, 80 S.Ct. 266, 4 L.Ed.2d 188 (1959); People v. Billups, 132 A.D.2d 612, 613, 518 N.Y.S.2d 9, 11 (2d Dep't), appeal denied, 70 N.Y.2d 873, 523 N.Y.S.2d 500, 518 N.E.2d 11 (1987).

28. See Schabel v. Onseyga Realty Co., 233 App.Div. 208, 213–14, 251 N.Y.S. 280, 287 (4th Dep't 1931).

29. See People v. Mason, 186 A.D.2d 984, 590 N.Y.S.2d 811 (4th Dep't 1992)(defendant failed to make offer of proof showing "the relevancy of the testimony and what he intended to prove by its introduction").

30. McCormick § 51, at 196.

31. Id. § 51, at 195–96.

must be "clear and unambiguous."[32]

No reported cases in New York appear to have explicitly applied the exception recognized in Rule 103(a)(2) of the Federal Rules of Evidence that the failure to make an offer of proof may be excused if "the substance of the evidence * * * was apparent from the context within which questions were asked."[33]

Another potential remedy for the party whose attempted introduction of evidence has met with opposition is to offer the evidence "subject to connection."[34] The argument to be made is that even if the relevance of the evidence is not apparent, or the foundation is not complete, it will be made so upon the introduction of additional evidence in the due course of the trial.[35] If the judge admits the evidence at this point, she is doing so on the condition that the evidence later will in fact be connected up. The burden then lies on the opponent to make a motion to strike, accompanied by a request for appropriate jury instructions, if and when it becomes clear that the promised connection will not materialize.[36]

Library References:

West's Key No. Digests, Criminal Law ⚖670; Trial ⚖44.

d. Motions *in Limine*

Most rulings regarding the admissibility of evidence are made during the course of trial. In recent years, however, the motion *in limine* (from the Latin, meaning "at the threshold") has become an increasingly prevalent procedural mechanism for resolving some evidentiary issues prior to trial. Of course, not all issues of evidence lend themselves to such pretrial resolution. Routine questions of relevance, prejudice, cumulativeness, hearsay and impeachment often can be effectively resolved only in the context in which they arise at trial.

Nevertheless, New York courts have long entertained motions *in limine* in criminal cases on certain matters. Pretrial motions for the suppression of illegally obtained evidence, for example, are regulated by

---

32. People v. Williams, 6 N.Y.2d 18, 23, 187 N.Y.S.2d 750, 754, 159 N.E.2d 549, 552, cert. denied, 361 U.S. 920, 80 S.Ct. 266, 4 L.Ed.2d 188 (1959). The court stated as follows:

It is a cardinal and well-settled principle that offers of proof must be made clearly and unambiguously. "Before a party excepts on account of the rejection of evidence, he should make the offer in such plain and unequivocal terms as to leave no room for debate about what was intended. If he fail to do so, and leave the offer fairly open to two constructions, he has no right to insist, in a court of review, upon that construction which is most favorable to himself, *unless it appears that it was so understood by the court which rejected the evidence.*"

Id. (quoting Daniels v. Patterson, 3 N.Y. 47, 51 (1849))(emphasis added by court).

33. See § 103.2(a) infra.

34. See D. Siegel, N.Y. Practice § 396, at 596 (2d ed.1991).

35. Marks v. King, 64 N.Y. 628, 629 (1876)(admitting evidence subject to connection goes to order of proof, which lies in court's discretion). See also Platner v. Platner, 78 N.Y. 90, 98, 99–100 (1879).

36. United States Vinegar Co. v. Schlegel, 143 N.Y. 537, 544, 38 N.E. 729, 731 (1894); Jarvis v. Metropolitan St. Ry. Co., 65 App.Div. 490, 491–92, 72 N.Y.S. 829, 830–31 (2d Dep't 1901); Village of Croton-on-Hudson v. State of New York, 48 Misc.2d 1092, 1094, 266 N.Y.S.2d 567, 570 (Ct.Cl.1966).

§ 103.1   GENERAL PRINCIPLES   Ch. 1

statute.[37] The Court of Appeals has also created pretrial motions for the resolution of such issues as the admissibility of uncharged crimes used as circumstantial evidence of the defendant's guilt;[38] the admissibility of prior bad acts and convictions for the purpose of impeaching the defendant should she elect to testify at trial;[39] the admissibility of novel scientific evidence;[40] and the scope of permissible testimony of a witness who has been hypnotized.[41]

In civil cases there are no statutory provisions or Court of Appeals decisions explicitly authorizing pretrial rulings on evidentiary issues. The lower courts, however, appear to have assumed the existence of an inherent authority[42] to entertain *in limine* motions to decide such questions as whether a witness was incompetent to testify under the "Dead Man's Statute;"[43] whether certain portions of medical records qualified for admission under the hearsay exception for business records;[44] whether a witness who had been hypnotized could testify to her post-hypnotic recollections;[45] whether expert testimony would be permitted concerning the rape trauma syndrome;[46] and whether expert testimony concerning medical malpractice should be precluded due to the proponent's failure to give timely notice of intent to introduce such testimony.[47]

Objections to the results of *in limine* motions should be renewed at trial to insure preservation of the issue for appellate review.[48]

Library References:

West's Key No. Digests, Criminal Law ⟶632(4); Pretrial Procedure ⟶3.

37. N.Y.Crim.Proc.Law Article 710.

38. People v. Ventimiglia, 52 N.Y.2d 350, 438 N.Y.S.2d 261, 420 N.E.2d 59 (1981).

39. People v. Sandoval, 34 N.Y.2d 371, 357 N.Y.S.2d 849, 314 N.E.2d 413 (1974). Unlike federal practice (see § 103.2, at note 23, infra, and § 609.2 infra), a defendant in New York need not actually testify at trial in order to preserve error on a pretrial ruling regarding such impeachment. See, e.g., People v. Mattiace, 77 N.Y.2d 269, 567 N.Y.S.2d 384, 568 N.E.2d 1189 (1990).

40. People v. Wesley, 83 N.Y.2d 417, 611 N.Y.S.2d 97, 633 N.E.2d 451 (1994).

41. People v. Tunstall, 63 N.Y.2d 1, 479 N.Y.S.2d 192, 468 N.E.2d 30 (1984).

42. Although the court in Belmar v. City of Syracuse, 100 A.D.2d 745, 473 N.Y.S.2d 624 (4th Dep't 1984), stated that trial courts in civil cases may not properly rule on evidentiary questions prior to trial, the same court has subsequently passed upon the merits of in limine motions without comment. See cases cited in notes 44 and 45 infra.

43. Endervelt v. Slade, 214 A.D.2d 456, 625 N.Y.S.2d 210 (1st Dep't 1995).

44. Passino v. DeRosa, 199 A.D.2d 1017, 606 N.Y.S.2d 107 (4th Dep't 1993).

45. Bennett v. Saeger Hotels, Inc., 209 A.D.2d 946, 619 N.Y.S.2d 424 (4th Dep't 1994).

46. Gutierrez v. Iulo, 156 Misc.2d 79, 591 N.Y.S.2d 711 (Sup.Ct.N.Y.Co.1992).

47. Bauernfeind v. Albany Medical Center, 195 A.D.2d 819, 600 N.Y.S.2d 516 (3d Dep't), leave to appeal dismissed, 82 N.Y.2d 885, 610 N.Y.S.2d 140, 632 N.E.2d 450 (1993).

48. There is very little New York authority on the preservation question. See, e.g., People v. Zayas, 202 A.D.2d 324, 609 N.Y.S.2d 9 (1st Dep't), appeal denied, 83 N.Y.2d 973, 616 N.Y.S.2d 26, 639 N.E.2d 766 (1994)("Defendant's *in limine* application to the trial court did not outline any specific proposed questioning of the complainant based upon the witness' employment records, and thus defendant did not preserve by appropriate record his current claim that the trial court improperly restricted his cross-examination of the complainant.").

The approach taken by federal courts is described in § 103.2, at notes 24–25, infra.

e. Harmless Error

A judge's erroneous ruling on a question of evidence, even if the point was properly preserved for appeal, will not necessarily result in reversal. The Court of Appeals recently summarized New York law on the harmless error doctrine in the context of criminal cases as follows:

> [Criminal Procedure Law] 470.05(1) directs us to "determine an appeal without regard to technical errors or defects which do not affect the substantial rights of the parties." Further, there exists a large body of case law establishing the standards to be used in determining whether a particular legal error requires reversal in light of the evidence and issues presented in an individual case. How demanding these standards are depends, at least in part, upon whether the error in question is of constitutional magnitude. As a general matter, the standard for nonconstitutional error, which is governed solely by State law, requires reversal if the properly admitted evidence was not "overwhelming" *and* there is a "significant probability * * * that the jury would have acquitted the defendant had it not been for the error or errors which occurred." * * * Constitutional error, in contrast, must lead to reversal unless there is no reasonable possibility that the error might have contributed to the conviction. * * * Even this highly exacting harmless-error standard, however, does not demand that guilt be proven "indisputably" * * *.[49]

In civil cases, CPLR 2002 states that "[a]n error in a ruling of the court shall be disregarded if a substantial right of a party is not prejudiced." With respect to evidentiary errors, it has been suggested that reversal is appropriate only if the error probably had a "substantial influence" on the outcome.[50]

Library References:

West's Key No. Digests, Appeal and Error ⚖1047–1059; Criminal Law ⚖1168–1170.

§ 103.2 Federal

a. Objections and Motions to Strike

Rule 103 of the Federal Rules of Evidence sets forth a comprehensive scheme governing rulings on evidence:

---

49. People v. Ayala, 75 N.Y.2d 422, 431, 554 N.Y.S.2d 412, 416, 553 N.E.2d 960 (1990), cert. denied, ___ U.S. ___, 115 S.Ct. 232, 130 L.Ed.2d 156 (1994)(citations omitted)(emphasis in original). See generally Preiser, Practice Commentaries, McKinney's N.Y.Crim.Proc.Law § 470.05.

50. McLaughlin, Practice Commentaries, McKinney's Civil Practice Law and Rules § 2002, at 450. Compare Barbagallo v. Americana Corp., 25 N.Y.2d 655, 306 N.Y.S.2d 466, 254 N.E.2d 768 (1969)(reversal ordered where court could not conclude as matter of law that jury would not have been influenced by evidence that was improperly excluded), and Badr v. Hogan, 75 N.Y.2d 629, 637, 555 N.Y.S.2d 249, 253, 554 N.E.2d 890, 894 (1990)(in light of emphasis given to improperly admitted evidence in connection with critical issue, error was "sufficiently prejudicial" to warrant new trial), with Fishman v. Scheuer, 39 N.Y.2d 502, 384 N.Y.S.2d 716, 349 N.E.2d 815 (1976)(no reversal where improperly admitted evidence was of "quibbling nature").

(a) Effect of erroneous ruling. Error may not be predicated upon a ruling which admits or excludes evidence unless a substantial right of the party is affected, and

(1) Objection. In case the ruling is one admitting evidence, a timely objection or motion to strike appears of record, stating the specific ground of objection, if the specific ground was not apparent from the context; or

(2) Offer of proof. In case the ruling is one excluding evidence, the substance of the evidence was made known to the court by offer or was apparent from the context within which questions were asked.

(b) Record of offer and ruling. The court may add any other or further statement which shows the character of the evidence, the form in which it was offered, the objection made, and the ruling thereon. It may direct the making of an offer in question and answer form.

(c) Hearing of jury. In jury cases, proceedings shall be conducted, to the extent practicable, so as to prevent inadmissible evidence from being suggested to the jury by any means, such as making statements or offers of proof or asking questions in the hearing of the jury.

(d) Plain error. Nothing in this rule precludes taking notice of plain errors affecting substantial rights although they were not brought to the attention of the court.

Federal Rule 103(a)(1), like New York law, requires that objections and motions to strike be timely interposed in order to avoid waiver or forfeiture of evidentiary issues and to insure preservation of error for appeal. Formal exceptions to the court's ruling, however, are not required so long as the party has made known to the court the action sought.[1] In general, Rule 103(a) is strictly applied in the Second Circuit.[2] Only the "plain error" doctrine[3] will save a party from the failure to timely register proper objections to the admission or exclusion of evidence.[4]

§ 103.2

1. Fed.R.Civ.P. 46; Fed.R.Crim.Proc. 51.

2. United States v. Hutcher, 622 F.2d 1083, 1087 (2d Cir.), cert. denied, 449 U.S. 875, 101 S.Ct. 218, 66 L.Ed.2d 96 (1980). See, e.g., United States v. Weiss, 930 F.2d 185, 198–99 (2d Cir.), cert. denied, 502 U.S. 842, 112 S.Ct. 133, 116 L.Ed.2d 100 (1991)(by withdrawing objection at trial, counsel waived right of appeal).

3. Fed.R.Evid. 103(d). See also Fed. R.Crim.P. 52(b).

4. See, e.g., Hutchinson v. Groskin, 927 F.2d 722, 725 (2d Cir.1991)(even if counsel's objection was untimely, trial court's failure to exclude expert testimony based on improper hearsay was plain error); United States v. Check, 582 F.2d 668, 676–78 (2d Cir.1978)(despite nonspecific objection, trial court's admission of hearsay was plain error). See generally United States v. Yu-Leung, 51 F.3d 1116, 1121 (2d Cir.1995)(quoting United States v. Viola, 35 F.3d 37, 41 (2d Cir.1994), cert. denied, ___ U.S. ___, 115 S.Ct. 1270, 131 L.Ed.2d 148 (1995))(in criminal cases, application of plain error exception requires three-part showing: "First, there must be 'error,' or deviation from a legal rule which has not been waived [i.e., intentionally relinquished]. Second, the error must be 'plain,' which at a minimum means 'clear under current law.' Third, the plain error must * * * 'affect[] substantial rights,'

As to timeliness, the Second Circuit generally enforces the rule that an objection must be made before the witness answers.[5] "[T]his rule is not inflexible," however;[6] the test is whether the objection or motion to strike is "made as soon as the ground of it is known, or reasonably should have been known to the objector."[7] Furthermore, in a pre-Rules decision, the court held that an objection once made need not be repeated throughout the course of a witness' testimony if the evidence concerns the same line of inquiry to which the objection was directed and court and counsel have made their positions clear.[8]

Library References:

West's Key No. Digests, Criminal Law ⚖ 690–698; Federal Civil Procedure ⚖ 2017.

b. General vs. Specific Objections

Federal Rule 103(a)(1) has virtually abolished the utility of general objections in federal practice. The rule requires that, in order to preserve error, the "specific ground of objection" must be stated unless such specific ground "was * * * apparent from the context." If a general objection is overruled, no ground for appeal will lie except possibly that of total irrelevancy.[9] The opponent and trial judge are entitled to be apprised of the particular ground of objection so that potential curative steps can be taken and evaluated at the trial court level.[10] On the other hand, the context at trial may make the ground of an otherwise general objection apparent and therefore save the point for appeal.[11]

Assuming the objection is specific, it preserves only the ground named. If the objection is overruled on that ground (e.g., relevance outweighed by prejudice), the objector may not be heard to complain on appeal that the evidence should have been excluded on some other ground that was not articulated at trial (e.g., improper impeachment by

which normally requires a showing of prejudice.")(citations omitted).

5. See, e.g., United States v. Armedo–Sarmiento, 545 F.2d 785, 795 (2d Cir.1976), cert. denied, 430 U.S. 917, 97 S.Ct. 1330, 51 L.Ed.2d 595 (1977). With respect to real evidence, the objection must be made when the item is offered, not after it has been admitted. See United States v. Gomez, 921 F.2d 378, 385 (1st Cir.1990).

6. Hutchinson v. Groskin, 927 F.2d 722, 725 (2d Cir.1991).

7. United States v. Check, 582 F.2d 668, 676 (2d Cir.1978)(quoting 21 C. Wright and K. Graham, Federal Practice and Procedure: Evidence § 5037, at 188 (1977)).

8. Keen v. Overseas Tankship Corp., 194 F.2d 515, 519 (2d Cir.), cert. denied, 343 U.S. 966, 72 S.Ct. 1061, 96 L.Ed. 1363 (1952). See also United States v. Gomez–Norena, 908 F.2d 497, 500 n.1 (9th Cir.), cert. denied, 498 U.S. 947, 111 S.Ct. 363, 112 L.Ed.2d 326 (1990).

9. United States v. Rubin, 609 F.2d 51, 62–63 (2d Cir.1979), aff'd, 449 U.S. 424, 101 S.Ct. 698, 66 L.Ed.2d 633 (1981); United States v. Klein, 488 F.2d 481, 482 (2d Cir. 1973), cert. denied, 419 U.S. 1091, 95 S.Ct. 683, 42 L.Ed.2d 684 (1974).

10. United States v. Klein, 488 F.2d 481, 482–83 (2d Cir.1973), cert. denied, 419 U.S. 1091, 95 S.Ct. 683, 42 L.Ed.2d 684 (1974). See also United States v. Benitez, 920 F.2d 1080, 1088 (2d Cir.1990); United States v. Mangan, 575 F.2d 32, 44 (2d Cir.), cert. denied, 439 U.S. 931, 99 S.Ct. 320, 58 L.Ed.2d 324 (1978).

11. See, e.g., United States v. Musacchia, 900 F.2d 493, 497 (2d Cir.1990), cert. denied, 501 U.S. 1250, 111 S.Ct. 2887, 115 L.Ed.2d 1052 (1991), vacated in part on other grounds, 955 F.2d 3 (2d Cir.1991).

§ 103.2   GENERAL PRINCIPLES   Ch. 1

inquiry into prior bad acts).[12] Furthermore, even if an objection on a specific ground might have been erroneously overruled (e.g., insufficient foundation for the coconspirator hearsay exception), the ruling may be affirmed on appeal if some other valid ground supported admission of the evidence (e.g., satisfaction of the requirements for the declaration against interest hearsay exception).[13]

When evidence is excluded over a protest that admissibility was proper on some specified ground (e.g., residual hearsay exception), the protestor may not be heard to complain on appeal that some other ground, not brought to the trial court's attention, supported admissibility (e.g., declaration against interest hearsay exception).[14] This rule is closely related to the offer-of-proof requirement, which is discussed in the next subdivision.

Library References:

> West's Key No. Digests, Criminal Law ⚛=695; Federal Civil Procedure ⚛=2017.

c. Offer of Proof and Offer to "Connect Up"

When evidence is excluded, Rule 103(a)(2) requires the proponent, in most instances, to make an offer of proof as to the substance of the evidence in order to preserve error for appeal.[15] Two exceptions may be applicable. The Rule itself excuses the proponent's failure to make an offer of proof if the substance of the excluded evidence was "apparent from the context."[16] A judge-made exception was applied by the Second

---

12. United States v. Mennuti, 679 F.2d 1032, 1036 (2d Cir.1982). See also United States v. Rubin, 609 F.2d 51, 61–63 (2d Cir.1979), aff'd, 449 U.S. 424, 101 S.Ct. 698, 66 L.Ed.2d 633 (1981)(objection to agent-witness' notes on ground that they were a paraphrase of what other person said rather than a verbatim quote was insufficient to preserve hearsay objection); United States v. Ruffin, 575 F.2d 346, 355 (2d Cir. 1978)(when ground of objection was that of irrelevancy, objector may not assert hearsay objection on appeal).

13. United States v. Cruz, 797 F.2d 90, 97 n.2 (2d Cir.1986).

14. United States v. Pugliese, 712 F.2d 1574, 1580–81 (2d Cir.1983) ("Unless the basis for proposed admission is obvious, it is the burden of counsel who seeks admission to alert the [trial] court to the legal basis for his proffer.").

15. See Fortunato v. Ford Motor Co., 464 F.2d 962, 967 (2d Cir.), cert. denied, 409 U.S. 1038, 93 S.Ct. 517, 34 L.Ed.2d 487 (1972)(content of excluded evidence must be made known to trial court; purposes of requirement are to enable reviewing court to determine if exclusion affected party's substantial rights and to permit trial judge to reconsider his ruling). See also § 103.1, at notes 28–32 supra.

16. See, e.g., United States v. Espinoza, 406 F.2d 733, 735 (2d Cir.1969)(offer of proof unnecessary where context of proposed cross-examination was sufficient to apprise court of relevancy). See also Massachusetts Mutual Life Ins. Co. v. Brei, 311 F.2d 463, 465 n.1 (2d Cir.1962). Compare Marrone v. United States, 355 F.2d 238, 240–41 (2d Cir.1966)(offer of proof required where significance of excluded evidence was not obvious); Shaw v. Scoville, 369 F.2d 909, 912 (2d Cir.1966) (purpose of evidence was not obvious).

The context is likely to make the purpose clear where substantial portions of the evidence have already been admitted, and the objection is belatedly raised by way of a motion to strike. See, e.g., United States v. Barash, 365 F.2d 395, 400–01 (2d Cir.1966), appeal after remand, 412 F.2d 26 (2d Cir.), cert. denied, 396 U.S. 832, 90 S.Ct. 86, 24 L.Ed.2d 82 (1969) (offer of proof excused where cross-examiner, after asking several impeaching questions, was told by district court, upon prosecutor's belated objection, to "cut it out").

Circuit where the proponent was effectively stymied by the trial court in his effort to develop a basis for the proposed evidence.[17]

When evidence that apparently is irrelevant or lacks a foundation faces possible exclusion, counsel's offer to "connect it up" at a later point in the trial is another potential response to an opponent's objection. The trial court has discretion to allow admission of the evidence conditionally upon counsel's representation that the necessary connection will be made.[18] If the connection is not made, the opponent must move to strike the evidence lest the original objection be waived.[19] The motion should be accompanied by a request that the jury be instructed to ignore the stricken evidence.[20]

Library References:

West's Key No. Digests, Criminal Law ⇌670; Federal Civil Procedure ⇌2013.

d. Motions *in Limine*

Motions *in limine*, seeking pretrial rulings on evidentiary issues that can be effectively determined outside the context of trial,[21] have become common in federal practice.[22] Two potential problems can arise in connection with such motions. First, in a criminal case, a pretrial ruling on the convictions that can be used for impeachment purposes if the defendant elects to testify cannot be reviewed on appeal unless the defendant actually takes the stand at trial.[23] Second, an unfavorable ruling on an *in limine* motion may not be preserved for appeal unless the aggrieved party raises the issue anew at trial. The Second Circuit, for

---

17. See United States v. Dennis, 843 F.2d 652, 655–56 (2d Cir.1988).

18. United States v. Kellerman, 431 F.2d 319, 323–24 (2d Cir.), cert. denied, 400 U.S. 957, 91 S.Ct. 356, 27 L.Ed.2d 266 (1970)("During the trial of every case, the proof has to be introduced step by step and through individual witnesses. It is often impossible to foresee the relevance of testimony or an exhibit—particularly in the early stages of the trial. Hence the necessity of receiving the testimony or exhibit 'subject to connection' * * *.").

19. See, e.g., United States v. Dougherty, 895 F.2d 399, 403–04 (7th Cir.1990).

20. United States v. Kellerman, 431 F.2d 319, 324 (2d Cir.), cert. denied, 400 U.S. 957, 91 S.Ct. 356, 27 L.Ed.2d 266 (1970)(court must assume that jury will follow instructions to disregard stricken evidence except in "extreme cases").

21. See generally § 103.1(d) supra.

22. See, e.g., United States v. Valencia, 826 F.2d 169, 171–72 (2d Cir.1987)(whether to entertain government's motion in limine to admit certain evidence at trial lies in court's discretion; despite absence of statutory authority for such motion, its availability has been tacitly approved by courts); In re Japanese Electronic Products Antitrust Litigation, 723 F.2d 238, 260 (3d Cir.1983), rev'd on other grounds, 475 U.S. 574, 106 S.Ct. 1348, 89 L.Ed.2d 538 (1986), on remand, 807 F.2d 44 (3d Cir.1986), cert. denied, 481 U.S. 1029, 107 S.Ct. 1955, 95 L.Ed.2d 527 (1987)(motion in limine is "a procedure which should, in a trial court's discretion, be used in appropriate cases"; in instant case, pretrial motion was more efficient than deferring rulings until trial and permitted more thorough briefing and argument of issues).

23. Luce v. United States, 469 U.S. 38, 105 S.Ct. 460, 83 L.Ed.2d 443 (1984)(appellate court cannot effectively review trial court's balancing of probative value and prejudice without reference to defendant's actual trial testimony). See § 609.2 infra. See also United States v. Weichert, 783 F.2d 23, 25 (2d Cir.), cert. denied, 479 U.S. 831, 107 S.Ct. 117, 93 L.Ed.2d 64 (1986)(appellate review precluded of in limine determination of proposed impeachment of defendant with prior bad acts (Fed.R.Evid. 608(b)) where defendant did not testify at trial).

example, has held that if the evidentiary issue is one which depends upon context, such as the balancing of relevance and prejudice, *in limine* objections must be raised again in the actual setting of the trial.[24] On the other hand, if the question is "not contextually bound," a motion *in limine* may preserve a question that "(1) is fairly presented to the district court, (2) is the type of issue that can be finally decided in a pretrial hearing, and (3) is ruled upon without equivocation by the trial judge."[25]

Library References:

West's Key No. Digests, Criminal Law ⚖632(4); Federal Civil Procedure ⚖2011.

e. Harmless Error

The harmless error doctrine is implicit in Rule 103(a) of the Federal Rules of Evidence and is explicitly codified in other provisions of federal law.[26] The Second Circuit has summarized the test for harmless error as follows:

> Erroneous evidentiary rulings alone do not lead to automatic reversal. We will reverse only where the improper admission or exclusion of evidence affects "a substantial right" of one of the parties. * * * Making this determination involves an "assessment of the likelihood that the error affected the outcome of the case." * * * "[I]f one cannot say, with fair assurance, * * * that the judgment was not substantially swayed by the error, it is impossible to conclude that substantial rights were not affected."[27]

The harmless error standard is less tolerant, however, where a criminal defendant's constitutional rights are at issue.[28]

Library References:

West's Key No. Digests, Criminal Law ⚖1168–1170; Federal Courts ⚖896–901.

---

24. United States v. Birbal, 62 F.3d 456, 465 (2d Cir.1995); United States v. Yu–Leung, 51 F.3d 1116, 1120 (2d Cir.1995).

25. United States v. Yu–Leung, 51 F.3d 1116, 1121 (2d Cir.1995)(quoting United States v. Mejia–Alarcon, 995 F.2d 982, 986 (10th Cir.), cert. denied, ___ U.S. ___, 114 S.Ct. 334, 126 L.Ed.2d 279 (1993)). See also Robinson v. Shapiro, 646 F.2d 734, 742 (2d Cir.1981)(court suggested, without deciding, that alleged error in pretrial ruling allowing evidence to be admitted at trial pursuant to residual hearsay exception was preserved for appeal).

26. 28 U.S.C.A. § 2111; Fed.R.Civ.P. 61; Fed.R.Crim.Proc. 52(a).

27. Phoenix Associates III v. Stone, 60 F.3d 95, 104–05 (2d Cir.1995) (aggregate of erroneous evidentiary rulings justified reversal). See also United States v. Harris, 733 F.2d 994, 1005 (2d Cir.1984)(court is less likely to find error harmless where defendant's sole means of defense is impaired).

28. Compare Chapman v. California, 386 U.S. 18, 87 S.Ct. 824, 17 L.Ed.2d 705, rehearing denied, 386 U.S. 987, 87 S.Ct. 1283, 18 L.Ed.2d 241 (1967)(federal constitutional error cannot be held harmless unless it is harmless "beyond a reasonable doubt"), with Kotteakos v. United States, 328 U.S. 750, 66 S.Ct. 1239, 90 L.Ed. 1557 (1946)(nonconstitutional error is not harmless unless appellate court can say with "fair assurance" that result was not affected).

104 Preliminary Rulings

§ 104.1 New York

a. Respective Responsibilities of Judge and Jury, In General

It is a familiar and long-standing principle that the trial judge decides questions of law and the jury decides questions of fact.[1] The admissibility of evidence, for example, falls within the judge's province, whereas the weight to be given such evidence, once admitted, is for the jury.[2] A trial judge decides such questions as whether evidence is relevant (or whether the probative value of such evidence would be outweighed by its unduly prejudicial effect),[3] whether a privilege based on a confidential communication applies,[4] whether a witness is competent,[5] whether impeachment techniques are proper,[6] whether an expert has adequate qualifications,[7] whether an out-of-court statement is hearsay and if so whether there is an exception,[8] whether a copy of a writing is admissible as secondary evidence under the best evidence rule,[9] and whether sufficient authentication has been established for the admission of physical evidence.[10] These examples are, of course, only illustrative and do not exhaust the admissibility questions detailed in the chapters ahead.

It is apparent from the examples given that some questions of admissibility are dependent on factual determinations. For instance, whether a husband-wife conversation can come into evidence over an objection based on privilege may turn on the question whether a third party was in the presence of the spouses when they spoke, thus destroying the required element of confidentiality. The court will decide this preliminary question of fact.[11] Similarly, a copy of a writing may be inadmissible over an objection based on the best evidence rule unless the proponent offers some legally recognized excuse for nonproduction of the original, such as its loss or good-faith destruction.[12] The judge will decide any factual questions relating to the proponent's excuse and allow the copy to be admitted if such excuse is proven to the court's satisfaction.[13] In short, the court decides the preliminary questions of fact upon which the admissibility of evidence turns.

---

§ 104.1

1. People v. Walker, 198 N.Y. 329, 334, 91 N.E. 806, 808 (1910).
2. See, e.g., Meiselman v. Crown Heights Hospital, 285 N.Y. 389, 398, 34 N.E.2d 367, 372 (1941)(judge decides whether witness is qualified to give expert opinion—a question of the competency of the witness and the admissibility of her testimony—but jury may take extent of expert's qualifications into account in deciding weight to give the testimony).
3. Chapter 4 infra.
4. Chapter 5 infra.
5. Chapter 6, at §§ 601.1–606.2, infra.
6. Chapter 6, at §§ 607.1–610.2, infra.
7. Chapter 7 infra.
8. Chapter 8 infra.
9. Chapter 10 infra.
10. Chapters 9 and 11 infra.
11. See § 503.3 infra.
12. See §§ 1004.1 and 1008.1 infra.
13. Schozer v. William Penn Life Ins. Co., 84 N.Y.2d 639, 644, 620 N.Y.S.2d 797, 799, 644 N.E.2d 1353, 1355 (1994).

§ 104.1   GENERAL PRINCIPLES   Ch. 1

One of the better explanations of the judge's role is found in *People v. Marks*,[14] where the prosecutor urged that the victim's statement identifying his assailant should be admitted under the excited utterance exception to the hearsay rule. Whether or not the utterance was spontaneous depends on one or more factors including the length of time between the startling event and the statement, and whether declarant had a motive and the opportunity to reflect and contrive. All these questions were held to be for the trial judge to decide, the court stating:

> This New York rule is not only well grounded in practice but is also sound in principle. The admissibility of evidence may depend upon complicated, collateral fact issues, which would be confusing in jury trials. If, in addition to the questions of fact which are directly involved, any number of collateral issues must be tried in order to determine the admissibility of evidence upon the principal issue, it would obstruct rather than facilitate the administration of justice.[15]

In the course of the discussion in *Marks*, cases were noted which involved the admissibility of a document,[16] whether declarant was a partner of the party so that the declarant's admission could also be used against the party,[17] and whether all the requirements for a dying declaration had been met.[18]

Ordinarily, the relevance of evidence, i.e., its tendency to increase the probabilities of the existence or nonexistence of a disputed issue of fact,[19] is a question exclusively for the trial judge.[20] The principle of "conditional relevancy," however, may give the jury a role to play.[21] An example often used by commentators is that of notice or warning to a particular person: under the applicable law the fact that notice was sent may be relevant only if the notice was received.[22] If the judge can conclude that the proponent has introduced sufficient evidence upon

---

14. 6 N.Y.2d 67, 188 N.Y.S.2d 465, 160 N.E.2d 26 (1959), cert. denied, 362 U.S. 912, 80 S.Ct. 662, 4 L.Ed.2d 620 (1960).

15. Id. at 75, 188 N.Y.S.2d at 471, 160 N.E.2d at 30. Consider the problem were the trial to stop at each point where evidence is offered so the jury could retire and deliberate upon its admissibility. A more recent case involving an excited utterance is People v. Torres, 175 A.D.2d 635, 636, 572 N.Y.S.2d 269, 270 (4th Dep't 1991)(question was whether details in prompt rape complaint could come in since the complaint also qualified as an excited utterance). See also People v. Acomb, 87 A.D.2d 1, 9, 450 N.Y.S.2d 632, 637 (4th Dep't 1982)("whether the utterance was made with the requisite spontaneity, is for the trial court to determine * * *.").

16. Roberge v. Winne, 144 N.Y. 709, 715, 39 N.E. 631, 633 (1895)("It is apparent, therefore, that before the paper offered could have been admitted the court had to decide a preliminary question of fact whether the plaintiff had such knowledge of the contents of the unsigned papers as to make it binding upon him as evidence * * *.").

17. Harris v. Wilson, 7 Wend. 57 (1832).

18. People v. Kraft, 36 N.Y.S. 1034, 1035, 91 Hun. 474, 475 (1st Dep't 1895), aff'd, 148 N.Y. 631, 43 N.E. 80 (1896)(whether the declarations were made in apprehension of death and after the declarant had lost all hope of recovery is to be determined by the judge). Another case involving a dying declaration is People v. Liccione, 63 A.D.2d 305, 316, 407 N.Y.S.2d 753, 759 (4th Dep't 1978)(court noted that there was no reason to have a pretrial hearing to deal with the admissibility of a dying declaration).

19. See § 401.1 infra.

20. People v. Feldman, 299 N.Y. 153, 169–70, 85 N.E.2d 913, 921 (1949).

21. McCormick § 53, at 215.

22. Id.; Mueller and Kirkpatrick § 1.13, at 56–57. See Advisory Committee's Note, Fed.R.Evid. 104(b).

which the jury rationally could base a finding of receipt, the matter should go to the jury for its determination as to whether the notice was actually received.[23] If the proponent seeks to introduce the pertinent evidence out of sequence, the court has discretion to admit it subject to the proponent's eventual "connecting up" of the linking evidence.[24]

Voice identification provides an example of the application of conditional relevancy principles in New York. In *People v. Lynes*,[25] the issue was whether the recipient of a telephone call could identify the caller by circumstantial evidence. The court said that admissibility of the telephone call depended upon "whether a sufficient foundation had been laid to permit a finding that the conversation was one with the party against whom it was offered. Putting the issue another way, in this case was the proof such that a jury could find that defendant was indeed the caller?"[26]

Unlike the practice under Rule 104 of the Federal Rules of Evidence,[27] New York has no uniform approach to the question of conditional relevancy. Each rule must be examined separately.[28] Subdivision (b)

---

23. Lilly § 2.6, at 40–42; McCormick § 53, at 215. See also § 104.2, at notes 1–7, infra. But see note 16 supra.

24. See § 103.1, at notes 34–36, supra. See also Lilly § 2.6, at 42–43; Mueller and Kirkpatrick § 1.13, at 56.

25. 49 N.Y.2d 286, 425 N.Y.S.2d 295, 401 N.E.2d 405 (1980).

26. Id. at 291, 425 N.Y.S.2d at 297, 401 N.E.2d at 407.

27. See § 104.2 infra.

28. Compare People v. McGee, 49 N.Y.2d 48, 60, 424 N.Y.S.2d 157, 163, 399 N.E.2d 1177, 1183 (1979)(implying that judge alone determines authenticity of tape recordings), with Schozer v. William Penn Life Ins. Co., 84 N.Y.2d 639, 645–46, 620 N.Y.S.2d 797, 800, 644 N.E.2d 1353, 1356 (accuracy of copy of original writing is determined preliminarily by trial judge as precondition to admissibility but weight and "final determination" are for jury). See § 900.1, at note 16, infra; § 1008.1, at note 4, infra.

The proposed New York Evidence Code, in § 104, draws upon various components of Federal Rule 104 (see § 104.2 infra), as well as some particularized rules under current New York law, to provide a detailed approach:

§ 104. Preliminary questions [PROPOSED]

(a) **Questions of relevance.** Preliminary questions as to the relevance of offered evidence shall be determined by the court. When the relevance of the offered evidence depends upon the fulfillment of a condition of fact, the court shall admit it after, or may admit it subject to, introduction of evidence sufficient to support a finding of the fulfillment of the condition.

(b) **Other preliminary questions.** This subdivision governs determination of preliminary questions other than those governed by subdivision (a) of this section.

(1) **Preliminary questions for the court.** Preliminary questions as to the admissibility of offered evidence, the qualifications of a person to be a witness, and the applicability of a privilege or an exception to a privilege shall be determined by the court. In a jury trial such preliminary questions shall not, except as otherwise provided by statute, be submitted to the jury for its determination. The jury shall not be informed of any factual determination made by the court in deciding preliminary questions.

(2) **Evidence in determining preliminary questions.**

(A) **General rule.** Except in accordance with section 710.60 of the criminal procedure law, in making its determination of a preliminary question under this subdivision, the court is not bound by the other provisions of this chapter other than the provisions with respect to privileges.

(B) **Admissions.** When the preliminary question concerns the admissibility of an authorized admission pursuant to paragraph three of subdivision (b) of section 803 of this chapter, the court may not consider the content of the statement being offered in determining

§ 104.1   GENERAL PRINCIPLES   Ch. 1

below describes some particular New York rules on the judge-jury allocation of fact-finding responsibility in frequently recurring situations.

b. Admissions; Confessions; Illegally Seized Evidence; Privileges

A hearsay exception provides that if an employee or agent makes an admission it is admissible against his employer or principal provided the agent was authorized to make such statements.[29] This is the so-called "speaking agent" rule in New York. A question for the court is whether the declarant had the requisite authority. In determining this question, the court may not use the agent's out-of-court statement.[30] A similar rule applies with regard to the admissibility of a coconspirator's state-

authority to speak or the existence of the employment or the agency.

(C) Co-conspirator's statements. When the preliminary question concerns the admissibility of a statement of a co-conspirator pursuant to paragraph four of subdivision (b) of section 803 of this chapter, the court may not consider the content of the statement being offered in determining the existence of the conspiracy or the participation of the declarant or the accused in the conspiracy.

(D) Privileges. When the preliminary question concerns the applicability of a privilege, other than the privilege against self-incrimination, or the applicability of an exception to such a privilege, other than the privilege against self-incrimination, and the court is unable to make the determination without disclosure of the communication or matter claimed to be privileged, the court may require the person from whom disclosure is sought or the person claiming the privilege, or both, to disclose the communication or matter claimed to be privileged out of the hearing of all persons except the person claiming the privilege and such other persons as the person claiming the privilege is willing to have present.

(3) Determining preliminary questions: burdens; order of proof.

(A) Burden of proof, findings of fact and conclusions of law. Except as otherwise provided by statute or the common law, the burden of showing that evidence is admissible or a witness is qualified shall be upon the party offering the evidence or calling the witness, but the burden of showing that a communication or matter is privileged shall be upon the person claiming the privilege. Unless a higher burden is required by statute or decisional law, the court's determination shall be based upon a preponderance of evidence. Whenever an inquiry is made or a hearing held, the court shall state on the record findings of fact and conclusions of law.

(B) Admission subject to connection. The court may admit offered evidence subject to later introduction of evidence sufficient to satisfy the burdens imposed by this paragraph but may do so with respect to a co-conspirator's statement offered by the prosecution in a criminal case under paragraph four of subdivision (b) of section 803 of this chapter only upon an offer of proof establishing the existence of the conspiracy, the defendant's participation in the conspiracy and that the offered statements were made during the course and in furtherance of the conspiracy.

(c) Hearing of jury. Hearings on preliminary questions shall be conducted out of the hearing or presence of the jury when required by statute, or in the interests of justice, or when an accused is a witness if the accused so requests.

(d) Testimony by accused. The accused in a criminal case does not become subject to cross-examination as to other issues in the case by testifying with respect to a preliminary question.

(e) Weight and credibility. This section does not limit the right of a party to introduce evidence relevant to weight or credibility before the trier of fact.

29. See § 802.2(f) infra.

30. Leary v. Albany Brewing Co., 77 App.Div. 6, 79 N.Y.S. 130 (4th Dep't 1902). The proposed New York Evidence Code, in § 104(b)(2)(B), codifies this rule. See note 28 supra. Note, however, that the agent may testify at trial to prove the authority.

ment, i.e., the statement is not admissible unless it was uttered in the context of an ongoing conspiracy.[31] The New York case law provides that the statement in issue may not be used by the court in determining the foundation question.[32]

The confessions and admissions of a criminal defendant provide an exception to the usual rule that preliminary fact questions are exclusively for the court. The voluntariness of a confession, if challenged, usually is determined by the judge in a pretrial hearing. If the confession is found admissible, the issue of voluntariness can be submitted to the trial jury all over again.[33] On the other hand, where the court determines in a closed suppression hearing that evidence was legally seized, no role is prescribed for the jury concerning the question of the legality of police procedures.[34]

Where the question is whether a statement or a conversation is protected by one of the privileges for confidential communications, the court may find it necessary to acquire evidence of the content of the communication. This can be accomplished in camera.[35]

Library References:

West's Key No. Digests, Criminal Law ⇐661–677; Trial ⇐32–39, 50.

Steuerwald v. Jackson, 123 App.Div. 569, 108 N.Y.S. 41 (2d Dep't 1908).

31. See § 802.2(g) infra.

32. See People v. Salko, 47 N.Y.2d 230, 238–40, 417 N.Y.S.2d 894, 899–900, 391 N.E.2d 976, 981–82 (1979). This rule is imported into the proposed New York Evidence Code as bearing on the consideration of preliminary matters. See Proposed New York Evidence Code § 104(b)(2)(C), note 28 supra.

33. See N.Y.Crim.Proc.Law § 710.70 (3). In People v. Marks, 6 N.Y.2d 67, 188 N.Y.S.2d 465, 160 N.E.2d 26 (1959), it was stated:

Submission to juries of the voluntariness of confessions by defendants in criminal cases is an exception to this general rule. The reason for making the exception is apparent. In such instances the confession or admission relates to the subject matter of the criminal action being tried, and the only collateral question is whether it was coerced by force or fear. That, in itself, has a bearing on the guilt or innocence of a defendant. An alleged confession or admission represents an endeavor to prove the charge at issue out of a defendant's mouth. It is advanced to prove recognition by the person charged with the crime that he himself did all or some of the things which constitute the crime charged. The voluntariness of such an admission or confession by a defendant is so intimately related to the merits of the controversy that it has become natural to submit to juries, along with the other issues on trial, whether defendants actually did say or write the damaging material which is ascribed to them. That is different from submitting to juries collateral issues of fact on which depend the admissibility of declarations by third parties.

Id. at 75–76, 188 N.Y.S.2d at 471, 160 N.E.2d at 30.

The rule and the governing procedure were established in People v. Huntley, 15 N.Y.2d 72, 255 N.Y.S.2d 838, 204 N.E.2d 179 (1965), which applied the ruling of the Supreme Court in Jackson v. Denno, 378 U.S. 368, 84 S.Ct. 1774, 12 L.Ed.2d 908 (1964). The issue of voluntariness need not go to the jury, however, if defendant does not offer some evidence challenging admissibility. People v. Cefaro, 23 N.Y.2d 283, 285–86, 296 N.Y.S.2d 345, 347–49, 244 N.E.2d 42, 44–45 (1968).

34. See N.Y.Crim.Proc.Law § 710.60(5).

35. See, e.g., Spectrum Systems International Corp. v. Chemical Bank, 78 N.Y.2d 371, 378, 575 N.Y.S.2d 809, 814, 581 N.E.2d 1055, 1060 (1991)(applicability of attorney-client privilege to documents; People v. Tissois, 72 N.Y.2d 75, 78, 531 N.Y.S.2d 228, 231, 526 N.E.2d 1086, 1089 (1988))(in sexual abuse case judge examined notes of interview with victims made by a social worker in order to determine whether they were privileged under CPLR 4508). The proposed New York Evidence Code, in

§ 104.2 Federal

In federal practice, Rule 104 of the Federal Rules of Evidence governs the division of labor between judge and jury on preliminary questions. Federal Rule 104 is as follows:

Rule 104. Preliminary Questions

(a) Questions of admissibility generally. Preliminary questions concerning the qualification of a person to be a witness, the existence of a privilege, or the admissibility of evidence shall be determined by the court, subject to the provisions of subdivision (b). In making its determination it is not bound by the rules of evidence except those with respect to privileges.

(b) Relevancy conditioned on fact. When the relevancy of evidence depends upon the fulfillment of a condition of fact, the court shall admit it upon, or subject to, the introduction of evidence sufficient to support a finding of the fulfillment of the condition.

(c) Hearing of jury. Hearings on the admissibility of confessions shall in all cases be conducted out of the hearing of the jury. Hearings on other preliminary matters shall be so conducted when the interests of justice require, or when an accused is a witness and so requests.

(d) Testimony by accused. The accused does not, by testifying upon a preliminary matter, become subject to cross-examination as to other issues in the case.

(e) Weight and credibility. This rule does not limit the right of a party to introduce before the jury evidence relevant to weight or credibility.

Subdivision (a) makes the judge the sole arbiter of factual questions upon which admissibility depends, such as whether a declaration is one against interest as required for that hearsay exception. Subdivision (b) governs matters of conditional relevancy, such as the question whether notice, although given, was ever received.[1] Subdivision (b) also contem-

---

§ 104(b)(2)(D) codifies this practice. See note 28 supra.

§ 104.2

1. See § 104.1, at notes 21–23, supra. The Advisory Committee's Note to Rule 104 explains the rationale of subdivision (b) as follows:

> If preliminary questions of conditional relevancy were determined solely by the judge, as provided in subdivision (a), the functioning of the jury as a trier of fact would be greatly restricted and in some cases virtually destroyed. These are appropriate questions for juries. Accepted treatment, as provided in the rule, is consistent with that given fact questions generally. The judge makes a preliminary determination whether the foundation evidence is sufficient to support a finding of fulfillment of the condition. If so, the item is admitted. If after all the evidence on the issue is in, pro and con, the jury could reasonably conclude that fulfillment of the condition is not established, the issue is for them. If the evidence is not such as to allow a finding, the judge withdraws the matter from their consideration. Morgan, supra; California Evi-

plates the admission of evidence subject to "connecting up."[2]

In *Huddleston v. United States*,[3] the Supreme Court applied Rule 104(b) to the admissibility of uncharged crimes under Rule 404(b) as proof of defendant's knowledge concerning the crime with which he was charged, i.e., selling video cassette tapes known to have been stolen. Crucial to the question of admissibility of the uncharged crimes—selling stolen televisions and appliances—was whether there indeed was proof that defendant had committed the uncharged acts. The Court ruled that the other crimes did not have to be proven to the judge's satisfaction before the judge could allow them in evidence. Rather,

> [i]n determining whether the Government has introduced sufficient evidence to meet Rule 104(b), the trial court neither weighs credibility nor makes a finding that the Government has proved the conditional fact by a preponderance of the evidence. The court simply examines all the evidence in the case and decides whether the jury could reasonably find the conditional fact—here, that the televisions were stolen—by a preponderance of the evidence.[4]

Thus, the trial judge need only decide that the jury could find by a preponderance that defendant committed the other crimes; the jury must actually be persuaded by a preponderance of the evidence in determining that question.[5] If the jury makes such a finding, it may then consider the other crimes as circumstantial evidence of some relevant aspect of the crime for which defendant is on trial.

A similar example of the application of Rule 104(b) is the Second Circuit's decision in *United States v. Sliker*.[6] This was an embezzlement case in which the government offered evidence of papers confiscated in a search of defendant's home tending to link him to the crimes charged. The question of authentication of the papers under Rule 901(a) prompted the court to state:

> The Advisory Committee's Notes [to Rule 901(a)] state that "[a]uthentication and identification represent a special aspect of relevancy ... The requirement ... falls in the category of

---

dence Code § 403; New Jersey Rule 8(2). See also Uniform Rules 19 and 67.

2. See Huddleston v. United States, 485 U.S. 681, 690 n.7, 108 S.Ct. 1496, 1501, 99 L.Ed.2d 771, 782–83 (1988), where the Court quotes the following passage from 21 C. Wright and K. Graham, Federal Practice and Procedure: Evidence § 5054, at 269–70 (1977)(footnotes omitted):

> When an item of evidence is conditionally relevant, it is often not possible for the offeror to prove the fact upon which relevance is conditioned at the time the evidence is offered. In such cases it is customary to permit him to introduce the evidence and "connect it up" later. Rule 104(b) continues this practice, specifically authorizing the judge to admit the evidence "subject to" proof of the preliminary fact. It is, of course, not the responsibility of the judge sua sponte to insure that the foundation evidence is offered; the objector must move to strike the evidence if at the close of the trial the offeror has failed to satisfy the condition.

See also § 103.2(c) supra.

3. 485 U.S. 681, 108 S.Ct. 1496, 99 L.Ed.2d 771 (1988).

4. Id. at 690, 108 S.Ct. at 1501, 99 L.Ed.2d at 782–83.

5. See further discussion of Huddleston at § 404.1(a) infra.

6. 751 F.2d 477 (2d Cir.1984), cert. denied sub nom., Buchwald v. United States,

relevancy dependent upon fulfillment of a condition of fact and is governed by the procedure set forth in Rule 104(b)" under which the judge may conditionally admit the evidence, subject to the jury's ultimate determination as to its genuineness. * * * Hence the rule requires the admission of evidence "if sufficient proof has been introduced so that a reasonable juror could find in favor of authenticity or identification." * * *

The type and quantum of evidence necessary for authentication is thus related to the purpose for which the evidence is offered.[7]

In contrast, determination of the foundation for admissibility of coconspirator statements (Fed.R.Evid. 801(d)(2)(E)) is governed by Rule 104(a). Thus, the Second Circuit explained in *United States v. Tracy*,[8] that the questions concerning whether declarant was part of a conspiracy and whether the statements were made in the course of and in furtherance of the conspiracy were for the judge alone.[9]

Whether evidence is inadmissible on a public policy ground[10] or whether it is inadmissible hearsay[11] are questions left to the judge; if he keeps the evidence out there is no role for the jury at all, and if he lets it in, the jury's job is simply to consider its weight. The qualifications of a witness to testify as an expert are for the court as a preliminary question under Rule 104(a),[12] but "evaluating witness credibility and weight of the evidence [is] the ageless role of the jury."[13]

Subdivisions (c), (d) and (e) of Rule 104 codify accepted practice. It bears noting that subdivision (d) does not address the subsequent use, if any, that may be made of testimony given by a defendant at a prelimi-

470 U.S. 1058, 105 S.Ct. 1772, 84 L.Ed.2d 832 (1985).

7. Id. at 488.

8. 12 F.3d 1186 (2d Cir.1993).

9. It was stated:

The decision as to whether the four prerequisites have been met, like all other preliminary questions of admissibility, see Fed.R.Evid.104 (a), is to be made by the court. Bourjaily v. United States, 483 U.S. at 181, 107 S.Ct. at 2781. If the government succeeds in persuading the court that the conditionally admitted coconspirator statements were made during and in furtherance of a conspiracy of which both the declarant and the defendant were members, the statements are allowed to go to the jury. If the court is not so persuaded, it either should instruct the jury to disregard the statements, or, if those statements were "so large a proportion of the proof as to render a cautionary instruction of doubtful utility," should declare a mistrial.

12 F.3d at 1199 (citing United States v. Geaney, 417 F.2d 1116, 1120 (2d Cir.1969), cert. denied, 397 U.S. 1028, 90 S.Ct. 1276, 25 L.Ed.2d 539 (1970)).

See the discussion concerning coconspirator's statements at § 802.3(d) infra. Note also that there is no necessity for an in limine hearing to determine the admissibility of coconspirators' statements. This can be done during trial outside the presence of the jury. United States v. Aguirre–Parra, 763 F.Supp. 1208, 1217 (S.D.N.Y.1991).

10. In Pierce v. F.R. Tripler & Co., 955 F.2d 820, 827 (2d Cir.1992), the court said that fact questions arising in connection with the admissibility of statements made during compromise negotiations (Fed. R.Evid. 408) are to be determined solely by the court pursuant to Rule 104(a).

11. The coconspirator situation discussed at notes 8–9 supra involves hearsay statements, even though such statements are labeled as nonhearsay under Rule 801(d)(2)(E).

12. United States v. Pugliese, 712 F.2d 1574, 1581 (2d Cir.1983).

13. McCullock v. H.B. Fuller Co., 61 F.3d 1038, 1045 (2d Cir.1995)(dispute over strength of experts' credentials, experience and methodology went to weight and credibility, not admissibility of experts' testimony).

nary hearing. According to the decision in *Harris v. New York*,[14] it appears that such testimony could be used to impeach the credibility of the defendant should he testify at trial. There, defendant's confession had been suppressed solely on *Miranda* grounds. When his trial testimony disclosed facts at odds with his confession, the prosecutor was allowed to use the confession for impeachment purposes. This suggests that contradictory testimony given at a suppression hearing might also be used to impeach defendant's trial testimony. Where, however, a confession is found to have been actually coerced, it may not be used for such impeachment purposes.[15]

Library References:

West's Key No. Digests, Criminal Law ⋘661–677; Federal Civil Procedure ⋘2011; Witnesses ⋘77–79.

105 Limited Admissibility

§ 105.1 New York

Evidence sometimes is admissible against one party but not another or for one purpose but not another. Such evidence is said to be of limited admissibility. For example, an out-of-court statement by defendant A may be admissible against A but not against defendant B;[1] an agent's unauthorized admission of negligence may be admissible to impeach the agent's trial testimony but not as evidence of the principal's liability;[2] evidence of a landowner's post-accident removal of a rotted tree from his property may be admissible as evidence of ownership and control of the property (if controverted) but not as evidence of negligence;[3] evidence of a testifying defendant's prior criminal conduct may be admissible to impeach his credibility but not as evidence of guilt of the crime with which he is currently charged;[4] and evidence of a defendant's improperly obtained confession may be admissible to impeach his exculpatory trial testimony but not as substantive evidence of guilt.[5]

In all such cases of limited admissibility, the party who might be prejudiced is entitled, upon request, to have the court instruct the jury concerning the limited use to which the evidence may be put. At

---

14. 401 U.S. 222, 91 S.Ct. 643, 28 L.Ed.2d 1 (1971).

15. New Jersey v. Portash, 440 U.S. 450, 99 S.Ct. 1292, 59 L.Ed.2d 501 (1979). See also § 607.8, at notes 10–12, infra.

§ 105.1

1. See, e.g., People v. Neal, 181 A.D.2d 584, 581 N.Y.S.2d 681 (1st Dep't), leave to appeal denied, 79 N.Y.2d 1052, 584 N.Y.S.2d 1020, 596 N.E.2d 418 (1992).

2. Wolfe v. Madison Avenue Coach Co., 171 Misc. 707, 709, 13 N.Y.S.2d 741, 743 (Sup.Ct.App.T., 1st Dep't 1939).

3. Harris v. Village of East Hills, 50 A.D.2d 921, 922, 377 N.Y.S.2d 619, 622 (2d Dep't 1975), aff'd, 41 N.Y.2d 446, 393 N.Y.S.2d 691, 362 N.E.2d 243 (1977). See also Brandon v. Caterpillar Tractor Corp., 125 A.D.2d 625, 627, 510 N.Y.S.2d 165, 167 (2d Dep't 1986)(in products liability action, defendant's "service letters" were admissible as evidence of duty to warn but not as evidence of design defect).

4. People v. Moorer, 77 A.D.2d 575, 577, 429 N.Y.S.2d 913, 916 (2d Dep't 1980).

5. People v. Grainger, 114 A.D.2d 285, 498 N.Y.S.2d 940 (4th Dep't 1986); People v. Patterson, 48 A.D.2d 933, 369 N.Y.S.2d 534 (2d Dep't 1975).

minimum, the limiting instruction should be given in the concluding jury charge.[6] Furthermore, upon counsel's request the instruction should be given when the evidence is first introduced.[7] Even in the absence of a request by counsel, it is the "better practice" for the court to give a contemporaneous instruction, sua sponte, describing the proper use of the evidence.[8] On the other hand, counsel's failure to request a limiting instruction is a waiver of any objection concerning the jury's improper use of the evidence.[9]

The proposed New York Evidence Code § 105 essentially codifies current law.[10]

It is, of course, a fundamental assumption of the jury system that jurors can and will obey a judge's limiting instructions.[11] This presumption is operative both in civil[12] and criminal[13] cases. In some circumstances, however, even the most forceful of limiting instructions cannot be trusted to overcome the potential for the jury's misuse of evidence.

The leading example is the Supreme Court's decision in *Bruton v. United States*.[14] It was there held that the admission of a nontestifying codefendant's confession which also implicated the defendant was viola-

6. People v. Moorer, 77 A.D.2d 575, 577, 429 N.Y.S.2d 913, 916 (2d Dep't 1980); Harris v. Village of East Hills, 50 A.D.2d 921, 922, 377 N.Y.S.2d 619, 622 (2d Dep't 1975), aff'd, 41 N.Y.2d 446, 393 N.Y.S.2d 691, 362 N.E.2d 243 (1977); Wolfe v. Madison Avenue Coach Co., 171 Misc. 707, 713, 13 N.Y.S.2d 741, 747 (Sup.Ct.App.T., 1st Dep't 1939).

7. See, e.g., Kish v. Board of Education, 76 N.Y.2d 379, 385, 559 N.Y.S.2d 687, 690, 558 N.E.2d 1159, 1162 (1990); People v. Marshall, 306 N.Y. 223, 227, 117 N.E.2d 265, 266–67 (1954). In criminal cases, contemporaneous limiting instructions are sometimes statutorily required without the need for a request. See, e.g., N.Y.Crim. Proc.Law § 60.35(2)(party's impeachment of her own witness with prior inconsistent statement); id. § 60.55(2)(statements made by defendant to psychiatrist in connection with insanity defense).

8. Wolfe v. Madison Avenue Coach Co., 171 Misc. 707, 713, 13 N.Y.S.2d 741, 747 (Sup.Ct.App.T., 1st Dep't 1939).

9. Hyde v. County of Rensselaer, 51 N.Y.2d 927, 434 N.Y.S.2d 984, 415 N.E.2d 972 (1980); People v. Williams, 50 N.Y.2d 996, 431 N.Y.S.2d 477, 409 N.E.2d 949 (1980).

10. The proposed code provision is as follows:

§ 105. Limited admissibility [PROPOSED]

When evidence that is admissible as to one party but not as to another or for one purpose but not for another is admitted, the court may, or upon request shall, restrict the evidence to its proper scope and instruct the jury accordingly at the time the evidence is admitted, and may, or upon request shall, so instruct as part of the court's charge to the jury. This section shall not preclude the court from excluding the evidence or taking any other action it deems appropriate when a limiting instruction will not adequately protect a party.

11. People v. Berg, 59 N.Y.2d 294, 299–300, 464 N.Y.S.2d 703, 705–06, 451 N.E.2d 450, 452 (1983). See also § 100.2, at note 6, supra.

12. See, e.g., Kish v. Board of Education, 76 N.Y.2d 379, 385, 559 N.Y.S.2d 687, 690, 558 N.E.2d 1159, 1162 (1990) (evidence that personal injury plaintiff had voluntarily retired did not prejudice plaintiff where jury was instructed to consider the evidence only on contested issue of possible malingering and not to speculate that plaintiff may have received retirement benefits).

13. See, e.g., People v. Paulino, 187 A.D.2d 736, 736, 590 N.Y.S.2d 532, 533 (2d Dep't 1992), leave to appeal denied, 81 N.Y.2d 792, 594 N.Y.S.2d 739, 610 N.E.2d 412 (1993)(evidence of codefendant's threats to a witness did not prejudice defendant where jury was instructed to consider such evidence only as showing codefendant's consciousness of guilt and not as evidence of defendant's guilt).

14. 391 U.S. 123, 88 S.Ct. 1620, 20 L.Ed.2d 476 (1968).

tive of the latter's right of confrontation. As to the defendant, the confession was hearsay, and telling the jury to consider the confession only as evidence against the confessor was viewed as an ineffective way to cure the defendant's inability to cross-examine the confessor.[15]

One obvious solution to the *Bruton* problem is severance of the trials of the codefendants. Alternatively, the Supreme Court has approved the admission of a redacted version of the nontestifying codefendant's confession, accompanied by limiting instructions, where no reference whatsoever to the defendant's name or existence remains in the confession.[16] The Court has not decided, however, whether the use of "a symbol or neutral pronoun" in place of the defendant's name will suffice.[17] In New York, the adequacy of substituting neutral pronouns as a redaction technique turns on a case-specific analysis of the risk that the jury will not be able to follow the court's limiting instructions and will "simply fill in the blanks found in the confessions."[18]

Library References:

West's Key No. Digests, Criminal Law ⚖=673(2); Trial ⚖=54.

§ 105.2 Federal

In federal practice, Rule 105 of the Federal Rules of Evidence entitles a party, upon request, to a cautionary jury instruction when evidence is admitted for limited purposes:

> When evidence is admissible as to one party or for one purpose but not admissible as to another party or for another purpose is admitted, the court, upon request, shall restrict the evidence to its proper scope and instruct the jury accordingly.

---

15. Id. at 135, 88 S.Ct. at 1627, 20 L.Ed.2d at 485 ("[T]here are some contexts in which the risk that the jury will not, or cannot, follow instructions is so great, and the consequences of failure so vital to the defendant, that the practical and human limitations of the jury system cannot be ignored.").

Section 105 of the proposed New York Evidence Code, in the concluding sentence, explicitly recognizes that limiting instructions may not always adequately protect a party from undue prejudice. See note 10 supra.

16. Richardson v. Marsh, 481 U.S. 200, 211, 107 S.Ct. 1702, 1709, 95 L.Ed.2d 176, 188 (1987).

An apparent exception to Bruton based on the existence of "interlocking confessions" by both defendants was rejected in Cruz v. New York, 481 U.S. 186, 107 S.Ct. 1714, 95 L.Ed.2d 162 (1987).

17. Richardson v. Marsh, 481 U.S. 200, 211 n.5, 107 S.Ct. 1702, 1709, 95 L.Ed.2d 176, 188 (1987).

18. People v. Khan, 200 A.D.2d 129, 138, 613 N.Y.S.2d 198, 203 (2d Dep't), appeal denied, 84 N.Y.2d 939, 621 N.Y.S.2d 536, 645 N.E.2d 1236 (1994)(substitution of pronouns was insufficient in multi-defendant case because all defendants were identified as perpetrators by one eyewitness). See also People v. Hussain, 165 A.D.2d 538, 568 N.Y.S.2d 966 (2d Dep't 1991)(substitution of general noun "cousin" insufficient in two-defendant case); People v. Sutter, 162 A.D.2d 644, 556 N.Y.S.2d 959 (2d Dep't), appeal denied, 76 N.Y.2d 897, 561 N.Y.S.2d 559, 562 N.E.2d 884 (1990)(substitution of pronouns was sufficient in case involving large numbers of defendants); People v. Marcus, 137 A.D.2d 723, 524 N.Y.S.2d 806 (2d Dep't), appeal denied, 72 N.Y.2d 862, 532 N.Y.S.2d 512, 528 N.E.2d 903 (1988)(substitution of pronoun was sufficient where several persons were potentially implicated).

Such instructions were held appropriate, for example, in a multi-defendant prosecution where evidence against one defendant was not relevant as against the others;[1] where a witness' prior inconsistent statement was admissible to impeach her credibility but not to prove the truth of the matter asserted in the statement;[2] and where a defendant's prior death threats were admissible to show his participation in a conspiracy but not as evidence of his violent character.[3]

The burden is on the affected party to request a limiting instruction when evidence of this nature is admitted. The failure to make a request waives the issue on appeal,[4] unless the appellant can show plain error.[5]

Often, trial judges within the Second Circuit will give a limiting instruction contemporaneously with the introduction of the evidence as well as in the final jury charge.[6] It is not necessarily error to decline the giving of a contemporaneous instruction, however, so long as limiting instructions are included in the final charge.[7] The timing question generally lies in the court's discretion.[8]

In most cases, it is assumed that juries will be able to comply with limiting instructions and that the potential "spill-over" effect of limited-purpose evidence will not prejudice a party.[9] As discussed in § 105.1

---

§ 105.2

1. United States v. Carson, 702 F.2d 351, 366–67 (2d Cir.), cert. denied, 462 U.S. 1108, 103 S.Ct. 2456, 77 L.Ed.2d 1335 (1983); United States v. Losada, 674 F.2d 167, 171–72 (2d Cir.), cert. denied, 457 U.S. 1125, 102 S.Ct. 2945, 73 L.Ed.2d 1341 (1982).

2. Gray v. Busch Entertainment Corp., 886 F.2d 14, 16 (2d Cir.1989).

3. United States v. Tracy, 12 F.3d 1186, 1195 (2d Cir.1993). See also United States v. Ramirez, 894 F.2d 565, 570 (2d Cir.1990) (evidence of defendant's other criminal activity admitted in narcotics prosecution with limiting instruction that it be considered only as circumstantial evidence of defendant's knowledge and not as evidence of general criminal propensity); United States v. Washington, 592 F.2d 680, 681 (2d Cir. 1979) (in prosecution for possession of deadly weapon by a convicted felon, trial judge erred in refusing to give defendant's requested jury charge that fact of his prior felony should not be considered as evidence of general criminal propensity).

4. See, e.g., Gray v. Busch Entertainment Corp., 886 F.2d 14, 16 (2d Cir.1989).

5. See United States v. Tracy, 12 F.3d 1186, 1195 (2d Cir.1993) (where limiting instruction has not been requested, "trial judge's failure to give such an instruction is a ground for reversal only if it constitutes an error that is 'egregious and obvious' and if reversal is 'necessary to redress a miscarriage of justice' ").

6. See, e.g., United States v. Ramirez, 894 F.2d 565, 570 (2d Cir.1990); United States v. Tutino, 883 F.2d 1125, 1130–31 (2d Cir.1989), cert. denied, 493 U.S. 1081, 110 S.Ct. 1139, 107 L.Ed.2d 1044 (1990).

7. See, e.g., United States v. Garcia, 848 F.2d 1324, 1334–35 (2d Cir.1988), rev'd on other grounds sub nom. Gomez v. United States, 490 U.S. 858, 109 S.Ct. 2237, 104 L.Ed.2d 923 (1989) (not error in multi-defendant case to refuse contemporaneous instructions in connection with admission of multiple items of physical evidence indicating particular defendant to which each item related; court had given contemporaneous limiting instructions with respect to coconspirator statements that were admissible against some—but not all—defendants, number of defendants was small, physical evidence easily lends itself to compartmentalized consideration, and final jury charge instructed jury to consider as against each defendant only the evidence that pertained to that defendant).

8. See United States v. Sliker, 751 F.2d 477, 487 (2d Cir.1984), cert. denied, 470 U.S. 1058, 105 S.Ct. 1772, 84 L.Ed.2d 832 (1985).

9. United States v. Teitler, 802 F.2d 606, 617 (2d Cir.1986) (jury is presumed to have heeded limiting instructions). See also United States v. Ramirez, 894 F.2d 565, 570 (2d Cir.1990); United States v. Tutino, 883 F.2d 1125, 1132 (2d Cir.1989), cert. denied, 493 U.S. 1081, 110 S.Ct. 1139, 107 L.Ed.2d 1044 (1990). But see Nash v.

supra, however, the *Bruton* rule[10] explodes this assumption in criminal cases where the confession of a nontestifying codefendant implicates another defendant. The Second Circuit has been fairly liberal, however, in allowing redacted confessions to be admitted in such cases, provided the jury is instructed to limit its use of such evidence to the confessor.[11]

Library References:
West's Key No. Digests, Criminal Law ⇔673(2); Federal Civil Procedure ⇔2011.

106 Rule of Completeness

§ 106.1 New York

The common law rule of completeness[1] is of long-standing vintage in New York, having found expression in several Court of Appeals decisions during the nineteenth century.[2] The following summary of the rule from *Grattan v. Metropolitan Life Insurance Co.*,[3] is illustrative:

> The rule appears to be firmly settled, both as to a conversation or writing, that the introduction of a part renders admissible so much of the remainder as tends to explain or qualify what has been received and that is to be deemed a qualification which rebuts and destroys the inference to be derived from or the use to be made of the portion put in evidence.[4]

The completeness doctrine, which is "founded upon the plainest principles of equity,"[5] helps to prevent distortion and false impressions.[6] The rule is frequently invoked when portions of a party's prior state-

---

United States, 54 F.2d 1006, 1007 (2d Cir.), cert. denied, 285 U.S. 556, 52 S.Ct. 457, 76 L.Ed. 945 (1932) (limiting instruction is "a mental gymnastic which is beyond not only [the jury's] powers, but anybody else's").

10. Bruton v. United States, 391 U.S. 123, 88 S.Ct. 1620, 20 L.Ed.2d 476 (1968). See § 105.1, at notes 14–15, supra.

11. In United States v. Tutino, 883 F.2d 1125 (2d Cir.1989), cert. denied, 493 U.S. 1081, 110 S.Ct. 1139, 107 L.Ed.2d 1044 (1990), the court held that "a redacted statement in which the names of co-defendants are replaced by neutral pronouns, with no indication to the jury that the original statement contained actual names, and where the statement standing alone does not otherwise connect co-defendants to the crimes, may be admitted without violating a co-defendant's *Bruton* rights." Id. at 1135. In a subsequent case, the court held that "the word 'friend' in the redacted * * * statement [was] a 'symbol' that serve[d] the office of a 'neutral pronoun' and thus [brought] this case within the rule in Tutino." United States v. Benitez, 920 F.2d 1080, 1087 (2d Cir.1990). See also United States v. Kyles, 40 F.3d 519, 526 (2d Cir. 1994), cert. denied, ___ U.S. ___, 115 S.Ct. 1419, 131 L.Ed.2d 302 (1995).

§ 106.1

1. Wigmore described the rule as follows: "[T]he opponent, against whom a part of an utterance has been put in, may in his turn complement it by putting in the remainder, in order to secure for the tribunal a complete understanding of the total tenor and effect of the utterance." 7 Wigmore § 2113, at 653.

2. See, e.g., Nay v. Curley, 113 N.Y. 575, 578–79, 21 N.E. 698, 699 (1889); Grattan v. Metropolitan Life Ins. Co., 92 N.Y. 274, 284 (1883); Rouse v. Whited, 25 N.Y. 170, 177 (1862).

3. 92 N.Y. 274 (1883).

4. Id. at 284.

5. Rouse v. Whited, 25 N.Y. 170, 177 (1862). See also People v. Gallo, 12 N.Y.2d 12, 15–16, 234 N.Y.S.2d 193, 195, 186 N.E.2d 399, 400 (1962) (fairness); Nay v. Curley, 113 N.Y. 575, 579, 21 N.E. 698, 699 (1889) ("obvious equity and justice").

6. See People v. Baker, 23 N.Y.2d 307, 324, 296 N.Y.S.2d 745, 756, 244 N.E.2d 232, 240 (1968); Grattan v. Metropolitan Life Ins. Co., 92 N.Y. 276, 284 (1883). See also 7 Wigmore § 2113, at 657 (purpose "is to be able to put a correct construction upon

§ 106.1   GENERAL PRINCIPLES   Ch. 1

ments have been introduced against her as admissions[7] or when a witness on cross-examination has been questioned about fragments of prior statements for impeachment purposes.[8] The aggrieved party in such cases may thereafter bring out omitted portions of the documents or conversations that tend to provide an explanation or qualification. CPLR 3117(b) carries forward this concept when an opponent reads only part of a deposition into evidence at trial.[9]

There are, of course, limits on the extent to which completion evidence may be admitted and the use to which it may be put. Drawing upon the early writings of Wigmore, the Court of Appeals identified those limits as follows:

> (a) No utterance irrelevant to the issue is receivable; (b) no more of the remainder of the utterance than concerns the same subject and is explanatory of the first part is receivable; (c) the remainder thus received merely aids in the construction of the utterance as a whole, and is not in itself testimony.[10]

The first limitation—relevancy—is self-explanatory. The second limitation precludes admission of remaining portions that relate to some other subject matter[11] or which fail to explain, modify or qualify that which was introduced by the opponent.[12] The third limitation, when strictly applied, disallows the completion evidence to be used as affirmative evidence in those situations in which it would be otherwise inadmissible.[13] As Wigmore explained, "The remainder of the utterance, regarded as an assertion of the facts contained in it, is merely a hearsay statement * * *. It is considered * * * merely in order to piece out and the part which the first party relies upon, and to avoid the danger of mistaking the effect of a fragment whose meaning is modified by a later or prior part").

7. See, e.g., People v. Dlugash, 41 N.Y.2d 725, 736, 395 N.Y.S.2d 419, 427, 363 N.E.2d 1155, 1162 (1977); People v. La Belle, 18 N.Y.2d 405, 410, 276 N.Y.S.2d 105, 109, 222 N.E.2d 727, 729 (1966); People v. Gallo, 12 N.Y.2d 12, 15–16, 234 N.Y.S.2d 193, 195, 186 N.E.2d 399, 400 (1962); Grattan v. Metropolitan Life Ins. Co., 92 N.Y. 276, 284 (1883).

8. People v. Torre, 42 N.Y.2d 1036, 1037, 399 N.Y.S.2d 203, 204, 369 N.E.2d 759, 760–61 (1977); Feblot v. New York Times Co., 32 N.Y.2d 486, 496–98, 346 N.Y.S.2d 256, 265–66, 299 N.E.2d 672, 678–79 (1973); People v. Regina, 19 N.Y.2d 65, 78, 277 N.Y.S.2d 683, 693, 224 N.E.2d 108, 115 (1966); People v. Baker, 23 N.Y.2d 307, 324, 296 N.Y.S.2d 745, 756, 244 N.E.2d 232, 240 (1968). See also § 607.5, at notes 19–20, infra (rehabilitation of impeached witnesses), and § 611.4 infra (scope of redirect testimony).

9. CPLR 3117(b) states as follows:

(b) **Use of part of deposition.** If only part of a deposition is read at the trial by a party, any other party may read any other part of the deposition which ought in fairness to be considered in connection with the part read.

10. People v. Schlessel, 196 N.Y. 476, 481, 90 N.E. 44, 45–46 (1909). See 7 Wigmore § 2113, at 656.

11. Rouse v. Whited, 25 N.Y. 170, 177 (1862). The Rouse court posits a hypothetical in which the defendant is sued on two promissory notes. As to note one the defense is forgery, and as to the other the defense is payment. If plaintiff proves a statement in which defendant admits to having signed note one, the rule of completeness does not entitle the defendant to introduce another statement made at the same time in which he said that he paid note two. Id. at 176.

12. Platner v. Platner, 78 N.Y. 90, 103 (1879). Judges may not always agree on whether the additional portions of a statement "explain, modify or qualify" that portion which the opponent introduced. See, e.g., People v. Spano, 57 A.D.2d 715, 395 N.Y.S.2d 548 (4th Dep't 1977) (difference of opinion between 3–judge majority and 2–judge concurrence).

13. See, e.g., Thrower v. Smith, 62 A.D.2d 907, 912, 406 N.Y.S.2d 513, 516 (2d Dep't 1978). See also Mravlja v. Hoke, 22 A.D.2d 848, 851, 254 N.Y.S.2d 162, 166–67

interpret the first fragment and ascertain whether as a whole the sense of the first becomes modified."[14]

In some cases, of course, the completion evidence might be independently admissible. Furthermore, in one older case the completion evidence was otherwise inadmissible not because it was hearsay, but because the witness was incompetent to testify in his own behalf under the "Dead Man's Statute" (CPLR 4519).[15] When this witness was called and examined by the adversary as to only a portion of a transaction with the decedent, fairness dictated that the bar of the statute be lifted and that he be allowed to describe the entire transaction as affirmative evidence of what transpired.[16]

As to the timing for introduction of completion evidence, it seems clear from the cases that when fragmentary statements are introduced or elicited during cross-examination, the appropriate time to complete the picture is on redirect of the witness.[17] When only portions of statements are introduced during a party's direct case, however, the question arises whether the opponent may insist upon contemporaneous presentation of the explanatory or qualifying portions, or whether she must wait until cross-examination or her own case. Some New York decisions imply that the opponent need not wait,[18] and the proposed New York Evidence Code would adopt this as a rule in all cases of written or recorded statements.[19] The rationale is that delayed repair of the case may be an inadequate remedy.[20]

Library References:

West's Key No. Digests, Criminal Law ⚖446; Evidence ⚖383(12).

§ 106.2 Federal

Rule 106 of the Federal Rules of Evidence is an incomplete codification of the common law rule of completeness:

(3d Dep't 1964) (dissenting opinion) (majority agreed that defendant's introduction of his own deposition exceeded permissible scope of rule but found no reversible error).

14. 7 Wigmore § 2113, at 659.

15. See Nay v. Curley, 113 N.Y. 575, 21 N.E. 698 (1889). See § 601.2, at notes 72–75, supra.

16. 113 N.Y. at 578–82, 21 N.E. at 699–700.

17. See authorities cited in note 8 supra.

18. See cases cited in note 7 supra. Contra, Villa v. Vetuskey, 50 A.D.2d 1093, 1094, 376 N.Y.S.2d 359, 363 (4th Dep't 1975) (when plaintiff read portions of defendant's deposition into evidence during plaintiff's case in chief, defendant was required to wait until his own case to read explanatory portions).

19. Proposed N.Y. Evid. Code § 106 provides as follows:

§ 106. **Completing a writing or recording [PROPOSED]**

When a writing or recorded statement or part thereof is introduced by a party, an adverse party may offer or may require the proponent at that time to introduce any other part or any other writing or recorded statement which is necessary for purposes such as understanding, assessment, explanation or clarification. When a writing or recording is admissible for impeachment purposes only, completing matter is admissible only to rehabilitate the witness and not as substantive evidence, unless the completing matter is admissible for substantive purposes independent of its admissibility under this section.

Requiring immediate completion of an oral conversation in all cases has been viewed as "impractical." Advisory Committee's Note, Fed.R.Evid. 106.

20. See § 106.2 infra.

Rule 106. Remainder of or Related Writings or Recorded Statements

When a writing or recorded statement or part thereof is introduced by a party, an adverse party may require the introduction at that time of any other part or any other writing or recorded statement which ought in fairness to be considered contemporaneously with it.

By its terms, the Federal Rule only applies to incomplete writings and recorded statements.[1] By allowing an opponent to insist upon immediate presentation of relevant omissions, the rule guards against the creation of misleading impressions and the inadequacy of delayed repair of one's case.[2] The same considerations obviously can apply to incomplete oral conversations, but the impracticality of contemporaneous completion of some conversations makes the procedure unsuitable for blanket inclusion within the rule.[3] The opponent may invoke common law principles,[4] however, to introduce omitted portions of conversations during cross-examination, as part of her own case,[5] and in some instances at the same time that the admitted portions come into evidence.[6]

In the Second Circuit, the applicability of Rule 106 turns on whether the excluded portions of written or recorded statements are "necessary to explain the admitted portion, to place the admitted portion in context, to avoid misleading the jury, or to ensure fair and impartial understanding of the admitted portion."[7] The Second Circuit has often said, however, that Rule 106 "does not render admissible evidence that is otherwise inadmissible."[8] It is submitted, however, that the appropriate

§ 106.2

1. "Recorded statements" include tape recordings. See, e.g., In re Air Crash Disaster at John F. Kennedy Int'l Airport, 635 F.2d 67, 72 (2d Cir.1980).

2. Advisory Committee's Note, Fed. R.Evid. 106.

3. Id. See also United States v. Castro, 813 F.2d 571, 576 (2d Cir.), cert. denied, 484 U.S. 844, 108 S.Ct. 137, 98 L.Ed.2d 94 (1987) ("Rule 106 governs only writings * * * since in practice verbal precision cannot be expected when the source of evidence as to an utterance is the memory of a witness").

4. See generally § 106.1 supra.

5. Advisory Committee's Note, Fed. R.Evid. 106. See also Beech Aircraft Corp. v. Rainey, 488 U.S. 153, 171–72, 109 S.Ct. 439, 451, 102 L.Ed.2d 445, 464–65 (1988).

6. Cf. United States v. Terry, 702 F.2d 299, 314 (2d Cir.), cert. denied, 461 U.S. 931, 103 S.Ct. 2095, 77 L.Ed.2d 304 (1983) (testimony that defendants refused to allow agent to fingerprint them (thus showing consciousness of guilt) should have been accompanied, upon request, by fact that they also told agent that they first wanted to consult with counsel (thus showing good-faith state of mind)).

7. United States v. Castro, 813 F.2d 571, 576 (2d Cir.), cert. denied, 484 U.S. 844, 108 S.Ct. 137, 98 L.Ed.2d 94 (1987). See also United States v. Rivera, 61 F.3d 131, 135–36 (2d Cir.1995) (criteria not satisfied); Phoenix Associates III v. Stone, 60 F.3d 95, 102 (2d Cir.1995) (criteria satisfied); United States v. Marin, 669 F.2d 73, 84–85 (2d Cir.1982) (criteria not satisfied).

8. United States v. Terry, 702 F.2d 299, 314 (2d Cir.), cert. denied, 461 U.S. 931, 103 S.Ct. 2095, 77 L.Ed.2d 304 (1983). See also Phoenix Associates III v. Stone, 60 F.3d 95, 103 (2d Cir.1995); United States v. Rivera, 61 F.3d 131, 136 (2d Cir.1995); United States Football League v. National Football League, 842 F.2d 1335, 1375–76 (2d Cir.1988); United States v. Weisman, 624 F.2d 1118, 1128–29 (2d Cir.), cert. denied, 449 U.S. 871, 101 S.Ct. 209, 66 L.Ed.2d 91 (1980).

analysis is that of the District of Columbia Circuit in *United States v. Sutton*,[9] where the court stated:

> Rule 106 can adequately fulfill its function only by permitting the admission of some otherwise inadmissible evidence when the court finds in fairness that the proffered evidence should be considered contemporaneously. A contrary construction raises the specter of distorted and misleading trials, and creates difficulties for both litigants and the trial court.[10]

Tension can sometimes become acute when the rule of completeness conflicts with the usual exclusionary rules of evidence. For example, in a joint trial of criminal defendants, the *Bruton* rule[11] disallows admission of a nontestifying codefendant's inculpatory statement if it also refers to the other defendant.[12] The codefendant, however, may have an argument based on completeness that deletion of any reference to the other participant may exaggerate or distort his own degree of culpability. Such was the situation in *United States v. Castro*,[13] where the trial judge devised a compromise that the Second Circuit found acceptable on the facts. When Castro was apprehended in a narcotics raid, he told an officer that cocaine was kept in a nearby bag that belonged to Acosta. At the joint trial of Castro and Acosta, the government was allowed to prove that Castro said he knew where the cocaine was located but that "in substance" he denied that the cocaine was his.[14] Acosta was thus protected against inculpation, and the rephrasing of Castro's deflection of blame, made at the same time as his admission of knowledge, sufficiently satisfied the rule of completeness.[15]

Library References:

West's Key No. Digests, Criminal Law ⚖446; Evidence ⚖383(12).

---

9. 801 F.2d 1346 (D.C.Cir.1986).

10. Id. at 1368. See also 21 C. Wright and K. Graham, Federal Practice and Procedure: Evidence § 5078 (1977).

With appropriate limiting instructions, the introduction of otherwise inadmissible portions of a statement that are necessary to explain, qualify or modify the admitted portions is consistent with traditional doctrine. See § 106.1, at notes 10–14, supra.

11. Bruton v. United States, 391 U.S. 123, 88 S.Ct. 1620, 20 L.Ed.2d 476 (1968).

12. See § 105.1, at notes 14–18, supra.

13. 813 F.2d 571 (2d Cir.), cert. denied, 484 U.S. 844, 108 S.Ct. 137, 98 L.Ed.2d 94 (1987).

14. Id. at 575–77.

15. Id. at 576 (trial court "reasonably accommodated these competing interests"). Separate trials may be the only alternative in some cases.

Chapter 2

JUDICIAL NOTICE

Table of Sections

200 INTRODUCTION
200.1 Judicial Notice, In General.

201 JUDICIAL NOTICE OF ADJUDICATIVE FACTS
201.1 New York.
    a. In General.
    b. Facts Subject to Judicial Notice.
    c. Examples.
    d. Procedure.
    e. Effect of Taking Judicial Notice.
    f. Proposed New York Evidence Code.
201.2 Federal.

202 JUDICIAL NOTICE OF LEGISLATIVE FACTS
202.1 New York and Federal.

203 JUDICIAL NOTICE OF LAW
203.1 New York.
203.2 Federal.

WESTLAW Electronic Research

See WESTLAW Electronic Research Guide preceding the Summary of Contents.

200 Introduction

§ 200.1 Judicial Notice, In General

The doctrine of judicial notice is analyzed under three separate headings: judicial notice of adjudicative facts, judicial notice of legislative facts and judicial notice of law.[1] All three types of judicial notice facilitate decision-making without the need for formal evidence.

"Adjudicative facts" are those facts which relate to the persons, places and events involved in the particular case: the who, what, when, where, how and why.[2] "Legislative facts" are the perceived social, political, economic and scientific realities that courts act upon in formulating judge-made rules of law or in assessing the meaning and validity

---

§ 200.1
1. See Advisory Committee's Note, Fed. R.Evid. 201.

2. McCormick § 328, at 385. See §§ 201.1–201.2 infra.

of legislation.[3] Taking "judicial notice of law" is simply a description of the informal process by which courts determine the law applicable to a particular case.[4] These three concepts of judicial notice are considered separately in the sections that follow.

Library References:

West's Key No. Digests, Criminal Law ⬛304; Evidence ⬛1–52.

201 Judicial Notice of Adjudicative Facts

§ 201.1 New York

a. In General

Courts are authorized in some circumstances to take judicial notice of adjudicative facts,[1] i.e., facts concerning the parties and events involved in a particular suit—matters that the jury ordinarily would determine.[2] The doctrine of judicial notice in this context is based on the principle that some matters of fact are so generally well established in the world outside the courtroom that the taking of evidence would be unnecessary and inefficient.[3] As to such matters, the court is justified "in declaring the truth of the proposition without requiring evidence from the party."[4]

Most often, judicial notice serves to relieve a party of the burden of producing evidence to prove a particular fact, thus filling a gap in the party's proof;[5] but it can also serve to prevent juries from making irrational findings.[6] *Hunter v. New York, Ontario and Western Railroad Co.*,[7] provides a dramatic illustration of the latter use of judicial notice. There, the plaintiff won a jury verdict in a negligence case on the basis of testimony that, due to inadequate warnings, he hit his head on an arch within a railroad tunnel entrance while he was sitting atop a moving boxcar. The proven dimensions of the tunnel entrance and boxcar, however, showed that the plaintiff would have to have been nine feet tall in order for the accident to have happened as he described it. The Court of Appeals took judicial notice that people generally do not grow to be nine feet tall and overturned the jury verdict.[8]

3. McCormick § 328, at 386. See § 202.1 infra.

4. McCormick § 335, at 413. See §§ 203.1–203.2 infra.

§ 201.1

1. See § 200.1, at note 2, supra.

2. See Lilly § 1.8, at 13.

3. McCormick § 329, at 388 ("The oldest and plainest ground for judicial notice is that the fact is so commonly known in the community as to make it unprofitable to require proof, and so certainly known as to make it indisputable among reasonable men.").

4. 9 Wigmore § 2565, at 693 (emphasis deleted).

5. See People v. Sowle, 68 Misc.2d 569, 571, 327 N.Y.S.2d 510, 514 (Fulton Co.Ct. 1971)("The effect of * * * judicial notice is to excuse the party having the burden of establishing the fact from the necessity of producing any proof of that fact by sworn witnesses or authenticated documents.").

6. See Lilly § 1.8, at 19.

7. 116 N.Y. 615, 23 N.E. 9 (1889).

8. Id. at 624, 23 N.E. at 11 ("Here the finding which must exist to support the judgment is so contrary to our general knowledge, and so far outside of common occurrence, that it may, in the absence of further proof, be regarded as contrary to nature, and hence untrue; and substantial justice will be done by reversing the judg-

b. Facts Subject to Judicial Notice

The type of adjudicative facts that are subject to judicial notice fall into two categories: (1) facts of general or common knowledge,[9] described in some opinions as "notorious" facts;[10] and (2) facts which can be ascertained by reference to readily available sources whose accuracy is not subject to reasonable dispute.[11] An example of a fact within the first category is that the usual period of human gestation is nine months.[12] Falling within the second category are such matters as the time of sunset on a particular day,[13] population statistics for a given locality,[14] and the scientific principle underlying radar.[15]

The second category of judicially cognizable facts is actually an outgrowth of the first. In older cases, it was said that courts could "refresh their recollection" about facts of general knowledge by consulting commonly used reference materials.[16] The standard which governs the acceptable sources that a court may consult to ascertain such facts is

ment and granting a new trial."). An alternative analysis is that the plaintiff's testimony was simply incredible as a matter of law. See § 300.3(a)(1), at note 36, infra, and § 607.1, at notes 4–6, infra.

Another example is People v. Genn, 144 Misc.2d 596, 545 N.Y.S.2d 478 (Sup.Ct. Bronx Co.1989), where the court rejected a police officer's testimony that, while standing outside a parked vehicle, he looked through the window and saw the seated defendant handling a clear plastic bag of white powder near his waist. The court took judicial notice that sundown occurred at 8:19 p.m. on the day in question. Since the observations occurred at 9:25 p.m., and there was no evidence that the exterior or interior of the car was illuminated by artificial lighting, it was not possible for the officer to have seen the bag and its contents. Id. at 602–03, 545 N.Y.S.2d at 483.

9. Hunter v. New York, Ontario and Western R.R. Co., 116 N.Y. 615, 621, 23 N.E. 9, 10 (1889)("facts which are a part of the general knowledge of the country"); Crater Club, Inc. v. Adirondack Park Agency, 86 A.D.2d 714, 715, 446 N.Y.S.2d 565, 567 (3d Dep't), aff'd, 57 N.Y.2d 990, 457 N.Y.S.2d 244, 443 N.E.2d 492 (1982)("common knowledge"); American Broadcasting Companies, Inc. v. Wolf, 76 A.D.2d 162, 169 n.2, 430 N.Y.S.2d 275, 280 n.2 (1st Dep't 1980), aff'd, 52 N.Y.2d 394, 438 N.Y.S.2d 482, 420 N.E.2d 363 (1981)("facts which are a part of the general knowledge of the public"); Ecco High Frequency Corp. v. Amtorg Trading Corp., 81 N.Y.S.2d 610, 617 (Sup.Ct.N.Y.Co.), aff'd, 274 App.Div. 982, 85 N.Y.S.2d 304 (1st Dep't 1948)("a matter of common and general knowledge").

10. See, e.g., People v. Alicea, 25 N.Y.2d 685, 686, 306 N.Y.S.2d 686, 688, 254 N.E.2d 915, 916 (1969). Wigmore also appears to have favored the term. 9 Wigmore § 2571, at 731.

11. Hunter v. New York, Ontario and Western R.R. Co., 116 N.Y. 615, 621, 23 N.E. 9, 10 (1889)(facts "which are generally known, and have been duly authenticated in repositories of facts, open to all"); People v. Jones, 73 N.Y.2d 427, 431, 541 N.Y.S.2d 340, 342, 539 N.E.2d 96, 98 (1989)("facts 'which are capable of immediate and accurate determination by resort to easily accessible sources of indisputable accuracy'") (quoting W. Richardson, Evidence § 9, at 6 (Prince 10th ed.1973)). See also text at notes 17–22 infra.

12. In re Wells' Will, 129 Misc. 447, 454, 221 N.Y.S. 714, 722 (Surr.Ct.Westchester Co.1927).

13. See, e.g., Montenes v. Metropolitan St. Ry. Co., 77 App.Div. 493, 495, 78 N.Y.S. 1059, 1060 (2d Dep't 1902).

14. See, e.g., Mackston v. State, 126 A.D.2d 710, 711, 510 N.Y.S.2d 912, 914 (2d Dep't 1987).

15. People v. Magri, 3 N.Y.2d 562, 566, 170 N.Y.S.2d 335, 337–38, 147 N.E.2d 728, 729 (1958).

16. See, e.g., Montenes v. Metropolitan St. Ry. Co., 77 App.Div. 493, 495, 78 N.Y.S. 1059, 1060 (2d Dep't 1902); Walton v. Stafford, 14 App.Div. 310, 314, 43 N.Y.S. 1049, 1052 (1st Dep't 1897). See generally McCormick § 330, at 393–95.

a flexible one, having been variously described as "repositories of facts open to all,"[17] "such documents and references as are worthy of confidence,"[18] "easily accessible sources of indisputable accuracy"[19] and "any means * * * which [the judge] may deem safe and proper."[20] The Federal Rules of Evidence[21] and the Proposed New York Evidence Code[22] express these ideas as a rule that allows recourse to "sources whose accuracy cannot reasonably be questioned." Caselaw examples of sources that courts have consulted include calendars,[23] official almanacs,[24] dictionaries,[25] textbooks and professional journals.[26]

Implicit in the early caselaw, but not expressly discussed, is the notion that any fact worthy of judicial notice must be essentially indisputable among reasonable persons.[27] More recent decisions in New York explicitly include a requirement that the fact be "well established and authoritatively settled, not doubtful or uncertain."[28] Both the Federal Rules of Evidence[29] and the Proposed New York Evidence Code[30] codify this concept with the statement that a judicially noticed fact "must be one not subject to reasonable dispute."

It should be apparent that the doctrine of judicial notice does not permit a judge to declare the existence of facts solely on the basis of her own personal knowledge.[31] The standard for judicial notice is an objective one: it is restricted to reasonably certain facts that are generally known. Also to be distinguished is the principle that juries may draw

17. Hunter v. New York, Ontario and Western R.R. Co., 116 N.Y. 615, 621, 23 N.E. 9, 10 (1889).

18. Id. at 622, 23 N.E. at 11.

19. People v. Jones, 73 N.Y.2d 427, 431, 541 N.Y.S.2d 340, 342, 539 N.E.2d 96, 98 (1989).

20. Brown v. Piper, 91 U.S. (1 Otto) 37, 42, 23 L.Ed. 200, 202 (1875). See also Walton v. Stafford, 14 App.Div. 310, 314, 43 N.Y.S. 1049, 1052 (1st Dep't 1897)(judge "may inform himself * * * in any way which he may deem best").

21. Fed.R.Evid. 201(b); § 201.2 infra.

22. See note 63 infra.

23. Schenectady Discount Corp. v. Dziedzic, 31 N.Y.S.2d 636, 638 (Schenectady Co.Ct.1941).

24. Montenes v. Metropolitan St. Ry. Co., 77 App.Div. 493, 495, 78 N.Y.S. 1059, 1060 (2d Dep't 1902).

25. Vadney v. United Traction Co., 193 App.Div. 329, 333, 183 N.Y.S. 926, 929 (3d Dep't 1920), aff'd, 233 N.Y. 643, 135 N.E. 952 (1922).

26. People ex rel. Butler v. McNeill, 30 Misc.2d 722, 727 n.11, 219 N.Y.S.2d 722, 727 (Sup.Ct.Dutchess Co.1961)(medical texts and journals). See also Stawski v. John Hancock Mutual Life Ins. Co., 7 Misc.2d 424, 426, 163 N.Y.S.2d 155, 157–58 (Sup.Ct.N.Y.Co.), appeal dismissed, 4 A.D.2d 940, 170 N.Y.S.2d 489 (1st Dep't 1957)(President's Report to Congress as source of details about publicly known terrorist attack on ship in foreign port).

27. See note 3 supra.

28. Wertling v. Manufacturers Hanover Trust Co., 118 Misc.2d 722, 726, 461 N.Y.S.2d 157, 160 (N.Y.C.Civ.Ct.1983)(quoting Ecco High Frequency Corp. v. Amtorg Trading Corp., 81 N.Y.S.2d 610, 617 (Sup. Ct.N.Y.Co.)), aff'd, 274 App.Div. 982, 85 N.Y.S.2d 304 (1st Dep't 1948). See also People v. Alicea, 25 N.Y.2d 685, 686, 306 N.Y.S.2d 686, 688, 254 N.E.2d 915, 916 (1969)("incontestable"); Abrevaya v. Palace Theatre & Realty Co., 25 Misc.2d 600, 603, 197 N.Y.S.2d 27, 30 (Sup.Ct.N.Y.Co. 1960)(not subject to "reasonable dispute").

29. Fed.R.Evid. 201(b); § 201.2 infra.

30. See note 63 infra.

31. See, e.g., People v. Weiss, 19 A.D.2d 900, 900, 244 N.Y.S.2d 914, 915 (2d Dep't 1963)(court could not base decision on personal observation of persons whose conduct was in issue); Gibson v. Von Glahn Hotel Co., 185 N.Y.S. 154, 155–56 (Sup.Ct.App.T., 1st Dep't 1920)(court improperly decided question of defendant's status as innkeeper on basis of personal knowledge that it was a "hotel").

upon their own general knowledge and common sense about the nature of things as they evaluate evidence that has been put before them.[32]

Library References:

West's Key No. Digests, Criminal Law ⚖304; Evidence ⚖1–50.

c. Examples

Wigmore aptly observed that generalizing and distinguishing the cases in which courts have and have not taken judicial notice of facts is "unprofitable, as well as impracticable" because "the notoriousness of a truth varies much with differences of period and of place."[33] Precedent is of only marginal value; "the spirit and example of the rulings" should be the guide.[34] What follows, therefore, is merely an illustrative list of the types of matters as to which New York courts have taken judicial notice:

1. Public records.[35]
2. The court's own records.[36]
3. Public officials.[37]
4. Census data.[38]

---

32. See Shaw v. Tague, 257 N.Y. 193, 195, 177 N.E. 417, 418 (1931)(in deciding whether plaintiff's hair turned white as result of accident, jurors could "draw their conclusions from their own knowledge or experience"); Oliver v. Bereano, 267 App. Div. 747, 749, 48 N.Y.S.2d 142, 143–44 (1st Dep't), aff'd, 293 N.Y. 931, 60 N.E.2d 134 (1944).

33. 9 Wigmore § 2580, at 797–805.

34. Id. § 2580, at 805.

35. See, e.g., Sommers v. Sommers, 203 A.D.2d 975, 976, 611 N.Y.S.2d 971, 973 (4th Dep't 1994)(government inflation statistics); Rex Paving Corp. v. White, 139 A.D.2d 176, 183 n.2, 531 N.Y.S.2d 831, 835 (3d Dep't 1988) (Governor's letter to agency was public record); Browne v. City of New York, 213 App.Div. 206, 233, 211 N.Y.S. 306, 330 (1st Dep't 1925)(notice taken of journals of assembly and senate). See also Siwek v. Mahoney, 39 N.Y.2d 159, 163 n.2, 383 N.Y.S.2d 238, 240, 347 N.E.2d 599, 601 (1976) ("Data culled from public records is * * * a proper subject of judicial notice."). But see Kissinger v. State, 126 A.D.2d 139, 144, 513 N.Y.S.2d 275, 278 (3d Dep't 1987)(state's highway design manual was not public record subject to judicial notice).

36. Matter of Ordway, 196 N.Y. 95, 97, 89 N.E. 474, 475 (1909). With respect to taking judicial notice of judicial proceedings in other courts, compare In re Justin "EE", 153 A.D.2d 772, 774, 544 N.Y.S.2d 892, 894 (3d Dep't 1989), appeal denied, 75 N.Y.2d 704, 552 N.Y.S.2d 109, 551 N.E.2d 602 (1990)(lies in court's discretion), with In re Estate of Bach, 81 Misc.2d 479, 486–87, 365 N.Y.S.2d 454, 462 (Surr.Ct.Dutchess Co.1975), aff'd, 53 A.D.2d 612, 383 N.Y.S.2d 653 (2d Dep't 1976)(it is "preferable" that formal proof be made of judicial records of other courts).

To the extent judicial notice is taken of records in other adjudicative proceedings, the assertions and findings of fact contained in the records are not a proper subject of judicial notice. Such findings constitute hearsay, and judicial notice cannot be used to circumvent limitations on the doctrine of collateral estoppel. Sleasman v. Sherwood, 212 A.D.2d, 868, 622 N.Y.S.2d 360, 361–62 (3d Dep't 1995). Judicial notice of such records should be limited to the fact of their existence and that of the other proceedings they represent. See § 201.2, at note 4, infra.

37. People v. Reese, 258 N.Y. 89, 98, 179 N.E. 305, 307 (1932)(public officers of the state, including their authority and signatures); City of New York v. Vanderveer, 91 App.Div. 303, 305, 86 N.Y.S. 659, 661 (1st Dep't 1904)(judicial notice of taxing branch of government, both state and local).

38. Mackston v. State, 126 A.D.2d 710, 711, 510 N.Y.S.2d 912, 914 (2d Dep't 1987); Trustees of Union College v. City of New York, 65 App.Div. 553, 557, 73 N.Y.S. 51, 54 (2d Dep't 1901), aff'd, 173 N.Y. 38, 65 N.E. 853 (1903).

Ch. 2   JUDICIAL NOTICE OF ADJUDICATIVE FACTS § 201.1

5. Geographical facts.[39]

6. Historical facts.[40]

7. Current Events.[41]

8. Days and Dates.[42]

9. Human characteristics.[43]

10. Animal characteristics.[44]

39. People v. Hillman, 246 N.Y. 467, 475–76, 159 N.E. 400, 403 (1927) (boundaries of state's territorial jurisdiction); Williams v. Brown, 53 App.Div. 486, 488, 65 N.Y.S. 1049, 1050 (2d Dep't 1900)(distance and travel time between places); Impagliazzo v. Nassau County, 123 N.Y.S.2d 819, 821 (Sup.Ct.Nassau Co.1953)("Merrick Road is a main traffic artery for east and west bound traffic"); Hartford v. Regal Shoe Store No. 162, Inc., 20 Misc.2d 1055, 1060, 192 N.Y.S.2d 167, 172 (N.Y.C.Mun.Ct. 1959), aff'd, 10 A.D.2d 622, 197 N.Y.S.2d 426 (1st Dep't 1960)("New York City is one of the world's great centers of art, music, culture and entertainment").

40. People ex rel. Rubin v. Tax Commission, 9 A.D.2d 47, 49, 189 N.Y.S.2d 784, 786 (3d Dep't 1959), aff'd, 8 N.Y.2d 922, 204 N.Y.S.2d 165, 168 N.E.2d 836 (1960)(1935–1938 were depression years); Stawski v. John Hancock Mutual Life Ins. Co., 7 Misc.2d 424, 426, 163 N.Y.S.2d 155, 158 (Sup.Ct.N.Y.Co.1957), appeal dismissed, 4 A.D.2d 940, 170 N.Y.S.2d 489 (1st Dep't 1957)(terrorist attack on ship in foreign harbor).

41. People v. Hines, 102 A.D.2d 713, 714, 476 N.Y.S.2d 851, 852 (1st Dep't 1984)(persons engaged in narcotics transactions at level above that of street-corner sales are often armed); American Broadcasting Companies, Inc. v. Wolf, 76 A.D.2d 162, 169, 430 N.Y.S.2d 275, 280 (1st Dep't 1980), appeal dismissed, 51 N.Y.2d 835, 433 N.Y.S.2d 759, 413 N.E.2d 1173, order aff'd, 52 N.Y.2d 394, 438 N.Y.S.2d 482, 420 N.E.2d 363 (1981)(local television sports announcer left one network and began appearing on competing network).

Compare Ecco High Frequency Corp. v. Amtorg Trading Corp., 81 N.Y.S.2d 610, 616–17 (Sup.Ct.N.Y.Co.), aff'd, 274 App.Div. 982, 85 N.Y.S.2d 304 (1st Dep't 1948)(refusal to take judicial notice of tense relations between United States and U.S.S.R.), with In re David T., 102 Misc.2d 956, 958–59, 424 N.Y.S.2d 842, 844 (Fam.Ct.N.Y. Co.1980)(recent "tragic events" in Indo-China adversely affected parent-child relationships).

42. Hunter v. New York, Ontario and Western R.R. Co., 116 N.Y. 615, 622, 23 N.E. 9, 11 (1889)("the course of time and the movements of the heavenly bodies, the coincidence of the days of the week with the days of the month, ordinary public feasts and festivals"). See also id. ("the time of the rising and setting of the sun and moon").

43. Hunter v. New York, Ontario and Western R.R. Co., 116 N.Y. 615, 622, 23 N.E. 9, 11 (1889)(proportions of human body); Erie County Board of Social Welfare v. Holiday, 14 A.D.2d 832, 220 N.Y.S.2d 679 (4th Dep't 1961)(usual period of human gestation); Sadowski v. Long Island R.R., 292 N.Y. 448, 456, 55 N.E.2d 497, 500 (1944)(silica dust is injurious to lungs); Boylhart v. Di Marco & Reimann, Inc., 270 N.Y. 217, 221, 200 N.E. 793, 794 (1936)(children are naturally curious about objects piled in street); In re Shirley C., 136 Misc.2d 843, 849, 519 N.Y.S.2d 328, 333 (Sup.Ct.Suffolk Co.1987)(individuals suffer some degree of trauma from loss of any body part). But see People v. Beard, 74 A.D.2d 926, 927, 426 N.Y.S.2d 90, 92 (2d Dep't 1980)(improper to take judicial notice of effects that marijuana would have on particular individual; also improper to assume that an observer would have knowledge of effects of marijuana on another individual).

44. Gaccione v. State of New York, 173 Misc. 367, 370, 18 N.Y.S.2d 161, 165 (Ct.Cl. 1940)(four-year-old bull is dangerous and unpredictable). Compare DeVaul v. Carvigo, Inc., 138 A.D.2d 669, 670, 526 N.Y.S.2d 483, 484 (2d Dep't), appeal dismissed, 72 N.Y.2d 914, 532 N.Y.S.2d 848, 529 N.E.2d 178, appeal denied, 72 N.Y.2d 806, 532 N.Y.S.2d 847, 529 N.E.2d 177 (1988)(refusal to take judicial notice that German Shepherds, as a breed, are vicious), and Abrevaya v. Palace Theatre and Realty Co., 25 Misc.2d 600, 603, 197 N.Y.S.2d 27, 30 (Sup.Ct.N.Y.Co.1960)(specific propensity of monkeys is not proper subject of judicial notice), with Garelli v. Sterling–Alaska Fur and Game Farms, Inc., 25 Misc.2d 1032, 1036, 206 N.Y.S.2d 130, 134 (Sup.Ct. Queens Co.1960)(monkeys are wild by nature).

§ 201.1 JUDICIAL NOTICE Ch. 2

11. Matters of commerce and trade.[45]
12. Scientific and mechanical facts.[46]

Library References:

West's Key No. Digests, Criminal Law ⚖304; Evidence ⚖1–50.

d. Procedure

New York caselaw contains very little guidance on the procedural aspects of judicial notice. The courts have repeatedly stressed, however, that the taking of judicial notice lies in the court's discretion.[47] It would seem that the party who wants the court to take judicial notice of a fact should make an explicit request, tendering whatever written materials may be necessary to demonstrate that the fact is a matter of general

---

45. See Elkaim v. Elkaim, 176 A.D.2d 116, 117, 574 N.Y.S.2d 2, 4 (1st Dep't), appeal dismissed, 78 N.Y.2d 1072, 576 N.Y.S.2d 222, 582 N.E.2d 605 (1991)(regularity with which customers' monthly bank statements are prepared); Miller v. Food Fair Stores, Inc., 63 A.D.2d 766, 767, 404 N.Y.S.2d 740, 741 (3d Dep't 1978)(customer who enters store will focus attention on prominent display); People v. Langlois, 122 Misc.2d 1018, 1021–22, 472 N.Y.S.2d 297, 300 (Sup.Ct.Suffolk Co.1984)(eligibility requirements for psychiatrist's certification as diplomate by American Board of Psychiatry); In re Pascal's Will, 15 Misc.2d 767, 768, 182 N.Y.S.2d 927, 928–29 (Sup.Ct. N.Y.Co.1959), aff'd, 10 A.D.2d 619, 197 N.Y.S.2d 424 (1st Dep't 1960), aff'd, 10 N.Y.2d 313, 222 N.Y.S.2d 324, 178 N.E.2d 723 (1961)(financial success of musical play "My Fair Lady"). But see People v. Alicea, 25 N.Y.2d 685, 686, 306 N.Y.S.2d 686, 688, 254 N.E.2d 915, 916 (1969)(values of used cars recorded in national market report are neither "notorious nor incontestable"); Wertling v. Manufacturers Hanover Trust Co., 118 Misc.2d 722, 726, 461 N.Y.S.2d 157, 160 (Sup.Ct.Kings Co.1983)("five-day rule" allegedly governing bank depositor's ability to draw on out-of-town check is not subject to judicial notice).

46. See, e.g., People v. Magri, 3 N.Y.2d 562, 566, 170 N.Y.S.2d 335, 338, 147 N.E.2d 728, 729 ("Almost daily, reproductions by photography * * * X rays, electroencephalograms, electrocardiograms, speedometer readings, time by watches and clocks, identity by fingerprinting, and ballistic evidence, among a variety of kindred scientific methods, are freely accepted in our courts for their general reliability, without the necessity of offering expert testimony as to the scientific principles underlying them. The use of radar for speed detection may now be said to fall in this category.").

When scientific principles and methods are used to interpret other data in the case, New York courts require a showing that the scientific evidence passes the so-called "Frye" test of general acceptance in the relevant scientific community. See § 702.1(b) infra. Until such time as the scientific principles are so well established as to merit the taking of judicial notice, expert testimony may be needed to show satisfaction of the general acceptance standard. § 702.1(b), at notes 19–20, infra.

Even if judicial notice is taken of the general reliability of a scientific technique as a means of interpreting data, evidence must be introduced to show that the equipment was in working condition and that it was operated correctly by a qualified and experienced person. See, e.g., People v. Knight, 72 N.Y.2d 481, 487, 534 N.Y.S.2d 353, 356, 530 N.E.2d 1273, 1276 (1988).

47. Hunter v. New York, Ontario and Western R.R. Co., 116 N.Y. 615, 621, 23 N.E. 9, 10 (1889)("Courts are not bound to take judicial notice of matters of fact. Whether they will do so or not depends on the nature of the subject, the issue involved and the apparent justice of the case."); Walton v. Stafford, 14 App.Div. 310, 314, 43 N.Y.S. 1049, 1052 (1st Dep't 1897)("The judge is not obliged to take judicial notice of the fact, but is at liberty to do so in his discretion."); Cole Fischer Rogow, Inc. v. Carl Ally, Inc., 29 A.D.2d 423, 426, 288 N.Y.S.2d 556, 561 (1st Dep't 1968), aff'd, 25 N.Y.2d 943, 305 N.Y.S.2d 154, 252 N.E.2d 633 (1969). But see Hoya Saxa, Inc. v. Gowan, 149 Misc.2d 191, 192, 571 N.Y.S.2d 179, 180 (Sup.Ct.App.T., 1st Dep't 1991)(trial court's refusal to take judicial notice of public records to which it had ready access was abuse of discretion).

knowledge and is not subject to reasonable dispute.[48] If the party does not volunteer such materials, the judge may ask her to supply them.[49] Courts also have the discretion to take judicial notice without a request by one of the parties.[50] When the court acts sua sponte, however, recent cases indicate that the parties should be notified in advance so that they may be heard on the matter.[51]

It has been said that judicial notice may be taken at any time during the course of a proceeding.[52] The most vivid example of this proposition is the 1889 *Hunter* case[53] in which the Court of Appeals took judicial notice on appeal and reversed a plaintiff's judgment because his version of events was physically impossible.[54] In a more recent decision, however, the court condemned the taking of judicial notice after the close of testimony in a criminal case where the purpose was to "salvage" the prosecution's insufficient case.[55]

Library References:

West's Key No. Digests, Criminal Law ⇌304; Evidence ⇌51.

e. Effect of Taking Judicial Notice

New York courts have not indicated the precise effect that the taking of judicial notice has on the process of adjudication. It seems clear that in a jury trial the judge's declaration that a particular fact has been judicially noticed should be brought to the jury's attention.[56] If this is to be the ruling, the question arises whether the opponent should be permitted to introduce contrary evidence or at least be allowed to suggest to the jury that they find otherwise.

48. See Walton v. Stafford, 14 App.Div. 310, 314, 43 N.Y.S. 1049, 1052 (1st Dep't 1897).

49. Id.

50. See, e.g., People v. Langlois, 122 Misc.2d 1018, 1021, 472 N.Y.S.2d 297, 300 (Suffolk Co.Ct.1984).

51. Chasalow v. Board of Assessors, 176 A.D.2d 800, 804, 575 N.Y.S.2d 129, 133 (2d Dep't 1991); In re Ronny, 40 Misc.2d 194, 204–05, 242 N.Y.S.2d 844, 855 (Fam.Ct. Queens Co.1963). See also In re Justin "EE," 153 A.D.2d 772, 774, 544 N.Y.S.2d 892, 894 (3d Dep't 1989), appeal denied, 75 N.Y.2d 704, 552 N.Y.S.2d 109, 551 N.E.2d 602 (1990)(trial court erred in taking judicial notice sua sponte after close of evidence because parties were deprived of opportunity to challenge facts).

52. Associated General Contractors of America v. Lapardo Bros. Excavating Contractors, Inc., 43 Misc.2d 825, 826, 252 N.Y.S.2d 486, 488 (Sup.Ct.Albany Co.1964).

53. Hunter v. New York, Ontario and Western R.R. Co., 116 N.Y. 615, 23 N.E. 9 (1889).

54. See text at notes 7–8 supra.

55. People v. Jones, 73 N.Y.2d 427, 431–32, 541 N.Y.S.2d 340, 342–43, 539 N.E.2d 96, 98–99 (1989)(in narcotics prosecution, government's expert failed to show basis for opinion that particular ingredient of Darvocet tablets was controlled substance; after close of testimony trial court took judicial notice of nature of the ingredient; Court of Appeals said that "judicial rescue of the People's inadequate case came too late"). Jones casts serious doubt on the precedential value of two cases in which appellate courts, for the first time on appeal, took judicial notice of sunset and sunrise on particular days to help sustain convictions of nighttime burglars. People v. Townes, 104 A.D.2d 1057, 480 N.Y.S.2d 962 (2d Dep't 1984); People v. Smith, 62 A.D.2d 1043, 404 N.Y.S.2d 48 (2d Dep't 1978). It is unclear from the opinions whether the evidence presented at the trial level would have been sufficient without such judicial notice.

56. See, e.g., 1 N.Y.Forms of Jury Instruction § 1.57 (1992).

Wigmore argued that a judicially noticed fact merely gives rise to a permissive inference that the adversary is free to contest.[57] Most modern authorities, however, take the position that once judicial notice is taken of a fact that is not subject to reasonable dispute, the matter is closed; the adversary may neither introduce contradictory evidence nor argue the contrary to the jury.[58] Logic suggests that if a fact is so well settled as to be subject to judicial notice, the jury reasonably could not find otherwise and therefore should not be given the opportunity to do so. This view, of course, makes it imperative that the "reasonably indisputable" element[59] of judicial notice be strictly applied. It also amplifies the need to give the parties an opportunity to be heard before judicial notice is taken. If the opponent can demonstrate that the matter is subject to reasonable dispute, taking judicial notice obviously is inappropriate.

The modern view is codified in Rule 201(g) of the Federal Rules of Evidence[60] and its proposed New York counterpart.[61] It is there provided that in civil cases, the jury is to be instructed that they must accept "as conclusive" any fact that has been judicially noticed. In criminal cases, on the other hand, Rule 201(g) prescribes an instruction that the jury may but is not required to find in accordance with a judicially noticed fact. The exception recognizes that a directed verdict may not be granted against the criminal defendant.[62]

Library References:

West's Key No. Digests, Criminal Law ⚖304; Evidence ⚖52.

f. Proposed New York Evidence Code

Section 201 of the Proposed New York Evidence Code, which is in the note,[63] is virtually identical to Rule 201 of the Federal Rules of

---

57. 9 Wigmore § 2567.

58. See, e.g., McCormick, "Judicial Notice," 5 Vand.L.Rev. 296, 321–22 (1952); Morgan, "Judicial Notice," 57 Harv.L.Rev. 269, 279–87 (1944).

59. See text at notes 27–30 supra.

60. See § 201.2 infra.

61. Proposed N.Y. Evidence Code § 201(g); note 63 infra.

62. People v. Walker, 198 N.Y. 329, 91 N.E. 806 (1910); § 300.3, at notes 39–40, infra. See also Sandstrom v. Montana, 442 U.S. 510, 516 n.5, 99 S.Ct. 2450, 2455, 61 L.Ed.2d 39, 46 (1979)("[V]erdicts may not be directed against defendants in criminal cases.").

63. § 201. Judicial notice of adjudicative facts [PROPOSED]

(a) Scope of section. This section governs only judicial notice of adjudicative facts. "Adjudicative facts" are the facts which but for this section would be determined by the trier of fact.

(b) Kinds of adjudicative facts which may be judicially noticed. To be judicially noticed, an adjudicative fact must be one not subject to reasonable dispute in that it is either: (1) generally known within the community where the trial court sits; or (2) capable of accurate and ready determination by resort to sources whose accuracy cannot reasonably be questioned.

(c) When judicial notice is mandatory. The court shall take judicial notice of an adjudicative fact if requested by a party and supplied with the information required by subdivision (b) of this section.

(d) When judicial notice is discretionary. The court may take judicial notice of an adjudicative fact, whether requested or not.

(e) Notice and opportunity to be heard. Before taking judicial notice, the court shall afford each party reasonable notice and an opportunity to be heard outside the presence of the jury as to the

Evidence.[64] It would codify most aspects of current New York Law except as follows: the facts which may be judicially noticed without the aid of extrinsic sources are limited to those generally known within the community in which the court sits;[65] judicial notice is mandatory, not merely discretionary, if the proponent supplies sufficient documentary support to satisfy the criteria for taking judicial notice; and the rule would require that the jury be instructed, in civil cases, to accept as conclusive any judicially noticed fact and, in criminal cass, to accept or reject the judicially noticed fact as they see fit.

§ 201.2 Federal

Rule 201 of the Federal Rules of Evidence sets forth a comprehensive scheme governing both the substance and procedure of judicial notice of adjudicative facts:

Rule 201. Judicial Notice of Adjudicative Facts

(a) Scope of rule. This rule governs only judicial notice of adjudicative facts.

(b) Kinds of facts. A judicially noticed fact must be one not subject to reasonable dispute in that it is either (1) generally known within the territorial jurisdiction of the trial court or (2) capable of accurate and ready determination by resort to sources whose accuracy cannot reasonably be questioned.

(c) When discretionary. A court may take judicial notice, whether requested or not.

(d) When mandatory. A court shall take judicial notice if requested by a party and supplied with the necessary information.

(e) Opportunity to be heard. A party is entitled upon timely request to an opportunity to be heard as to the propriety of taking judicial notice and the tenor of the matter noticed. In the absence of prior notification, the request may be made after judicial notice has been taken.

(f) Time of taking notice. Judicial notice may be taken at any stage of the proceeding.

(g) Instructing jury. In a civil action or proceeding, the court shall instruct the jury to accept as conclusive any fact judicially noticed. In a criminal case, the court shall instruct

---

matter to be noticed and the propriety of taking judicial notice.

(f) Time of taking notice. Judicial notice may be taken at any stage of the action or proceeding.

(g) Instructing jury. In a civil case, the court shall instruct the jury to accept as conclusive any adjudicative fact judicially noticed. In a criminal case, the court shall instruct the jury that it may accept as established any adjudicative fact judicially noticed.

64. See § 201.2 infra.

65. Cf. Varcoe v. Lee, 180 Cal. 338, 342–46, 181 P. 223, 225–26 (1919) (at trial in San Francisco, judicial notice that particular portion of Mission Street was business district was proper; judicial notice of location of public buildings in some other city or county might not be appropriate).

the jury that it may, but is not required to, accept as conclusive any fact judicially noticed.

In many respects, the federal approach to judicial notice is like that of New York. Subdivision (b) of Rule 201 authorizes federal courts to take judicial notice of two types of facts: (1) those which are generally known within the trial court's territorial jurisdiction, and (2) those which are readily verifiable in sources whose accuracy cannot reasonably be questioned.[1] As to both categories, any fact that is "subject to reasonable dispute" is beyond the scope of judicial notice.[2]

Within this framework,[3] federal courts in the Second Circuit have taken judicial notice of many of the same types of matters as their New York state counterparts, including public records,[4] geographical facts,[5]

---

§ 201.2

1. These two categories are essentially codifications of the common law rule, which was held to be applicable in federal courts in Brown v. Piper, 91 U.S. 37, 42, 23 L.Ed. 200, 202 (1875). The Supreme Court provided the following illustrations:

> Among the things of which judicial notice is taken are the law of nations; the general customs and usages of merchants; the notary's seal; things which must happen according to the laws of nature; the coincidences of the days of the week with those of the month; the meaning of words in the vernacular language; the customary abbreviations of Christian names; the accession of the Chief Magistrate to office, and his leaving it. In this country, such notice is taken of the appointment of members of the cabinet, the election and resignations of senators, and of the appointment of marshals and sheriffs, but not of their deputies. The courts of the United States take judicial notice of the ports and waters of the United States where the tide ebbs and flows, of the boundaries of the several States and judicial districts, and of the laws and jurisprudence of the several States in which they exercise jurisdiction.

Id. at 42, 23 L.Ed. at 201–02. In the case before it, the Court took judicial notice of the scientific and mechanical principles of the ice-cream freezer. Id. at 43, 23 L.Ed. at 202.

2. See, e.g., Pina v. Henderson, 752 F.2d 47, 50 (2d Cir.1985) (whether police officer actually prepared written record of statements made by particular arrestee, even though police practice might require report of this nature, was not proper subject of judicial notice).

3. See generally Graham §§ 201.2–201.3.

4. See, e.g., Liberty Mutual Ins. Co. v. Rotches Pork Packers, Inc., 969 F.2d 1384, 1388 (2d Cir.1992)(judicial records of another court); Kramer v. Time Warner Inc., 937 F.2d 767, 773–74 (2d Cir.1991)(documents required to be filed with federal agency and available for public inspection); Association Against Discrimination in Employment, Inc. v. City of Bridgeport, 647 F.2d 256, 277 (2d Cir.1981), cert. denied, 455 U.S. 988, 102 S.Ct. 1611, 71 L.Ed.2d 847 (1982)(municipality's published budget).

The Liberty Mutual case, however, recognized the following limitation on the taking of judicial notice of records filed in other judicial proceedings: "A court may take judicial notice of a document filed in another court 'not for the truth of the matters asserted in the other litigation, but rather to establish the fact of such litigation and related filings.'" Liberty Mutual, supra, 969 F.2d at 1388 (quoting Kramer v. Time Warner, Inc., supra, 937 F.2d at 744). Accord, United States v. Jones, 29 F.3d 1549, 1553–54 (11th Cir.1994)(factual assertions contained in records of other judicial proceedings are neither subject to judicial notice nor admissible pursuant to the hearsay exception for public records in Fed.R.Evid. 803(8)(C)).

5. See, e.g., United States v. Hernandez–Fundora, 58 F.3d 802, 811 (2d Cir.), cert. denied, ___ U.S. ___, 115 S.Ct. 2288, 132 L.Ed.2d 290 (1995)(" 'Geography has long been peculiarly susceptible to judicial notice for the obvious reason that geographic locations are facts which are not generally controversial * * *.' ")(quoting United States v. Piggie, 622 F.2d 486, 488 (10th Cir.), cert. denied, 449 U.S. 863, 101 S.Ct. 169, 66 L.Ed.2d 80 (1980)). See also note 7 infra.

Ch. 2   JUDICIAL NOTICE OF ADJUDICATIVE FACTS § 201.2

scientific facts,[6] matters of business, trade and commerce,[7] and miscellaneous aspects of human activity.[8]

Rule 201 is very specific in its procedural aspects. Judicial notice may be taken at any stage of the proceeding,[9] including on appeal,[10] upon the request of a party or by the court sua sponte.[11] The parties are entitled to be heard as to the propriety of taking judicial notice, thus guaranteeing fairness when the court acts sua sponte. The timing of this opportunity is flexible, however, inasmuch as the rule authorizes a post-notice hearing.[12] Assuming the criteria of subdivision (b) are satisfied, the taking of judicial notice becomes mandatory if a party's request is accompanied by the necessary source material.[13]

Rule 201(g) resolves the uncertainty that persists under New York law regarding the effect of taking judicial notice.[14] In civil actions, a fact that is judicially noticed becomes conclusive, and the jury must be so instructed.[15] In the interests of protecting the defendant's right to a jury trial, however, in criminal cases the jury must be told "that it may, but is not required to, accept as conclusive any fact judicially noticed."[16]

---

6. See, e.g., United States v. Lopez, 328 F.Supp. 1077, 1085 (E.D.N.Y.1971)(scientific principles of electronic weapons detector used at airports). See also note 1 supra.

7. See, e.g., United States v. Ramirez, 910 F.2d 1069, 1071 (2d Cir.), cert. denied, 498 U.S. 990, 111 S.Ct. 531, 112 L.Ed.2d 542 (1990)(fact that New York has no firearms manufacturers); Siderius v. M.V. Amilla, 880 F.2d 662, 667 (2d Cir.1989)(custom in maritime industry); United States v. Hing Shair Chan, 680 F.Supp. 521, 524 (E.D.N.Y.1988)("fact that Hong Kong's trade and service economy is sophisticated and its hotel business practices are much like those in the United States"); SEC v. Musella, 578 F.Supp. 425, 439 (S.D.N.Y. 1984)(fact that large law firms inform incoming employees of need to refrain from public discussions about clients); Sinatra v. Heckler, 566 F.Supp. 1354, 1356 (E.D.N.Y. 1983) (during weeks of Christmas and New Year's, large number of federal employees take vacations, office operations slow down, mails are heavily burdened and deliveries are sometimes slowed); United States v. Helgesen, 513 F.Supp. 209, 219 (E.D.N.Y. 1981), aff'd, 669 F.2d 69 (2d Cir.), cert. denied, 456 U.S. 929, 102 S.Ct. 1978, 72 L.Ed.2d 445 (1982)("Citibank, N.A. for 'National Association' is an FDIC-insured bank and, as one of the world's largest banking institutions, engages in interstate and foreign commerce"); Caulfield v. Board of Education, 486 F.Supp. 862, 885 (E.D.N.Y. 1979), aff'd, 632 F.2d 999 (2d Cir.1980), cert. denied, 450 U.S. 1030, 101 S.Ct. 1739, 68 L.Ed.2d 225 (1981)("fact that historically in New York City, a large percentage of the teaching force, particularly at the lower school levels, has been composed of women").

8. See, e.g., Eden Toys, Inc. v. Marshall Field & Co., 675 F.2d 498, 500 n.1 (2d Cir.1982)("traditional features of a snowman are known generally and thus appropriate for judicial notice"); United States v. Kahane, 396 F.Supp. 687, 692–93 (E.D.N.Y.1975)(Jewish dietary restrictions).

9. Fed.R.Evid. 201(f).

10. See, e.g., Browning–Ferris Industries South Jersey, Inc. v. Muszynski, 899 F.2d 151, 161 (2d Cir.1990)("Before an appellate court takes judicial notice it should advise the parties so they can object or furnish helpful documents.").

11. Fed.R.Evid. 201(c).

12. Id. 201(e).

13. Id. 201(d).

14. See § 201.1(e) supra.

15. See also Hardy v. Johns–Manville Sales Corp., 681 F.2d 334, 348 (5th Cir. 1982)(when judge decides to take judicial notice, no rebuttal evidence may be presented to jury).

16. See United States v. Mentz, 840 F.2d 315, 322 (6th Cir.1988) ("Rule 201(g) preserves the jury's 'traditional prerogative to ignore even uncontroverted facts in reaching a verdict,' and thereby prevents the trial court from transgressing the spirit, if not the letter, of the Sixth Amendment right to a jury trial by directing a partial verdict as to the facts"; trial court committed reversible error by not informing jury in bank robbery case that they could reject assumed fact that bank in question was FDIC-insured); United States v. Deckard,

Even in criminal cases, the jury's option to reject a judicially-noticed fact can be circumscribed if the matter is in the nature of a legislative fact,[17] rather than an adjudicative one. Only adjudicative facts are subject to Rule 201(g).[18] Thus, trial courts have been allowed to instruct juries to accept as conclusive the fact that a particular federal correctional institution is within the special maritime and territorial jurisdiction of the United States,[19] that Fort Benning, Georgia, is on land that is under United States jurisdiction,[20] and that cocaine hydrochloride is a derivative of coca leaves and therefore is a controlled substance under a federal statute.[21]

Assuming the fact in question is adjudicative in nature, the policy embodied in Rule 201(g) in criminal cases occasionally conflicts with the principle that judicial notice can be taken for the first time on appeal. Several appellate courts have refused to take judicial notice where the result would be to fill a missing gap in the prosecution's prima facie case.[22] Otherwise, it is reasoned, the jury would be deprived of their prerogative under Rule 201(g) to reject the fact. Some appellate courts in cases of this nature have been able to avoid the conflict by drawing liberal inferences from the trial testimony.[23]

Library References:

West's Key No. Digests, Criminal Law ⟲304; Evidence ⟲1–52.

816 F.2d 426, 428 (8th Cir.1987)(in prosecution for interception of wire communications, trial judge took judicial notice of interstate character of telephone company's services but properly told jury that it was not bound by judge's declaration).

17. See § 200.1, at notes 2–3, supra; § 202.1, at note 2, infra.

18. Fed.R.Evid. 201(a).

19. United States v. Hernandez–Fundora, 58 F.3d 802, 810–12 (2d Cir.), cert. denied, ___ U.S. ___, 115 S.Ct. 2288, 132 L.Ed.2d 290 (1995)(prosecution for assault on property within federal jurisdiction; "geographical/jurisdictional" fact is legislative fact to which judge may give conclusive effect, but where and whether the offense occurred are jury questions).

20. United States v. Bowers, 660 F.2d 527, 531 (5th Cir.1981)(unlike adjudicative fact, Fort Benning's status "does not change from case to case but, instead, remains fixed").

21. United States v. Gould, 536 F.2d 216, 219–21 (8th Cir.1976) (general nature of narcotic substance is legislative fact which bears on administration and application of narcotics statutes).

22. See United States v. Jones, 580 F.2d 219 (6th Cir.1978)(refusal to take judicial notice, for purpose of sustaining conviction, that telephone company was common carrier engaged in interstate communications, an element of the crime which was not proven at trial). Accord, United States v. Dior, 671 F.2d 351, 358 n.11 (9th Cir.1982); United States v. Thomas, 610 F.2d 1166, 1171 n.10 (3d Cir.1979). See also United States v. Bliss, 642 F.2d 390, 392 n.2 (10th Cir.1981).

23. See, e.g., United States v. Hernandez–Fundora, 58 F.3d 802, 808–09 (2d Cir.), cert. denied, ___ U.S. ___, 115 S.Ct. 2288, 132 L.Ed.2d 290 (1995)(witness' trial testimony given in June 1993 that correctional institution "is under concurrent [state and federal] jurisdiction" was sufficient to raise inference that it was under such jurisdiction at time of alleged crime in September 1992); United States v. Sliker, 751 F.2d 477, 484–85 (2d Cir.1984), cert. denied, 470 U.S. 1058, 105 S.Ct. 1772, 84 L.Ed.2d 832 (1985)(witness' testimony at trial that bank deposits "are" FDIC-insured was sufficient to raise inference that same situation prevailed at time of alleged crime); United States v. Thomas, 610 F.2d 1166, 1171–72 (3d Cir.1979)(trial witnesses' identification of bank as "First National Bank" was sufficient for jury to infer that bank was federally chartered).

202 Judicial Notice of Legislative Facts

§ 202.1 New York and Federal

Drawing upon the writings of Professor Kenneth Culp Davis,[1] McCormick explains judicial notice of legislative facts as follows:

> It is conventional wisdom today to observe that judges not only are charged to find what the law is, but must regularly make new law when deciding upon the constitutional validity of a statute, interpreting a statute, or extending or restricting a common law rule. The very nature of the judicial process necessitates that judges be guided, as legislators are, by considerations of expediency and public policy. They must, in the nature of things, act either upon knowledge already possessed or upon assumptions, or upon investigation of the pertinent general facts, social, economic, political, or scientific. An older tradition once prescribed that judges should rationalize their result solely in terms of analogy to old doctrines leaving the considerations of expedience unstated. Contemporary practice indicates that judges in their opinions should render explicit their policy- judgments and the factual grounds therefor. These latter have been helpfully classed as "legislative facts," as contrasted with the "adjudicative facts" which are historical facts pertaining to the incidents which give rise to lawsuits.[2]

The legislative facts upon which judges act ordinarily need not be formally proven.[3] Courts may rely upon data provided to them in the briefs of counsel or by "recourse to such [other] sources of information as [they] deem[] trustworthy."[4] There are no formal rules governing notice to the affected parties "other than those inherent in affording

---

§ 202.1

1. See, e.g., K. Davis and R. Pierce, Jr., Administrative Law Treatise §§ 10.5–10.6 (3d ed.1994).

2. McCormick § 331, at 398–99 (footnotes omitted). See Advisory Committee's Note, Fed.R.Evid. 201 ("Legislative facts * * * are those which have relevance to legal reasoning and the lawmaking process, whether in the formulation of a legal principle or ruling by a judge or court or in the enactment of a legislative body.").

3. See Advisory Committee's Note, Fed. R.Evid. 201(a).

Formal proof was deemed necessary, however, in a case involving the interpretation of the Articles of Confederation and certain treaties with the Oneida Indian Nation. Oneida Indian Nation of New York v. State of New York, 691 F.Supp. 1070, 1085–86 (2d Cir.1982), on remand, 649 F.Supp. 420 (N.D.N.Y.1986), aff'd, 860 F.2d 1145 (2d Cir.1988), cert. denied, 493 U.S. 871, 110 S.Ct. 200, 107 L.Ed.2d 154 (1989). The Second Circuit observed that analysis of legislative history usually is based on historical sources whose authenticity and accuracy are undisputed. In the instant case, however, the court held that an evidentiary hearing was needed "to clarify the meaning and context" of the miscellaneous records, correspondence, and histories that purported to explain the Articles of Confederation and pertinent treaties. Id. at 1086.

4. Viemeister v. White, 179 N.Y. 235, 240, 72 N.E. 97, 99 (1904). See also Bulova Watch Co. v. K. Hattori & Co., 508 F.Supp. 1322, 1328 (E.D.N.Y.1981)("A court's power to resort to less well known and accepted sources of data to fill in the gaps of its knowledge for legislative and general evidential hypothesis purposes must be accepted because it is essential to the judicial process.").

opportunity to hear and be heard and exchanging briefs."[5] Moreover, the data need not be indisputable.[6]

No court has ever defined the boundaries of the taking of judicial notice of legislative facts, and the drafters of the Federal Rules of Evidence made no attempt at codification.[7] Examples of the process, however, are in abundant supply. The common law evolution of the attorney-client privilege provides an illustration:[8] no one has ever demonstrated by indisputable empirical evidence that the privilege encourages candor between attorney and client.[9] Yet this is the perceived reality that courts have relied upon for over 200 years to justify the privilege as a rule of law.[10]

In the context of interpreting and applying one of New York's jurisdictional statutes,[11] Judge Weinstein took judicial notice of legislative facts concerning international commerce to conclude that a foreign corporation was "doing business" in New York.[12]

The New York Court of Appeals' decision in *Viemeister v. White*,[13] illustrates the process in the setting of judicial review of the constitutionality of legislation. There, a statute requiring vaccination of all public school children was upheld as a reasonable exercise of the state's police power because the Legislature had a right to rely upon the "common belief of the people of the state" that vaccination was an effective preventive of smallpox.[14] The court declared that "[a] common belief, like common knowledge, does not require evidence to establish its existence, but may be acted upon without proof by the Legislature and the courts."[15]

A federal court reached a different conclusion with respect to the constitutionality of a New York statute that prohibited the distribution

---

5. Advisory Committee's Note, Fed. R.Evid. 201(a). Cf. Bulova Watch Co. v. K. Hattori & Co., 508 F.Supp. 1322, 1328–29 (E.D.N.Y.1981)(because of extensive reliance on legislative facts in determining jurisdictional question, court invited parties to submit additional information in response to court's preliminary memorandum decision).

6. See McCormick § 331, at 400 ("While not necessarily indisputably true, it would appear that these legislative facts must at least appear to be more likely than not true if the opinion is going to have the requisite intellectual legitimacy upon which the authority of judge-made rules is ultimately founded."). See also text at notes 14–15 infra (courts may act upon "common beliefs").

7. The Advisory Committee's Note to Fed.R.Evid. 201 suggests that the drafters viewed the traditional flexibility of the doctrine as an argument against its codification.

8. See § 501.1 infra.

9. See Alexander, "The Corporate Attorney–Client Privilege: A Study of the Participants," 63 St. John's L.Rev. 191, 232–34, 260–70 (1989) (results of interview survey of 150 corporate lawyers and executives provide only partial support for traditional rationale of attorney-client privilege in corporate context).

10. 8 Wigmore §§ 2290–91. Perceptions about judge-made rules can change over time, of course, resulting in modifications of the common law. See, e.g., Scurti v. City of New York, 40 N.Y.2d 433, 439–42, 387 N.Y.S.2d 55, 57–59, 354 N.E.2d 794, 796–99 (1976)(old property law distinctions between licensees, trespassers and invitees held to be at odds with modern notions of landowner's responsibilities).

11. CPLR 301.

12. Bulova Watch Co. v. K. Hattori & Co., 508 F.Supp. 1322, 1327–29 (E.D.N.Y. 1981).

13. 179 N.Y. 235, 72 N.E. 97 (1904).

14. Id. at 241, 72 N.E. at 99.

15. Id. at 240, 72 N.E. at 99.

of contraceptives to persons under the age of 16.[16] The state's interest in deterring sexual activity by young persons was held to be insufficient to outweigh the burdens imposed on the constitutionally protected right of privacy. In considering the weight to be given the state's interest, the court took notice that some young persons under the age of 16 "do engage in sexual intercourse and that the consequence of such activity is often venereal disease, unwanted pregnancy, or both."[17]

The racial desegregation decision of the Supreme Court in *Brown v. Board of Education*,[18] is perhaps the quintessential example of the taking of judicial notice of legislative facts. The Court, relying upon various social science studies, found that "separate but equal" public education was inherently unequal and therefore violated the fourteenth amendment.

Library References:

West's Key No. Digests, Criminal Law ⚖304; Evidence ⚖1–50.

203 Judicial Notice of Law

§ 203.1 New York

When judges take judicial notice of law, they are determining, in an informal way, the law that applies to the particular cases before them.[1] This process relieves the parties of the need to prove the substance of such law. The judge simply consults available statutes, caselaw, treatises and any other relevant sources, aided but not confined by the briefs of counsel.[2] Determining the content of the law inherently is a judicial function; and even where formal proof may be necessary, as, for example, in a case based upon the law of a foreign country, the jury should play no role in the process.[3]

In New York, CPLR 4511 contains a comprehensive scheme governing the taking of judicial notice of law.[4]

---

16. Population Services International v. Wilson, 398 F.Supp. 321 (S.D.N.Y.1975), aff'd, 431 U.S. 678, 97 S.Ct. 2010, 52 L.Ed.2d 675 (1977).

17. Id. at 332–33.

18. 347 U.S. 483, 74 S.Ct. 686, 98 L.Ed. 873 (1954), supplemented 349 U.S. 294, 75 S.Ct. 753, 99 L.Ed. 1083 (1955).

§ 203.1

1. See Mueller and Kirkpatrick § 2.12, at 112–13; McCormick § 335, at 413.

2. See Morgan, "Judicial Notice," 57 Harv.L.Rev. 269, 270 (1944) ("In determining the content or applicability of a rule of domestic law, the judge is unrestricted in his investigation and conclusion. He may reject the propositions of either party or of both parties. He may consult the sources of pertinent data to which they refer, or he may refuse to do so. He may make an independent search for persuasive data or rest content with what he has or what the parties present."). See also CPLR 4511(d); note 4 infra.

3. See, e.g., CPLR 4511(c)(determination of law is made by court); note 4 infra; McCormick § 335, at 421.

4. CPLR 4511 provides as follows:

Rule 4511. Judicial notice of law

(a) When judicial notice shall be taken without request. Every court shall take judicial notice without request of the common law, constitutions and public statutes of the United States and of every state, territory and jurisdiction of the United States and of the official compilation of codes, rules and regulations of the state except those that relate solely to the organization or internal management of an agency of the state and of all local laws and county acts.

§ 203.1 JUDICIAL NOTICE

Pursuant to CPLR 4511(a), a New York court must take judicial notice of the following laws, without the need for a request by one of the parties:[5]

1. The constitution, public statutes and common law of the United States and of every territory and jurisdiction of the United States.

2. The constitution, public statutes and common law of every state, including New York.

3. All local laws and county acts within New York.

4. The official compilation of codes, rules and regulations of New York except those that relate solely to an agency's organization or internal management.

With respect to the following types of laws, subdivision (b) of CPLR 4511 provides that the court has discretion to take judicial notice regardless of whether a party so requests:[6]

1. Private acts and resolutions of the United States Congress or of the New York State Legislature.

2. Ordinances and regulations of officers, agencies or governmental subdivisions of New York or of the United States.

3. The law of foreign countries.

CPLR 4511(b) further provides that judicial notice of the foregoing becomes mandatory if a party makes a request supported by sufficient information to enable the court to comply and notifies the other parties of the request. Such notification must be made prior to trial—it may be

(b) **When judicial notice may be taken without request; when it shall be taken on request.** Every court may take judicial notice without request of private acts and resolutions of the congress of the United States and of the legislature of the state; ordinances and regulations of officers, agencies or governmental subdivisions of the state or of the United States; and the laws of foreign countries or their political subdivisions. Judicial notice shall be taken of matters specified in this subdivision if a party requests it, furnishes the court sufficient information to enable it to comply with the request, and has given each adverse party notice of his intention to request it. Notice shall be given in the pleadings or prior to the presentation of any evidence at the trial, but a court may require or permit other notice.

(c) **Determination by court; review as matter of law.** Whether a matter is judicially noticed or proof is taken, every matter specified in this section shall be determined by the judge or referee, and included in his findings or charged to the jury. Such findings or charge shall be subject to review on appeal as a finding or charge on a matter of law.

(d) **Evidence to be received on matter to be judicially noticed.** In considering whether a matter of law should be judicially noticed and in determining the matter of law to be judicially noticed, the court may consider any testimony, document, information or argument on the subject, whether offered by a party or discovered through its own research. Whether or not judicial notice is taken, a printed copy of a statute or other written law or a proclamation, edict, decree or ordinance by an executive contained in a book or publication, purporting to have been published by a government or commonly admitted as evidence of the existing law in the judicial tribunals of the jurisdiction where it is in force, is prima facie evidence of such law and the unwritten or common law of a jurisdiction may be proved by witnesses or printed reports of cases of the courts of the jurisdiction.

5. See note 4 supra.

6. See note 4 supra.

given in the pleadings, for example—or in accordance with the court's directions.[7]

As to foreign law, the request-and-notification component of CPLR 4511(b) is complemented by CPLR 3016(e). The latter provision requires that the substance of foreign law be stated in the pleading of the party who intends to rely upon it.[8] Compliance with the pleading requirement should be deemed to satisfy the request and notification aspects of CPLR 4511(b). Whether the pleading will also furnish the court "sufficient information" to take judicial notice of the foreign law will depend on the nature of the law in question. The more esoteric the law—and hence the greater the difficulty in locating it in a law library—the greater the need for specificity.

Subdivision (d) of CPLR 4511 gives courts latitude with respect to the sources they may consult in deciding whether to take judicial notice or in actually determining what the law is. The court is authorized to "consider any testimony, document, information or argument on the subject, whether offered by a party or discovered through its own research."[9] In ascertaining foreign law, a hearing for the purpose of taking expert testimony may be deemed necessary.[10]

Whether the law of another state is relevant to particular litigation is governed by choice-of-law rules. Although CPLR 4511 seemingly would mandate that judicial notice be taken of such out-of-state law, as a practical matter the parties to the action share in the responsibility of making the court aware in a timely manner of its relevance.[11]

Library References:

West's Key No. Digests, Criminal Law ⋘304; Evidence ⋘1-50.

---

7. CPLR 4511(b); note 4 supra. A party's failure to request the application of foreign law does not preclude the court from exercising its discretion to take judicial notice and apply such law sua sponte. Watts v. Swiss Bank Corp., 27 N.Y.2d 270, 276, 317 N.Y.S.2d 315, 320, 265 N.E.2d 739, 743 (1970). See also Lerner v. Karageorgis Lines, Inc., 66 N.Y.2d 479, 487–88, 497 N.Y.S.2d 894, 897, 488 N.E.2d 824, 827 (1985)(lower courts did not abuse discretion in declining to take judicial notice of foreign law sua sponte).

8. CPLR 3016(e)("Where a cause of action or defense is based upon the law of a foreign country or its political subdivision, the substance of the foreign law relied upon shall be stated [in the party's pleading].").

9. CPLR 4511(d); note 4 supra.

10. See, e.g., In re Will of Duysburgh, 154 Misc.2d 82, 85, 584 N.Y.S.2d 516, 518–19 (Surr.Ct.N.Y.Co.1992)(hearing deemed necessary to resolve disputed issue of French law where affidavits of parties' legal experts were inconclusive and contained "meager citation of authority").

11. See, e.g., Cousins v. Instrument Flyers, Inc., 44 N.Y.2d 698, 700, 405 N.Y.S.2d 441, 443, 376 N.E.2d 914, 915 (1978)(where parties tried case on assumption that New York law was applicable, plaintiff's request that law of another state be applied was untimely when made just before jury charge). See also Kucel v. Walter E. Heller & Co., 813 F.2d 67, 74 (5th Cir.1987)(although federal courts must take judicial notice of all states' laws, litigant had "obligation to call the applicability of another state's law to the court's attention in time to be properly considered").

On a related procedural point, a plaintiff can be required, upon demand, to identify in a bill of particulars the statutes, rules or regulations upon which she intends to rely even though CPLR 4511 may relieve her of the burden of proving the substance of such laws. See Vagelos v. Robinson, 37 A.D.2d 544, 322 N.Y.S.2d 384 (1st Dep't 1971); Sacks v. Town of Thompson, 33 A.D.2d 627, 304 N.Y.S.2d 729 (3d Dep't 1969).

§ 203.2 Federal

In federal practice, the rules governing judicial notice of law are mostly a product of caselaw. The Federal Rules of Evidence do not address the topic.

Federal courts are obligated to take judicial notice of federal law[1] and the statutory and judge-made law of all the states.[2] Federal regulatory law is also subject to mandatory judicial notice.[3] A rule of discretion appears to apply with respect to a state's administrative regulations.[4] If state regulatory law is not readily available in published form, a party may be required to prove the content of such law with documentary and testimonial evidence.[5]

Taking judicial notice of the law of foreign countries appears to lie in the court's discretion. The matter is handled as a rule of procedure. Under Rule 44.1 of the Federal Rules of Civil Procedure[6] and Rule 26.1 of the Federal Rules of Criminal Procedure,[7] a party who intends to raise an issue concerning foreign law must give "reasonable written notice" of such intent. Absent such notice, the court may choose to ignore the foreign law.[8] When the issue of foreign law is timely raised, the court "may consider any relevant material or source, including testimony, whether or not submitted by a party or admissible under the Federal Rules of Evidence."[9]

§ 203.2

1. Surprisingly, there is little authority for this obvious proposition. See In re Madeline Marie Nursing Homes, 694 F.2d 433, 445 (6th Cir.1982)("federal judges are presumed to know * * * the law of the United States").

2. Lamar v. Micou, 114 U.S. 218, 223, 5 S.Ct. 857, 859, 29 L.Ed. 94, 95 (1885); Schultz v. Tecumseh Prods., 310 F.2d 426, 433 (6th Cir.1962); Newman v. Clayton F. Summy Co., 133 F.2d 465, 467 n.3 (2d Cir. 1943). Hanley v. Donoghue, 116 U.S. 1, 6, 6 S.Ct. 242, 245, 29 L.Ed. 535, 537 (1885), however, held that on appeal from a state court, the Supreme Court's authority to take judicial notice of other state's laws is limited in scope to that of the court below.

3. Caha v. United States, 152 U.S. 211, 221–22, 14 S.Ct. 513, 517, 38 L.Ed. 415, 419 (1894). See also 44 U.S.C.A. § 1507 (judicial notice must be taken of contents of Federal Register).

4. See, e.g., Roemer v. Board of Public Works of Maryland, 426 U.S. 736, 743 n.4, 96 S.Ct. 2337, 2343, 49 L.Ed.2d 179, 185 (1976); 9 Wigmore § 2572, at 756 ("the doctrine applies at common law to *public or general statutes* of the Legislature only")(emphasis in original).

5. See, e.g., In re Madeline Marie Nursing Homes, 694 F.2d 433, 445–46 (6th Cir. 1982).

6. Fed.R.Civ.P. 44.1 states as follows:

A party who intends to raise an issue concerning the law of a foreign country shall give notice by pleadings or other reasonable written notice. The court, in determining foreign law, may consider any relevant material or source, including testimony, whether or not submitted by a party or admissible under the Federal Rules of Evidence. The court's determination shall be treated as a ruling on a question of law.

7. Fed.R.Crim.P. 26.1 provides as follows:

A party who intends to raise an issue concerning the law of a foreign country shall give reasonable written notice. The court, in determining foreign law, may consider any relevant material or source, including testimony, whether or not submitted by a party or admissible under the Federal Rules of Evidence. The court's determination shall be treated as a ruling on a question of law.

8. See, e.g., Ruff v. St. Paul Mercury Ins. Co., 393 F.2d 500, 502 (2d Cir.1968).

9. Fed.R.Civ.P. 44.1; Fed.R.Crim.P. 26.1; notes 6–7 supra. See, e.g., Overseas Development Disc Corp. v. Sangamo Construction Co., 840 F.2d 1319, 1324–25 (7th Cir.1988)(in determining foreign law, court may use any relevant source, including expert testimony). See also Application of Chase Manhattan Bank, 191 F.Supp. 206,

Library References:

West's Key No. Digests, Criminal Law ⇌304; Evidence ⇌1–50.

209 (S.D.N.Y.1961), on reargument, 192 F.Supp. 817, aff'd, 297 F.2d 611 (2d Cir. 1962)("The party relying on foreign law has the burden of proof. It must establish precisely what that law is and how it is interpreted.").

Chapter 3

BURDEN OF PROOF AND PRESUMPTIONS

Table of Sections

300 BURDEN OF PROOF

300.1 Burden of Proof, In General.
300.2 Allocation of Burden of Proof, In General.
300.3 Satisfying the Burden of Production.
    a. New York.
        1. The Test for Sufficiency.
        2. Shifting the Burden of Production.
    b. Federal.
300.4 Satisfying the Burden of Persuasion.
    a. In General.
    b. Civil Cases: New York.
        1. Preponderance of the Evidence.
        2. Clear and Convincing Evidence.
    c. Civil Cases: Federal.
    d. Criminal Cases: New York.
        1. Reasonable Doubt.
        2. Defenses and Affirmative Defenses.
    e. Criminal Cases: Federal.

301 PRESUMPTIONS IN CIVIL CASES

301.1 New York: Introduction.
301.2 The Meaning of a Presumption.
301.3 Rebuttable Presumptions.
301.4 Reasons for Presumptions; Illustrative Presumptions.
301.5 Effect of Presumptions in New York.
    a. In General.
        1. Thayer (the "Bursting Bubble" Rule).
        2. Morgan.
    b. New York Approach.
301.6 Res Ipsa Loquitur.
301.7 Prima Facie Evidence.
301.8 Effect of Presumptions in Federal Proceedings.
    a. Cases Governed by Federal Law.
    b. Cases Governed by State Law.

302 PRESUMPTIONS IN CRIMINAL CASES

302.1 New York.
    a. Constitutional Restraints.
    b. New York Approach.
302.2 Federal.

WESTLAW Electronic Research

See WESTLAW Electronic Research Guide preceding the Summary of Contents.

300 Burden of Proof

§ 300.1 Burden of Proof, In General

"Burden of proof," like its first cousin "presumptions," has been described as one of the "slipperiest member[s] of the family of legal terms."[1] It is now well recognized among evidence and procedure scholars that burden of proof encompasses two distinct concepts: burden of production and burden of persuasion.[2] The burden of production, sometimes called the "duty of going forward," is that burden which the law places on a party to introduce sufficient evidence to avoid an adverse judgment as a matter of law. The party with this burden on a particular matter must come forward with sufficient evidence to permit the fact-finder rationally to find in her favor. Whether this burden has been satisfied, i.e., whether the sufficiency standard has been met, is a question for the court to decide as a matter of law after the party rests her case. The court, in effect, screens the evidence to determine whether there is enough to let the matter "go to the jury."[3] Procedurally, the sufficiency question is raised by the modern equivalent of a motion for a directed verdict.[4]

The burden of persuasion is that burden which the law places on a party to actually convince the trier of facts that a proposition is true (or not true). The usual degree of persuasion, familiar to lawyers and laypersons alike, is that of a "preponderance of the evidence" in civil cases[5] and "beyond a reasonable doubt" in criminal cases.[6] Occasionally, an intermediate standard of "clear and convincing evidence" is applicable.[7] Such burdens of persuasion do not become operative unless and until the necessary burdens of production have been satisfied.[8] It is only then that the determination of disputed issues is reposed in the fact-finder. In a jury trial, the jury must be instructed that if the party with the burden of proof on a particular issue has not persuaded them to the requisite degree, they must find against that party. In a bench trial, the judge similarly must find against the party with the burden of proof if the judge is not convinced to the extent required by the applicable standard.

Neither the Federal Rules of Evidence nor the Proposed New York Evidence Code attempt to codify the law with respect to burdens of proof.

---

§ 300.1

1. McCormick § 342, at 449.
2. F. James, G. Hazard and J. Leubsdorf, Civil Procedure § 7.12 (4th ed.1992); McCormick § 336; 9 Wigmore §§ 2485–2487.
3. See 9 Wigmore § 2487, at 293.
4. See § 300.3(a)(1) infra.
5. See § 300.4(b)(1) infra.
6. See § 300.4 (d)(1) infra.
7. See § 300.4(b)(2) infra.
8. McCormick § 337, at 426 ("The burden of persuasion becomes a crucial factor only if the parties have sustained their burdens of producing evidence and only when all of the evidence has been introduced. It does not shift from party to party during the course of the trial simply because it need not be allocated until it is time for a decision.")

§ 300.1 BURDEN OF PROOF & PRESUMPTIONS Ch. 3

Library References:

West's Key No. Digests, Criminal Law ⚖=326; Evidence ⚖=90–98.

§ 300.2 Allocation of Burden of Proof, In General

Caselaw and statutes determine how burdens of proof are allocated between the parties. McCormick observes that "[i]n most cases, the party who has the burden of pleading a fact will have the burden of producing evidence and of persuading the jury of its existence as well."[1] This rule of thumb, which is riddled with exceptions, is borne out by New York law. In general, the plaintiff in a civil case must plead and prove (in both senses of the term) all of the elements of her cause of action,[2] and the defendant must do the same for affirmative defenses.[3] In a simple personal injury case based on negligence, for example, the plaintiff's complaint must allege the defendant's negligence, its causal relation to her injuries and damages.[4] At trial, plaintiff has the burden of producing evidence on these issues and persuading the fact-finder by the evidence that the facts are as contended by her.[5] The defendant, who has the burden of pleading plaintiff's contributory negligence if she wishes to assert it as an affirmative defense, must likewise produce

§ 300.2

1. McCormick § 337, at 427.

2. See, e.g., Farmers' Loan & Trust Co. v. Siefke, 144 N.Y. 354, 358–59, 39 N.E. 358, 359 (1895).

3. Id. at 359–60, 39 N.E. at 359. The rule governing the pleading, but not necessarily the proof, of affirmative defenses is set forth in CPLR 3018(b):

(b) **Affirmative defenses.** A party shall plead all matters which if not pleaded would be likely to take the adverse party by surprise or would raise issues of fact not appearing on the face of a prior pleading such as arbitration and award, collateral estoppel, culpable conduct claimed in diminution of damages as set forth in article fourteen-A, discharge in bankruptcy, facts showing illegality either by statute or common law, fraud, infancy or other disability of the party defending, payment, release, res judicata, statute of frauds, or statute of limitation. The application of this subdivision shall not be confined to the instances enumerated.

4. CPLR 3013 provides that a complaint "shall be sufficiently particular to give the court and parties notice of the transactions, occurrences, or series of transactions or occurrences, intended to be proved and the material elements of each cause of action * * *." CPLR 3017(a) requires the pleader to make "a demand for the relief to which the pleader deems himself entitled." In tort actions against municipalities and in medical malpractice actions, however, CPLR 3017(c) prohibits specification of the amount of damages so as to diminish the potential for pretrial sensationalism in such cases. See Braun v. Ahmed, 127 A.D.2d 418, 515 N.Y.S.2d 473 (2d Dep't 1987).

Form 12 of the "Official Forms" accompanying adoption of the CPLR is an example of a sufficient negligence complaint. See generally D. Siegel, New York Practice § 210 (2d ed.1991).

Special pleading rules may apply to the plaintiff in particular negligence actions, such as those seeking damages for personal injuries arising from an automobile accident. In such a case, plaintiff must demonstrate that her action falls outside the scope of New York's "no-fault" laws. Thus, she must allege (and prove) that she suffered "serious physical injuries" or "economic loss greater than basic economic loss" as defined by the Insurance Law. See CPLR 3016(g); Licari v. Elliott, 57 N.Y.2d 230, 455 N.Y.S.2d 570, 441 N.E.2d 1088 (1982).

As a result of other "tort reform" legislation, specialized pleading and proof requirements are imposed in multi-tortfeasor actions in which a defendant seeks to limit his liability to his own "equitable share of the culpability" and the plaintiff seeks to impose conventional joint-and-several liability. See CPLR §§ 1601–1603.

5. See, e.g., Schneider v. Kings Highway Hosp. Center, 67 N.Y.2d 743, 500 N.Y.S.2d 95, 490 N.E.2d 1221 (1986).

evidence of such negligence and persuade the fact-finder of its existence.[6]

There are some notable exceptions to the usual congruence between burden of pleading and burden of proof. This is particularly so in contract-related actions. For example, the plaintiff in an action for nonpayment ordinarily must plead nonpayment in order for the complaint to make any sense,[7] but defendant must plead and prove payment as an affirmative defense.[8] Nonperformance of a contractual condition precedent must be pleaded by the defendant, but the plaintiff must then prove her performance of the condition which has thus been put in issue.[9] Similarly, in an action on a negotiable instrument, the defendant who claims lack of effectiveness of the signature must explicitly deny, in her pleading, that the signature is valid.[10] Having thus raised the issue, however, the burden then falls on the plaintiff to prove the effectiveness of the signature.[11]

Various factors play a role in the judicial and legislative allocation of burdens of proof. Commentators have identified the following considerations as influencing, either individually or in combination, the apportionment of the burden of proof.[12]

(1) *Change in the status quo.* The party who invokes the court's jurisdiction for the purpose of demanding some sort of remedy or state action, the plaintiff in a civil case and the prosecutor in a criminal action, naturally can be expected to produce evidence in support of such demand.

(2) *Fairness.* Here again, the plaintiff or prosecutor should, in fairness, be required to come forward with her evidence before the defendant can be expected to defend. In the criminal sphere, the fairness factor assumes constitutional dimensions.[13]

(3) *Practicality and convenience.* Parties who rely upon defensive circumstances that have arisen after the maturing of a cause of action, such as release[14] or accord and satisfaction,[15] are in the most convenient

---

6. CPLR 1412. The common law rule that any amount of contributory negligence was a bar to plaintiff's recovery was changed by CPLR 1411 to provide for a rule of pure comparative negligence. The plaintiff's "culpable conduct," including contributory negligence or assumption of risk, will simply diminish the amount of her recovery. CPLR 1411.

7. Conkling v. Weatherwax, 181 N.Y. 258, 268, 73 N.E. 1028, 1031 (1905).

8. Id. See CPLR 3018(b); note 3 supra.

9. CPLR 3015(a). In contrast, performance of a statutorily-imposed condition precedent, such as service of a notice of claim in a tort action against a municipality, must be both alleged and proved by the plaintiff. See, e.g., Fullerton v. City of Schenectady, 285 App.Div. 545, 138 N.Y.S.2d 916 (3d Dep't), aff'd, 309 N.Y. 701, 128 N.E.2d 413 (1955).

10. CPLR 3015(d).

11. N.Y.Uniform Commercial Code § 3–307(1)(a). In proving the effectiveness of the signature, the plaintiff is aided in most cases by a presumption that it was genuine and authorized. Id. § 3–307(1)(b).

12. See James, Hazard and Leubsdorf § 7.16; McCormick § 337, at 428–32.

13. See § 300.4(d)(1) infra.

14. See, e.g., Fleming v. Ponziani, 24 N.Y.2d 105, 109–110, 299 N.Y.S.2d 134, 138–39, 247 N.E.2d 114, 118 (1969).

15. See, e.g., Reilly v. Barrett, 220 N.Y. 170, 173, 115 N.E. 453, 453 (1917); Conboy, McKay, Bachman & Kendall v. Armstrong, 110 A.D.2d 1042, 488 N.Y.S.2d 901 (4th Dep't 1985).

§ 300.2   BURDEN OF PROOF & PRESUMPTIONS   Ch. 3

position to prove such circumstances.[16] It is also said that the party who alleges the applicability of an exception to the enforcement of a statute or contract usually must prove the exception.[17] Similarly, the burden of proof lies on the party who claims that her opponent waived contractual rights[18] or should be estopped from asserting them.[19]

(4) *Access to evidence.* This factor frequently overlaps with fairness, practicality and convenience. The party who is likely to have "inside" knowledge about particular facts, such as whether a debt was paid, is often the party burdened with proving such facts.[20]

(5) *Probabilities.* A party who contends that her rights or obligations are dependent upon facts that are contrary to the normal course of events must often bear the burden of overcoming the probabilities.[21]

(6) *Policy.* Finally, policy considerations come into play with respect to claims or defenses that are favored or disfavored in the substantive law. Today, for example, significant burdens are placed on defamation plaintiffs,[22] and defendants who seek to avoid their obligations due only to the passage of time must prove the applicability of the statute of limitations.[23]

Many of the same factors identified above also underlie the creation of presumptions and the particular degree of persuasion that is imposed on the party with the burden of proof. In the final analysis, no one factor can be singled out as the universal determinant of which party

---

16. Murray v. Narwood, 192 N.Y. 172, 177–78, 84 N.E. 958, 959 (1908), holds that, in general, defenses based on facts arising subsequent to the execution of a contract must be proved by the party seeking to avoid enforcement of the contract.

17. See generally McCormick § 337, at 430. See, e.g., J.M. Rodriguez & Co. v. Moore–McCormack Lines, Inc., 32 N.Y.2d 425, 429–30, 345 N.Y.S.2d 993, 996, 299 N.E.2d 243, 245 (1973)(in order to benefit from contractual clause excusing delays due to strike, carrier had burden of proving that strike was cause of damage to goods).

18. See, e.g., City of New York v. State, 40 N.Y.2d 659, 669, 389 N.Y.S.2d 332, 340, 357 N.E.2d 988, 995 (1976).

19. See, e.g., Gratton v. Dido Realty Co., 89 Misc.2d 401, 402–03, 391 N.Y.S.2d 954, 955 (Sup.Ct.Queens Co.1977), aff'd, 63 A.D.2d 959, 405 N.Y.S.2d 1001 (2d Dep't 1978).

20. See notes 7–8 supra. See also Louis Harris and Associates, Inc. v. deLeon, 84 N.Y.2d 698, 705–06, 622 N.Y.S.2d 217, 221, 646 N.E.2d 438, 442 (1994)(in claim of employment discrimination based on disability, employer properly has burden of proving that he would be unable to reasonably accommodate employee or that any such accommodation would impose undue hardship; employer "is in the better position to assess the feasibility of possible accommodations and to know how they will impact [on] its business operations"). Obviously this factor is outweighed by other considerations in some cases, such as negligence, where each party must prove the other's conduct. See text at notes 4–6 supra.

21. In probate proceedings, for example, the party who claims that undue influence was exercised on the testator has the burden of proof on this issue. In re Kindberg's Will, 207 N.Y. 220, 228–29, 100 N.E. 789, 791 (1912).

22. See, e.g., Freeman v. Johnston, 84 N.Y.2d 52, 56, 614 N.Y.S.2d 377, 378, 637 N.E.2d 268, 269 (1994), cert. denied, ___ U.S. ___, 115 S.Ct. 576, 130 L.Ed.2d 492 (1994)(in defamation action brought by public figure, plaintiff must prove falsity of statement and defendant's knowledge of such falsity or reckless disregard as to truth or falsity).

23. Romano v. Romano, 19 N.Y.2d 444, 280 N.Y.S.2d 570, 227 N.E.2d 389 (1967). Conversely, the party who relies upon a toll or extension of the limitations period generally must prove its applicability. Brush v. Olivo, 81 A.D.2d 852, 853, 438 N.Y.S.2d 857, 859 (2d Dep't 1981); Doyon v. Bascom, 38 A.D.2d 645, 326 N.Y.S.2d 896 (3d Dep't 1971).

will be saddled with the burden of proof on a particular issue.[24]

A comprehensive cataloging of the burdens of proof in civil cases, and the law's allocation thereof to particular parties on particular issues, is beyond the scope of a one-volume evidence book. Questions in this regard must be answered by reference to the statutes and caselaw that govern the relevant areas of substantive law. With respect to criminal cases in New York, a relatively comprehensive scheme can be readily found in the provisions of the Penal Law.[25]

Library References:

West's Key No. Digests, Criminal Law ⟐326; Evidence ⟐90–98.

§ 300.3 Satisfying the Burden of Production

a. New York

1. The Test for Sufficiency

In general, the burden of production, which requires the burdened party to produce sufficient evidence of the fact she is trying to prove, may be satisfied by direct or circumstantial evidence. Direct evidence is that which, if believed, would prove the fact in issue.[1] Circumstantial evidence is evidence of collateral facts from which the fact in issue reasonably may be inferred.[2] Presumptions,[3] judicial notice[4] and admissions in the pleadings[5] may also help a party meet her burden of production.

Although a "scintilla" of evidence is not enough to satisfy the burden of production,[6] sufficiency is not necessarily a quantitative concept. Generally the testimony of one witness worthy of credit and with knowledge of the facts can be sufficient to satisfy a party's burden of production.[7] In a few instances, however, the law imposes a requirement of corroboration either because of the inherently "suspicious" nature of the testimony or for reasons of public policy.[8] Thus, for

---

24. 9 Wigmore § 2486, at 291.

25. Some of the specifics of allocation of burdens of proof in criminal cases are discussed in § 300.4(d)(New York) and § 300.4(e)(Federal) infra.

§ 300.3

1. See People v. Bretagna, 298 N.Y. 323, 325, 83 N.E.2d 537, 538, cert. denied, 336 U.S. 919, 69 S.Ct. 642, 93 L.Ed. 1082 (1949).

2. See Ridings v. Vaccarello, 55 A.D.2d 650, 651, 390 N.Y.S.2d 152, 153 (2d Dep't 1976); Markel v. Spencer, 5 A.D.2d 400, 407, 171 N.Y.S.2d 770, 777–78 (4th Dep't 1958), aff'd, 5 N.Y.2d 958, 184 N.Y.S.2d 835, 157 N.E.2d 713 (1959).

3. See §§ 301.1–301.8 and 302.1–302.2 infra.

4. See Chapter 2 supra.

5. See § 802.1, at notes 8–9, infra.

6. Laidlaw v. Sage, 158 N.Y. 73, 97, 52 N.E. 679, 687 (1899)("[T]his court has, in a long line of decisions, uniformly held that, to justify the submission to the jury of any issue, there must be sufficient proof to sustain the claim of the party upon whom the onus rests, and that mere conjecture, surmise, speculation, bare possibility or a mere scintilla of evidence, is not enough."). See also People v. Ledwon, 153 N.Y. 10, 17–18, 46 N.E. 1046, 1048 (1897).

7. Cf. People v. Reed, 40 N.Y.2d 204, 208–09, 386 N.Y.S.2d 371, 374–75, 352 N.E.2d 558, 561 (1976)(conviction cannot be based solely on testimony of one prosecution witness whose testimony consists only of "hopeless contradictions").

8. See People v. Daniels, 37 N.Y.2d 624, 628, 376 N.Y.S.2d 436, 439, 339 N.E.2d 139, 140 (1975):

Ordinarily the trier of fact is solely responsible for determining the credibility

example, no criminal defendant may be convicted solely on the basis of testimony by an accomplice[9] or by the unsworn testimony of a child under the age of 12.[10] Similarly, a defendant's out-of-court confession of guilt, although considered to be a form of direct evidence,[11] is not enough, standing alone, to convict.[12] Corroboration requirements also apply to a few particular types of crimes.[13] In the civil arena, a conspicuous example of a corroboration requirement is that which applies to the testimony of a spouse in a matrimonial action for an annulment.[14]

Although New York courts have said that circumstantial evidence generally is not of lower probative value than direct evidence,[15] the inferences that permissibly may be drawn from circumstantial evidence must be reasonable ones.[16] If the evidence is ambiguous and provides only equal support for entirely inconsistent conclusions, the jury may not properly draw either conclusion.[17] Conjecture and speculation are prohibited.[18]

Whether a party has met her burden of production is a question that is resolved by the court after the party has rested her case. As applied

of witnesses. However, the law looks askance at certain witnesses and, in order to insure fairness to the accused, requires that their testimony be supported by other proof if a conviction is to be had. This corroboration requirement exists to further considerations of public policy, and the amount of corroboration to be required varies with the policy sought to be served by the requirement.

9. N.Y.Crim.Proc.Law § 60.22.

10. Id. § 60.20(2)-(3). See § 601.1, at notes 38–43, infra.

11. People v. Bretagna, 298 N.Y. 323, 83 N.E.2d 537, cert. denied, 336 U.S. 919, 69 S.Ct. 642, 93 L.Ed. 1082 (1949).

12. N.Y.Crim.Proc.Law § 60.50.

13. See, e.g., Penal Law § 210.50 (perjury); id. § 255.30(1) (adultery); id. § 255.30(2)(incest). At one time, New York had very rigid statutory requirements of corroboration with respect to the testimony of victims of most sexual offenses. As a result of legislative reform recognizing that rape complainants who are women or children are not inherently untrustworthy witnesses, nearly all such corroboration requirements have been eliminated. See People v. Fuller, 50 N.Y.2d 628, 635–36, 431 N.Y.S.2d 357, 361, 409 N.E.2d 834, 838 (1980). Today, a general corroboration requirement applies only to sex offenses where the victim is incapable of consent due to mental defect or mental incapacity. N.Y.Crim.Proc.Law § 130.16. See generally Donnino, Practice Commentaries, McKinney's N.Y.Penal Law § 130.16.

14. See N.Y.Dom.Rel.Law § 144(2); DeBaillet–Latour v. DeBaillet–Latour, 301 N.Y. 428, 432–33, 94 N.E.2d 715, 716–17 (1950). The unsettled state of the law with respect to corroboration in divorce actions based on cruelty or adultery is discussed in Scheinkman, Practice Commentaries, McKinney's N.Y.Dom.Rel.Law § 170, at C170:4 (cruelty) and C170:11 (adultery).

In the related area of paternity proceedings, testimony of the respondent concerning "access by others" during the relevant time frame must be corroborated. N.Y.Fam.Ct.Act § 531.

15. See, e.g., People v. Kennedy, 47 N.Y.2d 196, 201, 417 N.Y.S.2d 452, 454, 391 N.E.2d 288, 290 (1979)("[T]here is much to be said for the argument that direct testimony may often be of more dubious value [than circumstantial evidence], as is indicated by the extensive literature on the lack of reliability of eyewitness testimony.").

16. See, e.g., Bernstein v. New York, 69 N.Y.2d 1020, 1022, 517 N.Y.S.2d 908, 909, 511 N.E.2d 52, 53 (1987); Schneider v. Kings Highway Hosp. Center, Inc., 67 N.Y.2d 743, 500 N.Y.S.2d 95, 490 N.E.2d 1221, (1986).

17. Bernstein v. New York, 69 N.Y.2d 1020, 1021–22, 517 N.Y.S.2d 908, 909, 511 N.E.2d 52, 53 (1987); Nieskes & Craig, Inc. v. Schoonerman, 40 A.D.2d 931, 932, 337 N.Y.S.2d 750, 752 (4th Dep't 1972).

18. Bernstein v. New York, 69 N.Y.2d 1020, 1021, 517 N.Y.S.2d 908, 909, 511 N.E.2d 52, 53 (1987); People v. Castillo, 47 N.Y.2d 270, 277, 417 N.Y.S.2d 915, 920, 391 N.E.2d 997, 1001 (1979).

§ 300.3   BURDEN OF PROOF   Ch. 3

to the plaintiff in a civil case or the prosecutor in a criminal case, the question is whether she has presented a "prima facie case." In civil cases, the procedural context, prior to submission of the case to the jury, is a motion by the opponent, pursuant to CPLR 4401, for judgment as a matter of law.[19] This is the modern equivalent of a motion for a directed verdict. If the question of sufficiency is addressed by the court after the jury has rendered a verdict, the procedural vehicle is a CPLR 4404(a) motion for judgment notwithstanding the verdict.[20] In both situations, the standard is the same, i.e., whether the burdened party presented sufficient evidence upon which reasonable persons could base a finding in her favor.[21]

The standard was described by the Court of Appeals in *Blum v. Fresh Grown Preserve Corp.*,[22] as follows: a directed verdict against the party with the burden of production is proper where "by no rational process could the trier of the facts base a finding in favor of the [burdened party] upon the evidence * * * presented."[23] Conversely, in *McDonald v. Metropolitan Street Railway Co.*,[24] the court said that a directed verdict against the burdened party must be denied where such party "has established facts or circumstances which would justify a

---

19. CPLR 4401 states as follows:

Rule 4401. Motion for judgment during trial

Any party may move for judgment with respect to a cause of action or issue upon the ground that the moving party is entitled to judgment as a matter of law, after the close of the evidence presented by an opposing party with respect to such cause of action or issue, or at any time on the basis of admissions. Grounds for the motion shall be specified. The motion does not waive the right to trial by jury or to present further evidence even where it is made by all parties.

20. CPLR 4404(a) states as follows:

(a) Motion after trial where jury required. After a trial of a cause of action or issue triable of right by a jury, upon the motion of any party or on its own initiative, the court may set aside a verdict or any judgment entered thereon and direct that judgment be entered in favor of a party entitled to judgment as a matter of law or it may order a new trial of a cause of action or separable issue where the verdict is contrary to the weight of the evidence, in the interest of justice or where the jury cannot agree after being kept together for as long as is deemed reasonable by the court.

21. When the issue arises after both sides have rested, the court's evaluation of the sufficiency of a particular party's case may take into account all the evidence, regardless of which party presented it. See, e.g., Lee v. City Brewing Corp., 279 N.Y. 380, 383, 18 N.E.2d 628, 630 (1939); Painton v. Northern Central Ry. Co. 83 N.Y. 7, 14 (1880).

A judge who is inclined to grant a preverdict motion for judgment may hesitate to do so for practical reasons. If the case is not actually sent to the jury, and the court's decision is reversed on appeal, a new trial must be ordered. If the judge instead grants a motion for judgment after the verdict, the appellate court can correct the trial judge's error in this regard by simply reinstating the verdict.

CPLR 4404(a) also permits the court to set aside a verdict and order a new trial on the ground that the verdict is against the weight of the evidence. Such action is based not on a finding of insufficiency of the evidence as a matter of law, but rather on a discretionary determination by the court that a more accurate result would be reached in a new trial. See generally Nicastro v. Park, 113 A.D.2d 129, 495 N.Y.S.2d 184 (2d Dep't 1985).

22. 292 N.Y. 241, 54 N.E.2d 809 (1944).

23. Id. at 245, 54 N.E.2d at 811. See also Pollock v. Pollock, 71 N.Y. 137, 153 (1877)("Insufficient evidence is, in the eye of the law, no evidence. 'When we say that there is no evidence to go to a jury, we do not mean literally none; but that there is none that ought reasonably to satisfy a jury, that the fact sought to be proved is established' * * *.")(citation omitted).

24. 167 N.Y. 66, 60 N.E. 282 (1901).

§ 300.3   BURDEN OF PROOF & PRESUMPTIONS   Ch. 3

finding in his favor[;] the right to have the issue of fact determined by a jury continues, and the case must ultimately be submitted to it."[25]

In a criminal case, the defendant may challenge the sufficiency of the prosecution's case with a motion for a "trial order of dismissal" under § 290.10(1) of the Criminal Procedure Law.[26] The Court of Appeals has said that "[i]n reviewing legal sufficiency we are required to view the evidence in the light most favorable to the prosecution and decide whether a rational trier of fact could have found the elements of the crime proved beyond a reasonable doubt."[27] The same standard is appropriate for the trial judge's determination of sufficiency.[28]

Until recently, the Court of Appeals imposed a stricter sufficiency standard for prosecutions based entirely on circumstantial evidence. Borrowing from the substance of the jury charge that is given in such cases,[29] it was said that a case based wholly on circumstantial evidence was not sufficient unless every reasonable hypothesis of innocence was excluded "to a moral certainty."[30] Recent cases, however, have rejected that standard and opted for a uniform approach to judicial review of sufficiency questions.[31] The test in all cases is whether the evidence before the jury, viewed in the light most favorable to the prosecution, could rationally lead them to the conclusion that all elements of the

---

25. Id. at 70, 60 N.E. at 283.

26. In pertinent part, N.Y.Crim.Proc. Law § 290.10(1) states:

At the conclusion of the people's case or at the conclusion of all the evidence, the court may, * * * upon motion of the defendant, (a) issue a "trial order of dismissal," dismissing any count of an indictment upon the ground that the trial evidence is not legally sufficient to establish the offense charged therein or any lesser included offense, or (b) reserve decision on the motion until after the verdict has been rendered and accepted by the court.

See generally Preiser, Practice Commentaries, McKinney's N.Y. Criminal Procedure Law § 290.10.

N.Y.Crim.Proc.Law § 70.10(1) defines "legally sufficient evidence" as "competent evidence which, if accepted as true, would establish every element of an offense charged and the defendant's commission thereof * * *." "Competent evidence" is simply "evidence not subject to an exclusionary rule." People v. Swamp, 84 N.Y.2d 725, 730, 622 N.Y.S.2d 472, 474, 646 N.E.2d 774 (1995).

27. People v. Foster, 64 N.Y.2d 1144, 1146, 490 N.Y.S.2d 726, 727–28, 480 N.E.2d 340, 341, cert. denied, 474 U.S. 857, 106 S.Ct. 166, 88 L.Ed.2d 137 (1985). See also People v. Contes, 60 N.Y.2d 620, 621, 467 N.Y.S.2d 349, 349–50, 454 N.E.2d 932, 932–33 (1983)(quoting Jackson v. Virginia, 443 U.S. 307, 319, 99 S.Ct. 2781, 2789, 61 L.Ed.2d 560, 573 (1979)).

28. See People v. Jackson, 65 N.Y.2d 265, 271 n.6, 491 N.Y.S.2d 138, 142, 480 N.E.2d 727, 731 (1985). The Jackson court quoted with approval Judge Prettyman's formulation of the trial judge's function in assessing legal sufficiency. Id. at 271–72, 491 N.Y.S.2d at 142–43, 480 N.E.2d at 731–32. See text at notes 54–57 infra.

29. See § 300.4(d)(1), at notes 46–49, infra.

30. See, e.g., People v. Benzinger, 36 N.Y.2d 29, 32, 364 N.Y.S.2d 855, 856, 324 N.E.2d 334, 335 (1974).

31. See People v. Norman, 85 N.Y.2d 609, 620–22, 627 N.Y.S.2d 302, 308–09, 650 N.E.2d 1303 (1995); People v. Williams, 84 N.Y.2d 925, 926, 620 N.Y.S.2d 811, 811–12, 644 N.E.2d 1367, 1367–68 (1994), appeal denied, 85 N.Y.2d 982, 629 N.Y.S.2d 742, 653 N.E.2d 638 (1995); People v. Wong, 81 N.Y.2d 600, 608, 601 N.Y.S.2d 440, 444, 619 N.E.2d 377, 381 (1993). The court has said that use of a "moral certainty" standard to evaluate legal sufficiency "blur[s] the important distinction between the role of the fact finder and that of the reviewing court. * * * The very term 'moral certainty' connotes that the decision-maker must possess a particular degree of conviction about the correctness of its conclusion, thereby demonstrating the test's unsuitability for the more objective legal sufficiency inquiry." Norman, supra, 85 N.Y.2d at 622, 627 N.Y.S.2d at 309, 650 N.E.2d at 1303.

crime have been proven beyond a reasonable doubt.[32] The concept that all reasonable hypotheses of innocence must be excluded to a moral certainty, however, is still a required component of the jury charge in a case based entirely on circumstantial evidence.[33]

In passing upon the sufficiency question, the court should give the party with the burden of production the benefit of every reasonable inference that may be drawn from the evidence.[34] The court may neither assess the credibility of a witness nor weigh conflicting evidence.[35] Such questions are for the jury. There is, of course, an exception to this rule when a witness' testimony is incredible as a matter of law because it is utterly contrary to physical facts, completely at odds with probabilities or simply impossible to believe.[36]

2. Shifting of the Burden of Production

We have seen that a party who fails to meet her burden of production will suffer an adverse ruling on the particular fact in issue or possibly will lose her entire case as a matter of law. The issue will never "get to the jury." What happens next, however, if sufficient evidence has been introduced to satisfy the burden of production? Does the burden of production then shift to the opponent?

Assume first that the party with the burden of production (the proponent) satisfied her burden but did nothing more than this, i.e., she presented sufficient but not conclusive evidence. In this scenario, no burden of production shifts to the opponent. If the opponent rests without offering any evidence to rebut that of the proponent, the matter will usually go to the fact-finder for acceptance or rejection of the proponent's evidence.[37] The opponent, in other words, can simply sit

---

32. People v. Wong, 81 N.Y.2d 600, 608, 601 N.Y.S.2d 440, 444, 619 N.E.2d 377, 381 (1993).

33. See, e.g., People v. Williams, 84 N.Y.2d 925, 926, 620 N.Y.S.2d 811, 811, 644 N.E.2d 1367, 1367 (1994), appeal denied, 85 N.Y.2d 982, 629 N.Y.S.2d 742, 653 N.E.2d 638 (1995)(moral certainty standard is to be used by trier of facts). See § 300.4(d)(1), at notes 46–49, infra.

34. See, e.g., People v. Way, 59 N.Y.2d 361, 365, 465 N.Y.S.2d 853, 855, 452 N.E.2d 1181, 1183 (1983); Meiselman v. Crown Heights Hosp., 285 N.Y. 389, 392, 34 N.E.2d 367, 369 (1941); McCloud v. Marcantonio, 106 A.D.2d 493, 495, 483 N.Y.S.2d 31, 33 (2d Dep't 1984).

35. See People v. Jackson, 65 N.Y.2d 265, 271–72, 491 N.Y.S.2d 138, 142–43, 480 N.E.2d 727, 731–32 (1985)(quoting Curley v. United States, 160 F.2d 229, 232–33 (D.C.Cir.), cert. denied, 331 U.S. 837, 67 S.Ct. 1512, 91 L.Ed. 1850 (1947)); Dolitsky v. Bay Isle Oil Co., 111 A.D.2d 366, 366, 489 N.Y.S.2d 580, 581 (2d Dep't 1985); Lipsius v. White, 91 A.D.2d 271, 276, 458 N.Y.S.2d 928, 933 (2d Dep't 1983); Bartkowiak v. St. Adalbert's Roman Catholic Church Soc'y, 40 A.D.2d 306, 309, 340 N.Y.S.2d 137, 141 (4th Dep't 1973). See also People v. Kennedy, 47 N.Y.2d 196, 204, 417 N.Y.S.2d 452, 456, 391 N.E.2d 288, 292 (1979)("it is for the jury to determine what evidence is to be believed and what evidence is to be discredited").

36. See, e.g., Loughlin v. City of New York, 186 A.D.2d 176, 587 N.Y.S.2d 732 (2d Dep't 1992), appeal denied, 81 N.Y.2d 704, 595 N.Y.S.2d 398, 611 N.E.2d 299 (1993); People v. Stroman, 83 A.D.2d 370, 372, 444 N.Y.S.2d 463, 465 (1st Dep't 1981); Tosto v. Marra Bros., Inc., 275 App.Div. 686, 86 N.Y.S.2d 549 (2d Dep't), aff'd, 299 N.Y. 700, 87 N.E.2d 74 (1949). See also § 607.1, at notes 4–6, infra.

37. Even undisputed evidence can raise conflicting inferences (George Foltis, Inc. v. City of New York, 287 N.Y. 108, 119–23, 38 N.E.2d 455, 459–63 (1941)), and uncontradicted testimony may still raise a question of credibility (Matter of Nowakowski, 2 N.Y.2d 618, 622, 162 N.Y.S.2d 19, 21, 142 N.E.2d 198, 200 (1957)).

§ 300.3   BURDEN OF PROOF & PRESUMPTIONS   Ch. 3

back and assume the risk that the fact-finder will not be persuaded that the facts are as contended by the proponent. Alternatively, the opponent is entitled to offer rebuttal evidence so as to increase the chances that the jury will reject the proponent's evidence. This does not mean that the burden of production is shifted to the opponent; the failure to offer such evidence would not result in a directed verdict against her.

Assume instead that the proponent has done more than merely satisfy her burden of production. She has presented evidence so compelling that, if unrebutted, a rational fact-finder could not reasonably reject her version of the facts.[38] In a case of this nature, the burden of production actually shifts to the opponent. If the opponent rests without offering any rebuttal evidence whatsoever, or that which she does offer is insufficient to detract from the conclusiveness of the evidence favoring the proponent, the proponent will be entitled to judgment as a matter of law. The burden on the opponent then would be, at minimum, to introduce sufficient rebuttal evidence to create reasonable disagreement over the fact in issue, thus sending the case to the jury. The opponent will thereby satisfy the burden of production that was shifted to her and save herself from a directed verdict.

In either of the above scenarios—proponent produces sufficient but not conclusive evidence, or proponent produces evidence which, if unrebutted, is conclusive—the opponent's rebuttal evidence itself may be so compelling as to overwhelm that of the proponent. In other words, it is possible for the opponent to shift the burden of production back again to the party upon whom the initial burden rested. At this point, if the proponent does not produce additional evidence, judgment as a matter of law should be granted to the opponent.

One major exception must be noted with respect to the potential shifting nature of the burden of production. In a criminal case, a directed verdict against the defendant on any element of the crime is impermissible no matter how conclusive the prosecution's evidence may seem.[39] In other words, the burden of production cannot shift to the defendant with respect to an element of the crime. She is entitled to have a jury pass upon the question of guilt regardless of the apparently conclusive nature of the case against her.[40] As to affirmative defenses, however, the defendant may bear the burden of production (and of persuasion).[41]

The foregoing discussion on the shifting nature of the burden of production uses terminology and concepts developed by the modern text

---

38. See Hull v. Littauer, 162 N.Y. 569, 572, 57 N.E. 102, 103 (1900) ("Where * * * the evidence of a party to the action is not contradicted by direct evidence, nor by any legitimate inferences from the evidence, and it is not opposed to the probabilities, nor in its nature, surprising or suspicious, there is no reason for denying to it conclusiveness.").

The same effect is achieved by the operation of a presumption. See §§ 301.2–301.3 infra.

39. People v. Walker, 198 N.Y. 329, 91 N.E. 806 (1910).

40. Id. at 334, 91 N.E. at 807–08.

41. See § 300.4(d)(2) infra.

writers on the law of evidence.[42] The problem in New York is that the courts continue to use ambiguous terminology in discussing the situations in which the burden of production does and does not shift. When the New York courts say that the "burden of going forward" shifts, the context in which the phrase is used and the actual effect described by the court must be carefully analyzed. Sometimes, the court means to describe, as we have done, an actual shifting of the burden of production. Thus, the court's statement that the duty or burden of going forward has shifted may mean that the compelling strength of the proponent's evidence will require the court to grant a motion for judgment as a matter of law against the opponent unless she literally introduces enough evidence to take the case to the jury.[43]

Other times, a court's statement that the burden of going forward has shifted signifies only that the proponent has presented sufficient evidence to get her case to the jury—that neither she nor the opponent are subject to an adverse judgment as a matter of law. The only thing that has shifted to the opponent is the risk that if she rests without producing any additional evidence, the jury may (but is not required) to find the proponent's evidence persuasive.[44] Discourse would be greatly

---

42. See James, Hazard and Leubsdorf § 7.15; McCormick § 338; 9 Wigmore §§ 2487–2489.

43. Powers v. Powers, 86 N.Y.2d 63, 629 N.Y.S.2d 984, 653 N.E.2d 1154 (1995), illustrates the point. Powers was a proceeding in which the petitioner (a mother of five) sought to have her former husband held in contempt for willfully failing to pay his obligations under a support order. An inability to pay, of course, would not warrant the sanction. At trial, the mother proved that the respondent was in arrears. By statute, such arrears, standing alone, constituted "prima facie evidence" of a willful violation of the support order, warranting contempt. N.Y.Fam.Ct.Act § 454(3)(a). After the mother rested her case, the father produced evidence showing only that he had spent his ample income on unnecessary things.

The Court of Appeals described this situation as one in which "the burden of going forward shifted to respondent to rebut petitioner's prima facie evidence of a willful violation." 86 N.Y.2d at 69, 629 N.Y.S.2d at 988, 653 N.E.2d at 1158. The respondent was then "*required* * * * to offer some competent, credible evidence of his inability to make the required payments." Id. at 69–70, 629 N.Y.S.2d at 988, 653 N.E.2d at 1158 (emphasis added). Thus, because respondent failed to satisfy his burden of going forward, judgment for the petitioner was proper.

44. In Meiselman v. Crown Heights Hospital, 285 N.Y. 389, 34 N.E.2d 367 (1941), for example, the plaintiff was nonsuited at the close of his evidence after seeking to show, circumstantially, negligence and medical malpractice by the defendants. The directed verdict was error, said the Court of Appeals, because plaintiff had made out a prima facie case. In one breath, the court said that "[s]ufficient evidence was presented to warrant a jury in awarding damages;" the jury "might" have found or inferred wrongdoing. Id. at 395–96, 34 N.E.2d at 370. The court went on to say, however, that "the burden of going forward with the case rested upon the defendants." Id. at 396, 34 N.E.2d at 370–71.

A more recent example is Matter of Philip M., 82 N.Y.2d 238, 604 N.Y.S.2d 40, 624 N.E.2d 168 (1993), in which the court analyzed the sufficiency of the evidence in a child abuse proceeding. Having proven sexual injuries to the child while in the custody of his parents, the petitioner was said to have made out a prima facie case of parental culpability. The court then stated that the "burden of going forward shift[ed] to respondents to rebut the evidence of parental culpability." Id. at 244, 604 N.Y.S.2d at 44, 624 N.E.2d at 172. The court went on to say, however:

> While the fact-finder *may* find respondents accountable for sexually abusing a child or allowing sexual abuse to occur after a prima facie case is established, it is *never required* to do so. * * *

Once a prima facie case has been established, respondents *may* simply rest without attempting to rebut the presumption [of parental culpability] and permit the court to decide the case on the strength

§ 300.3   BURDEN OF PROOF & PRESUMPTIONS   Ch. 3

simplified if the New York courts would confine their use of the phrase "shifting of the burden of going forward" to those situations in which the newly burdened party's failure to produce evidence will result, upon motion, in judgment as a matter of law against her.[45]

Library References:

West's Key No. Digests, Criminal Law ⇒326; Evidence ⇒90–98.

b. Federal

In federal practice, the concepts relating to burden of production and sufficiency of the evidence are applied in essentially the same way as under New York law.[46] In civil actions, the question of whether a party has met her burden of production is determined pursuant to a motion under Rule 50 of the Federal Rules of Civil Procedure.[47] The Second Circuit has said that a party fails to meet her burden if "the evidence is such that, without weighing the credibility of the witnesses or otherwise considering the weight of the evidence, there can be but one conclusion as to the verdict that reasonable [jurors] could have reached."[48]

In criminal cases, the matter is resolved in the context of a motion for judgment of acquittal under Rule 29 of the Federal Rules of Criminal Procedure.[49] With respect to corroboration requirements, federal law,

---

of petitioner's evidence or, alternatively, they *may* present evidence which challenges the establishment of the prima facie case.

Id. at 244, 604 N.Y.S.2d at 44, 624 N.E.2d at 172 (emphasis added).

45. See McCormick § 338, at 436.

46. See, e.g., Northwestern Mutual Life Ins. Co. v. Linard, 359 F.Supp. 1012, 1019 (S.D.N.Y.1973), aff'd, 498 F.2d 556 (2d Cir. 1974). See generally Graham §§ 301.2–301.4, 303.2; 1. C. Mueller and L. Kirkpatrick, Federal Evidence § 64 (2d ed.1994).

47. See generally 9A C. Wright and A. Miller, Federal Practice and Procedure: Civil §§ 2521–2540 (2d ed.1995).

Fed.R.Civ.P. 50(a)–(b) provides in pertinent part:

(a) Judgment as a Matter of Law.

(1) If during a trial by jury a party has been fully heard on an issue and there is no legally sufficient evidentiary basis for a reasonable jury to find for that party on that issue, the court may determine the issue against that party and may grant a motion for judgment as a matter of law against that party with respect to a claim or defense that cannot under the controlling law be maintained or defeated without a favorable finding on that issue.

(2) Motions for judgment as a matter of law may be made at any time before submission of the case to the jury. Such a motion shall specify the judgment sought and the law and the facts on which the moving party is entitled to the judgment.

(b) Renewal of Motion for Judgment After Trial; Alternative Motion for New Trial. Whenever a motion for a judgment as a matter of law made at the close of all the evidence is denied or for any reason is not granted, the court is deemed to have submitted the action to the jury subject to a later determination of the legal questions raised by the motion. Such a motion may be renewed by service and filing not later than 10 days after entry of judgment. * * *

48. Simblest v. Maynard, 427 F.2d 1, 4 (2d Cir.1970). See also In re Joint Eastern & Southern District Asbestos Litigation, 52 F.3d 1124, 1131–32 (2d Cir.1995); Stubbs v. Dudley, 849 F.2d 83, 85 (2d Cir.1988), cert. denied, 489 U.S. 1034, 109 S.Ct. 1095, 103 L.Ed.2d 230 (1989); Sirota v. Solitron Devices, Inc., 673 F.2d 566, 573 (2d Cir.), cert. denied, 459 U.S. 838, 103 S.Ct. 86, 74 L.Ed.2d 80 (1982).

49. See generally 2 C. Wright, Federal Practice and Procedure: Criminal §§ 461–469 (2d ed.1982). Fed.R.Crim.P. 29(a)-(b) provides as follows:

(a) Motion Before Submission to Jury. Motions for directed verdict are abolished and motions for judgment of acquittal shall be used in their place. The court on motion of a defendant or of its own motion shall order the entry of

Ch. 3 **BURDEN OF PROOF** § 300.3

like that of New York, will not allow a conviction to be based solely on a defendant's confession.[50] Unlike New York, however, federal law does not prohibit convictions based solely on the uncorroborated testimony of an accomplice.[51]

The Second Circuit has long used a single test for evaluating the sufficiency of the prosecution's case, regardless of whether it is based entirely on circumstantial evidence.[52] The question of guilt is for the jury so long as any rational trier of fact could find against the defendant beyond a reasonable doubt on each element of the charged offense.[53]

A classic description of the role of the trial judge in passing upon the sufficiency question in federal criminal cases is that of Judge Prettyman in *Curley v. United States*.[54] His analysis was applauded by the Supreme Court as "the prevailing criterion for judging motions for acquittal in federal criminal trials,"[55] and the Second Circuit has similarly recognized the cogency and lucidity of his formulation.[56] Although lengthy, Judge Prettyman's articulation of the standard is quoted below because of its continuing influence on federal and state courts alike:

> The functions of the jury include the determination of the credibility of witnesses, the weighing of the evidence, and the drawing of justifiable inferences of fact from proven facts. It is the function of the judge to deny the jury any opportunity to operate beyond its province. The jury may not be permitted to

judgment of acquittal of one or more offenses charged in the indictment or information after the evidence on either side is closed if the evidence is insufficient to sustain a conviction of such offense or offenses. If a defendant's motion for judgment of acquittal at the close of the evidence offered by the government is not granted, the defendant may offer evidence without having reserved the right.

(b) Reservation of Decision on Motion. The court may reserve decision on a motion for judgment of acquittal, proceed with the trial (where the motion is made before the close of all the evidence), submit the case to the jury and decide the motion either before the jury returns a verdict or after it returns a verdict of guilty or is discharged without having returned a verdict. If the court reserves decision, it must decide the motion on the basis of the evidence at the time the ruling was reserved.

50. See Opper v. United States, 348 U.S. 84, 89–91, 75 S.Ct. 158, 162–63, 99 L.Ed. 101, 106–08 (1954); Smith v. United States, 348 U.S. 147, 152–55, 75 S.Ct. 194, 197–98, 99 L.Ed. 192, 198–200 (1954). Opper and Smith extended the corroboration requirement that applies to confessions to admissions of fact made after the crime. But see United States v. Simmons, 923 F.2d 934, 954 (2d Cir.), cert. denied, 500 U.S. 919, 111 S.Ct. 2018, 114 L.Ed.2d 104 (1991)(Opper and Smith apply only to post-crime admissions made to law enforcement officers; no requirement of corroboration applies to testimony of coconspirator concerning admissions made to him).

51. United States v. Corallo, 413 F.2d 1306, 1323 (2d Cir.), cert. denied, 396 U.S. 958, 90 S.Ct. 431, 24 L.Ed.2d 422 (1969). Juries are instructed, however, to view accomplice testimony with caution. See, e.g., United States v. Agueci, 310 F.2d 817, 833 (2d Cir.1962), cert. denied, 372 U.S. 959, 83 S.Ct. 1013, 10 L.Ed.2d 11 (1963).

52. See, e.g., United States v. Botsch, 364 F.2d 542, 550 (2d Cir.1966), cert. denied, 386 U.S. 937, 87 S.Ct. 959, 17 L.Ed.2d 810 (1967); United States v. Taylor, 464 F.2d 240, 244 (2d Cir.1972).

53. See, e.g., United States v. Mariani, 725 F.2d 862, 865 (2d Cir.1984); United States v. Martinez, 54 F.3d 1040, 1042–43 (2d Cir.1995).

54. 160 F.2d 229 (D.C.Cir.), cert. denied, 331 U.S. 837, 67 S.Ct. 1511, 91 L.Ed. 1850 (1947).

55. Jackson v. Virginia, 443 U.S. 307, 318 n.11, 99 S.Ct. 2781, 2789, 61 L.Ed.2d 560, 573 (1979).

56. See, e.g., United States v. Mariani, 725 F.2d 862, 865 (2d Cir.1984); United States v. Taylor, 464 F.2d 240, 243 (2d Cir.1972).

conjecture merely, or to conclude upon pure speculation or from passion, prejudice or sympathy. The critical point in this boundary is the existence or non-existence of a reasonable doubt as to guilt. If the evidence is such that reasonable jurymen must necessarily have such a doubt, the judge must require acquittal, because no other result is permissible within the fixed bounds of jury consideration. But if a reasonable mind might fairly have a reasonable doubt or might fairly not have one, the case is for the jury, and the decision is for the jurors to make. The law recognizes that the scope of a reasonable mind is broad. Its conclusion is not always a point certain, but, upon given evidence, may be one of a number of conclusions. Both innocence and guilt beyond reasonable doubt may lie fairly within the limits of reasonable conclusion from given facts. The judge's function is exhausted when he determines that the evidence does or does not permit the conclusion of guilt beyond reasonable doubt within the fair operation of a reasonable mind.

The true rule, therefore, is that a trial judge, in passing upon a motion for directed verdict of acquittal, must determine whether upon the evidence, giving full play to the right of the jury to determine credibility, weigh the evidence, and draw justifiable inferences of fact, a reasonable mind might fairly conclude guilt beyond a reasonable doubt. If he concludes that upon the evidence there must be such a doubt in a reasonable mind, he must grant the motion; or, to state it another way, if there is no evidence upon which a reasonable mind might fairly conclude guilt beyond reasonable doubt, the motion must be granted. If he concludes that either of the two results, a reasonable doubt or no reasonable doubt, is fairly possible, he must let the jury decide the matter. In a given case, particularly one of circumstantial evidence, that determination may depend upon the difference between pure speculation and legitimate inference from proven facts. The task of the judge in such case is not easy, for the rule of reason is frequently difficult to apply, but we know of no way to avoid that difficulty.[57]

Library References:

West's Key No. Digests, Criminal Law ⚖326; Evidence ⚖90–98.

§ 300.4 Satisfying the Burden of Persuasion

a. In General

The burden of persuasion becomes critical after the parties have rested and the court has ascertained that reasonable persons may differ over the existence or nonexistence of the facts in dispute. The burden of persuasion specifies the level of certainty that the fact-finder must have in order to reach its decision. Unless she convinces the fact-finder to the

---

57. 160 F.2d at 232–33 (footnotes omitted).

requisite level, the party with the burden of persuasion must lose.[1] The required degree of certainty—whether measured by the preponderance, beyond-a-reasonable-doubt or clear-and-convincing standard—will differ depending upon the nature of the case and the particular issue. The New York Court of Appeals, drawing upon the writings of McCormick[2] and the United States Supreme Court,[3] has nicely summarized the role of the burden of persuasion in the truth-seeking process as follows:

> Because human fact finders lack the quality of omniscience, the process of determining the truth in adjudicative proceedings necessarily involves some margin of error * * *. The size of the margin of error that the law is willing to tolerate varies in inverse proportion to the importance to the party or to society of the issue to be resolved. On one end of the spectrum are most civil disputes, where, from a societal standpoint, "a mistaken judgment for the plaintiff is no worse than a mistaken judgment for the defendant" * * *. On the other end are criminal determinations of guilt or innocence, "[w]here one party has at stake an interest of transcendent value" * * *. The rules governing how persuasive the proof must be "[represent] an attempt to instruct the factfinder concerning the degree of confidence our society thinks * * * should [be had] in the correctness of factual conclusions for a particular type of adjudication" * * *.[4]

It should be apparent that a court's instruction to the jury on the burden of proof, both as to the party upon whom the burden falls and the standard to be applied, is one of the most important parts of the jury charge.[5]

Library References:

West's Key No. Digests, Criminal Law ⚖326, 549–572; Evidence ⚖90–98, 584–601.

b. Civil Cases: New York

1. Preponderance of the Evidence

The usual standard for the burden of persuasion in civil actions is

---

§ 300.4

1. In re Ballay, 482 F.2d 648, 662 (D.C.Cir.1973)("Broadly stated, the standard of proof reflects the risk of winning or losing a given adversary proceeding or, stated differently, the certainty with which the party bearing the burden of proof must convince the factfinder.").

2. McCormick § 341, at 445.

3. In re Winship, 397 U.S. 358, 370, 90 S.Ct. 1068, 1075–76, 25 L.Ed.2d 368, 378–79 (1970)(Harlan, J., concurring); Speiser v. Randall, 357 U.S. 513, 525, 78 S.Ct. 1332, 1342, 2 L.Ed.2d 1460, 1472 (1958).

4. People v. Geraci, 85 N.Y.2d 359, 367, 625 N.Y.S.2d 469, 473–74, 649 N.E.2d 817, 821–22 (1995)(citations omitted).

5. See Larson v. Jo Ann Cab Corp., 209 F.2d 929, 935 (2d Cir.1954). See also J. Baranello & Sons v. Chase Manhattan Bank, N.A., 119 A.D.2d 550, 500 N.Y.S.2d 727 (2d Dep't 1986)(failure to give jury charge on burden of proof is reversible error); Lentino v. Rosedale Gardens, Inc., 79 A.D.2d 554, 433 N.Y.S.2d 805 (1st Dep't 1980)(even if jury is instructed on burden of proof at outset of trial, such charge should be repeated before jury retires for deliberations).

§ 300.4   BURDEN OF PROOF & PRESUMPTIONS   Ch. 3

"preponderance of the evidence."[6] New York courts have traditionally described this standard in terms of weight: the evidence favoring the party with the burden of proof must outweigh that which favors the opponent.[7] The modern trend is to define preponderance as the "more likely" or "probable" account of what happened.[8] The Uniform Commercial Code, for example, defines "burden of establishing a fact" as "the burden of persuading the triers of fact that the existence of the fact is more probable than its nonexistence."[9]

It is not enough for a judge to simply tell the jury that they must be persuaded by a preponderance.[10] The jury must also be told that they are to rule against the party with the burden of proof if they find the evidence to be evenly balanced.[11] The judge must also explain that the "greater weight of the evidence" means the convincing force of the evidence, not the number of witnesses and exhibits.[12]

Under the so-called "*Noseworthy*" doctrine,[13] a slight modification of the preponderance charge is required in wrongful death actions. Because the decedent is unavailable to testify, the jury must be charged that the plaintiff is not held to as high a degree of proof as is an injured plaintiff who can herself describe the occurrence.[14] The *Noseworthy*

---

6. See, e.g., Rinaldi & Sons, Inc. v. Wells Fargo Alarm Service, Inc., 39 N.Y.2d 191, 194, 383 N.Y.S.2d 256, 257, 347 N.E.2d 618, 618 (1976); Jarrett v. Madifari, 67 A.D.2d 396, 404, 415 N.Y.S.2d 644, 649 (1st Dep't 1979).

Some of the older cases refer to a "fair preponderance of the evidence," see, e.g., Ward v. New York Life Ins. Co., 225 N.Y. 314, 322, 122 N.E. 207, 209 (1919), but it is doubtful that inclusion of the adjective "fair" in the charge adds much to juror comprehension.

7. Roberge v. Bonner, 185 N.Y. 265, 269, 77 N.E. 1023, 1024 (1906). Some judges mime the tipping of a set of scales to make the point. Id. See also James, Hazard and Leubsdorf § 7.14, at 339.

8. See note 35 infra. See also 3 E. Devitt, C. Blackmar and M. Wolff, Federal Jury Practice and Instructions: Civil § 72.01 (4th ed.1987); Morgan, "Instructing the Jury Upon Presumptions and Burden of Proof," 47 Harv.L.Rev. 59, 66 (1933). The conventional "greater weight of the evidence" explanation is recommended in 1 New York Pattern Jury Instructions—Civil § 1:60 (2d ed.1995 Supp.). An alternative which uses a "more likely to be true" formulation can be found in 1 New York Forms of Jury Instruction § 1.27 (1992).

9. N.Y.Uniform Commercial Code § 1–201(8).

10. Torem v. 564 Central Avenue Restaurant, Inc., 133 A.D.2d 25, 26, 518 N.Y.S.2d 620, 621–22 (1st Dep't 1987).

11. Roman v. Bronx–Lebanon Hosp. Center, 51 A.D.2d 529, 530, 379 N.Y.S.2d 81, 83 (1st Dep't), appeal denied, 39 N.Y.2d 709, 386 N.Y.S.2d 1027, 352 N.E.2d 597 (1976)(explaining to jury how to decide case when evidence is evenly balanced is "core" of burden of proof doctrine).

12. Torem v. 564 Central Avenue Restaurant, Inc., 133 A.D.2d 25, 26, 518 N.Y.S.2d 620, 622 (1st Dep't 1987).

13. Noseworthy v. City of New York, 298 N.Y. 76, 80 N.E.2d 744 (1948).

14. Id. at 80–81, 80 N.E.2d at 744–45. The court reasoned that such relaxed standard is a variant of the rule that an opponent with exclusive knowledge of facts has an obligation of explanation. The Noseworthy doctrine, however, does not itself shift any burden of proof to the defendant; it merely provides "a method of, or approach to, weighing evidence." Wank v. Ambrosino, 307 N.Y. 321, 324, 121 N.E.2d 246, 247 (1954).

The rule applies even if there are eyewitnesses to the event. See Schechter v. Klanfer, 28 N.Y.2d 228, 231, 321 N.Y.S.2d 99, 101–02, 269 N.E.2d 812, 814 (1971).

Recent cases, however, hold that the relaxed burden is inappropriate if the defendant did not himself witness the events and both parties are therefore "on equal footing" insofar as access to evidence of the occurrence is concerned. Wright v. New York City Housing Authority, 208 A.D.2d 327, 332, 624 N.Y.S.2d 144, 147 (1st Dep't 1995) (defendant-landlord did not witness

charge is also given in other types of tort actions when the plaintiff herself is unable to testify due to amnesia caused by the occurrence in issue.[15]

Library References:

West's Key No. Digests, Evidence ⟐598.

2. Clear and Convincing Evidence

As to some matters in civil cases, the burden of persuasion is higher than a preponderance of the evidence but less than the criminal standard of "beyond a reasonable doubt."[16] Courts have expressed this intermediate standard in a variety of ways, including "evidence of a very high order," "clear, positive and convincing evidence," "evidence of the clearest and most satisfactory character," and "proof of 'the most substantial and convincing character.'"[17] The trend, however, is to subsume all of these intermediate levels under the rubric of "clear and convincing evidence."[18]

Courts and legislatures have imposed the standard of clear and convincing evidence for the purpose of reducing the risk of an erroneous decision where the interests at stake are more substantial than in the usual civil case.[19] For example, allegations of criminal or quasi-criminal conduct such as fraud,[20] usury[21] and arson[22] often must be proved by the more demanding standard. Certain "disfavored" claims and defenses, or those as to which there is a "special danger of deception," may also be

decedent-tenant's murder); Lynn v. Lynn, ___ A.D.2d ___, ___, 628 N.Y.S.2d 667, 668 (1st Dep't 1995)(amnesiac plaintiff not entitled to application of Noseworthy rule where defendant did not witness the accident.).

15. Schechter v. Klanfer, 28 N.Y.2d 228, 321 N.Y.S.2d 99, 269 N.E.2d 812 (1971). Because amnesia can be feigned, expert testimony is required to establish plaintiff's condition and the fact that defendant's acts were a substantial factor in causing the condition. Sawyer v. Dreis & Krump Manufacturing Co., 67 N.Y.2d 328, 334, 502 N.Y.S.2d 696, 700, 493 N.E.2d 920, 924 (1986). Furthermore, the foundation must be proven to the jury by clear and convincing evidence. Id. at 334, 502 N.Y.S.2d at 699–700, 493 N.E.2d at 923. Only if these prerequisites are satisfied may greater latitude be used by the jury in weighing the evidence in support of plaintiff's case.

16. See In re Carter, 102 Misc.2d 867, 869, 424 N.Y.S.2d 833, 835 (Sup.Ct.Suffolk Co.1980).

17. See George Backer Management Corp. v. Acme Quilting Co., 46 N.Y.2d 211, 219–20, 413 N.Y.S.2d 135, 139, 385 N.E.2d 1062, 1066 (1978).

18. See, e.g., Ausch v. St. Paul Fire & Marine Ins. Co., 125 A.D.2d 43, 511 N.Y.S.2d 919 (2d Dep't), appeal denied, 70 N.Y.2d 610, 522 N.Y.S.2d 110, 516 N.E.2d 1223 (1987).

19. Addington v. Texas, 441 U.S. 418, 423–24, 99 S.Ct. 1804, 1808, 60 L.Ed.2d 323, 329 (1979). Soper v. Storar, 52 N.Y.2d 363, 379, 438 N.Y.S.2d 266, 274, 420 N.E.2d 64, 72, cert. denied, 454 U.S. 858, 102 S.Ct. 309, 70 L.Ed.2d 153 (1981)(when "particularly important personal interests are at stake").

The clear and convincing evidence standard is also applied to the threshold question of admissibility of certain evidence in criminal cases. See, e.g., People v. Geraci, 85 N.Y.2d 359, 366–69, 625 N.Y.S.2d 469, 473–75, 649 N.E.2d 817, 821–23 (1995)(defendant's causal connection to unavailability of prosecution witness as basis for introduction of such witness' grand jury testimony).

20. Simcuski v. Saeli, 44 N.Y.2d 442, 406 N.Y.S.2d 259, 377 N.E.2d 713 (1978).

21. Freitas v. Geddes Savings & Loan Ass'n, 63 N.Y.2d 254, 481 N.Y.S.2d 665, 471 N.E.2d 437 (1984).

22. Ausch v. St. Paul Fire & Marine Ins. Co., 125 A.D.2d 43, 511 N.Y.S.2d 919 (2d Dep't), appeal denied, 70 N.Y.2d 610, 522 N.Y.S.2d 110, 516 N.E.2d 1223 (1987).

§ 300.4 BURDEN OF PROOF & PRESUMPTIONS Ch. 3

governed by the higher burden of proof.[23] Examples include paternity,[24] reformation of a contract,[25] mistake as a basis of avoiding liability on a contract,[26] a claim that a decedent's pre-death transfer of property was a gift,[27] implied easements[28] and title by adverse possession.[29] Clear and convincing evidence is also required for the protection of some constitutional interests, as in certain defamation cases where the plaintiff is required by the first amendment to show that the defendant acted with malice.[30] Due process has also provided a basis for imposing the higher level of persuasion where deprivations of individual rights are at issue.[31]

It has been suggested that clear and convincing evidence be explained to the jury as evidence which makes the existence of a fact "highly probable" or "much more probable than its falsity."[32] New York courts appear to have approved this formulation.[33]

Library References:

West's Key No. Digests, Evidence ⇌596.

c. Civil Cases: Federal

Federal law on the burden of persuasion in civil cases is substantial-

---

23. See McCormick § 340, at 444.

24. Piccola v. Hibbard, 51 A.D.2d 674, 378 N.Y.S.2d 163 (4th Dep't), aff'd, 40 N.Y.2d 1035, 391 N.Y.S.2d 855, 360 N.E.2d 355 (1976).

25. George Backer Management Corp. v. Acme Quilting Co., 46 N.Y.2d 211, 413 N.Y.S.2d 135, 385 N.E.2d 1062 (1978).

26. Southard v. Curley, 134 N.Y. 148, 31 N.E. 330 (1892).

27. In re Love, 46 N.Y.2d 784, 413 N.Y.S.2d 919, 386 N.E.2d 830 (1978).

28. Huggins v. Castle Estates, Inc., 36 N.Y.2d 427, 369 N.Y.S.2d 80, 330 N.E.2d 48 (1975).

29. Mastin v. Village of Lima, 86 A.D.2d 777, 448 N.Y.S.2d 274 (4th Dep't 1982).

30. Rinaldi v. Holt, Rinehart & Winston, 42 N.Y.2d 369, 397 N.Y.S.2d 943, 366 N.E.2d 1299, cert. denied, 434 U.S. 969, 98 S.Ct. 514, 54 L.Ed.2d 456 (1977).

31. Santosky v. Kramer, 455 U.S. 745, 102 S.Ct. 1388, 71 L.Ed.2d 599 (1982)(termination of parental rights); Addington v. Texas, 441 U.S. 418, 99 S.Ct. 1804, 60 L.Ed.2d 323 (1979)(commitment to mental hospital); Woodby v. Immigration & Naturalization Service, 385 U.S. 276, 87 S.Ct. 483, 17 L.Ed.2d 362 (1966)(deportation); Schneiderman v. United States, 320 U.S. 118, 63 S.Ct. 1333, 87 L.Ed. 1796 (1943)(denaturalization).

Without explicitly imposing the enhanced standard as a requirement of due process, the Court of Appeals held that termination of artificial life support may not be effected except upon a showing by clear and convincing evidence that such were the wishes of the now-incompetent person. Soper v. Storar, 52 N.Y.2d 363, 379, 438 N.Y.S.2d 266, 274, 420 N.E.2d 64, 72, cert. denied, 454 U.S. 858, 102 S.Ct. 309, 70 L.Ed.2d 153 (1981).

Similarly, by statute a proceeding for the appointment of a guardian to manage the affairs of an allegedly incapacitated person is governed by the clear and convincing evidence standard. See N.Y.Mental Hygiene Law § 81.12(a).

32. McCormick § 340, at 442; McBaine, "Burden of Proof: Degrees of Belief," 32 Cal.L.Rev. 242, 246, 253–54 (1944); Morgan, "Instructing the Jury Upon Presumptions and Burden of Proof," 47 Harv.L.Rev. 59, 67 (1933).

33. Ausch v. St. Paul Fire & Marine Ins. Co., 125 A.D.2d 43, 45, 511 N.Y.S.2d 919, 921–22 (2d Dep't), appeal denied, 70 N.Y.2d 610, 522 N.Y.S.2d 110, 516 N.E.2d 1223 (1987)(court approved trial court's use of jury instruction that used "highly probable" language to describe clear and convincing evidence standard). See also In re Eichner, 73 A.D.2d 431, 469, 426 N.Y.S.2d 517, 546 (2d Dep't 1980)(court refers to clear and convincing evidence standard as requiring "a finding of high probability").

Suggested jury instructions on clear and convincing evidence can be found in 1 New York Pattern Jury Instructions—Civil

ly the same as under New York law.[34] With respect to the preponderance standard, the Second Circuit has approved the following definition: "The term 'preponderance' means that 'upon all the evidence * * * the facts asserted by the [proponent] are more probably true than false.' "[35] An instructive opinion by Judge Weinstein in *United States v. Fatico*,[36] describes various formulations of the intermediate "clear and convincing evidence" standard as applied in civil cases involving "moral turpitude"[37] and cases "where the various interests of society are pitted against restrictions on the liberty of the individual."[38]

Library References:

West's Key No. Digests, Evidence ⚖︎596–598.

d. Criminal Cases: New York

1. *Reasonable Doubt*

It is a fundamental principle of due process that the prosecution's case against a criminal defendant must be proved beyond a reasonable doubt.[39] Each element of the state's case is held to this standard.[40] Thus, the judge's instructions to the jury must neither expressly nor impliedly suggest that the defendant has any burden of disproving an element of the alleged crime.[41]

§ 1:64 (2d ed.1995 Supp.); 1 New York Forms of Jury Instruction § 1.28 (1992).

34. See generally Graham § 301.5; 1 C. Mueller and L. Kirkpatrick, Federal Evidence § 65 (2d ed.1994).

35. Nissho-Iwai Co., v. M/T Stolt Lion, 719 F.2d 34, 38 (2d Cir.1983)(citation omitted). See also United States v. Fatico, 458 F.Supp. 388, 403 (E.D.N.Y.1978), aff'd, 603 F.2d 1053 (2d Cir.1979), cert. denied, 444 U.S. 1073, 100 S.Ct. 1018, 62 L.Ed.2d 755 (1980) (preponderance represents a "more probably than not" standard).

In Larson v. Jo Ann Cab Corp., 209 F.2d 929 (2d Cir.1954), Judge Frank wrote a wry opinion lamenting the shortcomings of judicial attempts to articulate the meaning of "preponderance" for lay jurors. He observed that " '[p]reponderance' is but a long latinism for the short English words 'weigh more.' Today, it is merely a metaphor; it suggests that, when the jury considers the evidence, it is as if the evidence were weighed on a scale." Id. at 931. To describe preponderance to a jury in terms of "weight" and "scales," however, " 'is apt to lead the judicial discussion close to the danger line of the fallacious quantitative or numerical theory of testimony.' " Id. (quoting 9 Wigmore § 2498). The danger of the "weight" metaphor, therefore, is mitigated by "trial judges [who] often wisely inform the jurors * * * of the irrelevance of the mere 'number of witnesses or the quantity of exhibits.' " 209 F.2d at 933. Judge Frank, however, made no attempt, at least in the Larson case, to formulate any particular jury instruction.

36. 458 F.Supp. 388 (E.D.N.Y.1978), aff'd, 603 F.2d 1053 (2d Cir.1979), cert. denied, 444 U.S. 1073, 100 S.Ct. 1018, 62 L.Ed.2d 755 (1980).

37. Id. at 404. See also Barr Rubber Products Co. v. Sun Rubber Co., 425 F.2d 1114, 1120 (2d Cir.), cert. denied, 400 U.S. 878, 91 S.Ct. 118, 27 L.Ed.2d 115 (1970).

38. 458 F.Supp. at 405 (quoting In re Ballay, 482 F.2d 648, 662 (D.C.Cir.1973)). See also note 31 supra.

39. In re Winship, 397 U.S. 358, 361–64, 90 S.Ct. 1068, 1071–73, 25 L.Ed.2d 368, 373–75 (1970). See also N.Y.Crim.Proc. Law § 70.20 (prosecution must "establish[] beyond a reasonable doubt every element of [the] offense and the defendant's commission thereof").

40. People v. Kohl, 72 N.Y.2d 191, 198, 532 N.Y.S.2d 45, 48, 527 N.E.2d 1182, 1185 (1988).

41. See People v. Antommarchi, 80 N.Y.2d 247, 252, 590 N.Y.S.2d 33, 36, 604 N.E.2d 95, 98 (1992). In Antommarchi the trial judge charged the jury in a way which suggested that a juror's doubt would not be reasonable unless the juror, if questioned by other jurors, would be "willing and able" to give an explanation as to his position based on the evidence or lack thereof. Id. at 251, 590 N.Y.S.2d at 35, 604 N.E.2d at 97. This was error, said the Court of Appeals, because the instruction had the effect

§ 300.4   BURDEN OF PROOF & PRESUMPTIONS   Ch. 3

In charging the jury on the meaning of reasonable doubt, "[n]ecessarily, trial courts must use general terms to explain to the jury the important yet subtle difference between a reasonable doubt and one which is based on conjecture or caprice."[42] Instructions that speak of such doubt as a reasonable person may have after carefully reviewing and considering the evidence—it is not "a whim or a hunch"—will pass muster,[43] as will language defining reasonable doubt as "one for which a reason can be given."[44] The risk of error is greatest when a judge's instructions seek to improvise or otherwise deviate from pattern jury instructions that track the language of Court of Appeals caselaw.[45]

More demanding jury instructions are required when the prosecution's case is based entirely on circumstantial evidence.[46] It is said that such cases "often require the jury to undertake a more complex and problematical reasoning process than do cases based on direct evidence."[47] A perceived need exists, therefore, for the trial judge to make

of shifting the burden of proof to the defendant: "An instruction that requires jurors to supply concrete reasons 'based upon the evidence' for their inclination to acquit implicitly imposes on defendants the burden of presenting a defense that supplies the jurors with the arguments they need to legitimize their votes." Id. at 252, 590 N.Y.S.2d at 36, 604 N.E.2d at 98. A jury charge which describes reasonable doubt "as one which a juror could, if called upon to do so, express or articulate," is permissible, id. at 252, 590 N.Y.S.2d at 36, 604 N.E.2d at 98, but only if the effect is to define "the degree of clarity and coherence of thought necessary for the jurors to conclude they harbor a reasonable doubt." Id. at 251, 590 N.Y.S.2d at 36–37, 604 N.E.2d at 97–98. Instructions of this nature, therefore, should include "a clarifying statement that the jurors have no [affirmative] obligation to [specifically] articulate the basis for their doubts." Id. at 253, 590 N.Y.S.2d at 36, 604 N.E.2d at 98.

42. Antommarchi, supra note 41, 80 N.Y.2d at 251, 590 N.Y.S.2d at 36, 604 N.E.2d at 98.

43. See, e.g., People v. Antommarchi, 80 N.Y.2d 247, 252, 590 N.Y.S.2d 33, 36, 604 N.E.2d 95, 98 (1992); People v. Jones, 27 N.Y.2d 222, 226, 316 N.Y.S.2d 617, 619, 265 N.E.2d 446, 447 (1970); People v. Barker, 153 N.Y. 111, 115, 47 N.E. 31, 32 (1897).

44. People v. Antommarchi, 80 N.Y.2d 247, 252, 590 N.Y.S.2d 33, 36, 604 N.E.2d 95, 98 (1992). But see note 41 supra, regarding the qualifications to the use of such language.

45. See, e.g., 1 Criminal Jury Instructions, New York ¶ 6.20 (1991). Examples of failed attempts properly to describe the meaning of reasonable doubt include People v. Feldman, 296 N.Y. 127, 140, 71 N.E.2d 433, 439 (1947)(reasonable doubt "is not a doubt based upon sympathy or a whim or prejudice or bias or a caprice, or a sentimentality, or upon a reluctance of a weak-kneed, timid, jellyfish of a juror who is seeking to avoid the performance of a disagreeable duty * * *"); and People v. Wilds, 141 A.D.2d 395, 398, 529 N.Y.S.2d 325, 327 (1st Dep't 1988)(judge described prosecution's case as a jigsaw puzzle depicting a portrait of Abraham Lincoln and then said, "If it makes out its case beyond a reasonable doubt even though some questions are unanswered, even though there [are] some blank spaces in the jigsaw puzzle you will say so you are convinced beyond a reasonable doubt that this is a [portrait] of Abraham Lincoln"; instructions were improper because "the average American juror would recognize a jigsaw puzzle of Abraham Lincoln long before all of the pieces are in place.").

46. See, e.g., People v. Ford, 66 N.Y.2d 428, 497 N.Y.S.2d 637, 488 N.E.2d 458 (1985). Special instructions are not required, however, when the prosecution's case is a mix of both direct and circumstantial evidence. People v. Barnes, 50 N.Y.2d 375, 380, 429 N.Y.S.2d 178, 180, 406 N.E.2d 1071, 1073–74 (1980).

47. People v. Kennedy, 47 N.Y.2d 196, 201, 417 N.Y.S.2d 452, 455, 391 N.E.2d 288, 290 (1979). See People v. Benzinger, 36 N.Y.2d 29, 32, 364 N.Y.S.2d 855, 856, 324 N.E.2d 334, 335 (1974)("The reason for the * * * rule is not that circumstantial evidence is thought to be weaker than direct evidence, since the reverse is frequently true. Rather, the rule draws attention to the fact that proof by circumstantial evidence may require careful reasoning by the trier of facts.").

an extra effort to minimize the danger that the jury will "leap logical gaps in the proof offered and draw unwarranted conclusions based on probabilities of low degree."[48] Accordingly, the jury must be instructed "in substance that it must appear that the inference of guilt is the only one that can fairly and reasonably be drawn from the facts, and that the evidence excludes beyond a reasonable doubt every reasonable hypothesis of innocence."[49]

Library References:

West's Key No. Digests, Criminal Law ⟺561.

2. Defenses and Affirmative Defenses

New York Penal Law § 25.00 contains explicit directions with respect to burden-of-proof issues in the context of defenses interposed by the defendant:

§ 25.00 Defenses; burden of proof

1. When a "defense," other than an "affirmative defense," defined by statute is raised at a trial, the people have the burden of disproving such defense beyond a reasonable doubt.

2. When a defense declared by statute to be an "affirmative defense" is raised at a trial, the defendant has the burden of establishing such defense by a preponderance of the evidence.

Thus, as to statutorily-defined "defenses," no burden of persuasion shifts to the defendant. Justification defenses (self-defense and the like)[50] are the most prominent examples of defenses falling within this category.[51] Once a defense becomes an issue in the case, the prosecution's evidence must disprove the defense beyond a reasonable doubt. On the other hand, the defense issue need not be submitted to the jury unless the "evidence at trial viewed in the light most favorable to the

---

48. People v. Benzinger, 36 N.Y.2d 29, 32, 364 N.Y.S.2d 855, 856, 324 N.E.2d 334, 335 (1974).

49. People v. Sanchez, 61 N.Y.2d 1022, 1024, 475 N.Y.S.2d 376, 377, 463 N.E.2d 1228, 1229 (1984), appeal denied, 74 N.Y.2d 746, 545 N.Y.S.2d 121, 543 N.E.2d 764 (1989).

The concept, as originally put forward by the Court of Appeals, appeared to call for an instruction that the facts must exclude every reasonable hypothesis of innocence "to a moral certainty." See, e.g., People v. Cleague, 22 N.Y.2d 363, 365–66, 292 N.Y.S.2d 861, 863, 239 N.E.2d 617, 618 (1968); People v. Borrero, 26 N.Y.2d 430, 434–35, 311 N.Y.S.2d 475, 479, 259 N.E.2d 902, 905 (1970). More recent cases hold that the "moral certainty" language is unnecessary so long as the charge conveys the idea "that the facts proved must exclude every reasonable inference of innocence." People v. Ford, 66 N.Y.2d 428, 443, 497 N.Y.S.2d 637, 645, 488 N.E.2d 458, 466 (1985).

The "moral certainty" and "exclusion of every reasonable inference" concepts are used only in describing the reasonable doubt standard to the jury; they are not part of the standard to be used by trial or appellate courts in determining sufficiency of the evidence. See § 300.3, at notes 31–32 supra.

50. N.Y.Penal Law §§ 35.00–35.30.

51. Infancy is another statutory defense. Id. § 30.00. Although alibi is not defined in the Penal Law as a defense, it is treated as such for purposes of § 25.00(1). People v. Victor, 62 N.Y.2d 374, 377–78, 477 N.Y.S.2d 97, 99, 465 N.E.2d 817, 819 (1984). The prosecution must therefore disprove an alibi beyond a reasonable doubt, and the jury must be so charged. Id.

accused, sufficiently supports a claimed defense."[52] In other words, the burden of production with respect to a defense lies with the defendant:[53] Either the defendant herself must introduce evidence to support an inference of facts that would constitute a defense, or the prosecution's evidence itself must give rise to such an inference.[54] Only if sufficient evidence of the defense is in the record must the jury be informed that the defense is in issue,[55] in which case the jury must be instructed that the defense must be disproved beyond a reasonable doubt.

Statutorily-defined "affirmative defenses," such as duress,[56] entrapment[57] and insanity,[58] are another matter. In order to exculpate herself on such grounds, the defendant bears not only the burden of production but also the burden of persuasion by a preponderance.

May the state constitutionally shift the burden of persuasion to the defendant with respect to affirmative defenses? The Supreme Court gave an affirmative answer to this question in *Patterson v. New York*.[59] The Court there held that, in defending against a murder charge, the defendant properly could be required to prove "extreme emotional disturbance," which the New York Penal Law defines as an affirmative defense. Proof of such affirmative defense will exonerate the defendant of murder and expose him to guilt for the less serious crime of man-

---

52. People v. Watts, 57 N.Y.2d 299, 301, 456 N.Y.S.2d 677, 678, 442 N.E.2d 1188, 1189 (1982)(defendant's evidence of justification for shooting victim was insufficient to submit question to jury).

53. Cf. People v. Sandgren, 302 N.Y. 331, 334, 98 N.E.2d 460, 462 (1951)(in case predating Penal Law § 25.00(1), court stated: "Whether * * * homicide is justifiable or excusable has always been a matter of defense and the burden of going forward with evidence to show justifiableness or excusability or guilt of a lesser degree of the crime proved prima facie, shifts to the defendant. Whether or not the defendant avails himself of his right to go forward with evidence, the overall burden of establishing the guilt of the defendant beyond a reasonable doubt never shifts from the People who must bring the case within one of the statutory definitions of one of the divisions of punishable homicide.").

54. See People v. Steele, 26 N.Y.2d 526, 528–29, 311 N.Y.S.2d 889, 891, 260 N.E.2d 527, 528 (1970)("Of course, justification * * * need not be disproved in every case. Ordinarily, the possibility of the defense would not appear until injected by the defendant * * * but, here, the prosecution's case, viewed separately, warrants the requested charge. * * *").

55. See, e.g., id.; People v. Watts, 57 N.Y.2d 299, 301, 456 N.Y.S.2d 677, 678, 442 N.E.2d 1188, 1189 (1982)("A trial court need not charge a jury with respect to an accused's proffered defense of justification if no view of the evidence establishes the basic elements of the defense."); People v. Ortiz, 76 N.Y.2d 446, 447, 560 N.Y.S.2d 186, 186, 560 N.E.2d 162, 163 (1990)(in prosecution for selling narcotics, defendant was not entitled to submission of "agency defense" to jury because "no reasonable view of the evidence would support a finding that defendant, who directed a potential purchaser to a seller of narcotics, was acting as an agent of that purchaser").

A similar approach is taken in determining whether the jury should be instructed that they may consider defendant's intoxication (which is not a defense) as a factor "negativing" the intent element of the alleged crime. N.Y.Penal Law § 15.25. See People v. Rodriguez, 76 N.Y.2d 918, 920, 563 N.Y.S.2d 48, 49, 564 N.E.2d 658, 659 (1990)(" '[a] charge on intoxication should be given if there is sufficient evidence of intoxication in the record for a reasonable person to entertain a doubt as to the element of intent on that basis' ")(quoting People v. Perry, 61 N.Y.2d 849, 850, 473 N.Y.S.2d 966, 966–67, 462 N.E.2d 143, 143 (1984)).

56. N.Y.Penal Law § 40.00.

57. Id. § 40.05.

58. Id. at § 40.15 (mental disease or defect).

59. 432 U.S. 197, 97 S.Ct. 2319, 53 L.Ed.2d 281 (1977).

slaughter.[60] According to *Patterson*, the key to the constitutionality of a burden-shifting scheme is maintaining the requirement that the prosecution prove, beyond a reasonable doubt, all of the elements included in the definition of the crime.[61] This was accomplished in the *Patterson* case because the prosecution, in accordance with the Penal Law's definition of murder, was required to prove, and did in fact prove, that the defendant intentionally caused the death of another person. It appears to be the rule, therefore, that if no burden is shifted to the defendant with respect to an element of the crime charged, a state generally is free to impose on the defendant the burden of proving, as an affirmative defense, circumstances of an exculpatory or mitigating nature.[62]

In *People v. Kohl*,[63] the Court of Appeals applied the teachings of *Patterson* to the affirmative defense of insanity[64] and reached a similar finding of constitutionality.[65] The *Kohl* court noted, however, that when

---

60. See N.Y.Penal Law §§ 125.20(2) and 125.25(1)(a).

61. 432 U.S. at 205–11, 97 S.Ct. at 2324–27, 53 L.Ed.2d at 289–93.

62. Id. at 210–11, 97 S.Ct. at 2327, 53 L.Ed.2d at 292. The Court stated as follows:

We thus decline to adopt as a constitutional imperative, operative countrywide, that a State must disprove beyond a reasonable doubt every fact constituting any and all affirmative defenses related to the culpability of an accused. Traditionally, due process has required that only the most basic procedural safeguards be observed; more subtle balancing of society's interests against those of the accused have been left to the legislative branch. We therefore will not disturb the balance struck in previous cases holding that the Due Process Clause requires the prosecution to prove beyond a reasonable doubt all of the elements included in the definition of the offense of which the defendant is charged. Proof of the nonexistence of all affirmative defenses has never been constitutionally required; and we perceive no reason to fashion such a rule in this case and apply it to the statutory defense at issue here.

This view may seem to permit state legislatures to reallocate burdens of proof by labeling as affirmative defenses at least some elements of the crimes now defined in their statutes. But there are obviously constitutional limits beyond which the States may not go in this regard. * * *

Long before Winship, the universal rule in this country was that the prosecution must prove guilt beyond a reasonable doubt. At the same time, the long- accepted rule was that it was constitutionally permissible to provide that various affirmative defenses were to be proved by the defendant. This did not lead to such abuses or to such widespread redefinition of crime and reduction of the prosecution's burden that a new constitutional rule was required. This was not the problem to which Winship was addressed. Nor does the fact that a majority of the States have now assumed the burden of disproving affirmative defenses for whatever reasons mean that those States that strike a different balance are in violation of the Constitution.

Id. A thorough discussion of the constitutionality of affirmative defenses that shift the burden of proof to the defendant is beyond the scope of this work. A helpful exposition of the issues is contained in Mueller and Kirkpatrick § 3.12.

63. 72 N.Y.2d 191, 532 N.Y.S.2d 45, 527 N.E.2d 1182 (1988).

64. N.Y.Penal Law § 40.15 (mental disease or defect). Prior to 1984, insanity was defined as a "defense," thus requiring the prosecution to disprove insanity beyond a reasonable doubt. See 72 N.Y.2d at 195, 532 N.Y.S.2d at 46, 527 N.E.2d at 1183.

65. 72 N.Y.2d at 193–94, 532 N.Y.S.2d at 45, 527 N.E.2d at 1182 ("[T]here is no State constitutional violation because placing this burden on the defendant does not relieve or transform the People's primary and constant burden of proving, beyond a reasonable doubt, all the elements of the crimes charged, including all components of the applicable culpable mental state."). The defendant in Kohl challenged the New York scheme under the due process clause of the state constitution because the Supreme Court had previously rejected a federal constitutional challenge to burden-shifting on the insanity issue. Leland v. Oregon, 343 U.S. 790, 72 S.Ct. 1002, 96

§ 300.4   BURDEN OF PROOF & PRESUMPTIONS   Ch. 3

the jury is told, as it must be, that the prosecution must prove the defendant's criminal intent beyond a reasonable doubt, they should also consider the defendant's evidence of insanity in deciding whether the prosecution has met its own burden of proof with respect to the defendant's state of mind.[66] In other words, even if the evidence in support of defendant's affirmative defense of insanity does not persuade the jury by a preponderance, such evidence might still contribute to a reasonable doubt about the prosecution's satisfaction of the *mens rea* element of the crime.

Library References:

West's Key No. Digests, Criminal Law ⊙=569–572.

e. Criminal Cases: Federal

Federal courts obviously are bound by the constitutional requirement that each element of the crime charged against a defendant be proven beyond a reasonable doubt.[67] *Holland v. United States*,[68] is the Supreme Court decision most frequently cited as suggesting the proper way for federal judges to explain reasonable doubt to juries. From *Holland*, there has emerged a pattern jury instruction describing reasonable doubt as "a doubt based upon reason and common sense—the kind of doubt that would make a reasonable person hesitate to act * * * in the most important of his or her own affairs."[69] In *United States v. Ivic*,[70] the Second Circuit approved the "hesitate to act" instruction and cautioned against "improvise[d] variations upon it."[71]

L.Ed. 1302 (1952), rehearing denied, 344 U.S. 848, 73 S.Ct. 4, 97 L.Ed. 659 (1952)(requirement that defendant prove insanity beyond reasonable doubt did not violate fourteenth amendment).

66. 72 N.Y.2d at 199, 532 N.Y.S.2d at 49, 527 N.E.2d at 1186 (after charging jury as to prosecution's burden of proof on intent, "the trial court should also, after the primary instructions, sequentially advise the jury that defendant bears a different burden on insanity, and that evidence of insanity relating to whether defendant knew what he was doing must be considered by the jury in its consideration of the People's nontransferable satisfaction of its burden to prove intent beyond a reasonable doubt").

Such instructions will help preserve the constitutionality of burden-shifting where the nature of the affirmative defense tends to overlap with some definitional component of the crime. In Martin v. Ohio, 480 U.S. 228, 107 S.Ct. 1098, 94 L.Ed.2d 267 (1987), the Supreme Court upheld a state's allocation to the defendant of the burden of persuasion on an affirmative defense of self-defense, in part, because the jury was instructed that the defendant's evidence could be weighed by them in determining whether the prosecution's case was proven beyond a reasonable doubt. Id. at 233, 107 S.Ct. at 1101–02, 94 L.Ed.2d at 273–74.

67. In re Winship, 397 U.S. 358, 364, 90 S.Ct. 1068, 1073, 25 L.Ed.2d 368, 375 (1970).

68. 348 U.S. 121, 75 S.Ct. 127, 99 L.Ed. 150 (1954), rehearing denied, 348 U.S. 932, 75 S.Ct. 334, 99 L.Ed. 731 (1955).

69. The current version of this instruction is in 1 E. Devitt, C. Blackmar, and M. Wolff, Federal Jury Practice and Instructions: Criminal § 12.10 (4th ed.1987). The relevant paragraph of the instruction reads in full as follows:

It is not required that the government prove guilt beyond all possible doubt. The test is one of reasonable doubt. A reasonable doubt is a doubt based upon reason and common sense—the kind of doubt that would make a reasonable person hesitate to act. Proof beyond a reasonable doubt must, therefore, be proof of such a convincing character that a reasonable person would not hesitate to rely and act upon it in the most important of his or her own affairs.

70. 700 F.2d 51 (2d Cir.1983).

71. Id. at 69. See also United States v. Torres, 901 F.2d 205, 242–43 (2d Cir.), cert.

In contrast to New York practice,[72] no special jury instructions are used in cases based solely on circumstantial evidence. According to the Supreme Court, telling the jury that the prosecution must exclude every reasonable hypothesis other than guilt is "confusing and incorrect."[73]

Another difference between federal and state practice is in the treatment of defenses. With respect to nearly all matters of defense, including alibi, self-defense, entrapment and duress, the defendant's only burden is that of producing sufficient evidence to create an issue for submission to the jury.[74] When the defendant's burden of production is thus satisfied, the burden is then on the government to disprove the defense beyond a reasonable doubt.[75] This differs from the New York scheme in which certain "affirmative defenses" must be proven by the defendant by a preponderance.[76] The major exception to the rule in federal prosecutions is the defense of insanity. The relevant statute was amended in 1984 to place the burden on the defendant to prove insanity by clear and convincing evidence.[77]

Library References:

West's Key No. Digests, Criminal Law ⚖=549–572.

301 Presumptions in Civil Cases

§ 301.1 New York: Introduction

Searching for consistency in the law of presumptions in New York can be a frustrating exercise. The same might be said, of course, about the law of any state in which the topic has not been codified or at least definitively addressed by the courts.[1] Identifying the presumptions

---

denied, 498 U.S. 906, 111 S.Ct. 273, 112 L.Ed.2d 229 (1990).

72. See text at notes 46–49 supra.

73. Holland v. United States, 348 U.S. 121, 139–40, 75 S.Ct. 127, 137, 99 L.Ed. 150, 166–67 (1954), rehearing denied, 348 U.S. 932, 75 S.Ct. 334, 99 L.Ed. 731 (1955)("the better rule is that where the jury is properly instructed on the standards for reasonable doubt, such an additional instruction on circumstantial evidence is confusing and incorrect"). Accord, United States v. Botsch, 364 F.2d 542, 550 (2d Cir.1966), cert. denied, 386 U.S. 937, 87 S.Ct. 959, 17 L.Ed.2d 810 (1967) (quoting United States v. Woodner, 317 F.2d 649, 651 (2d Cir.), cert. denied, 375 U.S. 903, 84 S.Ct. 192, 11 L.Ed.2d 144 (1963)(circumstantial evidence is not inferior to direct evidence; it may be weighed by jury in same way as direct evidence)).

74. See, e.g., United States v. Burse, 531 F.2d 1151, 1152–53 (2d Cir.1976)(alibi); United States v. Jackson, 726 F.2d 1466, 1468–69 (9th Cir.1984)(self-defense); United States v. Brown, 43 F.3d 618, 623 (11th Cir.1995)(entrapment); United States v. Mitchell, 725 F.2d 832, 836 (2d Cir.1983)(duress). See generally 2 C. Wright, Federal Practice and Procedure: Criminal § 403 (2d ed.1982).

75. See United States v. Mitchell, 725 F.2d 832, 836 (2d Cir.1983)(in "general federal practice * * * once a criminal defendant satisfies an initial burden of producing sufficient evidence to warrant submission of a substantive defense to the jury, the prosecution must disprove at least an element of that defense beyond a reasonable doubt"). See also United States v. Durrani, 835 F.2d 410, 420 (2d Cir.1987)("An affirmative defense requires a defendant to produce 'some evidence' placing * * * [the defense] in issue; if he does so, the government would be required to prove its inapplicability beyond a reasonable doubt.")

76. See text at notes 50–66 supra.

77. 18 U.S.C.A. § 17.

§ 301.1

1. See, e.g., L. Packel and A. Paulin, Pennsylvania Evidence § 306, at 81 (1987)(law of presumptions in Pennsylvania

§ 301.1 BURDEN OF PROOF & PRESUMPTIONS

themselves is not necessarily a burdensome task; plentiful cases and statutes discuss the presumptions that apply in specific areas of the substantive law. Often, however, the operative effect that a particular presumption will have on the evidentiary burdens of the parties in a civil case cannot be predicted.

Despite these caveats, some of the fundamental concepts about presumptions in New York are sufficiently clear. Furthermore, the analytical framework developed by the leading theorists on the law of presumptions can serve as a helpful backdrop to comprehension of New York's approach to presumptions.

Library References:

West's Key No. Digests, Evidence ⌐53–89.

§ 301.2 The Meaning of a Presumption

At the outset of any review of the law of presumptions, one must contend with the problem of terminology. Properly used in the context of civil litigation, the term "presumption" refers to a rule of law that a particular inference must be drawn from particular facts unless the opponent, at minimum, introduces contrary evidence.[1] Schematically, upon proof of fact A (the basic fact), fact B (the presumed fact) automatically and compulsorily springs into existence and remains as the required finding in the absence of evidence of the nonexistence of B.[2] A common presumption, for example, provides that proof of proper mailing of a letter (fact A) establishes the addressee's receipt thereof (fact B).[3] Upon proof of proper mailing, the proponent will be entitled to a mandatory ruling that the letter was received unless evidence of nonreceipt is introduced.

Some older decisions accompany the term "presumption" with alternative prepositional phrases that radically affect the meaning of the word. Thus, a "presumption of law" has the mandatory effect just described,[4] whereas a "presumption of fact" is one as to which proof of fact A merely gives rise to a permissive inference of fact B. "In other

---

is "confused and frustrating"). See also McCormick § 342, at 449 (" 'presumption' is the slipperiest member of the family of legal terms, except its first cousin, 'burden of proof' "); Morgan, "Presumptions," 12 Wash.L.Rev. 255, 255 (1937)("Every writer of sufficient intelligence to appreciate the difficulties of the subject-matter has approached the topic of presumptions with a sense of hopelessness and has left with a feeling of despair.").

§ 301.2

[1]. Platt v. Elias, 186 N.Y. 374, 379, 79 N.E. 1, 2 (1906)("a presumption of law is a rule which requires that a particular inference *must* be drawn from an ascertained state of facts")(emphasis in original); McCormick § 342, at 450 (presumption is "a rule of law that, at a minimum, shifts the burden of producing evidence"); 9 Wigmore § 2491, at 305 ("[I]t must be kept in mind that the peculiar effect of a presumption 'of law' (that is, the real presumption) is merely to invoke a rule of law compelling the jury to reach the conclusion *in the absence of evidence to the contrary* from the opponent.")(emphasis in original).

[2]. See § 301.3 infra.

[3]. See, e.g., Engel v. Lichterman, 95 A.D.2d 536, 538, 467 N.Y.S.2d 642, 643 (2d Dep't 1983), aff'd, 62 N.Y.2d 943, 479 N.Y.S.2d 188, 468 N.E.2d 26 (1984)("It has long been recognized in the law of evidence that a letter properly mailed is presumed to have been received * * *.").

[4]. Platt v. Elias, 186 N.Y. 374, 379, 79 N.E. 1, 2 (1906).

words, a presumption of fact leaves the [fact-finder] at liberty to infer certain conclusions from a certain set of circumstances, but does not compel it to do so."[5]

In reading older cases in which the term "presumption" is used without any qualifying prepositional phrase, the researcher must carefully examine the outcome described by the court to ascertain the intended meaning.[6] In this book, the term "presumption" in the context of civil cases will be used in the modern sense, *i.e.*, to describe a rule of law that requires a finding of fact B upon proof of fact A. Where fact A merely permits the jury, through logic and reasoning, to arrive at the conclusion of fact B, we will simply use the term "inference" to describe fact A's effect.[7] On the other hand, in criminal cases "presumptions," whether judge-made or statutory, are treated as mere inferences.[8]

Another phrase that must be reckoned with is "prima facie evidence," which occasionally appears in New York statutes. Whether prima facie evidence has the effect of a presumption or mere inference is discussed in § 301.7 *infra*.

Library References:

West's Key No. Digests, Evidence ⚖53–89.

§ 301.3 Rebuttable Presumptions

Once it has been determined that particular circumstances give rise to a presumption, the next question is whether the presumption is rebuttable or conclusive. If the presumption is conclusive, the law prohibits the introduction of evidence to contradict the presumed fact.[1] An example is the common law presumption that a child under the age of seven is incapable of committing a crime.[2] Presumptions of this nature are rare and are really just another way of stating a substantive rule of law.[3] A six-year-old child, for example, is simply not subject to criminal liability.[4]

The usual type of presumption is rebuttable: The presumed fact (fact B) is deemed established upon proof of the basic fact (fact A) unless and until the existence of B is adequately rebutted. At minimum, a rebuttable presumption shifts to the opponent the burden of producing

---

5. Id.

6. See George Foltis, Inc. v. City of New York, 287 N.Y. 108, 121, 38 N.E.2d 455, 462 (1941)("A study of the opinions of the appellate courts of this State reveals that judges have used the terms 'inference' and 'presumption' indiscriminately and without recognition that an 'inference' and a 'presumption' are not identical in scope or effect. Judicial failure to note the distinction has led to confusion of thought and often to inconsistencies in judicial opinions and decisions.").

7. See McCormick § 342, at 450.

8. See § 302.1 infra.

§ 301.3

1. 9 Wigmore § 2492.

2. Id. § 2514.

3. Id. § 2492.

4. In New York, the defense of infancy to a charge of criminal liability is covered in N.Y.Penal Law § 30.00. Subdivision (1) of that statute provides, in general, that a person becomes subject to criminal responsibility at age 16. Subdivision (2) lowers the threshold of criminal responsibility to varying ages with respect to certain serious crimes.

sufficient evidence of the nonexistence of B, the presumed fact.[5] If the opponent's burden of production is not met, the proponent would be entitled to a ruling that fact B has been established as a matter of law. Using the mail-and-receipt presumption as an example,[6] upon the proponent's proof of proper mailing, the opponent, in order to avoid a directed verdict of receipt, would be required to produce evidence that is sufficient to at least create a question of fact concerning nonreceipt.

This shifting of the burden of production assumes that the basic fact giving rise to the presumed fact has been established.[7] The basic fact can be proven like any other fact: by judicial notice, formal admissions or stipulations, or evidence introduced by the proponent which the court determines to be conclusive or which the jury finds persuasive.[8] If the existence of fact A is in contention, the opponent's failure to introduce evidence of the nonexistence of B will have no adverse consequence unless and until the trier of fact is persuaded of the existence of A. The opponent might successfully defeat the presumption, in other words, simply by challenging the basic fact. This he could do by arguing to the jury that the evidence in support of fact A is unconvincing, and he would be free to bolster this argument by introducing rebuttal evidence of the nonexistence of A.[9]

Before undertaking a more detailed analysis of the effect of presumptions when the basic facts are established, it is necessary to consider the reasons for presumptions, the subject matter of § 301.4 *infra*.

Library References:

West's Key No. Digests, Evidence ⟺53–89.

§ 301.4 Reasons for Presumptions; Illustrative Presumptions

Four principal reasons underlie the legislative and judicial creation of presumptions: probability, social policy, procedural convenience, and

---

5. James, Hazard and Leubsdorf, § 7.17, at 347; McCormick § 342, at 450–51. 9 Wigmore § 2487, at 295.

6. See § 301.2, at note 3, supra.

7. See, e.g., Capra v. Lumbermens Mutual Casualty Co., 43 A.D.2d 986, 987, 352 N.Y.S.2d 58, 61 (3d Dep't 1974)("[A]ctual mailing must be established before the presumption of receipt arises. Thus, evidence of non-receipt is unnecessary before there has been presented sufficient evidence to invoke the presumption in the first instance."). See also Matter of Feinerman, 97 A.D.2d 920, 470 N.Y.S.2d 762 (3d Dep't 1983) (presumption of receipt did not arise where proof of mailing was insufficient).

8. For example, adequate evidence of the mailing upon which the presumption of receipt may arise may be based on direct testimony or evidence of an office practice and procedure, followed in the regular course of business, regarding the addressing and posting of mail. See, e.g., Nassau Ins. Co. v. Murray, 46 N.Y.2d 828, 830, 414 N.Y.S.2d 117, 118, 386 N.E.2d 1085, 1086 (1978). See also Engel v. Lichterman, 62 N.Y.2d 943, 944, 479 N.Y.S.2d 188, 189, 468 N.E.2d 26, 27 (1984)(with respect to litigation papers, "[a] properly executed affidavit of service raises a presumption that a proper mailing occurred"). In some situations, statutes may ease the burden of proving particular mailings. See, e.g., N.Y.Veh. and Traf.Law § 313(1)(b)(certificate of mailing, obtained from post office and thereafter kept in regular course of business of liability insurer, is "conclusive proof" of mailing requirement with respect to notice of termination of policy).

9. See McCormick § 344, at 460–61.

Ch. 3 PRESUMPTIONS IN CIVIL CASES **§ 301.4**

access to proof.[1] The same type of reasons influence the apportionment of burdens of proof, as previously discussed in § 300.2 *supra*.

(1) *Probability*. Some facts, by their nature, are probative of other facts. As a matter of common sense, therefore, the recognition of a presumption as to such matters is a logical way to save time. The presumption of receipt that arises upon proof of mailing is such a presumption.[2] Others include the rule that a status or condition once shown to exist is presumed to continue,[3] the presumption that the possessor of something is its owner,[4] the presumption that a person is mentally competent[5] and the presumption that public officials perform their tasks with regularity and in accordance with lawful procedure.[6]

(2) *Social Policy*. Presumptions often are created to advance socially desirable outcomes. Examples include presumptions of the legitimacy of children[7] and the validity of a marriage[8] and the presumption against

§ 301.4

1. See generally James, Hazard and Leubsdorf § 7.17, at 348–49; McCormick § 343; Morgan, "Instructing the Jury Upon Presumptions and Burden of Proof," 50 Harv.L.Rev. 59, 77–82 (1937).

2. Oregon Steam–Ship Co. v. Otis, 100 N.Y. 446, 452, 3 N.E. 485, 487 (1885), appeal dismissed, 116 U.S. 548, 6 S.Ct. 523, 29 L.Ed. 719 (1886) ("The great bulk of letters sent by mail reach their destination, and equally so the great bulk of telegrams. A failure in either case is an exception; possible, but rare."); § 301.2, at note 3, supra.

3. Wilkins v. Earle, 44 N.Y. 172, 192 (1870)("A partnership once established is presumed to continue. Life is presumed to exist. Possession is presumed to continue. The fact that a man was a gambler twenty months since, justifies the presumption that he continues to be one. An adulterous intercourse is presumed to continue. So of ownership and non-residence."); Pollock v. Rapid Industrial Plastics Co., 113 A.D.2d 520, 525–26, 497 N.Y.S.2d 45, 49 (2d Dep't 1985)(ownership is presumed to continue).

In a tort action seeking damages for the conscious pain and suffering of a decedent who died in the accident, would the presumption of "continuance of life" be sufficient to establish plaintiff's prima facie case that the decedent did not instantly lose consciousness? The Court of Appeals refused to answer this question in Cummins v. County of Onondaga, 84 N.Y.2d 322, 618 N.Y.S.2d 615, 642 N.E.2d 1071 (1994), due to the plaintiff-appellant's failure to raise the issue at trial. The Court of Appeals noted, however, that application of the presumption in this context "would affect longstanding and delicate burdens of proof and major risk and damage policy allocations." Id. at 326, 618 N.Y.S.2d at 617, 642 N.E.2d at 1073.

4. See, e.g., Benjamin v. Benjamin, 106 A.D.2d 599, 600, 483 N.Y.S.2d 418, 419 (2d Dep't 1984), aff'd, 65 N.Y.2d 756, 492 N.Y.S.2d 31, 481 N.E.2d 571 (winning lottery ticket, payable to bearer).

5. See, e.g., Matter of Estate of Obermeier, 150 A.D.2d 863, 864, 540 N.Y.S.2d 613, 613–14 (3d Dep't 1989)(party to contract was presumed competent at time of execution).

6. See, e.g., People v. Harrison, 85 N.Y.2d 794, 796, 628 N.Y.S.2d 939, 940, 652 N.E.2d 638 (1995)(judicial proceedings); People ex rel. Wallington Apartments, Inc. v. Miller, 288 N.Y. 31, 33, 41 N.E.2d 445, 446 (1942)(assessors' valuations); Deshong v. City of New York, 176 N.Y. 475, 485, 68 N.E. 880, 883 (1903)(record-keeping).

7. In re Matthews' Estate, 153 N.Y. 443, 448, 47 N.E. 901, 903 (1897) (without presumption of legitimacy, "[p]roperty rights would be rendered doubtful, and the fair fame of their ancestors might be destroyed, by the cupidity of remote heirs and next of kin. There might be others who would be willing to dishonor their ancestors and bastardize their relatives to increase their patrimony. * * * We have no hesitation in adhering to the principle that the law presumes legitimacy, and not illegitimacy; morality, and not immorality; social integrity, and not social dishonor * * *."). See also Buck v. Hunter (In re Fay), 44 N.Y.2d 137, 141, 404 N.Y.S.2d 554, 556, 375 N.E.2d 735, 737 (1978), appeal dismissed, 439 U.S. 1059, 99 S.Ct. 820, 59 L.Ed.2d 25, rehearing denied, 440 U.S. 968, 99 S.Ct. 1521, 59 L.Ed.2d 784 (1979).

8. Gall v. Gall, 114 N.Y. 109, 117–18, 21 N.E. 106, 108–109 (1889) (persons who cohabit as husband and wife, and are reputed to be such, are presumed to have been legally married); Esmond v. Thomas Lyons

suicide.[9]

(3) *Procedural Convenience.* Some otherwise insoluble dilemmas caused by the absence of affirmative evidence may be resolved by relevant presumptions that serve procedural convenience and thereby help to adjust substantive rights and obligations. For example, the continuous and unexplained absence of a person for three years or more gives rise to a statutory presumption that the person has died.[10] Another statutory presumption of this nature applies in the case of the apparently simultaneous death of two or more persons in a common disaster. To aid in the settlement of their estates, each decedent is presumed to have outlived the other for purposes of the distribution of her own property.[11]

(4) *Access to Proof.* The creation of some presumptions is heavily influenced by the recognition that the party with better access to relevant evidence on a particular matter should have the burden, at minimum, of coming forward with such evidence. The common law presumption in bailment cases, for example, holds that upon proof by the bailor of delivery of the chattel and the bailee's failure to return it upon demand, the bailee is presumed to have converted the chattel or to have

---

Bar & Grill, 26 A.D.2d 884, 884, 274 N.Y.S.2d 225, 227 (3d Dep't 1966) ("extremely strong presumption of validity arises from * * * a ceremonial marriage").

9. See Schelberger v. Eastern Savings Bank, 60 N.Y.2d 506, 510, 470 N.Y.S.2d 548, 549, 458 N.E.2d 1225, 1226 (1983)(presumption against suicide is based on "strong policy considerations" and "natural probability"); Wellisch v. John Hancock Mut. Life Ins. Co., 293 N.Y. 178, 184–85, 56 N.E.2d 540, 543 (1944)(presumption against suicide is based both on the principle that the law disfavors implications of "criminality or moral turpitude" and that suicide is "contrary to the general conduct of mankind").

10. N.Y.Est.Powers and Trusts Law § 2–1.7 states as follows:

§ 2–1.7 Presumption of death from absence; effect of exposure to specific peril

(a) A person who is absent for a continuous period of three years, during which, after diligent search, he or she has not been seen or heard of or from, and whose absence is not satisfactorily explained shall be presumed, in any action or proceeding involving any property of such person, contractual or property rights contingent upon his or her death or the administration of his or her estate, to have died three years after the date such unexplained absence commenced, subject to the following:

(1) The fact that such person was exposed to a specific peril of death may be a sufficient basis for determining that he or she died less than three years after the date his or her absence commenced.

(2) The three-year period provided herein shall not apply in any case in which a different period has been prescribed by statute.

The common law presumption of death based on disappearance fixed an arbitrary period of seven years' absence. See Butler v. Mutual Life Ins. Co. of New York, 225 N.Y. 197, 121 N.E. 758 (1919). The New York statute quoted above fixed the period at five years until a 1993 amendment reduced it to three.

The presumption does not take effect if the proponent fails to satisfy the prerequisites of subdivision (a). Thus, three years' absence raises no presumption of death "when there exist circumstances or facts which reasonably account for [the missing person's] not being heard of, or his absence and abstention from communication are reasonably explained without assuming his death, or where diligent inquiry as to whether he is alive or dead has not been made." Butler, supra, 225 N.Y. at 203, 121 N.E. at 760.

11. N.Y.Est.Powers and Trusts Law § 2–1.6(a). The statutory presumption arises only when there is insufficient evidence to prove that the deaths happened other than simultaneously. Id. A person is free to create a different rule in a will, trust, deed, or contract of insurance. Id. § 2–1.6(e).

negligently lost it.[12] The bailee, after all, had possession of the chattel and is more conveniently positioned than the bailor to ascertain what happened.[13]

Obviously, more than one consideration may play a role in providing the underpinning for a particular presumption.[14] Indeed, all presumptions other than those which serve merely the goal of procedural convenience are likely to have an element of probability to them. One frequently encountered multi-purpose presumption is the statutory rule in New York that the driver of an automobile is presumed to have been driving with the owner's permission at the time of an accident.[15] Such permission, of course, is a prerequisite to the owner's vicarious liability.[16] The presumption of permission is supported, in part, by probability (the driver is not likely to be a thief or an authorized driver who has exceeded the scope of consent), social policy (automobile owners, who must purchase insurance, are better risk bearers than injured victims) and access to proof (the owner is in the best position to produce evidence of the relationship between her and the driver).

Identifying the reasons for a particular presumption can be decisive in some cases because of the potential for conflict between presumptions. Situations of this nature often arise in the field of matrimonial litigation. Assume, for example, that one spouse seeks to annul the marriage on the ground that the other spouse was married to someone else at the time.[17] The plaintiff proves the fact of spouse number two's prior marriage and then rests her case. The presumption that a proven state of facts—the prior marriage—continues to exist favors the plaintiff's case, but the presumption of the validity of the second marriage favors the defendant's case. Which presumption, if either, should take precedence? In *Palmer v. Palmer*,[18] the Court of Appeals held that "[w]here there are conflicting presumptions of unequal weight, * * * the stronger will prevail."[19] Applying this approach in the conflicting marriages context, the presumption of validity of the second marriage would normally prevail because the conflicting presumption of continuance would result in a finding of bigamy.[20] If the presumptions are of equal weight, a

---

12. See, e.g., Hogan v. O'Brien, 212 App.Div. 193, 194, 208 N.Y.S. 477, 478 (3d Dep't 1925).

13. See ICC Metals, Inc. v. Municipal Warehouse Company, 50 N.Y.2d 657, 665, 431 N.Y.S.2d 372, 377, 409 N.E.2d 849, 854 (1980)("Since bailed property is in the possession of and under the sole control of the warehouse at the time of injury or loss * * * it is the warehouse which is in the best, if not the only, position to explain the loss of or damage to the property. Indeed, such information normally will be exclusively in the possession of the warehouse and will not be readily accessible to the bailor.")

14. See McCormick § 343, at 454–55.

15. Leotta v. Plessinger, 8 N.Y.2d 449, 461, 209 N.Y.S.2d 304, 312, 171 N.E.2d 454, 459 (1960).

16. N.Y.Veh. and Traf.Law § 388(1).

17. See, e.g., Fagin v. Fagin, 88 Misc. 304, 151 N.Y.S. 809 (Sup.Ct.Kings Co.1914).

18. 162 N.Y. 130, 56 N.E. 501 (1900).

19. Id. at 133, 56 N.E. at 501 (presumption of innocence of crime prevails over presumption of continuance). See also In re Werlich, 230 N.Y. 516, 520, 130 N.E. 632, 633 (1921)("Where the presumption against partial intestacy is in conflict with the presumption against disherison [disinheritance] * * *, the weaker must yield.").

20. Fagin v. Fagin, 88 Misc. 304, 306, 151 N.Y.S. 809, 810 (Sup.Ct.Kings Co.1914). See also Ventura v. Ventura, 53 Misc.2d 881, 885, 280 N.Y.S.2d 5, 9 (Sup.Ct. Queens Co.1967) (presumption of continu-

§ 301.4   BURDEN OF PROOF & PRESUMPTIONS   Ch. 3

possible solution is the disregarding of both presumptions and leaving the matter to be resolved on the basis of whatever inferences flow from the facts without the aid of presumptions.[21]

Dozens of presumptions are operative in New York, spanning the gamut of the substantive law. To catalogue all or even most of them, and to analyze the reasons for their creation, is beyond the scope of a one-volume evidence book. Presumptions are identifiable easily enough in the cases and statutes governing the relevant areas of law. We will turn our attention, instead, to the troubling issue of the effect that presumptions have on the trial process.

Library References:

West's Key No. Digests, Evidence ⟱53–89.

§ 301.5   Effect of Presumptions in New York

a. In General

Assuming the basic facts giving rise to a presumption are established, what must the opponent of the presumption do to effectively rebut it? What is the lingering effect, if any, of a presumption that has been met by rebuttal evidence? In New York, these are difficult questions to answer with any degree of authority. No uniform approach is apparent. Before examining the New York rules in detail, however, it may be helpful to provide a frame of reference by reviewing the two principal theoretical paradigms for the operation of presumptions.

1. Thayer (the "Bursting Bubble" Rule)

The Thayer rule, named for its chief advocate,[1] operates as follows: Upon proof of the basic fact (A), the presumed fact (B) must be found unless the opponent introduces sufficient evidence to support a finding of the nonexistence of B.[2] If the opponent introduces such evidence, the presumption is no longer in the case.[3] The issue as to the existence of B

---

ance of first marriage yields to presumption of validity of second marriage); Brown v. Brown, 51 Misc.2d 839, 840–41, 274 N.Y.S.2d 484, 486 (Fam.Ct.N.Y.Co. 1966)("in the case of conflicting marriages of the same spouse [the] presumption of validity operates in favor of the second marriage").

21. See McCormick § 344, at 465. See, e.g., Peoples National Bank of Rockland County v. Weiner, 129 A.D.2d 782, 785, 514 N.Y.S.2d 772, 774–75 (2d Dep't 1987)(where presumption of regularity of public employees' performance of duty conflicts with presumption of receipt upon proof of mailing, "both should be disregarded").

§ 301.5

1. See J. Thayer, A Preliminary Treatise on Evidence at the Common Law 346 (1898). Wigmore adopted Thayer's views on the effect of presumptions. See 9 Wigmore §§ 2487("c") and 2491(2). See generally McCormick § 344, at 462–63; Laughlin, "In Support of the Thayer Theory of Presumptions," 52 Mich.L.Rev. 195, 209–30 (1953). Whether the rule associated with Thayer's name is a wholly accurate reflection of his views is questioned in Gausewitz, "Presumptions," 40 Minn.L.Rev. 391, 406–08 (1956).

2. McCormick § 344, at 462.

3. 9 Wigmore § 2491, at 305 ("If the opponent *does* offer some evidence to the contrary (sufficient to satisfy the judge's requirement of some evidence), the presumption disappears as a rule of law and the case is in the jury's hands free from any rule * * *.")(emphasis in original).

is then to be decided solely on the evidence in the case, including whatever natural inferences flow from A, the basic fact.[4] The only effect of a presumption under the Thayer rule, therefore, is to shift the burden of production to the opponent.[5]

If the opponent's rebuttal evidence of non-B is such that rational persons could not reasonably reject it, the burden of production would shift back to the proponent. The proponent's failure at such point to introduce enough additional evidence to create a fact issue as to B would entitle the opponent to a directed verdict.[6] On the other hand, if the jury could still reasonably make a finding of B after both sides rest, the case would go to the jury based solely on the evidence before them. The burden of persuasion on the existence of B would remain where it began, i.e., on the proponent.[7] Under the orthodox Thayer approach, the jury is told nothing about the presumption.[8] The presumption made its exit from the case (the "bubble was burst") when the opponent introduced sufficient evidence of the nonexistence of the presumed fact.

As an example of the classic Thayer approach, consider the mail-and-receipt presumption.[9] When the mailing of the letter is established, the opponent will "burst the bubble" of receipt simply by taking the stand and testifying, "I did not receive the letter." The presumption is now out of the case. Whether anyone actually believes the opponent at this point is irrelevant.[10] Assuming, after both sides rest, that reasonable persons could still find that the letter was received,[11] the case will go to the jury with an instruction that the proponent has the burden of persuading them of such receipt. They will be told nothing about the mail-and-receipt presumption.

---

4. See Hogan v. O'Brien, 212 App.Div. 193, 195, 208 N.Y.S. 477, 479 (3d Dep't 1925)("[C]ertain presumptions are mere inferences of fact crystallized into legal rules by judicial authority. In any such case, when upon the appearance of proof to the contrary, the presumption disappears, the inference of fact may remain."); 9 Wigmore § 2491, at 304.

5. 9 Wigmore § 2487, at 295, and § 2491, at 305–06.

6. See, e.g., O'Brien v. Equitable Life Assur. Soc'y, 212 F.2d 383, 387–89 (8th Cir.), cert. denied, 348 U.S. 835, 75 S.Ct. 57, 99 L.Ed. 658 (1954)(in action on life insurance policy for payment of accidental death benefits, plaintiff's prima facie case was initially satisfied by presumption that violent death was accidental; after defendant's rebuttal evidence removed presumption (decedent was shown to have been engaged in criminal act), remaining inferences as to accidental death were insufficient to sustain plaintiff's burden of production).

7. James, Hazard and Leubsdorf § 7.17, at 350. See, e.g., Fleming v. Ponziani, 24 N.Y.2d 105, 111, 299 N.Y.S.2d 134, 140, 247 N.E.2d 114, 119 (1969)(presumption governed by Thayer rule has no effect on burden of persuasion).

8. James, Hazard and Leubsdorf § 7.17, at 352.

9. See § 301.2, at note 3, supra.

10. James, Hazard and Leubsdorf § 7.17, at 350 (opponent's testimony of nonreceipt would "*end the presumption even if everybody in the courtroom was convinced that the testimony was a lie*")(emphasis in original).

11. Id. ("If the trier rejects the testimony of nonreceipt as false and believes the testimony of proper mailing, it could and probably would find receipt as an inference from the mailing.").

2. Morgan

Courts[12] and commentators,[13] led chiefly by Professor Morgan,[14] have criticized the Thayer approach on the ground that it gives too little weight to the values and policies underlying presumptions. If a presumption is worth recognizing in the first place, why should it disappear from the case so easily?[15] In the mail-and-receipt example, the opponent's mere testimony, "I did not receive the letter," generally forces the exit of the presumption no matter how self-interested and improbable such testimony may be. Furthermore, as to some presumptions, the natural inferences of B that flow from the basic fact A may be weak. When the presumption vanishes, the proponent may either face a directed verdict[16] or her case will go to the jury in a greatly debilitated state. The values that the presumption was created to foster are thus undermined.[17]

The Morgan approach would therefore shift the burden of persuasion to the opponent: Upon proof of the basic fact (A), the presumed fact (B) must be found unless the opponent's evidence persuades the jury (ordinarily by a preponderance) of the nonexistence of B.[18] It is not enough that the opponent takes the stand and says she did not receive the letter. The jury will be instructed that, upon a finding that the letter was mailed, they must also find that it was received unless they are persuaded by the evidence favoring the opponent that it was not in fact received.[19]

---

12. See, e.g., Hinds v. John Hancock Mutual Life Ins. Co., 155 Me. 349, 362–65, 155 A.2d 721, 730–31 (1959).

13. See, e.g., Cleary, "Presuming and Pleading: An Essay on Juristic Immaturity," 12 Stan.L.Rev. 5, 16–20 (1959); Gausewitz, "Presumptions," 40 Minn.L.Rev. 391, 401–10 (1956).

14. See, e.g., Morgan and Maguire, "Looking Backward and Forward at Evidence," 50 Harv.L.Rev. 909, 913 (1937); Morgan, "Instructing the Jury Upon Presumptions and Burden of Proof," 47 Harv.L.Rev. 59, 82–83 (1933).

15. See, e.g., Hinds v. John Hancock Mutual Life Ins. Co., 155 Me. 349, 365, 155 A.2d 721, 731 (1959)("it seems pointless to create a presumption and endow it with coercive force, only to allow it to vanish in the face of evidence of dubious weight or credibility").

16. See, e.g., Fleming v. Ponziani, 24 N.Y.2d 105, 111, 299 N.Y.S.2d 134, 140, 247 N.E.2d 114, 119 (1969).

17. See McCormick § 344, at 463.

18. See Cleary, "Presuming and Pleading: An Essay on Juristic Immaturity," 12 Stan.L.Rev. 5, 20 (1959).

Morgan's views evolved over time. In one of his early articles on the subject, for example, he recommended a two-tiered approach: Most presumptions would continue to operate in the case unless and until the opponent persuaded the jury that the nonexistence of B was at least as probable as its existence (an approach adopted by the Hinds court, see note 12 supra), whereas presumptions based on important social policies would completely shift the burden of persuasion to the opponent. Morgan, "Instructing the Jury Upon Presumptions and Burden of Proof," 47 Harv.L.Rev. 59, 83 (1933).

He later questioned the practicality—"in the heat and hurry of the trial"—of classifying presumptions and giving to each the strength it deserves in light of the reasons for its creation. Morgan, "Presumptions," 12 Wash.L.Rev. 255, 280 (1937). Morgan thus sought to reconcile the need to give presumptions their appropriate effect with the need for a rule of practicality and ease of application. Id. at 280–81. He eventually concluded that "the better rule" for all presumptions is "that anything worthy of the name 'presumption' has the effect of fixing the burden of persuasion on the party contesting the existence of the presumed fact." McCormick § 344, at 470.

19. See McCormick § 344, at 469.

b. New York Approach

Which theory, that of Thayer or Morgan, governs the operation of presumptions in New York? It depends. Some presumptions appear to have a Thayer effect, some have a Morgan effect, and still others have a hybrid effect. The problem is that no definitive exposition has been provided by the Court of Appeals.

Some decisions, none very recent, describe the effect of presumptions in classic Thayerian terms. In *Fleming v. Ponziani*,[20] for example, the proponent of a release was favored with a presumption of regularity in its execution. To rebut this presumption, it was said that the opponent had to come forward with evidence of "fraud, duress or some other fact which will be sufficient to void the release."[21] The court then said: "Once this party puts in some evidence, the presumption is no longer in the case and * * * since the burden of persuasion does not shift throughout trial, the person who is [relying on the release] * * * must come forward with real evidence to sustain his burden as to the legality of the release or otherwise suffer a directed verdict."[22] In addition to such caselaw, § 1–201(31) of the New York Uniform Commercial Code explicitly adopts the Thayer model for presumptions that are identified as such by the terms of the Code: "'Presumption' or 'presumed' means that the trier of fact must find the existence of the fact presumed unless and until evidence is introduced which would support a finding of its nonexistence."[23]

---

20. 24 N.Y.2d 105, 299 N.Y.S.2d 134, 247 N.E.2d 114 (1969).

21. Id. at 111, 299 N.Y.S.2d at 140, 247 N.E.2d at 118–19.

22. Id. at 111, 299 N.Y.S.2d at 140, 247 N.E.2d at 119. In addition to prior New York caselaw, the court cites 9 Wigmore § 2491; see note 3 supra.

Other decisions of the Court of Appeals that appear to have expressed a preference for the Thayer rule include People v. Richetti, 302 N.Y. 290, 298, 97 N.E.2d 908, 912 (1951)(presumption of regularity in judicial proceedings "exists only until contrary substantial evidence appears. * * * It forces the opposing party * * * to go forward with proof but, once he does go forward, the presumption is out of the case."); People ex rel. Wallington Apartments, Inc. v. Miller, 288 N.Y. 31, 33, 41 N.E.2d 445, 446 (1942)(presumption of regularity that attaches to assessors' valuations "disappears" when opponent offers evidence to the contrary); In re Magna (State Industrial Board v. Hegeman Harris Co.), 258 N.Y. 82, 83–84, 179 N.E. 266, 266–67 (1932)(under workers' compensation statute, presumption concerning claimant's disability "fails" upon carrier's submission of "substantial evidence to the contrary"; case thereupon "ceases to be one for presumptions, and becomes a case for proof").

23. For example, N.Y.Uniform Commercial Code § 3–307(1)(b) provides that the signature on an instrument is "presumed to be genuine or authorized" except in cases involving signers who have died or become incompetent. The party who denies the signature's validity must therefore produce sufficient evidence from which a jury rationally could find invalidity. Upon the opponent's satisfaction of this burden, the proponent of the instrument would have to persuade the jury that the signature was in fact valid. Id. § 3–307(1)(a).

In those instances in which the U.C.C. intends to impose or shift the burden of persuasion, the term "presumption" is avoided and the phrase "burden of establishing" is used. See N.Y.Uniform Commercial Code § 1–201(8); § 300.4, at note 9, supra. The case of I.C.C. Metals, Inc. v. Municipal Warehouse Company, 50 N.Y.2d 657, 431 N.Y.S.2d 372, 409 N.E.2d 849 (1980), illustrates the application of § 1–201(8) in the context of warehouse bailments governed by N.Y. Uniform Commercial Code § 7–403(1)(b). The Court of Appeals there held that the bailor makes out a prima facie case of negligence or conversion by the warehouse upon proof that the goods were delivered but not returned upon demand. Pursuant to § 7–403(1)(b) the warehouse must "establish," i.e., persuade the fact-finder, that the loss was due to

§ 301.5   BURDEN OF PROOF & PRESUMPTIONS   Ch. 3

At the opposite extreme is the judicial treatment of the presumption against suicide. Here, the New York courts have abandoned the Thayer rule and approved an approach that amounts to a reallocation of the burden of persuasion. In *Schelberger v. Eastern Savings Bank*,[24] the defendant, seeking to avoid paying the proceeds of a life insurance policy on the ground of suicide, introduced substantial evidence tending to show that the insured took his own life. But such evidence did not "burst the bubble."[25] On the contrary, the Court of Appeals approved a jury instruction in which the trial judge explicitly told the jury, "You may make a finding of suicide only if you are satisfied from the evidence, and taking into consideration the presumption against suicide, that no conclusion other than suicide may reasonably be drawn."[26] The practical effect of such an instruction, obviously, is to place the burden of persuasion on the party against whom the presumption against suicide has been invoked.[27] Why such an effect in this situation? It would appear to be because "[t]he presumption springs from strong policy considerations as well as embodying natural probability."[28] The Court of Appeals has not specified how many other presumptions might merit

circumstances "for which the bailee is not liable." The burden is then on the bailor to "establish", i.e., persuade the fact-finder, that there was negligence or conversion. The court gave the following example: "[I]f the jury is persuaded that the goods were accidentally mislaid or destroyed in a fire or accident or stolen by a third party, the plaintiff cannot recover unless he has proven that the loss or the fire or the accident or the theft were the proximate result of either a purposive act or a negligent commission or omission by the warehouse." 50 N.Y.2d at 666, 431 N.Y.S.2d at 378, 409 N.E.2d at 855.

24. 60 N.Y.2d 506, 470 N.Y.S.2d 548, 458 N.E.2d 1225 (1983).

25. The Court of Appeals had already indicated in an earlier opinion that the presumption against suicide is not "the sort of 'presumption' that serves only to shift the burden of proof and disappears from the case as soon as evidence to the contrary is offered." Wellisch v. John Hancock Mutual Life Ins. Co., 293 N.Y. 178, 184, 56 N.E.2d 540, 543 (1944).

26. 60 N.Y.2d at 509, 470 N.Y.S.2d at 549, 458 N.E.2d at 1226. See 1 N.Y.Pattern Jury Instructions—Civil § 1:63.2 (1995 Supp.).

27. Arguably, Schelberger is a case that can be confined to its facts. In a claim for nonpayment of ordinary life insurance proceeds, as in Schelberger, death by suicide within two years of issuance of the policy is an affirmative defense as to which the insurer traditionally has borne the burden of persuasion, at least in theory. See 9 Wigmore § 2510, at 515. See, e.g., Wellisch v. John Hancock Mut. Life Ins. Co., 293 N.Y. 178, 183, 56 N.E.2d 540, 542 (in trial court's jury charge, jury was instructed that insurer had burden of establishing death by suicide).

Several years prior to Schelberger, however, the Court of Appeals in Begley v. Prudential Ins. Co. of America, 1 N.Y.2d 530, 154 N.Y.S.2d 866, 136 N.E.2d 839 (1956), held in effect that the burden of persuasion as to suicide also shifts to the insurer in a claim for accidental death benefits (double indemnity): "When death has resulted from violence, the presumption against suicide does more than shift the burden of proof and upon having done so disappears from the case; it continues to the end of the case and if a fair question of fact is presented as to whether death was due to suicide or accident, then the jury should answer accident." Id. at 533, 154 N.Y.S.2d at 868, 136 N.E.2d at 841. Begley was cited in Schelberger to support the court's holding that the jury instructions at issue in Schelberger were in accord with "the present law of New York." Schelberger, supra, 60 N.Y.2d at 509, 470 N.Y.S.2d at 549, 458 N.E.2d at 1226.

Taken together, these pronouncements of the Court of Appeals all point to the conclusion that the presumption against suicide has the effect of shifting the burden of persuasion regardless of the context in which the issue arises.

28. Schelberger, supra, 60 N.Y.2d at 510, 470 N.Y.S.2d at 549, 458 N.E.2d at 1226.

such treatment, but the presumptions of legitimacy and the validity of marriage are likely candidates.[29]

Another major deviation from the Thayer model is the hybrid approach that the Court of Appeals has applied in accident cases involving the presumption that the driver of an automobile was driving with the owner's permission at the time of the accident.[30] In such cases, testimony by the defendant-owner that such permission was lacking, even if corroborated by the driver and other persons, does not destroy the presumption. The presumption remains in the case unless and until the evidence of lack of consent is believed by the jury.[31] In practice, the jury typically is told that the accident victim has the burden of persuasion on the issue of consent, but that they may weigh the presumption of permission together with the other evidence in determining the question.[32]

---

29. It is generally agreed that these two presumptions can be rebutted only by "clear and convincing evidence." See, e.g., Jean P. v. Roger Warren J., 184 A.D.2d 1072, 1072, 584 N.Y.S.2d 256, 257 (4th Dep't 1992) (presumption of legitimacy of child must be "disproved by clear and convincing evidence"); Estate of Lowney, 152 A.D.2d 574, 575, 543 N.Y.S.2d 698, 700 (2d Dep't 1989)(presumption of valid marriage, "especially in a case involving legitimacy [of children], can be rebutted only by the most cogent and satisfactory evidence"); Penny "MM" v. Bruce "MM", 118 A.D.2d 979, 979, 500 N.Y.S.2d 199, 200 (3d Dep't 1986) (presumption of legitimacy is rebuttable "only on the basis of clear and convincing proof"); In re Erskine Edward Rudolph F., 100 A.D.2d 878, 878, 474 N.Y.S.2d 137, 138 (2d Dep't 1984)(presumption of child's legitimacy "may be overcome only by clear and convincing proof of illegitimacy"). See also Esmond v. Thomas Lyons Bar & Grill, 26 A.D.2d 884, 884, 274 N.Y.S.2d 225, 227 (3d Dep't 1966)("An extremely strong presumption of validity arises from * * * a ceremonial marriage which is overcome only by overwhelming proof to the contrary.").

The obvious implication is that these presumptions operate to place the burden of persuasion, not merely that of production, on the opponent. By its terms, the clear and convincing evidence standard refers to the convincing, i.e., persuasive, force of evidence. See § 300.4(b)(2) supra.

30. See § 301.4, at notes 15–16, supra.

31. See Leotta v. Plessinger, 8 N.Y.2d 449, 461, 209 N.Y.S.2d 304, 312, 171 N.E.2d 454, 459–60 (1960)(presumption of permission "continues until there is substantial evidence to the contrary. * * * However, even where the owner may escape liability, it is unquestionable that, unless the evidence has no merit whatsoever, the question of consent and authority is for the jury."); Piwowarski v. Cornwell, 273 N.Y. 226, 229, 7 N.E.2d 111, 112 (1937)(credibility of rebuttal testimony given by interested witnesses "was exclusively for the jury"). Cf. Chaika v. Vandenberg, 252 N.Y. 101, 104–05, 169 N.E. 103, 104 (1929) (defendant-owner's testimony that driver lacked permission "'was not sufficient in law to destroy the presumption of control, although it might have been in fact'"). But see St. Andrassy v. Mooney, 262 N.Y. 368, 372, 186 N.E. 867, 868 (1933)(where defendant's rebuttal testimony of permission was corroborated and uncontradicted, directed verdict for defendant should have been granted).

In the much earlier case of Potts v. Pardee, 220 N.Y. 431, 116 N.E. 78 (1917), the Court of Appeals had applied a "bursting bubble" rule to the presumption of an owner's responsibility for the manner in which his car was driven. The driver, who was alleged to be in the employ of the defendant-owner when the accident occurred, testified that this was not so. The court wrote as follows: "The presumption growing out of a prima facie case * * * remains only so long as there is no substantial evidence to the contrary. When that is offered the presumption disappears, and, unless met by further proof, there is nothing to justify a finding based solely upon it. * * * Here the presumption arising from the fact of ownership was entirely destroyed by the other evidence." Id. at 433, 116 N.E. at 79.

32. See 1 N.Y.Pattern Jury Instructions—Civil §§ 1:63 and 1:63.1 (Supp.1995). See, e.g., Ryder v. Cue Car Rental, Inc., 32 A.D.2d 143, 147, 302 N.Y.S.2d 17, 21 (4th Dep't 1969)(in weighing evidence jury "had the benefit of a presumption of permission").

In Rivera v. W. & R. Service Station, Inc., 34 A.D.2d 115, 116–18, 309 N.Y.S.2d 274,

§ 301.5   BURDEN OF PROOF & PRESUMPTIONS   Ch. 3

This modification of the Thayer rule was adopted by the Court of Appeals without any significant discussion of the reasons for doing so. It seems clear enough, however, that the court was unsatisfied with the rule that allowed the opponent's mere utterance of contrary words to destroy the presumption of permission.[33] Arguably, this is an important presumption in the state's effort to allocate risk in the area of automobile tort liability.[34] Indeed, lower courts have described the presumption of permission as "very strong."[35]

The hybrid approach, however, has not been confined to the presumption of permission. It was also approved by the Court of Appeals in *Bornhurst v. Massachusetts Bonding & Insurance Co.*,[36] a case involving the presumption of continuance. There, it was said that whenever the rebuttal of a presumption depends on the credibility of a witness, it is for the jury to determine whether such rebuttal evidence should be believed, i.e., it is "for the jury [not the court] to determine whether the presumption has been destroyed."[37] This cannot be taken as announcing a rule of general application, however, because *Fleming v. Ponziani*,[38] decided a year later, applied the orthodox Thayer rule to the presumption of due execution of releases.[39] Furthermore, the Uniform Commercial Code adheres to the Thayer model for cases governed by the Code.[40]

Yet another deviation from the Thayer model has been applied to the mail-and-receipt presumption. The opponent's testimonial denial of receipt, standing alone, is insufficient to rebut the presumption. She must also produce either rebuttal evidence addressed to the underlying fact of mailing or evidence of circumstances that corroborate the testimony of nonreceipt.[41] Without such evidence, the proponent is entitled to a

---

276–77 (1st Dep't 1970), it was held that a trial court committed reversible error in charging that the plaintiff had the burden of proof on the issue of the driver's permission without also advising the jury of the presumption of such permission.

33.   See Hinds v. John Hancock Mutual Life Ins. Co., 155 Me. 349, 362–63, 155 A.2d 721, 730 (1959)(critics of Thayer rule believe that "a presumption should not fall merely because words are uttered which nobody believes").

34.   See § 301.4, at notes 15–16 supra.

35.   See, e.g., Aetna Casualty and Surety Co. v. Santos, 175 A.D.2d 91, 92, 573 N.Y.S.2d 695, 696 (2d Dep't 1991); Aetna Casualty and Surety Co. v. Brice, 72 A.D.2d 927, 928, 422 N.Y.S.2d 203, 205 (4th Dep't 1979), aff'd, 50 N.Y.2d 958, 431 N.Y.S.2d 528, 409 N.E.2d 1000 (1980).

36.   21 N.Y.2d 581, 289 N.Y.S.2d 937, 237 N.E.2d 201 (1968).

37.   Id. at 586, 289 N.Y.S.2d at 941, 237 N.E.2d at 204 (quoting W. Richardson, Evidence § 57 (9th ed.Prince)(1964)).

38.   24 N.Y.2d 105, 299 N.Y.S.2d 134, 247 N.E.2d 114 (1969).

39.   See text at notes 20–22 supra.

40.   See text at note 23 supra.

41.   See Nassau Insurance Co. v. Murray, 46 N.Y.2d 828, 830, 414 N.Y.S.2d 117, 118, 386 N.E.2d 1085, 1086 (1978)(notice of cancellation of insurance policy); Engel v. Lichterman, 95 A.D.2d 536, 538, 467 N.Y.S.2d 642, 643–44 (2d Dep't 1983), aff'd, 62 N.Y.2d 943, 479 N.Y.S.2d 188, 468 N.E.2d 26 (1984)(attorney's receipt of litigation papers); Jonathan Woodner Co. v. Higgins, 179 A.D.2d 444, 578 N.Y.S.2d 561 (1st Dep't 1992) (receipt of regulatory agency's order); T.J. Gulf, Inc. v. New York State Tax Comm'n, 124 A.D.2d 314, 315–16, 508 N.Y.S.2d 97, 98–99 (3d Dep't 1986) (receipt of agency's notice of claim for unpaid taxes).

Cases in which the presumption of receipt was held to have been rebutted include Vita v. Heller, 97 A.D.2d 464, 464–65, 467 N.Y.S.2d 652, 653 (2d Dep't 1983)(attorney claiming nonreceipt also submitted affidavit of office secretary detailing her routine office practices regarding notations on office files and in office diary with respect to receipt of papers requiring response); DeFeo v. Merchant, 115 Misc.2d 286, 289–90,

directed verdict. The apparent solution here is to increase the quantum of evidence necessary for the opponent to meet its burden of production. If this burden is met, it is unclear whether, in sending the case to the jury, the judge should apply the Thayer rule (the presumption is now gone and the jury is told nothing about it) or the hybrid approach (the jury is told that the presumption of receipt may be considered by them in weighing the evidence).

Where does this leave the law of presumptions in New York? Where we suggested it was at the outset: in a state of uncertainty. Some presumptions, apparently those based on compelling policy considerations, such as the presumption against suicide, merit the application of Morgan's persuasion-shifting model. Others that are "strong," but not necessarily as weighty as the presumption against suicide, appear to be governed by the hybrid approach in which the opponent's rebuttal evidence must be believed in order for the presumption to be destroyed. Although the jury is instructed in such cases that the burden of persuasion is on the proponent, the presumption is explicitly brought to their attention and they are told that they may weigh it in their evaluation of the evidence. Finally, for presumptions that might be deemed of lesser importance,[42] and those governed by the Uniform Commercial Code, the Thayer model is operative.

In one sense, the current New York approach might be viewed as striving for the ideal. If fully developed, it apparently would assign to each presumption the most appropriate effect based on the reasons for the recognition of the particular presumption.[43] The problem is that such fine-tuning is ill-suited to the workaday world of civil trials.[44]

Recognizing the difficulties in presumption-by-presumption analysis, the drafters of the Proposed New York Evidence Code would provide, as a general rule in civil cases, that all presumptions have the effect of placing the burden of persuasion on those against whom such presumptions are operative.[45] The drafters argue that this approach would cause

454 N.Y.S.2d 576, 578–79 (City Ct.Mt.Vernon 1982)(in addition to denial of receipt, tenant showed evidence of "frequent failures by the Post Office to properly deposit the mail within the mailboxes" in tenant's building).

42. In addition to the cases cited in note 22, see Rawley v. Brown, 71 N.Y. 85, 89 (1877)(presumption of ownership that arises from possession is "the lowest species of evidence. It is merely presumptive, and liable to be overcome by any evidence showing the character of the possession, and that it is not necessarily as owner.")

43. See, e.g., O'Dea v. Amodeo, 118 Conn. 58, 170 A. 486, 487–88 (1934)(judicial classification of presumptions with prescribed rebuttal requirements based on nature of presumption); Calif.Evid.Code 600–606, 660–670 (legislative classification of presumptions in which policy-based presumptions shift burden of persuasion whereas those that implement no policy other than facilitation of disputed issues shift only the burden of production).

44. Morgan, noting that the rules on presumptions "must be applied by the trial judge in the heat and hurry of the trial," questioned whether it would be "practicable to classify presumptions and assign to each an effect dependent upon the considerations which caused the courts to create it[.] If such classification were made by statute with an enumeration of all presumptions, this might work." Morgan, "Presumptions," 12 Wash.L.Rev. 255, 280 (1937).

45. N.Y.Evidence Code § 302 [PROPOSED]:

A presumption is a rule of law requiring that if one (the "basic") fact or set of facts is established, the trier of fact must find that another (the "presumed") fact

no radical change in current practice.[46] Some presumptions already shift the burden of persuasion;[47] and the hybrid approach which is applied to the presumption of permission in automobile cases has the practical effect of shifting the burden of persuasion, notwithstanding the trial courts' jury instructions to the contrary.[48]

It seems to us that the drafters of the Proposed New York Evidence Code have a good argument that warrants the attention of the Court of Appeals. Across-the-board application of the Morgan rule would overcome the Thayer rule's inadequate promotion of the policies underlying presumptions, would be consistent in many cases with current practice, would be easy to apply by trial judges and "would abolish the prevailing confusion and complexities."[49] There is nothing to prevent the Court of Appeals from adopting a Morgan approach to presumptions as a uniform, judge-made rule subject only to specific statutes that provide otherwise.[50]

Library References:

West's Key No. Digests, Evidence ⇐85–89.

§ 301.6 Res Ipsa Loquitur

In New York, the doctrine of res ipsa loquitur creates an inference of negligence, not a presumption.[1] The plaintiff makes out a prima facie case of negligence upon a showing that: (1) the event is of the kind that ordinarily does not occur unless someone was negligent; (2) it was caused by an agency or instrumentality within the defendant's exclusive control; and (3) it was not due to any voluntary conduct on plaintiff's part.[2] In such a case, "an inference of negligence may be drawn solely from the happening of the accident upon the theory that 'certain occurrences contain within themselves a sufficient basis for an inference of negligence.'"[3]

also exists unless the trier of fact is persuaded that the presumed fact does not exist. The standard of persuasion shall be a preponderance of evidence, unless a higher burden is required by statute or decisional law.

The "unless" clause leaves room for the application of the "clear and convincing evidence" standard to such presumptions as legitimacy and validity of marriage. See note 29 supra.

It should be noted that the proposed Evidence Code provision fails to explicitly carve out an exception for the traditional Thayer approach that is codified in N.Y. Uniform Commercial Code § 1–201(31).

46. Comment, Proposed N.Y.Evidence Code § 302.

47. See text at notes 24–29 supra.

48. See text at notes 30–37.

49. Morgan, "Presumptions," 12 Wash. L.Rev. 255, 281 (1937).

50. See, e.g., Hinds v. John Hancock Mutual Life Ins. Co., 155 Me. 349, 360, 155 A.2d 721, 729 (1959)("[W]e have, * * * because of the conflicting expressions and the lack of any definitive announcement in our own opinions, some freedom in determining what procedural effect we will assign to disputable presumptions * * *.").

§ 301.6

1. Dermatossian v. New York City Transit Authority, 67 N.Y.2d 219, 226, 501 N.Y.S.2d 784, 788, 492 N.E.2d 1200, 1204 (1986); George Foltis, Inc. v. City of New York, 287 N.Y. 108, 119–22, 38 N.E.2d 455, 461–63 (1941).

2. Dermatossian v. New York City Transit Authority, 67 N.Y.2d 219, 226, 501 N.Y.S.2d 784, 788, 492 N.E.2d 1200, 1204 (1986).

3. Id. at 226, 501 N.Y.S.2d at 788, 492 N.E.2d at 1204 (quoting George Foltis, Inc. v. City of New York, 287 N.Y. 108, 116, 38 N.E.2d 455, 460 (1941)).

The court explained in *George Foltis, Inc. v. City of New York*,[4] that the burden of production does not shift to the defendant in the usual res ipsa case. Even if the defendant rests without offering any rebuttal evidence, she will not suffer a directed verdict.[5] The jury may, but is not required, to conclude that negligence by the defendant is the most probable cause of the accident,[6] and the burden of persuasion in this regard remains on the plaintiff.[7] The defendant is thus free to take the risk, regardless of whether she offers rebuttal evidence, that the jury will not be persuaded of her negligence.[8]

Library References:
West's Key No. Digests, Negligence ⚖121.2.

§ 301.7 Prima Facie Evidence

Various New York statutes provide that particular facts are "prima facie evidence" of other facts. A section of the New York Banking Law, for example, states that the opening of a bank account in joint names is "prima facie evidence" of the depositor's intent to create a joint tenancy.[1] Does such "prima facie evidence" have the same effect as a

---

4. 287 N.Y. 108, 38 N.E.2d 455 (1941).

5. Id. at 120, 122, 38 N.E.2d at 462, 463.

6. Id. at 122, 38 N.E.2d at 463 ("Where plaintiff establishes prima facie * * * that injury was caused by negligence of the defendant * * * the question of whether the defendant was in fault in what he did or failed to do is ordinarily one of fact to be determined by the jury unless the jury is waived.").

7. Id. at 118, 38 N.E.2d at 461.

8. There may be some res ipsa cases, of course, where the plaintiff's evidence, even though circumstantial, is so compelling that the burden of production will shift to the defendant. Id. at 121, 38 N.E.2d at 462. In such a case, the defendant's failure to introduce rebuttal evidence would result in a directed verdict for the plaintiff. See § 300.3(a)(2) supra. Conversely, the defendant might introduce "conclusive affirmative proof that the [defendant] had exercised all care reasonably possible," thus completely rebutting plaintiff's case and entitling defendant to a directed verdict unless additional evidence is forthcoming from the plaintiff. See George Foltis, Inc., supra, 287 N.Y. at 118, 38 N.E.2d at 461. See also § 300.3(a)(2) supra.

§ 301.7

1. N.Y. Banking Law § 675(b). Other examples include N.Y. Dom.Rel.Law § 14–a(4)(certified copy of marriage certificate is prima facie evidence of facts contained in record); N.Y.Public Health Law § 4103 (certified copy of birth or death record is prima facie evidence of contents of record); N.Y.Veh. and Traf.Law § 2108(c)(certificate of title of automobile is prima facie evidence that registrant is owner); N.Y.Uniform Commercial Code § 1–202 (any document, including bill of lading, insurance policy or inspector's certificate, which is authorized or required by contract to be issued by third party, is prima facie evidence of its own authenticity and of the facts stated in the document); N.Y.Worker's Compensation Law § 21(5)(medical reports submitted by claimant are prima facie evidence of facts contained in such reports).

Several statutory hearsay exceptions in Article 45 of the CPLR are described as creating prima facie evidence. Prominent examples include CPLR 4518(b)(hospital bills); CPLR 4518(c)(certified hospital, library and government records); CPLR 4518(d)(reports of blood genetic marker tests in Family Court proceedings); CPLR 4520 (certified public records); CPLR 4521 (certified statement concerning lack of public record); CPLR 4522 (ancient records regarding real property); CPLR 4525 (copy of statement under Article 9 of U.C.C.); CPLR 4526 (marriage certificate); CPLR 4527 (written finding of death pursuant to Federal Missing Persons Act); CPLR 4528 (U.S. Weather Bureau records); CPLR 4529 (U.S. Department of Agriculture inspection certificates); CPLR 4530(a)(U.S. census records); CPLR 4531 (affidavit of service by person who is unavailable to testify); CPLR 4533–a (itemized bill or invoice for services or repairs not exceeding $2,000); CPLR 4534 (surveyor's certificate of standard of measurement); CPLR 4540(a)(official's attestation that copy of public record is

presumption that shifts the burden of production to the opponent?[2] Or does "prima facie evidence," like the doctrine of res ipsa loquitur, create a mere inference that satisfies the proponent's burden of production but is not enough, even in the absence of rebuttal, to mandate a finding?[3] The apparent rule in civil cases is that prima facie evidence, as that term is used in a statute, generally shifts the burden of production.[4] The opponent must therefore introduce evidence that is sufficient to support a finding of the nonexistence of the facts to which the prima evidence gives rise. In the absence of such rebuttal, the proponent's establishment of the prima facie evidence will subject the opponent to a directed verdict.

Some doubt was thrown on the production-shifting interpretation, however, in the Court of Appeals' 1983 decision in *Commissioner of Social Services v. Philip De G.*[5] At issue was the evidentiary effect of entries in a certified hospital record, which CPLR 4518(c)(part of the hearsay exception for business records)[6] proclaims to be "prima facie evidence" of the facts contained in the record. The court said, "In the absence of contradictory evidence, these hospital entries were *sufficient to permit but not require* the trier of fact to find in accordance with the record."[7] Furthermore, three years later in *People v. Mertz*,[8] the court was confronted with a criminal statute making certain facts "presumptive evidence" of other facts.[9] The *Mertz* court stated as follows:

genuine copy); CPLR 4541 (contents of transcripts of proceedings of justice of peace).

2. See §§ 301.2–301.5 supra.

3. See § 301.6 supra.

4. Powers v. Powers, 86 N.Y.2d 63, 69, 629 N.Y.S.2d 984, 987–88, 653 N.E.2d 1154 (1995)("prima facie evidence" to which N.Y.Fam.Ct.Act § 454(3)(a) refers is not properly denominated a "presumption," but statute has effect of shifting burden of going forward); Punis v. Perales, 112 A.D.2d 236, 237–38, 491 N.Y.S.2d 451, 453 (2d Dep't 1985)("prima facie evidence" to which N.Y.Veh. and Traf.Law § 2108(c) refers creates rebuttable presumption of ownership). Cf. Trusts & Guarantee Co. v. Barnhardt, 270 N.Y. 350, 1 N.E.2d 459 (1936) (Canadian statute providing that notary's certificate of mailing was prima facie evidence of mailing had effect of entitling proponent to directed verdict in absence of sufficient evidence to the contrary).

The following cases appear to treat § 675(b) of the New York Banking Law (see text at note 1 supra) as a presumption that goes so far as to shift the burden of persuasion to the opponent: Estate of Harrison, 184 A.D.2d 42, 45, 590 N.Y.S.2d 318, 320–21 (3d Dep't 1992)("the party seeking to disprove the joint tenancy bears the burden of proving that it was intended to be an account of convenience or a tenancy in common"); Brezinski v. Brezinski, 94 A.D.2d 969, 969, 463 N.Y.S.2d 975, 976 (4th Dep't 1983)("the burden of proof is on the one challenging the presumption of joint tenancy"). Sometimes courts construing § 675(b) try to have it both ways. In one breath they say that the opponent's rebuttal burden is that of "clear and convincing evidence" (a standard relating to the burden of persuasion, see § 300.4(b)(2) supra) while in the other they say that the opponent's evidence must be "sufficient to support an inference that the joint account had been opened in that form only as a matter of convenience" (a standard relating merely to the burden of production, see § 300.3(a) supra). See, e.g., Krinsky v. Krinsky, 208 A.D.2d 599, 600, 618 N.Y.S.2d 36, 37–38 (2d Dep't 1994)(citing Brezinski v. Brezinski, supra, 94 A.D.2d at 969, 463 N.Y.S.2d at 976).

5. 59 N.Y.2d 137, 463 N.Y.S.2d 761, 450 N.E.2d 681 (1983).

6. See § 803(3).1(c) infra.

7. 59 N.Y.2d at 140, 463 N.Y.S.2d at 762, 450 N.E.2d at 682 (emphasis added).

8. 68 N.Y.2d 136, 506 N.Y.S.2d 290, 497 N.E.2d 657 (1986).

9. N.Y.Veh. and Traf.Law § 1194 (4)(c)(proof that breathalyzer analysis was made by person possessing permit issued by Department of Health is "presumptive evidence" that test was properly administered).

"Presumptive evidence, is, * * * like the prima facie evidence to which CPLR 4518(c) refers, evidence which permits but does not require the trier of fact to find in accordance with the 'presumed' fact, even though no contradictory evidence has been presented."[10]

Read together, *Philip De G.* and *Mertz* might be taken to stand for the proposition that any statute referring to "prima facie evidence" is to be treated as creating merely an inference rather than a rule that shifts the burden of production. *Mertz*, however, was a criminal case. In such cases, New York courts may not properly shift any burden of production to the defendant with respect to proof of the crime regardless of whether a statute creates a "presumption" or "prima facie evidence."[11] Furthermore, *Philip De G.*'s treatment of CPLR 4518(c) as an inference may simply be an aberration that is confined to that statute.[12]

In the 1995 decision of *Powers v. Powers*,[13] the Court of Appeals appears to have put things straight by treating prima facie evidence as a rule that shifts the burden of production. The statute in question provided that a spouse's nonpayment of his financial obligations under a support order was prima facie evidence of a "willful violation of the order."[14] Petitioner's proof at trial that her former husband was in arrears was described by the Court of Appeals as a situation in which "the burden of going forward shifted to respondent to rebut petitioner's prima facie evidence of a willful violation."[15] The respondent was then "*required* * * * to offer some competent, credible evidence of his inability to make the required payments."[16]

Thus, with the exception of criminal cases and the hearsay exception for certified hospital records (CPLR 4518(c)), statutes that create "prima

---

10. 68 N.Y.2d at 148, 506 N.Y.S.2d at 297, 497 N.E.2d at 663–64.

11. Id. at 148–49, 506 N.Y.S.2d at 297, 497 N.E.2d at 664. See generally § 302.1 infra.

12. The drafters of Article 45 of the CPLR, which contains § 4518(c) and several hearsay exceptions that constitute "prima facie evidence" (see note 1 supra), intended such evidence to have the same effect as a presumption. The Advisory Committee on Practice and Procedure wrote as follows: "The term 'prima facie' [as used in CPLR Article 45] * * * means a presumption which shifts the burden of coming forward and not the burden of persuasion. It is rebutted when evidence contrary to the presumed fact sufficient to support a finding of its negative has been introduced." N.Y.Adv.Comm.on Prac. and Proc., Second Prelim. Rep., Legis.Doc.No.13, p.267 (1958).

Philip De G.'s treatment of prima facie evidence in CPLR 4518(c) as a mere inference obviously is at odds with legislative intent. Technically, however, the court's interpretation of CPLR 4518(c) need not extend to the other hearsay exceptions in CPLR Article 45. CPLR 4518(c) was added to Article 45 in 1970, seven years after the CPLR was adopted. Thus, the drafters' interpretation of prima facie evidence as a presumption could still be considered operative with respect to the original hearsay provisions of CPLR Article 45. See generally Alexander, Practice Commentaries, McKinney's CPLR 4518, at C4518:9.

13. 86 N.Y.2d 63, 629 N.Y.S.2d 984, 653 N.E.2d 1154 (1995).

14. N.Y.Fam.Ct.Act § 454(3)(a).

15. 86 N.Y.2d at 69, 629 N.Y.S.2d at 988, 653 N.E.2d at 1158.

16. Id. at 69–70, 629 N.Y.S.2d at 988, 653 N.E.2d at 1158 (emphasis added). Interestingly, the court said that it would be inappropriate to refer to "prima facie evidence" in § 454(3)(a) as a "presumption." 86 N.Y.2d at 69, 629 N.Y.S.2d at 987, 653 N.E.2d at 1157. Nevertheless, when proof of a particular set of facts shifts the burden of production to the opponent to introduce sufficient evidence to justify a finding of the nonexistence of such facts, the *effect* is that of a presumption. See §§ 301.2–301.3 supra.

§ 301.7   BURDEN OF PROOF & PRESUMPTIONS   Ch. 3

facie evidence" would appear to shift to the opponent the burden of producing sufficient evidence to create a question of fact.

Library References:

West's Key No. Digests, Evidence ⚖=584(1).

§ 301.8   Effect of Presumptions in Federal Proceedings

a. Cases Governed by Federal Law

The Federal Rules of Evidence make no attempt to codify the many presumptions that have been created by federal statutory and decisional law. Rule 301, however, describes the effect of presumptions in civil cases governed by federal law:

> In all civil actions and proceedings not otherwise provided for by Act of Congress or by these rules, a presumption imposes on the party against whom it is directed the burden of going forward with evidence to rebut or meet the presumption, but does not shift to such party the burden of proof in the sense of the risk of nonpersuasion, which remains throughout the trial upon the party on whom it was originally cast.

In *St. Mary's Honor Center v. Hicks*,[1] The Supreme Court made clear that Rule 301 adopts, as a general rule, the "Thayer" or "bursting bubble" approach to presumptions.[2] Thus, a presumption ordinarily shifts to the opponent only the burden of producing evidence that contradicts the presumed fact. Rule 301 itself explicitly provides that in the usual case, the burden of persuasion does not shift.

The quantum of evidence necessary to rebut the presumption is that which would be sufficient for a reasonable jury to find the nonexistence of the presumed fact.[3] When this occurs, the "bubble is burst," and the

---

§ 301.8

1. ___ U.S. ___, 113 S.Ct. 2742, 125 L.Ed.2d 407 (1993). Hicks was an employment discrimination case under Title VII of the Civil Rights Act of 1964. 42 U.S.C.A. § 2000e–2(a)(1). In a majority opinion by Justice Scalia, the Court applied Rule 301 to the presumption of discrimination that arises from plaintiff's proof of a prima facie case. The presumption was said to place upon the defendant the burden of producing admissible evidence which, "'*if believed by the trier of fact*, would support a finding that unlawful discrimination was not the cause of the employment action.'" ___ U.S. at ___, 113 S.Ct. at 2747, 125 L.Ed.2d at 416 (quoting Texas Dep't of Community Affairs v. Burdine, 450 U.S. 248, 254–55 n.8, 101 S.Ct. 1089, 1094–95, 67 L.Ed.2d 207, 216 (1981))(emphasis in original). Once the defendant meets the burden of production, "'the presumption raised by the prima facie case is rebutted,' * * * and 'drops from the case.'" ___ U.S. at ___, 113 S.Ct. at 2747, 125 L.Ed.2d at 416 (quot-

ing Burdine, supra, 450 U.S. at 255 n.10, 101 S.Ct. at 1095, 67 L.Ed.2d at 216). The Court noted that "the fundamental principle of Rule 301 [is] that a presumption does not shift the burden of proof." ___ U.S. at ___, 113 S.Ct. at 2749, 125 L.Ed.2d at 419. Even Justice Souter's dissenting opinion agreed that Rule 301 shifts only the burden of production which, when satisfied, forces the presumption to drop out of the case. ___ U.S. at ___, 113 S.Ct. at 2759, 125 L.Ed.2d at 430 (dissent).

2. See § 301.5(a)(1) supra.

3. St. Mary's Honor Center v. Hicks, ___ U.S. ___, ___, 113 S.Ct. 2742, 2747, 2748, 125 L.Ed.2d 407, 416, 417 (1993)(evidence which, if believed by trier of facts, would permit finding of nonexistence of presumed fact); note 1 supra. See also Graham § 301.12, at 108–11; C. Mueller and L. Kirkpatrick, Federal Evidence § 71, at 333–35 (2d ed.1994); 1 Weinstein and Berger ¶ 301[02], at 301–28 and 301–32.

presumption drops out of the case.[4] Assuming sufficient evidence remains to create a jury question, the orthodox Thayer rule precludes any mention of the word "presumption" to the jury.[5] It has been suggested, however, that the trial judge may point out to the jury the natural inferences that may flow from the basic facts that originally gave rise to the presumption.[6]

The introductory phrase of Rule 301 explicitly provides that the Thayer effect codified in the Rule must defer to federal statutes that give presumptions a stronger effect. Thus, the persuasion-shifting "Morgan rule"[7] may be applicable in a given case. The presumption created by a particular federal statute may explicitly or implicitly shift to the opponent the burden of persuading the fact-finder that the presumed fact does not exist.[8]

b. Cases Governed by State Law

With respect to certain issues governed by state law, as in a diversity action, Rule 302 of the Federal Rules of Evidence requires deference to state law concerning the effect of presumptions:

> In civil actions and proceedings, the effect of a presumption respecting a fact which is an element of a claim or defense as to which State law supplies the rule of decision is determined in accordance with State law.

Rule 302 was motivated by a concern for the state interests that are reflected in the creation and operation of presumptions[9] and their effect on the resolution of state-based substantive rights and obligations.[10]

---

4. See St. Mary's Honor Center v. Hicks, __ U.S. __, __, 113 S.Ct. 2742, 2747, 125 L.Ed.2d 407, 416 (1993); note 1 supra. See generally § 301.5, at notes 1–11, supra.

5. See, e.g., Alpine Forwarding Co. v. Pennsylvania R.R. Co., 60 F.2d 734, 736 (2d Cir.1932)("If the trial is properly conducted, the presumption will not be mentioned at all"); § 301.5, at note 8, supra.

6. 1 Weinstein and Berger ¶ 301[02], at 301–33—301–34 ("The court may discuss with the jury the probative force—*i.e.*, normal inferential value—of the basic fact in assisting the jury to decide whether it is persuaded of the existence of the presumed fact. The specific instruction should avoid using the word 'presumption' because of the danger that the jury will mistakenly attribute effects to this term other than those described by the judge and prescribed by Rule 301."). Accord, C. Mueller and L. Kirkpatrick, Federal Evidence § 71, at 333–34 (2d ed.1994).

7. See § 301.5(a)(2) supra.

8. See, e.g., ACS Hospital Systems, Inc. v. Montefiore Hospital, 732 F.2d 1572, 1574–75 (Fed.Cir.1984)(burden of persuasion is on party who opposes presumption of validity of patent); Butts v. Secretary of Health & Human Services, 706 F.2d 107, 108 (2d Cir.1983)(under Social Security Act, absence of entry in Secretary's records as to wages allegedly paid by employer is "presumptive evidence" that no wages were paid, thus requiring claimant to prove his case by preponderance). See generally 1 Weinstein and Berger ¶ 301[03].

Aside from specific legislation that may create a persuasion-shifting presumption, it has been held that the adoption of Rule 301 did not alter the burdens previously established in the nonstatutory admiralty law. See James v. River Parishes Co., 686 F.2d 1129, 1131–33 (5th Cir.1982)(party whose boat causes damage while adrift is presumed to have been negligent, meaning that such party must, as under pre-Rules law, persuade fact-finder that he was not at fault).

9. See §§ 301.4–301.5 supra.

10. See 1 Weinstein and Berger ¶ 302[01], at 302–3. ("Rule 302 recognizes that the rationale of [Erie Railroad Co. v. Tompkins, 304 U.S. 64, 58 S.Ct. 817, 82 L.Ed. 1188 (1938)] * * * requires the effect of some presumptions in civil actions to be governed by state law * * *.").

Meckel v. Continental Resources Co.,[11] is an example of a federal case in the Second Circuit in which New York's rules governing the mail-and-receipt presumption[12] were applied to bar a claim that certain debenture holders did not receive timely notice of redemption.[13]

Library References:
West's Key No. Digests, Evidence ⚖︎85–89.

302 Presumptions in Criminal Cases

§ 302.1 New York

a. Constitutional Restraints

The controversy over the relative merits of the Thayer and Morgan approaches to presumptions[1] is largely moot in criminal cases. Significant constitutional limitations affect the way in which presumptions operate against criminal defendants. A trial court, for example, risks serious error if it charges the jury, on the contested issue of the defendant's intent, that "[a] person of sound mind and discretion is presumed to intend the natural and probable consequences of his act but the presumption may be rebutted."[2]

We have already seen that as a matter of due process, the state must prove every element of an alleged crime beyond a reasonable doubt.[3] The United States Supreme Court has held, therefore, that the Constitution precludes the application of a presumption in a way that suggests to the jury that the defendant has the burden of persuading them of the nonexistence of an element of the crime.[4] Whether the application of a presumption has improperly shifted the burden of persuasion to the defendant requires close analysis of the trial court's jury instructions "read in the context of the jury charge as a whole."[5] The constitutional question is whether the jury charge "could reasonably have been under-

---

11. 758 F.2d 811 (2d Cir.1985).

12. See § 301.2, at note 3, supra; § 301.3, at note 8, supra; and § 301.5, at note 41, supra.

13. 758 F.2d at 817–18. See also American Casualty Co. of Reading, Pennsylvania v. Nordic Leasing, Inc., 42 F.3d 725, 734 (2d Cir.1994) (application of Vermont rules regarding presumption of mail-and-receipt in case governed by substantive law of Vermont.)

§ 302.1

1. See § 301.5(a) supra.

2. See Francis v. Franklin, 471 U.S. 307, 309, 318, 105 S.Ct. 1965, 1968, 1973, 85 L.Ed.2d 344, 350, 356 (1985)("Standing alone, [such] language undeniably create[s] an unconstitutional burden-shifting presumption with respect to the element of intent."); Sandstrom v. Montana, 442 U.S. 510, 514–24, 99 S.Ct. 2450, 2454–59, 61 L.Ed.2d 39, 45–51 (1979)(instruction which bluntly tells jury that "the law presumes that a person intends the ordinary consequences of his voluntary acts," without any suggestion that jury may reject this conclusion, violates due process because effect is to shift burden of persuasion to defendant on issue of intent).

3. In re Winship, 397 U.S. 358, 364, 90 S.Ct. 1068, 1072, 25 L.Ed.2d 368, 375 (1970); § 300.4(d)(1) supra.

4. Francis v. Franklin, 471 U.S. 307, 317, 105 S.Ct. 1965, 1972–73, 85 L.Ed.2d 344, 355 (1985); Sandstrom v. Montana, 442 U.S. 510, 524, 99 S.Ct. 2450, 2459, 61 L.Ed.2d 39, 51 (1979); Patterson v. New York, 432 U.S. 197, 215, 97 S.Ct. 2319, 2329, 53 L.Ed.2d 281, 295 (1977); Mullaney v. Wilbur, 421 U.S. 684, 698–701, 95 S.Ct. 1881, 1889–90, 44 L.Ed.2d 508, 519–521 (1975).

5. Francis v. Franklin, 471 U.S. 307, 309, 105 S.Ct. 1965, 1968, 85 L.Ed.2d 344, 350 (1985).

stood as creating a presumption that relieves the State of its burden of persuasion on an element of an offense."[6]

On the other hand, the Supreme Court's decisions point to the conclusion that a "presumption" may be invoked against a defendant with respect to an element of the crime if two conditions are satisfied: (1) the presumption is explained to the jury in permissive terms, i.e., they are told that they may but are not required to draw certain inferences from specified basic facts proven by the prosecution;[7] and (2) in the circumstances of the case, "there is a 'rational connection' between the basic facts that the prosecution proved and the ultimate fact presumed, and the latter is 'more likely than not to flow from' the former."[8] The Court has also put the matter as follows: "A permissive inference violates the Due Process Clause only if the suggested conclusion is not one that reason and common sense justify in light of the proven facts before the jury."[9] Under the "rational connection" test, the constitutionality of a statutory permissive inference is assessed in light of all the facts at trial, not by an analysis of the statute on its face.[10]

Whether a presumption that shifts the burden of production to the defendant will pass constitutional muster is a close question that has not

---

6. Francis v. Franklin, 471 U.S. 307, 315, 105 S.Ct. 1965, 1971, 85 L.Ed.2d 344, 354 (1985). See also Sandstrom v. Montana, 442 U.S. 510, 514, 99 S.Ct. 2450, 2454, 61 L.Ed.2d 39, 45 (1979)("whether a defendant has been accorded his constitutional rights depends upon the way in which a reasonable juror could have interpreted the instruction").

Jury instructions that impermissibly shift the burden of persuasion to the defendant are nevertheless subject to harmless error analysis. Rose v. Clark, 478 U.S. 570, 580–84, 106 S.Ct. 3101, 3107–09, 92 L.Ed.2d 460, 472–74 (1986).

7. See County Court of Ulster County v. Allen, 442 U.S. 140, 157–63, 99 S.Ct. 2213, 2224–27, 60 L.Ed.2d 777, 792–95 (1979). See also Francis v. Franklin, 471 U.S. 307, 314, 105 S.Ct. 1965, 1971, 85 L.Ed.2d 344, 353 (1985)("A permissive inference does not relieve the State of its burden of persuasion because it still requires the State to convince the jury that the suggested conclusion should be inferred based on the predicate facts proved.").

8. County Court of Ulster County v. Allen, 442 U.S. 140, 165, 99 S.Ct. 2213, 2228–29, 60 L.Ed.2d 777, 797 (1979).

At issue in Allen was the application of a New York statute providing that the presence of an illegal firearm in an automobile is "presumptive evidence of its possession by all persons occupying such automobile at the time such weapon * * * is found." N.Y.Penal Law § 265.15(3). The defendants, three adult males and one 16-year-old girl, were charged with illegal possession of two large handguns. The guns were in the front passenger seat area of a car in which the defendants were riding when the car was stopped for speeding. The arresting officer, looking through the car window, saw the guns in the girl's open handbag, which was in close proximity to her.

In his jury instructions, the trial judge charged that the state had the burden of proving possession beyond a reasonable doubt, and that the statutory presumption of possession was "an element" of the state's proof. Id. at 162 n.19, 99 S.Ct. at 2227, 60 L.Ed.2d at 794. He explained the presumption in permissive terms: "[Y]ou may infer * * * that such prohibited weapon was possessed by each of the defendants * * *. The presumption * * * need not be rebutted by affirmative proof or affirmative evidence but may be rebutted by any evidence or lack of evidence in the case." Id. at 162 n.20, 99 S.Ct. at 227, 60 L.Ed.2d at 794. The Supreme Court concluded: "As applied to the facts of this case, the presumption of possession is entirely rational." Id. at 163, 99 S.Ct. at 2228, 60 L.Ed.2d at 795.

9. Francis v. Franklin, 471 U.S. 307, 314–15, 105 S.Ct. 1965, 1971, 85 L.Ed.2d 344, 353–54 (1985).

10. County Court of Ulster County v. Allen, 442 U.S. 140, 162–63, 99 S.Ct. 2213, 2227–28, 60 L.Ed.2d 777, 795 (1979); McCandless v. Beyer, 835 F.2d 58, 60 (3d Cir.1987).

been definitively answered by the Supreme Court.[11] For example, the presumption that a person with "unexplained" possession of recently stolen goods knows that they were stolen has been characterized, even when described to the jury in permissive terms, as having the "practical effect" of shifting "the burden of going forward with evidence to the defendant."[12] Nevertheless, the rationality of the presumption, when treated as a permissive inference and accompanied by an instruction that the defendant has no obligation to testify and that possession may be explained by any evidence in the record from any source, has saved it from constitutional condemnation.[13] It seems clear, however, that any presumption or inference that shifts the burden of production to the defendant may not properly result in the conventional consequence that befalls a party who fails to come forward with evidence: "[V]erdicts may not be directed against defendants in criminal cases."[14]

b. New York Approach

It is a long-standing tradition in the criminal law that a defendant is presumed innocent until proven guilty.[15] This presumption is really just another way of expressing the state's burden of proving guilt beyond a reasonable doubt.[16] Nevertheless, a defendant in New York is entitled to a jury instruction that explicitly describes the presumption of innocence.[17]

11. In County Court of Ulster County v. Allen, 442 U.S. 140, 99 S.Ct. 2213, 60 L.Ed.2d 777 (1979), the Court pronounced the following dictum: "To the extent that a presumption imposes an extremely low burden of production—e.g., being satisfied by 'any' evidence—it may well be that its impact is no greater than that of a permissive inference, and it may be proper to analyze it as such." Id. at 157 n.16, 99 S.Ct. at 2225, 60 L.Ed.2d at 792. This implies that the "rational connection" test, see text at notes 8–10 supra, is the standard for evaluating the constitutionality of a production-shifting inference.

The Third Circuit, on a habeas corpus petition, accepted the Supreme Court's suggestion and applied such analysis to a New Jersey presumption that permitted (but did not require) the jury to infer that a person in possession of a handgun lacked a carrying permit unless he introduced evidence to the contrary. McCandless v. Beyer, 835 F.2d 58 (3d Cir.1987). At the trial in question, the defendant offered no evidence concerning a permit; he simply testified that he never possessed the gun. This triggered a jury charge concerning the no-permit presumption, which the Third Circuit characterized as a permissive inference that shifted only a "minimal" burden of production without shifting the burden of persuasion. Id. at 61. The court then applied the "rational connection" test to the particular facts of the case and concluded that the jury rationally could have inferred that the defendant had not obtained a permit, thus satisfying due process. Id. at 61–63.

12. Barnes v. United States, 412 U.S. 837, 846 n.11, 93 S.Ct. 2357, 2363, 37 L.Ed.2d 380, 387 (1973).

13. Id. at 844–46, 93 S.Ct. at 2362–63, 37 L.Ed.2d at 386–87; United States v. Johnpoll, 739 F.2d 702, 711–12 (2d Cir.), cert. denied, 469 U.S. 1075, 105 S.Ct. 571, 83 L.Ed.2d 511 (1984), rehearing denied, 469 U.S. 1197, 105 S.Ct. 982, 83 L.Ed.2d 983 (1985); United States v. DeFillipo, 590 F.2d 1228, 1238–39 (2d Cir.), cert. denied, 442 U.S. 920, 99 S.Ct. 2844, 61 L.Ed.2d 288 (1979).

14. Sandstrom v. Montana, 442 U.S. 510, 516 n.5, 99 S.Ct. 2450, 2455, 61 L.Ed.2d 39, 46 (1979). A thorough discussion of the constitutionality of burden-shifting presumptions is beyond the scope of this book.

15. 9 Wigmore § 2511. See, e.g., People v. Sutherland, 252 N.Y. 86, 89, 168 N.E. 838, 838 (1929).

16. 9 Wigmore § 2511, at 530.

17. N.Y.Crim.Proc.Law § 300.10(2) (among "fundamental legal principles" that must be included in jury charge is "the presumption of defendant's innocence"). See also Taylor v. Kentucky, 436 U.S. 478, 98 S.Ct. 1930, 56 L.Ed.2d 468

As to the use of presumptions against the defendant, both decisional law and miscellaneous provisions of the Penal Law have created presumptions that are intended to help the prosecution establish its prima facie case. For example, a judge-made rule provides that a person in recent and exclusive possession of stolen goods may be presumed, in the absence of an explanation, to be either the thief or a receiver of the goods.[18] By statute, every person in an automobile that contains an illegal weapon may be presumed to be in possession thereof.[19]

If trial judges comply with the directions of the Court of Appeals, the employment of such presumptions against the defendant is not likely to offend the Constitution. The court has stated flatly, "Statutory presumptions in New York are permissive,"[20] thus bringing the law of New York well within the outer boundaries of the Constitution.[21] The court has indicated that a jury must be "clearly instructed" that presumptions are permissive[22]—that the jury may but is not required to find the presumed facts that flow from the state's proof. A conviction is likely to be reversed whenever "the jury may have understood from the charge as given that they were required" to make a particular finding.[23] Of course, even if the presumption is properly described in permissive terms, there must be a rational connection between the proven facts and the inferred facts.[24]

The same approach is taken with respect to judge-made presumptions. For example, as long ago as 1873, the Court of Appeals declared

(1978)(presumption of innocence is fundamental to fair trial; trial court's refusal to instruct jury on this presumption violated due process).

18. See People v. Baskerville, 60 N.Y.2d 374, 382, 469 N.Y.S.2d 646, 650–51, 457 N.E.2d 752, 756–57 (1983). See also text at notes 12–13 supra, and note 28 infra.

19. N.Y.Penal Law § 265.15(3)(presumption is subject to specified exceptions). See also note 8 supra.

Other examples of statutory presumptions in New York include the following: N.Y.Penal Law § 165.55(3)(person who possesses two or more stolen credit cards may be presumed to know they were stolen); id. § 220.25(2)(every person in "close proximity" to narcotics that are "in open view" in a room on private premises may be presumed to be in possession thereof, subject to specified exceptions); id. § 265.15(6) (any person in possession of five or more firearms may be presumed to possess them with the intent to sell); N.Y.Veh. and Traf. Law § 1194(4)(c) (proof that breathalyzer test was administered by person with permit issued by Department of Health is "presumptive evidence" that test was properly administered).

20. People v. McKenzie, 67 N.Y.2d 695, 696, 499 N.Y.S.2d 923, 924, 490 N.E.2d 842, 843 (1986).

21. See text at notes 4–8 supra.

22. People v. McKenzie, 67 N.Y.2d 695, 696, 499 N.Y.S.2d 923, 924, 490 N.E.2d 842, 843 (1986).

23. People v. Mertz, 68 N.Y.2d 136, 148–49, 506 N.Y.S.2d 290, 297, 497 N.E.2d 657, 664 (1986)(reversible error occurred when jury may have understood from judge's instructions that they were required to find that breathalyzer test had been properly administered based on "presumptive evidence" created by fact that test administrator had proper permit). See also People v. Gardner, 163 A.D.2d 892, 893, 559 N.Y.S.2d 63, 64 (4th Dep't 1990)(trial court committed reversible error in jury charge by reading statute containing presumption of possession of narcotics (Penal Law § 220.25(2)) without explaining that presumption was permissive).

24. See text at notes 8–10 supra. See also People v. Leyva, 38 N.Y.2d 160, 166 n.2, 379 N.Y.S.2d 30, 35, 341 N.E.2d 546, 550 (1975)("each presumption's rationality must be judged within its own context"). See, e.g., Young v. Abrams, 698 F.2d 131, 136–37 (2d Cir.1983)(statutory permissive inference that person who exhibits or advertises obscene films in course of business knows content and character of such films was rational in circumstances of case).

§ 302.1 BURDEN OF PROOF & PRESUMPTIONS Ch. 3

that the presumption that a person intends the natural and probable consequences of his acts is only a permissive inference.[25] In light of Supreme Court caselaw,[26] more recent decisions of the Court of Appeals have stressed the need for explaining this inference to the jury in a way that makes it clear that no burden on the issue of intent shifts to the defendant.[27] As to the judge-made presumption of criminality based on recent and exclusive possession of stolen goods, the court has said the following:

> [I]f [the jury] find[s] that defendant had possession of recently stolen property for the possession of which he has offered no explanation or an explanation which they find to be untrue, they may, although they are not required to, infer that defendant was guilty of a crime and must then weigh the evidence before them to determine whether it establishes beyond a reasonable doubt that the defendant participated in the theft of the property or received it after it was stolen with knowledge of that fact * * *.[28]

If the defendant in a criminal case introduces evidence to rebut a presumption, does the "bursting bubble" rule take the presumption out of the case and preclude any mention of it to the jury?[29] The apparent law in New York is that a presumption, at least one created by statute, ordinarily stays in the case:

> The statutory presumption establishes a prima facie case against the defendant which presumption he may, if he chooses, rebut by offering evidence. Generally, the presumption will

---

25. Stokes v. People, 53 N.Y. 164, 179 (1873). See People v. Getch, 50 N.Y.2d 456, 464, 429 N.Y.S.2d 579, 583, 407 N.E.2d 425, 429 (1980) (jury charge which stated that persons presumably intend consequences of their acts had impermissible effect of shifting burden of proof, warranting reversal; jury charge which explained same presumption as a permissible inference was proper).

26. See text at notes 2–6 supra.

27. People v. Green, 50 N.Y.2d 891, 893, 430 N.Y.S.2d 267, 268, 408 N.E.2d 675, 675, cert. denied, 449 U.S. 957, 101 S.Ct. 367, 66 L.Ed.2d 223 (1980); People v. Getch, 50 N.Y.2d 456, 466, 429 N.Y.S.2d 579, 584, 407 N.E.2d 425, 430 (1980).

28. People v. Baskerville, 60 N.Y.2d 374, 383, 469 N.Y.S.2d 646, 651, 457 N.E.2d 752, 757 (1983). The Baskerville court stressed that "the facts must shape the inference" as to the nature of the offense. Id. at 382, 469 N.Y.S.2d at 651, 457 N.E.2d at 757. If the defendant's exclusive possession is extremely close in time to the theft, the only charge that need be given is that he may be inferred to be the thief. Id. at 383, 469 N.Y.S.2d at 651, 457 N.E.2d at 757. At the opposite extreme are cases in which the possession is so remote in time to the theft, or the evidence shows so clearly that possession was merely shared, that "no inference instruction would be proper." Id. The cases in the middle, i.e., those in which the evidence could lead the jury reasonably to find either theft or subsequent receipt, are the ones to which the charge quoted in text is appropriate. Id.

The inference is not violative of the defendant's right not to testify because an explanation that refutes the inference may be put forward by evidence from other sources. The explanation, in other words, is not dependent on defendant's taking the stand. People v. Moro, 23 N.Y.2d 496, 501, 297 N.Y.S.2d 578, 582–83, 245 N.E.2d 226, 229 (1969). See also Barnes v. United States, 412 U.S. 837, 846–47, 93 S.Ct. 2357, 2363, 37 L.Ed.2d 380, 388 (1973); § 302.2, at note 6, infra; 1 Criminal Jury Instructions, New York ¶ 9.80 (1991)(example of charge which tells jury "[i]n deciding whether there exists any explanation other than guilty possession," they "must consider all the evidence in the case, from whatever source produced").

29. See § 301.5(a)(1) supra.

remain in the case for the jury to weigh even if contrary proof is offered but may be nullified if the contrary evidence is strong enough to make the presumption incredible. So too, if no contrary proof is offered, the presumption is not conclusive, but may be rejected by the jury.[30]

Library References:

West's Key No. Digests, Criminal Law ⚖︎305.

§ 302.2 Federal

Federal courts, like their state counterparts, are bound by due process limitations on the application of presumptions against criminal defendants.[1] Thus, when the prosecution relies on a judge-made[2] or statutory[3] presumption as part of its prima facie case, the presumption may neither expressly nor impliedly shift the burden of persuasion to the defendant with respect to an element of the crime.[4]

To avoid conflicts with this principle, the Second Circuit Court of Appeals has advised trial courts, in their jury instructions, to describe presumptions as merely permissive inferences, making it clear that the jury may reject the inferences.[5] Under this approach, for example, a jury charge that an inference of guilty knowledge may be drawn from the fact of recent and unexplained possession of stolen goods has passed constitutional muster on several occasions.[6]

Even if a presumption is described in permissive terms, due process may preclude the government's reliance on the presumption if there is an insufficient rational connection, in the particular case, between the

---

30. People v. Lemmons, 40 N.Y.2d 505, 510, 387 N.Y.S.2d 97, 100, 354 N.E.2d 836, 840 (1976). See also People v. Silver, 33 N.Y.2d 475, 482, 354 N.Y.S.2d 915, 921, 310 N.E.2d 520, 524 (1974)(common law presumption of sanity remains in case despite defendant's introduction of rebuttal evidence)(decision predates reallocation of burden of proof to defendant on issue of insanity; see N.Y.Penal Law § 40.15).

§ 302.2

1. See § 302.1(a) supra.

2. See, e.g., Barnes v. United States, 412 U.S. 837, 843–44, 93 S.Ct. 2357, 2362, 37 L.Ed.2d 380, 386–87 (1973)(defendant's possession of recently stolen property, if unexplained, is circumstance from which jury may draw inference that defendant knew the property was stolen).

3. See, e.g., 18 U.S.C.A. § 343(1)(operator of common carrier who has blood alcohol content of .10 percent or more is presumed to be under influence of alcohol).

4. Francis v. Franklin, 471 U.S. 307, 313–15, 105 S.Ct. 1965, 1970–71, 85 L.Ed.2d 344, 352–54 (1985). See generally § 302.1(a) supra.

5. See United States v. Crespo, 422 F.2d 718, 720–22 (2d Cir.), cert. denied, 398 U.S. 914, 90 S.Ct. 1716, 26 L.Ed.2d 77 (1970).

6. Barnes v. United States, 412 U.S. 837, 845–46, 93 S.Ct. 2357, 2362–63, 37 L.Ed.2d 380, 387 (1973); United States v. Johnpoll, 739 F.2d 702, 711–12 (2d Cir.), cert. denied, 469 U.S. 1075, 105 S.Ct. 571, 83 L.Ed.2d 511 (1984), rehearing denied, 469 U.S. 1197, 105 S.Ct. 982, 83 L.Ed.2d 983 (1985); United States v. DeFillipo, 590 F.2d 1228, 1238–39 (2d Cir.), cert. denied, 442 U.S. 920, 99 S.Ct. 2844, 61 L.Ed.2d 288 (1979). The Supreme Court in Barnes held that the "guilty knowledge" inference is rational and that it is consistent with the defendant's right to refrain from testifying where the jury is reminded of this right and instructed "that possession [can] be satisfactorily explained by evidence independent of [defendant's] testimony." 412 U.S. at 846–47, 93 S.Ct. at 2363, 37 L.Ed.2d at 388. The inference is one which, because of its rationality, may permissibly shift the burden of production to the defendant. United States v. Johnpoll, supra, 739 F.2d at 712. See § 302.1(a), at notes 11–14 supra.

basic facts proved by the prosecution and the fact to be inferred.[7]

Library References:

West's Key No. Digests, Criminal Law ⚷305.

7. See generally § 302.1(a), at notes 8–10 supra. Compare Young v. Abrams, 698 F.2d 131, 136–37 (2d Cir.1983)(in state prosecution, it was rational to apply permissive inference that one who exhibits or advertises obscene films in the course of a business knows the content and character of the films (N.Y.Penal Law § 235.10(1)), and United States v. Manarite, 448 F.2d 583, 594 (2d Cir.), cert. denied, 404 U.S. 947, 92 S.Ct. 281, 30 L.Ed.2d 264 (1971)(statutory inference that person who transports, in interstate commerce, two or more copies of obscene publication, or combined total of five such publications, intends to sell or distribute same (18 U.S.C.A. § 1465) was rational when applied to defendant who transported large number of lewd magazines), with United States v. Moore, 571 F.2d 76, 81–87 (2d Cir.1978)(permissive inference that kidnapper who fails to release victim within 24 hours of seizure has transported victim in interstate commerce (18 U.S.C.A. § 1201(b)) is irrational and deprived defendants of due process; court's holding seems sound on the facts, but analysis which concentrates on facial validity of statutory inference, rather than on application of inference in circumstances of particular case, is at odds with subsequent Supreme Court caselaw (see § 302.1(a), at notes 8–10, supra)).

Chapter 4

RELEVANCY

Table of Sections

400 INTRODUCTION

400.1 New York and Federal—Introduction.

401 RELEVANCY

401.1 New York.
    a. Probability.
    b. Factors Precluding Admissibility of Relevant Evidence—Prejudice and Exclusionary Rules.
    c. Proposed New York Evidence Code.
401.2 Federal.

402 CHARACTER EVIDENCE

402.1 New York.
    a. Introduction.
    b. Character in Issue.
    c. Character Evidence as Proof of Conduct in Civil Cases.
    d. Character Evidence as Proof of Conduct in Criminal Cases.
    e. The Effect of Character Evidence—Jury Charge.
    f. Character Trait of the Victim in a Homicide Case.
    g. Character Evidence Used to Impeach, Generally.
    h. Proposed New York Evidence Code.
402.2 Federal.

403 [RESERVED]

404 UNCHARGED CRIMES

404.1 New York.
    a. Generally.
    b. Motive.
    c. Intent.
    d. Absence of Accident or Mistake.
    e. Common Scheme or Plan.
    f. Identity.
    g. Background.
    h. Inextricably Intertwined.
    i. Multiple Counts.
    j. Sex Cases—"Amorous Design."
    k. Rebuttal.
    l. Civil Cases.
404.2 Federal.
    a. Generally.
    b. Procedure.
    c. Civil Cases.

405 SIMILAR OCCURRENCES

405.1 New York.
    a. Generally.
    b. Other Accidents.
    c. Other Business Transactions.
    d. Sales of Property.

405.2 Federal.
    a. Other Accidents.
    b. Other Business Transactions.
    c. Sales of Property.

406 HABIT AND CUSTOM

406.1 New York.
    a. Generally.
    b. Business and Professional Habit.
    c. Habit Evidence in the Workplace.
    d. Habit in Negligence Cases—Non–Workplace Situations.
    e. Eyewitnesses.
    f. Custom and Usage as a Standard of Care.

406.2 Federal.
    a. Business and Professional Habit.
    b. Evidence of Habit in Negligence Cases.
    c. Custom and Usage as a Standard of Care.

407 SUBSEQUENT REMEDIAL REMEDIES

407.1 New York.
    a. Generally.
    b. Negligence.
    c. Products Liability.
    d. Feasibility.
    e. Ownership, Control and Impeachment.
    f. Criminal Cases and Proposed New York Code Provision.

407.2 Federal.

408 COMPROMISES AND OFFERS TO COMPROMISE

408.1 New York.
408.2 Federal.

409 PAYMENT OF MEDICAL AND SIMILAR EXPENSES

409.1 New York.
409.2 Federal.

410 PLEAS AND PLEA DISCUSSIONS

410.1 New York.
410.2 Federal.

411 LIABILITY INSURANCE

411.1 New York.
411.2 Federal.

412 SHIELD LAWS

412.1 New York.
412.2 Federal.

413 DEFENDANT'S SEXUAL HISTORY

413.1 Federal.

400 Introduction

§ 400.1 New York and Federal—Introduction

The range of this chapter is extensive, covering at the outset the sometimes inexact rules for determining relevancy as a general proposition, all the way to matters of exact specification, such as legislative pronouncements regarding the inadmissibility of liability insurance, or the sexual history of a complaining witness. One of the most heavily litigated questions in criminal cases is whether the prosecutor may introduce, in his case in chief, evidence of defendant's participation in uncharged crimes. Although this is a matter of relevancy, it also is a matter of policy—the prejudice resulting from introduction of the uncharged crimes may outweigh the probative value of such evidence because the jury may decide defendant should be put away even if they really cannot find beyond a reasonable doubt that he committed the crime charged. Likewise, it is sometimes difficult to see why evidence of subsequent remedial measures is not perfectly relevant to aid plaintiff in the proof of his case, yet this sort of proof is hedged about with restrictions which differ in different jurisdictions. From direct evidence inferences are drawn, and much depends on the relevancy of those inferences.

Library References:

West's Key No. Digests, Criminal Law ⚖337–361; Evidence ⚖99–117.

401 Relevancy

§ 401.1 New York

The New York definition of relevance and limitations on the admissibility of relevant evidence are summarized as follows in *People v. Scarola*:[1]

> In New York, the general rule is that all relevant evidence is admissible unless its admission violates some exclusionary rule. * * * Evidence is relevant if it has any tendency in reason to prove the existence of any material fact, i.e., it makes determination of the action more probable or less probable than it would be without the evidence. * * * Not all relevant evidence is admissible as of right, however. Even where technically relevant evidence is admissible, it may still be excluded by the

§ 401.1
1. 71 N.Y.2d 769, 530 N.Y.S.2d 83, 525 N.E.2d 728 (1988).

§ 401.1   RELEVANCY   Ch. 4

trial court in the exercise of its discretion if its probative value is substantially outweighed by the danger that it will unfairly prejudice the other side or mislead the jury * * *.[2]

Thus, there are two broad factors to consider: probability and exclusionary factors.

a. Probability

Probative value must be contrasted with two other concepts, materiality and sufficiency. McCormick does this best where he points out that a case is proved item by item, each item depending for its admissibility on the degree of its relevance, i.e., its probative value. The item does not usually prove proponent's case conclusively, but is simply a link in the chain of proof. To be sufficient to sustain the proponent's case, there must be a sufficient number of links.[3] And, even if those links tend to establish the probability of an ultimate fact, that ultimate fact must be material to the issue in the case. Thus, as McCormick illustrates, "in a suit for worker's compensation evidence of contributory negligence would be immaterial, whether pleaded or not, since a worker's negligence does not affect the right of compensation."[4] Each item of evidence McCormick characterizes as a brick. "A brick [, however,] is not a wall."[5] Although the terms "relevant" and "material" have come often to be used interchangeably, the distinction is that, in McCormick's worker's compensation illustration, evidence of the worker's conduct would be relevant to whether or not he was careless, but whether or not he was careless is not material to any issue in the case.[6]

Does the fact that a person is observed looking at cars in a used car sales lot in the early morning hours while the sales office is being burgled by another make it probable that this person is an accomplice, a lookout? While this fact may have been relevant, it gave rise to no more than a mere suspicion of the person's involvement and without more could not be considered sufficient to sustain that person's conviction.[7] But where, in a similar situation, the person who seemed to be a lookout was joined by the burglar and the two made their departure together, the evidence was sufficient for conviction; the bricks formed a wall.[8] In

---

2. Id. at 777, 530 N.Y.S.2d at 86, 525 N.E.2d at 732.

3. McCormick § 185, at 776. "Whether the entire body of one party's evidence is sufficient to go to the jury is one question. Whether a particular item of evidence is relevant is quite another. It is enough if the item could reasonably show that a fact is slightly more probable than it would appear without the evidence."

4. McCormick § 185, at 773. It has been said elsewhere that the term "relevance" refers "to the required relationship between the evidence offered and the fact it is offered to prove; the term 'materiality' refers to the required relationship between that fact and an issue which is the proper subject of proof in the case." McLain, Maryland Evidence § 401.1, at 261 (West 1987).

5. McCormick § 185, at 776.

6. In White v. Molinari, 160 A.D.2d 302, 553 N.Y.S.2d 396 (1st Dep't 1990), the court held that defendant's license suspension for failing to have his vehicle inspected, and the citation for disorderly conduct he received for arguing with a police officer at the accident scene, were irrelevant to the issues of negligence and proximate cause pertaining to the accident itself.

7. People v. Cleague, 22 N.Y.2d 363, 292 N.Y.S.2d 861, 239 N.E.2d 617 (1968).

8. People v. Wachowicz, 22 N.Y.2d 369, 292 N.Y.S.2d 867, 239 N.E.2d 620 (1968).

both cases the ultimate fact sought to be proved by the bricks was material and admissible, but in the first case there were not enough bricks.

Relevant evidence can be either direct or circumstantial. In the illustrations just above, the evidence pointing to guilt was circumstantial. From the direct evidence—the observation by police of the person outside the premises—an inference would have to be drawn which would have to amount to more than a suspicion. As to the sufficiency of both direct and circumstantial evidence and the charges that must be given the jury, *see* § 300.3(a)(1) and 300.4(d)(1), *supra*.

Examples of the application of relevancy considerations—flight and suppression of evidence. A person's attempt to escape after being apprehended would be relevant as showing the probability that he was conscious of his guilt. This may not prove guilt of the crime charged, but it is a circumstantial brick. As stated in *People v. Bennett*:[9]

> Certain postcrime conduct is "indicative of a consciousness of guilt, and hence of guilt itself." (People v. Reddy, 261 N.Y. 479, 486). *Reddy*, a case involving evidence of flight, noted such evidence betrayed an awareness of guilt, citing Proverbs (ch XXVIII, VI): "The wicked flee, even when no man pursueth; but the righteous are bold as a lion." (*See also*, People v. Yazum, 13 N.Y.2d 302, 246 N.Y.S.2d 626, 196 N.E.2d 263; People v. Fiorentino, 197 N.Y. 560, 567.)

> Consciousness of guilt evidence has consistently been viewed as weak because the connection between the conduct and a guilty mind often is tenuous (*see*, People v. Yazum, 13 N.Y.2d, at 304, *supra*; People v. Leyra, 1 N.Y.2d, at 209, *supra*). Even innocent persons, fearing wrongful conviction, may flee or lie to extricate themselves from situations that look damning (*see*, People v. Moses, 63 N.Y.2d, at 308, *supra*).

> The issue here, however, is not sufficiency but admissibility of evidence. Even equivocal consciousness-of-guilt evidence may be admissible so long as it is relevant, meaning that it has a tendency to establish the fact sought to be proved—that defendant was aware of guilt (*see*, People v. Yazum, 13 N.Y.2d, at 304, *supra*).[10]

In the *Yazum* case[11] the court said that while circumstantial evidence must, in the aggregate, be inconsistent with all reasonable hypotheses of innocence, "each piece of circumstantial evidence is subject to no such rule. * * * That it is equivocal or that it is consistent with suppositions other than guilt does not render it inadmissible * * *"[12]

9. 79 N.Y.2d 464, 583 N.Y.S.2d 825, 593 N.E.2d 279 (1992).

10. Id. at 469–70, 583 N.Y.S.2d at 828–29, 593 N.E.2d at 282–83.

11. People v. Yazum, 13 N.Y.2d 302, 246 N.Y.S.2d 626, 196 N.E.2d 263 (1963), reargument denied, 15 N.Y.2d 679, 255 N.Y.S.2d 1027, 204 N.E.2d 217 (1964).

12. Id. at 304, 246 N.Y.S.2d at 628, 196 N.E.2d at 264.

§ 401.1

Similar situations, noted in the *Bennett* case,[13] include false statements or alibis,[14] coercion or harassment of witnesses,[15] and abandonment or concealment of evidence.[16] In each instance the act, while not conclusive on the question, is *some* evidence that defendant bore a consciousness of guilt. The facts in *Yazum* are particularly illustrative because in that case defendant, when he attempted escape, was wanted on more than one criminal charge. He argued that the escape attempt could not be shown to relate to consciousness of guilt of the crime for which he was on trial, and therefore materiality was lacking. The court stated: "We think there is obviously no justification for distinguishing in such a manner between an explanation urging that flight was not motivated by consciousness of guilt at all, and one which urges that it was prompted by consciousness of a different guilt."[17] The inference created by the flight evidence, or the evidence of witness intimidation, false statements, or of evidence spoliation, is a matter for the defense to neutralize if possible.[18]

But not all instances of suspect activity rise to the probability level necessary for admissibility. In *People v. Bennett*,[19] defendant, a state trooper, was on trial for raping a motorist who he had stopped on the highway, and the prosecutor wanted to show on defendant's cross-examination that he had tried, after he was charged, to obtain information from the files of the Department of Motor Vehicles concerning the complainant. Acknowledging the *Yazum* rule regarding admissibility of even equivocal consciousness-of-guilt evidence, the court said that here the proof of defendant's inquiry, standing alone, was not sufficient to show the probability that defendant intended to coerce, intimidate or harass the complainant.[20] This was only half a brick which could have been made whole had there been any showing of "the crucial 'next step'—that defendant actually intended to coerce the witness. Such a

---

13. 79 N.Y.2d at 469–70, 583 N.Y.S.2d at 829, 593 N.E.2d at 283.

14. People v. Moses, 63 N.Y.2d 299, 482 N.Y.S.2d 228, 472 N.E.2d 4 (1984); People v. Leyra, 1 N.Y.2d 199, 151 N.Y.S.2d 658, 134 N.E.2d 475 (1956).

15. People v. Shilitano, 218 N.Y. 161, 112 N.E. 733 (1916), reargument denied, 218 N.Y. 702, 113 N.E. 1064 (1916). See People v. Plummer, 36 N.Y.2d 161, 365 N.Y.S.2d 842, 325 N.E.2d 161 (1975).

16. People v. Alexander, 37 N.Y.2d 202, 371 N.Y.S.2d 876, 333 N.E.2d 157 (1975); People v. Butterly, 25 N.Y.2d 159, 303 N.Y.S.2d 57, 250 N.E.2d 340 (1969).

17. Yazum, 13 N.Y.2d at 305, 246 N.Y.S.2d at 629, 196 N.E.2d at 265. In addition, it was stated:

To require as a matter of law that the admissibility of flight evidence depends on its unequivocal connection with guilt feelings over the particular crime charged would, therefore, operate to exclude such evidence from many cases in which it has always been regarded as admissible as a matter of course. No one disputes the general rule, as stated by Wigmore, that ambiguities or explanations tending to rebut an inference of guilt do not render flight evidence inadmissible but, rather, must be introduced as part of the defense and submitted to the jury. (2 Wigmore, Evidence [3d ed.], § 276). The suggested distinction would mean that only alternative innocent explanations of the flight are matters of rebuttal within the supposedly general rule, while the special dispensation of absolute exclusion is reserved for those who could show multiple guilt.

Id. at 305, 246 N.Y.S.2d at 628–29, 196 N.E.2d at 264–65.

18. Id. at 305, 246 N.Y.S.2d at 629, 196 N.E.2d at 265.

19. 79 N.Y.2d 464, 583 N.Y.S.2d 825, 593 N.E.2d 279 (1992).

20. Id. at 470, 583 N.Y.S.2d at 829, 593 N.E.2d at 283.

conclusion would not be a reasonable inference from the attempt to obtain driving records, but would be pure speculation. Indeed, it is a common part of the defense process to investigate the background of adverse witnesses for potential impeachment material. Such efforts alone would generally not constitute a consciousness of guilt."[21]

The *Bennett* case prompts the observation that much is left to the judge's discretion in determining the probability quotient of a proffered item of evidence and its materiality to the issue to which it is directed. McCormick notes that "[ordinarily * * * the answer [to the question of relevancy] must lie in the judge's own experience, his general knowledge, and his understanding of human conduct and motivation]";[22] and the New York cases hold that questions of relevancy rest "largely in the discretion of the trial court."[23]

There are countless sui generis instances where the judge will have little precedent, but must bring logic to bear.[24]

Missing witness. Another recurring instance of circumstantial evidence demonstrating elements of relevancy not categorized elsewhere is a party's failure to call a witness he would have been expected to call. The rule is examined by the Court of Appeals in *People v. Gonzalez.*[25] In sum, if a witness has pertinent knowledge, and is available and under the "control" of a party who would normally be expected to call him, then failure to produce him should prompt a charge to the jury that an unfavorable inference may be drawn. The term "control" simply means that the witness would be expected to be favorable to one party and hostile to the other and therefore is someone who would have been called by that party if he had corroborative testimony.[26] It has been said that "[a] spouse or relative is perforce deemed to be under the defendant's control,"[27] and spouses of crime victims, because of their presumptive

21. Id.

22. McCormick § 185, at 778.

23. Radosh v. Shipstad, 20 N.Y.2d 504, 508, 285 N.Y.S.2d 60, 63, 231 N.E.2d 759, 762, reargument denied, 20 N.Y.2d 969, 286 N.Y.S.2d 860, 233 N.E.2d 862 (1967); Bodensteiner v. Vannais, 167 A.D.2d 954, 561 N.Y.S.2d 1017 (4th Dep't 1990).

24. See, e.g., White v. Molinari, 160 A.D.2d 302, 303, 553 N.Y.S.2d 396, 397 (1st Dep't 1990)(defendant's license suspension for failing to have his vehicle inspected, and the citation for disorderly conduct he received for arguing with the police officer at the accident scene, were "clearly irrelevant to the issues of negligence and proximate cause").

25. 68 N.Y.2d 424, 509 N.Y.S.2d 796, 502 N.E.2d 583 (1986).

26. Id. at 429, 509 N.Y.S.2d at 800, 502 N.E.2d at 587. It was noted in the Gonzalez opinion that the burden lies with the party seeking the charge to establish, prima facie, the foundation elements. The opposing party, if he is able, may then attempt to show that one or more of the necessary elements—knowledge, availability, control—are missing. See id. at 427–28, 509 N.Y.S.2d at 799, 502 N.E.2d at 586. "In order to allow for effective judicial review, it is imperative that all discussions regarding this matter be clearly set forth on the record so that the respective positions of each party are readily discernible. * * *" Id. at 428, 509 N.Y.S.2d at 799, 502 N.E.2d at 586.

27. People v. Macana, 84 N.Y.2d 173, 177, 615 N.Y.S.2d 656, 658, 639 N.E.2d 13, 15 (1994)(father of defendant). But see People v. Magett, 196 A.D.2d 62, 64–65, 608 N.Y.S.2d 434, 435–36 (1st Dep't 1994) ("[W]hile a familial relationship may, under certain circumstances, be sufficient to establish the necessary element of control, there must be evidence that such a relationship existed. * * * Here, [the missing witness'] mere status as defendant's stepsister * * * is insufficient by itself to give rise to a presumption that she was under his control.").

§ 401.1   RELEVANCY   Ch. 4

partiality, may be deemed under the prosecutor's control.[28] Strangers, of course, are not within a party's control.[29] As to the knowledge element, it must be shown that the missing witness was in a position to see or hear relevant matters.[30]

In *Gonzalez* the exact nature of the unfavorable inference was not specified; but in *People v. Paylor*,[31] the following explanation was offered:

> [T]he proper standard is that set forth in Criminal Jury Instructions (1 CJI [NY] 8.55, at 452), which provides that the fact finder may infer from defendant's failure to call a witness that if the witness had been called, he would not have supported the defense testimony on the issue of which he possessed knowledge. If the fact finder elects to draw an inference from the failure to produce a witness, it may not speculate about what the witness would have said, nor may it assume that the witness could have provided positive evidence corroborating or filling gaps in the People's proof. The inference is merely negative and allows the fact finder to infer that the missing witness would not have supported or corroborated defendant's evidence.[32]

From the references and citations so far, it is not to be taken that the missing witness rule is applicable only in criminal cases. The rule is equally applicable in civil cases,[33] with the added feature that an adverse

---

28. People v. Paulin, 70 N.Y.2d 685, 518 N.Y.S.2d 790, 512 N.E.2d 312 (1987); People v. Gonzalez, 68 N.Y.2d 424, 509 N.Y.S.2d 796, 502 N.E.2d 583 (1986). See also cases cited in note 30 infra (police officers or informants may be under "control" of prosecutor).

29. See, e.g., People v. Terry, 83 A.D.2d 491, 445 N.Y.S.2d 340 (4th Dep't 1981)(where defendant's alibi was that he was at social services agency when crime was committed, his failure to call agency employee to corroborate the alibi was not proper basis for missing witness charge). See also People v. Macana, 84 N.Y.2d 173, 177–80, 615 N.Y.S.2d 656, 658–59, 639 N.E.2d 13, 14–16 (1994)(missing witness charge is inappropriate where criminal defendant fails to call codefendant, accomplice or other person whose probable invocation of privilege against self-incrimination can be verified); Zeeck v. Melina Taxi Co., 177 A.D.2d 692, 576 N.Y.S.2d 878 (2d Dep't 1991)(error to allow missing witness charge where defendant's ex-employee had moved out of state, making him both unavailable and no longer in defendant's control).

30. See People v. Lyons, 81 N.Y.2d 753, 593 N.Y.S.2d 776, 609 N.E.2d 129 (1992)(the officer who made the arrest was called in after the drug sale, never saw the drug sale and had no knowledge of any facts material to the commission of the crime); People v. Kitching, 78 N.Y.2d 532, 577 N.Y.S.2d 231, 583 N.E.2d 944 (1991)(arresting officer's partner was near the arrest site where the drug sale was made at the time the crime was committed and should have been called to give his account of the events); People v. Dianda, 70 N.Y.2d 894, 524 N.Y.S.2d 381, 519 N.E.2d 292 (1987), reh. denied, 71 N.Y.2d 890, 527 N.Y.S.2d 772, 522 N.E.2d 1070 (1988) (informant not produced by the prosecution, but there was no showing that he was privy to any matters critical to the issues).

31. 70 N.Y.2d 146, 518 N.Y.S.2d 102, 511 N.E.2d 370 (1987).

32. Id. at 149, 518 N.Y.S.2d at 103, 511 N.E.2d at 371.

33. See, e.g., Noce v. Kaufman, 2 N.Y.2d 347, 161 N.Y.S.2d 1, 141 N.E.2d 529 (1957); Milio v. Railway Motor Trucking Co., 257 App.Div. 640, 15 N.Y.S.2d 73 (1st Dep't 1939). Examples of persons under the control of a party include employees (Grun v. Sportsman, Inc., 58 A.D.2d 802, 396 N.Y.S.2d 250 (2d Dep't 1977)); relatives (Jarrett v. Madifari, 67 A.D.2d 396, 415 N.Y.S.2d 644 (1st Dep't 1979)); treating physicians (Dukes v. Rotem, 191 A.D.2d 35, 599 N.Y.S.2d 915 (1st Dep't), appeal dismissed, 82 N.Y.2d 886, 609 N.Y.S.2d 563, 631 N.E.2d 569 (1993)).

inference may be drawn against a party in a civil action who fails to testify in support of his own case,[34] and counsel may, during summation, comment on a party's failure to testify or call a witness whether or not a sufficient foundation otherwise exists for the court's giving of the missing witness charge itself.[35]

The party against whom the missing witness inference is sought to be invoked has the burden of showing any one of five reasons in order to escape from the inference: (1) that the witness has no pertinent knowledge, (2) that there is no "control" over the party, (3) that the witness is unavailable for reasons of health, or his whereabouts are unknown, (4) that the witness' testimony, although relevant, would simply be unduly cumulative, or that (5) the witness' testimony would not be relevant in the first place.[36]

Library References:

West's Key No. Digests, Criminal Law ⚖338; Evidence ⚖99–117.

b. Factors Precluding Admissibility of Relevant Evidence— Prejudice and Exclusionary Rules

As stated in the quote from the *Scarola* case which opened this section, all relevant evidence is admissible unless it violates some exclusionary rule, or its prejudicial impact outweighs its probative value, or it would tend to mislead the jury. In *People v. Davis*,[37] defendant desired to introduce evidence that the accusatory statement of a potential witness, Smith, who the prosecutor did not call, was given under duress. This was to show that the police had attempted to procure false testimony because the witness was never called. Even assuming the evidence

---

34. See, e.g., Marine Midland Bank v. John E. Russo Produce Co., 50 N.Y.2d 31, 45, 427 N.Y.S.2d 961, 969, 405 N.E.2d 205, 212 (1980); Turner Press, Inc. v. Gould, 76 A.D.2d 906, 429 N.Y.S.2d 239 (2d Dep't 1980); Jarrett v. Madifari, 67 A.D.2d 396, 415 N.Y.S.2d 644 (1st Dep't 1979).

35. In People v. Tankleff, 84 N.Y.2d 992, 622 N.Y.S.2d 503, 646 N.E.2d 805 (1994), the prosecutor in summation commented on defendant's failure to call several witnesses who might be expected to have supported his defense that he had good relations with his parents and would not have killed them. Finding no error, the court stated:

* * * in these circumstances the People were not obliged to satisfy the burden * * * for establishing entitlement to a formal "missing witness" charge to be administered by the court. Since the disputed comments were not made in bad faith and were merely efforts to persuade the jury to draw inferences that supported the People's position, they were not improper even though there may have been some question as to whether all the uncalled witnesses were within defendant's "control" * * *. We note that there was no doubt that the witnesses in question, who included defendant's sister and brother-in-law and other relatives with personal knowledge of defendant's family, were available and had material, noncumulative information about the case * * *. We also note that defense counsel was not deprived of an opportunity to make his own summation comments on the subject.

Id. at 944–95, 622 N.Y.S.2d at 504–05, 646 N.E.2d at 806–07. See also Seligson, Morris & Neuburger v. Fairbanks Whitney Corp., 22 A.D.2d 625, 257 N.Y.S.2d 706 (1st Dep't 1965).

36. People v. Gonzalez, 68 N.Y.2d 424, 428, 509 N.Y.S.2d 796, 799, 502 N.E.2d 583, 586 (1986). Of course, if the witness is equally available to both parties and could be expected to testify just as favorably for one party as for the other, then generally no unfavorable inference may be drawn from the failure of either party to call the witness. Id. at 429, 50 N.Y.2d at 800, 502 N.E.2d at 587.

37. 43 N.Y.2d 17, 400 N.Y.S.2d 735, 371 N.E.2d 456 (1977).

§ 401.1   RELEVANCY   Ch. 4

was relevant to the quality of the prosecution's case, the court ruled that the trial judge was correct in keeping it out. "Since the attempt to introduce Smith's testimony on a collateral issue was for the obvious purpose of creating the impression that a substantial portion of the prosecution's proof was tainted in a fashion similar to the proffered Smith account, the probative value of the testimony could be outweighed by dangers that the main issue would be obscured, by prolongation of trial and by the solid possibility of undue prejudice to the prosecution."[38]

In a civil case, *Radosh v. Shipstad*,[39] plaintiff, a professional ice skater, sued for lost wages because of her dismissal by defendant employer on the ground she was overweight. The employer sought to introduce evidence of plaintiff's weight at the time of the trial, and the judge excluded it on the ground that plaintiff's weight at the time she was released was the only relevant question. The Court of Appeals stated: "Determination of relevancy and the conduct of a trial so as to avoid undue emphasis upon matters not really in issue * * * are matters largely in the discretion of the trial court. It is a close question whether the relevancy of plaintiff's then present weight was outweighed by the likelihood that introduction of such evidence would confuse or mislead the jury * * *, but, in any event * * * the exclusion of this evidence * * * was not sufficiently prejudicial to warrant reversal in this case."[40] And in the *Scarola* case, *supra*, defendant sought to take the stand only for the purpose of demonstrating the sound of his voice to the jury to show a speech problem not testified to by the complaining witness. Noting that the voice exemplar evidence would have been "broadly relevant," the Court of Appeals nevertheless recognized the trial court's proper exercise of discretion in keeping it out, "considering the inherent lack of trustworthiness * * * and the difficulty of testing the authenticity of any alleged speech impediment."[41]

In *People v. Lewis*,[42] a prosecution for incest, the trial court allowed evidence of 10 prior and uncharged acts of incest by defendant-father with his daughter. Saying that defendant's prior uncharged crimes may have "some probative value; indeed, Wigmore contends that such evidence is objectionable because juries attribute too much significance to it,"[43] the court nevertheless found their admission to be error since the prior crimes were not elements of the charge in issue, and they fit none of the *Molineux* exceptions.[44] Prohibition of uncharged crimes provides

38. Id. at 27, 400 N.Y.S.2d at 740, 371 N.E.2d at 460.

39. 20 N.Y.2d 504, 285 N.Y.S.2d 60, 231 N.E.2d 759 (1967).

40. Id. at 508, 285 N.Y.S.2d at 63, 231 N.E.2d at 762.

41. Scarola, 71 N.Y.2d at 777, 530 N.Y.S.2d at 86, 525 N.E.2d at 732. Note that in Radosh and Scarola the Court used the term relevance to mean materiality, illustrating how the terms have merged.

42. 69 N.Y.2d 321, 514 N.Y.S.2d 205, 506 N.E.2d 915 (1987).

43. Id. at 325, 514 N.Y.S.2d at 207, 506 N.E.2d at 916–17.

44. In People v. Molineux, 168 N.Y. 264, 273, 61 N.E. 286, 294 (1901), the court ruled that evidence of uncharged crimes could not be introduced simply to prove that the defendant was generally disposed toward criminal conduct, but held that such evidence is proper where it bears on motive, intent, absence of mistake or accident, common scheme or plan, or identity. The Molineux rules will be taken up in § 404.1 infra.

the prime example of categorical exclusion of otherwise relevant evidence on the ground that its prejudicial effect will outweigh its probative value.

Prejudice, of course, is a factor in disparate sorts of circumstances,[45] and the decision to admit or exclude the evidence rests within the discretion of the trial court.[46] The wealth of a defendant presents a good example of both initial irrelevancy in some cases and of the probative value-prejudicial effect equation in others.[47] Likewise, gruesome photographs or exhibits, while perhaps relevant, can be too prejudicial in some cases,[48] but perfectly admissible in others.[49]

---

45. See Kish v. Board of Educ., 76 N.Y.2d 379, 385, 559 N.Y.S.2d 687, 690, 558 N.E.2d 1159, 1162 (1990)(under collateral source rule proof of plaintiff's pension, while perhaps relevant to damages, is normally inadmissible, except that here it bore on another disputed issue and could be admitted with limiting instructions); People v. Conyers, 52 N.Y.2d 454, 458, 438 N.Y.S.2d 741, 743, 420 N.E.2d 933, 935 (1981)(evidence that defendant remained silent at time of arrest in the face of accusation has "minimal probative significance" and is outweighed by the resulting prejudice); O'Connell v. Jacobs, 181 A.D.2d 1064, 583 N.Y.S.2d 61 (4th Dep't 1992), aff'd, 81 N.Y.2d 797, 595 N.Y.S.2d 388, 611 N.E.2d 289 (1993) (psychiatric evidence that defendant was capable of committing an assault deemed prejudicial when the issue was whether he actually committed it); Arroyo v. City of New York, 171 A.D.2d 541, 567 N.Y.S.2d 257 (1st Dep't 1991)(evidence of defendant's drug and alcohol history prejudicial when there was no proof that he was intoxicated at the time of the accident).

46. Bodensteiner v. Vannais, 167 A.D.2d 954, 954, 561 N.Y.S.2d 1017, 1018 (4th Dep't 1990)("The decision whether to admit evidence that is logically relevant, but is so prejudicial that its probative value is outweighed, rests within the sound discretion of the court. * * *").

47. See, e.g., Dufresne v. Duemler, 108 A.D.2d 1102, 485 N.Y.S.2d 879 (3d Dep't 1985)(on issue of compensatory damages, financial resources of parties are irrelevant; wealth of defendant may be relevant, however, on issue of punitive damages). See also Weinstein and Berger ¶ 401[10], at 401-82-83:

Evidence of a defendant's wealth has been held irrelevant to the issue of compensatory damages, because the purpose of such damages is to make the plaintiff whole. On the other hand, some federal courts have allowed evidence of wealth to be introduced on the issue of punitive damages.

In Bower v. Weisman, 674 F.Supp. 113 (S.D.N.Y.1987), it was held that plaintiff, who sued defendant on an agreement based on a personal relationship, was entitled to introduce evidence of defendant's wealth because this would be relevant on the question of why she was allowed to sign defendant's name on sizable checks. The amount of those checks would appear small, and reasonable, when compared to defendant's enormous wealth. Id. at 117. In Matter of Joint Eastern and Southern Dist. Asbestos Lit., 798 F.Supp. 925, 934 (E. and S.D.N.Y.1992), rev'd on other grounds, 995 F.2d 343 (2d Cir.), rev'd on other grounds, Malcolm v. National Gypsum Co., 995 F.2d 346 (2d Cir.1993), defendant's wealth was deemed relevant to show that it had the resources to investigate whether its products were dangerous and whether it had a financial reason to want to suppress evidence of the dangers of its products. The balance under Rule 403 did not favor exclusion of this material, particularly since defendant was not shown to have been a particularly large or wealthy firm.

48. See Allen v. Stokes, 260 App.Div. 600, 601, 23 N.Y.S.2d 443, 444 (1st Dep't 1940)(prejudicial in negligence case to admit photograph of dead boy in coffin since his size and appearance could have been established by other evidence).

49. It appears that in criminal cases, if the exhibit has any relevance whatsoever, it will be admissible over the prejudice argument. See, e.g., People v. Wood, 79 N.Y.2d 958, 960, 582 N.Y.S.2d 992, 994, 591 N.E.2d 1178, 1180 (1992)(grisly photographs of crime victim should be excluded only if "sole purpose" is to arouse emotions of jury). See also People v. Bell, 63 N.Y.2d 796, 481 N.Y.S.2d 324, 471 N.E.2d 137 (1984); People v. Pobliner, 32 N.Y.2d 356, 345 N.Y.S.2d 482, 298 N.E.2d 637, reargument denied, 33 N.Y.2d 657, 348 N.Y.S.2d 1030, 303 N.E.2d 710 (1973), cert. denied, 416 U.S. 905, 94 S.Ct. 1609, 40 L.Ed.2d 110 (1974); People v. Bulger, 52 A.D.2d 682, 382 N.Y.S.2d 133 (3d Dep't 1976). See also People v. Hills, 140 A.D.2d 71, 532 N.Y.S.2d 269 (2d Dep't 1988), appeal dismissed, 73

Relevant evidence can be excluded because it is cumulative,[50] because of obfuscation of the main issue, delay and surprise,[51] because it is confusing,[52] or because it does not further public policy.[53] And the fact of relevancy does not guarantee admissibility since much relevant evidence is otherwise proscribed. The whole range of privileges, both constitutional and based on confidential communications, acts to thwart the admission of very relevant evidence. Similarly, limitations on the admissibility of evidence seized in violation of a person's fourth amendment rights act to keep out totally relevant, probative and material evidence.[54]

Library References:

West's Key No. Digests, Criminal Law ⚖337–361; Evidence ⚖99–156.

c. Proposed New York Evidence Code

Sections 401–403 of the proposed New York Evidence Code track the same sections of the Federal Rules in defining relevancy, stating that relevant evidence is admissible unless otherwise proscribed either by other evidence rules, or by practical considerations such as unfair prejudice, confusion of the issues, waste of time and, in the proposed New York Code § 403, surprise to the adverse party.[55] The

---

N.Y.2d 855, 537 N.Y.S.2d 502, 534 N.E.2d 340 (1988), where it was held that the prosecutor was not bound to accept defendant's offer to stipulate to the victim's serious injuries so as to keep out the People's evidence of the victim's injuries.

50. People v. Ely, 68 N.Y.2d 520, 532, 510 N.Y.S.2d 532, 539, 503 N.E.2d 88, 95 (1986)(disparaging remarks made by defendant regarding the victim, although "marginally probative," were cumulative and unduly prejudicial).

51. People v. Davis, 43 N.Y.2d 17, 27, 400 N.Y.S.2d 735, 740, 371 N.E.2d 456, 460 (1977), cert. denied, 435 U.S. 998, 98 S.Ct. 1653, 56 L.Ed.2d 88 (1978)(surprise, obfuscation and delay would be injected if defendant had been allowed to show that a potential prosecution witness was coerced to make a pretrial statement which was never sought to be introduced by the prosecution).

52. People v. Nitzberg, 287 N.Y. 183, 189, 38 N.E.2d 490, 493–494 (1941), reh. denied, 287 N.Y. 183, 40 N.E.2d 40 (1942)(testimony of non-accomplice witnesses to matters not disputed by defendant should not have been allowed because relevancy was remote "to say nothing * * * of the fact that such use of that testimony inevitably tended unnecessarily to confuse the real issues and unfairly to surprise the defendant to his prejudice").

53. Dermatossian v. New York City Trans. Auth., 67 N.Y.2d 219, 225, 501 N.Y.S.2d 784, 787, 492 N.E.2d 1200, 1204 (1986)(fact defendant paid no-fault benefits could not be used as proof of an admission of liability since this would run counter to the intent of the no-fault law and the spirit of the exclusion of offers to compromise). Compare Ando v. Woodberry, 8 N.Y.2d 165, 203 N.Y.S.2d 74, 168 N.E.2d 520 (1960), where the Court of Appeals, in a negligence case, had to decide whether a clearly relevant guilty plea to a traffic violation arising out of the same accident would be admissible over the argument that the plea would be hearsay and would violate public policy since many such pleas are simply made for reasons of expediency. The plea is an exception to the hearsay rule, being an admission, said the court, and the expediency aspect goes only to weight and not admissibility.

54. See, e.g., Katz v. United States, 389 U.S. 347, 88 S.Ct. 507, 19 L.Ed.2d 576 (1967)(relevant evidence suppressed where evidence obtained through illegal search and seizure).

55. § 401. Definition of relevant evidence [PROPOSED]

Relevant evidence means evidence having any tendency to make the existence of any fact that is material to the determination of the action more probable or less probable than it would be without the evidence.

§ 402. Relevant evidence generally admissible [PROPOSED]

All relevant evidence is admissible, except as otherwise provided by the consti-

ubiquitous balancing test pitting probative value against undue prejudice is found in proposed § 403 and applies with respect to all categories of evidence—not just aspects such as character evidence, or evidence of habit, custom or usage found in the rest of Article 4. These provisions, according to the comment to proposed article 4, are said to codify the present New York law with only "limited" changes.

§ 401.2 Federal

The New York rules set forth in the last section are equally applicable in the federal courts. Indeed, Federal Rules of Evidence 401, 402 and 403 are generally reflective of those common law precepts.[1] The relevancy of evidence is determined by the trial judge, who, using her discretion,[2] finds it relevant or irrelevant under Rule 401,[3] or inadmissi-

§ 403. **Exclusion of relevant evidence on grounds of prejudice, confusion, waste of time, or unfair surprise [PROPOSED]**

Although relevant, evidence may be excluded if its probative value is substantially outweighed by the danger that its admission would create undue prejudice to a party; or would confuse the issues and mislead the jury; or would prolong the trial to an unreasonable extent without any corresponding advantage to the offering party; or would unfairly surprise a party and no remedy other than exclusion could cure the prejudice caused by the surprise.

§ 401.2

1. Rule 401. Definition of "Relevant Evidence"

"Relevant evidence" means evidence having any tendency to make the existence of any fact that is of consequence to the determination of the action more probable or less probable than it would be without the evidence.

Rule 402. Relevant Evidence Generally Admissible: Irrelevant Evidence Inadmissible

All relevant evidence is admissible, except as otherwise provided by the Constitution of the United States, by Act of Congress, by these rules, or by other rules prescribed by the Supreme Court pursuant to statutory authority. Evidence which is not relevant is not admissible. tution of the United States or of this state, or this chapter or other statute. Evidence that is not relevant is not admissible.

Rule 403. Exclusion of Relevant Evidence on Grounds of Prejudice, Confusion, or Waste of Time

Although relevant, evidence may be excluded if its probative value is substantially outweighed by the danger of unfair prejudice, confusion of the issues, or misleading the jury, or by considerations of undue delay, waste of time, or needless presentation of cumulative evidence.

2. Robinson v. Shapiro, 646 F.2d 734, 741 (2d Cir.1981)(court well within its discretion in keeping out part of a contract the prejudicial effect of which outweighed any probative value); Fiacco v. City of Rensselaer, 783 F.2d 319, 327–28 (2d Cir.1986), cert. denied, 480 U.S. 922, 107 S.Ct. 1384, 94 L.Ed.2d 698 (1987)(trial judge has broad discretion to determine Rule 403 questions—here to allow evidence in civil rights case of police officers' prior use of force as relevant to questions in case); In Re Investors Funding Corp. of New York Securities Litigation, 635 F.Supp. 1262, 1265–66 (S.D.N.Y.1986)(fact of bribery scheme of little or no probative value, and highly prejudicial); In Re Agent Orange Products Liability Lit., 611 F.Supp. 1223, 1255 (E.D.N.Y.1985), aff'd, 818 F.2d 187 (2d Cir. 1987), cert. denied, Lombardi v. Dow Chem. Co., 487 U.S. 1234, 108 S.Ct. 2898, 101 L.Ed.2d 932 (1988)(trial courts are reluctant to exclude relevant evidence and will do so only when there are compelling reasons); Eng v. Scully, 146 F.R.D. 81 (S.D.N.Y.1993)(in civil rights case letters written by Prisoners' Legal Services to the Department of Corrections questioning incidents at a correctional facility were irrelevant to the issue of various officials' state of mind).

3. Purnell v. Lord, 952 F.2d 679, 685 (2d Cir.1992)(in inmate's civil rights suit, brought because his privilege of corresponding with a female inmate in another facility had been terminated, evidence of the female

ble although relevant under the provisions of Rules 402 and 403.[4]

The analytical approach was set forth by Judge Oakes of the Second Circuit Court of Appeals in his dissent in *United States v. Robinson*.[5] Rule 401 provides nothing more than a threshold test, "a starting point in the determination of admissibility."[6] If relevancy is found, the probative value of the evidence must be weighed against its prejudicial effect under Rule 403. "The probative value of evidence cannot, of course, be assessed in a vacuum; the value must always be measured in terms of the purpose for which the evidence was introduced."[7] In *Robinson* the defendant was arrested 10 weeks after the bank robbery for which he and others were tried. At the time of his arrest he possessed a .38–caliber handgun. Other evidence showed that the robbers used a shotgun, a .32–caliber gun, a .38–caliber gun and a gun that "looked like" a .38–caliber gun. The majority of an en banc court found that evidence of defendant's possession of the gun at the time of his arrest was relevant, and not outweighed by the attendant prejudice.[8] Extending the broadest area of discretion to the trial judge, the majority

---

inmate's propensity for violence, while prejudicial, was outweighed by its probative effect); Lamborn v. Dittmer, 873 F.2d 522, 528 (2d Cir.1989) (evidence of certain promissory notes, although prejudicial, nevertheless bore on questions of substance and credibility); S.E.C. v. Singer, 786 F.Supp. 1158, 1167 (S.D.N.Y.1992)(witness' recollection of events, although not certain, is admissible since nonconclusive evidence should be admitted if it makes a proposition more probable than not); Hoppe v. G.D. Searle & Co., 779 F.Supp. 1413, 1419 (S.D.N.Y.1991)(in suit alleging infertility due to use of defendant's IUD product, plaintiff cannot argue that evidence of her own or her husband's sexual history is irrelevant); Eng v. Scully, 146 F.R.D. 74, 80 (S.D.N.Y.1993)(in civil rights case, altercations between inmates relevant to question of supervisor's notice of danger, and evidence of correction officers' use of force on prior occasions relevant to officer's intent and motive); Amway Corp. v. Shapiro Ex. Co., 102 F.R.D. 564, 569 (S.D.N.Y.1984)(any facts tending to show that party really knew things he claimed not to know are relevant).

4. Berkovich v. Hicks, 922 F.2d 1018, 1023 (2d Cir.1991)(in civil rights suit against arresting officers, probative value of evidence of prior citizen complaints against officers was outweighed by the prejudicial effect); U.S. Football League v. National Football League, 842 F.2d 1335, 1374–75 (2d Cir.1988)(testimony of United States Senator concerning statements made by officials of professional football league to members of Congress properly excluded in antitrust action because prejudice outweighed probative value); Schneider v. Revici, 817 F.2d 987, 991 (2d Cir.1987)(in malpractice action against physician, book written by defendant should be kept out because of the prejudice occasioned thereby); Goldberg v. Nat. Life Ins. Co. of Vermont, 774 F.2d 559, 564–65 (2d Cir.1985)(relevant evidence which would have changed the theory of plaintiff's case and confused the jury was properly kept out); Contemp. Mission, Inc. v. Bonded Mailings, Inc., 671 F.2d 81, 83 (2d Cir.1982) (evidence which would have raised question as to plaintiff's religious status properly excluded since that point potentially extensive, confusing and prejudicial); Robinson v. Shapiro, 646 F.2d 734, 741 (2d Cir.1981) (where general contractor liable for worker's injuries under the New York Labor Law, introduction of the warranty clause in the contract could have confused and misled the jury); In Re Investors Funding Corp. of New York Securities Litigation, 635 F.Supp. 1262, 1265–66 (S.D.N.Y.1986)(proof of bribery scheme outweighed by prejudice and fact that it was of little or no relevance to the issue at hand); In re Agent Orange Product Liability Lit., 611 F.Supp. 1223, 1256 (E.D.N.Y.1985), aff'd, 818 F.2d 187 (2d Cir.1987), cert. denied, Lombardi v. Dow Chem., 487 U.S. 1234, 108 S.Ct. 2898, 101 L.Ed.2d 932 (1988)(physicians' testimony of low probative value with potential of misleading the jury and prolonging the litigation).

5. 560 F.2d 507, 519 (2d Cir.1977), cert. denied, 435 U.S. 905, 98 S.Ct. 1451, 55 L.Ed.2d 496 (1978).

6. Id.

7. Id.

8. Id. at 513.

found that the admission of the evidence was not erroneous; that "[t]he remarkable coincidence that he possessed a .38–caliber gun some weeks later thus tended directly to identify appellant as one of the participants * * *."[9] This case provides a good illustration of just how elusive the Rule 401–403 provisions can be. Judge Oakes in dissent found nothing remarkable about a person possessing a .38–caliber handgun in New York,[10] and that defendant's possession had little or no relevance to his presence at the bank robbery; and that even if there were any relevance it was so slight as to be easily overborne by the prejudicial effect.[11] Judge Gurfein, in his own dissent, regretted the decision to consider the case en banc since it would be of little help in dealing with future problems under Rules 401–403.[12]

By way of contrast, consider the situation in *United States v. Green*,[13] where there was other evidence that made defendant's possession of a gun when arrested particularly relevant. His wife, who was accused of robbing the bank with defendant, possessed a note in her handbag advising, " '[t]his is a stick up we have guns I went [sic] all the money don't push no button.' "[14] The court said: "The note and gun, both of which were found in [defendant's] constructive possession shortly after the events described in apparent pursuit of the common plan and scheme, are proof that [defendant] was accustomed in robbing banks to using a gun in conjunction with a note. Its relevancy can hardly be doubted."[15]

Rule 403 is thoroughly discussed by Judge Weinstein in *In Re Agent Orange Products Liability Lit.*,[16] where also is found a generous sampling of federal cases interpreting Rule 403.

Finally, the rules as to evidence of flight and missing witnesses in the federal courts are much the same as those employed in New York, as

9. Id. at 512.

10. Id. at 522.

11. Id. Judge Oakes distinguished other gun cases as follows:

The possession of a single gun of a common type is manifestly different from the situation in a case like United States v. Ravich [421 F.2d 1196, 1204 (2d Cir.), cert. denied, 400 U.S. 834, 91 S.Ct. 69, 27 L.Ed.2d 66 (1970)], where a number of handguns were found together with a large amount of ammunition * * *. Such an arsenal is unusual enough to give its finding some probative value on the question of opportunity or preparation. Similarly, the gun found in United States v. Wiener, 534 F.2d 15 (2d Cir.), cert. denied, 429 U.S. 820, 97 S.Ct. 66, 50 L.Ed.2d 80 (1976), was seized from a distinctive burlap bag that also contained the narcotics and paraphernalia which were the principal items of evidence in the case * * *. The gun in United States v. Campanile, 516 F.2d 288 (2d Cir.1975), was the particular gun that the defendant himself admitted taking to the area of the lobbies. Such guns, found in unusual situations or closely linked to the crimes in question, have a degree of probative value that is entirely missing in this case, where the gun was indistinctive and no evidence linked it to the commission of the crime.

Id. at 521.

12. Id. at 525.

13. 561 F.2d 423 (2d Cir.1977), cert. denied, 434 U.S. 1018, 98 S.Ct. 739, 54 L.Ed.2d 764 (1978).

14. Id. at 425.

15. Id. at 426.

16. 611 F.Supp. 1223, 1255 (E.D.N.Y. 1985), aff'd, 818 F.2d 187 (2d Cir.1987), cert. denied sub nom., Lombardi v. Dow Chem. Co., 487 U.S. 1234, 108 S.Ct. 2898, 101 L.Ed.2d 932 (1988).

§ 401.2 RELEVANCY Ch. 4

discussed in the last section. In *United States v. Amuso*,[17] the Second Circuit observed: "While trial judges should be aware of the limitations of flight as circumstantial evidence of guilt, the threshold decision on whether to admit such evidence in a particular case falls within the judge's sound discretion * * *."[18] Cases on the missing witness rule are collected in *United States v. Myerson*,[19] where the court determined what it termed an issue of first impression:[20] Is defendant entitled to the missing witness charge when the prosecutor refuses to immunize a witness who would claim his privilege against self-incrimination if put on the stand? The court held that where a prospective witness would invoke his fifth amendment rights, he is equally unavailable to both parties and defendant is not entitled to the charge. The refusal to immunize the witness is not necessarily an admission that the witness would not testify against the interests of defendant. There can be other legitimate reasons why the prosecutor does not want to confer immunity.[21]

Library References:

West's Key No. Digests, Criminal Law ⇔337–361; Evidence ⇔99–156.

402 Character Evidence

§ 402.1 New York

a. Introduction

The character of a person—whether, for example, she is peaceful, honest, law abiding, sober—can be relevant and admissible, but only in closely controlled circumstances.[1] The problem is that "the probative value is slight and the potential for prejudice large."[2] Character can be directly in issue under the substantive law applicable to a case, as, for example, in defamation[3] where plaintiff alleges damage to her reputation. Character evidence can be used to impeach the credibility of a witness,[4] and it can be used by defendant in a criminal case as evidence that he is not likely to have committed the crime charged. If the criminal defendant exercises the option of showing his good character, then the door is open for the prosecutor to rebut with evidence of defendant's bad character and cross-examine plaintiff's character wit-

---

17. 21 F.3d 1251 (2d Cir.), cert. denied, ___ U.S. ___, 115 S.Ct. 326, 130 L.Ed.2d 286 (1994).

18. Id. at 1258.

19. 18 F.3d 153, 157–60 (2d Cir.), cert. denied, ___ U.S. ___, 115 S.Ct. 159, 130 L.Ed.2d 97 (1994). See especially United States v. Torres, 845 F.2d 1165, 1169–70 (2d Cir.1988).

20. 18 F.3d at 158.

21. Id. at 159–60.

§ 402.1

1. People v. Mullin, 41 N.Y.2d 475, 479, 393 N.Y.S.2d 938, 941, 362 N.E.2d 571, 573–74 (1977).

2. McCormick § 186, at 786–87.

3. 1A Wigmore § 70. In a defamation case plaintiff sues for damage to her character. If her character was not much good to begin with, damages should be little or nothing.

4. Michelson v. United States, 335 U.S. 469, 69 S.Ct. 213, 93 L.Ed. 168 (1948). See § 402.1(g) infra.

ness with specific instances of defendant's bad conduct to impeach the witness' credibility.[5] Finally, a defendant in a homicide case may, with certain qualifications, prove the bad character of the victim to show that defendant acted in self-defense.[6] These categories of character evidence,[7] and the permissible methods of proving character where it is admissible, are taken up in the subparts that follow.

Library References:

West's Key No. Digests, Criminal Law ⟾369–381; Evidence ⟾106.

b. Character in Issue

New York cases involving the question of character evidence in defamation actions is extremely rare. Wigmore notes that such evidence might arise in three ways in such cases,[8] and points out that it is reputation, and not character, which plaintiff claims is damaged.[9] It is also noted in Wigmore that the right of a parent to retain custody of his child may depend on a finding of the fitness of that person as a parent.[10]

Cases of recent vintage in New York which reaffirm the use of character (reputation) evidence in defamation cases are noted below.[11]

---

5. Id.

6. People v. Miller, 39 N.Y.2d 543, 384 N.Y.S.2d 741, 349 N.E.2d 841 (1976).

7. McCormick states that character evidence serves two general purposes, depending on whether it is directly in issue or not, thus:

> If a person's character is itself an issue in the case, then character evidence is crucial. But if the evidence of character merely is introduced as circumstantial evidence of what a person did or thought, it is less critical. Other, and probably better, evidence of the acts or state of mind usually should be available. Exclusion is therefore much more likely when the character evidence is offered to help prove that a person acted in one way or another.

McCormick § 186, at 787–88.

8. See 1A Wigmore § 70, at 1483–84:

> 1. A plea of justification, alleging the truth of the defamatory statement, may make the character of the plaintiff material because of the nature of the defamatory statement, which may impugn the plaintiff's character.
>
> 2. A plea of justification, alleging the truth of the defamatory statement, may make material the question of whether the plaintiff engaged in misconduct that reflects adversely on the plaintiff's character. Evidence to prove such misconduct is relevant, and so is character evidence that shows that the plaintiff had an inclination or tendency to engage in such misconduct.
>
> 3. An action for defamation, by its definition, involves alleged injury to reputation, and evidence showing that this reputation is good or bad is relevant in the question of damages, by way of aggravation and mitigation respectively. However, the *character* of the plaintiff is not in issue unless it is put in issue by a plea of justification of a defamatory statement that asserts, directly or indirectly, that the character of the plaintiff is bad.

(Emphasis in original.)

9. See point 3 in note 8 supra.

10. Id. § 69.1, at 1457.

11. In Brennan v. Commonwealth Bank & Trust Co., 65 A.D.2d 636, 636–37, 409 N.Y.S.2d 266, 268 (3d Dep't 1978), the court, in dictum, said that "while evidence of a party's reputation is admissible where his character is in issue (e.g., actions based upon libel or slander), such evidence is not admissible where, as here, it is intended solely to create an inference as to who the aggressor was * * *." In Burdick v. Shearson American Express, Inc., 160 A.D.2d 642, 559 N.Y.S.2d 506 (1st Dep't), appeal denied, 76 N.Y.2d 706, 560 N.Y.S.2d 988, 561 N.E.2d 888 (1990), plaintiff sued defendant for having stated that plaintiff had been fired because he committed forgery in signing his wife's name to certain checks. The court stated: "The trial court properly permitted testimony on behalf of the defense as to the plaintiff's character, reputation and professional misconduct, which was relevant and probative to a determination of whether the plaintiff had, in fact,

§ 402.1   RELEVANCY   Ch. 4

A defendant's use of the entrapment defense in criminal cases is somewhat difficult to categorize since it raises the question whether defendant was predisposed to committing such crimes or whether he was inveigled into it by the authorities. In this sense the matter could be discussed along with the rules governing character evidence in criminal cases generally. But Wigmore considers this a situation where the chief issue is the question of defendant's character, introduced into the case by the defendant as her main defense.[12] It is material to the establishment of her defense. In *People v. Calvano*[13] the Court of Appeals ruled that the defense of entrapment puts the defendant's character in issue and opens the door to the prosecution to introduce evidence of other similar crimes, both prior and subsequent to the crime charged.

Character can also be directly in issue in the context of a claim that an employer was negligent in hiring a person who possessed careless or dangerous tendencies. For example, in *Georges v. American Export Lines, Inc.*,[14] plaintiff sued the owner of a ship on which he served for injuries sustained in an assault by a fellow seaman, a third-party defendant impleaded by defendant owner. The Appellate Division stated that "[w]henever the character or reputation of a party is material to the establishment of a claim or defense, * * * it is said to be in issue and may be proved."[15] Thus, it was proper for the trial judge to allow plaintiff to produce witnesses to attest to the unfriendly nature of the third-party defendant. But the judge erred in not allowing the third-party defendant an opportunity to call character witnesses on his own behalf.[16] In a forfeiture case brought against real property, evidence of the reputation of an occupant's drug dealing was admissible to refute the owner's "innocent owner" defense.[17] By contrast, *Fanelli v. di Lorenzo*,[18] was a civil assault case where defendant, the assaulter, claimed he was drunk and was permitted at trial to offer evidence that when drunk he was nonviolent and mellow. The Appellate Division stated: "Evidence of character is not admissible in a civil case to raise the inference that a party acted in conformity therewith on the date in question * * *. Because proof of [defendant's] character was not necessary to establish his defense to plaintiff's cause of action, it was error to admit the

---

forged his wife's name to a variety of important financial documents, as well as to whether his employers improperly fired him and cited forgery as the reason therefor." Id. at 642, 559 N.Y.S.2d at 508.

12. 1A Wigmore § 70.3, at 1527–45. In Sorrells v. United States, 287 U.S. 435, 451–52, 53 S.Ct. 210, 216, 77 L.Ed. 413, 422 (1932), the Court stated:

> [I]f the defendant seeks acquittal by reason of entrapment he cannot complain of an appropriate and searching inquiry into his own conduct and predisposition as bearing upon that issue. If in consequence he suffers a disadvantage, he has brought it upon himself by reason of the nature of the defense.

13. 30 N.Y.2d 199, 331 N.Y.S.2d 430, 282 N.E.2d 322 (1972).

14. 77 A.D.2d 26, 432 N.Y.S.2d 165 (1st Dep't 1980).

15. Id. at 32, 432 N.Y.S.2d at 170.

16. See also Park v. N.Y. Central & H.R.R.R. Co., 155 N.Y. 215, 49 N.E. 674 (1898).

17. United States v. Certain Real Property, 945 F.2d 1252, 1260 (2d Cir.1991), appeal after remand, 990 F.2d 1250 (2d Cir.1993).

18. 187 A.D.2d 1004, 591 N.Y.S.2d 658 (4th Dep't 1992).

testimony * * *."[19]

When character is directly in issue, specific instances of conduct indicating the character trait can be proved.[20]

Library References:

West's Key No. Digests, Criminal Law ⚖375; Evidence ⚖106.

c. Character Evidence as Proof of Conduct in Civil Cases

The *Fanelli* case in subsection b, above, states the following rule in civil cases: "Evidence of character is not admissible in a civil case to raise the inference that a party acted in conformity therewith * * *."[21] Evidence of character in civil cases is only admissible when it is necessary to the establishment of a claim or defense.[22] In this respect the *Georges* case,[23] discussed above in subsection b, contains a misleading aspect. In addition to condoning evidence of the employee's aggressive character to show the owner should not have hired him (a legitimate use of character evidence on the issue of negligent hiring), the court also allowed plaintiff to produce evidence of his own friendly character. Plaintiff's character could only be relevant to show that he acted in conformity with his benign nature at the time of the affray. The *Georges* decision thus seems to be half right and half wrong.

While evidence of the parties' character traits for peaceableness would seem just as relevant in civil assault cases, as in criminal assault cases,[24] current case law in New York bars such proof on the civil side. In addition to the *Fanelli* and *Georges* cases, see other cases cited below.[25] The impropriety of character evidence has also been noted

---

19. Id. at 1005, 591 N.Y.S.2d at 659.

20. In addition to People v. Calvano, 30 N.Y.2d 199, 331 N.Y.S.2d 430, 282 N.E.2d 322 (1972), see People v. Mann, 31 N.Y.2d 253, 336 N.Y.S.2d 633, 288 N.E.2d 595 (1972); Park v. N.Y. Central & H.R.R.R. Co., 155 N.Y. 215, 49 N.E. 674 (1898); McCormick § 187, at 790, 791. The proposed New York Evidence Code, in § 405(b), would make provision for use of specific conduct evidence:

Specific instances of conduct. Whenever the character or a trait of character of a person is, as a matter of substantive law, an essential element of a crime, charge, claim, or defense, proof may also be made of specific instances of that person's conduct.

21. 187 A.D.2d 1004, 1005, 591 N.Y.S.2d 658, 659 (4th Dep't 1992).

22. See § 402.1(b) supra.

23. See note 14 supra.

24. The Proposed New York Evidence Code would allow character evidence in civil assault cases with this provision:

§ 404. **Evidence of character and of other crimes not generally admissible to prove conduct [PROPOSED]**

* * *

(a)(2) **Character of a party in a civil case.** Evidence of a pertinent character trait of a party [may be] offered by that party in a civil case, in which the underlying cause of action is predicated upon knowing or intentional conduct of that party that also violates the penal law, or offered by the adverse party to rebut the same.

25. O'Connell v. Jacobs, 181 A.D.2d 1064, 1065, 583 N.Y.S.2d 61, 63 (4th Dep't 1992), aff'd, 81 N.Y.2d 797, 595 N.Y.S.2d 388, 611 N.E.2d 289 (1993) (where there was little or no evidence that defendant was the assaulter, testimony based on handwriting analysis that defendant possessed personality traits of sadism, narcissism and self-centeredness should not have been allowed since this depicted defendant's character as proof that he acted in conformity therewith); Taggart v. Alexander's, Inc., 90 A.D.2d 542, 543, 455 N.Y.S.2d 117, 119 (2d Dep't 1982)(it was error for defense counsel to put in evidence that defendant, the al-

where defendant physician in a medical malpractice case testified that he performed his services gratuitously,[26] in a suit brought against an insurer to recover for a fire loss where defendant produced proof of plaintiff's disposition toward his ex-wife who lived in the destroyed house,[27] and in a medical malpractice suit where defendant sought to prove that plaintiff, because of his alcoholism, used poor judgment in insisting on certain surgery.[28]

Sometimes it is difficult in civil cases to distinguish between character evidence and evidence of habit. In certain circumstances evidence of habit is admissible;[29] but where the evidence would simply describe traits, or disposition toward a certain behavioral pattern, we are dealing with character evidence and inadmissibility is the rule if the purpose is to prove conformity of conduct with character.[30]

Library References:

West's Key No. Digests, Evidence ⚖106.

d. Character Evidence as Proof of Conduct in Criminal Cases

As discussed in § 404.1(a) *infra*, the prosecutor in a criminal case may not introduce, during her case in chief, evidence of the defendant's general character or propensity for criminal behavior. The defendant, however, has the option to present evidence of a character trait that would tend to negate any idea of predisposition to the crime charged[31]— say, good reputation for peacefulness to dispel the notion that defendant would commit the charged assault. This tactic presents a risk because the door is then opened for the prosecutor to put on "bad" character

leged assaulter, was a minister, a church teacher, and a person who would never utter profanity). See also Beach v. Richtmyer, 275 App.Div. 466, 467–69, 90 N.Y.S.2d 332, 334–35 (3d Dep't 1949). The question in Beach was whether defendant's chauffeur was driving defendant's car with permission at the time of the accident in which the chauffeur was killed. Several witnesses, prominent in the community, were allowed to testify that the chauffeur's reputation for "general moral character" was good. This was ruled error since whatever relevance there might be in such evidence, the door should not be opened to it in civil cases.

26. Lium v. Ploski, 87 A.D.2d 860, 860, 449 N.Y.S.2d 297, 298 (2d Dep't 1982) ("We agree that this line of questioning was impermissible since character or reputation was not in issue * * * and evidence of Dr. Ploski's charitable nature could only serve to prejudice the jury in his favor.").

27. Liberto v. Worcester Mut. Ins., 87 A.D.2d 477, 479, 452 N.Y.S.2d 74, 76 (2d Dep't 1982)(the ex-wife's complaints were not admissible to show that plaintiff acted in conformity by setting the fire, and neither was the evidence admissible to prove his motive since it was based on double hearsay).

28. Davis v. Blum, 70 A.D.2d 583, 584, 416 N.Y.S.2d 57, 59 (2d Dep't 1979) ("In our opinion, such evidence is akin to evidence of character and habit which is generally inadmissible in civil cases to raise the inference that a party acted in a particular way on the occasion in issue * * *.").

29. See § 406.1 infra.

30. See McCormick § 189, at 795; Model Code of Evidence, at 190–91.

31. People v. Aharonowicz, 71 N.Y.2d 678, 681, 529 N.Y.S.2d 736, 737, 525 N.E.2d 458, 459 (1988). See 1A Wigmore § 56. Wigmore notes that character evidence is perfectly relevant (if, of course, related to the crime charged), but admissibility is closed to the prosecution initially because of its prejudicial effect. "Character being thus relevant, it follows that a *defendant may offer his good character* to evidence the improbability of his doing the act charged * * *." Id. at 450 (emphasis in original).

witnesses to rebut the defendant's witnesses,[32] and to cross-examine defendant's witnesses for impeachment purposes by asking them if they have heard of specific incidents of defendant's bad conduct,[33] none of which would have been permissible had defendant not ventured into the area.

Defendant's character—how proved. As a practical matter, the criminal defendant will not choose to exercise this option if her history is not relatively clear of convictions, bad acts, and even arrests.[34] Normally defendant will produce witnesses who will testify to defendant's *reputation* in the community for the character trait implicated by the crime in issue.[35] The character witness may not state an opinion or relate specific incidents which demonstrate the trait.[36] The "community" is "wherever an individual's associations are of such quantity and quality as to permit him to be personally observed by a sufficient number of individuals to give reasonable assurance of reliability";[37] one's "residential neighborhood" is regarded as too restrictive.[38]

New York doggedly adheres to the rule that defendant may prove only her *reputation* for sobriety, honesty, peaceableness, or whatever the pertinent character trait may be. The witness' own *opinion* as to defendant's character may not be voiced. This prompted a dissent from Judge Titone in *People v. Barber*,[39] in which he urged a change in this rule.[40]

---

32. McCormick § 191, at 815–16.

33. Michelson v. United States, 335 U.S. 469, 69 S.Ct. 213, 93 L.Ed. 168 (1948); People v. Kass, 25 N.Y.2d 123, 302 N.Y.S.2d 807, 250 N.E.2d 219 (1969); People v. Schwartzman, 24 N.Y.2d 241, 299 N.Y.S.2d 817, 247 N.E.2d 642, cert. denied, 396 U.S. 846, 90 S.Ct. 103, 24 L.Ed.2d 96 (1969); People v. Beaulieu, 40 A.D.2d 942, 339 N.Y.S.2d 234 (4th Dep't 1972).

34. Michelson, note 33 supra.

35. See People v. Miller, 35 N.Y.2d 65, 68, 358 N.Y.S.2d 733, 736, 315 N.E.2d 785, 787 (1974)("Thus, when a defendant introduces evidence of good character, such testimony must relate to the traits involved in the charge against him"). In People v. Sullivan, 177 A.D.2d 673, 576 N.Y.S.2d 599 (2d Dep't 1991), leave for appeal denied, 79 N.Y.2d 864, 580 N.Y.S.2d 736, 588 N.E.2d 771 (1992), defendant was charged with reckless endangerment and assault, and thus his proposal to have witnesses testify to his reputation for truth and veracity was property rejected. See also People v. Berge, 103 A.D.2d 1041, 478 N.Y.S.2d 433 (4th Dep't 1984)(it was improper for the character witness to testify that defendant was not a drug dealer or user since this was hearsay—witness could only testify to reputation for law abidingness, but not to the specific acts he mentioned).

36. People v. Barber, 74 N.Y.2d 653, 655–56, 543 N.Y.S.2d 365, 366–67, 541 N.E.2d 394, 395–96 (1989).

37. People v. Bouton, 50 N.Y.2d 130, 139, 428 N.Y.S.2d 218, 223, 405 N.E.2d 699, 704 (1980).

38. Id. at 140, 428 N.Y.S.2d at 223, 405 N.E.2d at 704.

39. 74 N.Y.2d 653, 655–56, 543 N.Y.S.2d 365, 366–67, 541 N.E.2d 394, 395–96 (1989).

40. Judge Titone states:

In this case involving an attempted murder charge, defendant contends that he should be afforded a new trial because of the trial court's errors in restricting his character witnesses' testimony to reputation evidence and in repeatedly precluding their testimony as to their own opinions of his character. While the existing precedent in this State may not support defendant's position, the weight of Federal and sister State authority, as well as simple common sense, does.

Under traditional evidentiary principles in New York, a defendant may attempt to establish his good character only by showing his general reputation in the community. The opinions of those who know him personally and have firsthand knowledge of his character are inadmissible (People v. Bouton, 50 N.Y.2d 130, 428 N.Y.S.2d 218, 405 N.E.2d 699 * * *). The rule is derived from People v. Van Gaasbeck (189 N.Y. 408, 82 N.E. 718),

§ 402.1 RELEVANCY Ch. 4

Since defendant is limited to proving her reputation when offering character to prove conduct in conformity therewith, her witnesses will testify that they are associated in the pertinent "community" and that defendant's reputation for the relevant character is good. The witness may, in effect, testify to a negative, i.e., that within the pertinent community she has never heard of defendant's reputation one way or the other and that therefore if her reputation is not bad, it must be good.[41]

Prosecution's cross-examination of defendant's character witnesses. In *Michelson v. United States*,[42] Justice Jackson wrote an extraordinary opinion in a case involving bribery of a federal revenue agent. Defendant put on five character witnesses, all of whom attested to his good reputation for honesty, truthfulness and for law abidingness. Each witness was asked on cross-examination whether he had ever heard that defendant had been arrested (at a time when they said they knew of his reputation) for receiving stolen goods. Each replied that he had not.

which was decided in 1907 and at a time when most American jurisdictions that had considered the question held that " 'character means the estimate in which the individual is held by the community and not the private opinion entertained of him by the witnesses who may be called to testify in reference to such fact' " (id., at 416, quoting Jackson v. State, 78 Ala. 471). The court adopted what was then the majority view because of "overwhelming considerations of practical convenience," namely the difficulty of ascertaining the truth of the specific occurrences underlying the witness's opinion and a concern that the admission of character evidence beyond reputation would lead to a proliferation of collateral factual disputes, thereby impeding the conduct of trial (People v. Van Gaasbeck, supra, at 417–418).

Whether it was the product of the pragmatic concerns of the time or, as one noted treatise argues (7 Wigmore, Evidence §§ 1981–1982, 1986 [Chadbourn rev ed]), the result of a cumulative misreading of prior precedent, the *Van Gaasbeck* restriction on proof of character has since been criticized as "archaic" and "paradoxical" (Michelson v. United States, 335 US 469, 486) and has been modified or rejected in a majority of jurisdictions, either by statute or judicial decision permitting opinion testimony as an alternative to reputation evidence * * *.

The *Van Gaasbeck* rule has fallen into disfavor because it, quite simply, does not promote the truth-seeking process. The rule is objectionable because it requires rejection of the more reliable form of proof, i.e., the opinions of those in a position to know the accused's character, while exposing the trier of fact to unverifiable hearsay of unknown origin. Further, it places the jury in the difficult position of having to evaluate the validity of so nebulous a concept as the opinion held of the defendant by the "general community," while the personal opinions of the testifying witnesses, which may readily be examined for credibility, bias and reliability through traditional forms of cross-examination, must be ignored. As Wigmore notes: "The Anglo-American rules of evidence have occasionally taken some curious twistings in the course of their development; but they have never done anything so curious in the way of shutting out evidential light as when they decided to exclude the person who knows as much as humanly can be known about the character of another, and have still admitted the secondhand, irresponsible product of multiplied guesses and gossip which we term 'reputation.' " (7 Wigmore, op. cit., at 244; accord, Jones, Evidence § 4:45, at 474; Morgan, Basic Problems of State and Federal Evidence, at 311 [Weinstein 5th ed.].) For these reasons, it has been said that "the rules * * * pertaining to the *method* of proving character [in New York] most urgently require reform * * *." [emphasis in original].

74 N.Y.2d at 655–56, 543 N.Y.S.2d at 336–67, 541 N.E.2d at 395–96.

The proposed New York Evidence Code § 405 provides that relevant character traits may be proved by either reputation or opinion.

41. People v. Van Gaasbeck, 189 N.Y. 408, 420, 82 N.E. 718, 722 (1907); Annot., 67 A.L.R. 1210 (negative proof of good character).

42. 335 U.S. 469, 69 S.Ct. 213, 93 L.Ed. 168 (1948).

Justice Jackson, in upholding the questioning, first recounted the rationale for the character evidence rule and the exception allowing a criminal defendant to introduce evidence of good character, and then pointed out that while this option is open to defendant, "it subjects his proof to tests of credibility designed to prevent him from profiting by a mere parade of partisans."[43] The prosecutor's cross-examination about the prior arrest, while certainly inadmissible for most any other purpose, did test the knowledge of the character witnesses as to defendant's reputation, with which they professed familiarity.[44] There is a potential for confusion here since this is one of the rare instances in which mere arrests may be inquired about as an impeachment technique. When a witness is cross-examined concerning his own prior conduct, mere arrests or indictments are irrelevant on the issue of that witness' character because they are only accusations.[45]

New York has adopted the *Michelson* rule. In *People v. Kuss*,[46] the Court of Appeals held that the prosecutor could ask defendant's character witnesses about specific instances in defendant's past to test their knowledge of defendant's character.[47] What basis must the prosecutor have to indicate that the specific incident actually took place? This question came up in *Kuss* where defendant challenged, but not very vigorously, the source of the prosecutor's information. The prosecutor's source appeared to be newspaper accounts, with respect to which the court stated:

> While persuasive arguments could be made as to the doubtful reliability of certain newspaper reports, these same considerations would apply with equal force to unsubstantiated rumors

---

43. Id. at 479, 69 S.Ct. at 220, 93 L.Ed. at 176.

44. Id. at 482–83, 69 S.Ct. at 221–22, 93 L.Ed. at 177. Justice Jackson stated:

A character witness may be cross-examined as to an arrest whether or not it culminated in a conviction, according to the overwhelming weight of authority. This rule is sometimes confused with that which prohibits cross-examination to credibility by asking a witness whether he himself has been arrested.

Arrest without more does not, in law any more than in reason, impeach the integrity or impair the credibility of a witness. It happens to the innocent as well as the guilty. Only a conviction, therefore, may be inquired about to undermine the trustworthiness of a witness.

Arrest without more may nevertheless impair or cloud one's reputation. * * *

The inquiry as to an arrest is permissible also because the prosecution has a right to test the qualifications of the witness to bespeak the community opinion. If one never heard the speculations and rumors in which even one's friends indulge upon his arrest, the jury may doubt whether he is capable of giving any very reliable conclusions as to his reputation. Id.

45. See § 608.2, at notes 19–20, infra. People v. Morrison, 195 N.Y. 116, 117–18, 88 N.E. 21, 22 (1909); People v. Cascone, 185 N.Y. 317, 334, 78 N.E. 287, 293 (1906); Dance v. Town of Southampton, 95 A.D.2d 442, 452–53, 467 N.Y.S.2d 203, 210 (2d Dep't 1983). The cross-examiner may, however, go into the misconduct underlying the arrest. See People v. Rahming, 26 N.Y.2d 411, 419, 311 N.Y.S.2d 292, 299, 259 N.E.2d 727, 732 (1970). See also Gedrin v. Long Island Jewish–Hillside Medical Center, 119 A.D.2d 799, 501 N.Y.S.2d 426 (2d Dep't 1986)(underlying facts of assault charge which resulted in adjournment in contemplation of dismissal and petit larceny charge which was reduced to disorderly conduct).

46. 32 N.Y.2d 436, 345 N.Y.S.2d 1002, 299 N.E.2d 249, reargument denied, 33 N.Y.2d 644, 347 N.Y.S.2d 1028, 301 N.E.2d 558 (1973), cert. denied, 415 U.S. 913, 94 S.Ct. 1408, 39 L.Ed.2d 467 (1974).

47. Id. at 443, 345 N.Y.S.2d at 1007, 294 N.E.2d at 213.

carried by the "grapevine," and in the past, the courts of this State have recognized no distinction between the report and the rumor. * * * The relevant consideration after all is not the truth or falsity of the particular account, but rather "the qualifications of the witness to bespeak the community opinion" [citing *Michelson*]. To this end the prosecutor may inquire of the witness to see if he has heard of a particular event which was likely to result in some comment in the community if not injury to the defendant's reputation.[48]

In *People v. Calvano*,[49] a character witness reported favorably on defendant's reputation for being "law abiding," and also testified to defendant's veracity because the credibility of defendant, who had also testified in his own behalf, had been impeached. On cross-examination of the character witness, the prosecutor asked whether the witness had heard that when defendant was ultimately arrested over a month after the date of the last crime charged, a hypodermic needle and a quantity of marijuana were found in his possession. Defendant argued that such acts subsequent to the times the crimes were committed were not relevant to the witness' knowledge of reputation as of the time of the crimes. The court evaded answering this question. Since the witness also testified as to defendant's veracity, he was reporting on defendant as of the time of the trial, thus validating questions as to his knowledge down to the time of the trial.[50]

The prosecutor may not ask the character witness whether she would change her mind about defendant's character if she knew that defendant committed the crime for which she was presently on trial.[51]

48. Id. at 444, 345 N.Y.S.2d at 1007–08, 299 N.E.2d at 253. See also People v. Alamo, 23 N.Y.2d 630, 298 N.Y.S.2d 681, 246 N.E.2d 496, cert. denied, 396 U.S. 879, 90 S.Ct. 156, 24 L.Ed.2d 137 (1969)(defendant's character witness was asked on cross-examination whether he had heard that defendant had been selling narcotics at Orchard Beach, and whether he had heard that defendant had been involved in four taxicab stickups, all of which was proper under the Michelson rule). In People v. Lediard, 80 A.D.2d 237, 438 N.Y.S.2d 540 (1st Dep't 1981), a character witness was asked whether he had heard that defendant had displayed a pistol to a bartender just prior to the crime charged. Aside from the fact there was no proof of this introduced at the trial, the question would not have tested the witness' knowledge of defendant's reputation and it was error to have allowed the prosecutor to ask the question. A similar situation is found in People v. Thompson, 75 A.D.2d 630, 426 N.Y.S.2d 829 (2d Dep't 1980), where the court held it error to allow the prosecutor to cross-examine the character witness concerning specific acts of misconduct occurring on the night the crime was committed.

The court in the Lediard case held on another point that cross-examination should be limited to questions concerning incidents involving the same character trait as the one in issue. 80 A.D.2d at 242, 438 N.Y.S.2d at 543. But see note 50 infra.

49. 30 N.Y.2d 199, 331 N.Y.S.2d 430, 282 N.E.2d 322 (1972).

50. Of course, this raises the question whether possession of the hypodermic needle and marijuana had any bearing on veracity. While the Legislature has said that character evidence may be rebutted by defendant's prior convictions of crimes which bear on the character trait in issue (Crim. Proc.Law § 60.40[2]), there is no such limitation on the sort of prior conviction that may be used to test a witness' knowledge of veracity. Thus, when a witness doubles as a character witness and a veracity witness, the *Calvano* court implies that he can be asked about whether he has heard of any of defendant's past indiscretions without regard to relatedness.

51. People v. Pryor, 70 A.D.2d 805, 806, 417 N.Y.S.2d 490, 492 (1st Dep't 1979). See also United States v. Oshatz, 912 F.2d 534 (2d Cir.1990), cert. denied, 500 U.S. 910, 111 S.Ct. 1695, 114 L.Ed.2d 89 (1991).

Such a question improperly assumes defendant's guilt of the crime charged.[52]

The character witness must be asked whether he *heard* of the specific incident, and not whether he had personal knowledge of it, since it is his knowledge of defendant's reputation that is being tested, not his own personal knowledge about the defendant.[53]

Prosecution's rebuttal. The prosecutor is permitted to rebut defendant's evidence of good character with witnesses who, assuming a proper foundation, will testify that defendant's reputation for the pertinent character trait is bad.[54] Additionally, Criminal Procedure Law § 60.40(2) provides:

> If a defendant in a criminal proceeding, through the testimony of a witness called by him, offers evidence of his good character, the people may independently prove any previous conviction of the defendant for an offense the commission of which would tend to negate any character trait or quality attributed to the defendant in such witness' testimony.

Thus, for example, a defendant in an assault case who introduces evidence of his good reputation for peacefulness opens the door to the prosecutor's use of defendant's prior convictions of violent crimes to rebut the character evidence.

Library References:

West's Key No. Digests, Criminal Law ⚖ 375.

e. The Effect of Character Evidence—Jury Charge

Where character evidence is in a case not as substantive evidence bearing on a claim or defense, but as proof that defendant acted in conformity with a pertinent good character trait, the question arises as to how the jury should treat the evidence. The answer is found in *People v. Miller*,[55] where defendant argued that the jury should be instructed that character evidence, standing alone, may be sufficient to create a reasonable doubt. In rejecting defendant's argument, the Court of Appeals adopted the views expressed in *People v. Trimarchi*:[56]

> Evidence of good character is not, of itself, sufficient to raise a reasonable doubt. Such evidence, in order to raise a reasonable doubt, must be believed by the jury. It then may, when considered with all the other evidence in the case, be sufficient to raise a reasonable doubt as to his guilt. This is upon the theory that good character may create a doubt against positive

---

52. People v. Lopez, 67 A.D.2d 624, 411 N.Y.S.2d 627 (1st Dep't), cert. denied, 444 U.S. 827, 100 S.Ct. 51, 62 L.Ed.2d 34 (1979).

53. People v. Lediard, 80 A.D.2d 237, 243, 438 N.Y.S.2d 540, 543–44 (1st Dep't 1981).

54. McCormick § 191, at 818. Such witnesses would have to meet the same qualifications as those called by the defendant. See notes 34–41 supra.

55. 35 N.Y.2d 65, 358 N.Y.S.2d 733, 315 N.E.2d 785 (1974).

56. 231 N.Y. 263, 131 N.E. 910 (1921). See also People v. Aharonowicz, 71 N.Y.2d 678, 529 N.Y.S.2d 736, 525 N.E.2d 458 (1988); People v. Gordon, 40 A.D.2d 835, 337 N.Y.S.2d 331 (2d Dep't 1972).

evidence, but this doubt against positive evidence is created only when in the judgment of the jury the character evidence is so good as to raise a doubt as to the truthfulness of the positive evidence tending to establish guilt.[57]

The *Miller* court refined this by stating:

> Character evidence does not exist in a vacuum, and its value, influence or the weight to be accorded it depends in great part upon the other evidence in the case. If accepted and believed, it becomes a fact to be weighed with the other facts. If the evidence of guilt against defendant is cumulative and reliable, the influence of contrary evidence of good character is likely to be slight. Under other circumstances, such evidence may be so good, if believed, as to create a reasonable doubt where without it none would exist.[58]

Library References:

West's Key No. Digests, Criminal Law ⚖︎776.

f. Character Trait of the Victim in a Homicide Case

In homicide cases where the defendant relies on self-defense, defendant may be able to show that the victim had a reputation for being a violent person. In *People v. Rodawald*,[59] the Court of Appeals held that evidence of the victim's reputation for violence was admissible on the issue of defendant's state of mind so long as the defendant knew the victim's reputation at the time of the affray. Similarly, in *People v. Miller*,[60] the court held that the victim's prior specific acts of violence against others, if known to the defendant, could be introduced to show defendant's state of mind. In *Matter of Robert S.*,[61] defendant was unaware of the victim's reputation or past acts at the time of the assault, but argued that the victim's past acts were nevertheless admissible to prove that in all probability he was the aggressor. The court was unwilling to so extend the rule. It is submitted, however, that the victim's aggressive nature is relevant and should be admissible to prove that his conduct conformed to his nature. In the latter situation, it would not matter whether defendant was aware of the victim's reputation.[62]

---

57. Trimarchi, 231 N.Y. at 266, 131 N.E. at 911.

58. Miller, 35 N.Y.2d at 69, 358 N.Y.S.2d at 736, 315 N.E.2d at 787. See also People v. Bouton, 50 N.Y.2d 130, 139, 428 N.Y.S.2d 218, 223, 405 N.E.2d 699, 704 (1980); 1 N.Y. Crim. Jury Instructions 691–94.

59. 177 N.Y. 408, 70 N.E. 1 (1904).

60. 39 N.Y.2d 543, 384 N.Y.S.2d 741, 349 N.E.2d 841 (1976).

61. 52 N.Y.2d 1046, 438 N.Y.S.2d 509, 420 N.E.2d 390 (1981).

62. Judge Cardamone, writing a concurrence in a habeas corpus review of a state conviction, said that in compelling cases trial judges ought to have discretion to admit evidence of the victim's propensity even though defendant knew nothing of it. He said that the New York restriction

not only, like sand thrown in the face of the wind, bucks the more enlightened modern trend, but also fails to recognize that the truth of whether a defendant is guilty or innocent is more likely to emerge by hearing the testimony of those possessing relevant facts, leaving the weight of such evidence to be determined, under proper instructions, by a jury.

Unlike Rule 404(a)(2) of the Federal Rules of Evidence, which specifically allows character evidence of the victim to prove action in conformity therewith, the Proposed New York Evidence Code § 404 makes no provision whatsoever regarding evidence of the victim's reputation. The comment states that "this evidence simply raises issues of relevancy under CE 401 and CE 403"[63] which would presumably leave the door open for a change in New York law by the Court of Appeals.

Library References:

West's Key No. Digests, Homicide ⚖188(2).

g. Character Evidence Used to Impeach, Generally

The use of character evidence as a general impeachment device is dealt with elsewhere in this work.[64] Witnesses may be impeached on the basis of their reputation for untruthfulness,[65] or on the basis of their prior convictions[66] or prior bad acts.[67] It has long been accepted that the fact that a witness has been convicted of a crime or has committed bad acts impeaches credibility by casting doubt on the witness' character for truthfulness.[68] If the witness is a criminal defendant, however, the decision in *People v. Sandoval*,[69] imposes certain limitations.

Library References:

West's Key No. Digests, Witnesses ⚖333-362.

h. Proposed New York Evidence Code

The pertinent proposed code provisions on the topic of character evidence are set forth in the note.[70]

Williams v. Lord, 996 F.2d 1481 (2d Cir. 1993), cert. denied, ___ U.S. ___, 114 S.Ct. 1073, 127 L.Ed.2d 391 (1994). The Second Circuit panel felt bound by the New York rule regarding the defendant's knowledge, seeing this as simply an evidence rule with no constitutional overtones.

The following hypothetical aids the argument for admissibility: Suppose that the defendant, immediately after a minor traffic accident, is assaulted by the driver of the other car who is a complete stranger. In self-defense, the defendant strikes a fatal blow. Should defendant be deprived of evidence concerning the victim's quick temper and past abusive and assaultive behavior?

63. Comment, Proposed New York Evidence Code, p. 44.

64. See §§ 608.0-609.2 infra.

65. § 608.1 infra.

66. §§ 609.1 and 609.2 infra.

67. § 608.2 infra.

68. Derrick v. Wallace, 217 N.Y. 520, 525, 112 N.E. 440, 442 (1916) ("Evidence of conviction * * * impeaches the general character for truth and veracity.")

69. 34 N.Y.2d 371, 357 N.Y.S.2d 849, 314 N.E.2d 413 (1974).

70. § 404. **Evidence of character and of other crimes not generally admissible to prove conduct [PROPOSED]**

(a) **Character evidence generally.** Evidence of a person's character or trait of character is not admissible for the purpose of proving that such person acted in conformity therewith on a particular occasion, except:

(1) **Character of accused in a criminal case.** Evidence of a pertinent trait of character of an accused offered by the accused, or by the prosecution to rebut the character evidence offered by the accused.

(2) **Character of a party in a civil case.** Evidence of a pertinent character trait or a party offered by that party in a civil case, in which the underlying cause of action is predicated upon knowing or intentional conduct of that party that also violates the penal law, or offered by the adverse party to rebut the same.

§ 402.2 Federal

Federal Rules of Evidence 404[1] and 405[2] contain fairly precise guidelines for the use of character evidence and the sort of proof involved. Rule 404(a)(1) codifies the traditional rules regarding character evidence in criminal cases by providing that the defendant is free to introduce evidence of his good character to show that he acted in accord

(3) Character of witness. Evidence of the character of a witness as provided in sections 607, 608 and 609 of this chapter.

* * *

§ 405. Methods of proving character [PROPOSED]

(a) Reputation or opinion. Whenever evidence of character or a trait of character of a person is admissible, proof may be made by testimony as to reputation or by testimony in the form of an opinion subject to the requirements of section 701 of this chapter.

(b) Specific instances of conduct. Whenever the character or a trait of character of a person is, as a matter of substantive law, an essential element of a crime, charge, claim, or defense, proof may also be made of specific instances of that person's conduct.

(c) Inquiry into specific acts and proof of prior convictions.

(1) Specific acts. On cross-examination of a character witness, a good faith inquiry upon a reasonable basis is allowable into relevant specific instances of conduct; provided, however, a character witness on behalf of an accused or a party may not be asked on cross-examination whether the witness's testimony would be different if the witness knew that the defendant or party committed the crime or act at issue in the instant trial.

(2) Prior convictions. Whenever an accused or a party offers evidence of a pertinent character trait, pursuant to paragraph one or two of subdivision (a) of section 404 of this article, the prosecution or the adverse party may offer to prove any conviction of the accused or the party for an offense the commission of which would tend to negate any character trait or quality attributed to the accused or the party in the character testimony offered by the accused or the party.

§ 402.2

1. Rule 404. Character Evidence Not Admissible to Prove Conduct; Exceptions; Other Crimes

(a) Character evidence generally. Evidence of a person's character or a trait of character is not admissible for the purpose of proving action in conformity therewith on a particular occasion, except:

(1) Character of accused. Evidence of a pertinent trait of character offered by an accused, or by the prosecution to rebut the same;

(2) Character of victim. Evidence of a pertinent trait of character of the victim of the crime offered by an accused, or by the prosecution to rebut the same, or evidence of a character trait of peacefulness of the victim offered by the prosecution in a homicide case to rebut evidence that the victim was the first aggressor;

(3) Character of witness. Evidence of the character of a witness, as provided in rules 607, 608, and 609.

(b) Other crimes, wrongs, or acts. Evidence of other crimes, wrongs, or acts is not admissible to prove the character of a person in order to show action in conformity therewith. It may, however, be admissible for other purposes, such as proof of motive, opportunity, intent, preparation, plan, knowledge, identity, or absence of mistake or accident, provided that upon request by the accused, the prosecution in a criminal case shall provide reasonable notice in advance of trial, or during trial if the court excuses pretrial notice on good cause shown, of the general nature of any such evidence it intends to introduce at trial.

2. Rule 405. Methods of Proving Character

(a) Reputation or opinion. In all cases in which evidence of character or a trait of character of a person is admissible, proof may be made by testimony as to reputation or by testimony in the form of an opinion. On cross-examination, inquiry is allowable into relevant specific instances of conduct.

(b) Specific instances of conduct. In cases in which character or a trait of character of a person is an essential element of a charge, claim, or defense, proof may also be made of specific instances of that person's conduct.

therewith. Virtually the same opportunities are then open to the prosecution to cross-examine the character witnesses and to rebut this evidence as discussed in the last section. The Federal Rules, however, have no analogue to New York Criminal Procedure Law § 60.40(2), which allows rebuttal by evidence of defendant's convictions. In federal courts, then, rebuttal is limited to evidence of defendant's bad reputation for the character trait in issue, or the witness' opinion regarding the character trait.[3] Rule 404(a)(2) permits the defendant to introduce evidence of the victim's pertinent character trait as circumstantial evidence that the victim acted in conformity with such character.[4] Furthermore, in homicide cases where defendant produces evidence that the victim was the first aggressor, whether by evidence of the victim's character or otherwise, the prosecution may offer evidence of the victim's character for peacefulness. This goes considerably beyond the New York case law discussed in the last section.[5]

Federal Rule 405(a) also exceeds the New York case law in allowing character to be proven by the witness' opinion as well as by reputation evidence. The second sentence of subdivision (a) incorporates the *Michelson* impeachment rule as discussed in the last section. Specific instances demonstrating a party's character may be offered under Rule 405(b) where character is in issue, i.e., "an essential element of a charge, claim, or defense." As is true under New York case law, certain issues in civil cases could be covered under this provision.[6]

The Second Circuit in *United States v. Pujana–Mena*,[7] discussed at length the question of jury instructions concerning character evidence in criminal cases and concluded that defendant is not entitled to a charge that reasonable doubt may be found from defendant's character evidence standing alone, even where defendant relies heavily or even entirely on

---

3. McCormick § 191, at 818. See United States v. Benedetto, 571 F.2d 1246, 1250 (2d Cir.1978).

4. On its face, the rule is applicable with respect to any type of crime, but Rule 412, described in § 412.2 infra, circumscribes evidence about the character of rape victims.

5. Williams v. Lord, 996 F.2d 1481 (2d Cir.1993), cert. denied, ___ U.S. ___, 114 S.Ct. 1073, 127 L.Ed.2d 391 (1994)(Judge Cardamone in concurring opinion criticized the New York rule which disallows evidence of the victim's character except where the defendant knew of it; such evidence is admissible only on the issue of defendant's state of mind). Under the Federal Rules, the victim's character, when offered as circumstantial evidence that the victim was the first aggressor, may be proven only by opinion or reputation. Fed.R.Evid. 405(a). See also United States v. Schatzle, 901 F.2d 252, 256 (2d Cir.1990)(district court did not abuse discretion in disallowing evidence of assault victim's prior specific act of aggression to prove that victim had quick-tempered personality and therefore instigated the assault). If the defendant contends that he acted reasonably based on what he knew about the victim, defendant should be able to prove knowledge of the victim's reputation and of specific instances of the victim's violent nature. Government of the Virgin Islands v. Carino, 631 F.2d 226, 229 (3d Cir.1980).

6. For example, in Sharon v. Time, Inc., 103 F.R.D. 86, 92–94 (S.D.N.Y.1984), the court discusses the propriety of evidence of similar instances or acts in defamation cases on the issue of actual malice and the right to punitive damages, citing Curtis Publishing Co. v. Butts and Associated Press v. Walker, 388 U.S. 130, 87 S.Ct. 1975, 18 L.Ed.2d 1094 (1967). In the Sharon case, however, the court ruled that defendant could not show instances of plaintiff's previous brutality toward Arabs in order to show that he acted in conformity on later occasions.

7. 949 F.2d 24 (2d Cir.1991).

character evidence. Although some support for a "standing alone" rule might be found in *Michelson v. United States*,[8] close analysis by the *Pujana-Mena* court resulted in approval of the following charge:

> You have heard testimony that the defendant has a good reputation for honesty in the community where he lives and works and for truthfulness. Along with all the other evidence you have heard, you may take into consideration what you believe about the defendant's honesty and truthfulness when you decide whether the government has proven, beyond a reasonable doubt, that the defendant committed the crime.[9]

Other points of particular interest in the Second Circuit caselaw are that defendant's character witness must be able to demonstrate her own familiarity with defendant's reputation, and not be just a private investigator who questions people at the barbershop and the church.[10] Nor can defendant offer proof of good character by witnesses who testify to his specific good acts.[11] The reputation attested to must be relevant to the character trait in issue,[12] and the prosecutor in cross-examining defendant's character witnesses may not ask their views concerning facts in the crime charged.[13] Merely by taking the stand defendant does not put her character in issue; she must call character witnesses.[14]

Library References:

West's Key No. Digests, Criminal Law ⚙ 375; Evidence ⚙ 106.

---

8. 335 U.S. 469, 476, 69 S.Ct. 213, 219, 93 L.Ed. 168, 174 (1948).

9. 949 F.2d at 27. Additionally, the court stated: "Even where it is accompanied by a charge instructing the jury to consider *all* the evidence in the case, a "standing alone" charge still unnecessarily flags character evidence and suggests to the jury that they give it heightened significance without regard to the other evidence." Id. at 31 (emphasis in original).

10. United States v. Perry, 643 F.2d 38, 52 (2d Cir.), cert. denied sub nom., Dewees v. United States, 454 U.S. 835, 102 S.Ct. 138, 70 L.Ed.2d 115 (1981).

11. United States v. Benedetto, 571 F.2d 1246, 1249, 1250 (2d Cir.1978) (improper character evidence submitted by defendant would not justify prosecution rebuttal evidence of specific bad acts); Sharon v. Time, Inc., 103 F.R.D. 86, 93, 94 (S.D.N.Y.1984)(defendant could not show instances of plaintiff's previous brutality toward Arabs in order to show that he acted in conformity on later occasions); United States v. Wilson, 586 F.Supp. 1011 (S.D.N.Y.1983), aff'd, 750 F.2d 7 (2d Cir. 1984), cert. denied, 479 U.S. 839, 107 S.Ct. 143, 93 L.Ed.2d 85 (1986).

12. United States v. Lamont, 565 F.2d 212, 226 (2d Cir.1977), cert. denied, 435 U.S. 914, 98 S.Ct. 1467, 55 L.Ed.2d 505 (1978)(defendant's reputation for truth and veracity not relevant to charge based on fraudulent use of the mails, and could only be used were she to testify and her testimony were impeached).

13. United States v. Oshatz, 912 F.2d 534 (2d Cir.1990), cert. denied, 500 U.S. 910, 111 S.Ct. 1695, 114 L.Ed.2d 89 (1991); United States v. Paccione, 949 F.2d 1183, 1202 (2d Cir.1991), cert. denied, 505 U.S. 1220, 112 S.Ct. 3029, 120 L.Ed.2d 900 (1992)(here the objectionable question to the character witness was: "Are you aware, Ms. Tanella, that on the permit application in the area, in the part of the permit application regarding the New Hanover Incinerator, John McDonald forged the name of another individual and wrote the name of another individual on that application?").

14. United States v. Tomaiolo, 249 F.2d 683 (2d Cir.1957), rev'd, 280 F.2d 411 (2d Cir.1960), rev'd, 286 F.2d 568 (2d Cir.1961), aff'd, 317 F.2d 324 (2d Cir.1963).

403 [Reserved]

404 Uncharged Crimes

§ 404.1 New York

a. Generally

As discussed in § 402.1(d) *supra*, a criminal defendant's character cannot be made the object of evidence offered by the prosecution during its direct case. As Judge Cardozo observed, "In a very real sense a defendant starts his life afresh when he stands before a jury, a prisoner at the bar."[1] The only object of such evidence would be to show the jury that defendant possessed a propensity for committing the crime charged, and this is not open to the prosecution in its case in chief.[2]

This section and the next take up the subject of the exceptions to the rule prohibiting the prosecutor from producing such evidence. In general terms, the question here is whether evidence of uncharged crimes may be introduced by the prosecutor based on its alleged relevance to a particular issue in the case, even when defendant does not offer exculpatory evidence of his good character.

The dangers of uncharged crimes evidence are set forth in *People v. Lewis*:[3]

> Evidence of a defendant's prior uncharged crimes may have some probative value; indeed, Wigmore contends that such evidence is objectionable because juries attribute too much significance to it * * *. For that reason it is usually excluded because it may (1) require defendant to meet a charge of which he had no notice; (2) raise collateral issues and direct the attention of the jury away from the crime charged; or (3) result in the proof of the prior offenses being taken by the jury as justifying a condemnation of the defendant irrespective of his guilt of the offenses charged * * *.[4]

Despite these reasons for excluding evidence of uncharged crimes, such evidence is often deemed admissible under certain exceptions. In his remarkably researched, instructive and entertaining opinion in *People v. Molineux*,[5] Judge Werner in 1901 analyzed the five main exceptions for the admission of uncharged crimes. In that case defendant was charged with the poisoning death of the hapless victim who took a potion disguised as Bromo Seltzer for a headache. At trial, the prosecution was

---

§ 404.1

1. People v. Zackowitz, 254 N.Y. 192, 197, 172 N.E. 466, 468 (1930).

2. Id. It was error, said Judge Cardozo, for the trial judge to have allowed the prosecutor to prove that defendant possessed several weapons in his apartment. Defendant admitted shooting the victim, and the issue was whether he shot the victim as the result of a premeditated plan, or in the heat of passion. Evidence of the weapons could serve only to prejudice the defendant in the eyes of the jury as one who was predisposed to violence.

3. 69 N.Y.2d 321, 514 N.Y.S.2d 205, 506 N.E.2d 915 (1987).

4. Id. at 325, 514 N.Y.S.2d at 207, 506 N.E.2d at 916–17.

5. 168 N.Y. 264, 61 N.E. 286 (1901).

§ 404.1

allowed to introduce evidence of an earlier poisoning death which was linked to the defendant. A majority of the Court of Appeals found this cause for reversal on the general rule that the prosecution cannot be allowed to prove an uncharged crime for the purpose of producing an inference that defendant must have committed the charged crime—the jury was as liable to convict him of the uncharged crime as the charged crime. However, if the uncharged crime had been relevant to some issue other than mere criminal propensity, there might have been grounds for admissibility. Thus, "evidence of other crimes is competent to prove the specific crime charged if it tends to establish (1) motive; (2) intent; (3) the absence of mistake or accident; (4) a common scheme or plan embracing the commission of two or more crimes so related to each other that proof of one tends to establish the other; (5) the identity of the person charged with the commission of the crime on trial."[6] It was noted that "these exceptions to the rule cannot be stated with categorical precision,"[7] and in recent times they have been held not to be exclusive.[8] In *Molineux* Judge Werner took up each of the exceptions in great detail.[9]

---

6. Id. at 293, 61 N.E. at 294.

7. Id.

8. See, e.g., People v. Stanard, 32 N.Y.2d 143, 344 N.Y.S.2d 331, 297 N.E.2d 77 (1973)(evidence of other criminal activity may sometimes be necessary to provide background so that the charged crime is more easily understood).

9. *Motive*: Example among many—"[O]n the trial of a husband for the murder of his wife, evidence of criminal proceedings against the defendant for failure to support his family, made ten months before the murder, was properly held admissible upon the question of motive." In Molineux, however, the earlier poisoning suggested no motive whatsoever. 168 N.Y. at 296, 61 N.E. at 295.

Intent: Example among many—"On the trial of an indictment for obtaining goods by false representations, similar representations made by the defendant to creditors from whom goods had been previously purchased by him were held admissible to prove intent." In Molineux, however, nothing about the earlier poisoning suggested why defendant should commit the second one. Id. at 298, 61 N.E. at 296.

Absence of mistake or accident: Example among many—"[T]he defendant was indicted for the murder of her child, an infant nine days old, whose death was caused by suffocation while he was in bed with his mother. The defense was accident. To rebut this defense, testimony was received to show that five other children of the defendant had all died in infancy." In Molineux, however, there was no need to produce such evidence; because of the way the crime was committed, there could be no defense of accident. Id. at 302–03, 61 N.E. at 298–99.

Common scheme or plan: Example among many—"[T]he defendant was indicted and tried for the crime of robbery in the first degree. The evidence disclosed that a number of masked men entered the apartment of the janitor of a bank and forcibly took his key to the bank. The bank was burglarized on the same occasion. The two crimes were held so connected that evidence of the burglary was deemed competent to connect the defendant with the robbery." In Molineux, however, no such integral connection was found between the two poisonings. Id. at 307, 61 N.E. at 301.

Identity: Example—Here there is a dearth of examples and in fact several are used which could more readily be placed under common scheme or plan. In recent years this exception has developed under the modus operandi theory, or the idea that the two crimes were committed in such a similar, and perhaps unique, manner as to identify the same person as the perpetrator of each. This will be further developed in the text. In Molineux, however, aside from the fact that each victim was dispatched with poison, and certain other similarities, there was no conclusive evidence that defendant had, in fact, committed the previous murder. Id. at 316, 61 N.E. at 303. The identity exception caused disagreement among the judges, three of them dissenting on this point and concluding that it should apply.

Before addressing the individual exceptions, the general framework governing the introduction of uncharged crimes will be reviewed. *People v. Ventimiglia*,[10] provides the modern cornerstone for this framework. First, even though evidence may fit one of the *Molineux* exceptions, it must also be tested by the prejudice vis-à-vis relevance balance. The evidence should be "directly probative" of some specific issue in the case other than the character of the defendant. Such probative value must then be weighed against the prejudicial effect, i.e., the danger that the jury will misuse the evidence as general propensity.[11] Additionally, if the evidence fits an exception, it should not be admissible if the point is established without it; in such case it would only be cumulative.[12] Furthermore, *Molineux* exceptions are "merely illustrative" and "not exhaustive."[13] After restating these principles, the court in *Ventimiglia* added a procedural feature: a hearing must be held to determine the admissibility of the uncharged crimes "[w]hether some time prior to trial, just before the trial begins or just before the witness testifies," depending on the circumstances. "The court should then assess how the evidence came into the case and the relevance and probativeness of, and necessity for it against its prejudicial effect, and either admit or exclude it in total, or admit it without the prejudicial parts when that can be done without distortion of its meaning. * * *"[14] The burden is on the prosecutor to furnish a basis for the introduction of such testimony.[15]

What degree of proof is needed to show that defendant was involved in the uncharged crime? In *People v. Robinson*,[16] the Court of Appeals adopted the clear and convincing standard, at least with respect to the identity exception, as a requisite for admissibility. It is not clear whether the preponderance standard might be permissible with respect to exceptions other than identity.[17] In *Robinson* it was noted that a

---

10. 52 N.Y.2d 350, 438 N.Y.S.2d 261, 420 N.E.2d 59 (1981).

11. Id. at 359, 438 N.Y.S.2d at 264, 420 N.E.2d at 62. See also People v. Hudy, 73 N.Y.2d 40, 538 N.Y.S.2d 197, 535 N.E.2d 250 (1988), where the court stated:

Admissibility of evidence under these principles is determined by reference to a two-part inquiry * * *. The first level of this inquiry requires the proponent of the evidence, as a threshold matter, to identify some issue, *other than mere criminal propensity*, to which the evidence is relevant * * *. Once such a showing is made, the court must go on to weigh the evidence's probative worth against its potential for mischief to determine whether it should ultimately be placed before the fact finder. This weighing process is discretionary, but the threshold problem of identifying a specific issue, other than propensity, to which the evidence pertains poses a question of law * * *.

Id. at 54, 538 N.Y.S.2d at 206, 535 N.E.2d at 258–59 (emphasis in original).

12. 52 N.Y.2d at 360, 438 N.Y.S.2d at 264, 420 N.E.2d at 62.

13. See notes 7–8 supra.

14. 52 N.Y.2d at 362, 438 N.Y.S.2d at 266, 420 N.E.2d at 64. Defendant has a right to be present at the hearing. People v. Spotford, 85 N.Y.2d 593, 627 N.Y.S.2d 295, 650 N.E.2d 1296 (1995).

15. People v. Colas, 206 A.D.2d 183, 187, 619 N.Y.S.2d 702, 705 (1st Dep't 1994), citing Ventimiglia, 52 N.Y.2d at 361–62, 438 N.Y.S.2d at 265, 420 N.E.2d at 63.

16. 68 N.Y.2d 541, 548–49, 510 N.Y.S.2d 837, 841, 503 N.E.2d 485, 489 (1986).

17. The best guess is that the clear and convincing test is applicable only in identity cases. In Robinson the court cited United States v. Beechum, 582 F.2d 898 (5th Cir. 1978), cert. denied, 440 U.S. 920, 99 S.Ct. 1244, 59 L.Ed.2d 472 (1979), for the proposition that a "much greater degree of similarity between the charged crime and the uncharged crime is required when the evidence of the other crime is introduced to prove identity than when it is introduced to prove state of mind." 68 N.Y.2d at 548, 510 N.Y.S.2d at 841, 503 N.E.2d at 489.

majority of the federal courts had applied the clear and convincing standard with respect to the identity exception.[18] But in a more recent case, *Huddleston v. United States*,[19] the United States Supreme Court prescribed the preponderance rule in a case involving the intent exception without any indication that a higher standard should be applied to the identity exception. The *Huddleston* court also said that the question of defendant's participation in the uncharged crime was to be determined by the jury, not the trial judge.[20] The New York rule on this is not clear, the *Robinson* court finding it unnecessary to decide the question.[21]

The Proposed New York Evidence Code § 404(b) codifies the *Molineux* rule and its exceptions and provides procedural detail for the prosecutor's giving notice of an intention to offer this evidence.[22]

b. Motive

People v. Mees,[23] is one of the few Court of Appeals cases illustrating this exception. There it was held proper for the trial court to have admitted evidence that a charge for assaulting the homicide victim was pending against defendant at the time of the homicide, since this would tend to demonstrate the motive for the homicide. *Terpstra v. Niagara*

---

18. 68 N.Y.2d at 548–59, 510 N.Y.S.2d at 841, 503 N.E.2d at 489.

19. 485 U.S. 681, 108 S.Ct. 1496, 99 L.Ed.2d 771 (1988).

20. Id. at 689, 108 S.Ct. at 1501, 99 L.Ed.2d at 782.

21. 68 N.Y.2d at 550 n.1, 510 N.Y.S.2d at 842, 503 N.E.2d at 490. It was stated: "But to the extent that the evidence of defendant's identity as the perpetrator of the uncharged crime is unclear, or is called into question by defendant's rebuttal evidence, the case becomes a trial within a trial which may result in jury confusion." Id.

22. § 404. **Evidence of character and of other crimes not generally admissible to prove conduct [PROPOSED]**

* * *

(b) **Other crimes, wrongs or acts.** Evidence of other crimes, wrongs or acts is not admissible to prove the character of a person in order to show that such person acted in conformity therewith on a particular occasion. It may, however, be admissible for other purposes, such as proving motive, opportunity, intent, preparation, common scheme or plan, knowledge, identity or absence of mistake or accident.

(1) **Notice.** Upon request of the opposing party, the proponent of evidence pursuant to this subdivision shall make known to all parties the proponent's intention to offer such evidence and its particulars sufficiently in advance of offering the evidence to provide them with a fair opportunity to meet it.

(2) **Criminal cases—notice.** After a request in a criminal case, when the prosecution or the accused intends to offer evidence pursuant to this subdivision, notification shall be made immediately prior to the commencement of jury selection, except that the court may, in its discretion, order such notification and make its determination within a period of three days, excluding Saturdays, Sundays and holidays, prior to the commencement of jury selection.

(3) **Time of determination and burden of proof.** At the request of the accused, or the prosecution, the determination of the admissibility of such evidence shall whenever practicable be made before the commencement of trial or hearing. The burden of proof governing the determination of a preliminary factual question under this subdivision shall be governed by paragraph three of subdivision (b) of section 104 of this chapter.

(4) **Remedy.** To remedy the prejudice from the failure to give notice, the court, pursuant to section 107 of this chapter, shall make any order the interests of justice require.

23. 47 N.Y.2d 997, 420 N.Y.S.2d 214, 394 N.E.2d 283 (1979).

Fire Ins. Co.,[24] is another example. The question whether an insurance claimant set the fire for which he sought to recover could be aided in its resolution by evidence that he had collected insurance on a series of previous fires. This evidence was said to bear on motive.[25] And where defendant would have been charged with a parole violation were he arrested, evidence of his parole status was admissible at his trial for shooting the officer who would have arrested him.[26]

There must, of course, be the necessary relationship between the crimes. In *People v. Ely*,[27] defendant was tried for the murder of her ex-husband and the prosecutor sought to prove her motive was to prevent him from visiting their son. The prosecutor produced tapes of telephone calls which tended to support this theory, but in those conversations there were references to a previous crime involving the defendant which had no relationship to the crime charged and thus should have been redacted. And in *People v. Napoletano*,[28] where defendants were on trial for torching a restaurant, the fact that they had previously stolen food from the restaurant bore no relevance on the question of motive.[29]

c. Intent

The chief problem with the intent exception is that sometimes other crimes are admitted by trial courts to prove intent when intent is not actually in issue. In *People v. Bayne*,[30] defendant was charged with embezzling a large sum by forging her boss' signature on checks and then cashing the checks. She denied doing the acts and claimed that large amounts of money accumulated by her came from family gifts. Intent was not in issue. But the court stated: "Here, the evidence of the 146 uncharged forged checks was offered to prove defendant's intent to commit the specific crimes charged. * * * The evidence did not amend or add to the charges in the indictment or submitted to the jury by the court, but rather served only as evidentiary support for the larceny count."[31] Since she denied the crime charged, this evidence, if admissible at all, would seem to have more closely fit the identity exception.

---

24. 26 N.Y.2d 70, 308 N.Y.S.2d 378, 256 N.E.2d 536 (1970).

25. Id. at 76, 308 N.Y.S.2d at 383, 256 N.E.2d at 539.

26. People v. Robinson, 200 A.D.2d 693, 606 N.Y.S.2d 908 (2d Dep't), appeal denied, 84 N.Y.2d 831, 617 N.Y.S.2d 152, 641 N.E.2d 173 (1994).

27. 68 N.Y.2d 520, 510 N.Y.S.2d 532, 503 N.E.2d 88 (1986).

28. 58 A.D.2d 83, 395 N.Y.S.2d 469 (2d Dep't 1977).

29. See also People v. Beckles, 128 A.D.2d 435, 512 N.Y.S.2d 826 (1st Dep't), appeal denied, 69 N.Y.2d 1001, 517 N.Y.S.2d 1033, 511 N.E.2d 92 (1987). Beckles was a peculiar case in which defendant's other crimes were sought to be used to rehabilitate a prosecution witness whose motives for testifying against defendant were questioned by defense counsel on cross-examination. She was allowed to testify on redirect that she wanted to see defendant incarcerated for all the crimes he had committed, charged and uncharged. The Appellate Division found this objectionable. The witness thus buttressed her own credibility by showing these additional reasons for her testimony. Her motive for testifying was adequately supported by her prompt reporting of the crime charged. Thus the prejudice outweighed the probative value.

30. 82 N.Y.2d 673, 601 N.Y.S.2d 464, 619 N.E.2d 401 (1993).

31. Id. at 676, 601 N.Y.S.2d at 465–66, 619 N.E.2d at 402–03. In People v. Alling, 69 N.Y.2d 637, 511 N.Y.S.2d 225, 503 N.E.2d 690 (1986), defendant charged with second degree manslaughter relied on the defenses of justification and self-defense in the killing of the victim. He did not put

§ 404.1   RELEVANCY   Ch. 4

Intent would be an issue, of course, if the defendant conceded doing the act but claimed an absence of criminal intent. In *People v. Alvino*,[32] for example, defendant was arrested in possession of a large quantity of drugs and charged with sale and possession. He claimed he was just a petty thief and had purchased the twenty-one bags for the purpose of feeding his own addiction. The prosecutor questioned the defendant on cross-examination about prior drug sales, which defendant denied, whereupon the prosecutor introduced a witness who testified to the uncharged crimes. Not only was this evidence admissible under the intent exception, but, since this was not impeachment on a collateral matter,[33] the extrinsic evidence of these events was perfectly admissible.[34]

A case which vividly points up the intent exception is *People v. Schwartzman*,[35] where defendant was tried for assigning an account receivable for the second time. During his testimony, defendant denied any intent in the matter, prompting the prosecutor to cross-examine him concerning previous shady dealings of a similar nature which defendant also denied. The prosecutor then produced extrinsic evidence of these prior events. Were the prosecutor merely impeaching defendant, this would be improper as a collateral issue;[36] but here the evidence was admissible as part of the prosecutor's evidence in chief under the *Molineux* intent exception, i.e., evidence of these other activities tended to prove that defendant knew exactly what he was doing at the time of the crime charged. There was no necessity that these crimes all be factually connected in any way, a relationship that the dissenter insisted was essential. The fact defendant had committed these other acts belied his protestations of an innocent state of mind at the time in question.[37]

intent in issue, which prompted the court to reverse his conviction since other crimes had been introduced pursuant to the intent exception. In People v. McKinney, 24 N.Y.2d 180, 185, 299 N.Y.S.2d 401, 405, 247 N.E.2d 244, 247 (1969), in reversing because of the introduction of other crimes evidence under the intent exception, it is stated: "Here, the alleged act of defendant in stabbing Belinda is unequivocal and his intention to inflict physical injury may be inferred from the act itself. Defendant did not contest the element of intention in the crime charged, but rather denied that he stabbed Belinda or assaulted her in any way." Similarly, in People v. Chamberlain, 38 A.D.2d 306, 329 N.Y.S.2d 61 (4th Dep't 1972), the acts of passing bad checks were unequivocal and thus evidence of other similar crimes was wrongly introduced.

32. 71 N.Y.2d 233, 525 N.Y.S.2d 7, 519 N.E.2d 808 (1987).

33. See § 607.3 infra.

34. The Alvino court noted, however, that "[i]n most drug cases involving criminal sale or drugs, intent is readily inferable from the sale itself and evidence of prior uncharged crimes is neither necessary nor permissible to establish it." 71 N.Y.2d at 246, 525 N.Y.S.2d at 14, 519 N.E.2d at 815 (1987). See also People v. Crandall, 67 N.Y.2d 111, 500 N.Y.S.2d 635, 491 N.E.2d 1092 (1986)(evidence of uncharged crimes offered on rebuttal ruled out in drug sale case where defendant denied intent; proof of sale was clear enough to establish intent without need for further embellishment).

35. 24 N.Y.2d 241, 299 N.Y.S.2d 817, 247 N.E.2d 642 (1969), cert. denied, 396 U.S. 846, 90 S.Ct. 103, 24 L.Ed.2d 96 (1969).

36. See generally § 608.2, at notes 14–17, infra. Extrinsic evidence concerning collateral matters may not be introduced for impeachment purposes.

37. In People v. Ingram, 71 N.Y.2d 474, 479, 527 N.Y.S.2d 363, 365, 522 N.E.2d 439, 441 (1988) it was stated: "In the case before us, defendant—by testifying that his purpose for being at the Mobil station on December 21, 1984 was to purchase gasoline and that he had no idea that Harrison was intending to commit a robbery—put the question of his criminal intent and state of mind directly in issue. Unquestionably, under our established case law pertaining to the Molineux intent exception, proof that

Similarly, when defendant raises the defense of entrapment he puts the question of intent directly in issue.[38]

It is not clear whether defendant could preclude the prosecution from introducing evidence of other crimes to prove intent by offering to stipulate to the requisite intent. In other contexts, the prosecution cannot be compelled to accept such an offer to stipulate.[39]

d. Absence of Accident or Mistake

There is an overlap between this exception and the intent exception. If a defendant contends that he did something by mistake, or that the events took place by accident, he is disclaiming any criminal intent. Nevertheless, several cases have been analyzed under the rubric of "absence of accident or mistake." In *People v. Alvino*,[40] defendant, a clerk in the Department of Motor Vehicles, was tried for accepting a bribe in return for issuing a false amended driver's license. The defendant argued that this had been a mistake because of the crush of work, and so the court approved the introduction of evidence of 15 prior events in which defendant had engaged in similar transactions. In *People v. Alling*,[41] a manslaughter case, accident or mistake was said by the prosecutor to have been disproved by evidence of defendant's arming himself on an earlier occasion in order to shoot the victim. The Court of Appeals, however, held that the issue of mistake, or intent, was not even in the case because defendant relied on the defenses of justification and self-defense. *People v. Henson*,[42] is an accident or mistake case as far removed from the intent category as can be found. Defendants, husband and wife, were tried for criminally negligent homicide for the death of

defendant and Harrison had acted together in another similar gas station holdup would be admissible." This confirms the majority view in Schwartzman that the crimes need not be factually related.

38. See, e.g., People v. Calvano, 30 N.Y.2d 199, 331 N.Y.S.2d 430, 282 N.E.2d 322 (1972)(other drug sales both before and after the one charged could be introduced to refute entrapment). See also People v. Mann, 31 N.Y.2d 253, 336 N.Y.S.2d 633, 288 N.E.2d 595 (1972)(defendant, charged with taking a deer out of season, claimed entrapment and so had no legitimate objection to evidence that he was an inveterate poacher).

39. People v. Hills, 140 A.D.2d 71, 532 N.Y.S.2d 269 (2d Dep't), appeal denied, 73 N.Y.2d 855, 537 N.Y.S.2d 502, 534 N.E.2d 340 (1988)(prosecutor was not obliged to accept defendant's stipulation as to the extent of the victim's injuries, and was free to introduce evidence of those extensive injuries).

40. 71 N.Y.2d 233, 525 N.Y.S.2d 7, 519 N.E.2d 808 (1987).

41. 69 N.Y.2d 637, 511 N.Y.S.2d 225, 503 N.E.2d 690 (1986). The Appellate Division majority had ruled that evidence of defendant's arming himself in anticipation of a visit from the victim was properly admitted. This act did not constitute another crime under Molineux and it tended to disprove accident or mistake. 118 A.D.2d 960, 500 N.Y.S.2d 186 (3d Dep't 1986). The Court of Appeals reversed on the basis of Justice Levine's dissenting opinion in the Appellate Division. He pointed out that Molineux exceptions are not limited to crimes per se, and that prior bad acts are the same as outright crimes under the Molineux rule. Next, absence of accident or mistake was not an issue in this case. Rather, self-defense and justification were what were being relied on by defendant. "The brandishing of the weapon upon the victim's arrival was admitted by the defense. Since defendant was not charged with murder, the theory of the prosecution had to be that the act of discharging the weapon into the victim's chest was unintentional, i.e., accidental." 118 A.D.2d at 964, 500 N.Y.S.2d at 189–90. Intent was simply not in issue which made absence of accident and mistake under the Molineux exception irrelevant.

42. 33 N.Y.2d 63, 349 N.Y.S.2d 657, 304 N.E.2d 358 (1973).

their four-year-old son. The defense was that the son's demise was due to a home accident. The prosecutor called witnesses who testified to seeing the child on prior occasions with multiple abrasions and that on numerous occasions the child suffered injuries similar to those causing his death. The court ruled this evidence perfectly admissible under the accident or mistake exception, especially in this sort of case where the crime charged occurred in the privacy of the home, making the facts especially difficult to obtain.[43]

e. Common Scheme or Plan

Judge Werner in *Molineux* took great pains to closely limit this exception to instances where the uncharged crime was bound up with the crime charged. He opened his explanation by stating: "It sometimes happens that two or more crimes are committed by the same person in pursuance of a single design or under circumstances which render it impossible to prove one without proving all."[44] In addition to the case of theft of the bank janitor's key so that the bank could be burglarized,[45] Judge Werner cites other examples. In an arson prosecution, evidence of defendant's aborted attempt to burn the same premises a few days before they actually burned was admissible as part of an integrated operation because this showed "a renewed purpose to accomplish the crime previously attempted and to identify the person who made both attempts."[46] There are few modern common scheme or plan cases, but only one is needed to illustrate that this exception is still very narrowly construed. In *People v. Fiore*,[47] defendant, president of the school board, was on trial for soliciting a kickback from the general contractor of a school construction project. The prosecutor was allowed to introduce evidence that previously the architect on the same project had made illegal payments to defendant. The prosecutor argued that this showed a common scheme on the part of defendant to extract these payments and thus was admissible to refute his denials. But the Court of Appeals would not allow it:

> Mere similarity * * * between the crime charged and the uncharged crime is not sufficient; much more is required. There must be "such a concurrence of common features that the various acts are naturally to be explained as caused by a general plan of which they are the individual manifestations" * * *. In this State, the courts have been particularly cautious in permit-

---

43. Another example is the notorious Joel Steinberg case (People v. Steinberg, 170 A.D.2d 50, 573 N.Y.S.2d 965 (1st Dep't 1991), aff'd, 79 N.Y.2d 673, 584 N.Y.S.2d 770, 595 N.E.2d 845 (1992)), in which Hedda Nussbaum, the defendant's battered live-in companion, testified that on previous occasions she had seen defendant severely beat Lisa, the six-year-old girl they were raising. Defendant was on trial for Lisa's death.

44. People v. Molineux, 168 N.Y. 264, 305, 61 N.E. 286, 298 (1901).

45. See note 9 supra.

46. 168 N.Y. at 308, 61 N.E. at 300, citing Kramer v. Commonwealth, 87 Pa.St. 301 (1878).

47. 34 N.Y.2d 81, 356 N.Y.S.2d 38, 312 N.E.2d 174 (1974).

Ch. 4 UNCHARGED CRIMES § 404.1

ting proof of uncharged criminal acts to establish a common scheme or plan. * * *[48]

The court then discussed *People v. Grutz*,[49] an arson case where the prosecutor sought to prove prior arsons with which defendant was connected. *Grutz*,[50] said the court, holds that it is impermissible to offer proof of uncharged crimes committed pursuant to a common plan unless the uncharged crimes support the inference that there exists a single inseparable plan encompassing both the charged and uncharged crimes, typically, but not exclusively, embracing uncharged crimes committed in order to effect the primary crime for which the accused has been indicted.[51]

f. Identity

Three classic identity cases warrant textual exposition. In the first, *People v. Kennedy*,[52] the victim was relieved of $2,000 from her bank account by the "handkerchief switch" ruse whereby the con men insinuated themselves into her confidence and talked her into withdrawing her money which was placed with theirs in a handkerchief which was then given to her for safekeeping—only, of course the handkerchief had been switched for another containing strips of newspaper while her attention had been distracted. In affirming the convictions the Court of Appeals wrote: "The introduction, over timely objection, of evidence of similar unrelated crimes was not error since the *modus operandi* was sufficiently unique, and thus properly admitted, to bear on the issue of identity. * * *"[53] In the second case, *People v. Condon*,[54] defendant was charged with a liquor store robbery and the prosecution was allowed to produce evidence of an unrelated liquor store robbery a week later which involved defendant. But the Court of Appeals pointed out that there was nothing unique in the way these crimes were committed; liquor store holdups are all too common and these were no exception. The point was made, however, that unless the evidence on identity from other witnesses is inconclusive, such evidence should not be admitted even if the uniqueness factor is present. And in the third case, *People v. Allweiss*,[55] defendant, charged with murder, had stabbed the victim and wrapped a

---

48. Id. at 84–85, 356 N.Y.S.2d at 42–43, 312 N.E.2d at 177.

49. 212 N.Y. 72, 105 N.E. 843 (1914).

50. In People v. Grutz, 212 N.Y. 72, 105 N.E. 843 (1914), discussed by the Fiore court, 34 N.Y.2d at 85, 356 N.Y.S.2d at 42, 312 N.E.2d at 177, the prosecution tried to get in proof that defendant had claimed insurance payments from nine incendiary fires preceding the one for which he was on trial. The other fires, however, were considered separate events and were not in pursuance of any general plan or design.

51. 34 N.Y.2d at 85, 356 N.Y.S.2d at 43, 312 N.E.2d at 177. Estate of Brandon, 55 N.Y.2d 206, 448 N.Y.S.2d 436, 433 N.E.2d 501 (1982), also illustrates the limitations of this exception. There, a nursing home operator was accused of bilking one of her patients out of her assets. Plaintiff sought to prove that on other occasions involving other patients she had done the same thing. The common scheme or plan exception was held inapplicable because all the incidents were separate acts. The intent exception did apply, however, because that element of the misconduct had not otherwise been conclusively established.

52. 27 N.Y.2d 551, 313 N.Y.S.2d 123, 261 N.E.2d 264 (1970).

53. Id. at 553, 313 N.Y.S.2d at 123, 261 N.E.2d at 265.

54. 26 N.Y.2d 139, 309 N.Y.S.2d 152, 257 N.E.2d 615 (1970).

55. 48 N.Y.2d 40, 421 N.Y.S.2d 341, 396 N.E.2d 735 (1979).

pair of pantyhose around her neck. The victim's dresser drawers had been disturbed with some articles left hanging out. The prosecutor called six women who all testified to being raped by defendant (he had pleaded guilty to all six crimes) and that in each case defendant had an uncommon interest in the victim's lingerie drawers, had utilized similar means in getting the victims from the elevators in their buildings to their apartments and had made certain verbal references about his wife similar to remarks known to have been made in connection with the charged crime. Here, of course, identity was the chief issue. The court stated: "In sum, the evidence was admissible not because it showed the defendant's propensity to commit the crime but because it demonstrated a distinctive repetitive pattern. * * *"[56] The identity exception[57] along with the intent exception appear from the reported cases to be the most heavily utilized of the *Molineux* exceptions.

As has been noted, the five *Molineux* exceptions are not exhaustive of the exceptions that may be employed. Herewith are others:

g. Background

So-called background evidence, evidence of a total situation which is sometimes necessary to orient the jury with respect to the narrow issue involved, had received minimal appellate attention until the Court of

---

56. Id. at 48, 421 N.Y.S.2d at 345, 396 N.E.2d at 739.

57. See also People v. Robinson, 68 N.Y.2d 541, 510 N.Y.S.2d 837, 503 N.E.2d 485 (1986)(evidence of defendant's participation in an uncharged bank holdup was not admissible at his trial for another bank holdup on the issue of identity because, even if there had been a unique modus operandi, the defendant's identity in the uncharged holdup had not been clearly established); People v. Beam, 57 N.Y.2d 241, 455 N.Y.S.2d 575, 441 N.E.2d 1093 (1982)(in prosecution for homosexual assaults, where assailant's identity was in issue, evidence of other homosexual assaults was admissible with respect to identity because of the unique modus operandi of the crimes including offering to share marijuana with young men in their late teens, luring them to an isolated location at which forcible sodomy and forcible kissing took place); People v. Ortiz, 156 A.D.2d 77, 554 N.Y.S.2d 107 (1st Dep't), leave for appeal denied, 76 N.Y.2d 793, 559 N.Y.S.2d 998, 559 N.E.2d 692 (1990)(defendant, charged with snatching a bill from the hand of a person approaching a subway booth to buy tokens, successfully objected to token booth clerk's testimony that minutes before he had seen the same defendant attempt to rob another transit customer); People v. Sanchez, 154 A.D.2d 15, 551 N.Y.S.2d 206 (1st Dep't 1990)(rape victim testified that defendant, whom she identified, had come to her door posing as a photographer; because identity was therefore not in issue it was error to allow another witness to testify that she was raped by defendant who posed as a photographer); People v. Neu, 126 A.D.2d 223, 513 N.Y.S.2d 531 (3d Dep't), appeal denied, 70 N.Y.2d 652, 518 N.Y.S.2d 1045, 512 N.E.2d 571 (1987)(to establish defendant's identity as perpetrator of a convenience store robbery, it was proper to offer evidence of another convenience store robbery in which defendant's participation was established by clear and convincing evidence; in each crime the perpetrator waited until the store was clear of customers, entered and shot the clerk in the head with a .22 revolver, and then emptied the cash register); People v. Sanza, 121 A.D.2d 89, 509 N.Y.S.2d 311 (1st Dep't 1986)(evidence of uncharged rapes committed by defendant was not admissible to establish defendant's identity as the perpetrator of a charged rape and murder because the common elements of gunpoint threats and theft of jewelry were neither unique nor uncommon in rape cases); People v. Battles, 83 A.D.2d 164, 443 N.Y.S.2d 932 (4th Dep't 1981)(because defendant's identity as the murderer had not been conclusively established, it was not error to allow a witness to testify that he was robbed by defendant on a previous occasion and that the gun he observed in defendant's hand was the same gun taken from defendant after the crime charged was committed).

Appeals decision in *People v. Stanard*.[58] Defendant, a police officer, was on trial for perjury stemming from his denial before a grand jury of having collected protection money. In his opening statement, the prosecutor said that he would paint a picture of the corruption of an entire police division, and he indeed painted that picture through the testimony of ex-officer Serpico,[59] who described in great detail specific instances of corrupt acts in which defendant and other officers had engaged—none of which involved the transaction concerning defendant's perjury. Judge Gabrielli, finding this error, reiterated the rule enunciated in *People v. Gleason*,[60] that while certain background evidence might be necessary for the jury's proper understanding of the charge before them, the use of such evidence must be closely controlled so that it does not distort the jury's evaluation of the critical evidence in the case.

In *People v. Jackson*,[61] a police officer testified that he observed a series of street corner drug transactions carried on for about an hour before the arrests were made. Defendant, when given money by a customer, would signal a woman who would then hand the customer the drugs. This string of transactions preceding the one for which defendant was charged was admissible to show how the two were acting in concert.[62]

h. Inextricably Intertwined

Sometimes references to uncharged crimes are made in testimony as to the unfolding of events, or in relation to conversations about which the witness testifies. The question is whether such references can be redacted or whether they are so intertwined with the rest of the account as to require that they remain. In *People v. Vails*,[63] references to prior uncharged drug sales in the undercover officer's conversation with defendant were admissible because the prior transactions concerned the

---

58. 32 N.Y.2d 143, 344 N.Y.S.2d 331, 297 N.E.2d 77 (1973).

59. See P. Maas, Serpico, The Cop Who Defied The System (1973).

60. 285 App.Div. 278, 136 N.Y.S.2d 220 (1st Dep't 1954).

61. 39 N.Y.2d 64, 382 N.Y.S.2d 736, 346 N.E.2d 537 (1976).

62. See also People v. Carter, 77 N.Y.2d 95, 564 N.Y.S.2d 992, 566 N.E.2d 119 (1990), cert. denied, 499 U.S. 967, 111 S.Ct. 1599, 113 L.Ed.2d 662 (1991)(court allowed evidence of series of drug sales to show how the defendants were acting in concert); People v. Castro, 101 A.D.2d 392, 475 N.Y.S.2d 840 (1st Dep't 1984), aff'd, 65 N.Y.2d 683, 491 N.Y.S.2d 623, 481 N.E.2d 255 (1985)(where defendant was tried for drug possession and possession of a weapon, much of the People's case consisted of evidence showing continuing police surveillance of a drug selling operation. According to police testimony, many comings and goings were reported, including the appearance of the previously unknown defendant. He was observed for an hour talking to various people outside a building before they entered. Defendant testified that he regularly jogged in the neighborhood and was simply in the wrong place at the wrong time. Was all the evidence of the drug selling operation going on around him, for which he was not charged, violative of Molineux? No, said the court majority. This evidence was admissible as background material because it was necessary to explain the context of the arrest; without it, defendant's arrest would exist in a vacuum.); People v. Rosado, 39 A.D.2d 871, 333 N.Y.S.2d 181 (1st Dep't 1972), aff'd, 32 N.Y.2d 649, 342 N.Y.S.2d 854, 295 N.E.2d 653 (1973)(arresting officer's testimony that he observed five or six other drug sales before he approached defendant to make the buy for which defendant was on trial was permissible, presumably as background).

63. 43 N.Y.2d 364, 401 N.Y.S.2d 479, 372 N.E.2d 320 (1977).

price and quality of the drugs which were the subject of the crime charged.[64] In a subsequent case, however, *People v. Crandall*,[65] the court seems to have tightened the reins where another drug sale conversation which included minor references to earlier transactions was held improperly admitted. Those references should have been redacted.[66] The *Ventimiglia* case[67] is equally strict. The prosecutor's witness, an accomplice, recounted a conversation he had with one of the defendants. In the conversation the defendant explained the plan to dispose of the body and stated the location of the burial spot. The defendant said that the group had disposed of bodies before, "just a couple of times." This was evidence of uncharged crimes coming from the mouth of a defendant, but the other occasions for which the group had used the burial location had no relevance to the charge at hand and should have been redacted. It was unnecessary to an understanding of the rest of the statement and was thus not inextricably interwoven.[68]

i. Multiple Counts

Where the prosecutor chooses to try a defendant for more than one crime under a single indictment, the danger is present that the jury will give undue weight to a count they ultimately reject in their appraisal of another count upon which they are inclined to convict. But in *People v. Brown*,[69] the Court of Appeals in a terse memorandum ruled that defendant had not been prejudiced as a matter of law, as held by the Appellate Division, by being charged and tried on counts upon which he was acquitted. Defendant was charged and tried on counts of felony murder, assault, possession of a weapon, attempted murder, robbery and reckless endangerment, all arising out of a continuing chain of events.

---

64. The court stated: "In this case the trial court admitted the evidence of the prior transaction because the process of buying and making preparations for the sale was inextricably interwoven into this one transaction. Reference to the prior sale was intrinsic to the bargaining between defendant and Officer Molfetta. It concerned the price to be paid and the quality of the drugs, providing highly probative evidence relating directly to the crime charged. When the conversation is so inextricably interwoven with the crime charged * * *, it may be received in evidence * * * where, as in this case, the value of the evidence clearly outweighs any possible prejudice." Id. at 368–369, 401 N.Y.S.2d at 482, 372 N.E.2d at 323.

65. 67 N.Y.2d 111, 500 N.Y.S.2d 635, 491 N.E.2d 1092 (1986).

66. The undercover officer had been permitted to testify that at the time of the charged transaction, he handed defendant $300 whereupon defendant produced the drugs and said: "Here's another seven for you. It's on the front seat. Don't let it melt. That's $650. See you later." The reference to the $300 should have been redacted said the court because it "was probative of nothing except to suggest an earlier transaction." Id. at 114–15, 500 N.Y.S.2d at 637, 491 N.E.2d at 1094.

67. People v. Ventimiglia, 52 N.Y.2d 350, 438 N.Y.S.2d 261, 420 N.E.2d 59 (1981). It was this case that gave rise to the Ventimiglia hearing. See notes 10–14 supra.

68. The error was harmless, however, because other statements that were admissible carried implications of prior crimes committed at the location of the crime. Id. at 361, 488 N.Y.S.2d at 265, 420 N.E.2d at 63. See also People v. Mitchell, 40 A.D.2d 117, 338 N.Y.S.2d 313 (3d Dep't 1972) (where defendant's conviction of bribery rested on a tape recording of the very conversation in which he offered the subject bribe and in which he talked of other crimes in which he had been involved, the Appellate Division regarded the conversation as a whole and said that the references to the other crimes were so inextricably interwoven with the charged crime as to make any attempt at redaction senseless).

69. 83 N.Y.2d 791, 610 N.Y.S.2d 956, 632 N.E.2d 1279 (1994).

In *People v. Lane*,[70] defendants were tried for two separate robberies charged in two separate indictments which occurred three days apart. Noting that the decision to consolidate separate indictments is within the trial judge's discretion, the court held consolidation proper where there is a relation between the crimes and defendant would not be prejudiced as he might where he wished to testify as to one charge, but not the other.[71] In *Lane* no such showing of prejudice was made, and the crimes were related because they both had been committed in a remarkably similar manner.[72] *People v. Streitferdt*,[73] presents interesting facts[74] and illustrates that the trial judge must keep close control in separating the counts for the jury's consideration, and, in fact, the jury's acquittal on some counts "demonstrates that they were able to segregate the evidence as it related to each count of the indictment. * * *"[75]

A related problem arises when the prosecutor elects to retry the defendant using some of the evidence introduced on another count upon which defendant had previously been acquitted. In *People v. Goodman*,[76] one event, the murder and robbery of an elderly woman, spawned multiple counts under one indictment. The defendant was acquitted of the homicide count but convicted of the larceny count. The Court of Appeals reversed the conviction because of an improperly received confession and ordered a new trial of the larceny count. The prosecutor's submission of the same evidence that was submitted on the homicide count, including the defendant's statements that he would kill for the woman's rings, was approved. The statements went to show defendant's intent to rob, and the other evidence tended to prove the victim's lack of consent in parting with her rings. But in the same volume of the

---

70. 56 N.Y.2d 1, 451 N.Y.S.2d 6, 436 N.E.2d 456 (1982).

71. The Lane court cited Baker v. United States, 401 F.2d 958, 977 (D.C.Cir.1968), cert. denied, 400 U.S. 965, 91 S.Ct. 367, 27 L.Ed.2d 384 (1970), calling it "the seminal decision governing defendant's contention in the context of a motion to sever counts of a single indictment." 56 N.Y.2d at 8, 451 N.Y.S.2d at 9, 436 N.E.2d at 459.

72. The court had to distinguish People v. Shapiro, 50 N.Y.2d 747, 431 N.Y.S.2d 422, 409 N.E.2d 897 (1980), where consolidation was held erroneous as a matter of law because prejudice was shown by defendant who was charged under three indictments, one of which charged 64 counts of sodomy.

73. 169 A.D.2d 171, 572 N.Y.S.2d 893 (1st Dep't), appeal denied, 78 N.Y.2d 1015, 575 N.Y.S.2d 823, 581 N.E.2d 1069 (1991).

74. The Appellate Division split on the question whether joining the separate counts in one prosecution violated Molineux principles. Three complainants charged the pastor of the True Church of God with violating them sexually in his church office on three separate, unrelated occasions. The majority found that evidence as to one incident would not color the jury's perception of the others. The proof as to each crime was presented separately, and the jury was instructed to consider each separately. The dissent on this point argued that this joinder directly violated the Molineux rule since if the jury would not have been quite convinced on the proof as to any one count, a convincing propensity could nevertheless be shown as to the others. 169 A.D.2d at 178–79, 572 N.Y.S.2d at 898.

75. Id. at 176, 572 N.Y.S.2d at 896. See also People v. Telford, 134 A.D.2d 632, 521 N.Y.S.2d 523 (2d Dep't 1987), appeal denied, 71 N.Y.2d 903, 527 N.Y.S.2d 1012, 523 N.E.2d 319 (1988)(defendant failed to make a showing that sex crime charge stemming from one incident should not be joined with others stemming from another incident); People v. Peterson, 42 A.D.2d 937, 348 N.Y.S.2d 137 (1st Dep't 1973), aff'd, 35 N.Y.2d 659, 360 N.Y.S.2d 640, 318 N.E.2d 796 (1974)(no error in joining three indictments involving 32 counts of robbery, burglary and larceny involving seven different victims on seven different occasions).

76. 69 N.Y.2d 32, 511 N.Y.S.2d 565, 503 N.E.2d 996 (1986).

§ 404.1   RELEVANCY   Ch. 4

New York reports appears *People v. Acevedo*.[77] Evidence of the other crime for which defendant had been acquitted at an earlier trial was introduced to impeach defendant's testimony as to his whereabouts on the night in question, and also some of this came in on the prosecutor's direct. The Court of Appeals seems to have banned all use of this evidence, Judge Kaye stating: "We perceive no meaningful difference in the unfairness to which a defendant is subjected when the State attempts to prove his guilt by relitigating a settled fact issue, once necessarily decided in his favor, whether it is a question of ultimate fact or evidentiary fact."[78] It is difficult, even though there are several distinctions, to reconcile *Goodman* and *Acevedo*.[79]

j. Sex Cases—"Amorous Design"

The now discredited amorous design exception allowed evidence of defendant's prior sexual encounters with the complaining witness to be offered by the prosecution in cases where consent was not in issue, such as statutory rape and incest cases. This exception was given prominence in *People v. Thompson*,[80] where the court ruled that in such cases prior sexual acts occurring between the parties was admissible to prove the act charged.[81] The Court of Appeals in *People v. Lewis*,[82] a case in which the trial judge allowed evidence of 10 previous sexual encounters between defendant father and his daughter, reasoned that since consent was not in issue it was not necessary to explain why the daughter had ceased to resist her father's advances. The evidence of the prior instances was irrelevant. In a subsequent case, *People v. Hudy*,[83] the Court of Appeals stated, "We recently held in *People v. Lewis* * * * that evidence of prior sexual contact with the same 'victim,' traditionally admitted under the rubric of 'amorous design,' was really no more than a form of propensity evidence hiding behind an assumed name and should no longer be permitted."[84] Hence, the amorous design rule voiced in *Thompson* is no longer considered viable.

77. 69 N.Y.2d 478, 515 N.Y.S.2d 753, 508 N.E.2d 665 (1987).

78. Id. at 486, 515 N.Y.S.2d at 759, 508 N.E.2d at 671.

79. In Goodman, the court held that evidentiary, as opposed to ultimate, facts would not be banned by collateral estoppel. 69 N.Y.2d at 38–40, 515 N.Y.S.2d at 570–71, 508 N.E.2d at 1001–02. In Acevedo, the court said no such distinction should be made and that it was all improper. 69 N.Y.2d at 486, 515 N.Y.S.2d at 759, 508 N.E.2d at 671. In neither case was there any discussion of there being a different standard of proof from one case to the next, a point prominently made in Dowling v. United States, 493 U.S. 342, 110 S.Ct. 668, 107 L.Ed.2d 708 (1990), taken up under the federal rule in the next section.

80. 212 N.Y. 249, 106 N.E. 78 (1914).

81. Id. at 251–52, 106 N.E. at 78.

82. 69 N.Y.2d 321, 514 N.Y.S.2d 205, 506 N.E.2d 915 (1987).

83. 73 N.Y.2d 40, 538 N.Y.S.2d 197, 535 N.E.2d 250 (1988).

84. Id. at 55, 538 N.Y.S.2d at 206, 535 N.E.2d at 259. Note that in N.Y.Crim. Proc.Law § 60.42, which limits evidence of the victim's prior sexual acts in sexual offense cases, an exception is carved out where the issue is consent and such evidence "(a) proves or tends to prove specific instances of the victim's prior sexual conduct with the accused." This statute is discussed in § 412.1, infra and, of course, has no pertinence to the discredited amorous design exception, which deals with defendant's prior acts to prove his conduct on a later occasion.

k. Rebuttal

The remaining way in which the prosecutor may introduce evidence of defendant's other criminal activity would be as rebuttal to a defense raised by defendant (in addition to the instances in which defendant raises any of the five traditional *Molineux* points). In *People v. Hudy*, noted just above, defendant claimed he was the victim of vicious rumors concerning his sexual proclivities with young boys. The prosecutor tried to rebut with evidence of uncharged instances of defendant's conduct with a young boy but was unsuccessful because the incident was irrelevant.[85] But in *People v. Santarelli*,[86] where defendant was on trial for fatally shooting his brother-in-law, an act which he conceded, his defense was insanity based upon the theory that he suffered a temporary "paranoid delusion" at the time he pulled the trigger. The prosecutor tried to show that defendant was not insane, but suffered from a mere "personality disorder" that manifested itself from time to time in "explosive" conduct. The Court of Appeals, noting that the *Molineux* exceptions were not exclusive, stated "that evidence of uncharged criminal or immoral conduct may be admitted as part of the People's case on rebuttal if it has a tendency to disprove the defendant's claim that he was legally insane at the time of the crime."[87]

l. Civil Cases

The Court of Appeals in *Matter of Brandon*,[88] stated: "A general rule of evidence, applicable in both civil and criminal cases, is that it is improper to prove that a person did an act on a particular occasion by showing that he did a similar act on a different, unrelated occasion."[89] But the court found the *Molineux* intent exception applicable where defendant was accused of using fraud and undue influence in obtaining the savings of an elderly woman under defendant's care. It was held proper to introduce evidence of two prior judgments entered against defendant which showed she had taken financial advantage of elderly people under her care. This evidence went to the question raised by her denial of any wrongdoing and showed that it was unlikely that the

---

85. 73 N.Y.2d 40, 55, 538 N.Y.S.2d 197, 206, 535 N.E.2d 250, 259 (1988).

86. 49 N.Y.2d 241, 425 N.Y.S.2d 77, 401 N.E.2d 199, motion for reargument denied, 49 N.Y.2d 918, 428 N.Y.S.2d 1028, 405 N.E.2d 712 (1980).

87. Id. at 248, 425 N.Y.S.2d at 82, 401 N.E.2d at 204. Two items of prior criminal conduct, however, were properly admitted: one witness related prior incidents in which the defendant reacted with violence to relatively mild provocation; and other testimony linked the defendant to organized crime. The other assaults tended to show his explosive personality, and the mob connection showed his rational anxiety at the time of the killing. Such facts would tend to disprove the defense of insane delusions. Some of the evidence of defendant's behavior was held to be irrelevant. The fact defendant had engaged in a barroom scuffle and had thrown glasses around a barroom was unsupported by any information showing what led to the altercations, or what it was that may have provoked defendant, thus not really tending to prove explosive behavior. Another incident in which defendant had assaulted another person, rather than showing explosive behavior, showed a purposeful, planned intent to beat up the victim.

88. 55 N.Y.2d 206, 448 N.Y.S.2d 436, 433 N.E.2d 501 (1982).

89. Id. at 210–11, 448 N.Y.S.2d at 438, 433 N.E.2d at 503.

current resident in defendant's home gave over her savings freely and voluntarily.[90]

Where the question is whether defendant acted fraudulently or made misrepresentations regarding the transaction at issue, plaintiff may be able to prove prior instances of fraud or misrepresentation on defendant's part. In *Terpstra v. Niagara Fire Ins. Co.*,[91] it was held relevant to the question of motive whether the claimant of fire insurance proceeds had submitted similar claims on two previous occasions.[92] Likewise, it has been held that previous insurance claims for vandalism and theft, similar to the claim in issue, were admissible as relevant to the issue of plaintiff's motive in light of plaintiff's admission as to his poor financial situation.[93]

Where defendant claims lack of intent or accident or mistake in a case where those issues are contested, plaintiff may be allowed to prove that because of prior similar claims, it is unlikely defendant could have acted innocently. Thus, in *Davis v. Solondz*,[94] a case brought for unauthorized dental treatment, plaintiff's discovery request for captions of previous lawsuits brought against defendant for unauthorized treatment was held proper on the question of intent or absence of accident or mistake. The court noted that if this were a malpractice action such evidence of prior similar acts would be irrelevant. But here, where defendant was charged with intentional unauthorized treatment, this evidence "would be admissible at trial to negate the existence of an innocent state of mind * * * and would likewise be relevant and, hence, discoverable."[95]

In *Kourtalis v. City of New York*,[96] however, the court held that in a false arrest case it would be improper "to prove that a person did an act on a particular occasion by showing that he did a similar act on a different, unrelated occasion."[97] Thus, plaintiff was barred from introducing evidence of other similar complaints made against the defendant police officer.[98]

---

90. In Brandon, the Surrogate ruled that the other occurrences were admissible under the common scheme or plan exception, but then charged the jury to consider them as relating to defendant's intent. The charge saved the case from reversal since this was not an example of a common scheme or plan. See subpart e of this section supra.

91. 26 N.Y.2d 70, 76, 308 N.Y.S.2d 378, 382, 256 N.E.2d 536, 539 (1970).

92. It was stated: "The court correctly charged that from the fact of the fires 'no inference can be drawn as bearing upon whether or not the plaintiff set fire to this house which is the subject of the action * * * [but] you may consider those prior fires and settlements therefrom as bearing upon any motive that the plaintiff may have had which you find has a bearing upon whether or not he set fire to the house which is the subject of this action.'" Id. at 76, 308 N.Y.S.2d at 383, 256 N.E.2d at 539.

93. Dlugosz v. New York Central Mut. Fire Ins. Co., 132 A.D.2d 903, 904, 518 N.Y.S.2d 237, 238 (3d Dep't), appeal denied, 70 N.Y.2d 612, 523 N.Y.S.2d 496, 518 N.E.2d 7 (1987).

94. 122 A.D.2d 401, 402, 504 N.Y.S.2d 804, 805 (3d Dep't 1986).

95. Id.

96. 191 A.D.2d 480, 481, 594 N.Y.S.2d 325, 327 (2d Dep't 1993).

97. Id.

98. The court noted also that the evidence of such other complaints was based on "unsubstantiated hearsay." Id.

Another case, not involving prior claims, but, rather, prior similar incidents bearing on defendant's intent in making a contract with plaintiff, is worthy of note.[99] Plaintiff, claiming defendant promised to hire him as a lawyer after he completed law school, was entitled to discovery of the names of all defendant's employees who were attorneys but who were not employed as such, and those among them who requested such employment. The court saw this as bearing on the question of defendant's intent, thus discoverable, and presumably admissible should discovery bear fruit.[100]

Library References:

West's Key No. Digests, Criminal Law ⚖369–374; Evidence ⚖129–142.

§ 404.2 Federal

Subdivision (b) of Federal Rule 404 provides:

(b) Other crimes, wrongs, or acts. Evidence of other crimes, wrongs, or acts is not admissible to prove the character of a person in order to show action in conformity therewith. It may, however, be admissible for other purposes, such as proof of motive, opportunity, intent, preparation, plan, knowledge, identity, or absence of mistake or accident, provided that upon request by the accused, the prosecution in a criminal case shall provide reasonable notice in advance of trial, or during trial if the court excuses pretrial notice on good cause shown, of the general nature of any such evidence it intends to introduce at trial.

a. Generally

In *Huddleston v. United States*,[1] the Supreme Court prescribed the steps to be taken by the trial judge when uncharged crime evidence is offered under Rule 404(b). The judge must (1) find a purpose for admission other than simply to show propensity, (2) find the evidence relevant under Rule 402, (3) find the Rule 403 probative value-prejudice test satisfied, and (4) instruct the jury that the evidence is to be considered only for the purpose for which it was admitted, i.e., for the appropriate inference to be drawn.[2]

The important question in *Huddleston* was whether the judge must make a preliminary finding under Rule 104(a) that the other crimes involved the defendant. Although the prosecutor must provide more than mere speculation that defendant is connected to the other crimes,[3]

---

99. Mangiaracina v. New York Telephone Co., 105 A.D.2d 695, 696, 481 N.Y.S.2d 134, 135 (2d Dep't 1984).

100. Id.

§ 404.2

1. 485 U.S. 681, 691–92, 108 S.Ct. 1496, 1502, 99 L.Ed.2d 771, 783–84 (1988).

2. Id. at 691–92, 108 S.Ct. at 1502, 99 L.Ed.2d at 783–84.

3. The court stated that the Government may not "parade past the jury a litany of potentially prejudicial similar acts" on the basis of "unsubstantiated innuendo that defendant is connected to them." The relevancy step of the judge's inquiry will settle this because the evidence would not be relevant if there were not reasonable evidence to conclude "that the act occurred

§ 404.2   RELEVANCY   Ch. 4

it is the jury that must find by a preponderance of the evidence that defendant was connected to the other crimes and only then may they draw any inferences. No preliminary Rule 104(a) ruling need be made by the trial judge; the judge must merely ascertain whether the jury reasonably could find the connection by a preponderance of the evidence.[4] The preponderance of evidence rule appears to be applicable regardless of which Rule 404(b) exception is involved since the *Huddleston* opinion, although it dealt with the intent or knowledge exception, made no distinctions. (It is to be noted that in New York the clear and convincing standard is to be applied with respect to the identity exception.[5] There has been no pronouncement in New York regarding the standard appropriate to the other exceptions.[6])

The Second Circuit, in *United States v. Gilan*,[7] applied the *Huddleston* criteria in a case involving the intent or knowledge exception and found error in admission of a prior, similar crime. "While the jury might reasonably conclude that the two crimes were planned and arranged by the same person, there was no evidence that [defendant] was that person or that he played any particular role in the uncharged crime."[8] The second prong of the *Huddleston* test was unsatisfied, i.e., relevancy could not be shown if defendant could not be linked to the prior crime.[9]

In another Supreme Court decision, *Dowling v. United States*,[10] the prosecution was allowed to introduce, on the issue of identity, evidence of a prior crime with a modus operandi similar to the crime charged. Defendant had been tried for that prior crime and acquitted. Those facts, he argued, could not be used against him again because of double jeopardy, collateral estoppel and due process. The Court disagreed. Collateral estoppel in the criminal context prohibits the government from relitigating ultimate facts that have already been determined,[11] but does not prevent the reintroduction of evidentiary facts.[12] Besides, here

and that the defendant was the actor." Id. at 689, 108 S.Ct. at 1501, 99 L.Ed.2d at 782.

4. Id. at 690, 108 S.Ct. at 1501, 99 L.Ed.2d at 782–83. The issue, therefore, is treated as one of conditional relevance under Rule 104(b). See also § 404.1(a), supra. See United States v. Ramirez, 894 F.2d 565, 569 (2d Cir.1990).

5. People v. Robinson, 68 N.Y.2d 541, 548–49, 510 N.Y.S.2d 837, 841, 503 N.E.2d 485, 489 (1986).

6. The best guess is that the clear and convincing test is applicable only in identity cases. In Robinson the court cited United States v. Beechum, 582 F.2d 898 (5th Cir. 1978), cert. denied, 440 U.S. 920, 99 S.Ct. 1244, 59 L.Ed.2d 472 (1979) for the proposition that "a much greater degree of similarity between the charged crime and the uncharged crime is required when the evidence of the other crime is introduced to prove identity than when it is introduced to prove state of mind." Robinson, 68 N.Y.2d at 549, 510 N.Y.S.2d at 84, 503 N.E.2d at 489, citing Beechum, 582 F.2d at 912 n.15.

7. 967 F.2d 776 (2d Cir.1992).

8. Id. at 781.

9. Id. at 780.

10. 493 U.S. 342, 110 S.Ct. 668, 107 L.Ed.2d 708 (1990).

11. See Ashe v. Swenson, 397 U.S. 436, 90 S.Ct. 1189, 25 L.Ed.2d 469 (1970). Several bandits robbed six men playing poker. Ashe was tried and acquitted of robbing one of them. He was then indicted and convicted of robbing one of the others. The conviction was reversed by the Supreme Court on grounds of collateral estoppel. The acquittal established the jury's view that Ashe was not one of the robbers. That was an ultimate fact and Ashe should not have been forced to retry the same issues.

12. 493 U.S. at 348, 110 S.Ct. at 672, 107 L.Ed.2d at 717.

it was not necessary for the government to prove the prior crime beyond a reasonable doubt; a lower standard of proof governed admissibility for identity purposes. As to the due process argument, it was noted that the jury had been fully informed of the prior acquittal and was left free to determine the significance of the evidence and to give it the weight they thought appropriate.[13] Similar questions arose in *United States v. Felix*,[14] where evidence of a prior crime for which defendant had been tried and convicted was allowed in a second trial to prove his intent.[15]

Several of the Rule 404(b) exceptions are illustrated by Second Circuit decisions as follows: intent,[16] absence of mistake,[17] identity,[18] motive,[19] and common plan[20] (which, from the cases, seems more loosely

---

13. Id. at 353, 110 S.Ct. at 674–75, 107 L.Ed.2d at 721.

14. 503 U.S. 378, 112 S.Ct. 1377, 118 L.Ed.2d 25 (1992).

15. In Felix, defendant was involved with manufacturing methamphetamine in Beggs, Oklahoma, and the crime of attempting to manufacture the same drug in Joplin, Missouri. There were two separate crimes. He was tried and convicted of the Missouri crime in the Western District of Missouri. Subsequently, he was tried and convicted for his Oklahoma activities in the Eastern District of Oklahoma. The charges involved conspiracy and substantive counts. In the first trial in Missouri, the government introduced evidence of defendant's activities in Beggs, Oklahoma, to show he knew what he was doing and thus had the necessary criminal intent over in Missouri. The question was whether the government was barred from prosecuting the Oklahoma crimes since the Oklahoma evidence had already been introduced against defendant in the Missouri trial. Relying on the Dowling case, the Court pointed out that two separate crimes were involved; defendant had never been prosecuted in Missouri for the Oklahoma crimes; and evidence of the Oklahoma activities had merely been introduced as circumstantial evidence under Federal Rule 404(b). The decision in Grady v. Corbin, 495 U.S. 508, 110 S.Ct. 2084, 109 L.Ed.2d 548 (1990), was distinguished because that was a case where the second prosecution on felony counts involved the same underlying facts for which defendant had already been convicted on guilty pleas in justice court. In Dowling and Felix, the evidence involved separate crimes:

> [O]ur precedents hold that a mere overlap in proof between two prosecutions does not establish a double jeopardy violation. The Court of Appeals relied on * * * language from our opinion in Grady v. Corbin in reaching its result. But we think that this is an extravagant reading of Grady, which disclaimed any intention of adopting a "same evidence" test. Our decision two Terms ago in Dowling * * * drives home this point.

Felix, 503 U.S. at 384, 112 S.Ct. at 1382, 118 L.Ed.2d at 34.

16. United States v. Oshatz, 912 F.2d 534, 541–42 (2d Cir.1990), cert. denied, 500 U.S. 910, 111 S.Ct. 1695, 114 L.Ed.2d 89 (1991)(evidence of prior fraudulent tax schemes permissible to show intent in relation to the crime charged even though the government failed to prove criminal intent as to the prior incidents); United States v. Arango–Correa, 851 F.2d 54, 59 (2d Cir. 1988)(in narcotics prosecution, the government could introduce defendant's records of prior narcotics transactions to rebut his defense of lack of knowledge with respect to the charged crime); United States v. Johnson, 382 F.2d 280, 281 (2d Cir.1967)(evidence of prior theft of an interstate shipment admissible to prove defendant's intent in the theft charged).

17. United States v. Ramirez, 894 F.2d 565, 569 (2d Cir.1990)(evidence of a narcotics sale occurring after the narcotics violation charged is permissible to show defendant knew what he was doing).

18. United States v. Sappe, 898 F.2d 878, 879, 880 (2d Cir.1990)(bank robberies committed by concealing gun with newspaper, but allowing teller to see the gun, unique enough modus operandi); United States v. Mills, 895 F.2d 897, 907 (2d Cir.), cert. denied, 495 U.S. 951, 110 S.Ct. 2216, 109 L.Ed.2d 541 (1990)(prior counterfeiting arrest and conviction to show defendant's intent and identity in charged counterfeiting act—crimes were committed in a "nearly identical" manner).

19. United States v. Birney, 686 F.2d 102, 106–07 (2d Cir.1982)(evidence of prior embezzlement could be introduced to show motive for making charged false entries in financial records); compare Berkovich v. Hicks, 922 F.2d 1018, 1021–22 (2d Cir.1991)(evidence of prior complaints against police officer said to show motive

20. See note 20 on page 156.

§ 404.2 RELEVANCY Ch. 4

applied than in New York). Lest one be led to believe that the exceptions have completely swallowed the rule, there is the occasional case in which no excuse for any exception can be found.[21]

There is also room for the introduction of prior crimes just outside the purview of the Rule 404(b) exceptions. In a RICO case, evidence that defendant engaged in a pattern of similar crimes that were part of the same conspiracy is admissible to establish guilt with regard to the crime in question.[22]

b. Procedure

In federal practice there is no decision comparable to New York's

---

for crime charged, but this evidence overly prejudicial since officer had been exonerated on most of prior charges).

20. United States v. Langford, 990 F.2d 65, 70 (2d Cir.1993)(prior acts of illegally dispensing narcotics admissible to show background, history and plan in relation to charged acts of illegal distribution since witness who testified was the originator of all the sales); United States v. Concepcion, 983 F.2d 369 (2d Cir.1992), cert. denied, ___ U.S. ___, 114 S.Ct. 163, 126 L.Ed.2d 124 (1993)(evidence of defendant's prior offer to arrange a murder tied in with charged crimes and was admissible); United States v. Brennan, 798 F.2d 581 (2d Cir.1986)), cert. denied, 490 U.S. 1022, 109 S.Ct. 1750, 104 L.Ed.2d 187 (1989)(evidence of prior fixing of cases by judge admissible to show pattern of conduct in fixing case for which he was charged); United States v. Carroll, 510 F.2d 507, 509 (2d Cir.1975), cert. denied, 426 U.S. 923, 96 S.Ct. 2633, 49 L.Ed.2d 378 (1976)(evidence of uncharged robbery admissible to show that defendants were ready and qualified to commit the charged robbery); Sharon v. Time, Inc., 103 F.R.D. 86 (S.D.N.Y.1984)(where plaintiff claimed he was libeled in defendant's article charging him with massacre of Palestinians in Beirut refugee camp, defendant could introduce evidence of plaintiff's prior conduct).

21. United States v. DeVillio, 983 F.2d 1185 (2d Cir.1993)(evidence of burglar tools found in defendant's home showed he was a professional burglar, and had no particular relevance to the charges of theft and transportation of goods in interstate commerce); Berkovich v. Hicks, 922 F.2d 1018, 1021–22 (2d Cir.1991)(in civil rights case charging police officer with certain abuses, evidence of prior complaints against officer would only show propensity and was rightly excluded); Cullen v. Margiotta, 811 F.2d 698, 716 (2d Cir.), cert. denied sub nom., Nassau County Republican Committee v. Cullen, 483 U.S. 1021, 107 S.Ct. 3266, 97 L.Ed.2d 764 (1987)(past conviction of defendant for obtaining kickback money from insurance companies doing business with the County not admissible where defendant and others charged with coercing political contributions from the county and city); Warner Bros. Inc. v. Dae Rim Trading, Inc., 677 F.Supp. 740 (S.D.N.Y.1988), appeal denied, 877 F.2d 1120 (2d Cir.1989)(where charge is copyright infringement, fact that defendants were previously sued in a trademark case had no relevance and was inadmissible).

22. Amendolare v. Schenkers Intern. Forwarders, Inc., 747 F.Supp. 162, 166 (E.D.N.Y.1990). While this seems to be close to the common scheme or plan exception it is not altogether clear but what a conspiracy situation might be yet another exception. The Court put it this way:

> Rule 404(b) of the Federal Rules of Evidence permits proof of other crimes or acts to show proof of opportunity, intent preparation, plan or knowledge. Under the "inclusionary" approach followed in this circuit, "evidence of prior crimes, wrongs, or acts is admissible for any purpose other than to show a defendant's criminal propensity * * * as long as it is relevant to some disputed issue in the trial and satisfies the probative-prejudice balancing test of Fed.R.Evid. 403." United States v. Brennan, 798 F.2d 581, 589 (2d Cir.1986)(citations omitted). Where, as here, there is evidence that a defendant engaged in a pattern or practice of similar crimes that were part of the same conspiracy, the courts in both criminal and civil actions have allowed proof of other crimes to help establish a defendant's involvement in the particular crime or scheme in question.

Id. at 166.

Ventimiglia,[23] which routinely requires a preliminary hearing for the trial judge's appraisal of other crimes evidence proffered by the prosecution. A 1991 amendment to Rule 404(b), however, does impose a "reasonable" pretrial notice requirement, activated by request of the defendant, pursuant to which the government must specify "the general nature of any such evidence it intends to introduce at trial."[24] The Advisory Committee's Note to the amendment indicates that the purpose is "to reduce surprise and promote early resolution on the issue of admissibility. * * * Nothing in the amendment precludes the court from requiring the government to provide it with an opportunity to rule *in limine* on 404(b) evidence before it is offered or even mentioned during trial."

The Second Circuit imposed some procedural guidelines of its own in two 1980 decisions. In *United States v. Figueroa,*[25] the government sought to admit evidence of defendant's prior narcotics conviction at the end of its case in chief, and before it had been ascertained that the defendants would rest without presenting evidence. Also, the government failed to inform the trial judge of the Rule 404(b) exception to which the evidence was claimed to be relevant. These maneuvers were deemed to constitute error.[26] In *United States v. Alessi,*[27] the Second Circuit said that evidence of uncharged crimes relating to defendant's mental state should not be admitted until the end of the defendant's case, "since by that time the court is in a better position to determine whether knowledge or intent is truly a disputed issue and whether the probative value of the evidence outweighs the risk of unfair prejudice."[28] The *Alessi* court also approved the following jury charge:

> You may not consider [other crime evidence] to prove the character of Mr. Alessi, in order to show that he acted in conformity with that. But you may consider it in determining Mr. Alessi's knowledge or intent or plan or motive.[29]

23. People v. Ventimiglia, 52 N.Y.2d 350, 438 N.Y.S.2d 261, 420 N.E.2d 59 (1981). See § 404.1, at notes 10–14, supra.

24. According to the Advisory Committee's Note:

The amendment requires the prosecution to provide notice, regardless of how it intends to use the extrinsic act evidence at trial, i.e., during its case-in-chief, for impeachment, or for possible rebuttal. The court in its discretion may, under the facts, decide that the particular request or notice was not reasonable, either because of the lack of timeliness or completeness. Because the notice requirement serves as condition precedent to admissibility of 404(b) evidence, the offered evidence is inadmissible if the court decides that the notice requirement has not been met.

25. 618 F.2d 934 (2d Cir.1980).

26. Noting that defendants frequently fail to disclose whether there will be defense evidence, and if so what it will be, the court said that "the safer course in offering similar act evidence that should normally await the prosecution's rebuttal case * * * is for the prosecution to rest, reserving, out of the presence of the jury, the right to reopen to present such evidence in the event the defendants rest without introducing evidence." 618 F.2d at 939 n.1. The court also stated that it is incumbent on the government to specify the precise Rule 404(b) exception(s) it seeks to invoke and it should not use the "inclusionary approach." Id. at n.2.

27. 638 F.2d 466 (2d Cir.1980).

28. Id. at 477.

29. Id. at 476.

§ 404.2   RELEVANCY   Ch. 4

It follows that prior bad acts can be used as rebuttal to a defense.[30] If a particular element of the crime, such as intent, is not in issue, there is no excuse for introducing the prior crime in order to prove intent.[31] The Second Circuit has allowed defendant to stipulate the intent issue out of the case, thus blocking the government's uncharged crime evidence.[32]

c. Civil Cases

Reputation or opinion evidence is not admissible under Rule 404(a) to prove, in a civil case, that a party acted in conformity with character,[33] but there is no prohibition on other-act evidence under in Rule 404(b) when it is probative of some issue other than mere propensity. Thus, for example, in an employment discrimination case evidence of prior acts of discrimination can be admissible;[34] and in a case involving racial discrimination, "it is clear that [under Rule 404(b)] the proffered evidence of past acts of racial discrimination was relevant to prove the landlord's motive in his action towards appellant."[35]

In *Leucadia, Inc. v. Reliance Ins. Co.*,[36] a suit on a fidelity bond, evidence of the employee's dishonesty prior to the period covered by the bond could not be introduced to show liability, but was admissible to show the employee's intent with respect to those acts that were committed during the bond period. In a civil rights claim against a police officer, evidence of his conduct concerning another person was admissible to show pattern and intent;[37] and in another civil rights claim evidence of a previous altercation between the claimant prisoner and a correction officer was held admissible on the issue of whether the officer's supervisor was on notice of the danger to the prisoner.[38] But relevance is not always shown. In *Cullen v. Margiotta*,[39] the fact political officials had extorted contributions from insurance brokers seeking business with the county could not be introduced to prove that county

---

30. United States v. Paccione, 949 F.2d 1183, 1199 (2d Cir.1991), cert. denied, 505 U.S. 1220, 112 S.Ct. 3029, 120 L.Ed.2d 900 (1992)(when defendant testified that he had no intent to violate the dumping law, the government was permitted to introduce evidence that at the time in question he had offered money to officers to "just go away").

31. United States v. Colon, 880 F.2d 650, 656–57 (2d Cir.1989).

32. United States v. Ortiz, 857 F.2d 900, 903–04 (2d Cir.1988), cert. denied, 489 U.S. 1070, 109 S.Ct. 1352, 103 L.Ed.2d 820 (1989)(intent is not in the case when defendant denies he committed the charged crime altogether, or if he stipulates that if found to have committed the charged crime, he had the requisite intent).

33. See § 402.2 supra; Nakasian v. Incontrade, Inc., 78 F.R.D. 229 (S.D.N.Y. 1978).

34. Hazelwood School Dist. v. United States, 433 U.S. 299, 309 n.15, 97 S.Ct. 2736, 2742, 53 L.Ed.2d 768, 778 (1977).

35. Miller v. Poretsky, 595 F.2d 780, 791 (D.C.Cir.1978).

36. 864 F.2d 964, 971 (2d Cir.1988), cert. denied, 490 U.S. 1107, 109 S.Ct. 3160, 104 L.Ed.2d 1023 (1989).

37. Ismail v. Cohen, 706 F.Supp. 243, 253 (S.D.N.Y.1989), aff'd, 899 F.2d 183 (2d Cir.1990); compare Otero v. Jennings, 698 F.Supp. 42 (S.D.N.Y.1988)(in civil rights case against police officer unsubstantiated complaints concerning officer's prior conduct were held inadmissible).

38. Eng v. Scully, 146 F.R.D. 74, 80 (S.D.N.Y.1993).

39. 811 F.2d 698 (2d Cir.1987), cert. denied sub. nom., Nassau Co. Republican Committee v. Cullin, 483 U.S. 1021, 107 S.Ct. 3266, 97 L.Ed.2d 764, 483 U.S. 1021 (1987).

employees had also been forced to make contributions. A previous trademark case brought against defendants was inadmissible to show willful infringement in a case brought for copyright infringement.[40] And in a negligence action the court found that while, if numerous enough, evidence of other negligent repairs might be admissible, where there was evidence of only one other unrelated repair, the probative value of the evidence was vastly outweighed by its prejudicial effect.[41]

Library References:

West's Key No. Digests, Criminal Law ⚖=369–374; Evidence ⚖=129–142.

405 Similar Occurrences

§ 405.1 New York

a. Generally

Related to the question of a person's or institution's habit or custom[1] is the question whether other occurrences not rising to the level of habit nevertheless are relevant to a disputed issue. There is some overlap with the *Molineux* exceptions since the other occurrence(s) may tend to show the actor's intent, absence of accident or mistake, common scheme or plan, motive or identity.[2] This topic is broken out of the *Molineux* section and the habit section, however, because the common law has tended to treat similar occurrences in civil cases on a separate basis, and often the evidence tends to prove a specific issue other than character, such as notice, condition or value. Hence, we will examine the admissibility of similar occurrences in accident cases, other business transactions, and other sales of similar property to prove value.

b. Other Accidents

As a general rule, proof of a party's involvement in prior accidents is inadmissible simply to show the party's propensity for carelessness, since this is akin to character evidence.[3] On the other hand, if the prior accident tends to prove notice of a dangerous condition, or simply the existence of a dangerous condition, it can become relevant and admissible. In *Hyde v. County of Rensselaer*,[4] it was stated: "It is well settled that proof of a prior accident, whether offered as proof of the existence of a dangerous condition or as proof of notice thereof, is admissible only upon a showing that the relevant conditions of the subject accident and

---

40. Warner Bros., Inc. v. Dae Rim Trading, Inc., 677 F.Supp. 740, 764 (S.D.N.Y. 1988), appeal denied, 877 F.2d 1120 (2d Cir.1989).

41. Strauss v. Douglas Aircraft Co., 404 F.2d 1152, 1158 (2d Cir.1968).

§ 405.1

1. See § 406.1 infra.

2. People v. Molineux, 168 N.Y. 264, 61 N.E. 286 (1901). See discussion in § 404.1 supra. See the discussion of civil cases in § 404.1(*l*).

3. Kourtalis v. City of New York, 191 A.D.2d 480, 481, 594 N.Y.S.2d 325, 327 (2d Dep't 1993); Feaster v. N.Y.C. Transit Auth., 172 A.D.2d 284, 568 N.Y.S.2d 380, 381 (1st Dep't 1991). Neither are similar acts of negligence considered admissible as habitual conduct. See § 406.1 infra.

4. 51 N.Y.2d 927, 434 N.Y.S.2d 984, 415 N.E.2d 972 (1980). See 21 A.L.R.4th 482.

§ 405.1   RELEVANCY   Ch. 4

the previous one were substantially the same."[5] Accordingly, in that case a state trooper's testimony that he had investigated a previous accident at the same location as the one involved in the case on trial was admissible to provide evidence of the condition of the shoulder of the road and the delineator posts "on the issue of constructive notice."[6] Additionally, evidence of other accidents may be admissible to show that a dangerous condition was the proximate cause of the subject accident.[7]

As indicated in the quote from *Hyde*, a foundation must be laid to the effect that conditions were substantially the same on the prior occasion as on the date of the incident in issue.[8] There must be a showing of the relevant conditions, such as weather,[9] time of day[10] and physical conditions at the accident scene.[11] In one case, for example, plaintiff, attempting to prove a dangerous street condition due in part to water accumulation, was allowed by the trial court to introduce computer records showing the prior accident history at the relevant location. This was held to be error because the records "did not list road conditions for the prior accidents and none listed water accumulation as a prime or contributing factor. Thus, the jury was improperly allowed to speculate."[12]

The occurrence of accidents after the accident in issue can be relevant on the issue of dangerous condition,[13] although not, of course,

---

5. 51 N.Y.2d at 929, 434 N.Y.S.2d at 985, 415 N.E.2d at 973.

6. Id. Apparently the witness improperly testified as to other details of the prior accident, but counsel's failure to request limiting instructions eliminated a basis for reversal.

7. Kaplan v. City of New York, 10 A.D.2d 319, 321, 200 N.Y.S.2d 261, 265 (1st Dep't 1960).

8. In addition to Hyde, see Gallagher v. City of New York, 30 A.D.2d 688, 292 N.Y.S.2d 139 (2d Dep't 1968); Jasinski v. New York Cent. R.R., 21 A.D.2d 456, 250 N.Y.S.2d 942 (4th Dep't 1964). Whether sufficient similarity of conditions exists is a preliminary question to be decided by the trial judge, not the jury. Vega v. Jacobs, 84 A.D.2d 813, 814, 444 N.Y.S.2d 132, 133 (2d Dep't 1981).

9. Castleberry v. Hudson Valley Asphalt Corp., 60 A.D.2d 878, 879, 401 N.Y.S.2d 278, 279 (2d Dep't 1978)("It was reversible error for the trial court to have permitted testimony that about 18 days prior to the accident, another individual had been injured as a result of his having slipped on the defendant's platform. On that date, unlike the day on which plaintiff * * * was injured, it had been raining heavily, thus making the oil soaked platform more slippery than usual.").

10. Gilliard v. Long Island Railroad Co., 45 N.Y.2d 996, 997, 413 N.Y.S.2d 116, 116, 385 N.E.2d 1044, 1044 (1978). ("The accident involving the plaintiff occurred in broad daylight whereas the prior accident occurred at night. There was no proof as to the speed of the approaching train at the time of the prior accident, whether or not the crossing whistle or bell were sounded, what the operator of the vehicle did or did not do before crossing the tracks, the direction or the speed of that vehicle.").

11. Hyde v. County of Rensselaer, 51 N.Y.2d 927, 929, 434 N.Y.S.2d 984, 985, 415 N.E.2d 972, 973 (1980).

12. Vega v. Jacobs, 84 A.D.2d 813, 814, 444 N.Y.S.2d 132, 134 (2d Dep't 1981). See also Dudley v. County of Saratoga, 145 A.D.2d 689, 690, 535 N.Y.S.2d 231, 233 (3d Dep't 1988), appeal denied, 73 N.Y.2d 710, 541 N.Y.S.2d 764, 539 N.E.2d 592 (1989)(no "foundation laid" in terms of similar conditions and the issue to be proved with respect to prior and subsequent accidents sought to be introduced by plaintiff).

13. Klatz v. Armor Elevator, 93 A.D.2d 633, 638, 462 N.Y.S.2d 677, 680 (2d Dep't 1983)("It has been consistently held by the courts of this state that proof of subsequent accidents at the same place and under the same conditions, while of no probative value on the question of notice, is admissible to establish the existence of a dangerous condition, instrumentality or place * * *.").

on the issue of notice.[14]

Defendant may introduce evidence that the accident site has been accident free in the past. This would tend to show the absence of a dangerous condition, as well as lack of notice. In *Orlick v. Granit Hotel*,[15] the Court of Appeals approved of the admissibility of such evidence provided there had been no change or alteration in the site over the period in question. The issue there was the trial court's charge. "In our opinion, the trial court should have charged that the evidence of no prior accidents (as scanty as it was) would merely be a *factor* for consideration and not in any way be conclusive on the issue of the nature of the condition of the stairway."[16] And in *De Salvo v. Stanley-Mark-Strand Corp.*,[17] the Court of Appeals dealt with plaintiff's claim that the balustrade guarding the mezzanine in a movie theater was not high enough to protect patrons from injury. In permitting evidence that showed no prior accidents had occurred, the Court quoted from an older case:[18] " 'No structure is ever so made that it may not be made safer. But as a general rule, when an appliance or machine or structure, not obviously dangerous, has been in daily use for years, and has uniformly proved adequate, safe and convenient, its use may be continued without the imputation of culpable imprudence or carelessness.' "[19]

c. Other Business Transactions

McCormick succinctly states the rule:

Evidence concerning other contracts or business dealings may be relevant to prove the terms of a contract, the meaning of these terms, a business habit or custom, and occasionally, the authority of an agent. As to many of these uses, there is little controversy. Certainly, evidence of other transactions between the same parties readily is received when relevant to show the meaning they probably attached to the terms of a contract.[20]

Perhaps because such evidence is so "readily received," there is a paucity of cases in New York which discuss the rule. This principle has been extended in the Second Circuit so that a plaintiff's business transactions with others can be used in interpreting a contract with the defendant.[21] McCormick is in agreement that prior transactions with third parties can also be relevant;[22] but the evidence of "parallelism" between the other transactions and the one in issue must be strong and

---

14. Id.; Bolm v. Triumph Corp., 71 A.D.2d 429, 438, 422 N.Y.S.2d 969, 975 (4th Dep't 1979)(evidence of another motorcycle accident similar to plaintiff's was admissible only on the question of faulty design, since the other accident happened after plaintiff's).

15. 30 N.Y.2d 246, 250, 331 N.Y.S.2d 651, 654, 282 N.E.2d 610, 612 (1972).

16. Id. (emphasis in original).

17. 281 N.Y. 333, 23 N.E.2d 457 (1939), reargument denied, 282 N.Y. 589, 25 N.E.2d 143 (1940).

18. Lafflin v. Buffalo and Southwestern R.R. Co., 106 N.Y. 136, 12 N.E. 599 (1887).

19. De Salvo, 281 N.Y. at 340, 23 N.E.2d at 459.

20. McCormick § 198, at 837–38.

21. Cibro Petroleum Products v. Sohio Alaska Petroleum, 602 F.Supp. 1520, 1551 (N.D.N.Y.1985), aff'd, 798 F.2d 1421 (Em. App.1986), cert. dismissed, 479 U.S. 979, 107 S.Ct. 562, 93 L.Ed.2d 568 (1986).

22. McCormick § 198, at 838, 839.

convincing—stronger than when the prior transaction is with the same party.[23]

In an 1893 case the Court of Appeals held, however, that past dealings with third parties would not be admissible to prove the transaction with the other party.[24]

d. Sales of Property

In eminent domain cases,[25] tax assessment cases,[26] and other cases where it is necessary to prove the value of real property,[27] evidence of comparable sales is admissible. The crucial question is whether prior sales are truly comparable in point of time, "relative size of the properties, their condition, the nature of the respective neighborhoods, and the circumstances of the sale."[28] If comparable, the other sales are "commonly the most accurate standard" available for valuation.[29] Comparable does not mean "identical" and so "dissimilarity in one or more respects should not necessarily render irrelevant a sale of an otherwise similar parcel of land."[30]

If a sale is to be comparable "the rule has evolved that the purchase price set in the course of an arm's length transaction of recent vintage, if not explained away as abnormal in any fashion, is evidence of the 'highest rank' to determine the true value of the property at that time * * *"[31]

The trial judge has discretion, so that rejection of evidence as to other properties which significantly differ both with respect to size and location will usually be affirmed.[32] The limits of the judge's discretion are wide, thus:

> In the case at bar, despite the rather large difference in size between the respondent's comparables (ranging from .83 to 1.51 acres), and that of the subject property (24.1 acres), and despite the different zoning classification of the respondents' fourth comparable, we hold that the properties were sufficiently alike in "character, situation, usability and improvements" * * * to have been relevant, with appropriate adjustments made for

---

23. Cibro, at 1551, citing Weinstein and Berger ¶ 406[03], at 406–18.

24. McLoghlin v. N.M.V. Bank, 139 N.Y. 514, 34 N.E. 1095 (1893)(to prove that plaintiff's account with defendant bank was an interest-bearing account, plaintiff wanted to show that all his accounts with other banks were interest-bearing).

25. Village of Lawrence v. Greenwood, 300 N.Y. 231, 90 N.E.2d 53 (1949).

26. Matter of 860 Fifth Ave. Corp. v. Tax Comm., 8 N.Y.2d 29, 31, 200 N.Y.S.2d 817, 819, 167 N.E.2d 455, 456 (1960).

27. See Plaza Hotel Associates v. Wellington Associates, Inc., 37 N.Y.2d 273, 372 N.Y.S.2d 35, 333 N.E.2d 346 (1975)(value of lease based on market value of land).

28. Matter of Katz v. Assessor, 82 A.D.2d 654, 658, 442 N.Y.S.2d 795, 798 (2d Dep't 1981).

29. Matter of Merrick Holding Corp. v. Board of Assessors, 45 N.Y.2d 538, 542, 410 N.Y.S.2d 565, 567, 382 N.E.2d 1341, 1342 (1978).

30. Matter of Katz, supra note 28, 82 A.D.2d at 658, 442 N.Y.S.2d at 798.

31. Plaza Hotel Associates, supra note 27, 37 N.Y.2d at 277, 372 N.Y.S.2d at 39, 333 N.E.2d at 34.

32. Niagara Falls Urban Renewal Agency v. 123 Falls Realty, 66 A.D.2d 1009, 411 N.Y.S.2d 752 (4th Dep't 1978). See also Matter of Katz, supra note 28, 82 A.D.2d at 658, 442 N.Y.S.2d at 797.

existing dissimilarities. Consequently, we are unable to say that Special Term, as a matter of law, could not consider these sales in arriving at its finding of value.[33]

As to personal property, there seems to be no reason why comparable sales should not be admissible to prove value since the Court of Appeals long ago set virtually no limits on the sort of evidence which could be admitted, and approved of evidence of the cost to plaintiff when she bought the items.[34]

If comparable sales of other properties provide an accurate guide, it follows that a recent sale of the subject property ought to be even more accurate. Generally, the best evidence of such value is "a recent sale of the subject property between a seller under no compulsion to sell and a buyer under no compulsion to buy."[35] But even in such a case the judge is not bound by such sale where, for instance, the value of the assembled properties is much greater than the sum paid for each property by claimant as he was building the assemblage.[36]

Library References:

West's Key No. Digests, Criminal Law ⊂⇒369–374; Evidence ⊂⇒129–142; Negligence ⊂⇒125.

§ 405.2 Federal

The rules governing prior similar acts in the Second Circuit conform to those discussed in the last section with regard to New York.

a. Other Accidents

Evidence of prior accidents, while not admissible to show the propensity of the actor,[1] is admissible to show the existence of a dangerous condition and notice of that condition. Thus, in *Fortunato v. Ford Motor Co.*,[2] where plaintiff alleged faulty equipment and Ford defended on the ground of dangerous road conditions, it was stated: "Ford's third contention is that it was unable to show the dangerous nature of the 'A' curve on the bridge, which would have supported its theory of the accident. Competent evidence of accidents similar to Fortunato's on that segment of the bridge would have been admissible. * * *"[3] In the other component of the *Fortunato* case involving the product, the court indi-

---

33. Matter of Katz, supra note 28, 82 A.D.2d at 659, 442 N.Y.S.2d at 798.

34. Jones v. Morgan, 90 N.Y. 4, 10 (1882). The court said that if there is no direct evidence of market value at the time in question, "then market value at some other time before or after may be proved." Id.

35. Allied Corp. v. Town of Camillus, 80 N.Y.2d 351, 356, 590 N.Y.S.2d 417, 419, 604 N.E.2d 1348, 1350 (1992)(tax certiorari proceeding).

36. Gold-Mark 35 Associates v. State, 210 A.D.2d 377, 620 N.Y.S.2d 110 (2d Dep't 1994).

§ 405.2

1. See Cereste v. New York, New Haven & Hartford R. Co., 231 F.2d 50, 57 (2d Cir.1956), cert. denied, 351 U.S. 951, 76 S.Ct. 848, 100 L.Ed. 1475 (1956).

2. 464 F.2d 962, 968 (2d Cir.1972), cert. denied, 409 U.S. 1038, 93 S.Ct. 517, 34 L.Ed.2d 487 (1972).

3. Id. The court cites Dist. of Columbia v. Arms, 107 U.S. 519, 2 S.Ct. 840, 27 L.Ed. 618 (1883); and Kaplan v. City of New York, 10 A.D.2d 319, 200 N.Y.S.2d 261 (1960).

§ 405.2 RELEVANCY Ch. 4

cated that while evidence of lack of complaints concerning the condition of the car would not be admissible where the claim is based on warranty (because warranty is based on the strict liability concept), it would be admissible were the claim grounded in negligence.[4]

In dictum in *McFarland v. Gregory*,[5] the court discussed principles related to the prior accident rule by stating:

> The continuity presumption [an existing condition is presumed to continue to exist] and the presumption of backward relation [if a situation exists at one point in time, it is to be presumed that it existed before that time] appear to be reasonable grounds on which to draw inferences where (1) a situation or the circumstances surrounding it do not go through an apparent material change and (2) the lapse of time is not great enough to suggest that unknown circumstances or causes, in the normal course of events, will have changed the situation.[6]

These so-called presumptions would seem to be useful in establishing the required foundation for the introduction of prior accident evidence that conditions were substantially the same.

Finally, in *Apicella v. McNeil Laboratories, Inc.*,[7] where plaintiff claimed to be disabled as a result of using defendant's drug, the court found that evidence of harm occurring to other persons because of the administering of this drug would be admissible. The court stated: "The fact that other persons suffered harm from the drug is relevant since it has a 'tendency to make the existence of * * * [a fact that is] of consequence to the determination of the action more probable * * * than it would be without the evidence.' Fed.R.Ev., Rule 401."[8] In *Becker v. American Airlines, Inc.*,[9] where plaintiff, in a case involving allegations of a faulty altimeter, sought to introduce evidence that a dozen identical altimeters malfunctioned before the accident and 25 malfunctioned after that date, the court ruled that the 12 prior malfunc-

---

4. 464 F.2d at 967 n.1.

5. 425 F.2d 443 (2d Cir.1970).

6. Id. at 447. In the same vein, see Keohane v. New York Central R.R. Co., 418 F.2d 478 (2d Cir.1969), where the court, considering whether evidence of the defective condition of an elevator would have a bearing on notice and dangerous condition, quoted from Lebrecht v. Bethlehem Steel Corp., 402 F.2d 585, 592 (2d Cir.1968), which, in turn, quoted from Wigmore and another Second Circuit case as follows:

> When the existence of an object, condition, quality, or tendency at a given time is in issue, the *prior existence* of it is in human experience some indication of its probable persistence of continuance *at a later period.* * * * Similar considerations affect the use of *subsequent existence* as evidence of existence at the time in issue. 2 Wigmore, Evidence § 437 (3d ed. 1940).

But in our opinion the trial court erred as a matter of law in failing to consider and apply the evidentiary principle that the subsequent existence of a fact supports the inference of its earlier existence, when the subsequent condition is one which ordinarily would not exist unless it had also existed at the earlier time. United States v. Consolidated Laundries Corp., 291 F.2d 563, 569 (2d Cir.1961).

418 F.2d at 481.

7. 66 F.R.D. 78 (E.D.N.Y.1975).

8. Id. at 82. In this case, however, evidence of the other incidents was sought from the editor of a medical magazine who claimed the journalist's privilege. Since the same information could be gained from other sources, the privilege was upheld.

9. 200 F.Supp. 243, 245 (S.D.N.Y.1961).

tions were relevant to the issues of notice and faulty product, but that the malfunctions occurring after the accident would be inadmissible because cumulative on the issue of faulty product.[10]

b. Other Business Transactions

When the meaning of a contract term or the conduct of a party to a business transaction is in issue, evidence of other transactions between the same parties is relevant to the intention of the parties on the occasion in issue.[11] This principle has been extended in the Second Circuit so that plaintiff's business transactions with others can be used in interpreting a contract with the defendant.[12] The *Cibro* court, however, added the admonition that "[s]ubsidiary evidence of parallelism must be strong and convincing when dealing with third party situations, and there is every reason to believe that standards of admissibility should be higher than when dealing with transactions between the same parties."[13] The *Cibro* court states that "[n]umerous federal courts are in agreement."[14]

c. Sales of Property

When the value of real property is in issue, as, for example, in condemnation cases, "[t]he best evidence of market value is comparable sales—*i.e.*, sales from a willing seller to a willing buyer of similar property in the vicinity of the taking at or about the same time as the taking."[15] Indeed, the "overwhelming weight of authority" in the federal courts permits such evidence with respect to either real or personal property when value is the issue.[16]

The New York rules set forth in the last section dealing with comparability also apply here, as does the observation that the trial judge possesses a great deal of discretion. *United States v. Michoud Industrial Facilities*,[17] however, demonstrates that an appellate court is free to find the evidence, due to lack of significant comparability, insufficient to establish a sustainable value.[18]

Library References:

West's Key No. Digests, Criminal Law ⟐369–374; Evidence ⟐129–142; Negligence ⟐125.

10. Id. at 245–46.
11. McCormick § 198, at 837–38.
12. Cibro Petroleum Products v. Sohio Alaska Petroleum, 602 F.Supp. 1520, 1551 (N.D.N.Y.1985), aff'd, 798 F.2d 1421 (Em. App.1986), cert. dismissed, 479 U.S. 979, 107 S.Ct. 562, 93 L.Ed.2d 568 (1986).
13. Id. at 1551.
14. Cited are: Federal Express Corp. v. Pan American World Airways, 623 F.2d 1297 (8th Cir.1980); Joseph v. Krull Wholesale Drug Co., 147 F.Supp. 250 (E.D.Pa. 1956), aff'd, 245 F.2d 231 (3d Cir.1957); and Amerine National Corporation v. Denver Feed Co., 493 F.2d 1275 (10th Cir. 1974). Cibro, 602 F.Supp. at 1551.
15. United States v. 8.41 Acres of Land, 680 F.2d 388 (5th Cir.1982).
16. United States v. Bloom, 237 F.2d 158, 163 (2d Cir.1956). In this case, the value of personal property was in issue— diamonds tied into an illegal promotion scheme.
17. 322 F.2d 698 (5th Cir.1963).
18. Id. at 706.

406 Habit and Custom

§ 406.1 New York

a. Generally

Whereas the general rule prohibits proof of character in civil cases to show that the party acted in conformity with the pertinent character trait,[1] the *habit* of a party might well be admissible as circumstantial evidence that she acted in accord with the habit at the time in question. The New York courts, for instance, have long followed the rule that allows evidence of business or professional habit, custom or usage to prove that the practice was followed on the occasion in question.[2] Character, on the other hand, goes to a person's general personality traits such as peacefulness or violence, carefulness or carelessness, honesty or dishonesty, sobriety or drunkenness. When a person is characterized as having a habit of carelessness, the word "habit" is really being used to show the person's general trait. As McCormick puts it, habit

> is more specific. It denotes one's regular response to a repeated situation. * * * A habit [as opposed to character] is the person's regular practice of responding to a particular kind of situation with a specific type of conduct. Thus, a person may be in the habit of bounding down a certain stairway two or three steps at a time, of patronizing a particular pub after each day's work, or of driving his automobile without using a seat belt.[3]

In contrast to the rule of admissibility with respect to business or professional habit, traditionally there has been a rule of inadmissibility in negligence cases arising outside the workplace.[4] Between these two extremes, and combining elements of both, is the situation where proof of a careless way of doing particular things in the workplace can be admitted as showing that the worker acted the same way at the time of the event in issue when it is shown that he is the sole actor.[5]

A separate and distinct topic is custom and usage as a standard of care. The latter relates not to whether a party acted in conformity with his own habits or traits, but to whether a party acted with due care compared to the care used by others in the same business or industry.[6] All of these topics are discussed below.

b. Business and Professional Habit

This category of habit evidence provides the context for judicial pronouncements that habit evidence is normally admissible. Thus, "one

---

§ 406.1

1. See § 402.1(c) supra.
2. Beakes v. Da Cunha, 126 N.Y. 293, 298, 27 N.E. 251, 252 (1891).
3. McCormick § 195, at 825–26.
4. Witherel v. Balling Construction, Inc., 99 A.D.2d 646, 647, 472 N.Y.S.2d 218, 219 (4th Dep't 1984); Hartley v. Szadkowski, 32 A.D.2d 550, 300 N.Y.S.2d 82 (2d Dep't 1969).
5. Halloran v. Virginia Chemicals, Inc., 41 N.Y.2d 386, 393 N.Y.S.2d 341, 361 N.E.2d 991 (1977).
6. Trimarco v. Klein, 56 N.Y.2d 98, 451 N.Y.S.2d 52, 436 N.E.2d 502 (1982).

who has demonstrated a consistent response under given circumstances is more likely to repeat that response when the circumstances arise again, [and therefore] evidence of habit has, since the days of the common-law reports, generally been admissible to prove conformity on specified occasions * * *."[7] New York has followed the rule allowing a business, professional or other institutional practice or custom to be used to show that such would have been followed under the same set of circumstances on a specific occasion.[8]

Consider these examples: To prove that notice was mailed on a specified day of the month, a witness was allowed to testify that he is in the habit of being home on that day of the month to transact such business.[9] To prove due execution of a will, a lawyer was allowed to testify that he always had wills executed according to statutory requirements.[10] Where a dispute arose whether the District Attorney's office conveyed a communication to the Legal Aid office, it was proper to allow the District Attorney's secretary to testify as to a routine for the transmittal of such messages over the years.[11] Where plaintiff sought to prove that the Lilly Company sold DES out of a certain drugstore in Owego, New York, during the mid-sixties, she was allowed to show that it was the practice of the wholesaler to stock the Buffalo distribution center with Lilly's DES, and from that it could be inferred that this practice also obtained with respect to the Syracuse distribution center from which the Owego store received its drug products.[12] But the court in another case, while recognizing that evidence of repetitive conduct would allow a nurse to establish her habit of proper sterilization practices (she had no recollection of the incident on trial), nevertheless found that she had not succeeded in establishing such a routine through proof of other instances.[13]

Helpful examples are also set forth in *Rigie v. Goldman*,[14] a case discussed below under subpart c.

7. People v. Culhane, 45 N.Y.2d 757, 763, 408 N.Y.S.2d 489, 494, 380 N.E.2d 315, 320, cert. denied, 439 U.S. 1047, 99 S.Ct. 723, 58 L.Ed.2d 706 (1978).

8. Soltis v. State, 188 A.D.2d 201, 203, 594 N.Y.S.2d 433, 434 (3d Dep't 1993)(here the dispute arose over the Court of Claims' refusal to receive evidence of the custom and practice of the physician's assistants and nurses at a prison clinic to advise inmates that the treating physicians were not state employees).

9. Beakes v. Da Cunha, 126 N.Y. 293, 298, 27 N.E. 251, 252 (1891).

10. Matter of Kellum, 52 N.Y. 517, 519–20 (1873).

11. People v. Johnson, 190 A.D.2d 910, 593 N.Y.S.2d 589 (3d Dep't 1993).

12. NY County DES Litigation, 171 A.D.2d 119, 124–25, 575 N.Y.S.2d 19, 23 (1st Dep't 1991).

13. Lindeman v. Slavin, 184 A.D.2d 910, 585 N.Y.S.2d 568 (3d Dep't 1992).

14. 148 A.D.2d 23, 26, 543 N.Y.S.2d 983, 984–85 (2d Dep't 1989):

As a general rule, evidence of habitual behavior or custom is admissible as circumstantial proof that the habit was followed on the occasion in question (see, Richardson, Evidence § 185 [Prince 10th ed.]). Traditionally, the admissibility of such evidence of habit was limited to situations involving the performance of routine business or professional tasks (see, Matter of Will of Kellum, 52 N.Y. 517 [evidence of habit of drawing a will in accordance with statutory requirements]; People v. Bombard, 5 A.D.2d 923, and People v. Bean, 284 App.Div. 922 [evidence of habit of advising defendants of their right to counsel]; Peninsula Natl. Bank v. Hill, 52 Misc.2d 903, aff'd, 30 A.D.2d 643 [evidence of process server's habit in making substituted service]). There is also some suggestion in the decisional law that in a criminal case evi-

§ 406.1 RELEVANCY Ch. 4

c. Habit Evidence in the Workplace

Halloran v. Virginia Chemicals,[15] contains a comprehensive discussion of habit evidence. The question concerned defendant manufacturer's liability where a can of freon exploded while being used by plaintiff automobile mechanic during the course of his work in servicing a customer's car. Other than the plaintiff there were no eyewitnesses. On the issue of contributory negligence, defendant produced testimony from plaintiff's co-employee that it was plaintiff's practice to place the freon can in water and then insert a heating coil in the water to rapidly heat the freon, thereby suggesting that this practice was being followed on the occasion when the can blew up.

The court first restated the general rule that "[b]ecause one who has demonstrated a consistent response under given circumstances is more likely to repeat that response when the circumstances arise again, evidence of habit has, since the days of common-law reports, generally been admissible to prove conformity on specified occasions. * * *"[16] While noting that habit traditionally is not allowed in negligence cases, the court found that routine practice of an individual in the course of employment could be admitted as an indicator of how the person acted at the time in question, especially given the fact that the person had sole control over the practice—here, the dangerous habit of overheating cans of freon while servicing automobile air conditioning units. The Court cautioned that when negligence is in issue it is normally error to admit similar specific acts of carelessness or carefulness; where, however, there is a "deliberate and repetitive" practice the necessary relevancy is heightened.[17] The Court cited business practice cases where habit and

---

dence of the defendant's "habitual" appearance (see, People v. Medina, 130 A.D.2d 515; People v. Gonzalez, 100 A.D.2d 852) or of the defendant's habit of carrying a particular weapon (see, People v. Paschall, 91 A.D.2d 645) may be admissible under appropriate circumstances.

15. 41 N.Y.2d 386, 393 N.Y.S.2d 341, 361 N.E.2d 991 (1977).

16. Id. at 391, 393 N.Y.S.2d at 345, 361 N.E.2d at 995.

17. The fact that the habit evidence in this case was for the purpose of showing plaintiff's negligence should not, said the court, disqualify it:

Hence, a lawyer, to prove due execution of a will, may testify that he always has wills executed according to statutory requirements * * *. So too, to prove that notice is mailed on a specified day of the month, one is allowed to testify that he is in the habit of being home on that day of the month to transact such business * * *.

When negligence is at issue, however, New York courts have long resisted allowing evidence of specific acts of carelessness or carefulness to create an inference that such conduct was repeated when like circumstances were again presented (e.g., Warner v. New York Cent. R.R. Co., 44 N.Y. 465, 472; Grenadier v. Surface Transp. Corp. of N.Y., 271 App. Div. 460, 461; Lefcourt v. Jenkinson, 258 App.Div.1080; Richardson, Evidence, § 186; Fisch, New York Evidence, § 202; cf. Cabezudo v. New York's Eldorado, 50 A.D.2d 794, 795). Hence, evidence of a plaintiff's habit of jumping on streetcars may not be offered to prove he was negligent on the day of the accident (Eppendorf v. Brooklyn City & Newtown R.R. Co., 69 N.Y. 195, 197). Nor could testimony that the deceased had usually looked both ways before crossing railroad tracks be introduced to establish his care on the particular occasion (Zucker v. Whitridge, 205 N.Y. 50, 58–66, supra). Whether a carry-over from the prohibition against using so-called "character" evidence in civil cases, or grounded on the assumption that even repeated instances of negligence or care do not sufficiently increase the probability of like conduct on a particular occasion, the statement that evidence of habit or regular usage is never admissible to establish negligence is

routine is often admissible and applied them to the previously-closed negligence area so that "[p]roof of a deliberate repetitive practice by one in complete control of the circumstances * * * should * * * be admissible because it is so highly probative."[18] The Appellate Division, in *Rigie v. Goldman*[19] applied *Halloran* to a dentist's habit of explaining risks to patients (where the patient claimed lack of informed consent). The court found that *Halloran* established an exception to the general rule forbidding habit evidence in negligence cases, and had no trouble fitting the dentist's evidence within that exception.[20] On the other hand, where a surgeon defending himself against a malpractice charge was allowed to augment his testimony by using a video of another operation he flawlessly performed, the trial judge was held to have committed error.[21] While the demonstration was ostensibly to educate the jury, its actual effect was to show the general "carefulness" and "thoroughness" of the surgeon. The *Halloran* exception was held inapplicable: "The manufacture or use of an inanimate object is scarcely analogous to that of a physician performing surgery wherein each patient and the nature of his or her medical condition is unique as are the actions of the operating doctor."[22]

d. Habit in Negligence Cases—Non-Workplace Situations

When negligence outside the workplace is at issue *Halloran* states that "New York courts have long resisted allowing specific acts of carelessness or carefulness to create an inference that such conduct was repeated when like circumstances were again presented."[23] The *Hallo-*

too broad (see 1 Wigmore, Evidence [3d ed.], § 97, esp. p.532).

At least, as in this kind of case, where the issue involves proof of a deliberate and repetitive practice, a party should be able, by introducing evidence of such habit or regular usage, to allow the inference of its persistence, and hence negligence on a particular occasion (see McCormick, Evidence [2d ed.], § 195, advocating an even more expansive approach; see, also, 1 Wigmore, Evidence [3d ed.], § 97). Far less likely to vary with the attendant circumstances, such repetitive conduct is more predictive than the frequency (or rarity) of jumping on streetcars or exercising stop-look-and-listen caution in crossing railroad tracks. On no view, under traditional analysis, can conduct involving not only oneself but particularly other persons or independently controlled instrumentalities produce a regular usage because of the likely variation of the circumstances in which such conduct will be indulged.

41 N.Y.2d at 391-92,, 393 N.Y.S.2d at 345-46, 361 N.E.2d at 995-96.

18. Id. at 392, 393 N.Y.S.2d at 346, 361 N.E.2d at 996. As to the method of proving habit, the court stated: "[A] party must be able to show on *voir dire*, to the satisfaction of the Trial Judge, that he expects to prove a sufficient number of instances of the conduct in question * * *." Id. at 392, 393 N.Y.S.2d at 346, 361 N.E.2d at 996.

19. 148 A.D.2d 23, 543 N.Y.S.2d 983 (2d Dep't 1989).

20. It was stated: "Moreover, Dr. Levin was in complete control of the circumstances in which the operative procedure was performed. Thus, while creating no presumption that the practice was followed in the particular instance at issue, the testimony of Dr. Levin as to his routine practice, corroborated by his dental assistant, was properly admissible to support an inference by the jury that the practice was followed on the particular occasion in question." 148 A.D.2d at 29, 543 N.Y.S.2d at 986-87.

21. Glusaskas v. John E. Hutchinson, 148 A.D.2d 203, 544 N.Y.S.2d 323 (1st Dep't 1989).

22. Id. at 206, 544 N.Y.S.2d at 325.

23. 41 N.Y.2d at 391, 393 N.Y.S.2d at 345, 361 N.E.2d at 995.

§ 406.1 RELEVANCY Ch. 4

ran opinion presents several illustrations.[24] The general rule in negligence cases would reject evidence in an automobile case that a party was either a careful or a careless driver. Thus, in *Hartley v. Szadkowski*,[25] it was error for the trial judge to allow defense counsel to examine plaintiff about a prior accident. The Appellate Division ruled such evidence incompetent "to show that plaintiff was generally careless."[26] Likewise, the trait of being generally a careful or careless person is considered an inadmissible character trait, and not an admissible habit.[27]

Other cases support the view that the general rule of inadmissibility in non-workplace negligence cases is still intact.[28] In *Ferrer v. Harris*,[29] the Court of Appeals held that it would not be proper to allow evidence that the mother of the four-year-old plaintiff had instructed the child repeatedly on safe procedures to be used in crossing the street. Presumably, this would have been offered to show that the child had acted on those instructions at the time in question rather than having run from between parked cars in the middle of the block into the street as asserted by defendant, with whose vehicle she collided. Although this is not evidence of how the child actually acted on other occasions and was introduced to "explore the knowledge and experience of the infant"[30] the court noted the *Halloran* holding and said that the mother's instructions to the infant were not proof that the infant had acted on them. But even if there had been evidence of prior carefulness at curb's edge, *Halloran* apparently would not have tolerated such evidence because other actors were involved and the child was not in sole control of the situation. Account must be taken of the following limiting sentence in *Halloran*: "On no view, under traditional analysis, can conduct involving not only oneself but particularly other persons or independently

---

24. Hence, evidence of a plaintiff's habit of jumping on streetcars may not be offered to prove he was negligent on the day of the accident (Eppendorf v. Brooklyn City & Newtown R.R. Co., 69 N.Y. 195, 197). Nor could testimony that the deceased had usually looked both ways before crossing railroad tracks be introduced to establish his care on the particular occasion (Zucker v. Whitridge, 205 N.Y. 50, 58–66, supra). Whether a carry-over from the prohibition against using so-called "character" evidence in civil cases, or grounded on the assumption that even repeated instances of negligence or care do not sufficiently increase the probability of like conduct on a particular occasion, the statement that evidence of habit or regular usage is never admissible to establish negligence is too broad (see 1 Wigmore, Evidence [3d ed.], § 97, esp. p. 532).
41 N.Y.2d at 391, 393 N.Y.S.2d at 345, 361 N.E.2d at 995.

25. 32 A.D.2d 550, 300 N.Y.S.2d 82 (2d Dep't 1969).

26. Id. at 550, 300 N.Y.S.2d at 84.

27. Zucker v. Whitridge, 205 N.Y. 50, 98 N.E. 209 (1912)(where pedestrian struck by trolley car, evidence that pedestrian was a careful person, that he usually looked both ways before entering the street, was not admissible).

28. Witherel v. Balling Construction, Inc., 99 A.D.2d 646, 646–47, 472 N.Y.S.2d 218, 219 (4th Dep't 1984)(habits of workmen on job site in regard to drinking not admissible, court stating: "Although habit testimony may be admissible in certain limited circumstances, such as where a worker always operates a particular device in a particular way, such testimony is not admissible where the habit is not 'a deliberate and repetitive practice'"); Davis v. Blum, 70 A.D.2d 583, 416 N.Y.S.2d 57 (2d Dep't 1979)(error to admit plaintiff's drinking habit to show he used poor judgment at time in question).

29. 55 N.Y.2d 285, 449 N.Y.S.2d 162, 434 N.E.2d 231 (1982).

30. Id. at 294, 449 N.Y.S.2d at 167, 434 N.E.2d at 236.

controlled instrumentalities produce a regular usage because of the likely variation of the circumstances in which such conduct will be indulged."[31]

The proposed New York Code provision, which would admit habit evidence without regard to the limitations suggested in *Halloran*, is cited in the note.[32]

e. Eyewitnesses

Some courts in other jurisdictions allow evidence of habitual conduct to prove that the party acted the same way at the time in question only when there are no eyewitnesses to the event in issue who can testify how the party conducted himself.[33] The older cases in New York, while apparently allowing habit evidence whether or not there were eyewitnesses to the event, were nevertheless unclear on the point.[34] The language of proposed New York Evidence Code § 406(a) makes habit evidence admissible "regardless of the presence of eyewitnesses."[35]

f. Custom and Usage as a Standard of Care

Somewhat related to habit evidence, but clearly distinct, is evidence which tends to show industry-wide practices. This is admissible to project a standard against which to measure whether a party acted with due care. "Proof of a generally accepted practice, custom or usage within a particular trade or industry is admissible as tending to establish

---

31. 41 N.Y.2d at 392, 393 N.Y.S.2d at 346, 361 N.E.2d at 996. Further, the Halloran court stated:

> At least, as in this kind of case, where the issue involves proof of a deliberate and repetitive practice, a party should be able, by introducing evidence of such habit or regular usage, to allow the inference of its persistence, and hence negligence on a particular occasion (see McCormick, Evidence [2d ed.], § 195, advocating an even more expansive approach; see, also, 1 Wigmore, Evidence [3d ed.], § 97). Far less likely to vary with the attendant circumstances, such repetitive conduct is more predictive than the frequency (or rarity) of jumping on streetcars or exercising stop-look-and-listen caution in crossing railroad tracks. On no view, under traditional analysis, can conduct involving not only oneself but particularly other persons or independently controlled instrumentalities produce a regular usage because of the likely variation of the circumstances in which such conduct will be indulged. Proof of a deliberate repetitive practice by one in complete control of the circumstances is quite another matter and it should therefore be admissible because it is so highly probative.

41 N.Y.2d at 392, 393 N.Y.S.2d at 346, 361 N.E.2d at 995–96.

32. **§ 406 Habit; routine practice [PROPOSED]**

(a) **Admissibility.** Evidence of the habit of a person or of the routine practice of an organization, whether corroborated or not and regardless of the presence of eyewitnesses, is relevant to prove that the conduct of the person or organization on a particular occasion was in conformity with the habit or routine practice.

(b) **Method of proving.** Habit or routine practice shall be proved by testimony in the form of an opinion, otherwise admissible under sections 701 and 702 of this chapter, or by specific instances of conduct sufficient in number to warrant a finding that the habit existed or that the practice was routine.

33. McCormick § 195, at 828.

34. See Gibson v. Casein Mfg. Co., 157 App.Div. 46, 47, 141 N.Y.S. 887, 888 (3d Dep't 1913), where the court construed two Court of Appeals' cases, Zucker v. Whitridge, 205 N.Y. 50, 98 N.E. 209 (1912), and Parsons v. Syracuse, Binghamton & N.Y. R.R. Co., 205 N.Y. 226, 98 N.E. 331 (1912), as allowing, in dicta at least, habit testimony regardless of whether there were eyewitnesses. Those cases involved classic contributory negligence situations and for that reason habit evidence would be inadmissible.

35. See note 32 supra.

a standard of care, and proof of a departure from that general custom or usage may constitute evidence of negligence."[36]

The rule was applied in *Trimarco v. Klein*,[37] where plaintiff's proof concerning defective glass in a shower door was accompanied by trade bulletins setting forth the type of material to be used and evidence of custom and practice in the contracting industry as to proper materials. This was admissible to show defendant had not met prevailing standards.[38] In *Cruz v. New York Transit Authority*,[39] it was held that plaintiff, who had fallen from a railing located at the landing of an exterior stairway leading to an elevated subway station, should have been allowed to show that railings at defendant's other stations had been fitted with impediments which would have prevented his perching on the railing in question. And in *Cramer v. Kuhns*,[40] where defendant was sued on the basis of faulty design of its motorcycle side stand apparatus, it was deemed error not to allow defendant to produce a chart containing a synopsis of a survey of 80 motorcycle models illustrating that only eight employed side stand safety features different from the ones used by defendant.

The mere fact that another enterprise uses different procedures does not, of course, prove defendant's negligence in not conforming. But where dangers are ameliorated by a customary procedure in the industry, then those procedures may be proved as some evidence of the nonconforming defendant's negligence.[41]

36. Cruz v. New York Transit Authority, 136 A.D.2d 196, 199, 526 N.Y.S.2d 827, 829 (2d Dep't 1988).

37. 56 N.Y.2d 98, 451 N.Y.S.2d 52, 436 N.E.2d 502 (1982).

38. It was stated:
It follows that, when proof of an accepted practice is accompanied by evidence that the defendant conformed to it, this may establish due care (Bennett v. Long Is. R.R. Co., 163 N.Y. 1, 4 [custom not to lock switch on temporary railroad siding during construction]), and, contrariwise, when proof of a customary practice is coupled with a showing that it was ignored and that this departure was a proximate cause of the accident, it may serve to establish liability (Levine v. Blaine Co., 273 N.Y. 386, 389 [custom to equip dumbwaiter with rope which does not splinter]). Put more conceptually, proof of a common practice aids in "formulat[ing] the general expectation of society as to how individuals will act in the course of their undertakings, and thus to guide the common sense or expert intuition of a jury or commission when called on to judge of particular conduct under particular circumstances" (Pound, Administrative Application of Legal Standards, 44 ABA Rep., 445, 456–457).
Id. at 105–6, 451 at 55, 436 N.E.2d at 505. See also Bailey v. Baker's Air Force Gas Corp., 50 A.D.2d 129, 376 N.Y.S.2d 212 (3d Dep't 1975), leave to appeal denied, 39 N.Y.2d 708, 386 N.Y.S.2d 1025, 352 N.E.2d 595 (1976)(it was not error to receive in evidence the National Board of Fire Underwriters pamphlet number 58 as evidence of the customary way of handling propane gas).

39. 136 A.D.2d 196, 526 N.Y.S.2d 827 (2d Dep't 1988).

40. 213 A.D.2d 131, 630 N.Y.S.2d 128 (3d Dep't 1995).

41. Garthe v. Ruppert, 264 N.Y. 290, 190 N.E. 643 (1934). In Garthe, plaintiff argued that defendant's locker room, where he slipped and fell, was not maintained in the same way as a competitor's locker room. The court stated:

The plaintiff proved, over objection and exception, that in another brewery the work was done in a better way than by Ruppert; that the necessary goods and grains were received and the waste discharged and carried away without dust upon the one hand and moisture upon the other. It was reasoned by the plaintiff that if other breweries could do this, then Ruppert should have done it. Such evidence is incompetent to prove negligence. One man is not obliged to run his business the same as some other man,

§ 406.2 Federal

Rule 406 of the Federal Rules of Evidence provides:

> Evidence of the habit of a person or of the routine practice of an organization, whether corroborated or not and regardless of the presence of eyewitnesses, is relevant to prove that the conduct of the person or organization on a particular occasion was in conformity with the habit or routine practice.

The federal rule makes no distinction between negligence cases and cases in which business or professional habit is involved. For purposes of analysis, however, this section is divided into those two categories, and the remotely related topic of custom and usage as a standard of care will also be noted.

a. Business and Professional Habit

A few examples will help illustrate the application of Rule 406 in business and professional settings. To refute charges of food adulteration a defendant may introduce evidence of routine practices, or "business habits," involving clean-up, and sanitation procedures under Rule 406;[1] evidence may be taken as to the regular practice in a United States Attorney's office as to filing papers with the court;[2] evidence of customary practices employed at the Naturalization Service office were admissible to show they had been followed at the time in question;[3] and where plaintiff sought to prove that he was injured by a protruding wire left on

---

nor can he be judged before the law according to the methods employed by others. When, however, a custom has prevailed in the trade or in the calling, or certain dangers have been removed by a customary way of doing things safely, this custom may be proved to show that a manufacturer or anyone else employing men has fallen below the required standard. Never, however, has it been permitted to take one or two instances as a gauge or guide in place of the custom of the trade. Ruppert was not obliged to change his factory or the methods of receiving and discharging his goods in his yard in order that the wash room off the locker room for his employees might be kept dry instead of wet.

General usage or custom may be shown in order to establish a standard of construction and equipment. When a question of negligence is involved, the general usage or practice is competent to show either ordinary care or the failure to exercise such care. Shannahan v. Empire Engineering Corp., 204 N.Y. 543, 98 N.E. 9, 44 L.R.A. (N.S.) 1185. One is not obliged, however, to use the best methods or to have the best equipment or the safest place, but only such as are reasonably safe and appropriate for the business. Bennett v. Long Island R.R. Co., 163 N.Y. 1, 57 N.E. 79; Miele v. Rosenblatt, 164 App.Div. 604, 150 N.Y.S. 323. What some other brewery did might have been better and safer than the ways of Ruppert, but there was no attempt to prove that what the other brewery or breweries did or had was the practice or custom or general usage in the business. For this reason it was incompetent.

Id. at 295–96, 296, 190 N.E. at 646.

§ 406.2

1. United States v. General Foods Corp., 446 F.Supp. 740, 752 (N.D.N.Y.), aff'd, 591 F.2d 1332 (2d Cir.1978).

2. United States v. Cirillo, 425 F.Supp. 1254, 1255 (S.D.N.Y.), aff'd, 554 F.2d 54 (2d Cir.), cert. dismissed, 434 U.S. 801, 98 S.Ct. 28, 54 L.Ed.2d 59 (1977).

3. United States v. Oddo, 314 F.2d 115 (2d Cir.), cert. denied, 375 U.S. 833, 84 S.Ct. 50, 11 L.Ed.2d 63 (1963).

§ 406.2 RELEVANCY Ch. 4

a gondola it was proper to allow evidence of a routine practice to tie cargo to the car with just such wire.[4] In *U.S. Football League v. National Football League*,[5] however, it was held that testimony concerning the "habitual disregard" of antitrust advice was inadmissible. This was neither habit evidence under Rule 406 (three or four episodes over a 20-year period did not constitute habit), nor was it otherwise admissible because it "would have put before the jury the precise evidence of prior antitrust judgments previously and correctly deemed inadmissible."[6] And in *United States v. Angelilli*,[7] New York City marshals were convicted of RICO violations of keeping some of the proceeds from judgment execution sales. From evidence that marshals, as a group, indulged in this practice, the prosecutor sought to prove defendants acted in conformity. Rule 406 would not permit such a leap, said the court, since the custom of a group cannot be used to show that individuals acted in accord.[8]

It has been held that Rule 406 evidence can be proved by a lay witness whose opinion, of course, must comply with Rule 701 which requires testimony that is rationally based on the witness' perception.[9]

b. Evidence of Habit in Negligence Cases

It appears that the federal courts, perhaps because of the apparent breadth of Rule 406, are more willing to allow evidence of past practices in negligence cases than are the New York courts. No particular distinction is made between workplace and non-workplace accidents.[10] In *Jones v. Southern Pacific R.R.*,[11] plaintiff argued that the trial judge erred in not allowing evidence of a train engineer's prior safety infractions to show that he operated his train negligently. It appears that the only reason the court did not agree was that nine infractions over a 29-year career did not rise to the level of habitual conduct.

The practice of a person to imbibe alcoholic beverages, rather than being classified as a general character trait, has been found admissible habitual conduct in two products liability cases where defendants were allowed to show plaintiffs' drinking habits as indicative of the condition they were in when operating the machinery.[12]

---

4. Mahoney v. New York Central Railroad, 234 F.2d 923, 925 (2d Cir.1956).

5. 842 F.2d 1335, 1373 (2d Cir.1988).

6. Id.

7. 660 F.2d 23 (2d Cir.1981), cert. denied sub nom., Ribotsky v. United States, 455 U.S. 910, 102 S.Ct. 1258, 71 L.Ed.2d 449, rehearing denied sub nom., Butler v. United States, 456 U.S. 939, 102 S.Ct. 1998, 72 L.Ed.2d 460 (1982).

8. 660 F.2d at 41. The Court stated in part: "It may be that the ambiguous structure of Rule 406—which does not link the conduct of a person expressly with proof as to the habit of that person, nor the conduct of an organization expressly with proof as to the routine practice of that organization, see 23 C. Wright and K. Graham, Federal Practice and Procedure § 5273, at 42 (1980)—was intended to make admissible the evidence of the practice of the organization to prove the conduct of any of its members."

9. Maynard v. Sayles, 817 F.2d 50, 52 (8th Cir.), rehearing granted, 823 F.2d 1277 (8th Cir.), opinion vacated, 831 F.2d 173 (8th Cir.1987).

10. See § 406.1(c) supra, for the New York rule regarding negligent conduct on the job.

11. 962 F.2d 447 (5th Cir.1992).

12. Loughan v. Firestone Tire & Rubber Co., 749 F.2d 1519 (11th Cir.1985); Keltner v. Ford Motor Co., 748 F.2d 1265 (8th Cir. 1984). The Advisory Committee Notes in-

In one case, evidence was admitted in a federal court which, if offered in a New York court, would surely be rejected under the current New York case law.[13] It was held in a wrongful death action that evidence of the decedent's "habitual" careful driving, that he was cautious and never exceeded the speed limit, was admissible.[14] Although this case was decided prior to the advent of Rule 406, and was based on an interpretation of Kansas law, there is nothing in Rule 406 that would inhibit such evidence.

Finally, in a civil rights case brought to recover for the death of the victim at the hands of the police, evidence was held admissible which showed that the victim habitually reacted violently when confronted by police officers.[15] This case vividly demonstrates the wide scope of Rule 406.

c. Custom and Usage as a Standard of Care

The rule that custom and usage can be proof of a proper standard of care is well established in the Second Circuit. Thus, over defendant's argument that circulars relating to operation of aircraft were only advisory and not intended to set standards of care, the court ruled the circulars admissible as relevant to the question of care;[16] where the question was as to the intended use of metal packing straps, evidence of the way in which they were customarily used would be admissible;[17] custom as to the disposition of fluids from service station storage tanks was held admissible on the question of care;[18] evidence of the customary practice of inspecting automobile wheels when they left the factory would be admissible;[19] and, in a case where plaintiff fell off a ladder while washing windows at an airport hangar claiming he was startled by the sudden "revving" of the engines on defendant's airplane, it was permissible to allow evidence of defendant's practice of warning in advance of the noisy procedure, plaintiff having come to rely on the warnings.[20] In *Lee v. Pennsylvania R. Co.*,[21] plaintiff, who was injured when caught in the moving parts of an escalator on defendant's premises, was held to have properly introduced evidence of generally accepted

---

dicate no intention that traits of intemperance or religious practices be included under Rule 406. Other than this, the Advisory Committee does not address the question of carelessness as habit. In Reyes v. Missouri Pacific R.R. Co., 589 F.2d 791 (5th Cir.1979), the court refused to allow plaintiff's convictions for intoxication to show he was intoxicated at the time of the accident.

13. See Hartley v. Szadkowski, 32 A.D.2d 550, 300 N.Y.S.2d 82 (2d Dep't 1969)(evidence that plaintiff had prior accident and was thus not a careful driver inadmissible).

14. Frase v. Henry, 444 F.2d 1228, 1232 (10th Cir.1971).

15. Perrin v. Anderson, 784 F.2d 1040 (10th Cir.1986). The court stated: "That Perrin might be proved to have a 'habit' of reacting violently to uniformed police officers seems rather extraordinary. We believe, however, that defendants did in fact demonstrate that Perrin repeatedly reacted with extreme aggression when dealing with uniformed officers." Id. at 1046.

16. In Re Air Crash Disaster, 635 F.2d 67, 76–77 (2d Cir.1980).

17. Avena v. Clauss & Co., 504 F.2d 469, 471–72 (2d Cir.1974).

18. Tropea v. Shell Oil Company, 307 F.2d 757, 763 (2d Cir.1962).

19. Cadillac Motor Car Co. v. Johnson, 221 F. 801, 804 (2d Cir.1915).

20. Kozman v. Trans World Airlines, 236 F.2d 527, 531 (2d Cir.1956), cert. denied, 352 U.S. 953, 77 S.Ct. 327, 1 L.Ed.2d 243 (1956).

21. 192 F.2d 226 (2d Cir.1951).

§ 406.2 RELEVANCY Ch. 4

equipment design differing from the subject escalator. Judge Clark, however, emphasized that the trial judge's charge must make it clear that such evidence is not conclusive on the issue of negligence and that a defendant is not obliged "to have the best equipment, or the safest place, but only such as are reasonably safe and appropriate for the business."[22]

Trade usage and custom may be introduced to explain the parties' agreement where a contract is ambiguous.[23]

Library References:

West's Key No. Digests, Criminal Law ⚖372; Customs and Usages ⚖19; Evidence ⚖138, 139.

407 Subsequent Remedial Measures

§ 407.1 New York

a. Generally

Where, after an accident, the owner of the premises where the accident occurred undertakes repairs or modifications to correct the condition which caused the accident, it might be inferred that the owner is thereby admitting the existence of a dangerous condition and that this ought to be admissible in a negligence action as an admission.[1] Likewise, the modification of a product either pre- or post-accident might be considered an acknowledgment by the manufacturer that there was a problem with the product, thus counting as an admission in either a negligence, strict liability, or failure-to-warn cause of action.[2] The general rule, however, is that such evidence is not admissible against the defendant. Two grounds are stated for the rule: First, the taking of subsequent remedial measures is only marginally relevant to prove prior neglect because such measures are often taken to improve a condition not in bad repair at the time of the accident; and the minimal probative worth would be clearly outweighed by the prejudicial effect it would have. Second, those in control of the offending premises or the instru-

---

22. Id. at 230. This opinion, even though looking to the law of New York, provides a sound, general statement of the law in the Second Circuit:

New York has adopted the generally honored rule that testimony of the practices of others may be adduced in order to place an allegation of negligence in a context of general usage, thus assisting the jury in formulating the standard of care of reasonable men. This rule is available to plaintiffs to show departure from and defendants to show adherence to an accepted standard. * * * But such custom or usage, when shown, is not conclusive on the issue of negligence. * * * Nor is the rule to be warped into a requirement that the defendant use the latest or safest equipment.

Id. at 229.

23. Cibro Petroleum Products, Inc. v. Sohio Alaska Petroleum Co., 602 F.Supp. 1520, 1547 (N.D.N.Y.1985), aff'd, 798 F.2d 1421 (Em.App.1986), cert. dismissed, 479 U.S. 979, 107 S.Ct. 562, 93 L.Ed.2d 568 (1986)(where the contract was not clear as to when notice of termination should be given, it was appropriate to resort to trade usage and custom to clear the ambiguity).

§ 407.1

1. McCormick § 267, at 200.

2. See Caprara v. Chrysler Corp., 52 N.Y.2d 114, 436 N.Y.S.2d 251, 417 N.E.2d 545, reargument denied, 52 N.Y.2d 1073, 438 N.Y.S.2d 1029, 420 N.E.2d 413 (1981).

mentality would be discouraged from making improvements were such evidence admissible against them.[3]

On the other hand, there may be purposes other than to show an admission of culpability for which evidence of remedial measures is admissible, such as to prove ownership, control, or feasibility of precautionary measures, where such issues are controverted, or for purposes of impeachment. These exceptions are discussed below.

b. Negligence

The older New York cases applied a rule of exclusion in circumstances such as the following: Evidence that a fence was constructed around a tree after an accident had occurred was incompetent to suggest there had been a negligent condition without the fence[4] as was evidence that after an accident occurred on the approach to a highway bridge, guards were erected.[5] The exclusionary rule in negligence cases remains firm in the modern era. In one case, evidence that defendant town erected road warning signs after plaintiff's accident was held to have been wrongly admitted.[6] In another case, evidence that shortly after plaintiff received an electrical shock in defendant's self-serve refrigerator an electrician came to repair it was held to have been properly excluded.[7] But where the repair was planned before the occurrence of the accident, and then was completed after the accident occurred, the court found that evidence of the repair was admissible to show a dangerous condition earlier recognized by defendant. Such evidence would not offend the relevancy rationale or contravene the policy favoring the making of repairs.[8]

The Court of Appeals, in *Caprara v. Chrysler Corp.*,[9] a products liability case discussed in subpart c, reiterated the rationale for the exclusionary rule in negligence cases:

> Now reaching the broader and more basic question of the role of postaccident change in this case, we start by reiterating the long accepted proposition that, in a negligence suit, proof of a defen-

---

3. 2 Wigmore § 283, at 151.

4. Corcoran v. Village of Peekskill, 108 N.Y. 151, 15 N.E. 309 (1888).

5. Getty v. Town of Hamlin, 127 N.Y. 636, 27 N.E. 399 (1891).

6. Ramundo v. Guilderland, 142 A.D.2d 50, 534 N.Y.S.2d 543 (3d Dep't 1988).

7. DiPaolo v. Somma, 111 A.D.2d 899, 490 N.Y.S.2d 803 (2d Dep't 1985).

8. Priolo v. Lefferts General Hospital, Inc., 54 Misc.2d 654, 656, 283 N.Y.S.2d 203, 206 (Sup.Ct.Kings Co.1967). The court noted that perhaps an injury will alert the owner for the first time that the premises need improvement and that "evidence of repair does not prove that the original condition was imperfect or unsafe or out of repair and only after an accident occurs may it for the first time become known that the danger is truly present. * * *" These reasons would not obtain where the owner already knew of the danger before the accident. See also Two Stables, Inc. v. Cornelius, 145 A.D.2d 685, 534 N.Y.S.2d 827 (3d Dep't 1988). Plaintiff sued for damages caused when a septic system installed by defendant failed. Plaintiff asserted two causes of action, one for breach of contract and the other for negligent performance. Evidence of subsequent repairs was permissible since the negligence count was dismissed and the case proceeded on the contract count which was not subject to the fault-based considerations inherent in negligence causes of action.

9. 52 N.Y.2d 114, 436 N.Y.S.2d 251, 417 N.E.2d 545, reargument denied, 52 N.Y.2d 1073, 438 N.Y.S.2d 1029, 420 N.E.2d 413 (1981).

§ 407.1 RELEVANCY Ch. 4

dant's postaccident repair or improvement ordinarily is not admissible. The reason for applying this rule of evidence to that kind of case is clear. Since at the heart of such an action is either affirmative conduct in creating a dangerous condition or a failure to perceive a foreseeable risk and take reasonable steps to avert its consequences, proof that goes to hindsight rather than foresight most often is entirely irrelevant and, at best, of low probative value.[10]

c. Products Liability

The exclusionary rule applicable in negligence cases to evidence of remedial measures also applies in products liability cases when they are based on design defects or failure to warn, i.e., fault-based claims. Causes of action based on the straightforward presence of a manufacturing defect, however, have been construed so as to allow the admission of subsequent changes. These rules were formulated by the Court of Appeals in *Caprara v. Chrysler Corp.*,[11] where the accident was allegedly caused by defective lower ball joints in the front end of the vehicle manufactured by defendant. The court found this to be a manufacturing defect and not a design defect, even though the evidence at issue was evidence that defendant had *redesigned* the lower ball joint system in these cars subsequent to the date of manufacture of plaintiff's vehicle. Regardless of the internal consistency of the holding,[12] the court found the evidence of the remedial measures taken by defendant to be admissible because "[evidence of subsequent repairs] tended * * * to indicate that the appellants themselves eventually formed the opinion that the ball joints * * * had a potential for movement when installed. And, it added to the probability that it was this defect rather than other causes that produced the accident."[13] This evidence, then, seems to have been approved for admissibility, not because it was an admission by defendant of a dangerous condition, but because it tended to prove the existence of the defect that caused the accident. Proof of manufacturing defects is notoriously difficult for plaintiffs to acquire, and so admissibility on this basis makes sense.[14]

But cases based on design defect and inadequate warnings are another matter. The dictum in the *Caprara* dissent, not disputed by the majority, is that liability for design defects is based on general negligence principles.[15] This is borne out in *Rainbow v. Albert Elia Building Co.*,[16]

10. Id. at 122, 436 N.Y.S.2d at 255, 417 N.E.2d at 549.

11. 52 N.Y.2d 114, 436 N.Y.S.2d 251, 417 N.E.2d 545, reargument denied, 52 N.Y.2d 1073, 438 N.Y.S.2d 1029, 420 N.E.2d 413 (1981).

12. The Caprara majority, while finding a manufacturing defect, nevertheless did not dispute this statement found in the dissent: "Indeed, it has been said that 'the standards for imposing liability for such unreasonably dangerous design defects are * * * general negligence principles.' [Citing to a determination in Bolm v. Triumph Corp., 33 N.Y.2d 151, 157–58, 350 N.Y.S.2d 644, 649, 305 N.E.2d 769, 772–72 (1973)]." 52 N.Y.2d at 129, 436 N.Y.S.2d at 259, 417 N.E.2d at 553.

13. 52 N.Y.2d at 125, 436 N.Y.S.2d at 257, 417 N.E.2d at 551.

14. The difficulty of proving manufacturing defects is discussed in the opinion at 52 N.Y.2d at 124–25, 436 N.Y.S.2d at 257, 417 N.E.2d at 551.

15. See note 12 supra.

16. 79 A.D.2d 287, 436 N.Y.S.2d 480 (4th Dep't 1981), aff'd mem., 56 N.Y.2d

Ch. 4   SUBSEQUENT REMEDIAL MEASURES   § 407.1

where evidence of a design change to the exterior of defendant's motorcycles was held inadmissible based on the historical prohibition of such evidence in negligence cases. The court reasoned that liability for design defect is based on the balancing of risk and utility factors which involve considerations of reasonable care. Where liability is based on a manufacturing defect, fault is not a factor. In the latter situation, the error in the manufacturing process is an objective determination to which the subsequent modification may be very relevant.[17] Other cases of interest involving design changes are in the notes.[18]

The Court of Appeals memorandum opinion in *Haran v. Union Carbide Corp.*,[19] states the court's position with respect to cases alleging inadequate warnings. In *Haran*, plaintiff sought to prove that defendant changed the label on its insecticide product in order to make the warning more detailed after the can which plaintiff purchased had been marketed. The court cited its decision in *Cover v. Cohen*,[20] and found that the feasibility exception (discussed in subpart d below) would not normally apply in warning cases. Where, however, the postmanufacture changes reveal a reason to warn those who had already purchased the product, plaintiff can introduce this evidence to show that defendant was at fault in not acting on the new knowledge. There is a continuing duty to warn about dangers in using products even after they have been manufactured and sold.[21]

550, 449 N.Y.S.2d 967, 434 N.E.2d 1345 (1982).

17. Id. at 292–94, 436 N.Y.S.2d at 484. The Appellate Division had decided an earlier motorcycle case, Bolm v. Triumph Corp., 71 A.D.2d 429, 422 N.Y.S.2d 969 (4th Dep't 1979), appeal dismissed, 50 N.Y.2d 801, 430 N.Y.S.2d 1025, 407 N.E.2d 1353 (1980), in which it ruled consistently that in a suit brought to recover damages for injuries incurred in the motorcycle accident plaintiff could not introduce evidence of a subsequent design change to eliminate protrusions from the machine claimed to have exacerbated plaintiff's injuries.

18. Perazone v. Sears, Roebuck and Co., 128 A.D.2d 15, 515 N.Y.S.2d 908 (3d Dep't 1987)(admission of design changes was error where plaintiff's proof showed that the battery, muffler and gas tank were placed too close to each other and lacked shielding, clearly a design problem); Opera v. Hyva, Inc., 86 A.D.2d 373, 450 N.Y.S.2d 615 (4th Dep't 1982)(evidence that ski binding manual had been changed concerning its instructions as to how to set the binding so it would release the ski in a fall should not have been admitted, especially since jury was charged this was evidence of an unsafe binding); Bartlett v. General Electric Co., 90 A.D.2d 183, 457 N.Y.S.2d 628 (3d Dep't 1982)(where infant was injured when he bit on an extension cord, evidence that design of cord was changed was approved by the Appellate Division as probative that such design could have been employed at the time of manufacture—an apparently erroneous interpretation as evidenced by other design cases where feasibility not in issue).

19. 68 N.Y.2d 710, 506 N.Y.S.2d 311, 497 N.E.2d 678 (1986).

20. 61 N.Y.2d 261, 473 N.Y.S.2d 378, 461 N.E.2d 864 (1984).

21. Power v. Crown Equip. Corp., 189 A.D.2d 310, 313, 596 N.Y.S.2d 38, 39 (1st Dep't 1993). Plaintiff sought to prove that defendant knew of the danger even before manufacture, and that it produced warning decals to be affixed to the equipment, but never distributed them to buyers like plaintiff's employer who purchased the equipment without the decals. And, in Brandon v. Caterpillar Tractor Corp., 125 A.D.2d 625, 627, 510 N.Y.S.2d 165, 167–68 (2d Dep't 1986), service letters issued by the manufacturer after the product was sold were admitted into evidence for the purpose of ascertaining whether the manufacturer had complied with its duty to warn. They could not, said the court, be considered by the jury as evidence of a defect. "[T]he jury should have been advised that these documents were relevant solely with respect to the plaintiffs' claim that the appellant did not fulfill its continuing duty to warn of subsequently discovered risks and hazards

On the question of the introduction of subsequent remedial repairs in products cases, most of the cases entail design and warning problems. Only two of the major cases in New York have been interpreted as involving manufacturing defects.[22]

In his opinion in *Cover v. Cohen*,[23] Judge Meyer concisely summarized the law with respect to manufacturing flaws, design defects and failure to warn:

> The combined effect of our decision in *Caprara v. Chrysler Corp.* * * * and *Rainbow v. Elia Bldg. Co.* * * * is to permit the introduction in a strict products liability case based upon a manufacturing defect of evidence of a manufacturer's subsequent modifications to establish defectiveness of the product when made, but to proscribe the use of such evidence to establish fault in a strict products liability case based upon a defect in design or the failure to warn or adequately instruct concerning the use of the product.[24]

d. Feasibility

Feasibility is an issue that may be raised in products liability cases based on a cause of action charging faulty design, i.e., whether or not there was a more feasible design known in the industry at the time the

---

or with regard to the issue of the feasibility of alternative design."

22. See Caprara v. Chrysler Corp., 52 N.Y.2d 114, 436 N.Y.S.2d 251, 417 N.E.2d 545 (1981)(faulty ball joints); Barry v. Manglass, 55 A.D.2d 1, 389 N.Y.S.2d 870 (2d Dep't 1976)(faulty engine mounts). It is not easy to determine in these two cases why the manufacture of the ball joints or engine mounts was at issue when the remedial measures seemed to be complete redesign of these units. As indicated in the text, this can only be explained on the ground that this evidence, rather than pertaining to a policy-forbidden or barely relevant admission, really is necessary to explain and prove the defect.

In Barry v. Manglass, the Appellate Division decided that it was proper for the plaintiff, suing for injuries sustained as the alleged result of faulty engine mounts in his car, to introduce evidence that the defendant had sent out letters to owners of cars of the same year and model recalling these cars for engine mount replacement. Over defendant's argument that this constituted inadmissible evidence of subsequent repairs, the court made the observation that the recall was not due to *this* particular accident and, more importantly, that in products liability cases as opposed to negligence cases plaintiff must prove that the defect existed not only at the time the accident occurred, but also at the time the product left the factory, thus making the relevancy of the recall letters outweigh any possible prejudice accruing to the defendant in its perceived duty to correct a production error. The court cited with approval the California Supreme Court's decision in Ault v. International Harvester Co., 13 Cal.3d 113, 528 P.2d 1148, 117 Cal.Rptr. 812 (1974), in which the negligence rule was held inapplicable to strict products liability cases because it is unrealistic to suppose that the manufacturer of mass-produced goods would forego making improvements since there would be numerous lawsuits resulting from injuries precisely because remedial measures were not taken. While, as will be seen, this view did not take hold with the Court of Appeals, the result in Barry may hold up on the alternate ground stated therein that recall letters are mandated by the Motor Vehicle Safety Act of 1966, and thus it was not a voluntary act on defendant's part to set about correcting a known, dangerous condition. 55 A.D.2d at 10, 389 N.Y.S.2d at 877.

23. 61 N.Y.2d 261, 473 N.Y.S.2d 378, 461 N.E.2d 864 (1984). In Cover, the main issue was whether a requirement for improvement of a Chevrolet throttle return spring, which appeared in federal motor safety standards after manufacture, could be introduced in a strict liability cause of action. Finding that this related to the design of the part, the evidence was ruled inadmissible.

24. Id. at 270, 473 N.Y.S.2d at 382, 461 N.E.2d at 868.

product in issue was designed. There is a fair amount of dicta in the New York cases relating to the admissibility of evidence of remedial measures, i.e., design changes, on the issue of feasibility but no modern appellate decisions where such evidence has actually been ruled admissible on that ground. The theory is that proof of a design change is relevant to show that it could have been executed at the time the offending product was originally designed and manufactured.[25]

If the defendant contests the issue of feasibility, then the door is open to plaintiff to introduce evidence of the subsequent redesign. In the opinion in *Cover v. Cohen*[26] Judge Meyer stated:

> Such evidence [of subsequent design change] may be admissible * * * to establish feasibility but, in view of the abstruse, subjective judgment involved in the balancing of risks and benefits necessary to determine whether the product as made and sold was reasonably safe * * * and the substantial risk that such evidence may be overemphasized by the jury, will not be admitted even for that purpose if the manufacturer concedes feasibility.[27]

Conceivably, feasibility could be an issue in a failure-to-warn case, but it is unlikely that there would be any incentive for a manufacturer to raise the flimsy contention that where a need to warn arose it was not feasible to issue the warning. In *Haran v. Union Carbide Corp.*,[28] the warning case noted in subpart c above, it was stated: "Feasibility was never in issue and, indeed, it is obvious that the modification of a warning label presents none of the difficulties typically involved in feasibility questions."[29]

e. Ownership, Control and Impeachment

In a case where an issue arises as to who was in control of the premises, or who had ownership at the time of the accident, there is strong relevancy in evidence that *A* rather than *B* undertook to remedy the condition. In *Scudero v. Campbell*,[30] for example, the court ruled that where the question was who had control of the premises, the landlord or the tenant, evidence that the landlord repaired the rotted step which had caused plaintiff's injury was admissible. It is not difficult to understand how such evidence can be used to impeach a witness who denies responsibility. Where the issue of ownership or control is in the case from the beginning, the evidence could be used as evidence in chief.

Where evidence of subsequent changes is introduced on the ownership or control issue, limiting instructions are in order. In the *Caprara*

---

25. See In Re Joint Eastern District & Southern District Asbestos Lit., 995 F.2d 343, 345–46 (2d Cir.1993).

26. 61 N.Y.2d 261, 473 N.Y.S.2d 378, 461 N.E.2d 864 (1984).

27. Id. at 270, 473 N.Y.S.2d at 382, 461 N.E.2d at 868.

28. 68 N.Y.2d 710, 506 N.Y.S.2d 311, 497 N.E.2d 678 (1986).

29. Id. at 712, 506 N.Y.S.2d at 312, 497 N.E.2d at 679.

30. 288 N.Y. 328, 43 N.E.2d 66 (1942).

case,[31] the court noted that "[w]here such evidence becomes admissible on some other theory or on another issue, such as control, impeachment or feasibility of precautionary measures, almost invariably Trial Judges have thought it best, lest the jury look upon it as an acknowledgment of negligence, to accompany its receipt with appropriate limiting instructions."[32]

f. Criminal Cases and Proposed New York Code Provision

The exclusionary rule for remedial measures has no application in criminal cases where altogether different concerns are operative. Thus, where the defense to a vehicular manslaughter charge was that the accident was caused because of a defect in the car, evidence of a postmanufacture design change was held admissible.[33]

Proposed New York Evidence Code § 407 is set forth in the note.[34]

Library References:

West's Key No. Digests, Evidence ⚖219(1); Negligence ⚖131.

§ 407.2 Federal

Federal Rule of Evidence 407 provides:

> When, after an event, measures are taken which, if taken previously, would have made the event less likely to occur, evidence of the subsequent measures is not admissible to prove negligence or culpable conduct in connection with the event. This rule does not require the exclusion of evidence of subsequent measures when offered for another purpose, such as proving ownership, control, or feasibility of precautionary measures, if controverted, or impeachment.

This exclusionary rule has deep roots in the federal system. In *Columbia P.S.R. Co. v. Hawthorne*,[1] the Supreme Court ruled inadmissible

---

31. Caprara v. Chrysler Corp., 52 N.Y.2d 114, 436 N.Y.S.2d 251, 417 N.E.2d 545, reargument denied, 52 N.Y.2d 1073, 438 N.Y.S.2d 1029, 420 N.E.2d 413 (1981).

32. Id. at 122, 436 N.Y.S.2d at 255, 417 N.E.2d at 549.

33. People v. Thomas, 70 N.Y.2d 823, 523 N.Y.S.2d 437, 517 N.E.2d 1323 (1987), affirming 121 A.D.2d 73, 509 N.Y.S.2d 668 (4th Dep't 1986). The Appellate Division stated:

> Subsequent design modifications, although inadmissible in some civil cases, may be admitted in criminal cases if relevant; the rationale underlying excluding such evidence in civil cases where the defendant is the accused culpable designer or manufacturer is ill-applied in criminal cases. Public policy does not justify the exclusion of this evidence where the manufacturer of the product cannot be prejudiced by its admission and the defendant has a constitutional right to present evidence.

121 A.D.2d at 80, 509 N.Y.S.2d at 673–74.

34. § 407. Subsequent remedial measures [PROPOSED]

> Evidence of measures taken after an event, which if taken before the event would have made injury or damage less likely to result, is not admissible to prove negligence or culpable conduct in connection with the event or to prove negligent or culpable conduct with respect to a product alleged to be defective. Evidence of such measures may, however, be admissible when offered to impeach or as proof on controverted issues such as ownership, control, or feasibility of precautionary measures.

§ 407.2

1. 144 U.S. 202, 12 S.Ct. 591, 36 L.Ed. 405 (1892).

evidence of remedial measures taken by defendant after the accident. The Court said that "the taking of such precautions against the future is not to be construed as an admission of responsibility for the past, has no legitimate tendency to prove that the defendant had been negligent before the accident happened, and is calculated to distract the minds of the jury from the real issue, and to create a prejudice against the defendant."[2]

As seen in the last section, the New York courts apply a common law version of Rule 407, and have extended the exclusionary rule to products cases insofar as recovery is sought on the basis of faulty design or lack of warning.[3] The federal courts are split on whether the exclusionary rule should extend to products cases. One view is that Rule 407 should not apply to products cases since mass market manufacturers are going to make remedial changes simply as a rational business practice irrespective of whether that evidence could be introduced at individual trials.[4]

The other view, adopted by the Second Circuit in *Cann v. Ford Motor Co.*,[5] applies Rule 407 in products cases. The plaintiff in *Cann* argued that in a negligence action the issue is the defendant's conduct, while in a strict liability case the issue is simply whether the product was defective and that the reasons behind Rule 407 only make sense when applied in a negligence action. The court rejected this argument, stating: "[T]he defendant must pay the judgment in both situations, regardless of where the jury's attention focused when they found against him. Since the policy underlying Rule 407 not to discourage persons from taking remedial measures is relevant to *defendants* sued under either theory, we do not see the significance of the distinction."[6] In the *Cann* case no distinction was drawn, as in New York,[7] between manufacturing defects on the one hand, and design defects and lack of warning on the other. Since Rule 407 broadly excludes evidence of subsequent

---

2. Id. at 207–08, 12 S.Ct. at 593, 36 L.Ed.2d at 407. The Court cites the English case Hart v. Lancashire & Yorkshire Railway, 21 Law Times (U.S.) 261, 263 and this quote from Baron Bramwell: "People do not furnish evidence against themselves simply by adopting a new plan in order to prevent the recurrence of an accident. I think that a proposition to the contrary would be barbarous. It would be, as I have often had occasion to tell juries, to hold that, because the world gets wiser as it gets older, therefore it was foolish before."

3. See § 407.1(c) supra; Cover v. Cohen, 61 N.Y.2d 261, 270, 473 N.Y.S.2d 378, 382, 461 N.E.2d 864, 868 (1984).

4. See, e.g., Farner v. Paccar, Inc., 562 F.2d 518 (8th Cir.1977). The theory that the exclusionary rule would serve no function as respects large manufacturers originated in Ault v. International Harvester Co., 13 Cal.3d 113, 528 P.2d 1148, 117 Cal.Rptr. 812 (1974). No consideration seems to have been given as to the probative value-prejudicial effect test.

5. 658 F.2d 54 (2d Cir.1981), cert. denied, 456 U.S. 960, 102 S.Ct. 2036, 72 L.Ed.2d 484 (1982).

6. 658 F.2d at 60 (emphasis in original). This conclusion seems to ignore the former major reason for the exclusionary rule which is the "hindsight-relevancy" notion expressed in the Columbia Railroad case, supra note 1, and elevates the formerly subordinate reason for the rule—that without the rule owners and manufacturers would be discouraged from taking remedial measures. This switching of priorities was accomplished in the Advisory Committee's Note to Rule 407 where the relevancy aspect is not even mentioned and the policy reason is featured.

7. See § 407.1(c) supra.

remedial measures to prove negligence "or culpable conduct," the Second Circuit is likely to apply Rule 407 in the latter types of cases as well.

As in New York, there are few reported cases where evidence of remedial measures has been offered to prove ownership, or control, where those issues are contested, and where evidence of who undertook the repair would be clearly relevant. The Second Circuit has, however, spoken to the question of the feasibility exception. This exception is designed to allow plaintiff to introduce evidence of remedial measures should defendant contend that the design of the offending product was the only feasible design, or that it would have been unfeasible to issue a timely warning. In *In re Joint Eastern District & Southern District Asbestos Litigation*,[8] the Second Circuit issued a forceful statement that the feasibility issue is the exception and not the rule. At trial, plaintiff was allowed to introduce evidence that the manufacturer first placed warnings on its asbestos products many years after decedent's exposures. Plaintiff argued that feasibility was in issue, but the appellate court stated:

> "Feasibility" is not an open sesame whose mere invocation parts Rule 407 and ushers in evidence of subsequent repairs and remedies. To read it that casually will cause the exception to engulf the rule. * * * Rule 407 states that a defendant must first contest the feasibility of a warning before the subsequent warning would become admissible. * * * The record is clear that [the manufacturer] at no point argued that it was unable to issue a warning. Instead, it vigorously denied that its product required a warning or was defective without a warning.[9]

In *Fish v. Georgia–Pacific Corp.*,[10] feasibility was discussed in another warning case, but the evidence of remedial measures was excluded. Defendant Georgia–Pacific warned its customers about formaldehyde emissions from its particle board product after plaintiff had been exposed. The court said that this evidence was not admissible on the question of whether it was feasible to issue an earlier warning. "Georgia–Pacific stated that it was willing to admit the feasibility of providing a warning in 1977 [before plaintiff's exposure]; it simply contended that it did not have a legal duty to do so. Because feasibility was not a contested issue, there was no reason to admit the evidence of the warning and it should have been excluded."[11]

Library References:

West's Key No. Digests, Evidence ⬅219(1); Negligence ⬅131.

408 Compromises and Offers to Compromise

§ 408.1 New York

The general rule prohibits evidence of compromise (settlement) or offers to compromise to prove liability or lack thereof for two main

8. 995 F.2d 343 (2d Cir.1993).
9. Id. at 345–46.
10. 779 F.2d 836 (2d Cir.1985).
11. Id. at 840.

Ch. 4   COMPROMISES & OFFERS TO COMPROMISE   § 408.1

reasons: First, the rule expresses a policy to encourage compromise and settlement, without fear that these efforts may be used as admissions of fault;[1] and second, willingness to compromise may well be irrelevant to fault where the party simply wants to be rid of the problem and finds it expedient in terms of cost, time and aggravation, to make it go away in this manner.[2]

The chief exception to this rule under New York law is that any admissions of fact made during compromise negotiations, separate from the offer to compromise or the compromise itself, will be admissible under the rule established in *White v. The Old Dominion S.S. Co.*[3] In New York, to avoid this trap, the parties should be careful to stipulate that the negotiations are "without prejudice," or at the very least be careful not to make any inculpatory statements.[4] In one case summary judgment was granted for plaintiff where plaintiff submitted a copy of a proposed settlement agreement in which defendants admitted "that they were personally served * * * and that they have no defenses to the complaint or any counterclaims against the plaintiff."[5] The court stated: "That the statement is contained in a settlement document is immaterial, for while evidence of settlement negotiations is generally inadmissible, admissions of fact made in connection with settlement

§ 408.1

1. In Dermatossian v. NYC Tr. Auth., 67 N.Y.2d 219, 501 N.Y.S.2d 784, 492 N.E.2d 1200 (1986) it was held that proof of payment of no-fault benefits could not be introduced as evidence of liability on the part of defendant. The statutory obligation to pay first-party benefits at a time when there is no reason for defendant not to accept the claim cannot be used as an admission of liability by the defendant, in this case a self-insurer. See also Universal Carloading & Distribution Co., Inc. v. Penn Central Transp. Co., 101 A.D.2d 61, 62–63, 474 N.Y.S.2d 502, 503 (1st Dep't 1984)("[A]n offer of settlement cannot be considered an admission of liability * * *. Such an offer of compromise, made for the purpose of procuring a settlement of a pending controversy, is not an admission of fact * * *"); Bigelow-Sanford, Inc. v. Spec. Comm. Floors of Rochester, Inc., 77 A.D.2d 464, 465, 433 N.Y.S.2d 931, 932 (4th Dep't 1980)("This rule 'is founded upon public policy, and with a view of encouraging and facilitating the settlement of legal controversies by compromise, which object is supposed to be obstructed by the fear entertained by litigants that such a negotiation may be converted into a trap to inveigle the unwary into hazardous admissions.'").

2. Tennant v. Dudley, 144 N.Y. 504, 506, 39 N.E. 644, 645 (1895)("The rule is well settled that no advantage can be taken by way of compromise; that a party may, with impunity, attempt to buy his peace."). In Esser v. Brophey, 212 Minn. 194, 3 N.W.2d 3 (1942), the Court added two other theories: First, it can be argued that compromise negotiations are privileged communications, the privilege being designed to encourage compromises (roughly equal to the simple policy reason), and second, exclusion might rest on an express or implied contract between the parties that the compromise negotiations are without prejudice.

3. 102 N.Y. 660, 6 N.E. 289 (1886)(during compromise negotiations, plaintiff admitted that he had seen cautionary lights, a fact damaging to his case).

4. Randall Elec., Inc. v. State, 150 A.D.2d 875, 876, 540 N.Y.S.2d 901, 902 (3d Dep't 1989)("'Admissions of fact explicitly or implicitly made "without prejudice" during settlement negotiations are protected from discovery pursuant to the public policy of encouraging and facilitating settlement'"); Crow–Crimmins–Wolff & Munier v. County of Westchester, 126 A.D.2d 696, 697, 511 N.Y.S.2d 117, 118 (2d Dep't 1987)(contents of a "confidential" discussion concerning compromise not admissible); Kollmer v. Slater Electric, Inc., 122 A.D.2d 117, 120, 504 N.Y.S.2d 690, 692 (2d Dep't 1986)(in settlement of an OSHA violation, language to the effect that the settlement was not to be taken as an admission protected it from admissibility).

5. Central Petroleum Corp. v. Kyriakoudes, 121 A.D.2d 165, 502 N.Y.S.2d 1017 (1st Dep't 1986), appeal dismissed, 68 N.Y.2d 807, 498 N.E.2d 437, 506 N.Y.S.2d 1037 (1986).

negotiations are admissible."[6] This exception is on the wane elsewhere because it tends to discourage a free exchange.[7] Federal Rule of Evidence 408, by way of contrast, expressly provides that evidence of conduct or statements made during negotiations are inadmissible. Settlements arrived at in claims other than the one at trial are also generally inadmissible to prove fault. Thus, in *Gilliam v. Lee*,[8] evidence that one passenger in a car involved in an accident settled with defendant's insurer cannot be introduced in the litigation brought by another passenger.[9] In *Keet v. Murrin*,[10] however, it was held permissible on cross-examination to prove that an adversary witness had settled a claim against the party calling him for the purpose of showing the witness' bias.[11]

The proposed New York Evidence Code § 408 restates the existing law except that it would change the *Old Dominion* rule and expressly protect conduct or statements made during the course of compromise negotiations.[12]

Library References:

West's Key No. Digests, Evidence ⚖212, 219(3).

6. Id. See also Bigelow–Sanford, Inc. v. Specialized Com'l Floors of Rochester, Inc., 77 A.D.2d 464, 466, 433 N.Y.S.2d 931, 933 (4th Dep't 1980)(where settlement between plaintiff and a third party contained no admission of fact, it was not admissible against plaintiff in an action arising out of the same subject matter as the settled claim); Union Bank v. Deshel, 139 App.Div. 217, 219, 123 N.Y.S. 585, 586 (2d Dep't 1910) (where defendant's letter to plaintiff contained an offer for less than that demanded by plaintiff it was clearly a compromise offer, and since the letter contained no admissions of fact, it was inadmissible under the general rule).

7. McCormick § 266, at 196. See also § 408.2, infra.

8. 32 A.D.2d 1058, 1059, 303 N.Y.S.2d 966, 968 (2d Dep't 1969).

9. Bevilacqua v. Gilbert, 143 A.D.2d 213, 532 N.Y.S.2d 15 (2d Dep't 1988) (prejudicial proof of settlements reached in two other, unrelated claims, where no admissions were established, were erroneously admitted especially since the instant claim would establish an additional aggravation of the condition involved in those settlements); Barnes v. Maguire, 62 A.D.2d 1076, 1077, 403 N.Y.S.2d 797, 799 (3d Dep't 1978)(evidence of Water Board's settlements with other riparian owners with respect to damages inadmissible as proof that damage also done to property in issue). See also Bigelow–Sanford v. Specialized Com'l Floors, 77 A.D.2d 464, 466, 433 N.Y.S.2d 931, 933 (4th Dep't 1980), note 7 supra.

10. 260 N.Y. 586, 184 N.E. 104 (1932).

11. See also Ryan v. Dwyer, 33 A.D.2d 878, 307 N.Y.S.2d 565 (4th Dep't 1969)(plaintiff's witness, a passenger in plaintiff's car at the time of the collision, testified, when asked on cross-examination, that she had settled her own claim (against plaintiff)); compare Catalfamo v. Boucher, 33 A.D.2d 1081, 307 N.Y.S.2d 678 (3d Dep't 1970)(the court, on facts similar to those in Ryan, held that the settlement evidence was inadmissible, but cited authority dealing with the general rule and not the impeachment exception).

12. **§ 408. Compromise of, and offers to compromise, disputed claims [PROPOSED]**

Evidence of (a) furnishing or offering or promising to furnish, or (b) accepting or offering or promising to accept, a valuable consideration in compromising or attempting to compromise a claim which was disputed as to either validity or amount, is not admissible to prove civil or criminal liability for, invalidity of, or the amount of the claim or any other claim. Evidence of conduct or statements made in compromise negotiations is likewise not admissible. This section does not, however, require the exclusion of evidence existing before the compromise negotiations merely because it is presented in the course of compromise negotiations. This section also does not require exclusion when the evidence is offered for another purpose, such as proving bias or prejudice of a witness, controverting a contention of undue delay, or proving an effort to obstruct a criminal investigation or prosecution.

§ 408.2 Federal

Federal Rule of Evidence 408 provides:

Evidence of (1) furnishing or offering or promising to furnish, or (2) accepting or offering or promising to accept, a valuable consideration in compromising or attempting to compromise a claim which was disputed as to either validity or amount, is not admissible to prove liability for or invalidity of the claim or its amount. Evidence of conduct or statements made in compromise negotiations is likewise not admissible. This rule does not require the exclusion of any evidence otherwise discoverable merely because it is presented in the course of compromise negotiations. This rule also does not require exclusion when the evidence is offered for another purpose, such as proving bias or prejudice of a witness, negativing a contention of undue delay, or proving an effort to obstruct a criminal investigation or prosecution.

The Second Circuit has taken a broad view of this rule so that it is immaterial which party seeks to introduce an offer of compromise. Thus in an age discrimination suit, the employer's evidence of a job offer made to the employee after he was denied promotion was inadmissible under Rule 408 even though the employer's purpose was to show that the employee in refusing the offer failed to mitigate damages.[1] The court stated that where a party is represented by counsel in a situation where litigation is threatened there will be a presumption that any offer made will be within the purview of Rule 408, and the party seeking admission must prove "convincingly" that the offer was other than a compromise offer.[2] Refusing to follow authority from the Supreme Court of Washington,[3] the court held that it makes no difference that it is the offeror who seeks the admission of this evidence. "We prefer to apply Rule 408 as written and exclude evidence of settlement offers to prove liability for or the amount of a claim regardless of which party attempts to offer the evidence."[4]

---

§ 408.2

1. Pierce v. F.R. Tripler & Co., 955 F.2d 820 (2d Cir.1992); compare Thomas v. Resort Health Related Facility, 539 F.Supp. 630 (E.D.N.Y.1982) (employer's offer to reinstate employee to his job without prejudice to employee's claim for back pay was admissible because reinstatement offer was not made to compromise claim for back pay in case where employee was seeking back pay).

2. 955 F.2d at at 827.

3. Bulaich v. AT & T Information Sys., 113 Wash.2d 254, 778 P.2d 1031 (1989).

4. Pierce, 955 F.2d at 828. In response to the employer's argument that the court had reached an opposite conclusion in Wrenn v. Secretary, Dep't of Veterans Affairs, 918 F.2d 1073 (2d Cir.1990), cert. denied, 499 U.S. 977, 111 S.Ct. 1625, 113 L.Ed.2d 721 (1991), it was stated:

In that case we held that an offer, to a plaintiff claiming race and age discrimination, of the same job that he claimed had been wrongly denied him, along with seniority and full back pay, supported the employer's race- and age-neutral reason for failing to hire the plaintiff initially—namely, that it believed the plaintiff was not interested in the job that was available. In Wrenn, however, we did not address whether the evidence of the offer was admissible under Rule 408. There is no indication that the issue ever was raised in that case. Id. at 828–829.

The implication seems to be that had the issue been raised, Rule 408 would have been applied to keep the evidence out. The court noted at the end of the above quote:

§ 408.2 RELEVANCY Ch. 4

Under the terms of Rule 408 the issue addressed by the offer to compromise, or the settlement itself, must be in dispute at the time.[5] Compromises, even though they relate to other disputes, will be inadmissible to prove liability in the dispute at hand,[6] and the mere threat of litigation is sufficient to put the question in dispute,[7] although it is sometimes difficult to determine if the communications had to do with efforts to compromise or settle.[8]

As provided in Rule 408, evidence of offers to compromise, or completed settlements, may be admissible on questions other than liability. For example, such evidence may be admitted where the parties' intent as to the meaning of a contract can be evidenced by the practical interpretation given during the parties' negotiations;[9] where the object is to show that an insurer is guilty of bad faith in refusing to settle an insurance claim;[10] where the date of settlement talks is crucial to the amount of damages;[11] and where the date of settlement negotiations marked the time from which prejudgment interest ought to be reckoned.[12] But in *Trebor Sportswear Co. v. The Ltd. Stores, Inc.*,[13] the

---

"Merely because evidence is relevant does not qualify it for admission under Rule 408."

See also American Ins. Co. v. North American Co. Etc., 697 F.2d 79 (2d Cir. 1982)(where primary insurer sought reimbursement from reinsurer based on settlement made on behalf of the insured, evidence that the reinsurer discussed commutation with another insurance company was barred under Rule 408); Olin Corp. v. Insurance Co. of North America, 603 F.Supp. 445, on rearg., 607 F.Supp. 1377 (S.D.N.Y. 1985)(where insured retained lawyer in anticipation of denial of insurance claims by insurers, discussions between insureds and insurers were protected by Rule 408).

5. In Re B.D. Intern. Discount Corp., 701 F.2d 1071 (2d Cir.1983), cert. denied, 464 U.S. 830, 104 S.Ct. 108, 78 L.Ed.2d 110 (1983)(entry in debtor's books, "Payable to Bank $7,269,052," was not excludable under Rule 408 because at the time of the negotiation to which the statement referred the debtor had not disputed the bank's claim, but was negotiating for an extension of time to pay).

6. Alpex Computer Corp. v. Nintendo Co., 770 F.Supp. 161 (S.D.N.Y.1991), on reconsideration, 1994 WL 139423 (S.D.N.Y. 1994), decision vacated in part, 1994 WL 381659 (S.D.N.Y.1994)(patent holder's offer to settle infringement claims against other companies cannot be used by alleged infringer in current action in its defense); Hawthorne v. Eckerson, Co., 77 F.2d 844 (2d Cir.1935)(evidence of defendant's settlement with another injured party was not admissible in claim brought by second injured party). See also Playboy Enterprises, Inc. v. Chuckleberry Pub., 486 F.Supp. 414, 423 n.10 (S.D.N.Y.1980)(plaintiff's copyright settlement with magazine A, was not admissible under Rule 408 in copyright litigation with magazine B to show that plaintiff's claim against B was unjustified).

7. Alpex Computer Corp. v. Nintendo Co., 770 F.Supp. 161, 164 (S.D.N.Y.1991), on reconsideration, 1994 WL 139423 (S.D.N.Y.1994), decision vacated in part, 1994 WL 381659 (S.D.N.Y.1994).

8. Olin Corp. v. Insurance Co. of North America, 603 F.Supp. 445, on rearg., 607 F.Supp. 1377 (S.D.N.Y.1985)(court decided that discussions were settlement-related and not merely business discussions because they concerned the rights and liabilities of the parties).

9. Gestetner Holdings, PLC v. Nashua Corp., 784 F.Supp. 78 (S.D.N.Y.1992) (meaning of the arbitration understood in the same way by both parties as evidenced by negotiations).

10. Olin Corp. v. Insurance Co. of North America, 603 F.Supp. 445, on rearg., 607 F.Supp. 1377 (S.D.N.Y.1985)(but in this case it was shown that there was no refusal to settle).

11. Thomas v. Resort Health Related Facility, 539 F.Supp. 630, 638 (E.D. N.Y.1982)("Defendant's purpose is to show that back pay otherwise recoverable after the date of its offer should not be allowed because the loss of back pay during that period is not attributable to defendant's determination").

12. Iberian Tankers Co. v. Gates Construction Corp., 388 F.Supp. 1190 (S.D.N.Y. 1975).

13. 865 F.2d 506 (2d Cir.1989).

Ch. 4   PAYMENT OF MEDICAL & SIMILAR EXPENSES   § 409.1

court, on a very close question, opted for exclusion where admissibility for another purpose was urged. The contract in litigation was subject to the statute of frauds and the writings in question were urged by plaintiffs as the necessary written evidence to satisfy the statute of frauds. Defendant argued that the documents were offers to compromise and should be excluded under Rule 408. The court found for defendant because of the public policy considerations favoring settlement attempts.[14] The Rule 408 prohibition applies only in civil litigation.[15]

In New York, as previously discussed, admissions of fact made during compromise negotiations are admissible.[16] This rule was seen by the Advisory Committee on the Federal Rules as inhibiting freedom of communication during negotiations, and so Rule 408 expressly provides for the exclusion of conduct or statements made during the negotiations. Sometimes, however, the "without prejudice" or hypothetical language used in New York to avoid the *Old Dominion* rule can be helpful in federal practice to identify a communication as a settlement communication where the nature of the communication would otherwise be doubtful.[17]

Library References:

West's Key No. Digests, Evidence ⟐212, 219(3).

409   Payment of Medical and Similar Expenses

§ 409.1   New York

As is the case with offers to compromise, or the taking of remedial measures, an offer to pay a person's medical expenses might be construed as an admission that the offeror was conceding his liability. But the law seeks to encourage such benevolence and so such an offer will be kept out of evidence. The law governing offers of payment for such expenses in New York is set forth in the seminal and still predominant

---

14. Id. at 510. The court stated:
Appellants urge that they sought to introduce the documents only in order to meet the statute of frauds. However, such a proffer presents two conflicting goals: proving the existence of a contract in compliance with the statute of frauds and overcoming the strictures of Rule 408. For appellants, satisfying the statute of frauds was the necessary first step to proving, ultimately, the validity of their claims of breach of contract. Since the two questions were so closely intertwined, admission of the documents even initially for the purpose of meeting the statute of frauds requirement would, under the circumstances of this case, militate against the public policy considerations which favor settlement negotiations and which underlie Rule 408. Cf.

Fiberglass Insulators, Inc. v. Dupuy, 856 F.2d 652, 655 (4th Cir.1988)(settlement offer from closely related litigation was properly excluded from evidence).

Id.

15. United States v. Baker, 926 F.2d 179 (2d Cir.1991)(evidence of defendant's desire to make a deal with investigators admissible); United States v. Gonzalez, 748 F.2d 74 (2d Cir.1984)(admissions made by defendant while negotiating settlement of a potential civil claim were admissible).

16. White v. Old Dominion Steamship Co., 102 N.Y. 660, 6 N.E. 289 (1886). See § 408.1 supra.

17. S. Leo Harmonay, Inc. v. Binks Mfg. Co., 597 F.Supp. 1014 (S.D.N.Y.1984), aff'd, 762 F.2d 990 (2d Cir.1985).

case, *Grogan v. Dooley*.[1] Plaintiff introduced evidence that defendants offered to pay his wages and medical bills while he was disabled because of his injury. In ruling this error Judge Cardozo stated: "The evidence was received as involving an admission of liability. We think it had no such significance. The defendants' offer was not made in response to any demand for compensation. It was not made in circumstances from which it might take form and color as a confession of fault. It was a voluntary act of mere benevolence."[2] Such an act was seen as a "humane recognition of an existing necessity, and not as an admission of the justice of a claim not then asserted."[3] Inherent in that position is the exception noted in § 408.1 *supra* with respect to offers of compromise generally—unless the offer is accompanied by "without prejudice" language, any admissions of liability accompanying the offer will be admissible.[4]

Grogan distinguishes *Brice v. Bauer*,[5] where the issue was whether defendant owned the dog that bit plaintiff. The Court of Appeals there ruled admissible a conversation initiated by defendant in which defendant offered plaintiff a small sum of money on account of plaintiff's injuries. Plaintiff refused the offer. The court pointed out that it did not appear that the offer to pay was in compromise of any dispute between the parties. "The disagreement was in reference only to the amount, and the transaction might well be regarded as a tacit admission of liability. In such a case even the offer of a sum by way of compromise is held to be admissible, unless stated to be confidential or made without prejudice."[6] Judge Cardozo found that in *Brice*, defendant's offer was not a spontaneous act of benevolence and was not an attempt to compromise a dispute. The *Brice* conversation was seen as an unprotected admission by defendant.[7]

Perhaps because the prohibition against medical payments is so specific, it has generated little further exposition in the cases.[8] Also, it seems to be understood that this evidence would be admissible for other purposes, such as proof of agency, ownership, or bias or prejudice of a witness, as set forth in the Proposed New York Evidence Code § 409.[9]

§ 409.1

1. 211 N.Y. 30, 105 N.E. 135 (1914).
2. Id. at 31, 105 N.E. at 136.
3. Id. at 32, 105 N.E. at 136.
4. See § 408.1, at note 4, supra.
5. 108 N.Y. 428, 15 N.E. 695 (1888).
6. Id. at 433, 15 N.E. at 697.
7. 211 N.Y. at 32, 105 N.E. at 136.

8. There are older cases: Smith v. Bailey, 14 App.Div. 283, 43 N.Y.S. 856 (1st Dep't 1897)(Defendant told victim he had just been hit with a street sweeper, that he would help him financially and later went to his house and gave him ten dollars—not admissible); Emery v. Litchard, 137 Misc. 885, 245 N.Y.S. 209 (Sup.Ct.Wyoming Co.1930)(payment to plaintiff not an admission of liability); Baldwin v. New York Cent. & H.R.R. Co., 56 N.Y.Super.Ct. 607, 2 N.Y.S. 481 (Super.Ct.N.Y.C.1888), aff'd, 121 N.Y. 684, 24 N.E. 1098 (1890) (defendant's procurement of a release, apparently on the basis of payment made, not admissible); 65 A.L.R.3d 941 (1975).

9. **§ 409. Payment of medical and similar expenses [PROPOSED]**

Evidence of furnishing or offering or promising to pay medical, hospital, or similar expenses occasioned by an injury is not admissible to prove civil or criminal liability for the injury. This section does not, however, require exclusion when the evidence is offered for another purpose, such as proof of agency, ownership, or control, or bias or prejudice of a witness.

Ch. 4   PLEAS & PLEA DISCUSSIONS   § 410.1

Indeed, since there was a question of ownership of the dog in the *Brice* case, defendant's conversation was used as proof on that issue. Note should be taken of the somewhat related rule in personal injury cases that the judge is to receive evidence of collateral payments, outside the presence of the jury, in order that she might reduce the economic loss damage award arrived at by the jury.[10]

Library References:

West's Key No. Digests, Evidence ⟲219(1).

§ 409.2 Federal

Federal Rule of Evidence 409 provides:

> Evidence of furnishing or offering or promising to pay medical, hospital, or similar expenses occasioned by an injury is not admissible to prove liability for the injury.

Here, unlike Rule 408, the exclusionary rule does not encompass conduct or statements made in connection with the payment or offer.[1] The rule codifies the law theretofore existing;[2] except that it is not clear whether the rule would allow this evidence for another purpose, such as to prove agency, ownership or control, or bias of a witness.

Library References:

West's Key No. Digests, Evidence ⟲219(1).

410 Pleas and Plea Discussions

§ 410.1 New York

As in the case of civil litigation, public policy encourages compromises on the criminal side to reduce the time and expense occasioned by criminal trials. This policy is promoted "by protecting from disclosure at trial not only the offer but also statements made during negotia-

---

The comment to the proposed rule points out that unlike proposed § 408 relating to compromises generally, this section does not exclude evidence of conduct or statements made in connection with the payment or offer.

10. CPLR 4545 provides for reduction of awards for economic loss when payments have been received from insurance, social security, workers' compensation, or employee benefit programs.

§ 409.2

1. The Advisory Committee's note states:

> Contrary to Rule 408, dealing with offers to compromise, the present rule does not extend to conduct or statements not a part of the act of furnishing or offering or promising to pay. This difference in treatment arises from fundamental differences in nature. Communication is es-

sential if compromises are to be effected, and consequently broad protection of statements is needed. This is not so in cases of payments or offers or promises to pay medical expenses, where factual statements may be expected to be incidental in nature.

2. In Arnold v. Owens, 78 F.2d 495, 497 (4th Cir.1935), plaintiff claimed that defendant came to his house and offered to pay his hospital expenses. The court ruled this evidence inadmissible to prove liability. "[A] voluntary offer of assistance made upon an impulse of benevolence or sympathy may not be considered an admission of culpable causation." See also Southern Railway Co. v. Madden, 235 F.2d 198, 201 (4th Cir.1956), cert. denied, 352 U.S. 953, 77 S.Ct. 328, 1 L.Ed.2d 244 (1956)(evidence that defendant offered to pay plaintiff's hospital bill inadmissible).

tions."[1] There are two chief areas of consideration: withdrawn guilty pleas, and statements and testimony given in connection with plea negotiations.

Withdrawn guilty plea. The plea of guilty is a direct acknowledgment that defendant committed a crime, whether the one charged or a reduced version thereof. Hence, it would follow that if that plea were withdrawn an admission would linger. But that admission may not be used against the defendant at trial in New York. The leading case is *People v. Spitaleri*,[2] where, at trial, the judge instructed the jury that defendant's withdrawn guilty plea was in the nature of a confession. In reversing the conviction the Court of Appeals stated:

> The question is not whether a plea of guilty is a confession of guilt and provable as such. Of course it is * * *. But we are inquiring into something quite different. We must say whether it is lawful in New York for a court, after allowing a guilty plea to be set at naught, to allow the jury to use that same plea as proof of guilt. Such a distortion of purpose should not be allowed.[3]

Reliance was placed on the United States Supreme Court's decision in *Kercheval v. United States*,[4] a unanimous determination squarely holding a withdrawn guilty plea to be inadmissible.

Statements made during the course of negotiations. The *Spitaleri* exclusionary rule with respect to the guilty plea itself is based entirely on basic elements of fairness.[5] Whether or not statements made before or during negotiations are admissible, therefore, turns on factors peculiar to each case.

Statements made prior to plea negotiations by the defendant, even if they provide the catalyst for the negotiations, are admissible. In *People v. Evans*,[6] the Court of Appeals held that defendant's voluntary "pre-plea incriminating statements"[7] were admissible. Defendant, with the presence and advice of counsel, made the inculpatory statements before entering into plea negotiations. There was no unfairness here since "[d]efendant had the opportunity, if he so desired, to express as a condition of his pleas that none of his statements and future testimony could be used against him * * *. This was entirely within his control. However, after consulting his attorney, he did not even attempt to so condition his plea."[8]

§ 410.1

1. McCormick § 266, at 1989.

2. 9 N.Y.2d 168, 212 N.Y.S.2d 53, 173 N.E.2d 35 (1961).

3. Id. at 172, 212 N.Y.S.2d at 55, 173 N.E.2d at 37. See also People v. Droz, 39 N.Y.2d 457, 463, 384 N.Y.S.2d 404, 408, 348 N.E.2d 880, 883 (1976).

4. 274 U.S. 220, 47 S.Ct. 582, 71 L.Ed. 1009 (1927).

5. People v. Curdgel, 83 N.Y.2d 862, 865, 611 N.Y.S.2d 827, 829, 634 N.E.2d 199, 201 (1994).

6. 58 N.Y.2d 14, 457 N.Y.S.2d 757, 444 N.E.2d 7 (1982).

7. Id. at 21, 457 N.Y.S.2d at 760 444 N.E.2d at 10.

8. Id. at 24, 457 N.Y.S.2d at 762, 444 N.E.2d at 12. The court went on: "Exclusion of evidence of defendant's guilty plea [under Spitaleri] provides all the protection necessary to assure that the court's decision to allow defendant to withdraw that plea is

Statements made during the plea negotiations themselves, however, can be used against defendant only if the prosecution exacts a waiver, i.e., "only if the People had specifically bargained for that use."[9] Thus, defendant's statements made during negotiations should be inadmissible. This is true even where defendant takes the stand and the prosecutor seeks to impeach him with those statements.[10]

Defendant's grand jury testimony against others, which is induced by his plea bargain, may be used against defendant if he breaches that bargain and is tried. In *People v. Curdgel*,[11] defendant pleaded guilty and then testified against accomplices before the grand jury. Later on television he said that he had lied to the grand jury. This negated his usefulness as a witness for the prosecution of those accomplices. The prosecutor was thus free not to honor the plea arrangements, and defendant's testimony, which also inculpated himself, could be used against him. It would be unfair to permit defendant to receive the benefit of the bargain (his reduced plea) and at the same time deprive the prosecutor of the bargained-for testimony.[12]

The Appellate Division in its opinion in *Curdgel* summed up the law nicely:

> While the People may not use a plea or the contents of a plea allocution on either their direct case or for impeachment, they may use statements made before plea negotiations and testimony given afterward * * *.[13]

The only loose end involves the situation where the prosecutor is somehow able to get defendant to permit use of all his statements, including those made after the negotiations have commenced through the plea allocution, and that case seems not to have arisen as yet.[14]

---

a meaningful one as required by Spitaleri. Providing an additional ground for exclusion of probative evidence serves only to denigrate the plea bargaining process and deprives a Judge or jury of evidence which is important to the truth-finding process." Id. at 25, 457 N.Y.S.2d at 762, 444 N.E.2d at 12. The Evans court also noted that had defendant exacted an agreement to immunize his statements, the prosecutor might well have bargained for an agreement by defendant not to appeal any suppression ruling. Since defendant had asked for no such condition, the prosecutor had no reason to impose such requirement on defendant. Id. at 23, n.2, 457 N.Y.S.2d at 761, 444 N.E.2d at 11.

9. People v. Curdgel, 83 N.Y.2d 862, 864, 611 N.Y.S.2d 827, 828, 634 N.E.2d 199, 200 (1994)(dictum).

10. People v. Moore, 66 N.Y.2d 1028, 1030, 499 N.Y.S.2d 393, 394, 489 N.E.2d 1295, 1296 (1985). See also People v. Papo, 80 A.D.2d 623, 436 N.Y.S.2d 65 (2d Dep't 1981); People v. Heffron, 59 A.D.2d 263, 399 N.Y.S.2d 501 (4th Dep't 1977); compare People v. Perez, 118 A.D.2d 431, 432, 499 N.Y.S.2d 716, 717 (1st Dep't), appeal denied, 67 N.Y.2d 1055, 504 N.Y.S.2d 1031, 495 N.E.2d 364 (1986)(defense counsel, in cross-examining police officer as to the plea of a codefendant, opened the door for the prosecution to introduce evidence of defendant's withdrawn plea).

11. 83 N.Y.2d 862, 611 N.Y.S.2d 827, 634 N.E.2d 199 (1994).

12. Id. at 865, 611 N.Y.S.2d at 201, 634 N.E.2d at 829.

13. 191 A.D.2d 743, 745, 594 N.Y.S.2d 410, 412 (3d Dep't 1993).

14. See People v. Ortiz, 141 Misc.2d 747, 755, 534 N.Y.S.2d 316, 321 (Sup.Ct.Richmond Co.1988)(factual admissions made by defendant as part of his plea process when charged with assault, could not be used against him under second indictment for murder after the victim died since prosecutor never bargained for a waiver for the use of those statements).

§ 410.1

The proposed New York Evidence Code § 410 is in the note.[15] It would seem, although there is no New York authority to this effect, that nolo contendere pleas made elsewhere would receive the same treatment as guilty pleas. Both Federal Rule 410 and Proposed New York Evidence Code § 410 include nolo contendere pleas in their coverage.

Library References:

West's Key No. Digests, Criminal Law ⟐406(4), 408; Evidence ⟐207(4), 212.

§ 410.2 Federal

In *Kercheval v. United States*,[1] the Supreme Court squarely held that a withdrawn guilty plea could not be used as an admission of guilt at trial.[2] Federal Rule of Evidence 410 excludes not only withdrawn guilty pleas, but also nolo contendere pleas and certain discussions made in connection with such pleas.[3]

---

15. **§ 410. Inadmissibility of pleas, plea discussions, and related statements [PROPOSED]**

Except as otherwise provided in this section, evidence of the following is not admissible in any civil or criminal case against the person who made the plea or was a participant in the plea discussions: (a) a plea of guilty which was later withdrawn or vacated; (b) a plea of nolo contendere validly made in any jurisdiction recognizing such pleas; (c) any statement made in the course of any judicial proceedings regarding either of the foregoing pleas; and (d) absent a waiver, any statement made in the course of plea discussions with an attorney for the prosecuting authority which do not result in a plea of guilty or which result in a plea of guilty later withdrawn or vacated. However, such a statement is admissible in any civil or criminal case in which another statement made in the course of the same plea or plea discussions has been introduced and the statement is necessary to complete, explain, assess, or make understood the previously introduced statement or in a criminal case for perjury or false statement if the statement was made by the defendant under oath, on the record, and in the presence of counsel.

§ 410.2

1. 274 U.S. 220, 47 S.Ct. 582, 71 L.Ed. 1009 (1927).

2. The Court stated:

A plea of guilty differs in purpose and effect from a mere admission or an extrajudicial confession; it is itself a conviction. Like a verdict of a jury it is conclusive. More is not required; the court has nothing to do but give judgment and sentence. Out of just consideration for persons accused of crime, courts are careful that a plea of guilty shall not be accepted unless made voluntarily after proper advice and with full understanding of the consequences. * * *

The effect of the court's order permitting the withdrawal was to adjudge that the plea of guilty be held for naught. Its subsequent use as evidence against petitioner was in direct conflict with that determination.

Id. at 223–24, 47 S.Ct. at 583, 71 L.Ed. at 1012.

3. Rule 410 provides:

Inadmissibility of Pleas, Plea Discussions, and Related Statements

Except as otherwise provided in this rule, evidence of the following is not, in any civil or criminal proceeding, admissible against the defendant who made the plea or was a participant in the plea discussions:

(1) a plea of guilty which was later withdrawn;

(2) a plea of nolo contendere;

(3) any statement made in the course of any proceedings under Rule 11 of the Federal Rules of Criminal Procedure or comparable state procedure regarding either of the foregoing pleas; or

(4) any statement made in the course of plea discussions with an attorney for the prosecuting authority which do not result in a plea of guilty or which result in a plea of guilty later withdrawn.

However, such a statement is admissible (i) in any proceeding wherein another statement made in the course of the same

In a prior version of Rule 410 any statement made "in connection with" a plea was considered inadmissible;[4] but the Rule was amended in 1980 so that now it is limited to statements made in plea discussions with an attorney for the prosecuting authority.[5] The question of preplea statements, and to whom made, has generated the bulk of the litigation. Where a government attorney was involved in the plea bargaining, but was not present when the incriminating statements were made, exclusion was required because the legislative history indicated that it would be enough that a government attorney "participated" in the plea process.[6] But where defendant simply offered to cooperate, without any expression of hope for a concession, the Rule was held not to apply.[7] And where defendant's false statements were sought to be used against him and were made by defendant on stipulation that anything said could be used against him, the "stipulations confirm that the interview was not a plea bargaining conference but an effort by him to convince the

plea or plea discussions has been introduced and the statement ought in fairness be considered contemporaneously with it, or (ii) in a criminal proceeding for perjury or false statement if the statement was made by the defendant under oath, on the record and in the presence of counsel.

4. United States v. Lawson, 683 F.2d 688, 690–93 (2d Cir.1982).

5. Federal Rule of Criminal Procedure 11(e)(6) is a companion rule, which was also amended accordingly. In United States v. Brooks, 536 F.2d 1137 (6th Cir.1976), defendant had offered to plead guilty to a postal inspector and the court ruled the offer inadmissible. It is doubtful that such a ruling would obtain today in light of the amendment to Rule 410. Likewise, in United States v. Herman, 544 F.2d 791 (5th Cir.), reh'g denied, 549 F.2d 204 (5th Cir. 1977), another pre-amendment case, defendant offered to plead guilty to postal inspectors and this evidence was held inadmissible.

6. United States v. Serna, 799 F.2d 842, 849 (2d Cir.1986).

7. United States v. Levy, 578 F.2d 896 (2d Cir.1978). The court stated:

Plea bargaining implies an offer to plead guilty upon condition. The offer by the defendant must, in some way, express the hope that a concession to reduce the punishment will come to pass. A silent hope, if uncommunicated, gives the officer or prosecutor no chance to reject a confession he did not seek. A contrary rule would permit the accused to grant retrospectively to himself what is akin to a use immunity. Id. at 901.

Note that the Levy case, which involved defendant's statements to the police, was decided prior to the amendment to the Rule. If the case arose today, it would be enough for admissibility that no government attorney was in the picture when the offer to cooperate was made.

In United States v. Arroyo–Angulo, 580 F.2d 1137 (2d Cir.), cert. denied, 439 U.S. 913, 99 S.Ct. 285, 58 L.Ed.2d 260 (1978), cert. denied sub nom., Moreno v. United States, 439 U.S. 1131, 99 S.Ct. 1052, 59 L.Ed.2d 93 (1979), the court said that evidence of a cooperation agreement, while not admissible to bolster the credibility of a witness, is admissible if the witness' credibility is attacked. 580 F.2d at 1146.

In United States v. Stirling, 571 F.2d 708, 731–32 (2d Cir.), cert. denied, 439 U.S. 824, 99 S.Ct. 93, 58 L.Ed.2d 116 (1978), defendant's statements were held admissible where he backed out of an agreement to plead guilty and testify against others. The D.C. Circuit adopted this approach in United States v. Davis, 617 F.2d 677, cert. denied sub nom., Gelestino v. United States, 445 U.S. 967, 100 S.Ct. 1659, 64 L.Ed.2d 244 (1980)(1979), stating: "Excluding [defendant's inculpatory] testimony made after—and pursuant to—the agreement would not serve the purpose of encouraging compromise. Indeed, such a rule would permit a defendant to breach his bargain with impunity: he could renounce the agreement and return to the status quo ante whenever he chose, even though the Government has no parallel power to rescind the compromise unilaterally." Davis, 617 F.2d at 685. In both Stirling and Davis the courts were construing Rule 11(e)(6) of the Federal Rules of Criminal Procedure, the companion to Fed.R.Evid. 410.

government that he was not guilty of any crime."[8]

When statements fall within the coverage of Rule 410 the Supreme Court has held they may be used to impeach defendant if he has knowingly waived his right to object to their use at trial.[9]

It has been held that a consent judgment between a federal agency and a private corporation is the equivalent of a plea of nolo contendere and therefore is inadmissible under Rule 410.[10]

It bears noting that the concluding portion of Rule 410 authorizes the use of plea-related statements made by defendant on the record, under oath, in the presence of counsel, where relevant in a perjury or false statement proceeding. Additionally, where a plea-related statement has been introduced, presumably by the defendant, a sort of waiver or door-opening occurs so as to allow other relevant statements made during plea discussions.

Library References:

West's Key No. Digests, Criminal Law ⚖️406(4), 408; Evidence ⚖️207(4), 212.

411 Liability Insurance

§ 411.1 New York

It is of no relevance whatsoever on the issues of negligence or strict liability whether the defendant is or is not insured. Because the prejudice quotient is obvious, the rule barring such evidence is one of the least controversial in the law of evidence. When rarely it comes up, the courts have not deviated from the rule as stated by the Court of Appeals in *Simpson v. Foundation Co.*:[1]

> Evidence that the defendant in an action for negligence was insured in a casualty company, or that the defense was conducted by an insurance company, is incompetent and so dangerous as to require a reversal even when the court strikes it from the record and directs the jury to disregard it, unless it clearly appears that it could not have influenced the verdict.[2]

---

8. United States v. Cunningham, 723 F.2d 217 (2d Cir.1983), cert. denied, 466 U.S. 951, 104 S.Ct. 2154, 80 L.Ed.2d 540 (1984).

9. United States v. Mezzanatto, ___ U.S. ___, 115 S.Ct. 797, 130 L.Ed.2d 697 (1995). Lower courts had previously decided otherwise. United States v. Lawson, 683 F.2d 688, 691–92 (2d Cir.1982). See also United States v. Udeagu, 110 F.R.D. 172, 174 (E.D.N.Y.1986), where the court relied upon legislative history to conclude that Rule 410 blocks the use of the statements even for impeachment purposes.

10. Lipsky v. Com. United Corp., 551 F.2d 887, 893 (2d Cir.1976). The court stated:

> This is a consent judgment between a federal agency and a private corporation which is not the result of an actual adjudication of any of the issues. Consequently, it can not be used as evidence in subsequent litigation between that corporation and another party. Fed. Rules Evid., Rule 410 * * * prohibits a plea of nolo contendere from being later used against the party who so pleaded. Although CUC did not, technically, plead nolo contendere to the SEC's complaint, nolo pleas have been equated with "consent decrees" for purposes of the proviso to § 5(a) of the Clayton Act.

§ 411.1

1. 201 N.Y. 479, 95 N.E. 10 (1911).

2. Id. at 490, 95 N.E.2d at 15.

Thus, reference by defendant's counsel in his summation to defendant's lack of insurance made to generate sympathy for defendant's plight if a large award were to be handed down could not be tolerated,[3] and even "oblique" attempts to suggest coverage or lack thereof will form grounds for reversal.[4]

Where issues other than those relating to fault or product defects are in the case, however, the fact of liability insurance coverage may be relevant. The fact of such coverage may be admissible, for example, where ownership or control of the instrumentality causing the accident is an issue.[5] Proof that a party insures an instrumentality is strong evidence showing ownership[6] or control.[7] Thus, where plaintiff was injured at a job site and the question arose whether defendant Melvit was the general contractor and in control of the premises, insurance coverage by Melvit "is strong proof that Melvit was in control of the project and was the 'general contractor.'"[8] The Appellate Division, Fourth Department, has placed limits on the exception relating to control and ownership.[9] If the probative value of the evidence of insurance coverage is outweighed by its prejudicial effect then it should be kept out. In that case, the question arose whether defendant Matie owned the car involved in the accident, or whether it was still owned by codefendant West Seneca Ford, a dealer which had either sold the car to Matie or was in the process of selling it. It was this question of whether the car had changed hands at the time of the accident that led the majority to view Matie's procurement of insurance as weak and prejudicial. The majority pointed out that it was necessary for Matie to obtain insurance in order to get temporary registration for the car.[10] A lower court has found, on the other hand, that New York law does not view the introduction of evidence of insurance as a question for balancing probative value against prejudice. "[O]nce the party seeking to offer the evidence has met the extremely high threshold showing of a necessity of

---

3. Rendo v. Schermerhorn, 24 A.D.2d 773, 263 N.Y.S.2d 743 (3d Dep't 1965). See also Thiele v. Hickey, 6 A.D.2d 939, 175 N.Y.S.2d 792 (3d Dep't 1958). Defense counsel in his summation indicated that his clients were uninsured. "Thus baited," said the court, "plaintiff's counsel in his summation strongly suggested that there was insurance, and said: 'and I don't believe they [plaintiff] will bring any harm to the defendants, if they win this case.' We condemn such practice by either party * * *." 6 A.D.2d at 939, 175 N.Y.S.2d at 793–94.

4. Wisniewski v. Jem Novelty Corp., 22 A.D.2d 10, 253 N.Y.S.2d 418 (1st Dep't 1964). When, in his summation, defense counsel referred to taking "money out of a man's pocket to pay for [plaintiff's injuries]," plaintiff's counsel interrupted and said, inter alia, "I want to have the right to make comment on the source of payment of judgment." All of this was deemed prejudicial error in a close case. Id. at 12–13, 253 N.Y.S.2d at 421.

5. Shutt v. Pooley, 43 A.D.2d 59, 61–62, 349 N.Y.S.2d 839, 843 (3d Dep't 1973). See also Leotta v. Plessinger, 8 N.Y.2d 449, 461–62, 209 N.Y.S.2d 304, 313, 171 N.E.2d 454, 460 (1960), rehearing denied, 9 N.Y.2d 688, 212 N.Y.S.2d 1025, 173 N.E.2d 246 (1961); Hoff v. State Farm Ins. Co., 48 A.D.2d 1001, 369 N.Y.S.2d 256 (4th Dep't 1975).

6. Ferris v. Sterling, 214 N.Y. 249, 253, 108 N.E. 406, 407 (1915); McGovern v. Oliver, 177 App.Div. 167, 169, 163 N.Y.S. 275, 277 (1st Dep't 1917).

7. Martyn v. Braun, 270 App.Div. 768, 59 N.Y.S.2d 588 (2d Dep't 1946).

8. Furia v. Mellucci, 143 Misc.2d 596, 598, 541 N.Y.S.2d 727, 728 (Sup.Ct.Bronx Co.1989).

9. Constable v. Matie, 199 A.D.2d 1004, 608 N.Y.S.2d 10 (4th Dep't 1993).

10. Id. at 1005, 608 N.Y.S.2d at 11.

§ 411.1

the proof on a relevant issue, possible prejudice to other parties is to be disregarded * * *."[11]

Issues other than ownership and control may arise which would make relevant the fact of insurance coverage. For instance, where an issue in a case involving a commercial truck accident was whether the lessee driver had breached his agreement by failing to furnish liability insurance, thus relieving the lessor of liability, evidence that the insurance had not been obtained was admissible.[12] Also, where the law of another jurisdiction permits actions directly against liability insurers, such law will be applied in New York under choice of law rules even though the jury thereby learns that there is insurance in the case.[13]

The Proposed New York Evidence Code restates the prevailing law.[14]

Library References:

West's Key No. Digests, Damages ⚖182; Trial ⚖127.

§ 411.2 Federal

Rule 411 of Federal Rule of Evidence provides:

> Evidence that a person was or was not insured against liability is not admissible upon the issue whether the person acted negligently or otherwise wrongfully. This rule does not require the exclusion of evidence of insurance against liability when offered for another purpose, such as proof of agency, ownership, or control, or bias or prejudice of a witness.

Prior to the enactment of Rule 411 the common law exclusionary "insurance rule" was well settled in the federal courts in cases where there were no issues to which such evidence could be relevant other than fault.[1] But where other issues have cropped up, evidence of insurance coverage can be introduced if relevant to those issues. Thus, evidence of defendant's insurance discussions with plaintiff's husband, to prove the

---

11. Furia v. Mellucci, 143 Misc.2d 596, 598, 541 N.Y.S.2d 727, 729 (Sup.Ct.Bronx Co.1989).

12. Leotta v. Plessinger, 8 N.Y.2d 449, 461, 209 N.Y.S.2d 304, 313, 171 N.E.2d 454, 459 (1960), rehearing denied, 9 N.Y.2d 688, 212 N.Y.S.2d 1025, 173 N.E.2d 246 (1961).

13. Oltarsh v. Aetna Ins. Co., 15 N.Y.2d 111, 256 N.Y.S.2d 577, 204 N.E.2d 622 (1965). The court noted that such evidence is inadmissible only where the sole reason for introducing it is to "improperly influence the jury," and where the fact of insurance is legitimately an issue in the case "there can be no ground for complaint." It was noted that it would be the rare individual who would not know that drivers are insured, a fact that must have been driven home by the advent of the law requiring compulsory liability insurance. Id. at 118, 119, 256 N.Y.S.2d at 582, 583, 204 N.E.2d at 626, 627.

14. § 411 Liability insurance [PROPOSED]

Evidence that a person was or was not insured against liability is not admissible upon the issue whether such person acted negligently or otherwise wrongfully or whether such person should be held strictly liable. This section does not, however, require exclusion when the evidence is offered for another purpose, such as proof of agency, ownership or control or bias or prejudice of a witness.

§ 411.2

1. See Brown v. Walter, 62 F.2d 798, 800 (2d Cir.1933)(plaintiff's persistent efforts to mention defendant's insurance coverage in the summation, and to ask defendant what he had told an insurance agent when there was no occasion for impeachment, resulted in reversal of jury verdict for plaintiff).

relevant fact that defendant had become entangled in the husband's business affairs, was admissible.[2] It has been held, however, that where evidence of insurance is relevant to an issue, it must be weighed under Rule 403 against its prejudicial effect.[3]

Other instances in which evidence of insurance has been held admissible are varied. Where a defense witness testified concerning the reputation for veracity of plaintiff's witness it would not be error to impeach the credibility of the defense witness by asking about his association with liability insurance companies, since he was employed by defendant's insurer;[4] where the issue was whether defendants had sent money to plaintiff, a material question was whether defendant had insured the shipment;[5] where defendant put in evidence a statement given by plaintiff it was proper for plaintiff to question the witness who took the statement concerning his employment by the defendant's insurance company so as to affect his credibility;[6] and where plaintiff's reference to insurance was "oblique," having been instigated by defendant's own witnesses and evidence (an insurance investigator and various insurance documents) there could be no grounds for upsetting the verdict.[7]

Library References:

West's Key No. Digests, Damages ⚖182; Trial ⚖127.

412 Shield Laws

§ 412.1 New York

New York's so-called "rape shield law," enacted in 1975, reads as follows:

---

2. Pinkham v. Burgess, 933 F.2d 1066, 1072 (1st Cir.1991). Plaintiff sued for legal malpractice, and the evidence of defendant's insurance inquiry tended to prove his involvement with her husband, which made it difficult for her to fire defendant as her lawyer. Furthermore, the insurance reference did not even suggest that defendant was covered by malpractice insurance.

3. Palmer v. Krueger, 897 F.2d 1529, 1538 (10th Cir.1990). Plaintiff in a wrongful death action against the pilot of a private plane sought to cross-examine the pilot's executor, plaintiff's stepbrother, concerning a family disagreement as to the ownership of the plane and to whom the insurance money for its loss was due and owing. The trial judge saw this as a collateral matter not sufficiently relevant to the issues of liability in the case and thus overcome by its prejudicial effect, and the circuit court affirmed.

4. Charter v. Chleborad, 551 F.2d 246, 248 (8th Cir.), cert. denied, 434 U.S. 856, 98 S.Ct. 176, 54 L.Ed.2d 128 (1977).

5. De Waay v. Dominick, 174 F.2d 204, 205 (2d Cir.1949).

6. Mideastern Contracting Corp. v. O'Toole, 55 F.2d 909, 912 (2d Cir.1932).

7. Cote v. Gentile, 257 F.Supp. 603, 606 (D.C.Conn.1966). In Cote, Judge Timbers stated:

> Moreover, Judge Hincks some years ago laid bare the shibboleth that knowledge on the part of jurors that a defendant in a negligence case is insured somehow softens a verdict out of considerations of sympathy or prejudice: "But only undue cynicism will support the thesis that knowledge of the presence of an insurer's interest will necessarily distort a juror's judgment." Schevling v. Johnson, 122 F.Supp. 87, 89–90 (D.Conn.1953), aff'd, 213 F.2d 959 (2d Cir.1954).

Id.

§ 412.1

Crim. Proc. Law § 60.42. Rules of evidence; admissibility of evidence of victim's sexual conduct in sex offense cases

Evidence of a victim's sexual conduct shall not be admissible in a prosecution for an offense or an attempt to commit an offense defined in article one hundred thirty of the penal law unless such evidence:

1. proves or tends to prove specific instances of the victim's prior sexual conduct with the accused; or

2. proves or tends to prove that the victim has been convicted of an offense under section 230.00 of the penal law within three years prior to the sex offense which is the subject of the prosecution; or

3. rebuts evidence introduced by the people of the victim's failure to engage in sexual intercourse, deviate sexual intercourse or sexual contact during a given period of time; or

4. rebuts evidence introduced by the people which proves or tends to prove that the accused is the cause of pregnancy or disease of the victim, or the source of semen found in the victim; or

5. is determined by the court after an offer of proof by the accused outside the hearing of the jury, or such hearing as the court may require, and a statement by the court of its findings of fact essential to its determination, to be relevant and admissible in the interests of justice.

This statute protects victims of sexual crimes[1] from cross-examination or other evidence as to their sexual background to suggest their consent to the sexual act with which defendant is charged. Aside from the questionable relevance of such background, exclusion serves to encourage the victim's testimony in prosecutions for such crimes.[2] In *People v. Williams*,[3] the Court of Appeals, noting that 47 other states had enacted rape shield laws, stated:

> The statute[s] put to rest the now-discredited rationale that a victim's past "unchastity" is probative of present consent and recognized that such evidence is typically of little or no rele-

---

§ 412.1

1. These are the crimes set forth in N.Y. Penal Law Art. 130, entitled "Sex Offenses." The 16 sections in the article cover rape, sodomy, sexual abuse, and sexual misconduct. The Proposed New York Evidence Code § 411 would also include offenses under Article 3, Family Court Act (Juvenile Delinquency).

2. The comment to Proposed New York Evidence Code § 411, which is almost identical to § 60.42, states:

This section restates CPL 60.42 which limits use of a victim's prior sexual conduct in a criminal case. "The basic twofold purpose of this enactment (CPL 60.42) is to bar harassment of victims with respect to irrelevant issues and to keep from the jury confusing and prejudicial matters which have no proper bearing on the issue of the guilt or innocence of the accused. It attempts to strike a reasonable balance between protecting the privacy and reputation of a victim and permitting an accused, when it is found relevant, to present evidence of a victim's sexual conduct." Bellacosa, Practice Commentary to Crim.Pro.Law § 60.42 (McKinney 1981).

3. 81 N.Y.2d 303, 598 N.Y.S.2d 167, 614 N.E.2d 730 (1993).

vance and may seriously prejudice the prosecution of sex crimes * * *. At the same time, by providing exceptions to the general evidentiary prohibition of section 60.42, our Legislature acknowledged that there are instances where evidence of a complainant's sexual history might be relevant and admissible.[4]

The fifth exception in § 60.42, the one most often invoked by defendants, is a constitutional safety valve that allows the trial judge to admit evidence of the victim's prior sexual conduct where, on the basis of an offer of proof or a hearing, it can be found that defendant is entitled to it "in the interests of justice." The *Williams* decision recognized that a balance must be struck between the victim's right to be protected under the statute against defendant's right of confrontation, noting that rape shield laws have the blessing of the United States Supreme Court.[5] On the facts of *Williams*, the court ruled that evidence of the victim's previous participation in group sex was properly kept out.[6] In another case, where, as the trial progressed, the victim's inconsistencies grew troublesome, it was held by the Appellate Division that the trial judge should have allowed the defendant to produce evidence of certain aspects of the victim's mental infirmities involving feelings of guilt because of her sexual promiscuity;[7] but the Court of Appeals reversed (holding § 60.42 constitutional in the process), so that not even in this perhaps more compelling situation could it be said that the interests of justice required the production of such evidence of her mental condition.[8]

---

4. Id. at 312, 598 N.Y.S.2d at 170, 614 N.E.2d at 733.

5. [I]t is settled that an accused's right to cross-examine witnesses and present a defense is not absolute * * *. Nor can the Sixth Amendment be read to "confer the right to present testimony free from the legitimate demands of the adversarial system" (United States v. Nobles, 422 U.S. 225, 241; accord, Michigan v. Lucas, 500 U.S. 145, 151–52, 111 S.Ct. 1743, 1747–48). Evidentiary restrictions are to be voided only if they are "arbitrary or disproportionate to the purposes they are designed to serve" (Rock v. Arkansas, supra, at 56; Michigan v. Lucas, 500 U.S. at 150, 111 S.Ct. at 1747, supra). A restriction is most likely to be found arbitrary when it is a per se rule, as in Rock, or when it is applied by a court without due consideration of the individualized circumstances and interests present in the matter before it, as in Chambers. Insofar as rape shield laws are concerned, the Supreme Court has recognized that they express the States' legitimate interest in giving rape victims "heightened protection against surprise, harassment and unnecessary invasions of privacy" (see, Michigan v. Lucas, 500 U.S. at 150, 111 S.Ct. at 1746, supra). Id. at 313, 598 N.Y.S.2d at 171, 614 N.E.2d at 734.

6. Defense counsel's offer of proof consisted of the argument that the victim's prior experience would explain her motive for testifying in this case, another instance of group sex; but the Court of Appeals held that this had no bearing on the issue of consent, which was the only relevant issue raised by the case. Id. at 315, 598 N.Y.S.2d at 173, 614 N.E.2d at 736.

7. People v. Mandel, 61 A.D.2d 563, 567, 572, 403 N.Y.S.2d 63, 66, 69–70 (2d Dep't 1978), rev'd on other grounds, 48 N.Y.2d 952, 425 N.Y.S.2d 63, 401 N.E.2d 185 (1979), cert. denied, 446 U.S. 949, 100 S.Ct. 2913, 64 L.Ed.2d 805, rehearing denied, 448 U.S. 908, 100 S.Ct. 3051, 65 L.Ed.2d 1138 (1980).

8. The Court of Appeals found error in allowing hospital records evidencing the victim's mental problems. It agreed with the Appellate Division that evidence of her past alleged false-rape complaints, a suggestive photograph of her, proof as to beatings administered by her father, and proof as to her prior vaginal condition should not be allowed. 48 N.Y.2d at 953, 954, 425 N.Y.S.2d at 64, 401 N.E.2d at 186, 187.

§ 412.1 RELEVANCY Ch. 4

Not all attempts to invoke the subdivision 5 exception have been futile. In a habeas corpus review, a federal district court ruled that defendant was entitled to cross-examine the complainants concerning sexual relations with other men.[9] "In this case," said the court, "the excluded evidence, when viewed in conjunction with the inconsistent identification testimony already on the record, could possibly have raised a reasonable doubt as to petitioner's guilt in the mind of the jurors."[10] In most other subdivision 5 cases, however, courts have been unwilling to find the purpose of the shield law outweighed by defendants' sixth amendment rights to confrontation and cross-examination.[11]

The first exception to the § 60.42 ban on evidence of the complaining witness' prior sexual history allows the court to admit evidence of specific instances of the victim's prior sexual history with the accused where the defense is based on consent. In *People v. Hauver*,[12] for example, consent was in issue, and the defendant was permitted to testify to two prior acts with the complaining witness. In *People v. Westfall*,[13] however, it was held that this was not a mandate and that the "threshold test of relevancy of such evidence should [not] be disregarded."[14] Here, two defendants, father and son, were on trial for rape, but the issue of consent was not in the case, thus ruling out any relevancy of evidence of prior sexual relations between one of the defendants and the complainant on that count. Defendant argued that remarks of the prosecutor in his summation opened the door to such evidence, and that

---

9. Latzer v. Abrams, 602 F.Supp. 1314, 1317–21 (E.D.N.Y.1985).

10. Id. at 1321.

11. People v. Naranjo, 194 A.D.2d 747, 748, 600 N.Y.S.2d 81, 82 (2d Dep't), appeal denied, 82 N.Y.2d 900, 610 N.Y.S.2d 167, 632 N.E.2d 477 (1993)(the court was spared the task of weighing defendant's request since the sexual history testimony would have been hearsay—but the prosecutor could offer proof of "child sexual abuse syndrome" to explain the victim's behavior); People v. Charlton, 192 A.D.2d 757, 759, 596 N.Y.S.2d 210, 212 (3d Dep't), leave to appeal denied, 81 N.Y.2d 1071, 601 N.Y.S.2d 590, 619 N.E.2d 668 (1993)(evidence as to victim's abuse by another person was properly excluded over defendant's argument that the victim confused that incident with the one in issue); People v. Neal, 191 A.D.2d 256, 595 N.Y.S.2d 17 (1st Dep't), leave to appeal denied, 82 N.Y.2d 723, 602 N.Y.S.2d 821, 622 N.E.2d 322 (1993)(trial court correct in allowing evidence of the victim's relationship with a friend of his mother's, but not allowing inquiry into the sexual aspects of the relationship); People v. Perryman, 178 A.D.2d 916, 917, 578 N.Y.S.2d 785, 786 (4th Dep't 1991), appeal denied, 79 N.Y.2d 1005, 584 N.Y.S.2d 460, 594 N.E.2d 954 (1992)(since evidence of prior sexual history generally bears on the issue of consent, there could be no reason for allowing it in a statutory rape case where consent is not a factor); People v. Lippert, 138 A.D.2d 770, 771, 525 N.Y.S.2d 390, 391 (3d Dep't 1988)(although prior alleged rape complaints do not literally come within the scope of § 60.42, the trial court can exclude such evidence); People v. Carroll, 117 A.D.2d 815, 816, 499 N.Y.S.2d 135, 136 (2d Dep't), appeal denied, 67 N.Y.2d 940, 502 N.Y.S.2d 1032, 494 N.E.2d 117 (1986)(where defendant never raised the issue of consent, any sexual history evidence would have been overly prejudicial); People v. Demerritt, 113 A.D.2d 898, 493 N.Y.S.2d 626 (2d Dep't), appeal denied, 66 N.Y.2d 918, 498 N.Y.S.2d 1033, 489 N.E.2d 778 (1985)(the trial court properly kept out defendant's offer to show complainant's sexual history, even though the prosecution introduced evidence that she was a lesbian and would not have consented).

12. 129 A.D.2d 889, 890, 514 N.Y.S.2d 814, 815 (3d Dep't), appeal denied, 70 N.Y.2d 712, 519 N.Y.S.2d 1047, 513 N.E.2d 1315 (1987).

13. 95 A.D.2d 581, 469 N.Y.S.2d 162 (3d Dep't 1983).

14. Id. at 583, 469 N.Y.S.2d at 164.

he should have been allowed to cross-examine complainant.[15] No reversible error was found since "the father was required on his cross-examination to testify to such relationship so the jury knew of its existence."[16] Other cases refusing to apply the first exception on various grounds are contained in the note.[17]

Exceptions 2 (victim has been convicted of a sexual offense) and 3 (rebuttal to People's evidence of victim's sexual abstinence) appear not to have arisen in the reported cases. There has been activity with respect to exception 4, however, which allows rebuttal where the People try to prove that defendant is the cause of pregnancy or disease of the victim, or the source of semen found in the victim. In *People v. Labenski*,[18] where defendant denied sexual contact with the complainant, the question was whether the semen in complainant's underpants was that of the defendant or complainant's boyfriend. The trial court was held to have correctly ruled that the fourth exception did not literally apply since the semen was not found "in" the victim. But the Appellate Division ruled that the evidence as it pertained to the boyfriend should have been admitted under the fifth exception else defendant would have been deprived of exploring the highly relevant question as to complainant's sexual contact with her boyfriend said to have occurred within hours of the alleged rape.[19]

The sexually-related activities of the complaining witness may be allowed for some impeachment purposes. Thus, in *People v. Harris*,[20] it was held error to preclude defendant from cross-examining complainant about her prior claims of rape "to demonstrate that the victim's prior claims were false."[21] If such complaints were made, they were not

---

15. The prosecutor said, "they ask you to believe that at 11:30 P.M. on a Sunday night they made an unannounced visit to the home of a single woman with whom they were only passingly acquainted." This remark was not challenged at trial. Id. at 584, 469 N.Y.S.2d at 164.

16. Id. at 585, 469 N.Y.S.2d at 165.

17. People v. Anderson, 184 A.D.2d 922, 584 N.Y.S.2d 946 (3d Dep't), appeal denied, 80 N.Y.2d 901, 588 N.Y.S.2d 826, 602 N.E.2d 234 (1992)(the question to the eight-year-old victim "When was the first time that *anyone* bad touched you?" was properly excluded as irrelevant to the first exception); People v. Goodwin, 179 A.D.2d 1046, 579 N.Y.S.2d 805 (4th Dep't), appeal denied, 79 N.Y.2d 948, 583 N.Y.S.2d 202, 592 N.E.2d 810 (1992)(a prior incident where defendant watched while another person had sexual contact with complainant was not within the scope of the first subdivision); People v. Martinez, 177 A.D.2d 600, 601, 575 N.Y.S.2d 938, 939 (2d Dep't), appeal denied, 79 N.Y.2d 829, 580 N.Y.S.2d 210, 588 N.E.2d 108 (1991)(defendant tried to establish through cross-examination of the complainant's mother that she "suspected" a sexual relationship between defendant and complainant—too speculative).

18. 134 A.D.2d 907, 908, 521 N.Y.S.2d 608, 609 (4th Dep't 1987).

19. Id. In People v. Maxwell, 122 A.D.2d 435, 504 N.Y.S.2d 832 (3d Dep't 1986), the court, in a cryptic memorandum held that the trial judge had not erred in excluding evidence of complainant's other sexual contacts where the prosecutor had introduced evidence of semen in her underpants. See also People v. Rivera, 158 A.D.2d 723, 552 N.Y.S.2d 171 (2d Dep't), appeal denied, 76 N.Y.2d 741, 558 N.Y.S.2d 903, 557 N.E.2d 1199 (1990) (evidence that nine-year-old complainant may have contracted venereal disease in 1986, irrelevant since defendant charged with crime in 1983).

20. 132 A.D.2d 940, 941, 518 N.Y.S.2d 269, 270 (4th Dep't 1987).

21. Id. See also People v. Harris, 151 A.D.2d 981, 542 N.Y.S.2d 71 (4th Dep't), appeal denied, 74 N.Y.2d 810, 546 N.Y.S.2d 568, 545 N.E.2d 882 (1989)(on retrial, the trial court again refused to allow cross-examination into complainant's prior rape

within the prohibition of § 60.42 in any event because they were not "sexual conduct."[22] It seems clear that in nearly all other impeachment contexts, inquiry into the victim's sexual activity will be foreclosed.[23]

In 1990 the Legislature added § 60.43 to the Criminal Procedure Law. This provision prohibits evidence of the victim's sexual conduct, "including the past sexual conduct of a deceased victim," in a prosecution for *any* offense, unless determined to be admissible in the interests of justice.[24] As is true with sex offense cases under § 60.42 (e.g., the semen cases under the fourth exception), it appears that to be admissible the victim's past sexual conduct must be directly relevant to the facts in the case, and not simply introduced for the purpose of generally attacking the morals of the victim. It seems unlikely that there will be many instances in non-sex offense cases where the necessary relevancy will be shown.[25] But in a lower court ruling, evidence of the murder victim's homosexual proclivities was held admissible where defendant in the murder prosecution sought to show that the victim had made an unwanted sexual advance giving rise to the defense of extreme emotional disturbance.[26]

In 1994, the Legislature added yet another protection against exploitation of the complainant's sexual conduct. Henceforth, under new § 60.48 of the Criminal Procedure Law, evidence as to how the complainant was dressed will be inadmissible in the trial of any sex offense

complaints and because of this and other errors the case was sent back for a second retrial).

22. The court noted, citing the Mandel case (see notes 7 and 8 supra) that prior rape allegations were not literally within the prohibition of § 60.42, and the judge in his discretion, should have allowed this line of questioning.

23. See, e.g., People v. Smith, 192 A.D.2d 806, 808, 596 N.Y.S.2d 539, 541 (3d Dep't), leave to appeal denied, 81 N.Y.2d 1080, 601 N.Y.S.2d 600, 619 N.E.2d 678 (1993)(complainant's psychiatric records could not be used by defendant both because they were remote in time and because they contained information regarding her sexual history); People v. Crawford, 143 A.D.2d 141, 142, 531 N.Y.S.2d 598, 599 (2d Dep't), appeal denied, 72 N.Y.2d 1044, 534 N.Y.S.2d 943, 531 N.E.2d 663 (1988)(cross-examination of complainant regarding her sexual history with other men improper); People v. Bergeron, 125 A.D.2d 927, 510 N.Y.S.2d 323 (4th Dep't 1986), appeal denied, 69 N.Y.2d 948, 516 N.Y.S.2d 1030, 509 N.E.2d 365 (1987)(evidence of sexual history not admissible to impeach complainant's testimony that she loved her husband with whom her relationship was "fine"); People v. Laundry, 122 A.D.2d 450, 451, 504 N.Y.S.2d 840, 841 (3d Dep't 1986)(the victim's sexual relationship with her boyfriend not admissible to show she concocted the sodomy story implicating defendant to get boyfriend's sympathy).

24. § 60.43. Rules of evidence; admissibility of evidence of victim's sexual conduct in non-sex offense cases

Evidence of the victim's sexual conduct, including the past sexual conduct of a deceased victim, may not be admitted in a prosecution for any offense, attempt to commit an offense or conspiracy to commit an offense defined in the penal law unless such evidence is determined by the court to be relevant and admissible in the interests of justice, after an offer of proof by the proponent of such evidence outside the hearing of the jury, or such hearing as the court may require, and a statement by the court of its findings of fact essential to its determination.

25. See People v. Culver, 192 A.D.2d 10, 598 N.Y.S.2d 832 (3d Dep't), leave to appeal denied, 82 N.Y.2d 716, 602 N.Y.S.2d 813, 622 N.E.2d 314 (1993)(no relevancy in fact that murder victim had been convicted of sexual abuse). See Professor Preiser's Practice Commentary to § 60.43 (McKinney 1992).

26. People v. Childs, 161 Misc.2d 749, 615 N.Y.S.2d 232 (Sup.Ct.Bronx Co.1994).

case unless the court can find admissibility in the interests of justice.[27] There seems to be no reported case of a judge in New York ever allowing such evidence to indicate complainant's consent.[28]

Library References:

West's Key No. Digests, Rape ⬡40.

§ 412.2 Federal

Federal Rule of Evidence 412[1] has undergone a drastic revision which took effect on December 1, 1994. The amended rule has less verbiage than its predecessor and clears up the tangled language previ-

---

27. § 60.48. **Rules of evidence; admissibility of evidence of victim's manner of dress in sex offense cases**

Evidence of the manner in which the victim was dressed at the time of the commission of an offense may not be admitted in a prosecution for any offense, or an attempt to commit an offense, defined in article one hundred thirty of the penal law, unless such evidence is determined by the court to be relevant and admissible in the interests of justice, after an offer of proof by the proponent of such evidence outside the hearing of the jury, or such hearing as the court may require, and a statement by the court of its findings of fact essential to its determination.

28. Professor Preiser in his Practice Commentary to § 60.48 (McKinney 1992) notes that the necessity for this provision was derived by its legislative sponsors from a newspaper account that a convicted Florida rapist remarked, "The way she was dressed she was asking for it."

§ 412.2

1. **Rule 412. Sex Offense Cases; Relevance of Alleged Victim's Past Behavior or Alleged Sexual Predisposition.**

   (a) Evidence Generally Inadmissible. The following evidence is not admissible in any civil or criminal proceeding involving alleged sexual misconduct except as provided in subdivision (b) and (c):

   (1) Evidence offered to prove that any alleged victim engaged in other sexual behavior.

   (2) Evidence offered to prove any alleged victim's sexual predisposition.

   (b) Exceptions.

   (1) In a criminal case, the following evidence is admissible, if otherwise admissible under these rules:

   (A) evidence of specific instances of sexual behavior by the alleged victim offered to prove that a person other than the accused was the source of semen, injury or other physical evidence;

   (B) evidence of specific instances of sexual behavior by the alleged victim with respect to the person accused of the sexual misconduct offered by the accused to prove consent or by the prosecution; and

   (C) evidence the exclusion of which would violate the constitutional rights of the defendant.

   (2) In a civil case, evidence offered to prove the sexual behavior or sexual predisposition of any alleged victim is admissible if it is otherwise admissible under these rules and its probative value substantially outweighs the danger of harm to any victim and of unfair prejudice to any party. Evidence of an alleged victim's reputation is admissible only if it has been placed in controversy by the alleged victim.

   (c) Procedure to Determine Admissibility.

   (1) A party intending to offer evidence under subdivision (b) must:

   (A) file a written motion at least 14 days before trial specifically describing the evidence and stating the purpose for which it is offered unless the court, for good cause requires a different time for filing or permits filing during trial; and

   (B) serve the motion on all parties and notify the alleged victim or, when appropriate, the alleged victim's guardian or representative.

   (2) Before admitting evidence under this rule the court must conduct a hearing in camera and afford the victim and parties a right to attend and be heard. The motion, related papers, and the record of the hearing must be sealed and remain under seal unless the court orders otherwise.

ously utilized.[2] The revision was drafted to apply in civil as well as criminal cases.[3]

Rule 412 provides essentially the same protection to the complaining witnesses as does its state counterpart, N.Y. Criminal Procedure Law § 60.42;[4] but there is no provision for defendants to counter the prosecution's evidence of the victim's chastity as there is in § 60.42(3) nor any specific provision allowing defendant to show complainant's recent convictions for prostitution, also found in the New York statute. Nevertheless, it is clear that the prosecutor in federal court would open the same door to evidence of the complainant's unchastity were evidence of chastity offered. In *Government of the Virgin Islands v. Jacobs,*[5] defendant was on trial for multiple rapes of his girlfriend's 12–year-old daughter. The government introduced evidence that the victim was a virgin prior to the rapes. On the basis of fairly solid evidence that the victim had prior incestuous relations with her brother, defendant was allowed to cross-examine the victim regarding these incidents. The court launched into a comprehensive discussion of the right to cross-examine generally and specifically as regards the right to raise facts otherwise barred by Rule 412. For instance, at least one circuit permits a defendant to prove his state of mind by showing that he was aware of the victim's reputation for promiscuity.[6] Rule 412 does not prevent a defendant in a sex crime case from introducing evidence as to complainant's lack of credibility so long as that evidence does not relate to her sexual background.[7] (Query: Complainant's conviction for prostitution could be used against her under the specific provisions of New York's Criminal Procedure Law § 60.42[2], but could it in federal court under the escape hatch in Rule 412 where no such specific exception is otherwise found in the Rule?) The *Jacobs* court was clearly disposed toward a liberal construction of subdivision (b)(1)(C)'s [formerly (b)(3)'s] constitutional provision, as are other courts.[8]

---

2. As the Advisory Committee Notes state: "Rule 412 has been revised to diminish some of the confusion engendered by the original rule." One of the areas of confusion noted was the "introductory phrase in subdivision (a) [which] was deleted because it lacked clarity and contained no explicit reference to the other provisions of law that were intended to be overridden."

3. The application of the rule prohibiting complainant's past sexual behavior in civil cases would have chief application in sexual harassment suits. See Meritor Sav. Bank v. Vinson, 477 U.S. 57, 106 S.Ct. 2399, 91 L.Ed.2d 49 (1986), where the issue in such cases was said to be whether the sexual advances were unwelcome. In determining this issue, evidence of complainant's sexually provocative speech or dress would be admissible.

4. See § 412.1 supra.

5. 634 F.Supp. 933, 937–40 (D.Virgin Islands 1986); compare Jeffries v. Nix, 912 F.2d 982, 986 (8th Cir.1990), cert. denied, 499 U.S. 927, 111 S.Ct. 1327, 113 L.Ed.2d 259, rehearing denied, 500 U.S. 930, 111 S.Ct. 2048, 114 L.Ed.2d 132 (1991)(questioning complainant as to her good works in the community did not open the question of her chastity).

6. Doe v. United States, 666 F.2d 43, 48 (4th Cir.1981).

7. Jacobs, supra note 5, 634 F.Supp. at 938.

8. United States v. Bear Stops, 997 F.2d 451 (8th Cir.1993)(where prosecutor introduced proof of the six-year-old male victim's behavioral manifestations of sexually abused child, defendant was entitled to show evidence of a sexual assault on the victim by three older boys); United States v. Begay, 937 F.2d 515, 520 (10th Cir. 1991)(where prosecutor introduced medical evidence showing the victim's abrasions and enlarged hymen, defendant was entitled to show the victim's recent sexual ac-

Nevertheless, cases which apply the Rule 412 prohibition predominate,[9] and this is demonstrated in part by the courts' reluctance to allow defendants to use complainant's prior allegedly false rape reports to attack her credibility.[10]

Library References:

West's Key No. Digests, Rape ⇒40.

413 Defendant's Sexual History

§ 413.1 Federal

On July 9, 1995 three new sections were added to article 4 of the Federal Rules of Evidence. Whereas Rule 412 is directed at evidence of the victim's sexual history and reputation, Rules 413,[1] 414,[2] and 415[3]

tivities with another); Doe v. United States, 666 F.2d 43, 47–48 (4th Cir.1981)(on the issue of consent, complainant's telephone calls to defendant prior to the charged offense, and her love letters to others and evidence given by other men pertaining to her, could be introduced, the latter to corroborate the former; but evidence of her general sexual reputation was held inadmissible); United States v. Saunders, 736 F.Supp. 698 (E.D.Va.1990), aff'd, 943 F.2d 388 (4th Cir.1991), cert. denied, 502 U.S. 1105, 112 S.Ct. 1199, 117 L.Ed.2d 439 (1992)(evidence of complainant's prior sexual relations with defendant held admissible, but her relations with others held not admissible).

9. See Weinstein and Berger ¶ 412[01].

10. United States v. Provost, 875 F.2d 172, 177 (8th Cir.), cert. denied, 493 U.S. 859, 110 S.Ct. 170, 107 L.Ed.2d 127 (1989)(trial judge correct in not allowing defendant to offer proof that previously complainant had falsely accused her brother of sexually molesting her—blocked under Rule 412 as bearing on her credibility); United States v. Cardinal, 782 F.2d 34, 36 (6th Cir.), cert. denied, 476 U.S. 1161, 106 S.Ct. 2282, 90 L.Ed.2d 724 (1986)(keeping out evidence of prior false rape reports within the spirit and intent of Rule 412); compare United States v. Bartlett, 794 F.2d 1285, 1292 (8th Cir.), cert. denied, 479 U.S. 934, 107 S.Ct. 409, 93 L.Ed.2d 361 (1986)(evidence of complainant's prior false rape reports went to issue of credibility and to defense of consent).

§ 413.1

1. Rule 413. Evidence of Similar Crimes in Sexual Assault Cases

(a) In a criminal case in which the defendant is accused of an offense of sexual assault, evidence of the defendant's commission of another offense or offenses of sexual assault is admissible, and may be considered for its bearing on any matter to which it is relevant.

(b) In a case in which the Government intends to offer evidence under this rule, the attorney for the Government shall disclose the evidence to the defendant, including statements of witnesses or a summary of the substance of any testimony that is expected to be offered, at least fifteen days before the scheduled date of trial or at such later time as the court may allow for good cause.

(c) This rule shall not be construed to limit the admission or consideration of evidence under any other rule.

(d) For purposes of this rule and Rule 415, "offense of sexual assault" means a crime under Federal law or the law of a State (as defined in section 513 of title 18, United States Code) that involved—

(1) any conduct proscribed by chapter 109A of title 18, United States Code;

(2) contact, without consent, between any part of the defendant's body or an object and the genitals or anus of another person;

(3) contact, without consent, between the genitals or anus of the defendant and any part of another person's body;

(4) deriving sexual pleasure or gratification from the infliction of death, bodily injury, or physical pain on another person; or

(5) an attempt or conspiracy to engage in conduct described in paragraphs (1)-(4).

2. Rule 414. Evidence of Similar Crimes in Child Molestation Cases

(a) In a criminal case in which the defendant is accused of an offense of child molestation, evidence of the defendant's

3. See note 3 on page 208.

focus on the *defendant's* other sexual indiscretions as evidence of his propensity. These Rules are thus closely related to Rule 404(b) which governs the admissibility of defendant's uncharged convictions and criminal activity as they may bear on the charged crime.[4]

The new provisions target sexual assault and child molestation cases and raise questions concerning the interplay with other Rules, chiefly Rules 404(b) and 403, and 405. For these reasons the Judicial Conference submitted a report urging that the new Rules not be enacted, or if enacted, with conforming amendments to Rules 404 and 405.[5] An excerpt from the report is found in the footnote.[6]

commission of another offense or offenses of child molestation is admissible, and may be considered for its bearing on any matter to which it is relevant.

(b) In a case in which the Government intends to offer evidence under this rule, the attorney for the Government shall disclose the evidence to the defendant, including statements of witnesses or a summary of the substance of any testimony that is expected to be offered, at least fifteen days before the scheduled date of trial or at such later time as the court may allow for good cause.

(c) This rule shall not be construed to limit the admission or consideration of evidence under any other rule.

(d) For purposes of this rule and Rule 415, "child" means a person below the age of fourteen, and "offense of child molestation" means a crime under Federal law or the law of a State (as defined in section 513 of title 18, United States Code) that involved—

(1) any conduct proscribed by chapter 109A of title 18, United States Code, that was committed in relation to a child;

(2) any conduct proscribed by chapter 110 of title 18, United States Code;

(3) contact between any part of the defendant's body or an object and the genitals or anus of a child;

(4) contact between the genitals or anus of the defendant and any part of the body of a child;

(5) deriving sexual pleasure or gratification from the infliction of death, bodily injury, or physical pain on a child; or

(6) an attempt or conspiracy to engage in conduct described in paragraphs (1)-(5).

3. Rule 415. Evidence of Similar Acts in Civil Cases Concerning Sexual Assault or Child Molestation

(a) In a civil case in which a claim for damages or other relief is predicated on a party's alleged commission of conduct constituting an offense of sexual assault or child molestation, evidence of that party's commission of another offense or offenses of sexual assault or child molestation is admissible and may be considered as provided in Rule 413 and Rule 414 of these rules.

(b) A party who intends to offer evidence under this Rule shall disclose the evidence to the party against whom it will be offered, including statements of witnesses or a summary of the substance of any testimony that is expected to be offered, at least fifteen days before the scheduled date of trial or at such later time as the court may allow for good cause.

(c) This rule shall not be construed to limit the admission or consideration of evidence under any other rule.

4. See § 404.2, supra.

5. See "Report Of The Judicial Conference On The Admission Of Character Evidence In Certain Sexual Misconduct Cases," February 9, 1995, West's Supreme Court Reporter, Adv. Sheet Vol. 115, No. 9, 3/1/95.

6. The report states in part:

The advisory committee believed that the concerns expressed by Congress and embodied in new Evidence Rules 413, 414, and 415 are already adequately addressed in the existing Federal Rules of Evidence. In particular, Evidence Rule 404(b) now allows the admission of evidence against a criminal defendant of the commission of prior crimes, wrongs, or acts for specified purposes, including to show intent, plan, motive, preparation, identity, knowledge, or absence of mistake or accident.

Furthermore, the new rules, which are not supported by empirical evidence, could diminish significantly the protections that have safeguarded persons accused in criminal cases and parties in civil cases against undue prejudice. These protections form a fundamental

Library References:

West's Key No. Digests, Criminal Law ⬳369.8; Rape ⬳42.

part of American jurisprudence and have evolved under long-standing rules and case law. A significant concern identified by the committee was the danger of convicting a criminal defendant for past, as opposed to charged, behavior or for being a bad person.

In addition, the advisory committee concluded that, because prior bad acts would be admissible even though not the subject of a conviction, mini-trials within trials concerning those acts would result when a defendant seeks to rebut such evidence. The committee also noticed that many of the comments received had concluded that the Rules, as drafted, were mandatory—that is, such evidence had to be admitted regardless of other rules of evidence such as the hearsay rule or the Rule 403 balancing test. The committee believed that this position was arguable because Rules 413–415 declare without qualification that such evidence "is admissible." In contrast, the new Rule 412, passed as part of the same legislation provided that certain evidence "is admissible if it is otherwise admissible under these Rules." Fed.R.Evid. 412(b)(2). If the critics are right, Rules 413–415 free the prosecution from rules that apply to the defendant—including the hearsay rule and Rule 403. If so, serious constitutional questions would arise.

The Advisory Committees on Criminal and Civil Rules unanimously, except for representatives of the Department of Justice, also opposed the new rules. Those committees also concluded that the new rules would permit the introduction of unreliable but highly prejudicial evidence and would complicate trials by causing mini-trials of other alleged wrongs. After the advisory committees reported, the Standing Committee unanimously, again except for the representative of the Department of Justice, agreed with the view of the advisory committees.

It is important to note the highly unusual unanimity of the members of the Standing and Advisory Committees, composed of over 40 judges, practicing lawyers, and academicians, in taking the view that Rules 413–415 are undesirable. Indeed, the only supporters of the Rules were representatives of the Department of Justice.

For these reasons, the Standing Committee recommended that Congress reconsider its decision on the policy questions embodied in new Evidence Rules 413, 414, and 415.

However, if Congress will not reconsider its decision on the policy questions, the Standing Committee recommended that Congress consider an alternative draft recommended by the Advisory Committee on Evidence Rules. That Committee drafted proposed amendments to existing Evidence Rules 404 and 405 that would both correct ambiguities and possible constitutional infirmities identified in New Evidence Rules 413, 414, and 415 yet still effectuate Congressional intent. In particular, the proposed amendments:

(1) expressly apply the other rules of evidence to evidence offered under the new rules;

(2) expressly allow the party against whom such evidence is offered to use similar evidence in rebuttal;

(3) expressly enumerate the factors to be weighed by a court in making its Rule 403 determination;

(4) render the notice provisions consistent with the provisions in existing Rule 404 regarding criminal cases;

(5) eliminate the special notice provisions of Rules 413–415 in civil cases so that notice will be required as provided in the Federal Rules of Civil Procedure; and

(6) permit reputation or opinion evidence after such evidence is offered by the accused or defendant.

It is to be noted that such conforming amendments were not made.

Chapter 5

PRIVILEGES

Table of Sections

500 INTRODUCTION

500.1 New York.
500.2 Federal.

501 ATTORNEY–CLIENT PRIVILEGE AND WORK PRODUCT

501.1 New York: Attorney–Client Privilege.
    a. In General.
    b. Attorney–Client Relationship.
    c. Communications.
    d. Legal Advice.
    e. Confidentiality.
    f. Application in the Corporate Context.
    g. Exceptions.
    h. Waiver.
501.2 Federal: Attorney–Client Privilege.
501.3 Work Product Immunities.
    a. In General.
    b. New York.
        1. Civil Cases.
        2. Criminal Cases.
        3. Waiver.
    c. Federal.

502 PHYSICIAN–PATIENT AND RELATED PRIVILEGES

502.1 New York.
    a. In General.
    b. Scope of the Physician–Patient Privilege.
    c. Waiver.
    d. Exceptions.
    e. Psychologists.
502.2 Federal.

503 SPOUSAL PRIVILEGES

503.1 New York: Generally.
503.2 New York: Incompetency in Adultery Cases.
503.3 New York: Privilege for Confidential Communications.
    a. Confidentiality.
    b. Induced by the Marital Relationship.
    c. Communication Made During the Marriage.
    d. Waiver.
    e. Exceptions.
503.4 New York: Parent–Child Privilege.
503.5 Federal.
    a. Testimonial Privilege.
    b. Marital Communications Privilege.

Ch. 5 **PRIVILEGES**

504 COMMUNICATIONS WITH CLERGY PRIVILEGE
504.1 New York.
504.2 Federal.

505 SOCIAL WORKER PRIVILEGE
505.1 New York.
505.2 Federal.

506 RAPE CRISIS COUNSELOR
506.1 New York.
506.2 Federal.

507 LIBRARY RECORDS
507.1 New York.
507.2 Federal.

508 JOURNALIST PRIVILEGE
508.1 New York.
508.2 Federal.

509 SELF-INCRIMINATION
509.1 New York State and Federal.
    a. Civil Cases.
    b. Criminal Proceedings.
       1. Testimony.
       2. Documents.
    c. Application of the Privilege During the Investigation Stage—Connection to the Trial.

510 THE INFORMER PRIVILEGE
510.1 New York.
510.2 Federal.

511 GOVERNMENT COMMUNICATIONS
511.1 New York.
511.2 Federal.

512 POLITICAL VOTE
512.1 New York.
512.2 Federal.

513 TRADE SECRETS
513.1 New York.
513.2 Federal Rule.

514 COMMENT UPON OR INFERENCE FROM CLAIM OF PRIVILEGE
514.1 New York.
514.2 Federal.

WESTLAW Electronic Research

See WESTLAW Electronic Research Guide preceding the Summary of Contents.

§ 500.1 PRIVILEGES Ch. 5

500 Introduction

§ 500.1 New York

The privileges based on confidential communications "are designed to encourage a particular form of behavior or to serve a certain desirable purpose. These privileges exact a heavy toll, however, because they tend to keep otherwise competent evidence from the reach of the Grand Jury and the courts (see 8 Wigmore, Evidence [McNaughton rev.], § 2380a). Accordingly, where the application of a privilege will not serve to further the legitimate purposes for which it was created, there is little reason to permit its invocation."[1] Insofar as the privileges are designed to encourage certain behavior they are perhaps substantive in nature, thus providing exceptions to the generality that the rules of evidence are geared to producing truthful and accurate evidence. The employment of the privileges acts to keep out perfectly accurate and reliable evidence.[2]

Be that as it may, the Legislature has seen fit to enact eight privileges in CPLR Article 45,[3] one in the Civil Rights Law,[4] and has implemented by statute the privilege against self-incrimination.[5] All of these, except the self-incrimination privilege, are based on the idea that certain kinds of desirable professional and personal relationships are helped by encouraging free disclosure of sensitive information made with enforceable assurances of confidentiality. In addition, there are four common law privileges based on confidentiality that will be noted in the following sections.[6]

The privileges, even those set forth in the CPLR, are applicable in criminal cases as well as civil cases[7] and ordinarily may be invoked at any stage of the proceedings.[8]

Library References:

West's Key No. Digests, Criminal Law ⚖627.5(6); Pretrial Procedure ⚖33–35; Witnesses ⚖184–223, 292–310.

It is to be noted that such conforming amendments were not made.

§ 500.1

1. Grand Jury Proceeding (Doe), 56 N.Y.2d 348, 352, 452 N.Y.S.2d 361, 363, 437 N.E.2d 1118, 1120 (1982). See also People ex rel. Vogelstein v. Warden of County Jail of New York County, 150 Misc. 714, 717, 270 N.Y.S. 362, 367 (Sup.Ct.N.Y.Co.), aff'd, 242 App.Div. 611, 271 N.Y.S. 1059 (1st Dep't 1934)("[E]xercise of the privilege may at times result in concealing the truth and in allowing the guilty to escape. That is an evil, however, which is considered to be outweighed by the benefit which results to the administration of justice generally").

2. McCormick § 72, at 269. See Trammel v. United States, 445 U.S. 40, 50, 100 S.Ct. 906, 912, 63 L.Ed.2d 186, 195 (1980)("privileges contravene the fundamental principle that 'the public * * * has a right to every man's evidence'").

3. CPLR §§ 4502 (spouse), 4503 (attorney), 4504 (physician), 4505 (clergy), 4507 (psychologist), 4508 (social worker), 4509 (library records) and 4510 (rape counselor).

4. N.Y. Civil Rights Law § 79–h.

5. CPLR 4501.

6. See infra §§ 510.1–510.2 (informer privilege), §§ 511.1–511.2 (government communications), §§ 512.1–512.2 (political vote), and §§ 513.1–513.2 (trade secrets).

7. N.Y.Crim.Proc.Law § 60.10; People v. Wilkins, 65 N.Y.2d 172, 176, 490 N.Y.S.2d 759, 761, 480 N.E.2d 373, 375 (1985).

8. See, e.g., Hughson v. St. Francis Hospital of Port Jervis, 93 A.D.2d 491, 498, 463 N.Y.S.2d 224, 229 (2d Dep't 1983)(physician-patient privilege applies during trial and pretrial discovery, in grand jury proceedings and in legislative proceedings). See also CPLR 3101(b).

§ 500.2 Federal

The Federal Rules of Evidence as proposed to Congress contained a full slate of privileges based on confidentiality. These still can be found in the appendices of the Federal Rules pamphlets, and to some extent are consulted as guides, but they were never enacted. While there were complex reasons for this result, the heart of the matter seems to be that because of their substantive nature, the privileges were left to state law, certainly in diversity cases, and in other cases where such interpretation would be dictated.[1] As a result we find only one rule—Rule 501—which leaves it to the federal courts to be governed by "the principles of the common law as they may be interpreted by the courts * * * in the light of reason and experience."[2] The Supreme Court has indicated that Congress's purpose, in federal cases, was to " 'provide the courts with the flexibility to develop rules of privilege on a case-by-case basis,' * * * and to leave the door open to change."[3] The Court, however, has also said that it is "disinclined to exercise this authority expansively."[4]

In diversity cases, a federal court must apply the relevant state privileges;[5] but otherwise it will follow the "reason and experience" rule. For example, in federal civil rights cases, federal rules of privilege and not those of the states apply.[6] State privileges, however, may

§ 500.2

1. See 2 Weinstein and Berger ¶ 501[01].

2. **Rule 501. General Rule**

Except as otherwise required by the Constitution of the United States or provided by Act of Congress or in rules prescribed by the Supreme Court pursuant to statutory authority, the privilege of a witness, person, government, State, or political subdivision thereof shall be governed by the principles of the common law as they may be interpreted by the courts of the United States in the light of reason and experience. However, in civil actions and proceedings, with respect to an element of a claim or defense as to which State law supplies the rule of decision, the privilege of a witness, person, government, State, or political subdivision thereof shall be determined in accordance with State law.

3. Trammel v. United States, 445 U.S. 40, 47, 100 S.Ct. 906, 910, 63 L.Ed.2d 186, 193 (1980)(modification of privilege against adverse spousal testimony in federal criminal trials).

4. University of Pennsylvania v. Equal Employment Opportunity Commission, 493 U.S. 182, 189, 110 S.Ct. 577, 582, 107 L.Ed.2d 571, 582 (1990) (rejection of privilege for university's peer review materials relating to tenure decisions).

Prior to the adoption of Fed.R.Evid. 501, the Supreme Court had refused to recognize a common law accountant-client privilege. Couch v. United States, 409 U.S. 322, 93 S.Ct. 611, 34 L.Ed.2d 548 (1973). Potential privileges that have not yet been passed upon by the Supreme Court include a "scholar's privilege" to withhold confidential information gathered in the course of research, In re Grand Jury Subpoena Dated January 4, 1984, 750 F.2d 223 (2d Cir.1984)(record inadequate to determine existence of any such privilege), and a privilege for information gathered by an organization for the purpose of "self-critical analysis," Dowling v. American Hawaii Cruises, Inc., 971 F.2d 423, 425 n.1 (9th Cir. 1992)("The Supreme Court and the circuit courts have neither definitively denied the existence of such a privilege, nor accepted it and defined its scope"). Other privileges of uncertain status under federal law are discussed in the sections that follow. See, e.g., § 502.2 infra (psychotherapist-patient privilege), § 503.5 infra (parent-child privilege).

5. See, e.g., Allen v. West Point–Pepperell Inc., 848 F.Supp. 423, 427 n.3 (S.D.N.Y. 1994)(state law on attorney-client privilege).

6. Breed v. United States Dist. Court For N.D. of Cal., 542 F.2d 1114, 1115 (9th Cir.1976)("The scope of an evidentiary privilege in a 42 U.S.C. § 1983 civil rights action is a question of federal law [citing Kerr v. United States District Court, 511 F.2d 192, 197 (9th Cir.1975), aff'd, 426 U.S. 394, 96 S.Ct. 2119, 48 L.Ed.2d 725 (1976)]. State law may provide a useful referent, but it is not controlling"). See also Morgan v.

"illustrate important privacy interests" that the federal court need not ignore.[7]

In consulting the ensuing sections dealing with the privileges under federal law the reader must keep in mind two things: First, the discussion concerns non-diversity situations, and second, where federal privilege rules are found in a codified format, they were only proposed, and never enacted.[8]

Library References:

West's Key No. Digests, Criminal Law ⬅627.5(6); Federal Civil Procedure ⬅1600; Witnesses ⬅184–223, 292–310.

501 Attorney–Client Privilege and Work Product

§ 501.1 New York: Attorney–Client Privilege

a. In General

The attorney-client privilege is probably the oldest of the common law privileges.[1] It is based on the premise that a client may be inclined to withhold information from her attorney if she fears that the attorney can be compelled to reveal her confidences. The lawyer, in turn, will be disabled from providing competent legal services due to insufficient knowledge of the facts. The privilege, therefore, is intended to "[foster] the open dialogue between lawyer and client that is deemed essential to effective representation."[2]

Although New York courts rely upon common law developments in

---

Labiak, 368 F.2d 338, 341 (10th Cir.1966)(opinion evidence admissible under broad federal guidelines then governed by Fed.R.Civ.P. 43(a)).

7. King v. Conde, 121 F.R.D. 180, 187–88 (E.D.N.Y.1988)(federal court in civil rights case may consider state privilege rules as factor in resolving discovery dispute, but federal substantive and procedural policies must be given priority).

8. Courts have held that the proposals on privilege provide a useful guide in federal cases. See, e.g., In re Bieter Company, 16 F.3d 929, 935 (8th Cir.1994); United States v. McPartlin, 595 F.2d 1321, 1337 (7th Cir.), cert. denied, 444 U.S. 833, 100 S.Ct. 65, 62 L.Ed.2d 43 (1979). But see United States v. Bizzard, 674 F.2d 1382, 1387 (11th Cir.), cert. denied, 459 U.S. 973, 103 S.Ct. 305, 74 L.Ed.2d 286 (1982).

§ 501.1

1. 8 Wigmore § 2290. The privilege first emerged in England during the reign of Elizabeth I. 9 W. Holdsworth, A History of English Law 201–02 (7th ed.1956).

2. Spectrum Systems International Corp. v. Chemical Bank, 78 N.Y.2d 371, 377, 575 N.Y.S.2d 809, 813, 581 N.E.2d 1055, 1059 (1991). See also People ex rel. Vogelstein v. Warden of County Jail of New York County, 150 Misc. 714, 717, 270 N.Y.S. 362, 367 (Sup.Ct.N.Y.Co.), aff'd, 242 App.Div. 611, 271 N.Y.S. 1059 (1st Dep't 1934)("[E]xercise of the privilege may at times result in concealing the truth and in allowing the guilty to escape. That is an evil, however, which is considered to be outweighed by the benefit which results to the administration of justice generally."). In criminal cases, the privilege may be bolstered by the fifth and sixth amendments. It has been argued that in order to obtain effective legal counsel, which requires full disclosure to one's lawyer, the defendant should not have to waive the right to remain silent, which would be the net effect of compelled testimony by the attorney. Hazard, "An Historical Perspective on the Attorney–Client Privilege," 66 Calif. L.Rev.1061, 1062–63 (1978).

applying the attorney-client privilege,[3] the basic contours of the privilege are codified in CPLR 4503:

(a) Confidential communication privileged; non-judicial proceedings. Unless the client waives the privilege, an attorney or his employee, or any person who obtains without the knowledge of the client evidence of a confidential communication made between the attorney or his employee and the client in the course of professional employment, shall not disclose, or be allowed to disclose such communication, nor shall the client be compelled to disclose such communication, in any action, disciplinary trial or hearing, or administrative action, proceeding or hearing conducted by or on behalf of any state, municipal or local governmental agency or by the legislature or any committee or body thereof. Evidence of any such communication obtained by any such person, and evidence resulting therefrom, shall not be disclosed by any state, municipal or local governmental agency or by the legislature or any committee or body thereof. The relationship of an attorney and client shall exist between a professional service corporation organized under article fifteen of the business corporation law to practice as an attorney and counselor-at-law and the clients to whom it renders legal services.

(b) Wills. In any action involving the probate, validity or construction of a will, an attorney or his employee shall be required to disclose information as to the preparation, execution or revocation of any will or other relevant instrument, but he shall not be allowed to disclose any communication privileged under subdivision (a) which would tend to disgrace the memory of the decedent.

The Proposed New York Evidence Code provision, § 504, contains essentially the same terms as CPLR 4503, but spells out a list of specific exceptions in subdivision (c).[4]

---

3. Spectrum Systems International Corp. v. Chemical Bank, 78 N.Y.2d 371, 377, 575 N.Y.S.2d 809, 813–14, 581 N.E.2d 1055, 1059–60 (1991). Thus, for example, the court in People v. Belge, 59 A.D.2d 307, 399 N.Y.S.2d 539 (4th Dep't 1977), relies upon a definition of the attorney-client privilege that appears in the frequently cited case of United States v. United Shoe Machinery Corp., 89 F.Supp. 357, 358–59 (D.Mass.1950):

The privilege applies only if (1) the asserted holder of the privilege is or sought to become a client; (2) the person to whom the communication was made (a) is a member of the bar of a court, or his subordinate and (b) in connection with this communication is acting as a lawyer; (3) the communication relates to a fact of which the attorney was informed (a) by his client (b) without the presence of strangers (c) for the purpose of securing primarily either (i) an opinion on law or (ii) legal services or (iii) assistance in some legal proceeding, and not (d) for the purpose of committing a crime or tort; and (4) the privilege has been (a) claimed and (b) not waived by the client.

4. § 504. Attorney-client privilege [PROPOSED]

(a) Confidential communication privileged. Unless the client waives the privilege, an attorney or the employee of an attorney or any person who obtains without the knowledge of the client evidence of a confidential communication made between the attorney or his or her employee and the client in the course of professional employment, shall not disclose, or be allowed to disclose, such communication, nor shall the client be com-

§ 501.1 PRIVILEGES Ch. 5

CPLR 4503(a) broadly permits invocation of the privilege in any type of judicial, administrative or legislative proceeding. Neither the attorney, the attorney's employees, the client nor any eavesdropper can be compelled in any such proceeding to disclose a protected communication unless the client himself has waived the privilege. Even if the client is not a party to the proceeding, the privilege can be invoked on his behalf by any of the participants in the litigation.[5] Furthermore, the privilege survives the client's death,[6] subject to the limited exception specified in CPLR 4503(b). On the other hand, the privilege has a potentially obstructive effect on the fact-finding process, which has led to the judicial admonition that the privilege should be restricted in scope "to that which is necessary to achieve its purpose."[7]

The court determines whether the requirements of the privilege

pelled to disclose such communication, in any action, disciplinary trial or hearing, or administrative action, proceeding or hearing conducted by or on behalf of any state, municipal or local governmental agency or by the legislature or any committee or body thereof. Evidence of any such communication obtained by any such person, and evidence resulting therefrom, shall not be disclosed by any state, municipal or local governmental agency or by the legislature or any committee or body thereof. The relationship of an attorney and client shall exist between a professional service corporation organized under article fifteen of the business corporation law to practice as an attorney and counselor-at-law and the clients to whom it renders legal services. An "attorney" is a person authorized or reasonably believed by the client to be authorized to practice law in this state or in any jurisdiction.

(b) Wills, deeds and other writings. In any action involving the probate, validity or construction of a will, a deed or other writing executed by a deceased client purporting to affect an interest in property, an attorney or his or her employee shall be required to disclose information as to the preparation, execution or revocation of a will, a deed, or other writing or other relevant instrument.

(c) Exceptions. The privilege in this section shall not apply when an exception is recognized by statute, or in other situations, where the policies underlying the privilege are absent, including but not limited to:

(1) Furtherance of crime or fraud. If the communications were made or obtained for the purpose of committing what the client knew or reasonably should have known to be a crime or fraud.

(2) Breach of duty by attorney or client. As to a communication relevant to an issue of breach of duty by the attorney to the client or by the client to the attorney.

(3) Joint clients. As to a communication relevant to a matter of common interest between or among two or more clients if the communication was made by any of them to an attorney retained or consulted in common, when offered in an action between or among any of the clients.

(4) Communication offered by an accused. In a criminal case or disciplinary proceeding in which the communication is offered by an accused who was one of the persons between whom the communication was made.

5. Bacon v. Frisbie, 80 N.Y. 394, 401 (1880)("The rule is in the nature of that which excludes evidence when the production of it would be prejudicial to the public interests"); Randy Intern., Ltd. v. Automatic Compactor Corp., 97 Misc.2d 977, 981, 412 N.Y.S.2d 995, 997 (N.Y.C.Civ.Ct. 1979).

6. Downey v. Owen, 98 App.Div. 411, 419, 90 N.Y.S. 280, 285 (4th Dep't 1904); In re Estate of Weinberg, 133 Misc.2d 950, 951, 509 N.Y.S.2d 240, 242 (Surr.Ct.N.Y.Co. 1986), order modified, 129 A.D.2d 126, 517 N.Y.S.2d 474 (1st Dep't 1987), reargument denied, 132 A.D.2d 190, 522 N.Y.S.2d 511, appeal dismissed, 71 N.Y.2d 994, 529 N.Y.S.2d 277, 524 N.E.2d 879 (1988).

7. Rossi v. Blue Cross and Blue Shield of Greater New York, 73 N.Y.2d 588, 593, 542 N.Y.S.2d 508, 510, 540 N.E.2d 703, 705 (1989). See also 8 Wigmore § 2291, at 554 (privilege should be "strictly confined within the narrowest possible limits consistent with the logic of its principle").

have been satisfied.[8] The threshold question is whether an attorney-client relationship existed at the time of the relevant communication.[9] The next level of analysis is whether the information sought to be protected was a confidential communication made for the purpose of obtaining or conveying legal advice or services.[10] The party who asserts the protection of the privilege has the burden of establishing its applicability.[11] When a claim of privilege is disputed with respect to documents, courts are authorized to conduct an in camera inquiry to determine the issue.[12]

b. Attorney–Client Relationship

An attorney-client relationship exists when a person has contacted an attorney in her capacity as such for the purpose of obtaining legal advice or assistance.[13] Courts examine the surrounding circumstances to determine any questions in this regard. Conclusory assertions by the attorney that someone was a client are insufficient.[14] Conversely, the attorney's disavowal that she was acting in the capacity of legal advisor is not dispositive. The client's belief is the principal factor.[15] If the person in whom the client confided was not licensed to practice law, but was reasonably believed to be, modern authorities would sustain a privilege claim.[16] Such rule would be both fair to unsuspecting laypersons and consistent with the candor-inducing policy behind the privilege.

---

8. Bacon v. Frisbie, 80 N.Y. 394, 399 (1880).

9. Matter of Priest v. Hennessy, 51 N.Y.2d 62, 68, 431 N.Y.S.2d 511, 514, 409 N.E.2d 983, 986 (1980); People v. O'Connor, 85 A.D.2d 92, 95, 447 N.Y.S.2d 553, 556 (4th Dep't 1982).

10. Matter of Priest v. Hennessy, 51 N.Y.2d 62, 68, 431 N.Y.S.2d 511, 514, 409 N.E.2d 983, 986 (1980); Rossi v. Blue Cross and Blue Shield of Greater New York, 73 N.Y.2d 588, 593, 542 N.Y.S.2d 508, 510–11, 540 N.E.2d 703, 706 (1989).

11. People v. Mitchell, 58 N.Y.2d 368, 373, 461 N.Y.S.2d 267, 270, 448 N.E.2d 121, 123 (1983).

12. Spectrum Systems International Corp. v. Chemical Bank, 78 N.Y.2d 371, 378, 575 N.Y.S.2d 809, 814, 581 N.E.2d 1055, 1060 (1991). See also People v. Belge, 59 A.D.2d 307, 399 N.Y.S.2d 539 (4th Dep't 1977)(attorney held in contempt, in part, for refusing to deliver subpoenaed documents to court for in camera resolution of privilege issue). As to oral communications, the court may conduct a voir dire outside the presence of the jury. See, e.g., People v. Mitchell, 58 N.Y.2d 368, 373–75, 461 N.Y.S.2d 267, 270, 448 N.E.2d 121, 124 (1983).

13. Matter of Priest v. Hennessy, 51 N.Y.2d 62, 68–69, 431 N.Y.S.2d 511, 514, 409 N.E.2d 983, 986 (1980). See also Bacon v. Frisbie, 80 N.Y. 394, 398–99 (1880)(existence of attorney-client relationship is not dependent on payment of a fee); People v. Belge, 59 A.D.2d 307, 309, 399 N.Y.S.2d 539, 540 (4th Dep't 1977)(privilege can extend to client or person who "sought to become a client").

14. Matter of Priest v. Hennessy, 51 N.Y.2d 62, 70, 431 N.Y.S.2d 511, 515, 409 N.E.2d 983, 987 (1980).

15. Bacon v. Frisbie, 80 N.Y. 394, 398–99 (1880). See also Doe v. Poe, 189 A.D.2d 132, 595 N.Y.S.2d 503 (2d Dep't), leave to appeal denied, 81 N.Y.2d 711, 600 N.Y.S.2d 442, 616 N.E.2d 1104 (1993)(under the circumstances, corporate executive could not have reasonably believed that he was a personal client of the corporation's attorneys); People v. O'Connor, 85 A.D.2d 92, 96, 447 N.Y.S.2d 553, 557 (4th Dep't 1982) (perpetrator of crime who called an assistant district attorney who had provided private counsel to the caller several years before knew that he could not receive such representation at time of call).

16. See, e.g., United States v. Rivera, 837 F.Supp. 565, 567 n.1 (S.D.N.Y.1993). See generally McCormick § 88. No New York cases have addressed this point, but § 504(a) of the Proposed New York Evidence Code defines an attorney, for purposes of the privilege, as a "person authorized or reasonably believed by the client to be authorized to practice law in this state or in any jurisdiction." See note 4 supra.

c. Communications

A privileged communication between attorney and client can take any form—conversation, writing or gesture.[17] The privilege, however, generally does not encompass an attorney's observations about the client such as the client's demeanor and mental capacity that would be ascertainable by anyone.[18] Furthermore, the privilege does not immunize the underlying factual information that the client may have communicated to the attorney.[19] In other words, a client need not reveal what he told his lawyer in confidence about an event, but he can be compelled to testify to his knowledge of the event.[20] Similarly, facts learned by the attorney from independent sources ordinarily are not within the attorney-client privilege, even if the attorney communicates the facts to the client.[21]

Preexisting documents in the hands of the client do not themselves become privileged communications merely by transfer to counsel.[22] Thus, if production of a document could be compelled if it were in the client's possession, the attorney can be compelled to produce it.[23] On the other hand, if the client himself could not be compelled to produce a document because doing so would be a self-incriminatory act, the attorney's acquisition of the document in the context of an attorney-client communication precludes its compelled production by the attorney.[24]

Tangible objects, such as the fruits or instrumentalities of a crime, do not become privileged when they are given to counsel for safekeep-

---

17. Matter of Vanderbilt, 57 N.Y.2d 66, 453 N.Y.S.2d 662, 439 N.E.2d 378 (1982)(tape-recorded message); Le Long v. Siebrecht, 196 App.Div. 74, 76, 187 N.Y.S. 150, 152 (2d Dep't 1921)(oral and written communications); People v. Investigation Into a Certain Weapon, 113 Misc.2d 348, 448 N.Y.S.2d 950 (Sup.Ct.Kings Co.1982)(delivery of object to counsel).

18. People v. Kinder, 126 A.D.2d 60, 512 N.Y.S.2d 597 (4th Dep't 1987)(in posttrial hearing to determine whether defendant was competent to stand trial, defendant's attorney could be compelled to testify to client's demeanor, attitude and ability to communicate).

19. Spectrum Systems International Corp. v. Chemical Bank, 78 N.Y.2d 371, 377, 575 N.Y.S.2d 809, 814, 581 N.E.2d 1055, 1060 (1991); Miranda v. Miranda, 184 A.D.2d 286, 584 N.Y.S.2d 818 (1st Dep't 1992).

20. Upjohn Co. v. United States, 449 U.S. 383, 395–96, 101 S.Ct. 677, 685–86, 66 L.Ed.2d 584, 595 (1981).

21. Kenford Co. v. County of Erie, 55 A.D.2d 466, 469, 390 N.Y.S.2d 715, 719 (4th Dep't 1977)(client-party can be compelled to state facts regardless of client's source of information). See also King v. Ashley, 179 N.Y. 281, 72 N.E. 106 (1904). To the extent information from non-privileged sources is incorporated into the lawyer's written advice or opinion, however, privilege may attach to the entire writing. Spectrum Systems International Corp. v. Chemical Bank, 78 N.Y.2d 371, 378–79, 575 N.Y.S.2d 809, 814–15, 581 N.E.2d 1055, 1060–61 (1991). Furthermore, the form in which counsel embodies information from third parties may fall within the work product immunities. See § 501.3 infra.

22. Spectrum Systems International Corp. v. Chemical Bank, 78 N.Y.2d 371, 379, 575 N.Y.S.2d 809, 815, 581 N.E.2d 1055, 1061 (1991)("an investigative report does not become privileged merely because it was sent to an attorney"); Matter of Bekins Record Storage Co., 62 N.Y.2d 324, 327, 476 N.Y.S.2d 806, 807, 465 N.E.2d 345, 346 (1984)("The mere circumstance that the documents were revealed in confidence to a lawyer does not of itself transform the papers into privileged communications.").

23. Jones v. Reilly, 174 N.Y. 97, 105, 66 N.E. 649, 651 (1903).

24. Fisher v. United States, 425 U.S. 391, 96 S.Ct. 1569, 48 L.Ed.2d 39 (1976)(combined effect of fifth amendment and attorney-client privilege); Matter of Vanderbilt, 57 N.Y.2d 66, 76–79, 453 N.Y.S.2d 662, 668–70, 439 N.E.2d 378, 383–85 (1982).

ing.[25] To be distinguished, however, is the client's act of delivery of such an item to counsel, which carries with it the implied statement, "This has been in my possession."[26]

In New York, the privilege encompasses not only confidential communications from client to attorney but also from attorney to client, provided they are made "for the purpose of facilitating the rendition of legal advice or services."[27] Furthermore, an attorney's legal advice to the client can qualify for privileged treatment even if it incorporates or recites facts that were obtained from third parties or other non-privileged sources.[28]

Facts relating to the client's engagement of counsel usually fall outside the scope of the privilege for the reason that they do not constitute confidential communications.[29] Thus, the fact that an attorney was consulted[30] and the amount of her fee[31] are not protected. Similarly, various considerations have produced a general rule that the identity of the client is not privileged: identity ordinarily is neither a confidential communication nor relevant to the obtaining of legal advice; knowledge of identity is necessary to ensure the existence of a bona fide attorney-client relationship; and litigants have a right to know who their opponents are.[32]

Despite the general rule requiring disclosure of a client's identity, the court in *In re Kaplan*,[33] recognized a policy-based exception where

---

25. Matter of Vanderbilt, 57 N.Y.2d 66, 80, 453 N.Y.S.2d 662, 670, 439 N.E.2d 378, 386 (1982)(attorney may not serve as repository for incriminating evidence held by client, such as physical evidence of a crime). Privilege may attach, however, to the client's confidential statements to counsel, after the completion of a crime, about the whereabouts of the corpus delicti. See People v. Belge, 83 Misc.2d 186, 372 N.Y.S.2d 798 (Sup.Ct.Onondaga Co.), aff'd, 50 A.D.2d 1088, 376 N.Y.S.2d 771 (4th Dep't 1975), order aff'd, 41 N.Y.2d 60, 390 N.Y.S.2d 867, 359 N.E.2d 377 (1976).

26. People v. Investigation Into a Certain Weapon, 113 Misc.2d 348, 448 N.Y.S.2d 950 (Sup.Ct.Kings Co.1982)(court suggested that it may be appropriate to shield the fact-finder from knowledge that the authorities acquired the physical evidence from the defendant's attorney).

27. Rossi v. Blue Cross and Blue Shield of Greater New York, 73 N.Y.2d 588, 593, 542 N.Y.S.2d 508, 511, 540 N.E.2d 703, 706 (1989). CPLR 4503(a), it bears noting, refers to communications "between" attorney and client.

28. Spectrum Systems International Corp. v. Chemical Bank, 78 N.Y.2d 371, 379, 575 N.Y.S.2d 809, 814–15, 581 N.E.2d 1055, 1060–61 (1991): "[T]he privilege is not narrowly confined to the repetition of confidences that were supplied to the lawyer by the client * * *. That cramped view of the attorney-client privilege is at odds with the underlying policy of encouraging open communication; it poses inordinate practical difficulties in making surgical separations so as not to risk revealing client confidences; and it denies that an attorney can have any role in fact-gathering incident to the rendition of legal advice and services."

29. Hoopes v. Carota, 74 N.Y.2d 716, 544 N.Y.S.2d 808, 543 N.E.2d 73 (1989).

30. Id.

31. Id.; Matter of Priest v. Hennessy, 51 N.Y.2d 62, 69, 431 N.Y.S.2d 511, 515, 409 N.E.2d 983, 986 (1980)(communication concerning fee is collateral, having no direct relevance to the legal advice to be given); People v. Belge, 59 A.D.2d 307, 399 N.Y.S.2d 539 (4th Dep't 1977) (retainer agreement not privileged).

32. In re Jacqueline F., 47 N.Y.2d 215, 219–20, 417 N.Y.S.2d 884, 887, 391 N.E.2d 967, 970 (1979); In re Kaplan, 8 N.Y.2d 214, 218–19, 203 N.Y.S.2d 836, 838–39, 168 N.E.2d 660, 661–62 (1960); People ex rel. Vogelstein v. Warden of County Jail, 150 Misc. 714, 717–19, 270 N.Y.S. 362, 367–69 (Sup.Ct.N.Y.Co.), aff'd, 242 App.Div. 611, 271 N.Y.S. 1059 (1st Dep't 1934).

33. 8 N.Y.2d 214, 203 N.Y.S.2d 836, 168 N.E.2d 660 (1960).

the client had complained to an attorney about the wrongdoing of others and requested that his identity be kept secret based on a fear of reprisal. Another exception shields the client's identity when revelation would have the effect of disclosing a confidential communication by the client.[34]

The client's address is normally not privileged while litigation is in progress.[35] In *In re Jacqueline F.,*[36] disclosure of a client's address was required, for policy reasons, even after the termination of certain child custody litigation. The client was frustrating a judicial decree and disclosure was in the best interests of the child who had been the subject of the prior litigation.

d. Legal Advice

To qualify for privileged treatment, the confidential communication between attorney and client must be made for the purpose of obtaining or rendering legal advice or services.[37] The privilege, however, is not restricted to communications involving litigation; it encompasses any matters that may call for legal advice or assistance.[38]

Attorney-client communications that relate solely to non-legal personal or business activities are not privileged.[39] A lawyer who is hired to perform commercial consulting services, for example, would be acting outside the role of legal advisor.[40] The issue is complicated, however, when the lawyer, in the course of providing legal services, combines business and other non-legal considerations in her advice. The rule that the New York courts have adopted for mixed communications of this nature is that references to non-legal matters will not vitiate the privilege if "the communication is primarily or predominantly of a legal character."[41] This rule was liberally applied in *Spectrum Systems Inter-*

---

34. Matter of D'Alessio, 205 A.D.2d 8, 617 N.Y.S.2d 484 (2d Dep't 1994) (attorney need not disclose identity of client who consulted attorney in confidence concerning his involvement in fatal hit-and-run accident).

35. CPLR 3118; In re Jacqueline F., 47 N.Y.2d 215, 220–21, 417 N.Y.S.2d 884, 887–88, 391 N.E.2d 967, 970–71 (1979).

36. 47 N.Y.2d 215, 417 N.Y.S.2d 884, 391 N.E.2d 967 (1979).

37. Matter of Bekins Record Storage Co., 62 N.Y.2d 324, 329, 476 N.Y.S.2d 806, 809, 465 N.E.2d 345, 348 (1984).

38. Root v. Wright, 84 N.Y. 72, 76 (1881); Bacon v. Frisbie, 80 N.Y. 394, 400 (1880).

39. Matter of Bekins Record Storage Co., 62 N.Y.2d 324, 329, 476 N.Y.S.2d 806, 809, 465 N.E.2d 345, 348 (1984). See also People v. O'Connor, 85 A.D.2d 92, 96, 447 N.Y.S.2d 553, 557 (4th Dep't 1982)(no privilege due, in part, to non-legal purpose of perpetrator's call to attorney to learn if victim was still alive, whether he could visit her in hospital and how he could best turn himself in to authorities).

40. Matter of Bekins Record Storage Co., 62 N.Y.2d 324, 329, 476 N.Y.S.2d 806, 809, 465 N.E.2d 345, 348 (1984). Matter of Levinsky's Will, 23 A.D.2d 25, 31, 258 N.Y.S.2d 613, 620 (2d Dep't), appeal denied, 16 N.Y.2d 484, 264 N.Y.S.2d 1026, 211 N.E.2d 654 (1965)(no privilege when lawyer acts as agent or negotiator in a business venture); Avery v. Lee, 117 App.Div. 244, 102 N.Y.S. 12 (1st Dep't 1907)(no privilege where attorney serves solely as negotiator in sale of property).

41. Rossi v. Blue Cross and Blue Shield of Greater New York, 73 N.Y.2d 588, 594, 542 N.Y.S.2d 508, 511, 540 N.E.2d 703, 706 (1989)("content and context" of house counsel's memorandum to corporate client demonstrated that the overall purpose was the rendering of legal advice). The Rossi court noted that "the inquiry is necessarily fact-specific." Id. at 593, 542 N.Y.S.2d at 510, 540 N.E.2d at 705.

national Corp. v. Chemical Bank,[42] where a law firm, after conducting an internal investigation of its corporate client's wrongdoing, submitted a report to the client discussing the results of the investigation. Although the report contained no legal research, it analyzed the facts and assessed the client's legal position. The predominant character of the report, therefore, was legal because it reflected the attorneys' professional skill and judgment.[43]

e. Confidentiality

One of the fundamental requirements of the attorney-client privilege is a showing that the client intended the communication with counsel to be confidential.[44] Thus, the known presence of a third party at the time of an attorney-client communication generally destroys any expectation of confidentiality.[45] In *People v. Harris*,[46] for example, the privilege did not attach where a client knew that a police officer was within earshot while she was speaking to her lawyer on the telephone.[47]

CPLR 4503(a), however, relieves a client of the need to ensure absolute secrecy. The statute prohibits disclosure of an attorney-client communication by any person who acquires evidence of the communication without the knowledge of the client.[48] Clients are thereby protected against eavesdroppers or interlopers who may secretly obtain possession of a written communication. The statute is consistent with the modern view that the privilege "depends on whether the client had a reasonable expectation of confidentiality under the circumstances."[49] Of course, if the client intended the attorney to convey the communication to others, the privilege is inapplicable.[50]

---

42. 78 N.Y.2d 371, 575 N.Y.S.2d 809, 581 N.E.2d 1055 (1991).

43. Id. at 379–80, 575 N.Y.S.2d at 815–16, 581 N.E.2d at 1061–62. In concluding that the report was motivated primarily by legal rather than business considerations, the court observed that "[t]he report offers no recommendations for desirable future business procedures or corruption prevention measures, or employee discipline." Id. at 380, 575 N.Y.S.2d at 815, 581 N.E.2d at 1061. See also Kraus v. Brandstetter, 185 A.D.2d 300, 586 N.Y.S.2d 270 (2d Dep't 1992).

44. People v. Harris, 57 N.Y.2d 335, 343, 456 N.Y.S.2d 694, 697, 442 N.E.2d 1205, 1208 (1982), cert. denied, 460 U.S. 1047, 103 S.Ct. 1448, 75 L.Ed.2d 803 (1983).

45. Baumann v. Steingester, 213 N.Y. 328, 332–33, 107 N.E. 578, 579–80 (1915)(privilege denied where friend of testatrix was present and within hearing while testatrix instructed her attorney regarding the desired contents of her will).

46. 57 N.Y.2d 335, 456 N.Y.S.2d 694, 442 N.E.2d 1205 (1982), cert. denied, 460 U.S. 1047, 103 S.Ct. 1448, 75 L.Ed.2d 803 (1983).

47. Improper government intrusion upon an otherwise confidential lawyer-client communication, however, may constitute a violation of due process. People v. Cooper, 307 N.Y. 253, 259–60, 120 N.E.2d 813, 816–17 (1954).

48. The provision in CPLR 4503(a) with respect to eavesdroppers was added to overrule the decision of the Court of Appeals in Lanza v. New York State Joint Legislative Committee, 3 N.Y.2d 92, 164 N.Y.S.2d 9, 143 N.E.2d 772 (1957), where a third party was allowed to disclose attorney-client communications that were surreptitiously overheard.

49. People v. Osorio, 75 N.Y.2d 80, 84, 550 N.Y.S.2d 612, 615, 549 N.E.2d 1183, 1186 (1989).

50. Rousseau v. Bleau, 131 N.Y. 177, 183–84, 30 N.E. 52, 53–54 (1892); Finn v. Morgan, 46 A.D.2d 229, 235, 362 N.Y.S.2d 292, 300 (4th Dep't 1974). The client's intent at the time of transmittal of the communication to counsel is determinative. Thus, in Matter of Vanderbilt, 57 N.Y.2d

Transmittal of attorney-client communications through or in the presence of employees of the attorney, such as secretaries or law clerks, does not destroy confidentiality.[51] The participation of such persons obviously is essential to the lawyer's performance of legal services. Similarly, the client may utilize an agent to convey a communication to counsel.[52] If the client and attorney speak different languages, the use of a hired interpreter to translate the communications will not vitiate confidentiality.[53] The Court of Appeals has also indicated its acceptance of the notion that a person, such as an accountant, who is retained by either the attorney or client to "facilitate" communication may participate in attorney-client discussions without a loss of privilege.[54] In the same vein, the Appellate Division concluded that an elderly client did not forfeit the privilege when she consulted counsel in the presence of her daughter, who was present for the purpose of helping her mother communicate.[55]

The privilege can also apply when two or more clients with a legal problem of common interest jointly consult the same lawyer. Third parties cannot compel disclosure of such communications.[56] On the other hand, if the two clients have a parting of the ways and become embroiled in litigation against each other, their prior communications to

66, 453 N.Y.S.2d 662, 439 N.E.2d 378 (1982), a client's tape-recorded message that was originally made for third parties was entitled to privilege because it remained confidential and in the client's possession until delivery to the attorney, at which time the client had no intent that it be passed on to others. Id. at 77, 435 N.Y.S.2d at 669, 439 N.E.2d at 384.

51. CPLR 4503(a); People v. Osorio, 75 N.Y.2d 80, 84, 550 N.Y.S.2d 612, 614–15, 549 N.E.2d 1183, 1185–86 (1989)(clients have reasonable expectation that such communications will be held in confidence and used solely for client's benefit). In People v. Mitchell, 58 N.Y.2d 368, 461 N.Y.S.2d 267, 448 N.E.2d 121 (1983), however, a client spoke openly in the reception area of his lawyer's office, where the status of the persons present (all but one of whom were nonemployees of the attorney), was unknown to the client. Since the client demonstrated no intention of confidentiality, the privilege did not apply.

52. Le Long v. Siebrecht, 196 App.Div. 74, 76, 187 N.Y.S. 150, 152 (2d Dep't 1921); In re Estate of Weinberg, 133 Misc.2d 950, 952, 509 N.Y.S.2d 240, 242 (Surr.Ct.N.Y.Co. 1986), order modified, 129 A.D.2d 126, 517 N.Y.S.2d 474 (1st Dep't 1987), reargument denied, 132 A.D.2d 190, 522 N.Y.S.2d 511, appeal dismissed, 71 N.Y.2d 994, 529 N.Y.S.2d 277, 524 N.E.2d 879 (1988). See also Hollien v. Kaye, 194 Misc. 821, 823–24, 87 N.Y.S.2d 782, 784–85 (Sup.Ct.Sullivan Co.1949)(privilege applied to motorist's statement to liability insurer which was later passed on to attorney selected by insurer to defend motorist).

53. People v. Osorio, 75 N.Y.2d 80, 84, 550 N.Y.S.2d 612, 615, 549 N.E.2d 1183, 1186 (1989). The interpreter in Osorio, however, was an accomplice-in-crime who was fortuitously present in the same jailroom at the time the client spoke with his lawyer. The "accommodation" by the interpreter did not, on the facts, create an agency or any other reasonable expectation of confidentiality on the part of the client. Id. at 85, 550 N.Y.S.2d at 615, 549 N.E.2d at 1186.

54. People v. Osorio, 75 N.Y.2d 80, 84, 550 N.Y.S.2d 612, 615, 549 N.E.2d 1183, 1186 (1989). The Osorio court cited United States v. Kovel, 296 F.2d 918 (2d Cir.1961), in which it was observed that an accountant retained by the attorney or client might serve as an "interpreter" with respect to technical accounting issues. The Kovel court would uphold the privilege in such cases on the principle that the use of such experts may be "necessary, or at least highly useful, for the effective consultation between the client and the lawyer." Id. at 922. But see People v. Edney, 39 N.Y.2d 620, 625, 385 N.Y.S.2d 23, 26, 350 N.E.2d 400, 403 (1976) (reliance on insanity defense is waiver of attorney-client privilege with respect to defendant's communications with defense-retained psychiatrist).

55. Stroh v. General Motors Corp., 213 A.D.2d 267, 623 N.Y.S.2d 873 (1st Dep't 1995).

56. Root v. Wright, 84 N.Y. 72 (1881).

counsel with respect to the matter of common interest are not privileged as between them.[57] Closely related to the joint-client rule is the joint-defense doctrine. Two or more parties with separate counsel may participate in joint attorney-client discussions for the purpose of preparing a common defense. Such communications are privileged against disclosure to outsiders.[58] If the separately-represented parties are not mounting a common defense, however, any expectations of confidentiality are deemed lacking.[59]

f. Application in the Corporate Context

Unquestionably corporate clients may claim the benefits of the attorney-client privilege in New York.[60] Furthermore, no distinction exists between house counsel and outside counsel as to the applicability of privilege so long as the attorney is acting as legal advisor.[61] If the corporation's staff counsel also performs business functions, the court must determine whether legal considerations were predominant in the particular communication.[62] An unresolved question in New York is how deep within the corporate hierarchy the privilege extends. In other words, which employees of the corporation can effectively "speak" on behalf of the corporate client for purposes of the privilege? Courts elsewhere have developed essentially two different approaches: the "control group" test and the "subject matter" test. Under the control group test, privilege applies only if the employee making the communication is "in a position to control or * * * take a substantial part in a decision about * * * action which the corporation may take upon the advice of the attorney, or if he is an authorized member of a body or group which has that authority."[63] The subject matter test provides a broader scope

---

57. Wallace v. Wallace, 216 N.Y. 28, 35–36, 109 N.E. 872, 873 (1915); Hurlburt v. Hurlburt, 128 N.Y. 420, 424, 28 N.E. 651, 652 (1891). The rationale appears to be that joint clients presumably intend their communications with counsel to be confidential as to outsiders but not as to each other. Finn v. Morgan, 46 A.D.2d 229, 235–36, 362 N.Y.S.2d 292, 300–01 (4th Dep't 1974).

58. People v. Osorio, 75 N.Y.2d 80, 85, 550 N.Y.S.2d 612, 615, 549 N.E.2d 1183, 1186 (1989).

59. Id. at 85, 550 N.Y.S.2d at 615, 549 N.E.2d at 1186.

60. Rossi v. Blue Cross and Blue Shield of Greater New York, 73 N.Y.2d 588, 542 N.Y.S.2d 508, 540 N.E.2d 703 (1989). See also Nicolo v. Greenfield, 163 A.D.2d 837, 558 N.Y.S.2d 371 (4th Dep't 1990) (attorney-client privilege available to government agencies).

Courts have recognized a discretionary exception, however, in shareholder derivative suits on the theory that corporate management owes fiduciary duties to the shareholders. Beard v. Ames, 96 A.D.2d 119, 468 N.Y.S.2d 253 (4th Dep't 1983). See generally notes 73–75 infra.

61. Rossi v. Blue Cross and Blue Shield of Greater New York, 73 N.Y.2d 588, 592, 542 N.Y.S.2d 508, 509, 540 N.E.2d 703, 705 (1989); Kraus v. Brandstetter, 185 A.D.2d 300, 586 N.Y.S.2d 270 (2d Dep't 1992). The Kraus court also held that no loss of confidentiality occurred when house counsel's investigatory report was circulated among a management group of the corporation that had a common interest in the investigation.

62. Compare Cooper–Rutter Associates, Inc. v. Anchor National Life Insurance Co., 168 A.D.2d 663, 563 N.Y.S.2d 491 (2d Dep't 1990)(house counsel's memoranda expressed "substantial non-legal concerns" of business transaction), with Quail Ridge Associates v. Chemical Bank, 174 A.D.2d 959, 571 N.Y.S.2d 648 (3d Dep't 1991)(memoranda by corporation's in-house attorneys, who performed no business functions, related primarily to the providing of legal advice).

63. City of Philadelphia v. Westinghouse Elec. Corp., 210 F.Supp. 483, 485

§ 501.1   PRIVILEGES   Ch. 5

to the corporate privilege. In essence, it extends the privilege to a confidential communication between the corporation's attorney and any employee, provided the subject matter of the communication concerns the employee's corporate duties and the purpose of the communication involves the providing of legal advice to the corporation.[64]

The control group test was rejected by the United States Supreme Court in proceedings based on federal claims,[65] but it is the governing standard in a few states.[66] The New York Court of Appeals has never squarely addressed the issue, but the trend of recent cases reveals an expansive attitude toward the attorney-client privilege in the corporate context.[67]

Regardless of whose communications qualify for the corporation's attorney-client privilege, the privilege ordinarily belongs solely to the corporation, not to the individual employee who spoke with counsel. Therefore, unless the corporation's attorney undertook joint representation, the employee has no control over the corporation's distribution of his communication.[68] The corporation may choose to waive the privilege, for example, and permit disclosure to outsiders, such as regulatory agencies or prosecuting authorities.[69]

(E.D.Pa.1962), mandamus denied sub nom. General Elec. Co. v. Kirkpatrick, 312 F.2d 742 (3d Cir.), cert. denied, 372 U.S. 943, 83 S.Ct. 937, 9 L.Ed.2d 969 (1963).

64. Diversified Industries, Inc. v. Meredith, 572 F.2d 596, 606–11 (8th Cir. 1977)(en banc); Harper & Row Publishers, Inc. v. Decker, 423 F.2d 487, 491–92 (7th Cir.1970), aff'd per curiam by an equally divided court, 400 U.S. 348, 91 S.Ct. 479, 27 L.Ed.2d 433, rehearing denied, 401 U.S. 950, 91 S.Ct. 917, 28 L.Ed.2d 234 (1971).

65. Upjohn Co. v. United States, 449 U.S. 383, 101 S.Ct. 677, 66 L.Ed.2d 584 (1981). See also § 501.2, at notes 29–34, infra.

66. See, e.g., Ark.R.Evid. 502(a)(2); Tex.R.Evid.—Civil and Crim. 503(a)(2); Claxton v. Thackston, 201 Ill.App.3d 232, 147 Ill.Dec. 82, 559 N.E.2d 82 (1990). The relative merits of the control group and subject matter tests are analyzed in Alexander, "The Corporate Attorney–Client Privilege: A Study of the Participants," 63 St. John's L.Rev. 191, 294–325 (1989).

67. See Spectrum Systems International Corp. v. Chemical Bank, 78 N.Y.2d 371, 575 N.Y.S.2d 809, 581 N.E.2d 1055 (1991)(upholding privilege for law firm's investigatory report on internal corporate wrongdoing); Rossi v. Blue Cross and Blue Shield of Greater New York, 73 N.Y.2d 588, 542 N.Y.S.2d 508, 540 N.E.2d 703 (1989)(upholding privilege for house counsel's memorandum to management). Additionally, in the context of identifying which employees of a corporation are protected by DR 7–104(A)(1)'s ethical prohibition against an opposing lawyer's ex parte communications, the court rejected a control group standard. Niesig v. Team I, 76 N.Y.2d 363, 559 N.Y.S.2d 493, 558 N.E.2d 1030 (1990). Opposing counsel is barred from ex parte contacts with employees "whose acts or omissions in the matter under inquiry are binding on the corporation * * * or imputed to the corporation for purposes of its liability, or employees implementing the advice of counsel." Id. at 374, 559 N.Y.S.2d at 498, 588 N.E.2d at 1035. The court, however, refrained from equating the scope of the ex parte contact rule with the attorney-client privilege. In dictum, the court stated: "As the Supreme Court recognized, a corporation's attorney-client privilege includes communications with low- and mid-level employees." Id. at 371, 559 N.Y.S.2d at 496–97, 558 N.E.2d at 1033–34.

68. Doe v. Poe, 189 A.D.2d 132, 595 N.Y.S.2d 503 (2d Dep't), leave to appeal denied, 81 N.Y.2d 711, 600 N.Y.S.2d 442, 616 N.E.2d 1104 (1993) (personally incriminating communications made by bank's CEO to bank's lawyers could be disclosed to a special committee of the bank's board of trustees over CEO's protest).

69. In the analogous context of a government lawyer's communications with a government employee, the court in Dooley v. Boyle, 140 Misc.2d 177, 186, 531 N.Y.S.2d 161, 167 (Sup.Ct.Suffolk Co.1988), refused to enjoin a county attorney from delivering a county officer's statements to

224

g. Exceptions

CPLR 4503(b) creates an exception to the attorney-client privilege for a deceased client's communications with counsel concerning the preparation, execution or revocation of a will or other relevant instrument in any action involving the probate, validity or construction of a will. The communications are subject to compelled disclosure under such circumstances on the theory that the now-deceased client would have wanted the information to be admitted into evidence to resolve a dispute over his will.[70] The statute, however, retains privilege for confidential communications concerning the client's will if disclosure would tend to disgrace the decedent's memory.

Several judge-made exceptions to the attorney-client privilege have been developed over the years. For reasons of public policy, the privilege is inapplicable when the client's communications were made in contemplation of a future crime or fraud.[71] The privilege is also lifted when a client sues his attorney for legal malpractice because of the attorney's need to defend herself against charges of wrongdoing.[72] An emerging exception permits the court, upon a particularized showing of "good cause," to order disclosure when the client, at the time of the relevant attorney-client communication, owed a fiduciary duty to the party seeking disclosure.[73] For example, the beneficiaries of a trust may be able to overcome the privilege that would otherwise exist for communications between the trustee and counsel regarding the legal affairs of the trust.[74] The good cause exception, however, is not likely to be applied to attorney-client communications made by the fiduciary for the

---

the district attorney. Practitioners should note DR 5–109 of the New York Code of Professional Responsibility, which provides that a lawyer for an organization must explain to employees and other "constituents" that she represents the organization, not the individual, if a potential conflict exists.

70. Matter of Levinsky's Will, 23 A.D.2d 25, 31, 258 N.Y.S.2d 613, 620 (2d Dep't), appeal denied, 16 N.Y.2d 484, 264 N.Y.S.2d 1026, 211 N.E.2d 654 (1965).

71. People ex rel. Vogelstein v. Warden of County Jail, 150 Misc. 714, 720–21, 270 N.Y.S. 362, 370–71 (Sup.Ct.N.Y.Co.), aff'd, 242 App.Div. 611, 271 N.Y.S. 1059 (1st Dep't 1934). See also Matter of Doe, 101 Misc.2d 388, 420 N.Y.S.2d 996 (Sup.Ct.N.Y.Co.1979)(attorney required to disclose whereabouts of client who, in violation of terms of plea bargaining agreement to undergo psychiatric treatment and return to court for sentencing, remained at large). Proof of the client's criminal or fraudulent intent need only be prima facie. In re Franklin Washington Trust Co., 1 Misc.2d 697, 699, 148 N.Y.S.2d 731, 734 (Sup.Ct.N.Y.Co.1956).

72. Finger Lakes Plumbing & Heating, Inc. v. O'Dell, 101 A.D.2d 1008, 476 N.Y.S.2d 670 (4th Dep't 1984). See also Glines v. Baird's Estate, 16 A.D.2d 743, 227 N.Y.S.2d 71 (4th Dep't 1962)(suit by attorney for fee). Cf. N.Y. Code of Professional Responsibility DR 4–101(C)(4). But see Jakobleff v. Cerrato, Sweeney & Cohn, 97 A.D.2d 834, 468 N.Y.S.2d 895 (2d Dep't 1983)(plaintiff in legal malpractice action against former attorneys may still assert privilege for communications with current attorney).

73. Hoopes v. Carota, 74 N.Y.2d 716, 544 N.Y.S.2d 808, 543 N.E.2d 73 (1989)(good cause shown); AMBAC Indemnity Corp. v. Bankers Trust Co., 151 Misc.2d 334, 573 N.Y.S.2d 204 (Sup.Ct. N.Y.Co.1991)(good cause not shown).

74. Hoopes v. Carota, 74 N.Y.2d 716, 544 N.Y.S.2d 808, 543 N.E.2d 73 (1989). See also Beard v. Ames, 96 A.D.2d 119, 468 N.Y.S.2d 253 (4th Dep't)(shareholder derivative action against corporate management). Cf. In re Estate of Baker, 139 Misc.2d 573, 528 N.Y.S.2d 470 (Surr.Ct.Nassau Co.1988)(privilege generally inapplicable in action by beneficiaries against executor of estate).

specific purpose of defending against the action brought by the beneficiary.[75]

The Court of Appeals has also stated, in general, that the attorney-client privilege may "yield in a proper case, where strong public policy requires disclosure."[76] The so-called public policy exception, however, has rarely been applied.[77]

h. Waiver

Confidentiality at the time of origination of an attorney-client communication is a factor that will determine whether the communication is privileged. Waiver involves a loss of confidentiality subsequent to the communication.[78] A client may waive the privilege for his confidential communications with an attorney, and such waiver will be deemed to occur if the client voluntarily testifies to the contents of the communication with counsel[79] or otherwise discloses it to others.[80] The client's testimony about the same events that he described to his lawyer, however, is not a waiver.[81] Such testimony, therefore, does not open the

---

75. In re Estate of Baker, 139 Misc.2d 573, 577, 528 N.Y.S.2d 470, 473 (Surr.Ct.Nassau Co.1988). The precise meaning of "good cause" has not been articulated by the New York courts. The relevant factors have been developed primarily in federal cases. See § 501.2, at notes 35–37, infra.

76. Matter of Priest v. Hennessy, 51 N.Y.2d 62, 69, 431 N.Y.S.2d 511, 514, 409 N.E.2d 983, 986 (1980). The exception originated in Matter of Jacqueline F., 47 N.Y.2d 215, 417 N.Y.S.2d 884, 391 N.E.2d 967 (1979), a custody dispute in which the attorney for a child's guardian was required to disclose the address of his client so that the child's best interests could be protected.

77. See, e.g., Spectrum Systems International Corp. v. Chemical Bank, 78 N.Y.2d 371, 380–81, 575 N.Y.S.2d 809, 816, 581 N.E.2d 1055, 1062 (1991) (public policy is furthered by preservation of privilege for counsel's investigatory report to corporate client); Rossi v. Blue Cross and Blue Shield of Greater New York, 73 N.Y.2d 588, 594, 542 N.Y.S.2d 508, 511, 540 N.E.2d 703, 706 (1989)(death of attorney-author of memorandum provided no basis for application of public policy exception). One court recognized that a criminal defendant's right of confrontation might occasionally provide something of a public policy exception where a prosecution witness has made potentially contradictory statements to her lawyer. People v. Radtke, ___ A.D.2d ___, 631 N.Y.S.2d 763 (2d Dep't 1995)(no basis for exception under the circumstances).

78. People v. Harris, 57 N.Y.2d 335, 343 n.1, 456 N.Y.S.2d 694, 697, 442 N.E.2d 1205, 1208 (1982), cert. denied, 460 U.S. 1047, 103 S.Ct. 1448, 75 L.Ed.2d 803 (1983).

79. People v. Patrick, 182 N.Y. 131, 175, 74 N.E. 843, 857, reargument denied, 183 N.Y. 52, 75 N.E. 963 (1905). See also Kaufman v. Rosenshine, 97 App.Div. 514, 90 N.Y.S. 205 (1st Dep't 1904), aff'd, 183 N.Y. 562, 76 N.E. 1098 (1906)(client who testified to contents of attorney-client communication did not waive privilege to extent of permitting attorney to testify to same communication because client's revelation occurred during cross-examination rather than on direct).

80. AMBAC Indemnity Corp. v. Bankers Trust Co., 151 Misc.2d 334, 340–41, 573 N.Y.S.2d 204, 208 (Sup.Ct.N.Y.Co.1991). In Matter of Pretino's Will, 150 Misc.2d 371, 373, 567 N.Y.S.2d 1009, 1011 (Surr.Ct.Nassau Co.1991), however, no waiver was found where a client disclosed the contents of an attorney-client communication to his wife, in confidence, because such disclosure occurred in a communication which was itself privileged.

81. People v. Lynch, 23 N.Y.2d 262, 271, 296 N.Y.S.2d 327, 334, 244 N.E.2d 29, 35 (1968)("testimony about an event * * * should not be construed as a waiver of the privilege, merely because the subject matter of the testimony may also have been discussed in the privileged communication"). This rule is a corollary of the principle that the privilege applies only to attorney-client communications, not the underlying facts. See text at notes 19–20 supra.

door to cross-examination into the attorney-client communications.[82] Nor should waiver occur merely because the client discloses the general subject matter of a particular communication with counsel.[83]

The potential for an implied waiver has been recognized in certain recurring situations. Reliance upon the advice of counsel to support a claim or defense on the merits will constitute a waiver as to all communications with counsel relating to the matter for which legal advice was sought.[84] Inadvertent disclosure of privileged documents during pretrial discovery may also be a waiver unless a showing is made that reasonable efforts were made to avoid such disclosure and the circumstances otherwise weigh in favor of preserving the privilege.[85] Refreshing the recollection of a witness with an attorney-client communication is another potential basis for a finding of waiver because the adversary ordinarily has a right of access to documents used to refresh recollection.[86] New York courts are divided over the waiver issue in this context.[87] The risk also exists that waiver will occur when attorney-client documents are carelessly left in the trash.[88]

People v. Cassas[89] provides protection against a finding of waiver based on counsel's informal disclosures. In *Cassas*, the trial court admitted into evidence the fact that, shortly after the shooting of defendant's wife, the defendant and his lawyer appeared at a police precinct where the lawyer told the police that his client had shot his wife and that the gun could be found in defendant's room. The defendant stood by silently. The Court of Appeals held that the trial judge committed reversible error because the record contained no evidence that the defendant had waived the attorney-client privilege. "The fact

---

82. People v. Shapiro, 308 N.Y. 453, 126 N.E.2d 559 (1955).

83. AMBAC Indemnity Corp. v. Bankers Trust Co., 151 Misc.2d 334, 340–41, 573 N.Y.S.2d 204, 208 (Sup.Ct.N.Y.Co.1991). See also Matter of Vanderbilt, 57 N.Y.2d 66, 76–77, 453 N.Y.S.2d 662, 668, 439 N.E.2d 378, 384 (1982)(outsider may be aware of subject matter of client's conversation with attorney but "she will be unable to discover the details of his discussion with his attorney").

84. Orco Bank, N.V. v. Proteinas Del Pacifico, S.A., 179 A.D.2d 390, 577 N.Y.S.2d 841 (1st Dep't 1992); Village Board of Village of Pleasantville v. Rattner, 130 A.D.2d 654, 515 N.Y.S.2d 585 (2d Dep't 1987).

85. John Blair Communications, Inc. v. Reliance Capital Group, L.P., 182 A.D.2d 578, 582 N.Y.S.2d 720 (1st Dep't 1992); Clark–Fitzpatrick, Inc. v. Long Island R.R. Co., 162 A.D.2d 577, 556 N.Y.S.2d 763 (2d Dep't 1990); Manufacturers and Traders Trust Co. v. Servotronics, Inc., 132 A.D.2d 392, 522 N.Y.S.2d 999 (4th Dep't 1987).

86. People v. Gezzo, 307 N.Y. 385, 121 N.E.2d 380 (1954). See § 612.1(b) infra.

87. Compare E.R. Carpenter Co. v. ABC Carpet Co., 98 Misc.2d 1091, 415 N.Y.S.2d 351 (N.Y.C.Civ.Ct.1979)(refreshing recollection prior to deposition with memorandum protected by attorney-client privilege constituted waiver under the circumstances), with Falk v. Kalt, 44 Misc.2d 172, 253 N.Y.S.2d 188 (Sup.Ct.Suffolk Co.1964)(no waiver where witness, during deposition, refreshed recollection with document protected by attorney-client privilege). Cf. Herrmann v. General Tire and Rubber Co., 79 A.D.2d 955, 435 N.Y.S.2d 14 (1st Dep't 1981)(use of attorney work product to refresh recollection prior to deposition constitutes waiver). But see Geffers v. Canisteo Central School District, 105 A.D.2d 1062, 482 N.Y.S.2d 635 (4th Dep't 1984)(witness' review of attorney work product prior to deposition is not a waiver).

88. See Suburban Sew 'N Sweep, Inc. v. Swiss–Bernina, Inc., 91 F.R.D. 254, 257–61 (N.D.Ill.1981). See also Matter of Victor, 422 F.Supp. 475, 476 (S.D.N.Y.1976)(loss of privilege for attorney-client papers left in public hallway).

89. 84 N.Y.2d 718, 622 N.Y.S.2d 228, 646 N.E.2d 449 (1995).

§ 501.1 PRIVILEGES Ch. 5

that the attorney is the agent of the client-principal does not alone equate to a waiver of this privilege. The specific authorization must come from defendant principal to attorney-agent to constitute a waiver of the attorney-client privilege."[90] The court stressed that strong evidence of waiver "is particularly important in criminal cases where a defendant retains the authority to make key choices about a defense against criminal charges."[91]

It bears noting that the lawyer's statements in *Cassas* were made in an informal setting, i.e., outside the context of papers filed in court or in statements made in a formal address to the court or jury. A finding of waiver may be more likely in the latter circumstances. For example, the *Cassas* court distinguished *People v. Rivera*,[92] where an attorney's affidavit, filed in support of a pretrial motion, was held admissible for the limited purpose of impeaching the client-defendant who testified at trial to a different version of the facts. The attorney in *Rivera*, who explicitly said in his affidavit that he had been informed of the facts by his client, was found to have filed the affidavit with the client's authority. The Second Circuit's decision in *United States v. McKeon*[93] was also distinguished. In *McKeon*, the attorney's opening statement in a prior trial of the defendant was held admissible against the defendant on the retrial because of clear inconsistencies in the facts alleged by the defense at the two trials. There, the lawyer's statements were found to have been the functional equivalent of "testimonial statements by the defendant."[94]

Library References:

West's Key No. Digests, Witnesses ⚖︎197, 219(3).

§ 501.2 Federal: Attorney–Client Privilege

The federal courts have developed a significant body of caselaw on the attorney-client privilege. One of the most frequently quoted formulations of the privilege in federal practice is that of Judge Wyzanski in *United States v. United Shoe Machinery Corp.*:[1]

> The privilege applies only if (1) the asserted holder of the privilege is or sought to become a client; (2) the person to whom the communication was made (a) is a member of the bar of a court, or his subordinate and (b) in connection with this communication is acting as a lawyer; (3) the communication relates to a fact of which the attorney was informed (a) by his client (b) without the presence of strangers (c) for the purpose of securing primarily either (i) an opinion on law or (ii) legal services or (iii) assistance in some legal proceeding, and not (d)

---

90. Id. at 724, 622 N.Y.S.2d at 230, 646 N.E.2d at 451.

91. Id. at 722, 622 N.Y.S.2d at 229, 646 N.E.2d at 450.

92. 58 A.D.2d 147, 396 N.Y.S.2d 26 (1st Dep't 1977), aff'd on opinion below, 45 N.Y.2d 989, 413 N.Y.S.2d 146, 385 N.E.2d 1073 (1978).

93. 738 F.2d 26 (2d Cir.1984).

94. 84 N.Y.2d at 723, 622 N.Y.S.2d at 230, 646 N.E.2d at 451.

§ 501.2

1. 89 F.Supp. 357 (D.Mass.1950).

for the purpose of committing a crime or tort; and (4) the privilege has been (a) claimed and (b) not waived by the client.[2]

Because the attorney-client privilege can be an obstacle to the ascertainment of truth, federal courts frequently concur with Wigmore's view that it should be "strictly confined within the narrowest possible limits consistent with the logic of its principle."[3] That principle, of course, is the promotion of candor by clients in their communications

---

2. Id. at 358. See Colton v. United States, 306 F.2d 633, 637 (2d Cir.1962). Some courts have relied upon the proposed Federal Rule on attorney-client privilege as instructive. See, e.g., In re Bieter Company, 16 F.3d 929, 935 (8th Cir.1994). Proposed Federal Rule of Evidence 503, which was not enacted, provides as follows:

(a) Definitions. As used in this rule:

(1) A "client" is a person, public officer, or corporation, association, or other organization or entity, either public or private, who is rendered professional legal services by a lawyer, or who consults a lawyer with a view to obtaining professional legal services from him.

(2) A "lawyer" is a person authorized, or reasonably believed by the client to be authorized, to practice law in any state or nation.

(3) A "representative of the lawyer" is one employed to assist the lawyer in the rendition of professional legal services.

(4) A communication is "confidential" if not intended to be disclosed to third persons other than those to whom disclosure is in furtherance of the rendition of professional legal services to the client or those reasonably necessary for the transmission of the communication.

(b) General rule of privilege. A client has a privilege to refuse to disclose and to prevent any other person from disclosing confidential communications made for the purpose of facilitating the rendition of professional legal services to the client, (1) between himself or his representative and his lawyer or his lawyer's representative, or (2) between his lawyer and the lawyer's representative, or (3) by him or his lawyer to a lawyer representing another in a matter of common interest, or (4) between representatives of the client or between the client and a representative of the client, or (5) between lawyers representing the client.

(c) Who may claim the privilege. The privilege may be claimed by the client, his guardian or conservator, the personal representative of a deceased client, or the successor, trustee, or similar representative of a corporation, association, or other organization, whether or not in existence. The person who was the lawyer at the time of the communication may claim the privilege but only on behalf of the client. His authority to do so is presumed in the absence of evidence to the contrary.

(d) Exceptions. There is no privilege under this rule:

(1) *Furtherance of crime or fraud.* If the services of the lawyer were sought or obtained to enable or aid anyone to commit or plan to commit what the client knew or reasonably should have known to be a crime or fraud; or

(2) *Claimants through same deceased client.* As to a communication relevant to an issue between parties who claim through the same deceased client, regardless of whether the claims are by testate or intestate succession or by *inter vivos* transaction; or

(3) *Breach of duty by lawyer or client.* As to a communication relevant to an issue of breach of duty by the lawyer to his client or by the client to his lawyer; or

(4) *Document attested by lawyer.* As to a communication relevant to an issue concerning an attested document to which the lawyer is an attesting witness; or

(5) *Joint clients.* As to a communication relevant to a matter of common interest between two or more clients if the communication was made by any of them to a lawyer retained or consulted in common, when offered in an action between any of the clients.

The burden of proving applicability of the privilege is upon the party claiming its benefits. In re Horowitz, 482 F.2d 72, 82 (2d Cir.), cert. denied, 414 U.S. 867, 94 S.Ct. 64, 38 L.Ed.2d 86 (1973); Bowne of New York City, Inc. v. AmBase Corp., 150 F.R.D. 465, 472–76 (S.D.N.Y.1993).

3. 8 Wigmore § 2291, at 554. See Fisher v. United States, 425 U.S. 391, 403, 96 S.Ct. 1569, 1577, 48 L.Ed.2d 39, 51 (1976);

§ 501.2   PRIVILEGES   Ch. 5

with counsel.[4] The attorney-client privilege, therefore, does not protect the underlying facts from disclosure,[5] nor does it provide immunity for pre-existing documents that come into the lawyer's possession[6] nor facts that come to the lawyer's attention from independent sources.[7]

In order for the confidential communications between attorney and client to be privileged, the parties must have entered into an attorney-client relationship[8] and the communications must relate to the client's seeking of legal advice or services.[9] Thus, lawyer-client communications relating solely to business matters are not privileged.[10] The lawyer's advice to the client is within the privilege if it would reveal, directly or

United States v. Goldberger & Dubin, P.C., 935 F.2d 501, 504 (2d Cir.1991).

4. Upjohn Co. v. United States, 449 U.S. 383, 389, 101 S.Ct. 677, 682, 66 L.Ed.2d 584, 591 (1981)(The purpose of the privilege is "to encourage full and frank communication between attorneys and their clients and thereby promote broader public interests in the observance of law and administration of justice. The privilege recognizes that sound legal advice or advocacy serves public ends and that such advice or advocacy depends upon the lawyer's being fully informed by the client."). See also United States v. Bilzerian, 926 F.2d 1285, 1292 (2d Cir.1991) (privilege "encourages the full and truthful revelation by the client of all the facts in his possession").

5. Upjohn Co. v. United States, 449 U.S. 383, 395–96, 101 S.Ct. 677, 685–86, 66 L.Ed.2d 584, 595 (1981). See also In re Six Grand Jury Witnesses, 979 F.2d 939, 944 (2d Cir.1992)("[T]he cloak of the privilege simply protects the communication from discovery[;] the underlying information contained in the communication is not shielded from discovery."); United States v. Cunningham, 672 F.2d 1064, 1073 n.8 (2d Cir.1982), cert. denied, 466 U.S. 951, 104 S.Ct. 2154, 80 L.Ed.2d 540 (1984)("The privilege attaches not to the information but to the communication of the information").

6. Colton v. United States, 306 F.2d 633, 639 (2d Cir.1962), cert. denied, 371 U.S. 951, 83 S.Ct. 505, 9 L.Ed.2d 499 (1963). But see Fisher v. United States, 425 U.S. 391, 96 S.Ct. 1569, 48 L.Ed.2d 39 (1976)(if client would be protected by fifth amendment from compelled production, attorney's acquisition of document in context of attorney-client communication precludes compelled production by attorney).

7. Hickman v. Taylor, 329 U.S. 495, 508, 67 S.Ct. 385, 392, 91 L.Ed. 451, 460–61 (1947); In re Sealed Case, 737 F.2d 94, 99 (D.C.Cir.1984); Carte Blanche (Singapore) PTE, Ltd. v. Diners Club International, Inc., 130 F.R.D. 28, 33 (S.D.N.Y.1990). The work product doctrine, however, may protect some forms of information obtained from third parties. See § 501.3 infra.

8. United States v. Dennis, 843 F.2d 652, 656–57 (2d Cir.1988)(privilege may attach during client's initial communications with attorney with a view toward professional employment, but privilege will not apply after attorney makes clear that she will not provide representation). Federal courts will apply the privilege when a would-be client communicates with an individual "in the genuine, but mistaken, belief that he is an attorney." United States v. Rivera, 837 F.Supp. 565, 567 n.1 (S.D.N.Y. 1993). The same approach is taken in Proposed Federal Rule of Evidence 503(a)(2). See note 2 supra.

9. In re Shargel, 742 F.2d 61, 62 (2d Cir.1984)(privilege is limited to communications necessary to obtain informed legal advice); In re John Doe Corp., 675 F.2d 482, 488 (2d Cir.1982)(privilege encompasses communications made "solely for the purpose of the [client] seeking legal advice and its counsel rendering it").

10. In re Grand Jury Subpoena Duces Tecum Dated September 15, 1983, 731 F.2d 1032, 1037 (2d Cir.1984); Colton v. United States, 306 F.2d 633, 638 (2d Cir.1962), cert. denied, 371 U.S. 951, 83 S.Ct. 505, 9 L.Ed.2d 499 (1963). See also Simon v. G.D. Searle & Co., 816 F.2d 397, 403–04 (8th Cir.), cert. denied, 484 U.S. 917, 108 S.Ct. 268, 98 L.Ed.2d 225 (1987) (counsel's attendance at business meeting does not automatically create privilege for communications exchanged at meeting). When legal and business considerations are commingled in attorney-client communications, privilege may still attach if the legal character of the communication is "predominant." Ohio–Sealy Mattress Mfg. Co. v. Kaplan, 90 F.R.D. 21, 34 (N.D.Ill.1980); Eutectic Corp. v. Metco, Inc., 61 F.R.D. 35, 39 (E.D.N.Y. 1973). See also Barr Marine Products Co. v. Borg–Warner Corp., 84 F.R.D. 631, 635 (E.D.Pa.1979)(test is whether communications were "primarily" concerned with seeking or giving legal advice).

indirectly, the client's communications, but federal courts are split over the question whether such advice, when based on data obtained from third parties, should also be privileged.[11]

The identity of a client and information about fees paid by the client generally do not fall within the scope of the privilege.[12] Occasionally, however, background information about the attorney-client relationship might be privileged if it would create an inference about the content of the communications.[13] It is also the rule in the Second Circuit that identity may be privileged where the substance, but not the source, of a confidential communication is already known and identifying the source would constitute prejudicial disclosure of a client communication.[14]

Communications made in furtherance of an ongoing or contemplated crime or fraud, of course, do not qualify for the privilege.[15] The proponent of the crime/fraud exception must show that there is "probable cause to believe that a crime or fraud [has] been committed and that the communications were in furtherance thereof."[16] Courts are autho-

---

11. Compare American Standard Inc. v. Pfizer, Inc., 828 F.2d 734, 745–46 (Fed.Cir.1987)(lawyer's advice privileged only if it would reveal substance of client's communication), with In re LTV Securities Litigation, 89 F.R.D. 595, 602 (N.D.Tex.1981)(privilege applies to attorney's advice regardless of whether it would reveal client's confidential communications). Cf. Upjohn Co. v. United States, 449 U.S. 383, 390, 101 S.Ct. 677, 683, 66 L.Ed.2d 584, 592 (1981)("[T]he privilege exists to protect not only the giving of professional advice to those who can act on it but also the giving of the information to the lawyer to enable him to give sound and informed legal advice.")

12. United States v. Goldberger & Dubin, P.C., 935 F.2d 501, 505 (2d Cir.1991); Colton v. United States, 306 F.2d 633, 637–38 (2d Cir.1962), cert. denied, 371 U.S. 951, 83 S.Ct. 505, 9 L.Ed.2d 499 (1963). The court in In re Shargel, 742 F.2d 61 (2d Cir.1984), reasoned as follows: The privilege encompasses "only those confidential communications necessary to obtain informed legal advice. * * * [D]isclosure of the identity of the client and fee information stand on a footing different from communications intended by the client to explain a problem to a lawyer in order to obtain legal advice. * * * [Identity and fee] information is not protected by the privilege even though the client may strongly fear the effects of disclosure, including incrimination." Id. at 62–63.

13. In re Shargel, 742 F.2d 61, 64 (2d Cir.1984).

14. Vingelli v. United States, Drug Enforcement Agency, 992 F.2d 449, 453 (2d Cir.1993); United States v. Pape, 144 F.2d 778, 783 (2d Cir.1944), cert. denied, 323 U.S. 752, 65 S.Ct. 86, 89 L.Ed. 602 (1944). Similarly, other circuit courts of appeals have held that the client's identity must be treated as privileged where the effect of revelation would be disclosure of the substance of a client's communication. Matter of Grand Jury Proceeding (Cherney), 898 F.2d 565, 568 (7th Cir.1990); United States v. Liebman, 742 F.2d 807, 809 (3d Cir. 1984); In re Grand Jury Subpoena for Osterhoudt, 722 F.2d 591, 593 (9th Cir.1983). See also In re Grand Jury Subpoena (Reyes Requena), 926 F.2d 1423, 1431–32 (5th Cir.1991)(incrimination of client is not proper rationale for protection of identity; privilege will apply, however, when identity is so intertwined with confidential communications that disclosure will reveal purpose for which legal advice was sought).

15. In re Grand Jury Subpoena Duces Tecum Dated September 15, 1983, 731 F.2d 1032, 1038 (2d Cir.1984)("'advice in furtherance of such goals is socially perverse, and the client's communications seeking such advice are not worthy of protection. * * * Such communications are properly excluded from the scope of the privilege even if the attorney is unaware that his advice is sought in furtherance of such an improper purpose."). The seeking of legal advice to defend against allegations of past crimes, of course, is entirely legitimate. Id. at 1041–42. Consulting counsel for the purpose of a cover-up, on the other hand, falls within the crime/fraud exception. In re John Doe Corp., 675 F.2d 482, 491–92 (2d Cir.1982).

16. In re Grand Jury Subpoena Duces Tecum Dated September 15, 1983, 731 F.2d 1032, 1039 (2d Cir.1984)(probable cause standard "require[s] that a prudent person have a reasonable basis to suspect the

rized to conduct an in camera inspection of attorney-client communications for the purpose of determining the applicability of the crime/fraud exception,[17] but the proponent must first make a threshold evidentiary showing "sufficient to support a reasonable belief that in camera review may yield evidence that establishes the exception's applicability."[18] Another exception to the privilege is recognized when the lawyer is compelled to defend against charges of wrongdoing made by the client or a third party.[19]

Confidentiality lies at the heart of the attorney-client privilege.[20] Thus, communications made in the known presence of third parties generally are not privileged.[21] Similarly, communications to an attorney that are intended to be disclosed to outsiders lack the requisite intent of confidentiality.[22] Communications through agents of the attorney or client, however, will not destroy confidentiality.[23] Federal courts have extended this principle to permit the participation of accountants and

perpetration of a crime or fraud"). See also In re Sealed Case, 754 F.2d 395, 399 (D.C.Cir.1985)(two-part showing is required: (1) prima facie showing of criminal or fraudulent purpose, and (2) relationship between the communication and the prima facie wrongdoing).

17. In re John Doe Corp., 675 F.2d 482, 490 (2d Cir.1982).

18. United States v. Zolin, 491 U.S. 554, 574–75, 109 S.Ct. 2619, 2632, 105 L.Ed.2d 469, 492 (1989). Only nonprivileged material may be considered by a court in making the preliminary determination to review the privileged communications in camera. Id. at 574, 109 S.Ct. at 2632, 105 L.Ed.2d at 492. In In re John Doe, Inc. 13 F.3d 633, 635–36 (2d Cir.1994), the Second Circuit held that the threshold inquiry required by Zolin may itself be conducted in camera if necessary to preserve the secrecy of grand jury proceedings that are in progress.

19. Meyerhofer v. Empire Fire & Marine Insurance Co., 497 F.2d 1190 (2d Cir.), cert. denied, 419 U.S. 998, 95 S.Ct. 314, 42 L.Ed.2d 272 (1974); First Federal Savings & Loan Ass'n v. Oppenheim, Appel, Dixon & Co., 110 F.R.D. 557, 560–68 (S.D.N.Y. 1986). But see Eckhaus v. Alfa–Laval, Inc., 764 F.Supp. 34 (S.D.N.Y.1991)(former house counsel not permitted to sue corporation for defamation because confidences would be disclosed; "poor performance review" of counsel did not amount to "an accusation of wrongful conduct" within the contemplation of the exception). Some courts have applied the exception prior to the commencement of an action or the filing of charges against the attorney. See, e.g., SEC v. Forma, 117 F.R.D. 516 (S.D.N.Y.1987)(attorney under investigation by administrative agency); In re Friend, 411 F.Supp. 776 (S.D.N.Y.1975) (attorney under investigation by grand jury). The attorney may also disclose confidences, if necessary, in a suit to collect her fee. First Federal Savings & Loan Ass'n v. Oppenheim, Appel, Dixon & Co., supra, at 560.

20. United States v. Tellier, 255 F.2d 441, 447 (2d Cir.), cert. denied, 358 U.S. 821, 79 S.Ct. 33, 3 L.Ed.2d 62 (1958)("It is of the essence of the attorney-client privilege that it is limited to those communications which are intended to be confidential.").

21. In re Grand Jury Subpoena Duces Tecum, 406 F.Supp. 381, 386 (S.D.N.Y. 1975).

22. United States v. Tellier, 255 F.2d 441, 447–48 (2d Cir.), cert. denied, 358 U.S. 821, 79 S.Ct. 33, 3 L.Ed.2d 62 (1958)(if client intended disclosure to third parties, privilege is lost even if such disclosure does not in fact occur). See also Colton v. United States, 306 F.2d 633, 638 (2d Cir.1962), cert. denied, 371 U.S. 951, 83 S.Ct. 505, 9 L.Ed.2d 499 (1963)(information to be included in tax return); United States v. White, 950 F.2d 426, 430 (7th Cir.1991)(information to be incorporated into bankruptcy petition); United States v. Rivera, 837 F.Supp. 565, 569–70 (S.D.N.Y.1993)(information to be conveyed to INS in application for amnesty). The mere possibility of third-party disclosure, however, will not vitiate the privilege for undisclosed material. In re Grand Jury Subpoena Duces Tecum Dated September 15, 1983, 731 F.2d 1032, 1037 (2d Cir.1984)(drafts of documents "the final version of which might eventually be sent to other persons" retained privilege because no showing was made that confidentiality was not intended at time of original communication).

23. McCormick § 91.

others whose expertise may be "necessary, or at least highly useful, for the effective consultation between the client and the lawyer."[24]

Another instance in which the presence of "third parties" is tolerated is that of joint representation of two clients by one lawyer with respect to a legal matter of common interest. Such communications between the lawyer and joint clients are protected from disclosure to outsiders,[25] but they are not protected in subsequent litigation between the two clients relating to the matter of common interest.[26] First cousin to the joint-client rule is the "joint defense" doctrine in which two or more parties, represented by separate lawyers, share a common interest in pending litigation. The clients' separate attorney-client communications may be shared among one another without loss of the privilege as against third parties.[27]

It is well settled that corporations may claim the benefits of the attorney-client privilege.[28] Furthermore, in *Upjohn Co. v. United*

24. United States v. Kovel, 296 F.2d 918, 922 (2d Cir.1961)(participation of accountant retained by attorney may be analogous to an interpreter). See also In re Grand Jury Proceedings Under Seal, 947 F.2d 1188, 1191 (4th Cir.1991)(communications by client with his own accountant may be protected by attorney-client privilege if made immediately prior to consultation with attorney and if communications were intended to aid in the obtaining of legal advice); United States v. Schwimmer, 892 F.2d 237, 244 (2d Cir.1989), cert. denied, 502 U.S. 810, 112 S.Ct. 55, 116 L.Ed.2d 31 (1991) (lawyer-retained accountant may assist multiple lawyers and clients in joint defense effort). But see In re J.K. Lasser & Co., 448 F.Supp. 103, 108 (E.D.N.Y.1978)(Kovel principle inapplicable when lawyer's use of accountant does not involve highly technical accounting issues).

25. In re Grand Jury Subpoena Duces Tecum Dated November 16, 1974, 406 F.Supp. 381, 386 (S.D.N.Y.1975)("it may reasonably be inferred that resultant disclosures are intended to be insulated from exposure beyond the confines of the group"). See also In re Grand Jury Proceedings (Auclair), 961 F.2d 65, 70 (5th Cir.1992)(group of persons may consult attorney without loss of privilege until such time as attorney declines joint representation due to conflict of interests).

26. In re Grand Jury Subpoena Duces Tecum Dated November 16, 1974, 406 F.Supp. 381, 386 (S.D.N.Y.1975)("what is divulged by and to the clients present at such a meeting cannot be deemed to be confidential inter sese"); Valente v. Pepsico, Inc., 68 F.R.D. 361, 368 (D.Del.1975)(in subsequent litigation, it would be unfair for one client to be favored over the other with respect to control over the attorney-client privilege). But see Eureka Investment Corp. v. Chicago Title Insurance Co., 743 F.2d 932, 937–38 (D.C.Cir.1984)(general rule recognized, but court held that privilege remained intact in subsequent litigation between former joint clients with respect to matters as to which their interests were adverse during the period of joint representation; counsel's improper representation of conflicting interests did not vitiate clients' expectations of confidentiality).

27. United States v. Schwimmer, 892 F.2d 237, 243–44 (2d Cir.1989), cert. denied, 502 U.S. 810, 112 S.Ct. 55, 116 L.Ed.2d 31 (1991)(also called the "common interest" rule). The Schwimmer court noted that it is not necessary for the lawyer who is representing the communicating party to be present when the other party's attorney receives the communication. Id. at 244.

28. Commodity Futures Trading Comm'n v. Weintraub, 471 U.S. 343, 348, 105 S.Ct. 1986, 1990, 85 L.Ed.2d 372, 378 (1985). It has been held that a corporation's attorney-client privilege does not yield even if the adversary is unable to obtain facts from individual corporate officers who assert their personal privilege against self-incrimination. Admiral Insurance Co. v. United States District Court, 881 F.2d 1486, 1494 (9th Cir.1989).

The unique problems raised by the applicability of the attorney-client privilege in the corporate context are analyzed in Alexander, "The Corporate Attorney–Client Privilege: A Study of the Participants," 63 St.John's L.Rev. 191, 220–28, 286–305, 319–25, 325–413 (1989)(ethical responsibilities of counsel, identification of employees whose communications are within the privilege, maintaining confidentiality within the corporation, mixed business and legal com-

§ 501.2 PRIVILEGES Ch. 5

States,[29] the Supreme Court held that the employees of a corporation whose communications with counsel qualify for the corporation's privilege are not limited to those in the corporate "control group."[30] Communications at lower levels of the corporate hierarchy are also eligible.[31] The Court, however, did not adopt any particular formula for determining precisely which corporate spokespersons should be covered by the attorney-client privilege.[32] The Court simply concluded that application of the privilege under the circumstances in *Upjohn* would be "[c]onsistent with the underlying purposes of the attorney-client privilege."[33] It is widely assumed, however, that the appropriate standard is a "subject matter" test that focuses on whether the corporate employee, of whatever rank, is communicating with the corporation's lawyer concerning the subject matter of her corporate responsibilities.[34]

munications, the "good cause" exception in shareholder actions, and potential qualified approach to the corporate attorney-client privilege).

29. 449 U.S. 383, 101 S.Ct. 677, 66 L.Ed.2d 584 (1981).

30. A member of the control group is someone who "is in a position to control or * * * to take a substantial part in a decision about any action which the corporation may take upon the advice of the attorney." City of Philadelphia v. Westinghouse Electric Corp., 210 F.Supp. 483, 485 (E.D.Pa. 1962), mandamus denied sub nom. General Electric Co. v. Kirkpatrick, 312 F.2d 742 (3d Cir.), cert. denied, 372 U.S. 943, 83 S.Ct. 937, 9 L.Ed.2d 969 (1963).

31. Upjohn Co. v. United States, 449 U.S. 383, 390–91, 101 S.Ct. 677, 683–84, 66 L.Ed.2d 584, 592 (1981). The Court reasoned that the control group standard frustrates counsel's ability to provide fully informed legal advice, which is needed to foster corporate compliance with the law. Id. at 390–93, 101 S.Ct. at 683–85, 66 L.Ed.2d at 592–93.

The Court was dealing with the privilege only as applied in federal litigation based on federal law. In diversity actions, Rule 501 of the Federal Rules of Evidence directs federal courts, subject to certain exceptions, to apply privileges in accordance with the relevant state law. See § 500.2 supra. For example, in Favala v. Cumberland Engineering Co., 17 F.3d 987, 989–90 (7th Cir. 1994), a federal district court in a diversity action in Illinois applied the control group standard, which is the rule applied by Illinois state courts.

32. The most that the Court would make clear was that the control group test was unacceptable as a basis for "govern[ing] the development of the law in this area." Upjohn Co. v. United States, 449 U.S. 383, 397, 101 S.Ct. 677, 686, 66 L.Ed.2d 584, 596 (1981).

33. Id. at 395, 101 S.Ct. at 685, 66 L.Ed.2d at 595. The Court found the following factors to be determinative: mid-level and lower-level employees had communicated with the corporation's counsel acting as such; they did so at the direction of their corporate superiors; the corporation was seeking legal advice; the necessary information for such advice was available only from such lower-echelon employees; the matters communicated were within the scope of the employees' corporate duties; the employees were aware that the purpose of the communications was to aid the corporation in obtaining legal advice; and confidentiality was requested and maintained. Id. at 394–95, 101 S.Ct. at 685, 66 L.Ed.2d at 594–95.

34. See, e.g., Diversified Industries, Inc. v. Meredith, 572 F.2d 596, 609 (8th Cir. 1977)(en banc). See also In re Bieter Company, 16 F.3d 929, 935–40 (8th Cir.1994)(subject matter test applied to a partnership; communications of counsel with an independent consultant for the partnership, under the circumstances, were held to be within the scope of the organization's privilege).

In a concurring opinion in Upjohn, Chief Justice Burger urged the adoption of his own version of a "subject matter" test: "[A]s a general rule, a communication is privileged at least when, as here, an employee or former employee speaks at the direction of the management with an attorney regarding conduct or proposed conduct within the scope of employment. The attorney must be one authorized by the management to inquire into the subject and must be seeking information to assist counsel in performing any of the following functions: (a) evaluating whether the employee's conduct has bound or would bind the corporation; (b) assessing the legal consequences, if any, of that conduct; or (c) formulating appropriate legal responses to

234

Federal courts have developed an exception to the corporate attorney-client privilege, however, in shareholder actions against officers and directors based on wrongdoing that is injurious to the shareholders' interests. *Garner v. Wolfinbarger*[35] held that in such actions, the privilege for communications between management and the corporation's lawyers is "subject to the right of stockholders to show cause why it should not be invoked in the particular instance."[36] *Garner* thus introduced the principle that plaintiff's status as a beneficiary of fiduciary obligations owed by the corporation's management is a factor in determining whether the privilege should apply.[37] Some courts have extended the "good cause" exception to other fiduciary relationships.[38]

actions that have been or may be taken by others with respect to that conduct." Upjohn Co. v. United States, 449 U.S. 383, 402–03, 101 S.Ct. 677, 689, 66 L.Ed.2d 584, 599–600 (1981)(Burger, C.J., concurring). Some adherents of the subject matter test would recognize privilege regardless of whether the corporate employees spoke at the direction of their superiors. See, e.g., Bruce v. Christian, 113 F.R.D. 554, 560 (S.D.N.Y.1986). But see Cuno, Inc. v. Pall Corp. 121 F.R.D. 198, 203 (E.D.N.Y.1988)(direction of superiors required).

35. 430 F.2d 1093 (5th Cir.1970), cert. denied, 401 U.S. 974, 91 S.Ct. 1191, 28 L.Ed.2d 323 (1971).

36. Id. at 1103–04. The court identified several factors to be considered in determining whether good cause exists for denial of the privilege in shareholder actions:

the number of shareholders and the percentage of stock they represent; the bona fides of the shareholders; the nature of the shareholders' claim and whether it is obviously colorable; the apparent necessity or desirability of the shareholders having the information and the availability of it from other sources; whether, if the shareholders' claim is of wrongful action by the corporation, it is of action criminal, or illegal but not criminal, or of doubtful legality; whether the communication related to past or to prospective actions; whether the communication is of advice concerning the litigation itself; the extent to which the communication is identified versus the extent to which the shareholders are blindly fishing; the risk of revelation of trade secrets or other information in whose confidentiality the corporation has an interest for independent reasons.

37. Id. at 1101–02. The Garner doctrine has been recognized as valid in both derivative actions and class actions. Fausek v. White, 965 F.2d 126, 129–33 (6th Cir.), cert. denied, ___ U.S. ___, 113 S.Ct. 814, 121 L.Ed.2d 686 (1992); In re Bairnco Corp. Securities Litigation, 148 F.R.D. 91, 98–99 (S.D.N.Y.1993); Cohen v. Uniroyal, Inc., 80 F.R.D. 480, 482–85 (E.D.Pa.1978); Panter v. Marshall Field & Co., 80 F.R.D. 718, 722–24 (N.D.Ill.1978); Valente v. Pepsico, Inc., 68 F.R.D. 361, 369–70 (D.Del. 1975).

Application of the good cause test, however, does not invariably result in compelled disclosure. See, e.g., Ward v. Succession of Freeman, 854 F.2d 780, 784–85 (5th Cir. 1988), cert. denied, 490 U.S. 1065, 109 S.Ct. 2064, 104 L.Ed.2d 629 (1989)(good cause lacking because transaction sued upon—stock redemption—involved inherent adversity between shareholders and management from outset, plaintiffs' aggregate stockholdings were less than 4%, and plaintiffs had made no attempt to obtain same information from other sources); Moskowitz v. Lopp, 128 F.R.D. 624, 636–37 (E.D.Pa.1989) (Garner inapplicable to communications made prior to plaintiff's purchase of stock); In re LTV Securities Litigation, 89 F.R.D. 595, 607–08 (N.D.Tex.1981)(communications at issue concerned preparation for defense of the shareholder litigation itself).

Furthermore, acceptance of Garner has not been universal. See Weil v. Investment/Indicators Research & Management, Inc., 647 F.2d 18, 23 (9th Cir.1981)(Garner rationale questioned when shareholders sue for their own benefit rather than solely on behalf of corporation); Shirvani v. Capital Investing Corp., 112 F.R.D. 389, 390–91 (D.Conn.1986)(rejection of Garner).

38. Nellis v. Air Line Pilots Ass'n, 144 F.R.D. 68, 70–71 (E.D.Va.1992) (union and its members); Helt v. Metropolitan District Comm'n, 113 F.R.D. 7, 9–11 (D.Conn.1986)(pension fund trustee and beneficiaries); Quintel Corp. N.V. v. Citibank, N.A., 567 F.Supp. 1357, 1363 (S.D.N.Y.1983) (investment adviser for purchaser in real estate acquisition). But see Colocotronis Tanker Securities Litigation, 449 F.Supp. 828, 833–34 (S.D.N.Y.1978)(no fiduciary relationship existed between lead

Federal courts have also made it clear that the corporation's privilege generally belongs only to the corporate client—not to the officers or employees who communicated with counsel on behalf of the corporation.[39] Thus, the corporation, despite the objections of the individual employee whose communications are involved, has the power to waive its privilege and permit disclosure to outsiders.[40] This point was underscored by the Supreme Court in *Commodity Futures Trading Commission v. Weintraub*,[41] in which a corporation's trustee in bankruptcy was held entitled to waive the privilege for management's pre-bankruptcy communications with counsel.[42] An individual employee may be able to preclude waiver by the corporation, however, upon a showing that the attorney had undertaken joint representation of both the corporation and the employee.[43]

Waiver of the attorney-client privilege—defined as "voluntary disclosure by the client to a third party"[44]—may occur in a variety of

lending bank and other banks that entered into participation agreements with lead bank). Some courts have held that the privilege simply does not apply in actions by beneficiaries against pension fund trustees. United States v. Evans, 796 F.2d 264, 265–66 (9th Cir.1986); Washington–Baltimore Newspaper Guild Local 35 v. Washington Star Co., 543 F.Supp. 906, 909–10 (D.D.C. 1982). See also Wildbur v. ARCO Chemical Co., 974 F.2d 631, 645–46 (5th Cir.1992)(no privilege for pension plan administrator's pre-litigation attorney-client communications, but work product immunity applies to such communications after suit has been filed).

39. In re Bevill, Bresler & Schulman Asset Management Corp., 805 F.2d 120, 124–25 (3d Cir.1986); In re Grand Jury Subpoenas Duces Tecum, 798 F.2d 32, 34 (2d Cir.1986); United States v. Keplinger, 776 F.2d 678, 699–701 (7th Cir.1985), cert. denied, 476 U.S. 1183, 106 S.Ct. 2919, 91 L.Ed.2d 548 (1986).

40. See, e.g., In re Grand Jury Proceedings (Jackier), 434 F.Supp. 648, 650 (E.D.Mich.1977), aff'd, 570 F.2d 562 (6th Cir.1978).

41. 471 U.S. 343, 105 S.Ct. 1986, 85 L.Ed.2d 372 (1985).

42. Id. at 349, 105 S.Ct. at 1991, 85 L.Ed.2d at 378–79 ("Displaced managers may not assert the privilege over the wishes of current managers, even as to statements that the former might have made to counsel concerning matters within the scope of their corporate duties."). See also Polycast Technology Corp. v. Uniroyal Inc., 125 F.R.D. 47, 49 (S.D.N.Y.1989)(control over privilege of divested subsidiary passes to new managers and owners); United States v. De Lillo, 448 F.Supp. 840, 841–43 (E.D.N.Y.1978)(chairman and former trustee of union pension fund cannot prevent waiver of privilege by current board of trustees).

43. SEC v. Forma, 117 F.R.D. 516, 522 (S.D.N.Y.1987); In re Grand Jury Proceedings (Jackier), 434 F.Supp. 648, 650 (E.D.Mich.1977), aff'd, 570 F.2d 562 (6th Cir.1978). Even in the absence of an express undertaking of joint representation, the employee may lay claim to privilege for her communications with counsel if the communications were made while the employee was attempting to become a personal client, In re Bevill, Bresler & Schulman Asset Management Corp., 805 F.2d 120, 124 n.1 (3d Cir.1986), or the employee reasonably believed that counsel was providing personal representation, Wylie v. Marley Co., 891 F.2d 1463, 1471–72 (10th Cir. 1989).

44. In re Sealed Case, 676 F.2d 793, 809 (D.C.Cir.1982). The attorney may possess implied authority to waive privilege on the client's behalf. In re von Bulow, 828 F.2d 94, 100–01 (2d Cir.1987). If disclosure of privileged communications is compelled by a court, there is no waiver with respect to subsequent litigation because waiver requires a voluntary act. Ward v. Succession of Freeman, 854 F.2d 780, 788–89 (5th Cir. 1988), cert. denied, 490 U.S. 1065, 109 S.Ct. 2064, 104 L.Ed.2d 629 (1989). See also Proposed Federal Rule of Evidence 512:

Rule 512. Privileged Matter Disclosed Under Compulsion or Without Opportunity to Claim Privilege [Not Enacted]

Evidence of a statement or other disclosure of privileged matter is not admissi-

circumstances. Examples include testimony by the client revealing the contents of the communication;[45] disclosure of the communication to third parties;[46] reliance upon counsel's advice in support of the client's claim or defense on the merits;[47] inadvertent production of privileged documents during pretrial discovery;[48] refreshing a witness's recollection with a privileged document during, and sometimes before, her testimony;[49] disclosure to government agencies in connection with regulatory investigations, thereby waiving the privilege as to third parties;[50] and carelessly leaving attorney-client documents in locations where third parties have access to them.[51]

Waiver will occasionally extend not only to the specific communication that was disclosed but also to all other attorney-client communica-

ble against the holder of the privilege if the disclosure was (a) compelled erroneously or (b) made without opportunity to claim the privilege.

45. United States v. Plache, 913 F.2d 1375, 1380 (9th Cir.1990).

46. In re von Bulow, 828 F.2d 94, 102 (2d Cir.1987)(conversations disclosed in book written by attorney); In re John Doe Corp., 675 F.2d 482, 488–89 (2d Cir.1982)(privileged documents shown to accountants for purpose of audit); In re Horowitz, 482 F.2d 72, 82 (2d Cir.), cert. denied, 414 U.S. 867, 94 S.Ct. 64, 38 L.Ed.2d 86 (1973)(files containing privileged documents were made available to accountants for business purposes).

47. Chevron Corp. v. Pennzoil Co., 974 F.2d 1156, 1162–63 (9th Cir.1992); Cruden v. Bank of New York, 957 F.2d 961, 972 (2d Cir.1992). Such waiver may also occur when a party's interjection of a particular legal or factual issue is deemed, as a matter of fairness, to entitle the adversary to inquire into the party's attorney-client communications. See, e.g., United States v. Bilzerian, 926 F.2d 1285, 1291–93 (2d Cir.), cert. denied, 502 U.S. 813, 112 S.Ct. 63, 116 L.Ed.2d 39 (1991). (defendant proposed to testify to good-faith belief in legality of his conduct). In general, however, a mere denial of the opponent's factual allegations of wrongful intent will not, standing alone, constitute an "advice-of-counsel" waiver. Cox v. Administrator United States Steel & Carnegie, 17 F.3d 1386, 1419 (11th Cir. 1994); Lorenz v. Valley Forge Insurance Co., 815 F.2d 1095, 1098 (7th Cir.1987).

48. Some courts apply a per se rule of waiver when privileged documents are inadvertently produced. See, e.g., In re Sealed Case, 877 F.2d 976, 980 (D.C.Cir.1989). Others apply a rule of discretion that takes into account such factors as the reasonableness of precautions taken to prevent disclosure, diligence in seeking to remedy the error, scope of discovery, extent of disclosure and considerations of fairness. See, e.g., Alldread v. City of Grenada, 988 F.2d 1425, 1433–35 (5th Cir.1993); Standard Chartered Bank v. Ayala International Holdings (U.S.) Inc., 111 F.R.D. 76, 85 (S.D.N.Y.1986); Lois Sportswear, U.S.A., Inc. v. Levi Strauss and Co., 104 F.R.D. 103, 105 (S.D.N.Y.1985).

49. Derderian v. Polaroid Corp., 121 F.R.D. 13, 15–16 (D.Mass.1988) (deponent's reliance upon privileged documents to refresh recollection prior to or during deposition may waive privilege, depending on circumstances); Leucadia, Inc. v. Reliance Insurance Co., 101 F.R.D. 674, 678–79 (S.D.N.Y.1983)(no waiver where, in preparation for deposition, executive looked at counsel's report but testimony did not appear to rely on report); Bailey v. Meister Brau, Inc., 57 F.R.D. 11, 13 (N.D.Ill.1972) (waiver as to documents used during deposition).

50. Westinghouse Electric Corp. v. Republic of the Philippines, 951 F.2d 1414, 1423–27 (3d Cir.1991). Cf. In re Steinhardt Partners, L.P., 9 F.3d 230, 233–36 (2d Cir.1993)(attorney work product). The rationale is that a client should not be able to "pick and choose" among its opponents. Permian Corp. v. United States, 665 F.2d 1214, 1221–22 (D.C.Cir.1981). But see Diversified Industries, Inc. v. Meredith, 572 F.2d 596, 611 (8th Cir.1977)(privilege should be preserved as to third parties in order to encourage voluntary cooperation with government regulatory efforts).

51. Suburban Sew 'N Sweep, Inc. v. Swiss–Bernina, Inc., 91 F.R.D. 254, 257–61 (N.D.Ill.1981)(papers left in trash); Matter of Victor, 422 F.Supp. 475, 476 (S.D.N.Y.1976)(papers left in public hallway).

tions relating to the same subject matter.[52] The extent to which a particular disclosure will result in such "subject matter waiver" is partly a function of the context in which the waiver occurs and its effect on the opposing party. The Second Circuit, for example, has held that subject matter waiver occurs only where the privilege-holder has made selective disclosure of privileged communications for some strategic advantage in litigation, thus prejudicing the opponent.[53]

Library References:

West's Key No. Digests, Witnesses ⚖197, 219(3).

§ 501.3 Work Product Immunities

a. In General

The work product immunity has its origins in the Supreme Court's 1947 decision in *Hickman v. Taylor*.[1] Following a tugboat accident, the owners of the tugboat hired a lawyer who interviewed several witnesses. In a wrongful death action against the owners, the plaintiff demanded pretrial discovery of the witnesses' statements and the lawyers' recollections thereof. The Court rejected the notion that the statements were protected by the attorney-client privilege but held that discovery was precluded nonetheless because the requested material constituted the "work product" of the attorney.[2] Such discovery, said the Court, would "[contravene] the public policy underlying the orderly prosecution and defense of legal claims."[3]

The *Hickman* Court reasoned that a lawyer should be able to perform her duties "with a certain degree of privacy, free from unnecessary intrusion by opposing parties and their counsel."[4] If trial preparation materials were available to the adversary upon demand, "much of

---

52. In re Sealed Case, 676 F.2d 793, 809 (D.C.Cir.1982). See 8 Wigmore § 2327 at 636 ("There is always also the objective consideration that when [the client's] conduct touches a certain point of disclosure, fairness requires that his privilege shall cease whether he intended that result or not. He cannot be allowed, after disclosing as much as he pleases, to withhold the remainder.").

53. In re von Bulow, 828 F.2d 94, 101–03 (2d Cir.1987)(lawyer's publication of book containing portions of confidential conversations with client did not constitute waiver as to balance of conversations in subsequent litigation: "[D]isclosures made in public rather than in court—even if selective—create no risk of legal prejudice until put in issue in the litigation by the privilege-holder."). See also Cox v. Administrator United States Steel & Carnegie, 17 F.3d 1386, 1417–18 (11th Cir.1994)(lawyer's limited disclosures in prior criminal proceeding did not result in implied waiver with respect to related, undisclosed communications because opponent failed to demonstrate unfairness or prejudice in subsequent civil litigation); United States v. Aronoff, 466 F.Supp. 855, 862–63 (S.D.N.Y.1979)(disclosure to prosecutors prior to indictment did not constitute waiver as to undisclosed communications because privilege-holder did not, by any affirmative act, put communications into issue in the actual prosecution).

§ 501.3

1. 329 U.S. 495, 67 S.Ct. 385, 91 L.Ed. 451 (1947).

2. Id. at 509–10, 67 S.Ct. at 393, 91 L.Ed. at 461–62.

3. Id. at 510, 67 S.Ct. at 393, 91 L.Ed. at 462. Subsequently, in United States v. Nobles, 422 U.S. 225, 95 S.Ct. 2160, 45 L.Ed.2d 141 (1975), the Court recognized the applicability of the work product doctrine in criminal cases, noting that "its role in assuring the proper functioning of the criminal justice system is even more vital" than in civil litigation. Id. at 238, 95 S.Ct. at 2170, 45 L.Ed.2d at 153.

4. 329 U.S. at 510, 67 S.Ct. at 393, 91 L.Ed. at 462.

what is now put down in writing would remain unwritten" and "[i]nefficiency, unfairness and sharp practices would inevitably develop in the giving of legal advice and in the preparation of cases for trial."[5]

Thus was born the work product immunity that has been codified in both New York State[6] and federal practice.[7] Whereas the purpose of the attorney-client privilege is to encourage clients to be candid in their communications with counsel, the work product immunity encourages lawyers to be diligent in their case preparation.[8]

b. New York

1. Civil Cases

In New York, the work product doctrine in civil cases is divided between two statutory provisions. First, CPLR 3101(c) gives the "work product of an attorney" an absolute exemption from discovery.[9] Because of its absolute nature, the immunity for attorney work product has been narrowly confined by courts to "those materials which are uniquely the product of a lawyer's learning and professional skills, such as materials which reflect his legal research, analysis, conclusions, legal theory or strategy."[10] A lawyer's recollections and notes of interviews with witnesses also fall within this category.[11] The work product immunity has been held applicable not only to material prepared for the litigation in progress but also to that which was prepared for prior litigation.[12]

The second type of work product immunity is described in CPLR 3101(d)(2) as "materials * * * prepared in anticipation of litigation or for trial by or for another party, or by or for that other party's

---

5. Id. at 511, 67 S.Ct. at 393–94, 91 L.Ed. at 462.

6. CPLR 3101(c) and (d); N.Y.Crim. Proc.Law § 240.10(2) and (3).

7. Fed.R.Civ.P. 26(b)(3) and (4); Fed. R.Crim.P. 16(a)(2) and (b)(2).

8. See In re Special September 1978 Grand Jury (II), 640 F.2d 49, 62 (7th Cir. 1980). In Hickman v. Taylor, 329 U.S. 495, 67 S.Ct. 385, 91 L.Ed. 451 (1947), the Supreme Court observed that "[p]roper preparation of a client's case demands that [the attorney] assemble information, sift what he considers to be the relevant from the irrelevant facts, prepare his legal theories and plan his legal strategy without undue and needless interference." Id. at 511, 67 S.Ct. at 393, 91 L.Ed. at 462.

9. Corcoran v. Peat, Marwick, Mitchell and Co., 151 A.D.2d 443, 542 N.Y.S.2d 642 (1st Dep't 1989). CPLR 3101(c) on its face does not require that the attorney's work product be prepared in anticipation of litigation in order to qualify for immunity, but such a requirement has been imposed by courts. See, e.g., Mahoney v. Staffa, 184 A.D.2d 886, 585 N.Y.S.2d 543 (3d Dep't), leave to appeal dismissed, 80 N.Y.2d 972, 591 N.Y.S.2d 140, 605 N.E.2d 876 (1992); Matter of Bekins Storage Co., 118 Misc.2d 173, 176–77, 460 N.Y.S.2d 684, 689–90 (Sup.Ct.N.Y.Co.1983), amended, 94 A.D.2d 643, 463 N.Y.S.2d 349, dismissal denied, 59 N.Y.2d 996, 466 N.Y.S.2d 682, 453 N.E.2d 1099, aff'd as modified on other grounds, 62 N.Y.2d 324, 476 N.Y.S.2d 806, 465 N.E.2d 345 (1984).

10. Hoffman v. Ro–San Manor, 73 A.D.2d 207, 211, 425 N.Y.S.2d 619, 622 (1st Dep't 1980). See also Bloss v. Ford Motor Co., 126 A.D.2d 804, 510 N.Y.S.2d 304 (3d Dep't 1987)(attorney's indexing of documents did not qualify as work product because uniquely legal skills were not required).

11. Corcoran v. Peat, Marwick, Mitchell and Co., 151 A.D.2d 443, 542 N.Y.S.2d 642 (1st Dep't 1989); People v. Marin, 86 A.D.2d 40, 448 N.Y.S.2d 748 (2d Dep't 1982).

12. Beasock v. Dioguardi Enterprises, Inc., 117 A.D.2d 1016, 499 N.Y.S.2d 560 (4th Dep't 1986). The rule may be different with respect to trial-preparation materials covered by the conditional immunity of CPLR 3101(d)(2). See, e.g., Milone v. General Motors Corp., 84 A.D.2d 921, 446 N.Y.S.2d 650 (4th Dep't 1981).

representative (including an attorney, consultant, surety, indemnitor, insurer or agent)." Unlike attorney work product, the trial-preparation materials encompassed by CPLR 3101(d)(2) are only conditionally immune from discovery. The immunity can be overcome "upon a showing that the party seeking discovery has substantial need of the materials in the preparation of the case and is unable without undue hardship to obtain the substantial equivalent of the materials by other means."[13] A statement obtained from a witness might be subject to discovery, for example, if the witness dies after giving the statement and the adversary cannot otherwise obtain the facts.[14] Even if the substantial need/undue hardship showing is made, however, "the court shall protect against disclosure of the mental impressions, conclusions, opinions or legal theories of an attorney or other representative of a party concerning the litigation."[15] In other words, redaction may be required for those portions of the material that are in the nature of analytical work product.

Courts have held that materials must be prepared solely for litigation in order to qualify for the immunity of CPLR 3101(d)(2).[16] Thus, investigatory reports that are motivated both by potential litigation and business considerations are not protected from discovery.[17] This has caused something of a quandary in the case of materials prepared by a casualty insurer while investigating a claim for a loss submitted by its insured. Inasmuch as claims evaluation is part of such an insurer's regular business, at what point, if any, should the investigatory activity be treated as having been conducted solely in anticipation of litigation?

---

13. CPLR 3101(d)(2).

14. See Barton v. Diesel Construction Co., 47 A.D.2d 729, 365 N.Y.S.2d 197 (1st Dep't 1975). See also Gaglia v. Wells, 112 A.D.2d 138, 490 N.Y.S.2d 829 (2d Dep't 1985)(defendant's statement to liability insurer was discoverable based upon showing that defendant could no longer recall accident and plaintiff suffered from amnesia); Barber v. Town of Northumberland, 88 A.D.2d 712, 451 N.Y.S.2d 291 (3d Dep't 1982) (photographs of accident scene taken by counsel shortly after accident could not be duplicated); Zimmerman v. Nassau Hospital, 76 A.D.2d 921, 429 N.Y.S.2d 262 (2d Dep't 1980)(where tests conducted for litigation purposes can no longer be duplicated, test reports are subject to discovery). But see Rosado v. Mercedes–Benz of North America, Inc., 90 A.D.2d 515, 454 N.Y.S.2d 759 (2d Dep't 1982)(plaintiff failed to make sufficient showing for discovery of test report where plaintiff had had ample time to conduct her own test prior to destruction of item to be tested).

15. CPLR 3101(d)(2). See, e.g., Matter of Lenny McN., 183 A.D.2d 627, 584 N.Y.S.2d 17 (1st Dep't 1992)(social worker who was retained by law guardian for infant in Family Court proceeding qualified as "representative" of party for purpose of heightened protection for opinion work product).

16. See, e.g., Carden v. Allstate Insurance Co., 105 A.D.2d 1048, 1049, 483 N.Y.S.2d 486, 487 (3d Dep't 1984). See also Hoenig v. Westphal, 52 N.Y.2d 605, 609, 439 N.Y.S.2d 831, 832, 422 N.E.2d 491, 492 (1981)(party claiming immunity under CPLR 3101(d) failed to demonstrate that reports of treating physicians concerning medical history, diagnosis and treatment were "material prepared primarily, if not solely, for litigation"); J.R. Stevenson Corp. v. Dormitory Authority of the State of New York, 112 A.D.2d 113, 119, 492 N.Y.S.2d 385, 390 (1st Dep't 1985)(audit report of company's expenditures was not immune because it was made in ordinary course of business).

17. See, e.g., Graf v. Aldrich, 94 A.D.2d 823, 463 N.Y.S.2d 124 (3d Dep't 1983)(plaintiff's report to treating physician was made for litigation purposes and to keep doctor abreast of plaintiff's condition); Carlo v. Queens Transit Corp., 76 A.D.2d 824, 428 N.Y.S.2d 298 (2d Dep't 1980) (multi-purpose report motivated both by litigation and considerations of efficiency and personnel discipline).

Courts have ruled that the immunity of CPLR 3101(d)(2) attaches only after the insurer has made a firm decision to reject the insured's claim.[18] With respect to materials prepared by a liability insurer, most courts have held that immunity attaches at the outset of the insurer's investigation of an accident in which its insured may be potentially liable.[19]

Statutory exceptions remove certain items from the work-product and trial-preparation immunities. A party to the litigation, for example, is entitled to obtain a copy of any statement he may have given to the opponent.[20] Accident reports prepared in the regular course of business operations are also subject to disclosure as a matter of right,[21] even if such reports were prepared in anticipation of litigation.[22] Another statutory exception requires disclosure of any films, photographs, video tapes or audio tapes, including transcripts or memoranda thereof, concerning any person whose conduct is involved in the litigation.[23]

---

18. Landmark Insurance Co. v. Beau Rivage Restaurant, Inc., 121 A.D.2d 98, 509 N.Y.S.2d 819 (2d Dep't 1986); Westhampton Adult Home, Inc. v. National Union Fire Insurance Co. of Pittsburgh, Pa., 105 A.D.2d 627, 481 N.Y.S.2d 358 (1st Dep't 1984); Mold Maintenance Service v. General Accident Fire and Life Assurance Corp., Ltd., 56 A.D.2d 134, 392 N.Y.S.2d 104 (4th Dep't 1977).

19. Lamberson v. Village of Allegany, 158 A.D.2d 943, 943, 551 N.Y.S.2d 104, 105 (4th Dep't 1990)(" '[O]nce an accident has arisen there is little or nothing that the [liability] insurer or its employees do with respect to an accident report except in contemplation and in preparation for eventual litigation or for a settlement which may avoid the necessity of litigation,' " quoting Kandel v. Tocher, 22 A.D.2d 513, 515, 256 N.Y.S.2d 898, 900 (1st Dep't 1965)). See also Sullivan v. Smith, 198 A.D.2d 749, 604 N.Y.S.2d 304 (3d Dep't 1993); James v. Metro North Commuter R.R., 166 A.D.2d 266, 560 N.Y.S.2d 459 (1st Dep't 1990); Vernet v. Gilbert, 90 A.D.2d 846, 456 N.Y.S.2d 93 (2d Dep't 1982). But see McKie v. Taylor, 146 A.D.2d 921, 536 N.Y.S.2d 893 (3d Dep't 1989)(insufficient showing was made that statements made by insured to liability insurer immediately after accident were motivated solely by litigation concerns).

20. CPLR 3101(e). See Sands v. News America Publishing Inc., 161 A.D.2d 30, 40–42, 560 N.Y.S.2d 416, 422–24 (1st Dep't 1990).

21. CPLR 3101(g). That subdivision provides as follows:

> Except as is otherwise provided by law, in addition to any other matter which may be subject to disclosure, there shall be full disclosure of any written report of an accident prepared in the regular course of business operations or practices of any person, firm, corporation, association or other public or private entity, unless prepared by a police or peace officer for a criminal investigation or prosecution and disclosure would interfere with a criminal investigation or prosecution.

22. Courts have held that subdivision (g), which was added to CPLR 3101 after the trial-preparation immunity of subdivision (d)(2) was well-established, was intended to supersede subdivision (d)(2) with respect to accident reports prepared as part of the regular internal operations of a business, even if the sole motive was potential litigation. James v. Metro North Commuter R.R., 166 A.D.2d 266, 560 N.Y.S.2d 459 (1st Dep't 1990); Pataki v. Kiseda, 80 A.D.2d 100, 437 N.Y.S.2d 692 (2d Dep't 1981), appeal dismissed, 54 N.Y.2d 606, 443 N.Y.S.2d 1029, 427 N.E.2d 514 (1981). The immunity of subdivision (d)(2) is still available, however, for accident reports made to a liability insurer in anticipation of litigation. James v. Metro North Commuter R.R., supra; Gavigan v. Otis Elevator Co., 117 A.D.2d 941, 499 N.Y.S.2d 253 (3d Dep't 1986); Vernet v. Gilbert, 90 A.D.2d 846, 456 N.Y.S.2d 93 (2d Dep't 1982). See also Goldstein v. New York Daily News, 106 A.D.2d 323, 482 N.Y.S.2d 768 (1st Dep't 1984)(accident report prepared upon request of attorney); Williams v. Metropolitan Transportation Authority, 99 A.D.2d 530, 471 N.Y.S.2d 310 (2d Dep't 1984)(accident report prepared by independent investigator for self-insured defendant).

23. CPLR 3101(i). Disclosure must include out-takes, not merely the material that the party intends to use. Id. The statute expands upon the judge-made exception that was recognized in DiMichel v. South Buffalo Ry. Co., 80 N.Y.S.2d 184, 590 N.Y.S.2d 1, 604 N.E.2d 63 (1992), cert. denied sub nom., Poole v. Consolidated Rail

Information compiled by experts who are consulted for litigation purposes generally falls within the immunity for trial preparation material.[24] Special discovery rules apply, however, with respect to an expert that a party expects to call as an expert witness at trial. Four types of data about an expert witness are subject to mandatory disclosure upon demand: (1) the expert's identity; (2) the subject matter on which the expert is expected to testify; (3) the substance of the facts and opinions on which the expert is expected to testify and the grounds for each opinion; and (4) the expert's qualifications.[25] The report of an expert who will not testify at trial is treated like any other trial-preparation material.[26]

The identity of ordinary witnesses is deemed neither attorney work product nor material prepared in anticipation of litigation and is therefore discoverable.[27]

2. Criminal Cases

In criminal proceedings, "attorneys' work product" is exempt from the material that must be disclosed pursuant to the discovery provisions of the Criminal Procedure Law.[28] The immunity for attorney work product in CPLR 3101(c) has also been held applicable in criminal

Corp., ___ U.S. ___, 114 S.Ct. 68, 126 L.Ed.2d 37 (1993), which held that plaintiffs in personal injury actions are entitled to discovery of surveillance films made by defendant's investigators. Although such materials are made in anticipation of litigation, a substantial need for pretrial discovery was said to exist because of the ease with which they may be altered, thus creating a risk of inadequate authentication and tainted trials. Id. at 196–97, 590 N.Y.S.2d at 6–7, 604 N.E.2d at 68–69. The court noted, however, the propriety of an order delaying discovery of the films until after plaintiff has given a deposition, thus minimizing the potential for tailored testimony. Id. at 197, 590 N.Y.S.2d at 6, 604 N.E.2d at 68.

24. Santariga v. McCann, 161 A.D.2d 320, 555 N.Y.S.2d 309 (1st Dep't 1990).

25. CPLR 3101(d)(1)(i). Any additional disclosure concerning trial experts generally requires a showing of special circumstances. CPLR 3101(d)(1)(iii). See, e.g., Rosario v. General Motors Corp., 148 A.D.2d 108, 109, 543 N.Y.S.2d 974, 974 (1st Dep't 1989)(destruction of physical evidence after one side's expert witness has inspected it but before adversary's expert has examined it "per se warrants disclosure directly from the expert concerning the facts surrounding his inspection").

The statute allows the identity of trial experts (but not the balance of the data described in the text) to be withheld in medical, dental and podiatric malpractice actions, presumably because of the fear that peer pressure might be brought to bear on experts in such cases to discourage their testimony. CPLR 3101(d)(1)(i).

26. Santariga v. McCann, 161 A.D.2d 320, 555 N.Y.S.2d 309 (1st Dep't 1990) (report of radiologist, a non-testifying expert consulted in preparation for defense of wrongful death action, was exempt under CPLR 3101(d)(2); plaintiff failed to demonstrate substantial need to overcome immunity). To the extent immunity for the report of a non-testifying expert is overcome based on a showing of substantial need and hardship, typically only the facts contained in the report, not the expert's opinion, will be discoverable. See e.g., Lundell v. Ford Motor Co., 120 A.D.2d 575, 502 N.Y.S.2d 63 (2d Dep't 1986).

27. Bombard v. County of Albany, 94 A.D.2d 910, 463 N.Y.S.2d 633 (3d Dep't 1983); Hoffman v. Ro–San Manor, 73 A.D.2d 207, 425 N.Y.S.2d 619 (1st Dep't 1980); O'Connor v. Larson, 74 A.D.2d 734, 425 N.Y.S.2d 702 (4th Dep't 1980).

28. Article 240 of the New York Criminal Procedure Law governs pretrial discovery in criminal proceedings. "Attorneys' work product" is defined as "the opinions, theories or conclusions of the prosecutor, defense counsel or members of their legal staffs." N.Y.Crim.Proc.Law § 240.10(2). Such work product is generally excluded from the material that a prosecutor must disclose, id. § 240.20, and from that which defense counsel must disclose, id. § 240.30.

cases.[29] The *Rosario* rule,[30] however, requires both prosecutors and defense counsel to disclose prior written or recorded statements of witnesses they intend to call[31] and any notes or memoranda summarizing the statements of such witnesses.[32]

3. Waiver

Waiver of the work product immunities may occur if the protected materials are disclosed to an adversary or the circumstances increase the opportunity for an adversary to obtain the materials.[33] Inadvertent disclosures in pretrial document production, therefore, can result in a waiver.[34] Immunity may also be lost if material prepared in anticipation

---

29. See People v. Edney, 39 N.Y.2d 620, 385 N.Y.S.2d 23, 350 N.E.2d 400 (1976)(in dicta, court observed that information disclosed by defense counsel to psychiatrist to aid in preparation of insanity defense would fall within work product immunity); People v. Marin, 86 A.D.2d 40, 448 N.Y.S.2d 748 (2d Dep't 1982)(work product immunity for lawyer's notes of interviews with witnesses took precedence over defendant's sixth amendment right of compulsory process).

The immunity for material prepared in anticipation of litigation (CPLR 3101(d)(2)), however, has been held to be unavailable as a basis for quashing a grand jury subpoena. Application to Quash a Subpoena Duces Tecum in Grand Jury Proceedings, 56 N.Y.2d 348, 452 N.Y.S.2d 361, 437 N.E.2d 1118 (1982).

30. People v. Rosario, 9 N.Y.2d 286, 213 N.Y.S.2d 448, 173 N.E.2d 881, cert. denied, 368 U.S. 866, 82 S.Ct. 117, 7 L.Ed.2d 64 (1961)(prosecution must give defendant, for use during cross-examination, any written or recorded statements of a prosecution witness relating to subject matter of witness's testimony).

31. Rosario was codified and expanded by § 240.45 of the Criminal Procedure Law to impose disclosure obligations on both prosecutors and defendants. The relevant portions of § 240.45 provide:

1. After the jury has been sworn and before the prosecutor's opening address, or in the case of a single judge trial after commencement and before submission of evidence, the prosecutor shall, subject to a protective order, make available to the defendant:

(a) Any written or recorded statement, including any testimony before a grand jury and an examination videotaped pursuant to section 190.32 of this chapter, made by a person whom the prosecutor intends to call as a witness at trial, and which relates to the subject matter of the witness's testimony;

* * *

Reports of physical or mental examinations and scientific tests or experiments may also be subject to discovery. N.Y.Crim.Proc. Law §§ 240.20(1)(c), 240.30(1)(a).

32. See People v. Consolazio, 40 N.Y.2d 446, 387 N.Y.S.2d 62, 354 N.E.2d 801 (1976), cert. denied, 433 U.S. 914, 97 S.Ct. 2986, 53 L.Ed.2d 1100 (1977)(work sheet compiled by prosecutor containing notes summarizing witness's statements); People v. Allen, 104 Misc.2d 136, 427 N.Y.S.2d 698 (Sup.Ct.Westchester Co.1980)(defense counsel's notes of witness's responses to questions). But see People v. Roberts, 178 A.D.2d 622, 577 N.Y.S.2d 672 (2d Dep't 1991), appeal denied, 79 N.Y.2d 952, 583 N.Y.S.2d 206, 592 N.E.2d 814 (1992)(prosecutor's notes made during interview were not subject to disclosure to extent they did not summarize witness's statements).

33. Will of Pretino, 150 Misc.2d 371, 567 N.Y.S.2d 1009 (Surr.Ct.Nassau Co.1991)(rationale of work product immunity is to protect against intrusion by opponent; disclosure to party or person with common interest, therefore, does not constitute waiver). See also Niagara Mohawk Power Corp. v. Stone & Webster Engineering Corp., 125 F.R.D. 578, 590 (N.D.N.Y. 1989)("[W]ork product protection is waived when protected materials are disclosed in a manner which is either inconsistent with maintaining secrecy against opponents or substantially increases the opportunity for a potential adversary to obtain the protected information"). Cf. § 501.1 supra, at note 88 (leaving papers protected by attorney-client privilege in location where third party has access).

34. See, e.g., Bras v. Atlas Construction Corp., 153 A.D.2d 914, 545 N.Y.S.2d 723 (2d Dep't 1989)(waiver based on failure to exercise due diligence in withholding documents protected by CPLR 3101(d)(2)). But see John Blair Communications, Inc. v. Reliance Capital Group, L.P., 182 A.D.2d 578, 582 N.Y.S.2d 720 (1st Dep't 1992)(no waiver where party who produced protected doc-

of litigation is used by a witness to refresh her recollection prior to or during the giving of testimony.[35] The rationale is that such disclosure is necessary, in fairness, to ensure meaningful cross-examination.[36]

c. Federal

In federal practice, a qualified immunity precludes discovery of materials prepared in anticipation of litigation in both civil and criminal proceedings.[37] As codified in Rule 26(b)(3) of the Federal Rules of Civil Procedure,[38] essentially two types of materials fall within the concept: "ordinary" work product and "opinion" work product. The former may include such items as statements of witnesses, investigative reports, photographs, diagrams and charts.[39] Opinion work product constitutes a more narrow field consisting of "mental impressions, conclusions, opinions or legal theories" about the litigation.[40]

---

uments had exercised reasonable precautions and promptly objected, and no prejudice to adversary was shown).

35. In the following cases, the immunity for material prepared in anticipation of litigation (CPLR 3101(d)(2)), was held to have been waived where the witness reviewed the material prior to being deposed: Rouse v. County of Greene, 115 A.D.2d 162, 495 N.Y.S.2d 496 (3d Dep't 1985); Herrmann v. General Tire and Rubber Co., 79 A.D.2d 955, 435 N.Y.S.2d 14 (1st Dep't 1981); Doxtator v. Swarthout, 38 A.D.2d 782, 328 N.Y.S.2d 150 (4th Dep't 1972).

The immunity for attorney work product (CPLR 3101(c)) was deemed waived in Grieco v. Cunningham, 128 A.D.2d 502, 512 N.Y.S.2d 432 (2d Dep't 1987), but not in Geffers v. Canisteo Central School District, 105 A.D.2d 1062, 482 N.Y.S.2d 635 (4th Dep't 1984). Attorney work product may be less susceptible to waiver, depending on the circumstances, due to the absolute nature of the immunity. See also Matter of Lenny McN., 183 A.D.2d 627, 584 N.Y.S.2d 17 (1st Dep't 1992)(opinion work product of social worker retained by law guardian of infant not subject to disclosure in Family Court custodial litigation even though she used case file to prepare for testimony).

36. Doxtator v. Swarthout, 38 A.D.2d 782, 782, 328 N.Y.S.2d 150, 152 (4th Dep't 1972).

37. United States v. Nobles, 422 U.S. 225, 238, 95 S.Ct. 2160, 2170, 45 L.Ed.2d 141, 153 (1975); Matter of Grand Jury Subpoenas Dated October 22, 1991, and November 1, 1991, 959 F.2d 1158, 1166 (2d Cir.1992). The immunity is unavailable for materials prepared in the ordinary course of business. Redvanly v. NYNEX Corp., 152 F.R.D. 460, 464–65 (S.D.N.Y.1993) ("It follows naturally from the purpose behind work product protection that material is not deserving of protection unless it was 'prepared in anticipation of litigation or for trial' ").

Once the immunity attaches, it has been held to survive the specific litigation for which it was generated. Republic Gear Co. v. Borg–Warner Corp., 381 F.2d 551, 557 (2d Cir.1967).

38. The rule provides, in pertinent part:

Subject to the provisions of subdivision (b)(4) of this rule, a party may obtain discovery of documents and tangible things otherwise discoverable under subdivision (b)(1) of this rule and prepared in anticipation of litigation or for trial by or for another party or by or for that other party's representative (including the other party's attorney, consultant, surety, indemnitor, insurer, or agent) only upon a showing that the party seeking discovery has substantial need of the materials in the preparation of the party's case and that the party is unable without undue hardship to obtain the substantial equivalent of the materials by other means. In ordering discovery of such materials when the required showing has been made, the court shall protect against disclosure of the mental impressions, conclusions, opinions, or legal theories of an attorney or other representative of a party concerning the litigation.

39. See Note, "The Work Product Doctrine," 68 Cornell L.Rev. 760, 791–98 (1983).

40. See Fed.R.Civ.P. 26(b)(3)(in ordering discovery, court "shall protect against disclosure of the mental impressions, conclusions, opinions or legal theories" of attorney or other representative of party). See, e.g., Shelton v. American Motors Corp., 805 F.2d 1323, 1327–29 (8th Cir.1986)(counsel's awareness of whether certain documents of the client existed was

Ordinary work product can lose its immunity upon a showing by the adversary of substantial need of the materials and an inability without undue hardship to obtain substantially equivalent materials through other means.[41] A higher threshold must be met to overcome the immunity for opinion work product, but the precise standard has never been definitively established.[42] Some courts have required "extraordinary" need and hardship,[43] while others have held the protection to be absolute.[44]

Special rules govern work product immunity for information relating to experts retained by a party in connection with civil litigation. A substantial amount of data is subject to discovery if the party may call the expert to give expert testimony at trial.[45] Information concerning a

opinion work product because counsel would likely remember only those documents considered important to counsel's legal theory); Sporck v. Peil, 759 F.2d 312, 316 (3d Cir.), cert. denied, 474 U.S. 903, 106 S.Ct. 232, 88 L.Ed.2d 230 (1985)(deponent could not be required to identify documents reviewed at counsel's request because counsel's selection and compilation of such documents would reveal counsel's understanding of case and, therefore, constituted opinion work product); Al–Rowaishan Establishment Universal Trading & Agencies, Ltd. v. Beatrice Foods Co., 92 F.R.D. 779, 779–80 (S.D.N.Y.1982)(deposition digest containing margin notes by attorney). But see Matter of Grand Jury Subpoenas Dated October 22, 1991 and November 1, 1991, 959 F.2d 1158 (2d Cir.1992)(discovery of party's telephone records in lawyer's possession would not reveal the specific telephone calls considered relevant by lawyer).

41. Fed.R.Civ.P. 26(b)(3). See, e.g., In re Grand Jury Investigation, 599 F.2d 1224, 1231–33 (3d Cir.1979)(sufficient need shown for statements to counsel made by now-deceased witness); Ehrlich v. Howe, 848 F.Supp. 482, 492–93 (S.D.N.Y.1994)(substantial need due to witnesses' inability, at deposition, to recall key event).

42. The Supreme Court has indicated only that opinion work product "cannot be disclosed simply on a showing of substantial need and inability to obtain the equivalent without undue hardship." Upjohn Co. v. United States, 449 U.S. 383, 401, 101 S.Ct. 677, 688, 66 L.Ed.2d 584, 599 (1981).

43. See, e.g., In re Sealed Case, 676 F.2d 793, 809–10 (D.C.Cir.1982); In re Murphy, 560 F.2d 326, 336 (8th Cir.1977). It has been said that an attorney's memorandum containing her account of interviews of witnesses will "rarely" be discoverable because it will reveal her mental impressions. In re Grand Jury Investigation, 599 F.2d 1224, 1231 (3d Cir.1979). Another court observed that "as the work product of the attorney becomes less a matter of creative legal thought and more a mere recognition of observed fact, the work product becomes increasingly susceptible to discovery." Duplan Corp. v. Deering Milliken, Inc., 397 F.Supp. 1146, 1199–1200 (D.S.C.1974).

The qualified nature of opinion work product was recognized in Holmgren v. State Farm Mutual Automobile Insurance Co., 976 F.2d 573 (9th Cir.1992) (in insured's action against liability insurer for bad-faith conduct in settlement of claim against insured, opinion work product of insurer's adjuster was discoverable because his mental impressions were directly "at issue" and plaintiff's need was compelling).

44. See, e.g., Duplan Corp. v. Moulinage et Retorderie de Chavanoz, 509 F.2d 730, 734 (4th Cir.1974), cert. denied, 420 U.S. 997, 95 S.Ct. 1438, 43 L.Ed.2d 680 (1975).

45. Fed.R.Civ.P. 26(a)(2) was amended, effective December 1, 1993, to provide as follows:

(A) In addition to the disclosures required by paragraph (1), a party shall disclose to other parties the identity of any person who may be used at trial to present evidence under Rules 702, 703, or 705 of the Federal Rules of Evidence.

(B) Except as otherwise stipulated or directed by the court, this disclosure shall, with respect to a witness who is retained or specially employed to provide expert testimony in the case or whose duties as an employee of the party regularly involve giving expert testimony, be accompanied by a written report prepared and signed by the witness. The report shall contain a complete statement of all opinions to be expressed and the basis and reasons therefor; the data or other information considered by the witness in forming the opinions; any exhibits to be used as a summary of or support for the opinions; the qualifications of the wit-

nontestifying expert who is retained merely for consultative purposes, on the other hand, is generally nondiscoverable in the absence of special circumstances.[46]

In a criminal case, reports or memoranda prepared by a prosecutor or defense counsel, or their agents, in connection with the case are immunized during pretrial discovery by Rules 16(a)(2) and (b)(2) of the Federal Rules of Criminal Procedure.[47] In *United States v. Nobles*,[48] the Supreme Court also recognized a common law work product immunity during the trial of criminal matters.[49] Prior statements of witnesses who are called to testify at trial, however, must be disclosed.[50] Reports

---

ness, including a list of all publications authored by the witness within the preceding ten years; the compensation to be paid for the study and testimony; and a listing of any other cases in which the witness has testified as an expert at trial or by deposition within the preceding four years.

(C) These disclosures shall be made at the times and in the sequence directed by the court. In the absence of other directions from the court or stipulation by the parties, the disclosures shall be made at least 90 days before the trial date or the date the case is to be ready for trial or, if the evidence is intended solely to contradict or rebut evidence on the same subject matter identified by another party under paragraph (2)(B), within 30 days after the disclosure made by the other party. The parties shall supplement these disclosures when required under subdivision (e)(1).

Fed.R.Civ.P. 26(b)(4)(A), as amended, provides further that those who are identified as expert witnesses may be deposed by any party.

In some federal districts, a party need not make the disclosures required by Fed. R.Civ.P. 26(a)(2) until such time as a discovery demand is made by the opponent. See Fed.R.Civ.P. 26(a)(1)(party is required to disclose, without awaiting a discovery request, certain specified items, including information about expert witnesses, "[e]xcept to the extent otherwise stipulated or directed by order or local rule").

46. Fed.R.Civ.P. 26(b)(4)(B) provides as follows:

A party may, through interrogatories or by deposition, discover facts known or opinions held by an expert who has been retained or specially employed by another party in anticipation of litigation or preparation for trial and who is not expected to be called as a witness at trial only as provided in Rule 35(b) or upon a showing of exceptional circumstances under which it is impracticable for the party seeking discovery to obtain facts or opinions on the same subject by other means.

47. Fed.R.Crim.P. 16(a)(2), in pertinent part, protects the government as follows:

[T]his rule does not authorize the discovery or inspection of reports, memoranda, or other internal government documents made by the attorney for the government or other government agents in connection with the investigation or prosecution of the case. Nor does the rule authorize the discovery or inspection of statements made by government witnesses or prospective government witnesses except as provided in 18 U.S.C. § 3500.

Fed.R.Crim.P. 16(b)(2) protects defendants as follows:

Except as to scientific or medical reports, this subdivision does not authorize the discovery or inspection of reports, memoranda, or other internal defense documents made by the defendant, or the defendant's attorneys or agents in connection with the investigation or defense of the case, or of statements made by the defendant, or by government or defense witnesses, or by prospective government or defense witnesses, to the defendant, the defendant's agents or attorneys.

48. 422 U.S. 225, 95 S.Ct. 2160, 45 L.Ed.2d 141 (1975).

49. The Court observed that "[d]isclosure of an attorney's efforts at trial, as surely as disclosure during pretrial discovery, could disrupt the orderly development and presentation of his case." Id. at 239, 95 S.Ct. at 2170, 45 L.Ed.2d at 154. In Nobles, however, the defense counsel was found to have waived the immunity for his investigator's notes when he elicited testimony from the investigator concerning the subject matter of the notes. Id. at 239–40, 95 S.Ct. at 2170–71, 45 L.Ed.2d at 154.

50. Fed.R.Crim.P. 26.2(a) states as follows:

After a witness other than the defendant has testified on direct examination, the court, on motion of a party who did not

concerning physical or mental examinations and scientific tests or experiments are also subject to disclosure.[51]

Waiver of the work product immunity will occur if voluntary disclosure is made to an adversary.[52] Such disclosure is inconsistent with the rationale of the immunity, i.e., to protect the attorney's litigation-related activity from intrusion by opponents.[53] Inadvertent disclosure during pretrial document production may also effect a waiver.[54] Waiver has also been held to occur, in many cases, when a witness reviews work product during or prior to his testimony.[55] Aside from waiver, work product protection may be rejected for materials that were prepared in further-

call the witness, shall order the attorney for the government or the defendant and the defendant's attorney, as the case may be, to produce, for the examination and use of the moving party, any statement of the witness that is in their possession and that relates to the subject matter concerning which the witness has testified. See also 18 U.S.C.A. § 3500 (government is obligated to disclose prior statements of prosecution witnesses after they testify at trial).

51. Fed.R.Crim.P. 16(a)(1)(D) and 16(b)(1)(B). The government must make such disclosure, upon request, if the items are "material to the preparation of the defense or are intended for use by the government as evidence in chief at the trial." Fed. R.Crim.P. 16(a)(D). The defendant, on the other hand, is required to make disclosure, upon request, only if the examinations or tests were made in connection with the particular case and the defendant intends to introduce the results as evidence in chief at trial or they were "prepared by a witness whom the defendant intends to call at the trial when the results or reports relate to his testimony." Fed.R.Crim.P. 16(b)(1)(B).

52. In re Steinhardt Partners, L.P., 9 F.3d 230, 235 (2d Cir.1993)(waiver found where memorandum containing counsel's legal theories was voluntarily submitted to a government agency that was in an adversarial position).

53. Id. at 234–35 ("The logic behind the work product doctrine is that opposing counsel should not enjoy free access to an attorney's thought processes. * * * Once a party allows an adversary to share the otherwise privileged thought processes of counsel, the need for the privilege disappears."); Niagara Mohawk Power Corp. v. Stone & Webster Engineering Corp., 125 F.R.D. 578, 590 (N.D.N.Y.1989)("work product protection is waived when protected materials are disclosed in a manner which is either inconsistent with maintaining secrecy against opponents or substantially increases the opportunity for a potential adversary to obtain the protected information").

In accordance with the logic of this rationale, disclosure of work product to a party with a common interest will not result in waiver. See, e.g., United States v. Gulf Oil Corp., 760 F.2d 292, 296 (Temp.Emer.Ct. App.1985); United States v. American Telephone and Telegraph Co., 642 F.2d 1285, 1299 (D.C.Cir.1980).

54. See, e.g., Lois Sportswear, U.S.A., Inc. v. Levi Strauss & Co., 104 F.R.D. 103 (S.D.N.Y.1985)(factors used in determining waiver include reasonableness of precautions to prevent disclosure, time taken to rectify error, scope and extent of discovery, and fairness).

55. See, e.g., Ehrlich v. Howe, 848 F.Supp. 482, 493–94 (S.D.N.Y.1994); In re Joint Eastern and Southern District Asbestos Litigation, 119 F.R.D. 4, 5 (E. & S.D.N.Y.1988); Berkey Photo, Inc. v. Eastman Kodak Co., 74 F.R.D. 613, 616–17 (S.D.N.Y.1977). But see Al–Rowaishan Establishment Universal Trading & Agencies, Ltd. v. Beatrice Foods Co., 92 F.R.D. 779, 780–81 (S.D.N.Y.1982)(attorney's opinion work product not subject to disclosure in absence of showing that adverse party would be hampered in testing accuracy of witness' testimony).

The principal justification for a finding of waiver in such circumstances is that effective cross-examination may depend upon the opponent's access to documents that have influenced the witness's testimony. See Fed.R.Evid. 612. See also United States v. Nobles, 422 U.S. 225, 239 n.14, 95 S.Ct. 2160, 2171, 45 L.Ed.2d 141, 154 (1975)(waiver occurred at trial when defense counsel called investigator whose written report contained inconsistent statements of prosecution witnesses: "[W]here * * * counsel attempts to make a testimonial use of [work product] materials the normal rules of evidence come into play with respect to cross-examination and production of documents.")

502 Physician-Patient and Related Privileges

§ 502.1 New York

a. In General

The physician-patient privilege was unknown at common law.[1] In 1828, however, New York became the first state to enact a statutory privilege for information acquired by physicians while treating patients.[2] The privilege serves "to protect those who are required to consult physicians from the disclosure of secrets imparted to them; to protect the relationship of patient and physician and to prevent physicians from disclosing information which might result in humiliation, embarrassment or disgrace to patients."[3] It has been said that the privilege encourages patients to seek medical attention and to be frank with their physicians, thus ensuring effective medical treatment.[4] Respect for a patient's privacy interests may also help to justify the privilege.[5]

The privilege is currently embodied in CPLR 4504, which encompasses not only a patient's communications with physicians but also with dentists, podiatrists, chiropractors, registered professional nurses and licensed practical nurses. A separate statutory provision applies to psychologists.[6] For discussion purposes, the professionals covered by CPLR 4504 will be referred to collectively in this chapter as "physicians." The complete text of CPLR 4504 is as follows:

---

56. In re John Doe Corp., 675 F.2d 482, 492 (2d Cir.1982).

§ 502.1

1. The Duchess of Kingston's Trial, 20 How.St.Trials 573 (1776).

2. See Dillenbeck v. Hess, 73 N.Y.2d 278, 284, 539 N.Y.S.2d 707, 711, 536 N.E.2d 1126, 1130 (1989). A majority of states have likewise adopted statutes creating a physician-patient privilege. See McCormick § 98.

3. Steinberg v. New York Life Insurance Co., 263 N.Y. 45, 48–49, 188 N.E. 152, 153 (1933).

4. Camperlengo v. Blum, 56 N.Y.2d 251, 254–55, 451 N.Y.S.2d 697, 698, 436 N.E.2d 1299, 1300 (1982). See also Williams v. Roosevelt Hospital, 66 N.Y.2d 391, 395, 497 N.Y.S.2d 348, 350, 488 N.E.2d 94, 96 (1985) (enactment of privilege "was based on the belief that fear of embarrassment or disgrace flowing from disclosure of communications made to a physician would deter people from seeking medical help and securing adequate diagnosis and treatment").

5. Dillenbeck v. Hess, 73 N.Y.2d 278, 285, 539 N.Y.S.2d 707, 711–12, 536 N.E.2d 1126, 1131 (1989). (" 'the value placed on privacy, manifested both by general concerns for privacy and by the specific concerns for an individual's bodily integrity found in constitutional, statutory, and common law doctrines, suggests a strong policy basis' for the privilege"), quoting Developments in the Law, "Privileged Communications," 98 Harv.L.Rev. 1450, 1548 (1985). The privacy rationale helps to answer critics of the doctor-patient privilege who question the empirical proposition that privilege in the courtroom promotes candor in the sickroom. See, e.g., Chafee, "Privileged Communications: Is Justice Served by Closing the Doctor's Mouth on the Witness Stand?," 52 Yale L.J. 607 (1943).

6. CPLR 4507. See subdivision(e) infra.

(a) **Confidential information privileged.** Unless the patient waives the privilege, a person authorized to practice medicine, registered professional nursing, licensed practical nursing, dentistry, podiatry or chiropractic shall not be allowed to disclose any information which he acquired in attending a patient in a professional capacity, and which was necessary to enable him to act in that capacity. The relationship of a physician and patient shall exist between a medical corporation, as defined in article forty-four of the public health law, a professional service corporation organized under article fifteen of the business corporation law to practice medicine, and the patients to whom they respectively render professional medical services.

A patient who, for the purposes of obtaining insurance benefits, authorizes the disclosure of any such privileged communication to any person shall not be deemed to have waived the privilege created by this subdivision. For purposes of this subdivision:

1. "person" shall mean any individual, insurer or agent thereof, peer review committee, public or private corporation, political subdivision, government agency, department or bureau of the state, municipality, industry, co-partnership, association, firm, trust, estate or any other legal entity whatsoever; and

2. "insurance benefits" shall include payments under a self-insured plan.

(b) **Identification by dentist; crime committed against patient under sixteen.** A dentist shall be required to disclose information necessary for identification of a patient. A physician, dentist, podiatrist, chiropractor or nurse shall be required to disclose information indicating that a patient who is under the age of sixteen years has been the victim of a crime.

(c) **Mental or physical condition of deceased patient.** A physician or nurse shall be required to disclose any information as to the mental or physical condition of a deceased patient privileged under subdivision (a), except information which would tend to disgrace the memory of the decedent, either in the absence of an objection by a party to the litigation or when the privilege has been waived:

1. by the personal representative, or the surviving spouse, or the next of kin of the decedent; or

2. in any litigation where the interests of the personal representative are deemed by the trial judge to be adverse to those of the estate of the decedent, by any party in interest; or

3. if the validity of the will of the decedent is in question, by the executor named in the will, or the surviving spouse or any heir-at-law or any of the next of kin or any other party in interest.

(d) Proof of negligence; unauthorized practice of medicine. In any action for damages for personal injuries or death against a person not authorized to practice medicine under article 131 of the education law for any act or acts constituting the practice of medicine, when such act or acts were a competent producing proximate or contributing cause of such injuries or death, the fact that such person practiced medicine without being so authorized shall be deemed prima facie evidence of negligence.

The Proposed New York Evidence Code provision, for the most part, simply restates CPLR 4504.[7]

7. **§ 507. Physician, nurse, dentist, and chiropractor-patient privilege. [PROPOSED]**

(a) **Confidential information privileged.** Unless the patient waives the privilege, a person authorized to practice medicine, registered professional nursing, licensed practical nursing, dentistry or chiropractics shall not be allowed to disclose any information acquired in attending a patient in a professional capacity, and which was necessary to enable the physician, nurse, dentist or chiropractor to act in that capacity. The relationship of a physician and patient shall exist between a medical corporation, as defined in article forty-four of the public health law, a professional service corporation organized under article fifteen of the business corporation law to practice medicine, and the patients to whom they respectively render professional medical services. For purposes of this section: "physician" shall mean a person who is licensed or reasonably believed by the patient to be licensed to practice medicine in this state or in any other jurisdiction; "nurse" shall mean a person who is authorized or reasonably believed by the patient to be authorized to practice registered professional nursing or licensed practical nursing in this state or in any other jurisdiction; "dentist" shall mean a person who is licensed or reasonably believed by the patient to be licensed to practice dentistry in this state or in any other jurisdiction; "chiropractor" shall mean a person who is authorized or reasonably believed by the patient to be authorized to practice chiropractics in this state or in any other jurisdiction.

(b) **Identification by dentist.** A dentist shall be required to disclose information necessary for identification of a patient.

(c) **Mental or physical condition of deceased patient.** A physician, dentist, chiropractor or nurse shall be required to disclose any information as to the mental or physical condition of a deceased patient privileged under subdivision (a) of this section, either in the absence of an objection by a party to the litigation or when the privilege has been waived: (1) by the personal representative, or the surviving spouse, or the next of kin of the decedent; or (2) in any litigation where the interests of the personal representative are deemed by the trial judge to be adverse to those of the estate of the decedent, by any party in interest; or (3) if the validity of the will of the decedent is in question, by the executor named in the will, or the surviving spouse or any heir-at-law or any of the next of kin or any other party in interest.

(d) **Exceptions.** The privilege in this section shall not apply when an exception is recognized by statute, or in other situations, where the policies underlying the privilege are absent, including but not limited to:

(1) **Furtherance of crime or fraud.** If the services of the physician, dentist, nurse, or chiropractor were sought for the purpose of committing what the patient knew or reasonably should have known to be a crime or a fraud, or to escape detection or apprehension after the commission of a crime or fraud.

(2) **Crime committed against patient under sixteen.** As to a communication relevant to a crime committed against a patient under the age of sixteen.

(3) **Examination by order of court.** As to a communication made in the course of a court-ordered examination of the physical condition of the patient, with respect to the particular purpose for which the examination is ordered, unless the court orders otherwise.

(4) **Condition in issue.** As to a communication relevant to the physi-

Supplementing CPLR 4504 with respect to HIV-related information is Article 27–F of the New York Public Health Law.[8] Special statutory protections are also provided for information about patients and doctors that is revealed in certain types of administrative proceedings. New York Public Health Law § 230 confers a general seal of confidentiality on proceedings relating to professional discipline of physicians. New York Education Law § 6527(3) generally protects against disclosure of the records of "peer review" proceedings conducted by hospitals and their accrediting organizations.

b. Scope of the Physician–Patient Privilege

Four elements must be satisfied to sustain a claim of privilege under CPLR 4504(a): (1) the relationship of physician and patient existed; (2) the information was acquired by the physician while attending the patient in a professional capacity; (3) the information was necessary for treatment; and (4) the patient intended that the information be kept confidential.[9] The proponent of the privilege bears the burden of establishing its applicability.[10]

With respect to the first element, privilege obviously will not attach unless the person who acquired information from a patient was one of the individuals listed in CPLR 4504(a). Pharmacists, for example, are excluded from coverage,[11] as are emergency medical technicians who are not acting as agents of a physician.[12]

A professional relationship exists if the physician attended the patient for the purpose of providing treatment. A leading case on this point is *People v. Decina*,[13] which held that an attending physician himself need not administer treatment if he examines the patient and makes a diagnosis for the use of other physicians.[14] *Decina* also suggest-

---

cal, mental or emotional condition of the patient in any action or proceeding in which the patient or the patient's representative relies upon that condition as an element of a claim or defense.

The proposed code provision differs from CPLR 4504 in three respects. First, it encompasses a patient's communications not only with a licensed physician (or other health care provider) but also one who "is reasonably believed by the patient to be authorized to practice." Second, the relevant health care providers may be located in New York or any other jurisdiction. (Caselaw already recognizes the privilege with respect to medical treatment rendered by out-of-state physicians. See Lorde v. Guardian Life Insurance Co. of America, 252 App.Div. 646, 300 N.Y.S. 721 (1st Dep't 1937)). Third, the proposed code provision contains a modified and expanded list of exceptions.

8. N.Y.Public Health Law §§ 2780–2787. But see note 64 infra.

9. State v. General Electric Co., 201 A.D.2d 802, 802, 607 N.Y.S.2d 181, 182 (3d Dep't 1994).

10. Williams v. Roosevelt Hospital, 66 N.Y.2d 391, 397, 497 N.Y.S.2d 348, 351, 488 N.E.2d 94, 97 (1985).

11. Matter of John Doe, Inc., Kuriansky, 120 Misc.2d 508, 466 N.Y.S.2d 202 (Sup.Ct.Bronx Co.1983).

12. People v. Ackerson, 149 Misc.2d 882, 566 N.Y.S.2d 833 (Monroe Co.Ct.1991)(emergency medical technicians were not gathering information for diagnosis or treatment by physician; rather, they were performing first aid). But see People v. Hanf, 159 Misc.2d 748, 611 N.Y.S.2d 85 (Monroe Co.Ct.1994)(emergency medical technician acted under direction and supervision of physician; nature of communication, however, was not within privilege).

13. 2 N.Y.2d 133, 157 N.Y.S.2d 558, 138 N.E.2d 799 (1956).

14. Id. at 142–43, 157 N.Y.S.2d at 567, 138 N.E.2d at 805 ("To say that in a hospi-

§ 502.1 PRIVILEGES Ch. 5

ed that the patient's reasonable expectations can be a factor in determining the existence of a physician-patient relationship. The court distinguished the case at bar from others in which "no evidence was adduced from which it might be found that the [patients] could reasonably have regarded the physician as acting in a professional capacity towards them."[15] Conversely, another Court of Appeals decision makes it clear that the requisite relationship can come into being from the fact alone of treatment, even if it is administered without the knowledge or, in the case of a suicide attempt, the consent of the patient.[16]

The second element of the privilege—information imparted in the course of professional services—can be satisfied if the physician was the recipient of communications "from the lips of the patient" or her knowledge was acquired from observation of the patient's appearance and symptoms.[17] The information acquired must flow from the application of professional skill or knowledge.[18] Thus, the privilege does not apply to the physician's observations of matters that would be obvious to laypersons.[19] Furthermore, the privilege protects only the physician-patient exchange itself, not the underlying facts of the patient's medical condition or history.[20] The patient, therefore, can be compelled to

tal, where there is division of duties among the staff, the relation of physician and patient does not arise with regard to those members of the staff who do not actually treat the patient is unsound."). In Rodriguez v. New York City Transit Authority, 151 Misc.2d 1027, 574 N.Y.S.2d 505 (Sup. Ct.Bronx Co.1991), a railway motorman was held to have had no physician-patient relationship with a laboratory that conducted a post-accident urine analysis to test for drug use pursuant to an employment contract. The employee, who was not injured, was seeking neither treatment nor diagnosis.

15. 2 N.Y.2d at 142, 157 N.Y.S.2d at 567, 138 N.E.2d at 805. In one of the cases distinguished by the Decina court, a doctor retained by law enforcement authorities had examined a defendant in jail solely to obtain information for prosecutorial purposes. People v. Sliney, 137 N.Y. 570, 33 N.E. 150 (1893). In another case, People v. Koerner, 154 N.Y. 355, 48 N.E. 730 (1897), the defendant had been explicitly told that the physician was not acting in his capacity as a doctor.

16. Meyer v. Supreme Lodge, Knights of Pythias, 178 N.Y. 63, 67, 70 N.E. 111, 112 (1904), aff'd, 198 U.S. 508, 25 S.Ct. 754, 49 L.Ed. 1146 (1905) (privilege applied where hotel guest who swallowed poison in suicide attempt protested treatment by physician summoned to scene by hotel employee: "When one who is sick unto death is in fact treated by a physician as a patient even against his will, he becomes the patient of that physician by operation of law. The same is true of one who is unconscious and unable to speak for himself.")

17. Edington v. Mutual Life Insurance Co., 67 N.Y. 185, 194 (1876).

18. Dillenbeck v. Hess, 73 N.Y.2d 278, 284 n.4, 539 N.Y.S.2d 707, 711, 536 N.E.2d 1126, 1130 (1989)(information obtained by physician in administering blood alcohol test was product of professional skill and knowledge). See also Lorde v. Guardian Life Insurance Co. of America, 252 App.Div. 646, 300 N.Y.S. 721 (1st Dep't 1937)(privilege applied to X-ray plates and photos made while physician attended plaintiff in professional capacity).

19. See, e.g., People v. Capra, 17 N.Y.2d 670, 269 N.Y.S.2d 451, 216 N.E.2d 610 (1966)(privilege inapplicable where emergency room doctor saw packet of heroin fall from one of patient's socks); People v. Hedges, 98 A.D.2d 950, 470 N.Y.S.2d 61 (4th Dep't 1983)(privilege inapplicable to emergency room doctor's observations concerning patient's slurred speech and odor of alcohol on his breath). Compare People v. Saaratu, 143 Misc.2d 1075, 541 N.Y.S.2d 889 (Sup.Ct.Bronx Co.1989)(physician's observation of heroin in balloons removed from patients's stomach during emergency operation was within privilege because discovery occurred as part of treatment itself), with note 67 infra.

20. Williams v. Roosevelt Hospital, 66 N.Y.2d 391, 396–97, 497 N.Y.S.2d 348, 351, 488 N.E.2d 94, 97 (1985)(mother of brain-damaged infant in child's medical malpractice action could be compelled to testify to

answer the question, "What is your medical condition and history?," but cannot be required to answer, "What did you and your doctor discuss about your medical condition and history?"[21] Similarly, the privilege does not encompass general facts about the physician-patient relationship, such as the identity of the patient, recognition that the patient was "sick" (provided the condition was observable by anyone), the fact that treatment was rendered (except as to the character of the treatment), and the dates of treatment.[22]

The third element of the privilege is a requirement that the information was "necessary" for treatment. The patient's narration of his prior medical history, for example, may be deemed necessary,[23] whereas details about an accident that are unrelated to treatment probably will not qualify.[24] In some cases, courts have taken a fairly broad view of the term "necessary," extending it to information about a patient's mental or physical condition that is not directly related to the particular condition being treated.[25] This is consistent with the notion that a competent medical practitioner treats "the whole person" even if referral to another doctor is necessary.[26]

The fourth element—confidentiality—is not explicitly mentioned in the text of CPLR 4504(a), but the term is used in the caption of the statute ("confidential information privileged") and courts have recognized that confidentiality is an inherent part of the privilege.[27] The presence of a third person during the doctor's meeting with the patient, however, will not necessarily prevent the privilege from attaching. The test is "whether in the light of all the surrounding circumstances, and particularly the occasion for the presence of the third person, the

such matters as existence of any physical or congenital problems of her children, whether she was in physician's care or took medication during particular time period, and facts surrounding an abortion).

21. Id.

22. Klein v. Prudential Insurance Co. of America, 221 N.Y. 449, 453, 117 N.E. 942, 943 (1917); Hughson v. St. Francis Hospital of Port Jervis, 93 A.D.2d 491, 499, 463 N.Y.S.2d 224, 229–30 (2d Dep't 1983). See also Rubin v. Alamo Rent-A-Car, 190 A.D.2d 661, 593 N.Y.S.2d 284 (2d Dep't 1993)(in doctor's personal injury action seeking damages for lost earnings, doctor could be compelled to disclose appointment books, billing invoices and patients' medical records to extent they reflected fees charged and payments made). But see In re Grand Jury Investigation of Onondaga County, 59 N.Y.2d 130, 135, 463 N.Y.S.2d 758, 760, 450 N.E.2d 678, 680 (1983)(grand jury's demand for "names and addresses of all persons treated for a knife wound" would result in disclosure of privileged information about diagnosis and treatment).

23. People v. Decina, 2 N.Y.2d 133, 143, 157 N.Y.S.2d 558, 568, 138 N.E.2d 799, 805–06 (1956).

24. Griffiths v. Metropolitan St.Ry.Co., 171 N.Y. 106, 112, 63 N.E. 808, 810 (1902)("There may be circumstances in which it is necessary for a physician to inquire of a patient how an accident happened in order to properly treat him. But that is not true in all cases, and no such necessity was shown in the case at bar.").

25. See Massachusetts Mutual Life Insurance Co. v. Brei, 311 F.2d 463, 467–69 (2d Cir.1962)(general practitioner learned of patient's suicidal tendency while treating patient's varicose veins). But see Polsky v. Union Mutual Stock Life Insurance Co., 80 A.D.2d 777, 436 N.Y.S.2d 744 (1st Dep't 1981)(patient's discussion of suicidal tendency with dentist was too remote from dental treatment).

26. Massachusetts Mutual Life Insurance Co. v. Brei, 311 F.2d 463, 469 (2d Cir.1962).

27. See, e.g., State v. General Electric Co., 201 A.D.2d 802, 607 N.Y.S.2d 181 (3d

§ 502.1 PRIVILEGES Ch. 5

communication was intended to be confidential."[28] If the third person is present to assist in the process of treatment-related communications between physician and patient, it can be argued that privilege should attach by analogy to agents who aid in attorney-client communications.[29]

A common law rule that apparently persists in New York would permit an unseen eavesdropper who overhears a physician-patient communication to testify to what she overheard, even though the privilege might still apply with respect to testimony by the physician and patient themselves.[30] This rule[31] obviously is out of step with the modern view that confidentiality should be measured by the reasonable expectations of the privilege-holder.[32]

If the elements of the privilege are satisfied, the information will be protected regardless of whether it is sought through the testimony of the parties or the production of medical records and files.[33] The patient is the privilege-holder,[34] but she is not the only person who may assert the privilege. For example, if the patient is not a party to the proceeding in which disclosure is sought, any party may assert the privilege on the patient's behalf unless the patient has waived the privilege.[35] For policy reasons, however, a criminal defendant may not assert his victim's physician-patient privilege in an attempt to conceal that he was the cause of the victim's harm.[36] Similarly, a hospital may not refuse to divulge information to a grand jury about its patients when the hospital

Dep't 1994); Farrow v. Allen, 194 A.D.2d 40, 608 N.Y.S.2d 1 (1st Dep't 1993).

28. People v. Decina, 2 N.Y.2d 133, 145, 157 N.Y.S.2d 558, 569, 138 N.E.2d 799, 807 (1956)(privilege upheld despite presence of police guard in doorway of patient's hospital room at time of communication.) Denaro v. Prudential Insurance Co. of America, 154 App.Div. 840, 843, 139 N.Y.S. 758, 761 (2d Dep't 1913)("communications necessary for the proper performance of the duties of a physician are not public, because made in the presence of his immediate family or those who are present because of the illness of the person").

29. See § 501.1 supra, at notes 51–55. See, e.g., People v. Hanf, 159 Misc.2d 748, 611 N.Y.S.2d 85 (Monroe Co.Ct.1994)(emergency medical technician acted under direction and supervision of physician). See also Edington v. Mutual Life Insurance Co., 67 N.Y. 185, 194 (1876) (information that may qualify for privilege includes "such knowledge as may be acquired * * * from the statement of others who may surround [patient] at the time").

30. Prink v. Rockefeller Center, Inc., 48 N.Y.2d 309, 315 n.2, 422 N.Y.S.2d 911, 915, 398 N.E.2d 517, 520 (1979).

31. Lanza v. New York State Joint Legislative Committee, 3 N.Y.2d 92, 97, 164 N.Y.S.2d 9, 12, 143 N.E.2d 772, 774, cert. denied, 355 U.S. 856, 78 S.Ct. 85, 2 L.Ed.2d 64 (1957)(common law rule applied to attorney-client privilege).

32. See People v. Decina, 2 N.Y.2d 133, 145, 157 N.Y.S.2d 558, 569, 138 N.E.2d 799, 807 (1956). The common law rule has been changed by statute in New York only in the case of the attorney-client privilege (CPLR 4503(a)) and illegal eavesdropping (CPLR 4506).

33. Williams v. Roosevelt Hospital, 66 N.Y.2d 391, 396, 497 N.Y.S.2d 348, 351, 488 N.E.2d 94, 97 (1985).

34. See Steinberg v. New York Life Insurance Co., 263 N.Y. 45, 49, 188 N.E. 152, 153 (1933)("privilege is personal to the patient").

35. CPLR 4504(a). See, e.g., In re Grand Jury Investigation of Onondaga County, 59 N.Y.2d 130, 135, 463 N.Y.S.2d 758, 760, 450 N.E.2d 678, 680 (1983)(in grand jury investigation of patient, hospital may assert privilege of patient to protect against disclosure of adverse medical information about patient); Moore v. St. John's Episcopal Hospital, 89 A.D.2d 618, 452 N.Y.S.2d 669 (2d Dep't 1982)(in personal injury action, hospital could assert privilege for medical information contained in records of patient who assaulted plaintiff's decedent in hospital).

36. People v. Lay, 254 App.Div. 372, 5 N.Y.S.2d 325 (2d Dep't 1938), aff'd, 279 N.Y. 737, 18 N.E.2d 686 (1939).

is under investigation for possible crimes against them.[37] The privilege generally survives the death of the patient,[38] subject to particularized rules of waiver that are described in the following subsection.

c. Waiver

Generally, the patient, as the privilege-holder, is the only person who can waive the physician-patient privilege.[39] Thus, waiver ordinarily will occur as to confidences that a patient authorizes her doctor to disclose to third parties,[40] but the privilege will remain intact if the doctor's disclosure is made without the patient's consent.[41] A contractual waiver, as, for example, in an application for life insurance, is enforceable and will outlive the patient's death.[42]

In the context of litigation, courts will find waiver where the patient voluntarily introduces documents or testimony, either his own or that of another, revealing privileged information.[43] Waiver will also occur if the

---

37. Application to Quash Subpoena Duces Tecum in Grand Jury Proceedings, 56 N.Y.2d 348, 353, 452 N.Y.S.2d 361, 363, 437 N.E.2d 1118, 1120 (1982) ("purpose of the privilege is to protect the patient, not to shield the criminal"; hospital was under investigation for selectively depriving patients of lifesaving measures).

38. See, e.g., Greene v. New England Mutual Life Insurance Co., 108 Misc.2d 540, 542–44, 437 N.Y.S.2d 844, 847–48 (Sup.Ct.N.Y.Co.1981).

39. Dillenbeck v. Hess, 73 N.Y.2d 278, 289, 539 N.Y.S.2d 707, 714, 536 N.E.2d 1126, 1133 (1989). The legal representative of a patient may also waive the patient's privilege. See, e.g., Scharlack v. Richmond Memorial Hospital, 102 A.D.2d 886, 477 N.Y.S.2d 184 (2d Dep't 1984)(parent of infant); Cook v. Cook, 8 A.D.2d 964, 190 N.Y.S.2d 955 (2d Dep't 1959) (guardian ad litem).

40. Farrow v. Allen, 194 A.D.2d 40, 43–44, 608 N.Y.S.2d 1, 3 (1st Dep't 1993)(patient authorized her psychiatrist to reveal certain treatment-related information in a letter to an organization that was participating in a criminal investigation).

The second paragraph of CPLR 4504(a), however, provides that a patient's authorization for disclosure of privileged communications for the purpose of obtaining insurance benefits does not constitute a waiver as to third parties. See also Henry v. Lewis, 102 A.D.2d 430, 478 N.Y.S.2d 263 (1st Dep't 1984)(patient's authorization of release of privileged information to insurance company did not constitute waiver as to state insurance investigatory authorities).

41. Prink v. Rockefeller Center, Inc., 48 N.Y.2d 309, 315, 422 N.Y.S.2d 911, 914–15, 398 N.E.2d 517, 520 (1979).

42. Lynch v. Mutual Life Insurance Co. of New York, 55 Misc.2d 179, 180, 284 N.Y.S.2d 768, 768 (Sup.Ct.Bronx Co.1967)(in life insurance application, insured waived "all provisions of law forbidding any physician or other person who has attended or examined, or who may attend or examine me or any other person covered by such insurance, from disclosing any knowledge or information which he thereby acquired"). See also Greene v. New England Mutual Life Insurance Co., 108 Misc.2d 540, 437 N.Y.S.2d 844 (Sup.Ct.N.Y.Co.1981)(narrow wording of waiver clause resulted in waiver only as to physician-patient communications that took place prior to patient's execution of insurance application).

Even if an insured does not waive the privilege by contract during her lifetime, as a practical matter beneficiaries of the policy will be compelled to waive it. See note 47 infra.

43. Hughson v. St. Francis Hospital of Port Jervis, 93 A.D.2d 491, 500, 463 N.Y.S.2d 224, 230 (2d Dep't 1983). See, e.g., Hethier v. Johns, 233 N.Y. 370, 135 N.E. 603 (1922)(patient testified to contents of consultation with doctor, thus entitling adversary to examine doctor on same subject); Steinberg v. New York Life Insurance Co., 263 N.Y. 45, 188 N.E. 152 (1933)(patient called doctor to testify to his examination of patient, thus entitling adversary to call other doctors who had examined patient during relevant time period).

Generally, a witness's testimony about the facts of her physical condition, standing alone, does not constitute a waiver because such information is not privileged. Compare Wepy v. Shen, 175 A.D.2d 124, 571 N.Y.S.2d 817 (2d Dep't 1991)(testimony

patient fails to object to the disclosure of privileged information introduced by other parties.[44] Such waivers extend beyond the particular litigation in which they occur.[45] On the other hand, if a privilege-holder reveals protected information during examination by the adversary, it has been held that no waiver occurs because such disclosure is not "voluntary."[46]

After the patient dies, CPLR 4504(c) authorizes waiver of the decedent's privilege by any one of the following individuals: (1) the personal representative, surviving spouse or next of kin of the decedent in any type of case; (2) any party in interest where the interests of the personal representative are adverse to those of the decedent's estate; or (3) the executor, surviving spouse, any heir-at-law, any next of kin or any other party in interest in a dispute over the validity of the decedent's will. Furthermore, the statute provides that a physician must disclose privileged information about the patient if no objection is raised by a party to the litigation.[47] No one may waive the privilege, however,

about "mere facts and incidents of medical history" was not a waiver), with DeSilva v. Rosenberg, 129 A.D.2d 609, 514 N.Y.S.2d 104 (2d Dep't 1987)(testimony that included disclosure of care and treatment constituted waiver). If the witness is a party who has affirmatively put her physical condition in controversy, however, implied waiver will occur even in the absence of the party's revelation of privileged information. See notes 50–58 infra.

44. See, e.g., Capron v. Douglass, 193 N.Y. 11, 17–18, 85 N.E. 827, 829 (1908)("when the privilege of the plaintiff has been once waived by him in court, either by his own testimony or by that of others given with his knowledge and consent, * * * the door is then thrown open for his opponent to give the facts as he understands them").

45. See, e.g., People v. Bloom, 193 N.Y. 1, 7, 85 N.E. 824, 825 (1908) (patient who failed to object to physician's testimony in civil case was bound by such waiver in subsequent criminal prosecution of patient for perjury: "when a waiver is once made it is general and not special, and its effect cannot properly be limited to a particular purpose or a particular person"); McKinney v. The Grand Street, P.P. & F.R. Co., 104 N.Y. 352, 355, 10 N.E. 544, 544 (1887)("consent having been once given and acted upon cannot be recalled, and the patient can never be restored to the condition which the statute, from motives of public policy, has sought to protect"); Will of Postley, 125 Misc.2d 416, 417, 479 N.Y.S.2d 464, 465 (Surr.Ct.Nassau Co.1984)(patient's waiver in conservatorship proceeding was held to apply in probate proceeding involving patient's will).

46. Hughes v. Kackas, 3 A.D.2d 402, 161 N.Y.S.2d 541 (3d Dep't 1957)(no waiver occurs where privilege-holder is called as witness by opponent or testifies on cross-examination). Query why disclosure in such circumstances should not be deemed voluntary in light of the privilege-holder's ability to object to inquiries that would elicit privileged information. See, e.g., CPLR 3101(b)(during pretrial discovery, privileged matter shall not be obtainable "upon objection by a person entitled to assert the privilege").

47. The "no-objection" provision can play a significant role in post-death insurance litigation. The beneficiary of a life insurance policy, for example, may not be one of the persons who is statutorily authorized to waive the decedent's privilege. If the beneficiary sues for nonpayment of the policy proceeds, however, the insurer, in support of a defense of misrepresentation by the insured concerning his physical condition, must be allowed to introduce evidence of the insured's privileged medical information in the absence of an objection by the beneficiary. Such an objection by the beneficiary would be unlikely due to the operation of § 3105(d) of the New York Insurance Law, which provides as follows:

> A misrepresentation that an applicant for life or accident and health insurance has not had previous medical treatment, consultation or observation, or has not had previous treatment or care in a hospital or other like institution, shall be deemed, for the purpose of determining its materiality, a misrepresentation that the applicant has not had the disease, ailment or other medical impairment for which such treatment or care was given or which was discovered by any licensed medical practi-

with respect to information "which would tend to disgrace the memory of the decedent."[48] Contemporary social standards play a role in the court's determination of whether particular information would disgrace the decedent's memory.[49]

Waiver by implication occurs when the patient affirmatively places his physical or mental condition in issue in litigation.[50] The rationale is one of fairness to adversaries: a party should be permitted to use the physician-patient privilege only as a shield, not as a sword.[51]

The plaintiff in a personal injury action is a paradigm of a party who has affirmatively put his physical or mental condition in controversy.[52]

tioner as a result of such consultation or observation. If in any action to rescind any such contract or to recover thereon, any such misrepresentation is proved by the insurer, and the insured or any other person having or claiming a right under such contract shall prevent full disclosure and proof of the nature of such medical impairment, such misrepresentation shall be presumed to have been material.

The practical effect of CPLR 4504(c) and Insurance Law § 3105(d) is to enable persons who claim the benefits of life, accident and health insurance policies to waive the physician-patient privilege. See, e.g., R.S. Saunders v. United Mutual Life Insurance Co., 9 Misc.2d 285, 172 N.Y.S.2d 443 (App. T., 2d Dep't 1957)(court had no authority to exclude privileged medical information about decedent-insured in absence of objection by a party); Roth v. Equitable Life Assurance Society of the United States, 186 Misc. 403, 59 N.Y.S.2d 707 (Sup.Ct.N.Y.Co. 1945), aff'd, 270 App.Div. 923, 62 N.Y.S.2d 612 (1st Dep't 1946)(beneficiary's objection to disclosure of privileged information by decedent-insured's doctors triggers adverse presumption).

48. CPLR 4504(c).

49. In a 1969 personal injury case, for example, a decedent's chronic alcoholism was found to be a disgracing fact that precluded the admissibility of privileged medical records relating to this condition despite an apparent waiver. Tinney v. Neilson's Flowers, Inc., 61 Misc.2d 717, 305 N.Y.S.2d 713 (Sup.Ct.Nassau Co.1969), aff'd, 35 A.D.2d 532, 314 N.Y.S.2d 161 (2d Dep't 1970)(3-2 decision). In a 1984 will contest, however, discovery was allowed because alcoholism was viewed as a mere illness that caused no disgrace to the decedent's memory. Will of Postley, 125 Misc.2d 416, 418, 479 N.Y.S.2d 464, 465-66 (Surr.Ct.Nassau Co.1984). See also Killip v. Rochester General Hospital, 1 Misc.2d 349, 351, 146 N.Y.S.2d 164, 167 (Sup.Ct.Monroe Co.1955)("people are today satisfied that * * * there is no more disgrace in being mentally ill than there is in suffering a heart ailment, poliomyelitis, or cancer").

50. See Koump v. Smith, 25 N.Y.2d 287, 294, 303 N.Y.S.2d 858, 864, 250 N.E.2d 857, 861 (1969).

51. Id. ("As a practical matter, a plaintiff or a defendant, who affirmatively asserts a mental or physical condition, must eventually waive the privilege to prove his case or his defense. To uphold the privilege would allow a party to use it as a sword rather than a shield").

52. See, e.g., Prink v. Rockefeller Center, Inc., 48 N.Y.2d 309, 315-17, 422 N.Y.S.2d 911, 915-916, 398 N.E.2d 517, 521-22 (1979)(waiver applies to medical information about plaintiff in personal injury action and decedent in wrongful death action). See also Apter v. Home Life Insurance Co. of New York, 266 N.Y. 333, 194 N.E. 846 (1935)(plaintiff who sued for nonpayment of proceeds of disability policy alleged disability due to tuberculosis and thereby waived privilege despite fact that he introduced no privileged medical evidence concerning his condition). McDonald v. McDonald, 196 A.D.2d 7, 608 N.Y.S.2d 477 (2d Dep't 1994)(in litigation involving child custody, party who actively contests custody puts his mental and emotional well-being into issue, but a showing must be made that resolution of custody issue requires revelation of privileged material).

A nominal plaintiff, such as a parent who sues solely in a representative capacity on behalf of her child or an executrix who sues for the wrongful death of her spouse, does not automatically place her own medical condition in issue. See, e.g., Scalone v. Phelps Memorial Hospital Center, 184 A.D.2d 65, 591 N.Y.S.2d 419 (2d Dep't 1992). If the alleged injuries to a child occurred while the infant was in utero, however, disclosure is required with respect to the mother's medical records during the period of the pregnancy because of the impossibility of severing the infant's prenatal condition from that of the mother. In re

Merely by bringing the action the plaintiff waives his physician-patient privilege for medical records and other information possessed by doctors and hospitals.[53] Such waiver, however, extends only to medical information that is relevant to the condition that has been put in issue.[54]

A defendant cannot be said to have affirmatively put her physical or mental condition in controversy simply by denying allegations that her condition played a role in the litigated event.[55] A denial merely puts the adversary to his burden of proof.[56] On the other hand, an implied waiver will be found if the defendant interposes an affirmative defense or offers testimony that seeks to excuse her conduct because of an impaired physical or mental condition.[57] The defendant who pleads insanity in a criminal case, for example, waives privilege for communications with her psychiatrist.[58]

When waiver occurs, its scope will be determined by the circumstances in which the disclosure took place and the impact on the opposing party.[59] Fairly broad waiver will occur, for example, where a party has affirmatively placed her condition in issue in a judicial setting.[60] As a matter of fairness, the opposing party in such a case may elicit any privileged information concerning the same or a related

---

New York County DES Litigation, 168 A.D.2d 44, 570 N.Y.S.2d 804 (1st Dep't 1991); Sibley v. Hayes 73 Corp., 126 A.D.2d 629, 511 N.Y.S.2d 65 (2d Dep't 1987).

53. See, e.g., Hoenig v. Westphal, 52 N.Y.2d 605, 439 N.Y.S.2d 831, 422 N.E.2d 491 (1981)(defendant entitled to discovery of medical reports of plaintiff's treating physicians). But see Cynthia B. v. New Rochelle Hospital Medical Center, 60 N.Y.2d 452, 470 N.Y.S.2d 122, 458 N.E.2d 363 (1983)(despite plaintiff-patient's waiver of privilege in action for damages for failed suicide attempt while under defendants' care, records of nonparty hospital concerning psychiatric treatment need not be disclosed if interests of patient, other persons, or hospital would be seriously harmed).

54. See, e.g., Zimmer v. Cathedral School of St. Mary and St. Paul, 204 A.D.2d 538, 611 N.Y.S.2d 911 (2d Dep't 1994)(suit for damages solely for physical injury did not constitute waiver with respect to psychiatric records); Iseman v. Delmar Medical–Dental Building, Inc., 113 A.D.2d 276, 495 N.Y.S.2d 747 (3d Dep't 1985)(in personal injury action for injuries to head, neck, hip and leg, plaintiff did not waive privilege with respect to prior treatment for eye disorder). See also Prink v. Rockefeller Center, Inc., 48 N.Y.2d 309, 317, 422 N.Y.S.2d 911, 916, 398 N.E.2d 517, 522 (1979)(in "extraordinary" circumstances of wrongful death action alleging accidental fall from 36th floor of office building, decedent's mental condition was deemed to have been put in issue with respect to potential suicide and, in addition, with respect to pecuniary loss suffered by distributees).

55. Dillenbeck v. Hess, 73 N.Y.2d 278, 539 N.Y.S.2d 707, 536 N.E.2d 1126 (1989)(in personal injury action, defendant who denied having been intoxicated at time of automobile accident could not be compelled to provide access to records of blood alcohol test conducted in hospital shortly after accident).

56. Id. at 289, 539 N.Y.S.2d at 714, 536 N.E.2d at 1133.

57. Id. at 288, 539 N.Y.S.2d at 713, 536 N.E.2d at 1132.

58. People v. Al–Kanani, 33 N.Y.2d 260, 264–65, 351 N.Y.S.2d 969, 971, 307 N.E.2d 43, 44 (1973), cert. denied, 417 U.S. 916, 94 S.Ct. 2619, 41 L.Ed.2d 220 (1974). Due to a quirk in the wording of the relevant statute, however, no such waiver occurs with respect to a defendant's communications with a psychologist. See text at notes 80–82 infra.

59. Farrow v. Allen, 194 A.D.2d 40, 45, 608 N.Y.S.2d 1, 4 (1st Dep't 1993).

60. See, e.g., Apter v. Home Life Insurance Co. of New York, 266 N.Y. 333, 337, 194 N.E. 846, 847 (1935)(plaintiff's voluntary disclosure of tuberculosis in support of action for nonpayment of disability benefits "destroy[ed] the seal of secrecy"; having "chosen the advantage that might follow from its disclosure," plaintiff could not preclude defendants from questioning plaintiff's physicians concerning the circumstances of their diagnosis of the condition).

condition so that a full picture of the matter can be obtained.[61] The waiver may be more limited, however, where the patient's disclosure occurred outside the context of a judicial proceeding. In that situation, the patient is not likely to have affirmatively used the privileged information in such a way as to gain a tactical litigation advantage over an adversary.[62]

d. Exceptions

Numerous statutory exceptions have been enacted with respect to the physician-patient privilege. CPLR 4504(b) specifies two such exceptions: dentists must disclose information necessary for identification of a patient, and other health care providers must disclose information indicating that a patient under the age of sixteen has been the victim of a crime. Another exception is contained in New York Family Court Act § 1046(a)(vii), which makes the physician-patient privilege inapplicable in child abuse and neglect proceedings. New York Social Services Law § 384–b(3)(h) eliminates the privilege in proceedings for guardianship and custody of children whose parents suffer from mental illness or retardation. New York Mental Hygiene Law § 81.09(d) authorizes courts to allow for an inspection of the medical records of an alleged incapacitated person.[63] Finally, New York Public Health Law § 2785(2) provides that a court may grant an order for the disclosure of HIV-related information upon an application showing a "compelling need" in judicial proceedings.[64]

Other statutes impose various reporting requirements on health care providers. Section 265.25 of the New York Penal Law requires the reporting of all gunshot wounds and knife wounds that could result in death.[65] New York Social Services Law §§ 413 and 415 provide that cases of suspected child abuse or maltreatment must be reported in writing and that such reports are admissible in any proceedings relating to child abuse or maltreatment.[66] New York Public Health Law

---

61. Farrow v. Allen, 194 A.D.2d 40, 46, 608 N.Y.S.2d 1, 4 (1st Dep't 1993).

62. Id. In Farrow, the petitioner sought to vacate her husband's adoption of two children. A third child, who was undergoing psychiatric treatment, had authorized her psychiatrist to reveal certain treatment-related information in a letter to an organization involved in a criminal investigation. Waiver was held to have occurred with respect to the letter, but the petitioner was denied access to the child's other physician-patient communications relating to the same subject matter. No one had attempted to use the letter against the petitioner in the adoption proceeding.

63. The court in In re Goldfarb, 160 Misc.2d 1036, 612 N.Y.S.2d 788 (Sup.Ct.Suffolk Co.1994), held that evidentiary use may be made of such records.

64. Plaza v. Wisser, 211 A.D.2d 111, 626 N.Y.S.2d 446 (1st Dep't 1995)(in suit for damages based on companion's transmittal of HIV virus to plaintiff, disclosure of companion's medical records was necessary to prove his HIV status and point in time at which he knew of such status).

65. See In re Grand Jury Investigation of Onondaga County, 59 N.Y.2d 130, 136, 463 N.Y.S.2d 758, 761, 450 N.E.2d 678, 681 (1983)(statute narrowly construed to preclude revelation of identity of clients who received knife wounds that were not life-threatening).

66. Courts are divided over the question whether these provisions create an exception that permits the use of otherwise privileged information outside the context of civil proceedings for child abuse. Compare People v. Bass, 140 Misc.2d 57, 529 N.Y.S.2d 961 (Sup.Ct.Bronx Co.1988) (exception inapplicable in criminal prosecutions), with People v. Gearhart, 148 Misc.2d 249, 560 N.Y.S.2d 247 (Nassau

§ 2101(1) contains a reporting requirement with respect to communicable diseases, and New York Public Health Law §§ 3372 and 3373 require the reporting of patients who are addicts or habitual users of narcotic drugs.[67]

New York courts have resisted the efforts of prosecutorial authorities to create any general "public interest" exception to the physician-patient privilege to aid in the investigation of criminal or fraudulent activity.[68] In *Camperlengo v. Blum*,[69] however, the court relied upon various federal and state Medicaid record-keeping and reporting requirements to imply an exception to the privilege in a case involving allegations of fraudulent Medicaid practices. Physicians, therefore, have been required to turn over diagnosis and treatment records of their Medicaid patients in response to subpoenas by appropriate state regulatory agencies[70] and grand juries[71] investigating Medicaid fraud.[72]

e. Psychologists

As noted previously, a separate statute governs the psychologist-client privilege. CPLR 4507 states:

> The confidential relations and communications between a psychologist registered under the provisions of article one hundred fifty-three of the education law and his client are placed on the same basis as those provided by law between attorney and client, and nothing in such article shall be construed to require any such privileged communications to be disclosed.

A client who, for the purpose of obtaining insurance benefits, authorizes the disclosure of any such privileged communica-

---

Co.Ct.1990)(doctor's reports of child abuse may be used in both civil and criminal proceedings).

67. It has been held that the statutory framework of the Public Health Law creates an exception to the physician-patient privilege so as to permit doctors to testify to the surgical removal of controlled substances swallowed by patients in balloons or condoms. People v. Figueroa, 173 A.D.2d 156, 568 N.Y.S.2d 957 (1st Dep't), appeal denied, 78 N.Y.2d 1075, 577 N.Y.S.2d 239, 583 N.E.2d 951 (1991).

68. Matter of Grand Jury Subpoena Duces Tecum Dated December 14, 1984, 69 N.Y.2d 232, 239, 513 N.Y.S.2d 359, 363, 505 N.E.2d 925, 928 (1987); Matter of Grand Jury Investigation of Onondaga County, 59 N.Y.2d 130, 135–36, 463 N.Y.S.2d 758, 760–61, 450 N.E.2d 678, 680–81 (1983)(existence of statutory exceptions indicates legislative intent to restrict creation of judge-made exceptions). A health care provider, however, cannot invoke the privilege to protect herself with respect to a crime committed against the patient. See supra notes 36–37.

69. 56 N.Y.2d 251, 451 N.Y.S.2d 697, 436 N.E.2d 1299 (1982).

70. Id.

71. Matter of Grand Jury Subpoena Duces Tecum Dated December 14, 1984, 69 N.Y.2d 232, 513 N.Y.S.2d 359, 505 N.E.2d 925 (1987). The Grand Jury Subpoena court, however, stressed that disclosure of the patient's records must be restricted to those charged with the investigation. Furthermore, in rare circumstances, a court may deny disclosure where "highly sensitive" patient information as to diagnosis and treatment is unnecessary to the investigation. Id. at 241, 513 N.Y.S.2d at 364, 505 N.E.2d at 929–30.

72. By analogy to the Medicaid cases, the court in People v. Bhatt, 160 Misc.2d 973, 611 N.Y.S.2d 447 (Sup.Ct.Queens Co.1994), created an exception in cases of alleged Medicare fraud. An exception with respect to investigation of conventional insurance fraud by the state superintendent of insurance was rejected, however, in Henry v. Lewis, 102 A.D.2d 430, 478 N.Y.S.2d 263 (1st Dep't 1984), because of the absence of any statutory or record-keeping requirements in the relevant statutes and regulations.

tion to any person shall not be deemed to have waived the privilege created by this section. For purposes of this section:

1. "person" shall mean any individual, insurer or agent thereof, peer review committee, public or private corporation, political subdivision, government agency, department or bureau of the state, municipality, industry, co-partnership, association, firm, trust, estate or any other legal entity whatsoever; and

2. "insurance benefits" shall include payments under a self-insured plan.

Justification for the psychologist-client privilege is based on the proposition that confidentiality is virtually essential for effective treatment of the mind and emotions.[73]

Caselaw is sparse with respect to the operation of the privilege,[74] but the language of CPLR 4507 makes clear that the attorney-client privilege, not the physician-patient privilege, is the appropriate model.[75] The communications, therefore, must have been made in confidence[76] and for the purpose of obtaining the psychologist's professional services.[77]

The psychologist's client may waive the privilege,[78] but the fact that the psychologist-client privilege is "placed on the same basis" as the

---

73. See Frederick R.C. v. Helene C., 153 Misc.2d 660, 662, 582 N.Y.S.2d 926, 928 (Sup.Ct.Suffolk Co.1992). See also United States v. Sessa, 806 F.Supp. 1063, 1070 (E.D.N.Y.1992)("People should be encouraged to speak fully and candidly with psychologists. Psychologists depend upon open communication to accomplish their valuable purpose of evaluating and improving the mental health of individual members of society.").

74. See, e.g., Matter of A–85–04–38, 138 Misc.2d 786, 525 N.Y.S.2d 479 (Sup.Ct.Albany Co.1988)(in professional disciplinary proceeding against a psychiatrist, privilege applied to records of a psychologist who had separately treated a patient of the psychiatrist; the patient had filed no charges against the psychiatrist and objected to the disciplinary board's subpoena); Matter of a Handicapped Child, 118 Misc.2d 137, 460 N.Y.S.2d 256 (Sup.Ct.Erie Co.1983)(school district's determination that a student was handicapped was challenged by student's parents; district's subpoena of a clinic's psychological testing and evaluation records of student was quashed on basis of privilege).

75. See CPLR 4504; § 501.1 supra.

76. CPLR 4507 itself refers to "confidential relations and communications." Absolute confidentiality may not be essential, however, if third persons are present to facilitate the communication process as it relates to counseling and treatment. See notes 28–29 supra. See also Yaron v. Yaron, 83 Misc.2d 276, 277–78, 372 N.Y.S.2d 518, 519 (Sup.Ct.N.Y.Co.1975)(with respect to counseling provided by clinic, court held that scope of psychologist-client privilege included "all of the other staff personnel of that agency by virtue of their relationship to the protected communications").

77. One court has held that the privilege protects more than just communications relating to treatment and encompasses the identity of the psychologist's clients. Frederick R.C. v. Helene C., 153 Misc.2d 660, 582 N.Y.S.2d 926 (Sup.Ct.Suffolk Co.1992). This reading of the psychologist-client privilege exceeds the scope of both the physician-patient and attorney-client privileges, neither of which, as a general matter, protect the identity of a patient or client. See text at note 22 supra and § 501.1, at note 32, supra. The court reasoned that identity, in this context, would automatically yield knowledge that the client sought counseling for mental health. 153 Misc.2d at 662 n.2. 582 N.Y.S.2d at 928. It might also be noted that the language of CPLR 4507 itself refers to confidential "relations," not merely communications.

78. See, e.g., Matter of Charles "RR," 166 A.D.2d 763, 563 N.Y.S.2d 123 (3d Dep't 1990)(client, who was fully represented by counsel in Family Court proceeding, failed to assert privilege when school psychologist presented adverse testimony). The statute provides, however, that a general waiver will not occur when a client authorizes disclosure in order to obtain insurance benefits.

attorney-client privilege[79] restricts the doctrine of implied waiver. This led to an unusual result in *People v. Wilkins*,[80] where the defendant asserted that his wounds had been inflicted by the victim. He put this in issue but then objected when the prosecution sought to produce his statements given to a psychologist in which he admitted that the wounds were self-inflicted. Had the physician-patient privilege been applicable, as, for example, if the defendant had consulted a psychiatrist, defendant would have impliedly waived his mental and physical condition.[81] The Court of Appeals, however, held that since an attorney could not be called in such a situation to contradict the client, neither could the psychologist.[82] This result would be corrected under § 508 of the Proposed New York Evidence Code, which creates an exception where the client of a psychologist puts a relevant condition in issue.[83]

Statutory exceptions to the psychologist-patient privilege are contained in New York Family Court Act § 1046(a)(vii), which makes the privilege inapplicable in child abuse and neglect proceedings;[84] New York Social Services Law § 384–b(3)(h), which eliminates the privilege in proceedings for guardianship and custody of children whose parents suffer from mental illness or retardation; and New York Social Services

---

79. See CPLR 4507.

80. 65 N.Y.2d 172, 490 N.Y.S.2d 759, 480 N.E.2d 373 (1985).

81. People v. Edney, 39 N.Y.2d 620, 385 N.Y.S.2d 23, 350 N.E.2d 400 (1976); Koump v. Smith, 25 N.Y.2d 287, 303 N.Y.S.2d 858, 250 N.E.2d 857 (1969). See notes 50–58 supra.

82. Wilkins casts doubt on Baecher v. Baecher, 58 A.D.2d 821, 396 N.Y.S.2d 447 (2d Dep't 1977), appeal denied, 43 N.Y.2d 645, 402 N.Y.S.2d 1026, 373 N.E.2d 995 (1978)(party who contests child custody puts mental condition in controversy and thereby waives psychologist-client privilege), and expressly rejects the holding in State of Florida v. Axelson, 80 Misc.2d 419, 363 N.Y.S.2d 200 (Sup.Ct.N.Y.Co.1974)(defendant's insanity plea was waiver of psychologist-client privilege).

83. § 508. Psychologist-client privilege [PROPOSED]

(a) **Confidential communications privileged.** The confidential relations and communications between a psychologist registered under the provisions of article one hundred fifty-three of the education law and a client are placed on the same basis as those provided by law between attorney and client, and nothing in such article shall be construed to require any such privileged communications to be disclosed. A "psychologist" shall mean a person who is licensed or reasonably believed by the client to be licensed to practice psychology in this state or any other jurisdiction.

(b) **Exceptions.** The privilege in this section shall not apply when an exception is recognized by statute, or in other situations, where the policies underlying the privilege are absent, including but not limited to:

(1) **Furtherance of crime or fraud.** If the services of the psychologist were sought or obtained for the purpose of committing what the patient knew or reasonably should have known to be a crime or a fraud or to escape detection or apprehension after the commission of a crime or fraud.

(2) **Crime committed against client under sixteen.** As to a communication relevant to a crime committed against a client under the age of sixteen.

(3) **Examination by order of court.** As to a communication made in the course of a court-ordered examination of the condition of the client with respect to the particular purpose for which the examination is ordered, unless the court orders otherwise.

(4) **Condition in issue.** As to a communication relevant to the physical, mental or emotional condition of the client in any action or proceeding in which the client or the client's representative relies upon that condition as an element of a claim or defense.

84. See, e.g., Rockland County Dep't of Social Services v. Brian McM, 193 A.D.2d 121, 602 N.Y.S.2d 416 (2d Dep't 1993).

Law §§ 413 and 415, which require the reporting of cases of suspected child abuse and authorize the use of such reports in proceedings relating to child abuse. Another form of exception is contained in New York Mental Hygiene Law § 33.13(c)(6), which authorizes psychologists in certain facilities licensed or operated by the state, when a client presents a "serious and imminent danger" to another person, to warn the endangered person and law enforcement authorities.[85] Judge-made exceptions have been recognized where the key witness against a criminal defendant had a history of psychological problems[86] and where a psychologist was under investigation for Medicaid fraud.[87]

Library References:

West's Key No. Digests, Witnesses ⇔207, 219(4).

§ 502.2 Federal

Federal law does not recognize a general physician-patient privilege.[1] While a few courts have recognized a limited psychotherapist-patient privilege,[2] others have continued to hold that no privilege of any kind exists between patients and physicians.[3] Proposed Federal Rule 504 would have created a psychotherapist-patient privilege.[4]

---

85. This statute served to free a psychologist from tort liability for breaching his client's confidences in Oringer v. Rotkin, 162 A.D.2d 113, 556 N.Y.S.2d 67 (1st Dep't 1990).

86. People v. Manzanillo, 145 Misc.2d 504, 546 N.Y.S.2d 954 (N.Y.C.Crim.Ct. 1989)(in child sex abuse prosecution, court ordered in camera inspection of complaining witness's mental health records to determine whether they contained any relevant and material information; court relied on defendant's sixth-amendment right of cross-examination and right of access to exculpatory material). See Pennsylvania v. Ritchie, 480 U.S. 39, 107 S.Ct. 989, 94 L.Ed.2d 40 (1987)(defendant in child sex abuse prosecution had right, under federal due process clause, to have court conduct in camera review of child abuse agency's otherwise privileged records and to release "material" information).

87. Doe v. Hynes, 104 Misc.2d 398, 428 N.Y.S.2d 810 (Sup.Ct.Monroe Co.1980). See also text at notes 69–72 supra.

§ 502.2

1. The Supreme Court has stated that "the physician-patient evidentiary privilege is unknown to the common law." Whalen v. Roe, 429 U.S. 589, 602 n.28, 97 S.Ct. 869, 877, 51 L.Ed.2d 64, 75 (1977). See also Hancock v. Dodson, 958 F.2d 1367, 1373 (6th Cir.1992); United States v. Moore, 970 F.2d 48, 50 (5th Cir.1992); United States v. Mullings, 364 F.2d 173, 176 n.3 (2d Cir. 1966). But see Mann v. University of Cincinnati, 824 F.Supp. 1190, 1197–98 (S.D.Ohio), aff'd, 152 F.R.D. 119 (S.D.Ohio 1993) (recognizing a doctor-patient privilege under federal law, and holding that medical records concerning plaintiff's mental and emotional health were protected).

2. See In re Zuniga, 714 F.2d 632, 639–40 (6th Cir.), cert. denied, 464 U.S. 983, 104 S.Ct. 426, 78 L.Ed.2d 361 (1983)(recognizing a qualified psychotherapist-patient privilege but holding that privilege did not protect identity of psychiatrist's patients and dates and duration of their treatment).

3. See, e.g., United States v. Burtrum, 17 F.3d 1299, 1302 (10th Cir.1994); United States v. Moore, 970 F.2d 48, 50 (5th Cir. 1992); In re Grand Jury Proceedings, 867 F.2d 562, 564–65 (9th Cir.), cert. denied, 493 U.S. 906, 110 S.Ct. 265, 107 L.Ed.2d 214 (1989); United States v. Corona, 849 F.2d 562, 567 (11th Cir.1988), cert. denied, 489 U.S. 1084, 109 S.Ct. 1542, 103 L.Ed.2d 846 (1989).

4. Although Congress declined to adopt it, Rule 504 would have provided:

(a) Definitions.

(1) A "patient" is a person who consults or is examined or interviewed by a psychotherapist.

(2) A "psychotherapist" is (A) a person authorized to practice medicine in any state or nation, or reasonably believed by the patient so to be, while engaged in the diagnosis or treatment of a mental or emotional condition, including drug addiction, or (B) a person licensed or certi-

The Second Circuit recognized a qualified psychotherapist-patient privilege in *In re Doe*.[5] The court reasoned that because psychotherapist-patient communications involve more highly personal and potentially embarrassing information than do ordinary physician-patient communications, the creation of a qualified privilege was justified.[6] The determination of whether testimony is subject to this privilege must be made on a case-by-case basis by balancing the witness's privacy interests against evidentiary needs.[7] In the case before it, the court concluded that the privilege did not protect the psychiatric records of a government witness whose credibility would be the central issue at defendant's extortion trial.[8] Subsequent decisions within the Second Circuit have upheld particular invocations of the privilege.[9]

fied as a psychologist under the laws of any state or nation, while similarly engaged.

(3) A communication is "confidential" if not intended to be disclosed to third persons other than those present to further the interest of the patient in the consultation, examination, or interview, or persons reasonably necessary for the transmission of the communication, or persons who are participating in the diagnosis and treatment under the direction of the psychotherapist, including members of the patient's family.

(b) General rule of privilege. A patient has a privilege to refuse to disclose and to prevent any other person from disclosing confidential communications, made for the purposes of diagnosis or treatment of his mental or emotional condition, including drug addiction, among himself, his psychotherapist, or persons who are participating in the diagnosis or treatment under the direction of the psychotherapist, including members of the patient's family.

(c) Who may claim the privilege. The privilege may be claimed by the patient, by his guardian or conservator, or by the personal representative of a deceased patient. The person who was the psychotherapist may claim the privilege but only on behalf of the patient. His authority so to do is presumed in the absence of evidence to the contrary.

(d) Exceptions.

(1) *Proceedings for hospitalization.* There is no privilege under this rule for communications relevant to an issue in proceedings to hospitalize the patient for mental illness, if the psychotherapist in the course of diagnosis or treatment has determined that the patient is in need of hospitalization.

(2) *Examination by order of judge.* If the judge orders an examination of the mental or emotional condition of the patient, communications made in the course thereof are not privileged under this rule with respect to the particular purpose for which the examination is ordered unless the judge orders otherwise.

(3) *Condition an element of claim or defense.* There is no privilege under this rule as to communications relevant to an issue of the mental or emotional condition of the patient in any proceeding in which he relies upon the condition as an element of his claim or defense, or, after the patient's death, in any proceeding in which any party relies upon the condition as an element of his claim or defense.

5. 964 F.2d 1325, 1328–29 (2d Cir.1992).

6. Id. at 1328 ("Nor can it be seriously disputed that unrestrained disclosure might discourage persons from seeking psychiatric help").

7. Id. at 1328–29 ("the privilege amounts only to a requirement that a court give consideration to a witness's privacy interests as an important factor to be weighed in the balance in considering the admissibility of psychiatric histories or diagnoses").

8. Id. at 1329.

9. United States v. Sessa, 806 F.Supp. 1063, 1070 (E.D.N.Y.1992) (government-retained psychologist who performed psychological evaluation of prosecution witness in connection with his possible placement in witness protection program could not be compelled by defendant to disclose her findings for purpose of attempted impeachment of witness' credibility; such testimony would have been of low probative value and would have unnecessarily intruded on witness' privacy interests); Misek-Falkoff v. International Business Machines Corp., 144 F.R.D. 48, 50–51 (S.D.N.Y.1992)(court approved a protective order that limited the

503 Spousal Privileges

§ 503.1 New York: Generally

There are two aspects to the spousal privilege, one based on incompetency of a spouse to testify against the other spouse about anything, and the second limited to the disclosure of confidential communications between them. The incompetency aspect has not been in the law of New York since the 1880s when it was eliminated by statute in both civil and criminal cases,[1] with a statutory exception relating to matrimonial proceedings based on adultery.[2] The second aspect, resting upon whether or not the communication was confidential, continues in full force and effect. The present law is codified in CPLR 4502 as follows:

(a) **Incompetency where issue adultery.** A husband or wife is not competent to testify against the other in an action founded upon adultery, except to prove the marriage, disprove the adultery, or disprove a defense after evidence has been introduced tending to prove such defense.

(b) **Confidential communication privileged.** A husband or wife shall not be required, or, without consent of the other if living, allowed, to disclosed a confidential communication made by one to the other during marriage.

Library References:

West's Key No. Digests, Witnesses ⚖51.

§ 503.2 New York: Incompetency in Adultery Cases

The subdivision (a) incompetency provision survives, although its rationale is unclear, especially since the grounds for divorce have multiplied beyond adultery. Wigmore says that the common law incompetency generally is cloaked in a "tantalizing obscurity,"[1] but that its best explanation is that there was a repugnance "to condemning a man by admitting to the witness stand against him those who lived under his roof, shared the secrets of his domestic life, depended on him for sustenance and were almost numbered among his chattels."[2] The reasons for retaining the adultery vestige do not necessarily flow from this unless the unseemliness involved in marital litigation based on

dissemination of defense-conducted psychiatric evaluation of plaintiff).

§ 503.1

1. People v. Daghita, 299 N.Y. 194, 198, 86 N.E.2d 172, 174 (1949). CPLR 4512 removes all testimonial incompetency "except as otherwise expressly prescribed."

2. CPLR 4502(a). A judge-made rule of incompetency also applies in some cases if a spouse seeks to testify to nonaccess by the other spouse during marriage. See § 601.1, at notes 23–26, infra.

§ 503.2

1. 8 Wigmore § 2227, at 211.
2. Id. at 212.

adultery is of the most extreme and that other devices should be found for the introduction of such proof.

In any event, the subdivision (a) prohibition is strictly and literally construed. It is a rule of substance and cannot be waived, at least not by a simple delay in voicing the objection.[3] It is applied only when one spouse attempts to testify *against* the other spouse in an action based on *adultery*. Hence, there is nothing to prevent a spouse from testifying to his or her own adultery,[4] and in an action based upon cruel and inhuman treatment one spouse may testify against the other spouse.[5] Where a spouse confesses his or her own adultery, however, there must be some form of corroboration in order to avoid the aspect of collusion.[6] Furthermore, a wife may not testify "to identify the husband's handwriting in the letter to her in which he confessed his adultery"[7] since she would then be testifying against him. A foundation for his letter would have to be made in some other way. Interestingly, the court noted that the privilege based on confidential communications was not implicated.[8]

Where the issue of child custody is paramount one court has held that the husband may testify in a divorce action concerning his wife's adultery.[9] Another has held that where the issue is legitimacy of a child, a wife's out-of-court admissions as to adultery are admissible, but she may not directly testify to the matter.[10] This holding stems also from the common law presumption of legitimacy, which forbids spousal testimony concerning nonaccess during the marriage.[11]

The three exceptions to the subdivision (a) prohibition—spousal testimony is allowed to prove the marriage, disprove the adultery, or disprove a defense—are straightforward and have produced little or no reported case law.

Library References:

West's Key No. Digests, Witnesses ⚍51.

§ 503.3 New York: Privilege for Confidential Communications

The privilege for confidential communications between spouses is litigated with some degree of frequency. Although certain black letter assertions can be made about it, its boundary lines are not entirely defined. The rationale for this branch of the privilege is that it furthers

---

3. Marrow v. Marrow, 124 A.D.2d 1000, 508 N.Y.S.2d 789 (4th Dep't 1986).

4. Rivett v. Rivett, 270 A.D. 878, 61 N.Y.S.2d 7 (4th Dep't 1946).

5. Lee v. Lee, 51 A.D.2d 576, 378 N.Y.S.2d 459 (2d Dep't 1976).

6. In Grobin v. Grobin, 184 Misc. 996, 55 N.Y.S.2d 32 (Sup.Ct.Bronx Co.1945), the court recounted the history of the corroboration requirement.

7. Id. at 1000, 55 N.Y.S. at 36.

8. It was stated: "The letter recognized a status of separation and a possible subsequent divorce, and therefore the confession could not be said to have been induced by the marital relationship or to have been confidential in character." Id.

9. Johnson v. Johnson, 47 Misc.2d 805, 263 N.Y.S.2d 404 (Sup.Ct.Westchester Co.1965), aff'd, 25 A.D.2d 672, 268 N.Y.S.2d 403 (2d Dep't 1966).

10. A.C. v. B.C., 12 Misc.2d 1, 176 N.Y.S.2d 794 (Sup.Ct.Chenango Co.1958).

11. See Wigmore §§ 134–137, at 1718–23. See also § 601.1, at notes 23–26, infra.

marital harmony and societal interest.¹ Its checkpoints are that there be a communication which (1) is confidential, (2) is induced by the marital relationship, and (3) is made during the marriage.² Waivers and exceptions will be noted below.

a. Confidentiality

A case that nicely bridges the space between incompetency based on adultery and the confidentiality privilege is *Poppe v. Poppe*,³ where the wife sued the husband for separation based on his abandonment. The husband testified that he left the home because she had told him of her adulterous relationships. This testimony would not be prohibited under subdivision (a) because the proceeding was not based on adultery. She alleged his abandonment, and he alleged her cruelty. Neither were her revelations considered confidential. Ordinarily, of course, confidentiality is found when spouses communicate with each other outside the known presence of other persons.⁴ The court observed, however, that "[t]he statute [then § 349 of the Civil Practice Act] does not render inadmissible all communications between husband and wife, even though made in privacy and when alone."⁵ The court went on to state: "It is * * * perfectly clear that the statute was never designed to forbid inquiry into the personal wrongs committed by one spouse against the other, or that it was ever intended to label confidential a communication aimed at destroying the marital relationship.* * *"⁶

Two classic New York cases well illustrate not only what is and what is not confidential, but also that the communication can be by acts as well as words. In *People v. Daghita*,⁷ defendant used his home as a repository for stolen goods with the full knowledge and apparent acquiescence of his wife. He was, in effect, confiding in her although there was no evidence that she was collaborating in a criminal enterprise.⁸ In

---

§ 503.3

1. The court in People v. Daghita, 299 N.Y. 194, 198, 86 N.E.2d 172, 174 (1949) stated: "The rule affecting husband and wife at common law had its foundation 'in the identity of their rights and concerns, the interest of civil society, and the sanctities of the marriage relation,' and it was enforced by the courts with much strictness. (People v. Houghton, supra [24 Hun 501], p. 501. The object was 'that the most entire confidence may exist between them, and that there may be no apprehension that such confidence can, at any time, or in any event, be violated, so far, at least, as regards any testimony or disclosure in a court of justice.' (Chamberlain v. People, 23 N.Y. 85, 89))." See also People v. Rodriguez, 38 N.Y.2d 95, 99–100 n.3, 341 N.E.2d 231, 232, 378 N.Y.S.2d 665, 667 (1975)(concise summary of the history of the privilege in New York).

2. Poppe v. Poppe, 3 N.Y.2d 312, 315, 165 N.Y.S.2d 99, 102, 144 N.E.2d 72, 74 (1957).

3. 3 N.Y.2d 312, 165 N.Y.S.2d 99, 144 N.E.2d 72 (1957).

4. People v. Ressler, 17 N.Y.2d 174, 269 N.Y.S.2d 414, 216 N.E.2d 582 (1966); People v. Melski, 10 N.Y.2d 78, 217 N.Y.S.2d 65, 176 N.E.2d 81 (1961).

5. 3 N.Y.2d at 314, 315, 165 N.Y.S.2d at 101, 144 N.E.2d at 73.

6. Id. at 315, 165 N.Y.S.2d at 102, 144 N.E.2d at 74.

7. 299 N.Y. 194, 86 N.E.2d 172 (1949).

8. In contrast to *Daghita* is People v. Wilson, 64 N.Y.2d 634, 485 N.Y.S.2d 40, 474 N.E.2d 248 (1984), where it was held that the mere fact of a spouse's presence or absence form his apartment was not within the privilege because such fact was not "a communication which would not have been made but for the marital relationship." Id. at 636, 485 N.Y.S.2d at 41, 474 N.E.2d at 249.

a later case, *People v. Melski*,[9] the wife surprised her husband early in the morning when she entered the kitchen to get milk for the baby. He was there with accomplices and the loot from the robbery they had completed. The court expressly reaffirmed its holding in *Daghita*, but held that here the husband's actions were not intended as confidential. Not only had he not intended that she make these observations, but his actions were made in the presence of others and thus were clearly not confidential.[10]

And then there is the sometimes overlooked point that seemingly confidential communications between spouses may occasionally be admissible regardless of the objection of one of the spouses. Subdivision (b) of CPLR 4502 may not protect against disclosure by a third party who secretly overhears the spouses.[11] Thus, recordings made by an authorized eavesdropping procedure might well be admissible, even if otherwise falling within the meaning of a confidential communication induced by the marital relationship.[12] Likewise, while the wife may not be allowed to testify to her observations of her husband's criminal activity within the home, evidence turned up as a result of the wife's invitation to the police to search the marital home will not be suppressed.[13]

b. Induced by the Marital Relationship

In *People v. Dudley*,[14] the husband committed a crime in the wife's presence and then threatened her with dire consequences if she did not remain quiet. The usual confidence induced by the marriage relationship did not inspire the criminal act[15] constituting the communication here, and so the wife was free to testify. Yet in a subsequent case,

---

9. 10 N.Y.2d 78, 217 N.Y.S.2d 65, 176 N.E.2d 81 (1961).

10. This prompted the dissenter to note that it was the presence of the third persons along with the loot that was "part of the very fact confidentially communicated." Id. at 84–85, 217 N.Y.S.2d at 71, 176 N.E.2d at 85–86.

11. People v. Watkins, 63 A.D.2d 1033, 406 N.Y.S.2d 343 (2d Dep't 1978), cert. denied, 439 U.S. 984, 99 S.Ct. 575, 58 L.Ed.2d 656 (1978).

12. Id. at 1034, 406 N.Y.S.2d at 344. The rule as to eavesdroppers is confirmed by the Court of Appeals in Prink v. Rockefeller Center, 48 N.Y.2d 309, 422 N.Y.S.2d 911, 398 N.E.2d 517 (1979), where the court noted that with respect to all of the article 45 CPLR privileges, only lawyer-client communications and communications overheard by illegal eavesdroppers are fully protected. Id. at 315 n.2, 422 N.Y.S.2d at 915, 398 N.E.2d at 520.

13. People v. Scull, 37 N.Y.2d 833, 378 N.Y.S.2d 30, 340 N.E.2d 466 (1975). In People v. Lifrieri, 157 Misc.2d 598, 597 N.Y.S.2d 580 (1993), the court reviewed the *Scull* case and other cases (People v. Kemp, 59 A.D.2d 414, 399 N.Y.S.2d 879 (1st Dep't 1977), and out-of-state authority cited at 157 Misc.2d at 602, 597 N.Y.S.2d at 583) in a situation where the police interviewed the wife, took the information gleaned from her and located homicide victims which were linked to defendant husband. The marital privilege, said the court, does not involve a constitutionally protected right and thus a breach of that privilege by the police will not give defendant a constitutional argument against introduction of the fruits of that breach.

14. 24 N.Y.2d 410, 301 N.Y.S.2d 9, 248 N.E.2d 860 (1969).

15. Defendant was convicted of killing an elderly woman and the defense agreed that up until the point the victim was actually dispatched, there could have been no confidentiality between husband and wife since a third person was present—the victim.

People v. Fields,[16] where the couple had been estranged for a prolonged period of time, and although the husband's confidence placed in his wife concerning his commission of a crime was accompanied by a threat to her life should he have to go to jail, the majority of the judges held the communication protected. That the issues in these cases turn on slight differentiation in the facts is well illustrated by *People v. Fediuk*,[17] which involved a telephone conversation between defendant and his estranged wife, defendant having killed his wife's male companion and having threatened her. The court said that there was a presumption of spousal confidentiality, even where the couple is estranged "for even in a stormy separation, disclosures to a spouse may be induced by absolute confidence in the marital relationship.* * *"[18]

These cases suggest that the court must make a collateral determination of strength of the marital relationship as a prerequisite to a ruling on the privilege issue. Perhaps the focus ought to be on the communication itself and the circumstances immediately surrounding it, given that the parties are, in fact, legally married.

c. Communication Made During the Marriage

One person's communication to another before they are married is not protected even at a time after they are married.[19] The communication must be made within the context of a legal marriage. Hence, if a valid common law marriage is entered into in a foreign state the privilege will be recognized in New York.[20] But where the couple are simply living together, even though raising a family, the privilege cannot obtain.[21] Bigamous relationships will not qualify for application of the privilege.[22] In *Matter of Vanderbilt*,[23] a communication was deemed to be made during the marriage where the husband made a tape recording just

---

16. 38 A.D.2d 231, 328 N.Y.S.2d 542 (1st Dep't), aff'd, 31 N.Y.2d 713, 337 N.Y.S.2d 517, 289 N.E.2d 557 (1972).

17. 66 N.Y.2d 881, 498 N.Y.S.2d 763, 489 N.E.2d 732 (1985).

18. Id. at 884, 498 N.Y.S.2d at 765, 489 N.E.2d at 734. The court held that here the substance of the conversation and the defendant's statements showed that he was "prompted by the affection, confidence and loyalty engendered by the marital relationship." Id. In contrast to *Fediuk*, see People v. Naylor, 120 A.D.2d 940, 502 N.Y.S.2d 856 (4th Dep't 1986) (wife permitted to testify where husband's communication, in the spirit of *Dudley*, was accompanied by fear and intimidation "and in pursuit of a criminal enterprise"); People v. D'Amato, 105 Misc.2d 1048, 430 N.Y.S.2d 521 (Sup. Ct.Bronx Co.1980)(communication not protected because it was made during a diatribe in conjunction with threatening and abusive behavior delivered when the relationship was in serious disrepair).

19. People v. Chirse, 132 A.D.2d 615, 517 N.Y.S.2d 772 (2d Dep't), appeal denied, 70 N.Y.2d 749, 520 N.Y.S.2d 1025, 514 N.E.2d 1377 (1987).

20. People v. Suarez, 148 Misc.2d 95, 560 N.Y.S.2d 68 (Sup.Ct.N.Y.Co.1990).

21. Id. In this case the couple had lived together since 1984 and were raising three children, two of their own and one of the woman's. They claimed that in 1985 they went to Ohio, a common law marriage state, where they made commitments to each other and exchanged vows. The court ordered an evidentiary hearing into whether or not an Ohio common law marriage existed.

22. People v. Mulgrave, 163 A.D.2d 538, 558 N.Y.S.2d 607 (2d Dep't), appeal denied, 76 N.Y.2d 989, 563 N.Y.S.2d 777, 565 N.E.2d 526 (1990).

23. 57 N.Y.2d 66, 453 N.Y.S.2d 662, 439 N.E.2d 378 (1982). The husband's suicide message was not destructive of the marriage because it may have been "a last attempt to preserve the affection that gave rise to the marriage and to explain the reason for the drastic act." Id. at 74, 453 N.Y.S.2d at 667, 439 N.E.2d at 382.

prior to attempting suicide, obviously contemplating that his wife would not hear it until after the marriage was terminated by his death.

d. Waiver

Prink v. Rockefeller Center[24] provides a most interesting lesson on the question of waiver. The wife brought a wrongful death action based on her husband's fall from his 36th floor office located in defendant's building. The defense was that deceased committed suicide and that the window had not been negligently maintained. At a pretrial deposition, the wife refused to testify as to what her husband had told her concerning the reason he was seeing a psychiatrist. The psychiatrist had, however, reported that the deceased was feeling tense and depressed before his death. This release of the information did not cause a waiver. The court emphasized the fact that the deceased is the person protected by the privilege. The persons to whom the information was given—the people who might be witnesses—do not possess the privilege and cannot waive it simply by revealing the information. Only the patient-husband could waive, and in this case his lips were sealed. In other words, the privilege belongs to the spouse against whom the other spouse's testimony is offered.[25] However, the wife's assertion of the privilege in *Prink* was rejected on a totally different ground. She was the plaintiff and could not, in fairness, use the privilege to suppress information about the claim.[26]

In another case with equally unusual facts, *Matter of Vanderbilt*,[27] a husband who survived his suicide attempt had recorded two taped messages, one to his wife and the other unaddressed, but apparently intended for a lawyer. The wife did not listen to the tape but delivered it instead it to a lawyer-friend. The fact that the wife parted with the tape and that it passed through several hands was not a waiver because none of the temporary custodians listened to the tape. Waiver consists of a revelation of the substance of a message, not merely the fact that the message existed.[28]

---

24. 48 N.Y.2d 309, 422 N.Y.S.2d 911, 398 N.E.2d 517 (1979).

25. People v. McCormack, 278 App.Div. 191, 104 N.Y.S.2d 139 (1st Dep't 1951), aff'd, 303 N.Y. 782, 103 N.E.2d 895 (1952). One spouse may not unilaterally waive the privilege. See People v. Wood, 126 N.Y. 249, 27 N.E. 362 (1891)(upon defendant-spouse's objection, witness-spouse should not have been permitted to waive privilege and testify to marital confidences).

26. To succeed in a wrongful death action, said the court, the plaintiff must show that the cause of action could have been maintained by the deceased had he lived. Under well established rules, the privileges can be used only as a shield, and thus the bringing of a personal injury action causes an automatic waiver of any privileged information relevant to the plaintiff's cause of action under the rule in Koump v. Smith, 25 N.Y.2d 287, 303 N.Y.S.2d 858, 250 N.E.2d 857 (1969). See § 502.1 supra at notes 50–51. Since the plaintiff in a wrongful death action in effect stands in the shoes of the deceased, and since the deceased's mental condition was an issue within the meaning of *Koump*, waiver occurs just as it would have had the action been one for personal injuries.

27. 57 N.Y.2d 66, 453 N.Y.S.2d 662, 439 N.E.2d 378 (1982).

28. Id. at 74, 453 N.Y.S.2d at 667, 439 N.E.2d at 382–83. The court noted that only the husband and justices of the lower courts, who had listened to the tape to ascertain its contents, knew the substance of its message. The second tape was held protected by the attorney-client privilege. Id. at 76–77, 453 N.Y.S.2d at 668–69, 439 N.E.2d at 384.

e. Exceptions

The so-called crime/fraud exception lifts the privilege for spousal communications made during the planning or commission of a crime in which both are collaborating.[29]

Another exception applies to the situation where one spouse commits a crime against the other, or against other family members,[30] or even where a civil wrong is perpetrated by one against the other.[31] Finally, the usual rule is that the privilege is sealed with the death of the spouse owning the privilege;[32] but as Wigmore states, there can be exceptions when the surviving spouse ought to be allowed to testify where it would have been in the deceased's interests to do so, or where it is necessary to exonerate the survivor from charges directed against him or her.[33]

These and other exceptions are incorporated into § 505 of the Proposed New York Evidence Code.[34]

Library References:

West's Key No. Digests, Witnesses ⇔187, 219(2).

---

29. People v. Watkins, 89 Misc.2d 870, 393 N.Y.S.2d 283 (Sup.Ct.Suffolk Co.1977), aff'd, 63 A.D.2d 1033, 406 N.Y.S.2d 343 (2d Dep't 1978), cert. denied, 439 U.S. 984, 99 S.Ct. 575, 58 L.Ed.2d 656 (1978).

30. People v. Allman, 41 A.D.2d 325, 342 N.Y.S.2d 896 (2d Dep't 1973). See N.Y.Family Ct.Act § 1046(a)(vii)(exception in proceedings for child abuse or neglect). See also People v. St. John, 74 A.D.2d 85, 426 N.Y.S.2d 863 (3d Dep't 1980).

31. In Poppe v. Poppe, 3 N.Y.2d 312, 315, 165 N.Y.S.2d 99, 102, 144 N.E.2d 72, 74 (1957), it is stated: "It is * * * perfectly clear that the statute was never designed to forbid inquiry into the personal wrongs committed by one spouse against the other, or that it was ever intended to label confidential a communication aimed at destroying the marital relation.* * *"

32. Prink v. Rockefeller Center, 48 N.Y.2d 309, 422 N.Y.S.2d 911, 398 N.E.2d 517 (1979).

33. 8 Wigmore § 2341 at 675.

34. § 505. **Spousal privilege [PROPOSED]**

(a) **Confidential communication privileged.** A husband or wife shall not be required, or without consent of the other if living, allowed, to disclose a confidential communication made by one to the other during marriage.

(b) **Exceptions.** The privilege in this section shall not apply when an exception is recognized by statute, or in other situations, where the policies underlying the privilege are absent, including but not limited to:

(1) **Furtherance of crime or fraud.** If the communication was made for the purpose of committing what the spouse knew or reasonably should have known to be a crime or fraud.

(2) **Crimes in the family.** In a criminal action or a family court proceeding in which one spouse is alleged to have committed an act against the person or property of (A) the other, (B) a child of either, or (C) a member of the same family or household.

(3) **Certain civil actions and proceedings.** In any civil action or proceeding brought by or on behalf of one spouse against the other, or in any civil action or proceeding involving custody of a child.

(4) **Communication offered by accused spouse.** In a criminal case in which the communication is offered by an accused who was one of the spouses between whom the communication was made.

(5) **Condition in issue.** As to a communication relevant to the physical, mental or emotional condition of the spouse in any action or proceeding in which the other spouse or the spouse's representative relies upon that condition as an element of a claim or defense.

§ 503.4 New York: Parent–Child Privilege

There is no parent-child privilege to be found in statutory form, but some courts have recognized such a privilege. In *In re A & M*[1] the court held that when a minor child confided to his father certain information implicating the child in the crime of arson, the communication was privileged and the father could claim that privilege in a grand jury hearing. The court stated that where the information divulged is for the purpose of gaining support, advice, or guidance, "the interest of society in protecting and nurturing the parent-child relationship is of such overwhelming significance that the State interest in fact-finding must give way."[2] This rule was extended to a confidential communication by a twenty-three-year-old to his father concerning an accident in which the son had run down two pedestrians, killing one of them. In *People v. Fitzgerald*[3] the court stated quite cogently that the underlying relationship of trust and confidence does not "cease at the stroke of midnight on the last day of the child's 17th year."[4]

Library References:

West's Key No. Digests, Evidence ⇔186; Witnesses ⇔66.

§ 503.5 Federal

The distinction between the spousal privilege based on incompetency, and the spousal privilege based on confidential communications, is nicely pointed up in *Trammel v. United States*.[1] Under the New York rule recounted in the previous sections, spouses have long been competent to testify against each other in general,[2] although confidential communications remain protected.[3] The federal rule as stated in *Hawkins v. United States*[4] prevented the testimony of one spouse against another in a criminal case, unless both consented, on any subject, not just confidential communications. *Hawkins* was drastically modified by *Trammel* where the rule was changed to provide that one spouse may testify against the other in a criminal case, if he or she chooses, concerning *non*-confidential matters.[5] The rule protecting confidential

§ 503.4

1. 61 A.D.2d 426, 403 N.Y.S.2d 375 (4th Dep't 1978).

2. Id. at 433–34, 403 N.Y.S.2d at 380.

3. 101 Misc.2d 712, 422 N.Y.S.2d 309 (Westchester Co.Court 1979).

4. Id. at 718, 422 N.Y.S.2d at 313. See also People v. Harrell, 87 A.D.2d 21, 450 N.Y.S.2d 501 (2d Dep't 1982)(officer barred from testifying to overheard communication between mother and son in police station). But see People v. Johnson, 84 N.Y.2d 956, 957, 620 N.Y.S.2d 822, 823, 644 N.E.2d 1378, 1379 (1994), where the court said that even if there were such a thing as a parent-child privilege it "would not even arguably apply in that defendant was 28 years old at the time of the conversation with his mother. * * *" Also, another person was present and the conversation concerned a crime against another family member.

§ 503.5

1. 445 U.S. 40, 100 S.Ct. 906, 63 L.Ed.2d 186 (1980).

2. CPLR 4512.

3. CPLR 4502(b).

4. 358 U.S. 74, 79 S.Ct. 136, 3 L.Ed.2d 125 (1958).

5. In *Trammel* it was said that "the ancient foundations for so sweeping a privilege have long since disappeared," and it was noted that women now have separate legal identities, which was not the case when the rule was formulated. Furthermore, "[t]he contemporary justification for affording an accused such a privilege is also

communications established in *Wolfle v. United States*[6] was specifically preserved in *Trammel*; but in *Trammel* the wife, in return for lenient treatment from the government, decided to testify against her husband concerning their role in a heroin distribution conspiracy, a topic clearly not protected by the confidential communications privilege.[7] Thus, the ability to waive the incompetency privilege, more commonly called the "testimonial privilege," rests with the witness, not the spouse against whom the testimony is directed. On the other hand, where the privilege is based on confidentiality, more commonly known as the "marital communications privilege," the witness may not testify over the objection of the other spouse.

Library References:
West's Key No. Digests, Witnesses ⬟51, 187, 219(2).

a. Testimonial Privilege

The rule precluding any testimony by one spouse against the other concerning any matter, applies only in the criminal area. Indeed, the proposed federal rule was expressly limited to criminal cases.[8] The privilege is inoperable when there is no bona fide marriage;[9] and there is no protection where the couple has been divorced even though the subject of the testimony arose during the marriage.[10] If the marriage is in such disrepair as to be "moribund,"[11] or if it is legally invalid,[12] there will be no privilege. It will not operate where one spouse is on trial for a

---

unpersuasive. When one spouse is willing to testify against the other in a criminal proceeding—whatever the motivation—their relationship is almost certainly in disrepair.* * *" 445 U.S. at 52, 100 S.Ct. at 913, 63 L.Ed.2d at 196.

6. 291 U.S. 7, 54 S.Ct. 279, 78 L.Ed. 617 (1934).

7. See also United States v. Robilotto, 828 F.2d 940 (2d Cir.1987)(wife's testimony in RICO case did not concern a confidential communication).

8. **Rule 505. Husband–Wife Privilege [Not Enacted]**

(a) **General rule of privilege.** An accused in a criminal proceeding has a privilege to prevent his spouse from testifying against him.

(b) **Who may claim the privilege.** The privilege may be claimed by the accused or by the spouse on his behalf. The authority of the spouse to do so is presumed in the absence of evidence to the contrary.

(c) **Exceptions.** There is no privilege under this rule (1) in proceedings in which one spouse is charged with a crime against the person or property of the other or of a child of either, or with a crime against the person or property of a third person committed in the course of committing a crime against the other, or (2) as to matters occurring prior to the marriage, or (3) in proceedings in which a spouse is charged with importing an alien for prostitution or other immoral purpose in violation of 8 U.S.C. § 1328, with transporting a female in interstate commerce for immoral purposes or other offense in violation of 18 U.S.C. §§ 2421–2424, or with violation of other similar statutes.

Note that the proposed rule does not incorporate the holding in Trammel. The proposal was drafted before Trammel was decided and there was no need to revisit it since it was not enacted as one of the Federal Rules.

9. Lutwak v. United States, 344 U.S. 604, 73 S.Ct. 481, 97 L.Ed. 593 (1953)(the marriage was arranged only for the purpose of getting alien brides into the United States).

10. Barsky v. United States, 339 F.2d 180 (9th Cir.1964). See United States v. Fisher, 518 F.2d 836 (2d Cir.), cert. denied, 423 U.S. 1033, 96 S.Ct. 565, 46 L.Ed.2d 407 (1975).

11. United States v. Byrd, 750 F.2d 585 (7th Cir.1984).

12. United States v. White 545 F.2d 1129 (8th Cir.1976).

crime against the other spouse or the children[13] (the *Trammel* rule leaves the spouse free to testify here anyway); and the privilege cannot be invoked where the couple were both carrying out criminal activity.[14]

b. Marital Communications Privilege

The federal courts, like the courts in New York, seem to take considerable interest in the viability of the marriage. Thus, if the relationship is beyond salvation and a guarantee of confidentiality would do nothing to remedy it, there is no point in granting the privilege.[15] This is almost formulaic in the Second Circuit where it was stated that "[t]he longer the period of estrangement at the time of the subject 'communications,' the easier it will be for the government to show that the couple, though still legally wed, had been in fact permanently separated and thus could not invoke the privilege."[16] The federal law respecting the marital communications privilege generally parallels the New York law. The crime/fraud exception and the exception operable where one spouse has committed a crime against the other apply;[17] the privilege survives the termination of the marriage;[18] the communication must, of course, have been confidential;[19] and in certain instances the privilege may be waived by the witness.[20] As is the case with the testimonial privilege, the marriage must be legal, and not just a sham.[21]

The status under federal law of any analogous parent-child privileges is uncertain. One federal district court upheld an adult son's refusal to testify before a grand jury concerning communications with his father on the ground that his right of privacy within the family unit outweighed the government's evidentiary needs.[22] The Second Circuit, however, rejected a claim of "family privilege" by a grand jury witness who sought to avoid testifying against his in-laws.[23]

---

13. United States v. Allery, 526 F.2d 1362 (8th Cir.1975).

14. Appeal of Malfitano, 633 F.2d 276 (3d Cir.1980). See also In re Grand Jury Subpoena United States, 755 F.2d 1022 (2d Cir.1985), cert. granted sub nom., United States v. Koecher, 474 U.S. 815, 106 S.Ct. 56, 88 L.Ed.2d 46 (1985), vacated as moot, 475 U.S. 133, 106 S.Ct. 1253, 89 L.Ed.2d 103 (1986)(opinion contains thorough discussion as to crime/fraud exception).

15. In re Witness Before Grand Jury, 791 F.2d 234 (2d Cir.1986) (communications occurred after there had been a four-year separation and husband had produced a child by another woman).

16. Id. at 238.

17. United States v. Estes, 793 F.2d 465 (2d Cir.1986); 2 Weinstein and Berger ¶ 505[03].

18. Pereira v. United States, 347 U.S. 1, 74 S.Ct. 358, 98 L.Ed. 435 (1954).

19. Id.; United States v. Parker, 834 F.2d 408 (4th Cir.1987), cert. denied, 485 U.S. 938, 108 S.Ct. 1118, 99 L.Ed.2d 279 (1988).

20. In United States v. Premises Known as 281 Syosset, Woodbury Road, 862 F.Supp. 847 (E.D.N.Y.1994), a civil drug forfeiture case, it was held that the wife waived the claim of privilege concerning discussions with her husband by raising an "innocent owner" defense to the government's claim on the property, and by testifying to part of the conversations with her husband. Beyond that, the crime-fraud exception would apply since the conversation sought to be protected involved ongoing criminal activity. The testimonial privilege was not available inasmuch as this was a civil proceeding.

21. See note 9 supra.

22. In re Agosto, 553 F.Supp. 1298 (D.Nev.1983)(recognition of parent-child testimonial privilege and confidential communications privilege).

23. In re Matthews, 714 F.2d 223 (2d Cir.1983).

504 Communications with Clergy Privilege

§ 504.1 New York

CPLR 4505 provides:

> Unless the person confessing or confiding waives the privilege, a clergyman, or other minister of any religion or duly accredited Christian practitioner, shall not be allowed [to] disclose a confession or confidence made to him in his professional character as spiritual advisor.

There was no common law "priest-penitent" privilege and no doubt many would confide in their spiritual advisors whether or not there was a legal privilege.[1] Nevertheless, the privilege is now firmly implanted in the law for a purpose similar to that inherent in the other privileges—to encourage sensitive communications without fear of reprisal.[2]

The two main elements of the privilege are that the communication be intended as confidential, and that it pass between the penitent and one who is acting in a spiritual advisory capacity. Despite the clear limitation to a spiritual relationship, the courts have had to deal with arguments urging a much broader coverage. In *Keenan v. Gigante*,[3] a priest unsuccessfully asserted the privilege when asked at a grand jury hearing whether he had attempted to obtain special treatment for a certain prisoner. In *B'Nai Jonah v. Kuriansky*,[4] a rabbi unsuccessfully sought to invoke the privilege when records kept on donors were subpoenaed; in *People v. Drelich*,[5] the rabbi was found to have been consulted, not as a spiritual advisor, but as an agent to procure a lawyer and help negotiate a beneficial plea bargain; and in *Matter of N. and G. Children*,[6] the priest initiated the contact by warning the "penitent" that he should discontinue sexual abuse of his children or lose custody, a communication clearly not covered by the privilege.

As to what constitutes waiver, the Court of Appeals in *People v.*

---

§ 504.1

1. McCormick § 76.2, at 286.

2. Matter of Keenan v. Gigante, 47 N.Y.2d 160, 417 N.Y.S.2d 226, 390 N.E.2d 1151, cert. denied sub nom., Gigante v. Lankler, 444 U.S. 887, 100 S.Ct. 181, 62 L.Ed.2d 118 (1979).

3. Id. Father Gigante was also a New York City Councilman and the inquiry involved, inter alia, his attempts to influence public officials in order to get special treatment for the prisoner. The questions put to the priest in no way involved disclosure of communications to or from a penitent, nor did the subject matter involved in the communication relate to the priest in his spiritual capacity.

4. 172 A.D.2d 35, 576 N.Y.S.2d 934 (3d Dep't 1991), appeal dismissed, 79 N.Y.2d 895, 581 N.Y.S.2d 659, 590 N.E.2d 244 (1992). Here, a grand jury issued subpoenas in a Medicaid fraud investigation, one to petitioner's bank for all records for a four-year period, and the other to petitioner's rabbi and spiritual leader to produce records for a five-year period listing donors, membership lists, mailing lists, and copies of all receipts given to any donors. The court could not see the subpoenaed material as coming "under the rubric of a 'confession or confidence' * * * or that it was 'made with the purpose of seeking religious counsel, advice, solace, absolution or ministration'. * * *" Id. at 38, 576 N.Y.S.2d at 936.

5. 123 A.D.2d 441, 506 N.Y.S.2d 746 (2d Dep't 1986).

6. 176 A.D.2d 504, 574 N.Y.S.2d 696 (1st Dep't 1991).

§ 504.1 PRIVILEGES Ch. 5

Carmona,[7] indicated that where the penitent tells detectives the same thing he told the clergy, and acknowledges that he had given the clergy this information, he would be deemed to have waived any claim of confidentiality.

So long as the clergyman is acting as a spiritual advisor it does not matter that he is not of the same congregation as the penitent[8] or that the communication is not a formal confession.[9] It is speculated that the privilege would hold even if the "clergyman" were not authentic, or did not fit the statutory description, if the penitent could have reasonably believed him to be a true spiritual advisor.[10] Also, it would seem that confidentiality would hold even where another person is present to assist the penitent, otherwise there would be a significant inconsistency with the major privileges.[11]

The Proposed New York Evidence Code generally expresses the prevailing law in New York.[12]

Library References:

West's Key No. Digests, Witnesses ⚞215.

7. 82 N.Y.2d 603, 606 N.Y.S.2d 879, 627 N.E.2d 959 (1993). The court found it unnecessary to decide the waiver question because the statements had been given the detectives in violation of defendant's right to counsel. To allow the statements in evidence on the waiver principle "would permit the People to do indirectly what they cannot do directly"—i.e., make positive use of an official illegal act. Such a "back door" use of an illegality would run counter to the underlying purpose of the suppression rule: to deter official misconduct by eliminating any benefit that may flow from it. Id. at 612, 606 N.Y.S.2d at 883, 627 N.E.2d at 963.

8. Kruglikov v. Kruglikov, 29 Misc.2d 17, 217 N.Y.S.2d 845 (Sup.Ct.Queens Co.1961), appeal dismissed, 16 A.D.2d 735, 226 N.Y.S.2d 931 (4th Dep't 1962); Matter of Fuhrer, 100 Misc.2d 315, 419 N.Y.S.2d 426 (Sup.Ct.Richmond Co.1979), aff'd, 72 A.D.2d 813, 421 N.Y.S.2d 906 (2d Dep't 1979). See also Anno., "Matters To Which The Privilege Covering Communications To Clergyman or Spiritual Advisor Extends," 71 A.L.R.3d 794 (1976).

9. Kruglikov, supra note 8 (disclosure concerned marital problems).

10. See Commentary to Proposed New York Evidence Code § 506, p.94. In Matter of Lewis v. N.Y. City Housing Auth., 151 A.D.2d 237, 542 N.Y.S.2d 165 (1st Dep't 1989), a housing policeman was also an ordained minister. Off duty, in his role as minister, he was given in confidence a .38 calibre gun. He was brought up on charges because, although he turned the gun into the police department, he had not followed procedures. His privilege claim was upheld because the "penitent" had reason to believe he was making a privileged communication to a clergyman.

11. See, e.g., § 501.1 supra, at note 55 (attorney-client); § 502.1 supra, at notes 28–29 (physician-patient).

12. § 506. **Privileged communication to the clergy [PROPOSED]**

(a) **Confidential communication privileged.** Unless the person confessing or confiding waives the privilege, a member of the clergy, or other minister of any religion or duly accredited Christian Science practitioner or a person reasonably believed to be so by the person confessing or confiding, shall not be allowed to disclose a confession or confidence received in a professional character as spiritual advisor.

(b) **Exceptions—Furtherance of crime or fraud.** The privilege in this section shall not apply when an exception is recognized by statute, or in other situations, where the policies underlying the privilege are absent, including but not limited to: if the confession or confidence was made for the purpose of committing what the person confiding or confession knew or reasonably should have known to be a crime or a fraud.

§ 504.2 Federal

The rule proposed for the federal courts with respect to clergy-penitent communications is somewhat different than the New York proposed code provision.[1] Although this privilege was not known at common law, and there is no statutory basis for it in federal law, the federal courts will employ it in cases based on federal law.[2]

Library References:
West's Key No. Digests, Witnesses ⇌215.

505 Social Worker Privilege

§ 505.1 New York

Sensitive communications pass between a social worker and client which call for the same protections as the other privileges, and for the same reason—to encourage the client to make full disclosure.[1] Thus CPLR 4508 contains a statutory scheme even more copious in detail than the venerable lawyer-client or spousal provisions.[2] It has been held that

§ 504.2

1. Rule 506. Communications to Clergymen [Not Enacted]

(a) Definitions. As used in this rule:

(1) A "clergyman" is a minister, priest, rabbi, or other similar functionary of a religious organization, or an individual reasonably believed so to be by the person consulting him.

(2) A communication is "confidential" if made privately and not intended for further disclosure except to other persons present in furtherance of the purpose of the communication.

(b) General rule of privilege. A person has a privilege to refuse to disclose and to prevent another from disclosing a confidential communication by the person to a clergyman in his professional character as spiritual adviser.

(c) Who may claim the privilege. The privilege may be claimed by the person, by his guardian or conservator, or by his personal representative if he is deceased. The clergyman may claim the privilege on behalf of the person. His authority so to do is presumed in the absence of evidence to the contrary.

2. In Trammel v. United States, 445 U.S. 40, 51, 100 S.Ct. 906, 912, 63 L.Ed.2d 186 (1980), a spousal privilege case, the Court in dictum stated: "The priest-penitent privilege recognizes the human need to disclose to a spiritual counselor, in total and absolute confidence, what are believed to be flawed acts or thoughts and to receive priestly consolation and guidance in return." In United States v. Gordon, 655 F.2d 478, 486 (2d Cir.1981), the court acknowledged the existence of the privilege but held that it would not obtain in that case where the communication related to business and not spiritual matters. And, in United States v. Wells, 446 F.2d 2 (2d Cir. 1971), defendant sought to bar evidence of a letter he sent to a priest requesting the priest to contact a certain FBI agent. In rejecting defendant's clergy-penitent argument, the court stated: "While the privilege has been recognized in the federal courts it appears to be restricted to confidential confessions or other confidential communications of a penitent seeking spiritual rehabilitation." Id. at 4.

§ 505.1

1. Grand Jury Proceeding (Doe), 56 N.Y.2d 348, 353, 452 N.Y.S.2d 361, 363, 437 N.E.2d 1118, 1120 (1982); Community Service Soc. v. Welfare Inspector General, 91 Misc.2d 383, 398 N.Y.S.2d 92 (Sup.Ct. N.Y.Co.1977), aff'd, 65 A.D.2d 734, 411 N.Y.S.2d 188 (1st Dep't 1978)(privilege said to equate with attorney-client, physician-patient and clergy-penitent).

2. § 4508. Social worker

(a) Confidential information privileged. A person duly registered as a certified social worker under the provisions of article one hundred fifty-four of the education law shall not be required to disclose a communication made by his client to him, or his advice given thereon, in the course of his professional employment, nor shall any clerk, stenographer or other person working for the same employer as

§ 505.1 PRIVILEGES Ch. 5

"client" means "client" and not the spouse of a client;[3] but it would seem, as has been held with respect to the lawyer-client privilege,[4] that where the spouse's presence (or anyone's presence for that matter) is necessary to enable the client to communicate, the privilege would be preserved.[5] The professional must be "duly registered as a certified social worker," and this has been strictly construed so that communications to an employee of a social agency who was not a bona fide social worker were deemed not privileged.[6] Given this interpretation, it is questionable whether the fact the client could reasonably have thought his confidante was a social worker would be enough to create a privilege.

Under the terms of the statute the fact the communication comes to the attention of agency employees will not destroy the privilege. Otherwise, the rules of confidentiality follow the same pattern as is found in the other privileges with regard to the presence of third parties[7] and the client's revealing the subject matter of the communication of his own accord, or, under the words of the statute, "as the client may authorize." Where claims are made for insurance benefits, the released information remains otherwise protected under CPLR 4508(b). Also, under the statute, where the client puts the subject matter of the counselling in issue, he will have waived any social worker privilege just as he would

the certified social worker or for the certified social worker be allowed to disclose any such communication or advice given thereon; except

1. that a certified social worker may disclose such information as the client may authorize;

2. that a certified social worker shall not be required to treat as confidential a communication by a client which reveals the contemplation of a crime or harmful act;

3. where the client is a child under the age of sixteen and the information acquired by the certified social worker indicates that the client has been the victim or subject of a crime, the certified social worker may be required to testify fully in relation thereto upon any examination, trial or other proceeding in which the commission of such crime is a subject of inquiry;

4. where the client waives the privilege by bringing charges against the certified social worker and such charges involve confidential communications between the client and certified social worker.

(b) Limitations on waiver. A client who, for the purpose of obtaining insurance benefits, authorizes the disclosure of any such privileged communication to any person shall not be deemed to have waived the privilege created by this section. For purposes of this subdivision:

1. "person" shall mean any individual, insurer or agent thereof, peer review committee, public or private corporation, political subdivision, government agency, department or bureau of the state, municipality, industry, co-partnership, association, firm, trust, estate or any other legal entity whatsoever; and

2. "insurance benefits" shall include payments under a self-insured plan.

3. Lichtenstein v. Montefiore Hospital & Medical Center, 56 A.D.2d 281, 392 N.Y.S.2d 18 (1st Dep't 1977).

4. Le Long v. Siebrecht, 196 A.D. 74, 187 N.Y.S. 150 (2d Dep't 1921); Hollien v. Kaye, 194 Misc. 821, 87 N.Y.S.2d 782 (Sup.Ct.Sullivan Co.1949).

5. Yaron v. Yaron, 83 Misc.2d 276, 372 N.Y.S.2d 518 (Sup.Ct.N.Y.Co.1975) (privilege intact where several family members consult concerning same issue).

6. Matter of Jeanne TT, 184 A.D.2d 895, 585 N.Y.S.2d 552 (3d Dep't 1992); People v. Bridges, 142 Misc.2d 789, 538 N.Y.S.2d 701 (Monroe Co.Ct.1989) (volunteer working at rape crisis center was not a certified social worker).

7. People v. Alaire, 148 A.D.2d 731, 539 N.Y.S.2d 468 (2d Dep't 1989) (no privilege where statement made by juvenile to social worker in police station was overheard by others); Humphrey v. Norden, 79 Misc.2d 192, 359 N.Y.S.2d 733 (Fam.Ct.Queens Co.1974)(in paternity proceeding statements made to social worker by putative

any other privilege.[8] The privilege can be waived at trial if not properly asserted.[9]

A "crime" exception is built into the statute where the client reveals the prospect of a future crime "or harmful act," and presumably an exception must exist should the client and the social worker conspire to commit a crime together. And where the communication in and of itself is part of a criminal transaction—where false statements are given in order to obtain welfare benefits—the privilege will fail.[10] The special exemption where the subject of the communication relates to a crime victim under the age of 16 complements Family Court Act § 1046(a)(vii) where there can be no privilege in child abuse or child neglect cases, and Social Services Law §§ 413 and 415, which require the reporting of suspected instances of child abuse.[11]

Cases involving children seem to have spawned the most case law concerning this privilege. In *People v. Tissois*,[12] defendant was prosecuted for rape and various counts of sexual abuse against young children who had been interviewed by a social worker. Defendant sought the social worker's interview notes as *Rosario* material,[13] which was denied since the statements had been made to the social worker and were not in the prosecutor's possession, and on the further ground that they were privileged under CPLR 4508. The court allowed that these impediments might have been overcome were defendant able to show that the notes had impeachment value, or that they contained exculpatory material,[14] which suggests that the privilege is not immutable and can be breached if a strong enough showing of the right to confrontation can be made.[15]

---

father in presence of mother are admissible).

8. Cf. Koump v. Smith, 25 N.Y.2d 287, 294, 303 N.Y.S.2d 858, 864, 250 N.E.2d 857, 861 (1969)(physician-patient privilege is "shield, not a sword").

9. People v. De Jesus, 69 N.Y.2d 855, 514 N.Y.S.2d 708, 507 N.E.2d 301 (1987). But see People v. Berkley, 157 A.D.2d 463, 549 N.Y.S.2d 392 (1st Dep't), appeal denied, 75 N.Y.2d 917, 555 N.Y.S.2d 35, 554 N.E.2d 72 (1990)(privilege preserved even though rape victim testified on direct and prosecutor neglected to assert the privilege).

10. People v. O'Gorman, 91 Misc.2d 539, 398 N.Y.S.2d 336 (Sup.Ct.Suffolk Co.1977)(misrepresentations in social service application that clients were tenants and not owners of their home was not protected).

11. The question has arisen whether the reporting requirements create an exception to the privilege in both civil and criminal proceedings. Compare People v. Bass, 140 Misc.2d 57, 529 N.Y.S.2d 961 (Sup.Ct. Bronx Co.1988)(exception applies only in civil cases), with People v. Gearhart, 148 Misc.2d 249, 560 N.Y.S.2d 247 (Nassau Co.Ct.1990)(exception applies in both).

12. 72 N.Y.2d 75, 531 N.Y.S.2d 228, 526 N.E.2d 1086 (1988).

13. People v. Rosario, 9 N.Y.2d 286, 213 N.Y.S.2d 448, 173 N.E.2d 881, cert. denied, 368 U.S. 866, 82 S.Ct. 117, 7 L.Ed.2d 64 (1961)(prosecutor must furnish defendant with any statements made by trial witnesses).

14. 72 N.Y.2d at 78, 531 N.Y.S.2d at 299, 526 N.E.2d at 1087. The trial judge had examined the notes in camera and found "nothing whatsoever exculpatory * * * that is inconsistent with the testimony of the children in direct examination." Id. at 78, 531 N.Y.S.2d at 231, 526 N.E.2d at 1089.

15. The Tissois court discussed several analogous non-social worker situations. In People v. Gissendanner, 48 N.Y.2d 543, 423 N.Y.S.2d 893, 399 N.E.2d 924 (1979), it was held that defendant was not entitled to personnel records where he could not show that the material could contain information that carried a potential for establishing the unreliability of either the criminal charge or the witness, and where there was no indication that the personnel records sought contained any exculpatory material. In Grattan v. People, 65 N.Y.2d 243, 491 N.Y.S.2d 125, 480 N.E.2d 714 (1985), the

§ 505.1   PRIVILEGES   Ch. 5

Matter of Koretta W.,[16] provides an interesting discussion on the question of whether the privilege is absolute. Wigmore's four factors for the recognition of privilege were applied:

(1) [c]ommunications must originate in the confidence that they will not be disclosed; (2) the element of confidentiality must be essential to the maintenance of the relationship between the parties; (3) the relation is one which in the opinion of the community ought to be fostered; and (4) the injury that would inure to the relationship as a result of disclosure must be greater than the benefit gained in regard to the correct disposal of litigation.[17]

The client, a juvenile charged with the crime of arson, had made inculpatory statements to a social worker, but the court held Wigmore's fourth point not to have been satisfied. "In one year the child will become part of the adult criminal court system if she has any further difficulties. * * * To shroud in secrecy what may well have been a cry for help now would be a cruel parody of justice."[18] Other courts have avoided the privilege in similar fashion.[19]

It is difficult to generalize from cases involving juveniles except to note that the privilege will be more easily broken when it would be in the child's interest to release the confidence. Questions that must be asked are: Who confided in the social worker—the defendant or the complaining witness? Who seeks disclosure? Who seeks the protection of the privilege? Can the person seeking the information show that the benefits from its disclosure will outweigh the maintenance of secrecy? Does the situation fall squarely within the purview of CPLR 4508(a)(3)?

information sought related to a sexually communicable disease and was protected under Public Health Law § 2306. It would not be revealed even though the 16-year-old girl had signed a release. There was no showing that the girl's contacts would not have been revealed by "less intrusive means." Finally, in Davis v. Alaska, 415 U.S. 308, 94 S.Ct. 1105, 39 L.Ed.2d 347 (1974), defendant's right to confrontation was violated where the protected background of a juvenile witness was not made available. Here, unlike the other cases, it could be shown that the material would have aided the defense.

In contrast to Tissois, see People v. Bass, 140 Misc.2d 57, 529 N.Y.S.2d 961 (Sup.Ct. Bronx Co.1990)(privilege could be invoked in child rape prosecution where it was the defendant who was the social worker's client).

16. 118 Misc.2d 660, 461 N.Y.S.2d 205 (Fam.Ct.N.Y.Co.1983).

17. Id. at 661, 461 N.Y.S.2d at 207 (citing 8 Wigmore § 2285).

18. Id. at 663, 461 N.Y.S.2d at 207–08.

19. See Humphrey v. Norden, 79 Misc.2d 192, 359 N.Y.S.2d 733 (Fam.Ct. Queens Co.1974)(in Family Court paternity proceeding, privilege was found not to be absolute where, under Wigmore's fourth criterion, the interests of the child were found to outweigh the application of the privilege); Perry v. Fiumano, 61 A.D.2d 512, 403 N.Y.S.2d 382 (4th Dep't 1978)(in custody case, privilege can be lifted where it would be in the child's best interests); People v. Easter, 90 Misc.2d 748, 395 N.Y.S.2d 926 (Albany Co.Ct.1977)(court discussed qualified nature of the privilege, but concluded that the child, not the father who made the statements to the social worker, was the client); Matter of Clear, 58 Misc.2d 699, 296 N.Y.S.2d 184 (Fam.Ct.N.Y.Co. 1969), rev'd on other grounds sub nom, Matter of Klug, 32 A.D.2d 915, 302 N.Y.S.2d 418 (1st Dep't 1969)(child, and not mother who made the statements, was client). But see Yaron v. Yaron, 83 Misc.2d 276, 372 N.Y.S.2d 518 (Sup.Ct.N.Y.Co. 1975)(court held the privilege was absolute and would not apply the Wigmore criteria; result criticized in Perry v. Fiumano, supra).

Section 509 of the Proposed New York Evidence Code "restates virtually verbatim CPLR 4508."[20]

Library References:

West's Key No. Digests, Witnesses ⚖214.5.

§ 505.2 Federal

No social worker-client privilege exists in cases based on federal law. In *Matter of Wood*,[1] it was stated: "A social worker has no privilege with respect to communications with a person who seeks his or her aid, Weinstein's Evidence ¶ 504[03] (1975). This Court is not free to extend the cloak of the priest-penitent privilege so far as to cover persons engaged in social work simply because the Hispanic Commission is affiliated with a religious organization."[2]

The proponent of such a privilege in a truly compelling case might advance the argument that Rule 501 of the Federal Rules of Evidence authorizes the privilege under "principles of the common law as they may be interpreted by the courts of the United States in the light of reason and experience."[3]

Library References:

West's Key No. Digests, Witnesses ⚖214.5.

506 Rape Crisis Counselor

§ 506.1 New York

This privilege became effective as CPLR 4510[1] in January, 1994, and covers the situation where a certified rape counselor might not otherwise

---

20. Comment to § 509, p. 105, Proposed New York Evidence Code.

§ 505.2

1. 430 F.Supp. 41, 46 (S.D.N.Y.1977).

2. Id. at 46.

3. See § 500.2 supra.

§ 506.1

1. § 4510. **Rape crisis counselor**

(a) Definitions. When used in this section, the following terms shall have the following meanings:

1. "Rape crisis program" means any office, institution or center which has been approved pursuant to subdivision fifteen of section two hundred six of the public health law, offering counseling and assistance to clients concerning sexual offenses, sexual abuses or incest.

2. "Rape crisis counselor" means any person who has been certified by an approved rape crisis program as having satisfied the training standards specified in subdivision fifteen of section two hundred six of the public health law, and who, regardless of compensation, is acting under the direction and supervision of an approved rape crisis program.

3. "Client" means any person who is seeking or receiving the services of a rape crisis counselor for the purpose of securing counseling or assistance concerning any sexual offenses, sexual abuse, incest or attempts to commit sexual offenses, sexual abuse, or incest, as defined in the penal law.

(b) Confidential information privileged. A rape crisis counselor shall not be required to disclose a communication made by his or her client to him or her, or advice given thereon, in the course of his or her services nor shall any clerk, stenographer or other person working for the same program as the rape crisis counselor or for the rape crisis counselor be allowed to disclose any such communication or advice given thereon nor shall any records made in the course of the services given to the client or recording of any

be a certified social worker, nurse, physician, or clergy.[2] The substance of the statute is much the same as CPLR 4508, which governs the social worker privilege, and it can be expected that the case law in that area will guide the courts with respect to the rape counselor privilege. The purposes of the statute, aside from filling a gap, are to foster full and open communications and insure privacy.[3]

It can be expected that this privilege will most often be invoked in criminal prosecutions when the defendant seeks disclosure of this information. In certain instances the privilege may be overcome by the defendant's confrontation rights, and if defendant can show that the information would be material to the defense he would be entitled to it.[4] In this vein, a companion statute was added to the Criminal Procedure Law, § 60.76, which provides:

> Where disclosure of a communication which would have been privileged pursuant to section forty-five hundred ten of the civil practice law and rules is sought on the grounds that the privilege has been waived or that disclosure is required pursuant to the constitution of this state or the United States, the party seeking disclosure must file a written motion supported by an affidavit containing specific factual allegations providing

communications made by or to a client be required to be disclosed, nor shall the client be compelled to disclose such communication or records, except:

1. that a rape crisis counselor may disclose such otherwise confidential communication to the extent authorized by the client;

2. that a rape crisis counselor shall not be required to treat as confidential a communication by a client which reveals the intent to commit a crime or harmful act;

3. in a case in which the client waives the privilege by instituting charges against the rape crisis counselor or the rape crisis program and such action or proceeding involves confidential communications between the client and the rape crisis counselor.

(c) Who may waive the privilege. The privilege may only be waived by the client, the personal representative of a deceased client, or, in the case of a client who has been adjudicated incompetent or for whom a conservator has been appointed, the committee or conservator.

(d) Limitation on waiver. A client who, for the purposes of obtaining compensation under article twenty-two of the executive law or insurance benefits, authorizes the disclosure of any privileged communication to an employee of the crime victims board or an insurance representative shall not be deemed to have waived the privilege created by this section.

2. In People v. Bridges, 142 Misc.2d 789, 538 N.Y.S.2d 701 (Monroe Co.Ct.1989) a rape victim confided in a volunteer counselor at Planned Parenthood rape crisis service. This counselor was not a certified social worker and thus the communications (which may have contained inconsistencies when compared with her testimony describing the attack) were not protected.

3. Executive Department memorandum, McKinney's 1993 Session Laws, p. 2619. It is also stated: "Moreover, many of a survivor's feelings in the aftermath of sexual assault might be prejudicial if revealed in court subject to misinterpretation by those unknowledgeable about various reactions that victims of sexual assault may experience." It is not clear why such feelings would be relevant in the criminal prosecution of the rapist, or what other context the drafters had in mind.

4. See People v. Tissois, 72 N.Y.2d 75, 531 N.Y.S.2d 228, 526 N.E.2d 1086 (1988)(defendant's request of social worker's notes denied since materiality not shown); People v. Gissendanner, 48 N.Y.2d 543, 423 N.Y.S.2d 893, 399 N.E.2d 924 (1979)(defendant not entitled to personnel records where he could not show that the material contained information that carried a potential for establishing the unreliability of either the criminal charge or the witness, and where there was no indication of exculpatory material in the records sought).

grounds that disclosure is required. Upon the filing of such motion and affidavit, the court shall conduct an in camera review of the communication outside the presence of the jury and of counsel for all parties in order to determine whether disclosure of any portion of the communication is required.[5]

One substantive difference between the social worker privilege and the rape counselor privilege is that the former contains an exception when the client is under age 16[6] and is the victim of a crime while the latter does not. Presumably, then, the privilege would hold with regard to communications of a child crime victim imparted to the rape counselor and the defendant would have to follow the procedure specified by Criminal Procedure Law § 60.76. Were the information favorable to the prosecution, and could escape the hearsay rule, it is reasonable to assume that the child would waive it.[7]

The rape counselor privilege is not necessarily confined to criminal proceedings, of course. It could conceivably arise in tort cases,[8] but is likely to arise more often in child abuse proceedings, which are quasi-criminal in nature. As is the case with the social worker privilege, Family Court Act § 1046(a)(vii) specifically provides that the rape counselor privilege may not be invoked in child abuse or neglect proceedings.

Library References:
West's Key No. Digests, Witnesses ⇐214.5.

§ 506.2 Federal

There is no federal rape counselor privilege. The practitioner who seeks to employ it can take what little can be found under the social worker and psychologist situations (including the privacy argument) and try to utilize whatever persuasive effect can be found under Rule 501 of the Federal Rules of Evidence where "reason and experience" would support the recognition of such a privilege.[1]

Library References:
West's Key No. Digests, Witnesses ⇐214.5.

507 Library Records

§ 507.1 New York

CPLR 4509 creates a privilege for library records. It is more of a privacy right than a testimonial privilege, although presumably a library client could prevent a librarian from testifying to the matters covered.

---

5. This in camera procedure coincides with that approved in Pennsylvania v. Ritchie, 480 U.S. 39, 107 S.Ct. 989, 94 L.Ed.2d 40 (1987). Professor Preiser's Practice Commentaries to § 60.76 of the Criminal Procedure Law, McKinney's Consolidated Laws of New York Annotated, are helpful.

6. CPLR 4508(a)(3).

7. CPLR 4510(b)(1).

8. Were the victim to sue an employer for its culpability due to its employee's harmful acts, for example, the privilege might arise.

§ 506.2

1. See § 500.2 supra.

At any rate, the statute, which has generated no reported caselaw, reads as follows:

§ 4509. Library records

Library records, which contain names or other personally identifying details regarding the users of public, free association, school, college and university libraries and library systems of this state, including but not limited to records related to the circulation of library materials, computer database searches, interlibrary loan transactions, reference queries, requests for photocopies of library materials, title reserve requests, or the use of audio-visual materials, films or records, shall be confidential and shall not be disclosed except that such records may be disclosed to the extent necessary for the proper operation of such library and shall be disclosed upon request or consent of the user or pursuant to subpoena, court order or where otherwise required by statute.[1]

§ 507.2 Federal

There is no library records privilege as such in the federal law except insofar as particular records might be protected under the omnibus provisions of proposed Rule 502 of the Federal Rules of Evidence.[1]

508 Journalist Privilege

§ 508.1 New York

New York's shield law—§ 79-h of the Civil Rights Law—is comprehensive and, since 1990, provides coverage for both confidential[1] and

§ 507.1

1. This provision is not unlike others scattered throughout the consolidated laws which create confidentiality rules with respect to records kept in public offices. See, e.g., N.Y. Public Health Law § 4138-c, which provides for the confidentiality of adoption records.

§ 507.2

1. Rule 502. **Required Reports Privileged By Statute [Not Enacted]**

A person, corporation, association, or other organization or entity, either public or private, making a return or report required by law to be made has a privilege to refuse to disclose and to prevent any other person from disclosing the return or report, if the law requiring it to be made so provides. A public officer of agency to whom a return or report is required by law to be made has a privilege to refuse to disclose the return or report if the law requiring it to be made so provides. No privilege exists under this rule in actions involving perjury, false statements, fraud in the return or report, or other failure to comply with the law in question.

§ 508.1

1. § 79-h.

* * *

(b) Exemption of professional journalists and newscasters from contempt: Absolute protection for confidential news. Notwithstanding the provisions of any general or specific law to the contrary, no professional journalist or newscaster presently or having previously been employed or otherwise associated with any newspaper, magazine, news agency, press association, wire service, radio or television transmission station or network or other professional medium of communicating news or information to the public shall be adjudged in contempt by any court in connection with any civil or criminal proceeding, or by the legislature or other body having contempt powers, nor shall a grand jury seek to have a

nonconfidential information received by the journalist.[2] The former is specifically made an absolute privilege while the latter is qualified. A three-prong test is set forth as to the qualified privilege so that nonconfidential information may be revealed only if it "(i) is highly material and relevant; (ii) is critical or necessary to the maintenance of a party's claim, defense or proof of an issue material thereto; and (iii) is not obtainable from any alternative source."

Statutory definitions of "professional journalists" and "newscasters" are included in the statute,[3] the basic test being whether the person

journalist or newscaster held in contempt by any court, legislature or other body having contempt powers for refusing or failing to disclose any news obtained or received in confidence or the identity of the source of any such news coming into such person's possession in the course of gathering or obtaining news for publication or to be published in a newspaper, magazine, or for broadcast by a radio or television transmission station or network or for public dissemination by any other professional medium or agency which has as one of its main functions the dissemination of news to the public, by which such person is professionally employed or otherwise associated in a news gathering capacity notwithstanding that the material or identity of a source of such material or related material gathered by a person described above performing a function described above is or is not highly relevant to a particular inquiry of government and notwithstanding that the information was not solicited by the journalist or newscaster prior to disclosure to such person.

2. Id.:

* * *

(c) Exemption of professional journalists and newscasters from contempt: Qualified protection for nonconfidential news. Notwithstanding the provisions of any general or specific law to the contrary, no professional journalist or newscaster presently or having previously been employed or otherwise associated with any newspaper, magazine, news agency, press association, wire service, radio or television transmission station or network or other professional medium of communicating news to the public shall be adjudged in contempt by any court in connection with any civil or criminal proceeding, or by the legislature or other body having contempt powers, nor shall a grand jury seek to have a journalist or newscaster held in contempt by any court, legislature, or other body having contempt powers for refusing or failing to disclose any unpublished news obtained or prepared by a journalist or newscaster in the course of gathering or obtaining news as provided in subdivision (b) of this section, or the source of any such news, where such news was not obtained or received in confidence, unless the party seeking such news has made a clear and specific showing that the news: (i) is highly material and relevant; (ii) is critical or necessary to the maintenance of a party's claim, defense or proof of an issue material thereto; and (iii) is not obtainable from any alternative source. A court shall order disclosure only of such portion, or portions, of the news sought as to which the above-described showing has been made and shall support such order with clear and specific findings made after a hearing. The provisions of this subdivision shall not affect the availability, under appropriate circumstances, of sanctions under section thirty-one hundred twenty-six of the civil practice law and rules.

3. Id.:

(a) Definitions. As used in this section, the following definitions shall apply:

(1) "Newspaper" shall mean a paper that is printed and distributed ordinarily not less frequently than once a week, and has done so for at least one year, and that contains news, article of opinion (as editorials), features, advertising, or other matter regarded as of current interest, has a paid circulation and has been entered at United States post-office as second-class matter.

(2) "Magazine" shall mean a publication containing news which is published and distributed periodically, and has done so for at least one year, has a paid circulation and has been entered at a United States post-office as second-class matter.

(3) "News agency" shall mean a commercial organization that collects and supplies news to subscribing newspapers, magazines, periodicals and news broadcasters.

gathering the information is doing it as a job from which she derives her livelihood. Not only is the journalist protected against contempt proceedings should she refuse to reveal information, but also "[a]ny information obtained in violation of the provisions of this section shall be inadmissible in any action or proceeding or hearing before any agency."[4] "The privilege contained within this section shall apply to supervisory or employer third person or organization having authority over the person described in this section."[5]

Although the journalist's privilege has first amendment overtones, it has a utilitarian basis. Thus:

> [t]he ability of the press freely to collect and edit news, unhampered by repeated demands for its resource materials, requires more protection than that afforded by the disclosure statute (CPLR 3101). The autonomy of the press would be jeopardized if resort to its resource materials, by litigants seeking to utilize the newsgathering efforts of journalists for their private purposes, were routinely permitted. * * * Moreover, because journalists typically gather information about accidents, crimes, and other matters of special interest that often give rise to litigation, attempts to obtain evidence by subjecting the press to discovery as a nonparty would be widespread if not restricted on a routine basis. The practical burdens on time and resources, as well as the consequent diversion of journalistic effort and disruption of newsgathering activity, would be particularly inimical to the vigor of a free press.[6]

Two cases were instrumental in forging the complete statutory scheme now found in § 79–h of the Civil Rights Law. In *Knight-Ridder v. Greenberg*,[7] the Court of Appeals held that § 79–h, which did not then contain the provision covering nonconfidential communications, did not extend its protection to such material. In that case the District Attor-

---

(4) "Press association" shall mean an association of newspapers and/or magazines formed to gather and distribute news to its members.

(5) "Wire service" shall mean a news agency that sends out syndicated news copy by wire to subscribing newspapers, magazines, periodicals or news broadcasters.

(6) "Professional journalist" shall mean one who, for gain or livelihood, is engaged in gathering, preparing, collecting, writing, editing, filming, taping or photographing of news intended for a newspaper, magazine, news agency, press association or wire service or other professional medium or agency which has as one of its regular functions the processing and researching of news intended for dissemination to the public; such person shall be someone performing said function either as a regular employee or as one otherwise professionally affiliated for gain or livelihood with such medium of communication.

(7) "Newscaster" shall mean a person who, for gain or livelihood, is engaged in analyzing, commenting on or broadcasting, news by radio or television transmission.

(8) "News" shall mean written, oral, pictorial, photographic, or electronically recorded information or communication concerning local, national or worldwide events or other matters of public concern or public interest or affecting the public welfare.

4. Id. § 79–h(d).

5. Id. § 79–h(f).

6. O'Neill v. Oakgrove Constr., Inc., 71 N.Y.2d 521, 526–27, 528 N.Y.S.2d 1, 3, 523 N.E.2d 277, 279 (1988).

7. 70 N.Y.2d 151, 518 N.Y.S.2d 595, 511 N.E.2d 1116 (1987).

ney sought outtakes from a videotape of a TV interview with a suspected murderer. But there was no showing by the TV station that the interview was given in confidence. Although the TV station made a first amendment argument, the courts focused only upon § 79–h, the Court of Appeals ultimately ruling that courts could not legislate to extend the statute's coverage. Shortly thereafter, the Court of Appeals entertained arguments in *O'Neill v. Oakgrove Construction, Inc.*,[8] where plaintiff in a personal injury action sought photographs taken of the accident scene by a journalist in the course of newsgathering. This was, of course, a nonconfidential situation, but this time the court dealt with the argument that the journalist was protected by the first amendment of the federal constitution and Article I, § 8 of the New York State Constitution, which governs press freedom. The court found a qualified protection and announced a tripartite test that is now found in subdivision (c) of the statute.[9]

As regards the absolute privilege covering confidential communications, the Court of Appeals in *Matter of Beach v. Shanley*[10] held the

---

8. 71 N.Y.2d 521, 528 N.Y.S.2d 1, 523 N.E.2d 277 (1988).

9. See note 2 supra. The Statement in Support of the 1990 bill (McKinney's 1990 Session Laws, p. 2331) states:

Decisions of state courts, and in particular Knight–Ridder Broadcasting v. Greenberg, 70 N.Y.2d 151, 518 N.Y.S.2d 595, 511 N.E.2d 1116 (1987) and O'Neill v. Oakgrove Construction, Inc., 71 N.Y.2d 521, 528 N.Y.S.2d 1, 523 N.E.2d 277 (1988), indicate a need to settle conflicting interpretations of the State's Shield Law.

By a 4–3 vote in 1987, the Court of Appeals held in *Knight-Ridder Broadcasting* that the Shield Law provided an exemption from contempt only for information or the source of information obtained by a journalist in confidence. The decision thus left unprotected unpublished non-confidential information and sources obtained by journalists. The following year in *O'Neill* the Court of Appeals addressed the question of whether, absent a statutory basis, there existed a federal or state constitutional basis to provide a privilege against compulsory disclosure of such non-confidential information and sources. There, the Court extended a non-statutory, constitutionally-predicated qualified journalist's privilege to unpublished non-confidential information and sources. *O'Neill* was a civil action, and the Court declined to state whether it would extend the qualified privilege in a criminal case.

Journalists, however, encounter the most problematic incursions into the integrity of the editorial process when they are drawn into the criminal justice system merely because they have reported on a crime. They run the risk of being used as investigative agents of the government or the defense. The need for protection of non-confidential information and sources is thus greatest in criminal cases. Accordingly, the bill codifies the Shield Law, the three-part test adopted in *O'Neill*, and makes clear that the same test applies to criminal proceedings.

In applying this standard to criminal proceedings, the bill does not override the right to a fair trial guaranteed to defendants in criminal proceedings by the United States and New York State Constitution. Thus, in People v. Troiano, 127 Misc.2d 738, 486 N.Y.S.2d 991 (Suffolk Cty. Court 1985), the court recognized that "[i]n appropriate circumstances, a reporter's privilege under the Shield Law may yield to the defendant's Sixth Amendment rights."

The waiver provision in the bill restates existing law and is designed to insure that if a journalist voluntarily reveals unpublished information or sources of news to a party to a litigation, other parties to that litigation are entitled to receive the same information.

10. 62 N.Y.2d 241, 476 N.Y.S.2d 765, 465 N.E.2d 304 (1984). In the course of the opinion Judge Cooke declined to place the basis of the privilege on constitutional grounds. "Courts should not decide constitutional questions when a case can be disposed of on a nonconstitutional ground. * * *" Id. at 254, 476 N.Y.S.2d at 772, 465 N.E.2d at 3411.

§ 508.1   PRIVILEGES   Ch. 5

privilege impervious even when the communication by the confidential source to the journalist may itself be a crime. In that case the reporter was leaked information regarding a sealed grand jury report, an act constituting a crime under § 215.70 of the Penal Law. In a comprehensive review of § 79–h from its original enactment in 1970 through its 1981 amendments, Chief Judge Cooke found the legislative intent clear that this was an absolute privilege.

When the person soliciting or receiving the information is not a professional journalist within the § 79–h definitions, there can be no privilege. Thus, in *von Bulow by Auersperg v. von Bulow*,[11] where there were no journalistic credentials to support the privilege claim by one taking notes at the von Bulow trial, § 79–h was not a factor and the discussion involved what, if any, federal constitutional protections applied.[12] Likewise, in *Blum v. Schlegel*,[13] a reporter for a student newspaper was not protected by § 79–h and had to make federal constitutional arguments.[14] Similarly, the author of a book does not achieve the status of a professional journalist under any definition found in § 79–h.[15]

The absolute privilege for news received in confidence covers only information imparted to the journalist by others and not to events that she personally observes.[16]

Library References:

West's Key No. Digests, Witnesses ⚮196.1.

§ 508.2 Federal

There is no federal statutory privilege for a journalist's sources. Whatever privilege there is in federal courts in nondiversity cases must take account of *Branzburg v. Hayes*,[1] where the Supreme Court held that newspaper reporters were not immune to inquiry concerning sources of their information and that no first amendment protection exists. Nevertheless, some lower federal courts, in reliance on Justice Powell's concurring opinion in *Branzburg*, have recognized a qualified journalist's privilege.[2]

---

11. 811 F.2d 136 (2d Cir.), cert. denied, 481 U.S. 1015, 107 S.Ct. 1891 95 L.Ed.2d 498 (1987).

12. See § 508.2 infra.

13. 150 F.R.D. 42 (W.D.N.Y.1993).

14. See § 508.2 infra.

15. In People v. LeGrand, 67 A.D.2d 446, 415 N.Y.S.2d 252 (2d Dep't 1979), the author, under contract with a publisher, was writing a book about a crime family. Defense counsel in a criminal proceeding involving the family subpoenaed the author to compel him to disclose information obtained during his interviews with witnesses. The § 79–h privilege was not applicable. To the extent the author had any first amendment protection, it was outweighed by defendant's due process rights.

16. People by Fischer v. Dan, 41 A.D.2d 687, 342 N.Y.S.2d 731 (4th Dep't), appeal dismissed, 32 N.Y.2d 764, 344 N.Y.S.2d 955, 298 N.E.2d 118 (1973); People v. Dupree, 88 Misc.2d 791, 388 N.Y.S.2d 1000 (Sup.Ct. N.Y.Co.1976).

§ 508.2

1. 408 U.S. 665, 92 S.Ct. 2646, 33 L.Ed.2d 626 (1972).

2. See, e.g., United States v. Criden, 633 F.2d 346, 357–58 (3d Cir.1980), cert. denied, 449 U.S. 1113, 101 S.Ct. 924, 66 L.Ed.2d 842 (1981); Zerilli v. Smith, 656 F.2d 705, 711–12 (D.C.Cir.1981). See O'Neill v. Oakgrove Constr., Inc., 71 N.Y.2d 521, 528 n.2, 523 N.E.2d 277, 281, 528 N.Y.S.2d 1, 5 (1988)("One commentator, in questioning any reliance on *Branzburg*, or on any other Supreme Court decision on

In the Second Circuit, the privilege was explored in *von Bulow by Auersperg v. von Bulow*,[3] a civil suit brought on behalf of the comatose Martha von Bulow alleging that her husband Claus had put her into her current state by injecting her surreptitiously with insulin and other drugs. The plaintiff sought discovery of three types of material: notes made by Claus's friend Andrea Reynolds at his second homicide trial, a manuscript being prepared by her for commercial publication concerning events surrounding the trial, and investigative reports on the lifestyles of Martha von Bulow's children that she had commissioned. Reynolds, who was not a professional journalist, turned over all but the manuscript and was found in contempt. Her journalist's privilege argument was not accepted by the Second Circuit. The issue was framed by the court as follows: "[W]e must decide whether one who gathers information initially for a purpose other than traditional journalistic endeavors and who later decides to author a book using such information may then invoke the First Amendment to shield the production of the information and manuscript."[4] This was seen as a question of first impression in the country.[5] The court laid down five principles for the determination of whether a person is of the class entitled to claim the privilege.[6] None of these tests were satisfied. In fact Reynolds remarked to the trial judge at one point that the notes she was taking (which led to the manuscript she refused to turn over) were "worthless doodles."[7]

In the later case of *Blum v. Schlegel*,[8] plaintiff, a SUNY Buffalo law professor who had been discharged, brought suit relating to his termination and subpoenaed a tape recording in the possession of a law student, Daniel Harris, who had written an article for the student newspaper. Harris resisted on the ground that New York State's shield

---

the subject, as a basis for finding a First Amendment reporter's privilege, has noted: 'Despite the holding in *Branzburg* and the discouraging tone of the majority opinion, the lower federal courts have consistently read the case to support some kind of qualified privilege for reporters' because five Justices apparently believed 'that the Constitution may at times protect the confidentiality of a journalist's sources' (Tribe, American Constitutional Law § 12–22, at 972 [2d ed.]).").

3. 811 F.2d 136 (2d Cir.), cert. denied, 481 U.S. 1015, 107 S.Ct. 1891, 95 L.Ed.2d 498 (1987).

4. Id. at 142. N.Y. Civil Rights Law § 79–h was not a factor since the case involved nonconfidential information.

5. 811 F.2d at 142.

6. The court stated:

We discern certain principles which we must use in determining whether, in the first instance, one is a member of the class entitled to claim the privilege. First, the process of newsgathering is a protected right under the First Amendment, albeit a qualified one. This qualified right, which results in the journalist's privilege, emanates from the strong public policy supporting the unfettered communication of information by the journalist to the public. Second, whether a person is a journalist, and thus protected by the privilege, must be determined by the person's intent at the inception of the information-gathering process. Third, an individual successfully may assert the journalist's privilege if he is involved in activities traditionally associated with the gathering and dissemination of news, even though he may not ordinarily be a member of the institutionalized press. Fourth, the relationship between the journalist and his source may be confidential or nonconfidential for purposes of the privilege. Fifth, unpublished resource material likewise may be protected.

Id.

7. Id.

8. 150 F.R.D. 42 (W.D.N.Y.1993).

law[9] was applicable; but Harris was not a professional journalist and so the only issue was whether federal constitutional protection might be available. Harris could have only a qualified privilege, and then only if the *von Bulow* requisites were satisfied. And they were. Harris could show the necessary initial intent to publish the gathered information in an organ designed to inform the public. Whether or not Harris was a professional journalist was irrelevant to the federal standard. Since plaintiff could not show that the information was not available from another source (he had not even tried to question the source himself), he could not insist on so much of the tape as was kept in confidence and not published. The court quoted from *Branzburg* as follows: "[A]ll reasonable attempts should be made to obtain information from non-press sources before there is any consideration of subpoenaing the press."[10]

Library References:

West's Key No. Digests, Witnesses ⚖︎196.1.

509 Self-incrimination

§ 509.1 New York State and Federal

a. Civil Cases

CPLR 4501, entitled Self-incrimination, provides:

> A competent witness shall not be excused from answering a relevant question, on the ground only that the answer may tend to establish that he owes a debt or is otherwise subject to a civil suit. This section does not require a witness to give an answer which will tend to accuse himself of a crime or to expose him to a penalty or forfeiture, nor does it vary any other rule respecting the examination of a witness.

Likewise, at the federal level the privilege against self-incrimination is applicable in civil cases.[1] *Malloy v. Hogan*[2] extended the fifth amendment protection to the states, and held that there should be uniform application of the protection in state and federal courts.[3] New York Constitution Article 1, § 6, provides a separate source implemented by CPLR 4501, quoted above.

---

9. N.Y. Civil Rights Law § 79–h.

10. 150 F.R.D. at 46, quoting Branzburg v. Hayes, 408 U.S. 665, 707 n.41, 92 S.Ct. 2646, 2669, 33 L.Ed.2d 626, 654 (1972). The *Branzburg* Court, in turn, quoted the Attorney General's Guidelines for Subpoenas to the News Media.

§ 509.1

1. McCormick § 116, at 428. See McCarthy v. Arndstein, 266 U.S. 34, 40, 45 S.Ct. 16, 17, 69 L.Ed. 158, 161 (1924):

> The Government insists, broadly, that the constitutional privilege against self-incrimination does not apply in any civil proceeding. The contrary must be accepted as settled. The privilege is not ordinarily dependent upon the nature of the proceeding in which the testimony is sought or is to be used. It applies alike to civil and criminal proceedings, wherever the answer might tend to subject to criminal responsibility him who gives it. The privilege protects a mere witness as fully as it does one who is also a party defendant.

2. 378 U.S. 1, 84 S.Ct. 1489, 12 L.Ed.2d 653 (1964).

3. Id. at 9–14, 84 S.Ct. at 1494–1497, 12 L.Ed.2d at 660–663.

Ch. 5   SELF–INCRIMINATION   § 509.1

The first sentence of CPLR 4501 eliminates any argument that the protection can apply to any danger short of exposure to criminal charges, or at the very least, penalties or forfeitures.[4] The protection applies, however, even though the danger of criminal prosecution lies in another jurisdiction;[5] and the privilege can be asserted in an administrative proceeding,[6] a legislative hearing[7] and in all stages of a civil suit.[8]

Invocation of the privilege by a party is on a question-by-question basis, i.e., a party cannot simply refuse to take the stand as can a defendant in a criminal matter.[9] Furthermore, an adverse inference can be drawn from the assertion of the privilege in a civil case,[10] meaning that even an occasional refusal to answer questions in private litigation can be devastating to that party's case. Dismissal of the action may result if the recalcitrant party is the plaintiff.[11]

---

4. It seems from sparse case law that penalties and forfeitures may simply be redundant language since criminal charges and the consequences flowing therefrom are the dangers against which the witness is protected. Application of Delehanty, 202 Misc. 40, 42, 115 N.Y.S.2d 610, 612 (Sup.Ct. N.Y.Co.), aff'd, 280 App.Div. 542, 115 N.Y.S.2d 614 (1st Dep't), aff'd, 304 N.Y. 725, 108 N.E.2d 46 (1952)(a penalty or forfeiture must be "a sanction essentially criminal in nature"); Busshart v. Park, 112 A.D.2d 787, 492 N.Y.S.2d 284 (4th Dep't 1985)(professional discipline cases do not qualify for the privilege); Cohen v. I. Goodman & Son, 205 App.Div. 312, 199 N.Y.S. 497 (1st Dep't), appeal dismissed, 236 N.Y. 642, 142 N.E. 317 (1923)(prospect of civil contempt will not invoke privilege).

5. It was established in Murphy v. Waterfront Commission, 378 U.S. 52, 84 S.Ct. 1594, 12 L.Ed.2d 678 (1964), that a witness in a state case can assert the privilege with respect to a federal crime and that a federal witness can assert the privilege as regards a state crime.

6. In LaChance v. Racing Bd., 118 A.D.2d 262, 504 N.Y.S.2d 635 (1st Dep't 1986), petitioner, a licensee of the New York State Racing and Wagering Board, had a right to assert the privilege at a Board hearing; and he would not be held to have waived the privilege because he made voluntary statements to government agents concerning the same subject matter at an earlier time. The court, invoking the rule reviewed in People v. Thomas, 51 N.Y.2d 466, 434 N.Y.S.2d 941, 415 N.E.2d 931 (1980), held that a binding waiver must occur in the same proceeding (i.e., hearing) in which petitioner attempts to assert the privilege.

7. Doyle v. Hofstader, 257 N.Y. 244, 177 N.E. 489 (1931).

8. See, e.g., Flushing National Bank v. Transamerica Ins. Co., 135 A.D.2d 486, 521 N.Y.S.2d 727 (2d Dep't 1987); Siegel v. Crawford, 266 App.Div. 878, 42 N.Y.S.2d 837, aff'd, 292 N.Y. 651, 55 N.E.2d 516 (1944).

9. "Unlike his counterpart in a criminal prosecution, the defendant in a civil suit has no inherent right to remain silent, or once on the stand, to answer only those inquiries which will have no adverse effect on his case." McDermott v. Manhattan Eye, Ear & Throat Hosp., 15 N.Y.2d 20, 28, 255 N.Y.S.2d 65, 72, 203 N.E.2d 469, 474 (1964). The witness, of course, may refuse to answer questions as they are put, thus instigating an inquiry into whether or not he has proper grounds for asserting the privilege. Slater v. Slater, 78 Misc.2d 13, 355 N.Y.S.2d 943 (Sup.Ct.Queens Co.1974). Upon invocation of the privilege, the issue is whether the witness has "reasonable cause to apprehend danger from a direct answer." State v. Carey Resources, Inc., 97 A.D.2d 508, 509, 467 N.Y.S.2d 876, 878 (2d Dep't 1983).

10. Marine Midland Bank v. John Russo Produce Co., 50 N.Y.2d 31, 427 N.Y.S.2d 961, 405 N.E.2d 205 (1980). See § 514.1 infra.

11. Levine v. Bornstein, 13 Misc.2d 161, 164, 174 N.Y.S.2d 574, 577 (Sup.Ct.Kings Co.1958), aff'd, 7 A.D.2d 995, 183 N.Y.S.2d 868 (2d Dep't 1959), aff'd, 6 N.Y.2d 892, 190 N.Y.S.2d 702, 160 N.E.2d 921 (1959) (privilege may not properly be used "to shield a plaintiff who with one hand seeks affirmative relief in court and with the other refuses to answer otherwise pertinent and proper questions which may have a bearing upon his right to maintain his action"). See also Gross v. United States Fire Ins. Co., 71 Misc.2d 815, 337 N.Y.S.2d 221 (Sup.Ct.Kings Co.1972), where an insured sued his fire insurer for nonpayment of his claim. At the time he was asked to submit to questions at a pretrial deposition,

§ 509.1   PRIVILEGES   Ch. 5

Under what circumstances will a witness or party in a civil case be deemed to waive the privilege? A partial answer is provided by the United States Supreme Court in *Brown v. United States*,[12] a denaturalization proceeding in which the defendant testified at length in her own behalf but asserted the self-incrimination privilege when asked questions on cross-examination that related to the same subject matter. This she had no right to do: "Petitioner, as a party to the suit, was a voluntary witness. She could not take the stand to testify in her own behalf and also claim the right to be free from cross-examination on matters raised by her own testimony on direct examination."[13] Otherwise, the fifth amendment would provide "a positive invitation to mutilate the truth a party offers to tell."[14]

In contrast to *Brown* is the situation presented in the New York case of *Steinbrecher v. Wapnick*,[15] where certain pretrial statements made by the defendant were not deemed a waiver. The defendant was sued by a used car dealer who alleged that the defendant and others had fraudulently sold him stolen automobiles. Defendant had been indicted on the same charges. In the civil action, defendant submitted four sworn affidavits denying his participation in the scheme in an effort to vacate a provisional order of civil arrest. Thereafter, defendant asserted the self-incrimination privilege in response to several questions posed by plaintiff at a pretrial deposition. Plaintiff argued that defendant had waived the privilege in his affidavits, i.e., having presented his version of the case he could not now remain silent when questioned. The trial court agreed and struck the defendant's answer, resulting in a default judgment.

The Court of Appeals, however, held that no waiver occurred. The defendant could still refuse to answer questions that would incriminate him because his posture in the case to that point had been strictly defensive. *Brown* was distinguished:

> This is not a case in which the defendant voluntarily chose to take the stand at a trial and present the jury with a one-sided view of the facts in order to gain an advantage over his adversary. On the contrary, the privilege was exercised at an examination before trial, at which the defendant had no choice but to appear and face questions chosen by his opponent solely for the latter's benefit. Nor is it relevant that, on a previous occasion

he was under indictment for arson regarding the same premises for which he was making the claim. His assertion of the privilege resulted in dismissal of the case. A similar result was reached in Federal Chandros v. Silverite Construction Co., 167 A.D.2d 315, 562 N.Y.S.2d 64 (1st Dep't 1990), appeal dismissed, 77 N.Y.2d 893, 568 N.Y.S.2d 910, 571 N.E.2d 80 (1991). Plaintiffs' main witness refused to answer any questions at a pretrial deposition and the court dismissed the complaint on the ground that "a party may not use a Fifth Amendment privilege as a shield to resist discovery while simultaneously pressing claims against the party seeking discovery. * * * This prohibition applies with equal force where the privilege is asserted by the principal of a corporate plaintiff. * * *" Id. at 316, 562 N.Y.S.2d at 65.

12. 356 U.S. 148, 78 S.Ct. 622, 2 L.Ed.2d 589 (1958).

13. Id. at 156, 78 S.Ct. at 627, 2 L.Ed.2d at 597.

14. Id.

15. 24 N.Y.2d 354, 300 N.Y.S.2d 555, 248 N.E.2d 419 (1969).

and for an entirely unrelated purpose, the defendant had made certain statements. It is true that the affidavits executed by the defendant were in support of his own motion but the purpose of that motion was purely defensive—to vacate an ex parte order previously obtained by the plaintiff. It was the latter who approached the court with an extensive exposition of the defendant's illegal activities and the defendant, in his own papers, was merely denying allegations already made. The essential fact is that at no time did the defendant ever attempt to use the privilege as a device to foreclose examination into facts which he himself had put in issue.[16]

In another passage in the *Steinbrecher* opinion, Chief Judge Fuld synthesized the law on waiver and made the point that the rules turn on the crucial distinction between criminal defendants on the one hand and witnesses and parties in civil cases on the other. The former waive the privilege by taking the stand to testify in their own defense while the latter generally waive only by answering questions as to matters that would have an incriminating effect.[17] Citing *Brown*, however, the Chief Judge went on to say that waiver will also occur where a witness or party in a civil action testifies to nonincriminating facts if such testimony is voluntary and a subsequent assertion of the privilege on the same subject would give the civil litigant an unfair advantage over her adversary.[18]

---

16. Id. at 363–64, 300 N.Y.S.2d at 564–65, 248 N.E.2d at 426.

17. The court explained:

In determining whether a person, by his previous acts or statements, has waived his privilege against self incrimination, the first important distinction to keep in mind is the difference between the privilege accorded an accused in a criminal case, who need not give any testimonial evidence whatsoever, and the privilege accorded the ordinary witness—including a party in a civil case—who may be compelled to testify as to any matter which does not actually tend to incriminate him. In the former case, where the scope of the privilege is the most sweeping, the courts have traditionally been more ready to find that there was a waiver. Thus, a defendant in a criminal prosecution who testifies at his trial may be compelled to answer questions as to all matters relevant to the case. * * *

On the other hand, an ordinary witness, including a party in a civil suit, does not waive his privilege by the mere act of testifying. The rule, as stated by the Supreme Court, is that, "where the previous disclosure by an ordinary witness is not an actual admission of guilt or incriminating facts, he is not deprived of the privilege of stopping short in his testimony whenever it may fairly tend to incriminate him." (McCarthy v. Arndstein, 262 U.S. 355, 359, 43 S.Ct. 562, 563, 67 L.Ed. 1023 * * *).

24 N.Y.2d at 360–61, 300 N.Y.S.2d at 561–62, 248 N.E.2d at 424.

18. Id. at 362, 300 N.Y.S.2d at 563, 248 N.E.2d at 425: "There is one important exception to the general rule that a witness is free to rely on the privilege unless he has waived it by voluntarily testifying to incriminating facts. Since the sole purpose of the privilege is to shield a witness against the incriminating effects of his testimony, the courts will not permit its use as a weapon to unfairly prejudice an adversary."

The Second Circuit Court of Appeals has articulated a similar test to determine waiver:

[W]e read the prior decisions of the Supreme Court and the courts of this Circuit to hold that a court should only infer a waiver of the fifth amendment's privilege against self-incrimination from a witness' prior statements if (1) the witness' prior statements have created a significant likelihood that the finder of fact will be left with and prone to rely on a distorted view of the truth, and (2) the witness had reason to know that his prior statements would be interpreted as a waiver of the fifth amendment's privilege against self-incrimination.

On the borderline between civil cases and criminal cases are civil commitment proceedings. In *In re Kenneth M.*,[19] at a hearing concerning the propriety of his detention,[20] which he requested, the patient sought a ruling that he would not have to take the stand if called by the state and hospital. Calling this an issue of first impression in New York, the court relied on *In re Gault*,[21] a juvenile delinquency proceeding, where it was held by the United States Supreme Court that the fifth amendment applied even though the case was not a full-blown criminal proceeding; the accused delinquent need not even take the stand. The *Gault* Court held that incarceration or deprivation of liberty is the same thing whether it occurs in a civil or criminal proceeding.[22]

Shortly after the *Kenneth M.* case, another state court held in *People ex rel. Anonymous v. Saribeyoglu*[23] that a patient, if called to the stand, must comply, but he may refuse to answer particular questions if they tended to implicate him in criminal activity. This court rejected the application of *Gault* and relied instead on the United States Supreme Court's language in *Addington v. Texas*[24] where it was held that different standards of proof are used in civil commitment proceedings as opposed to criminal proceedings because the former can "in no sense be equated to a criminal prosecution."[25] The *Saribeyoglu* court also relied on New York Court of Appeals dictum that not all deprivations of liberty will invoke the constitutional protections and that "[i]t is only those curtailments of liberty which serve the traditional purposes of the criminal law which require full protections of a criminal trial."[26] Left unanswered in *Saribeyoglu* is the applicability of the *Gault* language that incarceration against one's will is the same whether labeled criminal or civil.[27] There remains uncertainty in this area of fifth amendment litigation although the Court of Appeals in *People v. Fuller*,[28] a case dealing with mandatory drug treatment (which included commitment for treatment), held that since detention was not for punitive purposes, fifth amendment rights were not violated when evidence showing admissions of addiction were introduced.[29]

Klein v. Harris, 667 F.2d 274, 287 (2d Cir. 1981). Accord, United States v. Singer, 785 F.2d 228, 241 (8th Cir.), cert. denied, 479 U.S. 883, 107 S.Ct. 273, 93 L.Ed.2d 249 (1986).

19. 130 Misc.2d 217, 495 N.Y.S.2d 131 (Sup.Ct.Monroe Co.1985).

20. N.Y.Mental Hyg.Law § 9.27.

21. 387 U.S. 1, 87 S.Ct. 1428, 18 L.Ed.2d 527 (1967).

22. Id. at 50, 87 S.Ct. at 1456, 18 L.Ed.2d at 558.

23. 131 Misc.2d 647, 501 N.Y.S.2d 286 (Sup.Ct.Queens Co.1986).

24. 441 U.S. 418, 99 S.Ct. 1804, 60 L.Ed.2d 323 (1979).

25. Id. at 428, 99 S.Ct. at 1810, 60 L.Ed.2d at 332.

26. Saribeyoglu, 131 Misc.2d at 649, 501 N.Y.S.2d at 288 (quoting from People v. Fuller, 24 N.Y.2d 292, 303, 300 N.Y.S.2d 102, 108, 248 N.E.2d 17, 21 (1969)).

27. The Saribeyoglu court cited In Interest of Goodwin, 366 N.W.2d 809 (N.D. 1985), in which that court listed state and federal cases on both sides of the issue. Those finding commitment cases more civil than criminal seemed to predominate. See Saribeyoglu, 131 Misc.2d at 648, 501 N.Y.S.2d at 287.

28. 24 N.Y.2d 292, 300 N.Y.S.2d 102, 248 N.E.2d 17 (1969).

29. Id. at 303, 300 N.Y.S.2d at 108, 248 N.E.2d at 21, where it was stated: "For these reasons we conclude that the appellants' privilege against self incrimination and right to counsel were not violated when evidence was received of admissions of addiction made to examining physicians during the course of court ordered examinations."

b. Criminal Proceedings

Implementing the fifth amendment to the United States Constitution, and Article 1, § 6, of the New York Constitution, § 50.20 of the New York Criminal Procedure Law provides in part as follows:

> 1. Any witness in a legal proceeding, other than a grand jury proceeding, may refuse to give evidence requested of him on the ground that it may tend to incriminate him and he may not, except as provided in subdivision two, be compelled to give such evidence.[30]

Except for the coverage in subdivision c below, relating to trial use of pretrial confessions and defendant's silence, the procedures and protections applied in grand jury proceedings and other preliminary proceedings[31] are beyond the scope of this work, which is limited to the basic trial aspects of the privilege. For purposes of facilitating this discussion the application of the privilege is divided into two aspects—as it affects testimony, and as it affects documents.

1. Testimony.

Any attorney whose client has a substantial self-incrimination problem should steep himself in the late Henry J. Friendly's classic article "The Fifth Amendment Tomorrow: The Case For Constitution Change,"[32] one of the most useful law reviews article ever written. Although the author argues that the pretrial protections have become too broad, he has only respect for the classic rule that a defendant need not give evidence against himself at trial, and should not be forced to take the stand.[33] It is well settled that the defendant's failure to take

---

30. Subdivision 2 provides for the conferring of immunity and subdivision 5 refers to Crim.Proc.Law § 190.40 respecting grand jury procedures.

31. Since the privilege applies only to evidence that is testimonial in nature, it has no application to the gathering of physical evidence such as blood samples (Schmerber v. California, 384 U.S. 757, 86 S.Ct. 1826, 16 L.Ed.2d 908 (1966)), handwriting exemplars (United States v. Euge, 444 U.S. 707, 100 S.Ct. 874, 63 L.Ed.2d 141 (1980), rehearing denied, 446 U.S. 913, 100 S.Ct. 1845, 64 L.Ed.2d 267 (1980)), photographs (Simmons v. United States, 390 U.S. 377, 88 S.Ct. 967, 19 L.Ed.2d 1247 (1968)), or to cases where the person is exhibited for corporeal identification (United States v. Wade, 388 U.S. 218, 87 S.Ct. 1926, 18 L.Ed.2d 1149 (1967); People v. Rivera, 22 N.Y.2d 453, 293 N.Y.S.2d 271, 239 N.E.2d 873 (1968), cert. denied, 395 U.S. 964, 89 S.Ct. 2107, 23 L.Ed.2d 750 (1969); People v. Ballott, 20 N.Y.2d 600, 286 N.Y.S.2d 1, 233 N.E.2d 103 (1967)). See also Pennsylvania v. Muniz, 496 U.S. 582, 110 S.Ct. 2638, 110 L.Ed.2d 528 (1990)(videotape of slurred speech of arrested drunk-driving suspect when answering routine police-booking questions was admissible at trial, despite absence of *Miranda* warnings; compelled revelations of physical manner of speech is not testimonial).

32. 37 Cincinnati L.Rev. 671 (1968).

33. At pages 699–700, it is stated:

No defendant should ever be compelled to take the stand so long as the prosecution may bring out an entire criminal history, including crimes unrelated to that with which he is charged and having no real tendency to reflect on his veracity. * * * I agree * * * that many criminal defendants "are uneducated, unfortunate persons, frightened by their predicament—no match for the prosecutor or for the occasional sharp question from the judge." While such a person, if in fact innocent, may be making a serious mistake by not testifying, as Arthur Train said 30 years ago, he is entitled to his own decision when his life or liberty is at stake. It is no misuse of the term to say that to force such a man to the stand by use of the contempt power would be cruel. * * *

A recent study of over 3500 criminal jury trials showed that the defendant tes-

§ 509.1 PRIVILEGES Ch. 5

the stand "is not a factor from which any inference unfavorable to him may be drawn;"[34] but this need not be a part of the judge's jury charge unless requested by the defendant.[35] The rule is not without occasional exceptions, however. In one case it was held not to be error for a federal prosecutor in his closing argument to tell the jury that defendant could have taken the stand to explain his actions in light of defense counsel's argument that the government had not allowed the defendant to explain his side of the story.[36] And in another case, the New York Court of Appeals employed the harmless error doctrine where the prosecutor in his summation referred to the defendant's failure to testify.[37]

If the defendant chooses to take the stand, he generally waives any right to object to any material question, including questions asked for impeachment purposes, on self-incrimination grounds.[38] In *People v. Betts*,[39] however, the New York Court of Appeals discussed thoroughly the question of proper cross-examination of a criminal defendant, and stated: "The policy of protecting the defendant's opportunity to testify, while allowing the prosecution a balanced evidentiary response, is well served by the rule that the defendant's choice to testify in the case on trial does not, by itself, effect a waiver of the privilege against self-incrimination as to pending unrelated charges. This rule will not, on

tified in 82 percent and, where he had no criminal record, in 91 percent. Since the jury very likely draws an inference against him when he fails to testify, as a practical matter the sole significant adverse affect on the prosecution occurs where the testimony of the accused would produce what was needed to avoid the granting of a motion for acquittal.

34. N.Y.Crim.Proc.Law § 60.15(2). Although the rule against comment is codified in New York, it is mandated in any event by the federal constitution. Griffin v. California, 380 U.S. 609, 85 S.Ct. 1229, 14 L.Ed.2d 106 (1965). The fact the defendant stays off the stand may not be commented upon by the court or the prosecutor nor is any mention to be made of it unless the defendant asks for the charge under Crim. Proc.Law § 300.10(2). People v. Mirenda, 23 N.Y.2d 439, 457, 297 N.Y.S.2d 532, 546, 245 N.E.2d 194, 204 (1969); People v. McLucas, 15 N.Y.2d 167, 171–172, 256 N.Y.S.2d 799, 801, 204 N.E.2d 846, 848 (1965).

35. N.Y.Crim.Proc.Law § 300.10(2). If requested, the judge must confine the instructions to the statutory wording and may not elaborate, the point being that if too much is made of this the jury will be prone to recognize the negative inference where otherwise it might not have. See People v. Fitzgerald, 156 N.Y. 253, 266, 50 N.E. 846, 850 (1898). In People v. Vereen, 45 N.Y.2d 856, 410 N.Y.S.2d 288, 382 N.E.2d 1151 (1978), the defendant did not request the charge, but the judge gave it anyway. It was stated: "We do not read the statute (CPL § 300.10[2] which makes the charge mandatory when requested) conversely as establishing an absolute prohibition against the court exercising its discretion in submitting such a charge without a request from the defendant. This discretion, however, should be rarely exercised, since defense counsel, as a tactical matter, in many cases, may wish the charge not given." Id. at 857, 410 N.Y.S.2d at 289, 382 N.E.2d at 1151. The court went on to note that where a request for the charge is denied there could not be a finding of harmless error, while the giving of the charge without a request might be considered harmless if the evidence of guilt is overwhelming.

36. United States v. Robinson, 485 U.S. 25, 108 S.Ct. 864, 99 L.Ed.2d 23 (1988).

37. People v. Crimmins, 36 N.Y.2d 230, 237, 367 N.Y.S.2d 213, 218, 326 N.E.2d 787, 791 (1975).

38. People v. Shapiro, 308 N.Y. 453, 458, 126 N.E.2d 559, 561 (1955). See also Brown v. United States, 356 U.S. 148, 154–55, 78 S.Ct. 622, 626, 2 L.Ed.2d 589, 596 (1958)("If [a criminal defendant] takes the stand and testifies in his own defense, his credibility may be impeached and his testimony assailed like that of any other witness, and the breadth of his waiver is determined by the scope of relevant cross-examination").

39. 70 N.Y.2d 289, 295, 520 N.Y.S.2d 370, 514 N.E.2d 865 (1987).

the other hand, preclude prosecutors from inquiry into pending criminal charges if a defendant, in taking the stand, makes assertions that open the door and render those charges relevant for contradiction and response."[40]

In simply taking the stand defendant does not waive other privileges such as the attorney-client privilege[41] or the psychologist-client privilege.[42] There could, of course, be a separate waiver concerning such other privileges.[43]

In a trial where there are codefendants one defendant may not call the other to the stand; this would result in prejudice to the codefendant who assumes the stand and claims the privilege in the jury's presence. In *People v. Owens*,[44] it was held that a codefendant has no more right to force another defendant to the stand than does the prosecutor.

Ordinary witnesses in criminal trials generally must take the stand, but can assert the privilege as questions are asked.[45] An exception was recognized in a New York case where defense counsel wanted to call a witness who had made it known that on self-incrimination grounds he would not answer any questions. The trial court was warranted in excusing him from taking the stand where the jury would hear him repeatedly claim the privilege. "In the context of the instant case * * * there existed a very real danger that the jury would infer from Whitlock's refusal to testify that defendant's contention was correct and that

---

40. In Betts, defendant was tried for first degree rape. At a pretrial Sandoval hearing the trial judge held that he could be cross-examined for credibility purposes on a pending burglary charge and would, by reason of taking the stand, waive the right to assert his privilege against self-incrimination. The Court of Appeals agreed that the self-incrimination waiver allowed cross-examination on collateral matters for the purpose of testing credibility, but drew the line with respect to the pending criminal matter. A thorough discussion of the consequences of the defendant's decision to testify is found in this case, including full reaffirmation of the old case of People v. Tice, 131 N.Y. 651, 30 N.E. 494 (1892), where, on direct, defendant testified only to matters concerning his personal history. He was charged with homicide and entered an insanity defense. On cross-examination questions probed his state of mind at the time of the crime, his memory and his level of sanity. The Court of Appeals ruled that although the questions did not relate directly to defendant's testimony on direct, and did not relate to credibility, they were nevertheless relevant to the insanity issue. It was stated that when a defendant testifies, "he subjects himself voluntarily to the situation of any other witness, and if he is compelled to answer disparaging questions, or to give evidence relevant to the issue, which is injurious, it is the consequence of an election which he makes to become a witness, which involves a waiver on his part at that time, of the constitutional exemption." Id. at 656–657, 30 N.E. at 496. With regard to cross-examination on pending criminal matters see also People v. Bennett, 169 A.D.2d 369, 573 N.Y.S.2d 322 (3d Dep't), aff'd, 79 N.Y.2d 464, 583 N.Y.S.2d 825, 593 N.E.2d 279 (1992).

41. People v. Shapiro, 308 N.Y. 453, 459, 126 N.E.2d 559, 562 (1955).

42. People v. Wilkins, 65 N.Y.2d 172, 490 N.Y.S.2d 759, 480 N.E.2d 373 (1985).

43. In People v. Krawitz, 151 A.D.2d 850, 851, 542 N.Y.S.2d 824, 825 (3d Dep't 1989), it was stated: "Defendant waived the attorney-client privilege as to the subject matter of that testimony by placing in issue through his motion papers the communication between him and his former defense counsel and the quality of the representation he received * * * and by voluntarily testifying on privileged matter at the hearing on his motion. * * *"

44. 22 N.Y.2d 93, 291 N.Y.S.2d 313, 238 N.E.2d 715 (1968).

45. N.Y.Crim.Proc.Law § 60.15(1); Steinbrecher v. Wapnick, 24 N.Y.2d 354, 360–361, 300 N.Y.S.2d 555, 562, 248 N.E.2d 419, 424 (1969); People v. Bagby, 65 N.Y.2d 410, 415, 492 N.Y.S.2d 562, 565, 482 N.E.2d 41, 44 (1985).

it was Whitlock rather than defendant who had actually committed the * * * robbery."[46] Similarly, the Second Circuit Court of Appeals has stated, "The district court has the discretion to prevent a party from calling a witness solely to have him or her invoke the privilege against self-incrimination in front of the jury."[47]

As to waiver, once the witness testifies, she cannot claim the privilege when cross-examined on the same subject matter;[48] but the waiver applies only through the immediate proceeding and the privilege can be asserted in a subsequent proceeding.[49] By testifying to part of a transaction the witness will be deemed to have waived any objection to testifying as to the rest.[50] The Third Circuit Court of Appeals has held that even though a witness testified before the grand jury she could assert the privilege at the trial stage since "the setting in which the questions were asked of her had greatly changed and she could well have had apprehensions as to the incriminating effect of her requested testimony which she did not have on the earlier occasion."[51] The witness is the "sole arbiter" of what might be incriminating and "a particular witness' decision to refrain from testifying can never mean more than that the witness himself believes that something he might say would tend to implicate him with respect to some criminal wrongdoing of which only he is aware. It would thus be wholly improper in most situations to give the jurors an opportunity to speculate as to the nature of this wrongdoing by allowing a party to parade a witness before the jury for the sole purpose of eliciting in open court the witness' refusal to testify."[52] But "when the danger of incrimination is not readily apparent, the witness may be required to establish a factual predicate. * * *"[53]

Of course, if the prosecutor wants the testimony of a witness who will claim the privilege, immunity may be conferred in New York under the provisions of § 50.20(2) of the Criminal Procedure Law. In federal practice, the relevant immunity provisions are to be found in 18 U.S.C.A. §§ 6001–6003. If the prosecutor puts a witness on the stand who has said he will rely on his fifth amendment protection, forces the witness repeatedly to assert that right when asked questions crucial to defendant's culpability, and then pointedly makes references in her summa-

---

46. People v. Thomas, 51 N.Y.2d 466, 472, 434 N.Y.S.2d 941, 944, 415 N.E.2d 931, 934 (1980).

47. United States v. Deutsch, 987 F.2d 878, 883 (2d Cir.1993). In People v. Webb, 195 A.D.2d 614, 615, 601 N.Y.S.2d 127, 128 (2d Dep't 1993), it was stated: "[B]ecause any testimony which the witness might have given concerning the incident clearly could have tended to incriminate him, there was no need for the court to bring him into the courtroom to formally assert his Fifth Amendment privilege. * * *"

48. Brown v. United States, 356 U.S. 148, 156, 78 S.Ct. 622, 627, 2 L.Ed.2d 589, 597, rehearing denied, 356 U.S. 948, 78 S.Ct. 776, 2 L.Ed.2d 822 (1958).

49. People v. Cassidy, 213 N.Y. 388, 395–396, 107 N.E. 713, 715 (1915).

50. Rogers v. United States, 340 U.S. 367, 371, 71 S.Ct. 438, 440–441, 95 L.Ed. 344, 347–348 (1951); Klein v. Harris, 667 F.2d 274 (2d Cir.1981).

51. Matter of Neff, 206 F.2d 149, 152–153 (3d Cir.1953). See also People v. Bagby, 65 N.Y.2d 410, 413–414, 492 N.Y.S.2d 562, 564–565, 482 N.E.2d 41, 43–44 (1985).

52. People v. Thomas, 51 N.Y.2d 466, 472–473, 434 N.Y.S.2d 941, 944–945, 415 N.E.2d 931, 934 (1980).

53. State of New York v. Carey Resources, 97 A.D.2d 508, 509, 467 N.Y.S.2d 876, 878 (2d Dep't 1983).

tion to the connection between the witness' unwillingness to testify and defendant's involvement, there may be reversible error.[54]

2. Documents.

The fifth amendment states that no person "shall be compelled" to be a witness against himself. As a general rule, pre-existing documents are not a form of compelled testimony[55] (required reports are noted infra), and thus their introduction into evidence will not violate the maker's or the custodian's privilege. In *State of New York v. Carey Resources, Inc.,*[56] for example, plaintiffs requested that the corporate defendant identify or produce documents related to its operation and its transactions with other defendants. One of the grounds asserted by defendant in its motion for a protective order was that its self-incrimination privilege would be violated. The court held the motion should be denied and then stated the rules as follows:

> It is basic that the privilege against self incrimination is a personal right which cannot be invoked by, or on behalf of, a corporation (United States v. White, 322 U.S. 694, 698–699; James v. Hotel Gramatan, 251 App.Div. 748, 749). Similarly, an agent or officer of the corporation cannot invoke the privilege and decline to produce records and documents of the corporation over which he has custody in a representative capacity, even if the contents of the documents would personally incriminate him (Curcio v. United States, 354 U.S. 118, 122–123; United States v. White, *supra,* p. 699; Wilson v. United States, 221 U.S. 361; People v. MacLachlan, 58 A.D.2d 586; Bank of Buffalo v. Skinitis, 36 A.D.2d 891) and even if the officer is the sole shareholder of the corporation (Matter of Brennick v. Hynes, 68 A.D.2d 980, mot. for lv. to app. den. 47 N.Y.2d 706; Hair Ind. v. United States, 340 F.2d 510, cert. den. 381 U.S. 950; United States v. Fago, 319 F.2d 791, cert. den. 375 U.S. 906). Nonetheless, the person producing the books and records held in a representative capacity cannot be compelled to give oral testimony concerning them if his answers may incriminate

---

54. People v. Vargas, 86 N.Y.2d 215, 630 N.Y.S.2d 973, 654 N.E.2d 1221 (1995). The court, relying on Namet v. United States, 373 U.S. 179, 185–86, 83 S.Ct. 1151, 1154–55, 10 L.Ed.2d 278, 283 (1963), stated:

> Namet established the framework for courts to evaluate a challenge by a defendant regarding the prosecution's handling of the testimony of a witness who pleads the Fifth Amendment at trial. Essentially, this entails a determination of whether the probative value of the testimony of the witness who invoked the Fifth Amendment privilege in the presence of the jury outweighs any prejudice to the defendant. Important considerations which factor into this analysis include the prosecutor's conduct and intent in calling the witness, the number of questions asked, their significance to the state's case, whether the prosecutor draws any inference in closing arguments from the witness's assertion of the privilege and refusal to answer, the witness's relationship to defendant, and the jury instructions * * *.

55. See Doe v. United States, 487 U.S. 201, 210, 108 S.Ct. 2341, 2347, 101 L.Ed.2d 184, 197 (1988)("[I]n order to be testimonial [a witness'] communication must itself, explicitly or implicitly, relate a factual assertion or disclose information. Only then is a person compelled to be a 'witness' against himself.").

56. 97 A.D.2d 508, 467 N.Y.S.2d 876 (2d Dep't 1983).

§ 509.1   PRIVILEGES   Ch. 5

him (People v. MacLachlan, *supra*; Triangle Pub. v. Ferrare, 4 A.D.2d 591, 595; Bradley v. O'Hare, 2 A.D.2d 436, 441) and, of course, the privilege remains applicable to personal records (Bank of Buffalo v. Skinitis, *supra*).[57]

In *Curcio v. United States*,[58] the United States Supreme Court stated that compulsory production of corporate or association records by their custodian would not violate the custodian's privilege, but "forcing the custodian to testify orally as to the whereabouts of nonproduced records requires him to disclose the contents of his own mind. He might be compelled to convict himself out of his own mouth. That is contrary to the spirit and letter of the Fifth Amendment."[59] If the act of producing the documents is the only act by the custodian on behalf of the corporation, she would not incriminate herself; nor would the act of production cause her to incriminate herself so long as the government does not rely on her "truthtelling" to prove that the documents exist or that she has access to them.[60] The test is not whether the documents' contents would incriminate, but rather whether the incrimination would be the result of what the person would have to do in authenticating them.

In *In re Grand Jury Subpoenas Issued to Thirteen Corps.*,[61] Roe, the custodian, argued that the act of production and authentication would be testimonial in and of itself and would add to the government's evidence against him. But the Second Circuit held that the records would not be protected simply because somebody might be incriminated by them. By way of further explanation of this elusive concept, the United States Supreme Court has said that the thing, or the contents of the thing sought to be produced, is not protected since its existence was never compelled, but if the respondent would be incriminated by simply having it in his possession, then the fifth amendment could come into play.[62] The Second Circuit noted that such incrimination could come about only "(1) 'if the existence and location of the subpoenaed papers are unknown to the government'; or (2) where production would 'implicitly authenticate' the documents."[63]

In *United States v. Doe*,[64] the United States Supreme Court held that the owner of a sole proprietorship had fifth amendment protection

---

57. Id. at 508–09, 467 N.Y.S.2d at 878. The rule that a corporation cannot invoke the privilege is reiterated in EDP Medical Computer Systems, Inc. v. Sears, Roebuck and Co., 193 A.D.2d 645, 597 N.Y.S.2d 461 (2d Dep't 1993); and the rule that an agent or officer of an organization cannot invoke the privilege and decline to produce records and documents even if the contents would incriminate the agent or officer is reiterated in Matter of Rubin, 100 A.D.2d 850, 474 N.Y.S.2d 94 (2d Dep't 1984).

58. 354 U.S. 118, 77 S.Ct. 1145, 1 L.Ed.2d 1225 (1957).

59. Id. at 128, 77 S.Ct. at 1151, 1 L.Ed.2d at 1232.

60. In re Grand Jury Subpoenas, 959 F.2d 1158, 1165 (2d Cir.1992).

61. 775 F.2d 43 (2d Cir.1985), cert. denied, 475 U.S. 1081, 106 S.Ct. 1459, 89 L.Ed.2d 716 (1986).

62. United States v. Doe, 465 U.S. 605, 612, 104 S.Ct. 1237, 1242, 79 L.Ed.2d 552, 560 (1984).

63. In re Grand Jury Subpoena Duces Tecum Dated October 29, 1992, 1 F.3d 87, 92 (2d Cir.1993), cert. denied, ___ U.S. ___, 114 S.Ct. 920, 127 L.Ed.2d 214 (1994), (citing United States v. Fox, 721 F.2d 32, 36 (2d Cir.1983)).

64. 465 U.S. 605, 104 S.Ct. 1237, 79 L.Ed.2d 552 (1984).

against production of the business books and records since this would be akin to personal documents. The line has been drawn, however, at sole proprietorships. Family corporations, or close corporations, fall within the general rule, and the corporate custodian must produce the records.[65]

The Second Circuit is now in the throes of deciding whether *Boyd v. United States*,[66] which established the rule that a person has protection for his personal papers, still expresses the law. In a recent case[67] the majority of the Court of Appeals concluded that *Boyd* had been eroded over the years to the point of extinction. Doe was subpoenaed by a grand jury to produce a "calendar" which was a "breast-pocket appointment book which Doe used to record appointments, social engagements, chores, phone numbers and other reminders."[68] At the district court level this document was viewed as an "intimate personal document," protected by the fifth amendment.[69] On appeal, the majority reasoned that although *Boyd* has not been directly overruled it has been whittled away to the point it has no further authority.[70] The law as to private papers is somewhat unsettled in the Second Circuit, and clearly unsettled where, under New York State law, private papers would be protected under *Boyd*.[71] Of course, even if *Boyd* eventually proves to be overruled on the basis of sounder authority, New York could always preserve its stricter rule.

Where documents concerning a legitimate activity are required to be made and submitted to an agency of the government it is well settled that no privilege can be claimed should the contents tend to incriminate the maker.[72] Where, however, the requirement of self-reporting con-

---

65. Braswell v. United States, 487 U.S. 99, 109–10, 117–18, 108 S.Ct. 2284, 2290–91, 2295, 101 L.Ed.2d 98, 109, 114 (1988)(corporate agent's assumption of representative capacity of his solely-owned corporation led to certain obligations, including duty to produce corporate documents regardless of personally incriminating effect; however, agent's act of production could be used as evidence only against the corporation, not against the agent personally). See generally McCormick § 130.

66. 116 U.S. 616, 6 S.Ct. 524, 29 L.Ed. 746 (1886).

67. In re Grand Jury Subpoena Duces Tecum Dated October 29, 1992, 1 F.3d 87 (2d Cir.1993), cert. denied, __ U.S. __, 114 S.Ct. 920, 127 L.Ed.2d 214 (1994).

68. Id. at 88.

69. Id. at 90.

70. It was observed that in Fisher v. United States, 425 U.S. 391, 96 S.Ct. 1569, 48 L.Ed.2d 39 (1976), tax records and personal business records were held unprotected by the fifth amendment even if in the possession of the person who made them. See also Andresen v. Maryland, 427 U.S. 463, 96 S.Ct. 2737, 49 L.Ed.2d 627 (1976).

In the 1984 decision of the Supreme Court in United States v. Doe, 465 U.S. 605, 618, 104 S.Ct. 1237, 1245, 79 L.Ed.2d 552, 563 (1984), Justice O'Connor wrote a concurrence (not joined by any other justice) in which she said that Boyd was completely dead; that "[t]he Fifth Amendment provides absolutely no protection for the contents of private papers of any kind." Finally, the Second Circuit majority viewed Baltimore Dep't of Social Servs. v. Bouknight, 493 U.S. 549, 110 S.Ct. 900, 107 L.Ed.2d 992 (1990), as a sound indication that the entire Court would go along with Justice O'Connor. In Bouknight, the O'Connor concurrence in Doe was cited with approval; the facts, however, did not involve private papers, but rather the production of an infant in compliance with a juvenile court order.

71. See State of New York v. Carey Resources, 97 A.D.2d 508, 509, 467 N.Y.S.2d 876, 879 (2d Dep't 1983); Bank of Buffalo v. Skinitis, 36 A.D.2d 891, 320 N.Y.S.2d 304 (4th Dep't 1971).

72. California v. Byers, 402 U.S. 424, 91 S.Ct. 1535, 29 L.Ed.2d 9 (1971); Shapiro v. United States, 335 U.S. 1, 68 S.Ct. 1375, 92 L.Ed. 1787, rehearing denied, 335 U.S. 836, 69 S.Ct. 9, 93 L.Ed. 388 (1948).

cerning illegal conduct is concerned, the privilege may be invoked.[73] These principles are fully operable in New York.[74]

c. Application of the Privilege During the Investigation Stage—Connection to the Trial

It is beyond the scope of this work to deal with all the ramifications of a suspect's privilege against self-incrimination during police questioning, through arrest, arraignment and indictment. There are, however, several areas where pretrial events involving a suspect's constitutional protections may bear on the admissibility of evidence at trial.

People v. Harris[75] held that a confession that has been suppressed as a result of *Miranda* violations, while it may not be used by the prosecutor as evidence-in-chief, may nevertheless be used to impeach the defendant should he choose to take the stand and give testimony at variance with the confession. It is not necessary that the subject matter of the confession itself come up on direct examination in order for it to be usable on cross-examination. It is sufficient that the defendant on direct examination recounted the events to which the confession relates.[76] The *Harris* impeachment rule is applicable only where the confession was suppressed for simple failure of the authorities to observe the *Miranda* amenities. If the confession was involuntary because truly coerced it can have no trial value at all said the United States Supreme Court in *New Jersey v. Portash*,[77] where defendant testified in a grand jury proceeding after having been given immunity. At his subsequent trial he was informed that such prior testimony would be admissible for impeachment purposes. The Supreme Court held this to be error because of the essential involuntariness of testimony given under cover of immunity.

---

73. Marchetti v. United States, 390 U.S. 39, 88 S.Ct. 697, 19 L.Ed.2d 889 (1968)(where wagering violates state laws the privilege may be asserted when reporting is required); Grosso v. United States, 390 U.S. 62, 88 S.Ct. 709, 19 L.Ed.2d 906 (1968)(wagering excise tax provisions aimed at those involved in criminal activities); Haynes v. United States, 390 U.S. 85, 88 S.Ct. 722, 19 L.Ed.2d 923 (1968)(reporting involved taxation of classes of firearms used by persons engaged in criminal activities).

74. See Grand Jury v. Kuriansky, 69 N.Y.2d 232, 513 N.Y.S.2d 359, 505 N.E.2d 925, cert. denied, 482 U.S. 928, 107 S.Ct. 3211, 96 L.Ed.2d 698 (1987)(no privilege where psychiatrists were asked to produce required medical records in a Medicare fraud investigation); People v. Doe, 59 N.Y.2d 655, 657, 463 N.Y.S.2d 405, 406, 450 N.E.2d 211, 212 (1983)("In light of the fact that the physician appellants * * * were required to maintain the subject records * * * and, under certain circumstances, make them available for government inspection * * * we hold the appellants' personal privilege against self-incrimination does not apply to the records here sought"); Matter of Cappetta v. Santucci, 42 N.Y.2d 1066, 399 N.Y.S.2d 638, 369 N.E.2d 1172 (1977)(a school custodian was asked to produce certain financial and insurance reports that were deemed privilege-free on the dual grounds that certain of the documents were the school's, and that the custodian was required to keep records of public money received and dispensed); People v. Samuel, 29 N.Y.2d 252, 327 N.Y.S.2d 321, 277 N.E.2d 381 (1971)(self-reporting concerning a motor vehicle accident does not raise the privilege).

75. People v. Harris, 25 N.Y.2d 175, 303 N.Y.S.2d 71, 250 N.E.2d 349 (1969), aff'd, 401 U.S. 222, 91 S.Ct. 643, 28 L.Ed.2d 1 (1971).

76. People v. Wise, 46 N.Y.2d 321, 413 N.Y.S.2d 334, 385 N.E.2d 1262 (1978).

77. 440 U.S. 450, 99 S.Ct. 1292, 59 L.Ed.2d 501 (1979).

When a person remains silent in the face of an accusation, or by his silence apparently adopts the statement of another, his silence generally can be shown at trial because it amounts to an admission.[78] Where, however, the silence occurs at a time when a suspect is in custody, he has a fifth amendment right not to speak, thus rendering the usual rule of admissions inapplicable. In a case where the suspect was a police officer arrested for taking bribe money, the Court of Appeals held that while his silence could not be used as an admission, it could be used to impeach his credibility as a witness.[79] At trial he testified that he was in the process of completing his investigation and arrest of the complainant for bribe-giving when he was arrested. If that were the case, he would have been expected to speak up at the time and his silence was damning to his direct testimony. The United States Supreme Court held in *Doyle v. Ohio*,[80] however, that defendants who are given *Miranda* warnings upon arrest cannot be impeached by their post-arrest silence because silence is one of their *Miranda* rights.[81]

The *Conyers* cases, *Conyers I*[82] and *Conyers II*,[83] mark a departure on the admissibility, under New York law, of pre- and post-arrest silence. In *Conyers I* the New York Court of Appeals held that the defendant's silence at the point he ran into the police while being pursued by his victim could not be used to impeach his trial testimony that he, and not the pursuer, was the victim. It could be expected that during the interval of time it would take the police to sort out the situation such an explanation would have been forthcoming. Yet the court would not make the distinction suggested by the United States Supreme Court in *Doyle v. Ohio*[84] between pre- and post-*Miranda* warning silence. The Supreme Court granted certiorari in *Conyers I* and remanded the case[85] for the New York court's reappraisal in light of its intervening decision in *Jenkens v. Anderson*.[86] In *Jenkins* it was held that pre-arrest silence could be admissible to impeach because no warnings had been given by the police, meaning that the defendant would not have been told he could remain silent, unlike the situation in the previous *Doyle* case. The Supreme Court advised that each state remained free to formulate evidence rules defining the situation in which silence is viewed as more probative than prejudicial.[87] The New York court accepted this invita-

---

78. See § 802.2(b) & (e) infra.

79. People v. Rothschild, 35 N.Y.2d 355, 361 N.Y.S.2d 901, 320 N.E.2d 639 (1974).

80. 426 U.S. 610, 96 S.Ct. 2240, 49 L.Ed.2d 91 (1976).

81. Despite *Doyle*, in People v. Bowen, 65 A.D.2d 364, 411 N.Y.S.2d 573 (1st Dep't 1978), aff'd, 50 N.Y.2d 915, 431 N.Y.S.2d 449, 409 N.E.2d 924 (1980), a policeman testified that he was merely trying to aid the victim of a rape, but gave no such story at the time he was apprehended for the rape. The court held that a police officer had a special duty to give a full explanation and held the silence admissible.

82. People v. Conyers, 49 N.Y.2d 174, 424 N.Y.S.2d 402, 400 N.E.2d 342 (1980).

83. People v. Conyers, 52 N.Y.2d 454, 438 N.Y.S.2d 741, 420 N.E.2d 933 (1981).

84. 426 U.S. 610, 96 S.Ct. 2240, 49 L.Ed.2d 91 (1976).

85. New York v. Conyers, 449 U.S. 809, 101 S.Ct. 56, 66 L.Ed.2d 12 (1980).

86. 447 U.S. 231, 100 S.Ct. 2124, 65 L.Ed.2d 86 (1980).

87. Id. at 240, 100 S.Ct. at 2131, 65 L.Ed.2d at 98.

tion and adhered in *Conyers II* to its *Conyers I* determination. In *Conyers II*, emphasis was placed on the unreliability of such silence;[88] and the court clearly erased any distinction between pre- and post-arrest silence. It remains unclear what effect the *Conyers* cases might have on *Rothschild*, where the defendant was a policeman.

In a different situation, defendant testified in his own behalf and gave an exculpatory version of the events in issue. At the time of arrest he had not remained silent, but had told the police a story bearing little relation to that told from the stand. The court held that talking to the police was a voluntary act and could be fully used for impeachment as a prior inconsistent statement.[89]

It is also to be noted that a motorist's refusal to submit to a sobriety test is admissible at trial as an admission.[90]

Library References:

West's Key No. Digests, Witnesses ⚖=292–310.

510 The Informer Privilege

§ 510.1 New York

Those who are willing to give information to the authorities often will do so only on the guarantee of anonymity. Disclosure could result in harm to them or those close to them. The authorities, of course, are

---

88. At 52 N.Y.2d at 458–459, 438 N.Y.S.2d at 744, 420 N.E.2d at 935–936, it is stated:

As is evident from our opinion in *Conyers I*, our decision in that case, although based upon constitutional grounds, was heavily influenced by our conviction that evidence of an individual's pretrial failure to speak when confronted by law enforcement officials is of extremely limited probative worth. As noted in our earlier decision, the individual's silence in such circumstances may simply be attributable to his awareness that he is under no obligation to speak or to the natural caution that arises from his knowledge that anything he says might later be used against him at trial. Alternatively, the individual may refrain from speaking because he believes that efforts to exonerate himself under the circumstances would be futile. Finally, it is a lamentable but undeniable fact of modern society that some of our citizens harbor a mistrust for law enforcement authority which leads them to shun contact with the police even when the avoidance of contact is not in their own best interest. * * * Accordingly, evidence of a defendant's *pretrial* silence must be regarded as having minimal probative significance and as having a correspondingly low potential for advancing the truth-finding process even when offered solely for purposes of impeachment.

(Emphasis added).

89. People v. Savage, 50 N.Y.2d 673, 431 N.Y.S.2d 382, 409 N.E.2d 858, cert. denied, 449 U.S. 1016, 101 S.Ct. 577, 66 L.Ed.2d 475 (1980).

90. N.Y.Veh.and Traffic Law § 1194(4) specifically provides for admissibility. The constitutionality of this provision was upheld in People v. Thomas, 46 N.Y.2d 100, 412 N.Y.S.2d 845, 385 N.E.2d 584 (1978), appeal dismissed, 444 U.S. 891, 100 S.Ct. 197, 62 L.Ed.2d 127 (1979). If the motorist can constitutionally be compelled to take the test, as held in Schmerber v. California, 384 U.S. 757, 86 S.Ct. 1826, 16 L.Ed.2d 908 (1966), it follows that he has no constitutional right not to take it. It was suggested in Thomas that a simple refusal to submit to the test is not really testimonial in nature anyway; that it is more indicative of the person's behavior. 46 N.Y.2d at 106, 412 N.Y.S.2d at 848, 385 N.E.2d at 587. See also South Dakota v. Neville, 459 U.S. 553, 103 S.Ct. 916, 74 L.Ed.2d 748 (1983)(refusal to submit to blood-alcohol test may be used against defendant at trial; refusal is not a form of "compulsion").

more than willing to protect these informers to the extent possible.[1] Thus, case law gives the state a privilege to refuse to disclose the identity of a person who has furnished information or assistance to the police or prosecutor.[2] While this protection certainly benefits the informer, the privilege is a public interest privilege belonging to the state.[3]

Obviously this privilege appears most often in criminal cases, where the rights of the defendant must be observed. There are three exceptions to the privilege. First, the privilege vanishes when the informer reveals himself or when his identity is revealed at some stage by the authorities.[4] Second, if it appears that the informer possesses information crucial to the issue of guilt or innocence, his presence could be required at trial.[5] This determination turns on what defendant shows in support of the request for production of the informer and what the prosecutor can muster in opposition to the request.[6] Third, where the issue arises not at trial, but at a suppression hearing, there will be no privilege if the legality of the means by which evidence is obtained rests mainly on information said to have been given by an informer, and the

§ 510.1

1. 8 Wigmore § 2374, at 762. In People v. Darden, 34 N.Y.2d 177, 181, 356 N.Y.S.2d 582, 586, 313 N.E.2d 49, 52 (1974), it was stated: "The weighty considerations countervailing against disclosure of the identity of police informers are evident—'the furtherance and protection of the public interest in effective law enforcement' (Roviaro v. United States, 353 U.S. 53, 59). Assuring the desirable flow of useful information to the police will, of course, depend on predictable and reliable assurances that anonymity of informers will be preserved. The question as to when and in what manner, if at all, identity of the informer and verification of his communication should be established calls for a sensitive and wise balancing of the rights of the individual defendant and the interests of the public."

2. People v. Castillo, 80 N.Y.2d 578, 592 N.Y.S.2d 945, 607 N.E.2d 1050 (1992), cert. denied, ___ U.S. ___, 113 S.Ct. 1854, 123 L.Ed.2d 477 (1993); People v. Liberatore, 79 N.Y.2d 208, 581 N.Y.S.2d 634, 590 N.E.2d 219 (1992); People v. Ortega, 78 N.Y.2d 1101, 578 N.Y.S.2d 123, 585 N.E.2d 372 (1991); People v. Goggins, 34 N.Y.2d 163, 356 N.Y.S.2d 571, 313 N.E.2d 41, cert. denied, 419 U.S. 1012, 95 S.Ct. 332, 42 L.Ed.2d 286 (1974); People v. Darden, 34 N.Y.2d 177, 356 N.Y.S.2d 582, 313 N.E.2d 49 (1974); People v. Malinsky, 15 N.Y.2d 86, 255 N.Y.S.2d 850, 204 N.E.2d 188 (1965).

3. People v. Darden, note 1, supra.

4. This exception seems to have its origins in Roviaro v. United States, 353 U.S. 53, 60, 77 S.Ct. 623, 627, 1 L.Ed.2d 639, 644–45 (1957), where it is explained that the exception is invoked when "the identity of the informer has been disclosed to those who would have cause to resent the communication"; the disclosure must be such that it would normally come to defendant's attention. See also Harris v. United States, 371 F.2d 365 (9th Cir.1967)(informer became a government witness); Westinghouse Electric Corp. v. City of Burlington, 351 F.2d 762 (D.C.Cir.1965), (privilege sought to be applied regarding informants in criminal antitrust cases was destroyed when these people appeared in related civil antitrust proceedings); Advisory Committee's Note to proposed Fed.R.Evid. 510.

5. People v. Goggins, 34 N.Y.2d 163, 169, 170, 356 N.Y.S.2d 571, 576, 313 N.E.2d 41, 44 (1974). The court discussed what must be shown by defendant in order to gain knowledge of the informer's identity and said that bare assertions that the informer is a crucial witness will not suffice. "On this point the nature of the informant's role is of some significance. Undoubtedly the strongest case for disclosure is made out when it appears that the informant was an eyewitness or a participant * * *. When however he has played a marginal part by, for instance, merely furnishing a tip or some information to the police, the privilege should prevail absent an extremely strong showing of relevance." See also People v. Ortega, 78 N.Y.2d 1101, 585 N.E.2d 372, 578 N.Y.S.2d 123 (1991). For a discussion of circumstances under which an informer's tip needs corroboration, see People v. Elwell, 50 N.Y.2d 231, 428 N.Y.S.2d 655, 406 N.E.2d 471 (1980).

6. 34 N.Y.2d at 169–70, 356 N.Y.S.2d at 576, 313 N.E.2d at 44.

judge is not satisfied that there is an informer, or that the informer is reliable or credible.[7] In *People v. Darden*,[8] the court sanctioned the *in camera* hearing at suppression hearings, a device said by the court in the companion *Goggins* case to be inappropriate at trial.[9]

The Proposed New York Evidence Code, in § 514,[10] simply adopts these rules, but sets forth no criteria for determination of defendant's claims under either subdivision (b)(2) or (b)(3). In addition to the *Darden* case dealing with suppression hearings,[11] the court's decision in *People v. Jenkins*[12] is instructive as regards the trial and the difference between disclosure of the informer's identity and the production of the informer as a witness. In that case the informer had been sent to another state for her own safety and then she disappeared. There was no suggestion that the prosecutor was attempting thereby to make her unavailable for trial. Nevertheless, she was unavailable for production after defendant demonstrated her connection to the crime for which he was being prosecuted. The court held that under the *Goggins* requirements defendant proved that his demand for disclosure had some basis in that he showed the informer's connection to the crime and that his

---

7. People v. Castillo, 80 N.Y.2d 578, 592 N.Y.S.2d 945, 607 N.E.2d 1050 (1992); People v. Liberatore, 79 N.Y.2d 208, 581 N.Y.S.2d 634, 590 N.E.2d 219 (1992); People v. Darden, 34 N.Y.2d 177, 356 N.Y.S.2d 582, 313 N.E.2d 49 (1974).

8. 34 N.Y.2d at 181, 313 N.E.2d at 52, 356 N.Y.S.2d at 586 (1974). It was stated:

The prosecution [at the *in camera* hearing] should be required to make the informer available for interrogation before the Judge. The prosecutor may be present but not the defendant or his counsel. Opportunity should be afforded counsel for defendant to submit in writing any questions which he may desire the Judge to put to the informer. The Judge should take testimony, with recognition of the special need for protection of the interests of the absent defendant, and make a summary report as to the existence of the informer and with respect to the communications made by the informer to the police to which the police testify. That report should be made available to the defendant and to the People, and the transcript of testimony should be sealed to be available to the appellate courts if the occasion arises. At all stages of the procedure, of course, every reasonable precaution should be taken to assure that the anonymity of the informer is protected to the maximum degree possible.

9. People v. Goggins, 34 N.Y.2d 163, 169, 313 N.E.2d 41, 44, 356 N.Y.S.2d 571, 575 (1974).

10. § 514. Privilege for identity of person providing information to law enforcement [PROPOSED]

(a) **Nature of privilege.** The state, or a political subdivision, department, or agency thereof, has a privilege to refuse to disclose and to prevent any of its present or former officers or employees from disclosing the identity, or information which would lead to the identity, of a person who has furnished information concerning a violation of law to a law enforcement officer or prosecutor.

(b) **Exceptions.** Situations in which there is no privilege under this section include, but are not limited to:

(1) **Voluntary disclosure.** If the identity of the informant has been disclosed by the state or its employee or by the informant's own actions under circumstances which make it unnecessary to maintain confidentiality.

(2) **Trial on the merits.** When the informant's testimony will provide relevant testimony as to the guilt or innocence of an accused in a criminal proceeding.

(3) **In camera disclosure in suppression hearings.** Where there is insufficient evidence to establish the legality of the means by which evidence has been obtained, apart from testimony about communications received from an informer, and the issue of identity is raised by a defendant on a suppression motion in a criminal case, the court shall direct that the informant be produced before the court for in camera questioning.

11. See note 8 supra.

12. 41 N.Y.2d 307, 392 N.Y.S.2d 587, 360 N.E.2d 1288 (1977).

request was "not merely an angling in desperation for possible weaknesses in the prosecutor's investigation." However, said the court, the right of production, which was not in issue in *Goggins*, does not flow from the right to disclosure, and where the informer is unavailable for production due to no improper motives on the part of the prosecutor, defendant is not entitled to dismissal of the charges unless he can show that testimony by the informer would tend to be exculpatory or would create a reasonable doubt as to defendant's guilt. Thus, the court imposed an added burden on the defendant where the informer's whereabouts are unknown.

The Court of Appeals in 1992, in *People v. Castillo*,[13] had occasion to review most of the authorities and Judge Simons' opinion is helpful on almost any phase of the subject, although *Castillo* is a suppression case. Among the points made is that the informer's role at the trial stage affects defendant's basic rights to participate in his defense and confrontation, whereas the informer's role at the suppression stage goes to the question of whether probable cause existed for the gathering of evidence, a question of less gravity and one aimed at police conduct rather than whether the evidence is credible.[14]

Library References:

West's Key No. Digests, Witnesses ⚖216(4).

§ 510.2 Federal

The fount of the federal rules with respect to the privilege for informers' identities, and of the state rules insofar as defendant's due process rights are concerned, is *Roviaro v. United States*.[1] *Roviaro*

---

13. 80 N.Y.2d 578, 592 N.Y.S.2d 945, 607 N.E.2d 1050 (1992), cert. denied, ___ U.S. ___, 113 S.Ct. 1854, 123 L.Ed.2d 477 (1993).

14. 80 N.Y.2d at 582, 607 N.E.2d at 1051, 1052, 592 N.Y.S.2d at 946, 947. Later in the opinion Judge Simons described the suppression hearing process:
An examination of the record establishes that the court diligently protected defendant's rights in the case before us. In determining whether to disclose the informer's identity or statements, it followed the four-step procedure set forth in People v. Seychel (136 Misc.2d 310). In the first step the court reviewed the search warrant to determine whether it alleged probable cause in this case by application of the *Aguilar-Spinelli* test (see, People v. Griminger, 71 N.Y.2d 635), or whether it was perjurious on its face. If the supporting affidavit had appeared perjurious on its face, the court would have conducted an in camera hearing to determine if the affidavit contained perjury and if it did, would have given the People the choice of turning over the affidavit for a hearing or discontinuing the prosecution (see, Franks v. Delaware, 438 U.S. 154; People v. Alfinito, 16 N.Y.2d 181). Finding neither, the court next proceeded to conduct an in camera, ex parte inquiry of the informant and examined the People's exhibits to determine whether the informant's life and/or future investigations would be jeopardized by disclosure. Confidentiality was deemed necessary, and the court then proceeded to try and redact portions of the affidavit to conceal the informant's identity while giving the defendant a description of the information resulting in his arrest. It found this impossible and therefore ordered the People to produce the informant for a *Darden*-type inquiry in which it could evaluate credibility (see, People v. Darden, 34 N.Y.2d 177, supra).
80 N.Y.2d at 586, 607 N.E.2d at 1054, 592 N.Y.S.2d at 949.

§ 510.2

1. 353 U.S. 53, 77 S.Ct. 623, 1 L.Ed.2d 639 (1957). In Roviaro the court indicated areas of concern in determining whether the informer's identity should be revealed.

§ 510.2 PRIVILEGES Ch. 5

involved the trial stage, where the Supreme Court defined the privilege and the exceptions, prescribed the balancing test and, in the end, found that the defendant was entitled to the informer's identity. The reason for the privilege—that few will cooperate with authorities without a guarantee of anonymity—is found well stated in the Second Circuit[2] and the federal courts apply the *Roviaro* balancing test much the same as the New York courts apply the *Goggins*[3] and *Darden*[4] rules. Thus, in *DiBlasio v. Keane*[5] defendant was entitled to know the identity of the prosecution's informant who had arranged the drug sale and whose testimony would be relevant to the entrapment defense. But, in *United States v. Turbide*[6] the informer's anonymity was preserved since he was not present at the time the crime was committed and otherwise had little or no information that could be helpful to the defense. And in *Rugendorf v. United States*[7] defendant was unable to meet his burden of producing evidence showing how the informer's testimony would be helpful to his defense.

In *McCray v. Illinois*[8] the Supreme Court held that while a defendant does not have a constitutional right at the suppression stage to the informer's identity, he is entitled to the *Roviaro* balancing test so that if identity is material to the legality of the way in which evidence was obtained by the police he would be entitled to disclosure. This principle was applied in *United States v. Manley*[9] where it was held that the informant's identity need not be disclosed when the information is corroborated by other sources.

The informer's privilege or something like it also comes up in civil cases.[10] "Indeed, there is ample authority for the proposition that the strength of the privilege is greater in civil litigation than in criminal."[11]

Would the informer be a material witness, such as an eyewitness or perhaps a participant? Would the informer have information relevant to any element of the defense? 353 U.S. at 62–66, 77 S.Ct. at 629–631, 1 L.Ed.2d at 646–648. Other factors would also be of importance, such as the officer's credibility and the consequences to the informer and the government were his identity to be revealed.

2. United States v. Tucker, 380 F.2d 206, 213 (2d Cir.1967). See 2 Weinstein and Berger ¶ 510[02].

3. People v. Goggins, 34 N.Y.2d 163, 313 N.E.2d 41, 356 N.Y.S.2d 571 (1974).

4. People v. Darden, 34 N.Y.2d 177, 313 N.E.2d 49, 356 N.Y.S.2d 582 (1974).

5. 932 F.2d 1038 (2d Cir.1991).

6. 558 F.2d 1053 (2d Cir.), cert. denied, Perez v. United States, 434 U.S. 934, 98 S.Ct. 421, 54 L.Ed.2d 293 (1977).

7. 376 U.S. 528, 84 S.Ct. 825, 11 L.Ed.2d 887, rehearing denied, 377 U.S. 940, 84 S.Ct. 1330, 12 L.Ed.2d 303 (1964).

8. 386 U.S. 300, 87 S.Ct. 1056, 18 L.Ed.2d 62, rehearing denied, 386 U.S. 1042, 87 S.Ct. 1474, 18 L.Ed.2d 616 (1967).

9. 632 F.2d 978, 985 (2d Cir.1980), cert. denied, 449 U.S. 1112, 101 S.Ct. 922, 66 L.Ed.2d 841 (1981).

10. See, e.g., Dole v. Local 1942, International Brotherhood of Electrical Workers, AFL–CIO, 870 F.2d 368, 372 (7th Cir. 1989)(in action based on alleged improprieties in union election, defendant union failed to show sufficient need for identification of individual union members who assisted Department of Labor in its investigation).

11. In re United States, 565 F.2d 19, 22 (2d Cir.1977)(in action by Socialist Workers Party and others for damages and injunctive relief relating to alleged harassment by the government, plaintiffs failed to demonstrate sufficient need, prior to trial, for identification of persons who gave information to government, over course of several years, concerning plaintiffs' activities).

Proposed Federal Rule 510[12] provides essentially the same privilege and exceptions as the New York proposed rule with respect to informers, but is more elaborate in providing procedural detail. A departure from the New York proposed rule can be found in subdivision (c)(2) which specifically allows for an *in camera* hearing at the trial stage.

Library References:

West's Key No. Digests, Witnesses ⚷216(4).

12. **Rule 510. Identity of Informer [Not Enacted]**

(a) **Rule of privilege.** The government or state or subdivision thereof has a privilege to refuse to disclose the identity of a person who has furnished information relating to or assisting in an investigation of a possible violation of law to a law enforcement officer or member of a legislative committee or its staff conducting an investigation.

(b) **Who may claim.** The privilege may be claimed by an appropriate representative of the government, regardless of whether the information was furnished to an officer of the government or of a state or subdivision thereof. The privilege may be claimed by an appropriate representative of a state or subdivision if the information was furnished to an officer thereof, except that in criminal cases the privilege shall not be allowed if the government objects.

(c) **Exceptions.**

(1) **Voluntary disclosure; informer a witness.** No privilege exists under this rule if the identity of the informer or his interest in the subject matter of his communication has been disclosed to those who would have cause to resent the communication by a holder of the privilege or by the informer's own action, or if the informer appears as a witness for the government.

(2) **Testimony on merits.** If it appears from the evidence in the case or from other showing by a party that an informer may be able to give testimony necessary to a fair determination of the issue of guilt or innocence in a criminal case or of a material issue on the merits in a civil case to which the government is a party, and the government invokes the privilege, the judge shall give the government an opportunity to show in camera facts relevant to determining whether the informer can, in fact, supply that testimony. The showing will ordinarily be in the form of affidavits, but the judge may direct that testimony be taken if he finds that the matter cannot be resolved satisfactorily upon affidavit. If the judge finds that there is a reasonable probability that the informer can give the testimony, and the government elects not to disclose his identity the judge on motion of the defendant in a criminal case shall dismiss the charges to which the testimony would relate, and the judge may do so on his own motion. In civil cases, he may make any order that justice requires. Evidence submitted to the judge shall be sealed and preserved to be made available to the appellate court in the event of an appeal, and the contents shall not otherwise be revealed without consent of the government. All counsel and parties shall be permitted to be present at every stage of proceedings under this subdivision except a showing in camera, at which no counsel or party shall be permitted to be present.

(3) **Legality of obtaining evidence.** If information from an informer is relied upon to establish the legality of the means by which evidence was obtained and the judge is not satisfied that the information was received from an informer reasonably believed to be reliable or credible, he may require the identity of the informer to be disclosed. The judge shall, on request of the government direct that the disclosure be made in camera. All counsel and parties concerned with the issue of legality shall be permitted to be present at every stage of proceedings under this subdivision except a disclosure in camera, at which no counsel or party shall be permitted to be present. If disclosure of the identity of the informer is made in camera, the record thereof shall be sealed and preserved to be made available to the appellate court in the event of an appeal, and the contents shall not

511 Government Communications

§ 511.1 New York

The New York law on the official information or public interest privilege is set forth in the majority opinion in *Cirale v. 80 Pine St. Corp.*[1]:

> As part of the common law of evidence, "official information" in the hands of governmental agencies has been deemed in certain contexts, privileged. Such a privilege attaches to "confidential communications between public officers, and to public officers, in the performance of their duties, where the public interest requires that such confidential communications or the sources should not be divulged." (People v. Keating, 286 App.Div. 150, 153; see, generally, M.M. Carrow—Governmental Nondisclosure in Judicial Proceedings, 107 U. of Pa.L.Rev. 166.) The hallmark of this privilege is that it is applicable when the public interest would be harmed if the material were to to [sic] lose its cloak of confidentiality. (8 Wigmore, Evidence [McNaughton rev.], § 2378; Richardson, Evidence [10th ed.], § 456, p. 446; 1 Mottla, New York Evidence, Proof of Cases [2d ed.], § 394; Matter of Langert v. Tenney, 5 A.D.2d 586.) It has been said that the privilege is a qualified one, which may be ineffective when it appears that the disclosure of the privileged information is necessary to avoid the risk of false testimony or to secure useful testimony. (See People v. Keating, *supra*, at p. 153.) While this test may be appropriate in criminal cases, we would reject any such qualification in civil cases, since the privilege would become meaningless if it could be breached in order to secure "useful testimony." Any testimony, if relevant to the action at bar, may be said to be useful. While some commentators have argued that the privilege is qualified and requires a balancing of the needs of the litigants against the potential harm to the public interest that may result from disclosure (see 42 Fordham L.Rev. 807; 107 U. of Pa.L.Rev. 166), these, in reality, are two sides of the same coin. Public interest encompasses not only the needs of the government, but also the societal interests in redressing private wrongs and arriving at a just result in private litigation. Thus, the balancing that is required goes to the determination of the harm to the overall public interest. Once it is shown that disclosure would be more harmful to the interests of the government than the interests of the party seeking the information, the overall public interest on balance would then be better served by nondisclosure. While the need of a litigant for the information would present a strong

otherwise be revealed without consent of the government.

§ 511.1
1. 35 N.Y.2d 113, 359 N.Y.S.2d 1, 316 N.E.2d 301 (1974).

argument for disclosure, the court should balance such need against the government's duty to inquire into and ascertain the facts of a serious accident for the purposes of taking steps to prevent similar occurrences in the future.[2]

This privilege is qualified[3] and would not be operable where the information is relevant to the defense in a criminal case;[4] but the privilege is not otherwise easily dislodged.[5]

In *Cirale* it was noted that the then new Freedom of Information Law (FOIL)[6] "does not abolish the common-law privilege for official information";[7] but it would seem that FOIL would have the effect of limiting the privilege to the extent that information is required to be disclosed under FOIL. The provision protecting certain material under

---

2. Id. at 117–118, 359 N.Y.S.2d at 4, 5, 316 N.E.2d at 303.

3. The Court went on to state:

By our decision today, we do not hold that all governmental information is privileged or that such information may be withheld by a mere assertion of privilege. There must be specific support for the claim of privilege. Public interest is a flexible term and what constitutes sufficient potential harm to the public interest so as to render the privilege operable must of necessity be determined on the facts of each case. Such a determination is a judicial one and requires that the governmental agency come forward to show that the public interest would indeed be jeopardized by a disclosure of the information. Otherwise, the privilege could be easily abused, serving as a cloak for official misconduct. (8 Wigmore, Evidence [McNaughton rev.], § 2379, pp. 808–810; United States v. Reynolds, 345 U.S. 1; Stratford Factors v. New York State Banking Dept., 10 A.D.2d 66.) Of course, in some situations it may be difficult to determine if the assertion of the privilege is warranted without forcing a disclosure of the very thing sought to be withheld. In such situations, it would seem proper that the material requested be examined by the court *in camera*. (See United States v. Reynolds, supra; Stratford Factors v. New York State Banking Dept., supra.) However, it will be the rare case that *in camera* determinations will be necessary. A description of the material sought, the purpose for which it was gathered and other similar considerations will usually provide a sufficient basis upon which the court may determine whether the assertion of governmental privilege is warranted. Id. at 118–119, 359 N.Y.S.2d at 5,6, 316 N.E.2d at 304.

4. Application of Langert v. Tenney, 5 A.D.2d 586, 589, 173 N.Y.S.2d 665, 667 (1st Dep't), appeal denied, 6 A.D.2d 777, 175 N.Y.S.2d 154 (1st Dep't 1958), appeal dismissed, 5 N.Y.2d 875, 182 N.Y.S.2d 25, 155 N.E.2d 870 (1959).

5. In Martin A. v. Gross, 194 A.D.2d 195, 605 N.Y.S.2d 742 (1st Dep't 1993), the City was entitled to the privilege to protect an internal report by the New York City Human Resources Administration's Child Fatality Review Panel relating to the death of plaintiffs' sibling. Plaintiffs were pursuing various remedies based on alleged violation of duties pertaining to the City under the Child Welfare Reform Act. In Lowrance v. State of New York, 185 A.D.2d 268, 586 N.Y.S.2d 21 (2d Dep't 1992), a prison inmate was denied discovery of interviews conducted by the Inspector General's Office in pursuance of its investigation of grievances filed by the inmate. "Under the circumstances presented, the State's interest in maintaining the integrity of its internal investigations and protecting the confidentiality of sources who provide sensitive information within a prison context, outweighs any interest of the claimant in seeking access to the file. * * *" Id. at 269, 586 N.Y.S.2d at 22. See also Sanchez v. City of New York, 201 A.D.2d 325, 607 N.Y.S.2d 321 (1st Dep't 1994)(statements made by complaining witness to district attorney's office in rape investigation fell within public interest privilege; in witness' subsequent tort action against owner of premises where rape occurred, owner failed to demonstrate compelling and particularized need for access).

6. N.Y.Pub.Officers Law, Art. 6.

7. 35 N.Y.2d at 117 n.1, 359 N.Y.S.2d at 5, 316 N.E.2d at 304.

FOIL,[8] on the other hand, would tend to reinforce or extend the privileged area.

In *Application of Langert v. Tenney*,[9] petitioner wanted to bring a defamation action, but needed information to be gleaned from a communication made to the Commissioner of Investigation of the City of New York. Noting that the purpose of that office would be undermined were informer's communications made subject to disclosure (not just the identities of the informers, but the content of their communications as well) the court held the privilege as a bar. As to the qualified nature of the privilege, it was stated: "Generally, the information received or the records made thereof by public investigating officials is not subject to disclosure or inspection, but there are exceptions. * * * Thus, for instance, upon a criminal trial the court has power to compel disclosure of matter admissible in evidence, relevant to the innocence of the defendant, and not countervailed by a superior public interest. * * *"

The Proposed New York Evidence Code would essentially codify the caselaw.[10]

---

8. N.Y.Pub.Officers Law § 87(2) provides:

2. Each agency shall, in accordance with its published rules, make available for public inspection and copying all records, except that such agency may deny access to records or portions thereof that:

(a) are specifically exempted from disclosure by state or federal statute;

(b) if disclosed would constitute an unwarranted invasion of personal privacy under the provisions of subdivision two of section eighty-nine of this article;

(c) if disclosed would impair present or imminent contract awards or collective bargaining negotiations;

(d) are trade secrets or are maintained for the regulation of commercial enterprise which if disclosed would cause substantial injury to the competitive position of the subject enterprise;

(e) are compiled for law enforcement purposes and which, if disclosed, would:

 i. interfere with law enforcement investigations or judicial proceedings;

 ii. deprive a person of a right to a fair trial or impartial adjudication;

 iii. identify a confidential course or disclose confidential information relating to a criminal investigation; or

 iv. reveal criminal investigative techniques or procedures, except routine techniques and procedures;

(f) if disclosed would endanger the life or safety of any person;

(g) are inter-agency or intra-agency materials which are not:

 i. statistical or factual tabulations or data;

 ii. instructions to staff that affect the public;

 iii. final agency policy or determinations; or

 iv. external audits, including but not limited to audits performed by the comptroller and the federal government; or

(h) are examination questions or answers which are requested prior to the final administration of such questions.

9. 5 A.D.2d 586, 173 N.Y.S.2d 665 (1st Dep't), appeal denied, 6 A.D.2d 777, 175 N.Y.S.2d 154 (1st Dep't 1958), appeal dismissed, 5 N.Y.2d 875, 182 N.Y.S.2d 25, 155 N.E.2d 870 (1959). See also People v. Keating, 286 App.Div. 150, 141 N.Y.S.2d 562 (1st Dep't 1955); Fischer v. Citizens Comm., 72 Misc.2d 595, 339 N.Y.S.2d 853 (Sup.Ct.Wyoming Co.1973), aff'd, 42 A.D.2d 692, 346 N.Y.S.2d 217 (4th Dep't 1973)). In Fischer a special investigator, charged by the Governor to conduct a grand jury investigation of the Attica prison riots, sought to obtain information from the McKay Commission, also created by the Governor to investigate the uprising. The Commission's files contained records of nearly 3,000 interviews with persons, all of whom had been promised confidentiality. The court ruled that this information was protected by the privilege.

10. § 513. **Official information in the public interest privilege [PROPOSED]**

(a) **Nature of privilege.** The state, a political subdivision, department, agen-

§ 511.2 Federal

Proposed Federal Rule 509 combines the traditional protection for military and state secrets with the category called "Official Information."[1] The rule set forth with regard to official information approxi-

cy or bureau thereof or a governmental entity, has a privilege to refuse to disclose and to prevent any officer or employee from disclosing confidential official information when the court determines that the public interest in preserving the confidentiality of the official information outweighs the interests calling for disclosure in the particular proceeding. Provided, however, (1) an accused in a criminal proceeding is entitled to disclosure of relevant exculpatory evidence; and (2) in civil cases when a law enforcement agency is the repository of confidential information, the interest calling for disclosure in the particular proceeding must outweigh the public law enforcement interest in maintaining confidentiality.

(b) Official information defined. For purposes of this section, "official information" means confidential communications made to or confidential communications between public officers or employees in the performance of their duties, provided those communications are neither available to the public pursuant to article six of the public officers law or other statute, nor otherwise officially disclosed or intentionally made available to the public prior to the time the claim of privilege is made.

§ 511.2

1. Rule 509. Secrets of State and Other Official Information [Not Enacted]

(a) Definitions.

(1) Secret of state. A "secret of state" is a governmental secret relating to the national defense or the international relations of the United States.

(2) Official information. "Official information" is information within the custody or control of a department or agency of the government the disclosure of which is shown to be contrary to the public interest and which consists of: (A) intergovernmental opinions or recommendations submitted for consideration in the performance of decisional or policymaking functions, or (B) subject to the provisions of 18 U.S.C. § 3500, investigatory files compiled for law enforcement purposes and not otherwise available, or (C) information within the custody or control of a governmental department or agency whether initiated within the department or agency or acquired by it in its exercise of its official responsibilities and not otherwise available to the public pursuant to 5 U.S.C. § 552.

(b) General rule of privilege. The government has a privilege to refuse to give evidence and to prevent any person from giving evidence upon a showing of reasonable likelihood of danger that the evidence will disclose a secret of state or official information as defined in this rule.

(c) Procedures. The privilege for secrets of state may be claimed only by the chief officer of the government agency or department administering the subject matter which the secret information sought concerns, but the privilege for official information may be asserted by any attorney representing the government. The required showing may be made in whole or in part in the form of a written statement. The judge may hear the matter in chambers, but all counsel are entitled to inspect the claim and showing and to be heard thereon, except that, in the case of secrets of state, the judge upon motion of the government, may permit the government to make the required showing in the above form in camera. If the judge sustains the privilege upon a showing in camera, the entire text of the government's statements shall be sealed and preserved in the court's records in the event of appeal. In the case of privilege claimed for official information the court may require examination in camera of the information itself. The judge may take any protective measure which the interests of the government and the furtherance of justice may require.

(d) Notice to government. If the circumstances of the case indicate a substantial possibility that a claim of privilege would be appropriate but has not been made because of oversight or lack of knowledge, the judge shall give or cause notice to be given to the officer entitled to claim the privilege and shall stay further proceedings a reasonable time to afford opportunity to assert a claim of privilege.

Library References:

West's Key No. Digests, Witnesses ⊱216.

mates the New York common law rule.[2] The caselaw is not as cohesive as the New York caselaw in that the blanket privilege is not as well developed in the federal cases. Whereas in New York the *Cirale* rule[3] is pervasive (with aspects of the New York Freedom of Information Law (FOIL) closely connected), the federal cases deal with several categorical privileges such as those pertaining to the executive,[4] legislative[5] and judicial[6] branches, the public interest privilege generally (most often in the discovery stage of the lawsuit),[7] and Freedom of Information Act (FOIA) litigation.[8] Certainly these areas are overlapping, the balancing test being operative except where, in the FOIA, the statute prescribes certain protected areas.[9]

When the litigation concerns government malfeasance the courts are willing to find the privilege outweighed by the public need;[10] but the privilege will obtain when policy-making would otherwise be chilled.[11] Not even the President of the United States, however, has an unqualified privilege.[12]

As is the case at the state level, FOIA[13] bears on this privilege since,

(e) Effect of sustaining claim. If a claim of privilege is sustained in a proceeding to which the government is a party and it appears that another party is thereby deprived of material evidence, the judge shall make any further orders which the interests of justice require, including striking the testimony of a witness, declaring a mistrial, finding against the government upon an issue as to which the evidence is relevant, or dismissing the action.

2. The proposed Federal Rule is more detailed than the Proposed New York Evidence Code in its procedures and exceptions. For example, subdivision (a)(2) of the proposed Federal Rule makes investigatory files compiled for law enforcement purposes subject to the Jenks Act (18 U.S.C.A. § 3500), and to the Freedom of Information Act (5 U.S.C.A. § 552). Subdivision (b) specifically places the burden of justifying the privilege on the government. The government must be precise in proving its justification for invoking the privilege. See, e.g., Mobil Oil Corp. v. Department of Energy, 520 F.Supp. 414, 418 (N.D.N.Y.1981).

3. Cirale v. 80 Pine St. Corp., 35 N.Y.2d 113, 359 N.Y.S.2d 1, 316 N.E.2d 301 (1974).

4. United States v. Nixon, 418 U.S. 683, 94 S.Ct. 3090, 41 L.Ed.2d 1039 (1974).

5. Eastland v. United States Servicemen's Fund, 421 U.S. 491, 95 S.Ct. 1813, 44 L.Ed.2d 324 (1975).

6. In re Certain Complaints, 783 F.2d 1488 (11th Cir.), cert. denied, 477 U.S. 904, 106 S.Ct. 3273, 91 L.Ed.2d 563 (1986).

7. See, e.g., United States v. American Tel. and Tel. Co., 524 F.Supp. 1381 (D.D.C. 1981), where the court found attorneys' "deliberative process" and "work product" protected.

8. See, e.g., International Paper Co. v. Federal Power Comm'n, 438 F.2d 1349 (2d Cir.), cert. denied, 404 U.S. 827, 92 S.Ct. 61, 30 L.Ed.2d 56 (1971), where the privilege (actually a FOIA exemption) was upheld to protect memoranda sent to the Federal Power Commission from its general counsel and its Bureau of Natural Gas—typical examples of interagency communications.

9. See note 14 infra.

10. See, e.g., Socialist Workers Party v. Attorney General of United States, 458 F.Supp. 895 (S.D.N.Y.1978), reversed in part, 596 F.2d 58 (2d Cir.), cert. denied, 444 U.S. 903, 100 S.Ct. 217, 62 L.Ed.2d 141 (1979) (FBI files held not protected where there was relevance to FBI wrongdoing).

11. See International Paper Co. v. Federal Power Comm'n, 438 F.2d 1349 (2d Cir.), cert. denied, 404 U.S. 827, 92 S.Ct. 61, 30 L.Ed.2d 56 (1971).

12. See United States v. Nixon, 418 U.S. 683, 94 S.Ct. 3090, 41 L.Ed.2d 1039 (1974). The Court for the first time proclaimed that executive privilege claimed by the President was subject to judicial review. Utilizing this power, the Court went on to find that there were insufficient grounds shown for protecting the documents (the need to promote candor in government officials was lacking) and tapes sought, and the public interest would be better served by making the material available to the Watergate investigators.

13. 5 U.S.C.A. § 552.

aside from its purpose to make government information generally available, protected areas are carved out[14] based on the need for confidentiality.[15]

14. Subdivision (b) of § 552 provides:

(b) This section does not apply to matters that are—

(1)(A) specifically authorized under criteria established by an Executive order to be kept secret in the interest of national defense or foreign policy and (B) are in fact properly classified pursuant to such Executive order;

(2) related solely to the internal personnel rules and practices of an agency;

(3) specifically exempted from disclosure by statute (other than section 552b of this title), provided that such statute (A) requires that the matters be withheld from the public in such a manner as to leave no discretion on the issue, or (B) establishes particular criteria for withholding or refers to particular types of matters to be withheld;

(4) trade secrets and commercial or financial information obtained from a person and privileged or confidential;

(5) inter-agency or intra-agency memorandums or letters which would not be available by law to a party other than an agency in litigation with the agency;

(6) personnel and medical files and similar files the disclosure of which would constitute a clearly unwarranted invasion of personal privacy;

(7) records or information compiled for law enforcement purposes, but only to the extent that the production of such law enforcement records or information (A) could reasonably be expected to interfere with enforcement proceedings, (B) would deprive a person of a right to a fair trial or an impartial adjudication, (C) could reasonably be expected to constitute an unwarranted invasion of personal privacy, (D) could reasonably be expected to disclose the identity of a confidential source, including a State, local, or foreign agency or authority or any private institution which furnished information on a confidential basis, and, in the case of a record or information compiled by criminal law enforcement authority in the course of a criminal investigation or by an agency conducting a lawful national security intelligence investigation, information furnished by a confidential course, (E) would disclose techniques and procedures for law enforcement investigation or prosecutions, or would disclose guidelines for law enforcement investigations or prosecutions if such disclosure could reasonably be expected to risk circumvention of the law, or (F) could reasonably be expected to endanger the life of physical safety or any individual;

(8) contained in or related to examination, operating, or condition reports prepared by, on behalf of, or for the use of an agency responsible for the regulation or supervision of financial institutions; or

(9) geological and geophysical information and data, including maps, concerning wells.

15. In Renegotiation Board v. Grumman Aircraft, 421 U.S. 168, 186, 95 S.Ct. 1491, 1501, 44 L.Ed.2d 57, 72 (1975), it was held that a report that was made by an investigating board and then used by a higher level board for a final decision was protected by subdivision (b)(5) as an interagency memorandum: "The Regional Board Reports are thus precisely the kind of predecisional deliberative advice and recommendations contemplated by Exemption 5 which must remain uninhibited and thus undisclosed in order to supply maximum assistance to the Board in reaching its decision." In EPA v. Mink, 410 U.S. 73, 93 S.Ct. 827, 35 L.Ed.2d 119 (1973), members of Congress sought to obtain documents prepared by government officials for the President concerning underground nuclear testing, but this material, including that part not labeled top secret, was found to be protected under exemption 1 (protected by executive order in the interests of national defense or foreign policy) or under exemption 5 (interagency documents). See also Fischer v. IRS, 621 F.Supp. 835 (N.D.N.Y.1985)(exemption 5 protects IRS predecisional recommendations, deliberations, opinions and suggestions).

See also Proposed Federal Rule of Evidence 502, Required Reports Privileged By Statute:

A person, corporation, association, or other organization or entity, either public or private, making a return or report required by law to be made has a privilege to refuse to disclose and to prevent any other person from disclosing the return or report, if the law requiring it to be made so provides. A public officer or agency to whom a return or report is required by law to be made has a privilege to refuse to disclose the return or report if the law requiring it to be made so provides. No privilege exists under

§ 511.2   PRIVILEGES   Ch. 5

Library References:

West's Key No. Digests, Witnesses ⚖=216.

512   Political Vote

§ 512.1   New York

The rule of the secret ballot is provided for in the New York Constitution,[1] and is given implementation in the Election Law.[2] These provisions guarantee that a person may vote in secret, and caselaw has long held that she need not later reveal how her vote was cast.[3] As is the case with other privileges based on confidentiality, the voter may waive this privilege and reveal how her ballot was cast.[4] If the vote were cast illegally, the common law rule would allow for inquiry into charges of dishonesty at the polls.[5] The privilege against self-incrimination is available to a witness if her act of illegal voting constitutes a crime, but immunity can be conferred under the Election Law[6] in which case she could be compelled to testify how she voted.[7] Section 512 of the Proposed New York Evidence Code covers this privilege.[8]

Library References:

West's Key No. Digests, Elections ⚖=28.

§ 512.1

1. N.Y.Const. art. II, § 7.

2. Section 7-202 of the New York Election Law provides, inter alia, that voting machines must allow persons to vote "in absolute secrecy." Section 8-300(2) states: "The operating of the voting machine by the voter while voting or the marking of his ballot shall be secret and obscured from all other persons except as provided by this chapter in case of voting by assisted voters."

3. People ex rel. Judson v. Thacher, 55 N.Y. 525, 535 (1874); People v. Pease, 27 N.Y. 45, 71–72 (1863); 8 Wigmore § 2214; Nutting, "Freedom of Silence: Constitutional Protection Against Government Intrusion in Political Affairs," 47 Mich.L.Rev. 181 (1948).

4. Matter of Creedon, 264 N.Y. 40, 189 N.E. 773 (1934); People ex rel. Deister v. Wintermute, 194 N.Y. 99, 86 N.E. 818 (1909); Shaughnessy v. Monahan, 79 Misc.2d 648, 361 N.Y.S.2d 101 (Sup.Ct.Rensselaer Co.1974); Matter of Longo v. D'Apice, 154 A.D.2d 726, 727, 546 N.Y.S.2d 907, 908 (2d Dep't 1989). In Longo, the court, collecting what authority there is, ruled that the privilege "covers qualified voters only, and does not extend to those persons who the court determines were unqualified to vote. Such persons may be compelled to reveal for whom they voted so their votes may be discounted. * * *"

this rule in actions involving perjury, false statements, fraud in the return or report, or other failure to comply with the law in question.

See 2 Weinstein and Berger Evidence ¶¶ 502[01]-[06], which discusses the influence of this provision even though it was not enacted.

5. 8 Wigmore § 2214, at 163. See, e.g., McGuinness v. DeSapio, 9 A.D.2d 65, 71, 191 N.Y.S.2d 798, 804 (1st Dep't 1959)(court noted that while a contested election can be investigated to discern irregularities which could have affected the outcome, the petitioner's burden would not necessarily include showing how particular persons actually voted).

6. N.Y.Elec.Law § 17-146.

7. See 2 Weinstein and Berger ¶ 507[04].

8. § 512. Secrecy of the vote privilege [PROPOSED]

A person has a privilege to refuse to disclose and to prevent any other person from disclosing the tenor of that person's vote cast during an election conducted pursuant to the provisions of the election law unless the vote was cast illegally.

§ 512.2 Federal

The rule proposed for the federal courts with respect to the secrecy of one's vote is roughly the same as New York's proposed rule.[1] The privilege exists in the federal courts even though Rule 507 was not enacted.[2]

513 Trade Secrets

§ 513.1 New York

The protection against disclosure of trade secrets has long been a common law principle.[1] A trade secret can be any formula, device or information which gives one an advantage over competitors.[2] This principle is highly qualified in that the protection cannot be used to conceal fraud or wrongdoing. Certainly, where the defendant is charged with production and circulation of a dangerous compound, "the secrecy of its manufacture ought not to be protected."[3] The trade secret protection is operative, however, to prevent disclosure of a product's secret formula where knowledge of its ingredients, without the proportion of their combination, will give the plaintiff sufficient information for his personal injury action.[4] The Proposed New York Evidence Code § 511 would codify this privilege for the person who wishes to preserve the secret, or for that person's agent, employee, or exclusive licensee so long as invocation of the privilege will not tend to conceal fraud or work injustice.[5] Assertion of the protection comes most often, of course, at the discovery stage of the lawsuit and the courts can achieve partial protection by modifying orders to provide that evidence concerning the trade secret not become available to other than the parties to the suit.[6]

§ 512.2

1. **Rule 507. Political Vote [Not Enacted]**

Every person has a privilege to refuse to disclose the tenor of his vote at a political election conducted by secret ballot unless the vote was cast illegally.

2. In re Dinnan, 661 F.2d 426, 432 (5th Cir.1981), cert. denied, 457 U.S. 1106, 102 S.Ct. 2904, 73 L.Ed.2d 1314 (1982); 2 Weinstein and Berger ¶ 507[2].

§ 513.1

1. Drake v. Herrman, 261 N.Y. 414, 185 N.E. 685 (1933); Griffin Mfg. Co. v. Gold Dust Corp., 245 App.Div. 385, 282 N.Y.S. 931 (2d Dep't 1935); 8 Wigmore § 2212, at 158; Hutter, "Trade Secret Misappropriation: A Lawyer's Practical Approach to the Case Law," 1 Western New England L.Rev. 1 (1978).

2. Restatement of Torts § 757 (1939).

3. Drake v. Herrman, 261 N.Y. 414, 418, 185 N.E. 685, 686 (1933). See also Fibron Products v. Hooker Chem. Corp., 26 Misc.2d 779, 206 N.Y.S.2d 659 (Sup.Ct.Erie Co.1960)(knowledge of the proportion of ingredients was necessary to establish negligent manufacture).

4. Hyman v. Revlon, 277 App.Div. 1118, 100 N.Y.S.2d 937 (2d Dep't 1950).

5. **§ 511. Trade secrets privilege [PROPOSED]**

A person who owns a trade secret has a privilege, which may be claimed by that person or an agent, employee, or exclusive licensee, to refuse to disclose and to prevent any other person from disclosing that trade secret, unless recognition of the privilege would tend to conceal fraud or otherwise work injustice. When disclosure is directed, the court shall take protective measures as may be required by the interests of the holder of the privilege, of the parties and in furtherance of justice.

6. Meyer Bros., Inc. v. Higgins, 232 App. Div. 783, 249 N.Y.S. 921 (2d Dep't 1931); American Seal–Kap Corp. v. Smith Lee Co., 154 Misc. 176, 277 N.Y.S. 549 (Sup.Ct. Queens Co.1934), aff'd, 248 A.D. 617, 289 N.Y.S. 756 (1936).

The second sentence of proposed § 511 would permit the court just such use of discretion to fit the case at hand.

Although this privilege is not often used in personal injury cases, and can be expected to see increased use under the developing theory of products liability, it is also applicable in wrongful competition cases.[7] According to Wigmore, reliance on the privilege by defendants in such cases is common; but again the privilege's qualification comes into play since "[i]n such cases, it might amount practically to a legal sanction of the wrong if the court conceded to the alleged wrongdoer the privilege of keeping his doings secret from judicial investigation."[8]

Library References:

West's Key No. Digests, Pretrial Procedure ⚙︎33, 356.

§ 513.2 Federal Rule

Proposed Federal Rule 508[1] on trade secrets is virtually identical to § 511 of the Proposed New York Evidence Code and expresses the current practice in the federal courts.[2] In federal practice, during discovery, Federal Rule of Civil Procedure 26(c)(7) provides the necessary protection,[3] a feature not appearing in Article 31 of the New York CPLR, although trade secrets are listed as protected under the New York Freedom of Information Law.[4] The coverage of this protection is broad in the Second Circuit, ranging from financial records[5] through methods

---

[7] See, e.g., Interstate Cigar v. IBI Security Inc. Serv., 105 Misc.2d 179, 431 N.Y.S.2d 1016 (Sup.Ct.Nassau Co.1980), a "commercial espionage" case where "secondary sources" (sources from whom plaintiff receives products that he then distributes) were not seen by the court as inherently trade secrets. Plaintiff had to do more than make conclusory assertions to that effect.

[8] 8 Wigmore § 2212, at 156. In Carvel Corp. v. Lefkowitz, 106 Misc.2d 284, 291, 431 N.Y.S.2d 609, 614 (Sup.Ct.Westchester Co.1979), aff'd, 77 A.D.2d 872, 431 N.Y.S.2d 615 (2d Dept. 1980), it is stated: "As a general rule where the disclosure of trade secrets is essential to ascertaining the truth, the privilege must yield." In a "monopolistic practices" investigation the Attorney General was instructed as follows: "Although the secrets of the Carvel manner of doing business may be relevant to the present investigation, and may be properly protected * * * by [§ 343 Gen. Business Law], the secret formula developed by Carvel over a period of 40 years must be placed in a separate category. Not only is it irrelevant to the subject of the investigation but its preservation would be placed in irretrievable jeopardy." 106 Misc.2d at 291, 431 N.Y.S.2d at 614.

§ 513.2

[1] Rule 508. Trade Secrets [Not Enacted]

A person has a privilege, which may be claimed by him or his agent or employee, to refuse to disclose and to prevent other persons from disclosing a trade secret owned by him, if the allowance of the privilege will not tend to conceal fraud or otherwise work injustice. When disclosure is directed, the judge shall take such protective measure as the interests of the holder of the privilege and of the parties and the furtherance of justice may require.

[2] 2 Weinstein and Berger ¶ 508[03].

[3] A party may request "that a trade secret or other confidential research, development, or commercial information not be revealed or be revealed only in a designated way."

[4] N.Y.Public Officers Law § 87(2)(D).

[5] See Penthouse Intern., Ltd. v. Playboy Enterprises, 663 F.2d 371 (2d Cir.1981)(district judge was granted great discretion as to which documents should be protected and which not protected).

of picking locks,[6] to business contracts and customer lists.[7]

Library References:

West's Key No. Digests, Federal Civil Procedure ⟐1600(1).

514 Comment upon or Inference from Claim of Privilege

§ 514.1 New York

Under older law the invocation of a privilege based on confidential communications gave rise to an inference unfavorable to the party asserting it, which the jury would be allowed to consider.[1] This was true in both civil and criminal cases, although, of course, a defendant who invokes her fifth amendment right in a criminal prosecution is fully protected.[2] Since the opinion in *People v. Rodriguez*[3] was written, however, there is some doubt on the above generality as respects privileges based on confidential communications. *Rodriguez* is essentially a missing witness case, the missing witness being defendant's wife. This situation led to a discussion of the spousal privilege, and the court noted the question of whether comment could be made upon the assertion of the privilege, but found it unnecessary to decide it.[4] The footnote appended to this passage creates the doubt that still exists, at least in criminal cases.[5]

The Law Revision Commission would end this doubt in § 503 of the

---

6. See Segal Lock & Hardware Co. v. Federal Trade Comm'n, 143 F.2d 935 (2d Cir.), cert. denied, 323 U.S. 791, 65 S.Ct. 429, 89 L.Ed. 631 (1945). The FTC was looking into petitioner's claims that its locks were "pick proof." The judge had wide discretion in dealing with witnesses who claimed to have picked the locks so as to protect against the revelation of how the locks were picked, i.e., their trade secrets.

7. In Maritime Cinema Service Corp. v. Movies En Route, Inc., 60 F.R.D. 587, 590 (S.D.N.Y.1973), the court stated: "The information sought here is not a patent, a secret process, or a customer list, which the courts have rather carefully protected. See, e.g., American Oil Co. v. Pennsylvania Petroleum Prod. Co., 23 F.R.D. 680, 683–685 (D.R.I.1959). Defendants seek a protective order only against exposure of the license fees and the oral agreements with their customers; in essence, their own competitive stance. In a competitive economy, such information is often freely available, more so, certainly, than 'processes, formulas or methods.'"

§ 514.1

1. Deutschmann v. Third Ave. R.R., 87 App.Div. 503, 513–15, 84 N.Y.S. 887, 895 (1st Dep't 1903); In re Weaver's Estate, 58 Misc.2d 901, 297 N.Y.S.2d 201 (Surr.Ct.Albany Co.1969); New York Pattern Jury Instructions, 2d ed. § 1:76; "Propriety and Prejudicial Effect of Comment by Counsel as to Refusal to Permit Introduction of Privileged Testimony," 32 A.L.R.2d 906 (1970).

2. N.Y.Crim.Proc.Law §§ 60.15(2), 300.10(2). See § 509.1(b) supra.

3. 38 N.Y.2d 95, 378 N.Y.S.2d 665, 341 N.E.2d 231 (1975).

4. Id. at 100 n.3, 378 N.Y.S.2d at 670, 341 N.E.2d at 234.

5. Id. n. 3, which states: "Although one writer suggests that New York permits comment upon assertion of the privilege (Richardson, Evidence [10th ed.], op cit. § 457, pp. 447–448), at least one lower New York court has held to the contrary (People v. Afarian, 202 Misc. 199; see also, discussion in 4 Bender's NY Evidence, § 244.02, especially pp. 335–336, n.4; § 245.03, subd. [8]; see cases collected in Privilege—Presence of Jury—Request to Waive, Ann.144 ALR 1007; Calling Accused's Spouse as Witness, Ann., 76 ALR2d 920; Privilege Not to Testify—Comments on, Ann., 32 ALR3d 906; Privileged Testimony—Inference, Ann., 34 ALR3d 775)."

Proposed New York Evidence Code,[6] which would prohibit any inferences or comment, except that in a civil case a party would suffer the consequences of an adverse inference if he "claims a privilege as to a communication or matter necessary to the claim or defense of another party."[7]

Regardless of the proposed code, the rule expressed in *Marine Midland Bank v. Russo*,[8] as regards an inference arising when plaintiff called defendants to the stand and they asserted their self-incrimination privilege, might be applicable to confidential communications privileges. In that case, the plaintiff bank brought an action in fraud and conversion against the defendants who maintained a checking account with plaintiff, and who drew checks against deposits that had not yet cleared through the bank's collection process. The trial court instructed the jury that they could draw no inferences from the defendants' invocation of the fifth amendment. The Court of Appeals, recognizing that it had never before dealt with this point, held that the trial judge was in error in his instruction. The court reasoned that the situation becomes like the one "arising when a party fails or refuses to produce a material witness who is within his control. * * * It is now well established that such an event may be considered by a jury in assessing the strength of evidence offered by the opposite party on the issue which the witness was in a position to controvert. * * *"[9] The court, noting that in an attorney disciplinary hearing an adverse interest can be drawn from the attorney's refusal to testify,[10] said that a like result should result in a purely civil case. "For, here the parties are on an equal footing and the only disadvantage threatened is liability to compensate an adversary in damages."[11]

---

6. § 503. **Claim of privilege: without knowledge of jury; comment upon or inference from; jury instruction [PROPOSED]**

(a) **Claiming privilege without knowledge of jury.** In jury cases, proceedings shall be conducted, to the extent practicable, so as to facilitate the making of a claim of privilege without the knowledge of the jury.

(b) **Comment and inference.**

(1) **General rule.** Except as otherwise provided in paragraphs two of this subdivision, the valid claim of a privilege under this article whether in the present trial, proceeding, or hearing, or upon a prior occasion, is not a proper subject of comment by the court or counsel and the trier of fact shall draw no inference therefrom.

(2) **Claim of privilege by party in civil case.** In any civil case in which a party claims a privilege as to a communication or matter necessary to the claim or defense of another party, the court, when appropriate, may permit comment upon or an inference from the claim of privilege or the court, when appropriate, may grant other relief including dismissal of the claim for relief or the defense to which the privileged communication or matter would relate.

(c) **Jury instruction.** Upon request, any party against whom the jury might draw an impermissible adverse inference from a claim of a privilege is entitled to an instruction that no inference may be drawn therefrom.

7. Proposed New York Evidence Code § 503(2).

8. 50 N.Y.2d 31, 427 N.Y.S.2d 961, 405 N.E.2d 205 (1980).

9. Id. at 42, 427 N.Y.S.2d at 967, 405 N.E.2d at 211.

10. See Anonymous Attorneys v. Bar Ass'n of Erie County, 41 N.Y.2d 506, 393 N.Y.S.2d 961, 362 N.E.2d 592 (1977).

11. 50 N.Y.2d at 42, 427 N.Y.S.2d at 967, 405 N.E.2d at 211.

The Court of Appeals appears to be favorably disposed toward extension of this rationale to the communications privileges. In *Commissioner of Social Services v. Philip De G.*,[12] a paternity action, the court held that an adverse inference could be drawn against the putative father who refused to testify in his own defense. The court stated: "[I]t is now established that in civil proceedings an inference may be drawn against the witness because of his failure to testify or because he exercises his privilege to prevent another from testifying, whether the privilege is constitutional, * * * *or statutory*."[13]

Library References:

West's Key No. Digests, Witnesses ⟐309.

§ 514.2 Federal

Proposed Federal Rule 513 would prohibit inference or comment with respect to any privilege, without exception,[1] on the rationale that allowing such "cuts down on the privilege by making its assertion costly."[2] The Advisory Committee's Note indicates that the proposed rule against adverse inferences would extend to the communication privileges in both civil and criminal cases.[3]

Proposed Rule 513 is in accord with the weight of federal cases involving communications privileges, at least in the criminal sphere.[4]

---

12. 59 N.Y.2d 137, 463 N.Y.S.2d 761, 450 N.E.2d 681 (1983).

13. Id. at 141, 463 N.Y.S.2d at 763, 450 N.E.2d at 683 (emphasis added; court cites, as examples, the physician-patient and marital communications privileges). The Law Revision Commission, in its comment to § 503 of the Proposed New York Evidence Code, cites Philip De G. as expressing the New York law in civil cases. The comment argues that if an adverse inference is permissible with respect to a witness' invocation of the privilege against self-incrimination, "the same rule when appropriate should apply with equal or greater force to privileges within the article." Under the proposed rule (see note 6 supra), there remains a question of interpretation as to when a "matter necessary to the claim or defense of another party" is being thwarted by assertion of a privilege. In civil cases this exception, contained in proposed § 503(b)(2), could easily swallow up the general rule in § 503(b)(1) prohibiting inference or comment.

§ 514.2

1. **Rule 513. Comment Upon or Inference from Claim of Privilege; Instruction [Not Enacted]**

(a) **Comment or inference not permitted.** The claim of a privilege, whether in the present proceeding or upon a prior occasion, is not a proper subject of comment by judge or counsel. No inference may be drawn therefrom.

(b) **Claiming privilege without knowledge of jury.** In jury cases, proceedings shall be conducted, to the extent practicable, so as to facilitate the making of claims of privilege without the knowledge of the jury.

(c) **Jury instruction.** Upon request, any party against whom the jury might draw an adverse inference from a claim of privilege is entitled to an instruction that no inference may be drawn therefrom.

2. Griffin v. California, 380 U.S. 609, 614, 85 S.Ct. 1229, 1233, 14 L.Ed.2d 106, 110, rehearing denied, 381 U.S. 957, 85 S.Ct. 1797, 14 L.Ed.2d 730 (1965)(no comment on criminal defendant's failure to testify). See Advisory Committee's Note to proposed Fed.R.Evid. 513.

3. Advisory Committee's Note to proposed Rule 513, subdivision (a).

4. Courtney v. United States, 390 F.2d 521, 526, cert. denied, 393 U.S. 857, 89 S.Ct. 98, 21 L.Ed.2d 126 (9th Cir.1968). See also Tallo v. United States, 344 F.2d 467, 469 (1st Cir.1965)(a spousal privilege case in which the court listed state decisions to that date, most of which prohibited jury knowledge of the communications privilege, and federal cases which to that date also prohibited jury knowledge, including

§ 514.2 PRIVILEGES Ch. 5

The Second Circuit, however, has produced its counterpart of *Marine Midland Bank v. Russo*[5] in *Brink's, Inc. v. City of New York*[6] in the civil area. Plaintiff's employees, charged by the city in its counterclaim with having stolen parking meter receipts, claimed their self-incrimination right and the court upheld the judge's instruction that the jury could draw an adverse interest against their employer, the plaintiff, noting that the United States Supreme Court in *Baxter v. Palmigiano*[7] held that fifth amendment assertions in civil cases could properly call forth the appropriate inference.[8]

Whether the inference resulting from use of the fifth amendment in civil cases will influence the courts with respect to the communications privileges in civil cases as is the indication in New York, is problematical. There is no provision in the proposed Federal Rule 513 as there is in the Proposed New York Evidence Code § 514 that an exception can be made in civil cases, and the case law is sparse with respect to the inference question arising from assertion of the communications privileges in civil cases.[9]

Library References:

West's Key No. Digests, Witnesses ⚖︎309.

United States v. Tomaiolo, 249 F.2d 683, 690 [2d Cir.1957] [attorney-client and spousal]; McClanahan v. United States, 230 F.2d 919, 926 [5th Cir.1956], cert. denied, 352 U.S. 824, 77 S.Ct. 33, 1 L.Ed.2d 47 [1959] [attorney-client]; United States v. Cotter, 60 F.2d 689, 691 [2d Cir.], cert. denied 287 U.S. 666, 53 S.Ct. 291, 77 L.Ed. 575 [1932]; but see Bisno v. United States, 299 F.2d 711, 720–721 [9th Cir.1961], cert. denied 370 U.S. 952, 82 S.Ct. 1602, 8 L.Ed.2d 818 [1962]).

5. 50 N.Y.2d 31, 427 N.Y.S.2d 961, 405 N.E.2d 205 (1980).

6. 717 F.2d 700 (2d Cir.1983).

7. 425 U.S. 308, 96 S.Ct. 1551, 47 L.Ed.2d 810 (1976).

8. See also RAD Services Inc. v. Aetna Casualty & Surety Co., 808 F.2d 271, 275–77 (3d Cir.1986)("nothing forbids imputing to a corporation the silence of its personnel").

9. In United States v. Premises Known as 281 Syosset Woodbury Road, 862 F.Supp. 847 (E.D.N.Y.1994), the court, in a lengthy dictum, concluded that an adverse inference could be drawn against a party who, seeking to avoid forfeiture of property that was allegedly purchased with the proceeds of illegal drug trafficking, invoked the confidential marital communications privilege. Id. at 859–60.

Chapter 6

WITNESSES

Table of Sections

600 INTRODUCTION

600.1 Overview.

601 GENERAL RULE OF COMPETENCY

601.1 New York.
    a. In General.
    b. Interest.
    c. Spouses of Parties.
    d. Convictions.
    e. Children.
    f. Mental, Sensory or Communicative Infirmities.
    g. Alcohol and Drugs.
    h. Hypnotically–Induced Memory.
601.2 New York Dead Man's Statute.
    a. In General.
    b. Disqualified Witnesses.
    c. Protected Persons.
    d. Prohibited Subject Matter.
    e. Exceptions.
    f. Waiver.
    g. Inapplicability Before Trial.
601.3 Federal.

602 PERSONAL KNOWLEDGE

602.1 New York.
602.2 Federal.

603 OATH OR AFFIRMATION

603.1 New York.
603.2 Federal.

604 INTERPRETERS

604.1 New York.
604.2 Federal.

605 JUDGE'S COMPETENCY AS WITNESS

605.1 New York.
605.2 Federal.

606 JUROR'S COMPETENCY AS WITNESS

606.1 New York.
606.2 Federal.

607 IMPEACHMENT AND REHABILITATION OF WITNESSES

607.1 Credibility: New York and Federal.
607.2 Impeachment, In General: New York and Federal.
607.3 Contradiction; Collateral and Noncollateral Matters.

607.4 Party Impeachment of Her Own Witness.
    a. New York, In General.
    b. New York Exception for Prior Inconsistent Statements.
    c. Federal.
607.5 Support and Rehabilitation of Credibility.
    a. New York.
       1. Advance Accreditation.
       2. Rehabilitation.
          (a) Explanation.
          (b) Good Character for Truthfulness.
          (c) Prior Consistent Statements.
    b. Federal.
607.6 Impeachment by Bias and Similar Forms of Partiality.
    a. New York.
    b. Federal.
607.7 Impeachment by Mental or Sensory Impairment.
    a. New York.
    b. Federal.
607.8 Impeachment by Prior Inconsistent Statements.
    a. New York.
       1. In General.
       2. Nature of the Inconsistency.
       3. Foundation Requirements, Extrinsic Evidence.
    b. Federal.

608 IMPEACHMENT BY EVIDENCE OF UNTRUTHFUL CHARACTER AND PRIOR MISCONDUCT

608.0 In General.
608.1 Bad Character for Truthfulness.
    a. New York.
    b. Federal.
608.2 Prior Acts of Misconduct.
    a. New York.
    b. Federal.

609 IMPEACHMENT BY EVIDENCE OF CRIMINAL CONVICTIONS

609.1 New York.
    a. In General.
    b. Civil Cases.
    c. Criminal Cases.
609.2 Federal.

610 RELIGIOUS BELIEFS OR OPINIONS

610.1 New York.
610.2 Federal.

611 PRESENTATION OF TESTIMONY

611.1 New York: Order of Trial.
611.2 New York: Form of Questioning.
    a. In General.
    b. Leading Questions.
611.3 New York: Cross-Examination.
    a. In General.
    b. Scope of Cross-Examination.
    c. Judicial Discretion.
    d. Voir Dire of the Witness.
611.4 New York: Redirect and Recross Examination.

Ch. 6   INTRODUCTION   § 600.1

611.5   Federal: Mode and Order of Interrogation and Presentation.
        a. Order of Trial.
        b. Form of Questioning.
        c. Cross–Examination, Redirect and Recross.

612   REFRESHING THE WITNESS' RECOLLECTION

612.1   New York.
        a. In General.
        b. Adversary's Right of Inspection.
612.2   Federal.

613   [RESERVED]

614   *Calling and Questioning of Witnesses by the Court or Jury*

614.1   New York.
        a. Calling of Witnesses by the Court.
        b. Judicial Questioning of Witnesses.
        c. Questioning by Jurors.
614.2   Federal.

615   EXCLUSION OF WITNESSES FROM THE COURTROOM

615.1   New York.
615.2   Federal.

WESTLAW Electronic Research

See WESTLAW Electronic Research Guide preceding the Summary of Contents.

---

600   Introduction

§ 600.1. Overview

This chapter brings together a wide range of rules that focus principally upon testimonial evidence. Sections 601.1 through 606.2 deal with the competency of witnesses—their eligibility to testify. Sections 607.1 through 610.2 address credibility—the impeachment and rehabilitation of witnesses. The concluding sections, §§ 611.1–615.2, cover procedural rules governing the examination of witnesses—the order, scope, form and judicial control of testimonial evidence. The special problems associated with opinion testimony are taken up in Chapter 7.

In connection with the topics of impeachment and rehabilitation, it was necessary for us to deviate somewhat from the order of presentation in the Federal Rules of Evidence, which otherwise governs the organization of this book. The Federal Rules, for example, cover procedural aspects of prior inconsistent statements in Rule 613, which is out of sequence with other topics of impeachment. Rules relating to rehabilitation are divided between Rules 608(a)(2) and 801(d)(1)(B). Some forms of impeachment, such as bias and mental impairment, are not even touched upon in the Federal Rules. All of these stray rules relating to the credibility of witnesses are brought together here as subdivisions of

§ 607. Otherwise, the section headings of this chapter track the numbering system of Article 6 of the Federal Rules.

601 General Rule of Competency

§ 601.1 New York

a. In General

Competency of evidence is a term that is often used as a synonym for the admissibility of evidence.[1] With respect to witnesses, the term refers to the eligibility of a witness to testify.[2] The evidence itself may qualify for admission, as, for example, an out-of-court statement that falls within a hearsay exception, but the particular witness who is called to the stand may be incompetent to testify to the statement.[3] At the extreme, an incompetent witness may be precluded from taking the witness stand altogether; in other instances, the witness may be incompetent to testify only as to certain matters.[4]

In the early days of the common law, some witnesses were deemed incompetent as a matter of law based on their status or possession of particular characteristics or qualities. For example, a witness was incompetent if he was a party or had an interest in the outcome of the case, if he was the spouse of a party, if he did not have appropriate religious beliefs, if he was mentally disabled or if he was a convicted criminal.[5] Over time, these incompetencies were in large measure swept away in New York by legislative action[6] or enlightened caselaw,[7] presumably in recognition of the fact that they were "serious obstructions to the

---

§ 601.1

1. See People v. Swamp, 84 N.Y.2d 725, 730, 622 N.Y.S.2d 472, 474, 646 N.E.2d 774 (1995)(competent evidence means "evidence not subject to an exclusionary rule"); United States v. Sliker, 751 F.2d 477, 498 (2d Cir.1984), cert. denied, 470 U.S. 1058, 105 S.Ct. 1772, 84 L.Ed.2d 832 (1985)(question of competency of evidence concerns "evidence which is relevant but may be subject to exclusion by virtue of some principle of the law of evidence"). The discredited nonspecific objection, "I object on the grounds that the evidence is incompetent, immaterial, and irrelevant," is based, in part, on this usage of the term. Such an objection is insufficient to preserve a challenge to the competency of a witness to testify. See, e.g., Hoag v. Wright, 174 N.Y. 36, 39–40, 66 N.E. 579, 579–80 (1903)(objection that question posed to witness was "incompetent" did not preserve issue of witness' incompetency under the "Dead Man's Statute").

2. See E. Cleary, J. Strong, K. Broun, R. Mosteller, Evidence Cases and Materials 434 (4th ed.1988)("The term 'competent,' with reference to witnesses, is generally used to describe a person who is free of personal characteristics which would disable him from giving testimony before a court of law.").

3. See, e.g., CPLR 4519 (party in automobile accident case who is incompetent pursuant to "Dead Man's Statute" may not testify to statements made by deceased adversary). See § 601.2 infra.

4. See, e.g., People v. Hughes, 59 N.Y.2d 523, 466 N.Y.S.2d 255, 453 N.E.2d 484 (1983)(witness who has been hypnotized prior to trial for purpose of restoring memory is incompetent to testify to posthypnotic recollections but may be able to testify to matters remembered prior to hypnosis). See notes 60–69 infra.

5. See generally McCormick §§ 62–67.

6. CPLR 4512 eliminates the incompetency, in general, of parties, interested witnesses and spouses; and CPLR 4513 eliminates the incompetency of persons convicted of crimes. By constitutional provision, religious belief is abolished as a ground of incompetency. N.Y.Const., art. I, § 3.

7. See, e.g., Barker v. Washburn, 200 N.Y. 280, 283, 93 N.E. 958, 959 (1911)(even person who has been adjudicated incompetent may have sufficient intelligence to be truthful and to describe relevant facts).

ascertainment of truth."[8] Only a few lingering per se disqualifications of the common law remain, the chief one being the so-called "Dead Man's Statute" in CPLR 4519.[9] By modern standards, the general rule is that any person is a competent witness if she possesses sufficient powers of perception, memory and communication and appreciates the moral and legal duty to testify truthfully.[10] Today, nearly all adult witnesses are presumed competent,[11] thus placing on the opponent the burden of demonstrating incompetency.[12] Whenever the issue of competency arises, it is the trial judge alone who determines the question: "The resolution of the issue of witness competency is exclusively the responsibility of the trial court, subject to limited appellate review. It is the Trial Judge who has the opportunity to view the witness, to observe manner, demeanor and presence of mind, and to undertake such inquiries as are effective to disclose the witness' capacity and intelligence."[13]

Consideration of the principal issues of witness competency—perception, memory, communication and the capacity to appreciate the obli-

8. McCormick § 71, at 266. See, e.g., McDermott v. Manhattan Eye, Ear & Throat Hospital, 15 N.Y.2d 20, 26, 255 N.Y.S.2d 65, 70, 203 N.E.2d 469, 473 (1964)(parties were made eligible to testify "on the ground, no doubt, that 'plain sense and reason * * * obviously suggest that any living witness who could throw light upon a fact in issue should be heard to state what he knows, subject always to such observations as may arise as to his means of knowledge or his disposition to the truth' ").

9. See § 601.2 infra. Other isolated forms of incompetency are discussed in the balance of § 601.1.

10. McCormick § 62, at 247. See, e.g., Brown v. Ristich, 36 N.Y.2d 183, 189, 366 N.Y.S.2d 116, 122, 325 N.E.2d 533, 537 (1975)(witness must have "ability to observe, recall and narrate"); People v. Rensing, 14 N.Y.2d 210, 213, 250 N.Y.S.2d 401, 403, 199 N.E.2d 489, 490–91 (1964)(mentally ill person may testify so long as he has "sufficient intelligence to understand the nature of an oath and to give a reasonably accurate account of what he has seen and heard vis-a-vis the subject about which he is interrogated"); Senecal v. Drollette, 304 N.Y. 446, 449, 108 N.E.2d 602, 603 (1952)(witness must have ability to "observe, know and remember").

The Proposed New York Evidence Code states, in § 601: "Except as otherwise provided by this chapter or other statute, every person is competent to be a witness and no person is incompetent to testify to any matter." Section 602 of the proposed code goes on to describe five specific grounds of incompetency: (a) lack of personal knowledge; (b) inability to express oneself, either directly or through an interpreter; (c) inability to understand the nature of an oath or affirmation except where statutory exceptions exist; (d) incompetency of a spouse with respect to the issue of adultery; and (e) incompetency of an interested witness to testify to a personal transaction or communication with a decedent (the "Dead Man's Statute").

11. People v. Parks, 41 N.Y.2d 36, 45, 390 N.Y.S.2d 848, 856, 359 N.E.2d 358, 366 (1976)("all adults are presumed to be competent to testify"); Aguilar v. State, 279 App.Div. 103, 104, 108 N.Y.S.2d 456, 459 (3d Dep't 1951), amended, 279 App.Div. 1121, 112 N.Y.S.2d 779 (3d Dep't), appeal withdrawn, 304 N.Y. 616, 107 N.E.2d 94 (1952). Special presumptions apply in the case of children. See notes 33 and 38–44 and accompanying text infra.

12. Matter of Luz P., 189 A.D.2d 274, 282, 595 N.Y.S.2d 541, 546 (2d Dep't 1993); Bopple v. The Supreme Tent of the Knights of the Maccabees of the World, 18 App.Div. 488, 493, 45 N.Y.S. 1096, 1099 (4th Dep't 1897).

Objections relating to competency should refer specifically to the witness' incompetency to testify. See, e.g., Hoag v. Wright, 174 N.Y. 36, 39–40, 66 N.E. 579, 579–80 (1903)("An objection that the witness is incompetent or interested would, perhaps, be sufficient, but the simple objection that the evidence is incompetent is not specific enough to justify a reversal").

13. People v. Parks, 41 N.Y.2d 36, 46, 390 N.Y.S.2d 848, 856, 359 N.E.2d 358, 366 (1976). It has been said that judges have the inherent authority to examine witnesses to ascertain their competency. N.Y. Adv.Comm.on Prac. and Proc., Second Prelim.Rep., p.204 (1958).

gations of an oath—is best accomplished by analysis of the situations in which such issues most often arise. The balance of this section will be devoted to those situations. Incompetency due to interest under the "Dead Man's Statute" warrants coverage in a separate subsection, § 601.2. The requirement that a witness have personal knowledge, which is sometimes considered to be an aspect of competency, is discussed in § 602.1. The formalities of an oath or affirmation are described in § 603.1. The topic of interpreters, which is relevant to a witness's communicative capacity, is covered in § 604.1. Finally, the unique problems associated with testimony by judges and jurors are covered in §§ 605.1 and 606.1, respectively.

b. Interest

At early common law, a party or other person with an interest in the outcome of the particular case was incompetent to testify. Such witness was deemed untrustworthy as a matter of law.[14] CPLR 4512 abolishes interest as a disqualifying factor in the following terms: "Except as otherwise expressly prescribed, a person shall not be excluded or excused from being a witness, by reason of his interest in the event or because he is a party * * *." The vestigial exception to CPLR 4512 is the so-called "Dead Man's Statute," which is treated below in § 601.2.

It bears noting that CPLR 4512 not only permits a party to testify in his own behalf,[15] it also prohibits a party from declining to testify when called as a witness by his adversary.[16] In criminal cases, however, the defendant is protected by the right against self-incrimination from being called upon by the prosecution.[17]

Although interest has been abolished, in general, as a ground of incompetency, it is a fact that may be established for the purpose of impeaching the witness' credibility.[18] Furthermore, New York courts may explicitly advise the jury that a party or witness is interested in the outcome of the case as a factor to be considered in assessing credibility.[19]

c. Spouses of Parties

At early common law, just as a party to an action was incompetent

---

14. Coleman v. New York City Transit Auth., 37 N.Y.2d 137, 142, 371 N.Y.S.2d 663, 667, 332 N.E.2d 850, 853 (1975). See also Washington v. Texas, 388 U.S. 14, 21, 87 S.Ct. 1920, 1924, 18 L.Ed.2d 1019, 1024 (1967) (disqualifications for interest "rested on the unstated premises that the right to present witnesses was subordinate to the courts' interest in preventing perjury").

15. Regardless of CPLR 4512, the defendant in a criminal case has a constitutional right to take the stand in his own defense. Rock v. Arkansas, 483 U.S. 44, 49–53, 107 S.Ct. 2704, 2708–10, 97 L.Ed.2d 37, 44–47 (1987).

16. McDermott v. Manhattan Eye, Ear & Throat Hospital, 15 N.Y.2d 20, 26, 255 N.Y.S.2d 65, 70, 203 N.E.2d 469, 472–73 (1964).

17. See N.Y.Crim.Proc.Law § 60.15(2). See also § 509.1(b) supra.

18. Coleman v. New York City Transit Auth., 37 N.Y.2d 137, 142, 371 N.Y.S.2d 663, 667, 332 N.E.2d 850, 853 (1975).

19. See, e.g., People v. Demery, 60 A.D.2d 606, 607, 400 N.Y.S.2d 135, 136 (2d Dep't 1977). But see People v. Ochs, 3 N.Y.2d 54, 56, 163 N.Y.S.2d 671, 672, 143 N.E.2d 388, 389 (1957)(in instructing jury that criminal defendant's interest may be considered, judge may not tell jury that interested witness is more likely to lie). See also § 607.6, at note 8, infra.

to testify, so too a party's spouse was incompetent.[20] CPLR 4512 eliminates spousal incompetency as follows: "Except as otherwise expressly prescribed, a person shall not be excluded or excused from being a witness * * * because he is * * * the spouse of a party." CPLR 4512, however, is subject to two statutory qualifications: a spouse is precluded from testifying against the other spouse with respect to certain matters in matrimonial actions based on adultery,[21] and both spouses may invoke a privilege for confidential communications in any type of proceeding.[22] These two aspects of spousal testimony are treated in §§ 503.1–503.3.

A judge-made rule of spousal incompetency, however, appears to have survived the foregoing statutory modifications of the common law. Lord Mansfield announced in a 1777 case that for reasons of decency, morality and policy, spouses may not testify to nonaccess during marriage where the legitimacy of offspring would be adversely affected.[23] New York courts have continued to apply the common law rule that disallows spousal testimony of nonaccess,[24] except to the extent that the rule has been explicitly abolished by statute in paternity proceedings[25] and proceedings to enforce child support.[26]

d. Convictions

Conviction of a crime, although a ground of incompetency at early common law, no longer renders a witness ineligible to testify.[27] A witness' prior convictions, however, may be admissible to impeach the credibility of the witness.[28]

e. Children

A witness' youth, standing alone, does not render her incompetent.[29] The Court of Appeals has succinctly declared, "Age alone is no testimonial infirmity."[30] Thus, reversible error has been found in cases where trial courts have summarily precluded children from testifying without conducting a preliminary examination into their capacity and knowl-

20. See Trammel v. United States, 445 U.S. 40, 43–47, 100 S.Ct. 906, 909–10, 63 L.Ed.2d 186, 190–92 (1980).

21. CPLR 4502(a).

22. CPLR 4502(b).

23. Goodright v. Moss, 2 Cowp. 591, 98 Eng.Rep. 1257 (1777).

24. See, e.g., In re Diaz–Albertini's Estate, 153 N.Y.S.2d 261, 265 (Surr.Ct. N.Y.Co.), aff'd, 2 A.D.2d 671, 154 N.Y.S.2d 422 (1st Dep't 1956). The Proposed New York Evidence Code would eliminate spousal incompetency altogether with respect to nonaccess. See comment to Proposed N.Y.Evid.Code § 601: "The [common law] rule is detrimental to the ascertainment of the truth. The goals of the rule are adequately achieved by the presumption favoring legitimacy, which can be overcome only through clear and convincing evidence to the contrary."

25. N.Y.Fam.Ct.Act § 531.

26. N.Y.Fam.Ct.Act § 436.

27. CPLR 4513.

28. Id.; N.Y.Crim.Proc.Law § 60.40(1). See § 609.1 infra.

29. See, e.g., Jensen v. Shady Pines, Inc., 32 A.D.2d 648, 300 N.Y.S.2d 746 (2d Dep't 1969)(infant plaintiff who was six years old at time of event in controversy was not per se incompetent to testify).

30. People v. Fuller, 50 N.Y.2d 628, 636, 431 N.Y.S.2d 357, 361, 409 N.E.2d 834, 838 (1980)(10-year-old child properly sworn as witness). See also People v. Nisoff, 36 N.Y.2d 560, 565, 369 N.Y.S.2d 686, 690, 330 N.E.2d 638, 641 (1975)("There is no precise age at which a child is deemed competent to testify under oath in a criminal proceeding").

edge.[31] In addition to a showing that children can remember and relate what they observed, children, like all witnesses, must ordinarily demonstrate sufficient understanding of the duty imposed by an oath or affirmation to testify truthfully.[32] A preliminary examination into these issues is appropriate whenever children of "tender years" are called to the stand.[33]

The nature of a trial court's inquiry into the testimonial capacity of a child has been described by the Court of Appeals as follows: "The preliminary examination by the presiding justice as to the competency of a witness of tender years * * * is for the consideration of the court only, not of the jury. It is usually an informal conversation upon indifferent subjects, designed to put the child at ease so that he will speak naturally. His intelligence and ability to tell the truth are tested by noting his answers and his general appearance."[34] In another case, the court said, "The tests as to the infant's testimonial capacity and ability to understand the nature of an oath are necessarily individualistic in nature and are to be determined by 'the capacity and intelligence of the child, his appreciation of the difference between truth and falsehood, as well as his duty to tell the former.'"[35] The trial court's determination on the issue of a child's competency will not be disturbed on appeal in the absence of an abuse of discretion.[36]

---

31. Kapuscinski v. Kapuscinski, 75 A.D.2d 576, 426 N.Y.S.2d 582 (2d Dep't 1980)(improper to exclude testimony of 14-year-old child based on age without first conducting a preliminary examination); Rittenhouse v. Town of North Hempstead, 11 A.D.2d 957, 205 N.Y.S.2d 564, reargument denied, 11 A.D.2d 1071, 207 N.Y.S.2d 1019, appeal and reargument denied, 12 A.D.2d 490, 210 N.Y.S.2d 493 (2d Dep't 1960)(trial court should not have excluded testimony of nine-and-one-half-year-old child without preliminary examination).

32. Olshansky v. Prensky, 185 App.Div. 469, 470, 172 N.Y.S. 856, 856 (2d Dep't 1918).

33. Id. See also Jensen v. Shady Pines, Inc., 32 A.D.2d 648, 300 N.Y.S.2d 746 (2d Dep't 1969)(preliminary examination of infant who was six at time of operative events should be conducted prior to testimony). The Olshansky court noted the existence of a common law presumption that children under 14 years of age are incompetent to testify. 185 App.Div. at 470, 172 N.Y.S. at 856. Regardless of whether that presumption has any continuing vitality in civil cases, child witnesses in criminal cases are presumed, by statute, to be incompetent if they are under the age of 12. N.Y.Crim.Proc.Law § 60.20(2). See notes 38–39 and accompanying text infra.

34. People v. Johnson, 185 N.Y. 219, 228, 77 N.E. 1164, 1167 (1906).

35. People v. Nisoff, 36 N.Y.2d 560, 566, 369 N.Y.S.2d 686, 690–91, 330 N.E.2d 638, 641 (1975)(quoting Wheeler v. United States, 159 U.S. 523, 524, 16 S.Ct. 93, 93, 40 L.Ed. 244, 247 (1895)).

36. See, e.g., People v. Yonko, 34 N.Y.2d 825, 359 N.Y.S.2d 54, 316 N.E.2d 338 (1974). See also People v. Parks, 41 N.Y.2d 36, 46, 390 N.Y.S.2d 848, 857, 359 N.E.2d 358, 366 (1976).

The following cases illustrate both the deference that is paid to a trial court's determination and the flexible criteria that have been used to ascertain a child's understanding of the oath: People v. McDaniel, 165 A.D.2d 817, 817–18, 560 N.Y.S.2d 160, 161 (2d Dep't), appeal denied, 76 N.Y.2d 1023, 565 N.Y.S.2d 773, 566 N.E.2d 1178 (1990)("The [eight-year-old] complainant understood the meaning of telling a lie, that it was wrong to lie, and that she would be 'punished' for lying. She also indicated that she understood that it was incumbent upon her to tell the truth on the stand and that she would not lie in court. Moreover, she indicated that she goes to church, believes in God, and believes that God would punish her if she lied. Thus, the complainant was cognizant of a moral duty to tell the truth and she accepted the concept of divine retribution as a consequence of lying. Under the circumstances, it was not required that the complainant be able to define the meaning of an oath, nor was the court required to determine whether the witness was aware that criminal sanctions could be imposed for giving false testimo-

In civil actions, the usual rule is that a child may not testify unless she does so under oath or pursuant to affirmation.[37] In criminal actions, on the other hand, § 60.20(2) of the New York Criminal Procedure Law provides that a child under 12 years old who does not understand the nature of an oath may give "unsworn evidence" provided the court is "satisfied that the witness possesses sufficient intelligence and capacity to justify the reception thereof."[38] In effect, § 60.20(2) creates a rebuttable presumption in criminal cases that a child under 12 is incompetent to testify.[39] The judge is duty-bound, therefore, to conduct a preliminary inquiry to ascertain whether, and how, such child will be permitted to

ny."); People v. Mercado, 157 A.D.2d 457, 457, 549 N.Y.S.2d 383, 383 (1st Dep't), appeal denied, 75 N.Y.2d 922, 555 N.Y.S.2d 40, 554 N.E.2d 77 (1990)(testimony of 10-year-old witness properly received where he "told the court that he attended church and had been taught about God, that he had sworn on the Bible previously and had told the truth, and that he understood the importance of telling the truth and believed the judge, his parents and God would punish him if he failed to do so. While Louis was unable to articulate a concept of God or of an oath, or to indicate specifically how he would be punished if he lied, the law does not require that children define abstract concepts with the sophistication of an adult."); People v. Sinatra, 134 A.D.2d 738, 739–40, 521 N.Y.S.2d 551, 552 (3d Dep't 1987), appeal denied, 70 N.Y.2d 1011, 526 N.Y.S.2d 946, 521 N.E.2d 1089 (1988) ("Although County Court neglected to apprise the victim of the penalty for perjury and afforded her little opportunity to demonstrate that she understood what 'oath' meant, after the court had explained it to her, it did conduct a searching inquiry into the victim's ability to differentiate between truth and falsity, her belief that lying is a sin punishable by God, and her understanding of the courtroom proceedings * * *. In the course of the inquiry, the victim manifested an awareness of a moral duty to testify truthfully and the possibility of punishment for lying * * *."). But see People v. Maldonado, 199 A.D.2d 563, 563, 606 N.Y.S.2d 258, 259 (2d Dep't 1993)(trial court erred in accepting sworn testimony of nine-year-old witness where appellate court was "not satisfied that her perfunctory, one-word, or nonverbal responses to the mostly leading questions demonstrate that she understood that there is a special moral duty to tell the truth while under oath").

37. Stoppick v. Goldstein, 174 App.Div. 306, 160 N.Y.S. 947 (2d Dep't 1916); People v. Murray, 158 Misc.2d 952, 954, 601 N.Y.S.2d 1019, 1021 (Sup.Ct.Kings Co.1993). If the child is incapable of understanding an oath, she is equally incapable of testifying by way of affirmation.

Salmon v. Sunday, 134 Misc. 475, 235 N.Y.S. 672 (Sup.Ct.App.T.1929).

An exception is contained in § 152(b) of the New York Family Court Act, which provides that "[i]n conducting a hearing under this act, a judge may dispense with the formality of placing a minor under oath before taking his testimony." It has been held, however, that a quasi-criminal adjudication in Family Court, such as a finding of juvenile delinquency, cannot be based solely on the unsworn evidence of a child. In re H., 41 A.D.2d 817, 342 N.Y.S.2d 696 (1st Dep't 1973). Analogy is made to the practice with respect to unsworn evidence in criminal cases. In re Steven B., 30 A.D.2d 442, 293 N.Y.S.2d 946 (1st Dep't 1968).

38. The full text of N.Y.Crim.Proc.Law § 60.20 is as follows:

1. Any person may be a witness in a criminal proceeding unless the court finds that, by reason of infancy or mental disease or defect, he does not possess sufficient intelligence or capacity to justify the reception of his evidence.

2. Every witness more than twelve years old may testify only under oath unless the court is satisfied that such witness cannot, as a result of mental disease or defect, understand the nature of an oath. A child less than twelve years old may not testify under oath unless the court is satisfied that he understands the nature of an oath. If the court is not so satisfied, such child or such witness over twelve years old who cannot, as a result of mental disease or defect, understand the nature of an oath may nevertheless be permitted to give unsworn evidence if the court is satisfied that the witness possesses sufficient intelligence and capacity to justify the reception thereof.

3. A defendant may not be convicted of an offense solely upon unsworn evidence given pursuant to subdivision two.

39. People v. Nisoff, 36 N.Y.2d 560, 565–66, 369 N.Y.S.2d 686, 690, 330 N.E.2d 638, 641 (1975); People v. Klein, 266 N.Y. 188, 189, 194 N.E. 402, 403 (1935).

give evidence.[40] If the child can understand the nature of an oath as well as recall and relate prior events, sworn testimony is to be given.[41] If the child cannot appreciate an oath, her unsworn statements may be received if she has sufficient intelligence and capacity.[42] The statute provides, however, that a defendant cannot be convicted solely on the basis of a child's unsworn evidence, i.e., there must be corroboration.[43] A witness who is over 12 years of age generally must be able to testify pursuant to an oath.[44]

Child victims and witnesses in sex-crime cases, even if competent to testify, may encounter extreme psychological stress as a result of the courtroom experience. Statutory provisions have been enacted to permit such witnesses to testify from a separate testimonial room by means of live, two-way closed-circuit television.[45]

f. Mental, Sensory or Communicative Infirmities

The fact that a potential witness is mentally ill or mentally deficient, even if he has been confined to a mental institution or adjudicated incapable of handling his affairs, is not a per se basis of incompetency.[46] The court may allow a mentally infirm person to testify if the witness "has sufficient intelligence to understand the nature of an oath and to give a reasonably accurate account of what he has seen and heard vis-a-

---

40. People v. Morales, 80 N.Y.2d 450, 452–53, 591 N.Y.S.2d 825, 827, 606 N.E.2d 953, 955 (1992). The preliminary examination may be conducted before or during trial. Id.

41. Id. at 452–53, 591 N.Y.S.2d at 827, 606 N.E.2d at 955.

42. Id. See, e.g., People v. Nisoff, 36 N.Y.2d 560, 369 N.Y.S.2d 686, 330 N.E.2d 638 (1975)(trial court properly found, on voir dire, that 10-year-old child was competent to give sworn testimony and that eight-year-old child, who did not understand nature of oath, nevertheless had requisite capacity and intelligence to give unsworn testimony).

43. N.Y.Crim.Proc.Law § 60.20(3). See, e.g., People v. Groff, 71 N.Y.2d 101, 109–110, 524 N.Y.S.2d 13, 18, 518 N.E.2d 908, 912–13 (1987)(when witness is unsworn, prosecution must present legally sufficient corroborative evidence which tends to establish the crime and that the defendant committed it). It has been held that the requirement of corroboration applies only to the prosecution's case; unsworn exculpatory evidence offered in defendant's behalf need not be corroborated. People v. Murray, 158 Misc.2d 952, 601 N.Y.S.2d 1019 (Sup.Ct.Kings Co.1993).

44. N.Y.Crim.Proc.Law § 60.20(2). If the witness is over 12 years old, the oath may be dispensed with only if the witness "cannot, as a result of mental disease or defect, understand the nature of an oath." Id. A mentally diseased or mentally defective witness, therefore, is treated in the same manner as a child under 12: Unsworn evidence may be received from such witness "if the court is satisfied that the witness possesses sufficient intelligence and capacity to justify the reception thereof." Id.

45. N.Y.Crim.Proc.Law art. 65. As a prerequisite, the child (12 years old or under) must be declared "vulnerable" by the court based on a showing "by clear and convincing evidence that it is likely, as a result of extraordinary circumstances, that such child witness will suffer severe mental or emotional harm if required to testify * * * without the use of live, two-way closed circuit television * * *." Id. § 65.10(1). The constitutionality of the procedure was upheld in People v. Cintron, 75 N.Y.2d 249, 552 N.Y.S.2d 68, 551 N.E.2d 561 (1990).

46. People v. Rensing, 14 N.Y.2d 210, 213, 250 N.Y.S.2d 401, 403, 199 N.E.2d 489, 490–91 (1964)(insanity); Barker v. Washburn, 200 N.Y. 280, 283, 93 N.E. 958, 959 (1911); People v. Chan, 110 A.D.2d 158, 161, 493 N.Y.S.2d 778, 780 (2d Dep't), appeal denied, 66 N.Y.2d 920, 498 N.Y.S.2d 1035, 489 N.E.2d 780 (1985); Aguilar v. State, 279 App.Div. 103, 104, 108 N.Y.S.2d 456, 459 (3d Dep't 1951).

vis the subject about which he is interrogated."[47] The mental infirmity, of course, may be considered by the fact-finder on the issue of credibility.[48]

It has been settled for some time that the trial court, in making its determination as to the competency of a mentally infirm witness, may consider the testimony of physicians or other persons who are in a position to "shed light on the capacity and intelligence of the prospective witness."[49] *People v. Parks*[50] took this notion one step further by holding that the trial court, in its discretion, may also let the jury hear testimony by an expert or another person familiar with the particular witness's infirmity to assist them in evaluating the testimony of the witness.[51]

In criminal cases, statutory provision has been made for the receipt of unsworn evidence by a witness who, "as a result of mental disease or defect, [cannot] understand the nature of an oath" provided the court is satisfied that such witness "possesses sufficient intelligence and capacity to justify the reception thereof."[52] Presumably, a mentally infirm witness may not testify in a civil case unless he is able to do so under oath.[53]

The competency of a witness with a physical infirmity that affects the power of communication, such as deafness, severe speech impediment or the inability to speak altogether, raises related but distinct problems.[54] The legislature and the courts in recent years have shown sensitivity to this issue, and have sought to accommodate communication-impaired witnesses by authorizing the use of reliable interpreters, or their functional equivalents, to facilitate such witnesses' courtroom testimony.[55]

47. People v. Rensing, 14 N.Y.2d 210, 213, 250 N.Y.S.2d 401, 403, 199 N.E.2d 489, 490–91 (1964).

48. Id. at 213–14, 250 N.Y.S.2d at 404, 199 N.E.2d at 491. See § 607.7 infra.

49. People v. Parks, 41 N.Y.2d 36, 46, 390 N.Y.S.2d 848, 857, 359 N.E.2d 358, 366 (1976). See Aguilar v. State, 279 App.Div. 103, 105, 108 N.Y.S.2d 456, 459 (3d Dep't 1951).

50. 41 N.Y.2d 36, 390 N.Y.S.2d 848, 359 N.E.2d 358 (1976).

51. Id. at 47, 390 N.Y.S.2d at 857–58, 359 N.E.2d at 367. The decision as to whether the witness was competent to testify was that of the judge alone, said the court, but the jury still had the job of determining whether and to what extent the witness' testimony should be credited. Thus, the teacher's testimony provided "an objective analytical framework" for the jury's evaluative process. Two limitations on the introduction of such expert testimony were stressed by the court: the effect of the witness' physical or mental infirmity must be in issue, and the expert must confine her testimony to objective physical and psychological analysis without expressing any opinion on the credibility of the witness. Id. at 48–49, 390 N.Y.S.2d at 858–59, 359 N.E.2d at 367–68. See also § 702.1(d) infra.

52. Crim.Proc.Law § 60.20(2). See note 38 supra.

53. See text at note 37 supra. Cf. People v. Parks, 41 N.Y.2d 36, 45, 390 N.Y.S.2d 848, 856, 359 N.E.2d 358, 365–66 (1976)(prior to amendment of Crim.Proc. Law § 60.20(2), mentally infirm witnesses over 12 years old could testify in criminal cases only under oath).

54. The Proposed New York Evidence Code would provide, in § 602(b): "A person may not testify if the court finds such person is incapable of expressing herself or himself concerning the matter so as to be understood by the trier of fact either directly or though interpretation by one who can understand such person."

55. See N.Y.Jud.Law § 390 (court must appoint sign language interpreter for deaf party or witness); Matter of Luz P., 189 A.D.2d 274, 595 N.Y.S.2d 541 (2d Dep't 1993)(trial court should have conducted pragmatic test to determine whether "facili-

g. Alcohol and Drugs

A witness who is under the influence of alcohol or narcotics while on the witness stand raises two concerns relating to competency: testimonial qualification and the dignity of the judicial proceedings. An early nineteenth-century case held that a heavily intoxicated witness should not be permitted to testify[56] while a more recent case held that a witness who was under the influence of narcotics could give testimony, his consumption of drugs being a factor merely affecting credibility.[57] It seems that the matter lies in the court's discretion: If the witness can adequately recall, communicate and appreciate the obligation of an oath, he may testify unless the breach of courtroom decorum exceeds the bounds of tolerance.[58]

In theory, a witness who was under the influence of alcohol or drugs at the time of the events about which he proposes to testify could have been so seriously impaired as to negate the powers of perception, memory and personal knowledge, rendering him incompetent to testify. The cases, however, have treated intoxication and drug use at the time of the operative event only as a basis for impeachment.[59]

---

tator" could reliably convey answers of autistic, mentally-retarded nonverbal child); People v. Miller, 140 Misc.2d 247, 530 N.Y.S.2d 490 (Rochester City Ct.1988)(court permitted speech therapist to interpret responses of adult witness with cerebral palsy who was incapable of normal verbal communication). See also People v. Rodriguez, 145 Misc.2d 105, 546 N.Y.S.2d 769 (Sup.Ct.Queens Co.1989) (sign-language interpreter for deaf and speech-impaired witness must be qualified in the particular signing method known by the witness). Cf. People v. Thompson, 34 A.D.2d 561, 309 N.Y.S.2d 861 (2d Dep't 1970), aff'd, 28 N.Y.2d 616, 320 N.Y.S.2d 77, 268 N.E.2d 804 (1971)(trial court permitted speech therapist to convey answers by deaf and illiterate witness who did not know sign language but was able to read lips; defendant's acquittal of relevant charge eliminated issue on appeal).

56. Hartford v. Palmer, 16 Johns. (N.Y.) 142, 144 (Sup.Ct.1819)("[E]very Court must necessarily have the power to decide, from their own view of the situation of the witness offered, whether he be intoxicated to such a degree, as that he ought not to be heard.").

57. People v. Sorrentini, 26 A.D.2d 827, 273 N.Y.S.2d 981 (2d Dep't 1966). See also People v. Freeland, 36 N.Y.2d 518, 525, 369 N.Y.S.2d 649, 653, 330 N.E.2d 611, 614 (1975)(addiction to narcotics at time of trial is admissible to impeach credibility if it tends to show that witness is under the influence of drugs while testifying or that witness' powers of perception or recollection have been impaired by the habit).

58. An instructive decision is that of the Second Circuit in United States v. Van Meerbeke, 548 F.2d 415 (2d Cir.1976), cert. denied, 430 U.S. 974, 97 S.Ct. 1663, 52 L.Ed.2d 368 (1977). See § 601.3 infra. There, a prosecution witness ingested small bits of opium on two occasions while on the witness stand. Defense counsel vigorously cross-examined the witness about the incidents, but defendant's motion to strike the witness' testimony was denied. The Court of Appeals chastised the trial judge for "serious abdication of his responsibility to maintain order and to control the proceedings." Id. at 418. The trial judge, said the court, could have suspended the witness' testimony for the day, ordered a medical examination to determine the witness' capacity to continue testifying, and issued a stern warning to the witness. Id. The appellate court, nevertheless, indicated that the witness was competent and that his credibility was for the jury. Id. at 418 n.3.

59. See, e.g., People v. Goddard, 153 A.D.2d 758, 545 N.Y.S.2d 42 (2d Dep't), appeal denied, 74 N.Y.2d 896, 548 N.Y.S.2d 429, 547 N.E.2d 956 (1989)(use of drugs); People v. Watson, 85 A.D.2d 920, 446 N.Y.S.2d 775 (4th Dep't 1981)(consumption of alcohol). See also People v. Freeland, 36 N.Y.2d 518, 525, 369 N.Y.S.2d 649, 653, 330 N.E.2d 611, 614 (1975) ("narcotic addiction is admissible to impeach a witness' credibility if tending to show that she was under the influence of drugs * * * at the time of the events to which she testified, or that her powers of perception or recollection, were actually impaired by the habit"). See generally § 607.7 infra.

h. Hypnotically–Induced Memory

Hypnosis is sometimes used to help restore or enhance a person's memory for purposes of medical treatment or to aid in a criminal investigation. May a person who has undergone hypnosis thereafter testify in a judicial proceeding to matters that were recalled as a result of the hypnosis? The Court of Appeals answered this question in the negative in *People v. Hughes*.[60]

In *Hughes*, the victim of a rape was unable to positively identify her attacker until after she had been hypnotized. The trial court permitted the witness to testify to all that she remembered as of the date of trial, holding that hypnosis is simply a method of refreshing recollection and that any weaknesses in the methodology could be considered on the issue of credibility.[61] The Court of Appeals disagreed, holding that witnesses are incompetent to testify to posthypnotic recollections.[62] The court deferred to the prevailing views of the scientific community that hypnosis is not a reliable method of restoring memory.[63] It is an inherently suggestive procedure that taints a potential witness in three ways: (1) the witness may be susceptible to suggestions given by the hypnotist or others present during the session; (2) the witness may confabulate or intentionally fabricate facts to fill memory gaps; and (3) the witness may acquire an artificially enhanced confidence in her prehypnotic memory of events, thereby impairing the opponent's ability to cross-examine the witness.[64]

---

60. 59 N.Y.2d 523, 466 N.Y.S.2d 255, 453 N.E.2d 484 (1983).

61. The trial court's view as to the evidentiary effect of hypnotically-induced memory was based on a line of authority that began with Harding v. State, 5 Md. App. 230, 246 A.2d 302 (1968), cert. denied, 395 U.S. 949, 89 S.Ct. 2030, 23 L.Ed.2d 468 (1969).

62. 59 N.Y.2d at 545, 466 N.Y.S.2d at 266, 453 N.E.2d at 495. The court acknowledged in a footnote that, after hypnosis, a witness might occasionally remember new facts about an event independently of the influence of the hypnosis. Testimony about such facts might be permissible provided a pretrial or voir dire hearing established "that any such delayed recall was unaffected by and not a product of the hypnosis." Id. at 547 n.38, 466 N.Y.S.2d at 267, 453 N.E.2d at 496. The Hughes rule of incompetency applies in both criminal and civil proceedings. Bennett v. Saeger Hotels, Inc., 209 A.D.2d 946, 619 N.Y.S.2d 424 (4th Dep't 1994).

63. 59 N.Y.2d at 543, 466 N.Y.S.2d at 265, 453 N.E.2d at 494 ("it has been scientifically demonstrated that [hypnosis] produces recollections which may contain a mixture of accurate recall, fantasy or pure fabrication in unknown quantities"). The court applied the Frye rule requiring general acceptance in the scientific community as a prerequisite to the admissibility of scientific evidence. See § 702.1(b) infra.

64. 59 N.Y.2d at 534–36, 466 N.Y.S.2d at 260–61, 453 N.E.2d at 489–90. In subsequent decisions, the court has made it clear that any out-of-court statements that embody recollections based on hypnotic therapy are also inadmissible, even if such statements might otherwise overcome a hearsay objection. See People v. Schreiner, 77 N.Y.2d 733, 570 N.Y.S.2d 464, 573 N.E.2d 552 (1991)(prosecution may not use defendant's hypnotically-induced statement against him); People v. Hults, 76 N.Y.2d 190, 557 N.Y.S.2d 270, 556 N.E.2d 1077 (1990)(defendant may not impeach credibility of witness with inconsistent statements made by witness during hypnosis). The reasoning is the same as that in Hughes: hypnosis is an inherently unreliable procedure. But see People v. Santana, 159 Misc.2d 301, 604 N.Y.S.2d 1016 (Sup.Ct. Queens Co.1993)(in support of insanity defense, psychiatrist may testify to statements made by criminal defendant during hypnosis in order to explain basis of psychiatrist's opinion that defendant was insane).

Hughes rejected the approach taken in State v. Hurd, 86 N.J. 525, 432 A.2d 86 (1981), which would allow a witness to testify to posthypnotic recollections if sufficient procedural safeguards were used dur-

Prior hypnosis however, does not necessarily render a witness wholly incompetent. She may testify to matters that she had recalled prior to being hypnotized provided the hypnosis did not substantially impair the opponent's ability to cross-examine the witness.[65] A pretrial hearing must be conducted to establish the extent of the witness' prehypnotic memory, thus marking the permissible testimonial boundaries, and to examine the circumstances of the hypnotic session to ascertain whether the procedures used may have unduly tainted the prehypnotic recollection.[66] The witness should be precluded from testifying to prehypnotic recollections to the extent the opponent's ability to meaningfully cross-examine has been unfairly impaired.[67]

Hughes' apparent per se rule that a witness is incompetent to testify to posthypnotic recollections is circumscribed by constitutional considerations if the witness in question is a criminal defendant. The Supreme Court held in *Rock v. Arkansas*,[68] that a criminal defendant who has been hypnotized cannot be deprived of the right to testify in her own defense so long as a particularized inquiry concerning the reliability of the hypnotic process that produced the recollections was conducted in a reliable manner.[69]

Library References:

West's Key No. Digests, Witnesses ⚖=35–79.

---

ing the hypnotic session to minimize the potential for suggestion by the hypnotist. Even if such procedures eliminated all external suggestions, said the Hughes court, they would have no effect on the risk that the subject would confabulate or fantasize to fill in memory gaps. 59 N.Y.2d at 543–44, 466 N.Y.S.2d at 265–66, 453 N.E.2d at 494–95.

65. "[T]he People should assume the burden of demonstrating by clear and convincing proof that the testimony of the witness as to his or her prehypnotic recollection will be reliable and that there has been no substantial impairment of the defendant's right of cross-examination." 59 N.Y.2d at 547, 466 N.Y.S.2d at 267, 453 N.E.2d at 497. See, e.g., People v. Lozado, 210 A.D.2d 83, 620 N.Y.S.2d 32 (1st Dep't 1994), appeal denied, 85 N.Y.2d 976, 629 N.Y.S.2d 736, 653 N.E.2d 632 (1995) (prosecution met burden of showing that eyewitnesses' prehypnotic memory was not affected by hypnosis). By analogy to the hypnosis cases, one court has held that a child who has been exposed to unduly suggestive questioning about alleged sexual abuse may not testify to the abuse except to the extent the witness is shown to have an independent recollection. People v. Michael M., 162 Misc.2d 803, 618 N.Y.S.2d 171 (Sup.Ct. Kings Co.1994).

66. Id. at 546, 466 N.Y.S.2d at 267, 453 N.E.2d at 496. "[D]etailed proof should be introduced as to the precise procedures that were followed in the particular instance, including measures taken to reduce the risk of impermissible suggestiveness." Id. at 547, 466 N.Y.S.2d at 267, 453 N.E.2d at 496.

67. People v. Tunstall, 63 N.Y.2d 1, 8–9, 479 N.Y.S.2d 192, 195–96, 468 N.E.2d 30, 33–34 (1984).

68. 483 U.S. 44, 107 S.Ct. 2704, 97 L.Ed.2d 37 (1987)(criminal defendant could not recall important exculpatory facts until after hypnosis).

69. Id. at 56–62, 107 S.Ct. at 2712–14, 97 L.Ed.2d at 49–53 ("A State's legitimate interest in barring unreliable evidence does not extend to per se exclusions that may be reliable in an individual case. Wholesale inadmissibility of a defendant's testimony is an arbitrary restriction on the right to testify in the absence of clear evidence by the State repudiating the validity of all post-hypnosis recollections.") In People v. Hults, 76 N.Y.2d 190, 557 N.Y.S.2d 270, 556 N.E.2d 1077 (1990), the court found no constitutional violation in a trial court's rejection of the defendant's request to impeach the credibility of a prosecution witness with prior inconsistent statements that the witness had made during hypnosis. The defendant himself had conceded that the witness' hypnotically-induced statements were unreliable.

§ 601.2 New York Dead Man's Statute

a. In General

The so-called "Dead Man's Statute"—CPLR 4519—carries forward, in civil trials, the common law rule of incompetency based on interest where the testimony is that of an interested witness concerning a transaction or communication with a decedent or mentally ill person. Such testimony is presumed untrustworthy as a matter of law. Thus, when death or mental illness has sealed the lips of one of the parties to a transaction, CPLR 4519 seals the lips of the surviving party.[1] Transactions or communications between an interested witness and the decedent or mentally ill person generally can be established only through documentary evidence and the testimony of disinterested witnesses.

Statutes of the type exemplified by CPLR 4519 have been criticized for seeking to cure injustice to one side by creating injustice to the other.[2] Less drastic solutions have been proposed to level the playing ground.[3] Nevertheless, the Dead Man's Statute "remains a part of the law of [New York]."[4] The complete text of CPLR 4519 is as follows:

§ 4519. Personal transaction or communication between witness and decedent or mentally ill person

Upon the trial of an action or the hearing upon the merits of a special proceeding, a party or a person interested in the event, or a person from, through or under whom such a party or interested person derives his interest or title by assignment or otherwise, shall not be examined as a witness in his own behalf or interest, or in behalf of the party succeeding to his title or interest against the executor, administrator or survivor of a deceased person or the committee of a mentally ill person, or a

---

§ 601.2

1. In re Estate of Wood, 52 N.Y.2d 139, 144, 436 N.Y.S.2d 850, 851–52, 418 N.E.2d 365, 366–67 (1981)("One of the main purposes of the rule was to protect the estate of the deceased from claims of the living who, through their own perjury, could make factual assertions which the decedent could not refute in court.").

2. McCormick § 65, at 251. "The fear that interested parties may deviate from the truth should generally be viewed as affecting the weight, rather than the admissibility, of evidence." Estate of Isaacs, 86 Misc.2d 954, 957, 383 N.Y.S.2d 976, 979 (Surr.Ct.N.Y.Co.1976).

3. Proposed alternatives include a requirement that the survivor's testimony be corroborated, the allowance of hearsay statements by the decedent, and a higher burden of proof on the estate's adversary. McCormick § 65; N.Y.Adv.Comm.on Prac. and Proc., Second Prelim.Rep., Legis.Doc. No.13, pp. 269–70 (1958).

4. In re Estate of Wood, 52 N.Y.2d 139, 144, 436 N.Y.S.2d 850, 852, 418 N.E.2d 365, 367 (1981). It may be of some consolation that the party asserting the protection of CPLR 4519 has the burden of proving its applicability. Stay v. Horvath, 177 A.D.2d 897, 899, 576 N.Y.S.2d 908, 910 (3d Dep't 1991).

Although the statute is firmly imbedded in New York jurisprudence, one court has aptly observed that the complexity of the rule, together with an inclination toward "leniency or distinction in application" in cases of perceived injustice, "has led to innumerable contradictory decisions both at the trial and appellate court levels." Hadley v. Clabeau, 140 Misc.2d 994, 997, 532 N.Y.S.2d 221, 223 (Sup.Ct.Cattaraugus Co.1988), aff'd, 161 A.D.2d 1141, 555 N.Y.S.2d 951 (4th Dep't 1990). An effort to avoid the applicability of the statute on due process grounds was rejected in In re Estate of Hamburg, 151 Misc.2d 1034, 574 N.Y.S.2d 914 (Surr.Ct.Bronx Co.1991).

§ 601.2 WITNESSES

person deriving his title or interest from, through or under a deceased person or mentally ill person, by assignment or otherwise, concerning a personal transaction or communication between the witness and the deceased person or mentally ill person, except where the executor, administrator, survivor, committee or person so deriving title or interest is examined in his own behalf, or the testimony of the mentally ill person or deceased person is given in evidence, concerning the same transaction or communication. A person shall not be deemed interested for the purposes of this section by reason of being a stockholder or officer of any banking corporation which is a party to the action or proceeding, or interested in the event thereof. No party or person interested in the event, who is otherwise competent to testify, shall be disqualified from testifying by the possible imposition of costs against him or the award of costs to him. A party or person interested in the event or a person from, through or under whom such a party or interested person derives his interest or title by assignment or otherwise, shall not be qualified for the purposes of this section, to testify in his own behalf or interest, or in behalf of the party succeeding to his title or interest, to personal transactions or communications with the donee of a power of appointment in an action or proceeding for the probate of a will, which exercises or attempts to exercise a power of appointment granted by the will of a donor of such power, or in an action or proceeding involving the construction of the will of the donee after its admission to probate.

Nothing contained in this section, however, shall render a person incompetent to testify as to the facts of an accident or the results therefrom where the proceeding, hearing, defense or cause of action involves a claim of negligence or contributory negligence in an action wherein one or more parties is the representative of a deceased or incompetent person based upon, or by reason of, the operation or ownership of a motor vehicle being operated upon the highways of the state, or the operation or ownership of aircraft being operated in the air space over the state, or the operation or ownership of a vessel on any of the lakes, rivers, streams, canals or other waters of this state, but this provision shall not be construed as permitting testimony as to conversations with the deceased.

Reduced to its essentials, CPLR 4519 consists of three elements: (1) Any person "interested in the event," or a predecessor in interest of such person, may not testify in her own behalf or that of the successor in interest against (2) certain protected persons with a specified relationship to a decedent or mentally ill person (3) concerning a transaction or communication with the decedent or mentally ill person.

It bears emphasizing that the statute, by its terms, applies only to the testimony of witnesses, not to documentary evidence. Thus, an adverse party's introduction of a document written by the decedent is not, standing alone, testimony against the estate.[5] On the other hand, if authentication of a document depends upon testimony concerning a transaction or communication with the decedent, such as observation of the decedent in the process of writing, only a competent witness may provide the authentication.[6] Similarly, records that describe a transaction with a decedent may be admitted pursuant to the hearsay exception for business records only if a competent witness can testify to the necessary foundation concerning preparation of the records.[7]

b. Disqualified Witnesses

Two types of witnesses may be rendered incompetent by the statute: (1) a party or person interested in the event; and (2) a person from, through or under whom such a party or person derived her interest by assignment or otherwise. Both types of witnesses are disqualified from giving testimony in their own behalf, or that of parties succeeding to their interest, concerning a personal transaction or communication with a decedent or mentally ill person when such testimony is offered against the class of persons protected by the statute.

A party or person "interested in the event" is one who has such an interest that the witness "will either gain or lose by the direct legal operation and effect of the judgment, or * * * the record will be legal evidence for or against him in some other action. It must be a present, certain, and vested interest, and not an interest uncertain, remote or contingent."[8] A common example of persons interested in the event are the contestants in a probate dispute. Beneficiaries under the will are

---

5. Kiser v. Bailey, 92 Misc.2d 435, 438–39, 400 N.Y.S.2d 312, 313–14 (N.Y.C.Civ.Ct. 1977). See also Yager Pontiac, Inc. v. Fred A. Danker and Sons, Inc., 69 Misc.2d 546, 330 N.Y.S.2d 409, aff'd, 41 A.D.2d 366, 343 N.Y.S.2d 209 (3d Dep't 1973), aff'd, 34 N.Y.2d 707, 356 N.Y.S.2d 860, 313 N.E.2d 340 (1974).

6. Wilber v. Gillespie, 127 App.Div. 604, 112 N.Y.S. 20 (1st Dep't 1908); Estate of Isaacs, 86 Misc.2d 954, 383 N.Y.S.2d 976 (Surr.Ct.N.Y.Co.1976) (contract written and executed by decedent was properly authenticated by disinterested witness).

7. William L. Mantha Co. v. De Graff, 242 App.Div. 666, 273 N.Y.S. 384 (2d Dep't 1934), aff'd, 266 N.Y. 581, 195 N.E. 209 (1935). DeGraff was an action by a corporation against a decedent's estate in which the corporation's bookkeeper was permitted to provide the foundation for admissibility of the corporation's records. Even though the clerk was a shareholder, and therefore interested in the event, his testimony as to the authenticity and method of preparation of the records did not involve a transaction between the bookkeeper and the decedent. See also In re Schaff's Estate, 274 App.Div. 1020, 85 N.Y.S.2d 147 (3d Dep't 1948) (necessary foundation for business records could be made by interested party's spouse). A contrary result was reached in the case of a nurse who sought to authenticate her own business records containing evidence of the services she performed for the decedent. In re Mulderig, 196 Misc. 527, 91 N.Y.S.2d 895 (Surr.Ct.Broome Co.1949).

8. Laka v. Krystek, 261 N.Y. 126, 130, 184 N.E. 732, 733 (1933). A person can be interested in the event, even if not a party in the action, if she stands to gain or lose by the direct legal operation of the judgment. See, e.g., Kerwood v. Hall, 201 App.Div. 89, 193 N.Y.S. 811 (3d Dep't 1922)(second mortgagee of property held incompetent to give adverse testimony concerning transaction with deceased first mortgagee in foreclosure action by estate of first mortgagee against mortgagor because invalidation of first mortgage would improve security of second mortgage); Carpenter v. Romer and Tremper Co., 48 App.Div. 363, 63 N.Y.S. 274 (3d Dep't 1900)(nonparty witness who was under contractual duty to indemnify defendant was "interested in the event"). See also Kwoh v. Delum Builders and Suppliers, Inc., 173 A.D.2d 326, 575 N.Y.S.2d 465 (1st Dep't 1991)(witness stood to lose right of occupancy of real property that was allegedly misappropriated by decedent). But see Stay v. Horvath, 177 A.D.2d 897, 899, 576 N.Y.S.2d 908, 910 (3d Dep't 1991)(judgment creditor of plaintiff was not shown to be sufficiently interested).

usually incompetent to testify in support of the will to transactions or communications with the decedent.[9] Statutory distributees are incompetent to testify to their dealings with the decedent for the purpose of defeating the will.[10] An executor, however, is not disqualified from testifying to a transaction with the decedent in support of the will unless he is also a beneficiary.[11] On the other hand, if the executor or administrator has a personal claim against the estate, he may not testify to a transaction or communication with the decedent in support of that claim.[12]

The shareholder of a corporation may not testify on behalf of the corporation to a transaction or communication with a decedent whose estate is suing or being sued by the corporation. Stock ownership is deemed to give the stockholder a direct pecuniary interest in the judgment.[13] (The statute contains an exception applicable only to shareholders of banking corporations). Officers, directors and employees of the corporation, however, are not incompetent to testify unless they also happen to be shareholders.[14] Such individuals may be biased, but a judgment for or against the corporation usually will have no direct operative effect on them. Similarly, an agent may testify to a transaction between the decedent and the agent's principal because the agent is not interested in the event.[15]

Relationship by blood or marriage to an interested party does not, standing alone, make the relative an incompetent witness under CPLR 4519.[16] In *Duncan v. Clarke*,[17] for example, a mother was held competent to testify in support of her child's action against the estate of the child's deceased father to enforce an oral support agreement made by the child's grandmother and father. The mother had been present when the agreement was made. The *Duncan,* court held that the mother was not a person interested in the event because the judgment in the action would have no direct legal effect on her. She may have had an interest "in the question" inasmuch as a favorable judgment for the child would have relieved her own financial burdens. Such an interest made her a biased witness—something the fact-finder could take into account in weighing her testimony—but it did not disqualify her from testifying. Furthermore, her status as the child's guardian ad litem, a nominal party in the action, did not make her a party interested in the event.

Similarly, a party's spouse is not per se disqualified by the statute. A husband, for example, could testify to his wife's meeting with a

---

9. In re Sheehan's Will, 51 A.D.2d 645, 378 N.Y.S.2d 141 (4th Dep't 1976).

10. In re Aievoli's Will, 272 App.Div. 544, 74 N.Y.S.2d 29 (2d Dep't 1947).

11. The executor's right to commissions is not deemed a disqualifying interest because commissions are a statutory entitlement, not a gift from the decedent. In re Will of Wilson, 103 N.Y. 374, 8 N.E. 731 (1886).

12. In re Van Valkenburgh's Will, 164 Misc. 295, 298 N.Y.S. 819 (Surr.Ct.Kings Co.1937).

13. Friedrich v. Martin, 294 N.Y. 588, 63 N.E.2d 586 (1945).

14. Jewell v. Irvmac Shoe Shops, Inc., 19 Misc.2d 815, 187 N.Y.S.2d 412 (Sup.Ct.Nassau Co.1959).

15. Nearpass v. Tilman, 104 N.Y. 506, 10 N.E. 894 (1887).

16. Laka v. Krystek, 261 N.Y. 126, 184 N.E. 732 (1933).

17. 308 N.Y. 282, 125 N.E.2d 569 (1955).

decedent in which the decedent allegedly made a gift of property to the wife,[18] or to his wife's performance of services for a decedent who failed to pay for the services.[19] On the other hand, if an alleged gift from a decedent were made to the spouses jointly, or if an alleged debt were jointly owed to the decedent by both spouses, both of them would be incompetent to testify against the decedent's estate with respect to their dealings with the decedent.[20]

The second type of incompetent witness is a predecessor in interest—a person from, through or under whom a party or interested person derived her interest or title in the subject matter at issue in the action. In such case, the assignor or predecessor presumably would be "morally and indirectly, if not legally and directly, interested in maintaining the validity and integrity of the assignment."[21]

The original promisee of an oral third-party beneficiary contract, for example, would be incompetent to testify to the making of the contract in support of the beneficiary's claim against the deceased promisor's estate. The promisee is the person "from, through or under whom" the third-party beneficiary derives her interest.[22] In cases of this nature, however, the predecessor in interest is incompetent only when the title or interest that passed to the party is the subject matter of the litigation.[23]

For a person to be interested in the event, the disqualifying interest must exist at the time the testimony is offered. Therefore, a potential witness' divestiture of his interest prior to testifying generally will restore the witness' competency. For example, in *Friedrich v. Martin*,[24] the shareholder of a corporation who sold his stock just moments before

18. Murray v. Smith, 155 A.D.2d 963, 547 N.Y.S.2d 774 (4th Dep't 1989).

19. Hamar v. Isachsen, 58 A.D.2d 988, 397 N.Y.S.2d 485 (4th Dep't 1977).

20. Slusarczyk v. Slusarczyk, 41 A.D.2d 593, 340 N.Y.S.2d 250 (4th Dep't 1973).

21. Abbott v. Doughan, 204 N.Y. 223, 226, 97 N.E. 599, 600 (1912).

22. Duncan v. Clarke, 308 N.Y. 282, 285, 125 N.E.2d 569, 570 (1955). In Duncan, which is described in the text at note 17 supra, the grandmother of the plaintiff child was disqualified because it was through the grandmother that the child acquired her contractual claim. See also Estate of Isaacs, 86 Misc.2d 954, 383 N.Y.S.2d 976 (Surr.Ct.N.Y.Co.1976).

23. Stay v. Horvath, 177 A.D.2d 897, 899, 576 N.Y.S.2d 908, 910 (3d Dep't 1991). The plaintiff in Stay, who had leased property from the defendant's decedent, was the franchisee of an automobile rental business. The action alleged that the decedent had tortiously interfered with the business. Plaintiff's franchisor was not incompetent under the "from, through or under whom" clause to testify in plaintiff's behalf because the claim did not concern plaintiff's title or interest in the franchise. The Stay court relied on Abbott v. Doughan, 204 N.Y. 223, 97 N.E. 599 (1912), where a seller of jewelry was deemed competent to testify on behalf of the buyer in the latter's action against the estate of an alleged converter of the jewelry. The Abbott court distinguished the situation of a transferee who has become an outright title holder of property from that of a transferee of a mere chose in action. Only in the latter situation is an assignor likely to feel compelled to give favorable testimony on behalf of the assignee and therefore deemed to have a continuing "interest" in the matter. Id. at 226, 97 N.E. at 600–01. The court made the pertinent observation that the statute should be construed by keeping in mind "its fundamental purpose." The seller of property "did not come within the spirit of the provision concerning assignors. He made no assignment or transfer to plaintiff which was involved in this action." Id. at 226, 97 N.E. at 600.

24. 294 N.Y. 588, 63 N.E.2d 586 (1945).

testifying on behalf of the corporation became competent because he had no interest at the time of the testimony.[25] On the other hand, incompetency will persist if the witness, after having divested the interest, is a person "from, through or under whom" some other interested person derives her interest. This issue has arisen in probate contests. For example, a residuary legatee who renounces her bequest under a will, thereby increasing the shares of other legatees, is no longer interested in the event. But is the renouncing legatee a person "from, through or under whom" the remaining residuary legatees derive their increased interests? The courts have answered in the negative, holding that the increased interest of the others is deemed to flow from the testator, not from the renouncing legatee.[26] The renouncing legatee, therefore, may testify to her dealings with the testator in support of the will.

A different analysis has been applied to distributees. The court in *In re Aievoli's Will*,[27] held that a distributee who renounced his distributive share did not become competent to testify in opposition to the will. Although the renouncing distributee no longer had an interest in the event, he was deemed to be the person from whom the other distributees acquired their increased interest in the estate. A counter-argument to *Aievoli* might be based on § 2–1.11(d) of the New York Estates, Powers and Trusts Law, which provides that a person who duly renounces a distributive share is to be treated as having predeceased the decedent. The increase in the other distributees' shares, therefore, could be deemed to flow from the decedent.

Even if a witness is interested in the event according to the foregoing criteria, CPLR 4519 applies only when the witness is being examined in his own behalf or that of his successor in interest. Thus, testimony given in opposition to the witness' interest or that of the successor is permitted.[28] For example, the residuary legatee under a will may testify in support of an alleged inter vivos gift made by the testator to third parties because the gift would diminish the residuary bequest.[29]

c. Protected Persons

The persons who are entitled to invoke CPLR 4519 against interested witnesses fall into three categories: (1) the executor or administrator

---

25. See also Bechard v. Eisinger, 105 A.D.2d 939, 481 N.Y.S.2d 906 (3d Dep't 1984)(plaintiff's wife dropped her derivative suit and thereby became competent to testify in support of her husband's medical malpractice claim against the estate of a deceased doctor).

Just as divesting one's interest prior to testifying may serve to qualify a previously incompetent witness, acquiring the interest after the transaction in question may serve to invoke the incompetency. Thus, in Oneida National Bank and Trust Co. of Central New York v. Kranz, 70 Misc.2d 595, 334 N.Y.S.2d 336 (Sup.Ct.Oneida Co.1972), a wife who had assumed an interest in property with her husband as co-mortgagor was incompetent to testify to cash payments that she and her husband had made to the decedent-mortgagee even though the payments had been made prior to her assumption of the mortgage.

26. In re Will of Wilson, 103 N.Y. 374, 8 N.E. 731 (1886).

27. 272 App.Div. 544, 74 N.Y.S.2d 29 (2d Dep't 1947).

28. Harrington v. Schiller, 231 N.Y. 278, 132 N.E. 89 (1921).

29. In re Estate of Tremaine, 156 A.D.2d 862, 549 N.Y.S.2d 857 (3d Dep't 1989). See also Brezinski v. Brezinski, 84 A.D.2d 464, 468, 446 N.Y.S.2d 833, 836 (4th Dep't 1982)(potentially disqualified witness is not being examined in her own behalf when called by adverse party).

of the decedent's estate or the committee of a mentally ill person; (2) a "survivor" of the decedent; and (3) a person deriving her title or interest from, through or under the decedent or mentally ill person.

The executor or administrator of a decedent's estate may invoke the statute regardless of whether the fiduciary is defending a claim against the estate or prosecuting a claim on behalf of the estate.[30] A judicially-appointed committee for a person who has been adjudicated incompetent also has standing to invoke the statute. The scope of protection for a mentally ill person who has not been formally adjudicated incompetent is less clear. One court has held that only the committee of an adjudicated incompetent falls within the statute,[31] while others have held that the guardian ad litem of a person hospitalized for mental illness is also within its coverage.[32]

The second type of protected party, the "survivor" of a decedent, is narrowly interpreted. It does not mean a relative who outlives the decedent.[33] Rather, it means the surviving member of a partnership or joint venture of which the decedent was a member.[34] The surviving debtor on a joint debt has also been said to fall within the meaning of the term.[35]

The third individual entitled to assert the protection of CPLR 4519 is a person who derives her title or interest from, through or under a decedent or mentally ill person. For example, a challenge to the title of a person's property will trigger the applicability of the statute and bar testimony by an interested party who dealt with any decedent who was a

---

30. De Laurent v. Townsend, 243 N.Y. 130, 152 N.E. 699 (1926); In re Estate of Hamburg, 151 Misc.2d 1034, 574 N.Y.S.2d 914 (Surr.Ct.Bronx Co.1991). The statute applies even if the personal representative's official status has not yet been established. Schoonmaker v. Wolford, 20 Hun. 166 (N.Y. 1880).

31. Clark v. Dada, 183 App.Div. 253, 171 N.Y.S. 205 (4th Dep't 1918).

32. In re Musczak, 196 Misc. 364, 92 N.Y.S.2d 97 (Surr.Ct.N.Y.Co.1949); In re Harkavy, 184 Misc. 742, 56 N.Y.S.2d 700 (Surr.Ct.N.Y.Co.1945). A liberal reading of the term "committee" furthers the purpose of the statute.

Article 81 of the New York Mental Hygiene Law, which took effect in 1993, abolished incompetency proceedings and created a proceeding for the appointment of a "guardian for personal needs or property management" of an incapacitated person. Diverse forms of incapacity, not merely mental illness, are encompassed by the proceeding. Committees appointed under the old system are continued until such time as their powers are judicially modified or abrogated pursuant to the new Article 81. See N.Y.Laws of 1992, ch. 698, § 4. Of particular significance to the application of CPLR 4519 is the following provision in the implementing legislation for Article 81: "Wherever a statute uses the terms conservators or committees, such statute shall be construed to include the term guardian * * * unless the context otherwise requires." N.Y.Laws of 1992, ch. 698, § 4.

33. Agluzzi v. Aluzzo, 286 App.Div. 399, 402, 143 N.Y.S.2d 51, 53 (4th Dep't 1955). See also Ehrlich v. American Moninger Greenhouse Manufacturing Corp., 26 N.Y.2d 255, 257–58, 309 N.Y.S.2d 341, 342–43, 257 N.E.2d 890, 891–92 (1970)(in plaintiff-wife's action on promissory note payable to wife, defendant-promisor was not barred by CPLR 4519 from testifying to transaction with plaintiff's deceased husband regarding consideration for note; plaintiff was suing solely in individual capacity, not as representative of husband's estate or as survivor of the deceased).

34. Agluzzi v. Aluzzo, 286 App.Div. 399, 402, 143 N.Y.S.2d 51, 53 (4th Dep't 1955). See, e.g., Clift v. Moses, 112 N.Y. 426, 20 N.E. 392 (1889).

35. Melkon v. H.B. Kirk and Co., 220 App.Div. 180, 220 N.Y.S. 551 (1st Dep't 1927).

prior owner of the person's property.[36] In *Brundige v. Bradley*,[37] the "from, through or under" clause protected successor trustees who were being sued in their representative capacity for a judgment to dissolve the trust on the ground that plaintiffs had been defrauded in conveying their property to the original trustee, now deceased. The plaintiffs were barred from testifying to their dealings with the deceased trustee because he was a predecessor in title to the persons against whom the testimony was offered.[38]

The "from, through or under" clause rarely applies in cases involving deceased agents. A principal does not take title or interest in the subject matter of litigation from, through or under the agent who negotiated the relevant transaction. An agent ordinarily owns no property interest in the matter for which she acted on behalf of the principal and therefore has no title or interest to transfer. Thus, in *Rodenhouse v. American Casualty Co. of Pennsylvania*,[39] a corporate defendant could not bar the plaintiff from testifying to his dealings with the defendant's now-deceased agent. The principal is also free to testify to her own dealings with the now-deceased agent because the adversary likewise takes no title or interest in the matter from, through or under the agent.[40]

Another limitation on the "from, through or under" clause was identified in *Ward v. New York Life Insurance Co.*[41] In disputed claims to the proceeds of a life insurance policy, it was held that the beneficiaries named in the policy did not derive their title from the deceased insured and therefore lacked standing to invoke the statute against adverse claimants. Since the decedent himself did not own the proceeds during his lifetime, nothing passed through him.[42] *Ward* was distinguished, however, in *Poslock v. Teachers' Retirement Board of the Teachers Retirement System*,[43] which involved a dispute between contesting beneficiaries of a decedent's retirement death benefits and pension funds. During his lifetime, the decedent possessed several incidents of ownership in the funds in question,[44] making him the person from whom

---

36. Pope v. Allen, 90 N.Y. 298 (1882).

37. 294 N.Y. 345, 62 N.E.2d 385 (1945).

38. Although the decedent's estate did not stand to gain or lose by the suit, the court found no requirement in the statute for any such threat to the estate. Id. at 349–50, 62 N.E.2d at 386. See also Carpenter v. Romer and Tremper Steamboat Co., 48 App.Div. 363, 63 N.Y.S. 274 (3d Dep't 1900) (successor executor).

39. 20 A.D.2d 620, 244 N.Y.S.2d 856 (4th Dep't 1963).

40. Jones v. Maloney, 277 N.Y. 437, 14 N.E.2d 782 (1938).

41. 225 N.Y. 314, 122 N.E. 207 (1919).

42. The principle that property does not pass from a decedent who himself lacked title prior to death is responsible for the addition in 1935 of the statutory language relating to powers of appointment. The problem is discussed in Matter of Carroll, 153 Misc. 649, 275 N.Y.S. 911 (Surr.Ct. N.Y.Co.1934), modified, 247 App.Div. 11, 286 N.Y.S. 307 (1st Dep't 1936), modified, 274 N.Y. 288, 8 N.E.2d 864 (1937). Interested witnesses are now explicitly prohibited from testifying in their own behalf with respect to personal transactions or communications with the donee of a power of appointment in probate proceedings involving the will in which the power of appointment was exercised.

43. 209 A.D.2d 87, 624 N.Y.S.2d 574 (1st Dep't 1995).

44. The decedent had the right to invade contributions he had made to the plan, to select the particular funds to which his contributions would be allocated, and to be paid the full amount of accumulated deductions if he resigned his membership in the

the beneficiaries would receive their interest in the proceeds. To the extent the rationale of CPLR 4519 has validity, one would expect it to be fully operative in a dispute over a decedent's intended disposition of life insurance proceeds or similar death benefits. *Poslock* thus represents a realistic evaluation of a decedent's pre-death interest in such assets.

d. Prohibited Subject Matter

An interested witness may not testify against a member of the protected class "concerning a personal transaction or communication between the witness and the deceased person or mentally ill person." The broad scope that courts have given to "transaction or communication" with the decedent is illustrated by the following passage from the 1884 case of *Holcomb v. Holcomb*:[45] "Transactions and communications embrace every variety of affairs which can form the subject of negotiation, interviews, or actions between two persons, and include every method by which one person can derive impressions or information from the conduct, condition, or language of another."[46]

An interested witness can be disqualified even if he is not a participant in the matter that he observed.[47] In *Griswold v. Hart*,[48] for example, the issue was whether the decedent had made a gift of certain bank instruments to his daughter. The trial court allowed the decedent's son-in-law, who had become an interested party through inheritance, to testify that he had fortuitously passed through the room in which the decedent and his daughter were conversing and saw the decedent give the instruments to his daughter. The Court of Appeals held that the testimony was inadmissible. The statute was said to "[exclude] the testimony of an interested witness to any knowledge which he has gained by the use of his senses from the personal presence of the deceased."[49]

"Negative" testimony by an interested witness concerning things a decedent did not say or do is just as objectionable as testimony describing affirmative conduct by the decedent.[50] Similarly, indirect proof of a

retirement association. Id. at 93–94, 624 N.Y.S.2d at 578.

45. 95 N.Y. 316 (1884)(interested witness forbidden to testify to his observations of decedent's mental and physical condition).

46. Id. at 325. See, e.g., Sklaire v. Estate of Turner, 12 A.D.2d 386, 212 N.Y.S.2d 389 (3d Dep't 1961)(in action by physician against estate for value of medical services rendered to decedent, physician was barred by CPLR 4519 from testifying to nature and value of services).

47. See Hadley v. Clabeau, 140 Misc.2d 994, 995–98, 532 N.Y.S.2d 221, 222–24 (Sup.Ct.Cattaraugus Co.1988), aff'd, 161 A.D.2d 1141, 555 N.Y.S.2d 951 (4th Dep't 1990).

48. 205 N.Y. 384, 98 N.E. 918 (1912).

49. Id. at 395, 98 N.E. at 921. In another portion of the opinion, the court provided an alternative phrasing of the test as any testimony "which the deceased person if living could contradict or explain." Id. at 397, 98 N.E. at 922.

50. See, e.g., Endervelt v. Slade, 162 Misc.2d 975, 618 N.Y.S.2d 520 (Sup.Ct. N.Y.Co.), aff'd, 214 A.D.2d 456, 625 N.Y.S.2d 210 (1st Dep't 1995)(plaintiffs were barred from testifying that decedent, an attorney whose estate was being sued for fraud, had concealed information from plaintiffs). See also Boyd v. Boyd, 164 N.Y. 234, 242–44, 58 N.E. 118, 121 (1900)(testimony of "negative fact" is barred); Grey v. Grey, 47 N.Y. 552 (1872)(bar of statute applied where interested witness sought to testify to receipt of gift from "no one else" but the decedent).

§ 601.2

transaction or communication with the deceased is barred, as illustrated in *Clift v. Moses*.[51] In *Clift*, the issue was whether promissory notes payable to the decedent had been delivered by the decedent to the defendant following defendant's payment. The notes themselves could not be found. Defendant's wife (a noninterested witness) was properly permitted to testify that she had seen the decedent give the notes to her husband. The defendant-husband, however, was barred from testifying that he had subsequently seen the notes among his household possessions because such possession was derived from his receipt of the notes. The court declared that an interested witness may not indirectly prove his own transaction or communication with a decedent by offering testimony "which, on its face, relates to an independent fact, when it is disclosed by other evidence that the fact had its origin in and directly resulted from a personal transaction."[52] The *Clift* court's reference to "independent facts" may provide an escape from the rule against indirect testimony by interested witnesses concerning their dealings with the decedent. Thus, testimony describing some forms of activity performed solely by the witness outside the presence of the decedent has been permitted, even if it reflects on the nature of a transaction with the decedent.[53] The cases, however, are in conflict.[54]

Dealings between the interested witness and the agent of the decedent provide another escape from the statute. In such circumstances, the transaction or communication is not "with the decedent."[55] This holds true even if the decedent is present when the communication with the agent takes place (assuming the decedent remains silent and plays no role in the transaction).[56]

e. Exceptions

The principal exception to the incompetency that would otherwise result from the operation of CPLR 4519 is contained in the second paragraph of the statute.[57] Interested witnesses may testify against

---

51. 112 N.Y. 426, 20 N.E. 392 (1889).
52. Id. at 437, 20 N.E. at 396.
53. See, e.g., Matter of Estate of Tremaine, 156 A.D.2d 862, 549 N.Y.S.2d 857 (3d Dep't 1989)(court permitted recipient of alleged inter vivos gift of furniture from decedent to testify to his "rearrangement, storage and disposal" of the furniture while living with the decedent); Brezinski v. Brezinski, 84 A.D.2d 464, 466, 446 N.Y.S.2d 833, 835 (4th Dep't 1982) (party who unilaterally opened joint bank account in name of decedent and herself (outside presence of decedent) should have been permitted to testify to her own intent to create account solely for her own convenience rather than to make gift to decedent; witness' mental state was not "derived from or dependant upon any conversation, transaction or communication with the deceased").
54. In contrast to the cases cited in note 53 supra, see In re O'Neil's Estate, 20 A.D.2d 741, 246 N.Y.S.2d 892 (3d Dep't 1964)(action on alleged express contract with decedent to provide services cannot be proven through testimony by provider as to what services consisted of even if decedent was not present when services were performed); Gurski v. Sapowitch, 276 App.Div. 821, 93 N.Y.S.2d 159 (4th Dep't 1949)(plaintiff could not testify to placing of cedar chest in decedent's locked trunk as to which plaintiff had no key; apparent inference was that plaintiff obtained key from decedent).
55. McCarthy v. Stanley, 151 App.Div. 358, 136 N.Y.S. 386 (3d Dep't 1912); Warth v. Kastriner, 114 App.Div. 766, 100 N.Y.S. 279 (2d Dep't 1906).
56. In re Ryder's Will, 279 App.Div. 1131, 112 N.Y.S.2d 601 (4th Dep't 1952).
57. The statute also provides that the stockholder of a banking corporation shall not be deemed an interested witness in litigation between the bank and parties oth-

representatives of a decedent or mentally ill person with respect to "the facts of an accident" involving negligence arising out of the operation or ownership of a motor vehicle, aircraft or vessel in New York. This exception, however, does not encompass testimony concerning conversations with the decedent. Thus, an interested witness could testify that he saw the decedent run a red light but not that the decedent admitted the violation to the witness.

Another important exception is contained in § 5–1.1(b)(3) of the New York Estates, Powers and Trusts Law, which provides that a surviving spouse is competent to testify regarding the spouses' respective contributions to property jointly owned with the deceased spouse.

Another exception, of sorts, is contained in the hearsay exception for former testimony. By statute, testimony given by an interested witness in a prior trial can be used against the estate at a subsequent trial.[58] Some courts have extended this notion so as to admit the "former testimony" of an otherwise incompetent witness given during a pretrial deposition in the pending action, provided the decedent had been alive at the time of the deposition and participated therein.[59] CPLR 4519 technically does not preclude the introduction of such deposition testimony against the decedent's estate. The statute provides only that, upon the trial, a disqualified witness "shall not be examined as a witness in his own behalf or interest." The court in *Siegel v. Waldbaum*,[60] where this evasion of CPLR 4519 was first validated, reasoned that the statute is premised on the inability of a decedent to contradict an interested witness' testimony. This policy is not frustrated if the decedent was able to "confront and cross-examine" the interested party during the pretrial deposition.[61]

f. Waiver

Waiver of the incompetency created by CPLR 4519 can occur in any one of four situations: (1) no objection is interposed at trial to the

---

erwise protected by the statute. Another exception is that the potential for the award or imposition of costs is not a disqualifying interest.

58. CPLR 4517. A witness who is incompetent under the Dead Man's Statute is deemed to be "unavailable" at the subsequent trial. Id. Presumably, the decedent was alive at the time of the former trial; otherwise, such testimony would have been subject to exclusion, upon objection, at the prior trial.

If the prior proceeding was something other than a trial, the common law hearsay exception, which coexists with CPLR 4517, may be applicable. Fleury v. Edwards, 14 N.Y.2d 334, 251 N.Y.S.2d 647, 200 N.E.2d 550 (1964).

59. Compare Siegel v. Waldbaum, 59 A.D.2d 555, 397 N.Y.S.2d 144 (2d Dep't 1977)(pretrial deposition of interested party was admissible at trial of action against decedent's estate pursuant to common law hearsay exception for former testimony; decedent had attended deposition and had been an active participant in cross-examination of interested party), with In re Estate of Mead, 129 A.D.2d 1008, 514 N.Y.S.2d 581 (4th Dep't 1987), appeal denied, 70 N.Y.2d 609, 522 N.Y.S.2d 109, 516 N.E.2d 1222 (1987)(pretrial deposition of interested party inadmissible; although decedent was alive at time of deposition, he was confined in nursing home), and Rosenberg v. Grace, 158 Misc.2d 32, 600 N.Y.S.2d 425 (Sup.Ct.N.Y.Co.1993)(pretrial deposition of interested party inadmissible where decedent, although alive at time of deposition, was recuperating from stroke and apparently did not attend).

60. 59 A.D.2d 555, 397 N.Y.S.2d 144 (2d Dep't 1977).

61. Id. at 555, 397 N.Y.S.2d at 146.

§ 601.2 WITNESSES Ch. 6

interested witness' incompetency; (2) the protected party testifies at trial in his own behalf concerning a transaction or communication with the decedent or mentally ill person; (3) the protected party examines the disqualified witness concerning the transaction or communication; or (4) testimony about the transaction or communication by the decedent or mentally ill person given on a prior occasion is introduced into evidence at trial.

The clearest sort of waiver of the protection of CPLR 4519 occurs when a party who is entitled to invoke the statute fails to object at trial to the incompetency of a disqualified witness who testifies in his own behalf concerning a transaction or communication with the decedent or mentally ill person.[62] The objection may be made, however, at any point in the testimony; failure to object at the outset of the testimony is not an irrevocable waiver.[63] Furthermore, because CPLR 4519 is applicable only at trial,[64] the fact that the protected party does not object to the incompetency of an interested witness at the investigatory phase of a surrogate's proceeding or in pretrial testimony, such as a deposition, does not preclude an objection to such incompetency at trial.[65] The same right of objection exists at trial even if the protected party himself elicited incompetent testimony from the interested witness prior to trial.[66]

The second basis for waiver is explicitly described in CPLR 4519: testimony in his own behalf by either the estate representative, survivor, or person deriving title or interest from the decedent (or mentally ill person) concerning a personal transaction or communication between the interested witness and the decedent opens the door to testimony by the interested witness regarding the same transaction or communication. Waiver under this part of the statute obviously is based on a principle of fairness,[67] but the scope of the provision has been narrowly interpreted by the courts.

62. See In re Estate of Mastrianni, 55 A.D.2d 784, 389 N.Y.S.2d 914 (3d Dep't 1976). To be effective, the objection must be specifically directed to the incompetency of the witness. See § 601.1, at notes 1 & 12, supra. If there is to be a waiver of the statute at a trial in which several members of the protected class are participants, such as a probate contest, the decision to waive must be unanimous. For example, the executor's willingness to allow a beneficiary to testify in support of the will cannot prevent a contesting distributee (who derives her title or interest from, through or under the decedent) from precluding such testimony.

63. In re Honigman's Will, 8 N.Y.2d 244, 251–52, 203 N.Y.S.2d 859, 864, 168 N.E.2d 676, 679 (1960).

64. See Phillips v. Joseph Kantor and Co., 31 N.Y.2d 307, 313, 338 N.Y.S.2d 882 887, 291 N.E.2d 129, 132 (1972)(plaintiff's evidence in opposition to defendant's motion for summary judgment would have been barred by CPLR 4519 if presented at trial but was sufficient to avoid pretrial dismissal).

65. In re Van Volkenburgh, 254 N.Y. 139, 143–44, 172 N.E. 269, 270 (1930).

66. In re Schulman's Estate, 189 Misc. 672, 72 N.Y.S.2d 239 (Surr.Ct.Kings Co.1947).

67. "Once having introduced testimony concerning [a personal transaction of his adversary with the deceased] into evidence, [the protected party] cannot thereafter prevent his adversary from testifying to the details of the same transaction, for to do so would give the estate an unfair advantage not intended by the statute." In re Estate of Wood, 52 N.Y.2d 139, 145, 436 N.Y.S.2d 850, 852, 418 N.E.2d 365, 367 (1981).

In re Estate of Wood,[68] for example, makes clear that this waiver provision is triggered only when the protected party testifies and his testimony concerns a personal transaction or communication between the adversary and the decedent. In *Wood*, the executor of an estate sought to prove that respondents were liable for having withdrawn and retained money from decedent's bank accounts. The defense was that the money had been returned personally to the decedent in his sickbed. The executor introduced bank statements and the testimony of a bank officer to prove the withdrawals. The executor himself testified that he had not found the proceeds during his search of the decedent's effects. Despite respondents' arguments that the withdrawal and return of the money were part of one overall transaction, the evidence introduced by the executor in his own behalf did not open the door to testimony by the respondents that they had returned the money to the decedent. The bank statements and testimony of the bank officer did not constitute testimony by the executor, and the executor himself did not testify to a transaction between the respondents and the decedent: he spoke only about his search of the decedent's property after death.

The narrow scope of the waiver clause is also illustrated by cases holding that it is only when testimony about a transaction with the decedent is given by a protected party in his own behalf that waiver will occur. Testimony elicited from the protected party by an adversary does not open the door.[69] Furthermore, if the protected party gives pretrial testimony about a transaction with the decedent, no waiver occurs even if the protected party is testifying in his own behalf. This is because CPLR 4519, including its waiver provision, applies only at trial.[70] Finally, opening the door with respect to one transaction with the decedent does not waive the bar of the statute with respect to other transactions.[71]

The third type of waiver is not explicitly mentioned in CPLR 4519. It occurs when a protected party examines an interested witness at trial concerning the witness' dealings with a decedent or mentally ill person. *Nay v. Curley*[72] held that once a portion of a transaction with a decedent has been elicited by an executor from an interested witness, that witness must be permitted to testify to the whole of the transaction. This equitable result flows from the common law "rule of completeness" and the principle that the Dead Man's Statute may be used only as a shield not a sword.[73] The waiver principle of *Nay v. Curley* also encompasses an executor's introduction at trial of his examination of the interested

---

68. 52 N.Y.2d 139, 436 N.Y.S.2d 850, 418 N.E.2d 365 (1981). See also In re Callister, 153 N.Y. 294, 307, 47 N.E. 268, 271 (1897)(executor's proof of a transaction between interested party and decedent through testimony of neutral witness did not constitute waiver).

69. Corning v. Walker, 100 N.Y. 547, 3 N.E. 290 (1885). See, e.g., Sklaire v. Estate of Turner, 12 A.D.2d 386, 388, 212 N.Y.S.2d 389, 391–92 (3d Dep't 1961)(executor's testimony on cross-examination concerning physician's treatment of decedent did not "open the door" to testimony by physician in latter's action for services rendered to decedent).

70. In re Van Volkenburgh, 254 N.Y. 139, 172 N.E. 269 (1930).

71. Martin v. Hillen, 142 N.Y. 140, 36 N.E. 803 (1894).

72. 113 N.Y. 575, 21 N.E. 698 (1889).

73. In re Estate of Wood, 52 N.Y.2d 139, 145, 436 N.Y.S.2d 850, 852, 418 N.E.2d 365, 367 (1981); Estate of Dunbar, 139 Misc.2d 955, 956, 529 N.Y.S.2d 452, 452–53 (Surr. Ct.Bronx Co.1988).

party at a pretrial deposition concerning that party's transaction with the decedent.[74] In such circumstances, the executor "forced" the interested party to testify at the deposition to otherwise forbidden matter. Fairness dictates that when such forced testimony is offered at trial, the interested party should be given an opportunity to explain.[75]

The fourth ground for waiver occurs, by the terms of CPLR 4519, when "the testimony of the mentally ill person or deceased person is given in evidence." The otherwise incompetent party is then free to testify to the same transaction or communication that forms the subject matter of the decedent's or mentally ill person's testimony. The term "testimony" has been narrowly interpreted to mean a "sworn statement * * * made in a judicial proceeding, where there was opportunity for an opposing party to cross-examine."[76] Testimony of the decedent admitted pursuant to the former testimony hearsay exception[77] or the rules governing pretrial depositions[78] undoubtedly triggers the waiver. Introduction of documents written by the decedent or nontestimonial declarations of the decedent, on the other hand, do not open the door to permit trial testimony by an otherwise incompetent witness concerning the relevant transaction.[79]

Older authorities have assumed that the fourth basis for waiver is dependent upon introduction of the decedent's testimony by a member of the protected class.[80] Recent decisions have held, however, that the testimony of the decedent given at a pretrial deposition may be introduced by an interested party at the subsequent trial with the same effect, i.e., freeing the interested witness to testify at trial to the same matters described by the decedent.[81] These courts have concluded that CPLR 4519 contains no explicit limitation as to whose introduction of the decedent's testimony will lift the bar of incompetency. The statutory ambiguity, said the courts, should be resolved in favor of the judicial search for truth—letting the jury hear more, not less, relevant evidence.

g. Inapplicability Before Trial

By its terms, CPLR 4519 is operative only "upon the trial of an action or the hearing upon the merits of a special proceeding." Since

---

74. In re Radus, 140 A.D.2d 348, 349, 527 N.Y.S.2d 840, 841 (2d Dep't 1988).

75. See In re Estate of Wood, 52 N.Y.2d 139, 145, 436 N.Y.S.2d 850, 852, 418 N.E.2d 365, 367 (1981)(Nay v. Curley applies where interested party has been "forced" to testify). Sternberg v. Sternberg, 81 A.D.2d 1010, 440 N.Y.S.2d 96 (4th Dep't 1981), however, holds that no waiver occurs where the executor offers prior testimony given by the interested party in some unrelated proceeding in which the estate was not a party. In such circumstances the executor did not "force" the interested party to testify about a transaction with the decedent.

76. Farmers' Loan and Trust Co. v. Wagstaff, 194 App.Div. 757, 762, 185 N.Y.S. 812, 816 (2d Dep't 1921).

77. See CPLR 4517.

78. CPLR 3117(a)(3)(i).

79. In re Callister, 153 N.Y. 294, 306–08, 47 N.E. 268, 271–72 (1897); Farmers' Loan and Trust Co. v. Wagstaff, 194 App. Div. 757, 762, 185 N.Y.S. 812, 816 (2d Dep't 1921). But see In re Boesenberg's Estate, 265 App.Div. 484, 39 N.Y.S.2d 418 (1st Dep't 1943)(letter written by decedent).

80. Potts v. Mayer, 86 N.Y. 302, 305–06 (1881)(dicta); Miller v. Adkins, 9 Hun. 9 (N.Y.1876)(holding).

81. Tepper v. Tannenbaum, 65 A.D.2d 359, 363, 411 N.Y.S.2d 588, 591 (1st Dep't 1978), rehearing denied, 67 A.D.2d 882, 413 N.Y.S.2d 1019 (1979), later appeal, 83 A.D.2d 541, 441 N.Y.S.2d 470 (1981); Ward v. Kovacs, 55 A.D.2d 391, 390 N.Y.S.2d 931 (2d Dep't 1977).

the statute applies only during the trial phase of an action or special proceeding, interested witnesses may freely testify during the pretrial phase concerning their transactions or communications with the decedent or mentally ill person. No valid objection may be raised at that point.[82] A corollary to the inapplicability of CPLR 4519 in pretrial proceedings is that a protected party's own testimony or elicitation of testimony from interested witnesses during such proceedings does not, standing alone, serve as a waiver of the statute in the subsequent trial or hearing.[83]

Library References:

West's Key No. Digests, Witnesses ⟬125–183½.

§ 601.3 Federal

Witness competency in federal courts is governed, in general, by Rule 601 of the Federal Rules of Evidence, which states as follows:

> Every person is competent to be a witness except as otherwise provided in these rules. However, in civil actions and proceedings, with respect to an element of a claim or defense as to which State law supplies the rule of decision, the competency of a witness shall be determined in accordance with State law.

The second sentence of the rule incorporates state law with respect to issues of witness competency in diversity cases. For example, the New York "Dead Man's Statute"[1] is operative in diversity actions brought in federal district courts in New York.[2]

In actions based on federal law, however, neither state Dead Man's Statutes nor any other interest-based disqualifications apply.[3] Indeed,

---

82. Phillips v. Joseph Kantor and Co., 31 N.Y.2d 307, 313, 338 N.Y.S.2d 882, 887, 291 N.E.2d 129, 132 (1972). Such preliminary testimony might be given, for example, during a pretrial deposition or in one of the various inquisitorial proceedings under the Surrogate's Court Procedure Act. See, e.g., N.Y.Surr.Ct.Proc.Act § 2211 (examination of fiduciary); N.Y.Surr.Ct.Proc.Act §§ 2103–2104 (examination of person in possession of estate property). If the preliminary matter "metamorphoses" into a trial or hearing, however, the statute becomes fully operative. In re Estate of Detweiler, 121 Misc.2d 453, 467 N.Y.S.2d 766 (Surr.Ct.Cattaraugus Co.1983). Because CPLR 4519 applies only at trial, testimony or affidavits concerning transactions with the decedent by witnesses who would be incompetent at trial may be used to defeat a motion for summary judgment. Phillips v. Joseph Kantor and Co., supra; Tancredi v. Mannino, 75 A.D.2d 579, 426 N.Y.S.2d 577 (2d Dep't 1980).

83. In re Van Volkenburgh, 254 N.Y. 139, 143–44, 172 N.E. 269, 270 (1930); De Laurent v. Townsend, 243 N.Y. 130, 133–34, 152 N.E. 699, 700 (1926).

§ 601.3

1. CPLR 4519. See § 601.2 supra.

2. See, e.g., Wagner v. Tucker, 517 F.Supp. 1248, 1250 (S.D.N.Y.1981). But see Brand v. Brand, 811 F.2d 74, 79–80 (2d Cir.1987)(in bench trial, district judge did not commit reversible error in allowing testimony by witness who was incompetent under New York Dead Man's Statute; judge gave little or no weight to the witness' testimony).

Aside from the Dead Man's Statute, there are few rules of incompetency under New York law that are likely to be relevant in federal diversity actions. One other potential situation is that of a witness who has undergone hypnosis for the purpose of reviving her memory. Under New York law, such witness is incompetent to testify to her posthypnotic recollections. See § 601.1, at notes 60–67, supra.

3. Advisory Committee's Note, Fed. R.Evid. 601 ("The Dead Man's Acts are surviving traces of the common law disqualification of parties and interested persons. They exist in variety too great to convey

§ 601.3 WITNESSES Ch. 6

the Advisory Committee's Note describes Rule 601 as a "ground-clearing" that "eliminates all grounds of incompetency not specifically recognized in the succeeding rules of this Article [Article VI]."[4] The only explicit bases for a finding of incompetency, therefore, would appear to be lack of personal knowledge (Fed.R.Evid. 602),[5] refusal to take an oath (Fed.R.Evid. 603),[6] and status as a judge or juror (Fed.R.Evid. 605 and 606).[7] Neither mental nor moral qualifications for testifying are specified in Rule 601. The Advisory Committee's Note states that any mental infirmities of the witness bear only on weight and credibility, and the moral obligation of truth-telling can be regulated in connection with administration of the oath.[8]

Despite the text of Rule 601 and the Advisory Committee's analysis, federal courts have been willing to entertain challenges to the competency of witnesses on such grounds as mental infirmity,[9] youth,[10] and drug

---

conviction of their wisdom and effectiveness. These rules contain no provision of this kind. * * *"). See also Donohoe v. Consolidated Operating Production Corp., 736 F.Supp. 845, 860 (N.D.Ill.1990), aff'd in part, vacated in part, 982 F.2d 1130 (7th Cir.1992), on remand, 833 F.Supp. 719 (N.D.Ill.1993), aff'd, 30 F.3d 907 (7th Cir. 1994)(in action involving mixture of state and federal claims, court refused to apply state Dead Man's Statute).

4. Advisory Committee's Note, Fed. R.Evid. 601 ("This general ground-clearing eliminates all grounds of incompetency not specifically recognized in the succeeding rules of this Article. Included among the grounds thus abolished are religious belief, conviction of crime, and connection with the litigation as a party or interested person or spouse of a party or interested person."). At minimum, Rule 601 creates a presumption that all witnesses are competent to testify. See United States v. Blankenship, 923 F.2d 1110, 1116 (5th Cir.), cert. denied, 500 U.S. 954, 111 S.Ct. 2262, 114 L.Ed.2d 714 (1991).

5. See § 602.2 infra.

6. See § 603.2 infra.

7. See §§ 605.2 and 606.2 infra.

8. Advisory Committee's Note, Fed. R.Evid. 601:

No mental or moral qualifications for testifying as a witness are specified. Standards of mental capacity have proved elusive in actual application. A leading commentator observes that few witnesses are disqualified on that ground. Weihofen, Testimonial Competence and Credibility, 34 Geo.Wash.L.Rev. 53 (1965). Discretion is regularly exercised in favor of allowing the testimony. A witness wholly without capacity is difficult to imagine. The question is one particularly suited to the jury as one of weight and credibility, subject to judicial authority to review the sufficiency of the evidence. 2 Wigmore §§ 501, 509. Standards of moral qualification in practice consist essentially of evaluating a person's truthfulness in terms of his own answers about it. Their principal utility is in affording an opportunity on voir dire examination to impress upon the witness his moral duty. This result may, however, be accomplished more directly, and without haggling in terms of legal standards, by the manner of administering the oath or affirmation under Rule 603.

9. See, e.g., United States v. Devin, 918 F.2d 280, 291–92 (1st Cir.1990) (district court conducted hearing into potential effect of witness' 14–year-old psychiatric episode and concluded that witness was competent to testify).

It has been said, however, that "the Federal Rules of Evidence strongly disfavor barring witnesses on competency grounds due to mental incapacity." United States v. Phibbs, 999 F.2d 1053, 1068 (6th Cir. 1993), cert. denied, ___ U.S. ___, 114 S.Ct. 1070, 127 L.Ed.2d 389 (1994). The court in United States v. Odom, 736 F.2d 104, 111 (4th Cir.1984), articulated the following guidelines with respect to mental incapacity:

Neither feeble-mindedness nor insanity renders a witness incompetent or disqualified. * * * The only grounds for disqualifying a party as a witness under Rule 601 are that the witness "does not have knowledge of the matters about which he is to testify, that he does not have the capacity to recall, or that he does not understand the duty to testify truthfully." [United States v. Lightly, 677 F.2d 1027, 1028 (4th Cir.1982)]. * * * Whether the witness has such competency is a matter for determination by

---

10. See note 10 on page 353.

usage.[11] Courts occasionally conduct hearings into such matters,[12] but there is no requirement that they do so.[13]

The authority for judicial inquiry into witness competency has been posited principally on the notion that evidence by persons who lack sufficient testimonial capacity may be excluded as an exercise of discretion pursuant to Rule 403.[14] In practice, however, the courts seem disinclined to exercise any such exclusionary authority. The trend is simply to permit evidence of mental infirmities for their impeachment value.[15] A bizarre case in this regard arose in the Second Circuit, where

the trial judge after such examination as he deems appropriate and his exercise of discretion in this regard is to be reversed only for clear error.

10. See, e.g., United States v. Spotted War Bonnet, 882 F.2d 1360, 1363 (8th Cir. 1989), cert. granted and judgment vacated on other grounds, 497 U.S. 1021, 110 S.Ct. 3267, 111 L.Ed.2d 777 (1990), on remand, 933 F.2d 1471 (8th Cir.1991), cert. denied, 502 U.S. 1101, 112 S.Ct. 1187, 117 L.Ed.2d 429 (1992) ("It is appropriate for the court to conduct a preliminary voir dire to determine the competency of young children. * * * Our decisions, however, do not require the court to conduct such a determination."). Cf. United States v. Thai, 29 F.3d 785, 809 (2d Cir.1994)(child witness was found competent where she "struck [judge] as a very intelligent child, a bright child who understood the process and knew what this was about").

11. See, e.g., United States v. Hyson, 721 F.2d 856, 863–64 (1st Cir.1983) (district court struck testimony of witness shown by medical examinations to have been on drugs at time of testimony, but permitted witness to be recalled at later date); United States v. Roach, 590 F.2d 181, 185–86 (5th Cir.1979)(at conclusion of voir dire of witness, district court ruled that witness who was emotionally disturbed and used drugs was competent to testify). In United States v. Hickey, 917 F.2d 901, 904 (6th Cir.1990), the court acknowledged that a witness' addiction to drugs might have impaired his perceptive abilities to such an extent as to deprive him of personal knowledge (Fed. R.Evid. 602) but stressed that the personal knowledge requirement has a "low threshold." See § 602.2 infra.

12. See cases cited in notes 9–11 supra.

13. United States v. Phibbs, 999 F.2d 1053, 1069 (6th Cir.1993), cert. denied, ___ U.S. ___, 114 S.Ct. 1070, 127 L.Ed.2d 389 (1994)(district court was not required to conduct special examination into competency of witness with psychiatric problems); United States v. Roach, 590 F.2d 181, 186 (5th Cir.1979)("there seems no longer to be any occasion for judicially-ordered psychiatric examinations or competency hearings of witnesses—none, at least, on the theory that a preliminary determination of competency must be made by the district court"); United States v. Odom, 736 F.2d 104, 111 (4th Cir.1984)("[A] district judge has great latitude in the procedure he may follow in determining the competency of a witness to testify. Neither the authorities nor the Rules require an in camera hearing"). But see United States v. Gutman, 725 F.2d 417, 420 (7th Cir.), cert. denied, 469 U.S. 880, 105 S.Ct. 244, 83 L.Ed.2d 183 (1984)("a district judge has the power, and in an appropriate case the duty, to hold a hearing to determine whether a witness should not be allowed to testify because insanity has made him incapable of testifying in a competent fashion").

14. Fed.R.Evid. 403 (relevant evidence may be excluded if probative value is substantially outweighed by danger of undue prejudice, confusion of issues, misleading jury, or by considerations of undue delay, waste of time or needless presentation of cumulative evidence). See United States v. Ramirez, 871 F.2d 582, 584 (6th Cir.), cert. denied, 493 U.S. 841, 110 S.Ct. 127, 107 L.Ed.2d 88 (1989):

The authority of the court to control the admissibility of the testimony of persons so impaired in some manner that they cannot give meaningful testimony is to be found outside of Rule 601. For example, the judge always has the authority under Rule 403 to balance the probative value of testimony against its prejudicial effect. Similarly, under Rule 603, the inability of a witness to take or comprehend an oath or affirmation will allow the judge to exclude that person's testimony. An argument can also be constructed that a person might be impaired to the point that he would not be able to satisfy the "personal knowledge" requirement of Rule 602.

15. See, e.g., United States v. Phibbs, 999 F.2d 1053, 1070 (6th Cir.1993), cert. denied, ___ U.S. ___, 114 S.Ct. 1070, 127 L.Ed.2d 389 (1994)(court, which declined to

a witness who consumed opium while on the stand was found to be a competent witness whose drug consumption was a matter properly left to the jury on the issue of credibility.[16]

With respect to testimony by children in criminal cases, Congress adopted statutory rules in 1990 providing that children are presumptively competent witnesses and that "competency examinations" of children may be conducted only when "compelling reasons exist."[17]

conduct preliminary examination into competency of witness with mental infirmities, permitted adversary "to use the psychiatric records [of the witnesses], as well as other indicia of their mental capacity, to vigorously attack their credibility. * * * As long as a witness appreciates his duty to tell the truth, and is minimally capable of observing, recalling, and communicating events, his testimony should come in for whatever it is worth."); United States v. Peyro, 786 F.2d 826, 831 (8th Cir.1986)(trial court conducted voir dire of "emotionally unbalanced" witness with substantial memory problems and concluded that while witness could not recall detail, she had "broad, general recollection"; court did not err in refusing to strike the testimony "for [her] recall and emotional problems were laid bare for the jury's consideration"). See also United States v. Bedonie, 913 F.2d 782, 799–801 (10th Cir.1990), cert. denied, 501 U.S. 1253, 111 S.Ct. 2895, 115 L.Ed.2d 1059 (1991)(rejection of argument that witness, because of numerous inconsistent statements, was so untrustworthy as to be wholly incompetent to testify; jury is capable of making credibility determination). See generally § 607.7 infra.

16. United States v. Van Meerbeke, 548 F.2d 415, 418 n.3 (2d Cir.1976), cert. denied, 430 U.S. 974, 97 S.Ct. 1663, 52 L.Ed.2d 368 (1977). The district judge refused to grant a motion for a mistrial after the witness in question had completed his second day of testimony. In response to defense counsel's argument that the witness was incompetent, the trial judge ruled that the witness had been coherent and that the question of credibility that was raised by drug consumption was for the jury. The Court of Appeals agreed. The appellate court, however, criticized the trial judge, who had seen the witness ingest the opium, for permitting such a breach of courtroom decorum. The Court of Appeals suggested that a recess could have been called, followed by "suspension of testimony for the day, a medical examination to determine the witness's capacity to continue with his testimony, and a stern warning to the witness outside the jury's hearing, that such behavior would not be tolerated." Id. at 418.

17. 18 U.S.C.A. § 3509(c):

(c) **Competency examinations.**—

(1) **Effect on federal rules of evidence.**—Nothing in this subdivision shall be construed to abrogate rule 601 of the Federal Rules of Evidence.

(2) **Presumption.**—A child is presumed to be competent.

(3) **Requirement of written motion.**—A competency examination regarding a child witness may be conducted by the court only upon written motion and offer of proof of incompetency by a party.

(4) **Requirement of compelling reasons.**—A competency examination regarding a child may be conducted only if the court determines, on the record, that compelling reasons exist. A child's age alone is not a compelling reason.

(5) **Persons permitted to be present.**—The only persons who may be permitted to be present at a competency examination are—

(A) the judge;

(B) the attorney for the government;

(C) the attorney for the defendant;

(D) a court reporter; and

(E) persons whose presence, in the opinion of the court, is necessary to the welfare and well-being of the child, including the child's attorney, guardian ad litem, or adult attendant.

(6) **Not before jury.**—A competency examination regarding a child witness shall be conducted out of the sight and hearing of a jury.

(7) **Direct examination of child.**—Examination of a child related to competency shall normally be conducted by the court on the basis of questions submitted by the attorney for the Government and the attorney for the defendant including a party acting as an attorney pro se. The court may permit an attorney but not a party

Unlike the approach taken in New York,[18] a witness who has undergone hypnosis is not necessarily incompetent to testify to posthypnotic memory in federal proceedings.[19] The Second Circuit has adopted a case-by-case approach that focuses on the "totality of the circumstances" in determining the reliability of the testimony.[20]

Library References:

West's Key No. Digests, Witnesses ⌦35–223.

602 Personal Knowledge

§ 602.1 New York

The requirement that a witness have personal knowledge of the facts to which she testifies is fundamental in the law of evidence.[1] Wigmore defined personal knowledge as "an impression derived from the exercise of [the witness'] own senses, not from the reports of others."[2]

Judicial discourse on this topic is thin in New York, but a few decisions illustrate the point. In one case, proof that the plaintiff had shipped certain goods was held to be wholly inadequate because the only witness who testified to the facts surrounding the shipments was shown

acting as an attorney pro se to examine a child directly on competency if the court is satisfied that the child will not suffer emotional trauma as a result of the examination.

(8) Appropriate questions.—The questions asked at the competency examination of a child shall be appropriate to the age and developmental level of the child, shall not be related to the issues at trial, and shall focus on determining the child's ability to understand and answer simple questions.

(9) Psychological and psychiatric examinations.—Psychological and psychiatric examinations to assess the competency of a child witness shall not be ordered without a showing of compelling need.

A child is defined as a person under the age of eighteen. Id. § 3509(a)(2). Subdivision (b)(1) of the same statute permits testimony of a child victim by means of closed circuit television "if the child is unable to testify in open court in the presence of the defendant" for such reasons as fear or emotional trauma. Additionally, subdivision (e) authorizes closure of the courtroom when any child witness testifies, if open-court testimony "would cause substantial psychological harm to the child or would result in the child's inability to effectively communicate."

18. See § 601.1, at notes 60–69, supra.

19. See, e.g., United States v. Kimberlin, 805 F.2d 210, 219 (7th Cir.1986), cert. denied, 483 U.S. 1023, 107 S.Ct. 3270, 97 L.Ed.2d 768 (1987)(court declined to adopt any per se rules, opting instead to scrutinize circumstances to assess reliability and impact of posthypnotic memory); Sprynczynatyk v. General Motors Corp., 771 F.2d 1112, 1123 (8th Cir.1985), cert. denied, 475 U.S. 1046, 106 S.Ct. 1263, 89 L.Ed.2d 572 (1986)(use of procedural safeguards should be examined by trial court to ascertain whether posthypnotic memory is sufficiently reliable and probative value outweighs prejudicial effect). See also United States v. Awkard, 597 F.2d 667, 669 (9th Cir.), cert. denied, 444 U.S. 885, 100 S.Ct. 179, 62 L.Ed.2d 116 (1979)(use of hypnosis to refresh recollection does not make witness incompetent; it merely presents a question of credibility). But see text at notes 1–2 supra (state rules of competency apply to issues governed by state law).

20. Borawick v. Shay, 68 F.3d 597 (2d Cir.1995).

§ 602.1

1. See McCormick § 10. See, e.g., People v. Di Loretto, 150 A.D.2d 920, 922, 541 N.Y.S.2d 260, 261 (3d Dep't), appeal denied, 74 N.Y.2d 739, 545 N.Y.S.2d 113, 543 N.E.2d 756 (1989)(witnesses who had "firsthand knowledge" of a conversation could testify thereto after refreshing their recollection by referring to a transcript).

2. 2 Wigmore § 657, at 889.

§ 602.1 WITNESSES Ch. 6

on cross-examination to have lacked personal knowledge of the matter.[3] The witness, therefore, was "not competent," and the testimony should have been stricken on defendant's motion.[4] In another case of similar import, a trial judge was held to have committed error in allowing a witness to testify that certain horses had been moved from his property where it was shown that he was relying on information imparted to him by his daughter rather than on his own observations.[5] Conversely, other cases indicate that if a witness testifies that she had the opportunity to see and actually did see a particular event, the testimony should be admitted.[6] Any shortcomings in the witness' opportunity to observe should be a matter for the jury to consider in assessing credibility.[7]

An expert witness, of course, is not confined to opinions based on personal knowledge.[8] Also to be distinguished is the witness who testifies to an out-of-court statement that is not barred by the hearsay rule. In such case the witness must have actually heard what was said by the out-of-declarant but she need not have personal knowledge of the subject matter of the out-of-court statement.[9]

§ 602.2 Federal

Rule 602 of the Federal Rules of Evidence carries forward the common law rule that a witness may testify only to facts of which she has personal knowledge:

> A witness may not testify to a matter unless evidence is introduced sufficient to support a finding that the witness has

---

3. Turkel v. American Ry. Express Co., 188 N.Y.S. 207 (Sup.Ct.App.T., 1st Dep't 1921).

4. Id. at 208.

5. Hallenbeck v. Vogt, 9 A.D.2d 836, 192 N.Y.S.2d 945 (3d Dep't 1959). See also Overseas Trust Bank v. Poon, 181 A.D.2d 762, 763, 581 N.Y.S.2d 92, 93 (2d Dep't 1992)(trial court properly excluded testimony of defendant's husband concerning wife's overseas travels during certain time period where it was "clear" that husband lacked personal knowledge).

6. See Senecal v. Drollette, 304 N.Y. 446, 448–49, 108 N.E.2d 602, 603 (1952)(trial court should not have excluded 12-year-old witness from testifying to type of car that hit him where witness said that he "got a glance at it just before it hit him").

Section 602(a) of the Proposed New York Evidence Code summarizes the law as follows:

§ 602. Incompetencies [PROPOSED]

(a) Lack of personal knowledge. Except as otherwise provided by this chapter or other statute, a person may not testify to a matter unless evidence is introduced sufficient to support a finding that such person has personal knowledge of the matter. Evidence to prove personal knowledge may, but need not, consist of the witness's own testimony.

The proposed New York rule is virtually identical to Fed.R.Evid. 602. See § 602.2 infra.

7. Cf. People v. Regina, 19 N.Y.2d 65, 68–70, 277 N.Y.S.2d 683, 685–89, 224 N.E.2d 108, 109–12 (1966)(murder witness, who was riding in car with victim, testified that during five-second time period, he saw perpetrators pull alongside in their vehicle and fire two shots; court held that such testimony was not "incredible as a matter of law.")

8. See, e.g., People v. Keough, 276 N.Y. 141, 145, 11 N.E.2d 570, 572 (1937)(expert opinion may be based upon facts personally known by expert or upon facts in evidence that are made known to expert at trial); People v. Sugden, 35 N.Y.2d 453, 459, 363 N.Y.S.2d 923, 929, 323 N.E.2d 169, 173 (1974)(expert opinion may rely, in part, on hearsay if it "is of a kind accepted in the profession as reliable in forming a professional opinion"). See generally § 703.1 infra.

9. 2 Wigmore § 657. See also § 602.2 infra.

personal knowledge of the matter. Evidence to prove personal knowledge may, but need not, consist of the witness' own testimony. This rule is subject to the provisions of Rule 703, relating to opinion testimony by expert witnesses.[1]

A witness has the necessary knowledge if she "had an opportunity of personal observation and did get some impressions from this observation."[2] Whether a witness meets these qualifications is an issue of conditional relevancy,[3] i.e., the trial judge should permit the witness to testify if there is a sufficient basis for the fact-finder to conclude that the witness had an opportunity and did in fact perceive the matter about which she testifies.[4] If the requisite threshold is met, the credibility question is for the jury.[5] The witness' own testimony that she has the requisite knowledge can satisfy the foundation requirement.[6]

The witness need not be certain of her perceptions. The rule tolerates testimony in the form of "I think" or "I believe," provided the witness had an opportunity to observe and obtained some impressions from those observations.[7] Mere speculation or conjecture, however, is beyond the pale.[8]

If a witness asserts a fact at trial as though it were based on her own perception, when in fact the assertion is based on what someone else told her, the personal knowledge requirement obviously is not met.[9]

§ 602.2

1. The rule's cross-reference to Fed. R.Evid. 703 recognizes that expert opinions need not be based on the expert witness' personal knowledge. See § 703.2 infra.

2. United States v. Evans, 484 F.2d 1178, 1181 (2d Cir.1973), quoting 2 Wigmore § 658.

3. Fed.R.Evid. 104(b); § 104.2 supra.

4. Folio Impressions, Inc. v. Byer California, 937 F.2d 759, 764 (2d Cir. 1991)("test is whether a reasonable trier of fact could believe the witness had personal knowledge"); United States v. Owens–El, 889 F.2d 913, 915 (9th Cir.1989)("role of the judge is to determine 'not whether the witness did perceive the matter, but whether a jury or other trier of fact could reasonably believe that the witness perceived it' ").

5. United States v. Owens–El, 889 F.2d 913, 915 (9th Cir.1989).

6. Fed.R.Evid. 602. But see McCrary-El v. Shaw, 992 F.2d 809, 811 (8th Cir.1993)(witness' testimony that he saw an event was belied by evidence of his physical location and the presence of visual obstructions; trial judge did not abuse discretion in determining that "no reasonable person could conclude that [the witness] was able to see anything of relevance").

7. SEC v. Singer, 786 F.Supp. 1158, 1167–68 (S.D.N.Y.1992)(witness, who had long-standing business relationship with defendant, believed that it was "inconceivable" that he did not tell defendant about a particular fact; "[t]estimony can be admissible under Rule 602 even if the witness has only a broad general recollection of the subject matter"). See also United States v. Rodriguez, 968 F.2d 130, 143 (2d Cir.), cert. denied, ___ U.S. ___, 113 S.Ct. 139, 121 L.Ed.2d 92 (1992)("lack of certainty is a matter to be argued to the jury rather than a reason for excluding the evidence"); Folio Impressions, Inc. v. Byer California, 937 F.2d 759, 764 (2d Cir.1991)(statement of "belief," if based on general observation and knowledge, will suffice); M.B.A.F.B. Federal Credit Union v. Cumis Insurance Soc'y, Inc., 681 F.2d 930, 932–33 (4th Cir.1982)(equivocal nature of witness' knowledge went to weight of testimony).

8. Folio Impressions, Inc. v. Byer California, 937 F.2d 759, 764 (2d Cir.1991)(witness' belief may not properly be based on "conjecture or hearsay"). See also United States v. Kupau, 781 F.2d 740, 745 (9th Cir.), cert. denied, 479 U.S. 823, 107 S.Ct. 93, 93 L.Ed.2d 45 (1986) (witness could not speculate as to other person's unexpressed state of mind).

9. See, e.g., Kaczmarek v. Allied Chemical Corp., 836 F.2d 1055, 1060–61 (7th Cir.1987)(witness could not have had personal knowledge of safety practices used by his employer five years prior to witness'

On the other hand, if the witness testifies that another person said so-and-so, the personal knowledge rule is not necessarily violated. The witness will satisfy the personal knowledge rule if she actually heard what the other person said.[10] Whether the statement of the other person may be repeated by the witness turns on the rules governing hearsay.[11] The personal knowledge rule is relevant in this context, however, because the other person usually must be shown to have had personal knowledge of the subject matter asserted in the statement if it is offered to prove the truth of the assertion.[12]

Library References:

West's Key No. Digests, Witnesses ⊕37.

603 Oath or Affirmation

§ 603.1 New York

Subject to certain limited exceptions,[1] every witness who testifies in court must swear to or affirm the truth of her testimony. The oath (or its equivalent) serves two purposes: "to alert the witness to the moral duty to testify truthfully and to deter false testimony by establishing a legal basis for a perjury prosecution."[2] The witness' capacity to understand the nature of an oath relates to the witness' competency, which is determined by the court.[3]

employment; he was relying on the say-so of other people and "a witness cannot offer the contents of a hearsay statement as *his* personal knowledge") (emphasis in original).

10. See Advisory Committee's Note, Fed.R.Evid. 602 ("This rule does not govern the situation of a witness who testifies to a hearsay statement as such, if he has personal knowledge of the making of the statement").

11. See Chapter 8 infra.

12. The relationship between the personal knowledge rule and the hearsay rule has been described as follows: "[T]he personal knowledge requirement of Rule 602 applies at two levels: first, the witness who testifies must have personal knowledge of the making of the out-of-court statement, and second, the person who made the out-of-court statement must have had personal knowledge of the events on which he based his statement." United States v. Owens-El, 889 F.2d 913, 915 (9th Cir.1989). The Second Circuit explained the matter as follows:

> When A testifies that B told him of an event, A usually has personal knowledge only of B's report. It is B who has personal knowledge of the event. Thus, the hearsay rules require that the *declarant*, B in our example, have personal knowledge of the events recounted, not that the witness have such personal knowledge.

United States v. Stratton, 779 F.2d 820, 829 (2d Cir.1985)(emphasis in original), cert. denied, 476 U.S. 1162, 106 S.Ct. 2285, 90 L.Ed.2d 726 (1986).

The personal knowledge requirement is relaxed, however, when the out-of-court statement is that of an adverse party. See Advisory Committee's Note, Fed.R.Evid. 801(d)(2).

§ 603.1

1. See § 601.1, at notes 38–44 (children in criminal cases) and 52–53 (mental disease or defect in criminal cases), supra.

2. People v. Parks, 41 N.Y.2d 36, 45, 390 N.Y.S.2d 848, 856, 359 N.E.2d 358, 366 (1976).

3. See § 601.1, at notes 10–13, supra. See also Olshansky v. Prensky, 185 App. Div. 469, 470, 172 N.Y.S. 856, 857 (2d Dep't 1918)("[A] witness must be under pressure of some influence arising out of the solemnity of the occasion, beyond the ordinary obligation of truth telling. * * * Of this the witness must have some conception; and to determine whether he has or not is the function and duty of the court, and not of the jury.").

CPLR 2309(b) states that "[a]n oath or affirmation shall be administered in a form calculated to awaken the conscience and impress the mind of the person taking it in accordance with his religious or ethical beliefs."[4] The statute makes clear that an affirmation is the functional equivalent of an oath,[5] and courts have prohibited comments on a witness' preference for one or the other.[6] Obviously a witness need not believe in a Supreme Being in order to affirm that her testimony is truthful.[7]

Despite the importance of the oath, a party's failure to object to the receipt of unsworn testimony generally constitutes a waiver.[8] New York Courts, however, have taken the position that a determination cannot be based solely on unsworn testimony.[9]

Library References:

West's Key No. Digests, Witnesses ⊙—45, 227.

§ 603.2 Federal

In federal courts, Rule 603 of the Federal Rules of Evidence requires that all witnesses, without exception, testify under oath or pursuant to affirmation:

> Before testifying, every witness shall be required to declare that the witness will testify truthfully, by oath or affirmation administered in a form calculated to awaken the witness' conscience and impress the witness' mind with the duty to do so.

A witness has a right to affirm, rather than swear, even if she is a member of an organized religion.[1] With respect to formalities, the

---

4. Section 603(a) of the Proposed New York Evidence Code restates the general requirement that all testimony be sworn and incorporates the language of CPLR 2309(b):

> Except as otherwise provided in subdivision (b) of this section [exceptions in some proceedings, for children and persons with mental disease or defect] or other statute, every person shall be required before testifying to declare that such person will testify truthfully by oath or affirmation administered in a form calculated to awaken such person's conscience and impress such person's mind in accordance with such person's religious or ethical beliefs.

5. People v. Wood, 66 N.Y.2d 374, 378, 497 N.Y.S.2d 340, 342, 488 N.E.2d 86, 88 (1985).

6. Id.

7. N.Y.Const. art. I, § 3 ("no person shall be rendered incompetent to be a witness on account of his opinions on matters of religious belief").

8. Brown v. Ristich, 36 N.Y.2d 183, 189, 366 N.Y.S.2d 116, 122, 325 N.E.2d 533, 538 (1975); Razauckas v. New York Dugan Bros., Inc., 263 App.Div. 1002, 33 N.Y.S.2d 411 (2d Dep't), aff'd, 289 N.Y. 592, 43 N.E.2d 722 (1942); People v. Theodore Zaleski General Contractor, Inc., 46 Misc.2d 993, 261 N.Y.S.2d 325 (Schenectady Co.Ct.), aff'd, 16 N.Y.2d 733, 262 N.Y.S.2d 111, 209 N.E.2d 727 (1965).

9. Napiearlski v. Pickering, 278 App. Div. 456, 106 N.Y.S.2d 28 (4th Dep't 1951), motion to dismiss appeal denied, 303 N.Y. 905, 105 N.E.2d 492 (1952); Scherback v. Stern, 246 App.Div. 746, 283 N.Y.S. 804 (2d Dep't 1935); Ranofsky v. Frank, 208 App. Div. 213, 203 N.Y.S. 160 (1st Dep't 1924).

§ 603.2

1. United States v. Kalaydjian, 784 F.2d 53 (2d Cir.1986)(Muslim need not take oath on the Koran).

A witness who refuses to take an oath or to affirm on the ground that both acts are a form of swearing prohibited by the witness' religion, must be given an opportunity to make an alternative statement. Ferguson v. Commissioner of Internal Revenue, 921 F.2d 588 (5th Cir.1991)(abuse of discretion for district judge to refuse to consider wit-

§ 603.2 WITNESSES Ch. 6

Advisory Committee's Note to Rule 603 defines an affirmation as "simply a solemn undertaking to tell the truth; no special verbal formula is required." Courts have recognized the flexibility afforded by Rule 603,[2] especially in cases involving child witnesses.[3]

The failure of a party to object to unsworn testimony constitutes a waiver of the requirements of Rule 603.[4] Any question as to a witness' understanding of the duty to testify truthfully can be addressed by the court, upon request, by a voir dire outside the presence of the jury.[5]

Library References:

West's Key No. Digests, Witnesses ⊙═45, 227.

604 Interpreters

§ 604.1 New York

By facilitating communication, interpreters can help shore up the competency of a witness who might otherwise be disqualified. The use of interpreters in court proceedings is governed by statute. The Judiciary Law provides both for the appointment of official interpreters[1] and the temporary appointment of interpreters at the discretion of courts as the need arises.[2] New York courts have construed the Judiciary Law as providing judges with the discretion to appoint interpreters when necessary either for witnesses to be understood or for parties to understand

ness' alternative proposal, based on religious objection, to "declare" that the facts about to be given were accurate, correct and complete; on appeal, witness also indicated willingness to add sentence acknowledging that she was subject to penalty of perjury). See also Gordon v. State of Idaho, 778 F.2d 1397, 1400–01 (9th Cir.1985)(at pretrial deposition, "any statement indicating that the deponent is impressed with the duty to tell the truth and understands that he or she can be prosecuted for perjury for failure to do so satisfies the requirement for an oath or affirmation"; court also held that deponents need not raise their hands if doing so would "[impinge] on sincerely-held religious beliefs' ").

2. See, e.g., United States v. Salim, 855 F.2d 944, 952 (2d Cir.1988)(at deposition conducted in France, "French judge took pains to impress upon [the witness] the need to answer truthfully, and the witness promised that she would do so. That is essentially all that Rule 603 requires."). The Advisory Committee's Note to Rule 603 states: "The rule is designed to afford the flexibility required in dealing with religious adults, atheists, conscientious objectors, mental defectives, and children."

3. See, e.g., United States v. Thai, 29 F.3d 785, 811–12 (2d Cir.1994)(after asking child several questions to establish that he understood difference between truth and falsehood and the impropriety of lying, court obtained "promise" from witness that he would tell the truth); Spigarolo v. Meachum, 934 F.2d 19, 24 (2d Cir.1991)("When children testify, the trial court may fashion an oath or affirmation that is meaningful to the witness.").

4. United States v. Odom, 736 F.2d 104, 114–16 (4th Cir.1984)("[T]he swearing of a witness is waived by failure to raise the point during the witness' testimony, thus denying the trial court an opportunity to correct what has been characterized as an 'irregularity.' ").

5. See United States v. Kalaydjian, 784 F.2d 53, 55 (2d Cir.1986)(defendant waived right to assert, an appeal, that witness' affirmation was sham by failing to request trial court to determine if witness appreciated duty to testify truthfully). See also § 601.3, at note 8, supra. Competency hearings with respect to child witnesses are governed by 18 U.S.C.A. § 3509(c). See § 601.3, at note 17, supra.

§ 604.1

1. N.Y.Jud.Law §§ 106, 107, 386.

2. N.Y.Jud.Law § 387.

the proceedings.[3] This discretion has been held to include the appointment of interpreters for parties or witnesses with English language deficiencies,[4] physical and mental disabilities,[5] and hearing impairments.[6]

The right to obtain an interpreter, however, can be waived if the defendant fails to make a timely demonstration to the court of the need for an interpreter.[7] Moreover, no matter what type of disability necessitates the appointment of an interpreter, the interpreter must be judged competent by the court.[8]

3. Berthoumieux v. We Try Harder, Inc., 170 A.D.2d 248, 566 N.Y.S.2d 240 (1st Dep't 1991), held that the trial court properly appointed an interpreter for the plaintiff whose proficiency with the English language was so limited that the jury had trouble understanding him. Id. at 249, 566 N.Y.S.2d at 241. In People v. Johnny P., 112 Misc.2d 647, 445 N.Y.S.2d 1007 (N.Y.C.Crim.Ct.1981), the court held that criminal defendants have an absolute right to an interpreter when one is necessary to understand the proceeding. Id. at 650, 445 N.Y.S.2d at 1010.

4. People v. Ramos, 26 N.Y.2d 272, 274, 309 N.Y.S.2d 906, 908, 258 N.E.2d 197, 198 (1970)(criminal defendant who cannot understand English is entitled to appointment of an interpreter who speaks language that the defendant understands).

5. People v. Miller, 140 Misc.2d 247, 250, 530 N.Y.S.2d 490, 492 (Rochester City Ct.1988). See also Matter of Luz P., 189 A.D.2d 274, 277, 595 N.Y.S.2d 541, 543 (2d Dep't 1993)("deaf mute, similar to a witness unable to speak English, may testify through a person who can understand and communicate with the witness"). See § 601.1, at note 55, supra.

6. Section 390 of the Judiciary Law provides in relevant part:

> Whenever any deaf person is a party to a legal proceeding of any nature, or a witness therein, the court in all instances shall appoint a qualified interpreter who is certified by a recognized national or New York state credentialing authority as approved by the chief administrator of the courts to interpret the proceeding to, and the testimony of, such deaf person; provided, however, where compliance with this section would cause unreasonable delay in court proceedings, the court shall be authorized to temporarily appoint an interpreter who is otherwise qualified to interpret the proceedings to, and the testimony of, such deaf person until a certified interpreter is available. In any criminal action in a state-funded court, the court shall also appoint such an interpreter to interpret the proceedings to a deaf person who is the victim of the crime or may appoint such interpreter for the deaf members of the immediate family (parent or spouse) of a victim of the crime when specifically requested to do so by such victim or family member.

See also People v. Doe, 158 Misc.2d 863, 866–67, 602 N.Y.S.2d 507, 509 (N.Y.C.Crim.Ct.1993)(holding on due process grounds that hearing-impaired criminal defendant is entitled to appointment by court of sign language interpreter).

7. People v. Ramos, 26 N.Y.2d 272, 274, 309 N.Y.S.2d 906, 908, 258 N.E.2d 197, 198 (1970). Unless there is an obvious indication to the court that the defendant cannot understand English, or there is a specific request, the court has no obligation to appoint an interpreter. Id. at 275, 309 N.Y.S.2d at 908, 258 N.E.2d at 199. See, e.g., Catholic Guardian Society of Diocese of Brooklyn, Inc. v. Elba V., __ A.D. __, 628 N.Y.S.2d 796 (2d Dep't 1995); People v. Calizaire, 190 A.D.2d 857, 593 N.Y.S.2d 879 (2d Dep't 1993); People v. Ortiz, 198 A.D.2d 912, 604 N.Y.S.2d 462 (4th Dep't 1993); People v. Pineda, 160 A.D.2d 649, 559 N.Y.S.2d 266 (1st Dep't 1990). See also People v. Perez, 198 A.D.2d 446, 447, 604 N.Y.S.2d 152, 153 (2d Dep't 1993) appeal denied, 82 N.Y.2d 929, 610 N.Y.S.2d 181, 632 N.E.2d 491 (1994)(holding that criminal defendant may not challenge qualification of interpreter when defendant failed to make any complaint during trial).

8. People v. Catron, 143 A.D.2d 468, 468, 532 N.Y.S.2d 589, 590 (3d Dep't), appeal denied, 73 N.Y.2d 853, 537 N.Y.S.2d 500, 534 N.E.2d 338 (1988)("the determination that a particular interpreter is 'qualified' lies within the sound discretion of the trial court").

When a court makes a temporary appointment pursuant to § 387 of the Judiciary Law, an inquiry as to the qualifications of the interpreter must be made on the record. People v. Miller, 140 Misc.2d 247, 250, 530 N.Y.S.2d 490, 492 (N.Y.C.Crim.Ct. 1988). The focus of the inquiry should be on whether the interpreter can provide the witness or party with meaningful understanding of the proceeding and whether the interpreter can translate word for word

§ 604.1 WITNESSES Ch. 6

Library References:

West's Key No. Digests, Courts ⚖︎56; Criminal Law ⚖︎642; Trial ⚖︎22; Witnesses ⚖︎230.

§ 604.2 Federal

The authority to appoint interpreters in federal proceedings is contained in Rule 43(f) of the Federal Rules of Civil Procedure,[1] Rule 28 of the Federal Rules of Criminal Procedure[2] and, in proceedings instituted by the United States, the Federal Court Interpreters Act.[3] The determination as to whether an interpreter should be appointed either to facilitate a particular witness' testimony[4] or to aid a party's comprehension of the proceedings[5] ordinarily lies within the district court's discretion.[6] Rule 604 of the Federal Rules of Evidence provides that "[a]n

what a witness or party says. Id. When language deficiencies provide the basis for appointment of an interpreter, the court must not only ensure that the interpreter speaks the same language as the witness but also the same dialect. See Santana v. New York City Transit Authority, 132 Misc.2d 777, 505 N.Y.S.2d 775 (Sup.Ct. N.Y.Co.1986). Similarly, where the witness or party suffers from a mental or physical disability, the court must be satisfied that the interpreter is capable of understanding and conveying the communications of the handicapped witness or party. See People v. Webb, 157 Misc.2d 474, 476–77, 597 N.Y.S.2d 565, 567–68 (St.Lawrence Co.Ct. 1993); People v. Rodriguez, 145 Misc.2d 105, 109, 546 N.Y.S.2d 769, 772 (Sup.Ct. Queens Co.1989)

§ 604.2

1. Fed.R.Civ.P. 43(f) provides, in relevant part, that "[t]he court may appoint an interpreter of its own selection and may fix the interpreter's reasonable compensation."

2. Fed.R.Crim.P. 28 states, in relevant part, that "[t]he court may appoint an interpreter of its own selection and may fix the reasonable compensation for such interpreter."

3. 18 U.S.C.A. § 1827. Subdivision (d)(1) provides:

The presiding judicial officer, with the assistance of the Director of the Administrative Office of the United States Courts, shall utilize the services of the most available certified interpreter, or when no certified interpreter is reasonably available, as determined by the presiding judicial officer, the services of an otherwise qualified interpreter, in judicial proceedings instituted by the United States, if the presiding judicial officer determines on such officer's own motion or on the motion of a party that such party (including a defendant in a criminal case), or a witness who may present testimony in such judicial proceedings—

(A) speaks only or primarily a language other than the English language; or

(B) suffers from a hearing impairment (whether or not suffering also from a speech impairment)

so as to inhibit such party's comprehension of the proceedings or communication with counsel or the presiding judicial officer, or so as to inhibit such witness' comprehension of questions and the presentation of such testimony.

4. See, e.g., United States v. Ball, 988 F.2d 7, 9 (5th Cir.1993)(no abuse of discretion to appoint government witness' wife as interpreter where witness was deaf and severely speech-impaired); United States v. Frank, 494 F.2d 145, 157–58 (2d Cir.), cert. denied, 419 U.S. 828, 95 S.Ct. 48, 42 L.Ed.2d 52 (1974)(no abuse of discretion to appoint interpreter for partially bilingual government witness during cross-examination despite fact that testimony on direct was given in English); Suarez v. United States, 309 F.2d 709, 712 (5th Cir.1962)(no abuse of discretion to refuse appointment of interpreter for defendant-witness who had sufficient command of English language).

5. See, e.g., United States v. Rodriguez, 424 F.2d 205, 206 (4th Cir.1970) (no abuse of discretion to refuse appointment of interpreter to assist criminal defendant at second trial where interpreter had been appointed but was not used at first trial, defendant indicated his understanding of all that transpired at first trial, and defendant's attorney advised court that he had no difficulty communicating with defendant without interpreter).

6. If a criminal defendant does not speak or understand English, the appointment of a translator or interpreter may be constitutionally mandated. See, e.g., United States ex rel. Negron v. State of New

362

interpreter is subject to the provisions of [the Federal Rules] relating to qualification as an expert and the administration of an oath or affirmation to make a true translation."[7]

Library References:

West's Key No. Digests, Courts ⚖56; Criminal Law ⚖642; Federal Civil Procedure ⚖1951; Witnesses ⚖230.

605 Judge's Competency as Witness

§ 605.1 New York

It is well settled in New York that a judge is incompetent to testify in any trial over which she presides.[1] The roles of judge and witness in the same case are simply inconsistent, and the matter is rife with the potential for prejudice to the parties.[2] A judge may, however, testify as a witness to events that she observed while presiding in a prior proceeding.[3] In *Estate of Sheen*,[4] for example, a judge who presided over pretrial

York, 434 F.2d 386 (2d Cir.1970). But see United States v. Bennett, 848 F.2d 1134, 1141 (11th Cir.1988)(court's refusal to appoint multiple interpreters, rather than one interpreter, in multi-defendant criminal case was matter of discretion that did not violate Court Interpreters Act or sixth amendment).

7. See, e.g., United States v. Salim, 855 F.2d 944, 952–53 (2d Cir.1988) (certified experts under French law who translated statements of witnesses made to French judge "represented to the French Judge on the record that they were making verbatim translations, thereby satisfying Fed.R.Evid. 604").

§ 605.1

1. People v. Dohring, 59 N.Y. 374, 378 (1874)("where the judge, who is called to the witness box, is actually trying the cause, and his continuance in action as judge is necessary to the seemly and proper trial of the cause, then he may not become a witness; it is error so to do, and if objection be made, and exception taken, it is fatal error"). People ex rel. Singer v. Rogers, 254 App.Div. 865, 866, 4 N.Y.S.2d 905, 907 (2d Dep't 1938), appeal denied, 278 N.Y. 741, 16 N.E.2d 805 (1938); People v. McDermott, 180 Misc. 247, 248, 40 N.Y.S.2d 456, 457 (Sup.Ct.Rockland Co.1943).

The Proposed New York Evidence Code would codify this rule in § 605, as follows: "The testimony of a judge shall not be admissible at a trial, proceeding, or hearing at which the judge is presiding. No objection need be made in order to preserve the point." The proposal to eliminate the need for an objection, which is based on Fed. R.Evid. 605, is "so that a party faced with the testimony of the judge need not be compromised in a belief that the judge would feel that his or her integrity had been attacked by such an objection, and thus be prejudiced against the objecting party for the balance of the trial." Comment, Proposed N.Y.Evid.Code § 605.

2. Morss v. Morss, 11 Barb. (N.Y.) 510, 511 (1851)("The two characters are inconsistent with each other and their being united in one person is incompatible with the fair and safe administration of justice"). See also Advisory Committee's Note, Fed. R.Evid. 605, quoted in § 605.2, at note 1, infra.

3. See, e.g., People v. Carpus, 2 A.D.2d 653, 152 N.Y.S.2d 27 (4th Dep't 1956)(sentencing judge is competent to testify as witness at hearing for post-conviction relief).

4. 145 Misc.2d 920, 548 N.Y.S.2d 618 (Surr.Ct.Bronx Co.1989). The Sheen court summarized the law as follows:

> The common law in New York has evolved to allow a judge to testify as a witness to matters which he observed while performing his judicial function in the same way that any other citizen who might have been present and observed the same events would be competent to testify. In other words, a judge is competent, in a subsequent proceeding over which he is not presiding, to testify as a witness to events which transpired before him in a prior proceeding provided that the information sought to be elicited does not involve findings of fact or conclusions of law made solely as a result of his judicial status.

Id. at 925, 548 N.Y.S.2d at 622.

§ 605.1   WITNESSES   Ch. 6

settlement negotiations was held competent to testify about the contents of those negotiations in a subsequent proceeding to set aside the settlement.

The rule that prohibits a judge from testifying at the trial over which she is presiding must be distinguished from the doctrine of judicial notice, discussed in Chapter 2 *supra*. When matters of common knowledge are not subject to reasonable dispute, the court may take judicial notice and rule from the bench that such facts have been established.

Library References:

West's Key No. Digests, Witnesses ⟲68, 69.

§ 605.2 Federal

Rule 605 of the Federal Rules of Evidence creates a blanket rule of incompetency with respect to testimony by judges in cases over which they are presiding: "The judge presiding at the trial may not testify in that trial as a witness. No objection need be made in order to preserve the point."[1] A party is freed of the necessity of objecting to testimony by a judge in order to avoid the prejudice that might result to her case from the making of an objection.[2]

The judge's incompetency as a witness extends as well to the judge's law clerks.[3] Furthermore, a judge's comments from the bench may be deemed to violate the rule even though the judge has not taken the witness stand.[4]

---

§ 605.2

1. The blanket approach of Rule 605 rejects distinctions that might otherwise be attempted between testimony by judges as to "material" matters (thus requiring disqualification) and "formal" or "inconsequential" matters (thus allowing the judge to testify in her discretion). See, e.g., 6 Wigmore § 1909.

The reasons for the blanket rule of incompetency are contained in the Advisory Committee's Note:

> The solution here presented is a broad rule of incompetency, rather than such alternatives as incompetency only as to material matters, leaving the matter to the discretion of the judge, or recognizing no incompetency. The choice is the result of inability to evolve satisfactory answers to questions which arise when the judge abandons the bench for the witness stand. Who rules on objections? Who compels him to answer? Can he rule impartially on the weight and admissibility of his own testimony? Can he be impeached or cross-examined effectively? Can he, in a jury trial, avoid conferring his seal of approval on one side in the eyes of the jury? Can he, in a bench trial, avoid an involvement destructive of

impartiality? The rule of general incompetency has substantial support. * * *

See also Brown v. Lynaugh, 843 F.2d 849, 850 (5th Cir.1988)("It is difficult to see how the neutral role of the court could be more compromised, or more blurred with the prosecutor's role, than when the judge serves as a witness for the state").

2. See Advisory Committee's Note, Fed. R.Evid. 605:

> The rule provides an "automatic" objection. To require an actual objection would confront the opponent with a choice between not objecting, with the result of allowing the testimony, and objecting, with the probable result of excluding the testimony but at the price of continuing the trial before a judge likely to feel that his integrity had been attacked by the objector.

3. Kennedy v. Great Atlantic & Pacific Tea Co., 551 F.2d 593, 598–99 (5th Cir. 1977). See also Price Brothers Co. v. Philadelphia Gear Corp., 629 F.2d 444 (6th Cir. 1980), cert. denied, 454 U.S. 1099, 102 S.Ct. 674, 70 L.Ed.2d 641 (1981)(in bench trial, judge should not send law clerk to gather evidence outside the record).

4. See, e.g., United States v. Pritchett, 699 F.2d 317, 318–20 (6th Cir.1983)(judge's

Ch. 6   JUROR'S COMPETENCY AS WITNESS   § 606.1

Testimony by a judge who is no longer presiding over the case, although presenting the danger of an appearance of partiality, has been permitted.[5]

Library References:

West's Key No. Digests, Witnesses ⚖︎68, 69.

606   Juror's Competency as Witness

§ 606.1   New York

An early New York case states that jurors are competent to testify to facts in issue in cases in which they have been impaneled.[1] This view, however, is contrary to modern authority.[2]

When a verdict has been reached, the law is well settled that a juror generally is incompetent to give testimony that would impeach the verdict.[3] Thus, jurors will not be allowed to testify to improper procedures, errors concerning the merits or misconduct, such as incivility and intimidation, that occurred during the deliberations.[4] The rule of incom-

comment from bench confirmed that person with whom defendant had a relationship was a convicted cocaine dealer, a fact that prosecutor was improperly seeking to prove). See also Jones v. Benefit Trust Life Ins. Co., 800 F.2d 1397 (5th Cir. 1986)(judge's pretrial ruling on summary judgment motion on issue of contract interpretation should not be introduced on issue of fact before a jury). But see United States v. Sanchez, 790 F.2d 245 (2d Cir.1986)(trial court's jury instruction that flight or nonappearance of defendant being tried in absentia could be considered evidence of guilt did not constitute "implied testimony" in violation of Rule 605).

5. United States v. Frankenthal, 582 F.2d 1102, 1107–08 (7th Cir.1978) (prior to trial, judge recused himself after defense witness made ex parte communication with judge; contents of communication were material issue with respect to witness' credibility at trial). The judge, however, may not testify to the mental processes that led to her findings of fact or conclusions of law in a prior matter. Fayerweather v. Ritch, 195 U.S. 276, 306–07, 25 S.Ct. 58, 67–68, 49 L.Ed. 193, 213 (1904)(judge's testimony with respect to prior judicial business is limited to historical facts).

§ 606.1

1. People v. Dohring, 59 N.Y. 374, 378 (1874).

2. See § 606.2 infra. The Proposed New York Evidence Code, in § 606(a), would change the apparent common law rule, as follows: "A member of the jury may not testify as a witness before that jury in the trial of the case in which such member is sitting as a juror."

As McCormick points out, the issue is not one that will arise with any frequency if a thorough voir dire is conducted during jury selection. McCormick § 68, at 258 n.14.

3. Alford v. Sventek, 53 N.Y.2d 743, 744, 439 N.Y.S.2d 339, 340, 421 N.E.2d 831, 832 (1981); People v. De Lucia, 20 N.Y.2d 275, 276–77, 282 N.Y.S.2d 526, 527, 229 N.E.2d 211, 212 (1967); People v. Redd, 164 A.D.2d 34, 36, 561 N.Y.S.2d 439, 440 (1st Dep't 1990); Lundgren v. McColgin, 96 A.D.2d 706, 707, 464 N.Y.S.2d 317, 318 (4th Dep't 1983).

4. See, e.g., Kaufman v. Eli Lilly & Co., 65 N.Y.2d 449, 460, 492 N.Y.S.2d 584, 591, 482 N.E.2d 63, 70 (1985)(jurors are incompetent to impeach verdict with testimony that verdict was a compromise); People v. Redd, 164 A.D.2d 34, 37, 561 N.Y.S.2d 439, 440 (1st Dep't 1990)(escalated tempers, obscenities, threats and belligerent exchanges resulting in coercive atmosphere during deliberations were not permissible subject of postverdict testimony by jurors); People v. Maddox, 139 A.D.2d 597, 598, 527 N.Y.S.2d 89, 91 (2d Dep't), appeal denied, 72 N.Y.2d 862, 532 N.Y.S.2d 512, 528 N.E.2d 903 (1988)(juror not permitted to impeach verdict by testimony recounting personal attacks, harassment and intimidation by other jurors); Fahey v. South Nassau Communities Hospital, 197 Misc. 490, 492, 95 N.Y.S.2d 842, 844 (Sup.Ct.Nassau Co.), aff'd, 277 App.Div. 774, 97 N.Y.S.2d 711 (2d Dep't 1950)(affidavit of juror not receivable to impeach "for mistake or error in respect of the merits of the case").

§ 606.1   WITNESSES   Ch. 6

petency is said to promote frank jury deliberations, to protect against posttrial harassment and to produce finality.[5]

The Court of Appeals stressed in *Sharrow v. Dick Corporation*,[6] however, that "[a]n inquiry [by the trial court] to clarify a verdict before discharging a jury must be distinguished from an attempt to impeach a jury's verdict after discharge."[7] If the polling process discloses "an inconsistency or ambiguity" in the verdict, the trial court is permitted to make "limited inquiry" of the jurors to ascertain whether corrective action is needed.[8] Thus, in *Sharrow* the trial judge was held to have committed reversible error for failing to interrogate a juror who apparently had not participated in certain portions of the jury's deliberations, thereby depriving the defendants of the right to trial by a full six-member jury.[9] In other cases, jurors have been permitted to give testimony showing that the verdict was incorrectly reported to the court.[10]

In addition to allowing juror testimony to clarify a verdict, New York courts have also recognized an exception to the anti-impeachment rule in cases involving improper external influences.[11] Outside influences occur less frequently and are more susceptible to adequate proof than potential defects in the substance of jury deliberations.[12] Examples include improper communications by court officers,[13] unauthorized visits to crime scenes,[14] independent research using sources not admitted in

---

5. See People v. De Lucia, 20 N.Y.2d 275, 278, 282 N.Y.S.2d 526, 529, 229 N.E.2d 211, 213 (1967)("The policy reason for the present rule is, of course, that we do not wish to encourage the posttrial harassing of jurors for statements which might render their verdicts questionable. With regard to juryroom deliberations, scarcely any verdict might remain unassailable, if such statements were admissible. Common experience indicates that at times articulate jurors may intimidate the inarticulate, the aggressive may unduly influence the docile. Some jurors may 'throw in' when deliberations have reached an impasse. Others may attempt to compromise. Permitting jurors to testify regarding such occurrences would create chaos."); People v. Redd, 164 A.D.2d 34, 36–37, 561 N.Y.S.2d 439, 440 (1st Dep't 1990)(rule was intended to protect against harassment of jurors, to secure secrecy so as to promote frank and free deliberations, and to achieve finality of judgment).

6. 86 N.Y.2d 54, 629 N.Y.S.2d 980, 653 N.E.2d 1150 (1995).

7. Id. at 60, 629 N.Y.S.2d at 983, 653 N.E.2d at 1153.

8. Id. at 61, 629 N.Y.S.2d at 983, 653 N.E.2d at 1153.

9. Id. at 62, 629 N.Y.S.2d at 983, 653 N.E.2d at 1153. The right to jury trial in civil actions is constitutionally guaranteed (N.Y.Const. art. I, § 2), and CPLR 4104 states that "[a] jury shall be composed of six persons." Although CPLR 4113(a) authorizes a five-sixths verdict, Sharrow held that "the constitutional right to a jury trial contemplates that all six jurors participate in the deliberative process." 86 N.Y.2d at 59, 629 N.Y.S.2d at 982, 653 N.E.2d at 1152.

10. See, e.g., Dalrymple v. Williams, 63 N.Y. 361, 364 (1875); Pache v. Boehm, 60 A.D.2d 867, 401 N.Y.S.2d 260 (2d Dep't 1978); Rose v. Thau, 45 A.D.2d 182, 357 N.Y.S.2d 201 (3d Dep't 1974).

11. People v. De Lucia, 20 N.Y.2d 275, 279, 282 N.Y.S.2d 526, 530, 229 N.E.2d 211, 214 (1967).

12. Id.

13. People v. Rukaj, 123 A.D.2d 277, 277–78, 506 N.Y.S.2d 677, 678 (1st Dep't 1986)(without authorization, officer stated in loud voice that if jury did not reach quick verdict, it might be sequestered for entire weekend or possibly five or six weeks). See also Parker v. Gladden, 385 U.S. 363, 87 S.Ct. 468, 17 L.Ed.2d 420 (1966)(bailiff's statement about merits of case).

14. People v. De Lucia, 20 N.Y.2d 275, 282 N.Y.S.2d 526, 229 N.E.2d 211 (1967). Such unauthorized visits are deemed inherently prejudicial in criminal cases, but civil cases are examined on a case-by-case basis to determine the extent of prejudice. Al-

evidence[15] and performing out-of-court experiments.[16] One court held that racial bias was "a corrupt outside influence" that fell within the exception where expressions of such bias permeated the jury's deliberations.[17] The line between inquiries into "the tenor" of deliberations (juror incompetency) and external influences (juror competency) is not always easy to draw, making the articulation of precise guidelines impossible.[18]

Library References:

West's Key No. Digests, Witnesses ⚖︎68, 69.

ford v. Sventek, 53 N.Y.2d 743, 439 N.Y.S.2d 339, 421 N.E.2d 831 (1981).

15. People v. Dashnau, 187 A.D.2d 966, 591 N.Y.S.2d 124 (4th Dep't 1992), leave to appeal denied, 81 N.Y.2d 838, 595 N.Y.S.2d 737, 611 N.E.2d 776 (1993)(juror looked up defense counsel's name in phone book to ascertain that he was private attorney; juror suggested to other jurors that since defendant had funds to hire private counsel, he must have sold drugs, as charged in indictment); People v. Thomas, 184 A.D.2d 1069, 584 N.Y.S.2d 706 (4th Dep't 1992)(in case in which defendant's defense was based on lack of intent due to consumption of cocaine and alcohol, juror did library research on the effects of such consumption, the results of which he shared with other jurors); Maslinski v. Brunswick Hosp. Center, Inc., 118 A.D.2d 834, 500 N.Y.S.2d 318 (2d Dep't 1986)(in medical malpractice action, juror looked up definitions of malpractice in medical dictionaries and read definitions to other jurors).

16. People v. Brown, 48 N.Y.2d 388, 423 N.Y.S.2d 461, 399 N.E.2d 51 (1979) (juror "tested" police officer's testimony that he could see defendant from vehicle in which he was riding; after purporting to recreate the circumstances using her own vehicle, she described results of experiment to other jurors).

17. People v. Rukaj, 123 A.D.2d 277, 279–81, 506 N.Y.S.2d 677, 678–80 (1st Dep't 1986)(jury was composed entirely of blacks and Hispanics while defendant and his counsel were white; throughout deliberations, some jurors allegedly expressed racial animosity and urged other jurors to vote for conviction based on race of defendant and his lawyer).

Racial bias was also a basis for allowing juror impeachment of the verdict in a case where the juror revealed to defense counsel, after trial, that he had lied during voir dire as to his propensity for bias. People v. Leonti, 262 N.Y. 256, 258, 186 N.E. 693, 694 (1933). But see People v. Morales, 121 A.D.2d 240, 503 N.Y.S.2d 374 (1st Dep't 1986), appeal withdrawn, 68 N.Y.2d 766, 506 N.Y.S.2d 1041, 498 N.E.2d 151 (1986) (stressing that Leonti did not involve revelations concerning contents of jury's deliberations themselves, court disallowed juror A from testifying to statements made by juror B during deliberations where such statements showed that B had lied during voir dire about his status as a crime victim).

18. People v. Brown, 48 N.Y.2d 388, 394, 423 N.Y.S.2d 461, 463, 399 N.E.2d 51, 53 (1979). ("Because juror misconduct can take many forms, no ironclad rule of decision is possible. In each case the facts must be examined to determine the nature of the material placed before the jury and the likelihood that prejudice would be engendered.").

The Proposed New York Evidence Code § 606(b) would codify the New York rules regarding juror competence to impeach the verdict as follows:

(b) **Inquiry into the validity of verdict. [PROPOSED]** Except as otherwise provided by statute, upon an inquiry into the validity of a verdict, a juror may not testify as to any matter or statement occurring during the course of the jury's deliberations, or to the effect of anything upon such juror's or any other juror's mind or emotions as influencing such juror to assent to or dissent from the verdict, or concerning such juror's mental processes in connection therewith. The juror's affidavit or evidence of any statement by such juror concerning a matter about which such juror would be precluded from testifying is likewise not admissible. A juror may, however, testify on the question whether extraneous prejudicial information, regardless of its source, had been brought to the jury's attention or any outside influence or other influence that violates the constitutional right to a jury trial was improperly brought to bear upon any juror.

§ 606.2 Federal

In federal proceedings, a juror is incompetent to testify to the facts in a trial in which she has been impaneled.[1] With respect to impeachment of the verdict, federal law parallels that of New York: juror testimony concerning internal deliberations is off limits while testimony concerning external influences is permitted. Rule 606(b) of the Federal Rules of Evidence codifies the law on juror impeachment as follows:

(b) Inquiry into validity of verdict or indictment. Upon an inquiry into the validity of a verdict or indictment, a juror may not testify as to any matter or statement occurring during the course of the jury's deliberations or to the effect of anything upon that or any other juror's mind or emotions as influencing the juror to assent to or dissent from the verdict or indictment or concerning the juror's mental processes in connection therewith, except that a juror may testify on the question whether extraneous prejudicial information was improperly brought to the jury's attention or whether any outside influence was improperly brought to bear upon any juror. Nor may a juror's affidavit or evidence of any statement by the juror concerning a matter about which the juror would be precluded from testifying be received for these purposes.[2]

As in New York, the federal courts have not articulated a precise definition as to what constitutes an "extraneous prejudicial influence."[3] Examples of such influences include bribery of a juror,[4] exposure to external communications,[5] and the conducting of improvised experiments.[6] Incompetency is the norm, however, with respect to misconduct

---

§ 606.2

1. Fed.R.Evid. 606(a) states:

(a) **At the trial.** A member of the jury may not testify as a witness before that jury in the trial of the case in which the juror is sitting. If the juror is called so to testify, the opposing party shall be afforded an opportunity to object out of the presence of the jury.

2. The Advisory Committee's Note to Fed.R.Evid. 606(b) indicates that Rule 606(b) offers an accommodation between the values promoted by a rule of juror incompetency—freedom of deliberation, finality of verdicts and protection against annoyance—and the notion that verdicts should not be totally insulated from irregularity and injustice. Furthermore, the "rule does not purport to specify the substantive grounds for setting aside verdicts for irregularity; it deals only with the competency of jurors to testify concerning those grounds."

Although jurors may not testify to internal deliberations that would "impeach" the verdict, they may testify that the verdict was incorrectly reported: "The permissibility of juror testimony hinges upon the purpose for which it is offered. Where the court seeks to correct the mistaken transmission of the verdict from the jury, evidence may be received." Attridge v. Cencorp Division of Dover Technologies Internat'l, Inc., 836 F.2d 113, 117 (2d Cir.1987).

3. The external/internal distinction is "not based on whether the juror was literally inside or outside the jury room when the alleged irregularity took place; rather, the distinction [is] based on the nature of the allegation." Tanner v. United States, 483 U.S. 107, 117, 107 S.Ct. 2739, 2746, 97 L.Ed.2d 90, 104 (1987).

4. Remmer v. United States, 347 U.S. 227, 74 S.Ct. 450, 98 L.Ed. 654 (1954).

5. Parker v. Gladden, 385 U.S. 363, 87 S.Ct. 468, 17 L.Ed.2d 420 (1966) (bailiff's statement to juror that defendant was guilty); Mattox v. United States, 146 U.S. 140, 150–51, 13 S.Ct. 50, 53, 36 L.Ed. 917, 920–21 (1892)(exposure to newspaper article about case).

6. In re Beverly Hills Fire Litigation, 695 F.2d 207, 214–15 (6th Cir.1982), cert. denied, 461 U.S. 929, 103 S.Ct. 2090, 77 L.Ed.2d 300 (1983), on remand, 583 F.Supp. 1163 (E.D.Ky.1984).

or errors in the deliberation process.[7] Juror intoxication straddles the line. In *Tanner v. United States*,[8] however, voluntary drug and alcohol consumption by some of the jurors was said to be "no more an 'outside influence' than a virus, poorly prepared food or a lack of sleep."[9] A narrow approach to the exception for outside influences is supported by the policies that undergird the rule of incompetency: "to avoid harassment of jurors, inhibition of deliberation in the jury room, a deluge of post-verdict applications mostly without real merit, and an increase in opportunities for jury tampering; [and] also to prevent jury verdicts from being made more uncertain."[10]

Library References:

West's Key No. Digests, Witnesses ⊙=68, 69.

Even if the impeachment involves an external influence, the juror may not testify to the effect that the information had on the juror's mental processes or the jury's deliberations. The court makes an independent determination, using an objective standard, as to whether the external information "would have a substantial and injurious impact on the verdict of a reasonable jury." Bibbins v. Dalsheim, 21 F.3d 13, 17 (2d Cir.1994).

7. The Advisory Committee's Note to Fed.R.Evid. 606(b) collects illustrative cases that preceded adoption of the Federal Rule:

Under the federal decisions the central focus has been upon insulation of the manner in which the jury reached its verdict, and this protection extends to each of the components of deliberation, including arguments, statements, discussions, mental and emotional reactions, votes, and any other feature of the process. Thus testimony or affidavits of jurors have been held incompetent to show a compromise verdict, Hyde v. United States, 225 U.S. 347, 382, 32 S.Ct. 793, 807, 56 L.Ed. 1114 (1912); a quotient verdict, McDonald v. Pless, 238 U.S. 264, 35 S.Ct. 783, 59 L.Ed. 1300 (1915); speculation as to insurance coverage, Holden v. Porter, 405 F.2d 878 (10th Cir.1969), Farmers Co-op. Elev. Ass'n v. Strand, 382 F.2d 224, 230 (8th Cir.1967), cert. denied 389 U.S. 1014, 88 S.Ct. 589, 19 L.Ed.2d 659; misinterpretation of instructions, Farmers Coop. Elev. Ass'n v. Strand, supra; mistake in returning verdict, United States v. Chereton, 309 F.2d 197 (6th Cir.1962); interpretation of guilty plea by one defendant as implicating others, United States v. Crosby, 294 F.2d 928, 949 (2d Cir.1961).

More recent decisions of the same tenor include United States v. Norton, 867 F.2d 1354, 1366 (11th Cir.), cert. denied, 491 U.S. 907, 109 S.Ct. 3192, 105 L.Ed.2d 701 (1989)(duress by one juror against another juror is not a proper subject of juror testimony); Robles v. Exxon Corp., 862 F.2d 1201, 1204–09 (5th Cir.), cert. denied, 490 U.S. 1051, 109 S.Ct. 1967, 104 L.Ed.2d 434 (1989)(testimony as to misunderstanding of judge's instructions not permitted); Ohanian v. Avis Rent A Car System, Inc., 779 F.2d 101, 110 (2d Cir.1985)(juror's notes indicating confusion on computation of damages is inadmissible).

8. 483 U.S. 107, 107 S.Ct. 2739, 97 L.Ed.2d 90 (1987).

9. Id. at 122, 107 S.Ct. at 2748, 97 L.Ed.2d at 107. See also Government of the Virgin Islands v. Nicholas, 759 F.2d 1073, 1080 (3d Cir.1985), on remand, 639 F.Supp. 486 (D.V.I.1986), aff'd, 819 F.2d 1133 (3d Cir.1987) (juror's hearing impairment was not an external factor).

Federal courts have applied the rule to preclude testimony by one juror that another juror revealed racial prejudice during the deliberations. Shillcutt v. Gagnon, 827 F.2d 1155, 1158 (7th Cir.1987); Wright v. United States, 559 F.Supp. 1139, 1151–52 (E.D.N.Y.1983), aff'd, 732 F.2d 1048 (2d Cir.1984), cert. denied, 469 U.S. 1106, 105 S.Ct. 779, 83 L.Ed.2d 774 (1985)(juror testimony about racial prejudice restricted to extraordinary cases). See § 606.1, at note 17, supra.

10. King v. United States, 576 F.2d 432, 438 (2d Cir.), cert. denied, 439 U.S. 850, 99 S.Ct. 155, 58 L.Ed.2d 154 (1978). The Supreme Court observed in Tanner: "There is little doubt that postverdict investigation into juror misconduct would in some instances lead to the invalidation of verdicts reached after irresponsible or improper juror behavior. It is not at all clear, however, that the jury system could survive such

607 Impeachment and Rehabilitation of Witnesses

§ 607.1 Credibility: New York and Federal

The credibility of a witness is an important and frequently decisive issue in the fact-finding process. As discussed in the foregoing sections of this chapter, a witness may be competent to testify because she has adequate powers of perception, memory and communication and understands the duty to testify truthfully.[1] The fact-finder, however, must determine the accuracy with which the witness exercised her cognitive and perceptual capacity, the strength of her memory and the actual truthfulness of her testimony.[2]

Various factors may be considered in assessing credibility, including the witness' physical and mental capacity, opportunity for observation, narrative ability and any interest or bias as well as the inherent probabilities of the testimony when evaluated in the light of other evidence in the case. Another key datum in the assessment of credibility is "demeanor evidence," i.e., the appearance and attitude of the witness while testifying.[3] Credibility ordinarily is a question of fact for the jury.[4]

efforts to perfect it." 483 U.S. at 120, 107 S.Ct. at 2747, 97 L.Ed.2d at 106.

§ 607.1

1. See §§ 601.1, 601.3, 603.1, 603.2, supra.

2. See McCormick § 33, at 111 n.1 ("Credibility is dependent upon the willingness of the witness to tell the truth and upon his ability to do so.").

3. People v. Carter, 37 N.Y.2d 234, 239, 371 N.Y.S.2d 905, 909–10, 333 N.E.2d 177, 180 (1975)("[T]he appearance, attitude and demeanor of a witness upon being questioned and while before the court are matters to be taken into consideration in testing veracity and in determining the weight to be accorded his or her testimony. * * * Indeed, the opportunity of observation often affords the most accurate method of ascertaining the truth."). According to Wigmore, "The *demeanor of the witness on the stand* may always be considered by the jury in their estimation of his credibility." 3A Wigmore § 946, at 783 (emphasis in original). See also The William J. Riddle, 102 F.Supp. 884, 887 (S.D.N.Y.), aff'd, 200 F.2d 608 (2d Cir.1952)("The demeanor of a witness is always assumed to be in evidence").

The importance of demeanor evidence helps to explain the deference paid by appellate courts to credibility determinations made at the trial court level. See, e.g., People v. Gaimari, 176 N.Y. 84, 94, 68 N.E. 112, 115–16 (1903)("[The jury] could look into the faces of the various witnesses as they gave their versions of the transaction and decide, so far as human judgment can tell, not only who intended to speak the truth, but who in fact spoke the truth. Representing the average judgment of mankind, they could separate the true from the false with a degree of accuracy which, according to the theory of our law founded on the experience of many generations, cannot be attained by reviewing judges. The memory, motive, mental capacity, accuracy of observation and statement, truthfulness and other tests of the reliability of witnesses can be passed upon with greater safety by those who see and hear than by those who simply read the printed narrative.").

4. People v. Regina, 19 N.Y.2d 65, 72, 277 N.Y.S.2d 683, 688, 224 N.E.2d 108, 111 (1966)(credibility is a jury question "to be determined, not only from the words, but also from the demeanor, interest and motives of the witnesses"); Kelly v. Watson Elevator Co., 309 N.Y. 49, 51, 127 N.E.2d 802, 803 (1955)("[W]here there is a conflict in the evidence as to the issues controverted, matters of credibility and weight are for the jury to determine or, if the trial be without a jury, for the trier of the facts."). See also United States v. Richter, 826 F.2d 206, 208 (2d Cir.1987)(because questions of credibility are for jury, prosecutor may not properly press defendant, during cross-examination, into characterizing government witnesses as liars). Accord, People v. Montgomery, 103 A.D.2d 622, 481 N.Y.S.2d 532 (4th Dep't 1984). But see United States v. Gaind, 31 F.3d 73, 77 (2d Cir.1994)(no error

Ch. 6 IMPEACHMENT & REHABILITATION § 607.1

Even testimony that is uncontradicted may be disbelieved by the jury.[5] Occasionally, however, the credibility (or lack thereof) of a witness' testimony may be determined by the court as a matter of law.[6]

Zealous advocates, of course, will do their best to cast doubt on the credibility of their opponents' witnesses and to shore up the credibility of their own witnesses.[7] The law of impeachment regulates the former process while that of bolstering and rehabilitation governs the latter. In principle, any relevant evidence bearing on a witness' credibility should be admissible, subject to limitations imposed by considerations of potential confusion, consumption of time, unfair surprise, or undue prejudice.[8]

---

found where prosecutor asked defendant whether testimony of government witnesses, none of whom were police officers, was "mistaken").

A court's jury instructions usually will apprise the jury of the various factors to be considered in assessing credibility. See, e.g., 1 New York Forms of Jury Instruction § 1.25[1] (1992); Pattern Jury Instructions of the U.S. Eleventh Circuit District Judges Association—Civil Cases, Basic Instruction No. 3 (1990). A classic jury charge with respect to credibility is that of Judge Medina in United States v. Foster, 9 F.R.D. 367, 388 (S.D.N.Y.1949):

> This judging of testimony is very like what goes on in real life. People may tell you things which may or may not influence some important decisions on your part. You consider whether the people you deal with had the capacity and the opportunity to observe or be familiar with and to remember the things they tell you about. You consider any possible interest they may have, and any bias or prejudice. You consider a person's demeanor, to use a colloquial expression, you "size him up" when he tells you anything; you decide whether he strikes you as fair and candid or not. Then you consider the inherent believability of what he says, whether it accords with your own knowledge or experience. It is the same thing with witnesses. You ask yourself if they know what they are talking about. You watch them on the stand as they testify and note their demeanor. You decide how their testimony strikes you.

5. Matter of Nowakowski, 2 N.Y.2d 618, 622, 162 N.Y.S.2d 19, 21, 142 N.E.2d 198, 200 (1957).

6. Courts may find, from time to time, that testimony is incredible as a matter of law. See Caperna v. Williams–Bauer Corp., 184 Misc. 192, 197, 53 N.Y.S.2d 295, 300 (Sup.Ct.App.T., 1st Dep't 1945)("Testimony is incredible when it is so extraordinarily in conflict with probability, or so utterly hostile to reason and intelligence, as to become so nearly impossible that it ought not to be believed by the trier of the facts."). See also Loughlin v. City of New York, 186 A.D.2d 176, 587 N.Y.S.2d 732 (2d Dep't 1992), appeal denied, 81 N.Y.2d 704, 595 N.Y.S.2d 398, 611 N.E.2d 299 (1993), (defendant's motion for directed verdict should have been granted because plaintiff's testimony was a "physical impossibility"); People v. Stroman, 83 A.D.2d 370, 372, 444 N.Y.S.2d 463, 465 (1st Dep't 1981) (testimony will be rejected as incredible as matter of law when it is "impossible" to believe).

Conversely, and with much less frequency, a court may find that a witness' testimony, at least in a civil action, cannot reasonably be doubted. See, e.g., Hull v. Littauer, 162 N.Y. 569, 572, 57 N.E. 102, 103 (1900) ("Generally, the credibility of a witness who is a party to the action, and therefore interested in its result, is for the jury * * *. Where, however, the evidence of a party to the action is not contradicted by direct evidence, nor by any legitimate inferences from the evidence, and it is not opposed to the probabilities; nor, in its nature, surprising or suspicious, there is no reason for denying to it conclusiveness.").

7. On occasion, a party may wish to discredit her own witness, an issue that is discussed in § 607.4 infra.

8. See 3 Weinstein and Berger ¶ 607[02]. Modern decisions of the New York Court of Appeals recognize that relevance is the governing standard. See, e.g., § 607.2, at notes 8–13, infra. "Relevant evidence means 'evidence having any tendency to make the existence of any fact that is of consequence to the determination of the action more probable or less probable than it would be without the evidence.'" People v. Davis, 43 N.Y.2d 17, 27, 400 N.Y.S.2d 735, 740, 371 N.E.2d 456, 460 (1977), cert. denied, 435 U.S. 998, 98 S.Ct. 1653, 56 L.Ed.2d 88, and 438 U.S. 914, 98 S.Ct. 3143, 57 L.Ed.2d 1160 (1978), quoting Unif.R.Evid. 401. Since credibility is a fact "of consequence" in a trial, "circumstantial evidence bearing on the credibility of a witness is relevant." Graham § 607.1, at 414.

§ 607.1

Several crystallized rules have evolved, however, marking the boundaries, in most cases, of permissible methods of attacking and supporting credibility. Those boundaries are explored in the remaining subsections of § 607 and §§ 608, 609 and 610.

Slight deviation from the order of presentation contained in the Federal Rules of Evidence, which otherwise governs the methodology of this book, was necessitated by the desire to treat the topics of impeachment and rehabilitation as an integrated unit. In the Federal Rules of Evidence, for example, procedures relating to prior inconsistent statements are covered in Rule 613, which is out of sequence with other topics of impeachment in the Federal Rules. Furthermore, some impeachment issues, such as bias and mental impairment, are nowhere touched upon in the Federal Rules, and the issue of rehabilitation is divided between Rules 608(a)(2) and 801(d)(1)(B). All of these stray topics have been brought together in this chapter as subsections of § 607. In this manner, parallelism with the numerical system of the Federal Rules is kept essentially intact.

Library References:

West's Key No. Digests, Witnesses ⇔311–416.

§ 607.2 Impeachment, In General: New York and Federal

Impeachment is the process of discrediting a witness. An attack on credibility may be directed either at the witness' capacity and opportunity to observe, remember and narrate or the witness' honesty, or both. The traditional methods of impeachment in New York are as follows: (1) showing that the witness is biased in favor of or against a party, has an interest in the outcome of the case, or has been corrupted in connection with his testimony;[1] (2) showing an impairment in the witness' mental capacity or powers of perception;[2] (3) revealing inconsistencies between prior statements of the witness and his trial testimony;[3] (4) showing the witness' bad reputation for truthfulness;[4] (5) exposing prior vicious, immoral or criminal acts;[5] and (6) proving prior criminal convictions of the witness.[6] In addition, the introduction of evidence that contradicts the testimony of a witness, when permitted, indirectly serves to impeach the witness' credibility.[7]

Even relevant evidence may be excluded, however, if it would prolong the trial, confuse or mislead the jury, or surprise or prejudice a party to such an extent that its probative value is outweighed. People v. Davis, supra, 43 N.Y.2d at 27, 400 N.Y.S.2d at 740, 371 N.E.2d at 460.

The Proposed New York Evidence Code, in § 607(a), explicitly embraces the view that general principles of relevance should govern all credibility evidence: "Except as otherwise provided by this chapter or other statute, the trier of fact may consider in determining the credibility of a witness any matter that has any tendency in reason to prove or disprove the truthfulness of the witness's testimony."

§ 607.2

1. See § 607.6(a) infra.
2. See § 607.7(a) infra.
3. See § 607.8(a) infra.
4. See § 608.1(a) infra.
5. See § 608.2(a) infra.
6. See § 609.1 infra.
7. See § 607.3 infra.

Ch. 6   IMPEACHMENT & REHABILITATION   § 607.2

The traditional categories of impeachment are justified by their probative value on the issue of credibility either in general or with respect to the particular matter about which the witness is testifying.[8] As will be seen in the coverage of the individual categories of impeachment (§§ 607.6, 607.7, 607.8, 608, and 609, *infra*) the probative value of the evidence frequently must be weighed against potentially countervailing factors of confusion, unfair surprise, consumption of time and undue prejudice, thereby resulting in exclusion or limitation in individual cases. It is well settled that the trial court's discretion plays a pervasive role in matters of impeachment.[9]

Furthermore, the traditional categories of impeachment do not represent a closed universe. The New York Court of Appeals has made it clear that trial courts should be guided by general principles of relevance in determining whether particular facts may be introduced to impeach credibility. In *People v. Walker*,[10] for example, the court upheld cross-examination of a criminal defendant with respect to his prior use of aliases, an impeaching fact that did not fall within the conventional category of "immoral, vicious or criminal acts." The court reasoned that a witness' conduct "may be a proper subject for impeachment questioning where it demonstrates an untruthful bent or 'significantly reveal[s] a willingness or disposition on the part of the particular [witness] voluntarily to place the advancement of his individual self-interest ahead of principle or of the interests of society.'"[11] The use of a false name, said the court, "is an indication of dishonesty that goes to the very heart of the question of that individual's testimonial credibili-

---

8. See, e.g., People v. Pavao, 59 N.Y.2d 282, 291, 464 N.Y.S.2d 458, 463, 451 N.E.2d 216, 221 (1983)(in analyzing the continuing appropriateness of impeachment by showing the witness' bad reputation for honesty and truthfulness, the court "reaffirm[ed] * * * the rule * * * which permits the introduction of relevant evidence which is probative of a witness' credibility * * * but does not carry with it the danger that numerous collateral issues will have to be resolved, causing the trial to become unnecessarily protracted and clouding the main issues").

9. People v. Hudy, 73 N.Y.2d 40, 56, 538 N.Y.S.2d 197, 207, 535 N.E.2d 250, 259 (1988)("trial courts have broad discretion to keep the proceedings within manageable limits and to curtail exploration of collateral matters"); People v. Coleman, 56 N.Y.2d 269, 273, 451 N.Y.S.2d 705, 707, 436 N.E.2d 1307, 1309 (1982)("The determination of what evidence may be introduced for purposes of impeachment lies within the sound discretion of the trial court"); People v. Caviness, 38 N.Y.2d 227, 232, 379 N.Y.S.2d 695, 700, 342 N.E.2d 496, 500 (1975)("the extent to which disparaging questions, not relevant to the issues but bearing on the credibility of a witness may be put upon cross-examination is discretionary with the trial court and its rulings are not subject to review, unless it clearly appears that the discretion has been abused").

10. 83 N.Y.2d 455, 611 N.Y.S.2d 118, 633 N.E.2d 472 (1994).

11. Id. at 461, 611 N.Y.S.2d at 122, 633 N.E.2d at 476, quoting People v. Sandoval, 34 N.Y.2d 371, 377, 357 N.Y.S.2d 849, 855, 314 N.E.2d 413, 417 (1974).

A similar analysis was applied in People v. Coleman, 56 N.Y.2d 269, 451 N.Y.S.2d 705, 436 N.E.2d 1307 (1982), where the court permitted cross-examination of a criminal defendant with respect to prior publications of a printing company in which the defendant was a principal officer and shareholder. The books explained how to cheat on taxes and telephone services. Although such impeachment fell outside the conventional category of "immoral, vicious or criminal acts," the court held that the evidence "was both relevant and material to the credibility, veracity and honesty of defendant." 56 N.Y.2d at 273, 451 N.Y.S.2d at 707, 436 N.E.2d at 1309.

§ 607.2   WITNESSES   Ch. 6

ty."[12] The witness was free, of course, to explain any mitigating or innocent circumstances surrounding the use of the aliases.[13]

Federal courts recognize the relevance, in general, of impeachment by one variant or another of the traditional methods. The Federal Rules of Evidence, however, explicitly address only some of the traditional forms of impeachment,[14] leaving the balance of impeachment issues for analysis in accordance with common law principles and the general relevance/prejudice framework of Rules 401, 402 and 403.[15] *Outley v. City of New York*,[16] for example, illustrates that impeachment evidence of weak probative value may be overcome by considerations of confusion, undue time consumption and the like. In *Outley*, prior "litigiousness" of the plaintiff was held to be insufficiently probative of a dishonest bent,[17] and to the extent it may have been marginally relevant on the issue of bias (the prior lawsuits, like the pending case, were brought by plaintiff, an African–American, against white police officers), the inquiry would have been distracting, time-consuming and confusing.[18]

---

12. 83 N.Y.2d at 461, 611 N.Y.S.2d at 112, 633 N.E.2d at 476.

13. The court observed:

The existence of * * * potential "innocent" explanations for a name discrepancy, however, is not a sufficient basis to treat alias evidence differently or to carve out a special exception to the general rule that the nature and extent of cross-examination are matters that are entrusted to the sound discretion of the trial court. * * * Whether a particular discrepancy in the name an arrested individual has given is indicative of dishonesty or is instead the product of some other noncorrupt circumstance is a question the trier of fact can readily resolve as part of its over-all function to weigh the evidence and resolve credibility issues. In this regard, alias evidence is no different from any other factual information elicited in an effort to impeach a witness's credibility. Like any other form of impeachment evidence, the probative worth of this class of evidence may effectively be challenged through such conventional methods as explanation and rehabilitation. * * * Once all of the evidence is placed before the fact finder, the truth-seeking process itself can be trusted to sort out the relevant variables and arrive at the proper conclusion.

Id. at 462–63, 611 N.Y.S.2d at 122–23, 633 N.E.2d at 476–77 (footnote omitted).

14. Rule 608(a) governs evidence of a witness' bad character for truth and veracity, Rule 608(b) addresses prior bad acts that may impugn a witness' propensity for truthfulness, Rule 609 covers prior convictions, and Rule 610 prohibits impeachment on the basis of the witness' beliefs on matters of religion. Rule 613 governs the procedure, but not the substance, of prior inconsistent statements, and Rule 801(d)(1)(A) deals only with the hearsay status of prior inconsistent statements.

15. See 3 Weinstein and Berger ¶ 607[02]. For example, in United States v. Abel, 469 U.S. 45, 105 S.Ct. 465, 83 L.Ed.2d 450 (1984), the Supreme Court upheld use of the traditional impeachment technique of exposing a witness' bias. The Court found no intent by the drafters of the Federal Rules to "scuttle" pre-Rules law with respect to bias, observed that bias is relevant and therefore admissible under Rules 401 and 402, and agreed with the proposition that the common law may serve as a source of guidance. 469 U.S. at 50–52, 105 S.Ct. at 468–69, 83 L.Ed.2d at 456–57. The Court also concluded that the district court, having weighed the probative value of the particular bias evidence in the case at hand against its potential for prejudice, properly exercised its discretion in favor of admissibility in accordance with Rule 403. 469 U.S. at 53–55, 105 S.Ct. at 470, 83 L.Ed.2d at 458–59.

16. 837 F.2d 587 (2d Cir.1988).

17. The court stressed that the previous actions brought by the plaintiff were not shown to have been fraudulent. Id. at 592, 594.

18. Id. at 595 ("In order for a jury properly to consider [the other lawsuits], the particular details of each action, and the extent to which the bringing of each action was justified, must be before the jury. Opening up this area thus invites detailed inquiries, denials, and explanations, likely to lead to multifariousness and a confusion of issues. * * * As such, at least in this case, it is an area of examination better left closed.").

In both state and federal courts, all of the permissible impeachment techniques may be employed by questioning the witness on cross-examination.[19] Some of the techniques may also be exploited by the introduction of extrinsic evidence, i.e., documents or the testimony of other witnesses, to prove the impeaching facts. For example, if the witness denies the impeaching fact on cross-examination, the cross-examiner thereafter (usually during the next affirmative phase of the cross-examiner's case) may introduce other evidence to prove the point.

Impeaching facts that traditionally may be proven by extrinsic evidence are bias, interest, corrupting influences, mental and sensory impairments, bad reputation for truthfulness and prior criminal convictions.[20] As to such matters, the introduction of independent evidence apparently is deemed appropriate either because the fact is highly probative of credibility in the particular case, or the impeaching matter, even though it may be of lesser probative value, is relatively quick and easy to prove. Prior vicious and immoral acts that have not resulted in a conviction, on the other hand, are not provable by extrinsic evidence where the sole purpose is to impeach on the basis of bad character for truthfulness.[21] Whether prior inconsistent statements[22] or other contradictory facts[23] may be proven by extrinsic evidence depends on whether they are collateral or noncollateral, an issue that is introduced in § 607.3 *infra*.

When impeaching facts are not provable by extrinsic evidence, the cross-examiner must "take the answer"[24] of the witness, meaning that the witness' denial, after attempts to press the witness into changing the answer have been exhausted, ends further pursuit of the matter.[25] The admissibility of extrinsic evidence with respect to each type of impeachment is discussed in the sections that follow.

Library References:

West's Key No. Digests, Witnesses ⇛311–416.

19. 3A Wigmore §§ 944, 1006. See also Davis v. Alaska, 415 U.S. 308, 316, 94 S.Ct. 1105, 1110, 39 L.Ed.2d 347, 353 (1974)("Cross-examination is the principal means by which the believability of a witness and the truth of his testimony are tested. Subject always to the broad discretion of a trial judge to preclude repetitive and unduly harassing interrogation, the cross-examiner is not only permitted to delve into the witness' story to test the witness' perceptions and memory, but the cross-examiner has traditionally been allowed to impeach, i.e., discredit the witness"); Fed.R.Evid. 611(b)("Cross-examination should be limited to the subject matter of the direct examination and matters affecting the credibility of the witness").

In practice, a witness' bad reputation for truthfulness is proven through other witnesses without prior cross-examination of the witness regarding his reputation.

20. See §§ 607.6, 607.7, 608.1 and 609 infra.

21. Badr v. Hogan, 75 N.Y.2d 629, 635, 555 N.Y.S.2d 249, 252, 554 N.E.2d 890, 893 (1990). See § 608.2 infra. But see § 607.3, at notes 9–12, infra (prior bad acts may be proven by extrinsic evidence where independently relevant on some issue other than character for truthfulness), and § 607.6, at notes 12–14, 17–19 and 24, infra (bad acts that are probative of bias may be proven).

22. See § 607.8 infra.

23. See § 607.3 infra.

24. McCormick § 49, at 182.

25. See, e.g., People v. Sorge, 301 N.Y. 198, 201, 93 N.E.2d 637, 639 (1950).

§ 607.3 Contradiction; Collateral and Noncollateral Matters

One of the functions of cross-examination is to expose inaccuracies and falsehoods in the witness' direct testimony. Thus, if the witness is shown to have made a mistake or to have lied on a particular point, a permissible inference is that the witness is not worthy of belief, either as to other parts or the whole of his testimony.[1] Such impeachment will be accomplished if the witness, as a result of skillful cross-examination, admits the contrary fact. If the witness steadfastly denies any error or falsehood, may the cross-examiner introduce extrinsic evidence, i.e., documents or testimony by other witnesses, to prove the contrary fact? The admissibility of extrinsic evidence of a contradictory fact turns on the nature of the fact sought to be contradicted: Extrinsic evidence to contradict for the purpose of impeachment is prohibited with respect to collateral matters but is admissible with respect to noncollateral matters.

Two considerations underlie the rule against extrinsic evidence of collateral matters for purposes of impeachment: (1) insignificant or trivial errors or falsehoods are simply not very probative of credibility;[2] and (2) impeachment evidence on collateral matters may catch the witness by unfair surprise, confuse and distract the fact-finder, or unduly prolong the trial.[3]

Assume, for example, that a witness to an automobile accident testified that he observed defendant's automobile run a red light. On cross-examination the witness denied that he was intoxicated at the time of his observations, denied that the traffic light was not functioning and insisted that the type of tree at the relevant street corner was a maple tree. The witness' denial of intoxication could be contradicted by extrinsic evidence because sensory impairment traditionally is a noncollateral impeaching fact.[4] The nonfunctioning of the traffic light would be considered noncollateral, and therefore subject to extrinsic proof, because it bears on a key issue in the case—the defendant's negligence.

---

§ 607.3

1. Despite the impeaching value of contradiction, fact-finders are not bound by the common law maxim, "Falsus in uno, falsus in omnibus,"—a person who speaks falsely as to one matter will speak falsely as to all. See 3A Wigmore § 1008. A fact-finder may disbelieve part of a witness' testimony and accept the balance. See, e.g., Accardi v. City of New York, 121 A.D.2d 489, 490–91, 503 N.Y.S.2d 818, 819 (2d Dept 1986)("jury was not required to disregard all of the testimony of the witnesses appearing on behalf of the plaintiffs when, apparently, it disbelieved a part of their testimony").

2. 3A Wigmore § 1001. See also People v. Schwartzman, 24 N.Y.2d 241, 245, 299 N.Y.S.2d 817, 821, 247 N.E.2d 642, 645 (1969), cert. denied, 396 U.S. 846, 90 S.Ct. 103, 24 L.Ed.2d 96 (1969)("testimonial errors concerning distant and unconnected points are of inferior probative value").

3. 3A Wigmore § 1002. See People v. Pavao, 59 N.Y.2d 282, 289, 464 N.Y.S.2d 458, 461, 451 N.E.2d 216, 219–20 (1983)("[I]f extrinsic evidence which is otherwise inadmissible is allowed to be introduced to contradict each and every answer given by a witness solely for the purpose of impeaching that witness, numerous collateral minitrials would arise involving the accuracy of each of the witness' answers. The resulting length of the trial would by far outweigh the limited probative value of such evidence."); People v. Wise, 46 N.Y.2d 321, 328, 413 N.Y.S.2d 334, 338, 385 N.E.2d 1262, 1266 (1978)("The obvious and salutary purpose of this rule is to prevent needless multiplication of issues in a case so as not to confuse the jury").

4. See § 607.7 infra.

On the other hand, the fact that it was an oak tree at the corner, rather than a maple tree, although perhaps a fair question on cross-examination,[5] undoubtedly would be considered collateral and therefore not subject to extrinsic evidence.[6]

A wholly satisfactory delineation of collateral and noncollateral matters has never been articulated. Influenced by Wigmore,[7] however, the New York Court of Appeals in *People v. Schwartzman* [8] identified two categories of facts that are noncollateral and therefore subject to proof by extrinsic evidence to contradict a witness: (1) facts that traditionally may be proven by extrinsic evidence to impeach credibility, such as bias, interest, sensory impairment and the like; and (2) facts that are relevant to an issue in the case other than mere credibility.[9] The rationale for permitting extrinsic evidence with respect to the second category of facts seems clear enough:

> [T]he objection of confusion of issues is inapplicable if the evidence is admissible for any purpose other than contradiction. Likewise, it is not unfair to expect a party to refute testimonial errors when the subject of the error is a material issue in the case, for upon such subjects the parties should in any event come prepared. * * *

---

5. See Feldsberg v. Nitschke, 49 N.Y.2d 636, 643, 427 N.Y.S.2d 751, 755, 404 N.E.2d 1293, 1297 (1980)(trial court has discretion to restrict cross-examination into collateral matters); 3A Wigmore § 1006 (cross-examiner may question witness on collateral points, subject to trial court's discretion to limit such inquiries). See also § 611.3, at notes 29–32, infra (judicial discretion to curtail cross-examination).

6. See Simmons, Inc. v. Pinkerton's, Inc., 762 F.2d 591, 604–05 (7th Cir.1985):

> Impeachment by contradiction simply involves presenting evidence that part or all of a witness' testimony is incorrect. Thus if an eyewitness to an auto accident testifies that the car that caused the accident was red, impeachment by contradiction relies on evidence that the car actually was yellow. The inference to be drawn is not that the witness was lying, but that the witness made a mistake of fact, and so perhaps her testimony may contain other errors and should be discounted accordingly.
>
> Of course, a particular misstatement may or may not be probative of the witness' general accuracy, depending on the circumstances, and thus may or may not be worth the time it takes to establish it. For this reason the collateral evidence rule developed. In the above example, assuming the color of the car was not directly relevant to any substantive issue in the case (e.g., if the identity of the car were stipulated), it presumably would not be worth the fact finder's time to entertain a "mini-trial" on the issue of the car's color, simply to prove that the witness was mistaken as to this fact. Thus, while the accuracy of a witness' perception or memory can always be tested through traditional cross-examination techniques, the collateral evidence rule limits the extent to which the witness' testimony about non-essential matters may be contradicted by extrinsic proof. In short, if a matter is collateral (that is, if it could not be introduced into evidence as substantive proof) then it cannot be proven simply to contradict the witness' testimony for impeachment purposes.

See also United States v. Rovetuso, 768 F.2d 809, 817–18 (7th Cir.1985), cert. denied, 474 U.S. 1076, 106 S.Ct. 838, 88 L.Ed.2d 809, and 476 U.S. 1106, 106 S.Ct. 1951, 90 L.Ed.2d 360 (1986)(witness' statement on cross-examination that he had once been a Panamanian police officer could not be contradicted by extrinsic evidence because of its collateral nature under the circumstances).

7. 3A Wigmore §§ 1004–1005.

8. 24 N.Y.2d 241, 299 N.Y.S.2d 817, 247 N.E.2d 642, cert. denied, 396 U.S. 846, 90 S.Ct. 103, 24 L.Ed.2d 96 (1969).

9. Id. at 245, 299 N.Y.S.2d at 821, 247 N.E.2d at 644. The Schwartzman court characterized the two classes of facts as "exceptions" to the rule against extrinsic evidence of collateral matters whereas Wigmore defined them simply as "noncollateral" matters. 3A Wigmore §§ 1004–1005.

§ 607.3 WITNESSES Ch. 6

Thus, when a witness testifies concerning a fact material to the case, he may be contradicted either by cross-examination or by introduction of other evidence.[10]

In *Schwartzman*, a prosecution for larceny based on misrepresentation, the defendant's denial on cross-examination of several prior instances of fraudulent conduct for which he had not been prosecuted did not foreclose the introduction of evidence of the other conduct. Although prior bad acts ordinarily may not be proved by extrinsic evidence for impeachment purposes,[11] such proof in the instant case did more than merely contradict the witness. It was independently probative of a material issue in the case, i.e., the fraudulent intent with which the defendant had acted in the crime charged.[12]

Contradictory evidence which is independently probative of a material issue in the case may sometimes be admissible for impeachment purposes despite constitutionally-based exclusionary rules that might otherwise apply. For example, in *United States v. Havens*,[13] a defendant on trial for importing cocaine testified on cross-examination that he had nothing to do with sewing make-shift pockets on T-shirts. Such pockets had been used by the defendant's accomplice, however, to hold the cocaine. The prosecutor then asked the defendant about the contents of his suitcase, which had been suppressed because of an illegal search and seizure. The suitcase contained a T-shirt from which the cloth for the accomplice's T-shirt pockets had been cut. On rebuttal, the prosecutor introduced testimony that the shirt was found in defendant's luggage and was permitted to admit the shirt into evidence, limited to the purpose of impeaching defendant's credibility. The Supreme Court upheld the procedure, stressing that a defendant has an obligation to testify truthfully.[14]

---

10. 24 N.Y.2d at 245–46, 299 N.Y.S.2d at 821–22, 247 N.E.2d at 645.

11. See § 608.2 infra.

12. 24 N.Y.2d at 246–49, 299 N.Y.S.2d at 822–25, 247 N.E.2d at 645–47. See § 404.1 at notes 29–38, supra. The extrinsic evidence therefore could be weighed by the jury on the issue of intent as well as credibility.

The "material issue" analysis is also applied when the cross-examiner seeks to prove through extrinsic evidence that a witness has made a prior statement that is inconsistent with his testimony. See § 607.8 infra.

13. 446 U.S. 620, 100 S.Ct. 1912, 64 L.Ed.2d 559 (1980).

14. Id. at 626–27, 100 S.Ct. at 1916, 64 L.Ed.2d at 566. The point addressed in Havens had already been established with respect to introduction of illegally-obtained evidence to contradict specific statements made by a defendant during his direct testimony. Walder v. United States, 347 U.S. 62, 74 S.Ct. 354, 98 L.Ed. 503 (1954). The complicating aspect of Havens was that the precise matter—defendant's possession of a T-shirt that had been cut up to facilitate the importation scheme—was first raised by the prosecutor during cross-examination. The cross-examination, however, was within the scope of defendant's direct testimony, in which he affirmatively volunteered that he had engaged in no activity concerning the concealment of cocaine on the accomplice's body. See § 611.5, at note 15, infra (scope of cross-examination). When questions that are put to a defendant on cross-examination are reasonably suggested by his direct examination, "[he] must testify truthfully or suffer the consequences," 446 U.S. at 626, 100 S.Ct. at 1916, 64 L.Ed.2d at 565–66. The policy considerations underlying the exclusionary rule, said the Court, are vindicated by precluding use of the tainted evidence on the government's direct case as substantive evidence of guilt. Id. at 627–28, 100 S.Ct. at 1916–17, 64 L.Ed.2d at 566.

The same reasoning supports impeachment by prior inconsistent statements of a

Professor McCormick argued that there is a third basis for the introduction of contradictory evidence with respect to a matter that might otherwise seem collateral: Contradiction should be allowed as to "any part of the witness's account of the background and circumstances of a material transaction, which as a matter of human experience he would not have been mistaken about if his story were true."[15] One of the cases cited by McCormick to illustrate his point was an 1859 decision of the New York Court of Appeals in which the defendant was on trial for poisoning his wife with arsenic.[16] Defendants' witnesses testified that arsenic had been purchased by or on behalf of the defendant for the purpose of killing rats in a cellar where provisions were kept. The prosecutor was allowed to prove through other witnesses that no provisions had been kept in the cellar because the matter was "not strictly collateral."[17]

New York courts have not explicitly acknowledged McCormick's third category of extrinsic contradiction evidence. The Second Circuit, however, on a habeas corpus petition, held that a criminal defendant in a New York state trial should have been allowed to introduce evidence to contradict the testimony of a key prosecution witness regarding the background circumstances under which he allegedly observed the crime.[18]

---

defendant that were obtained in violation of the defendant's Miranda rights. See § 607.8, at notes 10–12, infra.

15. McCormick on Evidence § 47, at 112 (3d ed.1984). It bears noting that the quotation in the text is from the third edition of McCormick's treatise. The fourth edition carries forward the argument but in truncated form. See McCormick § 49, at 184. The earlier edition explains the point as follows:

> Suppose a witness has told a story of a transaction crucial to the controversy. To prove him wrong in some trivial detail of time, place or circumstance is "collateral." But to prove untrue some fact recited by the witness that if he were really there and saw what he claims to have seen, he could not have been mistaken about, is a convincing kind of impeachment, that the courts must make place for * * *. To disprove such a fact is to pull out the linchpin of the story.

McCormick on Evidence, § 47, at 111–12 (3d ed.1984). See also Lilly § 8.6, at 371 ("In close cases, * * * it is important to consider whether the challenged evidence cast sufficient doubt—albeit indirectly—upon important testimony that goes to a central issue in the case").

16. Stephens v. People, 19 N.Y. 549 (1859).

17. Id. at 572. Another case cited by McCormick to illustrate his point was East Tennessee, Virginia & Georgia Ry. Co. v. Daniel, 91 Ga. 768, 18 S.E. 22, 22 (1893)(witness testified that he was at accident scene as result of having left home to buy some tobacco, had bought the tobacco at certain store and was on his way home when he saw the accident; opponent should have been allowed to introduce testimony by the shopkeeper that the witness had purchased no tobacco: "it was indirectly material because it contradicted the witness as to the train of events which led him to be present").

18. Rosario v. Kuhlman, 839 F.2d 918, 925–26 (2d Cir.1988). The defendant was identified by the prosecution's sole eyewitness as having committed murder during the course of a robbery. The witness testified that he had been in the company of his girlfriend, one Eva Lopez, at the time he observed the crime. The defense was not allowed at trial to prove that the witness did not even know Lopez at the time of the crime. Precluding such extrinsic evidence was error, said the Second Circuit, because it was relevant impeachment by contradiction on a matter as to which the witness could not have been mistaken if his witnessing of the crime were true. Id. at 926.

The Rosario court noted that the Second Circuit itself had endorsed McCormick's third category of contradictory extrinsic evidence in federal trials in United States v. Robinson, 544 F.2d 110, 114 (2d Cir.1976), cert. denied, 434 U.S. 1050, 98 S.Ct. 901, 54 L.Ed.2d 803 (1978)(alibi witness testified

§ 607.3   WITNESSES   Ch. 6

"Door opening" is a fourth potential rationale for the introduction of extrinsic evidence of contradiction. New York courts have held that the volunteering of collateral information on direct examination may, in some circumstances, make the information "material," thereby opening the door to contradiction.[19] The scope of the rule is unclear. In some of the cases, the facts that were held to be properly contradicted might readily have been classified as falling within either the second category identified in *Schwartzman* (facts bearing on a material issue in the case)[20] or the third category advocated by McCormick (facts which the witness could not have been mistaken about if her story were true).[21] In another line of cases, contradiction by party *A* was allowed after party *B* affirmatively sought to prove collateral matters that *A* had merely inquired about for attempted impeachment during cross-examination of *B*.[22] Federal courts have occasionally invoked the "door opening" rubric

that he remembered the day in question because he had picked up unemployment check on that day; government could prove through extrinsic evidence that witness had not been issued unemployment check on that day).

19. Halloran v. Virginia Chemicals, Inc., 41 N.Y.2d 386, 393, 393 N.Y.S.2d 341, 347, 361 N.E.2d 991, 996–97 (1977); People v. Castro, 101 A.D.2d 392, 398, 475 N.Y.S.2d 840, 843–44 (1st Dep't 1984), aff'd, 65 N.Y.2d 683, 491 N.Y.S.2d 623, 481 N.E.2d 255 (1985). The "door opening" concept has also been used to permit cross-examination, as contrasted with extrinsic proof of contradictory facts, into matters that might otherwise be inadmissible, such as a defendant-witness' prior criminal record. See People v. Fardan, 82 N.Y.2d 638, 646, 607 N.Y.S.2d 220, 224, 628 N.E.2d 41, 45 (1993); §§ 608.2(a) and 609.1 infra.

20. In Halloran v. Virginia Chemicals, Inc., 41 N.Y.2d 386, 393 N.Y.S.2d 341, 361 N.E.2d 991 (1977), the plaintiff alleged that he was injured while using defendant's product. On direct testimony, he described how, on numerous prior occasions, he had used the product in accordance with the manufacturer's instructions. On cross-examination, he denied the defendant's insinuations that his actual practice in using the product was contrary to his testimony.

The trial court was held to have erred in precluding defendant, on rebuttal, from proving that plaintiff's prior usage of the product was routinely improper. The Court of Appeals held that because the proffered evidence of plaintiff's habit was probative of his conduct at the time of injury, it was noncollateral and therefore could have been introduced on defendant's direct case. The court's discussion of plaintiff's "door opening" was made in the context of an analysis of whether defendant had preserved the question of habit evidence for appeal in light of defendant's argument at the trial court level that the evidence was admissible for the limited purpose of impeaching plaintiff's credibility. Id. at 393–94, 393 N.Y.S.2d at 346–47, 361 N.E.2d at 996–97.

21. In People v. Castro, 101 A.D.2d 392, 475 N.Y.S.2d 840 (1st Dep't 1984), aff'd, 65 N.Y.2d 683, 491 N.Y.S.2d 623, 481 N.E.2d 255 (1985), the defendant explained, on direct examination, that he was at the crime scene, a beer distributorship, innocently drinking a soda which he had purchased from the distributorship. During rebuttal, the prosecution was allowed to prove that there was no soda for sale at the distributorship at the time in question. Id. at 395, 398, 475 N.Y.S.2d at 842, 843–44.

22. People v. Leonardo, 199 N.Y. 432, 441–42, 92 N.E. 1060, 1064 (1910) (on cross-examination, defendant denied insinuation that he had stolen certain jewelry, a collateral criminal act with which the prosecutor sought to impeach defendant's credibility; thereafter defendant introduced the testimony of another witness in an effort to disprove any involvement in the theft that the prosecutor had asked about; court held that no prejudice occurred when, on rebuttal, prosecution attempted to elicit from another witness facts that contradicted defendant's witness because defendant had "voluntarily assumed to make the collateral issue a material one"); Osnato v. New York City Transit Auth., 172 A.D.2d 597, 599, 568 N.Y.S.2d 821, 823 (2d Dep't 1991)(during liability phase of personal injury action, plaintiff insisted, in response to questions raised on cross-examination, that he had not worked since the accident; on redirect, plaintiff reiterated that he had not worked and introduced photographs to support his statement; defendant was thereafter allowed to introduce testimony of an investigator to contradict plaintiff; the matter was

to permit proof by contradiction with respect to otherwise collateral matters volunteered by criminal defendants for strategic advantage during their direct testimony.[23]

Wigmore argued that door opening through volunteered testimony, standing alone, is a questionable basis for the introduction of extrinsic contradictory evidence.[24] Although the "unfair surprise" factor is inoperative in such cases (the witness herself has tendered the point), the potential for confusion and delay may still be present. Nevertheless, the allowance of contradiction for purposes of impeachment may be justified in some "door opening" situations by legitimate interests in preventing a party from unfairly presenting a distorted picture of the facts or of her credibility.

Library References:

West's Key No. Digests, Witnesses ⚖︎405.

§ 607.4 Party Impeachment of Her Own Witness

a. New York, In General

There comes a time in the life of virtually every trial lawyer when she must call to the stand a witness with knowledge of certain facts that must be placed before the fact-finder but whose account of an event may be otherwise quite harmful to the party the lawyer represents. This is almost certain to happen when the adverse party himself is called. Even a witness who is expected to be helpful, perhaps because of prior statements, may disappoint counsel with unhelpful or damaging testimony. In these circumstances may the lawyer proceed to impeach her own witness in an effort to neutralize or mitigate the harm? The answer of the New York courts, as a general matter, is in the negative.

The origins of the common law rule against impeaching one's own witness are obscure,[1] but the persistence of the rule in New York is

collateral but plaintiff's "testimony on redirect opened the door to the issue of his employment after the accident").

23. See, e.g., United States v. Garcia, 900 F.2d 571, 575 (2d Cir.), cert. denied, 498 U.S. 862, 111 S.Ct. 169, 112 L.Ed.2d 133 (1990)(on redirect testimony, defendant sought to create false impression that a prior arrest had not involved drugs; prosecutor thereafter could prove the arrest record); United States v. Babbitt, 683 F.2d 21, 25 (1st Cir.1982) (prosecutor could prove two remote arrests after defendant testified on direct that he had no police record); United States v. Colletti, 245 F.2d 781, 782 (2d Cir.), cert. denied, 355 U.S. 874, 78 S.Ct. 125, 2 L.Ed.2d 78 (1957)(prosecutor could prove prior assault convictions after defendant testified on direct that he had never been convicted of any crime; defendant himself had put his previous good conduct into issue). In United States v. Beno, 324 F.2d 582 (2d Cir.1963), the court explained, "[W]here a defendant in his direct testimony, falsely states a specific fact, the prosecution will not be prevented from proving, either through cross-examination or by calling its own witnesses, that he lied *as to that fact*. * * * [E]ven if the issue is irrelevant or collateral, a defendant should not be allowed to profit by a gratuitously offered misstatement." Id. at 588 (emphasis in original). See also United States v. Wright, 542 F.2d 975, 980 (7th Cir.1976), cert. denied, 429 U.S. 1073, 97 S.Ct. 810, 50 L.Ed.2d 790 (1977)(government could prove prior misconduct where defendant volunteered facts concerning the matter during cross-examination).

24. 3A Wigmore § 1007.

§ 607.4

1. Wigmore hypothesizes that the rule may have been a carryover from the ancient trial practice of calling partisan oath-helpers, rather than fact witnesses, to swear to

§ 607.4   WITNESSES   Ch. 6

clear.[2] The usual justification is that a party who has voluntarily selected a witness vouches for that witness' credibility and should not be heard thereafter to attack his credibility.[3] Apparently, the notion is that a party has no one to blame but herself if the witness' testimony turns out to be unfavorable and that it is somehow unfair to let the party indulge in impeachment.[4] Another justification is that a party should not have it within her power to intimidate or coerce her own witness into giving favorable testimony under threat of exposing damaging facts about the witness' character that bear on credibility. A witness has enough to fear in that regard from the adversary.[5]

Modern authorities elsewhere have rejected this reasoning and permit the impeachment of one's own witness by any relevant impeachment technique.[6] New York courts, however, have not retreated from the rule

---

the truth of the party's cause. 3A Wigmore § 896. For a party to impeach the credibility of her own oath-helper obviously would make no sense. See People v. Fitzpatrick, 40 N.Y.2d 44, 49, 386 N.Y.S.2d 28, 30, 351 N.E.2d 675, 677–78 (1976).

2. See, e.g., People v. Saez, 69 N.Y.2d 802, 513 N.Y.S.2d 380, 505 N.E.2d 945 (1987)(state's witness could not be impeached by prosecutor except to limited extent permitted by statute); Spampinato v. A.B.C. Consolidated Corp., 35 N.Y.2d 283, 287, 360 N.Y.S.2d 878, 880, 319 N.E.2d 196, 198 (1974)("party may not generally impeach, that is, attack the general or specific credibility of his own witness").

3. Carlisle v. Norris, 215 N.Y. 400, 409, 109 N.E. 564, 567 (1915)(by calling witness, party vouches for his reliability and credibility); People v. Sexton, 187 N.Y. 495, 509, 80 N.E. 396, 401 (1907)("the party who calls a witness certifies his credibility"); Pollock v. Pollock, 71 N.Y. 137, 152 (1877)("It is fair to judge a party by his own witness. * * * If a party puts upon the stand a witness who is for any reason assailable, that party asserts or admits the credibility of that witness.").

The validity of the voucher concept is undermined by the rule that a party may contradict her own witness' version of material facts through the testimony of other witnesses for the purpose of showing that the facts are different from those related by her own witness. See notes 17–19 infra; N.Y.Jud.Council, Second Ann.Rep. 179–80 (1936).

4. The counterargument is that parties as a practical matter are not free to pick and choose witnesses. See N.Y.Jud.Council, Second Ann.Rep. 179 (1936). The circumstances of the case will dictate the witnesses that must be called based on their supposed knowledge of the facts. In any event, as Wigmore argued: "[T]he ends of truth are not to be subserved by binding the parties with guarantees and vouchings, and * * * it is the business of a court of justice, in mere self-respect, to seek all sources of correct information, whatever foolish guarantees a party may or may not have chosen to make." 3A Wigmore § 898, at 662.

5. People v. Minsky, 227 N.Y. 94, 100, 124 N.E. 126, 128 (1919)("A witness of bad character has enough to fear from the adverse party without being intimidated by the party calling him. The power to coerce a witness may as reasonably be expected to beget a lie as to force the truth from unwilling lips."). Although Wigmore favored total abolition of the anti-impeachment rule, he conceded that there was some force to the coercion rationale. 3A Wigmore § 899. Assuming the validity of a rule that would protect the party's own witness from tactical revelation of his bad character, however, Wigmore found no justification for prohibiting impeachment on the grounds of bias or prior inconsistent statements, neither of which would "disgrace" the witness. Id. §§ 899, 901, 902. See also note 29 infra.

6. See text at notes 45–47 infra. Section 607(b) of the Proposed New York Evidence Code would permit impeachment of any witness, subject to certain limitations:

(b) Who may impeach. [PROPOSED] Except as otherwise provided in subdivision (c) of section 613 of this article, the credibility of a witness may be attacked by any party, including the party calling that witness. Provided, however, a party may not call a witness for the sole purpose of impeaching the credibility of that witness unless that witness has previously testified or a hearsay statement of that witness has previously been admitted into evidence.

The comment of the Law Revision Commission to proposed § 607(b) states that the

that a party may not show the bias or interest of her witness[7] or bring out facts that demonstrate her witness' bad character for truthfulness.[8] Furthermore, it remains the general rule that prior inconsistent statements of the party's own witness may not be proven for impeachment purposes.[9] There has been a modicum of legislative reform with respect to prior inconsistent statements, but impeachment is permitted only if the prior statement was in a signed writing or was given orally under oath.[10]

A party generally makes a witness her own, including in a civil case the opponent himself,[11] by calling the witness to the stand at trial and eliciting testimony from him on some material issue in the case.[12] By statute, however, the mere taking of a pretrial deposition of a witness does not make the witness that of the party who took the deposition.[13] On the other hand, if deposition testimony is introduced at trial as

voucher concept is based on false premises and is at odds with "the practical exigencies of litigation." The cross-reference to § 613(c) in proposed § 607(b) would preserve the substance of current limits on the use of prior inconsistent statements in criminal cases. See text at notes 26–44 infra.

7. Carlisle v. Norris, 215 N.Y. 400, 408–09, 109 N.E. 564, 567 (1915) (interest); Jones v. State, 93 Misc.2d 916, 924, 403 N.Y.S.2d 691, 697 (Ct.of Cl.1978)(bias).

8. Hanrahan v. New York Edison Co., 238 N.Y. 194, 197, 144 N.E. 499, 500 (1924)(party's own witness may not be impeached by "general evidence of bad character"; improper to question witness about prior conviction); People v. Minsky, 227 N.Y. 94, 99, 124 N.E. 126, 127–28 (1919)(having called witness and thereby presented him as worthy of belief, party "must not thereafter attack the credibility of the witness by general character evidence tending to show him to be untruthful and unworthy of belief"; prosecutor improperly inquired of his witness, after she gave disappointing testimony, whether she was a prostitute and had several venereal diseases).

Whether the rule against impeachment also prohibits the party from showing a sensory or mental impairment of her witness has not been discussed in the cases.

9. See note 31 infra.

10. CPLR 4514; N.Y.Crim.Proc.Law § 60.35. The details of the statutory exceptions are described in the text at notes 26–43 infra.

A criminal defendant may be able to make a case for a broader right of impeachment of his own witness on due process or confrontation grounds. See note 44 infra.

11. See, e.g., Cross v. Cross, 108 N.Y. 628, 629, 15 N.E. 333, 334 (1888); Jordan v. Parrinello, 144 A.D.2d 540, 534 N.Y.S.2d 686 (2d Dep't 1988).

12. It has been held that the mere swearing of a witness followed by a few preliminary questions on background matters will not make the witness that of the party who called him to the stand. Fall Brook Coal Co. v. Hewson, 158 N.Y. 150, 52 N.E. 1095 (1899)(witness called to stand by defendant was asked preliminary questions and then excused; defendant was permitted to impeach the witness when he was subsequently called by plaintiff). The Fall Brook court stated:

[T]he rule [against impeachment of one's own witness] is not properly applicable, save in cases where a party attempts to elicit, from a witness called to the stand, testimony material to the issues upon trial; that until such an attempt is made, the party has done nothing that can by any possibility affect the trial either to his own benefit or to the harm of his opponent, and, therefore, he has not offered a witness in proof of his cause and is not within the reason of the rule that burdens him with the necessity of supporting the character of the witness to the end of the trial.

Id. at 155, 52 N.E. at 1096–97. See also Valenti v. Mesinger, 175 App.Div. 398, 162 N.Y.S. 30 (1st Dep't 1916)(party did not make witness his own by asking questions that had no bearing on litigated issues).

Where compulsion of law has dictated the calling of a particular witness, such as an attesting witness to a will, impeachment is permitted. Conselyea v. Walker, 2 Dem. 117 (N.Y.1884), aff'd sub nom. In re Bogart's Estate, 33 Hun 665 (1884). See also 3A Wigmore § 918 (witness called by judge is open to impeachment by either party).

13. CPLR 3117(d).

affirmative evidence, the deponent become the witness of the party who introduced it.[14]

Once ownership of a witness attaches, the calling of the witness by the opponent does not free the original owner from the prohibition against impeachment.[15] In such circumstances, both parties are precluded from impeaching the witness. Furthermore, if the witness was originally called by the opponent, cross-examination into material matters that exceed the scope of the direct testimony makes the witness that of the cross-examiner as well as that of the opponent.[16]

The harshness of the rule against impeachment of one's own witness is mitigated by its limitations, the most important of which is that the concept of impeachment in this context is confined to a direct personal attack on the witness' credibility. *Contradiction* of the witness on material issues with evidence from other sources is not prohibited.[17] Put another way, a party is not bound by her own witness' version of events.[18] Assume, for example, that A in an auto accident case testifies

---

14. CPLR 3117(d) provides that "[t]he introduction in evidence of the deposition or any part thereof for any purpose other than that of contradicting or impeaching the deponent makes the deponent the witness of the party introducing the deposition * * *." The statute goes on to provide an exception where the deposition which is introduced is that of the adverse party. Prior statements of an adverse party are usually admissible as affirmative evidence against the party pursuant to the hearsay exception for party admissions even if he has become the witness of the opponent. See note 32 infra.

15. Hanrahan v. New York Edison Co., 238 N.Y. 194, 197–98, 144 N.E. 499, 500 (1924).

16. Bennett v. Crescent Athletic–Hamilton Club, 270 N.Y. 456, 458, 1 N.E.2d 963, 964 (1936); Kay v. Metropolitan Street Ry. Co., 163 N.Y. 447, 451–52, 57 N.E. 751, 752 (1900).

17. Becker v. Koch, 104 N.Y. 394, 403, 10 N.E. 701, 704 (1887)("[A]ll the cases concur in the right of a party to contradict his own witness by calling witnesses to prove a fact material to the issue to be otherwise than as sworn to by him, even when the necessary effect is to impeach him."); People v. Figueroa, 153 A.D.2d 576, 584, 544 N.Y.S.2d 618, 624 (2d Dep't 1989)("[W]hile, ordinarily, a party may not impeach the credibility of its own witness * * *, this rule does not prevent a party from proving a material fact by another witness even if the effect is to implicitly contradict its own witness."). Similarly, when a party introduces the contents of a pretrial deposition as affirmative evidence, he makes the deponent his own witness (unless the deponent is the adverse party), but CPLR 3117(d) explicitly provides that "any party may rebut any relevant evidence contained in a deposition, whether introduced by him or by any other party."

18. Spampinato v. A.B.C. Consolidated Corp., 35 N.Y.2d 283, 287, 360 N.Y.S.2d 878, 880–81, 319 N.E.2d 196, 198 (1974)(by calling defendant to testify, plaintiff made him his own witness, but "it does not follow from this * * * that the plaintiff adopted, or became bound by, the witness's version of the facts. No party is ever limited by the witnesses he produces, or examines, from establishing the facts in issue. A party may not generally impeach, that is, attack the general or specific credibility of his own witness, but impeachment is not to be confused with 'binding' testimony * * *."). See also Gonzalez v. Medina, 69 A.D.2d 14, 22, 417 N.Y.S.2d 953, 958–59 (1st Dep't 1979).

In Becker v. Koch, 104 N.Y. 394, 10 N.E. 701 (1887), contradictory evidence was contained in the witness' own business records, which he explained as containing inaccurate descriptions of transactions. The court held that the jury was free to disbelieve the witness' explanation: "Why should not the right exist to show that a portion of the evidence of your own witness is untrue, by comparing it with another portion of the evidence of the same witness and with the other facts in the case?" Id. at 403, 10 N.E. at 704.

Of course, in a practical sense a party is bound by her own witness if his testimony contains no self-contradictions, contradictory evidence from other sources is not introduced, and the witness' account is free from inherent ambiguity or improbability. See,

for plaintiff that the defendant was driving while intoxicated but had a green light. *B*'s contradictory testimony for plaintiff that the color of the traffic light was red, while obviously having an indirect impeaching effect on *A*'s credibility, would not put the plaintiff in the position of directly assailing witness *A*'s character for truthfulness or showing *A*'s own self-contradictions. Plaintiff's counsel could ask the jury to accept a portion of *A*'s testimony, such as *A*'s statement that defendant had been intoxicated, and to reject the balance.[19]

In addition, when the party's own witness is adverse or hostile, the rule against impeachment does not prohibit the use of leading questions.[20] It is said that in such cases, the witness may be questioned as if on cross-examination.[21] Furthermore, a prior inconsistent statement of the witness, even if it does not qualify for impeachment purposes under a statutory exception,[22] can be shown to the witness in an effort to refresh his recollection and induce a change in testimony.[23] Moreover, in civil actions, a party may do more than silently confront the witness with his prior statement. If the party is surprised by her witness' testimony, the witness may be interrogated in the presence of the jury about prior inconsistent statements both to refresh the witness' memory and to help explain why the party called the witness in the first place.[24]

e.g., Carlisle v. Norris, 215 N.Y. 400, 408–11, 109 N.E. 564, 567–68 (1915)(plaintiff suffered directed verdict where his witness, whose interest in defendant's favor could not properly be considered to impeach credibility, gave testimony that was neither improbable nor contradicted in any manner by other evidence in the case).

19. See People v. Minsky, 227 N.Y. 94, 100, 124 N.E. 126, 128 (1919) ("The People were not bound by [their witness'] denial. They could, without impeaching the witness, ask the jury to infer that she did not tell the whole truth and nothing but the truth."); Koester v. Rochester Candy Works, 194 N.Y. 92, 97, 87 N.E. 77, 79 (1909)("[Party] may prove by competent testimony that the facts material to the issue are the exact reverse of those testified to by his witness, and may ask the jury to disbelieve his statement, and credit that of the later witnesses."); Becker v. Koch, 104 N.Y. 394, 404, 10 N.E. 701, 705 (1887)(party "may ask a jury to believe in part and to disbelieve the residue" of testimony of adverse witness called by party; credibility is jury question).

20. Becker v. Koch, 104 N.Y. 394, 401, 10 N.E. 701, 703 (1887)("An adverse witness may be cross-examined, and leading questions may be put to him by the party calling him, for the very sensible and sufficient reason that he is adverse and that the danger arising from such a mode of examination by the party calling a friendly or unbiased witness does not exist.")

21. Id. See also People v. Minsky, 227 N.Y. 94, 98, 124 N.E. 126, 127 (1919)(trial court, in its discretion, properly allowed prosecutor to "cross-examine" hostile witness he had called to stand); People v. Sexton, 187 N.Y. 495, 509, 80 N.E. 396, 401 (1907)("when a witness proves hostile or unwilling, the party calling him may probe his conscience or test his recollection, to the end that the whole truth may be laid bare"); Jordan v. Parrinello, 144 A.D.2d 540, 541, 534 N.Y.S.2d 686, 687 (2d Dep't 1988)(adverse party, called by opponent, is presumed hostile, and in court's discretion "direct examination may assume the nature of cross-examination by the use of leading questions").

22. See text at notes 26–43 infra.

23. Bullard v. Pearsall, 53 N.Y. 230 (1873)(rule in civil cases); N.Y.Crim.Proc. Law § 60.35(3)(rule in criminal cases).

24. Bullard v. Pearsall, 53 N.Y. 230, 231 (1873). The Bullard court justified the procedure as follows:

The further question has frequently arisen whether the party calling the witness should, upon being taken by surprise by unexpected testimony, be permitted to interrogate the witness in respect to his own previous declarations, inconsistent with his evidence. Upon this point there is considerable conflict in the authorities. We are of opinion that such questions may be asked of the witness for the purpose of probing his recollection, recalling to his mind the statements he has previ-

§ 607.4　　　　　WITNESSES　　　　　Ch. 6

Finally, a party is not deemed to impeach her witness by revealing prior convictions or other adverse facts about the witness during direct examination where the purpose is simply to soften the blow of anticipated cross-examination on such matters.[25]

b. New York Exception for Prior Inconsistent Statements

CPLR 4514 and New York Criminal Procedure Law § 60.35 have modified the general rule against impeachment of one's own witness by allowing a party to show that the witness has made certain types of statements that are inconsistent with his trial testimony. CPLR 4514, applicable in civil actions, provides that "any party may introduce proof that any witness has made a prior statement inconsistent with his testimony if the statement was made in a writing subscribed by him or was made under oath." In criminal cases, § 60.35 of the Criminal Procedure Law also allows a party to impeach his own witness with prior inconsistent statements that are in a signed writing or were made orally under oath, but the statute contains additional qualifications:

§ 60.35 Rules of evidence; impeachment of own witness by proof of prior contradictory statement

1. When, upon examination by the party who called him, a witness in a criminal proceeding gives testimony upon a material issue of the case which tends to disprove the position of such party, such party may introduce evidence that such witness has previously made either a written statement signed by him or an oral statement under oath contradictory to such testimony.

2. Evidence concerning a prior contradictory statement introduced pursuant to subdivision one may be received only for the purpose of impeaching the credibility of the witness with

---

ously made, and drawing out an explanation of his apparent inconsistency. This course of examination may result in satisfying the witness that he has fallen into error and that his original statements were correct, and it is calculated to elicit the truth. It is also proper for the purpose of showing the circumstances which induced the party to call him. Though the answers of the witness may involve him in contradictions calculated to impair his credibility, that is not a sufficient reason for excluding the inquiry. Proof by other witnesses that his statements are incorrect would have the same effect, yet the admissibility of such proof cannot be questioned. It is only evidence offered for the mere purpose of impeaching the credibility of the witness, which is inadmissible when offered by the party calling him. Inquiries calculated to elicit the facts, or to show to the witness that he is mistaken and to induce him to correct his evidence, should not be excluded simply because they may result unfavorably to his credibility. In case he should deny having made previous statements inconsistent with his testimony, we do not think it would be proper to allow such statements to be proved by other witnesses; but where the questions as to such statements are confined to the witness himself, we think they are admissible. As a matter of course, such previous unsworn statements are not evidence, and when the trial is before a jury that instruction should be given."

Id. at 231–32.

Such interrogation is prohibited in criminal cases by § 60.35(3) of the New York Criminal Procedure Law. See note 26 infra.

25. People v. Minsky, 227 N.Y. 94, 98, 124 N.E. 126, 127 (1919)("The law does not * * * compel a party to conceal the bad record of his witnesses from the jury, to have it afterwards revealed by the opposing party with telling effect. Such a rule would be unfair alike to the party calling the witness and the jury.").

respect to his testimony upon the subject, and does not constitute evidence in chief. Upon receiving such evidence at a jury trial, the court must so instruct the jury.

3. When a witness has made a prior signed or sworn statement contradictory to his testimony in a criminal proceeding upon a material issue of the case, but his testimony does not tend to disprove the position of the party who called him and elicited such testimony, evidence that the witness made such prior statement is not admissible, and such party may not use such prior statement for the purpose of refreshing the recollection of the witness in a manner that discloses its contents to the trier of the facts.[26]

Both statutes were enacted "to correct the inequities occasioned by the fact that in many cases both sides were unfairly hampered by their inability to impeach unreliable witnesses upon whom they were compelled to rely."[27] Prior inconsistent statements were singled out for the exception probably because they are the most effective of the impeachment techniques[28] and because they do not impugn a witness' character or have much of a coercive effect on a witness who is committed to certain testimony.[29] The statutory requirement of a signed writing or an oral statement under oath helps ensure that the prior statement was made with a fair degree of deliberation on the part of the witness and that a relatively quick and easy means of proof is available.[30] Prior

---

26. Subdivision (3) of the statute regulates the use of prior inconsistent statements to refresh the recollection of a party's own witness when such statements do not qualify for impeachment. Any attempt to refresh recollection with such statements must be done in such a way that the statements are not disclosed to the trier of fact. This procedure was imposed to eliminate the danger that the jury will misuse the statements as substantive evidence. See People v. Fitzpatrick, 40 N.Y.2d 44, 50–51, 386 N.Y.S.2d 28, 31–32, 351 N.E.2d 675, 678–79 (1976). For example, in the jury's presence a prosecutor may not, under the guise of memory refreshment, engage in a line-by-line reading of statements that do not qualify under § 60.35(1), asking at each interval whether the witness remembers making the statement. Cf. People v. Welch, 16 A.D.2d 554, 229 N.Y.S.2d 909 (4th Dep't 1962). Although § 60.35(3) on its face prohibits revelation only of non-qualifying written statements and oral statements under oath, the spirit of the rule should foreclose inquiry in the jury's presence as to any type of prior inconsistent statement. See People v. Fitzpatrick, supra, 40 N.Y.2d at 51, 386 N.Y.S.2d at 32, 351 N.E.2d at 679 (§ 60.35(3) "also bars the traditional [refreshment-of-recollection] exception for material which is neither signed nor sworn and which otherwise may not be used to impeach"; dictum).

27. People v. McCormick, 278 App.Div. 410, 413, 105 N.Y.S.2d 571, 575 (1st Dep't 1951), aff'd, 303 N.Y. 403, 103 N.E.2d 529 (1952). See generally N.Y.Jud.Council, Second Ann.Rep. 177–84 (1936).

28. See McCormick § 38. The probative value of impeachment by self-contradiction is discussed in § 607.8 infra.

29. See 3A Wigmore § 902. To the extent the anti-impeachment rule is justified by fairness to the witness, see note 5 supra, Wigmore argued that "exposure of a self-contradiction * * * [carries] no necessary implication of bad character, no smirching of reputation, no exposure of misdeeds on cross-examination, nothing that could fairly operate to coerce either an honest or a dishonest witness to persist in an incorrect story through fear of the party calling him." 3A Wigmore § 902, at 669.

30. Cf. N.Y.Jud.Council, Second Ann. Rep. 180, 184 (1936). The Proposed New York Evidence Code, in § 613(c), preserves the substance of Crim.Proc.Law § 60.35 but would expand the exception to include prior inconsistent statements recorded on "videotape, audiotape or their technological equivalent" because such statements, like those under current law, leave "no room for doubt" that the statements were made. Comment, N.Y.Proposed Evid.Code § 613.

§ 607.4   WITNESSES   Ch. 6

inconsistent statements that do not meet one of these criteria cannot be used to impeach the credibility of the party's own witness.[31] Of course, if the adverse party himself has been called by the opponent in a civil case, any type of prior inconsistent statement on a material issue may be used as substantive evidence against the party as an admission, independent of the rules on impeachment.[32]

In criminal cases, § 60.35(1) of the Criminal Procedure Law restricts impeachment to inconsistencies that emerge during the party's own examination of her witness; inconsistencies on the opponent's cross-examination cannot be proven even if they might otherwise qualify.[33] Furthermore, in a criminal case the testimony must "tend to disprove" the party's case. In *People v. Fitzpatrick*,[34] the Court of Appeals interpreted this language as requiring affirmative damage to the party's case; a mere lack of recollection of the events in question will not trigger the right to impeach.[35] The court reasoned that the Legislature intended an affirmative-damage limitation in order to inhibit parties from calling witnesses as a mere subterfuge for bringing otherwise inadmissible statements to the jury's attention. Even with the requirement in subdivision (2) of § 60.35 that the jury be instructed to consider prior inconsistencies only on the issue of credibility, not as substantive evidence,[36] the danger still exists that a jury will misuse the prior

---

31. Jenkins v. 313–321 W. 37th Street Corp., 284 N.Y. 397, 402–03, 31 N.E.2d 503, 505 (1940), reh'g denied, 285 N.Y. 614, 33 N.E.2d 547 (1941) ("The recent amendment to [the predecessor of the CPLR] permitting impeachment of one's own witness is in derogation of the common law and must be strictly construed. Such construction does not admit of the use of other than signed statements or statements made under oath to impeach one's own witness."); People v. Jordan, 59 A.D.2d 746, 747, 398 N.Y.S.2d 556, 558 (2d Dep't 1977)("The requirement [of Crim.Proc.Law § 60.35(1)] that the previous statement be either signed or sworn to is absolute.").

No such restrictions are applicable, of course, to impeachment of an opponent's witness. See § 607.8, at note 7, infra. On the other hand, the procedural requirement that a witness be confronted with his prior inconsistent statement before it may be proven is operative regardless of whose witness is being impeached. See § 607.8 at notes 28–30, infra.

32. Koester v. Rochester Candy Works, 194 N.Y. 92, 97–98, 87 N.E. 77, 79 (1909)(defendant, assuming he made plaintiff his own witness through overly broad cross-examination, was free to introduce a material statement that contradicted plaintiff's testimony because the statement was a party admission: "When * * * it is said that one cannot impeach his own witness by contradictory statements made out of court, this statement must be limited to the case of a witness who is not the adverse party.").

33. People v. Fuller, 50 N.Y.2d 628, 638, 431 N.Y.S.2d 357, 362, 409 N.E.2d 834, 839–40 (1980)(prosecutor's impeachment with prior statement based on inconsistency during cross-examination did not comply with statute; harmless error under the circumstances).

34. 40 N.Y.2d 44, 386 N.Y.S.2d 28, 351 N.E.2d 675 (1976).

35. Id. at 52, 386 N.Y.S.2d at 32, 351 N.E.2d at 679 ("neutral testimony [that the witness did not recall a particular transaction], in and of itself, merely failed to corroborate or bolster the prosecutor's case; it did not contradict or disprove any testimony or other factual evidence presented by the prosecution here").

36. In People v. Romandette, 111 A.D.2d 1040, 490 N.Y.S.2d 347 (3d Dep't 1985), limiting instructions at the time of introduction of a prosecution witness' prior inconsistent statements were insufficient to avoid reversible error where the prosecutor, during summation, was allowed repeatedly to refer to the witness' prior statements as "direct evidence of * * * defendant's participation by an eyewitness." Id. at 1041–42, 490 N.Y.S.2d at 349.

CPLR 4514, unlike its counterpart in the Criminal Procedure Law, does not explicitly restrict the use of prior inconsistent statements to the credibility issue. The poten-

Ch. 6 IMPEACHMENT & REHABILITATION § 607.4

statements. Such danger should be risked, said the court, only when the testimony at trial has caused affirmative damage to the case of the party who called the witness.[37]

Interestingly, neither § 60.35(1) nor the courts have required the party to be "surprised" by her witness' damaging testimony as a prerequisite to impeachment with prior inconsistent statements.[38] Elsewhere, modifications of the common law rule often contain a "surprise" requirement as a further check on abuse of the impeachment privilege.[39] Despite the absence of a "surprise" requirement in New York, the courts

---

tial use of some prior inconsistent statements as substantive evidence in civil actions is undergoing evolution in New York. See § 801(1).2(a) infra.

37. 40 N.Y.2d at 51, 386 N.Y.S.2d at 32, 351 N.E.2d at 679. The three-judge dissent in Fitzpatrick took a broader view of the statutory language, arguing that the witness' "claimed inability to recall the incident at trial cast doubt upon the ability of the prosecution to prove defendant guilty and, therefore, 'tended to disprove' the prosecution case." Id. at 58, 386 N.Y.S.2d at 36, 351 N.E.2d at 683.

Not surprisingly, satisfaction of the affirmative-damage standard is a frequently litigated issue in the appellate courts. Affirmative damage was found in the following cases: People v. Barber, 186 A.D.2d 483, 589 N.Y.S.2d 409 (1st Dep't 1992), appeal denied, 81 N.Y.2d 836, 595 N.Y.S.2d 735, 611 N.E.2d 774 (1993)(witness denied at trial that defendant pulled out a gun, which contradicted prior sworn statement that he saw defendant pull a gun and shoot victim); People v. Mercado, 162 A.D.2d 722, 557 N.Y.S.2d 123 (2d Dep't 1990), appeal denied, 77 N.Y.2d 841, 567 N.Y.S.2d 210, 568 N.E.2d 659 (1991)(witness at trial recanted prior written statement that defendant was shooter and identified someone other than defendant as the perpetrator); People v. Romandette, 111 A.D.2d 1040, 490 N.Y.S.2d 347 (3d Dep't 1985)(witness testified that she and defendant drove to site of burglary where defendant said he was going inside to apply for employment and emerged a few minutes later empty-handed; in prior statement witness had said that defendant ran from premises with goods, telling her that he had stolen them; conviction was reversed, however, because prior statement was presented to jury as affirmative evidence of defendant's guilt); People v. De Jesus, 101 A.D.2d 111, 112–13, 475 N.Y.S.2d 19, 21–22 (1st Dep't 1984), aff'd, 64 N.Y.2d 1126, 490 N.Y.S.2d 188, 479 N.E.2d 824 (1985)(witness' testimony at trial that defendant "looked like" but was not the perpetrator could be impeached by witness' prior identification of defendant in photo array at grand jury).

Affirmative damage was found lacking in the following cases: People v. Saez, 69 N.Y.2d 802, 513 N.Y.S.2d 380, 505 N.E.2d 945 (1987)(in robbery prosecution in which defendant's display of object that "appeared" to be firearm was sufficient to convict, witness' prior statement that he saw shotgun barrel could not be used to impeach trial testimony that defendant pulled out an object wrapped in paper and stuck it in witness' side; another witness testified to seeing gun barrel); People v. Andre, 185 A.D.2d 276, 585 N.Y.S.2d 792 (2d Dep't 1992)(witness' testimony that he did not witness an argument between defendant and victim or see defendant shoot victim could not be contradicted by testimony from prior trial in which witness stated that defendant had been the shooter); People v. Comer, 146 A.D.2d 794, 537 N.Y.S.2d 272 (2d Dep't), appeal denied, 73 N.Y.2d 976, 540 N.Y.S.2d 1009, 538 N.E.2d 361 (1989)(at trial, witness testified that he did not know who shot victim because he had been in another room at the time; witness' absence of knowledge could not be impeached by prior grand jury testimony in which he identified defendant as the perpetrator).

38. People v. Magee, 128 A.D.2d 811, 811, 513 N.Y.S.2d 514, 515 (2d Dep't 1987)(fact that prosecutor was not surprised by his witness' testimony did not bar impeachment); People v. DeJesus, 101 A.D.2d 111, 114, 475 N.Y.S.2d 19, 22 (1st Dep't 1984), aff'd, 64 N.Y.2d 1126, 490 N.Y.S.2d 188, 479 N.E.2d 824 (1985)("CPL § 60.35 includes no requirement that the party calling the witness be surprised by the testimony of the witness.").

39. United States v. Miles, 413 F.2d 34 (3d Cir.1969). appeal after remand, 468 F.2d 482 (3d Cir.1972)(version of federal common law exception prior to adoption of Fed.R.Evid. 607); Poole v. State, 290 Md. 114, 118, 123, 428 A.2d 434, 437, 439 (1981), appeal after remand, 295 Md. 167, 453 A.2d 1218 (1983)(judge-made rule that applied prior to statutory elimination of rule against party's impeachment of her own witness).

§ 607.4 WITNESSES Ch. 6

have held that a prosecutor must act in good faith in calling a witness whom she anticipates impeaching.[40] The good faith standard is likely to be violated, for example, if the prosecutor, with advance knowledge of a witness' unequivocal refusal to give substantive testimony against the defendant, persists in calling the witness for the sole purpose of impeaching his credibility with a prior statement that implicates the defendant.[41] In such circumstances any argument by the prosecutor that "hope springs eternal" would ring hollow.[42] On the other hand, if the prosecutor reasonably expects to elicit at least some testimony that incriminates the defendant, anticipation of additional evidence that will harm the state's case should not preclude impeachment.[43]

On the face of § 60.35, the "affirmative damage" prerequisite and all other limitations on the use of prior inconsistent statements apply to prosecutors and defendants alike. A criminal defendant, however, might in some circumstances have a due process claim to a broader right of impeachment with prior inconsistent statements of defense witnesses.[44]

---

40. The concept appears to have first been articulated in People v. DeJesus 101 A.D.2d 111, 114, 475 N.Y.S.2d 19, 22 (1st Dep't 1984), aff'd, 64 N.Y.2d 1126, 490 N.Y.S.2d 188, 479 N.E.2d 824 (1985), where the court said, "[T]here may * * * be circumstances in which the absence of surprise may raise a question as to the good faith of a District Attorney in calling a witness." In De Jesus, the witness, before trial, had expressed "apprehension in testifying and * * * intimated that she might not tell her story in court." Id. at 114, 475 N.Y.S.2d at 22. The court held that it was not bad faith to call such witness.

41. See, e.g., People v. Russ, 79 N.Y.2d 173, 177–78, 581 N.Y.S.2d 152, 154–55, 589 N.E.2d 375, 377–78 (1992).

42. Id. at 177, 581 N.Y.S.2d at 154, 589 N.E.2d at 377.

43. See, e.g., People v. Wieber, 202 A.D.2d 789, 791, 609 N.Y.S.2d 398, 400 (3d Dep't), appeal denied, 84 N.Y.2d 834, 617 N.Y.S.2d 155, 641 N.E.2d 176 (1994)(before trial, witness recanted only a portion of her grand jury testimony against defendant; prosecutor "could reasonably anticipate" that witness would supply other evidence that incriminated defendant). See also People v. Brisbane, 203 A.D.2d 89, 90, 610 N.Y.S.2d 223, 223 (1st Dep't), appeal denied, 83 N.Y.2d 909, 614 N.Y.S.2d 391, 637 N.E.2d 282 (1994)(no bad faith where "witness was not called merely with the hope of evoking an inference of guilt by way of impeachment"); People v. Magee, 128 A.D.2d 811, 812, 513 N.Y.S.2d 514, 515 (2d Dep't 1987)(absence of bad faith where prosecution witness, although denying seeing defendant at crime scene, "gave significant independent testimony which incriminated the defendant's brother and codefendant in this case").

44. See Chambers v. Mississippi, 410 U.S. 284, 294, 93 S.Ct. 1038, 1045, 35 L.Ed.2d 297, 308 (1973)("The rights to confront and cross-examine witnesses and to call witnesses in one's own behalf have long been recognized as essential to due process"). In Chambers, the defendant called a witness, one McDonald, who had confessed to defendant's counsel in a sworn statement that he had committed the murder for which defendant was on trial. On direct examination, the defendant was able to prove the confession. On cross-examination, however, McDonald repudiated the confession. The trial court did not allow defendant thereafter to seek to discredit McDonald's repudiation by "cross-examining" him or introducing the testimony of three other witnesses that McDonald had made oral confessions shortly after the crime. The state's evidentiary rule against impeaching one's own witness and the hearsay rule were said to preclude the defendant. The Supreme Court, however, severely criticized the voucher rule and held that it unduly interfered with the defendant's right to confront and cross-examine witnesses and to develop his defense. Id. at 295–98, 93 S.Ct. at 1046, 35 L.Ed.2d at 309–10. The Court also rejected the state's invocation of the hearsay rule as a proper basis for excluding the other confessions, holding that they were reliable and fell within a relaxed version of the exception for declarations against interest.

c. Federal

Rule 607 of the Federal Rules of Evidence represents a total repudiation of the common law. The rule states simply, "The credibility of a witness may be attacked by any party, including the party calling the witness." The Advisory Committee's Note explains as follows:

> The traditional rule against impeaching one's own witness is abandoned as based on false premises. A party does not hold out his witnesses as worthy of belief, since he rarely has a free choice in selecting them. Denial of the right leaves the party at the mercy of the witness and the adversary.[45]

Rule 607 imposes no restrictions on the type of impeachment technique that a party may use to discredit her own witness.[46] Unlike New York law, for example, a prior inconsistent statement in any form may qualify. Furthermore, the witness' testimony need not "affirmatively damage" the party's case as a prerequisite to impeachment with a prior inconsistent statement.[47] On the other hand, several federal courts have held in criminal cases that the prosecutor may not impeach her witness with prior inconsistent statements where the primary purpose in calling the witness is merely to bring otherwise inadmissible evidence to the jury's attention.[48] The approach is similar to that taken by New

---

45. The Second Circuit had already condemned the voucher rule in United States v. Freeman, 302 F.2d 347, 351 (2d Cir. 1962), cert.denied, 375 U.S. 958, 84 S.Ct. 448, 11 L.Ed.2d 316 (1963)(criminal defendant was free to impeach credibility of government agents he had called to stand to establish portion of defense). The Supreme Court had the following to say about the voucher rule in Chambers v. Mississippi, 410 U.S. 284, 93 S.Ct. 1038, 35 L.Ed.2d 297 (1973):

> Whatever validity the "voucher" rule may have once enjoyed, and apart from whatever usefulness it retains today in the civil trial process, it bears little present relationship to the realities of the criminal process. It might have been logical for the early common law to require a party to vouch for the credibility of witnesses he brought before the jury to affirm his veracity. Having selected them especially for that purpose, the party might reasonably be expected to stand firmly behind their testimony. But in modern criminal trials, defendants are rarely able to select their witnesses: they must take them where they find them.

Id. at 296, 93 S.Ct. at 1046, 35 L.Ed.2d at 309. (footnotes omitted). A majority of jurisdictions appear to have joined the movement toward abolition. See Rowe v. Farmers Ins. Co., 699 S.W.2d 423, 424–25 (Mo. 1985).

46. See, e.g., Robinson v. Watts Detective Agency, Inc., 685 F.2d 729, 739–40 (1st Cir.1982), cert. denied, 459 U.S. 1105, 103 S.Ct. 728, 74 L.Ed.2d 953 (1983)(prior conviction); United States v. Hedman, 630 F.2d 1184, 1198–99 (7th Cir.1980), cert. denied, 450 U.S. 965, 101 S.Ct. 1481, 67 L.Ed.2d 614 (1981)(bias).

47. See United States v. Webster, 734 F.2d 1191, 1193 (7th Cir.1984).

48. United States v. Hogan, 763 F.2d 697, 702 (5th Cir.1985)(prosecutor may not, under guise of impeachment, introduce prior statement where "primary purpose" is to "[place] before the jury substantive evidence which is not otherwise admissible"); United States v. Webster, 734 F.2d 1191, 1192 (7th Cir.1984)("it would be an abuse of the rule, in a criminal case, for the prosecution to call a witness that it knew would not give it useful evidence, just so it could introduce hearsay evidence against the defendant in the hope that the jury would miss the subtle distinction between impeachment and substantive evidence—or, if it didn't miss it, would ignore it"); United States v. Morlang, 531 F.2d 183, 190 (4th Cir.1975)("impeachment by prior inconsistent statement may not be permitted where employed as a mere subterfuge to get before the jury evidence not otherwise admissible"). See also Whitehurst v. Wright, 592 F.2d 834, 839–40 (5th Cir.1979)(in civil rights action, court held that it was proper to preclude plaintiff from impeaching her witness with prior inconsistent statement where plaintiff knew that witness's testimo-

§ 607.4   WITNESSES   Ch. 6

York state courts, which require good faith on the part of the prosecutor.[49]

Library References:

West's Key No. Digests, Witnesses ⟐320, 380(5), 399.

§ 607.5 Support and Rehabilitation of Credibility
a. New York
1. Advance Accreditation

It is a general rule in the law of evidence that a party may not bolster the credibility of his witness in advance of impeachment by the opponent.[1] For example, the fact that the witness has made prior statements consistent with his trial testimony may not be proven for the purpose of enhancing credibility unless and until his credibility has been impeached in a way that would make such statements relevant.[2] Similarly, the witness' good character for truthfulness may not be proven in the absence of an attack on such character.[3]

---

ny would be unfavorable and expressly called witness solely for purpose of impeachment).

In United States v. DeLillo, 620 F.2d 939, 946–47 (2d Cir.), cert. denied, 449 U.S. 835, 101 S.Ct. 107, 66 L.Ed.2d 41 (1980), the Second Circuit Court of Appeals held that a prosecutor who knows in advance that her witness will give a certain amount of unfavorable testimony may still properly call the witness and impeach him with prior inconsistent statements where the witness is also reasonably expected to give testimony that is favorable to the government's case.

49. See text at notes 40–43 supra.

§ 607.5

1. See McCormick § 47, at 172. It is customary, however, for the court to permit the elicitation of a certain amount of introductory information about a witness at the outset of direct examination. The peripheral effect of such testimony is to bolster the witness' credibility. J. Weinstein, J. Mansfield, N. Abrams and M. Berger, Evidence Cases and Materials 487 (8th ed.1988). See also note 49 infra.

2. People v. Jung Hing, 212 N.Y. 393, 401, 106 N.E. 105, 108 (1914) ("[W]hen a witness has not been discredited or impeached there is no reason for resorting to his prior consistent statements. In such circumstances 'his testimony under oath is better evidence than his confirmatory declarations not under oath; and the repetition of his assertions does not carry his credibility further * * *.' "); People v. McDaniel, 81 N.Y.2d 10, 19–20, 595 N.Y.S.2d 364, 370, 611 N.E.2d 265, 271 (1993)(prosecutor's elicitation of complaining witness' prior consistent statements prior to cross-examination was "premature"). See also 4 Wigmore § 1124, at 255 (proof of prior consistent statements is "unnecessary and valueless" during direct examination of witness; even if witness' testimony is questionable, "it is not made more probable or more trustworthy by any number of repetitions of it").

A witness' prior statement may be admissible or direct examination, however, if it falls within a recognized hearsay exception. See, e.g., People v. Caviness, 38 N.Y.2d 227, 379 N.Y.S.2d 695, 342 N.E.2d 496 (1975) (witness permitted to testify to her own excited utterance made at crime scene); People v. Buie, ___ N.Y.2d ___, 634 N.Y.S.2d 415, 658 N.E.2d 192 (1995) (witness' prior statement in a 911–telephone call while crime was in progress fell within present sense impression hearsay exception; no error to admit statement where it had evidentiary value beyond "simple bolstering"). In such cases, the prior statement is not merely a credibility-booster; it is affirmative evidence of facts in issue.

3. People v. Gay, 7 N.Y. 378, 381 (1852); Kravitz v. Long Island Jewish–Hillside Medical Center, 113 A.D.2d 577, 583, 497 N.Y.S.2d 51, 56 (2d Dep't 1985). See 4 Wigmore § 1104, at 233 ("[T]here is no reason why time should be spent in proving that which may be assumed to exist. Every witness may be assumed to be of normal moral character for veracity, just as he is assumed to be of normal sanity.").

In People v. Parks, 41 N.Y.2d 36, 390 N.Y.S.2d 848, 359 N.E.2d 358 (1976), however, a school teacher was permitted to explain to the jury the mental capacity of a retarded child—the complaining witness—

Nevertheless, three principal exceptions to the rule against pre-impeachment accreditation have been recognized in New York. First, the party who calls a witness with a criminal record may make mention of the conviction on direct examination in order to take the "sting" out of potential cross-examination.[4]

Second, in sexual assault cases, the "prompt outcry" or "fresh complaint" doctrine permits the prosecutor to show, prior to any impeachment, that the complaining witness reported the assault shortly after it occurred.[5] The justification for admissibility is that some jurors inevitably will doubt a victim's claim of rape or sexual assault if she did not promptly report it, "such conduct being 'natural' for an 'outraged female.'"[6] If the foundation is met, the victim's prompt complaint is admissible "to corroborate the allegation that an assault took place."[7] To be admissible, the report must have been made "at the first suitable opportunity."[8] A limitation on the prompt complaint doctrine is that

before the child herself took the stand. See § 601.1, at notes 50–51, supra, and § 702.1, at notes 66–70, infra. Two members of the court characterized the teacher's testimony as a violation of the rule against advance accreditation of character. 41 N.Y.2d at 51–52, 390 N.Y.S.2d at 860, 359 N.E.2d at 370.

4. People v. Minsky, 227 N.Y. 94, 98, 124 N.E. 126, 127 (1919).

5. People v. McDaniel, 81 N.Y.2d 10, 16–17, 595 N.Y.S.2d 364, 367–69, 611 N.E.2d 265, 268–69 (1993). The fact that the report was made may be established during the direct examination of the complaining witness or, as in McDaniel, by the testimony of the person to whom the report was made, before the complaining witness takes the stand. Implicit in the rule is the requirement that the victim is (or will be) a witness at trial. Baccio v. People, 41 N.Y. 265, 268 (1869); Matter of Angel F., 166 A.D.2d 890, 560 N.Y.S.2d 549 (4th Dep't 1990). If the report was promptly made by the victim while still under the influence of the traumatic event, however, it might qualify for admission pursuant to the excited utterance hearsay exception regardless of whether the victim testifies. See § 803(1).1(b) infra.

6. People v. McDaniel, 81 N.Y.2d 10, 16, 595 N.Y.S.2d 364, 368, 611 N.E.2d 265, 269 (1993), quoting People v. Rice, 75 N.Y.2d 929, 931, 555 N.Y.S.2d 677, 678, 554 N.E.2d 1265, 1266 (1990). If the complaining witness did not make a prompt complaint, explanatory expert testimony on the "rape trauma syndrome" may be admitted. See § 702.1, at notes 59–62, infra.

Occasionally, the prompt outcry concept has been invoked outside the context of sexual assaults. See, e.g., People v. Alex, 260 N.Y. 425, 428–29, 183 N.E. 906, 907–08 (1933)(defendant who opposed admissibility of his confession on grounds that it was induced by police beating had right to prove that he complained of mistreatment at first opportunity because of its direct bearing upon truth of his claim of brutality). See also People v. Wooden, 66 A.D.2d 1004, 411 N.Y.S.2d 759 (4th Dep't 1978) (fact that victim-witness of larceny by threat promptly reported theft was permissible, but details of report should not have been allowed).

7. People v. McDaniel, 81 N.Y.2d 10, 16, 595 N.Y.S.2d 364, 367, 611 N.E.2d 265, 268 (1993).

8. Id. at 17, 595 N.Y.S.2d at 368, 611 N.E.2d at 269, quoting People v. O'Sullivan, 104 N.Y. 481, 486, 489, 10 N.E. 880, 883, 884 (1887). In People v. McDaniel, supra, the court held that a child's report to her mother on the morning after alleged molestation by the mother's boyfriend was sufficiently prompt. Statements made "days later" to the police, however, did not qualify. 81 N.Y.2d at 17, 595 N.Y.S.2d at 368, 611 N.E.2d at 269. Promptness, said the court, "is a relative concept dependent on the facts." Id. at 17, 595 N.Y.S.2d at 368, 611 N.E.2d at 269. In People v. O'Sullivan, supra, the court held that delay in reporting may be excused "as when the prosecutrix is under the physical control of the defendant; when she is among strangers, and there is no one in whom she can confide; when she is induced to silence by threats, and is so far within the power or reach of the defendant that the threats may be executed." 104 N.Y. at 489–90, 10 N.E. at 884. In O'Sullivan, however, the court found nothing to justify an 11-month delay. See People v. Hollaway, 132 A.D.2d 940, 518 N.Y.S.2d 487 (4th Dep't), appeal denied, 70 N.Y.2d 800, 522 N.Y.S.2d 117, 516 N.E.2d

§ 607.5 WITNESSES Ch. 6

the prosecutor may not elicit the details that were reported by the victim; only the fact that a complaint was made is admissible.[9] Proof of the details of the report would exceed the limited purpose of countering the presumed skepticism of the jury about the complaining witness' credibility.[10]

A third exception to the rule against advance accreditation permits the witness in a criminal case in which identity is in issue to corroborate her in-court identification of the defendant by testifying that she previously identified the same person under nonsuggestive circumstances, as, for example, in a properly-conducted lineup.[11] By statute, evidence of such identification is an outright hearsay exception, thus permitting it to be used by the jury as affirmative evidence.[12] Evidence of prior identification is discussed in greater detail in connection with the hearsay rule, § 801(2).1 *infra*.

On a related point, the court in *People v. Huertas*,[13] where the identity of a rapist was in issue, permitted the complaining witness to testify on direct examination to a prior description of her attacker which she had given to the police shortly after the assault. Testimony of the prior description was admissible, said the court, not to prove the truth of the details of the description, but rather for the limited nonhearsay purpose of showing that she had possessed the "ability to observe and

1230 (1987)(five-day delay was too late); People v. Vincent, 34 A.D.2d 705, 706, 309 N.Y.S.2d 690, 692 (3d Dep't), aff'd, 27 N.Y.2d 964, 318 N.Y.S.2d 498, 267 N.E.2d 273 (1970), appeal denied, 28 N.Y.2d 583, 319 N.Y.S.2d 1029, 268 N.E.2d 332 (1971)(one-month delay was adequately explained).

9. People v. McDaniel, 81 N.Y.2d 10, 17, 595 N.Y.S.2d 364, 368, 611 N.E.2d 265, 269 (1993). The general substance of the report may be revealed, however, if the fact that it was a complaint about a sexual attack is not obvious from the context. Thus, in McDaniel the rule against detail was not violated where the mother of a young girl testified to her daughter's report that "defendant 'bothered her,' 'attacked her' and 'tried to molest her.'" Id. at 14, 595 N.Y.S.2d at 366, 611 N.E.2d at 267. On the other hand, in People v. Rice, 75 N.Y.2d 929, 555 N.Y.S.2d 677, 554 N.E.2d 1265 (1990), the rule was violated where the complaining witness, in testifying to her prompt report of the rape to the police, repeated the description of the assailant which she had given the police. See also People v. Deitsch, 237 N.Y. 300, 142 N.E. 670 (1923)(details which included description of assailant).

10. People v. McDaniel, 81 N.Y.2d 10, 17, 595 N.Y.S.2d 364, 368, 611 N.E.2d 265, 269 (1993). Depending on the circumstances, however, the details of the report may be admissible under alternative theories. For example, if the defendant's identity is the key issue, evidence of a prompt description may help establish that the complaining witness had the capacity to observe and remember her attacker. See text at notes 13–16 infra. Furthermore, a prompt complaint might qualify as affirmative evidence under the hearsay exception for excited utterances. See § 803(1).1(b) infra. Finally, if the complaining witness' testimony is assailed on cross-examination as a recent fabrication, her prompt complaint, including the details, may be admissible on redirect for rehabilitation as a prior consistent statement, provided it predated the onset of the alleged reason to fabricate. See text at notes 29–46 infra. Obviously close distinctions must be drawn in such cases.

11. N.Y.Crim.Proc.Law § 60.30. Additional testimony by another witness, such as a police officer, of the prior identification is considered improper bolstering. On the other hand, if the witness cannot identify the defendant at trial due to a failed memory, another witness would be permitted to show that identification was made on a prior occasion. N.Y.Crim.Proc.Law § 60.25. See People v. Quevas, 81 N.Y.2d 41, 595 N.Y.S.2d 721, 611 N.E.2d 760 (1993).

12. N.Y.Crim.Proc.Law §§ 60.25 and 60.30. See People v. Huertas, 75 N.Y.2d 487, 493–94, 554 N.Y.S.2d 444, 448, 553 N.E.2d 992, 996 (1990).

13. 75 N.Y.2d 487, 554 N.Y.S.2d 444, 553 N.E.2d 992 (1990).

remember the features of the perpetrator."[14] The *Huertas* court determined, in effect, that the witness' credibility could be bolstered by the description evidence before any direct impeachment by the defendant[15] in order to "[assist] the jury in evaluating the witness' opportunity to observe at the time of the crime, and the reliability of her memory at the time of the corporeal identification."[16]

2. Rehabilitation

After a witness has been impeached, rehabilitation of the witness may be attempted by three traditional techniques: explanation, proof of good character for truthfulness, and proof of prior consistent statements. The particular form of rehabilitation, however, must be relevant in countering the particular form of impeachment.

(a) Explanation

Several New York precedents illustrate that a witness on redirect may explain impeaching facts that have been brought out on cross-examination. In a recent decision, for example, the Court of Appeals "assumed" the right of a witness to explain why he used an alias, an impeaching fact that reflected adversely on his propensity for truthfulness.[17] An older case held that when a cross-examiner had created an innuendo that certain conduct of the witness was an attempt to bribe another witness, the impeached witness should have been permitted to show the motive behind his conduct "for it might have rebutted the

---

14. Id. at 492, 554 N.Y.S.2d at 447, 553 N.E.2d at 995. The court explained how the description evidence could be probative of credibility without being considered by the jury for the impermissible purpose of its truth: "[T]he fact that such a description was given would tend to demonstrate that the particular conditions at least allowed the witness to make observations, whether accurate or not." Id. at 492, 554 N.Y.S.2d at 447, 553 N.E.2d at 995. The trial court's jury charge explained that the description evidence was to be " 'considered by you in assessing the witness' capacity to observe and remember.' " Id. at 491, 554 N.Y.S.2d at 446–47, 553 N.E.2d at 994–95.

15. The description evidence in Huertas was elicited on direct examination of the complaining witness. Id. at 490, 554 N.Y.S.2d at 446, 553 N.E.2d at 994. The Huertas opinion does not indicate whether the defense had raised the issue of her capacity to observe and remember in an opening statement. See id. at 493, 554 N.Y.S.2d at 447, 553 N.E.2d at 995 (in summation, defense counsel stressed discrepancies between complainant's out-of-court description and defendant's appearance).

16. Id. at 493, 554 N.Y.S.2d at 448, 553 N.E.2d at 996. It is difficult to reconcile Huertas with another case decided on the same day, People v. Rice, 75 N.Y.2d 929, 555 N.Y.S.2d 677, 554 N.E.2d 1265 (1990). In Rice, the details of a complaining witness' description of her attacker shortly after a rape were held to have been erroneously admitted where the prosecutor sought to justify admissibility solely under the prompt complaint doctrine. See text at notes 9–10 supra. Another distinguishing aspect of Rice is that the prior description evidence was introduced not only by the complaining witness but also by three police officers to whom the description was given. The additional testimony of the police officers would appear to be an improper form of cumulative bolstering. Cf. People v. Trowbridge, 305 N.Y. 471, 476–77, 113 N.E.2d 841, 843 (1953) (complaining witness' testimony of prior identification of defendant may not properly be bolstered by additional testimony of police officers who were present during prior identification).

17. People v. Walker, 83 N.Y.2d 455, 463 n.1, 611 N.Y.S.2d 118, 123, 633 N.E.2d 472, 477 (1994)("We assume that, upon request and a proper offer of proof by the defense, the trial court will ordinarily exercise its discretion in favor of permitting a cross-examined defendant to explain his or her prior use of an alias.").

§ 607.5   WITNESSES   Ch. 6

inference to be drawn from the cross-examination."[18]

If a prior inconsistent statement or conduct is established on cross-examination, the witness on redirect may "endeavor to explain away the effect of the supposed inconsistency by relating whatever circumstances would naturally remove it."[19] Similarly, if only part of an impeaching statement is brought out on cross-examination, other parts may be introduced on redirect to explain or correct a false impression.[20] Impeachment by proof of a witness' criminal conviction may be answered by an explanation of "the facts and circumstances surrounding [the] conviction."[21] Whether the witness may deny his guilt in the face of a conviction, however, is unsettled.[22]

---

18. Gray v. Metropolitan St. Ry. Co., 165 N.Y. 457, 459, 59 N.E. 262, 263 (1901). See also People v. Buchanan, 145 N.Y. 1, 24, 39 N.E. 846, 853, error dismissed, 158 U.S. 31, 15 S.Ct. 723, 39 L.Ed. 884 (1895)("a witness may be re-examined by the party calling him upon all topics on which he has been cross-examined, for the purpose of explaining any new facts which came out; * * *. He may be questioned to show the meaning of his expressions, or of his motive in using them.").

Aside from explanation, facts that have been introduced to prove bias or interest may be denied or rebutted with facts tending to negate the bias or interest. See, e.g., Ryan v. Dwyer, 33 A.D.2d 878, 879, 307 N.Y.S.2d 565, 566 (4th Dep't 1969)(plaintiff's witness was shown to have settled her claim against plaintiff arising out of same occurrence; similar settlement with defendant could be proved); Clapp v. Wilson, 5 Denio (N.Y.) 286 (1848)(witness for defense was shown to be defendant's son-in-law; court allowed counter-evidence that defendant and witness were on unfriendly terms).

19. People v. Buchalter, 289 N.Y. 181, 202, 45 N.E.2d 225, 235 (1942), aff'd, 319 U.S. 427, 63 S.Ct. 1129, 87 L.Ed. 1492 (1943), quoting 3A Wigmore § 1044, at 1062. See also People v. Russell, 179 A.D.2d 521, 522, 579 N.Y.S.2d 18, 20 (1st Dep't), appeal denied, 79 N.Y.2d 952, 583 N.Y.S.2d 206, 592 N.E.2d 814 (1992); Ryan v. Dwyer, 33 A.D.2d 878, 879, 307 N.Y.S.2d 565, 566 (4th Dep't 1969). In People v. Dawson, 50 N.Y.2d 311, 428 N.Y.S.2d 914, 406 N.E.2d 771 (1980), where the prosecutor was allowed to impeach an alibi witness by showing the witness' failure to have come forward with the alibi at an earlier date, the court observed that "the witness or the party for whom he was sworn always remains free to explain the witness' prior conduct or attempt to reconcile it with the witness' present testimony." Id. at 322, 428 N.Y.S.2d at 921, 406 N.E.2d at 778. Similarly, in People v. Regina, 19 N.Y.2d 65, 277 N.Y.S.2d 683, 224 N.E.2d 108 (1966), a detective was forced to admit on cross-examination that he had not made any notes of defendant's participation in a crime on the night of the occurrence. On redirect, he was allowed to testify that he had done so three days later, for he "did no more than to explain, clarify and fully elicit a question only partially examined by the defense." Id. at 78, 277 N.Y.S.2d at 693, 224 N.E.2d at 115.

20. People v. Melendez, 55 N.Y.2d 445, 451–52, 449 N.Y.S.2d 946, 950, 434 N.E.2d 1324, 1328 (1982). See, e.g., People v. Baker, 23 N.Y.2d 307, 324, 296 N.Y.S.2d 745, 756, 244 N.E.2d 232, 240 (1968)(on issue of identification, cross-examiner brought out that witness had told grand jury she did not recognize certain persons running on street; on redirect, prosecutor was allowed to show that in another part of same grand jury testimony, witness had identified these persons from photographic array, an otherwise impermissible form of evidence). See also CPLR 3117(b)("If only part of a deposition is read at the trial by a party, any other party may read any other part of the deposition which ought in fairness to be considered in connection with the part read.").

21. People v. Tait, 234 App.Div. 433, 439, 255 N.Y.S. 455, 461 (1st Dep't 1932), aff'd, 259 N.Y. 599, 182 N.E. 197 (1932). See 3A Wigmore § 1117, at 251 ("it would seem a harmless charity to allow the witness to make such protestations on his own behalf as he may feel able to make with a due regard to the penalties of perjury"). The witness may also testify that he has subsequently led a reformed life. Conley v. Meeker, 85 N.Y. 618, 619 (1881).

22. In Sims v. Sims, 75 N.Y. 466 (1878), the Court of Appeals upheld the right of a witness to assert his innocence despite a judgment of conviction. Subsequent decisions of the Appellate Divisions, however, have restricted the convicted witness to an explanation of mitigating circumstances surrounding the conviction. People v. Tait,

(b) Good Character for Truthfulness

After a witness has been impeached in a way that directly calls his general character for truthfulness into question, rehabilitation traditionally may be attempted by showing his good character for truthfulness.[23] What constitutes an attack on the witness' general character for truthfulness so as to permit this form of rehabilitation? Obviously testimony by character witnesses that the witness to be impeached has a bad reputation for truth and veracity should qualify.[24] Impeachment by the showing of a prior conviction is also considered an attack on the witness' general character for truthfulness, thus permitting the witness to show that his current reputation is good.[25] In logic the same sort of rehabilitation should be allowed when the witness admits on cross-examination to a prior vicious, immoral or criminal act inasmuch as the purpose of such impeachment is to call into doubt the witness' character for truthfulness.[26] On the other hand, impeachment by a prior inconsistent statement ordinarily carries no necessary imputation of bad character, thus precluding evidence of good character to rehabilitate.[27] Categorical

---

234 App.Div. 433, 439, 255 N.Y.S. 455, 461 (1st Dep't 1932), aff'd, 259 N.Y. 599, 182 N.E. 197 (1932); People v. Michaels, 168 App.Div. 258, 259, 153 N.Y.S. 796, 797–98 (2d Dep't 1915). See 4 Wigmore § 1116, at 250 (conclusiveness of judgment of conviction should preclude denial of guilt).

23. See Kravitz v. Long Island Jewish–Hillside Medical Center, 113 A.D.2d 577, 583, 497 N.Y.S.2d 51, 56 (2d Dep't 1985). In general, a rehabilitation witness on the issue of character may testify only to the impeached witness' reputation for truthfulness; a character witness' direct opinion on the matter apparently is still prohibited under New York law. Id. at 582–83, 497 N.Y.S.2d at 55–56. Section 608(a) of the Proposed New York Evidence Code, however, would permit a character witness to give her opinion on an impeached witness' character for truthfulness. See note 28 infra. Even under existing precedents, a rehabilitation witness may testify, based on her personal knowledge of the impeached witness, that she would believe him under oath. Adams v. Greenwich Ins. Co., 70 N.Y. 166, 170 (1877). If the rehabilitation witness knows other people with whom the impeached witness associates, she may testify that she has never heard his veracity called into question. People v. Davis, 21 Wend. (N.Y) 309 (1839).

24. Derrick v. Wallace, 217 N.Y. 520, 523, 112 N.E. 440, 441 (1916). See § 608.1 infra.

Certain language in People v. Pavao, 59 N.Y.2d 282, 464 N.Y.S.2d 458, 451 N.E.2d 216 (1983), however, suggests that the ability to rehabilitate with evidence of good character for truthfulness is subject to the court's discretion. After affirming the traditional right to impeach a key witness with evidence of his bad reputation for truthfulness, the court stated: "Whether the opposing party may call witnesses to rebut the impeaching witness' statement is a question best left to the discretion of the Trial Judge for it is he who can best assess whether doing so may result in confusion or cause the trial to be unduly extended in length." Id. at 290, 464 N.Y.S.2d at 462, 451 N.E.2d at 220.

25. Derrick v. Wallace, 217 N.Y. 520, 525, 112 N.E. 440, 442 (1916) ("[T]he only purpose for which conviction can be shown is to affect credibility by suggesting general bad reputation. Evidence of conviction thus impeaches the general character for truth and veracity, and may be met by evidence of general good character."). See also Conley v. Meeker, 85 N.Y. 618, 619 (1881)(witness who had been convicted was permitted to state that he had been reformed and now led an honest and orderly life).

26. McCormick § 47, at 174; 4 Wigmore § 1106. See §§ 608.0 and 608.2 infra. But see Derrick v. Wallace, 217 N.Y. 520, 525, 112 N.E. 440, 442 (1916)("misconduct thus confessed cannot be said to discredit character generally in the community, in the sense that proof of conviction discredits it") Id. at 525, 112 N.E. at 442.

27. Frost v. McCarger, 29 Barb. (N.Y.) 617 (1859). Inconsistencies may simply be the result of human error. 4 Wigmore § 1108. See also People v. Rector, 19 Wend. 569 (1838)(introduction of evidence which contradicts witness does not open door to rehabilitation with character evidence); Kravitz v. Long Island Jewish–Hillside Medical Center, 113 A.D.2d 577, 584,

§ 607.5 WITNESSES Ch. 6

rules, however, provide a less satisfactory approach than an analysis which focuses on the question whether inconsistencies and contradictions in the particular case are aimed at impugning the witness' general character for truthfulness.[28]

(c) Prior Consistent Statements

A long line of New York cases allows rehabilitation by proof of a witness' prior consistent statements where his trial testimony has been attacked as a recent fabrication.[29] The prior consistent statements must have been made before the motive to fabricate existed or before corrupting influences were brought to bear.[30] This restrictive approach is premised on the notion that prior consistent statements are not particularly probative of credibility where impeachment of the witness is general in nature, such as a showing of bias based solely on personal relationship, bad character for truthfulness or prior inconsistent statement.[31] Repetition of a lie or mistake simply does not increase a witness' veracity.[32]

---

497 N.Y.S.2d 51, 56 (2d Dep't 1985)(opponent's focus on "contradictions and improbabilities * * * did not constitute an attempt to prove bad character").

28. See McCormick § 47, at 175–76. Section 608(a) of the Proposed New York Evidence Code would restate New York law as follows:

(a) **Opinion and reputation evidence of character.** [PROPOSED] The credibility of a witness may be attacked or supported by evidence in the form of opinion or reputation, subject to these limitations:

(1) **Only evidence of character for truthfulness.** The evidence may refer only to character for truthfulness; and

(2) **Evidence of truthful character only after an attack on truthfulness.** Evidence of truthful character is admissible only after the character of the witness for truthfulness has been attacked by opinion or reputation evidence, or the witness has been attacked in any other manner as a person unworthy of belief because of an untruthful character and not because the witness is mistaken, confused, forgetful, or inaccurate with respect to her or his testimony on this particular occasion.

The proposed rule's principal difference from current law is that it would allow character for truthfulness to be proved by opinion as well as by reputation. See § 608.1 infra.

29. People v. Seit, 86 N.Y.2d 92, 629 N.Y.S.2d 998, 653 N.E.2d 1168 (1995); People v. McDaniel, 81 N.Y.2d 10, 19, 595 N.Y.S.2d 364, 369, 611 N.E.2d 265, 270 (1993); People v. McClean, 69 N.Y.2d 426, 428, 515 N.Y.S.2d 428, 429–30, 508 N.E.2d 140, 141 (1987); People v. Davis, 44 N.Y.2d 269, 277, 405 N.Y.S.2d 428, 432, 376 N.E.2d 901, 905 (1978); Moore v. Leventhal, 303 N.Y. 534, 537–38, 104 N.E.2d 892, 894 (1952); People v. Singer, 300 N.Y. 120, 123, 89 N.E.2d 710, 711 (1949); Crawford v. Nilan, 289 N.Y. 444, 450–51, 46 N.E.2d 512, 515 (1943); Ferris v. Sterling, 214 N.Y. 249, 254, 108 N.E. 406, 408 (1915); People v. Katz, 209 N.Y. 311, 339–40, 103 N.E. 305, 315 (1913).

30. See cases cited in note 29 supra.

31. Crawford v. Nilan, 289 N.Y. 444, 450, 46 N.E.2d 512, 515 (1943) ("testimony of an impeached or discredited witness may not be supported and bolstered by proving that he has made similar declarations out of court"). See also People v. Caserta, 19 N.Y.2d 18, 24–25, 277 N.Y.S.2d 647, 652, 224 N.E.2d 82, 85–86 (1966)(showing of police officer's general interest in promotion and the solving of crimes does not amount to charge of recent fabrication, thus precluding officer from testifying on redirect to prior identification of defendant in photo array); People v. Katz, 209 N.Y. 311, 338, 103 N.E. 305, 313 (1913)(general rule is that testimony of contradicted, impeached or discredited witness may not be bolstered by proof of prior consistent statements).

32. People v. McClean, 69 N.Y.2d 426, 428, 515 N.Y.S.2d 428, 429, 508 N.E.2d 140, 141 (1987)("an untrustworthy statement is not made more trustworthy by repetition"). The rule has also been justified by the fact that testimony under oath is superior to out-of-court confirmatory declarations and the notion that litigation should not develop into a contest as to which party can obtain

If the witness is charged with giving false testimony as the result of corrupting influences or a recently-developed motive, however, proof that the witness said the same thing before any such factors came into play naturally tends to rebut the inference of fabrication at trial.[33] Obviously, the propriety of prior consistent statements as rehabilitative evidence under this theory is highly fact-specific. Examples abound in Court of Appeals decisions of recent vintage. An instructive case is *People v. McDaniel*,[34] in which an accused child molester sought to establish on cross-examination that the child's step-father, the police and the district attorney had influenced her story during conversations with her. Accusatory statements made by the child to her mother on the mornings after the alleged incidents, all of which predated her conversations with the step-father and the authorities, were admissible to rebut the implied charge of recent fabrication.[35] Conversely, the child's consistent statements to the police and district attorney subsequent to the tainting

the latest version of a witness' story. Crawford v. Nilan, 289 N.Y. 444, 451, 46 N.E.2d 512, 516 (1943).

33. People v. McDaniel, 81 N.Y.2d 10, 18, 595 N.Y.S.2d 364, 369, 611 N.E.2d 265, 270 (1993)("This exception is rooted in fairness; it would be unjust to permit a party to suggest that a witness, as a result of interest, bias or influence, is fabricating a story without allowing the opponent to demonstrate that the witness had spoken similarly even before the alleged incentive to falsify arose."); People v. McClean, 69 N.Y.2d 426, 428, 515 N.Y.S.2d 428, 429, 508 N.E.2d 140, 141 (1987)("[I]f the cross-examiner seeks to impeach the witness by evidence tending to show that his testimony is of recent invention, given under motives of interest or bias, the party calling the witness, in order to rebut that inference, may show that the witness made statements similar to his trial testimony at some earlier time when he was free from the alleged bias"); People v. Davis, 44 N.Y.2d 269, 277, 405 N.Y.S.2d 428, 432, 376 N.E.2d 901, 905 (1978)("prior consistent statements made at a time when there was no motive to falsify are admissible to repel the implication or charge").

As explained by Wigmore, when a consistent statement predated the onset of the alleged motive to fabricate, the testimony will appear to be "independent of the discrediting influence." 4 Wigmore § 1128, at 268.

34. 81 N.Y.2d 10, 595 N.Y.S.2d 364, 611 N.E.2d 265 (1993).

35. Id. at 19, 595 N.Y.S.2d at 369, 611 N.E.2d at 270.

Other decisions in which prior consistent statements were held to have been properly admitted because they were made prior to the onset of an alleged reason to fabricate include the following: People v. Boyd, 58 N.Y.2d 1016, 462 N.Y.S.2d 435, 448 N.E.2d 1346 (1983)(in drug prosecution, defendant's cross-examination of police-agent showed omission of defendant's name in witness' "buy reports" of October 31 and November 28, 1974; because of "implicit assertion" of recent fabrication, prosecutor was permitted to show inclusion of defendant's name in buy report of October 24, 1974); People v. Coffey, 11 N.Y.2d 142, 146, 227 N.Y.S.2d 412, 414, 182 N.E.2d 92, 94 (1962)(defendant sought to charge identification witness with recent fabrication contrived after defendant's arrest; prosecution was allowed to show that prior to picking out defendant in lineup, witness had described perpetrator to police artist who made sketch that closely resembled defendant's appearance); Moore v. Leventhal, 303 N.Y. 534, 537, 104 N.E.2d 892, 894 (1952)(police officer's testimony for defendant that plaintiff had made damaging admissions at scene of accident, which was attacked as recent fabrication, was properly rebutted by showing that officer had included the admissions in official accident report filed by him); Ferris v. Sterling, 214 N.Y. 249, 254, 108 N.E. 406, 407–08 (1915)(in personal injury action against father based on son's negligent operation of vehicle allegedly owned by father, defense contended that documentation showing father's ownership was mistake; plaintiff contended that denial of ownership was fabricated following accident; correspondence between son and state authorities discussing mistake three months before accident was properly admitted).

Cases involving prior consistent statements by accomplices of a criminal defendant are contained in note 39 infra.

§ 607.5 WITNESSES Ch. 6

events were inadmissible.[36]

Another illustrative case is *People v. McClean*,[37] where the defendant's accomplices incriminated him in their testimony for the prosecution. On cross-examination, the defendant sought to establish that the accomplices' testimony was a recent fabrication that resulted from police pressure during custodial interrogation and the hope for leniency. The prosecutor's subsequent introduction of consistent statements given to the police by the accomplices shortly after their arrest was error, said the court, because "[t]he hope for preferred treatment, * * * which was the only motive charged by the defense, was precisely the same at the time of arrest as it was at the time of trial."[38] The fact that the accomplices had not yet entered into a plea bargain at the time of their statements did not neutralize the fact that these witnesses were seeking to curry favor with the authorities from the moment of their arrest.[39]

The Court of Appeals explained the meaning of recent fabrication in *People v. Singer*:[40] " 'Recent' * * * has a relative, not an absolute meaning. It means * * * that the [cross-examiner] is charging the witness not with mistake or confusion, but with making up a false story well after the event * * *. 'Recently fabricated' means the same thing as fabricated to meet the exigencies of the case."[41] The cross-examiner's charge of recent fabrication may consist of an explicit characterization of

---

36. 81 N.Y.2d at 19, 595 N.Y.S.2d at 369, 611 N.E.2d at 270. See also People v. Davis, 44 N.Y.2d 269, 405 N.Y.S.2d 428, 376 N.E.2d 901 (1978) (in narcotics prosecution, undercover officer's trial testimony was attacked as fabrication; officer's official post-arrest report did not serve to rehabilitate because defense theory was that charges had been falsely concocted prior to arrest); People v. Perez, 193 A.D.2d 630, 597 N.Y.S.2d 445 (2d Dep't), appeal denied, 82 N.Y.2d 724, 602 N.Y.S.2d 822, 622 N.E.2d 323 (1993)(defendant's friend, impeached for bias, had same motive to favor defendant at time of prior consistent statement as at time of trial).

37. 69 N.Y.2d 426, 515 N.Y.S.2d 428, 508 N.E.2d 140 (1987).

38. Id. at 429–30, 515 N.Y.S.2d at 430, 508 N.E.2d at 142.

39. McClean is one of the few decisions in which the rehabilitation of an accomplice with a prior consistent statement was held improper. A critical issue in such cases is pinpointing when the alleged motive to fabricate arose. In many of the cases, the accomplice's motives are mixed, requiring focus on the nature of the cross-examination and the relative strength of the particular motive to falsify at the time of the making of the prior consistent statement. See People v. Baker, 23 N.Y.2d 307, 322–23, 296 N.Y.S.2d 745, 754–55, 244 N.E.2d 232, 238–39 (1968) (accomplice's prior consistent statement, made while being interrogated by detective held admissible; although accomplice had motive from outset to cast blame on others, defendant's cross-examination stressed particular motive to falsify based on favors accomplice received from police subsequent to his statement, such as witness fees and free food); People v. Feld, 305 N.Y. 322, 329–30, 113 N.E.2d 440, 442–43 (1953)(giver of bribe to defendant, a police officer, made prior consistent statement during wire-tapped phone conversation with co-conspirator prior to arrests; held admissible); People v. Singer, 300 N.Y. 120, 89 N.E.2d 710 (1949)(accomplice to illegal abortion was impeached on ground that he was seeking clemency from prosecutor; prior consistent statement made to father of victim on day following abortion held admissible); People v. Katz, 209 N.Y. 311, 336–43, 103 N.E. 305, 312–15 (1913)(accomplice's testimony was attacked as recent fabrication based on plea bargain in which accomplice was promised immunity in exchange for his testimony; prior consistent statement, made shortly after arrest and one year before any discussion with prosecutor about immunity, held admissible).

40. 300 N.Y. 120, 89 N.E.2d 710 (1949).

41. Id. at 124, 89 N.E.2d at 711. See, e.g., People v. Regina, 19 N.Y.2d 65, 78, 277 N.Y.S.2d 683, 692, 224 N.E.2d 108, 115 (1966)(suggestion that it was too dark for detective to have seen occurrence is not a charge of recent fabrication).

the witness' testimony or it may come about through implication and insinuation.[42] The particular impeachment technique—showing bias, interest, or prior inconsistent statements—is not determinative; it is the inference created by the cross-examiner's questioning that governs the issue. "[N]ot every inconsistency developed on cross-examination triggers the exception"[43] and "minor point[s] of cross-examination" will not suffice.[44]

Assuming a prior consistent statement is admissible to rebut a charge of recent fabrication, it may be proven by the impeached witness himself or by the testimony of the person to whom the statement was made.[45] The proper purpose of admission is "not to prove or disprove any of the facts in issue, but to aid in establishing the credibility of the witness."[46]

In some circumstances, a prior consistent statement may be admissible for a rehabilitative purpose other than rebuttal of a charge of recent fabrication. For example, it might be relevant in clarifying or explaining a statement of the witness that is apparently inconsistent with his testimony.[47] Similarly, if the witness denies having made a prior inconsistent statement, the fact that he made a relatively contemporaneous statement which is consistent with his testimony would tend to corroborate the denial.[48]

---

42. People v. McDaniel, 81 N.Y.2d 10, 18, 595 N.Y.S.2d 364, 369, 611 N.E.2d 265, 270 (1993)("either directly or inferentially"); People v. McClean, 69 N.Y.2d 426, 428, 515 N.Y.S.2d 428, 429, 508 N.E.2d 140, 141 (1987)("cross-examiner has created the inference of, or directly characterized the testimony as, a recent fabrication").

43. People v. Davis, 44 N.Y.2d 269, 277, 405 N.Y.S.2d 428, 432–33, 376 N.E.2d 901, 905 (1978).

44. People v. Baker, 23 N.Y.2d 307, 323, 296 N.Y.S.2d 745, 755, 244 N.E.2d 232, 239 (1968). See, e.g., People v. Caserta, 19 N.Y.2d 18, 26–27, 277 N.Y.S.2d 647, 653–54, 224 N.E.2d 82, 87 (1966)(general bias of police officers based on desire for job promotion and successful solving of crimes is not a sufficiently specific charge of recent fabrication to permit officer to prove prior identification of defendant from photo array). See also People v. Seit, 86 N.Y.2d 92, 96, 629 N.Y.S.2d 998, 1000, 653 N.E.2d 1168 (1995)("The implication that the testimony was recently fabricated arises only if it appears that the cross examiner believes and wants the jury to believe that the witness is testifying falsely to 'meet the exigencies of the case' * * *.").

45. People v. Mirenda, 23 N.Y.2d 439, 451–52, 297 N.Y.S.2d 532, 541, 245 N.E.2d 194, 200 (1969)("Normally a witness is rehabilitated by either offering a document or by third-party testimony. Occasionally the witness himself testifies to something contained in a written instrument present in court or to which a third party later testifies. * * * We see no reason why a witness cannot attempt to rehabilitate himself by testifying to prior consistent statements after a claim of recent fabrication. It is open to the adversary, of course, to point out to the jury that this rehabilitation testimony is a less reliable indication of veracity than if independent verification of the prior statements had been offered, and, therefore, the witness' testimony should be viewed circumspectly.").

46. People v. McClean, 69 N.Y.2d 426, 428, 515 N.Y.S.2d 428, 430, 508 N.E.2d 140, 141 (1987). The fact that the statement was made, regardless of the truth of its content, is what makes the statement a relevant form of rebuttal.

47. See text at notes 19–20 supra.

48. See Donovan v. Moore–McCormack Lines, Inc., 266 App.Div. 406, 42 N.Y.S.2d 441 (1st Dep't 1943)(prior consistent statement made within a few days of the alleged inconsistent statement). See also note 67 infra.

Since the purpose of admission in such cases is not to rebut a charge of recent fabrication, it should not matter that the statement was made after an alleged motive to fabricate existed.

b. Federal

For the most part, federal law parallels that of New York with respect to support and rehabilitation of witness credibility. In general, accreditation of a witness in advance of impeachment is disallowed.[49] It is well settled, however, that counsel may seek to take the "sting" out of an opponent's anticipated cross-examination by eliciting discrediting information about his witness on direct examination.[50] In criminal cases, for example, it is permissible for the prosecution to establish that coconspirators and accomplices who testify for the government have pleaded guilty[51] or entered into cooperation agreements.[52] In the Second Circuit, however, the inclusion of truth-telling provisions in such agreements may not be used for bolstering purposes until after credibility has been attacked.[53] A witness' prior identification of a person is admissible

49. United States v. Bolick, 917 F.2d 135, 138–39 (4th Cir.1990); United States v. Cosentino, 844 F.2d 30, 32–33 (2d Cir.), cert. denied, 488 U.S. 923, 109 S.Ct. 303, 102 L.Ed.2d 322 (1988).

Within limits, a party may elicit background information about the witness' employment, which may have the indirect effect of bolstering credibility. See Raysor v. Port Authority of New York & New Jersey, 768 F.2d 34, 40 (2d Cir.1985), cert. denied, 475 U.S. 1027, 106 S.Ct. 1227, 89 L.Ed.2d 337 (1986)(personal information about witness' religion, faithful and long marriage and financial support of children's college education exceeded permissible scope of background rule). Compare Government of Virgin Islands v. Grant, 775 F.2d 508, 513 (3d Cir.1985)(criminal defendants commonly are permitted to testify to absence of criminal record but no abuse of discretion to prohibit such testimony in particular case), with United States v. Hicks, 748 F.2d 854, 859 (4th Cir.1984)(prosecution witness should not be allowed to testify to absence of criminal record).

50. United States v. Cosentino, 844 F.2d 30, 33 (2d Cir.), cert. denied, 488 U.S. 923, 109 S.Ct. 303, 102 L.Ed.2d 322 (1988)("It may sometimes be useful * * * to develop impeaching matter in direct examination of a 'friendly' witness in order to deprive an adversary of the psychological advantage of revealing it to the jury for the first time during cross-examination."). See also United States v. Ewings, 936 F.2d 903, 909–10 (7th Cir.1991); United States v. Medical Therapy Sciences, Inc., 583 F.2d 36, 39–40 (2d Cir.1978), cert. denied, 439 U.S. 1130, 99 S.Ct. 1049, 59 L.Ed.2d 91 (1979).

51. United States v. Davis, 766 F.2d 1452, 1456 (10th Cir.), cert. denied, 474 U.S. 908, 106 S.Ct. 239, 88 L.Ed.2d 240 (1985)(guilty plea may be shown to support witness' claim of first-hand knowledge, to deflect potential impeachment and to repel suggestion that government and witness have something to hide; trial judge should instruct jury that plea is to be used solely to assess credibility of witness and not as substantive evidence against defendant). See also United States v. Kroh, 915 F.2d 326, 331 (8th Cir.1990); United States v. Freeman, 302 F.2d 347, 350 (2d Cir.1962), cert. denied, 375 U.S. 958, 84 S.Ct. 448, 11 L.Ed.2d 316 (1963).

52. See, e.g., United States v. Cosentino, 844 F.2d 30 (2d Cir.), cert. denied, 488 U.S. 923, 109 S.Ct. 303, 102 L.Ed.2d 322 (1988)(participants in kickback scheme agreed to testify in return for guilty pleas on reduced charges). Plea bargains and cooperation agreements provide fertile ground for impeachment on the basis that the beneficiaries of such agreements "cannot be believed because they are under pressure to deliver convictions and correspondingly tempted to twist facts to do so." Id. at 32. See also United States v. Melia, 691 F.2d 672, 675–76 (4th Cir.1982), appeal after remand, 741 F.2d 70 (4th Cir.1984), cert. denied, 471 U.S. 1135, 105 S.Ct. 2674, 86 L.Ed.2d 693 (1985)(prosecution may, under some circumstances, establish that witness is participant in witness protection program, but caution is required where jury might believe defendant is source of death threats to witness).

53. United States v. Cosentino, 844 F.2d 30, 33 (2d Cir.), cert. denied, 488 U.S. 923, 109 S.Ct. 303, 102 L.Ed.2d 322 (1988). Accord, United States v. Cohen, 888 F.2d 770, 774–75 (11th Cir.1989). "Truth-telling" provisions typically include promises by the witness to testify truthfully and penalties for failure to do so, such as prosecution for perjury and reinstatement of charges that may have been dropped. Cosentino, 844 F.2d at 32. Several other circuits eschew the drawing of distinctions between those aspects of a cooperation agreement that

on direct examination pursuant to Rule 801(d)(1)(C) of the Federal Rules of Evidence.[54]

After impeachment, rehabilitation may be attempted by denial, rebuttal or explanation, as appropriate.[55] The introduction of the witness' good character for truthfulness is governed by Rule 608(a) of the Federal Rules of Evidence, which provides as follows:

(a) **Opinion and reputation evidence of character.** The credibility of a witness may be attacked or supported by evidence in the form of opinion or reputation, but subject to these limitations: (1) the evidence may refer only to character for truthfulness or untruthfulness, and (2) evidence of truthful character is admissible only after the character of the witness for truthfulness has been attacked by opinion or reputation evidence or otherwise.

Thus, an attack on the witness' character for truthfulness is a prerequisite to rehabilitation by evidence of good character for truthful-

---

serve to impeach (the motive to falsify inherent in a plea bargain) and those which bolster credibility (truth-telling provisions) and allow the substance of the entire agreement to be admitted on direct examination of the witness. See, e.g., United States v. Lord, 907 F.2d 1028, 1029–31 (10th Cir. 1990); United States v. Drews, 877 F.2d 10, 12 (8th Cir.1989); United States v. Dadanian, 818 F.2d 1443, 1445 (9th Cir.1987).

Although the Second Circuit allows admission of truth-telling provisions only for rehabilitative purposes after an attack on credibility, such attack may occur during defense counsel's opening statement, thereby opening the door to admission during the witness' direct examination. Cosentino, 844 F.2d at 33. See also United States v. Gaind, 31 F.3d 73, 77–78 (2d Cir.1994).

54. See § 801(2).2 infra.

In federal practice, there is nothing comparable to the development under New York law of the "prompt outcry" doctrine in sexual assault cases. See text at notes 5–10 supra. The doctrine is so well settled at common law that undoubtedly it may be used in a federal prosecution to bolster the credibility of a rape victim before impeachment. See McCormick § 272.1. Most of the attention in recent years has been focused on the admissibility of a rape victim's prior complaint under the excited utterance hearsay exception in Fed.R.Evid. 803(2). See, e.g., United States v. Iron Shell, 633 F.2d 77, 85–86 (8th Cir.1980), cert. denied, 450 U.S. 1001, 101 S.Ct. 1709, 68 L.Ed.2d 203 (1981).

55. See, e.g., United States v. Mitchell, 556 F.2d 371, 380 (6th Cir.), cert. denied, 434 U.S. 925, 98 S.Ct. 406, 54 L.Ed.2d 284 (1977) (explanation and rebuttal of facts suggesting bias); United States v. Brown, 547 F.2d 438, 445–46 (8th Cir.), cert. denied, 430 U.S. 937, 97 S.Ct. 1566, 51 L.Ed.2d 784 (1977)(facts rebutting hostility); United States v. Holland, 526 F.2d 284, 285 (5th Cir.1976)(witness impeached by a prior inconsistency in grand jury testimony may seek to explain it away by showing that such testimony was corrected in later appearance before grand jury).

Federal courts are divided over the question whether a witness may explain his prior criminal conviction. Compare United States v. Plante, 472 F.2d 829, 832 (1st Cir.1973), cert. denied, 411 U.S. 950, 93 S.Ct. 1932, 36 L.Ed.2d 411 (1973)(details of conviction may not be developed because issue is collateral and opponent may be at evidentiary disadvantage in rebutting the witness' explanation), with United States v. Crisafi, 304 F.2d 803, 804 (2d Cir.1962)(rehabilitation may be attempted by brief explanation of conviction "in the control of the trial court"; trial court did not err in precluding defendant from testifying that he had pleaded guilty "to save his sixteen year old sister who was involved in the charges" where defense counsel himself made same explanation to jury). In Zinman v. Black & Decker (U.S.), Inc., 983 F.2d 431, 435–36 (2d Cir.1993), the court found no abuse of discretion where plaintiff, whose conviction was admitted to impeach his credibility, was precluded from testifying to his subsequent law-abiding and community-minded behavior.

§ 607.5   WITNESSES   Ch. 6

ness.[56] The Advisory Committee's Note states that "[o]pinion or reputation that the witness is untruthful specifically qualifies as an attack under the rule, and evidence of misconduct, including conviction of crime, and of corruption also fall within this category. Evidence of bias or interest does not."[57] As to other forms of impeachment, such as prior inconsistent statements or contradiction, commentators have argued in favor of judicial discretion to admit rebuttal evidence of good character for truthfulness when the cross-examination has the net effect of an attack on general character for truthfulness.[58] The Second Circuit favored this view in *United States v. Medical Therapy Sciences, Inc.*[59]

---

56. "Character evidence in support of credibility is admissible under the rule only after the witness' character has first been attacked, as has been the case at common law. * * * The enormous needless consumption of time which a contrary practice would entail justifies the limitation." Advisory Committee's Note, Fed.R.Evid. 608. The rule allows proof of character for truthfulness only by opinion or reputation evidence. Subdivision (b) of Rule 608 specifically prohibits evidence of specific instances of conduct to support the witness' credibility. See, e.g., United States v. Melia, 691 F.2d 672, 674 (4th Cir.1982), appeal after remand, 741 F.2d 70 (4th Cir.1984), cert. denied, 471 U.S. 1135, 105 S.Ct. 2674, 86 L.Ed.2d 693 (1985)(prosecution witnesses were improperly supported by evidence of specific acts of cooperation and assistance to government in solving crimes).

57. Advisory Committee's Note, Fed. R.Evid. 608. See, e.g., United States v. Medical Therapy Sciences, Inc., 583 F.2d 36, 40–41 (2d Cir.1978), cert. denied, 439 U.S. 1130, 99 S.Ct. 1049, 59 L.Ed.2d 91 (1979)(prosecution witness was subjected to sharp questioning on cross-examination about prior convictions; although she denied cross-examiner's allegations of embezzling money from defendant, the imputation of misconduct amounted to charge of corruption rather than mere bias).

58. See McCormick § 47, at 176 ("[T]he judge should consider in each case whether a particular impeachment for inconsistency or a conflict in testimony, or either of them, amounts in net effect to an attack on character for truth and should exercise his discretion accordingly to admit or exclude the character-support."); 3 Weinstein and Berger ¶ 608[08], at 608–68 and–69 (Consideration of the circumstances in the particular case "should be used in deciding whether to admit rehabilitating evidence after the witness has been contradicted by the testimony of other witnesses. Wigmore points out that 'the insinuation against Moral Character is here more remote' than in the case of prior inconsistent statements and McCormick states that most courts do not view contradiction as an attack on character. Nevertheless, the mandate in Rule 401 to admit all relevant evidence should be construed to authorize—but not to require—the admission of supportive character evidence if the trial judge finds in the circumstances of the particular case that the contradiction amounted to an attack on veracity.")(footnotes omitted). See also Advisory Committee's Note, Fed.R.Evid. 608 ("Whether evidence in the form of contradiction is an attack upon the character of the witness must depend upon the circumstances.").

59. 583 F.2d 36 (2d Cir.1978), cert. denied, 439 U.S. 1130, 99 S.Ct. 1049, 59 L.Ed.2d 91 (1979). This was a prosecution for Medicare billing fraud in which one of the government's chief witnesses, a former employee of defendant, was cross-examined as to hostility based on her alleged embezzlement from the defendant. Although she denied the embezzlement, the court concluded that her character for truthfulness had been sufficiently "attacked" within the meaning of Rule 608(a):

[T]he defense attack here went far beyond mere accusation by cross-examination and denial. Other witnesses were called to contradict Russell's denials in order to support the defense's theory that Russell had the motive to commit the frauds, on her own, and for her own purposes—that she could have submitted false claims to cover up for her embezzlement. Though contradiction cannot usually be characterized as an "attack" on character, Weinstein and Berger, supra, ¶ 608[08], at 608–43, citing McCormick, Evidence § 49, here the contradiction specifically implicated Russell's veracity.

As Judge Weinstein and Professor Berger suggest,

"the mandate in Rule 401 to admit all relevant evidence should be construed to authorize—but not to require—the admission of supportive character evidence if the trial judge finds in the circumstances of the particular case

Several other courts, however, have shown a conservative attitude.[60]

Pursuant to Rule 801(d)(1)(B) of the Federal Rules of Evidence, the prior consistent statement of a witness is admissible "to rebut an express or implied charge against the [witness] of recent fabrication or improper influence or motive." When the requirements of the rule are met, the prior consistent statement is nonhearsay, meaning that it can be used as substantive evidence.[61] Lower federal courts have disagreed over the question whether the rule preserved the common law requirement that the consistent statement must predate the onset of the improper influence or motive to fabricate.[62] The Supreme Court re-

---

that the contradiction amounted to an attack on veracity." ¶ 608[08], at 608–43.

This suggestion, in essence, is the conclusion we adopt today. Accord, Advisory Committee Note to Rule 608. We think that trial judges should be permitted, under Rule 608, to exercise sound discretion to permit or deny a party the use of character evidence to support veracity. As is always the case, the balancing test under Rule 403 must be considered before any such evidence is permitted over objection. Furthermore, it is always open to the trial judge to deny a party the opportunity to present only cumulative evidence bearing solely on credibility. See United States v. Augello, 452 F.2d 1135, 1140 (2d Cir.1971)(character evidence should be used with great circumspection, and may be disallowed), cert. denied, 406 U.S. 922, 92 S.Ct. 1787, 32 L.Ed.2d 122 (1972), and cert. denied, 409 U.S. 859, 93 S.Ct. 145, 34 L.Ed.2d 105 (1972).

583 F.2d at 41 n.6. See also Beard v. Mitchell, 604 F.2d 485, 503 (7th Cir.1979)(use of prior inconsistent statements may constitute attack on truthfulness); United States v. Scholle, 553 F.2d 1109, 1123 (8th Cir.), cert. denied, 434 U.S. 940, 98 S.Ct. 432, 54 L.Ed.2d 300 (1977) ("evidence of good character for truth is logically relevant to meet an impeachment accomplished through slashing cross-examination carrying strong accusations of misconduct and bad character, which, as here, the witness' denial would not remove from the jury's mind")(dictum). Cf. United States v. Lechoco, 542 F.2d 84, 86–89 (D.C.Cir.1976)(credibility of nontestifying defendant could have been bolstered by character evidence where experts who testified in support of insanity defense had relied on defendant's out-of-court statements, and "vigorous" cross-examination of experts had stressed defendant's motive to lie when such statements were made).

60. See United States v. Dring, 930 F.2d 687, 691–92 (9th Cir.1991), cert. denied, ___ U.S. ___, 113 S.Ct. 110, 121 L.Ed.2d 68 (1992)(emphasis on defendant's interest in case and inconsistencies between his testimony and that of other witnesses did not impugn general character for truthfulness); United States v. Thomas, 768 F.2d 611, 618 (5th Cir.1985) ("Vigorous cross-examination and/or the fact that a witness is contradicted by other evidence in the case does not constitute [an attack on truthful character]."); United States v. Danehy, 680 F.2d 1311, 1314 (11th Cir.1982)("pointing out inconsistencies in testimony and arguing that the accused's testimony is not credible does not constitute an attack on the accused's reputation for truthfulness"); United States v. Jackson, 588 F.2d 1046, 1055 (5th Cir.) rehearing denied, 591 F.2d 1343, cert. denied, 442 U.S. 941, 99 S.Ct. 2882, 61 L.Ed.2d 310 (1979)(mere fact of contradiction by other evidence in case does not constitute attack on character for truthfulness).

61. See § 801(1).3(b) infra.

62. See text at notes 30–39 supra. Fed. R.Evid. 801(d)(1)(B) does not explicitly indicate when the prior statement must have been made. Some federal courts, therefore, concluded that general principles of relevancy should govern on a case-by-case basis as to whether a prior consistent statement serves to rebut a charge of recent fabrication or improper influence or motive. See, e.g., United States v. Lawson, 872 F.2d 179, 182 (6th Cir.), cert. denied, 493 U.S. 834, 110 S.Ct. 110, 107 L.Ed.2d 72 (1989). Other federal courts concluded that the common law rule is inherent in Fed.R.Evid. 801(d)(1)(B) because a prior consistent statement rebuts a charge of recent fabrication or improper influence only if it was made before the corrupting influence existed. Otherwise, a prior consistent statement is nothing more than a repetition of the same story, which adds nothing to the witness' veracity. See, e.g., United States v. Vest, 842 F.2d 1319, 1329–30 (1st Cir.), cert. denied, 488 U.S. 965, 109 S.Ct. 489, 102 L.Ed.2d 526 (1988); United States v. Quinto, 582 F.2d 224, 233–34 (2d Cir.1978).

solved the matter in *Tome v. United States:* [63] "The language of [Rule 801(d)(1)(B)], in its concentration on rebutting charges of recent fabrication, improper influence and motive to the exclusion of other forms of impeachment, as well as in its use of wording which follows the language of the common-law cases, suggests that it was intended to carry over the common-law pre-motive rule."[64]

The *Tome* Court explicitly stated that its "holding is confined to the requirements for admission under Rule 801(d)(1)(B)."[65] Thus, the decision does not necessarily unravel a line of authority in the Second Circuit which holds that a prior consistent statement may, in some circumstances, be admitted for the limited nonsubstantive purpose of rehabilitating a witness' credibility after impeachment with a prior inconsistent statement regardless of whether the requirements of Rule 801(d)(1)(B) have been met.[66] In particular, where impeachment consists of an allegation of self-contradiction by the witness, a prior consistent statement may "cast doubt on whether the prior inconsistent statement was made or on whether the impeaching statement is really inconsistent with the trial testimony," or the consistent statement may

---

63. ___ U.S. ___, 115 S.Ct. 696, 130 L.Ed.2d 574 (1995). Tome was a prosecution of a father for sexual abuse of his young daughter over whom he shared custody with his former wife. On cross-examination of the child, the defense contended that she had been motivated to incriminate the defendant by a desire to live permanently with the mother. The trial court allowed the prosecution thereafter to prove that the child had made several prior accusatory statements to the mother, a babysitter, a social worker and three doctors, all at a time when the alleged custody-based motive already existed. The Tenth Circuit affirmed, holding that the child's alleged motive to lie was "not particularly strong" and that the statements had "probative force apart from mere repetition." 3 F.3d 342, 351 (10th Cir.1993).

64. ___ U.S. at ___, 115 S.Ct. at 702, 130 L.Ed.2d at 584. The Court observed that "the forms of impeachment within the Rule's coverage are the ones in which the temporal requirement makes the most sense. * * * A consistent statement that predates the motive [to fabricate] is a square rebuttal of the charge that the testimony was contrived as a consequence of that motive. By contrast, prior consistent statements carry little rebuttal force when most other types of impeachment are involved." Id. at ___, 115 S.Ct. at 701, 130 L.Ed.2d at 582–83. Conceding that prior consistent statements postdating the onset of an alleged motive to fabricate may occasionally "have some probative force" in rebutting the charge, the rebuttal effect is "less direct and forceful." Id. at ___, 115 S.Ct. at 701, 130 L.Ed.2d at 583. If Congress had intended a broader relevance test, however, it could have done so by the use of language less tied to common law tradition.

65. Id. at ___, 115 S.Ct. at 705, 130 L.Ed.2d at 588. The four-Justice dissent also noted that the majority opinion dealt only with the admissibility of prior consistent statements for the purpose of rebutting charges of recent fabrication. The dissent identified three other potential ways in which prior consistent statements may serve to rehabilitate a witness: "(a) placing a claimed inconsistent statement in context; (b) showing that an inconsistent statement was not made; (c) indicating that the witness' memory is not as faulty as a cross-examiner has claimed." Id. at ___, 115 S.Ct. at 707, 130 L.Ed.2d at 590, citing United States v. Rubin, 609 F.2d 51, 68 (2d Cir.1979)(Friendly, J., concurring).

66. See United States v. Pierre, 781 F.2d 329, 331 (2d Cir.1986)("Of course, not every prior consistent statement has much force in rebutting the effect of a prior inconsistent statement, and the issue ought to be whether the particular prior consistent statement sought to be used has some rebutting force beyond the mere fact that the witness has repeated on a prior occasion a statement consistent with his trial testimony."). See also United States v. Castillo, 14 F.3d 802, 805–07 (2d Cir.1994); United States v. Khan, 821 F.2d 90, 94 (2d Cir. 1987); United States v. Brennan, 798 F.2d 581, 587–89 (2d Cir.1986).

"amplify or clarify the allegedly inconsistent statement."[67] Admission in such cases, which turns on the court's discretion,[68] renders the criteria of Rule 801(d)(1)(B) irrelevant because the rehabilitative purpose is different from that of rebutting a charge of recent fabrication or improper motive.

Library References:

West's Key No. Digests, Witnesses ⟲361, 395, 410–416.

§ 607.6 Impeachment by Bias and Similar Forms of Partiality

a. New York

A time-honored method of impeachment is to show the witness' bias in favor of a party, hostility toward a party, interest in the outcome of the case, exposure to coercive influences or corruption with respect to her own testimony or that of another. Such matters suggest that the witness has a motive to give false, or at least slanted, testimony in the particular case.[1] "Untrustworthy partiality," as Wigmore put it, may be inferred from a witness' relationship to one of the parties or the subject matter of the action or from her statements or conduct.[2]

As to particular types of partiality, bias may be the product of family, business or close social relationships.[3] Employees, for example,

---

67. United States v. Pierre, 781 F.2d 329, 333 (2d Cir.1986). In Pierre, a government agent was impeached by the fact that his handwritten notes concerning defendant's arrest, made immediately after the arrest, did not mention certain incriminating conduct about which the agent had testified. On redirect, the agent was allowed to testify that the incriminating conduct had been included in his formal, typewritten arrest report prepared three days after the arrest, thus suggesting that the omission in the handwritten notes was merely an oversight. The cases of United States v. Khan, 821 F.2d 90 (2d Cir.1987), and United States v. Brennan, 798 F.2d 581 (2d Cir.1986), also permitted rehabilitation with prior consistent statements that tended to overcome the impeaching effect of prior conduct in which witnesses had neglected to incriminate the defendants. In United States v. Castillo, 14 F.3d 802 (2d Cir.1994), a prior consistent statement was held to be admissible to "clarify" an alleged inconsistency. Castillo was a narcotics prosecution in which the arresting officer testified that he snorted cocaine at the time of the transaction as a result of one of the perpetrator's coercive display of a handgun. On cross-examination, the defense contended that the officer lied about the presence of the gun to justify snorting the cocaine and stressed the discrepancy between the officer's testimony that he saw the gun in the perpetrator's "waistband" and his debriefing by his supervisor in which he said he had been "at gunpoint." The officer and his supervisor thereafter were allowed to testify that the officer had told the supervisor that the gun was in the waistband to help the jury evaluate whether the officer's various statements actually meant the same thing.

68. United States v. Pierre, 781 F.2d 329, 333 (2d Cir.1986).

§ 607.6

1. "[P]artiality * * * is * * * always relevant as discrediting the witness and affecting the weight of his testimony." 3A Wigmore § 940, at 775. Whereas criminal convictions, prior bad acts and bad reputation for truthfulness are aimed at discrediting the witness' general character for honesty, the showing of bias is a particularized attack on the motives of the witness "as they may relate directly to issues or personalities in the case at hand." Davis v. Alaska, 415 U.S. 308, 316, 94 S.Ct. 1105, 1110, 39 L.Ed.2d 347, 354 (1974).

2. 3A Wigmore § 945, at 782.

3. Coleman v. New York City Transit Auth., 37 N.Y.2d 137, 142, 371 N.Y.S.2d 663, 668, 332 N.E.2d 850, 853 (1975); People v. Webster, 139 N.Y. 73, 85, 34 N.E. 730, 733–34 (1893).

§ 607.6   WITNESSES   Ch. 6

are likely to be biased in favor of their employers,[4] as are experts who testify for a fee.[5] Another example of a potentially biased witness is one who has settled his own claim against a party and thereafter testifies for such party.[6] The mirror image of bias for a party is hostility toward another party as a result of spite, ill will, personal animosity, jealousy or a desire for revenge.[7]

An interested witness is one who has a personal stake, financial or otherwise, in the outcome of the litigation.[8] Parties to an action obviously are interested witnesses.[9] So, too, are witnesses who may be

---

4. Coleman v. New York City Transit Auth., 37 N.Y.2d 137, 142, 371 N.Y.S.2d 663, 663, 332 N.E.2d 850, 853 (1975).

5. Zimmer v. Third Avenue R.R. Co., 36 App.Div. 273, 55 N.Y.S. 314 (2d Dep't 1899).

6. Pretto v. Leiwant, 80 A.D.2d 579, 580, 435 N.Y.S.2d 778, 780 (2d Dep't 1981); Ryan v. Dwyer, 33 A.D.2d 878, 878–79, 307 N.Y.S.2d 565, 566 (4th Dep't 1969). See also Gilleo v. Elizabeth A. Horton Memorial Hosp., 196 A.D.2d 569, 570, 601 N.Y.S.2d 332, 333 (2d Dep't 1993)(party against whom claim was discontinued testified for prior adversary).

7. Schultz v. Third Avenue R.R. Co., 89 N.Y. 242, 249 (1882)("It is always competent to show that a witness produced upon the trial of an action is hostile in his feelings toward the party against whom he is called to testify or that he entertains malice toward that party * * *"; discharged employee testified against former employer with respect to facts of an accident). See also Brink v. Stratton, 176 N.Y. 150, 151–54, 68 N.E. 148, 148–49 (1903)(defendant was entitled to show that witnesses who testified to his bad reputation for truth and veracity may have been hostile due to business competition and matters printed about them in defendant's newspaper); Garnsey v. Rhodes, 138 N.Y. 461, 34 N.E. 199 (1893)(hostility toward plaintiff's architects (nonparties) where alleged conspiracy between plaintiff and architects was material issue); People v. Brooks, 131 N.Y. 321, 30 N.E. 189 (1892)(defendant's step-daughter, who testified for prosecution, was properly cross-examined as to altercations and ill will between her and defendant); People v. Bonilla, 102 A.D.2d 739, 739, 476 N.Y.S.2d 573, 574 (1st Dep't 1984)(error not to permit defendant to show complaining witness' hostility based on defendant's attention to witness' lady friend).

8. Coleman v. New York City Transit Auth., 37 N.Y.2d 137, 142, 371 N.Y.S.2d 663, 667, 332 N.E.2d 850, 853 (1975); Noseworthy v. City of New York, 298 N.Y. 76, 79–80, 80 N.E.2d 744, 745 (1948). See also People v. Agosto, 73 N.Y.2d 963, 967, 540 N.Y.S.2d 988, 990, 538 N.E.2d 340, 342 (1989)(defendant in criminal case was interested witness as matter of law; jury could determine whether defendant's wife was also interested); In re Snelling's Will, 136 N.Y. 515, 519–20, 32 N.E. 1006, 1007 (1893) (will contestant should have been permitted to show that subscribing witness received or was promised monetary reward for testifying in support of will because "the interest which a witness has in the subject of the controversy is a material inquiry").

Although bias and interest are closely related concepts, the impeaching party may gain a slight advantage by having the trial judge, in her jury instructions, differentiate the particular witnesses who are interested. See, e.g., Coleman v. New York City Transit Auth., 37 N.Y.2d 137, 142–43, 371 N.Y.S.2d 663, 667–68, 332 N.E.2d 850, 852–53 (1975)(trial court correctly charged jury that employee of defendant who was responsible for accident was interested witness; other employees who testified for defendant were merely biased and should have been described as such). Trial courts, however, may not properly tell juries that the testimony of an interested witness is entitled to less weight than that of a disinterested witness. People v. Gerdvine, 210 N.Y. 184, 186, 104 N.E. 129, 130 (1914); People v. Whitmore, 123 A.D.2d 336, 336, 506 N.Y.S.2d 231, 232 (2d Dep't), appeal denied, 68 N.Y.2d 919, 508 N.Y.S.2d 1040, 501 N.E.2d 613 (1986); People v. Demery, 60 A.D.2d 606, 607, 400 N.Y.S.2d 135, 136 (2d Dep't 1977). See also People v. Isidron, 209 A.D.2d 718, 619 N.Y.S.2d 329 (2d Dep't 1994)(error to charge jury that criminal defendant had "deep personal interest * * * of a character * * * possessed by no other witness"). On the other hand, in criminal cases, the jury may be advised to "carefully scrutinize" the testimony of a prosecution witness who has received leniency for his own misconduct in exchange for his testimony. See note 13 infra.

9. See, e.g., People v. Agosto, 73 N.Y.2d 963, 967, 540 N.Y.S.2d 988, 990, 538 N.E.2d 340, 342 (1989)(defendant is interested witness as matter of law).

subject to liability for the same misconduct that is charged against a party.[10] For example, in a personal injury suit against an employer on the theory of respondeat superior, the employee who engaged in the allegedly tortious conduct is an interested witness even if she was not named as a codefendant.[11] Accomplices of a criminal defendant who have received or may hope to receive leniency or some other consideration as a result of testifying for the prosecution also may be viewed as interested, or at least biased, witnesses.[12] Similarly, a prosecution witness who has engaged in unrelated misconduct has a motive to curry favor with the authorities.[13]

Coercive influences on the witness also provide a basis for an inference of partiality. Persons in custody, on bail, or on probation may be under pressure—real or imagined—to testify favorably for the prosecution.[14] Persons threatened by violence may give testimony that is

10. See, e.g., Coleman v. New York City Transit Auth., 37 N.Y.2d 137, 142, 371 N.Y.S.2d 663, 667, 332 N.E.2d 850, 853 (1975)("an actor in the transaction at issue, having a motive to shield himself from blame, would be an interested witness, even though not a party to the action").

11. Id.; Noseworthy v. City of New York, 298 N.Y. 76, 79–80, 80 N.E.2d 744, 745 (1948). See also Noble v. Marx, 298 N.Y. 106, 111, 81 N.E.2d 40, 42 (1948)(in tort action against landlord based on failure to repair, real estate agents who managed defendant's property and who allegedly assured tenant that repairs would be made were interested witnesses).

12. See, e.g., Ryan v. The People, 79 N.Y. 593, 600 (1880)(prosecution witness who had been indicted as participant in same incident forming basis of charges against defendant "might therefore have an interest in the litigation, and a feeling of prejudice or bias which was proper for the consideration of the jury in weighing his evidence"); People v. Capuano, 15 A.D.2d 400, 401–02, 225 N.Y.S.2d 252, 254–55 (4th Dep't 1962) (error to preclude defendant from cross-examining accomplice, who had been indicted for same crime and received suspended sentence, as to whether accomplice hoped to receive benefit from testifying). Ordinarily, the fact that a witness was indicted on some prior occasion is not a permissible form of impeachment because it has no bearing on the witness' general character for truthfulness. See § 608.2, at notes 19–20, infra. In the present context, however, the matter is relevant to the witness' possible motive to falsify in the particular case.

13. See, e.g., People v. Inniss, 83 N.Y.2d 653, 657–58, 612 N.Y.S.2d 360, 362, 634 N.E.2d 961, 963 (1994)(pursuant to cooperation agreement, witness' indictment on unrelated charges was dismissed; because terms of agreement were fully explored on cross-examination, trial court's refusal to admit documentary evidence of agreement was not error); People v. Jackson, 74 N.Y.2d 787, 790, 545 N.Y.S.2d 95, 96–97, 543 N.E.2d 738, 739 (1989)(informant-witness, whose cooperation was obtained only after receipt of reduced jail term on unrelated charge, had "obvious interest"); People v. Chin, 67 N.Y.2d 22, 30–31, 499 N.Y.S.2d 638, 645, 490 N.E.2d 505, 512 (1986)(fact that other charges were pending against prosecution witness was proper subject of cross-examination on issue of motive to curry favor with law enforcement authorities; if witness had denied existence of another charge, it could have been proven because "interest or bias is not collateral").

Where such witness has received some form of favorable treatment from the prosecuting authorities, the defendant is entitled to a special jury instruction to the effect that the witness' testimony "should be scrutinized carefully and a determination made as to whether any benefit he received affected the truthfulness of that testimony." People v. Jackson, supra, 74 N.Y.2d at 790, 545 N.Y.S.2d at 96–97, 543 N.E.2d at 739. But see People v. Inniss, supra, 83 N.Y.2d at 659, 612 N.Y.S.2d at 363, 634 N.E.2d at 363 (failure to give "careful scrutiny" charge was harmless error where witness' interest was "hammered at by the defense in opening, cross-examination and in summation, not seriously disputed" and trial court advised jury, in general, that it could consider the bias or interest of any witness).

14. See, e.g., People v. Stridiron, 33 N.Y.2d 287, 291, 352 N.Y.S.2d 179, 181, 307 N.E.2d 242, 244 (1973)("If the witness is in custody, such cross-examination may tend to show that the witness' testimony was affected by fear or promise of favor growing

§ 607.6 WITNESSES Ch. 6

tainted by fear or intimidation.[15] The testimony of young children is suspect when they have been exposed to potentially coercive or suggestive interrogation concerning the subject matter of their testimony.[16] Finally, corrupt activity by the witness in the form of bribing or pressuring other witnesses[17] or soliciting or receiving a bribe for himself[18] provides a strong inference of partiality.[19]

The foregoing list of possible causes of bias or partiality obviously is nonexclusive. Although evidence of partiality for impeachment purposes ordinarily is liberally allowed, trial courts have discretion to exclude such evidence when it is remote.[20] In *People v. Thomas*,[21] for example, a criminal defendant was precluded at trial from attempting to impeach

out of his detention * * *."); People v. Glennon, 175 N.Y. 45, 52, 67 N.E. 125, 127 (1903) ("If the witness had been arrested and his bail raised so that he could not get at liberty, and he was testifying under what may be termed duress so as to save himself, it was competent to show it.").

15. People v. Portelli, 15 N.Y.2d 235, 257 N.Y.S.2d 931, 205 N.E.2d 857 (1965), cert. denied, 382 U.S. 1009, 86 S.Ct. 612, 16 L.Ed.2d 524 (1966) (prosecution witness held in custody overnight and allegedly beaten and tortured by police); People v. Rodriguez, 143 A.D.2d 854, 855, 533 N.Y.S.2d 331, 332 (2d Dep't), appeal denied, 73 N.Y.2d 859, 537 N.Y.S.2d 506, 534 N.E.2d 344 (1988)(defense witness who gave exculpatory evidence was properly cross-examined by prosecutor as to defendant's threatening and violent conduct toward witness). The Rodriguez case makes the point that the probative value of threatening conduct by the defendant as it relates to the issue of a witness' credibility may overcome the general rule against evidence of a defendant's uncharged crimes. See § 404.1(a) supra.

16. People v. Hudy, 73 N.Y.2d 40, 57, 538 N.Y.S.2d 197, 207, 535 N.E.2d 250, 260 (1988)(in child sexual abuse prosecution, trial court erred in precluding defense from examining investigators concerning their interrogation of complaining witnesses; defense had right to explore "possible reason for fabrication by these impressionable witnesses, i.e., the investigators' suggestive comments"). One court has held that unduly suggestive questioning of a child may result in complete exclusion of the child's testimony except as to those facts shown by the prosecution, in a pretrial hearing, to be based on the child's independent recollection. People v. Michael M., 162 Misc.2d 803, 618 N.Y.S.2d 171 (Sup.Ct.Kings Co.1994).

17. See, e.g., People v. Michalow, 229 N.Y. 325, 331–33, 128 N.E. 228, 230 (1920)(defendant should have been allowed to show that prosecution witness was pressuring other witnesses to testify against him).

18. See, e.g., In re Snelling's Will, 136 N.Y. 515, 519–20, 32 N.E. 1006, 1007 (1893)(contestant of will had right to attempt to show that subscribing witness had been paid for her testimony); People v. Acomb, 87 A.D.2d 1, 7–9, 450 N.Y.S.2d 632, 636–37 (4th Dep't 1982)(defendant's right of confrontation was violated when he was precluded from cross-examining prosecution witness concerning witness' solicitation of bribe from defense investigator in exchange for agreement not to testify at trial).

19. See Hoag v. Wright, 174 N.Y. 36, 45–46, 66 N.E. 579, 582 (1903)("The relations which a witness has to the case, or to a party, threats made by him, the fact that a party tried to bribe him, the fabrication, destruction or concealment of evidence and the like, may be shown.").

20. See Schultz v. Third Avenue R.R. Co., 89 N.Y. 242, 250 (1882)("The evidence to show the hostile feelings of a witness * * * should be direct and positive, and not very remote and uncertain, for the reason that the trial of the main issues in the case cannot be properly suspended to make out the case of hostile feeling by mere circumstantial evidence from which such hostility or malice may or may not be inferred."); 3A Wigmore § 949, at 784 ("circumstances [that prove bias] should have some clearly apparent force, as tested by experience of human nature, or, as it is usually put, they should not be too remote"). See also People v. Stewart, 188 A.D.2d 626, 627, 591 N.Y.S.2d 483, 484 (2d Dep't 1992), appeal denied, 81 N.Y.2d 977, 598 N.Y.S.2d 778, 615 N.E.2d 235 (1993) (inquiry into motive to fabricate may be foreclosed if proof is remote or speculative or if good-faith basis lacking).

21. 46 N.Y.2d 100, 412 N.Y.S.2d 845, 385 N.E.2d 584 (1978), appeal dismissed, 444 U.S. 891, 100 S.Ct. 197, 62 L.Ed.2d 127 (1979).

the arresting officers on the ground of hostility by inquiring into their awareness of the fact that defendant had previously filed a civilian complaint against one of their fellow officers. The trial court did not abuse its discretion, said the Court of Appeals, in finding the evidence "too remote" on the issue of hostility.[22] A different case would have been presented if defendant's complaint had been filed against the witnesses themselves.[23]

Impeachment by bias and related forms of partiality ordinarily is pursued during cross-examination of the witness to be impeached. If the witness denies the bias or the facts upon which it is based, extrinsic evidence may be introduced to prove the matter because it is considered a noncollateral issue.[24] Although courts have discretion to limit the extent of the evidence to be admitted in proof of bias,[25] they may not properly exclude it entirely.[26] Furthermore, in criminal cases the defendant's sixth amendment right of confrontation ensures him the opportunity, at least on cross-examination, to expose the facts upon which an inference of partiality or motive to fabricate may be based.[27]

---

22. Id. at 105, 412 N.Y.S.2d at 848, 385 N.E.2d at 586.

23. The court noted that the action taken against the fellow police officer was "a significant step removed" from any complaint against the witnesses. In addition, no showing was made as to any special relationship between the witnesses and the other officer or the character or seriousness of the complaint. Id. at 105, 412 N.Y.S.2d at 848, 385 N.E.2d at 586.

24. People v. Chin, 67 N.Y.2d 22, 31, 499 N.Y.S.2d 638, 645, 490 N.E.2d 505, 512 (1986)(if witness had denied facts suggestive of interest or bias, opponent would have been entitled to call other witnesses to prove such facts because "interest or bias is not collateral"); Potter v. Browne, 197 N.Y. 288, 291–92, 90 N.E. 812, 813 (1910)("[W]hen the witness unqualifiedly admits his hostility there is neither necessity nor propriety in further pursuing the inquiry. But when he denies it absolutely, or * * * admits it with qualifications, the party invoking the rule may properly supplement the denial or qualified admission by giving testimony tending to show affirmative acts or declarations of hostility."); Brink v. Stratton, 176 N.Y. 150, 152, 68 N.E. 148, 149 (1903)("it was competent to prove the hostility of any or all of these witnesses * * * by their cross-examination or by other testimony").

The functional difference between collateral and noncollateral facts in connection with impeachment is discussed in § 607.2, at notes 19–25, supra, and in § 607.3 supra.

It has been held, however, that courts have discretion to exclude extrinsic evidence bearing on bias or interest where such evidence is not "direct and positive."

See, e.g., People v. Justice, 172 A.D.2d 851, 569 N.Y.S.2d 456 (2d Dep't), appeal denied, 78 N.Y.2d 923, 573 N.Y.S.2d 476, 577 N.E.2d 1068 (1991). See also Schultz v. Third Avenue R.R. Co., 89 N.Y. 242, 250 (1882)(trial of main issue should not be suspended for purpose of proving hostility where proof thereof is based on "mere circumstantial evidence").

25. People v. Brooks, 131 N.Y. 321, 325–27, 30 N.E. 189, 190–91 (1892) (complaining witness, on cross-examination, admitted to several facts showing hostility toward defendant and defendant was permitted to testify to an altercation with such witness; preclusion of further testimony by defendant on issue of hostility, however, caused no harm because "ample evidence" of the matter had been introduced). See also People v. Inniss, 83 N.Y.2d 653, 657–59, 612 N.Y.S.2d 360, 362, 634 N.E.2d 961, 963 (1994) (interest of witness was sufficiently established on cross-examination).

26. People v. McDowell, 9 N.Y.2d 12, 15, 210 N.Y.S.2d 514, 515, 172 N.E.2d 279, 280 (1961)(trial court has discretion only to limit quantity of evidence of hostility).

27. Davis v. Alaska, 415 U.S. 308, 318, 94 S.Ct. 1105, 1111, 39 L.Ed.2d 347, 355 (1974)(defendant's right of confrontation was denied where he was precluded from showing, on cross-examination, that prosecution witness was on probation in connection with juvenile adjudication: "While counsel was permitted to ask [the witness] *whether* he was biased, counsel was unable to make a record from which to argue *why* [the witness] might have been biased or otherwise lacked that degree of impartiality expected of a witness at trial.")(emphasis in

Although the rule is different in some other jurisdictions,[28] New York courts do not require preliminary questioning of the witness as a prerequisite to the introduction of extrinsic evidence of conduct or statements that reveal the witness' partiality.[29]

b. Federal

Although impeachment by bias is not expressly covered in the Federal Rules of Evidence, the Supreme Court in *United States v. Abel*[30] held that such evidence is relevant and therefore admissible pursuant to Rules 401 and 402.[31] Furthermore, the criminal defendant has a constitutional right, on cross-examination, to expose facts suggestive of partiality by prosecution witnesses.[32]

The same types of partiality that have been recognized in the New York caselaw[33] have been found relevant in federal decisions. Thus, a "bias inquiry" may expose facts "such as pecuniary interest in the trial, * * * personal animosity or favoritism toward [a party], * * * or the

---

original). See also People v. Hudy, 73 N.Y.2d 40, 57, 538 N.Y.S.2d 197, 207, 535 N.E.2d 250, 260 (1988)("both the constitutional and the evidentiary rules were breached" when defendant was precluded from examining police officers about their potentially suggestive interrogation of complaining witnesses, which could have shown possible reason for fabrication by such witnesses); People v. Ashner, 190 A.D.2d 238, 246–48, 597 N.Y.S.2d 975, 980–81 (2d Dep't 1993)(defendant had constitutional right to show, on cross-examination, that witness' financial circumstances provided motive to shift suspicion for larceny and forgery away from herself and onto defendant).

28. See McCormick § 39, at 134. See also notes 38–39 infra.

29. People v. Michalow, 229 N.Y. 325, 331, 128 N.E. 228, 230 (1920)(no requirement that allegedly hostile witness be confronted on cross-examination with statement showing such hostility); Brink v. Stratton, 176 N.Y. 150, 152, 68 N.E. 148, 149 (1903)("it is not necessary that the witness should first be examined as to his hostility before calling other witnesses"); People v. Brooks, 131 N.Y. 321, 325, 30 N.E. 189, 190 (1892)("There can be no reason for holding that the witness must first be examined as to his hostility, and that then, and not till then, witnesses may be called to contradict him * * *.").

30. 469 U.S. 45, 105 S.Ct. 465, 83 L.Ed.2d 450 (1984).

31. Id. at 50–52, 105 S.Ct. at 468–69, 83 L.Ed.2d at 456–57. The Court found no intent by the drafters of the Federal Rules to "scuttle" the common law tradition. "Proof of bias," said the Court, "is almost always relevant because the jury, as finder of fact and weigher of credibility, has historically been entitled to assess all evidence which might bear on the accuracy and truth of a witness' testimony." Id. at 52, 105 S.Ct. at 469, 83 L.Ed.2d at 457. Thus, in Abel it was held proper for the government to have proved, through extrinsic evidence, that a defense witness belonged to an organization whose members, which included the defendant, had agreed to "lie, cheat, steal [and] kill" for each other. Id. at 48, 105 S.Ct. at 467, 83 L.Ed.2d at 454–55.

32. Delaware v. Van Arsdall, 475 U.S. 673, 106 S.Ct. 1431, 89 L.Ed.2d 674 (1986)(state's dismissal of charges against witness in unrelated matter); Davis v. Alaska, 415 U.S. 308, 94 S.Ct. 1105, 39 L.Ed.2d 347 (1974) (witness on probation in connection with unrelated matter). The Second Circuit summarized the defendant's rights in this regard in Henry v. Speckard, 22 F.3d 1209, 1214–15 (2d Cir.), cert. denied, ___ U.S. ___, 115 S.Ct. 606, 130 L.Ed.2d 517 (1994):

> The motivation of a witness in testifying, including her possible self-interest and any bias or prejudice against the defendant, is one of the principal subjects for cross-examination. * * * Thus, though the Confrontation Clause does not deprive the trial judge of all discretion to set limits on the cross-examination of a prosecution witness for potential bias, * * * the court "must allow some cross-examination of a witness to show bias." * * * A complete bar on examination into bias would impermissibly deny the jury information "central to assessing [the witness's] reliability."

33. See text at notes 3–19 supra.

Ch. 6   BIAS   § 607.6

witness' plea agreement with the government."[34] Evidence of partiality may be excluded or limited in scope, however, if it is "too remote"[35] or its probative value is outweighed by the potential for unfair prejudice.[36]

As under common law rules, a witness' denial of facts indicative of bias may be proven by extrinsic evidence.[37] Federal courts, however, impose a foundational requirement that prior to extrinsic proof of a witness' statements showing bias, the witness must be given an opportu-

---

34. United States v. Greenwood, 796 F.2d 49, 54 (4th Cir.1986)(citations omitted). In United States v. Abel, 469 U.S. 45, 105 S.Ct. 465, 83 L.Ed.2d 450 (1984), the Supreme Court observed as follows:

> Bias is a term used in the "common law of evidence" to describe the relationship between a party and a witness which might lead the witness to slant, unconsciously or otherwise, his testimony in favor of or against a party. Bias may be induced by a witness' like, dislike, or fear of a party, or by the witness' self-interest. Proof of bias is almost always relevant because the jury, as finder of fact and weigher of credibility, has historically been entitled to assess all evidence which might bear on the accuracy and truth of a witness' testimony.

Id. at 52, 105 S.Ct. at 469, 83 L.Ed.2d at 457.

Cooperation agreements between law enforcement officials and prosecution witnesses are so highly probative of bias that prosecutors are permitted to elicit the existence of such agreements on direct examination in order to take the sting out of cross-examination. See, e.g., United States v. Cosentino, 844 F.2d 30, 33 (2d Cir.), cert. denied, 488 U.S. 923, 109 S.Ct. 303, 102 L.Ed.2d 322 (1988). See also § 607.5, at notes 51–52, supra.

35. Outley v. City of New York, 837 F.2d 587, 594–95 (2d Cir.1988) (defendant should not have been allowed to impeach plaintiff, an African–American, on ground that his prior civil actions against white police officers showed a grudge or prejudice against such officers; bias of this nature was more akin to "character evidence," which is prohibited by Fed.R.Evid. 404(a), and its relevance on the issue of partiality was too remote). Cf. United States v. Greenwood, 796 F.2d 49, 54 (4th Cir.1986)(prosecution witness' erroneous statement to grand jury was not sufficiently probative of animosity or favoritism, and "thumbs up" signal to another prosecution witness was too ambiguous to be indicative of bias).

36. United States v. Weiss, 930 F.2d 185, 197–98 (2d Cir.), cert. denied, 502 U.S. 842, 112 S.Ct. 133, 116 L.Ed.2d 100 (1991)(trial court's curtailment of cross-examination on issue of witness' hostility was proper because further questioning would have been cumulative and would have entailed unnecessary delay). In United States v. Abel, 469 U.S. 45, 105 S.Ct. 465, 83 L.Ed.2d 450 (1984), the Supreme Court observed that the trial court weighed potential prejudice against the probative value of the particular bias evidence in that case, see note 31 supra, and had properly exercised its discretion in favor of admissibility in accordance with Fed.R.Evid. 403. 469 U.S. at 53–55, 105 S.Ct. at 469–70, 83 L.Ed.2d at 458–59. See also United States v. Frankenthal, 582 F.2d 1102, 1106–07 (7th Cir.1978)(trial judge has discretion to limit proof of bias or interest where the evidence is cumulative or its probative value is outweighed by unfair prejudice).

37. United States v. Abel, 469 U.S. 45, 52, 105 S.Ct. 465, 469, 83 L.Ed.2d 450, 457 (1984)(common law, which serves as source of guidance in applying Federal Rules, permits proof of bias by extrinsic evidence). The Abel Court also observed that although extrinsic evidence of a witness' misconduct is prohibited if the only purpose is to show general bad character for truthfulness, see Fed.R.Evid. 608(b), such evidence may be admissible for the more particularized purpose of showing bias. 469 U.S. at 55–56, 105 S.Ct. at 471, 83 L.Ed.2d at 459–60 (defense witness and defendant were shown to be fellow members of organization whose tenets included duty of members to lie, cheat, steal and murder on each other's behalf). See also United States v. Marzano, 537 F.2d 257, 264 (7th Cir.1976), cert. denied, 429 U.S. 1038, 97 S.Ct. 734, 50 L.Ed.2d 749 (1977)("Evidence of prior illegal acts not resulting in convictions is not admissible to show a witness' general lack of character. Such evidence is admissible to show bias."). But see United States v. Atherton, 936 F.2d 728, 733–34 (2d Cir. 1991), cert. denied, 502 U.S. 1101, 112 S.Ct. 1187, 117 L.Ed.2d 429, (1992)(proof of unrelated criminal conduct of prosecution witness to suggest witness' motive to curry favor with government may be excluded if authorities were unaware of such conduct).

§ 607.6 WITNESSES Ch. 6

nity to explain the statements.[38] It is unsettled as to whether proof of nonverbal conduct that reveals bias must also be preceded by preliminary questioning.[39]

Library References:

West's Key No. Digests, Witnesses ⟞363-378.

§ 607.7 Impeachment by Mental or Sensory Impairment

a. New York

Impairments in a witness' mental or sensory capacities, even if they do not render him incompetent to testify,[1] are factors that may be considered in weighing the witness' credibility.[2] While problems of memory or perception ordinarily have no relevance to the witness' willingness to tell the truth, they bear on the potential for human error in what the witness purports to have seen or heard. Thus, they are a proper basis of impeachment.

Mental or sensory deficiencies may be explored on cross-examination, but because they are considered noncollateral matters, they also may be proven by extrinsic evidence.[3] A leading case is *Ellarson v.*

---

38. United States v. Harvey, 547 F.2d 720, 722 (2d Cir.1976); United States v. Marzano, 537 F.2d 257, 265 (7th Cir.1976), cert denied, 429 U.S. 1038, 97 S.Ct. 734, 50 L.Ed.2d 749 (1977). In Harvey, the Second Circuit analogized to the rule governing impeachment by prior inconsistent statements: "Extrinsic evidence of a prior inconsistent statement by a witness is not admissible unless the witness is afforded an opportunity to explain or deny the same and the opposite party is afforded an opportunity to interrogate the witness thereon, or the interests of justice otherwise require." Fed.R.Evid. 613(b). In a subsequent case, however, the Second Circuit gave a more flexible reading to Fed.R.Evid. 613(b), holding that confrontation of a witness with a prior inconsistent statement need not always precede proof of such statement. United States v. Praetorius, 622 F.2d 1054, 1065 (2d Cir.1979), cert. denied, 449 U.S. 860, 101 S.Ct. 162, 66 L.Ed.2d 76 (1980). See § 607.8, at notes 48-50, infra.

39. See 3 Weinstein and Berger ¶ 607[03], at 607-52 to 607-54. Prior to adoption of the Federal Rules, the Second Circuit required foundation questioning in the case of statements showing bias, but imposed no such restriction with respect to conduct suggestive of bias. See Comer v. Pennsylvania R.R. Co., 323 F.2d 863 (2d Cir.1963) The McCormick treatise argues that a preferable approach is one that either eliminates prior confrontation as to both statements and conduct or generally requires it as to both, with discretion in the latter situation to dispense with prior confrontation when the practicalities of the case so demand. McCormick § 39, at 134-35.

§ 607.7

1. See § 601.1, at notes 46-59, supra.

2. See Ellarson v. Ellarson, 198 App. Div. 103, 106, 190 N.Y.S. 6, 9 (3d Dep't 1921)("Having passed the examination by the court and been sworn, the mental capacity of the witness may be tested and considered as bearing upon her credibility and her degree of intelligence.").

3. People v. Freeland, 36 N.Y.2d 518, 525, 369 N.Y.S.2d 649, 653, 330 N.E.2d 611, 615 (1975)(influence of narcotic addiction); Ellarson v. Ellarson, 198 App.Div. 103, 106, 190 N.Y.S. 6, 10 (3d Dep't 1921)(mental illness). See also McCormick § 44, at 160 ("Any deficiency of the senses, such as deafness, or color blindness or defect of other senses which would substantially lessen the ability to perceive the facts which the witness purports to have observed, should of course be provable to attack the credibility of the witness, either upon cross-examination or by producing other witnesses to prove the defect."). The Proposed New York Evidence Code § 608(b)(3) would codify the rule that extrinsic evidence is admissible on the issue of a witness' ability to perceive or remember.

The distinction between collateral and noncollateral facts in connection with impeachment is discussed in § 607.2, at notes 19-25 supra, and § 607.3 supra.

Demeanor evidence, of course, also plays a role in the assessment of the witness'

Ellarson,[4] in which the court held that proof could be made of a witness' history of mental illness at or about the time of the events to which she testified or at the time of trial.[5] In another case, error was found where a defendant was precluded from cross-examining a key prosecution witness with respect to a documented history of serious psychiatric problems that might have affected his capacity to perceive and recall.[6] As noted by the *Ellarson* court, however, "[i]t must appear that, in the interests of truth and justice, such inquiry is necessary," and the court has discretion to determine the extent to which the inquiry may go.[7]

Where evidence of serious mental illness has been held admissible, testimony by experts with knowledge of the witness' condition has been authorized.[8] Where no such experts with prior knowledge are available, the question has arisen, usually in cases of alleged sexual misconduct, whether a court has the power to order a psychiatric evaluation of the witness. The issue is unresolved in New York,[9] but even if courts have such discretionary authority, it would appear that they may exercise it

---

mental and sensory capacities. See People v. Williams, 6 N.Y.2d 18, 29, 187 N.Y.S.2d 750, 759, 159 N.E.2d 549, 555, cert. denied, 361 U.S. 920, 80 S.Ct. 266, 4 L.Ed.2d 188 (1959); § 607.1, at note 3, supra.

4. 198 App.Div. 103, 190 N.Y.S. 6 (3d Dep't 1921).

5. Id. at 106, 190 N.Y.S. at 10. Ellarson should be contrasted with People v. Nieves, 186 A.D.2d 276, 588 N.Y.S.2d 305 (2d Dep't 1992), in which reversible error was found as a result of the prosecutor's cross-examination of the defendant about a psychiatric history that was remote to the cause of the crime and to the issue of credibility.

6. People v. Knowell, 127 A.D.2d 794, 794–95, 512 N.Y.S.2d 190, 192 (2d Dep't 1987). See also People v. Rensing, 14 N.Y.2d 210, 213–14, 250 N.Y.S.2d 401, 404, 199 N.E.2d 489, 491 (1964)(new trial ordered where prosecution witness was diagnosed insane shortly after trial).

7. 198 App.Div. at 107, 190 N.Y.S. at 10. See, e.g., People v. Ely, 115 A.D.2d 171, 172, 495 N.Y.S.2d 240, 242 (3d Dep't 1985), rev'd on other grounds, 68 N.Y.2d 520, 510 N.Y.S.2d 532, 503 N.E.2d 88 (1986), appeal after remand, 164 A.D.2d 442, 563 N.Y.S.2d 890 (3d Dep't 1990), appeal denied, 77 N.Y.2d 905, 569 N.Y.S.2d 937, 572 N.E.2d 620 (1991)(trial court's preclusion of questioning about prosecution witness' past psychiatric examinations was proper exercise of discretion where her testimony was not crucial and no showing was made that witness had ever been diagnosed as having mental disease or disorder).

8. See, e.g., People v. Dudley, 167 A.D.2d 317, 317–18, 562 N.Y.S.2d 66, 67 (1st Dep't 1990)("The People's case rested solely upon the eyewitness testimony of the complainant who had a long history of psychiatric illness. Thus, the trial court should have permitted the defense to offer expert testimony as to the witness' medical condition and treatment, and as to the effect, if any, his condition had upon his capacity at the time of the incident."). The Dudley court relied principally upon People v. Parks, 41 N.Y.2d 36, 390 N.Y.S.2d 848, 359 N.E.2d 358 (1976), where the prosecution was allowed, in effect, to bolster the credibility of a mentally infirm witness by introducing the testimony of experts familiar with the witness' condition and capable of providing "an objective analytical framework" for the evaluation of the witness' credibility. Id. at 48, 390 N.Y.S.2d at 858, 359 N.E.2d at 367. See § 601.1, at notes 50–51, supra and § 702.1(d) infra. But see People v. Kampshoff, 53 A.D.2d 325, 330–31, 385 N.Y.S.2d 672, 677 (4th Dep't 1976), cert. denied, 433 U.S. 911, 97 S.Ct. 2979, 53 L.Ed.2d 1096 (1977)(no error in excluding psychiatrist's testimony concerning witness' mental infirmity where sufficient evidence of this fact was elicited on cross-examination).

9. Compare People v. Earl, ___ A.D.2d ___, 632 N.Y.S.2d 689 (3d Dep't 1995) (no authority for court-ordered psychiatric evaluation of complaining witness), with People v. Griffin, 138 Misc.2d 279, 284, 524 N.Y.S.2d 153, 156–57 (Sup.Ct.Kings Co.1988)(court has authority to order psychiatric evaluation but insufficient grounds shown in case at bar).

only for compelling reasons.[10] The principal factor courts have focused upon is the strength of the preliminary showing that the witness has a relevant mental or psychiatric condition.[11]

A witness' consumption of alcohol or drugs either at the time of the events about which the witness is testifying or at the time of trial is another permissible basis of impeachment with respect to memory and perception.[12] Here again, it may be possible to supplement the impeaching evidence with expert testimony as to how particular substances could impair the ability to perceive and remember, but only if the expert is sufficiently familiar with the witness' circumstances.[13]

Addiction to abusive substances may also be admissible if it has sufficient probative force. In *People v. Freeland*,[14] the Court of Appeals ruled that evidence of addiction to narcotics is admissible if it tends to show "that [the witness] was under the influence of drugs while testifying, or at the time of the events to which she testified, or that her powers of perception or recollection were actually impaired by the

10. The court in People v. Griffin, 138 Misc.2d 279, 524 N.Y.S.2d 153 (Sup.Ct. Kings Co.1988), stated as follows:

[A]n examination can only be ordered in light of the particular facts of a given case and only where compelling reason is present. We must recognize that even while the complainant's credibility is in issue, he himself is not on trial, and a balance must be struck between the necessity to protect the rights of those with possible mental impairment and the rights of the defendants to a fair trail * * *.

Id. at 284, 524 N.Y.S.2d at 157.

11. See People v. Passenger, 175 A.D.2d 944, 945, 572 N.Y.S.2d 972, 974 (3d Dep't 1991)(no abuse of discretion to refuse to order sex-abuse victim to undergo psychiatric testing in absence of compelling proof of mental or emotional instability); People v. Blanche, 152 A.D.2d 770, 772, 543 N.Y.S.2d 548, 550 (3d Dep't)(no indication that victim was mentally unstable), appeal denied, 74 N.Y.2d 894, 548 N.Y.S.2d 427, 547 N.E.2d 954 (1989); People v. Griffin, 138 Misc.2d 279, 284–85, 524 N.Y.S.2d 153, 157 (Sup.Ct.Kings Co.1988)(conclusory and speculative allegations of mental illness were insufficient to order "drastic relief" of court-ordered psychiatric evaluation).

12. People v. Webster, 139 N.Y. 73, 87, 34 N.E. 730, 734 (1893)(if witness "was then under the influence of a powerful narcotic, whose well-known properties are to distort the vision and induce mental confusion, it was material to show it"; if witness denied the matter on cross-examination, opponent could prove it with extrinsic evidence); People v. Wrigglesworth, 204 A.D.2d 758, 611 N.Y.S.2d 678 (3d Dep't 1994) (cross-examination properly elicited witness' consumption of alcohol during evening of crime); People v. Watson, 85 A.D.2d 920, 446 N.Y.S.2d 775 (4th Dep't 1981)(state of sobriety or drunkenness on night of crime was properly explored on cross-examination); People v. Knatz, 76 A.D.2d 889, 428 N.Y.S.2d 709 (2d Dep't 1980)(defendant should have been permitted to fully explore witness' ingestion of narcotics on day of crime and at time of witness' testimony). In some circumstances, the consumption of alcohol or drugs at the time of trial might preclude the witness from testifying. See § 601.1, at notes 56–58 supra.

13. See, e.g., People v. Billups, 132 A.D.2d 612, 612–13, 518 N.Y.S.2d 9, 11 (2d Dep't 1987), appeal denied, 70 N.Y.2d 873, 523 N.Y.S.2d 500, 518 N.E.2d 11 and 70 N.Y.2d 1004, 526 N.Y.S.2d 939, 521 N.E.2d 1082 (1988) (although evidence concerning testimonial capacity is not collateral, proposed experts on effects of methadone maintenance for former heroin addicts were not shown to have knowledge of dosage prescribed for witnesses in question). See also People v. Benson, 206 A.D.2d 674, 614 N.Y.S.2d 808 (3d Dep't 1994), appeal denied, 84 N.Y.2d 1029, 623 N.Y.S.2d 185, 647 N.E.2d 457(1995)(expert opinion on effects of drug ingestion would have been merely speculative where time and amount of witness' consumption of cocaine and alcohol were not established). People v. Williams, 6 N.Y.2d 18, 187 N.Y.S.2d 750, 159 N.E.2d 549, cert. denied, 361 U.S. 920, 80 S.Ct. 266, 4 L.Ed.2d 188 (1959), however, would prohibit a direct opinion by the expert as to the witness' credibility. See note 18 infra.

14. 36 N.Y.2d 518, 369 N.Y.S.2d 649, 330 N.E.2d 611 (1975).

habit."[15] Thus, in *Freeland* the defendant should have been allowed to introduce hospital records showing that the prosecution's chief witness had a long history of heroin addiction up to and including the month before the crime because the evidence was probative of her impaired powers of observation and recollection on the date of the events to which she testified.[16]

The standard for impeachment on the basis of drug addiction may also be applicable, by analogy, to alcoholism.[17] Impeachment by substance abuse may not be reinforced, however, with expert testimony that the particular witness, or a person in general who is addicted to the same type of substance, is "unworthy of belief."[18]

b. Federal

Although no specific Federal Rule of Evidence addresses the point, federal courts, like their New York counterparts, generally permit impeachment by showing impairment of a witness' ability to perceive and remember.[19] Thus, mental infirmities at the time of trial or the time of events to which the witness testifies are a proper subject of cross-examination as well as extrinsic evidence.[20] Courts have discretion

---

15. Id. at 525, 369 N.Y.S.2d at 653, 330 N.E.2d at 614.

16. Id., 369 N.Y.S.2d at 654, 330 N.E.2d at 615. Freeland should be contrasted with People v. Bellamy, 97 A.D.2d 654, 655, 469 N.Y.S.2d 181, 183 (3d Dep't 1983), where no showing was made that the witness might have been affected by drugs at the relevant times. The witness denied, on cross-examination, to using drugs during the past two years and no independent evidence was proffered to show otherwise.

17. See People v. Walker, 116 A.D.2d 948, 951, 498 N.Y.S.2d 521, 524 (3d Dep't), appeal denied, 67 N.Y.2d 952, 502 N.Y.S.2d 1046, 494 N.E.2d 131 (1986)(trial court held to have properly disallowed introduction of hospital records relating to witness' chronic alcoholism where seriousness of condition had decreased and witness was no longer hallucinating at time of most recent hospitalization); People v. Fappiano, 134 Misc.2d 693, 696–97, 512 N.Y.S.2d 301, 304 (Sup.Ct. Kings Co.1987), aff'd, 139 A.D.2d 524, 526 N.Y.S.2d 620 (2d Dep't), appeal denied, 72 N.Y.2d 918, 532 N.Y.S.2d 852, 529 N.E.2d 182 (1988)(alcoholism, standing alone, may not be introduced to infer intoxication at time of event or at trial).

18. People v. Williams, 6 N.Y.2d 18, 25, 187 N.Y.S.2d 750, 757, 159 N.E.2d 549, 553, cert. denied, 361 U.S. 920, 80 S.Ct. 266, 4 L.Ed.2d 188 (1959). The court reasoned that an opinion as to the particular witness' credibility would intrude upon the jury's province as sole arbiter of such questions, and as to drug addicts in general, no consensus existed in the scientific community, at least at the time of the decision, that addicts are generally unworthy of belief. See also People v. Kampshoff, 53 A.D.2d 325, 330, 385 N.Y.S.2d 672, 676 (4th Dep't 1976), cert. denied, 433 U.S. 911, 97 S.Ct. 2979, 53 L.Ed.2d 1096 (1977)(psychiatrist could not properly give opinion, based on informal diagnosis of witness' psychopathic personality, that witness had lied on stand).

19. See United States v. Pryce, 938 F.2d 1343, 1346 (D.C.Cir.1991), cert. denied, 503 U.S. 941, 112 S.Ct. 1488, 117 L.Ed.2d 629 (1992)("Physical impairments—a witness's being blind or deaf, or just myopic or hard of hearing—have long been proper subjects of impeachment. * * * Courts have extended that principle to evidence of mental illnesses that do not directly impair a witness's perception, reasoning that such evidence also affects a witness's credibility, though more obliquely."); Advisory Committee's Note, Fed.R.Evid. 601 ("Interest in the outcome of litigation and mental capacity are, of course, highly relevant to credibility and require no special treatment to render them admissible along with other matters bearing upon the perception, memory, and narration of witnesses.").

20. United States v. Pryce, 938 F.2d 1343, 1346 (D.C.Cir.1991), cert. denied, 503 U.S. 941, 112 S.Ct. 1488, 117 L.Ed.2d 629 (1992)(witness' hallucinations in September were probative of same problem in December, the time of the operative events); United States v. Phibbs, 999 F.2d 1053, 1070 (6th Cir.1993), cert. denied, ___ U.S. ___, 114 S.Ct. 1070, 127 L.Ed.2d 389 (1994) (psychiatric records could be used to attack

§ 607.7

pursuant to Rule 403, however, to exclude or limit such evidence when probative value is outweighed by considerations of prejudice, confusion, time-consumption and the like.[21] Such discretion was held to have been abused, however, in a Second Circuit decision in which hospital records concerning the plaintiff-witness' paranoid schizophrenia had been excluded by the trial judge despite their proximity in time and the fact that plaintiff's credibility was a key issue in the case.[22] Authority for a court-imposed psychiatric examination of a mentally-impaired witness to aid in the impeachment process is recognized but rarely exercised.[23]

Consumption of drugs or alcohol at the time of trial or when operative events occurred is also grounds for impeachment,[24] but evi-

credibility); United States v. Lindstrom, 698 F.2d 1154, 1159–63 (11th Cir.1983)(restrictions on defendant's cross-examination of prosecution witness' history of mental disorders violated sixth amendment); United States v. Partin, 493 F.2d 750, 762–64 (5th Cir.1974), appeal after remand, 552 F.2d 621 (5th Cir.), cert. denied, 434 U.S. 903, 98 S.Ct. 298, 54 L.Ed.2d 189 (1977)(hospital records and expert testimony admissible on issue of insanity and mental derangement); United States v. Hiss, 88 F.Supp. 559, 559–60 (S.D.N.Y.1950)(psychiatrist who observed witness in courtroom permitted to testify to alleged pathology of witness).

One court has held that impeachment on the basis of mental illness should be restricted to serious disorders. United States v. Butt, 955 F.2d 77, 82–83 (1st Cir.1992)("federal courts appear to have found mental instability relevant to credibility only where, during the time-frame of the events testified to, the witness exhibited a pronounced disposition to lie or hallucinate, or suffered from a severe illness, such as schizophrenia, that dramatically impaired her ability to perceive and tell the truth").

21. See, e.g., United States v. Sasso, 59 F.3d 341, 347–48 (2d Cir.1995) (witness' mild depression and use of medications following vehicular accident in which fellow worker was killed was not likely to have altered her ability to perceive events about which she testified); United States v. Bari, 750 F.2d 1169, 1178–79 (2d Cir.1984), cert. denied, 472 U.S. 1019, 105 S.Ct. 3482, 87 L.Ed.2d 617 (1985)(probative value of 10-year-old hospitalization of witness for psychiatric trouble was outweighed by its confusing, time-consuming and cumulative nature; more cogent grounds for impeachment were available and were utilized); United States v. Lopez, 611 F.2d 44, 45–47 (4th Cir.1979)(Rule 403 gives courts power to protect witnesses from cross-examination that has little value in impairing credibility but damages reputation, invades privacy and assaults personality).

22. Chnapkova v. Koh, 985 F.2d 79, 80–82 (2d Cir.1993)(hospitalization occurred slightly over one year after operative events, and final out-patient entry in records was made slightly over three years before trial; contents of hospital records were also relevant to material fact in issue, i.e., presence or absence of substantial scars on plaintiff's face).

23. United States v. Gutman, 725 F.2d 417, 420 (7th Cir.), cert. denied, 469 U.S. 880, 105 S.Ct. 244, 83 L.Ed.2d 183 (1984)(district courts may condition testimony of mentally ill prosecution witness on witness' agreement to take psychiatric examination and to share results with defendant, but the power "should be exercised sparingly" because of intrusive and intimidating consequences; in instant case, defendant already had unlimited use of prior psychiatric reports concerning witness); United States v. Roach, 590 F.2d 181, 186 n.9 (5th Cir.1979) (examination might be ordered to help reveal "severely troubled witness' unreliability in distinguishing truth from fantasy," but defendant already had access to recent reports and other information); United States v. Pacelli, 521 F.2d 135, 141 n.5 (2d Cir.1975), cert. denied, 424 U.S. 911, 96 S.Ct. 1106, 47 L.Ed.2d 314 (1976)(district court has discretion to order psychiatric examination of witness).

24. United States v. DiPaolo, 804 F.2d 225, 229 (2d Cir.1986)("It is * * * within the proper scope of cross-examination to determine whether a witness was under the influence of drugs or narcotics or alcohol at the time of observation of events in dispute, * * * or at the time the witness is testifying, * * *."). See also Rheaume v. Patterson, 289 F.2d 611 (2d Cir.1961)(intoxication at time of operative events proven by extrinsic evidence). But see Smalley v. United States, 798 F.2d 1182, 1188–89 (8th Cir. 1986)(court acknowledged general rule permitting evidence of drug or alcohol use at

dence of mere addiction or general usage is seldom permitted.[25]

Library References:
West's Key No. Digests, Witnesses ⌾327, 328.

§ 607.8 Impeachment by Prior Inconsistent Statements

a. New York

1. In General

One of the most effective techniques of impeachment is showing self-contradiction by the witness in the form of a prior statement or conduct that is inconsistent with his testimony at trial. The impeaching effect becomes apparent when the testimony and the prior inconsistent statement are juxtaposed. Inasmuch as both versions cannot be correct, the inference is that the witness is either mistaken, confused, forgetful or dishonest.[1] For impeachment purposes, therefore, relevance turns not on the truth of the prior statement but the fact that the inconsistent statement was made. Thus, there is no violation of hearsay principles.[2] Indeed, the traditional common law rule is that a prior inconsistent statement generally may not be presented to the fact-finder as evidence of the truth asserted in the statement.[3] This remains the basic rule in New York,[4] but as discussed in § 801(1).2(a), *infra*, the trend in civil actions is to permit certain types of prior inconsistent statements to be

time of occurrence or at trial, but disallowed expert testimony concerning effects of witness' consumption of tranquilizer at time of testimony where such effects did not include potential for falsehood or mental disorientation; the attempted impeachment was irrelevant).

25. United States v. DiPaolo, 804 F.2d 225, 230 (2d Cir.1986) (cross-examination into witness' alcoholism not permitted where no showing was made that witness was under influence at time of events or at trial); United States v. Cameron, 814 F.2d 403, 405 (7th Cir.1987)(prior use of illegal drugs properly excluded as prejudicial pursuant to Fed.R.Evid. 403); United States v. Sampol, 636 F.2d 621, 667 (D.C.Cir.1980) (narcotics addiction should be excluded in absence of foundation that witness was influenced by narcotics during testimony or at time of events testified to). See also United States v. Kizer, 569 F.2d 504, 505–06 (9th Cir.), cert. denied, 435 U.S. 976, 98 S.Ct. 1626, 56 L.Ed.2d 71 (1978) (proper to exclude past drug use and hospitalization for drug addiction when offered on issue of witness' motive to testify favorably for law enforcement agencies in absence of showing of payment or other consideration; "drug addiction is an issue fraught with potential prejudice").

As in the case of mental illness in general, see note 23 supra, courts have the discretion to compel psychiatric examinations of witnesses who have a history of drug use but they seldom do so. See, e.g., United States v. Ramirez, 871 F.2d 582, 584–85 (6th Cir.), cert. denied, 493 U.S. 841, 110 S.Ct. 127, 107 L.Ed.2d 88 (1989); United States v. Jackson, 576 F.2d 46, 48–49 (5th Cir.1978).

§ 607.8

1. See 3A Wigmore § 1017, at 993. See also Larkin v. Nassau Electric R.R. Co., 205 N.Y. 267, 269, 98 N.E. 465, 466 (1912)("Repugnant statements or contraries cannot be true, and the fact that the witness has made them tends to show that he is untrustworthy through carelessness, an uncertain memory, or dishonesty.").

2. 3A Wigmore § 1018, at 995–96.

3. See Larkin v. Nassau Electric R.R. Co., 205 N.Y. 267, 269, 98 N.E. 465, 466 (1912)(prior inconsistent statement is admissible "not as substantive proof of the truth of such statement, but as tending to discredit [the witness]").

4. Id. See also Fitzgibbons Boiler Co. v. National City Bank of New York, 287 N.Y. 326, 330, 39 N.E.2d 897, 899 (1942); Roge v. Valentine, 280 N.Y. 268, 276–77, 20 N.E.2d 751, 754 (1939). Cf. N.Y.Crim. Proc.Law § 60.35(2) (prior inconsistent statement used by party to impeach his own witness "does not constitute evidence in chief").

admitted for their truth.[5] Furthermore, if the prior inconsistent statement is that of an adverse party, the statement is usually admissible against the party as substantive evidence pursuant to the hearsay exception for party admissions.[6] The focus of the present section, however, is solely on the impeachment function of prior inconsistent statements.

As a general rule, the prior inconsistent statement may be in any form—oral or written, sworn or unsworn.[7] Prior conduct that is inconsistent with the witness' testimony may also be used to impeach.[8] Obviously, the prior statement or conduct must be that of the witness himself or a person authorized to speak or act on his behalf.[9] If the

---

5. See, e.g., Letendre v. Hartford Accident & Indem. Co., 21 N.Y.2d 518, 522, 289 N.Y.S.2d 183, 186–87, 236 N.E.2d 467, 469 (1968)(prior statement in writing made by plaintiff's employee admitting embezzlement admissible against fidelity bond insurer where employee denied theft at trial); Vincent v. Thompson, 50 A.D.2d 211, 223–24, 377 N.Y.S.2d 118, 130 (2d Dep't 1975); (prior statement of doctor in products liability action admitted to show use of defective drug when doctor denied such use at trial because doctor was available for cross-examination); Campbell v. City of Elmira, 198 A.D.2d 736, 738, 604 N.Y.S.2d 609, 611 (3d Dep't 1993), aff'd, 84 N.Y.2d 505, 620 N.Y.S.2d 302, 644 N.E.2d 993 (1994) (deposition testimony of defendant's employee).

6. See Koester v. Rochester Candy Works, 194 N.Y. 92, 97, 87 N.E. 77, 79 (1909).

7. Hanlon v. Ehrich, 178 N.Y. 474, 479–80, 71 N.E. 12, 14 (1904)("[A] witness * * * may be discredited by his own contradictory oral or written statements. * * * Letters, affidavits, written statements, verified pleadings, depositions, and previous testimony of a witness are admissible to impeach him * * *.") To the extent a party is authorized to impeach his own witness, however, the party is restricted to prior written statements signed by the witness or oral statements under oath. CPLR 4514; N.Y.Crim.Proc.Law § 60.35(1). See § 607.4(b) supra.

8. People v. Dawson, 50 N.Y.2d 311, 318, 428 N.Y.S.2d 914, 919, 406 N.E.2d 771, 775 (1980)("an inconsistency in a witness' prior conduct or statements may be used as a means of impeaching his testimony at trial"). See, e.g., Service Fire Insurance Co. of New York v. Lederman, 279 App.Div. 319, 320, 109 N.Y.S.2d 812, 813 (3d Dep't), aff'd, 304 N.Y. 658, 107 N.E.2d 588 (1952)(witness whose testimony tended to show defendant was not negligent was properly impeached by fact that she had previously instituted her own action in negligence against defendant).

9. Compare People v. Dickerson, 70 A.D.2d 623, 623, 416 N.Y.S.2d 622, 623 (2d Dep't 1979)(defendant's alibi witness could not properly be impeached by prior inconsistent statement made by third party), with Carriage House Motor Inn, Inc. v. City of Watertown, 136 A.D.2d 895, 896, 524 N.Y.S.2d 930, 932 (4th Dep't), aff'd, 72 N.Y.2d 990, 534 N.Y.S.2d 663, 531 N.E.2d 295 (1988)(appraiser who gave opinion on value at trial could be impeached by prior inconsistent opinion given by another member of same appraisal firm).

Inconsistent statements made by a party's attorney may be used to impeach the party's trial testimony only if the court finds that the attorney was authorized to make the statements. See, e.g., Service Fire Insurance Co. of New York v. Lederman, 279 App.Div. 319, 320, 109 N.Y.S.2d 812, 813 (3d Dep't 1952)(witness acknowledged that she authorized attorney to draft complaint which was inconsistent with her testimony). Compare People v. Rivera, 58 A.D.2d 147, 148, 396 N.Y.S.2d 26, 27–28 (1st Dep't 1977), aff'd, 45 N.Y.2d 989, 413 N.Y.S.2d 146, 385 N.E.2d 1073 (1978)(attorney's affidavit filed in same action specifically indicated that client had informed him of certain facts), with People v. Jones, 190 A.D.2d 31, 33–34, 596 N.Y.S.2d 811, 812 (1st Dep't 1993)(attorney's source of information for affidavit was ambiguous). Cf. People v. Cassas, 84 N.Y.2d 718, 721–24, 622 N.Y.S.2d 228, 229–30, 646 N.E.2d 449, 450–51 (1995) (attorney's out-of-court oral statement to third party could not be used as admission of attorney's client in absence of showing that client authorized the statement and thereby waived attorney-client privilege). See also Hageman v. Jacobson, 202 A.D.2d 160, 608 N.Y.S.2d 180 (1st Dep't 1994)(lawyer's written response on behalf of defendant disclosing information about trial expert's opinion could not be used as prior inconsistent statement of defendant or expert where neither participated in drafting the response).

prior inconsistent statement is that of a criminal defendant who has elected to testify, it may be used to impeach his credibility even if it was obtained in violation of *Miranda* or the right to counsel.[10] On the other hand, an involuntary statement may not be used for impeachment of a criminal defendant[11] or any other witness.[12]

2. Nature of the Inconsistency

What degree of inconsistency is required? The Court of Appeals has taken a broad view of the meaning of inconsistency. In the 1912 case of *Larkin v. Nassau Electric R.R. Co.*,[13] the court said that "[d]irect and positive contradiction" is unnecessary; "[i]t is enough that the testimony and the statements are inconsistent and tend to prove differing facts."[14] More recently, in *People v. Wise*[15] the court said, "In case of

---

10. Harris v. New York, 401 U.S. 222, 91 S.Ct. 643, 28 L.Ed.2d 1 (1971)(Miranda violation); Oregon v. Hass, 420 U.S. 714, 95 S.Ct. 1215, 43 L.Ed.2d 570 (1975)(Miranda violation); Michigan v. Harvey, 494 U.S. 344, 110 S.Ct. 1176, 108 L.Ed.2d 293 (1990)(violation of sixth amendment right to counsel); People v. Ricco, 56 N.Y.2d 320, 325–26, 452 N.Y.S.2d 340, 343, 437 N.E.2d 1097, 1100 (1982)(right to counsel under New York State Constitution). See generally People v. Maerling, 64 N.Y.2d 134, 140–41, 485 N.Y.S.2d 23, 25, 474 N.E.2d 231, 232 (1984). Miranda, of course, holds that statements obtained by official interrogation of a criminal defendant while he is in custody may not be used against him as evidence in chief unless he was warned of his right to remain silent and his right to counsel. Miranda v. Arizona, 384 U.S. 436, 86 S.Ct. 1602, 16 L.Ed.2d 694 (1966). In Harris, however, the Supreme Court held that the Miranda rule should not be "perverted into a license to use perjury by way of a defense, free from the risk of confrontation with prior inconsistent utterances." 401 U.S. at 226, 91 S.Ct. at 646, 28 L.Ed.2d at 5.

Prior inconsistent statements of such nature may be used for impeachment of the defendant both during cross-examination and, assuming a proper foundation is laid, by extrinsic proof during rebuttal. People v. Moshier, 181 A.D.2d 800, 581 N.Y.S.2d 369 (2d Dep't 1992). Limiting instructions to the jury are necessary to prevent misuse of the prior statement as evidence in chief. People v. Grainger, 114 A.D.2d 285, 498 N.Y.S.2d 940 (4th Dep't 1986).

11. People v. Maerling, 64 N.Y.2d 134, 140, 485 N.Y.S.2d 23, 25, 474 N.E.2d 231, 233 (1984); People v. Walker, 110 A.D.2d 730, 732, 487 N.Y.S.2d 613, 615 (2d Dep't 1985), aff'd, 67 N.Y.2d 776, 500 N.Y.S.2d 643, 491 N.E.2d 1100 (1986). See Mincey v. Arizona, 437 U.S. 385, 98 S.Ct. 2408, 57 L.Ed.2d 290 (1978)(Harris rule does not encompass impeachment by involuntary statement taken from wounded, semi-conscious defendant in hospital). See also New Jersey v. Portash, 440 U.S. 450, 99 S.Ct. 1292, 59 L.Ed.2d 501 (1979)(prior testimony which was compelled by grant of use immunity could not be used to impeach defendant at subsequent trial).

The issue of voluntariness may also arise outside the context of official interrogation or compulsion. In People v. Gelikkaya, 84 N.Y.2d 456, 618 N.Y.S.2d 895, 643 N.E.2d 517 (1994), the defendant contended that his grand jury testimony, as to which he waived immunity, should not have been admissible to impeach his credibility at trial because shortly after his grand jury appearance he had been diagnosed as suffering from a psychiatric disorder and was temporarily unfit to stand trial. The Court of Appeals concluded, however, that defendant failed to rebut the presumption that he was mentally competent at the time of the grand jury appearance. The trial court's explicit finding that the defendant had had a "reasonable degree of rational understanding" of the grand jury proceedings was tantamount to a determination of voluntariness of the statements made during those proceedings.

12. See People v. Hults, 76 N.Y.2d 190, 198, 557 N.Y.S.2d 270, 274–75, 556 N.E.2d 1077, 1081–82 (1990)(complaining witness could not be impeached with inconsistent statements made during hypnosis: "A hypnotic statement * * * may be the product of suggestion or confabulation and thus not fairly the witness' own. Even if such a statement is inconsistent with a witness' trial testimony, because of the statement's unreliability, the inconsistency simply is not probative of the truth or falsity of the witness' subsequent trial testimony.").

13. 205 N.Y. 267, 98 N.E. 465 (1912).

14. Id. at 269, 98 N.E. at 466.

15. 46 N.Y.2d 321, 413 N.Y.S.2d 334, 385 N.E.2d 1262 (1978).

§ 607.8

doubt, * * * the balance should be struck in favor of admissibility, leaving to the jury the function of determining what weight should be assigned the impeachment evidence."[16]

The facts in *Wise* illustrate the liberal approach. The witness there testified that he had neither fired a gun nor been in the room in which the gun was fired and only later saw another person handling the weapon. In a prior statement, however, he had told someone "the gun must have had a hair trigger; it went off accidentally, or it just went off." The "hair trigger" remark was sufficiently inconsistent, said the court, because it suggested not only that the witness had seen the shooting but also that he himself had fired the gun. Although not a direct contradiction, the statement tended to establish "a differing version of the facts."[17]

If the testimony is in the form of an opinion, as in the case of expert testimony, a prior contrary opinion by the witness on the same matter obviously serves to impeach.[18] Furthermore, fact-based testimony by a layperson may be impeached by the witness' prior opinion relating to the same facts, even though such opinion would not be an admissible form of evidence if the witness were to give the opinion in court.[19] The jury is not being asked to accept the prior opinion for its truth, and it is clearly relevant to impeach if it suggests an inconsistent belief in the mind of the speaker.[20]

---

16. Id. at 327, 413 N.Y.S.2d at 337, 385 N.E.2d at 1265. See also Champagne v. Shop Rite Supermarkets, 203 A.D.2d 410, 610 N.Y.S.2d 559 (2d Dep't 1994)(in case of doubt, issue of whether witness' prior deposition testimony was inconsistent was properly submitted to jury); People v. Stavris, 75 A.D.2d 507, 508, 426 N.Y.S.2d 741, 743 (1st Dep't 1980)(where question of consistency is arguable, "court should not have decided the question of consistency as a matter of law but should have passed it to the jury to decide, with a proper instruction, as an issue of fact bearing on credibility").

17. 46 N.Y.2d at 327, 413 N.Y.S.2d at 337–38, 385 N.E.2d at 1266.

18. See, e.g., Brooks v. Rochester Ry. Co., 156 N.Y. 244, 50 N.E. 945 (1898)(physician's contradictory opinions as to extent of personal injuries); Garces v. Hip Hospital, Inc., 201 A.D.2d 615, 608 N.Y.S.2d 237 (2d Dep't 1994)(fact that expert gave contrary opinion in another case is proper impeachment); Carriage House Motor Inn, Inc. v. City of Watertown, 136 A.D.2d 895, 524 N.Y.S.2d 930 (4th Dep't), aff'd, 72 N.Y.2d 990, 534 N.Y.S.2d 663, 531 N.E.2d 295 (1988)(appraiser's opinion of value was inconsistent with prior opinion of another member of same appraisal firm); Wachs v. Commercial Travelers Mut. Acc. Ass'n of America, 283 App.Div. 29, 125 N.Y.S.2d 857 (1st Dep't 1953)(physician's opinion at trial as to cause of heart ailment was inconsistent with opinion on cause given during worker's compensation board hearing). See also In re Oates' Will, 171 App.Div. 679, 157 N.Y.S. 646 (2d Dep't 1916)(subscribing witness to will, who gave opinion at trial that testator had been of sound mind, on prior occasion had told someone that testator's mind had been unsound).

19. Judson v. Fielding, 227 App.Div. 430, 433, 237 N.Y.S. 348, 352 (3d Dep't 1929), aff'd, 253 N.Y. 596, 171 N.E. 798 (1930)(witness for plaintiff who testified at trial to facts tending to show that bus was in illegal position in road was properly impeached by statement made to a trooper immediately after accident that "the bus was not to blame"); Wolfe v. Madison Avenue Coach Co., Inc., 171 Misc. 707, 708, 13 N.Y.S.2d 741, 743 (Sup.Ct.App.T.1939)(bus driver's trial testimony describing facts suggesting due care could be impeached by driver's prior statement, "I admit it is my fault").

Lay witnesses are generally precluded, of course, from giving trial testimony in the form of an opinion. See § 701.1 infra.

20. See McCormick § 35, at 117 ("[W]hen the out-of-court statement is not offered at all as evidence of the fact asserted, but only to show the asserter's inconsis-

Ch. 6 PRIOR INCONSISTENT STATEMENTS § 607.8

An omission in a prior account of the facts to which the witness has testified is also considered an inconsistent statement "when given circumstances make it most unnatural to omit certain information."[21] A complete failure to speak may also constitute a form of prior inconsistent statement, as in the case of a defendant's alibi witness who failed to inform the authorities of the alibi, despite a motive and opportunity to do so, shortly after the defendant's arrest.[22] The admissibility of an alibi witness' prior silence, however, is subject to several court-imposed limitations.[23] Furthermore, silence of the defendant himself in the presence

tency, the whole purpose of the opinion rule, to improve the objectivity and hence reliability of testimonial assertions, is quite inapplicable."). See also Larkin v. Nassau Electric R.R. Co., 205 N.Y. 267, 269, 98 N.E. 465, 466 (1912)("If it is sought to prove the expression of an opinion inconsistent with the testimony, it is enough if the opinion is so incompatible with the facts testified to by the witness that an honest mind knowing the facts would not be likely to entertain the opinion.").

21. People v. Savage, 50 N.Y.2d 673, 679, 431 N.Y.S.2d 382, 384, 409 N.E.2d 858, 861, cert. denied, 449 U.S. 1016, 101 S.Ct. 577, 66 L.Ed.2d 475 (1980)(when confessing to police that he shot victim during dispute, defendant omitted to state fact—to which he later testified at trial—that he shot victim unintentionally while victim was attempting to rob him); People v. Bishop, 206 A.D.2d 884, 615 N.Y.S.2d 163 (4th Dep't), appeal denied, 84 N.Y.2d 933, 621 N.Y.S.2d 530, 645 N.E.2d 1230 (1994)(police officer's official report, which omitted to mention that pattern on sneaker-sole imprints at crime scene was visible, was sufficiently inconsistent with trial testimony that such imprints had been clearly visible); Hoberman v. Lane, 85 A.D.2d 595, 444 N.Y.S.2d 704 (2d Dep't 1981)(defendant in auto negligence case testified that he had swerved in order to avoid a bicyclist; plaintiff should have been permitted to show that in narrative of accident to police, defendant made no mention of bicyclist).

Despite the wisdom of the flexible rule announced in Savage, another line of New York authority holds that omissions in a witness' prior narrative of events are not a proper basis of impeachment unless it is shown that at the prior time the witness' attention was called to the matter when the statement was made and that he was specifically asked about the facts embraced in the question propounded at trial. People v. Bornholdt, 33 N.Y.2d 75, 88, 350 N.Y.S.2d 369, 380, 305 N.E.2d 461, 468 (1973), cert. denied, 416 U.S. 905, 94 S.Ct. 1609, 40 L.Ed.2d 109 (1974); People v. Jones, 136 A.D.2d 740, 741, 524 N.Y.S.2d 79, 81 (2d Dep't), appeal denied, 71 N.Y.2d 969, 529 N.Y.S.2d 81, 524 N.E.2d 435 (1988). The Bornholdt formula is unnecessarily rigid. It is inconsistent not only with Savage's standard of "human experience," 50 N.Y.2d at 679, 431 N.Y.S.2d at 385, 409 N.E.2d at 861, but also with the guideline in People v. Wise, 46 N.Y.2d 321, 413 N.Y.S.2d 334, 385 N.E.2d 1262 (1978), that doubts concerning the existence of an inconsistency should be resolved in favor of admissibility. See notes 15–16 supra.

22. People v. Dawson, 50 N.Y.2d 311, 428 N.Y.S.2d 914, 406 N.E.2d 771 (1980). Although the prior silence of the alibi witness had no bearing on the witness' credibility in general, it cast doubt on the veracity of the witness' exculpatory story at trial: "[F]ailure to assert a fact, when it would have been natural to assert it, amounts in effect to an assertion of the nonexistence of the fact." Id. at 318, 428 N.Y.S.2d at 919, 406 N.E.2d at 775 (quoting 3A Wigmore § 1042, at 1056).

23. The prosecutor must lay a foundation showing that the witness was aware of the charges against the defendant, had reason to recognize that he possessed exculpatory information, had a reasonable motive to act to exonerate the defendant, and was familiar with the means of bringing such information to the attention of the authorities. People v. Dawson, 50 N.Y.2d 311, 321 n.4, 428 N.Y.S.2d 914, 921, 406 N.E.2d 771, 777 (1980). In addition, the jury must be advised that citizens have no civil or moral duty to volunteer exculpatory information and that the sole relevance of the silence is the doubt it may cast on the veracity of the witness' statements at trial. At the outset of the prosecutor's questioning, the court must ascertain in a bench conference whether the witness' prior silence was the product of counsel's advice, in which case the silence is inadmissible. Finally, ordinarily no adverse inferences may be drawn from a witness' failure to report the alibi to a grand jury unless the witness was summoned to appear before the grand jury. Id. at 322–23, 428 N.Y.S.2d at 922, 406 N.Y.2d at 778-79.

In cases where the proper foundation for an alibi witness' silence has been made, the

of the police ordinarily is considered too ambiguous a form of contradiction, and too prejudicial in any event, to be admissible to impeach his exculpatory trial testimony.[24]

A witness who purports to recall particular facts and testifies to them at trial may be impeached with his prior statement that he had no recollection of those facts.[25] On the other hand, courts have excluded a witness' prior statement that contains a recitation of facts where the witness claims a lack of recollection at trial.[26] It is said that no inconsistency with respect to the testimony exists in such circumstances. Furthermore, there is a danger that the jury will consider the prior statement for its truth, rather than simply for impeachment, because there is no testimonial statement of fact by the witness against which to juxtapose his prior statement.[27]

3. Foundation Requirements; Extrinsic Evidence

Under New York law, impeachment with a prior inconsistent statement may not proceed until after the witness has been confronted with the prior inconsistent statement.[28] The following foundation is a prereq-

---

prosecutor may prove such silence with extrinsic evidence, despite the witness' denial on cross-examination, because the matter is noncollateral. People v. Knight, 80 N.Y.2d 845, 587 N.Y.S.2d 588, 600 N.E.2d 219 (1992). See text at notes 39–43 infra.

24. People v. De George, 73 N.Y.2d 614, 543 N.Y.S.2d 11, 541 N.E.2d 11 (1989); People v. Conyers, 52 N.Y.2d 454, 438 N.Y.S.2d 741, 420 N.E.2d 933 (1981). Both De George and Conyers are based on New York state rules of evidence rather than constitutional law. The De George court explained that the silence of the defendant is ambiguous "because an innocent person may have many reasons for not speaking," including knowledge that he is under no obligation to speak, a belief that efforts at exoneration would be futile, or mistrust or fear of law enforcement officials. 73 N.Y.2d at 618–19, 543 N.Y.S.2d at 13, 541 N.E.2d at 13. In addition to the low probative value of the accused's silence, "[j]urors, who may not be sensitive to the wide variety of alternative explanations for a defendant's pretrial silence, may assign much more weight to it than is warranted and thus the evidence may create a substantial risk of prejudice." Id. at 619, 543 N.Y.S.2d at 13, 541 N.E.2d at 13. The DeGeorge court distinguished People v. Rothschild, 35 N.Y.2d 355, 361 N.Y.S.2d 901, 320 N.E.2d 639 (1974), where a police office charged with larceny testified in his defense that he had been engaged in an undercover operation. He was properly impeached with his silence at the time of arrest, said the court, because he had an employment-related duty to explain that he was engaged in such an operation.

25. See People v. Schainuck, 286 N.Y. 161, 164, 36 N.E.2d 94, 95 (1941); McCormick § 34, at 115.

26. See, e.g., Varela v. Previti, 64 A.D.2d 560, 406 N.Y.S.2d 830 (1st Dep't 1978). Cf. People v. Fitzpatrick, 40 N.Y.2d 44, 386 N.Y.S.2d 28, 351 N.E.2d 675 (1976) (under N.Y.Crim.Proc.Law § 60.35(1), party in criminal case may not impeach his own witness with prior inconsistent statement unless testimony "tends to disprove" party's case; mere lack of recollection does not tend to disprove case); Brown v. Western Union Telegraph Co., 26 A.D.2d 316, 319, 274 N.Y.S.2d 52, 55 (4th Dep't 1966) (witness who could not recall either the event or her own prior statement about the event could not be "impeached" with prior statement because "[t]here [was] no testimony of this witness altogether different in essential and material points from and at variance with that contained in the signed statement").

27. See Varela v. Previti, 64 A.D.2d 560, 406 N.Y.S.2d 830 (1st Dep't 1978). See also 3A Wigmore § 1043, at 1059. Wigmore urged discretion to admit such statements, at least in the case of the opponent's witness, noting that the "unwilling witness often takes refuge in a failure to remember, and the astute liar is sometimes impregnable unless his flank can be exposed to an attack of this sort." Id. § 1043, at 1061.

28. Larkin v. Nassau Electric R.R. Co., 205 N.Y. 267, 269, 98 N.E. 465, 466 (1912). See also People v. Duncan, 46 N.Y.2d 74, 80–81, 412 N.Y.S.2d 833, 838, 385 N.E.2d 572, 576 (1978), cert. denied, 442 U.S. 910, 99 S.Ct. 2823, 61 L.Ed.2d 275 (1979)("[I]t is

uisite to questioning the witness about the prior statement: If the statement was oral, the time, place, persons present and substance of the statement must be described for the witness coupled with the question whether he made the statement;[29] if the statement was written, the writing must be shown to the witness or the relevant contents read to him.[30]

An admission by the witness of the making of the statement ordinarily will render additional proof of the statement unnecessary. Once the prior inconsistency is acknowledged by the witness, the self-contradiction is complete.[31] On the other hand, if the witness denies making

necessary that the witness be clearly and fairly apprised of the statements which may be subject to impeachment").

29. People v. Wise, 46 N.Y.2d 321, 326, 413 N.Y.S.2d 334, 337, 385 N.E.2d 1262, 1265 (1978)("To set the stage for the prior inconsistency, the questioner must first inform the witness of the circumstances surrounding the making of the statement, and inquire of him whether he in fact made it."); Larkin v. Nassau Electric R.R. Co., 205 N.Y. 267, 269, 98 N.E. 465, 466 (1912)("In case the statements are oral, the warning is given by asking the witness, in substance and effect, if he did not at a given time and place in the presence of or to a person or persons specified make the alleged contradictory statements."); People v. Dachille, 14 A.D.2d 554, 554, 218 N.Y.S.2d 156, 158–59 (2d Dep't 1961)(preferred practice is to quote exact words of alleged prior statement but "rule is flexible" and "[i]t is not necessary that the question used as the foundation be in the exact words of the prior statement" so long as "substance and effect" are disclosed). See, e.g., People v. Duncan, 46 N.Y.2d 74, 81, 412 N.Y.S.2d 833, 838, 385 N.E.2d 572, 577 (1978), cert. denied, 442 U.S. 910, 99 S.Ct. 2823, 61 L.Ed.2d 275 (1979)(on cross-examination witness was asked only whether she had previously said that she wanted money from aunt; proof of prior statement that she would kill aunt if necessary was properly excluded); People v. Bernal, 162 A.D.2d 362, 557 N.Y.S.2d 319 (1st Dep't), leave to appeal denied, 76 N.Y.2d 984, 563 N.Y.S.2d 772, 565 N.E.2d 521 (1990)(inadequate foundation where witness was asked only general questions as to whether he had previously spoken with an officer and no questions were asked as to substance of statement to officer); People v. Watford, 146 A.D.2d 590, 536 N.Y.S.2d 835 (2d Dep't), appeal denied, 73 N.Y.2d 984, 540 N.Y.S.2d 1018, 538 N.E.2d 370 (1989)(error to allow detective to prove witness' statement to him where witness was never asked if he had in fact made such statement to detective).

30. Larkin v. Nassau Electric R.R. Co., 205 N.Y. 267, 269, 98 N.E. 465, 466 (1912)("In case the statements are in writing and unsubscribed, the paper must be shown or read to the witness and marked for identification and, if subscribed, the signature, and, in case he so demands, the paper must be shown to him.").

31. Hanlon v. Ehrich, 178 N.Y. 474, 479–80, 71 N.E. 12, 14 (1904)("If the witness, without explanation or qualification, admits having made the statement, that is the end of the inquiry, because the witness has discredited himself, and there is no need for contradiction."); Stein v. Lebowitz–Pine View Hotel, Inc., 111 A.D.2d 574, 489 N.Y.S.2d 635, 638 (3d Dep't), appeal denied, 65 N.Y.2d 611, 494 N.Y.S.2d 1026, 484 N.E.2d 1053 (1985).

Some cases have authorized extrinsic evidence of inconsistent statements given in prior testimony notwithstanding the witness' admission of such inconsistencies on cross-examination. See People v. Schainuck, 286 N.Y. 161, 165, 36 N.E.2d 94, 96 (1941)(in prior testimony at fire marshal's investigation, witnesses denied knowledge of fire but subsequently accused defendants of setting it; on cross-examination the witnesses admitted the inconsistencies: "Should not there have been an opportunity to compare, detail for detail, the conflicting versions, and to spread them both before the jury? * * * We adopt the view that the right to scrutinize prior inconsistent statements cannot be cut off by the mere admission by the witness that he has been guilty of inconsistency."); Wachs v. Commercial Travelers Mut. Acc. Ass'n of America, 283 App.Div. 29, 31, 125 N.Y.S.2d 857, 858 (1st Dep't 1953)(although doctor admitted having given inconsistent opinion at prior workers' compensation board hearing, jury should have been permitted to scrutinize the transcript of the hearing).

It has been suggested that the usual practice should be one of exclusion of extrinsic evidence when a witness admits his prior inconsistency so as to save time and mini-

§ 607.8 WITNESSES Ch. 6

the statement or is unable to recall whether he made the statement, the impeaching party may prove the statement with extrinsic evidence, i.e., testimony by other witnesses or documentary proof, during the next phase of his case.[32]

Thus, the ability to prove a prior inconsistent statement with extrinsic evidence is contingent upon prior disclosure of the alleged statement to the witness during cross-examination.[33] The confrontation foundation is intended to avoid surprise and give the witness timely opportunity to deny, clarify or explain the inconsistency either immediately or upon redirect.[34] The rule also serves to minimize the consumption of time inasmuch as an acknowledgement of the statement will eliminate the need for introducing extrinsic evidence.[35] The confrontation policy is so strong in New York that it has been applied to self-contradiction by a hearsay declarant whose former testimony or deposition is read into evidence at trial pursuant to a hearsay exception.[36] If the now-unavailable declarant was not confronted with the inconsistent

mize the calling of witnesses on a mere question of credibility. On the other hand, the trial judge should have discretion in the matter, especially if the prior inconsistency is in writing. McCormick § 37, at 120–21 n.10. A rule of discretion appears to be the governing standard in New York. See People v. Piazza, 48 N.Y.2d 151, 163–65, 422 N.Y.S.2d 9, 16–17, 397 N.E.2d 700, 707–08 (1979)(trial court acted within its discretion in disallowing introduction into evidence of inconsistent affidavit where detailed contents of affidavit were entered into record during cross-examination of witness; this was not a case "in which the subtleties of expression or the omissions and inclusions in the statement required particularly close study of the detail and refinements of composition").

32. Hanlon v. Ehrich, 178 N.Y. 474, 480, 71 N.E. 12, 14 (1904). With respect to a writing, the witness may not be cross-examined concerning its contents and it may not be read to the jury until it has been admitted into evidence either as a result of the witness' admission that the writing is his or upon extrinsic proof that it is his. Larkin v. Nassau Electric R.R. Co., 205 N.Y. 267, 269–70, 98 N.E. 465, 466 (1912). To the extent the writing contains matters that are irrelevant to the inconsistency or are otherwise inadmissible, the document should not be given to the jury for its inspection without redaction. If necessary, the contradictory passages of the document can simply be read into the record. Blackwood v. Chemical Corn Exchange Bank, 4 A.D.2d 656, 658–59, 168 N.Y.S.2d 335, 338–39 (1st Dep't 1957), appeal denied, 5 A.D.2d 768, 170 N.Y.S.2d 504 (1st Dep't), appeal dismissed, 4 N.Y.2d 675, 171 N.Y.S.2d 1028, 148 N.E.2d 916 (1958).

33. Proposed New York Evidence Code § 613(a)-(b) would codify existing law as follows:

(a) Examining witness concerning prior inconsistent statement. [PROPOSED] In examining a witness concerning a prior inconsistent statement made by such witness, whether written or not, the statement should be shown or its contents disclosed to such witness at that time.

(b) Extrinsic evidence of prior inconsistent statement of witness. Except when the interests of justice otherwise require, extrinsic evidence of a prior inconsistent statement by a witness is not admissible unless the witness is first afforded an opportunity to explain or deny the statement and the opposing party is afforded an opportunity to interrogate the witness thereon. This provision does not apply to admissions of a party-opponent as defined in subdivision (b) of section 803 of this chapter.

34. People v. Duncan, 46 N.Y.2d 74, 81, 412 N.Y.S.2d 833, 838, 385 N.E.2d 572, 576 (1978), cert. denied 442 U.S. 910, 99 S.Ct. 2823, 61 L.Ed.2d 275 (1979); Larkin v. Nassau Electric R.R. Co., 205 N.Y. 267, 269, 98 N.E. 465, 466 (1912).

35. McCormick § 37, at 120.

36. People v. Hines, 284 N.Y. 93, 115, 29 N.E.2d 483, 494 (1940), overruled on other grounds, People v. Kohut, 30 N.Y.2d 183, 331 N.Y.S.2d 416, 282 N.E.2d 312 (1972); Stacy v. Graham, 14 N.Y. 492, 498–500 (1856); Harding v. Conlon, 159 App. Div. 441, 450–51, 144 N.Y.S. 663, 669–70 (1st Dep't 1913).

statement at the time of his prior testimony, the inconsistency may not be used at trial to impeach his credibility.[37]

The foregoing foundation requirements are inoperative, however, when the prior inconsistent statement is that of an adverse party. Such statement may be proved as a party admission regardless of whether the adverse party is confronted with the statement at the time of his testimony.[38]

In addition to the confrontation prerequisite, the introduction of extrinsic evidence is further limited by the rule against independent proof of collateral matters.[39] As discussed in § 607.3 *supra,* the distinction between collateral and noncollateral matters is imprecise. In general, a witness' prior inconsistent statement is noncollateral when it contradicts the witness' testimony on a "material issue in the case,"[40] i.e., an issue that has relevance beyond mere impeachment of the witness.[41]

Obviously, the question whether a particular inconsistency is material is a case-specific inquiry. In *People v. Beavers,*[42] for example, the defendant's alibi witness, his mother, testified that her son had been home with her at the time of the crime. When questioned by the police a few days after the crime, however, the witness said she had not seen her son for several weeks. This inconsistency, which the witness denied making, was noncollateral and subject to proof by extrinsic evidence, said the court, because it directly contradicted the alibi defense that defendant had sought to establish through his mother's testimony.[43]

---

37. On this point, Proposed New York Evidence Code § 809 would change current law by eliminating the foundation requirement that the hearsay declarant be given an opportunity to deny or explain an inconsistent statement. See § 806.1(a), at note 3, infra. See also McCormick § 37, at 124 (arguing that even under traditional rule, court should dispense with foundation requirement if inconsistent statement was made after the prior testimony was given).

38. Mindlin v. Dorfman, 197 App.Div. 770, 189 N.Y.S. 265 (1921); McCormick § 37, at 124–25 (little danger of surprise with respect to adverse party, and party has adequate opportunity for denial or explanation after statement is proved).

39. See, e.g., People v. Jones, 190 A.D.2d 31, 33, 596 N.Y.S.2d 811, 812 (1st Dep't 1993)(prosecutor was barred from proving prior inconsistent statement, when it was denied by witness, because "the purported inconsistency was on matters collateral to the material issues in the case, and extrinsic evidence may not be introduced to impeach on collateral facts solely for the purpose of determining credibility").

40. People v. Knight, 80 N.Y.2d 845, 847–48, 587 N.Y.S.2d 588, 590, 600 N.E.2d 219, 221 (1992); People v. Cade, 73 N.Y.2d 904, 905, 539 N.Y.S.2d 287, 288, 536 N.E.2d 616, 616–17 (1989).

41. People v. Wise, 46 N.Y.2d 321, 328, 413 N.Y.S.2d 334, 338, 385 N.E.2d 1262, 1266 (1978)("Evidence is not collateral * * * when it is relevant to some issue other than credibility"); People v. Beavers, 127 A.D.2d 138, 141, 514 N.Y.S.2d 235, 238 (1st Dep't), appeal denied, 70 N.Y.2d 642, 518 N.Y.S.2d 1034, 512 N.E.2d 560 (1987)("Nor is evidence collateral when it tends to impeach a witness's credibility with respect to the very issues the jury is asked to resolve."). See also § 607.3, at notes 9–12, supra.

42. 127 A.D.2d 138, 514 N.Y.S.2d 235 (1st Dep't), appeal denied, 70 N.Y.2d 642, 518 N.Y.S.2d 1034, 512 N.E.2d 560 (1987).

43. Id. at 142–43, 514 N.Y.S.2d at 238–39. The Court of Appeals cited Beavers with approval in another alibi witness case, People v. Cade, 73 N.Y.2d 904, 539 N.Y.S.2d 287, 536 N.E.2d 616 (1989). In Cade, the defendant's brother testified at trial that he and the defendant had been playing basketball at the time the crime was committed. The prosecution was held to have properly proved with extrinsic evidence that a few days after defendant's arrest, the brother told the police that defendant "might have

§ 607.8 WITNESSES Ch. 6

b. Federal

The Federal Rules of Evidence indirectly endorse the use of prior inconsistent statements as a basis for impeachment of a witness by providing, in Rule 613, procedural rules for the admission of such statements. Furthermore, Rule 801(d)(1)(A) permits certain types of prior inconsistent statements under oath to be used as evidence in chief, not merely for the purpose of impeachment. The substantive use of prior inconsistent statements under the Federal Rules is discussed in § 801(1).3(a), *infra,* whereas the present section is confined to the issues of impeachment and procedures for the proof of prior inconsistent statements.

Whether a witness' prior statement is inconsistent with her testimony, and thereby serves to impeach, is largely a discretionary decision for the court.[44] It has been said that "inconsistency is not limited to diametrically opposed answers but may be found in evasive answers, inability to recall, silence, or changes of position."[45]

---

committed the robbery." The contradiction was noncollateral because it went "to a material, core issue in the case—defendant's whereabouts at the time of the crime." Id. at 905, 539 N.Y.S.2d at 287, 536 N.E.2d at 616–17. Accord, People v. Knight, 80 N.Y.2d 845, 847, 587 N.Y.S.2d 588, 589, 600 N.E.2d 219, 220 (1992)(alibi witness' silence at time of defendant's arrest was noncollateral and therefore provable by extrinsic evidence because it was "clearly relevant to a material issue that the jury [was] obligated to resolve").

44. United States v. Agajanian, 852 F.2d 56, 58 (2d Cir.1988); United States v. Gravely, 840 F.2d 1156, 1163 (4th Cir. 1988); United States v. Causey, 834 F.2d 1277, 1282 (6th Cir.1987), cert. denied, 486 U.S. 1034, 108 S.Ct. 2019, 100 L.Ed.2d 606 (1988); United States v. Dennis, 625 F.2d 782, 795 (8th Cir.1980); United States v. Insana, 423 F.2d 1165, 1170 (2d Cir.), cert. denied, 400 U.S. 841, 91 S.Ct. 83, 27 L.Ed.2d 76 (1970).

45. United States v. Dennis, 625 F.2d 782, 795 (8th Cir.1980). See also United States v. Gravely, 840 F.2d 1156, 1163 (4th Cir.1988)("It is enough if the 'proffered testimony, taken as a whole, either by what it says or by what it omits to say' affords some indication that the fact was different from the testimony of the witness whom it sought to contradict."). See, e.g., United States v. Causey, 834 F.2d 1277, 1282–83 (6th Cir.1987), cert. denied, 486 U.S. 1034, 108 S.Ct. 2019, 100 L.Ed.2d 606 (1988)(witness claimed to be unable to recall facts at trial); United States v. Carr, 584 F.2d 612, 618 (2d Cir.1978), cert. denied, 440 U.S. 935, 99 S.Ct. 1280, 59 L.Ed.2d 494 (1979)(prior silence of witness); United States v. Insana, 423 F.2d 1165, 1170 (2d Cir.), cert. denied, 400 U.S. 841, 91 S.Ct. 83, 27 L.Ed.2d 76 (1970)(witness disavowed memory at trial so as "not to hurt anyone").

With respect to prior statements that omit facts described at trial, the court in United States v. Stock, 948 F.2d 1299 (D.C.Cir.1991), held that inconsistency turns on whether "it would have been 'natural' for the witness to include them in the earlier statement. * * * The test is plainly elastic, as the 'naturalness' of a witness's decision to omit a point may depend on nuances of the prior statement's context as well as on his own loquacity." Id. at 1301. Compare United States v. Strother, 49 F.3d 869, 874–75 (2d Cir.1995)(omissions in memoranda were inconsistent with trial testimony because it would have been "natural" for author-witness to have included certain matters in memoranda), with United States v. Leonardi, 623 F.2d 746, 756 (2d Cir.), cert. denied, 447 U.S. 928, 100 S.Ct. 3027, 65 L.Ed.2d 1123, and cert. denied sub nom. Berland v. United States, 449 U.S. 884, 101 S.Ct. 236, 66 L.Ed.2d 109 (1980) (omissions were "simply too ambiguous to have any probative force")

The use of a criminal defendant's prior silence to impeach is circumscribed by constitutional limitations. Compare Doyle v. Ohio, 426 US. 610, 96 S.Ct. 2240, 49 L.Ed.2d 91 (1976)(prosecution may not impeach defendant's exculpatory trial testimony with fact of defendant's silence in presence of law enforcement officers following arrest and receipt of Miranda warnings), with Jenkins v. Anderson, 447 U.S. 231, 100 S.Ct. 2124, 65 L.Ed.2d 86 (1980)(use of defendant's prearrest silence to impeach does not violate Constitution), and Fletcher

The prior inconsistent statement must be shown to be that of the witness herself, and if the statement was supposedly recorded in another person's business records, such as a public official's written report, the statement must have been recorded verbatim.[46] If the witness denies or fails to recall having made the prior inconsistent statement, generally it may be proven with extrinsic evidence unless the court determines that the inconsistency relates to a collateral matter.[47]

As illustrated by New York Law, discussed above,[48] a fairly rigid ritual applies to the common law process of impeachment with prior inconsistent statements. When a witness is being questioned about her prior inconsistent statement, the contents and circumstances of the statement must be disclosed to the witness at the outset of such questioning. Furthermore, confrontation of the witness is a prerequisite to the introduction of extrinsic evidence of the statement, thereby enabling the witness immediately to deny or explain the inconsistency. Rule 613 of the Federal Rules of Evidence departs from the common law by adding an element of flexibility to the procedure:

> **(a) Examining witness concerning prior statement.** In examining a witness concerning a prior statement made by the witness, whether written or not, the statement need not be shown nor its contents disclosed to the witness at that time, but on request the same shall be shown or disclosed to opposing counsel.
>
> **(b) Extrinsic evidence of prior inconsistent statement of witness.** Extrinsic evidence of a prior inconsistent statement by a witness is not admissible unless the witness is afforded an opportunity to explain or deny the same and the opposite party is afforded an opportunity to interrogate the witness thereon, or the interests of justice otherwise require. This provision does not apply to admissions of a party-opponent as defined in rule 801(d)(2).

Subdivision (a) of Rule 613 eliminates the common law requirement that the prior inconsistent statement be disclosed to the witness before questioning about it may proceed.[49] The only limitation is that opposing

---

v. Weir, 455 U.S. 603, 102 S.Ct. 1309, 71 L.Ed.2d 490 (1982)(use of defendant's post-arrest silence to impeach does not violate Constitution if Miranda warnings were not given).

46. United States v. Almonte, 956 F.2d 27, 29–30 (2d Cir.1992)("If a third party's notes reflect only that note-taker's summary characterization of a witness's prior statement, then the notes are irrelevant as an impeaching prior inconsistent statement, and thus inadmissible"). A witness may also be deemed to have made a prior inconsistent statement reported in a third party's memorandum if she "subscribed" to the third party's characterization of her statement. United States v. Strother, 49 F.3d 869, 875 (2d Cir.1995). See also United States v. Chavez, 979 F.2d 1350, 1355 (9th Cir.1992)(insufficient proof that witness to be impeached was author of inconsistent notation on police diagram of crime scene).

47. United States v. Grooms, 978 F.2d 425, 428–29 (8th Cir.1992)("a witness may not be impeached on a collateral matter by the use of extrinsic evidence; 'self-contradiction of a witness by prior inconsistent statements may be shown only on a matter material to the substantive issues of the case' "). See generally § 607.3 supra.

48. See notes 28–35 supra.

49. But see United States v. Marks, 816 F.2d 1207, 1210–11 (7th Cir.1987) (district judge "is entitled to conclude that in particular circumstances the older approach

§ 607.8 WITNESSES Ch. 6

counsel is entitled to disclosure of the statement upon request "to protect against unwarranted insinuations that a statement has been made when the fact is to the contrary."[50]

Subdivision (b) of Rule 613 loosens up the traditional foundation requirements with respect to extrinsic evidence of prior inconsistent statements. Although Rule 613(b) still generally requires that the witness be given an opportunity to explain or deny a prior inconsistent statement,[51] there is no "specification of any particular time or sequence."[52] Thus, for example, the impeaching party may introduce extrinsic evidence of a prior inconsistent statement without first confronting the witness with it, provided the witness has an opportunity thereafter to return to the stand to refute or explain the statement.[53]

should be used in order to avoid confusing witnesses and jurors"; trial judge required counsel to show witnesses FBI interview reports which contained witnesses' alleged inconsistent statements because witnesses' denials of the statements might unfairly imply that witnesses were lying when in fact FBI might have garbled their stories).

50. Advisory Committee's Note, Fed. R.Evid. 613. See. e.g., United States v. Lawson, 683 F.2d 688, 694 (2d Cir.1982).

51. In at least three situations, however, no opportunity for denial or explanation need be given. The prior inconsistent statement of a party who testifies at trial usually will qualify as a party admission that may be proven against the party without any obligation to give the party-witness an opportunity to deny or explain it. Fed. R.Evid. 613(b) (last sentence). Nor does the rule apply when the prior inconsistency is in the form of conduct rather than a statement. Advisory Committee's Note, Fed.R.Evid. 613. Finally, Rule 613(b) provides that the court may dispense with the opportunity of denial and explanation when "the interests of justice otherwise require." The Advisory Committee's Note explains that such discretion is conferred "to allow for such eventualities as the witness becoming unavailable by the time the statement is discovered." See Wammock v. Celotex Corp., 793 F.2d 1518, 1523-27 (11th Cir.1986)("interests of justice" exception inapplicable where impeaching party, although unaware of witness' particular prior inconsistent statements, had sufficient knowledge of "inconsistent past performance" of witness; witness' unavailability for purpose of explanation therefore precluded use of extrinsic evidence to prove prior statements with which witness had not been confronted while on stand).

In United States v. Bibbs, 564 F.2d 1165 (5th Cir.1977), cert. denied, 435 U.S. 1007, 98 S.Ct. 1877, 56 L.Ed.2d 388 (1978), the court held that Rule 613(b)'s requirement of an opportunity for denial or explanation did not apply with respect to an inconsistent statement made by the witness subsequent to her trial testimony. Alternatively, the court noted that the aggrieved party could have requested that the witness be recalled. Id. at 1169.

52. Advisory Committee's Note, Fed. R.Evid. 613.

53. See, e.g., United States v. Hudson, 970 F.2d 948, 955-56 (1st Cir.1992)(during defense, defendant should have been allowed to prove prior inconsistent statement of prosecution witness despite absence of confrontation during cross-examination of witness because no showing was made by prosecution that witness was not available for recall; "the foundation requirements of 613(b) do not require that the witness be confronted with the statement while on the witness stand, but rather, only that the witness be available to be recalled in order to explain the statement during the course of the trial"); Wilmington Trust Co. v. Manufacturers Life Ins. Co., 749 F.2d 694, 699 (11th Cir.1985)(court properly allowed extrinsic proof, during rebuttal, of a witness' prior inconsistent statement despite absence of confrontation during cross-examination of witness; opponent waived opportunity for denial or explanation by not requesting recall of witness for surrebuttal or reopening of case); United States v. Praetorius, 622 F.2d 1054, 1065 (2d Cir.1979), cert. denied sub nom. Lebel v. United States, 449 U.S. 860, 101 S.Ct. 162, 66 L.Ed.2d 76 (1980)(defendant should have been permitted to prove witness' prior inconsistent statement with extrinsic evidence without prior confrontation of witness). But see Wammock v. Celotex Corp., 793 F.2d 1518, 1523 (11th Cir.1986)(trial court's exclusion of extrinsic evidence of witness' prior inconsistent statement was proper where witness was not confronted while on stand and thereafter was unavailable for recall).

Despite the flexibility authorized by Rule 613(b), it has been said that the common law approach of prior confrontation is the "preferred method" in practice.[54] Furthermore, another court has observed that Rule 611(a) of the Federal Rules of Evidence "allows the trial judge to control the mode and order of interrogation and presentation of evidence, giving him or her the discretion to impose the common-law 'prior foundation' requirement when such an approach seems fitting."[55]

Library References:

West's Key No. Digests, Witnesses ⊗379–397.

608 Impeachment by Evidence of Untruthful Character and Prior Misconduct

§ 608.0 In General

Despite the general rule against evidence of a person's character to prove her conduct on a particular occasion, which is discussed in § 402.1 *supra*, the law has long allowed character-related evidence on the issue of witness credibility. It is said that a witness whose character is flawed with respect to the trait of truthfulness is less likely than other persons to testify truthfully on the stand.

Proof of character may be made in a relatively direct manner through the testimony of other witnesses who are familiar with the reputation of the witness to be impeached or indirectly by evidence of the witness' prior misconduct or criminal convictions. Sections 608.1 and 608.2 treat the first two types of character-related impeachment. Convictions are the subject of §§ 609.1 and 609.2 *infra*.

§ 608.1 Bad Character for Truthfulness

a. New York

New York courts traditionally have permitted evidence of a witness' bad character for truthfulness as a method of impeachment on the theory that a dishonest person is less likely to testify truthfully than one who is reputed to be honest.[1] In the 1983 decision of *People v. Pavao*,[2] the Court of Appeals reaffirmed the tradition, holding that "a party has a right to call a witness to testify that a key opposing witness, who gave

---

54. Wammock v. Celotex Corp., 793 F.2d 1518, 1522 (11th Cir.1986).

55. United States v. Hudson, 970 F.2d 948, 956 n.2 (1st Cir.1992). Accord, United States v. Sutton, 41 F.3d 1257, 1260 (8th Cir.1994). The Hudson court also said, "[A] trial court is free to use its informed discretion to exclude extrinsic evidence of prior inconsistent statements on grounds of unwarranted prejudice, confusion, waste of time, or the like." 970 F.2d at 956 n.2. See also United States v. King, 560 F.2d 122, 128 n.2 (2d Cir.), cert. denied, 434 U.S. 925, 98 S.Ct. 404, 54 L.Ed.2d 283, and cert. denied sub nom. Boucher v. United States, 434 U.S. 925, 98 S.Ct. 404, 54 L.Ed.2d 283 (1977)("Although admissible under 613 the papers could be excluded under 403").

§ 608.1

1. People v. Hinksman, 192 N.Y. 421, 435, 85 N.E. 676, 681 (1908).

2. 59 N.Y.2d 282, 464 N.Y.S.2d 458, 451 N.E.2d 216 (1983).

§ 608.1

substantive evidence and was not called for purposes of impeachment, has a bad reputation in the community for truth and veracity."[3] It bears noting, however, that *Pavao* explicitly limits the use of character evidence to impeachment of "key" witnesses of the opponent who have given "substantive evidence." This standard was satisfied in *Pavao*, where a prosecution witness testified to a damaging admission allegedly made by the defendant. The trial court's exclusion of evidence that the prosecution witness had a bad reputation for truthfulness was said to deprive the jury of "evidence which would assist them in evaluating the credibility of this important witness."[4]

Assuming the conditions have been met for the introduction of character evidence to impeach a witness' credibility, such evidence must refer to the particular character trait of untruthfulness; the witness' general bad moral character is not admissible.[5] Furthermore, New York courts continue to insist that the witness' character be proved by evidence of her reputation for truth and veracity.[6] The impeaching witness may not give her own personal opinion of the untruthful character of the witness to be impeached.[7] By tradition, however, after reporting the reputation of the witness to be impeached, the impeaching witness may be asked whether she would believe the other witness under oath.[8]

---

3. Id. at 290, 464 N.Y.S.2d at 462, 451 N.E.2d at 220. The court reasoned that character evidence is probative on the issue of credibility and that proof of such character through other witnesses does not implicate the usual concerns that weigh against extrinsic evidence on collateral matters:

> When the use of extrinsic impeaching testimony is limited to a general statement that the witness' reputation in the community for truth and veracity is bad, there is no fear that trials will become unnecessarily protracted affairs involving numerous minitrials over whether or not a witness' answer was accurate or whether a witness did a particular act. Nor will the introduction of this evidence divert the jury's attention from the main issues involved in the trial.

Id. at 289–90, 464 N.Y.S.2d at 462, 451 N.E.2d at 220.

4. Id. at 291, 464 N.Y.S.2d at 462, 451 N.E.2d at 221. See also People v. Streitferdt, 169 A.D.2d 171, 175, 572 N.Y.S.2d 893, 896 (1st Dep't), appeal denied, 78 N.Y.2d 1015, 575 N.Y.S.2d 823, 581 N.E.2d 1069 (1991)(defendant had right to show bad reputation for truthfulness of complaining witnesses in prosecution for sexual misconduct).

5. People v. Pavao, 59 N.Y.2d 282, 289, 464 N.Y.S.2d 458, 462, 451 N.E.2d 216, 220 (1983); People v. Hinksman, 192 N.Y. 421, 435, 85 N.E. 676, 681 (1908); People v. Lyde, 160 A.D.2d 817, 818, 554 N.Y.S.2d 74, 75 (2d Dep't 1990).

6. See People v. Bouton, 50 N.Y.2d 130, 139, 428 N.Y.S.2d 218, 222, 405 N.E.2d 699, 703 (1980)("reputation—the aggregate tenor of what others say or do not say about him—is the raw material from which that character may be established").

7. See Kravitz v. Long Island Jewish–Hillside Medical Center, 113 A.D.2d 577, 581–82, 497 N.Y.S.2d 51, 55 (2d Dep't 1985). The Court of Appeals refused to reconsider the rule against opinions in the analogous context of character evidence offered by an accused as circumstantial evidence that he did not commit the crime with which he is charged. People v. Barber, 74 N.Y.2d 653, 543 N.Y.S.2d 365, 541 N.E.2d 394 (1989). In a dissenting opinion, however, Judge Titone argued that opinion evidence by a witness with first-hand knowledge of a person's character is superior to reputation evidence, which is merely "unverifiable hearsay of unknown origin." Id. at 657, 543 N.Y.S.2d at 367, 541 N.E.2d at 396. Proposed New York Evidence Code § 608(a) would explicitly change current law by allowing proof of a witness' untruthful character by reputation or opinion. See note 16 infra.

8. Elmendorf v. Ross, 221 App.Div. 376, 377, 222 N.Y.S. 737, 738 (3d Dep't 1927). See People v. Streitferdt, 169 A.D.2d 171, 174–75, 572 N.Y.S.2d 893, 895 (1st Dep't), appeal denied, 78 N.Y.2d 1015, 575 N.Y.S.2d 823, 581 N.E.2d 1069 (1991).

The impeaching witness may not describe specific instances of untruthful conduct by the witness to be impeached.[9] Such evidence is barred by the rule against extrinsic evidence of collateral matters.[10] On the other hand, the impeaching witness probably can be cross-examined as to whether or not she has heard of specific instances of honest or truthful conduct of the principal witness in an effort to challenge her evaluation of the principal witness' reputation.[11] The impeaching witness may also be impeached by such matters as bias or partiality,[12] but not by evidence that she herself has a bad reputation for truthfulness.[13]

Presumably, the same qualifications that apply to other types of character witnesses[14] also apply to those who testify to untruthful character for impeachment purposes. Thus, the character witness need not live in the same residential neighborhood as that of the witness to be impeached.[15] It should be enough that she is familiar with the witness' reputation for truthfulness in a circle of associations "of such quantity and quality as to permit [the principal witness] to be personally observed by a sufficient number of individuals to give reasonable assurance of reliability."[16]

---

9. See, e.g., People v. Majeed, 204 A.D.2d 986, 613 N.Y.S.2d 69 (4th Dep't 1994).

10. See People v. Pavao, 59 N.Y.2d 282, 288–89, 464 N.Y.S.2d 458, 461, 451 N.E.2d 216, 219–20 (1983). See generally § 607.3 supra.

11. See Proposed N.Y.Evid.Code § 608(b)(2), quoted in note 16 infra. In the analogous context of a reputation witness whose testimony is offered as circumstantial evidence that a defendant did not commit the crime with which he is charged, the prosecutor, if acting on reasonable grounds and in good faith, may cross-examine the reputation witness as to whether she has heard reports or rumors of specific instances of misconduct of the defendant that reflect adversely on the character trait in issue. People v. Kuss, 32 N.Y.2d 436, 443, 345 N.Y.S.2d 1002, 1007, 299 N.E.2d 249, 253 (1973), cert. denied, 415 U.S. 913, 94 S.Ct. 1408, 39 L.Ed.2d 467 (1974). Such questioning would bear on the credibility of the reputation witness as follows: If the impeaching witness has not heard of the specific instances of truthful conduct by the principal witness, she is not very knowledgeable about the reputation of which she speaks; if she has heard of them, her judgment about the reputation is called into question. See Michelson v. United States, 335 U.S. 469, 478, 481, 69 S.Ct. 213, 220, 221, 93 L.Ed. 168, 175, 176 (1948).

12. See People v. Streitferdt, 169 A.D.2d 171, 175–76, 572 N.Y.S.2d 893, 896 (1st Dep't), appeal denied, 78 N.Y.2d 1015, 575 N.Y.S.2d 823, 581 N.E.2d 1069 (1991).

13. People v. Pavao, 59 N.Y.2d 282, 290, 464 N.Y.S.2d 458, 462, 451 N.E.2d 216, 220 (1983) See text at note 3 supra.

Whether the witness with the allegedly bad reputation may be rehabilitated by rebuttal evidence of witnesses who can attest to her good reputation for truthfulness apparently lies in the discretion of the trial court. People v. Pavao, supra, 59 N.Y.2d at 290, 464 N.Y.S.2d at 462, 451 N.E.2d at 220; see § 607.5, at note 24, supra.

14. See generally § 402.1, at notes 35–41, supra.

15. People v. Bouton, 50 N.Y.2d 130, 139–40, 428 N.Y.S.2d 218, 223, 405 N.E.2d 699, 704 (1980).

16. Id. at 139, 428 N.Y.S.2d at 223, 405 N.E.2d at 704 (reputation at school, in military unit, in veterans's organization, in business community). Proposed New York Evidence Code § 608(a)(1) and (b)(2) and (3) would codify the rules on impeachment by character for untruthfulness as follows:

§ 608. **Evidence of character and conduct of witness [PROPOSED]**

(a) **Opinion and reputation evidence of character.** The credibility of a witness may be attacked or supported by evidence in the form of opinion or reputation, subject to these limitations:

(1) **Only evidence of character for truthfulness**. The evidence may refer only to character for truthfulness; and

* * *

(b) **Specific instances of conduct.**

* * *

§ 608.1 WITNESSES Ch. 6

b. Federal

Federal Rule of Evidence 608(a)(1) carries forward the common law rule that allows an attack upon a witness' credibility by means of character evidence from the lips of a qualified character witness.[17] The federal rule goes beyond current New York practice, however, by authorizing opinion evidence as well as traditional reputation evidence. Rule 608(a)(1) states, in relevant part: "The credibility of a witness may be attacked * * * by evidence in the form of opinion or reputation, but subject to these limitations: (1) the evidence may refer only to character for truthfulness or untruthfulness * * *."

If the character witness proposes to testify to the principal witness' bad reputation for truthfulness,[18] a foundation must be shown that the character witness has such knowledge of the witness, his community and his circle of associations as to be able to "speak with authority of the terms in which generally he is regarded."[19] The relevant time frame of the witness' reputation is at or about the time of trial.[20] After reporting on the reputation of the witness to be impeached, the reputation witness may be asked whether she would believe the other witness under oath.[21]

If qualified, a character witness may give a direct opinion that the witness to be impeached has a bad character for truthfulness. The foundation is satisfied by a showing that the character witness has

(2) Inquiry of character witness. A witness who has been examined and testified about the truthful character of another witness may be asked, if asked on reasonable grounds and good faith, about specific instances of conduct bearing on the truthfulness of that other witness. A character witness may be asked whether, based upon that witness's knowledge or opinion, he or she would believe the other witness under oath. A character witness on behalf of a criminal defendant, however, may not be asked on cross-examination whether the witness's testimony would be different if the witness knew that defendant had committed the crime charged.

(3) Extrinsic evidence. For the purpose of attacking or supporting the truthfulness of a witness under this section, specific instances of the conduct of the witness not resulting in a criminal conviction may not be proved by extrinsic evidence, provided, however, nothing in this subdivision shall preclude extrinsic proof bearing on matters such as a witness's bias, prejudice, interest, motive, hostility, or ability to perceive or remember.

As discussed in notes 6–7 supra, New York law does not currently allow a character witness to give her own opinion of the principal witness' character for truthfulness.

17. See, e.g., Wilson v. City of Chicago, 6 F.3d 1233, 1239 (7th Cir.1993), cert. denied, ___ U.S. ___, 114 S.Ct. 1844, 128 L.Ed.2d 470 (1994).

18. Fed.R.Evid. 608(a)(1), on its face, limits the relevant character trait to that of truth and veracity. See United States v. Greer, 643 F.2d 280, 283 (5th Cir.), cert. denied, 454 U.S. 854, 102 S.Ct. 300, 70 L.Ed.2d 147 (1981).

19. United States v. Watson, 669 F.2d 1374, 1381 (11th Cir.1982), quoting Michelson v. United States, 335 U.S. 469, 478, 69 S.Ct. 213, 219, 93 L.Ed. 168, 175 (1948). The concept of "community," of course, is not restricted to one's place of residence. Courts have permitted evidence of a witness' reputation "in the community in which he works," United States v. Mandel, 591 F.2d 1347, 1370 (4th Cir.1979), cert. denied, 445 U.S. 961, 100 S.Ct. 1647, 64 L.Ed.2d 236 (1980), and the school he attends, United States v. Bedonie, 913 F.2d 782, 802 (10th Cir.1990), cert. denied, 501 U.S. 1253, 111 S.Ct. 2895, 115 L.Ed.2d 1059 (1991). See also Cooper v. Asplundh Tree Expert Co., 836 F.2d 1544, 1552 (10th Cir. 1988).

20. United States v. Watson, 669 F.2d 1374, 1382 n.5 (11th Cir.1982).

21. United States v. Davis, 787 F.2d 1501, 1504 (11th Cir.), cert. denied, 479 U.S. 852, 107 S.Ct. 184, 93 L.Ed.2d 118 (1986); United States v. Lollar, 606 F.2d 587, 588–89 (5th Cir.1979).

personal knowledge of the principal witness.[22] Familiarity with the witness' community reputation is unnecessary.[23]

Neither reputation nor opinion witnesses may buttress their testimony by recounting their knowledge of specific instances of conduct of the witness to be impeached for the purpose of demonstrating his untruthful character. Such extrinsic evidence is prohibited both by the language of Rule 608(a)(1) and by the rule against extrinsic evidence of specific acts on the issue of character, as discussed in § 608.2 *infra*.

Library References:

West's Key No. Digests, Witnesses ⊕=333–362.

§ 608.2 Prior Acts of Misconduct

a. New York

Eliciting an admission from a witness that she has engaged in specific acts of misconduct of a certain type impeaches credibility by indirectly attacking the witness' character for truthfulness. New York has been categorized as a jurisdiction that takes a liberal view of the types of prior acts that reflect adversely on truthfulness.[1]

The leading case is *People v. Sorge*,[2] in which a defendant charged with performing an illegal abortion took the stand in her own defense. The prosecutor was held to have properly cross-examined the defendant by asking whether she had performed illegal abortions on four other women. The court declared that a witness may be questioned upon cross-examination about " 'any vicious or criminal act of his life' that has a bearing on his credibility as a witness."[3] The court also included "immoral acts" that bear on credibility.[4] In all cases of immoral, vicious or criminal acts, "the inquiry must have some tendency to show moral turpitude to be relevant on the credibility issue."[5] With respect to a criminal defendant who testifies, the standard has been phrased, alternatively, in terms of whether the misconduct of the witness would reveal a willingness "to place the advancement of his individual self-interest ahead of principle or of the interests of society," thereby suggesting a readiness to do so again on the witness stand.[6] Furthermore, the Court

---

22. United States v. Watson, 669 F.2d 1374, 1382 (11th Cir.1982).

23. Id. See also United States v. Lollar, 606 F.2d 587, 589 (5th Cir.1979)(no requirement of long acquaintance or recent information; shortcomings in degree of familiarity may be explored on cross-examination). But see United States v. Dotson, 799 F.2d 189, 192–94 (5th Cir.1986)(improper to allow law enforcement officials, based solely on investigatory activity, to express opinion that defendant-witness was "liar").

§ 608.2

1. McCormick § 41, at 138 n.6.

2. 301 N.Y. 198, 93 N.E.2d 637 (1950).

3. Id. at 200, 93 N.E.2d at 638, quoting People v. Webster, 139 N.Y. 73, 84, 34 N.E. 730, 733 (1893).

4. 301 N.Y. at 200, 93 N.E.2d at 638. See Badr v. Hogan, 75 N.Y.2d 629, 634, 555 N.Y.S.2d 249, 251, 554 N.E.2d 890, 892 (1990)("a witness may be cross-examined with respect to specific immoral, vicious or criminal acts which have a bearing on the witness's credibility").

5. Badr v. Hogan, 75 N.Y.2d 629, 634, 555 N.Y.S.2d 249, 251, 554 N.E.2d 890, 892 (1990).

6. People v. Walker, 83 N.Y.2d 455, 461, 611 N.Y.S.2d 118, 122, 633 N.E.2d 472, 476 (1994); People v. Coleman, 56 N.Y.2d 269, 273, 451 N.Y.S.2d 705, 707, 436 N.E.2d

§ 608.2   WITNESSES   Ch. 6

of Appeals has recently ventured beyond its "immoral-vicious-or-criminal" formula to include prior conduct suggestive simply of the witness' "untruthful bent," such as using an alias[7] or publishing books on how to cheat on taxes and telephone services.[8]

Whether a particular type of conduct falls within the foregoing standards is within the sound discretion of the trial court.[9] Not surprisingly, the caselaw reflects a broad spectrum of application.[10] As to prior

---

1307, 1309 (1982); People v. Duffy, 36 N.Y.2d 258, 262, 367 N.Y.S.2d 236, 240, 326 N.E.2d 804, 807, amended, 36 N.Y.2d 857, 370 N.Y.S.2d 919, 331 N.E.2d 695, cert. denied, 423 U.S. 861, 96 S.Ct. 116, 46 L.Ed.2d 88 (1975); People v. Sandoval, 34 N.Y.2d 371, 377, 357 N.Y.S.2d 849, 855, 314 N.E.2d 413, 417 (1974).

7. People v. Walker, 83 N.Y.2d 455, 461–62, 611 N.Y.S.2d 118, 122, 633 N.E.2d 472, 476 (1994)("a suspect's use of a false name or other inaccurate pedigree information is an indication of dishonesty that goes to the very heart of the question of that individual's testimonial credibility").

8. People v. Coleman, 56 N.Y.2d 269, 273, 451 N.Y.S.2d 705, 707, 436 N.E.2d 1307, 1308 (1982)(trial court properly exercised discretion in determining that witness' publication of books advocating cheating was relevant and material to witness' credibility, veracity and honesty).

9. Id. at 273, 451 N.Y.S.2d at 707, 436 N.E.2d at 1308 (1982); People v. Schwartzman, 24 N.Y.2d 241, 244, 299 N.Y.S.2d 817, 820, 247 N.E.2d 642, 644, cert. denied, 396 U.S. 846, 90 S.Ct. 103, 24 L.Ed.2d 96 (1969).

10. In addition to the cases cited in notes 2, 7 and 8 supra, the following cases illustrate allowable impeachment: Martin v. Alabama 84 Truck Rental, Inc., 47 N.Y.2d 721, 417 N.Y.S.2d 56, 390 N.E.2d 774 (1979) (plaintiff's failure to renew his driver's license); People v. Duffy, 36 N.Y.2d 258, 262, 367 N.Y.S.2d 236, 239–40, 326 N.E.2d 804, 806, amended, 36 N.Y.2d 857, 370 N.Y.S.2d 919, 331 N.E.2d 695, cert. denied, 423 U.S. 861, 96 S.Ct. 116, 46 L.Ed.2d 88 (1975)(defendant's use and possession of heroin); People v. Jones, 193 A.D.2d 696, 598 N.Y.S.2d 40 (2d Dep't 1993) (police officer's brutality and false arrests); People v. Squires, 171 A.D.2d 893, 567 N.Y.S.2d 555 (2d Dep't 1991)(defendant's concealment of income and assets from department of social services); People v. Harris, 151 A.D.2d 981, 542 N.Y.S.2d 71 (4th Dep't), appeal denied, 74 N.Y.2d 810, 546 N.Y.S.2d 568, 545 N.E.2d 882 (1989)(in sex offense prosecution, complaining witness' prior false complaints of rape); People v. Charkow, 142 A.D.2d 734, 735, 531 N.Y.S.2d 120, 121 (2d Dep't 1988)(defendant's failure to pay taxes and practice of paying employees "off the books"); People v. Jones, 136 A.D.2d 740, 524 N.Y.S.2d 79 (2d Dep't), appeal denied, 71 N.Y.2d 969, 529 N.Y.S.2d 81, 524 N.E.2d 435 (1988)(defendant's falsification of employment application in which he denied prior conviction); People v. Batista, 113 A.D.2d 890, 493 N.Y.S.2d 608 (2d Dep't 1985), appeal denied, 67 N.Y.2d 648, 499 N.Y.S.2d 1044, 490 N.E.2d 560 (1986)(prosecution witness' failure to carry green card and participation in illegal gambling activities); People v. Dukett, 110 A.D.2d 940, 487 N.Y.S.2d 875 (3d Dep't 1985)(defendant giving woman drink containing five tranquilizers qualified as vicious act); People v. Rivera, 101 A.D.2d 981, 477 N.Y.S.2d 732 (3d Dep't 1984), aff'd, 65 N.Y.2d 661, 491 N.Y.S.2d 621, 481 N.E.2d 253 (1985)(defendant's receipt of social service checks and benefits to which she was not entitled); Batease v. Dion, 275 App.Div. 451, 90 N.Y.S.2d 851 (3d Dep't 1949) (attorney's disbarment or suspension from practice of law).

In the following cases the attempted cross-examination was considered improper: People v. Dorthy, 156 N.Y. 237, 241, 50 N.E. 800, 801 (1898) (expulsion from church, society or club); People v. Grier, 162 A.D.2d 416, 557 N.Y.S.2d 68 (1st Dep't), appeal denied, 76 N.Y.2d 1021, 565 N.Y.S.2d 771, 566 N.E.2d 1176 (1990)(prosecution witness' employment in pornography industry); People v. Kelly, 124 A.D.2d 825, 509 N.Y.S.2d 44 (2d Dep't 1986), appeal denied, 69 N.Y.2d 829, 513 N.Y.S.2d 1036, 506 N.E.2d 547 (1987)(complaining witness' loss of custody of her child); People v. Buggs, 109 A.D.2d 1052, 487 N.Y.S.2d 202 (4th Dep't 1985) (defense witness' failure to pay rent); People v. Moore, 42 A.D.2d 268, 272, 346 N.Y.S.2d 363, 368 (2d Dep't 1973)(defendant's act of vandalism at age 12 did not show moral turpitude); Hamby v. Bonventre, 36 A.D.2d 648, 649, 318 N.Y.S.2d 178, 181 (3d Dep't 1971)(violation of college rule prohibiting operation of motorcycle on campus); People v. Hyman, 284 App. Div. 347, 350, 131 N.Y.S.2d 691, 695 (1st Dep't 1954), aff'd, 308 N.Y. 794, 125 N.E.2d 597 (1955)(card player who also bet on horses).

sexual misconduct, the court's discretion is circumscribed by New York Criminal Procedure Law § 60.42, which generally prohibits evidence of specific instances of sexual conduct of the victim in a sex offense prosecution, and New York Criminal Procedure Law § 60.43, which generally prohibits evidence of the sexual conduct of a victim in all other types of criminal prosecutions.[11]

The cross-examiner must have a reasonable basis in fact for his questions about prior misconduct and must act in good faith.[12] The nature and extent of the cross-examination is within the trial court's discretion.[13] Perhaps the most important limit on the use of prior misconduct for impeachment purposes is the rule that such misconduct may not be proven by extrinsic evidence.[14] Inquiry may be made on cross-examination, and if the witness admits the misconduct, the impeachment has been achieved. If the witness denies the conduct, however, the cross-examiner is bound by the witness' answer. Where such misconduct has not resulted in a conviction, it is usually considered collateral.[15] The cross-examiner, therefore, ordinarily may not prove the conduct through the testimony of other witnesses or documentary evidence.[16] The most that the cross-examiner may do is press the witness

---

11. See § 412.1 supra. A victim's prior false accusations of rape, however, may qualify as an impeaching fact that falls outside the exclusionary rule of § 60.42 or § 60.43. See People v. Harris, 151 A.D.2d 981, 542 N.Y.S.2d 71 (4th Dep't), appeal denied, 74 N.Y.2d 810, 546 N.Y.S.2d 568, 545 N.E.2d 882 (1989). Furthermore, if the witness is not the victim of the crime, the admissibility of her sexual misconduct turns on the court's discretion. See, e.g., La Beau v. People, 34 N.Y. 222, 230 (1866)(trial court properly excluded questioning of victim's wife concerning her adulterous acts).

12. People v. Kass, 25 N.Y.2d 123, 125–26, 302 N.Y.S.2d 807, 809, 250 N.E.2d 219, 221 (1969); People v. Sorge, 301 N.Y. 198, 200, 93 N.E.2d 637, 639 (1950); People v. Steele, 168 A.D.2d 937, 938, 565 N.Y.S.2d 339, 339–40 (4th Dep't), appeal denied, 77 N.Y.2d 967, 570 N.Y.S.2d 501, 573 N.E.2d 589 (1991); People v. Dellarocco, 115 A.D.2d 904, 905, 496 N.Y.S.2d 801, 802 (3d Dep't 1985), appeal denied, 67 N.Y.2d 941, 502 N.Y.S.2d 1033, 494 N.E.2d 118 (1986).

13. People v. Walker, 83 N.Y.2d 455, 462, 611 N.Y.S.2d 118, 122, 633 N.E.2d 472, 476 (1994); Badr v. Hogan, 75 N.Y.2d 629, 634, 555 N.Y.S.2d 249, 251, 554 N.E.2d 890, 892 (1990).

In People v. Sorge, 301 N.Y. 198, 200–02, 93 N.E.2d 637, 638–40 (1950), it was observed that the trial court's allowance of inquiry into several other acts that were similar to the crime with which the defendant-witness was charged was not an abuse of discretion. See text at notes 2–4 supra.

14. Badr v. Hogan, 75 N.Y.2d 629, 635, 555 N.Y.S.2d 249, 252, 554 N.E.2d 890, 893 (1990); People v. Zabrocky, 26 N.Y.2d 530, 535, 311 N.Y.S.2d 892, 896, 260 N.E.2d 529, 532 (1970).

15. See generally § 607.3, at notes 1–6, supra.

16. Badr v. Hogan, 75 N.Y.2d 629, 635, 555 N.Y.S.2d 249, 252, 554 N.E.2d 890, 893 (1990); People v. Pavao, 59 N.Y.2d 282, 288–89, 464 N.Y.S.2d 458, 461, 451 N.E.2d 216, 219 (1983). See also People v. Grant, 210 A.D.2d 166, 620 N.Y.S.2d 358 (1st Dep't 1994), appeal denied, 85 N.Y.2d 862, 624 N.Y.S.2d 381, 648 N.E.2d 801 (1995)(where defendant-witness denied prior misconduct about which prosecutor made inquiry for impeachment purposes, trial court was said to have acted properly in immediately instructing jury that counsel's questions did not constitute evidence).

Extrinsic evidence of prior misconduct in the face of a witness' denial may be admissible, however, when it is probative of a material issue in the case, not merely the witness' credibility. See People v. Schwartzman, 24 N.Y.2d 241, 245–49, 299 N.Y.S.2d 817, 821–25, 247 N.E.2d 642, 645–47, cert. denied, 396 U.S. 846, 90 S.Ct. 103, 24 L.Ed.2d 96 (1969)(evidence of defendant-witness' prior fraudulent activity was independently probative of crime with which he was currently charged). See § 607.3, at notes 7–12, supra. Even unrelated misconduct may be provable by extrinsic evidence if the witness herself "opens the door" by affirmatively seeking to disprove it after the

§ 608.2   WITNESSES   Ch. 6

in an effort to convince her to retract her denial.[17] When such effort is exhausted, the cross-examiner must end the pursuit.

Unlike convictions,[18] mere arrests or indictments are irrelevant on the issue of character because they are only accusations.[19] Thus, the witness may be questioned about the misconduct underlying an arrest, but not the fact of the arrest itself.[20] Another limitation is that the witness may refuse to admit or deny collateral criminal conduct by invoking her privilege against self-incrimination.[21] Furthermore, if the witness has already been tried and acquitted of other criminal conduct, New York law prohibits any inquiry about that conduct.[22]

Additional procedural protections have been prescribed for criminal defendants. A criminal defendant, of course, is not immune from impeachment if she elects to testify in her own defense, and such impeachment may include inquiries into other immoral, vicious or criminal acts that bear on credibility.[23] There is a danger, however, that the

---

cross-examiner has raised the issue. See § 607.3, at notes 19–24, supra. See also note 31 infra.

17. See People v. Sorge, 301 N.Y. 198, 200–01, 93 N.E.2d 637, 639 (1950) ("[A] negative response will not fob off further interrogation of the witness himself, for, if it did, the witness would have it within his power to render futile most cross-examination. * * * [T]here is no prohibition against examining the witness himself further on the chance that he may change his testimony or his answer.").

The line between "further interrogation" and "proof by extrinsic evidence" was crossed in Badr v. Hogan, 75 N.Y.2d 629, 555 N.Y.S.2d 249, 554 N.E.2d 890 (1990). Badr was a personal injury case in which the plaintiff-witness denied on cross-examination that she had received and retained welfare payments to which she was not entitled. Such payments were unrelated to the issue of damages. The cross-examiner nevertheless confronted her with her confession of judgment as to the payments (a civil judgment, not a conviction), which was improperly admitted into evidence as an exhibit after she admitted signing it: "It was error to admit this extrinsic proof for the sole purpose of contradicting her testimony on that collateral issue." Id. at 636, 555 N.Y.S.2d at 253, 554 N.E.2d at 894.

18. See § 609.1 infra.

19. People v. Morrison, 195 N.Y. 116, 117–18, 88 N.E. 21, 22 (1909); People v. Cascone, 185 N.Y. 317, 334, 78 N.E. 287, 293 (1906); Dance v. Town of Southampton, 95 A.D.2d 442, 452–53, 467 N.Y.S.2d 203, 210 (2d Dep't 1983).

20. See People v. Rahming, 26 N.Y.2d 411, 419, 311 N.Y.S.2d 292, 299, 259 N.E.2d 727, 732 (1970). See also Gedrin v. Long Island Jewish–Hillside Medical Center, 119 A.D.2d 799, 501 N.Y.S.2d 426 (2d Dep't 1986) (underlying facts of assault charge which resulted in adjournment in contemplation of dismissal and petit larceny charge which was reduced to disorderly conduct).

In criminal proceedings, however, the fact that a prosecution witness has been arrested, is in custody, is on bail or is under indictment, is admissible for the separate purpose of showing the witness' possible partiality toward the prosecution. See § 607.6, at notes 12–14, supra.

21. Potter v. Browne, 197 N.Y. 288, 293, 90 N.E. 812, 814 (1910)("A witness may upon cross-examination be compelled to disclose any vicious or criminal act of his life, unless he asserts his privilege.") Cf. People v. Johnston, 228 N.Y. 332, 340, 127 N.E. 186, 188 (1920)(assuming privilege against self-incrimination may be invoked with respect to collateral misconduct affecting credibility, the privilege must be asserted by the witness). In People v. Sorge, 301 N.Y. 198, 93 N.E.2d 637 (1950), discussed in text at notes 2–4 supra, the court's failure to mention limitations imposed by the privilege against self-incrimination has been characterized as an oversight. McCormick § 41, at 141 n.25.

22. People v. Santiago, 15 N.Y.2d 640, 641, 255 N.Y.S.2d 864, 864, 204 N.E.2d 197, 198 (1964).

23. People v. Betts, 70 N.Y.2d 289, 292, 520 N.Y.S.2d 370, 371, 514 N.E.2d 865, 866 (1987)("[A] criminal defendant, as a witness, places himself or herself in the position of any other witness, having the same duties and exposures * * *. The rule includes a defendant-witness being 'asked questions disclosing his past life and con-

jury will confuse evidence of prior misconduct as it relates to credibility with defendant's general propensity for wrongdoing and improperly apply the impeachment evidence to the underlying question of guilt or innocence.[24] In addition, the defendant may be deterred from testifying altogether if evidence of other misconduct may be elicited on cross-examination.[25]

Thus, *People v. Sandoval*[26] created a right to a pretrial ruling, upon motion of the defendant, as to which of the defendant's immoral, vicious or criminal acts may be used in the prosecution's cross-examination of the defendant should she elect to testify at trial.[27] *Sandoval* also articulated a "frame of reference" for the balancing process to be employed by the trial court in weighing the probative value of the defendant's prior misconduct on the issue of credibility against the potential for prejudice.[28] The Court of Appeals has also stressed that the right to a pretrial ruling is limited to criminal defendants who themselves are contemplating testifying; no other witness may claim such

duct, and thus impairing his credibility'" * * *.)(quoting People v. Casey, 72 N.Y. 393, 398–99 (1878)); People v. Sorge, 301 N.Y. 198, 200, 93 N.E.2d 637, 638 (1950) ("There can, of course, be no doubt as to the propriety of cross-examining a defendant concerning the commission of other specific criminal or immoral acts.").

24. See People v. McGee, 68 N.Y.2d 328, 332, 508 N.Y.S.2d 927, 929, 501 N.E.2d 576, 578 (1986); People v. Allen, 67 A.D.2d 558, 560, 416 N.Y.S.2d 49, 50–51 (2d Dep't 1979), aff'd, 50 N.Y.2d 898, 430 N.Y.S.2d 588, 408 N.E.2d 917 (1980)("evidence of prior criminal or immoral acts of a *defendant*-witness tends to portray the defendant as having a propensity to commit crimes in general, and the crime charged in particular, thereby raising to a high degree of probability the likelihood of unfairly prejudicing the jury against the defendant") (emphasis in original).

25. People v. Ocasio, 47 N.Y.2d 55, 58, 416 N.Y.S.2d 581, 582, 389 N.E.2d 1101, 1102 (1979)("fear of the probable effect of the introduction of testimony of this character often will cause a defendant to hide behind his or her privilege not to take the stand, thereby blotting out what may be the only available source of material testimony in support of the defense").

26. 34 N.Y.2d 371, 357 N.Y.S.2d 849, 314 N.E.2d 413 (1974).

27. Id. at 374–75, 357 N.Y.S.2d at 853–54, 314 N.E.2d at 416–17. The "Sandoval motion," which applies to prior convictions as well as other misconduct, may also be made during trial. People v. Mackey, 49 N.Y.2d 274, 282, 425 N.Y.S.2d 288, 292, 401 N.E.2d 398, 403 (1980).

With respect to the trial court's exercise of discretion, the defendant has the burden of "demonstrating that the prejudicial effect of the admission of evidence [of misconduct] for impeachment purposes would so far outweigh the probative worth of such evidence on the issue of credibility as to warrant its exclusion." 34 N.Y.2d at 378, 357 N.Y.S.2d at 856, 314 N.E.2d at 418. The Sandoval opinion imposed the additional burden on the defendant of disclosing all convictions and other misconduct as to which the defendant desired an advance ruling. Id. This created a dilemma with respect to uncharged crimes inasmuch as the defendant understandably would not want to raise matters that might be unknown to the prosecutor. N.Y. Crim.Proc. Law § 240.43 modified this aspect of Sandoval in 1987 by requiring the prosecutor, upon defendant's request, to notify the defendant of "all specific instances of a defendant's prior uncharged criminal, vicious or immoral conduct of which the prosecutor has knowledge and which the prosecutor intends to use at trial for purposes of impeaching the credibility of the defendant." The defendant still has the burden, however, of identifying convictions and pending charges as to which he fears cross-examination.

28. 34 N.Y.2d at 376–78, 357 N.Y.S.2d at 854–56, 314 N.E.2d at 417–18. The frame of reference identified in Sandoval is discussed in § 609.1, at notes 17–29, infra, in connection with the use of convictions to impeach the criminal defendant. The same weighing process applies to immoral, vicious or criminal acts that have not resulted in a conviction. People v. Kennedy, 47 N.Y.2d 196, 205–06, 417 N.Y.S.2d 452, 457, 391 N.E.2d 288, 293 (1979).

entitlement.[29]

Another unique protection for the criminal defendant is operative when her unrelated misconduct is the subject of separate charges that are still pending at the time of the trial in which she plans to testify. Rather than imposing on the defendant the burden of invoking her privilege against self-incrimination[30] should the prosecutor question her about the substance of the pending charges, the prosecutor is precluded outright from cross-examining her about them.[31] If the defendant's unrelated misconduct is not the subject of pending charges, but criminal prosecution is still possible, the defendant should be able to invoke her privilege against self-incrimination in response to individual questions.[32]

Proposed New York Evidence Code § 608(b) would preserve most aspects of current practice with respect to impeachment by evidence of prior misconduct.[33]

---

29. People v. Ocasio, 47 N.Y.2d 55, 59, 416 N.Y.S.2d 581, 583, 389 N.E.2d 1101, 1103 (1979)("[U]nlike the dilemma posed for a defendant, the focus of the impeachment of a witness is credibility, not guilt or innocence. It was these distinctions that called upon us to formulate the *Sandoval* procedure. For the same reasons, we take the opportunity presented by this case to make explicit that it is inapplicable to witnesses who are not defendants."). As to witnesses who are nondefendants, the trial court may, in its discretion, entertain a motion in limine to determine the permissible scope of cross-examination as to prior misconduct, but it is not obligated to do so. Id.

Sandoval has been further limited to cross-examination by the prosecutor. Thus, in cases involving multiple defendants, a defendant cannot claim the benefits of a Sandoval motion with respect to potential cross-examination by a codefendant. People v. McGee, 68 N.Y.2d 328, 332–33, 508 N.Y.S.2d 927, 929–30, 501 N.E.2d 576, 578–79 (1986). A severance may be appropriate in such cases. Id. at 333, 508 N.Y.S.2d at 930, 501 N.E.2d at 579.

30. See People v. Johnston, 228 N.Y. 332, 336, 127 N.E. 186, 188 (1920).

31. People v. Betts, 70 N.Y.2d 289, 291, 520 N.Y.S.2d 370, 370, 514 N.E.2d 865, 865 (1987). See also People v. Bennett, 79 N.Y.2d 464, 468–69, 583 N.Y.S.2d 825, 828, 593 N.E.2d 279, 282 (1992). The Betts court noted, however, that the rule against prosecutorial inquiry into defendant's pending unrelated charges may yield "if a defendant, in taking the stand, makes assertions that open the door and render those charges relevant for contradiction and response." 70 N.Y.2d at 295, 520 N.Y.S.2d at 373, 514 N.E.2d at 868. See, e.g., People v. Lugo, 202 A.D.2d 248, 608 N.Y.S.2d 632 (1st Dep't 1994)(fact that defendant carried gun and participated in homicide with friend, which were subject of other pending charges, was proper cross-examination where defendant testified that he feared his friend).

32. See note 21 supra.

33. Proposed New York Evidence Code § 608(b) would change current law by: (1) making relevance on the issue of "credibility" the sole determinant of the appropriate type of misconduct for impeachment; (2) altering the burden of proof with respect to the weighing of probative value against prejudice in the case of the criminal defendant; and (3) imposing a 15-year-old cap on the misconduct that can be inquired about unless probative value substantially outweighs prejudice.

The proposed rule reads in pertinent part as follows:

(b) Specific instances of conduct [PROPOSED]

(1) General rule. A witness may be asked, if asked on reasonable grounds and in good faith, about specific instances of conduct bearing on that witness's credibility, provided, however, a witness may not be asked about conduct that was the subject of criminal charges of which the witness was acquitted.

* * *

(3) Extrinsic evidence. For the purpose of attacking or supporting the truthfulness of a witness under this section, specific instances of the conduct of the witness not resulting in a criminal conviction may not be proved by extrinsic evidence, provided, however, nothing in this subdivision shall preclude extrinsic proof bearing on matters such as a witness's bias, prejudice, interest, motive, hostility, or ability to perceive or remember.

b. Federal

Federal law is more circumscribed than that of New York with respect to inquiry into prior misconduct of a witness that did not result in a conviction. The first paragraph of Federal Rule of Evidence 608(b) provides, in pertinent part, as follows:

> **(b) Specific instances of conduct.** Specific instances of the conduct of a witness, for the purpose of attacking or supporting the witness' credibility, other than conviction of crime as provided in rule 609, may not be proved by extrinsic evidence. They may, however, in the discretion of the court, if probative of truthfulness or untruthfulness, be inquired into on cross-examination of the witness (1) concerning the witness' character for truthfulness or untruthfulness, or (2) concerning the character for truthfulness or untruthfulness of another witness as to which character the witness being cross-examined has testified.

Rule 608(b) explicitly restricts the cross-examiner to questions regarding conduct that is "probative of untruthfulness," which is much

(4) The accused in a criminal case. In a criminal case, specific instances of conduct bearing on the credibility of the accused offered by the prosecution are not admissible if the prejudicial effect of the evidence, including the effect the evidence would have in deterring the accused from testifying, outweighs the probative worth of the evidence on the accused's credibility. Upon request, the prosecutor shall, pursuant to section 240.43 of the criminal procedure law, inform the accused before the commencement of trial of the specific acts of conduct of the accused about which it intends to inquire if the accused chooses to testify. To remedy the prejudice from the failure to give notice, the court, pursuant to section 107 of this chapter, shall make any order the interests of justice require. At the request of the accused, the determination pursuant to this subdivision of the admissibility of evidence of specific instances of conduct of the accused shall be made before the commencement of trial.

(5) A party in a civil case. Subject to section 403 of this chapter, a party in a civil case may be asked about specific instances of conduct bearing on the credibility of that party.

(c) Instances of conduct more than fifteen years old.

(1) General rule. Evidence of a specific act of conduct under this section is not admissible if a period of more than fifteen years, excluding any period of incarceration, has elapsed since the date of the occurrence of the act, unless the court determines that the probative worth of the specific act on the witness's credibility substantially outweighs its prejudicial effect. The proponent of evidence of a specific act of conduct more than fifteen years old shall make known to all parties the proponent's intention to offer the evidence and its particulars sufficiently in advance of offering the evidence to provide them with a fair opportunity to meet it. To remedy the prejudice from the failure to give notice, the court, pursuant to section 107 of this chapter, shall make any order the interests of justice require.

(2) The accused in a criminal case. Upon request the prosecutor, pursuant to section 240.43 of the criminal procedure law, shall inform the accused before the commencement of trial of the specific instances of the accused's conduct more than fifteen years old about which it intends to inquire. At the request of the accused, the determination pursuant to this subdivision of the admissibility of such evidence shall be made before the commencement of trial.

(d) Self-incrimination. The giving of testimony, whether by an accused or by any other witness, does not operate as a waiver of such person's privilege against self-incrimination when examined with respect to matters which relate only to credibility. A witness who properly invokes the privilege against self- incrimination may be required to testify only if there is compliance with the require-

§ 608.2   WITNESSES   Ch. 6

narrower than the New York standard of "immoral, vicious or criminal acts."[34] Rule 608(b) also gives federal courts a large measure of discretion as to whether to admit such impeaching evidence. In this regard, the Advisory Committee's Note to Rule 608 states: "[T]he overriding protection of Rule 403 requires that probative value not be outweighed by danger of unfair prejudice, confusion of issues or misleading the jury, and that of Rule 611 bars harassment and undue embarrassment." A trial judge's decision to exclude evidence of prior misconduct will be reversed in the Second Circuit only in the "rare instance" of an abuse of discretion.[35]

In general, most of the caselaw reflects judicial deference to the apparent congressional intent that Rule 608(b) be narrowly applied.[36] In the Second Circuit, cross-examination of witnesses concerning the following types of conduct bearing on truthfulness has been upheld: fraud and embezzlement;[37] false statements in applications for employment, housing, licenses, loans, credit cards and association memberships;[38] apparently false testimony in prior proceedings;[39] destruction of personal and business records;[40] and disbarment of an attorney.[41] Conversely, the Second Circuit has upheld the exclusion of such misconduct as sodomy of a minor[42] and failure to repay loans.[43] A more controversial decision is that of *Chnapkova v. Koh*,[44] in which the trial judge was held to have abused his discretion in disallowing inquiry concerning the plaintiff-witness' eight-year failure to file income tax returns.[45]

In *United States v. Schwab*,[46] the Second Circuit ruled that cross-examination of a criminal defendant about an 18-year-old fraud prosecu-

ments of section 50.20 of the criminal procedure law.

34. See notes 2-5 supra.

35. United States v. Tillem, 906 F.2d 814, 827 (2d Cir.1990).

36. See generally 3 Weinstein and Berger ¶ 608[03].

37. United States v. Schwab, 886 F.2d 509, 514 (2d Cir.1989), cert. denied, 493 U.S. 1080, 110 S.Ct. 1136, 107 L.Ed.2d 1041 (1990).

38. United States v. Jones, 900 F.2d 512, 520-21 (2d Cir.), cert. denied, 498 U.S. 846, 111 S.Ct. 131, 112 L.Ed.2d 99 (1990). See also United States v. Sperling, 726 F.2d 69, 75 (2d Cir.), cert. denied, 467 U.S. 1243, 104 S.Ct. 3516, 82 L.Ed.2d 824 (1984).

39. United States v. Bagaric, 706 F.2d 42, 65 (2d Cir.), cert. denied, 464 U.S. 840, 104 S.Ct. 134, 78 L.Ed.2d 128, and cert. denied, 464 U.S. 917, 104 S.Ct. 283, 78 L.Ed.2d 261 (1983)(in prior proceeding, administrative judge found witness' testimony "not credible"); United States v. Terry, 702 F.2d 299, 316 (2d Cir.), cert. denied, 461 U.S. 931, 103 S.Ct. 2095, 77 L.Ed.2d 304, and cert. denied, 464 U.S. 992, 104 S.Ct. 482, 78 L.Ed.2d 680 (1983)(in prior case, judge declared that expert witness had "guessed under oath").

40. United States v. Clemente, 640 F.2d 1069, 1082 (2d Cir.), cert. denied, 454 U.S. 820, 102 S.Ct. 102, 70 L.Ed.2d 91 (1981).

41. United States v. Weichert, 783 F.2d 23, 25-26 (2d Cir.), cert. denied, 479 U.S. 831, 107 S.Ct. 117, 93 L.Ed.2d 64 (1986).

42. United States v. Rabinowitz, 578 F.2d 910, 912 (2d Cir.1978).

43. United States v. Lanza, 790 F.2d 1015, 1020 (2d Cir.), cert. denied, 479 U.S. 861, 107 S.Ct. 211, 93 L.Ed.2d 141 (1986).

44. 985 F.2d 79 (2d Cir.1993).

45. Id. at 82-83. The court noted that "plaintiff's credibility in this unusual case was of * * * crucial importance." Id. at 83. Other circuits have split over the question whether the failure to file tax returns is a crime of "dishonesty or false statement" in the analogous situation of impeachment by prior convictions under Fed. R.Evid. 609(a)(2). See § 609.2, at note 14, infra.

46. 886 F.2d 509 (2d Cir.1989), cert. denied, 493 U.S. 1080, 110 S.Ct. 1136, 107 L.Ed.2d 1041 (1990).

Ch. 6 PRIOR ACTS OF MISCONDUCT § 608.2

tion that ended in an acquittal was an abuse of discretion. Although the court stressed the circumstances of the particular case, including the bad faith of the prosecutor,[47] *Schwab* is persuasive authority for the proposition that every witness ordinarily should be immune from impeachment of her character for truthfulness on the basis of prior misconduct that resulted in an acquittal.[48]

Rule 608(b), like the common law, restricts impeachment evidence of prior bad acts to cross-examination. If the witness admits the misconduct, the impeachment is accomplished. If she denies it, however, the cross-examiner is bound by the denial. Extrinsic evidence may not be introduced to prove, on the issue of character for truthfulness, prior bad acts that did not result in convictions.[49] On the other hand, Rule 608(b) does not preclude extrinsic evidence of a witness' bad acts where they are relevant to some issue other than the witness' character. For example, the witness' misconduct may bear on her bias,[50] or the misconduct may be independently probative of some issue in the case other than credibility.[51]

---

47. The prosecutor knew of the acquittal prior to trial, did not advise the trial court in advance of his intent to pursue "such novel questioning," and had no independent information to indicate that the defendant was in fact guilty of the prior tax fraud. Id. at 513. The court was also troubled by the "ancient" nature of the prior misconduct. Although Rule 608(b) has no 10-year time limit like its Rule 609 counterpart with respect to prior convictions, see § 609.2 infra, the court suggested that a trial judge should be alerted in advance when cross-examination on the basis of old misconduct is contemplated. Id. at 513–14.

48. Schwab was decided on the ground that undue prejudice to the defendant outweighed the probative value of misconduct as to which there had been an acquittal. Id. at 513. The court stated as follows:

> Whether or not an acquittal technically estops the prosecution from eliciting the fact of prior misconduct, it will normally alter the balance between probative force and prejudice, which is already a close matter in many cases where prior misconduct of a defendant is offered. * * * Moreover, there is the blunt reality that a witness who has been acquitted will almost certainly deny the misconduct, either because he did no wrong or because he may understandably believe that when asked about it after an acquittal, he is entitled to have the law regard him as innocent. Thus, the only purpose served by permitting the inquiry is to place before the jury the allegation of misconduct contained in the prosecutor's question, an allegation the jury will be instructed has no evidentiary weight. To permit the inquiry risks unfair prejudice, which is not justified by the theoretical possibility that the witness, though acquitted, will admit to the misconduct. When the witness is the defendant, the significance of the prejudice is magnified.

Id. Schwab was decided before Dowling v. United States, 493 U.S. 342, 110 S.Ct. 668, 107 L.Ed.2d 708 (1990), in which the Supreme Court held that constitutional considerations do not preclude proof of a defendant's prior criminal conduct for a permissible purpose under Fed.R.Evid. 404(b) where the defendant was acquitted of the prior crime. See § 404.2, at notes 10–13, supra. Dowling is not directly applicable to the trial court's discretionary authority under Fed.R.Evid. 608(b).

49. See, e.g., United States v. Aponte, 31 F.3d 86, 88 (2d Cir.1994) (trial court properly excluded documentary evidence containing witness' false statements offered solely to impeach); United States v. Smith, 727 F.2d 214, 221 (2d Cir.1984)(trial court erred in permitting extrinsic evidence of witness' prior misappropriation of stock).

50. See United States v. Schwab, 886 F.2d 509, 511 (2d Cir.1989), cert. denied, 493 U.S. 1080, 110 S.Ct. 1136, 107 L.Ed.2d 1041 (1990)(when relevant to issue of bias, witness' misconduct is not limited by strictures of Rule 608(b)). See also § 607.6, at note 37, supra.

51. See, e.g., United States v. Smith, 727 F.2d 214, 221 (2d Cir.1984) (defendant-witness' prior fraudulent acts were independently admissible under Fed.R.Evid. 404(b) on issue of intent in crime charged).

§ 608.2   WITNESSES   Ch. 6

To the extent the cross-examiner makes inquiry into prior misconduct solely to attack the witness' credibility, the witness may be entitled to avoid answering by invoking her privilege against self-incrimination.[52] The final paragraph of Rule 608(b) explicitly recognizes such protection as follows: "The giving of testimony, whether by an accused or by any other witness, does not operate as a waiver of the accused's or the witness' privilege against self-incrimination when examined with respect to matters which relate only to credibility."

Library References:

West's Key No. Digests, Witnesses ⚖︎333–362.

609 Impeachment by Evidence of Criminal Convictions

§ 609.1 New York

a. In General

The fact that a witness has been convicted of a crime impeaches credibility by casting doubt on the witness' character for truthfulness.[1] Inquiry about criminal convictions is undertaken on cross-examination. Unlike impeachment by immoral, vicious or criminal acts that have evaded prosecution,[2] convictions are not subject to the rule against extrinsic evidence. Thus, if the witness denies a conviction or gives an equivocal answer, the cross-examiner may prove the conviction.[3] Such difference in treatment is appropriate because a conviction represents an official act of public condemnation, thereby enhancing its probative value on the issue of credibility. A conviction is also relatively quick and easy to prove.[4] Regardless of whether the witness admits the conviction or it

---

52. See, e.g., Air Et Chaleur, S.A. v. Janeway, 757 F.2d 489, 496 (2d Cir.1985)(witness properly invoked privilege against self-incrimination when asked on cross-examination about nonpayment of taxes because inquiry related solely to collateral issue of credibility).

§ 609.1

1. Derrick v. Wallace, 217 N.Y. 520, 525, 112 N.E. 440, 442 (1916)("Evidence of conviction * * * impeaches the general character for truth and veracity * * *.").

2. See § 608.2, at notes 14–17, supra.

3. CPLR 4513, applicable in civil actions, provides as follows:

A person who has been convicted of a crime is a competent witness; but the conviction may be proved, for the purpose of affecting the weight of his testimony, either by cross-examination, upon which he shall be required to answer any relevant question, or by the record. The party cross-examining is not concluded by such persons's answer.

In criminal actions, proof by extrinsic evidence is authorized by N.Y.Crim.Proc.Law § 60.40(1), which states:

If in the course of a criminal proceeding, any witness, including a defendant, is properly asked whether he was previously convicted of a specified offense and answers in the negative or in an equivocal manner, the party adverse to the one who called him may independently prove such conviction. If in response to proper inquiry whether he has ever been convicted of any offense the witness answers in the negative or in an equivocal manner, the adverse party may independently prove any previous conviction of the witness.

4. See, e.g., N.Y.Crim.Proc.Law § 60.60(1)("A certificate issued by a criminal court, or the clerk thereof, certifying that a judgment of conviction against a designated defendant has been entered in such court, constitutes presumptive evidence of the facts stated in such certificate."); People v. Beale, 73 A.D.2d 547, 423 N.Y.S.2d 6 (1st Dep't 1979)(certificate of

is independently proven, the cross-examiner generally may question the witness about the essential facts of the underlying crime.[5]

Youthful offender and juvenile delinquency adjudications may not be introduced to show bad character for the simple reason that they are not convictions.[6] Nevertheless, the cross-examiner may elicit the underlying facts of such adjudications pursuant to the rule allowing for inquiry into prior immoral, vicious or criminal acts.[7] An analogous approach is taken with respect to arrests and indictments, which are merely formal accusations that have no inherent impeachment value.[8]

b. Civil Cases

In civil actions, statutory guidance is found in CPLR 4513, which states that a witness' conviction "of a crime" may be proven "for the purpose of affecting the weight of his testimony."[9] Courts have interpreted this provision broadly, holding that witnesses in civil actions may be impeached by convictions for crimes of any type.[10] Some decisions

---

conviction is appropriate means of proving witness' prior conviction). A certified copy of the official record of conviction could also be used. See CPLR 4540. If the defendant denies that he is the person named in the record of conviction, it may be necessary to introduce fingerprint evidence. N.Y.Crim. Proc.Law § 60.60(2).

5. People v. Sorge, 301 N.Y. 198, 201, 93 N.E.2d 637, 639 (1950) (knowledge of acts underlying conviction "casts light upon the degree of turpitude involved and assists the jury in evaluating the witness' credibility"). See also People v. Bennette, 56 N.Y.2d 142, 149, 451 N.Y.S.2d 647, 650, 436 N.E.2d 1249, 1252 (1982)("court may * * * permit further questioning for the purpose of determining, at least in general terms, what conduct gave rise to the conviction"); Dance v. Town of Southampton, 95 A.D.2d 442, 452, 467 N.Y.S.2d 203, 210 (2d Dep't 1983). Such inquiry is sometimes circumscribed in the case of a criminal defendant who testifies in his own behalf. See note 40 infra.

6. People v. Duffy, 36 N.Y.2d 258, 264, 367 N.Y.S.2d 236, 241, 326 N.E.2d 804, 807, cert. denied, 423 U.S. 861, 96 S.Ct. 116, 46 L.Ed.2d 88 (1975); People v. Sarra, 283 App.Div. 876, 129 N.Y.S.2d 201 (2d Dep't 1954), aff'd, 308 N.Y. 302, 125 N.E.2d 580 (1955). But see People v. Gray, 84 N.Y.2d 709, 622 N.Y.S.2d 223, 646 N.E.2d 444 (1995)(Maryland conviction of 15-year-old boy whose acts would have resulted in juvenile delinquency adjudication under New York law may be used for impeachment in subsequent New York trial).

If the witness in question is testifying for the prosecution in a criminal case, however, defendant's right of confrontation may entitle him to elicit the adjudication to show the witness' potential motive for cooperating with the government. See § 607.6, at note 27, supra.

7. People v. Greer, 42 N.Y.2d 170, 177, 397 N.Y.S.2d 613, 617, 366 N.E.2d 273, 277 (1977); People v. Doane, 208 A.D.2d 971, 973, 617 N.Y.S.2d 232, 234 (3d Dep't 1994).

8. See § 608.2, at notes 18–20, supra.

9. See note 3 supra. By its terms, CPLR 4513 is limited to convictions of "crimes," i.e., felonies or misdemeanors. See N.Y.Penal Law § 10.00(6). The rule is broader in criminal cases, where the relevant statute permits convictions of "offenses" in general. See note 3 supra and note 13 infra. Traffic infractions, however, are explicitly disallowed for impeachment purposes in civil and criminal actions. N.Y.Veh. and Traf.Law § 155.

A lawyer's disbarment or suspension from practice may be admitted to impeach although it is civil in nature. Batease v. Dion, 275 App. Div. 451, 90 N.Y.S.2d 851 (3d Dep't 1949).

10. Vernon v. New York City Health and Hospitals Corp., 167 A.D.2d 252, 561 N.Y.S.2d 751 (1st Dep't 1990)("Any of plaintiff's criminal convictions [involving marijuana] would have been admissible under CPLR 4513, which grants a civil litigant broad authority to use the criminal convictions of an adverse witness to impeach the credibility of that witness."); Able Cycle Engines, Inc. v. Allstate Insurance Co., 84 A.D.2d 140, 143, 445 N.Y.S.2d 469, 471–72 (2d Dep't 1981), appeal denied, 57 N.Y.2d 607, 455 N.Y.S.2d 1027, 442 N.E.2d 69 (1982)("Pursuant to CPLR 4513, any conviction of a crime may be introduced to impeach the credibility of a witness at a civil trial.").

§ 609.1 WITNESSES Ch. 6

suggest that a trial judge has virtually no discretion to consider the probative value of the particular prior crime on the issue of credibility.[11] One court has held, however, that if the defendant in a civil action is sued for acts that are criminal in nature, it is appropriate for the court to exercise the same discretionary balancing of relevance and prejudice that would apply if the defendant were being prosecuted.[12]

c. Criminal Cases

The leading case in New York on impeachment by prior convictions[13] in criminal cases is the 1974 decision of the Court of Appeals in *People v. Sandoval*.[14] The witness whose prior convictions were at issue in *Sandoval* was the defendant himself, who was on trial for murder. He made a motion for a pretrial ruling as to which, if any, of his prior convictions could be used by the prosecutor for impeachment purposes in the event the defendant took the stand to testify in his own behalf. The trial judge entertained the motion and determined that the defendant could be cross-examined with his prior convictions of disorderly conduct and assault but not his convictions of contributing to the delinquency of a minor or driving while intoxicated.

The Court of Appeals gave its seal of approval to the procedure used by the trial court to provide the defendant with a prospective ruling with respect to the prosecutor's use of convictions for impeachment purposes. Thus was born the "*Sandoval* motion," which serves to inform the defendant of the impeachment risks he faces should he decide to take the stand.[15] The Court of Appeals also affirmed the trial court's particular

---

11. Matter of Linda O., 95 Misc.2d 744, 408 N.Y.S.2d 308 (Fam.Ct.Queens Co.1978); Guarisco v. E.J. Milk Farms, 90 Misc.2d 81, 393 N.Y.S.2d 883 (Sup.Ct.Queens Co.1977). One decision implies that a trial court may not even properly place limits on the number of a witness' convictions that may be admitted. Vernon v. New York City Health and Hospitals Corp., 167 A.D.2d 252, 561 N.Y.S.2d 751 (1st Dep't 1990)(plaintiff complained on appeal that trial court had admitted three of his eight marijuana-related convictions; appellate court said "any" of the convictions would have been admissible).

It is arguable that despite CPLR 4513, courts retain some degree of discretion with respect to impeachment by prior convictions in light of the oft-repeated general rule that "[t]he nature and extent of cross-examination have always been subject to the sound discretion of the Trial Judge." People v. Sandoval, 34 N.Y.2d 371, 374, 357 N.Y.S.2d 849, 853, 314 N.E.2d 413, 416 (1974).

12. Evans v. Willson, 133 Misc.2d 1079, 509 N.Y.S.2d 296 (N.Y.C.Civ.Ct.1986)(in personal injury action arising out of defendant's hit-and-run conduct, court restricted cross-examination to elicitation of fact of defendant's prior unrelated conviction of "a misdemeanor" without disclosure that it was for drunken driving).

13. In criminal cases, N.Y.Crim.Proc. Law § 60.40(1) authorizes impeachment by proof of "offenses," a generic term that includes violations as well as misdemeanors and felonies. See N.Y.Penal Law § 10.00(1)-(5). Thus, a conviction for harassment, a mere "violation," was held admissible for impeachment purposes in People v. Gray, 41 A.D.2d 125, 341 N.Y.S.2d 485 (3d Dep't 1973), aff'd, 34 N.Y.2d 903, 359 N.Y.S.2d 286, 316 N.E.2d 719, cert. denied, 419 U.S. 1055, 95 S.Ct. 637, 42 L.Ed.2d 652 (1974). By statute, however, convictions of traffic infractions may not be used far impeachment purposes. N.Y.Veh. and Traf.Law § 155.

An order of disbarment or suspension of a lawyer may also be elicited. See Batease v. Dion, 275 App.Div. 451, 90 N.Y.S.2d 851 (3d Dep't 1949).

14. 34 N.Y.2d 371, 357 N.Y.S.2d 849, 314 N.E.2d 413 (1974).

15. Id. at 374, 357 N.Y.S.2d at 853, 314 N.E.2d at 416 ("We now hold that * * * a Trial Judge may * * * make an advance ruling as to the use by the prosecutor of prior convictions or proof of the prior com-

ruling as to the convictions that could be used to impeach Mr. Sandoval, finding "no abuse of discretion."[16]

Aside from endorsing a new rule of procedure, *Sandoval* is important for its analysis of the balancing process that a trial court must undertake in determining the extent to which a particular defendant-witness may be impeached with his prior convictions. The court rejected the notion that precise guidelines could be articulated but offered an "illustrative and suggestive" frame of reference for the trial court's exercise of discretion in individual cases.[17]

The court began with the observation that the prosecutor has a legitimate interest in testing the credibility of the defendant in his role as a witness. Thus, evidence of the defendant's prior bad acts and convictions generally should be admitted if they "bear logically and reasonably on the issue of credibility."[18] Two important interests of the defendant, however, must be weighed against those of the prosecutor. First, the danger exists, even with careful limiting instructions,[19] that impeachment of a criminal defendant with his prior bad acts and convictions will have a disproportionate impact on the fact-finder, will be misused as evidence of guilt of the crime for which he is now on trial, or will lead the jury to convict simply because he is a bad person.[20] Second, a defendant may be deterred from testifying altogether based on the fear of such effects, thus depriving the fact-finder, in some cases, of significant evidence.[21] Thus, the trial court must weigh the relevance of the prior convictions on the issue of credibility against these two potential prejudicial effects on the defendant. In this process, the defendant has

mission of specific criminal, vicious or immoral acts for the purpose of impeaching a defendant's credibility."). A Sandoval motion may also be entertained during the trial. People v. Mackey, 49 N.Y.2d 274, 282, 425 N.Y.S.2d 288, 292, 401 N.E.2d 398, 403 (1980). The motion is not available, however, to a potential defendant who is contemplating testifying before a grand jury. People v. Thomas, 213 A.D.2d 73, 628 N.Y.S.2d 707 (2d Dep't 1995).

Two of the Appellate Divisions are divided over whether a defendant is entitled to a Sandoval ruling in a nonjury trial. Compare People v. Oglesby, 137 A.D.2d 840, 842, 525 N.Y.S.2d 304, 305 (2d Dep't 1988), appeal dismissed, 72 N.Y.2d 831, 530 N.Y.S.2d 549, 526 N.E.2d 40 (1988) ("Inasmuch as the Court of Appeals did not limit Sandoval to jury trials, the defendant is entitled to a prior determination of his Sandoval application, by a trial court sitting as the trier of fact."), with People v. Stevenson, 163 A.D.2d 854, 855, 558 N.Y.S.2d 383, 384 (4th Dep't 1990)("To require a trial court to conduct a Sandoval hearing in every nonjury trial would be a wasteful expenditure of the court's time and effort.").

Unlike federal practice, see § 609.2, at notes 8–9, infra, a defendant in New York need not actually testify at trial in order to preserve the relevance/prejudice balancing issue for appeal. See, e.g., People v. Mattiace, 77 N.Y.2d 269, 567 N.Y.S.2d 384, 568 N.E.2d 1189 (1990).

16. 34 N.Y.2d at 373, 357 N.Y.S.2d at 852, 314 N.E.2d at 415.

17. Id. at 376, 357 N.Y.S.2d at 854, 314 N.E.2d at 417.

18. Id., 357 N.Y.S.2d at 855, 314 N.E.2d at 417.

19. When convictions are used solely for impeachment purposes, the defendant is entitled to a limiting instruction that such convictions must not be used as evidence of guilt of the crime for which defendant is now on trial. People v. Moorer, 77 A.D.2d 575, 429 N.Y.S.2d 913 (2d Dep't 1980).

20. People v. Sandoval, 34 N.Y.2d 371, 375–76, 357 N.Y.S.2d 849, 853–55, 314 N.E.2d 413, 416–17 (1974). See also People v. Williams, 56 N.Y.2d 236, 240, 451 N.Y.S.2d 690, 692, 436 N.E.2d 1292, 1294 (1982)(danger that defendant may be convicted for past criminal record rather than for crime now charged.)

21. 34 N.Y.2d at 375–76, 357 N.Y.S.2d at 853–55, 314 N.E.2d at 416–17.

the burden of "demonstrating that the prejudicial effect of the admission of evidence [of bad acts and convictions] for impeachment purposes would so far outweigh the probative worth of such evidence on the issue of credibility as to warrant its exclusion."[22]

The court made some specific observations about the relevance component of the balancing process. Prior "perjury or other crimes or acts of individual dishonesty or untrustworthiness" were said to be of "material relevance" in most cases.[23] Other types of crimes are relevant on the issue of credibility to the extent they "significantly [reveal] a willingness or disposition on the part of the particular defendant voluntarily to place the advancement of his individual self-interest ahead of principle or of the interests of society," thereby "suggest[ing] his readiness to do so again on the witness stand."[24] Crimes of impulsive violence or crimes resulting from addiction or uncontrollable habit were identified as having less probative value.[25] Lapse of time was also said to be a factor that diminishes probative value.[26]

On the prejudice side of the equation, the court noted that special risks are presented when the defendant's prior crimes are similar in nature to that with which he is currently charged.[27] The court also indicated that trial courts should be especially sensitive to the needs of the fact-finding process if the defendant is "the only available source of material testimony in support of his defense."[28]

The Court of Appeals stressed that its frame of reference for the trial court's balancing of relevance and prejudice was neither categorical nor mandatory and that other factors and considerations undoubtedly will be identified as caselaw evolves.[29] In subsequent opinions, the court has indicated that appellate review of a particular exercise of discretion by a trial court usually "ends in the intermediate appellate court."[30] Further review in the Court of Appeals is restricted to cases where "the trial court ha[s] either abused its discretion or exercised none at all."[31]

---

22. Id. at 378, 357 N.Y.S.2d at 856, 314 N.E.2d at 418.

23. Id. at 377, 357 N.Y.S.2d at 856, 314 N.E.2d at 418.

24. Id., 357 N.Y.S.2d at 855, 314 N.E.2d at 417.

25. Id. at 376–77, 357 N.Y.S.2d at 855, 314 N.E.2d at 417–18.

26. Id. at 376, 357 N.Y.S.2d at 855, 314 N.E.2d at 417.

27. Id. at 377–78, 357 N.Y.S.2d at 856, 314 N.E.2d at 418.

28. Id. at 378, 357 N.Y.S.2d at 856, 314 N.E.2d at 418.

29. Id. at 376, 378, 357 N.Y.S.2d at 854, 856, 314 N.E.2d at 417, 418.

30. People v. Pollock, 50 N.Y.2d 547, 550, 429 N.Y.S.2d 628, 629, 407 N.E.2d 472, 473 (1980).

31. People v. Walker, 83 N.Y.2d 455, 459, 611 N.Y.S.2d 118, 120, 633 N.E.2d 472, 474 (1994), quoting People v. Williams, 56 N.Y.2d 236, 238, 451 N.Y.S.2d 690, 691, 436 N.E.2d 1292, 1293 (1982). In Williams, the record of the Sandoval hearing showed that the trial judge, who permitted 20 of defendant's 22 convictions to be used for impeachment, did not weigh relevance against prejudice. See also People v. Mayrant, 43 N.Y.2d 236, 401 N.Y.S.2d 165, 372 N.E.2d 1 (1977)(trial court applied wrong legal standard in determining relevance of convictions for impeachment purposes); People v. Caviness, 38 N.Y.2d 227, 232–33, 379 N.Y.S.2d 695, 700–01, 342 N.E.2d 496, 500–01 (1975)(in case where trial predated Sandoval decision, trial judge erroneously concluded that he had no discretion to exclude defendant's 22-year-old conviction for gun possession in homicide prosecution where defendant testified that he did not possess the gun that fired the fatal shot; the error was not harmless because of significant probability that jury misused the prior conviction as evidence of guilt of the homicide).

A review of some of the principal post-*Sandoval* cases that have reached the Court of Appeals demonstrates that each instance of a trial court's balancing of prejudice against probative value is sui generis. To illustrate, an abuse of discretion was found in *People v. Dickman*,[32] a reckless driving prosecution in which the trial court permitted impeachment of the defendant with a two-year-old conviction for reckless driving. The risk was too great, said the Court of Appeals, that the jury misused the prior conviction as proof of guilt rather than as a reflection on credibility.[33]

Conversely, no abuse of discretion was found in *People v. Mattiace*,[34] a four-to-three decision involving a prosecution for a hazardous waste disposal crime committed by the defendant and the corporation of which he was the president and chief stockholder. The defendant complained on appeal that the trial court erroneously ruled that he could be impeached, if he chose to testify, with his two prior convictions for pollution crimes as well as two convictions of his corporation for hazardous waste storage and transport. The majority held that the similarity of the prior convictions to the current charges was not a per se ground of exclusion.[35] In addition the court upheld the proposed impeachment of the defendant personally with the convictions of the small, closely-held corporation which had been jointly indicted and tried with him.[36] Nor was discretion found to have been abused in *People v. Bennette*,[37] a prosecution for robbery, burglary and assault, in which the defendant was impeached with a recent conviction for sodomizing a 10-year-old child. The prior conviction was highly relevant to veracity, said the court, because it showed defendant's willingness to place self-interest above the interests of society.[38]

32. 42 N.Y.2d 294, 397 N.Y.S.2d 754, 366 N.E.2d 843 (1977).

33. Id. at 297–98, 397 N.Y.S.2d at 756–57, 366 N.E.2d at 845. See also People v. Carmack, 44 N.Y.2d 706, 707, 405 N.Y.S.2d 446, 447, 376 N.E.2d 919, 919 (1978)(trial court abused discretion in prosecution for sale of narcotics by allowing extensive cross-examination on prior charges of drug possession; danger was too great that "the evidence would tend to demonstrate a propensity to commit the very crime for which the defendant was on trial")(4–3 decision).

34. 77 N.Y.2d 269, 567 N.Y.S.2d 384, 568 N.E.2d 1189 (1990).

35. Id. at 275–76, 567 N.Y.S.2d at 387, 568 N.E.2d at 1192 ("We have eschewed per se rules in this Sandoval field and no reason is evident here—whether we would agree in the first instance with the trial court's inclusions or exclusions ourselves—to embark on a path of establishing automatic categories, e.g., as to the similar nature of prior convictions or the particular party relationships."). See also People v. Pavao, 59 N.Y.2d 282, 292, 464 N.Y.S.2d 458, 463, 451 N.E.2d 216, 221 (1983) ("questioning concerning other crimes is not automatically precluded simply because the crimes to be inquired about are similar to the crimes charged").

36. Id. at 276, 567 N.Y.S.2d at 387–88, 568 N.E.2d at 1192–93. The three-judge dissent found no basis in the record for presuming that the defendant had personally participated in the corporate crimes that the trial court would have authorized for impeachment of the defendant personally. Id. at 276–77, 567 N.Y.S.2d at 388, 568 N.E.2d at 1193.

37. 56 N.Y.2d 142, 451 N.Y.S.2d 647, 436 N.E.2d 1249 (1982).

38. Id. at 148, 451 N.Y.S.2d at 650, 436 N.E.2d at 1252 ("A person ruthless enough to sexually exploit a child may well disregard an oath and resort to perjury if he perceives that to be in his self-interest."). The court noted that this was not a case where defendant's credibility was capable of being impeached by the use of other less inflammatory incidents. Id. at 148, 451 N.Y.S.2d at 650, 436 N.E.2d at 1252.

§ 609.1 WITNESSES Ch. 6

People v. Walker,[39] a recent example of the Court of Appeals' deference to trial court discretion, is noteworthy for its approval of what has been termed the "*Sandoval* compromise": If the defendant's prior convictions are similar in nature to the crime with which he is now charged, prejudice can be minimized by restricting the prosecutor to elicitation of the number and dates of prior convictions without disclosure of the nature of the convictions or their underlying facts.[40] The trial court in *Walker* had used this procedure in permitting impeachment with two felonies and 17 misdemeanors. The Court of Appeals noted that the trial judge might have been more selective in light of the age of some of the convictions and their number, but it refused to second-guess the lower court's conclusion.[41] The Court of Appeals stated that "there are no per se rules requiring preclusion because of the age, nature and number of a defendant's prior crimes."[42]

As a general matter, once the trial court has made a *Sandoval* ruling excluding particular prior convictions, fairness dictates that the court adhere to its decision if the defendant, in reliance on the ruling, actually takes the stand.[43] Courts have recognized an exception, however, where the defendant "opens the door" to the admissibility of otherwise precluded convictions. Such door-opening can occur if the defendant testifies that he has never engaged in any prior criminal conduct, volunteers misleading information about convictions or creates a misimpression concerning the number of his prior convictions.[44] In *People v. Fardan*,[45]

---

39. 83 N.Y.2d 455, 611 N.Y.S.2d 118, 633 N.E.2d 472 (1994).

40. See, e.g., People v. Carrasquillo, 204 A.D.2d 735, 612 N.Y.S.2d 424 (2d Dep't), appeal denied, 84 N.Y.2d 866, 618 N.Y.S.2d 12, 642 N.E.2d 331 (1994)(trial court properly made "Sandoval compromise" by allowing prosecutor to inquire whether defendant had been convicted of a felony without eliciting the underlying facts). See also People v. Lewis, 196 A.D.2d 742, 602 N.Y.S.2d 6 (1st Dep't), appeal denied, 82 N.Y.2d 898, 610 N.Y.S.2d 165, 632 N.E.2d 475 (1993)(prejudice was minimized by trial court's limiting of prosecutor's inquiry into facts underlying the convictions). Another means of minimizing prejudice is limiting the number of convictions that may be used where there are multiple convictions for similar crimes.

41. 83 N.Y.2d at 458–59, 611 N.Y.S.2d at 120, 633 N.E.2d at 474.

42. Id. at 459, 611 N.Y.S.2d at 120, 633 N.E.2d at 474. See also People v. Mackey, 49 N.Y.2d 274, 281–82, 425 N.Y.S.2d 288, 292, 401 N.E.2d 398, 402–03 (1980)(in rape and burglary prosecution, trial court ruled that defendant could be impeached with prior convictions for disorderly conduct, petit larceny, attempted possession of drugs, robbery and criminal trespass; Court of Appeals found no abuse of discretion, although it indicated that exclusion of the convictions for disorderly conduct or petit larceny, both of which occurred when defendant was 13 years old, might have been appropriate).

43. People v. Fardan, 82 N.Y.2d 638, 646, 607 N.Y.S.2d 220, 224, 628 N.E.2d 41, 45 (1993); People v. Owens, 203 A.D.2d 106, 107, 610 N.Y.S.2d 485, 486 (1st Dep't), appeal denied, 84 N.Y.2d 871, 618 N.Y.S.2d 16, 642 N.E.2d 335 (1994).

44. See, e.g., People v. Morgan, 171 A.D.2d 698, 567 N.Y.S.2d 166 (2d Dep't), appeal denied, 78 N.Y.2d 971, 574 N.Y.S.2d 950, 580 N.E.2d 422 (1991)(after trial court limited prosecutor to inquiry about one prior conviction, defense counsel elicited testimony from defendant falsely suggesting that this was his only conviction). Compare People v. Gordon, 202 A.D.2d 166, 608 N.Y.S.2d 192 (1st Dep't), appeal denied, 83 N.Y.2d 911, 614 N.Y.S.2d 393, 637 N.E.2d 284 (1994)(defendant's testimony that he "never put a knife to anyone's throat," made in response to prosecutor's question about using knife in current case, opened door to cross-examination about two prior incidents involving use of knife that otherwise would have been precluded by Sandoval ruling), with People v. Evans, 202 A.D.2d 377, 610 N.Y.S.2d 192 (1st Dep't), appeal denied, 83 N.Y.2d 966, 616 N.Y.S.2d 19, 639 N.E.2d 759 (1994)(defendant's testimony that he had told police he was "not

45. See note 45 on page 451.

the door-opening rationale was extended to the prosecutor's cross-examination of a defense-retained psychologist who had testified that defendant had been a "nonviolent type of individual * * * throughout his life."[46] To impeach the expert's opinion, the prosecutor was permitted to ask the psychologist whether defendant had told him that he had committed a robbery seventeen years ago, even though the robbery conviction previously had been precluded pursuant to a pretrial *Sandoval* motion. The defense opens the door, said the court, "when the defendant or a witness for the defense testifies to facts that are in conflict with the precluded evidence."[47]

Neither the *Sandoval* motion nor the particular balancing of relevance and prejudice suggested in *Sandoval* are required with respect to witnesses other than the criminal defendant himself. The two dangers of impeachment-by-conviction identified in *Sandoval*—misuse of defendant's prior convictions as evidence of guilt and deterrence of defendant's right to testify—are not implicated when prosecution witnesses and other defense witnesses testify.[48] Thus, as to such witnesses, the "usual rules of evidence" apply.[49] Few restrictions have been articulated with respect to the use of convictions to impeach nondefendant witnesses. The Court of Appeals has stated only that a trial court has discretion to control the nature and extent of cross-examination[50] and that a witness' prior immoral, vicious or criminal acts must be relevant on the issue of credibility.[51]

into robbery," when read in context, was not an assertion that he had never committed robbery and therefore did not warrant a change in original Sandoval ruling precluding inquiry into prior robbery).

45. 82 N.Y.2d 638, 607 N.Y.S.2d 220, 628 N.E.2d 41 (1993).

46. Id. at 646, 607 N.Y.S.2d at 223, 628 N.E.2d at 44.

47. Id. at 646, 607 N.Y.S.2d at 224, 628 N.E.2d at 45.

48. People v. Ocasio, 47 N.Y.2d 55, 59, 416 N.Y.S.2d 581, 583, 389 N.E.2d 1101, 1103 (1979)(defense witness other than defendant); People v. Allen, 67 A.D.2d 558, 560, 416 N.Y.S.2d 49, 51 (2d Dep't 1979), aff'd, 50 N.Y.2d 898, 430 N.Y.S.2d 588, 408 N.E.2d 917 (1980)(prosecution witnesses).

49. People v. McGee, 68 N.Y.2d 328, 332, 508 N.Y.S.2d 927, 929, 501 N.E.2d 576, 578 (1986). McGee held that a defendant who is tried jointly with a co-defendant cannot claim the protections of Sandoval with respect to potential cross-examination by the co-defendant. In relation to the co-defendant, the defendant is the functional equivalent of a prosecution witness. Severance is a potential remedy in such cases. Id. at 333, 508 N.Y.S.2d at 930, 501 N.E.2d at 579.

50. See, e.g., People v. Schwartzman, 24 N.Y.2d 241, 244, 299 N.Y.S.2d 817, 820, 247 N.E.2d 642, 644 (1969), cert. denied, 396 U.S. 846, 90 S.Ct. 103, 24 L.Ed.2d 96 (1969).

51. See, e.g., People v. Allen, 67 A.D.2d 558, 560, 416 N.Y.S.2d 49, 51 (2d Dep't 1979), aff'd, 50 N.Y.2d 898, 430 N.Y.S.2d 588, 408 N.E.2d 917 (1980)(trial court should have allowed defendant to cross-examine prosecution witnesses with all recent convictions for attempted rape, robbery, burglary, parole violation, drugs possession, weapons possession, assault, attempted murder as well as 30-year-old convictions for housebreaking and burglary; cross-examination is allowed "as to any immoral, vicious or criminal act committed by them which may affect their character and show them to be unworthy of belief"); People v. Ocasio, 47 N.Y.2d 55, 60, 416 N.Y.S.2d 581, 584, 389 N.E.2d 1101, 1104 (1979)(trial court did not abuse discretion in allowing impeachment of defendant's alibi witness with her 32-year-old conviction of manslaughter for the fatal stabbing of her mother because "it was important the jury know who and what she was").

On a procedural note, Ocasio held that a trial court has the discretion, but is not mandated, to entertain an in limine motion for a ruling on the permissible scope of cross-examination as to a nonparty's prior immoral, vicious or criminal acts. 47 N.Y.2d at 59, 416 N.Y.S.2d at 583, 389 N.E.2d at 1103.

Proposed New York Evidence Code § 609 would codify New York practice with respect to impeachment by evidence of convictions but with some modifications.[52]

[52]. Principal changes in the proposed code provision include: (1) allowance of convictions of "offenses" in both civil and criminal cases; (2) reducing the burden of proof with respect to the showing of prejudice that must be made by the defendant-witness in a criminal case to exclude evidence of his convictions; (3) explicitly requiring a balancing test for convictions of party-witnesses in civil actions; (4) imposing a 15-year-old time limit on the convictions that can be inquired about unless probative value substantially outweighs prejudice; and (5) explicitly providing for the treatment to be accorded pardons and vacated convictions based on findings of innocence, sealed and nullified convictions and convictions as to which an appeal is pending. The text of the proposed rule is as follows:

§ 609. Evidence of conviction of crime [PROPOSED]

(a) General rule. For the purpose of attacking the credibility of a witness, when that witness is properly asked whether he or she was previously convicted of a specified offense and answers in the negative or in an equivocal manner, the party adverse to the one who called the witness may independently prove that conviction. If in response to proper inquiry whether the witness has ever been convicted of any offense, the witness answers in the negative or in an equivocal manner, the adverse party may independently prove any previous conviction of the witness. The party examining the witness may inquire into the nature of the criminal conduct underlying the conviction and is not precluded from making that inquiry by the witness's answer concerning the conviction.

(b) The accused in a criminal case and parties in a civil case

(1) Criminal cases. In a criminal case, evidence offered by the prosecution that the accused has been convicted of an offense, or evidence of the nature of an offense, is not admissible if the prejudicial effect of the evidence, including the effect the evidence would have in deterring the accused from testifying in his or her own behalf, substantially outweighs the probative worth of the evidence on the accused's credibility. Upon request, the prosecutor shall, pursuant to section 240.43 of the criminal procedure law, inform the court and the accused of the convictions of the accused about which the prosecutor intends to inquire. At the request of the accused, determination pursuant to this subdivision shall be made before the commencement of trial.

(2) Civil cases. Subject to section 403 of this chapter, evidence that a party in a civil case has been convicted of an offense is admissible under subdivision (a) of this section.

(c) Convictions more than fifteen years old.

(1) General rule. Evidence of a conviction under this section is not admissible if a period of more than fifteen years, excluding any period of incarceration, has elapsed since the date of the conviction or the release of the witness from the confinement imposed for that conviction, whichever is the later date, unless the court determines that the probative worth of the conviction on the witness's credibility substantially outweighs its prejudicial effect. The proponent of evidence of a conviction more than fifteen years old as calculated herein shall make known to all parties the proponent's intention to use the conviction sufficiently in advance of offering the evidence to provide them with a fair opportunity to contest the use of such evidence. To remedy the prejudice from the failure to give notice, the court, pursuant to section 107 of this chapter, shall make any order the interests of justice require.

(2) The accused in a criminal case. Upon request, the prosecutor, pursuant to section 240.43 of the criminal procedure law, shall inform the accused before the commencement of trial of the specific convictions more than fifteen years old about which it intends to inquire. At the request of the accused, the determination pursuant to this subdivision of the admissibility of such evidence shall be made before the commencement of trial.

(d) Effect of pardon, vacated convictions and findings of innocence. Evidence of a conviction is not admissible under this section if the conviction has been set aside pursuant to law, vacated, or has been the subject of a pardon on a finding of innocence or other equivalent procedure based on a finding of innocence.

Library References:
West's Key No. Digests, Witnesses ⟺337, 345.

§ 609.2 Federal

The federal approach to the admissibility of convictions[1] for impeachment purposes is more formalistic than that of New York. Rule 609 of the Federal Rules of Evidence, as amended in 1990, provides as follows:

Rule 609. Impeachment by Evidence of Conviction of Crime

(a) General rule. For the purpose of attacking the credibility of a witness,

(1) evidence that a witness other than an accused has been convicted of a crime shall be admitted, subject to Rule 403, if the crime was punishable by death or imprisonment in excess of one year under the law under which the witness was convicted, and evidence that an accused has been convicted of such a crime shall be admitted if the court determines that the probative value of admitting this evidence outweighs its prejudicial effect to the accused; and

(2) evidence that any witness has been convicted of a crime shall be admitted if it involved dishonesty or false statement, regardless of the punishment.

(b) Time limit. Evidence of a conviction under this rule is not admissible if a period of more than ten years has elapsed since the date of the conviction or of the release of the witness from the confinement imposed for that conviction, whichever is the later date, unless the court determines, in the interests of justice, that the probative value of the conviction supported by specific facts and circumstances substantially outweighs its prejudicial effect. However, evidence of a conviction more than 10 years old as calculated herein, is not admissible unless the proponent gives to the adverse party sufficient advance written notice of intent to use such evidence to provide the adverse

(e) Sealed and nullified convictions, youthful offender, and juvenile delinquency adjudications. For purposes of this section, a conviction sealed and deemed nullified pursuant to sections 160.50, 160.55 and 160.60 of the criminal procedure law or other equivalent procedure, an adjudication as a youthful offender under article seven hundred twenty of the criminal procedure law or an adjudication as a juvenile delinquent under article three of the family court act or an adjudication as a person in need of supervision under article seven of the family court act is not admissible. Subject to subdivisions (b) and (c) of section 608 of this article, the party examining the witness may, however, inquire into the facts underlying the conviction or adjudication.

(f) Pendency of appeal. Evidence of a conviction is admissible under this section even though an appeal is pending therefrom. Evidence of the pendency of the appeal is admissible.

§ 609.2

1. In United States v. Vanderbosch, 610 F.2d 95 (2d Cir.1979), the Second Circuit held that a guilty verdict qualifies as a conviction for purposes of Fed.R.Evid. 609(a) even prior to entry of judgment.

party with a fair opportunity to contest the use of such evidence.

(c) Effect of pardon, annulment, or certificate of rehabilitation. Evidence of a conviction is not admissible under this rule if (1) the conviction has been the subject of a pardon, annulment, certificate of rehabilitation, or other equivalent procedure based on a finding of the rehabilitation of the person convicted, and that person has not been convicted of a subsequent crime which was punishable by death or imprisonment in excess of one year, or (2) the conviction has been the subject of a pardon, annulment, or other equivalent procedure based on a finding of innocence.

(d) Juvenile adjudications. Evidence of juvenile adjudications is generally not admissible under this rule. The court may, however, in a criminal case allow evidence of a juvenile adjudication of a witness other than the accused if conviction of the offense would be admissible to attack the credibility of an adult and the court is satisfied that admission in evidence is necessary for a fair determination of the issue of guilt or innocence.

(e) Pendency of appeal. The pendency of an appeal therefrom does not render evidence of a conviction inadmissible. Evidence of the pendency of an appeal is admissible.

By way of overview, Rule 609(a) authorizes the use of two types of convictions to attack a witness' credibility: (1) conviction of a crime punishable by death or imprisonment in excess of one year (usually a felony); and (2) conviction of a crime involving dishonesty or false statement without regard to the severity of punishment. Convictions of the first type are subject to the trial court's discretionary balancing of relevance and prejudice (the nature of which turns on whether the witness is a criminal defendant), while convictions involving dishonesty or false statement are automatically admissible.[2] Both types of convictions, however, are subject to the time limitation in subdivision (b), which prohibits the use of convictions over 10 years old unless probative value "substantially outweighs" prejudicial effect. Subdivisions (c), (d) and (e) resolve issues concerning pardons, juvenile adjudications and

---

2. The court in Campbell v. Greer, 831 F.2d 700 (7th Cir.1987), explained the relevance of felony convictions on the issue of credibility as follows:

> Rule 609 and the common law tradition out of which it evolved rest on the common-sense proposition that a person who has flouted society's most fundamental norms, as embodied in its felony statutes, is less likely than other members of society to be deterred from lying under oath in a trial by the solemnity of the oath, the (minuscule) danger of prosecution for perjury, or internalized ethical norms against lying. If so, this is something a jury should be permitted to take into account in evaluating a witness's believability.

Id. at 707. Nevertheless, the "degree of relevance" of felony convictions, in general, is less than that of convictions for crimes involving dishonesty or false statement, thus explaining the rule of automatic admissibility for the latter, Fed.R.Evid. 609(a)(2), and the rule of discretion for the former, Fed.R.Evid. 609(a)(1). United States v. Hawley, 554 F.2d 50, 52 (2d Cir. 1977).

pendency of appeals. The trial court's discretion governs the point in the trial at which impeaching convictions may be proven, although in practice such proof usually occurs during cross-examination.[3]

With respect to a felony conviction that does not involve dishonesty or false statement (subdivision (a)(1)), the Rule currently provides for special protection against prejudice to the criminal defendant who proposes to testify in his own behalf. Such a conviction may be used for impeachment only if the government shows that its probative value on the issue of the defendant's credibility outweighs the prejudicial effect to him.[4] The reason for this approach is the same as that which motivated New York's *Sandoval* motion:[5] the danger exists that convictions intended only for impeachment purposes will be misused as evidence of defendant's guilt.[6]

Federal courts have identified five principal factors to be weighed in the relevance/prejudice balancing as it applies to criminal defendants: (1) impeachment value of the prior crime; (2) lapse of time between the conviction and the current trial; (3) similarity between the prior crime and the current charges; (4) importance of the defendant's testimony; and (5) the centrality of credibility to the resolution of the case.[7]

It should be noted that in federal practice, the defendant's failure to testify because of an unfavorable ruling concerning impeachment with prior convictions waives the ability to assert error as to this issue on

---

3. The 1990 amendment to Rule 609(a) removed language that purported to restrict proof of convictions to cross-examination, "a limitation that virtually every circuit has found to be inapplicable. It is common for witnesses to reveal on direct examination their convictions to 'remove the sting' of the impeachment." Advisory Committee's Note to 1990 Amendment to Fed.R.Evid. 609.

In proving a conviction for impeachment purposes, the cross-examiner is restricted to the name of the crime, date of conviction and disposition; the underlying facts may not be elicited. Campbell v. Greer, 831 F.2d 700, 707–08 (7th Cir.1987).

4. See United States v. Hayes, 553 F.2d 824, 828 (2d Cir.), cert. denied, 434 U.S. 867, 98 S.Ct. 204, 54 L.Ed.2d 143 (1977)(government has burden of showing that probative value outweighs prejudice); Advisory Committee's Note to 1990 Amendment to Fed.R.Evid. 609 (Rule 609(a)(1) requires government to show that probative value outweighs prejudicial effect). The defendant, however, has the burden of raising the balancing issue as a basis for exclusion. United States v. Vanderbosch, 610 F.2d 95, 98 (2d Cir.1979).

5. See § 609.1, at notes 14–28, supra.

6. Advisory Committee's Note to 1990 Amendment to Fed.R.Evid. 609.

7. See United States v. Pritchard, 973 F.2d 905, 908–09 (11th Cir.1992); United States v. Hawley, 554 F.2d 50, 53 n.5 (2d Cir.1977). See generally 3 Weinstein and Berger ¶ 609[3]. The balancing factors have their origins in Luck v. United States, 348 F.2d 763, 769 (D.C.Cir.1965), and Gordon v. United States, 383 F.2d 936, 940–41 (D.C.Cir.1967), cert. denied, 390 U.S. 1029, 88 S.Ct. 1421, 20 L.Ed.2d 287 (1968). Other factors occasionally have been deemed relevant to the inquiry. See, e.g., United States v. Hayes, 553 F.2d 824, 828 (2d Cir.), cert. denied, 434 U.S. 867, 98 S.Ct. 204, 54 L.Ed.2d 143 (1977)(fact that defendant testified at the trial which resulted in his prior conviction implies that defendant perjured self).

Within the Second Circuit, a trial court's exercise of discretion under Fed.R.Evid. 609(a)(1) is "virtually unreviewable." United States v. Pedroza, 750 F.2d 187, 202 (2d Cir.1984). The Court of Appeals has upheld impeachment of criminal defendants with felony convictions of attempted burglary, United States v. Hawley, supra, importation of cocaine, United States v. Hayes, supra, and heroin sales, United States v. Ortiz, 553 F.2d 782 (2d Cir.), cert. denied, 434 U.S. 897, 98 S.Ct. 277, 54 L.Ed.2d 183 (1977).

§ 609.2 WITNESSES Ch. 6

appeal. In *Luce v. United States*,[8] the Supreme Court reasoned that appellate review is not possible in the absence of a trial record in which the probative value and prejudicial effect of the impeaching convictions can be examined in relation to the defendant's actual testimony.[9]

As to all witnesses other than the criminal defendant, i.e., other defense witnesses and prosecution witnesses in criminal cases and all witnesses in civil actions, Rule 609(a)(1) now provides for balancing under the standard of Rule 403.[10] It would appear, therefore, that as to all witnesses other than the criminal defendant, a felony conviction within 10 years is prima facie admissible to impeach unless its probative value is substantially outweighed by considerations of unfair prejudice to the litigants, confusion, cumulativeness and the like.

The second category of impeaching convictions—those that "involved dishonesty or false statement" regardless of the punishment, i.e., misdemeanors as well as felonies (subdivision (a)(2))—enjoy a favored status: such convictions "shall" be admitted. In other words, no balancing of relevance and prejudice is to be undertaken by trial courts in individual cases; Congress has already struck the balance in favor of

---

8. 469 U.S. 38, 105 S.Ct. 460, 83 L.Ed.2d 443 (1984).

9. Id. at 42–43, 105 S.Ct. at 463–64, 83 L.Ed.2d at 447.

10. Cf. United States v. Pedroza, 750 F.2d 187, 203 (2d Cir.1984)(in multi-defendant criminal case in which a prior conviction is potentially admissible to impeach one defendant, the prejudicial effect on other defendants must be taken into account). The following excerpts from the Advisory Committee's Note to the 1990 Amendment to Rule 609 reveal the drafters' purpose:

Rule 403 now clearly protects against unfair impeachment of any defense witness other than the defendant. There are cases in which a defendant might be prejudiced when a defense witness is impeached. Such cases may arise, for example, when the witness bears a special relationship to the defendant such that the defendant is likely to suffer some spill-over effect from impeachment of the witness.

The amendment also protects other litigants from unfair impeachment of their witnesses. The danger of prejudice from the use of prior convictions is not confined to criminal defendants. Although the danger that prior convictions will be misused as character evidence is particularly acute when the defendant is impeached, the danger exists in other situations as well. The amendment reflects the view that it is desirable to protect all litigants from the unfair use of prior convictions, and that the ordinary balancing test of Rule 403, which provides that evidence shall not be excluded unless its prejudicial effect substantially outweighs its probative value, is appropriate for assessing the admissibility of prior convictions for impeachment of any witness other than a criminal defendant.

* * *

* * * There are cases in which impeachment of government witnesses with prior convictions that have little, if anything, to do with credibility may result in unfair prejudice to the government's interest in a fair trial and unnecessary embarrassment to a witness. Fed.R.Evid. 412 already recognizes this and excluded certain evidence of past sexual behavior in the context of prosecutions for sexual assaults.

* * *

The probability that prior convictions of an ordinary government witness will be unduly prejudicial is low in most criminal cases. Since the behavior of the witness is not the issue in dispute in most cases, there is little chance that the trier of fact will misuse the convictions offered as impeachment evidence as propensity evidence. Thus, trial courts will be skeptical when the government objects to impeachment of its witnesses with prior convictions. Only when the government is able to point to a real danger of prejudice that is sufficient to outweigh substantially the probative value of the conviction for impeachment purposes will the conviction be excluded.

admissibility. Moreover, automatic admissibility applies even as to criminal defendants.[11]

Problems of application, however, have arisen under Rule 609(a)(2). It seems clear enough that the rule encompasses convictions that would be classified at common law as *crimen falsi*, i.e., crimes having a definitional element of deceit, such as fraud, perjury or false statement.[12] At the other extreme, the second category excludes crimes of violence, such as assault, murder and rape.[13] Courts have split, however, over the question whether convictions for theft-related crimes may properly be included in category two.[14] The Second Circuit appears to have a

---

11. See United States v. Hayes, 553 F.2d 824, 827 (2d Cir.), cert. denied, 434 U.S. 867, 98 S.Ct. 204, 54 L.Ed.2d 143 (1977)(convictions within subdivision (a)(2) "must be admitted, with the trial court having no discretion, regardless of the seriousness of the offense or its prejudice to the defendant"). See also United States v. Noble, 754 F.2d 1324, 1331 (7th Cir.), cert. denied, 474 U.S. 818, 106 S.Ct. 63, 88 L.Ed.2d 51 (1985) (in counterfeiting prosecution, trial court properly admitted defendant's prior counterfeiting conviction to impeach his credibility because no balancing of relevance and prejudice would have been appropriate); United States v. Toney, 615 F.2d 277, 279–80 (5th Cir.), cert. denied, 449 U.S. 985, 101 S.Ct. 403, 66 L.Ed.2d 248 (1980)(in mail fraud prosecution, trial court had no discretion to exclude defendant's prior mail fraud conviction for impeachment purposes despite its similarity to current charge).

12. See United States v. Hayes, 553 F.2d 824, 827 (2d Cir.), cert. denied, 434 U.S. 867, 98 S.Ct. 204, 54 L.Ed.2d 143 (1977)("Because [Rule 609(a)(2)] is quite inflexible, allowing no leeway for consideration of mitigating circumstances, it was inevitable that Congress would define narrowly the words 'dishonesty or false statement,' which, taken at their broadest, involve activities that are part of nearly all crimes. Hence Congress emphasized that the second prong was meant to refer to convictions 'peculiarly probative of credibility,' such as those for 'perjury or subornation of perjury, false statement, criminal fraud, embezzlement, or false pretense, or any other offense in the nature of crimen falsi, the commission of which involves some element of deceit, untruthfulness, or falsification bearing on the accused's propensity to testify truthfully.' "), quoting Conference Report on Fed.R.Evid., 1974 U.S.Code Cong. and Ad.News 7098, 7102. See also United States v. Tracy, 36 F.3d 187, 192 (1st Cir.1994)(uttering false prescription); Altobello v. Borden Confectionary Products, Inc., 872 F.2d 215, 217 (7th Cir.1989) (meter tampering); United States v. Noble, 754 F.2d 1324, 1331 (7th Cir.), cert. denied, 474 U.S. 818, 106 S.Ct. 63, 88 L.Ed.2d 51 (1985) (counterfeiting).

13. Czajka v. Hickman, 703 F.2d 317, 319 n.1 (8th Cir.1983)(rape); United States v. Harvey, 588 F.2d 1201, 1203 (8th Cir.1978)(assault). See also United States v. Cameron, 814 F.2d 403, 405–06 (7th Cir. 1987) (possession of switchblade); United States v. Mansaw, 714 F.2d 785, 789 (8th Cir.), cert. denied, 464 U.S. 986, 104 S.Ct. 434, 78 L.Ed.2d 366 (1983)(prostitution); United States v. Lewis, 626 F.2d 940, 946 (D.C.Cir.1980)(heroin distribution); Reyes v. Missouri Pacific R.R. Co., 589 F.2d 791, 795 n.10 (5th Cir.1979)(public intoxication).

14. The following cases are illustrative of an expansive interpretation of Rule 609(a)(2): United States v. Del Toro Soto, 676 F.2d 13, 18 (1st Cir.1982)(grand larceny conviction falls within Fed.R.Evid. 609(a)(2)); United States v. Kinslow, 860 F.2d 963, 968 (9th Cir.1988), cert. denied, 493 U.S. 829, 110 S.Ct. 96, 107 L.Ed.2d 60 (1989)(armed robbery is crime of dishonesty). It should be noted that Kinslow was disavowed by the Ninth Circuit in United States v. Brackeen, 969 F.2d 827, 829 (9th Cir.1992)(en banc)(bank robbery is not necessarily a crime of dishonesty).

The following cases illustrate a strict view: United States v. Pritchard, 973 F.2d 905, 909 n.6 (11th Cir.1992)(burglary does not involve dishonesty or false statement); McHenry v. Chadwick, 896 F.2d 184, 188 (6th Cir.1990)(shoplifting does not fall within Fed.R.Evid. 609(a)(2)); United States v. Yeo, 739 F.2d 385, 387 (8th Cir.1984)(theft, although it involves stealth, does not require an element of deceit or false statement); United States v. Mehrmanesh, 689 F.2d 822, 833 (9th Cir.1982) (smuggling of narcotics is surreptitious but does not necessarily involve fraud or deceit); United States v. Grandmont, 680 F.2d 867, 870 (1st Cir.1982)(robbery is not, on its face, crime of dishonesty); United States v. Smith, 551 F.2d 348, 361–65 (D.C.Cir.1976)(attempted robbery is not a crime of dishonesty or false statement).

negative view toward the automatic admissibility of such convictions.[15] On the other hand, some courts, including the Second Circuit,[16] have indicated a willingness to permit the prosecutor to go behind the title of a conviction. If the name of the crime does not on its face bespeak the notion of dishonesty or false statement, but the underlying facts of the crime are shown by the government to have involved deceit in furtherance of the crime, the conviction may qualify for automatic admissibility.[17]

Assuming a prior conviction satisfies one or the other of the two tests in Rule 609(a), it may be admitted if it occurred within 10 years (or if the witness' release from confinement for that conviction occurred within 10 years).[18] Additional requirements must be satisfied, however, if more than 10 years have elapsed: The court must determine "in the interests of justice" that the conviction's probative value "substantially outweighs its prejudicial effect," and the proponent must give "sufficient advance written notice" to the adversary of the intent to use such conviction.[19] Although Congress appears to have intended stale convic-

---

Courts have also divided over the characterization of a conviction for willful failure to file income tax returns. Compare Cree v. Hatcher, 969 F.2d 34, 37–38 (3d Cir.), cert. dismissed, __ U.S. __, 113 S.Ct. 1147, 121 L.Ed.2d 577 (1992)(not within subdivision (a)(2)), with Dean v. Trans World Airlines, Inc., 924 F.2d 805, 811 (9th Cir.1991)(falls within subdivision (a)(2)), and United States v. Gellman, 677 F.2d 65, 66 (11th Cir.1982)(falls within subdivision (a)(2)).

15. In United States v. Hayes, 553 F.2d 824 (2d Cir.), cert. denied, 434 U.S. 867, 98 S.Ct. 204, 54 L.Ed.2d 143 (1977), the Second Circuit expressed the view that Congress intended a narrow definition of the types of crimes that qualify for automatic admissibility under subdivision (a)(2): "The use of the second prong of Rule 609(a) is thus restricted to convictions that bear directly on the likelihood that the defendant will testify truthfully (and not merely on whether he has a propensity to commit crimes). It follows that crimes of force, such as armed robbery or assault, * * * or crimes of stealth, such as burglary * * * or petit larceny, * * * do not come within this clause." Id. at 827. See also note 12 supra.

16. United States v. Hayes, 553 F.2d 824, 827 (2d Cir.), cert. denied, 434 U.S. 867, 98 S.Ct. 204, 54 L.Ed.2d 143 (1977)(conviction for importation of narcotics could qualify as crime of dishonesty or false statement if witness used false shipping documents).

17. The courts that have indicated the appropriateness of an inquiry into the manner in which the crime was committed have done so in dicta. See Altobello v. Borden Confectionary Products, Inc., 872 F.2d 215, 216–17 (7th Cir.1989); United States v. Yeo, 739 F.2d 385, 388 (8th Cir.1984); United States v. Grandmont, 680 F.2d 867, 871 (1st Cir.1982); United States v. Glenn, 667 F.2d 1269, 1273 (9th Cir.1982).

The permissibility of an inquiry into the underlying facts appears to have been rejected in Cree v. Hatcher, 969 F.2d 34, 38 n.2 (3d Cir.), cert. dismissed, __ U.S. __, 113 S.Ct. 1147, 121 L.Ed.2d 577 (1992)(manner of commission of crime is irrelevant; "what matters is whether dishonesty or false statement is an element of the statutory offense"), and United States v. Lewis, 626 F.2d 940, 946 (D.C.Cir.1980)(manner in which crime was committed has no bearing on admissibility pursuant to Fed.R.Evid. 609(a)(2)).

18. The Weinstein and Berger treatise argues that the time of the witness' testimony is the correct point from which the 10-year backward measurement should be made. 3 Weinstein and Berger ¶ 609[07], at 609–74.

19. See, e.g., United States v. Colletti, 984 F.2d 1339, 1343 (3d Cir.1992)(no abuse of discretion occurred where defendants were precluded from cross-examining prosecution witness with 22-year-old conviction for disorderly conduct; defendants also failed to give advance notice of intent to use the conviction). Compare United States v. Livingston, 816 F.2d 184, 190 (5th Cir. 1987)(stale conviction properly excluded where no advance notice given), with Zinman v. Black & Decker (U.S.), Inc., 983 F.2d 431, 435 (2d Cir.1993)(by declining

tions to be admitted only on rare occasions,[20] a fair number of cases have upheld the admissibility, in particular circumstances, of convictions over 10 years old.[21]

Library References:

West's Key No. Digests, Witnesses ⚖ 337, 345.

610 Religious Beliefs or Opinions

§ 610.1 New York

As discussed in preceding sections relating to competency, a witness' religious beliefs have no bearing on his testimonial qualifications.[1] Furthermore, a witness is free to affirm the truth of his testimony rather than take an oath.[2] Just as one's religious beliefs are irrelevant on the question of one's qualifications to tell the truth, they are likewise irrelevant on the question whether the witness has in fact told the truth. The Court of Appeals, therefore, has declared, "With limited exceptions * * *, any attempt to discredit * * * a witness because of his religious beliefs or for the exercise of his right to affirm the truth of his testimony is improper, because those factors are irrelevant to the issue of credibility."[3] By the same token, a witness' religious beliefs may not properly be elicited for the purpose of bolstering his credibility.[4]

On rare occasions, however, religious beliefs may be relevant on some issue in the case other than the witness' propensity for truthfulness.[5] It has also been suggested that one's religious affiliation might in

court's offer of mistrial, party waived objection to insufficiency of notice).

20. See Zinman v. Black & Decker (U.S.), Inc., 983 F.2d 431, 434 (2d Cir.1993).

21. See, e.g., United States v. Pritchard, 973 F.2d 905, 909 (11th Cir.1992)(13-year-old burglary conviction was properly admitted against defendant in bank robbery case pitting credibility of defendant against one prosecution witness whose own criminal record was admissible to impeach); United States v. Gilbert, 668 F.2d 94, 97 (2d Cir. 1981), cert. denied, 456 U.S. 946, 102 S.Ct. 2014, 72 L.Ed.2d 469 (1982)(trial court did not abuse discretion in securities fraud prosecution by ruling that defendant could be impeached with mail fraud conviction over 10 years old; defendant's credibility was crucial issue, impeachment value of conviction was high, crimes were not so similar as to invite improper inference of guilt, and age of conviction in light of defendant's post-conviction history did not suggest abandonment of defendant's earlier ways). The court in Pritchard observed that cases finding an abuse of discretion often involve prior crimes that are of an inflammatory nature, are extremely old, or lack strong probative value on the issue of credibility, 973 F.2d at 909 n. 7.

§ 610.1

1. See § 601.1, at note 6, supra.

2. See § 603.1, at notes 4–7, supra.

3. People v. Wood, 66 N.Y.2d 374, 379, 497 N.Y.S.2d 340, 343, 488 N.E.2d 86, 89 (1985), aff'd, 79 N.Y.2d 958, 582 N.Y.S.2d 992, 591 N.E.2d 1178 (1992). See, e.g., People v. Thomas, 91 A.D.2d 857, 858, 458 N.Y.S.2d 383, 384 (4th Dep't 1982)(improper for prosecutor to cross-examine alibi witness concerning religious beliefs); People v. Forchalle, 88 A.D.2d 645, 646, 450 N.Y.S.2d 220, 222 (2d Dep't 1982)(prosecutor improperly sought to discredit defendant by showing affiliation with church group which had unorthodox views). See also People v. Valdivia, 108 A.D.2d 885, 886, 485 N.Y.S.2d 580, 582 (2d Dep't 1985)(improper to cross-examine witness concerning taking of affirmation rather than oath, but not per se reversible error).

4. People v. Mercado, 188 A.D.2d 941, 944, 592 N.Y.S.2d 75, 78 (3d Dep't 1992).

5. See, e.g., Toomey v. Farley, 2 N.Y.2d 71, 82, 156 N.Y.S.2d 840, 848, 138 N.E.2d 221, 227 (1956)(in defamation action based on accusation that plaintiff was communist, evidence of plaintiff's devotion to church was relevant on issue of damages).

§ 610.1 WITNESSES Ch. 6

some circumstances be relevant on the issue of bias.[6]

By extension of the rule against impeachment on the ground of religious belief, some courts have recognized a general prohibition on the use of a witness' group affiliation as a basis of impeachment.[7] Unless a witness' associations clearly reflect on credibility in the particular case, as, for example, demonstrating bias,[8] their relevance would seem to be remote[9] and the potential for prejudice strong.[10]

Library References:

West's Key No. Digests, Witnesses ⟺340(2).

§ 610.2 Federal

Federal Rule of Evidence 610 states: "Evidence of the beliefs or opinions of a witness on matters of religion is not admissible for the purpose of showing that by reason of their nature the witness' credibility is impaired or enhanced." As explained by one court: "The purpose of the rule is to guard against the prejudice which may result from disclosure of a witness's faith. The scope of the prohibition includes unconventional or unusual religions."[1] The Advisory Committee's Note observes that the rule bars inquiry into religions beliefs only as they bear on a witness' character for truthfulness,[2] which of course is the usual driving force behind such questioning. If the purpose is to show

---

6. See Brink v. Stratton, 176 N.Y. 150, 162, 68 N.E. 148, 152 (1903) (concurring opinion)("Experience teaches us that we may be biased in favor of our associates, whether in a church, in a club or in business institution.") But see Saunders v. Champlain Bus Corp., 263 App.Div. 683, 34 N.Y.S.2d 447 (3d Dep't 1942)(questioning two witnesses concerning their shared ethnic background was an improper appeal to prejudice and passion).

The comment to Proposed New York Evidence Code § 610 states that inquiry into religious beliefs may show interest or bias, and cites as an example the witness' membership in a church which is a party to the action. The code section itself, § 610, provides as follows: "Evidence of the beliefs or opinions of a witness on matters of religion is not admissible for the purpose of showing that by reason of their nature credibility is impaired or enhanced."

7. People v. Hambrick, 122 A.D.2d 163, 164, 504 N.Y.S.2d 540, 541 (2d Dep't), appeal denied, 69 N.Y.2d 712, 512 N.Y.S.2d 1038, 504 N.E.2d 406 (1986)("attempt to discredit the defendant, whether by reason of his religious beliefs or because of his affiliation with a group held in general disfavor, was improper"). See also People v. Torres, 72 A.D.2d 754, 755, 421 N.Y.S.2d 275, 276 (2d Dep't 1979)("attempt to impeach the defendants through the alleged acts of an organization with which they associated [street gang] constitutes reversible error in this case, in which the credibility of the witnesses was critical").

8. See, e.g., United States v. Abel, 469 U.S. 45, 105 S.Ct. 465, 83 L.Ed.2d 450 (1984)(proper to show that defense witness and defendant were fellow members of organization whose members had agreed to lie, cheat, steal and kill for each other). See generally § 607.6(a) supra.

9. See § 607.6(a), at notes 20–23, supra.

10. Cf. Saunders v. Champlain Bus Corp., 263 App.Div. 683, 34 N.Y.S.2d 447 (3d Dep't 1942)(stressing of shared ethnic background of witnesses was improper appeal to "prejudice and passion").

§ 610.2

1. United States v. Sampol, 636 F.2d 621, 666 (D.C.Cir.1980)(improper for defense counsel to elicit that prosecution witness was member of unconventional religion and "consulted with spirits of his religion before taking certain actions"). See also United States v. Kalaydjian, 784 F.2d 53, 56–57 (2d Cir.1986)(no cross-examination permitted concerning witness' decision to affirm rather than take oath). The rule also prohibits questioning about religions beliefs for the purpose of supporting credibility. See Government of the Virgin Islands v. Petersen, 553 F.2d 324, 328 (3d Cir.1977).

2. Advisory Committee's Note, Fed. R.Evid. 610.

bias, as, for example, in the case of a witness who is a member of a church which is a party to the litigation, Rule 610 is inapplicable.[3] The mere fact that a witness and the party for whom he testifies share the same religious affiliation or beliefs, however, is probably insufficient to overcome rule 610.[4]

Library References:

West's Key No. Digests, Witnesses ⚖︎340(2).

611 Presentation of Testimony

§ 611.1 New York: Order of Trial

Insofar as the presentation of evidence is concerned, a trial usually proceeds in the following order:

1. Plaintiff's (or prosecutor's) case in chief;
2. Defendant's case in defense;
3. Plaintiff's (or prosecutor's) rebuttal;
4. Defendant's surrebuttal (or rejoinder).[1]

---

3. Id.

4. See Malek v. Federal Insurance Co., 994 F.2d 49, 54–55, 59–60 (2d Cir.1993)(violation of Rule 610 occurred where plaintiff was Hasidic and cross-examination of plaintiff's accountant elicited fact that witness had several other Hasidic clients and was faculty member of Jewish-based university system; whereas majority viewed the inquiries as improper character impeachment on religious grounds, dissent saw cross-examination as legitimate impeachment for bias). Evidence of bias based simply on the fact that the witness and a party share the same religious affiliation may be inappropriate on grounds of remoteness. See § 607.6(b), at notes 35–36, supra. Much will depend on the strength of the relationship between the witness and the party and the nature of the shared beliefs. Cf. United States v. Abel, 469 U.S. 45, 105 S.Ct. 465, 83 L.Ed.2d 450 (1984)(defense witness was subject to impeachment on ground of bias because of membership with defendant in small organization whose members were dedicated to lying, cheating and killing on each other's behalf).

On occasion, an adverse witness' religious beliefs or affiliation might raise a permissible inference of hostility toward a party. Cf. United States v. Teicher, 987 F.2d 112, 118–19 (2d Cir.), cert. denied, ___ U.S. ___, 114 S.Ct. 467, 126 L.Ed.2d 419 (1993)(after eliciting from witness that, as a Jew, he would not seek to "turn other Jews over," district court concluded that witness had no bias against defendants, who were also Jewish; witness' "messianic beliefs" were therefore irrelevant for impeachment purposes).

§ 611.1

1. See generally McCormick § 4. The presentation of evidence is preceded by counsel's opening statements, which are merely outlines of what the parties intend to prove and do not constitute evidence. People v. Musmacher, 133 A.D.2d 352, 353, 519 N.Y.S.2d 253, 253 (2d Dep't), appeal denied, 70 N.Y.2d 802, 522 N.Y.S.2d 120, 516 N.E.2d 1233 (1987). After both parties have presented their evidence and rested, counsel make their closing arguments, in which they summarize and interpret the evidence. If the case is being tried to a jury, the judge will then instruct the jury on the applicable law. CPLR 4110–b.

The plaintiff, because she has the burden of proof, ordinarily delivers the first opening argument and the last closing argument. See CPLR 4016. On rare occasions, the defendant may have conceded every aspect of a plaintiff's case, making trial necessary only as to an affirmative defense or counterclaim. In such a case, the defendant would have the right to make the first opening statement and final closing argument. See generally Heilbronn v. Herzog, 165 N.Y. 98, 58 N.E. 759 (1900); Lake Ontario Nat'l Bank v. Judson, 122 N.Y. 278, 25 N.E. 367 (1890); American Union Line v. Oriental Navigation Corp., 199 App. Div. 513, 192 N.Y.S. 154 (1st Dep't 1922).

In criminal cases, § 260.30 of the New York Criminal Procedure Law prescribes the entire order of trial:

§ 611.1   WITNESSES   Ch. 6

The plaintiff (or prosecutor) assumes the burden during her case in chief of presenting sufficient evidence to support a finding in her favor.[2] During the defense, the defendant may present evidence that seeks to refute the plaintiff/prosecutor's version of events, impeach the credibility of the plaintiff/prosecutor's witnesses (to the extent impeachment evidence is permitted by extrinsic evidence)[3] and affirmatively prove defensive matters.

Rebuttal generally is restricted to evidence that refutes new matters raised during the defense and impeaches the credibility of the defendant's witnesses.[4] Generally the plaintiff/prosecutor may not, during rebuttal, present evidence that merely reinforces her case in chief.[5] In other words, if evidence could have been properly admitted during the case in chief, ordinarily it should not be admissible during rebuttal. On the other hand, to the extent the testimony of a defense witness is subject to contradiction,[6] the plaintiff/prosecutor may be able to introduce evidence in rebuttal that might also have been admitted during the case in chief.[7] Furthermore, a trial court exercises discretion to modify

---

The order of a jury trial, in general, is as follows:

1. The jury must be selected and sworn.
2. The court must deliver preliminary instructions to the jury.
3. The people must deliver an opening address to the jury.
4. The defendant may deliver an opening address to the jury.
5. The people must offer evidence in support of the indictment.
6. The defendant may offer evidence in his defense.
7. The people may offer evidence in rebuttal of the defense evidence, and the defendant may then offer evidence in rebuttal of the people's rebuttal evidence. The court may in its discretion permit the parties to offer further rebuttal or surrebuttal evidence in this pattern. In the interest of justice, the court may permit either party to offer evidence upon rebuttal which is not technically of a rebuttal nature but more properly a part of the offering party's original case.
8. At the conclusion of the evidence, the defendant may deliver a summation to the jury.
9. The people may then deliver a summation to the jury.
10. The court must then deliver a charge to the jury.
11. The jury must then retire to deliberate and, if possible, render a verdict.

See also N.Y.Crim.Proc.Law § 320.20(3)(order in nonjury trial).

2. With respect to the burden of producing evidence, see § 300.3(a)(1) supra.

3. See § 607.2, at notes 19–25, supra.

4. People v. Harris, 57 N.Y.2d 335, 345, 456 N.Y.S.2d 694, 698, 442 N.E.2d 1205, 1209 (1982), cert. denied, 460 U.S. 1047, 103 S.Ct. 1448, 75 L.Ed.2d 803 (1983); Ankersmit v. Tuch, 114 N.Y. 51, 55, 20 N.E. 819, 820 (1889); Marshall v. Davies, 78 N.Y. 414, 420 (1877); People v. Brown, 126 A.D.2d 657, 658, 511 N.Y.S.2d 86, 87 (2d Dep't), appeal denied, 70 N.Y.2d 703, 519 N.Y.S.2d 1037, 513 N.E.2d 714 (1987).

5. See Hutchinson v. Shaheen, 55 A.D.2d 833, 834, 390 N.Y.S.2d 317, 319 (4th Dep't 1976)("A party holding the affirmative of an issue is bound to present all the evidence on his side of the case before he closes his proof and may not add to it by the device of rebuttal evidence * * *. He may not hold back some evidence and then submit it to bolster his case after defendant has rested * * *."). See also Kapinos v. Alvarado, 143 A.D.2d 332, 333, 532 N.Y.S.2d 416, 417–18 (2d Dep't 1988)(trial court properly refused to allow rebuttal evidence where ample opportunity for presentation had been afforded during case in chief).

6. Contradiction of a witness' testimony is circumscribed by limits on extrinsic evidence of collateral matters. See § 607.3 supra.

7. People v. Harris, 57 N.Y.2d 335, 345, 456 N.Y.S.2d 694, 698, 442 N.E.2d 1205, 1209 (1982), cert. denied, 460 U.S. 1047, 103 S.Ct. 1448, 75 L.Ed.2d 803 (1983);

Ch. 6 PRESENTATION OF TESTIMONY § 611.1

the order of proof,[8] and in appropriate circumstances a party may be permitted to introduce evidence during rebuttal that otherwise should have been brought out during the case in chief.[9] The same pattern applies to the defendant's case in surrebuttal, i.e., the defendant generally is restricted to addressing new matters that were introduced on rebuttal.

When each party has finished presenting evidence in support of her particular phase of the case, she announces that she rests. Here again, the trial court has inherent discretion to permit a party to reopen her case to present additional evidence after she has rested.[10] Indeed, "[t]he common-law power of the trial court to alter the order of proof 'in its discretion and in furtherance of justice' remains at least up to the time the case is submitted to the jury.'"[11] The same discretion extends to the

Ankersmit v. Tuch, 114 N.Y. 51, 55, 20 N.E. 819, 820 (1889).

8. See Feldsberg v. Nitschke, 49 N.Y.2d 636, 643, 427 N.Y.S.2d 751, 755, 404 N.E.2d 1293, 1297 (1980)("order of introducing evidence and the time when it may be introduced are matters generally resting in the sound discretion of the trial court"); People v. Schwartzman, 24 N.Y.2d 241, 249–50, 299 N.Y.S.2d 817, 825, 247 N.E.2d 642, 647, cert. denied, 396 U.S. 846, 90 S.Ct. 103, 24 L.Ed.2d 96 (1969)(trial court has broad discretion "to vary the prescribed order of the trial and the normal order of proof").

9. In criminal cases, N.Y.Crim.Proc.Law § 260.30(7) specifically allows the court to "permit either party to offer evidence upon rebuttal which is not technically of a rebuttal nature but more properly a part of the offering party's original case." See note 1 supra. The provision was applied in People v. Harris, 57 N.Y.2d 335, 456 N.Y.S.2d 694, 442 N.E.2d 1205 (1982), cert. denied, 460 U.S. 1047, 103 S.Ct. 1448, 75 L.Ed.2d 803 (1983), where a prosecution witness was allowed to testify during rebuttal to a telephone conversation of the defendant even though the conversation would have been provable during the prosecutor's case in chief. The witness had been unable to identify the defendant's voice until after defendant testified during the defense. Id. at 345–46, 456 N.Y.S.2d at 698, 442 N.E.2d at 1209. See also People v. Alvino, 71 N.Y.2d 233, 248, 525 N.Y.S.2d 7, 15, 519 N.E.2d 808, 816 (1987)(evidence of uncharged crimes, which could have been admitted during prosecutor's case in chief, admissible on rebuttal in court's discretion).

10. Feldsberg v. Nitschke, 49 N.Y.2d 636, 643, 427 N.Y.S.2d 751, 755, 404 N.E.2d 1293, 1297 (1980); People v. Ventura, 35 N.Y.2d 654, 655, 360 N.Y.S.2d 419, 420, 318 N.E.2d 609, 609 (1974). See, e.g., People v. Hinkley, 178 A.D.2d 800, 581 N.Y.S.2d 253 (3d Dep't 1991)(not abuse of discretion to allow prosecution to reopen, after summations, to allow testimony by informant who could not previously be located); Veal v. New York City Transit Auth., 148 A.D.2d 443, 444–45, 538 N.Y.S.2d 594, 596 (2d Dep't 1989)(in circumstances of particular case, trial court abused discretion by not allowing defendant to reopen case to introduce recently-obtained documentary evidence). But see King v. Burkowski, 155 A.D.2d 285, 286, 547 N.Y.S.2d 48, 49 (1st Dep't 1989)("trial court's discretion to reopen a case after a party has rested should be sparingly exercised").

The reopening issue often arises in criminal cases in which the defendant expresses a last-minute desire to take the stand in his own behalf. See, e.g., People v. Washington, 71 N.Y.2d 916, 528 N.Y.S.2d 531, 523 N.E.2d 818 (1988)(no abuse of discretion to decline to reopen after counsel's closing arguments but before court's jury charge); People v. Farrow, 176 A.D.2d 130, 574 N.Y.S.2d 17 (1st Dep't), appeal denied, 79 N.Y.2d 826, 580 N.Y.S.2d 207, 588 N.E.2d 105 (1991)(no abuse of discretion to decline to reopen where request was made during jury instructions); People v. Hendricks, 114 A.D.2d 510, 494 N.Y.S.2d 729 (2d Dep't 1985)(denial of defendant's request was abuse of discretion where made after defense counsel's summation but prior to prosecutor's summation).

11. People v. Olsen, 34 N.Y.2d 349, 353, 357 N.Y.S.2d 487, 490, 313 N.E.2d 782, 784 (1974). See, e.g., People v. Smith, 166 A.D.2d 385, 561 N.Y.S.2d 189 (1st Dep't 1990), aff'd, 79 N.Y.2d 779, 579 N.Y.S.2d 648, 587 N.E.2d 286 (1991)(trial court did not abuse discretion in permitting prosecutor to delay close of case in chief until after testimony of expert whose availability was delayed until after defendant's case began; defendant was apprised in advance of substance of expert's proposed testimony).

recalling of witnesses.[12]

Within each phase of the trial, as described above, the parties are free to call witnesses in the order that suits them, "subject to the general supervisory discretion of the court."[13] The examination of each witness unfolds as follows:

1. Direct examination of the witness by the party who called her;
2. Cross-examination by the opponent;
3. Redirect;
4. Recross.

The sections which follow will concentrate on the particulars of the questioning of witnesses.

Library References:

West's Key No. Digests, Witnesses ⊂⊃224–265.

The recurring theme throughout the caselaw governing order of proof is one of judicial discretion. The principle of judicial control would be codified in § 611(a) of the New York Proposed Evidence Code as follows:

(a) Control by court. The court shall exercise reasonable control over the mode and order of examining witnesses and presenting evidence so as to: (1) make the examination and presentation effective for the ascertainment of the truth; (2) avoid prolonging the trial to an unreasonable extent without any corresponding advantage to the examining party; and (3) protect witnesses from harassment, humiliation or danger. Cross-examination may be limited under paragraphs two and three of this subdivision only if the probative value of that cross-examination is substantially outweighed by the interest in limiting cross-examination.

12. Feldsberg v. Nitschke, 49 N.Y.2d 636, 643–44, 427 N.Y.S.2d 751, 755, 404 N.E.2d 1293, 1297 (1980):

Nor can it be doubted that recall of a witness for redirect examination is subject to the discretion of the court * * *. Generally, sound trial practice demands that every witness be questioned in the first instance on all relevant matters of which he has knowledge and be excused at the completion of this testimony. In this manner, the litigation is contained within reasonable limits, the adversary is aware of the evidence he will have to meet and the jury is not unnecessarily confused. Recall at a later point in the trial not only may inject untoward administrative burdens into the litigation by reopening the whole range of prior testimony, but may also unfairly disadvantage the adversary in his ability to meet the proof or unnecessarily divert the jury's attention away from the material issues of the case. In certain situations, however, the trial court may find it necessary to depart from this general rule and may do so in its discretion * * *.

See, e.g., People v. Canonico, 187 A.D.2d 267, 589 N.Y.S.2d 868 (1st Dep't), leave to appeal denied, 81 N.Y.2d 761, 594 N.Y.S.2d 723, 610 N.E.2d 396 (1992)(no abuse of discretion to preclude defendant from retaking stand after defense rested); People v. Beecher, 122 A.D.2d 407, 505 N.Y.S.2d 222 (3d Dep't 1986)(no abuse of discretion where prosecution was allowed to recall a witness after both sides had rested); People v. Frieson, 103 A.D.2d 1009, 478 N.Y.S.2d 213 (4th Dep't 1984)(no abuse of discretion to preclude defense from calling prosecution witness for further cross-examination after prosecution rested; defense made no showing that information could not have been discovered earlier).

13. People v. Parks, 41 N.Y.2d 36, 48–49, 390 N.Y.S.2d 848, 858, 359 N.E.2d 358, 368 (1976)(court has discretion to permit testimony of mentally disabled witness to be preceded by that of expert with information that will shed light on capacity and intelligence of disabled witness).

§ 611.2 New York: Form of Questioning

a. In General

"[W]ith respect to the examination of all witnesses, the scope and manner of interrogation are committed to the Trial Judge in the exercise of his responsibility to supervise and to oversee the conduct of the trial."[1] Subject to the court's discretion, the lawyers for the parties have a fair amount of leeway as to the form of questioning witnesses. The usual method for eliciting testimony from a witness is the asking of specific questions that call for answers on specific points. Narrative testimony, in which the witness is directed to a given time and place and is simply asked to state "what happened" without interruption, is an alternative that is sometimes used on direct examination. The use of narrative, however, presents certain tactical problems. The proponent must be prepared to follow up with specific questions when omissions occur. The opponent, for his part, must be alert to interdict objectionable evidence by quickly moving to strike.[2] The trial court exercises discretion regarding the extent to which narrative testimony may be used.[3]

Assuming the usual question-and-answer methodology is employed, certain types of questions may be objectionable as to form. For example, argumentative questions, such as asking the witness to characterize disputed facts, should not be used.[4] Similarly, questions that assume the truth of facts not in evidence are improper.[5] The court may circumscribe "unnecessarily repetitive" questioning.[6] Questions that

---

§ 611.2

1. Bernstein v. Bodean, 53 N.Y.2d 520, 529, 443 N.Y.S.2d 49, 53, 426 N.E.2d 741, 745 (1981).

2. See generally McCormick § 5. One of the principal advantages of the question-and-answer format is that counsel can control the order in which facts are presented and can systematically supplement the testimony with demonstrative evidence. An advantage of narrative testimony is that it gives the impression of spontaneity. Id.

3. See Watson v. State, 53 A.D.2d 798, 799, 385 N.Y.S.2d 170, 172 (3d Dep't 1976).

4. See, e.g., People v. Ellis, 94 A.D.2d 652, 652, 462 N.Y.S.2d 212, 213 (1st Dep't 1983)(prosecutor improperly asked defendant whether he thought prosecution witnesses were lying); Sturgeon v. Delaware & Hudson R.R. Corp., 2 A.D.2d 725, 725, 152 N.Y.S.2d 371, 373 (3d Dep't 1956)(improper to press expert into stating whether he agreed or disagreed with opinion of another expert). See also People v. Mackell, 47 A.D.2d 209, 220, 366 N.Y.S.2d 173, 184 (2d Dep't 1975), aff'd, 40 N.Y.2d 59, 386 N.Y.S.2d 37, 351 N.E.2d 684 (1976)(argumentative questions are improper).

5. See, e.g., Gray v. Brooklyn Heights R. Co., 175 N.Y. 448, 451–52, 67 N.E. 899, 900 (1903)(in personal injury case in which dispute centered on whether plaintiff suffered miscarriage as result of accident, improper to ask plaintiff, in effect, "How long did you continue to bleed after the miscarriage?"; question assumed fact not proved); People v. Mather, 4 Wend. (N.Y.) 229, 249 (1830)("even on cross examination it is not allowable to put a question which assumes a fact proved which is not."); Zeleznik v. Jewish Chronic Disease Hospital, 47 A.D.2d 199, 204, 366 N.Y.S.2d 163, 169 (2d Dep't 1975)(in medical malpractice case, asking expert whether "time delay" between onset of symptoms and surgery contributed to plaintiff's condition "assumed the very matter in issue," i.e., whether time lapse constituted "delay").

6. Feldsberg v. Nitschke, 49 N.Y.2d 636, 643, 427 N.Y.S.2d 751, 755, 404 N.E.2d 1293, 1297 (1980). See also People v. Johnson, 172 A.D.2d 329, 329, 568 N.Y.S.2d 611, 612 (1st Dep't), appeal denied, 78 N.Y.2d 923, 573 N.Y.S.2d 476, 577 N.E.2d 1068 (1991)(cross-examination was properly curtailed where it became repetitive); People v. Wright, 159 A.D.2d 282, 282–83, 552 N.Y.S.2d 285, 285–86 (1st Dep't), appeal denied, 76 N.Y.2d 745, 558 N.Y.S.2d 907, 557 N.E.2d 1203 (1990)(cross-examination was properly curtailed where defense coun-

§ 611.2 WITNESSES Ch. 6

serve merely to harass, humiliate, embarrass or endanger the witness are also subject to the court's control.[7] The propriety of leading questions is discussed below.

Regardless of whether a question is in proper form, an answer that is nonresponsive may provide the basis for a motion to strike the answer.[8]

b. Leading Questions

A leading question is one which suggests the answer that the questioner wants to elicit, as, for example, "Did the defendant, holding a four-inch knife, lunge at the victim while her back was turned?"[9] If a suggestive question asks for a "yes" or "no" answer or specifies the details of an event and then asks whether that is how it happened, the question is likely to be characterized as leading.[10] Form, alone, however, is not always determinative; the content, context and circumstances, including the tone and inflection of counsel's voice, play a role in evaluating suggestiveness.[11]

The general rule is that leading questions may not be used during the direct examination of a witness. This rule is explained by the likelihood that a witness will be friendly, or at least nonhostile, toward the party who called her and therefore susceptible to mouthing the version of events sought to be proved by that party.[12] Thus, to help

sel asked "essentially the same questions"). But see § 608.2, at note 17, supra (cross-examiner may "press" witness to admit prior bad acts that reflect adversely on credibility).

7. See § 611.3, at notes 30–32, infra. Cf. People v. Stanard, 42 N.Y.2d 74, 84, 396 N.Y.S.2d 825, 831, 365 N.E.2d 857, 863, cert. denied, 434 U.S. 986, 98 S.Ct. 615, 54 L.Ed.2d 481 (1977)(in criminal case, factors identified in text must be balanced against defendant's right to cross-examine prosecution witnesses).

8. See, e.g., People v. Rivera, 172 A.D.2d 1059, 1060, 569 N.Y.S.2d 316, 317 (4th Dep't 1991)(unresponsive answer should have been stricken, but error was harmless). Compare Helmken v. City of New York, 90 App.Div. 135, 136, 85 N.Y.S. 1048, 1049 (1st Dep't 1904)(in response to question calling for "yes" or "no" answer, witness responded with speculative answer containing inadmissible evidence; answer should have been stricken on motion), with People v. Vincent, 34 A.D.2d 705, 706, 309 N.Y.S.2d 690, 692–93 (3d Dep't), aff'd, 27 N.Y.2d 964, 318 N.Y.S.2d 498, 267 N.E.2d 273 (1970), appeal denied, 28 N.Y.2d 583, 319 N.Y.S.2d 1029, 268 N.E.2d 332 (1971)(question was so broad that striking of answer as nonresponsive would have been inappropriate).

9. See People v. Mather, 4 Wend. (N.Y.) 229, 247 (1830)("A question is leading which puts into a witness' mouth the words that are to be echoed back, or plainly suggest the answer which the party wishes to get from him.").

10. Id. See also Downs v. N.Y. Central R.R. Co., 47 N.Y. 83, 87–88 (1871) (leading question: "Did he state on that occasion * * * that the way the accident happened was, that he was standing on the threshold of the car and that the cars were jerked up and threw him under the train and that they ran over him, or in substance that?"). See generally McCormick § 6, at 17–18 ("It is sometimes supposed that a question which can be answered yes or no is by that fact marked as leading, and the beginner may seek refuge in the form of a neutral alternative ('State whether or not * * *') to escape the charge of leading. But quite often the former kind of question will not be leading and equally often the latter kind will be. The whole issue is whether an ordinary man would get the impression that the questioner desired one answer rather than another.").

11. Enfield, "Direct Examination of Witnesses," 15 Ark.L.Rev. 32, 35 (1960)("an otherwise unobjectionable question may become leading merely by the tone or inflection of voice in which it is asked").

12. See Denroche, "Leading Questions," 6 Crim.L.Q. 21, 22 (1963)(three reasons for disallowing leading questions on direct are:

insure that the fact-finder hears the facts as they are known by the witness, not by counsel, leading questions are generally prohibited on direct.[13] On timely objection, such questions should be rephrased. Conversely, on cross-examination a witness usually is of an uncooperative frame of mind and is more likely to resist the suggestions of the cross-examiner. Therefore, leading questions ordinarily are allowed on cross-examination.[14]

With respect to direct examination, there are four exceptions to the prohibition on leading questions. First, in the interest of trial efficiency, a leading question may be used to focus the attention of the witness on a particular time, place or matter.[15] Second, a leading question may be permissible, within limits, in an attempt to jog the memory of a witness whose recollection has been exhausted.[16] Third, leading questions may be the only expedient means of examining a child or a witness with diminished mental capacity.[17] Finally, a witness who demonstrates reluctance, unwillingness or hostility may be examined, in the court's discretion, with leading questions as if on cross-examination.[18] When a party is compelled by the necessities of his case to call an opposing party to the stand, hostility is assumed and leading questions should be

"[F]irst, that the witness is presumed to have a bias in favour of the party calling him; secondly that the party calling a witness, knowing what that witness may prove, might by leading bring out only that portion of the witness' story favourable to his own case; and, thirdly, that a witness, intending to be entirely fair and honest, might assent to a leading question which did not express his real meaning").

13. See, e.g., People v. Mather, 4 Wend. (N.Y.) 229, 247–48 (1830).

14. See McCormick § 20. In some instances, however, counsel may be "cross-examining" a friendly witness, such as his own client, who has been called to the stand by the opponent, thus reversing the usual assumptions and calling for disallowance of leading questions. 3 Wigmore § 773, at 166.

15. People v. Mather, 4 Wend. (N.Y.) 229, 247–48 (1830); Cope v. Sibley, 12 Barb. (N.Y.) 521, 524–25 (1850). See also Sloan v. New York Central R.R. Co., 45 N.Y. 125, 127–28 (1871)(leading question may be used to elicit from witness A proof of prior inconsistent statement made by witness B).

16. Cheeney v. Arnold, 18 Barb. (N.Y.) 434, 439 (1854), aff'd, 15 N.Y. 345 (1857). See also O'Hagan v. Dillon, 76 N.Y. 170, 173 (1879).

17. See, e.g., People v. Tyrrell, 101 A.D.2d 946, 475 N.Y.S.2d 937 (3d Dep't 1984)(eight-year-old victim of sex crime);

People v. Yarusevich, 81 A.D.2d 528, 438 N.Y.S.2d 94 (1st Dep't 1981)("mentally slow" witness); People v. Greenhagen, 78 A.D.2d 964, 966, 433 N.Y.S.2d 683, 685–86 (4th Dep't 1980)("in view of [children's] age and the intimate and embarrassing nature of the crimes, the court did not abuse its discretion in permitting the prosecutor to use leading questions to examine them"); Cheeney v. Arnold, 18 Barb. (N.Y.) 434, 438–39 (1854), aff'd, 15 N.Y. 345 (1857)(visually impaired witness, where issue involved contents of documents).

18. Becker v. Koch, 104 N.Y. 394, 401, 10 N.E. 701, 703 (1887)("An adverse witness may be cross-examined, and leading questions may be put to him by the party calling him, for the very sensible and sufficient reason that he is adverse and that the danger arising from such a mode of examination by the party calling a friendly or unbiased witness does not exist"); People v. Rozanski, 209 A.D.2d 1018, 1018–19, 619 N.Y.S.2d 441, 442 (4th Dep't 1994), appeal denied, 84 N.Y.2d 1038, 623 N.Y.S.2d 194, 647 N.E.2d 466 (1995)(leading questions were proper during prosecutor's direct examination of defendant's wife, who was "patently reluctant and hostile"); People v. Arhin, 203 A.D.2d 62, 62, 609 N.Y.S.2d 604, 605 (1st Dep't), appeal denied, 83 N.Y.2d 908, 614 N.Y.S.2d 390, 637 N.E.2d 281 (1994)(court had discretion to permit prosecutor to lead complaining witness (defendant's wife) "given the complainant's reluctance to testify").

allowed as a matter of course.[19] As to other witnesses, the trial judge must determine whether the witness is sufficiently reluctant or hostile to permit the direct examination to proceed with leading questions.[20]

A trial judge's "sufferance" of an occasional leading question in inappropriate circumstances will seldom, by itself, serve as a basis for reversal.[21] An excessive use of leading questions, however, may contribute to the overall unfairness of a trial, thus producing a reversal.[22]

Library References:

West's Key No. Digests, Witnesses ⚖︎224–265.

§ 611.3 New York: Cross–Examination

a. In General

Cross-examination generally serves two purposes: (1) to test and attack the credibility of the witness; and (2) to elicit additional information relating to matters about which the witness testified on direct.[1] Wigmore described cross-examination as "beyond any doubt the greatest legal engine ever invented for the discovery of truth."[2] Cross-examina-

---

19. Jordan v. Parrinello, 144 A.D.2d 540, 541, 534 N.Y.S.2d 686, 687 (2d Dep't 1988)("[W]hen an adverse party is called as a witness, it may be assumed that such adverse party is a hostile witness, and, in the discretion of the court, direct examination may assume the nature of cross-examination by the use of leading questions."); Cornwell v. Cleveland, 44 A.D.2d 891, 891, 355 N.Y.S.2d 679, 681 (4th Dep't 1974) (trial court should have allowed use of leading questions when defendant was called by plaintiff as part of plaintiff's case); Arlene W. v. Robert D., 36 A.D.2d 455, 456, 324 N.Y.S.2d 333, 334 (4th Dep't 1971)("A party who calls as a witness an adverse party * * * should be permitted to lead and cross-examine him, he being obviously a hostile witness.").

20. See, e.g., People v. Mather, 4 Wend. (N.Y.) 229, 247 (1830)("If it is apparent that the witness is in the interest of the adverse party, the court will be justified in going so far as to permit the direct examination to take the character of a cross-examination."). See also cases cited in note 18 supra.

Proposed New York Evidence Code § 611(c) would codify current practice with respect to leading questions as follows:

(c) **Leading questions.** Leading questions should not be used on the direct examination of a witness except as may be necessary to develop the witness's testimony. Ordinarily, leading questions should be permitted on cross-examination. When a party calls a hostile witness, an adverse party, or a witness identified with an adverse party, or when a witness turns hostile, examination may be by leading questions.

21. See Downs v. N.Y. Central R.R. Co., 47 N.Y. 83, 88 (1871)(trial court had discretion to "suffer a question, leading in form, to be put, and the judgment will not be reversed for an error in that respect"); Cope v. Sibley, 12 Barb. (N.Y.) 521, 523–24 (1850)("[N]o one, I apprehend, would contend, even admitting the questions to be clearly leading, that such decision would be good cause of a motion for a new trial, or of reversing the judgment. Such questions are, of necessity, left very much to the discretion of the judge at the trial, and unless it appears that he has abused the discretion, so that injustice has been done, his decision will not be disturbed."). Of course, if the evidence elicited by the leading question is otherwise inadmissible, reversal may occur for that reason. Downs v. N.Y. Central R.R. Co., supra, at 88.

22. See, e.g., People v. Mackell, 47 A.D.2d 209, 220, 366 N.Y.S.2d 173, 184 (2d Dep't 1975), aff'd, 40 N.Y.2d 59, 386 N.Y.S.2d 37, 351 N.E.2d 684 (1976).

§ 611.3

1. McCormick § 29. See text at notes 16–28 infra. See People v. Chin, 67 N.Y.2d 22, 28, 499 N.Y.S.2d 638, 643, 490 N.E.2d 505, 510 (1986) ("cross-examiner may delve deep in order to attack credibility and present an alternate view of the facts").

2. 5 Wigmore § 1367, at 32. See also Davis v. Alaska, 415 U.S. 308, 316, 94 S.Ct. 1105, 1110, 39 L.Ed.2d 347, 353

tion is considered so fundamental to the adversary system of trial that it has assumed the status of a right.[3] Furthermore, in criminal cases, cross-examination is a key ingredient of the defendant's sixth amendment right to confront the witnesses against him.[4]

If the opponent is deprived of the opportunity to cross-examine through no fault of her own, an appropriate remedy is the striking of the witness' direct testimony.[5] This is the rule that is applied when the witness unjustifiably refuses to undergo cross-examination or becomes unavailable for cross-examination as a result of death or illness.[6] On the other hand, if a portion of the cross-examination has been completed before the witness becomes unavailable, it may be possible, depending on the circumstances, to preserve that portion of the direct testimony to which the cross-examination relates.[7] Furthermore, the right of cross-examination may be waived if the party refuses to accept a mistrial and proceeds with the trial despite the witness' refusal to submit to cross-examination.[8]

A witness' invocation of her privilege against self-incrimination is another situation in which cross-examination may be stymied, thereby potentially requiring the striking of direct testimony.[9] In *People v. Chin*,[10] the Court of Appeals summarized the state of the law on this point in the context of a criminal defendant's right of confrontation: "Decisional law generally distinguishes between invoking the privilege on matters that are collateral to the direct examination, which does not require the striking of direct testimony * * * and invoking the privilege

(1974)("Cross-examination is the principal means by which the believability of a witness and the truth of his testimony are tested.").

3. Friedel v. Board of Regents of the University of New York, 296 N.Y. 347, 352, 73 N.E.2d 545, 547 (1947)("Cross-examination of adverse witnesses is a matter of right in every trial of a disputed issue of fact."). See also N.Y.Crim.Proc.Law § 60.15(1)(prosecutor and defendant each "may cross-examine every witness called by the other party").

4. Kentucky v. Stincer, 482 U.S. 730, 736, 107 S.Ct. 2658, 2662, 96 L.Ed.2d 631, 641 (1987); Davis v. Alaska, 415 U.S. 308, 315–16, 94 S.Ct. 1105, 1109–10, 39 L.Ed.2d 347, 353–54 (1974); People v. Chin, 67 N.Y.2d 22, 27, 499 N.Y.S.2d 638, 643, 490 N.E.2d 505, 510 (1986).

5. People v. Cole, 43 N.Y. 508, 512–13 (1871). It may be necessary in some cases to declare a mistrial.

6. Id. (prosecution witness became ill immediately after direct examination and remained unavailable). Diocese of Buffalo v. McCarthy, 91 A.D.2d 213, 220, 458 N.Y.S.2d 764, 768 (4th Dep't), appeal denied, 59 N.Y.2d 605, 466 N.Y.S.2d 1025, 453 N.E.2d 550 (1983)(without excuse, witness failed to return to court after direct examination).

7. Matter of Mezger's Estate, 154 Misc. 633, 636–38, 278 N.Y.S. 669, 673–74 (Surr.Ct.Monroe Co.1935)(partially-completed cross-examination may be adequate to permit some portions of direct testimony to stand; in circumstances of case, however, all of direct testimony stricken). See also Schwartz v. 38 Town Associates, 187 A.D.2d 377, 589 N.Y.S.2d 487 (1st Dep't 1992), leave to appeal dismissed, 82 N.Y.2d 845, 606 N.Y.S.2d 594, 627 N.E.2d 516 (1993)(direct testimony stricken in whole where witness failed to return to court after cross-examination "had barely begun").

8. Cf. People v. Chan, 110 A.D.2d 158, 493 N.Y.S.2d 778 (2d Dep't), appeal denied, 66 N.Y.2d 920, 498 N.Y.S.2d 1035, 489 N.E.2d 780 (1985)(waiver occurred where defendant who complained of inadequate cross-examination declined order of mistrial).

9. See, e.g., People v. Schneider, 36 N.Y.2d 708, 366 N.Y.S.2d 419, 325 N.E.2d 877 (1975), adopting dissenting opinion in 44 A.D.2d 845, 356 N.Y.S.2d 214 (2d Dep't 1974); People v. Acomb, 87 A.D.2d 1, 7–9, 450 N.Y.S.2d 632, 636–37 (4th Dep't 1982).

10. 67 N.Y.2d 22, 499 N.Y.S.2d 638, 490 N.E.2d 505 (1986).

on matters directly related to the direct examination, which entitles the defendant to have the direct testimony stricken."[11] The troublesome cases are those in which the cross-examination is on matters relating solely to credibility. Some forms of impeachment, such as prior bad acts of the witness, may very well be collateral,[12] which means that the direct testimony may stand despite the witness' refusal on cross-examination to answer questions about those acts.[13] On the other hand, facts relating to the witness' bias or hostility, which also bear on credibility, are considered noncollateral.[14] Whether the witness' invocation of privilege as to such matters will require a striking of the direct testimony will depend on whether the defendant has had an adequate opportunity to test the witness' credibility in other ways: "If bias or interest has been fully explored through other means * * *, or the precluded area involved cumulative matter already presented * * *, there generally has been no infringement of the right of confrontation."[15]

b. Scope of Cross–Examination

As discussed in preceding sections of this chapter, a principal function of cross-examination is to elicit facts that tend to impeach the credibility of the witness.[16] So long as such facts fall within accepted standards of relevance on the issue of credibility, and subject to the trial court's discretion, it matters not that the cross-examiner covers "new" matters that were not touched upon during the witness' direct examination. Beyond impeachment of credibility, however, the scope of cross-examination, as a general rule, is restricted to development of matters about which the witness testified on direct. The New York cases are not entirely clear on this point, but the foregoing rule appears to be the accepted practice in civil actions.[17]

---

11. Id. at 28, 499 N.Y.S.2d at 643, 490 N.E.2d at 510.

12. See § 608.2, at notes 14–17, supra.

13. See, e.g., People v. Patterson, 165 A.D.2d 886, 560 N.Y.S.2d 357 (2d Dep't), appeal denied, 76 N.Y.2d 989, 563 N.Y.S.2d 778, 565 N.E.2d 527 (1990)(error to strike direct testimony of witness where witness refused to respond to questions about tax returns, a collateral matter relating solely to credibility).

14. See § 607.6, at notes 24–27, supra.

15. 67 N.Y.2d at 29, 499 N.Y.S.2d at 644, 490 N.E.2d at 511. In Chin, the trial court was held not to have abused its discretion in declining to strike the direct testimony of a key prosecution witness. Although the witness invoked privilege in response to cross-examination concerning misconduct probative of his motive to favor the prosecution, he had been fully cross-examined as to all matters to which he testified on direct, and "all collateral facts relevant to the witness' bias, credibility, and motive were established through the cross examination of [the witness] and through the testimony of other witnesses." Id. at 32, 499 N.Y.S.2d at 646, 490 N.E.2d at 513.

16. See §§ 607.1 through 610.2 supra.

17. See, e.g., Grcic v. City of New York, 139 A.D.2d 621, 626, 527 N.Y.S.2d 263, 267 (2d Dep't), motion denied, 73 N.Y.2d 702, 536 N.Y.S.2d 743, 533 N.E.2d 673 (1988)(trial court did not abuse discretion when it restricted cross-examination of plaintiff's treating physicians to matters raised by them on direct examination); Hall v. Allemannia Fire Insurance Co. of Pittsburgh, 175 App.Div. 289, 292, 161 N.Y.S. 1091, 1093 (4th Dep't 1916)(trial court properly disallowed cross-examination into issues not covered on direct). A case for broader treatment of the scope of cross-examination might be based on a cryptic statement in Langley v. Wadsworth, 99 N.Y. 61, 1 N.E. 106 (1885), that cross-examination may be pursued as "matter of right" if it "relates either to facts in issue or relevant facts." Id. at 63, 1 N.E. at 107.

The reason for the rule relates to orderliness in the presentation of evidence: "The rule that the scope of cross-examination must be limited to that of the direct examination exists chiefly to prevent the cross-examiner from cluttering up the direct examiner's case with unfavorable and extraneous facts when he could make the witness his own."[18] A defendant, for example, should not be allowed to begin proving an affirmative defense during cross-examination of a witness called by the plaintiff if the facts underlying such defense are unrelated to anything the witness testified about on direct. To say that the scope of cross-examination is limited to matters covered on direct, however, should not be interpreted to mean that the cross-examiner is confined "to the precise details brought out on direct examination."[19] The "implications" of an event or transaction may be pursued[20] as well as an explanation and clarification of matters only partially disclosed on direct.[21]

Cross-examination may sometimes cross over into entirely new matters, however, either because no objection is made by the adversary or the proponent requests and is granted judicial permission to do so. A potentially serious consequence of going into new matters is that the cross-examiner makes the witness his own, thereby hampering the ability to impeach the witness[22] and precluding the use of leading questions.[23]

In criminal cases, the New York courts are not of one mind. The Appellate Division, Second Department, has declared, "[I]t is well-settled that in a criminal case a party may prove through cross-examination any relevant proposition, regardless of the scope of the direct examination."[24] On the other hand, the First Department suggested that the scope of cross-examination is restricted to the same subject matter as the direct, but observed that "this rule is often relaxed in criminal proceedings where the testimony would be material to major issues in the case."[25] Other criminal cases imply that the scope of cross is limited to that of direct by holding that the cross-examiner makes the witness his own when cross-examination goes into new matters.[26] The Court of Appeals

18. People v. Hadden, 95 A.D.2d 725, 725–26, 464 N.Y.S.2d 134, 135 (1st Dep't 1983). See also McCormick § 27, at 93–94.

19. Crawford v. Nilan, 264 App.Div. 46, 51, 35 N.Y.S.2d 33, 37–38 (3d Dep't 1942), rev'd on other grounds, 289 N.Y. 444, 46 N.E.2d 512 (1943).

20. Id. (witness who testified on direct that he had been in automobile at time of accident could be asked what he understood to be the intended destination).

21. People v. Ayala, 194 A.D.2d 547, 598 N.Y.S.2d 318 (2d Dep't 1993).

22. Bennett v. Crescent Athletic–Hamilton Club, 270 N.Y. 456, 458, 1 N.E.2d 963, 964 (1936).

23. People ex rel. Phelps v. Court of Oyer and Terminer of the County of New York, 83 N.Y. 436, 459–60 (1881).

24. People v. Kennedy, 70 A.D.2d 181, 186, 420 N.Y.S.2d 23, 26 (2d Dep't 1979).

25. People v. Hadden, 95 A.D.2d 725, 726, 464 N.Y.S.2d 134, 135 (1st Dep't 1983). See also People v. Fowler, 46 A.D.2d 838, 839, 361 N.Y.S.2d 408, 409 (3d Dep't 1974), aff'd, 37 N.Y.2d 100, 371 N.Y.S.2d 471, 332 N.E.2d 338, cert. denied, 423 U.S. 950, 96 S.Ct. 372, 46 L.Ed.2d 287 (1975) (trial court did not abuse discretion in allowing prosecution to cross-examine a defense witness on matters relating to narcotics sale that were not brought out on direct examination).

26. People v. Maerling, 64 N.Y.2d 134, 141, 485 N.Y.S.2d 23, 25–26, 474 N.E.2d 231, 233 (1984)(when defense counsel's cross-examination of police officer exceeded scope of direct examination, "defense coun-

has not thoroughly explored the issue in over 100 years.[27] The majority approach elsewhere is to confine the scope of cross-examination to that of direct in both civil and criminal cases, subject to the court's discretionary authority to allow cross-examination into new matter.[28]

c. Judicial Discretion

An overarching rule is that "once the right [of cross-examination] has been accorded, the extent of cross-examination rests largely in the discretion of the tribunal, whose exercise thereof is not reviewable unless abused."[29] In exercising her supervisory role, the trial judge may curtail cross-examination that is repetitive or cumulative, overly collateral, marginally relevant, abusive, harassing, embarrassing or otherwise prejudicial.[30] The trial court's discretion is circumscribed in criminal cases, however, by the defendant's constitutional right to confront prosecution witnesses.[31] Legitimate concerns about protecting the witness and the trial process must then be balanced against the extent to which the sought-after testimony is material to the issue of guilt or innocence.[32]

---

sel agreed to take [him] as her own witness and to be bound by the rules governing direct examination"); People v. Dolan, 172 A.D.2d 68, 75–76, 576 N.Y.S.2d 901, 905 (3d Dep't 1991), appeal denied, 79 N.Y.2d 946, 583 N.Y.S.2d 200, 592 N.E.2d 808 (1992)(when defendant's cross-examination of police officers exceeded scope of prosecutor's direct examination, officers became defense witnesses).

27. In People v. Tice, 131 N.Y. 651, 30 N.E. 494 (1892), the court held that a prosecutor, without violating the defendant's privilege against self-incrimination, could freely question him during cross-examination about matters relevant to the case even though the defendant had not raised them during his direct testimony. The court stated that "it is the constant practice in civil and criminal trials to permit the plaintiff or the people to fortify their own case by facts elicited on cross-examination of the witnesses for the defense. The matter is subject to the regulation and discretion of the trial judge." Id. at 658. The cases cited in notes 25–26 supra suggest that the practice may not be so "constant."

28. See McCormick § 21, at 83. Federal Rule of Evidence 611(b), which adopted the majority rule, is discussed in § 611.5, at notes 15–17, infra. Proposed New York Evidence Code § 611(b), which is identical to the Federal Rule, would provide as follows:

(b) Scope of cross-examination. Cross-examination should be limited to the subject matter of the direct examination and matters affecting the credibility of the witness. The court may, in the exercise of discretion, permit inquiry into additional matters as if on direct examination.

Advocates of a rule of "wide-open" cross-examination argue that fact-finding is promoted by allowing a witness to testify to all that she knows about the issues when initially called to the stand and that wide-open cross-examination is easy to administer. McCormick § 27, at 94–95; 6 Wigmore § 1888.

29. Friedel v. Board of Regents of University of New York, 296 N.Y. 347, 352, 73 N.E.2d 545, 548 (1947). See also People v. Schwartzman, 24 N.Y.2d 241, 244, 299 N.Y.S.2d 817, 820, 247 N.E.2d 642, 644, cert. denied, 396 U.S. 846, 90 S.Ct. 103, 24 L.Ed.2d 96 (1969)("The nature and extent of cross-examination is subject to the sound discretion of the Trial Judge.")

30. See Bernstein v. Bodean, 53 N.Y.2d 520, 529, 443 N.Y.S.2d 49, 53, 426 N.E.2d 741, 745 (1981); Friedel v. Board of Regents of University of New York, 296 N.Y. 347, 352, 73 N.E.2d 545, 548 (1947); Gutierrez v. City of New York, 205 A.D.2d 425, 427, 613 N.Y.S.2d 627, 629 (1st Dep't 1994). Proposed New York Evidence Code § 611(a) would codify existing judicial standards regarding the court's discretionary control over cross-examination. See § 611.1, at note 11, supra.

31. Kentucky v. Stincer, 482 U.S. 730, 737–39, 107 S.Ct. 2658, 2663–64, 96 L.Ed.2d 631, 642–43 (1987); Davis v. Alaska, 415 U.S. 308, 316, 94 S.Ct. 1105, 1110, 39 L.Ed.2d 347, 353–54 (1974); People v. Hudy, 73 N.Y.2d 40, 57, 538 N.Y.S.2d 197, 207, 535 N.E.2d 250, 260 (1988).

32. People v. Stanard, 42 N.Y.2d 74, 83–84, 396 N.Y.S.2d 825, 831–32, 365 N.E.2d

d. Voir Dire of the Witness

As noted in § 611.1 *supra*, cross-examination ordinarily occurs only after a witness' direct examination has been completed. In certain instances, however, direct testimony may be interrupted, in the court's discretion, by a form of cross-examination known as "voir dire" of the witness.[33] Such voir dire may be requested when the opponent wishes to challenge the foundation for the introduction (or exclusion) of evidence. Examples include questions concerning the qualifications of an expert witness, competency of a witness, the facts upon which a claim of privilege is based, and authentication of evidence.[34] If the court permits such voir dire, the questioning obviously should be confined to the sufficiency of the foundation. Depending on the nature of the evidence, it may be appropriate to conduct the voir dire outside the jury's presence.[35] If the voir dire exposes a fatal defect in the foundation, inadmissible evidence can be excluded without ever coming to the fact-finder's attention.

Library References:

West's Key No. Digests, Witnesses ⇔266–284.

§ 611.4 New York: Redirect and Recross Examination

Both redirect and recross examination are generally intended to allow a party to meet new matters that were brought out during the immediately preceding examination.[1] Redirect examination, for exam-

---

857, 863, cert. denied, 434 U.S. 986, 98 S.Ct. 615, 54 L.Ed.2d 481 (1977). Compare People v. Ashner, 190 A.D.2d 238, 246–48, 597 N.Y.S.2d 975, 980–82 (2d Dep't 1993)(defendant's interest in exposing prosecution witness' financial motive to commit crime with which defendant was charged outweighed state's interest in protecting witness from embarrassing questions), with People v. Tai, 145 Misc.2d 599, 603–10, 547 N.Y.S.2d 989, 993–97 (Sup.Ct.N.Y.Co.1989)(current name and address of prosecution witness, a confidential informant, could be withheld where witness' life was endangered; court required prosecutor to disclose witness' prior criminal record to defendant to facilitate alternative impeachment).

33. See generally Graham § 611.4, at 523, and § 611.9; Mueller and Kirkpatrick § 6.21.

34. See, e.g., Halloran v. Virginia Chemicals, Inc., 41 N.Y.2d 386, 392, 393 N.Y.S.2d 341, 346, 361 N.E.2d 991, 996 (1977)(proponent of evidence of person's habit must show sufficient number of instances of relevant conduct to infer habit); Archer v. N.Y., N.H. & H.R.R. Co., 106 N.Y. 589, 603, 13 N.E. 318, 324 (1887)(accuracy of photograph); People v. Laws, 203 A.D.2d 34, 610 N.Y.S.2d 196 (1st Dep't 1994)(qualifications of expert witness); Finn v. Morgan, 46 A.D.2d 229, 235, 362 N.Y.S.2d 292, 300 (4th Dep't 1974)(basis for exception to attorney-client privilege).

35. See, e.g., People v. Mitchell, 58 N.Y.2d 368, 373–75, 461 N.Y.S.2d 267, 270, 448 N.E.2d 121, 124 (1983)(jury excused during voir dire of witnesses concerning circumstances surrounding allegedly privileged communications).

§ 611.4

1. People v. Buchanan, 145 N.Y. 1, 24, 39 N.E. 846, 853 (1895)("The re-examination of a witness is, largely, in the discretion of the court. The proper limitations upon it are that it shall relate to the subject-matter of the cross-examination and bear upon the question at issue. He cannot be asked as to new matter."); People v. Bethune, 105 A.D.2d 262, 269, 484 N.Y.S.2d 577, 583 (2d Dep't 1984)("once the parties have proceeded to redirect and recross-examination, inquiry as of right is limited to new matters brought out on the preceding examination, and the scope of examination otherwise rests within the sound discretion of the trial court"). Bethune illustrates the usual operation of the rule. On cross-examination of an expert on bite-mark identification evidence, defendant conducted a demonstration to question the feasibility of the victim's biting of the defendant. On

ple, provides an opportunity to rehabilitate a witness who was impeached on cross-examination.[2] It has been held that a witness has a right to explain or clarify new matters elicited on cross-examination and to give a full account of a transaction or conversation only partially disclosed on cross.[3]

In *People v. Melendez*,[4] the Court of Appeals described the scope of entitlement to redirect in terms of the extent to which the cross-examiner "opened the door" to "matters not touched upon during the direct examination."[5] As to limits on such redirect, the court observed that the raising of new issues on cross-examination does not permit the introduction of "all evidence, no matter how remote or tangential to the subject matter opened up."[6] Door opening "does not provide an independent basis for introducing new evidence on redirect; nor does it afford a party the opportunity to place evidence before the jury that should have been brought out on direct examination."[7] Any additional evidence on redirect should be confined to that which was made "necessary" by the cross-examination.[8]

---

redirect, the prosecutor simply confirmed that the expert's opinion had not changed as a result of the demonstration. Thus, on recross examination, the defendant was properly precluded from questioning the expert about his ability to evaluate bite marks that were over two years old because the age factor had not been raised on redirect. 105 A.D.2d at 269, 484 N.Y.S.2d at 583.

2. See § 607.5, at notes 17–22 and 29–48, supra.

3. People v. Melendez, 55 N.Y.2d 445, 451, 449 N.Y.S.2d 946, 949, 434 N.E.2d 1324, 1327–28 (1982). The Melendez court provided the following illustrations of permissible redirect:

[A]pparent inconsistencies or contradictions in a witness' statements or acts brought out on cross-examination to discredit his testimony may be reconciled on redirect by relating to the jury the relevant surrounding circumstances. * * * Similarly, where cross-examination raises the inference that the witness' testimony was the product of a recent fabrication, a party on redirect can refute this allegation either by introducing consistent statements made by the witness at a time when there was no motive to lie or by having the witness explain why the information was not disclosed earlier. * * * In addition, in situations where only a part of a statement has been brought out on cross-examination, the other parts may be introduced on redirect examination for the purpose of explaining or clarifying the statement.

Id. at 451–52, 449 N.Y.S.2d at 950, 434 N.E.2d at 1328. See also People v. Buchanan, 145 N.Y. 1, 24, 39 N.E. 846, 853 (1895)(witness "may be questioned to show the meaning of his expressions, or of his motive in using them")(dictum); People v. Anderson, 184 A.D.2d 1005, 584 N.Y.S.2d 349 (4th Dep't), appeal denied, 80 N.Y.2d 926, 589 N.Y.S.2d 854, 603 N.E.2d 959 (1992)(in rape case, defendant elicited from complainant's mother on cross-examination that daughter did not tell her that defendant "raped" her or "had sex" with her; on redirect, mother was permitted to relate that daughter told her defendant "entered her").

4. 55 N.Y.2d 445, 449 N.Y.S.2d 946, 434 N.E.2d 1324 (1982).

5. Id. at 451, 449 N.Y.S.2d at 949, 434 N.E.2d at 1327.

6. Id. at 452, 449 N.Y.S.2d at 950, 434 N.E.2d at 1328. See also People v. Zigouras, 163 N.Y. 250, 256, 57 N.E. 465, 466 (1900)(although trial court may not entirely preclude explanation of new matter raised on cross-examination, "the range in details to which the re-examination may extend should rest largely in the discretion of the court, to the end that immaterial issues may not arise").

7. 55 N.Y.2d at 452, 449 N.Y.S.2d at 950, 434 N.E. at 1328.

8. Id. The issue in Melendez arose because the defendant, on cross-examination of an arresting officer, asked whether the officer had also considered another individual to be a suspect. On redirect, the prosecutor elicited detailed hearsay information upon which the officer based his conclusion that both the defendant and the other individual were the perpetrators. This went too far, said the Court of Appeals. While the officer should have been allowed on

Aside from new matters as to which a right of further examination exists, the extent of reexamination of witnesses lies in the "sound discretion of the trial court."[9]

Library References:

West's Key No. Digests, Witnesses ⃕285–291.

§ 611.5 Federal: Mode and Order of Interrogation and Presentation

a. Order of Trial

In federal practice, the rules governing order of trial and order and mode of examination of witnesses are generally the same as under New York law, as set out in §§ 611.1–611.4 *supra*.[1] Federal Rule of Evidence 611(a) essentially codifies a long-standing tradition of judicial control over the presentation of evidence.[2] The rule states:

> **(a) Control by court.** The court shall exercise reasonable control over the mode and order of interrogating witnesses and presenting evidence so as to (1) make the interrogation and presentation effective for the ascertainment of the truth, (2) avoid needless consumption of time, and (3) protect witnesses from harassment or undue embarrassment.

Within this framework, conventional rules of trial practice are generally applied by federal courts. Thus, for example, a plaintiff/prosecutor's rebuttal case generally is restricted to new matters raised during the defense.[3] Whether a party may reopen her case[4] or recall witnesses[5] lies within the court's discretion. Similarly, a court has discretion to

redirect to amplify the basis for his suspicions as to the other individual, it was error to permit the prosecutor "to explore the entire ambit of the officer's investigation, including all information connecting the defendant with the homicide." Id. at 453, 449 N.Y.S.2d at 950, 434 N.E.2d at 1328.

9. Id. at 451, 449 N.Y.S.2d at 949, 434 N.E.2d at 1327. See also note 1 supra.

§ 611.5

1. A detailed exposition of the order and mode of presenting evidence in federal trials can be found in Graham §§ 611.1–611.13.

2. See Advisory Committee's Note, Fed. R.Evid. 611 ("Item (1) restates in broad terms the power and obligation of the judge as developed under common law principles."). In an early pre-Rules case, the Second Circuit observed: "[The court] has a right to determine the order in which evidence shall be introduced by the parties, the time and mode of examining the witness, the form and propriety of the questions, the manner in which questions may be put, and the extent to which the witness may be examined, especially with respect to collateral matters." Fire Association of Philadelphia v. Oneida County Macaroni Co., 294 F. 633, 639 (2d Cir.1923).

3. Weiss v. Chrysler Motors Corp., 515 F.2d 449, 457–59 (2d Cir.1975). See also United States v. Vivero, 413 F.2d 971, 972 (2d Cir.1969), cert. denied, 396 U.S. 1017, 90 S.Ct. 583, 24 L.Ed.2d 509 (1970)(rebuttal evidence with respect to collateral matters is discretionary with trial judge).

4. See, e.g., Air Et Chaleur, S.A. v. Janeway, 757 F.2d 489, 495 (2d Cir.1985)(trial court's discretionary decision to deny defendant's motion to reopen case was not cause for reversal in absence of surprise regarding issue raised by plaintiff and offer of proof as to additional evidence that would have been presented if reopening had been granted). See also United States v. Rodriguez, 43 F.3d 117, 125 (5th Cir.1995).

5. See, e.g., United States v. Rivera, 971 F.2d 876, 886 (2d Cir.1992).

§ 611.5   WITNESSES   Ch. 6

allow witnesses to be called out of order.[6] Rule 611(a)(2) explicitly allows the court to curb "needlessly" time-consuming evidence, but the imposition of arbitrary time limits has been criticized.[7]

b. Form of Questioning

Rule 611(a) confers substantial discretion on the courts to allow (or restrict) the various forms of questioning that the litigants may wish to utilize. Narrative questioning, for example, is permissible as an alternative to the usual question-and-answer format.[8] The trial court may, of course, restrict questions that are argumentative, misleading, unintelligible, repetitive and the like.[9] Furthermore, Rule 611(a)(3) explicitly provides for protection of witnesses from "harassment or undue embarrassment."

Leading questions are regulated by Rule 611(c), which provides as follows:

> **(c) Leading questions.** Leading questions should not be used on the direct examination of a witness except as may be necessary to develop the witness' testimony. Ordinarily leading questions should be permitted on cross-examination. When a party calls a hostile witness, an adverse party, or a witness identified with an adverse party, interrogation may be by leading questions.

As under New York law, leading questions generally are disallowed on direct examination, subject to four exceptions: (1) for preliminary and introductory matters;[10] (2) to assist in the elicitation of facts from children and others with diminished mental capacity;[11] (3) to refresh a witness' recollection;[12] and (4) as a means of coping with reluctant, frightened, unresponsive or hostile witnesses.[13] As suggested in the last

---

6. See, e.g., United States v. DeLuna, 763 F.2d 897, 911–12 (8th Cir.), cert. denied, 474 U.S. 980, 106 S.Ct. 382, 88 L.Ed.2d 336 (1985) (testimony given in three installments, with cross-examination at end of each installment); Berroyer v. Hertz, 672 F.2d 334, 339 (3d Cir.1982) (expert allowed to testify out of order to accommodate schedule). See also Loinaz v. EG & G Inc., 910 F.2d 1, 6–10 (1st Cir.1990)(under circumstances, refusal to permit witness to testify out of order was abuse of discretion).

7. Johnson v. Ashby, 808 F.2d 676, 678 (8th Cir.1987).

8. United States v. Young, 745 F.2d 733, 760–61 (2d Cir.1984), cert. denied sub nom. Myers v. United States, 470 U.S. 1084, 105 S.Ct. 1842, 85 L.Ed.2d 142 (1985).

9. See generally Graham §§ 611.16–611.22; McCormick § 7. See, e.g., United States v. Clark, 613 F.2d 391, 406–07 (2d Cir.1979), cert. denied, 449 U.S. 820, 101 S.Ct. 78, 66 L.Ed.2d 22 (1980)(confusing question was properly excluded).

10. See, e.g., Shultz v. Rice, 809 F.2d 643, 654–55 (10th Cir.1986); McClard v. United States, 386 F.2d 495, 501 (8th Cir. 1967), cert. denied, 393 U.S. 866, 89 S.Ct. 149, 21 L.Ed.2d 134 (1968), rehearing denied, 393 U.S. 1045, 89 S.Ct. 638, 21 L.Ed.2d 598 (1969).

11. See, e.g., United States v. Castro–Romero, 964 F.2d 942, 943–44 (9th Cir. 1992)(eight-year-old reluctant witness); Litherland v. Petrolane Offshore Construction Services, Inc., 546 F.2d 129, 134 (5th Cir.1977) (mentally handicapped witness).

12. See, e.g., United States v. McGovern, 499 F.2d 1140, 1142 (1st Cir.1974).

13. See, e.g., United States v. Grey Bear, 883 F.2d 1382, 1393 (8th Cir.1989), cert. denied, 493 U.S. 1047, 110 S.Ct. 846, 107 L.Ed.2d 840 (1990)("unusually softspoken and frightened witness"); United States v. Wiley, 846 F.2d 150, 156 (2d Cir.1988)(unresponsive hostile witness); United States v. Tunnell, 667 F.2d 1182, 1187–88 (5th Cir.1982)(witness' hostility was apparent by demeanor).

sentence of Rule 611(c), hostility is presumed in the case of an adverse party or a person "identified with an adverse party."[14]

On cross-examination, leading questions are ordinarily allowed, a traditional rule that is carried forward by the second sentence of Rule 611(c).

c. Cross–Examination, Redirect and Recross

Aside from impeachment of the witness' credibility, Federal Rule of Evidence 611(b) limits the scope of cross-examination to the subject matter of the direct testimony:

> **(b) Scope of cross-examination.** Cross-examination should be limited to the subject matter of the direct examination and matters affecting the credibility of the witness. The court may, in the exercise of discretion, permit inquiry into additional matters as if on direct examination.

The "subject matter" rule has been interpreted to allow inquiry into "all inferences and implications arising from the [direct] testimony."[15] Although Rule 611(b) permits the court in its discretion to authorize cross-examination beyond the scope of direct,[16] it has been held that such discretion should be sparingly exercised.[17]

Cross-examination is a right that is enforced by striking the witness' direct testimony when a complete deprivation occurs.[18] Despite the general entitlement to cross-examination, courts have the discretion to curtail the interrogation if it becomes repetitive, confusing, or harassing or pursues only marginally relevant matters.[19] Consistent with a criminal defendant's right of confrontation, however, the court may not impose a blanket prohibition on "exploration of an area that is central to

---

14. See, e.g., Haney v. Mizell Memorial Hospital, 744 F.2d 1467, 1477–78 (11th Cir.1984)(plaintiff should have been allowed to use leading questions on direct examination of defendant's employee).

15. United States v. Arnott, 704 F.2d 322, 324 (6th Cir.), cert. denied, 464 U.S. 948, 104 S.Ct. 364, 78 L.Ed.2d 325 (1983). See also United States v. Segal, 534 F.2d 578, 583 (3d Cir.1976)("That specific evidence could have been a part of the defense does not preclude its development on cross-examination if the prosecution makes the subject matter part of its direct testimony.").

16. See, e.g., United States v. Alvarez, 833 F.2d 724, 729 (7th Cir.1987).

17. Lis v. Robert Packer Hospital, 579 F.2d 819, 822–23 (3d Cir.), cert. denied, 439 U.S. 955, 99 S.Ct. 354, 58 L.Ed.2d 346 (1978)(Fed.R.Evid. 611(b) contemplates "special circumstances" before cross-examination should be expanded beyond subject matter of direct).

18. See United States v. Cardillo, 316 F.2d 606, 611–13 (2d Cir.), cert. denied, 375 U.S. 822, 84 S.Ct. 60, 11 L.Ed.2d 55 (1963). A striking of only a portion of the direct may suffice if the cross-examination was adequate as to the remaining parts. Id. at 613.

19. United States v. Maldonado–Rivera, 922 F.2d 934, 956 (2d Cir.1990), cert. denied, 501 U.S. 1211, 111 S.Ct. 2811, 115 L.Ed.2d 984 (1991)(trial court may impose limits on cross-examination based on concerns about time-consumption, confusion, misleading of jury, repetitiveness and marginal relevance); United States v. Christian, 786 F.2d 203, 212–13 (6th Cir.1986)("trial judge may limit cross-examination where interrogation becomes repetitious or unduly harassing, * * * where the cross- examination is irrelevant to the credibility of the witness, * * * or to protect the witness' constitutional immunity from self-incrimination").

§ 611.5   WITNESSES   Ch. 6

an assessment of the [prosecution] witness's reliability."[20]

Redirect and recross examination are generally limited to the meeting of new facts elicited in the immediately preceding examination and to rehabilitating a witness whose credibility has been impeached.[21] Assuming a litigant is given ample opportunity to address new matters, the scope of redirect and recross is within the trial court's discretion.[22]

Library References:

West's Key No. Digests, Witnesses ⟲224–310.

612   Refreshing the Witness' Recollection

§ 612.1   New York

a. In General

As discussed in §§ 601.1(a) and 602.1 *supra*, a witness ordinarily must testify on the basis of personal knowledge and memory. A witness is not permitted to prepare a written statement and simply walk into the courtroom and read the statement into the record. It may be necessary,

---

20. United States v. Maldonado–Rivera, 922 F.2d 934, 955 (2d Cir.1990), cert. denied, 501 U.S. 1211, 111 S.Ct. 2811, 115 L.Ed.2d 984 (1991). See also United States v. Mayer, 556 F.2d 245, 250 (5th Cir.1977)(trial court's "discretionary authority to limit cross-examination comes into play only after there has been permitted as a matter of right sufficient cross-examination to satisfy the Sixth Amendment"); § 607.6, at notes 27 and 32, supra; § 611.3, at notes 31–32, supra. Cf. United States v. Singh, 628 F.2d 758, 763 (2d Cir.), cert. denied, 449 U.S. 1034, 101 S.Ct. 609, 66 L.Ed.2d 496 (1980)("In determining whether a trial judge has abused his discretion in the curtailment of cross-examination of government witnesses, the test is whether the jury was already in possession of sufficient information to make a discriminating appraisal of the particular witness's possible motives for testifying falsely in favor of the government.").

21. See, e.g., United States v. Henry, 47 F.3d 17, 22 (2d Cir.1995)(trial court did not abuse discretion in precluding redirect where cross-examination did not raise new matters); United States v. Braidlow, 806 F.2d 781, 783 (8th Cir.1986)("The trial court does not abuse its discretion by allowing the use of evidence on redirect examination to clarify an issue that was opened up by the defense on cross-examination—even when this evidence would otherwise be inadmissible."); United States v. Walker, 613 F.2d 1349, 1353 n. 5 (5th Cir.), cert. denied, 446 U.S. 944, 100 S.Ct. 2172, 64 L.Ed.2d 800 (1980) (scope of redirect is "limited to the subject matter of the cross-examination"; cross-examination as to portion of transaction enables party on redirect to elicit evidence as to whole of transaction "at least to the extent that it relates to the same subject"); F.H. Krear & Co. v. Nineteen Named Trustees, 810 F.2d 1250, 1257 (2d Cir.1987)(because redirect examination of witness did not include questioning with respect to certain contracts, trial court did not commit error in disallowing recross examination as to such contracts); United States v. Caudle, 606 F.2d 451, 458 (4th Cir.1979)("where, as here, new matter is brought out on redirect examination the defendant's first opportunity to test the truthfulness, accuracy, and completeness of that testimony is on recross examination. * * * To deny recross examination on matter first drawn out on redirect is to deny the defendant the right of any cross-examination as to that new matter.").

22. See United States v. Braidlow, 806 F.2d 781, 783 (8th Cir.1986) (redirect); F.H. Krear & Co. v. Nineteen Named Trustees, 810 F.2d 1250, 1257 (2d Cir.1987)(recross); United States v. Caudle, 606 F.2d 451, 458–59 (4th Cir.1979)(trial court has no discretion to curtail recross examination until after questioner has had reasonable opportunity to address new matters raised on redirect). As in the case of cross-examination, a court's discretion to limit recross examination by a criminal defendant is subject to the sixth amendment right of confrontation. See, e.g., United States v. Ross, 33 F.3d 1507, 1517–18 (11th Cir.1994)(defendant has limited right of recross examination where new matter is brought out on redirect).

however, to stimulate or revive the witness' memory, a process that has come to be known as refreshing the witness' recollection. The use of a leading question, discussed in § 611.2 *supra*, is one permissible means of jogging a witness' recollection.[1] The most common method, however, is showing the witness a writing. The breadth of the rule is illustrated by the following passage from an 1852 decision of the Court of Appeals:

> [A witness] is permitted to assist his memory by the use of any written instrument, memorandum or entry in a book, and it is not necessary that such writing should have been made by the witness himself, or that it should be an original writing, provided, after inspecting it, he can speak to the facts from his own recollection.[2]

It is clear, therefore, that virtually any type of writing may be shown to the witness to refresh her recollection.[3] It need not have been written by the witness[4] nor made at the time of the events recorded in the document.[5] This liberal approach is explained, in part, by the concomitant rule that a writing used merely to refresh recollection is not, in itself, evidence; only the testimony of the witness whose memory has been refreshed constitutes evidence.[6] Thus, unless some independent basis of admissibility is established, a writing used to refresh recollection may not be introduced into evidence by the proponent of the witness' testimony, either as an exhibit or by a reading to the jury.[7] To avoid

§ 612.1

1. See § 611.2, at note 16, supra.

2. Huff v. Bennett, 6 N.Y. 337, 338 (1852)(in libel action, witness was properly allowed to look at newspaper article to refresh recollection).

3. It has been said elsewhere that literally anything, not just a writing, may be used to refresh a witness' recollection. See § 612.2, at note 2, infra.

4. See, e.g., People v. Di Loretto, 150 A.D.2d 920, 922, 541 N.Y.S.2d 260, 261–62 (3d Dep't), appeal denied, 74 N.Y.2d 739, 545 N.Y.S.2d 113, 543 N.E.2d 756 (1989)(officers who monitored tape recording of conversation between undercover agent and defendant refreshed their recollections of the conversation by reviewing transcript of recording prepared by the agent); People v. Goldfeld, 60 A.D.2d 1, 11–12, 400 N.Y.S.2d 229, 235–36 (4th Dep't 1977)(accomplice-witness referred to bill of particulars prepared by district attorney and notes prepared jointly by accomplice and district attorney).

Frequently, of course, the writing is a memorandum prepared by the witness herself or a document or transcript containing the witness' prior statements or testimony. See, e.g., People v. Ferraro, 293 N.Y. 51, 56, 55 N.E.2d 861, 863 (1944)(proper to use witnesses' prior out-of-court statements and grand jury testimony to refresh their recollection); People v. DeLong, 206 A.D.2d 914, 916, 615 N.Y.S.2d 168, 170 (4th Dep't 1994)(witness' prior statement to police).

5. See, e.g., People v. Ferraro, 293 N.Y. 51, 56, 55 N.E.2d 861, 863 (1944)(witness' grand jury testimony).

6. Howard v. McDonough, 77 N.Y. 592, 593 (1879); People v. Reger, 13 A.D.2d 63, 70, 213 N.Y.S.2d 298, 307 (1st Dep't 1961).

7. People v. Reger, 13 A.D.2d 63, 70–71, 213 N.Y.S.2d 298, 307 (1st Dep't 1961). See also Grow Tunneling Corp. v. Consolidated Edison Co., 195 A.D.2d 325, 326, 600 N.Y.S.2d 30, 32 (1st Dep't 1993); Matter of Adoption of Baby Boy B., 163 A.D.2d 673, 675, 558 N.Y.S.2d 281, 283 (3d Dep't), appeal denied, 76 N.Y.2d 710, 563 N.Y.S.2d 62, 564 N.E.2d 672 (1990). In an older case, however, a trial court was held to have properly admitted into evidence a lengthy list of goods and their values which the witness had prepared to refresh his recollection while testifying in support of an action for wrongful seizure of the goods. Howard v. McDonough, 77 N.Y. 592 (1879). The Court of Appeals said that the list was admissible "not as proving anything of itself, but as a detailed statement of the items testified to by the witness." Id. at 594. The court appears to have viewed the list as a form of demonstrative evidence illustrative of the witness' testimony. See § 1103.1 infra.

§ 612.1

transgressions in this regard, the proponent usually should disclose the writing to the witness in such manner that the jury is not made aware of its contents.[8]

To be distinguished is the hearsay exception for past recollection recorded, which allows for admissibility of the contents of a writing, in some circumstances, when showing the writing to the witness fails to refresh her recollection.[9] The foundation for past recollection recorded is discussed in § 803(2).1 *infra*.

Safeguards have been developed by the courts to confine the process of refreshing recollection to its proper bounds. The danger in the process, of course, is that the witness' memory may not be truly refreshed by the writing, resulting in effect in a reading of the document into evidence in the guise of testimony.[10] Worse yet, the witness may never have had personal knowledge of the events and may be simply mouthing the proponent's wished-for version of the facts.[11]

To limit the potential for abuse, courts have required a showing that the witness' current memory is exhausted before the examining party may be allowed to resort to memory prods.[12] Courts also perform a supervisory role to assure that the witness really has an independent

---

8. See, e.g., People v. Kellogg, 210 A.D.2d 912, 913–14, 621 N.Y.S.2d 418, 421 (4th Dep't 1994)(improper for prosecutor to read into evidence titles of book chapters for purpose of refreshing witness' recollection as to whether she had read the book in a college course); Berkowsky v. New York City Ry. Co., 127 App.Div. 544, 546, 111 N.Y.S. 989, 990 (1st Dep't 1908) (improper to read to jury memorandum used to refresh witness' recollection)(dictum). In criminal cases, when an inadmissible prior inconsistent statement is used to refresh the recollection of the examining party's witness, N.Y.Crim.Proc.Law § 60.35(3) explicitly prohibits the examining party from using the statement in a way that would disclose its contents to the jury. See § 607.4, at note 26, supra.

9. McCarthy v. Meaney, 183 N.Y. 190, 193–94, 76 N.E. 36, 37–38 (1905) (distinguishing between use of memorandum to refresh recollection and use thereof as past recollection recorded; neither rule was satisfied); Brown v. Western Union Telegraph Co., 26 A.D.2d 316, 318, 274 N.Y.S.2d 52, 54–55 (4th Dep't 1966)(same).

10. See Brown v. Western Union Telegraph Co., 26 A.D.2d 316, 320, 274 N.Y.S.2d 52, 56 (4th Dep't 1966).

11. See, e.g., People v. Ramos, 141 Misc.2d 930, 936, 535 N.Y.S.2d 663, 668 (Sup.Ct.N.Y.Co.1988)(police officer who reviewed chart of narcotics transactions prepared by prosecutor had no independent recollection of at least one of the transactions).

12. People v. Reger, 13 A.D.2d 63, 70, 213 N.Y.S.2d 298, 307 (1st Dep't 1961). For the witness' current memory to be "exhausted," however, is not the same thing as being nonexistent. In other words, it should be permissible to use a writing to refresh recollection even where the witness purports to remember an event, as, for example, to help the witness remember additional facts or to modify her testimony. See, e.g., People v. Ferraro, 293 N.Y. 51, 56, 55 N.E.2d 861, 863 (1944)(prosecution witnesses whose trial testimony was far less inculpatory of the defendant than was their grand jury testimony could be shown their prior statements in effort to refresh recollection); Brown v. Western Union Telegraph Co., 26 A.D.2d 316, 319, 274 N.Y.S.2d 52, 55 (4th Dep't 1966)("A witness' memory may be refreshed by directing attention to a prior inconsistent statement in order to induce a correction of testimony or to explain an apparent inconsistency."); McCormick § 9, at 33–34. Some of the New York cases, however, might be read as imposing an overly strict interpretation of the rule. Nappi v. Gerdts, 103 A.D.2d 737, 737, 477 N.Y.S.2d 202, 203 (2d Dep't 1984)(improper to seek to refresh recollection of witness unless witness indicates current inability to recall sufficient facts to testify from memory); People v. Boice, 89 A.D.2d 33, 35, 455 N.Y.S.2d 859, 860 (3d Dep't 1982)(witness who "unequivocally" testified that defendant was driving motorcycle at "30–45 miles per hour" should not have been shown grand jury testimony in which she testified that speed was "40 miles per hour").

recollection and that the material is being used merely to refresh that recollection.[13] The governing test appears to be whether the writing was used "in good faith and whether it is at all likely to stimulate the memory of the witness."[14] The most important safeguard of all, perhaps, is the right of the adversary to inspect any writing used to refresh the recollection of the witness while on the stand. That issue is addressed in the next subdivision.

b. Adversary's Right of Inspection

An adversary is entitled to inspect, and use on cross-examination, a writing that was reviewed by a witness to refresh her recollection while testifying.[15] The adversary's right of access helps protect against the introduction of "false, forged or manufactured evidence"[16] and provides a potential basis for discrediting the witness' assertions of a restored memory.[17] Further, the adversary, unlike the proponent of the witness' testimony, may introduce the writing into evidence for purposes of impeachment.[18] To be distinguished from the rule under discussion is the *Rosario* rule,[19] the codified form of which gives either party in a criminal case the right to inspect any written statement that the opponent's witness made prior to trial regardless of whether the witness has relied on the statement to refresh her recollection.[20]

---

13. People v. Reger, 13 A.D.2d 63, 70, 213 N.Y.S.2d 298, 307 (1st Dep't 1961)(writing used to refresh witness' recollection must "actually [serve] that purpose"). See also McCormick § 9, at 31 ("It is a preliminary question for [the judge's] decision whether the memorandum actually does refresh, and from the nature of the memorandum and the witness's testimony she may find that it does not.")

14. Brown v. Western Union Telegraph Co., 26 A.D.2d 316, 320, 274 N.Y.S.2d 52, 56 (4th Dep't 1966). See also People v. Di Loretto, 150 A.D.2d 920, 922, 541 N.Y.S.2d 260, 262 (3d Dep't), appeal denied, 74 N.Y.2d 739, 545 N.Y.S.2d 113, 543 N.E.2d 756 (1989)(good-faith standard); People v. Goldfeld, 60 A.D.2d 1, 11, 400 N.Y.S.2d 229, 236 (4th Dep't 1977) (good-faith standard).

15. People v. Gezzo, 307 N.Y. 385, 393–94, 121 N.E.2d 380, 384 (1954); People v. Reger, 13 A.D.2d 63, 71, 213 N.Y.S.2d 298, 307 (1st Dep't 1961); Miller v. Greenwald Petticoat Co., 192 App.Div. 559, 562, 183 N.Y.S. 97, 99 (1st Dep't 1920). Cf. Hayes v. Henault, 131 A.D.2d 930, 933–34, 516 N.Y.S.2d 798, 801 (3d Dep't 1987)(writing need not be turned over to opponent until witness uses it to refresh recollection; error occurred where plaintiff called defense witness during plaintiff's case in chief and trial court ordered defendant to turn over witness' prior statement). Proposed New York Evidence Code § 612(c) would limit the right of inspection to those portions of the writing that are "related to the subject matter" of the witness' testimony. See note 23 infra.

16. Tibbetts v. Sternberg, 66 Barb. (N.Y.) 201, 203 (1870). Inspection of the document enables the opponent to make an informed decision as to the appropriateness of objecting to its use as a refreshment device. See, e.g., People v. Ramos, 141 Misc.2d 930, 936, 535 N.Y.S.2d 663, 668 (Sup.Ct.N.Y.Co.1988)(mistrial declared where defendant, after inspecting chart prepared by prosecutor to refresh police officer's testimony, showed that use of chart presented danger of officer's adoption of facts either contrary to his recollection or previously unknown to him).

17. See McCormick § 9, at 32 ("With the memorandum before her, the cross-examiner has a good opportunity to test the credibility of the witness's claim that her memory has been revived, and to search out any discrepancies between the writing and the testimony.").

18. Caupain v. Johnson, 20 A.D.2d 712, 713, 247 N.Y.S.2d 345, 346 (2d Dep't 1964); People v. Reger, 13 A.D.2d 63, 71, 213 N.Y.S.2d 298, 307 (1st Dep't 1961).

19. People v. Rosario, 9 N.Y.2d 286, 213 N.Y.S.2d 448, 173 N.E.2d 881, cert. denied, 368 U.S. 866, 82 S.Ct. 117, 7 L.Ed.2d 64 (1961).

20. See § 501.3, at notes 30–32, supra.

§ 612.1   WITNESSES   Ch. 6

In recent years, New York courts have expanded the adversary's right of inspection to include documents that the witness reviewed for refreshment purposes prior to testifying even if the documents were not shown to the witness during her testimony.[21] The fact that the witness engaged in pretestimonial review of documents to refresh recollection can be established on cross-examination and the demand for production can be made at that time. Much like Federal Rule of Evidence 612,[22] the Proposed New York Evidence Code would explicitly recognize the adversary's interest in examining such writings but would restrict disclosure to cases where the "interests of justice" require it.[23] Such judicial discretion would safeguard against undue burdens on the opponent, fishing expeditions into the opponent's files and incursions on privilege claims.[24]

21. Chabica v. Schneider, 213 A.D.2d 579, 581, 624 N.Y.S.2d 271, 273 (2d Dep't 1995). See also Stern v. Aetna Casualty & Surety Co., 159 A.D.2d 1013, 552 N.Y.S.2d 730 (4th Dep't 1990); Rouse v. County of Greene, 115 A.D.2d 162, 495 N.Y.S.2d 496 (3d Dep't 1985); Herrmann v. General Tire and Rubber Co., 79 A.D.2d 955, 956, 435 N.Y.S.2d 14, 16 (1st Dep't 1981); Doxtator v. Swarthout, 38 A.D.2d 782, 328 N.Y.S.2d 150 (4th Dep't 1972). This approach was advocated by McCormick and Wigmore for the same reasons that justify the right of inspection of materials used by the witness while on the stand. McCormick § 9, at 32–33; 3 Wigmore § 72, at 140. See also 3 Weinstein and Berger ¶ 612[01] (even greater danger of misuse of materials is present during pretrial refreshment of recollection than at trial).

22. See § 612.2 infra.

23. Proposed N.Y. Evidence Code § 612(b). The complete text of the proposed code provision is as follows:

§ 612. Writing or object used to refresh memory [PROPOSED]

(a) **While testifying.** Any writing or object may be used by a witness to refresh the witness's memory while testifying. If, while a witness is testifying, a writing or object is used by the witness to refresh the witness's own memory, an adverse party is entitled upon request, subject to subdivision (c) of this section, to inspect the writing or object, to cross-examine the witness thereon, and to introduce in evidence those portions which relate to the testimony of the witness.

(b) **Before testifying.** If a witness, immediately before testifying, uses a writing or object to refresh the witness's memory solely for the purpose of testifying, unless the court determines that the interests of justice require otherwise, an adverse party is, subject to subdivision (c) of this section, entitled upon request: (1) to have the writing or object produced at the trial, proceeding, or hearing; (2) to inspect it; (3) to cross-examine the witness thereon; and (4) to introduce in evidence those portions which relate to the testimony of the witness.

(c) **Claims of privilege or irrelevance.** If it is claimed that the writing or object contains matters not related to the subject matter of the testimony, the court shall examine it in camera, excise any portions not so related, and order delivery of the remainder to the party entitled thereto. Any portion withheld over objection shall be preserved and made available to the appellate court in the event of an appeal. If it is claimed that the writing or object contains privileged communications or matters, or that use of a writing or object to refresh recollection before testifying is privileged and thus not subject to cross-examination, the court shall rule on any claim of privilege raised.

(d) **Failure to produce.** If a writing or object is not produced or delivered pursuant to order under this section, to remedy such failure of production or delivery, the court, pursuant to section 107 of this chapter, shall make any order the interests of justice require [e.g., continuance, adverse inference instruction, striking of testimony, mistrial].

24. Comment, Proposed N.Y. Evid. Code § 612(b):

Flexibility is necessary, for example, in a case in which the witness has reviewed a considerable number of documents, or when the attorney might not have immediate access to all of the materials reviewed by the witness prior to trial. Of course, ordering a brief delay to secure the documents is well within the discre-

Most authorities agree that the use of a writing to refresh recollection while the witness is on the stand waives any privilege otherwise applicable to the writing.[25] Whether automatic waiver should occur with respect to privileged documents reviewed by a witness prior to her testimony is more controversial.[26] Nevertheless, in this context some New York courts have found waiver of the attorney-client privilege[27] and the immunity for material prepared in anticipation of litigation.[28] A commendable limitation on the waiver principle, however, is a required showing that the witness' testimony was actually based on the privileged writing,[29] thus constituting in effect an affirmative use of the privileged material.[30] Furthermore, the balance was struck in favor of preserving

tion of the trial court. Additionally, discretion is necessary in order to prevent the adverse party from embarking on a "roving tour" through the other party's files. * * * Furthermore, the grant of discretion gives the court the ability to assess properly a claim that the writing or object of which production and inspection is sought is exempt from discovery under CPL 240.10(2), (3) or CPLR 3101(c), (d), i.e., "attorney's work product," "material prepared for litigation," and thus should not be ordered produced * * *.

25. McCormick § 9, at 35; Mueller and Kirkpatrick § 6.26, at 567. But see Falk v. Kalt, 44 Misc.2d 172, 253 N.Y.S.2d 188 (Sup.Ct.Suffolk Co.1964) (no waiver where witness, during deposition, refreshed recollection with document protected by attorney-client privilege).

26. See Marcus, "The Perils of Privilege: Waiver and the Litigator," 84 Mich. L.Rev. 1605, 1642–48 (1986); Ward, "The Litigator's Dilemma: Waiver of Core Work Product Used in Trial Preparation," 62 St. John's L.Rev. 515, 530–47 (1988).

27. E.R. Carpenter Co. v. ABC Carpet Co., 98 Misc.2d 1091, 415 N.Y.S.2d 351 (N.Y.C.Civ.Ct.1979). See also Slotnik v. State, 129 Misc.2d 553, 493 N.Y.S.2d 731 (Ct.Cl.1985)(waiver of privilege for medical review committee meetings).

28. Stern v. Aetna Casualty & Surety Co., 159 A.D.2d 1013, 552 N.Y.S.2d 730 (4th Dep't 1990); Rouse v. County of Greene, 115 A.D.2d 162, 495 N.Y.S.2d 496 (3d Dep't 1985); Merrill Lynch Realty Commercial Services, Inc. v. Rudin Management Co., 94 A.D.2d 617, 462 N.Y.S.2d 16 (1st Dep't 1983); Doxtator v. Swarthout 38 A.D.2d 782, 328 N.Y.S.2d 150 (4th Dep't 1972). It bears noting that the immunity for trial-preparation materials (CPLR 3101(d)(2)) is a qualified privilege. See § 501.3 supra. A claim for stronger protection might be made for attorney work product, i.e., materials reflecting counsel's opinions, conclusions and strategies, which has the status of an absolute privilege under CPLR 3101(c). See, e.g., Geffers v. Canisteo Central School District No. 463201, 105 A.D.2d 1062, 482 N.Y.S.2d 635 (4th Dep't 1984)(no waiver). See also Matter of Lenny McN., 183 A.D.2d 627, 584 N.Y.S.2d 17 (1st Dep't 1992)(no waiver for conclusions, mental impressions of social worker, a "representative" of the party within the meaning of CPLR 3101 (d)(2)). Although Herrmann v. General Tire and Rubber Co., 79 A.D.2d 955, 956, 435 N.Y.S.2d 14, 16 (1st Dep't 1981), states that the privilege for "attorney's work product" is waived when the witness reviews such material before testifying, the reported facts suggest that the item in question, a tape recording of a witness' interview made by an insurance carrier, was merely material prepared for litigation.

29. See Stern v. Aetna Casualty & Surety Co., 159 A.D.2d 1013, 1014, 552 N.Y.S.2d 730, 730 (4th Dep't 1990)(claim of privilege is waived when witness uses writing to refresh recollection and "bases his deposition testimony on that writing"); Rouse v. County of Greene, 115 A.D.2d 162, 162, 495 N.Y.S.2d 496, 497 (3d Dep't 1985)(waiver occurs when witness reviews writing and "bases her deposition testimony on that writing"); Merrill Lynch Realty Commercial Services, Inc. v. Rudin Management Co., 94 A.D.2d 617, 617, 462 N.Y.S.2d 16, 17 (1st Dep't 1983)(privilege is waived when writing "becomes the basis of pretrial testimony").

30. See Doxtator v. Swarthout, 38 A.D.2d 782, 782, 328 N.Y.S.2d 150, 152 (4th Dep't 1972). The comment to Proposed N.Y. Evidence Code § 612 urges consideration of the following factors in the court's determination of whether waiver should be found with respect to pretestimonial review of privileged materials: "the significance of the testimony, the availability of other evidence for impeachment purposes, and the extent to which the witness consulted or relied on the writing or object."

§ 612.1   WITNESSES   Ch. 6

privilege in *Matter of Lenny McN.*,[31] where "the confidentiality and sensitivity of Family Court custodial litigation" was found to outweigh a litigant's interest in seeing the case file of a social worker who reviewed her file prior to testifying.[32]

Library References:

West's Key No. Digests, Witnesses ⚿253.

§ 612.2 Federal

No Federal Rule of Evidence addresses the entire process of refreshing the recollection of a witness. The use of leading questions is only indirectly treated in Rule 611.[1] Rule 612, quoted below, deals only with the adversary's right to inspect a writing that has been used to refresh a witness' recollection. Thus, federal caselaw predating the adoption of the Federal Rules of Evidence continues to serve as a guide. In general, federal law on this topic differs little from that of New York, which is described in the immediately preceding section.

The wide range of material that may be used to refresh a witness' recollection is reflected in an oft-quoted passage from a Second Circuit decision: "Anything may in fact revive a memory: a song, a scent, a photograph, [an] allusion, even a past statement known to be false."[2] In general, a writing used to refresh need not have been written by the witness,[3] and its time of preparation is immaterial.[4] Federal courts have even permitted illegally or unethically obtained evidence to be used to refresh recollection.[5] Exclusionary principles are not offended by the use of such material because of the general rule that an item used to refresh a witness' recollection is not admissible at the behest of the party using it. Only the refreshed testimony of the witness, not the memory prod, constitutes admissible evidence.[6] The preferred practice, there-

---

31. 183 A.D.2d 627, 584 N.Y.S.2d 17 (1st Dep't 1992).

32. Id. at 627–28, 584 N.Y.S.2d at 18.

§ 612.2

1. § 611.5, at note 12, infra.

2. United States v. Rappy, 157 F.2d 964, 967 (2d Cir.), cert. denied, 329 U.S. 806, 67 S.Ct. 501, 91 L.Ed. 688 (1947). See also United States v. Lombardozzi, 335 F.2d 414, 417 (2d Cir.1964), cert. denied, 379 U.S. 914, 85 S.Ct. 261, 13 L.Ed.2d 185 (1964)(witness was shown photograph to refresh recollection).

3. United States v. Landof, 591 F.2d 36, 39 (9th Cir.1978)(prosecutor properly refreshed recollection of witness with FBI report describing agent's interview of witness: "[T]he law is clear that recollection can be refreshed from documents made by persons other than the witness."). But see Berkovich v. Hicks, 922 F.2d 1018, 1025 (2d Cir.1991)(trial court did not abuse discretion in precluding refreshment use of FBI report summarizing witness' interview with FBI agent).

4. See, e.g., Bankers Trust Co. v. Publicker Industries, Inc., 641 F.2d 1361, 1363 (2d Cir.1981)(chronology of two-year-old events prepared by witness shortly before trial).

5. United States v. Kusek, 844 F.2d 942, 949 (2d Cir.), cert. denied, 488 U.S. 860, 109 S.Ct. 157, 102 L.Ed.2d 128 (1988)(tape recording seized in violation of search warrant); 20th Century Wear v. Sanmark-Stardust Inc., 747 F.2d 81, 93 n.17 (2d Cir.1984), cert. denied, 470 U.S. 1052, 105 S.Ct. 1755, 84 L.Ed.2d 818 (1985)(tape recording unethically made by attorney); United States v. Baratta, 397 F.2d 215, 221–22 (2d Cir.), cert. denied, 393 U.S. 939, 89 S.Ct. 293, 21 L.Ed.2d 276 (1968)(statement obtained from defendant-witness in violation of Miranda).

6. United States v. Riccardi, 174 F.2d 883, 889 (3d Cir.), cert. denied, 337 U.S. 941, 69 S.Ct. 1519, 93 L.Ed. 1746 (1949).

Ch. 6   REFRESHING WITNESS' RECOLLECTION   § 612.2

fore, is to show the refreshing material to the witness without disclosure to the jury.[7]

Refreshing the recollection of a witness with a writing carries with it the danger of improper suggestion or outright fabrication of evidence.[8] Thus, courts exercise discretion to control the process in at least two ways. First, the court must be satisfied that the witness' current memory is exhausted.[9] Second, the witness' recollection must be actually refreshed so that the writing is not merely being read into evidence under the guise of testimony.[10] It is proper for the two-part foundation

See also 20th Century Wear, Inc. v. Sanmark–Stardust Inc., 747 F.2d 81, 93 n.17 (2d Cir.1984), cert denied, 470 U.S. 1052, 105 S.Ct. 1755, 84 L.Ed.2d 818 (1985)(where witness' recollection is refreshed by tape recording, "[r]eliance on the tape recording without having the witness repeat in his own words what he remembered * * * is not proper"). Of course, the material used to refresh recollection may be admissible on independent grounds. Furthermore, the contents of a memorandum which fails to refresh the witness' recollection may be admissible pursuant to the hearsay exception for past recollection recorded. See § 803(2).2 infra.

7. See New Mexico Savings & Loan Ass'n v. United States Fidelity and Guaranty Co., 454 F.2d 328, 337 (10th Cir.1972)("best practice would be for the trial court to require that the witness silently reread his pertinent deposition testimony, so that deposition answers which are not admissible as evidence will not be heard by the jury"; no error in instant case, however, where opponent raised no objection). See also Gaines v. United States, 349 F.2d 190, 192 (D.C.Cir.1965)(error, but no basis for reversal, where prosecutor read witnesses' prior statements aloud in presence of jury); Goings v. United States, 377 F.2d 753, 762 (8th Cir.1967), appeal after remand, 393 F.2d 884 (8th Cir.), and cert. denied, 393 U.S. 883, 89 S.Ct. 191, 21 L.Ed.2d 158 (1968)(reversible error where prosecutor read witness' prior statement aloud ostensibly to refresh recollection but where motive was "to inject hearsay evidence into the case as substantive proof").

8. See United States v. Riccardi, 174 F.2d 883, 889 (3d Cir.), cert. denied, 337 U.S. 941, 69 S.Ct. 1519, 93 L.Ed. 1746 (1949)("[I]t is in complication thereof that a cooperative witness, yielding to suggestion, deceives himself, that a hostile witness seizes an opportunity, or that a writing is used to convey an improper suggestion.").

9. United States v. Morlang, 531 F.2d 183, 191 (4th Cir.1975); Goings v. United States, 377 F.2d 753, 760 (8th Cir.1967); Thompson v. United States, 342 F.2d 137, 139 (5th Cir.), cert. denied, 381 U.S. 926, 85 S.Ct. 1560, 14 L.Ed.2d 685 (1965). See also Hall v. American Bakeries Co., 873 F.2d 1133, 1136 (8th Cir.1989)(absence of foundation regarding witness' "need" to refresh his memory).

10. 20th Century Wear, Inc. v. Sanmark–Stardust, Inc., 747 F.2d 81, 93 n.17 (2d Cir.1984), cert. denied, 470 U.S. 1052, 105 S.Ct. 1755, 84 L.Ed.2d 818 (1985)("The court must ensure * * * that the witness actually has a present recollection and that otherwise inadmissible evidence does not slip in inadvertently for its truth."); NLRB v. Federal Dairy Co., 297 F.2d 487, 488 (1st Cir.1962)(upon objection, witness should first testify that paper "does in fact have [the] effect" of refreshing recollection).

When the evidence consists of detailed information or a lengthy itemization, the court has discretion, assuming the witness' memory is actually refreshed, to permit the witness to continue referring to the writing while she testifies. United States v. Riccardi, 174 F.2d 883, 890 (3d Cir.), cert. denied, 337 U.S. 941, 69 S.Ct. 1519, 93 L.Ed. 1746 (1949) (prosecution for interstate transportation of stolen household objects: "the items of property involved were so numerous that in the ordinary course of events no one would be expected to recite them without having learned a list by rote memory"). See also United States v. Rinke, 778 F.2d 581, 588 (10th Cir.1985)(trial court did not abuse discretion in allowing witness repeatedly to refer to notes while testifying where embellishments and additional facts contained in testimony demonstrated that witness had independent recollection); Goings v. United States, 377 F.2d 753, 761 n. 11 (8th Cir.1967), appeal after remand, 393 F.2d 884 (8th Cir.), and cert. denied, 393 U.S. 883, 89 S.Ct. 191, 21 L.Ed.2d 158 (1968) ("The trial court in many instances should liberally allow a witness to refer to records, accounting sheets and reports in testifying. Generally, doctors, engineers, accountants and other lay witnesses testifying should be allowed continuously to refer to data on their reports, etc. * * * However, the trial court should exercise caution to

§ 612.2   WITNESSES   Ch. 6

to be established explicitly by the witness,[11] but no "ritualistic formula" is required.[12] Furthermore, "the trial judge has broad discretion to organize or limit the use of evidence to refresh recollection."[13]

Another critical safeguard against impropriety is the adversary's right to inspect writings that have been used to refresh a witness' recollection, to use them on cross-examination and to have relevant portions admitted into evidence. The "search of credibility and memory" is thereby promoted.[14] Federal Rule of Evidence 612 is the current source of authority on this issue:

> Except as otherwise provided in criminal proceedings by section 3500 of title 18, United States Code, if a witness uses a writing to refresh memory for the purpose of testifying, either—
>
> > (1) while testifying, or
> >
> > (2) before testifying, if the court in its discretion determines it is necessary in the interests of justice,
>
> an adverse party is entitled to have the writing produced at the hearing, to inspect it, to cross-examine the witness thereon, and to introduce in evidence those portions which relate to the testimony of the witness. If it is claimed that the writing contains matters not related to the subject matter of the testimony the court shall examine the writing in camera, excise any portions not so related, and order delivery of the remainder to

---

assure that the memorandum is not a written summary made specifically for use in court. It cannot be a mere subterfuge for suggestion."); McCormick § 9, at 34 (rule that witness must testify "independently of the writing seems too inflexible, and it is believed that the matter is discretionary and that the trial judge may properly permit the witness to consult the memorandum as she speaks, especially where it is so lengthy and detailed that even a fresh memory would be unable to recite all the items unaided").

11. Goings v. United States, 377 F.2d 753, 760–61 (8th Cir.1967), appeal after remand, 393 F.2d 884 (8th Cir.), and cert. denied, 393 U.S. 883, 89 S.Ct. 191, 21 L.Ed.2d 158 (1968)(when court is satisfied that witness' recollection is exhausted and that writing will help refresh memory, "[i]t then becomes proper to have the witness, if it is a fact, to say that his memory is refreshed and, independent of the exhibit, testify what *his present recollection is*")(emphasis in original); NLRB v. Federal Dairy Co., 297 F.2d 487, 488–89 (1st Cir. 1962)("The witness should first testify, if there is objection, that the paper [used to refresh recollection] does in fact have that effect. * * * Equally important, the witness, unless opposing counsel waives it, should not refresh his recollection until he has been examined without leading, if it is direct examination, and has testified that his recollection is exhausted.")

12. Bankers Trust Co. v. Publicker Industries, Inc. 641 F.2d 1361, 1363 (2d Cir.1981)(trial court properly exercised discretion in permitting witness to refer to written chronology recently prepared by witness herself where she indicated it would "enhance my memory since a lot of this happened two years ago"). See also Thompson v. United States, 342 F.2d 137, 140 (5th Cir.), cert. denied, 381 U.S. 926, 85 S.Ct. 1560, 14 L.Ed.2d 685 (1965)("[T]he court properly supervised the use of the statement to refresh [the witness'] recollection; and, where there was an absence of the customary formalistic wording to show inability to recollect without aid and the refreshing effect of the writing, the context of the specific queries, the witness' spoken reaction and the trial judge's opportunity to observe the witness' demeanor, leave no occasion to find reversible error in his rulings on these objections.")

13. 20th Century Wear, Inc. v. Sanmark–Stardust Inc., 747 F.2d 81, 93 n.17 (2d Cir.1984), cert. denied, 470 U.S. 1052, 105 S.Ct. 1755, 84 L.Ed.2d 818 (1985). See also United States v. Riccardi, 174 F.2d 883, 889–90 (3d Cir.), cert. denied, 337 U.S. 941, 69 S.Ct. 1519, 93 L.Ed. 1746 (1949).

14. Advisory Committee's Note, Fed. R.Evid. 612.

the party entitled thereto. Any portion withheld over objections shall be preserved and made available to the appellate court in the event of an appeal. If a writing is not produced or delivered pursuant to order under this rule, the court shall make any order justice requires, except that in criminal cases when the prosecution elects not to comply, the order shall be one striking the testimony or, if the court in its discretion determines that the interests of justice so require, declaring a mistrial.

The Rule creates a double standard: The right of inspection apparently is absolute with respect to writings that have been used to refresh recollection while the witness is on the stand; the court's discretion, however, determines whether inspection is "necessary in the interests of justice" with respect to writings that were reviewed by the witness prior to her testimony.[15] It bears noting that the rights of inspection in Rule 612 are independent of the rules of discovery in criminal cases governing pretrial statements made by a party's witness.[16] The latter rules apply regardless of whether the witness used her statement to refresh recollection during or before her testimony.

If a document used to refresh the recollection of a witness while she is on the stand is subject to a privilege, such as work product or attorney-client privilege, courts appear to be in agreement that the privilege is waived.[17] Waiver has also been found with respect to privileged documents used to refresh recollection prior to testifying,[18] although a more discriminating balancing of interests is often applied.[19]

---

15. See, e.g., United States v. Blas, 947 F.2d 1320, 1327–28 (7th Cir.1991), cert. denied, 502 U.S. 1118, 112 S.Ct. 1234, 117 L.Ed.2d 468 (1992)(at sentencing hearing, trial court did not abuse discretion in refusing to order production of large volume of material reviewed by witness prior to testifying; defendant's cross-examination of witness was adequate to test credibility and memory); United States v. Finkielstain, 718 F.Supp. 1187, 1192 (S.D.N.Y.1989)(noting sparsity of authority as to meaning of "interests of justice" under Fed.R.Evid. 612, court refused to order production of documents reviewed by witness prior to deposition where materiality of documents was not shown and opponent failed to obtain the documents when the opportunity presented itself).

Relevant considerations in the court's exercise of discretion are suggested in § 612.1, at note 24, supra.

16. See § 501.3, at note 50, supra.

17. Derderian v. Polaroid Corp., 121 F.R.D. 13, 15 (D.Mass.1988) (deponent's use of document to refresh recollection while testifying waives "any privilege or protection"); Bailey v. Meister Brau, Inc., 57 F.R.D. 11, 13 (N.D.Ill.1972)(waiver of attorney-client privilege for documents used to refresh recollection during deposition). See also United States v. Nobles, 422 U.S. 225, 239 n.14, 95 S.Ct. 2160, 2171, 45 L.Ed.2d 141, 154 (1975)(waiver of work product privilege occurred at trial when defense counsel called investigator whose written report contained inconsistent statements of prosecution witnesses: "[W]here * * * counsel attempts to make a testimonial use of [work product] materials the normal rules of evidence come into play with respect to cross-examination and production of documents.").

18. See, e.g., Ehrlich v. Howe, 848 F.Supp. 482, 493–94 (S.D.N.Y.1994) (work product and attorney-client privilege; waiving party, however, was allowed to submit privileged document to court for determination of appropriateness and feasibility of redacting particular portions containing "solely an attorney's mental impressions, conclusions, opinions and legal theories").

19. Id.; In re Joint Eastern and Southern District Asbestos Litigation, 119 F.R.D. 4, 5–6 (E.D.N.Y., S.D.N.Y.1988)(with respect to work product, "[t]he rules may be reconciled because the 'interests of justice' standard of Rule 612 incorporates as part of the balancing analysis the protection afford-

Courts have stressed that Rule 612 itself imposes the prerequisite of a showing that a privileged document, like all material used to jog a witness' memory, had "an impact" on the testimony.[20]

Library References:

West's Key No. Digests, Witnesses ⚷253.

613 [Reserved]

(The topic of impeachment by prior inconsistent statements is covered in § 607.8 *supra*.)

614 Calling and Questioning of Witnesses by the Court or Jury

§ 614.1 New York

It is a fundamental precept of the adversary system that the litigants themselves decide what witnesses to call and what questions to ask them. Nevertheless, a New York trial judge has discretion to intervene in the questioning of witnesses to a limited extent and for limited purposes. Jurors likewise may be allowed to interrogate witnesses. Whether the judge may call a witness whom the parties have chosen not to call, however, is less certain.

a. Calling of Witnesses by the Court

Wigmore posited a common law right of trial courts to call witnesses as "auxiliary" to their power to administer cases.[1] The court itself might wish clarification of the facts, or a party, not wishing to be associated with a particular witness, might prefer that the individual be called as a "court's witness."[2] New York courts have recognized, but rarely exercised, an inherent power to appoint expert witnesses despite

---

ed by the work-product doctrine, * * * while the 'substantial need' requirement of Rule 26 [Fed.R.Civ.P.] can take into account the need for disclosure under Rule 612"); In re Atlantic Financial Management Securities Litigation, 121 F.R.D. 141, 143 (D.Mass.1988)("The question of whether disclosure is necessary must be resolved with a recognition of the competing policy concerns underlying Fed.R.Evid. 612 and Fed.R.Civ.P. 26(b)(3) [work product immunity]."). See generally Marcus, "The Perils of Privilege: Waiver and the Litigator," 84 Mich.L.Rev. 1605, 1642–48 (1986).

20. Sporck v. Peil, 759 F.2d 312, 317–18 (3d Cir.), cert. denied, 474 U.S. 903, 106 S.Ct. 232, 88 L.Ed.2d 230 (1985); Berkey Photo, Inc. v. Eastman Kodak Co., 74 F.R.D. 613, 615–16 (S.D.N.Y.1977). Cf. Advisory Committee's Note, Fed.R.Evid. 612 ("The purpose of [Rule 612's introductory] phrase 'for the purpose of testifying' is to safeguard against using the rule as a pretext for wholesale exploration of an opposing party's files and to insure that access is limited only to those writings which may fairly be said in fact to have an impact upon the testimony of the witness.")

§ 614.1

1. 9 Wigmore § 2484, at 277. The court's inherent authority to call witnesses was recognized by federal courts even prior to the adoption of Fed.R.Evid. 614(a). See § 614.2 infra.

2. See McCormick § 8, at 26–27. In the case of a court-called witness, the party would be freed from the strictures of the "voucher rule," which generally prohibits a party from impeaching her own witness. See § 607.4, at notes 1–10, supra. A court-called witness should be subject to cross-examination and impeachment by either party. See Fed.R.Evid. 614(a). See also Proposed N.Y.Evid.Code § 614(a), quoted in note 21 infra.

the absence of explicit statutory authorization.[3] Very little New York precedent exists, however, for the court's calling of a lay witness. In a 1970 decision of the Appellate Division, First Department, the trial court's sua sponte recalling of the defendant for further questioning by the court after the parties had rested was upheld, thus suggesting that the power exists.[4]

More recently, however, the judge presiding at a bench trial in a contract dispute was held by the First Department to have had no authority to order the parties, after both sides had rested, to conduct depositions of two witnesses located in France and to present their deposition testimony to the court.[5] The trial judge said, on the record, that he wanted to find out who was "committing blatant perjury in this case" so that appropriate action could be taken.[6] The First Department found that the trial judge had improperly "arrogated to himself the function of advocate, thus abandoning the impartiality required of his office."[7] If the witnesses had been subject to the court's jurisdiction,[8] and the purpose had been simply to elucidate the facts rather than investigate perjury,[9] it is arguable that the trial judge had discretion to call the witnesses himself. The First Department did not expressly disavow the existence of inherent power in the courts to call witnesses, but it noted that no "provision" authorized such action by the court in the instant case.[10] The paucity of New York caselaw on this subject suggests that neither courts nor litigants have perceived any crying need

---

3. See § 706.1 infra. See also Matter of Estate of Atkinson, 117 A.D.2d 843, 844, 498 N.Y.S.2d 543, 544 (3d Dep't 1986)(Surrogate has inherent power to appoint expert witness, but no abuse of discretion in refusal to do so in circumstances of case).

4. Thom v. Jaymee Fashions, Inc., 35 A.D.2d 946, 316 N.Y.S.2d 595 (1st Dep't 1970), aff'd, 29 N.Y.2d 534, 324 N.Y.S.2d 86, 272 N.E.2d 577 (1971).

5. Carroll v. Gammerman, 193 A.D.2d 202, 602 N.Y.S.2d 841 (1st Dep't 1993) (writ of prohibition granted). There is precedent in federal practice for a judge's sua sponte order that the parties conduct a deposition of a particular witness. Cunningham v. Housing Authority of the City of Opelousas, 764 F.2d 1097, 1100–01 (5th Cir.), cert. denied, 474 U.S. 1007, 106 S.Ct. 530, 88 L.Ed.2d 461 (1985). Such order can be viewed as the functional equivalent of the court's calling of its own witness, which is explicitly authorized in federal cases by Fed.R.Evid. 614(a).

6. 193 A.D.2d at 206, 602 N.Y.S.2d at 844.

7. Id. The First Department stated that the trial judge's proper role was simply to resolve fact questions based on the evidence presented. If one party's evidence was unworthy of belief or its burden of proof was not satisfied, judgment should have been made accordingly. Id. at 206, 602 N.Y.S.2d at 844.

There is a postscript to the case. When the proceedings resumed, one of the relevant witnesses appeared in court to testify, and the trial court's reopening of the record for this purpose was affirmed. Birch v. Carroll, 210 A.D.2d 119, 620 N.Y.S.2d 56 (1st Dep't 1994).

8. A New York court's subpoena power is confined to the state's borders. N.Y.Const. art. VI, § 1(c); N.Y.Judiciary Law § 2–b(1).

9. "[T]he examination of witnesses to ascertain whether a basis exists for prosecution is the province of the District Attorney's Office and the Grand Jury, not a civil trial court." 193 A.D.2d at 206, 602 N.Y.S.2d at 844.

10. Id. at 205, 602 N.Y.S.2d at 843. See also Dentes v. Zimmerman, 159 Misc.2d 415, 418, 605 N.Y.S.2d 188, 190 (Sup.Ct.Tompkins Co.1993)(writ of prohibition granted against town justice for issuing numerous judicial subpoenas on her own motion, "thus injecting the court into the production of evidence without reference to counsel" and "without any threshold showing of relevance").

§ 614.1   WITNESSES   Ch. 6

for the exercise of judicial power to call a court's witness.[11]

b. Judicial Questioning of Witnesses

Although the court's power to call a witness is uncertain, it is clear in New York that the adversary system does not preclude a trial judge from "assuming an active role in the resolution of the truth."[12] Thus, the court may participate in the questioning of witnesses called by the parties when "necessary to elicit significant facts, to clarify or enlighten an issue or merely to facilitate the orderly and expeditious progress of the trial."[13]

The Court of Appeals has repeatedly warned, however, that judicial interrogation of witnesses should be conducted sparingly[14] and with caution.[15] "[T]he Bench must be scrupulously free from and above even the appearance or taint of partiality."[16] The danger in the process of judicial interrogation is that the judge, through words, conduct or demeanor, may be perceived by the jury as having an opinion concerning the merits or the credibility of a witness. Reversals have occurred, for example, when the extent, tone, phrasing or timing of judicial questioning evinced the trial court's belief or disbelief of one side's witnesses[17] or

---

11. The Proposed New York Evidence Code, in § 614(a), would specify certain procedures to be followed when the court calls a witness. See note 21 infra. The code provision itself would not serve as a source of authority for the judicial calling of witnesses, leaving that aspect of the law in the same state of uncertainty that currently exists. Curiously, proposed § 614(a) generally provides that the jury should not be told that the witness was called by the court. Federal practice is to the contrary. See United States v. Karnes, 531 F.2d 214, 217 (4th Cir.1976)(trial court erred in not telling jury why witnesses were called by court and that their credibility was no greater than that of other witnesses).

12. People v. De Jesus, 42 N.Y.2d 519, 523, 399 N.Y.S.2d 196, 199, 369 N.E.2d 752, 755 (1977).

13. People v. Mendes, 3 N.Y.2d 120, 121, 164 N.Y.S.2d 401, 402, 143 N.E.2d 806, 807 (1957). See, e.g., People v. Bennette, 56 N.Y.2d 142, 149, 451 N.Y.S.2d 647, 650, 436 N.E.2d 1249, 1252 (1982)(during prosecutor's cross-examination of defendant about prior sodomy conviction, trial court did not act improperly by intervening with questions designed to obtain more responsive answers regarding details of the crime); People v. Jamison, 47 N.Y.2d 882, 884, 419 N.Y.S.2d 472, 473, 393 N.E.2d 467, 468 (1979)(trial court's questioning of witnesses was evenhanded, temperate, infrequent, and restricted to aiding jury in understanding issues). See also People v. Yut Wai Tom, 53 N.Y.2d 44, 58, 439 N.Y.S.2d 896, 904, 422 N.E.2d 556, 564 (1981)(as illustration of appropriate intervention by trial judge, it was said that judge may "properly question witnesses to insure that a proper foundation is made for the admission of evidence").

14. People v. Jamison, 47 N.Y.2d 882, 883, 419 N.Y.S.2d 472, 473, 393 N.E.2d 467, 468 (1979).

15. People v. Mendes, 3 N.Y.2d 120, 121, 164 N.Y.S.2d 401, 402, 143 N.E.2d 806, 807 (1957).

16. People v. De Jesus, 42 N.Y.2d 519, 524, 399 N.Y.S.2d 196, 199, 369 N.E.2d 752, 755 (1977).

17. See, e.g., People v. Carter, 40 N.Y.2d 933, 934, 389 N.Y.S.2d 835, 836, 358 N.E.2d 517, 519 (1976)("The Trial Judge engaged in prolonged questioning of a defense witness during which he appeared to display an inordinate amount of skepticism in the witness' testimony which was crucial to the defense * * *."); People v. Mendes, 3 N.Y.2d 120, 121, 164 N.Y.S.2d 401, 402, 143 N.E.2d 806, 807 (1957)("a number of questions by the Trial Judge, many of them rhetorical, directed at defendant's witnesses were of such a nature as to indicate a communicable disbelief of their testimony"); People v. Arabadjis, 78 A.D.2d 614, 616, 432 N.Y.S.2d 391, 393 (1st Dep't 1980)("slanted" questioning by judge unfairly buttressed People's case and showed disbelief of defense witnesses); People v. Santana, 73 A.D.2d 977, 977, 424 N.Y.S.2d 237, 238 (2d Dep't 1980)(judge asked 64% of the questions posed to complaining witness on direct examination, thus providing "unnecessarily extensive assistance" to the

created tactical disadvantage to one of the parties.[18]

In *People v. Yut Wai Tom*,[19] the court observed that counsel, in order to make a record for appeal, need not object to judicial questioning "until it is clear that the Judge intends to exceed his permissible role and assume the advocate's function."[20] To preserve the issue, it is sufficient that counsel "[enter] an objection to the improper conduct at a meaningful time during the trial."[21]

c. Questioning by Jurors

New York courts have held that a trial judge has discretion to permit jurors to ask questions of witnesses.[22] The practice has its problems, of course, because lay jurors may ask improper questions, and counsel may be hesitant to object for fear of alienating the jury.[23] The preferred practice, therefore, is for jurors to submit any questions to the trial judge in writing, thereby allowing the judge to strike or modify those that are inappropriate, and for the judge to then pose the questions to the witnesses.[24]

---

prosecution); Livant v. Adams, 17 A.D.2d 784, 784, 232 N.Y.S.2d 641, 642 (1st Dep't 1962)(court's derogatory cross-examination of defense witnesses "openly evinced disbelief in the testimony").

18. People v. Yut Wai Tom, 53 N.Y.2d 44, 57–61, 439 N.Y.S.2d 896, 904–05, 422 N.E.2d 556, 564–65 (1981)(trial court elicited significant testimony from prosecution witnesses during their direct examination and repeatedly interrupted defense counsel's cross-examination in a way that amounted to a "running redirect examination"); People v. De Jesus, 42 N.Y.2d 519, 521, 399 N.Y.S.2d 196, 197, 369 N.E.2d 752, 754 (1977)(during defense counsel's cross-examination, court used caustic, snide and sarcastic remarks to denigrate counsel in jury's presence).

19. 53 N.Y.2d 44, 439 N.Y.S.2d 896, 422 N.E.2d 556 (1981).

20. Id. at 55, 439 N.Y.S.2d at 902, 422 N.E.2d at 562.

21. Id. at 56, 439 N.Y.S.2d at 903, 422 N.E.2d at 563.

The Proposed New York Evidence Code would codify the calling and questioning of witnesses by the court as follows:

§ 614. Calling and examination of witnesses by court [PROPOSED]

(a) Calling by court. When authorized by law, the court may, on its own motion or at the request of a party, call witnesses. Before calling a witness on its own, the court must afford the parties reasonable notice and the opportunity to be heard outside of the presence of the jury. Unless both sides agree, the jury shall not be told that a witness has been called by the court. All parties are entitled to cross-examine witnesses called by the court.

(b) Examination by court. When necessary to aid the jury in understanding the legal and factual issues, the court may examine witnesses, whether called by itself or by a party, provided that the court: should not generally conduct extended examination of a witness, should not assume the role of an advocate, and should refrain from exhibiting hostility, partiality, or bias.

(c) Objections. Objections to the calling of witnesses by the court or to examination by it may be made at the time or at the next available opportunity when the jury is not present.

22. People v. Bacic, 202 A.D.2d 234, 235, 608 N.Y.S.2d 452, 452 (1st Dep't), appeal denied, 83 N.Y.2d 1002, 616 N.Y.S.2d 483, 640 N.E.2d 151 (1994); People v. Wilds, 141 A.D.2d 395, 397, 529 N.Y.S.2d 325, 326 (1st Dep't 1988); People v. Knapper, 230 App.Div. 487, 492, 245 N.Y.S. 245, 251 (1st Dep't 1930); Sitrin Brothers, Inc. v. Deluxe Lines, Inc., 35 Misc.2d 1041, 1043, 231 N.Y.S.2d 943, 946 (Oneida Co.Ct. 1962).

23. People v. Knapper, 230 App.Div. 487, 492, 245 N.Y.S. 245, 251 (1st Dep't 1930). See also § 614.2, at notes 9–12, infra.

24. People v. Bacic, 202 A.D.2d 234, 235, 608 N.Y.S.2d 452, 452 (1st Dep't), appeal denied, 83 N.Y.2d 1002, 616 N.Y.S.2d 483, 640 N.E.2d 151 (1994); People v.

§ 614.1

Library References:

West's Key No. Digests, Witnesses ⚖246.

§ 614.2 Federal

The calling and examination of witnesses by the court is treated in Rule 614 of the Federal Rules of Evidence as follows:

(a) Calling by Court

The court may, on its own motion or at the suggestion of a party, call witnesses, and all parties are entitled to cross-examine witnesses thus called.

(b) Interrogation by court.

The court may interrogate witnesses, whether called by itself or by a party.

(c) Objections.

Objections to the calling of witnesses by the court or to interrogation by it may be made at the time or at the next available opportunity when the jury is not present.

Subdivision (a)'s conferral of authority on the court to call a witness on its own motion codifies an inherent discretion that was recognized prior to the adoption of the Federal Rules of Evidence.[1] Both before and after Rule 614(a), the authority has been exercised sparingly.[2]

Regardless of who calls a witness, subdivision (b) authorizes the court to participate in the interrogation. The Second Circuit has said that " 'the questioning of witnesses by a trial judge, if for a proper purpose such as clarifying ambiguities, correcting misstatements, or obtaining information needed to make rulings, is well within' the court's 'active responsibility to insure that issues clearly are presented to the

---

Wilds, 141 A.D.2d 395, 397, 529 N.Y.S.2d 325, 326 (1st Dep't 1988).

§ 614.2

1. See, e.g., United States v. Marzano, 149 F.2d 923, 925 (2d Cir.1945)("It is permissible, though it is seldom very desirable, for a judge to call and examine a witness whom the parties do not wish to call. * * * A judge is more than a moderator; he is charged to see that the law is properly administered, and it is a duty which he cannot discharge by remaining inert."); United States v. Browne, 313 F.2d 197, 199 (2d Cir.), cert. denied, 374 U.S. 814, 83 S.Ct. 1707, 10 L.Ed.2d 1037, rehearing denied, 375 U.S. 874, 84 S.Ct. 35, 11 L.Ed.2d 105 (1963).

2. See United States v. Marzano, 149 F.2d 923, 925 (2d Cir.1945); United States v. Ostrer, 422 F.Supp. 93, 103 n.11 (S.D.N.Y.1976).

Illustrations of the application of Federal Rule of Evidence 614(a) include the following: United States v. Agajanian, 852 F.2d 56, 58 (2d Cir.1988)(in bench trial for criminal contempt, trial judge acted within discretion in calling witness and having parties cross-examine her without preliminary direct examination by judge); Cunningham v. Housing Authority of the City of Opelousas, 764 F.2d 1097, 1100–01 (5th Cir.), cert. denied, 474 U.S. 1007, 106 S.Ct. 530, 88 L.Ed.2d 461 (1985)(court acted within discretion in directing parties to conduct deposition of witness after both sides had rested; order was equivalent to court's calling its own witness); United States v. Herring, 602 F.2d 1220, 1226–27, rehearing denied, 606 F.2d 321 (5th Cir.1979), cert. denied, 444 U.S. 1046, 100 S.Ct. 734, 62 L.Ed.2d 732 (1980)(court did not abuse discretion in refusing to call court's witness, at defendant's suggestion, on collateral issue); United States v. Karnes, 531 F.2d 214, 216–17 (4th Cir.1976) (trial court abused discretion in calling witnesses to fill gaps in prosecution's case; court also erred by failing to tell jury why witnesses were called by court

Ch. 6 QUESTIONING BY COURT OR JURY § 614.2

jury.'"[3] The trial judge, however, must neither assume the role of advocate[4] nor "convey the court's view about the merits of a party's claim."[5] Obviously, appellate review of alleged abuse is highly fact-specific.[6] Subdivision (c) of Rule 614 specifies that preserving the issue of abusive questioning by the judge requires an objection "either at the

and that their credibility was no greater than that of any other witness).

3. United States v. Victoria, 837 F.2d 50, 54 (2d Cir.1988), quoting United States v. Pisani, 773 F.2d 397, 403 (2d Cir.1985), rehearing denied, 787 F.2d 71 (2d Cir.1986).

4. Advisory Committee's Note, Fed. R.Evid. 614(b). See United States v. Fernandez, 480 F.2d 726, 737 (2d Cir.1973), quoting United States v. Marzano, 149 F.2d 923, 926 (2d Cir.1945)("while the judge may examine witnesses, or occasionally even call them, 'he must not enter the lists'").

5. Berkovich v. Hicks, 922 F.2d 1018, 1025 (2d Cir.1991).

6. Helpful guideposts were articulated by the Sixth Circuit in United States v. Hickman, 592 F.2d 931, 933–34 (6th Cir. 1979):

As is apparent, determining when a trial judge oversteps is difficult. Numerous factors need be considered. First, the nature of the issues at trial. In a lengthy, complex trial, intervention by the judge is often needed to clarify what is going on. * * *

Second, the conduct of counsel. If the attorneys in a case are unprepared or obstreperous, judicial intervention is often called for. If the facts are becoming muddled and neither side is succeeding at attempts to clear them up, the judge performs an important duty by interposing clarificatory comments or questions. * * *

Third, the conduct of witnesses. It is often impossible for counsel to deal with a difficult witness without judicial intervention. * * * Similarly, a witness' testimony may be unbelievable and counsel may fail to adequately probe. * * * More commonly, judicial intervention will operate to clear up inadvertent witness confusion. * * *

Assuming that a trial judge has good reason to interject himself into the trial, the manner in which he does so is crucial. Thus, an objective demeanor is important. Outright bias or belittling of counsel is ordinarily reversible error. * * * However, under some circumstances, misconduct by a trial judge may not mandate reversal. * * *

More common is the appearance of partiality which can easily arise if the judge intervenes continually on the side of one of the parties. Our system of criminal jurisprudence hinges upon the advocacy role played by opposing counsel. Although a trial is a quest for the truth, and a federal trial judge is more than a neutral arbiter[,] interference with the presentations of counsel has the potential of making a mockery of a defendant's right to a fair trial, even in the absence of open hostility. * * * Also present is the danger that undue interference with cross examination rights will result if a judge takes over examination by counsel.

* * *

The following is a sampling of Second Circuit precedents: Berkovich v. Hicks, 922 F.2d 1018, 1025 (2d Cir.1991)(no reversal where trial judge's questioning of plaintiff was "appropriate effort" to clarify answers, had little bearing on significant issues and court posed "equally challenging questions" to defendant); Johnson v. Celotex Corp., 899 F.2d 1281, 1290 (2d Cir.), cert. denied, 498 U.S. 920, 111 S.Ct. 297, 112 L.Ed.2d 250 (1990)(no reversal where judge's questions sought clarification; despite counsel's expression of concern over "manner" of judge's questioning, jury instructions "cured even the appearance of any impropriety"); United States v. Mazzilli, 848 F.2d 384, 388 (2d Cir.1988)(reversal where court's "intensive questioning" of defendant left jury with "indelible impression" that court did not believe defendant, and jury instruction not to be swayed by court's questioning "did not mitigate the adverse impact of [the court's] active intervention"); United States v. Victoria, 837 F.2d 50, 54–55 (2d Cir.1988)(reversal where court's questioning of defendants was in nature of cross-examination which "clearly implied" court's skepticism concerning their credibility); United States v. DiTommaso, 817 F.2d 201, 220 (2d Cir.1987)(no reversal where trial court's reprimands of defense counsel reflected on handling of case, rather than merits, and occurred either outside jury's presence or were accompanied by jury instructions not to draw adverse inferences against attorney's client; limited questioning of witnesses served to clarify testimony, did not reveal judge's opinion and was accompanied by appropriate jury instruction).

§ 614.2　　　　　　WITNESSES　　　　　　Ch. 6

time or at the next available opportunity when the jury is not present."[7]

Questioning by jurors is not explicitly addressed by the Federal Rules of Evidence.[8] Although the Second Circuit "strongly discourage[s]" the practice,[9] the court has held that a trial judge has discretion to permit such questioning in "extraordinary or compelling circumstances" for the purpose of clarifying the issues.[10] In *United States v. Bush*,[11] the court prescribed the following procedures to be followed by trial courts: "(1) jurors should be instructed to submit their questions in writing to the judge; (2) outside the presence of the jury, the judge should review the questions with counsel, who may then object; and (3) the court itself should put the approved questions to the witnesses."[12]

Library References:

West's Key No. Digests, Witnesses ⚷246.

615　Exclusion of Witnesses from the Courtroom

§ 615.1　New York

It is a time-honored practice for the trial judge, upon a party's request, to exclude witnesses from the courtroom prior to their testimony.[1] The purpose is to prevent the tailoring of testimony and to facilitate counsel's exposure of inconsistencies, inaccuracies and falsehoods.[2] In New York practice, however, the sequestration of witnesses,

---

7. See, e.g., United States v. Vega, 589 F.2d 1147, 1153 (2d Cir.1978) (even if error was committed by judge with respect to questioning of witness, counsel failed to object either at time of questioning or later in trial; appeals court suggested that counsel request bench conference to avoid objecting in jury's presence).

8. Cf. Fed.R.Evid. 611(a)("court shall exercise control over the mode * * * of interrogating witnesses").

9. United States v. Bush, 47 F.3d 511, 515 (2d Cir.1995).

10. Id. at 516. In United States v. Ajmal, 67 F.3d 12 (2d Cir.1995), the district court was held to have abused its discretion by encouraging extensive juror questioning in a routine case. See also DeBenedetto v. Goodyear Tire Rubber Co., 754 F.2d 512, 515–16 (4th Cir.1985)(propriety of jury's questioning of witnesses is within trial judge's discretion but practice should be restricted to "compelling circumstances"); United States v. Callahan, 588 F.2d 1078, 1086, rehearing denied, 591 F.2d 1343 (5th Cir.), cert. denied, 444 U.S. 826, 100 S.Ct. 49, 62 L.Ed.2d 33 (1979)("occasional" questions by jurors are within court's discretion to clarify point in the proof).

The Second Circuit listed the dangers inherent in juror questioning: (1) it is difficult for jurors to remain neutral observers when they become "active participants in the adversary process"; (2) jury questioning risks premature commencement of deliberations; (3) jurors generally lack knowledge of the rules of evidence and may therefore ask prejudicial or improper questions; and (4) attorneys who openly object to improper juror questions risk alienating the jury. United States v. Bush, supra, 47 F.3d at 515.

11. 47 F.3d 511(2d Cir.1995).

12. Id. at 516.

§ 615.1

1. People v. Felder, 39 A.D.2d 373, 379–80, 334 N.Y.S.2d 992, 999 (2d Dep't 1972), aff'd, 32 N.Y.2d 747, 344 N.Y.S.2d 643, 297 N.E.2d 522, appeal dismissed, 414 U.S. 948, 94 S.Ct. 299, 38 L.Ed.2d 204 (1973), reargument denied, 39 N.Y.2d 743, 384 N.Y.S.2d 1029, 349 N.E.2d 892 (1976).

2. See Perry v. Leeke, 488 U.S. 272, 281–82, 109 S.Ct. 594, 600, 102 L.Ed.2d 624, 634 (1989)("[W]itnesses may be sequestered to lessen the danger that their testimony will be influenced by hearing what other witnesses have to say, and to increase the likelihood that they will confine themselves to truthful statements

or "putting the witnesses under the rule," as it is sometimes called,[3] is not mandatory; it has always been in the trial court's discretion.[4] Appellate courts have encouraged the granting of exclusion orders,[5] but reversals for abuse of discretion are rare.[6]

A trial court's authority to exclude a witness from the courtroom would seem to carry with it the implied power to direct the witness not to discuss her testimony with others or to read a transcript until the trial is over.[7] The power of sequestration, however, is limited when it comes to the parties themselves. Both criminal defendants[8] and parties in civil actions[9] have a constitutional right to be present in the court-

based on their own recollections."); Philpot v. Fifth Avenue Coach Co., 142 App.Div. 811, 813, 128 N.Y.S. 35, 37 (1st Dep't 1911)("What is important is that each person's impression of the occurrence should be stated—not suggested or colored by what he has heard others testify to * * *."); McCormick § 50, at 188 ("[T]he cross-examiner will find it more difficult to expose fabrication, collusion, inconsistencies or inaccuracies with respect to witnesses who have heard others testify.").

3. People v. Cooke, 292 N.Y. 185, 191, 54 N.E.2d 357, 360 (1944).

4. Id.

5. Id. at 190–91, 54 N.E.2d at 360; People v. Felder, 39 A.D.2d 373, 380, 334 N.Y.S.2d 992, 999 (2d Dep't 1972), aff'd, 32 N.Y.2d 747, 344 N.Y.S.2d 643, 297 N.E.2d 522, appeal dismissed, 414 U.S. 948, 94 S.Ct. 299, 38 L.Ed.2d 204 (1973), reargument denied, 39 N.Y.2d 743, 384 N.Y.S.2d 1029, 349 N.E.2d 892 (1976); Philpot v. Fifth Avenue Coach Co., 142 App.Div. 811, 813, 128 N.Y.S. 35, 37 (1st Dep't 1911).

The Proposed New York Evidence Code § 615(a), which is quoted in note 10 infra, would make the exclusion of witnesses mandatory upon a party's request.

6. See, e.g., Levine v. Levine, 56 N.Y.2d 42, 49, 451 N.Y.S.2d 26, 29, 436 N.E.2d 476, 479 (1982)(in wife's action to rescind separation agreement, court did not abuse discretion in refusing to exclude attorney who drafted agreement for both parties); People v. Torres, 118 A.D.2d 821, 822, 500 N.Y.S.2d 178, 179 (2d Dep't 1986)(not abuse of discretion to permit police witnesses to remain in courtroom).

7. See Perry v. Leeke, 488 U.S. 272, 281, 109 S.Ct. 594, 600, 102 L.Ed.2d 624, 634 (1989)(judge's instruction to witness to refrain from discussing her testimony with others is "corollary of the broader rule that witnesses may be sequestered."); McCormick § 50, at 191.

New York authority on this question, as it applies in the case of ordinary witnesses, is virtually nonexistent. In one civil action in which the witnesses were excluded from the courtroom, apparently without any explicit prohibition on speaking to others about their testimony, the court held that defense counsel "in the circumstances here presented" was not precluded from speaking to the witnesses during recess. Capitol Cab Corp. v. Anderson, 194 Misc. 21, 24, 85 N.Y.S.2d 767, 770 (N.Y.C.Mun.Ct.1949), aff'd, 197 Misc. 1035, 100 N.Y.S.2d 39 (Sup. Ct.App.T., 1st Dep't 1950). Federal precedents are cited in § 615.2, at notes 8–10, infra. To avoid uncertainties, counsel should ask the court to make the scope of its order of exclusion clear from the outset. In any event, a criminal defendant's right to counsel circumscribes prohibitions on consulting with defense counsel. See note 8 infra.

8. See People v. Dokes, 79 N.Y.2d 656, 659, 584 N.Y.S.2d 761, 763, 595 N.E.2d 836, 838 (1992)(criminal defendant has confrontation and due process rights under both federal and state constitutions to be present during trial). The criminal defendant's right to counsel also entitles her to discuss her testimony with her attorney during overnight recesses. Geders v. United States, 425 U.S. 80, 88–89, 96 S.Ct. 1330, 1335–36, 47 L.Ed.2d 592, 599 (1976). See also People v. Joseph, 84 N.Y.2d 995, 997–98, 622 N.Y.S.2d 505, 506–07, 646 N.E.2d 807, 808 (1994)(weekend recess). On the other hand, a short-term bar on defendant's ability to discuss her testimony with counsel, such as during a luncheon recess in the prosecution's cross-examination of the defendant, is permissible. People v. Enrique, 80 N.Y.2d 869, 587 N.Y.S.2d 598, 600 N.E.2d 229 (1992). See also Perry v. Leeke, 488 U.S. 272, 284, 109 S.Ct. 594, 602, 102 L.Ed.2d 624, 635–36 (1989)(barring defendant from consulting with counsel during 15-minute interlude between direct and cross-examination did not violate sixth amendment).

9. Radjpaul v. Patton, 145 A.D.2d 494, 497–98, 535 N.Y.S.2d 743, 745–46 (2d Dep't

room throughout the trial. It follows that an organizational party, such as a corporation, should be entitled to designate a representative to remain with the party's counsel even if that representative will be a witness.[10] A party's right to be present at trial, however, is subject to waiver or "unusual circumstances."[11] Some courts, for example, have authorized the exclusion of profoundly injured plaintiffs from the liability phase of a bifurcated jury trial, i.e., a trial of liability issues prior to damages, where such plaintiffs have no ability to communicate with counsel and the prejudice to defendants would be serious.[12]

What consequences should flow from a witness' violation of a proper order of exclusion? New York courts have shown no inclination to disqualify the witness from testifying.[13] She may be punished for contempt,[14] and her credibility may be impeached by showing that prior

---

1988); Lunney v. Graham, 91 A.D.2d 592, 593, 457 N.Y.S.2d 282, 283 (1st Dep't 1982); Carlisle v. County of Nassau, 64 A.D.2d 15, 18, 408 N.Y.S.2d 114, 116 (2d Dep't 1978). ("[T]he fundamental constitutional right of a person to have a jury trial in certain civil cases includes therein the ancillary right to be present at all stages of such a trial, except deliberations of the jury. * * * Such right is basic to due process of law. * * *").

10. Cf. Sherman v. Irving Merchandise Corp., 26 N.Y.S.2d 645 (Sup.Ct.App.T., 1st Dep't 1941)(exclusion of defendant-corporation's president, who had responsibility for "looking after the corporation's interests at trial," was prejudicial error: "Great caution should be exercised in considering an application to exclude the officers of corporations, or a representative in charge of the matters litigated.").

Proposed New York Evidence Code § 615(b) would explicitly exempt an organizational party's designated representative from the rule of exclusion (except the state in a criminal case). Subdivision (c) of the proposed code rule would also permit a party to show that a witness is "necessary to assist the attorney or the party" in presenting the case. The complete text of the proposed rule is as follows:

§ 615. Exclusion of witnesses [PROPOSED]

The court may, or upon request shall, order prospective witnesses excluded so that they cannot hear the testimony of other witnesses. This section does not authorize exclusion of:

(a) a party who is a natural person except that in a child custody proceeding the court may examine the child out of the presence of the parties;

(b) an officer or employee of a party, other than the state in a criminal case, which is not a natural person if that officer or employee is designated as the representative of the party by its attorney: or

(c) a person whose presence the court determines to be necessary to assist the attorney or the party, including the state in a criminal case in the presentation of a party's cause.

The proposed code provision is similar to Fed.R.Evid. 615. See § 615.2 infra.

11. Lunney v. Graham, 91 A.D.2d 592, 593, 457 N.Y.S.2d 282, 283 (1st Dep't 1982). In criminal cases, a criminal defendant may be excluded for disruptive conduct. N.Y.Crim.Proc.Law § 260.20.

12. See Caputo v. Joseph J. Sarcona Trucking Co., 204 A.D.2d 507, 507–08, 611 N.Y.S.2d 655, 656 (2d Dep't 1994)("Although the physical condition of a plaintiff, in and of itself, is not enough to justify his involuntary exclusion from any phase of the trial, * * *, when a plaintiff is both physically and mentally incapable and his mental incapacity prevents him from assisting counsel in any meaningful way, then the decision to exclude the plaintiff from the liability phase of a trial lies within the sound discretion of the trial court * * *. Here, [plaintiff's] presence in the courtroom would have impaired the jury's ability to objectively perform its task because he physically appeared to be in a state of unawareness * * *."); Monteleone v. Gestetner Corp., 140 Misc.2d 841, 531 N.Y.S.2d 857 (Sup.Ct.N.Y.Co.1988). See also § 615.2, at note 2, infra.

13. See e.g., People v. Rivera, 182 A.D.2d 1092, 583 N.Y.S.2d 78 (4th Dep't), appeal denied, 80 N.Y.2d 896, 587 N.Y.S.2d 927, 600 N.E.2d 654 (1992).

14. People v. Gifford, 2 A.D.2d 634, 634, 151 N.Y.S.2d 980, 981 (3d Dep't 1956).

to testifying she heard the testimony of the other witnesses.[15]

Library References:

West's Key No. Digests, Criminal Law ⚖=665; Trial ⚖=41.

§ 615.2 Federal

In contrast to the rule of discretion in New York,[1] Federal Rule of Evidence 615 makes the exclusion of witnesses mandatory upon the request of any party. The text of Rule 615 is as follows:

> At the request of a party the court shall order witnesses excluded so that they cannot hear the testimony of other witnesses, and it may make the order of its own motion. This rule does not authorize exclusion of (1) a party who is a natural person, or (2) an officer or employee of a party which is not a natural person designated as its representative by its attorney, or (3) a person whose presence is shown by a party to be essential to the presentation of the party's cause.

The Rule contains three exemptions. First, any party who is a natural person has a right to be present.[2] Second, the attorney for an organizational party, including the government, may designate an officer or employee to serve as its representative.[3] The designated representative may then remain in the courtroom (usually at counsel's table) throughout the trial even if she will be a witness. Third, the court may exempt a witness whose presence is shown to be "essential to the presentation of the party's cause."[4]

In criminal cases, prosecutors have been allowed to maintain the presence of two agent-witnesses, one as a representative of the government (Rule 615(2)), and the other as a person whose expertise has been shown to be essential in presenting the government's case (Rule 615(3)).[5] Moreover, the Second Circuit has held that a district judge has discretion

---

15. Id. See also People v. Lloyde, 106 A.D.2d 405, 405–06, 482 N.Y.S.2d 326, 327 (2d Dep't 1984). Federal trial courts have discretion, in egregious cases, to exclude the testimony of a disobedient witness. See § 615.2, at note 12, infra.

§ 615.2

1. See § 615.1, at note 4, supra.

2. It has been held, however, that exclusion of a plaintiff during the liability phase of a personal injury trial is permissible, in the court's discretion, where the jury's viewing of the plaintiff would seriously prejudice the defendant and the plaintiff is shown to be incapable of assisting counsel and understanding the proceedings. Helminski v. Ayerst Laboratories, 766 F.2d 208, 217–18 (6th Cir.), cert. denied, 474 U.S. 981, 106 S.Ct. 386, 88 L.Ed.2d 339 (1985). See also In re Bendectin Litigation, 857 F.2d 290, 322–24 (6th Cir.1988), cert.denied, 488 U.S. 1006, 109 S.Ct. 788, 102 L.Ed.2d 779 (1989).

3. In criminal trials, the chief investigative agent who supervised the case is often designated as the government's representative. See, e.g., United States v. Rivera, 971 F.2d 876, 889 (2d Cir.1992).

4. See, e.g., Malek v. Federal Insurance Co., 994 F.2d 49, 54 (2d Cir.1993)(expert witness "whose assistance was important to the presentation of plaintiffs' case * * * should have been permitted to remain in the courtroom").

On a related point, 18 U.S.C.A. § 3509(i) provides that a child-victim of physical or sexual abuse or a child-witness to such crimes has a right to the continued presence in the courtroom of an adult attendant while the child testifies.

5. See United States v. Jackson, 60 F.3d 128, 134 (2d Cir.1995); United States v. Rivera, 971 F.2d 876, 890 (2d Cir.1992).

to authorize more than one exemption per subparagraph of Rule 615.[6] The prosecution might be able to establish, for example, that the technical and administrative complexities of the case necessitate the continuing presence of two agent-witnesses in addition to the supervisory agent-witness who is serving as the government's representative.[7]

Implicit in the court's authority to sequester witnesses is the authority to direct them not to talk about the case to third persons or to read transcripts.[8] Some courts have taken the position that a general order of exclusion, standing alone, impliedly prohibits out-of-court communications among witnesses or the reading of transcripts.[9] Such courts nevertheless have encouraged counsel to obtain instructions from the trial judge concerning the precise scope of an exclusion order.[10]

---

6. United States v. Jackson, 60 F.3d 128, 134–35 (2d Cir.1995). The court noted, however, that because Rule 615 "carries a strong presumption in favor of sequestration * * * [t]he party opposing sequestration * * * has the burden of demonstrating why the pertinent Rule 615 exception applies." Id. at 135.

Some other circuits have restricted the government to one agent per exception. United States v. Pulley, 922 F.2d 1283, 1285–86 (6th Cir.), cert. denied, 502 U.S. 815, 112 S.Ct. 67, 116 L.Ed.2d 42 (1991); United States v. Farnham, 791 F.2d 331, 334–35 (4th Cir.1986).

7. United States v. Jackson, 60 F.3d 128, 135–37 (2d Cir.1995) (government's showing at trial of need for two agent-witnesses to manage volume of evidence and electronic equipment was meager, but government carried its burden on appeal of demonstrating that any error was harmless under the circumstances).

8. Perry v. Leeke, 488 U.S. 272, 281–82, 109 S.Ct. 594, 600–01, 102 L.Ed.2d 624, 634 (1989)(nondiscussion order is corollary of trial court's authority to exclude witnesses from courtroom); United States v. Bautista, 23 F.3d 726, 732 (2d Cir.), cert. denied, ___ U.S. ___, 115 S.Ct. 174, 130 L.Ed.2d 110, (1994)(defendant could have requested trial judge to instruct government witness not to discuss case with prosecutor or others during recess).

A criminal defendant, on the other hand, has a constitutional right to consult with her attorney during overnight recesses. Geders v. United States, 425 U.S. 80, 88–89, 96 S.Ct. 1330, 1335–36, 47 L.Ed.2d 592, 599 (1976). On the other hand, a trial court's short-term prohibition on consultation between defendant and counsel during a fifteen-minute break between direct and cross-examination was held to be constitutionally permissible. Perry v. Leeke, 488 U.S. 272, 283–85, 109 S.Ct. 594, 601–02, 102 L.Ed.2d 624, 635–36 (1989).

9. See United States v. Buchanan, 787 F.2d 477, 484 (10th Cir.1986), cert. denied, 494 U.S. 1088, 110 S.Ct. 1829, 108 L.Ed.2d 958 (1990)(although prohibition on witness-to-witness communication is not within explicit wording of Rule 615, "it is necessary to prevent a circumvention of the Rule"); United States v. Johnston, 578 F.2d 1352, 1355 (10th Cir.), cert. denied, 439 U.S. 931, 99 S.Ct. 321, 58 L.Ed.2d 325 (1978) ("circumvention of the rule does occur where witnesses indirectly defeat its purpose by discussing testimony they have given and events in the courtroom with other witnesses who are to testify"); Miller v. Universal City Studios, Inc., 650 F.2d 1365, 1373 (5th Cir.1981)(where court made general order of sequestration, witness' reading of daily transcripts was violation of general sequestration order: "The harm [of tailored testimony] may be even more pronounced with a witness who reads trial transcript than with one who hears the testimony in open court, because the former need not rely on his memory of the testimony but can thoroughly review and study the transcript in formulating his own testimony.").

The Second Circuit has not definitively adopted a position. See United States v. Friedman, 854 F.2d 535, 568 (2d Cir.1988), cert. denied, 490 U.S. 1004, 109 S.Ct. 1637, 104 L.Ed.2d 153 (1989)(reading of transcript "may" be violative of general exclusion order).

10. United States v. Buchanan, 787 F.2d 477, 485 (10th Cir.1986), cert. denied, 494 U.S. 1088, 110 S.Ct. 1829, 108 L.Ed.2d 958 (1990)("The witnesses should be clearly directed, when the Rule is invoked, that they must all leave the courtroom (with the exceptions the Rule permits), and that they are not to discuss the case or what their testimony has been or would be or what occurs in the courtroom with anyone other than counsel for either side. * * * Counsel know, and are responsible to the court, not to cause any indirect violation of the Rule

When violation of an exclusion order occurs, the usual remedy is to permit impeachment of the witness' credibility on this basis.[11] The trial judge has discretion to exclude the testimony of the disobedient witness altogether, but such disqualification has been reserved for cases involving "connivance" by the witness or counsel coupled with a showing of actual prejudice.[12]

Library References:

West's Key No. Digests, Criminal Law ⚖︎665; Federal Civil Procedure ⚖︎2012.

by themselves discussing what has occurred in the courtroom with the witnesses.")

11. See, e.g., United States v. Friedman, 854 F.2d 535, 568–69 (2d Cir.1988), cert. denied, 490 U.S. 1004, 109 S.Ct. 1637, 104 L.Ed.2d 153 (1989); United States v. Buchanan, 787 F.2d 477, 485 (10th Cir.1986), cert. denied, 494 U.S. 1088, 110 S.Ct. 1829, 108 L.Ed.2d 958 (1990).

12. United States v. Friedman, 854 F.2d 535, 568 (2d Cir.1988)(trial court properly allowed witness to testify); United States v. Gibson, 675 F.2d 825, 836 (6th Cir.), cert. denied, 459 U.S. 972, 103 S.Ct. 305, 74 L.Ed.2d 285 (1982)(disqualification of witness was justified). See also Miller v. Universal City Studios, Inc., 650 F.2d 1365, 1373 (5th Cir.1981) (disqualification of expert witness was "reasonable" where counsel had permitted expert to read daily transcripts despite general sequestration order).

Chapter 7

OPINIONS AND EXPERT TESTIMONY

Table of Sections

700 OPINION TESTIMONY: INTRODUCTION
700.1 New York and Federal.

701 OPINION TESTIMONY BY LAY WITNESSES
701.1 New York.
701.2 Federal.

702 EXPERT TESTIMONY
702.1 New York.
    a. Generally.
    b. Novel Scientific Theories and Methods.
    c. Recurring Problems of Expert Testimony.
    d. The "Interested Observer."
    e. Qualifications.
    f. Impeachment of Experts.
702.2 Federal.
    a. Generally.
    b. Scientific Evidence.

703 BASIS OF EXPERT OPINION TESTIMONY
703.1 New York.
703.2 Federal.

704 OPINION ON ULTIMATE ISSUES
704.1 New York.
704.2 Federal.

705 DISCLOSURE OF FACTS AND DATA UNDERLYING EXPERT OPINION
705.1 New York.
705.2 Federal.

706 COURT-APPOINTED EXPERTS
706.1 New York.
706.2 Federal.

WESTLAW Electronic Research

See WESTLAW Electronic Research Guide preceding the Summary of Contents.

700 Opinion Testimony: Introduction

§ 700.1 New York and Federal

Perhaps there is no other area in the law of evidence so open to construction and so honored in the breach than the area of opinion evidence. Certain guidelines have been historically imposed which purport to limit the way in which witnesses may express themselves on the stand. Ordinary witnesses, including eyewitnesses, are in a different category from witnesses with special knowledge and skills, or expert witnesses. The former shall not invade the province of the latter, and the latter shall not invade the province of the jury—or so it is handed down to us. Likewise, the expert witness should not be employed to testify on a matter which really needs no expertise and which can be fully dealt with by a lay witness.

Article 7 of the Federal Rules of Evidence contains the current general guidelines that are followed closely in the Proposed New York Evidence Code. This framework to a large extent expresses the law now being applied by the state courts in New York and thus provides a good reference even though the proposed New York Code has not been adopted.

Library References:

West's Key No. Digests, Criminal Law ⚖️448–506; Evidence ⚖️470–574.

701 Opinion Testimony by Lay Witnesses

§ 701.1 New York

The common law opinion rule posits that a lay witness may testify only as to facts and may not indulge in rendering an opinion.[1] Historically, opinion was equated with "conjecture," a jurisprudential mistake resulting from mixing the issue of competency (whether the witness has personal knowledge) with mode of expression.[2] The point is that more often than not the witness is incapable of describing an event without resorting to testimony that can only be described literally as opinion. The Proposed New York Evidence Code § 701 acknowledges there is still such a thing as the opinion rule, but would open it up to the wide use of discretion:

> If a witness is not testifying as an expert, the testimony of the witness in the form of opinions or inferences is limited to

---

§ 701.1

1. Morehouse v. Mathews, 2 N.Y. 514, 515–16 (1849)("[W]itnesses must be confined to the communication of *facts*, and not *opinions* or conclusions which they have formed from facts, whether known to themselves, or derived from the testimony of others. It is the special duty of the jury to draw *conclusions*, and not of the witness.") (emphasis in original).

2. McCormick, §§ 10, 11, at 39–42. Carried to its logical extreme the opinion rule would not let a witness say he had seen a cow. He would have to testify that he saw a four-legged animal that weighed around 700 pounds, ate grass, had horns and an udder and was colored black and white.

those opinions or inferences which are difficult to describe in more concrete terms, rationally based on the perception of the witness, and helpful to a clear understanding of the testimony of the witness or the determination of a fact in issue.

This warms to McCormick's view that today, quibbling objections concerning whether the lay witness' testimony is an "opinion" should be summarily overruled, at least if that is the only basis for the objection. The question should be whether the witness' testimony is based on personal knowledge and will assist the jury in understanding the facts.[3] The proposed New York Code provision does not go as far to fulfill this objective as does Rule 701 of the Federal Rules of Evidence, discussed in § 701.2 below, but the New York courts have long adopted a relatively liberal approach in any event.[4] Certainly it has long been established that objections will not be brooked when the witness is testifying to ordinary perceptions such as color, weight, and height on the ground that technically such observations call for an opinion.[5] Permissible testimony on such matters, however, ends at the point that the witness is in an area calling for special knowledge which it is not shown he possesses. In *Larsen v. Vigliarolo Brothers, Inc.*,[6] the court would not let the witness testify to the speed of a motorcycle because "[w]hile it is true that a witness will ordinarily be allowed to testify as to the estimated speed of an automobile * * * such rule is premised upon the prevalence of automobiles in our society and the frequency with which most people have to view them at various speeds. However, the same may not be said about motorcycles."[7] This holding is typical of the fairly unpredict-

---

3. McCormick § 11, at 44–45. It is there stated: "It is believed that the standard actually applied by many of the trial judges of today includes the principle espoused by Wigmore, namely that opinions of laymen should be rejected only when they are superfluous in the sense that they will be of no value to the jury. * * * It seems fair to observe that the prevailing practice in respect to the admission of the opinions of non-expert witnesses may well be described, not as a rule excluding opinions, but as a rule of preference. The more concrete description is preferred to the more abstract."

4. See People v. Adorno, 128 Misc.2d 389, 393–94, 489 N.Y.S.2d 441, 444 (N.Y.C.Crim.Ct.1984)("Since the time of the Morehouse decision [note 1 supra], the courts have expanded their views regarding the admission of testimony of ordinary witnesses to include those items which are recognizable through everyday experience. This expansionist trend can be attributed to the fact that the difference between a statement of conclusion, inadmissible as evidence and an admissible statement of fact is in many cases 'shadowy and difficult to define.'").

5. See 7 Wigmore § 1919. See, e.g., People v. Fernandez, 35 N.Y. 49, 60–62 (1866)(lay witness may testify that stains on garments appeared to be blood: "Matter of common observation may ordinarily be proved by those who witness them, without resorting to mechanical or scientific tests to verify them with definite precision").

6. 77 A.D.2d 562, 429 N.Y.S.2d 273 (2d Dep't), leave to appeal denied, 52 N.Y.2d 702, 437 N.Y.S.2d 1025, 418 N.E.2d 679 (1980).

7. The court cited Marcucci v. Bird, 275 App.Div. 127, 88 N.Y.S.2d 333 (3d Dep't 1949), for the proposition that witnesses can testify concerning automobile speeds. The witness in *Larsen*, however, was allowed to state that just before the accident he observed plaintiff's motorcycle travel 70 feet in one second. Another witness, one with "special knowledge," in response to a hypothetical question containing that observation, gave an opinion that the plaintiff was going 47¾ miles per hour at the time. This was approved by the Appellate Division.

able gray area along the line separating ordinary knowledge from specialized knowledge.[8]

8. In People v. Kenny, 30 N.Y.2d 154, 331 N.Y.S.2d 392, 282 N.E.2d 295 (1972), the court was unwilling to hold that the alcohol rule could be extended to marijuana. The alcohol rule simply provides that ordinary witnesses can testify that a drink was alcoholic. People v. Leonard, 8 N.Y.2d 60, 201 N.Y.S.2d 509, 167 N.E.2d 842 (1960). The world was seen as being much more experienced with alcohol than with narcotics; only an expert could identify the latter.

Recurring subjects of lay testimony that implicate the opinion rule are as follows:

Handwriting. Provided a foundation is laid that the witness is familiar with the person's handwriting by having received correspondence from that person, or otherwise having observed the person's writing, he may testify that he views the document in evidence to have been written or signed by that person. People v. Corey, 148 N.Y. 476, 484, 42 N.E. 1066, 1069 (1896); People v. Clark, 122 A.D.2d 389, 390, 504 N.Y.S.2d 799, 800 (3d Dep't), appeal denied, 68 N.Y.2d 913, 508 N.Y.S.2d 1033, 501 N.E.2d 606 (1986). The lay witness may not, however, without such a foundation, testify that in his opinion a signature in issue was made by the same person whose specimen signature is offered for comparison. Such a comparison can only be made by a handwriting expert. Matter of Collins v. Wyman, 38 A.D.2d 600, 328 N.Y.S.2d 725 (2d Dep't 1971). Wigmore's history of the handwriting rule is incredibly rich. See 7 Wigmore §§ 1991–2028, especially § 2007. Handwriting comparison is discussed again at § 901.2(a), infra.

Speed. In addition to Larsen v. Vigliarolo Brothers, Inc., 77 A.D.2d 562, 429 N.Y.S.2d 273 (2d Dep't), leave to appeal denied, 52 N.Y.2d 702, 437 N.Y.S.2d 1025, 418 N.E.2d 679 (1980)(discussed in the text), see People v. Olsen, 22 N.Y.2d 230, 292 N.Y.S.2d 420, 239 N.E.2d 354 (1968), which held that a speeding conviction could rest on the uncorroborated estimate of a police officer as to the speed of defendant's vehicle: "The rule is well settled in this State that opinion evidence with regard to the speed of moving vehicles is admissible provided that the witness who testifies first shows some experience in observing the rate of speed of moving objects or some other satisfactory reason or basis for his opinion." Id. at 231–32, 292 N.Y.S.2d at 421, 239 N.E.2d at 355. The rule, since it is based on the idea that the witness must have sufficient experience with the vehicle in question, could apply to the speed of any vehicle, including motorcycles (see Swoboda v. We Try Harder, Inc., 128 A.D.2d 862, 513 N.Y.S.2d 781 (2d Dep't 1987), and airplanes. As to the latter, special knowledge and experience would probably be required.

Sanity. Although the lay witness may not render an opinion that another person was sane or insane, or appeared sane or insane, he may testify that the actions and words of the person appeared rational or irrational. People v. Kohlmeyer, 284 N.Y. 366, 369, 31 N.E.2d 490, 492 (1940); Gomboy v. Mitchell, 57 A.D.2d 916, 916, 395 N.Y.S.2d 55, 56 (2d Dep't 1977). An exception to this rule is expressed in the older cases so that it is permissible for a subscribing witness to a will to testify, based on his observations of the testator at the time the will was signed, that the testator was either of sound or unsound mind. Matter of Coleman, 111 N.Y. 220, 19 N.E. 71 (1888). In any case, it seems that the witness must preface his opinion by describing the acts and words of the subject which led to the conclusion reached by the witness. People v. Pekarz, 185 N.Y. 470, 78 N.E. 294 (1906).

Intoxication, Physical Appearance. Under the rule in People v. Leonard, 8 N.Y.2d 60, 201 N.Y.S.2d 509, 167 N.E.2d 842 (1960), reinforced in People v. Kenny, 30 N.Y.2d 154, 331 N.Y.S.2d 392, 282 N.E.2d 295 (1972), a lay witness may testify to whether a person was sober or intoxicated based on his observations and foundation experience. See also Allan v. Keystone Nineties, Inc., 74 A.D.2d 992, 427 N.Y.S.2d 107 (4th Dep't 1980); Burke v. Tower East Restaurant, 37 A.D.2d 836, 326 N.Y.S.2d 32 (2d Dep't 1971); Donahue v. Meagley, 220 App. Div. 469, 221 N.Y.S. 707 (4th Dep't 1927). It follows that observations as to less intense conditions such as that the person looked sick, sad, angry or jovial is admissible (7 Wigmore § 1974) as is testimony concerning a physical infirmity which would have been observable by anyone (Id. §§ 568, 1975). Compare Blake v. People, 73 N.Y. 586, 587 (1878)(lay witness may characterize emotions of another person) with Pearce v. Stace, 207 N.Y. 506, 512, 101 N.E. 434, 436 (1913)(lay witness may not opine that two people appeared to be in love). Under the rule in the *Kenny* case it seems unlikely that lay testimony can be used to identify narcotics. Whether such a witness can testify that from her observations she concluded that a person was under the influence of narcotics or a particular narcotic is questionable.

Age, Race. Estimation of age based on physical appearance can generally be given

That the describing of observations by the witness is permissible even if technically in opinion form, assuming the topic lies within lay competence, makes up only part of the problem. The other aspect of concern is that the witness should testify only to those observations and not go on to draw conclusions such as "that certainly was negligent," or "I know he intended to pull the trigger."[9] These, of course, are truly "ultimate" questions for the fact-finder, and while a qualified expert might be permitted occasionally to broach such conclusions, the lay witness may not.[10] There are also witness-by-witness determinations where testimony is challenged because of its equivocal nature. For instance, when the witness prefaces his statement by "I think," "I believe," "my impression is," "I cannot be positive, but I think," "to the best of my recollection," or "it is my understanding," the judge is simply put to the task of evaluating such limitations in light of all the circumstances.[11] The question of how the testimony is framed bears close connection to the extent of the witness' personal knowledge and soundness of recollection, points that are discussed in §§ 601.1–602.2 *supra*.

Library References:

West's Key No. Digests, Criminal Law ⚖449; Evidence ⚖470–503.

§ 701.2 Federal

Rule 701 of the Federal Rules of Evidence, "Opinion Testimony By Lay Witnesses," states:

> If the witness is not testifying as an expert, the witness' testimony in the form of opinions or inferences is limited to those opinions or inferences which are (a) rationally based on the perception of the witness and (b) helpful to a clear understanding of the witness' testimony or the determination of a fact in issue.

This provision offers the trial judge wide latitude in evaluating the way in which testimony is expressed.[1] The Advisory Committee, in

---

by a lay witness. Hartshorn v. Metropolitan Life Ins. Co., 55 App. Div. 471, 67 N.Y.S. 13 (4th Dep't 1900); 2 Wigmore § 222. Likewise, if possessing the necessary experience, a witness may testify as to a person's race (1 Wigmore § 167).

9. A witness may, however, testify to his own intent. People v. Levan, 295 N.Y. 26, 33–34, 64 N.E.2d 341, 345 (1945).

10. Hartley v. Szadkowski, 32 A.D.2d 550, 300 N.Y.S.2d 82 (2d Dep't 1969) (witness should not have been allowed to testify that highway was "dangerous"). Loaded words such as "stolen" should normally be stricken; but where in context the word is relatively innocuous the fact that it, like other words such as "discriminate," "accident," and "assault," expresses a legal conclusion, often the "ultimate" question, its use will not be fatal. See Weinstein and Berger ¶ 701[02], at 701–27, 28. See also Stone v. United States, 385 F.2d 713 (10th Cir.1967), cert. denied, 391 U.S. 966, 88 S.Ct. 2038, 20 L.Ed.2d 880 (1968). Cf. Strauch v. Hirschman, 40 A.D.2d 711, 336 N.Y.S.2d 678 (2d Dep't 1972)(testimony that a certain basketball drill that caused injury to the infant plaintiff was "dangerous and improper" was held to have "invaded the province of the jury").

11. The illustrations are taken from 3 Weinstein and Berger ¶ 701[02], at 701–29–30 n.32, quoting from Ladd, "Expert and Other Opinion Testimony," 40 Minn.L.Rev. 437, 440 (1956).

§ 701.2

1. The "rational-basis" component of the Rule is derived from the requirement that a witness have personal knowledge of the matter. United States v. Rivera, 22 F.3d 430, 434 (2d Cir.1994). See § 602.2 supra.

effect, disavowed the common law opinion rule and opted for a common-sense rule for the admission of testimony whether in the form of opinion or not.[2] In this respect it is more liberal than the Proposed New York Evidence Code § 701, discussed in § 701.1, above, which limits opinion testimony to situations where it would be difficult for the witness to testify "in more concrete terms."

In practical application of the lay opinion rule, there seems little variation between New York state and federal cases. The several recurring categories listed in § 701.1 at note 8 could be repeated here with even more liberality. For instance, a lay witness may testify (assuming the necessary knowledge and experience) that another was of a certain age[3] or was intoxicated,[4] that handwriting in issue is that of defendant,[5] that what the witness smelled seemed like marijuana,[6] that a person appeared to be "nervous,"[7] that a vehicle moved at a certain speed,[8] and that a person appeared sane or insane.[9] The witness' expression that she "thinks" or "believes" need not be fatal.[10]

The Second Circuit has adopted the broad position that "a lay witness may testify about his conclusions if they are based upon his perceptions and if they aid the jury in understanding the witness' testimony."[11] One area that the court has emphatically declared to be beyond the scope of Rule 701 is witness credibility: "As a matter of law, '[t]he credibility of witnesses is exclusively for the determination [of] the jury, and witnesses may not opine as to the credibility of the testimony of other witnesses at the trial.' "[12]

---

2. The Advisory Committee states, in part: "While the courts have made concessions in certain recurring situations, necessity as a standard for permitting opinions and conclusions has proved too elusive and too unadaptable to particular situations for purposes of satisfactory judicial administration. McCormick § 11. Moreover, the practical impossibility of determining by rule what is a 'fact,' demonstrated by a century of litigation of the question of what is a fact for purposes of pleading under the Field Code, extends into evidence also. 7 Wigmore § 1919. The rule assumes that the natural characteristics of the adversary system will generally lead to an acceptable result, since the detailed account carries more conviction than the broad assertion, and a lawyer can be expected to display his witness to the best advantage."

3. United States v. Stanley, 896 F.2d 450, 452 (10th Cir.1990).

4. Singletary v. Secretary of Health, Education and Welfare, 623 F.2d 217, 219 (2d Cir.1980).

5. United States v. Barker, 735 F.2d 1280, 1283 (11th Cir.), cert. denied, 469 U.S. 933, 105 S.Ct. 329, 83 L.Ed.2d 266 (1984).

6. United States v. Arrasmith, 557 F.2d 1093, 1094 (5th Cir.1977).

7. United States v. Mastberg, 503 F.2d 465 (9th Cir.1974).

8. United States v. Thompson, 708 F.2d 1294, 1305–06 (8th Cir.1983).

9. United States v. Lawson, 653 F.2d 299, 303 (7th Cir.1981), cert. denied, 454 U.S. 1150, 102 S.Ct. 1017, 71 L.Ed.2d 305 (1982).

10. United States v. Freeman, 619 F.2d 1112, 1120 (5th Cir.1980), cert. denied, 450 U.S. 910, 101 S.Ct. 1348, 67 L.Ed.2d 334 (1981).

11. Brady v. Chemical Const. Corp., 740 F.2d 195, 200–201 (2d Cir.1984) (the witness, who had personally investigated the business affairs of a former employee, was permitted to testify to the uncovered facts, and to his conclusions drawn therefrom). See also United States v. Rivera, 22 F.3d 430 (2d Cir.1994)(former employee of organization involved in manufacture and distribution of heroin had personal knowledge of record-keeping practices of the organization and could therefore interpret the records and explain their contents).

12. United States v. Forrester, 60 F.3d 52, 63 (2d Cir.1995)(quoting United States v. Scop, 846 F.2d 135, 142 (2d Cir.), rev'd in part on other grounds, 856 F.2d 5 (2d Cir. 1988)).

702 Expert Testimony

§ 702.1 New York

a. Generally

People v. Kenny[1] provides a bridge from lay to expert testimony. A Court of Appeals majority held that a lay witness could not identify a substance which he saw, smoked and smelled as marijuana. The substance had not been preserved as evidence and so the prosecutor had to rely on this witness' testimony. The Court held that "up to now the world is much more experienced with alcohol than with narcotics,"[2] even though the witness described the way the substance looked and that he became "high" and "dizzy" from inhaling it. The fact the conviction rested on this evidence alone helps explain the decision, but one wonders whether today it can categorically be said that the identification of marijuana must be made by an expert, a witness with special knowledge.[3] *Kenny* illustrates the gray area giving rise to the question whether a subject of testimony requires the witness to have special knowledge.

The problem works both ways. If the subject does not require expertise, and a so-called expert testifies, error results because the jury could have been unduly swayed by the witness' qualifications in a matter about which anyone could have testified and which the jury would be competent to analyze without any help.[4] On the other hand, if the subject requires special knowledge, testimony by an unqualified witness will result in error because of the witness' incompetence.[5] While probably still true, the former edict rests on ever weakening ground. In *De Long v. County of Erie*,[6] a housewife was murdered by a prowler after defendant's employees had mishandled her 911 call. On the issue of damages in the wrongful death action, plaintiff offered an economist as

---

§ 702.1

1. 30 N.Y.2d 154, 331 N.Y.S.2d 392, 282 N.E.2d 295 (1972).

2. Id. at 157, 331 N.Y.S.2d at 395, 282 N.E.2d at 297.

3. See United States v. Arrasmith, 557 F.2d 1093, 1094 (5th Cir.1977).

4. See, e.g., Kulak v. Nationwide Mut. Ins. Co., 40 N.Y.2d 140, 386 N.Y.S.2d 87, 351 N.E.2d 735 (1976)(in action against liability insurer for bad-faith refusal to settle personal injury claim within policy limits, testimony by attorney-experts was unnecessary and improper with respect to viability of insured's particular defenses, likelihood of verdict in excess of policy limits and estimation of probable outcome of personal injury trial; testimony should have been confined to expert's knowledge of factors used by insurers, in general, in evaluating claims for settlement purposes).

5. Larsen v. Vigliarolo Bros., 77 A.D.2d 562, 429 N.Y.S.2d 273 (2d Dep't 1980)(speed of a motorcycle held beyond lay competence); Stafford v. Mussers Potato Chips, Inc., 39 A.D.2d 831, 333 N.Y.S.2d 139 (4th Dep't 1972)(state trooper, not qualified as an expert, should not have rendered an opinion as to where the vehicular impact occurred); compare Lee v. Decarr, 36 A.D.2d 554, 317 N.Y.S.2d 226 (3d Dep't 1971)(trooper who investigated scene of the accident before cars had been removed allowed to testify as to point of impact).

6. 60 N.Y.2d 296, 307–08, 469 N.Y.S.2d 611, 617–18, 457 N.E.2d 717, 723 (1983).

an expert witness on the monetary value of a housewife's services. The Court of Appeals found this proper:

> Undoubtedly most jurors have at least a general awareness of the various services performed by a housewife. It is doubtful, however, that they are equally knowledgeable with respect to the monetary equivalent of those services. Although it was once thought that this was not a subject which would lend itself to scientific inquiry and analysis * * * that can no longer be said today. It is now apparent, as a majority of courts have held * * * that qualified experts are available and may aid the jury in evaluating the housewife's services not only because jurors may not know the value of those services, but also to dispel the notion that what is provided without financial reward may be considered of little or no financial value in the marketplace.[7]

The *DeLong* decision can be seen as a departure from early New York law, which restricted expert testimony to cases in which such testimony was necessary in order for the jury to be able to draw conclusions.[8] *DeLong* opens the way for testimony by witnesses with any sort of "extra" knowledge that could assist the jury on subjects formerly considered to partake of common knowledge. The *DeLong* court announced that expert testimony is appropriate "when it would help to clarify an issue calling for professional or technical knowledge possessed by the expert and beyond the ken of the typical juror."[9] Although Rule 702 of the Federal Rules of Evidence was not cited in *DeLong*, the decision clearly approaches the federal standard, which places the emphasis on whether the testimony "will assist the trier of

---

7. Id. See also Selkowitz v. County of Nassau, 45 N.Y.2d 97, 408 N.Y.S.2d 10, 379 N.E.2d 1140 (1978). A county patrolman stationed his car so as to block a car being chased by other police, thus blocking the escape route and forcing the fleeing car to crash into plaintiff's car at an intersection. In plaintiff's suit based on the patrolman's negligence, a retired police officer testified as an expert in emergency traffic procedures and said that the patrolman should not have positioned his car as he did. Although acknowledging that the reasonable operation of vehicles would be within the understanding of most jurors, the court found the expert's opinion admissible to aid the jury's perception of the standards governing high speed chases. Both Selkowitz and DeLong seem greatly to undermine the Court's earlier decision in Kulak, cited in note 4 supra.

8. See Dougherty v. Milliken, 163 N.Y. 527, 533–34, 57 N.E. 757, 759 (1900).

9. 60 N.Y.2d at 307, 469 N.Y.S.2d at 617, 457 N.E.2d at 722. See also People v. Cronin, 60 N.Y.2d 430, 433, 470 N.Y.S.2d 110, 111, 458 N.E.2d 351, 352 (1983)(trial court decides whether jurors "would be benefited by the specialized knowledge of an expert witness").

Examples of admissible expert testimony under the modern standard include People v. Garcia, 196 A.D.2d 433, 601 N.Y.S.2d 482 (1st Dep't 1993), aff'd, 83 N.Y.2d 817, 611 N.Y.S.2d 490, 633 N.E.2d 1094 (1994)(undercover police officer's explanation of terminology used in narcotics transactions); Sitaras v. James Ricciardi & Sons, Inc., 154 A.D.2d 451, 545 N.Y.S.2d 937 (2d Dep't 1989), appeal denied, 75 N.Y.2d 708, 554 N.Y.S.2d 833, 553 N.E.2d 1343 (1990)(accident reconstruction expert could give opinion as to how accident happened and effect of collision even though most jurors have general understanding of auto accidents); Franck v. Minisink Valley School District, 136 A.D.2d 588, 523 N.Y.S.2d 573 (2d Dep't 1988)(expert could testify to standards of school playground supervision). But see Nevins v. Great Atlantic and Pacific Tea Co., 164 A.D.2d 807, 559 N.Y.S.2d 539 (1st Dep't 1990)(proper procedures for removal of snow and ice from sidewalks is not proper subject for expert testimony).

§ 702.1   OPINIONS & EXPERT TESTIMONY   Ch. 7

fact to understand the evidence."[10] Section 702 of the Proposed New York Evidence Code rests on essentially the same basis although its wording is more precise:

> (a) Testimony by experts. A witness qualified as an expert by knowledge, skills, experience, training, education, or otherwise may testify in the form of an opinion or otherwise concerning scientific, technical, or other specialized knowledge that is beyond the understanding or will dispel misconceptions of the typical trier of fact, thereby helping the trier of fact to understand the evidence or to determine a fact in issue. * * *[11]

The urge to encourage the use of expert testimony on just about any subject (not discouraged, certainly, by the *DeLong* case) was curbed by

---

10. See § 702.2 infra.

11. Proposed New York Evidence Code § 702 continues as follows:

(b) **Scientific testimony.** Testimony concerning scientific matters, or testimony concerning the result of a scientific procedure, test or experiment is admissible provided: (1) there is general acceptance within the relevant scientific community of the validity of the theory or principle underlying the matter, procedure, test or experiment; (2) there is general acceptance within the relevant scientific community that the procedure, test or experiment is reliable and produces accurate results; and (3) the particular test, procedure or experiment was conducted in such a way as to yield an accurate result. Upon request of a party, a determination pursuant to this subdivision shall be made before the commencement of trial.

(c) **Psychiatric testimony in certain criminal cases.**

(1) **Diagnosis and opinion as to defendant's criminal responsibility.** When, in connection with the affirmative defense of lack of criminal responsibility by reason of mental disease or defect, a psychiatrist or licensed psychologist testifies at a trial concerning the defendant's mental condition at the time of the conduct charged to constitute a crime, such psychiatrist or licensed psychologist must be permitted to make a statement as to the nature of any examination of the defendant, the diagnosis of the mental condition of the defendant and the opinion of such psychiatrist or licensed psychologist as to the extent, if any, to which the capacity of the defendant to know or appreciate the nature and consequence of such conduct, or its wrongfulness, was impaired as a result of mental disease or defect at that time.

The psychiatrist or licensed psychologist must be permitted to make any explanation reasonably serving to clarify the diagnosis and opinion of such psychiatrist or licensed psychologist, and may be cross-examined as to any matter bearing on the competency, credibility or the validity of the diagnosis or opinion of such psychiatrist or licensed psychologist.

(2) **Use of statements made by defendant in course of examination.** Any statement made by the defendant to a psychiatrist or licensed psychologist during the examination of the defendant by such psychiatrist or licensed psychologist shall be inadmissible in evidence on any issue other than that of the affirmative defense of lack of criminal responsibility by reason of mental disease or defect. The statement shall, however, be admissible upon the issue of the affirmative defense of lack of criminal responsibility by reason of mental disease or defect, whether or not it would otherwise be deemed a privileged communication. Upon receiving the statement in evidence, the court must instruct the jury that the statement is to be considered only on the issue of such affirmative defense and may not be considered by it in its determination of whether the defendant committed the act constituting the crime charged.

Subdivision (b) of the proposed code provision is similar, but not identical, to the approach to scientific evidence that was articulated by the Court of Appeals in People v. Wesley, 83 N.Y.2d 417, 611 N.Y.S.2d 97, 633 N.E.2d 451 (1994), which is described in the text at notes 17–21 infra. Subdivi-

the Appellate Division in *Matter of Luz P.*[12] where it was held that an expert was not needed to qualify and explain the testimony of a nonverbal, autistic child by use of "facilitated communication" through a keyboard.[13]

b. Novel Scientific Theories and Methods

New York courts still adhere to the so-called *Frye* standard of admissibility for new scientific theories and methodologies. In *Frye v. United States*,[14] it was held that the results of a systolic blood pressure deception test, a form of lie detector, were inadmissible because the theory—truth is spontaneous while lying involves thought which is reflected in the subject's blood pressure—had not been fully accepted in the scientific community. The court stated:

> Somewhere in this twilight zone [between experimental and accepted] the evidential force of the principle must be recognized, and while courts will go a long way in admitting expert testimony deduced from a well-recognized scientific principle or discovery, the thing from which the deduction is made must be sufficiently established to have gained general acceptance in the particular field in which it belongs.[15]

Despite the rejection in federal courts of the *Frye* standard,[16] the Court of Appeals in *People v. Wesley*[17] unanimously affirmed its continuing vitality in New York.[18] Whether the *Frye* standard has been satisfied with respect to particular types of scientific evidence is for the trial judge to decide. The court may be able to make its determination by reference to scientific literature or judicial opinions.[19] If these are insufficient, the

---

sion (c) is a restatement of N.Y.Crim.Proc. Law § 60.55.

12. 189 A.D.2d 274, 595 N.Y.S.2d 541 (2d Dep't 1993).

13. The trial judge insisted that a Frye hearing (see text at notes 14–21 infra) was necessary to validate the acceptance of facilitated communication in the scientific community, and that expert testimony was needed in order to decide whether the child could even testify in the first place given her autism. It was stated in the Appellate Division:

> A determination of these questions does not require expert testimony. To the contrary, the proffered facilitated communication lends itself to empirical rather than scientific proof. Thus, the test proposed by the County Attorney, whereby the court could question Luz [the child] outside the presence of the facilitator and then hear her responses through facilitated communication, should adequately establish whether this is a reliable and accurate means of communication by Luz.

Id. at 279, 280, 595 N.Y.S.2d at 545.

14. 293 F. 1013 (D.C.Cir.1923).

15. Id. at 1014.

16. See § 702.2 infra.

17. 83 N.Y.2d 417, 611 N.Y.S.2d 97, 633 N.E.2d 451 (1994). Wesley involved the admissibility of the RFLP technique of DNA identification analysis. The technique was found to be generally accepted in the relevant scientific community.

18. Id. at 422–23, 611 N.Y.2d at 100, 633 N.E.2d at 454. In a concurring opinion, Chief Judge Kaye succinctly explained the value of the Frye standard of general acceptance: "It is not for a court to take pioneering risks on promising new scientific techniques, because premature admission both prejudices litigants and short-circuits debate necessary to determination of the accuracy of a technique." Id. at 437 n.4, 611 N.Y.S.2d at 108, 633 N.E.2d at 462 (concurring opinion). Thus, the scientific community, not the court, is the "gatekeeper" for the admissibility of scientific evidence.

19. See, e.g., People v. Middleton, 54 N.Y.2d 42, 49–50, 444 N.Y.S.2d 581, 584–

court must conduct a hearing at which expert testimony will be taken on the issue of general acceptance in the relevant scientific community.[20]

In *Wesley*, the court outlined the following procedural framework for the admissibility of scientific evidence: First, the trial judge must determine whether the *Frye* standard has been met, either pretrial or at trial outside the presence of the jury. Second, the proponent of the scientific evidence must present a testimonial description of the procedures that were used to produce the evidence in question. If the trial judge determines that an adequate foundation has been made, the third step is the presentation of the expert's opinion on the scientific results, which may then be considered by the jury.[21]

The track record under *Frye* of various scientific principles and methods can be found among the particularized areas of expert testimony described below.

c. Recurring Problems of Expert Testimony

There probably is no end to the subject matter that either requires[22] or permits[23] expert testimony, but certain areas of evidence involving experts recur often enough to be sketched as follows:

Medical Testimony. This speciality, which includes testimony as to mental as well as physical conditions, is undoubtedly the most often

---

85, 429 N.E.2d 100, 103–104 (1981)(bitemark identification).

20. See, e.g., People v. Jeter, 80 N.Y.2d 818, 821, 587 N.Y.S.2d 583, 585, 600 N.E.2d 214, 216 (1992)(spectrograph voice identification). Unanimous indorsement by the scientific community is not required; "general acceptance" is sufficient. People v. Middleton, 54 N.Y.2d 42, 49, 444 N.Y.S.2d 581, 584, 429 N.E.2d 100, 103 (1981).

21. People v. Wesley, 83 N.Y.2d 417, 428–29, 611 N.Y.S.2d 97, 103–04, 633 N.E.2d 451, 457–58 (1994). Assuming the foundation for admissibility is determined by the trial court to be adequate, any flaws or shortcomings with respect to procedures used in the collection and analysis of the data go to the weight of the evidence. 83 N.Y.2d at 429, 611 N.Y.S.2d at 104, 633 N.E.2d at 458.

22. Expert testimony is required if the particular factual issue transcends the realm of knowledge possessed by laypersons. See, e.g., Sawyer v. Dreis & Krump Manufacturing Co., 67 N.Y.2d 328, 334, 502 N.Y.S.2d 696, 700, 493 N.E.2d 920, 924 (1986)(in order for plaintiff to take advantage of reduced burden of proof where he suffers amnesia caused by accident, expert testimony is necessary to show causal relationship between amnesia and defendant's conduct). Expert testimony, therefore, is often required with respect to the standard of care in particular trades or professions or as to the functioning of mechanical devices.

See, e.g., Viacom Intern., Inc. v. Midtown Realty Co., 193 A.D.2d 45, 602 N.Y.S.2d 326 (1st Dep't 1993)(whether well-maintained fire alarm system would have reacted in time); Iannelli v. Powers, 114 A.D.2d 157, 498 N.Y.S.2d 377 (2d Dep't), appeal denied, 68 N.Y.2d 604, 506 N.Y.S.2d 1027, 497 N.E.2d 707 (1986)(deficiencies in security of building and safety measures that should have been taken). But see Food Pageant, Inc. v. Consolidated Edison, 54 N.Y.2d 167, 445 N.Y.S.2d 60, 429 N.E.2d 738 (1981) (even if matter usually involves scientific or technical complexity, thus requiring expertise as to standard of care, e.g., medical malpractice, expert testimony is not required if jurors can reach opinion on basis of common sense and ordinary experience).

23. See text at notes 9–10 above. An example of an extraordinary expert witness is Peter L. Borchelt, Ph.D., Director of the Animal Behavior Therapy Clinic of the Animal Medical Center of New York City. Dr. Borchelt testified for the defendant (whose name, ironically, is Goodfriend) who was being tried for rape. The victim owned a dog which defendant theorized would have tried to protect her had he forced himself on her. Dr. Borchelt was allowed to testify concerning the breed of the dog and its emotional tendencies, but the court refused to order a reenactment of the encounter to put the dog to what could only be described as a truly clinical test. People v. Good-

utilized area of expert testimony. The question arising here is not so much whether expertise is needed as it is whether the proffered witness is qualified. The courts seem willing to stretch on this point[24] leaving the evaluation of the testimony to the fact-finder.[25] But where the opinion appears to be based on speculation the court may disallow it altogether.[26] These rules of qualification are closely tied to the question of the basis of the expert's opinion treated in § 703.1, below, and of course are applicable to all expert witnesses, not just those in the medical field. Psychiatric testimony on the issue of insanity in criminal cases is governed, in part, by § 60.55 of the New York Criminal Procedure Law.[27]

Handwriting. Whereas under the lay witness handwriting rule the witness renders his opinion based on familiarity with the subject's handwriting,[28] a handwriting expert, qualified by training and experience as an expert, compares the writing in issue to a sample known to have been written by the subject. This approach is currently codified in CPLR 4536,[29] and the New York cases are to the effect that such comparisons can be made, not just by experts, but also by the jury,[30] or judge in a bench trial.[31] The authenticity of the specimen, if not stipulated, can be proved by an admission, testimony by the adversary, testimony by a witness who saw the specimen being written or to whom the subject acknowledged authenticity, testimony by a witness familiar with the subject's handwriting, or proof that the subject had purposefully acted on the basis of the specimen.[32] The court will determine the

friend, 106 Misc.2d 989, 436 N.Y.S.2d 826 (Sup.Ct.N.Y.Co.1981).

24. See, e.g., Hoagland v. Kamp, 155 A.D.2d 148, 552 N.Y.S.2d 978 (3d Dep't 1990)(oral and maxillofacial surgeon who practiced exclusively in New York City could testify as to standards governing general dentistry applying elsewhere); Anderson v. Donis, 150 A.D.2d 414, 541 N.Y.S.2d 25 (2d Dep't 1989)(orthopedist could testify as to methods used by podiatrist); Riley v. Wieman, 137 A.D.2d 309, 528 N.Y.S.2d 925 (3d Dep't 1988)(California radiologist could testify concerning the practices of New York radiologist despite the rule in malpractice actions that the defendant need only conform to the procedures commonly followed in the locality where defendant practices); compare Taormina v. Goodman, 63 A.D.2d 1018, 406 N.Y.S.2d 350 (2d Dep't 1978)(medical doctor with limited knowledge of chiropractic not qualified to testify in action for chiropractor's negligence); McDonnell v. Nassau County, 129 Misc.2d 228, 492 N.Y.S.2d 699 (Sup.Ct.Nassau Co.1985)(psychologist unqualified to testify concerning psychiatric standard of care at a time when the witness was not even a licensed psychologist).

25. See, e.g., De Luca v. Kameros, 130 A.D.2d 705, 515 N.Y.S.2d 819 (2d Dep't 1987).

26. Miller v. National Cabinet Co., 8 N.Y.2d 277, 282, 204 N.Y.S.2d 129, 132–133, 168 N.E.2d 811, 813 (1960)(the court cautioned that the use of qualifying words such as "could produce" or "it is possible," would not necessarily negate the opinion provided there were other indications that the opinion was soundly based). Matott v. Ward, 48 N.Y.2d 455, 423 N.Y.S.2d 645, 399 N.E.2d 532 (1979)(pursuant to pragmatic analysis, physician need not explicitly state that opinion is made with "a reasonable degree of medical certainty" if it is reasonably apparent that expert is not speculating and shows sufficient confidence in his conclusions).

27. See note 11 supra.

28. See § 701.1, at note 8, supra.

29. CPLR 4536 provides as follows:

Comparison of a disputed writing with any writing proved to the satisfaction of the court to be the handwriting of the person claimed to have made the disputed writing shall be permitted.

30. People v. Hunter, 34 N.Y.2d 432, 358 N.Y.S.2d 360, 315 N.E.2d 436 (1974).

31. Ibanez v. Pfeiffer, 76 Misc.2d 363, 350 N.Y.S.2d 964 (N.Y.C.Civ.Ct.1973).

32. People v. Molineux, 168 N.Y. 264, 328, 61 N.E. 286, 307 (1901).

§ 702.1   OPINIONS & EXPERT TESTIMONY   Ch. 7

specimen's authenticity,[33] and the fact-finder, as in any other case involving expert opinion, has the discretion to accept it or not.[34] There is some authority that in criminal cases the jury also has the discretion to reject the specimen;[35] and a specimen cannot be used which was created for purposes of the litigation by the party who created it,[36] even if created while the subject is on the witness stand.[37] In *Felt v. Olson*,[38] the Court of Appeals offers an interesting appraisal of one judge's consideration of an expert's opinion.

Blood Alcohol Test. Alcohol content in the blood is commonly determined by either of two accepted methods—analysis of a blood sample, or the results of a breathalyzer test.[39] Section 1194 of the New York Vehicle and Traffic Law provides that a motor vehicle operator is deemed to have given his consent "to a chemical test, of his breath, blood, urine, or saliva." This statute has long been upheld as constitutional,[40] and the provision that a person's refusal to submit to a test can be used as an admission against that person in subdivision (2)(d)(3)(f), added in 1973, was upheld within a few years thereafter.[41] Evidence from a test performed on an unconscious driver is admissible since without an express refusal he is deemed under the statute to have given his consent.[42] Section 1194 provides that the test must be administered within two hours after the arrest, but if the driver consents to the test

33. Clark v. Douglass, 5 App.Div. 547, 40 N.Y.S. 769 (3d Dep't 1896) (authenticity of the specimen should be beyond doubt in order for it to be used).

34. Matter of Sylvestri, 44 N.Y.2d 260, 405 N.Y.S.2d 424, 376 N.E.2d 897 (1978); Heller v. Murray, 112 Misc.2d 745, 447 N.Y.S.2d 348 (N.Y.C.Civ.Ct.1981), aff'd, 118 Misc.2d 508, 464 N.Y.S.2d 391 (Sup.Ct.App. T.1983).

35. People v. Molineux, 168 N.Y. 264, 329–30, 61 N.E. 286, 308 (1901).

36. Id.

37. Nelson v. Brady, 268 App.Div. 226, 50 N.Y.S.2d 582 (1st Dep't 1944).

38. 51 N.Y.2d 977, 979, 435 N.Y.S.2d 708, 709, 416 N.E.2d 1043, 1044 (1980). It was stated, speaking of a judge as the trier of fact:

Although he received [the opinion of the handwriting expert] in evidence, he was not bound to credit it. In deciding whether to do so or not, it would be unrealistic to expect that, as a fact finder, he would not be influenced in the exercise of his judgment by the general experience and education that in the course of his life had shaped him as a person. In the case of a Trial Judge that will almost always have included impressions that he had garnered in the course of presiding over trials. It goes without saying that does not mean that personal knowledge of a probative fact under consideration may be used to decide a case. But the reference by the trial court to expert opinions to which the Judge had been exposed in the past need not be taken as more than a candid unveiling of some of the inner thoughts that, perhaps unavoidably, ran through his mind as he pondered the factual questions he had to determine. It does not compel the conclusion that it was a declaration that he was applying an erroneous legal standard. This view is reinforced by the very language in which, in weighing the handwriting evidence, in the end he goes no further than to talk of "difficulty" on this score and then proceeds with an analysis based on the assumption that the handwriting testimony had sufficed to make out a prima facie case.

39. The breathalyzer passed the Frye test in People v. Donaldson, 36 A.D.2d 37, 319 N.Y.S.2d 172 (4th Dep't 1971), and another machine, the intoxilyzer, has passed muster in two lower courts. People v. Summa, 140 Misc.2d 763, 531 N.Y.S.2d 993 (Dist.Ct.Suffolk Co.1988); People v. Jones, 118 Misc.2d 687, 461 N.Y.S.2d 962 (Albany Co.Ct.1983).

40. People v. Craft, 28 N.Y.2d 274, 321 N.Y.S.2d 566, 270 N.E.2d 297 (1971).

41. People v. Thomas, 46 N.Y.2d 100, 412 N.Y.S.2d 845, 385 N.E.2d 584 (1978), appeal dismissed, 444 U.S. 891, 100 S.Ct. 197, 62 L.Ed.2d 127 (1979).

42. People v. Kates, 53 N.Y.2d 591, 444 N.Y.S.2d 446, 428 N.E.2d 852 (1981).

the two-hour provision does not apply and the test may be administered beyond that time.[43] The witness testifying to the breath test is usually a police officer who conducted the test and simply reports the results determined by the machine. The crucial aspect of this testimony is that a proper foundation must be laid with respect to the accuracy of the machine and the training of the operator.[44] The taking and testing of blood is difficult to challenge since § 1194(4)(c) creates a presumption[45] that the test was properly given if it was administered by a person possessing a Department of Health permit, and this includes people ranging from a physician to a laboratory technician.[46] In a related situation it has been held that radioimmunoassay analysis (RIA) of human hair passed *Frye* and could be used to test individuals to determine whether they had been using controlled substances.[47]

The Polygraph and Other Tests and Devices. The polygraph, or lie detector, has never passed the *Frye* test in New York[48] and, as a consequence, is only useful for investigation purposes. Likewise, the voice stress evaluator, another lie detecting technique, has failed to pass *Frye* muster.[49] The radar gun has long been accepted.[50] The vulnerability lies, if at all, with its operation. The Court of Appeals has made no determination as to the admissibility of the results of a voice identification machine (spectrograph) since the lower court failed to conduct a *Frye* hearing.[51] A lower court accepted the neutron activation analysis (NAA) many years ago.[52] NAA provides a qualitative and quantitative method for determining the elemental composition of substances such as hair, glass, paint and gunshot residue. This test does not appear to have been dealt with as yet in the New York appellate courts. The use of hypnosis to restore memory was rejected in *People v. Hughes.*[53] The results of positron emission tomograph (PET) and skin conductance response (SCR), tests of the autonomic nervous system, were held admissible by a lower court in a homicide case where the defense was lack of criminal responsibility because of mental disease.[54] For expanded

---

43. People v. Atkins, 85 N.Y.2d 1007, 630 N.Y.S.2d 965, 654 N.E.2d 1213 (1995).

44. See People v. Freeland, 68 N.Y.2d 699, 506 N.Y.S.2d 306, 497 N.E.2d 673 (1986); People v. Dembeck, 145 Misc.2d 442, 546 N.Y.S.2d 936 (Dist.Ct.Suffolk Co.1989).

45. This presumption is really a permissive inference. People v. Mertz, 68 N.Y.2d 136, 506 N.Y.S.2d 290, 497 N.E.2d 657 (1986).

46. N.Y.Veh. and Traf.Law § 1194(4)(a).

47. Matter of Baby Boy L., 157 Misc.2d 353, 596 N.Y.S.2d 997 (Fam.Ct.Suffolk Co.1993).

48. People v. Leone, 25 N.Y.2d 511, 307 N.Y.S.2d 430, 255 N.E.2d 696 (1969); cf. People v. Daniels, 102 Misc.2d 540, 422 N.Y.S.2d 832 (Sup.Ct.Westchester Co.1979). In Daniels, the court construed Leone as having been decided simply on the inexperience of the examiner—a questionable interpretation as evidenced by the refusal of another judge in People v. Vinson, 104 Misc.2d 664, 428 N.Y.S.2d 832 (Sup.Ct.Westchester Co.1980) to follow that rationale.

49. People v. Tarsia, 50 N.Y.2d 1, 427 N.Y.S.2d 944, 405 N.E.2d 188 (1980).

50. People v. Magri, 3 N.Y.2d 562, 170 N.Y.S.2d 335, 147 N.E.2d 728 (1958).

51. People v. Jeter, 80 N.Y.2d 818, 587 N.Y.S.2d 583, 600 N.E.2d 214 (1992).

52. People v. Pieropan, 72 Misc.2d 770, 340 N.Y.S.2d 31 (Oneida Co.Ct.1973).

53. 59 N.Y.2d 523, 466 N.Y.S.2d 255, 453 N.E.2d 484 (1983). See § 601.1(h) supra.

54. People v. Weinstein, 156 Misc.2d 34, 591 N.Y.S.2d 715 (Sup.Ct.N.Y.Co.1992). The court, while allowing experts to testify

§ 702.1   OPINIONS & EXPERT TESTIMONY   Ch. 7

discussion of these and related matters of scientific technique, the reader is directed elsewhere.[55]

Blood Grouping—DNA. If blood relationship is at issue, CPLR 3121 authorizes procurement of a blood examination as part of the discovery process and is applicable in cases where the more precise provisions of § 418 of the New York Family Court Act is not.[56] Section 418 of the Family Court Act is authority for blood genetic marker tests to be applied to the mother, child and putative father in paternity proceedings. The results of the conventional blood genetic marker test are admissible only when the paternity of the putative father is excluded by the test. The statute also provides for the admissibility of the results of the human leucocyte blood tissue test and, pursuant to a 1994 amendment, the DNA genetic test. Even without statutory authorization, the results of the RFLP technique of DNA analysis have been held admissible on the issue of identification in criminal cases.[57] A significant problem with DNA evidence is the laboratory procedure used to analyze the blood (or other bodily fluid); a solid foundation must be shown.[58]

Rape Trauma Syndrome. The classic and ancient rule regarding the prompt reporting of rape is that if the complaining witness had really been raped she would have made a prompt complaint.[59] A great deal has happened to the nature of proof in rape cases,[60] not the least of which is that delayed complaint can now be explained by the phenomenon known as rape trauma syndrome, i.e., a reaction of humiliation and fear which stifles the victim's willingness to report. In *People v. Taylor,*[61] the Court of Appeals held that this could be explained to the jury by a psychologist to account for the victim's behavior following the attack; but in a companion case it was held that such evidence cannot be used to prove commission of the crime itself, i.e., that because the victim suffered from rape trauma syndrome, she must therefore have been raped.[62]

---

as to the results of the tests which depicted certain cyst and metabolic imbalances in defendant's brain, would not allow them to explain that these abnormalities cause violent behavior because the theory had not been accepted in the scientific community. Id. at 46–48, 591 N.Y.S.2d at 724–25.

55. See Giannelli and Imwinkelried, Scientific Evidence (2d ed.), chapters 8–18.

56. Prof. Siegel in his Practice Commentaries on CPLR 3121 states, at C3121:2, that a blood examination "may also be sought in cases in which no blood relationship is involved at all."

57. People v. Wesley, 83 N.Y.2d 417, 611 N.Y.S.2d 97, 633 N.E.2d 451 (1994).

58. See People v. Castro, 144 Misc.2d 956, 545 N.Y.S.2d 985 (Sup.Ct.Bronx Co.1989)(certain portions of DNA test results excluded due to inadequacy of foundation with respect to testing procedures).

59. Baccio v. People, 41 N.Y. 265 (1869).

60. The corroboration requirement has disappeared (Penal Law § 130.15, providing that a conviction could not rest on the uncorroborated testimony of the alleged victim, was repealed by L.1974, ch. 14) and the victim's sexual history is closed to defense counsel, subject to certain exceptions (N.Y.Crim.Proc.Law § 60.42).

61. 75 N.Y.2d 277, 552 N.Y.S.2d 883, 552 N.E.2d 131 (1990). In a similar vein, a psychiatrist's opinion as to the range of psychological reactions of a child sex-crime victim was upheld in People v. Keindl, 68 N.Y.2d 410, 509 N.Y.S.2d 790, 502 N.E.2d 577 (1986). See also People v. Torres, 128 Misc.2d 129, 488 N.Y.S.2d 358 (Sup.Ct. Bronx Co.1985)(battered woman syndrome).

62. People v. Banks, 75 N.Y.2d 277, 293, 552 N.Y.S.2d 883, 891, 552 N.E.2d 131, 139 (1990).

The Eyewitness Expert. A budding area for expertise has developed from attempts to impeach eyewitness identification testimony by having a psychologist testify as to the unreliability of such testimony. Thus far, the Court of Appeals has not expressly accepted or rejected this technique. In *People v. Mooney,*[63] the Court of Appeals upheld the trial court's refusal to allow a defense expert to testify as to the factors that can affect the recollection of an eyewitness regarding the defendant's identity. The trial court based the decision on three grounds. First, such testimony had not met the *Frye* test in that it was not accepted in the scientific community; second, such testimony would be cumulative since the relevant factors would be explored in cross-examination of the eyewitness anyway; and third, factors influencing identity and recollection are not beyond the ken of the ordinary juror and thus no expertise was required. In a 5–2 decision, the Court of Appeals held that the determination to exclude this evidence could not be disturbed because it was made in the sound discretion of the trial court. The majority specifically declined to pass on the admissibility of the expert's testimony, and Judge Kaye wrote a strong dissent on the ground the trial judge abused his discretion.[64] The lower courts are at odds over whether this form of eyewitness impeachment testimony is admissible.[65]

d. The "Interested Observer"

In *People v. Parks,*[66] the victim of a rape suffered from a mental deficiency, yet was competent to testify. The Court of Appeals held it proper for the victim's teacher to testify concerning the nature of the victim's deficiency in order to provide a framework within which the victim's testimony and behavior could be evaluated by the jury. The teacher could not, however, render an opinion as to the victim's credibility. Building on the authority of *Parks,* the judge in *People v. Acklin*[67] held that the prosecutor could put a school psychologist on the stand, not to render an opinion regarding the retarded victim's credibility, but simply to explain the nature of the victim's problem. The judge called this the doctrine of the "interested observer" who does not testify as an expert, but merely as one who can enlighten the jury as to the victim's background.[68] This testimony normally would be received before the victim or impaired witness takes the stand. The judge set forth five

---

63. 76 N.Y.2d 827, 560 N.Y.S.2d 115, 559 N.E.2d 1274 (1990).

64. As to the Frye test Judge Kaye thought the Court ought to grapple with the question whether that test should be applied. As to the finding that the expert testimony would be cumulative, she concluded that cross-examination was inherently limited. As to whether any expertise was needed at all, she reviewed the thesis of more recent years that informed testimony can always assist the jury. 76 N.Y.2d at 829–832, 560 N.Y.S.2d at 116–118, 559 N.E.2d at 1275–1277.

65. Compare People v. Wright, 161 A.D.2d 743, 558 N.Y.S.2d 842 (2d Dep't 1990)(inadmissible), with People v. Wong, 150 Misc.2d 554, 568 N.Y.S.2d 1020 (Sup. Ct.Queens Co.1991)(testimony allowed).

66. 41 N.Y.2d 36, 390 N.Y.S.2d 848, 359 N.E.2d 358 (1976).

67. 102 Misc.2d 596, 424 N.Y.S.2d 633 (Sup.Ct.N.Y.Co.1980).

68. Id. at 600–01, 424 N.Y.S.2d at 638.

§ 702.1   OPINIONS & EXPERT TESTIMONY   Ch. 7

conditions for the reception of such testimony.[69] So far, the interested observer has been used only to prepare the way for the testimony of impaired witnesses.[70] Somewhat related are those cases where experts testify as to what effect certain external stimuli would have had on the subject.[71]

e. Qualifications

If expertise of some sort would be helpful to the factfinder then it follows that the witness must be qualified by training, experience or education to give such help. There are two basic points here which overlap. The first involves the judge's discretion in deciding whether a witness is qualified, and the second goes to the question of the sort of training, experience or education possessed by the proposed witness. The opinion in *Meiselman v. Crown Heights Hospital*,[72] contains the rules as to both aspects:

> The prevailing rule is that the question of the qualification of a witness to testify as an expert is for determination, in his reasonable discretion, by the trial court, which discretion, when exercised, is not open to review unless in deciding the question the trial court has made a serious mistake or committed an error of law or has abused his discretion.[73]

As to the nature of the witness' background and the jury's role, it is stated:

> No precise rule has been formulated and applied as to the exact manner in which such skill and experience must be acquired. Long observation and actual experience, though without actual study of the subject, qualify a witness as an expert in that subject. * * * Likewise, a physician may qualify himself from study of the subject alone. * * * The extent of the expert's qualifications is always a proper subject for the jury on the question of the weight to be given to his testimony.[74]

Thus, training, or experience, or education, or any combination, can be taken into account by the judge in his threshold consideration

---

69. First, the handicapped witness must be found legally competent to testify. Second, the witness must actually testify. Third, this testimony must be crucial to the case. Fourth, the ability of the witness to testify must be in question so that testimony of the interested observer is not used simply as a bolstering device. Fifth, the witness' testimony must be otherwise admissible. Id. at 602–03, 424 N.Y.S.2d at 639.

70. See also Matter of Luz P., 189 A.D.2d 274, 595 N.Y.S.2d 541 (2d Dep't 1993)(court held that an expert witness was not needed to qualify and explain the testimony of a nonverbal, autistic child by use of "facilitated communication" through a keyboard).

71. See, e.g., People v. Cronin, 60 N.Y.2d 430, 470 N.Y.S.2d 110, 458 N.E.2d 351 (1983)(where issue was intent to commit the crime a psychiatrist could testify as to the effects drugs and alcohol would have on defendant's brain); People v. Whitehead, 142 A.D.2d 745, 531 N.Y.S.2d 48 (3d Dep't 1988)(an expert was allowed to testify to the rape victim's actions under the rape trauma syndrome when the victim at first denied having been raped).

72. 285 N.Y. 389, 34 N.E.2d 367 (1941).

73. Id. at 398–99, 34 N.E.2d at 372.

74. Id. at 398, 34 N.E.2d at 371.

whether to let the witness testify,[75] and these factors can also be considered by the jury in determining how much weight to give the testimony.[76] These questions can turn on narrow interpretations,[77] and can tie in with whether expertise is necessary in the first place.[78]

With respect to the necessary experience, training, and education, we find a high degree of flexibility as exemplified by this passage from *Caprara v. Chrysler Corp.*:[79]

> As may be true, for example, of a knowledgeable music critic who has never written a note, Burrill's competency [gained from education and some experience] could just as well have derived from the real world of everyday use as from that of the laboratory. As the court said in *Meiselman* * * *, "[l]ong observation and actual experience, though without actual study [may] qualify a witness as an expert" (see, also, Delair v. Gaudet, 4 A.D.2d 736, 737, 163 N.Y.S.2d 685 [engineer qualified by education and experience to give expert testimony on the adequacy of the installation of a heating plant, despite having never installed one]).

A sampling of the cases demonstrates the liberality with which qualifications are appraised.[80] It is worth noting that the trial court

---

75. See Werner v. Sun Oil Co., 65 N.Y.2d 839, 493 N.Y.S.2d 125, 482 N.E.2d 921 (1985)(trial judge should have allowed plaintiff to lay a foundation for qualification of a witness with special knowledge as to gas pumps). There is no requirement that a trial judge explicitly "certify" a witness as an expert as a prerequisite to the testimony. People v. Gordon, 202 A.D.2d 166, 608 N.Y.S.2d 192 (1st Dep't 1994)(trial court's overruling of adversary's objection to expert testimony is implicit indication that court has exercised discretion in favor of expert's qualifications).

76. See Topel v. Long Island Jewish Medical Center, 55 N.Y.2d 682, 690, 446 N.Y.S.2d 932, 937, 431 N.E.2d 293, 298 (1981)("Of course in the end, the weight to be given the testimony of such a witness, as with the testimony of all witnesses, is for the jury or other trier of the facts * * *.") (dissenting opinion).

77. See People v. Diaz, 51 N.Y.2d 841, 842, 433 N.Y.S.2d 751, 752, 413 N.E.2d 1166, 1166 (1980)(a witness with a B.A. in psychology and 27 years experience in psychological testing was qualified to testify about tests administered to defendant, but it was not error for the trial judge to refuse to allow the witness to go on and render an opinion as to defendant's mental condition at the time the crime was committed since "the witness' expertise in interpretations of this nature had not been satisfactorily established").

78. People v. Kehn, 109 A.D.2d 912, 486 N.Y.S.2d 380 (3d Dep't 1985) (there was no abuse of discretion by the judge in refusing to allow defendant's alcoholism counselor to testify as an expert on the subject of alcohol blackouts since, although she was qualified "and it is settled that expert medical testimony need not come from a licensed doctor," this was an issue the jury could deal with without special explanation).

79. 52 N.Y.2d 114, 121, 436 N.Y.S.2d 251, 254, 417 N.E.2d 545, 548–549 (1981).

80. People v. Duchowney, 166 A.D.2d 769, 563 N.Y.S.2d 524 (3d Dep't 1990) (policeman with basic police training in identification of counterfeit money, and experience on three or four occasions dealing with counterfeit money, found qualified to give an opinion as to $20 bill in issue); People v. Curry, 157 A.D.2d 623, 550 N.Y.S.2d 641 (1st Dep't 1990) (police chemist with 13 years' experience analyzing controlled substances who had performed over 1,200 tests for the narcotic PCP was qualified to identify substance in issue as PCP "through both practical experience and academic study"); Gutierrez v. Iulo, 156 Misc.2d 79, 591 N.Y.S.2d 711 (Sup.Ct.N.Y.Co.1992)(witness holding an MSW was allowed to testify as an expert on rape trauma syndrome); People v. Greene, 153 A.D.2d 439, 552 N.Y.S.2d 640 (2d Dep't 1990), leave to appeal denied, 76 N.Y.2d 735, 558 N.Y.S.2d 897, 557 N.E.2d 1193 (1990), cert. denied, 498 U.S. 947, 111 S.Ct. 363, 112 L.Ed.2d 326 (1990)(wood fracture analysis was a subject about which the witness could testify since, although he had not previously dealt specif-

§ 702.1   OPINIONS & EXPERT TESTIMONY   Ch. 7

cannot compel the proponent of expert testimony to accept the adversary's offer to stipulate to the expert's qualifications.[81]

Library References:

West's Key No. Digests, Criminal Law ⟲477; Evidence ⟲535–546.

Library References:

West's Key No. Digests, Criminal Law ⟲477; Evidence ⟲535–546.

f. Impeachment of Experts

An expert may, of course, be impeached in the same way as other witnesses, and certainly the most effective impeachment technique would be to demonstrate weaknesses, omissions and contradictions inherent in the very subject about which he testified on direct examination.[82] A unique impeachment technique deserving of special mention here is that involving the use of a learned treatise which is at odds with the witness' testimony. As stated in *Labate v. Plotkin*:[83]

> It is well settled that on cross-examination an expert witness may be confronted with a passage from a treatise or book which contradicts the opinion the expert witness previously expressed on the stand, only after the expert witness has accepted the

---

ically with wood, he had had two weeks of forensic training concerning fracture pattern analysis and said that the pattern of fractures is the same regardless of the substance); Anderson v. Donis, 150 A.D.2d 414, 541 N.Y.S.2d 25 (2d Dep't 1989)(orthopedist held competent to testify as to podiatric procedure); Bellinzoni v. Seland, 128 A.D.2d 580, 512 N.Y.S.2d 846 (2d Dep't 1987)(judge abused his discretion in not allowing witness with experience in design and construction of wood structures to testify as to workmanship in construction); People v. Battease, 124 A.D.2d 807, 509 N.Y.S.2d 39 (2d Dep't 1986)(police officer, having completed course in accident investigation and reconstruction, and having investigated over 400 motor vehicle accidents, was qualified to testify as to the point of impact of vehicles); People v. Donaldson, 107 A.D.2d 758, 484 N.Y.S.2d 123 (2d Dep't 1985)(police officer who had acquired some training in fingerprint analysis had received no degree, but had lifted "thousands" of fingerprints, was qualified by "practical experience" to testify that defendant had water on his hand at the time the impression was left). Compare People v. Ciervo, 178 A.D.2d 486, 577 N.Y.S.2d 140 (2d Dep't 1991)(no abuse of discretion for judge to refuse to qualify an electrical engineer as an expert in the operation of electric meters since he had no experience with these devices); Goldman v. County of Nassau, 170 A.D.2d 648, 567 N.Y.S.2d 360 (2d Dep't 1991)(no abuse of discretion in rejecting witness since although he had extensive experience in the area of safety in scholastic sports, he lacked sufficient expertise in designing facilities of a park).

81. Counihan v. J.H. Werbelovsky's Sons, 5 A.D.2d 80, 168 N.Y.S.2d 829 (1st Dep't 1957).

82. See, e.g., Herring v. Hayes, 135 A.D.2d 684, 684, 522 N.Y.S.2d 583, 584 (2d Dep't 1987)("The trier of fact is not required to accept an expert's opinion to the exclusion of the facts and circumstances disclosed by other testimony and/or the facts disclosed on cross-examination of the expert witness. The plaintiff's expert was equivocal upon cross-examination as to whether the competent producing cause of the plaintiff's injuries was the accident in question. As instructed by the court, the jury was at liberty to reject the expert's opinion if it found the facts to be different from those which formed the basis for the opinion or if, after careful consideration of all the evidence in the case, it disagreed with the opinion."). See also Garces v. Hip Hospital, Inc., 201 A.D.2d 615, 608 N.Y.S.2d 237 (2d Dep't 1994)(fact that expert had given contrary opinion in another case was proper impeachment).

83. 195 A.D.2d 444, 445, 600 N.Y.S.2d 144, 145 (2d Dep't 1993).

treatise or book as authoritative.[84]

The court in *Labate* held it reversible error for defense counsel to have cross-examined the expert with material from a book the expert refused to acknowledge as authoritative.[85] Assuming the contradictory material has been acknowledged by the witness as authoritative it may be used to impeach, but is not admissible for its truth.[86]

Rule 803(18) of the Federal Rules of Evidence creates a hearsay exception which would admit passages from learned treatises as evidence-in-chief if relied on by an expert in his direct testimony and if shown to be reliable authority. Treatises can also be used on cross-examination of an expert for impeachment purposes, and there is no requirement that the witness acknowledge the work's reliability. These liberalizations have not occurred in New York either through caselaw or the proposed code.

Library References:

West's Key No. Digests, Criminal Law ⚖489, 490; Evidence ⚖560.
West's Key No. Digests, Criminal Law ⚖468; Evidence ⚖505–534.

§ 702.2 Federal

a. Generally

Rule 702 of the Federal Rules of Evidence, "Testimony By Experts," provides:

> If scientific, technical, or other specialized knowledge will assist the trier of fact to understand the evidence or to determine a fact issue, a witness qualified as an expert by knowledge, skill, experience, training or education, may testify thereto in the form of an opinion or otherwise.

This is said to be a codification of pre-existing federal case law.[1] The Second Circuit has said, "For an expert's testimony to be admissible under this Rule, * * * it must be directed to matters within the witness' scientific, technical, or specialized knowledge and not to lay matters which a jury is capable of understanding and deciding without the expert's help."[2] If there is any dissimilarity with the New York state law discussed in the last section, it would be that the federal courts are more liberal in determining what will be of help to the fact-finder. Thus, for example, experienced narcotics officers may give their opinion

---

84. The court cited Mark v. Colgate Univ., 53 A.D.2d 884, 385 N.Y.S.2d 621 (2d Dep't 1976).

85. See also Walsh v. Staten Island Obstetrics, 193 A.D.2d 672, 598 N.Y.S.2d 17 (2d Dep't), motion for lv. to appeal denied, 82 N.Y.2d 845, 606 N.Y.S.2d 595, 627 N.E.2d 517 (1993), where the court noted the same problem, but that it had not been preserved for appellate review.

86. Hastings v. Chrysler Corp., 273 App. Div. 292, 77 N.Y.S.2d 524 (1st Dep't 1948).

§ 702.2

1. 3 Weinstein and Berger ¶ 702[01] at 702–7.

2. Andrews v. Metro North Commuter R.R. Co., 882 F.2d 705, 708 (2d Cir.1989).

§ 702.2   OPINIONS & EXPERT TESTIMONY   Ch. 7

that what they saw was a drug sale,[3] auctioneers may testify as to custom and practice of city marshals in running auctions,[4] dress buyers may testify as to preferences of defendant's clientele,[5] and an experienced patent agent should be allowed to testify on a matter of patent infringement even though he had received no formal training in patent law.[6] There are limits, however. It is for the trial judge, not an expert, to instruct the jury respecting applicable principles of law;[7] a tugboat captain should not have been allowed to testify as to adequacy of the lighting at the place where a barge-pleasure boat collision occurred;[8] an expert witness should not have given his opinion, in an action involving the breach of a stock agreement, as to the obligations of the parties under the contract,[9] and an expert on drug sales should not have been permitted to testify about "typical" sales where the only purpose and effect was to bolster the credibility of fact-witnesses who had observed the events in issue.[10] The question of expert testimony concerning the reliability of eyewitness identification does not appear to have come up in the New York federal courts. Such testimony is generally rejected in other circuits.[11]

Each case contains different considerations, and generalization beyond the language of Rule 702 is impossible, except that trial judges have broad discretion in these matters.[12] Furthermore, even if expert testi-

3. United States v. Young, 745 F.2d 733 (2d Cir.1984), cert. denied, 470 U.S. 1084, 105 S.Ct. 1842, 85 L.Ed.2d 142 (1985).

4. United States v. Angelilli, 660 F.2d 23 (2d Cir.1981), cert. denied, 455 U.S. 910, 102 S.Ct. 1258, 71 L.Ed.2d 449, cert. denied, 455 U.S. 945, 102 S.Ct. 1442, 71 L.Ed.2d 657, reh. den., 456 U.S. 939, 102 S.Ct. 1998, 72 L.Ed.2d 460 (1982).

5. McGregor-Doniger, Inc. v. Drizzle, Inc., 599 F.2d 1126 (2d Cir.1979).

6. N.V. Maatschappij Voor Industriele Waarden v. A.O. Smith Corp., 590 F.2d 415 (2d Cir.1978).

7. F.H. Krear & Co. v. Nineteen Named Trustees, 810 F.2d 1250 (2d Cir.1987).

8. Stissi v. Interstate and Ocean Transport Co., 765 F.2d 370 (2d Cir.1985). Cf. Martell v. Boardwalk Enterprises, Inc., 748 F.2d 740 (2d Cir.1984)(expert testimony in products liability case that craft operated by a boy was unstable at certain speeds was more probative than prejudicial).

9. Marx & Co., Inc. v. Diners' Club, Inc., 550 F.2d 505 (2d Cir.), cert. denied, 434 U.S. 861, 98 S.Ct. 188, 54 L.Ed.2d 134 (1977).

10. United States v. Cruz, 981 F.2d 659, 663–64 (2d Cir.1992)(where expert's testimony mirrors facts as related by fact-witness, such testimony may create improper inference "that a law enforcement specialist * * * believes the government's [witnesses] to be credible and the defendant to be guilty").

11. See, e.g., United States v. Rincon, 28 F.3d 921, 923–26 (9th Cir.), cert. denied, ___ U.S. ___, 115 S.Ct. 605, 130 L.Ed.2d 516 (1994)(eyewitness identification expert's opinion was not shown to have been based on scientific method as required by Supreme Court's Daubert decision (see notes 17–27 infra) nor would it have assisted jury); United States v. Harris, 995 F.2d 532 (4th Cir.1993); cf. United States v. Moore, 786 F.2d 1308 (5th Cir.1986)(such opinion is proper in some cases).

12. See, e.g., United States v. Amuso, 21 F.3d 1251, 1263 (2d Cir.), cert. denied, ___ U.S. ___, 115 S.Ct. 326, 130 L.Ed.2d 286 (1994)("A district court has broad discretion under Fed.R.Evid. 702 whether to admit expert testimony, and that discretion will be disturbed only if it was manifestly erroneous"); Fiatauruolo v. United States, 8 F.3d 930, 941 (2d Cir.1993) (trial judge has discretion in determining satisfaction of helpfulness standard). In United States v. DiDomenico, 985 F.2d 1159, 1163 (2d Cir. 1993), the court observed: "There has been a palpable ebb and flow in judicial attitudes toward expert testimony * * *. Yet, there has been one recurrent tide coursing through the cases: the admissibility of such evidence is generally best left to trial judges."

The trial court's discretion encompasses decisions regarding the "specialized knowl-

mony might be of assistance to the jury in understanding the evidence, the trial court has discretion under Rule 403 of the Federal Rules of Evidence to exclude the testimony where its probative value is substantially outweighed by its prejudicial, confusing, misleading or cumulative nature.[13]

b. Scientific Evidence

Beginning in 1923, the *Frye* rule for the admissibility of scientific evidence—"general acceptance in the scientific community"—took hold in the federal and state courts.[14] New York courts have steadfastly adhered to this test.[15] Following the adoption of the Federal Rules of Evidence, however, doubt as to its continued viability arose in the federal courts.[16] Finally, in *Daubert v. Merrell Dow Pharmaceuticals*,[17] the United States Supreme Court decided that Rule 702 replaced the *Frye* rule as the test for admissibility of scientific evidence.

As seen above, Rule 702 is virtually standardless.[18] Justice Blackmun noted in *Daubert* that not only is the general acceptance standard not in Rule 702, but that "[t]he drafting history makes no mention of *Frye*, and a rigid 'general acceptance' requirement would be at odds with the 'liberal thrust' of the Federal Rules and their 'general approach of relaxing the traditional barriers' to 'opinion testimony.'"[19] The basis of the *Daubert* decision is that the *Frye* test has been superseded by a more flexible test based on relevance and reliability.[20] Where the majority and dissent part company is over the majority's prescription for a test that should be applied by the trial judge.[21] The dissenters felt that the announcement of rules in the abstract was unnecessary and dangerous and that such rules should be fashioned as cases arise.[22]

---

edge" and helpfulness components of Rule 702 as well as those concerning the adequacy of the expert's qualifications. See McCulloch v. H.B. Fuller Co., 61 F.3d 1038, 1042–44 (2d Cir.1995).

13. In re Air Disaster at Lockerbie Scotland, 37 F.3d 804, 824 (2d Cir.1994), cert. denied sub nom., Pan American World Airways v. Pagnucco, ___ U.S. ___, 115 S.Ct. 934, 130 L.Ed.2d 880 (1995)(trial court has discretion to exclude expert testimony if court deems testimony to be unhelpful, cumulative, confusing to jury or more prejudicial than probative); United States v. Castillo, 924 F.2d 1227, 1232 n.9 (2d Cir.1991)(expert testimony that satisfies Rule 702 may still be excluded pursuant to Rule 403); F.H. Krear & Co. v. Nineteen Named Trustees, 810 F.2d 1250, 1257 (2d Cir.1987)(even if expert testimony might assist jury in determining disputed facts, trial court has discretion under Rule 403 to exclude the evidence).

14. Frye v. United States, 293 F. 1013, 1014 (D.C.Cir.1923).

15. See People v. Wesley, 83 N.Y.2d 417, 611 N.Y.S.2d 97, 633 N.E.2d 451 (1994).

16. See United States v. Downing, 753 F.2d 1224 (3d Cir.1985).

17. ___ U.S. ___, 113 S.Ct. 2786, 125 L.Ed.2d 469 (1993), on remand, 43 F.3d 1311 (9th Cir.1995).

18. The Judicial Conference Advisory Committee on Civil Rules has proposed an amendment to FRE 702 which would give courts more discretion to evaluate the quality of the evidence. Expert testimony would be allowed only if "the information is reasonably reliable and will substantially assist the trier of fact to understand the evidence or to determine a fact in issue."

19. ___ U.S. at ___, 113 S.Ct. at 2794, 125 L.Ed.2d at 480, citing Beech Aircraft Corp. v. Rainey, 488 U.S. 153, 109 S.Ct. 439, 102 L.Ed.2d 445 (1988).

20. ___ U.S. at ___, 113 S.Ct. at 2797, 125 L.Ed.2d at 484.

21. ___ U.S. at ___, 113 S.Ct. at 2796–97, 125 L.Ed.2d at 483.

22. Id. at ___, 113 S.Ct. at 2799–2800, 125 L.Ed.2d at 486–487.

§ 702.2   OPINIONS & EXPERT TESTIMONY   Ch. 7

The *Daubert* majority declared that the language of Rule 702 must be the focal point for the trial judge's determination of admissibility: (1) the expert's testimony must reflect "scientific knowledge"; and (2) the testimony must be of assistance to the fact-finder, i.e., there must be a connection or "fit" between the testimony and the issues of the particular case.[23] With respect to the "scientific knowledge" component, the testimony must be grounded in the methods and procedures of science: "Proposed testimony must be supported by appropriate validation—i.e., 'good grounds,' based on what is known."[24]

The trial judge serves as a "gatekeeper" who must make "a preliminary assessment of whether the reasoning or methodology underlying the testimony is scientifically valid and of whether that reasoning or methodology properly can be applied to the facts in issue."[25] The Court identified four nonexclusive areas of inquiry for the trial judge to consider: (1) whether the scientific theory or method can and has been tested; (2) whether it has been subjected to peer review and publication; (3) the potential rate of error and the existence of standards controlling the operation of the technique; and (4) the extent of "general acceptance" in the relevant scientific community.[26] The focus, said the Supreme Court, "must be solely on principles and methodology, not on the conclusions that they generate."[27]

A thorough exploration of the applications and ramifications of *Daubert* is beyond the scope of this work.[28] Suffice it to say that federal courts have warmed to the flexible standards of *Daubert* in determining the admission[29] and exclusion[30] of scientific evidence. The Second Circuit Court of Appeals, however, has held that the district judge's gate-

---

23. Id. at ___, 113 S.Ct. at 2795–96, 125 L.Ed.2d at 480–82.

24. Id. at ___, 113 S.Ct. at 2795, 125 L.Ed.2d at 481.

25. Id. at ___, 113 S.Ct. at 2796, 125 L.Ed.2d at 482.

26. Id. at ___, 113 S.Ct. at 2796–97, 125 L.Ed.2d at 482–84. Interestingly, Frye's emphasis on general acceptance is not irrelevant; it remains as a factor to be considered in determining the reliability of scientific evidence. The Supreme Court also noted that Fed.R.Evid. 403 (unfair prejudice, confusion, misleading the jury) may be taken into account as a basis for excluding scientific evidence that is otherwise relevant. Id. at ___, 113 S.Ct. at 2798, 125 L.Ed.2d at 484.

On remand in Daubert, the Ninth Circuit added another inquiry to the Supreme Court's list: Was the expert's opinion the product of independent research or was it developed solely for purposes of testifying? Daubert v. Merrell Dow Pharmaceuticals, Inc., 43 F.3d 1311, 1317 (9th Cir.1995).

27. Id. at ___, 113 S.Ct. at 2797, 125 L.Ed.2d at 484. But see In re Paoli Railroad Yard PCB Litigation, 35 F.3d 717, 746 (3d Cir.1994):

Daubert requires the judge's admissibility decision to focus not on the expert's conclusions but on his or her principles and methodology. * * * But we think that this distinction has only limited practical import. When a judge disagrees with the conclusions of an expert, it will generally be because he or she thinks that there is a mistake at some step in the investigative or reasoning process of that expert. If the judge thinks that the conclusions of some other expert are correct, it will likely be because the judge thinks that the methodology and reasoning process of the other expert are superior to those of the first expert.

28. Helpful analyses can be found in Berger, "Procedural Paradigms for Applying the Daubert Test," 78 Minn.L.Rev. 1345 (1994); Symposium, "Scientific Evidence After the Death of Frye," 15 Cardozo L.Rev. 1745–2294 (1994).

29. The Daubert standards were met in the following sampling of cases: Pioneer Hi–Bred Int'l v. Holden Foundation Seeds, Inc., 35 F.3d 1226 (8th Cir.1994)(electrophoresis, liquid chromatography, and grow-out testing); United States v. Quinn, 18 F.3d 1461 (9th Cir.), cert. denied, ___ U.S.

30. See note 30 on page 523.

keeping role in evaluating the reliability of scientific evidence applies only to the threshold question of admissibility.[31] Once the scientific evidence is determined to be admissible, traditional standards apply to the question whether the proponent's case, as a whole, is sufficient to withstand an opponent's motion for judgment as a matter of law.[32] The Second Circuit has also suggested that *Daubert* is confined to problems of "junk science," and is inapplicable to routine issues of technical expertise.[33]

Library References:

West's Key No. Digests, Criminal Law ⚖468–494; Evidence ⚖505–560.

703 Basis of Expert Opinion Testimony

§ 703.1 New York

An expert must base her opinion on facts; speculation, conjecture

___, 114 S.Ct. 2755, 129 L.Ed.2d 871 (1994)(photogrammetry to identify individual's height); Hopkins v. Dow Corning Corp., 33 F.3d 1116 (9th Cir.1994) (ability of silicone to cause immune disorders in humans, based on animal studies and biophysical data).

As a result of Daubert, the Eleventh Circuit held in United States v. Posado, 57 F.3d 428 (5th Cir.1995), that its prior per se rule of exclusion of polygraph evidence was no longer viable. The district court was therefore directed to reevaluate the issue in accordance with the Daubert standards. Id. at 436.

30. In the following sampling of cases, expert testimony failed to pass muster under Daubert: Sorensen v. Shaklee Corp., 31 F.3d 638 (8th Cir.1994)(insufficient scientific basis for experts' conclusion that parents' consumption of chemically treated alfalfa tablets caused mental retardation of subsequently-born infants); Claar v. Burlington Northern R.R. Co., 29 F.3d 499 (9th Cir.1994)(experts' methodology in concluding that link existed between plaintiff's injuries and exposure to chemicals in the workplace lacked scientific basis); United States v. Jones, 24 F.3d 1177 (9th Cir. 1994)(voice comparison technique lacked scientific basis); Porter v. Whitehall Laboratories, Inc., 9 F.3d 607 (7th Cir.1993) (experts' opinions concerning ibuprofen-induced kidney failure were not based on scientific methodology).

31. In re Joint Eastern & Southern District Asbestos Litigation, 52 F.3d 1124, 1131–33 (2d Cir.1995).

32. Id. The standards within the Second Circuit for evaluating the sufficiency of a party's case are discussed in § 300.3(b) supra. In the case at hand, the district judge was held to have erred in granting defendant's motion for judgment notwithstanding the verdict based on the judge's own evaluation of the weight of certain epidemiological studies that had been admitted in evidence in support of plaintiff's case. Id. at 1133–37. The Second Circuit stated that the proper approach is as follows:

> Applied to epidemiological studies, the question is not whether there is some dispute about the validity or force of a given study, but rather, whether it would be unreasonable for a rational jury to rely on that study to find causation by a preponderance of the evidence. * * * Unlike admissibility assessments, which involve decisions about individual pieces of evidence, sufficiency assessments entail a review of the sum total of a plaintiff's evidence.

Id. at 1133.

33. Iacobelli Construction, Inc. v. County of Monroe, 32 F.3d 19, 25 (2d Cir.1994). Iacobelli was an action arising out of a contract to construct a sewage tunnel in which the trial court relied on Daubert as the basis for rejecting affidavits of a geotechnical consultant and an underground construction consultant. This was error, said the court of appeals, because the experts "[relied] upon the type of methodology and data typically used and accepted in construction-litigation cases." Id. But see Frymire–Brinati v. KPMG Peat Marwick, 2 F.3d 183, 186-87 (7th Cir.1993)(where accounting expert in securities fraud action does not adhere to methodology that valuation experts find essential in forming basis for opinion, accounting expert's opinion should be excluded under Daubert rule); Imwinkelried, "The Next Step After Daubert: Developing a Similarly Epistemological Approach to Ensuring the Reliability of Nonscientific Expert Testimony," 15 Cardozo L.Rev. 2271 (1994).

and unsupported assumptions are impermissible.[1] From what sources does an expert learn the facts? In this regard, there are generally two kinds of experts—those who have personal knowledge of the subject, such as a treating physician, and those who are hired to testify on the basis of data created by others who may well not be witnesses. The latter category may involve an expert who is not altogether detached from the subject such as a physician who at least examined the subject. The treating physician, or the mechanic who worked on the car, or the engineer who designed the subject instrumentality, can testify from direct knowledge, thus seldom causing concern as to the basis of their opinions. The witness hired as an expert, however, may seek to base his opinion on a variety of facts, some of which may have been introduced at trial and others that are not in the record, including hearsay.

A line of New York cases traces the evolution from inadmissibility to admissibility of expert opinions based on data not in evidence. In *People v. Keough*,[2] it was held that an expert may testify only on the basis of facts personally known by the expert or upon facts supported by independent evidence in the trial record. *People v. DiPiazza*,[3] and *People v. Stone*[4] indicated a relaxed attitude, but neither opinion was clear in defining the limits to be placed on such bases. Finally, in *People v. Sugden*,[5] the Court of Appeals broke new ground. The court relied upon *Keogh* as stating the general rule that an expert's opinion must be based on facts in evidence. But then two exceptions were carved out. First, if people interviewed by the expert testify at trial, the expert may rely on their information.[6] Second, it was stated that the expert may rely, in part, on material not in evidence if it "is of a kind accepted in the profession as reliable in forming a professional opinion."[7] The court

§ 703.1

1. See, e.g., Neidert v. Austin S. Edgar, Inc., 204 A.D.2d 1030, 612 N.Y.S.2d 529 (4th Dep't 1994)(meteorologist's knowledge of weather conditions in a general vicinity on a particular date could not serve as basis for opinion that there was "black ice" on roads in that area); Dulin v. Maher, 200 A.D.2d 707, 607 N.Y.S.2d 67 (2d Dep't 1994)(foundation insufficient for testimony by accident reconstruction expert who did not inspect accident site until three years after event and who was not familiar through other sources with condition of site at time of accident); Kracker v. Spartan Chemical Co., 183 A.D.2d 810, 585 N.Y.S.2d 216 (2d Dep't 1992)(expert opinion is "worthless" if not based on facts). Cf. Sawyer v. Dreis & Krump Manufacturing Co., 67 N.Y.2d 328, 502 N.Y.S.2d 696, 493 N.E.2d 920 (1986)(expert was unable to substantiate plaintiff's claim that defendant's conduct caused his amnesia because of absence of evidence as to what happened when plaintiff injured his hand while operating machine manufactured by defendant).

2. 276 N.Y. 141, 11 N.E.2d 570 (1937).

3. 24 N.Y.2d 342, 300 N.Y.S.2d 545, 248 N.E.2d 412 (1969). In DiPiazza psychiatric experts relied on hospital records not in evidence. The court allowed the testimony since it comprised but a part of the testimonial basis and the witnesses were thoroughly cross-examined.

4. 35 N.Y.2d 69, 358 N.Y.S.2d 737, 315 N.E.2d 787 (1974). In this case, the court approved an expert opinion that was confirmed, said the psychiatrist, by interviews with 12 people, four of whom did not testify. The court said the Keogh rule imposed an undue limitation on an expert's investigation which ought to be thorough and unhampered by the fact all sources might not get into evidence. It was said that the expert's opinion must be substantially, if not exclusively, resting on facts in evidence.

5. 35 N.Y.2d 453, 363 N.Y.S.2d 923, 323 N.E.2d 169 (1974).

6. Id. at 461, 363 N.Y.S.2d at 929, 323 N.E.2d at 169.

7. Id. at 460, 363 N.Y.S.2d at 929, 323 N.E.2d at 169. The rationale for the exception, at least in cases involving expert testi-

Ch. 7   BASIS OF EXPERT OPINION TESTIMONY   § 703.1

cited Rule 703 of the Federal Rules of Evidence, which expressly provides for expert reliance on non-record material if of a sort "reasonably relied upon by experts in the particular field."[8] The court found no violation of defendant's right to confrontation in the particular case.[9]

All of the foregoing cases involved testimony by psychiatrists; indeed the "professional reliance" rule has seldom been discussed in any other sort of case.[10] Perhaps there is something about the science of the mind that, unlike other aspects of medicine, requires a range of data, not all of which can practically be introduced in evidence. At any rate, most cases adhere to the *Keogh* rule which requires the basis for expert opinion to be in evidence, except where one of the *Sugden* exceptions has been satisfied.[11] The Proposed New York Evidence Code § 703 codifies

---

mony by physicians, was articulated by Justice Yesawich of the Appellate Division in his concurring opinion in Borden v. Brady, 92 A.D.2d 983, 984, 461 N.Y.S.2d 497, 498 (3d Dep't 1983): "The underlying rationale is that since physicians make life and death decisions in reliance upon medical reports filed by other doctors and medical personnel, those reports, though not independently admissible in evidence, enjoy a singular trustworthiness (Advisory Committee Note to Federal Rules of Evidence 703)."

8. 35 N.Y.2d at 459, 363 N.Y.S.2d at 927, 323 N.E.2d at 172. See § 703.2 infra.

9. Id. at 460, 363 N.Y.S.2d at 929, 323 N.E.2d at 169. Sugden involved an insanity defense. The psychiatrist who testified for the prosecution had interviewed the defendant and had examined a psychologist's report rendered when defendant was age seven, together with other psychiatric and medical reports, defendant's written confession and written statements of four persons involved in the crime. Only one of these people did not testify. The psychiatrist also examined a statement given to the police by an accomplice who testified. All of this data was sufficient as a basis for his testimony. Had the accomplice not testified it is doubtful the expert could have used her prior statement as a basis for his opinion.

10. See, e.g., Matter of Omar B., 175 A.D.2d 834, 573 N.Y.S.2d 301(1991) (court-appointed psychiatrist could express opinion based, in part, on medical records not in evidence). An exception is found in Marulli v. Pro Sec. Serv., 151 Misc.2d 1077, 1078–79, 583 N.Y.S.2d 870, 871 (Sup.Ct.App.T. 1992), where it was stated: "The court properly permitted limited reference by plaintiff's succeeding treating physicians to the contents of the report of plaintiff's non-testifying original treating physician which provided background information as to the conservative care that was furnished to plaintiff for a short time after the accident [citing Sugden]." See also Holshek v. Stokes, 122 A.D.2d 777, 505 N.Y.S.2d 664 (2d Dep't 1986).

11. See Hambsch v. New York City Transit Auth., 63 N.Y.2d 723, 480 N.Y.S.2d 195, 469 N.E.2d 516 (1984)(expert's opinion inadmissible where based on X-ray not in evidence and out-of-court discussion with radiologist because no evidence was presented "establishing the reliability of the out-of-court material"); Lee v. Shields, 188 A.D.2d 637, 591 N.Y.S.2d 522 (2d Dep't 1992)(a physician's opinion that deceased's death was due to hypertension was inadmissible because he relied on reports not in evidence and not known personally by him); Tucker v. Salomon Elimelech, 184 A.D.2d 636, 584 N.Y.S.2d 895 (2d Dep't 1992), (expert testified that based on his observations a guard rail was not maintained at the required height, but ran afoul of the general rule when he went on to calculate angles and distances involving the accident from reports not in evidence); Kracker v. Spartan Chemical Co., 183 A.D.2d 810, 585 N.Y.S.2d 216 (2d Dep't 1992)(physician's deposition offered in opposition to defendant's motion to dismiss not sufficient since no sound basis for his opinions); cf. Schozer v. William Penn Life Ins. Co., 84 N.Y.2d 639, 620 N.Y.S.2d 797, 644 N.E.2d 1353 (1994) (radiologist's analysis of X-ray admissible where X-ray itself missing under excusable circumstances—see § 1004.1 infra); Natale v. Niagara Mohawk Power Corp., 135 A.D.2d 955, 522 N.Y.S.2d 364 (3d Dep't 1987), appeal denied, 71 N.Y.2d 804, 528 N.Y.S.2d 829, 524 N.E.2d 149 (1988)(expert may base opinion on the testimony of other witnesses who are subject to cross-examination); Holshek v. Stokes, 122 A.D.2d 777, 505 N.Y.S.2d 664 (2d Dep't 1986) (physician's opinion based on X-ray not in evidence was allowed under the "professional reliance" exception; court noted that "[additionally], while not in evidence,

§ 703.1   OPINIONS & EXPERT TESTIMONY   Ch. 7

the *Sugden* exceptions[12] and is a bit more detailed than Federal Rule of evidence 703.

The foundation for expert testimony based on out-of-court material requires a showing, to the trial judge's satisfaction, that the material is reliable.[13] Even if such foundation is made, the expert may not rely exclusively on out-of-court material.[14] Furthermore, there are limits on the use that may be made of the material at trial. In *Borden v. Brady*,[15] for example, the plaintiff's treating orthopedic surgeon opined that the plaintiff's condition was permanent in reliance on a neurologist's report that was not independently admissible in evidence. After the surgeon identified the report and explained its significance in forming his opinion, the plaintiff was permitted to admit the report into evidence and to have it read to the jury. Admission into evidence went too far, said the Appellate Division, because the *Sugden* case "was not intended to carve out such a new exception to the hearsay rule."[16] The *Borden* case, however, fails to provide precise guidelines regarding the extent to which an expert may discuss, in his own testimony, how and why he relied on the out-of-court material.[17] Where the defendant's insanity is asserted

the defendant had a copy of both the X-ray and the report; accordingly he was not foreclosed from effective cross-examination"); Rodolitz v. Boston–Old Colony Ins. Co., 74 A.D.2d 821, 425 N.Y.S.2d 353 (2d Dep't 1980)(lack of personal knowledge goes to weight of expert's testimony and testimony may be based on facts proven, or reasonably inferable, from testimony of other witnesses).

12. § 703. Bases of opinion testimony by experts [PROPOSED]

The facts or data in the particular case upon which an expert bases an opinion or inference may be those perceived by or made known to the expert at or before the trial, proceeding, or hearing. The facts or data need not be admissible in evidence if of a reliable type upon which experts in the particular field reasonably rely in forming opinions or inferences upon the subject or if the facts or data come from a person with personal knowledge who testifies and is subject to cross-examination at trial. The facts or data relied on pursuant to this section do not constitute substantive evidence, unless otherwise admissible as such evidence.

13. Hambsch v. New York City Transit Auth., 63 N.Y.2d 723, 726, 480 N.Y.S.2d 195, 196, 469 N.E.2d 516, 518 (1984)("In order to qualify for the 'professional reliability' exception, there must be evidence establishing the reliability of the out-of-court material"). See also Borden v. Brady, 92 A.D.2d 983, 984, 461 N.Y.S.2d 497, 498 (3d Dep't 1983) ("Reliability of the material is the touchstone; once reliability is established, the medical expert may testify about it even though it would otherwise be considered inadmissible hearsay.")(concurring opinion).

14. O'Shea v. Sarro, 106 A.D.2d 435, 482 N.Y.S.2d 529 (2d Dep't 1984); Borden v. Brady, 92 A.D.2d 983, 461 N.Y.S.2d 497 (3d Dep't 1983).

15. 92 A.D.2d 983, 461 N.Y.S.2d 497 (3d Dep't 1983).

16. Id. at 984, 461 N.Y.S.2d at 4998.

17. A concurring opinion in Borden found no fault in the reading of the report to the jury: "If the dependability of the neurosurgeon's report had been established, passages relevant to the orthopedic surgeon's opinion could properly have been brought to the jury's attention." Id. The error, according to the concurrence, was in the absence of any independent evidence of the reliability of the report. See note 13 supra. Cf. People v. Jones, 73 N.Y.2d 427, 430, 541 N.Y.S.2d 340, 342, 539 N.E.2d 96, 98 (1989)(jury must be informed of extrajudicial material upon which expert relied so that it can judge its reliability).

Courts in other jurisdictions are divided over the question as to how far the expert may go in describing the hearsay upon which he relied. See § 703.2, at note 11, infra.

A related question is whether the "professional reliance" exception eviscerates the rule in New York that only a treating physician, not an expert retained solely for trial purposes, may testify to the patient's out-of-court statements concerning physical condition. See Davidson v. Cornell, 132 N.Y. 228, 30 N.E. 573 (1892); § 803(1).1(d), at note 68, infra.

as an affirmative defense in a criminal case, however, courts have interpreted § 60.55 of the New York Criminal Procedure Law to permit expert psychiatric witnesses to testify to any extrajudicial facts and sources that were utilized in forming their opinions.[18]

Library References:
West's Key No. Digests, Criminal Law ⊕=486; Evidence ⊕=555.

§ 703.2 Federal

Rule 703 of the Federal Rules of Evidence is similar to New York law with respect to the permissible bases of expert testimony. Rule 703 states:

> The facts or data in the particular case upon which an expert bases an opinion or inference may be those perceived by or made known to the expert at or before the hearing. If of a type reasonably relied upon by experts in the particular field in forming opinions or inferences upon the subject, the facts or data need not be admissible in evidence.

The basic rule still requires that the data upon which the expert bases his opinion be in evidence or that the expert testify from personal knowledge.[1] The expert may rely upon facts or data that are not admissible in evidence only if such information is of a kind that is reasonably relied upon by other experts in the relevant field.[2] In no

---

18. See People v. Rudd, 196 A.D.2d 666, 667, 601 N.Y.S.2d 933, 934 (2d Dep't), appeal denied, 82 N.Y.2d 853, 606 N.Y.S.2d 605, 627 N.E.2d 526 (1993)(prosecution psychiatrist was permitted to describe interviews conducted with friends and family of victim; court took note "that the jury was instructed that testimony concerning the statements made by the victim's friends and family members to the psychiatrist was being admitted for the limited purpose of enabling them to understand the basis for the psychiatrist's opinion, and not for the truth of these statements"). N.Y.Crim. Proc.Law § 60.55(1) provides that, on the issue of insanity, "[t]he psychiatrist or licensed psychologist must be permitted to make any explanation reasonably serving to clarify his diagnosis and opinion." Subdivision (2) of the statute explicitly permits the expert to testify to statements made by the defendant to the expert to the extent such statements bear on the issue of insanity.

§ 703.2

1. Pennsylvania Dental Ass'n v. Medical Service Ass'n, 745 F.2d 248 (3d Cir.1984), cert. denied, 471 U.S. 1016, 105 S.Ct. 2021, 85 L.Ed.2d 303 (1985)(expert made conclusory statements not based on any evidence in the record); DiRose v. PK Management Corp., 691 F.2d 628 (2d Cir.1982), cert. denied, 461 U.S. 915, 103 S.Ct. 1896, 77 L.Ed.2d 285 (1983)(appraisals that "rest upon conclusory and subjective opinions will not suffice").

The Second Circuit's decision in United States v. Scop, 846 F.2d 135 (2d Cir.1988), modified in part on other grounds, 856 F.2d 5 (2d Cir.1988), imposes a limitation on an expert's ability to rely upon testimony introduced by other experts. In Scop, the government qualified an expert in a securities fraud trial, one Whitten, who had been investigating the case for four years and who assisted in the preparation of the indictment. Nevertheless, he professed to base his opinions on evidence adduced at the trial including testimony from other government witnesses whose credibility provided a jury question. This was held to be improper: "Our holding * * * is that witness *A* may not offer an opinion as to relevant facts based on *A*'s assessment of the trustworthiness or accuracy of witness *B* where *B*'s credibility is an issue to be determined by the trier of fact. Were we to rule otherwise, triers of fact would be called upon either to evaluate opinion testimony in ignorance of an important foundation for that opinion or to hear testimony that is otherwise inadmissible and highly prejudicial." Id. at 142.

2. Compare International Adhesive Coating Co. v. Bolton Emerson Int'l, Inc., 851 F.2d 540, 544–45 (1st Cir.1988)(expert

§ 703.2   OPINIONS & EXPERT TESTIMONY   Ch. 7

event may the expert speculate or testify on the basis of unsupported assumptions.[3]

When an expert relies on out-of-court material, does the expert have the final word on whether such material is reliable or should the trial judge play a screening role? Judge Jack Weinstein thoroughly analyzed Rule 703 in *In re "Agent Orange" Product Liability Litigation*[4] and concluded that the trial court should make an independent evaluation of the reliability of the data upon which the expert relies. He states:

> Rule 703 permits experts to rely upon hearsay. The guarantee of trustworthiness is that it be of the kind normally employed by experts in the field. The expert is assumed, if he meets the test of Rule 702, to have the skill to properly evaluate the hearsay, giving it probative force appropriate to the circumstances. Nevertheless, the court may not abdicate its independent responsibilities to decide if the bases met minimum standards of reliability as a condition of admissibility.[5]

The Second Circuit Court of Appeals, under the influence of *Daubert*,[6] has determined that Judge Weinstein's approach to the matter is the proper one.[7] The Third Circuit, which originally left the question of reliability to the expert alone,[8] has also concluded that *Daubert* requires independent scrutiny of the expert's out-of-court sources.[9]

---

accountant's testimony based on buyer's financial and business records, and on interviews with company personnel, was properly admitted because testimony was type of information reasonably relied on by accountants), with United States v. Scrima, 819 F.2d 996, 1002 (11th Cir.1987)(on issue of client's net worth, no showing was made that accountants customarily rely on conversations between client and casual business acquaintances), and Soden v. Freightliner Corp., 714 F.2d 498, 502–05 (5th Cir.1983)(testimony of defendant's expert was properly excluded because it was based on statistical material not reasonably relied upon by experts in same field).

3. Shatkin v. McDonnell Douglas Corp., 727 F.2d 202, 208 (2d Cir.1984) (expert may not properly rely upon unrealistic and contradictory assumptions). See also Washington v. Armstrong World Indus., Inc., 839 F.2d 1121, 1123–24 (5th Cir.1988)(expert's testimony was properly excluded where expert never examined plaintiff but relied on other experts whose examinations produced different conclusions; testimony as to cause of death was "pure speculation").

4. 611 F.Supp. 1223 (E.D.N.Y.1985), aff'd, 818 F.2d 187 (2d Cir.1987), cert. denied, 487 U.S. 1234, 108 S.Ct. 2898, 101 L.Ed.2d 932 (1988).

5. Id. at 1245. See also Shu–Tao Lin v. McDonnell Douglas Corp., 574 F.Supp. 1407 (S.D.N.Y.1983), aff'd in part and rev'd in part, 742 F.2d 45 (2d Cir.1984)(court may examine hearsay basis for purpose of determining its reliability).

6. See § 702.2(b) supra.

7. United States v. Locascio, 6 F.3d 924, 938–39 (2d Cir.1993), cert. denied, ___ U.S. ___, 114 S.Ct. 1645, 128 L.Ed.2d 365 (1994)(Daubert "makes clear" that "district court is not bound to accept expert testimony based on questionable data simply because other experts use such data in the field"; however, trial judge need not necessarily conduct a trustworthiness hearing or make an explicit ruling on the record: trustworthiness analysis may be performed sub silentio).

8. In re Japanese Electronic Products Antitrust Litigation, 723 F.2d 238, 277 (3d Cir.1983), rev'd on other grounds sub nom. Matsushita Elec. Indus. Co. v. Zenith Radio Corp., 475 U.S. 574, 106 S.Ct. 1348, 89 L.Ed.2d 538 (1986)(proper inquiry for trial court is not what court deems reliable but what experts in same field deem reliable).

9. In re Paoli Railroad Yard PCB Litigation, 35 F.3d 717 (3d Cir.1994), cert. denied, ___ U.S. ___, 115 S.Ct. 1253, 131 L.Ed.2d 134 (1995):

> Judge Weinstein's view is extremely persuasive, and we are free to express our agreement with it because we think that our former view is no longer tenable in light of Daubert. * * * Daubert makes clear for the first time at the Supreme

Inadmissible hearsay, even if properly relied upon by the expert in forming his opinion, may not be admitted as affirmative proof of facts.[10] At most, the expert on direct examination may describe the out-of-court data to explain the basis of his opinion, and the opponent is entitled to a limiting instruction that such material is not to be considered for its truth.[11]

Library References:

West's Key No. Digests, Criminal Law ⌬486; Evidence ⌬555.

704 Opinion on Ultimate Issues

§ 704.1 New York

The pendulum seems to swing in New York from decisions holding that a witness should not invade the province of the jury by voicing an opinion on an ultimate jury question, to cases which reflect the more liberal view embodied in the Proposed New York Evidence Code § 704.[1]

Court level that courts have to play a gatekeeping role with regard to experts.
* * *
We now make clear that it is the judge who makes the determination of reasonable reliance, and that for the judge to make the factual determination under Rule 104(a) that an expert is basing his or her opinion on a type of data *reasonably* relied upon by experts, the judge must conduct an independent evaluation into reasonableness. The judge can of course take into account the particular expert's opinion that experts reasonably rely on that type of data, as well as the opinions of other experts as to its reliability, but the judge can also take into account other factors he or she deems relevant.

Id. at 748 (emphasis in original).

10. See, e.g., Hutchinson v. Groskin, 927 F.2d 722, 725–26 (2d Cir.1991) (trial court improperly allowed expert to testify that his opinion was "consistent" with those of three other experts whose written statements he relied upon, in part, in forming his own opinion; such testimony converted the out-of-court statements into affirmative evidence); Paddack v. Dave Christensen, Inc., 745 F.2d 1254, 1261–62 (9th Cir.1984). In criminal cases, the defendant's right of confrontation may be implicated. See, e.g., United States v. Lawson, 653 F.2d 299, 302 (7th Cir.1981), cert. denied, 454 U.S. 1150, 102 S.Ct. 1017, 71 L.Ed.2d 305 (1982)("An expert's testimony that was based entirely on hearsay reports, while perhaps satisfying Rule 703, would nevertheless violate a defendant's constitutional right to confront adverse witnesses.").

11. See, e.g., Engebretsen v. Fairchild Aircraft Corp., 21 F.3d 721, 728–29 (6th Cir.1994); United States v. Affleck, 776 F.2d 1451, 1456–58 (10th Cir.1985). Cf. O'Gee v. Dobbs Houses, Inc., 570 F.2d 1084, 1088–89 (2d Cir.1978)(trial court did not abuse discretion in permitting expert to describe hearsay to explain basis of expert opinion where opposing counsel was aware of content of hearsay material and had opportunity to cross-examine expert).

Some authorities, insisting that limiting instructions are ineffective to prevent improper use of the hearsay by the jury, would restrict the expert, on direct examination, to a cursory reference to the material that was relied upon. The specifics could be disclosed only at the adversary's option on cross-examination. See, e.g., First Southwest Lloyds Ins. Co. v. MacDowell, 769 S.W.2d 954, 957–58 (Tex.Ct.App.1989). Cf. Nachtsheim v. Beech Aircraft Corp., 847 F.2d 1261, 1271–72 (7th Cir.1988)(expert will not be permitted to give testimony otherwise inadmissible to explain basis for expert opinion if trial court determines that potential prejudice outweighs probative value under Fed.R.Evid. 403). See generally Carlson, "In Defense of a Constitutional Theory of Experts," 87 Northwest.U.L.Rev. 1182 (1993).

§ 704.1

1. § 704. Opinion on ultimate issue [PROPOSED]

Testimony in the form of an opinion or inference otherwise admissible pursuant to a section of this article is not objectionable because it embraces an ultimate issue to be decided by the trier of fact.

Under what now appears to be the former rule a fire marshal, after testifying as to his investigation of the origins of a fire, should not have concluded by stating that the fire was "set;"[2] attorneys could testify as experts as to the usual practice in settling cases, but overstepped their bounds when giving opinions as to the validity of the procedures followed in the particular case;[3] and, while plaintiff's witness could testify as to the substances left on the floor, he invaded the jury's province when he went on to say that the spillage created the hazardous condition that caused the accident.[4] These questions naturally overlap with those discussed in § 702.1 *supra*, concerning whether any expertise is needed in the first place.[5]

Illustrative of the modern trend is *DeLong v. County of Erie*,[6] discussed in § 702.1 *supra*, where an economist was allowed to testify not only to a seemingly ordinary matter such as the monetary value of a housewife's services, but also out of necessity had to reach conclusions if the testimony was to be comprehensive. In *Selkowitz v. County of Nassau*,[7] a police expert had to reach certain ultimate conclusions in assessing a county patrolman's actions in an emergency situation, but

---

2. People v. Grutz, 212 N.Y. 72, 105 N.E. 843 (1914). Compare Vigilant Ins. Co. v. Rippner Elec. Construc. Co., 196 A.D.2d 494, 601 N.Y.S.2d 137 (2d Dep't 1993)(fire marshal and engineer should have been permitted to testify to cause of fire).

3. Kulak v. Nationwide Ins. Co., 40 N.Y.2d 140, 386 N.Y.S.2d 87, 351 N.E.2d 735 (1976).

4. Vispetto v. Bassuk, 41 A.D.2d 958, 343 N.Y.S.2d 988 (2d Dep't 1973).

5. The Comment to Proposed New York Evidence Code § 704 contains a sampling of such cases, and also those which present both views of the extent to which the witness can go:

Ofttimes, an expert opinion on an ultimate issue, including issues of fact[,] simply will not satisfy the general section 702 standard for expert testimony because the jury is fully capable of reaching its own conclusion on the ultimate issue including issues of fact after being supplied with information by the expert and other sources. See, e.g., People v. Ciaccio, 47 N.Y.2d 431, 438–39, 418 N.Y.S.2d 371, 374, 391 N.E.2d 1347 (1970)(excluding testimony that was nothing more than a judgment on a witness' credibility); Chafoulias v. 240 E. 55th St. Ten. Corp., 141 A.D.2d 207, 533 N.Y.S.2d 440 (1st Dep't 1988)(no need for an expert to assess whether color and arrangement of building vestibule was dangerous or defective); compare People v. Grutz, 212 N.Y. 72, 105 N.E. 843 * * *.

Present New York law seemingly rejects the restriction on expressing an otherwise permissible opinion that might or does embrace the ultimate issue. See People v. Cronin, 60 N.Y.2d 430, 470 N.Y.S.2d 110, 458 N.E.2d 351 (1983); People v. Keindl, 68 N.Y.2d 410, 422, 509 N.Y.S.2d 790, 796, 502 N.E.2d 577 (1986); Broun v. Equitable Life Assur. Soc., 69 N.Y.2d 675, 512 N.Y.S.2d 12, 504 N.E.2d 379 (1986); Sitaras v. Ricciardi & Sons, Inc., 154 A.D.2d 451, 545 N.Y.S.2d 937 (2d Dep't 1989); Doukas v. America On Wheels, 154 A.D.2d 426, 545 N.Y.S.2d 928 (2d Dep't 1989). Older cases expressly rejected the ultimate issue restriction. See Van Wycklyn v. Brooklyn, 118 N.Y. 424, 429, 24 N.E. 179, 180–81 (1890). Several later decisions resurrected the prohibition. See People v. Creasy, 236 N.Y. 205, 222, 140 N.E. 563, 569 (1923); People v. Grutz, supra; Kulak v. Nationwide Mutual Ins. Co., 40 N.Y.2d 140, 386 N.Y.S.2d 87, 351 N.E.2d 735 (1976); Nelson v. X–Ray Systems, Inc., 46 A.D.2d 995, 361 N.Y.S.2d 468 (4th Dep't 1974); Vispetto v. Bassuk, 41 A.D.2d 958, 343 N.Y.S.2d 988 (2d Dep't 1973); Strauch v. Hirschman, 40 A.D.2d 711, 336 N.Y.S.2d 678 (2d Dep't 1972); Bearss v. Westbury Hotel, Inc., 33 A.D.2d 47, 304 N.Y.S.2d 894 (1st Dep't 1969). Other decisions, often without comment on the matter, allow opinions which embrace the issue to be decided by the jury. See Spier v. Barker, 35 N.Y.2d 444, 363 N.Y.S.2d 916, 323 N.E.2d 164 (1974); General Accident Fire & Life Assur. Corp. v. Krieghbaum, 46 A.D.2d 713, 360 N.Y.S.2d 310 (3d Dep't 1974).

6. 60 N.Y.2d 296, 469 N.Y.S.2d 611, 457 N.E.2d 717 (1983).

7. 45 N.Y.2d 97, 408 N.Y.S.2d 10, 379 N.E.2d 1140 (1978).

this was permissible to aid the jury's perception of the standards governing high speed chases. *People v. Cronin*[8] is a good example of the Court of Appeals correcting a trial judge who applied the "other" rule by not allowing a forensic psychiatrist to testify to the effect drugs and alcohol would have on defendant's brain, although he allowed the witness to testify that these substances would have a certain effect on an abstract human brain. The Court of Appeals stated:

> In a sense, opinion testimony of an expert witness necessarily enters upon the jury's province, since the expert and not the jury draws conclusions from the facts, which the jury is then asked to adopt. Such testimony, however, is admissible where the conclusions "to be drawn from the facts" * * * depend upon professional or scientific knowledge or skill not within the range of ordinary training or intelligence.[9]

Further, the Court stated:

> While controversy about opinion testimony going to the ultimate questions has brewed elsewhere, in this State the test has been different. For testimony regarding both the ultimate questions and those of lesser significance, admissibility turns on whether, given the nature of the subject, "the facts cannot be stated or described to the jury in such a manner as to enable them to form an accurate judgment thereon, and no better evidence than such opinions is attainable."[10]

This cannot really be said to be a new rule since the cases quoted from in the above passages are ancient. The problem may have been that lay conclusions as to ultimate issues got mixed up with expert opinions.[11] At any rate, where the subject demands some level of expertise, and the opinion would be helpful, the witness should be allowed to voice a conclusion even if the fact-finder must decide the same issue.[12]

---

8. 60 N.Y.2d 430, 470 N.Y.S.2d 110, 458 N.E.2d 351 (1983).

9. Id. at 432, 470 N.Y.S.2d at 111, 458 N.E.2d at 352, quoting Dougherty v. Milliken, 163 N.Y. 527, 533, 57 N.E. 757, 759 (1900).

10. 60 N.Y.2d at 432–33, 470 N.Y.S.2d at 111, 458 N.E.2d at 352, quoting Van Wycklen v. City of Brooklyn, 118 N.Y. 424, 429, 24 N.E. 179, 180 (1890).

11. See, e.g., Nelson v. X–Ray Systems, Inc., 46 A.D.2d 995, 361 N.Y.S.2d 468 (4th Dep't 1974)(lay opinion as to who was giving supervision invaded the province of the jury); Strauch v. Hirschman, 40 A.D.2d 711, 336 N.Y.S.2d 678 (2d Dep't 1972)(plaintiff's "experts" erroneously testified concerning dangerousness of a basketball drill, a topic within the understanding of the jury). But Proposed New York Evidence Code § 704 is not confined to expert witnesses, and those cases in which the courts continue to talk about the jury's province can usually be explained as cases where the topic is so common as not to require any interpretation by a witness— any kind of a witness.

12. See, e.g., Broun v. Equitable Life Assur. Soc., 69 N.Y.2d 675, 512 N.Y.S.2d 12, 504 N.E.2d 379 (1986)(even though the jury's job was to decide whether or not death was due to suicide, it was proper for the expert to testify that in his opinion suicide was the cause); People v. Keindl, 68 N.Y.2d 410, 509 N.Y.S.2d 790, 502 N.E.2d 577 (1986) (psychiatrist properly testified as to how children suffer psychologically from repeated sexual abuse by a relative); Torelli v. City of New York, 176 A.D.2d 119, 574 N.Y.S.2d 5 (1st Dep't 1991), appeal denied, 79 N.Y.2d 754, 581 N.Y.S.2d 282, 589 N.E.2d 1264 (1992)(toxicologist should have been allowed to testify as to level of awareness a person would have who had a blood-alcohol count of .18 as did the plaintiff's deceased); Sitaras v. Ricciardi & Sons, Inc.,

§ 704.1 OPINIONS & EXPERT TESTIMONY Ch. 7

A troublesome situation can arise, however, when the witness tailors his opinion to conform to a legal definition. Such opinions often do not provide assistance to the fact-finder.[13] Nevertheless, in *Dufel v. Green*[14] the Court of Appeals found no problem where plaintiff's experts testified that plaintiff suffered a "permanent consequential limitation" and "a significant limitation" of the use of a body member, function, organ or system,[15] the very words of the Insurance Law describing a basis for exemption from the no-fault rule.[16] The court said that an opinion on such an ultimate issue may be admissible when it concerns a subject requiring expertise even though the trial judge framed the question in his charge in exactly the same language. The court stated: "The test is one of need as applied to the unique circumstances of each case. If the jury requires the benefit of the expert's specialized knowledge, the expert's opinion should be allowed even when it bears on the ultimate question * * *." Thus, the question before the court distills to whether a "permanent consequential limitation" or a "significant limitation" of use of a body function, organ or system lie within the medical expert's specialized knowledge.[17] If there is no necessity for framing an expert's testimony so that the opinion is rendered in statutory language or otherwise to have the expert give a conclusory opinion "tailored to meet statutory standards,"[18] the practitioner is advised to steer clear of this practice.[19] Additional examples of the problem are also found in § 704.2, below.

Library References:

West's Key No. Digests, Criminal Law ⚖450; Evidence ⚖506.

154 A.D.2d 451, 545 N.Y.S.2d 937 (2d Dep't 1989)(accident reconstruction expert properly allowed to give his opinion as to how accident happened).

13. See § 701.1, at notes 9–10; § 702.1, at notes 9–10, supra.

14. 84 N.Y.2d 795, 622 N.Y.S.2d 900, 647 N.E.2d 105 (1995); accord, Robillard v. Robbins, 168 A.D.2d 803, 563 N.Y.S.2d 940 (3d Dep't 1990), aff'd, 78 N.Y.2d 1105, 578 N.Y.S.2d 126, 585 N.E.2d 375 (1991).

15. 84 N.Y.2d at 797, 622 N.Y.S.2d at 901, 647 N.E.2d at 107.

16. N.Y.Ins.Law § 5102(d). Other bases of serious injury include death, dismemberment, disfigurement, fractures, loss of fetus.

17. 84 N.Y.2d at 798, 622 N.Y.S.2d at 902, 647 N.E.2d at 107. Compare Lopez v. Senatore, 65 N.Y.2d 1017, 1019, 494 N.Y.S.2d 101, 102, 484 N.E.2d 130, 131 (1985), where the court stated that an expert should not express "conclusory assertions tailored to meet statutory standards." But in Dufel, unlike Lopez, there was other objective evidence of plaintiff's condition. 84 N.Y.2d at 798, 622 N.Y.S.2d at 902, 647 N.E.2d at 107. See also People v. Forcione,

156 A.D.2d 952, 952, 549 N.Y.S.2d 248, 248 (4th Dep't 1989), appeal denied, 75 N.Y.2d 919, 555 N.Y.S.2d 37, 554 N.E.2d 74 (1990)("while the physician was competent to testify concerning the nature, extent, treatment, prognosis and permanency of the victim's injuries, the ultimate determination whether those injuries satisfied the statutory definition [serious physical injury] was not beyond the ken of the typical juror. * * *").

18. Lopez v. Senatore, 65 N.Y.2d 1017, 1019, 494 N.Y.S.2d 101, 102, 484 N.E.2d 130, 131 (1985). The distinction between Dufel and Lopez noted in note 17 seems very thin.

19. See People v. Cronin, 60 N.Y.2d 430, 433 n.2, 470 N.Y.S.2d 110, 111, 458 N.E.2d 351, 352 (1983)(expert may not properly testify in legal terms); Roman v. Vargas, 182 A.D.2d 543, 582 N.Y.S.2d 1020 (1st Dep't 1992)(no expert is permitted to testify that a party was "negligent"); People v. McCart, 157 A.D.2d 194, 555 N.Y.S.2d 954 (4th Dep't), appeal denied, 76 N.Y.2d 861, 560 N.Y.S.2d 1000, 561 N.E.2d 900 (1990)(expert may not testify that defendant's conduct was a "link in the chain"—the language of the legal standard—of the causes of victim's death).

§ 704.2 Federal

The federal courts have long been committed to the practice of allowing experts and lay witnesses to give opinions on ultimate issues.[1] Rule 704(a) of the Federal Rules of Evidence provides for this unequivocally.[2] As with the New York construction, however, there is one sticky point: Testimony that expresses a conclusion with purely legal terminology should be excluded. In *United States v. Scop*,[3] we find perhaps the best example of the problem:

> Had Whitten merely testified that controlled buying and selling of the kind alleged here can create artificial price levels to lure outside investors, no sustainable objection could have been made. Instead, however, Whitten made no attempt to couch the opinion testimony at issue in even conclusory factual statement, but drew directly upon the language of the statute and accompanying regulations concerning "manipulation" and "fraud." * * * In essence, his opinions were legal conclusions that were highly prejudicial and went well beyond his province as an expert in securities trading.[4]

The *Scop* court cited portions of the Advisory Committee's Note,

---

§ 704.2

1. 3 Weinstein and Berger ¶ 704[01], at 704–6, notes that the reasons for abandoning the "jury province" rule were that (1) the distinction between ultimate and non-ultimate facts was impossible to make; (2) witnesses found it difficult if not impossible to give meaningful testimony without giving ultimate conclusions; (3) jurors are free to make their own determinations and do not have to accept witness's opinions; (4) opinions on issues of law and fact are often impossible to separate, e.g., "if the witness expresses an opinion about a party's sanity or negligence or capacity to make a will or his intention to defraud, is he talking about factual findings or is he drawing legal conclusions"?

As an example of the modern approach, see Karns v. Emerson Elec. Co., 817 F.2d 1452, 1459 (10th Cir.1987)(in products liability action, trial court properly allowed expert to testify that product was unreasonably dangerous even though testimony embraced ultimate issue of case; expert explained basis of opinion in sufficient detail for jury to evaluate reliability of opinion, and trial court instructed jury that it could disregard expert opinion if it found basis to be unsound).

2. **Rule 704. Opinion on Ultimate Issue**

(a) Except as provided in subdivision (b), testimony in the form of an opinion or inference otherwise admissible is not objectionable because it embraces an ultimate issue to be decided by the trier of fact.

(b) No expert witness testifying with respect to the mental state or condition of a defendant in a criminal case may state an opinion or inference as to whether the defendant did or did not have the mental state or condition constituting an element of the crime charged or of a defense thereto. Such ultimate issues are matters for the trier of fact alone.

3. 846 F.2d 135, 140, modified in part on other grounds, 856 F.2d 5 (2d Cir.1988).

4. The court also offers this example: "None of our prior cases, however, has allowed testimony similar to Whitten's repeated use of statutory and regulatory language indicating guilt. For example, telling the jury that a defendant acted as a 'steerer' or participated in a narcotics transaction differs from opining that the defendant 'possessed narcotics, to wit, heroin with intent to sell,' or 'aided and abetted the possession of heroin with intent to sell,' the functional equivalent of Whitten's testimony in a drug case." Compare In re Air Disaster at Lockerbie Scotland, 37 F.3d 804, 826–27 (2d Cir.1994), cert. denied sub nom., Pan American World Airways, Inc., v. Pagnucco, ___ U.S. ___, 115 S.Ct. 934, 130 L.Ed.2d 880 (1995)(expert's testimony that he thought party engaged in "fraud" and "deceit" was not improper because context indicated that he used the terms in nonlegal sense; however, expert should not have been allowed to testify that party violated FAA regulation).

§ 704.2   OPINIONS & EXPERT TESTIMONY   Ch. 7

which is also helpful.[5] Similarly, in *Hygh v. Jacobs*,[6] the expert wrongly discussed the party's use of force in statutory terms, i.e., "deadly physical force," "force which is readily capable of causing death or other serious physical injury"; and in *Marx & Co., Inc. v. Diners' Club, Inc.*,[7] the trial court should not have allowed an expert to give his opinion as to the legal obligations under a contract.[8]

As is true in the case of New York law,[9] there are federal cases which find error when the expert witness invades the jury's province—when it is not helpful under Rule 702—usually because the jury needs no help in the first place.[10]

Subdivision (b) of Rule 704 presents a specific exception to the general rule and restores the old rule with respect to a psychiatrist's testimony concerning whether a defendant had such a mental condition as would constitute an element of the crime charged, or a defense such as insanity. The Senate Judiciary Committee Report fully explains this 1984 amendment as a product of the American Psychiatric Association's concern that psychiatrists, experts in medicine and not in law, should be limited to testifying about "defendant's mental state and motivation and to explain in detail the reason for his medical-psychiatric conclusions."[11] The Second Circuit Court of Appeals had occasion to apply Rule 704(b) in *United States v. DiDomenico*,[12] where it upheld the trial court's exclusion of psychiatric testimony offered by the defendant to show that, due to psychological factors, she could not have "known" that certain property was stolen: "The plain language of the rule, however, means that the expert cannot expressly 'state the inference,' but must leave the

---

5. The Advisory Committee's Note to Fed.R.Evid. 704 states:

The abolition of the ultimate issue rule does not lower the bars so as to admit all opinions. Under Rules 701 and 702, opinions must be helpful to the trier of fact, and Rule 403 provides for exclusion of evidence which wastes time. These provisions afford ample assurances against the admission of opinions which would merely tell the jury what result to reach, somewhat in the manner of the oath-helpers of an earlier day. They also stand ready to exclude opinions phrased in terms of inadequately explored legal criteria. Thus the question, "Did T have capacity to make a will?" would be excluded, while the question, "Did T have sufficient mental capacity to know the nature and extent of his property and the natural objects of his bounty and to formulate a rational scheme of distribution?" would be allowed. McCormick § 12 at 50–51, n.22.

6. 961 F.2d 359, 364 (2d Cir.1992).

7. 550 F.2d 505 (2d Cir.), cert. denied, 434 U.S. 861, 98 S.Ct. 188, 54 L.Ed.2d 134 (1977).

8. But see Fiataruolo v. United States, 8 F.3d 930, 941–42 (2d Cir.1993) (taxpayers sought refund of tax penalties assessed against them as "responsible persons"—the legal standard—for construction contractor's unpaid withholding taxes; taxpayer's expert's testimony that plaintiff was not "responsible person" was upheld because expert gave lengthy explanation of context for opinion).

9. See § 704.1, at note 11, supra.

10. See United States v. Schatzle, 901 F.2d 252, 257 (2d Cir.1990)("The district court concluded that the jury was capable of assessing the reasonableness of Schatzle's conduct on its own and that Desmedt's 'expert' opinion on the issue might confuse the jury"); Andrews v. Metro North Commuter R. Co., 882 F.2d 705 (2d Cir.1989)(testimony of "forensic engineer" as to condition of station platform and distance walked by pedestrian was error since these were matters that the jury could handle).

11. The Judiciary Committee Report can be found with the Advisory Committee's Note to Rule 704.

12. 985 F.2d 1159 (2d Cir.1993).

inference, however obvious, for the jury to draw."[13]

Library References:

West's Key No. Digests, Criminal Law ⟜450; Evidence ⟜506.

705 Disclosure of Facts and Data Underlying Expert Opinion

§ 705.1 New York

Those experts who do not testify from personal knowledge, but who form an opinion based on facts that are in evidence, often do so on the basis of a hypothetical question, posed by counsel, containing those facts. The cumbersomeness of this technique, together with the opportunity it affords counsel to summarize the facts in a slanted manner, led to the enactment of CPLR 4515. The statute provides:

> Unless the court orders otherwise, questions calling for the opinion of an expert witness need not be hypothetical in form, and the witness may state his opinion and reasons without first specifying the data upon which it is based. Upon cross-examination, he may be required to specify the data and other criteria supporting the opinion.[1]

The hypothetical question is not outlawed by the statute and may still be used, subject to judicial control. Normally, counsel will want to buttress the expert's opinion by laying out a solid basis for it. If no such background is forthcoming during the expert's direct testimony, opposing counsel could well be risking providing support for the opinion by delving into its basis on cross-examination. What, then, is the purpose for this curious provision? May the expert simply give an opinion without ever introducing a basis for it? The Court of Appeals in *Tarlowe v. Metropolitan Ski Slopes*[2] did not quite answer this question. The witness was asked a hypothetical question as to what force would be transmitted to plaintiff's leg had he failed in a certain maneuver while skiing—that being in evidence. The expert's answer was unaccompanied by any explanation as to how he reached it. *Tarlowe* provided the first major explanation of CPLR 4515 and it was held that the expert need not give a basis for his opinion on direct examination; that this may be left for cross-examination; and that the extent to which he elaborates on his opinion only affects its weight. *Tarlowe* contained no statement that at some point the basis for the opinion would have to be

---

13. Id. at 1165.

§ 705.1

1. The Proposed New York Evidence Code § 705 is virtually identical, but adds a third sentence: "Provided, however, an expert, pursuant to section 703 of this article, may not render an opinion on an essential element of a crime, defense or cause of action based upon information not introduced at trial unless the basis for that opinion is first elicited from the expert."

When, under § 703 of the Proposed Code, the witness bases an opinion partly on data "of a reliable type upon which experts in the particular field reasonably rely," the basis would first have to be disclosed by the expert. This is a proposed codification of the apparent rule under New York caselaw. See text at notes 5–7 infra.

2. 28 N.Y.2d 410, 322 N.Y.S.2d 665, 271 N.E.2d 515 (1971).

§ 705.1   OPINIONS & EXPERT TESTIMONY   Ch. 7

entered into the record. This finally came in *Caton v. Doug Urban Construction Co.*:[3]

> [A]lthough CPLR 4515 permits an expert witness to state an opinion without specifying the data upon which it is based, it does not avoid the necessity for presentation of such data. Its purpose is, rather, to make the expert's presentation more readily understandable by permitting the opinion to be stated on direct, and leaving the development of the data on which it is based for cross-examination. * * * It does not, however, change the basic principle that an expert's opinion not based on facts is worthless.

It would appear from these two cases that the underlying facts giving rise to the need for an opinion in the first place (e.g., how the skier fell) must at some point be introduced in evidence, but the rationale employed by the witness in reaching his opinion relating to those underlying facts need not be explained, a factor which will affect weight, but not admissibility.[4]

A third major case, *People v. Jones*,[5] affects the construction of CPLR 4515 even though the statute is not mentioned in the majority opinion. Defendant was charged with selling Darvocet as a controlled substance, but the prosecution's expert, testifying as to the chemical makeup of Darvocet, never made it clear that the compound was on the list of controlled substances. Such testimony could be said to be admissible under CPLR 4515, although this was not discussed in the majority opinion. The problem seems to be that this is a case of sufficiency of the evidence needed to prove the crime, and not a question of admissibility.[6] In dicta, the court declared that when an expert relies on facts within personal knowledge that are not already in the trial record, he "is required to testify to those facts prior to rendering the opinion."[7]

---

3. 65 N.Y.2d 909, 911, 493 N.Y.S.2d 453, 454, 483 N.E.2d 128, 129 (1985).

4. The Advisory Committee on Practice and Procedure, which drafted the statute, stated: "[T]he rule is designed to provide the trial judge with the discretion necessary to obtain the maximum benefits from the use of witnesses by limiting the abuse of hypothetical questions. It will permit the expert to state what he knows in a natural way; at the same time, it gives the cross-examiner full opportunity to discredit him." N.Y.Adv.Comm.on Prac. and Proc., Second Prelim.Rep., Legis.Doc.No.13, p.263 (1958). Note that the statute separates "reasons" from "facts or data" and implies that reasons are expected.

5. 73 N.Y.2d 427, 541 N.Y.S.2d 340, 539 N.E.2d 96 (1989).

6. This point is made in the concurring opinion where there is concern that the majority opinion could be construed as going to admissibility because of the discussion of what can be relied upon by an expert in formulating the opinion. 73 N.Y.2d at 432–33, 541 N.Y.S.2d at 342–43, 539 N.E.2d at 99. Indeed, this caused one writer to speculate that the liberal provisions of CPLR 4515 were being cut back. See Capra, "Permissible Bases of Expert Testimony," N.Y.L.J., July 14, 1989, p.3, col.1. It is doubtful that this is the case. The expert's testimony was admissible, but the built-in ambiguity simply caused a failure of proof. Had the expert pinned down the substance she was talking about, and had it been the controlled substance, the prosecution would have had a prima facie case.

7. 73 N.Y.2d at 430, 541 N.Y.S.2d at 342, 539 N.E.2d at 98.

Ch. 7   DISCLOSURE OF FACTS & DATA   § 705.1

When the basis of the expert's opinion does come in it must, of course, be sound. The opinion must be founded on evidence in the record with the exception of the limited "professional reliance" rule discussed in § 703.1 *supra*, and certainly cannot be based entirely on hearsay.[8] So, too, a speculative opinion is without worth.[9]

If the plaintiff cannot describe the happening of the accident because of claimed amnesia, and there is no other proof of how the accident happened, the plaintiff needs to support his amnesia claim with an expert medical witness. Otherwise, it is improper for an engineer to testify as to the improper design of the machine which injured plaintiff based on his own surmise of how the accident might have happened.[10]

Finally, the way in which the opinion is expressed must show a degree of confidence in its correctness. In *Matott v. Ward*,[11] a physician, appearing as an expert witness, testified that he possessed a "degree" of medical certainty as to causal relationship, but could not state this with absolute certainty. Defendant argued that an opinion must be rendered with at least a "reasonable degree of medical certainty." The Court of Appeals disagreed, stating that the test is whether the expert "exhibited a degree of confidence in his conclusions sufficient to satisfy accepted

---

8. See Easley v. City of New York, 189 A.D.2d 599, 592 N.Y.S.2d 690 (1st Dep't 1993)(nontreating physician should not testify as to how the accident happened on the strength of what the patient told him); Borden v. Brady, 92 A.D.2d 983, 461 N.Y.S.2d 497 (3d Dep't 1983)(opinion based solely upon another expert's report not in evidence improper). Cf. Karashik v. Brenner, 111 A.D.2d 150, 489 N.Y.S.2d 9 (2d Dep't 1985) (examining physician can base his opinion on his own observations, and absence of medical history in the record is immaterial); Buck Construction Corp. v. 200 Genesee Street Corp., 109 A.D.2d 1056, 487 N.Y.S.2d 198 (4th Dep't 1985)(expert's opinions as to value of services bereft of "data upon which his opinions are based" was proper under CPLR 4515; in addition, the expert was prevented by defendant's objections from explaining his opinions).

9. See Carringi v. Int'l. Paper Co., 184 A.D.2d 137, 591 N.Y.S.2d 600 (3d Dep't 1992)(motion for summary judgment not aided by defendant's expert's affidavit reciting that he had reviewed the records and concluded that plaintiff's affliction was not caused by the accident); Espinosa v. A & S Welding & Boiler Repair, Inc., 120 A.D.2d 435, 502 N.Y.S.2d 451 (1st Dep't 1986), appeal denied, 69 N.Y.2d 604, 512 N.Y.S.2d 1027, 504 N.E.2d 698 (1987)(where expert had not examined the faulty mechanism, where no other witness testified as to it, and where no manufacturer's brochures were introduced, it was improper for expert to voice a conclusion based on "blind speculation").

10. Sawyer v. Dreis & Krump Manufacturing, 67 N.Y.2d 328, 502 N.Y.S.2d 696, 493 N.E.2d 920 (1986). Had the amnesia claim been supported, plaintiff would have been aided by a relaxation in his burden of proof. It was stated:

The rule is intended to avoid unfairness to a plaintiff who has suffered amnesia as a result of the accident and who, because he cannot testify to the event, might otherwise be prejudiced by an instruction to the jury that it may draw the strongest inferences against a party who fails to testify or who withholds evidence. (Citation omitted.) It is also based, at least in part, on the belief that since the plaintiff is not able to testify, it is unfair to permit defendant to stand mute and defeat the claim. (Citation omitted.) The rule does not entitle the jury to presume [that the plaintiff] exercised due care at the time of the accident nor does it shift the burden of proof; plaintiff must still establish a prima facie case. It merely describes a method or approach to weighing evidence and permits the jury greater latitude in drawing inferences favorable to plaintiff (citation omitted). * * * In New York, contrasted with some other states, the rule may come into play even if there are eyewitnesses.

Id. at 333–34, 502 N.Y.S.2d at 699, 493 N.E.2d at 923.

11. 48 N.Y.2d 455, 423 N.Y.S.2d 645, 399 N.E.2d 532 (1979).

§ 705.1 OPINIONS & EXPERT TESTIMONY Ch. 7

standards of reliability."[12] While that standard may be satisfied by "a reasonable degree of medical certainty," said the court, it does not have to be stated that way. What is important is that the expert's confidence in his conclusions can be ascertained "by any formulation from which it can be said that the witness's 'whole opinion' reflects an acceptable level of certainty. * * *"[13]

Library References:

West's Key No. Digests, Criminal Law ⬄486; Evidence ⬄555.

§ 705.2 Federal

Rule 705 of the Federal Rules of Evidence provides:

> The expert may testify in terms of opinion or inference and give reasons therefor without prior disclosure of the underlying facts or data unless the court requires otherwise. The expert may in any event be required to disclose the underlying facts or data on cross-examination.

Other than omission of any reference to abolition of the hypothetical question as a prerequisite to the expert's opinion, this provision is essentially the same as CPLR 4515.[1] The reasons prompting its enactment are similar.[2]

As to the basis upon which the opinion rests, the federal courts may be a bit more liberal than New York courts. In *Delaware v. Fensterer*,[3] the witness, testifying as to whether hair was forcibly removed, could not remember which one of three tests was employed and made certain concessions reflecting on his certitude. This only goes to weight, said the Supreme Court and certainly does not deprive defendant, who has the full force of cross-examination, of his confrontation right. And the

---

12. Id. at 459, 423 N.Y.S.2d at 647, 399 N.E.2d at 534.

13. Id. at 460, 423 N.Y.S.2d at 647, 399 N.E.2d at 534. See also People v. Bethune, 105 A.D.2d 262, 484 N.Y.S.2d 577 (2d Dep't 1984)(although expert was unable to testify with reasonable certainty as to whether bite mark was made by a certain person, he could identify the bite marks as having been made by six upper and three lower human teeth, and to that extent his opinion was admissible).

§ 705.2

1. See § 705.1 supra.

2. The Advisory Committee's Note to Fed.R.Evid. 705 mentions the abuse of the hypothetical question and the fact that the idea for eliminating the necessity for a preliminary recitation of data goes back at least to 1937. 3 Weinstein and Berger ¶ 705[01] traces the idea back to Wigmore. The permissive language of Rule 705 still allows a hypothetical question to be used to elicit the expert's opinion if counsel so chooses.

The section was given literal application in Symbol Technologies, Inc. v. Opticon, Inc., 935 F.2d 1569 (Fed.Cir.1991), where a co-inventor who was claiming patent infringements testified on the ultimate issue of infringement but did not detail how he arrived at that conclusion. The court said that the responsibility for challenging the "factual underpinnings" of this testimony fell to the alleged infringer on cross-examination. See also International Adhesive Coating Co., Inc. v. Bolton Emerson Int'l, Inc., 851 F.2d 540, 544 (1st Cir.1988)(basis for expert opinion need not be disclosed as condition of admissibility; burden is on opposing counsel to demonstrate weaknesses in basis for expert opinion by cross-examining expert). It is written elsewhere that through the discovery process opposing counsel should have the information necessary for conducting such a cross-examination so that the statutory provision is not unfair in this regard. 3 Weinstein and Berger ¶ 705[01], at 705-10, 11.

3. 474 U.S. 15, 106 S.Ct. 292, 88 L.Ed.2d 15 (1985).

Second Circuit in *In re Joint Eastern & Southern District Asbestos Litigation*[4] held that plaintiff's doctor's statements of causal relationship between her husband's colon cancer and asbestos exposure were sufficient to defeat defendant's summary judgment motion. The clinical evidence relied on by the witnesses was the deceased's own records plus plaintiff's statement that his diet was not high in fat content. Abstract epidemiological studies were relied on in part by the witnesses, but the court stated: "[P]laintiff did not need to provide epidemiological evidence of a certain magnitude in order to defeat a summary judgment motion because she did not rely on epidemiological studies alone."[5] On the other hand, at trial a stock trader testified as to the value of a corporation based solely on the price at which its shares were sold, a wholly inadequate basis. "Because substantial adjustments have to be made, the expert witness must explain the factors upon which he based his judgment."[6]

Library References:

West's Key No. Digests, Criminal Law ⚖486; Evidence ⚖555.

706 Court-appointed Experts

§ 706.1 New York

New York courts have inherent power to appoint experts,[1] parties can stipulate to such appointments,[2] and appointments can be made pursuant to statute.[3] On the civil side most appointments occur in the

---

4. 964 F.2d 92 (2d Cir.1992).

5. Id. at 97.

6. DiRose v. PK Management Corp., 691 F.2d 628, 631–32 (2d Cir.1982), cert. denied, 461 U.S. 915, 103 S.Ct. 1896, 77 L.Ed.2d 285 (1983). See also Shatkin v. McDonnell Douglas Corp., 565 F.Supp. 93 (1983)(court has a duty to inquire into trustworthiness of data underlying expert testimony); cf. Fogel v. Chestnutt, 668 F.2d 100 (2d Cir.1981), cert. denied, 459 U.S. 828, 103 S.Ct. 65, 74 L.Ed.2d 66, reh. den., 459 U.S. 1059, 103 S.Ct. 478, 74 L.Ed.2d 625 (1982)(investment fund expert could base his opinion on a sample of the fund's transactions and need not examine all of the hundreds of transactions).

§ 706.1

1. Kesseler v. Kesseler, 10 N.Y.2d 445, 455, 225 N.Y.S.2d 1, 8, 180 N.E.2d 402, 407 (1962); Zirinsky v. Zirinsky, 138 A.D.2d 43, 529 N.Y.S.2d 298 (1st Dep't 1988).

2. Kesseler v. Kesseler, 10 N.Y.2d 445, 455, 225 N.Y.S.2d 1, 8, 180 N.E.2d 402, 407 (1962)

3. New York Judiciary Law § 35 provides in subdivision (4) for the appointment of psychiatrists, psychologists and physicians in the instances described in subdivision (1)(a) as follows:

1. a. When a court orders a hearing in a proceeding upon a writ of habeas corpus to inquire into the cause of detention of a person in custody in a state institution, or when it orders a hearing in a civil proceeding to commit or transfer a person to or retain him in a state institution when such person is alleged to be mentally ill, mentally defective or a narcotic addict, or when it orders a hearing for the commitment of the guardianship and custody of a child to an authorized agency by reason of the mental illness or mental retardation of a parent, or when it orders a hearing to determine whether consent to the adoption of a child shall be required of a parent who is alleged to be mentally ill or mentally retarded, or when it orders a hearing to determine the best interests of a child when the parent of the child revokes a consent to the adoption of such child and such revocation is opposed or in any adoption or custody proceeding if it determines that assignment of counsel in such cases is mandated by the constitution of this state or of the United States, the court may assign counsel to represent such person if it is satisfied that he is financially unable to obtain counsel. Upon an appeal taken from an order entered in any such pro-

§ 706.1 OPINIONS & EXPERT TESTIMONY Ch. 7

area of domestic relations[4] but can also occur in tort litigation such as a products liability case.[5] The court's inherent power naturally includes the use of discretion to refuse to make an appointment.[6] Proposed New York Evidence Code § 706[7] would simply provide the procedures for such appointment.

ceeding, the appellate court may assign counsel to represent such person upon the appeal if it is satisfied that he is financially unable to obtain counsel.

The Uniform Civil Rules for the Supreme Court and the County Court, in § 202.18 (22 N.Y.C.R.R. § 202.18), also provide authority in Domestic Relations situations, to wit:

202.18 Testimony of court-appointed expert witness in matrimonial action or proceeding. In any action or proceeding tried without a jury to which section 237 of the Domestic Relations Law applies, the court may appoint a psychiatrist, psychologist, social worker or other appropriate expert to give testimony with respect to custody or visitation, and may appoint an accountant, appraiser, actuary or other appropriate expert to give testimony with respect to equitable distribution or a distributive award. The cost of such expert witness shall be paid by a party or parties as the court shall direct.

4. See Match v. Match, 146 Misc.2d 986, 553 N.Y.S.2d 626 (Sup.Ct.N.Y.Co.1990), rev'd on other grounds, 168 A.D.2d 226, 562 N.Y.S.2d 115 (1st Dep't 1990), where it was stated:

Designation of an expert without objection was a relatively widely employed technique in IAS matrimonial parts, but it did not receive the imprimatur of appellate approval until Justice Jacqueline Silbermann's thorough decision in Zirinsky v. Zirinsky (138 Misc.2d 775 [Sup Ct, NY County]) was appealed and affirmed (138 A.D.2d 43 [1st Dep't 1988]). Designation of experts in all fields in accordance with *Zirinsky* is now standard practice in matrimonial cases.

5. In Kaplowitz v. Borden, Inc., 189 A.D.2d 90, 594 N.Y.S.2d 744 (1st Dep't 1993), the claim was that the infant plaintiff was injured in utero by her mother's exposure to defendant's spray paint. Medical records were submitted which were dealt with as follows:

[W]e remand the matter to the trial court for the appointment of a medical expert (see Zirinsky v. Zirinsky, 138 A.D.2d 43, 529 N.Y.S.2d 298) to review, in camera, all the medical records pertaining to the plaintiff mother's subsequent pregnancies and to render an opinion based upon the expert's medical training and expertise as to whether they contain any information bearing on whether the infant plaintiff's birth defects are the result of a genetic disorder.

6. In Haymes v. Haymes, 157 A.D.2d 506, 549 N.Y.S.2d 698 (1st Dep't 1990), the question was whether an appraiser should be appointed. The court said:

While clearly the Supreme Court has the power to appoint an independent appraiser * * *, nevertheless, the denial of such relief under the circumstances of this case did not constitute an abuse of discretion. * * * The action is at an early stage, with discovery still in progress. Further, the plaintiff has already obtained an expert and, at least at this point, has not established that the husband's affairs are so complex that it is necessary for the court to appoint an appraiser.

7. **§ 706. Court-appointed experts [PROPOSED]**

(a) Appointment. When authorized by law, the court on its own motion or on the motion of any party may appoint one or more expert witnesses. The court may appoint any expert witness agreed upon by the parties or may appoint an expert witness of its own selection. Reasonable notice shall be given to the parties of the names and addresses of the experts proposed for appointment. Before appointing its own expert, the court must afford the parties reasonable notice and an opportunity to be heard outside of the presence of the jury. An expert witness shall not be appointed by the court unless the expert consents to act. The duties of a witness so appointed shall be communicated to such witness by the court in writing, a copy of which shall be furnished to each party, or at a conference in which the parties shall have the opportunity to participate. The findings, if any, of a witness so appointed shall be communicated by such witness to the parties; the deposition of such witness may be taken by any party; and such witness may be called to testify by the court or any party. A witness so appointed shall be subject to cross-examination by each party, including a party calling that person as a witness.

Ch. 7   COURT–APPOINTED EXPERTS   § 706.2

Library References:

West's Key No. Digests, Criminal Law ⚖=641.12(3); Trial ⚖=18.

§ 706.2   Federal

Rule 706 of the Federal Rules of Evidence provides the authority for a court to appoint experts with no apparent limitation as to the kind of litigation in which the procedure would be suitable.[1] Unlike its proposed New York counterpart, which only offers a procedure for effectuating the power found elsewhere,[2] the federal rule empowers district judges to make appointments and provides the necessary procedure, rules for compensation, and restrictions. This authorization seems simply to codify[3] the well-established inherent power of the federal courts to appoint expert witnesses.[4]

The Advisory Committee's Note illuminates the fact that while the marketing of hired experts can result in "venality," the use of court-appointed experts is relatively infrequent.[5] Experts have been appointed

(b) **Disclosure of appointment.** With the consent of all parties, the court may authorize disclosure to the jury of the fact that the court appointed the expert witness.

(c) **Parties' experts of own selection.** Nothing in this section limits the parties in calling expert witnesses of their own selection.

§ 706.2

1. **Rule 706. Court Appointed Experts**

(a) **Appointment.** The court may on its own motion or on the motion of any party enter an order to show cause why expert witnesses should not be appointed, and may request the parties to submit nominations. The court may appoint any expert witnesses agreed upon by the parties, and may appoint expert witnesses of its own selection. An expert witness shall not be appointed by the court unless the witness consents to act. A witness so appointed shall be informed of the witness' duties by the court in writing, a copy of which shall be filed with the clerk, or at a conference in which the parties shall have opportunity to participate. A witness so appointed shall advise the parties of the witness' findings, if any; the witness' deposition may be taken by any party; and the witness may be called to testify by the court or any party. The witness shall be subject to cross-examination by each party, including a party calling the witness.

(b) **Compensation.** Expert witnesses so appointed are entitled to reasonable compensation in whatever sum the court may allow. The compensation thus fixed is payable from funds which may be provided by law in criminal cases and civil actions and proceedings involving just compensation under the fifth amendment. In other civil actions and proceedings the compensation shall be paid by the parties in such proportion and at such time as the court directs, and thereafter charged in like manner as other costs.

(c) **Disclosure of appointment.** In the exercise of its discretion, the court may authorize disclosure to the jury of the fact that the court appointed the expert witness.

(d) **Parties' experts of own selection.** Nothing in this rule limits the parties in calling expert witnesses of their own selection.

2. See § 706.1 supra.

3. A similar authorization was enacted in 1946 in Rule 28 of the Federal Rules of Criminal Procedure but was never so enacted for civil cases until the advent of Rule 706. See Advisory Committee's Note to Fed.R.Evid.706.

4. See, e.g., Scott v. Spanjer Bros., Inc., 298 F.2d 928, 930 (2d Cir.1962)(personal injury action where physician was appointed to examine infant plaintiff; the court stated: "Appellate courts no longer question the inherent power of a trial court to appoint an expert under proper circumstances, to aid it in the just disposition of a case").

5. The Note states in part:

The practice of shopping for experts, the venality of some experts, and the reluctance of many reputable experts to in-

§ 706.2   OPINIONS & EXPERT TESTIMONY   Ch. 7

to help the judge "in dismantling the intricacies of computer science,"[6] in helping on issues of patent construction,[7] in estimating the volume of future asbestos claims,[8] and in the weighing of complex factors relating to school desegregation.[9] This diverse sampling of the cases shows that court appointment of experts at the federal level is much more diverse, if not more frequent, than at the state level.

Library References:

West's Key No. Digests, Criminal Law ⛌641.12(3); Federal Civil Procedure ⛌1951.

---

volve themselves in litigation, have been matters of deep concern. Though the contention is made that court appointed experts acquire an aura of infallibility to which they are not entitled, Levy, Impartial Medical Testimony—Revisited, 34 Temple L.Q. 416 (1961), the trend is increasingly to provide for their use. While experience indicates that actual appointment is a relatively infrequent occurrence, the assumption may be made that the availability of the procedure in itself decreases the need for resorting to it. The ever-present possibility that the judge *may* appoint an expert in a given case must inevitably exert a sobering effect on the expert witness of a party and upon the person utilizing his services.

(Emphasis in original).

6. Computer Associates Intern., Inc. v. Altai, Inc., 982 F.2d 693 (2d Cir.1992).

7. Unique Concepts, Inc. v. Brown, 659 F.Supp. 1008 (S.D.N.Y.1987) (illustrated also in this case is the practice common in patent cases of deposing the appointed witness as expressly provided for in Rule 706); Leesona Corp. v. Varta Batteries, Inc., 522 F.Supp. 1304 (S.D.N.Y.1981).

8. In Re Joint Eastern & Southern Districts Asbestos Litigation, 830 F.Supp. 686 (E.D.N.Y. and S.D.N.Y.1993).

9. Hart v. Community School Board of Brooklyn, 383 F.Supp. 699 (E.D.N.Y.1974), aff'd, 512 F.2d 37 (2d Cir.1975).

Chapter 8

HEARSAY

Table of Sections

801 HEARSAY, NEW YORK AND FEDERAL—GENERALLY

801.1 Introduction
    a. The Nature of Hearsay.
    b. Assertions.
    c. Operative Words (Verbal Acts).
    d. State of Mind.
    e. Indirect Hearsay.

801(1) STATEMENTS NOT HEARSAY

801(1).1 Generally.
801(1).2 Prior Statements—New York.
    a. Inconsistent Statements.
    b. Prior Consistent Statements.
801(1).3 Prior Statements—Federal.
    a. Inconsistent Statements.
    b. Consistent Statements.

801(2) IDENTIFICATION

801(2).1 New York.
801(2).2 Federal.

802 ADMISSIONS

802.1 New York & Federal—Introduction.
802.2 A Party's Statement—New York.
    a. Admission by a Party's Conduct.
    b. Admissions by Silence.
    c. Privity.
    d. Representative Capacity.
    e. Adoptive Admissions.
    f. Statements by the Party's Agent or Servant.
    g. Coconspirator's Statements.
802.3 A Party's Statement—Federal.
    a. Pleadings.
    b. Admissions by a Party, by Statements, Acts, Adoption or in a Representative Capacity.
    c. Statements Made by an Agent or Servant, and Statements Otherwise Authorized.
    d. Coconspirator's Statements.

803 HEARSAY EXCEPTIONS WHERE AVAILABILITY OF THE DECLARANT IS IMMATERIAL

803.1 New York and Federal, In General.

HEARSAY Ch. 8

803(1) SPONTANEOUS STATEMENTS, STATEMENTS EVIDENCING A STATE OF MIND OR PHYSICAL CONDITION, AND STATEMENTS MADE FOR PURPOSES OF MEDICAL DIAGNOSIS OR TREATMENT

803(1).1 New York.
    a. Present Sense Impression.
    b. Excited Utterance.
    c. State of Mind or Physical Condition.
    d. Statements Made for Purposes of Medical Diagnosis or Treatment.

803(1).2 Federal.
    a. Present Sense Impression.
    b. Excited Utterance.
    c. State of Mind or Physical Condition.
    d. Statements Made for Purposes of Medical Diagnosis or Treatment.

803(2) RECORDED RECOLLECTION

803(2).1 New York.
803(2).2 Federal.

803(3) REGULARLY KEPT RECORDS

803(3).1 New York.
    a. General Principles, Accident Reports.
    b. Agency Documents Offered by the Prosecution in Criminal Cases.
    c. Records of Hospitals, Libraries, and Other Government Bureaus.
    d. The Proposed New York Evidence Code.

803(3).2 Federal.

803(4) ABSENCE OF RECORD

803(4).1 New York.
    a. Business Records.
    b. Public Records.

803(4).2 Federal.

803(5) PUBLIC RECORDS

803(5).1 New York.
    a. Common Law Exception and Business Entry Exception.
    b. CPLR 4520.
    c. Investigatory Reports Made by Government Agencies.
    d. Ancient Maps and Real Property Records.
    e. Records of Sister State Real Property Conveyances.
    f. Marriage Certificates.
    g. Presumption of Death or of Being Missing.
    h. Birth and Death Certificates.
    i. Weather Records.
    j. Agriculture Inspection Certificates.
    k. Certificate of Population.
    l. Surveyor's Standard.
    m. Justice of the Peace Proceedings.
    n. Absence of Public Record.
    o. Criminal Judgments of Conviction.
    p. Records of Religious Organizations.

803(5).2 Federal.
    a. Public Records Generally.
    b. Vital Statistics.
    c. Documents Affecting Interests In Real Property.
    d. Judgment of Previous Conviction; Judgment as Proof of Family History and Boundaries.
    e. Absence of Public Record.
    f. Records of Religious Organizations.

Ch. 8   **HEARSAY**

803(6) LEARNED TREATISES, MARKET REPORTS AND COMMERCIAL PUBLICATIONS

803(6).1   New York.
803(6).2   Federal.

803(7) ANCIENT DOCUMENTS, AND REPUTATION

803(7).1   New York.
         a. Family Records.
         b. Ancient Documents.
         c. Reputation.
803(7).2   Federal.
         a. Family Records.
         b. Ancient Documents.
         c. Reputation.

804 HEARSAY STATEMENTS ADMISSIBLE IF DECLARANT UNAVAILABLE

804.1   Unavailability—New York and Federal.

804(1) FORMER TESTIMONY

804(1).1   New York.
         a. Civil Cases.
         b. Criminal Cases.
804(1).2   Federal.

804(2) DYING DECLARATIONS

804(2).1   New York.
804(2).2   Federal.

804(3) DECLARATIONS AGAINST INTEREST

804(3).1   New York.
         a. Civil Cases.
         b. Criminal Cases.
804(3).2   Federal.

804(4) PEDIGREE

804(4).1   New York.
804(4).2   Federal.

804(5) RESIDUAL HEARSAY EXCEPTION

804(5).1   New York.
804(5).2   Federal.

805 HEARING WITHIN HEARSAY

805.1   New York.
805.2   Federal.

806 ATTACKING AND SUPPORTING DECLARANT'S CREDIBILITY

806.1   New York and Federal.

807 ADMISSIBILITY OF HEARSAY WHERE PARTY CAUSES DECLARANT'S UNAVAILABILITY

807.1   New York and Federal.

WESTLAW Electronic Research

See WESTLAW Electronic Research Guide preceding the Summary of Contents.

801 Hearsay, New York and Federal—Generally

§ 801.1 Introduction

a. The Nature of Hearsay

The definition of hearsay is set forth in Rule 801 of the Federal Rules of Evidence:

Rule 801. Definitions

(a) Statement. A "statement" is (1) an oral or written assertion or (2) nonverbal conduct of a person, if it is intended by the person as an assertion.

(b) Declarant. A "declarant" is a person who makes a statement.

(c) Hearsay. "Hearsay" is a statement, other than one made by the declarant while testifying at the trial or hearing, offered in evidence to prove the truth of the matter asserted.

* * *

The New York definition, stated in a less analytical fashion, is as follows: "Out-of-court statements which are offered for the truth of their content constitute hearsay, and may not be admitted unless they come within an exception to the hearsay rule."[1]

The rule prohibiting hearsay evidence was developed to insure that the declarant had the opportunity to *perceive* the event, had the *memory* necessary to recall the event, and had the ability to *accurately narrate* the event.[2] Where the account of the event originates from firsthand knowledge of the witness at trial, these essential factors can be tested by cross-examination. Where, however, the witness is testifying as to a fact or event which she only heard about, and the testimony is being offered to prove the truth of the fact or that the event happened, then the essential factors of perception, memory and accurate narration cannot be tested because the declarant—the source—is not available for cross-examination.

The simplicity of the definition of hearsay belies complex interpretations. Out-of-court statements can come into evidence in two ways. First, they can be construed as not being hearsay because they are not being offered to prove the truth of the matters asserted in the statements. Second, even though coming in for their truth, such statements have certain characteristics tending to insure trustworthiness and are considered exceptions to the rule. The exceptions are taken up in subsequent sections in this chapter. The basic distinctions between hearsay and nonhearsay will be taken up in this section.

---

§ 801.1
1. People v. Slaughter, 189 A.D.2d 157, 159, 596 N.Y.S.2d 22, 24 (1st Dep't 1993).

2. McCormick § 245, at 93.

Wigmore draws the distinction between hearsay and nonhearsay when he writes that when a statement is offered "as evidence of the truth asserted in it, the credit of the assertor becomes the basis of our inference. * * * If, therefore, an extrajudicial utterance is offered, not as an assertion to evidence the matter asserted, but *without reference to the truth of the matter asserted*, the hearsay rule does not apply."[3]

Since some of the best examples of hearsay and nonhearsay come from jurisdictions beyond New York and the Second Circuit we should be free to roam. Consider a slip-and-fall case based on a broken bottle of ketchup in the supermarket aisle. A witness could testify, on the issue of contributory negligence, that she heard the store manager yell, "Lady, please don't step in that ketchup."[4] This is not hearsay because the witness is merely testifying that she heard a warning to the plaintiff—the words used are not coming into evidence to prove that there was ketchup in the aisle. If the warning was relevant, as it would be on the issue of due care, then the person who heard it can testify to hearing it since we are relying on the witness' perceptions and the witness can be cross-examined fully on what she heard. If we change the facts, however, and have the witness testify that although she did not hear a warning, the manager told her right after plaintiff slipped in the ketchup, "I told her to look out for the ketchup," we have a different situation. If the evidence is offered to prove that a warning was given, the declarant's statement is being relayed for the truth of its content. Here, we must rely on the declarant's (manager's) veracity concerning whether or not a warning was issued and the declarant is not on the stand to be cross-examined.

Sometimes nonhearsay is characterized as being admissible simply "for the fact it was said," without regard to the truth of its content. The key question is, for what purpose is the statement being introduced? For example, plaintiff, testifying as to his mental suffering resulting from drinking a bottle of soda containing broken glass, said that his physician told him of the extensive stomach surgery that might have to take place. This was ruled admissible as nonhearsay because it was offered to show the effect on plaintiff's state of mind.[5] The truth or non-truth of the physician's statement was not important. The point was that it was said, and plaintiff claimed it had an effect on his state of mind. In another case, the physician's advice to plaintiff that she might develop cancer was admissible, not to prove that she would get cancer, but to show why she developed cancerphobia.[6] On the other hand, where a plaintiff testified to what her physician told her to prove the malady that the physician discussed, the physician's statement was coming in for its truth and was inadmissible.[7]

3. 6 Wigmore § 1766, at 250 (emphasis in original).

4. Safeway Stores, Inc. v. Combs, 273 F.2d 295 (5th Cir.1960).

5. Brown v. Coca–Cola Bottling, Inc., 54 Wash.2d 665, 344 P.2d 207 (1959).

6. Ferrara v. Galluchio, 5 N.Y.2d 16, 176 N.Y.S.2d 996, 152 N.E.2d 249, reh. denied, 5 N.Y.2d 793, 180 N.Y.S.2d 1025, 154 N.E.2d 581 (1958).

7. Dolan v. United Casualty Co., 259 App.Div. 784, 18 N.Y.S.2d 387 (4th Dep't 1940). See also Rosenberg v. Equitable

As a final illustration, we have the New York Court of Appeals' decision in *People v. Huertas*.[8] There it was held that a rape victim's identification of defendant 12 days after the rape, made to the police right after she had seen him on the street, could be testified to because it was not introduced for its truth. Rather, it was admissible as corroboration of the victim's *ability* to describe the defendant to the police immediately following the crime.[9]

b. Assertions

Rule 801(a) of the Federal Rules of Evidence defines a statement as an oral or written assertion, or nonverbal conduct if intended as an assertion, and subdivision (c) brands the statement hearsay if offered to prove the truth of the matter asserted. Again, the problem is best dealt with if we concentrate on why the statement is sought to be introduced. What is sought to be proved? This discussion must start with the venerable case of *Wright v. Doe d. Tatham*,[10] where the testator's mental capacity to make a will was drawn in question. To prove him a man of sufficient capacity and intelligence, several letters which had been written to him were introduced to show their content. The messages discussed various matters, including business affairs, and it was argued that such letters would not have been written to a person of diminished mental capacity. The court, however, held that this was hearsay, and inadmissible as such because the letters should be treated as though they had contained direct and positive statements as to the recipient's competency. In recent times this has become a controversial holding, and would not comport with Rule 801's requirement that the statement be intended as an assertion—an assertion of the point sought to be proved. If the letter writers had formulated any opinion at all concerning the

---

Life Assur. Soc., 148 A.D.2d 337, 538 N.Y.S.2d 551 (1st Dep't 1989)(where decedent had been given a stress test, his later statements concerning the pain and fatigue caused by the test would only be relevant if introduced to prove these conditions and thus were inadmissible).

8. 75 N.Y.2d 487, 554 N.Y.S.2d 444, 553 N.E.2d 992 (1990).

9. It was noted that the victim's identification was the chief issue in controversy, and that the later identification was "evidence that assists the jury in evaluating the witness's opportunity to observe at the time of the crime, and the reliability of her memory at the time of the corporeal identification—both important aspects of the critical issue. Thus, the description testimony was properly admitted for this nonhearsay purpose and, that being so, defendant's contention that it was inadmissible as a prior consistent statement is irrelevant." Id. at 493, 554 N.Y.S.2d at 448, 553 N.E.2d at 946. See also United States v. Detrich, 865 F.2d 17 (2d Cir.1988), where defendant, who had brought a suit of clothes from India with heroin sewn into the lining, argued that he had no knowledge of the heroin and brought the suit into the United States for a friend, Dawood, to wear at Dawood's wedding. Defendant wanted to get into evidence Dawood's statement to a DEA agent that he was getting married. The court stated:

> Without regard to the truth of Dawood's marriage plans, the jury could draw from the statement an important inference as to what [defendant] knew—or thought he knew. From this affirmative statement by Dawood to the authorities that he was getting married, a jury could infer that appellant had also been told that Dawood was getting married and therefore believed that Dawood was a prospective groom who needed the wedding suit in a few weeks.

865 F.2d at 21.

10. 7 Ad. and E. 313, 112 Eng.Rep. 488 (Court of Exchequer Chamber, 1837).

testator's mental competency it was certainly not asserted and it seems clear that what they did write was not intended as an assertion of his mental powers. If anything, the content of the letters showed unexpressed assumptions on the part of testator's correspondents that he must be competent or else they would not have written such letters. In this light they would be nonhearsay. They are relevant as bearing on testator's competency simply because they were written.

The idea of a relevant nonassertion being admissible as nonhearsay is succinctly summed up as follows:

> [I]t is clear that evidence of conduct must be taken as freed from at least one of the hearsay dangers, i.e., mendacity. A man does not lie to himself. Put otherwise, if in doing what he does a man has no intention of asserting the existence or nonexistence of a fact, it would appear that the trustworthiness of evidence of this conduct is the same whether he is an egregious liar or a paragon of veracity.[11]

From this comes the oft-repeated hypothetical concerning the witness who may testify, to prove that it was raining on the day in question, that she saw a person open his umbrella as he stepped out the door. In opening the umbrella he had no intention of making an assertion to the world that it was raining. He simply desired to avoid getting wet. Yet the act of opening the umbrella is relevant to the issue of the weather and comes in simply because it was done. The only credibility that needs testing is that of the witness who saw the opening of the umbrella.

When would conduct be assertive and inadmissible? Consider a case in which the issue is the nature of the patient's disease. Evidence of the treatment rendered by the physician (which would indirectly indicate the disease being treated) was held in an old New York case to be hearsay because it was no different than had the witness testified that the physician verbally announced to all in attendance what ailed the patient.[12] Would such treatment be considered an assertion under Rule 801 were the issue to arise today? The one example of conduct admitting of no doubt as to its assertive nature is where a person (declarant), in response to the question, "Who is the culprit?" simply points at an individual.[13] Clearly the act of pointing would have been intended as an assertion and would not be admissible through the testimony of a witness who was present and observed the matter.

---

11. Falknor, "The 'Hear-Say' Rule as a 'See-Do' Rule: Evidence of Conduct," 33 Rocky Mtn.L.Rev. 133, 136–37 (1961). But see Professor Morgan's view defending the rationale of the Wright case. "Basic Problems of Evidence," Vol.2, pp.219-20 (ALI, 1954).

12. Thompson v. Manhattan R. Co., 11 App.Div. 182, 42 N.Y.S. 896 (2d Dep't 1896); Central of Georgia Railway Co. v. Reeves, 288 Ala. 121, 257 So.2d 839 (1972).

13. See People v. Nieves, 67 N.Y.2d 125, 501 N.Y.S.2d 1, 492 N.E.2d 109 (1986); United States v. Ross, 321 F.2d 61, 69 (2d Cir.), cert. denied, 375 U.S. 894, 84 S.Ct. 170, 11 L.Ed.2d 123 (1963)(testimony that a person pointed to a list of salesmen described act within the hearsay rule because

In *People v. Salko*,[14] the Court of Appeals gave an example of admissible nonassertive conduct where a police officer described a lawyer's bribe attempt. The lawyer's approach, their meetings, and the transfer of money were deemed nonassertive. "The distinction has long been made between acts and declarations. The hearsay rule interdicts the introduction of an out-of-court statement offered to establish the truth of its assertion; it has, as a general rule, no application to an act which is not intended to serve as an expressive communication."[15]

Finally, if the modern view is that a statement or act must be expressly assertive and not just impliedly assertive to qualify as hearsay, it would seem to follow that silence or a failure to act could not be considered hearsay. Historically under the *Wright* rule, evidence of customers' failure to complain about a product would be considered hearsay and inadmissible to prove there was nothing wrong with the product.[16] But this view would seem outmoded under the approach used by the federal and proposed state codifications. Better reasoning lies in cases where, for example, a lack of complaints by other passengers in a railroad car was admissible as circumstantial evidence to refute plaintiff's charge that the car was too cold,[17] and where the fact no guests complained about a heater in a motel was admissible to show there was no indication that anything was wrong with the heater.[18]

In sum, nonassertive conduct is admissible under the clear wording and intendment of Federal Rule 801(a) and the interpreting federal cases.[19] In New York, the *Salko* opinion gives a strong indication of the acceptance of this modern view in New York.

c. Operative Words (Verbal Acts)

So-called "operative words" or "verbal acts" are not hearsay. The classic example is where a witness testifies to what he heard parties say in the formation of a verbal agreement. The words can be considered, not for any truth inherent in them, but simply because they were uttered. The words themselves have a legally operative effect in the

---

the act was in response to a question going to the substance of the case).

14. 47 N.Y.2d 230, 417 N.Y.S.2d 894, 391 N.E.2d 976, reh. denied, 47 N.Y.2d 1012, 420 N.Y.S.2d 1025, 394 N.E.2d 308 (1979).

15. Id. at 239, 417 N.Y.S.2d at 899, 391 N.E.2d at 982. See also People v. Jones, 135 A.D.2d 652, 522 N.Y.S.2d 228 (2d Dep't 1987), aff'd, 73 N.Y.2d 902, 539 N.Y.S.2d 286, 536 N.E.2d 615, reh. denied, 74 N.Y.2d 651, 542 N.Y.S.2d 520, 540 N.E.2d 715 (1989)(officer could properly testify that defendant was called "Fat Man" and that he responded to that appellation).

16. James K. Thomson Co., Inc. v. International Compositions Co., Inc., 191 App. Div. 553, 181 N.Y.S.2d 637 (1st Dep't 1920).

17. Silver v. New York Cent. R. Co., 329 Mass. 14, 105 N.E.2d 923 (1952).

18. Cain v. George, 411 F.2d 572 (5th Cir.1969).

19. See, e.g., Headley v. Tilghman, 53 F.3d 472, 477 (2d Cir.1995)(in prosecution for drug sales, telephone caller's statements during phone call to defendant's premises were admissible as nonassertive verbal conduct to prove that defendant used beeper to receive requests for drugs); United States v. Zenni, 492 F.Supp. 464, 469 (E.D.Ky. 1980)(in bookmaking prosecution statements made by persons who telephoned defendant's premises and gave directions for placing bets were nonassertive verbal conduct, offered as relevant to support inference that bets could be placed at defendant's premises, and as such were admissible).

formation of a legal obligation.[20] From this basic premise variations abound. Thus, where the issue was whether an insurance policy was in effect at the time of the accident, an insurance company employee could testify that the insured said that he wanted to cancel the policy, whereupon it was cancelled. Whether the insured was really telling the truth when he issued these instructions is beside the point. The words were said, and they amounted to operative instructions.[21] In a liquor board hearing based on charges that the licensed establishment was used as a house of prostitution, it was permissible to allow the government's agent to testify that he had conversations with Pattie and Jean in the bar and that he had been solicited by them both by words and acts. The hearsay objection foundered because the women's statements proved the critical issue—the use of the premises for illegal purposes. The truth of the statements was unimportant because they had the operative effect, simply because they were said, of defining the use to which the premises were being put.[22] In a similar case, where agents had raided and secured premises from which drugs had been sold, customers continued to appear and the agents sold drugs to them. The actions and words of the customers were admissible to show the use of the premises, and any truth in their statements was immaterial.[23] And the distinction between hearsay and nonhearsay is set forth in a Second Circuit case where a telephone conversation between coinventors as to the operation of their creation was deemed admissible under the verbal act doctrine. Thus, the witness, who was with one of the parties to the conversation could testify to what that party said; but he should not be allowed to testify to what that party told him the other party said.[24]

---

20. See Sheedy v. Stall, 255 Or. 594, 468 P.2d 529 (1970); Kosinski v. Woodside Const. Corp., 77 A.D.2d 674, 429 N.Y.S.2d 783 (3d Dep't 1980).

21. Creaghe v. Iowa Home Mutual Casualty Co., 323 F.2d 981 (10th Cir.1963).

22. Los Robles Motor Lodge, Inc. v. Department of Alcoholic Beverage Control, 246 Cal.App.2d 198, 54 Cal.Rptr. 547 (Cal. Dist.Ct.App.3d Dist.1966). The testimony of undercover agents as to the statements and actions of their quarry is usually held admissible since they have the operative effect of proving the crime. See also State v. Forsythe, 243 La. 460, 144 So.2d 536 (1962).

23. People v. Charles, 137 Misc.2d 111, 519 N.Y.S.2d 921 (Sup.Ct.Kings Co.1987). See also People v. Clark, 203 A.D.2d 935, 611 N.Y.S.2d 387 (4th Dep't 1994)(in forgery and larceny prosecution deposit slips and withdrawal slips were not hearsay because not offered for truth of assertions therein; the documents were made in furtherance of the crime); DeLuca v. Ricci, 194 A.D.2d 457, 599 N.Y.S.2d 267 (1st Dep't 1993) (person who accepted summons on defendant's behalf lied about her identity; such statement was verbal act not offered for its truth but as evidence of fraud); People v. Barnhart, 66 Cal.App.2d 714, 153 P.2d 214 (Cal.Dist.Ct.App.1944)(police continued to man phones in a raided betting parlor and could testify as to the statements of bettors in order to show the nature of the operation); United States v. Zenni, 492 F.Supp. 464, 469 (E.D.Ky.1980)(in bookmaking prosecution statements made by persons who telephoned defendant's premises and gave directions for placing bets were nonassertive verbal conduct, offered as relevant to support inference that bets could be placed at defendant's premises, and as such were admissible).

24. Knorr v. Pearson, 671 F.2d 1368, 1372–73 (Cust. & Pat.App.1982). It was stated:

We are persuaded that the conversation between the coinventors was a "verbal act" affecting the legal rights of the parties. Evidence of what the coinventors said to each other is not offered to prove the truth of the statements themselves. Whether the holes in the outer layer and the space between the layers actually function to create a "chimney effect" and cool the stud during a fire is irrelevant; rather, the question is whether the ideas

§ 801.1   HEARSAY   Ch. 8

While it seems that many statements are admissible as nonhearsay, the courts remain assiduous in observing the rule when there is no point to the offered statement other than to prove the truth.[25]

Another body of caselaw concerns the nonhearsay status of verbal parts of acts. Where the person's actions would seem to be relevant, but they are ambiguous, clarifying words accompanying the acts would be admissible. The late Dean Jerome Prince illustrated this by the example of a professor handing her student twenty dollars. The act is ambiguous because we do not know why the money was proffered. Was it to pay a debt or was it a gift? The professor's words, spoken as the money is given, "This is your reward for achieving the highest grade in the examination," can come into evidence to clear up the ambiguity. On point is the holding in *United States v. Romano*,[26] where a question concerned the nature of payments made by wholesalers to union members and where it was stated that "the requests to give the money to the 'boys in the union' were admissible as 'an utterance which was contemporaneous with an independently nonverbal act * * * and which relates to that act and throws some light upon it.' "[27] In another case, tape-recorded statements tending to explain defendant's possession of cocaine as possession with intent to sell were admissible precisely because they shed light on the nature of the possession.[28]

were communicated, the *communication* (as opposed to the truth) having legal significance. * * * However * * * Buergin's [coinventor] statements to Rutkowski [the witness] regarding what Pearson [other coinventor] said * * * are hearsay when offered by Rutkowski.

(Emphasis in original). See also United States v. Katz, 425 F.2d 928, 932 (2d Cir.1970)(contents of application for FHA loan admissible as verbal act not requiring laying of a business record foundation); United States v. Payden, 622 F.Supp. 915, 918 (S.D.N.Y.), mot. to vacate denied, 623 F.Supp. 1148 (S.D.N.Y.1985)(statements accompanying drug deal deemed verbal acts); Morgan Guar. Trust Co. v. Hellenic Lines Ltd., 621 F.Supp. 198, 219 (S.D.N.Y.1985)(shareholders agreement admissible as nonhearsay to prove its terms—although not admissible to "prove the truth of the statements contained therein").

25. United States v. Harwood, 998 F.2d 91, 97 (2d Cir.), cert. denied, ___ U.S. ___, 114 S.Ct. 456, 126 L.Ed.2d 388 (1993)(codefendant's statement to newspaper reporter to the effect defendant was an innocent bystander was inadmissible because the only relevance it could have had at trial would have been the truth of it); United States v. Rea, 958 F.2d 1206, 1225 (2d Cir.1992)(government's introduction of admissible incriminating statements made by defendant in no way served to open the door to defendant's other statements since the only reason for getting them in evidence would be to prove their truth); United States v. Cardascia, 951 F.2d 474, 487 (2d Cir.1991)(defendant's letter of resignation would be hearsay if offered to prove the truth of the reasons stated therein); Branch v. Ogilvy & Mather, Inc., 765 F.Supp. 819, 822 (S.D.N.Y.1990)(in copyright case letters, book reviews and advertisements not admissible to prove value of the allegedly copied book); United States v. Garcia–Duarte, 718 F.2d 42, 45 (2d Cir.1983)(introduction of a book containing names of drug dealer's clientele was error where it could not qualify under the business entry rule or as a coconspirator's statement).

26. 684 F.2d 1057, 1066 (2d Cir.), cert. denied, 459 U.S. 1016, 103 S.Ct. 375, 74 L.Ed.2d 509 (1982).

27. Id. at 1066. The court cited United States v. Glasser, 443 F.2d 994, 999 (2d Cir.), cert. denied, 404 U.S. 854, 92 S.Ct. 96, 30 L.Ed.2d 95 (1971)(where defendant was charged with damaging a store owner's window, a note that was left demanding that the window be replaced with "union glass" was admissible as a contemporaneous utterance).

28. United States v. Giraldo, 822 F.2d 205, 213 (2d Cir.), cert. denied, 484 U.S. 969, 108 S.Ct. 466, 98 L.Ed.2d 405 (1987). See also People v. Thompson, 186 A.D.2d 768, 589 N.Y.S.2d 68 (2d Dep't 1992), leave to appeal denied, 81 N.Y.2d 848, 595 N.Y.S.2d 747, 611 N.E.2d 786 (1993) (ac-

The Court of Appeals in *People v. Salko*,[29] having found a lawyer's bribe attempts admissible nonassertive conduct, went on to hold that the lawyer's statements accompanying those acts were also admissible to flesh out the otherwise somewhat ambiguous actions of the lawyer.[30]

d. State of Mind

There are two types of state of mind "exceptions" to the hearsay rule. The first is not an exception because it really is not hearsay in the first place. The statement does not come in for its truth, but simply because it was uttered. An example, previously discussed in subdivision a, is that of a malpractice plaintiff, suing for damages for cancerphobia.[31] The fact she was told she might develop cancer is relevant to her state of mind, regardless of the truth of the statement. This nonhearsay type of state of mind statement will be taken up here.

The true exception is where a declarant makes a direct assertion of her state of mind ("I love Jim," "I intend to live here forever," "I despise my professor") and the statement is offered to prove the truth of the assertion.[32] Such statements are taken up under the exceptions discussed in § 803(1).1(c).

Another example of nonhearsay is *Garsten v. MacMurray*,[33] where plaintiff wanted to explain away at trial the notation on his accident report that his vehicle had skidded on an oil slick. He said the only reason he put that down was because his wife told him she heard a radio report that an oil slick was involved in the accident. The evidence would be inadmissible to prove that an oil slick was involved, but it could come in to show the information upon which the plaintiff based his belief, which he subsequently discovered was mistaken. As stated by the Appellate Division: "[t]he appellants thereby sought to demonstrate [plaintiff's] state of mind rather than the truth of the statements that there was any oil slick. Hence, the proffered testimony would not have been hearsay and the court's ruling [keeping it out] was erroneous."[34]

There are, in New York, two venerable old cases which illustrate the two types of state-of-mind nonhearsay. In *Loetsch v. New York City Omnibus Corp.*,[35] defendant was sued for causing the death of plaintiff's wife, and defendant, in an attempt to prove the husband of the deceased

---

complice's statements accompanying equivocal gestures provided "interpretations" indicating that drug transaction was in progress).

29. 47 N.Y.2d 230, 417 N.Y.S.2d 894, 391 N.E.2d 976, rearg. denied, 47 N.Y.2d 1012, 420 N.Y.S.2d 1025, 394 N.E.2d 308 (1979).

30. It was stated: "Without these statements Lindenhauer's [the lawyer's] acts—his approach of Galvin, their meetings and even the transfer of money by Lindenhauer to Galvin—would remain equivocal and without legal significance. None of Lindenhauer's statements, except those in which he referred to defendant, were offered for the truth of their assertions." Id. at 239–40, 417 N.Y.S.2d at 900, 391 N.E.2d at 982. It also seems that these acts and words constituted the crime itself and would be admissible on the same basis as the prostitutes' solicitations.

31. Ferrara v. Galluchio, 5 N.Y.2d 16, 176 N.Y.S.2d 996, 152 N.E.2d 249 (1958).

32. Mutual Life Ins. Co. v. Hillmon, 145 U.S. 285, 12 S.Ct. 909, 36 L.Ed. 706 (1892).

33. 133 A.D.2d 442, 519 N.Y.S.2d 563 (2d Dep't 1987).

34. Id. at 443, 519 N.Y.S.2d at 564.

35. 291 N.Y. 308, 52 N.E.2d 448 (1943).

would have profited little had there not been the accident, offered in evidence the wife's will in which there was a passage disparaging the husband and leaving him one dollar. This was admissible since, regardless of the truth of the statement, it certainly showed the wife's feelings toward her husband. That example illustrates admissibility as relevant to the declarant's state of mind. The other old case exemplifies admissibility to show the state of mind of the person who heard the statement. In *People v. Harris*,[36] defendant husband was on trial for killing his wife and his defense was that he had formed no intent to kill, but had acted in the heat of passion. He was properly allowed to testify that he went into a rage when his wife told him she had become pregnant by another man. By whom she had become pregnant, or whether she was even pregnant at all, were factors beside the point, the point being that the mere utterance of the words were sufficient to cause a drastic alteration in the state of defendant's mind.

Typically admissible are statements introduced to demonstrate the declarant's mental defects,[37] statements offered to explain declarant's acts,[38] and statements intended to show why the person who heard the statement acted as he did.[39] But if the statement could also be used as

---

36. 209 N.Y. 70, 102 N.E. 546 (1913).

37. People v. Ricco, 56 N.Y.2d 320, 328, 452 N.Y.S.2d 340, 345, 437 N.E.2d 1097, 1102 (1982)(defendant's delusional statements to his mother were admissible, not to prove he saw spaceships through his telescope, but to show the condition of his mind).

38. In addition to Loetsch v. New York City Omnibus Corp., supra note 35, see People v. Boyling, 84 A.D.2d 892, 893, 444 N.Y.S.2d 760, 762 (3d Dep't 1981)(statements made by defendant during activities which the People charged as burglary were admissible to evidence the nature of these activities inside the building).

39. In addition to People v. Harris, supra note 35, see also People v. Felder, 37 N.Y.2d 779, 780–81, 375 N.Y.S.2d 98, 98, 337 N.E.2d 606, 606 (1975)(the testimony that a bystander said to one Brunson "This Joe is going to take your money" was admissible to explain Brunson's conduct in jumping on a table and running away from the premises); Matter of Bergstein v. Board of Educ., 34 N.Y.2d 318, 323, 357 N.Y.S.2d 465, 469, 313 N.E.2d 767, 769–70 (1974)(school board members could testify as to statements made by them regarding a candidate's fitness for tenure to show why they voted as they did); Provenzo v. Sam, 23 N.Y.2d 256, 261–62, 296 N.Y.S.2d 322, 326, 244 N.E.2d 26, 29 (1968)(plaintiff's statement to his wife concerning erratic actions of driver ahead of them admissible to show why, after the other car had crashed, plaintiff stopped, got out of his car, and rushed across the road); Rivera v. City of New York, 200 A.D.2d 379, 606 N.Y.S.2d 193 (1st Dep't 1994)(in action for medical malpractice a statement by the comatose plaintiff's niece to a medical technician that plaintiff had used crack cocaine was admissible to show basis upon which technician acted); Splawn v. Lextaj Corp., 197 A.D.2d 479, 603 N.Y.S.2d 41 (1st Dep't 1993), leave to appeal denied, 83 N.Y.2d 753, 612 N.Y.S.2d 107, 634 N.E.2d 603 (1994)(on issue of hotel's inadequate security, prior reports to hotel of burglaries and thefts on premises were not hearsay because they were not offered to prove that prior crimes occurred but rather to prove that hotel was on notice of criminal activity); People v. Black, 180 A.D.2d 806, 580 N.Y.S.2d 444 (2d Dep't), appeal denied, 80 N.Y.2d 828, 587 N.Y.S.2d 912, 600 N.E.2d 639 (1992)(in support of entrapment defense, statements of undercover officer to defendant were not hearsay because they were offered to show defendant's state of mind); Piehnik v. Graff, 158 A.D.2d 863, 864, 551 N.Y.S.2d 656, 657 (3d Dep't 1990)(as bearing on the question of mitigation of damages, it was proper in medical malpractice case to allow plaintiff to testify as to what others told him about the risks of undergoing a laminectomy); Doreen J. v. Thomas John F., 101 A.D.2d 862, 476 N.Y.S.2d 10 (2d Dep't 1984)(proper for petitioner's mother to testify as to instructions she gave petitioner prior to petitioner's testifying at a Social Services hearing to show petitioner's state of mind); Veras v. Truth Verification Corp., 87 A.D.2d 381, 386–87, 451 N.Y.S.2d 761, 765 (1st Dep't), aff'd, 57 N.Y.2d 947, 457 N.Y.S.2d 241, 443 N.E.2d 489 (1982)(in false arrest case statements of a private

evidence of the truth of its substance,[40] or would be irrelevant as evidencing the state of the wrong person's mind,[41] then, of course, it could be kept out.

Second Circuit cases concerning the hearer's state of mind,[42] and the declarant's state of mind,[43] are wholly consistent. A sharp eye must be kept for the instance where the statement's effect as a state-of-mind statement is overborne by its effect in conveying the truth of its content to the jury.[44]

e. Indirect Hearsay

In *Duffy v. The People*,[45] decided in 1863, a detective was allowed to testify that, as a result of what defendant had told him, he located the stolen property. The district attorney specifically cautioned the witness not to relate what the defendant had said, but only the occurrences following the receipt of that communication. The Court of Appeals

investigator made to police were admissible to show the basis upon which the police acted); People v. Etheridge, 71 A.D.2d 861, 419 N.Y.S.2d 188 (2d Dep't 1979)(proper for defendant to testify that others told him that certain persons were out to get him—to explain his sudden departure to Florida).

40. People v. Melendez, 55 N.Y.2d 445, 452–53, 449 N.Y.S.2d 946, 950, 434 N.E.2d 1324, 1328 (1982)(evidence that a "concerned citizen" had informed the detective that defendant was involved in the shooting, while it might explain why defendant was arrested, was also hearsay evidence showing defendant's guilt).

41. People v. Seit, 86 N.Y.2d 92, 629 N.Y.S.2d 998, 653 N.E.2d 1168 (1995)(regarding a claim of self-defense, testimony as to a 911 call made by murder defendant's son in which son stated that there was a person [the victim] with a gun present, was not admissible to show defendant's state of mind, but was admissible to rehabilitate the son as a witness since the telephone message was consistent with his testimony and was made before he would have had any motive to fabricate.).

42. United States v. Puzzo, 928 F.2d 1356, 1365 (2d Cir.1991)(defendant's testimony as to what another party told him concerning the package defendant was to take from Italy to New York was admissible to show defendant's motivations in the matter); United States v. Kohan, 806 F.2d 18, 22 (2d Cir.1986)(codefendant's statements to defendant concerning nature of payments admissible by defendant in defense of his position that he believed codefendant to be acting legitimately); United States v. Reed, 639 F.2d 896, 907 (2d Cir.1981)(in mail fraud prosecution letter from bank informing defendant he was behind in his mortgage payments was not introduced to prove the nonpayments, but rather to show why defendant would have a motive to participate in fraudulent scheme); United States v. Kanovsky, 618 F.2d 229, 231 (2d Cir.1980)(introduction of statements made by U.S. Attorney to defendant admissible since coming into evidence merely to show they were made to refresh defendant's recollection); United States v. Dunloy, 584 F.2d 6, 11 (2d Cir.1978)(defendant's testimony as to what he was told concerning the contents of a package admissible to show his motivations); United States v. Press, 336 F.2d 1003, 1011 (2d Cir.1964), cert. denied, 379 U.S. 965, 85 S.Ct. 658, 13 L.Ed.2d 559 (1965)(evidence of complaints being made concerning defendant's services, while not admissible to prove the truth of the complaints, was admissible to show defendant's reaction or lack thereof); Mendez v. United States, 732 F.Supp. 414, 423 (S.D.N.Y.1990)(in medical malpractice case hospital record showing guardian's understanding of minor's medical problem admissible to prove what guardian knew regarding minor's condition).

43. United States v. Southland Corp., 760 F.2d 1366, 1375–76 (2d Cir.), cert. denied, 474 U.S. 825, 106 S.Ct. 82, 88 L.Ed.2d 67 (1985)(corporate defendant's counsel's notes regarding transaction in issue admissible to show defendants' understanding of the transaction); United States v. Harris, 733 F.2d 994, 1004 (2d Cir.1984)(defendant's statements to the effect others were after him were admissible to show defendant's state of mind).

44. United States v. Check, 582 F.2d 668, 678 (2d Cir.1978)(since the undercover agent's testimony as to what the informant told him simply amounted to outright evidence of defendant's criminal activities, it was inadmissible hearsay).

45. 26 N.Y. 588 (1863).

allowed this testimony without discussing its hearsay ramifications.[46]

The better disposition for such an end run around the hearsay rule is found in *Commonwealth v. Farris*,[47] where this exchange occurred:

> Q. As a result of what Gary Moore told you, what if anything did you do?
>
> A. I arrested Emanuel Farris.

In ruling this testimony inadmissible, the court stated:

> Had the detective testified flat-out, "Moore told me that one of the men involved was Farris," it would be clear beyond reasonable argument that the testimony would have been hearsay: it would have been an assertion by someone not in court * * * offered for its truth * * * and thus depending for its value upon the credibility of the out-of-court asserter.[48]

In *People v. Bent*[49] the prosecutor asked his witnesses their side of the conversation with the homicide victim prior to the assault that killed her. The prosecutor argued that this was not hearsay because the victim's words were not being relayed into court.[50] A unanimous court ruled that the effect of this line of questioning put the substance of the victim's hearsay before the jury just as surely as if her words had been introduced.[51]

Library References:

West's Key No. Digests, Criminal Law ⚖︎419–421; Evidence ⚖︎314–324.

801(1) Statements Not Hearsay

§ 801(1).1 Generally

Federal Rule of Evidence 801, subdivision (d), provides as follows:

> **(d) Statements which are not hearsay.** A statement is not hearsay if—
>
> **(1) Prior statement by witness.** The declarant testifies at the trial or hearing and is subject to cross-examination concerning the statement, and the statement is (A) inconsistent with the declarant's testimony, and was given under oath sub-

---

46. The court was concerned with the problem that defendant's statement posed as a confession. The statement could not come in since it was tainted by the detective's promise of leniency. But credibility was established when the detective uncovered the contraband. Id. at 590. Much of the law in Duffy has undergone great change (e.g., the "fruit of the poisonous tree" doctrine developed in Wong Sun v. United States, 371 U.S. 471, 488, 83 S.Ct. 407, 417, 9 L.Ed.2d 441, 455 (1963)).

47. 251 Pa.Super. 277, 380 A.2d 486 (1977).

48. Id. at 282, 380 A.2d at 488–89.

49. 160 A.D.2d 1176, 555 N.Y.S.2d 454 (3d Dep't), appeal denied, 76 N.Y.2d 937, 563 N.Y.S.2d 66, 564 N.E.2d 676 (1990).

50. One witness testified that she had a conversation with the victim, and in response to a statement by the victim said, "[i]f I was in fear of my life, I wouldn't be considering transferring ownership or title to her property." Another witness testified that she told the victim, "[w]hy don't you just pack up and leave, and if he's getting physical with you call the police." Appellant's brief, p.22.

51. 160 A.D.2d at 1178, 555 N.Y.S.2d at 455.

ject to the penalty of perjury at a trial, hearing, or other proceeding, or in a deposition, or (B) consistent with the declarant's testimony and is offered to rebut an express or implied charge against the declarant of recent fabrication or improper influence or motive, or (C) one of identification of a person made after perceiving the person; or

(2) Admission by party-opponent. The statement is offered against a party and is (A) the party's own statement, in either an individual or a representative capacity or (B) a statement of which the party has manifested an adoption or belief in its truth, or (C) a statement by a person authorized by the party to make a statement concerning the subject, or (D) a statement by the party's agent or servant concerning a matter within the scope of the agency or employment, made during the existence of the relationship, or (E) a statement by a coconspirator of a party during the course and in furtherance of the conspiracy.

Proposed New York Evidence Code § 803, subdivisions (a)(1) and (2) and (b)(1), (2), (3) and (4), generally provides for admissibility of the same types of statements, but denominates them as exceptions to the hearsay rule. Regardless of whether such statements are called nonhearsay or hearsay exceptions, under either label they can be admitted into evidence. The current caselaw in New York, however, is not altogether in accord with the various parts of Federal Rule 801(d). The distinctions will be duly noted in the following sections which cover prior statements, identification evidence and admissions.

Library References:

West's Key No. Digests, Criminal Law ⚖419–421; Evidence ⚖314–324.

§ 801(1).2 Prior Statements—New York

a. Inconsistent Statements

Prior inconsistent statements can be used to impeach a witness' testimony. They can be introduced, not for their truth, but to damage the credibility of the witness (see § 607.8(a), *supra*). Here, however, the issue is whether prior inconsistent statements of a witness can be used as evidence in chief. After all, the declarant is now a witness and thus is available for cross-examination both as to his current testimony and his prior statement. But, it is noted that Federal Rule 801(d)(1)(A) places a strict limitation on the use of such statements. They must have been made "under oath subject to the penalty of perjury at a trial, hearing or other proceeding, or in a deposition." The New York rule is, at best, sketchy. There seems to be a willingness on the part of the Court of Appeals, as indicated in the *Letendre* case discussed below, to permit prior inconsistent statements of a witness as evidence in chief in civil cases but there has been little since the *Letendre* decision in the way of a development of such a rule.

Historically, there has been a resistance to letting any prior inconsistent statement in for its truth because it was said that cross-examination, to be effective, must be contemporaneous with the statement.[1] Further, the witness was not under oath when the prior statement was uttered. But this perhaps overly intellectualized appraisal of the timing of the cross-examination is not the modern view. The United States Supreme Court has found that the in-court opportunity to cross-examine concerning the prior statement satisfies a criminal defendant's right to confrontation,[2] and the New York Court of Appeals, at least in civil cases, seems willing to entertain the prior statement as substantive evidence under certain circumstances.

In *Letendre v. Hartford Accident and Indemnity Co.*[3] suit was against the bonding company which covered plaintiff's employees. An employee, Tremblay, was accused by plaintiff of stealing money from the till. On the witness stand Tremblay denied that he had done so. The only evidence implicating him were two statements taken by the insurer's representative during an investigation, in which Tremblay gave varying accounts, but essentially admitted thefts. On Tremblay's cross-examination those statements could come in to impeach, but unless they also had substantive value plaintiff would not have made out a prima facie case. The Court of Appeals, first noting that the statements were preserved in writing so there could be no question as to their accuracy or whether they were made, said that Tremblay's availability for cross-examination was sufficient reason to allow the statements in for their truth. It was pointed out that had Tremblay died or otherwise become unavailable, the statements would have been admissible as statements against his pecuniary interests.[4] A second aspect of this case is that the Court overturned longstanding precedent holding admissions by a principal not binding on the surety if not made contemporaneously with the act to which they relate.[5] The *Letendre* case was given an extremely broad application by the Appellate Division in *Vincent v. Thompson*,[6] where it was held that any prior statement may be admitted if the declarant testifies at trial. Regarding other New York authority, one case specifically allowed a witness' prior sworn statement in for its truth where it was inconsistent with his testimony,[7] and another case allowed in a prior oral inconsistent statement for its truth at an administrative

§ 801(1).2

1. See the classic discussion of the dilemma in Ruhala v. Roby, 379 Mich. 102, 150 N.W.2d 146 (1967), the basic tenet of which is that when the witness denies the truthfulness or accuracy of the prior statement, as he often will, cross-examination upon the prior statement is foreclosed since the witness has precluded any such effective cross-examination. In effect, the cross-examiner is not really cross-examining as to the prior statement—he would like to see the witness reaffirm it, thereby destroying the effect of the in-court testimony. (Id. at 125, 150 N.W.2d at 156).

2. California v. Green, 399 U.S. 149, 153, 90 S.Ct. 1930, 1932, 26 L.Ed.2d 489, 494 (1970).

3. 21 N.Y.2d 518, 289 N.Y.S.2d 183, 236 N.E.2d 467 (1968).

4. Id. at 524, 289 N.Y.S.2d at 188, 236 N.E.2d at 470.

5. Hatch v. Elkins, 65 N.Y. 489 (1875).

6. 50 A.D.2d 211, 224, 377 N.Y.S.2d 118, 130 (2d Dep't 1975).

7. Campbell v. City of Elmira, 198 A.D.2d 736, 738, 604 N.Y.S.2d 609, 611 (3d Dep't 1993), aff'd, 84 N.Y.2d 505, 620 N.Y.S.2d 302, 644 N.E.2d 993 (1994)(where fire truck driver testified at a deposition that the first time he looked in plaintiff's direction was when his truck was in the middle of the intersection, that statement was admissible for its truth where at trial the driver testified he looked in all directions before entering the intersection).

hearing.[8] In a third case the court, without citing *Letendre*, held that the jury should have been instructed "that prior inconsistent statements of the witness [apparently oral] could have been considered by them, not as substantive testimony or direct proof, but only for the purpose of impeaching the credibility of the witnesses."[9]

On the criminal side, prior inconsistent statements can be used only for impeachment purposes. The Criminal Procedure Law, § 60.35, prohibits a party from impeaching his own witness with prior inconsistent statements unless the testimony actually disproves the position of the party who called him (see § 607.4(b) *supra*) and even if that stringent condition[10] is met, the statement can only be used to impeach. As to cross-examination of the other party's witness, the Court of Appeals has adopted Wigmore's view that statements contrary to the witness' testimony may only be used to impeach the witness,[11] and the Appellate Division has left no doubt as to this limitation.[12]

When a prior inconsistent statement is used for impeachment purposes a certain foundation must be laid. (See § 607.8[a][3] *supra*.) That foundation consists of reminding the witness of the circumstances

---

8. Whitman Delicatessen, Inc. v. State Liquor Authority, 83 A.D.2d 963, 964, 443 N.Y.S.2d 14, 16 (2d Dep't 1981)(where, in a State Liquor Authority hearing, a minor testified that he purchased beer at petitioner's store, his prior statement that he had purchased the beer elsewhere could come in for its truth; and the court added dictum that the statement would be equally admissible in a civil action).

9. Millington v. New York City Transit Auth., 44 A.D.2d 542, 353 N.Y.S.2d 469 (1st Dep't 1974).

10. See People v. Fitzpatrick, 40 N.Y.2d 44, 386 N.Y.S.2d 28, 351 N.E.2d 675 (1976). Note 1 in Fitzpatrick provides an interesting comment on the use of prior inconsistent statements as substantive evidence, together with the citation of pertinent authority:

1. A number of authorities have pointed out that the potential for prejudice in the out-of-court statements may be exaggerated in cases where the person making the statement is in court and available for cross-examination and, under such circumstances, favor their admission as evidence-in-chief. (See Note, Impeaching One's Own Witness, 49 Va LJ 996, 1008–1009; Note, Prior Statements of One's Own Witness to Counteract Surprise Testimony: Hearsay and Impeachment Under the "Damage" Test, 62 Yale LJ 650, 658–661; 3A Wigmore, Evidence, § 1018; McCormick, The Turncoat Witness: Previous Statements as Substantive Evidence, 25 Tex L Rev 573; Morgan, Hearsay Dangers and the Application of the Hearsay Concept, 62 Harv L Rev 177; Di Carlo v. United States, 6 F.2d 364, cert. den. 268 U.S. 706; United States v. Freeman, 302 F.2d 347, 351; cf. Letendre v. Hartford Acc. & Ind. Co., 21 N.Y.2d 518, 289 N.Y.S.2d 183, 236 N.E.2d 467.) The objection that material intended to bear only on credibility might be utilized by the jury for more than that limited purpose would, of course, then be academic. We do not comment on these proposals other than to note them, since we are bound by CPL 60.35, the statute before us, which makes the admissibility of such material turn on criteria other than its hearsay nature.

40 N.Y.2d at 50, 386 N.Y.S.2d at 31, 351 N.E.2d at 678.

11. People v. Freeman, 9 N.Y.2d 600, 605, 217 N.Y.S.2d 5, 8, 176 N.E.2d 39, 41 (1961), citing 3 Wigmore § 1018.

12. People v. Raja, 77 A.D.2d 322, 325, 433 N.Y.S.2d 200, 202 (2d Dep't 1980). In this case the prior statement was written and was allowed as substantive evidence, the witness having confirmed its accuracy, as past recollection recorded. The court emphasized that were the statement introduced to contradict the witness' testimony it could only have an impeaching effect and could not be considered for its truth. See also People v. Nieto, 97 A.D.2d 774, 776, 468 N.Y.S.2d 504, 506 (2d Dep't 1983) (prior statements useable only for impeachment); People v. Summers, 49 A.D.2d 611, 612, 370 N.Y.S.2d 204, 206 (2d Dep't 1975)(trial judge not clear in his charge that prior statements could only be considered on the question of the witness' credibility).

under which an oral statement was made,[13] and showing him the document if the prior statement was written;[14] and of giving the witness the opportunity to explain or deny the statement before he is questioned about it. Were one attempting to get such statements in evidence pursuant to the authority found in *Letendre*, or even in *Vincent*, such a foundation should be laid. This simply requires, under *Larkin v. Nassau Elec. R.R. Co.*,[15] that the witness be oriented as to the time and place the statement was made and reminded of any other people who were in attendance.

b. Prior Consistent Statements

Prior consistent statements of a witness, when offered to prove the truth of the matter asserted therein, fall within the definition of hearsay under New York law. Such statements therefore are generally inadmissible. The usual ground of objection is that they improperly bolster the witness' testimony.[16] As discussed in § 607.5(a)(2)(c) *supra*, however, prior consistent statements may be admissible to rehabilitate the credibility of a witness whose testimony has been impeached as a recent fabrication. When the witness' testimony is thus attacked, the fact that the witness said the same thing on a prior occasion and before there was any motive to fabricate lends credence to the testimonial version.

Details as to the circumstances under which a prior consistent statement may be admitted to rebut a charge of recent fabrication are set forth in § 607.5(a)(2)(c) *supra*. The issue here is the evidentiary status of the prior consistent statement when the proper foundation for

---

13. People v. Wise, 46 N.Y.2d 321, 326, 413 N.Y.S.2d 334, 337, 385 N.E.2d 1262, 1265 (1978)("To set the stage for the prior inconsistency, the questioner must first inform the witness of the circumstances surrounding the making of the statement, and inquire of him whether he in fact made it."); Larkin v. Nassau Electric R.R. Co., 205 N.Y. 267, 269, 98 N.E. 465, 466 (1912)("In case the statements are oral, the warning is given by asking the witness, in substance and effect, if he did not at a given time and place in the presence of or to a person or persons specified make the alleged contradictory statements."); People v. Dachille, 14 A.D.2d 554, 554, 218 N.Y.S.2d 156, 158–59 (2d Dep't 1961)(preferred practice is to quote exact words of alleged "prior statement" but "rule is flexible" and "[i]t is not necessary that the question used as the foundation be in the exact words of the prior statement" so long as "substance and effect" are disclosed). See, e.g., People v. Duncan, 46 N.Y.2d 74, 81, 412 N.Y.S.2d 833, 838, 385 N.E.2d 572, 577 (1978), cert. denied, 442 U.S. 910, 99 S.Ct. 2823, 61 L.Ed.2d 275 (1979)(on cross-examination witness was asked only whether she had previously said that she wanted money from aunt; proof of statement that she would kill aunt if necessary was properly excluded); People v. Bernal, 162 A.D.2d 362, 557 N.Y.S.2d 319 (1st Dep't), leave to appeal denied, 76 N.Y.2d 984, 563 N.Y.S.2d 772, 565 N.E.2d 521 (1990)(inadequate foundation where witness was asked only general questions as to whether he had previously spoken with an officer and no questions were asked as to substance of statement to officer); People v. Watford, 146 A.D.2d 590, 536 N.Y.S.2d 835 (2d Dep't), appeal denied, 73 N.Y.2d 984, 540 N.Y.S.2d 1018, 538 N.E.2d 370 (1989)(error to allow detective to prove witness' statement to him where witness was never asked if he had in fact made such statement to detective).

14. Larkin v. Nassau Electric R.R. Co., 205 N.Y. 267, 269, 98 N.E. 465, 466 (1912)("In case the statements are in writing and unsubscribed, the paper must be shown or read to the witness and marked for identification and, if subscribed, the signature, and, in case he so demands, the paper must be shown to him.").

15. 205 N.Y. 267, 269, 98 N.E. 465, 466 (1912).

16. Fishman v. Scheuer, 39 N.Y.2d 502, 504, 384 N.Y.S.2d 716, 717, 349 N.E.2d 815, 816 (1976); Crawford v. Nilan, 289 N.Y. 444, 451, 46 N.E.2d 512, 516 (1943).

admissibility has been met. The Court of Appeals has characterized the admissibility of prior consistent statements as an "exception" to the hearsay rule,[17] but this should not be taken as an indication that a prior consistent statement is admissible for the truth of the matter asserted. The court has clearly indicated the contrary: "The prior consistent statements antedating the motive to fabricate are not introduced to prove or disprove the facts in issue, but to rehabilitate the credibility of the witness."[18] Thus, the only permissible purpose of a prior consistent statement used to rebut a charge of recent fabrication is to lend credibility to the witness' testimony; it may not properly serve as additional evidence in chief. Whether a jury can appreciate this distinction is another matter. Federal Rule of Evidence 801(d)(1)(B), as discussed in § 801(1).3, subdivision b, *infra*, discards the pretense and allows the admission of prior consistent statements as affirmative evidence. The Proposed New York Evidence Code would do the same.[19]

Even under current New York law, some types of "prior consistent statements" may be admissible to prove the truth of the matter asserted if an independent, genuine hearsay exception is operative. A witness' prior identification of a criminal defendant, for example, may constitute evidence in chief, as discussed in § 801(2).1 *infra*. Similarly, a witness' out-of-court excited utterance, the substance of which duplicates her in-court testimony, may be admissible as affirmative evidence.[20]

The relevant provisions of the proposed New York Evidence Code are in the note below.[21]

---

17. People v. Seit, 86 N.Y.2d 92, 629 N.Y.S.2d 998, 653 N.E.2d 1168 (1995).

18. Id. at 96, 629 N.Y.S.2d at 1000, 653 N.E.2d at 1170.

19. See Proposed N.Y. Evid. Code § 803(a)(2); note 21 infra.

20. See People v. Caviness, 38 N.Y.2d 227, 379 N.Y.S.2d 695, 342 N.E.2d 496 (1975)(witness was permitted to testify to prior spontaneous utterance made at crime scene even though her in-court testimony described same event; court did not discuss bolstering effect of prior statement.). See also People v. Buie, ___ N.Y.2d ___, ___ N.Y.S.2d ___, ___ N.E.2d ___, 1995 WL 626482 (1995) (witness' prior statement that qualifies as present sense impression hearsay exception may be admitted even if duplicative of witness' trial testimony).

21. Proposed New York Evidence Code § 803(a)(1), (2) provides:

§ 803. **Hearsay exceptions; prior statement by witness; admission by party-opponents; availability of declarant immaterial**

(a) Prior statement by witness. The following are not excluded by the hearsay rule if the declarant testifies at the trial, proceeding, or hearing and is subject to cross-examination concerning a statement previously made by the declarant unless the party objecting to the statement establishes its untrustworthiness by proof of circumstances involving the making of the statement, including but not limited to a motive to falsify by the declarant:

(1) **Prior inconsistent statement.** In a civil case when the requirements of subdivision (b) of section 613 of this chapter are satisfied, a statement by the declarant inconsistent with the declarant's testimony regarding any fact material to the determination of the action, provided that the prior statement by the declarant was in a writing signed by such declarant or recorded on videotape, audiotape or their technological equivalent, or the statement was made under oath and subject to the penalty of perjury.

(2) **Prior consistent statement.** A statement by the declarant consistent with the declarant's testimony if offered to rebut an express or implied charge of recent fabrication, including one based upon improper influence or motive and if made prior to the circumstances supporting that charge.

Library References:
West's Key No. Digests, Witnesses ⊙⇒395, 397, 414(2).

§ 801(1).3 Prior Statements—Federal

a. Inconsistent Statements

Federal Rule of Evidence 801(d)(1)(A) provides that a witness' prior inconsistent statement is admissible for its truth provided it "was given under oath subject to the penalty of perjury at a trial, hearing or other proceeding, or in a deposition." Prior to the enactment of the Federal Rules, the United States Supreme Court and the Second Circuit had accepted the principle that where the declarant was also a witness and subject to cross-examination there would not necessarily be any violation of defendant's confrontation right. In *California v. Green*,[1] the chief prosecution witness, Porter, proved uncooperative on the witness stand at trial, and suffered a memory loss. The prosecutor reminded Porter of statements made at a preliminary hearing, apparently to refresh his recollection; but the prior testimony, basically inconsistent with Porter's posture at trial, was allowed as substantive evidence. The court discussed the orthodox hearsay rule which rejects the efficacy of belated cross-examination (see § 801(1).2, *supra*) and held that regardless of whether or not a state adheres to the orthodox rule,[2] the confrontation right can be satisfied even though the opportunity to cross-examine is not contemporaneous with the making of the statement.[3] In *Green*, Porter acknowledged his prior statements, but could not remember those events when presented with them at trial. What if a witness denies making the prior statement and proceeds to testify favorably for defendant? In *Nelson v. O'Neil*,[4] the Supreme Court held that the prior statement would still be admissible. "We conclude that where a codefendant takes the stand in his own defense, denies making an alleged out-of-court statement implicating the defendant, and proceeds to testify favorably to the defendant concerning the underlying facts, the defendant has been denied no rights protected by the Sixth and Fourteenth Amendments."[5] The Second Circuit in *United States v. Pacelli*,[6] citing *Green*, ruled admissible the prior inconsistent statement of a witness, but noted that there was other evidence to the same effect. In an earlier case the Second Circuit held that where a witness curtailed his testimony because he did not want "to hurt anyone" the court had the

---

§ 801(1).3

1. 399 U.S. 149, 90 S.Ct. 1930, 26 L.Ed.2d 489 (1970).

2. California Evidence Code § 1235 provides the modern rule allowing the prior statement for its truth.

3. 399 U.S. at 159, 90 S.Ct. at 1935, 26 L.Ed.2d at 497. Had Porter not been available to testify it is altogether possible that the testimony given at the preliminary hearing, where he was subjected to cross-examination by defendant's counsel, would have been admissible under the prior testimony exception. The court noted its decisions in Barber v. Page, 390 U.S. 719, 88 S.Ct. 1318, 20 L.Ed.2d 255 (1968), and Pointer v. Texas, 380 U.S. 400, 85 S.Ct. 1065, 13 L.Ed.2d 923 (1965), cases in which there had been no opportunity to cross-examine the witness or in which the showing of unavailability had not been made.

4. 402 U.S. 622, 91 S.Ct. 1723, 29 L.Ed.2d 222 (1971).

5. Id. at 629–30, 91 S.Ct. at 1727, 29 L.Ed.2d at 228.

6. 470 F.2d 67, 69–70 (2d Cir.1972), cert. denied, 410 U.S. 983, 93 S.Ct. 1501, 36 L.Ed.2d 178 (1973).

discretion to admit a prior sworn statement which the witness did not deny making.[7] Other pre-Rule 801(d)(1)(A) Second Circuit cases are in accord,[8] *United States v. De Sisto*[9] providing especially potent derision of the orthodox rule:

> The rule limiting the use of prior statements by a witness subject to cross-examination to their effect on his credibility has been described by eminent scholars and judges as "pious fraud," "artificial," "basically misguided," "mere verbal ritual," and an anachronism "that still impede(s) our pursuit of the truth." * * * The sanctioned ritual seems peculiarly absurd when a witness who has given damaging testimony on his first appearance at a trial denies any relevant knowledge on his second; to tell a jury it may consider the prior testimony as reflecting on the veracity of the later denial of relevant knowledge but not as the substantive evidence that alone would be pertinent is a demand for mental gymnastics of which jurors are happily incapable. Beyond this the orthodox rule defies the dictate of common sense that "The fresher the memory, the fuller and more accurate it is."[10]

Second Circuit cases utilizing Federal Rule 801(d)(1)(A) are exemplified by *United States v. Marchand*,[11] where, in relation to a witness' prior identification of defendant, it was stated: "[I]f a witness has testified to such facts [pertaining to identification] before a grand jury and forgets or denies them at trial, his grand jury testimony or any fair representation of it falls squarely within Rule 801(d)(1)(A)."[12]

What constitutes another "proceeding" as providing the necessary context for the prior statement is not clear. Grand jury proceedings qualify,[13] as do immigration proceedings, at least according to the Ninth Circuit.[14] In order to qualify under Rule 801(d)(1)(A), the prior inconsis-

---

7. United States v. Insana, 423 F.2d 1165, 1170 (2d Cir.1970), cert. denied, 400 U.S. 841, 91 S.Ct. 83, 27 L.Ed.2d 76 (1970).

8. See United States v. Blitz, 533 F.2d 1329, 1345 (2d Cir.), cert. denied, 429 U.S. 819, 97 S.Ct. 65, 50 L.Ed.2d 79 (1976)("Since Orpheus testified at trial and was available for cross-examination, and since his trial testimony was inconsistent with his grand jury testimony, we hold that the jury properly was permitted to consider the evidence in question in the case against Drew," citing previous Second Circuit cases); United States v. Klein, 488 F.2d 481, 483 (2d Cir.1973), cert. denied, 419 U.S. 1091, 95 S.Ct. 683, 42 L.Ed.2d 684 (1974)(inconsistent grand jury testimony allowed in for truth); United States v. Terrell, 390 F.Supp. 371, 373 (S.D.N.Y.1975)(prior sworn trial testimony of witness admissible as affirmative evidence).

9. 329 F.2d 929 (2d Cir.1964), cert. denied, 377 U.S. 979, 84 S.Ct. 1885, 12 L.Ed.2d 747 (1964).

10. Id. at 933.

11. 564 F.2d 983 (2d Cir.1977), cert. denied, 434 U.S. 1015, 98 S.Ct. 732, 54 L.Ed.2d 760 (1978).

12. Id. at 999. The court noted that even though the specific identification exception provided in Rule 801(d)(1)(C) was not applicable because corporeal or photographic identification must be made after the crime, Rule 801(d)(1)(A) could nevertheless be utilized. Id. at 998, 999.

13. United States v. Blitz, 533 F.2d 1329, 1345 (2d Cir.1976).

14. United States v. Castro–Ayon, 537 F.2d 1055 (9th Cir.), cert. denied, 429 U.S. 983, 97 S.Ct. 501, 50 L.Ed.2d 594 (1976). Aliens, stopped at a border station, gave statements later sought to be introduced under Rule 801(d)(1)(A). The court compared this questioning session with a grand jury proceeding. "[B]oth are investigatory, ex parte, inquisitive, sworn, basically prosecutorial, held before an officer other than

tent statement must be "subject to the penalty of perjury." Thus, statements made at police station inquisitions would seem beyond the pale. Presumably, statements given under oath at a civil or administrative proceeding would qualify.

b. Consistent Statements

Federal Rule of Evidence 801(d)(1)(B) provides:

> **(d) Statements which are not hearsay.** A statement is not hearsay if—
>
> > **(1) Prior statement by witness.** The declarant testifies at the trial or hearing and is subject to cross-examination concerning the statement, and the statement is * * * (B) consistent with the declarant's testimony and is offered to rebut an express or implied charge against the declarant of recent fabrication or improper influence or motive * * *.

If the criteria of Rule 801(d)(1)(B) are met, the prior consistent statement is admissible to prove the truth of the matter asserted in the prior statement. The McCormick treatise notes the absence of any sound reason for denying substantive effect to such statements, stressing that the witness is subject to cross-examination and that limiting instructions to the jury are "needless and useless."[15]

The issue in most cases is whether the prior consistent statement was made before any motive to falsify arose, and so the quest becomes fact-specific from case to case. *United States v. Quinto*[16] set the tone for the Second Circuit when, in interpreting Rule 801(d)(1)(B), the court promulgated three tests: First, the prior statement had to be clearly consistent. Second, fabrication must be charged by the cross-examiner. Third, the statement must have been made before the motive to fabricate arose.[17] All of these requisites comport with the common law rule even though the federal codification does not by its own terms require the third component of the *Quinto* test.[18]

---

the arresting officer, recorded, and held in circumstances of some legal formality." Id. at 1058.

15. McCormick § 251, at 122.

16. 582 F.2d 224 (2d Cir.1978).

17. Id. at 234.

18. United States v. Khan, 821 F.2d 90 (2d Cir.1987). See also United States v. Estes, 793 F.2d 465, 468 (2d Cir.1986)(prior consistent statements made to attorney admissible); United States v. Wilkinson, 754 F.2d 1427, 1433 (2d Cir.1985), cert. denied, 472 U.S. 1019, 105 S.Ct. 3482, 87 L.Ed.2d 617 (1985)(prior consistent statement made "long before [declarant] had entered into any agreement with the U.S. Attorney"); United States v. Hall, 739 F.2d 96, 101 (2d Cir.1984)(while the recent fabrication element was missing, the prior statement was nevertheless admissible because the witness-declarant was cross-examined as if it were inconsistent—that opened door for prosecutor to introduce the statement to show its consistency); United States v. James, 609 F.2d 36, 49–50 (2d Cir.1979), cert. denied, 445 U.S. 905, 100 S.Ct. 1082, 63 L.Ed.2d 321 (1980)(grand jury testimony admissible as prior consistent statement since defense counsel indicated that witness had a motivation to falsify which came after that); United States v. McGrath, 558 F.2d 1102, 1107 (2d Cir.1977), cert. denied, 434 U.S. 1064, 98 S.Ct. 1239, 55 L.Ed.2d 765 (1978)(where witness was charged with recent fabrication because of criminal charges against him, prior consistent statement admissible); United States v. Obayagbona, 627 F.Supp. 329, 337 (E.D.N.Y.1985) (consistent statement made by witness, FBI agent, immediately after arrest not as strong a motive to fabricate as later arose). Compare Felice v. Long Island Railroad Co., 426 F.2d 192, 198 (2d Cir.), cert. denied,

The third *Quinto* factor had not been universally adopted in the federal courts.[19] The Supreme Court resolved the matter in *Tome v. United States*:[20] "The language of [Rule 801(d)(1)(B)], in its concentration on rebutting charges of recent fabrication, improper influence and motive to the exclusion of other forms of impeachment, as well as its use of wording which follows the language of the common-law cases, suggests that it was intended to carry over the common-law pre-motive rule."[21]

The *Tome* court explicitly stated that its "holding is confined to the

400 U.S. 820, 91 S.Ct. 37, 27 L.Ed.2d 47 (1970)(prior consistency not admissible since statement made six weeks after the action commenced and any motive to falsify would have arisen); Alexander v. Kramer Bros. Freight Lines, Inc., 273 F.2d 373 (2d Cir.1959)(driver of truck had motive to falsify from the time the accident happened and thus statements consistent with his testimony would not be admissible).

19. Fed.R.Evid. 801(d)(1)(B) does not explicitly indicate when the prior statement must have been made. Some federal courts, therefore, concluded that general principles of relevancy should govern on a case-by-case basis as to whether a prior consistent statement serves to rebut a charge of recent fabrication or improper influence or motive. See, e.g., United States v. Lawson, 872 F.2d 179, 182 (6th Cir.), cert. denied, 493 U.S. 834, 110 S.Ct. 110, 107 L.Ed.2d 72 (1989). Other federal courts concluded that the common law rule is inherent in Fed.R.Evid. 801(d)(1)(B) because a prior consistent statement rebuts a charge of recent fabrication or improper influence only if it was made before the corrupting influence existed. Otherwise, a prior consistent statement is nothing more than a repetition of the same story, which adds nothing to the witness' veracity. See, e.g., United States v. Vest, 842 F.2d 1319, 1329–30 (1st Cir.), cert. denied, 488 U.S. 965, 109 S.Ct. 489, 102 L.Ed.2d 526 (1988).

Judge Weinstein was prompted to write on this point:

The third Quinto criterion—that the statement must have been made before a motive to fabricate arose—also comports with the facts of this case. It should be noted that this Second Circuit addition to the test does not appear in Rule 801(d)(1)(B) itself, and it has properly met with criticism in other circuits as an unnecessary impediment to control of the trial in a search for the truth. * * * Generally, it would seem useful to drop this third element of the Quinto test. There is no warrant for it in the language of the rule and it unnecessarily complicates the court's problems in administering trials.

Rules 401 to 403 provide a better and more flexible guarantee of fairness.

United States v. Obayagbona, 627 F.Supp. 329, 337 (E.D.N.Y.1985).

20. __ U.S. __, 115 S.Ct. 696, 130 L.Ed.2d 574 (1995). Tome was a prosecution of a father for sexual abuse of his young daughter over whom he shared custody with his former wife. On cross-examination of the child, the defense contended that she had been motivated to incriminate the defendant by a desire to live permanently with the mother. The trial court allowed the prosecution thereafter to prove that the child had made several prior accusatory statements to the mother, a babysitter, a social worker and three doctors, all at a time when the alleged custody-based motive already existed. The Tenth Circuit affirmed, holding that the child's alleged motive to lie was "not particularly strong" and that the statements had "probative force apart from mere repetition." 3 F.3d 342, 351 (10th Cir.1993).

21. __ U.S. at __, 115 S.Ct. at 702, 130 L.Ed.2d at 584. The court observed that "the forms of impeachment within the Rule's coverage are the ones in which the temporal requirement makes the most sense. * * * A consistent statement that predates the motive [to fabricate] is a square rebuttal of the charge that the testimony was contrived as a consequence of that motive. By contrast, prior consistent statements carry little rebuttal force when mostly other types of impeachment are involved." Id. at __, 115 S.Ct. at 701, 130 L.Ed.2d at 582–83. Conceding that prior consistent statements postdating the onset of an alleged motive to fabricate may occasionally "have some probative force" in rebutting the charge, the rebuttal effect is "less direct and forceful." Id. at __, 115 S.Ct. at 701, 130 L.Ed.2d at 583. If Congress had intended a broader relevance test, however, it could have done so by the use of language less tied to common law tradition.

§ 801(1).3   HEARSAY   Ch. 8

requirements for admission under Rule 801(d)(1)(B).''[22] Thus, the decision does not necessarily unravel a line of authority in the Second Circuit which holds that a prior consistent statement may, in some circumstances, be admitted for the limited nonsubstantive purpose of rehabilitating a witness' credibility after impeachment with a prior inconsistent statement regardless of whether the requirements of Rule 801(d)(1)(B) have been met.[23] In particular, where impeachment consists of an allegation of self-contradiction by the witness, a prior consistent statement may "cast doubt on whether the prior inconsistent statement was made or on whether the impeaching statement is really inconsistent with the trial testimony," or the consistent statement may "amplify or clarify the allegedly inconsistent statement."[24] Admission in such cases, which turns on the court's discretion,[25] renders the criteria of Rule 801(d)(1)(B) irrelevant because the rehabilitative purpose is different from that of rebutting a charge of recent fabrication or improper motive.

---

22. Id. at ___, 115 S.Ct. at 705, 130 L.Ed.2d at 588. The four-Justice dissent also noted that the majority opinion dealt only with the admissibility of prior consistent statements for the purpose of rebutting charges of recent fabrication. The dissent identified three other potential ways in which prior consistent statements may serve to rehabilitate a witness: "(a) placing a claimed inconsistent statement in context; (b) showing that an inconsistent statement was not made; (c) indicating that the witness' memory is not as faulty as a cross-examiner has claimed." Id. at ___, 115 S.Ct. at 707, 130 L.Ed.2d at 590, citing United States v. Rubin, 609 F.2d 51, 68 (2d Cir.1979)(Friendly, J., concurring), aff'd, 449 U.S. 424, 101 S.Ct. 698, 66 L.Ed.2d 633 (1981).

23. See United States v. Pierre, 781 F.2d 329, 331 (2d Cir.1986)("Of course, not every prior consistent statement has much force in rebutting the effect of a prior inconsistent statement, and the issue ought to be whether the particular prior consistent statement sought to be used has some rebutting force beyond the mere fact that the witness has repeated on a prior occasion a statement consistent with his trial testimony."). See also United States v. Castillo, 14 F.3d 802, 805–07 (2d Cir.), cert. denied, ___ U.S. ___, 115 S.Ct. 101, 130 L.Ed.2d 50 (1994); United States v. Khan, 821 F.2d 90, 94 (2d Cir.1987); United States v. Brennan, 798 F.2d 581, 587–89 (2d Cir.1986).

24. United States v. Pierre, 781 F.2d 329, 333 (2d Cir.1986). In Pierre, a government agent was impeached by the fact that his handwritten notes concerning defendant's arrest, made immediately after the arrest, did not mention certain incriminating conduct about which the agent had testified. On redirect, the agent was allowed to testify that the incriminating conduct had been included in his formal, typewritten arrest report prepared three days after the arrest, thus suggesting that the omission in the handwritten notes was merely an oversight. The cases of United States v. Khan, 821 F.2d 90 (2d Cir.1987), and United States v. Brennan, 798 F.2d 581 (2d Cir.1986), also permitted rehabilitation with prior consistent statements that tended to overcome the impeaching effect of prior conduct in which witnesses had neglected to incriminate the defendants. In United States v. Castillo, 14 F.3d 802 (2d Cir.), cert. denied, ___ U.S. ___, 115 S.Ct. 101, 130 L.Ed.2d 50 (1994), a prior consistent statement was held to be admissible to "clarify" an alleged inconsistency. Castillo was a narcotics prosecution in which the arresting officer testified that he snorted cocaine at the time of the transaction as a result of a perpetrator's coercive display of a handgun. On cross-examination, the defense contended that the officer lied about the presence of the gun to justify snorting the cocaine and stressed the discrepancy between the officer's testimony that he saw the gun in the perpetrator's "waistband" and his debriefing by his supervisor in which he said he had been "at gunpoint." The officer and his supervisor thereafter were allowed to testify that the officer had told the supervisor that the gun was in the waistband to help the jury evaluate whether the officer's various statements actually meant the same thing.

25. United States v. Pierre, 781 F.2d 329, 333 (2d Cir.1986).

801(2) Identification

§ 801(2).1 New York

In many criminal trials the complaining witness will be asked to make an in-court identification of the person who she claims committed the crime. The question arises as to whether this testimony can be aided by the witness' prior identifications of the suspect, either at line-ups, show-ups, or just on the street. Such testimony would constitute prior consistent statements and serve to buttress the witness' in-court identification. In *People v. Trowbridge*,[1] a prosecution witness made an in-court identification of defendant as the culprit. Another prosecution witness testified that he was present when the witness made another positive identification of defendant as the culprit. This was held to be error since it was a classic instance of a prior consistent statement being used to buttress testimony. A similar situation arises where the witness testifies that she is unable to make the in-court identification because of the lapse of time since the commission of the crime, or because the suspect has altered his appearance. Then it becomes crucial for the prosecution to produce evidence of her prior identification.

In New York there is a comprehensive statutory scheme that provides for these situations. Section 60.30 of the Criminal Procedure Law,[2] enacted after the *Trowbridge* decision, permits a witness to bolster her own identification testimony, but makes no provision for bolstering by others. Companion section 60.25[3] provides that, if the witness

---

§ 801(2).1

1. 305 N.Y. 471, 113 N.E.2d 841 (1953).

2. § 60.30. **Rules of evidence; Identification by means of previous recognition, in addition to present identification**

In any criminal proceeding in which the defendant's commission of an offense is in issue, a witness who testifies that (a) he observed the person claimed by the people to be the defendant either at the time and place of the commission of the offense or upon some other occasion relevant to the case, and (b) on the basis of present recollection, the defendant is the person in question and (c) on a subsequent occasion he observed the defendant, under circumstances consistent with such rights as an accused person may derive under the constitution of this state or of the United States, and then also recognized him as the same person whom he had observed on the first or incriminating occasion, may, in addition to making an identification of the defendant at the criminal proceeding on the basis of present recollection as the person whom he observed on the first or incriminating occasion, also describe his previous recognition of the defendant and testify that the person whom he observed on such second occasion is the same person whom he had observed on the first or incriminating occasion. Such testimony constitutes evidence in chief.

3. § 60.25. **Rules of evidence; identification by means of previous recognition in absence of present identification**

1. In any criminal proceeding in which the defendant's commission of an offense is in issue, testimony as provided in subdivision two may be given by a witness when:

(a) Such witness testifies that:

(i) He observed the person claimed by the people to be the defendant either at the time and place of the commission of the offense or upon some other occasion relevant to the case; and

(ii) On a subsequent occasion he observed, under circumstances con-

identifies the defendant at the time of the crime, and affirms the identification on a subsequent occasion, but is unable to make an identification at the trial, *then* another person who observed the earlier identification may testify to it. Thus, in *People v. Mobley*,[4] it was error to allow a police witness to testify that the victim of a robbery pointed at defendants shortly after the robbery, when the victim had already identified the defendants by her in-court testimony. Had she testified as to her own prior identification that would have been permissible under § 60.30. Proposed New York Evidence Code § 805 adopts both sections verbatim.

In addition to its bolstering effect, evidence of prior identification technically is hearsay,[5] but both sections 60.25 and 60.30 state that "[s]uch [prior identification evidence] constitutes evidence in chief."

It has been argued that § 60.25 does not allow testimony by other witnesses that defendant was actually identified; that the other witnesses may only testify as to "the sameness of the defendant and the person identified."[6] That argument was called "strained reasoning" and disposed of accordingly.[7] On the other hand, § 60.25 has been strictly construed so that the witness' failure to make the in-court identification must be due to lack of recollection, and not to fear of retribution should

sistent with such rights as an accused person may derive under the constitution of this state or of the United States, a person whom he recognized as the same person whom he had observed on the first or incriminating occasion; and

(iii) He is unable at the proceeding to state, on the basis of present recollection, whether or not the defendant is the person in question; and

(b) It is established that the defendant is in fact the person whom the witness observed and recognized on the second occasion. Such fact may be established by testimony of another person or persons to whom the witness promptly declared his recognition on such occasion.

2. Under circumstances prescribed in subdivision one, such witness may testify at the criminal proceeding that the person whom he observed and recognized on the second occasion is the same person whom he observed on the first or incriminating occasion. Such testimony, together with the evidence that the defendant is in fact the person whom the witness observed and recognized on the second occasion, constitutes evidence in chief.

4. 56 N.Y.2d 584, 450 N.Y.S.2d 302, 435 N.E.2d 672 (1982).

5. People v. Bolden, 58 N.Y.2d 741, 743, 459 N.Y.S.2d 22, 23, 445 N.E.2d 198, 199 (1982). ("The rationale behind the Trowbridge rule is twofold. First, the statement of the third-party witness is hearsay. An out-of-court statement of the declarant, communicated at trial by a third party, is generally hearsay if it is offered for the truth of the fact asserted in the statement * * *. In the Trowbridge situation, the out-of-court declaration of the eyewitness is offered primarily for the truth of the identification statement.").

6. People v. Nival, 33 N.Y.2d 391, 394–95, 353 N.Y.S.2d 409, 411–12, 308 N.E.2d 883–85, cert. denied, 417 U.S. 903, 94 S.Ct. 2597, 41 L.Ed.2d 208 (1974)(the robbery victim could not identify defendant at trial, but she testified as to her previous identification of men who were in her store, and a detective properly testified that defendant was one of those identified at that time in his presence).

7. Id. See also People v. Lagana, 36 N.Y.2d 71, 74, 365 N.Y.S.2d 147, 148, 324 N.E.2d 534, 535 (1975)(a witness, who could not identify defendant at trial, testified that shortly after the crime she picked out a person sitting in a hospital ward as the person who had been arguing with the victim, thus legitimizing the detective's testimony that it was defendant that she had identified. The court stated: "Our holding in People v. Nival * * * makes it clear that CPL 60.25 overrules the effect of People v. Trowbridge * * * by permitting the fact of the prior identification to be established by the testimony of another person when the identifying witness is unable to make an identification at trial.").

she testify.[8] Normally, the witness' recollection is affected because of lapse of time or because defendant's appearance has changed.[9] In *People v. Quevas*,[10] however, the recollection foundation was not laid because the victim, who was retarded, was unable to state why he could not make an in-court identification. In another case, where defendant absented himself from the courtroom during the eyewitness' testimony, there was no reason not to allow evidence of their prior identification, the in-court identification having been rendered impossible.[11]

In order for the intermediate identification conducted under police auspices to be admissible there must have been compliance with defendant's due process rights, i.e, the circumstances cannot have been arranged so as to be suggestive to the witness and defendant's right to counsel must have been satisfied.[12] Where the police simply videotaped various people in the street and showed the tape to the victim, the victim's identification of defendant could be testified to because none of defendant's rights were violated.[13] This case also illustrates an exception to the rule that an identification witness may testify only to prior corporeal identifications. Ordinarily, the witness may not testify that on a previous occasion he identified a photograph of defendant,[14] or testify that he described the defendant to a police artist who offered the sketch

---

8. People v. Bayron, 66 N.Y.2d 77, 81–82, 495 N.Y.S.2d 24, 26, 485 N.E.2d 231, 233 (1985)(where the witness was fearful to testify, rather than being unable to remember, the court stated: "We decline to extend CPL 60.25 to the present situation because to do so would require us to read out of the statute the unambiguous prerequisite that the witness be unable to make the identification 'on the basis of present recollection.' ").

9. Id. See also People v. Marrero, 183 A.D.2d 728, 729, 583 N.Y.S.2d 468, 470 (2d Dep't), appeal denied, 80 N.Y.2d 906, 588 N.Y.S.2d 831, 602 N.E.2d 239 (1992)(the witness' not being "100% certain" of defendant's identity at trial did not allow for the introduction of his prior identification).

10. 81 N.Y.2d 41, 45, 595 N.Y.S.2d 721, 723, 611 N.E.2d 760, 762 (1993) (the court said that in order to lay a proper foundation for CPL 60.25 testimony by another person, the witness must testify, either at trial, or at a hearing to suppress identification testimony, that she has no present recollection; the reason for failure to identify in court cannot be ambiguous, and cannot rest solely on the ground of the witness' mental retardation).

11. People v. Torres, 184 A.D.2d 605, 606, 584 N.Y.S.2d 631, 632 (2d Dep't), appeal denied, 80 N.Y.2d 934, 589 N.Y.S.2d 862, 603 N.E.2d 967 (1992). (The court stated: "The two eyewitnesses were unable to identify the defendant at trial not because they could not recognize him due to the lapse of time or the defendant's changed appearance, but simply because the defendant voluntarily absented himself from the courtroom at the time their testimony was elicited. 'Bolstering' was never a problem at trial. Since the defendant was absent during the People's case, the eyewitnesses' in-court identifications at the Wade hearing were properly admitted.").

12. See People v. Edmonson, 75 N.Y.2d 672, 676–77, 555 N.Y.S.2d 666, 668, 554 N.E.2d 1254, 1256, reargument denied, 76 N.Y.2d 846, 560 N.Y.S.2d 130, 559 N.E.2d 1289, cert. denied, 498 U.S. 1001, 111 S.Ct. 563, 112 L.Ed.2d 570 (1990).

13. Id.

14. People v. Cioffi, 1 N.Y.2d 70, 150 N.Y.S.2d 192, 133 N.E.2d 703 (1956). See also People v. Wright, 21 N.Y.2d 1011, 1012, 290 N.Y.S.2d 930, 931–32, 238 N.E.2d 330, 331 (1968), where it was error to allow victim to testify that he selected photographs from police files, and then for a police witness to confirm this as the inference was that these were photographs of the defendants. It was stated that "There was a resulting inference the photographs in police files were those of defendants. In the context of the record reception of the proof was prejudicial." Id. at 1012, 290 N.Y.S.2d at 931–32, 238 N.E.2d at 331. This is a rare expression of the reason for the rule involving photographs. Also, identifying a photograph is not literally identifying the "person" within the meaning of Crim.Proc.Law §§ 60.30 and 60.25. People v. Hagedorny, 272 App.Div. 830, 70 N.Y.S.2d 511, 512 (2d Dep't 1947).

in evidence.[15] Another exception to the rule was recognized where the defendant's appearance was different at trial. Individuals acquainted with defendant, but who were not witnesses to the crime, were allowed to testify that they identified defendant as the person displayed on a bank surveillance film. Their testimony concerning defendant's facial hair supported the prosecutor's contention that defendant had altered his appearance after the bank robbery.[16]

In other cases the question has arisen whether the witness' in-court testimony is tainted because of the previous viewing of a photograph. Thus, where a witness, an undercover officer who dealt with the defendant in a drug deal, picked defendant's picture out of a mug book two days later the court ruled that "the photographic identification by the undercover officer was merely confirmatory, and could not have tainted the in-court identification";[17] and where defendant stole a car from a dealer on the pretext of trying it out, the dealer's identification testimony was not tainted because she viewed an improper photo display, the court stating, "[a]n in-court identification is not precluded * * * so long as clear and convincing evidence establishes that the in-court identification derives from an independent basis which preceded the improper procedure."[18] But in another case a witness' identification of defendant's picture at an improper mug shot display would have improperly tainted his in-court identification.[19] Situations involving identification through the use of photographs arise in a variety of ways.[20]

---

15. People v. Griffin, 29 N.Y.2d 91, 93, 323 N.Y.S.2d 964, 965, 272 N.E.2d 477, 478 (1971). The court said that the photograph rule applies in the case of a sketch, but that sketches may nevertheless be useful at suppression hearings on issues of probable cause. Defendant may introduce a sketch on cross-examination of the witness to show inconsistencies between the in-court identification and the description given the artist. Likewise, where the witness' identification testimony is challenged as a recent fabrication, her description given to a police sketch artist before any motive to falsify would have arisen is admissible. People v. Coffey, 11 N.Y.2d 142, 146, 227 N.Y.S.2d 412, 414, 182 N.E.2d 92, 94 (1962).

16. People v. Russell, 165 A.D.2d 327, 328–29, 567 N.Y.S.2d 548, 549 (2d Dep't), appeal denied, 78 N.Y.2d 926, 573 N.Y.S.2d 479, 577 N.E.2d 1071 (1991).

17. People v. Johnson, 173 A.D.2d 734, 735, 570 N.Y.S.2d 616, 617 (2d Dep't), appeal denied, 78 N.Y.2d 1012, 575 N.Y.S.2d 820, 581 N.E.2d 1066 (1991).

18. People v. Stacey, 173 A.D.2d 960, 961, 569 N.Y.S.2d 470, 471 (3d Dep't 1991), appeal denied, 79 N.Y.2d 832, 580 N.Y.S.2d 213, 588 N.E.2d 111 (1991).

19. People v. Moss, 80 N.Y.2d 857, 858, 587 N.Y.S.2d 593, 594, 600 N.E.2d 224, 225 (1992). Immediately after the robbery of a store the owner and his clerk described the perpetrator to police. Four days later the owner saw defendant on the street and called police. The clerk saw defendant being chased by police and recognized him as the perpetrator. The next day he picked out defendant from a mug shot display. This was impermissible since notice pursuant to CPL 710.30 had not been given. This would have tainted his observation of defendant being chased and so any in-court identification testimony, or any testimony as to the chase was improperly introduced. However, "his description of the robber given to the police prior to the potentially tainted identification procedure," was held to be properly introduced.

20. People v. Wilson, 195 A.D.2d 493, 494, 600 N.Y.S.2d 113, 114 (2d Dep't 1993)(defendant's cross-examination of witness opened door for evidence that witness had previously identified defendant's photograph; but it was error to allow witness to select from a photo array in court); People v. Boyd, 189 A.D.2d 433, 440–41, 596 N.Y.S.2d 760, 765 (1st Dep't), appeal denied, 82 N.Y.2d 714, 602 N.Y.S.2d 811, 622 N.E.2d 312 (1993)(the detective's answer to a question on cross-examination that he met the witness "to view a photo array," was insufficient to open the door on redirect to show the identification made by the witness).

A peculiar situation can arise in rape prosecutions. In *People v. Rice*,[21] the Court of Appeals, in a memorandum opinion, held that a victim's prompt report of a rape to the police is an exception to the hearsay rule and is fully admissible. Testimony as to the details of the victim's description of the culprit, however, if testified to by the police who heard the complaint, is not admissible as an exception.[22] In a companion case, *People v. Huertas*,[23] a distinction was made. There, the victim promptly reported the crime to the police and described her assailant. At trial she testified not only to her in-court identification, but also as to the description she gave police. This was not hearsay because it was not offered for its truth. Rather, it was offered by the prosecutor "because it bore upon the accuracy and reliability of the identification of defendant, and was a factor mentioned in the standard charge on identification in a one-witness identification case."[24] It was further stated: "It is not the accuracy or truth of the description that establishes relevance. It is, rather, the comparison of the prior description and the features of the person later identified by the witness as the perpetrator that is the ground of the relevance."[25] Had the evidence been presented for this purpose in *Rice*, perhaps its admission would not have been error. It appears from these cases that evidence of the prompt report, while its content does not come in for its truth, is nevertheless "probative"[26] evidence simply because it was made.

The prior buttressing identification may have taken place at a previous trial and can be introduced even though the prosecutor served no notice of intention to use prior identification as provided for under Criminal Procedure Law § 710.30.[27] The notice requirement is not applicable where the identification was made in court and defendant was represented by counsel.[28]

21. 75 N.Y.2d 929, 555 N.Y.S.2d 677, 554 N.E.2d 1265 (1990).

22. Id. at 931–32, 555 N.Y.S.2d at 678, 554 N.E.2d at 1266.

23. 75 N.Y.2d 487, 554 N.Y.S.2d 444, 553 N.E.2d 992 (1990).

24. Id. at 490, 554 N.Y.S.2d at 446, 553 N.E.2d at 994. The pattern jury instruction is as follows:

[i]n evaluating the witness's capacity to observe and remember, you may consider the "description" of the perpetrator which he gave to the police soon after the commission of the crime. If that "description" does not match the physical characteristics of the defendant, that factor must be considered by you in making your determination of the witness's capacity and ability to observe and remember the physical features of the perpetrator. On the other hand, an accurate matching "description" may be considered by you in assessing the witness's capacity to observe and remember.

Id. at 491, 554 N.Y.S.2d at 446–47, 553 N.E.2d at 994–95 (quoting 1 Crim.Jury Instructions NY § 10.01, at 586).

25. Huertas, 75 N.Y.2d at 492, 554 N.Y.S.2d at 447, 553 N.E.2d at 995.

26. Id. at 493, 554 N.Y.S.2d at 448, 553 N.E.2d at 996.

27. People v. White, 73 N.Y.2d 468, 541 N.Y.S.2d 749, 539 N.E.2d 577, cert. denied, 493 U.S. 859, 110 S.Ct. 170, 107 L.Ed.2d 127 (1989).

28. Id. at 474, 541 N.Y.S.2d at 752, 539 N.E.2d at 580. It was stated:

[A]t a prior in-court identification, a Wade hearing, preliminary felony hearing, or previous trial * * * defendant knows of the identification and the notice purpose of the statute is not implicated. More importantly, defense counsel is present and has the ability to challenge the suggestive nature of the identification at the time it is taking place.

Id.

§ 801(2).1   HEARSAY   Ch. 8

In some instances the complainant gives a description of defendant to the police to aid apprehension. In one case,[29] detectives did not testify that the informant identified the defendant by pointing him out in a lineup or a photo array, but said that they had arrested defendant based on information given them by the informant concerning the culprit's clothing, build and skin coloring. This was held proper.[30] In a similar situation in another case the court stated: "[T]he undercover officer's testimony, together with the testimony of the arresting officers who received the description, provided a necessary explanation of the events which precipitated the defendant's arrest * * *."[31] But in yet other circumstances it was held error to have allowed "testimony from a detective which indicated that, following the lineup viewings, the defendant was arrested."[32] This, in effect, constituted an end run around the *Trowbridge* rule. The distinction in this case is the fact of the lineup identification.

In more than a few instances error by the trial court in allowing identification evidence has been deemed harmless in light of the overwhelming evidence of guilt and no significant possibility that the jury would have acquitted if it had not heard the objectionable identification evidence.[33]

Library References:

West's Key No. Digests, Criminal Law ⚖︎339.5; Witnesses ⚖︎318, 414(2).

29. People v. Sydney, 195 A.D.2d 763, 600 N.Y.S.2d 358 (3d Dep't 1993).

30. Id. at 765, 600 N.Y.S.2d at 360.

31. People v. Kanston, 192 A.D.2d 721, 722, 597 N.Y.S.2d 152, 153 (2d Dep't), appeal denied, 81 N.Y.2d 1074, 601 N.Y.S.2d 594, 619 N.E.2d 672 (1993). To the same effect, see People v. Byrd, 187 A.D.2d 724, 590 N.Y.S.2d 511 (2d Dep't 1992), appeal denied, 81 N.Y.2d 968, 598 N.Y.S.2d 769, 615 N.E.2d 226 (1993).

32. People v. Stanley, 185 A.D.2d 827, 828, 586 N.Y.S.2d 649, 650 (2d Dep't), appeal denied, 80 N.Y.2d 977, 591 N.Y.S.2d 146, 605 N.E.2d 882 (1992).

33. See People v. Johnson, 57 N.Y.2d 969, 970, 457 N.Y.S.2d 230, 230, 443 N.E.2d 478, 478 (1982)(where victim identified defendant in court, it was error to allow specific bolstering by corroborating testimony of victim's companion, and implicit corroboration of testimony by police officers; but two-step test for harmless error satisfied here while (1) the proof of defendant's guilt without the evidence erroneously admitted is overwhelming, and (2) there is no significant probability that the jury would have acquitted had it not been for this evidence); People v. Mobley, 56 N.Y.2d 584, 585, 450 N.Y.S.2d 302, 303, 435 N.E.2d 672, 673 (1982)(where the victim had identified defendant in court it was error, though harmless, for police witnesses to have testified that shortly after the robbery the victim pointed at defendant as the perpetrator); People v. Johnson, 32 N.Y.2d 814, 816, 345 N.Y.S.2d 1011, 299 N.E.2d 256 (1973) (where victim's neighbor observed defendant for two or three minutes while committing the crime, a subsequent identification from a photo array would have tainted her in-court identification; but this was harmless in light of all the other evidence); People v. Gordillo, 191 A.D.2d 455, 456, 594 N.Y.S.2d 60, 61 (2d Dep't), appeal denied, 81 N.Y.2d 1014, 600 N.Y.S.2d 202, 616 N.E.2d 859 (1993)(testimony of arresting officer that he arrested defendant after conferring with complainant, was inferential bolstering, but harmless in this case); People v. Stanley, 185 A.D.2d 827, 829, 586 N.Y.S.2d 649, 651 (2d Dep't), appeal denied, 80 N.Y.2d 977, 591 N.Y.S.2d 146, 605 N.E.2d 882 (1992)(testimony of officer that defendant was arrested as a result of the witness' identification at lineup was error, but harmless); People v. Marrero, 183 A.D.2d 728, 729, 583 N.Y.S.2d 468, 470 (2d Dep't), appeal denied, 80 N.Y.2d 906, 588 N.Y.S.2d 831, 602 N.E.2d 239 (1992)(where witness testified in court that he was not "absolutely sure" of his identification of defendant, it was error to allow officer to testify to a prior identification under § 60.25, but error harmless).

§ 801(2).2 Federal

The federal rule regarding evidence of previous identification, unlike New York Criminal Procedure Law §§ 60.25 and 60.30,[1] is, on the face of it, without limitation. Federal Rule 801(d)(1)(C) provides that a statement is not hearsay if it is "one of identification of a person made after perceiving the person," and the declarant, of course, testifies and is subject to cross-examination. The United States Supreme Court has long been of the view that a witness' prior identification is desirable evidence in chief because it occurred closer in time to the event in issue and hence is much more reliable than the in-court identification.[2]

The question of most concern in the federal system is whether the previous identification was made with full observance of defendant's due process and sixth amendment rights. If in-court identification testimony is to be admitted there must be a determination that the witness was not unduly influenced by an improper lineup, showup or photo array.[3] Much discretion is left to the trial court since the "totality of the

---

§ 801(2).2

1. See § 801(2).1 supra.

2. Gilbert v. California, 388 U.S. 263, 87 S.Ct. 1951, 18 L.Ed.2d 1178 (1967). The Court, in footnote 3 of the opinion, quoted from People v. Gould, 54 Cal.2d 621, 626, 354 P.2d 865, 867, 7 Cal.Rptr. 273, 275 (1960) as follows:

Evidence of an extrajudicial identification is admissible, not only to corroborate an identification made at the trial * * * but as independent evidence of identity. Unlike other testimony that cannot be corroborated by proof of prior consistent statements unless it is first impeached * * * evidence of an extrajudicial identification is admitted regardless of whether the testimonial identification is impeached, because the earlier identification has greater probative value than an identification made in the courtroom after the suggestions of others and the circumstances of the trial may have intervened to create a fancied recognition in the witness' mind. * * * The failure of the witness to repeat the extrajudicial identification in court does not destroy its probative value, for such failure may be explained by loss of memory or other circumstances. The extrajudicial identification tends to connect the defendant with the crime, and the principal danger of admitting hearsay evidence is not present since the witness is available at the trial for cross-examination.

388 U.S. at 274, 87 S.Ct. at 1957, 18 L.Ed.2d at 1186.

See also United States v. Barbati, 284 F.Supp. 409 (E.D.N.Y.1968). In this case a barmaid, who reported defendants to police as having passed counterfeit bills, could not identify them at trial whereupon evidence of her original identification was introduced through the testimony of the arresting officer. This was admissible as substantive evidence, Judge Weinstein stating:

We should not blind ourselves to what the law has learned by bitter experience—identification in court is frequently an almost worthless formality. * * * By the time of trial positions have often become fixed and memory so attenuated and distorted by subsequent events that witnesses seldom make identifications on the basis of their raw recollection of the original event. Their apparent certitude is often misleading and not infrequently less reliable than earlier reactions. We cannot permit the mechanical and unreasoned application of the hearsay rule to deny evidence vital to our search for truth.

284 F.Supp. at 413.

3. Gilbert v. California, 388 U.S. 263, 272–73, 87 S.Ct. 1951, 1956–57, 18 L.Ed.2d 1178, 1186 (1967). Companion cases, United States v. Wade, 388 U.S. 218, 87 S.Ct. 1926, 18 L.Ed.2d 1149 (1967), and Stovall v. Denno, 388 U.S. 293, 87 S.Ct. 1967, 18 L.Ed.2d 1199 (1967), laid down the rules governing witness identification procedures, chief among which is that the procedure should not be unduly suggestive, and that at any lineup the suspect be afforded the presence of counsel. Violation of these rules could, under these three cases, result in inadmissibility of in-court identification if not duly formed on an independent basis such as full opportunity to observe the culprit at the time of the commission of the crime.

circumstances" may dictate that even a one-suspect showup would not have violated defendant's rights.[4] The degree of liberality with which the Supreme Court treats the identification rule is demonstrated by its decision in *United States v. Owens*.[5] John Foster, a correctional counselor, was attacked in a federal prison and severely beaten. As a result, his memory was greatly impaired. Mansfield, an FBI agent, visited Foster and showed him a photograph of an inmate Foster identified as his assailant. Foster testified to this identification at trial. On cross-examination defense counsel tried to get Foster to remember that at one time he had named another person as the assailant, but Foster was unable to recall. Over the argument that there was no opportunity for meaningful cross-examination, agreed with by the Ninth Circuit,[6] Justice Scalia, writing for a majority of the Supreme Court, stated that the confrontation clause only guarantees the opportunity for cross-examination, not necessarily successful cross-examination.[7] The fact there was an out-of-court identification was of no consequence because under Rule 801(d)(1)(C) it is sufficient if a declarant is present at the trial and subject to unrestricted cross-examination.[8]

In *United States v. Jacobowitz*,[9] the Second Circuit applied these rules in a typical case where the witnesses had been shown photo arrays. The court stated:

> Generally, pretrial photographic identification procedures violate due process only if they are "so impermissibly suggestive as to give rise to a very substantial likelihood of irreparable misidentification." [Citing Simmons v. United States, 390 U.S. 377, 384, 88 S.Ct. 967, 971, 19 L.Ed.2d 1247 (1968)]. * * * [W]e note that the reliability of each witness's identification was indicated by virtually all of the factors listed in Neil v. Biggers, 490 U.S. at 199–200, 93 S.Ct. at 382–83, to wit, "opportunity of the witness to view the criminal at the time of the crime, the witness' degree of attention, the accuracy of the witness' prior description of the criminal [and] the level of certainty demonstrated by the witness at the confrontation" * * *.

---

4. See Neil v. Biggers, 409 U.S. 188, 93 S.Ct. 375, 34 L.Ed.2d 401 (1972). Where the victim had ample opportunity to view her assailant at the time of the crime, and had given the police his description, a showup seven months after the crime at the police station, with defendant the only person displayed, was not unduly prejudicial. In the Stovall case cited in note 3 supra, a showup in the victim's hospital room was proper under the circumstances, which included the fact the victim was in critical condition. See also Coleman v. Alabama, 399 U.S. 1, 90 S.Ct. 1999, 26 L.Ed.2d 387 (1970); and Simmons v. United States, 390 U.S. 377, 88 S.Ct. 967, 19 L.Ed.2d 1247 (1968). Compare Foster v. California, 394 U.S. 440, 89 S.Ct. 1127, 22 L.Ed.2d 402 (1969), where the police all but used coercive procedures to worm an identification out of the witness and the circumstances thus dictated inadmissibility.

5. 484 U.S. 554, 559–563, 108 S.Ct. 838, 842–44, 98 L.Ed.2d 951, 957–60 (1988).

6. 789 F.2d 750, 755–56 (9th Cir.1986), rev'd, 484 U.S. 554, 108 S.Ct. 838, 98 L.Ed.2d 951 (1988).

7. 484 U.S. at 560, 108 S.Ct. at 843, 98 L.Ed.2d at 958.

8. Id., citing California v. Green, 399 U.S. 149, 90 S.Ct. 1930, 26 L.Ed.2d 489 (1970).

9. 877 F.2d 162 (2d Cir.), cert. denied, 493 U.S. 866, 110 S.Ct. 186, 107 L.Ed.2d 141 (1989).

These rules seem uniformly to be applied in the Second Circuit.[10]

Unlike the rule in New York (see § 801(2).1, *supra*) there is no prohibition in the federal courts against using evidence of prior identification of a photograph.[11] Also, evidence of prior identification can be used as rebuttal evidence when the witness' identification testimony is impeached on cross-examination.[12]

Library References:
West's Key No. Digests, Criminal Law ⚷339.5; Witnesses ⚷318, 414(2).

802 Admissions

§ 802.1 New York & Federal—Introduction

Unlike the supposed guarantee of trustworthiness which undergirds hearsay exceptions generally (or other sorts of nonhearsay statements set forth in Federal Rule of Evidence 801(d)(1), where the declarant is present at trial) the only requirement for the admissibility of an admission is simply that it be a statement or an act done or made by a party which cuts against his interest at the time of litigation. The statement could well be in the party's interest when made (lacking any particular degree of trustworthiness), the classic example being the case of the property owner who puts a low value on his property for tax assessment purposes, but then contends for a much higher value when the land is taken by the process of eminent domain.[1] Furthermore, the party need have no personal knowledge of whether the statement is true.[2] Perhaps,

---

10. See United States v. Sanchez, 603 F.2d 381, 384–86 (2d Cir.1979)(even though 15 months elapsed between the crime and the in-court identification, and even under the assumption that photographic identification procedures were suggestive, the in-court identification was admissible because there was not a very substantial likelihood of irreparable misidentification); United States v. Moskowitz, 581 F.2d 14, 21 (2d Cir.), cert. denied, 439 U.S. 871, 99 S.Ct. 204, 58 L.Ed.2d 184 (1978)(sketch made by police artist at direction of witness to a bank robbery was admissible as was the witness' in-court identification which was held untainted from a series of pretrial identifications); United States v. Marchand, 564 F.2d 983, 995 (2d Cir.1977), cert. denied, 434 U.S. 1015, 98 S.Ct. 732, 54 L.Ed.2d 760 (1978)(nine month delay in viewing the photo array and fact defendant's appearance was distinct in certain respects from that of others in the photographs did not create irreparable misidentification); United States v. Miller, 381 F.2d 529, 538 (2d Cir.1967), cert. denied, 392 U.S. 929, 88 S.Ct. 2273, 20 L.Ed.2d 1387, reh. denied, 393 U.S. 902, 89 S.Ct. 66, 21 L.Ed.2d 188 (1968) (eyewitness' impeachment in court not fatal to government's case since prosecutor could show witness' positive pretrial identification).

11. United States v. Lewis, 565 F.2d 1248, 1251–52 (2d Cir.1977), cert. denied, 435 U.S. 973, 98 S.Ct. 1618, 56 L.Ed.2d 66 (1978)(the term "person" in Rule 801(d)(1)(C) as the object of identification is not limited to corporeal identification and can include photographs).

12. United States v. De Sisto, 329 F.2d 929, 932–33 (2d Cir.), cert. denied, 377 U.S. 979, 84 S.Ct. 1885, 12 L.Ed.2d 747 (1964)(long before enactment of Rule 801(d)(1)(C)) court held prior identification could be used as evidence in chief where witness is impeached on cross-examination; compare United States v. Jenkins, 496 F.2d 57, 68–70 (2d Cir.1974), cert. denied, 420 U.S. 925, 95 S.Ct. 1119, 43 L.Ed.2d 394 (1975)(pretrial photo identification through testimony of an officer who was present not admissible where witness did not testify to it at trial leaving defendant with no opportunity for cross-examination on the point).

§ 802.1

1. East Kentucky Rural Electric Co-op. Corp. v. Phelps, 275 S.W.2d 592, 595 (Ky. 1955).

2. McCormick § 254, at 140.

§ 802.1   **HEARSAY**   Ch. 8

then, the rationale is that the inability to cross-examine a declarant, a chief reason why hearsay is prohibited, is not present because a declarant-party cannot complain of the inability to cross-examine himself.[3]

The landmark New York case concerning admissions is *Reed v. McCord*,[4] where the defendant at a coroner's inquest made statements concerning the negligently maintained machine which had caused plaintiff's intestate's death. Defendant had no firsthand knowledge of the machine's condition, but had simply adopted facts told to him by others. Had he merely repeated that he had heard these facts without adopting them "then it would only have amounted to an admission that he had heard the statement which he repeated and not to an admission of the facts included in it."[5] The court stated in these oft-quoted words: "In a civil action the admissions by a party of any fact material to the issue are always competent evidence against him, wherever, whenever or to whomsoever made."[6] A party's admission may be made by his conduct[7] as well as his words.

Judicial admissions. Stipulations as to facts for purposes of litigation,[8] and statements in pleadings upon which the parties go to trial are considered formal, binding commitments which will brook no denial.[9] Indeed, as McCormick states: "Judicial admissions are not evidence at all. Rather, they are formal concessions in the pleadings in the case or stipulations by a party or its counsel that have the effect of withdrawing

---

3. Id., citing 4 Wigmore § 1048. See also McCormick § 254, at 141 ("the most satisfactory justification of the admissibility of admissions is that they are the product of the adversary system"); United States v. McKeon, 738 F.2d 26, 32 (2d Cir.1984)(hearsay exception for party admissions is product of "older, rough and ready view of the adversary process which leaves each party to bear the consequences of its own acts, no matter how unreliable these acts may be as proof").

4. 160 N.Y. 330, 54 N.E. 737 (1899).

5. Id. at 341, 54 N.E. at 740.

6. Id.

7. E.g., People v. Thomas, 46 N.Y.2d 100, 412 N.Y.S.2d 845, 385 N.E.2d 584 (1978), appeal dismissed, 444 U.S. 891, 100 S.Ct. 197, 62 L.Ed.2d 127 (1979)(motorist's refusal to submit to blood-alcohol test considered an admission of intoxication); United States v. Heitner, 149 F.2d 105, 107 (2d Cir.), cert. denied, 326 U.S. 727, 66 S.Ct. 33, 90 L.Ed. 432, reh. denied, 326 U.S. 809, 66 S.Ct. 164, 90 L.Ed. 494 (1945)(flight, like spoliation of papers, is a legitimate ground for the inference of guilt).

8. See CPLR 3222 (Agreed Statement of Facts) and CPLR 3123 (Notice to Admit). Note that CPLR 3014 permits separate causes of action or defenses to be pleaded "regardless of consistency." Such pleading would not raise the specter of creating formal admissions. Collins v. Caldor of Kingston, Inc., 73 A.D.2d 708, 709, 422 N.Y.S.2d 524, 525 (3d Dep't 1979) (where plaintiff, accidentally shot in the eye with pellet gun manufactured by Crosman and sold by Caldor, Caldor's allegation in its unverified, third-party complaint against Crosman that the gun was unsafe and not of merchantable quality, did not constitute admissions of fact by Caldor, but were merely inconsistent pleadings which are permissible).

9. In People v. Rivera, 45 N.Y.2d 989, 991, 413 N.Y.S.2d 146, 385 N.E.2d 1073 (1978), it was held that defendant's admission, in an affidavit drawn by his lawyer, that defendant had possession of marked currency, would qualify, not as a formal judicial admission with binding effect, but as an informal judicial admission with substantive evidentiary effect. It is not indicated for what purpose the affidavit was made. Compare Pok Rye Kim v. Mars Cup Co., Inc., 102 A.D.2d 812, 476 N.Y.S.2d 381 (2d Dep't 1984)(statements in opposition to a motion for summary judgment held to be formal and binding); East Egg Associates v. Diraffaele, 158 Misc.2d 364, 600 N.Y.S.2d 999 (N.Y.C.Civ.Ct.N.Y.Co.1993)(unqualified statements in pleadings constitute formal judicial admissions; compare allegations "upon information and belief"), order affirmed, 160 Misc.2d 667, 614 N.Y.S.2d 102 (Sup.Ct.N.Y.Co.1994).

a fact from issue and dispensing wholly with the need for proof of the fact."[10] Where, however, a complaint in one law suit is used as an admission against the pleader's position in a second lawsuit, the admission is deemed informal and not binding.[11]

Evidentiary admissions. Everything else falls into the category of "evidentiary admissions," and whatever the nature of the inculpatory words or acts, they are not binding and the party can try to neutralize their effect.[12] The weight of authority is that inculpatory statements in a party's own testimony are of evidentiary weight, and not binding on the party.[13]

To be distinguished from admissions are confessions, statements against interest and withdrawn guilty pleas:

Confessions. Confessions are inclusive statements normally made in custody in which a criminal suspect implicates himself in the details of the commission of a crime.[14] An admission may simply be an act or a remark done or made at any time which tends to be incriminating to some degree or indicates culpability.

Statements against interest. Statements against interest comprise a separate hearsay exception in the common law and under Federal Rule of Evidence 804(b)(3), and are statements made by those who are not parties. Unlike admissions, declarations against interest must be

---

10. McCormick § 254, at 142. The binding effect of such pleadings or stipulations can last throughout the litigation, even on a retrial. See Stemmler v. Mayor, 179 N.Y. 473, 482, 72 N.E. 581, 584 (1904)("A stipulation made by the parties or their attorneys with respect to the facts in a case for the purpose of evidence, is general and not limited in respect of time or occasion, but stands in the case for all purposes until the litigation is ended, unless the court upon application shall relieve either or both of the parties from its operation.") But see People v. Ortiz, 141 Misc.2d 747, 534 N.Y.S.2d 316 (Sup.Ct.Richmond Co.1988) (defendant's admissions made at a plea allocution in an assault case were held not admissible when defendant was charged later with murder, the victim having ultimately died—this was not part of his bargain with the prosecutor).

11. Cramer v. Kuhns, 213 A.D.2d 131, 630 N.Y.S.2d 128 (3d Dep't 1995)(in suit against motorcycle manufacturer based on alleged faulty design of the machine, plaintiff's notice of claim against the state filed in the Court of Claims alleging that the accident was caused by defective roadway would be considered an informal admission).

12. Statements in superseded pleadings lose their effect as formal admissions, but can persist as evidentiary admissions. See Vermeule v. City of Corning, 186 App.Div. 206, 210, 174 N.Y.S. 220, 223 (4th Dep't 1919), aff'd, 230 N.Y. 585, 130 N.E. 903 (1920).

13. McCormick § 258. See Skelka v. Metro Tr. Auth., 76 A.D.2d 492, 497, 430 N.Y.S.2d 840, 843–44 (2d Dep't), appeal denied, 51 N.Y.2d 709, 434 N.Y.S.2d 1025, 415 N.E.2d 984 (1980), where the court, drawing on authority from other jurisdictions, discussed thoroughly the effect of a party's own testimony and ruled that it should be treated as would testimony from any other witness, and not as a binding judicial admission. The testimony can occur at trial or at a deposition. Answers to interrogatories, and statements in affidavits and bill of particulars also considered evidentiary. Payne v. New Hyde Park Dodge, 163 A.D.2d 285, 557 N.Y.S.2d 152 (2d Dep't 1990). The United States Supreme Court has ruled that testimony given at a prior trial is admissible, Harrison v. United States, 392 U.S. 219, 88 S.Ct. 2008, 20 L.Ed.2d 1047 (1968), but in that case the prior testimony had been induced by coerced confessions. In United States v. GAF Corp., 928 F.2d 1253, 1259 (2d Cir. 1991), it was held that where the government's bill of particulars in a prior prosecution was inconsistent with its present theory the jury was entitled to know what the government previously claimed.

14. McCormick devotes a long chapter to the topic of confessions. See McCormick § 144 et seq.

§ 802.1 HEARSAY Ch. 8

against the declarant's interest at the time uttered. That is the guarantee of trustworthiness, for it is supposed that a person would not declare against his pecuniary, proprietary or criminal interest unless the declaration were true. A basic condition for the admission into evidence of a declaration against interest is that the declarant be unavailable as a trial witness.[15]

Withdrawn guilty plea. In *People v. Spitaleri*,[16] the Court of Appeals ruled that a withdrawn guilty plea may not be used against the defendant even as an evidentiary admission. The same result was reached by the United States Supreme Court in *Kercheval v. United States*.[17] But a guilty plea (not withdrawn) may be used as an evidentiary admission in a civil action based on the same facts.[18] See §§ 410.1 and 410.2, *supra*.

The format used in discussing the various sorts of admissions in the ensuing section will be in accord with the classifications set forth in Federal Rule of Evidence 801(d)(2):

(A) the party's own statement, in either an individual or a representative capacity or (B) a statement of which the party has manifested an adoption or belief in its truth, or (C) a statement by a person authorized by the party to make a statement concerning the subject, or (D) a statement by the party's agent or servant concerning a matter within the scope of the agency or employment, made during the existence of the relationship, or (E) a statement by a coconspirator of a party during the course and in furtherance of the conspiracy.

The proposed New York Code of Evidence provisions concerning admissions are different enough to be separately set forth.[19]

---

15. See § 804(3).1 infra.

16. 9 N.Y.2d 168, 212 N.Y.S.2d 53, 173 N.E.2d 35 (1961).

17. 274 U.S. 220, 47 S.Ct. 582, 71 L.Ed. 1009 (1927).

18. Ando v. Woodberry, 8 N.Y.2d 165, 203 N.Y.S.2d 74, 168 N.E.2d 520 (1960)(defendant's plea of guilty to traffic offense can be used against him in related civil liability case as evidentiary admission; fact that such pleas are often made on grounds of expediency can be shown by defendant to affect weight).

19. § 803. Hearsay exceptions: prior statement by witness; admission by party-opponent; availability of declarant immaterial [PROPOSED]

* * *

(b) Admission by party-opponent. The following are not excluded by the hearsay rule if offered against a party:

(1) By party in individual or representative capacity. The party's own statement made in the party's individual or representative capacity and offered against the party in that capacity, and statements made by a person through whom a party claims by representation.

(2) Adoptive. A statement which the party has adopted or in which the party has manifested belief in its truth.

(3) Authorized. A statement by an agent or employee of a party authorized by that party to make a statement concerning the subject, provided that authorized statements to the employer or principal are made on the basis of personal knowledge.

(4) Co-conspirator. Subject to a determination made pursuant to paragraph two of subdivision (b) of section 104 of this chapter [court cannot consider content of statement in determining the authority by which the admission was made], and subject to decisional law requirements of unavailability, if any, a statement by a co-conspirator of the party made during the course and in furtherance of the conspiracy.

§ 802.2 A Party's Statement—New York

A party's statement in a letter,[1] after an accident,[2] in an affidavit or deposition[3]—"wherever or whenever" made in the words of *Reed v. McCord*[4]—can be introduced against the party as an admission. Basic classifications of admissions are set forth in § 802.1, *supra*; but further variations need to be discussed such as admissions by a party's conduct, by his silence, in pleas, or in settlement negotiations. Another question is whether an admission made by one in privity with others is binding on the others. A related question is whether the declarant speaks in an individual or representative capacity and whether his statement can be used against his principal, employer or coconspirator.

a. Admission by a Party's Conduct

In *People v. Thomas*,[5] the Court of Appeals held that a motorist's refusal to submit to a blood-alcohol test could be introduced against him at a related proceeding—that a 1973 amendment to § 1194 of the New York Vehicle and Traffic Law which provided for such admissibility was constitutional.[6] Since the motorist's choice not to take such test is not compelled, there can be no violation of his fifth amendment right.[7] It has subsequently been held that delaying the test while the motorist tries to contact his lawyer is tantamount to a refusal and can be introduced against him.[8] This is the sort of contextual conduct which amounts to an admission even without statutory authorization. Likewise, a party's attempt to scuttle evidence or procure false testimony,[9] or

---

§ 802.2

1. Dattner v. Pokoik, 81 A.D.2d 572, 437 N.Y.S.2d 425 (2d Dep't 1981), appeal dismissed, 54 N.Y.2d 750, 442 N.Y.S.2d 996, 426 N.E.2d 491 (1981)(letter to newspaper); Columbia Pictures Industries, Inc. v. Stein for Senator Campaign, 77 A.D.2d 836, 431 N.Y.S.2d 23 (1st Dep't 1980) (unsuccessful candidate's letter stating responsibility for certain campaign costs constituted admission).

2. Rosario v. New York City Transit Auth., 73 A.D.2d 912, 423 N.Y.S.2d 254 (2d Dep't 1980)(admissions contained in MV 104, accident report); compare Thrower v. Smith, 62 A.D.2d 907, 406 N.Y.S.2d 513 (2d Dep't), aff'd, 46 N.Y.2d 835, 414 N.Y.S.2d 124, 386 N.E.2d 1091 (1978), amended, 68 A.D.2d 896, 414 N.Y.S.2d 294 (2d Dep't), appeal dismissed, 47 N.Y.2d 1011, 420 N.Y.S.2d 223, 394 N.E.2d 292 (1979)(statement by driver in MV 104, deceased at time of trial, that he hit car in front of him, admissible as an admission).

3. People v. Rivera, 45 N.Y.2d 989, 413 N.Y.S.2d 146, 385 N.E.2d 1073 (1978)(admission in affidavit had evidentiary effect).

4. 160 N.Y. 330, 341, 54 N.E. 737, 740 (1899).

5. 46 N.Y.2d 100, 412 N.Y.S.2d 845, 385 N.E.2d 584 (1978), appeal dismissed, 444 U.S. 891, 100 S.Ct. 197, 62 L.Ed.2d 127 (1979).

6. Id. at 103, 412 N.Y.S.2d at 846, 385 N.E.2d at 585.

7. Id. at 107–108, 412 N.Y.S.2d at 849–850, 385 N.E.2d at 587–588. See also Bazza v. Banscher, 143 A.D.2d 715, 533 N.Y.S.2d 285 (2d Dep't 1988).

8. People v. O'Rama, 78 N.Y.2d 270, 574 N.Y.S.2d 159, 579 N.E.2d 189 (1991).

9. People v. Davis, 43 N.Y.2d 17, 400 N.Y.S.2d 735, 371 N.E.2d 456 (1977), cert. denied, 435 U.S. 998, 98 S.Ct. 1653, 56 L.Ed.2d 88, cert. denied sub nom., New York v. James, 438 U.S. 914, 98 S.Ct. 3143, 57 L.Ed.2d 1160 (1978)(the false testimony procured by the prosecution was not introduced by the prosecution, but defendant wanted to bring out that the prosecution had made such an attempt as an admission that the whole case was tainted; but this,

§ 802.2   HEARSAY   Ch. 8

his advancement of a false alibi,[10] or any such attempt at a coverup[11] would tend to prove his culpability. Such acts are indicative of consciousness of guilt, another expression of which is flight.[12] Whether expressed as circumstantial evidence or as an admission makes little difference, except that relevance plays a part when a suspect, subject to criminal charges in two jurisdictions, tries to escape, and it is not clear as to which charge he thereby expressed a consciousness of guilt.[13] A good discussion of the flight charge is found in *People v. Anglin*[14] where the trial court applied the principle to a defendant who simply absented himself from the trial, could not be found, and so was tried in absentia.

A defendant's attempt to intimidate a witness into not testifying against him may result in more than simply an admission that can be used against defendant. In *People v. Geraci*,[15] the Court of Appeals ruled that the grand jury testimony of the intimidated witness who refused to testify at trial could be introduced as an exception to the hearsay rule. The court held that there must be a foundation supported by clear and convincing evidence that the witness was, in fact, intimidated since, as with any hearsay evidence, defendant suffers the loss of his right to confrontation.[16] The court did not base this new[17] hearsay exception on any inherent trustworthiness in the grand jury testimony, but rather invoked it on policy grounds so that a defendant cannot profit from his own wrong.[18]

For policy reasons discussed in § 408.1 *supra*, the fact that a party entered into settlement negotiations, or offered to compromise a claim, is inadmissible as an admission.[19] However, under the current New York rule any inculpatory words uttered by the party during those negotiations may well be admissions that can be used against the party.[20]

although relevant, was outweighed by the prospect of confusion and prolongation of the trial).

10. People v. Moses, 63 N.Y.2d 299, 482 N.Y.S.2d 228, 472 N.E.2d 4 (1984) (false alibi, although an admission against declarant, is insufficient standing alone to corroborate the testimony of an accomplice).

11. Changing one's appearance, assuming a false name, resisting arrest, attempting to bribe and suicide attempts all comprise conduct amounting to admissions. McCormick § 263, at 182.

12. McCormick § 263: "The wicked flee when no one pursues," citing Proverbs 28:1.

13. People v. Yazum, 13 N.Y.2d 302, 246 N.Y.S.2d 626, 196 N.E.2d 263 (1963), reargument denied, 15 N.Y.2d 679, 255 N.Y.S.2d 1027, 204 N.E.2d 217 (1964)(evidence of flight admissible and burden on defendant to explain reason for flight).

14. 136 Misc.2d 987, 519 N.Y.S.2d 586 (Sup.Ct.Kings Co.1987).

15. 85 N.Y.2d 359, 625 N.Y.S.2d 469, 649 N.E.2d 817 (1995).

16. Noting that the Second Circuit in United States v. Mastrangelo, 693 F.2d 269, 272–73 (2d Cir.1982), cert. denied, 467 U.S. 1204, 104 S.Ct. 2385, 81 L.Ed.2d 343 (1984), had adopted such a hearsay exception, Judge Titone in Geraci decided against the preponderance of the evidence standard used in Mastrangelo and opted for the clear and convincing test.

17. This hearsay exception had been used previously in Matter of Holtzman v. Hellenbrand, 92 A.D.2d 405, 460 N.Y.S.2d 591 (2d Dep't 1983) and federal cases, in addition to Mastrangelo, cited by the court. 85 N.Y.2d at 366, 625 N.Y.S.2d at 473, 649 N.E.2d at 821.

18. 85 N.Y.2d at 367–68, 625 N.Y.S.2d at 474, 649 N.E.2d at 822.

19. Bigelow Sanford, Inc. v. Spec. Comm. Floors of Rochester, Inc., 77 A.D.2d 464, 465, 433 N.Y.S.2d 931, 932 (4th Dep't 1980).

20. White v. Old Dominion Steamship Company, 102 N.Y. 660, 6 N.E. 289 (1886)(during compromise negotiations plaintiff admitted that he had seen cautionary lights, a fact damaging to his case).

An additional aspect[21] of the effect of a person's plea to a criminal charge, or a charge to a traffic infraction is that it can be used as an informal admission in related litigation. Thus, in *Augustine v. Village of Interlaken*,[22] the Appellate Division ruled that a guilty plea to a traffic infraction could be used in the personal injury action which arose out of the resulting accident. The court held also, that while the plea was admissible, the conviction would have no collateral estoppel effect in the tort litigation.[23] This was not a new rule, having been enunciated previously in *Montalvo v. Morales*[24] where the court pointed out that it would not be desirable for traffic courts to become the crucial forums in negligence suits.[25] Note, however, that pleas to felony charges can have estoppel effect in related civil litigation.[26] Since pleas to minor charges in related litigation are only evidentiary admissions, the defendant is free to explain why they were entered.[27]

b. Admissions by Silence

A party's silence in the face of an accusation is generally considered an admission.[28] It must be shown, of course, that where a party remains silent or reacts nonchalantly to charges or questions he must have heard the charge and understood it.[29] The largest obstacle to the admission of silence evidence in criminal cases is the fifth amendment, i.e., if the suspect had a right to remain silent, then that silence may not be used against him. In New York this right obtains from the moment the suspect encounters the police,[30] even before he is apprised of his *Miranda* rights.[31] See the discussion at § 509.1 *supra*. The rule may be some-

---

21. A criminal plea can be a formal and binding judicial admission to the charge to which it relates, but a withdrawn plea will have no effect as an admission in that litigation or any other. See discussion at §§ 802.1 and 410.1, supra.

22. 68 A.D.2d 705, 418 N.Y.S.2d 683 (4th Dep't 1979), appeal dismissed, 48 N.Y.2d 608, 424 N.Y.S.2d 1025, 399 N.E.2d 1205 (1979). See also Ando v. Woodberry, 8 N.Y.2d 165, 203 N.Y.S.2d 74, 168 N.E.2d 520 (1960) (defendant's plea of guilty to traffic offense can be used against him in related civil case as evidentiary admission; fact that such pleas often made on grounds of expediency can be shown by defendant to affect weight).

23. Id. at 710, 418 N.Y.S.2d at 685.

24. 18 A.D.2d 20, 239 N.Y.S.2d 72 (2d Dep't 1963).

25. Id. at 26, 239 N.Y.S.2d at 77.

26. S.T. Grand, Inc. v. City of New York, 32 N.Y.2d 300, 344 N.Y.S.2d 938, 298 N.E.2d 105 (1973), reargument denied, 33 N.Y.2d 658, 348 N.Y.S.2d 1030, 303 N.E.2d 710 (1973)(contractor's suit against city for breach of a public works contract, dismissed under rules of collateral estoppel since contractor had been convicted for offering a bribe to obtain this very contract).

27. Guarino v. Woodworth, 204 A.D.2d 391, 611 N.Y.S.2d 638 (2d Dep't 1994) (jury verdict for defendant upheld since he satisfactorily explained his guilty plea in traffic court by pointing out that it was easier to plead and pay rather than travel all the way from New York to Maine); compare McGraw v. Ranieri, 202 A.D.2d 725, 608 N.Y.S.2d 577 (3d Dep't 1994) (defendant's plea of guilty to violation of N.Y. Veh. and Traffic Law § 1141 is an admission, and in the absence of any explanation for the guilty plea summary judgment properly entered for plaintiff).

28. McCormick § 262, at 176, citing 4 Wigmore § 1071.

29. People v. Lourido, 70 N.Y.2d 428, 522 N.Y.S.2d 98, 516 N.E.2d 1212 (1987)(doubt as to whether defendant even understood English and so the proper foundation was not laid).

30. People v. Conyers, 52 N.Y.2d 454, 438 N.Y.S.2d 741, 420 N.E.2d 933 (1981).

31. The federal rule differs in that the right to remain silent does not obtain until the Miranda warnings are given. Jenkins v. Anderson, 447 U.S. 231, 100 S.Ct. 2124, 65 L.Ed.2d 86 (1980). See also Doyle v. Ohio, 426 U.S. 610, 96 S.Ct. 2240, 49 L.Ed.2d 91 (1976).

§ 802.2   HEARSAY   Ch. 8

what different when the suspect is a police officer.[32] Beyond the constitutional limitations, it has been said that evidence of an individual's failure to speak when he might have been expected to do so "must be regarded as having minimal probative significance and as having a correspondingly low potential for advancing the truth finding process even when offered solely for purposes of impeachment."[33]

On the civil side the same principles (minus the constitutional considerations) may apply with respect to acquiescence in bills which are sent by a creditor;[34] but simple failure to respond to correspondence or to contest it will normally not rise to the level of an admission.[35]

c. Privity

It is the current rule in New York that the statements of a person in a relationship of privity with another—joint-owner,[36] grantor,[37] joint obligor[38]—are admissible not only against the speaker, but also against the other person in the relationship, when the statement concerns the joint interest. This principle is represented by such sparse and antiqu-

---

32. In People v. Rothschild, 35 N.Y.2d 355, 361 N.Y.S.2d 901, 320 N.E.2d 639 (1974), decided prior to Conyers, supra note 30, it was held that where the officer maintained at trial that he was about to make an arrest for bribe-giving when apprehended, his silence at that time, while not an admission, could nevertheless be used to cast doubt on his story at trial. See also People v. Bowen, 65 A.D.2d 364, 411 N.Y.S.2d 573 (1st Dep't 1978), aff'd, 50 N.Y.2d 915, 431 N.Y.S.2d 449, 409 N.E.2d 924 (1980) (police officer made no statement at scene of crime and this could be used to impeach his trial testimony).

33. People v. Conyers, 52 N.Y.2d 454, 459-59, 438 N.Y.S.2d 741, 743, 420 N.E.2d 933, 935 (1981).

34. American Lith. Co. v. Dorrance-Sullivan & Co., 241 N.Y. 306, 150 N.E. 125 (1925)(in response to plaintiff's statement of charges, defendant wrote a letter, but did not question the correctness of the charges, and this constituted an admission). The operative word is "acquiesce." In Gurney, Becker & Bourne, Inc. v. Benderson Development Co., Inc., 47 N.Y.2d 995, 420 N.Y.S.2d 212, 394 N.E.2d 282 (1979), because there was no express or implied assent to its correctness, and there were unfulfilled conditions which resulted in an incomplete statement, no admission could be found. See also Bernstein v. Tisch, 102 A.D.2d 778, 477 N.Y.S.2d 149 (1st Dep't 1984), where the claim was characterized as an "account stated." Defendant's silence could not be construed as an assent where the account stated was only an approximation and some aspects of plaintiff's services had not been completed.

35. Matter of Barnes, 37 Misc.2d 833, 836, 237 N.Y.S.2d 183, 186-87 (Surr.Ct. N.Y.Co.1962)("There is 'no rule of law which requires a person to enter into correspondence with another in reference to a matter in dispute between them, or which holds that silence should be regarded as an admission against the party to whom the letter is addressed'"(citing Gray v. Kaufman Dairy & Ice-Cream Co., 162 N.Y. 388, 398, 56 N.E. 903, 905 (1900)). See also George v. State of New York, 134 A.D.2d 847, 521 N.Y.S.2d 593 (4th Dep't 1987)(in taking case, state's use of claimant's appraisal report in formulating its own appraisal was not an acquiescence or an admission as to the correctness of claimant's report); Paulsen v. Catherwood, 27 A.D.2d 493, 280 N.Y.S.2d 491 (3d Dep't 1967) (where claimant for unemployment benefits did not respond when accused by employer of intoxication, his silence did not amount to an admission).

36. Hayes v. Claessens, 234 N.Y. 230, 137 N.E. 313 (1922)(letters written by one owner of bank account were competent as admissions both as against her and as against the other owner that their interest was joint and not as tenants in common).

37. Chadwick v. Fonner, 69 N.Y. 404 (1877)(oral admission made by one who at the time he held title to land, to the effect he had contracted by parol to sell the land to another, and had received compensation, is competent evidence against all persons claiming title under or through him).

38. Murdock v. Waterman, 145 N.Y. 55, 39 N.E. 829 (1895)(admissions by a joint obligor are not automatically admissible against the other joint obligor—they would had to have been authorized).

ated New York authority, and such a questionable rationale, that Professor Morgan was prompted to say:

> The dogma of vicarious admissions, as soon as it passes beyond recognized principles of representation, baffles the understanding. Joint ownership, joint obligation, privity of title, each and all furnish no criterion of credibility, no aid in the evaluation of testimony.[39]

McCormick points out that the doctrine does not apply to tenants in common, colegatees or codevisees.[40] The Proposed New York Code of Evidence makes no provision for privity as a basis of admissibility and it is stated in the comment to Proposed New York Evidence Code § 802(b)(1) that the privity basis should be abandoned.[41]

In the relationship of principal and surety, admissions of the former are admissible against the latter when suit is brought on the bond. The rule in *Hatch v. Elkins*[42] was that only statements that were made concurrently with the acts of the principal's defalcations could be used; but in *Letendre v. Hartford Accident and Indemnity Co.*,[43] the rule was modified to allow the principal's admissions to the police made after the events to come in against the surety.[44]

d. Representative Capacity

Both the federal[45] and proposed state rules[46] provide for the admissibility of statements made by a party in his individual and representative capacity. Unlike the Federal Rule, which allows the statement in *either* an individual or representative capacity, the proposed New York rule would limit the statement to use against the party in the capacity in which it was made, i.e., if the declarant is the executor of an estate, statements made by him that he was obligated on a note would be admissible against him individually, but not admissible against the estate.[47] Presumably under the federal rule the admission would have a dual effect.[48]

39. Morgan, "Admissions," 12 Wash. L.Rev. 181, 202 (1937).

40. McCormick § 260, at 170.

41. It is noted in the comment that such statements might be admissible as statements against interest under that hearsay excepted, provided, of course, that the declarant is unavailable and the statement was against interest at the time made.

42. 65 N.Y. 489 (1879).

43. 21 N.Y.2d 518, 289 N.Y.S.2d 183, 236 N.E.2d 467 (1968).

44. The Letendre case is more prominent for its holding that the principal's statements to the police could be introduced as substantive evidence because the principal was on the stand and could be cross-examined. Id. at 522, 289 N.Y.S.2d at 187, 236 N.E.2d at 469 (1968). See § 801(1).2(a), supra.

45. Federal Rule 801(d)(2)(A).

46. Proposed New York Evidence Code § 803(b)(1).

47. Commercial Trading Co., Inc. v. Tucker, 80 A.D.2d 779, 437 N.Y.S.2d 86 (1st Dep't 1981).

48. This distinction is somewhat hard to make. Thus, for instance, if a guardian makes an admission that he had neglected to pay a medical bill occasioned by the ward's injuries, how does one know in which capacity he made the statement? In the Commercial Trading case, note 47 supra, the court noted that the executor made the admission in answers to interrogatories addressed to him individually. 80 A.D.2d at 780, 437 N.Y.S.2d at 87.

§ 802.2   HEARSAY   Ch. 8

e. Adoptive Admissions

Upon hearing a commotion outdoors the owner steps outside and then returns, telling her guest that she is sorry but her dog bit one of the guest's children. Declarant obviously was told this by someone on the scene, but her adoption of that account makes it hers and seals its admissibility against her.[49] But if declarant had said that her children had told her that the dog bit the visitor's child, we could have a different outcome. In *Cox v. State*,[50] an entry in a hospital report sought to be used against defendant as an admission was ruled out since it was reported in the statement that another patient told the entrant that plaintiff's incompetent had been pushed. That entry was clearly based on acknowledged hearsay and was in no way adopted. This distinction was recognized early on in *Reed v. McCord*,[51] where it was held that no admission would result were the declarant to acknowledge that she was given the information by another;[52] but in *Reed* itself the court was willing to accept as an unqualified admission the party's straightforward statement concerning the condition of a machine even though the declarant had been informed by another.

A good deal of litigation arises in cases involving life and accident policies where statements made by insureds or insureds' physicians are sought to be used against the insurer on the premise that the insurer, the party, somehow adopted them.[53] Thus, where the insurance company submitted papers as part of its case, it adopted the insured's physician's statement contained therein as proof of death, even though this was contrary to the beneficiary's own statement.[54] In a similar case, defendant's adjuster's estimate of plaintiff's loss wound up in papers submitted by the insurer on a motion and was thus considered adopted by the insurer.[55]

Adoption of another's statement or position by the hearer can also be manifested by silence in a situation calling for a contrary statement by the hearer. This is discussed in subdivision b, above.

f. Statements by the Party's Agent or Servant

Federal Rules of Evidence 801(d)(2)(C) and (D) provide two very closely related categories of statements made by an agent. Subpart (C) refers to statements by a person authorized by a party to make statements concerning a subject, and subpart (D) refers to statements by

---

49. See Berkowitz v. Simone, 96 R.I. 11, 188 A.2d 665 (1963).

50. 3 N.Y.2d 693, 171 N.Y.S.2d 818, 148 N.E.2d 879 (1958).

51. 160 N.Y. 330, 54 N.E. 737 (1899).

52. See also Flynn v. Manhattan & Bronx Surface Transit Operating Auth., 61 N.Y.2d 769, 473 N.Y.S.2d 154, 461 N.E.2d 291 (1984)(bus driver's statement that he had been told by passenger that he had hit the bicyclist not an admission).

53. Rudolph v. John Hancock Mut. Life Ins. Co., 251 N.Y. 208, 167 N.E. 223 (1929).

See also Yannon v. RCA Corp., 100 A.D.2d 966, 475 N.Y.S.2d 107 (2d Dep't 1984)(statements contrary to defendant's interests were submitted on motion for summary judgment and were ruled adopted as admissions against defendant).

54. Miller v. Nationwide Mutual Fire Ins. Co., 100 A.D.2d 727, 473 N.Y.S.2d 658 (4th Dep't 1984).

55. Taylor v. Commercial Bank, 174 N.Y. 181, 66 N.E. 726 (1903); McCormick § 259, at 157.

agents or servants concerning an employment-related matter made during the employment relationship. A fundamental difference between the existing New York state rule on agency statements and Federal Rule 801(d)(2)(D) is that virtually *all* statements made by an agent must have been authorized by the principal under the state rule, whereas the Federal Rule admits any statement made by a servant or agent whether authorized or not, so long as it was made during the relationship and concerns a matter within the scope of that relationship.

The New York rule that the agent's statement must have been authorized, the so-called "speaking agent" rule, is of ancient origin.[56] The Federal Rules' abandonment of this restriction is part of a trend to broaden the rule[57] which has not, however, persuaded the New York Court of Appeals. The Court of Appeals in *Loschiavo v. Port Authority of New York*[58] perpetuated the speaking agent rule on these facts: After plaintiff tripped and fell over a loose carpet in the "jetway" extending from defendant's airplane to the terminal, defendant's employee stated that other persons had tripped and fallen in the same place. Under the prevailing New York rule adhered to in this case, the statement was inadmissible against the employer because the employee had no authority to make such statements. The Court of Appeals noted that the rule has been widely criticized but said any modification is a legislative matter.[59]

The necessary authorization may, of course, be express, such as where the agent's job description includes the authority to speak for the principal. It may not, however, be deduced from the agent's own out-of-court statements.[60] The speaking authority may be drawn from circumstantial evidence. Thus, in *Spett v. President Monroe Bldg. & Manufacturing Corp.*,[61] where a statement harmful to the defendant building owner was uttered by her husband, the "general foreman," the Court of Appeals reversed exclusion of the evidence stating:

> In the instant case Albert Levine's authority as agent for his wife, the defendant here, seems clearly to have been broad enough to include an admission of Harvey's responsibility for placement of the skid receivable against the defendant. Though called merely "general foreman," Levine was apparently the person who *ran* Harvey, in whom complete managerial responsibility for the enterprise was vested.[62]

The speaking agent rule, which is strictly applied in criminal cases,[63] may not be as rigidly applied in civil cases. *Nowack v. Metropolitan St.*

---

56. McCormick § 259, at 156–57.

57. Id. at 158.

58. 58 N.Y.2d 1040, 462 N.Y.S.2d 440, 448 N.E.2d 1351 (1983).

59. Id. at 1041–42, 46 N.Y.S.2d at 441, 448 N.E.2d at 1352.

60. Leary v. Albany Brewing Co., 77 App.Div. 6, 79 N.Y.S. 130 (4th Dep't 1902). But in Steuerwald v. Jackson, 123 App.Div. 569, 108 N.Y.S. 41 (2d Dep't 1908), it was held that the agent's testimony at trial was competent to prove the agency.

61. 19 N.Y.2d 203, 278 N.Y.S.2d 826, 225 N.E.2d 527 (1967).

62. Id. at 206, 278 N.Y.S.2d at 829, 225 N.E.2d at 529 (emphasis in original).

63. See People v. Buzzi, 238 N.Y. 390, 144 N.E. 653 (1924)(unauthorized bribe attempt not admissible in criminal case).

§ 802.2　　　　　　　HEARSAY　　　　　　　Ch. 8

Ry. Co.[64] is the seminal authority for the proposition that where a corporate party to a lawsuit gave authority to an investigator to "see to" witnesses, he need not have been given specific authority to offer them bribes in order for the bribe attempts to be used as admissions. The court based this holding on the rule that corporate principals are vicariously liable for the torts of their agents committed within the scope of the agency even though the agents were not authorized to commit torts. This would seem to be a sound basis upon which the Court of Appeals could broaden the rule generally to conform to the federal rule. But the holding in *Nowak*, the civil case, was confined to its own facts in the criminal case, *People v. Buzzi*,[65] where the court held that the rule allowing agents' statements without evidence of express authorization to speak should be limited to instances where the principal is a corporation.[66] There was no language to the effect that only in criminal cases would proof be needed of authorization to make bribe attempts or suborn evidence, yet at least one court has so construed the case.[67] A sampling of more recent cases shows that the *Buzzi* authorization requirement is indeed applied in criminal cases;[68] but the language in one of those cases would seem to justify its application in non-corporate party civil cases as well: "In the absence of such knowledge, efforts by friends to suppress evidence has no tendency to justify an inference of consciousness of guilt by defendant."[69]

Two other areas should be treated separately from the general rule as expressed in *Loschiavo*. Lawyers, unless the lawyer-client privilege is implicated,[70] seem clothed with enough authority by their clients so that their utterances, even if not binding as they would be in pleadings (*see* § 802.1 *supra*), can at least serve as admissions against the clients.[71]

64. 166 N.Y. 433, 60 N.E. 32 (1901).

65. 238 N.Y. 390, 398–399, 144 N.E. 653, 656 (1924).

66. Id.

67. Nieves v. City of New York, 109 N.Y.S.2d 556, 559 (Sup.Ct.N.Y.Co.1951), aff'd, 280 App.Div. 972, 116 N.Y.S.2d 927 (1st Dep't 1952)("Whatever may be the rule in criminal cases, People v. Buzzi, supra, it is my opinion that, in civil cases, subornation of perjury by an attorney is chargeable to the client he represents, and that this is particularly true where, as here, the client permits the same attorney to represent him after he has knowledge of the charges against the lawyer.").

68. See, e.g., People v. Kress, 284 N.Y. 452, 464, 31 N.E.2d 898, 904 (1940) ("The unauthorized acts of third parties may not be used to connect defendant with the commission of the crime."); People v. Upshaw, 138 A.D.2d 761, 762, 526 N.Y.S.2d 575, 576 (2d Dep't 1988)(since there was no evidence defendant had asked C to "speak to" the complaining witness about dropping the charges, there was no basis for admitting that evidence against defendant); People v. Murphy, 128 A.D.2d 177, 183, 515 N.Y.S.2d 895, 899 (3d Dep't 1987), order affirmed, 70 N.Y.2d 969, 525 N.Y.S.2d 834, 520 N.E.2d 552 (1988)(where defendant's clothing would appear to bear on the issues, defendant's failure to produce it could not be deemed to show consciousness of guilt without evidence showing that defendant somehow authorized its loss or destruction).

69. People v. Pignataro, 263 N.Y. 229, 237, 188 N.E. 720, 722 (1934).

70. In People v. Cassas, 84 N.Y.2d 718, 622 N.Y.S.2d 228, 646 N.E.2d 449 (1995), the client conferred with his lawyer shortly after killing his wife. The lawyer took the client to the police station, after verifying the murder, and explained to the police that the client killed his wife and explained where the gun with the client's fingerprints could be found. Since there was no showing of any waiver by the client of the privilege, the court held that the attorney's statements should have been suppressed.

71. McCormick § 259, at 163–64. One is left to speculate whether, had the individual's agent in the Nieves case (note 67, supra) not been a lawyer, the agent's unau-

Beyond that, where lawyers engage in settlement negotiations, they have "apparent authority" to bind the client, even if they have not been given express authority to settle for a certain amount.[72] Here, the viewpoint is that of the adversary who, because of the lawyer's representation in the case up to the settlement point, could reasonably believe the lawyer to have the necessary authority.[73] The second area is where a partner's admission can be used against the partnership,[74] but this grows out of a special relationship which might also have been included under the privity category, above.

Except for these three categories—subornation attempts in civil cases, lawyers' representations, and partners' statements—the *Loschiavo* rules remain rigidly adhered to.[75] On occasion, an agent's statement can be admitted on other grounds.[76] Finally, on the question whether the

thorized subornation attempt would have been admissible against the individual.

72. Hallock v. State of New York, 64 N.Y.2d 224, 231–32, 485 N.Y.S.2d 510, 514, 474 N.E.2d 1178, 1182 (1984)(this case defines the authority of the lawyer to speak for the client, but does not involve the question of whether an admission by the lawyer is binding on the client).

73. Id. at 231, 485 N.Y.S.2d at 513, 474 N.E.2d at 1181. See also Henry v. Gutenplan, 197 A.D.2d 608, 604 N.Y.S.2d 757 (2d Dep't 1993)(attorney had authority to bind client to a stipulation); Arvelo v. Multi Trucking, Inc., 194 A.D.2d 758, 759, 599 N.Y.S.2d 301 (2d Dep't 1993)(attorney had authority to bind client to settlement); Buckingham Manufacturing Co., Inc. v. Frank J. Koch, Jr., 194 A.D.2d 886, 888, 599 N.Y.S.2d 155, 156 (3d Dep't), leave to appeal denied, 82 N.Y.2d 658, 604 N.Y.S.2d 556, 624 N.E.2d 694 (1993)(settlement by attorney binding on client).

74. McCormick § 259, at 164.

75. See Risoli v. Long Island Lighting Co., 195 A.D.2d 543, 544, 600 N.Y.S.2d 497, 498 (2d Dep't), leave to appeal denied, 82 N.Y.2d 661, 605 N.Y.S.2d 7, 625 N.E.2d 592 (1993)(where plaintiff injured in gas explosion in defendant's restaurant, assistant manager's statement that a waitress had earlier reported the smell of gas not admissible); Kelleher v. F.M.E. Auto Leasing Corp., 192 A.D.2d 581, 583, 596 N.Y.S.2d 136, 138 (2d Dep't 1993)(statement of taxi driver that dispatcher told him to get rid of fare, an elderly man who was ejected into the snow and froze to death, not admissible as an admission against the taxi company, but could be admitted as a declaration against the driver's interest); Fruin–Colnon Corp. v. Niagara Frontier Transportation Auth., 180 A.D.2d 222, 234, 585 N.Y.S.2d 248, 256 (4th Dep't 1992)(an inculpatory letter not admissible where written by "subconsultants who had been asked to express an opinion to defendant, not to make liability concessions on his behalf"); Nordhauser v. N.Y. City Health and Hospitals Corp., 176 A.D.2d 787, 791, 575 N.Y.S.2d 117, 120 (2d Dep't 1991)(emergency room nurse's statement to investigators as to time plaintiff entered emergency room, not admissible against hospital since she was not a "speaking agent"); Sherman v. Tamarack Lodge, 146 A.D.2d 767, 768, 537 N.Y.S.2d 249, 250 (2d Dep't), appeal denied, 74 N.Y.2d 613, 547 N.Y.S.2d 847, 547 N.E.2d 102 (1989) (statement by an unidentified employee of defendant made to a busboy that the busboy was to have cleaned up, not admissible).

In People v. Romero, 78 N.Y.2d 355, 575 N.Y.S.2d 802, 581 N.E.2d 1048 (1991), it was held that an interpreter's translation of statements made by a non-English-speaking opponent are admissible on an agency theory unless the interpreter has a motive to falsify.

76. Spontaneous Statements: Compare Golden v. Horn & Hardart Co., 244 App. Div. 92, 278 N.Y.S. 385 (1st Dep't 1935), aff'd, 270 N.Y. 544, 200 N.E. 309 (1936)(assistant manager's statement to employee about directions to clean stairs admissible as spontaneous statement against defendant restaurant), with Sherman v. Tamarack Lodge, 146 A.D.2d 767, 768, 537 N.Y.S.2d 249, 250 (2d Dep't 1989)(here, statement by an unidentified employee to busboy to clean up was ruled not admissible as spontaneous statement). Declaration against interest: Kelleher v. F.M.E. Auto Leasing Corp., 192 A.D.2d 581, 583, 596 N.Y.S.2d 136, 138 (2d Dep't 1993) (taxi driver's statement to police that he was ordered by dispatcher to eject fare from cab admissible as declaration against interest where driver was unavailable). See also Kasper v. Buffalo Bills, 42 A.D.2d 87, 345

§ 802.2　　　　　　　　HEARSAY　　　　　　　　Ch. 8

principal-agent relationship exists, the Appellate Division has held that a victim's statement harmful to the prosecution's case is not an admission against the People in its case against defendant.[77]

g. Coconspirator's Statements

As a special application of the agency rule, New York courts have long allowed the declaration of a conspirator made during the course of and in furtherance of the conspiracy to be admitted against a coconspirator.[78] The statement can be used not only to prove the coconspirator committed the crime of conspiracy but also to prove a coconspirator's commission of another crime for which the conspiracy was formed.[79] It is not necessary that in order for the statement to be admissible the declarant or the defendant have been charged with the crime of conspiracy.[80] "The basis for the rule permitting vicarious statements is the joint enterprise relationship between the parties and the assurance of truthfulness derived from the fact that the statement is against the declarant's penal interest."[81] There are essentially three components to the rule. In addition to the two already noted—that the statement must have been made during the ongoing conspiracy and in furtherance thereof—the third, that there must be a prima facie showing that a conspiracy existed independent of the conspirator's statements sought to be admitted, has been raised most often in the cases and will be dealt with first.

Undoubtedly the premier case in New York dealing with a coconspirator's statements is *People v. Salko*.[82] The Appellate Division had found that there was insufficient admissible evidence apart from declarant's statements implicating defendant to establish the needed prima facie showing of a conspiracy.[83] The Court of Appeals, however, identified some of declarant's conduct as nonassertive and declarant's words as "verbal parts of acts" (*see* § 801.1(b), (c), *supra*), all of which was said to satisfactorily make out the conspiracy independent of the words of the

---

N.Y.S.2d 244 (4th Dep't 1973) (employee's admission was held inadmissible against his employer by the trial court because not spontaneous, but the Appellate Division held that the scope of the employee's authority had not been fully explored; that perhaps he was in a position of sufficient authority so that he could be found to be a speaking agent); Strauch v. Hirschman, 40 A.D.2d 711, 336 N.Y.S.2d 678 (2d Dep't 1972)(defendant's physical education director's admission was inadmissible against defendant because it did not fit within the spontaneous declarations exception, and no mention was made as to any possible speaking authority).

77. People v. Esteves, 152 A.D.2d 406, 412–13, 549 N.Y.S.2d 30, 34 (2d Dep't 1989), appeal denied, 75 N.Y.2d 918, 555 N.Y.S.2d 37, 554 N.E.2d 74 (1990).

78. People v. Salko, 47 N.Y.2d 230, 237, 417 N.Y.S.2d 894, 898, 391 N.E.2d 976, 980, reargument denied, 47 N.Y.2d 1012, 420 N.Y.S.2d 1025, 394 N.E.2d 308 (1979).

79. Id.

80. People v. Stewart, 173 A.D.2d 877, 570 N.Y.S.2d 834 (2d Dep't), appeal denied, 78 N.Y.2d 1081, 577 N.Y.S.2d 245, 583 N.E.2d 957 (1991).

81. People v. Liccione, 63 A.D.2d 305, 320, 407 N.Y.S.2d 753, 761 (4th Dep't 1978), aff'd, 50 N.Y.2d 850, 430 N.Y.S.2d 36, 407 N.E.2d 1333, reargument denied, 51 N.Y.2d 770, 432 N.Y.S.2d 1029, 411 N.E.2d 799 (1980).

82. 47 N.Y.2d 230, 417 N.Y.S.2d 894, 391 N.E.2d 976 (1979).

83. Salko, People v., 60 A.D.2d 307, 310, 401 N.Y.S.2d 494, 496 (1st Dep't 1978).

declarant that actually linked defendant to the conspiracy.[84] Beyond that, however, defendant himself had made statements to an assistant district attorney and the arresting officer which made out a conspiracy; these statements were perfectly admissible and could have established the conspiracy without need for the aforementioned nonassertive acts and statements.[85] Many years later it was noted by the Court of Appeals that in *Salko* the statements by defendant would indeed have been sufficient to make out the conspiracy.[86] The *Salko* court also held that the coconspirator's rule posed no affront to the defendant's right of confrontation.[87] Despite this ruling, the Appellate Division, First Department, in *People v. Persico*[88] held that, as a prerequisite to admissibility of a coconspirator's out-of-court declaration, the prosecutor must either call the declarant to the stand or establish the declarant's unavailability.[89] Although the United States Supreme Court had held that unavailability was not required under the federal right of confrontation, as discussed in § 802.3(d) *infra*, the First Department concluded that the New York State Constitution imposed a stricter standard. The Court of Appeals has not passed on this, and the *Persico* decision has been questioned.[90]

Note that only a prima facie showing of the conspiracy need be made,[91] not a showing by a preponderance of the evidence,[92] and certainly not a showing beyond a reasonable doubt.[93]

---

84. 47 N.Y.2d at 238–40, 417 N.Y.S.2d at 899–900, 391 N.E.2d at 981–82.

85. Id.

86. People v. Bac Tran, 80 N.Y.2d 170, 179–80, 589 N.Y.S.2d 845, 851, 603 N.E.2d 950, 956 (1992), reargument denied, 81 N.Y.2d 784, 594 N.Y.S.2d 721, 610 N.E.2d 394 (1993).

87. Salko, 47 N.Y.2d at 241, 417 N.Y.S.2d at 901, 391 N.E.2d at 983. In a prior case, People v. Rastelli, 37 N.Y.2d 240, 244, 371 N.Y.S.2d 911, 914, 333 N.E.2d 182, 183–84, cert. denied, 423 U.S. 995, 96 S.Ct. 421, 46 L.Ed.2d 369 (1975), the court held that the coconspirator's hearsay exception did not violate the confrontation right; that the rule announced in Bruton v. United States, 391 U.S. 123, 88 S.Ct. 1620, 20 L.Ed.2d 476 (1968), involved the admissibility of a nontestifying codefendant's confession implicating defendant, which was quite different. Dutton v. Evans, 400 U.S. 74, 91 S.Ct. 210, 27 L.Ed.2d 213 (1970), held that the confrontation right did not apply to a conspirator's statement. These cases predate refinements of the rationale developed in the 1980s, supporting the holding that the confrontation right is not violated by coconspirators' statements. See United States v. Inadi, 475 U.S. 387, 106 S.Ct. 1121, 89 L.Ed.2d 390 (1986), and Bourjaily v. United States, 483 U.S. 171, 107 S.Ct. 2775, 97 L.Ed.2d 144 (1987), both discussed in § 802.3(d) infra.

88. 157 A.D.2d 339, 349, 556 N.Y.S.2d 262, 269 (1st Dep't), appeal denied, 76 N.Y.2d 895, 561 N.Y.S.2d 558, 562 N.E.2d 883 (1990).

89. Id.

90. See People v. Cook, 159 Misc.2d 430, 436–38, 603 N.Y.S.2d 979, 983–84 (Sup.Ct.Kings Co.1993), where the court referred to White v. Illinois, 502 U.S. 346, 112 S.Ct. 736, 116 L.Ed.2d 848 (1992), and other more recent rulings in New York including People v. Brown, 80 N.Y.2d 729, 594 N.Y.S.2d 696, 610 N.E.2d 369 (1993), the present sense impression case discussed in § 803(1).1(a) infra.

91. Salko, 47 N.Y.2d at 237, 417 N.Y.S.2d at 898, 391 N.E.2d at 980.

92. People v. Bell, 48 N.Y.2d 913, 915, 425 N.Y.S.2d 52, 53, 401 N.E.2d 175, 176 (1979), reargument denied, 49 N.Y.2d 801, 426 N.Y.S.2d 1029, 403 N.E.2d 466 (1980)(even though the preponderance rule was not applicable, the district attorney failed to object to the judge's preponderance charge and was thereby bound by that standard, which had not been satisfied).

93. People v. Malagon, 50 N.Y.2d 954, 431 N.Y.S.2d 460, 409 N.E.2d 934 (1980)(even though the reasonable doubt rule was not applicable, the district attorney neglected to take exception to the court's reasonable doubt charge).

§ 802.2 HEARSAY Ch. 8

The element of an independent showing of the conspiracy is frequently passed upon by the courts.[94] The other two elements—that the statements be made in furtherance of the conspiracy and during the course thereof—seem rarely to raise issues in the New York cases. As to the "in furtherance" requirement, *People v. Liccione*[95] is probably the most prominent, albeit inconclusive, example. Must the statement be an operative element of the conspiracy, or only pertain to the fact that a conspiracy is afoot? The second theory seems to have been adopted by the Appellate Division majority. In that case, as the hired assailant attacked the victim, he told her that her husband had hired him for the job. The dissent would not have allowed that statement (admissible through the victim's dying declaration) because it was unnecessary to the carrying out of the conspiracy.[96] The majority conceived of the statements as being part of the "res gestae"—words accompanying the commission of the crime—stating: "The act was in furtherance of the conspiracy, the words in explanation of the act were part of the res gestae, and the assailant's statements were admissible against defendant [husband] as declarations of a coconspirator * * *."[97] In its memorandum order of affirmance, the Court of Appeals noted the argument that the statement was not made in the furtherance of the conspiracy, but declined to pass on it since it had not been preserved for review.[98]

As to the "course of the conspiracy," certainly statements made "where the transaction, the criminal design, is still pending and unaccomplished"[99] qualify. The problem is determining when the conspiracy has ended. The Court of Appeals in *People v. Storrs*,[100] adopted the rule that the conspiracy continues even past the accomplishment of the planned crime where statements " 'were not recitals of past occurrences, but were connected with acts done evidently to shield the conspirators from the consequences of their crime.' "[101] Also, "[i]n the case of a larceny perpetrated by two or more, the conspiracy continues so long as

---

94. People v. Bac Tran, 80 N.Y.2d 170, 179, 589 N.Y.S.2d 845, 850–51, 603 N.E.2d 950, 955–56 (1992), reargument denied, 81 N.Y.2d 784, 594 N.Y.S.2d 721, 610 N.E.2d 394 (1993)(in a bribery case evidence that coconspirator paid undercover investigator $100 to influence investigator's handling of hotel safety violations did not show that defendant was involved in scheme, and thus the foundation was not laid for other statements by the coconspirator implicating defendant); People v. Alwadish, 67 N.Y.2d 973, 974, 502 N.Y.S.2d 989, 990, 494 N.E.2d 94, 95 (1986)(defendant's statements to an undercover officer concerning his collaboration with D provided the necessary prima facie independent showing of the conspiracy so that D's statements implicating defendant would be admissible under the rule); People v. Sanders, 56 N.Y.2d 51, 62–63, 451 N.Y.S.2d 30, 34, 436 N.E.2d 480, 484, reargument denied, 57 N.Y.2d 674, 454 N.Y.S.2d 1032, 439 N.E.2d 1247 (1982)(defendant's own statements established the prima facie case of conspiracy allowing in a coconspirator's statements implicating him); People v. Berkowitz, 50 N.Y.2d 333, 341–342, 428 N.Y.S.2d 927, 931, 406 N.E.2d 783, 787 (1980)(defendant's own actions made out the conspiracy).

95. 63 A.D.2d 305, 407 N.Y.S.2d 753 (4th Dep't 1978), aff'd, 50 N.Y.2d 850, 430 N.Y.S.2d 36, 407 N.E.2d 1333 (1980), reargument denied, 51 N.Y.2d 770, 432 N.Y.S.2d 1029, 411 N.E.2d 799 (1980).

96. Id. at 324, 407 N.Y.S.2d at 764.

97. Id. at 323, 407 N.Y.S.2d at 763.

98. 50 N.Y.2d 850, 851, 430 N.Y.S.2d 36, 37, 407 N.E.2d 1333, 1334 (1980).

99. People v. Storrs, 207 N.Y. 147, 158, 100 N.E. 730, 733 (1912); see also People v. Marshall, 306 N.Y. 223, 226, 117 N.E.2d 265, 266 (1954).

100. Storrs, supra note 99.

101. Id. at 159, 100 N.E. at 733 (quoting Commonwealth v. Smith, 151 Mass. 491, 496 (1890)).

the stolen property has not been divided or disposed of according to the plan of the conspirators."[102] This latter dictum was utilized recently where the Appellate Division stated: "Additionally, because the statement was made prior to disposition of the proceeds of the larceny according to the conspirator's plan, it was made during the course of the conspiracy * * *."[103] One case casts some doubt on the extent to which post-crime activities can perpetuate the conspiracy;[104] and another provides an excellent example of when a conspiracy has definitely ended.[105]

Library References:

West's Key No. Digests, Criminal Law ⟢405–410, 419(8), 422–428; Evidence ⟢200–265.

§ 802.3 A Party's Statement—Federal

a. Pleadings

Having established the basic distinction between judicial and evidentiary admissions in § 802.1 we note here that insofar as pleadings are concerned:

[a] pleading prepared by an attorney is an admission by one presumptively authorized to speak for his principal * * *. When a pleading is amended or withdrawn, the superseded portion ceases to be a conclusive judicial admission; but it still

---

102. 207 N.Y. at 159, 100 N.E.2d at 734.

103. People v. Rivera, 192 A.D.2d 363, 364, 595 N.Y.S.2d 782 (1st Dep't), leave to appeal denied, 82 N.Y.2d 758, 603 N.Y.S.2d 1000, 624 N.E.2d 186 (1993).

104. People v. Wisan, 132 Misc.2d 691, 693, 505 N.Y.S.2d 361, 362 (Sup.Ct.Richmond Co.1986). After the murder of defendant's husband was accomplished the weapon was disposed of, the parties escaped the scene, and the money was paid the defendant. These acts did not extend the conspiracy, said the court, relying on Grunewald v. United States, 353 U.S. 391, 400–406, 77 S.Ct. 963, 974, 1 L.Ed.2d 931, 941–44 (1957); Lutwak v. United States, 344 U.S. 604, 615–20, 73 S.Ct. 481, 490, 97 L.Ed. 593, 602–605 (1953). The court stated in Wisan that the Supreme Court had held that the mere existence of a conspiracy to commit a crime does not imply a continuing conspiracy to conceal its detection and apprehension of the conspirators after the main object of the conspiracy has been accomplished. The court noted that there was some uncertainty in this state regarding the question of whether the payment of money to a coconspirator as a quid pro quo for his participation can be considered an act committed in furtherance of the conspiracy. See People v. Teeter, 62 A.D.2d 1158, 404 N.Y.S.2d 210 (4th Dep't 1978), aff'd, 47 N.Y.2d 1002, 420 N.Y.S.2d 217, 394 N.E.2d 286 (1979); People v. Wolff, 24 A.D.2d 828, 264 N.Y.S.2d 40 (4th Dep't 1965); People v. De Cabia, 10 Misc.2d 923, 122 N.Y.S.2d 1004 (Sup.Ct.Nassau Co.1958), aff'd, 8 A.D.2d 825, 190 N.Y.S.2d 142 (2d Dep't), aff'd, 7 N.Y.2d 823, 196 N.Y.S.2d 701, 164 N.E.2d 720 (1959); People v. Hines, 168 Misc. 453, 6 N.Y.S.2d 2 (Sup.Ct.New York Co.1938), aff'd, 258 App. Div. 466, 17 N.Y.S.2d 141 (1st Dep't), modified, 284 N.Y. 93, 29 N.E.2d 483 (1940).

It was stated further in Wisan that even in People v. Ortiz, 100 A.D.2d 6, 473 N.Y.S.2d 288 (4th Dep't), leave to appeal denied, 62 N.Y.2d 809, 477 N.Y.S.2d 1034, 465 N.E.2d 1277 (1984), where the court favored the idea that payments made after the formation of the conspiracy were part of the conspiracy, "confines itself solely to the 'payment [of money] to a coconspirator for his *prospective services* in carrying out the object of the conspiracy' * * *." 132 Misc.2d at 692–94, 505 N.Y.S.2d at 362–363 (emphasis in original).

105. In People v. Gotti, 146 Misc.2d 793, 552 N.Y.S.2d 485 (Sup.Ct.N.Y.Co. 1990), after completion of the crime and resulting arrests, an informant secretly recorded a conversation with a gang member at Rikers Island Jail and the People unsuccessfully argued that a continuing conspiratorial relationship validated use of the statement.

remains as a statement once seriously made by an authorized agent, and as such it is competent evidence of the facts stated, though controvertible, like any other extra-judicial admission made by a party or his agent * * *. If the agent made the admission without adequate information, that goes to its weight, not to its admissibility.[1]

On the basis of this fundamental rule, the Second Circuit has held that statements in superseded opening statements[2] and superseded bills of particulars,[3] while having lost any binding effect they may have had as originally presented, may retain value as evidentiary admissions. Also, the inculpatory testimony of a defendant can be introduced against him at a second trial, even though he does not take the stand.[4] Withdrawn guilty pleas in criminal cases, of course, have no further effect.[5]

The remainder of this section will be devoted to evidentiary admissions as provided for in Federal Rule 801(d)(2).[6]

b. Admissions by a Party, by Statements, Acts, Adoption or in a Representative Capacity

Under concepts set forth in § 802.1 *supra*, we know that a party's statement in order to be an admission need not necessarily be trustworthy. It merely needs to be antithetical to the party's interest at trial. Thus, the United States Supreme Court, relying on Rule 801(d)(2)(A), stated, "* * * [W]e fail to understand why, on any approach to the case, the out-of-court representations of respondent himself that he and Gayle Graff were husband and wife were considered to be inadmissible against him. * * * [T]he respondent's own out-of-court admissions would surmount all objections * * * and would be admissible for whatever inferences the trial judge could reasonably draw concerning joint occupancy of the east bedroom."[7] In another typical case it was held that where a document submitted by a party stated accrued interest, that could be

---

§ 802.3

1. United States v. GAF Corp., 928 F.2d 1253, 1259–60 (2d Cir.1991) (quoting Kunglig Jarnvagsstyrelsen v. Dexter and Carpenter, Inc., 32 F.2d 195, 198 (2d Cir.), cert. denied, 280 U.S. 579, 50 S.Ct. 32, 74 L.Ed. 629 (1929)).

2. United States v. McKeon, 738 F.2d 26, 30–33 (2d Cir.1984). But see text at note 23 infra.

3. United States v. GAF Corp., 928 F.2d 1253, 1259–60 (2d Cir.1991).

4. Edmonds v. United States, 273 F.2d 108 (D.C.Cir.1959), cert. denied, 362 U.S. 977, 80 S.Ct. 1062, 4 L.Ed.2d 1012 (1960). This case was decided long before enactment of Federal Rule of Evidence 804(b)(1), the prior testimony exception, which may account for the court's placing admissibility on the ground that it contained admissions.

5. Kercheval v. United States, 274 U.S. 220, 47 S.Ct. 582, 71 L.Ed. 1009 (1927). See § 410.2 supra.

6. Fed.R.Evid. 801(d)(2):

(2) Admission by party-opponent. The statement is offered against a party and is (A) the party's own statement, in either an individual or a representative capacity or (B) a statement of which the party has manifested an adoption or belief in its truth, or (C) a statement by a person authorized by the party to make a statement concerning the subject, or (D) a statement by the party's agent or servant concerning a matter within the scope of the agency or employment, made during the existence of the relationship, or (E) a statement by a coconspirator of a party during the course and in furtherance of the conspiracy.

7. United States v. Matlock, 415 U.S. 164, 172, 94 S.Ct. 988, 994, 39 L.Ed.2d 242, 250 (1974).

taken as an admission on that point, even though the document would not be "persuasive" as a business record under Federal Rule of Evidence 803(6),[8] and where a party's statement would not qualify as a coconspirator's statement, it was nevertheless admissible as a party's own statement offered against him.[9] The liberality with which the admission is treated in the Second Circuit is illustrated in *O'Neal v. Morgan*,[10] where it was held that plaintiff's showing that one of several defendants made an admission over the telephone cast the burden on each defendant to show that he was not the declarant.[11] This was a 42 U.S.C. § 1983 civil rights case, and it remains questionable whether this holding would extend so as to force each of several defendants in a criminal case to explain why he was not the declarant.[12]

The Second Circuit annals suffer no lack of examples of admissions as evidenced by the party's acts,[13] and admissions by way of adoption.[14]

As to statements made in a representative capacity, Federal Rule 801(d)(2)(A) is not as narrow as the New York rule (*see* § 802.2(d) *supra*). The Advisory Committee's Note following Rule 801 states:

> A party's own statement is the classic example of an admission. If he has a representative capacity and the statement is offered against him in that capacity, no inquiry whether he was acting

---

8. Omar Intern. v. ALAF, 817 F.Supp. 394, 399 (S.D.N.Y.1993).

9. United States v. Pedroza, 750 F.2d 187, 202 (2d Cir.1984), cert. denied sub nom., Osorno v. United States, 479 U.S. 842 107 S.Ct. 151, 93 L.Ed.2d 92 (1986).

10. 637 F.2d 846, 850–52 (2d Cir.1980), cert. denied, 451 U.S. 971, 101 S.Ct. 2050, 68 L.Ed.2d 351 (1981).

11. Id. The answering codefendant was identified, although he did not give his name, because he identified himself as the codefendants' partner.

12. Id. The court drew an analogy from tort law and Prosser's illustration of the plaintiff hit by a bullet which could have been fired by either of several shooters and the burden falls on each of the latter to show he was not the culprit. Prosser, Law of Torts 243 and nn.54–57 (4th ed.1971).

13. See Hellenic Lines Ltd. v. Gulf Oil Corp., 340 F.2d 398, 401 (2d Cir. 1965)("[The letter] was affirmative proof of the assertions contained in it and Gulf's reply could be found to imply concurrence or, to the extent it failed to respond to these assertions, under circumstances which reasonably called for a reply, could be found to constitute an admission by silence"); Harrington v. Sharff, 305 F.2d 333, 338 (2d Cir.1962)(in both civil and criminal cases "evidence of flight from the scene of a [crime] accident is admissible * * * tending to prove that the fleer believes himself to be responsible for the mishap"); United States v. Heitner, 149 F.2d 105, 107 (2d Cir.), cert. denied sub. nom., Cryne v. U.S., 326 U.S. 727, 66 S.Ct. 33, 90 L.Ed. 432, reh. denied, 326 U.S. 809, 66 S.Ct. 164, 90 L.Ed. 494 (1945)(while an out-and-out presumption of guilt may not be derived from evidence of flight, such evidence at least gives rise to an inference of guilt).

14. See United States v. Shulman, 624 F.2d 384, 390 (2d Cir.1980)(good discussion of adoptive admissions, holding that declarant's statement need not necessarily incriminate the adopting defendant to be admissible against defendant); United States v. Costanzo, 581 F.2d 28, 34 (2d Cir.1978), cert. denied, 439 U.S. 1067, 99 S.Ct. 833, 59 L.Ed.2d 32 (1979) (statements by taxpayer's son, made in taxpayer's presence with his concurrence, were admissible against taxpayer); United States v. DiGiovanni, 544 F.2d 642, 645 (2d Cir.1976)(testimony of defendant's cellmate "relating a three-way conversation in which latter two described their roles in a bank robbery consisted of direct admissions or adoptions and was admissible"); United States v. Torres, 519 F.2d 723, 726, n.10 (2d Cir.), cert. denied, 423 U.S. 1019, 96 S.Ct. 457, 46 L.Ed.2d 392 (1975)(codefendant's response "all right" to narrative statement by another, seen as adopting that statement); Brownko Intern., Inc. v. Ogden Steel Co., 585 F.Supp. 1432, 1438 (S.D.N.Y.1983)(where minutes of board meeting not called to party's attention, it cannot be said that party adopted them or acquiesced in them).

§ 802.3   HEARSAY   Ch. 8

in the representative capacity in making the statement is required; the statement need only be relevant to representative affairs.

This is illustrated in the Third Circuit decision in *Matter of Special Federal Grand Jury*,[15] where it was held that even if an individual produced subpoenaed corporate records as a representative of the corporation, his individual fifth amendment rights could be jeopardized, and so he could assert the "act of production" protection (*see* discussion of the fifth amendment privilege in § 509.1 *supra*).

c. Statements Made by an Agent or Servant, and Statements Otherwise Authorized

Federal Rule 801(d)(2)(C) and (D) differ from the New York rule which requires that agents have "speaking authority" in order for their statements to be used against their principals (*see* § 802.2(f) *supra*). The Federal Rule requires only that the statement be made about matters within the scope of the agency and during the agency relationship.

Zaken v. Boerer,[16] a civil rights case charging pregnancy discrimination, illustrates the Second Circuit's liberal approach to the agency question. At trial, plaintiff was not allowed to introduce testimony of a former employee that defendant's vice-president of sales had told her that she was fired because of her pregnancy. On appeal this was seen as error since the agency relationship existed and, since hiring and firing was within declarant's province, the statement concerned a matter within the scope of the agency. Evidence that the declarant had been plotting against the defendant at the time the statement was made would go only to the weight to be given the statement.[17]

The statement sought to be introduced may not be relied upon to establish the agency relationship, but this may be proved by circumstantial evidence, said the court in *Pappas v. Middle Earth Condominium Ass'n*.[18] With respect to the declarant's availability at trial, the court stated:

> Nor is availability of the declarant relevant under Fed. R. Evid. 801(d)(2)(D). Although such availability may be a critical issue where dealing with hearsay statements that are otherwise generally inadmissible, *see* Fed. R. Evid. 804, Rule 801 defines certain statements *as not being hearsay*. It follows therefore that whether plaintiff should have made greater efforts to depose the unidentified declarant has no bearing on the issue of the proffered testimony's admissibility.[19]

---

15. 819 F.2d 56, 58–59 (3d Cir.1987).

16. 964 F.2d 1319, 1322–24 (2d Cir.), cert. denied, ___ U.S. ___, 113 S.Ct. 467, 121 L.Ed.2d 375 (1992).

17. Id. at 1323. See also Meschino v. Intern. Tel. and Tel. Corp., 563 F.Supp. 1066, 1072 (S.D.N.Y.1983)(statements similar to those in Zaken made in age discrimination suit).

18. 963 F.2d 534, 538 (2d Cir. 1992)(where plaintiff fell on icy walk owned by defendant, proof that declarant arrived at the scene with a shovel and bucket was proof enough of the necessary relationship).

19. Id. at 538 (emphasis in original).

The agency can arise out of nontraditional relationships,[20] but the usual case is unremarkable.[21] *United States v. Valencia*[22] is instructive with respect to statements by attorneys on behalf of their clients in criminal cases. The court refused to allow a defense lawyer's statements made during informal discussions with the prosecutor concerning defendant's bail because of the casual nature of the discussion, and because they threatened to chill the prospects for plea negotiations. The court distinguished its decision in *United States v. McKeon*,[23] where it was held that a lawyer's opening statement from a prior trial could be used as an admission:

> This Court has recognized that "[s]tatements made by an attorney concerning a matter within his employment *may* be admissible against the party retaining the attorney." *United States v. Margiotta, supra*, 662 F.2d at 142 (emphasis added)(citations omitted). However, in *United States v. McKeon*, 738 F.2d 26 (2d Cir.1984), we emphasized that care must be exercised in the criminal context in determining under what circumstances attorney statements may be used against a client, and we declined "to subject such statements to the more expansive practices sometimes permitted under the rule allowing use of admissions by a party-opponent." *Id.* at 31. Our concern arose because the routine use of attorney statements against a criminal defendant risks impairment of the privilege against self-incrimination, the right to counsel of one's choice, and the right to the effective assistance of counsel. In *McKeon* we considered whether an attorney's description of facts during his opening statement in a criminal trial was admissible against his client on retrial to show consciousness of guilt arising from a change in the defense claim between the first trial and the retrial. Noting the analogous example of superseded pleadings in civil cases, which are viewed as admissions of a party-opponent and are admissible in both the original and subsequent cases, we concluded that opening statements were not per se inadmissible in criminal cases. Nevertheless, "to avoid trenching upon other important policies," * * * we declined to permit expansive use of prior jury argument at a prior trial. Only after canvassing

---

20. See, e.g., United States v. Pilarinos, 864 F.2d 253, 256 (2d Cir.1988) (statements by middleman in bribery attempt can be used against his principal, the person who is the briber).

21. See, e.g., Hartford Fire Ins. Co. v. M/V "Savannah," 756 F.Supp. 825, 828 (S.D.N.Y.1991)(receipt made by defendant's stevedore held admissible against defendant); Guccione v. Hustler Magazine, Inc., 632 F.Supp. 313, 320 (S.D.N.Y.), rev'd on other grounds, 800 F.2d 298 (2d Cir.1986), cert. denied, 479 U.S. 1091, 107 S.Ct. 1303, 94 L.Ed.2d 158 (1987)(magazine owner's statements indicating disregard for the truth admissible against corporation); Westmoreland v. CBS, Inc., 601 F.Supp. 66, 68 (S.D.N.Y.1984)(defamation action in which statements in an investigation report made by defendant's senior executive producer held admissible against defendant); Carl Wagner and Sons v. Appendagez, Inc., 485 F.Supp. 762, 773–74 (S.D.N.Y.1980)(defendant's employees' statements to plaintiff admissible against defendant as proof of antitrust violations).

22. 826 F.2d 169, 172 (2d Cir.1987).

23. 738 F.2d 26 (2d Cir.1984).

§ 802.3   HEARSAY   Ch. 8

the precise circumstances of the case did we approve the admission at retrial of counsel's opening argument at the prior trial.[24]

Statements in notes made by an attorney in a civil setting may not be so stringently protected.[25]

The general rule allowing agents' admissions under Rule 801(d)(2)(C) and (D) does not obtain in criminal cases where the agent is a government employee and his statements are sought to be used against the government. In *United States v. Santos*,[26] it was stated:

> [I]nconsistent out-of-court statements or actions of a government agent said or done in the course of his employment take on quite a different probative character in a government criminal case from that which inconsistent out-of-court acts of agents acting within the scope of their employment generally take on at trial. Though a government prosecution is an exemplification of the adversary process, nevertheless, when the government prosecutes, it prosecutes on behalf of all the people of the United States; therefore all persons, whether law enforcement agents, government investigators, complaining prosecuting witnesses, or the like, who testify on behalf of the prosecution, and who, because of an employment relation or other personal interest in the outcome of the prosecution, may happen to be inseparably connected with the government side of the adversary process, stand in relation to the United States and in relation to the defendant no differently from persons unconnected with the effective development of or furtherance of the success of, the prosecution.
>
> * * *
>
> This apparent discrimination is explained by the peculiar posture of the parties in a criminal prosecution—the only party on the government side being the government itself whose many agents and actors are supposedly uninterested personally in the outcome of the trial and are historically unable to bind the sovereign.[27]

There is little authority in relation to whether a government em-

---

24. Valencia, 826 F.2d at 172–73.

25. Litton Systems, Inc. v. American Tel. & Tel. Co., 700 F.2d 785, 816–17 (2d Cir.1983), cert. denied, 464 U.S. 1073, 104 S.Ct. 984, 79 L.Ed.2d 220 (1984)(court indicated that had proper showing of agency been made, statements in notes made by attorney assigned to an internal investigation could be used against the client—no mention of attorney work product or attorney-client privilege).

26. 372 F.2d 177 (2d Cir.1967), cited and discussed in United States v. Durrani, 659 F.Supp. 1183, 1185 (D.Conn.1987), aff'd, 835 F.2d 410 (2d Cir.1987)(report of President's Special Review Board inadmissible against government).

27. Santos, at 180. Santos was relied on in a case decided after Rule 801(d)(2) came into effect. In United States v. Kampiles, 609 F.2d 1233, 1246 (7th Cir.1979), cert. denied, 446 U.S. 954, 100 S.Ct. 2923, 64 L.Ed.2d 812 (1980), the court refused to allow, against the government, evidence that a CIA employee made certain statements to a court reporter which, under the Santos rule, were inadmissible, and not of the sort Rule 801(d)(2)(D) would allow.

ployee's statement is admissible against the government in a civil case.[28] In one case, statements by government employees were considered inadmissible because they would not be considered parties under the disciplinary rule (DR 7–104) prohibiting interviews by adversary lawyers, the statements apparently having been gathered from the interviews.[29] Related is the rule that a grand jury is not an agency of the government, so that findings in superseded indictments cannot be used as admissions against the government.[30]

Even in the absence of an established agency or employment relationship, statements specifically authorized to be made may, by the terms of Rule 801(d)(2)(C), be admissible against the person giving the authorization. Thus, in *United States v. Iaconetti*,[31] Judge Weinstein held that where defendant solicited a bribe from X he authorized X to confer with his associates thereby making X's statements to them admissible against defendant.

Interpreters can be treated either as agents, or as persons specially authorized to repeat the subject's statements.[32]

Finally, it is not altogether clear in the Second Circuit whether the agent-declarant must have personal knowledge of the facts underlying his vicarious admission in order for it to be admissible. In *Oreck Corp. v. Whirlpool Corp.*,[33] discussed below as a coconspirator case, the argument was made that declarant had no personal knowledge of that about which he spoke. The court did not have to answer the question since it found no independent evidence of a conspiracy upon which to base any hearsay statements.[34] The Eighth Circuit in *Mahlandt v. Wild Canid*

---

28. United States v. D.K.G. Appaloosas, Inc., 630 F.Supp. 1540, 1564 (E.D.Tex. 1986), aff'd, 829 F.2d 532 (5th Cir.1987), cert. denied sub nom., One 1984 Lincoln Mark VII Two Door v. United States, 485 U.S. 976, 108 S.Ct. 1270, 99 L.Ed.2d 481 (1988). The court in that case states:

> As a general rule, statements made by an attorney concerning any matter within the scope of his employment are admissible. United States v. McKeon, 738 F.2d 26, 30 (2d Cir.1984); Fed.R.Evid. 801(d)(2)(D). Government attorneys in criminal cases are exempt from this rule, since they supposedly are uninterested in the outcome of the trial. In civil cases, however, where the adversarial process insures trustworthiness, statements by government attorneys are admissible. United States v. Santos, 372 F.2d 177, 180 (2d Cir.1967)(explaining difference between civil and criminal cases). See also United States v. American Tel. & Tel. Co., 498 F.Supp. 353, 359 (D.D.C. 1980); Burkey v. Ellis, 483 F.Supp. 897, 911 n.13 (N.D.Ala.1979)(statements by government agents are admissible).

29. Frey v. Dept. of Health and Human Services, 106 F.R.D. 32 (E.D.N.Y.1985). The court noted that plaintiff could not have it both ways, i.e., interview the employees as non-parties, and then argue that their statements were admissible against the Department. Perhaps the court might better have simply utilized the Santos rule.

30. United States v. Salerno, 937 F.2d 797, 811 (2d Cir.1991), modified on other grounds, 952 F.2d 623, rev'd and remanded on other grounds, 505 U.S. 317, 112 S.Ct. 2503, 120 L.Ed.2d 255 (1992).

31. 406 F.Supp. 554, 558 (E.D.N.Y.), aff'd, 540 F.2d 574 (2d Cir.1976), cert. denied, 429 U.S. 1041, 97 S.Ct. 739, 50 L.Ed.2d 752, rehearing denied, 430 U.S. 911, 97 S.Ct. 1186, 51 L.Ed.2d 589 (1977).

32. United States v. Da Silva, 725 F.2d 828, 831–32 (2d Cir.1983).

33. 639 F.2d 75, 80 (2d Cir.1980), cert. denied, 454 U.S. 1083, 102 S.Ct. 639, 70 L.Ed.2d 618 (1981).

34. Id. at 80 n.3.

§ 802.3 HEARSAY Ch. 8

Survival & Research Center, Inc.[35] rejected any "implied condition" of personal knowledge under Rule 801(d)(2).

d. Coconspirator's Statements

There are two major differences between the New York rule concerning coconspirator's statements and Federal Rule of Evidence 801(d)(2)(E): in New York the underlying conspiracy can be established by a simple prima facie showing (*see* § 802.2(g) *supra*), while the federal standard requires a preponderance of evidence;[36] and whereas in New York the statements sought to be introduced may not be used to prove the underlying conspiracy (*see* § 802.2(g) *supra*), the federal cases tolerate the use of such statements as an ingredient in establishing the needed preponderance.[37] Otherwise the rules are the same in that they both require for admissibility that the statements be made during the course of the conspiracy and in furtherance of the conspiracy.

In *United States v. Inadi*,[38] the United States Supreme Court referred to the unique character of coconspirators' statements as follows:

> Because they are made while the conspiracy is in progress, such statements provide evidence of the conspiracy's context that cannot be replicated, even if the declarant testifies to the same matters in court * * * [the statement often will derive its significance from the circumstances in which it was made.] Conspirators are likely to speak differently when talking to each other in furtherance of their illegal aims than when testifying on the witness stand * * *. [C]o-conspirator statements derive much of their value from the fact they are made in a context very different from trial, and therefore are usually irreplaceable as substantive evidence.[39]

On this basis the *Inadi* court held that there was no violation of the right of confrontation, and no need for a showing of the declarant's unavailability at trial.[40]

In *Bourjaily v. United States*,[41] defendant argued that the government should not be allowed to help lay the foundation for admissibility of the coconspirator's declaration by using the hearsay statement sought

---

35. 588 F.2d 626 (8th Cir.1978)(declarant, an employee of defendant, was told that a wolf belonging to defendant, which he was keeping at his house, had bitten a neighbor's child and he repeated this as, in effect, an adopted admission; held admissible against defendant employer since declarant spoke about matter within scope of employment).

36. Bourjaily v. United States, 483 U.S. 171, 175–76, 107 S.Ct. 2775, 2778, 97 L.Ed.2d 144, 152–53 (1987); State of N.Y. v. Hendrickson Bros., Inc., 840 F.2d 1065, 1073 (2d Cir.1988), cert. denied, 488 U.S. 848, 109 S.Ct. 128, 102 L.Ed.2d 101 (1988); Maritime Ventures Int'l, Inc. v. Caribbean Trading & Fidelity, Ltd., 722 F.Supp. 1032, 1035 (S.D.N.Y.1989).

37. Bourjaily v. United States, 483 U.S. 171, 181, 107 S.Ct. 2775, 2782, 97 L.Ed.2d 144, 156 (1987).

38. 475 U.S. 387, 106 S.Ct. 1121, 89 L.Ed.2d 390 (1986).

39. Id. at 395, 106 S.Ct. at 1126, 89 L.Ed.2d at 398.

40. Id. at 398, 106 S.Ct. at 1128, 89 L.Ed.2d at 401.

41. 483 U.S. 171, 107 S.Ct. 2775, 97 L.Ed.2d 144 (1987).

to be admitted.[42] This, in fact, had been squarely held by the court in an older case as being an impermissible "bootstrap" operation.[43] Chief Justice Rehnquist held in *Bourjaily*, however, that the effect of that ruling had been overcome by Rule 104(a) of the Federal Rules of Evidence, which lodges admissibility questions with the judge who "is not bound by the rules of evidence except those with respect to privilege."[44] The Court expressly declined to decide whether the content of the statement could provide the *sole* evidence of the conspiracy.[45] Instead, the Court held that the statement could be considered, along with other evidence, in the determination of whether or not a conspiracy existed.[46] The Chief Justice cemented the *Inadi* holding that there need be no independent evidence in order to establish reliability because "firmly rooted" hearsay exceptions (which apparently include coconspirators' statements), are presumptively reliable.[47] Clearly, the right of confrontation is not offended by application of the coconspirator's rule.[48]

No hard and fast objective rule describes the amount of evidence needed to constitute a preponderance, and on a case-to-case basis the federal rule probably differs from the New York prima facie standard only in the abstract. Needless to say, not every association is a conspiracy.[49]

On the question of procedure, the Second Circuit is governed by its decision in *United States v. Geaney*[50] which, even though decided before the Federal Rules of Evidence were enacted, continues to guide the handling of statements attributed to a coconspirator. Thus, in *United States v. Tracy*[51] the court reiterated *Geaney*'s foundation requirements (proof of the underlying conspiracy, defendant and declarant were mem-

---

42. Id. at 174, 107 S.Ct. at 2778, 97 L.Ed.2d at 152.

43. See Glasser v. United States, 315 U.S. 60, 62 S.Ct. 457, 86 L.Ed. 680 (1942). The court stated, "Such declarations are admissible over the objection of an alleged co-conspirator, who was not present when they were made, only if there is proof aliunde that he is connected with the conspiracy * * *. Otherwise, hearsay would lift itself by its own bootstraps to the level of competent evidence." Id. at 74–75, 62 S.Ct. at 467, 86 L.Ed. at 701.

44. Bourjaily, 483 U.S. at 178, 107 S.Ct. at 2780, 97 L.Ed.2d at 154.

45. Id. at 175, 107 S.Ct. at 2778, 97 L.Ed.2d at 152.

46. Id. at 176, 107 S.Ct. at 2779, 97 L.Ed.2d at 153.

47. Id. at 183, 107 S.Ct. at 2783, 97 L.Ed.2d at 157.

48. Earlier, the Supreme Court in Dutton v. Evans, 400 U.S. 74, 91 S.Ct. 210, 27 L.Ed.2d 213 (1970), held that the introduction of a coconspirator's statement was not a violation of the right of confrontation, and the supporting rationale was refined in the Inadi and Bourjaily cases. Bruton v. United States, 391 U.S. 123, 88 S.Ct. 1620, 20 L.Ed.2d 476 (1968), posed no threat to the coconspirator hearsay exception since that case involved the admissibility of a nontestifying codefendant's confession implicating defendant.

49. See, e.g., Maritime Ventures Int'l, Inc. v. Caribbean Trading & Fidelity, Ltd., 722 F.Supp. 1032, 1035 (S.D.N.Y. 1989)(where it was just as likely that declarant spoke in his role of government agent as that he spoke as a collaborator in a private venture for his own benefit, there was insufficient evidence of a conspiracy even taking into account the content of the statements sought to be introduced); Oreck Corp. v. Whirlpool Corp., 639 F.2d 75, 80 (2d Cir.1980), cert. denied, 454 U.S. 1083, 102 S.Ct. 639, 70 L.Ed.2d 618 (1981)("The mere showing of a close association between defendants is not sufficient to satisfy the independent proof requirement").

50. 417 F.2d 1116, 1120 (2d Cir.1969), cert. denied sub nom., Lynch v. U.S., 397 U.S. 1028, 90 S.Ct. 1276, 25 L.Ed.2d 539 (1970).

51. 12 F.3d 1186 (2d Cir.1993).

bers, and the statements were made during the course of and in furtherance of the conspiracy)[52] and held that under the *Geaney* rule "statements proffered as coconspirator statements may be admitted in evidence on a conditional basis, subject to the later submission of the necessary evidence of those four prerequisites."[53] The trial judge in *Tracy* handled this properly, except that he was criticized for explaining to the jury the facts that convinced him that the foundation requirements had been met.[54] The Second Circuit has also held that "once a conspiracy is established, only slight, even circumstantial evidence is needed to link another defendant with it";[55] and that application of the coconspirator rule is not conditioned on the presence of a conspiracy count in the indictment.[56]

In furtherance of the conspiracy. The question of what constitutes a statement that furthers the conspiracy seems no closer to resolution in the federal courts than it does in New York (*see* § 802.2(g) *supra*). Thus, where one defendant offered to obtain a lawyer for another defendant while both were incarcerated awaiting trial, declarant's statement was an admission against himself, and a coconspirator's statement admissible against the other defendant "[s]ince the jury could infer that they were in furtherance of the common objective of preventing convictions of both defendants. Coconspirator statements may include attempts to cover up an ongoing conspiracy after the participants have been arrested."[57] In another case, statements characterized as "idle chatter" were held to be in furtherance of the conspiracy since "we have recognized that '[s]tatements between conspirators which provide reassurance, serve to maintain trust and cohesiveness among them, or inform each other of the current status of the conspiracy, further the ends of [a] conspiracy.' "[58] And, as another example of the loose constraints put on this requisite consider the following excerpt from *United States v. Maldonado–Rivera*:[59]

> To be in furtherance of the conspiracy, a statement must be more than a "mere narrative" description by one coconspirator of the acts of another. * * * Rather, the statements must be such as to prompt the listener—who need not be a coconspirator—to respond in a way that promotes or facilitates the carrying out of a criminal activity.[60]

---

52. Id. at 1199.

53. Id.

54. Id. at 1200.

55. United States v. Cota, 953 F.2d 753, 758 (2d Cir.1992).

56. United States v. DeVillio, 983 F.2d 1185, 1193 (2d Cir.1993).

57. United States v. Roldan–Zapata, 916 F.2d 795, 804 (2d Cir.1990), cert. denied, 499 U.S. 940, 111 S.Ct. 1397, 113 L.Ed.2d 453 (1991). Conspiracy was charged and so this explains why the "in furtherance" question would be considered by the jury here.

58. United States v. Simmons, 923 F.2d 934, 945 (2d Cir.), cert. denied, 500 U.S. 919, 111 S.Ct. 2018, 114 L.Ed.2d 104 (1991). Compare United States v. Paone, 782 F.2d 386, 390 (2d Cir.1986), where although "idle chatter" was seen as not furthering the conspiracy, the statements were nevertheless admitted as statements against interest.

59. 922 F.2d 934 (2d Cir.1990), cert. denied, 501 U.S. 1233, 111 S.Ct. 2858, 115 L.Ed.2d 1025 (1991).

60. Id. at 958.

On that basis, the *Maldonado-Rivera* court held that the "in furtherance" requirement was satisfied where a communique issued by a revolutionary group claiming responsibility for a robbery was issued a year after the robbery. The tone of the communique was said to convey an ongoing operation contemplating the use of the proceeds of the robbery. It also would tend to give coconspirators information as to the organization's status and solvency and encourage them for future operations.[61]

Other cases on this point are noted below.[62]

Course of conspiracy. There is overlap between the "in furtherance" and "in the course of" requisites since if the statement is seen to be made in the furtherance of the conspiracy it would follow that the conspiracy would not have ended. The cases which do focus more on the duration of the conspiracy are as scattered as those interpreting when statements are "in furtherance." In *Krulewitch v. United States*,[63] the Supreme Court ruled that statements made after a prostitution ring had dissolved were inadmissible. The government's argument that the conspiracy survives through the concealment phase[64] was rejected by the Court which saw this as unduly expanding the exception.[65] This strict rule was adhered to in *Lutwak v. United States*[66] where it was held that while post-conspiracy statements would not be admissible under the rule, post-conspiracy nonassertive acts could be admitted to prove the conspiracy.[67] In *Dutton v. Evans*,[68] the court noted that while the

---

61. Id. at 959.

62. See United States v. Amato, 15 F.3d 230 (2d Cir.1994)(statement by A to B concerning loan to C was admissible in loan sharking prosecution since it furthered the conspiracy by apprising another member of the status of a particular loan); United States v. Lopez, 937 F.2d 716, 724 (2d Cir.1991)(testimony by witness who did not speak Spanish concerning statements made by Spanish-speaking conspirator through interpreter admissible since it apprised a coconspirator of the progress of the conspiracy and the interpreter was also a conspiracy member); United States v. Vanwort, 887 F.2d 375, 388 (2d Cir.1989), cert. denied sub nom., Chapoteau v. United States, 495 U.S. 906, 110 S.Ct. 1927, 109 L.Ed.2d 290 (1990)(coconspirator's computer printout containing names and addresses of other conspirators admissible with no discussion of how this was in furtherance); United States v. Beech–Nut Nutrition Corp., 871 F.2d 1181, 1199 (2d Cir.), cert. denied sub nom., Lavery v. United States, 493 U.S. 933, 110 S.Ct. 324, 107 L.Ed.2d 314 (1989)(statements made by corporation managers who misbranded adulterated apple juice were made in furtherance of adulteration conspiracy because designed to cover up distribution of adulterated juice); compare this older case, United States v. Birnbaum, 337 F.2d 490, 495 (2d Cir. 1964)(court would not accept government's argument that coconspirator's statement, on its face merely recounting the facts of another conspirator's past activities, was made to induce L to honor his part of the bribery scheme by paying money he owed—too tenuous, said the court).

63. 336 U.S. 440, 69 S.Ct. 716, 93 L.Ed. 790 (1949).

64. The elements comprising the concealment phase are not free from doubt. The Supreme Court in Grunewald v. United States, 353 U.S. 391, 399–406, 77 S.Ct. 963, 971–75, 1 L.Ed.2d 931, 940–44 (1957), held that a new agreement to conceal a conspiracy is not necessarily part of the predecessor conspiracy. As stated in United States v. Teitler, 802 F.2d 606, 615 (2d Cir.1986), "There instead may be a separate conspiracy to conceal the predecessor conspiracy. Members of the original conspiracy may not be convicted for the conspiracy to conceal unless they actually participated in the conspiracy to conceal."

65. Krulewitch, 336 U.S. at 443, 69 S.Ct. at 718, 93 L.Ed. at 794.

66. 344 U.S. 604, 73 S.Ct. 481, 97 L.Ed. 593 (1953).

67. Id. at 618, 73 S.Ct. at 489, 97 L.Ed. at 604.

§ 802.3   HEARSAY   Ch. 8

Krulewitch concealment phase restriction was applicable in federal court, it was not a constitutional mandate, and states could choose to admit statements made during the concealment phase.[69] (New York seems to have so chosen. *See* § 802.2(g) *supra*).

These precepts become muddled when, from case-to-case, it is sought to be determined whether the conspiracy has ended for purposes of deciding the admissibility of the declarant's statements—or as in one case,[70] whether the conspiracy had yet begun when the statements were made. In another case, *United States v. Persico*,[71] the Second Circuit found a continuing conspiracy after members had been arrested and jailed. By way of explaining its reasoning, the court stated: "The very purpose of one of the bribe schemes charged was to ensure that Carmine Persico would have ready access to a telephone while in prison, so that he could continue to conduct the Columbo Family's affairs while incarcerated."[72] The court's explanation in another case was that although a conspiracy would end upon the arrest of one or more of the conspirators, "that is not necessarily the case here. Morgan remained free after his arrest, and his statements to the police do not indicate the conspiracy's objectives had been met or that they were over."[73] But in a case where the nature of the conspiracy was apparently not so clouded, the court said that while post-arrest statements could be used as admissions against the declarant, they could not be used against a (former) coconspirator since the arrest ended the conspiracy.[74] After acknowledging the post-conspiracy rule, the court stated: "On the other hand, it is fair to say that where a general objective of the conspirators is money, the conspiracy does not end, of necessity, before the spoils are divided among the miscreants."[75]

Dividing the spoils, concealing the conspiracy, and arrests, are, of course, distinguishable events. That the permutations are probably infinite is indicated in another case where after the objects of the conspiracy had been accomplished, the conspirators gathered together with W, who had not been a coconspirator, to destroy the car used to effectuate the conspiracy. It was proposed by the prosecutor that W testify as to what one of the coconspirators said about the main conspira-

68. 400 U.S. 74, 91 S.Ct. 210, 27 L.Ed.2d 213 (1970).

69. Id. at 81, 91 S.Ct. at 215, 27 L.Ed.2d at 222.

70. See United States v. Casamento, 887 F.2d 1141, 1171 (2d Cir.1989), cert. denied, 493 U.S. 1081, 110 S.Ct. 1138, 107 L.Ed.2d 1043 (1990) ("Post-statement events may be used to prove that a statement was made during the course of the conspiracy").

71. 832 F.2d 705 (2d Cir.1987), cert. denied, 486 U.S. 1022 108 S.Ct. 1995, 100 L.Ed.2d 227 (1988).

72. Id. at 715–16. See also United States v. Arrington, 867 F.2d 122, 130 (2d Cir.), cert. denied sub nom., 493 U.S. 817, 110 S.Ct. 70, 107 L.Ed.2d 37 (1989)(conspiracy not seen as ended even though some of the conspirators indicted and incarcerated).

73. United States v. Kusek, 647 F.Supp. 1150, 1154 (S.D.N.Y.1986).

74. United States v. Lam Lek Chong, 544 F.2d 58, 69 (2d Cir.1976), cert. denied sub nom., Liganoza v. United States, 429 U.S. 1101, 97 S.Ct. 1124, 51 L.Ed.2d 550 (1977).

75. United States v. Knuckles, 581 F.2d 305, 313 (2d Cir.), cert. denied, 439 U.S. 986, 99 S.Ct. 581, 58 L.Ed.2d 659 (1978); United States v. Kahan, 572 F.2d 923 (2d Cir.), cert. denied, 439 U.S. 833, 99 S.Ct. 112, 58 L.Ed.2d 128 (1978)(conspiracy in progress through sale of hijacked goods.).

cy as the group burned the car. Rejecting this, the court stated: "To include in the conspiracy an event, no matter how proximately related, occurring after the main objectives of a conspiracy have been accomplished would unnecessarily blur the relatively clear line drawn by the Supreme Court's decisions on this subject."[76]

A sharp eye must be kept to make sure that a post-conspiracy statement (or a statement not meeting any of the other requisites) might alternatively be admissible under another hearsay exception[77] or as a different kind of nonhearsay—not for its truth, but simply because there is relevance in the fact that it was said.[78]

Library References:
> West's Key No. Digests, Criminal Law ⟸405–410, 419(8), 422–428; Evidence ⟸200–265.

803 Hearsay Exceptions Where Availability of the Declarant Is Immaterial

§ 803.1 New York and Federal, In General

Federal Rule of Evidence 803 sets forth hearsay exceptions applicable when it is immaterial whether the declarant is available to testify.

The hearsay exceptions gathered under Federal Rule 803 are for the most part recognized in New York either in caselaw or by statute. Each exception is based on the notion that the circumstances in which the declarations are made lend a degree of trustworthiness to them—that the declarations are probably true because it would be unlikely for a person to falsify under the circumstances necessary for the particular exception. As the Federal Rules Advisory Committee states:

> The present rule proceeds upon the theory that under appropriate circumstances a hearsay statement may possess circumstantial guarantees of trustworthiness sufficient to justify nonproduction of the declarant in person at the trial even though he may be available. The theory finds vast support in the many exceptions to the hearsay rule developed by the common law in which unavailability of the declarant is not a relevant factor. The present rule is a synthesis of them, with revision where modern developments and conditions are believed to make that course appropriate.

---

76. United States v. Floyd, 555 F.2d 45, 48 (2d Cir.), cert. denied, 434 U.S. 851, 98 S.Ct. 163, 54 L.Ed.2d 120 (1977).

77. See, e.g., United States v. Lam Lek Chong, 544 F.2d 58, 69 (2d Cir.1976), cert. denied sub nom., Liganoza v. United States, 429 U.S. 1101, 97 S.Ct. 1124, 51 L.Ed.2d 550 (1977)(admission usable against declarant); United States v. Kusek, 647 F.Supp. 1150, 1154 (S.D.N.Y.1986) (statement against penal interest under Federal Rule 804[b][3]).

78. See United States v. Lopez, 584 F.2d 1175, 1179 (2d Cir.1978)("While Romero's taped telephone conversation may be said to have occurred after the conspiracy ended, because Romero was already arrested and the narcotics seized * * * it was offered not to prove the truth of the declarations but to prove that Romero and Lopez knew each other.").

§ 803.1　　　　　　　HEARSAY　　　　　　　Ch. 8

In the interest of efficient organization of the material, several of the 803 exceptions are gathered under one section of this chapter (§ 803(1)). Also, for ease of reference, the 803 exceptions are distinguished from 804 exceptions, discussed later, which can be utilized only when the declarant is unavailable.[1]

§ 803(1) Spontaneous Statements, Statements Evidencing a State of Mind or Physical Condition, and Statements Made for Purposes of Medical Diagnosis or Treatment

§ 803(1).1　New York

This section deals with statements of present sense impressions, excited utterances, statements as to state of mind or physical condition, and statements made for purposes of medical diagnosis or treatment. The trustworthiness in these statements is found in the fact either that the declarant had little or no time to reflect on the content of the statement before it was made, or that the statement or expression more accurately shows the declarant's condition at the time in question than testimony coming forth much later at trial.[1] There is something of the *"res gestae"* rule to all of these exceptions, i.e., the statements and expressions were contemporaneous with the transaction at issue;[2] but the more precise terminology and analysis as set forth in the Federal Rules of Evidence and various state codes are the source of guidance now, rather than that ancient, vague and overused phrase. And even though there is no code in New York, these exceptions are accepted and applied by the courts.

It is in the *res gestae* area, as observed by Wigmore, that the greatest confusion exists between statements or expressions which are admissible simply because they are made (the verbal act doctrine discussed in § 801.1(c), *supra*), and contemporaneous statements which are introduced for their truth.[3] McCormick reminds us of such distinctions with these examples relating to the declarant's state of mind:

> But many so-called spontaneous statements are in fact not assertive statements or, if assertive, are not offered to prove the truth of the assertions made. For example, it is clear that the statements, "I plan to spend the rest of my life here in New

---

§ 803.1

1. McCormick states that in the 803 group of exceptions "the availability or unavailability of the declarant is not a relevant factor: the exception is applied without regard to it." The theory behind the 803 exception is that the statement "is at least as reliable as would be [declarant's] testimony in person, so that producing him would involve pointless delay and inconvenience." The theory behind the 804 exceptions is that "while it would be preferable to have live testimony, if the declarant is unavailable, the out-of-court statement will be accepted." McCormick § 253, at 130.

§ 803(1).1

1. See McCormick § 268, at 206–208.
2. Id.
3. 6 Wigmore § 1745.

York" and "I have lost my affection for my husband" are hearsay, when offered to prove the plan to remain in New York or the loss of affection. On the other hand, statements such as "I have been happier in New York than in any other place," when offered to show the speaker's intent to remain in New York, and "My husband is a detestable wretch," offered to show lack of affection for the husband, will or will not be classed as hearsay, depending upon the position taken with respect to the long debated question whether "implied assertions" are to be classed as hearsay.[4]

Similarly, declarant's words while formulating a contract, handing over money to another, or in soliciting a bribe would not be hearsay under the verbal act doctrine (see § 801.1(c), *supra*), because they are a part of the transaction itself. In the next several sections, emanating from the ancient res gestae doctrine, we will be concerned with relatively contemporaneous statements and expressions which are assertive, very often describing the event being witnessed, or just having been witnessed, or a bodily condition being experienced. That event would have and could have happened independently of the descriptive words. The words are offered for their truth to prove that the event happened.

a. Present Sense Impression

This is the most recent hearsay exception to find acceptance in New York. It is a spontaneous statement in the sense that it describes an event at the time the event is happening or very shortly thereafter. It differs from an excited utterance precisely because the declarant is dispassionate and unexcited. Three elements sustain this exception: (1) since the statement is simultaneous with the event there is no memory problem; (2) for the same reason there is no time for a calculated misstatement; and (3) there must be some corroboration.[5]

The 911 telephone call is the best example of the present sense impression and, in fact, is the situation involved in *People v. Brown*,[6] where the Court of Appeals announced the new rule. Previously, in *People v. Luke*,[7] the exception had been allowed by the trial judge where the declarant described in a 911 call a burglary she was watching out of her window. In a comprehensive opinion the court explored the views of Thayer, Wigmore and Morgan.[8] The caller's description was validated by what the police found when they arrived at the scene.[9] The convic-

---

4. McCormick § 269, at 208.

5. People v. Brown, 80 N.Y.2d 729, 736, 594 N.Y.S.2d 696, 700, 610 N.E.2d 369, 373 (1993).

6. Id.

7. 136 Misc.2d 733, 519 N.Y.S.2d 316 (Sup.Ct.Bronx Co.1987), affirmed sub nom., People v. Duke, 147 A.D.2d 990, 538 N.Y.S.2d 886 (1st Dep't), appeal denied, 74 N.Y.2d 663, 543 N.Y.S.2d 406, 541 N.E.2d 435 (1989).

8. Id. at 735, 519 N.Y.S.2d at 318. According to the court, Thayer fully justified the present sense impression exception, while Wigmore felt it untrustworthy. See id. at 735, 519 N.Y.S.2d at 318. Morgan agreed with Thayer as to the viability of the exception, and so these evidence giants split two to one on the issue. See id. at 735–36, 519 N.Y.S.2d at 317–18.

9. Id. at 739, 519 N.Y.S.2d at 320.

§ 803(1).1   HEARSAY   Ch. 8

tion was upheld on appeal.[10] The facts in *Brown* differed little from those in *Luke*. A 911 caller who identified himself only as "Henry" described an unfolding burglary attempt and this was substantially verified by the police when they arrived. Over defendant's argument that the corroboration requirement could only be satisfied by the testimony of another eyewitness,[11] it was held that the observation of the police provided enough corroboration. If there is such an available eyewitness "there is certainly no pressing need for the hearsay testimony."[12] It was further stated: "Insisting that the declarant's descriptions of the events must be corroborated in court by a witness who was present with the declarant and who observed the very same events would deprive the exception of most, if not all, of its usefulness."[13] Corroboration there must be, but what satisfies that requirement will vary from case to case and will largely be left to the trial judge's discretion.[14]

Under Federal Rule of Evidence 803(1) it does not matter whether the declarant is available or not for his present sense impression to be admissible. The court in *Brown* did not discuss the availability question since not only was it clear that declarant was unavailable, he was unavailable because nobody even knew who he was. If declarant is available can his statement also come in? It has long been established that a trial witness' prior excited utterance is admissible;[15] but a lower court has held that in order for a present sense statement to be admissible declarant's unavailability must be established.[16] The Court of Appeals, however, has held that unavailability is not a requisite for admission in a case where declarant was a trial witness and his 911 call was admissible because of its independent evidentiary significance.[17]

---

10. People v. Duke, 147 A.D.2d 990, 538 N.Y.S.2d 886.

11. Such a corroboration standard was set forth by the Appellate Division in People v. Watson, 100 A.D.2d 452, 474 N.Y.S.2d 978 (2d Dep't 1984). This was probably the first case in New York where the present sense impression was treated seriously. The trial judge allowed a witness to testify that the victim told her over the telephone at or about the time she was murdered that the "super" had come to fix a leak. The building superintendent was on trial for the declarant's murder and the statement was introduced against him. The Appellate Division, citing Weinstein and Berger (¶ 803[a][o]), held that the corroboration rule could only be satisfied by another witness who saw or experienced the same event as the victim. 100 A.D.2d at 466–69, 474 N.Y.S.2d at 987–89.

12. 80 N.Y.S.2d at 736, 594 N.Y.S.2d at 700, 610 N.E.2d at 373.

13. Id.

14. Id. at 737, 594 N.Y.S.2d at 701, 610 N.E.2d at 374. The Luke case had been relied on by the Appellate Division in its affirmance in Brown (179 A.D.2d 485, 486, 579 N.Y.S.2d 15, 16 (1st Dep't 1992)) and it was referred to with approval in the Court of Appeals' Brown opinion (80 N.Y.S.2d at 733, n.2, 594 N.Y.S.2d at 699, 610 N.E.2d at 372).

15. People v. Caviness, 38 N.Y.2d 227, 379 N.Y.S.2d 695, 342 N.E.2d 496 (1975).

16. People v. Cook, 159 Misc.2d 430, 603 N.Y.S.2d 979 (Sup.Ct.Kings Co.1993). The present sense statement may not be a firmly rooted hearsay exception as is the excited utterance. Firm roots resolves any claim to the confrontation right that may be raised by defendant. See United States v. Inadi, 475 U.S. 387, 106 S.Ct. 1121, 89 L.Ed.2d 390 (1986); Bourjaily v. United States, 483 U.S. 171, 107 S.Ct. 2775, 97 L.Ed.2d 144 (1987).

17. People v. Buie, ___ N.Y.2d ___, ___ N.Y.S.2d ___, ___ N.E.2d ___, 1995 WL 626482 (1995). A notable aspect of the *Buie* case is that the witness had identified the defendant to the police, to which he was permitted to testify, but then misidentified the defendant at trial. See also People v. Victor R., 161 Misc.2d 212, 613 N.Y.S.2d 567 (Sup.Ct.Kings Co.1994)(victim's excited utterance statement in a 911 call admissible in addition to her testimony).

In criminal cases, there may still be an unresolved issue with respect to present sense statements, one not specifically addressed in the *Brown* opinion. Can a hearsay exception adopted in 1993 be considered a firmly-rooted hearsay exception so as to fall within the Supreme Court's edict that reliability is inherent thus obviating defendant's potential confrontation objection?[18] Perhaps the firmly-rooted status derives from the fact that the exception "has been accepted in some form by the majority of States and has now been widely approved by legal commentators."[19] Is there an added confrontation concern where, as in *Brown*, declarant's identity is unknown?

New York cases on the present sense impression are beginning to proliferate.[20] The current version of the proposed New York code, however, omits any provision for this hearsay exception. The earlier version of the proposed code did include the exception in a provision identical to the Federal Rule.[21]

b. Excited Utterance

This well-established hearsay exception finds its modern New York footing in the Court of Appeals' opinion in *People v. Caviness*.[22] There, a witness to a shooting was allowed to testify that immediately after the victim was shot—an occurrence to which she was in close proximity—she said "Burnis shot Earl," as the victim fell to the ground. Defendant argued that an excited utterance, to be admissible, had to be made by a participant in the event—that a bystander's words would not qualify. This was rejected by the court, which held that an excited utterance was

---

18. See United States v. Inadi, and Bourjailly v. United States, supra, note 16.

19. Brown, 80 N.Y.2d at 733–34, 594 N.Y.S.2d at 699, 610 N.E.2d at 372.

20. See Taft v. New York City Transit Authority, 193 A.D.2d 503, 597 N.Y.S.2d 374 (1st Dep't 1993)(relying on the Brown present sense impression holding, the court ruled that a statement made by an "agitated" declarant right after a person fell under a subway train was admissible and was corroborated by circumstances surrounding the finding of the body); Griggs v. Children's Hospital, Inc., 193 A.D.2d 1060, 599 N.Y.S.2d 197 (4th Dep't 1993)(witness' testimony as to conversation with decedent who related what doctor had told her to do to ease her physical condition, was not admissible since it was double hearsay and was not a present sense impression under the Brown rule); People v. Slaughter, 189 A.D.2d 157, 596 N.Y.S.2d 22 (1st Dep't), leave to appeal denied, 81 N.Y.2d 1080, 601 N.Y.S.2d 600, 619 N.E.2d 678 (1993)(victim's statement after hanging up telephone that "[defendant] is going to kill me" not admissible under any exception including present sense impression); People v. Cook, 159 Misc.2d 430, 603 N.Y.S.2d 979 (Sup.Ct. Kings Co.1993) (911 tape admissible and court discussed whether declarant needs to be unavailable, reviewing all the "firmly rooted" cases [present sense impression said not to be such] from United States v. Inadi, 475 U.S. 387, 106 S.Ct. 1121, 89 L.Ed.2d 390 (1986), through White v. Illinois, 502 U.S. 346, 112 S.Ct. 736, 116 L.Ed.2d 848 (1992) and most if not all of the New York Court of Appeals cases dealing with hearsay exceptions vis a vis confrontation rights); Berger v. City of New York, 157 Misc.2d 521, 597 N.Y.S.2d 555 (Sup.Ct.N.Y.Co.1993)(unknown person's 911 call describing plaintiff as having been knocked from her bicycle by a city streetsweeper, not admissible since court could find no corroborating evidence, direct or circumstantial).

21. Proposed New York Evidence Code § 803(1) provided in the 1982 version:

Present Sense Impression. A statement describing or explaining an event or condition made while the declarant was perceiving the event or condition, or immediately thereafter.

22. 38 N.Y.2d 227, 379 N.Y.S.2d 695, 342 N.E.2d 496 (1975).

just as trustworthy coming from the lips of an observer as from a participant.[23] Judge Cooke described the exception as follows:

> Spontaneous declarations, frequently referred to with some inexactitude as *res gestae* declarations * * * form an exception to the hearsay rule. It is established that spontaneous declarations made by a participant while he is under the stress of nervous excitement resulting from an injury or other startling event, while his reflective powers are stilled and during the brief period when considerations of self-interest could not have been brought fully to bear by reasoned reflection and deliberation, are admissible as true exceptions to the hearsay rule * * *. The question whether a declaration conforms to the spontaneity requirements of the rule is a preliminary question to be determined by the Trial Judge, not the jury, the test being whether the declarant was so influenced by the excitement and shock of the event that it is probable that he or she spoke impulsively and without reflection rather than reflectively and with deliberation * * *.[24]

The question arising most frequently in the cases is whether the utterance is sufficiently close in time to the event. The generalization can be made that it depends on the duration of the declarant's state of excitement, i.e., the test is concerned more with the condition of the declarant's psyche than with the amount of time that has elapsed between the happening of the event and the utterance. Early on, the Court of Appeals applied the time factor strictly. Two classic cases are *People v. Del Vermo*[25] and *Greener v. General Electric Co.*[26] In *Del Vermo* the victim was walking with the witness and defendant. The victim slumped to the ground and the witness asked him what happened as defendant ran off. The witness testified that the victim said, "Del Vermo stabbed me with a knife."[27] In the context of the incident this statement was deemed admissible.[28] It apparently was of no concern that the statement was in response to a question. In *Greener* plaintiff fell from a ladder. His partner, hearing the commotion, asked plaintiff what had happened. Plaintiff responded, "my feet is broke, the ladder

---

23. Id. at 231–32, 379 N.Y.S.2d at 700, 342 N.E.2d at 499–500.

24. Id. at 230–31, 379 N.Y.S.2d at 698–99, 342 N.E.2d at 499. See also People v. Victor R., 161 Misc.2d 212, 613 N.Y.S.2d 567 (Sup.Ct.Kings Co.1994)(victim's excited utterance statement in a 911 call admissible in addition to her testimony). McCormick notes that while the requirement of immediacy of the statement may guarantee the lack of reflectiveness, the shock created by the startling event may well produce a distorted perception of what actually happened. McCormick § 272, at 216.

25. 192 N.Y. 470, 85 N.E. 690 (1908).

26. 209 N.Y. 135, 138, 102 N.E. 527, 528 (1913).

27. 192 N.Y. at 476, 102 N.E. at 692 (1908).

28. Del Vermo, 192 N.Y. at 483, 85 N.E. at 695. See People v. Wortherly, 68 A.D.2d 158, 160, 416 N.Y.S.2d 594, 596 (1st Dep't 1979), where the victim's statement, "Ziggy stabbed me," uttered within three minutes of the stabbing in response to a question, was held admissible. This case is remarkably similar to Del Vermo where the statement was made immediately after the stabbing, and where the court indicated that any lapse of time would be a crucial factor. Del Vermo, 192 N.Y. at 484, 85 N.E. at 695. It is clear that the time rule has been liberalized, as seen in Wortherly and the other modern cases discussed in this section.

bent over."[29] This was ruled inadmissible. It was a narrative statement of what had occurred, it was made when declarant's reflective processes might well have become operative and it was in response to a question.[30]

The Court of Appeals' more modern assessment of this exception is found in *People v. Brown*,[31] where the statements of a seriously wounded victim as to who shot him were held admissible (as spontaneous statements, not as dying declarations)[32] when made in a hospital emergency room 30 minutes after the shooting. Given that declarant was in great pain and the surrounding circumstances showed that the statements would not have been made as a result of "studied reflection," the statements were considered trustworthy.[33] Again, the spontaneity was not affected by the fact the utterance was made in response to a question. Judge Hancock surveyed the landmark decisions[34] and stated that the court would not try to define a permissible time period,[35] since this would be in conflict with the by-then established rule which looks to a continuing state of shock and stress and its effect on the declarant's ability to reflect on the situation and possibly make self-serving statements.[36] Thus, the requirements for admission have evolved consider-

---

29. Greener, 209 N.Y. at 137, 102 N.E. at 528.

30. Id. at 138, 102 N.E. at 528.

31. 70 N.Y.2d 513, 522 N.Y.S.2d 837, 517 N.E.2d 515 (1987).

32. Could the statements be considered dying declarations? In Brown the question was not reached because the statements came in as spontaneous utterances. As shown in People v. Nieves, 67 N.Y.2d 125, 501 N.Y.S.2d 1, 492 N.E.2d 109 (1986), it is more difficult to qualify a statement as a dying declaration than as an excited utterance because there must be proof of a settled expectation of death with regard to the former (see § 804(2).1 infra). Beyond that, the Nieves court was skeptical of the reliability of dying declarations generally, and it was hinted that on retrial the prosecutor might seek to introduce the statements as excited utterances. Id. at 136–37, 501 N.Y.S.2d at 8, 492 N.E.2d at 116.

33. Id. at 522, 522 N.Y.S.2d at 842, 517 N.E.2d at 520. On the way to the hospital the victim told his mother who the assailant was.

34. In addition to the Del Vermo and Greener cases, see People v. Marks, 6 N.Y.2d 67, 188 N.Y.S.2d 465, 160 N.E.2d 26 (1959), cert. denied, 362 U.S. 912, 80 S.Ct. 662, 4 L.Ed.2d 620 (1960)(a statement about a past transaction could be admitted as an excited utterance where shock and stress continue so that the reflective faculties could have no influence); People v. Edwards, 47 N.Y.2d 493, 497, 419 N.Y.S.2d 45, 47, 392 N.E.2d 1229, 1231 (1979)(the fact the statement was in response to a question would not rule out the element of spontaneity, nor would the fact there was an appreciable lapse of time; the test was whether or not the statement was made under "the impetus of studied reflection"); Compare People v. Smith, 52 N.Y.2d 802, 436 N.Y.S.2d 867, 418 N.E.2d 382 (1980) (where the declarant was one of four like-minded individuals, the witness was not sure which of the four uttered the racial slur at the victim who was fatally attacked, and it was held not admissible because it could not be attributed to defendant).

35. Brown, 70 N.Y.2d at 520–21, 522 N.Y.S.2d at 841, 517 N.E.2d at 519.

36. Id. at 519, 522 N.Y.S.2d at 840, 517 N.E.2d at 518. The Appellate Division made a similar determination seven years prior to Brown in People v. McCullough, 73 A.D.2d 310, 425 N.Y.S.2d 982 (1st Dep't 1980), where it ruled admissible the victim's statement naming the defendant given in response to a question some 10 minutes after the shooting. The court stated: "[r]ealistically viewed, the trauma produced by the shooting was as acute 10 minutes after the shooting as it was in the first moments." Id. at 314, 425 N.Y.S.2d at 985. Compare People v. Sostre, 70 A.D.2d 40, 418 N.Y.S.2d 662 (2d Dep't 1979), aff'd, 51 N.Y.2d 958, 435 N.Y.S.2d 702, 416 N.E.2d 1038 (1980), where the complainant, intended victim, shot the defendant, his would-be assailant, in the arm and leg. The statement made by the wounded assailant, as the police came on the scene two to five minutes after the shooting, that complainant had shot him "for nothing," was held to be inadmissible either as an excited utterance, or as part of the res gestae, or as

§ 803(1).1 HEARSAY Ch. 8

ably since the decision in *Del Vermo* and *Greener*. The proposed New York Evidence Code offers a provision covering this exception[37] which conforms to the current New York case law.

The excited utterance exception appears in a variety of contexts.[38]

c. State of Mind or Physical Condition

There are two types of state of mind "exceptions" to the hearsay rule. The first is not an exception because it really is not hearsay in the first place. The statement does not come in for its truth; its mere utterance provides circumstantial evidence of something else. For example, where defendant was on trial for killing his wife, her statement to him that she was pregnant by another man was admissible as proof in his defense that he had formed no intent to kill but had acted in the heat of passion.[39] By whom the victim had become pregnant, or whether she was even pregnant at all were factors beside the point, the point being that the mere utterance of the words was sufficient to cause a drastic alteration in the defendant's state of mind. These and other examples of this nonhearsay type of statement, showing the declarant's state of mind, or the hearer's state of mind, are discussed in § 801.1(d) *supra*.

In this section, we discuss the exception to the hearsay rule which allows the statement as evidence of the truth contained in it. Here again there is a division between those statements which evidence the

a verbal act, or as a state of mind expression. Id. at 43, 418 N.Y.S.2d at 663. Characterizing the statement as self-serving, the court recognized that it was an outgrowth of an exciting event, but stated that "the interval of time between the event and the statement, and other factors, clearly negate any contention that the statement was prompted by the incident without time to reflect, and thus was dominated by the nervous excitement of the event." Id. at 45, 418 N.Y.S.2d at 665. This does not seem inconsistent with McCullough. The wounds in Sostre were less severe and, although the time lapse was less, the nature of the statement was such as to raise an obvious question as to its motivation, thus undermining its trustworthiness.

37. § 803(c)(1) [PROPOSED]: "Excited utterance. A statement relating to a startling event or condition made while the declarant was under the stress of excitement caused by the event or condition, that stilled the reflective powers of the declarant."

38. In People v. Miklejohn, 184 A.D.2d 735, 585 N.Y.S.2d 454 (2d Dep't 1992), responding to a question, the dying victim told police shortly after he had been beaten that he did not know the identity of his assailant. Defendant sought to have the statement admitted as he and the victim had known each other for 15 years. The court found that the statement satisfied the requirements and allowed it in. In People v. Norton, 164 A.D.2d 343, 563 N.Y.S.2d 802 (1st Dep't 1990), aff'd, 79 N.Y.2d 808, 580 N.Y.S.2d 174, 588 N.E.2d 72 (1991), one Roldos approached the police and complained that he had been stabbed. All of his statements after that were in response to police questioning. None of them were admissible since it did not appear that declarant was seriously wounded or that he was in a state of shock. In People v. Knapp, 139 A.D.2d 931, 527 N.Y.S.2d 914 (4th Dep't), appeal denied, 72 N.Y.2d 862, 532 N.Y.S.2d 512, 528 N.E.2d 902 (1988) the four-year-old victim's mother found her with the defendant at which point the victim said words to the effect that defendant had sexually molested her. This was admissible. The traumatic and emotional nature of the event indicated that the statement was made while the child was still in a state of excitement. And, in Flynn v. Manhattan & Bronx Surface Transit Operating Auth., 94 A.D.2d 617, 462 N.Y.S.2d 17 (1st Dep't 1983), aff'd, 61 N.Y.2d 769, 473 N.Y.S.2d 154, 461 N.E.2d 291 (1984), the court allowed the use of plaintiff's crucial statement, "The bus hit me," made as bystanders went to his aid.

39. People v. Harris, 209 N.Y. 70, 102 N.E. 546 (1913).

thoughts a person has at the time she speaks, where this would be relevant, and those statements which evidence an intention to do something, go somewhere, or meet someone. Most of the New York cases under the first category are of the nonhearsay type, i.e., statements as to declarant's mental state,[40] statements offered to explain declarant's acts,[41] and statements to show why the person who heard the declarant acted the way she did.[42] Some statements concerning a present physical condition are also admissible for the truth, e.g., expressions of pain introduced to show declarant was in pain.[43]

---

40. People v. Ricco, 56 N.Y.2d 320, 328, 452 N.Y.S.2d 340, 345, 437 N.E.2d 1097, 1102 (1982)(defendant's delusional statements to his mother were admissible, not to prove he saw spaceships through his telescope, but to show the condition of his mind).

41. Loetsch v. New York City Omnibus Corp., 291 N.Y. 308, 52 N.E.2d 448 (1943)(in an attempt to prove the plaintiff husband would have profited little from his wife's death, defendant introduced the wife's will which disparaged her husband and left him one dollar since regardless of the truth of the statement, it showed the wife's attitude toward her husband); People v. Boyling, 84 A.D.2d 892, 444 N.Y.S.2d 760 (3d Dep't 1981) (statements made by defendant during activities which the People charged as burglary were admissible to evidence the nature of these activities inside the building).

42. In addition to People v. Harris, note 39 supra, see People v. Felder, 37 N.Y.2d 779, 375 N.Y.S.2d 98, 337 N.E.2d 606 (1975)(the testimony that a bystander said to one Brunson "This Joe is going to take your money" was admissible to explain Brunson's conduct in jumping on a table and running away from the premises). There is one notable old case where the statement seems to be admitted for its truth. A tenant's statement that he was leaving the premises because of construction of the elevated railroad outside his window could be used by the landlord in his suit against the railroad for damages. Hine v. N.Y. Elevated R.R. Co., 149 N.Y. 154, 43 N.E. 414 (1896).

43. The rule in New York regarding expressions of pain is contained in Roche v. Brooklyn City & Newtown R.R. Co., 105 N.Y. 294, 11 N.E. 630 (1887), where it was held that involuntary expressions of pain such as screams or groans are admissible, but that literate references regarding pain, such as an outright statement that the declarant is suffering pain, are not. The court stated: "But evidence of simple declarations of a party made some time after the injury and not to a physician for the purpose of being attended to professionally, and simply making the statement that he or she is then suffering pain, is evidence of a totally different nature, is easily stated, liable to gross exaggeration and of a most dangerous tendency while the former necessity for its admission [common law rule that the parties could not testify] has wholly ceased." 105 N.Y. at 298, 11 N.E. at 632. The literate statement as to pain may, however, be admitted if the declarant has since died. Tromblee v. North American Accident Ins. Co., 173 App.Div. 174, 158 N.Y.S. 1014 (3d Dep't 1916), aff'd, 226 N.Y. 615, 123 N.E. 892 (1919). The proposed New York Code § 803(c)(2) seems to preserve the Roche rule since it refers to "involuntary expressions of pain or physical condition"; but voluntary expressions of pain are provided for in proposed § 804 where the declarant is unavailable.

The full text of proposed New York Evidence Code § 803(c)(2) is as follows:

(2) Then-existing mental, emotional, or physical condition. An involuntary expression of pain or physical condition, a statement of a declarant's then-existing state of mind, emotion (such as intent, plan, motive, design, mental feeling). Provided, however, none of the foregoing statements may include a statement of memory or belief to prove the fact remembered or believed and the admissibility of a declaration of intent to prove the conduct of a person other than the declarant shall be governed by paragraph five of subdivision (b) of section 804 of this article.

Proposed § 804(b)(4)(declarant unavailable) provides for "a statement of a then-existing sensation or physical condition (such as pain or bodily condition.)" The comment states: "This subdivision includes voluntary statements of a declarant's present bodily feelings * * *. This slightly changes present law which admitted declarations of present pain, conditions, or symptoms only when the declarant was dead. * * * Broadening the grounds of unavailability reflects a modest but desirable change in the law."

§ 803(1).1   HEARSAY   Ch. 8

The prime requisite to any of these statement is that they be expressions of current thought or feeling. References to past thoughts or feelings will not be admissible. Thus, in *People v. Reynoso*[44] defendant argued that he should be allowed to introduce a statement, made to his sister two hours after the shooting, that he believed the victim had been armed. The court held the statement irrelevant unless offered to prove its truth, and in that respect it would be inadmissible hearsay. "While such declarations may be received to show the declarant's state of mind at the time the statement was made, they are not admissible to establish the truth of past facts contained in them * * *."[45] In other words, the expression of the state of mind must be made contemporaneously with the thought giving rise to the expression—a close adherence to the old *res gestae* doctrine. Under Federal Rule of Evidence 803(3) there is an exception so that statements as to facts remembered or believed are admissible when relating to the execution, revocation, identification, or terms of declarant's will. No such exception appears in the Proposed New York Evidence Code, and this is said by the drafters to be in accord with present New York law.[46]

Expressions of intent. These declarations can be treated as a unit since many cases have evolved from the United States Supreme Court's decision in *Mutual Life Insurance Co. v. Hillmon*,[47] a case that shook the hearsay world in its day.[48] In that case, an insurance company was attempting to prove that a body found at Crooked Creek, Kansas, was that of Walters and not that of Hillmon, the insured, who the insurance company suspected of perpetrating a fraud. To aid this proof the insurer sought to introduce letters written by Walters in which he said he was going to Crooked Creek with Hillmon. "[T]he letters in question," said the court, "were competent * * * as evidence that * * * [Walters] had the intention of going, and of going with Hillmon, which made it more probable both that he did go and that he went with Hillmon."[49]

The most prominent New York manifestation of the *Hillmon* rule is found in *People v. Malizia*[50] where Malizia denied his complicity in a gangland-style slaying. The victim's brother, the prosecution's chief witness, was allowed to testify that his brother told him that he was

---

44. 73 N.Y.2d 816, 537 N.Y.S.2d 113, 534 N.E.2d 30 (1988).

45. Id. at 819, 537 N.Y.S.2d at 114, 534 N.E.2d at 31. To include memories of past events within the state-of-mind exception would eviscerate the hearsay rule.

46. Cited in the comment are the following cases: In re Will of Bonner, 17 N.Y.2d 9, 266 N.Y.S.2d 971, 214 N.E.2d 154 (1966); In re Kennedy's Will, 167 N.Y. 163, 60 N.E. 442 (1901); Waterman v. Whitney, 11 N.Y. 157 (1854); In re Kent's Will, 169 App.Div. 388, 155 N.Y.S. 894 (4th Dep't 1915); and N.Y.Surrogates Court Procedure Act § 1407.

47. 145 U.S. 285, 12 S.Ct. 909, 36 L.Ed. 706 (1892).

48. See McCormick § 276, at 241, to the effect that the Hillmon decision, as stated in Shepard v. United States, 290 U.S. 96, 105, 54 S.Ct. 22, 26, 78 L.Ed. 196 (1933), "marks the high water line beyond which courts have been unwilling to go." See also Maguire, "The Hillmon Case—Thirty-three Years After," 38 Harvard L.Rev. 709 (1925).

49. 145 U.S. at 295–96, 12 S.Ct. at 912–13, 36 L.Ed. at 710.

50. 92 A.D.2d 154, 460 N.Y.S.2d 23 (1st Dep't 1983), aff'd, 62 N.Y.2d 755, 476 N.Y.S.2d 825, 465 N.E.2d 364, cert. denied, 469 U.S. 932, 105 S.Ct. 327, 83 L.Ed.2d 264 (1984).

going to meet Malizia in order to pay him a large sum of money in connection with a narcotics transaction. If this were all there was to it an almost pure *Hillmon* situation would arise except that the inference the jury would have to draw was that Malizia also intended this meeting, did show up, and killed the victim. This might be warranted under a liberal reading of *Hillmon*. In *Malizia*, however, there was more. The brother drove the victim to the meeting place, observed a car linked to Malizia, and was himself shot at as the other car sped away with the victim inside. The evidence concerning the statement of intent was not broached in the Court of Appeals' affirmance of the conviction since the question had not been properly preserved for review.[51] The *Hillmon* rule was again implicated in *People v. Chambers*,[52] where the victim had telephoned Resnick and told him that she had received a call from defendant, who stated that he intended to visit her within about an hour. The victim was murdered and her statement was sought to be introduced against defendant through Resnick's testimony. The majority found this inadmissible. There were no surrounding circumstances which gave credence to defendant's purported statement. The double hearsay nature of the evidence prevented cross-examination of the person who spoke to the defendant. That person, the deceased, was called a passive actor. It was not her intent to have a meeting. She simply repeated what was reputed to be somebody else's intent.[53] In *Malizia*, by contrast, the witness heard the expression of intent directly from one of the persons who intended a meeting, and there was abundant corroboration. Thus, the line seems reasonably to have been drawn in the *Chambers* case. But questions remain. *Hillmon* and *Malizia* both entailed expressions as to what someone else would do, i.e., the relevance of the statement in *Malizia* was that someone other than the speaker also attended the meeting. *Hillmon* did not go quite that far since there, Walter's statements as to his own intentions were introduced chiefly to show he fulfilled them. The fact that Hillmon's name was included might indicate that Hillmon also went to Crooked Creek, but the insurer wanted mainly to show Walter's presence there. *Malizia* thus seems questionable had there been no corroborating evidence of the other person's conduct.[54] The proposed New York Evidence Code would delineate the *Hillmon* rule as applied in *Malizia*.[55]

---

51. 62 N.Y.2d at 757, 476 N.Y.S.2d at 827, 465 N.E.2d at 366. In the opinion at the Appellate Division it was stated: "We are persuaded that a statement by a deceased that he intends to meet another is admissible where the statement is made under circumstances that make it probable that the expressed intent was a serious one, and that it was realistically likely that such a meeting would in fact take place." 92 A.D.2d at 160, 460 N.Y.S.2d at 27.

52. 125 A.D.2d 88, 512 N.Y.S.2d 89 (1st Dep't), appeal dismissed, 70 N.Y.2d 694, 518 N.Y.S.2d 1031, 512 N.E.2d 557 (1987).

53. Id. at 95, 512 N.Y.S.2d at 93.

54. The Proposed New York Evidence Code § 803(c)(2) provides that if the purpose is to show the intent of a person other than the declarant, then the provisions regarding trustworthiness of statements made by unavailable declarants under proposed section 804(b)(5) must govern. With respect to the question whether the Hillmon rule extends to the actions of others besides the declarant, see the Second Circuit's construction of Hillmon as discussed in § 803(1).2(c) infra.

55. § 804(b)(5) [PROPOSED]
(5) Intent to engage in conduct with another. A declaration of intent to engage in conduct with another person to establish the conduct of that other person

Older cases have established the admissibility of statements of intent in more prosaic circumstances;[56] but one of more recent vintage illustrates the lengths to which *Hillmon* is sought to be stretched.[57] A defendant's threats are admissible to show his state of mind and probable conduct,[58] and threats to the defendant, where the defense of self-defense is raised, are admissible as showing the victim's state of mind and probable conduct regardless of whether the defendant knew of the threats.[59] The instance where, in self-defense cases, threats are admitted as circumstantial evidence of the victim's alleged provocation should be distinguished from those instances where the victim's reputation for acts of violence would have to be known by defendant in order to show defendant's state of mind.[60] (*See* § 402.1(f) *supra* for a discussion of character evidence in self-defense cases.)

made under circumstances that make it: probable that the expressed intent was a serious one; realistically likely that the person other than the declarant would engage in the conduct; and the statement is corroborated by other evidence tending to show that the person other than the declarant engaged in the conduct in question.

The comment states: "Crucially, the hearsay declaration must reflect the intent of the declarant and not the intent of the other person who may have spoken to the declarant."

56. See Healy v. Rennert, 9 N.Y.2d 202, 209, 213 N.Y.S.2d 44, 49, 173 N.E.2d 777, 780 (1961)(evidence contained in letters and statements of witness that he had moved to Arizona with no intention of returning admissible to show his unavailability for purposes of introducing his testimony from a previous trial); Crawford v. Nilan, 289 N.Y. 444, 448–49, 46 N.E.2d 512, 514 (1943)(statement as to where declarant and others were intending to go in car admissible); People v. Conklin, 175 N.Y. 333, 343, 67 N.E. 624, 627 (1903)(testimony would be proper from a defense witness in a murder case that victim said, three years prior to her death, that she intended to commit suicide); Sees v. Massachusetts Bonding & Ins. Co., 243 App.Div. 400, 402–03, 277 N.Y.S. 198, 201 (1st Dep't 1935)(to prove insured committed suicide, it was proper to admit letter evidencing his state of mind written two months before his death); Landon v. Preferred Acc. Ins. Co., 43 App.Div. 487, 490, 60 N.Y.S. 188, 190 (2d Dep't 1899), aff'd, 167 N.Y. 577, 60 N.E. 1114 (1901)(declaration of deceased that he intended to go to Staten Island, and the finding of his body off its shores, tended to prove accidental death).

57. In People v. Lauro, 91 Misc.2d 706, 709–10, 398 N.Y.S.2d 503, 505 (Sup.Ct. Westchester Co.1977), the prosecutor, in order to show husband's motive for killing his wife, proffered evidence that the wife said she intended to confront her husband with a financial ultimatum, but the court would not allow it since it would be stretching Hillmon too far to allow the jury to draw this series of inferences: "(1) that Angie Lauro did *perform the act intended*, i.e., confront the defendant with her 'ultimatum' financial offer; (2) that he reacted adversely to such a proposal; which in turn, (3) provided the defendant with a motive to kill; and (4) ultimately led him to actually kill his wife Angie with a shotgun" (emphasis in original).

58. People v. O'Sullivan, 104 N.Y. 481, 484, 10 N.E. 880, 881 (1887)(in rape prosecution it is permissible to show that defendant had declared his intent to commit the crime); People v. St. John, 74 A.D.2d 85, 89, 426 N.Y.S.2d 863, 866 (3d Dep't 1980)("A threat to do an act is some evidence that the act threatened was at least attempted;" here, defendant stated to his wife that he intended to "break in" his daughters by having sexual relations with them).

59. People v. Miller, 39 N.Y.2d 543, 549, 384 N.Y.S.2d 741, 745, 349 N.E.2d 841, 845 (1976); People v. Dixon, 138 A.D.2d 929, 930, 526 N.Y.S.2d 269, 270 (4th Dep't 1988)(defendant's girlfriend could testify that the victim had threatened defendant because defendant was black and his girlfriend was Hispanic, even though defendant had not heard these threats).

60. In People v. Miller, note 59 supra, it was stated:

"The character of the deceased with reference to violence, when known to the accused, enables him to judge of the danger and aids the jury in deciding whether he acted in good faith and upon the honest belief that his life was in peril. It shows the state of his mind as to the necessity of defending himself." (People

d. Statements Made for Purposes of Medical Diagnosis or Treatment

Expressions of present bodily feelings and functions when made to a treating physician are admissible in New York.[61] This is a very limited rule because it does not provide for (1) expressions of past bodily feelings and functions, and (2) statements made to people other than a treating physician such as hospital attendants, ambulance personnel, members of the family, and perhaps even paramedics.[62] Federal Rule of Evidence 803(4) is not curtailed by such limitations; and Proposed New York Evidence Code § 803(c)(3) would allow for statements as to past bodily condition, keeping, however, the rule that the statement, to be admissible, must be made to a physician and expanding this a bit to include an agent of a physician.[63]

The opinion in the 1892 case of *Davidson v. Cornell*,[64] remains the fount of the current New York rule. In that case, the trial court allowed the patient-declarant's doctor to testify to what declarant told him concerning the loss of his sexual powers and other disabilities caused by the accident. The doctor was not the treating physician, but one who was apparently consulted for purposes of expert testimony. The Court of Appeals reversed plaintiff's verdict holding that statements made by the prospective plaintiff for trial purposes would not conform to the general rule that allows statements made for purposes of treatment. In the latter situation, there is a "strong inducement for the patient to speak truly of his pains and sufferings while it may be otherwise when medically examined for the purpose of creating evidence in his own behalf."[65] The court also stated that, to be admissible, the expressions by declarant must relate to present and not past pain.[66]

---

v. Rodawald, 177 N.Y. 408, 423, 70 N.E. 1; see, generally, Evidence—Self Defense—Reputation, Ann. 1 ALR3d 571). Similarly, the threats of the deceased against the defendant are admissible, whether communicated to the defendant or not. Even if the defendant was not aware of the threat, the threat still is probative of the deceased's state of mind and bears, thus, on whether the deceased was the aggressor. (Stokes v. People, 53 N.Y. 164, 174.)

Miller, 39 N.Y.2d at 549, 384 N.Y.S.2d at 745, 349 N.E.2d at 845.

61. Davidson v. Cornell, 132 N.Y. 228, 30 N.E. 573 (1892).

62. But see People v. Caccese, 211 A.D.2d 976, 621 N.Y.S.2d 735 (3d Dep't 1995)(statement made to nurse for purposes of treatment held admissible).

63. Proposed § 803(c)(3) states:

(3) Statements for purposes of medical diagnosis or treatment. Statements, reasonably pertinent to diagnosis or treatment of the declarant, made to a physician or an agent of a physician describing medical history, or past or present symptoms, pain, or sensations, or the inception or general character or the cause or external source thereof, made with the expectation that they will be relied upon by a treating physician for purposes of medical diagnosis or treatment.

Whether or not an ambulance attendant, a paramedic, or others who initially attend to the declarant are a physician's agent would presumably have to be decided on a case-by-case basis, but physician's assistants would presumably be acting at the direction of a physician. These people are intended as possible agents under the proposed rule as indicated in the related comment.

64. 132 N.Y. 228, 30 N.E. 573 (1892).

65. Id. at 237, 30 N.E. at 576.

66. Id. These rules have been perpetuated. See De Luca v. Kameros, 130 A.D.2d 705, 515 N.Y.S.2d 819 (2d Dep't 1987); Nissen v. Rubin, 121 A.D.2d 320, 321, 504 N.Y.S.2d 106, 107 (1st Dep't 1986); Lessin v. Direct Delivery Service, 10 A.D.2d 624, 196 N.Y.S.2d 751 (1st Dep't 1960).

§ 803(1).1   HEARSAY   Ch. 8

The rule excluding statements made to an expert medical witness who was not also a treating physician is circumscribed by the rule that in rendering an opinion a medical witness may rely on, *inter alia*, the history of the event as related by the plaintiff. Thus, in *Daliendo v. Johnson*,[67] the court stated:

> The corporate defendants' argument overstates the rule of law in New York that a nontreating physician, hired only to testify as an expert, may not state the history of an accident as related by a party or testify as to the party's medical complaints * * *. This rule was designed to prevent unfair bolstering of a party's credibility and does not preclude such a witness from testifying as to a relevant medical opinion.[68]

This expresses the rule in *People v. Keough*,[69] updated by the decision in *People v. Sugden*,[70] concerning the testimony of expert witnesses. (See § 703.1 *supra*.) *Keough* concerned an expert's testimony as to defendant's sanity and cautioned that while the expert's opinion could be based on his interview with defendant, his opinion should not be based on information imparted by non-testifying third parties.[71] Older cases would appear to have limited the expert's reliance on the subject's expressions of past mental condition;[72] but that rule seems to have been swallowed up in the more contemporary views regarding what can be relied on by an expert. It is not unthinkable that the New York courts, when given the opportunity, might note the somewhat confusing nature of this situation where statements made to a nontreating physician are inadmissible on their own as substantive evidence, but where they can be introduced when the nontreating physician explains the basis for her opinion. This distinction has been abolished under Federal Rule 803(4). (See § 803(1).2(d), *infra*.)

The proposed New York Evidence Code § 803(c)(3) provides that in addition to the expression of present bodily condition as related by the patient, the attending physician may also testify concerning the patient's statement as to the "cause or external source thereof" meaning, it is presumed, that the witness may testify that the patient said he was struck by broken glass, stabbed with a knife, shot by a pellet gun, or whatever the cause of his malady might have been. The comment to the proposed code provision cautions that this should be limited to the immediate cause, and not include facts unnecessary for diagnosis and

---

67. 147 A.D.2d 312, 543 N.Y.S.2d 987 (2d Dep't 1989).

68. Id. at 320, 543 N.Y.S.2d at 992.

69. 276 N.Y. 141, 11 N.E.2d 570 (1937).

70. 35 N.Y.2d 453, 363 N.Y.S.2d 923, 323 N.E.2d 169 (1974).

71. Keough, 276 N.Y. at 145–46, 11 N.E.2d at 572.

72. See People v. Hawkins, 109 N.Y. 408, 410, 17 N.E. 371, 372 (1888) ("The prisoner's declaration [to a doctor] in November as to his condition in September was not competent as evidence of his actual condition at that time, nor could it be the basis of a scientific opinion as to whether he was sane or insane at that period."); People v. Hill, 195 N.Y. 16, 25, 87 N.E. 813, 816 (1909)("an expert witness cannot be permitted to give an opinion as to the mental condition of a person at the time of the commission of a criminal act, based upon a statement not in evidence, made by a party in his own behalf after the commission of the act, which pertains to his past conduct"). See also People v. Raizen, 211 App. Div. 446, 459–60, 208 N.Y.S. 185, 198 (2d Dep't 1925).

treatment such as the identity of the perpetrator. This rule stems from the opinion in *Williams v. Alexander*[73] where it was held that a medical record could qualify as evidence under the business entry rule only insofar as it related to information necessary for diagnosis and treatment, and that the patient's relation of events leading up to the accident (which would tend to fix liability) was not necessary for diagnosis and treatment and thus would be inadmissible. This remains the general rule[74] and would seem to govern the extent to which the treating physician may testify to what the patient told him; except that any admissions made by the patient ought to be considered admissible, when offered by the opponent, under the rules applying to admissions (*see* § 802.2 *supra*).

Even without passage of proposed New York Evidence Code § 803(c)(3), it might well be that the courts could be persuaded to modernize the law so as to include statements of past condition,[75] and perhaps even to extend the rule so that people other than physicians called on to aid a person in mental or physical distress could testify as to statements made, at least with respect to expressions of current distress. If, as originally recognized in *Davidson v. Cornell*,[76] the guarantee of truthfulness lies in the patient's recognition that he can only get meaningful help if he gives accurate information, it should not matter that the person trying to help is not a physician.

Library References:

West's Key No. Digests, Criminal Law ⊂⇒362–368, 419(2.15, 2.20); Evidence ⊂⇒118–128, 268.

§ 803(1).2 Federal

The introductory material in the last section is applicable here. The distinguishing aspect of the Federal Rules is that they have liberalized to some extent the *res gestae* concept in respect to several of the exceptions. Of these exceptions, the boldest stroke was the recognition of the present sense impression which, until enactment of the rule, had had minimal case law acceptance.[1]

---

73. 309 N.Y. 283, 129 N.E.2d 417 (1955).

74. The recent case of People v. Caccese, 211 A.D.2d 976, 621 N.Y.S.2d 735 (3d Dep't 1995), appears to have relaxed the rule by allowing a nurse to testify to an injured child's statement identifying a foster parent as the person who injured him. Arguably, in child abuse situations the identity of the abuser is very pertinent to the psychological treatment and diagnosis of the child.

75. See McCormick § 277, at 247. This would be "generally sound, as patients are likely to recognize the importance to their treatment of accurate statements as to past, as well as present, symptoms."

76. 132 N.Y. 228, 237, 30 N.E. 573, 576 (1892). See text at note 65 supra.

§ 803(1).2

1. See, e.g., Houston Oxygen Co. v. Davis, 139 Tex. 1, 161 S.W.2d 474 (Sup.Ct.Texas 1942). A passenger in a car remarked as another car sped past that if that speed was sustained the other car would wind up in a wreck, and of course this prophecy was fulfilled a short way down the road. Holding the statement admissible, the court stated: "Such a comment, as to a situation then before the declarant, does not have the safeguard of impulse, emotion or excitement, but there are other safeguards. In the first place, the report at the moment of the thing seen, heard, etc., is safe from any error from defect or memory of the declarant. Secondly, there is little or no time for calculated misstatement, and thirdly, the statement

§ 803(1).2   HEARSAY   Ch. 8

a. Present Sense Impression

Federal Rule of Evidence 803(1) renders admissible:

A statement describing or explaining an event or condition made while the declarant was perceiving the event or condition, or immediately thereafter.

United States v. Medico[2] is a case indicating that the Second Circuit was prepared early on to treat this provision with liberality. A bank employee testified that five minutes after robbers had fled the bank, he was in the process of locking the entrance glass door when an unknown person knocked and shouted the make and license number of the getaway car. Another person sitting in a car at the curb was giving the speaker this information and he relayed it to the witness, the bank employee. The evidence was ruled admissible at the trial under the residuary provision of Federal Rule 804, i.e., Rule 804(b)(5), which permits hearsay from an unavailable declarant when the statement does not satisfy all of the requirements of the other Rule 804 exceptions but has sufficient earmarks of trustworthiness (*see* § 804(5).2 *infra*). On appeal the court affirmed the ruling and said in dictum that the statements fit all the requirements of the present sense impression.[3] The court noted the Advisory Committee's comment that the new provision did not conform to some case law that held that the identity of the declarant ought to be known.[4] It appears that that court would have affirmed had the trial judge used the present sense impression exception; but affirmance was based on the residuary exception since it fit there also.[5] The dissenter stressed the double hearsay nature of the message through the closed door and found that it lacked the necessary guarantees of trustworthiness.[6]

The present sense impression exception has been held to apply to statements made by a government agent recorded on his body recorder in response to questions shortly after arrests in the transaction in which he was involved;[7] to a statement testified to by the witness as to limited

---

will usually be made to another (the witness who reports it) who would have equal opportunities to observe and hence to check a misstatement." 139 Tex. at 6, 161 S.W.2d at 476–77. The last point quoted relating to the presence of a second witness could not be fulfilled where the report comes over the telephone, and the New York Court of Appeals in People v. Brown, 80 N.Y.2d 729, 594 N.Y.S.2d 696, 610 N.E.2d 369 (1993), held such a requirement unnecessary, but retained the notion that there must be some sort of corroboration. See the discussion of Brown in § 803(1).1(a) supra. See also Emens v. Lehigh Valley R. Co., 223 F. 810, 825–27 (N.D.N.Y.1915)(bystander's statement, "Why don't the train whistle?" as she watched the train nearing the intersection held admissible).

2. 557 F.2d 309 (2d Cir.), cert. denied, 434 U.S. 986, 98 S.Ct. 614, 54 L.Ed.2d 480 (1977).

3. Id. at 315.

4. Id. This is the enigmatic Advisory Committee statement: "However, when declarant is an unidentified bystander, the cases indicate hesitancy in upholding the statement alone as sufficient, Garrett v. Howden, 73 N.M. 307, 387 P.2d 874 (1963); Beck v. Dye, 200 Wash. 1, 92 P.2d 1113 (1939), a result which would under appropriate circumstances be consistent with the rule."

5. 557 F.2d at 315.

6. Id. at 319–22.

7. United States v. Obayagbona, 627 F.Supp. 329, 339 (E.D.N.Y.1985).

access to a dangerous work area;[8] and to the reaction of an audience to the rendition of a musical performance.[9] And in *United States v. Mejia-Velez,*[10] we find what appears to be the first reported case in the Second Circuit involving a 911 call. Here, two witnesses who saw the event gave their testimony at trial, and the court allowed the tape of their consistent 911 calls to be played, pursuant to Rule 803(1). It does not appear that a 911 case such as New York's *Brown*[11] case has arisen where the identity of the declarant is unknown; but the *Medico* dictum indicates that the Rule would accommodate that circumstance.

b. Excited Utterance

Federal Rule of Evidence 803(2) makes admissible:

> A statement relating to a startling event or condition made while the declarant was under the stress of excitement caused by the event or condition.

The Advisory Committee points out that this provision is somewhat broader than the present sense impression since, while they do overlap, a statement under Rule 803(1) is limited to a description of the event being witnessed while under Rule 803(2) the statement need only *relate* to the startling event.[12]

That the excited utterance exception is treated with extreme liberality in the Second Circuit is illustrated in *United States v. Scarpa,*[13] where the statement in question, made to a police officer and naming declarant's attackers, came after a lapse of five to six hours from the time declarant was beaten. Over defendants' argument that the requisite stress would have been alleviated by that time, the court stated:

> We disagree. An excited utterance need not be contemporaneous with the startling event to be admissible under rule 803(2). * * * The length of time between the event and the utterance is only one factor to be taken into account in determining whether

---

8. Robinson v. Shapiro, 484 F.Supp. 91, 94–95 (S.D.N.Y.1980), aff'd, 646 F.2d 734 (2d Cir.1981)(the witness testified that the decedent told him that the building superintendent had told him, decedent, that access to the work site could only be by a certain way; this was not double hearsay because the superintendent's statement was a verbal act, and the decedent's statement was made immediately upon hearing it).

9. MCA, Inc. v. Wilson, 425 F.Supp. 443, 450–51 (S.D.N.Y.1976), aff'd, 677 F.2d 180 (2d Cir.1981)(in copyright infringement case audience responses to song were admissible since "their spontaneity provides their reliability and cures any hearsay infirmities").

10. 855 F.Supp. 607, 613 (E.D.N.Y. 1994).

11. People v. Brown, 80 N.Y.2d 729, 594 N.Y.S.2d 696, 610 N.E.2d 369 (1993). See discussion of this case in § 803(1).1(a) supra.

12. As illustrations of this distinction, the Advisory Committee cites 6 Wigmore §§ 1750, 1754, and states: "See Sanitary Grocery Co. v. Snead, 67 App.D.C. 129, 90 F.2d 374 (D.C.App.1937), slip-and-fall case sustaining admissibility of clerk's statement, 'That has been on the floor for a couple of hours,' and Murphy Auto Parts Co., Inc. v. Ball, 101 U.S.App.D.C. 416, 249 F.2d 508 (C.A.D.C.1957), cert. denied, 355 U.S. 932, 78 S.Ct. 413, 2 L.Ed.2d 415 (1958) upholding admission, on issue of driver's agency, of his statement that he had to call on a customer and was in a hurry to get home. Quick, Hearsay, Excitement, Necessity and the Uniform Rules: A Reappraisal of Rule 63(4), 6 Wayne L.Rev. 204, 206–209 (1960)."

13. 913 F.2d 993 (2d Cir.1990).

the declarant was, within the meaning of rule 803(2), "under the stress of excitement caused by the event or condition."[14]

The court, however, is watchful of the foundation requirements, i.e., that there be proof that the declarant actually saw the event about which he spoke. Thus, in *Cummiskey v. Chandris, S.A.*,[15] on the issue whether a dangerous condition existed on defendant's ship, plaintiff sought to introduce a statement by an unknown declarant that the site of the accident was wet. Finding the statement inadmissible under Rule 804, the court turned to Rule 803(2), but could not qualify the statement there either, noting that when the declarant is both unknown and unidentified the proponent of the evidence has a greater burden of establishing perception of the event by the purported declarant.[16]

In Judge Weinstein's opinion in *United States v. Obayagbona*,[17] there is found a prime example of the excited utterance where the statements were made shortly after the arrest of the culprits with whom declarant had been dealing.[18]

Recent cases from other circuits are also instructive.[19]

c. State of Mind or Physical Condition

Federal Rule of Evidence 803(3) provides that a statement is admissible if it is:

> A statement of the declarant's then existing state of mind, emotion, sensation, or physical condition (such as intent, plan, motive, design, mental feeling, pain, and bodily health), but not including a statement of memory or belief to prove the fact

---

14. Id. at 1017. The court cited Gross v. Greer, 773 F.2d 116, 119–20 (7th Cir. 1985)(court properly admitted evidence of statement made 12 hours after startling event).

15. 719 F.Supp. 1183 (S.D.N.Y.1989), aff'd, 895 F.2d 107 (2d Cir.1990).

16. Id. at 1187. The court indicated that the happening of the event normally cannot be proved by the statement itself. Id.

17. 627 F.Supp. 329 (E.D.N.Y.1985).

18. Declarant, with another FBI agent, had engaged defendants in a drug sale. Declarant was equipped with a tape recorder which kept running after defendants were led away. At this point declarant recounted what had occurred as the situation climaxed. Judge Weinstein stated:

> Determination of excitement is facilitated by the recording. On tape Agent Turner's voice is exultant—he has just completed his job, a successful arrest has been made, and the pent-up tension of his performance in the role of "Joe" has just come to an abrupt end. Testimony, and Turner's recording, depict a quick and somewhat chaotic arrest that would continue the excitement of receiving and testing the sample. Such a situation engenders excitement. Listening to the tape, the court determined that these were valid psychological guarantees against fabrication. It is not likely that the witness was deliberately fabricating evidence. He was too excited to do so.

Id. at 338–39.

19. See United States v. Moses, 15 F.3d 774, 777–78 (8th Cir.), cert. denied, ___ U.S. ___, 114 S.Ct. 2691, 129 L.Ed.2d 822 (1994) (statement by prisoner as to the identity of defendant who prisoner said had attacked the victim admissible where made immediately after the attack); United States v. Fontenot, 14 F.3d 1364, 1371 (9th Cir.), cert. denied, ___ U.S. ___, 115 S.Ct. 431, 130 L.Ed.2d 343 (1994)(declarant's statement, made four days after receiving an apparently "terrifying" telephone call ruled not within the excitement zone); People of Territory of Guam v. Ignacio, 10 F.3d 608, 614–15 (9th Cir.1993)(statement by child to defendant's wife that defendant had molested her, made about an hour after the event, ruled admissible as the court could "assume" that the child would still be under the stress of it).

remembered or believed unless it relates to the execution, revocation, identification, or terms of declarant's will.

As noted in § 803(1).1(c) *supra*, the Federal Rule is more liberal than its proposed New York counterpart in that the latter speaks of "involuntary" expressions of physical condition, bars all statements of memory or belief, and relegates statements introduced to show the intent of a person other than the declarant to the residuary exception under the unavailability provisions of proposed section 804(b)(5).

As was discussed in § 803(1).1(c) *supra*, declarations of present state of mind, introduced for the purpose of proving the state of mind as of the time of the declaration, can come in as either nonhearsay, or under the Rule 803(3) exception. In *United States v. Southland Corp.*,[20] holding that a person's notes made during a meeting were admissible to show his understanding of the substance of the meeting, the court stated:

> When a declaration is admitted only to prove a relevant state of mind, it does not appear to matter * * * whether admissibility is predicated on the declaration not being hearsay because it was not offered to prove the truth of the matter asserted, FRE 801(c), or under the hearsay exception for declaration of states of mind, FRE 803(3). Under either theory, "[a] state of mind can be proved circumstantially by statements ... which are not intended to assert the truth of the fact being proved,"* * *.[21]

Rule 803(3) has been used to show suspects' protestations when asked for palm prints by the authorities;[22] customers' statements as to their reasons for not dealing with a seller or supplier;[23] defendant's belief as to the person with whom he was dealing in a drug transaction;[24] plaintiff's expression, in a letter, of his then physical condition;[25] and a broker's statements accompanying his solicitations.[26] Decided before the

---

20. 760 F.2d 1366 (2d Cir.1985), cert. denied, 474 U.S. 825, 106 S.Ct. 82, 88 L.Ed.2d 67 (1985).

21. Id. at 1376. The court cited Metzler v. United States, 64 F.2d 203, 208 (9th Cir.1933), where a letter to a district attorney charging that the county sheriff was taking protection money was admissible, not to prove the sheriff was taking money, but as proof that the district attorney had knowledge.

22. United States v. Terry, 702 F.2d 299, 314 (2d Cir.), cert. denied sub nom. Williams v. United States, 461 U.S. 931, 103 S.Ct. 2095, 77 L.Ed.2d 304 (1983), where suspects had no constitutional right not to submit to giving palm prints, their refusals with accompanying statements were admissible as proof of consciousness of guilt.

23. Hydrolevel Corp. v. Am. Soc. of Mech. Engineers, 635 F.2d 118, 128 (2d Cir.1980), aff'd, 456 U.S. 556, 102 S.Ct. 1935, 72 L.Ed.2d 330 (1982)(in private antitrust action responses of customer, apparently occasioned by defendant's acts, admissible to show effects of defendant's acts).

24. United States v. Harris, 733 F.2d 994, 1004–05 (2d Cir.1984). Defendant's statement to his parole officer during conspiracy that he was dealing with government agents admissible as to his existing belief.

25. Harrigan v. New England Mut. Life Ins. Co., 693 F.Supp. 1531, 1532 (S.D.N.Y.1988)(doctor's letter contained assertion that plaintiff complained of headaches—admissible as "a memorialization of a statement of a then existing mental, emotional, or physical condition.").

26. United States v. Valentine, 637 F.Supp. 196, 198 (S.D.N.Y.1986), rev'd on other grounds, 820 F.2d 565 (2d Cir.1987). Here the court states that the broker's statements come within Rule 803(3) as evidence of intent, plan and motive, but then refers to them as verbal acts admissible to shed light on the rest of the transaction.

enactment of Rule 803(3), but consistent with it, is a case holding that answers to survey questions are admissible under the state of mind exception.[27] The proscription in Rule 803(3) barring statements of memory and belief (except such statements as might bear on matters concerning a will) has been given effect where defendant sought to admit a statement made by a cohort three weeks before trial that defendant was in the wrong place at the wrong time;[28] where defendant tried to introduce evidence that he had said to others, after receiving telephone calls, that his life was in danger;[29] and where defendant's letter of resignation contained his reasons for disagreeing with the employer's policies.[30]

Two cases illustrate the sometimes delicate distinction between statements as to present state of mind, and statements which are retrospective and express a point remembered or believed. In *Shepard v. United States*[31] declarant, before she died, said to her nurse that her husband was poisoning her. This was not, said Justice Cardozo, a declaration expressing her then existing state of mind, but, rather, her belief as to an external, past event.

> [The Government] did not use the declarations by Mrs. Shepard to prove her present thoughts and feelings, or even her thoughts and feelings in times past. It used the declarations as proof of an act committed by someone else, as evidence that she was dying of poison given by her husband.
>
> * * *
>
> The testimony now questioned faced backward and not forward * * *. What is even more important, it spoke to a past act, and more than that, to an act by someone not the speaker.[32]

But, in *United States v. DiMaria*[33] the result was different where, in a prosecution for possession of stolen cigarettes, defendant told government agents, "I thought you guys were just investigating white collar crime; what are you doing here? I only came here to get some cigarettes real cheap."[34] The court said that this statement had none of

---

27. Zippo Manufacturing Company v. Rogers Imports, Inc., 216 F.Supp. 670, 682–83 (S.D.N.Y.1963).

28. United States v. Harwood, 998 F.2d 91, 97–98 (2d Cir.1993). "[Declarant's] statements were not offered to prove his state of mind, but were intended to be used by the jury to support an inference about conduct that had occurred five months earlier." Id. at 98.

29. United States v. Fontenot, 14 F.3d 1364 (9th Cir.), cert. denied, ___ U.S. ___, 115 S.Ct. 431, 130 L.Ed.2d 343 (1994). Defendant argued that this showed his state of mind, but the court found that it was a forbidden expression of belief. This appears a very close question in view of some of the other cases noted above.

30. United States v. Cardascia, 951 F.2d 474, 488 (2d Cir.1991). The court said defendant made a statement of memory or belief to prove he had not agreed with decisions at the time they were made. Defendant was trying to introduce this to show he lacked criminal intent as pertaining to the matters involved in those decisions. The court seemed to doubt any inherent trustworthiness.

31. 290 U.S. 96, 54 S.Ct. 22, 78 L.Ed. 196 (1933).

32. Id. at 104, 106, 54 S.Ct. at 25, 26, 78 L.Ed. at 201, 202, 203.

33. 727 F.2d 265 (2d Cir.1984).

34. Id. at 270.

the characteristics of the statement in *Shepard*; that, rather, his existing state of mind was to possess bootleg cigarettes, not stolen cigarettes:

> It was not offered to prove that the cigarettes were not stolen cigarettes but only to show that DiMaria did not think they were. It would defy reality to predicate any contrary conclusion on the use of the words "I came" rather than "I am." DiMaria's remark was not a statement, like Mrs. Shepard's, of what he or someone else had done in the past. It was a statement of what he was thinking in the present.[35]

Expressions of intent. Since the decision in *Mutual Life Insurance Co. v. Hillmon* [36] is at the root of this part of the state of mind exception, its summarization will be repeated here.[37] In *Hillmon* the insurance company was attempting to prove that a body found at Crooked Creek, Kansas, was that of Walters and not that of Hillmon, the insured, who the insurance company suspected of perpetrating a fraud. To aid this proof the insurer sought to introduce letters written by Walters in which he said he was going to Crooked Creek with Hillmon. "[T]he letters in question," said the court, "were competent * * * as evidence that * * * [Walters] had the intention of going, and of going with Hillmon, which made it more probable both that he did go and that he went with Hillmon."[38]

The Second Circuit has accepted Rule 803(3) as the embodiment of the *Hillmon* rule. This is summed up nicely as follows:

> Burnell contends that Fed.R.Evid. 803(3) was approved by Congress with the understanding that it be construed to limit the *Hillmon* rule to render statements of intent by a declarant admissible only to prove *his* future conduct, not that of a third person. See H.R.Rep.No. 93–650, 93d Cong., 2d Sess., *reprinted in* [1974] U.S.Code Cong.4 Admin.News, pp.7075, 7087. As the Government points out, however, the Advisory Committee Note to Rule 803(3) left the *Hillmon* doctrine "undisturbed," and the courts have held that *Hillmon* declarations of intent are admissible as evidence of actions of the declarant and others.[39]

Even before the enactment of Rule 803(3) the statement of intent was accepted as admissible in the Second Circuit,[40] and the question most bothersome seems to be the extent to which it can be used as proof

---

35. Id. at 271.
36. 145 U.S. 285, 12 S.Ct. 909, 36 L.Ed. 706 (1892).
37. See the discussion of Hillmon in § 803(1).1(c).
38. 145 U.S. at 295–96, 12 S.Ct. at 912–13, 36 L.Ed. at 710.
39. United States v. Moore, 571 F.2d 76, 82 n.3 (2d Cir.1978)(emphasis in original)(having found the Hillmon rule viable, the court nevertheless found that declarant's statement concerning his intent to take the kidnap victim out of state inadmissible as it was uncorroborated). Cited as support for the finding of Hillmon's continuing viability is United States v. Stanchich, 550 F.2d 1294, 1297–98 n.1 (2d Cir. 1977)(threats were admitted under coconspirator exception, but the court indulged in dictum which seems to base admissibility on the presence of corroboration).

40. See United States v. Annunziato, 293 F.2d 373, 377 (2d Cir.), cert. denied, 368 U.S. 919, 82 S.Ct. 240, 7 L.Ed.2d 134 (1961)(declarant's statement, "This money I'm sending up to Annunziato," admissible as proof that it was probable that the money was so dispatched).

of the actions of those other than the declarant. As indicated in the quote just above, despite some opposition, the *Hillmon* rule was intended to be left intact as proof of the declarant's intent as well as the intent of anyone else included in the statement. In some instances the court has sidestepped the question, such as in *United States v. Mangan,* [41] where the court noted confusion as to how *Hillmon* should be applied to the intent of others than the declarant, and characterized the Advisory Committee's acceptance of full application as a gloss over the disparate views involved.[42] In a later case, the court found that the actions of another party could be proved independently of declarant's expression of intent and that thus there was no need to enter the "debate" over the reach of *Hillmon*.[43]

The current status of this situation in the Second Circuit seems to be enunciated in *United States v. Sperling,* [44] where the statement made by an informant that she and others would engage in a drug transaction at a certain time was admissible against the others, not to show their intent, but to show declarant's, and that this evidence, together with other evidence corroborating the fact that the transaction took place would be admissible in tandem.[45]

It appears, then, that the Second Circuit uses a qualified *Hillmon* rule, i.e., that declarant's statement is admissible to evidence his own intent, but it is not admissible to show the intentions of others who might be included in the statement unless there is independent evidence as to the others.[46]

---

41. 575 F.2d 32, 43, n.12 (2d Cir.), cert. denied, 439 U.S. 931, 99 S.Ct. 320, 58 L.Ed.2d 324 (1978). Noting that the Hillmon rule affected not only what Walters was going to do, but also what Hillmon was going to do, the court noted "confusion" as to the extent to which this should be applied, and found the statement admissible as being in furtherance of a conspiracy. Id. at 44.

42. Id. at 43.

43. United States v. Cicale, 691 F.2d 95 (2d Cir.1982), cert. denied, 460 U.S. 1082, 103 S.Ct. 1771, 76 L.Ed.2d 344 (1983). It was stated:

On three separate occasions, we have declined to hold that Hillmon statements illuminate only the actions of the declarant. United States v. Mangan, 575 F.2d 32, 43 n.12 (2d Cir.), cert. denied, 439 U.S. 931, 99 S.Ct. 320, 58 L.Ed.2d 324 (1978); United States v. Moore, 571 F.2d 76, 82 n.3 (2d Cir.1978); Stanchich, 550 F.2d at 1297-98 n.1. On several other occasions we have recognized that Hillmon allows the implication to be drawn from a declarant's statement that he had "relations" with the other persons implicated which made his criminal plans "feasible," thereby rendering such statements admissible "to show the existence of a conspiracy" from which a third party's participation may be inferred. Stanchich, 550 F.2d at 1297-98 n.1, United States v. D'Amato, 493 F.2d 359, 363 (2d Cir.), cert. denied, 419 U.S. 826, 95 S.Ct. 43, 42 L.Ed.2d 50 (1974), United States v. Annunziato, 293 F.2d 373, 377-78 (2d Cir.), cert. denied, 368 U.S. 919, 82 S.Ct. 240, 7 L.Ed.2d 134 (1961).

Id. at 104.

44. 726 F.2d 69, 73-74 (2d Cir.), cert. denied, 467 U.S. 1243, 104 S.Ct. 3516, 82 L.Ed.2d 824 (1984).

45. Id. at 74. The court relied on its decision in the Cicale case, note 43 supra, where the declarant's statement as to what was intended, together with other evidence indicating that others participated in fulfilling that intent, could be used together to prove the entire transaction.

46. See 4 Weinstein and Berger, ¶ 803(3)[04], p.803-128. See also United States v. Nersesian, 824 F.2d 1294, 1325 (2d Cir.), cert. denied, 484 U.S. 958, 108 S.Ct. 357, 98 L.Ed.2d 382 (1987). The court stated:

Hearsay statements reflecting a declarant's intentions or future plans are admissible against the declarant to prove

Finally, in *United States v. Torres*,[47] the court held, in effect, that trial judges have no discretion to exclude declarations of intent if they qualify under the letter of Rule 803(3). In *Torres*, in order to establish an alibi, a defense witness proposed to testify that defendant had said he would take her (the witness) to the beach on the following day. The trial judge found the testimony inherently untrustworthy. The Second Circuit, however, ruled that the adoption of Rule 803(3) removed the judge's prerogative in these situations, citing the *DiMaria* case[48] as referred to in *United States v. Lawal*,[49] as follows:

> *DiMaria* held that relevant declarations which fall within the parameters of Rule 803(3) are *categorically* admissible, even if they are self-serving and made under circumstances which undermine their trustworthiness * * *.[50]

d. Statements Made for Purposes of Medical Diagnosis or Treatment

As noted in § 803(1).1(d) *supra*, Federal Rule of Evidence 803(4) has opened wide the doors for the admissibility of statements of those seeking medical aid. The Rule renders admissible

> statements made for purposes of medical diagnosis or treatment and describing medical history, or past or present symptoms, pain, or sensations, or the inception or general character of the cause or external source thereof insofar as reasonably pertinent to diagnosis or treatment.

Thus, the statements can be made to almost anyone trying to be of assistance (the Advisory Committee states that family members might be included); the statements can relate to past symptoms (the Advisory Committee noted that the motivation for giving accurate information is no less when the statements relate to past conditions); statements can include an account of the cause of the problem if pertinent to diagnosis

---

subsequent acts under Fed.R.Evid. 803(3). * * * More importantly, declarations of intention or future plans are admissible against a nondeclarant when they are linked with independent evidence that corroborates the declaration. Id. at 1325.

47. 901 F.2d 205, 239 (2d Cir.), cert. denied sub nom. Cruz v. United States, 498 U.S. 906, 111 S.Ct. 273, 112 L.Ed.2d 229 (1990).

48. United States v. DiMaria, 727 F.2d 265, 270–72 (2d Cir.1984).

49. 736 F.2d 5, 8 (2d Cir.1984).

50. Torres, 901 F.2d at 240, citing Lawal, 736 F.2d at 8. The court also cited this quote from Judge Friendly's opinion in DiMaria:

> It is doubtless true that all the hearsay exceptions in Rules 803 and 804 rest on a belief that declarations of the sort there described have "some particular assurance of credibility." See Introductory Note, supra. But the scheme of the Rules is to determine that issue by categories; if a declaration comes within a category defined as an exception, the declaration is admissible without any preliminary finding of probable credibility by the judge, save for the "catch-all" exceptions of Rules 803(24) and 804(b)(5) and the business records exception of Rule 803(6) . . ., even though this excludes certain hearsay statements with a high degree of trustworthiness and admits certain statements with a low one. This evil was doubtless thought preferable to requiring preliminary determinations of the judge with respect to trustworthiness, with attendant possibilities of delay, prejudgment and encroachment on the province of the jury.

Torres, 901 F.2d at 239, 240, citing DiMaria, 727 F.2d at 272.

§ 803(1).2

and treatment (the Advisory Committee would not include statements fixing fault); and statements to a nontreating physician in preparation for her testimony as an expert are admissible (the Advisory Committee said it was unrealistic to prohibit a patient's statements as substantive evidence, and then to permit such statements under conventional doctrine if introduced as the basis for an expert's opinion). (*See* discussion of this point in § 803(1).1(d) *supra*.)

It does not appear that the Second Circuit has had an opportunity to test the outer limits of these innovations,[51] but in other circuits the rule is liberally construed.[52] Since the Second Circuit historically has implemented the common law predecessor of Rule 803(4),[53] there is no reason to think that the Rule's wide parameters would not be used by the courts in the Second Circuit.

Library References:

West's Key No. Digests, Criminal Law ⚖362–368, 419(2.15, 2.20); Evidence ⚖118–128, 268.

803(2) Recorded Recollection

§ 803(2).1 New York

If a witness with limited memory of an event in issue memorialized that event in a writing, or perhaps some other form of recording, at or

---

51. In O'Gee v. Dobbs Houses, Inc., 570 F.2d 1084, 1089 (2d Cir.1978), the court recognized the change in the rule relating to statements made to nontreating physicians, and stated: "Rule 803(4) clearly permits the admission into evidence of what O'Gee told Dr. Koven about her condition, so long as it was relied on by Dr. Koven in formulating his opinion—a foundation that was properly laid." This does not clearly address the question whether the patient's statements to this nontreating physician would be admissible separate and apart from his expert opinion. As a practical matter, of course, when a nontreating physician testifies it is for the purpose of stating her opinion and thus the patient's statements would almost always be admissible in this context. And in Mendez v. United States, 732 F.Supp. 414, 423–24 (S.D.N.Y. 1990), the court found that Rule 803(4) accommodated the situation where the guardian of an infant made statements to a treating physician concerning the infant's condition.

52. See United States v. Farley, 992 F.2d 1122, 1125 (10th Cir.1993) (statements to nontreating physician admissible); United States v. Balfany, 965 F.2d 575, 579–580 (8th Cir.1992)(the court stretched the Rule 803(4) provision allowing evidence of the external cause of the injury so that statements of a sexually abused child made to a physician could be introduced to the extent that details of the rape, and the identity of the rapist came in); Wilson v. Zapata Off-Shore Co., 939 F.2d 260, 272 (5th Cir.1991)(statements concerning patient's condition made by her sister admissible under the rule); Navarro de Cosme v. Hospital Pavia, 922 F.2d 926, 932 (1st Cir.1991)(statements to social worker admissible where made for the purpose of obtaining medical treatment); United States v. Iron Shell, 633 F.2d 77, 85 (8th Cir.1980), cert. denied, 450 U.S. 1001, 101 S.Ct. 1709, 68 L.Ed.2d 203 (1981)(child's statements to treating physician concerning details of rape attempt admissible under Rule 803(4).

53. See Stewart v. Baltimore & O.R. Co., 137 F.2d 527, 530 (2d Cir.1943) (statements to treating physician admissible, not as spontaneous utterances, but under the rule that finds trustworthiness in the patient's incentive to be accurate when seeking medical help); Reid v. Quebec Paper Sales & Transportation Company, 340 F.2d 34, 38 (2d Cir.1965)(statements to nontreating physician concerning past ailments admissible, but court noted that "the testimony was not introduced to establish the fact that Reid had experienced these headaches, but rather to show the basis of the doctor's diagnosis," this being characterized as a "non-hearsay purpose").

about the time of the event, and the writing does not refresh her memory (see § 612.1 *supra*), she can attest to its accuracy on the witness stand, and the memorandum or recording can be admitted for its truth. The Appellate Division in *People v. Raja*,[1] set forth the requirements as follows:

> If * * * even after reading the memorandum, the witness remains unable or unwilling to testify as to its contents, the memorandum itself is admissible as substantive evidence of the truth of its contents, provided that otherwise competent testimony establishes that (1) the witness once had knowledge of the contents of the memorandum, (2) the memorandum was prepared by the witness, or at his direction, (3) the memorandum was prepared when the knowledge of the contents was fresh in the mind of the witness, and (4) the witness intended, when the memorandum was made, that it be accurate.[2]

The rule respecting past recollection recorded commands a hearsay exception under Federal Rule of Evidence 803(5), and Proposed New York Evidence Code § 803(c)(4). Currently in New York, of course, the rules are to be found in caselaw, an early guide being *People v. Weinberger*.[3] There, the Court of Appeals reversed a conviction for producing an obscene theatrical production because the trial judge had refused to admit defendant producer's offer of a transcript of the play copied from an actor's script and compared "word for word" with the production version during the time in issue. The trial judge had ruled that the witness' present recollection must be exhausted before his recorded recollection could be introduced, and also denied admissibility because the document was prepared after the indictment was handed up. Judge Lehman said that any rule requiring exhaustion of memory "has not been universally accepted or approved. There are times when the record of a past recollection, if it exists, is more trustworthy and desirable than

---

§ 803(2).1

1. 77 A.D.2d 322, 433 N.Y.S.2d 200 (2d Dep't 1980).

2. Id. at 325–26, 433 N.Y.S.2d at 202. When witnesses testified that they could not recall certain crucial details concerning the commission of the crime, the trial court allowed their statements made to the police at the time of the arrests, to be read into evidence, the witnesses confirming their probable accuracy. All the requirements were clearly satisfied in Raja, except as to the fourth one concerning the belief that the document when made was true and accurate. Although the witnesses testified that they had not read their statements, and they were upset when they made them, they did affirm from the stand that they intended accuracy and "imagined" that the statements were true and honest. Based on these somewhat conflicting signals, the Appellate Division deferred to the trial judge's use of discretion in allowing the statements in. Id. at 327, 433 N.Y.S.2d at 203. See also People v. Barber, 186 A.D.2d 483, 589 N.Y.S.2d 409 (1st Dep't 1992), leave to appeal denied, 81 N.Y.2d 836, 595 N.Y.S.2d 735, 611 N.E.2d 774 (1993), where the witness denied on the stand that he saw defendant pull out a gun. He was properly impeached under Crim.Proc.Law § 60.35 by his prior statement that he had seen defendant pull out a gun and shoot the victim. The witness later testified that he did not recall seeing defendant pull out a gun, but he affirmed the making of the statement and said he had tried to be accurate. Even though he testified on cross-examination that he was frightened by the police when he made the statement, the trial judge had discretion to admit the statement as a past recollection recorded.

3. 239 N.Y. 307, 146 N.E. 434 (1925).

§ 803(2).1 HEARSAY Ch. 8

a present recollection of greater or less vividness * * *."[4]

In the case of a jointly-prepared past recollection recorded, the witness to the event in issue must be able to affirm that she reported accurately to the recorder, and either the witness-reporter or the recorder must be able to affirm that an accurate memorandum of the report was made. In *People v. Taylor*[5] a citizen telephoned the police and gave a detective a crucial license plate number which she could not remember at trial. She testified to this. But the detective on the stand had no recollection of that call or of having made the memorandum in which he recorded the number. Thus, the necessary foundation as to the accuracy of the memorandum could not be laid.[6]

If the witness cannot remember making her own memorandum, the document will not qualify as a past recollection recorded.[7] Where, however, the witness has forgotten the event, or at least some of it,[8] but does recall making a memorandum, and can affirm that the memorandum must have been true and accurate, then the document may qualify. But where the witness will not attest to truth and accuracy the document cannot be admitted under this exception[9] (although under the

---

4. Id. at 311, 146 N.E. at 435.

5. 80 N.Y.2d 1, 586 N.Y.S.2d 545, 598 N.E.2d 693 (1992).

6. Ordinarily, a memorandum made from facts provided by another is not included within this hearsay exception. The memorandum in Taylor might have been admissible had the detective upheld his end, since both the giver and receiver of the information testified. See Muth v. J & T Metal Products Co., 74 A.D.2d 898, 425 N.Y.S.2d 858 (2d Dep't 1980). See also text at note 13 infra.

Judge Hancock stated in Taylor:

Thus, he could not state that what he wrote down was what he had been told * * *. He could state only that because the memorandum was in his handwriting he must have taken the message and that it was his habit to take messages as accurately as possible. * * *

Thus, there can be no more than supposition on the critical question of whether what was observed and sent corresponded with what was heard by the recorder and written down. Without some verification by the observer-sender that what was recorded accurately reflected her observations when made, the record of those observations should not have been received against defendant as substantive incriminating evidence.

80 N.Y.2d at 10–11, 586 N.Y.S.2d at 549, 598 N.E.2d at 697. Compare People v. Blyden, 142 A.D.2d 959, 960, 531 N.Y.S.2d 72 (4th Dep't), appeal denied, 72 N.Y.2d 955, 534 N.Y.S.2d 668, 531 N.E.2d 300 (1988), where the witness testified he could not recall what had happened, and the court held his statement to be admissible with this curious statement: "In our view, it was properly within the trial court's discretion to discount the witness's present disclaimer of his prior sworn statement to the police and find the statement admissible as past recollection recorded for whatever weight the jury saw fit to give it * * *." Id. at 960, 531 N.Y.S.2d at 72.

7. See Brown v. Western Union Tel. Co., 26 A.D.2d 316, 319, 274 N.Y.S.2d 52, 55 (4th Dep't 1966)(where witness professed to have no recollection whatsoever of making the prior statement it had no substantive or impeachment value).

8. People v. Briggs, 190 A.D.2d 995, 996, 593 N.Y.S.2d 622, 623 (4th Dep't), leave to appeal denied, 81 N.Y.2d 1011, 600 N.Y.S.2d 199, 616 N.E.2d 856 (1993)("Although the witness had some general memory of the events, he was unable to remember a number of facts recited in the memorandum and, therefore, the memorandum was properly admitted to augment his memory as past recollection recorded * * *.").

9. People v. Fields, 151 A.D.2d 598, 599, 542 N.Y.S.2d 356, 358 (2d Dep't 1989)(witness must be able to assert the accuracy of the record, and where witness would not do this on the ground he was under the influence of drugs at the time he made it and in fear of the police because of his parolee status the document could not be admitted).

right circumstances the prior statement if inconsistent with the witness' testimony could be admitted for impeachment purposes).[10] The document is likewise inadmissible where the delay between the event and the making of it is too great.[11] It would appear that any form of memorandum can qualify as the necessary evidence.[12] It has been held that the memorandum need not be in the witness' handwriting or even signed by the witness provided that when the matter was fresh in mind he read the document and found it correct.[13]

The past recollection recorded exception has also served to provide identification of a criminal defendant where the witness has been unable to make positive identification on the stand.[14] This is consistent with the rule under Criminal Procedure Law § 60.25 which allows proof of prior identification where the witness has no courtroom recollection. (*See* § 801(2).1 *supra*).

Finally, unlike Federal Rule 803(5) which states that the memorandum may not be received as an exhibit, Proposed New York Evidence Code § 803(c)(4) contains no such restriction, the comment indicating that the memoranda admissible under the exception should be treated like any other exhibit which currently can be examined by the jury.[15]

Library References:

West's Key No. Digests, Criminal Law ⚖=435; Evidence ⚖=355(6).

§ 803(2).2 Federal

Federal Rule of Evidence 803(5) renders admissible:

> A memorandum or record concerning a matter about which a witness once had knowledge but now has insufficient recollection to enable the witness to testify fully and accurately, shown to have been made or adopted by the witness when the matter was fresh in the witness' memory and to reflect that knowledge correctly. If admitted, the memorandum or record may be read

---

10. See Raja, 77 A.D.2d at 325, 433 N.Y.S.2d at 201. See also People v. Barber, 186 A.D.2d 483, 589 N.Y.S.2d 409 (1st Dep't 1992), leave to appeal denied, 81 N.Y.2d 836, 595 N.Y.S.2d 735, 611 N.E.2d 774 (1993); note 2 supra.

11. See Calandra v. Norwood, 81 A.D.2d 650, 651, 438 N.Y.S.2d 381, 382 (2d Dep't 1981)(four and one half month gap between the accident and the statement disqualifies statement for admission in evidence).

12. See, e.g., People v. Caprio, 25 A.D.2d 145, 268 N.Y.S.2d 70 (2d Dep't), aff'd, 18 N.Y.2d 617, 272 N.Y.S.2d 385, 219 N.E.2d 204 (1966) (witness' confession, made 28 hours after crimes, was affirmed by witness on stand).

13. Clark v. Nat. Shoe & Leather Bank, 164 N.Y. 498, 503, 58 N.E. 659, 660 (1900).

This case blends the book entry rule with the past recollection recorded rule since plaintiff's bookkeeper made the entries, but plaintiff could testify and say he confirmed accuracy at the time of the entries.

14. People v. Almestica, 42 N.Y.2d 222, 225, 397 N.Y.S.2d 709, 711, 366 N.E.2d 799, 801 (1977).

15. Proposed New York Evidence Code § 803(c)(4) states:

> Recorded recollection. A memorandum or record concerning a matter about which a witness once had knowledge but now has insufficient recollection to enable the witness to testify fully and accurately, shown to have been made when the matter was fresh in the memory of the witness and to reflect that knowledge correctly.

§ 803(2).2 HEARSAY Ch. 8

into evidence but may not itself be received as an exhibit unless offered by an adverse party.

The terms of this provision leave little or no room for doubt as to the requisites for its implementation. Clearly, the witness need not be completely devoid of all recollection about the transaction at issue and can rely on the timely made memorandum in order to render a full and complete account. As indicated in the Advisory Committee's comments, a contemporaneous memorandum will be more accurate than the present testimony of a witness with a hazy memory.[1] This hearsay exception is most helpful with respect to events that occur in routine fashion, are jotted down, and then much later are seen as relevant links in a chain of evidence. Thus, a telephone number, which the witness would not be expected to recall from the witness stand, can be received in evidence on the paper upon which it was written at the time received;[2] likewise, in a pre-Rule 803(5) case, a message left by a telephone caller and written down by the person who received the call and who could not fully remember the message was admissible to prove the message.[3] Not all recorded information is of such seeming inconsequence at the time written down. The exception has also been found applicable where the witness, a jeweler, could not remember his valuation of a stolen diamond ring, but where he could confirm the accuracy of the appraisal report he wrote at the time of his valuation.[4]

The argument has arisen in criminal cases that the fact that the witness has little or no recollection of the event makes cross-examination futile, thus depriving defendant of the right of confrontation. This argument has consistently been rejected, first in *United States v. Kelly*,[5] where a former bank employer could not remember specifics of his conference with defendant concerning appointment of the bank as a co-transfer agent of certain stock, but had made contemporaneous notes of the conference, and then in *United States v. Smalls*,[6] where government narcotics agents could not remember the transactions at issue which had occurred over five years earlier, but who had made notes at the time. The *Kelly* court cited a host of cases and authorities for the proposition that the past recollection recorded exception "has long been favored by the federal and practically all the state courts that have had occasion to decide the question,"[7] and, of course, the witness involved was on the stand and available for cross-examination. This view as to nonviolation of the right of confrontation in such circumstances was confirmed by the

§ 803(2).2

1. The Advisory Committee agrees that this rationale is just as forceful where the witness says she can testify from present memory; but the "insufficient recollection" requirement is retained to prevent the calculated drafting of memoranda with an eye toward litigation.

2. United States v. Cambindo Valencia, 609 F.2d 603 (2d Cir.1979), cert. denied sub nom. Prado v. U.S., 446 U.S. 940, 100 S.Ct. 2163, 64 L.Ed.2d 795 (1980).

3. United States v. Allied Stevedoring Corp., 241 F.2d 925 (2d Cir.), cert. denied, 353 U.S. 984, 77 S.Ct. 1282, 1 L.Ed.2d 1143 (1957).

4. D'Angelo v. Columbia Fire Ins. Co. of Ohio, 118 F.Supp. 474, 477 (E.D.N.Y.1954).

5. 349 F.2d 720, 770 (2d Cir.1965), cert. denied, 384 U.S. 947, 86 S.Ct. 1467, 16 L.Ed.2d 544 (1966).

6. 438 F.2d 711, 714 (2d Cir.1971), cert. denied, 403 U.S. 933, 91 S.Ct. 2261, 29 L.Ed.2d 712 (1971).

7. 349 F.2d at 770.

Supreme Court in *United States v. Owens*.[8]

Library References:

West's Key No. Digests, Criminal Law ⚖=435; Evidence ⚖=355(6).

§ 803(3) Regularly Kept Records

§ 803(3).1 New York

a. General Principles, Accident Reports

The common law hearsay exception known as the shop book rule proved to be too cumbersome for proving routine transactions in twentieth century litigation,[1] and thus in 1927 the Legislature enacted § 374–a of the Civil Practice Act, now CPLR 4518(a):

> **Rule 4518. Business records**
>
> **(a) Generally.** Any writing or record, whether in the form of an entry in a book or otherwise, made as a memorandum or record of any act, transaction, occurrence or event, shall be admissible in evidence in proof of that act, transaction, occurrence or event, if the judge finds that it was made in the regular course of any business and that it was the regular course of such business to make it, at the time of the act, transaction, occurrence or event, or within a reasonable time thereafter. All other circumstances of the making of the memorandum or record, including lack of personal knowledge by the maker, may be proved to affect its weight, but they shall not affect its admissibility. The term business includes a business, profession, occupation and calling of every kind.

The trustworthiness upon which the admissibility of such records is based is their routineness. "The essence of the business records exception to the hearsay rule is that records systematically made for the conduct of a business as a business are inherently highly trustworthy because they are routine reflections of day-to-day operations and because the entrant's obligation is to have them truthful and accurate for purposes of the conduct of the enterprise * * *."[2] Foundation requirements are:

> *first*, that the record be made in the regular course of business—essentially, that it reflect a routine, regularly conducted business activity, and that it be needed and relied on in the performance of functions of the business; *second*, that it be the

---

8. 484 U.S. 554, 108 S.Ct. 838, 98 L.Ed.2d 951 (1988)(witness previously identified defendant as his assailant, but had no recollection on stand).

§ 803(3).1

1. Prior to 1928 an account could be proved by introducing the books, but the foundation required was difficult. It had to be shown "that there were regular dealings between the parties, that the plaintiff kept honest and fair books, that some of the articles charged had been delivered, and that the plaintiff kept no clerk." Johnson v. Lutz, 253 N.Y. 124, 126, 170 N.E. 517, 517 (1930).

2. People v. Kennedy, 68 N.Y.2d 569, 579, 510 N.Y.S.2d 853, 859, 503 N.E.2d 501, 507 (1986).

§ 803(3).1   HEARSAY   Ch. 8

regular course of such business to make the record (a double requirement of regularity)—essentially, that the record be made pursuant to established procedures for the routine, habitual, systematic making of such a record; and *third*, that the record be made at or about the time of the event being recorded—essentially, that recollection be fairly accurate and the habit or routine of making the entries assured.[3]

To establish these three requirements it is not necessary to call the person who actually made the record. It is enough that an employee familiar with the office routine can testify that such records are routinely made and that it is regular business practice to make such records.[4] It is unnecessary to show that the maker of the records is unavailable.[5] Unless the parties stipulate to admissibility, or the court takes judicial notice,[6] the proponent of business records must usually produce a foundation witness from within the business itself. The prime example is offered by the Court of Appeals' decision in *People v. Kennedy*,[7] where the proffered records were a loan shark's little black books containing cryptic records of his transactions. The prosecution was for conspiracy and criminal usury, and the People sought to introduce the books through an expert witness, a retired police officer whose expertise centered around the area of criminal usury. He testified that in his opinion the books were master business records kept in the sort of jargon common to loan sharks. The court was thus faced with the question whether foundation testimony can be given by a stranger, even though an expert. Noting that records of a criminal enterprise might well be covered under CPLR 4518(a), the court ruled that this testimony was insufficient to establish the necessary aspect of routineness.[8] The court left the door open a crack since it was unwilling to hold that there never could be circumstances in which an expert's testimony would

---

3. Id. at 579–80, 510 N.Y.S.2d at 859–60, 503 N.E.2d at 507–8.

4. See Vermont Commissioner of Banking & Insurance v. Welbilt Corp., 133 A.D.2d 396, 519 N.Y.S.2d 390 (2d Dep't 1987), appeal dismissed, 70 N.Y.2d 1002, 526 N.Y.S.2d 438, 521 N.E.2d 445 (1988); McClure v. Baier's Automotive Service Center, Inc., 126 A.D.2d 610, 511 N.Y.S.2d 50 (2d Dep't 1987). If necessary, a subpoena can be served on the necessary witness. Hefte v. Bellin, 137 A.D.2d 406, 406–8, 524 N.Y.S.2d 42, 44 (1st Dep't 1988).

5. Napolitano v. Branks, 141 A.D.2d 705, 529 N.Y.S.2d 824 (2d Dep't 1988). See also Clark v. New York City Transit Authority, 174 A.D.2d 268, 273, 580 N.Y.S.2d 221, 225 (1st Dep't 1992). In Clark a fire marshal's record of investigation of injuries to two homeless men who sued the city showed they were intoxicated and that their condition was the proximate cause of their injuries. This was a routine report and admissible under CPLR 4518 even though the fire marshal was available to testify. There may, however, be a confrontation problem in criminal cases, as discussed in subdivision (b), infra.

6. See Elkaim v. Elkaim, 176 A.D.2d 116, 117, 574 N.Y.S.2d 2, 4 (1st Dep't), appeal dismissed, 78 N.Y.2d 1072, 576 N.Y.S.2d 222, 582 N.E.2d 605 (1991)(bank statements inherently trustworthy); compare Tomanelli v. Lizda Realty Ltd., 174 A.D.2d 889, 571 N.Y.S.2d 171 (3d Dep't 1991)(bank employee must lay proper foundation for bank statements). It was stated in People v. Kennedy that judicial notice could be used only when the record would otherwise be self-authenticating. 68 N.Y.2d 569, 577, n.4, 510 N.Y.S.2d 853, 858, 503 N.E.2d 501, 506 (1986).

7. 68 N.Y.2d 569, 510 N.Y.S.2d 853, 503 N.E.2d 501 (1986).

8. Id. at 581–82, 510 N.Y.S.2d at 861, 503 N.E.2d at 509.

suffice;[9] but it is difficult to think of a situation in which an expert, otherwise having no relationship to the enterprise and its records, could supply the missing element of personal knowledge.[10]

Since the foundation witness must be familiar with the circumstances in which the records were made, a recipient of someone else's records ordinarily would not be able to lay the necessary foundation. Thus, a trial court was held to have erred in allowing introduction of freight bills received from common carriers which shipped the merchandise sought to be proved. Even though plaintiff routinely filed these bills when they were received, they were made by the carriers, and so it would be necessary to produce proof by someone with personal knowledge that they were made routinely by the carriers.[11] Where, however, an independent contractor acts on behalf of an agency in writing routine reports that are used by the agency, the foundation can be laid by an agency employee who is sufficiently familiar with the general circumstances under which the contractor's reports are prepared.[12]

Routine information fed into a computer and stored there can qualify under CPLR 4518(a);[13] and there is no argument that the process of retrieving the data amounts to producing records specifically for litigation, which might otherwise disqualify them for admissibility.[14]

---

9. Id. at 578, 510 N.Y.S.2d at 858, 503 N.E.2d at 506.

10. Perhaps the testimony that was given in this case could be combined with testimony of someone with personal knowledge of the way in which the books were kept, such as an accomplice, or perhaps even a victim. In People v. Macklowitz, 135 Misc.2d 232, 514 N.Y.S.2d 883 (Sup.Ct. N.Y.Co.1987) it was held that records of drug sales were admissible as business records on the foundation testimony of an accomplice. The federal counterpart of CPLR 4518(a), Federal Rule of Evidence 803(6), requires foundation testimony by a "custodian or other qualified witness."

11. Standard Textile Co. v. National Equipment Rental Ltd., 80 A.D.2d 911, 437 N.Y.S.2d 398 (2d Dep't 1981). See also People v. Pierre, 157 A.D.2d 750, 751, 550 N.Y.S.2d 44, 46 (2d Dep't 1990)(bank statement, although routinely filed by person who received it, lacked necessary foundation regarding making of record).

12. See People v. Cratsley, 86 N.Y.2d 81, 629 N.Y.S.2d 992, 653 N.E.2d 1162 (1995), where the issue concerned proof as to a mentally retarded victim's ability to consent to sexual intercourse. The New York State Office of Vocational Rehabilitation routinely received psychological evaluation reports made by an outside psychologist concerning the IQ of those being considered for admission into the program. Such reports were admissible as proof of the victim's IQ on the testimony of the agency employee who received and kept them.

13. Ed Guth Realty, Inc. v. Gingold, 34 N.Y.2d 440, 358 N.Y.S.2d 367, 315 N.E.2d 441 (1974). Judge Gabrielli stated: "Certainly, compiling and feeding data into a computer in the context we have before us would seem to be as routine a function as could be imagined and should be included under CPLR 4518." Id. at 451, 358 N.Y.S.2d at 374, 315 N.E.2d at 446. See also Comment, "Computer Print–Outs of Business Records and Their Admissibility in New York," 31 Albany L.Rev. 61 (1967).

14. See text at notes 30–31 infra. In Briar Hill Apartments v. Teperman, 165 A.D.2d 519, 568 N.Y.S.2d 50 (1st Dep't 1991), the question was whether the premises constituted defendant's primary residence. Plaintiff landlord, seeking to evict defendant from a rent-stabilized apartment, produced Consolidated Edison's computer-generated records, along with a foundation witness from Con Ed who testified that they were kept in the ordinary course of business. The records showed little or no use of any electricity in the apartment. The fact the foundation witness was not asked the other two formulaic questions— was it the ordinary course of Con Ed's business to make these records and were the records made contemporaneously or within a reasonable time after the events recorded—was held of no consequence since opposing counsel took no notice, and the testimony taken as a whole provided affir-

§ 803(3).1   HEARSAY   Ch. 8

The contents of the records, in order to be admissible under CPLR 4518(a), must have been recorded as a routine procedure of the business, and the person entering the material must have had a business duty to enter it. Furthermore, the contents are admissible only if one of the following requirements is met: (1) the maker of the record had personal knowledge of the matter recorded; (2) the maker relied upon information supplied by a person with a "business duty" to supply accurate information; or (3) the maker recorded a statement that is not hearsay or qualified as an independent hearsay exception. These requirements are a product of the Court of Appeals' landmark interpretation of the 1928 statute in *Johnson v. Lutz*.[15] There, a report made by a police officer concerning an intersection accident was held inadmissible because much of the information contained therein was gathered from bystanders' statements. These people, while perhaps having a civic duty to aid the police, had no business duty so to do. It could be surmised from the opinion in this case that accident reports simply were never intended to be included within the scope of the legislation. The citation to Wigmore dealt with the statute's usefulness in "mercantile and industrial life."[16] On the other hand, such reports were not foreclosed in so many words, and it has eventuated, of course, that police accident reports are admissible if the source of the information and the entrant are the same person with the requisite business duty in making the record;[17] where the source, even though a different person (such as another officer) also had a business duty to impart the information;[18] if the source is sustainable under a separate hearsay exception (such as an admission by a party);[19] or where, regardless of the nature of the source, the content is relevant as nonhearsay, simply because it was made.[20] (This, of course, would be the case with any business record, not just accident reports.)

In *Kelly v. Wasserman*,[21] the Court of Appeals upheld the admissibility of a welfare investigator's report containing information imparted by

---

mative answers in any event. Id. at 521, 568 N.Y.S.2d at 52. As to the argument that the records were prepared for litigation, the court noted that obtaining printouts from a computer was no different than going to a file cabinet and extracting the documents stored there. Id. at 522, 568 N.Y.S.2d at 52. See also People v. Weinberg, 183 A.D.2d 932, 934, 586 N.Y.S.2d 132, 134 (2d Dep't 1992)(clerical testimony that data originally entered in computer in regular course of business at or about the time of the events recorded, qualified this data, when retrieved, for admissibility).

15. 253 N.Y. 124, 170 N.E. 517 (1930).

16. Id. at 128–29 170 N.E. at 518–19, citing 3 Wigmore § 1530, at 278 (1923 ed.).

17. Johnson v. Lutz, 253 N.Y. at 128–29, 170 N.E. at 518–19. See also Lee v. Decarr, 36 A.D.2d 554, 317 N.Y.S.2d 226 (3d Dep't 1971)(trooper's report contained diagram of accident scene made from his own observations).

18. Johnson v. Lutz, 253 N.Y. at 128, 170 N.E. at 518. In Quaglio v. Tomaselli, 99 A.D.2d 487, 470 N.Y.S.2d 427 (2d Dep't 1984), plaintiff's account of an accident and corroboration by her passenger found its way into the police report and the introduction of this report in support of plaintiff's case was held to be error.

19. Toll v. State of New York, 32 A.D.2d 47, 49–50, 299 N.Y.S.2d 589, 592 (3d Dep't 1969).

20. Splawn v. Lextaj Corp. NV., 197 A.D.2d 479, 603 N.Y.S.2d 41 (1st Dep't 1993), leave to appeal denied, 83 N.Y.2d 753, 612 N.Y.S.2d 107, 634 N.E.2d 603 (1994)(hotel logbook entries of guests' complaints admissible to show management had notice of problems involving security).

21. 5 N.Y.2d 425, 185 N.Y.S.2d 538, 158 N.E.2d 241 (1959).

the welfare recipient's landlord. This was a puzzlement in light of *Johnson v. Lutz*, since the landlord's business duty to give this information was not evident. But in a later case, *Toll v. State of New York*,[22] it was pointed out that the landlord's statement, in the context of an action against the landlord, amounted to an admission by the landlord. In the *Toll* case, an errant driver's statement to the investigating officer, included in his report, was likewise found to have the necessary independent basis under the hearsay exception for party admissions because the report was introduced against the driver. In contrast, note the ruling of inadmissibility in *Cover v. Cohen*[23] where the driver's statement to the officer that his accelerator stuck was self-serving and thus not admissible through the officer's report when offered by the driver; the ruling in *Matter of Leon*,[24] where social services files relating to a child were in large part inadmissible because many entries were the result of information given by people with no requisite business duty and largely made up of rumor and speculation;[25] and the holding in *Cox v. State of New York*,[26] where the statement in a hospital record that a patient was pushed by another patient was not admissible since it was given by that patient who had no business duty in the affair.

22. 32 A.D.2d 47, 299 N.Y.S.2d 589 (3d Dep't 1969). See also Ferrera v. Poranski, 88 A.D.2d 904, 450 N.Y.S.2d 596 (2d Dep't 1982)(plaintiff's statement that she must have fallen asleep at wheel of car admissible by defendant through the police report).

23. 61 N.Y.2d 261, 473 N.Y.S.2d 378, 461 N.E.2d 864 (1984).

24. 48 N.Y.2d 117, 421 N.Y.S.2d 863, 397 N.E.2d 374 (1979).

25. See also Matter of Dept. of Social Services v. Waleska M., 195 A.D.2d 507, 600 N.Y.S.2d 464 (2d Dep't), leave to appeal denied, 82 N.Y.2d 660, 605 N.Y.S.2d 6, 625 N.E.2d 591 (1993), a child abuse proceeding, where the foster care agency's certified records were challenged. The court noted that the people who prepared them had a business duty to record all matters concerning the condition of the children, and that the records were admitted pursuant to Family Court Act § 1046(a)(iv), which is like CPLR 4518(a), but tailored to child abuse proceedings. Matter of Leon was distinguished because it was a termination proceeding, because the records were admitted pursuant to CPLR 4518(a), and because of the hearsay information contained in the record. 195 A.D.2d at 510, 600 N.Y.S.2d at 467. In addition see Matter of F. Children, 199 A.D.2d 81, 604 N.Y.S.2d 956 (1st Dep't 1993)(in hearing dealing with placement of children Uniform Case Records properly admitted under CPLR 4518[a]); Matter of Christopher B., 192 A.D.2d 180, 184, 600 N.Y.S.2d 531, 533 (4th Dep't 1993)(Leon followed where the document was nothing more than a statement written by an officer as to what someone with no business duty told him). See also Kelly v. Diesel Constr., Morse, Inc., 35 N.Y.2d 1, 358 N.Y.S.2d 685, 315 N.E.2d 751 (1974)(information given by an employee on a construction site to a public safety inspector inadmissible since the employee had no requisite business duty, and he had not been authorized to make admissions against his employer).

26. 3 N.Y.2d 693, 171 N.Y.S.2d 818, 148 N.E.2d 879 (1958). The statement entered by a hospital attendant could not serve as an admission since it was merely relayed into the report and not adopted. Id. at 697, 171 N.Y.S.2d at 821, 148 N.E.2d at 881. See also Stevens v. Kirby, 86 A.D.2d 391, 450 N.Y.S.2d 607 (4th Dep't 1982), where plaintiff sued defendant tavern for injuries suffered in a brawl in the parking lot. To prove foreseeability, plaintiff was permitted to introduce a Liquor Authority investigation report based on an investigation of local police reports concerning prior fights at the premises. Various opinion and conclusions were taken verbatim into the report, one reciting that the owner "cannot control his patrons and allows them to drink until they become intoxicated and then trouble breaks out." Id. at 393, 450 N.Y.S.2d at 610. The Appellate Division found this to be error. That the report was prepared as part of the liquor authority's routine practice did not take away from the fact that the underlying police reports were filled with information provided by informants with no business duty to provide the information. Id. at 395, 396, 450 N.Y.S.2d at 611.

§ 803(3).1   HEARSAY   Ch. 8

A sampling of other such cases is found in the notes,[27] but one, *Taft v. New York City Transit Authority*,[28] is especially instructive. A bystander, described as being agitated, made a statement describing a subway accident about one minute after it had occurred. A transit authority employee relayed this to other employees who entered it in the company's accident report. The report was admissible, said the court, since at each stage there was a hearsay exception. The bystander's statement qualified as an excited utterance, and the transit employee who heard it had a business duty to pass it on.[29]

In contrast to reports made by the authorities, consider those made by the injured party or the defendant in pursuit of its practice of investigating accidents occurring on its premises or in the use of its equipment. The question is whether or not such reports are made for business purposes within the contemplation of CPLR 4518(a), or whether they are made for purposes of litigation. This issue was raised in the United States Supreme Court's 1943 decision in *Palmer v. Hoffman*,[30] where the Court held inadmissible an accident report of a railroad

---

27. See Miller v. Alagna, 203 A.D.2d 264, 609 N.Y.S.2d 650 (2d Dep't), leave to appeal denied, 84 N.Y.2d 805, 618 N.Y.S.2d 7, 642 N.E.2d 326 (1994)(conclusion in policeman's report as to cause of accident admissible since it was his opinion based on his own observations); Lindsay v. Academy Broadway Corp., 198 A.D.2d 641, 642, 603 N.Y.S.2d 622, 623 (3d Dep't 1993)("The police report is hearsay but, contrary to plaintiff's contention, it is admissible under the business record exception of CPLR 4518(a) inasmuch as the witnesses who gave the statements were police officers at the scene with a duty to report their observations to the reporting officer"); Abbe v. Board of Education, 186 A.D.2d 102, 103, 587 N.Y.S.2d 707, 708 (2d Dep't 1992)(where issue was whether two baseball practice sessions were run simultaneously on the same field, the injured student's mother's statement that her son told her that such was the case, not admissible as found in report of the accident since no duty and otherwise no hearsay exception); Clarke v. New York City Transit Authority, 174 A.D.2d 268, 273, 580 N.Y.S.2d 221, 225 (1st Dep't 1992)(report of fire marshal after he interviewed plaintiffs containing their statements that they had been drinking before the accident properly admitted under CPLR 4518(a) even though the fire marshal was available to testify); Hayes v. State of New York, 50 A.D.2d 693, 694, 376 N.Y.S.2d 647, 649 (3d Dep't 1975), order aff'd, 40 N.Y.2d 1044, 392 N.Y.S.2d 282, 360 N.E.2d 959 (1976)(information furnished by other patients disqualifies hospital report as a business entry); Donohue v. Losito, 141 A.D.2d 691, 692, 529 N.Y.S.2d 813, 814 (2d Dep't), appeal denied, 72 N.Y.2d 810, 534 N.Y.S.2d 938, 531 N.E.2d 658 (1988)(although document did not satisfy all the requirements of CPLR 4518[a], a statement therein was admissible for purposes of impeachment); Casey v. Tierno, 127 A.D.2d 727, 728, 512 N.Y.S.2d 123, 124–25 (2d Dep't 1987)(statement given by defendant to officer regarding accident was not admissible since she had no duty, and the statement did not conform to any hearsay exception); Bracco v. Mabstoa, 117 A.D.2d 273, 277, 502 N.Y.S.2d 158, 161 (1st Dep't 1986)(reports by defendant's dispatcher and a police officer that they observed slush on steps of bus where plaintiff fell, admissible since these were their own observations); Cornier v. Spagna, 101 A.D.2d 141, 147, 148, 475 N.Y.S.2d 7, 12 (1st Dep't 1984)(police report of vehicular accident erroneously admitted without any foundation testimony as to source of information); Chemical Leaman Tank Lines, Inc. v. Stevens, 21 A.D.2d 556, 251 N.Y.S.2d 240 (3d Dep't 1964)(statements by defendant properly admissible in officer's report as admissions); Zaulich v. Thompkins Square Holding Co., 10 A.D.2d 492, 496, 497, 200 N.Y.S.2d 550, 554, 555 (1st Dep't 1960)(police report containing information gathered from the officer's own observations admissible, but in this earlier case court found it necessary also to find report admissible to rebut a charge of recent fabrication).

28. 193 A.D.2d 503, 597 N.Y.S.2d 374 (1st Dep't 1993).

29. Id. at 504–05, 597 N.Y.S.2d at 375.

30. 318 U.S. 109, 63 S.Ct. 477, 87 L.Ed. 645, rehearing denied, 318 U.S. 800, 63 S.Ct. 757, 87 L.Ed. 1163 (1943).

accident prepared by a railroad employee before he died and offered into evidence by the railroad. The primary purpose of the report, said Justice Douglas, was for litigating, not for railroading.[31] But *Palmer* is rarely followed:[32] The rule has emerged that where the report has more than a single purpose it may well qualify under CPLR 4518(a). For example, such reports may routinely be made for purposes of improving plant safety.

Although *People v. Foster*[33] does not deal with an employment accident report, it does state the applicable rule. That case involved the question whether a police cruiser speedometer deviation record, which can provide a foundation for testimony in speeding cases, was a document prepared for litigation. Noting that deviation tests and resulting records must be made on a routine basis, and not in preparation for any particular litigation, the court stated:

> This is a classic example of making records in the regular course of business; and, it is probably the regular course of police business in maintaining highway safety to make such records at the time of the test. While it is true that such records may later be used in litigation, such was not the sole purpose when they were made, and, therefore, they should not be excluded merely because this was a possible future use.[34]

Although the Court of Appeals has not had the occasion specifically to apply the same or similar rationale to accident reports prepared as part of routine company practice, the Appellate Divisions have.[35] The fact such reports will more often than not be self-serving is not an obstacle.[36]

---

31. Id. at 114, 63 S.Ct. at 481, 87 L.Ed. at 650.

32. See criticism of the case in 59 Harvard L.Rev. 566, 567 (1946). See also Fagan v. Newark, 78 N.J.Super. 294, 314, 188 A.2d 427, 438 (1963), where it is stated: "The effect of some subsequent decisions, particularly in the federal courts, and notably in the Second Circuit, has been to whittle down the authority of the Douglas opinion in Palmer to strongly self-exculpatory accident reports offered by defendants to rebut negligence or fault."

33. 27 N.Y.2d 47, 313 N.Y.S.2d 384, 261 N.E.2d 389 (1970).

34. Id. at 52, 313 N.Y.S.2d at 388, 261 N.E.2d at 391–92.

35. See Galanek v. New York Transit Authority, 53 A.D.2d 586, 586, 385 N.Y.S.2d 62–64 (1st Dep't 1976). "The [trial] court admitted into evidence a report of the accident made by the motorman on the day of the accident. The report was admitted as an entry in the regular course of business under CPLR 4518 (subd [a]). In Palmer v. Hoffman * * * the United States Supreme Court held such a report not to be admissible under the analogous Federal statute. However, in a number of cases the receipt in evidence of similar reports has been approved by the Appellate Divisions of this State. (Toll v. State of New York, 32 A.D.2d 47, 299 N.Y.S.2d 589; Bishin v. New York Cent. R.R. Co., 20 A.D.2d 921). On its face the statute would seem to render such reports admissible." Id. But where a doctor's report is requested by counsel, it is not relevant for diagnosis and treatment, and therefore not admissible. Wilson v. Bodian, 130 A.D.2d 221, 519 N.Y.S.2d 126 (2d Dep't 1987).

36. Bishin v. New York Central R.R. Co., 20 A.D.2d 921, 922, 249 N.Y.S.2d 778, 780 (2d Dep't 1964). Compare National States Electric Corp. v. LFO Constr. Corp., 203 A.D.2d 49, 50 609 N.Y.S.2d 900, 901 (1st Dep't 1994) (where a contractor made a one-page summary of damages relating to a certain incident, the document was not a routine business record, but prepared for purposes of possible litigation).

§ 803(3).1   HEARSAY   Ch. 8

b. Agency Documents Offered by the Prosecution in Criminal Cases

Logically, law enforcement records might be considered under CPLR 4520, covered in the next section, which deals with reports required of public officers. Under Federal Rule of Evidence 803(8) reports and documents generated by public agencies are qualifiedly admissible, except for those records based on "matters observed by police officers and other law enforcement personnel." But in New York, perhaps because police reports have been treated as business records in accident cases, law enforcement records in criminal cases are dealt with under CPLR 4518(a), and there is no special bar to their introduction except as defendant's confrontation rights might be affected.

There are two broad categories of such reports: First, those that are produced on a regular basis recording equipment tests, and the like, and, second, those that bear specifically on the guilt of the accused. *People v. Foster*, discussed just above, which dealt with the report of a speedometer deviation test,[37] is a prime example of the first category, as is *People v. Farrell*,[38] where the Court of Appeals held that reports of tests of sample chemical ampoules used in breathalyzers were admissible under CPLR 4518(a).[39] Representative of the second category is *People ex rel. McGee v. Walters*[40] where the Court of Appeals ruled in a parole revocation hearing that proof of the violations could not be proved by means of the parole officer's report, a record routinely made, unless the unavailability of the parole officer could be established and an informed evaluation made whether the report could be admitted on its own.[41] In an

---

37. 27 N.Y.2d 47, 313 N.Y.S.2d 384, 261 N.E.2d 389 (1970).

38. 58 N.Y.2d 637, 458 N.Y.S.2d 514, 444 N.E.2d 978 (1982).

39. In People v. Gower, 42 N.Y.2d 117, 397 N.Y.S.2d 368, 366 N.E.2d 69 (1977), the court noted that there are foundation requirements necessary to show that the subject breathalyzer was in proper condition at the time defendant took the test. This requires proof of ampoule analysis results, calibration test results, and simulator solution analysis results. In Gower, certificates of these tests, simply signed by officials from various testing places, were held inadequate to satisfy the requirements of CPLR 4518(a). Their source was not represented and there was no showing that the tests were made in the regular course of the business of the testing agencies. The court indicated that observance of the requirements of subdivision (c) of CPLR 4518 would solve the problem. That subdivision is discussed at notes 58–59 infra and essentially provides that live business record foundation testimony may be dispensed with where the reports emanate from a public office and where the report is certified to comply with the routineness and time requirements of subdivision (a).

In a later case, People v. Mertz, 68 N.Y.2d 136, 506 N.Y.S.2d 290, 497 N.E.2d 657 (1986), the defendant could show there was no proper foundation for the introduction of his breathalyzer test results because the foundation testimony establishing the logs for the breathalyzer, simulator and ampoule, failed to note that it was the regular course of business to make such records at the time of the tests or within a reasonable time thereafter. In People v. Miller, 199 A.D.2d 692, 694, 605 N.Y.S.2d 160, 162 (3d Dep't 1993), a facsimile copy of a memorandum provided to show the officer administering the breathalyzer test was qualified was not admissible pursuant to CPLR 4518(a), although the court, apparently overlooking the hearsay factor, said it was admissible under the best evidence rule since an excuse was shown for non-production of the original.

40. 62 N.Y.2d 317, 476 N.Y.S.2d 803, 465 N.E.2d 342 (1984).

41. The court stated:

In the matter now under review, the State's only proffered reason for dispensing with the need to produce the officer who had prepared the subject report was that he was no longer employed by the

earlier case, *People v. Nisonoff*,[42] decided before the sixth amendment was held to apply to the states,[43] it was stated: "The right of an accused in a criminal action to be confronted by the witnesses who testify against him, is not violated by the introduction of so-called public documents or official records required to be kept."[44] In that case the document in question was an autopsy report, the maker having died before trial, and the business entry statute was held applicable.[45]

A neutral ground seems to exist somewhere between those records in the first category which do not affect the defendant directly, and those in the second category which do. In this median zone the confrontation right does not appear to be a problem. Thus, properly prepared certifications of narcotics tests are admissible[46] unaccompanied by the maker's testimony, and a teletype printout was held admissible which established that defendant's vehicle bore the license plate written down by the victim.[47] And, the Court of Appeals in *People v. Guidice*[48] ruled that

Division of Parole. In determining that the report would be admitted notwithstanding the preparer's absence, the hearing officer did not consider general policies favoring confrontation, the objective or subjective nature of the contents of the particular report, the potential assistance that cross-examination of the parole officer would lend to the fact-finding process, whether the evidence was cumulative, or what burden would be entailed in requiring that the parole officer be made available to testify. Indeed the hearing officer made no specific finding of good cause to dispense with the production of the witness whose statements comprised the only evidence offered by the State.
62 N.Y.2d at 323, 476 N.Y.S.2d at 806, 465 N.E.2d at 345.

42. 293 N.Y. 597, 59 N.E.2d 420 (1944), cert. denied, 326 U.S. 745, 66 S.Ct. 22, 90 L.Ed. 445 (1945).

43. Id. at 602, 59 N.E.2d at 422.

44. Id.

45. Subsequently, in People v. Hampton, 38 A.D.2d 772, 327 N.Y.S.2d 961 (3d Dep't 1972), another case concerning an autopsy report, it appears that there was no foundation witness and the court ruled its admission error, stating: "This report contained the statement that death was caused by (1) traumatic shock and (2) battered child syndrome. It is an established principle of law that certain public records may be received into evidence without offending the hearsay rule or right of confrontation. An autopsy report is such a public record and, therefore admissible. Our courts, however, have not extended the rule to include opinions as to the cause of death contained in such reports. (People v. Nisonoff, 267 App.Div. 356, 369, aff'd. 293 N.Y. 597, 59 N.E.2d 420.) On such an issue a defendant may not be deprived of the right of confrontation and cross-examination." Id. at 773, 327 N.Y.S.2d at 962. Would this remain true under McGee were it to be shown that the person who conducted the autopsy was unavailable? This point was not broached in Nisonoff.

46. People v. Montgomery, 195 A.D.2d 886, 887, 600 N.Y.S.2d 814, 816 (3d Dep't 1993). See also People v. Torres, 213 A.D.2d 797, 623 N.Y.S.2d 645 (3d Dep't 1995)(admission of chemist's lab report containing finding that substance was cocaine did not violate defendant's confrontation rights despite chemist's failure to testify; the report, which was prepared contemporaneously with "mechanically objective tests," possessed "particular indicia of reliability"). Under the proposed New York Evidence Code fingerprint records are specifically provided for:

New York Evidence Code § 803(c)(7)(B)(ii) [PROPOSED]

(ii) Certificates of fingerprint identification. A report of a public employee charged with the custody of official fingerprint records which contains a certification that the fingerprints of a designated person who has previously been convicted of an offense are identical with those of a defendant in a criminal case constitutes evidence of the fact that such person has previously been convicted of such offense.

47. People v. Miller, 150 A.D.2d 910, 541 N.Y.S.2d 257 (3d Dep't), appeal denied, 74 N.Y.2d 815, 546 N.Y.S.2d 573, 545 N.E.2d 887 (1989).

48. 83 N.Y.2d 630, 612 N.Y.S.2d 350, 634 N.E.2d 951 (1994). "Linesheets" rec-

"linesheet" entries made during police surveillance were admissible as business entries.

It must be remembered that although the person who made the record need not testify, there is generally a need for a foundation witness to establish the requirements of routineness and timeliness. In one case a police report made on the basis of computer information that defendant's license had been suspended was held inadmissible because there was no CPLR 4518(a) foundation supplied for the computer printout.[49] A 25-year-old medical report regarding the cause of the victim's death was not admissible pursuant to CPLR 4518(a) since it was contained in a letter written by a consultant to the State Police who had no business duty.[50] And, proof that defendants were unlicensed vendors based on an officer's testimony that he scanned the city records and did not find their names, was insufficient since there was no CPLR 4518(a) foundation to qualify the city records.[51]

The last word on the confrontation question as it relates to the introduction of law enforcement records in criminal prosecutions has yet to be written. In *People v. Sugden*[52] the Court of Appeals, in dictum, stated: "The right to confront witnesses in a criminal case is not one without narrow and cautious exceptions. The book entries and public records rules, available on the civil side, are also available on the criminal side * * *."[53] But the *McGee* case warns us that where at all possible, the person who collected the information or who ran the test ought to be provided as a witness.[54]

ord the date, sequential number of call and times when conversations began and ended as respects recordings of telephone conversations. The court stated: "We note that the linesheets served an important administrative function in the daily conduct of a police surveillance operation; they were required to be made pursuant to a court order, their purpose was to maintain an inventory of the tapes and to safeguard them against tampering; and they were included in the progress reports that were filed regularly with the Judge supervising the wiretap order." Id. at 635, 612 N.Y.S.2d at 352, 634 N.E.2d at 953.

49. People v. Pierre, 157 Misc.2d 812, 814, 599 N.Y.S.2d 412, 414 (N.Y.C.Crim.Ct. 1993).

50. People v. Ruff, 185 A.D.2d 454, 457, 586 N.Y.S.2d 327, 330 (3d Dep't 1992), aff'd, 81 N.Y.2d 330, 599 N.Y.S.2d 221, 615 N.E.2d 611 (1993).

51. People v. Sylla, 154 Misc.2d 112, 118, 584 N.Y.S.2d 985, 989 (N.Y.C.Crim.Ct. 1992). See also In re Gregory M., 184 A.D.2d 252, 254, 585 N.Y.S.2d 193, 195 (1st Dep't 1992), aff'd, 82 N.Y.2d 588, 606 N.Y.S.2d 579, 627 N.E.2d 500 (1993)(ballistics report improperly allowed in evidence since there was nothing to indicate that entries were either contemporaneous with the testing or were made within a reasonable time thereafter).

52. 35 N.Y.2d 453, 363 N.Y.S.2d 923, 323 N.E.2d 169 (1974).

53. Id. at 460, 363 N.Y.S.2d at 928, 323 N.E.2d at 173.

54. The comment to the Proposed New York Evidence Code § 803(c)(5)(A)(iii) which provides that documents offered to establish guilt can be used only where the person who furnished the information testifies, or is unavailable, states: "Thus, for example, an otherwise qualified business record detailing a police officer's personal recollection of a statement satisfying a hearsay exception, a chemist's report that tested substances are illegally controlled substances, or fingerprint report reciting that the fingerprints of defendant match the fingerprints found at the crime scene are all reports that require the declarant's

c. Records of Hospitals, Libraries, and Other Government Bureaus

Bills. Measures that greatly ease foundation requirements are found in subdivisions (b), (c), (d) and (e) of CPLR 4518. These will be taken up in order. First, subdivision (b) provides that a properly certified hospital bill may be introduced in evidence and will be prima facie evidence of its contents.[55] This is for the purpose of facilitating proof in personal injury actions,[56] and does not apply, by its express terms, where the hospital itself is suing a patient for payment of bills. CPLR 4533–a allows for the submission of properly certified and verified bills for the rendition of services and repairs of any kind where the amount does not exceed $2,000.[57] These documents are self-authenticating and the necessary foundation can be laid without need of a live witness. Of course, if plaintiff seeks to go beyond the mere submission of the bill and present evidence as to causation and other matters requiring expertise, he will need to provide the necessary witness.

Government and Hospital Records. Subdivision (c) of CPLR 4518 allows for admission of certified records described in CPLR 2306 and 2307, i.e., medical records of a hospital or other government entity concerning the condition and treatment of a patient; and also records of a library, or municipal or state department or bureau, which are not confined to medical matters.[58] The prescribed certification must be testimony or a showing of unavailability as that term is defined in CE 804(a)."

55. CPLR 4518 * * *

(b) **Hospital bills.** A hospital bill is admissible in evidence under this rule and is prima facie evidence of the facts contained, provided it bears a certification by the head of the hospital or by a responsible employee in the controller's or accounting office that the bill is correct, that each of the items was necessarily supplied and that the amount charged is reasonable. This subdivision shall not apply to any proceeding in a surrogate's court nor in any action instituted by or on behalf of a hospital to recover payment for accommodations or supplies furnished or for services rendered by or in such hospital, except that in a proceeding pursuant to section one hundred eighty-nine of the lien law to determine the validity and extent of the lien of a hospital, such certified hospital bills are prima facie evidence of the fact of services and of the reasonableness of any charges which do not exceed the comparable charges made by the hospital in the care of workmen's compensation patients.

56. 1950 N.Y. Law Rev. Comm'n Report, Leg.Doc.No. 65(B), p.56.

57. CPLR 4533–a. Prima facie proof of damages

An itemized bill or invoice, receipted or marked paid, for services or repairs of an amount not in excess of two thousand dollars is admissible in evidence and is prima facie evidence of the reasonable value and necessity of such services or repairs itemized therein in any civil action provided it bears a certification by the person, firm or corporation, or an authorized agent or employee thereof, rendering such services or making such repairs and charging for the same, and contains a verified statement that no part of the payment received therefor will be refunded to the debtor, and that the amounts itemized therein are the usual and customary rates charged for such services or repairs by the affiant or his employer; and provided further that a true copy of such itemized bill or invoice together with a notice of intention to introduce such bill or invoice into evidence pursuant to this rule is served upon each party at least ten days before the trial. No more than one bill or invoice from the same person, firm or corporation to the same debtor shall be admissible in evidence under this rule in the same action.

58. CPLR 4518 * * *

(c) **Other records.** All records, writings and other things referred to in sections 2306 and 2307 are admissible in evidence under this rule and are prima facie evidence of the facts contained, provided they bear a certification or authentication by the head of the hospital, laboratory, department or bureau of a munic-

§ 803(3).1   HEARSAY   Ch. 8

supplied and the document becomes prima facie evidence of its content without need for a foundation witness. The certificate, in addition to authenticating the document, must also show that the document was timely made, and made in the regular course of the business, and that it was the regular course of the business to make such records.[59] The documents submitted need not be originals, but may be photostatic copies, as prescribed in CPLR 2306(a) and 2307(b). And in the case of warehoused hospital records, there would seem to be the need for two certifications in addition to the other necessary statements, one by the hospital's agent, stating that the subject record was warehoused with the required permission of the state health commissioner, and the other by the manager of the warehouse concerning the nature of the custody.

It has been held that in the case of a medical record, a physician's opinion contained therein is perfectly admissible along with the rest of the record.[60]

Subdivision (c) does not purport to prescribe the exclusive procedure for the introduction of these records. They can still be admitted, as would records of a private business, by a foundation witness such as a custodian of the record, or someone with the personal knowledge to supply the necessary information concerning timeliness and routineness.[61] It has been argued that subdivision (c) can only apply to records which are subpoenaed because CPLR 2306 and 2307 specifically provide

ipal corporation or of the state, or by an employee delegated for that purpose or by a qualified physician. Where a hospital record is in the custody of a warehouse, or "warehouseman" as that term is defined by paragraph (h) of subdivision one of section 7–102 of the uniform commercial code, pursuant to a plan approved in writing by the state commissioner of health, admissibility under this subdivision may be established by a certification made by the manager of the warehouse that sets forth (i) the authority by which the record is held, including but not limited to a court order, order of the commissioner, or order or resolution of the governing body or official of the hospital, and (ii) that the record has been in the exclusive custody of such warehouse or warehousemen since its receipt from the hospital or, if another has had access to it, the name and address of such person and the date on which and the circumstances under which such access was had. Any warehouseman providing a certification as required by this subdivision shall have no liability for acts or omissions relating thereto, except for intentional misconduct, and the warehouseman is authorized to assess and collect a reasonable charge for providing the certification described by this subdivision.

59. See People v. Gower, 42 N.Y.2d 117, 397 N.Y.S.2d 368, 366 N.E.2d 69 (1977),
and People v. Mertz, 68 N.Y.2d 136, 506 N.Y.S.2d 290, 497 N.E.2d 657 (1986), both discussed in note 39 supra.

60. People v. Kohlmeyer, 284 N.Y. 366, 369–70, 31 N.E.2d 490, 492 (1940) (in aid of his insanity defense defendant wanted to show that his paternal grandmother was insane; court ruled trial court in error in not allowing hospital records showing grandmother's condition).

61. See People v. Mertz, 68 N.Y.2d 136, 506 N.Y.S.2d 290, 497 N.E.2d 657 (1986), at note 39. See also People v. Kinne, 71 N.Y.2d 879, 880, 527 N.Y.S.2d 754, 755, 522 N.E.2d 1052, 1052 (1988), which points out that it is the document sought to be admitted which must have been timely made. The certificate prepared for purposes of subdivision (c) can be made at any time. And, in People ex rel. Saafir v. Mantello, 163 A.D.2d 824, 825, 558 N.Y.S.2d 356, 359 (4th Dep't 1990) it is stated: "The report of [urine] tests performed by a private laboratory was hearsay evidence. It did not qualify as a business record because the Division of Parole failed to produce a witness to lay a proper foundation * * * under CPLR 4518(a)." See Marigliano v. City of New York, 196 A.D.2d 533, 601 N.Y.S.2d 161 (2d Dep't 1993)(where source of information not explainable, record inadmissible); and People v. Khadaidi, 201 A.D.2d 585, 608 N.Y.S.2d 471 (2d Dep't 1994)(source of information not ascertainable).

for the subpoenaing of such material. But it has been held that subdivision (c) covers material voluntarily submitted in evidence as well.[62]

The extent to which information in a hospital record is admissible (regardless of whether it is certified or admitted through a foundation witness) continues to be governed by the Court of Appeals' decision in *Williams v. Alexander*.[63] A hospital's business is to diagnose and treat, and so the recording of information in a hospital record which is necessary for diagnosis and treatment is admissible. But in this case, where plaintiff sued A for running into him at an intersection, A could not use information in the record concerning plaintiff's statement to a doctor that B rear-ended A, forcing A to strike plaintiff, because this was not necessary for diagnosis or treatment.[64] Of course had the physician who took this information testified she could have reported this statement as an admission by plaintiff.[65]

In *Wilson v. Bodian*,[66] the Appellate Division held that a physician's *office records* could qualify under CPLR 4518(a), given the necessary foundation. Noting that the rule had previously been otherwise, the court pointed to its decision in *McClure v. Baier's Auto Serv. Center*,[67] where it held that entries in the office records germane to diagnosis and treatment are admissible, including medical opinions and conclusions.[68]

Genetic marker and DNA reports in paternity proceedings. Subdivision (d) of CPLR 4518 provides that certified reports of these blood tests, as performed pursuant to sections 418 and 532 of the Family Court Act, are prima facie evidence of their contents; and if at least 95 percent probability of paternity is shown, the report will create a rebuttable presumption of paternity. Subdivision (e) provides that such reports are

---

62. See People v. Montgomery, 195 A.D.2d 886, 887, 600 N.Y.S.2d 814, 815–16 (3d Dep't), appeal denied, 82 N.Y.2d 851, 606 N.Y.S.2d 603, 627 N.E.2d 525 (1993)(records of narcotics tests, properly authenticated and certified, can be produced voluntarily); Joyce v. Kowalcewski, 80 A.D.2d 27, 437 N.Y.S.2d 809 (4th Dep't 1981)(plaintiff's medical records, properly authenticated, admissible on basis of voluntary production).

63. 309 N.Y. 283, 129 N.E.2d 417 (1955). See also DeJesus v. City of New York, 199 A.D.2d 139, 140, 605 N.Y.S.2d 253, 254 (1st Dep't 1993)(cause of fall not necessary for diagnosis and treatment).

64. Id. at 287–88, 129 N.E.2d at 419.

65. See Barzaghi v. Maislin Transport, 115 A.D.2d 679, 687, 497 N.Y.S.2d 131, 137 (2d Dep't 1985), appeal dismissed, 67 N.Y.2d 852, 501 N.Y.S.2d 660, 492 N.E.2d 788 (1986)(social worker who took information from plaintiff could testify to admission that was made). See also Passino v. DeRosa, 199 A.D.2d 1017, 606 N.Y.S.2d 107 (4th Dep't 1993)(plaintiff's admission in hospital report inadmissible in that form, and physician to whom statement given could not recall whether plaintiff or someone else had given him damaging statement, hence, inadmissible).

66. 130 A.D.2d 221, 519 N.Y.S.2d 126 (2d Dep't 1987).

67. 126 A.D.2d 610, 511 N.Y.S.2d 50, 51 (2d Dep't 1987). The court embarked on a lengthy discussion of the admissibility of physician's office records. The earlier authority to the contrary was Rodriguez v. Zampella, 42 A.D.2d 805, 346 N.Y.S.2d 558 (3d Dep't 1973), where the court refused to allow a physician's report since it contained opinion and diagnosis. The Second Department in Wilson disagreed.

68. See also Dayanim v. Unis, 171 A.D.2d 579, 580, 567 N.Y.S.2d 673, 674 (1st Dep't 1991)(with foundation witness, office records admissible); Fanelli v. di Lorenzo, 187 A.D.2d 1004, 591 N.Y.S.2d 658 (4th Dep't 1992) (letter written by treating physician to psychiatrist concerning patient admissible). But reports prepared on instruction of counsel are material prepared for litigation. Wilson v. Bodian, 130 A.D.2d 221, 519 N.Y.S.2d 126 (2d Dep't 1987).

admissible "without the need for foundation testimony or further proof of authenticity or accuracy unless objections * * * are made * * *."[69]

DNA tests used in criminal prosecutions presumably will have to be supported by a foundation witness, or they might be admissible under subdivision (c) if the test is conducted in a laboratory operated by a bureau of the government. The Court of Appeals' decision in *People v. Wesley*,[70] while approving, in general, the use of DNA evidence in criminal cases, requires the laying of a detailed foundation in each case concerning the procedures used in the testing process.[71] Admissibility on the basis of certification alone in paternity cases is perhaps justified by the controlled circumstances in which the blood is obtained, and the tests made. DNA evidence in criminal cases often is collected in fragmentary samples from a crime scene and can consist of bodily fluids other than blood.

69. CPLR 4518 * * *

(d) Any records or reports relating to the administration and analysis of a blood genetic marker or DNA test administered pursuant to sections four hundred eighteen and five hundred thirty-two of the family court act are admissible in evidence under this rule and are prima facie evidence of the facts contained provided they bear a certification or authentication by the head of the hospital, laboratory, department or bureau of a municipal corporation or of the state or by an employee delegated for that purpose, or by a qualified physician. If such record or report relating to the administration and analysis of a blood genetic marker or DNA test or tests administered pursuant to sections four hundred eighteen and five hundred thirty-two of the family court act indicates at least a ninety-five percent probability of paternity, the admission of such record or report shall create a rebuttable presumption of paternity, and shall, if unrebutted, establish the paternity of and liability for the support of a child pursuant to articles four and five of the family court act.

(e) Notwithstanding any other provision of law, a record or report relating to the administration and analysis of a blood genetic marker or DNA test certified in accordance with subdivision (d) of this rule and administered pursuant to sections four hundred eighteen and five hundred thirty-two of the family court act is admissible in evidence under this rule without the need for foundation testimony or further proof of authenticity or accuracy unless objections to the record or report are made in writing no later than twenty days before a hearing at which the record or report may be introduced into evidence or thirty days after receipt of the test results, whichever is earlier.

(f) Notwithstanding any other provision of law, records or reports of support payments and disbursements maintained pursuant to title six-A of article three of the social services law by the department of social services or the fiscal agent under contract to the department for the provision of centralized collection and disbursement functions are admissible in evidence under this rule, provided that they bear a certification by an official of a social services district attesting to the accuracy of the content of the record or report of support payments and that in attesting to the accuracy of the record or report such official has received confirmation from the department of social services or the fiscal agent under contract to the department for the provision of centralized collection and disbursement functions pursuant to section one hundred eleven-h of the social services law that the record or report of support payments reflects the processing of all support payments in the possession of the department or the fiscal agent as of a specified date, and that the document is a record or report of support payments maintained pursuant to title six-A of article three of the social services law. If so certified, such record or report shall be admitted into evidence under this rule without the need for additional foundation testimony. Such records shall be the basis for a permissive inference of the facts contained therein unless the trier of fact finds good cause not to draw such inference.

70. 83 N.Y.2d 417, 611 N.Y.S.2d 97, 633 N.E.2d 451 (1994). See discussion at § 702.1(b) supra.

71. See also People v. Castro, 144 Misc.2d 956, 545 N.Y.S.2d 985 (Sup.Ct. Bronx Co.1989).

Prima facie evidence. As has been noted, hospital bills under CPLR 4518, subdivision (b), the various government and hospital records under subdivision (c), and the blood genetic marker and DNA material under subdivision (d) and (e), are designated as "prima facie evidence"; under subdivision (d) if the blood sample shows at least 95 percent probability of paternity, a rebuttable presumption of paternity will be established.

The distinction, if any, between prima facie evidence and a rebuttable presumption, creates uncertainty as to what was intended by the legislature. It might be argued that prima facie evidence is evidence that, although it satisfies the proponent's duty to make out a case, can be accepted or rejected by the factfinder whether rebutted or not. The perhaps careless use of the term "presumptive evidence" may be intended to have the same effect. Where, however, the term "rebuttable presumption" is used, as it is in subdivision (d) with respect to the 95 percent requirement, paternity will be established if the evidence is unrebutted.

Despite the intermingling of these terms it seems clear that the original intention of the drafters of CPLR 4518 was that "prima facie evidence" have the same effect as "rebuttable presumption,"[72] so that in either case the evidence must be accepted if unrebutted. The Court of Appeals, however, has held that the term "prima facie evidence" in CPLR 4518(c) refers to evidence which is "sufficient to permit but not require the trier of fact to find in accordance with the record."[73] But 12 years later the Court of Appeals in *Powers v. Powers*[74] said, in another context, that prima facie evidence must be accepted if left unrebutted. See the detailed discussion of this problem in § 301.7 *supra*.

X-rays. CPLR 4532–a provides for the introduction of X-rays in personal injury cases without the need for a foundation witness. This provision now also covers the magnetic resonance image, computed axial tomograph, positron emission tomograph, electromyogram, sonogram and fetal heart rate monitor strips.

To take advantage of the rule, three requirements must be met: (1) a photographic inscription on the X-ray must state the name of the injured person, the date taken, the identifying number, and the name and address of the physician under whose supervision the X-ray was taken; (2) at least ten days prior to trial, notice must be served upon all parties who have appeared in the action (see CPLR 2103[e]) stating that the X-ray will be offered and authorizing an inspection of the X-ray at

---

72. See note of the Advisory Committee on Practice and Procedure to CPLR 4518(b), N.Y.Adv.Comm. on Prac. and Proc., Second Prelim.Rep., Legis.Doc.No.13, p.267 (1958).

73. Commissioner of Social Services v. Philip De G., 59 N.Y.2d 137, 141, 463 N.Y.S.2d 761, 762, 450 N.E.2d 681, 682 (1983)(certified hospital records under CPLR 4518(c)); see also People v. Mertz, 68 N.Y.2d 136, 148, 506 N.Y.S.2d 290, 296–97, 497 N.E.2d 657, 663 (1986)(certified results of police breathalyzer test). See Alexander, Practice Commentaries on CPLR 4518, at C4518:9, McKinney's Consolidated Laws of New York Annotated.

74. 86 N.Y.2d 63, 629 N.Y.S.2d 984, 653 N.E.2d 1154 (1995).

the serving attorney's office; and (3) the notice must be accompanied by an affidavit of the physician under whose supervision the X-ray was taken identifying the X-ray, attesting to the information inscribed on the X-ray and attesting that he or she would so testify if called as a witness at trial.

If the X-ray has been lost, and its unavailability is established, a physician's report and his testimony based on his examination of the X-ray may be introduced as secondary evidence of what the X-ray displayed without violating the best evidence rule.[75] This also illustrates the point that normally a physician will have to testify anyway in order to explain the X-ray, and that CPLR 4532-a essentially provides a device for authentication.[76]

The last unnumbered paragraph of CPLR 4532-a provides that X-rays may be admitted in evidence by other authorized means. This is borne out in *Hoffman v. City of New York*,[77] where it was held that an X-ray could be offered as part of plaintiff's hospital records under CPLR 4518. "Indeed," said the court, "if X-rays contained in the medical records pertain to diagnosis and treatment of plaintiff's alleged injuries it would be error to exclude them."[78]

---

75. Schozer v. William Penn Life Insurance Co., 84 N.Y.2d 639, 620 N.Y.S.2d 797, 644 N.E.2d 1353 (1994).

76. CPLR Rule 4532-a. X-rays, magnetic resonance images, computed axial tomographs, positron emission tomographs, electromyograms, sonograms and fetal heart rate monitor strips in personal injury actions

In an action in which a claim for personal injuries is asserted, an X-ray, magnetic resonance image, computed axial tomograph, positron emission tomograph, electromyogram, sonogram or fetal heart rate monitor strips of any party thereto is admissible in evidence provided:

(1) that there is photographically inscribed on such X-ray, magnetic resonance image, computer axial tomograph, positron emission tomograph, electromyogram, sonogram or fetal heart rate monitor strips the name of the injured party, the date when taken, the identifying number thereof, and the name and address of the physician under whose supervision the same was taken;

(2) that at least ten days before the date of trial of the action, the attorney for the party intending to offer such X-ray, magnetic resonance image, computed axial tomograph, positron emission tomograph, electromyogram, sonogram or fetal heart rate monitor strips, serve upon the attorney or attorneys for the party or parties against whom said X-ray, magnetic resonance image, computed axial tomograph, positron emission tomograph, electromyogram, sonogram or fetal heart rate monitor strips is to be offered, a notice of his intention to offer such X-ray, magnetic resonance image, computed axial tomograph, positron emission tomograph, electromyogram, sonogram or fetal heart rate monitor strips in evidence during the trial and that the same is available for inspection at his office, provided that such X-ray, magnetic resonance image, computed axial tomograph, positron emission tomograph, electromyogram, sonogram or fetal heart rate monitor strips has or have not been previously so examined; and

(3) that the notice aforesaid is accompanied by an affidavit of such physician identifying the X-ray, magnetic resonance image, computed axial tomograph, positron emission tomograph, electromyogram, sonogram or fetal heart rate monitor strips and attesting to the information inscribed thereon, and further attesting that, if called as a witness in the action, he would so testify.

Nothing contained in this section, however, shall prohibit the admissibility of an X-ray, magnetic resonance image, computed axial tomograph, positron emission tomograph, electromyogram, sonogram or fetal heart rate monitor strips in evidence in a personal injury action where otherwise admissible.

77. 141 Misc.2d 893, 535 N.Y.S.2d 342 (Sup.Ct.Kings Co.1988).

78. Id. at 894, 535 N.Y.S.2d at 342.

d. The Proposed New York Evidence Code

The proposed New York Evidence Code § 803(c)(5) is found below.[79]

79. (5) Business records. [PROPOSED]

(A) General rule. Any writing or record, whether in the form of an entry in a book or otherwise, made as a memorandum or record of any act, transaction, occurrence or event, shall be admissible in evidence in proof of that act, transaction, occurrence or event, if it was made in the regular course of any business and that it was the regular course of such business to make it, at the time of the act, transaction, occurrence or event, or within a reasonable time thereafter.

(i) Exceptions and other circumstances. Records or reports prepared solely for purposes of litigation are not admissible under this paragraph. All other circumstances of the making of the memorandum or record, including lack of personal knowledge by the maker, may be proved to affect its weight, but they shall not affect its admissibility.

(ii) Businesses included. The term business includes a business, profession, occupation and calling of every kind.

(iii) Law enforcement records in criminal cases. In a criminal case, a business record of a law enforcement agency offered by the prosecution under this paragraph to prove directly an element of the crime charged or other crucial facts establishing guilt is admissible: (a) when the person who provided the information set forth in the writing or record testifies, or is unavailable to testify within the meaning of subdivision (a) of section 804 of this article, and (b) when the writing or record contains an expert opinion, if the person who rendered that opinion testifies, or if that person is unavailable to testify within the meaning of subdivision (a) of section 804 of this article and there is available no other witness who can provide equivalent testimony.

(B) Hospital bills. A hospital bill is admissible as evidence of the facts contained therein, provided it bears a certification by the head of the hospital or by a responsible employee in the controller's or accounting office that the bill is correct, that each of the items was necessarily supplied, and that the amount charged is reasonable. This paragraph shall not apply to any proceeding in a surrogate's court nor in any action instituted by or on behalf of a hospital to recover payment for accommodations or supplies furnished or for services rendered by or in such hospital, except that in a proceeding pursuant to section 189 of the lien law to determine the validity and extent of the lien of a hospital, such certified hospital bills are admissible as evidence of the fact of services and of the reasonableness of any charges which do not exceed the comparable charges made by the hospital in the care of workers' compensation patients.

(C) Records of hospital, library, or department or bureau of a municipal corporation or of the state. All records, writings, and other things referred to in sections 2306 and 2307 of the civil practice law and rules and any record and report relating to the administering and analysis of a blood genetic marker test administered pursuant to sections 418 and 532 of the family court act are admissible as evidence of the facts contained therein without testimony of the custodian or other qualified witness, provided they bear a certification or authentication by the head of the hospital, laboratory, library, or department or bureau of a municipal corporation or of the state, or by an employee delegated for that purpose or by a qualified physician.

(D) Bill for services or repairs. An itemized bill or invoice, receipted or marked paid, for services or repairs of an amount not in excess of two thousand dollars is admissible as evidence of the reasonable value and necessity of such services or repairs itemized therein in any civil case, provided it bears a certification by the person, firm, or corporation, or an authorized agent or employee thereof, rendering such services or making such repairs and charging for the same, and contains a verified statement that no part of the payment received therefor will be refunded to the debtor, and that the amounts itemized therein are the usual and customary rates charged for such services or repairs by the affiant or the affiant's employer. No more than one bill or invoice from the same person, firm, or corporation to the same debtor shall be admissible under this paragraph in the same case.

(E) X-rays in personal injury and wrongful death actions. In an action for personal injury, or for wrongful death, an X-ray of any party thereto or the decedent is admissible provided: (i) that there is photographically inscribed on such X-ray the name of the injured person, the date when taken, the identifying number thereof, and the name and ad-

§ 803(3).1　　　　　HEARSAY　　　　　Ch. 8

Library References:

West's Key No. Digests, Criminal Law ⟺429–446; Evidence ⟺325–383.

§ 803(3).2　Federal

Unlike New York's CPLR 4518, which contains a general rule for admissibility of business records and also provides for several discrete situations where records may be admitted without the necessity for foundation testimony, Federal Rule 803(6) provides only a general rule:

(6) Records of regularly conducted activity. A memorandum, report, record, or data compilation, in any form, of acts, events, conditions, opinions, or diagnoses, made at or near the time by, or from information transmitted by, a person with knowledge, if kept in the course of a regularly conducted business activity, and if it was the regular practice of that business activity to make the memorandum, report, record, or data compilation, all as shown by the testimony of the custodian or other qualified witness, unless the source of information or the method or circumstances of preparation indicate lack of trustworthiness. The term "business" as used in this paragraph includes business, institution, association, profession, occupation, and calling of every kind, whether or not conducted for profit.

The Federal Rule pointedly avoids the use of the word "business" in the title so as not to restrict the rule to activities of a commercial type. In the last sentence, the rule gives a much broader reach to the term "business" than is found in the body of the provision,[1] and there is no indication that New York's CPLR 4518(a) is any less expansively applied.[2] Another distinction in the wording of CPLR 4518(a) and Federal Rule 803(6), which creates no distinction in practice, is the requirement in the Federal Rule that the source of information be trustworthy. This point was added to the state rule, in effect, by the opinion in *Johnson v. Lutz*.[3] Likewise, the more specific Federal Rule refers to foundation testimony by "the custodian or other qualified witness," which is an unspoken requirement of CPLR 4518(a).

Johnson v. Lutz held that if the maker of the record lacked personal knowledge, the person providing the information to the maker had to have a business duty to impart the information so as to insure the necessary element of reliability. *Johnson v. Lutz* is cited in the Advisory

---

dress of the physician under whose supervision the same was taken; (ii) that the X-ray is accompanied by an affidavit of such physician identifying the X-ray and attesting to the information inscribed thereon, and further attesting that, if called as a witness in the action, such physician would so testify; and (iii) nothing contained in this section, however, shall prohibit the admissibility of an X-ray in evidence in a personal injury action where otherwise admissible.

§ 803(3).2

1. See the Advisory Committee's note to Rule 803(6).

2. The last sentence of CPLR 4518(a) defines business as meaning "a business, profession, occupation and calling of every kind." The Federal Rule's last sentence adds the words institution and association, and "whether or not conducted for profit."

3. 253 N.Y. 124, 170 N.E. 517 (1930), discussed in § 803(3).1(a) supra.

Committee's note to Rule 803(6), with an indication that the informant in a record governed by Rule 803(6) ordinarily must have been under a duty to provide the information.

The federal and state rules thus are essentially applied in the same general way, except that material generated by law enforcement agencies for use in criminal prosecutions, dealt with at the state level under CPLR 4518, are handled at the federal level under the public records provisions of Federal Rule 803(8).

Yates v. Bair Transport, Inc.[4] is to the Federal Rule in the Second Circuit what *Johnson v. Lutz* is to the state rule. Concerning a police officer's report of an accident, Judge Tenney explained that such could be considered a business record, but that in the case at hand there was no indication of where or from whom the officer obtained his information, thus precluding admissibility.[5] Judge Tenney's interpretation, which was based on a federal statute that preceded adoption of the Federal Rules of Evidence, has not changed with the advent of Rule 803(6). Thus the source of the information was a crucial factor where, in a § 1983 civil rights case, progress notes concerning an inmate in a correctional institution were involved;[6] where case notes were made by a social worker;[7] and where the entrant gathered information from fellow employees.[8] If the information recorded would be admissible under another hearsay exception, or would be relevant not for its truth, but for

4. 249 F.Supp. 681 (1965).

5. Id. at 687–88. Judge Tenney stated:

Based on the foregoing authorities, it appears that the Business Records Act overcomes the initial hurdle to the admissibility of evidence, but goes no further. Thus the hearsay statement (of a volunteer) contained in the police officer's report is no more admissible than the testimony of the police officer on the stand as to the hearsay statement made at the scene of the accident. If the making of the statement itself is relevant, it can be proved both by the report, which is a record kept in the ordinary course of business, as well as by the in-Court testimony of the officer. However, if the report is offered to prove the truth of the statement contained therein, the statement must either have been made in the regular course of business of the person making it, or must have an independent ground of admissibility such as an admission, etc., the same as the in-Court testimony of the officer as to the statements made, offered to prove the truth of what was said, must have an independent ground of admissibility, since all that can be shown under the Business Records Act is that in the regular course of business of the officer he wrote that X made the following statement to prove the truth of the fact that X made the statement, not the proof of the facts contained in the statement.

Accordingly, without knowing who made the statements and under what circumstances they were made, an insufficient foundation has presently been laid upon which to admit the proffered report over objection. Id.

6. Romano v. Howarth, 998 F.2d 101, 107–108 (2d Cir.1993)(information imparted by a corrections officer to a nurse was not admissible because it did not appear that the corrections staff had a business duty to give information to the medical staff, and there was also an issue of trustworthiness since the officer was a defendant and reported an admission said to have been made by the plaintiff).

7. Malek v. Federal Ins. Co., 994 F.2d 49, 53, 57–58 (2d Cir.1993) (whereas majority considered these notes admissible under Rule 803(6), a sharp dissent could find no support for a trustworthy source).

8. United States v. Re, 336 F.2d 306, 313 (2d Cir.), cert. denied, 379 U.S. 904, 85 S.Ct. 188, 13 L.Ed.2d 177 (1964)(fact entrant had no personal knowledge of all information received was no bar to admissibility when information imparted from fellow employees with requisite business duty).

the fact it was said, then it ought to be admissible if the other regularity requirements for the making of the record are satisfied.[9]

Concerning those other requirements, the Second Circuit in *United States v. Freidin*[10] had occasion to analyze the scope of Rule 803(6). This was a prosecution for income tax violations. The government offered a memorandum in defendant's office file which recorded the diversion of funds from an income classification. But this memorandum was not filed in the regular course of business. It was made on special instructions, and the office custodian of records testified that it was not routine to prepare memoranda pertaining to capital accounts. Nevertheless, the memorandum appeared trustworthy and the court was urged to find it admissible anyway since that money, through some office practice, had to be kept track of. The court recognized the liberality with which the rule had been interpreted in the Second Circuit,[11] but noted that Rule 803(6), in addition to other requirements, stated that it should be the regular course of business to make the memorandum. Could that requirement, and all the others, simply be "collapsed" into one—"the showing of sufficient indicia of trustworthiness"?[12] While sympathetic to this view, the court was unwilling to implement it.

> In the end, though we believe the better rule would permit admission of the Colasanti memorandum, we must respect Congress's addition of the phrase ["regular practice of that business activity to make the memorandum"] * * *. As such, since the Colasanti memorandum was not shown to have been made pursuant to a "regular practice" of Touche Ross, it must be held inadmissible.[13]

The mere foundation statement that the document was made in the regular course of business is insufficient,[14] but there is no requirement that the person whose firsthand knowledge was the basis for the entry need be known, so long as it was the entity's regular practice to gather and record such information.[15] An exception to the usual foundation rule can occur where the document is required to be made and kept by law and witnesses testify that they "are integrated into an office's records and relied upon in its day-to-day operations."[16] "Although an

---

9. See Judge Tenney's discussion in Yates, note 5 supra. See also United States v. Sackett, 598 F.2d 739, 742 (2d Cir.1979), discussed at notes 23 and 24 infra.

10. 849 F.2d 716 (2d Cir.1988).

11. Id. at 722.

12. Id.

13. Id. at 723.

14. Ortho Pharmaceutical Corp. v. Cosprophar, Inc., 828 F.Supp. 1114, 1120 (S.D.N.Y.1993), aff'd, 32 F.3d 690 (2d Cir.1994)(report summarizing market survey was not admissible as a business record because, although such market research is regularly conducted, the source of the information was not shown to be objective and there was no showing of any controls placed on her methodology).

15. Saks Intern., Inc. v. M/V "Export Champion," 817 F.2d 1011, 1014 (2d Cir.1987)(loading tallies prepared by shoreside stevedores admissible under Rule 803(6) to establish quantity of coffee loaded—even though they are records of entity other than one of the parties, and even though foundation is laid by witness who is not an employee of entity that prepared them).

16. United States v. Mendel, 746 F.2d 155, 166 (2d Cir.1984), cert. denied, 469 U.S. 1213, 105 S.Ct. 1184, 84 L.Ed.2d 331 (1985). In this case, reports of livestock brucellosis eradication program had to be

employee of the preparing business normally lays the foundation required by Rule 803(6), no such employee need testify when circumstances otherwise demonstrate trustworthiness."[17]

The reach of Rule 803(6) can extend to a drug dealer's customer book where there is proof that the entries were made in identified handwriting because "[i]t is not unreasonable to expect that one who keeps the records of a multi-million dollar business does so with care and precision";[18] but where such a customer book is simply found with nothing connecting it to the participants involved in the prosecution inadmissibility is the result.[19]

A record made and kept in a foreign country is admissible in a federal criminal proceeding under the Comprehensive Crime Control Act of 1984, 18 U.S.C.A. § 3505, and "the statute establishes the requisite conditions for determining the records' reliability by analogy to those in Rule 803(6)."[20]

Medical records. Whether from the files of a hospital, a physician or an employer, medical records and reports are treated no differently than other regularly made records, and foundation testimony will be necessary unless an instance arises where trustworthiness can be established by other proof.[21] With respect to the scope of the term "diagnosis and treatment" the Second Circuit seems not as strict as the New York Court of Appeals, which allows only so much of such records as relate *directly* to diagnosis and treatment.[22] In *United States v. Sackett*,[23] the

submitted to Agriculture Department by law. The reports were on the government's own forms and completed at its request. These circumstances "manifestly demonstrate trustworthiness," said the court, and there was no need for an employee to lay the usual foundation.

17. Id. See Zenith Radio Corp. v. Matsushita Elec. Ind. Co., 505 F.Supp. 1190, 1233–36 (E.D.Pa.1980), rev'd on other grounds, 723 F.2d 238 (3d Cir.1983), rev'd on other grounds, 475 U.S. 574, 106 S.Ct. 1348, 89 L.Ed.2d 538 (1986). Here the court was willing to dispense with the custodian's testimony where proponent could show regularity of practice in some other manner, either by external evidence or from documents themselves plus surrounding circumstances.

18. United States v. McGrath, 613 F.2d 361, 368 (2d Cir.1979), cert. denied, 446 U.S. 967, 100 S.Ct. 2946, 64 L.Ed.2d 827 (1980).

19. United States v. Garcia–Duarte, 718 F.2d 42, 45 (2d Cir.1983). Another case illustrating that the recorded activity, in order to be admissible under Rule 803(6), need not necessarily be legal, is United States v. Cohen, 384 F.2d 699 (2d Cir.1967), where lists made by employer's bookkeeper of illegal payments by the employer to union representatives were held admissible.

20. United States v. Hing Shair Chan, 680 F.Supp. 521, 523 (E.D.N.Y.1988) (Hong Kong hotel records admissible in prosecution for conspiracy to import heroin).

21. See Zenith Radio Corp. v. Matsushita Elec. Ind. Co., 505 F.Supp. 1190, 1233–36 (E.D.Pa.1980), rev'd on other grounds, 723 F.2d 238 (3d Cir.1983), rev'd on other grounds, 475 U.S. 574, 106 S.Ct. 1348, 89 L.Ed.2d 538 (1986).

22. See Williams v. Alexander, 309 N.Y. 283, 129 N.E.2d 417 (1955), discussed in § 803(3).1, at notes 63–64 supra. In Central Railroad Co. v. Jules S. Sottnek Co., 258 F.2d 85 (2d Cir.1958), cert. denied, 359 U.S. 913, 79 S.Ct. 588, 3 L.Ed.2d 574 (1959), it was stated in connection with approval of a fire marshal's report: "The federal courts generally apply the more liberal evidentiary rule between the federal and state rules so as to favor the reception of evidence." Id. at 88. The court then noted, citing inter alia Williams v. Alexander, that this report would not be admissible in a New York court. In another case, Sugarman v. New England Mutual Life Insurance Co., 201 F.Supp. 759, 761 n.1 (E.D.N.Y.1962), it was stated, "The hospital record, corroborating the testimony of one witness, was admissible to show that the wife did not report a 'fall' to the attending physician. See Williams v. Alexander * * *"

23. See note 23 on page 652.

history portion of the hospital's medical record, which recorded that the family thought the patient was "pre-terminal," was relevant to the son's loan application and was held admissible, "[b]ecause the statements at issue have some relevance to diagnosis or treatment, [and] they were kept 'in the course of' the regularly conducted business activity of the hospital."[24]

The Second Circuit early on, in dealing with the business entry statute under the predecessor of Rule 803(6),[25] ruled liberally with respect to doctors' reports so that the report of a doctor retained by defendant's insurer to examine plaintiff was admissible when offered by the plaintiff even to the extent it referred to X-rays of plaintiff taken by another doctor which were not included in the report.[26] In another case an outpatient record, containing an intake form recording defendant's answers to certain questions including those seeking information as to his use of drugs, was held admissible as a business record;[27] and a plastic surgeon who was sued for malpractice, his defense being that plaintiff's scars resulted from other surgery performed subsequent to his, could introduce plaintiff's psychiatric records, compiled after his surgery, and containing no complaints concerning the defendant's surgery.[28] But where a doctor's report was offered to show the patient's prior consistent statement and was made two months after the injury and after the patient would have had a motive to falsify, it was held not admissible "even if [it] would have been admissible under the Federal Business Records Act."[29]

Medical records are considered reliable by the United States Supreme Court,[30] and can routinely be received in administrative hearings.[31]

---

23. 598 F.2d 739, 742 (2d Cir.1979).

24. Id. at 742. The court also found that this information was not necessarily introduced for its truth anyway since the fact of what the family thought was relevant was simply to show state of mind. This coincides with McCormick's analysis which is that unless the information is relevant to the question of diagnosis and treatment, the information would have to be a separate hearsay exception, such as an admission. McCormick § 293, at 279–80. This states a broader rule than is found in New York where Williams v. Alexander, 309 N.Y. 283, 129 N.E.2d 417 (1955), would not allow any hearsay exception to come in through the hospital report, unless the information was directly related to diagnosis and treatment. See § 803(3).1(c) supra.

25. Then 28 U.S.C.A. § 1732, the old Federal Business Records Act.

26. White v. Zutell, 263 F.2d 613, 614–15 (2d Cir.1959). There is no discussion on the point, but what if defendant had sought to introduce this report as a business record? See text at notes 32–38 infra.

27. United States v. Maddox, 444 F.2d 148, 150 (2d Cir.1971).

28. Chnapkova v. Koh, 985 F.2d 79 (2d Cir.1993). Compare Lewis v. Velez, 149 F.R.D. 474, 484 (S.D.N.Y.1993), where psychiatric records were not allowed when offered for the purpose of showing plaintiff's general credibility. In footnote 5 of the opinion, the court notes that in addition to being admissible under Rule 803(6), medical records, where they record statements by patients for purposes of diagnosis and treatment, are also admissible under Rule 803(4), "Statements for purposes of diagnosis and treatment."

29. Felice v. Long Island Railroad Company, 426 F.2d 192 (2d Cir.), cert. denied, 400 U.S. 820, 91 S.Ct. 37, 27 L.Ed.2d 47 (1970).

30. Richardson v. Perales, 402 U.S. 389, 402, 91 S.Ct. 1420, 1428, 28 L.Ed.2d 842, 853 (1971).

31. Id. See also Gullo v. Califano, 609 F.2d 649, 650 (2d Cir.1979) (where the court held medical records improperly considered since they were received after the

Palmer v. Hoffman—material prepared for litigation. The "litigation-records" doctrine of *Palmer v. Hoffman* is discussed in § 803(3).1(a), *supra*. In the Second Circuit, *Yates v. Bair Transport, Inc.*[32] serves as a modern anchor. The court discussed the admissibility of doctors' reports made after examinations of plaintiff pursuant to provisions of the Worker's Compensation Law. Some of the doctors examined plaintiff on behalf of the defendant's insurer, others were plaintiff's own doctors. Plaintiff sought to introduce all of the reports, and defendant argued that all were barred under *Palmer v. Hoffman*[33] because prepared for litigation purposes. Judge Tenney ruled that only the reports made on defendant's behalf were admissible as business records stating that "what must be found * * * is an added element of trustworthiness which will counterbalance the fact that these reports were prepared in clear anticipation of litigation."[34] Judge Tenney referred to *Pekelis v. Transcontinental & W. Air, Inc.*,[35] which restricted the rule in *Palmer v. Hoffman* to instances where the report is self-serving, made in anticipation of litigation, and has no element of trustworthiness.[36] Thus, the reports made by plaintiff's doctors were inadmissible when offered by plaintiff: "No case * * * has been found or cited wherein a plaintiff was permitted to introduce self-serving reports made by doctors of his own choosing, in anticipation of litigation to shore up his own case."[37] But where the doctors made their reports as a routine practice, and the reports were offered *against* the party responsible for their preparation, admissibility of the reports was virtually assured.[38]

claimant's social security hearing, thereby depriving him of a chance to challenge them).

32. 249 F.Supp. 681 (S.D.N.Y.1965).

33. 318 U.S. 109, 63 S.Ct. 477, 87 L.Ed. 645, rehearing denied, 318 U.S. 800, 63 S.Ct. 757, 87 L.Ed. 1163 (1943)(accident report made by employee of defendant railroad held to be in anticipation of litigation).

34. Yates, 249 F.Supp. at 689–90.

35. 187 F.2d 122 (2d Cir.), cert. denied, 341 U.S. 951, 71 S.Ct. 1020, 95 L.Ed. 1374 (1951).

36. Yates, 249 F.Supp. at 690. A quotation construing Pekelis was taken from United States v. New York Foreign Trade Zone Operators, 304 F.2d 792, 798 (2d Cir. 1962). Korte v. New York, N.H. & H.R.R.Co., 191 F.2d 86 (2d Cir.), cert. denied, 342 U.S. 868, 72 S.Ct. 108, 96 L.Ed. 652 (1951), was also cited in the quote. This emphasized that Palmer v. Hoffman is not offended where reports are introduced against the party for whom the reports were prepared.

37. Yates, 249 F.Supp. at 691. Judge Tenney cited Taylor v. Baltimore & Ohio R.R., 344 F.2d 281, 286 (2d Cir.1965), cert. denied, 382 U.S. 831, 86 S.Ct. 72, 15 L.Ed.2d 75 (1965), by way of contrast, for this quote:

> The report here was made when, so far as the record shows, no one thought Taylor had suffered any serious injury, and it can hardly be assumed that a freight agent would appreciate the witty diversity whereby the difference of a few feet in the place of an employee's injury would result in the imposition of a distinct legal regime.

249 F.Supp. at 691.

The Taylor case indeed construes the Palmer v. Hoffman rule as one which should be limited to the facts there found where the employee makes the report knowing that he will use it to advance his claim. In Taylor a key issue was where Taylor was when he was injured. If he was on the gangplank, the Longshoreman's Compensation Act would not apply. If he was a few feet away on the bulkhead, a location covered under the Act, he could recover. The employer's accident report had him on the gangplank and the jury found against him. The verdict was affirmed since the report was fully admissible.

38. See in addition to cases already noted above, Terrasi v. South Atlantic Lines,

§ 803(3).2

Accident reports made by company employees, when offered by the company, edge closer to *Palmer v. Hoffman,* but even here they will be admissible if it is the routine practice to investigate and report on accidents, and such activity is motivated by purposes other than possible litigation. Thus, in *Lewis v. Baker,*[39] an FELA case, reports made by employees pursuant to company and ICC rules were admissible under the business entry rule. The court stated:

> In addition to their use by the railroad in making reports to the ICC, the reports here were undoubtedly of utility to the employer in ascertaining whether the equipment involved was defective so that future accidents might be prevented. These factors, we think, are sufficient indicia of trustworthiness to establish the admissibility of the reports into evidence under the Federal Business Records Act.[40]

A like result was reached in *United States v. New York Foreign Trade Zone Operators,*[41] where a statutorily required report relating to the personal injury suffered by a ship's employee, made by the employee's superior who simply filled in the blanks, was held admissible over a *Palmer v. Hoffman* objection. While in both of these cases some emphasis was placed on the fact the reports were required by law, it appears that without this ingredient the results would have been the same. This is not to say, however, that all employer investigatory reports will be admissible. In *Lewis v. Velez,*[42] a § 1983 civil rights case brought on charges of alleged injuries suffered at the hands of prison guards, the "incident report" made by the very guards who would be likely defendants fell under the *Palmer v. Hoffman* proscription. With respect to governmental investigatory reports mandated by law, Rule 803(8)(C), as discussed in § 803(5).2, *infra,* may prove to be more applicable than Rule 803(6).

Library References:

West's Key No. Digests, Criminal Law ⊜429–446; Evidence ⊜325–383.

§ 803(4) Absence of Record

§ 803(4).1 New York

Public records and private business records have been treated differently from each other in New York in terms of whether their absence can be introduced to prove that the transaction in issue did not occur.

a. Business Records

The apparent rule in New York, enunciated in somewhat antiquated lower court cases, is that proof of the absence of a record where one

226 F.2d 823, 825 (2d Cir.1955), cert. denied, 350 U.S. 988, 76 S.Ct. 475, 100 L.Ed. 855 (1956)(in action against ship line by passenger alleging he was struck by an assailant, ship's doctor's report that passenger said he had been caught by sudden dizziness and fell was held admissible as business entry).

39. 526 F.2d 470 (2d Cir.1975).
40. Id. at 474.
41. 304 F.2d 792, 797 (2d Cir.1962).
42. 149 F.R.D. 474 (S.D.N.Y.1993).

would normally be found if the transaction in issue had occurred, is not admissible. In a case where defendant sought to prove nondelivery of concrete, for which plaintiff was suing, by showing there were no entries in its records, the court said: "Neither [defendant's affidavit] nor the books of the defendant corporation could be used as evidence that the deliveries were not received. Such evidence, completely negative, has uniformly been held to be hearsay in character and incompetent and irrelevant."[1]

There may have been other reasons for rejecting this evidence, but New York seems to be one of the few if not the only remaining jurisdictions that would not recognize such a hearsay exception,[2] trustworthiness otherwise being indicated. The proposed New York Evidence Code § 803(c)(6) would prescribe a change.[3]

It would seem that records as reliable as bank records[4] could be introduced to show, for instance, that a deposit or withdrawal was not made, despite the rule of the older cases.

b. Public Records

CPLR 4521[5] creates a hearsay exception for a signed statement by an authorized public employee that after a diligent search of official

§ 803(4).1

1. Gravel Prods. v. Sunnydale Acres, 10 Misc.2d 323, 325, 171 N.Y.S.2d 519, 521–22 (Sup.Ct.Erie Co.1958). See also Roe v. Nichols, 5 App.Div. 472, 474, 38 N.Y.S. 1100 (2d Dep't 1896)(bank passbook not competent, because of lack of entry, to show decedent never received money due on a note, both because such evidence per se not competent, and also because lack of deposit would not necessarily prove that the sum had not been paid); Boor v. Moschell, 8 N.Y.S. 583, 584 (Sup.Ct.5th Dep't 1889)(in action on note defendant could not prove that his books did not show the existence of the debt for which the note was alleged to have been written, or that bill-book contained no memorandum of such a note, since this was inadmissible hearsay); Bernstein v. Holtz, 34 Misc. 795, 69 N.Y.S. 892 (N.Y.C.Municipal Ct.1901)(evidence that certain checks had not been written, shown by lack of any checkbook stubs, inadmissible since payments could have been made by cash; decision thus based on lack of relevancy more than disapproval of negative evidence); Winder v. Pollack, 151 N.Y.S. 870 (App.Term 1st Dep't 1915)(in action for goods sold, defendant's books of account, containing no entry of receipt of certain goods, and the testimony of bookkeeper that the books contained no such entry, inadmissible to show goods not delivered).

2. McCormick § 287, at 268–69.

3. § 803(c)(6) Absence of entry in records kept in accordance with the provisions of paragraph five of this subdivision. [PROPOSED.]

Evidence that a matter is not included in the writings, records, or data compilations kept in accordance with the provisions of paragraph five of this subdivision [regular entry rule], to prove the nonoccurrence or nonexistence of the matter, if the matter was of a kind of which otherwise a writing, record, or data compilation would have been regularly made and preserved.

4. See Elkaim v. Elkaim, 176 A.D.2d 116, 117, 574 N.Y.S.2d 2, 4 (1st Dep't 1991)(bank records considered so reliable as to warrant judicial notice without need for independent foundation of reliability). See also text at notes 12–13 infra.

5. Rule 4521. Lack of record

A statement signed by an officer or a deputy of an officer having legal custody of specified official records of the United States or of any state, territory of jurisdiction of the United States, or of any court thereof, or kept in any public office thereof, that he has made diligent search of the records and has found no record or entry of a specified nature, is prima facie evidence that the records contain no such record of entry, provided that the statement is accompanied by a certificate that legal custody of the specified official records belongs to such person, which certificate shall be made by a person described in rule 4540.

records over which she has legal custody she has been unable to locate a particular record of entry. The statement must be certified in accordance with CPLR 4540. Upon satisfaction of these requirements, the statement is "prima facie evidence" that no such record or entry ever existed.[6] CPLR 4521 undoubtedly has its origins in the common law presumption that a public official will not do anything contrary to official duty or omit anything required to be done by official duty.[7]

CPLR 4521 and its predecessors have provided an expeditious method of proving such matters as the failure of a married couple to have obtained a divorce decree,[8] failure of a landowner to have obtained a building permit,[9] and the failure of a contractor to have obtained a license to do business.[10] To ensure that the evidentiary benefit of CPLR 4521 is obtained, the public employee's certificate should state explicitly that she made a "diligent search."[11]

The existence of CPLR 4521 should not preclude recognition of a common law hearsay exception for the absence of a public record. Under the common law, regularly prepared government records are deemed sufficiently trustworthy to justify their admission as affirmative proof of the truth of their contents under CPLR 4520. By a parity of reasoning, the absence of a record or entry therein is sufficiently trustworthy as proof of a negative.[12] Thus, a public employee's in-court testimony (as opposed to a certified statement) that she has been unable to locate a particular record or entry among government documents in her custody should be admissible as evidence of the nonexistence of the record or nonoccurrence of the event that otherwise would have appeared as an entry in the record.[13] Since CPLR 4521 is limited by its

---

6. See discussion of the meaning of "prima facie evidence" in § 803(3).1(c) and § 301.7 supra.

7. See Mandeville v. Reynolds, 68 N.Y. 528, 534 (1877)(in action on a judgment where judgment roll missing and where county clerk testified that he would not have docketed the judgment had he not had the judgment roll—admissible to prove the judgment because of presumption of regularity of public officials' functions; not a case involving lack of a record in context involved here).

8. Matter of Brown's Estate, 40 N.Y.2d 938, 390 N.Y.S.2d 59, 358 N.E.2d 883 (1976)(presumption in favor of validity of second marriage overcome by evidence of lack of any record of divorce from first marriage).

9. Deshong v. City of New York, 176 N.Y. 475, 68 N.E. 880 (1903)(where party relies on continuing validity of building permit issued years previously, presumption of continuing validity dispelled by proof that no permit or any index of any such index exists).

10. Dartmouth Plan, Inc. v. Valle, 117 Misc.2d 534, 537, 458 N.Y.S.2d 848, 850 (Sup.Ct.Kings Co.1983)(where shown that no license ever issued "it is incumbent upon plaintiff to come forward with proof of contradictory evidentiary facts showing the existence of a genuine and substantial issue").

11. See Briggs v. Waldron, 83 N.Y. 582 (1881).

12. See Chesapeake & Delaware Canal Co. v. United States, 250 U.S. 123, 39 S.Ct. 407, 63 L.Ed. 889 (1919)(under public records hearsay exception, evidence of nonpayment may be inferred from absence of entry of payment in book designed to record all payments; entry of payment naturally would have been found in such book if payment had been made).

13. See, e.g., People v. Niang, 160 Misc.2d 500, 609 N.Y.S.2d 1017 (N.Y.C.Crim.Ct.1994). But see People v. Ebramha, 157 Misc.2d 222, 596 N.Y.S.2d 295 (N.Y.C.Crim.Ct.1993)(court was unwilling to recognize the common law rule where it was relied upon to prove that defendant had not procured a street vendor's license).

terms to public officials within the United States, the common law exception should also embrace the absence of a record in a foreign government's office.[14]

See a discussion complementary to this in § 803(5).1(n), *infra*, regarding CPLR 4521.

Library References:

West's Key No. Digests, Criminal Law ⚖︎429–446; Evidence ⚖︎325, 333(1), 351.

§ 803(4).2 Federal

Unlike the situation in New York, there is clear authority in the Federal Rules of Evidence for proof based on the absence of private business records. Rule 803(7) is as follows:

> (7) Absence of entry in records kept in accordance with the provisions of paragraph (6). Evidence that a matter is not included in the memoranda, reports, records, or data compilations in any form, kept in accordance with the provisions of paragraph (6), to prove the nonoccurrence or nonexistence of the matter, if the matter was of a kind of which a memorandum, report, record, or data compilation was regularly made and preserved, unless the sources of information or other circumstances indicate lack of trustworthiness.

The Second Circuit appears bereft of any important cases interpreting this rule, which, rather than being a hearsay exception, is more akin to circumstantial evidence. A sampling from the other circuits demonstrates instances where such proof has satisfied the requirements of the rule,[1] and instances where it has not.[2] One case indicates a preference for admissibility even where some problems are present.[3]

---

14. See Brill v. Brill, 10 N.Y.2d 308, 222 N.Y.S.2d 321, 178 N.E.2d 720 (certificates of foreign officials that search of court records revealed no divorce action between particular parties was evidence that no such divorce had occurred).

§ 803(4).2

1. United States v. Gentry, 925 F.2d 186, 188 (7th Cir.1991)(where defendant was prosecuted for giving false report of pin in candy, manufacturer can demonstrate through its business records that no other such complaints received); Hunt v. Liberty Lobby, 720 F.2d 631, 651 (11th Cir.1983)(affidavits of CIA officials that they searched records and failed to locate certain documents admissible under Rule 803(10), relating to absence of public documents); United States v. Lanier, 578 F.2d 1246, 1254–55 (8th Cir.), cert. denied, 439 U.S. 856, 99 S.Ct. 169, 58 L.Ed.2d 163 (1978)(testimony by USDA auditor that he searched records of bank and failed to find crucial deposits admissible under Rule 803[7]); United States v. Zeidman, 540 F.2d 314, 319 (7th Cir.1976)(account manager properly testified to search for particular check which was not found).

2. Fury Imports, Inc. v. Shakespeare Co., 554 F.2d 1376, 1381 (5th Cir.1977), cert. denied, 450 U.S. 921, 101 S.Ct. 1369, 67 L.Ed.2d 349 (1981)(trial judge's reliance on Rule 803[7] for proof that contract did not exist was misplaced insofar as the jury verdict was set aside because, while absence of records might be a factor, there were other facts also to be considered by the jury); United States v. Robinson, 544 F.2d 110, 115 (2d Cir.1976), cert. denied, 434 U.S. 1050, 98 S.Ct. 901, 54 L.Ed.2d 803 (1978)(absence of records insufficient proof that particular payment had not been made where foundation witness acknowledged records were confused and indefinite, and that payment might well have been made even if not recorded).

3. In United States v. Hutson, 821 F.2d 1015, 1020 (5th Cir.1987) the court stated, over defendant's arguments as to lack of

§ 803(4).2   HEARSAY   Ch. 8

There must be foundation testimony, even though not specified in Rule 803(7), that the records which are reported to be devoid of the entry in issue were regularly kept.[4]

A discussion of Federal Rule 803(10), the absence of a public record or entry, is found in § 803(5).2(e), *infra*.

Library References:

West's Key No. Digests, Criminal Law ⚖︎429–446; Evidence ⚖︎325, 333(1), 351.

803(5)   Public Records

§ 803(5).1   New York

In New York there is a hodgepodge of sources authorizing introduction of records kept in public offices. The common law public records hearsay exception remains viable, aided but not limited by CPLR 4520, "Certificate or affidavit of public officer." In addition there are provisions for ancient filed maps (CPLR 4522), records of out-of-state real property conveyances (CPLR 4524), marriage certificates (CPLR 4526), presumption of death (CPLR 4527), weather reports (CPLR 4528), agricultural inspection certificates (CPLR 4529), certificates of population (CPLR 4530), standard of measurement used by surveyor (CPLR 4534), birth and death certificates (Pub.Health Law § 4103[3]), and proof of proceedings before a justice of the peace (CPLR 4541). All of these are noted below in addition to the problem presented by investigatory reports.

a. Common Law Exception and Business Entry Exception

Whereas the Legislature enacted a comprehensive business entry rule in CPLR 4518, it enacted a cramped and narrow provision regarding public records in CPLR 4520 which will be taken up just below. There is thus reason to consider the admission of public records either under

---

trustworthiness "under Rule 803(6) or (7)" due to the way records were kept:

This court rejected a similar argument in United States v. Tafoya, 757 F.2d 1522 (5th Cir.), cert. denied, 474 U.S. 921, 106 S.Ct. 252, 88 L.Ed.2d 259 (1985). Evidence in Tafoya showed that billing memoranda were sometimes falsified. Id. at 15, 28–29. This court found the evidence admissible under Rule 803(6). Id. at 1529. The district court is given great latitude on the issue of trustworthiness. Miss. Grain Elevator, Inc., 659 F.2d at 1319. Since access to the computer was restricted, we affirm the district court's admission of the computer records.

4. See United States v. Rich, 580 F.2d 929, 938, 939 (9th Cir.), cert. denied, 439 U.S. 935, 99 S.Ct. 330, 58 L.Ed.2d 331 (1978), where it was stated:

Rule 803(7), which governs admission of evidence of the absence of entries in business records, does not specifically require the testimony of a custodian or another qualified witness. For the purpose of our opinion here, we assume, without deciding, that such a foundation is a necessary predicate to the admission of evidence of the absence of entries and that this requirement was not met.

Id. at 938–39.

In this case a police officer testified that he had checked public records and regularly maintained business records neither of which disclosed a name relevant to defendant's alibi. Although the court found an insufficient foundation as to the regularity of these records, defendant did not show that this evidence was inaccurate, and the conviction was not reversed.

the auspices of CPLR 4518 subdivision (a) which is certainly broad enough, and subdivision (c) which, *inter alia*, specifically includes by reference records of a library, and records of a department or bureau of a municipal corporation or of the state (*see* discussion in § 803(3).1(c), *supra*), or under the established common law exception which has not been usurped by any of these provisions.[1]

Although the Court of Appeals has not had the occasion to comment on the use of the common law hearsay exception for public records,[2] the lower courts have accepted it, although the cases are few. Where exhibits (unnamed, but apparently gleaned from a government office) did not qualify for admission under CPLR 4520, they were admissible under the common-law hearsay exception for official written statements, often called the "official entries" or "public document" rule.[3] In a case where the results of a breathalyzer test were sought to be introduced, the court allowed the report under the common law rule because "there was no demonstration of compliance with CPLR 4520, nor was the court requested to take judicial notice of the same"[4] and in a somewhat curious decision, the court held that although a Department of Motor Vehicles report was not admissible under CPLR 4518 for lack of the proper foundation, it was admissible under CPLR 4520 and the common law rule.[5]

When the document is admissible under the common law rule (and is not a document covered under CPLR 4518(c)) it must be based on foundation testimony and authenticated.[6] It is suggested that judicial

---

§ 803(5).1

1. See Consolidated Midland Corp. v. Columbia Pharmaceutical Corp., 42 A.D.2d 601, 345 N.Y.S.2d 105 (2d Dep't 1973). CPLR 4543 states: "Nothing in this article prevents the proof of a fact or a writing by any method authorized by any applicable statute or by the rule of evidence at common law."

2. Cf. Saranac Land and Timber Co. v. Roberts, 208 N.Y. 288, 299, 101 N.E. 898, 901 (1913); People v. Nisonoff, 293 N.Y. 597, 600–01, 59 N.E.2d 420, 421–22 (1944), cert denied, 326 U.S. 745, 66 S.Ct. 22, 90 L.Ed.2d 445 (1945).

3. Consolidated Midland Corp., 42 A.D.2d 601, 345 N.Y.S.2d 105 (2d Dep't 1973). The court added that since the exhibits were not admissible under CPLR 4520 they would not constitute prima facie evidence.

4. People v. Hoats, 102 Misc.2d 1004, 1009, 425 N.Y.S.2d 497, 501 (Monroe Co.Ct. 1980). The court, citing Chesapeake & Delaware Canal Co. v. United States, 250 U.S. 123, 128–29, 39 S.Ct. 407, 409, 63 L.Ed. 889, 893 (1919) stated:

The rationale for this exception is that these records are usually made by persons having no motive to suppress or distort the truth or manufacture evidence, and, moreover, are made in the discharge of a public duty, and almost always under the sanction of an official oath. * * * Under the common-law exception, when a public officer is authorized by the nature of this official duty to keep records of transactions occurring in the course of his duty, the record so made by him or under his supervision is admissible in evidence * * *.

Id. at 1009–10, 425 N.Y.S.2d at 501.

5. People v. Kollore, 151 Misc.2d 384, 388, 573 N.Y.S.2d 357, 360 (City Ct.of Mount Vernon 1991).

6. People v. Garneau, 120 A.D.2d 112, 116, 507 N.Y.S.2d 931, 935 (4th Dep't 1986), appeal denied, 69 N.Y.2d 880, 515 N.Y.S.2d 1028, 507 N.E.2d 1098 (1987). Here, a breathalyzer report was kept out because it was unaccompanied by any information concerning its origin. Also concerned with the necessary foundation for this sort of evidence is People v. Gower, 42 N.Y.2d 117, 397 N.Y.S.2d 368, 366 N.E.2d 69 (1977), where the court specified foundation requirements for the introduction of breathalyzer records. (See discussion in § 803(3).1(b), at note 39).

§ 803(5).1   HEARSAY   Ch. 8

notice might be taken in certain cases,[7] but the Court of Appeals has severely restricted this option.[8]

b. CPLR 4520

This enactment states:

CPLR 4520. Certificate or affidavit of public officer

Where a public officer is required or authorized, by special provision of law, to make a certificate or an affidavit to a fact ascertained, or an act performed, by him in the course of his official duty, and to file or deposit it in a public office of the state, the certificate or affidavit so filed or deposited is prima facie evidence of the facts stated.

The six requirements set forth[9] are not easily satisfied and thus many if not most public records fall outside the statute's coverage, which is unfortunate in many cases since no foundation testimony is required and the document would provide prima facie proof. The Court of Appeals has not construed CPLR 4520, and the few opinions in the lower courts are parsimonious.[10] This statute seems to a large degree to be outmoded in light of CPLR 4518, subdivision (c) of which, enacted in 1970, covers what CPLR 4520 purports to cover and much more (*see* § 803(3).1(c), *supra*).

---

7. See, in addition to the Hoats case, cited in note 4, People v. D'Agostino, 120 Misc.2d 437, 442, 465 N.Y.S.2d 834, 839 (Monroe Co.Ct.1983), where the same county judge who wrote the Hoats opinion again voiced his view that judicial notice was a possibility.

8. People v. Kennedy, 68 N.Y.2d 569, 577 n.4, 510 N.Y.S.2d 853, 858, 503 N.E.2d 501, 506 (1986). In order for judicial notice to suffice the document would have to be so "patently trustworthy as to be self-authenticating." Such an instance is found in Elkaim v. Elkaim, 176 A.D.2d 116, 117, 574 N.Y.S.2d 2, 4 (1st Dep't), appeal dismissed, 78 N.Y.2d 1072, 576 N.Y.S.2d 222, 582 N.E.2d 605 (1991), where it was held in a business records case under CPLR 4518 that judicial notice could be taken of bank records, procured by court order from the banks where they originated, and whose authenticity was not challenged.

9. To be admissible the record

(1) must be made by a public officer

(2) it must be in the form of a "certificate" or "affidavit"

(3) It must be required or authorized "by special provision of law"

(4) it must be made in the course of the officer's official duty

(5) it must be a record of a fact ascertained or an act performed by the officer

(6) it must be on file or deposit in a public office of the state (which apparently excludes offices of lesser municipalities).

10. See Loughran v. Markle, 242 App. Div. 331, 275 N.Y.S. 721 (2d Dep't 1934), aff'd, 266 N.Y. 601, 195 N.E. 219 (1935)(record of receipts and disbursements of highway department prepared by county treasurer pursuant to statute and filed with board of supervisors covered); Richards v. Robin, 178 App.Div. 535, 165 N.Y.S. 780 (1st Dep't 1917)(verified statement of bank's assets and liabilities prepared by Superintendent of Banks and filed with county clerk under statute covered); but see Eighth Judicial District Asbestos Litigation, 152 Misc.2d 338, 341, 576 N.Y.S.2d 757, 759–60 (Sup.Ct.Erie Co.1991)(EPA rule dealing with asbestos, promulgated in the Federal Register, containing EPA's conclusions based on research of other agencies, not admissible under CPLR 4520 which is strictly interpreted and was not designed for this sort of document; nor is it admissible under common law rule).

The term "prima facie evidence" in CPLR 4520 has the effect of creating a rebuttable presumption. (*See* discussion in § 803(3).1(c) and § 301.7 *supra*.)

The proposed New York Evidence Code § 803(c)(7)(A), although not the same as Federal Rule of Evidence 803(8), nevertheless would provide broad coverage.[11]

c. Investigatory Reports Made by Government Agencies

Unlike the provision in Federal Rule of Evidence 803(8)(C)(*see* discussion in § 803(5).2, *infra*), there is no statutory authority in New York specifically covering government investigatory reports, and such case law as there is does not provide a clear rule. Such reports, as found in *Steven v. Kirby*,[12] depend often on information gathered outside the agency, which presents separate hearsay problems, and then there are propounded findings, conclusions and opinions which might be considered as prejudicing the factfinder in the action or proceeding in which the report is sought to be introduced.

The Appellate Division in *Kozlowski v. City of Amsterdam*,[13] however, approved the admission in evidence of an investigative report made by a medical review commission of the State Commission of Corrections which had been made under statutory mandate. The suit was in wrongful death because deceased had committed suicide while in the city jail and in the report was a finding that the jailers had violated an administrative rule. The court found the common law public document exception applicable and stated:

> Contrary to defendant's contention that admission of the report would serve to preempt the jury's function, a violation of an administrative rule is simply some evidence of negligence which

---

11. **(7) Public records and reports.** **[PROPOSED]**

(a) **General rule.** Records, reports, or other writings or data compilations of public offices not prepared solely for purposes of litigation setting forth: (i) the activities of the office; or (ii) matters observed pursuant to a duty imposed by law as to which matters there was a duty to report, except that in a criminal case a law enforcement record or report offered by the prosecution under this paragraph to prove directly an element of the crime charged or other crucial facts established guilt is admissible: (a) when the person who provided the information set forth in the record or report testifies, or is unavailable to testify within the meaning of subdivision (a) of section 804 of this article; and (b) when the record or report contains an expert opinion, if the person who rendered that opinion testifies, or if that person is unavailable to testify within the meaning of subdivision (a) of section 804 of this article and there is available no other witness who can provide equivalent testimony; or (iii) in civil actions and proceedings, factual findings resulting from an investigation made pursuant to authority granted by law.

12. 86 A.D.2d 391, 395–96, 450 N.Y.S.2d 607, 611–12 (4th Dep't 1982). Here the State Liquor Authority report of a brawl which occurred in the parking lot of a tavern was based on the investigator's review of police reports, his interviews with police and his examination of court records. It summarized the information and stated opinions and conclusions drawn by the investigator. The court stated:

> It is the sole province of the jury to draw inferences from the facts. The opinions of the individual deputies summarized by the Liquor Authority investigator are conclusions which only the jury could draw after having heard the evidence * * *

Id. at 396, 450 N.Y.S.2d at 612.

13. 111 A.D.2d 476, 488 N.Y.S.2d 862 (3d Dep't 1985).

§ 803(5).1   **HEARSAY**   Ch. 8

a jury is free to disregard even where the adverse party offers no evidence on the point * * *.[14]

Certainly, trustworthiness is stronger in *Kozlowski*, where the investigation seems to have been fairly closed and professional, than in *Stevens* where information was gathered from many sources and where the business duties were suspect. Thus, the law in New York remains largely unformed in this area, but *Kozlowski* affords an opening where trustworthiness is inherent in the report.[15]

Part (iii) of the proposed New York Evidence Code § 803(c)(7)(A) provides for investigatory reports (*see* note 11 *supra*).

d. Ancient Maps and Real Property Records

CPLR 4522. Ancient filed maps, surveys and records affecting real property

All maps, surveys and official records affecting real property, which have been on file in the state in the office of the register of any county, any county clerk, any court of record or any department of the city of New York for more than ten years, are prima facie evidence of their contents.

This CPLR provision envisions the element of trustworthiness as inherent in the care with which documents pertaining to real property are normally prepared. That aspect, added to the fact such records have been on file for 10 years, thus qualifying as a kind of ancient document,[16] make these records as trustworthy if not more so than any others kept in a public office.[17]

Where the document fails to meet any of the three statutory requirements (must be a map, survey or official record, must be on file in a specified office, must have been there for at least 10 years), the court will require other support such as foundation testimony, or perhaps an affidavit of the person who made the map or survey.[18] Where the requirements are met, where they undoubtedly are in scores of unreport-

---

14. Id. at 478, 488 N.Y.S.2d at 864.

15. Such trustworthiness was found lacking in Cramer v. Kuhns, 213 A.D.2d 131, 630 N.Y.S.2d 128 (3d Dep't 1995) where plaintiff sought to introduce a study produced by the National Highway Traffic Safety Administration regarding the safety of the side stand apparatus of 14 models of motorcycles including defendant's. The court found that its probative value would be outweighed by its prejudicial effect because the study was preliminary, brief in nature, and provided little detail as to the actual tests conducted. Of general interest is this statement:

As a starting point, the study itself was hearsay and, as such, needed to fall within a recognized exception to the hearsay doctrine in order to be admissible. In this regard, we note that inasmuch as no one from the NHTSA testified at trial, the study could not have been admitted as a business record (see CPLR 4518). As to whether the study could have been admitted under the public document exception (see CPLR 4520), we note that the admissibility of a government investigative report under this provision has not been definitively addressed in this State (see Alexander, Practice Commentaries, McKinney's Cons Laws of NY, Book 7B, CPLR C4520:3, at 245–247).

213 A.D.2d at 135, 630 N.Y.S.2d at 131.

16. McCormick § 323.

17. Note that the period for qualifying for ownership under the rule of adverse possession is 10 years. CPLR 212.

18. See Greenberg v. Manlon Realty, Inc., 43 A.D.2d 968, 352 N.Y.S.2d 494 (2d Dep't 1974).

662

ed cases and cases where the issue does not arise, CPLR 4522 provides a streamlined method of proof.[19]

Other hearsay exceptions exist pertaining to real property records.[20]

The term "prima facie evidence" has the effect in these provisions of creating a rebuttable presumption. (*See* discussion in § 803(3).1(c) and § 301.7 *supra*.)

The proposed New York Evidence Code contains three provisions that could be applied here.[21]

e. Records of Sister State Real Property Conveyances

CPLR 4524. Conveyance of real property without the state

A record of a conveyance of real property situated within another state, territory or jurisdiction of the United States, recorded therein pursuant to its laws, is prima facie evidence of conveyance and as due execution.

This simple provision expedites proof of sister-state real property conveyances and, if it has spawned any issues in litigation, they seem scarce or nonexistent. The record should be certified in accordance with CPLR 4540.

The term "prima facie evidence" has the effect in these provisions of creating a rebuttable presumption. (*See* discussion in § 803(3).1(c) and § 301.7 *supra*.)

f. Marriage Certificates

CPLR 4526. Marriage certificate

An original certificate of a marriage made by the person by whom it was solemnized within the state, or the original entry

---

19. See City of New York v. Wilson & Co., 278 N.Y. 86, 94, 15 N.E.2d 408, 412, reargument denied, 278 N.Y. 702, 16 N.E.2d 850 (1938).

20. Real Property Actions and Proceedings Law § 331 (after 10 years from sheriff's sale, certain records referring to the execution pursuant to which sale made are prima facie evidence of execution); Real Property Actions and Proceedings Law § 341 (in instruments of conveyance over 10 years old recitals of heirship and survivorship presumptive evidence of those facts); Real Property Actions and Proceedings Law § 342 (in judgments affecting title to real property recitals of jurisdiction-conferring acts presumptive evidence of those acts).

21. New York Evidence Code § 803 [PROPOSED].

(12) **Records of documents affecting an interest in property.** The record of a document purporting to establish or affect an interest in property, as proof of the content of the original recorded document and its execution and delivery by each person by whom it purports to have been executed, if the record is a record of a public office and an applicable statute authorized the recording of documents of that kind in that office.

(13) **Statements in documents affecting an interest in property.** A statement contained in a document purporting to establish or affect an interest in property if the matter stated was relevant to the purpose of the document, unless dealings with the property since the document was made have been inconsistent with the truth of the statement or the purport of the document.

(14) **Statements in ancient documents.** Statements in a document in existence twenty years or more, the authenticity of which is established, if the statement has been acted upon as true by persons having an interest in the matter.

thereof made pursuant to law in the office of the clerk of a city or a town within the state, is prima facie evidence of the marriage.

Marriage certificates are thus routinely admissible to prove the fact of the marriage. If it is sought to prove other facts recited in the certificate such as age or place of birth, § 14–a of the Domestic Relations Law can be utilized.[22]

Where a foreign marriage certificate is sought to be proved, it can be admitted under the certification provisions of CPLR 4542. While this will not guarantee it a hearsay exception the court may be prevailed upon to consider it inherently trustworthy, or as a business or public record generally.[23]

The term "prima facie evidence" has the effect in these provisions of creating a rebuttable presumption. (*See* discussion in § 803(3).1(c) and § 301.7 *supra.*)

Under the proposed New York Evidence Code, marriage certificates are separately provided for.[24]

g. Presumption of Death or of Being Missing

CPLR 4527. Death or other status of missing person

(a) Presumed death. A written finding of presumed death, made by any person authorized to make such findings by the federal missing persons act is prima facie evidence of the death, and the date, circumstances and place of disappearance. In the case of a merchant seaman, a written finding of presumed death, made by the maritime war emergency board or by the war shipping administration or the successors or assigns of such board or administration in connection with war risk insurance is prima facie evidence of the death, and the date, circumstances and place of disappearance.

(b) Death, internment, capture and other status. An official written report or record that a person is missing, missing in action, interned in a neutral country, or beleaguered, besieged or captured by an enemy, or is dead, or is alive, made by an officer or employee of the United States authorized by law of the United States to make it is prima facie evidence of such fact.

---

22. Certified under this provision, the marriage certificate seems to be admissible to prove all facts therein recited.

23. See De Yong v. De Yong, 263 App. Div. 291, 294, 32 N.Y.S.2d 505, 508 (1st Dep't 1942).

24. New York Evidence Code § 803 [PROPOSED]

(11) **Marriage, baptismal, and similar certificates.** Statements in a certificate that the maker performed a marriage or other ceremony or administered a sacrament, made by a member of the clergy, public official, or other person authorized by the rules or practices of a religious organization or by law to perform the act certified, and purporting to have been issued at the time of the act or within a reasonable time thereafter.

This provision ties in with federal legislation providing for finding and reporting of death which makes such finding presumptive proof of death, or under subdivision (b), that a person is missing. Since the federal statutes (5 U.S.C.A. § 5561, et seq. and 37 U.S.C.A. § 551, et seq.) are limited to the reporting of deaths of federal civilian employees, and their dependents, and military personnel and their dependents, the coverage of CPLR 4527 is limited accordingly except that subdivision (a) adds the deaths of merchant seamen.

The scope of subdivision (a) is limited so that the report is proof of the fact of death and "the date, circumstances and place of disappearance."[25] From this information the court might well draw an inference as to the date of death, and whether that coincides with the date fixed by a federal department for other purposes.[26] Note that Estates, Powers and Trusts Law § 2-1.7(a)(1) provides that death can be presumed after an unexplained absence of three years except that if the missing person was involved in any sort of life threatening incident at the time of disappearance, the court can find that death occurred at that time.[27]

Subdivision (b) simply makes the official report of the status of a missing person proof of the status given by the report to that person (missing, missing in action, interned, captured by an enemy, or dead or alive).

The term "prima facie evidence" has the effect in these provisions of creating a rebuttable presumption. (*See* discussion in § 803(3).1(c) and § 301.7 *supra*.)

h. Birth and Death Certificates

Public Health Law § 4103. Vital statistics; evidence

1. [Certified copies of birth certificates authorized for school and employment purposes].

* * *

2. Any copy of the record of a birth or of a death or any certificate of registration of birth or any certification of birth, when properly certified by the local registrar, shall be prima facie evidence of the facts therein stated in all courts and places and in all actions, proceedings, or applications, judicial, administrative or otherwise, and any such certificate of registration of birth or any such certification of birth shall be accepted with

---

25. These are the words of CPLR 4527(a), as adhered to in Risikoff v. Metropolitan Life Ins. Co., 188 Misc. 768, 769, 66 N.Y.S.2d 878, 879 (Sup.Ct.Kings Co.1946).

26. In Matter of Cuthell, 193 Misc. 226, 229, 83 N.Y.S.2d 902, 904 (Sup.Ct.Westchester Co.1948), the War Department determined that deceased's plane was shot down in the Pacific Ocean on January 28, 1944, but that his date of death was January 17, 1946, for certain administrative purposes. The question before the court was whether death occurred before deceased reached age 30 in which case trust benefits would inure to the remainderman. Rather than relying on the then seven-year presumption, or the War Department's finding, the court found that death occurred on the date the plane went down.

27. Id. See Connor v. New York Life Ins. Co., 179 App.Div. 596, 598, 166 N.Y.S. 985, 987 (2d Dep't 1917).

the same force and effect with respect to the facts therein stated as the original certificate of birth or a certified copy thereof.

3. A certified copy of the record of a birth or death, a certification of birth or death, a transcript of a birth or death certificate, a certificate of birth data or a certificate of registration of birth, when properly certified by the commissioner or persons authorized to act for him, shall be prima facie evidence in all courts and places of the facts therein stated.

These two subdivisions provide for admission of a certified copy of the original record, or for admission of a copy of the record of a birth or a death certificate when that is duly certified.

Despite the clear wording that the certificates will be "prima facie evidence in all courts and places of the facts therein stated," there is caselaw to the effect that the birth certificate is not admissible to show parentage.[28] Caselaw with respect to death certificates indicates that they are admissible to prove the cause of death, or the time of death[29] as well as the fact of death.

There appears to be more of a trustworthiness problem regarding the parentage aspect of the birth certificate than regarding collateral facts found in a death certificate since the latter are made by those with a disinterested business duty, while the circumstances under which birth information is given can be conducive to falsifying the identity of the father. Nevertheless, those circumstances can be shown to rebut the presumption which otherwise ought to be utilized with respect to parentage in the interests of efficiency.

---

28. See Matter of Lock v. Fisher, 104 Misc.2d 656, 662, 428 N.Y.S.2d 868, 873 (Family Ct.Westchester Co.1980); Matter of Meyer, 206 Misc. 368, 371, 132 N.Y.S.2d 825, 828 (Surr.Ct.N.Y.Co.1954). But compare Lewis v. Lewis, 85 Misc.2d 610, 612, 381 N.Y.S.2d 631, 633 (Sup.Ct.Kings Co.1976), where the court finds the presumptive finding of parentage under § 4103 overcome by other proof. In the Lock case the father found proof of the father's identity under Public Health Law §§ 4135 and 4138 dealing with corrected birth certificates which require duly verified consent of the putative father and mother, to the entry of the name of the father.

See also Anonymous v. Mellon, 91 Misc.2d 375, 379, 398 N.Y.S.2d 99, 102 (Sup.Ct.N.Y.Co.1977), where the court ruled that the Director of the Bureau of Vital Statistics was not required to issue a second birth certificate, corrected as to sex, upon the application of a person who had undergone a sex change operation.

29. See Matter of Whitaker, 120 Misc.2d 1021, 466 N.Y.S.2d 947 (Surr.Ct.Rensselaer Co.1983), where the question was whether the daughter predeceased her father where both bodies were found together. The court stated:

Subdivision 3 of section 4103 of the Public Health Law provides in part that "a * * * death certificate * * * shall be prima facie evidence in all courts and places of the facts therein stated." There has been some question as to whether a death certificate is admissible to prove any facts other than the fact of death. * * *

This court is persuaded by the reasoning of Surrogate Bennett as expressed in Matter of Esther T. (86 Misc.2d 452) and follows its own thinking in Matter of Bausch (100 Misc.2d 817) and holds that the death certificates offered by petitioner are admissible in evidence together with the collateral facts stated therein and not solely for the proof of death. Id. at 1022, 466 N.Y.S.2d at 948.

Having said that, the court found the times set forth in the certificates overcome by other proof submitted by the medical examiner as to the condition of the bodies.

See also Anderson v. Commercial Travelers Mut. Acc. Ass'n., 73 A.D.2d 769, 423 N.Y.S.2d 542 (3d Dep't 1979)(cause of death); Regan v. National Postal Trans. Ass'n., 53 Misc.2d 901, 907, 280 N.Y.S.2d 319, 326 (N.Y.C.Civil Ct.1967).

The term "prima facie evidence" has the effect in these provisions of creating a rebuttable presumption. (*See* discussion in § 803(3).1(c) and § 301.7 *supra*.)

The proposed New York Evidence Code provides a section for such vital statistics.[30]

i. Weather Records

CPLR 4528. Weather conditions

Any record of the observations of weather, taken under the direction of the United States weather bureau, is prima facie evidence of the facts stated.

These records are routinely introduced, and the only thing that makes CPLR 4528 more attractive as a vehicle than CPLR 4518 or the common law public record exception, is that here they offer prima facie proof.

The term "prima facie evidence" has the effect in these provisions of creating a rebuttable presumption. (*See* discussion in § 803(3).1(c) and § 301.7 *supra*.)

j. Agriculture Inspection Certificates

CPLR 4529. Inspection certificate issued by United States department of agriculture

An inspection certificate issued by the authorized agents of the United States department of agriculture on file with the United States secretary of agriculture is prima facie evidence of the facts stated.

These records are routinely introduced, and the only thing that makes CPLR 4529 more attractive as a vehicle than CPLR 4518 or the common law public interest exception, is that here they offer prima facie proof.

The term "prima facie evidence" has the effect in these provisions of creating a rebuttable presumption. (*See* discussion in § 803(3).1(c) and § 301.7 *supra*.)

k. Certificate of Population

CPLR 4530. Certificate of population

(a) **Prima facie evidence.** A certificate of the officer in charge of the census of the United States, attested by the United States secretary of commerce, giving the result of the census is, except as hereinafter provided, prima facie evidence of such result.

---

30. New York Evidence Code § 803 [PROPOSED]

(8) **Records of vital statistics.** Records in any form of births, fetal deaths, deaths, or marriages, if the report thereof was made to a public office pursuant to requirements of law.

(b) Conclusive evidence. Where the population of the state or a subdivision, or a portion of a subdivision of the state is required to be determined according to the federal or state census or enumeration last preceding a particular time, a certificate of the officer in charge of the census of the United States, attested by the United States secretary of commerce, as to such population as shown by such federal census, or a certificate of the secretary of state as to such population as shown by such state enumeration, is conclusive evidence of such population.

Census data are admissible as prima facie evidence under subdivision (a) in ordinary litigation, but subdivision (b) provides for conclusive evidence where the nature of the litigation requires the latest census figures, such as a legislative reapportionment case.[31]

This information is subject to judicial notice in any event,[32] and the reports can be used for collateral information such as family relationships based upon the court's assessment of trustworthiness.[33]

The term "prima facie evidence" has the effect in these provisions of creating a rebuttable presumption. (*See* discussion in § 803(3).1(c) and § 301.7 *supra*.) The Proposed New York Evidence Code § 803(c)(22) is identical to subdivision (b) of CPLR 4530.

1. Surveyor's Standard

CPLR 4534. Standard of measurement used by surveyor

An official certificate of any state, county, city, village or town sealer elected or appointed pursuant to the laws of the state, or the statement under oath of a surveyor, that the chain or measure used by him conformed to the state standard at the time a survey was made is prima facie evidence of conformity, and an official certificate made by any sealer that the implement used in measuring such chain or other measure was the one provided the sealer pursuant to the provisions of the laws of the state is prima facie evidence of that fact.

This provision, like the weather report and the agricultural inspection certificate is so noncontroversial as to engender no noticeable questions.

The term "prima facie evidence" has the effect in these provisions of creating a rebuttable presumption. (*See* discussion in § 803(3).1(c) and § 301.7 *supra*.) Proposed New York Evidence Code § 803(c)(21) is nearly identical. It differs mainly in that the certificate provides merely evidence and not prima facie evidence.

---

31. Seaman v. Fedourich, 16 N.Y.2d 94, 104, 262 N.Y.S.2d 444, 451–52, 209 N.E.2d 778, 783–84 (1965).

32. Trustees of Union College v. City of New York, 65 App.Div. 553, 73 N.Y.S. 51 (2d Dep't 1901), aff'd, 173 N.Y. 38, 65 N.E. 853 (1903).

33. Estate of Kirkby, 57 Misc.2d 982, 293 N.Y.S.2d 1008 (Surr.Ct.N.Y.Co.1968), reconsideration denied, 59 Misc.2d 584, 299 N.Y.S.2d 873 (Surr.Ct.N.Y.Co.1969).

m. Justice of the Peace Proceedings

CPLR 4541. Proof of proceedings before justice of the peace

(a) **Of the state.** A transcript from the docket-book of a justice of the peace of the state, subscribed by him, and authenticated by a certificate signed by the clerk of the county in which the justice resides, with the county seal affixed, to the effect that the person subscribing the transcript is a justice of the peace of that county, is prima facie evidence of any matter stated in the transcript which is required by law to be entered by the justice in his docket-book.

(b) **Of another state.** A transcript from the docket-book of a justice of the peace of another state, of his minutes of the proceedings in a cause, of a judgment rendered by him, of an execution issued thereon or of the return of an execution, when subscribed by him, and authenticated as prescribed in this subdivision is prima facie evidence of his jurisdiction in the case and of the matters shown by the transcript. The transcript shall be authenticated by a certificate of the justice to the effect that it is in all respects correct and that he had jurisdiction of the cause; and also by a certificate of the clerk or prothonotary of the county in which the justice resides, with his official seal affixed, to the effect that the person subscribing the certificate attached to the transcript is a justice of the peace of that county.

This provides for self-authentication of Justice Court docket books and creates a hearsay exception as respects their contents. Note that records from all other courts would be authenticated under CPLR 4540 and find their hearsay exception under CPLR 4518 or 4520. Subdivision (b) is more liberal as respects sister state Justice Court records than subdivision (a) is with respect to New York Justice Court records. Subdivision (b) provides that the authentication not only makes the record prima facie evidence of its contents, but also serves as proof of the court's jurisdiction. Subdivision (a) provides no authentication as to jurisdiction. This seems to be a perhaps unwitting carryover from previous legislation (Civil Practice Act §§ 387(1) and 394.) However, Justice Court jurisdiction in subdivision (a) seems appropriate for judicial notice.[34] While probably not of high priority considering its noncontroversial history, redrafting of this section might profitably be considered.

The term "prima facie evidence" has the effect in these provisions of creating a rebuttable presumption. (*See* discussion in § 803(3).1(c) and § 301.7 *supra*.)

The proposed New York Evidence Code contains a provision which is

---

34. See CPLR 4511(a).

§ 803(5).1   HEARSAY   Ch. 8

related to, but does not seem to supplant CPLR 4541.[35]

n. Absence of Public Record

CPLR 4521. Lack of record

A statement signed by an officer or a deputy of an officer having legal custody of specified official records of the United States or of any state, territory or jurisdiction of the United States, or of any court thereof, or kept in any public office thereof, that he has made diligent search of the records and has found no record or entry of a specified nature, is prima facie evidence that the records contain no such record or entry, provided that the statement is accompanied by a certificate that legal custody of the specified official records belongs to such person, which certificate shall be made by a person described in rule 4540.

As discussed in § 803(4).1(a) *supra*, the common law rule in New York apparently does not recognize the admissibility of proof of the absence of a private business record where, if the transaction had occurred, one would normally be found. The absence of a public record, however, is prima facie evidence that there is no such record. Apparently the trustworthiness of the public official is considered superior to that of the functionary in the private sector.[36] Certainly this speeds the process of proof where otherwise custodians of public records would have to be called to testify to the same information. CPLR 4521 has been used in a variety of ways.[37]

If the requirements of the statute are not satisfied, a parallel common law hearsay exception would permit the custodian to give testimony that he made the prescribed "diligent" search,[38] thus providing evidence that the necessary document does not exist.[39] The common

---

35. New York Evidence Code § 803(c)(7)(B)(i) [PROPOSED]

* * *

(B) Certificates concerning judgment of conviction and fingerprints.

(i) Certificates of judgment. A certificate issued by a criminal court, or the clerk thereof, certifying that a judgment of conviction against a designated defendant has been entered in such court constitutes evidence of the facts stated therein.

36. See Mandeville v. Reynolds, 68 N.Y. 528, 534 (1877)(in action on a judgment where judgment roll missing and where county clerk testified that he would not have docketed judgment had he not had the judgment roll—admissible to prove the judgment because of presumption of regularity of public officials functions; not a case involving lack of a record in the context involved here).

37. See, e.g., Matter of Brown's Estate, 40 N.Y.2d 938, 390 N.Y.S.2d 59, 358 N.E.2d 883 (1976)(presumption in favor of validity of second marriage overcome by evidence of any record of divorce from first marriage); Dartmouth Plan, Inc. v. Valle, 117 Misc.2d 534, 537, 458 N.Y.S.2d 848, 850 (Sup.Ct. Kings Co.1983)(when shown that no license was ever issued, "it is incumbent upon plaintiff to come forward with proof of contradictory evidentiary facts showing the existence of a genuine and substantial issue").

38. The words prescribed in the statute ought to be used, especially "diligent search." Briggs v. Waldron, 83 N.Y. 582 (1881).

39. See People v. Niang, 160 Misc.2d 500, 609 N.Y.S.2d 1017 (N.Y.C.Crim.Ct. 1994). But see People v. Ebramha, 157 Misc.2d 222, 596 N.Y.S.2d 295 (N.Y.C.Crim. Ct.1993)(court was unwilling to recognize common law exception where it was relied upon to prove that defendant had not procured a street vendor's license).

law rule can be utilized to prove the absence of a record in a foreign country's government office[40] since CPLR 4521 by its terms applies only to public offices in the United States.

The proposed New York Evidence Code contains a provision for proof of the absence of a public record.[41] See also the discussion of the absence of public records, which parallels this discussion, in § 803(4).1(b), *supra*.

o. Criminal Judgments of Conviction

Where a person is convicted of a felony, the New York cases hold that, at the very least, facts necessary for the conviction can be introduced in a civil action where relevant,[42] and that the conviction can act as collateral estoppel against the criminal defendant in a related civil case where central issues are identical.[43] In the *S.T. Grand* case[44] plaintiff sued the city for payment for services rendered in cleaning a city reservoir pursuant to contract. Plaintiff and its president, however, had been convicted of bribery in the obtaining of that very contract. The city moved for summary judgment arguing that the illegality of the contract had been established by the criminal conviction. The Court of Appeals agreed. A conviction based on a plea of guilty to a felony will also bind the defendant in a subsequent civil case.[45] Care must be taken in ascertaining exactly what was established in the criminal proceeding. A plea of guilty to statutory rape, for instance, would not show that force had been used and so that conviction could not be collateral estoppel in the victim's civil action based on assault and battery.[46] But a conviction based on a so-called *Serrano*[47] plea, where defendant chooses not to contest the underlying facts, but whose version of events differs from the

---

40. See Brill v. Brill, 10 N.Y.2d 308, 222 N.Y.S.2d 321, 178 N.E.2d 720 (1961)(search of foreign records revealed lack of claimed divorce records, and this was proof that divorce had not been obtained).

41. New York Evidence Code § 803 [PROPOSED]

(9) **Absence of public record or entry.** To prove the absence of a record, report, or other writing or data compilation or the nonoccurrence or nonexistence of a matter of which otherwise a record, report, or other writing or data compilation would have been regularly made and preserved by a public office, testimony or a certificate authenticated in accordance with section 902 of this chapter, that diligent search failed to disclose the record, report, or other writing or data compilation, or entry therein.

42. Schindler v. Royal Ins. Co., 258 N.Y. 310, 179 N.E. 711 (1932). See also Matter of Suffolk Department of Social Services v. James M., 83 N.Y.2d 178, 608 N.Y.S.2d 940, 630 N.E.2d 636 (1994), where it was held that stepfather's conviction for abusing children was conclusive in Family Court on the question of his abuse and neglect. See also Hudson v. Varney, 196 A.D.2d 856, 857, 602 N.Y.S.2d 176, 177 (2d Dep't), appeal dismissed, 82 N.Y.2d 888, 610 N.Y.S.2d 153, 632 N.E.2d 463 (1993), cert. denied, ___ U.S. ___, 115 S.Ct. 62, 130 L.Ed.2d 19, rehearing denied, ___ U.S. ___, 115 S.Ct. 615, 130 L.Ed.2d 524 (1994)("In the present case the plaintiff asserts the very same right to an easement over his neighbor's land he had earlier asserted as a defense in the criminal action, which issue was considered by the jury and resolved against him").

43. S.T. Grand, Inc. v. City of New York, 32 N.Y.2d 300, 344 N.Y.S.2d 938, 298 N.E.2d 105 (1973).

44. Id.

45. See Merchants Mutual Ins. Co. v. Arzillo, 98 A.D.2d 495, 472 N.Y.S.2d 97 (2d Dep't 1984).

46. Stavroula S. v. Guerriera, 193 A.D.2d 796, 797, 598 N.Y.S.2d 300, 301 (2d Dep't 1993); Preston v. State of New York, 152 A.D.2d 943, 944, 543 N.Y.S.2d 823, 824 (4th Dep't 1989).

47. People v. Serrano, 15 N.Y.2d 304, 258 N.Y.S.2d 386, 206 N.E.2d 330 (1965).

§ 803(5).1   HEARSAY   Ch. 8

crime charged, will have collateral estoppel effect with regard to the establishment of the underlying facts.[48]

Where, however, the conviction for a "petty offense" was sought to be used in a related civil suit for damages based on alleged assault, the *S.T. Grand* rule was held inapplicable.[49] The Court of Appeals noted that the harassment charge of which defendant had been convicted in city court was even below the grade of misdemeanor, a far cry from the felony involved in *S.T. Grand*. Defendant had no right to a jury trial, there was far less reason to mount a vigorous defense and the charge might be prosecuted in a perfunctory manner. If such proceedings were deemed to provide binding results there would be "an incentive to potential plaintiffs to file a minor charge before commencing a civil action."[50]

The Court of Appeals has not addressed the question of the effect a misdemeanor conviction might have. It could be argued that many of the same reasons barring a "petty offense" conviction could be applied to misdemeanor convictions as well. Judgments of acquittal would have no bearing on related civil proceedings because of the high degree of proof required to convict in a criminal case.[51]

The proposed New York Evidence Code contains a provision covering judgments of conviction.[52]

p. Records of Religious Organizations

Such records are of a quasi-public nature since they are kept by an institution, but one which may not be covered by the business entry rule since those who provide the information concerning relationships and dates are not usually under any business duty. Federal Rule of Evidence 803(11) (discussed in § 803(5).2(f) *infra*) provides for admissibility of the contents of "regularly kept" records; but in New York there is very little on this rule save a lower court decision which limited proof of a baptismal record to the fact of the baptism.[53] Other facts in the certificate, such as the subject's date of birth, could not be proved in this

---

48. Kuriansky v. Professional Care, Inc., 158 A.D.2d 897, 899, 551 N.Y.S.2d 695, 696 (3d Dep't 1990).

49. Gilberg v. Barbieri, 53 N.Y.2d 285, 441 N.Y.S.2d 49, 423 N.E.2d 807 (1981).

50. Id. at 294, 441 N.Y.S.2d at 52, 423 N.E.2d at 810. See also Montalvo v. Morales, 18 A.D.2d 20, 239 N.Y.S.2d 72 (2d Dep't 1963)(proof of conviction of violation of failure to yield right of way not admissible in civil suit concerning the accident at the intersection).

51. Schindler v. Royal Insurance Co., 258 N.Y. 310, 313, 179 N.E. 711, 712 (1932).

52. § 803 [PROPOSED]
* * *

(22) **Judgment of previous conviction.** Evidence of a final judgment, entered after trial or upon a plea of guilty (but not upon a plea of nolo contendere or its equivalent), adjudging a person guilty of a crime, to prove any fact essential to sustain the judgment, but not including judgments against persons other than the accused when offered by the prosecution in a criminal case for purposes other than impeachment. The pendency of an appeal may be shown but does not affect admissibility.

53. Abbondola v. Church of St. Vincent De Paul, 205 Misc. 353, 355, 123 N.Y.S.2d 32, 34 (Sup.Ct.Kings Co.1953).

fashion. The proposed New York Evidence Code carries a provision similar to the federal rule.[54]

Library References:

West's Key No. Digests, Criminal Law ⬚429; Evidence ⬚325–337.

§ 803(5).2 Federal

a. Public Records Generally

Federal Rule of Evidence 803(8) states:

(8) Public records and reports. Records, reports, statements, or data compilations, in any form, of public offices or agencies, setting forth (A) the activities of the office or agency, or (B) matters observed pursuant to duty imposed by law as to which matters there was a duty to report, excluding, however, in criminal cases matters observed by police officers and other law enforcement personnel, or (C) in civil actions and proceedings and against the Government in criminal cases, factual findings resulting from an investigation made pursuant to authority granted by law, unless the sources of information or other circumstances indicate lack of trustworthiness.

This useful statute provides for the introduction of public records unencumbered with the need for foundation testimony if they qualify for authentication under Rule 902(4).[1] The Rule, since it applies to any public officer, not just a federal officer,[2] seems especially useful in diversity litigation.

Rule 803(8) specifies three sorts of reports. Part (A) is quickly dealt with since it encompasses the most traditional of all public records—those that record the activities of the office itself.[3] Part (B) describes

---

54. § 803(11) Records of religious organizations. Statements of births, marriages, divorces, deaths, legitimacy, ancestry, or relationship by blood or marriage contained in a regularly kept record of a religious organization.

§ 803(5).2

1. Rule 902(4) states:

Extrinsic evidence of authenticity as a condition precedent to admissibility is not required with respect to the following:

* * *

(4) Certified copies of public records. A copy of an official record or report or entry therein, or of a document authorized by law to be recorded or filed and actually recorded or filed in a public office, including data compilations in any form, certified as correct by the custodian or other person authorized to make the certification, by certificate complying with paragraph (1), (2), or (3) of this rule or complying with any Act of Congress or rule prescribed by the Supreme Court pursuant to statutory authority.

See 4 Weinstein and Berger ¶ 803(8)(01), at 803–262.

2. See 4 Weinstein and Berger ¶ 803(8)(01), at 803–262.

3. See Chesapeake & Delaware Canal Co. v. United States, 250 U.S. 123, 128–29, 39 S.Ct. 407, 409, 63 L.Ed. 889, 893 (1919), where Treasury Department books showing government receipts and disbursements were held admissible, the court stating:

Thus, their character as public records required by law to be kept, the official character of their contents entered under the sanction of public duty, the obvious necessity for regular contemporaneous entries in them and the reduction to a minimum of motive on the part of public officials and employees to either make false entries or to omit proper ones, all unite to make these books admissible as unusually trustworthy sources of evidence. Id. at 128–29, 39 S.Ct. at 409, 63 L.Ed.2d at 893.

§ 803(5).2

reports of observations made by public officials performing their official duties,[4] and part (C) provides for evaluative, or investigatory reports.[5] Parts (B) and (C) are taken up separately. Included in both are discussions of the ramifications in criminal cases. Unlike New York practice where records made by prosecutorial authorities are analyzed under the business entry provisions, under the Federal Rules reports relevant to criminal prosecutions are covered under this provision.

Part (B), reports made pursuant to duty. The controversial aspects of this category involve the use of police reports and records in criminal cases. An exception to admissibility is made in the statute which bars reports of matters observed by police officers or other law enforcement personnel. What sort of "personnel" are contemplated? In *United States v. Oates*,[6] the Second Circuit gave this an extremely rigid construction in holding that the report of a United States Customs Service chemist concerning analysis of a substance determined to be heroin was not admissible under rule 803(8) since he fell within the category of law enforcement personnel. It was stated: "We would thus construe 'other law enforcement personnel' to include, at the least, any officer or employee of a governmental agency which has law enforcement responsibilities."[7] Yet, this strict interpretation was not in evidence just prior to the *Oates* decision where in *United States v. Grady*,[8] the court ruled that police records of Northern Ireland were admissible to prove "the routine function of recording serial numbers and receipt of certain weapons."[9] *Oates* was followed shortly after it was decided,[10] but subsequent cases

See also United States v. Lechuga, 975 F.2d 397, 398–99 (7th Cir.1992) (court records); United States v. Lumumba, 794 F.2d 806, 815 (2d Cir.1986), cert. denied, 479 U.S. 855, 107 S.Ct. 192, 93 L.Ed.2d 125 (1986)(transcript of trial); Conn. Light & Power Co. v. Federal Power Com'n, 557 F.2d 349, 356 (2d Cir.1977)("Evidence contained in public records and reports, recorded deeds affecting interest in real property and learned historical treatises are exceptions to the hearsay rule."); LeRoy v. Sabena Belgian World Airlines, 344 F.2d 266, 273 (2d Cir.), cert. denied, 382 U.S. 878, 86 S.Ct. 161, 15 L.Ed.2d 119 (1965) (report of recording made by Italian aircraft controller between pilot and ground just prior to accident). Compare Lindsay v. Ortho Pharmaceutical Corp., 637 F.2d 87, 94 (2d Cir.1980)(labeling changes on toxic product made by FDA deal with medical opinions, not routine government record keeping and are not admissible since they could cause undue prejudice and confusion).

4. See United States v. Brown, 9 F.3d 907 (11th Cir.1993), cert. denied, ___ U.S. ___, 115 S.Ct. 152, 130 L.Ed.2d 91 (1994)(property receipt issued by police department for confiscation of a firearm admissible since issued routinely before this defendant even apprehended).

5. See Beech Aircraft v. Rainey, 488 U.S. 153, 109 S.Ct. 439, 102 L.Ed.2d 445 (1988)(report of military board of investigation of fatal military aircraft accident admissible in civil suit).

6. 560 F.2d 45, 68–69 (2d Cir.1977).

7. Id. at 68.

8. 544 F.2d 598, 604 (2d Cir.1976). See also United States v. Sawyer, 607 F.2d 1190 (7th Cir.1979), cert. denied, 445 U.S. 943, 100 S.Ct. 1338, 63 L.Ed.2d 776 (1980)(admitted an IRS agent's report of a telephone conversation with defendant since agent appeared and testified; but he only testified to foundational facts and could not be cross-examined as to the substance of the conversation because he had no recollection of it).

9. Id. at 604. See also United States v. Agustino-Hernandez, 14 F.3d 42 (11th Cir.1994)(records of deportations and records showing defendant had been warned of penalties for re-entry into country admissible since records were filed in routine fashion and prior to prosecution).

10. United States v. Ruffin, 575 F.2d 346, 355–56 (2d Cir.1978)(printout of an IRS report inadmissible under Oates since IRS agents were law enforcement personnel). Compare Ruffin with Sawyer, note 8, supra.

have been more liberal.[11] In *United States v. Rosa*,[12] the court refused to interpret the phrase "law enforcement personnel" as applying to the Medical Examiner's Office and held that autopsy reports ought to be admissible under Rule 803(8). The court did indeed attempt to distinguish *Oates* by finding that the responsibilities of a medical examiner were less law enforcement oriented than those of a Customs Service chemist;[13] but *Oates* does not seem now to be as it first appeared. The problem, of course, is determining where the court will draw the line on the *Oates* erosion.[14] In the meantime, it would seem that routine reports or certificates made and filed at a time disassociated with a particular defendant's prosecution should be admissible under either the (A) or (B) part of Rule 803(8).[15] One aspect of the holding in *Oates* seems clearly to be correct, and that is that if a public record would not be admissible because of the proscriptions in Rule 803(8), then it should not alternatively be admissible under the business entry exception of Rule 803(6).[16]

Part (C), investigatory reports. Prior to the United States Supreme Court's 1988 decision in *Beech Aircraft v. Rainey*,[17] courts in the Second Circuit were taking a measured approach to the admissibility of investigatory or evaluative reports, as was warranted from the two key elements of part (C). The reports were made admissible for their "factual findings," and were made expressly subject to discretionary review for overall trustworthiness. In *Complaint of American Export Lines, Inc.*,[18] the court reviewed the legislative history of the provision with respect to the term "factual findings" and concluded that the term did not include evaluative conclusions or opinions contained in a Coast Guard report of a marine accident.[19] Prior to 1988 there are varied instances of reports being kept out on grounds of untrustworthiness,[20] or simply because not

---

11. In United States v. Yakobov, 712 F.2d 20, 24–25 (2d Cir.1983), the government sought to prove that defendant was not licensed to sell firearms by introducing a certificate produced by the Bureau of Alcohol, Tobacco and Firearms, that its records were searched and that no license was found on file. In response to defendant's Oates argument, the court stated: "Although our language was indeed sufficiently broad to encompass the blanket foreclosure contended for by Yakobov, we regard any implicit application of that language to rule 803(10) as obiter, and we believe that Oates should not be applied to exclude on remand a certificate that meets the requirements of Rule 803(10)." Id. at 25. The court went on to closely analyze Oates, and while it did not overrule its application to Rule 803(8), it was decisively dismissed as having any bearing on Rule 803(10)(absence of a public record).

12. 11 F.3d 315, 332–33 (2d Cir.1993), cert. denied, ___ U.S. ___, 114 S.Ct. 1565, 128 L.Ed.2d 211 (1994).

13. Id. at 332.

14. In United States v. Gotti, 641 F.Supp. 283, 290–91 (E.D.N.Y.1986), the court discussed the limitations placed on Oates and ruled that Rule 803(8) would allow the report of a judge taking a guilty plea since the court is a public office, and the judge, who is not in law enforcement, as a public officer had the duty to report the plea.

15. See, e.g., the Brown and Augustino-Hernandez cases at notes 4 and 9 supra. Such routine reports lack the adversarial bias that can taint the report of a "cop on the beat." See also Alexander, "The Hearsay Exception for Public Records in Federal Criminal Trials," 47 Albany Law Rev. 699 (1983).

16. Oates, 560 F.2d at 74.

17. 488 U.S. 153, 109 S.Ct. 439, 102 L.Ed.2d 445 (1988).

18. 73 F.R.D. 454 (S.D.N.Y.1977).

19. Id. at 457–58.

20. See United States v. Durrani, 835 F.2d 410, 425 (2d Cir.1987)(U.S. Senate report on the Iran Contra affair, the Tower report, lacked sufficient indicia of trustworthiness); United States v. MacDonald, 688 F.2d 224, 229–30 (4th Cir.1982), cert. de-

§ 803(5).2   HEARSAY   Ch. 8

the kind of report contemplated by the rule in the first place.[21] In evaluating trustworthiness:

> Factors to consider in deciding whether to admit the evaluative findings of the Report under Rule 803(8)(C) are "the timeliness of the investigation, [the special skill or experience of the reporter,] whether a hearing was held in conjunction with [the investigation], and the motivation of the officials conducting the investigation."[22]

The annals prior to 1988 are also replete with cases in which investigatory reports were deemed perfectly admissible;[23] but in 1988, in

---

nied, 459 U.S. 1103, 103 S.Ct. 726, 74 L.Ed.2d 951 (1983)(military investigation into death of officer's family sought to be introduced by defendant against the government in a criminal prosecution, ruled untrustworthy by trial judge, whose discretion was confirmed even though appellate panel stated that the report met the requirements of Rule 803(8)); Anderson v. City of New York, 657 F.Supp. 1571, 1578 (S.D.N.Y.1987)(a congressional report concerning police misconduct in the City of New York, not admissible by plaintiff in § 1983 civil rights case since untrustworthy).

21. See City of New York v. Pullman Inc., 662 F.2d 910, 914 (2d Cir.1981), cert. denied sub nom., Rockwell International Corp. v. City of N.Y., 454 U.S. 1164, 102 S.Ct. 1038, 71 L.Ed.2d 320 (1982)(transportation agency report concerning condition and maintenance of equipment not admissible because it was an "interim staff" report subject to revision and review); Lerner v. Seaboard Coast Line R. Co., 594 F.Supp. 963, 973 (S.D.N.Y.1984)(police officer's notation on an accident report that railroad crossing "needs railroad crossing arms," not admissible, since officer not qualified as a safety expert and inference prejudicial).

22. Anderson v. City of New York, 657 F.Supp. 1571, 1578 (S.D.N.Y.1987), citing 4 Weinstein and Berger, ¶ 803(8)[03], at 254. In this case the report sought to be admitted was a congressional report on alleged misconduct of New York City police and was the result of hearings which lacked procedural due process protections and stated findings based not on personal knowledge of the reporter but on highly charged interviews with interested parties. This was not admissible based on the stated criteria.

23. See Chandler v. Roudebush, 425 U.S. 840, 863 n.39, 96 S.Ct. 1949, 1961, 48 L.Ed.2d 416, 432 (1976)(court endorsed admissibility of an administrative adjudicatory finding in a subsequent civil proceeding involving same substantive matters); FAA v. Landy, 705 F.2d 624, 633 (2d Cir.1983)(telex sent to FAA by German government concerning air traffic incorporated in FAA report was made "pursuant to authority granted by law" and was "admissible as a public record and report" under Fed. R.Evid. 803(8)(B), (C)); Litton Systems, Inc. v. American Tel. & Tel. Co., 700 F.2d 785, 818 (2d Cir.1983), cert. denied, 464 U.S. 1073, 104 S.Ct. 984, 79 L.Ed.2d 220 (1984)(FCC reports appraising reasonableness of tariff rates admissible "as factual findings resulting from an investigation made pursuant to authority granted by law"); Miller v. New York Produce Exchange, 550 F.2d 762 (2d Cir.1977), cert. denied, 434 U.S. 823, 98 S.Ct. 68, 54 L.Ed.2d 80 (1977)(report made by Commodity Exchange Authority containing data concerning cottonseed oil purchases which included statements alleged to be conclusory, was held admissible with the statement, "[i]t is often difficult to distinguish between what is fact and what is opinion"); In re Agent Orange Product Liability Lit., 611 F.Supp. 1223, 1240 (E.D.N.Y.1985), aff'd, 818 F.2d 187, cert. denied sub nom., Lombardi v. Dow Chemical Co., 487 U.S. 1234, 108 S.Ct. 2898, 101 L.Ed.2d 932 (1988)(epidemiological studies conducted by the government admissible under Rule 803(8)); Revlon, Inc. v. Carson Products Co., 602 F.Supp. 1071, 1079 (S.D.N.Y.1985), aff'd, 803 F.2d 676, (Fed.Cir.), cert. denied, 479 U.S. 1018, 107 S.Ct. 671, 93 L.Ed.2d 722 (1986)(report in the form of official's affidavit giving findings pursuant to investigation concerning trade secret status of product, admissible as public record); Doe v. New York University, 511 F.Supp. 606, 610 (S.D.N.Y.1981)(in suit for reinstatement to medical school, HEW's report of investigation into the matter offered by plaintiff admissible unless defendant can establish the report unreliable); Elwood v. City of New York, 450 F.Supp. 846, 872 (S.D.N.Y. 1978), rev'd on other grounds sub nom, Badgley v. City of New York, 606 F.2d 358 (2d Cir.1979), cert. denied sub nom., Badgley v. City of New York, 447 U.S. 906, 100 S.Ct. 2989, 64 L.Ed.2d 855 (1980)(in envi-

the *Beech Aircraft* case, the Supreme Court took a big step in liberally construing the term "factual findings." All the Justices opted for a broad interpretation, and agreed that the findings of a military investigation board that a fatal aircraft accident was due to pilot error would be admissible in the trial of an action brought against the plane's manufacturer based on the theory of equipment malfunction.[24] The accident occurred on a training flight, and both the trainee and the instructor were killed. Justice Brennan, in interpreting Rule 803(8), found that although the House report stated that the term "factual finding" should be strictly construed,[25] the Senate report rejected this and adopted the Advisory Committee's interpretation, which provided that "in the first instance of evaluative reports, they are not admissible if, as the rule states, 'the sources of information or other circumstances indicate lack of trustworthiness.' "[26] Justice Brennan found the Advisory Committee's comments important in that "they contain no mention of any dichotomy between statements of 'fact' and 'opinions' or 'conclusions.' What was on the Committee's mind was simply whether what it called 'evaluative reports' should be admissible."[27] The trial judge had found the evaluative report trustworthy, and stated: "[r]ather than requiring that we draw some inevitably arbitrary line between the various shades of fact/opinion that invariably will be presented in investigatory reports, we believe the Rule instructs us—as its plain language states—to admit 'reports * * * setting forth * * * factual findings.' "[28] Certainly such reports will influence the civil jury as appears to be the case in *Beech Aircraft* where the jury found for defendant; but the court has obviously gone beyond the argument that the jury should not know of another body's conclusions on the very issues they are to decide.

Although the term "factual findings" has been construed to include opinions and conclusions,[29] the trustworthiness aspect of part (C) remains of concern in each case[30] and, of course, the report must be found to be relevant.[31] Thus, Rule 803(8)(C) admissibility has been found

ronmental litigation, report issued by N.Y. Environmental Conservation Department containing factual material concerning water release practices from the New York City reservoir system offered by plaintiffs ruled admissible).

24. Beech Aircraft, 488 U.S. at 169, 109 S.Ct. at 450, 102 L.Ed.2d at 463.

25. H.R.Rep.No.650, 93d Cong., 2d Sess. 14, reprinted in 1974 U.S.Code Cong. and Admin.News 7065, 7088.

26. S.Rep.No.1277, 93d Cong., 2d Sess. 18, reprinted in 1974 U.S.Code Cong. and Admin.News 7051, 7064.

27. Beech Aircraft, 488 U.S. at 166, 109 S.Ct. at 448, 102 L.Ed.2d at 461.

28. Id. at 169, 109 S.Ct. at 449, 102 L.Ed.2d at 463.

29. In Gentile v. County of Suffolk, 926 F.2d 142, 148 (2d Cir.1991), the court held that there was a presumption of admissibility which "extends not merely to factual findings in the narrow sense, but also to conclusions or opinions that are based upon a factual investigation."

30. See United Air Lines, Inc. v. Austin Travel Corp., 867 F.2d 737, 743 (2d Cir.1989)(Congressional reports relating to computerized reservation system were interim, and inconclusive in nature and thus did not meet the trustworthiness test); Lewis v. Velez, 149 F.R.D. 474, 487 (S.D.N.Y.1993) (report of investigation into prison incident containing information by correction officers involved offered by defendant cannot be admitted in a § 1983 civil rights case brought by inmate).

31. Janetka v. Dabe, 892 F.2d 187, 190 (2d Cir.1989)(report critical of Suffolk County police officers, offered by plaintiff in malicious prosecution action, held not relevant where plaintiff unable to show connections to his case); Ricciuti v. New York City

§ 803(5).2   HEARSAY   Ch. 8

where a Coast Guard accident investigation report was concerned,[32] where a report relating to product regulatory requirements was admitted in a products liability suit,[33] where a departmental internal investigatory report was offered by plaintiff in a malicious prosecution action;[34] and where the court was concerned with the conditions in a mental institution, it would consider the findings of state and federal certifying agencies.[35]

Perhaps the foremost Second Circuit case dealing with part (C) is *Gentile v. County of Suffolk*[36] where the court, in addition to confirming the *Beech Aircraft* determination that "factual findings" included opinions and conclusions,[37] stated: "Reports such as those issued by the Commission are presumed to be 'admissible in the first instance,' * * * and the 'party opposing the introduction of a report bears the burden of coming forward with enough negative factors to persuade a court that a report should not be admitted.'"[38]

In criminal cases, as specified in part (C), investigatory reports can be used only against the government.

b. Vital Statistics

Federal Rule of Evidence 803(9) makes admissible:

(9) Records of vital statistics. Records or data compilations, in any form, of births, fetal deaths, deaths, or marriages, if the report thereof was made to a public office pursuant to requirements of law.

There appears to be little controversy concerning the admissibility of such records. The feature to be marked here is that, unlike public records generally, the person furnishing the information—clergy, physician, hospitals—are not usually public officials and thus this category of

Transit Authority, 754 F.Supp. 980, 984–85 (S.D.N.Y.1990), vacated on other grounds, 941 F.2d 119 (2d Cir.1991)(several investigatory reports concerning Transit Authority police held irrelevant to plaintiff's § 1983 civil rights action). Compare Gentile v. County of Suffolk, 129 F.R.D. 435, 447–49 (E.D.N.Y.1990), where Judge Weinstein found relevance under similar circumstances.

32. Strehle v. United States, 860 F.Supp. 136, 138 (S.D.N.Y.1994), aff'd, 54 F.3d 765 (2d Cir.1995)(in statutory action against government for death of seaman killed in the performance of duties aboard ship the official Coast Guard investigatory report was admissible under Rule 803(8); but the investigator's opinions and conclusions could not be considered since this would lead to tendency to downplay errors committed by Coast Guard).

33. Contini v. Hyundai Motor Co., 840 F.Supp. 22, 24 (S.D.N.Y.1993) (whether product measured up to government requirements is a factor to be considered on the question of whether the product was defective and public sector studies supporting regulatory requirements would be relevant and admissible under Rule 803(8)).

34. Tveraas v. Coffey, 818 F.Supp. 75, 77–78 (D.Vt.1993), appeal dismissed, 9 F.3d 1536 (2d Cir.1993)(official letter of reprimand written to defendant at close of agency's internal investigation, including statements of both fact and opinion, qualifies under Rule 803(8)).

35. Society For Good Will For Retarded Children, Inc. v. Cuomo, 718 F.Supp. 139, 140–41 (E.D.N.Y.1989), rev'd on other grounds, 902 F.2d 1085 (2d Cir.1990)(in litigation seeking relief from alleged unconstitutional conditions, and violations of statutes, reports of state and federal certifying agencies admissible under Rule 803(8)).

36. 926 F.2d 142 (2d Cir.1991).

37. Id. at 148.

38. Id., quoting from Masemer v. Delmarva Power and Light Co., 723 F.Supp. 1019, 1021 (D.Del.1989).

records needs a special exception. Although it is unlikely that questions of paternity will be directly in issue in the federal courts, should they arise, a party wishing to contest certainly may seek to disprove the contents of the birth record.[39] The contents of these records are not even designated as prima facie evidence as are the contents of their New York counterparts. (See § 803(5).1(h).) The other area of possible doubt is that part of the death certificate as lists the cause of death. McCormick treats this as follows:

> As to routine matters, such as place and date of birth or death and "immediate" cause of death, such as drowning or gunshot wound, admissibility is seldom questioned. However, entries in death certificates as to the "remote" cause of death, such as suicide, accident, or homicide, usually are made on the basis of information obtained from other persons and predictably involve the questions that have been raised with regard to investigative reports generally, and courts have divided on admissibility. When conclusions of this type are involved, the provisions of Rule 803(8), which is equally applicable and involves a much more careful treatment of the issues, should be applied. Thus, the restrictions on using police and investigative reports against accused persons * * * should be applied to this aspect of records of vital statistics.[40]

The Second Circuit probably would be receptive to a liberal application of this provision.[41]

c. Documents Affecting Interests In Real Property

Federal Rule of Evidence 803(14) makes admissible:

(14) Records of documents affecting an interest in property. The record of a document purporting to establish or affect an interest in property, as proof of the content of the original recorded document and its execution and delivery by each person by whom it purports to have been executed, if the record is a record of a public office and an applicable statute authorizes the recording of documents of that kind in that office.

Again, a special rule is needed where the information in the record is not based on the personal knowledge of a public official, but where it makes good sense to provide for admissibility because the odds in favor of trustworthiness are high. Since questions relating to title questions are matters of local law, the provision incorporates by reference the local law requirements, whatever they may be.[42]

---

39. See 4 Weinstein and Berger ¶ 803(9)[01], at 803-314.

40. McCormick § 297, at 295 (footnotes omitted).

41. See Hunter v. Derby Foods, 110 F.2d 970, 972–73 (2d Cir.1940)(in food poisoning case brought against canned meat distributor, statement in death certificate, "accident—eating canned meat—enteritis with an acute nephritis," ruled admissible).

42. 4 Weinstein and Berger ¶ 803(14)[01], at 803-344, 345.

In *United States v. Ruffin*,[43] the government offered evidence against defendant in a tax evasion case concerning the expenditure of income which had not been reported. The expenditure was for the purchase of a real property mortgage. Instead of introducing the records concerning this transaction, a witness testified as to what he had reviewed in the county clerk's office, but this was error, the Second Circuit stating:

> On the initial level the mortgage which Ruffin allegedly purchased in his own name by use of Rugore corporate funds would itself satisfy Fed.R.Evid. 803(14), the hearsay exception for "[r]ecords of documents affecting an interest in property" but Hamel's recitation of the contents of the documents, if offered, as it was here, to prove the truth of the matters asserted in the mortgage, cannot satisfy any hearsay exception set forth in Fed.R.Evid. 803 or 804.

d. Judgment of Previous Conviction; Judgment as Proof of Family History and Boundaries

Federal Rule of Evidence 803(22) makes admissible—

> **(22) Judgment of previous conviction.** Evidence of a final judgment entered after a trial or upon a plea of guilty (but not upon a plea of nolo contendere), adjudging a person guilty of a crime punishable by death or imprisonment in excess of one year, to prove any fact essential to sustain the judgment, but not including, when offered by the Government in a criminal prosecution for purposes other than impeachment, judgments against persons other than the accused. The pendency of an appeal may be shown but does not affect admissibility.

Where a jury finds defendant guilty of a felony beyond a reasonable doubt, or where defendant pleads guilty to a felony, an event occurs which is considered reliable enough to allow for admissibility in subsequent litigation involving any of the facts undergirding the judgment of conviction. Thus, where the government brought an action prior to enactment of Rule 803(22) for conversion of government property, criminal convictions based on false statements made by defendant's agents in connection with the converted property were admissible under the common law rule.[44] Judge Weinstein, in a case applying Rule 803(22), gave it full force and effect.[45] In this case plaintiff sued defendant for damages accruing to plaintiff because of defendant's allegedly false testimony at a criminal trial where plaintiff was convicted of robbing defendant. The court ruled that defendant's credibility had been conclusively established in the criminal trial. Judge Weinstein stated:

---

43. 575 F.2d 346, 357 (2d Cir.1978).

44. United States v. Fabric Garment Co., 366 F.2d 530, 534 (2d Cir.1966). See concurring opinion in New York & Cuba Mail S.S. Co. v. Continental Ins. Co., 117 F.2d 404, 411 (2d Cir.1941), cert. denied, 313 U.S. 580, 61 S.Ct. 1103, 85 L.Ed. 1537 (1941), for a discussion of the older cases which precluded the use of judgments of conviction, and the trend toward allowing such evidence.

45. Warren v. Applebaum, 526 F.Supp. 586 (E.D.N.Y.1981).

The function of Rule 803(22) is evidentiary. It operates to admit prior convictions but it does not by itself insulate the evidence from rebuttal. * * * Thus, it must be distinguished from doctrines of collateral estoppel applied as a matter of policy, particularly in actions in which convicted criminals attempt to reap the benefit of their own wrongs or to avoid responsibility for them. * * * Nevertheless, the effect of Rule 803(22) is to provide evidence of such overpowering probative force in the context of a case such as the one before us as to be, in effect, conclusive; "there is no way to refuse it."[46]

Not all cases call for the invocation of Rule 802(22) as clearly as this one; instances arise where the criminal judgment simply will not measure up to the requirement of simple relevancy.[47] Judgments of acquittal are not admissible because they are much less probative than judgments of convictions.[48] Pleas, however, whether to felonies or misdemeanors may be admissible as admissions.[49]

Rule 803(23) makes admissible:

(23) Judgment as to personal, family, or general history, or boundaries. Judgments as proof of matters of personal family or general history, or boundaries, essential to the judgment, if the same would be provable by evidence of reputation.

This rule relates to the three reputation exceptions found in Rule 803(19) (reputation among family members as to family and personal relationships, or concerning birth, adoption, marriage, death, etc.), (20)(reputation concerning boundaries and events of "general history") and (21) (reputation as to character). These exceptions are treated in § 803(7).2, *infra*. Thus, a judgment can be used for its essential facts which prove the same things. The judgment could be either civil or criminal, and "judgment" can include determinations by boards and agencies.[50]

---

46. Id. at 588. See also S. T. Grand v. City of New York, 32 N.Y.2d 300, 344 N.Y.S.2d 938, 298 N.E.2d 105 (1973), reargument denied, 33 N.Y.2d 658, 348 N.Y.S.2d 1030, 303 N.E.2d 710 (1973), where the plaintiff's suit against the city for breach of a construction contract, was interdicted by proof that plaintiff had procured the contract through bribery. Plaintiff's conviction for bribery was held as collateral estoppel to the civil suit.

47. See Index Fund, Inc. v. Hagopian, 677 F.Supp. 710, 720 (S.D.N.Y.1987) (in securities suit for market manipulation, plaintiff not entitled to prove defendant's conviction based on a different transaction and for the crime of embezzlement, not bribery which would have been more pertinent to the civil suit).

48. See United States v. Viserto, 596 F.2d 531, 536–37 (2d Cir.), cert. denied, 444 U.S. 841, 100 S.Ct. 80, 62 L.Ed.2d 52 (1979)("A judgment of acquittal is relevant to the legal question of whether the prosecution is barred by the constitutional doctrine of double jeopardy or of collateral estoppel. But [it] * * * is not usually admissible to rebut inferences that may be drawn from the evidence that was admitted.").

49. See United States v. Gotti, 641 F.Supp. 283, 289–90 (E.D.N.Y.1986) (misdemeanor guilty plea admissible in criminal proceedings); Hinshaw v. Keith, 645 F.Supp. 180, 182–83 (D.Me.1986)(misdemeanor guilty plea admissible in civil litigation).

50. In the absence of Second Circuit activity regarding this exception we cite by way of example the Tenth Circuit case of United States v. Mid–Continent Petroleum Corp., 67 F.2d 37, 43 (10th Cir.1933), cert. denied, 290 U.S. 702, 54 S.Ct. 346, 78 L.Ed.

e. Absence of Public Record

Federal Rule 803(10) provides:

> **(10) Absence of public record or entry.** To prove the absence of a record, report, statement, or data compilation, in any form, or the nonoccurrence or nonexistence of a matter of which a record, report, statement, or data compilation, in any form, was regularly made and preserved by a public office or agency, evidence in the form of a certification in accord with rule 902, or testimony, that diligent search failed to disclose the record, report, statement, or data compilation, or entry.

This provision can be used to prove simply that a particular record was never filed or recorded, if that is the issue; and it can also be used to prove the often more significant allegation that a particular transaction, evidence of which would normally have been filed or recorded had it occurred, never happened. The requirement that a "diligent" search be made is not to be taken lightly. In *United States v. Yakobov*,[51] defendant was charged with unlawful dealing in firearms and the government introduced a certificate made by an employee of the Bureau of Alcohol, Tobacco and Firearms stating that a diligent search had been made, but that no record of any license to deal in firearms was found issued to defendant. The court found the certificate defective on its face:

> An essential requirement of Rule 803(10) is that evidence of the absence of a record be the result of a "diligent search." * * * The diligence requirement is one of substance, not form. It is not satisfied merely by a ritual incantation that the certificate results from a "diligent search." * * * Rather, "if, in a particular instance, the circumstances indicate a lack of trustworthiness, the evidence should be excluded," and the result of "a search that has been less than diligent is inadmissible to prove the absence of a record." United States v. Robinson, *supra*, 544 F.2d at 115.[52]

Under the *Yakobov* rule, it appears that the custodian must actually describe his search and what he looked for. The court determined this search to be inadequate because all the variations of defendant's name had not been checked out.[53]

Challenges to the admissibility of such evidence on the ground that it violates the right to confrontation have been rejected.[54]

---

603 (1933) and the Ninth Circuit case of Jung Yen Loy v. Cahill, 81 F.2d 809, 812 (9th Cir.1936). In the former, records of a commission that enrolled Indians was held admissible on question of pedigree which was relevant to dispute over Indian lands. In the latter, determinations by immigration authorities as to person's citizenship, while not res judicata, nevertheless are admissible. These cases predate Rule 803(23), and are not even judgments; but otherwise, there are no cases construing this rule.

51. 712 F.2d 20 (2d Cir.1983).

52. Id. at 24.

53. Id.

54. United States v. Metzger, 778 F.2d 1195, 1202 (6th Cir.1985), cert. denied, 477 U.S. 906, 106 S.Ct. 3279, 91 L.Ed.2d 568 (1986).

f. Records of Religious Organizations

Federal Rule 803(11) creates an exception for:

> **(11) Records of religious organizations.** Statements of births, marriages, divorces, deaths, legitimacy, ancestry, relationship by blood or marriage, or other similar facts of personal or family history, contained in a regularly kept record of a religious organization.

As indicated in the Advisory Committee's Note, there is no reason to limit this sort of evidence so that only the fact represented (e.g., a baptism) can be proved, but not other facts contained in the record such as the age of the subject. "In view of the unlikelihood that false information would be furnished on occasions of this kind, the rule contains no requirement that the informant be in the course of [business] activity." The Second Circuit has held Rule 803(11) inapplicable to prove the amount of monetary donations to the church through receipts issued by the church.[55]

Related to this provision is Federal Rule 803(12) which provides for:

> **(12) Marriage, baptismal, and similar certificates.** Statements of fact contained in a certificate that the maker performed a marriage or other ceremony or administered a sacrament, made by a clergyman, public official, or other person authorized by the rules or practices of a religious organization or by law to perform the act certified, and purporting to have been issued at the time of the act or within a reasonable time thereafter.

Although some of this information can be gleaned from public records, some of it cannot, and as the Advisory Committee puts it "[t]he area covered by the rule is, however, substantially larger and extends the certification procedure to clergymen and the like who perform marriages and other ceremonies or administer sacraments." This provision seems to overlap Rule 803(11), except that this provides for the introduction of certificates for proof of the fact that the event was performed. Had there been an intent to provide for proof of other facts contained in the document, as included under Rule 803(11), such provision would likely have been made.

The only federal case in which Rule 803(12) is cited is *McMorrow v. Schweiker*,[56] which involved a woman seeking widow's insurance benefits under Title II of the Social Security Act. While the widow lacked any tangible proof of marriage and was denied benefits, the court cited Rule 803(12) as follows:

> The most common mode of proof of a ceremonial marriage, oddly enough, is by hearsay, namely the marriage certificate issued by the performing official, and such hearsay is regularly

---

55. Ruberto v. Commissioner of Internal Revenue, 774 F.2d 61, 63 (2d Cir.1985), judgment affirmed after remand, 873 F.2d 1436 (2d Cir.1989). In order to be admissible church receipts for contributions would have to come in under Rule 803(6), as regular business entries.

56. 561 F.Supp. 584 (D.N.J.1982).

§ 803(5).2   HEARSAY   Ch. 8

received despite the availability of the declarant. See, 5 Wigmore, "Evidence," I 1644, 1645 (Chadbourn rev.1974); Fed.Ev. Rule 8G3(12); N.J.Ev.Rule 63(18); Balazinski v. Lebid, 65 N.J.Super. 483, 168 A.2d 209 (App.Div.1961).[57]

Library References:
West's Key No. Digests, Criminal Law ⟹429; Evidence ⟹325–337.

803(6)   Learned Treatises, Market Reports and Commercial Publications

§ 803(6).1   New York

In New York the use of learned treatises is confined to impeachment of expert witnesses (*see* discussion at § 702.1(f), *supra*). Unlike Federal Rule 803(18), there is no learned treatise hearsay exception included in the proposed New York Evidence Code.

As for market reports, CPLR 4533 provides:

> A report of a regularly organized stock or commodity market published in a newspaper or periodical of general circulation or in an official publication or trade journal is admissible in evidence to prove the market price or value of any article regularly sold or dealt in on such market. The circumstances of the preparation of such a report may be shown to affect its weight, but they shall not affect its admissibility.

Although newspapers and periodicals are self-authenticating under CPLR 4532, trade journals and official publications will need a foundation in the absence of a stipulation. Unlike many of the other evidence provisions in CPLR Art. 45, these reports simply provide evidence, not prima facie evidence. Only one case bears notation with reference to CPLR 4533;[1] but a common law rule has long allowed admission of such compilations and tables as mortality tables,[2] price lists,[3] statistical abstracts,[4] and books of registry.[5] With respect to these common law

---

57. Id. at 589.

§ 803(6).1

1. Auld v. Estridge, 86 Misc.2d 895, 906–07, 382 N.Y.S.2d 897, 904–05 (Sup.Ct.Nassau Co.1976), aff'd, 58 A.D.2d 636, 395 N.Y.S.2d 969 (2d Dep't), appeal denied, 43 N.Y.2d 641, 401 N.Y.S.2d 1025, 371 N.E.2d 830 (1977)("pink sheets" published by the National Quotation Bureau, held admissible under CPLR 4533).

2. Matter of Keenan, 302 N.Y. 417, 421, 99 N.E.2d 219, 221 (1951)(court reaffirmed admissibility of mortality tables and on that basis approved admissibility of remarriage tables).

3. Whelan v. Lynch, 60 N.Y. 469, 474 (1875)(although affirming the admissibility of price lists, the court enunciated the requirement that there be a foundation showing the source of the information and how it was compiled).

4. Matter of B. Altman & Co. v. City of White Plains, 57 N.Y.2d 904, 906, 456 N.Y.S.2d 755, 756, 442 N.E.2d 1266, 1267 (1982)(lower court's reliance on expert's real property appraisal of shopping center property using nationwide abstracts of percentage lease rates in calculating income affirmed since the expert testified that such statistical data is usually relied on in the shopping center trade); Adcor Realty Corp. v. Srogi, 54 A.D.2d 1096, 388 N.Y.S.2d 962 (4th Dep't 1976), appeal denied, 41 N.Y.2d 806, 396 N.Y.S.2d 1025, 364 N.E.2d 850 (1977)(admission of nationwide statistical abstracts of department store percentage leases relied on by the witness affirmed, since witness testified that these bulletins

---

5. See note 5 on page 685.

exceptions a foundation must be laid as to reliability, and it is likely that the courts will be receptive to broadening the scope of this rule in accord with the comprehensive approach used in Federal Rule 803(17) discussed in the next section. A section covering market reports and commercial publications is included in the proposed New York Code.[6]

Library References:

West's Key No. Digests, Criminal Law ⬩434, 439; Evidence ⬩360.

§ 803(6).2 Federal

Federal Rule 803(18) makes the following admissible:

> **(18) Learned treatises.** To the extent called to the attention of an expert witness upon cross-examination or relied upon by the expert witness in direct examination, statements contained in published treatises, periodicals, or pamphlets on a subject of history, medicine, or other science or art, established as a reliable authority by the testimony or admission of the witness or by other expert testimony or by judicial notice. If admitted, the statements may be read into evidence but may not be received as exhibits.

Unlike the New York rule, which confines a learned treatises to the realm of impeachment, and then only if the witness is willing to recognize it as authoritative (see § 702.1(f), *supra*), Rule 803(18) provides that the relevant passage can be used as evidence in chief. And, of course, the treatise can also be used for impeachment even if the witness is not willing to recognize it as authoritative. Authoritativeness can be established in the other ways set forth in the rule. It is anomalous that New York does not recognize this exception, or that it is not even proposed, since it is arguable that few other hearsay exceptions have a greater degree of trustworthiness;[1] and to limit the effect of such evidence to impeachment struck the Federal Rules Advisory Committee as unrealistic.[2] The last sentence of the rule was included "to prevent a jury from rifling through a learned treatise and drawing improper inferences from technical language it might not be able properly to

---

were carefully compiled and relied on by real estate consultants).

5. Slocovich v. Orient Mut. Ins. Co., 108 N.Y. 56, 63–64, 14 N.E. 802, 805 (1888)(ship's registry book which recorded character, condition, age, tonnage, and the materials of which ship was constructed admissible to establish value; registry relied on by underwriters, merchants and buyers and sellers of ships).

6. New York Code of Evidence § 803(c)(15) [PROPOSED] states:

(15) Market reports, commercial publications. Market quotations, tabulations, lists, directories, or other published compilations, generally used and relied upon by the public or by persons in particular occupations.

§ 803(6).2

1. The Advisory Committee's Note to Rule 803(18) observes that "a high standard of accuracy is engendered by various factors: the treatise is written primarily and impartially for professionals, subject to scrutiny and exposure for inaccuracy, with the reputation of the writer at stake."

2. The Advisory Committee's Note to Rule 803(18) states that "[the exception] avoids the unreality of admitting evidence for the purpose of impeachment only, with an instruction to the jury not to consider it otherwise."

understand without expert guidance."[3]

The Second Circuit cases point up the necessity for strict adherence to all the rule's requirements, and hold that the relevance/prejudice provision of Rule 403 can be a factor;[4] and that there can be a connection with Rule 703, which concerns an expert's reliance on facts or data not in evidence.[5]

Rule 803(17) provides for the admission of

(17) Market reports, commercial publications. Market quotations, tabulations, lists, directories, or other published compilations, generally used and relied upon by the public or by persons in particular occupations.

This provides broader coverage than its New York counterpart (CPLR 4533), which refers only to reports of the stock and commodity markets. Under Rule 803(17) the contents of all published compilations can come into evidence since trustworthiness lies in the fact that these lists are made by professionals under pressure to be accurate, and necessity lies in the obvious burden of otherwise having to assemble as witnesses all those who participated in the origin, assembling and publishing of the information.[6]

McCormick's survey names the following as being included within the scope of Rule 803(17), along with newspapers and other regularly published reports: "publications such as reports of market prices, professional directories, city and telephone directories, and mortality and annuity tables used by life insurance companies,"[7] and in addition, price lists, mercantile credit reports, safety codes and opinion polls can be

---

3. United States v. Mangan, 575 F.2d 32, 48 n.19 (2d Cir.), cert. denied, 439 U.S. 931, 99 S.Ct. 320, 58 L.Ed.2d 324 (1978). In Mangan, however, the treatise material consisted of charts abstracted from a treatise which the trial court held could be read to the jury, but not admitted into evidence, but which the appellate court found could well have been admitted since it was hard to see how a chart could be "read into evidence."

4. See Schneider v. Revici, 817 F.2d 987, 991 (2d Cir.1987)(here, defense counsel failed to produce any evidence that the book was authoritative or reliable, and the lack of objectivity was compounded by the fact that the book was written by defendant, which the court saw as bringing Rule 403 into play as well); Tart v. McGann, 697 F.2d 75, 78 (2d Cir.1982)(where plaintiff sought to use tables of recommended heart rates published by the American Medical Association on cross-examination of defendant's expert, counsel did not assert Rule 803(18) as his authority thus justifying the trial judge's exclusion of the evidence which also admitted of a relevancy problem);

Walker v. North Dakota Eye Clinic, Ltd., 415 F.Supp. 891, 894 (D.N.D.1976).

5. See Apicella v. McNeil Laboratories, Inc., 66 F.R.D. 78, 85–86 (E.D.N.Y.1975), where Judge Weinstein dealt with plaintiff's attempts to confront defendant drug manufacturer with a medical newsletter reporting other deaths related to the subject drug. After reviewing the Rule 703 and Rule 803(18) rules regarding such material, the court held that it could not be used. One problem was that the source of the information in the newsletter could not be ascertained, thus complicating defendant's attempts to refute it. Furthermore, Judge Weinstein found that the problem had Rule 403 implications since the newsletter material "unlike a treatise, deals not with general background information, but with precisely the question which will be before the jury, the dangerous nature of this particular drug when used as directed by the manufacturer." Id. at 86.

6. 4 Weinstein and Berger ¶ 803(17)[01], at 803–360, 361.

7. McCormick § 321, at 353.

counted in.[8] The lists certainly do not exhaust the possibilities.[9]

There are, of course, limits. In *White Indus., Inc. v. Cessna Aircraft Co.*,[10] a party sought to introduce documents filed with the SEC by a distributor of a product—10–K forms and a prospectus. The district court held that the documents failed to qualify as market reports or commercial publications because they were not "published," and because the kinds of publications Rule 803(17) encompasses deals with compilations of objective facts, not with the kind of subjective analysis of information contained in prospectuses and 10–K forms.[11] Objectivity could be found, however, in *Ellis v. International Playtex*,[12] where it was held that Rule 803(17) permitted evidence of findings by the Center for Disease Control concerning toxic shock syndrome, even though the findings were based on reports from doctors who interviewed patients. The rationale given for permitting the exception to cover multiple levels of hearsay was the inherent reliability of the underlying statements and the impossibility of calling each of the patients whose comments contributed to the study.[13]

Library References:

West's Key No. Digests, Criminal Law ⇔434, 439; Evidence ⇔360.

803(7) Ancient Documents, and Reputation

§ 803(7).1 New York

Several minor common law exceptions are listed below.

a. Family Records

Unlike Federal Rule 803(13), which provides for statements of family history, whether declarant is available or not, the rule in New York, as it presently stands, includes this sort of information in the pedigree exception premised on the declarant's being dead. The pedi-

---

8. 4 Weinstein and Berger ¶ 803(17)[01], at 803–361–65.

9. In Caten v. Salt City Movers & Storage Co., 149 F.2d 428 (2d Cir.1945) plaintiffs submitted a letter from a dealer of glassware of the kind for which plaintiffs were claiming damages, to prove the value of their loss. The court stated: "We think this letter was like a price list issued by a dealer in such property and that it was admissible as evidence of value." Id. at 433. In Zippo Manufacturing Company v. Rogers Imports, Inc., 216 F.Supp. 670, 680–84 (S.D.N.Y.1963), in a case charging defendant with marketing knock-offs of plaintiff's lighter, the court held admissible a consumer survey offered by plaintiff which showed that those asked confused defendant's lighter with plaintiff's. This opinion provides a valuable analysis of the admissibility of such polling results (much the same as public opinion polls) and adds that the state of mind exception provides an additional reason for admissibility. Id. at 683.

10. 611 F.Supp. 1049 (W.D.Mo.1985).

11. Id. at 1069. See also In re Richardson–Merrell, Inc. Bendectin Products Liability Litigation, 624 F.Supp. 1212, 1231 (S.D.Ohio 1985), aff'd, 857 F.2d 290 (6th Cir.1988), cert. denied sub nom., Hoffman v. Merrell Dow Pharmaceuticals, Inc., 488 U.S. 1006, 109 S.Ct. 788, 102 L.Ed.2d 779 (1989)(holding that excerpts from the Physicians Desk Reference were not admissible under Rule 803(17) to show side effects of drugs similar to Bendectin).

12. 745 F.2d 292 (4th Cir.1984).

13. Id. at 303.

gree exception is taken up in § 804(4).1 *infra*.[1] It is not beyond the realm of possibility that the rule could be broadened in New York to include entries in bibles, inscriptions on rings, or any other reliable source as to age and relationships whether or not the declarant is available, under the persuasive effect of the Federal Rule, or by ultimate enactment of a statutory provision.[2]

A person may testify as to his own age, citizenship, and legitimacy.[3]

b. Ancient Documents

If a document is 30 years old or more, it is self-authenticating.[4] The question is whether this is simply an authentication rule, or whether the content of the document can be admitted for its truth as a hearsay exception. Under Federal Rule 803(16) statements in documents 20 years old or more "the authenticity of which is established" come in as hearsay exceptions, and this would no doubt be influential in persuading the New York courts clearly to enunciate such a rule. As it is, statements in old deeds are admissible for their truth, but it must be shown that ownership has been undisturbed over a long period of time.[5] And there is some dictum alluding to an ancient document exception in other cases.[6] The movement toward recognition as a genuine hearsay exception was greatly advanced in *Tillman v. Lincoln Warehouse Corp.*[7] where, in order to prove the contents of an art collection, plaintiff offered an inventory list compiled over 30 years previously, and the court ruled it admissible stating:

> Under the "ancient document" rule, a record or document which is found to be more than 30 years of age and which is proven to have come from proper custody and is itself free from any indication of fraud or invalidity "proves itself." * * * This rule dispenses with the proof of the execution of a record or

---

§ 803(7).1

1. See Aalholm v. People, 211 N.Y. 406, 412–13, 105 N.E. 647, 649 (1914)("The admissibility of such declarations is subject to three conditions: 1. The declarant must be deceased. 2. They must have been made * * * at the time when there was no motive to distort the truth. 3. The declarant must be related either by blood or affinity to the family concerning which he speaks.").

2. The New York Evidence Code, § 803(c)(16) [PROPOSED] states:

(16) **Reputation concerning personal or family history.** Reputation, existing before the controversy, among members of a person's family by blood, adoption, or marriage, or among a person's associates, or in the community, concerning such person's birth, adoption, marriage, divorce, death, legitimacy, relationship by blood, adoption or marriage, ancestry, or other similar fact of such person's personal or family history.

3. 2 Wigmore § 667.

4. 7 Wigmore § 2138. See § 901.8(a) infra.

5. McKinnon v. Bliss, 21 N.Y. 206, 211 (1860). Other statutory provisions relating to documents affecting real property are Real Property Actions and Proceedings Law §§ 331 (sheriff's certificate of sale over 10 years old) and 341 (recitals as to heirship in instruments related to the conveyance of real property which are more than 10 years old), and CPLR 4522 (making admissible maps, surveys and official records on file as proof of contents if document over 10 years old—discussed at § 803(5).1(d), supra).

6. See Matter of Barney, 185 App.Div. 782, 802, 174 N.Y.S. 242, 253 (1st Dep't 1919). See 5 Wigmore § 1573, where only limited instances of the ancient document rule being used as a hearsay exception are discussed.

7. 72 A.D.2d 40, 423 N.Y.S.2d 151 (1st Dep't 1979).

document in the proof of its antiquity. It presumes that the entrant of the record or document is dead after the passage of 30 years. * * * If the genuineness of an ancient document is established, it may be received to prove the truth of the facts that it recites.* * *[8]

The court, after noting that the inventory constituted some evidence to support plaintiff's claim added: "In passing, it should be observed that the inventory was also admissible as a business record."[9]

c. Reputation

There is little case law of any consequence in New York concerning the admissibility of facts repeated often enough that they take on the aspect of common knowledge in the community or the family. There is no reason to believe that the New York courts would not be receptive to the common law rule outlined by Wigmore where it is noted that the ancient rule regarding reputation evidence has been refined to the following topics:

(1) land boundaries and land customary rights and verdicts in other litigation,

(2) events of general history,

(3) marriage and other facts of family history, and

(4) personal character.[10]

Land boundaries. The reputation must be ancient, whatever that means now that the time period with regard to related matters has been reduced from 30 years, to 20 years to 10 years,[11] and the fact must be borne out by reputation, not just an individual assertion.[12] Presumably, the witness testifying would have to state that he established the boundary lines because the information reached him through more than one source; but, there being no reason to doubt trustworthiness generally, the witness ought to be able to state that his source told him that this was the common understanding.[13] While it seems to be assumed that the source of the witness' information is deceased at the time of trial,[14]

---

8. Id. at 44–45, 423 N.Y.S.2d at 153.

9. Id. at 45, 423 N.Y.S.2d at 153. See also Fairchild v. Union Ferry Co., 121 Misc. 513, 201 N.Y.S. 295 (Sup.Ct.Kings Co.1923), a case concerned with rights to docks and piers in New York harbor. The court stated:

Upon the trial, proof was offered by the plaintiffs and received over objection. This consisted of old writings and book entries and was, I believe, properly received under the ancient document rule. This rule is that a record or document which is found to be more than thirty years of age and which is proved to have come from proper custody and is itself free from any indication of fraud or invalidity proves itself.

Id. at 518, 201 N.Y.S. at 300.

Why would these writings and book entries be admitted if not to prove their content?

10. 5 Wigmore § 1580, at 544.

11. See, e.g., CPLR 4522 (provides for authentication of old maps, deeds and surveys more than 10 years old), Real Property Actions and Proceedings Law §§ 331 (alternate proof of sheriff's sale occurring more than 20 years ago) and 341 (recitals as to heirships in conveyances more than 15 years old), noted at note 5 supra.

12. 5 Wigmore § 1584, at 548.

13. Id. at 549, 550.

14. Id. at 548.

§ 803(7).1   HEARSAY   Ch. 8

this would not appear to be an essential element. The crucial aspect is that the reputation has existed for a long period of time, and that it relate to matters of general interest, i.e., not the declarant's expression of his own understanding, but his expression of the general understanding.[15] The source of the information need not be an individual, but may be old deeds, maps and surveys, the admissibility of which is provided for under CPLR 4522 if they are more than 10 years old. Apart from reputation evidence as to boundaries, there is also the rule that the declaration of an individual as to the boundaries of his land are admissible if he is dead and had no reason to misrepresent.[16] Although there is some authority that if an individual is speaking of his own land he must be pointing out the boundary lines at the time, this is not the rule in New York; but he may have to be "on the scene."[17]

Events of general history. The general rules enunciated just above could be utilized to facilitate the admissibility of any relevant information, not just boundary lines, so long as the topic was of general interest. Wigmore lists no examples in the text, but subjects of community interest listed in the footnoted cases range from inscriptions on monuments in public places, through community residence, to landmarks.[18] Again, the reputation must have been of long standing, i.e., "it must be a matter concerning a former generation."[19]

Marriage and other facts of family history. Community reputation as to a couple's marital status has been held admissible in New York.[20] Generally, the conditions necessary to proving boundaries would apply here, except that it is not necessary that the reputation be of ancient origin.[21] Other matters concerning families which can be shown to be of public knowledge such as race, legitimacy, birth and death are also subject to admissibility under this rule.[22]

Moral character. This sort of reputation evidence is confined in New York to criminal cases in which defendant chooses to open the question of his character;[23] or in civil cases where character is directly in issue.[24] These matters are dealt with in § 402.1 *supra.*

Miscellaneous. In *McKinnon v. Bliss,*[25] itself of ancient origin, there is dictum applicable to reputation evidence generally:

> That hearsay or reputation is admissible as evidence, upon questions of pedigree or family relationships, and also upon

---

15. Id. § 1586, at 551.

16. Hannah v. Baylon Holding Corp., 28 N.Y.2d 89, 92, 320 N.Y.S.2d 35, 37–38, 268 N.E.2d 775, 776 (1971).

17. In Hannah the court stated: "There is discussion in some of these cases about the need for 'pointing out' the boundary. The physical means by which the boundary is indicated could not itself be decisive. It is good enough if the declarant, on the scene and in possession of the land, tells the witness where the boundary is." Id. at 92, 320 N.Y.S.2d at 38, 268 N.E.2d at 776.

18. 5 Wigmore §§ 1597–99, at 561–67.

19. Id. § 1597, at 561.

20. Badger v. Badger, 88 N.Y. 546, 552 (1882).

21. 5 Wigmore § 1602, at 567.

22. Id. §§ 1605, 1606, at 571–78.

23. See People v. Bouton, 50 N.Y.2d 130, 428 N.Y.S.2d 218, 405 N.E.2d 699 (1980).

24. In defamation or malicious prosecution cases, for instance, plaintiff's character is directly in issue. See § 402.1, supra.

25. 21 N.Y. 206 (1860), note 5, supra.

questions respecting the boundaries of lands, is a familiar doctrine. But there are, no doubt, other cases in which the same kind of evidence may be received, for the purpose of establishing a mere private right, when the fact to be proved is one of a *quasi* public nature, that is, one which interests a multitude of people, or an entire community * * *.[26]

The reputation provisions in the proposed New York Evidence Code, in addition to the family history provision at note 2, are set forth below.[27]

Library References:

West's Key No. Digests, Criminal Law ⚖︎429–446; Evidence ⚖︎325–383.

§ 803(7).2 Federal

a. Family Records

Federal Rule 803(13) provides for admissibility concerning

(13) Family records. Statements of fact concerning personal or family history contained in family Bibles, genealogies, charts, engravings on rings, inscriptions on family portraits, engravings on urns, crypts, or tombstones, or the like.

Unlike the cramped and vague New York rule, Rule 803(13) opens up this avenue with no limitations such as unavailability of the declarant.

Related to this provision is Federal Rule 803(12), which provides for marriage, baptismal, and similar certificates, noted in § 803(5).2(f), *supra*.

Although much of this information can be gleaned from public records, some of it cannot, and as the Advisory Committee puts it, "[t]he area covered by the rule is * * * substantially larger and extends the certification procedure to clergymen and the like who perform marriages and other ceremonies or administer sacraments." This provision seems to overlap Rule 803(12), except under Rule 803(12) the act to be proved is represented by a certificate.

b. Ancient Documents

Federal Rule 803(16) provides admissibility for

(16) Statements in ancient documents. Statements in a document in existence twenty years or more the authenticity of which is established.

---

26. Id. at 217. There is an error in pagination. This quote is from the second page 217. This case involves untangling title going back to a land grant to Sir William Johnson prior to 1774.

27. New York Evidence Code §§ 803(c)(19), (20) and (21) [PROPOSED] provide:

(17) **Reputation concerning boundaries or general history.** Reputation in a community, existing before the controversy, as to boundaries of, or customs affecting, lands in the community, and reputation as to events of general history important to the community or state or nation in which the events took place.

(18) **Reputation as to character.** Reputation of a person's character among the person's associates or in the community.

The Advisory Committee Note explains the conscious decision to extend this beyond a mere rule of authentication.[1] In the Second Circuit, the rule has been applied to such disparate material as memoranda,[2] catalogues,[3] and photographs.[4] Certainly the court has discretion to limit or foreclose admissibility where circumstances show a lack of trustworthiness, or prejudice would outweigh probative value under Federal Rule 403.[5] The common law requirements that the document must have come from proper custody and be free of any indication of fraud or invalidity, while not carried forward in Rule 803(16), would naturally be factors in any appraisal of admissibility. (*See* § 901.8(b) *infra*.)

A somewhat related concept applies to statements in instruments affecting property. Federal Rule 803(15) provides for:

(15) Statements in documents affecting an interest in property. A statement contained in a document purporting to establish or affect an interest in property if the matter stated was relevant to the purpose of the document, unless dealings with the property since the document was made have been inconsistent with the truth of the statement or the purport of the document.

The Advisory Committee's Note explains that because of the care and exactitude with which dispositive instruments are prepared and executed, there is small danger of error. For example, deeds may recite a power of attorney or facts of heirship, which might be at issue later on. These instruments do not have to be "ancient." In one case, for instance, the court found that recitals in two warranty deeds proved the fact that Dave and Nettie Lewis were husband and wife.[6]

c. Reputation.

Land boundaries or general history. Federal rule 803(20) provides for

(20) Reputation concerning boundaries or general history. Reputation in a community, arising before the controversy, as to boundaries of or customs affecting lands in the

---

§ 803(7).2

1. The Committee notes the rule is applied to "all sorts of documents, including letters, records, contracts, maps, and certificates, in addition to title documents;" and that "[a]s pointed out in McCormick § 298, danger of mistake is minimized by authentication requirements, and age affords assurance that the writing antedates the present controversy."

2. George v. Celotex Corp., 914 F.2d 26, 30 (2d Cir.1990)(unpublished 1947 report of an asbestos study).

3. Jeanneret v. Vichey, 693 F.2d 259, 264 n.7 (2d Cir.1982)(art catalogue from the 1920's would have been admissible had counsel properly authenticated it).

4. DeWeerth v. Baldinger, 658 F.Supp. 688, 695 n.12 (S.D.N.Y.1987), rev'd on other grounds, 836 F.2d 103 (2d Cir.1987), cert. denied, 486 U.S. 1056, 108 S.Ct. 2823, 100 L.Ed.2d 924 (1988)(relevant 1943 photograph admissible as ancient document).

5. George v. Celotex Corp., 914 F.2d 26, 30–31 (2d Cir.1990)(1947 report on dangers of asbestos admissible as ancient document and withstands application of the Rule 403 test).

6. Compton v. Davis Oil Company, HPC, 607 F.Supp. 1221 (D.Wyo.1985).

community, and reputation as to events of general history important to the community or State or nation in which located.

There is no requirement that the reputation be "ancient," but trustworthiness is furthered by the requirement that it be abroad prior to "the controversy." The Advisory Committee Note states that the rule is intended "to include private as well as public boundaries." The Second Circuit has had occasion to apply the rule.[7] As to "events of general history" the Rule was found inapplicable in a civil rights action to prove defendant's practices discriminatory.[8]

Personal or family history. Federal Rule 803(19) provides for

(19) Reputation concerning personal or family history. Reputation among members of a person's family by blood, adoption, or marriage, or among a person's associates, or in the community, concerning a person's birth, adoption marriage, divorce, death, legitimacy, relationship by blood, adoption, or marriage, ancestry, or other similar fact of his personal or family history.

There has been little interpretation concerning this rule except for a Third Circuit case finding that a witness' testimony as to his own birth can be admitted under it.[9]

Character. Federal Rule 803(21) provides for

(21) Reputation as to character. Reputation of a person's character among associates or in the community.

This provision, according to the Advisory Committee's Note, applies only to provide a hearsay exception. Otherwise, character evidence is dealt with in terms of the instances in which admissible under Federal Rules 404, 405 and 608. (*See* discussions in §§ 402.2 and 608.1(b), *supra.*)

Library References:

West's Key No. Digests, Criminal Law ⚖︎429–446; Evidence ⚖︎325–383.

804 Hearsay Statements Admissible If Declarant Unavailable

§ 804.1 Unavailability—New York and Federal

Certain hearsay statements are admissible only if the declarant is unavailable. Categories include prior testimony, dying declarations,

---

7. Connecticut Light & Power Co. v. Federal Power Commission, 557 F.2d 349, 355–56 (2d Cir.1977)(historical data admissible to determine navigability of a river).

8. United States v. Ocampo, 650 F.2d 421, 427–28 (2d Cir.1981)(the rule did not cover the situation where a witness testified that defendant was known as "Negro" Pablon). See also Abrams v. Ocean Club, Inc., 602 F.Supp. 489, 491 (E.D.N.Y.1984), where plaintiffs sued swim club on grounds it discriminated against Jews. Plaintiffs tried to introduce evidence of the club's reputation for such discrimination, but the court disallowed it on the ground that the reputation was not ancient, even though the rule carries no such requirement. Perhaps the court was reluctant to permit such hearsay to be used to prove the central issue in the case.

9. Government of Virgin Islands v. Joseph, 765 F.2d 394, 397 n.5 (3d Cir.1985).

§ 804.1 HEARSAY Ch. 8

declarations against interest and pedigree declarations, each of which is discussed in the following sections. Unavailability is required for this group of exceptions because of the notion, historically perpetuated, that it would be more desirable to have live testimony in these matters, but that the hearsay statement, having certain attributes of trustworthiness, is better than nothing. As McCormick puts it:

> The theory of the first group [of exceptions not requiring unavailability] is that the out-of-court statement is at least as reliable as would be [declarant's] testimony in person, so that producing him would involve pointless delay and inconvenience. The theory of the second group [of exceptions requiring unavailability] is that, while it would be preferable to have live testimony, if the declarant is unavailable, the out-of-court statement will be accepted.[1]

The preliminary question exists as to circumstances that constitute unavailability. Definitions are set forth in Federal Rule 804(a):

(a) Definition of unavailability. "Unavailability as a witness" includes situations in which the declarant—

> (1) is exempted by ruling of the court on the ground of privilege from testifying concerning the subject matter of the declarant's statement; or
>
> (2) persists in refusing to testify concerning the subject matter of the declarant's statement despite an order of the court to do so; or
>
> (3) testifies to a lack of memory of the subject matter of the declarant's statement; or
>
> (4) is unable to be present or to testify at the hearing because of death or then existing physical or mental illness or infirmity; or
>
> (5) is absent from the hearing and the proponent of the declarant's statement has been unable to procure the declarant's attendance (or in the case of a hearsay exception under subdivision (b)(2), (3) or (4), the declarant's attendance or testimony) by process or other reasonable means.

A declarant is not unavailable as a witness if exemption, refusal, claim of lack of memory, inability, or absence is due to the procurement or wrongdoing of the proponent of a statement for the purpose of preventing the witness from attending or testifying.[2]

---

§ 804.1

1. 2 McCormick § 253, at 130.

2. The one perhaps questionable ground of unavailability listed is lack of memory in (a)(3). As to this, the Advisory Committee states:

> The position that a claimed lack of memory by the witness of the subject matter of his statement constitutes unavailability likewise finds support in the cases, though not without dissent. * * * If the claim is successful, the practical effect is to put the testimony beyond reach, as in the other instances. In this instance, however, it will be noted that the lack of memory must be established by the testimony of the witness himself, which clear-

694

It is not beyond the realm of possibility to suppose that the New York Court of Appeals would adopt all of these grounds of unavailability; but simple refusal to testify or a claimed lack of memory have not been tested.[3] Statutory grounds of unavailability are set forth in CPLR 4517 with regard to the admission of prior testimony.[4] In *People v. Brown*,[5] the Court of Appeals extended the statement against (pecuniary or propriety) interest to criminal cases (statements against one's "penal" interest) and also "modernized" the unavailability rule to include failure to testify by reason of asserting the privilege against self-incrimination.[6] Theretofore the accepted grounds had been death or absence. Thus in New York it was finally recognized that it is the unavailability of the testimony and not necessarily of the witness that is the crucial factor. Judge Bergan's dictum indicates that the court may indeed be willing to extend New York's unavailability rules to match those listed in Federal Rule 804(a). Thus:

> The rule on admissions against interest was based on the absence of the witness; and usually this meant that he was dead. But whether the person is dead, or beyond the jurisdiction, or will not testify, and cannot be compelled to testify because of a constitutional privilege, all equally spell out unavailability of trial testimony.[7]

Since the *Brown* determination rests on unavailability by way of assertion of the fifth amendment privilege, the question lingers whether the assertion of privileges based on confidential communications under Article 45 of the CPLR would also serve as a basis for an unavailability finding. The assertion of such privileges is contemplated under Federal Rule 804(a)(1) as providing the basis for a finding of unavailability.[8]

Absence from the jurisdiction. Absence from the court's reach provides one of the chief bases for the finding of unavailability. Litigation over the sufficiency of the proponent's showing of absence has been the focal point of several Supreme Court decisions regarding the criminal defendant's right of confrontation. In *Barber v. Page*,[9] a prosecution in Oklahoma state court, the prosecution introduced against defendant in a

---

ly contemplates his production and subjection to cross-examination.

The Advisory Committee found the simple refusal to testify akin to the situation created when the witness claims a privilege and thus included (a)(2).

3. The Proposed New York Evidence Code does not include these grounds, but "leaves it to decisional law to decide whether these grounds are appropriate in the particular case."

4. Prior testimony is discussed at § 804(1).1 infra. The grounds set forth in CPLR 4517 are "privilege, death, physical or mental illness, absence beyond the jurisdiction of the court * * * or absence because the proponent of his statement does not know and with diligence has been unable to ascertain his whereabouts, or because he is incompetent to testify by virtue of section 4519 * * *."

5. 26 N.Y.2d 88, 308 N.Y.S.2d 825, 257 N.E.2d 16 (1970).

6. Id. at 94, 308 N.Y.S.2d at 829, 257 N.E.2d at 18.

7. Id.

8. See United States v. Lilley, 581 F.2d 182, 189 (8th Cir.1978), where the witness claimed the spousal privilege. The court would have used this as a basis for a finding of unavailability except that one of the requirements for valid assertion of the privilege was lacking.

9. 390 U.S. 719, 88 S.Ct. 1318, 20 L.Ed.2d 255 (1968).

criminal trial the transcript of prior testimony by a declarant who was housed in a federal prison outside of Oklahoma. There had been no attempt by the prosecution to produce the declarant's presence. This violated the defendant's right of confrontation, the Supreme Court held, because the prosecution failed to show that a good faith effort was made to procure the declarant's presence.[10] But in *Mancusi v. Stubbs*,[11] another state court prosecution, the declarant was residing in Sweden, which released the state from making good faith, but useless, efforts to procure his presence. Thus, unavailability could be premised on a somewhat more relaxed standard than that which was required in *Barber v. Page*.[12] In *Ohio v. Roberts*,[13] unavailability was established, and the right of confrontation was thus satisfied, where the prosecutor served several subpoenas at the declarant's parents' home, and had made inquiries of those in declarant's family who would be expected to know her whereabouts. The Supreme Court described the good faith test as requiring the prosecutor to take measures to explore all possibilities, no matter how remote, to locate and produce the declarant. But "the law does not require the doing of a futile act,"[14] and all feasible measures were taken in *Roberts* to satisfy this burden.

The Second Circuit has found the burden satisfied where it was shown that declarant was in Columbia,[15] where the government offered to pay the witness' expenses to come to the United States from Europe,[16] where the witnesses were deported aliens and the prosecutor tried to prevent their deportation by the INS,[17] and where the witness was incarcerated in a country with which there was no extradition treaty.[18]

In New York, where cases on the question of unavailability are sparse, it has been held that unavailability is not established merely by showing that the witness is in prison.[19] The court pointed out that no attempt to depose the prisoner was made, and no request was made for the court to seek to compel the prisoner to attend the trial.[20] In a Family Court case a physician's prior testimony could be introduced in a custody proceeding where the petitioner, who had qualified for appoint-

10. Id. at 724, 725, 88 S.Ct. at 1322, 20 L.Ed.2d at 2601.

11. 408 U.S. 204, 92 S.Ct. 2308, 33 L.Ed.2d 293 (1972).

12. Id. at 212, 92 S.Ct. at 2313, 33 L.Ed.2d at 301.

13. 448 U.S. 56, 100 S.Ct. 2531, 65 L.Ed.2d 597 (1980).

14. Id. at 74, 100 S.Ct. at 2543, 65 L.Ed.2d at 2531.

15. United States v. Losada, 674 F.2d 167, 172 (2d Cir.), cert. denied, 457 U.S. 1125, 102 S.Ct. 2945, 73 L.Ed.2d 1341 (1982)(since witness was in foreign country he was not procurable, but defendant argued unsuccessfully that since he testified at prior trial in this country, the government should produce him at the second trial).

16. United States v. Sindona, 636 F.2d 792, 804 (2d Cir.1980), cert. denied, 451 U.S. 912, 101 S.Ct. 1984, 68 L.Ed.2d 302 (1981)(since the government could not entice witnesses to come and testify through good faith efforts, they were properly declared unavailable).

17. United States v. Seijo, 595 F.2d 116, 120 (2d Cir.1979)(there was no evidence the deported aliens were absent due to the prosecutor's wrongdoing).

18. United States v. Salim, 664 F.Supp. 682 (E.D.N.Y.1987), aff'd, 855 F.2d 944 (2d Cir.1988)(the good faith requirement is satisfied when the prosecution shows the lack of the treaty).

19. 2641 Concourse v. City Univ., 135 Misc.2d 464, 515 N.Y.S.2d 994 (Ct.of Claims 1987).

20. Id. at 467, 515 N.Y.S.2d at 996.

ment of counsel, could not afford to pay the physician's expert witness fee.[21] Noting that CPLR 4517 requires unavailability by reason of "privilege, death, physical or mental illness, or absence beyond the jurisdiction of the court" in order to qualify the prior testimony, the court found the physician unavailable because petitioner could not pay for his appearance.[22] The court noted that the physician could be subpoenaed to give facts, but not to render an opinion, which is what petitioner sought.[23]

In a personal injury case it was sufficient as a ground of unavailability that the declarant had moved his domicile to Arizona.[24]

Assertion of the privilege against self-incrimination. Assertion of the fifth amendment privilege forms the basis for a finding of unavailability in many cases;[25] and it is no argument at the federal level that the witness is available where the government has refused to grant immunity.[26] There is a lower court case in New York, however, in which it is stated: "After all, if the cause for the unavailability of the witness is due to the failure of the People to fulfill a condition (conferral of immunity) the People may not rely on this unavailability * * *."[27] It is not necessary that the witness assume the stand and actually assert the privilege so long as it is clear that she would assert it if called.[28] Where the witness lacks a legitimate claim to fifth amendment protection, such as where he has pleaded guilty to the subject crime, the People have to establish that he would refuse to testify in any event.[29]

The court will not find unavailability so as to admit prior testimony where the defendant herself, who testified at her first trial, chooses not to do so at her second trial and thereby claims she is now unavailable.[30]

---

21. Palma S. v. Carmine S., 134 Misc.2d 34, 509 N.Y.S.2d 527 (Family Ct.Kings Co.1986).

22. Id. at 36, 509 N.Y.S.2d at 528.

23. Id. at 37, 509 N.Y.S.2d at 529.

24. Healy v. Rennert, 9 N.Y.2d 202, 213 N.Y.S.2d 44, 173 N.E.2d 777 (1961)(proof of domicile was satisfied by showing the witness' Arizona mailing address and by statements made by the witness that he lived in Arizona).

25. See, e.g., United States v. Matthews, 20 F.3d 538, 545 (2d Cir.1994) (where co-defendant did not take the stand, his out-of-court declarations against interest implicating objecting co-defendant admissible since co-defendant declarant was unavailable); United States v. Rodriguez, 706 F.2d 31, 40 (2d Cir.1983)(defendant's witness claimed the privilege thus rendering her unavailable and allowing admissibility of her statements against penal interest).

26. United States v. Lang, 589 F.2d 92, 95–96 (2d Cir.1978).

27. People v. Goetz, 135 Misc.2d 888, 891, 516 N.Y.S.2d 1007, 1009 (Sup.Ct. N.Y.Co.1987).

28. United States v. Williams, 927 F.2d 95, 98 (2d Cir.), cert. denied sub nom., Davis v. United States, 502 U.S. 911, 112 S.Ct. 307, 116 L.Ed.2d 250 (1991)(where accomplices all indicated they would claim privilege at trial of defendant, it was not necessary to put them on the stand in order to assert the privilege); People v. Comfort, 151 A.D.2d 1019, 1020, 542 N.Y.S.2d 84, 85 (4th Dep't 1989)(where witness declares intent to claim privilege it appears not to be necessary to call him to stand to make him actually claim it).

29. See People v. Crampton, 107 A.D.2d 998, 999, 484 N.Y.S.2d 721, 722 (3d Dep't 1985).

30. See People v. Ely, 164 A.D.2d 442, 563 N.Y.S.2d 890 (3d Dep't 1990). Defendant, charged with arranging for the murder of her husband sought under Crim. Proc.Law § 670.10(1)(h) to have her prior testimony read in since her fifth amendment protection amounted to an "incapacity" within the meaning of the statute which creates the hearsay exception only when "the witness is unable to attend * * * by reason of death, illness of incapacity, or cannot with due diligence be found * * *."

Refusal to testify. Where the witness has no legitimate fifth amendment privilege, but persists in her refusal to testify after being ordered by the court to do so on pain of contempt, she will be deemed unavailable.[31]

Lack of memory. In *United States v. Garris*,[32] the defendant's sister appeared and gave some testimony, but professed to have forgotten other details. "After hearing Phyllis' testimony and inspecting Kirchenbauer's notes, the district court ruled that Phyllis's lack of memory of her statement made her an 'unavailable' witness under Fed.R.Evid. 804(a)(3), that the statements had been against her penal interest, and that therefore, after Phyllis testified before the jury as to her lack of memory, Kirchenbauer could testify as to her statement * * *."[33] This was approved on appeal.[34]

Death or illness. There is no more convincing ground of unavailability than that the declarant is dead. Illness and disability can also be a ground for unavailability, depending on the nature and duration of the malady. The criteria have been set forth as follows:

> Moreover, since witness availability affects the court's ability to manage its cases, the trial court's decision to refuse an adjournment and to admit prior testimony must be treated with respectful deference. In exercising discretion a trial court must consider all relevant circumstances, including: the importance of the absent witness for the case; the nature and extent of cross-examination in the earlier testimony; the nature of the illness; the expected time of recovery; the reliability of the evidence of the probable duration of the illness; and any special circumstances counselling against delay.[35]

The court noted that the choice whether or not to take the stand was hers. In fact she did testify at the second trial after her "ploy," as the court put it, came to naught "which seems to support our conclusion that she was not incapacitated." Id. at 446, 563 N.Y.S. at 893.

31. United States v. Zappola, 646 F.2d 48, 54 (2d Cir.1981), cert. denied sub nom., Melli v. U.S., 459 U.S. 866, 103 S.Ct. 145, 74 L.Ed.2d 122 (1982)("It is clear that in this case, the district court did not order Marano to testify. Instead, the district court relied on his assertion that he would refuse to testify even if ordered to by the court. The procedure that should have been followed by the court when faced with Marano's refusal to testify was (1) the issuance of an order, outside the presence of the jury, directing him to testify and (2) a warning that continued refusal to testify despite the court's order would be punishable by contempt."); see also United States v. Oliver, 626 F.2d 254, 261 (2d Cir. 1980)(judicial pressure without an order to testify is insufficient to create unavailability where witness persists in refusing to testify).

In a Seventh Circuit case, United States v. Boulahanis, 677 F.2d 586, 588 (7th Cir.), cert. denied, 459 U.S. 1016, 103 S.Ct. 375, 74 L.Ed.2d 509 (1982), the witness was found unavailable upon refusing to testify out of fear. It was not necessary, said the court, for him to have been ordered on pain of contempt to testify.

32. 616 F.2d 626 (2d Cir.), cert. denied, 447 U.S. 926, 100 S.Ct. 3021, 65 L.Ed.2d 1119 (1980).

33. Id. at 629.

34. Id. at 633.

35. United States v. Faison, 679 F.2d 292, 297 (3d Cir.1982). Application of this rule can be found in United States v. Donaldson, 978 F.2d 381 (7th Cir.1992), where the court allowed in evidence a videotaped deposition of a bank teller in a prosecution for bank robbery. The teller had given birth shortly before she was scheduled to testify and was in the hospital on the day of her scheduled testimony. Obviously this was not a long term disability, but the ruling was affirmed since defendant had been represented at the taking of the depo-

804(1) Former Testimony

§ 804(1).1 New York

a. Civil Cases

The rule against hearsay evidence is premised on the notion that the fact-finding process is best served when a witness testifies under oath and subject to cross-examination in the presence of the fact-finder. However, if a person has given sworn testimony, subject to cross-examination, on the same subject matter in a prior proceeding involving the same parties, and that person is now unavailable to testify, the prior testimony may be an acceptable substitute. This exception was recognized at common law, and CPLR 4517 has codified the essential common law doctrine.[1] The Advisory Committee on Practice and Procedure

The requirements for unavailability set forth in the Proposed New York Evidence Code are in the footnote.[36]

---

sition knowing that deponent might be unavailable.

36. § 804. Hearsay exceptions: declarant unavailable [PROPOSED]

(a) Definition of unavailability. "Unavailability as a witness," except for subparagraph (B) of paragraph one of subdivision (b) of this section, includes but is not limited to situations in which the declarant:

(1) is exempted by ruling of the court on the ground of privilege or incompetency from testifying concerning the subject matter of the statement;

(2) is unable to be present or to testify at the trial, proceeding, or hearing because of death or then existing physical or mental illness or infirmity; or

(3) is absent from the trial, proceeding, or hearing and the proponent of the statement has been unable to procure the declarant's attendance by process or other reasonable means. A declarant is not unavailable as a witness if the declarant's exemption, inability, or absence is procured by the proponent of the statement, or results from the proponent's culpable neglect or wrongdoing.

(b) Hearsay exceptions. The following are not excluded by the hearsay rule if the declarant is unavailable as a witness, provided (i) the declarant had personal knowledge, where such knowledge is required by the particular exception, and (ii) when the statement is a lay opinion, that opinion is rationally based on the perception of the declarant and is helpful to a clear understanding of the statement or to the determination of a fact in issue, or when the statement is an expert opinion it satisfies section 702 of this chapter, unless (iii) the party objecting to the statement establishes its untrustworthiness by proof of circumstances involving the making of the statement, including but not limited to a motive to falsify by the declarant.

The specific exceptions follow in the proposed § 804, which are taken up separately in the following sections.

§ 804(1).1

1. CPLR 4517. Prior testimony by unavailable witness

In a civil action, if a witness' testimony is not available because of privilege, death, physical or mental illness, absence beyond the jurisdiction of the court to compel appearance by its process or absence because the proponent of his statement does not know and with diligence has been unable to ascertain his whereabouts, or because he is incompetent to testify by virtue of section 4519, his testimony, taken or introduced in evidence at a former trial, together with all exhibits and documents introduced in connection with it, may be introduced in evidence by any party upon any trial of the same subject-matter in the same or another action between the same parties or their representatives, subject to any objection to admissibility other than hearsay. Such testimony may not be used if the witness' unavailability was procured by, or through the culpable neglect or wrongdoing of, the proponent of his statement. The original stenographic notes of testimony taken by a stenographer who has since died or become incompetent may be read in evidence by any person whose

§ 804(1).1　　HEARSAY　　Ch. 8

stated: "The prior testimony exception to the hearsay rule offers the maximum guarantee of trustworthiness since the original statement was made in court, under oath and subject to cross-examination by a party who had the same motive to expose falsehood and inaccuracy as does the opponent in the trial where the testimony is sought to be used."[2]

Because of the preference for live testimony, a showing of unavailability of the present testimony is a prerequisite to the use of the former testimony.[3] Whereas at early common law death was the only ground of unavailability,[4] CPLR 4517 specifies a range of grounds: death, claim of privilege; physical or mental illness; absence due to the inability of the proponent, with the use of due diligence, to ascertain the witness' whereabouts; or incompetency because the witness would be barred from testifying under the "Dead Man's Statute" (CPLR 4519).[5] And, CPLR 4517 states the obvious, that unavailability cannot be established where unavailability was procured by the proponent of the prior testimony.

In addition to a showing of unavailability, it must also be demonstrated that the former testimony carries indicia of reliability, and this can only occur when the party against whom the former testimony is now offered had adequate opportunity and incentive to cross-examine the witness in the prior proceeding.[6] CPLR 4517 therefore contains the key common law requirements that the prior testimony and the current trial concern the "same subject matter" and "same parties or their representatives."

The most significant New York case on the question of prior testimony is *Fleury v. Edwards*,[7] where it was held that CPLR 4517 (actually its predecessor, Civil Practice Act § 348) did not provide the exclusive rule for the admission of prior testimony—that the common law rule continued to co-exist and could provide a basis for admissibility where the statute might not. Under CPLR 4517 the prior testimony

competency to read them accurately is established to the satisfaction of the court.

2. N.Y.Adv.Comm.on Prac. and Proc., Second Prelim.Rep., Legis.Doc.No.13, p.265 (1958).

3. It may appear anomalous that a hearsay statement so thoroughly protected as to accuracy by the oath and the opportunity for cross-examination is relegated to the category of exceptions requiring unavailability rather that the category where availability is of no concern because the hearsay is arguably as reliable as the declarant's current testimony would be. On the other hand, as between two testimonial versions of the same story, the law prefers the one in which the declarant is in the presence of the current fact-finder.

4. Fleury v. Edwards, 14 N.Y.2d 334, 337–38, 251 N.Y.S.2d 647, 650, 200 N.E.2d 550, 552 (1964).

5. In a Family Court case a physician's prior testimony could be introduced in a custody proceeding where the petitioner, who had qualified for appointment of counsel, could not afford to pay the physician's expert witness fee. Noting that CPLR 4517 requires unavailability by reason of "absence beyond the jurisdiction of the court," among other grounds, the court found the physician unavailable because petitioner could not pay for his appearance, and he was needed to render opinions, and not facts for which the court could issue a subpoena. Thus his prior testimony was held admissible. Palma S. v. Carmine S., 134 Misc.2d 34, 509 N.Y.S.2d 527 (Family Ct. Kings Co.1986).

6. Healy v. Rennert, 9 N.Y.2d 202, 208–09, 213 N.Y.S.2d 44, 48–49, 173 N.E.2d 777, 780 (1961).

7. 14 N.Y.2d 334, 251 N.Y.S.2d 647, 200 N.E.2d 550 (1964).

must have been given in "a former trial," which was interpreted as being a prior action or proceeding.[8] In *Fleury* the former testimony was taken at a hearing conducted pursuant to the Vehicle and Traffic Law concerning an automobile accident at which both parties to the accident were represented and had the opportunity to cross-examine. Thereafter Fleury, one of the parties, died and his estate sued Edwards for wrongful death as a result of the same accident. Fleury's estate sought to admit testimony he had given at the administrative hearing, but the lower courts found that the statute for former testimony was inapplicable because it contained no provision for prior testimony given in an administrative proceeding. The Court of Appeals invoked the common law rule and found it flexible enough to accommodate this prior testimony since the necessary requisites of "same subject matter" and "same parties" were satisfied.[9] It is in the *Fleury* case that Judge Fuld's well-known call for general expansion of hearsay exceptions is found in his concurring opinion.[10]

This is not to say that CPLR 4517 itself cannot be liberally interpreted, especially with respect to the "same parties" requirement. In *Healy v. Rennert*,[11] another key holding, the court held that testimony by a now-deceased witness given in a criminal proceeding should have been admitted against the defendant in a subsequent civil action based on the same facts, *viz.*, defendant's alleged traffic violation. The parties were not identical inasmuch as the state had prosecuted the defendant in the first action and a private litigant sought damages in the second. The court's opinion makes clear that the rule does not require exact identity of parties. The key inquiry is whether "the party against whom the testimony is offered had an adequate opportunity to cross-examine the witness."[12] As to the similarity of subject matter, the court indicated that the inquiry should focus on whether "the issue was so nearly identical that the cross-examination in both instances would normally cover the same field."[13]

Concerning the opportunity to cross-examine, the question arises whether the opportunity alone is sufficient, or whether there must also have been an incentive to cross-examine. In *In re White's Will*,[14] testimony given during a prior incompetency proceeding was held properly admitted 30 years later in a probate proceeding concerning whether the now-deceased incompetent had the capacity to make a will. Those concerned in the probate proceeding had been cited as respondents at the incompetency proceeding and the subject matter was the same. Judge Van Voorhis dissented, stating that the respondents at the incom-

---

8. Id. at 338, 251 N.Y.S.2d at 650 200 N.E.2d at 552.

9. Id. at 339, 251 N.Y.S.2d at 651, 200 N.E.2d at 553.

10. Id. at 339–41, 251 N.Y.S.2d at 651–53, 200 N.E.2d at 553–59. See § 804(5).1, at note 3, infra.

11. 9 N.Y.2d 202, 213 N.Y.S.2d 44, 173 N.E.2d 777 (1961).

12. Id. at 208, 213 N.Y.S.2d at 48, 173 N.E.2d at 780.

13. Id. at 209, 213 N.Y.S.2d at 49, 173 N.E.2d at 780.

14. 2 N.Y.2d 309, 160 N.Y.S.2d 841, 141 N.E.2d 416 (1957).

§ 804(1).1   **HEARSAY**   Ch. 8

petency hearing had no motive to cross-examine the testator.[15] He later wrote the opinion in *Healy* in which he was satisfied, under different circumstances, that the party against whom the former testimony was offered "had the opportunity *and the inducement* to cross-examine [the witness] concerning the same aspects of the accident which were relevant upon [the subsequent] trial."[16] It should be noted that Federal Rule 804(b)(1), discussed in § 804(1).2 *infra*, requires there to have been a motive, in addition to an opportunity, to cross-examine, as does § 804(b)(1)(A) of the proposed New York Evidence Code.[17]

The statement in CPLR 4517 that the former testimony is "subject to any objection to admissibility other than hearsay" can only mean that had the prior testimony, when uttered violated an evidentiary rule such as irrelevance, the opinion rule, or even that it was itself hearsay, such objections can be raised based on the defect in the original testimony. Obviously it could not be objectionable at the subsequent trial, the hearsay exception for former testimony having been satisfied, that it is now hearsay.

While the nature of the prior proceeding or hearing at which the testimony was given is immaterial so long as the same subject matter is involved and the party against whom it is now offered had an opportunity and an inducement or motive to cross-examine,[18] testimony given by way of deposition does not fall under the rule. The admissibility of deposition testimony is governed by CPLR 3117. However, if a deposition were properly read into evidence at the former proceeding, it would seem that either CPLR 3117 or CPLR 4517 could provide access for this evidence at the subsequent trial.[19]

---

15. Id. at 317, 160 N.Y.S.2d at 847, 141 N.E.2d at 420.

16. Healy, 9 N.Y.2d at 208–09, 2113 N.Y.S.2d at 49, 173 N.E.2d at 780 (emphasis added). Other cases seem to ignore the motive element. See Matter of Will of Goldberg, 153 Misc.2d 560, 582 N.Y.S.2d 617 (Sur.Ct.N.Y.Co.1992)(opportunity to cross-examine is enough where parties' positions in both proceedings the same); Overseas Nat. Airways, Inc. v. General Elec. Co., 119 Misc.2d 72, 462 N.Y.S.2d 984 (Sup.Ct.Queens Co.1983)(opportunity to cross-examine was afforded, and if not taken, cross-examination deemed waived).

17. New York Code of Evidence [PROPOSED]:

§ 804

* * *

(b)(1) Former testimony.

(A) Civil cases. In a civil case, testimony given as a witness at another trial, proceeding, or hearing of the same subject matter in the same or in a different case, or in a deposition taken in compliance with statute in the course of the same or another proceeding, if the party against whom the testimony is now offered, or a person in privity with that party, had an opportunity and motive to develop or limit the testimony by direct, cross, or redirect examination. Former testimony may be proved by an authenticated transcript or recording; if an authenticated transcript or recording cannot be obtained by the exercise of reasonable diligence, other evidence of the testimony may be admitted.

18. In addition to the Fleury and Healy cases, see also Rothman v. City of New York, 273 App.Div. 780, 75 N.Y.S.2d 151 (2d Dep't 1947)(in action for personal injuries suffered as a consequence of being struck by trolley, examination before city comptroller was properly received where claimant died before trial; it is assumed the other requisites were satisfied, although this does not appear in the terse memorandum).

19. See Sigman–Weiss Consultants, Inc. v. Raiff, 149 Misc.2d 111, 563 N.Y.S.2d 618 (Sup.Ct.Kings Co.1990)(party's deposition of self could be used at trial where adverse party since deceased); see note 23, infra.

Ch. 8   FORMER TESTIMONY   § 804(1).1

The "same subject matter" requirement has been given varying interpretations,[20] as has the unavailability requirement[21] and the variants of absence,[22] the Dead Man's incompetency,[23] and mental incompetency.[24]

The last sentence of CPLR 4517 provides that the prior testimony may be presented at trial through the transcript if the stenographer has since died; but surely the transcript could be used even if the stenographer is not dead[25] under the public records hearsay exception (see § 803(5).1 supra). And there appears no reason why, as permitted under the common law, any person who heard the testimony could not

---

20. See Monahan v. Monahan, 29 A.D.2d 1046, 289 N.Y.S.2d 812 (4th Dep't 1968)(in divorce action where wife sought to prove husband's adultery, it was improper to admit testimony given at husband's criminal trial that the witness spent several nights at a hotel with the husband; subject matter was different and defense counsel did not have same motive to cross-examine the witness); Sabathie v. Russo, 21 A.D.2d 911, 252 N.Y.S.2d 15 (2d Dep't 1964)(testimony at a previous Motor Vehicle hearing, unlike the testimony in Fleury, not admissible since other requirements not met); Turner v. Sunshine Taxi Corp., 269 App.Div. 997, 58 N.Y.S.2d 422 (2d Dep't 1945)(testimony given in Magistrate's Court improperly admitted in wrongful death action, where defendant had not been a party in Magistrate's Court).

21. See National Hotel Management Corp. v. Shelton Towers Assoc., 188 A.D.2d 305, 590 N.Y.S.2d 476 (1st Dep't 1992) (privilege ground for unavailability not recognized where the witness at trial refused to answer all questions and not just those which could have been incriminating; moreover, where, as here, the witness is the party, he cannot successfully claim his own "unavailability" at second trial by asserting the fifth amendment).

22. See City of Buffalo v. J.W. Clement Co., Inc., 45 A.D.2d 620, 360 N.Y.S.2d 362 (4th Dep't 1974), appeal denied, 35 N.Y.2d 645, 366 N.Y.S.2d 1025, 324 N.E.2d 560, appeal dismissed, 36 N.Y.2d 713, 366 N.Y.S.2d 1029, 325 N.E.2d 883 (1975). The court stated: CPLR 4517 "does not require that any efforts, let alone diligent efforts as maintained by the City, be made to secure the attendance of such a witness. In this case, there was adequate foundation laid for the absence of the two Clement witnesses whose testimony is objected to by the City." Presumably, although it is not in the opinion, the witnesses were no longer employed by the proponent and their whereabouts were unknown. See also Rohrmayr v. City of New York, 33 A.D.2d 920, 307 N.Y.S.2d 539 (2d Dep't 1970)(witness who testified at vehicular homicide hearing unavailable at precise time of trial of personal injury action, but his testimony not admissible because he could be produced within two weeks; court properly refused to adjourn trial and was not required to admit former testimony).

23. See Matter of Estate of Mead, 129 A.D.2d 1008, 514 N.Y.S.2d 581 (4th Dep't), appeal denied, 70 N.Y.2d 609, 522 N.Y.S.2d 109, 516 N.E.2d 1222 (1987). In this case a party had become incompetent to testify by reason of the "Dead Man's Statute" (CPLR 4519) and wanted to introduce a deposition taken in connection with a prior proceeding. But the now-deceased party had been unable to cross-examine the deponent at the prior time. Compare Siegel v. Waldbaum, 59 A.D.2d 555, 397 N.Y.S.2d 144 (2d Dep't 1977), where a party was permitted under the common law rule to read in evidence his deposition concerning a transaction with the now-deceased opposing party because at the time of the deposition the other party was alive and present to confront. See also Sigman–Weiss Consultants, Inc. v. Raiff, 149 Misc.2d 111, 563 N.Y.S.2d 618 (Sup.Ct.Kings Co.1990)(party's deposition of self may qualify as former testimony if adverse party dies between time of deposition and trial); Rosenberg v. Grace, 158 Misc.2d 32, 600 N.Y.S.2d 425 (Sup.Ct. N.Y.Co.1993)(plaintiff not permitted to introduce his own deposition where now-deceased defendant had not appeared at deposition and had not given his own deposition).

24. Aguilar v. State, 279 App.Div. 103, 108 N.Y.S.2d 456, amended on other grounds, 279 App.Div.1121, 112 N.Y.S.2d 779 (3d Dep't 1952), appeal withdrawn, 304 N.Y. 616, 107 N.E.2d 94 (1952)(incarceration in a mental institution does not prove unavailability; it must be shown that witness is incompetent to testify).

25. See Palma S. v. Carmine S., 134 Misc.2d 34, 37, 509 N.Y.S.2d 527, 529 (Family Ct.Kings Co.1986).

§ 804(1).1   HEARSAY   Ch. 8

relay its substance at the second trial, perhaps aided by the transcript as a memory refreshment device.

b. Criminal Cases

The rule respecting the use of prior testimony in criminal trials is very different from that governing this hearsay exception in civil trials. Due to the concern for protection of the criminal defendant's confrontation rights,[26] the Legislature enacted Criminal Procedure Law § 670.10,[27] which is much more limited in scope than its civil counterpart, CPLR 4517, and is not augmented by aspects of the common law rule as is CPLR 4517.[28]

By the terms of § 670.10(1) the only usable prior testimony must have been given in a *related*[29] prior criminal trial, preliminary hearing, or a hearing under Article 660 of the Criminal Procedure Law, which provides for the taking of testimony for future use when there is a good chance the witness will not be available at the trial because he will leave the state or will be physically ill or incapacitated.[30] There is no allowance here for testimony given in some other criminal proceeding (supposing the present defendant was there represented and entitled to cross-examine),[31] or unaccountably, even in other sorts of hearings in the same criminal proceeding such as suppression hearings where defendant

---

26. People v. Arroyo, 54 N.Y.2d 567, 446 N.Y.S.2d 910, 431 N.E.2d 271 (1982).

27. § 670.10 **Use in a criminal proceeding of testimony given in a previous proceeding; when authorized**

1. Under circumstances prescribed in this article, testimony given by a witness at (a) a trial of an accusatory instrument, or (b) a hearing upon a felony complaint conducted pursuant to section 180.60, or (c) an examination of such witness conditionally, conducted pursuant to article six hundred sixty, may, where otherwise admissible, be received into evidence at a subsequent proceeding in or relating to the action involved when at the time of such subsequent proceeding the witness is unable to attend the same by reason of death, illness or incapacity, or cannot with due diligence be found, or is outside the state or in federal custody and cannot with due diligence be brought before the court. Upon being received into evidence, such testimony may be read and any videotape or photographic recording thereof played. Where any recording is received into evidence, the stenographic transcript of that examination shall also be received.

2. The subsequent proceedings at which such testimony may be received in evidence consist of:

(a) Any proceeding constituting a part of a criminal action based upon the charge or charges which were pending against the defendant at the time of the witness's testimony and to which such testimony related; and

(b) Any post-judgment proceeding in which a judgment of conviction upon a charge specified in paragraph (a) is challenged.

28. See Fleury v. Edwards, 14 N.Y.2d 334, 251 N.Y.S.2d 647, 200 N.E.2d 550 (1964), discussed in text at notes 7–10 supra.

29. Certainly if the prior hearing is part of the prosecution of the same charge, the relatedness requirement is satisfied. In People v. Prince, 106 A.D.2d 521, 483 N.Y.S.2d 57 (2d Dep't 1984), aff'd, 66 N.Y.2d 935, 498 N.Y.S.2d 797, 489 N.E.2d 766 (1985), the court allowed the use of testimony "taken at a preliminary hearing to be introduced into evidence at a subsequent trial on a related, but separate, crime." Id. at 522, 483 N.Y.S.2d at 58. There is no further explanation of the nature of the relation.

30. N.Y.Crim.Proc.Law § 660.20.

31. People v. Harding, 37 N.Y.2d 130, 371 N.Y.S.2d 493, 332 N.E.2d 354 (1975). See note 33 infra.

would be represented and entitled to cross-examine.[32]

Testimony from any of the three approved contexts, by terms of subdivision 2 of the statute, may be used in *any* subsequent phase of the same criminal proceeding including post-judgment proceedings such as a habeas corpus hearing.

Pursuant to subdivision 1, declarant, of course, must be unavailable to testify again at the subsequent hearing, and such unavailability can be established by reason of death, illness or incapacity, or absence without reasonable likelihood either of locating him or, if locatable, of procuring his presence by use of due diligence.

Even though the Court of Appeals has been unwilling to stretch the statute's coverage[33] and insists that even in otherwise covered proceedings there must have been full and fair opportunity to cross-examine,[34] it was willing in *People v. Arroyo*[35] to affirm a conviction based almost wholly on the missing victim's preliminary hearing testimony. Defendant's "common-law wife" was the victim of multiple stab wounds. She cooperated with the police and gave testimony at a preliminary hearing accusing defendant of the assault. Just before the trial she disappeared. The trial judge found the prosecutor had employed due diligence to locate her and that her testimony was necessary. The prosecutor had no other witnesses. The preliminary hearing had been conducted in an open manner and "delved into substantially the same subject matter as did the trial on which it later was to be used."[36] There was nothing to support defendant's claim that the hearing judge had been "too restrictive" in his rulings on certain aspects of the cross-examination.[37]

---

32. People v. Ayala, 75 N.Y.2d 422, 554 N.Y.S.2d 412, 553 N.E.2d 960 (1990). See note 38 infra.

33. See People v. Harding, 37 N.Y.2d 130, 371 N.Y.S.2d 493, 332 N.E.2d 354 (1975). The witness in Harding testified against a police officer in an administrative disciplinary hearing brought on bribery charges. The witness died thereafter, and her testimony was sought to be used at the trial of an indictment against the officer based on the same charges. Id. at 132, 371 N.Y.S.2d at 494, 332 N.E.2d at 355. The court noted that § 670.10 by its terms did not cover testimony taken at an administrative hearing and refused to judicially extend it as had been done in the case of its civil counterpart, CPLR 4517.

34. See People v. Simmons, 36 N.Y.2d 126, 365 N.Y.S.2d 812, 325 N.E.2d 139 (1975)(court refused to allow testimony taken at a preliminary hearing held in the same prosecution because the hearing judge had closely restricted the scope of defense counsel's cross-examination of the then missing-witness).

35. 54 N.Y.2d 567, 446 N.Y.S.2d 910, 431 N.E.2d 271 (1982).

36. Id. at 575, 446 N.Y.S.2d at 915, 431 N.E.2d at 276.

37. Id. Defense counsel in this case attempted a ploy whereby she argued that she had a right to strike her cross-examination of the witness at the preliminary hearing, apparently because she had some sort of proprietary right over her questions. The court rejected this argument, however, stating that, "[o]nce uttered, the testimony was not the exclusive property of either party." Id. at 577, 446 N.Y.S.2d at 916, 431 N.E.2d at 277. The court also rejected the defendant's argument that a criminal conviction could not rest solely on uncorroborated hearsay. Judge Fuchsberg briefly reviewed the corroboration rules and pointed out that such was not necessary to validate a victim's testimony even if admitted as prior testimony. He stated further:

There may be instances in which, though the circumstances surrounding prior testimony have rendered it admissible, in the context of the entire case as it develops, the prior testimony, by itself, will be found insufficient to support a guilty verdict beyond a reasonable doubt. But here, the people not only met the test of trustworthiness posed by the confrontation issue, but, on the record already detailed, the prior testimony could serve as a basis on which to uphold the conviction.

The *Arroyo* case conformed to the literal requirements of the statute, and satisfied the additional court-made test requiring adequate opportunity to cross-examine even in a hearing otherwise covered under the statute. But where the prior testimony stems from a related suppression hearing,[38] a related grand jury hearing,[39] or a related administrative hearing,[40] it will not be admissible. It has been expressly stated that § 670.10 is the exclusive vehicle for admitting prior testimony *qua* prior testimony;[41] but the content of a statement rendered in the form of prior testimony might be admissible under another hearsay exception.[42]

Unavailability and due diligence. The decision in the *Arroyo* case sets quite reasonable standards for establishing whether due diligence was employed in trying to produce the witness. There, even though the complainant decided after her preliminary hearing testimony that she wanted to "drop the charges" the prosecutor kept her on a long leash. When she disappeared on the eve of trial it became clear that the

---

Id. at 578, 446 N.Y.S.2d at 917, 431 N.E.2d at 276.

38. In People v. Ayala, 75 N.Y.2d 422, 554 N.Y.S.2d 412, 553 N.E.2d 960 (1990), defendant was charged with stabbing the victim, and the chief evidence against him consisted of eyewitness testimony plus several out-of-court statements. The first such testimony was given at a Wade hearing by Zina Everett, who was unavailable at trial. She testified that she saw an object in defendant's hand when he attacked the victim. The two other statements came from witnesses questioned by the police after the crime was committed. None of the statements should have been admitted. The Wade testimony was not the sort of prior testimony included under § 670.10 because it fit none of the listed categories. Such a hearing is not a part of the trial, which begins after the jury is sworn. By definition a Wade hearing cannot be part of the trial because it is a pretrial suppression hearing. Even though there was ample opportunity for defense counsel to cross-examine Everett at the hearing, this alone cannot supplant the clear provisions of the statute. Id. at 429, 554 N.Y.S.2d at 415, 553 N.E.2d at 963.

Although admission of the Wade testimony was error, it only involved the misapplication of a statute and was not a constitutional violation. Id. at 431, 554 N.Y.S.2d at 416, 553 N.E.2d at 964.

39. In People v. Green, 78 N.Y.2d 1029, 576 N.Y.S.2d 75, 581 N.E.2d 1330 (1991), it was held reversible error for a trial judge to have allowed a witness' grand jury testimony identifying defendant as the murderer. The witness was a nine-year-old boy who, since his grand jury experience, had lost all recollection of the murder committed in his presence. And even though there was abundant other evidence of defendant's guilt, "[u]nder the circumstances of this case, in which identification was the central issue, [the court could not] conclude that the error was harmless." Id. at 1030, 576 N.Y.S.2d at 76, 581 N.E.2d at 1331.

40. See People v. Harding, 37 N.Y.2d 130, 371 N.Y.S.2d 493, 332 N.E.2d 354 (1975), supra notes 31, 33.

41. Judge Titone made this clear in People v. Ayala, 75 N.Y.2d 422, 429, 554 N.Y.S.2d 412, 415, 553 N.E.2d 960, 963 (1990), supra, note 32.

42. In a case decided several months before Ayala came down there was an intimation in People v. Morgan, 151 A.D.2d 221, 547 N.Y.S.2d 711 (4th Dep't 1989), aff'd, 76 N.Y.2d 493, 561 N.Y.S.2d 408, 562 N.E.2d 485 (1990), that § 670.10 was not the exclusive route for such testimony. Defendant argued, for the first time on appeal, that a witness' grand jury testimony could not come in as prior testimony under § 670.10. In a footnote it was stated: "[t]he claim is not persuasive * * * because while the statute mentions specific instances where prior testimony may be used in a criminal proceeding it does not prohibit testimony from being admitted by other means * * *." Id. at 224 n.1, 547 N.Y.S.2d at 712. If the court was referring to common law prior testimony exceptions this was wrong in light of the later statement in Ayala. If, however, this was a reference to the same statements coming in under another hearsay exception, then it would be correct. It appears in Morgan that the question was whether grand jury testimony was a statement against penal interest, a point discussed by the Court of Appeals in its affirmance.

See also People v. Ferraro, 293 N.Y. 51, 55 N.E.2d 861 (1944), where grand jury statements were used to impeach.

prosecutor should have done more to insure her attendance at trial. Nevertheless, the court was unwilling to penalize the prosecutor for what appeared in hindsight to be questionable judgment (although all during the period leading up to the trial the witness seemed cooperative), and found that the procurement of a material witness order and investigation by police constituted reasonable attempts to locate her.

Although unavailability due to an assertion of privilege is not listed in § 670.10, the Appellate Division has held refusal to testify on fifth amendment grounds as satisfying the unavailability requirements of the statute.[43] A defendant, however, was not allowed to present her testimony from her first trial when at her second trial she decided not to take the stand.[44]

Absence of the witness constitutes probably the most frequent basis of unavailability. The proponent of the prior testimony must not be responsible for the witness' absence and must have used due diligence in trying to procure the witness' presence. Thus, where a prosecution witness was on an extended trip in what was then Yugoslavia when the second trial commenced, the court allowed the use of his testimony given at the first trial, since the prosecutor bore no fault in the matter.[45] In another case, admissibility was decreed where a reluctant witness disappeared, there was no indication the prosecution had anything to do with the disappearance, and it was found that additional efforts to locate the witness would be futile.[46]

---

43. People v. Varsos, 182 A.D.2d 508, 509, 582 N.Y.S.2d 193, 194 (1st Dep't 1992)("The court properly admitted the sworn testimony of the shooter, given at defendant's first trial herein which terminated with a hung jury, on the ground that the refusal of this witness to testify at the instant trial, based upon his Fifth Amendment privilege, rendered him an 'unavailable' witness within the meaning of CPL 670.10.").

44. In People v. Ely, 164 A.D.2d 442, 563 N.Y.S.2d 890 (3d Dep't 1990), the court agreed that assertion of the privilege could constitute unavailability under the statute (citing People v. Muccia, 139 A.D.2d 838, 839, 527 N.Y.S.2d 620, 621 (3d Dep't 1988)), but held that in this situation defendant could not create her own unavailability by refusing to take the stand at the second trial. She had the choice, and in fact did testify at her second trial after her "ploy," as the court put it, came to naught "which seems to support our conclusion that she was not incapacitated." Id. at 446, 563 N.Y.S.2d at 893. The court went on: "nor is there any merit in defendant's claim that she was compelled to testify by the denial of her motion [to use her prior testimony]. As noted * * * she was under no compulsion to testify when she made the motion and the proper denial of her motion did not alter that fact." Id.

45. People v. Carracedo, 147 Misc.2d 1093, 1097, 559 N.Y.S.2d 784, 787 (Sup.Ct. Bronx Co.1990). ("The People should not be forced into a position of delaying a three-year-old case for at least an additional five months to await the unascertainable arrival of a peripheral witness and shoulder the additional heavy burden of rescheduling the appearance of 19 witnesses who are presently ready to proceed.").

46. People v. Wiggins, 189 A.D.2d 908, 910, 593 N.Y.S.2d 62, 63 (2d Dep't 1993). See also People v. Nucci, 162 A.D.2d 725, 726, 557 N.Y.S.2d 422, 423–24 (2d Dep't 1990)(court conducted hearing and was satisfied that reluctant witness could not be produced despite best efforts of the prosecutor); People v. Nettles, 118 A.D.2d 875, 876, 500 N.Y.S.2d 361, 363 (2d Dep't), appeal denied, 68 N.Y.2d 671, 505 N.Y.S.2d 1037, 496 N.E.2d 695 (1986)(it was enough that "once the witness failed to appear at the trial, a material witness order was issued, and an investigator from the prosecutor's office made extensive efforts over the course of three days to locate her"); People v. Tumerman, 133 A.D.2d 714, 715, 519 N.Y.S.2d 880, 881 (2d Dep't), appeal denied, 70 N.Y.2d 938, 524 N.Y.S.2d 690, 519 N.E.2d 636 (1987), cert. denied, 485 U.S. 969, 108 S.Ct. 1245, 99 L.Ed.2d 443, on reconsideration appeal denied, 72 N.Y.2d

Defendant's waiver of the statutory requirements. Where the defendant procures the absence of a prosecution witness, as, for example, through threats and intimidation, the strict requirements of § 670.10 cease to apply. The prosecution may then introduce prior testimony from such sources as grand jury testimony upon clear and convincing proof of defendant's tampering activity.[47] So held the Court of Appeals in *People v. Geraci*,[48] discussed at § 807.1 *infra*.

Similarly, where the witness attends the trial, claims amnesia, and it can be shown that the loss of memory was brought on by defendant's threats, the witness will be treated as unavailable and his grand jury testimony allowed.[49] The court must hold a hearing to determine whether the prosecutor can prove defendant's waiver of his § 670.10 protection, and hence of a part of his confrontation rights.[50] The guiding force for these rules is found in the Second Circuit's opinion in *United States v. Mastrangelo*.[51]

Defendant's right to produce prior testimony. The statute does not specify that it pertains only to prosecution witnesses. It sometimes happens that a defense witness is unavailable to testify, in which case defendant's constitutional right to present a defense would outweigh the limitations of § 670.10.[52]

867, 532 N.Y.S.2d 517, 528 N.E.2d 908 (1988)(it was enough that the missing witness was not under the People's control and the prosecutor stated that he had ascertained from the witness' closest relatives that she was in Europe and that her whereabouts there and her return date were unknown).

47. See People v. Tuzzio, 201 A.D.2d 595, 596, 608 N.Y.S.2d 226, 227 (2d Dep't 1994), appeal denied, 83 N.Y.2d 877, 613 N.Y.S.2d 137, 635 N.E.2d 306 (1994)(the People proved by "clear and convincing evidence" that defendant had threatened the complaining witness, stalked her and effectively scared her off thus permitting her grand jury testimony to be admitted); People v. Small, 177 A.D.2d 669, 576 N.Y.S.2d 595, 596 (2d Dep't 1991), appeal denied, 79 N.Y.2d 953, 583 N.Y.S.2d 207, 592 N.E.2d 815 (1992)(the prosecutor produced evidence from several sources of defendant's threats, and the fact the witness believed that in other instances defendant had "put out contracts" on witnesses who had testified against him).

48. 85 N.Y.2d 359, 625 N.Y.S.2d 469, 649 N.E.2d 817 (1995).

49. People v. Pappalardo, 152 Misc.2d 364, 367, 576 N.Y.S.2d 1001, 1003 (Sup.Ct. Kings Co.1991).

50. Matter of Holtzman v. Hellenbrand, 92 A.D.2d 405, 460 N.Y.S.2d 591 (2d Dep't 1983)("whenever the People allege specific facts which demonstrate a 'distinct possibility' * * * that a criminal defendant's misconduct has induced a witness' unlawful refusal to testify at trial or has caused the witness' disappearance or demise, the People shall be given the opportunity to prove that misconduct at an evidentiary hearing * * * [at which] the burden shall be upon the People to prove defendant's misconduct by clear and convincing evidence * * * and * * * upon an affirmative finding by the court on the issue of defendant's misconduct, the defendant will be deemed to have waived any objection to the admissibility of the witness' prior Grand Jury testimony and said testimony may be admitted as direct evidence at the defendant's trial." Id. at 415, 460 N.Y.S.2d at 597).

51. 693 F.2d 269 (2d Cir.1982). The Mastrangelo court reviewed an array of authority dealing with a defendant's waiver of trial rights either by consent or misconduct. Id. at 272–73.

52. See People v. Legrande, 176 A.D.2d 351, 352, 574 N.Y.S.2d 780, 782 (2d Dep't 1991). The court noted that defendant had exercised due diligence in attempting to procure the presence of his alibi witness, and cited and quoted from the Second Circuit habeas corpus case Rosario v. Kuhlman, 839 F.2d 918 (2d Cir.1988) as follows:

The right to present a defense is one of the "minimum essentials of a fair trial." * * * It is a right which derives not only from the general fairness requirements of the due process clause of the fourteenth

§ 804(1).2 Federal

Federal Rule of Evidence 804(b)(1) provides:

> **(1) Former testimony.** Testimony given as a witness at another hearing of the same or a different proceeding, or in a deposition taken in compliance with law in the course of the same or another proceeding, if the party against whom the testimony is now offered, or, in a civil action or proceeding a predecessor in interest, had an opportunity and similar motive to develop the testimony by direct, cross, or redirect examination.

Remembering that unavailability is a requisite for all the Rule 804 hearsay exceptions, we note several points of interest in comparing Rule 804(b)(1) with its New York counterparts CPLR 4517, and Criminal Procedure Law § 670.10, discussed in the last section. First, Rule 804(b)(1) applies to both civil and criminal cases. Second, both New York provisions require that the testimony have been given in a trial of the same subject matter, or upon the same criminal charge, whereas under Rule 804(b)(1) the source of the testimony may be the same or a different proceeding. And third, whereas the state rules are silent about the opportunity for cross-examination (the case decisions filling that omission), the Federal Rule is very specific in stating that the party against whom the testimony is offered must have had "an opportunity and similar motive to develop the testimony by direct, cross, or redirect examination."

Ironically, it is this specificity with regard to examination of the witness at the prior trial that has caused the most turmoil in the Second Circuit.

Opportunity and motive to cross-examine at the first trial. In *United States v. Salerno*,[1] the question was whether testimony given by two mob witnesses before a grand jury which tended to exonerate the defendant could be used at defendant's trial by defendant where the witnesses were unavailable to testify because of the assertion of their fifth amendment rights, and the prosecutor's refusal to confer immunity. The trial judge amendment but also, and more directly, from the compulsory process clause of the sixth amendment. It is a right which comprehends more than the right to present the direct testimony of live witnesses, and includes the right, under certain circumstances, to place before the jury secondary forms of evidence, such as hearsay or, as here, prior testimony.

Id. at 924. See also People v. Tinh Phan, 150 Misc.2d 435, 568 N.Y.S.2d 498 (Sup.Ct. Kings Co.1990). The Tinh Phan court followed the Second Department's Rosario rationale just above quoted and found that defendant would ordinarily be entitled to use the grand jury testimony of a missing alibi witness, except that here he had not proved due diligence in procuring the presence of the witness: "The extent of the investigation, consisting of ringing doorbells, visiting one relative of the witness, and telephone calls, does not satisfy this court that the witness is unavailable." Id. at 441, 568 N.Y.S.2d at 503.

§ 804(1).2

1. 505 U.S. 317, 112 S.Ct. 2503, 120 L.Ed.2d 255 (1992).

§ 804(1).2   HEARSAY   Ch. 8

found that the prosecutor did not have a similar motive to develop the testimony at the grand jury stage because the investigatory stage of the criminal process provides different motives for producing testimony than does the trial stage.

The Second Circuit reversed, ruling that the similar motives requirement was not applicable where there would be "adversarial [un]fairness" were the evidence excluded.[2] If this prior testimony were kept out the prosecutor would have an unfair advantage by simply refusing to confer immunity at trial thus forcing defendant to forego any use of this favorable evidence.

The Supreme Court reversed, holding that the similar motives requirement cannot simply be disregarded on the basis of abstract fairness. The party against whom the prior testimony is offered, here the prosecutor, must have had a similar motive on the earlier occasion to develop the testimony. The case was sent back for a determination on that point.[3]

Under the new title *United States v. DiNapoli*,[4] the court, *en banc*, decided that the similar motive requirement was not met and that the former grand jury testimony was properly excluded. This overruled a panel decision, made pursuant to the Supreme Court remand, that what the prosecutor did with these witnesses at the grand jury stage is what he would have done at trial.[5] Likening this to the principle that bars the use of issue preclusion when the first suit is not of the stature of the second suit,[6] the *en banc* court said the rule must turn on the question whether there is a substantially similar degree of interest on that issue at each occasion. While holding that there is no *per se* rule against the later use of grand jury testimony by the defendant,[7] the court said that the prosecutor is not normally the "opponent" of a grand jury witness and is merely trying to develop the facts to see if an indictment is warranted. The inquiry in each case must be "fact specific," and the motivation in dealing with witnesses will vary from grand jury to grand jury.[8]

Of course the prosecution can never seek to use grand jury testimony pursuant to Rule 804(b)(1) because defense counsel would have had no opportunity to cross-examine[9] (although it might be admissible for

---

2. United States v. Salerno, 937 F.2d 797, 806 (2d Cir.1991).

3. 505 U.S. at 324–25, 112 S.Ct. at 2508–09, 120 L.Ed.2d at 260–62.

4. 8 F.3d 909 (2d Cir.1993).

5. United States v. Salerno, 974 F.2d 231 (2d Cir.1992).

6. 8 F.3d at 912.

7. Id. at 913.

8. Id. at 914. Applying these principles, the court found, first, that in this case defendants had already been indicted, thus lessening any interest in impeaching the witness' testimony at that point. Id. at 915. Second, the prosecutor had been advised by grand jurors that they did not believe the witnesses anyway, thus virtually eliminating any motivation the prosecutor might have to go after the witnesses. Id. Three judges from the en banc group of 11 dissented, finding that the majority had changed the statutory requirement of "similar motive" to a judge-made requirement of "same motive."

9. See United States v. Jones, 402 F.2d 851 (2d Cir.1968)(codefendant's grand jury testimony inadmissible against defendant under the newly decided case of Bruton v. United States, 391 U.S. 123, 88 S.Ct. 1620, 20 L.Ed.2d 476 (1968); would be inadmissible under later enacted Rule 804(b)(1) sim-

710

Ch. 8   **FORMER TESTIMONY**   **§ 804(1).2**

other purposes such as for impeachment or under another hearsay exception; or defendant may have procured the witness' absence in which case he might well be deemed to have waived his objection to use of the testimony).[10] While the situation in *Salerno-DiNapoli* should not occur often, the opinions in that case offer helpful guidelines for the more common situations involving testimony at preliminary hearings and suppression hearings, and of course at other trials, where the party against whom the testimony is offered was represented. Motive ought to be more easily analyzed in those contexts, and indeed the courts seem to have had little trouble even before these opinions.

Thus, in separate trials of defendants involved in the same or related crimes or in civil proceedings, motives to examine or cross-examine may well shift and change;[11] and this ties in with the problem of differences in the issues in the two situations.[12] As respects depositions, to which reference is made in Rule 804(b)(1), if they are sought to be introduced under Rule 804(b)(1) rather than Rule 32 of the Federal Rules of Civil Procedure, all of the requirements for Rule 804(b)(1)

---

ply because there was no opportunity, much less any motivation, to cross-examine).

10. See discussion in § 804(1).1(b) supra. Grand jury testimony of a deceased prosecution witness might be admissible under the residual provisions of Rule 804(b)(5). United States v. Yonkers Contracting Co., Inc., 701 F.Supp. 431, 437 (S.D.N.Y.1988). See discussion of this case in § 804(5).2, in text at note 13, infra.

11. See United States v. Serna, 799 F.2d 842 (2d Cir.1986), cert. denied sub nom., Cinnante v. United States, 481 U.S. 1013, 107 S.Ct. 1887, 95 L.Ed.2d 494 (1987), where coconspirators were tried separately. Chupurdy testified at his own trial. Serna, at his trial, wanted to use Chupurdy's testimony since it tended to exonerate Serna, and Chupurdy would assert the fifth amendment at Serna's trial. The court pointed out that since it was clear Chupurdy's denial of a key issue in his trial would not be shaken "the prosecutor, wisely we think, chose to focus his cross-examination on the details [of another issue]." Id. at 849. The court approved of the trial court's offer to allow defendant to use Chupurdy's testimony on condition that the Serna jury be advised that obviously the Chupurdy jury did not believe Chupurdy inasmuch as they convicted him, an offer rejected by defense counsel. The court found no abuse of discretion in the judge's offer since this would have been a legitimate credibility attack on hearsay evidence under Federal Rule 806. Id. at 850.

See also Pacelli v. Nassau County Police Dept., 639 F.Supp. 1382 (E.D.N.Y.1986), a civil rights suit where plaintiff charged the police with fabricating evidence against him. In a previous criminal prosecution one Lipsky rendered a perjurious confession which implicated Pacelli and supposedly encouraged the police to produce evidence to corroborate Lipsky's confession. Plaintiff wanted to produce Lipsky's testimony from the criminal trial, but the court pointed out that the prosecutor's objectives in redirect examination of Lipsky at that trial were different than would be defense counsel's objectives at the civil rights trial. Id. at 1386.

In Matter of Sterling Nav. Co., Ltd., 444 F.Supp. 1043 (S.D.N.Y.1977), it was found that in bankruptcy proceedings a rule X1–4 hearing was a non-adversary proceeding which lacked defined issues and that hence testimony given at such a hearing could not be introduced at a later hearing where relief was sought against a bankrupt corporation. There was no similar motive to cross-examine the witness. Id. at 1046.

12. See United States v. Wingate, 520 F.2d 309 (2d Cir.1975), cert. denied, 423 U.S. 1074, 96 S.Ct. 858, 47 L.Ed.2d 84 (1976), where it was stated: "The issue at the suppression hearing in this case was not whether Wingate was guilty or innocent but rather whether Smith's confession was made voluntarily so that it could be used in the Government's case against him. The Government therefore had no meaningful opportunity to cross-examine Smith as to Wingate's involvement in a narcotics conspiracy, which was the issue on which Wingate later sought to introduce his testimony." Id. at 316.

§ 804(1).2   HEARSAY   Ch. 8

admission must be satisfied.[13]

A closely related factor concerns the scope of the hearing in which the prior testimony was given. The Supreme Court has had several opportunities to appraise the use of prior testimony in state court criminal cases in light of the confrontation requirement. In *Barber v. Page*,[14] the Court said that "[a] preliminary hearing is ordinarily a much less searching exploration into the merits of a case than a trial simply because its function is the more limited one of determining whether probable cause exists to hold the accused for trial."[15] But in a later case, *Ohio v. Roberts*,[16] the Court approved the use of preliminary hearing testimony where there are "sufficient indicia of reliability," and the hearsay exception, such as the prior testimony exception, is "firmly rooted."[17] The *Roberts* Court declined to decide whether it is sufficient if counsel merely has the opportunity to cross-examine, or whether there must be actual cross-examination in order to protect the confrontation right.[18] Defense counsel had, in fact, partaken of cross-examination. But the Court did quote with apparent approval language from its earlier decision in *California v. Green*,[19] which indicated that the opportunity to cross-examine, whether utilized or not, would be an adequate protection of the confrontation right.[20] Where the testimony of a prosecution witness was taken at defendant's prior trial, rather than at a preliminary hearing, the Supreme Court in *Mancusi v. Stubbs*[21] had no trouble in finding it admissible at defendant's second trial when it was shown that the witness was unavailable. It was observed in the opinion that the witness had been cross-examined at the first trial,[22] although there is no indication in the opinion that this would have been a requisite.

What with the concern for the nature and quality of the cross-examination in the prior proceeding, and with whether the opportunity alone satisfies the rule (so long as motives remained similar), one would expect there to be great concern with the scope of a discovery proceeding at which a deposition was taken, to say nothing of counsel's motive for

---

13. See United States v. Intern. Business Machines Corp., 90 F.R.D. 377 (S.D.N.Y.1981): "Although Rule 804 is an independent basis for admission of a deposition, it will not provide a basis for the admission of the depositions here offered by IBM. IBM has not demonstrated that the depositions meet any of the unavailability criteria under Rule 804. It has stated only that the deponents are beyond a distance of 100 miles from the courthouse, which is an insufficient assertion to demonstrate unavailability under Rule 804." Id. at 384. Presumably, the requirements respecting cross-examination would also apply to depositions.

14. 390 U.S. 719, 88 S.Ct. 1318, 20 L.Ed.2d 255 (1968).

15. Id. at 725, 88 S.Ct. at 1322, 20 L.Ed.2d at 260. It was also not shown in Barber v. Page that the witness was unavailable.

16. 448 U.S. 56, 100 S.Ct. 2531, 65 L.Ed.2d 597 (1980).

17. Id. at 66, 100 S.Ct. at 2539, 65 L.Ed.2d at 608.

18. Id. at 70, 100 S.Ct. at 2541, 65 L.Ed.2d at 610.

19. 399 U.S. 149, 90 S.Ct. 1930, 26 L.Ed.2d 489 (1970).

20. Ohio v. Roberts, 448 U.S. at 69, 100 S.Ct. at 2540, 65 L.Ed.2d at 609-10.

21. 408 U.S. 204, 92 S.Ct. 2308, 33 L.Ed.2d 293 (1972).

22. Id. at 216, 92 S.Ct. at 2315, 33 L.Ed.2d at 303.

Expert witnesses. There are cases in the Second Circuit signalling different requirements where the testimony sought to be introduced was given by an expert witness. Thus, in *Carter-Wallace, Inc. v. Otte*,[24] a pre-Rule case, the court discussed at length the obligations of a party who sought admission of the expert's prior testimony and concluded that in addition to showing the expert's unavailability the proponent must also show that no other expert with equivalent qualifications is available.[25] It would not seem that the later enactment of Rule 804(b)(1) would affect this ruling in any way. In *Hoppe v. G.D. Searle & Co.*,[26] a products liability case decided under Rule 804(b)(1), the court would not allow the testimony of physicians given at the trial of another case, both because there was no explanation of why they refused to testify in plaintiff's case, and because there was no showing that the facts in the other case were the same or that there was similar motive to testify.[27] But an absent expert's prior affidavit was allowed where the witness' unavailability was caused by defendant, the government, and the government had made no objection when plaintiff had included his name on her original witness list.[28] Admissibility was posited on Rule 804(b)(5), the catchall provision, however, and not on Rule 804(b)(1).

Library References:

West's Key No. Digests, Criminal Law ☞419(5), 539–548; Evidence ☞575–583.

23. See Wright Root Beer Co. v. Dr. Pepper Co., 414 F.2d 887, 889–91 (5th Cir. 1969)(where deponent at trial, and deposition read in, it was error for the trial judge to have instructed the jury to give the testimony little weight)(discussed in 4 Weinstein and Berger, ¶ 804(b)(1)[02], at 804–97.)

See also United States v. Salim, 664 F.Supp. 682, 687 (E.D.N.Y.1987), aff'd, 855 F.2d 944 (2d Cir.1988)(where deposition taken of defendant's accomplice in France specifically for use at defendant's trial pursuant to the requirements of French law, where the same motive to cross-examine existed, deposition admissible even though counsel was not able directly to cross-examine the witness, but had to submit questions in writing).

24. 474 F.2d 529 (2d Cir.1972), cert. denied, 412 U.S. 929, 93 S.Ct. 2753, 37 L.Ed.2d 156 (1973).

25. Id. at 535–37. In a patent infringement case, counsel was allowed to use evidence earlier admitted in another action against the United States in the Court of Claims. But the appellate court balked at the use of the testimony of an expert absent from the second trial by reason of the fact he resided more than 100 miles from the courthouse. While noting that this might be sufficient to show unavailability of an ordinary witness in a civil case, more was required where the witness had been paid to render an opinion and normally appeared in the first action pursuant to voluntary arrangements. The court stated: "It seems to us, therefore, that before the former testimony of an expert witness can be used, there should be some showing not only that the witness is unavailable, but that no other expert of similar qualifications is available or that the unavailable expert has some unique testimony to contribute." Id. at 536–37.

26. 779 F.Supp. 1413 (S.D.N.Y.1991).

27. Id. at 1417.

28. Barrett v. United States, 651 F.Supp. 606 (S.D.N.Y.1986). In this civil rights action involving a claim that the government had illegally used human subjects for chemical warfare experimentation, the court utilized the catchall provisions of Rule 804(b)(5) to admit the affidavit. Apparently the government had intimidated the expert into not testifying at trial.

804(2) Dying Declarations

§ 804(2).1 New York

In a homicide prosecution (and in no other case) the words of the dying victim may be admissible to identify his killer if it is clear that the victim-declarant had a settled expectation of death and was actually in extremis. The statement must be confined to what declarant believed to be the cause or circumstances of his impending death.[1] If it appears that declarant had the slightest expectation of recovery, his words will not be allowed.[2] The rule's rationale lies in the idea that "the mind, impressed with the awful idea of approaching dissolution, acts under a sanction equally powerful with that which it is presumed to feel by a solemn appeal to God upon an oath."[3]

On the other hand, "[d]ying declarations are dangerous, because made with no fear of prosecution for perjury and without the test of cross-examination * * *. Such evidence is the mere statement of what was said by a person not under oath, usually made when the body is in pain, the mind agitated and the memory shaken by the certainty of impending death."[4]

The upshot of these competing views is that dying declarations are admissible, if the necessary foundation is scrupulously adhered to; but the victim's statements provide weak evidence and normally, if left uncorroborated, will not alone support a conviction.[5] It has been stated that the Court of Appeals "has always regarded dying declarations with a degree of skepticism."[6]

Declarant must be the victim of a homicide. In *People v. Becker*,[7] defendant, a police officer, was charged with arranging the killing of a petty gambler with whom defendant had been criminally involved. The hit men had previously been convicted and had been executed. One of them just before his execution stated that so far as he knew defendant had nothing to do with the killing. Defendant sought to admit that statement as a dying declaration. But the declarant, while he may have sensed impending death, was not speaking of the perpetrator of *his* death.[8]

§ 804(2).1

1. McCormick § 311, at 330.
2. People v. Bartelini, 285 N.Y. 433, 440, 35 N.E.2d 29, 32 (1941).
3. People v. Sarzano, 212 N.Y. 231, 234–35, 106 N.E. 87, 87–88 (1914).
4. People v. Falletto, 202 N.Y. 494, 499, 96 N.E. 355, 357 (1911).
5. People v. Ludkowitz, 266 N.Y. 233, 240, 194 N.E. 688, 690 (1935). In People v. Johnson, 163 Misc.2d 256–61, 620 N.Y.S.2d 200, 204 (Sup.Ct.Bronx Co.1994, order reversed on other grounds 632 N.Y.S.2d 547 (1995)), the court, while holding that the dying declaration could not support the conviction because uncorroborated, qualified this by noting that the statement was ambiguous. The implication is that an unambiguous statement might well support a conviction, even if it is the only evidence.
6. People v. Nieves, 67 N.Y.2d 125, 133, 501 N.Y.S.2d 1, 6, 492 N.E.2d 109, 114 (1986).
7. 215 N.Y. 126, 109 N.E. 127 (1915).
8. Id. at 145, 109 N.E. at 133. It was stated: "The declaration must be a statement by the *victim of the crime* * * * and however cogent may be the reasoning in favor of admitting proof of declarations by any witness about to die and aware of his approaching dissolution, it suffices to say that up to the present time evidence of dying declarations has never been admissi-

Declarant must have a settled expectation of death. This requirement is difficult because seldom are the victim's expressions totally unequivocal. "There is no unyielding ritual of words to be spoken by the dying."[9] "If, however, it appears that the declarant 'had any expectation or hope of recovery, however slight it may have been, and though death ensued in an hour afterwards, the declarations are inadmissible.'"[10]

Where declarant was asked a series of questions which elicited the name of his attacker, the evidence was admissible since he stated, "Papa, I die," and in another conversation with a police officer he said, "Don't you see I am going out? I feel rotten. * * * I mean I am going to die."[11] In another case the victim, riddled with 12 bullets, lay in a hospital. In response to the question, "Do you believe you are about to die?" he answered "Yes." He had also been told by a surgeon that he would not live. This was deemed sufficient.[12] The settled expectation requirement was also found to be satisfied where an elderly man whose throat was seriously cut and whose lungs were filling with blood received the last rites, made an oral will to his gathered family and said, "I don't know what I have done in this world to deserve such an end."[13]

In *People v. Liccione*,[14] the victim related that her killer told her as he attacked her that her husband had hired him to kill her. She first told this to neighbors who came to her aid, and later to detectives at the hospital. These statements were found admissible. There was medical evidence that declarant was in extremis and she repeatedly told the neighbors that she was dying and she was rapidly losing blood through multiple stab wounds. Her statements at the hospital were made after she had received the last rites, had undergone major surgery and had repeatedly said that she was dying.[15]

The statement was not admissible in *People v. Allen*,[16] where the wife, stabbed and bleeding, accused her intoxicated husband in his presence of assaulting her (because of his condition his silence was not deemed an adopted admission), and she also stated the same thing to her mother in the hospital some four days later. There was evidence that declarant had received the last rites, that she asked for the removal of an oxygen tent since she was "going to die anyway, that she told a relative she did not think she would recover, and that on several occasions down

---

ble * * * unless the declaration proceeded from the victim of the assault, the alleged perpetrator of which was on trial." Id. at 145, 146, 109 N.E. at 133 (emphasis in original).

9. People v. Bartelini, 285 N.Y. 433, 440, 35 N.E.2d 29, 32 (1941)(quoting Shepard v. United States, 290 U.S. 96, 100, 54 S.Ct. 22, 24, 78 L.Ed. 196 (1933)).

10. Bartelini, 285 N.Y. at 440, 35 N.E.2d at 32 (quoting Commonwealth v. Roberts, 108 Mass. 296, 301 (1871)).

11. Bartelini, 285 N.Y. at 439–41, 35 N.E. at 32–33.

12. People v. Ludkowitz, 266 N.Y. 233, 237–39, 194 N.E. 688, 689–90 (1935) (although the dying declaration was deemed admissible, the conviction rested on that evidence alone, and so the conviction was reversed).

13. People v. Falletto, 202 N.Y. 494, 497–98, 96 N.E. 355, 357 (1911).

14. 63 A.D.2d 305, 407 N.Y.S.2d 753 (4th Dep't 1978).

15. Id. at 317, 318, 407 N.Y.S.2d at 759, 760.

16. 300 N.Y. 222, 90 N.E.2d 48 (1949).

§ 804(2).1   HEARSAY   Ch. 8

to the night of her death she told a nephew that she knew she would die because all her relatives had visited her."[17] But the court ruled the evidence inadmissible:

> Here there was not shown any certainty on declarant's part that she was about to die, and more conspicuously, there was absent the slightest intimation that her statements to her mother, as to her husband's stabbing her, were made under a sense of, or because of, or were controlled by, any such belief. Not only were her predictions of death made casually and not solemnly, but her accusation was not shown to have any near relation, in time or thought, to those earlier expressions as to nearness of death.[18]

Where declarant was questioned at the hospital by police and named defendant as his attacker the statement was ruled inadmissible because he had pleaded with the officers to help him.[19] "There is nothing in this to indicate that [declarant] believed he was going to die; much less that he had given up all hope of recovery. He may have thought the chances were against him. But that certainly is as far as we should go in the realm of conjecture and that is not inconsistent with the hope that he might live."[20] In *People v. Arnold*,[21] the victim's statement inculpating defendant failed to meet the hopelessness test since she asked the officers to take her to the hospital.

It is seen from these cases that the question of whether declarant expected imminent death can be ascertained from his own words, the nature of his wounds, what the doctor or others told him, or a combination of some or all of these factors.[22]

Procedural aspects. There is no requirement that there be a hearing outside the presence of the jury to determine admissibility[23] (although the trial judge would seem free to order such a hearing, especially where an offer of proof is sought to be made). Where, however, police have arranged for a showup in the dying victim's hospital room, it has been held that defendant is entitled to a *Wade* hearing;[24] "a foundation for reception of the evidence must be established before the jury hears the declaration and decides the weight to be attributed to it."[25] As to jury instructions: "[T]he defendant is entitled to have the jury instructed * * * that dying declarations are not to be regarded by the jurors as

---

17. Id. at 226, 90 N.E. at 50.
18. Id. at 227–28, 90 N.E. at 50–51.
19. People v. Mikulec, 207 App.Div. 505, 508, 202 N.Y.S. 551, 553 (3d Dep't 1924).
20. Id. at 508, 202 N.Y.S. at 553.
21. 34 N.Y.2d 548, 354 N.Y.S.2d 106, 309 N.E.2d 875 (1974).
22. McCormick § 310, at 327.
23. People v. Liccione, 63 A.D.2d 305, 316, 407 N.Y.S.2d 753, 759 (4th Dep't 1978).
24. People v. Mendez, 155 Misc.2d 368, 589 N.Y.S.2d 268 (Sup.Ct.N.Y.Co.1992). The court stated: "When no police-arranged procedure is used to procure an identification, the possibility of unduly suggestive activity by the police is not a concern. Therefore, no pre-trial Wade hearing is required to ascertain the reliability of an identification that is not the product of police-arranged procedures * * *." Id. at 369, 589 N.Y.S.2d at 270. For purposes of the decision, the judge assumed that the victim's identification was a dying declaration. Id.
25. Id.

having the same value and weight as sworn testimony given in open court, the accuracy of which the defendant may challenge, by cross-examination * * *."[26]

It has been said that dying declarations may be proved for the facts contained in them, but not for opinions or conclusions.[27] This rule, however, seems not to be rigidly applied. The court in the *Liccione* case quoted from Justice Cardozo in *Shepard v. United States*[28] as follows:

"He murdered me," [by putting poison in the whiskey bottle] does not cease to be competent as a dying declaration because in the statement of the act there is also an appraisal of the crime * * *. One does not hold the dying to the observance of all the niceties of speech to which conformity is exacted from a witness on the stand. What is decisive is something deeper and more fundamental than any difference of form. The declaration is kept out if the setting of the occasion satisfies the judge, or in reason ought to satisfy him, that the speaker is giving expression to suspicion or conjecture, and not to known facts.[29]

In the *Liccione* case, while some of the victim's statements were incompetent because she gave a somewhat detailed account of what happened, including some assumptions, the court said that the victim's declaration that the assailant told her he had been hired by her husband were admissible.[30]

Dying declarations as excited utterances. Perhaps if statements made by a dying victim do not qualify as dying declarations they can come into evidence as excited utterances. Thus, in *People v. Nieves*,[31] the stabbed victim survived for awhile and for a period of 20 to 25 minutes was lucid in the emergency room. She was asked by the doctor what happened, and she replied that defendant had stabbed her. Although the requisites for a dying declaration were not shown,[32] the case was sent back with the suggestion that on a second trial, the People might seek to admit the statement as an excited utterance.[33] See § 803(1).1(b) *supra*.

---

26. Id.

27. Liccione, 63 A.D.2d at 319, 407 N.Y.S.2d at 761.

28. 290 U.S. 96, 101, 54 S.Ct. 22, 24, 78 L.Ed. 196, 197 (1933).

29. Liccione, 63 A.D.2d at 319, 407 N.Y.S.2d at 761.

30. Id. at 319, 320, 407 N.Y.S.2d at 761, 762. The court held that the double hearsay nature of the victim's dying declaration was overcome by the fact that the attacker's statement to the victim fell under the coconspirator hearsay exception. Id. at 320–22, 407 N.Y.S.2d at 761–63. While the statement was made during the conspiracy, it is debatable that it was made in furtherance thereof. See § 802.2(g) supra.

31. 67 N.Y.2d 125, 501 N.Y.S.2d 1, 492 N.E.2d 109 (1986).

32. The victim expressed the hope that she would not die, no one told her she might, nor did she evidence any thought that she would. Id. at 127–28, 501 N.Y.S.2d at 3–4, 492 N.E.2d at 112.

33. Id. at 136–37, 501 N.Y.S.2d at 8, 492 N.E.2d at 116. See also People v. Brown, 70 N.Y.2d 513, 522 N.Y.S.2d 837, 517 N.E.2d 515 (1987), where the statements of a seriously wounded victim as to who shot him were held admissible as spontaneous statements and not as dying declarations, when made in a hospital emergency room 30 minutes after the shooting. Given that declarant was in great pain and the surrounding circumstances showed that the statements would not have been made as a result of "studied reflection," the statements could be considered trustworthy.

§ 804(2).1 HEARSAY Ch. 8

The proposed New York Evidence Code provision. The proposed New York Code § 804(b)(2) codifies the existing law and extends it to wrongful death actions.[34]

Library References:

West's Key No. Digests, Criminal Law ⚖︎366, 415(2), 419(6); Evidence ⚖︎275½.

§ 804(2).2 Federal

Federal Rule of Evidence 804(b)(2) states as a hearsay exception:

(2) Statement under belief of impending death. In a prosecution for homicide or in a civil action or proceeding, a statement made by a declarant while believing that the declarant's death was imminent, concerning the cause or circumstances of what the declarant believed to be impending death.

Note that the dying declaration hearsay exception is extended to civil cases, and not only to wrongful death actions as provided under the proposed New York Code rule (*see* § 804(2).1 *supra*). This implies that in a civil action which is not a wrongful death action, the unavailable declarant need not have actually died in order for the statement to be admitted.[1]

Although the rule provides that declarant must believe death to be imminent, thus connoting something less than a settled expectation of death, the latter test probably supplies the standard still to be applied. There is no indication that the drafters intended to depart from Justice Cardozo's declaration of the common law rule in his opinion in *Shepard v. United States*[2] where he stated: "To make out a dying declaration, the declarant must have spoken without hope of recovery and in the shadow of impending death."[3] The question was posed, but not an-

---

34. § 804(b)(2) [PROPOSED]

(2) Statement under belief of impending death. In a homicide prosecution or wrongful death action, a statement, based upon personal knowledge, made by a declarant in extremis, while under a sense of impending death with no hope of recovery, concerning the cause or circumstances of what the declarant believed to be the declarant's impending death.

§ 804(2).2

1. With respect to this extension it is stated in the Advisory Committee's Notes:

The common law required that the statement be that of the victim, offered in a prosecution for criminal homicide. Thus declarations by victims in prosecutions for other crimes, e.g. a declaration by a rape victim who dies in childbirth, and all declarations in civil cases were outside the scope of the exception. * * * While the common law exception no doubt originated as a result of the exceptional need for the evidence in homicide cases, the theory of admissibility applies equally in civil cases. * * * Unavailability is not limited to death.

2. 290 U.S. 96, 54 S.Ct. 22, 78 L.Ed. 196 (1933).

3. Id. at 99, 54 S.Ct. at 23, 78 L.Ed. at 199. In Shepard the victim, wife of the defendant, believed he had put poison in her whiskey, and said so to her maid at a time when she seemed to be in remission from her sickness. Later, when again in the throes of severe illness she said to a doctor "You will get me well, won't you?" These facts did not bring her statement to the maid within the exception. Nor was her statement admissible for the nonhearsay purpose of showing her state of mind inconsistent with the suggestion she may have been suicidal. There was no indication at trial that this could be a ground for admission, and defendant would be prejudiced were such a ground offered for the first time on appeal. Moreover, her accusa-

swered, as to whether the sick wife's accusation that her husband had poisoned her would be admissible were the proper foundation for a dying declaration laid. Her statement may have been the product of speculation and conjecture rather than of a fact of which she was aware.[4]

The Second Circuit Court of Appeals has contributed little to the literature on this hearsay exception, except that in *United States v. Sacasas*,[5] the court dismissed out of hand defendant's assertion of the exception where it was not remotely applicable.[6]

A classic instance where the exception applied in a federal case appears in *United States v. Etheridge*,[7] where all the circumstances taken together showed that declarant must have expected imminent death, even though he asked that an ambulance be called.[8] In another case,

---

tion expressed a belief as to a past act by someone else, and not an expression of a present feeling or intent of her own. Id. at 102–03, 54 S.Ct. at 25, 78 L.Ed. at 201.

4. Id. at 101–02, 54 S.Ct. at 25–25, 78 L.Ed. at 200.

5. 381 F.2d 451 (2d Cir.1967).

6. The court stated:

According to one Boyle, a fellow inmate of the Federal House of Detention with Richard Mahan, who had been indicted with appellant, and who, there awaiting trial, died before trial, told Boyle ten minutes before Mahan finally lost consciousness, "If anything happens to me tell him that the Greek had nothing to do with the job." Appellant seeks to persuade that this hearsay evidence should be admissible under the "dying declaration" exception to the exclusion of hearsay. Of course the exception is inapplicable here—Mahan was not dying following a homicidal attack, and neither appellant, "the Greek," nor Mahan had been prosecuted for homicide.

Id. at 454.

It might be added that from those facts there is no indication that declarant had a settled expectation of death.

7. 424 F.2d 951 (6th Cir.1970), cert. granted sub nom., Bostic v. U.S., 400 U.S. 991, 91 S.Ct. 462, 27 L.Ed.2d 437, cert. dismissed sub nom., Bostic v. U.S., 402 U.S. 547, 91 S.Ct. 2174, 29 L.Ed.2d 102, reh. denied sub nom., Bostic v. U.S., 404 U.S. 875, 92 S.Ct. 32, 30 L.Ed.2d 122 (1971).

8. The facts in this case are illustrative:

As to the dying declaration of Ferguson, which we have quoted above, the District Judge was well within the discretion vested in him when he admitted it into evidence. * * * Ferguson had been shot five times in the head and body with a .38 caliber pistol. His own statements indicated that he contemplated death and, indeed, he died very shortly after making the declaration.

In ruling the declaration admissible, the District Judge said:

"In this case, all of the facts, as I recall them, as testified to by this witness, proposed witness, are indicative of rationality, rational mind and of a consciousness of impending death with one exception which I will note in a moment."

"First we have the fact that here was a man who was shot five times, five bullets from a revolver having entered his body. We have the fact that he drove the car up to the house. He blew the horn to get the attention of someone in the house. He got out of the car and leaned over against the car door. He then made his way to the front porch and was able to knock on the door several different times. Then he made the declarations which were attributed to him to the effect that he wanted to make a confession, and I believe some statement to the effect, referring to God or to the Lord, and then he made a statement identifying his assailant, the person who shot him, and then the reason for the shooting. Then he made a statement to the effect that at least open the door and call an ambulance."

"In this pattern of circumstances, the only possible statement that I see that would indicate that the deceased may at that time have had some lingering hope of survival was the statement that he would like for an ambulance to be called. Certainly all of these circumstances taken together would indicate a rational mind, not an irrational mind."

"I find a Missouri case quoted in the footnote in 'Underhill's Criminal Evi-

§ 804(2).2   HEARSAY   Ch. 8

although the declarant never expressed his hopelessness, his injuries were so severe that he must have known he could not survive. A physician testified that in his opinion the declarant knew that his chances for living were "very slim."[9] And, where declarant was in a hospital suffering from third degree burns and said that she was going to die because she was in "too much pain," the necessary foundation was laid.[10]

The dying declaration hearsay exception, although not considered among the most reliable of the exceptions,[11] nevertheless passes muster under the confrontation clause. It is certainly a deeply rooted exception,[12] and the Supreme Court has specifically listed it as resistant to confrontation challenge.[13] Presumably, if the foundation is in place for admission of the statement under the rules governing the hearsay exception, defendant's confrontation objection would be rejected.

There are at least two federal cases where the dying declaration exception has been implicated on the civil side.

dence,' 5th Edition, Section 288, page 931, referring to a Missouri case, State v. Evans, 124 Missouri 397, [28 S.W. 8] where it was said:"

"The mere fact that the victim, while writing under the torments of a murderous blow, seeks relief from anguish by sending for a physician is not indicative of a hope of life, but a natural desire to be relieved of pain."

"When I take all of these circumstances together in this case, the reference to the ambulance, I think, could be given no greater significance than the statement in this Missouri case in which the declarant asked for a physician."

"So I am satisfied first that these statements were made at the time when the declarant was of rational mind; secondly that they were made without any hope of survival, that this man had knowledge of the fact that he was going to die, that death was imminent. All of the circumstances together indicate that clearly in my mind."

Like the District Judge, we have no doubt that under the facts of this case the statements previously noted from Ferguson were dying declarations.

424 F.2d at 965–66.

9. United States v. Mobley, 421 F.2d 345, 347–48 (5th Cir.1970). The court stated:

The admissibility of dying declarations, on behalf of and against an accused has long been recognized by the Supreme Court as an exception to hearsay evidence. Such declarations are admissible to the fact of a homicide and to the person by whom it was committed, contingent, however, upon a showing that the declarer was aware of impending death at the time the statement was made. Mattox v. United States, 146 U.S. 140, 151, 13 S.Ct. 50, 53, 36 L.Ed. 917 (1892).

Id. at 347.

10. United States v. Barnes, 464 F.2d 828, 831, 150 U.S.App.D.C. 319, 322 (D.C.Cir.), cert. denied, 410 U.S. 986, 93 S.Ct. 1514, 36 L.Ed.2d 183 (1973).

11. McCormick § 314, at 333.

12. See Mattox v. United States, 146 U.S. 140, 152, 13 S.Ct. 50, 53–54, 36 L.Ed. 917, 921 (1892). In this case the trial court refused to admit the victim's statement in response to a question that defendant was not among those who shot him. This was held to be error since, "[i]n this case the lapse of time [between the attack and death] was but a few hours. The wounds were three in number, and one of them of great severity. The patient was perfectly conscious, and asked the attending physician his opinion, and was told that the chances were all against him, and that the physician thought there was no 'show for you [him] at all.'" Id. at 152, 13 S.Ct. at 54, 36 L.Ed.2d at 922. The court reached back to the English cases for the origin of the exception. Id.

13. Pointer v. Texas, 380 U.S. 400, 406, 85 S.Ct. 1065, 1069, 13 L.Ed.2d 923, 927

Ch. 8   DECLARATIONS AGAINST INTEREST § 804(3).1

In *Pfeil v. Rogers*,[14] the father of a murder victim brought a 42 U.S.C.A. § 1983 civil rights action against deputy sheriffs and other county officials claiming they had caused his son's death. Deceased's neighbor, Betty Zajec, claimed to have seen defendants at the scene and became distraught when she felt threatened by defendants. She committed suicide, but before doing so told members of her family that defendants had killed plaintiff's son. The court might have disposed of the matter by noticing that these statements had nothing to do with declarant's own death; but the determination denying admissibility was based on the fact that the statements were not made in contemplation of death.[15] Neither were the statements admissible under the present sense impression or excited utterance exceptions.[16] In *Pau v. Yosemite Park and Curry Co.*,[17] suit was brought against a bicycle rental company by the family of a bicyclist who died in an accident. The bicyclist fell into a coma and died several days later; but on the second day she awoke long enough to say "the brakes failed." The trial judge at first kept this out, but then decided that under Rule 804(b)(2) it would be admissible in a civil case. This never got beyond an offer of proof at trial, however, and plaintiffs failed to raise it on appeal since, apparently, they felt they had better hearsay exceptions to argue.[18] It would have been interesting, had the dying declaration exception been pursued, to see whether a person waking from a coma can have a settled expectation of impending death.

Library References:

West's Key No. Digests, Criminal Law ⚖︎366, 415(2), 419(6); Evidence ⚖︎275½.

§ 804(3)   Declarations Against Interest

§ 804(3).1   New York

Since a person would not ordinarily utter a statement against his interest were it untrue, such a statement is imbued with an aura of trustworthiness, and if the declarant is unavailable for trial the statement ought to be admissible.[1] Historically this exception was utilized mostly in civil cases because the interests to which the exception applied were one's pecuniary interest (which would normally include one's civil liability interest), and one's proprietary interest, and to satisfy the unavailability requirement the declarant must have died. In *People v.*

(1965). Pointer concerned the admissibility of testimony given at a preliminary hearing.

14. 757 F.2d 850 (7th Cir.1985), cert. denied, 475 U.S. 1107, 106 S.Ct. 1513, 89 L.Ed.2d 912 (1986).

15. Id. at 861.

16. "[R]ather, the affidavits relate to conversations that took place some period of time before her death but sometime after [the son's] demise." Id.

17. 928 F.2d 880 (9th Cir.1991).

18. Id. at 889–90. The court found the statement not to be an excited utterance, a present sense impression statement, or a statement generally reliable under the catchall provisions of Rule 803(24).

§ 804(3).1

1. See McCormick § 316, at 335–37. McCormick observes that "people generally do not lightly make statements that are damaging to their interests." He notes that the interest must not be too indirect and remote and that declarant must have

§ 804(3).1   HEARSAY   Ch. 8

Brown,[2] the Court of Appeals expanded the hearsay exception to include declarations against penal interest and increased the grounds of unavailability. Subsequent to the decision in *Brown*, application of the exception in criminal cases has dominated the landscape. The expansion of the grounds of unavailability beyond the ground of death, however, appears equally applicable to civil cases.[3]

The declaration against interest differs from an admission in four respects: First, the declaration against interest could have been made by a nonparty; second, the statement must have been against the declarant's interest when made and not, as is the case of a party's admission, against the party's interest as it appears at the trial;[4] third, the declaration against interest exception, unlike that of admissions, contains an unavailability requirement; and fourth, the person who makes a declaration against interest must have personal knowledge of the facts.

In the case of a declaration against interest, courts are also careful to examine any motive to falsify that the declarant might have had.[5] For example, in *People v. Shortridge*,[6] statements made by defendant's deceased father inculpating himself and tending to exculpate defendant were inadmissible because the father did not want to see his son sent to prison.[7]

a. Civil Cases

Declarations against pecuniary interest.

had firsthand knowledge of that about which he spoke.

2. 26 N.Y.2d 88, 308 N.Y.S.2d 825, 257 N.E.2d 16 (1970).

3. See Jamison v. Walker, 48 A.D.2d 320, 369 N.Y.S.2d 469 (2d Dep't 1975), where inability to locate the declarant was deemed sufficient.

4. See discussion at § 802.1, supra.

5. See Mills v. Davis, 113 N.Y. 243, 21 N.E. 68 (1889). Evidence that a creditor acknowledged part payment on a note by the debtor, while against the creditor's pecuniary interest, nevertheless is suspect since it was in his interest to keep the statute of limitations running for payment of the whole amount, and partial payment keeps the time open. Of course, the element of motive to falsify is of paramount concern in the criminal cases which will be examined infra.

6. 65 N.Y.2d 309, 491 N.Y.S.2d 298, 480 N.E.2d 1080 (1985).

7. The statements were in the form of letters written by the father, nine months after the death with which the son was charged. The court used the phrase "intrinsic trustworthiness" and found it lacking here.

While the admissibility of declarations against penal interest is predicated upon the theory that their reliability can generally be presumed because a person does not ordinarily reveal facts which jeopardize his interests * * * nevertheless, that generalization must be tempered with a recognition of the limitations upon its validity under particular circumstances. Indeed, certain considerations may be fatal to the reliability of a declaration and thereby render the out-of-court statement inadmissible.

These considerations include the declarant's motivation—e.g., whether the statement was designed to exculpate a loved one or inculpate an enemy. Important also is the declarant's personality—e.g., whether he suffers psychological or emotional instability of whether he is a chronic or pathological liar. Additionally, the declarant's spontaneity or hesitancy, promptness or tardiness in making the statement may shed light on its authenticity. Likewise, the internal consistency and coherence of the declaration, or its lack thereof, may reflect on its bona fides. Most critical in some cases, is the availability of supporting evidence—that is, some proof, independent of the declaration itself, which tends to confirm the truth of the facts asserted therein. Regardless of how self-incriminatory a particular declaration against penal interest might be, all or any of the foregoing may affect its reliability.

The Court of Appeals in *Kwiatkowski v. John Lowry, Inc.*,[8] noting that a statement made by the driver of a car concerning the accident he was involved in could be used against his estate in the resulting wrongful death action, did not need to decide whether the statement was a privity admission, or a declaration against interest.[9] Citing abundant authority from many jurisdictions supporting both theories, the court simply held that the statements should not have been excluded from evidence.[10] The Court of Appeals dealt with a case where the statements contained in partnership books were labeled declarations against interest, the partners having died. But they might have been privity admissions, also, since the entries were made by clerks and "[a]ll partners are supposed to have knowledge of entries in their books made by their clerks in the regular course of business."[11] Were that case to have arisen after enactment of the statutory business entry rule, there might have been three options.[12]

There is authority in New York, in *Livingston v. Arnoux*,[13] that declarations against interest are admissible in a civil case as "evidence after the death of the party who made them, * * * of the fact against his interest, [and] of the other incidental and collateral facts and circumstances mentioned, and are admissible irrespective of the fact whether any privity exists between the person who made them and the party against whom they are offered."[14] This is not the rule in criminal cases in New York, nor under the Federal Rule.[15]

In *Livingston v. Arnoux*, the issuance of a receipt by the sheriff for fees received in connection with a sheriff's sale constituted a statement against his interest since it obligated him to account for the money.[16] This is illustrative of the fact that the declaration concerning pecuniary

---

Id. at 312–13, 491 N.Y.S.2d at 300, 480 N.E.2d at 1082.

8. 276 N.Y. 126, 133, 11 N.E.2d 563, 566 (1937)(after the accident decedent made statements which exonerated the defendant in the wrongful death action from all responsibility).

9. Id. at 132–33, 11 N.E.2d at 566.

10. Id. at 134, 11 N.E.2d at 567.

11. Kittredge v. Grannis, 244 N.Y. 168, 175, 155 N.E. 88, 90 (1926).

12. See Chenango Bridge Co. v. Paige, 83 N.Y. 178 (1880), where the declaration against interest exception might not have been necessary had there been a business entry rule. "The amount of tolls received by the Binghamton Bridge Company was sufficiently proved. The book kept by the treasurer of the company was produced, and that was the book in which such tolls were entered. The entries were made by the treasurer, who was dead at the time of the trial, and such entries were against his interest, as they charged him with the amount of such tolls. They were, therefore, admissible for the purpose of showing the amount of tolls received by that company." Id. at 192.

13. 56 N.Y. 507 (1874). Here, as part of the proof in showing the transfer of property a sheriff's receipt was admitted which evidenced a sheriff's sale. The court found the issuance of the receipt to be a declaration against interest on the deceased sheriff's part. "The officer thereby charged himself with the money, and rendered himself accountable for it to the creditor. It was an admission against his interest, made in respect to a matter pertaining to his official duty." Id.

14. Id. at 519.

15. See discussions in subdivision (b) of this section with respect to the admissibility of collateral matters.

16. Livingston v. Arnoux, 56 N.Y. at 519. A similar analysis was made in McDonald v. Wesendonck, 30 Misc. 601, 605, 62 N.Y.S. 764, 767 (Sup.Ct.App.Term 1900), where the declarant wrote a letter in which he obligated his company to be responsible for expense money being paid certain salesmen. The acknowledgment of this obli-

liability can be somewhat indirect. Sometimes the pathway to the declarant's pecuniary liability is not straight. Thus, in *Martorella v. Prudential Insurance Co.*,[17] defendant raised the defense of suicide to a claim for the proceeds of a life policy made by the beneficiary of the policy. Defendant was permitted to show that deceased had made statements after she had ingested the poison that she took it intentionally because she did not care to live. The court found this not to have been an admission because declarant "seems not to have been in privity (in a legal sense) with the plaintiff, the beneficiary."[18] But the court went on to find a declaration against her pecuniary interest. "As, however, the insured had reserved the right, under the policy, to change the beneficiary, her statement implying the existence of a suicidal intent was clearly a declaration made by a person now deceased against her own pecuniary or proprietary interest, namely, her interest in the policy because of her power to change the beneficiary. This power was a beneficial power. She could have named her own estate as beneficiary or for a consideration could have named someone else. Her declaration, as proved by the defendant, was against this beneficial interest."[19]

That "pecuniary interest" translates to "civil liability" is illustrated in *Jamison v. Walker*,[20] where the driver of the car that struck decedent, one Cunningham, admitted the incident to the police. The defendant was an automobile dealer whose plates were on Cunningham's car, but defendant denied that it owned the car. Even if Cunningham was not in privity with the dealer so that his statement would be an admission, it constituted a declaration against interest since Cunningham was nowhere to be found at the time of trial.[21] As to declarant's unavailability, the court stated that absence from the state, an accepted ground, "should be equated with inability to locate the declarant with due diligence within the State."[22]

Statements against proprietary interest.

In *Lyon v. Ricker*,[23] it was stated:

The court receives declarations of a deceased person against his interest because of the likelihood of their being true, of their general freedom from any reasonable probability of fraud, and because they cannot be set up or proven until the death of the party making them.

We think it plain that the declarations of the deceased grantor were admissible against the defendant, although the latter claimed nothing under the grantor, and was not, therefore, strictly in privity with him.[24]

This case is illustrative of what constitutes a statement adverse to propriety interest. Plaintiff was demanding conveyance of property

gation was viewed as a declaration against the writer's pecuniary interest.

17. 238 App.Div. 532, 264 N.Y.S. 751 (4th Dep't 1933).

18. Id. at 533, 264 N.Y.S. at 753.

19. Id. at 534, 264 N.Y.S. at 753.

20. 48 A.D.2d 320, 369 N.Y.S.2d 469 (2d Dep't 1975).

21. Id. at 323, 369 N.Y.S.2d at 472.

22. Id.

23. 141 N.Y. 225, 36 N.E. 189 (1894).

24. Id. at 231, 36 N.E. at 191.

from defendant. As proof that he was entitled to the property plaintiff produced statements by his deceased father, who had given deeds to the property to defendant, that upon his, the father's death, defendant was to deliver the deeds to plaintiff and his brother. Observe that this was against the father's interest simply because he was thereby parting with his proprietary interest in the property. The fact that he wanted to do this, and did it intentionally is beside the point.

More readily apparent as a statement against proprietary interest is where declarant, record owner of the property, states that it actually belongs to someone else.[25] A second example is where one Hall wrote, "The bond and mortgage assigned to me by Prince & Whitely, for the sum of $20,400, does not belong to me [but to Sarah A. Jarvis]. * * *"[26] The problem with the second example, however, is that on the facts of the *Hall* case, the declarant never claimed to have any interest in the bond and mortgage. "The [hearsay] exception does not apply here because these statements of Hall were, when made, against the interests of Mary H. Jarvis and not against his interest. He never at any time claimed to hold the mortgage as his own, and never in fact owned it, and the defendants, upon the trial, did not claim he ever owned it, or that they had any interest in it. If these statements were allowed as evidence they would simply tend to show that the money in controversy belonged to Sarah A. Jarvis, and not to Mary H. Jarvis, and hence they are not within the reason of the exception * * *."[27]

The hearsay exception also applies to statements concerning chattels.[28]

b. Criminal Cases

Prior to 1970 New York did not recognize a declaration against penal interest as a hearsay exception, nor could unavailability be based on anything other than declarant's death. In *People v. Brown*,[29] however, Judge Bergan added penal interest to the accepted list and expanded the bases of unavailability to include absence from the jurisdiction and

---

25. New York Water Co. v. Crow, 110 App.Div. 32, 96 N.Y.S. 899 (2d Dep't 1905), aff'd, 187 N.Y. 516, 79 N.E. 1112 (1907)(in action brought by water company to establish rights in land as against heirs and judgment creditors of deceased record holder, deceased's statements could be used since they were in "disparagement of his title." 110 App.Div. at 34, 96 N.Y.S. at 901).

26. Brennan v. Hall, 131 N.Y. 160, 29 N.E. 1009 (1892).

27. Id. at 166, 29 N.E. at 1010.

28. See Tompkins v. Fonda Glove Lining Co., 188 N.Y. 261, 80 N.E. 933 (1907). This was an action for the conversion of machinery in which one issue was whether defendant had knowledge of plaintiff's claim to the machinery. A stockholder and director of defendant, Sheard, had made statements prior to his death showing he knew of plaintiff's interest. "The fact that Sheard was a director and officer of the defendant did not render his admissions or declarations admissible as against the defendant. * * * They were admissible, however, on another ground of which his connection with the defendant forms no factor, except that it was through that connection that the declarations made were against the interest of the declarant." Id. at 264, 80 N.E. at 934. Thus, while declarant's statements were not binding on the defendant as admissions, they were allowed as evidence under the rubric announced in Lyon v. Ricker, supra, note 23, i.e., that qualifying declarations are admissible even though the declarant and the party against whom they are used are not in privity.

29. 26 N.Y.2d 88, 308 N.Y.S.2d 825, 257 N.E.2d 16 (1970).

declarant's refusal to testify based on assertion of fifth amendment rights.

Brown's defense was self-defense. He claimed that the victim had produced a gun whereupon he, defendant, shot the victim. The problem with this defense, however, was that no gun was found in the victim's possession. Brown sought to admit a statement by one Seals that Seals had picked up a gun at the scene shortly after the mishap and run off to commit a robbery with it. This was properly kept out of evidence under the prevailing rule which disallowed statements against penal interest. Besides, Seals was available in the sense that, although he refused to testify on grounds of self-incrimination, he was not dead. Pointing to the absurdity of permitting evidence of statements against propriety interest, but prohibiting statements against penal interest, Judge Bergan stated: "Yet the distinction which would authorize a court to receive proof that a man admitted he never had title to an Elgin watch, but not to receive proof that he had admitted striking Jones over the head with a club, assuming equal relevancy of both statements, does not readily withstand analysis."[30] As to the question of unavailability:

> The rule on admissions against interest was based on the absence of the witness; and usually this meant that he was dead. But whether the person is dead, or beyond the jurisdiction, or will not testify, and cannot be compelled to testify because of a constitutional privilege, all equally spell out unavailability of trial testimony. If the rule is to be changed to include penal admissions against interest, it ought to embrace unavailability because of the assertion of constitutional right which might be fairly common in the area of penal admissions.[31]

In *People v. Maerling*,[32] a unanimous Court of Appeals agreed that, conceptually, the prosecutor could introduce declarations against penal interest to incriminate the defendant.[33] In *Maerling*, however, the only statements made by the declarant that could be considered as being against her penal interest were not related to the crime for which defendant was being tried.[34] Part of her statement was that she had overheard defendant and others plotting the crime. This was not a declaration against her penal interest because it indicated that she had nothing to do with the commission of the crime. Her statements about other crimes not involving defendant were collateral. Thus, the court held that a declaration against penal interest is admissible only if

---

30. Id. at 91, 308 N.Y.S.2d at 827, 257 N.E.2d at 17.

31. Id. at 93, 308 N.Y.S.2d at 828, 257 N.E.2d at 18. There is no reason to think that expansion of the unavailability rules would not apply to the pecuniary and proprietary rules as well. See Jamison v. Walker, 48 A.D.2d 320, 369 N.Y.S.2d 469 (2d Dep't 1975), where inability to locate the declarant was deemed sufficient in a pecuniary interest case. The question whether the rule extends to privileges founded on confidential communications is taken up in United States v. Lilley, 581 F.2d 182 (8th Cir.1978), where the witness claimed the spousal privilege. The court would have used this as a basis for a finding of unavailability except that it was found that there was no valid marriage.

32. 46 N.Y.2d 289, 413 N.Y.S.2d 316, 385 N.E.2d 1245 (1978).

33. Id. at 297, 413 N.Y.S.2d at 321, 385 N.E.2d at 1249.

34. Id. at 300, 413 N.Y.S.2d at 323, 385 N.E.2d at 1251.

relevant to the question of the defendant's guilt. If the part of the statement that inculpates defendant is collateral to the declarant's expression of her own culpability, then the statement's trustworthiness "may be expected to be open to question."[35]

Important also are the circumstances under which the statement is made. In *Maerling* the reliability of the statements was suspect, because at the time that declarant made them she was seeking leniency from the authorities in connection with an unrelated crime.[36]

Reliability is also a factor, of course, when defendant offers the declarations for exculpatory purposes. It has been said, however, that statements offered by the prosecution to inculpate the defendant are subject to a higher standard of proof as to reliability.[37] Where the prosecutor offers the statement there must be a "high probability" of truthfulness. Where defendant offers the statement it is sufficient if there is a "reasonable possibility" that the statement might be true.[38] In *People v. Settles*,[39] where defendant sought to introduce the evidence, the court imposed the rule that, in order to insure reliability of the declaration, "[t]here must be some evidence, independent of the declaration itself, which fairly tends to support the facts asserted therein."[40] In other words, a foundation must be provided that puts the declarations in a context of reliability. The court listed four requisites to admission:

1. The declarant must be unavailable.

2. When the statement was made, the declarant was aware that it was adverse to his penal interest.

3. The declarant must have had competent knowledge of the facts and no motive to misrepresent.

---

35. Id. If, for example, declarant stated that she and the defendant committed a burglary, that would be inextricably mixed up with declarant's own penal interest and would not seem to be collateral in the sense discussed in Maerling. If, however, the declarant talks about his own commission of a burglary, and then adds that the defendant burgled the same premises at a later time, the inculpatory reference to defendant would be collateral and probably inadmissible. There is no indication that the somewhat vaguely stated rule in Maerling as to collateral matter comes anywhere near the radical interpretation of collateral matter rendered by the Supreme Court in Williamson v. United States, ___ U.S. ___, 114 S.Ct. 2431, 129 L.Ed.2d 476 (1994), discussed in § 804(3).2.

36. Id. at 301, 413 N.Y.S.2d at 323, 385 N.E.2d at 1252.

37. See People v. Fonfrias, 204 A.D.2d 736, 738, 612 N.Y.S.2d 421, 423 (2d Dep't 1994).

38. Id. For examples of cases offered for exculpatory purposes, see: People v. Defares, 209 A.D.2d 875, 877, 619 N.Y.S.2d 375, 377 (3d Dep't 1994), appeal denied, 84 N.Y.2d 1030, 623 N.Y.S.2d 186, 647 N.E.2d 458 (1995)(declarant's statement that drugs found by police were his, offered by defendant, not admissible since at the time made declarant had been acquitted of charges concerning those drugs); People v. Barbieri, 207 A.D.2d 554, 555, 616 N.Y.S.2d 80, 81 (2d Dep't 1994), appeal denied, 85 N.Y.2d 905, 627 N.Y.S.2d 328, 650 N.E.2d 1330 (1995)(offer of statement to exculpate defendant unsuccessful since there was no showing that declarant knew his statement was against his penal interest when he made it); People v. Fonfrias, 204 A.D.2d 736, 737–38, 612 N.Y.S.2d 421, 422–23 (2d Dep't 1994)(defendant deprived of a fair trial where third party's confessions not allowed in evidence; circumstances showed a reasonable possibility of truthfulness).

39. 46 N.Y.2d 154, 412 N.Y.S.2d 874, 385 N.E.2d 612 (1978).

40. Id. at 168, 412 N.Y.S.2d at 883, 385 N.E.2d at 620.

4. Supporting circumstances, independent of the statement itself, attest to its trustworthiness.[41]

By way of illustration of the last point, the court stated that evidence placing the declarant at or near the scene of the crime about which he speaks, or proof of his possession of fruits of the crime or instrumentalities used to commit it, would be sufficient.[42] This surrounding evidence of trustworthiness must be laid as a foundation to admissibility. Thus, it is the practice for the trial judge to hold a hearing outside the presence of the jury, known as a *Settles* hearing, to assess these matters.[43]

The trustworthiness requirement is particularly difficult to satisfy where the prosecution offers a declaration against interest that was made to the police while the declarant was in custody. In *People v. Geoghegan*,[44] for example, the declarant had been arrested for murder. He made a confession which implicated the defendant, but the court held the confession inadmissible because the declarant could easily have been motivated to implicate the defendant in hopes of obtaining immunity or a reduced charge.[45] This case creates something of a rebuttable presumption that in-custody statements will not satisfy the second *Settles* requirement, i.e., that the defendant was aware that it was against his penal interest to make the statement.[46]

---

41. Id. at 167, 412 N.Y.S.2d at 882, 385 N.E.2d at 619.

42. Id. at 169, 412 N.Y.S.2d at 884, 385 N.E.2d at 620–21. In the Settles case one Boalds had given the police a statement in which he implicated himself and another, but not Settles, in the crime for which Settles was on trial.

43. See People v. Brensic, 70 N.Y.2d 9, 17, 517 N.Y.S.2d 120, 124, 509 N.E.2d 1226, 1230 (1987).

44. 51 N.Y.2d 45, 431 N.Y.S.2d 502, 409 N.E.2d 975 (1980).

45. Id. at 49, 431 N.Y.S.2d at 504, 409 N.E.2d at 976.

46. But there are purposes to which some in-custody statements can be put. In People v. Thomas, 68 N.Y.2d 194, 507 N.Y.S.2d 973, 500 N.E.2d 293 (1986), cert. denied, 480 U.S. 948, 107 S.Ct. 1609, 94 L.Ed.2d 794 (1987), the defendant was tried for crimes involving the snatching of gold chains from people's necks. He was aided by one Rucker who decided to plead guilty to a lesser felony charge. At his plea allocution Rucker gave an account of the crimes which implicated himself and the defendant. At trial, where Rucker asserted fifth amendment rights, the court allowed the plea allocution statement, not to prove directly defendant's guilt, but for the limited purpose of clarifying the testimony of other eyewitnesses whose stories were less than clear as to whether more than one person committed the crime. All references to defendant by name were redacted. The Court of Appeals upheld this ruling. The court noted that the jury was twice informed that the statement was to be considered solely with respect to the issue of whether more than one person was involved. Beyond that, Rucker should have been fully aware that the statement was against his interest. "We simply cannot accept," said Judge Kaye, "defendant's cynical assertion that, in an admission of guilt sworn to in open court, a declarant will say anything necessary for a favorable plea bargain." Id. at 198, 507 N.Y.S.2d at 975–76, 500 N.E.2d at 295–96. It was noted that by pleading to a felony a person faces immediate conviction, he establishes a criminal record, and he faces increased punishment if convicted of future crimes. Here Rucker was made fully aware of these grim consequences during the plea process. Nor did it seem that his statement was at the defendant's expense. It was not so colored as to minimize Rucker's participation and enhance the defendant's. The other Settles requisites were satisfied, including the fact that there were circumstances independent of the statement which corroborated the statement's contents.

The Appellate Division in People v. Shannon, 207 A.D.2d 727, 728, 616 N.Y.S.2d 615, 616 (1st Dep't 1994), appeal denied, 84 N.Y.2d 1038, 623 N.Y.S.2d 194, 647 N.E.2d 466 (1995), allowed in evidence a statement against interest uttered by an indicted code-

In a case where the *Settles* requirements are satisfied by the prosecution, there would not appear to be a confrontation problem. Although it could be argued that the declaration against *penal* interest is of comparatively recent origin in New York and thus should not be considered a "deeply rooted" hearsay exception, the Court of Appeals' discussions in *Settles*, *Geoghegan* and *Maerling* indicate no concern over this issue, and the Supreme Court's position as expressed in *Ohio v. Roberts*[47] (prior testimony), *United States v. Inadi*[48] (coconspirator's statement), and *Bourjaily v. United States*[49] (coconspirator's statement) show that no confrontation problems under the federal constitution are apparent where the statement is established as trustworthy. The Second Circuit Court of Appeals in *United States v. Katsougrakis*,[50] has ruled on the point and stated that once a statement qualifies as one against penal interest it "usually will survive Confrontation Clause

fendant during his plea allocution, relying on the Thomas decision.

To be compared with Thomas is People v. Morgan, 76 N.Y.2d 493, 561 N.Y.S.2d 408, 562 N.E.2d 485 (1990), where the court refined the conditions under which a custodial declaration would be admissible. One Flihan agreed to waive immunity and testify before the grand jury in return for being permitted to plead to a lesser charge. He testified before the grand jury but balked at the trial of defendant. Ruling him unavailable, the trial judge admitted the grand jury testimony under the authority of People v. Thomas. The Court of Appeals, however, found distinctions and held the grand jury testimony inadmissible because Flihan's testimony may well have been motivated by the prospect of a lesser charge and his conviction and punishment were not in the immediate offing. Except for the immediacy of the consequences of speaking against penal interest, there is little to distinguish the two cases. They are both cases in which the declaration was made after the declarant was in custody and when more often than not declarations will not have all the attributes of being against interest.

In People v. Brensic, 70 N.Y.2d 9, 517 N.Y.S.2d 120, 509 N.E.2d 1226 (1987), however, where the Appellate Division had found the Settles tests satisfied, the Court of Appeals disagreed. A group of four juveniles assaulted and killed a 13-year-old. One of the juveniles, 15-year-old Peter Quartato, gave several confessions to detectives. One statement, given in the presence of his mother, implicated defendant. At trial Peter refused to testify and the statement was allowed in evidence as a declaration against penal interest. Defendant's name was deleted and the jury was told to consider the statement only in their appraisal of the testimony of the other witnesses as to their accounts of the crime. A unanimous Court of Appeals reversed, holding as a matter of law that the statement was unreliable.

Given this substantial evidence that the confession was but one of several, each containing material differences, that it was obtained from a juvenile after lengthy custodial questioning and that it was given under circumstances which suggest that it was induced by the hope of leniency, the confession should not have been placed before the jury as evidence of defendant's guilt. Nor is the argument for reliability stronger because part of Peter's confession was consistent with other evidence before the jury. The test is whether the confession was truly against the declarant's penal interests and the People failed, as a matter of law, to establish in this case that it was.

Id. at 22, 517 N.Y.S.2d at 127, 509 N.E.2d at 1233.

The rule was reiterated that in cases such as this a hearing must be had to determine whether the statement satisfies the Settles requisites and, in fact, referred to this as a "Settles hearing." Id. at 17, 517 N.Y.S.2d at 124, 509 N.E.2d at 1230. In a companion case to Brensic, People v. Young, bearing the same citation, the trial judge did not hold a Settles hearing and all the Huntley hearing evidence indicated that the statement used against the defendant was clothed with an unrebutted presumption of unreliability. See Young, 70 N.Y.2d at 25–26, 517 N.Y.S.2d at 128–29, 509 N.E.2d at 1234–35.

47. 448 U.S. 56, 100 S.Ct. 2531, 65 L.Ed.2d 597 (1980).

48. 475 U.S. 387, 106 S.Ct. 1121, 89 L.Ed.2d 390 (1986).

49. 483 U.S. 171, 107 S.Ct. 2775, 97 L.Ed.2d 144 (1987).

50. 715 F.2d 769 (2d Cir.1983).

scrutiny because the 'trustworthiness' issue has already been decided in favor of admissibility."[51]

Where the statement against interest is in a codefendant's in-custody confession which implicates defendant, *Bruton v. United States*[52] may also prohibit introduction of the confession on confrontation grounds.

Not all declarations sought to be introduced are made after declarant is in custody. Often non-custodial declarations are found wanting in light of the *Settles* requirements.[53] The penal interest exception is not necessarily confined to criminal cases,[54] and, as to a particular statement, more than one hearsay exception may apply.[55]

---

51. Id. at 776. Defendant, tried on charges stemming from arson, had allegedly hired Chrisanthou and another to set the fire. Chrisanthou was fatally injured in the fire, but before he died he was visited in the hospital by a friend. The friend testified that Chrisanthou could not talk, but nodded affirmatively when asked whether he had been paid to set the fire. See also People v. Piazza, 48 N.Y.2d 151, 422 N.Y.S.2d 9, 397 N.E.2d 700 (1979) (without discussion of confrontation issue, court allowed statements by deceased arsonist who incriminated self and alleged employer).

52. 391 U.S. 123, 88 S.Ct. 1620, 20 L.Ed.2d 476 (1968). See § 105.1, at notes 14–15, supra.

53. See People v. Williams, 142 A.D.2d 310, 536 N.Y.S.2d 814 (2d Dep't 1988), appeal denied, 73 N.Y.2d 1023, 541 N.Y.S.2d 778, 539 N.E.2d 606 (1989), where defendant sought admission of a statement made by another defendant, Singleton, that he, Singleton, was in a taxi with two others when they, without his prior knowledge, robbed the driver at gunpoint. This statement would be helpful to defendant since he was not named as one of the other two. This was ruled inadmissible since it was supported by only three of the four Settles requisites. There were no circumstances independent of the statement to provide the needed context of reliability.

In People v. Presler, 134 A.D.2d 866, 521 N.Y.S.2d 920 (4th Dep't 1987), defendant and his friend Kirshner fled from their car after a high-speed chase. Defendant was tried, Kirshner having died in the meantime. Defendant, in order to show Kirshner was the driver, wanted to get in Kirshner's statement, made to an acquaintance shortly after the escape, that he did not "want a DWI." A majority of three justices affirmed the trial court's refusal to admit the statement because "there does not exist sufficient proof independent of the declaration to insure its reliability." Id. at 866, 521 N.Y.S.2d at 921. This was not explained. The dissenter pointed out that the prosecutor never called Kirshner while he was still alive to testify before the grand jury. Id. at 868, 521 N.Y.S.2d at 922. Moreover, some reliability ought to be accorded since the statement was made while Kirshner was in the process of escaping, or shortly thereafter.

Compare People v. Smith, 195 A.D.2d 112, 606 N.Y.S.2d 656 (1st Dep't), appeal denied, 83 N.Y.2d 876, 613 N.Y.S.2d 137, 635 N.E.2d 306 (1994) (statement that exculpated defendant was reliable); People v. Gotti, 146 Misc.2d 793, 552 N.Y.S.2d 485 (Sup.Ct.N.Y.Co.1990) (statement that incriminated defendant was reliable).

54. In Kelleher v. F.M.E. Auto Leasing Corp., 192 A.D.2d 581, 596 N.Y.S.2d 136 (2d Dep't 1993), defendant cab company and its driver were sued for the wrongful death of a 72-year-old man who the driver bodily ejected from the cab and who then froze to death in the snow. The driver told police that he had done this on orders of the dispatcher when he could not locate the old man's home and other fares were waiting. The court held the statement admissible, not as an admission against the company since the driver lacked the authority to bind the company, but as a declaration against the driver's penal interest. Despite the fact the driver made the statements to the police, the court, with no discussion as to his possible self-interest in implicating his employer, simply said that "he had no possible motive to misrepresent the facts." Id. at 583, 596 N.Y.S.2d at 138.

55. In People v. Egan, 78 A.D.2d 34, 434 N.Y.S.2d 55 (4th Dep't 1980), the prosecution's witness testified that he was awakened by a sound. James Egan and his wife Mavis appeared in the room and James said: "'We blew the sucker away,'" and "'Mavis makes the first hit woman in the world.'" Id. at 35, 434 N.Y.S.2d at 57. Mavis then said she was "glad it was over and done with." Id. This testimony arose during Mavis' trial for murder; James had

§ 804(3).2 Federal

Federal Rule of Evidence 804(b)(3) provides:

(3) Statement against interest. A statement which was at the time of its making so far contrary to the declarant's pecuniary or proprietary interest, or so far tended to subject the declarant to civil or criminal liability, or to render invalid a claim by the declarant against another, that a reasonable person in the declarant's position would not have made the statement unless believing it to be true. A statement tending to expose the declarant to criminal liability and offered to exculpate the accused is not admissible unless corroborating circumstances clearly indicate the trustworthiness of the statement.

The application of this rule and its common law predecessor is, like that in New York (see § 804(3).1 *supra*), predominantly in criminal cases with regard to the declaration against penal interest. Nevertheless, several lessons are to be learned from the civil cases.

Civil Cases. Pecuniary and proprietary interests include interests concerning one's job. So said the court in *Gichner v. Antonio Troiano Tile & Marble Co.*[1] In this case an off-duty employee returned to his employer's premises with friends to drink and smoke. Later that night the building went up in flames. The employee's statement to the fire department investigator that he had been smoking at the scene was deemed a declaration against his pecuniary and proprietary interest and thereby admissible in a suit brought by the building owner and its insurer against declarant's employer, the lessee of the building.[2]

The rule in the federal courts is applied as it is in New York in civil cases; and the two chief requisites for admissibility, aside from unavaila-

---

been tried separately and convicted, but he refused to testify at Mavis' trial apparently because his case was on appeal. His statements, as testified to by the witness, were admissible for three reasons. First, because Mavis received James' comments without protest, the statements were admissible to show her admission by silence. Second, James' first statement implicating himself and Mavis could be considered a declaration against penal interest. Third, the statements could be considered spontaneous declarations made immediately following an exciting event. Id. at 36–37, 434 N.Y.S.2d at 57–58.

§ 804(3).2

1. 410 F.2d 238, 242 (D.C.Cir.1969).
2. The court stated:

Here Fauld's [the employee] statement is an important link in providing a basis for concluding that Faulds and the other nighttime visitors to the warehouse were responsible for starting the fire; the possibility of civil liability against him arising from the statement is thus evident. * * * Further, even though Troiano did not have a rule against smoking on the premises, Fauld's admission that he had been there after hours, for a purpose unrelated to his employment, and while there did something which may have caused the destruction of his employer's stock in trade, reflects on his responsibility and trustworthiness, and can reasonably be said to jeopardize his standing with his employer.

Id. at 242.

bility, are that the statement actually be against declarant's interest in the context in which made, and that the declarant know that it is against his interest.

Illustrative of the first point is *Donovan v. Chrisostomo*,[3] a suit brought by the Secretary of Labor seeking sanctions against an employer for overtime payments due its employees. The employer sought to admit statements made by employees to government investigators that they did not work overtime. These statements would be technically against declarants' pecuniary interests since, of course, they would be entitled to more money had they worked overtime. The court noted that to be admissible under Rule 804(b)(3) the statement had to be so "decidedly against the declarant's interest 'that a reasonable man in his position would not have made the statement unless he believed it to be true.' "[4] The statements in question might well have been in declarants' interest in order "to avoid the wrath of [the] employer."[5]

An employee's statement which seemed to implicate his employer in a price-fixing conspiracy would not be admissible in the absence of any evidence that declarant had any understanding of vertical price-fixing when he made the statement.[6] This case illustrates the second chief requisite—that declarant be aware that the statement is against his interest. In another such case it would have been against a partner's interest to admit that dancing was permitted on the partnership premises, but "there is nothing to indicate he was aware of this fact at the time the statements were made."[7]

Criminal cases. There is a curious aspect to Rule 804(b)(3) in regard to criminal matters. The rule specifies that when defendant desires to admit a declaration against interest that would tend to exonerate him he must show corroborating circumstances "clearly indicating the trustworthiness of the statement."[8] The rule is silent as to any corroboration or trustworthiness requirements when the prosecutor

---

3. 689 F.2d 869 (9th Cir.1982).
4. Id. at 877.
5. Id.
6. Pink Supply Corp. v. Hiebert, Inc., 612 F.Supp. 1334, 1345 (D.Minn.1985), aff'd, 788 F.2d 1313 (8th Cir.1986).
7. Filesi v. United States, 352 F.2d 339, 344 (4th Cir.1965). Filesi concerned the imposition of federal cabaret excise taxes. The statements were also ruled out as admissions made by a partner and binding on the partnership since they were made three years after the partnership was dissolved.
8. The Advisory Committee's Note explains this as follows:

> The exception discards the common law limitation and expands to the full logical limit. One result is to remove doubt as to the admissibility of declarations tending to establish a tort liability against the declarant or to extinguish one which might be asserted by him, in accordance with the trend of the decisions in this country. McCormick, § 254, pp.548–549 * * *. And finally, exposure to criminal liability satisfies the against-interest requirement. The refusal of the common law to concede the adequacy of a penal interest was no doubt indefensible in logic, see the dissent of Mr. Justice Holmes in Donnelly v. United States, 228 U.S. 243, 33 S.Ct. 449, 57 L.Ed. 820 (1913), but one senses in the decisions a distrust of evidence of confessions by third persons offered to exculpate the accused arising from suspicions of fabrication either of the fact of the making of the confession or in its contents, enhanced in either instance by the required unavailability of the declarant. Nevertheless, an increasing amount of decisional law recognizes exposure to punishment for crime as a sufficient stake.

offers a statement tending to inculpate the defendant.[9] As discussed in the prior section, in New York there is a heavy burden on the prosecutor to prove the trustworthiness of the statement, and that it was actually against declarant's interest when, as is often the case, the statement was made while declarant was in custody.

There is no doubt, despite the lack of any explicit requirement in Rule 804(b)(3), that trustworthiness must also be established when the federal prosecutor offers the statement. The confrontation aspect becomes an issue here and the federal courts, including the Second Circuit, have insisted on a showing of reliability,[10] especially when the declarant was in custody when he made the statement.[11] The indicia of reliability of a hearsay statement necessary to satisfy the confrontation clause is

---

9. This is dealt with by the Advisory Committee as follows:

Ordinarily the third-party confession is thought of in terms of exculpating the accused, but this is by no means always or necessarily the case: it may include statements implicating him, and under the general theory of declarations against interest they would be admissible as related statements. Douglas v. Alabama, 380 U.S. 415, 85 S.Ct. 1074, 13 L.Ed.2d 934 (1965), and Bruton v. United States, 389 U.S. 818, 88 S.Ct. 126, 19 L.Ed.2d 70 (1967), both involved confessions by codefendants which implicated the accused. While the confession was not actually offered in evidence in Douglas, the procedure followed effectively put it before the jury, which the Court ruled to be error. Whether the confession might have been admissible as a declaration against penal interest was not considered or discussed. Bruton assumed the inadmissibility, as against the accused, of the implicating confession of his codefendant, and centered upon the question of the effectiveness of a limiting instruction. These decisions, however, by no means require that all statements implicating another person be excluded from the category of declarations against interest. Whether a statement is in fact against interest must be determined from the circumstances of each case. Thus a statement admitting guilt and implicating another person, made while in custody, may well be motivated by a desire to curry favor with the authorities and hence fail to qualify as against interest. See the dissenting opinion of Mr. Justice White in Bruton. On the other hand, the same words spoken under different circumstances, e.g., to an acquaintance, would have no difficulty in qualifying. The rule does not purport to deal with questions of the right of confrontation.

10. See United States v. Oliver, 626 F.2d 254, 260 (2d Cir.1980)(a statement may be received as one against penal interest under Rule 804(b)(3) if it is shown that (1) the declarant is unavailable as a witness, (2) the statement must so far tend to subject the declarant to criminal liability that a reasonable person in the declarant's position would not have made the statement unless he or she believed it to be true, and (3) corroborating circumstances clearly indicate the trustworthiness of the statement). Accord, United States v. Riley, 657 F.2d 1377, 1383 (8th Cir.1981), cert. denied, 459 U.S. 1111, 103 S.Ct. 742, 74 L.Ed.2d 962 (1983); United States v. Palumbo, 639 F.2d 123, 131 (3d Cir.), cert. denied, 454 U.S. 819, 102 S.Ct. 100, 70 L.Ed.2d 90 (1981); United States v. Oliver, 626 F.2d 254, 260 (2d Cir.1980).

11. See United States v. Oliver, 626 F.2d 254, 261 (2d Cir.1980) (in-custody statement untrustworthy when declarant is under arrest and told that if she cooperates leniency will be suggested); United States v. Boyce, 849 F.2d 833, 836–37 (3d Cir. 1988)(codefendant's statement made while in custody was not a declaration against interest and there was no showing that it was not made to curry favor); United States v. Palumbo, 639 F.2d 123, 127–28 (3d Cir.), cert. denied, 454 U.S. 819, 102 S.Ct. 100, 70 L.Ed.2d 90 (1981)(no indication that declarant not trying to curry favor). Accord, United States v. Sarmiento-Perez, 633 F.2d 1092, 1104 (5th Cir.1981), cert. denied, 459 U.S. 834, 103 S.Ct. 77, 74 L.Ed.2d 75 (1982); United States v. McClendon, 454 F.Supp. 960, 962 (W.D.Pa. 1978), aff'd, 601 F.2d 577 (3d Cir.), cert. denied sub nom., Jones v. United States, 444 U.S. 952, 100 S.Ct. 427, 62 L.Ed.2d 323 (1979).

§ 804(3).2   HEARSAY   Ch. 8

set forth in a Fifth Circuit case.[12]

A definitive Second Circuit discussion of a statement inculpating declarant and defendant (although not made in custody) is found in *United States v. Katsougrakis*[13] where declarant, on his deathbed in a hospital after being caught in a fire he had set, nodded affirmatively to a friend when asked whether defendant had hired him to commit arson. Finding that the nod was a declaration against interest, the court stated: "Moreover, circumstances surrounding the conversation confirmed the reliability of the hearsay declaration and Chrisanthou's belief in its truth. The declarant was approaching death and was talking privately with his friend when the challenged admission was made. He was not conversing with police or other government agents whose favor he might be expected to curry."[14] Similarly, in *United States v. Matthews*,[15] trustworthiness was found where "[t]he statements were not made to law enforcement authorities, were not made in response to questioning, and were not made in a coercive atmosphere. Rather, they were volunteered by [declarant] to his girl-friend, an intimate and confidante, in the private recesses of their home."[16] The footnote contains additional examples of admissible noncustodial statements.[17]

The element of trustworthiness is no less a factor when defendant is attempting to introduce a declaration against interest which tends to

---

12. In United States v. Sarmiento–Perez, 633 F.2d 1092 (5th Cir.1981), cert. denied, 459 U.S. 834, 103 S.Ct. 77, 74 L.Ed.2d 75 (1982), the court referred to California v. Green, 399 U.S. 149, 90 S.Ct. 1930, 26 L.Ed.2d 489 (1970), Dutton v. Evans, 400 U.S. 74, 91 S.Ct. 210, 27 L.Ed.2d 213 (1970) and Ohio v. Roberts, 448 U.S. 56, 100 S.Ct. 2531, 65 L.Ed.2d 597 (1980), and concluded that more often than not, if the statement reaches that level of reliability sufficient to permit admission as a hearsay exception, it will also have qualified under the confrontation clause. Id. at 1099–1100. Subsequent pronouncements in similar situations have issued from the Supreme Court in United States v. Inadi, 475 U.S. 387, 106 S.Ct. 1121, 89 L.Ed.2d 390 (1986), and Bourjaily v. United States, 483 U.S. 171, 107 S.Ct. 2775, 97 L.Ed.2d 144 (1987), both dealing with coconspirators' statements.

13. 715 F.2d 769 (2d Cir.1983), cert. denied, 464 U.S. 1040, 104 S.Ct. 704, 79 L.Ed.2d 169 (1984).

14. Id. at 775.

15. 20 F.3d 538 (2d Cir.1994).

16. Id. at 546. Judge Kearse discusses at length the requirements for reliability needed to surmount the confrontation obstacles, and stated: "Thus, ordinarily, 'a confession of an accomplice resulting from formal police interrogation cannot be introduced as evidence of the guilt of an accused, absent some circumstance indicating authorization or adoption.'" Id. at 545, quoting from Lee v. Illinois, 476 U.S. 530, 541–42, 106 S.Ct. 2056, 2062, 90 L.Ed.2d 514 (1986).

17. Examples of noncustodial declarations against interest which have been deemed admissible are found in United States v. Bakhtiar, 994 F.2d 970 (2d Cir.), cert. denied sub nom., McDonald v. U.S., ___ U.S. ___, 114 S.Ct. 554, 126 L.Ed.2d 455 (1993)(accomplice's statements to government informant admissible where it did not appear that he tried to shift responsibility from defendant to himself); United States v. Casamento, 887 F.2d 1141, 1160–61 (2d Cir.1989), cert. denied, 493 U.S. 1081, 110 S.Ct. 1138, 107 L.Ed.2d 1043 (1990)(statements made to former business associate reliable within context made); United States v. Koskerides, 877 F.2d 1129, 1135–36 (2d Cir.1989)(statements made to IRS agent admissible since declarant's wife present, declarant was not in custody, and context indicated trustworthiness); United States v. Cruz, 797 F.2d 90, 97 (2d Cir. 1986)(statements by declarant just prior to drug sale made to detective admissible as to the drug operation, his role in it, and the role of "the big man," apparently meaning defendant); United States v. Stratton, 779 F.2d 820, 829 (2d Cir.1985), cert. denied, 476 U.S. 1162, 106 S.Ct. 2285, 90 L.Ed.2d 726 (1986)(declarant thought he was talking to coconspirators and not to authorities and there was no reason to believe he would be falsifying, so statements admissible).

exculpate him.[18] There is the occasional situation where the custodial, inculpatory statement can be used by the prosecutor.[19] Sometimes, the statement is simply not against declarant's interest when made.[20]

The Williamson Case. Much of the federal case law just noted is affected by the Supreme Court's holding in *Williamson v. United States*,[21] where it was announced by Justice O'Connor that only so much of the declaration as was actually against declarant's interest could be admitted, assuming there remained any relevancy to it. In other words, everything else in the statement, including references to the activities of others, must be deleted from the statement. This is the ultimate invocation of the rule that collateral matters in a declaration against interest will be inadmissible.[22] The facts in *Williamson*[23] indicate that

18. See United States v. DeVillio, 983 F.2d 1185, 1189–90 (2d Cir.1993) (where declarant was wired and was cooperating with police his statement exculpating defendant not reliable); United States v. Bahadar, 954 F.2d 821, 828–29 (2d Cir.), cert. denied, ___ U.S. ___, 113 S.Ct. 149, 121 L.Ed.2d 101 (1992)(declarant's statements regarding defendant's involvement inconsistent with each other, and there was no corroboration of trustworthiness to warrant admitting statements); United States v. Salvador, 820 F.2d 558, 561–62 (2d Cir.), cert. denied, 484 U.S. 966, 108 S.Ct. 458, 98 L.Ed.2d 398 (1987)(statement given U.S. Attorney not trustworthy where witness could have had a reason to help defendant, and where, with only an informal plea agreement, declarant not obligated to tell the truth—plus, statement at odds with all the other evidence in the case); United States v. Ford, 771 F.2d 60, 62 (2d Cir.1985)(postarrest statements offered to exculpate defendant untrustworthy where contradicted by observations of undercover officers).

19. In United States v. Williams, 927 F.2d 95, 98–99 (2d Cir.), cert. denied sub nom., Davis v. United States, 502 U.S. 911, 112 S.Ct. 307, 116 L.Ed.2d 250 (1991), four of the original defendants pleaded guilty and in their plea allocutions named defendant as being involved. These statements were allowed in at defendant's trial, although defendant's name had been redacted, to aid the jury in determining whether there was a conspiracy and to describe the criminal activity. It is not clear how, after declarants had plea bargained, these statements were against their interests. Compare United States v. Scopo, 861 F.2d 339, 348 (2d Cir.1988), cert. denied, 490 U.S. 1048, 109 S.Ct. 1957, 104 L.Ed.2d 426 (1989), where it was held that a statement given in a plea allocution was not against penal interest since made pursuant to a plea bargain.

20. In United States v. Harwood, 998 F.2d 91 (2d Cir.1993), Harwood had been arrested along with McKee for drug possession. They were tried together. Harwood's defense was that the drugs all belonged to McKee. The drugs were found in Harwood's van and the circumstantial evidence of his complicity with McKee was substantial. Shortly after the arrests Maynard, a newspaper reporter, had interviewed McKee. Maynard told Harwood's lawyer that McKee had told him that "Harwood was in the wrong place at the wrong time," and "the same would have happened to any person driving a vehicle in which he [McKee] was a passenger." Judge McLaughlin found no point to these statements other than to come in for their truth and no hearsay exceptions could be found. The statements, rather than exposing McKee to criminal liability "seem only to suggest that Harwood was arrested at an inopportune time." Id. at 98. But even if the statements could be seen as incriminating, they were not supported by the corroboration needed under Rule 804(b)(3). Id.

21. ___ U.S. ___, 114 S.Ct. 2431, 129 L.Ed.2d 476(1994).

22. As was noted in § 804(3).1(a), in New York collateral matter in statements against pecuniary and propriety interest is admissible (Livingston v. Arnoux, 56 N.Y. 507, 519 (1874)). As regards statements against penal interest, in New York, the Court of Appeals in People v. Maerling, 46 N.Y.2d 289, 413 N.Y.S.2d 316, 385 N.E.2d 1245 (1978), spoke of collateral matter not being admissible, but there the court seems to have been dealing with matters of relevancy since several of declarant's statements dealt with crimes other than the one in issue. The New York courts have not applied the rule regarding collateral matters as has the Williamson court so as to per se bar all of the statement except so much of it as is directly against declarant's interest.

23. See note 23 on page 736.

the Court could have simply disposed of the matter on the ground that the statement was unreliable since made after declarant was in custody.[24]

Justice O'Connor, in response to the charge that her interpretation "eviscerates" the penal interest exception,[25] argued that the exception retains utility. If declarant stated that "John and I robbed the bank," the words "John and" must be deleted because collateral to that part of the statement directly against declarant's own interest.[26] Justice O'Connor states that what is left of that statement might be relevant when coupled with a witness' testimony that she saw declarant and defendant drive away from the bank together at the crucial time.[27] In other words, if some sort of linkage can be found between the inculpatory words of the declarant and the actions of the defendant then the words might be admissible. That such instances are likely to be rare is shown by the fact that the hypothetical situations used to illustrate the utility left in the hearsay exception are just that—hypotheticals, without citation to instances in which such facts have actually occurred.[28]

---

23. Harris was caught with a trunkload of cocaine. His first story to the DEA agent was that he was to have deposited the dope in a dumpster where Williamson, the defendant, would pick it up. His second story, prompted by the agent's suggestion that he go through with the mission (enabling agents to nab Williamson at the pick-up site), was that he was transporting the dope from Fort Lauderdale to Atlanta for Williamson, that Williamson was driving ahead of him and had seen Harris' apprehension when he doubled back on the road. At Williamson's trial Harris refused to testify and the trial judge allowed in evidence Harris' statements since they were against his penal interest, he was unavailable, and there seemed to be corroborating circumstances.

24. Although Justices Ginsburg, Blackmun, Stevens and Souter agreed that the strict collateral rule should be applied, they would also have ruled the statement inherently unreliable since it was in Harris' interest to shift as much blame as possible to defendant (__ U.S. at __, 114 S.Ct. at 2439, 129 L.Ed.2d at 488); and Justice Kennedy, joined by Chief Justice Rehnquist and Justice Thomas, would have remanded the case for a factual determination as to the nature of Harris' interest (__ U.S. at __, 114 S.Ct. at 2445, 129 L.Ed.2d at 496). The latter group saw no reason for the rule on collateral matter adopted by the majority. Justice Scalia agreed with Justice O'Connor's strict interpretation.

25. Justice Kennedy, id. at __, 114 S.Ct at 2443, 129 L.Ed.2d at 493.

26. Justice Kennedy, id. at __, 114 S.Ct. at 2441, 129 L.Ed.2d at 490.

27. Id. at __, 114 S.Ct. at 2436, 129 L.Ed.2d at 485.

28. Justice O'Connor writes:

For instance, a declarant's squarely self-inculpatory confession—"Yes, I killed X"—will likely be admissible under Rule 804(b)(3) against accomplices of his who are being tried under a co-conspirator liability theory. See Pinkerton v. United States, 328 U.S. 640, 647, 66 S.Ct. 1180, 1184, 90 L.Ed. 1489 (1946). Likewise, by showing that the declarant knew something, a self-inculpatory statement can in some situations help the jury infer that his confederates knew it as well. And when seen with other evidence an accomplice's self-inculpatory statement can inculpate the defendant directly: "I was robbing the bank on Friday morning," coupled with someone's testimony that the declarant and the defendant drove off together Friday morning, is evidence that the defendant also participated in the robbery.

Id. at __, 114 S.Ct. at 2436, 129 L.Ed.2d at 485.

The Pinkerton case is not a case where a coconspirator's statement was used to create an inference that others were involved. At the page cited is found dictum illustrating the nature of a conspiracy and the fact that words and acts in connection therewith can be admissible. Coconspirators' statements made during the conspiracy and in furtherance thereof are not hearsay under Rule 801(d)(2)(E) and would be admissible on that ground anyway. It is conceivable that a conspirator's statement not made during the conspiracy or in furtherance thereof might be admissible as a declaration

This sharp curtailment of the use of declarations against penal interest affects not only custodial inculpatory statements, as in *Williamson*, but also all statements having an exculpatory effect, and noncustodial statements having an inculpatory effect.[29] Further interpretation lies ahead. For instance, where the declaration against interest consists of a nod of the head, as in the *Katsougrakis* case noted above, it can be conjectured that the nod will be inadmissible, despite its apparent trustworthiness, because the question asked implicated not just declarant, but also the defendant.

Library References:

West's Key No. Digests, Criminal Law ⇐412, 417(15), 422(5); Evidence ⇐272.

804(4) Pedigree

§ 804(4).1 New York

It sometimes occurs that when family relationships are in issue it is impossible to produce direct evidence of lineage because those having knowledge of such events are long dead. The traditional test for the pedigree hearsay exception has it that the declarant must be dead, the statements must have been made prior to the occurrence of any motive to distort the truth, and the declarant must be related by blood or marriage to the family of which he speaks.[1] Pedigree declarations are statements attesting to matters of "lineage, descent and succession of families;"[2] but this does not necessarily include statements as to a family member's age.[3] (This is not to be confused with the rule that a

against interest which could implicate the others through some linking evidence creating an inference, but Pinkerton is not such a case.

Justice O'Connor gives further hypothetical circumstances:

> Even statements that are on their face neutral may actually be against the declarant's interest. "I hid the gun in Joe's apartment," may not be a confession of a crime; but if it is likely to help the police find the murder weapon, then it is certainly self-inculpatory. "Sam and I went to Joe's house" might be against the declarant's interest if a reasonable person in the declarant's shoes would realize that being linked to Joe and Sam would implicate the declarant in Joe and Sam's conspiracy.

Id. at __, 114 S.Ct. at 2436-37, 129 L.Ed.2d at 485.

Justice Scalia who was fully in accord with Justice O'Connor and wrote only to answer Justice Kennedy's opinion, also recites an example of how the new, revised statement against penal interest may be used, equally hypothetical.

29. There is nothing in Justice O'Connor's opinion which limits it to custodial, inculpatory statements.

§ 804(4).1

1. Aalholm v. People, 211 N.Y. 406, 412–13, 105 N.E. 647, 649 (1914).

2. Washington v. Bank For Savings, 171 N.Y. 166, 173, 63 N.E. 831, 833 (1902).

3. See People v. Lammes, 208 App.Div. 533, 534–35, 203 N.Y.S. 736, 738 (4th Dep't 1924). The question in this statutory rape case was the age of the victim. The prosecution sought to introduce evidence of a statement by the victim's deceased mother as to her age. The court stated: "This affidavit was hearsay evidence pure and simple. It was received on the theory that it established the pedigree of the complainant. It could not be properly received for any such purpose for age is not essential to establish pedigree, and the question of pedigree was not necessarily involved in the case." Id.

See also Bowen v. Preferred Accident Ins. Co., 68 App.Div. 342, 74 N.Y.S. 101 (2d Dep't 1902). In an action on a life insur-

person may testify as to his own age.)[4]

"Declarations in regard to pedigree, although hearsay, are admitted on the principle that they are the natural effusions of persons who must know the truth and who speak on occasions when their minds stand in an even position without any temptation to exceed or fall short of the truth."[5] Also, "[t]he exception regarding the admission of hearsay evidence in case of pedigree is not confined to ancient facts, but extends also to matters of pedigree which have recently transpired; and the hearsay as to deceased witnesses is admitted as to facts which have occurred in the presence of living witnesses."[6]

Pedigree includes not only descent and relationship, but also "the facts of birth, marriage and death, and the times when these events happened."[7] Moreover, the declarant need not have firsthand knowledge of that about which he speaks. "Thus evidence that a deceased [or otherwise unavailable] member of the family said that he heard from others of his family the facts which he states is admissible."[8]

The ancient requirement that the declarant be dead, recited also in more recent cases,[9] probably misstates the rule. The Court of Appeals in 1901 in *Young v. Shulenberg*,[10] stated: "Therefore, before the declarations can be received * * * as evidence of pedigree, it must appear that the person making them was a member of the family and that he is dead, incompetent, or beyond the jurisdiction of the court."[11] That, taken together with modern concepts of unavailability as stated in the various codifications of the rules[12] virtually assures that admissibility today would not be confined only to instances where declarant was dead.[13]

The requirement that the declarant be a family member cannot, except where declarant spoke of his own relationship,[14] be satisfied by

ance policy the defense was that the insured misrepresented his age when he applied for the policy. Plaintiff offered a letter written by the insured's deceased brother offering his opinion on the age of the insured. The Appellate Division ruled that the reception of the letter was error stating: "The error was due to the conclusion that a question of age is one of pedigree, or, perhaps, to the confusion of age with pedigree. A question of pedigree may, of course, involve a question of age; but a case which involves age is not necessarily one of pedigree." Id. at 344, 74 N.Y.S. at 102.

4. See Koester v. Rochester Candy Works, 194 N.Y. 92, 97, 87 N.E. 77, 78 (1909); People v. Mishlanie, 24 Misc.2d 277, 278, 204 N.Y.S.2d 450, 451 (Oneida Co.Ct.1960)(in a prosecution for selling beer to a minor the court allowed the purchaser to testify to his own age stating: "A witness may * * * testify to his own age even though based essentially on hearsay evidence, upon the theory that it is common knowledge in the family.")

5. Aalholm v. People, 211 N.Y. 406, 412, 105 N.E. 647, 649 (1914).

6. Eisenlord v. Clum, 126 N.Y. 552, 563, 27 N.E. 1024, 1027 (1891).

7. Id. at 564, 27 N.E. at 1027.

8. Id. at 565, 27 N.E. at 1028.

9. See, e.g., Matter of Esther T., 86 Misc.2d 452, 455, 382 N.Y.S.2d 916, 919 (Surr.Ct.Nassau Co.1976).

10. 165 N.Y. 385, 59 N.E. 135 (1901).

11. Id. at 388, 59 N.E. at 136.

12. See § 804.1 supra.

13. But see the recitation that declarant must be deceased in the later case of Aalholm v. People, 211 N.Y. 406, 412, 105 N.E. 647, 649 (1914). In Matter of Strong, 168 Misc. 716, 6 N.Y.S.2d 300 (Surr.Ct.N.Y.Co. 1938), aff'd, 256 App.Div. 971, 11 N.Y.S.2d 225 (1st Dep't 1939), the court recognized the conflict and opted to accept testimony concerning statements of a parent who was alive, but beyond the court's jurisdiction. 168 Misc. at 719–20, 11 N.Y.S.2d at 303.

14. McCormick § 322, at 354.

Ch. 8   PEDIGREE   § 804(4).1

the declarations sought to be admitted. Unless the relationship is conceded,[15] there must be some independent evidence of the relationship;[16] but such proof need only be "slight."[17] In tune with Federal Rule 804(b)(4) and proposed New York Evidence Code § 804(6)(A)(ii), the court might be persuaded that statements made by one "intimately associated" with the subject family would be admissible.

The declaration of pedigree, if meeting the requirements, can be in any form. As was stated in *Matter of Whalen*:[18] "The rules * * * apply to all pedigree declarations regardless of the form in which they are presented, whether as ancient documents, entries in a family bible, inscriptions on tombstones, etc."[19] Oral statements by family members are at issue in some cases,[20] while statements in documents are at issue in others.[21]

---

15. Matter of Findlay, 253 N.Y. 1, 11, 170 N.E. 471, 474 (1930).

16. Aalholm v. People, 211 N.Y. 406, 413, 105 N.E. 647, 649 (1914).

17. Id. at 415, 105 N.E. at 650. See also Young v. Shulenberg, 165 N.Y. 385, 388, 59 N.E. 135, 136 (1901)(excerpts from deeds, proper custody of deeds, and an immigration acknowledgment before a United States minister found to be sufficient corroboration); Matter of Morris, 277 App.Div. 211, 215, 98 N.Y.S.2d 997, 1001 (3d Dep't 1950)(sufficient corroboration rested on a "single and a rather casual remark fifty-six years before the trial attributed to the decedent by a neighbor, a statement by her husband in her presence, and several other like statements"); Matter of Whalen, 146 Misc. 176, 190, 261 N.Y.S. 761, 776 (Surr. Ct.N.Y.Co.1932) (insufficient evidence of relationship: similarity of name and religion are too common to be probative).

In the case of In re Estate of Riggs, 68 Misc.2d 760, 328 N.Y.S.2d 138 (Surr.Ct. N.Y.Co.1972), petitioner claimed the position of distributee in the estate of decedent who was alleged to have been a paternal first cousin. Petitioner's father and Leon Corey Riggs were brothers and the question was whether decedent was the adopted daughter of Leon Corey Riggs. Petitioner relied on a statement in Riggs' will, admitted to probate in 1920, referring to decedent as "* * * my daughter Helen whom I have legally and lawfully adopted * * * *" Id. at 762, 328 N.Y.S.2d at 140. Of the requisites for the admission of such evidence two are present: the declarant was dead and the declaration was made ante litem motam. The third requisite, that declarant be related to the family of which he speaks, involved in part the very declaration sought to be introduced. This technical point did not detain the surrogate who held that the declaration was admissible, but was not enough, standing alone, to establish the crucial fact of legal adoption. He said that the whereabouts of the family was known at all times and proper investigation would locate an adoption order if, in fact, a legal adoption had occurred. The pedigree question was thus one of weight and not admissibility.

18. 146 Misc. 176, 261 N.Y.S. 761 (Surr. Ct.N.Y.Co.1932).

19. Id. at 189, 261 N.Y.S. at 775.

20. See Aalholm v. People, 211 N.Y. 406, 412, 105 N.E. 647, 649 (1914) (petitioner, asserting claim to estate, offered statements of relationship made to him by his mother, and statements of children of a half sister—not admissible because no independent proof of relationship of declarant); Washington v. Bank For Savings, 171 N.Y. 166, 172–73, 63 N.E. 831, 833 (1902)(witness who knew declarant in her lifetime permitted to testify as to statements that she had no children—to prove that bank account was set up in fictitious names of children); Eisenlord v. Clum, 126 N.Y. 552, 563, 27 N.E. 1024, 1027 (1891)(where question was whether H was married to W, proper to introduce deceased's H's statements to that effect even though no other evidence that the couple ever cohabited); Matter of Morris, 277 App.Div. 211, 213, 98 N.Y.S.2d 997, 999 (3d Dep't 1950)(a witness who was a first cousin of intestate testified that her mother told her when she was a child that intestate's mother and she were sisters, thus establishing kinship—aided by similar statements made by other deceased relatives).

21. See Young v. Shulenberg, 165 N.Y. 385, 388, 59 N.E. 135, 136 (1901) (where plaintiff's title to land challenged by defendant in trespass action, plaintiff can offer evidence of statements in deeds showing relationship to grantor); Farmers' Loan & Trust Co. v. Wagstaff, 194 App.Div. 757, 761, 185 N.Y.S. 812, 815 (2d Dep't

§ 804(4).1 HEARSAY Ch. 8

Family facts and relationships may be proved by circumstantial evidence consisting of a chain of related records and events, and not just on the basis of statements made by family members.[22]

Of course if the declarant's statement does not meet all the requirements of the pedigree rule, it might be admissible under another hearsay exception,[23] or as nonhearsay.[24]

The pedigree rules found in the proposed New York Evidence Code are in the footnote.[25] The proposed code restates the various aspects of

1921)(deceased's statement in income tax returns that he was single, admissible in opposition to plaintiff's claim that she was his wife); Young v. Shulenberg, 35 App.Div. 79, 80, 54 N.Y.S. 419 (3d Dep't 1898), aff'd, 165 N.Y. 385, 59 N.E. 135 (1901)(recitals in deeds established necessary link in relationships claimed by plaintiff to establish title in trespass action); In re Estate of Riggs, 68 Misc.2d 760, 328 N.Y.S.2d 138 (Surr.Ct.N.Y.Co.1972)(statement in will which had been admitted to probate that person was his daughter Helen who he had legally adopted was admissible).

22. Surrogate Foley in Matter of Hayden, 176 Misc. 1078, 29 N.Y.S.2d 852 (Surr. Ct.N.Y.Co.1941) stated:

The rules applicable to pedigree cases involving proof of the identity of a person have been frequently stated. Their object is to lead the trier of the facts to a reasonable conclusion. Pedigree is the lineage, descent and succession of families. (Washington v. Bank for Savings, 171 N.Y. 166, 63 N.E. 831.) The primary rule of evidence emphasizes the progressive value of proved coincidences and circumstances based upon undisputed facts, all pointing to only one conclusion. * * * A single and independent undisputed fact or coincidence is seldom of value. The accumulation of coincidences and undisputed facts and records, when bound together, multiplies the convincing quality of the entire case. (Wigmore on Principles of Judicial Proof, p.64.) In cases of this kind the pieces of evidence fit together in a perfect picture, like a mosaic, when status is established. On the other hand, where correlation or co-ordination of the pieces is absent, the fictitious nature of the claim of the pretender to kinship is revealed. (Matter of Wendel, 146 Misc. 260.)

176 Misc. at 1080, 29 N.Y.S. at 854.

In establishing heirship the court considered the pension application and army service record of decedent's father, Chicago directories containing the names of decedent's father and petitioner's father in the same locality, and a baptismal record showing the decedent's father as one of the sponsors and godfather of a son of petitioner's father. The decedent's father's first name was Loftus, an unusual enough name so that he could be linked to other family members in order to establish the necessary link to petitioner. Id. at 1080–81, 29 N.Y.S. at 854.

23. The comment to proposed New York Evidence Code § 804(b)(6) states: "Even if certain evidence is not admissible under this paragraph, the evidence may be admissible under one or more of the exceptions of CE 803, e.g., 803(c)(5)(business records); 803(c)(7)(public records and reports); 803(c)(8)(records of vital statistics); 803(c)(10)(records of religious organizations); 803(c)(11)(marriage, baptismal, and similar certificates); 803(c)(14)(statements in ancient documents); 803(c)(16) (reputation concerning personal or family history); and 804(b)(4)(B) (family records)."

24. In Matter of Findlay, 253 N.Y. 1, 11–12, 170 N.E. 471, 474–75 (1930), Judge Cardozo found a deceased mother's statements admissible as verbal acts in a case involving the question of legitimacy of children, where the proof showing illegitimacy overcame the presumption of legitimacy.

25. § 804 New York Code of Evidence [PROPOSED].

(6) Statement of personal or family history and family records.

(A) Family History.

(i) Statement relating to declarant's family. A statement, made prior to the controversy, concerning declarant's own birth, adoption, marriage, divorce, legitimacy, relationship by blood, adoption or marriage, ancestry, or other similar fact of personal or family history, even though declarant had no means of acquiring personal knowledge of the matter stated.

(ii) Statement relating to another family. A statement, made prior to the controversy, concerning any of the foregoing matters or the death of another person, if the declarant was related to the other by blood, adoption, or marriage or was so intimately associated with the oth-

the existing rule found in the cases and broadens them in several respects.[26]

Library References:

West's Key No. Digests, Criminal Law ⬅411–418.10; Evidence ⬅285–297.

§ 804(4).2 Federal

Federal Rule 804(b)(4) describes the pedigree exception as follows:

(4) Statement of personal or family history. (A) A statement concerning the declarant's own birth, adoption, marriage, divorce, legitimacy, relationship by blood, adoption, or marriage, ancestry, or other similar fact of personal or family history, even though declarant had no means of acquiring personal knowledge of the matter stated; or (B) a statement concerning the foregoing matters, and death also, of another person, if the declarant was related to the other by blood, adoption, or marriage or was so intimately associated with the other's family as to be likely to have accurate information concerning the matter declared.

Not surprisingly, cases in which genealogical issues arise are few in the federal courts. Contests over estates, trespass cases and family disputes are confined chiefly to state courts. Nevertheless, Rule 804(b)(4) provides a complete guide when the issue does arise. It departs from its proposed state counterpart in eliminating the necessity that the statement be made before any controversy arose.[1]

er's family as to be likely to have accurate information concerning the matter declared.

(B) Family records. Statements of fact concerning personal or family history, made prior to the controversy and contained in family bibles, engravings on rings, inscriptions on family portraits, engravings on urns, crypts, or tombstones, or the like.

26. In the Comment it is stated:

The subparagraph [(b)(6)(A)(i)] also broadens the present exception by expanding the types of statements to which the exceptions apply. Traditionally, pedigree had to be directly at issue, i.e., the controversy had to be essentially genealogical. * * * This paragraph, on the other hand, follows the trend of recent judicial decisions and expands the exception "to encompass the whole area of family history." See 4 Berger and Weinstein ¶ 804[6][4][01].

* * *

As to subparagraph (b)(6)(A)(ii) it is stated:

When the statement sought to be admitted relates to the personal history of one other than the declarant, the provision requires additionally that the declarant's competency be established by a showing that he probably had knowledge of the matters of which he spoke, either because of relationship or intimate association. This broadens present law, which admitted this type of pedigree statement only upon independent evidence of relationship.

§ 804(4).2

1. The Advisory Committee's Note is as follows:

Exception [4]. The general common law requirement that a declaration in this area must have been made *ante litem motam* has been dropped, as bearing more appropriately on weight than admissibility. See 5 Wigmore § 1483. Item (i) specifically disclaims any need of firsthand knowledge respecting declarant's own personal history. In some instances it is self-evident (marriage) and in others impossible and traditionally not required (date of birth). Item (ii) deals with declarations concerning the history of another person. As at common law, declarant is qualified if related by blood or marriage. 5 Wigmore, § 1489. In addition, and contrary to the common law, declarant qualifies by virtue of intimate association with the family. Id., § 1487.

As illustrative of an instance where the pedigree rule might be raised in federal practice we have Judge Weinstein's decision in *Brown for Brown v. Bowen*,[2] which involved a child's claim for Social Security payments based on the death of her father. The question was whether Otis Fulton, 20 years old when he was hit and killed by a passing motorist, was the child's father. He and the child's mother were not married. The facts were proved at an administrative hearing which might have eliminated the need to find hearsay exceptions, but Judge Weinstein nevertheless stated that Rule 804(b)(4) would allow for Otis Fulton's mother's testimony that Otis had told her he was the child's father[3] and that he had signed an acknowledgment of paternity at the Department of Social Services.[4]

Underscoring the fact that the pedigree rule has reached beyond a narrow focus on issues of lineage and now encompasses all family matters is the pre-Rule 804(b)(4) case of *Bank of New York v. United States*.[5] There, in a situation where the subject's death was sought to be established by his long, unexplained absence, the court stated that weight must be given the statement of the subject's deceased mother in her will that she had not heard from the subject, her son, for many years.[6]

The Supreme Court in *Fulkerson v. Holmes*[7] long ago set forth the traditional common law pedigree exception which required the conditions that the statement regarding genealogy be made by a since deceased person, that declarant be a family member, and that where the statement concerns others in the family some slight independent evidence of relationship be produced.[8] By 1959 the Ninth Circuit Court of

The requirement sometimes encountered that when the subject of the statement is the relationship between two other persons the declarant must qualify as to both is omitted. Relationship is reciprocal. Id., § 1491.

2. 668 F.Supp. 146 (E.D.N.Y.1987).

3. Id. at 148, 150.

4. Id.

5. 174 F.Supp. 911 (S.D.N.Y.1957).

6. Id. at 915. But see United States v. Carvalho, 742 F.2d 146, 151 (4th Cir.1984), where the court ruled that the pedigree exception governs matters of fact, not evidence of "motive or purpose, or [other] highly debatable or controversial matters," and excluded statements relating to one's motives and reasons for getting married. See also United States v. Medina–Gasca, 739 F.2d 1451, 1454 (9th Cir.1984), where the court held that testimony by an immigration officer that an illegal alien had made statements concerning his foreign birth and ancestry would be excluded because it was sought to be used against a criminal defendant and tended to prove "a critical element of the crimes charged."

7. 117 U.S. 389, 6 S.Ct. 780, 29 L.Ed. 915 (1886).

8. Id. at 397, 6 S.Ct. at 784, 29 L.Ed.2d at 918. This was an ejectment action where heirship was sought to be established by statements in deeds. The court stated:

The question is therefore fairly presented whether the recitals made in the deed of Samuel C. Young to John Holmes, to the effect that Samuel Young, the patentee, had died intestate, leaving one child only, namely, the said Samuel C. Young, the grantor, were admissible in evidence against the defendants, who did not claim title under the deed. The fact to be established is one of pedigree. The proof to show pedigree forms a well-settled exception to the rule which excludes hearsay evidence. This exception has been recognized on the ground of necessity; for as in inquiries respecting relationship or descent facts must often be proved which occurred many years before the trial, and were known to but few persons, it is obvious that the strict enforcement in such cases of the rules against hearsay evidence would frequently occasion a failure of justice. * * * Traditional evidence

Appeals was willing to consider whether declarants could be non-family members who were nevertheless intimately associated with the family,[9] and, of course, Rule 804(b)(4) has broadened the rules governing unavailability and the contents of the statements.

Federal Rules 803(13)[10] and 803(19)[11] complement the pedigree exception.

Library References:

West's Key No. Digests, Criminal Law ⌹411–418.10; Evidence ⌹285–297.

804(5) Residual Hearsay Exception

§ 804(5).1 New York

Under Federal Rules 803(24) and 804(b)(5), discussed in the next section, and Proposed New York Evidence Code § 806,[1] are found

is therefore admissible. * * * The rule is that declarations of deceased persons who were *de jure* related by blood or marriage to the family in question may be given in evidence in matters of pedigree. * * * A qualification of the rule is that before a declaration can be admitted in evidence the relationship of the declarant with the family must be established by some proof independent of the declaration itself. * * * But it is evident that but slight proof of the relationship will be required, since the relationship of the declarant with the family might be as difficult to prove as the very fact in controversy.

Applying these rules, we are of opinion that the recital in the deed of Samuel C. Young to John Holmes, supported as it was by the circumstances of the case shown by the evidence, was admissible, as tending to prove the facts recited, namely, that Samuel Young, the patentee, was dead, and Samuel C. Young, the grantor, was his only child and heir.

Id. at 397–98, 6 S.Ct. at 784, 29 L.Ed.2d at 918.

9. Young Ah Chor v. Dulles, 270 F.2d 338, 344–45 (9th Cir.1959)(the declarant, while an acquaintance, was far from being intimately associated with the family and thus his statements in a citizenship proceeding to establish petitioner as the son of an American citizen were inadmissible).

10. **Rule 803(13) Family records.**

Statements of fact concerning personal or family history contained in family Bibles, genealogies, charts, engravings on rings, inscriptions on family portraits, engravings on urns, crypts, or tombstones, or the like.

See § 803(7).2 supra.

11. **Rule 803(19) Reputation concerning personal or family history.**

Reputation among members of a person's family by blood, adoption, or marriage, or among a person's associates, or in the community, concerning a person's birth, adoption, marriage, divorce, death, legitimacy, relationship by blood, adoption, or marriage, ancestry, or other similar fact of his personal or family history.

See § 803(7).2 supra.

§ 804(5).1

1. **§ 806. Unenumerated exceptions to the hearsay rule [PROPOSED]**

In a criminal case a statement of an unavailable declarant, or in a civil case a statement of a declarant, regardless of that person's availability, not specifically encompassed by sections 803, 804 or 805 of this article and not intentionally excluded from those sections because of its unreliability, is not excluded by the hearsay rule if the court determines that the statement: (i) is within a definable category of statements that possesses substantial guarantees of trustworthiness and that is separate and distinct from the categories set forth in this article; (ii) has substantial guarantees of trustworthiness; and (iii) there is a substantial need for the statement to establish an essential part of the proponent's case. In admitting a statement under this section, the court shall make specific findings of the facts and circumstances supporting the substantial guarantees of trustworthiness and the substantial need for receipt of the particular statement as well as specific conclusions of law demonstrating the substantial guarantees of trustworthiness of the general category encompassing the particular statement. The decision to

§ 804(5).1 HEARSAY Ch. 8

provisions allowing in evidence hearsay not otherwise covered under any of the other exceptions. Sometimes these rules are referred to as the "residual" or "catchall" hearsay exceptions, but they are hedged about with strict limitations. There must be strong guarantees of trustworthiness, and the hearsay must be more probative than other available evidence making it, in effect, a rule of necessity.

Currently New York has no cohesive catchall rule even in the caselaw; but there are indications in scattered cases that, given the right circumstances, the courts would be willing to expand the admissibility of hearsay. Thus, in *Fleury v. Edwards*,[2] in broadening the prior testimony rule to cover testimony taken in an administrative proceeding, the court was chiefly concerned with the high degree of trustworthiness of the offered evidence.[3] In *Letendre v. Hartford Acc. & Ind. Co.*,[4] in allowing a witness' prior inconsistent statements in evidence not just for impeachment purposes, but also for their truth,[5] the court stated: "Often hearsay evidence has far more probative value than testimonial evidence. There was nothing in Tremblay's [prior] statements or in the circumstances under which they were given which made them less reliable than his testimony in court."[6] Later, in *People v. Brown*,[7] the Court of Appeals broadened the statement against interest rule to cover statements against penal interest and opened the unavailability rule to absences beyond those caused by death. And, in *People v. Arnold*,[8] in finding declarant's accusatory statement not to be admissible as a dying declaration, but finding its admission harmless error, it was stated: "Were it necessary to determine whether the deceased's utterance fit within an exception to the hearsay rule, it is observed that this court has in recent years emphasized that the hearsay doctrine has been too restrictively applied to exclude otherwise reliable evidence from the jury * * *. The issue, however, is not determined now and may be reserved

recognize a new category or the decision to expand, restrict or modify a category recognized under this section is solely a question of law. A statement may not be admitted under this section unless the proponent of it makes known to all parties the proponent's intention to offer the statement and its particulars, including the name and address of the declarant, sufficiently in advance of offering the statement to provide them with a fair opportunity to meet it.

2. 14 N.Y.2d 334, 251 N.Y.S.2d 647, 200 N.E.2d 550 (1964).

3. Id. at 339, 200 N.Y.S.2d at 553, 251 N.E.2d at 651. Judge Fuld in a concurring opinion stated:

Whether prior testimony before an administrative body would have been admissible in 1879, when the predecessor of CPLR 4517 was adopted, is not significant. The common law of evidence is constantly being refashioned by the courts of this and other jurisdictions to meet the demands of modern litigation.

Exceptions to hearsay rules are being broadened and created where necessary. * * * Absent some strong public policy or a clear act of pre-emption by the Legislature, rules of evidence should be fashioned to further, not frustrate, the truth-finding function of the courts in civil cases.

4. 21 N.Y.2d 518, 289 N.Y.S.2d 183, 236 N.E.2d 467 (1968).

5. Without these prior statements made by plaintiff's employee given to investigators, plaintiff would have had no evidence to make out a prima facie case against the bonding company for reimbursement for the employee's defalcations. See § 801(1).2(a) supra.

6. 21 N.Y.2d at 525, 289 N.Y.S.2d at 189, 236 N.E.2d at 470.

7. 26 N.Y.2d 88, 308 N.Y.S.2d 825, 257 N.E.2d 16 (1970).

8. 34 N.Y.2d 548, 354 N.Y.S.2d 106, 309 N.E.2d 875 (1974).

for resolution in a case which would require such resolution."[9] In *People v. Geraci*,[10] the Court of Appeals allowed otherwise inadmissible grand jury testimony. Defendant had waived his objection by intimidating the witness into not testifying at trial.

It is arguable that the Court of Appeals in *People v. Nieves*[11] decided the residual hearsay question in the negative. The *Nieves* court, however, did not cite *Arnold* much less discuss the dictum quoted just above. *Nieves* involved the issue whether certain accusatory statements constituted dying declarations and it was decided they did not because declarant had no settled expectation of impending death. On appeal, the prosecution argued that the statements were inherently reliable and should be admissible on that basis alone, citing *Arnold*. The court stated:

> Miss Gonzalez's statements, of course, constituted hearsay evidence, as they were made out of court and were sought to be introduced for the truth of what she asserted * * *. Accordingly, they were admissible only if the People demonstrated that they fell within one of the exceptions to the hearsay rule. Although the People now contend that the statements should be admissible as long as they are deemed "reliable," without regard to whether they fit into any such exception, they made no such argument before the trial court. Furthermore, we are not prepared at this time to abandon the well-established reliance on specific categories of hearsay exceptions in favor of an amorphous "reliability" test, particularly in criminal cases where to do so could raise confrontation clause problems * * *.[12]

Where, however, it is the defendant who wishes to introduce such generic hearsay, the courts have been creative. Thus, in the trial court's opinion in *People v. Ortiz*,[13] it was pointed out that defense counsel wished to examine a detective in order to inquire about a lineup eyewitness who was not produced to testify for the prosecution. The detective's testimony would be hearsay as to the eyewitness' responses and would not fit any known hearsay exception. The court noted the relaxation of the hearsay rule at the federal level, surveyed key cases in New York and elsewhere that took a liberal approach,[14] set forth eight factors to be weighed concerning the admissibility of hearsay,[15] and

---

9. Id. at 549–50, 354 N.Y.S.2d at 107, 309 N.E.2d at 875.

10. 85 N.Y.2d 359, 625 N.Y.S.2d 469, 649 N.E.2d 817 (1995). See discussion of this case at § 807.1.

11. 67 N.Y.2d 125, 501 N.Y.S.2d 1, 492 N.E.2d 109 (1986) (victim of stabbing named defendant as attacker in response to questions by emergency room doctor). See the discussion of this case at § 804(2).1, at notes 31–32 supra.

12. Id. at 131, 501 N.Y.S.2d at 4–5, 492 N.E.2d at 112. The confrontation problem is taken up in the next section.

13. 119 Misc.2d 572, 463 N.Y.S.2d 713 (Sup.Ct.Bronx Co.1983).

14. Chief among these is Chambers v. Mississippi, 410 U.S. 284, 93 S.Ct. 1038, 35 L.Ed.2d 297 (1973), which held that the hearsay rule could not be applied mechanically to keep out hearsay statements circumstantially trustworthy and vital to the defense and essential to due process.

15. Courts should consider the following factors:

discussed Wigmore's dictum that the hearsay element does not necessarily make a statement worthless.[16] The detective's testimony in this case, however, proved to be a double-edged sword since once the detective testified that the lineup witness would not identify the defendant, the way was opened for the prosecution to ask him *why* the witness refused to make the identification.[17]

Where hearsay statements are not "critical" to the defense, the trial judge is warranted in keeping them out.[18] Statements which are critical to the defense will still be inadmissible where basic trustworthiness is

(a) Is the evidence material and relevant to a central issue in the case or is it collateral?

(b) Is the proffered hearsay probative of a disputed fact or would it be merely cumulative?

(c) What is the form of hearsay, i.e. does the witness claim to have heard the ultimate declarant or is his information third-party hearsay?

(d) Is the witness credible and disinterested or is there independent corroboration of his testimony?

(e) Did the declarant of the statement have firsthand knowledge of the facts?

(f) Has the proponent of the hearsay made reasonable attempts to procure the attendance of the declarant or has the proponent in fact prevented the declarant from testifying or procured or attempted to procure his absence?

(g) Is the right of the party against whom the hearsay is offered to cross-examine or otherwise controvert the evidence protected as far as possible?

(h) Would the admission of the procured hearsay otherwise serve the interests of justice?

Ortiz, 119 Misc.2d at 577, 463 N.Y.S.2d at 717.

16. The court stated:

Wigmore's cautionary language to the contrary, the rule * * * has often been applied in a pedantic and wooden manner and probative and reliable testimony has often been excluded merely because it did not qualify under one of the recognized exceptions to the hearsay rule. To make matters worse the exceptions themselves were often rigidly construed. Thus much time has been spent considering whether challenged documentary evidence is a "business entry" or whether a statement is sufficiently "spontaneous." Such effort would have been better directed towards analyzing the value of the evidence itself.

Ortiz, 119 Misc.2d at 575–75, 463 N.Y.S.2d at 716.

Wigmore stated:

No one could defend a rule which pronounced that all statements thus untested by cross-examination are *worthless*; for all historical truth is based on un-cross-examined assertions; and every day's experience of life gives denial to such an exaggeration. What the Hearsay Rule implies—and with profound verity—is that all testimonial assertions *ought to be* tested by cross-examination, as the best attainable measure; and it should not be burdened with the pedantic implication that they must be rejected as worthless if the test is unavailable.

2 J. Wigmore, Evidence § 8c, at 644 (Tillers rev.ed.1983), quoted in Ortiz, 119 Misc.2d at 574, 463 N.Y.S.2d at 715–16 (emphasis in original).

17. It was because the witness complained that he had been threatened and warned not to testify. The court ruled that if the defense wanted evidence that the eyewitness did not identify the defendant, then it must expect evidence as to why there was no identification. Ortiz, 119 Misc.2d at 579, 463 N.Y.S.2d at 718.

18. See People v. Esteves, 152 A.D.2d 406, 413–14, 549 N.Y.S.2d 30, 36 (2d Dep't 1989)(where defendant charged with acting with another in shooting the victim, victim's statement that defendant did not fire the shot, inadmissible under any hearsay exception, would not otherwise be admissible since there was no distinction between defendant's liability as a principal or an accomplice); People v. Clark, 178 A.D.2d 258, 260, 577 N.Y.S.2d 790, 792 (1st Dep't 1991)(trial court warranted in barring detective's testimony of eyewitness' failure to identify defendant at lineup, since the eyewitness testified at the trial and "unlike the circumstances found in People v. Ortiz * * *, [the witness] not only told the jury that she could not say who she had picked out at the lineup, but she failed to identify defendant at the trial").

lacking.[19]

Out-of-court statements made by children in child abuse cases often will not fit any hearsay exception, and if they are to be admitted in evidence must come in under the catchall category.[20] The Supreme Court in *Idaho v. Wright*[21] put a crimp in this practice by requiring that circumstances immediately surrounding the giving of the statements show trustworthiness.[22] This, of course, involves a confrontation problem, and *Wright* will be discussed on that point in the next section.

Worthy of note is a Westchester County Family Court decision in which the judge refused to apply *Idaho v. Wright* in a civil child protective proceeding. In *In re Linda S.*,[23] a child abuse expert was allowed to testify as to what the child told him concerning the attentions paid by her father. The proceeding was brought under article 10 of the Family Court Act, § 1046(a) of which provides that a child's out-of-court hearsay statements can be admitted if corroborated by any relevant evidence.[24] The Court of Appeals had held in *In re Nicole V.*,[25] that a child's hearsay statements could be received pursuant to § 1046(a) if corroborated, and corroboration was provided in that case by the testimony of an expert as to the consistency and specificity of the description of the acts and the details exhibited by the child.

The child's testimony at the proceeding is not necessary to establish abuse,[26] but if the child does testify, can that testimony provide the necessary corroboration for the out-of-court statements? In *In re Christina F.*,[27] the Court of Appeals answered affirmatively. While out-

19. In People v. Brunson, 151 A.D.2d 303, 542 N.Y.S.2d 571 (1st Dep't), appeal dismissed, 74 N.Y.2d 894, 548 N.Y.S.2d 426, 547 N.E.2d 953 (1989), the victim, shot in the head, paralyzed from the neck down and sedated, purportedly responded to questions by blinking her eyes, one blink for yes, two for no. The person who established this means of communication with her would testify that she exonerated defendant in her shooting. Recognizing this as fitting the catchall provision of the proposed New York Evidence Code, the court nevertheless held that the element of trustworthiness was lacking. It was doubtful, because of the wound, that the victim, who later died, had any memory. Moreover, the witness was clearly biased in defendant's favor, and it appeared that the blinking system of communication may well have been misunderstood, or not understood at all, by the victim.

20. See McCormick § 324, at 367.

21. 497 U.S. 805, 110 S.Ct. 3139, 111 L.Ed.2d 638 (1990).

22. Id. at 819–20, 110 S.Ct. at 3148, 111 L.Ed.2d at 654–55. The court stated:

> We think the Supreme Court of Idaho properly focused on the presumptive unreliability of the out-of-court statements and on the suggestive manner in which Dr. Jambura conducted the interview. Viewing the totality of the circumstances surrounding the younger daughter's responses to Dr. Jambura's questions, we find no special reason for supposing that the incriminating statements were particularly trustworthy.

23. 148 Misc.2d 169, 560 N.Y.S.2d 181 (Fam.Ct.Westchester Co.1990).

24. Section 1046(a)(vi) of the Family Court Act provides by implication that corroborated out-of-court statements by the child can be enough to substantiate a finding of abuse or neglect. Other types of admissible evidence provided for include injuries sustained (subparagraph ii), parents' drug use (subparagraph iii), hospital records (subparagraph iv), child abuse reports (subparagraph v), and statements of parents (subparagraph vii). For further exposition of article 10 proceedings, see Matter of Philip M., 82 N.Y.2d 238, 604 N.Y.S.2d 40, 624 N.E.2d 168 (1993).

25. 71 N.Y.2d 112, 524 N.Y.S.2d 19, 518 N.E.2d 914 (1987).

26. Family Court Act § 1046(a)(vi).

27. 74 N.Y.2d 532, 549 N.Y.S.2d 643, 548 N.E.2d 1294 (1989).

of-court statements cannot corroborate each other for purposes of making any of them admissible, the child's in-court testimony will provide corroboration so that the hearsay can be admitted.[28] The reason for the distinction lies in the guarantees of reliability attending the taking of the testimony subject to cross-examination and judicial supervision.[29]

Library References:

West's Key No. Digests, Criminal Law ⚖=419(2.5); Evidence ⚖=314(1).

§ 804(5).2 Federal

Identical provisions for the admission of residuary hearsay are found in Rule 803(24) (declarant's unavailability irrelevant), and Rule 804(b)(5) (declarant unavailable):

> **Other exceptions.** A statement not specifically covered by any of the foregoing exceptions but having equivalent circumstantial guarantees of trustworthiness, if the court determines that (A) the statement is offered as evidence of a material fact; (B) the statement is more probative on the point for which it is offered than any other evidence which the proponent can procure through reasonable efforts; and (C) the general purposes of these rules and the interests of justice will best be served by admission of the statement into evidence. However, a statement may not be admitted under this exception unless the proponent of it makes known to the adverse party sufficiently in advance of the trial or hearing to provide the adverse party with a fair opportunity to prepare to meet it, the proponent's intention to offer the statement and the particulars of it, including the name and address of the declarant.

The Senate Committee report indicates that these provisions should be used "very rarely, and only in exceptional circumstances."[1]

---

28. Id. at 537, 549 N.Y.S.2d at 646, 548 N.E.2d at 1297.

29. Id. See also Matter of Jessica G., 200 A.D.2d 906, 607 N.Y.S.2d 156 (3d Dep't 1994), a post-Idaho v. Wright case in which the court held that the testimony of an unsworn child provided sufficient corroboration for her out-of-court statements.

§ 804(5).2

1. This portion of the Senate report states:

It is intended that the residuary hearsay exceptions will be used very rarely, and only in exceptional circumstances. The committee does not intend to establish a broad license for trial judges to admit hearsay statements that do not fall within one of the other exceptions contained in rules 803 and 804(b). The residuary exceptions are not meant to authorize major judicial revisions of the hearsay rule, including its present exceptions. Such major revisions are best accomplished by legislative action. It is intended that in any case in which evidence is sought to be admitted under these subsections, the trial judge will exercise no less care, reflection and caution than the courts did under the common law in establishing the now-recognized exceptions to the hearsay rule.

See Mitchell v. Hoke, 930 F.2d 1, 2 (2d Cir.1991)(police testimony as to a witness' lineup identification of defendant not admissible under the residuary clause because of the confrontation problem, and because this was not an exceptional instance). In United States v. American Cyanamid Co., 427 F.Supp. 859, 865–66 (S.D.N.Y.1977), the question was whether letters written to the Justice Department in response to an inquiry as to accepted industry use of the term "production capacity" would be admissible under the catchall clause. In ruling the letters admissible, the court stated:

A district court in New York was on record prior to the inception of the Federal Rules of Evidence as advocating a liberal approach to the admissibility of hearsay not otherwise provided for under a recognized exception. In *United States v. Barbati*,[2] Judge Weinstein dealt with the admissibility of an officer's testimony that a barmaid, who could not identify defendant at trial, had identified him in a showup as having passed counterfeit money. He found her out-of-court identification admissible.[3] Among the cases cited by Judge Weinstein was *Dallas County v. Commercial Union Assurance Co.*,[4] a holding which can be considered the inspiration for the catchall provisions in the Rules.[5] The

The Government argued at the trial, that the hearsay exception of Rule 803(24) was meant to apply only in exceptional cases. This argument is based on a reading of the Senate Judiciary Committee Report which limits the application of this section to exceptional cases. Neither the Rule, nor the cases in this Circuit interpreting the Rule, however, impose any express limitation concerning exceptional cases. To every criminal defendant, his own case is exceptional. Rule 803(24) establishes sufficient express criteria which must be satisfied before an item of hearsay will be admissible. Since the exhibits listed above conform to these criteria, they should be received. There is no requirement that the Court find a case to be "exceptional," whatever that means, in order to receive any evidence. To imply such a provision, as suggested by the Judicial Committee, supra, would negate the requirement of Rule 102, F.R.Evid. that "[t]hese rules shall be construed to secure fairness in administration, elimination of unjustifiable expense and delay, and promotion of growth and development of the law of evidence to the end that the truth may be ascertained and proceedings justly determined." And it would bring into each trial, the foot of the Chancellor, an historical enemy of our liberties.

427 F.Supp. at 865–66.

The defendant's confrontation right was not discussed.

2. 284 F.Supp. 409, 412 (E.D.N.Y.1968).

3. Judge Weinstein stated:

The current clear tendency is for federal courts to ask whether admissibility will tend to aid in the search for truth. Hearsay is admitted when it is highly reliable, highly probative, and where the opponent has an adequate opportunity to attack it. See, e.g., United States v. Castellana, 349 F.2d 264, 276 (2d Cir.1965), cert. denied, 383 U.S. 928, 86 S.Ct. 935, 15 L.Ed.2d 847 (1966)("we are loath to reduce the corpus of hearsay rules to a strait-jacketing, hypertechnical body of semantical slogans to be mechanically invoked regardless of the reliability of the proffered evidence"); Dallas County v. Commercial Union Assurance Co., 286 F.2d 388, 398 (5th Cir.1961)(hearsay "admissible because it is necessary and trustworthy"); United States v. Schwartz, 252 F.Supp. 866 (E.D.Pa.1966). Cf. United States v. Nuccio, 373 F.2d 168, 174 (2d Cir.), cert. denied, 387 U.S. 906, 87 S.Ct. 1688, 18 L.Ed.2d 623 (1967)("the notion that evidentiary use of anything emerging from the mouth is banned unless it comes within an exception to the hearsay rule is as fallacious as it is durable").

284 F.Supp. at 412.

4. 286 F.2d 388, 398 (5th Cir.1961).

5. Dallas County sued an insurance carrier claiming that the clock tower on the county courthouse had collapsed because struck by lightning, a covered hazard. The insurance company maintained that the tower, weakened by a fire during construction many years earlier, had simply collapsed of its own weight. Charred timbers found in the rubble might indicate either explanation. The insurance company was allowed to introduce a newspaper clipping written during the building's construction which reported the fire. Judge Wisdom stated:

There is no procedural canon against the exercise of common sense in deciding the admissibility of hearsay evidence. In 1901 Selma, Alabama, was a small town. Taking a common sense view of this case, it is inconceivable to us that a newspaper reporter in a small town would report there was a fire in the dome of the new courthouse—if there had been no fire. He is without motive to falsify, and a false report would have subjected the newspaper and him to embarrassment in the community. The usual dangers inherent in hearsay evidence, such as lack of memory, faulty narration, intent to influence the court proceedings, and plain lack of truthfulness are not present here. To our minds, the article published in the

Second Circuit Court of Appeals in *United States v. Iaconetti*[6] readily utilized Rule 803(24). This was a prosecution of an employee of a government agency for soliciting and receiving a bribe from the president of a successful corporate bidder on a government contract. Testimony of the president's lawyer relating what the president told him about relevant statements made by the defendant was held admissible under the Rule.[7] The Second Circuit followed this case with its decision in *United States v. Medico*,[8] a bank robbery prosecution in which double hearsay was held to be admissible under Rule 804(b)(5). A bank employee testified that five minutes after the robbery, and while he was locking the entrance door, a bank customer knocked on the door and proceeded to relay license plate numbers being given by a man sitting in a car at the curb. The plate numbers were linked to defendant. The court reasoned that technically the statements could have been allowed under Rule 803(1) as present sense impressions, but that since the bystanders' identities were unknown, Rule 804(b)(5) would cover the situation.[9] The *Iaconetti* and *Medico* cases indicate a liberal approach to the catchall provisions in the Second Circuit. This is not the universal approach. The Third Circuit, for instance, has given them a "narrow focus."[10]

A systematic approach to the scope of the residuary clauses would recognize five criteria: (1) the "equivalent circumstantial guarantees of trustworthiness"; (2) probative value of the evidence; (3) the notice requirement; (4) the confrontation problem; (5) the court's discretion.

The equivalent guarantees of trustworthiness. The catchall provisions require that the statements carry at least as much reliability as is inherent in the other hearsay exceptions. Since some of those exceptions provide for more reliable evidence than others, it might be argued that hearsay to be admissible under the catchall provisions need only be as trustworthy as the least of the other exceptions. But it seems clear that the evidence should bear a "sufficient indicia of reliability."[11]

Selma Morning-Times on the day of the fire is more reliable, more trustworthy, more competent evidence than the testimony of a witness called to the stand fifty-eight years later.
286 F.2d at 397.

6. 540 F.2d 574, 578 (2d Cir.1976), cert. denied, 429 U.S. 1041, 97 S.Ct. 739, 50 L.Ed.2d 752, cert. denied, 430 U.S. 911, 97 S.Ct. 1186, 51 L.Ed.2d 589 (1977).

7. 540 F.2d at 578. The court found sufficient indicia of reliability surrounding this evidence, and also that it was the best available evidence to corroborate the testimony of the government's chief witness.

8. 557 F.2d 309, 314–16 (2d Cir.1977), cert. denied, 434 U.S. 986, 98 S.Ct. 614, 54 L.Ed.2d 480 (1977).

9. 557 F.2d at 315. It was stated: "The fact however, that the statement meets all the specific standards for admission under 803(1) but fails to meet all the criteria set forth in the supportive judicial rationale [unknown declarants] surely brings it within the grant of discretion which 804(b)(5) accords to a trial judge, consonant with the legislative purposes which the residual exception was designed to achieve."

10. See In re Japanese Elec. Products Antitrust Litig., 723 F.2d 238, 301 (3d Cir. 1983), rev'd on other grounds, 475 U.S. 574, 106 S.Ct. 1348, 89 L.Ed.2d 538 (1986). Compare United States v. Furst, 886 F.2d 558, 573 (3d Cir.1989), cert. denied, 493 U.S. 1062, 110 S.Ct. 878, 107 L.Ed.2d 961 (1990), where the court held Rule 803(24) available when the proponent fails to meet the standards set forth in other exceptions.

11. United States v. Iaconetti, 540 F.2d 574 at 578.

Interpreting this, of course, is a case specific proposition.[12] In *United States v. Yonkers Contracting Co., Inc.*,[13] in assessing the admissibility of grand jury testimony of a deceased witness under Rule 804(b)(5), the court noted that the Second Circuit "has not spelled out the inquiry to be followed in assessing the trustworthiness of hearsay,"[14] and went on to list criteria established in other circuits,[15] and found that this grand jury testimony satisfied most, if not all of the factors. It does not appear to be necessary that all of these factors need be satisfied, and, indeed, some of them would not apply to hearsay which is not grand jury testimony.

---

12. In Sherrell Perfumers, Inc. v. Revlon, Inc., 524 F.Supp. 302 (S.D.N.Y.1980), an antitrust action, the question was whether a highly probative taped conversation between defendant's president and the president of another corporation could be allowed in under Rule 803(24). The court stated:

> The factors supporting admissibility include the fact that the statement by Greif was strongly against penal and economic interest and would not have been made by a reasonable person unless true, the absence of intoxication, sickness or duress of Greif at the time the statements were made, the recording of Greif's remarks, thereby removing any issue as to authenticity, Greif's admission that the story was not fabricated pursuant to prior plan and that he would have been concerned had Chanel or Revlon learned of his remarks, and the availability of both Greif and Woolard for testimony at trial so that the jury will have a direct opportunity to assess whether the statements attributed to Woolard were in fact made. Under the tests set forth in United States v. Iaconetti * * * and United States v. Medico * * *, there are sufficient circumstantial guarantees of trustworthiness to admit the conversation under Rule 803(24) despite the subsequent disavowals by Greif and Woolard.

But in Branch v. Ogilvy & Mather, Inc., 765 F.Supp. 819, 822 (S.D.N.Y.1990), a copyright case, letters, book reviews, and advertisements offered to show the value of the assertedly copied book were held inadmissible under Rule 803(24). The court summarily held, without explanation, that the exception was inapplicable since those items did not have the needed equivalent guarantee of trustworthiness.

In United States v. Cardascia, 951 F.2d 474, 489 (2d Cir.1991), a letter of resignation sent by defendant to the bank president was not admissible under the catchall provision in his prosecution for bank fraud since there were insufficient guarantees of trustworthiness.

13. 701 F.Supp. 431, 437 (S.D.N.Y. 1988).

14. Id. at 437.

15. Id. The list is as follows:

a. Testimony was under oath. United States v. Curro, 847 F.2d 325, 327 (6th Cir.), cert. denied, 488 U.S. 843, 109 S.Ct. 116, 102 L.Ed.2d 90 (1988); United States v. Boulahanis, 677 F.2d 586, 588 (7th Cir.), cert. denied, 459 U.S. 1016, 103 S.Ct. 375, 74 L.Ed.2d 509 (1982); United States v. Carlson, 547 F.2d 1346, 1354 (8th Cir.1976), cert. denied sub nom. Hofstad v. United States, 431 U.S. 914, 97 S.Ct. 2174, 53 L.Ed.2d 224 (1977);

b. Witness was represented by counsel. United States v. Marchini, 797 F.2d 759, 764 (9th Cir.1986), cert. denied, 479 U.S. 1085, 107 S.Ct. 1288, 94 L.Ed.2d 145 (1987);

c. Testimony concerns personal knowledge. Marchini, 797 F.2d at 764; Carlson, 547 F.2d at 1354; United States v. Barlow, 693 F.2d 954, 962 (6th Cir.1982), cert. denied, 461 U.S. 945, 103 S.Ct. 2124, 77 L.Ed.2d 1304 (1983);

d. Witness did not recant testimony. Curro, 847 F.2d at 327; Marchini, 797 F.2d at 764; Carlson, 547 F.2d at 1354;

e. Witness had no motive to falsify given witness's relationship to the Government and defendants. United States v. Guinan, 836 F.2d 350, 355 (7th Cir.), cert. denied, 487 U.S. 1218, 108 S.Ct. 2871, 101 L.Ed.2d 907 (1988); Barlow, 693 F.2d at 962; and

f. Corroborating evidence is available. Curro, 847 F.2d at 327; United States v. Papadakis, 572 F.Supp. 1518 (S.D.N.Y.1983)(Weinfeld, J.)(court noted that testimony was consistent with notes of witness's statement previously taken by law enforcement officers), aff'd, 739 F.2d 784 (2d Cir.1984).

701 F.Supp. at 437.

§ 804(5).2   HEARSAY   Ch. 8

The Supreme Court in *Idaho v. Wright*,[16] discussed under the confrontation heading below, may well have eliminated the relevance of corroboration in criminal cases since the test is narrowed in that case to trustworthiness immediately concerned with the making of the out-of-court statements.

Probative value. The Rules require that the hearsay be "more probative on the point for which it is offered than any other evidence which the proponent can procure through reasonable efforts." This means pretty much what it says. If the proponent has readily admissible evidence of equal or greater quality on the point in issue, then there is no need to resort to the farthest reach of the hearsay exceptions. In *Parsons v. Honeywell, Inc.*,[17] a products liability case, an eyewitness to a gas explosion gave a statement to the police sometime later. But the statement did not qualify as a present sense impression or an excited utterance, and so it was proffered under Rule 803(24). The court stated: "Brongo [the eyewitness] apparently is able to testify in person. We agree * * * that the evidence should be used only to refresh Brongo's recollection. In this manner, both sides will have the opportunity to examine and cross-examine the witness, and his veracity can be judged first-hand by the trier of the facts."[18] But in *Robinson v. Shapiro*,[19] a wrongful death action brought on behalf of a worker killed on a construction site, testimony of decedent's coworker as to what decedent told him concerning a conversation with a building superintendent was properly admitted under Rule 804(b)(5).[20] It stands to reason that the odds of admissibility are greater under Rule 804(b)(5) than under Rule 803(24), since in the latter instance the declarant will be available. But where that declarant is on the witness stand, but cannot recall the events in issue, and her memory is not refreshed by reviewing a statement she had given to a government agent, the court, while it would not find her unavailable, held that the prior statement was admissible under Rule 803(24).[21] That unavailability does not guarantee admissibility under Rule 804(b)(5) is well illustrated in *United States v. Gotti*,[22] where the court would not admit a murder victim's statements that defendant and friends had threatened him if he testified against the defendant. This evidence was not more probative than other evidence which the government had as proof that defendant knew of declarant's

---

16. 497 U.S. 805, 110 S.Ct. 3139, 111 L.Ed.2d 638 (1990).

17. 929 F.2d 901, 907–08 (2d Cir.1991).

18. Id. at 908.

19. 646 F.2d 734, 742 (2d Cir.1981).

20. The court stated: "There is no dispute that the evidence was material, nor can there be any serious argument that the statement was not 'more probative on the point for which it [was] offered' than other reasonably available evidence. Castro's [the co-worker] testimony was the only evidence indicating that a Village Towers employee who was clearly aware of the condition of the gate prohibited the crew from removing the obstruction or using a safe passage." Id. at 742.

21. In re Drake, 786 F.Supp. 229, 233 (E.D.N.Y.1992). The court stated: "This court is satisfied that these statements not only exhibit indicia of trustworthiness equivalent to those of the other hearsay exceptions under Rule 803 but also that they are material and more probative than any other source of this evidence and, finally, that the general purposes of the federal evidence rules, as well as the interests of justice, will best be served by their admission." Id. at 233.

22. 641 F.Supp. 283 (E.D.N.Y.1986).

potential as a government witness.[23] Also, in the *Gotti* case it was held that misdemeanor convictions, which are not covered under Rule 803(22),[24] could be admitted under the catchall provisions provided they were probative and relevant.[25]

The notice requirement. The rules require the proponent of evidence proposed to be admitted under the residual hearsay exception to notify his adversary of this intention and to give the name and address of the declarant "sufficiently in advance of the trial or hearing to provide the adverse party with a fair opportunity to prepare to meet it." This provision may be bent,[26] but not broken.[27]

The confrontation problem. In civil cases the courts can take a more relaxed attitude toward the catchall provisions. Criminal cases present different considerations. In *Idaho v. Wright*,[28] the prosecutor succeeded in admitting testimony of a pediatrician concerning his interview with a two and one-half year old child in regard to the child's assertions of abuse by the defendant. The child was deemed incapable of testifying and so was unavailable. The evidence was allowed by the trial judge under Idaho's residual hearsay exception, but the Supreme Court found a violation of the sixth amendment. Although unavailability was not an issue, the Supreme Court, in dictum, stated that as a general rule unavailability had to be established to override defendant's confrontation

---

23. Id. at 287. The victim's prior testimony at a hearing at which he was cross-examined by defense counsel would be admissible on the same point.

In a similar vein, see Mitchell v. Hoke, 930 F.2d 1, 2 (2d Cir.1991). Where an eyewitness made a lineup identification and then recanted, the detective could not testify to the identification, the court stating: "Even if we were to regard the residual exception as sufficiently 'firmly rooted,' to satisfy the Sixth Amendment right to confrontation, [the detective's] testimony would not be admissible under it. The residual exception is limited to hearsay statements with 'highly probative value' and is to 'be used very rarely, and only in exceptional circumstances.'" The eyewitness was available, but, of course, was of little use to the government at the trial. His prior identification was characterized as not being of "high probative value." Id. at 3.

24. Rule 803(22):

Judgment of previous conviction. Evidence of a final judgment, entered after a trial or upon a plea of guilty (but not upon a plea of nolo contendere), adjudging a person guilty of a crime punishable by death or imprisonment in excess of one year, to prove any fact essential to sustain the judgment, but not including, when offered by the Government in a criminal prosecution for purposes other than impeachment, judgments against persons other than the accused. The pendency of an appeal may be shown but does not affect admissibility.

See discussion of Rule 803(22) at § 803(5).2(d), supra.

25. 641 F.Supp. at 289.

26. In United States v. Iaconetti, 540 F.2d 574 (2d Cir.1976), cert. denied, 429 U.S. 1041, 97 S.Ct. 739, 50 L.Ed.2d 752, reh. denied, 430 U.S. 911, 97 S.Ct. 1186, 51 L.Ed.2d 589 (1977), defendant was given no notice of the government's Rule 803(24) evidence until three days before the statements were admitted. "While strict compliance with the rule is lacking, we agree with Judge Weinstein that the defendant was given sufficient notice here, and that some latitude must be permitted in situations like this in which the need does not become apparent until after the trial has commenced." 540 F.2d at 578.

27. In United States v. Oates, 560 F.2d 45 (2d Cir.1977), the defense was unaware of the government's intention to offer residuary hearsay until the witness was called to the stand. "In other words, not only did the defense not receive notice in advance of trial, it did not receive any notice at all until the actual appearance of witness Harrington in the late afternoon of the fourth day of trial." Id. at 72–73 n.30.

28. 497 U.S. 805, 110 S.Ct. 3139, 111 L.Ed.2d 638 (1990).

argument.[29] Furthermore, if the hearsay does not fall within a firmly rooted exception, a particularized showing of reliability must be made.[30] The majority, in an opinion by Justice O'Connor, held that the residual hearsay exception was not a firmly rooted exception and that there were no particularized guarantees of trustworthiness surrounding the child's statements to the doctor.[31] The test is not whether all the circumstances in the case indicated that the statements were probably true;[32] rather, it is whether the circumstances immediately surrounding the giving of the statements showed trustworthiness.[33] Thus, it appears that under this test circumstantial corroboration cannot be used to support the trustworthiness of the statement.

Wright has thus constrained the admissibility of residual hearsay against criminal defendants in two respects: Declarants usually must be unavailable and the search for trustworthiness must be made without reliance upon corroborating evidence. It remains to be seen the extent to which the Court's trustworthiness analysis may have undermined the decisions in the criminal cases noted elsewhere in this section.[34] As to the unavailability element, the necessity for the evidence may help override defendant's confrontation argument.[35] The extent to which this

29. Id. at 813–14, 110 S.Ct. at 3143, 111 L.Ed.2d at 657.

30. It was stated:
[Quoting from Ohio v. Roberts, 448 U.S. 56, 65, 100 S.Ct. 2531, 2538, 65 L.Ed.2d 597, 608 (1980)]: "First, in conformance with the Framers' preference for face-to-face accusation, the Sixth Amendment establishes a rule of necessity. In the usual case * * *, the prosecution must either produce or demonstrate the unavailability of the declarant whose statement it wishes to use against the defendant. * * * Second, once a witness is shown to be unavailable, 'his statement is admissible only if it bears adequate "indicia of reliability." ' Reliability can be inferred without more in a case where the evidence falls within a firmly rooted hearsay exception."
Wright, 497 U.S. at 814–15, 110 S.Ct. at 3146, 111 L.Ed.2d at 651–52.

31. Id. at 816, 110 S.Ct. at 3146, 111 L.Ed.2d at 652–53.

32. 497 U.S. at 819–20, 110 S.Ct. at 3148, 111 L.Ed.2d at 655. The trial judge found it relevant that there was proof of physical abuse, proof of defendant's opportunity to commit the crime and proof of corroborating statements by a sister. 497 U.S. at 825–26, 110 S.Ct. at 3152, 111 L.Ed.2d at 659.

33. The majority stated: "We think the Supreme Court of Idaho properly focused on the presumptive unreliability of the out-of-court statements and on the suggestive manner in which Dr. Jambura conducted the interview. Viewing the totality of the circumstances surrounding the younger daughter's responses to Dr. Jambura's questions, we find no special reason for supposing that the incriminating statements were particularly trustworthy." Id. at 819–20, 110 S.Ct. at 3148, 111 L.Ed.2d at 655.

34. In United States v. Yonkers Contracting Co., Inc., 701 F.Supp. 431, 436, 437 (S.D.N.Y.1988) (see text at notes 13–15 supra), the court's rationale seems in jeopardy because it lists circumstantial corroboration as sufficient to buttress trustworthiness.

35. Unavailability is not always required in order to satisfy the sixth amendment. The Court cited with approval its decision in United States v. Inadi, 475 U.S. 387, 106 S.Ct. 1121, 89 L.Ed.2d 390 (1986), where, in a case concerning the coconspirator's exception, it was held that such exception was deeply rooted and that the statements, rendered during the ongoing conspiracy, had particular contextual significance and trustworthiness. For these reasons also, unavailability of declarant would not be required when defendant raised the confrontation issue. See also Bourjaily v. United States, 483 U.S. 171, 107 S.Ct. 2775, 97 L.Ed.2d 144 (1987); and Justice Scalia's dissent in Maryland v. Craig, 497 U.S. 836, 110 S.Ct. 3157, 111 L.Ed.2d 666 (1990), where he stated: "We have permitted a few exceptions [to the unavailability rule], e.g., for co-conspirators' statements, whose effect cannot be replicated by live testimony because they 'derive [their] significance from the circumstances in which [they

aspect of *Wright* undermines decisions discussed elsewhere in this section [36] also remains to be seen.

The court's discretion. "A determination that evidence is not admissible under the Rule 803(24) exception to the hearsay rule is reviewed under an abuse of discretion standard."[37]

If evidence is received under a catchall provision, that fact should be in the record.[38]

Library References:

West's Key No. Digests, Criminal Law ⚖419(2.5); Evidence ⚖314(1).

805 Hearsay Within Hearsay

§ 805.1 New York

A hearsay statement contained within another hearsay statement is admissible only if both statements come within exceptions to the rule barring hearsay. Most often, the multiple hearsay situation is presented when a business record or a public record, itself admissible as a hearsay exception, contains a statement sought to be proved for its truth. For example, if a police report, otherwise admissible under the business entry exception, contains a statement by a party to the action which qualifies as an admission, then the document can be allowed in evidence.[1] But if the statement contained in the business record is not

---

were] made.'" 497 U.S. at 865, 110 S.Ct. at 3174, 111 L.Ed.2d at 691.

See also White v. Illinois, 502 U.S. 346, 112 S.Ct. 736, 116 L.Ed.2d 848 (1992) (unavailability of declarant not required by sixth amendment with respect to excited utterances and statements made for purposes of medical treatment because such statements are made in context that provides substantial guarantees of trustworthiness).

36. In United States v. Medico, 557 F.2d 309, 314 (2d Cir.1977), cert. denied, 434 U.S. 986, 98 S.Ct. 614, 54 L.Ed.2d 480 (1977) (see text at notes 8–9 supra), for instance, the court stated that "[e]xperience has taught that the stated exceptions now codified in the Federal Rules of Evidence meet [the conditions necessary to override the confrontation argument]." 557 F.2d at 314, n. 4. The result in Medico might well be the same, however, since declarants were, in fact, unavailable.

37. United States v. Cardascia, 951 F.2d 474, 489 (2d Cir.1991). See also Toys R Us, Inc. v. Canarsie Kiddie Shop, Inc., 559 F.Supp. 1189, 1205 (E.D.N.Y.1983), where, in keeping out evidence of public opinion surveys in a trademark infringement case, the court stated: "Accepting necessity and genuine guarantees of trustworthiness to be the correct bases for receiving survey evidence, Rules 803(24), 804(b)(5), Fed. R.Evid., it is for the court to determine whether those bases are present." 559 F.Supp. at 1205.

38. In United States v. Nixon, 779 F.2d 126, 134 (2d Cir.1985) it was stated: "Further, any attempt to bring the telex within the catch-all exception * * * must fail for lack of specific findings on the record that it was being received under that exception." Id. at 134.

§ 805.1

1. See § 803(3).1(a) supra. In Chemical Leaman Tank Lines v. Stevens, 21 A.D.2d 556, 557, 251 N.Y.S.2d 240, 241–42 (3d Dep't 1964), the driver of a car involved in an accident told the officer she turned in front of the oncoming car. This statement was reported in the officer's accident report. The report was admissible as a business record under CPLR 4518, and the driver's statement was admissible against the driver as an admission.

Although the Court of Appeals in Kelly v. Wasserman, 5 N.Y.2d 425, 185 N.Y.S.2d 538, 158 N.E.2d 241 (1959), never articulated its rationale in allowing in a citizen's statement contained in a business report made by a social worker in apparent violation of the rule in Johnson v. Lutz, 253 N.Y. 124, 170 N.E. 517 (1930)(see § 803(3).1(a), supra), its decision can be

§ 805.1 HEARSAY Ch. 8

separately supported by a hearsay exception, then the record may not be admitted for the purpose of proving the truth of the statement.[2]

Sometimes the court will allow in evidence double or triple hearsay, even though there appear to be no hearsay exceptions supporting the underlying statements.[3]

The Court of Appeals, however, has little regard for blatant double hearsay. In *Cover v. Cohen*,[4] defendant told the investigating officer that his accelerator stuck, causing the accident, thus putting the blame on General Motors and off himself. Since the statement was exculpatory and not inculpatory there was no hearsay exception to support it,[5] and it could not be admitted in support of defendant's case via the officer's written report.

explained on the same basis. When the social worker telephoned the landlord concerning the wellbeing of Miss Kelly, an elderly tenant, the landlord acknowledged she had a tenancy for life. Subsequently the landlord tried to evict Miss Kelly and the social worker's record, admissible as a business record, could come in against the landlord for the landlord's admission reported in it. See also Penn v. Kirsh, 40 A.D.2d 814, 338 N.Y.S.2d 161 (1st Dep't 1972)(plaintiff's statement to police contained in police report concerning the manner in which the accident happened "is an admission or declaration against interest and as such admissible into evidence. The report was made by the police officer whose duty it was to interview plaintiff at the scene of the accident and to record his answer. The statement was relevant to the department's investigation and to its business."). Id. at 814, 338 N.Y.S.2d at 162.

2. In Toll v. State of New York, 32 A.D.2d 47, 49–50, 299 N.Y.S.2d 589, 592 (3d Dep't 1969), the officer's accident report contained details of the accident given the officer by others. But there was no showing that these people had a business duty to impart this information under the rule in Johnson v. Lutz, 253 N.Y. 124, 170 N.E. 517 (1930)(see § 803(3).1(a), supra), or that the information was made up of admissions or conformed to any other hearsay exception. The report was thus ruled inadmissible. See also Hayes v. State, 50 A.D.2d 693, 694, 376 N.Y.S.2d 647, 648–49 (3d Dep't 1975), aff'd, 40 N.Y.2d 1044, 392 N.Y.S.2d 282, 360 N.E.2d 959 (1976)(information in hospital report not shown to be independently supportable as having been given by one with a business duty, nor was the information covered under another hearsay exception).

3. In Feinstein v. Goebel, 144 Misc.2d 462, 544 N.Y.S.2d 968 (Sup.Ct.Queens Co.1989), the plaintiff sued the defendant physicians for malpractice, contending that their negligence caused his severely deteriorated condition. Defendants contended that his condition was due to other causes, including excessive use of alcohol. As evidence in support of their contentions, defendants proffered the contents of a hospital record which contained an entry by a staff doctor that the plaintiff's son had told the doctor that the plaintiff "drank heavy" on the night he was involved in a car accident. The son, however, had no direct knowledge of this and must have been so informed by his mother. His mother had, in fact, called one of the defendants and told him that she had had an altercation with the plaintiff, that he was drinking heavily, and that he had left the house and had been involved in an accident. The plaintiff pointed out that this was "hearsay within hearsay within hearsay." The first hearsay was the statement in the hospital record, the second was the statement by the son which found its way into the hospital record, and the third was the mother's statement to the son. According to the court the son had a "filial" duty to relate the information. Apparently, the mother's duty to inform the son was a "maternal" duty, but this part of the opinion becomes obscure. Although these duties are not exactly recognized duties under the business entry exception, the court felt that these factors all contributed to the essential element of trustworthiness. Id. at 466, 544 N.Y.2d at 970. The catchall hearsay exception might also be considered here.

4. 61 N.Y.2d 261, 274, 473 N.Y.S.2d 378, 384, 461 N.E.2d 864, 870 (1984).

5. The idea that defendant's statement might be an excited utterance had not been raised at the trial and could not be considered on appeal. 61 N.Y.2d at 274, 473 N.Y.S.2d at 384, 461 N.E.2d at 870.

Of course, double hearsay can arise outside the scope of the business entry rule. In *Flynn v. Manhattan and Bronx Surface Transit Operating Auth.*,[6] the court stated:

> Appellant correctly argues that it was error to have admitted the testimony of Sergeant Hansen, the investigating officer, that the driver of the bus (who was deceased at the time of the trial) told him at the scene "that an unidentified passenger had come up to him after he had passed the guy on the bike, and the unidentified passenger said that he had struck the person on the bike." This was properly objected to as hearsay. Indeed, Sergeant Hansen's testimony as to the statement of the unidentified passenger was double hearsay, not within any of the exceptions to the hearsay rule.[7]

The proposed New York Evidence Code provides that hearsay within hearsay is admissible provided each component satisfies an exception.[8] This expresses the current law as noted above and as applied in *Taft v. New York City Transit Authority*,[9] an action brought for the wrongful death of a passenger trying to board defendant's subway. To prove the deceased's predicament which allegedly should have been noticed by the operator of the train, plaintiff sought to introduce defendant's own accident report which recorded the statement of the platform conductor that an "extremely agitated," unidentified man told him that he had just seen a woman try to board the train, that she slipped and was hanging on as the train left the station. This was all held admissible since the conductor had a business duty to report, and the statement he reported could qualify as an excited utterance.[10]

It may be that the internal statement is not to be introduced for its truth, but only for the fact it was said; it may amount to a verbal act or express a state of mind.[11] Since the statement is not hearsay there is no

---

6. 61 N.Y.2d 769, 473 N.Y.S.2d 154, 461 N.E.2d 291 (1984).

7. Id. at 770–71, 473 N.Y.S.2d at 156, 461 N.E.2d at 293. Even if the bus driver's statement to the officer could be construed as an admission, there seems to be no exception in support of the passenger's statement to the bus driver. Compare People v. Liccione, 63 A.D.2d 305, 407 N.Y.S.2d 753 (4th Dep't 1978), where the victim's dying declaration that her husband arranged the attack on her was premised on statements made by the hired killer as he attacked her. His statements were said to be admissible as statements of a coconspirator.

8. New York Code of Evidence [PROPOSED]

§ 808. Hearsay within hearsay

Hearsay included within hearsay is not excluded by the hearsay rule if each part of the combined statement conforms to an exception to the hearsay rule provided by statute or the code of evidence.

9. 193 A.D.2d 503, 597 N.Y.S.2d 374 (1st Dep't 1993).

10. Id. at 504–04, 597 N.Y.S.2d at 375–76.

11. Toll v. State, 32 A.D.2d 47, 49, 299 N.Y.S.2d 589, 592 (3d Dep't 1969) ("[T]he record may be admitted * * * to prove that the statement recorded therein was made by the outsider * * *"). A good example is found in Splawn v. Lextaj Corp., 197 A.D.2d 479, 603 N.Y.S.2d 41 (1st Dep't 1993), appeal denied, 83 N.Y.2d 753, 612 N.Y.S.2d 107, 634 N.E.2d 603 (1994), where hotel logbook entries showing burglaries and thefts on the premises were admissible even though the information had been gathered from reports by those who had no duty to report. The entries were admissible not for their truth, but to show the hotel had notice of criminal activity.

§ 805.1 HEARSAY Ch. 8

multiple hearsay problem and the primary statement, supported by an exception, can serve to get the internal statement into evidence.

Library References:

West's Key No. Digests, Criminal Law ⟐419(13); Evidence ⟐314–324.

§ 805.2 Federal

The application of the hearsay-within-hearsay rule in the Second Circuit is virtually identical to its application in the New York courts. Perhaps the definitive federal opinion written on the matter is that by Judge Tenney in *Yates v. Bair Transport, Inc.*[1] in which he adopted the New York cases discussed in the last section.[2] *Yates* involved the classic situation of an admissible police report containing details of the accident given by persons unknown. Since the internal statement could not be validated under a hearsay exception, and since it was sought to be introduced for its truth, and not simply for the fact it was said, or for impeachment purposes, Judge Tenney held the report inadmissible.[3]

Federal Rule 805 provides:

> Hearsay included within hearsay is not excluded under the hearsay rule if each part of the combined statements conforms with an exception to the hearsay rule provided in these rules.

The Second Circuit is very careful with multiple hearsay[4] even when

---

§ 805.2

1. 249 F.Supp. 681 (S.D.N.Y.1965).

2. Starting with Johnson v. Lutz, 253 N.Y. 124, 170 N.E. 517 (1930), the line of cases includes Chemical Tank Lines, Inc. v. Stevens, 21 A.D.2d 556, 251 N.Y.S.2d 240 (3d Dep't 1964), and the decision in Kelly v. Wasserman, 5 N.Y.2d 425, 185 N.Y.S.2d 538, 158 N.E.2d 241 (1959), later explained in Toll v. State, 32 A.D.2d 47, 299 N.Y.S.2d 589 (3d Dep't 1969), decided after Yates v. Bair Transport, Inc., as involving a double hearsay situation in which each statement qualified as an exception.

3. Judge Tenney summed up the rule as follows:

> Based on the foregoing authorities, it appears that the Business Records Act overcomes the initial hurdle to the admissibility of evidence, but goes no further. Thus the hearsay statement (of a volunteer) contained in the police officer's report is no more admissible than the testimony of the police officer on the stand as to the hearsay statement made at the scene of the accident. If the making of the statement itself is relevant, it can be proved both by the report, which is a record kept in the ordinary course of business, as well as by the in-Court testimony of the officer. However, if the report is offered to prove the truth of the statement contained therein, the statement must either have been made in the regular course of business of the person making it, or must have an independent ground of admissibility such as an admission, etc., the same as the in-Court testimony of the officer as to the statements made, offered to prove the truth of what was said, must have an independent ground of admissibility. Since all that can be shown under the Business Records Act is that in the regular course of business of the officer he wrote that X made the following statement to prove the truth of the fact that X made the statement, not the proof of the facts contained in the statement.

Id. at 687–88.

Other pre-rule 805 cases are in accord: United States v. Maddox, 444 F.2d 148, 151 (2d Cir.1971)(an out-patient record, admissible as a business entry, contained admission by defendant as to his use of narcotics); Felice v. Long Island Railroad Co., 426 F.2d 192, 197 (2d Cir.1970) (since patient's statement concerning how the accident occurred, contained in a hospital report, was not necessary for diagnosis and treatment, this part of the report would not be admissible under the business entry rule in the first place).

4. In United States v. Cruz, 894 F.2d 41 (2d Cir.), cert. denied sub nom., Olivier v. U.S., 498 U.S. 837, 111 S.Ct. 107, 112

Ch. 8   **HEARSAY WITHIN HEARSAY**   **§ 805.2**

the catchall provisions are urged.[5]

A peculiar situation can arise under Rule 805 which would not be a problem under state law. There are some out-of-court statements admissible under Federal Rule 801(d), which are labeled as nonhearsay. These include admissions, witness' prior statements, identification statements and coconspirators' statements. (See §§ 801(1).1–802.3, *supra*.) Thus, if a business entry contained an admission, it could be argued that since an admission is not a hearsay exception Rule 805 would provide no authority for its admission. Since under state law an admission is a hearsay exception the argument could not be made. The appropriate resolution of this problem at the federal level would be to treat the internal statement as if it were a hearsay exception.[6]

The result is not clear when the arrangement is in reverse, i.e., where statements are contained in a Rule 801(d) nonhearsay statement. Thus where a coconspirator's statement, admissible as nonhearsay under Rule 801(d)(2)(E), contains other nonhearsay statements made to declarant by others, the whole thing may come in not apparently under Rule 805 (there seems to be no hearsay exception to support the internal statements), but simply under Rule 801(d)(2)(E). The rationale of the Second Circuit is not entirely clear on this precise point, except that it seems that the internal statements were admissible for the fact made

---

L.Ed.2d 77 (1990), defendant sought to introduce inconsistent versions of the report of his arrest containing accounts given by others. First, there was a serious question whether the report itself conformed to the business records or public document exceptions. But even if it did there were no exceptions for the rest of it. "Whether the investigation reports are public or business records, prior inconsistent statements, or proof of fabrication, the reports remain inadmissible because Geisel's recording of what Hunt told him Perez said constitutes multiple hearsay." Id. at 44.

In United States Football League v. National Football League, 842 F.2d 1335 (2d Cir.1988), there seemed to be no exception in support of either leg of the hearsay. "First, no foundation was laid to introduce handwritten notes of an NFL official allegedly reflecting the comments of an NFL players union official at an NFL meeting. Second, these notes were * * * being offered for their truth, not simply for the fact that the statements were made, and were properly excluded as multiple hearsay under Fed.R.Evid. 805." Id. at 1376.

In United States v. Lang, 589 F.2d 92 (2d Cir.1978), the government was erroneously allowed to introduce a tape recording of a conversation between an undercover agent and the person reputed to have supplied defendant with the counterfeit bills he possessed when arrested. This was double hearsay since neither participant in the conversation was available for cross-examination and there was no hearsay exception to support admission of the tape, or the statements contained in it. The attempt to characterize the supplier's statements as declarations against interest failed because there was no indication he had firsthand knowledge of that about which he spoke. Id. at 98–99.

5. In Parsons v. Honeywell, Inc., 929 F.2d 901 (2d Cir.1991), where a police report containing the statement of a bystander as to the occurrence of an explosion was proffered, the court found it unacceptable since there was no exception relating to the statement. Neither was it admissible under the residual exception since the declarant was available and could use his prior statement to refresh his recollection. Id. at 907–08.

6. McCormick states: "One answer has been that admissions are within the spirit and purpose of the rule. [Citing United States v. Lang, 589 F.2d 92, 99 n.2 (2d Cir.1978).] An easier answer may be that only one level of hearsay exists since an admission is not hearsay under the Federal Rules, and if the other statement satisfies an exception, no further hearsay difficulty remains." McCormick § 324.1, at 370.

§ 805.2   HEARSAY   Ch. 8

and not for their truth.[7]

The court had no problem when a coconspirator's statement was contained within a coconspirator's statement. The same reasons underlying Rule 805 would govern this situation and the package would be admissible.[8]

Library References:

West's Key No. Digests, Criminal Law ⟨→419(13); Evidence ⟨→314–324.

806 Attacking and Supporting Declarant's Credibility

§ 806.1 New York and Federal

Hearsay evidence is not immune from impeachment. The credibility of the declarant may be attacked in any of the usual ways, including showing declarant's prior convictions, his bias or interest, his character for truthfulness and his inconsistent statements.[1] Federal Rule of Evidence 806 expresses this rule and does away with the requirement normally applied in connection with prior inconsistent statements that an opportunity be given declarant to explain the inconsistency.[2]

---

7. In State of New York v. Hendrickson Bros., Inc., 840 F.2d 1065 (2d Cir.), cert. denied, 488 U.S. 848, 109 S.Ct. 128, 102 L.Ed.2d 101 (1988), the court stated:

> We find no merit in the contention that the court should have excluded Farino's statements pursuant to Fed.R.Evid. 805 because they themselves contained hearsay statements by other unidentified declarants. Rule 805 provides for the exclusion of "[h]earsay included within hearsay" unless the included statement, as well as the encompassing statement, is covered by some exception to the hearsay rule. Whether or not Rule 805 is applicable when the encompassing statement is defined as nonhearsay, as is true of coconspirator statements, and the only hearsay is a statement contained in the nonhearsay statement, compare Cedeck v. Hamiltonian Federal Savings & Loan Ass'n, 551 F.2d 1136, 1138 (8th Cir.1977)(hearsay within co-conspirator statement excludable unless it meets a hearsay exception), with United States v. McLernon, 746 F.2d 1098, 1106 (6th Cir.1984)(upholding admissibility without reference to such exceptions), we reject appellant's contention because the challenged contents of Farino's statements were not themselves hearsay.

Id. at 1074–75.

Having presented that apparent conflict between the sixth and eighth circuits, the court went on to say that its case was different because the internal statements were not hearsay since they were being offered not for their truth, but to show they were made. One statement was characterized as a verbal act. Id. at 1075.

8. In United States v. Gotti, 644 F.Supp. 370 (E.D.N.Y.1986), the court stated:

> The tape of one of the conversations shows a coconspirator statement of Ruggiero that John Gotti had said to him that it is "an administrative thing" that Dellacroce should know of the interim appointment by Caiazza. This statement of Gotti is also a coconspirator statement and not hearsay, within the definition of Rule 801(d)(2)(E). While Rule 805, providing for the admission of hearsay within hearsay, does not in terms apply, the same criteria should apply to the admissibility of one extrajudicial statement within another.

Id. at 375.

§ 806.1

1. McCormick § 324.2, at 371.

2. The Advisory Committee's Note states:

> The principal difference between using hearsay and an actual witness is that the inconsistent statement will in the case of the witness almost inevitably of necessity in the nature of things be a *prior* statement, which it is entirely possible and feasible to call to his attention, while in the case of hearsay the inconsistent state-

Rule 806 provides:

> When a hearsay statement, or a statement defined in rule 801(d)(2)(C), (D), or (E), has been admitted in evidence, the credibility of the declarant may be attacked, and if attacked may be supported, by any evidence which would be admissible for those purposes if declarant had testified as a witness. Evidence of a statement or conduct by the declarant at any time, inconsistent with the declarant's hearsay statement, is not subject to any requirement that the declarant may have been afforded an opportunity to deny or explain. If the party against whom a hearsay statement has been admitted calls the declarant as a witness, the party is entitled to examine the declarant on the statement as if under cross-examination.[3]

The rule applies to all the hearsay possibilities under Rules 803 and 804, and specifies also all the nonhearsay possibilities listed in Rule 801(d)(2), (C), (D) and (E), i.e., admissions and coconspirator's statements. It has been held that nonhearsay statements admitted for the fact said, and not for their truth, are not subject to impeachment under Rule 806.[4]

New York has traditionally allowed for impeachment of hearsay declarants. The basis was laid in *Matter of Hesdra*,[5] where the Court of Appeals allowed impeachment of the credibility of a subscribing witness to a will;[6] and in *People v. Ricken*,[7] the Appellate Division held that the credibility of an author of a dying declaration could be attacked by proof

---

ment may well be a *subsequent* one, which practically precludes calling it to the attention of the declarant. The result of insisting upon observation of this impossible requirement in the hearsay situation is to deny the opponent, already barred from cross-examination, any benefit of this important technique of impeachment. The writers favor allowing the subsequent statement. McCormick, § 37, p. 69; 3 Wigmore § 1033.

(Emphasis in original). In this connection see the cases at notes 11–13, infra.

3. Proposed New York Evidence Code § 809 is similar:

§ 809. Attacking and supporting credibility of declarant [PROPOSED]

When a hearsay statement has been admitted in evidence, the credibility of the declarant may be attacked, and if attacked may be supported, by any evidence which would be admissible for those purposes if the declarant had testified as a witness. Evidence of a statement or conduct by the declarant at any time, inconsistent with the declarant's hearsay statement, is not subject to any requirement that the declarant be afforded an opportunity to deny or explain. If the party against whom a hearsay statement has been admitted calls the declarant as a witness, the party is entitled to examine the declarant on the statement as if on cross-examination.

4. United States v. Price, 792 F.2d 994, 996–97 (11th Cir.1986)(taped conversations between defendant and informant, showing that defendant gave informant drugs for delivery were admissible, not for the truth, but for the purpose of lending background so the jury could put the operative facts in proper perspective—thus, since not hearsay, not covered by Rule 806).

5. 119 N.Y. 615, 23 N.E. 555 (1890).

6. Id. at 616, 23 N.E. at 556. The presumption of regularity created by signatures on a will "may be rebutted, and, hence, the propriety and even necessity of permitting him to be impeached in the usual mode, as if he were living and had testified at the trial to what his signature imports." Id.

7. 242 App.Div. 106, 273 N.Y.S. 470 (3d Dep't 1934).

§ 806.1   HEARSAY   Ch. 8

that he had been convicted of a crime.[8]

In *People v. Hines*,[9] however, the Court of Appeals ruled that where a witness, deceased at the time of trial, gave testimony at a prior hearing and was cross-examined by counsel for defendant, his credibility was immune to attack at the second trial where the witness' testimony was read in under the prior testimony exception. Defendant wanted to show that the witness' suicide impinged on the credibility of his testimony. In approving the disallowance of this evidence, the Court of Appeals put emphasis on the fact that the witness had already been cross-examined;[10] but, of course, there could have been no cross-examination as to the subsequent act of suicide.

Hines is out of step with the modern view, assuming there was any impeachment value in the act of suicide, and seemingly at odds with earlier authority.[11] In a case involving the statement of a patient contained in a hospital report admitted as a business record, the Appellate Division reviewed the authorities and concluded that the patient's subsequent inconsistent statements would be admissible to impeach her credibility.[12] There was no opportunity to confront declarant with her inconsistencies since she had died from the attack for which defendant was on trial. Noting cases involving dying declarations, the court stated:

> The case for permitting impeachment of dying declarations by proof of the declarant's contradictory statement is surely no stronger than that for allowing hearsay contradiction of the far less solemn recital of a history of injury, by a decedent equally unavailable from cross-examination. In view, therefore, of the strong analogy furnished by dying declarations, it is worthy of note that the great weight of judicial authority in the United States renders such declarations susceptible to impeachment by

---

8. Id. at 109–10, 273 N.Y.S. at 473. It is there stated:

Professor Wigmore in the second edition of his work on Evidence, section 1446, states that the declarant is open to impeachment and discrediting in the same way as other witnesses so far as such a process is feasible. Had the declarant appeared in person as a witness upon the trial, such conviction could properly have been shown. The situation is not changed by the fact that he is not personally present. It strengthens the claim of the defendant to the right of impeachment. He has been deprived of his strongest arm of defense—cross-examination, and to now deprive him of the benefits of impeachment would be carrying the exception to unwarranted limits.

9. 284 N.Y. 93, 29 N.E.2d 483 (1940).

10. Id. at 115–16, 29 N.E. at 493–94.

11. The court in Hines cited Hubbard v. Briggs, 31 N.Y. 517, 536–37, (1865); Stacy v. Graham, 14 N.Y. 492, 498–50 (1856); and Mattox v. United States, 156 U.S. 237, 248–50, 15 S.Ct. 337, 341–42, 39 L.Ed. 409, 412–13 (1895). As in Hines, the cases involved prior testimony, and in all of them the courts decried the practice of introducing inconsistencies without declarant having an opportunity to explain. Not only has this rule been specifically altered in Federal Rule 806, but it does not really fit the Hines case where declarant could not possibly have been questioned about his suicide. Also, much of the effect of the Mattox case was overcome in Carver v. United States, 164 U.S. 694, 17 S.Ct. 228, 41 L.Ed. 602 (1897), where it was held that statements inconsistent with a dying declaration should have been allowed.

12. People v. Conde, 16 A.D.2d 327, 228 N.Y.S.2d 69 (3d Dep't 1962), aff'd, 13 N.Y.2d 939, 244 N.Y.S.2d 314, 194 N.E.2d 130 (1963).

proof of contradictory statements for which, of course, the conventional foundation has not been laid by cross-examination.[13]

Impeachment devices other than inconsistent statements or actions have precedent in New York. *People v. Ricken*, noted above, is not the only instance where a criminal conviction has been allowed for impeachment of a hearsay declarant. In *Sansevere v. United Parcel Service*,[14] a deponent's statement was read in at trial. He was unavailable because he had been committed to jail. His was the only eyewitness evidence as to the happening of the accident. The trial court's refusal to allow evidence of declarant's extensive criminal background was held error on appeal.[15] It was not necessary that he have been cross-examined at the taking of the deposition as to this since it was not anticipated that he would not testify at the trial.[16] In another case, defendant, in order to counter damaging coconspirator's statements, was allowed to call witnesses to impeach the character of the declarant.[17]

The federal circuits apply Rule 806 with liberality,[18] although occasionally the rule is found inapplicable to the facts.[19]

---

13. 16 A.D.2d at 331–32, 228 N.Y.S.2d at 72. A more recent case involving a dying declaration is People v. Canady, 186 A.D.2d 749, 589 N.Y.S.2d 184 (2d Dep't 1992), appeal denied, 81 N.Y.2d 786, 594 N.Y.S.2d 732, 610 N.E.2d 405 (1993)(defendant introduced X's exculpatory dying declarations; prosecution entitled to impeach with X's inconsistent statements).

14. 181 A.D.2d 521, 581 N.Y.S.2d 315 (1st Dep't 1992).

15. Id. at 522, 581 N.Y.S.2d at 316.

16. Id. at 523, 581 N.Y.S.2d at 317.

17. People v. Tai, 145 Misc.2d 599, 603–05, 547 N.Y.S.2d 989, 992–93 (Sup.Ct. N.Y.Co.1989)(the court cited Federal Rule 806 in support of the holding).

18. The occasion for Rule 806 impeachment seems to arise most often upon the introduction of coconspirator' statements. See United States v. Vegas, 27 F.3d 773, 782 (2d Cir.1994)(contradictory testimony of coconspirator as to his knowledge of source of heroin properly admitted to impeach coconspirator's hearsay statements exonerating defendant); United States v. Wali, 860 F.2d 588, 591 (3d Cir.1988)(coconspirator's statements properly used to show inconsistency with coconspirator's statements admitted in evidence); United States v. Serna, 799 F.2d 842, 849–50 (2d Cir.1986), cert. denied sub nom., Cinnante v. U.S., 481 U.S. 1013, 107 S.Ct. 1887, 95 L.Ed.2d 494 (1987)(trial judge did not abuse discretion by making admission of coconspirator's statements conditional on the adversary's right to produce evidence of declarant's criminal activities). In one case, evidence of the demeanor of the declarant observed at a prior trial was allowed in to impeach the testimony given at that trial, now offered under the prior testimony exception. United States v. Salim, 664 F.Supp. 682, 692 (E.D.N.Y.1987)("This commonsensical result is supported by Rule 806 * * *. It permits evidence on 'credibility of the declarant' to the same extent as 'if declarant had testified as a witness.' ").

19. United States v. Friedman, 854 F.2d 535, 569–70 (2d Cir.1988), cert. denied, 490 U.S. 1004, 109 S.Ct. 1637, 104 L.Ed.2d 153 (1989)(where coconspirator's statements admitted to prove the crime charged, evidence that declarant had lied to police on another matter was not inconsistent and was properly excluded under Rule 403 since its probative value was outweighed by the danger of confusion of the issues); United States v. Katsougrakis, 715 F.2d 769, 778–79 (2d Cir.1983), cert. denied, 464 U.S. 1040, 104 S.Ct. 704, 79 L.Ed.2d 169 (1984)(normally Rule 806 would provide the authority for impeaching hearsay declarants, whose statements were allowed under the coconspirator exception, except that here there was no good faith basis shown for the impeaching evidence); United States v. Mejia–Velez, 855 F.Supp. 607, 615 (E.D.N.Y.1994)(where there was no inconsistency between the hearsay evidence and the impeachment evidence there would be no excuse for the invocation of Rule 806 and every reason for the invocation of Rule 403 under which the impeachment value would be outweighed by confusion of issues).

§ 806.1 HEARSAY Ch. 8

There appear to be no cases interpreting the last sentence of Rule 806, which authorizes the calling and cross-examining of the declarant and very little on the authorization for evidence in support of the hearsay after it is impeached.[20]

Library References:

West's Key No. Digests, Witnesses ⟜311–416.

807 Admissibility of Hearsay Where Party Causes Declarant's Unavailability

§ 807.1 New York and Federal

Hearsay which is otherwise inadmissible because falling under no hearsay exception may nevertheless be admissible where declarant's absence from the trial is caused by the party against whom he would have testified. The Court of Appeals in *People v. Geraci*,[1] noted that this is often labeled "waiver by misconduct," but was also a forfeiture dictated by public policy.[2] In *Geraci* there was evidence that defendant had intimidated a grand jury witness so that the witness was unavailable for the trial. The use of the witness' grand jury testimony was approved by the court mainly on a policy basis. The court first noted the maxim that a person should not be allowed to take advantage of his own wrong, and then stated:

> Additionally, the rule is invoked to "[protect] the integrity of the adversary process by deterring litigants from acting on strong incentives to prevent the testimony of an adverse witness" * * *. Like all of the other courts that have adopted and applied the rule, we conclude that out-of-court statements, including Grand Jury testimony, may be admitted as direct evidence where the witness is unavailable to testify at trial and the proof establishes that the witness's unavailability was procured by misconduct on the part of the defendant.[3]

The court went on to decide that such misconduct had to be proved by clear and convincing evidence before the hearsay would be allowed,[4] and that such can be made out partially or entirely by circumstantial evidence[5] developed at a fact-based hearing called a *Sirois* hearing.[6]

---

20. See United States v. Bernal, 719 F.2d 1475, 1479 (9th Cir.1983)(where declarant's coconspirator's statement was impeached with an inconsistent statement, the court allowed introduction of a third statement consistent with his first statement).

§ 807.1

1. 85 N.Y.2d 359, 625 N.Y.S.2d 469, 649 N.E.2d 817 (1995).

2. Id. at 366, 625 N.Y.S.2d at 473, 649 N.E.2d at 821.

3. Id.

4. Id. at 366–70, 625 N.Y.S.2d at 473–75, 649 N.E.2d at 821–23. The clear and convincing standard had been applied 11 years earlier in People v. Sweeper, 122 Misc.2d 386, 388, 471 N.Y.S.2d 486, 488 (Sup.Ct.N.Y.Co.1984).

5. Id. at 369–71, 625 N.Y.S.2d at 475–76, 649 N.E.2d at 822–24.

6. It was stated: "This type of hearing has been named after the defendant in People v. Sirois, the criminal case that was considered in Matter of Holtzman v. Hellenbrand (92 AD2d 405). In that case, the

The Court of Appeals had broached this rule on a prior occasion, but had no reason to define all its aspects;[7] and the lower courts had recognized and applied the rule so that hearsay evidence was admitted.[8]

Although there is no Federal Rule of Evidence governing this forfeiture rule,[9] the Second Circuit has adopted it, noting Supreme Court precedent.[10] The Second Circuit rule varies markedly from the rule set forth in *Geraci*, however, in that the Second Circuit has settled on the preponderance of evidence test as a standard to establish the foundation

Second Department outlined the procedure to be followed 'whenever the People allege specific facts which demonstrate a "distinct possibility" * * * that a criminal defendant's misconduct had induced a witness' unlawful refusal to testify * * * or has caused the witness' "disappearance or demise" (92 AD2d at 415).'" 85 N.Y.2d at 363, 625 N.Y.S.2d at 471, 649 N.E.2d at 819.

The court took pains to note that misconduct need not be proved beyond a reasonable doubt. That standard has no application in a Sirois hearing, "where the trier of fact is called upon to resolve a subsidiary evidentiary question and the burden of proof is measured by the lesser 'clear and convincing evidence'" test. Id. at 371, 625 N.Y.S.2d at 476, 649 N.E.2d at 824.

The court added that the judge at the Sirois hearing is involved in fact-finding, and not of reviewing the weight of evidence, and that "it was bound to consider the circumstantial evidence as a whole and to determine for itself whether it was clearly and convincingly persuaded. This required something more than an assessment of whether defendant's involvement was more probable than not and something less than a determination that all of the innocent inferences could be excluded to a 'moral certainty' * * *. It required a fact-based inquiry that is generically different in kind from the legal assessment of whether the inference of guilt could be rationally drawn * * *." Id.

7. In People v. Hamilton, 70 N.Y.2d 987, 526 N.Y.S.2d 421, 521 N.E.2d 428 (1988), the People had produced no evidence that defendant had intimidated the witness and so there was a complete lack of any foundation. Id. at 988, 526 N.Y.S.2d at 421–22, 521 N.E.2d at 428–29.

8. Holtzman v. Hellenbrand, 92 A.D.2d 405, 460 N.Y.S.2d 591 (2d Dep't 1983)(grand jury testimony); People v. Okafor, 130 Misc.2d 536, 495 N.Y.S.2d 895 (Sup.Ct.Bronx Co.1985)(former testimony given in Family Court proceeding).

9. There is, however, a proposed New York Evidence Code section, which provides as follows:

§ 807. **Rendering hearsay admissible by causing the unavailability of a witness [PROPOSED]**

(a) **Misconduct causing unavailability.** Reliable statements by a potential witness which would otherwise be inadmissible hearsay are admissible as direct evidence against a party whose criminal misconduct has caused that witness to be unavailable within the meaning of subdivision (a) of section 804 of this article.

(b) **Misconduct causing a change in testimony.** When the criminal misconduct of a party has caused a witness in a criminal case to give testimony upon a material issue of the case which tends to disprove the position of the party who called the witness, prior contradictory reliable statements of that witness are admissible as evidence in chief, without regard to the limitations contained in subdivision (c) of section 613 of this chapter.

(c) **Procedure.** Whenever a party alleges specific facts based upon reliable sources of information which demonstrate reasonable cause to believe that another party's misconduct has caused a witness to be unavailable or to change his or her testimony under the circumstances outlined in subdivision (a) and (b) of this section, the court shall hold a hearing pursuant to subdivision (b) of section 104 of this chapter. The determination of whether a defendant has engaged in criminal misconduct shall be based upon clear and convincing evidence.

(d) **Evidence of misconduct.** Nothing in this section precludes the admission of evidence of misconduct when it is otherwise relevant.

10. United States v. Mastrangelo, 693 F.2d 269 (2d Cir.1982), cert. denied, 467 U.S. 1204, 104 S.Ct. 2385, 81 L.Ed.2d 343 (1984). The court cited Snyder v. Massachusetts, 291 U.S. 97, 106, 54 S.Ct. 330, 332–33, 78 L.Ed. 674 (1934); Diaz v. United States, 223 U.S. 442, 452–53, 32 S.Ct. 250, 252–53, 56 L.Ed. 500 (1912), and other cases of similar nature (693 F.2d at 272).

§ 807.1   HEARSAY   Ch. 8

rather than the clear and convincing test adopted by the *Geraci* court.[11] The circuits are not in accord on the appropriate standard of proof.[12]

Library References:

West's Key No. Digests, Criminal Law ⚖419(5); Evidence ⚖266–313.

11. The Mastrangelo court stated:

Since the right of confrontation is closely related to the reliability of testimonial evidence, the clear and convincing test may well apply to issues of admissibility arising under it. However, waiver by misconduct is an issue distinct from the underlying right of confrontation and not necessarily governed by the same rules concerning burden of proof. We see no reason to impose upon the government more than the usual burden of proof by a preponderance of the evidence where waiver by misconduct is concerned. Such a claim of waiver is not one which is either unusually subject to deception or disfavored by the law. * * * To the contrary, such misconduct is invariably accompanied by tangible evidence such as the disappearance of the defendant, disruption in the courtroom or the murder of a key witness, and there is hardly any reason to apply a burden of proof which might encourage behavior which strikes at the heart of the system of justice itself.

693 F.2d at 273.

12. Compare United States v. Thevis, 665 F.2d 616, 631 (5th Cir.), cert. denied, 459 U.S. 825, 103 S.Ct. 57, 74 L.Ed.2d 61 (1982)(requires clear and convincing evidence), with Steele v. Taylor, 684 F.2d 1193, 1202 (6th Cir.1982)(requires only a preponderance of the evidence).

CHAPTER 9

AUTHENTICATION AND IDENTIFICATION

Table of Sections

900 INTRODUCTION

900.1 Authentication and Identification In General—New York and Federal.

901 COMMON INSTANCES REQUIRING AUTHENTICATION OR IDENTIFICATION

901.1 Testimony of Witness with Knowledge.
  a. New York.
  b. Federal.
901.2 Lay Opinion on Handwriting.
  a. New York.
  b. Federal.
901.3 Comparisons by Trier or Expert Witness.
  a. New York.
  b. Federal.
901.4 Circumstantial Evidence of Authenticity.
  a. New York.
  b. Federal.
901.5 Voice Identification.
  a. New York.
  b. Federal.
901.6 Telephone Conversations.
  a. New York.
  b. Federal.
901.7 Public Records.
  a. New York.
  b. Federal.
901.8 Ancient Documents.
  a. New York.
  b. Federal.
901.9 Process or System.
  a. New York.
  b. Federal.
901.10 Methods Provided by Statute or Rule.
  a. New York.
  b. Federal.

902 SELF–AUTHENTICATION

902.1 Self–Authentication.
  a. New York.
  b. Federal.

903 SUBSCRIBING WITNESSES

903.1 Subscribing Witnesses—New York and Federal.

900 Introduction

§ 900.1 Authentication and Identification In General—New York and Federal

When a writing or an item of physical proof is sought to be introduced in evidence it must be authenticated in the sense that a showing is required that the item is what its proponent claims it to be.[1] Likewise, testimony concerning a conversation with another person, either in person or by telephone, normally requires identification of the person speaking, and this is also true where the conversation comes into evidence by way of a recording.[2] A sound recording would require, in addition, evidence of the accuracy, completeness and unaltered condition of the tape on which the conversation is preserved.[3]

Authentication and identification of physical evidence, writings and voices "represent a special aspect of relevance."[4] Judge Friendly put the matter as follows: "Authentication is perhaps the purest example of a rule respecting relevance: evidence admitted as something can have no probative value unless that is what it really is."[5] An inculpatory statement of the defendant, for example, is not relevant unless it is shown that defendant was the speaker. There may be instances, howev-

---

§ 900.1

1. See, e.g., People v. McGee, 49 N.Y.2d 48, 59, 424 N.Y.S.2d 157, 163, 399 N.E.2d 1177, 1183 (1979)(where the admissibility question related to the authenticity of tape recordings, the court said that accuracy and authenticity "is established by proof that the offered evidence is genuine and that there has been no tampering with it * * *."); People v. Corey, 148 N.Y. 476, 488, 42 N.E. 1066, 1070 (1896)("Until [handwriting] genuineness was established to the entire satisfaction of the court, it was not admissible for the purpose of comparison * * * and the trial court may well have characterized it as alleged to be genuine instead of being genuine"); United States v. Sliker, 751 F.2d 477, 497 (2d Cir.1984), cert. denied sub nom., Buchwald v. United States, 470 U.S. 1058, 105 S.Ct. 1772, 84 L.Ed.2d 832, and cert. denied sub nom., Carbone v. United States, 471 U.S. 1137, 105 S.Ct. 2679, 86 L.Ed.2d 697 (1985)("In order for a piece of evidence to be of probative value, there must be proof that it is what its proponent says it is. The requirement of authentication is thus a condition precedent to admitting evidence.").

2. People v. Lynes, 49 N.Y.2d 286, 291–93, 425 N.Y.S.2d 295, 297–98, 401 N.E.2d 405, 407–08 (1980)(telephone conversation); United States v. Sliker, 751 F.2d 477, 499–500 (2d Cir.1984), cert. denied sub. nom., Buchwald v. United States, 470 U.S. 1058, 105 S.Ct. 1772, 84 L.Ed.2d 832, and cert. denied sub nom., Carbone v. United States, 471 U.S. 1137, 105 S.Ct. 2679, 86 L.Ed.2d 697 (1985)(tape recording).

3. See, e.g., People v. Ely, 68 N.Y.2d 520, 528, 510 N.Y.S.2d 532, 537, 503 N.E.2d 88, 93 (1986). United States v. Fuentes, 563 F.2d 527, 531–32 (2d Cir.1977).

4. Federal Rule of Evidence 901(a), Advisory Committee's Note; 7 Wigmore § 2129 (requirement of authentication is "an inherent logical necessity").

5. Sliker, 751 F.2d at 499. Sliker contains several authentication issues, the chief one concerning the identification of defendant's voice on a tape recording. The court noted that the jury could make its own voice comparison between the voice of the defendant who testified and the voice on the tape. Id. at 500.

er, when the contents of a statement, whether in writing or made in person or in a telephone call, will be relevant regardless of the identity of the speaker and will be admissible if the evidence is shown to be authentic in other necessary respects.[6]

The process of authentication and identification, often called laying a foundation, is relatively clear under federal practice. Rule 901(a) of the Federal Rules of Evidence provides:

General Provision. The requirement of authentication or identification as a condition precedent to admissibility is satisfied by evidence sufficient to support a finding that the matter in question is what its proponent claims.

The Advisory Committee's Note to Rule 901(a) states that the requirement of authentication and identification "falls in the category of relevancy dependent upon fulfillment of a condition of fact and is governed by the procedure set forth in Rule 104(b)."[7] In *United States v. Sliker*,[8] Judge Friendly said: "[U]nder [Rule 104(b)] * * * the judge may conditionally admit the evidence, subject to the jury's ultimate determination as to its genuineness. * * * Hence the rule requires the admission of evidence 'if sufficient proof has been introduced so that a reasonable juror could find in favor of authenticity of identification.' "[9] To admit the matter into evidence, therefore, the trial judge personally need not be persuaded of its authenticity so long as the jury rationally could be so persuaded. If the jury is not in fact convinced of authenticity, it should disregard the evidence.

The standard to be used by the trial judge in federal court in deciding whether to admit evidence over an authentication objection is whether the jury could find authenticity by a preponderance of the evidence.[10] For the authentication of sound recordings in criminal cases,

---

6. See, e.g., People v. Brown, 80 N.Y.2d 729, 594 N.Y.S.2d 696, 610 N.E.2d 369 (1993), where the substance of a 911 call satisfied the present sense impression exception to the hearsay rule. The fact the caller's identity was unknown was not important since his call was verified by police who substantiated his description by observing events at the scene when they arrived. (See discussion of Brown at § 803(1).1(a) supra.)

See also Sliker, 751 F.2d at 488, where commercial paper was offered to prove a part of the scheme that created a sham offshore bank. The court observed: "The papers were relevant no matter who their author was. All that was needed was sufficient proof for a jury to find that they were connected to the bank that issued the checks * * *."

7. See the discussion of Federal Rule 104(b) in § 104.2 supra.

8. 751 F.2d 477 (2d Cir.1984), cert. denied, 470 U.S. 1058, 105 S.Ct. 1772, 84 L.Ed.2d 832, and cert. denied sub. nom., Carbone v. United States, 471 U.S. 1137, 105 S.Ct. 2679, 86 L.Ed.2d 697 (1985).

9. Id. at 488, quoting 5 Weinstein and Berger ¶ 901(a)[01]. See also United States v. Ruggiero, 928 F.2d 1289, 1303 (2d Cir. 1991).

10. Huddleston v. United States, 485 U.S. 681, 690, 108 S.Ct. 1496, 1501, 99 L.Ed.2d 771, 782–83 (1988). See § 404.2(a) for a discussion of Huddleston's construction of Federal Rule 404(b)(admissibility of other crimes or acts).

Presumably this is what is meant by the Second Circuit panels in United States v. Gelzer, 50 F.3d 1133, 1140–41 (2d Cir.1995)("authentication seeks to establish that the evidence offered is what its proponent claims it to be, and must be shown by a preponderance of the evidence"), and United States v. Grant, 967 F.2d 81, 82 (2d Cir.1992)(Federal Rule 901 "requires as a condition precedent to admissibility a showing, by a preponderance of evidence, that the thing offered is what its proponent claims it to be").

however, the Second Circuit has imposed the higher burden of "clear and convincing evidence" because of the unique susceptibility of such evidence to alteration.[11]

In New York, the applicable standard of proof on issues of authentication, as well as the allocation of responsibility between judge and jury, is less clear than in federal practice. In *People v. McGee*,[12] the Court of Appeals made the following statement: "In determining whether a proper foundation has been laid for the introduction of real evidence, the accuracy of the object itself is the focus of inquiry, which must be demonstrated by clear and convincing evidence."[13] The evidence in issue in *McGee* was a sound recording, the very type of evidence singled out by the Second Circuit for application of the clear and convincing standard.[14] But the Court of Appeals indicated that the clear and convincing standard was "applicable to any real evidence sought to be admitted."[15] It is questionable, however, that the *McGee* standard was intended to apply in civil actions where life, liberty and other important public interests are not at stake.

McGee also implies that the trial judge himself must be persuaded of the authenticity of real evidence by clear and convincing evidence as a precondition to admissibility.[16] Thus, contrary to federal practice, the New York judge performs more than a mere preliminary screening to ascertain whether there is enough for the jury to find authenticity. Under the apparent New York rule the evidence is not admitted at all

---

The court in United States v. Hon, 904 F.2d 803, 809 (2d Cir.1990), described the standard of proof for the judge's preliminary determination as that of a "rational basis." Accord: United States v. Inserra, 34 F.3d 83, 90 (2d Cir.1994). See also United States v. Neal, 36 F.3d 1190, 1210 (1st Cir.1994)("reasonable probability").

11. United States v. Ruggiero, 928 F.2d 1289, 1303 (2d Cir.1991). It was stated: "Recognizing, however, that 'recorded evidence is likely to have a strong impression upon a jury and is susceptible to alteration, we have adopted a general standard, namely, that the government 'produce clear and convincing evidence of authenticity and accuracy" as a foundation for the admission of such recordings.' United States v. Fuentes, 563 F.2d 527, 532 (2d Cir.)(quoting "United States v. Knohl, 379 F.2d 427, 440 (2d Cir.), cert. denied, 389 U.S. 973, 88 S.Ct. 472, 19 L.Ed.2d 465 (1967)), cert. denied, 434 U.S. 959, 98 S.Ct. 491, 54 L.Ed.2d 320 (1977)." See the discussion of sound recordings at § 1104.2(c), infra.

12. 49 N.Y.2d 48, 424 N.Y.S.2d 157, 399 N.E.2d 1177 (1979).

13. Id. at 59, 424 N.Y.S.2d at 163, 399 N.E.2d at 1183. See also § 1101.1 infra.

14. The McGee court cited the Second Circuit's decision in United States v. Fuentes, 563 F.2d 527 (2d Cir.1977).

15. 49 N.Y.2d at 59, 424 N.Y.S.2d at 163, 399 N.E.2d at 1183. In People v. Ely, 68 N.Y.2d 520, 527, 510 N.Y.S.2d 532, 536, 503 N.E.2d 88, 92 (1986), the Court of Appeals reiterated that the clear and convincing standard applies to sound recordings, and some lower courts in criminal cases have applied the same standard to other types of physical evidence. See, e.g., People v. Moyer, 186 A.D.2d 997, 998, 588 N.Y.S.2d 457, 458 (4th Dep't 1992), leave to appeal denied, 81 N.Y.2d 844, 595 N.Y.S.2d 743, 611 N.E.2d 782 (1993)(drugs); People v. Branch, 161 A.D.2d 776, 556 N.Y.S.2d 122 (2d Dep't 1990)(victim's coat).

16. 49 N.Y.2d at 60, 424 N.Y.S.2d at 163, 399 N.E.2d at 1183. It was stated: "Proof that the evidence has not been altered may be established in a similar fashion [by testimony of a participant in the conversation]. This testimony, if credited by the Trial Judge, is sufficient to establish that the taped conversation accurately and fairly represents the event to which it refers." See also People v. Ely, supra note 15, where the court states: "Admissibility of tape-recorded conversation requires proof of the accuracy or authenticity of the tape by 'clear and convincing evidence' establishing 'that the offered evidence is genuine and that there has been no tampering.'" 68 N.Y.2d at 527, 510 N.Y.S.2d at 532, 503 N.E.2d at 92.

unless the judge is convinced of the authenticity of the evidence, at least in criminal cases.[17] Giving the judge a strong supervisory role in the admission of real evidence can be justified in criminal cases since it can be difficult for defense counsel effectively to expose bogus prosecution evidence.[18]

It is not suggested that the jury in a criminal case is bound to accept the judge's determination of authenticity. The Court of Appeals has stated: "If the court * * * adjudges the papers genuine, it then becomes the duty of the jury in its turn, at the proper time, * * * to examine the testimony respecting the genuineness * * * and to decide for itself, under proper legal instruction from the court, whether their genuineness has been established."[19]

The foregoing procedures regarding real evidence, however, have not been applied to all issues of authentication. In *People v. Lynes*,[20] a different approach was taken with respect to the identification of voices. In *Lynes*, the issue was whether the recipient of a telephone call could identify the caller, whose identity was disputed, by circumstantial evidence. The court said that admissibility of the telephone call depended upon "whether a sufficient foundation had been laid to permit a finding that the conversation was one with the party against whom it was offered. Putting the issue another way, in this case was the proof such that a jury could find that defendant was indeed the caller?"[21] Furthermore, the court implied that the standard of proof was that of a preponderance: "From all this emerges the rule that * * * in the first instance the Judge who presides over the trial must determine that the proffered proof permits the drawing of inferences which make it improbable that the caller's voice belongs to anyone other than the purported caller."[22] As to the identification of voices, therefore, the New York approach appears consistent with that taken in the federal courts.

The Proposed New York Evidence Code apparently adopted the federal standard for all issues of authentication and identification.[23]

---

17. See People v. Molineux, 168 N.Y. 264, 330, 61 N.E. 286, 308 (1901), where it was stated that "the genuineness of the papers offered as standards is a preliminary point to be determined in the first instance by the court before permitting the papers to go to the jury." In Clark v. Douglass, 5 App.Div. 547, 550–551, 40 N.Y.S. 769, 771–772 (3d Dep't 1896) the court said: "Without intending to lay down any inflexible rule, we are of the opinion that unless the evidence of the genuineness of the standard is so clear that if it were one of the issues in the case for the jury to determine a verdict should be directed in favor of its genuineness by the court, it may not properly be allowed in evidence."

18. See Lilly § 13.3, at 518 ("The possibility that false or altered evidence may be produced by the prosecution under circumstances not easily exposed by a defendant may justify the policy.").

19. People v. Molineux, 168 N.Y. 264, 330, 61 N.E. 286, 308 (1901). There appears to be no standard criminal jury instruction precisely on this point. See 1 Criminal Jury Instructions, New York.

20. 49 N.Y.2d 286, 425 N.Y.S.2d 295, 401 N.E.2d 405 (1980).

21. Id. at 291, 425 N.Y.S.2d at 297, 401 N.E.2d at 407.

22. Id. at 292, 425 N.Y.S.2d at 298, 401 N.E.2d at 408.

23. Proposed New York Evidence Code § 901(a):

(a) **General provision.** A requirement of authentication or identification as a condition precedent to admissibility is satisfied by evidence sufficient to support a finding that the offered evidence is what its proponent claims.

The Comment to proposed § 104(a), which delineates the judge's role in the

§ 900.1   AUTHENTICATION & IDENTIFICATION   Ch. 9

During the process of authentication and identification, both state and federal courts will permit limited cross-examination, known as voir dire, prior to the conclusion of the direct testimony of the witness who is providing the foundation evidence.[24] Some matters, however, are self-authenticating, thereby reducing and in some cases eliminating the need for foundation testimony.[25] Furthermore, a party may be able to avoid the need for foundation evidence if the adversary is willing to stipulate to authenticity,[26] makes an admission in the pleadings,[27] or an admission as to genuineness is obtained.[28]

The authentication requirements for particular types of physical evidence other than writings are covered in detail in chapter 11, which deals with real and demonstrative evidence.[29] The present chapter focuses on general principles and methods for the authentication and identification of writings, voices and other miscellaneous items of evidence as to which genuineness, authorship or source is a critical aspect of relevance.

Authentication is only one of several factors applied in the determination of admissibility. The evidence, of course, must be relevant,[30] if written it must comply with the best evidence rule,[31] and the hearsay rules must be looked to when the evidence consists of statements.[32]

Library References:

West's Key No. Digests, Criminal Law ⟐444; Evidence ⟐366–383.

901 Common Instances Requiring Authentication or Identification

§ 901.1 Testimony of Witness with Knowledge

Federal Rule of Evidence 901(b) offers 10 illustrations of recurring situations where certain rules have evolved as to the requirement and

introduction of evidence, states: "Thus, the court's function in ruling on admissibility is only to decide that the evidence has probative force." An example given is that "when an issue arises concerning the authenticity of offered documentary evidence, e.g., CE 901(a), the court admits the evidence if there is a sufficient showing of authorship (or genuineness), and the jury is then free to decide for itself whether that condition (authorship or genuineness) is fulfilled * * *." The Comments to the Proposed Code make no reference to the apparent discrepancy between the approach in McGee to real evidence, and the Lynes approach to voice identification.

24. See § 611.3(d) supra.

25. E.g., ancient documents discussed in § 901.8 infra, and public documents discussed in § 902.1 infra.

26. See, e.g., CPLR 2104, providing for written and subscribed stipulations, or stipulations made in open court.

27. See § 802.1 supra.

28. CPLR 3123 provides for the notice to admit, which can result in sanctions should the adversary unreasonably refuse to admit.

29. See §§ 1100.1 (general principles), 1101.1–1101.2 (tangible objects, including chain of custody of fungible items), 1103.1–1103.2 (models, charts and diagrams), and 1104.1–1104.2 (photographs, x-rays, sound recordings, motion pictures and videotape).

30. See §§ 401.1 and 401.2 supra.

31. See chapter 10 infra.

32. See chapter 8 supra.

process for authenticity or identification. The first illustration is that of a foundation laid by "[t]estimony that a matter is what it is claimed to be."

a. New York

A person who has personal knowledge of the genuineness of a writing, or an object, or a voice may so testify. The Court of Appeals in *People v. McGee*[1] made an important distinction between a tape recording and fungible material such as drugs. Because they have no distinguishing characteristics, drugs must be authenticated by establishing a chain of custody so that their identity from the time taken from defendant until returned to the prosecutor after laboratory testing can be accounted for.[2] But the conversation on a tape is unique, and participants can attest to its accuracy. "A foundation may be established by a participant to the conversation who testifies that the conversation has been accurately and fairly reproduced * * *. Proof that the evidence has not been altered may be established in a similar fashion."[3]

Of course, testimonial evidence is no less important in proving a chain of custody where the exhibit is a fungible substance since the chain can only be established through the testimony of the custodians.[4]

Examples of testimonial authentication are endless. For instance, a mugging victim's testimony that the gun found at the scene "was like the one placed against his chest" was sufficient to link the gun to defendant;[5] testimony that eyeglasses found at the site of the crime "resembled" glasses owned by defendant was sufficient foundation;[6] in authenticating the voice of a person on the telephone, the witness' testimony that he recognized the voice was enough to prove identity;[7] a witness' testimony that a photograph was a fair and accurate representation of a particular scene was enough to establish the authenticity and identity of the photograph;[8] and a witness' testimony that he saw a party write a document, or sign it, will lay the foundation for authorship of the document.[9]

An exception to the requirement that the foundation witness have personal knowledge of the authenticity or identity of a writing applies where the writing is being offered under CPLR 4518, the business entry statute; the witness need have only general knowledge as to office

§ 901.1

1. 49 N.Y.2d 48, 424 N.Y.S.2d 157, 399 N.E.2d 1177 (1979).

2. People v. Julian, 41 N.Y.2d 340, 392 N.Y.S.2d 610, 360 N.E.2d 1310 (1977); see the discussion concerning chain of custody in § 1101.1, at notes 18–24, infra.

3. McGee, 49 N.Y.2d at 60, 424 N.Y.S.2d at 163, 398 N.E.2d at 1183.

4. People v. Julian, 41 N.Y.2d 340, 342–43, 392 N.Y.S.2d 610, 612–13, 360 N.E.2d 1310, 1312–13 (1977).

5. People v. Randolph, 40 A.D.2d 806, 338 N.Y.S.2d 229 (1st Dep't 1972).

6. People v. Mirenda, 23 N.Y.2d 439, 452–53, 297 N.Y.S.2d 532, 542, 245 N.E.2d 194, 201 (1969).

7. People v. Lynes, 49 N.Y.2d 286, 291, 425 N.Y.S.2d 295, 297, 401 N.E.2d 405, 407 (1980).

8. Archer v. New York, N.H. & H.R.R.Co., 106 N.Y. 589, 603, 13 N.E. 318, 324 (1887).

9. People v. Molineux, 168 N.Y. 264, 328, 61 N.E. 286, 307 (1901).

§ 901.1   AUTHENTICATION & IDENTIFICATION   Ch. 9

practices.[10]

Proposed New York Evidence Code § 901(b)(1) is identical to Federal Rule 901(b)(1), and the Comment to the New York provision states that it "codifies existing law."

b. Federal

Second Circuit cases provide several examples of the applicability of Federal Rule of Evidence 901(b)(1). In *United States v. Almonte*,[11] defendant sought to discredit DEA agents' testimony concerning his admissions by introducing notes made by an Assistant United States Attorney during a debriefing of one of the agents. The question was whether these notes were an accurate reflection of what the agent had said, or were the prosecuting attorney's own characterization of what he said. The court noted that the burden of proving that notes reflect the witness' own words rather than the note-taker's characterization falls on the party seeking to introduce the notes and that the trial judge in this case had not abused his discretion in keeping the notes out because that burden had not been met. The trial judge commented that the notes "look and sound not like a memorialization of Traver's exact words, but like a quickly jotted summary."[12]

Police practices assure in many cases that crime evidence will have a secure foundation at trial. In *United States v. Sabater*,[13] confiscated currency used by an undercover agent in a narcotics buy found its way safely into evidence because when it was taken from defendant, its numbers having been prerecorded, and the bills photocopied, the officer's initials were inscribed and the bill was stamped and recorded with the police property clerk. The officer had no trouble in court identifying the currency. Since premarked currency is not fungible in the way that drugs are, there was no necessity for proving a chain of custody.[14] The chain of custody routine was utilized, however, where a gun was admitted into evidence and the issue was whether the gap in the chain was so wide as to result in inadmissibility.[15] While it is true that unlike money used to buy drugs, the gun could not be prerecorded and photographed, it would nevertheless seem that it could have identifying marks and characteristics enabling identification without establishing a full chain of custody.[16]

---

10. See, e.g., Jezowski v. Beach, 59 Misc.2d 224, 225–26, 298 N.Y.S.2d 360, 361–62 (Sup.Ct.Oneida Co.1968)(where deceased doctor's widow testified that doctor's office cards, relating to patients and kept in his handwriting, were regularly kept in his office they were authenticated sufficiently to be admissible under CPLR 4518). See the discussion of the business entry rule at §§ 803(3).1 and 803(3).2, supra.

11. 956 F.2d 27 (2d Cir.1992).

12. Id. at 29–30.

13. 830 F.2d 7 (2d Cir.1987).

14. Id. at 10–11.

15. United States v. Gelzer, 50 F.3d 1133, 1141 (2d Cir.1995).

16. Defendant had waived his objection to introduction of the gun, but the court ruled that despite the gap there was sufficient evidence "to establish that it is more likely than not that the revolver offered at trial was the same as that recovered by Officer Staub." 50 F.3d at 1141.

New York cases allow introduction of a gun on the strength of the victim's testimony that it looks like the gun used by defendant. See, e.g., People v. Randolph, 40 A.D.2d 806, 338 N.Y.S.2d 229 (1st Dep't 1972); see also People v. Capers, 105

Unless exhibits are self-authenticating, a witness will have to testify in some fashion to authenticity, and thus the provisions of Rule 901(b)(1) pervade every civil and criminal trial. In some instances personal knowledge is not required, as where the witness is testifying to the keeping of business records, but normally the witness will have to be a person with knowledge of that about which he testifies.[17]

Library References:
> West's Key No. Digests, Criminal Law ⊙404.10, 444; Evidence ⊙188, 366–383.

§ 901.2 Lay Opinion on Handwriting

a. New York

Provided a foundation is laid that the witness is familiar with the person's handwriting by having received correspondence from that person,[1] having seen the person write,[2] or otherwise having observed the person's writing,[3] he may testify that he believes the document in question to have been written or signed by that person.[4] The degree to which the witness is familiar with the handwriting normally goes to weight and not admissibility,[5] but familiarity can be found to be so lacking that the testimony ought not be allowed at all.[6]

The witness' familiarity with the handwriting must have been gained in the normal course of events, and cannot have been acquired for

---

A.D.2d 842, 482 N.Y.S.2d 37 (2d Dep't 1984)(gun marked with police officer's initials).

17. In United States v. Inserra, 34 F.3d 83, 90 (2d Cir.1994), defendant argued that probation reports (apparently not linked to him by their contents) had no proper foundation; but the court found that the probation officer's testimony connecting those reports to defendant was sufficient to overcome the objection.

§ 901.2

1. See Gross v. Sormani, 50 App.Div. 531, 534, 64 N.Y.S. 300, 302–03 (2d Dep't 1900).

2. See Hammond v. Varian, 54 N.Y. 398, 400 (1873).

3. See Hynes v. McDermott, 82 N.Y. 41, 52–54 (1880). The court stated:

> Testimony as to handwriting is testimony of opinion. Any person acquainted with it may be permitted to give his opinion of it. The acquaintance need not come from having seem the person write. It may be formed from seeing writing under such circumstances as put it beyond doubt that it was a true signature.

Id. at 52–53.

4. In People v. Molineux, 168 N.Y. 264, 61 N.E. 286 (1901), the court listed the ways in which handwriting could be proved, one of which is "by witnesses familiar with the handwriting of the person charged to be the writer, and who were able to testify from their familiarity with his handwriting to a belief respecting the genuineness of the handwriting in question." Id. at 321, 61 N.E. at 305. See also People v. Clark, 122 A.D.2d 389, 390, 504 N.Y.S.2d 799, 800 (3d Dep't), appeal denied, 68 N.Y.2d 913, 508 N.Y.S.2d 1033, 501 N.E.2d 606 (1986).

5. In Hammond v. Varian, 54 N.Y. 398 (1873), the court stated: "They had some means, although slight, of enabling them to judge whether the signature was that of the defendant, yet sufficient, in their belief, to express an opinion in reference thereto. The extent of their knowledge, and the weight or effect to be given to their opinion, were proper matters for the consideration of the jury." Id. at 400.

In Hynes v. McDermott, 82 N.Y. 41 (1880), the court stated: "The competency of a witness is not determined by the degree of his knowledge. If he has had means of becoming acquainted with the handwriting in question, he is competent to speak, and the weight of his testimony is for the jury." Id. at 53.

6. See People v. Corey, 148 N.Y. 476, 483, 42 N.E. 1066, 1069 (1896) (witness who professed to know defendant's handwriting was shown to be illiterate).

§ 901.2 AUTHENTICATION & IDENTIFICATION Ch. 9

the purposes of litigation.[7] In-court comparison of the writing in issue with a specimen writing can only be made by an expert.[8] The Proposed New York Evidence Code § 901(b)(2) would codify these rules.[9]

Lay opinion testimony generally in New York is discussed in chapter 7.[10]

b. Federal

Federal Rule of Evidence 901(b)(2) provides:

Nonexpert opinion on handwriting. Nonexpert opinion as to the genuineness of handwriting, based upon familiarity not acquired for purposes of the litigation.

Prior to adoption of the Federal Rules, the Supreme Court had enunciated this standard with a liberal construction in a common law framework.[11] In *United States v. Tipton*,[12] the Seventh Circuit construed Rule 901(b)(2) for the first time and ruled in a prosecution for embezzlement and tax evasion that defendant's co-workers who had previously observed his writing could testify as to his signature on the phony documents in issue.[13] In reaching its conclusion, the court reviewed cases in the Fifth[14] and Eleventh[15] Circuits which had allowed such

---

7. In Hynes v. McDermott, 82 N.Y. 41 (1880), the court pointed out the distinction "between the testimony of a witness who, intending to be a witness, has inspected genuine documents, for the purpose of forming an acquaintance with the characteristics of a certain handwriting, and that of one who, in the course of business, without having in view the being a witness, has used the same documents, and thus got an acquaintance." Id. at 54. The former was held inadmissible.

8. Matter of Collins v. Wyman, 38 A.D.2d 600, 328 N.Y.S.2d 725 (2d Dep't 1971).

9. The section provides:

(2) Nonexpert opinion on handwriting. Nonexpert opinion as to handwriting based upon familiarity not acquired for purposes of litigation.

10. See § 701.1 supra. Wigmore's history of the handwriting rule is incredibly rich. See 7 Wigmore §§ 1991–2028, especially § 2007.

11. In Rogers v. Ritter, 79 U.S. (12 Wall.) 317, 20 L.Ed. 417 (1870), the Court stated:

The witnesses in this case were conversant with the signature of Sanchez, and swore to their belief, not by comparing a disputed with an acknowledged signature, but from the knowledge they had previously acquired on the subject. The textwriters all agree, that a witness is qualified to testify to the genuineness of a controverted signature if he has the proper knowledge of the party's handwriting. The difficulty has been in determining what is proper knowledge, and how it shall be acquired. It is settled everywhere that if a person has seen another write his name but once he can testify, and that he is equally competent, if he has personally communicated with him by letter, although he has never seen him write at all. But is the witness incompetent unless he has obtained his knowledge in one or the other of these modes? Clearly not, for in the varied affairs of life there are many modes in which one person can become acquainted with the handwriting of another, besides having seen him write or corresponded with him. There is no good reason for excluding any of these modes of getting information, and if the court, on the preliminary examination of the witness, can see that he has that degree of knowledge of the party's handwriting which will enable him to judge of its genuineness, he should be permitted to give to the jury his opinion on the subject.

Id. at 322.

12. 964 F.2d 650 (7th Cir.1992).

13. Id. at 655.

14. United States v. Whittington, 783 F.2d 1210, 1214–15 (5th Cir.), cert. denied, 479 U.S. 882, 107 S.Ct. 269, 93 L.Ed.2d 246 (1986)(court allowed testimony of co-workers because even though they had not seen defendant sign the document, they were familiar with his handwriting).

---

15. See note 15 on page 777.

testimony.[16]

The degree of familiarity with the subject handwriting according to the *Tipton* court goes to the weight to be given the opinion[17] unless, of course, it is shown that the witness in fact has very little or no familiarity. Where the exhibit consists of a multi-page printed document, it is not necessary that the witness testify that she is familiar with the contents of each page. If the point in issue is the signature at the end of the document, then that is all the witness need be familiar with.[18]

An example of familiarity acquired for the purposes of the litigation is found in *United States v. Pitts*,[19] where the issue was the authenticity of a signature appearing on a sales receipt. It was proposed that a lawyer appearing for defendant in another proceeding testify that he compared the signature in question with a sample signature. In agreeing that the trial judge correctly kept out this testimony, the court stated: "Such one-shot comparisons made for purposes of the litigation lack the extent of familiarity contemplated by 901(b)(2)."[20] The court might also have observed that such comparisons can only be made by witnesses qualified as experts.

Lay opinion testimony in the federal courts is discussed in Chapter 7.[21]

Library References:

West's Key No. Digests, Criminal Law ⊶452(4), 458; Evidence ⊶474(14), 480.

§ 901.3 Comparisons by Trier or Expert Witness

a. New York

The comparison category of authentication is not limited to handwriting comparisons, although, of course, handwriting exemplars are included.[1] Whereas under the lay witness handwriting rule the witness renders his opinion based on familiarity with the subject's handwriting,[2] a handwriting expert, qualified by training and experience as an expert, compares the writing in issue to a sample known to have been written by the subject. This approach is codified under CPLR 4536,[3] and the New

---

15. United States v. Barker, 735 F.2d 1280, 1283 (11th Cir.), cert. denied, 469 U.S. 933, 105 S.Ct. 329, 83 L.Ed.2d 266 (1984)(co-workers familiar with defendant's handwriting could testify that in their opinion the handwriting in question was defendant's).

16. 964 F.2d at 655. The testimony was not rendered inadmissible because the witness could not say he was "certain" of his opinion.

17. 964 F.2d at 655.

18. United States v. Whittington, supra note 14. The court observed that "were it necessary for a witness to a document to identify every page of the document as a condition of admissibility, few documents would be admissible." 783 F.2d at 1215.

The court also noted that the witness' absolute certainty is not required, and that the weight of the evidence authenticated, and the authentication itself, is for the jury. Id.

19. 569 F.2d 343 (5th Cir.1978), cert. denied, 436 U.S. 959, 98 S.Ct. 3076, 57 L.Ed.2d 1125 (1978).

20. 569 F.2d at 348.

21. See § 701.2 supra.

§ 901.3

1. See People v. Molineux, 168 N.Y. 264, 328, 61 N.E. 286, 307 (1901).

2. See § 901.2 supra.

3. CPLR 4536 provides as follows:

Comparison of a disputed writing with any writing proved to the satisfaction of

§ 901.3 AUTHENTICATION & IDENTIFICATION Ch. 9

York cases are to the effect that such comparisons can be made, not just by experts, but also by the jury,[4] or judge in a bench trial.[5]

Since more sophisticated forms of evidence will be beyond the abilities of ordinary jurors to appraise, reliance must be placed on experts. Thus, authentication by expert comparison and analysis is common with respect to voiceprints,[6] ballistics[7] and fingerprints.[8] The role of experts is discussed in Chapter 7.[9]

The chief concern under CPLR 4536, and with samples other than handwriting as well, is that they be accepted by the judge as genuine. The authenticity of the specimen, if not stipulated, can be proved by an admission, testimony by the adversary, testimony by a witness who saw the specimen being written or to whom the adversary acknowledged the genuineness of the sample, testimony by a witness who is familiar with the author's handwriting, or proof that the author had purposefully acted on the basis of the specimen.[10] The court will determine the specimen's authenticity,[11] and in civil cases it would appear that the jury has the power to accept it or not.[12] As discussed in § 900.1 *supra*, it seems in New York that in criminal cases the judge is the final arbiter of the specimen's authenticity, subject to the jury's right to reject the judge's finding of genuineness.[13] A specimen cannot be used which was created for purposes of the litigation[14] even if created while the subject is on the witness stand.[15] Samples of writings are often obtained from reliable sources such as tax returns,[16] or writings prepared for other official use.[17]

The proposed New York Evidence Code § 903(b)(3) is found below.[18]

the court to be the handwriting of the person claimed to have made the disputed writing shall be permitted.

4. People v. Hunter, 34 N.Y.2d 432, 358 N.Y.S.2d 360, 315 N.E.2d 436 (1974).

5. Ibanez v. Pfeiffer, 76 Misc.2d 363, 350 N.Y.S.2d 964 (N.Y.C.Civ.Ct.1973).

6. See People v. Jeter, 80 N.Y.2d 818, 587 N.Y.S.2d 583, 600 N.E.2d 214 (1992). The lower court in this case neglected to conduct a Frye hearing with regard to the "spectrograph."

7. People v. Soper, 243 N.Y. 320, 153 N.E. 433 (1926).

8. People v. Roach, 215 N.Y. 592, 109 N.E. 618 (1915).

9. See § 702.1 supra.

10. People v. Molineux, 168 N.Y. 264, 328, 61 N.E. 286, 307 (1901).

11. Clark v. Douglass, 5 App.Div. 547, 40 N.Y.S. 769 (3d Dep't 1896) (authenticity of the specimen should be beyond doubt in order for it to be used).

12. Matter of Estate of Sylvestri, 44 N.Y.2d 260, 405 N.Y.S.2d 424, 376 N.E.2d 897 (1978); Heller v. Murray, 112 Misc.2d 745, 447 N.Y.S.2d 348 (N.Y.C.Civ.Ct.1981), aff'd, 118 Misc.2d 508, 464 N.Y.S.2d 391 (Sup.Ct.App.T.1983).

13. § 900.1, in text at note 19, supra.

14. People v. Molineux, 168 N.Y. 264, 329–30, 61 N.E. 286, 308 (1901).

15. Nelson v. Brady, 268 App.Div. 226, 50 N.Y.S.2d 582 (1st Dep't 1944).

16. See United States v. Mangan, 575 F.2d 32, 41–42 (2d Cir.), cert. denied, 439 U.S. 931, 99 S.Ct. 320, 58 L.Ed.2d 324 (1978).

17. See Scharfenberger v. Wingo, 542 F.2d 328, 336–37 (6th Cir.1976) (where the authenticity of Dr. Salb's signature was in issue the court could use his signature affixed to documents in the state personnel files as exemplars since there was no reason not to assume their regularity).

18. New York Evidence Code § 901(b)(3) [PROPOSED]

Comparison by court or expert witness. Comparison by the court or by an expert witness of the offered evidence with a specimen which the court has determined to be authentic.

778

b. Federal

Federal Rule of Evidence 901(b)(3) provides:

Comparison by trier or expert witness. Comparison by the trier of fact or by expert witnesses with specimens which have been authenticated.[19]

With respect to the role of judge and jury in appraising genuineness, and with respect to the standard to be applied by the judge in allowing use of the specimen, the Advisory Committee Notes are explicit: The provisions of Rule 104(b) are to be applied so that the specimen can be admitted if the judge finds that the jury could accept it as genuine.[20] (*See* discussion in § 900.1 *supra*.)

The cases applying the rule, both before and after its codification, typically are fact specific. For example, in a case brought to recover for death due to asbestos exposure during employment, company documents were held to have been authenticated by the company's employee who compared the documents in issue with other company documents which had been authenticated and admitted without objection.[21] A specimen of a prisoner's handwriting was adequately authenticated by a prison official who had often seen the prisoner write and who verified samples in the prison records.[22] Although no witnesses testified that they had seen the subject write the exemplars, the court properly admitted his writing on tax returns and personnel files, there being a presumption of genuineness of signatures under Int.Rev.Code § 6064.[23] A "strong infer-

---

19. Note that comparison by the "trier of fact" is not provided for under the proposed New York § 901(b)(3), supra note 18. Rather, the term "court" is used. This discrepancy is not noted in the Comment to the proposed section, and, in fact, the Comment discusses the comparison by "triers of fact" as traditional and unchanged.

20. The Advisory Committee Note states, in part:

Example (3). The history of common law restrictions upon the technique of proving or disproving the genuineness of a disputed specimen of handwriting through comparison with a genuine specimen, by either the testimony of expert witnesses or direct viewing by the triers themselves, is detailed in 7 Wigmore §§ 1991–1994. In breaking away, the English Common Law Procedure Act of 1854, 17 and 18 Vict., c. 125, § 27, cautiously allowed expert or trier to use exemplars "proved to the satisfaction of the judge to be genuine" for purposes of comparison. The language found its way into numerous statutes in this country, e.g., California Evidence Code §§ 1417, 1418. While explainable as a measure of prudence in the process of breaking with precedent in the handwriting situation, the reservation to the judge of the question of the genuineness of exemplars and the imposition of an unusually high standard of persuasion are at variance with the general treatment of relevancy which depends upon fulfillment of a condition of fact. Rule 104(b). No similar attitude is found in other comparison situations, e.g., ballistics comparison by jury, as in Evans v. Commonwealth, 230 Ky. 411, 19 S.W.2d 1091 (1929), or by experts, Annot., 26 A.L.R.2d 892, and no reason appears for its continued existence in handwriting cases. Consequently Example (3) sets no higher standard for handwriting specimens and treats all comparison situations alike, to be governed by Rule 104(b). This approach is consistent with 28 U.S.C. § 1731: "The admitted or proved handwriting of any person shall be admissible, for purposes of comparison, to determine genuineness of other handwriting attributed to such person."

21. Fagiola v. National Gypsum Co. AC & S., Inc., 906 F.2d 53, 58 (2d Cir.1990).

22. United States v. Mauchlin, 670 F.2d 746, 749 (7th Cir.1982).

23. United States v. Mangan, 575 F.2d 32, 41 (2d Cir.1978), cert. denied, 439 U.S. 931, 99 S.Ct. 320, 58 L.Ed.2d 324 (1978).

ence" of the regularity of a student's handwriting appearing in the university student records was sufficient for authentication.[24] Where the issue was which of three claimants was entitled to death benefits, the signature on the designation of beneficiary card could be compared with deceased's concededly authentic signature on a separation agreement.[25] And in a bankruptcy proceeding where signatures on certain documents were in dispute, it was permissible to use, for comparison purposes, signatures on two checks previously admitted in evidence without objection.[26]

Library References:

West's Key No. Digests, Criminal Law ⚖=491; Evidence ⚖=561–567.

§ 901.4 Circumstantial Evidence of Authenticity

a. New York

Authentication of a document or tangible item may be based on characteristics which alone, or with other evidence, aid in its identification. Many examples available to illustrate this rule are also appropriate under the first illustration outlined in § 901.1 *supra*, concerning the testimony of a witness. Thus, a gun,[1] eyeglasses,[2] an iron bar broken in a prison escape identifiable because of its wrappings,[3] or a voice on the telephone,[4] can all be authenticated because the witness recognizes certain characteristics about the object or sound.

Indeed, a document or telephone message may be proved by its content if no one but the author or speaker would have had access to that information.[5] And even where the content would have been known by relatively few, that together with other circumstances ought to be competent to identify the author.[6] Where reference is made to facts which only the subject would know, the proper linkage and hence authentication can be made.[7]

24. United States v. Swan, 396 F.2d 883, 885 (2d Cir.), cert. denied, 393 U.S. 923, 89 S.Ct. 254, 21 L.Ed.2d 259 (1968).

25. Brandon v. Collins, 267 F.2d 731, 733 (2d Cir.1959).

26. In re Goldberg, 91 F.2d 996, 997 (2d Cir.1937).

§ 901.4

1. People v. Randolph, 40 A.D.2d 806, 338 N.Y.S.2d 229 (1st Dep't 1972).

2. People v. Mirenda, 23 N.Y.2d 439, 297 N.Y.S.2d 532, 245 N.E.2d 194 (1969).

3. People v. Flanigan, 174 N.Y. 356, 368, 66 N.E. 988, 992 (1903).

4. People v. Lynes, 49 N.Y.2d 286, 425 N.Y.S.2d 295, 401 N.E.2d 405 (1980).

5. Id. at 292, 425 N.Y.S.2d at 298, 401 N.E.2d at 408. See also Dave Levine & Co. v. Wolf's Package Depot, 29 Misc.2d 1085, 1088, 138 N.Y.S.2d 427, 431 (Sup.Ct. N.Y.Co.1955), aff'd, 1 A.D.2d 874, 150 N.Y.S.2d 543 (1st Dep't), appeal denied, 1 A.D.2d 949, 151 N.Y.S.2d 601 (1st Dep't 1956) ("Circumstantial evidence is permissible to authenticate the voice heard over the telephone when the message reveals that the speaker had knowledge of facts that only he would likely know, or if other confirmatory circumstances make it probable that he was the speaker.").

6. See United States v. Mangan, 575 F.2d 32, 41–42 (2d Cir.), cert. denied, 439 U.S. 931, 99 S.Ct. 320, 58 L.Ed.2d 324 (1978)(court indicated that it should not be necessary that only one person would know the matter involved).

7. Lynes, supra note 4, 49 N.Y.2d at 292, 425 N.Y.S.2d at 298, 401 N.E.2d at 408.

The place of custody can help authenticate an item,[8] and the fact a letter is a reply to another communication and refers to that communication[9] are further illustrations of the principle.

The proposed New York Evidence Code § 901(b)(4) is in the note.[10]

b. Federal

Federal Rule of Evidence 902(b)(4) provides:

Distinctive characteristics and the like. Appearance, contents, substance, internal patterns, or other distinctive characteristics, taken in conjunction with circumstances.

The Federal Rule's broad provision will accommodate endless authentication possibilities, examples of which are as follows: A message by a revolutionary group was sufficiently shown to be a document written by one or more of defendant conspirators since it bore the group's logo, it claimed responsibility for the subject robbery, was consistent with statements made by defendants, and it was found with another document from the group.[11] Distinctive jargon found in documents helped identify them along with other evidence as loansharking records belonging to the conspirators.[12] Where a notebook was found in a hotel room recently occupied by X and contained distinctive information linking X and defendant, its authenticity was established.[13] A letter which could be identified only by its contents was shown to be a letter written by A to B because of the references, the language used and the deciphering of the signature.[14] Where the name on the check offered by the prosecution was the same as defendant's, and where other evidence indicated the source of the drug conspiracy was a town in Mexico which was the place to which the check was sent and where defendant was known to be involved in the narcotics enterprise, the check was sufficiently authenticated.[15] And where proof consisted of an aggregate of circumstances showing it extremely improbable that anyone other than defendant could have been the telephone caller, his identity was authen-

---

8. United States v. Ward, 173 F.2d 628 (2d Cir.1949), and Tameling v. Commissioner, 43 F.2d 814 (2d Cir.1930), deal with records kept in official government offices.

9. McCormick § 225, at 50.

10. **New York Evidence Code § 904(b)(4) [PROPOSED]**

(4) **Circumstantial evidence.** Distinctive facts and circumstances, such as appearance, contents, substance, internal patterns, or other identifying characteristics.

11. United States v. Maldonado–Rivera, 922 F.2d 934, 957–58 (2d Cir.1990), cert. denied, 501 U.S. 1233, 111 S.Ct. 2858, 115 L.Ed.2d 1026 (1991).

12. United States v. Orena, 32 F.3d 704, 715 (2d Cir.), aff'd sub nom., U.S. v. Sessa, 41 F.3d 1501 (2d Cir.1994).

13. United States v. Calbas, 821 F.2d 887, 893 (2d Cir.1987), cert. denied, 485 U.S. 937, 108 S.Ct. 1114, 99 L.Ed.2d 275 (1988). See also United States v. Natale, 526 F.2d 1160, 1173 (2d Cir.1975), cert. denied, 425 U.S. 950, 96 S.Ct. 1724, 48 L.Ed.2d 193 (1976)(facts which showed that notebook belonged to defendants were that it was found where defendants were present and had had business dealings and an entry in the notebook referring to a particular loan to a witness at trial whose testimony corroborated the linkage).

14. United States v. Bagaric, 706 F.2d 42, 67 (2d Cir.), cert. denied, 464 U.S. 840, 104 S.Ct. 133, 78 L.Ed.2d 128 (1983).

15. United States v. Gutierrez, 576 F.2d 269, 276 (10th Cir.), cert. denied, 439 U.S. 954, 99 S.Ct. 351, 58 L.Ed.2d 345 (1978).

§ 901.4   AUTHENTICATION & IDENTIFICATION   Ch. 9

ticated.[16]

Library References:

West's Key No. Digests, Criminal Law ⚖404.10, 444; Evidence ⚖188, 366–383.

§ 901.5 Voice Identification

a. New York

It has long been the rule in New York that a witness may testify that he recognized a person's voice as being that of X, whether he heard it in person, over the telephone, or by some other mechanical or electronic means.[1] The scant New York caselaw on the point deals mostly with the identification of telephone callers. Identification of those *to whom* calls are made is the subject of § 901.6.

Judge Cardozo in *People v. Dunbar Contracting Co.*,[2] laid down the simple rule that a voice heard "may be compared with the voice of a speaker whom one meets for the first time thereafter as well as with the voice of a speaker whom one has known before."[3] Although this was a "telephone" case the principle has been extended to voices on tape recordings;[4] and the rule was applicable where a police officer having overheard the conversation accompanying a drug buy transmitted by a wired informant, testified that he recognized defendant's voice in the transmission having heard him speak when he was arrested a few months later.[5]

A telephone caller's identity may also be established, circumstantially, by the substance of the conversation, as, for example, where the caller refers to matters that only a particular person could have known about.[6]

The proposed New York Evidence Code § 901(b)(5), according to the accompanying comment, codifies the New York law, and is found in the note.[7]

---

16. United States v. Lo Bue, 180 F.Supp. 955, 956 (S.D.N.Y.1960).

§ 901.5

1. People v. Dunbar Contracting Co., 215 N.Y. 416, 422, 109 N.E. 554, 556 (1915).

2. Id.

3. Id. at 422, 109 N.E. at 556.

4. See People v. Dinan, 15 A.D.2d 786, 787, 224 N.Y.S.2d 624, 627 (2d Dep't), aff'd, 11 N.Y.2d 350, 229 N.Y.S.2d 406, 183 N.E.2d 689, cert. denied, 371 U.S. 877, 83 S.Ct. 146, 9 L.Ed.2d 115 (1962)(in ascertaining identity of the voice on tape "[t]he remoteness of the personal conversations between the identifying witness and defendant from the time of the voice identification affected the weight rather than the competency of the evidence").

5. In People v. Rivera, 59 A.D.2d 874, 399 N.Y.S.2d 662 (1st Dep't 1977), the policeman so testified, but the majority found the tape of the conversation largely inaudible and garbled with other voices and background noises so that the evidence fell below any reasonable standard of admissibility. Id. at 875, 399 N.Y.S.2d at 664.

6. People v. Lynes, 49 N.Y.2d 286, 292, 425 N.Y.S.2d 295, 298, 401 N.E.2d 405, 408 (1980).

7. New York Evidence Code § 901(b)(5) [PROPOSED]

(5) Nonexpert opinion of voice identification. Identification of a voice, whether heard firsthand or through mechanical or electronic transmission or recording, by opinion based upon familiarity with the voice of the person identified as the speaker, provided that such familiarity was not acquired for purposes of litigation.

Authentication of the sound recording as an accurate representation is discussed in Chapter 11,[8] where particular emphasis is given to the Court of Appeals' decision in *People v. Ely*.[9] Extracting voice exemplars from criminal defendants is also noted in Chapter 11.[10]

b. Federal

Federal Rule of Evidence 901(b)(5) provides:

Voice identification. Identification of a voice, whether heard firsthand or through mechanical or electronic transmission or recording, by opinion based upon hearing the voice at any time under circumstances connecting it with the alleged speaker.[11]

The wording of this illustration contemplates testimony by a witness as to his opinion[12] of similarity. But in *United States v. Sliker*,[13] Judge Friendly noted that the Rule is only an illustration, and there is no reason why the jury cannot make its own comparison based on hearing the voice on the tape and hearing the person's testimony.[14]

The fact a caller identifies himself, without more, is not sufficient to prove that person's identity.[15] On the other hand, self-identification by the caller, when combined with the content of the communication[16] or other circumstances,[17] may be sufficient circumstantial evidence of identity.

Where the question is whether the overheard voice is male or female there will be no obstacle to opinion testimony,[18] and the witness may

---

8. See § 1104.1(c) infra.

9. 68 N.Y.2d 520, 510 N.Y.S.2d 532, 503 N.E.2d 88 (1986).

10. See § 1102.1, at note 4, infra.

11. Note that the Federal Rule omits the phrase contained in the state rule counterpart, supra note 7, "provided that such familiarity was not acquired for purposes of litigation." It is difficult to understand why a witness should not be able to familiarize himself for trial purposes with the person's voice in order to testify that either the voice was or was not that of the person whose identity is at issue. The Advisory Committee's Notes indicate that this sort of identification is meant to parallel that of visual identification. Such is often performed for purposes of litigation.

12. United States v. Cambindo Valencia, 609 F.2d 603, 640 (2d Cir.1979), cert. denied sub nom., Prado v. United States, 446 U.S. 940, 100 S.Ct. 2163, 64 L.Ed.2d 795 (1980)(voice identification not considered an area where expertise is important).

13. 751 F.2d 477 (2d Cir.1984), cert. denied sub nom., Buchwald v. United States, 470 U.S. 1058, 105 S.Ct. 1772, 84 L.Ed.2d 832 (1985).

14. Id. at 500.

15. Van Riper v. United States, 13 F.2d 961, 968 (2d Cir.), cert. denied sub nom., Ackerson v. United States, 273 U.S. 702, 47 S.Ct. 102, 71 L.Ed. 848 (1926). United States v. Hyatt, 565 F.2d 229, 232 (2d Cir. 1977)(the statement is hearsay where the witness attempts to prove the caller was X by repeating the caller's statement, "I am X"; but the witness' testimony that he received calls from someone calling himself X could be admissible for the limited purpose of showing that calls were being made).

16. Van Riper, 13 F.2d at 968.

17. In United States v. Ross, 321 F.2d 61, 69 (2d Cir.1963), cert. denied, 375 U.S. 894, 84 S.Ct. 170, 11 L.Ed.2d 123 (1963), the caller's self-identification together with telephone company records and business records from the caller's office made the authentication.

18. United States v. Wilkes, 451 F.2d 938, 941 (2d Cir.1971)("Even in this age of specialization most people are confident of their ability generally to identify the sex of an unseen adult by hearing the voice; indeed, with today's habits of hair and dress, there may be instances when determination of sex by voice is more reliable than by casual observation of appearance.").

§ 901.5   AUTHENTICATION & IDENTIFICATION   Ch. 9

testify to his opinion where he was familiar with the voices of both an informer and the defendant, even though he made the comparison through listening to a tape of a telephone conversation to which he was not a party.[19] In one case the crime victim identified defendant's voice at a show-up within an hour of having been attacked, and the court found the evidence admissible over the argument that, as with a visual one-person show-up, the situation was overly suggestive.[20] And, as a final example of the various ways in which the rule of voice identification arises, a police officer's identification of defendant as a participant in a telephone conversation was not unduly suggestive because, after hearing the voice during a wiretap, the officer went to the bar where the conversation originated and overheard defendant's voice.[21]

The use of the spectrograph (voice identification device) is not within this rule. It has passed the *Frye* test in the Second Circuit in a case where defendant gave voice exemplars which were then matched with the voice of defendant taped in a telephone conversation with the aid of expert interpretation of the spectrograph results.[22]

Library References:

West's Key No. Digests, Criminal Law ⟺386, 444, 453; Evidence ⟺148, 380, 475.

§ 901.6 Telephone Conversations

a. New York

Identification of the voice of a person who made a telephone call is discussed in § 901.5 *supra*. The subject matter of the present section is identification of the person to whom a telephone call has been made.

When a witness testifies to the identity of a person to whom he has placed a call, he may be able to make the identification on the basis of familiarity with the recipient's voice.[1] Alternatively, even if the witness has developed no familiarity with the recipient's voice, identification may be possible on the basis of circumstantial evidence. In *People v. Lynes*[2] the court stated: "Thus, in part on the theory that the customary mode of operation of telephone users provides some assurance of reliability, in some instances the placing of a call to a number listed in a directory or other similarly responsible index of subscribers, coupled with an un-

---

19. United States v. Bonanno, 487 F.2d 654, 659 (2d Cir.1973).

20. Burtis v. Dalsheim, 536 F.Supp. 805, 807 (S.D.N.Y.1982).

21. United States v. Albergo, 539 F.2d 860 (2d Cir.), cert. denied, 429 U.S. 1000, 97 S.Ct. 529, 50 L.Ed.2d 611 (1976).

22. United States v. Williams, 583 F.2d 1194, 1197 (2d Cir.1978), cert. denied, 439 U.S. 1117, 99 S.Ct. 1025, 59 L.Ed.2d 77 (1979).

§ 901.6

1. People v. Dunbar, 215 N.Y. 416, 422, 109 N.E. 554, 555 (1915). See also People v. McDermott, 160 Misc.2d 769, 773, 610 N.Y.S.2d 984, 986 (Dist.Ct.Nassau Co.1994)("If the witness was not acquainted with the speaker, and, therefore, did not recognize his voice at the time of the telephone conversation, the telephone conversation is admissible if the witness testifies that she met the speaker thereafter and then recognized his voice as the voice she had heard over the telephone").

2. 49 N.Y.2d 286, 425 N.Y.S.2d 295, 401 N.E.2d 405 (1980).

forced acknowledgment by the one answering that he or she is the one so listed, has been held to constitute an adequate showing."[3]

It can be seen that the rule as thus expressed partakes in large part of the rule noted in § 901.4, *supra*, relating to authentication by use of circumstantial evidence.

The rule was given an interesting application in *Russell v. New York State Elec. & Gas Corp.*[4] where the question was whether the power company had been notified of a fallen wire. A police officer testified that he called the number listed for the power company and was told by "someone" who answered that they had already been informed. Noting the objection to this evidence on the question of notice, the court stated: "The ordinary rule of evidence applied to telephone conversations [i.e., requirement of familiarity with recipient's voice] should not apply in this case where an emergency existed and a police officer in the discharge of his official duty had called upon the telephone operator to connect him with the power company. The jury had a right to believe under such circumstances that the company had notice without proof of the identity of the listener."[5] In point of fact, the telephone rule embodied in proposed New York Evidence Code § 901(b)(6), said in the Comment to codify New York law, would seem to contemplate the testimony in *Russell* as within the rule, rather than as an exception to it.[6]

b. Federal

Federal Rule of Evidence 901(b)(6) provides:

> **Telephone conversations.** Telephone conversations, by evidence that a call was made to the number assigned at the time by the telephone company to a particular person or business, if (A) in the case of a person, circumstances, including self-identification, show the person answering to be the one called, or (B) in the case of a business, the call was made to a place of business and the conversation related to business reasonably transacted over the telephone.

In *Van Riper v. United States*,[7] Judge Learned Hand marshaled the common law rule in part as follows:

> The decisions hold, though not with entire unanimity, that when a witness calls up at the proper number in a telephone

---

3. Id. at 292, 425 N.Y.S.2d at 297–98, 401 N.E.2d at 407.

4. 276 App.Div. 44, 48–49, 93 N.Y.S.2d 3, 8 (3d Dep't 1949).

5. Id. at 48–49, 92 N.Y.S.2d at 8.

6. New York Evidence Code § 901(b)(6) [PROPOSED]

(6) Identification of recipient of telephone call. Identification of a recipient of a telephone call, by evidence that a call was made to the number assigned at the time by the telephone company to a particular person or business, if: (A) in the case of a person, self-identification or other circumstances show the person answering to be the one called; or (B) in the case of a business, the call was made to a place of business and the conversation related to that business.

7. 13 F.2d 961, 967 (2d Cir.), cert. denied sub nom., Ackerson v. United States, 273 U.S. 702, 47 S.Ct. 102, 71 L.Ed. 848 (1926).

book the person whose admissions are relevant, and gets an answer from one professing to be the person called, it is prima facie proof of identity; that is, that the proof is equal to an interview with some one found at the office of the party in question. * * * The case is not the same, to be sure, when the declarant calls up the witness, for the declaration of the speaker cannot establish his identity; but even then as we have suggested, the substance of the communication may itself be enough to make prima facie proof.[8]

Sometimes additional evidence must be introduced to authenticate the identity of the person called.[9]

The Advisory Committee's Notes provide a nice summary of the rule's coverage.[10]

Library References:

West's Key No. Digests, Criminal Law ⟸386; Evidence ⟸148.

§ 901.7 Public Records

a. New York

The network of provisions in New York's Civil Practice Law and Rules assure that the best evidence rule, the hearsay rule and the rules of authentication will be satisfied when a certified copy of a public record, attested by officials in the office where it is kept, is offered in evidence. The hearsay question concerning the contents of public rec-

---

8. 13 F.2d at 968. See also United States v. Benjamin, 328 F.2d 854, n.3 (2d Cir.1964).

9. In United States v. Alessi, 638 F.2d 466, 480 (2d Cir.1980), one Ferrera claimed that his identity as the person called was not authenticated because the caller said that the person who answered identified himself as "Corky." Other evidence, however, showed that the witness had dialed the number listed in the name of Ferrara's wife at their residence and that Ferrera's nickname was "Corky."

10. It is stated:

Example (6). The cases are in agreement that a mere assertion of his identity by a person talking on the telephone is not sufficient evidence of the authenticity of the conversation and that additional evidence of his identity is required. The additional evidence need not fall in any set pattern. Thus the content of his statements or the reply technique, under Example (4), supra, or voice identification under Example (5), may furnish the necessary foundation. Outgoing calls made by the witness involve additional factors bearing upon authenticity. The calling of a number assigned by the telephone company reasonably supports the assumption that the listing is correct and that the number is the one reached. If the number is that of a place of business, the mass of authority allows an ensuing conversation if it relates to business reasonably transacted over the telephone, on the theory that the maintenance of the telephone connection is an invitation to do business without further identification. Mattan v. Hoover Co., 350 Mo. 506, 166 S.W.2d 557 (1942); City of Pawhuska v. Crutchfield, 147 Okl. 4, 293 P. 1095 (1930); Zurich General Acc. & Liability Ins. Co. v. Baum, 159 Va. 404, 165 S.E. 518 (1932). Otherwise, some additional circumstance of identification of the speaker is required. The authorities divide on the question whether the self-identifying statement of the person answering suffices. Example (6) answers in the affirmative on the assumption that usual conduct respecting telephone calls furnish adequate assurances of regularity, bearing in mind that the entire matter is open to exploration before the trier of fact. In general, see McCormick § 193; 7 Wigmore § 2155; Annot., 71 A.L.R. 5, 105 id. 326.

ords is addressed by CPLR 4518 and 4520, which are covered in Chapter 8.[1] The best evidence question is noted in Chapter 10.[2]

Here we are concerned with authentication under CPLR 4540[3] and 4542.[4] Such records are those kept by the agency, bureau or court in the regular course of its official activities (e.g., tax assessment records, court

§ 901.7

1. § 803(5).1 supra.

2. § 1005.1 infra.

3. **CPLR 4540. Authentication of official record of court or government office in the United States**

(a) **Copies permitted.** An official publication, or a copy attested as correct by an officer or a deputy of an officer having legal custody of an official record of the United States or of any state territory or jurisdiction of the United States, or of any of its courts, legislature, offices, public bodies or boards is prima facie evidence of such record.

(b) **Certificate of officer of the state.** Where the copy is attested by an officer of the state, it shall be accompanied by a certificate signed by, or with a facsimile of the signature of, the clerk of a court having legal custody of the record, and, except where the copy is used in the same court or before one of its officers, with the seal of the court affixed; or signed by, or with a facsimile of the signature of, the officer having legal custody of the original, or his deputy or clerk, with his official seal affixed; or signed by, or with a facsimile of the signature of, the presiding officer, secretary or clerk of the public body or board and, except where it is certified by the clerk or secretary of either house of the legislature, with the seal of the body or board affixed. If the certificate is made by a county clerk, the county seal shall be affixed.

(c) **Certificate of officer of another jurisdiction.** Where the copy is attested by an officer of another jurisdiction, it shall be accompanied by a certificate that such officer has legal custody of the record, and that his signature is believed to be genuine, which certificate shall be made by a judge of a court of record of the district or political subdivision in which the record is kept, with the seal of the court affixed; or by and [sic] public officer having a seal of office and having official duties in that district or political subdivision with respect to the subject matter of the record, with the seal of his office affixed.

(d) **Printed tariff or classification subject to public service commission, commissioner of transportation or interstate commerce commission.** A printed copy of a tariff or classification which shows a public service commission or commissioner of transportation number of this state and an effective date, or a printed copy of a tariff or classification which shows an interstate commerce commission number and an effective date, is admissible in evidence, without certification, and is prima facie evidence of the filed original tariff or classification.

4. **CPLR 4542. Proof of foreign records and documents**

(a) **Foreign record.** A foreign official record, or an entry therein, when admissible for any purpose, may be evidenced by an official publication thereof; or a copy thereof, attested by a person, authorized to make the attestation, and accompanied by a final certification as to the genuineness of the signature and official position

1. of the attesting person, or

2. of any foreign official whose certificate of genuineness of signature and official position

(i) relates to the attestation, or

(ii) is in a chain of certificates of genuineness of signature and official position relating to the attestation.

(b) **Final certification.** A final certification may be made by a secretary of an embassy or legation, consul general, consul, vice consul, or consular agent of the United States, or a diplomatic or consular official of the foreign country assigned or accredited to the United States. If reasonable opportunity has been given to all parties to investigate the authenticity and accuracy of the documents, the court may, for good cause shown, admit an attested copy without final certification, or permit the foreign official record to be evidenced by an attested summary with or without a final certification.

(c) **Lack of record.** A written statement that after diligent search no record or entry of a specified tenor was found to exist in the foreign records designated by the statement, authenticated in compliance with the requirements set forth in subdivisions (a) and (b) for a copy of a

§ 901.7   AUTHENTICATION & IDENTIFICATION   Ch. 9

orders, motor vehicle records), and those records normally found in a public office (e.g., birth records, deeds, wills and mortgages).

Certified photocopies of such records kept in a public office in New York are self-authenticating if the statutory formalities are followed. The public official attests by his certification under CPLR 4540(a) that the document is a true copy of the original, and the attested copy becomes "prima facie evidence" of the genuineness of the record.[5] The attestation (certification) must be a statement by an officer or his deputy that he has legal custody of the document, that the copy has been compared to the original and that the copy is accurate. The official's legal authority in the matter must also be shown on the copy, and that is accomplished in one of the three ways under CPLR 4540(b). First, the affixing of the official's signature and official seal will do the job (this is in addition to the certification); second, if the record is a court record, the signature of the clerk and the court's seal will do the job (in addition to the certification); and, three, copies of records of boards or public bodies are self-authenticating with the seal of the body or board and the signature of the presiding officer, secretary or clerk (in addition to the certification).

If the subject document is an official publication, rather than a copy, no attestation is required since an official publication is deemed prima facie authentic (CPLR 4540(a)).

CPLR 4540(d) makes copies of certain printed tariffs prima facie evidence and eliminates the need for certification. Such copies are both self-authenticating and admissible to prove the truth of their contents.[6]

CPLR 4540(c) deals with copies of public records from jurisdictions other than New York, and the requirements are more demanding. The signature, certification and seal of the official must be accompanied by a certificate of another authorized person, such as a judge if a court record is involved, or a public officer having a seal and having official duties in the certifying official's district who will, in turn, attest to the first official's authority. Whether subdivision (c) applies to federal records is not clear. On its face it does, but sections 399 and 400 of the predecessor Civil Practice Act allowed attestation of the custodial official alone. This would seem the better rule, but no court has dealt with the question. The requirements of subdivision (c) have been strictly applied in criminal cases.[7]

Official records of foreign nations are covered under CPLR 4542, subdivision (a) of which provides for self-authentication of an official publication, and for certification by officials with respect to official

foreign record is admissible as evidence that the records contain no such record or entry.

5. CPLR 4540(a); note 3 supra. The meaning of "prima facie evidence" is discussed in § 301.7 supra.

6. See Newman v. Consolidated Edison Co., 79 Misc.2d 153, 360 N.Y.S.2d 141 (Sup. Ct.App.T.2d Dep't 1973)(uncertified but printed copy of such filed tariff, showing Public Service Commission's number and effective date, admissible).

7. See, e.g., People v. Acebedo, 156 A.D.2d 369, 548 N.Y.S.2d 324 (2d Dep't 1989); People v. Hines, 90 A.D.2d 621, 456 N.Y.S.2d 235 (3d Dep't 1982); People v. Gonzalez, 64 A.D.2d 534, 406 N.Y.S.2d 488 (1st Dep't 1978).

documents as follows: First, the copy is attested to by the custodial official and, second, a "final certification" is made with respect to the genuineness of the signature and official position either of (a) the person who attested the copy or (b) of any other foreign official who made a certification concerning the attestation. The purpose of such "chain" authentication is to ensure that the person who first attested as to genuineness had the requisite authority.[8]

Subdivision (b), authorizing final certification by a United States foreign service official, will prove useful in many situations. Subdivision (b) also authorizes authentication solely by an attested copy or an attested summary of the record (a common practice in some countries) if "good cause" is shown and if all parties are given reasonable opportunity to investigate the authenticity and accuracy of the documents.[9]

Normally the CPLR 4542 provisions are flexibly applied;[10] and they might be bypassed entirely if the foreign country is a signatory to the Convention Abolishing the Requirement of Legalization for Foreign Public Documents.[11]

Subdivision (c) of CPLR 4542 provides a hearsay exception for a statement by a foreign public official that after diligent search no record or entry of a particular kind could be found.[12] This is analogous to the hearsay exception in CPLR 4521 relating to domestic searches for public records, but, unlike the provision in CPLR 4521 making the official's statement prima facie evidence of no record, here the foreign official's statement is merely "admissible as evidence."[13]

The proposed New York Evidence Code § 901(b)(7) is in the note and according to the Comment would apply to both domestic and foreign

---

8. See Estate of McDermott, 112 Misc.2d 308, 447 N.Y.S.2d 107 (Surr.Ct. Bronx Co.1982).

9. But see Estate of Rohner, 94 Misc.2d 596, 404 N.Y.S.2d 1017 (Surr.Ct.Orange Co.1978)(abstract of Swiss birth records is inadmissible since it is merely certifying officer's version of original papers).

10. See, e.g., Matter of Will Eggers, 122 Misc.2d 793, 471 N.Y.S.2d 570 (Surr.Ct.Nassau Co.1984)(officially signed foreign death, marriage and birth certificates lacked attestation but were sufficiently authenticated by expert testimony and final certification); Estate of Birsten, 104 Misc.2d 345, 428 N.Y.S.2d 392 (Surr.Ct.N.Y.Co.1980)(attested copies of foreign documents were sufficiently authenticated by expert testimony and "affidavit of authenticity submitted in lieu of certification").

11. 33 U.S.T. (part 1) 883, T.I.A.S. No. 10072 (entered into force for U.S., Oct. 15, 1981). The records of signatories may be proved by a simplified "apostille" certificate, requiring only one signature as prescribed by the Convention. The court's discussion in Estate of McDermott, 112 Misc.2d 308, 447 N.Y.S.2d 107 (Surr.Ct. Bronx Co.1982), is helpful with respect to this Convention. As of January 1, 1994, signatory countries are: Antigua and Barbados, Argentina, Armenia, Austria, The Bahamas, Belarus, Belgium, Belize, Bosnia–Herzegovina, Botswana, Brunei, Croatia, Cyprus, Fiji, Finland, Former Yugoslav Republic of Macedonia, France, Fed. Rep. Germany, Greece, Hungary, Israel, Italy, Japan, Lesotho, Liechtenstein, Luxembourg, Malawi, Malta, Marshall Is., Mauritius, Netherlands, Norway, Panama, Portugal, Russian Fed., Seychelles, Slovenia, Spain, Suriname, Swaziland, Switzerland, Tonga, Turkey, Union of Soviet Socialist Reps., United Kingdom, United States and Yugoslavia.

12. This codifies the decision in Brill v. Brill, 10 N.Y.2d 308, 222 N.Y.S.2d 321, 178 N.E.2d 720 (1961)(report of no record of divorce was evidence that no divorce occurred).

13. The meaning of "prima facie evidence" is discussed in § 301.7 supra.

records.[14]

Finally, it bears noting that the methods of authenticating public documents contained in CPLR 4540 and CPLR 4542 are not exclusive. CPLR 4543 provides, "Nothing in this article prevents the proof of a fact or a writing by any method authorized by any applicable statute or by the rules of evidence at common law."[15] CPLR 4541 covers proof of proceedings before a justice of the peace.

b. Federal

Federal Rule of Evidence 901(b)(7) provides:

> **Public records or reports.** Evidence that a writing authorized by law to be recorded or filed and in fact recorded or filed in a public office, or a purported public record, report, statement, or data compilation, in any form, is from the public office where items of this nature are kept.

This provision makes no specification as to the nature of the proof required other than a showing of public custody. The Rule was devised to make authentication of public records relatively easy because of the unlikelihood that the grave risks necessary to falsify public records would be taken.[16] Certainly custodial attestations (certifications) will suffice without the necessity for "chain" certifications or official seals required in certain situations in New York under the CPLR.[17] One court allowed authentication simply on the testimony of a witness who had firsthand knowledge that the record was kept in the proper public office,[18] and in some cases judicial notice can be taken.[19] The rules are open to reasonable interpretation,[20] although limitations sometimes must be drawn.[21]

---

14. New York Evidence Code § 901(b)(7) [PROPOSED]

(7) **Public records.** Evidence that a record, report, or other writing or data compilation authorized by statute to be recorded or filed and actually recorded or filed in a public office is from that public office.

15. Examples of statutes providing alternative authenticating methods, not exclusively pertaining to public records, are Business Corp. Law § 107 (corporate seal is prima facie evidence of execution and authority); CPLR 2105 (certification of copy by attorney); Domestic Relations Law § 14-a (marriage certificate issued by town and city clerks).

16. 5 Weinstein and Berger ¶ 901(b)(7)[01] at 901–117.

17. See § 901.7(a) supra.

18. Wausau Sulphate Fibre Co. v. Commissioner of Internal Revenue, 61 F.2d 879 (7th Cir.1932). Tax waivers were offered in evidence with no indication they were signed by the person whose signature appeared nor any indication they were taken from the proper public office. Over objection the court allowed them in on the testimony of the counsel in charge of the case that the waivers were taken from the files of the IRS and who otherwise verified them from his own knowledge. Id. at 880–81.

19. See Maroon v. Immigration and Naturalization Service, 364 F.2d 982, 984 (8th Cir.1966); Chapter 2, supra.

20. In United States v. Matusow, 244 F.2d 532, 533–34 (2d Cir.), cert. denied, 354 U.S. 942, 77 S.Ct. 1406, 1 L.Ed.2d 1540 (1957), the document presented was a photocopy of a typed copy of a teleprinted record of a conversation heard by an F.B.I. agent, after deletion of F.B.I. numbers, symbols and administrative data, added to the typed copy by someone other than the agent who heard the talk. That agent explained that the deleted material had nothing to do with the substance of the conversation and the court approved the document's admission in evidence.

21. In Dowling v. Jones, 67 F.2d 537, 540 (2d Cir.1933), Judge Learned Hand ruled error the admission of an abstract of

Public documents will normally be admitted in evidence under the self-authentication provisions of Federal Rule 902(1)-(5), taken up in § 902.1 *infra*.

Library References:

West's Key No. Digests, Criminal Law ⚖︎444; Evidence ⚖︎366.

§ 901.8 Ancient Documents

a. New York

Under the case law in New York a writing is authenticated if it is at least 30 years old, free from any suspicion of inaccuracy or fraud, and is found where it be likely to be found.[1] The rationale for this sort of authentication is that any document that has been in existence for such a long period of time without dispute over its terms or authenticity is probably genuine. Furthermore, as the years pass it becomes more difficult to provide authenticating evidence in other ways.[2]

It is not beyond reason to think that the Court of Appeals could be persuaded to shorten the time period to 20 years in view of the fact that Federal Rule 901(b)(8) so provides, as does proposed New York Evidence Code § 901(b)(8).[3]

With respect to documents evidencing title to real property, the common law rule required the additional condition that there be proof of possession of the property.[4] None of the codes continue this requirement, and the courts might likewise be persuaded to abandon that rule. The common law rule applies to all kinds of writings, public and private,[5] and the proposed New York Evidence Code would extend coverage to recordings and photographs.

the original document stating: "But an abstract is not a 'copy'; the difference may be material, as it is here, for the abstract does not show that the acknowledgment followed the statute, except in so far as that may be inferred from the fact that the assignments were recorded. Unless so acknowledged not even the originals were competent." Id. at 540.

§ 901.8

1. Tillman v. Lincoln Warehouse Corp., 72 A.D.2d 40, 44–45, 423 N.Y.S.2d 151, 153 (1st Dep't 1979).

2. See McCormick § 223.

3. **New York Evidence Code § 901(b)(8) [PROPOSED]**

(8) Ancient writings, recordings and photographs. Evidence that a writing, recording, or photograph, as those terms are defined in section 1001 of this chapter: (A) is in such condition as to create no suspicion concerning its authenticity; (B) was in a place where it, if authentic, would likely be; and (C) has been in existence twenty years or more at the time it is offered into evidence.

4. The most recent expression of this rule is found in Porter v. State of New York, 5 Misc.2d 28, 34, 159 N.Y.S.2d 549, 556 (Ct.of Claims 1957).

5. Dodge v. Gallatin, 130 N.Y. 117, 132–33, 29 N.E. 107, 111 (1891)(old maps and leases); Matter of Barney's Will, 185 App. Div. 782, 799–800, 174 N.Y.S. 242, 254–55 (1st Dep't 1919)(old hospital records); Coleman v. Bruch, 132 App.Div. 716, 717, 117 N.Y.S. 582, 583 (1st Dep't 1909); Beisheim v. People, 26 Misc.2d 684, 695, 39 N.Y.S.2d 333, 344 (Sup.Ct.Monroe Co.1942) (old maps); Cobb v. County of Monroe, 7 Misc.2d 141, 146, 165 N.Y.S.2d 583, 588 (Sup.Ct.Monroe Co.1957)(documents establishing the way a highway was laid out); Fairchild v. Union Ferry Co., 121 Misc. 513, 518, 201 N.Y.S. 295, 300 (Sup.Ct.Kings Co.1923), aff'd, 212 App.Div. 823, 207 N.Y.S. 835, aff'd, 240 N.Y. 666, 148 N.E. 750 (1925)(old book entries).

§ 901.8   AUTHENTICATION & IDENTIFICATION   Ch. 9

At common law in New York, the ancient document rule was only a rule of authentication, and presumably an independent hearsay exception would have to be found if the contents were to be admissible. It is not clear that the courts always observed this distinction since it seemed the only question for full admissibility under the rule was whether the document was ancient.[6] Under the codes, satisfaction of the ancient document rule also provides a hearsay exception.[7]

b. Federal

Federal Rule of Evidence 901(b)(8) provides:

> **Ancient documents or data compilation.** Evidence that a document or data compilation, in any form, (A) is in such condition as to create no suspicion concerning its authenticity, (B) was in a place where it, if authentic, would likely be, and (C) has been in existence 20 years or more at the time offered.

Changes from the common law rules include reduction of the time period to 20 years, removal of the requirement for proof of possession as regards real property documents,[8] and the addition of "data compilation, in any form." Whether, as is the case with the proposed New York Evidence Code, photographs and recordings are within Rule 901(b)(8)'s coverage is not clear, and there appear to have been no cases calling for this construction.[9]

If a date does not appear on the evidence sought to be admitted, age may be proved by expert witnesses either with respect to the contents, or the age of the paper, ink, or typewriting.[10]

The ancient document rule rarely appears in the recent cases.[11] Once a document is authenticated under Rule 901(b)(8) its contents will be admissible as an exception to the hearsay rule pursuant to Rule 803(16).[12]

Library References:

West's Key No. Digests, Criminal Law ⚷444; Evidence ⚷372.

§ 901.9   Process or System

a. New York

Federal Rule of Evidence 901(b)(9) and its proposed New York

---

6. See Tillman v. Lincoln Warehouse Corp., supra note 1, 72 A.D.2d at 44–45, 423 N.Y.S.2d at 153.

7. See §§ 803(7).1(b) and 803(7).2(b) supra.

8. See Wilson v. Snow, 228 U.S. 217, 221, 33 S.Ct. 487, 489, 57 L.Ed. 807, 811 (1913)(possession should be consistent with terms in the documents).

9. See 5 Weinstein and Berger ¶ 901(b)(8)[01], at 901–123.

10. See Mueller and Kirkpatrick § 9.10, at 1140; 5 Weinstein and Berger ¶ 901(b)(8)[01], at 901–124.

11. But see George v. Celotex Corp., 914 F.2d 26, 30 (2d Cir.1990), an asbestos exposure case, where an unpublished scientific report setting forth the dangers of asbestos was admitted under the ancient document rule.

12. See discussion of Rule 803(16) at § 803(7).2(b) supra.

counterpart[1] in effect incorporate the requirements discussed in Chapter 7[2] with regard to expert and scientific evidence. Thus, authentication of the results of an experiment or a laboratory test would require the use of methods and controls set forth by the Court of Appeals in *People v. Wesley*.[3] In many instances the *Frye* standard[4] will be applied.[5]

The processes underlying the production of blood-alcohol results,[6] radar speed results,[7] and blood grouping test results,[8] are examples of the kind of proof subject to the foundation required under the *Wesley* rule.

b. Federal

Federal Rule of Evidence 901(b)(9) provides:

> **Process or system.** Evidence describing a process or system used to produce a result and showing that the process or system produces an accurate result.

What is needed to authenticate a given piece of scientific or technical evidence which is the end product of some process or system will be a case-specific problem. The Advisory Committee's Notes give two examples—X-rays and computer data.[9]

With respect to scientific and technical evidence that must be authenticated, the United States Supreme Court has replaced the *Frye* rule with the approach announced in *Daubert v. Merrell Dow Pharma-*

---

§ 901.9

1. New York Evidence Code § 901(b)(9) [Proposed] provides:

(9) Process, system and scientific test or experiment. Subject to the requirements of subdivision (b) of section 702 of this chapter, evidence that a process, system, or scientific test or experiment is reliable and accurate, and was properly employed or applied on the particular occasion.

2. See §§ 702.1 and 703.1 supra.

3. 83 N.Y.2d 417, 611 N.Y.S.2d 97, 633 N.E.2d 451 (1994). Wesley involve the admissibility of the RFLP technique of DNA identification analysis. The technique was found to be generally accepted in the relevant scientific community. It was emphasized that in each case the proponent of such evidence, even though it has generally been accepted under the Frye test, must prove that all the procedures were correctly followed in that case. In sum, first, the trial judge must determine whether the Frye standard has been met, either pretrial or at trial outside the presence of the jury. Second, the proponent of the scientific or technical evidence must present a testimonial description of the procedures that were followed to produce the evidence in question. If the trial judge determines that an adequate foundation has been made, the third step is the presentation of the expert's opinion on the scientific or technical results, which may then be considered by the jury. Id. at 428–29, 611 N.Y.S.2d at 103–04, 633 N.E.2d at 457.

4. Frye v. United States, 293 F. 1013 (D.C.Cir.1923).

5. See § 702.1(b) supra.

6. See People v. Freeland, 68 N.Y.2d 699, 506 N.Y.S.2d 306, 497 N.E.2d 673 (1986); People v. Dembeck, 145 Misc.2d 442, 546 N.Y.S.2d 936 (Dist.Ct.Suffolk Co.1989). Although Veh. and Traffic Law § 1194 provides that the blood-alcohol test must be administered within two hours of the arrest, results are admissible even if that time is exceeded where the driver has given his consent to the test. People v. Atkins, 85 N.Y.2d 1007, 630 N.Y.S.2d 965, 654 N.E.2d 1213 (1995).

7. See People v. Magri, 3 N.Y.2d 562, 170 N.Y.S.2d 335, 147 N.E.2d 728 (1958).

8. See in addition to Wesley, People v. Castro, 144 Misc.2d 956, 545 N.Y.S.2d 985 (Sup.Ct.Bronx Co.1989)(certain portions of DNA test results excluded due to inadequacy of foundation with respect to testing procedures).

9. See also § 1104.2(b)(X-rays) and § 1106.1 (computer-generated graphics), infra.

§ 901.9   AUTHENTICATION & IDENTIFICATION

ceuticals,[10] which the Court felt better interpreted Federal Rule of Evidence 702.[11]

The results of a computer's operation will normally have to be accompanied by the testimony of a knowledgeable witness whose explanation will vary with the complexity of the computer operation and the interpretation that the results require.[12] *Rosado v. Wyman*[13] exemplifies the sort of case that can be almost wholly dependent on computer proof. *Rosado* is instructive on the value and use of samples and poll results,[14] which would be the sort of proof for which a foundation as respects process or system would have to be laid.

Library References:

West's Key No. Digests, Criminal Law ⟐388; Evidence ⟐150.

§ 901.10   Methods Provided by Statute or Rule

a. New York

CPLR 4543 provides that the methods of authentication specified in Article 45 of the CPLR are not preemptive.

CPLR 4543. Proof of facts or writing by methods other than those authorized in this article.

Nothing in this article prevents the proof of a fact or a writing by any method authorized by any applicable statute or by the rules of evidence at common law.

Other statutes provide for self-authentication of certain documents e.g., Business Corporation Law § 107 (corporate seal is prima facie evidence of execution and authority); CPLR 2105 (certification of copy by an

---

10. __ U.S. __, 113 S.Ct. 2786, 125 L.Ed.2d 469 (1993). See § 702.2(b) supra.

11. The Court identified four nonexclusive areas of inquiry for the trial judge to consider: (1) whether the scientific theory or method can and has been tested; (2) whether it has been subjected to peer review and publication; (3) the potential rate of error and the existence of standards controlling the operation of the technique; and (4) the extent of "general acceptance" in the relevant scientific community. Methodology used in each instance, of course, must be validated. __ U.S. at __, 113 S.Ct. at 2796–97, 125 L.Ed.2d at 482–84.

12. See 5 Weinstein and Berger ¶ 901(b)(9)[02], at 901-133–901-138.

13. 322 F.Supp. 1173 (E.D.N.Y.), aff'd, 437 F.2d 619 (2d Cir.1970), aff'd, 402 U.S. 991, 91 S.Ct. 2169, 29 L.Ed.2d 157 (1971). It was necessary in this case to determine the value of "special needs" as this related to the application of New York's Social Services Law. Noting that it was impossible to review all the case records (the monthly average number of cases was 186,629), Judge Weinstein approved the use of proof of the universe by canvassing a representative sample. Id. at 1181. All this information was stored on electronic data processing tapes as revealed in a prior determination in the same case. (Rosado v. Wyman, 304 F.Supp. 1350, 1353 (E.D.N.Y.)), rev'd, 414 F.2d 170 (2d Cir.1969), rev'd, 397 U.S. 397, 90 S.Ct. 1207, 25 L.Ed.2d 442 (1970)).

14. In the course of his discussion Judge Weinstein recounted a list of the sorts of questions lending themselves to mathematical and statistical methods of analysis citing, by way of example, Zippo Manufacturing Co. v. Rogers Imports, Inc., 216 F.Supp. 670 (S.D.N.Y.1963)(unfair competition; sample of consumers); Iannucci v. Board of Supervisors, 20 N.Y.2d 244, 282 N.Y.S.2d 502, 229 N.E.2d 195 (1967)(reapportionment problems); and Campbell v. Board of Education, 310 F.Supp. 94 (E.D.N.Y.1970)(election procedures); together with a long list of articles dealing with such evidence. 322 F.Supp. at 1180–81.

attorney); Domestic Relations Law § 14–a (marriage certificate issued by town and city clerks).

Ordinary common law, common sense measures may also be resorted to. Thus, where an issue concerned whether there was a Philippine divorce, but the records were unavailable because of wartime loss and destruction, the divorce could be proved by the Philippine judge's deposition that such an uncontested matter would have gone to final decree, and the testimony of a relative that he had seen the divorce decree;[1] where records of births, marriages and baptism were kept by the parish pastor in Germany and not found in any public office there, they were admissible since there was every indication of regularity in that the pastor made an attestation as to the genuineness of the copies made for admission and they appeared to be without change or erasure;[2] but where a plaintiff testified that a photograph depicted the slippery stair step on which he fell, authentication was lacking in the absence of proof of when the photograph was taken so that a determination could be made whether the slippery substance would likely have been on the step at the time of the accident.[3]

The proposed New York Evidence Code § 901(b)(10) simply provides for authentication by "[a]ny method of authentication or identification provided by this chapter or other statute."[4]

b. Federal

Federal Rule of Evidence 901(b)(10) provides:

> **Methods provided by statute or rule.** Any method of authentication or identification provided by Act of Congress or by other rules prescribed by the Supreme Court pursuant to statutory authority.

Aside from the self-authentication provisions of Federal Rule 902 pertaining mainly to public documents, discussed in § 902.2 *infra*, there are other specialized federal provisions allowing for self-authentication. For instance, the Federal Business Records Act provides that documents shown to have been made in the regular course of business can be admitted without the need for further authentication,[5] and court reporters may certify transcripts for admission.[6] Federal Rule of Civil Procedure 30(f)(1) specifies procedures for the authentication of deposition transcripts.

Library References:

West's Key No. Digests, Criminal Law ⚖404.10, 444; Evidence ⚖188, 366–383.

§ 901.10

1. Estate of Gonzalez, 6 Misc.2d 118, 156 N.Y.S.2d 28 (Surr.Ct.N.Y.Co.1956).

2. Jacobi v. Order of Germania, 73 Hun. 602, 26 N.Y.S. 318 (1893).

3. Melendez v. N.Y. City Transit Auth., 196 A.D.2d 460, 601 N.Y.S.2d 489 (1st Dep't 1993).

4. Examples of other provisions for authentication would presumably be found under § 803(c)(7)(B)(i), (ii) of the proposed code (certificates of judgments issued by the clerk of a court, or a fingerprint certification issued by a custodial employee).

5. 28 U.S.C.A. § 1732.

6. Fed.R.Civ.P. 80(c).

902 Self-Authentication

§ 902.1 Self-Authentication

a. New York

Evidence that can be authenticated or identified without a foundation witness is said to be self-authenticating. Where, for example, a public document under seal and certified as to accuracy is offered, it comes into evidence unless seriously challenged (*see* § 901.7 *supra*) as would also a document duly acknowledged by the signature of a notary. In some instances, of course, judicial notice may be taken that the evidence is genuine and admissible.[1]

Following is a list of evidentiary items conforming to the list appearing in the proposed New York Evidence Code § 902, which have been traditionally self-authenticating:

Public records, both domestic and foreign. Public records were dealt with in § 901.7 *supra*, and the reader is referred to that description of the provisions of CPLR 4540 (domestic public documents) and CPLR 4542 (foreign public documents), which provide for self-authentication given the appropriate seals and certifications. Those provisions expressly provide for the use of copies so that the originals need not be removed from the public office.

Official publications. CPLR 4511(d) provides that judicial notice may be taken of a "printed copy of a statute or other written law or proclamation, edict, decree or ordinance by an executive contained in a book or publication, purporting to have been published by a government or commonly admitted as evidence of the existing law in the judicial tribunals of the jurisdiction where it is in force * * *." CPLR 4540 and 4542 also include official publications among the sort of documents which are self-authenticating under those provisions.

Newspapers and periodicals. The unlikelihood of the presentation of forged copies of regularly published newspapers and periodicals permits their routine authentication simply on the strength of their layout and masthead. Whether the contents are admissible or not is another question. Certainly there is no hearsay problem when routine market reports are sought to be admitted,[2] but it is unlikely that news stories or feature articles will be admissible to prove the truth of their contents.[3] In one ancient case a newspaper was allowed to be used by a witness to refresh his recollection.[4] CPLR 4532 provides for the self-authentication of newspapers and periodicals of general circulation.

§ 902.1

1. See Chapter 2 supra.
2. See CPLR 4533. Market reports are exempt from the hearsay bar. See § 803(6).1 supra.
3. But see Dallas Cty. v. Commercial Union Assur. Co., 286 F.2d 388, 398 (5th Cir.1961), discussed at § 804(5).2, at notes 4–5, supra.
4. Huff v. Bennett, 6 N.Y. 337 (1852). See also, Blanding v. Cohen, 101 App.Div. 442, 92 N.Y.S. 93 (1905), aff'd, 184 N.Y. 538, 76 N.E. 1089 (1906).

Ch. 9 SELF–AUTHENTICATION § 902.1

Trade inscriptions. A product which is identified by a sign, mark, tag or label "affixed in the course of business"[5] is self-authenticating. Certainly where the identifying name is imprinted, embossed or stitched the "affixed in the course of business" requirement would seem to be satisfied. The situation becomes less certain where a handwritten tag is involved. This provision aids in the identification of products,[6] but it need not be limited to products since trade inscriptions can appear on publications, business records, contracts, bills, and the like.

Acknowledged documents. CPLR 4538 provides that acknowledgment of any document (other than a will) according to the manner prescribed by law for acknowledgment of signatures on documents for the conveyance of real property will self-authenticate the document.[7] Real Property Law §§ 248–312 provide such procedures. The acknowledgment typically consists of a notary's certificate, appearing on the document in question, stating that the person who executed the document personally appeared before the notary and acknowledged that he executed it. The certificate must indicate that the person is known to the notary and known to be the person described in and who executed the document.[8] The certified acknowledgment, under the terms of CPLR 4538, becomes prima facie evidence that the writing was executed by the person who acknowledged having done so. This has been held to create a presumption of genuineness rebuttable only by clear and convincing evidence.[9] In other cases it has been stated that such presumption can only be rebutted "by proof credible to the trier of fact."[10] It has been held that the acknowledgment can be taken for purposes of litigation, i.e., if the author of a document swears to a notary that the signature on the document is his, the notary can acknowledge this and the document will be self-authenticated.[11] The second sentence of CPLR 4538 is limited to conveyances of real property located in another state,

---

5. Using the terms of proposed New York Evidence Code § 902(a)(7). See note 13 infra.

6. In Weiner v. Mager & Throne, 167 Misc. 338, 3 N.Y.S.2d 918 (N.Y.C.Mun.Ct. 1938), plaintiff bit into a wormy slice of bread. The judge stated: "This defendant's trade label, affixed to the loaf, is some evidence that it manufactured the bread; and unless rebutted, or at least contested by evidence, gives rise to a reasonable inference that the owner of the trade label manufactured the article to which it was affixed." Id. at 340, 3 N.Y.S.2d at 920.

7. **CPLR 4538. Acknowledged, proved or certified writing; conveyance of real property without the state**

Certification of the acknowledgment or proof of a writing, except a will, in the manner prescribed by law for taking and certifying the acknowledgment or proof of a conveyance of real property within the state is prima facie evidence that it was executed by the person who purported to do so. A conveyance of real property, situated within another state, territory or jurisdiction of the United States, which has been duly authenticated, according to the laws of that state, territory or jurisdiction, so as to be read in evidence in the courts thereof, is admissible in evidence in the state.

Proof of wills is governed by N.Y. Surrogate's Court Procedure Act §§ 1404–1407.

8. N.Y. Real Property Law § 303.

9. In re Goodman's Will, 2 A.D.2d 558, 563, 157 N.Y.S.2d 109, 115 (1st Dep't 1956). See also § 301.7 supra.

10. Langford v. Cameron, 73 A.D.2d 1001, 1002, 424 N.Y.S.2d 41, 43 (3d Dep't 1980)(summary judgment denied where defendant denied he signed promissory note); Dart Associates v. Rosal Meat Market, Inc., 39 A.D.2d 564, 564, 331 N.Y.S.2d 853, 855 (2d Dep't 1972).

11. Holbrook v. New Jersey Zinc Co., 57 N.Y. 616, 624 (1874); Wetterer v. Soubirous, 22 Misc. 739, 741–42, 49 N.Y.S. 1043, 1045 (1898).

§ 902.1 AUTHENTICATION & IDENTIFICATION Ch. 9

territory or jurisdiction of the United States. If such conveyance has been authenticated according to the laws of the state, territory or jurisdiction of location, so as to be admissible in evidence in the out-of-state court, it will be admissible in New York. Presumably, any other sort of document acknowledged outside New York will need additional proof for authentication.

Tariff or classification. CPLR 4540(d) provides:

> **Printed tariff or classification subject to public service commission, commissioner of transportation or interstate commerce commission.** A printed copy of a tariff or classification which shows a public service commission or commissioner of transportation number of this state and an effective date, or a printed copy of a tariff or classification which shows an interstate commerce commission number and an effective date, is admissible in evidence, without certification, and is prima facie evidence of the filed original tariff or classification.

Self-authentication by other statutes. There are various statutes which provide for self-authentication of certain kinds of documents which under the provisions of CPLR 4543 have in no way been superseded by other CPLR provisions in Article 45. These have been marshaled in the Comment to proposed New York Evidence Code § 902(a)(10).[12]

Proposed New York Evidence Code. The proposed New York Evidence Code § 902 provides for the foregoing categories and is reproduced in the note.[13]

---

12. The Comment states:
This paragraph is intended to make clear that methods of self-authentication provided by other statutes are not superseded. The paragraph is to the same effect as CPLR 4543. Statutes that remain in effect include: Ag. and Mkt.Law § 96 (certificates of registry and transfer of domestic animals under seal of appropriate organization); Bank. Law §§ 1006, 9012 (corporate seal *prima facie* evidence of execution and authority); BCL § 107 (corporate seal *prima facie* evidence of execution and authority); N.Y.City Uninc.Bus.Income Tax Act § 124(a),(b) (signature on tax return *prima facie* evidence of execution and authority); CPLR 2105 (certification by attorney); Executive Law § 137 (certificate of notary admissible as presumptive evidence of the facts contained); Gen'l City Law § 25–a, Model Local Law § 33(a)(signature on return or other document is *prima facie* evidence document signed by purported signer); Mental Hygiene Law § 23.21(d)(certified statement by bank, etc., covering assets of drug-dependent person admissible in any action or proceeding); N.Y.City Civ. Ct.Act § 1102(b)(signature to instrument pleaded shall be deemed genuine unless opponent denies specifically and demands proof); Uniform City Ct.Act § 1102(b)(same); Uniform Dist.Ct.Act § 1102(b)(same); Uniform Justice Ct.Act § 1102(b) (same); Not-for-Profit Corp. Law § 107 (corporate seal *prima facie* evidence document executed by authority of corporation); Tax Law §§ 287, 367, 429, 505, 653 (signature on return *prima facie* evidence it was actually signed by persons named); Uniform Commercial Code § 3–307(1) (signatures on negotiable instruments).

13. § 902. Self-authentication [PROPOSED]

(a) **General provision.** Extrinsic evidence of authenticity as a condition precedent to admissibility is not required with respect to the following:

(1) **Public documents bearing official seals.** A public document bearing a seal purporting to be the official seal of (A) this state, or a political subdivision, department, agency, bureau, officer, or employee thereof; (B) the United States, or a department, agency, bureau, officer, or employee thereof; or (C) any state, territory, or

798

b. Federal

Federal Rule of Evidence 902 provides as follows:

jurisdiction of the United States, or a political subdivision, department, agency, bureau, officer, or employee thereof.

(2) Public documents bearing official signatures. A public document bearing a signature purporting to be the signature in the official capacity of an officer or employee of: (A) this state, or a political subdivision, department, agency, or bureau thereof; (B) the United States, or a department, agency, or bureau thereof; or (C) any state, territory, or jurisdiction of the United States, or a political subdivision, department, agency, or bureau thereof.

(3) Foreign public documents. A foreign public document purporting to be executed or attested in a person's official capacity by a person authorized by the laws of a foreign country to make the execution or attestation, and accompanied by a final certification as to the genuineness of the signature and official position of the executing or attesting person, or of any foreign official whose certificate of genuineness of signature and official position relates to the execution or attestation or is in a chain of certificates of genuineness of signature and official position relating to the execution or attestation. A final certification may be made by a secretary of an embassy or legation, consul general, consul, vice consul, or consular agent of the United States, or a diplomatic or consular official of the foreign country assigned or accredited to the United States. If reasonable opportunity has been given to all parties to investigate the authenticity and accuracy of a foreign public document, the court may, for good cause shown, order that they be admitted as authentic without final certification or permit them to be evidenced by an attested summary with or without final certification.

(4) Certified copies of public records. A copy of a record, report, or other writing or data compilation produced by a public office or authorized by statute to be recorded or filed and actually recorded or filed in a public office, certified as correct by the custodian or other person authorized to make the certification, by certificate complying either with paragraph one, two or three of this subdivision, or with any other statute.

(5) Official publications. Books, pamphlets, or other publications purporting to be issued by public authority.

(6) Newspapers and periodicals. Printed material purporting to be newspapers or periodicals of general circulation; provided, however, nothing herein shall be deemed to preclude or limit the right of a party to challenge the authenticity of such printed material, by extrinsic evidence or otherwise, prior to admission by the court or to raise the issue of authenticity as an issue of fact.

(7) Trade inscriptions and the like. Inscriptions, signs, marks, tags, or labels purporting to have been affixed in the course of business and indicating ownership, control, or origin.

(8) Acknowledged documents. Documents, except wills, accompanied by a certificate of acknowledgment or of proof executed in the manner provided by statute by a notary public or other person authorized by law to take an acknowledgment or proof.

(9) Tariff or classification subject to public service commission, commissioner of transportation, or interstate commerce commission. A printed copy of a tariff or classification which shows a public service commission or commissioner of transportation number of this state and an effective date, or a printed copy of a tariff or classification which shows an interstate commerce commission number and an effective date.

(10) Self-authentication by statute. Any signature, document, or other matter declared by statute presumptively or prima facie genuine or authentic.

(b) Notice. The proponent of evidence under this section shall make known to all parties the proponent's intention to offer the evidence and its particulars sufficiently in advance of offering the evidence to provide them with a fair opportunity to meet it. To cure the prejudice from the failure to give such notice, the court, pursuant to section 107 of this chapter, shall make any order the interests of justice require.

Rule 902. Self–Authentication

Extrinsic evidence of authenticity as a condition precedent to admissibility is not required with respect to the following:

(1) Domestic public documents under seal. A document bearing a seal purporting to be that of the United States, or of any State, district, Commonwealth, territory, or insular possession thereof, or the Panama Canal Zone, or the Trust Territory of the Pacific Islands, or of a political subdivision, department, officer, or agency thereof, and a signature purporting to be an attestation or execution.

(2) Domestic public documents not under seal. A document purporting to bear the signature in the official capacity of an officer or employee of any entity included in paragraph (1) hereof, having no seal, if a public officer having a seal and having official duties in the district or political subdivision of the officer or employee certifies under seal that the signer has the official capacity and that the signature is genuine.

(3) Foreign public documents. A document purporting to be executed or attested in an official capacity by a person authorized by the laws of a foreign country to make the execution or attestation, and accompanied by a final certification as to the genuineness of the signature and official position (A) of the executing or attesting person, or (B) of any foreign official whose certificate of genuineness of signature and official position relates to the execution or attestation or is in a chain of certificates of genuineness of signature and official position relating to the execution or attestation. A final certification may be made by a secretary of embassy or legation, consul general, consul, vice consul, or consular agent of the United States, or a diplomatic or consular official of the foreign country assigned or accredited to the United States. If reasonable opportunity has been given to all parties to investigate the authenticity and accuracy of official documents, the court may, for good cause shown, order that they be treated as presumptively authentic without final certification or permit them to be evidenced by an attested summary with or without final certification.

(4) Certified copies of public records. A copy of an official record or report or entry therein, or of a document authorized by law to be recorded or filed and actually recorded or filed in a public office, including data compilations in any form, certified as correct by the custodian or other person authorized to make the certification, by certificate complying with paragraph (1), (2), or (3) of this rule or complying with any Act of Congress or rule prescribed by the Supreme Court pursuant to statutory authority.

(5) Official publications. Books, pamphlets, or other publications purporting to be issued by public authority.

(6) Newspapers and periodicals. Printed materials purporting to be newspapers or periodicals.

(7) Trade inscriptions and the like. Inscriptions, signs, tags, or labels purporting to have been affixed in the course of business and indicating ownership, control, or origin.

(8) Acknowledged documents. Documents accompanied by a certificate of acknowledgment executed in the manner provided by law by a notary public or other officer authorized by law to take acknowledgments.

(9) Commercial paper and related documents. Commercial paper, signatures thereon, and documents relating thereto to the extent provided by general commercial law.

(10) Presumptions under Acts of Congress. Any signature, document, or other matter declared by Act of Congress to be presumptively or prima facie genuine or authentic.

Domestic and foreign public documents. The self-authentication provision of Rule 902(1), (2), (3) and (4), relating to public documents, are laid out with more precision than their counterparts in CPLR 4540 and 4542. Under CPLR 4540(b) if the custodial official affixes his seal to his certification, authentication is complete. But if the custodial official has no seal there is no further provision in CPLR 4540 for accomplishment of the authentication. Under Rule 902 there is provision for documents under seal (in which case the seal itself is all that is needed), and documents not under seal (in which case another public officer in the same district who does not have a seal may certify that the custodial official has the capacity claimed and that the signature is his). Presumably this technique could be used to fill the void under CPLR 4540(b) since a similar process can be used to authenticate custodial signatures on foreign documents under CPLR 4542. The federal provision in Rule 902(2) allows custodial signatures by officials low on the totem pole and ought specifically to be provided for in New York by an appropriate amendment to CPLR 4540(b).[14]

The New York and federal schemes also differ in that CPLR 4540 and 4542 make indigenous provisions for copies in each category, i.e., copies are specified across the board whether the record is domestic, from another state, or from a foreign country. Federal Rule 902(4) makes a special provision for certified copies so long as the other requirements specified in subdivisions (1), (2) and (3) are met. In other words, a certified copy is permissible so long as the custodial officer has a

---

14. In People v. Brown, 128 Misc.2d 149, 488 N.Y.S.2d 559 (Co.Ct.Madison Co.1985), photocopies of breathalyzer test reports were improperly certified. Noting that New York has a "welter" of rules regarding formal execution of certificates, the court stated:

Thus, under CPLR 4540(b) in order for a copy of a public document to be admissible "it shall be accompanied by a certificate signed by, or with a facsimile of the signature of * * * the officer having legal custody of the original, or his deputy or clerk, with his official seal affixed." The attachment of a seal has been termed a "requisite of admissibility" under CPLR 4540(b) * * * and if the certifier has no seal the document cannot be introduced under this section.

Id. at 153, 488 N.Y.S.2d at 563.

seal or if he does not have a seal so long as his signature is attested to by an officer up the line who does have a seal. The reason for the separate subdivision relating to copies apparently stems from the fact that there may be some public records which could only be presented in their original form,[15] although it is not clear what these records might be. Otherwise, subdivision (4) is pervasive in its application to most public documents.[16]

A good deal of flexibility is accorded in subdivision (3) for authentication of foreign public documents which differs little from its CPLR 4542 counterpart. A foreign public document is self-authenticated if the custodial signature is certified by a United States consular or embassy official; or, if the custodial signature is the first in a chain of certifications required in the country, the certification by the United States official, called the "final certification," must apply to the whole chain. The last sentence of subdivision (3) dispenses with the need for final certification if the parties have had a reasonable opportunity to investigate authenticity and accuracy.[17]

Official publications. This category provides for self-authentication for the usual items such as official case reporters, agency pamphlets, legislative reports and statistics, but also for items as disparate as the Army Field Manual, "Field Hygiene and Sanitation,"[18] and reports by the Department of Health and Human Services regarding Medicaid reimbursement rates for California laboratories.[19] This provision does not provide for self-authentication of a commercially published book, although if the work were done under government contract it would seem that it should qualify. Parallel provisions for the admissibility of

---

15. See 5 Weinstein and Berger ¶ 902(4)[01], at 902–31.

16. See, e.g., United States v. Lumumba, 794 F.2d 806, 815 (2d Cir.), cert. denied, 479 U.S. 855, 107 S.Ct. 192, 93 L.Ed.2d 125 (1986) (certified copy of transcript of trial was a public record and was thus prima facie correct statement of testimony and properly admitted into evidence in contempt hearing).

17. In Raphaely Intern., Inc. v. Waterman S.S. Corp., 972 F.2d 498 (2d Cir.1992), cert. denied, ___ U.S. ___, 113 S.Ct. 1271, 122 L.Ed.2d 666 (1993), an official certificate of inspection, apparently properly executed or attested, had not been finally certified. The court stated:

Waterman had nine years preceding trial to challenge the authenticity of these certificates. This time period provided Waterman with a reasonable opportunity to investigate the authenticity and accuracy of the certificates, satisfying the first condition for excuse of the certification requirement. The second prerequisite to excuse the certification requirement was satisfied by Waterman's delay in challenging the documents and its failure to adduce at trial any evidence casting doubt upon the certificate's authenticity.

Id. at 502.

18. In United States v. The Rainbow Family, 695 F.Supp. 314, 330 n.5 (E.D.Tex. 1988), where the government sought an injunction against a gathering of persons in a national forest, the court held the hygiene manual admissible under Rule 902(5).

19. In California Ass'n of Bioanalysts v. Rank, 577 F.Supp. 1342, 1355 n.23 (C.D.Cal.1983), in a suit brought by licensed clinical laboratories to challenge reduction of state Medicaid rates, the court admitted an HEW study entitled "Lessons Learned Report, Project Integrity II, Laboratories, California," which noted the practice of dual pricing, for the purpose "of establishing the conceivable state of mind of the legislature in enacting the 25% reduction." Id. at 1355 n.23. The court found the reports admissible stating: "As a result of the facsimile of the official seal of the USDHHS on its cover page, suggesting that it was printed by authority of that agency, Exhibit 54 is self-authenticating under Rule 902(5)." * * *. Id.

such items are found in Federal Rules of Civil Procedure § 44(a)(1). Even though the publication is self-authenticating, a hearsay exception must be found pursuant to which the contents can be introduced.

Newspapers and periodicals. Such items, published on a regular basis, are self-authenticating, except that the contents may encounter a valid hearsay objection,[20] or the origins of a particular article may be questionable.

Trade inscriptions. The premier federal case dealing with trade inscriptions is *United States v. Hing Shair Chan*,[21] where the admissibility of Hong Kong hotel records was in issue, defendant arguing that there should have been an authenticating witness to lay a foundation. Judge Weinstein found several grounds for authentication, stating: "The records are authenticated under Rule 901 * * * because the sworn statement of Mr. Lee [hotel office manager] supports a finding that the documents are what the government claims them to be. Both the records and Mr. Lee's stamped, sealed declaration are also authenticated under Rule 902, because the sworn statement is a foreign public document under Rule 902(3), and because the hotel records bear printed and embossed trade inscriptions indicating their origin in the Hotel Regal Meridien under Rule 902(7). In addition, internal evidence supports both authenticity and reliability under Rule 901(4)."[22] A further reason for assuming the authenticity of a branded product was expressed by the dissenting judge in the oft-cited case *Keegan v. Green Giant Co.*:[23] the misuse of trademarks and the misbranding of products constitute serious offenses under federal statutes and regulations.[24] The Advisory Committee's Note adds that "[i]nscriptions on trains and vehicles are held to be prima facie evidence of ownership or control," and that under 19 U.S.C.A. § 1615(2) "marks, labels, brands, or stamps indicating foreign origin are prima facie evidence of foreign origin of merchandise."[25]

Acknowledged documents. The Advisory Committee's Note cites CPLR 4538 as an example of a liberal provision for self-authentication by acknowledgment of signatures. Since the language of Rule 902(8) allows acknowledgments "executed in the manner provided by law,"[26] the

20. In addition to the items at notes 2, 3 and 4, supra, there is New England Mut. Life Ins. Co. v. Anderson, 888 F.2d 646, 650 (10th Cir.1989), where a newspaper was offered unsuccessfully to prove the substance of a story in which a wife admitted a conspiracy to kill her husband.

21. 680 F.Supp. 521 (E.D.N.Y.1988).

22. Id. at 526.

23. 150 Me. 283, 110 A.2d 599 (Me. 1954). The case is oft-cited because of the wrong-headed determination of the majority that the label identifying a can as having contained Green Giant peas provided an insufficient showing of authenticity. This is the case which prompted the code provisions. The case is cited in the Advisory Committee Note.

24. Id. at 601.

25. In this respect, see United States v. Blackwood, 47 F.2d 849 (1st Cir.), cert. denied, 284 U.S. 627, 52 S.Ct. 12, 76 L.Ed. 534 (1931). There, labels on bottles of liquor indicated foreign origination (id. at 850), providing justification for the Coast Guard's seizure, and the prosecution for violation of a federal statute which prohibited unloading foreign products on Sunday. Indirectly, the court indicated that the labels also satisfied the government's burden at trial to prove the foreign origination Id. at 851.

26. The Report of the House Committee on the Judiciary, accompanying the Advisory Committee's Note, notes that "the Rule merely requires that the document be executed in the manner prescribed by State law."

coverage would be coextensive with that provided under CPLR 4538, i.e., any document acknowledged by a notary "or other person authorized by law," in the manner prescribed for the acknowledgment of a deed will be self-authenticating.

Commercial paper. This category is not specifically included in the proposed New York Evidence Code § 902, but would fall under the provision recognizing self-authentication as provided in other statutes— here the Uniform Commercial Code. The "general commercial law" set forth as the guidepost in Federal Rule 902(9), is intended as meaning the U.C.C.[27] There are five U.C.C. provisions which relate to authentication,[28] which would be commonly used.

Presumptions under acts of Congress. The Rule 902 provisions are not exclusive and authentication may proceed according to specific rules for authentication set forth elsewhere.[29] Certainly in many cases the provisions of Rule 902 will overlap with a specialized statute and there appears no reason why the authority of Rule 902 could not be used if it would provide an easier way to authenticate.

Copies. If there is any problem with 902 it would be its lack of clarity as to whether it was meant to cover copies of the subject items. Subdivision (4) allows for certified copies of public records; but what if an uncertified copy of a public record is presented under subdivision (2) where a public officer of higher rank with a seal has put his imprimatur on the uncertified copy (i.e., uncertified by the custodial signer)? And what about copies of items other than public documents such as newspapers, commercial paper or photocopies of products bearing trade inscriptions? There is some authority to the effect that such copies would be self-authenticating given no serious question as to genuineness.[30]

Library References:

West's Key No. Digests, Criminal Law ☞430, 444; Evidence ☞338–349, 366–383.

27. The Advisory Committee's Note states in part: "In these situations, resort to the useful authentication provisions of the Uniform Commercial Code is provided for. While the phrasing is in terms of 'general commercial law,' in order to avoid the potential complications inherent in borrowing local statutes, today one would have difficulty in determining the general commercial law without referring to the Code."

28. The most useful provision is under § 3–307(1)(b) which makes a signature on an instrument presumptive evidence of authenticity, with certain exceptions. Section 8–105(3)(b) provides the same recognition for a signature on a security. The date on an instrument is presumed correct (§ 3–114(3)), and bills of lading, certificates of insurance, inspector's certificates and other documents are prima facie authentic (§ 1–202). Section 3–510 provides that a stamp indicating that the drawee dishonors a check is a presumption of dishonor.

29. The Advisory Committee's Note cites as examples 15 U.S.C.A. § 77f(a) (signature on SEC registration presumed genuine) and 26 U.S.C.A. § 6064 (signature on tax return prima facie genuine). Other examples are court transcripts (28 U.S.C.A. § 753(b)), naturalization records (8 U.S.C.A. § 1454(e)), and authorization for embassy or legation officers to perform notarial services (22 U.S.C.A. § 4221).

30. See AMFAC Distribution Corp. v. Harrelson, 842 F.2d 304 (11th Cir. 1988)(copy of state court judgment admissible since it carried a stamp which satisfied the necessary indication of reliability otherwise requiring the signature and seal); United States v. Hitsman, 604 F.2d 443 (5th Cir.1979)(copy of college transcript self-authenticating because it carried the university seal and otherwise had every internal mark of reliability).

903 Subscribing Witnesses

§ 903.1 Subscribing Witnesses—New York and Federal

CPLR 4537. Proof of writing subscribed by witness

Unless a writing requires a subscribing witness for its validity, it may be proved as if there was no subscribing witness.

CPLR 4537 abolishes, for the most part, the common law rule that the authenticity of a document bearing the signatures of subscribing or attesting witnesses can be proved only by the testimony of those witnesses.[1] Under CPLR 4537, even if a document was attested by a subscribing witness, its authenticity may be proved without the need for testimony by that witness by using any authorized method. The exception to this—a writing requiring a subscribing witness for its validity—is, of course, a will, the probate of which cannot go forward without at least affidavits by the witnesses, or proof of their unavailability.[2]

Federal Rule of Evidence 903 is to the same effect as CPLR 4537, and the Advisory Committee's Note refers to CPLR 4537. Proposed New York Evidence Code § 903 is substantially the same. There seems to be no federal statute requiring subscribing witnesses to be called to testify and so this rule seldom comes up.[3]

Library References:

West's Key No. Digests, Criminal Law ⟜444; Evidence ⟜374.

§ 903.1

1. Fox v. Reil, 3 Johns 477 (1808).
2. N.Y. Surrogate's Court Procedure Act §§ 1404, 1405; N.Y. Estates, Powers and Trusts Law § 3–2.1. A contract of marriage also requires subscribing witnesses. N.Y. Domestic Relations Law § 11(4).
3. But see Zenith Radio Corp. v. Matsushita Elec. Indus. Co., 505 F.Supp. 1190, 1223 (E.D.Pa.1980)(absence of a subscribing witness no hindrance to authentication).

CHAPTER 10

BEST EVIDENCE

Table of Sections

1001 BEST EVIDENCE

1001.1 The Best Evidence Rule—New York and Federal.
    a. Generally.
    b. Federal Rule of Evidence 1001—Definitions.

1002 ORIGINALS

1002.1 Originals—New York and Federal.

1003 DUPLICATES

1003.1 Duplicates—New York and Federal.

1004 SECONDARY EVIDENCE

1004.1 Secondary Evidence—New York and Federal.
    a. Loss or Destruction.
    b. Original Not Obtainable.
    c. Original in Possession of Opponent.
    d. Collateral Matters.

1005 PUBLIC RECORDS

1005.1 New York and Federal.
    a. New York.
    b. Federal.

1006 SUMMARIES

1006.1 Summaries—New York and Federal.
    a. New York.
    b. Federal.

1007 TESTIMONY OR WRITTEN ADMISSION OF PARTY

1007.1 Admission as to Genuineness—New York and Federal.

1008 FUNCTIONS OF COURT AND JURY

1008.1 Functions of Court and Jury.
    a. New York.
    b. Federal.

WESTLAW Electronic Research

See WESTLAW Electronic Research Guide preceding the Summary of Contents.

1001 Best Evidence

§ 1001.1 The Best Evidence Rule—New York and Federal

a. Generally

The best evidence rule provides that when the terms of a writing are to be proved, the original document must be produced unless the proponent can show it to be unavailable for reasons other than his own fault.[1] If the absence of the original can be satisfactorily accounted for, secondary evidence will be admissible.

Several questions must be answered in considering whether the best evidence rule applies to a particular offer of written evidence. First, is the content of the writing sought to be admitted for its substantive value?[2] Second, what constitutes an original?[3] Third, if the contents are sought to be proved and there is no original, what is a sufficient foundation for the introduction of secondary evidence?[4] Fourth, what constitutes admissible secondary evidence?[5] These and other points will be addressed in the chapter sections which follow.

The best evidence rule applies to the contents of writings, recordings and photographs.[6] The temptation has been to extend the rule to all

---

§ 1001.1

1. McCormick § 2320, at 61.

2. The best evidence rule is applicable only in those instances where a party seeks to prove the contents of a writing. It has no application where the fact to be proved is independent of the writing. Universal Grain Corp. v. Lamport & Holt Line, 54 N.Y.S.2d 53 (Sup.Ct.App.T.1st Dep't 1945)(plaintiff relied upon direct testimony of witnesses having independent knowledge; fact that laboratory records containing same information were not produced was of no consequence). See also Herzig v. Swift & Co., 146 F.2d 444 (2d Cir.1945)(partnership's earnings existed apart from the account books in which such earnings were recorded; earnings could therefore be proved by testimony even if account books were available).

3. At common law, the distinction between "original" and "duplicate" or "copy" was not always obvious. For example, a duplicate contract was considered an original. Sarasohn v. Kamaiky, 193 N.Y. 203, 86 N.E. 20 (1908); but where duplicate wills have been executed, the duplicate was not considered an original. In re Robinson's Will, 257 App.Div. 405, 13 N.Y.S.2d 324 (4th Dep't 1939). At common law, blotter-press or letter press reproductions were not included as originals, Foot v. Bentley, 44 N.Y. 166 (1870), nor were photostated bills of lading. Toho Bussan Kaisha, Ltd. v. American President Lines, Ltd., 265 F.2d 418 (2d Cir.1959).

4. The more important the document, the stricter the evidentiary foundation will be for the introduction of secondary evidence. People v. Dolan, 186 N.Y. 4, 78 N.E. 569 (1906).

5. The "best" secondary evidence would, of course, be a copy of the original, but a witness' recollection of what the document stated may have to suffice. It is the rule in New York that more reliable forms of secondary evidence need not be produced if evidence of lesser worth is also available. Why, as a tactical matter, the proponent would not want to produce the "best" secondary evidence at hand would not in most cases be clear. The New York rule allowing any form of secondary evidence is open to construction from case to case. Compare Rosenbaum v. Podolsky, 97 Misc. 614, 162 N.Y.S. 227 (Sup.Ct.App.T.1st Dep't 1916)(court rejected argument that oral evidence of contents of writing should be excluded where a copy of the writing existed), with Lazzaro v. Maugham, 10 Misc. 230, 30 N.Y.S. 1066 (N.Y.City Ct.1894)(court disallowed testimony of witness regarding contents of letter where a copy existed).

6. See Schozer v. William Penn Life Ins. Co., 84 N.Y.2d 639, 620 N.Y.S.2d 797, 644 N.E.2d 1353 (1994)(photographs—more particularly X-rays); People v. Graham, 57 A.D.2d 478, 394 N.Y.S.2d 982 (4th Dep't

§ 1001.1

forms of evidence, but the rule is meant to apply only to writings, recordings and photographs.[7]

Perhaps the most subtle part of the rule is that which involves proof of an event that exists independent of a writing that memorializes the event. The payment of a debt, for example, may be evidenced by a written receipt. Nevertheless, the debtor may testify that he paid the debt without producing the receipt or accounting for its absence. The payment is an independent event not dependent for its validity on the receipt. Thus, the best evidence rule does not apply, and no foundation need be laid for the admission of the debtor's testimony as to payment.[8] If, however, title to property is in dispute and the deed is not produced, a foundation will have to be laid for the production of secondary evidence. This is because a transfer of property does not exist independent of the deed. The deed, unlike the receipt, is a dispositive instrument.[9] The transfer is inherently a written transaction.

In the payment example, the debtor will probably choose to prove payment by producing the receipt if he has it. Now the best evidence rule will apply and he must introduce the original, or give a satisfactory explanation as to why he has only a copy. In other words, where the proponent decides to use a writing as proof, then he must deal with the best evidence rule because he is seeking to prove the contents of a writing.[10] Similarly, a witness who heard the testimony of an individual ordinarily may testify to his recollection of that testimony; but if the testimony is to be proved by the transcript, then the best evidence rule

1977), aff'd, 44 N.Y.2d 768, 406 N.Y.S.2d 36, 377 N.E.2d 480 (1978)(tape recordings); Ed Guth Realty, Inc. v. Gingold, 34 N.Y.2d 440, 358 N.Y.S.2d 367, 315 N.E.2d 441 (1974)(computer printouts).

7. McCormick § 229, at 60–61. The misconception that the rule extends beyond writings finds expression in Judge Prettyman's dissent in Meyers v. United States, 171 F.2d 800 (D.C.Cir.1948), cert. denied, 336 U.S. 912, 69 S.Ct. 602, 93 L.Ed. 1076 (1949). "There is * * * a legal cliche that the best evidence rule applies only to documentary evidence * * *. The rationale of the so-called 'best evidence rule' requires that a party having available evidence which is relatively certain may not submit evidence which is far less certain." Id. at 816. Meyers was a perjury case with the majority holding that a witness' testimony as to a defendant's prior testimony under oath was admissible even though a transcript of that testimony was available. See also U.S. Homes, Inc. v. Yates, 174 N.W.2d 402, 403 (Iowa 1970)(the best evidence which is within the power of the party to produce must always be produced for every disputed fact); Padgett v. Brezner, 359 S.W.2d 416, 422 (Mo.Ct.App.1962) ("It is an elementary principle of law that the best evidence of which the case in its nature is susceptible and which is within the power of the party to produce, or is capable of being produced, must always be produced in proof of every disputed fact").

Although clearly erroneous, this reasoning has a certain appeal. Judge Prettyman's rationale in Myers refers to an earlier day when the rule was applied more extensively than it is now. Initially, the best evidence rule required that a party seeking to prove his case produce the best evidence that the circumstances of the case would allow. Over the years, the best evidence rule became the term for a number of specific rules. The chief use of the phrase, and the one that has survived, is that the terms of a document must be proved by the production of that document. Other uses of the phrase have been in connection with the hearsay rule, and to denote which testimony of certain witnesses is preferred. 4 Wigmore § 1174, at 400. Perhaps the reason for the entrenchment of the application of the best evidence rule regarding documents is that they have always carried a sense of formalism and solemnity. Id. § 1177, at 406.

8. Steele v. Lord, 70 N.Y. 280 (1877). See also note 2 supra.

9. McCormick § 233, at 66.

10. Id.

applies.[11] A written confession may be recounted by a witness who heard it dictated, but if the party seeks to prove the confession with the writing, the best evidence rule applies.[12]

It may be stated, therefore, with reasonable certainty, that there are two instances where the rule applies: (1) where the object of proof is a written transaction (a deed, will, judgment or other dispositive instrument)[13] or (2) where, although the object of proof is not a written transaction, the event has been memorialized in a writing (or tape or photograph) and the proponent chooses to use the graphic or aural evidence as the proof. But where the mere existence of a document is to be proved, i.e., "where evidence concerning a document is introduced to prove something other than content"[14] the best evidence rule is inappli-

11. Meyers v. United States, 171 F.2d 800 (D.C.Cir.1948), cert. denied, 336 U.S. 912, 69 S.Ct. 602, 93 L.Ed. 1076 (1949). In McRorie v. Monroe, 203 N.Y. 426, 430, 96 N.E. 724, 725 (1911), it was held that whenever a witness' testimony is to be proved it can be recounted by any person who heard it and could undertake to narrate it correctly. "There is no rule of law which makes the stenographic reporter the only competent witness in such a case." This was followed in People v. Colon, 281 App.Div. 354, 356, 119 N.Y.S.2d 503, 505 (1st Dep't 1953), where it was held that the stenographer's minutes reporting a court hearing were not within the best evidence rule, for what was sought to be proved was what the witness said, and not what the stenographer wrote. But see Crim.Proc.Law § 670.20(1) which provides that in any criminal action or proceeding other than a grand jury proceeding, a party, if he desires to offer testimony given at a previous action or proceeding, must make a motion and submit an authenticated transcript to the court.

12. People v. Giro, 197 N.Y. 152, 160, 90 N.E. 432, 435 (1910)(the written confession and the recollection of a witness as to its substance were both allowed). Compare Gray v. State, 181 Md. 439, 30 A.2d 744 (1943)(court held that written confession should be introduced rather than witness' recollection).

In United States v. White, 223 F.2d 674 (2d Cir.1955), the question was whether a witness could testify as to defendant's confession when a recording of the confession was available. The court stated: "Since the matter at issue regarding the confession was not the contents of the tape recording but what the appellant had said, the best evidence rule did not require that the recording be produced and oral testimony of what had been said was admissible." Id. at 675.

13. In Cullinan v. Horan, 116 App.Div. 711, 713, 102 N.Y.S. 132, 134 (2d Dep't 1907), the issue was whether or not the county treasurer had issued a liquor tax certificate. The court held that the fact could be proved by the treasurer's testimony and that written records were not necessary. In its discussion, however, the court noted that a divorce is an event that does not exist independent of a court's written decree. The court cited with approval Commonwealth v. Dill, 156 Mass. 226, 30 N.E. 1016 (1892), stating:

In that case objection was taken to the oral proof of marriage on the ground that the record should be produced, and the court, per Holmes, J., said: "It is true that the record by statute is presumptive evidence of the marriage * * * but the record of a marriage is not like the record of a divorce, or other judgment or decree. It is a mere memorandum or declaration of the fact which effected the result, not itself the fact, nor that which has been constituted the only evidence of the fact. There is no reason why the oath of the person who did the act should be deemed inferior evidence to a written statement by him or another."

Id. at 713, 102 N.Y.S. at 134.

Compare Matter of Spondre, 98 Misc. 524, 527, 162 N.Y.S. 943, 946 (Surr.Ct. N.Y.Co.1917), where the court held that a Jewish divorce, a "get," could be proved without producing documentation.

14. See, e.g., United States v. Jones, 958 F.2d 520, 521 (2d Cir.1992). In Jones the issue was not the content of defendant's tax return, but whether she had engaged in conduct inconsistent with the theory of her defense. The IRS transcript sheet concerning her tax account proved that she had acted inconsistently with that defense. The court added: "For example, in United States v. Sliker, 751 F.2d 477, 483–84 (2d Cir.1984), cert. denied, 470 U.S. 1058, 105 S.Ct. 1772, 84 L.Ed.2d 832 (1985) we held that oral testimony about an insurance poli-

cable.[15]

Professors Cleary and Strong in their oft-cited article[16] note that the original justification for the rule was that it prevented fraud; that when something other than the original was offered in evidence a presumption of fraud arose.[17] Although the presumption has long since disappeared, the rule does indeed serve as a fraud preventive, and that idea continues to form part of the foundation for the rule.[18] The main support for the rule, however, consists of the notion that accuracy in proof of a writing is of the utmost importance.[19]

One may question the need for continuing the best evidence rule.[20] Modern rules of pretrial discovery help to achieve objectives formerly sought to be obtained under the best evidence rule in the sense that documents in the hands of the adversary must now be turned over under the provisions of Rule 34 of the Federal Rules of Civil Procedure and Article 31 of the New York CPLR. Moreover, modern advances in photography, sound recording and photocopying have largely eliminated the concern over inaccurate copying.[21] Nevertheless, Article 10 of the Federal Rules of Evidence and Article 10 of the proposed New York Evidence Code, which in all important respects follows federal Article 10, continue the rule, although in a liberalized form.

It is because the New York common law, the Federal Rules of Evidence and the proposed New York Evidence Code are so homogenous, and because there is every reason to believe the New York courts will follow these codified rules, that the two jurisdictions will continue to be treated together in much of the remainder of this chapter.

b. Federal Rule of Evidence 1001—Definitions

Rule 1001 of the Federal Rules of Evidence states as follows:

cy was properly admitted to prove the existence of insurance, in contrast to proving the terms of the policy." Id. at 521. See also Cullinan v. Horan, 116 App.Div. 711, 713, 102 N.Y.S. 132, 134 (2d Dep't 1907); note 13 supra.

15. See also Universal Grain Corp. v. Lamport & Holt Line, 54 N.Y.S.2d 53 (Sup. Ct.App.T.1st Dep't 1945); note 2, supra. See also Wolper v. New York Water Service Corp., 276 App.Div.1106, 1107, 96 N.Y.S.2d 647, 649 (2d Dep't 1950)("The Trial Justice erroneously ruled that the customer of plaintiffs could not testify as to ownership of bonds or real property without the production of the bonds or deeds. The terms of the bonds or deeds were not in issue.").

16. Cleary and Strong, "The Best Evidence Rule: An Evaluation in Context," 51 Iowa L.Rev. 825 (1966).

17. Id. at 826–27.

18. Id. The text of the Cleary and Strong article reveals a competing policy view advanced by Professor Wigmore which focuses on the inherent value of the written word in its original form. 4 Wigmore § 1179, at 417. This view emphasizes the law's preference for the written word, and the extrinsic value found in the original words as compared to any other form. "As between a supposed literal copy and the original, the copy is always liable to errors on the part of the copyist * * *. This wholly disappears when the original is produced. Moreover, the original may contain, and the copy will lack, such features of handwriting, paper and the like * * *. 4 Wigmore § 1179, at 417."

The copying process has advanced to the point where, as discussed infra, photocopies are classified as originals. All of this reasoning has become quaint.

19. Cleary and Strong, supra note 16, at 828. See also McCormick § 231, at 62–63.

20. McCormick § 231, at 63.

21. See Cleary and Strong, note 16, supra.

Ch. 10 BEST EVIDENCE § 1001.1

For purposes of this article the following definitions are applicable:

(1) Writings and recordings. "Writings" and "recordings" consist of letters, words, or numbers, or their equivalent, set down by handwriting, typewriting, printing, photostating, photographing, magnetic impulse, mechanical or electronic recording, or other form of data compilation.

(2) Photographs. "Photographs" include still photographs, X-ray films, video tapes, and motion pictures.

(3) Original. An "original" of a writing or recording is the writing or recording itself or any counterpart intended to have the same effect by a person executing or issuing it. An "original" of a photograph includes the negative or any print therefrom. If data are stored in a computer or similar device, any printout or other output readable by sight, shown to reflect the data accurately, is an "original."

(4) Duplicate. A "duplicate" is a counterpart produced by the same impression as the original, or from the same matrix, or by means of photography, including enlargements and miniatures, or by mechanical or electronic re-recording, or by chemical reproduction, or by other equivalent techniques which accurately reproduces the original.

The definitions in subdivision (1) clearly pinpoint the items that are subject to the best evidence rule. An important federal precedent on the meaning of the "equivalent" of a writing for purposes of the best evidence rule is *Seiler v. Lucasfilm, Ltd.*[22] There, it was alleged that film-maker George Lucas had infringed the plaintiff-artist's copyright on drawings of certain science fiction characters. The best evidence rule applied to the drawings, the court concluded, because "[just] as a contract objectively manifests the subjective intent of the makers, so [plaintiff's] drawings are objective manifestations of the creative mind."[23] The court reasoned that the rule should be applied in a way that furthers its purposes, i.e., to take account of the centrality of written materials to legal issues, to prevent fraud and to guard against faulty memory.[24]

Whether such considerations will bring an inscription-bearing chattel within the rule cannot always be predicted. It can be argued that whenever an inscription on an object is relevant for the substance of its content, the chattel ought to be treated as a writing. Courts apparently exercise discretion on this issue, the rule of thumb being that the more central the inscription is to the merits of the case, the more likely a court is to insist upon the chattel's production.[25] On the other hand,

22. 808 F.2d 1316 (9th Cir.1986), cert. denied, 484 U.S. 826, 108 S.Ct. 92, 98 L.Ed.2d 53 (1987).

23. Id. at 1320.

24. Id. at 1319–20.

25. McCormick states:

Thus, when an object such as a policeman's badge, a flag, or a tombstone bears

§ 1001.1 BEST EVIDENCE Ch. 10

distinctive and easily-remembered labels and trademarks are often held to be exempt from the rule.[26]

In New York the burden is on the proponent to satisfy the best evidence rule, and not on the adversary to call for such satisfaction.[27]

a number or legend the terms of which are relevant the problem is raised as to whether the object shall be treated as a chattel or a writing. It is here clearly unwise to adopt a purely semantic approach and to classify the object according to whether its written component predominates sufficiently to alter the label attached to it in common parlance. At the same time, however, it would seem also unnecessary to classify as writings * * * any object which carries an inscription of any sort whatsoever. In the final analysis, it is perhaps impossible to improve upon Wigmore's suggestion [4 Wigmore § 1182], followed by a number of courts, that the judge shall have discretion to apply the present rule to inscribed chattels or not in light of such factors as the need for precise information as to the exact inscription, the ease or difficulty of production, and the simplicity or complexity of the inscription.

McCormick § 232, at 64–65.

The cases are fact-specific. In United States v. Duffy, 454 F.2d 809, 812 (5th Cir.1972), for example, the court ruled that where a shirt containing the laundry mark "D–U–F" would tend to link defendant to the crime, the shirt was not a writing and need not be produced. A witness could simply testify to having seen the laundry mark. The court reasoned that the abbreviation was "simple," thus reducing the danger of inaccurate memory by the witness. The court also noted that in terms of the substantial case against Duffy, the laundry mark was not critical.

In other cases, courts have insisted on production of the chattel. See, e.g., United States v. Marcantoni, 590 F.2d 1324, 1329–30 (5th Cir.), cert. denied, 441 U.S. 937, 99 S.Ct. 2063, 60 L.Ed.2d 666 (1979)(best evidence rules applies to a witness' testimony concerning serial numbers on stolen money so that testimony allowed only after showing of the unavailability of the money); Davenport v. Ourisman–Mandell Chevrolet, Inc., 195 A.2d 743 (D.C.App.1963)(rule bars testimony stating mileage on automobile service sticker since the sticker itself ought to be produced, or an explanation given as to its unavailability).

26. In addition to United States v. Duffy, note 25 supra, see United States v. Yamin, 868 F.2d 130, 134 (5th Cir.), cert. denied, 492 U.S. 924, 109 S.Ct. 3258, 106 L.Ed.2d 603 (1989)(in prosecution for the sale of watches bearing counterfeit trademarks, the court dismissed the argument that the watches ought to be produced on the premise that the viewing of a simple and recognized trademark is not likely to be remembered inaccurately); Carroll v. Gimbel Brothers, New York, 195 App.Div. 444, 451, 186 N.Y.S. 737, 741 (1st Dep't 1921), appeal dismissed, 234 N.Y. 528, 138 N.E. 433 (1922)(error to exclude testimony offered by store owner's employees that drug articles found in alleged shoplifter's bag all bore employer's trademark and tag).

27. In Mahaney v. Carr, 175 N.Y. 454, 67 N.E. 903 (1903), plaintiff tried to prove an agreement to adopt a child and give it a certain share of the adoptive father's property. The court stated:

Whatever proof the plaintiff gave was of a verbal agreement and the finding which has been considered in the product of these rulings. It would seem to be a plain violation of one of the most elementary rules of evidence to permit the plaintiff to prove her case by the very vague and inconclusive testimony of her father, consisting of conversations with the grandfather who was dead, so long as it appeared that the transaction was in writing and there was no attempt made to produce the papers, account for their loss or destruction, or to give secondary proof of their contents. The answer of the learned counsel for the plaintiff to this objection is, substantially, that the defendant's counsel omitted to call for the papers. He was under no obligation to do so. The plaintiff's counsel was bound to prove his case by competent evidence, and when it appeared that the transaction was in writing it was incumbent upon him to produce it, or show that it was lost or destroyed. He would then be required to confine the proof to secondary evidence of the contents of the papers.

Id. at 462, 461–62, 67 N.E. at 905–06.

In Mastan Company, Inc. v. Weil, 84 A.D.2d 657, 659, 444 N.Y.S.2d 315, 318 (3d Dep't 1981), there was an issue with respect to the balance due on mortgages. The court held that the mortgage documents in question should have been produced and that the defendant's failure to demand those documents in no way lessened the fact that plaintiff's proof failed because it neglected to produce the documents.

Examples of writings covered by the rule, where the proponent's purpose is to prove terms or content, include contracts,[28] computer printouts,[29] mortgage documents,[30] letters,[31] convictions[32] and plot plans.[33] Tape

The Second Circuit in Andrew Crispo Gallery, Inc. v. Commissioner, 16 F.3d 1336, 1343 (2d Cir.1994), held that where the taxpayer, who has the burden of proving his right to deductions, cannot submit documentary proof because the government confiscated and lost his records, he is entitled to produce secondary evidence to support deductions. On remand, the Tax Court was to consider whether to draw inferences that the true facts were as alleged by the taxpayer. Compare Ruberto v. Commissioner, 774 F.2d 61, 64 (2d Cir.1985), where the taxpayers were held not to have satisfied their burden of sustaining deductions by offering in evidence photocopies of cancelled checks since problems inhered in matching the fronts and backs of the various copies. But in United States v. Kushner, 135 F.2d 668, 674 (2d Cir.), cert. denied, 320 U.S. 212, 212, 63 S.Ct. 1449, 87 L.Ed. 1850, reh'g denied, 320 U.S. 808, 64 S.Ct. 32, 88 L.Ed. 488 (1943), a pre-Rules case, photostatic copies of bank statements were allowed as not violative of the best evidence rule. Evidently there was no problem regarding the reverse side as there would be with photocopies of cancelled checks. In United States v. Manton, 107 F.2d 834, 845 (2d Cir.1939), cert. denied, 309 U.S. 664, 60 S.Ct. 590, 84 L.Ed. 1012 (1940), the court allowed photostatic copies of the face of checks to prove payment.

28. Trombley v. Seligman, 191 N.Y. 400, 403, 84 N.E. 280, 281 (1908)(in action to recover for materials and labor under a building contract, shipping bills were best evidence of what was delivered and it was improper to allow witness' recollection where no attempt was made to explain why the bills could not be produced); Butler v. Mail & Express Pub. Co., 171 N.Y. 208, 211, 63 N.E. 951, 952 (1902)(in an action against a publisher to recover amount of bills which it had agreed to pay in advertising, the absence of the stipulation embodying this agreement had to be explained before plaintiff could testify to it).

29. Ed Guth Realty v. Gingold, 34 N.Y.2d 440, 451–52, 358 N.Y.S.2d 367, 374, 315 N.E.2d 441, 446 (1974). Here, the court held that computer printouts satisfied the business records hearsay exception and also the best evidence rule. "As for the best evidence rule, the 'voluminous writings' exception to that rule would apply. That permits the admission of summaries of voluminous records of entries where, if requested, the party against whom it is offered can have access to the original data." Id. at 451, 358 N.Y.S.2d at 374, 315 N.E.2d at 441.

In Briar Hill Apts v. Teperman, 165 A.D.2d 519, 568 N.Y.S.2d 50 (1st Dep't 1991), the court stated:

The third aspect of tenant's argument, i.e., that the records, by being responsive to subpoena, somehow lost their character as business records, seems to us to lack sufficient appreciation of the benefits conferred upon the world in general, and litigation in particular, by modern computer technology. Mr. Hogan stated that he obtained the records from the company data bank by pressing the appropriate key or keys on his office computer. This would appear to be no different in its legal consequences from normal practice in the precomputer age where business records reposed in a steel file instead of a mainframe computer data bank, and would be subject to retrieval by a file clerk and placed on Mr. Hogan's desk manually, rather than electronically.

Id. at 522, 568 N.Y.S.2d at 52.

30. Mastan Co., Inc. v. Weil, 84 A.D.2d 657, 659, 444 N.Y.S.2d 315, 318 (3d Dep't 1981)(where mortgage documents were available they should have been produced to prove balances due; plaintiff could not rely on testimony of witness on this point).

31. People v. Pennick, 204 A.D.2d 988, 612 N.Y.S.2d 723 (4th Dep't), appeal denied, 83 N.Y.2d 970, 616 N.Y.S.2d 23, 639 N.E.2d 763 (1994)(The court stated: "County Court erred in permitting a codefendant to testify during the prosecutor's direct case regarding the contents of a letter that was not produced. The admission of that testimony violates the 'best evidence rule,' which 'requires that one who desires to prove the contents of a writing, do so by producing the writing itself unless sufficient reason is shown for its absence.'" Id. at 988, 612 N.Y.S.2d at 724.

32. People v. Conklin, 102 A.D.2d 829, 476 N.Y.S.2d 602 (2d Dep't 1984). The court stated: "The People relied on a Pennsylvania judgment of conviction which was not properly certified (see CPLR 4540, subd. [c]; People v. Hines, 90 A.D.2d 621, 456 N.Y.S.2d 235) and the testimony of a police officer who witnessed defendant's conviction. While the officer's testimony presents hearsay and best evidence problems, it was admitted without objection and

33. See note 33 on page 814.

§ 1001.1 BEST EVIDENCE Ch. 10

recordings[34] and photographs[35] are also now included within the rule. Records and memoranda used for memory refreshment (*see* §§ 612.1 and 612.2, *supra*) are not within the best evidence rule because the purpose is not to prove the terms or contents of such writings.[36]

Library References:

West's Key No. Digests, Criminal Law ⚖=398–404; Evidence ⚖=157–187.

1002 Originals

§ 1002.1 Originals—New York and Federal

Federal Rule of Evidence 1002 provides:

> To prove the content of a writing, recording, or photograph, the original writing, recording, or photograph is required, except as otherwise provided in these rules or by Act of Congress.

That simply restates the best evidence rule. The inquiry in this section is to try and discern what an original is in certain commonly presented situations.

---

was therefore properly considered * * * as proof of a prior conviction * * *." Id. at 829, 476 N.Y.S.2d at 603.

33. In re Estate of Marks, 33 A.D.2d 1029, 307 N.Y.S.2d 950 (2d Dep't 1970). The court held that the Surrogate should not have approved the sale of property where there was a dispute as to dimensions stated in plot plans submitted to the Village. The letter of the Village acknowledging the plot plans did "not serve to exclude the possibility, as charged by appellants, that the plot plan submitted by the purchaser misstated the true dimensions of the tract * * *. Although the best evidence of the contents of the plot plan submitted is the plan itself, the purchaser has failed to produce it." Id. at 1029, 307 N.Y.S.2d at 951.

34. People v. Graham, 57 A.D.2d 478, 394 N.Y.S.2d 982 (4th Dep't 1977), aff'd, 44 N.Y.2d 768, 406 N.Y.S.2d 36, 377 N.E.2d 480 (1978)(if the tape is available it is the best evidence of its contents and the principal problem is authenticating it. Were the tape inaudible or missing, it would seem that a participant in the conversation, or one who overheard it, could testify as to its content. In People v. Torres, 118 A.D.2d 821, 500 N.Y.S.2d 178 (2d Dep't 1986)), however, the court held that there was no error in allowing a detective to testify as to a taped conversation even when the tape itself was in evidence. "Since what was sought to be proven by the testimony was the content of a conversation, a fact existing independently of the tape recording, the best evidence rule was inapplicable and the conversation could be testified to by anyone who heard it." Id. at 822, 500 N.Y.S.2d at 180. See also text at notes 8–15, supra.

35. Schozer v. William Penn Life Ins. Co., 84 N.Y.2d 639, 620 N.Y.S.2d 797, 644 N.E.2d 1353 (1994)(X-rays are within the rule; foundation must therefore be laid for secondary evidence if X-ray lost); Sirico v. Cotto, 67 Misc.2d 636, 638, 324 N.Y.S.2d 483, 486 (N.Y.City Civil Ct.1971)(Judge Irving Younger stated: "A 'document,' within the meaning of the best evidence rule, is any physical embodiment of information or ideas—a letter, a contract, a receipt, a book of account, a blueprint, or an x-ray plate."). When photographs are available for admission into evidence, the question as to whether they are the "originals" is really a question of authentication. See People v. Byrnes, 33 N.Y.2d 343, 347–48, 352 N.Y.S.2d 913, 916, 308 N.E.2d 435, 437 (1974). The Advisory Committee's Note to Fed.R.Evid. 1001 observes that the negative is the only true original of a photograph but that "practicality and common usage require that any print from the negative be regarded as an original." The second sentence of Rule 1001(3) states: "An 'original' of a photograph includes the negative or any print therefrom."

36. In People v. Murray, 90 A.D.2d 640, 456 N.Y.S.2d 445 (3d Dep't 1982), the prosecution's expert testified as to tests revealing the substance found in defendant's possession to be heroin. It was stated: "Nor is there any 'best evidence' issue here; the records and materials used by the expert merely recorded his personal observations and were not, in themselves, legally operative documents * * *." Id. at 640, 456 N.Y.S.2d at 447.

We start with the Rule 1001(3) definition which is that an original is "the writing or recording itself or any counterpart intended to have the same effect by a person executing or issuing it." (*See* § 1001.1(b) *supra*.) Often the original will be the document which was produced first, or the document which is signed, or notarized, or bears the original seal. Copies and duplicates may later be made, but that which was produced first is the writing "itself." However, there may be instances in which the first-produced document is not the relevant document. Where, for instance, a defendant was prosecuted for submitting false charge card receipts for reimbursement, the relevant documents were the photocopies of the receipts that the defendant actually submitted. These photocopies, therefore, constituted the originals.[1] And where a defendant submitted photocopies of checks in support of a false loan application, the photocopies were the originals in the context of that case.[2] Thus, if the duplicates or copies are the focus of the lawsuit, or the issue in the lawsuit, they become the originals for purposes of the best evidence rule. In the case last noted, since the photocopies of the checks could not be produced, a foundation was laid for secondary evidence.[3]

Where, as in most cases, the original is the first and operative document, reasons for insisting on its production have lessened greatly with the advances in the technology for the reproduction of that original. Starting with the error-prone efforts of the scrivener, through the letter press process,[4] the advent of carbon paper and the mimeograph machine and ending with computer printouts, photocopies and microfilm, an evolving acceptance of the reproduction process has emerged. There has been acceptance of carbon copies as originals in New York[5] and the codes now recognize that at the very least reproductions from the same matrix (document produced from the same set of type, plates or mats) qualify as originals under Rule 1001(3). It has long been the rule that all executed copies of dispositive instruments are deemed originals[6] (with the exception of wills which will be taken up in § 1003.1 *infra*), and that where multiple copies are produced at the same time, as with carbons or on a

§ 1002.1

1. United States v. Rangel, 585 F.2d 344, 346 (8th Cir.1978).

2. United States v. Gerhart, 538 F.2d 807, 810 n.4 (8th Cir.1976).

3. Id. at 809 (photocopy of a photocopy of bank check admissible as secondary evidence).

4. See Foot v. Bentley, 44 N.Y. 166, 171 (1870). It was held that letter press copies of correspondence were not originals and that a foundation had to be laid for secondary evidence of the correspondence.

5. In People v. Kolp, 49 A.D.2d 139, 373 N.Y.S.2d 681 (3d Dep't 1975), defendant signed a four-copy carbon copy waiver of rights form. At trial the first or white copy was missing, but a colored carbon copy was offered in evidence. The court stated: "On such multi-copy forms, all duplicates or counterparts are regarded as originals and any such duplicate copies are admissible as originals without the necessity of either producing or accounting for the absence of the other." Id. at 141, 373 N.Y.S.2d at 683. Accord, Campbell v. Pure Oil Co., 92 Ga. App. 523, 524, 88 S.E.2d 630, 631 (1955)(carbons could be considered originals since produced with "the same stroke of the pen or typewriter)". But see in Shirer v. O.W.S. & Associates, 253 S.C. 232, 169 S.E.2d 621 (1969) (rejection of any general rule that carbons could be viewed as originals).

6. Sarasohn v. Kamaiky, 193 N.Y. 203, 86 N.E. 20 (1908).

§ 1002.1 BEST EVIDENCE Ch. 10

printing press, all are considered originals.[7]

Business Records. By statute, duplicates that are made and kept in the regular course of business are admissible as originals in both New York[8] and federal[9] courts. The statutory provisions eliminate the best evidence problem in many situations. For example, if a document is admissible under the business records hearsay exception (CPLR 4518(a); Federal Rule of Evidence 803(6)), the best evidence rule will be satisfied if the record is either the original or a duplicate made in the regular course of business. The rule reflects the reality that copies are relied upon without question in the business world and that modern reproduction processes produce trustworthy copies.[10] Computer printouts are easily includable under this category provided the original data are comprised of regularly kept business matters.[11]

---

7. McCormick § 236, at 73.

8. CPLR 4539 provides:

Reproductions of original

If any business, institution, or member of a profession or calling, in the regular course of business or activity has made, kept or recorded any writing, entry, print or representation and in the regular course of business has recorded, copied, or reproduced it by any process which accurately reproduces or forms a durable medium for reproducing the original, such reproduction, when satisfactorily identified, is as admissible in evidence as the original, whether the original is in existence or not, and an enlargement or facsimile of such reproduction is admissible in evidence if the original reproduction is in existence and available for inspection under direction of the court. The introduction of a reproduction does not preclude admission of the original.

The last sentence of proposed New York Evidence Code § 1001(c) states: "A duplicate of a writing, recording, or photograph, made in the regular course of business or activity and preserved as part of the records of any business, institution, or member of a profession or calling, is an 'original.'" This sentence does not appear in the federal counterpart, Rule 1001(3).

9. § 28 U.S.C.A. § 1732 provides:

Record made in regular course of business; photographic copies

If any business, institution, member of a profession or calling, or any department or agency of government, in the regular course of business or activity has kept or recorded any memorandum, writing, entry, print, representation or combination thereof, of any act, transaction, occurrence, or event, and in the regular course of business has caused any or all of the same to be recorded, copied, or reproduced by any photographic, photostatic, microfilm, micro-card, miniature photographic, or other process which accurately reproduces or forms a durable medium for so reproducing the original, the original may be destroyed in the regular course of business unless its preservation is required by law. Such reproduction, when satisfactorily identified, is as admissible in evidence as the original itself in any judicial or administrative proceeding whether the original is in existence or not and an enlargement or facsimile of such reproduction is likewise admissible in evidence if the original reproduction is in existence and available for inspection under direction of court. The introduction of a reproduced record, enlargement, or facsimile does not preclude admission of the original. This subsection shall not be construed to exclude from evidence any document or copy thereof which is otherwise admissible under the rules of evidence.

10. See, e.g., People v. May, 162 A.D.2d 977, 557 N.Y.S.2d 203 (4th Dep't), appeal denied, 76 N.Y.2d 861, 560 N.Y.S.2d 1000, 561 N.E.2d 900 (1990)(photocopies and fax copies of record of vehicle identification number of stolen car admissible under CPLR 4539); People v. Flores, 138 A.D.2d 512, 526 N.Y.S.2d 125 (2d Dep't), appeal denied, 72 N.Y.2d 859, 532 N.Y.S.2d 509, 528 N.E.2d 899 (1988)(photocopies of laboratory forms which accompanied packets of cocaine through series of laboratory tests properly admitted under CPLR 4539 since kept in the regular course of business).

11. See Ed Guth Realty v. Gingold, 34 N.Y.2d 440, 451–52, 358 N.Y.S.2d 367, 374, 315 N.E.2d 441, 445–46 (1974). Here, the court held that computer printouts satisfied the business records hearsay exception and also the best evidence rule. It would seem that if the original data are in the comput-

The routineness of the copy-making is crucial. Copies made solely for the litigation in question traditionally have not qualified as "routine."[12] Under Federal Rule of Evidence 1003, however (see § 1003.1 infra), business records that have been copied for litigation may still satisfy the best evidence rule. It is uncertain whether New York courts would treat business-related duplicates in like manner.

Correspondence. Depending on what is sought to be proved, the original will be either the copy received, the copy sent, or the copy retained by the sender. If the issue is whether notice was received then, of course, the original is the copy received. If the issue concerns the sender's intent, then his retained copy becomes the original.[13] The old "telegram rule" relating to offers and acceptances is that the original of the offer is the copy given the telegraph company. If the issue concerns whether the offer or acceptance was received, the original would be the copy delivered by the telegraph company; and if the issue lies in a dispute between the sender and the telegraph company, the original is the copy given the company.[14]

Photographs. Federal Rule 1001(3) states that an original of a photograph includes the negative or any print therefrom. The proposed New York Evidence Code § 1001(c) makes the same provision, and this,

---

er, instead of a file folder, their retrieval would constitute original material. In Ed Guth the printouts seem to have been a recapitulation of the pertinent records since the court stated: "As for the best evidence rule, the 'voluminous writings' exception to that rule would apply. That permits the admission of summaries of voluminous records of entries where, if requested, the party against whom it is offered can have access to the original data." Id. at 452, 358 N.Y.S.2d at 374, 315 N.E.2d at 446.

In Briar Hill Apts. v. Teperman, 165 A.D.2d 519, 522, 568 N.Y.S.2d 50, 52 (1st Dep't 1991), in response to the argument that computer records lost their character as business records when printed out for trial, the court stated: "This would appear to be no different in legal consequences from normal practice in the precomputer age where business records reposed in a steel file instead of a mainframe computer data bank, and would be subject to retrieval by a file clerk and placed on Mr. Hogan's desk manually, rather than electronically." Id.

12. See, e.g., Toho Bussan Kaisha, Ltd. v. American President Lines, Ltd., 265 F.2d 418 (2d Cir.1959)(in this pre-Rules case, where originals were kept in Japan, later-produced photocopies would not be accepted as originals since there were dangers of fraud in the use of photocopies prepared for trial, thus raising genuine questions as to accuracy).

13. The rule expressed in Foot v. Bentley, 44 N.Y. 166, 171 (1870), that letter press copies of correspondence are not originals and must be proved as secondary evidence, was premised on the nature of the copying technique of that day. This is recognized in the proposed New York Evidence Code § 1003, which treats duplicates as originals if no serious question is raised as to their accuracy and there is no "unfairness" in using duplicates. See § 1003.1, at note 8, infra.

14. See Anheuser–Busch Brewing Co. v. Hutmacher, 127 Ill. 652, 21 N.E. 626 (1889)(as between sender and receiver, the written message delivered to receiver is the original when the sender takes initiative in using telegraph, and there is no evidence of error in the transmission of the message); Oregon Steam–Ship Co. v. Otis, 100 N.Y. 446, 453, 3 N.E. 485, 487–88 (1885), appeal dismissed, 116 U.S. 548, 6 S.Ct. 523, 29 L.Ed. 719 (1886)(to prove receipt of telegram from its sending, the copy delivered to recipient is not the original; there must be proof of the copy given by the sender to the telegraph office); Hartzell v. United States, 72 F.2d 569, 578 (8th Cir.), cert. denied, 293 U.S. 621, 55 S.Ct. 216, 79 L.Ed. 708 (1934)(in criminal prosecution circumstantial evidence sufficient to prove defendant was sender of cablegrams).

§ 1002.1   BEST EVIDENCE   Ch. 10

according to the accompanying comment, codifies New York law.[15] Photographs include X-rays.[16] If there is any problem with the admissibility of photographs, it would normally involve authentication. (*See* §§ 1104.1(a) and 1104.2(a) *infra*.)

Recordings. The original of a disk or tape recording would be the original transcription. Copies made and kept in the regular course of business would qualify for admission under CPLR 4539 or 28 U.S.C. § 1732.[17] Recordings are routinely admitted,[18] and the chief problems would be clarity and authentication. (*See* §§ 1104.1(c) and 1104.2(c) *infra*.)

Library References:

West's Key No. Digests, Criminal Law ⇔398–404; Evidence ⇔157–187.

1003 Duplicates

§ 1003.1 Duplicates—New York and Federal

Federal Rule 1003 provides:

> A duplicate is admissible to the same extent as an original unless (1) a genuine question is raised as to the authenticity of the original or (2) in the circumstances it would be unfair to admit the duplicate in lieu of the original.[1]

From the discussion in the last section[2] we know that resort to Federal Rule 1003 is necessary only where the copy is not made as part of a routine business ritual. Also, we know from the definition in Federal Rule 1001(4) that a duplicate is either made in the same process that produced the original (where it would be treated as an original under caselaw in any event),[3] or is made by a photographic, mechanical or other process "which accurately reproduces the original."[4]

Under Rule 1003, the proponent of the duplicate need only offer it into evidence, and the burden falls on the adversary to challenge the duplicate on either of the two grounds specified in the Rule: (1) a

---

15. See People v. Byrnes, 33 N.Y.2d 343, 348, 352 N.Y.S.2d 913, 916, 308 N.E.2d 435, 437 (1974)(photographs admissible as proof that defendant was involved in an incestuous relationship with daughter).

16. Schozer v. William Penn Life Ins. Co., 84 N.Y.2d 639, 620 N.Y.S.2d 797, 644 N.E.2d 1353 (1994)(if X-ray is lost, secondary evidence of its content is admissible); Sirico v. Cotto, 67 Misc.2d 636, 638, 324 N.Y.S.2d 483, 486 (N.Y.C.Civ.Ct.1971).

17. See notes 8 and 9 supra.

18. See, e.g., People v. Torres, 118 A.D.2d 821, 822, 500 N.Y.S.2d 178, 180 (2d Dep't), appeal denied, 68 N.Y.2d 672, 505 N.Y.S.2d 1039, 496 N.E.2d 697 (1986)(although the tape is admissible it may not be necessary if a witness can testify as to the recorded conversation); People v. Graham, 57 A.D.2d 478, 480, 394 N.Y.S.2d 982, 984 (4th Dep't 1977), aff'd, 44 N.Y.2d 768, 406 N.Y.S.2d 36, 377 N.E.2d 480 (1978)(where tape only partially inaudible, it could nevertheless be admitted).

§ 1003.1

1. The proposed New York Evidence Code version makes the same provision and adds a subdivision (2) which requires that notice be given of intent to use a duplicate.

2. § 1002.1, at notes 8–12, supra.

3. McCormick § 236, at 73.

4. See § 1001.1(b) supra.

genuine question exists as to the authenticity of the original,[5] or (2) it would be "unfair" to admit the duplicate.[6] If the opponent meets this burden, the original must be produced, or a satisfactory excuse must be given for not doing so.

The New York courts have not yet embraced the notion, embodied in Rule 1003, that duplicates, in general, should be prima facie admissible regardless of whether they are made in the regular course of business.[7] The proposed New York Evidence Code favors the federal approach.[8]

The admissibility of certified photocopies of public records is discussed in § 1005.1(a) *infra*.

A rule somewhat related to questions arising over the use of duplicates is peculiar to wills. Where there is an original and an executed duplicate of a will, only the original need be admitted to probate, but the duplicate must be produced or its absence explained since the possibility exists that the testator may have purposely destroyed the duplicate with the intent to revoke the will.[9]

Library References:

West's Key No. Digests, Criminal Law ⚖=398–404; Evidence ⚖=157–187.

---

5. Compare United States v. Haddock, 956 F.2d 1534, 1545–46 (10th Cir.), cert. denied, ___ U.S. ___, 113 S.Ct. 88, 121 L.Ed.2d 50 (1992) (question raised as to whether originals were forgeries), with United States v. Balzano, 687 F.2d 6 (1st Cir.1982)(no genuine issue raised as to authenticity of original tape recording).

6. See, e.g., Ruberto v. C.I.R., 774 F.2d 61, 64 (2d Cir.1985), where the taxpayers were held not to have satisfied their burden of sustaining deductions (it was agency's burden to challenge the photocopies, although the court sua sponte could have found them insufficient) by offering in evidence photocopies of cancelled checks. Problems inhered in matching the fronts and backs of the various copies. See also Myrick v. United States, 332 F.2d 279 (5th Cir.), cert. denied sub nom., Bergman v. United States, 377 U.S. 952, 84 S.Ct. 1630, 12 L.Ed.2d 497 (1964).

7. See § 1002.1, at notes 8–12, supra.

8. **§ 1003. Admissibility of duplicates [PROPOSED]**

(a) General provision. Except as otherwise provided by section 1005 of this article, a duplicate is admissible to the same extent as an original unless: (1) a genuine question is raised as to the authenticity of the original; or (2) under the circumstances it would be unfair to admit the duplicate in lieu of the original.

(b) Notice. The proponent of a duplicate shall make known to all parties the proponent's intention to offer the duplicate and its particulars sufficiently in advance of offering the evidence to provide them with a fair opportunity to meet it. Upon request of the other party, the proponent shall make the original available for inspection if it exists and is in the proponent's possession. If the original no longer exists or is not in the possession of the proponent, the proponent shall so notify the requesting party and advise that party of the location of the original, if known. To remedy the prejudice from the failure to give such notice, the court, pursuant to section 107 of this chapter, shall make any order the interests of justice require.

9. Crossman v. Crossman, 95 N.Y. 145, 149–50, 30 Hun. 385 (1884); Matter of Robinson's Will, 257 App.Div. 405, 407, 13 N.Y.S.2d 324, 326 (4th Dep't 1939); See N.Y.Surrogate's Court Procedure Act § 1407.

1004 Secondary Evidence

§ 1004.1 Secondary Evidence—New York and Federal

Federal Rule of Evidence 1004 provides for the introduction of secondary evidence when the original (or a duplicate deemed an original under Rule 1003) cannot be produced. Rule 1004[1] provides:

> The original is not required, and other evidence of the contents of a writing, recording, or photograph is admissible if—
>
> **(1) Originals lost or destroyed.** All originals are lost or have been destroyed, unless the proponent lost or destroyed them in bad faith; or
>
> **(2) Original not obtainable.** No original can be obtained by any available judicial process or procedure; or
>
> **(3) Original in possession of opponent.** At a time when an original was under the control of the party against whom offered, that party was put on notice, by the pleadings or otherwise, that the contents would be a subject of proof at the hearing, and that party does not produce the original at the hearing; or
>
> **(4) Collateral matters.** The writing, recording, or photograph is not closely related to a controlling issue.

New York and federal law are generally in accord as to the necessary foundation for the use of secondary evidence.

a. Loss or Destruction

Where the original is not available because of excusable loss or destruction[2] the door is open to the use of other evidence to prove the

---

§ 1004.1

1. Proposed New York Evidence Code § 1004 is substantially the same.

§ 1004. Admissibility of other evidence of contents [PROPOSED]

The original is not required, and, except as otherwise provided by section 1005 of this article, other evidence of the contents of a writing, recording, or photograph is admissible if:

(a) **Originals lost or destroyed.** All originals are lost or have been destroyed, unless the proponent lost or destroyed them in bad faith;

(b) **Original not reasonably obtainable.** An original cannot be obtained by any available judicial process or procedure, or the utility of producing the original is substantially outweighed by considerations of difficulty, expense, or the like;

(c) **Original in control of opponent.** At a time when an original was under the control of the party against whom offered, that party was put on notice, by the pleadings or otherwise, that the contents would be a subject of proof, and that party does not produce the original; or

(d) **Collateral matters.** The writing, recording, or photograph is not closely related to a controlling issue.

2. See Steele v. Lord, 70 N.Y. 280, 283–84 (1877)(the fact that plaintiffs routinely destroyed drafts received from the bank without fraudulent intent did not deprive plaintiffs of the opportunity of proving acceptance and payment of drafts without producing them); Cole v. Canno, 168 App. Div. 178, 182, 153 N.Y.S. 957, 960 (3d Dep't 1915)(insufficient showing that letter crucial to the issues was lost or could not be produced); United States v. Bueno–Risquet, 799 F.2d 804, 811 (2d Cir.1986)(where bags of heroin and their identifying markings had been stolen from government safe through no fault of the prosecutor, it was

contents of the missing original.[3] If the document is missing it must be shown that the proponent made reasonable efforts to locate it.[4] There is no order of preference as to the use of secondary evidence. Thus, a witness' recollection of the contents can be presented without showing why a copy known to have been made is not introduced.[5] A document destroyed by the proponent with the sole intent of establishing a foundation for the use of secondary evidence is, in effect, spoliation (*see* § 401.1(a) and § 802.2(a) *supra*) thus precluding the use of the secondary evidence.[6]

permissible for witnesses to use property request forms to refresh their recollection as to markings on bags, and forms could also be used as secondary evidence). In United States v. Jacobs, 475 F.2d 270, 285 (2d Cir.), cert. denied sub nom., Lavelle v. United States, 414 U.S. 821, 94 S.Ct. 116, 38 L.Ed.2d 53 (1973), three conspirators had agreed to share the gains of their enterprise in a certain way and the arrangement was put in writing. But when the enterprise had to be called off, the three decided to destroy the writings. One of the conspirators, however, not the one who ordered the document's destruction, had made a photocopy and the question was whether this was admissible over the objection that the original had been purposely destroyed. The prosecutor brought this out on cross-examination of one of the coconspirators and another coconspirator objected on the ground the original had purposely been destroyed. The court ruled the copy admissible stating:

> The view now generally accepted is that (1) a destruction in the ordinary course of business, and, of course, a destruction by mistake, is sufficient to allow the contents to be shown as in other cases of loss, and that (2) a destruction otherwise made will equally suffice, provided the proponent first removes to the satisfaction of the judge, any reasonable suspicion of fraud.

Id. at 285.

The coconspirator on the witness stand with the copy had not ordered the original's destruction and, besides, the prosecutor should not be precluded from getting in this secondary evidence any more than any other secondary evidence.

In United States v. Maxwell, 383 F.2d 437 (2d Cir.1967), cert. denied, 389 U.S. 1043, 88 S.Ct. 786, 19 L.Ed.2d 835 (1968), the tape was erased because it was legitimately thought that it would not be needed again. But prior to this, shorthand notes had been taken while the witness listened to the tape and the notes had been transcribed. The witness testified that the transcript was an accurate representation of the contents of the tape and thus it was held admissible.

3. Schozer v. William Penn Life Ins. Co., 84 N.Y.2d 639, 644, 620 N.Y.S.2d 797, 799–800, 644 N.E.2d 1353, 1355–56 (1994).

4. Id. The court stated: "Indeed, the more important the document to the resolution of the ultimate issue in the case, 'the stricter becomes the requirement of the evidentiary foundation [establishing loss] for the admission of secondary evidence' (Harmon v. Matthews, 27 N.Y.2d 656, 663, citing People v. Dolan, 186 N.Y. 4, 13, 78 N.E. 569)." Id. See also Kearney v. Mayor of New York, 92 N.Y. 617, 621 (1883).

In United States v. Ross, 321 F.2d 61, 70 (2d Cir.), cert. denied, 375 U.S. 894, 84 S.Ct. 170, 11 L.Ed.2d 123 (1963), Judge Friendly stated that great deference is accorded the trial judge's decision as to the reasonableness of the efforts to locate the original.

In State of New York v. Blank, 820 F.Supp. 697, 703 (N.D.N.Y.1993), the insurer from whom contribution was sought argued there was no proof of any policy covering the risk. A showing was made that a diligent but unsuccessful search for the policy had been made. The permissible secondary evidence consisted of testimony by an insurance broker interpreting the "Declarations Page" of the subject policy and this together with certain concessions made by the fourth-party defendant constituted sufficient secondary evidence to establish the prima facie existence of the policy.

But in In re 716 Third Avenue Holding Corp., 225 F.Supp. 268, 272 (S.D.N.Y.), rev'd on other grounds, 340 F.2d 42 (2d Cir.1964), the bare testimony that the party's books had disappeared was not sufficient. "There was no showing that a diligent search for the books had been made or of the circumstances under which they disappeared." Id.

5. Schozer, 84 N.Y.2d at 645, 620 N.Y.S.2d at 798, 644 N.E.2d at 1353. See also § 1000.1, at note 5, supra.

6. See People v. Betts, 272 App.Div. 737, 741, 74 N.Y.S.2d 791 (1st Dep't 1947),

§ 1004.1   BEST EVIDENCE   Ch. 10

Despite the general rule that authentic and reliable secondary evidence is generally admissible when the original is satisfactorily shown to be unavailable, the New York Court of Appeals in *Schozer v. William Penn Life Ins. Co.*[7] was confronted with the argument that there can be no secondary evidence with respect to a missing X-ray; that the only acceptable evidence of what an X-ray shows is the X-ray itself. The argument was derived from the case of *Hambsch v. New York City Transit Auth.*,[8] where it was held error to have allowed a physician to testify as to his reading of an X-ray without producing the X-ray itself; that the witness' testimony had to have been based on evidence in the record, and the X-ray was not in the record. The Court of Appeals majority in *Schozer* was unwilling to apply that rationale where the record showed an excuse for the absence of the X-ray. The majority said that *Hambsch* "does not per se preclude a party from introducing secondary evidence of an X-ray, if the necessary showing of unavailability is made."[9]

In reaching its conclusion, the majority reviewed and helpfully updated the pertinent aspects of the best evidence rule. Its ultimate holding seems bottomed on the general rule recited by the court as follows:

> Such a mitigating principle [the allowance of secondary evidence] is necessary since a strict requirement of the original writing would serve to extinguish otherwise valid legal claims or defenses where a party has, through no mischief or bad faith, lost or destroyed an original. As stated by one commentator, the failure to excuse the loss of an original "would in many instances mean a return to the bygone and unlamented days in which to lose one's paper was to lose one's right."[10]

b. Original Not Obtainable

Even though the original is not lost or destroyed, it nevertheless may be beyond the reach of the proponent. For example, the document may be in the possession of a third party beyond the court's jurisdiction so that its procurement would be overly expensive or time consuming;[11]

---

aff'd, 297 N.Y. 1000, 80 N.E.2d 456 (1948)(where police officer purposefully destroyed notes he could have used to refresh his recollection court likened this to the situation where, under the best evidence rule, one may not benefit from the use of inferior evidence where the higher evidence has been willfully destroyed); West v. N.Y. Central & H.R.R.R.Co., 55 App.Div. 464, 467, 67 N.Y.S. 104, 106 (4th Dep't 1900) (trial court properly refused to receive secondary evidence where the circumstances raised a strong presumption that original was destroyed with the intention of furnishing an excuse for the use of the secondary evidence).

7. 84 N.Y.2d 639, 620 N.Y.S.2d 797, 644 N.E.2d 1353 (1994).

8. 63 N.Y.2d 723, 725, 480 N.Y.S.2d 195, 196, 469 N.E.2d 516, 517 (1984). See also Marion v. B. G. Coon Constr. Co., 216 N.Y. 178, 182, 110 N.E. 444, 445–46 (1915), for a holding similar to that in Hambsch.

9. Schozer, 84 N.Y.2d at 647, 620 N.Y.S.2d at 801, 644 N.E.2d at 1357.

10. Id. at 644, 620 N.Y.S.2d at 800, 644 N.E.2d at 1355–56, citing McCormick § 237, at 76.

11. The Advisory Committee's Note to Federal Rule 1004(2) states:

> When the original is in the possession of a third person, inability to procure it from him by resort to process or other judicial procedure is a sufficient explanation of nonproduction. Judicial proce-

or the writing may be imprinted on an immovable object such as a building or a tombstone.[12]

c. Original in Possession of Opponent

If the original document is possessed by the proponent's adversary, all the proponent need do is notify the adversary of his intention to rely on the evidence. This is called a "notice to produce." If the adversary fails to produce the original, the foundation is laid for the proponent to use secondary evidence. Of course, if the proponent has no secondary evidence, only a subpoena will do. Furthermore, the notice to produce is ineffective as a means of overcoming the best evidence rule when the writing is in the hands of a stranger to the litigation.[13]

The fact that notice can be implied from the pleadings (where it is made clear that the contents of the document will be in issue) demonstrates that the burden is heavily on the adversary to produce the original, or suffer the consequences of proponent's secondary evidence.[14]

When the proponent specifically notifies the adversary to produce the document, this is not to be taken as a discovery device. Such notice simply serves to lay the foundation for secondary evidence at trial.[15] Nor is a notice to produce to be confused with the "notice to admit," a discovery device contained in CPLR 3121 and Federal Rule of Civil Procedure 36.

If the question arises whether the adversary possesses the document, the proponent must prove such possession through ordinary methods of proof.[16]

---

dure includes subpoena duces tecum as an incident to the taking of a deposition in another jurisdiction. No further showing is required.

12. The Comment to Proposed New York Evidence Code § 1004(b) states in part:

Furthermore, this subdivision grants a court some discretion to excuse production of the original, even if obtainable by subpoena, if such production is "substantially outweighed by considerations of difficulty, expense or the like." Such variables as the need for establishing the exact terms, and the difficulty and expense of bringing the original into court will enter into the court's determination of whether production of the original should be excused. As one court has observed: "If a sign were painted on a house, it would hardly be contended that the house would have to be produced, nor can it be said that the law converts the courtroom into a receptacle for wagons, boxes, tombstones, and the like, on which one's name may be written." Kansas Pacific Ry. Co. v. Miller, 2 Colo. 442, 462 (1874). This provision codifies present law.

13. See generally Graham § 1004.4; D. Siegel, New York Practice § 387 (2d ed.1991).

14. See A.F.L. Falck, S.p.A. v. E.A. Karay Co., 722 F.Supp. 12 (S.D. N.Y.1989)(pleading can satisfy notice requirement).

15. The Advisory Committee's Note to Federal Rule 1004(3) states:

A party who has an original in his control has no need for the protection of the rule if put on notice that proof of contents will be made. He can ward off secondary evidence by offering the original. The notice procedure here provided is not to be confused with orders to produce or other discovery procedures, as the purpose of the procedure under this rule is to afford the opposite party an opportunity to produce the original, not to compel him to do so.

16. If proponent could, for instance, establish that he mailed the original to his adversary he would succeed in his proof. See William Gardam & Son v. Batterson, 198 N.Y. 175, 91 N.E. 371 (1910)(here, however, proponent failed to establish the necessary proof as to office mailing practice).

§ 1004.1 BEST EVIDENCE Ch. 10

An older New York case holds that because a notice to produce may not properly be served on a criminal defendant for self-incrimination reasons, the prosecution may automatically rely upon secondary evidence of a document in defendant's possession.[17] Modern authorities, however, have stressed that a pretrial notice to produce has no actual self-incriminating impact on the defendant, meaning that a notice to produce can and should be served as a prerequisite to the prosecution's use of secondary evidence.[18]

d. Collateral Matters

Where, technically, the best evidence rule could be said to apply to certain proof, compliance with the rule may be excused where the writing is not of crucial importance. McCormick states that it is impossible neatly to categorize situations where a writing could be deemed collateral or unimportant,[19] but he provides a working concept:

> At nearly every turn in human affairs some writing—a letter, a bill of sale, a newspaper, a deed—plays a part. Consequently any narration by a witness is likely to include many references to transactions consisting partly of written communications or other writings. A witness to a confession, for example, identifies the date as being the day after the crime because he read of the crime in the newspaper that day, or a witness may state that he was unable to procure a certain article because it was patented. It is apparent that it is impracticable to forbid such references except upon condition that the writings (e.g., the newspaper and the patent) be produced in court. Recognition of an exception exempting "collateral writings" from the operation of the basic rule has followed as a necessary concession to expedition of trials and clearness of narration, interests which outweigh, in the case of merely incidental references to documents, the need for perfect exactitude in the presentation of these documents' contents.[20]

Thus, where it was proved that *A* had loaned *B* money by a written order to *C*, who owed *A* money, it was not necessary to produce the written order;[21] and where, in an action for nonpayment for publishing defendant's advertisement, plaintiff's witness could testify that he knew that the advertisement had been published, there was no need to produce the newspaper carrying the advertisement.[22] These cases overlap those in which it was found unnecessary to apply the best evidence

---

17. People v. Gibson, 218 N.Y. 70, 112 N.E. 730 (1916).

18. McCormick § 239, at 81–82; Comment, Proposed N.Y. Evidence Code § 1104(c).

19. McCormick § 234, at 70.

20. Id. at 69.

21. Daniels v. Smith, 130 N.Y. 696, 698, 29 N.E. 1098, 1099 (1892). It was stated: "In view, therefore, of the temporary nature of the order, the length of time since its use, the fact that it had long before accomplished its purpose and its collateral character, parol evidence characterizing the writing and stating the amount for which it was drawn was admissible." Id. at 698, 29 N.E. at 1099.

22. Foster-Holcomb Inv. Co. v. Little Rock Pub. Co., 151 Ark. 449, 451–52, 236 S.W. 597, 598 (1922).

rule either because the existence of the writing was the only thing in issue or for other reasons the contents of the writing were not in issue.[23]

Library References:

West's Key No. Digests, Criminal Law ⊃398–404; Evidence ⊃157–187.

1005 Public Records

§ 1005.1 New York and Federal

a. New York

In New York, CPLR 4540 and 4542 provide for the authentication of domestic and foreign official documents respectively.[1] These authentication procedures are discussed in § 901.7 *supra*. There is no separate best evidence provision governing public records, but it has been held that satisfaction of these CPLR provisions would satisfy the best evidence rule as well.[2] The proposed New York Evidence Code provides separate best evidence authorization under proposed section 1005.[3]

Other separate provisions for the admission of certified copies of public records are noted in the Comment to proposed New York Evidence Code § 1005.[4]

---

23. See Wolper v. New York Water Service Corp., 276 App.Div.1106, 1107, 96 N.Y.S.2d 647, 649 (2d Dep't 1950), where it was stated: "The Trial Justice erroneously ruled that the customer of plaintiffs could not testify as to ownership of bonds or real property without the production of the bonds or deeds. The terms of the bonds or deeds were not in issue." Id. at 1107, 96 N.Y.S.2d at 649. See also the cases discussed in § 1001.1 at notes 2, 13 and 14.

§ 1005.1

1. CPLR 4540(a)–(c) provides for the self-authentication (and therefore admission) of public documents by certified copies issued by officials in New York or other jurisdictions (where an additional attestation must be made that the official is who he purports to be). Subdivision (d) of CPLR 4540 allows the admission of uncertified printed copies of tariffs if imprinted with a Public Service Commission or Interstate Commerce Commission number.

CPLR 4542 provides for a somewhat more complicated process for the authentication of public records from foreign countries.

The admissibility of the contents of public documents as an exception to the hearsay rule is discussed in §§ 803(5).1 and 803(5).2, supra.

2. Chanler v. Manocherian, 151 A.D.2d 432, 435, 543 N.Y.S.2d 671, 673 (1st Dep't 1989)(in personal injury action against general contractor it was error for trial judge to refuse to admit certified copy of defendant's construction permit since "CPLR 4540(a), in effect, excepts official records from the mandates of the best evidence rule (see also, CPLR 4518[c])").

3. § 1005. Public Records [PROPOSED]

The contents of a record, report, or other writing or data compilation produced by a public office or authorized by statute to be recorded or filed and actually recorded or filed in a public office may be proved by a copy that is certified as correct in accordance with the provisions of paragraph four of subdivision (a) of section 902 of this chapter, or testified to be correct by a witness who has compared it with the original, or authenticated in any manner prescribed by statute. If a copy complying with the foregoing cannot be obtained by the exercise of reasonable diligence, other evidence of the contents may be admitted.

4. The Comment cites Banking Law § 11(3)(b)(reports required by the Superintendent); Education Law §§ 106, 312 (papers under seal; Commissioner's papers in review proceedings under seal); and General Municipal Law § 51–a(2)(certified copies of records kept by municipal departments—REPEALED, L.1987, c.737, § 5). Illustrative of other statutes which excuse production of the original are: Banking Law § 256 (photocopies of bank records); County Law § 208(5)(should be § 208(1)—certified copies of records which have become unfit for

825

§ 1005.1   BEST EVIDENCE   Ch. 10

The reason public records are given special treatment is that such documents should not be removed from the public offices, nor should custodial employees be constantly called to court to authenticate them.[5]

What is a public record? Generally, a public record is a document kept in a local, state or federal office which pertains to the regular business of that office, whether it relates to reports made by public employees in the course of their duties, or records such as deeds, mortgages and birth certificates which are recorded in the public office.[6] As regards such "private" recorded documents, either the certified copy from the public office[7] or, of course, the original which would have been returned after recordation, would be considered "originals."

b. Federal

Federal Rule of Evidence 1005 provides:

> The contents of an official record, or of a document authorized to be recorded or filed and actually recorded or filed, including data compilations in any form, if otherwise admissible, may be proved by copy, certified as correct in accordance with rule 902 or testified to be correct by a witness who has compared it with the original. If a copy which complies with the foregoing cannot be obtained by the exercise of reasonable diligence, then other evidence of the contents may be given.

Note that this is the one instance where a hierarchy of secondary evidence is provided for, i.e., unless there is no way to obtain with due diligence a certified or compared copy, other evidence of what the record contains may not be admitted.

Not every document kept in a public office is a public record under

---

public inspection); General Business Law § 394–a (where negotiable instrument lost while in possession of creditor, contents may be proved by parol or other secondary evidence); Indian Law § 71 (certified copies of leases granted by Senecas); Public Lands Law § 5 (certified copies of letters patent); Public Services Law § 17 (certified copies of all official documents of Public Service Commission); Real Property Law § 399 (certificate of title, and any certified copy); and Transportation Law §§ 69, 88 (reproduction of records of Utica Transit Authority).

It is also noted in the comment to proposed § 1002 that copies of public records are admissible for proof of their contents when the procedures in 28 U.S.C.A. §§ 1739 and 1740 are complied with. Section 1739 requires that the records be duly certified by the custodian together with certification by a judge or governor or secretary of state that the custodian's certification is in proper form. This provides a means whereby the official records of one state may be authenticated for use in the court of another state. Section 1740 provides that authenticated copies of official documents kept in United States consulates are admissible as originals. The comment points out that public records would also be admissible pursuant to CPLR 4540 and 4542.

5. McCormick § 240, at 82.

6. One of CPLR 4540's predecessor statutes, Civil Practice Act § 382, specifically authorized admissibility of a certified copy of any paper filed or recorded "pursuant to law in a public office of the state," and it seems to be assumed that this is carried into CPLR 4540 although that specific provision has been dropped from the language of the statute.

7. Sudlow v. Warshing, 108 N.Y. 520, 522, 15 N.E. 532, 533–34 (1887) ("The rule * * * as sanctioned by the statutory enactment, is to allow a deed, which has been recorded, to be read as presumptive evidence of the truth of the record itself and of the fact of the conveyance of the title.")

826

the rule. In *Amoco Production Co. v. United States*[8] the Tenth Circuit pointed out in a quiet title action concerning a deed given by the United States to plaintiffs years earlier that a file copy of the deed kept by the government in its working file was not a public record. The copy of the deed recorded and kept in the county recorder's office would be the public record.[9] Had a certified copy of the deed recorded in the county office not been procurable (the original was lost, but the recorded version was in evidence) the government's file copy may have qualified as secondary evidence under Federal Rule 1004. The circuit court reasoned that the file copy should come in anyway since there was a genuine issue as to whether the government had retained mineral rights, and the original deed had manually been recorded in the county office by typewriting. This case is a good illustration that the literal provisions of Rule 1005 can be circumvented when the issues require more certitude. The document at issue here was the original deed and whether or not it contained a mineral reservation clause. The recorded version might well have lacked the clause through inadvertence of the typist.

Otherwise the public document rule has been administered routinely. Even before the advent of Rule 1005 the Second Circuit allowed copies of foreign census records,[10] foreign country marriage records,[11] and letters required by law to be kept in the files of the Navy Department in Washington, D.C.[12]

Library References:

West's Key No. Digests, Criminal Law ⚖︎398–404; Evidence ⚖︎157–187.

1006 Summaries

§ 1006.1 Summaries—New York and Federal

Federal Rule of Evidence 1006 provides:

> The contents of voluminous writings, recordings, or photographs which cannot conveniently be examined in court may be presented in the form of a chart, summary, or calculation. The originals, or duplicates, shall be made available for examination or copying, or both, by other parties at reasonable time and place. The court may order that they be produced in court.

The proposed New York Evidence Code provides the same exception

---

8. 619 F.2d 1383, 1390–91 (10th Cir. 1980).

9. Id. at 1391 note 7.

10. United States v. Ghaloub, 385 F.2d 567, 571 (2d Cir.1966) (authenticity of defendant's United States birth certificate belied by census records from Syria properly authenticated under then existing federal rules).

11. United States v. D'Agostino, 338 F.2d 490, 492 (2d Cir.1964)(in denaturalization proceeding foreign marriage documents admissible).

12. Cohn v. United States, 258 Fed. 355, 362 (2d Cir.1919)(documents used as evidence in naval court marshal, and required by statute to be transmitted to Navy Department and kept on file for two years, are "official records" while so kept, and authenticated copies may be admitted in evidence).

to the best evidence rule and adds a notice requirement.[1]

a. New York

The summaries exception currently is governed by case law which, to the extent it has been developed, is in accord with the code versions. Also known as the "voluminous writings" rule, the exception simply recognizes the practical inconvenience of requiring the production in court of a large number of records (usually business records) where a summary of their content would serve the proof requirement just as well, and the party against whom the summaries are offered has an adequate opportunity to inspect the originals upon which the summary is based.[2] The trial judge must decide whether the original batch of records would be too cumbersome to introduce into evidence.[3]

Modern approval for the use of summaries, and also of computer printouts which comprise the summary, can be found in the Court of Appeals' decision in *Ed Guth Realty, Inc. v. Gingold*.[4] The holding was without elaboration,[5] so the case is not particularly helpful in fleshing out details of the rule.

Instructive is the opinion in *People v. Weinberg*,[6] where defendants, who operated a clinic, were tried for submitting bogus Medicaid bills for payment. The false bills were made up by hand, and then sent to a computer service named Dataline where they were placed on magnetic tape. Later, the original false bills were entered directly into a computer at the clinic from which they were transmitted directly to Dataline's computer. At trial, a Dataline employee produced computer printouts to establish the false bills presented between 1984 and 1987. The court first held these printouts to be admissible under CPLR 4518(a) (business records exception) and, further, that they came within the voluminous writings exception to the best evidence rule. Prior to trial defendants

---

§ 1006.1

1. § 1006. Summaries [PROPOSED]

The contents of voluminous writings, recordings, or photographs which cannot conveniently be examined in court may be presented in the form of a chart, summary, or calculation. The proponent of such evidence shall make known to all parties the proponent's intention to offer the evidence and its particulars sufficiently in advance of offering it to provide them with a fair opportunity to meet it. To remedy the failure of the proponent to give notice, the court, pursuant to section 107 of this chapter, shall make any order the interests of justice require. The originals or duplicates shall be made available for examination or copying, or both, by other parties at a reasonable time and place. The court may order that they be produced in court.

2. McCormick § 233, at 67–68.

3. See Von Sachs v. Kretz, 72 N.Y. 548, 552, 10 Hun. 95 (1878)("It would not have been error for the referee to have allowed a witness, with the books before him, to give a summary of their contents; but this was a question of convenience simply, and a matter within his discretion.").

4. 34 N.Y.2d 440, 358 N.Y.S.2d 367, 315 N.E.2d 441, (1974).

5. The court, after finding computer printouts were admissible under the business records rule (citing Federal Rule of Evidence 803(6)), stated: "nowhere in the present case * * * did the city challenge the routineness of this data storage. As for the best evidence rule, the 'voluminous writings' exception to that rule would apply. That permits the admission of summaries of voluminous records or entries where, if requested, the party against whom it is offered can have access to the original data." 34 N.Y.2d at 451–52, 358 N.Y.S.2d at 373–74, 315 N.E.2d at 445.

6. 183 A.D.2d 932, 933–34, 586 N.Y.S.2d 132, 134–35 (2d Dep't 1992).

were provided copies of Dataline's tapes and given permission to hire, at state expense, an expert to examine the tapes. The fact the summaries were produced for use at trial after the criminal proceedings were commenced was held to be of no consequence to admissibility.[7]

In *Briar Hill Apts. v. Teperman*,[8] the presentation of computer summaries went smoothly because they were accompanied by the testimony of an employee under the business records rule. This was a holdover proceeding where the defendant claimed he lived in a rent-stabilized apartment. Plaintiff produced Consolidated Edison's senior customer service representative along with the printouts which showed that defendant could not have been living in the apartment since there had been no electricity consumption during the time in question.[9]

It will be noted that there is always the threshold question in these cases whether the underlying data qualifies for admission as a hearsay exception, usually under the business records exception or the public documents exception.

In applying the voluminous writings exception to the best evidence rule, New York courts likely will be guided by Federal Rule 1006 and the cases noted in subdivision b *infra*. Certainly, when summaries are contemplated as evidence, it would be wise to notify the adversary so that there can be no complaint of an insufficient opportunity to prepare to meet the evidence.[10]

A summary of voluminous records that cannot conveniently be examined in court must be distinguished from a summary, chart or schedule that is used to illustrate documentary exhibits that have been admitted in evidence. The former type of summary is substantive evidence and is subject to special foundation requirements as a discretionary exception to the best evidence rule: the originals are voluminous, introducing them in evidence would be inconvenient, and the adversary has a right of inspection. A summary of admitted evidence, on the other hand, is a form of demonstrative evidence. As discussed in § 1103.1 *infra*, the foundation requires a showing that the summary, chart or schedule is a fair representation of testimony or documents in evidence, and the court must determine that the summary will assist the jury in determining the issues.[11]

b. Federal

Summaries of voluminous documents are admissible as long as the underlying material would be admissible.[12] Any hearsay objection re-

---

7. Id. at 934, 586 N.Y.S.2d at 134–35.

8. 165 A.D.2d 519, 568 N.Y.S.2d 50 (1st Dep't 1991).

9. Id. at 521–22, 568 N.Y.S.2d at 51–52.

10. Very probably the underlying data will have been examined under the discovery process, but the creation of the summary will occasion further reasons for inspection and comparison. In People v. Weinberg, supra notes 6 and 7, the fact of pretrial notification was mentioned in the opinion. 183 A.D.2d at 934, 586 N.Y.S.2d at 134.

11. See, e.g., Public Operating Corp. v. Weingart, 257 App.Div. 379, 13 N.Y.S.2d 182 (1st Dep't 1939). See also § 1103.1, at note 6, infra.

12. Tamarin v. Adam Caterers, Inc., 13 F.3d 51, 53 (2d Cir.1993) (accountant's summary and projection of employer's pay-

§ 1006.1　　　　　BEST EVIDENCE　　　　　Ch. 10

garding summary evidence requires a finding that the underlying evidence would be admissible.[13] The production of a summary for the purposes of trial therefore does not eliminate the need to scrutinize the character of the underlying data.

Summaries of documents must be based on adequate foundation testimony. In *Fagiola v. National Gypsum Co. AC & S, Inc.*,[14] suit was brought to recover for death alleged to have been caused by asbestos exposure from products manufactured by defendants. Defendants' position was that their products had not been used at deceased's place of employment. To prove this, defendants submitted a summary compiled by their witness, Jackson, who testified that the underlying business documents showed no sales by defendants to deceased's employer. The documents were not complete and the witness had to make some projections. Many of the underlying documents had also been admitted in evidence. The Second Circuit held the summary admissible. Jackson's methods were explained, he was available for cross-examination, the underlying documents had been the object of discovery, and many were in evidence.[15]

Perhaps the most difficult part of applying Rule 1006 is determining whether the summary is being used as substantive evidence or simply to illustrate other evidence that is independently in the record. The latter type of summary is a form of demonstrative evidence, which as discussed in § 1103.2 *infra*, is governed by separate foundation requirements. In *Gomez v. Great Lakes Steel Div., Nat. Steel Corp.*[16] it was stated:

> Contents of charts or summaries admitted as evidence under Rule 1006 must fairly represent and be taken from underlying documentary proof which is too voluminous for convenient in-court examination, and they must be accurate and nonprejudicial. * * * Such summaries or charts admitted *as evidence* under Rule 1006 are to be distinguished from summaries or charts used as pedagogical devices which organize or aid the jury's examination of testimony or documents which are them-

roll record [a business record] sufficient to support summary judgment for unpaid ERISA benefits to union vacation fund where employer failed to produce any evidence on the motion creating a question of fact); United States v. Conlin, 551 F.2d 534, 538 (2d Cir.), cert. denied, 434 U.S. 831, 98 S.Ct. 114, 54 L.Ed.2d 91 (1977)(the summary was of the testimony of witnesses who had already testified).

Calling it "secondary evidence," Judge Learned Hand fully approved the admission of a summary of sales of sheet music since "to produce the books themselves would have been cumbersome and dilatory, and Fox consented to let the plaintiffs examine them at length in his office." Pallma v. Fox, 182 F.2d 895, 902 (2d Cir.1950). See also United States v. Mortimer, 118 F.2d 266, 269 (2d Cir.1941), where Judge Clark approved admission of charts made up from tax records for the purpose of showing defaults in the payment of taxes. The procurement of the tax books or even certified copies "would have been a practical impossibility," and "the records themselves, in official custody, were equally open to inspection by the defense." Id. at 269.

13. See, e.g., United States v. Johnson, 594 F.2d 1253, 1255 (9th Cir.1979), cert. denied, 444 U.S. 964, 100 S.Ct. 451, 62 L.Ed.2d 376 (1979)(underlying data consisting of records seized by the government were not supported as business records and hence the document purporting to summarize them was inadmissible).

14. 906 F.2d 53 (2d Cir.1990).

15. Id. at 57.

16. 803 F.2d 250, 257 (6th Cir.1986).

830

selves admitted into evidence. * * * Such pedagogical devices "are more akin to argument than evidence * * *. Quite often they are used on summation.". Generally, such a summary is, and should be, accompanied by a limiting instruction which informs the jury of the summary's purpose and that it does not itself constitute evidence.[17]

Thus, if the summary is actually the evidentiary equivalent of underlying admissible documentation it becomes the evidence and should go to the jury room.[18] The trial court can allow the parties to use charts or other visual aids that summarize or organize testimony or documents already in evidence, "but charts of this nature are not themselves evidence and, absent the consent of all parties, they should not be sent to the juryroom with the other exhibits."[19]

However, it cannot be taken from this authority that in all cases where documents or testimony are already in evidence that summarizations cannot also be considered evidence. In *United States v. Pinto*[20] the Second Circuit allowed summaries as evidence when "[t]he ten-week trial in this case involved numerous witnesses and voluminous evidence, including references to 66 wiretaps of telephone calls placed to some 35 telephone numbers."[21] The summaries included the names of participants in the telephone conversations, addresses and telephone numbers. The trial judge had admonished the jury that they had to determine whether the charts accurately reflected the evidence presented. The Second Circuit held that the admissibility of such summaries of evidence otherwise admitted was within the trial judge's discretion,[22] and the Seventh Circuit has held similarly.[23]

---

17. Id. at 257–58 (emphasis in original). In this case plaintiff presented for the first time at trial a "summary of actual damages" which the trial court erroneously admitted into evidence along with other primary evidence going to the question of damages. See also § 1103.2, at note 1, infra.

18. Pierce v. Ramsey Winch Co., 753 F.2d 416, 431 (5th Cir.1985).

19. Id. at 431. In this case charts organizing sales data were prepared during the trial and were held to be pedagogical devices by the court.

See also United States v. Wood, 943 F.2d 1048, 1053 (9th Cir.1991)(chart filled in by defense counsel during trial outlining his version of correct tax calculations not admissible as evidence).

20. 850 F.2d 927, 935 (2d Cir.), cert. denied, 488 U.S. 867, 109 S.Ct. 174, 102 L.Ed.2d 143 (1988).

21. 850 F.2d at 935.

22. Id.

23. United States v. Howard, 774 F.2d 838, 844 (7th Cir.1985). Here the court allowed the government to summarize all the evidence of forged ballot applications by using charts. The court had no trouble approving the admission of the charts as within the trial judge's discretion. A footnote is appended which draws the distinction between charts used merely as pedagogical devices and charts as evidence:

4. The defendants argue that the chart was inadmissible under Fed.R.Evid. 1006, which allows the admission of charts summarizing the contents of "voluminous writings, recordings, or photographs that cannot conveniently be examined in court." Regardless of whether the chart fell within the precise confines of this Rule, the trial court nevertheless had discretion to permit the government to use it as a "pedagogical device [] to summarize or organize testimony or documents which have themselves been admitted in evidence." 5 Weinstein's Evidence ¶ 1006[07], at 1006–15 (1983). We note, however, that when a trial court authorizes the use of such charts as a teaching device rather than as substantive evidence under Rule 1006, the preferred practice would be for the court to give a limiting instruction regarding this pur-

§ 1006.1   BEST EVIDENCE   Ch. 10

The Second Circuit's decision in *Pinto* is tempered by other holdings from that court drawing clear distinctions between charts as mere aids, and charts as evidence.[24] If a generalization can be drawn from these somewhat hazy edicts it would be this: Properly drawn and supported summaries of underlying data not in evidence because of volume and complexity can be considered evidence and admitted as such pursuant to Rule 1006. Summaries which are abstracts of voluminous underlying data, some or all of which are in evidence, but too complex to be examined and understood by the jury, in the court's discretion can be considered evidence and admitted as such provided the adversary has ample opportunity to inspect both the data and the summary. Summaries which are used as pedagogical aids to help the jury in understanding the voluminous or complex underlying data otherwise in evidence should not be accorded the status of evidence, and the jury should be so instructed. The distinction between the last two categories is vague, and the correct handling of the summaries in such cases must be determined on a case-to-case basis.

The summary rule is not confined to written data; it has been applied to allow a composite tape recording of numerous underlying tapes.[25]

Sometimes attempts are made to use Rule 1006 for the purpose of excluding testimony on the pretext that the testimony is based on underlying data that cannot be checked.[26]

Library References:

West's Key No. Digests, Criminal Law ⚖︎398–404; Evidence ⚖︎157–187.

pose. Id. at 1006-15 to 1006-16. Accord, United States v. Scales, 594 F.2d 558, 563–64 (6th Cir.), cert. denied, 441 U.S. 946, 99 S.Ct. 2168, 60 L.Ed.2d 1049 (1979).

774 F.2d at 844.

24. United States v. Conlin, 551 F.2d 534, 538 (2d Cir.), cert. denied, 434 U.S. 831, 98 S.Ct. 114, 54 L.Ed.2d 91 (1977). Here the government prepared a chart summarizing the testimony of defendant's taxpayer clients. Defense counsel had ample opportunity to examine it, and it seems to have been "received in evidence." Copies of the exhibit were distributed to the jury "to assist them in following the testimony of the witnesses." A mistake in the exhibit rendered it prejudicial, but not so prejudicial as to cause a reversal. It is difficult to discern whether or not the trial judge's instruction that the exhibit had no independent evidentiary value was agreed with.

But, in United States v. Nathan, 536 F.2d 988 (2d Cir.1976), cert. denied, 429 U.S. 930, 97 S.Ct. 337, 50 L.Ed.2d 300 (1976), there seems to be a clear expression that a trial chart summarizing other evidence has no independent evidentiary value and that juries should be so instructed.

25. See United States v. Nunez, 658 F.Supp. 828, 838 (D.Colo.1987), aff'd, 877 F.2d 1470 (10th Cir.), cert. denied, 493 U.S. 981, 110 S.Ct. 513, 107 L.Ed.2d 515 (1989)("Since evidence in this case includes approximately 112 tape recordings, I will allow composite tapes to be presented at trial provided they are representative and in proper context.").

26. See, e.g., Accent Designs, Inc. v. Jan Jewelry Designs, Inc., 827 F.Supp. 957, 970–71 (S.D.N.Y.1993). In this patent infringement case defendants sought to preclude plaintiff's testimony as a summary of underlying data, but there was no evidence that there were any documents or that any documents had been destroyed. This was unlike another case, Square Liner 360°, Inc. v. Chisum, 691 F.2d 362 (8th Cir.1982), discussed by the Accent Designs court, where the witness' testimony was based on documents and where the testimony "relating to such documentation" would be unfair. The Accent Designs court said that Rule 1006 and the Square Liner holding were "inapposite." "This is not the sort of situation Rule 1006 was designed to address." Evidently the witness in Accent Designs had direct knowledge of that about which he testified and was not, in fact,

832

1007 Testimony or Written Admission of Party

§ 1007.1 Admission as to Genuineness—New York and Federal

Federal Rule of Evidence 1007 provides:

> Contents of writings, recordings, or photographs may be proved by the testimony or deposition of the party against whom offered or by the party's written admission, without accounting for the nonproduction of the original.

Proposed New York Evidence Code § 1007, which is identical to the Federal Rule, apparently restates current practice.[1]

The testimony referred to need not be restricted to testimony given at the time the evidence is offered, but may have been given at any prior hearing or proceeding at which the party testified under oath.[2]

The only cautionary note to this clear and unlitigated provision is the observance of its limitation to written or testimonial provisions. This limitation devolves from Professor McCormick's disagreement with an 1840 English case[3] which held that oral admissions would be sufficient to trigger this exception to the best evidence rule. "Upon reflection," says McCormick, "it will be seen that Baron Parke's decision squares rather poorly with the primary modern day policy in favor of obtaining the contents of writings with accuracy."[4]

Certainly the admissibility of documentary evidence, whether the original or a duplicate, or even secondary evidence, can be stipulated to by the parties; and where there can be no genuine controversy concerning the accuracy of the document it would seem that the proponent could serve a notice to admit under the auspices of CPLR 3123 or Federal Rule of Civil Procedure 36.[5]

relying on or summarizing underlying documents.

§ 1007.1

1. See comment to the proposed New York Evidence Code § 1007.

2. The comment to the proposed New York Evidence Code states this explicitly. The Advisory Committee's Note to Federal Rule 1007 refers to McCormick's edict that the admissions exception to the best evidence rule ought to be limited to those admissions made in the course of giving testimony or in writing. Reference to McCormick discloses that the contemplated testimony would be given "in this or some other trial or hearing." McCormick § 242, at 86.

3. Slatterie v. Pooley, 6 M. & W. 665, 151 Eng.Rep. 579 (Exch.1840).

4. McCormick § 242, at 85–86. Should the original of the subject document be unobtainable, the oral admission would be considered secondary evidence and admissible as such under Rule 1004, or Rule 1005 were the document a public record. Cociancich v. Vazzoler, 48 App.Div. 462, 467, 62 N.Y.S. 893, 894–95 (2d Dep't 1900)(in this case the court noted that New York law was not in accord with Slatterie v. Pooley).

5. The purpose of a notice to admit is not to obtain discovery of documents, but only to eliminate from contention matters that are not in dispute. Johantgen v. Hobart Mfg. Co., 64 A.D.2d 858, 859–60, 407 N.Y.S.2d 355, 357 (4th Dep't 1978).

1008 Functions of Court and Jury

§ 1008.1 Functions of Court and Jury

a. New York

It seems relatively clear in New York that most preliminary fact questions relating to the application of the best evidence rule are to be decided solely by the trial judge. The Court of Appeals, for example, recently stated that "secondary evidence of the contents of an unproduced original may be admitted upon threshold factual findings by the trial court that the proponent of the substitute has sufficiently explained the unavailability of the primary evidence * * * and has not procured its loss or destruction in bad faith."[1] Two nineteenth-century cases likewise held that such matters present questions of fact for the trial judge.[2] By analogy, other foundation questions relating to the admissibility of secondary evidence are exclusively for the court, such as whether a duplicate photocopy was made in the regular course of business, whether an original was in the possession of a party who received sufficient notice to produce it and whether original documents are so voluminous as to justify the use of summaries.[3]

As to the accuracy of the secondary evidence, the Court of Appeals has explained the allocation of fact-finding between judge and jury as follows:

> [T]he proponent of such derivative proof has the heavy burden of establishing, preliminarily to the court's satisfaction, that it is a reliable and accurate portrayal of the original. Thus, as a threshold matter, the trial court must be satisfied that the proffered evidence is authentic and "correctly reflects the contents of the original" before ruling on its admissibility * * *. For example, when oral testimony is received to establish the contents of an unavailable writing, the proponent of that proof must establish that the witness is able to recount or recite, from

---

§ 1008.1

1. Schozer v. William Penn Life Ins. Co., 84 N.Y.2d 639, 644, 620 N.Y.S.2d 797, 799, 644 N.E.2d 1353, 1355 (1994).

2. Kearney v. The Mayor, Aldermen and Commonality of the City of New York, 92 N.Y. 617, 620 (1883)(whether proponent of oral testimony concerning contents of writing had lost writing and diligently tried to find it "presented a question to be determined by [the trial judge] as matter of fact"); Mason v. Libbey, 90 N.Y. 683, 685 (1882)(where letters allegedly had been destroyed in good faith, "the sufficiency of the explanation presented a question of fact for the trial judge").

3. The comment to proposed New York Evidence Code § 1008 (note 5 infra) gives the following examples:

> Thus, the court should decide * * * such issues as: (1) whether a given writing, recording or photograph is an "original"; (2) whether a given writing, recording or photograph is a "duplicate"; (3) whether a genuine question is raised as to the authenticity of the original for purposes of CE 1003; (4) whether it would be unfair to admit a duplicate as provided for in CE 1003; (5) whether an original is lost or destroyed; (6) whether the proponent lost or destroyed an original in bad faith; (7) whether an original can be reasonably obtained; (8) whether proper notice was given to a party in control of an original; (9) whether the writing, recording or photograph goes to a collateral matter or to a controlling issue; and (10) whether a certified copy of a public record is obtainable by the exercise of reasonable diligence.

personal knowledge, "substantially and with reasonable accuracy" all of its contents * * *. Once a sufficient foundation for admission is presented, the secondary evidence is "subject to an attack by the opposing party not as to admissibility but to the weight to be given the evidence, with [the] final determination left to the trier of fact" * * *.[4]

Section 1008 of the proposed New York Evidence Code adopts essentially the same approach as that of the caselaw.[5]

b. Federal

Federal Rule of Evidence 1008 provides:

When the admissibility of other evidence of contents of writings, recording, or photographs under these rules depends upon the fulfillment of a condition of fact, the question whether the condition has been fulfilled is ordinarily for the court to determine in accordance with the provisions of rule 104. However, when an issue is raised (a) whether the asserted writing ever existed, or (b) whether another writing, recording, or photograph produced at the trial is the original, or (c) whether other evidence of contents correctly reflects the contents, the issue is for the trier of fact to determine as in the case of other issues of fact.

A leading federal case decided under Rule 1008 is *Seiler v. Lucasfilm, Ltd.*,[6] a copyright infringement action where plaintiff Seiler, because he had no originals of the drawings he alleged had been copied, sought to introduce secondary evidence in the form of reconstructions. The trial judge determined after a lengthy hearing that the best evidence rule applied, and that plaintiff had lost or destroyed the originals in bad faith. Plaintiff's case was thus dismissed on a motion for summary

---

4. Schozer v. William Penn Life Ins. Co., 84 N.Y.2d 639, 645–46, 620 N.Y.S.2d 797, 800, 644 N.E.2d 1353, 1356 (1994)(quoting, inter alia, United States v. Gerhart, 538 F.2d 807, 809 (8th Cir.1976)).

5. The proposed state provision is as follows:

§ 1008. Functions of court and jury [PROPOSED]

Whenever the admissibility of other evidence of contents of writings, recordings, or photographs depends upon the fulfillment of a condition of fact, the question whether the condition has been fulfilled is ordinarily for the court to determine in accordance with the provisions of subdivision (b) of section 104 of this chapter. However, when an issue is raised whether (a) the asserted writing ever existed, or (b) another writing, recording, or photograph produced at the trial, proceeding, or hearing is the original, or (c) other evidence of contents correctly reflects the contents, the issue is for the trier of fact to determine in accordance with the provisions of subdivision (a) of section 104 of this chapter.

As explained in the comment to proposed § 1008, the three exceptions to the court's exclusive fact-finding responsibility—(a) whether the writing ever existed, (b) whether another writing is the original, and (c) whether the secondary evidence accurately portrays the original—should be treated as matters of conditional relevancy. See §§ 104.1 and 104.2 supra. Thus, as to the three exceptions, the comment states that "the court determines only whether there is sufficient evidence to support a finding [by the jury] of the fulfillment of the condition of fact." This appears to be consistent with the approach endorsed by the Schozer court. See quotation in text at note 4 supra. See also note 10 infra.

6. 808 F.2d 1316 (9th Cir.1986), cert. denied, 484 U.S. 826, 108 S.Ct. 92, 98 L.Ed.2d 53 (1987).

judgment. Plaintiff argued that under Rule 1008 a question remained for the jury whether the reconstructions correctly reflected the content of the originals. Plaintiff, however, confused the threshold question of admissibility of the reconstructions with the weight that should be given them if they were admitted.[7] It was stated:

> In the instant case, the condition of fact which Seiler needed to prove was that the originals were not lost or destroyed in bad faith. Had he been able to prove this, his reconstructions would have been admissible and then their accuracy would have been a question for the jury.[8]

As under New York law, therefore, the judge alone decides preliminary fact questions relating to the foundation for the admissibility of secondary evidence.[9] The jury becomes a participant in the fact-finding process only as to the ultimate issue of the accuracy of the secondary evidence. On that question, the judge's task is to determine whether the proponent has introduced sufficient evidence "so that a 'reasonable juror could be convinced' that the secondary evidence correctly reflects the contents of the original."[10]

Library References:

West's Key No. Digests, Criminal Law ⊙=398–404; Evidence ⊙=187.

---

7. Id. at 1321.

8. Id.

9. See text at notes 1–3 supra. Relevant pre-Rules federal cases include United States v. Jacobs, 475 F.2d 270, 285 n.31 (2d Cir.), cert. denied, 414 U.S. 821, 94 S.Ct. 116, 38 L.Ed.2d 53 (1973)(although the trial judge mistakenly gave the jury the question whether the originals had intentionally been destroyed, there had been no objection and the error, in effect, gave appellant a "second bite at the apple" so there could have been no prejudice); Sylvania Electronics Products, Inc. v. Flanagan, 352 F.2d 1005, 1008 (1st Cir.1965)(trial judge must make preliminary finding concerning circumstances surrounding loss of original).

10. United States v. Gerhart, 538 F.2d 807, 809 (8th Cir.1976).

The same judge-jury allocation of responsibility also applies to a question that may lie at the heart of the merits of the controversy, namely, whether the original writing ever existed. Fed.R.Evid. 1008(a). The Advisory Committee's Note to Rule 1008 explains: "[P]laintiff offers secondary evidence of the contents of an alleged contract, after first introducing evidence of loss of the original, and defendant counters with evidence that no such contract was ever executed." The issue goes to the jury because "[i]f the judge decides that the contract was never executed and excludes the secondary evidence, the case is at an end without ever going to the jury on a central issue." The jury also decides which of two documents is the original if such an issue arises. Fed.R.Evid. 1008(b).

CHAPTER 11

REAL AND DEMONSTRATIVE EVIDENCE

Table of Sections

1100 INTRODUCTION
1100.1 Real and Demonstrative Evidence, In General: New York and Federal.

1101 TANGIBLE OBJECTS
1101.1 New York.
1101.2 Federal.

1102 PERSONS: PHYSICAL FEATURES, INJURIES AND THEIR EFFECTS
1102.1 New York.
1102.2 Federal.

1103 DRAWINGS, DIAGRAMS AND MODELS
1103.1 New York.
1103.2 Federal.

1104 PHOTOGRAPHIC AND RELATED FORMS OF EVIDENCE
1104.1 New York.
    a. Photographs.
    b. X-rays and Analogous Medical Pictorial Processes.
    c. Sound Recordings.
    d. Motion Pictures and Videotapes.
1104.2 Federal.
    a. Photographs.
    b. X-rays.
    c. Sound Recordings.
    d. Motion Pictures and Videotapes.

1105 EXPERIMENTS AND DEMONSTRATIONS
1105.1 New York.
1105.2 Federal.

1106 COMPUTER–GENERATED GRAPHICS
1106.1 Computer–Generated Graphics: New York and Federal.

1107 JURY VIEWS
1107.1 New York.
1107.2 Federal.

1108 TAKING EXHIBITS INTO THE JURY ROOM; JURY EXPERIMENTATION
1108.1 New York.
1108.2 Federal.

1100 Introduction

§ 1100.1 Real and Demonstrative Evidence, In General: New York and Federal

The terms "real" and "demonstrative" evidence are often used interchangeably to describe physical evidence, animate or inanimate, that is exhibited to the fact-finder.[1] To the extent the terms are differentiated, "real evidence" most frequently refers to objects or persons that played an actual role in the litigated event, such as the alleged murder weapon or the personal injury plaintiff's scarred body.[2] In New York, sound recordings of original events, such as conversations among criminal conspirators, are also treated as a form of real evidence.[3] "Demonstrative evidence," on the other hand, most commonly refers to that which illustrates or demonstrates a witness' testimony about the occurrence in issue, such as a model of the human skeleton, a photograph of the accident scene, or a demonstration as to how an object works.[4] In either case, such evidence is intended to help the fact-finder better comprehend whether or how an event happened by appealing directly to the fact-finder's senses.[5] Rather than rely solely upon the testimony of a witness about her perception of something, the judge and jury look and listen for themselves.[6] "Seeing is believing," as the saying goes.[7]

From a practical perspective, the types and uses of real and demonstrative evidence are constrained only be the limits of counsel's creativity and the client's financial resources. From a legal perspective, the constraints are those of (1) relevance; (2) potential countervailing con-

---

§ 1100.1

1. Lilly § 13.1.

2. McCormick § 212, at 7–8. Writings, which might also fall within this definition, are treated in Chapter 9.

3. People v. McGee, 49 N.Y.2d 48, 59–60, 424 N.Y.S.2d 157, 163, 399 N.E.2d 1177, 1183 (1979), cert. denied sub nom. Waters v. New York, 446 U.S. 942, 100 S.Ct. 2166, 64 L.Ed.2d 797 (1980). See § 1101.1, at note 10, infra.

4. McCormick § 212, at 9. The McCormick treatise has no separate chapter or section entitled "real evidence"; all physical evidence is treated under the caption of "demonstrative evidence." See id. ch. 21. Terminology is not as important as the nature of the physical evidence and the particular purpose for which it is offered. These variables will determine the showing needed to establish relevance and authentication of the evidence.

5. Id. § 212, at 3. See People v. Acevedo, 40 N.Y.2d 701, 704, 389 N.Y.S.2d 811, 813, 358 N.E.2d 495, 497 (1976)(with demonstrative evidence, "judges and juries can themselves form perceptions through the direct use of their own senses").

6. See, e.g., King v. N.Y. Central & Hudson River R.R. Co., 72 N.Y. 607, 609 (1878)("[I]n this case, there was or was not something visible in the piece of iron which plaintiff's counsel called cross-cracks. The eyes of the jury were as good to see whether they were there, as the eyes of a witness, and the testimony of their eyes would be as satisfactory to them as that given by a witness.").

7. McCormick § 212, at 3.

siderations of undue prejudice, confusion, cumulativeness, time-consumption and the like; and (3) the need for proper authentication, or identification, of the evidence in question, which is usually referred to as laying the foundation. The first two requirements require a particularized application of the relevance/prejudice balancing discussed in Part 401 of this work. The foundation requirement carries forward the general principles of authentication discussed in § 900.1 of Chapter 9: There must be sufficient evidence that an item of evidence is what its proponent claims it to be. The reader is also referred to that section for the general rules governing burdens of proof and the allocation of responsibility between judge and jury in determining issues of authentication.

The admissibility of real and demonstrative evidence is governed for the most part by caselaw. Neither the Federal Rules of Evidence[8] nor the Proposed New York Evidence Code[9] contain any specific provisions on this form of evidence. Although issues of relevance, prejudice and authentication are present to a greater or lesser degree in virtually all proffers of physical evidence, they are best analyzed in the context of specific types of such evidence. The balance of this chapter therefore addresses particularized issues of admissibility associated with the principal generic forms of real and demonstrative evidence other than writings. Authentication issues concerning writings are covered in Chapter 9.[10]

Library References:

West's Key No. Digests, Criminal Law ⚖404.5–404.85; Evidence ⚖188–198.

1101 Tangible Objects

§ 1101.1 New York

As noted in the introduction, the term "real evidence" is frequently used to describe a tangible object that played an actual role in the occurrence that is the subject matter of the litigation. The object may be related to the issues either as direct or circumstantial evidence. A ripped and blood-stained jacket retrieved from the body of a homicide victim, for example, may show directly the physical results of multiple piercings of the fabric and circumstantially the type of instrument used,

---

8. The Advisory Committee's Note to Fed.R.Evid. 401 simply recognizes that "[c]harts, photographs, views of real estate, murder weapons" fall in the category of relevant evidence that can serve "as an aid to understanding." Fed.R.Evid. 901(a) simply specifies the general standard for authentication as "evidence sufficient to support a finding that the matter in question is what its proponent claims." See § 900.1 supra.

9. On the issue of authentication, the comment to § 901(b)(1) of the Proposed New York Evidence Code states simply that real and demonstrative evidence can be admitted on the basis of testimony by a witness with knowledge that the item in question is what it purports to be, such as the murder weapon found by the witness at the crime scene. "Fungible" items, such as drugs, can be authenticated pursuant to a chain of custody, as developed in the caselaw. See § 1101.1 infra.

10. See §§ 900.1–901.4 supra, and §§ 901.7–903.1, supra.

§ 1101.1   REAL & DEMONSTRATIVE EVIDENCE   Ch. 11

the manner in which the piercings occurred and the state of mind of the person who did it.[1]

The physical object, of course, must be relevant.[2] For example, on the issue whether defendant was the perpetrator of a crime, an object found near the crime scene[3] or in defendant's possession[4] must be sufficiently connected both to the crime and to the defendant in order to be probative of his identity.[5] As with all questions of relevance, there is no requirement that the particular piece of real evidence lead to only one inference.[6] Such dangers as unfair prejudice, undue cumulativeness or misleading the jury must be considered by a trial court in exercising discretion on the issue of admissibility; but assuming the feasibility of bringing the object into the courtroom, anything shown to have played a material role in the occurrence is likely to pass muster.[7] Whether a

§ 1101.1

1. Cf. People v. Pobliner, 32 N.Y.2d 356, 370, 345 N.Y.S.2d 482, 494, 298 N.E.2d 637, 646 (1973), cert. denied, 416 U.S. 905, 94 S.Ct. 1609, 40 L.Ed.2d 110 (1974)(photograph showing clustered bullet holes near homicide victim's left temple indicated "marksmanship and deliberateness in the killing").

2. Cf. People v. Julian, 41 N.Y.2d 340, 342, 392 N.Y.S.2d 610, 612, 360 N.E.2d 1310, 1312 (1977). ("To be admissible, any piece of real evidence must be shown to accurately portray a relevant and material element of the case."). See, e.g., Uss v. Town of Oyster Bay, 37 N.Y.2d 639, 376 N.Y.S.2d 449, 339 N.E.2d 147 (1975)(street sign that fell on plaintiff's head); People v. Benoit, 8 A.D.2d 626, 185 N.Y.S.2d 622 (2d Dep't 1959) (burglar's tools, found in defendant's possession, which he allegedly intended to use for commission of burglaries).

3. See, e.g., People v. Mirenda, 23 N.Y.2d 439, 452–54, 297 N.Y.S.2d 532, 541–43, 245 N.E.2d 194, 200–02 (1969)(sunglasses found near crime scene were "sufficiently connected with the defendants" to be relevant; accomplice testified that the glasses resembled ones he had once kept in his car, had offered to give to defendant on occasion prior to crime while defendant was in the car, and had later discovered were missing; "there were enough surrounding circumstances to permit the jury to infer that these glasses were actually the glasses which [the accomplice] offered [the defendant]"); People v. O'Bryan, 36 A.D.2d 548, 317 N.Y.S.2d 34 (3d Dep't 1971)(car jack handle found at site of attack on victim, nature of injuries, and absence of any jack in defendant's car at time of apprehension were sufficient to raise inference that defendant used the jack to perpetrate the crime).

4. See, e.g., People v. Neufeld, 165 N.Y. 43, 47, 58 N.E. 786, 788 (1900) (dark suit found in defendant's closet, although not directly shown to have been worn by defendant on day of crime, was said by witnesses to be similar to one worn by defendant on that day).

5. See People v. Mirenda, 23 N.Y.2d 439, 453, 297 N.Y.S.2d 532, 543, 245 N.E.2d 194, 201 (1969)(test for admissibility of object found at crime scene as circumstantial evidence that defendant was perpetrator requires "evaluation of how close is the connection between the object and the defendant. If it is not so tenuous as to be improbable, it is admissible as is any other evidence which is relevant to an issue in the prosecution.")

6. Id. ("The admission of this item into evidence is not dependent * * * upon a showing that the evidence adduced permits only one inference. * * * Though the glasses [found near the crime scene] were of a common variety the possibility that they were dropped in the roadway by someone other than the defendants was not so great as to make their introduction irrelevant."). See also cases cited in notes 3–4 supra. See generally § 401.1 supra.

7. See, e.g., People v. White, 211 A.D.2d 982, 986, 621 N.Y.S.2d 728, 732–33 (3d Dep't 1995), appeal denied, 85 N.Y.2d 944, 627 N.Y.S.2d 1006, 651 N.E.2d 931 (1995) (in rape prosecution, identification of rapist was based on DNA analysis of aborted fetus which defendant allegedly fathered; remains of fetal tissue were held properly admitted as exhibit to help confirm chain of custody relating to DNA evidence). See also People v. Singer, 300 N.Y. 120, 122, 89 N.E.2d 710, 710–11 (1949)(in prosecution for manslaughter arising from abortion, admission was upheld of mangled parts of fetus and organs of aborted woman).

It has been said that an item of real evidence may be introduced to give a full

tangible object that has been displayed to the jury may also be used in a courtroom experiment is governed by principles discussed in § 1105.1 *infra*.[8]

Assuming the relevance test is satisfied, a proper foundation must be laid for introduction of the exhibit into evidence: If offered as the actual object,[9] it must be authenticated as such through the testimony of one or more sponsoring witnesses. In *People v. McGee*,[10] the Court of Appeals summarized the authentication requirements as follows:

> In determining whether a proper foundation has been laid for the introduction of real evidence, the accuracy of the object itself is the focus of inquiry, which must be demonstrated by clear and convincing evidence * * *. Accuracy or authenticity is established by proof that the offered evidence is genuine and that there has been no tampering with it * * *. The foundation necessary to establish these elements may differ according to the nature of the evidence sought to be admitted. For instance, a chain of custody is employed when "the evidence itself is not patently identifiable or is capable of being replaced or altered" * * *. Mere identification by one familiar with the object, however, will be sufficient "when the object possesses unique characteristics or markings" and any material alteration would be readily apparent * * *.[11]

The foundation requirements thus vary depending on whether the object has unique characteristics that a witness can readily observe, or whether it is generic and fungible, making particularized recognition impossible. In either case, the requirement is twofold: identifying the object and accounting for its condition.

Examples of "unique" objects that have been admitted on the basis of a witness' in-court identification include a piece of cracked iron that was part of some broken machinery that caused the plaintiff's injuries;[12] an iron bar and rope that were used by a defendant in escaping from

---

picture or "background" of an event "as an aid to understanding" even if the matter is not actually disputed. Advisory Committee's Note, Fed.R.Evid. 401. In such case, however, potential undue prejudice or time consumption may weigh against admissibility. Id.

8. See also People v. Benoit, 8 A.D.2d 626, 185 N.Y.S.2d 622 (2d Dep't 1959)(in prosecution for possession of burglar's tools, display of tools found in defendant's possession was appropriate but prosecution's demonstration of use of tools to break open safes was prejudicial error; defendant conceded obvious capacity of the seized tools to perform such tasks, leaving as the only real issue for the jury his intent to use the tools for criminal purposes; demonstration of hypothetical safecracking crime was therefore unnecessary and inflammatory).

9. If the actual object is not available, a "duplicate" or "model" of the object, i.e., an object of the same type as that described by a witness, may be admissible to help the fact-finder visualize what happened. See § 1103.1 infra.

10. 49 N.Y.2d 48, 424 N.Y.S.2d 157, 399 N.E.2d 1177 (1979), cert. denied sub nom. Waters v. New York, 446 U.S. 942, 100 S.Ct. 2166, 64 L.Ed.2d 797 (1980). At issue in McGee was the standard of admissibility for sound recordings, which the court said was "that [which is] applicable to any real evidence sought to be admitted." Id. at 59, 424 N.Y.S.2d at 163, 399 N.E.2d at 1183.

11. Id. at 59–60, 424 N.Y.S.2d at 163, 399 N.E.2d at 1183. The burden-of-proof issue to which the McGee court alludes at the outset of the quoted passage is discussed in § 900.1 supra.

12. King v. N.Y. Central & Hudson R.R. Co., 72 N.Y. 607 (1878).

prison;[13] labelled suits stolen from a department store;[14] and a gun marked with a police officer's initials.[15] As noted by the court in *People v. Flanigan*,[16] it is not essential that such objects be in the precise condition they were in at the time of the operative events; it is sufficient that the witness can recognize the exhibit and testify that it is in "substantially" the same condition.[17]

The authentication of "fungible" items, most commonly narcotics or liquids but including any item that is not readily identifiable by observation alone, is accomplished by the presentation of testimony showing the chain of custody from the time of the operative events to the courtroom proffer. The chain evidence must also show that the fungible item is in substantially the same condition, thereby ruling out contamination, tampering or other alteration.[18]

In *People v. Julian*,[19] the Court of Appeals held that a missing link in the custodial chain of a fungible item may be excused so long as the "circumstances provide reasonable assurances" of identity and unchanged condition.[20] In *Julian*, for example, a complete chain of custody was established for drugs from the time of an officer's seizure through initial chemical analysis followed by deposit in the police property clerk's vault. Three years later, however, the officer went to the vault to

---

13. People v. Flanigan, 174 N.Y. 356, 368, 66 N.E. 988, 992 (1903).

14. People v. Washington, 96 A.D.2d 996, 997, 467 N.Y.S.2d 87, 88–89 (3d Dep't 1983), appeal denied, 68 N.Y.2d 673, 505 N.Y.S.2d 1039, 496 N.E.2d 697 (1986). See also People v. Branch, 161 A.D.2d 776, 556 N.Y.S.2d 122 (2d Dep't 1990)(theft victim was able to identify her coat).

15. People v. Capers, 105 A.D.2d 842, 482 N.Y.S.2d 37 (2d Dep't 1984).

16. 174 N.Y. 356, 66 N.E. 988 (1903).

17. Id. at 368, 66 N.E. at 992 (iron bar and rope used by defendant to escape from prison were identifiable and admissible; fact that rope was now slightly torn was due to handling by reporters and others). See also People v. Connelly, 35 N.Y.2d 171, 174, 359 N.Y.S.2d 266, 269, 316 N.E.2d 706, 707 (1974)(fact that object "might have passed through several hands in the interim is of little significance when the object possesses unique characteristics or markings and is not subject to material alteration which is not readily apparent"); People v. Taylor, 206 A.D.2d 904, 905, 616 N.Y.S.2d 116, 117 (4th Dep't), appeal denied, 84 N.Y.2d 940, 621 N.Y.S.2d 537, 645 N.E.2d 1237 (1994)("uncertainties about the identification of [a unique] item of real evidence and whether it is adequately connected to defendant go to the weight, not the admissibility of the challenged item.")

18. Showing a chain of custody with respect to a fungible item may be necessary regardless of whether the substance itself is introduced as an exhibit, as, for example, in the case of a chemical analysis as to which only the results are offered into evidence. See, e.g., Amaro v. City of New York, 40 N.Y.2d 30, 35–36, 386 N.Y.S.2d 19, 22, 351 N.E.2d 665, 668–69 (1976)(laboratory report on blood sample lacked adequate foundation due to insufficient showing of custody of sample between time of collection and analysis).

19. 41 N.Y.2d 340, 392 N.Y.S.2d 610, 360 N.E.2d 1310 (1977).

20. Id. at 343, 392 N.Y.S.2d at 613, 360 N.E.2d at 1313. Drawing upon the prior precedents of People v. Connelly, 35 N.Y.2d 171, 359 N.Y.S.2d 266, 316 N.E.2d 706 (1974), and Amaro v. City of New York, 40 N.Y.2d 30, 386 N.Y.S.2d 19, 351 N.E.2d 665 (1976), the Julian court stated as follows:

[T]he admissibility of a fungible item "generally requires that all those who have handled the item 'identify it and testify to its custody and unchanged condition.'" * * * That is not to say, however, that the chain of custody requirement should be extended to unreasonable limits. * * * In Amaro v. City of New York * * * we recognized that failure to establish a chain of custody may be excused "where the circumstances provide reasonable assurances of the identity and unchanged condition" of the evidence.

41 N.Y.2d at 343, 392 N.Y.S.2d at 612–13, 360 N.E.2d at 1312–13.

retrieve the drugs for trial only to discover that they had been transferred to the police laboratory six months prior thereto by some unknown person for a second analysis by another chemist. There was thus a gap in the chain during the period between the deposit in the vault and the reanalysis.

The Court of Appeals, however, found that the gap was "adequately bridged" by the circumstances: During the period in question, all drugs in the vault had been removed for inventory and reanalysis pursuant to a police administrative directive, thus suggesting that the drugs had been in police control at all times, and the particular drugs were in the same labelled containers and identifiable suitcases in which they had been placed at the time of the first analysis.[21] The question of potential alteration was answered by the fact that the first chemical analysis, which was performed prior to the gap in the chain of custody, established the narcotic content, and the slight variations in content that were revealed in the second analysis were within the range of normal deviation.[22] The court concluded by noting that so long as the "reasonable assurances" standard is satisfied, deficiencies in the chain of custody merely serve to "discredit the weight of the real evidence."[23]

The "reasonable assurances" standard has been applied to countless chain-of-custody issues, obviously producing varying outcomes.[24]

---

21. 41 N.Y.2d at 343–44, 392 N.Y.S.2d at 613, 360 N.E.2d at 1313.

22. Id. at 344, 392 N.Y.S.2d at 613, 360 N.E.2d at 1313.

23. Id., 392 N.Y.S.2d at 613, 360 N.E.2d at 1313.

24. In addition to Julian, cases illustrating findings of reasonable assurances include People v. Moyer, 186 A.D.2d 997, 588 N.Y.S.2d 457 (4th Dep't 1992), leave to appeal denied, 81 N.Y.2d 844, 595 N.Y.S.2d 743, 611 N.E.2d 782 (1993)(testimony of police officer who seized drugs and one of the chemists who analyzed them, both of whom relied on their markings on packages containing drugs, was sufficient despite absence of testimony by another police employee who also analyzed them); People v. Jiminez, 100 A.D.2d 629, 473 N.Y.S.2d 593 (2d Dep't 1984)(absence of first chemist who analyzed drugs was excusable where laboratory supervisor could trace chain of custody based on lab records and chemist who reanalyzed the sample testified to her findings); People v. Arthur, 99 A.D.2d 595, 471 N.Y.S.2d 412 (3d Dep't 1984)(absence of one member of sheriff's office who had brief custody of sealed blood sample that was mailed to laboratory excused where evidence established that sample was still sealed at time of mailing and was received in that condition by laboratory). The court in People v. Steiner, 148 A.D.2d 980, 981, 539 N.Y.S.2d 217, 218 (4th Dep't 1989), listed some additional permissible gaps in the chain of custody of narcotics as follows: "[I]t is not necessary for the People to call * * * the postal employees who handled the mailing of the evidence to the laboratory or the evidence clerk who received the package, nor is it required for the People to 'establish the precise day-by-day location of the narcotics within the laboratory.'"

Cases illustrating insufficient assurances of identity or unchanged condition include Amaro v. City of New York, 40 N.Y.2d 30, 35, 386 N.Y.S.2d 19, 22, 351 N.E.2d 665, 668 (1976)(blood sample taken by doctor from fire fighter was given to chauffeur, who was not produced at trial, and sample was not delivered to laboratory until 36 hours later, "leaving over 36 hours of custody completely unaccounted for"); People v. Rutter, 202 A.D.2d 123, 135–36, 616 N.Y.S.2d 598, 606–07 (1st Dep't 1994), appeal dismissed, 85 N.Y.2d 866, 624 N.Y.S.2d 385, 648 N.E.2d 805 (1995) (blood-stained carpet in car used in crime was not sufficiently connected to crime where tests performed shortly after crime did not detect blood on carpet and car was used again and involved in an unrelated accident before new test detected presence of blood); People v. Steiner, 148 A.D.2d 980, 539 N.Y.S.2d 217 (4th Dep't 1989)(testimony failed to explain why cocaine, white and powdery at time of purchase, had become reddish powder with white chunks at time of first analysis and reddish powder with no chunks at time of second analysis, thus failing to show

§ 1101.2 Federal

Federal law with respect to the admissibility of tangible objects is based on principles similar to those that govern New York law. Relevancy, of course, is a fundamental requirement. Obviously, items that played a direct and actual role in the litigated event, such as an alleged murder weapon,[1] illegal narcotics,[2] or the fruits of a crime[3] are likely to be relevant. In other cases, the object may serve as circumstantial evidence of some other disputed issue. A criminal defendant's possession upon arrest of particular tangible objects, for example, might bear on the issue of his participation in the crime. Examples in the Second Circuit include clothing or jewelry matching the description of that worn by the perpetrator,[4] large quantities of cash after a crime of theft[5] or narcotics activity,[6] weapons like those used in the crime,[7] or simply tools

that substance purchased from defendant was in unchanged condition).

§ 1101.2

1. See, e.g., United States v. Gonzalez, 922 F.2d 1044, 1056 (2d Cir.), cert. denied, 502 U.S. 1014, 112 S.Ct. 660, 116 L.Ed.2d 751 (1991)(defendant was seen throwing gun into vacant lot; ballistics test showed that gun was used in homicide with which defendant was charged and acquaintances of defendant identified gun as belonging to him).

2. See, e.g., United States v. Arango–Correa, 851 F.2d 54, 58 (2d Cir.1988)(display of 500 pounds of cocaine imported in narcotics conspiracy).

3. See, e.g., United States v. Messina, 507 F.2d 73, 78 (2d Cir.1974), cert. denied, 420 U.S. 993, 95 S.Ct. 1433, 43 L.Ed.2d 676 (1975)(stolen sweaters found in defendant's possession).

4. See, e.g., United States v. Gonzalez, 922 F.2d 1044, 1056 (2d Cir.), cert. denied, 502 U.S. 1014, 112 S.Ct. 660, 116 L.Ed.2d 751 (1991)(chain; medallion and Rolex watch).

5. See, e.g., United States v. Ravich, 421 F.2d 1196, 1204 cert. denied, 400 U.S. 834, 91 S.Ct. 69, 27 L.Ed.2d 66 (1970)("Sudden possession of considerable sums of money has long been recognized as relevant to a charge of theft * * *.")

See also United States v. Fisher, 455 F.2d 1101, 1103 (2d Cir.1972) (possession of large sum of cash in getaway car seized five days after bank robbery, together with two federal reserve bank straps (used to fasten large bundles of money), was relevant despite absence of showing of defendant's prior economic status and absence of bait money).

6. See, e.g., United States v. Gonzalez, 922 F.2d 1044, 1056 (2d Cir.), cert. denied, 502 U.S. 1014, 112 S.Ct. 660, 116 L.Ed.2d 751 (1991)(murder suspect's possession of large sum of cash tended to show he was major drug dealer who had motive to kill government informant).

7. See, e.g., United States v. Ravich, 421 F.2d 1196, 1204 (2d Cir.), cert. denied, 400 U.S. 834, 91 S.Ct. 69, 27 L.Ed.2d 66 (1970)(following bank robbery in which perpetrators used three pistols, agents found six pistols and boxes of ammunition in defendants' possession: "[A] jury could infer from the possession of a large number of guns at the date of arrest that at least some of them had been possessed for a substantial period of time, and therefore that the defendants had possessed guns on and before the date of the robbery. * * * Direct evidence of such possession would have been relevant to establish opportunity or preparation to commit the crime charged, and thus would have tended to prove the identity of the robbers * * *. Circumstantial evidence of such possession was therefore also relevant."); United States v. Medico, 557 F.2d 309, 313 (2d Cir.), cert. denied, 434 U.S. 986, 98 S.Ct. 614, 54 L.Ed.2d 480 (1977)(following bank robbery in which one of the perpetrators used shotgun and the other used a rifle, agents found, at defendant's apartment, bullet-riddled walls and pair of red pants pierced with "pellet holes possibly from a shotgun": red pants tended to identify defendant as perpetrator because jury could infer from condition of pants that defendant possessed, at time of robbery, the weapon that was used to shoot holes in the walls and pants and that such weapon was used in the robbery).

of the particular "trade" in question.[8] In some cases, the connection of such items to the defendant may be challenged, thus raising an issue of authentication that can be met by direct or circumstantial evidence.[9] Of course, even a relevant tangible object may be excluded if the trial court, in its discretion, determines that probative value is outweighed by the considerations in Rule 403.[10]

Authentication—proof that an item is what its proponent claims it to be[11]—may be made by a witness who recognizes it.[12] If the object lacks unique identifying characteristics, evidence of its chain of custody[13]

See also United States v. Robinson, 560 F.2d 507, 512–16 (2d Cir.1977)(en banc), cert. denied, 435 U.S. 905, 98 S.Ct. 1451, 55 L.Ed.2d 496 (1978), discussed in § 401.2, at notes 5–12, supra.

8. See, e.g., United States v. Terry, 702 F.2d 299, 318 (2d Cir.), cert. denied, 464 U.S. 992, 104 S.Ct. 482, 78 L.Ed.2d 680, cert. denied, 461 U.S. 931, 103 S.Ct. 2095, 77 L.Ed.2d 304 (1983)(gun and special ammunition found in basement of bar rather than in bar itself supported inference that gun was used by tavern owner in narcotics business, not tavern keeping); United States v. Wiener, 534 F.2d 15, 18 (2d Cir.), cert. denied, 429 U.S. 820, 97 S.Ct. 66, 50 L.Ed.2d 80 (1976) ("Experience on the trial and appellate benches has taught that substantial dealers in narcotics keep firearms on their premises as tools of the trade almost to the same extent as they keep scales, glassine bags, cutting equipment and other narcotics equipment.") See also United States v. Montalvo, 271 F.2d 922, 927 (2d Cir.1959), cert. denied, 361 U.S. 961, 80 S.Ct. 589, 4 L.Ed.2d 543 (1960)(on issue of defendant's intent, at time of arrest, to meet with coconspirator to engage in narcotics transaction, defendant's possession of penknife caked with small quantity of heroin was relevant).

9. See United States v. Orena, 32 F.3d 704, 715 (2d Cir.1994)(firearms found under wooden deck of house where appellant resided were sufficiently connected to him: "'Proof of the connection of an exhibit to the defendants may be made by circumstantial evidence. And the prosecution need only prove a rational basis from which to conclude that the exhibit did, in fact, belong to the appellant[].' * * * A trial judge has broad discretion to determine whether an exhibit has been authenticated properly.")(citation omitted); United States v. Montalvo, 271 F.2d 922, 925 (2d Cir.1959), cert. denied, 361 U.S. 961, 80 S.Ct. 589, 4 L.Ed.2d 543 (1960)(bag containing heroin (which matched description of witness who saw defendant with bag), shirtsleeve containing heroin, and narcotics paraphernalia, all found in basement closet of defendant's apartment building, to which defendant had access, reasonably could have been found by jury to have been possessed by him: "it was not necessary to exclude all other possibilities in order to establish sufficient authentication to make the bag [and other items] admissible").

10. See, e.g., United States v. Medico, 557 F.2d 309, 317 (2d Cir.), cert. denied, 434 U.S. 986, 98 S.Ct. 614, 54 L.Ed.2d 480 (1977)("Rule 403 directs the trial judge to weigh the probative value of [real] evidence against its prejudicial effect on the jury * * *. This balancing is 'a matter generally left within the wide, and wise, discretion of the trial court.'"); United States v. Ravich, 421 F.2d 1196, 1204–05 (2d Cir.), cert. denied, 400 U.S. 834, 91 S.Ct. 69, 27 L.Ed.2d 66 (1970)(trial court might properly have concluded that relevance of guns and ammunition possessed by defendant at time of arrest was outweighed by potential to confuse or inflame jury; jury's seeing of real evidence has potential for giving undue strength to questionable inferences). See also United States v. Arango-Correa, 851 F.2d 54, 58 (2d Cir.1988)(trial court did not abuse discretion in allowing display of 500 pounds of cocaine allegedly imported by defendants, despite their offer to stipulate to quantity, purity and manner of packaging; prejudicial impact was minimized by court's limiting of duration of display); United States v. Robinson, 560 F.2d 507, 515–16 (2d Cir.1977)(en banc), cert. denied, 435 U.S. 905, 98 S.Ct. 1451, 55 L.Ed.2d 496 (1978)(in admitting testimony that defendant possessed gun like that used in robbery, trial court minimized potential for prejudice by excluding introduction of gun itself). See generally § 401.2 supra.

11. See § 900.1 supra.

12. See, e.g., United States v. Sabater, 830 F.2d 7, 10–11 (2d Cir.1987) (officer was able to identify $5 bill used in undercover operation based on serial number and markings made on bill; chain of custody not required). See also § 901.1(b) infra.

13. United States v. Grant, 967 F.2d 81, 82–83 (2d Cir.1992), cert. denied, ___ U.S. ___, 113 S.Ct. 1293, 122 L.Ed.2d 684

§ 1101.2   REAL & DEMONSTRATIVE EVIDENCE   Ch. 11

is used to authenticate it.[14] A break in the chain of custody will not preclude admissibility[15] provided a sufficient showing is made that "it is improbable that the original item ha[s] been exchanged with another or otherwise tampered with."[16] Burdens of proof in the authentication process are discussed in greater detail in § 900.1 *supra*.

Library References:

West's Key No. Digests, Criminal Law ⇐XVII(K); Evidence ⇐188–198.

1102 Persons: Physical Features, Injuries and Their Effects

§ 1102.1 New York

How a person looks or acts may bear directly or circumstantially on some issue of fact, suggesting the potential relevance of displaying the person to the fact-finder without regard to whether the person testifies as a witness.[1] Thus, assuming the threshold test of relevance is satisfied,[2] a person can constitute real or demonstrative evidence.

(1993)("Chain of custody is usually an issue where a party attempts to introduce a piece of physical evidence. * * * [I]f the government seeks to introduce a bag of drugs into evidence, it must first establish that the bag is what the government asserts it to be— the bag found at the scene of the crime. One way to establish that fact is to show the 'chain of custody' of the bag, that is, where the bag has been from the moment it was seized until the moment it is offered into evidence.").

14. See, e.g., id. (narcotics); United States v. Gelzer, 50 F.3d 1133, 1140–41 (2d Cir.1995)(revolver allegedly used in robbery and discarded during car chase); United States v. Hon, 904 F.2d 803, 810 (2d Cir. 1990), cert. denied, 498 U.S. 1069, 111 S.Ct. 789, 112 L.Ed.2d 851 (1991) (wristwatches sold in violation of commercial counterfeiting laws); United States v. Mendel, 746 F.2d 155, 166–67 (2d Cir.1984), cert. denied, 469 U.S. 1213, 105 S.Ct. 1184, 84 L.Ed.2d 331 (1985)(blood samples).

15. See, e.g., United States v. Gelzer, 50 F.3d 1133, 1141 (2d Cir.1995).

16. United States v. Grant, 967 F.2d 81, 83 (2d Cir.1992), cert. denied, ___ U.S. ___, 113 S.Ct. 1293, 122 L.Ed.2d 684 (1993)(quoting United States v. Howard–Arias, 679 F.2d 363, 366 (4th Cir.), cert. denied, 459 U.S. 874, 103 S.Ct. 165, 74 L.Ed.2d 136 (1982)).

In Grant, the chain-of-custody issue arose in connection with a chemist's testimony of his analysis of alleged narcotics. Although the drugs themselves were not offered into evidence, chain of custody evidence was necessary in order for the chemist's analysis to be relevant: "[T]here must be some likelihood that the substance tested by the chemist was the substance seized at the airport." Id. at 83.

§ 1102.1

1. Photographs or films of a person may also be relevant. See, e.g., People v. Webster, 139 N.Y. 73, 83, 34 N.E. 730, 733 (1893)(photograph showing physique of homicide victim prior to death would permit jury to draw inferences concerning defendant's claim of self-defense); Matter of Burack, 201 A.D.2d 561, 607 N.Y.S.2d 711 (2d Dep't 1994)(videotape of testator in act of executing will admissible in probate proceeding on issue of testamentary capacity).

The related but distinct issue of demeanor evidence as a factor in the evaluation of a witness' credibility is discussed in § 607.1, at note 3, supra.

2. Corporeal or photographic evidence of persons was found irrelevant or outweighed by prejudice in the following illustrative cases: Radosh v. Shipstad, 20 N.Y.2d 504, 507, 285 N.Y.S.2d 60, 63, 231 N.E.2d 759, 761 (1967)(in action by ice skater against employer for suspension based on alleged overweightness, permitting plaintiff to display self to jury in costume overemphasized weight at time of trial rather than at time of suspension); Smith v. Lehigh Valley R.R. Co., 177 N.Y. 379, 384, 69 N.E. 729, 730 (1904)(in wrongful death action in which solely pecuniary damages to next of kin were recoverable, photograph of decedent prior to death should not have been admitted because "personal element" of her death was irrelevant); People v.

§ 1102.1

The criminal defendant, for example, can be displayed to the jury for a witness' identification of him as the perpetrator.[3] Similarly, a criminal defendant can be compelled to display scars or tattoos to which an identifying witness has testified.[4] By parity of reasoning, to suggest mistaken identity the defendant may be permitted to display to the jury another suspect who resembles him.[5] Whether the defendant may display his own scars, tattoos or other physical features is dependent on foundation evidence that he had such features on or before the day of the crime and that they would have been visible to the witness whose testimony he is seeking to rebut.[6]

Rios, 191 A.D.2d 722, 595 N.Y.S.2d 524 (2d Dep't), leave to appeal denied, 81 N.Y.2d 1079, 601 N.Y.S.2d 599, 619 N.E.2d 677 (1993)(in sex abuse prosecution, display of six-year-old victim was more prejudicial than relevant on issue of forcible compulsion); Allen v. Stokes, 260 App.Div. 600, 23 N.Y.S.2d 443 (1st Dep't 1940)(in wrongful death action, probative value of photograph of deceased boy in coffin on issue of size and appearance was outweighed by potential for improper influence on jury's emotions).

3. See, e.g., People v. Green, 121 A.D.2d 739, 504 N.Y.S.2d 460 (2d Dep't), appeal denied, 68 N.Y.2d 813, 507 N.Y.S.2d 1030, 499 N.E.2d 879 (1986)(no abuse of discretion in permitting witness to leave stand and approach defendant to identify him).

4. Id. (where witness testified that one of perpetrator's eyes was blind or crossed, defendant was properly required to remove dark glasses to show his eye). See also People v. Herr, 203 A.D.2d 927, 928, 611 N.Y.S.2d 389, 391 (4th Dep't), appeal granted, 84 N.Y.2d 908, 621 N.Y.S.2d 525, 645 N.E.2d 1225 (1994)(trial court did not abuse discretion in compelling defendant to display his tattoos in lieu of using "less prejudicial" alternative of photographs). Compelling a defendant to exhibit himself or to speak designated words is not violative of the privilege against self-incrimination because the defendant in such circumstances is not being compelled to "testify"; he is merely producing real evidence. See People v. Scarola, 71 N.Y.2d 769, 776–77, 530 N.Y.S.2d 83, 85–86, 525 N.E.2d 728, 731–32 (1988); People v. Allen, 140 A.D.2d 229, 232, 528 N.Y.S.2d 380, 382 (1st Dep't), appeal denied, 72 N.Y.2d 1043, 534 N.Y.S.2d 942, 531 N.E.2d 662 (1988); § 509.1, at note 31, supra.

With respect to potential evidence of defendant's physical characteristics, such as the fact that he is left-handed, the prosecutor may not, during summation, properly ask the jury to reflect upon their observations of defendant taking notes at the defense table in the absence of a formal demonstration during the trial. This would constitute an improper reference to facts not in evidence. People v. Ferguson, 82 N.Y.2d 837, 606 N.Y.S.2d 145, 626 N.E.2d 930 (1993).

5. People v. Smith, 195 A.D.2d 112, 606 N.Y.S.2d 656 (1st Dep't), appeal denied, 83 N.Y.2d 876, 613 N.Y.S.2d 137, 635 N.E.2d 306 (1994)(defendant should have been allowed to display his brother, whom he resembled, where brother had confessed to same crime but refused to testify); People v. Diaz, 111 Misc.2d 1083, 445 N.Y.S.2d 888 (Sup.Ct.N.Y.Co.1981)(in support of defense that X was the real killer, defendant was allowed to display X, who resembled defendant and allegedly more closely matched the eyewitness' description of the perpetrator). See also People v. Malphurs, 111 A.D.2d 266, 270, 489 N.Y.S.2d 102, 106 (2d Dep't), appeal denied, 66 N.Y.2d 616, 494 N.Y.S.2d 1039, 485 N.E.2d 243 (1985) (where two assailants robbed victim but only one of them raped her, victim had said that rapist was shorter than other assailant and that other assailant had a mole; defendant, charged with the rape, could display X, who had no mole and was shorter than defendant, only upon a showing that X had been charged as one of the assailants).

6. People v. Rodriguez, 64 N.Y.2d 738, 741, 485 N.Y.S.2d 976, 978, 475 N.E.2d 443, 445 (1984)(defendant's request to display tattooed hands properly denied in absence of proof that he had the tattoos on day of crime); People v. Allen, 140 A.D.2d 229, 528 N.Y.S.2d 380 (1st Dep't), appeal denied, 72 N.Y.2d 1043, 534 N.Y.S.2d 942, 531 N.E.2d 662 (1988) (rape victim testified that assailant had a chipped upper-right tooth; defendant should have been allowed to display tooth because dental results and expert witness tended to prove there had been no chip at time of crime or any subsequent alteration); People v. Shields, 81 A.D.2d 870, 438 N.Y.S.2d 885 (2d Dep't 1981)(rape defendant should have been permitted to show 14–16 inch abdominal scar upon proof such scar predated rape). See also People v. Sugrue, 103 A.D.2d 785, 477 N.Y.S.2d 425 (2d Dep't 1984)(no error in

More problematic is the question whether a defendant should be permitted to give a demonstration of his voice to show, for example, that he has a unique manner of speech which is at odds with the identification testimony against him. Accents and speech impediments can be easily feigned, and trial courts have discretion, as with all courtroom demonstrations,[7] to exclude such voice exemplars when they lack sufficient trustworthiness or their relevance is outweighed by unfair prejudice or the danger of misleading the jury.[8] Part of the driving force behind a defendant's request to display his body parts or manner of speech is the desire to avoid taking the stand in support of a mistaken identity defense. Because such displays to the jury constitute real evidence, the defendant would not be "testifying"[9] and he thereby could avoid cross-examination.

Another controversial form of real evidence is the exhibition of two or more persons to the fact-finder for the purpose of proving family relationship. New York courts appear to have adopted a per se rule of exclusion on the ground that such evidence is too unreliable.[10] When the

refusing to permit defendant to show that his tattoo would not be visible if he had been wearing a tank top shirt, as described by witness, where shirt sought to be used in demonstration was not shown to be substantially same style as that allegedly worn at time of crime).

A person's physical features may also be relevant to issues in civil litigation. See, e.g., De Baillet–Latour v. De Baillet–Latour, 301 N.Y. 428, 433–34, 94 N.E.2d, 715, 717 (1950)(in annulment action, to impeach husband's testimony that he had normal sexual relations with wife, wife was allowed to exhibit conspicuous scars the existence of which husband had denied).

7. See § 1105.1 infra.

8. People v. Scarola, 71 N.Y.2d 769, 776–79, 530 N.Y.S.2d 83, 85–87, 525 N.E.2d 728, 731–33 (1988)(trial courts in two unrelated cases did not abuse discretion in excluding defendants' proposed voice exemplars that were intended to demonstrate speech impediments; victims did not rely on voice identification and defendants failed to rule out possibility of fabrication); People v. Veal, 158 A.D.2d 633, 635, 551 N.Y.S.2d 602, 604 (2d Dep't 1990)(no abuse of discretion in precluding defendant from giving voice exemplar to establish southern drawl rather than Jamaican accent; although victim said assailant had Jamaican accent, identification was visual, and faking of accent was possible); People v. Williams, 130 Misc.2d 773, 497 N.Y.S.2d 849 (Sup.Ct. Kings Co.1986)(in one-witness identification case, voice exemplar consisting of reading of randomly selected newspaper paragraph permitted where defendant's relatives established long-standing existence of heavy Jamaican accent). See also People v. Taylor, 186 A.D.2d 367, 588 N.Y.S.2d 156 (1st Dep't), leave to appeal denied, 80 N.Y.2d 1030, 592 N.Y.S.2d 680, 607 N.E.2d 827 (1992)(no abuse of discretion to preclude defendant from demonstrating "speaking style" to display gold tooth; straightforward display of tooth was sufficient to support defense of misidentification).

Defendants in cases of this nature often seek to offer voice exemplars in lieu of testifying so as to avoid cross-examination. See also note 6 supra.

9. See note 4 supra.

10. Bilkovie v. Loeb, 156 App.Div. 719, 141 N.Y.S. 279 (1st Dep't 1913) (in civil action for assault and rape, on issue of identification of defendant as perpetrator, trial court erred in allowing display of child who was alleged to be a product of the rape: "[s]uch evidence is neither accurate nor reliable"). See also Dep't of Public Welfare v. Hamilton, 282 App.Div.1025, 126 N.Y.S.2d 240 (1st Dep't 1953)(on issue of paternity, trial court properly excluded testimony by putative father as to absence of physical resemblance to child; scientific evidence, however, would be admissible to show impossibility of child having certain racial characteristics if defendant were the father); Matter of Wendel's Estate, 146 Misc. 260, 267–69, 262 N.Y.S. 41, 49–51 (Surr.Ct.N.Y.Co.1933) (in probate proceeding, testimony as to physical resemblance between decedent and alleged adult son was inadmissible).

Other jurisdictions have taken a variety of approaches to resemblance evidence, and Wigmore urged that trial courts should

age of a child is in issue, however, CPLR 4516 expressly permits the child to be displayed to the fact-finder to permit determination of age on the basis of observation.[11]

Exhibition of the injured portion of a tort plaintiff's body may be relevant as direct evidence of the nature and extent of the injury or as circumstantial evidence of such matters as how the injury occurred and pain and suffering.[12] Courts have said that a display of injuries can make testimonial evidence about the matter "more intelligible" to the jury.[13] In addition to a courtroom display by the plaintiff herself, the trend is to permit the use of properly authenticated photographs taken shortly after the accident.[14] The relevance of such corporeal or photographic evidence is weighed against the danger that it will be unfairly prejudicial because of the potential for unduly influencing the jury's sympathies and emotions, thereby diverting them from rational decision-making.[15] Admissibility lies in the court's discretion, but assuming

have discretion to admit such evidence in paternity cases. See 1 Wigmore § 166.

11. CPLR 4516 states as follows: "Whenever it becomes necessary to determine the age of a child, he may be produced and exhibited to enable the court or jury to determine his age by a personal inspection." Even without statutory authority, the approximate age of an adult may be determined by visual inspection. See Wellington Associates v. Vandee Enterprises Corp., 75 Misc.2d 330, 332, 347 N.Y.S.2d 788, 791 (N.Y.C.Civ.Ct.1973)(general rule, in absence of statute, is that age may be determined by courtroom observation).

12. See Butez v. Fonda, Johnstown & Gloversville R.R. Co., 20 Misc. 123, 124, 45 N.Y.S. 808, 808 (Sup.Ct.1897)(it is "competent to exhibit an injured member to a jury which is to pass upon the gravity as well as the method of the infliction of the injury even though there has been a lapse of time which has changed to some extent the condition of the injured member, it being assumed that such change would be taken into consideration by a jury in determining the probable cause or permanence of the effect of the injury itself").

13. Mulhado v. Brooklyn City R.R. Co., 30 N.Y. 370, 372 (1864)(exhibition of injured arm "tended to make the description of the injury more intelligible"); Perry v. Metropolitan Street Ry. Co., 68 App.Div. 351, 353, 74 N.Y.S. 1, 2 (2d Dep't 1902)(exhibition of bared rib cage "was necessary to a demonstration of the deformity testified to by the physician, and tended to make the description of the injury more intelligible to the jury"). See also cases cited in note 14 infra.

14. See, e.g., Axelrod v. Rosenbaum, 205 A.D.2d 722, 722–23, 613 N.Y.S.2d 707, 708 (2d Dep't 1994)("Photographs that fairly and accurately represent the plaintiff shortly after an accident are admissible when they aid the jury in their assessment of the medical testimony and plaintiff's pain and suffering."); Rivera v. City of New York, 160 A.D.2d 985, 985, 554 N.Y.S.2d 706, 707 (2d Dep't 1990)(three photographs of burn victim's feet shortly after accident "aided" jury in assessing "both the medical testimony and the infant plaintiff's pain and suffering"); Gallo v. Supermarkets General Corp., 112 A.D.2d 345, 349, 491 N.Y.S.2d 796, 799 (2d Dep't), appeal denied, 66 N.Y.2d 605, 498 N.Y.S.2d 1025, 489 N.E.2d 770 (1985)(photographs of plaintiff's burn-scarred body taken in hospital "reveal[ed] some rather unsightly injuries, [but] they were introduced only during the damages phase of the trial, where they were clearly relevant to the jury's assessment of [plaintiff's] pain and suffering, and helped the jury to understand the medical testimony relating to [plaintiff's] treatment").

The requirements for authenticating photographs are discussed in § 1104.1(a) infra.

15. See, e.g., Rost v. Brooklyn Heights R.R. Co., 10 App.Div. 477, 481, 41 N.Y.S. 1069, 1072 (2d Dep't 1896)(rule authorizing exhibition "is without force when the legitimate purpose for which the exhibition may be made is slight and the strong tendency is to work improper and illegitimate results"; amputated foot, which was preserved in glass jar, may have been relevant to show age of child at time of accident or proximate cause of accident (apparent burns on foot suggested electrical current on defendant's train had not been shut off), but relevance was "far" outweighed by tendency of exhibit "to arouse the prejudice and inflame the passions of the jury into an angry resentment against the author of the misfor-

§ 1102.1   REAL & DEMONSTRATIVE EVIDENCE   Ch. 11

relevance, most reported opinions suggest a presumption in favor of admissibility.[16]

In criminal cases, New York courts have been particularly liberal in allowing the showing of a victim's wounds,[17] including photographs of the victim taken at the crime scene itself.[18] If viewing the victim's injured body would be at all relevant in determining some material issue, such as the manner in which the crime was committed or the mental state of the person who inflicted the wounds, gruesomeness is not likely to be a basis for exclusion. The leading case is *People v. Pobliner*,[19] which held that photographs of a homicide corpse "are admissible if they tend to prove or disprove a disputed or material issue, to illustrate or elucidate other relevant evidence, or to corroborate or disprove some other evidence offered or to be offered."[20] As to potential prejudice, the court broadly ruled that "[p]hotographic evidence should be excluded

tune"); Butez v. Fonda, Johnstown & Gloversville R.R. Co., 20 Misc. 123, 124–25, 45 N.Y.S. 808, 808–09 (Sup.Ct.1897) (display of child's injured leg to jury was improper where child cried loudly during exhibition, thus likely affecting jury's judgment "on doubtful questions in [plaintiff's] favor"). See also Allen v. Stokes, 260 App.Div. 600, 23 N.Y.S.2d 443 (1st Dep't 1940)(in wrongful death action, minimal probative value of photograph of boy in coffin on issues of size and appearance was outweighed by prejudice).

Occasionally, profoundly injured plaintiffs who are incapable of communicating with counsel are completely excluded from the courtroom during the liability phase of bifurcated trials where seeing the plaintiff has no relevance on the issue of liability and the potential for prejudice is strong. See § 615.1, at note 12, supra.

16. See Mulhado v. Brooklyn City R.R. Co., 30 N.Y. 370, 372 (1864)(court refused to assume, in general or in instant case, that display of injured arm would unduly influence or excite jury's feelings); McNaier v. Manhattan Ry. Co., 4 N.Y.S. 310 (Sup.Ct. 1889), aff'd, 123 N.Y. 664, 26 N.E. 750 (1890) (plaintiff was allowed to show jury his injured eye, which still oozed pus). See also cases cited in note 14 supra. Compare New v. Cortright, 32 A.D.2d 576, 577, 299 N.Y.S.2d 43, 45 (3d Dep't 1969)(photographs of plaintiff in hospital, which showed lacerations and sutures on face, were "not inflammatory" and "contributed to the presentation and understanding of the medical evidence"), with Garcia v. City of New York, 23 A.D.2d 734, 737, 258 N.Y.S.2d 213, 217 (1st Dep't 1965)(photographs of plaintiff while undergoing hospital treatment made such "slight" contribution to presentation or understanding of issues that appellate court "deem[ed] their introduction an excessive effort to capture jury sympathy").

17. See, e.g., People v. Dananel, 183 A.D.2d 778, 584 N.Y.S.2d 485 (2d Dep't), appeal denied, 80 N.Y.2d 902, 588 N.Y.S.2d 827, 602 N.E.2d 235 (1992)(in assault case, no abuse of discretion for victim to display scars on chest and stomach to demonstrate seriousness of injury); People v. Hunter, 131 A.D.2d 877, 517 N.Y.S.2d 234 (2d Dep't), appeal denied, 70 N.Y.2d 875, 523 N.Y.S.2d 502, 518 N.E.2d 13 (1987)(in attempted robbery case, no abuse of discretion for victim to display scars on chest to demonstrate seriousness of injury).

18. See cases cited in notes 19–21 infra.

19. 32 N.Y.2d 356, 345 N.Y.S.2d 482, 298 N.E.2d 637 (1973), cert. denied, 416 U.S. 905, 94 S.Ct. 1609, 40 L.Ed.2d 110 (1974)(30" x 40" color photograph of victim in bed where she was shot, plus two photographs of victim at morgue).

20. Id. at 369, 345 N.Y.S.2d at 493, 298 N.E.2d at 645 (three clustered bullet holes in corpse's left temple showed marksmanship and deliberateness). See also People v. Wood, 79 N.Y.2d 958, 582 N.Y.S.2d 992, 591 N.E.2d 1178 (1992)(to counter defense of extreme emotional disturbance, photographs of corpse illustrated severity and calculated nature of wounds); People v. Stevens, 76 N.Y.2d 833, 560 N.Y.S.2d 119, 559 N.E.2d 1278 (1990)(photographs of corpse showed nature of injury and tended to prove that assailant acted with intent to inflict serious injury; prosecutor was not restricted to reliance on medical testimony).

Photographs of a homicide victim while alive were held to be irrelevant in People v. Stevens, supra, and People v. Daughtry, 202 A.D.2d 686, 610 N.Y.S.2d 54 (2d Dep't), appeal dismissed, 84 N.Y.2d 906, 621 N.Y.S.2d 524, 645 N.E.2d 1224 (1994).

only if its sole purpose is to arouse the emotions of the jury and to prejudice the defendant."[21]

Courtroom demonstrations of the effects of an injury are also admissible in the court's discretion. As with all types of evidence of demonstrations and experiments,[22] the Court of Appeals has cautioned trial courts to be "alert to the danger that, when ill-designed or not properly relevant to the point at issue, instead of being helpful [demonstrations] may serve but to mislead, confuse, divert or otherwise prejudice the purposes of the trial."[23] Within this framework, a trial court was held to have acted within its discretion in permitting an injured plaintiff to demonstrate drinking water from a glass and writing his name for the purpose of illustrating testimony that his injury resulted in a hand tremor.[24] In another case, the trial judge did not abuse discretion by permitting a severely brain-damaged plaintiff, who was apparently incapable of testifying, to be questioned in front of the jury on mundane matters for the purpose of showing the effect of the accident on his cognitive abilities.[25]

"Day-in-the-life" films or videotapes, prepared prior to trial and showing the impact of an injury on the plaintiff's routine activities, have also been held admissible, subject to the same balancing of relevance and

---

21. 32 N.Y.2d at 370, 345 N.Y.S.2d at 493, 298 N.E.2d at 645. The Pobliner standard, which excludes grisly photographs only when the "sole purpose" is to inflame the jury, all but eliminates a balancing of relevance and prejudice. When the Pobliner test was reaffirmed in People v. Wood, 79 N.Y.2d 958, 960, 582 N.Y.S.2d 992, 993, 591 N.E.2d 1178, 1179 (1992), a dissenting opinion by Judge Titone argued that photographs of a homicide victim "even if relevant to a material issue in the case, are admissible only if, on balance, their probative value can be said to outweigh their prejudicial effect." Id. at 961, 582 N.Y.S.2d at 994, 591 N.E.2d at 1180.

While rejecting the balancing urged by Judge Titone, the majority in Wood did note that an offer of multiple photographs may raise a legitimate question of undue cumulativeness. In Wood itself, however, no abuse of discretion was found where the trial judge concluded that each of 44 photographs of the corpse was "relevant and necessary to refute defendant's claim of extreme emotional disturbance." Id. at 960, 582 N.Y.S.2d at 994, 591 N.E.2d at 1180.

22. See § 1105.1 infra.

23. Harvey v. Mazal American Partners, 79 N.Y.2d 218, 224, 581 N.Y.S.2d 639, 642, 590 N.E.2d 224, 227 (1992)(quoting People v. Acevedo, 40 N.Y.2d 701, 704, 389 N.Y.S.2d 811, 814–15, 358 N.E.2d 495, 497 (1976)).

24. Clark v. Brooklyn Heights R.R. Co., 177 N.Y. 359, 360–62, 69 N.E. 647, 647 (1904)(demonstration "was on the border line" of an abuse of discretion because acting out of nervous affection was "under the sole control of the witness himself"). See also Sutherland v. County of Nassau, 190 A.D.2d 664, 593 N.Y.S.2d 287 (2d Dep't 1993)(plaintiff was properly permitted to partially disrobe and redress in presence of jury to demonstrate limiting effect of disabled arm and hand; there was no indication of faking or exaggeration and value of evidence outweighed potential for prejudice); Riddle v. Memorial Hospital, 43 A.D.2d 750, 349 N.Y.S.2d 855 (3d Dep't 1973)(where plaintiff's capacity to play violin was allegedly impaired by injury to wrist, conductor who was familiar with violin playing and with plaintiff's recent performances was permitted to demonstrate the difficulties he had observed plaintiff experiencing when she played).

25. Harvey v. Mazal American Partners, 79 N.Y.2d 218, 223–25, 581 N.Y.S.2d 639, 641–43, 590 N.E.2d 224, 226–27 (1992). The Court of Appeals stated that it would have been "preferable" for the trial judge to conduct a rehearsal of the exhibition outside the presence of the jury before letting them see it, but the failure to do so in this case was not an abuse of discretion. Id. at 224, 581 N.Y.S.2d at 642, 590 N.E.2d at 227.

§ 1102.1   REAL & DEMONSTRATIVE EVIDENCE   Ch. 11

prejudice.[26] By the same token, defense-prepared surveillance films showing the absence of a disabling condition have equal probative value.[27] The authentication process for such photographic evidence is discussed in § 1104.1 *infra*.

Library References:

West's Key No. Digests, Criminal Law ⚖404.5–404.85; Evidence ⚖188–198.

§ 1102.2 Federal

Federal courts have permitted persons to be displayed to the jury, either by corporeal exhibition or by means of photographic evidence,[1] where relevant on such issues as age of the person,[2] absence of physical abuse,[3] demeanor while giving allegedly perjurious testimony,[4] mistaken identity[5] and, in a wrongful death action, the type of person the decedent was before she died.[6] On the issue of voice identification, however, the Second Circuit held that a criminal defendant was properly precluded from giving a nontestimonial demonstration of his heavy foreign accent

---

26. Caprara v. Chrysler Corp., 71 A.D.2d 515, 522–23, 423 N.Y.S.2d 694, 698–99 (3d Dep't 1979), aff'd, 52 N.Y.2d 114, 436 N.Y.S.2d 251, 417 N.E.2d 545 (1981)(probative value of 10-minute silent movie narrated by plaintiff's brother outweighed prejudice; fact that uncontradicted medical testimony establishes nature and extent of plaintiff's injuries does not alone prevent "showing to the jury a motion picture illustrating in an 'informative and non-inflammatory manner the impact that the accident has had on his or her life'"). See also § 1104.1(d), at notes 48–50, infra.

27. See, e.g., Boyarsky v. G.A. Zimmerman Corp., 240 App.Div. 361, 270 N.Y.S. 134 (1st Dep't 1934); Haley v. Hockey, 199 Misc. 512, 103 N.Y.S.2d 717 (Sup.Ct.Jefferson Co.1950). See also People v. Perez, 300 N.Y. 208, 216, 90 N.E.2d 40, 44 (1949), cert. denied, 338 U.S. 952, 70 S.Ct. 483, 94 L.Ed. 588 (1950)(photograph of defendant taken immediately after confession to police could have been sufficient to persuade jury of falsity of defendant's claims of assault and abuse by police).

§ 1102.2

1. The authentication of photographic evidence in federal courts is treated in § 1104.2(a) and (c) infra.

2. United States ex rel. Fong On v. Day, 54 F.2d 990, 991 (2d Cir.1932) (contention of immigration applicant that he was 12½ years old was belied by his height and mature appearance as shown in photograph and as observed by triers of fact in immigration tribunal).

3. United States v. Valdes, 417 F.2d 335, 338 (2d Cir.1969), cert. denied, 399 U.S. 912, 90 S.Ct. 2206, 26 L.Ed.2d 566 (1970)(defendant's testimony that he was beaten by federal agents at time of arrest was belied by photograph of defendant taken at station house shortly after arrest).

4. United States v. Moran, 194 F.2d 623, 626 (2d Cir.), cert. denied, 343 U.S. 965, 72 S.Ct. 1058, 96 L.Ed. 1362 (1952)(in perjury prosecution, movie taken of defendant while giving allegedly perjured testimony was relevant to show defendant's demeanor).

5. United States v. Bay, 748 F.2d 1344, 1346–47 (9th Cir.), modified on rehearing, 762 F.2d 1314 (9th Cir.1984)(upon foundation showing that defendant had tattoos on backs of his hands at time of robbery, display of hands to jury would be relevant to counter identification testimony by witnesses who saw hands of perpetrator but recalled no tattoos).

6. Drinon v. Wilson, 113 F.2d 654 (2d Cir.1940). The only compensable damages in the wrongful death action at issue in Drinon were the pecuniary losses to the decedent's parents, i.e., the financial aid that the decedent would have given them had she lived: "Her contributions in money or its equivalent for their benefit depended much upon the kind of girl she was and her photograph was certainly some evidence to aid the jury in determining that." Id. at 655. The Drinon court rejected an older decision in New York which held that such a photograph would have no relevance except to show the survivors' grief and sorrow, a "personal element" not compensable under the wrongful death statute. See Smith v. Lehigh Valley R.R. Co., 177 N.Y. 379, 69 N.E. 729 (1904); § 1102.1, at note 2, supra.

because of the lack of inherent trustworthiness of such evidence, the difficulty in testing the authenticity of the accent, and the potential for prejudicing the prosecution and misleading the jury.[7]

Injuries and wounds of tort plaintiffs and crime victims may be shown to the jury, either in person or by photographic evidence, subject to the court's discretionary balancing of relevance and prejudice.[8] Demonstrations of the effects of such injuries are also permitted.[9] Most of the reported cases within the Second Circuit appear to favor admissibility, but in *Ryan v. United Parcel Service*,[10] the trial judge was found to have erred in admitting a grisly photograph of the body of a wrongful death victim at the accident scene. The victim had died instantly, and defendant conceded the cause of death. The only remaining issues concerned the defendant's and the victim's respective negligent driving, as to which the position of the dead body had little or no relevance. The photograph thus served only to inflame the jury.[11]

1103 Drawings, Diagrams, and Models

§ 1103.1 New York

Drawings, maps, diagrams, charts or mechanical models are a classic form of demonstrative evidence to which a witness may be allowed to

---

7. United States v. Esdaille, 769 F.2d 104, 108 (2d Cir.), cert. denied, 474 U.S. 923, 106 S.Ct. 258, 88 L.Ed.2d 264 (1985) (probative value was slight because government witness' identification was based on observation, not sound of voice, and defendant was able to present testimony of acquaintance that defendant had heavy accent; trial judge's decision that prejudice outweighed relevance "was neither arbitrary nor irrational"). Similar considerations have guided New York courts. See § 1102.1, at notes 7–9, supra.

8. See, e.g., Rich v. Ellerman & Bucknall S.S. Co., 278 F.2d 704, 707–08 (2d Cir.1960)(trial court should not have precluded plaintiff from exhibiting scarred shoulder (or photographs thereof) to jury because such evidence "is always proper, unless reasons of policy apply to exclude it"; the photographs here showed "nothing gruesome or revolting about [the injuries], or any likelihood that they would inflame or bias a jury"); Slattery v. Marra Bros., 186 F.2d 134, 138 (2d Cir.), cert. denied, 341 U.S. 915, 71 S.Ct. 736, 95 L.Ed. 1351 (1951)(trial judge did not abuse discretion in allowing plaintiff to display injured leg to jury: "It is sometimes said that the jury should not be allowed to see repulsive injuries since they may excite their emotions. That may at times be true; but ordinarily it would seem that the very hideousness of the deformity was a part of the suffering of the victim, and could not rationally be excluded in the assessment of his damages.");

United States v. Lee, 800 F.2d 903, 904 (9th Cir.1986)(location and size of bite victim's scar "were directly probative of the severity of the wound the defendant inflicted and of the accuracy of the conflicting theories of the government and the defense as to how the altercation proceeded. Defendant made no showing that the scar was so gruesome that it tended unfairly to inflame the jury's passions.").

See also Martin v. The Maintenance Co., 588 F.2d 355, 357 (2d Cir.1978) (admission of photographs of child's foot showing its condition immediately after accident was within trial court's discretion); Whelan v. Penn Central Co., 503 F.2d 886, 891 (2d Cir.1974)(photographs of plaintiff taken at various stages of medical treatment were relevant to pain and suffering).

9. See, e.g., Allen v. Seacoast Products, Inc., 623 F.2d 355, 365 n.23 (5th Cir. 1980)(victim who lost eye in accident was properly permitted to demonstrate removal and replacement of artificial eye in front of jury: "[T]he Trial Judge did not abuse his discretion in determining that the demonstration's probative value (in showing the daily regimen which [plaintiff] must endure) outweighed its prejudicial effect.").

With respect to "day-in-the-life" films, see § 1104.1, at note 49, infra.

10. 205 F.2d 362 (2d Cir.1953).

11. Id. at 364.

§ 1103.1   REAL & DEMONSTRATIVE EVIDENCE   Ch. 11

refer while on the stand to help the fact-finder visualize her testimony.[1] Examples include a diagram of the electrical wiring in a building,[2] a human skull,[3] and an anatomical doll.[4] The test of relevance for demonstrative evidence of this nature is whether the item will be of "assistance to understanding."[5] Charts that summarize the evidence may also be used by counsel.[6] A prosecutor went too far, however, when he used a chart in an overly "dramatic" way that could have misled the jury into thinking that certain facts had been conclusively proved.[7]

The foundation for admissibility of an item used solely for illustrative purposes differs from that of objects that played an actual role in the litigated event.[8] With respect to an illustrative drawing or model, it should be sufficient for the witness to declare, in substance, that the item is a "fair representation" of the matter she is describing and that use of the item will help explain her testimony.[9]

§ 1103.1

1. People v. Del Vermo, 192 N.Y. 470, 482, 85 N.E. 690, 694–95 (1908)(maps, diagrams, drawings, photographs and models "enable the jury to use their eyes as well as their ears in order to gain an intelligent comprehension of the case"); Archer v. New York, N.H. & H.R.R. Co., 106 N.Y. 589, 603, 13 N.E. 318, 324 (1887)(maps, diagrams and drawings are "uniformly received * * * to enable courts and juries to comprehend readily the question in dispute"). See generally McCormick § 213.

2. See Flah's, Inc. v. Richard Rosette Electric, Inc., 155 A.D.2d 772, 547 N.Y.S.2d 935 (3d Dep't 1989)(engineering expert was properly permitted to use diagram of mall's electrical system and components to explain how and where explosion occurred).

3. McNaier v. Manhattan Ry. Co., 4 N.Y.S. 310 (Sup.Ct. 1889), aff'd, 123 N.Y. 664, 26 N.E. 750 (1890)(physician was properly permitted to use skull to explain nature of injury to plaintiff's eye).

4. See N.Y. Crim.Proc.Law § 60.44:

Any person who is less than sixteen years old may in the discretion of the court and where helpful and appropriate, use an anatomically correct doll in testifying in a criminal proceeding based upon conduct prohibited by article one hundred thirty, article two hundred sixty or section 255.25 of the penal law [sex-related crimes].

The foregoing statute, adopted in 1986, is not exclusive. See People v. Herring, 135 Misc.2d 487, 515 N.Y.S.2d 954 (Sup.Ct. Queens Co.1987)(sodomy victim who was over 70 and had difficulty in speaking was properly allowed to use anatomical doll to explain what happened).

5. People v. Feld, 305 N.Y. 322, 332, 113 N.E.2d 440, 444 (1953). See also note 1 supra.

6. Carroll v. Roman Catholic Diocese of Rockville Centre, 26 A.D.2d 552, 553, 271 N.Y.S.2d 7, 11 (2d Dep't 1966), aff'd, 19 N.Y.2d 658, 278 N.Y.S.2d 626, 225 N.E.2d 217 (1967); Public Operating Corp. v. Weingart, 257 App.Div. 379, 381–82, 13 N.Y.S.2d 182, 185 (1st Dep't 1939); Haley v. Hockey, 199 Misc. 512, 513, 103 N.Y.S.2d 717, 718 (Sup.Ct.Jefferson Co.1950).

7. People v. Workman, 308 N.Y. 668, 670, 124 N.E.2d 314, 315 (1954). Workman was a perjury prosecution in which the defendant was accused of having failed to disclose 20 items in his possession in his response to a grand jury questionnaire. The inappropriate "drama" consisted of the following:

[T]he prosecution employed a chart at the top of which appeared the legend "It is claimed that the defendant failed to list," and underneath this were listed twenty items, together with their alleged value. When this chart was first presented, the names of these twenty items were concealed by paper covering strips, which strips were removed one by one by the prosecuting attorney as testimony was elicited to prove that defendant had possessed the items.

Id. The conviction was affirmed, however, on harmless error grounds.

8. See § 1102.1 supra.

9. Archer v. New York, N.H. & H.R.R. Co., 106 N.Y. 589, 603, 13 N.E. 318, 324 (1887); People v. Knapper, 168 A.D.2d 234, 234, 562 N.Y.S.2d 475, 476 (1st Dep't 1990), appeal denied, 77 N.Y.2d 908, 569 N.Y.S.2d 940, 572 N.E.2d 623 (1991). See generally McCormick § 213, at 11–12.

More than one witness may be used to lay the foundation for admissibility. See, e.g., Flah's, Inc. v. Richard Rosette Electric, Inc.,

When a "somewhat exceptional" object that was actually involved in a litigated event is not available, the court might allow the display of a duplicate in order to give the jury a "more accurate idea of [the original's] true character."[10] Models might also be admissible in conjunction with courtroom experiments, a topic that is covered in § 1105.1 *infra*.

Library References:

West's Key No. Digests, Criminal Law ⚖404.5–404.85, 437; Evidence ⚖188–198, 358; Witnesses ⚖252.

§ 1103.2 Federal

Drawings, charts and diagrams may be used in federal trials as "visual representations of information or data as set forth in the testimony of a witness or in documents that are exhibits in evidence."[1] The witness upon whose testimony the picture or diagram is based may authenticate its accuracy, regardless of who did the artwork.[2] The purpose, of course, is to assist the jury in understanding the evidence.[3]

155 A.D.2d 772, 773, 547 N.Y.S.2d 935, 937 (3d Dep't 1989). Furthermore, slight variations between a diagram and the matter being depicted are permitted when brought to the jury's attention. Id.

10. People v. Del Vermo, 192 N.Y. 470, 482, 85 N.E. 690, 694 (1908) (knife of same pattern and character owned by defendant and used in homicide); People v. Taylor, 197 A.D.2d 841, 602 N.Y.S.2d 255 (4th Dep't 1993)(shotgun similar to one purchased by defendant; variations between model and original went to weight, not admissibility); People v. Pike, 131 A.D.2d 890, 517 N.Y.S.2d 246 (2d Dep't)("stungun," which was similar in appearance to gun used on assault victim; appeal denied, 70 N.Y.2d 711, 519 N.Y.S.2d 1046, 513 N.E.2d 1314, and 70 N.Y.2d 716, 519 N.Y.S.2d 1052, 513 N.E.2d 1320 (1987).

In People v. Mirenda, 23 N.Y.2d 439, 453, 297 N.Y.S.2d 532, 542, 245 N.E.2d 194, 201 (1969), the court suggested that it is inappropriate for a court to admit a model where the object under discussion, such as a pair of sunglasses, "is not so difficult to visualize that a model is required to assist the jury in understanding the witness' testimony."

§ 1103.2

1. See United States v. Goldberg, 401 F.2d 644, 647–48 (2d Cir.1968), cert. denied, 393 U.S. 1099, 89 S.Ct. 895, 21 L.Ed.2d 790 (1969)(charts and summaries of transactions based on witness' testimony and business records); Cohen v. Kindlon, 366 F.2d 762, 763–64 (2d Cir.1966)(sketch of accident scene which illustrated witness' testimony). The language quoted in text was approved by the Goldberg court as an appropriate jury instruction. 401 F.2d at 647.

The use of summaries as demonstrative evidence must be distinguished from the introduction of summaries of voluminous records as an exception to the best evidence rule pursuant to Fed.R.Evid. 1006. See § 1006.1 supra. Summaries used to illustrate the contents of other writings that have been admitted have no evidentiary significance beyond the underlying data represented, whereas summaries admitted under Fed.R.Evid. 1006 constitute independent substantive evidence. See, e.g., United States v. Howard, 774 F.2d 838, 844 n.4 (7th Cir.1985)(urging use of limiting instruction when chart is used as "teaching device"); United States v. Goldberg, 401 F.2d 644, 647 (2d Cir.1968), cert. denied, 393 U.S. 1099, 89 S.Ct. 895, 21 L.Ed.2d 790 (1969)("court carefully charged the jury that these resumes were not themselves independent evidence").

2. Cohen v. Kindlon, 366 F.2d 762, 763–64 (2d Cir.1966). A sketch need only be "approximate," and its probative value is for the jury. Id. at 764.

3. See United States v. Ellenbogen, 365 F.2d 982, 988 (2d Cir.1966), cert. denied, 386 U.S. 923, 87 S.Ct. 892, 17 L.Ed.2d 795 (1967). See also United States v. Altruda, 224 F.2d 935, 938–39 (2d Cir.1955)(in tax evasion prosecution, "accounting schedules" introduced by government failed to assist jury in understanding evidence: "It would take a jury of mathematicians to ascertain the facts out of the confusion created by these schedules * * *.")

§ 1103.2   REAL & DEMONSTRATIVE EVIDENCE   Ch. 11

Analogous reasoning supports the admissibility of models or duplicates of objects that played an actual role in the litigated event.[4]

Admissibility of drawings, charts and models lies in the discretion of the trial judge.[5] Factors that the judge should take into account include the potentially misleading nature of the particular chart or diagram[6] and the danger, especially where the underlying facts are controverted, that its "dramatic and impressive" effect may cause the jury to lose sight of the contested nature of the evidence.[7]

In criminal prosecutions, government-prepared charts that purport to summarize the evidence must be screened by the court to ascertain the "fairness" of the representation.[8] If the chart consists of numerical calculations, as is common in tax fraud cases, the government's foundation must contain an explanation as to how the figures were derived from the evidence in the record.[9]

Library References:

West's Key No. Digests, Criminal Law ⟶404.5–404.85, 437; Evidence ⟶188–198, 358; Witnesses ⟶252.

4. See United States v. Moret, 334 F.2d 887, 890 (2d Cir.1964), cert. denied, 379 U.S. 993, 85 S.Ct. 707, 13 L.Ed.2d 612 (1965)(binoculars of the same type that were used by federal agents during surveillance of narcotics activity; because foundation demonstrated that the exhibits had same size, structure, shape and capacity as those actually used, there was no need for testimony that they were "in the same condition").

5. In re Air Crash Disaster at John F. Kennedy International Airport, 635 F.2d 67, 72–73 (2d Cir.1980); United States v. Ellenbogen, 365 F.2d 982, 988 (2d Cir. 1966), cert. denied, 386 U.S. 923, 87 S.Ct. 892, 17 L.Ed.2d 795 (1967).

6. In re Air Crash Disaster at John F. Kennedy International Airport, 635 F.2d 67, 73 (2d Cir.1980)(in airplane accident case, national safety board chart comparing standard "glide slope path" with actual path of aircraft was properly excluded pursuant to Fed.R.Evid. 403 because thickness of lines on chart and times of conversation marked on chart did not match stipulated conversation times, thereby potentially misleading jury); United States v. Citron, 783 F.2d 307, 316 (2d Cir.1986), rev'd on other grounds, 853 F.2d 1055 (2d Cir.1988)(summary charts that are more likely to confuse or mislead jury than to assist it should be excluded under Fed.R.Evid. 403).

7. United States v. Ellenbogen, 365 F.2d 982, 988 (2d Cir.1966), cert. denied, 386 U.S. 923, 87 S.Ct. 892, 17 L.Ed.2d 795 (1967). In criminal cases, juries are customarily given a limiting instruction to the effect that charts and summaries are no better than the evidence upon which they are based and that the underlying data must control in the event any conflict is perceived between the chart and the evidence. See, e.g., id.; United States v. Goldberg, 401 F.2d 644, 647–48 (2d Cir. 1968), cert. denied, 393 U.S. 1099, 89 S.Ct. 895, 21 L.Ed.2d 790 (1969).

8. See, e.g., United States v. Citron, 783 F.2d 307, 316 (2d Cir.1986); United States v. Conlin, 551 F.2d 534, 538–39 (2d Cir. 1977)("A chart submitted by the prosecution is a very persuasive and powerful tool and must be fairly used, since, by its arrangement and use, it is an argument to the jury during the course of the trial. * * * A chart which for any reason presents an unfair picture can be a potent weapon for harm, and permitting the jury to consider it is error.")

9. United States v. Citron, 783 F.2d 307, 316–17 (2d Cir.1986), rev'd on other grounds, 853 F.2d 1055 (2d Cir.1988).

1104 Photographic and Related Forms of Evidence

§ 1104.1 New York

a. Photographs

The principal theory for the admissibility of photographs is the same as that which underlies drawings and diagrams:[1] they are demonstrative evidence that illustrates the testimony of a witness.[2] Thus, assuming relevance of the matter about which the witness is testifying, a sufficient foundation is laid when the witness testifies that the photograph is a fair and accurate representation of the persons, places or objects in question.[3] If the witness is able to verify that the photograph is an accurate depiction of something she has observed, the authentication process does not require testimony by the photographer.[4] Nor is there any need for expert testimony showing the chain of custody of the film. Furthermore, slight imperfections or lack of clarity in the picture usually go only to the weight of the evidence.[5]

New York courts have recognized that a photograph can do more than merely illustrate a witness' description; it can also serve as "independent probative evidence of what it shows."[6] Furthermore, the "illustrative" basis of authentication, i.e., testimony that the photograph accurately illustrates the witness' personal observations, is not the

---

§ 1104.1

1. See § 1103.1 supra.

2. Alberti v. New York, Lake Erie & Western R.R. Co., 118 N.Y. 77, 88, 23 N.E. 35, 38 (1889)(photograph described by witness as correct representation of plaintiff's limbs was "competent as a map or diagram"); Archer v. New York, N.H. & H.R.R. Co., 106 N.Y. 589, 603, 13 N.E. 318, 324 (1887)(photograph said by witness to be fair description of accident site was likened to map or diagram which serves "to explain or illustrate and apply testimony").

3. People v. Byrnes, 33 N.Y.2d 343, 347, 352 N.Y.S.2d 913, 916, 308 N.E.2d 435, 437 (1974)(sufficient authentication was shown where witness with personal knowledge "identified the subjects and verified that the photographs accurately represented the subject matter depicted").

4. Id. See also Stiasny v. Metropolitan Street Ry. Co., 58 App.Div. 172, 175, 68 N.Y.S. 694, 696 (1st Dep't 1901)(foundation for introduction of person's photo could be laid by anyone able to testify that it was a correct likeness).

5. See, e.g., People v. Moody, 195 A.D.2d 1016, 600 N.Y.S.2d 581 (4th Dep't 1993)(whether "fuzzy" photographs, printed from a videotape, were sufficiently clear went to weight, not admissibility). Obviously, there will be cases where the quality of a photograph is so poor that it cannot fairly be described as an accurate representation of the matter. See, e.g., People v. Tortorice, 142 A.D.2d 916, 531 N.Y.S.2d 414 (3d Dep't 1988).

6. People v. Byrnes, 33 N.Y.2d 343, 348, 352 N.Y.S.2d 913, 917, 308 N.E.2d 435, 437 (1974)(photographs of child sexual abuse in progress). See also Taylor v. New York City Transit Auth., 48 N.Y.2d 903, 904, 424 N.Y.S.2d 888, 889, 400 N.E.2d 1340, 1341 (1979)(by observing photograph of stairway step, jury could infer from appearance of defect that condition was long-standing and that owner therefore had constructive notice); People v. Perez, 300 N.Y. 208, 216, 90 N.E.2d 40, 44 (1949), cert. denied, 338 U.S. 952, 70 S.Ct. 483, 94 L.Ed. 588 (1950)(photograph of defendant taken immediately after confession to police might "in itself" have persuaded jury that defendant's assertions of assault and abuse by police were false); People v. Webster, 139 N.Y. 73, 83, 34 N.E. 730, 733 (1893)(jury was properly instructed that it could look at photograph of deceased homicide victim to ascertain victim's physical features as bearing on defendant's claim of self-defense).

§ 1104.1   REAL & DEMONSTRATIVE EVIDENCE   Ch. 11

exclusive means. *People v. Byrnes*[7] embraced what has become known as the "silent witness" theory of authentication,[8] which may be used when no witness is able to testify to having seen the subject matter shown in the photograph. This approach, which obviously underlies the admissibility of X-rays,[9] can be satisfied, for example, with foundation evidence describing the date, time and location of filming, the mechanics and operation of the camera, and expert testimony that there has been no alteration of the film or prints.[10] Chain-of-custody evidence might serve as a sufficient substitute for expert testimony on the issue of alteration.[11]

No New York court has established specific requirements for authenticating photographic evidence under the silent witness theory. It was said in an instructive opinion from another jurisdiction that it would be "neither possible nor wise" to do so "since the context in which the photographic evidence was obtained and its intended use at trial will be different in virtually every case."[12] The standard is simply one which requires the presentation of sufficient foundation evidence to demonstrate that the photographs in question accurately depict what they purport to show.[13]

Even if a photograph is properly authenticated as an accurate representation of a matter, it is inadmissible unless the matter depicted is relevant to the case and such relevance is not outweighed by the dangers of unfair prejudice, confusion of issues, misleading the jury or undue cumulativeness. A photograph of an accident site, for example, usually is inadmissible unless the conditions at the time of the taking of the photograph were substantially the same as at the time of the accident.[14] In general, the relevance-prejudice balancing that occurs

---

7. 33 N.Y.2d 343, 346–49, 352 N.Y.S.2d 913, 915–17, 308 N.E.2d 435, 436–38 (1974). The Byrnes court relied upon several California cases. See People v. Doggett, 83 Cal.App.2d 405, 188 P.2d 792 (1948); People v. Bowley, 59 Cal.2d 855, 860–61, 382 P.2d 591, 594–95, 31 Cal.Rptr. 471, 474–75 (1963); People v. Samuels, 250 Cal.App.2d 501, 512, 58 Cal.Rptr. 439, 446 (1967).

8. See generally McCormick § 214, at 14–16.

9. See text at notes 19–20 infra.

10. Byrnes, 33 N.Y.2d at 346–49, 352 N.Y.S.2d at 915–17, 308 N.E.2d at 436–38.

11. Cf. People v. Ely, 68 N.Y.2d 520, 527–28, 510 N.Y.S.2d 532, 536–37, 503 N.E.2d 88, 92–93 (1986)("chain of custody" is one means of authenticating sound recordings); see text at notes 23–24 infra. See also § 1101.1, at notes 10–24, supra ("chain of custody" can be used to authenticate "fungible" objects not identifiable by observation).

12. Fisher v. State, 7 Ark.App. 1, 8, 643 S.W.2d 571, 575 (1982). In Fisher, a store manager was held to have properly laid a foundation for a videotape of employees in the act of stealing merchandise. He testified to setting up the camera, starting it, checking its operation, leaving the activated camera unattended, returning later to find the camera untouched, and removing the film and maintaining continuous custody thereof. Neither the manager nor any other witness saw the theft while it was happening.

13. See People v. Byrnes, 33 N.Y.2d 343, 349, 352 N.Y.S.2d 913, 917, 308 N.E.2d 435, 438 (1974).

14. See, e.g., Niles v. State, 201 A.D.2d 774, 777, 607 N.Y.S.2d 480, 483 (3d Dep't 1994)(photographs of highway exit ramp, taken five days after accident, were properly excluded in absence of testimony that they "fairly and accurately depicted the scene on the day of the accident"); Leven v. Tallis Department Store, 178 A.D.2d 466, 577 N.Y.S.2d 132 (2d Dep't 1991)(employee of department store, who was out of country for several weeks prior to and after accident, should not have been allowed to verify that photograph of store, taken two years later, showed same conditions that existed on day of accident).

with respect to courtroom exhibitions of objects[15] and persons[16] applies to photographs of such matters taken before trial. Under the standard developed in the leading case of *People v. Pobliner*,[17] the balance is usually struck in favor of admissibility:

> [P]hotographs are admissible if they tend "to prove or disprove a disputed or material issue, to illustrate or elucidate other relevant evidence, or to corroborate or disprove some other evidence offered or to be offered." They should be excluded "only if [their] *sole purpose* is to arouse the emotions of the jury and to prejudice the defendant" * * *.[18]

b. X-rays and Analogous Medical Pictorial Processes

Since the unaided eyes of a physician cannot see what is depicted in an X-ray, such images are authenticated by means of the "silent witness" approach.[19] Thus, an adequate foundation probably can be laid with testimony, including a showing of the chain of custody, that the X-ray, produced by specific machinery that was properly operated by a qualified technician at a given location on a given date, is that of a particular person's anatomy and that there has been no alteration.[20]

If the prerequisites of CPLR 4532–a are met, an X-ray, as well as the results of six other modern medical processes, can be authenticated in a

---

Depending on the matter sought to be proven, the time when the photograph was taken will make no difference if the witness is in a position to verify that the photograph is an accurate representation of the matter as it existed at a relevant point in time. See, e.g., Taylor v. New York City Transit Auth., 48 N.Y.2d 903, 424 N.Y.S.2d 888, 400 N.E.2d 1340 (1979)(jury could have found that photographs of concrete surface, "whenever taken," were "a fair and accurate representation of the condition of the penultimate step on the stairway as of the time of the occurrence"); People v. Buddenseick, 103 N.Y. 487, 500, 9 N.E. 44, 47 (1886)(photograph of fallen structure, taken while trial was in progress, was admissible for purpose of showing relevant condition of walls where witness verified that conditions depicted in photo were same as those that existed when structure collapsed or soon thereafter). But see Melendez v. New York City Transit Auth., 196 A.D.2d 460, 601 N.Y.S.2d 489 (1st Dep't 1993)(plaintiff who fell on stairway allegedly due to presence of substance consisting of mixture of spilled beer and soda failed to establish time of taking of post-accident photograph of stairway, thus making photograph inadmissible because of "ephemeral" nature of the alleged defect).

15. See § 1101.1 supra.

16. See § 1102.1 supra.

17. 32 N.Y.2d 356, 345 N.Y.S.2d 482, 298 N.E.2d 637 (1973), cert. denied, 416 U.S. 905, 94 S.Ct. 1609, 40 L.Ed.2d 110 (1974).

18. People v. Wood, 79 N.Y.2d 958, 960, 582 N.Y.S.2d 992, 993, 591 N.E.2d 1178, 1179 (1992)(emphasis in original)(quoting People v. Pobliner, 32 N.Y.2d 356, 369–70, 345 N.Y.S.2d 482, 493, 298 N.E.2d 637, 645 (1973), cert. denied, 416 U.S. 905, 94 S.Ct. 1609, 40 L.Ed.2d 110 (1974)). The Wood court recognized, however, that prejudice may ensue when the number of photographs of the same gruesome matter becomes excessive. See § 1102.1, at note 21, supra. With respect to posed photographs of experiments or reenactments, see text at notes 48–50 infra.

19. See text at notes 7–11 supra. The applicability of the best evidence rule to X-rays is discussed in § 1004.1, in text at notes 7–10, supra.

20. See, e.g., Mueller and Kirkpatrick § 9.16, at 1152. No reported New York cases have specifically addressed the authentication requirements for X-rays. Analogy can be drawn to the "chain-of-custody" method of authentication as applied to sound recordings in People v. Ely, 68 N.Y.2d 520, 527–28, 510 N.Y.S.2d 532, 536–37, 503 N.E.2d 88, 92–93 (1986). See text at notes 23–24 infra.

One case held that an X-ray could be authenticated as part of the business records of a hospital or physician. Hoffman v. City of New York, 141 Misc.2d 893, 535 N.Y.S.2d 342 (Sup.Ct.Kings Co.1988).

§ 1104.1 REAL & DEMONSTRATIVE EVIDENCE Ch. 11

personal injury action without the need for foundation testimony.[21] The statute specifies the type of identifying inscriptions that must appear on the image, and an affidavit must be provided by the physician under whose supervision the procedure was performed.[22]

c. Sound Recordings

Sound recordings of relevant events are admissible upon a proper foundation. In *People v. Ely*,[23] the Court of Appeals identified four alternative ways to authenticate sound recordings of conversations:

> Admissibility of tape-recorded conversation requires proof of the accuracy or authenticity of the tape by "clear and convincing evidence" establishing "that the offered evidence is genuine and that there has been no tampering with it" * * *. The neces-

---

21. CPLR 4532-a provides as follows:

Rule 4532-a. X-rays, magnetic resonance images, computed axial tomographs, positron emission tomographs, electromyograms, sonograms and fetal heart rate monitor strips in personal injury actions

In an action in which a claim for personal injuries is asserted, an X-ray, magnetic resonance image, computed axial tomograph, positron emission tomograph, electromyogram, sonogram or fetal heart rate monitor strips of any party thereto is admissible in evidence provided:

(1) that there is photographically inscribed on such X-ray, magnetic resonance image, computed axial tomograph, positron emission tomograph, electromyogram, sonogram or fetal heart rate monitor strips the name of the injured party, the date when taken, the identifying number thereof, and the name and address of the physician under whose supervision the same was taken;

(2) that at least ten days before the date of trial of the action, the attorney for the party intending to offer such X-ray, magnetic resonance image, computed axial tomograph, positron emission tomograph, electromyogram, sonogram or fetal heart rate monitor strips is to be offered, a notice of his intention to offer such X-ray, magnetic resonance image, computed axial tomograph, positron emission tomograph, electromyogram, sonogram or fetal heart rate monitor strips in evidence during the trial and that the same is available for inspection at his office, provided that such X-ray, magnetic resonance image, computed axial tomograph, positron emission tomograph, electromyogram, sonogram or fetal heart rate monitor strips has or have not been previously so examined; and

(3) that the notice aforesaid is accompanied by an affidavit of such physician identifying the X-ray, magnetic resonance image, computed axial tomograph, positron emission tomograph, electromyogram, sonogram or fetal heart rate monitor strips and attesting to the information inscribed thereon, and further attesting that, if called as a witness in the action, he would so testify.

Nothing contained in this section, however, shall prohibit the admissibility of an X-ray, magnetic resonance image, computed axial tomograph, positron emission tomograph, electromyogram, sonogram or fetal heart rate monitor strips in evidence in a personal injury action where otherwise admissible.

Parties relying on CPLR 4532-a have been held to strict compliance with its requirements. See Galuska v. Arbaiza, 106 A.D.2d 543, 545, 482 N.Y.S.2d 846, 848 (2d Dep't 1984). Shortcomings in this regard will require authentication by some other means. See, e.g., text at note 20 supra. Furthermore, even if foundation testimony is not needed to authenticate an X-ray admitted pursuant to CPLR 4532-a, expert testimony will undoubtedly be necessary to interpret the X-ray for the jury. See Marion v. B.G. Coon Construc. Co., 216 N.Y. 178, 181–82, 110 N.E. 444, 445 (1915)(X-rays unexplained by expert "may tend to mislead rather than to aid"); Vander Wel v. Palazzo, 155 A.D.2d 387, 548 N.Y.S.2d 14 (1st Dep't 1989).

22. CPLR 4532-a; note 21 supra.

23. 68 N.Y.2d 520, 510 N.Y.S.2d 532, 503 N.E.2d 88 (1986).

sary foundation may be provided in a number of different ways. Testimony of a participant in the conversation that it is a complete and accurate reproduction of the conversation and has not been altered * * * or of a witness to the conversation or to its recording, such as the machine operator, to the same effect * * * are two well-recognized ways. Testimony of a participant in the conversation together with proof by an expert witness that after analysis of the tapes for splices or alterations there was, in his or her opinion, no indication of either * * * is a third available method.

A fourth, chain of custody, though not a requirement as to tape recordings * * *, is also an available method * * *. It requires, in addition to evidence concerning the making of the tapes and identification of the speakers, that within reasonable limits those who have handled the tape from its making to its production in court " 'identify it and testify to its custody and unchanged condition' "* * *.[24]

The fourth method, which may be used when no auditor of the conversation is available, is analogous to the "silent witness" approach that is sometimes used to authenticate photographic evidence.[25]

Other cases establish the principle that exclusion is required if a sound recording "is so inaudible and indistinct that a jury must speculate as to its contents."[26] The prevailing test of sufficiency with respect to audibility is whether an "independent third [party] can listen to [the recording] and produce a reasonable transcript."[27] If the overall tape is sufficiently audible, fair and accurate as to material events recorded thereon, the presence of some inaudible portions will not preclude admissibility.[28] Such infirmities "go to the weight of the evidence, not its admissibility."[29]

---

24. Id. at 527–28, 510 N.Y.S.2d at 536–37, 503 N.E.2d at 92–93 (citations omitted). The burden-of-proof issue to which the court alludes at the outset of the quoted passage is discussed in § 900.1 supra.

25. See text at notes 7–11 supra. Chain of custody evidence is not required under the first three methods because a particular conversation, like a nonfungible object, usually is a unique event that a participant or witness with personal knowledge can readily identify. See People v. McGee, 49 N.Y.2d 48, 60, 424 N.Y.S.2d 157, 163, 399 N.E.2d 1177, 1183 (1979), cert. denied sub nom. Waters v. New York, 446 U.S. 942, 100 S.Ct. 2166, 64 L.Ed.2d 797 (1980).

A sound recording of noises other than a conversation, however, might be more in the nature of fungible matter, thus requiring a chain of custody. See generally § 1101.1, at notes 10–24, supra.

26. People v. Carrasco, 125 A.D.2d 695, 696, 509 N.Y.S.2d 879, 881 (2d Dep't 1986); People v. Harris, 199 A.D.2d 636, 636, 604 N.Y.S.2d 1005, 1006 (3d Dep't 1993), appeal denied, 83 N.Y.2d 872, 613 N.Y.S.2d 133, 635 N.E.2d 302 (1994).

27. People v. Carrasco, 125 A.D.2d 695, 696, 509 N.Y.S.2d 879, 881 (2d Dep't 1986).

28. See, e.g., People v. Morgan, 175 A.D.2d 930, 932, 573 N.Y.S.2d 765, 767 (2d Dep't 1991), appeal denied, 79 N.Y.2d 861, 580 N.Y.S.2d 733, 588 N.E.2d 768 (1992); People v. Harris, 199 A.D.2d 636, 636, 604 N.Y.S.2d 1005, 1006 (3d Dep't 1993), appeal denied, 83 N.Y.2d 872, 613 N.Y.S.2d 133, 635 N.E.2d 302 (1994).

29. People v. McGee, 49 N.Y.2d 48, 60, 424 N.Y.S.2d 157, 164, 399 N.E.2d 1177, 1183 (1979), cert. denied sub nom. Waters v. New York 446 U.S. 942, 100 S.Ct. 2166, 64 L.Ed.2d 797 (1980); People v. Wilson, 207 A.D.2d 463, 463, 615 N.Y.S.2d 769, 770 (2d Dep't 1994).

Identification of the voices on the tape, of course, is another condition to the admissibility of a sound recording. That aspect of the authentication process is discussed in § 901.5 and § 901.6 *supra*.

If a sound recording is determined to be admissible, it is common for the court to allow the jury to look at a transcript of the recording while listening to it.[30] The transcript is considered another form of demonstrative evidence, like a drawing or model, which "illustrates" the recording.[31]

d. Motion Pictures and Videotapes

As early as 1934, New York courts acknowledged the capacity of motion pictures accurately to depict "the true conditions sought to be shown."[32] No New York appellate case has explicitly noted the equal level of verisimilitude achieved by videotape, but the matter appears to have been assumed in numerous modern cases.[33] On the other hand, the Court of Appeals recently observed that films and videotapes can be easily altered and manipulated to produce a distorted image.[34] Even without deliberate manipulation, misleading impressions can be created by camera angles, lighting conditions, and uneven speeds. Nevertheless, a relevant movie or videotape can be admitted, in the court's discretion, on the basis of testimony by a witness who observed the matter that it fairly and accurately reproduces the filmed event and does not appear to have been altered.[35] The showing of a chain of custody, although helpful

---

30. See, e.g., People v. Tapia, 114 A.D.2d 983, 984, 495 N.Y.S.2d 93, 94 (2d Dep't 1985), appeal denied, 67 N.Y.2d 951, 502 N.Y.S.2d 1045, 494 N.E.2d 130 (1986)("A jury may use a transcript as an aid to understanding a tape recorded conversation when there is sufficient proof as to the accuracy of the transcript.").

31. People v. Feld, 305 N.Y. 322, 331–32, 113 N.E.2d 440, 444 (1953). See also People v. Robinson, 158 A.D.2d 628, 629, 551 N.Y.S.2d 599, 599 (2d Dep't 1990) ("court instructed the jury that the transcripts were not in evidence but were for their assistance only").

32. Boyarsky v. G.A. Zimmerman Corp., 240 App.Div. 361, 365, 270 N.Y.S. 134, 138 (1st Dep't 1934).

33. See, e.g., cases cited in notes 35–40 and 43–47 infra.

The taking of pretrial depositions by videotape has been statutorily authorized in civil cases, see CPLR 3113(b), and the administrative rules regulating the procedure for videotaped depositions contemplate their eventual use at trial in accordance with existing law governing the admissibility of evidence, in general, and deposition testimony in particular. See N.Y. Uniform Rules for the Supreme Court and the County Court 22 NYCRR 202.15(i).

34. DiMichel v. South Buffalo Ry. Co., 80 N.Y.2d 184, 196–97, 590 N.Y.S.2d 1, 6, 604 N.E.2d 63, 68 (1992), cert. denied sub nom. Poole v. Consolidated Rail Corp., ___ U.S. ___, 114 S.Ct. 68, 126 L.Ed.2d 37 (1993). DiMichel involved a personal injury plaintiff's request for pretrial discovery of defendant's surveillance films secretly taken of the plaintiff. The court ruled that plaintiffs have a practical need to view such films before trial in order to test their accuracy and authenticity. This can also be done, of course, during a voir dire at trial. See § 611.3(d) supra. The court observed, however, that "[a]uthentication of surveillance films can be a slow and painstaking process" and that a plaintiff would almost certainly be entitled to a continuance for examination purposes if confronted with such films for the first time at trial. 80 N.Y.2d at 196, 590 N.Y.S.2d at 6, 604 N.E.2d at 68. Interests in trial efficiency and protection against prejudice thus supported pretrial discovery of the films. The holding in DiMichel was codified (and expanded to include still photographs and audio recordings) in CPLR 3101(i). See § 501.3, at note 23, supra.

35. See, e.g., Matter of Burack, 201 A.D.2d 561, 561, 607 N.Y.S.2d 711, 712 (2d Dep't 1994). As in the case of a sound recording, see text at notes 30–31 supra, the court may allow the jury to use an

in support of authentication, apparently is unnecessary.[36] A more elaborate foundation would be required, however, if no witness observed the matter that was filmed and the proponent relies upon the "silent witness" theory of authentication.[37] Under any method of authentication, the presence of a few inaudible or unviewable segments of a film or videotape will not necessarily render the exhibit inadmissible,[38] but exclusion is appropriate if the deficiencies are so extensive "that a jury would have to speculate as to its contents."[39]

Even if the film is authenticated, admissibility ultimately turns on whether the matter depicted in the movie is relevant. For example, a videotape of a snarling, lunging pit bull filmed a few hours after the dog menaced police officers was held to be relevant in establishing the dog's vicious nature at the time of the incident.[40] On the other hand, a videotape of an apparently gentle border collie herding sheep three years after the dog's attack on a child was held to be too remote in time to be probative of defendant's lack of prior knowledge of the dog's allegedly vicious propensities.[41]

Furthermore, the court, in exercising its discretion, may find that such factors as delay, confusion, exaggeration or undue cumulativeness outweigh relevance.[42] New York courts have been especially receptive to movies taken of original, unrehearsed events such as a crime scene,[43] a crime in progress,[44] a defendant's confession to the police,[45] an allegedly

accurate transcript of the audio portion of a film "as an aid to understanding." See, e.g., People v. Dyla, 169 A.D.2d 777, 778, 565 N.Y.S.2d 143, 143–44 (2d Dep't), appeal denied, 77 N.Y.2d 994, 571 N.Y.S.2d 920, 575 N.E.2d 406 (1991).

36. See, e.g., People v. Fondal, 154 A.D.2d 476, 546 N.Y.S.2d 26 (2d Dep't), appeal denied, 75 N.Y.2d 770, 551 N.Y.S.2d 912, 551 N.E.2d 113 (1989)(testimony that videotape accurately depicted events observed by witness was "adequate foundation"). Cf. People v. Ely, 68 N.Y.2d 520, 527–28, 510 N.Y.S.2d 532, 536–37, 503 N.E.2d 88, 92–93 (1986)(description of available methods of authenticating sound recordings); text at note 24 supra.

37. See text at notes 7–13 supra.

38. See, e.g., People v. Harrell, 187 A.D.2d 453, 589 N.Y.S.2d 531 (2d Dep't 1992), leave to appeal denied, 81 N.Y.2d 789, 594 N.Y.S.2d 736, 610 N.E.2d 409 (1993); People v. Bazelais, 98 A.D.2d 802, 470 N.Y.S.2d 25 (2d Dep't 1983).

39. See, e.g., People v. Williams, 206 A.D.2d 917, 614 N.Y.S.2d 842 (4th Dep't), appeal denied, 84 N.Y.2d 911, 621 N.Y.S.2d 529, 645 N.E.2d 1229 (1994).

40. People v. Garraway, 187 A.D.2d 761, 589 N.Y.S.2d 942 (3d Dep't 1992), leave to appeal denied, 81 N.Y.2d 886, 597 N.Y.S.2d 947, 613 N.E.2d 979 (1993).

41. Austin v. Bascaran, 185 A.D.2d 474, 585 N.Y.S.2d 859 (3d Dep't 1992).

42. See Caprara v. Chrysler Corp., 71 A.D.2d 515, 523, 423 N.Y.S.2d 694, 698 (3d Dep't 1979), aff'd, 52 N.Y.2d 114, 436 N.Y.S.2d 251, 417 N.E.2d 545 (1981) ("Whether a motion picture is admissible is a matter within the sound discretion of the trial court * * *, and depends upon the facts and circumstances of each case."); Boyarsky v. G.A. Zimmerman Corp., 240 App. Div. 361, 270 N.Y.S. 134 (1st Dep't 1934)(in exercise of discretion, court may consider degree of assistance to jury, delay, sensationalism, physical difficulty, cumulativeness, risk of misleading jury, exaggeration of facts sought to be proved); McCormick § 214, at 18–20.

43. People v. Bernard, 214 A.D.2d 576, 625 N.Y.S.2d 67 (2d Dep't 1995), appeal denied, 85 N.Y.2d 969, 629 N.Y.S.2d 729, 653 N.E.2d 625 (1995).

44. People v. Harrell, 187 A.D.2d 453, 589 N.Y.S.2d 531 (2d Dep't 1992), leave to appeal denied, 81 N.Y.2d 789, 594 N.Y.S.2d 736, 610 N.E.2d 409 (1993) (sale of narcotics); People v. Fondal, 154 A.D.2d 476, 546 N.Y.S.2d 26 (2d Dep't), appeal denied, 75 N.Y.2d 770, 551 N.Y.S.2d 912, 551 N.E.2d 113 (1989)(shoplifting).

45. People v. Bazelais, 98 A.D.2d 802, 470 N.Y.S.2d 25 (2d Dep't 1983).

§ 1104.1   REAL & DEMONSTRATIVE EVIDENCE   Ch. 11

intoxicated driver shortly after his arrest[46] and an unsuspecting plaintiff, who is allegedly disabled, engaged in vigorous activity.[47] Movies of staged events, such as experiments, reenactments and demonstrations of products, skills or the effects of physical injuries, present a greater risk that the jury will be misled,[48] but precedent for admissibility exists here as well.[49] In assessing probative value, courts must pay close attention to the purpose for which such a film is offered and the fairness of the manner in which it seeks to achieve that end.[50]

46. People v. Strozier, 116 Misc.2d 103, 455 N.Y.S.2d 217 (Justice Ct.Monroe Co. 1982).

47. Boyarsky v. G.A. Zimmerman Corp., 240 App.Div. 361, 270 N.Y.S. 134 (1st Dep't 1934); Haley v. Hockey, 199 Misc. 512, 103 N.Y.S.2d 717 (Sup.Ct.Jefferson Co.1950).

48. Boyarsky v. G.A. Zimmerman Corp., 240 App.Div. 361, 366–67, 270 N.Y.S. 134, 140 (1st Dep't 1934). See generally McCormick § 214, at 16–20 (posed photographs and staged movies portraying proponent's version of facts present risk of unduly emphasizing only one side's testimony and confusing art with reality).

General principles governing evidence of tangible objects, the physical condition of persons, and experiments and reenactments are discussed in §§ 1101.1 and 1102.1 supra, and § 1105.1 infra, respectively. The admissibility of such evidence becomes more complex when presented through the medium of film with its potential for visual distortion or exaggeration of the matter.

49. Caprara v. Chrysler Corp., 71 A.D.2d 515, 522–23, 423 N.Y.S.2d 694, 698–99 (3d Dep't 1979), aff'd, 52 N.Y.2d 114, 436 N.Y.S.2d 251, 417 N.E.2d 545 (1981) (10–minute "day-in-the-life" film showing impact of personal injury on plaintiff; probative value outweighed any prejudice where film illustrated "a portion of the typical daily routine of plaintiff being tended to at his parents' home * * * in an informative and noninflammatory manner."). Factors that a trial court should consider in exercising its discretion with respect to the admissibility of day-in-the-life films are suggested in Bannister v. Town of Noble, Oklahoma, 812 F.2d 1265, 1269–70 (10th Cir.1987).

A videotape of a testator in the act of executing his will straddles the line between an original event and a staged performance. Such evidence was held to have been properly admitted in a probate proceeding on the issue of the decedent's testamentary capacity in Matter of Burack, 201 A.D.2d 561, 607 N.Y.S.2d 711 (2d Dep't 1994).

50. In the following cases, films of staged events were held to be inadmissible because of their low probative value and misleading nature with respect to the facts in issue: Austin v. Bascaran, 185 A.D.2d 474, 585 N.Y.S.2d 859(3d Dep't 1992)(in dog-bite case alleging defendant's prior knowledge of dog's vicious nature, 20–minute videotape of dog following defendant's commands and herding sheep, made for trial over three years after attack, was of "questionable probative value" and "highly prejudicial"); Mercatante v. Hyster Co., 159 A.D.2d 492, 552 N.Y.S.2d 364 (2d Dep't 1990)(in products liability action alleging design defect, videotape of machine, prepared for trial and introduced ostensibly for instructional purpose of showing its safe operational functions, "was of questionable probative value" where it depicted operator using machine in manner different from that involved in plaintiff's action; court noted that machine was at courthouse and available for inspection and demonstration during trial); Glusaskas v. Hutchinson, 148 A.D.2d 203, 544 N.Y.S.2d 323 (1st Dep't 1989)(in medical malpractice action alleging negligent and hastily performed incision during heart surgery for valve replacement, trial court erred in admitting videotape of defendant made for trial six years after accident, showing him performing surgical incision on another patient with different physical and medical condition; court observed that videotape can sometimes serve instructional purpose as to how particular medical procedures are performed, but here, the circumstances were too dissimilar, the film tended to show defendant's general "carefulness" (a prohibited form of character evidence, see §§ 402.1 and 406.1 supra), and record indicated that defendant was much slower and deliberate on videotape than during surgery at issue); Mechanick v. Conradi, 139 A.D.2d 857, 527 N.Y.S.2d 586 (3d Dep't 1988) (in vehicular collision case alleging defendant's improper left-hand turn in front of motorcycle approaching from opposite direction, videotape offered by plaintiff to show "sight distance" from defendant's point of view was properly excluded due to potential misleading of jury: large van, rather than motorcycle, was used to represent plaintiff's vehicle; large red cones, not present at time of accident, were

As part of the authentication process, a trial judge may conduct a preliminary viewing before the film is shown to the jury.[51] Such procedure helps to guard against the potential for undue prejudice in the event sufficient relevance or authenticity is not established.[52]

Library References:

West's Key No. Digests, Criminal Law ⚖438, 438.1; Evidence ⚖359.

§ 1104.2 Federal

a. Photographs

Photographs of relevant matters may be admitted as demonstrative evidence of a witness' testimony. Authentication can be satisfied in such cases by the testimony of the witness that the photograph is a fair and accurate representation of what she observed.[1] Federal courts within the Second Circuit have also endorsed the "silent witness" principle,[2] pursuant to which photographic evidence which is shown to have been produced by proper procedures and preserved unaltered may be admitted without the need for eyewitness testimony concerning the matter depicted in the photograph.[3] Assuming proper authentication, admissibility turns on the trial court's discretionary balancing of the relevance of the matter depicted against the considerations of Rule 403.[4]

b. X-Rays

X-rays are admissible in federal court pursuant to the "silent witness" theory of authentication.[5]

c. Sound Recordings

Sound recordings of relevant events are admissible upon sufficient foundation evidence of authenticity of the recording and identification of the speakers. Methods of voice identification are covered in §§ 901.5 and 901.6 *supra*. As to authentication, a relatively early opinion by a federal district court in New York formulated a list of foundation

placed on side of road as visual markers; use of telephoto lens "enhanced defendant's alleged sight distance"; and van was shown traveling at speeds no greater than 55 m.p.h., which was consistent with motorcyclist's testimony but contradictory of state trooper's testimony (and radar reading) that motorcyclist was traveling at 70 m.p.h.).

51. Caprara v. Chrysler Corp., 71 A.D.2d 515, 523, 423 N.Y.S.2d 694, 699 (3d Dep't 1979), aff'd, 52 N.Y.2d 114, 436 N.Y.S.2d 251, 417 N.E.2d 545 (1981); Boyarsky v. G.A. Zimmerman Corp., 240 App. Div. 361, 366, 270 N.Y.S. 134, 139 (1st Dep't 1934).

52. The same need for a private screening seldom exists in the case of still photographs, which usually can be shielded from the jury's view until the authentication process is complete.

§ 1104.2

1. United States v. Valdes, 417 F.2d 335, 338 (2d Cir.1969), cert. denied, 399 U.S. 912, 90 S.Ct. 2206, 26 L.Ed.2d 566 (1970)(witness who was present when photograph of defendant was taken testified that photograph was fair representation of defendant as he appeared at that time).

2. See § 1104.1, at notes 7–13, supra.

3. United States v. Pageau, 526 F.Supp. 1221, 1224 (N.D.N.Y.1981) (videotape recording was sufficiently authenticated by testimony of proper installation, activation and operation of camera and by chain of custody of tape). See also note 18 infra.

4. See, e.g., §§ 1101.2 and 1102.2 supra. See generally § 401.2 supra.

5. See § 1104.1, at notes 19–20, supra. See also Graham § 401.8.

§ 1104.2   REAL & DEMONSTRATIVE EVIDENCE   Ch. 11

requirements for sound recordings that included a showing of the mechanics of the particular recording process, chain of custody, absence of alteration and testimony as to the accuracy of the recording.[6] Several years later, however, the Second Circuit in *United States v. Fuentes*[7] declined to adopt the list, stating that "inflexible criteria applicable to all cases" should be avoided.[8] On the other hand, *Fuentes* held that the authenticity of sound recordings must be established by clear and convincing evidence because "recorded evidence is likely to have a strong impression on a jury and is susceptible to alteration."[9]

Recent cases outside the Second Circuit suggest that a recording can be authenticated in either of two ways. It is sufficient that a witness who participated in or overheard the conversation can testify that the recording is a fair and accurate reproduction.[10] Alternatively, the recording can be authenticated by a showing of the mechanics and procedures that were followed, together with a chain of custody and evidence that no tampering occurred.[11] Recordings that contain inaudible seg-

---

6. United States v. McKeever, 169 F.Supp. 426, 430 (S.D.N.Y.1958), rev'd on other grounds, 271 F.2d 669 (2d Cir.1959):

[B]efore a sound recording is admitted into evidence, a foundation must be established by showing the following facts:

(1) That the recording device was capable of taking the conversation now offered in evidence.

(2) That the operator of the device was competent to operate the device.

(3) That the recording is authentic and correct.

(4) That changes, additions or deletions have not been made in the recording.

(5) That the recording has been preserved in a manner that is shown to the court.

(6) That the speakers are identified.

(7) That the conversation elicited [in a criminal case] was made voluntarily and in good faith, without any kind of inducement.

The Eighth Circuit adopted the McKeever court's formulation in Slatinsky v. Bailey, 330 F.2d 136, 140–41 (8th Cir.1964), and continues to follow it. See United States v. Buchanan, 985 F.2d 1372, 1378–79 (8th Cir. 1993), cert. denied, __ U.S. __, 114 S.Ct. 2727, 129 L.Ed.2d 850 (1994).

7. 563 F.2d 527 (2d Cir.), cert. denied, 434 U.S. 959, 98 S.Ct. 491, 54 L.Ed.2d 320 (1977).

8. Id. at 532. The court said that the McKeever list, quoted in note 6 supra, should simply be regarded "as a valuable formulation of the factors a trial judge should consider in making an initial determination whether a sufficient foundation for the admissibility of the tape recordings has been established." Id.

9. Id. The applicability of a clear-and-convincing-evidence standard to the authentication of tape recordings was reaffirmed in United States v. Ruggiero, 928 F.2d 1289, 1303 (2d Cir.1991), cert. denied, 502 U.S. 938, 112 S.Ct. 372, 116 L.Ed.2d 324 (1991). See also § 900.1 supra.

In United States v. Bryant, 480 F.2d 785, 789 (2d Cir.1973), the court indicated that the correct procedure is for the trial judge to have sound recordings first played outside the presence of the jury so that rulings on objections can be made before the jury hears the tapes. Similarly, any transcript of a recording should be compared with the tape before the transcript is given to the jury.

10. United States v. Lance, 853 F.2d 1177, 1181 (5th Cir.1988) (authentication was adequate where participants in taped conversation "testified that, according to their memories, the audio and video tapes contained accurate recordings of the conversations that occurred."). See also § 1104.1, at notes 23–24, supra.

11. United States v. Rengifo, 789 F.2d 975, 978–79 (1st Cir.1986) (government agent who supervised wiretap recording operation, but did not personally hear conversation, sufficiently authenticated tapes by giving detailed testimony describing recording procedures that were followed, including testing of equipment, labelling and custody of tapes; agent's testimony raised "presumption of official regularity").

This methodology of authentication is analogous to the "silent witness" approach to the authentication of photographic evi-

ments can still be admitted unless the inaudible portion is so substantial as to render the recording untrustworthy.[12] Properly authenticated composite recordings are permitted,[13] and transcripts, if stipulated to be accurate, may be used by the jury while listening to tapes.[14] Furthermore, in the Second Circuit the trial court, in its discretion, may permit the jury to take transcripts of a recording into the jury room during deliberations.[15]

d. Motion Pictures and Videotape

Motion pictures and videotapes of relevant events can be authenticated by either: (1) the testimony of a witness who observed the event and is able to say that the film is a fair and accurate representation thereof,[16] or (2) the "silent witness" approach,[17] which may be satisfied by testimony of "the proper installation, activation and operation of the camera and by the chain of possession of the tape."[18]

The Second Circuit has indicated its agreement with Wigmore that a contemporaneous film of the actual event involved in the litigation lacks the "special risk of misleading" that inheres in a staged reenactment and therefore should be admissible with the same ease as photographs.[19]

---

dence. See generally § 1104.1, at notes 7–13, supra. See also note 3 supra, and note 18 infra.

12. United States v. Bryant, 480 F.2d 785, 790 (2d Cir.1973). See also United States v. Arango–Correa, 851 F.2d 54, 58 (2d Cir.1988)("Our decisions in this area reveal a clear preference for the admission of recordings notwithstanding some ambiguity or inaudibility, as long as the recordings are probative.").

13. See, e.g., United States v. Rengifo, 789 F.2d 975, 979–80 (1st Cir.1986).

14. See United States v. Bryant, 480 F.2d 785, 790–91 (2d Cir.1973); United States v. Koska, 443 F.2d 1167, 1169 (2d Cir.), cert. denied, 404 U.S. 852, 92 S.Ct. 92, 30 L.Ed.2d 92 (1971). In United States v. Carson, 464 F.2d 424, 437 (2d Cir.), cert. denied, 409 U.S. 949, 93 S.Ct. 268, 34 L.Ed.2d 219 (1972), the transcript given to the jury reflected a stipulation as to which words on the tape both sides could agree upon and which portions were to be marked "inaudible"; as to disputed segments, each side gave a version believed to be accurate.

15. See United States v. Carson, 464 F.2d 424, 437 (2d Cir.), cert. denied, 409 U.S. 949, 93 S.Ct. 268, 34 L.Ed.2d 219 (1972). See also United States v. Rengifo, 789 F.2d 975, 980–83 (1st Cir.1986).

16. Mikus v. United States, 433 F.2d 719, 725 (2d Cir.1970)(bank teller testified that movie was fair and accurate representation of robbery that occurred in her presence); Louis Vuitton S.A. v. Spencer Handbags Corp., 765 F.2d 966, 973–74 (2d Cir.1985)(participant in private sting operation testified that videotape accurately depicted meeting between participant and defendants: "Where, as here, no well-founded accusation of impropriety or inaccuracy is made, testimony as to authentication is sufficient.").

17. See § 1104.1, at notes 7–13, supra.

18. United States v. Pageau, 526 F.Supp. 1221, 1224 (N.D.N.Y.1981)(prison official, upon hearing noises in particular gallery of prison, activated video camera which recorded defendant's assault on prisoner; the official, who did not see the entire event, testified in detail as to how he operated the camera, and substantial evidence was presented as to technical aspects of installation and recording capabilities of cameras and microphones located in the area where the events occurred). See also Mikus v. United States, 433 F.2d 719, 722, 725–26 (2d Cir.1970) (wall-mounted camera recorded aspects of bank robbery not seen by bank teller who testified that movie was fair and accurate representation of robbery; teller, who was behind teller's counter, testified that robber was short and movie, taken from different vantage point, showed that suspect was bent over).

19. Mikus v. United States, 433 F.2d 719, 725 (2d Cir.1970), quoting 3 Wigmore § 798–a, at 203 (movie of bank robbery in progress). In addition to the cases cited in notes 16 and 18, supra, movies of original events were held to be admissible in the following cases: United States v. Birnbaum, 337 F.2d 490, 496 (2d Cir.1964)(passing of bribe money to federal agent); United

Assuming authenticity, admissibility lies in the discretion of the trial judge, who balances probative value against potential prejudicial effects.[20] A Tenth Circuit decision urges special caution with respect to videotape animations offered to illustrate expert testimony concerning theoretical reconstructions of particular accidents.[21]

Library References:
West's Key No. Digests, Criminal Law ⚷438, 438.1; Evidence ⚷359.

1105 Experiments and Demonstrations

§ 1105.1 New York

The results of experiments and demonstrations may be relevant to help prove (or disprove) factual assertions relating to mechanical principles or qualities, physical properties or characteristics, and human capacities or behavior under particular conditions.[1] New York courts, for example, have permitted evidence of experiments to show whether the striking of a metal pole with the human hand could cause the fall of a particular street sign mounted on top of the pole;[2] whether a fire that was ignited by a particular source could have caused certain effects;[3] and whether a train motorman could have seen a person lying on the tracks

---

States v. Moran, 194 F.2d 623, 626 (2d Cir.), cert. denied, 343 U.S. 965, 72 S.Ct. 1058, 96 L.Ed. 1362 (1952)(film of defendant's allegedly perjurious testimony before Senate subcommittee showed defendant's demeanor).

20. United States v. Birnbaum, 337 F.2d 490, 496 (2d Cir.1964).

In determining admissibility, the trial judge typically views the movie and receives foundation testimony before it is shown to the jury. The supporting testimony may then be repeated in the jury's presence. See, e.g., Mikus v. United States, 433 F.2d 719, 725 (2d Cir.1970); Veliz v. Crown Lift Trucks, 714 F.Supp. 49, 52 (E.D.N.Y.1989). Such preliminary authentication of a film may also be considered in a pretrial hearing. See, e.g., United States v. Pageau, 526 F.Supp. 1221, 1223 (N.D.N.Y.1981).

The Federal Rules of Civil Procedure explicitly permit the taking of depositions by videotape. Fed.R.Civ.P. 30(b)(2). Assuming satisfaction of one of the grounds for admissibility at trial under Fed.R.Civ.P. 32(a), a videotaped deposition offered as substantive evidence "shall" be admitted in its videotaped form, rather than by transcript, upon the request of any party in a jury trial "unless the court for good cause orders otherwise." Fed.R.Civ.P. 32(c).

21. Robinson v. Missouri Pacific R.R. Co., 16 F.3d 1083, 1086–89 (10th Cir.1994). Robinson involved the admissibility of a two-minute silent color video prepared by an accident reconstruction expert who used miniatures of a car, train and crossing gate to depict, in animated form, the expert's theory as to how a railroad crossing accident must have happened in light of the physical evidence. There was no abuse of discretion in admitting the animated film, said the appellate court, because of its solely illustrative purpose, the trial court's limiting instructions and the opportunity for cross-examination of the expert. The court nevertheless observed, "Because of its dramatic power, trial judges should carefully and meticulously examine proposed animation evidence for proper foundation, relevancy and the potential for undue prejudice." Id. at 1988. See also § 1106.1 infra.

§ 1105.1

1. See generally McCormick §§ 202 and 215. Demonstrations of the effects of human injuries are discussed in § 1102.1, at notes 22–26, supra.

2. Uss v. Town of Oyster Bay, 37 N.Y.2d 639, 376 N.Y.S.2d 449, 339 N.E.2d 147 (1975)(courtroom experiment). See also Washington v. Long Island R.R. Co., 13 A.D.2d 710, 214 N.Y.S.2d 115 (2d Dep't 1961)(stopping distance of train; out-of-court experiment).

3. Goldner v. Kemper Insurance Co., 152 A.D.2d 936, 544 N.Y.S.2d 396 (4th Dep't 1989), apppeal denied, 75 N.Y.2d 704, 552 N.Y.S.2d 109, 551 N.E.2d 602 (1990) (out-of-court experiment).

Ch. 11   EXPERIMENTS & DEMONSTRATIONS   § 1105.1

ahead of him at a certain distance.[4] Sometimes demonstrations, like drawings or diagrams, may be useful simply to help the fact-finder visualize a witness' testimony.[5]

The same basic rules govern admissibility regardless of whether the experiment or demonstration is performed in the courtroom or in an out-of-court setting and then described in court.[6] A fundamental prerequisite, of course, is relevance, which is measured principally by the similarity between the conditions under which the experiment or demonstration was performed and those that existed at the time of the event at issue.[7]

The degree to which similarity will be required is largely dependent on the purpose for which the evidence is offered. It would seem that the more limited the purpose of the experiment, the less need there is for exactitude of circumstances so long as sufficient similarity exists to fairly

---

4. Norfleet v. New York City Transit Auth., 124 A.D.2d 715, 508 N.Y.S.2d 468 (2d Dep't 1986), appeal denied, 69 N.Y.2d 605, 513 N.Y.S.2d 1026, 505 N.E.2d 953 (1987)(out-of-court experiment). See also People v. Mariner, 147 A.D.2d 659, 538 N.Y.S.2d 61 (2d Dep't), appeal denied, 74 N.Y.2d 666, 543 N.Y.S.2d 409, 541 N.E.2d 438 (1989)(police officer's ability to see exchange of glassine envelopes through binoculars at distance of 40 feet; courtroom experiment); Thomas v. Central Greyhound Lines, Inc., 6 A.D.2d 649, 653–54, 180 N.Y.S.2d 461, 466–67 (1st Dep't 1958) (whether bus passenger seated on left-hand side of bus and looking out passenger's window could see center line of highway 6–12 inches to left of bus; out-of-court experiment).

5. See, e.g., People v. Barnes, 175 A.D.2d 695, 572 N.Y.S.2d 686 (1st Dep't 1991), aff'd, 80 N.Y.2d 867, 587 N.Y.S.2d 597, 600 N.E.2d 228 (1992) (during cross-examination of defense witness, two court officers were permitted to demonstrate relative positions of defendant and victim at time of shooting according to witness' testimony). See also Glusaskas v. Hutchinson, 148 A.D.2d 203, 208, 544 N.Y.S.2d 323, 326 (1st Dep't 1989) (in dictum, court suggested that film showing how expert witness commonly carries out particular medical procedure could serve valid instructional purpose in medical malpractice trial; in case at hand, however, film showing defendant doctor operating on different patient using different procedures was misleading and prejudicial); § 1102.1, at notes 22–26, supra (demonstration of effects of personal injuries).

6. Additional problems of authentication and potential prejudice are raised when testimonial descriptions of out-of-court experiments or reenactments are augmented by filmed versions. See § 1104.1(d), supra.

There is some indication in the cases that demonstrations or experiments that are not feasible in the courtroom may be performed for the jury, under judicial supervision, at other locations on the courthouse grounds. See Mercatante v. Hyster Co., 159 A.D.2d 492, 493, 552 N.Y.S.2d 364, 365 (2d Dep't 1990)(court noted that machine "was available for inspection and demonstration at the courthouse during the pendency of the trial"). See also Veliz v. Crown Lift Trucks, 714 F.Supp. 49, 51 (E.D.N.Y.1989) (court permitted supervised demonstration of operation of lift truck, in jury's presence, in courthouse basement).

7. Hoover v. Durkee, 212 A.D.2d 839, 841, 622 N.Y.S.2d 348, 350 (3d Dep't 1995)(results of out-of-court tests or experiments "would only be admissible so long as the conditions under which the test or experiment was conducted were sufficiently similar to those existing at the time in issue to make the results achieved relevant at trial"); People v. Mariner, 147 A.D.2d 659, 660, 538 N.Y.S.2d 61, 62 (2d Dep't), appeal denied, 74 N.Y.2d 666, 543 N.Y.S.2d 409, 541 N.E.2d 438 (1989)(in reviewing propriety of courtroom experiment, court applied the following standard: "Demonstrative evidence is admissible, in the court's discretion, provided that the conditions under which the experiment are conducted are similar to those existing at the time of the incident at issue.") See also People v. Cohen, 50 N.Y.2d 908, 910, 431 N.Y.S.2d 446, 448, 409 N.E.2d 921, 922 (1980), cert. denied, 461 U.S. 930, 103 S.Ct. 2092, 77 L.Ed.2d 302 (1983)(results of test-firing of murder weapon at various distances to show effect on human tissue would be inadmissible absent showing of substantial similarity between skin tissue of animals used in test and that of humans).

demonstrate the proposition in question. Nonessential variations may simply affect the weight of the evidence rather than its admissibility.[8] Furthermore, dissimilarities are most likely to be tolerated when the test conditions would make it more difficult for the proponent to prove her point.[9] New York courts have also said that the danger of a jury's giving undue weight to an experiment that lacks absolute similarity can be mitigated by giving the opponent "unrestricted opportunity for cross-examination."[10] Nevertheless, dozens of decisions excluding evidence of experiments and demonstrations attest to the continuing vitality of the similarity requirement.[11] As a practical matter, and depending on the

---

8. People v. Mariner, 147 A.D.2d 659, 660, 538 N.Y.S.2d 61, 62 (2d Dep't), appeal denied, 74 N.Y.2d 666, 543 N.Y.S.2d 409, 541 N.E.2d 438 (1989); Thomas v. Central Greyhound Lines, Inc., 6 A.D.2d 649, 654, 180 N.Y.S.2d 461, 466 (1st Dep't 1958).

9. The leading New York case for this proposition is Thomas v. Central Greyhound Lines, Inc., 6 A.D.2d 649, 180 N.Y.S.2d 461 (1st Dep't 1958). At issue was the credibility of a bus passenger who testified that while riding on the left-hand side of the bus, he looked down at the road out the window and saw the highway divider line, which was 6–12 inches to the left of the bus gradually disappear from view, suggesting that the bus had veered to the left. In an experiment conducted in the bus company's garage, the passenger's angle of vision on the left-hand side of the bus was tested from several possible vantage points with the result that it would have been physically impossible for the passenger to have seen a divider line 6–12 inches to the left. The conditions under which the experiment was conducted were more likely to result in a finding of visibility than those which existed at the accident site: the weather was rainy and misty at the time of the accident, whereas the test was indoors, and the ground was flat and level in the garage whereas the road at the accident site was crowned for drainage purposes. The crowned road, unlike the garage floor, would have tilted the bus in a way that would have reduced the passenger's field of vision. Id. at 653–54, 180 N.Y.S.2d at 466–67. See also Norfleet v. New York City Transit Auth., 124 A.D.2d 715, 717, 508 N.Y.S.2d 468, 469 (2d Dep't 1986), appeal denied, 69 N.Y.2d 605, 513 N.Y.S.2d 1026, 505 N.E.2d 953 (1987).

10. Uss v. Town of Oyster Bay, 37 N.Y.2d 639, 641, 376 N.Y.S.2d 449, 450–51, 339 N.E.2d 147, 149 (1975)("By effective exploitation of the dissimilarities between the model and the original it was thus open to counsel to minimize the significance to be attached to the demonstration."); Norfleet v. New York City Transit Auth., 124 A.D.2d 715, 717, 508 N.Y.S.2d 468, 469 (2d Dep't 1986), appeal denied, 69 N.Y.2d 605, 513 N.Y.S.2d 1026, 505 N.E.2d 953 (1987)(opponent's attorney "emphatically highlighted" variations, both in cross-examination and in summation).

11. In the following illustrative cases, the similarity prerequisite was not satisfied: People v. Acevedo, 40 N.Y.2d 701, 389 N.Y.S.2d 811, 358 N.E.2d 495 (1976)(trial court properly excluded courtroom experiment which sought to test ability of robbery victim, who allegedly identified voice of masked defendant, to recognize voice of defendant's brother: on day of robbery, victim had been in recent contact with defendant, whereas at time of trial two years had elapsed since she had last heard the brother's voice; extent of familiarity with brother had been limited; exposure to defendant's voice during robbery lasted 20 minutes whereas proposed demonstration contemplated brother's utterance of two short sentences; and victim had been able to observe masked robber, thereby adding visual component to identification, whereas victim would have been blindfolded for experiment); Hoover v. Durkee, 212 A.D.2d 839, 841, 622 N.Y.S.2d 348, 350 (3d Dep't 1995)(in nuisance action, noise levels of race track at time of test were not shown to be similar to usual occasions); People v. Gregg, 203 A.D.2d 188, 611 N.Y.S.2d 151 (1st Dep't), appeal denied, 83 N.Y.2d 911, 614 N.Y.S.2d 393, 637 N.E.2d 284 (1994) (whether defendant's dropping of small tin canister could have sounded to police officer like dropping of small caliber gun was not testable due to uniqueness of surrounding circumstances); Austin v. Bascaran, 185 A.D.2d 474, 585 N.Y.S.2d 859 (3d Dep't 1992)(in dog-bite case, videotape of dog calmly herding sheep and following owner's commands three years after event was too dissimilar and remote to actual circumstances); Mercatante v. Hyster Co., 159 A.D.2d 492, 552 N.Y.S.2d 364 (2d Dep't 1990)(videotape showing operation of allegedly defective machinery in manner different from circumstances of accident); Mechanick v. Conradi, 139 A.D.2d 857, 527 N.Y.S.2d 586 (3d Dep't 1988)(driver's abili-

issue, it may be more difficult to achieve sufficient similarity of conditions in the courtroom than in an out-of-court experiment.[12]

The trial court's "sound discretion" ultimately governs admissibility.[13] This exercise of discretion includes the usual weighing of probative value against factors of distraction, delay, cumulativeness and the potential for misleading or confusing the jury.[14]

Library References:

West's Key No. Digests, Criminal Law ⚖388, 650; Evidence ⚖150; Trial ⚖27.

---

ty to see oncoming motorcycle could not properly be demonstrated by test that used van instead of motorcycle and failed to take account of dispute in testimony concerning speed of cycle); Weinstein v. Daman, 132 A.D.2d 547, 548–49, 517 N.Y.S.2d 278, 280 (2d Dep't), motion for leave to appeal dismissed, 70 N.Y.2d 872, 523 N.Y.S.2d 498, 518 N.E.2d 8 (1987), and appeal dismissed, 70 N.Y.2d 951, 524 N.Y.S.2d 678, 519 N.E.2d 624 (1988)(ability of plaintiff with injury in right eye to see defense counsel's table could not be tested by having each juror sit in witness stand and close right eye); People v. Bethune, 105 A.D.2d 262, 272, 484 N.Y.S.2d 577, 585 (2d Dep't 1984)(defense counsel's proposed placing of arm around neck of defendant to show that victim could not have bitten attacker's arm was improper in absence of evidence as to how neck of actual victim was held); People v. Sugrue, 103 A.D.2d 785, 477 N.Y.S.2d 425 (2d Dep't 1984)(visibility of defendant's tattoos if he had been wearing particular type of shirt could not be tested without showing that shirt used in test was same type as that worn by perpetrator).

12. See, e.g., People v. Esquilin, 207 A.D.2d 686, 616 N.Y.S.2d 364 (1st Dep't), appeal denied, 84 N.Y.2d 907, 621 N.Y.S.2d 524, 645 N.E.2d 1224 (1994)(because of variations in conditions of courtroom and moving train, court properly precluded demonstration of defendant's struggle with decedent). Some experiments simply may not be safe or feasible in the courtroom. See also note 6 supra.

13. People v. Acevedo, 40 N.Y.2d 701, 704, 389 N.Y.S.2d 811, 814, 358 N.E.2d 495, 497 (1976); Uss v. Town of Oyster Bay, 37 N.Y.2d 639, 641, 376 N.Y.S.2d 449, 450, 339 N.E.2d 147, 149 (1975). See also Goldner v. Kemper Insurance Co., 152 A.D.2d 936, 937, 544 N.Y.S.2d 396, 397 (4th Dep't 1989), appeal denied, 75 N.Y.2d 704, 552 N.Y.S.2d 109, 551 N.E.2d 602 (1990)("The trial court has broad discretion with respect to the admission of [test] evidence, especially with reference to the question of the similarity of conditions. The most broadly stated or recognized standard is whether the evidence tends to enlighten rather than to mislead the jury.").

14. People v. Acevedo, 40 N.Y.2d 701, 704, 389 N.Y.S.2d 811, 813–14, 358 N.E.2d 495, 497 (1976)(although tests and demonstrations can play "a positive and helpful role in the ascertainment of truth, courts must be alert to the danger that, when ill-designed or not properly relevant to the point at issue, instead of being helpful they may serve but to mislead, confuse, divert or otherwise prejudice the purposes of the trial"); Uss v. Town of Oyster Bay, 37 N.Y.2d 639, 641, 376 N.Y.S.2d 449, 451, 339 N.E.2d 147, 149 (1975)(factors weighing against admissibility include deception, sensationalism, disruption and conjectural conditions). See, e.g., People v. Walstatter, 53 N.Y.2d 871, 440 N.Y.S.2d 615, 423 N.E.2d 38 (1981)(in rape prosecution where defense was based on consent, trial court properly precluded defendant from using live models for in-court demonstration of events); People v. Benoit, 8 A.D.2d 626, 185 N.Y.S.2d 622 (2d Dep't 1959)(in prosecution for possession of burglar's tools, prejudice outweighed relevance where police officer demonstrated use of seized tools to break open safes to show capacity and suitability of tools for burglary; capacity of tools in question was obvious and had been conceded by defendant, leaving defendant's intent to use the tools for criminal purposes as the only real issue and making demonstration of hypothetical safecracking unnecessary and inflammatory); McCormick § 214, at 19–20 (staged reproductions of events presented through medium of film may have tendency to unduly emphasize one side's testimony and lead jury to confuse art with reality); § 1104.1, at notes 42–50, supra.

§ 1105.2 Federal

Surprisingly, only a handful of cases within the Second Circuit touch upon the federal standards for the admissibility of demonstrations and experiments. A district judge in New York, in the context of a products liability case, drew upon cases from other circuits to articulate the following basic rules:

> It is, of course, firmly established that the decision whether to admit evidence of experimental tests or demonstrations is a matter left to the sound discretion of the trial judge. * * * "[A] court may properly admit experimental evidence if the tests were conducted under conditions substantially similar to the actual conditions. Admissibility, however, does not depend on perfect identity between actual and experimental conditions. Ordinarily, dissimilarities affect the weight of the evidence, not its admissibility." * * * The notion underlying the admission of such evidence in a products liability case is that it fosters a better understanding by the jury of the product, issues, and often abstruse expert testimony involved. * * *
>
> To be sure, there are certain dangers inherent in the admission of demonstrations, as there exists the possibility of juror confusion about the precise purpose of the demonstrations. Courts have recognized, however, that when accompanied by limiting instructions or testimony detailing the dissimilarities between the demonstration and actual conditions, it is not error to admit demonstrations that are substantially similar to, but do not mirror, the actual conditions involved. * * *[1]

Some courts have drawn a distinction between experiments and demonstrations that purport to reenact the actual event and those that are used merely to demonstrate general scientific, physical or mechanical principles. To the extent an experiment is more like a reenactment, the requirement of similarity of conditions is more strictly enforced in order to avoid the risk of misleading the jury.[2] With respect to more generalized demonstrations, the similarity requirement is less strictly enforced, provided no suggestion is made that simulation of actual events was

---

§ 1105.2

1. Veliz v. Crown Lift Trucks, 714 F.Supp. 49, 51–52 (E.D.N.Y.1989) (quoting Champeau v. Fruehauf Corp., 814 F.2d 1271, 1278 (8th Cir.1987)) (other citations and quotations omitted). Other cases cited by the district court are Szeliga v. General Motors Corp., 728 F.2d 566 (1st Cir.1984); Randall v. Warnaco, Inc., 677 F.2d 1226 (8th Cir.1982); Nanda v. Ford Motor Co., 509 F.2d 213 (7th Cir.1974); Millers' National Ins. Co. v. Wichita Flour Mills Co., 257 F.2d 93 (10th Cir.1958). In Veliz, the plaintiff alleged, inter alia, that defendant's lift truck had an excessive stopping distance. The court admitted videotapes showing the operation of a lift truck carrying various loads to demonstrate the physical and mechanical principles involved in braking. The court also supervised a brief live demonstration of the same type of machine in the courthouse basement. Veliz, 714 F.Supp. at 51–54.

2. Fusco v. General Motors Corp., 11 F.3d 259, 264 (1st Cir.1993). Accord, McKnight v. Johnson Controls, Inc., 36 F.3d 1396, 1402–03 (8th Cir.1994); Four Corners Helicopters, Inc., v. Turbomeca, S.A., 979 F.2d 1434, 1442 (10th Cir.1992).

intended and the jury is carefully instructed concerning the limited purposes for which the evidence is offered.[3]

A 1972 dictum of the Second Circuit would impose the following constraint on experiments conducted outside of court: "Test results should not even be admissible as evidence, unless made by a qualified, independent expert or unless the opposing party has the opportunity to participate in the test."[4]

Library References:

West's Key No. Digests, Criminal Law ⚖︎388, 650; Evidence ⚖︎150; Federal Civil Procedure ⚖︎2011.

1106   Computer-Generated Graphics

§ 1106.1   Computer–Generated Graphics: New York and Federal

Computer-generated graphics can produce an especially compelling form of demonstrative evidence that litigants with the necessary resources can be expected increasingly to exploit. Such evidence has been used successfully in conjunction with expert testimony. For example, an accident reconstruction specialist, after developing an opinion as to how an accident occurred, may work with a computer technician to develop an animated pictorial representation on videotape that reflects the expert's opinion.

---

3. Gilbert v. Cosco Inc., 989 F.2d 399, 402–04 (10th Cir.1993); McKnight v. Johnson Controls, Inc., 36 F.3d 1396, 1402–03 (8th Cir.1994). The district court in Veliz v. Crown Lift Trucks, 714 F.Supp. 49 (E.D.N.Y.1989), used jury instructions that seem well-suited to the task of clarification for the jury. Id. at 52–53.

One of the few decisions of the Second Circuit Court of Appeals on experiments and demonstrations suggests that the court would agree with the more relaxed standard of similarity for experiments that show isolated aspects of mechanical principles. Lobel v. American Airlines, 205 F.2d 927, 931 (2d Cir.1953)(overly strict requirement of identity of conditions "would mean * * * that no showing by experiment in a field of mechanical operation would ever be possible, since the conditions could not so be duplicated, and hence jury and court would be deprived of helpful and informative illustrative evidence").

Courts in criminal cases have also applied the similarity requirement. See, e.g., United States v. Wanoskia, 800 F.2d 235, 237–39 (10th Cir.1986)(human model with arm length approximating that of homicide victim was allowed to demonstrate how gun would have to have been held in order for victim to shoot self in head); Pacheco v. United States, 367 F.2d 878, 881 (10th Cir. 1966)(to discredit agent's testimony that he was able to hear conversation while hiding in trunk of automobile, counsel conducted experiment using tape recorder in trunk of same car; results were inadmissible because experiment was conducted at different location, different voices were involved and, unlike actual event, "hush-hush" speaking levels were used).

4. Fortunato v. Ford Motor Co., 464 F.2d 962, 966 (2d Cir.), cert. denied, 409 U.S. 1038, 93 S.Ct. 517, 34 L.Ed.2d 487 (1972). The statement is dicta because the issue was whether defendant was entitled to judgment as a matter of law on the grounds that the tests in question had conclusively established the physical impossibility of plaintiff's version of events. There appears to be some support elsewhere, however, for the proposition that the adversary should be in attendance. See, Hall v. General Motors Corp., 647 F.2d 175, 180–81 (D.C.Cir.1980)(trial court properly exercised discretion in excluding results of one of defendant's experiments because, inter alia, plaintiffs' representative, having attended earlier tests, was not present for later one).

To date, caselaw on the evidentiary use of such computer graphics is sparse. In one of the earliest reported opinions, a trial judge in New York likened computer graphics of this nature to a chart or diagram, which can be admitted regardless of whether it is "hand drawn or mechanically drawn by means of a computer."[1] The requirements for admissibility, said the court, consist of a showing that the presentation is relevant, that it "fairly and accurately reflect the oral testimony offered and that it be an aid to the jury's understanding of the issue."[2] A few years later, a federal district judge in New York similarly admitted a computer-generated animation that depicted an engineer's opinion as to where a fire inside an airplane engine began and how it spread.[3] The court explained to the jury that the computer animation was not intended to be a reenactment of the accident and that it was being admitted for the limited purpose of helping them to understand the expert's opinion.[4]

Error, however, was committed by a trial judge in Arizona who allowed one side's counsel to show a computer animation of an accident during summation without having connected the animation to any expert testimony during the trial.[5] The appellate court ruled that computer graphics representing an expert's theory as to how an event happened cannot be admitted under the guise of counsel's "summary" of the evidence; the expert must testify to her opinion, with an opportunity for cross-examination, and explain that the computer animation fairly and accurately depicts the expert's opinion.[6]

If the foregoing guidelines are followed, the use of computer-generated animations to illustrate expert testimony is likely to be readily accepted by New York state courts and federal courts. In the exercise of discretion, however, courts should be sensitive to the dangers that a jury may "confuse art with reality."[7] The matter becomes even more com-

§ 1106.1

1. People v. McHugh, 124 Misc.2d 559, 560, 476 N.Y.S.2d 721, 722 (Sup.Ct.Bronx Co.1984)(computer reenactment of car crash based on expert's analysis).

2. Id. at 560, 476 N.Y.S.2d at 723. See also Feaster v. New York City Transit Auth., 172 A.D.2d 284, 285, 568 N.Y.S.2d 380, 381 (1st Dep't 1991) (admissibility of computer-generated simulation of accident is in trial court's discretion).

3. Datskow v. Teledyne Continental Motors Aircraft Products, 826 F.Supp. 677, 685–86 (W.D.N.Y.1993).

4. Id. at 685. The opponent argued that the jury would be misled into thinking that the animation was an actual recreation of the event, as to which the necessary showing of similarity of conditions was lacking. See generally § 1105.2, at note 2, supra. The court, however, responded that its jury instructions had made clear that the jury was not seeing a repeat of the actual event, but rather was "seeing an illustration of someone else's *opinion* of what happened." Id. at 686 (emphasis in original). Since that distinction was made clear, "there is no reason for them to credit the illustration any more than they credit the underlying opinion." Id. Various differences between the conditions shown on the tape and those of the actual flight went only to the weight of the animation, not its admissibility. Id.

5. Bledsoe v. Salt River Valley Water Users' Ass'n, 179 Ariz. 469, 471–72, 880 P.2d 689, 691–92 (App.1994).

6. Id. at 472, 880 P.2d at 692.

7. See McCormick § 214, at 19 (the "extreme vividness and verisimilitude of pictorial evidence" depicting a party's staged reproduction of events creates "the danger that the jury may confuse art with reality"). See generally § 1104.1, at notes 48–49, supra and § 1104.2, at notes 19–21, supra (motion pictures and videotapes), and §§ 1105.1 and 1105.2 supra (experiments and demonstrations).

plex if the computer-generated animation does more than merely illustrate a theory that the expert has independently developed through her own use of models and principles of mathematics and physics. If the computer itself contributes to the expert's opinion by means of a program that accepts data, performs an analysis and predicts a result, the computer may be producing an independent form of scientific evidence. Courts in other states that have considered this issue have required a showing of the scientific reliability of the particular computer program and its output.[8] If this view were to take hold in New York, the proponent of expert testimony incorporating computer analysis would have to satisfy the *Frye* standard for the admissibility of scientific evidence.[9] In federal court, the *Daubert* criteria would have to be met.[10]

Library References:

West's Key No. Digests, Criminal Law ⚖404.80, 438; Evidence ⚖195, 359; Witnesses ⚖252.

In Datskow, notes 3–4 supra, the court sought to minimize the danger that the jury would mistake the animation for a reenactment by disallowing the proponent simultaneously to play the soundtrack, which consisted of the actual radio communications between the aircraft involved in the accident and the airport control tower. 826 F.Supp. at 685.

8. See Commercial Union Insurance Co. v. Boston Edison Co., 412 Mass. 545, 548–53, 591 N.E.2d 165, 167–70 (1992)(in building owner's action against utility for overcharges for steam usage, owner's expert relied, in part, on computer calculations to estimate actual steam usage of building during relevant time period based on architecture and location of building, operating characteristics of building's ventilation and heating equipment, and weather history); Starr v. Campos, 134 Ariz. 254, 256–58, 655 P.2d 794, 796–98 (Ct.App.1982)(computerized analysis of vehicular accident); Schaeffer v. General Motors Corp., 372 Mass. 171, 177–78, 360 N.E.2d 1062, 1066–67 (1977)(computer-generated determination of speed of vehicles at time of impact based on operating characteristics of vehicles, friction coefficient of pavement, lengths and nature of skid marks).

9. See § 702.1(b) supra. In Commercial Union Insurance Co. v. Boston Edison Co., 412 Mass. 545, 591 N.E.2d 165 (1992), the court provided the following Frye-related guidelines for the admissibility of expert testimony that relies on computer analyses:

[W]e treat computer-generated models or simulations like other scientific tests, and condition admissibility on a sufficient showing that: (1) the computer is functioning properly; (2) the input and underlying equations are sufficiently complete and accurate (and disclosed to the opposing party, so that they may challenge them); and (3) the program is generally accepted by the appropriate community of scientists.

Id. at 549, 591 N.E.2d at 168. See also Starr v. Campos, 134 Ariz. 254, 257–58, 655 P.2d 794, 797–98 (Ct.App.1982)(admissibility of computer-based analysis of automobile accident requires trial court to determine "whether the procedure used to obtain that evidence is generally accepted among scientists in relevant fields, including accident reconstruction and automotive engineering"; trial court may take judicial notice of properly programmed computer's ability to perform mathematical computations and of basic principles of physics, but must assure general acceptance of computer program's application of those principles to automobile collisions).

10. See § 702.2(b) supra.

In Perma Research & Development v. Singer Co., 542 F.2d 111 (2d Cir.), cert. denied, 429 U.S. 987, 97 S.Ct. 507, 50 L.Ed.2d 598 (1976), the Second Circuit, on a procedural point, suggested that an expert whose opinion is based on the results of a computer analysis could be required to disclose, in advance of trial, the underlying data and the manner in which the computer was programmed in order to avoid "belabored discussion" at trial and to resolve potential disputes over the protection of proprietary secrets. Id. at 115. In the particular case, however, the court found no abuse of discretion in admitting expert testimony in the absence of such disclosure, either before or during trial, because the opponent had an adequate basis for cross-examination. Id.

1107 Jury Views

§ 1107.1 New York

By statute, a trial court in New York may direct that the jury be taken to the actual location where some relevant event occurred so that the jurors may see the place for themselves. In criminal cases, jury views are governed by § 270.50 of the New York Criminal Procedure Law,[1] and in most civil cases CPLR 4110–c is the governing statute.[2]

Both statutes contain the same basic standards. The view may be ordered where the court is of the opinion that it "will be helpful to the jury in determining any material factual issue."[3] The decision to order a view lies in the court's discretion. An important consideration is wheth-

---

§ 1107.1

1. N.Y. Crim. Proc. Law § 270.50 provides as follows:

§ 270.50 Trial jury; viewing of premises

1. When the court is of the opinion that a viewing or observation by the jury of the premises or place where an offense on trial was allegedly committed, or of any other premises or place involved in the case, will be helpful to the jury in determining any material factual issue, it may in its discretion, at any time before the commencement of the summations, order that the jury be conducted to such premises or place for such purpose in accordance with the provisions of this section.

2. In such case, the jury must be kept together throughout under the supervision of an appropriate public servant or servants appointed by the court, and the court itself must be present throughout. The prosecutor, the defendant and counsel for the defendant may as a matter of right be present throughout, but such right may be waived.

3. The purpose of such an inspection is solely to permit visual observation by the jury of the premises or place in question, and neither the court, the parties, counsel nor the jurors may engage in discussion or argumentation concerning the significance or implications of anything under observation or concerning any issue in the case.

2. CPLR 4110–c provides as follows:

§ 4110–c. Trial jury; viewing of premises

1. When during the course of a trial the court is of the opinion that a viewing or observation by the jury of the premises or place where alleged injuries to person or property were sustained in an accident or occurrence claimed to have been the cause thereof or of any other premises or place involved in the case will be helpful to the jury in determining any material factual issue, it may in its discretion, at any time before the commencement of the summations, order that the jury be conducted to such premises or place for such purpose in accordance with the provisions of this section.

2. In such case, the jury must be kept together throughout under the supervision of an appropriate public servant or servants appointed by the court, and the court itself must be present throughout. The parties to the action and counsel for them may as a matter of right be present throughout, but such right may be waived.

3. The purpose of such an inspection is solely to permit visual observation by the jury of the premises or place in question and neither the court, the parties, counsel nor the jurors may engage in discussion or argumentation concerning the significance or implications of anything under observation or concerning any issue in the case.

For the most part, the breadth of CPLR 4110–c moots the question whether trial courts have inherent authority to order a jury view. Compare Manuta v. Lazarus, 104 Misc. 134, 136, 171 N.Y.S. 1076, 1077 (N.Y.C.City Ct.1918) (courts have inherent power), with Buffalo Structural Steel Co. v. Dickinson, 98 App. Div. 355, 360, 90 N.Y.S. 268, 271 (4th Dep't 1904)(no authority in absence of statute).

Two additional statutory provisions provide for views. In actions for waste, views are authorized by N.Y. Real Prop.Actions and Proc.Law § 821; and in condemnation proceedings, N.Y. Eminent Domain Proc. Law § 510(A) provides that the trial court must view the property in question unless the parties stipulate otherwise.

3. N.Y. Crim.Proc.Law § 270.50(1); CPLR 4110–c(1).

er physical conditions at the location have changed substantially or would otherwise be too different in relevant respects from those that existed at the time of the matter in issue.[4] In some cases, the fact that the appearance of the premises has been made known to the jury through photographic evidence will weigh against the time and distraction involved in a view;[5] in other situations, a visit by the jury may be worth the effort.[6]

As to matters of procedure, the statutes[7] provide as follows: the view may be conducted at any time before summations begin,[8] the jury must be kept together and properly supervised, the trial judge must accompany them, the parties and their counsel have a right to be present at all times[9] (although this right may be waived),[10] and there is to be no discussion or argumentation by anyone during the inspection. The fact that the express statutory purpose of a view is to help the jury "determine" issues, that the court must attend, and that the parties and counsel have a right to be present suggests that a jury view today constitutes the perception of real evidence with independent evidentiary significance.[11] The view is not merely an aid to "understanding" testi-

---

4. People v. McCurdy, 86 A.D.2d 493, 496, 450 N.Y.S.2d 507, 509 (2d Dep't 1982)(in exercising discretion, trial court must insure "that the scene has not significantly changed in any relevant respect"; abuse of discretion to order view where issue was one of visibility from vestibule door window of apartment building and subsequent changes to door, color of wallpaint and lighting, together with other factors, made view inappropriate). See also People v. Santiago, 197 A.D.2d 756, 602 N.Y.S.2d 732 (3d Dep't 1993), appeal denied, 83 N.Y.2d 876, 613 N.Y.S.2d 136, 635 N.E.2d 305 (1994)(on issue of identification witness' ability to see defendant, court refused to order view of scene where arson of car occurred; events occurred at night and visibility was affected by flash of cigarette lighter and car bursting into flames; replication of conditions was impossible); People v. Rao, 107 A.D.2d 720, 484 N.Y.S.2d 76 (2d Dep't 1985)(no abuse of discretion to deny request for view of location where police observed defendant; differences in season, natural light, illumination from street lamps and storefronts and foliage would render view of no assistance); People v. Purcell, 103 A.D.2d 938, 938–39, 479 N.Y.S.2d 768, 770–71 (3d Dep't 1984)(although events occurred at night, rather than during day, location of buildings and roads that played role in crime made view appropriate); People v. Hamel, 96 A.D.2d 644, 466 N.Y.S.2d 748 (3d Dep't 1983)(although some changes had occurred in apartment where homicide took place, court-ordered view was appropriate where judge explained changes to jury and directed them to concentrate only on physical layout).

5. See, e.g., Schechtman v. Lappin, 161 A.D.2d 118, 121–22, 554 N.Y.S.2d 846, 849 (1st Dep't 1990)(jury was sufficiently made aware of scene by photographs introduced by both sides).

6. See, e.g., People v. Purcell, 103 A.D.2d 938, 938, 479 N.Y.S.2d 768, 770 (3d Dep't 1984)(view would help jury relate actual layout to photographs and diagrams); People v. Hamel, 96 A.D.2d 644, 645, 466 N.Y.S.2d 748, 749 (3d Dep't 1983)(reliance solely upon verbal descriptions and photographs of apartment layout would create "perplexing image").

7. See notes 1–2 supra.

8. See People v. White, 53 N.Y.2d 721, 439 N.Y.S.2d 333, 421 N.E.2d 825 (1981)(view of premises after summations did not constitute error where defendant and prosecutor both consented).

9. People v. Morton, 189 A.D.2d 488, 494, 596 N.Y.S.2d 783, 788 (1st Dep't 1993)(defendant has statutory "right to see everything the jury sees"; trial court's refusal to permit defendant to attend view is reversible error without regard to showing of actual prejudice).

10. N.Y. Crim.Proc.Law § 270.50(2); CPLR 4110–c(2).

11. See People v. Morton, 189 A.D.2d 488, 495, 596 N.Y.S.2d 783, 788 (1st Dep't 1993)(requirement of attendance by judge makes jury view a part of the trial itself). See also Tubular Products, Inc. v. Jacobson, 138 A.D.2d 371, 525 N.Y.S.2d 655 (2d Dep't

mony that is presented in the courtroom.[12]

Obviously, the controls imposed by the statutes would be meaningless if jurors were to engage in sightseeing on their own. Thus, in criminal cases, the jury must be told in the court's introductory charge not to visit any location involved in the case.[13] No similar charge is required in civil cases; but if the conditions at a given place are likely to be an important issue, such a charge would be well advised. An unauthorized visit may be deemed an improper influence that "tends to put the jury in possession of evidence not introduced at trial."[14] In criminal cases, an unauthorized visit to the scene of the crime or some other location that figured prominently in trial testimony is likely to be treated as inherently prejudicial and, if not discovered until after the trial, an automatic basis for setting aside a conviction.[15] In civil cases, a

1988)(in case involving dispute over condition of custom-made railings installed in defendant's home, trial court properly ordered view to help resolve conflict in testimony); Manuta v. Lazarus, 104 Misc. 134, 136, 171 N.Y.S. 1076, 1077 (N.Y.C.City Ct.1918)(where no change of conditions has occurred, jury view is logical way to ascertain truth of disputed matter).

12. The "illustrative" theory of jury views was articulated by the Court of Appeals in People v. Thorn, 156 N.Y. 286, 298, 50 N.E. 947, 951 (1898) ("the sole purpose and object of the view is to enable the jurors to more accurately and more fully appreciate the testimony of witnesses given before them"). McCormick attributes this approach, in part, to the "consideration that facts garnered by the jury from a view are difficult or impossible to embody in the written record, thus rendering review of questions concerning weight or sufficiency of the evidence impracticable." McCormick § 216, at 27–28. Although the trend is to treat jury views as independent evidence, id. § 216, at 28, McCormick suggests that "where the question is one of sufficiency, a view alone cannot logically be considered to constitute sufficient evidence of a fact the establishment of which ordinarily requires the introduction of expert testimony." Id. Cf. In re City of New York, West Park (Manhattan Town) Clearance Project, 1 N.Y.2d 428, 432, 154 N.Y.S.2d 1, 4, 136 N.E.2d 478, 480 (1956)(in condemnation case, judge may not properly base decision solely upon view of premises in disregard of expert testimony).

13. N.Y. Crim.Proc.Law § 270.40.

14. People v. Brown, 48 N.Y.2d 388, 393, 423 N.Y.S.2d 461, 463, 399 N.E.2d 51, 53 (1979). See also People v. Huntley, 87 A.D.2d 488, 492, 452 N.Y.S.2d 952, 955 (4th Dep't 1982), aff'd, 59 N.Y.2d 868, 465 N.Y.S.2d 929, 452 N.E.2d 1257 (1983)(juror who had not actually viewed scene of crime told other jurors that he had done so, and made statements that bolstered credibility of prosecution witness and undermined defendant's credibility; juror improperly became unsworn witness against defendant). External influences of this nature are an exception to the rule that ordinarily renders jurors incompetent to testify to matters that would impeach the verdict. See § 606.1 supra.

15. The "inherent prejudice" rule was announced in People v. De Lucia, 20 N.Y.2d 275, 282 N.Y.S.2d 526, 229 N.E.2d 211 (1967), where several jurors not only visited the crime scene on their own but also reenacted the alleged crime. The court said that "[i]n this type of case," there was no need for a showing as to how the unauthorized visit may have affected the deliberations: "Such a visit, in and of itself, constitutes inherent prejudice to the defendants." Id. at 280, 282 N.Y.S.2d at 529, 229 N.E.2d at 214. Similarly, in People v. Crimmins, 26 N.Y.2d 319, 310 N.Y.S.2d 300, 258 N.E.2d 708 (1970), the court held that a visit by three jurors to a location where an eyewitness testified to having seen and heard incriminating acts by the defendant was inherently prejudicial.

In the context of improvised experiments by individual jurors, however, the Court of Appeals has said that "not every misstep by a juror rises to the inherently prejudicial level at which reversal is required automatically." People v. Brown, 48 N.Y.2d 388, 394, 423 N.Y.S.2d 461, 463, 399 N.E.2d 51, 53 (1979). This potential tempering of the inherent prejudice rule as applied to unauthorized jury views may be necessary to reach common sense results where, for example, jurors fortuitously see a relevant location or the events occurred at a public place known to the community at large. Cf. People v. Thorn, 156 N.Y. 286, 298, 50 N.E. 947, 951 (1898)(extrajudicial "taking

showing of actual prejudice is required for such post-verdict relief.[16] Related problems arising from ad hoc experiments conducted by jurors are discussed in § 1108.1 *infra*.

Library References:

West's Key No. Digests, Criminal Law ⚖651; Trial ⚖28.

§ 1107.2 Federal

No statute or specific provision of the Federal Rules of Evidence addresses jury views in federal practice. By tradition, however, federal trial courts have the discretion to order views of relevant locations in both criminal[1] and civil[2] cases. As under New York state practice, factors include the extent to which conditions at the location have changed in relevant respects[3] and the sufficiency of photographic evidence to convey physical appearances.[4] Federal courts have also said that considerations of safety and inconvenience may weigh against a view.[5] There is no clear consensus among federal courts as to whether a jury view should be treated as merely an aid to the understanding of other evidence in the record or whether it constitutes the taking of

of evidence" does not occur merely because juror is familiar with locality where crime took place).

If an improper view is discovered before the jury begins its deliberations, it may be possible to avoid a mistrial by curative instructions or by a court-supervised view. See, e.g., People v. Sher, 24 N.Y.2d 454, 457–58, 301 N.Y.S.2d 46, 47–48, 248 N.E.2d 887, 888–89, cert. denied, 396 U.S. 837, 90 S.Ct. 96, 24 L.Ed.2d 87 (1969)(where improper communications to jurors were discovered before deliberations began, trial court was able to "sterilize" jury); People v. Purcell, 103 A.D.2d 938, 938, 479 N.Y.S.2d 768, 770 (3d Dep't 1984)(court ordered a view, in part, to minimize prejudice from possible viewing of area by two jurors).

16. Alford v. Sventek, 53 N.Y.2d 743, 439 N.Y.S.2d 339, 421 N.E.2d 831 (1981).

§ 1107.2

1. See United States v. Passos–Paternina, 918 F.2d 979, 986 (1st Cir.1990), cert. denied, 499 U.S. 982, 111 S.Ct. 1637, 113 L.Ed.2d 732 (1991)(federal courts have "inherent power to permit a jury view of places or objects outside the courtroom"); Schonfeld v. United States, 277 F. 934, 938 (2d Cir.1921), cert. denied, 258 U.S. 623, 42 S.Ct. 317, 66 L.Ed. 796 (1922)("Permitting a jury to view the scene of the crime is within the discretion of the court.").

2. See Clemente v. Carnicon–Puerto Rico Management Associates, L.C., 52 F.3d 383, 385 (1st Cir.1995)(trial judge had discretion to order jury view of hotel site where guest slipped and fell); Auto Owners Ins. Co. v. Bass, 684 F.2d 764, 769 (11th Cir.1982)("Whether to allow the jury to visit the scene was in the discretion of the district court"); Northwestern National Casualty Co. v. Global Moving & Storage, Inc., 533 F.2d 320, 323 (6th Cir.1976)(no abuse of discretion where judge in bench trial viewed scene of warehouse fire just before trial, on notice to defense counsel).

3. United States v. Culpepper, 834 F.2d 879, 883 (10th Cir.1987) (condition of field over which defendant allegedly exercised dominion and control had changed substantially as result of heavy rainfall; photographs taken day after relevant event were sufficient).

4. See, e.g., id.; Auto Owners Ins. Co. v. Bass, 684 F.2d 764, 769 (11th Cir.1982)(no abuse of discretion not to conduct view of scene of fire: 16 months had elapsed, fire occurred 30–35 miles away from courthouse and over 100 photographs taken shortly after fire had been admitted into evidence).

5. See, e.g., United States v. Passos–Paternina, 918 F.2d 979, 986 (1st Cir.1990), cert. denied, 499 U.S. 982, 111 S.Ct. 1637, 113 L.Ed.2d 732 (1991)(jury view of seagoing vessel properly denied where court found that conditions were dangerous and testimonial descriptions were sufficient); Stokes v. Delcambre, 710 F.2d 1120, 1129 (5th Cir.1983) (judge properly denied request for view of jail in light of security problems, risk of comment by prisoners and adequacy of evidence at trial regarding layout).

independent evidence.[6] Procedural safeguards for jury views in civil actions were outlined in a recent First Circuit decision.[7]

Library References:

West's Key No. Digests, Criminal Law ⚖︎651; Federal Civil Procedure ⚖︎1968.

1108 Taking Exhibits into the Jury Room; Jury Experimentation

§ 1108.1 New York

Trial courts have discretion to permit exhibits to be taken into the jury room during deliberations.[1] In criminal cases, the practice is authorized by § 310.20(1) of the Criminal Procedure Law, which states that jurors may take with them "[a]ny exhibits received in evidence at the trial which the court, after according the parties an opportunity to be heard upon the matter, in its discretion permits them to take."[2] No

---

6. See 22 C. Wright & K. Graham, Federal Practice and Procedure: Evidence § 5176, at 140 n. 6 (1978). A 1921 decision of the Second Circuit held that no error was committed where a jury had been permitted to view a crime scene without the judge in attendance because the view did not constitute the taking of testimony; its purpose was merely to enable the jury to understand the courtroom evidence. Schonfeld v. United States, 277 F. 934, 938 (2d Cir. 1921), cert. denied, 258 U.S. 623, 42 S.Ct. 317, 66 L.Ed. 796 (1922). On the other hand, in Leo Spear Construction Co. v. Fidelity and Casualty Co. of New York, 446 F.2d 439 (2d Cir.1971), a judge in a bench trial was held to have properly allowed his view of a construction site to influence his decision as to the value of a contractor's materials and labor. Id. at 444.

In Lillie v. United States, 953 F.2d 1188 (10th Cir.1992), the court held that it was error for a judge in the bench trial of a tort case to view the accident scene without giving counsel prior notice and an opportunity to attend, in part, because "a view should always be considered evidence." Id. at 1192. See also In re Application to Take Testimony in Criminal Case Outside District, 102 F.R.D. 521, 524 (E.D.N.Y.1984) ("Authorities now generally agree that the view provides independent evidence. * * * The defendant as well as his counsel should be present.").

7. Clemente v. Carnicon—Puerto Rico Management Associates, L.C., 52 F.3d 383, 386–87 (1st Cir.1995)(counsel should be given prior notice and opportunity to be heard as to appropriateness of view; jury should be instructed concerning purpose of view; counsel should be given opportunity to attend view; judge ordinarily should attend view; events at view should be recorded, such as by court reporter; procedural omissions or improprieties should be brought to court's attention in timely fashion).

§ 1108.1

1. Levy v. Corn, 191 App.Div. 56, 57, 180 N.Y.S. 794, 795 (1st Dep't 1920); Raynolds v. Vinier, 125 App.Div. 18, 20–21, 109 N.Y.S. 293, 295 (4th Dep't 1908). See also Uss v. Town of Oyster Bay, 37 N.Y.2d 639, 641, 376 N.Y.S.2d 449, 450, 339 N.E.2d 147, 148 (1975)(street sign and model of metal pole, introduced into evidence and used during courtroom experiment, were taken into jury room without objection).

2. See also N.Y. Crim.Proc.Law § 310.30 (during deliberations, jury may request further "information" concerning "any trial evidence"). Obviously, potential exhibits that have not been admitted into evidence should not go to the jury room. In People v. Bouton, 50 N.Y.2d 130, 428 N.Y.S.2d 218, 405 N.E.2d 699 (1980), for example, a court officer delivered to the jury a stack of admitted exhibits together with documents that had been ruled inadmissible by the trial judge and merely marked for identification. The inadmissible papers contained prejudicial information about defendant's uncharged criminal activity. The court held this to be reversible error, stating, "Since an unadmitted exhibit has not undergone the test of cross-examination, its consideration by the jury directly infringes on the defendant's right of confrontation." Id. at 137, 428 N.Y.S.2d at 221, 405 N.E.2d at 702.

People v. Scott, 120 Misc.2d 313, 465 N.Y.S.2d 819 (Monroe Co.Ct.1983), is an

cases have provided guidelines to govern the court's discretion, but liberality in the sending of exhibits to the jury room seems to be prevalent. In one case of interest, the jury's use of a magnifying glass during deliberations to "enhance the clarity" of photographic exhibits was approved on the theory that magnification is the functional equivalent of using reading glasses.[3] Documentary exhibits, of course, may be particularly useful for the jury to peruse during deliberations because the written word can often be of critical importance in resolving a dispute.[4] When only a portion of a document has been admitted, the inadmissible parts must be effectively concealed if the document is to be given to the jury.[5]

In the exercise of discretion, New York courts have allowed accurate transcripts of tape recordings that have been admitted into evidence to be sent to the jury room.[6] On a related point, courts have the discretion to permit jurors to make written notes concerning testimony and exhibits during the trial and to refer to such notes during deliberations provided the court cautions the jury as to the limited use that may be made of such notes.[7]

---

unusual case in which the jury, during deliberations, discovered an undisclosed knife inside a pocket of a pair of pants that had been admitted into evidence. When this was made known to the court, the newly discovered knife was admitted as an additional exhibit, and the case was reopened to give both sides an opportunity to submit additional testimony and to make additional summations regarding the new exhibit.

3. People v. Moody, 195 A.D.2d 1016, 1017, 600 N.Y.S.2d 581, 582 (4th Dep't 1993).

4. See generally McCormick § 217, at 29–30.

5. People v. Epps, 21 A.D.2d 650, 651, 249 N.Y.S.2d 639, 640 (1st Dep't), cert. denied, 379 U.S. 940, 85 S.Ct. 347, 13 L.Ed.2d 350 (1964)(cards signed by defendant as handwriting exemplars also contained inadmissible notes below signature line; notes were covered by paper or cardboard stapled to cards in such manner that jurors' unauthorized look at hidden portion was possible; such possibility, however, was insufficient to disturb conviction where defendant was aware of manner in which cards were sent to jury and requested no cautionary instructions).

6. People v. Kuss, 81 A.D.2d 427, 430, 442 N.Y.S.2d 313, 315 (4th Dep't 1981)(no abuse of discretion in allowing jury to use transcripts of tape recordings during deliberations where accuracy of transcripts had been sufficiently established and tapes and transcripts had both been received as exhibits; trial court had advised jury that the tapes, not the transcripts, were the real evidence and that the tapes should be relied upon in the event of any perceived discrepancies between the transcripts and the tapes). See also People v. Tapia, 114 A.D.2d 983, 495 N.Y.S.2d 93 (2d Dep't 1985), appeal denied, 67 N.Y.2d 951, 502 N.Y.S.2d 1045, 494 N.E.2d 130 (1986).

7. People v. DiLuca, 85 A.D.2d 439, 445, 448 N.Y.S.2d 730, 735 (2d Dep't 1982). Accord, People v. Tucker, 153 A.D.2d 164, 167–69, 550 N.Y.S.2d 1, 2–3 (1st Dep't 1990), aff'd, 77 N.Y.2d 861, 568 N.Y.S.2d 342, 569 N.E.2d 1021 (1991). The DiLuca court prescribed the following guidelines for instructing the jury on note-taking:

[M]andatory cautionary instructions require an explanation to the jury that they should not permit their note-taking to distract them from the ongoing proceedings; that their notes are only an aid to their memory and should not take precedence over their independent recollection; that those jurors who do not take notes should rely on their independent recollection of the evidence and not be influenced by the fact that another juror has taken notes; and that the notes are for the note-taker's own personal use in refreshing his recollection of the evidence. The jury must be reminded that should any discrepancy exist between their recollection of the evidence and their notes, they should request that the record of the proceedings be read back and that it is the transcript that must prevail over their notes. We would also point out that in certain cases additional cautionary instructions may be required. Thus, for example, if one juror is a highly skilled note-taker, as a stenographer or secretary may be, then it might be appro-

§ 1108.1   REAL & DEMONSTRATIVE EVIDENCE   Ch. 11

A factor that courts probably should consider in connection with the jury's possession of exhibits is the risk, especially with tangible objects, that improvised experimentation will occur.[8] Two principal dangers in such experimentation are the absence of control over similarity of conditions (the standard for the admissibility of evidentiary experiments)[9] and the absence of adversarial scrutiny.[10] Inappropriate experimentation can constitute an improper influence, with the potential for a mistrial or setting aside of the verdict. In the context of experiments performed by the jury out of court, *People v. Brown*[11] stated that the standard for determining impropriety is whether the conduct "tends to put the jury in possession of evidence not introduced at trial."[12] On the other hand, an "experiment" that involves nothing more than the "application of everyday experience" apparently is acceptable.[13] The same standards undoubtedly apply to experimentation both inside and outside the jury room and regardless of whether the experiment includes the use of tangible objects.[14]

Caselaw demonstrates that the standard for impropriety can be difficult to apply except in the clearest of cases. The jury experiment at issue in *Brown*, for example, fell within the prohibited class. There, a juror sought to assess the credibility of a police officer who testified that while sitting in the back of a van, he could see the defendant in the driver's seat of a car that was stopped alongside the van at a traffic light. The juror performed a sight test using her own van (a different model from that used by the witness) at a different location and under different lighting conditions, and then reported to the jury that it was indeed

priate to instruct the other jurors that they need not pay special attention to that one juror's notes.

85 A.D.2d at 445–46, 448 N.Y.S.2d at 735.

Whether jurors may properly be allowed to take notes during the court's charge to the jury is more problematic. See, e.g., People v. Morales, 159 A.D.2d 86, 559 N.Y.S.2d 869 (1st Dep't 1990)(note-taking by two jurors during supplemental charge was improper where counsel objected and cautionary instructions were inadequate). See also N.Y. Crim.Proc.Law § 310.30 (court may not give text of statute to jury without consent of parties).

8. See generally McCormick § 217, at 30–31.

9. See § 1105.1, at notes 7 and 11, supra.

10. See note 2 supra and § 1107.1, at note 14, supra.

11. 48 N.Y.2d 388, 423 N.Y.S.2d 461, 399 N.E.2d 51 (1979).

12. Id. at 393, 423 N.Y.S.2d at 463, 399 N.E.2d at 53.

13. Id. at 394, 423 N.Y.S.2d at 463, 399 N.E.2d at 53. See also People v. Smith, 87 A.D.2d 357, 359, 451 N.Y.S.2d 429, 431 (1st Dep't 1982), aff'd, 59 N.Y.2d 988, 466 N.Y.S.2d 662, 453 N.E.2d 1079 (1983)(quoting People v. Brown, supra, 48 N.Y.2d at 393, 423 N.Y.S.2d at 461, 399 N.E.2d at 51) ("If * * * the jurors' conduct 'was no more than the application of everyday perceptions and common sense to the issues presented in the trial', such conduct does not taint a subsequent verdict.").

14. Apparently, there are no New York cases discussing juror experimentation with tangible objects. In addition to the federal cases cited in § 1108.2 infra, an instructive decision is Geo. C. Christopher & Son, Inc. v. Kansas Paint & Color Co., 215 Kan. 185, 523 P.2d 709, modified, 215 Kan. 510, 525 P.2d 626 (1974), a breach of warranty action involving the quality of certain paint. During deliberations, the jury foreman used a pocket knife to scrape paint from a paint sample that had been received as an exhibit. A similar test apparently had been performed by the litigants in the courtroom. The court found no error in the jury's conduct stating, "An experiment or demonstration is proper when conducted by the jury with the use of exhibits properly submitted to it for the purpose of testing the truth of statements made by witnesses or duplicat-

possible to see an adjacent driver. The court found this to be prejudicial error.[15] A different result was reached in *People v. Smith*,[16] where a juror, while going to and from the courthouse during deliberations, looked into the rear windows of cars to test the credibility of police officers who testified that they had seen the defendant in the back seat of a car brandishing a gun. In this case, the juror's test was characterized as having been based on "everyday experience."[17] Unlike the juror in *Brown*, the *Smith* juror had performed no calculated or extraordinary test, having merely seen "what every other juror could have seen had they chosen to do so."[18] In another case, the "everyday experience" characterization served to justify an attempted reenactment of a crime by the jury "in accordance with their own recollection of the testimony."[19] Obviously, the standards articulated in *Brown* can produce outcomes that are hard to reconcile.

Library References:

West's Key No. Digests, Criminal Law ⟾858–861; Trial ⟾307–310.

§ 1108.2 Federal

Federal courts, like their New York state counterparts, may permit jurors to take exhibits to the jury room.[1] The court's discretion in this regard extends to transcripts of tape recordings that were played during the trial.[2] If only a portion of a document was admitted into evidence, the inadmissible segment must be adequately excised before the jury is given possession.[3]

---

ing tests made by witnesses in open court." Id. at 186, 523 P.2d at 711.

15. 48 N.Y.2d at 394–95, 423 N.Y.S.2d at 463–64, 399 N.E.2d at 53–54.

16. 87 A.D.2d 357, 451 N.Y.S.2d 429 (1st Dep't 1982), aff'd, 59 N.Y.2d 988, 466 N.Y.S.2d 662, 453 N.E.2d 1079 (1983).

17. Id. at 360, 451 N.Y.S.2d at 432 ("All he did was to assess the credibility of the officers on the basis of an everyday experience—peering into a car through its rear window.").

18. Id. at 361, 451 N.Y.S.2d at 432.

19. People v. Harris, 84 A.D.2d 63, 105, 445 N.Y.S.2d 520, 546 (2d Dep't 1981), aff'd, 57 N.Y.2d 335, 456 N.Y.S.2d 694, 442 N.E.2d 1205 (1982), cert. denied, 460 U.S. 1047, 103 S.Ct. 1448, 75 L.Ed.2d 803 (1983) (quoting People v. Brown, 48 N.Y.2d 388, 393, 423 N.Y.S.2d 461, 463, 399 N.E.2d 51, 53 (1979))("where the jurors attempt to reenact the crime during their deliberations in accordance with their own recollection of the testimony, their conduct constitutes nothing more than an 'application of everyday perceptions and common sense to the issues presented in the trial.' ").

§ 1108.2

1. United States v. Thomas, 521 F.2d 76, 81–82 (8th Cir.1975); United States v. Parker, 491 F.2d 517, 521–22 (8th Cir. 1973); Dallago v. United States, 427 F.2d 546, 553 (D.C.Cir.1969).

2. United States v. Rengifo, 789 F.2d 975, 980–83 (1st Cir.1986); United States v. Carson, 464 F.2d 424, 437 (2d Cir.), cert. denied, 409 U.S. 949, 93 S.Ct. 268, 34 L.Ed.2d 219 (1972). See generally § 1104.2(c) supra.

3. See, e.g., United States v. Camporeale, 515 F.2d 184, 187–89 (2d Cir.1975)(reversible error where court clerk, without first consulting counsel, gave jury an unredacted exhibit that contained inadmissible passages that were highly prejudicial to defendant); Dallago v. United States, 427 F.2d 546, 553 (D.C.Cir.1969)(reversible error where clerk provided jury with unrequested documents including highly prejudicial order which should have been extracted from document packet before it was forwarded to jury); United States v. Strassman, 241 F.2d 784, 785–86 (2d Cir.1957)(inadvertently providing jury with inadmissible portions of ship's log was not reversible error where evidence from log was cumulative, and counsel failed to check the documents before they went to the jury). See also United States v. Burket, 480 F.2d 568, 571 (2d Cir.1973)(both sides share responsi-

§ 1108.2   REAL & DEMONSTRATIVE EVIDENCE   Ch. 11

As to note-taking by jurors, federal courts have held that the trial judge may allow the jury to make notes during the trial and to refer to them during deliberations.[4]

The propriety of jury experimentation with exhibits during deliberations depends on whether the experiment is "within the scope or purview of the evidence introduced at the trial, or whether it amounts to the taking of evidence outside the presence of the parties."[5] Caselaw on experimentation with exhibits is sparse, but two cases illustrate the distinction. In *Taylor v. Reo Motors, Inc.*,[6] a "heat exchanger" was the alleged cause of a fire in a motor-freight tractor. During the trial, the heat exchanger was admitted into evidence and was disassembled and reassembled in open court by manufacturing experts. The jury's disassembling of the exhibit during deliberations was held to have been proper "for the purpose of testing the validity of statements made in open court in respect thereto."[7]

In *United States v. Beach*,[8] the defendant was on trial for perjury based on his statement to a grand jury that he had not heard adding machines being operated at a friend's house which he frequently visited. The jury's running of the adding machines in the jury room to test their noise level would be error, said the court, because "[t]he law is well settled that a case must be decided upon evidence submitted in court during the trial and not upon private experiments of the jurors."[9] Apparently no similar experiment had been conducted during the trial because of the obvious difficulty of recreating the physical circumstances surrounding the defendant's presence at his friend's house. The *Beach* case thus demonstrates one of the principal vices of improvised juror

---

bility of insuring that only proper exhibits are sent to jury room).

4. See, e.g., United States v. Bertolotti, 529 F.2d 149, 159–60 (2d Cir.1975)(no abuse of discretion to permit note-taking and use of notes during deliberations in lengthy trial; judge advised jury to use notes solely as memory aids and to disregard such notes where they were in conflict with jurors' independent memory of facts). Accord, United States v. Polowichak, 783 F.2d 410, 413 (4th Cir.1986).

5. Taylor v. Reo Motors, Inc., 275 F.2d 699, 705 (10th Cir.1960).

6. 275 F.2d 699 (10th Cir.1960).

7. Id. at 706. The court likened the jury's duplication of the experiment to the use of a magnifying glass "for the purpose of scrutinizing critical language" in a document. Id. See also Imperial Meat Co. v. United States, 316 F.2d 435, 438 (10th Cir.), cert. denied, 375 U.S. 820, 84 S.Ct. 57, 11 L.Ed.2d 54 (1963)(jury was held to have properly performed computations on adding machine during deliberations because machine "accomplished the same result that the jury would have with pens and pencils which it can be safely assumed they had in their possession").

8. 296 F.2d 153 (4th Cir.1961).

9. Id. at 158. The issue came before the appellate court based solely on the trial judge's having granted the jury's request for an electric drop cord during deliberations. The case was remanded for a hearing as to whether the jury had actually performed the noise-level experiment, in which case the defendant would be entitled to a new trial. Id. at 160.

Cf. Wilson v. United States, 116 F. 484, 486 (9th Cir.1902)(jury was improperly directed by trial judge to test contents of tin can during deliberations to ascertain if it contained opium; no testimony had been introduced and no experiment had been conducted during trial as to contents of the exhibit: "It is contrary to fundamental principles to permit jurors to receive evidence without the presence of the defendant to the prosecution. They must and can only properly decide the question of his guilt or innocence upon evidence introduced at the trial.")

experimentation: the inability to control the similarity of conditions upon which the relevance of experiments depends.[10]

Library References:

West's Key No. Digests, Criminal Law ⚖︎858–861; Federal Civil Procedure ⚖︎1974.

10. See § 1105.2 supra. See generally McCormick § 217, at 30–31.

*

TABLE OF STATUTES

NEW YORK, MCKINNEY'S CONSTITUTION

Art.	This Work Sec.	Note
I, § 2	606.1	9
I, § 3	601.1	6
	603.1	7
I, § 6	509.1	
I, § 8	508.1	
II, § 7	512.1	1
VI, § 1(c)	614.1	8

NEW YORK, MCKINNEY'S BANKING LAW

Sec.	This Work Sec.	Note
11(3)(b)	1005.1	4
256	1005.1	4
675(b)	301.7	1
	301.7	4

NEW YORK, MCKINNEY'S BUSINESS CORPORATION LAW

Sec.	This Work Sec.	Note
107	901.7	15
	901.10	

NEW YORK, MCKINNEY'S CIVIL PRACTICE LAW AND RULES

Sec.	This Work Sec.	Note
212	803(5).1	17
301	202.1	11
1411	300.2	6
1412	300.2	6
1601—1603	300.2	4
2002	103.1	
2103(e)	803(3).1	
2104	900.1	26
2105	901.7	15
	901.10	
2306	803(3).1	
2306(a)	803(3).1	
2307	803(3).1	
2307(b)	803(3).1	
2309(b)	602.2	
	603.1	4
3013	300.2	4
3014	802.1	8
3015(a)	300.2	9
3015(d)	300.2	10
3016(e)	203.1	

NEW YORK, MCKINNEY'S CIVIL PRACTICE LAW AND RULES

Sec.	This Work Sec.	Note
3016(e) (Cont'd)	203.1	8
3016(g)	300.2	4
3017(a)	300.2	4
3017(c)	300.2	4
3018(b)	300.2	3
	300.2	8
Art. 31	513.2	
	1001.1	
3101(1)(b)	500.1	8
3101(b)	502.1	46
3101(c)	501.3	
	501.3	6
	501.3	9
	501.3	35
	612.1	28
3101(d)	501.3	6
	501.3	16
3101(d)(1)(i)	501.3	25
3101(d)(1)(iii)	501.3	25
3101(d)(2)	501.3	
	501.3	12
	501.3	13
	501.3	15
	501.3	22
	501.3	26
	501.3	29
	501.3	34
	501.3	35
	612.1	28
3101(e)	501.3	20
3101(g)	501.3	21
	501.3	22
3101(i)	501.3	23
	1104.1	34
3113(b)	1104.1	33
3117	804(1).1	
3117(a)(3)(i)	601.2	78
3117(b)	106.1	
	106.1	9
	607.5	20
3117(d)	607.4	13
	607.4	14
	607.4	17
3118	501.1	35
3121	702.1	
	702.1	56
	1004.1	
3123	802.1	8
	900.1	28
	1007.1	
3222	802.1	8
3509(a)(2)	601.3	17

887

TABLE OF STATUTES

NEW YORK, MCKINNEY'S CIVIL PRACTICE LAW AND RULES

Sec.	This Work Sec.	Note
3509(b)(1)	601.3	17
4016	611.1	1
4017	103.1	
	103.1	4
	103.1	8
4103	803(5).1	
	803(5).1	28
4104	606.1	9
4110-b	103.1	4
	611.1	1
4110-c	1107.1	
	1107.1	2
4110-c(1)	1107.1	3
4110-c(2)	1107.1	10
4113(a)	606.1	9
4401	300.3	
	300.3	19
4404	300.3	21
4404(a)	300.3	
	300.3	20
Art. 45	100.1	
	301.7	1
	301.7	12
	500.1	
	503.3	12
	803(6).1	
	804.1	
	901.10	
	902.1	
4501	500.1	5
	509.1	
4502	500.1	3
	503.1	
4502(a)	503.1	2
	503.2	
	601.1	21
4502(b)	503.3	
	503.5	3
	601.1	22
4503	500.1	3
	501.1	
4503(a)	501.1	
	501.1	27
	501.1	48
	501.1	51
	502.1	32
4503(b)	501.1	
4504	500.1	3
	502.1	
	502.1	7
	502.1	75
4504(a)	502.1	
	502.1	35
	502.1	40
4504(b)	502.1	
4504(c)	502.1	
	502.1	48
4505	500.1	3
	504.1	
4506	502.1	32
4507	500.1	3

NEW YORK, MCKINNEY'S CIVIL PRACTICE LAW AND RULES

Sec.	This Work Sec.	Note
4507 (Cont'd)	502.1	
	502.1	6
	502.1	76
	502.1	77
	502.1	79
4508	104.1	35
	500.1	3
	505.1	
	505.1	2
	506.1	
4508(a)(3)	505.1	
	506.1	6
4508(b)	505.1	
4509	500.1	3
	507.1	
4510	500.1	3
	506.1	
	506.1	1
4510(b)(1)	506.1	7
4511	203.1	
	203.1	4
	203.1	11
4511(a)	203.1	
	803(5).1	34
4511(b)	203.1	
	203.1	7
4511(c)	203.1	3
4511(d)	203.1	
	203.1	2
	203.1	9
	902.1	
4512	503.1	1
	503.5	2
	601.1	
	601.1	6
	601.1	15
4513	601.1	6
	601.1	27
	601.1	28
	609.1	
	609.1	3
	609.1	9
	609.1	11
4514	607.4	
	607.4	10
	607.4	36
	607.8	7
4515	705.1	
	705.1	6
	705.1	8
	705.2	
4516	1102.1	
	1102.1	11
4517	601.2	58
	601.2	77
	804.1	
	804.1	4
	804(1).1	
	804(1).1	1
	804(1).1	5
	804(1).1	33

888

TABLE OF STATUTES

NEW YORK, MCKINNEY'S CIVIL PRACTICE LAW AND RULES

Sec.	This Work Sec.	Note
4517 (Cont'd)	804(1).2	
4518	803(3).1	
	803(3).1	5
	803(3).1	55
	803(3).1	58
	803(3).1	69
	803(3).1	73
	803(3).2	
	803(5).1	
	803(5).1	8
	805.1	1
	901.1	
	901.1	10
	901.7	
4518(a)	803(3).1	
	803(3).1	10
	803(3).1	25
	803(3).1	27
	803(3).1	35
	803(3).1	39
	803(3).2	
	803(3).2	2
	803(5).1	
	1002.1	
	1006.1	
4518(b)	301.7	1
	803(3).1	
4518(c)	301.7	
	301.7	1
	301.7	12
	803(3).1	
	803(3).1	39
	803(3).1	61
	803(3).1	73
	803(5).1	
4518(d)	301.7	1
	803(3).1	
4518(e)	803(3).1	
4519	106.1	
	601.1	
	601.1	3
	601.2	
	601.2	4
	601.2	32
	601.2	33
	601.2	46
	601.2	64
	601.3	1
	804(1).1	
	804(1).1	23
4520	301.7	1
	803(3).1	
	803(4).1	
	803(5).1	
	803(5).1	3
	901.7	
4520(a)	901.7	5
4520(b)	901.7	
4521	301.7	1
	803(4).1	
	803(4).1	5

NEW YORK, MCKINNEY'S CIVIL PRACTICE LAW AND RULES

Sec.	This Work Sec.	Note
4521 (Cont'd)	803(5).1	
	901.7	
4522	301.7	1
	803(5).1	
	803(7).1	
	803(7).1	5
	803(7).1	11
4524	803(5).1	
4525	301.7	1
4526	301.7	1
	803(5).1	
4527	301.7	1
	803(5).1	
4527(a)	803(5).1	
	803(5).1	25
4527(b)	803(5).1	
4528	301.7	1
	803(5).1	
4529	301.7	1
	803(5).1	
4530	803(5).1	
4530(a)	301.7	1
	803(5).1	
4530(b)	803(5).1	
4531	301.7	1
4532	803(6).1	
	902.1	
4532–a	803(3).1	
	803(3).1	76
	1104.1	
	1104.1	21
	1104.1	22
4533	803(6).1	
	803(6).1	1
	803(6).2	
	902.1	2
4533–a	301.7	1
	803(3).1	
	803(3).1	57
4534	301.7	1
	803(5).1	
4536	702.1	
	702.1	29
	901.3	
	901.3	3
4537	903.1	
4538	902.1	
	902.1	7
4539	1002.1	
	1002.1	8
	1002.1	10
4540	609.1	4
	803(4).1	
	901.7	
	901.7	3
	902.1	
	1005.1	
	1005.1	1
	1005.1	4
	1005.1	6
4540(a)	301.7	1

889

TABLE OF STATUTES

NEW YORK, MCKINNEY'S CIVIL PRACTICE LAW AND RULES

Sec.	This Work Sec.	Note
4540(a) (Cont'd)	901.7	
4540(b)	902.1	
4540(c)	901.7	
	1001.1	32
4540(d)	901.7	
	902.1	
	1005.1	1
4541	301.7	1
	803(5).1	
	901.7	
4541(a)	803(5).1	
4541(b)	803(5).1	
4542	901.7	
	901.7	4
	902.1	
	1005.1	
	1005.1	1
	1005.1	4
4542(a)	901.7	
4542(b)	901.7	
4542(c)	901.7	
4543	803(5).1	1
	901.7	
	901.10	
	902.1	
4545	409.1	10
5501(a)	103.1	7
5501(a)(3)	103.1	
	103.1	5

NEW YORK, MCKINNEY'S CIVIL RIGHTS LAW

Sec.	This Work Sec.	Note
79–h	500.1	4
	508.1	
	508.1	1
	508.1	2
	508.1	3
	508.1	15
	508.2	4
	508.2	5
	508.2	9
79–h(c)	508.1	
79–h(d)	508.1	4
79–h(f)	508.1	5

NEW YORK CIVIL PRACTICE ACT

Sec.	This Work Sec.	Note
348	804(1).1	
349	503.3	
374–a	803(3).1	
382	1005.1	6
399	901.7	
400	901.7	

NEW YORK, MCKINNEY'S COUNTY LAW

Sec.	This Work Sec.	Note
208(1)	1005.1	4
208(5)	1005.1	4

NEW YORK, MCKINNEY'S CRIMINAL PROCEDURE LAW

Sec.	This Work Sec.	Note
50.20	509.1	
50.20(2)	509.1	
	509.1	30
50.20(5)	509.1	30
Art. 60	100.1	
60.10	100.1	1
	500.1	7
60.15(1)	509.1	45
	611.3	3
60.15(2)	509.1	34
	514.1	2
	601.1	17
60.20	601.1	38
60.20(1)	601.1	33
60.20(2)	601.1	
	601.1	44
	601.1	52
	601.1	53
60.20(3)	601.1	43
60.22	300.3	9
60.25	607.5	11
	607.5	12
	801(2).1	
	801(2).1	3
	801(2).1	10
	801(2).1	14
	801(2).1	33
	801(2).2	
	803(2).1	
60.30	607.5	11
	607.5	12
	801(2).1	
	801(2).1	2
	801(2).1	14
	801(2).2	
60.35	607.4	
	607.4	10
	607.4	30
	801(1).2	
	801(1).2	10
	803(2).1	2
60.35(1)	607.4	
	607.4	26
	607.4	31
	607.8	7
	607.8	26
60.35(2)	105.1	7
	607.4	
	607.8	4
60.35(3)	607.4	23
	607.4	24
	607.4	26
	612.1	8
60.40(1)	601.1	28
	609.1	3

890

TABLE OF STATUTES

NEW YORK, MCKINNEY'S CRIMINAL PROCEDURE LAW

Sec.	This Work Sec.	Note
60.40(1) (Cont'd)	609.1	13
60.40(2)	402.1	
	402.1	50
	402.2	
60.42	404.1	84
	412.1	
	412.1	2
	412.1	11
	412.1	22
	412.2	
	608.2	
	608.2	11
	702.1	60
60.42(2)	412.2	
60.42(3)	412.2	
60.42(5)	412.1	
60.43	412.1	
	412.1	24
	608.2	
	608.2	11
60.44	1103.1	4
60.48	412.1	
	412.1	27
60.50	300.3	12
60.55	702.1	
	702.1	11
	703.1	
60.55(1)	703.1	18
60.55(2)	105.1	7
	703.1	18
60.60(1)	609.1	4
60.60(2)	609.1	4
60.76	506.1	
Art. 65	601.1	45
65.10(1)	601.1	45
70.10(1)	300.3	26
70.20	300.4	39
130.16	300.3	13
190.40	509.1	30
Art. 240	501.3	28
240.10(2)	501.3	6
	501.3	28
240.10(3)	501.3	6
240.20	501.3	28
240.20(1)(c)	501.3	31
240.30	501.3	28
240.30(1)(a)	501.3	31
240.43	608.2	27
240.45	501.3	31
260.20	615.1	11
260.30	611.1	1
260.30(7)	611.1	9
270.40	1107.1	13
270.50	1107.1	
	1107.1	1
270.50(1)	1107.1	3
270.50(2)	1107.1	10
290.10(1)	300.3	
	300.3	26
300.10	509.1	34
300.10(2)	302.1	17
	509.1	35

NEW YORK, MCKINNEY'S CRIMINAL PROCEDURE LAW

Sec.	This Work Sec.	Note
300.10(2) (Cont'd)	514.1	2
310.20(1)	1108.1	
310.30	1108.1	2
	1108.1	7
320.20(3)	611.1	1
470.05(2)	103.1	
	103.1	6
	103.1	8
470.15(3)(c)	103.1	7
Art. 660	804(1).1	
660.20	804(1).1	30
670.10	804(1).1	
	804(1).1	27
	804(1).1	33
	804(1).1	38
	804(1).1	42
	804(1).2	
670.10(1)	804(1).1	
670.10(1)(h)	804.1	30
670.10(2)	804(1).1	
670.20(1)	1001.1	11
706.10	804(1).1	
Art. 710	103.1	37
710.30	801(2).1	
	801(2).1	19
710.60(5)	104.1	34
710.70(3)	104.1	33

NEW YORK, MCKINNEY'S DOMESTIC RELATIONS LAW

Sec.	This Work Sec.	Note
11(4)	903.1	2
14–a	803(5).1	
	901.7	15
	901.10	
14–a(4)	301.7	1
144(2)	300.3	14

NEW YORK, MCKINNEY'S EDUCATION LAW

Sec.	This Work Sec.	Note
106	1005.1	4
312	1005.1	4
6527(3)	502.1	

NEW YORK, MCKINNEY'S EMINENT DOMAIN PROCEDURE LAW

Sec.	This Work Sec.	Note
510(A)	1107.1	2

NEW YORK, MCKINNEY'S ELECTION LAW

Sec.	This Work Sec.	Note
7–202	512.1	2

TABLE OF STATUTES

NEW YORK, MCKINNEY'S ELECTION LAW

Sec.	This Work Sec.	Note
8–300(2)	512.1	2
17–146	512.1	6

NEW YORK, MCKINNEY'S ESTATES, POWERS AND TRUSTS LAW

Sec.	This Work Sec.	Note
2–1.6(a)	301.4	11
2–1.6(e)	301.4	11
2–1.7	301.4	10
2–1.7(a)(1)	803(5).1	
2–1.11(d)	601.2	
3–2.1	903.1	2
5–1.1(b)(3)	601.2	

PROPOSED NEW YORK EVIDENCE CODE

Sec.	This Work Sec.	Note
103	103.1	1
104	104.1	28
104(b)(2)(B)	104.1	30
104(b)(2)(C)	104.1	32
104(b)(2)(D)	104.1	35
105	105.1	
	105.1	10
	105.1	15
106	106.1	19
201	201.1	
	201.1	63
201(g)	201.1	61
302	301.5	45
302, Comment	301.5	46
Art. 4	401.1	
401	401.1	55
401—403	401.1	
402	401.1	55
403	401.1	
	401.1	55
404	402.1	
	402.1	24
	402.1	70
	404.1	22
404(b)	404.1	
405	402.1	40
	402.1	70
405(b)	402.1	20
406	406.1	32
406(a)	406.1	
407	407.1	
	407.1	34
408	408.1	
	408.1	12
	409.1	9
409	409.1	
	409.1	9
410	410.1	
	410.1	15
411	411.1	14

PROPOSED NEW YORK EVIDENCE CODE

Sec.	This Work Sec.	Note
411 (Cont'd)	412.1	1
411, Comment	412.1	2
503	501.2	2
	514.1	
	514.1	6
	514.1	13
503(b)(2)	514.1	7
503(b)(1)	514.1	13
503(b)(2)	514.1	13
504	501.1	
	501.1	4
504(a)	501.1	16
504(c)	501.1	
505	503.3	
	503.3	34
506	504.1	12
507	502.1	7
508	502.1	
	502.1	83
509	505.1	
	511.2	
	511.2	1
509(a)(2)	511.2	2
509(b)	511.2	2
511	513.1	
	513.1	5
	513.2	
512	512.1	
	512.1	8
513	511.1	10
514	510.1	
	510.1	10
	514.2	
514(b)(2)	510.1	
514(b)(3)	510.1	
601	601.1	10
601, Comment	601.1	24
602	601.1	10
602(a)	602.1	6
602(b)	601.1	54
603(a)	603.1	4
605	605.1	1
606(a)	606.1	2
606(b)	606.1	18
607	600.1	
607(a)	607.1	8
607(b)	607.4	6
608	608.1	16
608(a)	607.5	23
	607.5	28
	608.1	7
608(a)(1)	608.1	16
608(b)	608.2	
	608.2	33
608(b)(2)	608.1	11
	608.1	16
608(b)(3)	607.7	3
	608.1	16
609	609.1	
	609.1	52
610, Comment	610.1	6
611(a)	611.1	11

892

TABLE OF STATUTES

PROPOSED NEW YORK EVIDENCE CODE

Sec.	This Work Sec.	Note
611(a) (Cont'd)	611.3	30
611(b)	611.3	28
611(c)	611.2	20
612	612.1	23
612, Comment	612.1	30
612(b)	612.1	23
612(b), Comment	612.1	24
612(c)	612.1	15
613, Comment	607.4	30
613(a)—(b)	607.8	33
613(c)	607.4	6
	607.4	30
614	614.1	21
614(a)	614.1	2
	614.1	11
615	615.1	10
615(a)	615.1	5
615(b)	615.1	10
615(c)	615.1	10
701	701.1	
	701.2	
702	702.1	
	702.1	11
702(b)	702.1	11
702(c)	702.1	11
703	703.1	
	703.1	12
	705.1	1
704	704.1	
	704.1	1
	704.1	11
704, Comment	704.1	5
705	705.1	1
706	706.1	
	706.1	7
802(b)(1), Comment	802.2	
803	802.1	19
	803(5).1	21
	803(5).1	24
	803(5).1	30
	803(5).1	41
803(1)	803(1).1	21
803(a)(1)	801(1).1	
	801(1).2	21
803(a)(2)	801(1).1	
	801(1).2	19
	801(1).2	21
803(b)(1)	801(1).1	
	802.2	46
803(b)(2)	801(1).1	
803(b)(3)	801(1).1	
803(b)(4)	801(1).1	
803(c)(1)	803(1).1	37
803(c)(2)	803(1).1	43
	803(1).1	54
803(c)(3)	803(1).1	
	803(1).1	63
803(c)(4)	803(2).1	
	803(2).1	15

PROPOSED NEW YORK EVIDENCE CODE

Sec.	This Work Sec.	Note
803(c)(5)	803(3).1	
	803(3).1	79
803(c)(5)(A)(iii)	803(3).1	54
803(c)(6)	803(4).1	
	803(4).1	3
803(c)(7)	803(5).1	11
803(c)(7)(A)	803(5).1	
803(c)(7)(B)(i)	803(5).1	35
	901.10	4
803(c)(7)(B)(ii)	803(3).1	46
	901.10	4
803(c)(15)	803(6).1	6
803(c)(16)	803(7).1	2
803(c)(19)	803(7).1	27
803(c)(20)	803(7).1	27
803(c)(21)	803(5).1	
	803(7).1	27
803(c)(22)	803(5).1	
804	803(1).1	43
	804.1	36
	804(1).1	17
	804(4).1	25
804(6)(A)(ii)	804(4).1	
804(b)(1)(A)	804(1).1	
804(b)(2)	804(1).2	
	804(2).1	34
804(b)(4)	803(1).1	43
804(b)(5)	803(1).1	54
	803(1).1	55
	803(1).2	
804(b)(6), Comment	804(4).1	23
805	801(2).1	
806	804(5).1	
	804(5).1	1
807	807.1	9
808	805.1	8
809	607.8	37
	806.1	3
901(a)	900.1	23
901(b)(1)	901.1	
901(b)(1), Comment	1100.1	9
901(b)(2)	901.2	
901(b)(3)	901.3	18
	901.3	19
901(b)(4)	901.4	
901(b)(5)	901.5	
	901.5	7
901(b)(6)	901.6	
	901.6	6
901(b)(7)	901.7	
	901.7	14
901(b)(8)	901.8	
	901.8	3
901(b)(9)	901.9	1
901(b)(10)	901.10	
902	902.1	
	902.1	13
902(a)(7)	902.1	5

TABLE OF STATUTES

PROPOSED NEW YORK EVIDENCE CODE

Sec.	This Work Sec.	Note
902(a)(10), Comment	902.1	
903	903.1	
903(b)(3)	901.3	
904(b)(4)	901.4	10
Art. 10	1001.1	
1001, Comment	1005.1	
1001(c)	1002.1	
	1002.1	8
1002, Comment	1005.1	4
1003	1002.1	13
	1003.1	8
1004	1004.1	1
1004(b), Comment	1004.1	12
1005	1005.1	
	1005.1	3
1006	1006.1	1
1007	1007.1	
1007, Comment	1007.1	1
1008	1008.1	
	1008.1	5
1008, Comment	1008.1	3
	1008.1	5
1104(c), Comment	1004.1	18

NEW YORK, MCKINNEY'S GENERAL BUSINESS LAW

Sec.	This Work Sec.	Note
343	513.1	8
394–a	1005.1	4

NEW YORK, MCKINNEY'S GENERAL MUNICIPAL LAW

Sec.	This Work Sec.	Note
51–a(2) (repealed)	1005.1	4

NEW YORK, MCKINNEY'S INDIAN LAW

Sec.	This Work Sec.	Note
71	1005.1	4

NEW YORK, MCKINNEY'S INSURANCE LAW

Sec.	This Work Sec.	Note
3105(d)	502.1	47
5102(d)	704.1	16

NEW YORK, MCKINNEY'S JUDICIARY LAW

Sec.	This Work Sec.	Note
2–b(1)	614.1	8
35(1)(a)	706.1	3

NEW YORK, MCKINNEY'S JUDICIARY LAW

Sec.	This Work Sec.	Note
35(4)	706.1	3
106	604.1	1
107	604.1	1
386	604.1	1
387	604.1	2
	604.1	8
390	601.1	55
	604.1	6

NEW YORK, MCKINNEY'S FAMILY COURT ACT

Sec.	This Work Sec.	Note
152(b)	601.1	37
Art. 3	412.1	1
418	702.1	
	803(3).1	
436	601.1	26
454(3)(a)	300.3	43
	301.7	4
	301.7	14
	301.7	16
531	300.3	14
	601.1	25
532	803(3).1	
Art. 10	804(5).1	
	804(5).1	24
1046(a)	804(5).1	
1046(a)(ii)	804(5).1	24
1046(a)(iii)	804(5).1	24
1046(a)(iv)	803(3).1	25
	804(5).1	24
1046(a)(v)	804(5).1	24
1046(a)(vi)	804(5).1	24
	804(5).1	26
1046(a)(vii)	502.1	
	505.1	
	506.1	
	804(5).1	24
1046(a)(viii)	503.3	30

NEW YORK, MCKINNEY'S MENTAL HYGIENE LAW

Sec.	This Work Sec.	Note
9.27	509.1	20
33.13(c)(6)	502.1	
Art. 81	601.2	32
81.09(d)	502.1	
81.12(a)	300.4	31

NEW YORK, MCKINNEY'S PENAL LAW

Sec.	This Work Sec.	Note
10.00(1)—(5)	609.1	13
10.00(6)	609.1	9
15.25	300.4	55
25.00	300.4	

TABLE OF STATUTES

NEW YORK, MCKINNEY'S PENAL LAW

Sec.	This Work Sec.	Note
25.00(1)	300.4	51
	300.4	53
30.00	300.4	51
	301.3	4
30.00(1)	301.3	4
30.00(2)	301.3	4
35.00—35.30	300.4	50
40.00	300.4	56
40.05	300.4	57
40.15	300.4	58
	300.4	64
	302.1	30
125.20(2)	300.4	60
125.25(1)(a)	300.4	60
Art. 130	412.1	1
130.15	702.1	60
165.55(3)	302.1	19
210.50	300.3	13
215.70	508.1	
220.25(2)	302.1	19
	302.1	23
235.10(1)	302.2	7
255.30(1)	300.3	13
255.30(2)	300.3	13
265.15(3)	302.1	8
	302.1	19
265.15(6)	302.1	19
265.25	502.1	

NEW YORK, MCKINNEY'S PUBLIC HEALTH LAW

Sec.	This Work Sec.	Note
27–F	502.1	
230	502.1	
2101(1)	502.1	
2306	505.1	15
2780—2787	502.1	8
2785(2)	502.1	
3372	502.1	
3373	502.1	
4103	301.7	1
4103(3)	803(5).1	
4135	803(5).1	28
4138	803(5).1	28
4138–c	507.1	1

NEW YORK, MCKINNEY'S PUBLIC LANDS LAW

Sec.	This Work Sec.	Note
5	1005.1	4

NEW YORK, MCKINNEY'S PUBLIC OFFICERS LAW

Sec.	This Work Sec.	Note
Art. 6	511.1	6
87(2)	511.1	8

NEW YORK, MCKINNEY'S PUBLIC OFFICERS LAW

Sec.	This Work Sec.	Note
87(2)(D)	513.2	4

NEW YORK, MCKINNEY'S PUBLIC SERVICE LAW

Sec.	This Work Sec.	Note
17	1005.1	4

NEW YORK, MCKINNEY'S REAL PROPERTY LAW

Sec.	This Work Sec.	Note
248—312	902.1	
303	902.1	8
399	1005.1	4

NEW YORK, MCKINNEY'S REAL PROPERTY ACTIONS & PROCEEDINGS LAW

Sec.	This Work Sec.	Note
331	803(5).1	20
	803(7).1	5
	803(7).1	11
341	803(5).1	20
	803(7).1	5
	803(7).1	11
342	803(5).1	20
821	1107.1	2

NEW YORK, MCKINNEY'S SOCIAL SERVICES LAW

Sec.	This Work Sec.	Note
413	502.1	
	505.1	
415	502.1	
425	505.1	
384–b(3)(h)	502.1	

NEW YORK, MCKINNEY'S SURROGATE'S COURT PROCEDURE ACT

Sec.	This Work Sec.	Note
1404	903.1	2
1404—1407	902.1	7
1405	903.1	2
1407	803(1).1	46
	1003.1	9
2103—2104	601.2	82
2211	601.2	82

NEW YORK, MCKINNEY'S TRANSPORTATION LAW

Sec.	This Work Sec.	Note
69	1005.1	4

895

TABLE OF STATUTES

NEW YORK, MCKINNEY'S TRANSPORTATION LAW

Sec.	This Work Sec.	Note
88	1005.1	4

NEW YORK, MCKINNEY'S UNIFORM COMMERCIAL CODE

Sec.	This Work Sec.	Note
1–201(8)	300.4	9
	301.5	23
1–201(31)	301.5	
	301.5	45
1–202	301.7	1
3–307(1)(a)	300.2	11
	301.5	23
3–307(1)(b)	300.2	11
	301.5	23
7–403(1)(b)	301.5	23
Art. 9	301.7	1

NEW YORK, MCKINNEY'S VEHICLE AND TRAFFIC LAW

Sec.	This Work Sec.	Note
155	609.1	9
	609.1	13
313(1)(b)	301.3	8
388(1)	301.4	16
1141	802.2	27
1184(2)(d)(3)(f)	702.1	
1194	702.1	
	802.2	
	901.9	6
1194(4)	509.1	90
1194(4)(a)	702.1	46
1194(4)(c)	301.7	9
	302.1	19
	702.1	
2108(c)	301.7	1
	301.7	4

NEW YORK, MCKINNEY'S WORKERS' COMPENSATION LAW

Sec.	This Work Sec.	Note
21(5)	301.7	1

NEW YORK LAWS

Year	This Work Sec.	Note
1974, ch. 14	702.1	60
1987, ch. 737, § 5	1005.1	4
1992, ch. 698, § 4	601.2	32

UNITED STATES

UNITED STATES CONSTITUTION

Amend.	This Work Sec.	Note
1	300.4	
	508.1	
	508.2	
4	401.1	
5	401.2	
	501.1	24
	501.2	6
	509.1	
	509.1	47
	509.1	70
	514.1	
	514.2	
	802.2	
	802.3	
	804.1	
	804.1	30
	804(1).1	
	804(1).2	
	804(1).2	11
	804(3).1	
	804(3).1	46
6	412.1	5
	501.3	29
	502.1	86
	604.2	6
	607.7	20
	607.8	10
	611.3	
	804(1).1	21
14	202.1	

UNITED STATES CODE ANNOTATED

5 U.S.C.A.—Government Organization and Employees

Sec.	This Work Sec.	Note
552	511.2	2
	511.2	13
552(b)	511.2	14
552(b)(5)	511.2	15
5561 et seq.	803(5).1	

8 U.S.C.A.—Aliens and Nationality

Sec.	This Work Sec.	Note
1454(e)	902.1	29

15 U.S.C.A.—Commerce and Trade

Sec.	This Work Sec.	Note
77f(a)	902.1	29

18 U.S.C.A.—Crimes and Criminal Procedure

Sec.	This Work Sec.	Note
17	300.4	77
343(1)	302.2	3

TABLE OF STATUTES

UNITED STATES CODE ANNOTATED
18 U.S.C.A.—Crimes and Criminal Procedure

Sec.	This Work Sec.	Note
1201(b)	302.2	7
1465	302.2	7
1827(d)(1)	604.2	3
3500	501.3	50
	511.2	2
3505	803(3).2	
3509(c)	601.3	17
	603.2	5
3509(i)	615.2	4
6001—6003	509.1	

19 U.S.C.A.—Customs and Duties

Sec.	This Work Sec.	Note
1615(2)	902.1	

22 U.S.C.A.—Foreign Relations and Intercourse

Sec.	This Work Sec.	Note
4221	902.1	29

26 U.S.C.A.—Internal Revenue Code

Sec.	This Work Sec.	Note
6064	902.1	29

28 U.S.C.A.—Judiciary and Judicial Procedure

Sec.	This Work Sec.	Note
753(b)	902.1	29
1732	803(3).2	25
	901.10	5
	1002.1	
	1002.1	9
1739	1005.1	4
1740	1005.1	4
2111	103.2	26

UNITED STATES CODE ANNOTATED
37 U.S.C.A.—Pay and Allowances of the Uniformed Services

Sec.	This Work Sec.	Note
551 et seq.	803(5).1	

42 U.S.C.A.—The Public Health and Welfare

Sec.	This Work Sec.	Note
1983	802.3	
	803(3).2	
	804(2).2	
2000e–2(a)(1)	301.8	1

44 U.S.C.A.—Public Printing and Documents

Sec.	This Work Sec.	Note
1507	203.2	3

POPULAR NAME ACTS

CIVIL RIGHTS ACT OF 1964

Tit.	This Work Sec.	Note
VII	301.8	1

SOCIAL SECURITY ACT

Sec.	This Work Sec.	Note
Tit. II	803(5).2	

UNIFORM COMMERCIAL CODE

Sec.	This Work Sec.	Note
1–202	902.1	28
3–114(3)	902.1	28
3–307(1)(b)	902.1	28
3–510	902.1	28
8–105(3)(b)	902.1	28

TABLE OF RULES

DISCIPLINARY RULES OF THE NEW YORK CODE OF PROFESSIONAL RESPONSIBILITY

Rule	This Work Sec.	Note
4–101(C)(4)	501.1	72
5–109	501.1	69
7–104	802.3	
7–104(A)(1)	501.1	67

OFFICIAL COMPILATION OF CODES, RULES AND REGULATIONS OF THE STATE OF NEW YORK

Tit.	This Work Sec.	Note
22, § 202.15(i)	1104.1	33
22, § 202.18	706.1	3

U.S. DISTRICT COURTS OF N.Y.–SOUTHERN AND EASTERN DISTRICTS–BANKRUPTCY RULES

Rule	This Work Sec.	Note
X1–4	804(1).2	11

FEDERAL RULES OF CIVIL PROCEDURE

Rule	This Work Sec.	Note
10(c)	901.10	
26(a)(1)	501.3	45
26(a)(2)	501.3	45
26(b)(3)	501.3	
	501.3	7
	501.3	40
	501.3	41
26(b)(4)	501.3	7
26(b)(4)(A)	501.3	45
26(b)(4)(B)	501.3	46
26(c)(7)	513.2	
30(b)(2)	1104.2	20
30(f)(1)	901.10	
32	804(1).2	
32(a)	1104.2	20
32(c)	1104.2	20
34	1001.1	
36	1004.1	
	1007.1	
43(a)	500.1	6
43(f)	604.2	
	604.2	1
44(a)(1)	902.1	
44.1	203.2	
	203.2	6
	203.2	9

FEDERAL RULES OF CIVIL PROCEDURE

Rule	This Work Sec.	Note
46	103.2	1
50	300.3	
50(a)—(b)	300.3	47
61	103.2	26
80(c)	901.10	6

FEDERAL RULES OF CRIMINAL PROCEDURE

Rule	This Work Sec.	Note
11(e)(6)	410.2	5
	410.2	7
16(a)(1)(D)	501.3	51
16(a)(2)	501.3	
	501.3	7
	501.3	47
16(b)(1)(B)	501.3	51
16(b)(2)	501.3	
	501.3	7
	501.3	47
26.1	203.2	
	203.2	7
	203.2	9
26.2(a)	501.3	50
28	604.2	
	604.2	2
	706.2	3
29	300.3	
29(a)—(b)	300.3	49
51	103.2	1
52(a)	103.2	26
52(b)	103.2	3

PROPOSED FEDERAL RULES OF EVIDENCE

Rule	This Work Sec.	Note
502	507.2	
	507.2	1
	511.2	15
503(a)(2)	501.2	8
504	502.2	
	502.2	4
505	503.5	8
506	504.2	1
507	512.2	
	512.2	1
508	513.2	
	513.2	1
510	510.2	
	510.2	12

899

TABLE OF RULES

PROPOSED FEDERAL RULES OF EVIDENCE

Rule	This Work Sec.	Note
510(c)(2)	510.2	
512	501.2	44
513	514.2	
	514.2	1

FEDERAL RULES OF EVIDENCE

Rule	This Work Sec.	Note
103	103.1	1
	103.2	
103(a)	103.2	
103(a)(1)	103.2	
103(a)(2)	103.1	
	103.2	
103(d)	103.2	3
104	104.1	
	104.1	28
	104.2	
104(a)	104.2	
	104.2	9
	104.2	10
	404.2	
	802.3	
104(b)	104.1	
	104.2	
	404.2	4
	602.2	3
	900.1	7
104(c)	104.2	
104(d)	104.2	
104(e)	104.2	
105	105.2	
106	106.2	
201	201.1	
	201.2	
201(a)	201.2	18
201(b)	201.1	21
	201.1	29
	201.2	
201(c)	201.2	11
201(d)	201.2	13
201(e)	201.2	12
201(f)	201.2	9
201(g)	201.1	
	201.2	
301	301.8	
	301.8	1
	301.8	8
302	301.8	
Art. 4	413.1	
401	401.2	
	401.2	1
	607.2	
	607.2	15
	607.6	
401—403	401.2	
402	401.2	
	401.2	1
	404.2	
	607.2	
	607.2	15

FEDERAL RULES OF EVIDENCE

Rule	This Work Sec.	Note
402 (Cont'd)	607.6	
403	401.1	47
	401.2	
	401.2	1
	401.2	2
	404.2	
	411.2	
	413.1	
	601.3	
	601.3	14
	607.2	
	607.2	15
	607.6	36
	607.7	
	607.7	21
	607.7	25
	609.2	
	702.2	
	702.2	13
	702.2	26
	703.2	11
	803(6).2	
	803(6).2	4
	803(7).2	
	803(7).2	
	806.1	19
	1101.2	
	1103.2	6
	1104.2	
404	402.2	
	402.2	1
	413.1	
	803(7).2	
404(a)	404.2	
	607.6	35
404(a)(1)	402.2	
404(a)(2)	402.1	
	402.2	
404(b)	104.2	
	404.2	
	404.2	15
	404.2	26
	413.1	
	608.2	48
	608.2	51
	900.1	10
405	402.2	
	402.2	2
	413.1	
	803(7).2	
405(a)	402.2	
	402.2	5
405(b)	402.2	
406	406.2	
407	407.2	
408	104.2	10
	408.1	
	408.2	
	408.2	4
	408.2	5
	408.2	6
	409.2	
409	409.2	

900

TABLE OF RULES

FEDERAL RULES OF EVIDENCE

Rule	This Work Sec.	Note
410	410.1	
	410.2	
	410.2	3
	410.2	5
	410.2	7
	410.2	9
411	411.2	
412	402.2	4
	412.2	
	412.2	1
	412.2	10
	413.1	
412(b)(1)(C)	412.2	
413	413.1	
	413.1	1
414	413.1	
	413.1	2
415	413.1	
	413.1	3
501	500.2	
	500.2	2
	500.2	4
	501.2	31
	505.2	
	506.2	
Art. 6	600.1	
601	601.3	
	601.3	4
602	601.3	
	601.3	11
	602.1	6
	602.2	
	602.2	6
603	601.3	
	603.2	
604	604.2	
605	601.3	
	605.1	1
	605.2	
	605.2	1
	605.2	4
606	601.3	
606(a)	606.2	1
606(b)	606.2	
	606.2	2
607	607.4	
	607.4	39
608	803(7).2	
608(a)	607.2	14
	607.5	
	607.5	59
608(a)(1)	608.1	
	608.1	18
608(a)(2)	600.1	
	607.1	
608(b)	103.2	23
	607.2	14
	607.5	56
	607.6	37
	608.2	
	608.2	47
	608.2	48
	608.2	50

FEDERAL RULES OF EVIDENCE

Rule	This Work Sec.	Note
609	607.2	14
	608.2	47
	609.2	
609(a)	609.2	
	609.2	1
	609.2	3
609(a)(1)	609.2	
	609.2	2
	609.2	4
	609.2	7
609(a)(2)	608.2	45
	609.2	
	609.2	2
	609.2	11
	609.2	12
	609.2	14
	609.2	15
	609.2	17
610	607.2	14
	610.2	
	610.2	4
611	612.2	
611(a)	607.8	
	611.5	
	614.2	8
611(a)(2)	611.5	
611(a)(3)	611.5	
611(b)	607.2	19
	611.3	28
	611.5	
	611.5	17
611(c)	611.5	
612	501.3	55
	612.1	
	612.2	
	612.2	15
	612.2	20
613	600.1	
	607.1	
	607.2	14
	607.8	
613(a)	607.8	
613(b)	607.6	38
	607.8	
	607.8	51
614	614.2	
614(a)	614.1	1
	614.1	5
	614.2	
	614.2	2
614(b)	614.2	
614(c)	614.2	
615	615.1	10
	615.2	
	615.2	6
	615.2	9
615(2)	615.2	
615(3)	615.2	
Art. 7	700.1	
701	406.2	
	701.1	
	701.2	
702	702.1	

901

TABLE OF RULES

FEDERAL RULES OF EVIDENCE

Rule	Sec.	Note
702 (Cont'd)	702.2	
	702.2	12
	702.2	13
	702.2	18
	704.2	
	901.9	
703	602.2	1
	703.1	
	703.2	
	803(6).2	
	803(6).2	5
704	704.2	2
704(a)	704.2	
704(b)	704.2	
705	705.2	
	705.2	2
706	706.2	
	706.2	1
	706.2	3
	706.2	7
801	801.1	
801(a)	801.1	
801(c)	801.1	
801(d)	801(1).1	
	805.2	
801(d)(1)	802.1	
801(d)(1)(A)	607.2	14
	607.8	
	801(1).2	
	801(1).3	
	801(1).3	12
	801(1).3	14
801(d)(1)(B)	600.1	
	607.1	
	607.5	
	607.5	62
	801(1).2	
	801(1).3	
	801(1).3	19
801(d)(1)(C)	607.5	
	801(1).3	12
	801(2).2	
	801(2).2	11
	801(2).2	12
801(d)(2)	802.1	
	802.3	
	802.3	6
	802.3	27
	806.1	
801(d)(2)(A)	802.2	45
	802.3	
801(d)(2)(C)	802.2	
	802.3	
	806.1	
801(d)(2)(D)	802.2	
	802.3	
	802.3	28
	803.3	27
	806.1	
801(d)(2)(E)	104.2	
	104.2	11
	802.3	
	804(3).2	28

FEDERAL RULES OF EVIDENCE

Rule	Sec.	Note
801(d)(2)(E) (Cont'd)	805.2	
	806.1	
803	803.1	
	803.1	1
	803(5).1	52
	806.1	
803(1)	803(1).1	
	803(1).2	
	804(5).2	
803(2)	607.5	54
	803(1).2	
	803(1).2	52
803(3)	803(1).1	
	803(1).2	
	803(1).2	26
803(4)	803(1).1	
	803(1).2	
	803(1).2	52
	803(3).2	28
803(5)	803(2).1	
	803(2).2	
803(6)	802.3	
	803(3).1	10
	803(3).2	
	803(3).2	7
	803(3).2	15
	803(3).2	19
	803(3).2	28
	803(5).2	55
	1002.1	
	1006.1	5
803(7)	803(4).2	
	803(4).2	2
803(8)	803(3).1	
	803(3).2	
	803(5).1	
	803(5).2	
	803(5).2	14
	803(5).2	23
	803(5).2	32
	803(5).2	33
	803(5).2	34
	803(5).2	35
803(8)(B)	803(5).2	23
803(8)(C)	201.2	4
	803(3).2	
	803(5).1	
	803(5).2	
	803(5).2	23
803(9)	803(5).2	
803(10)	803(4).2	
	803(4).2	1
	803(5).2	
	803(5).2	11
803(11)	803(5).1	
	803(5).1	54
	803(5).2	
803(12)	803(5).2	
	803(7).2	
803(13)	803(7).1	
	803(7).2	
	804(4).2	
	804(4).2	10

902

TABLE OF RULES

FEDERAL RULES OF EVIDENCE

Rule	This Work Sec.	Note
803(14)	803(5).2	
803(15)	803(7).2	5
803(16)	803(7).1	
	803(7).2	
	901.8	
	901.8	12
803(17)	803(6).1	
	803(6).2	
	803(6).2	11
803(18)	702.1	
	803(6).1	
	803(6).2	
	803(6).2	4
	803(6).2	5
803(19)	803(5).2	
	803(7).2	
	804(4).2	
	804(4).2	11
803(20)	803(5).2	
	803(7).2	
803(21)	803(5).2	
	803(7).2	
803(22)	803(5).2	
	804(5).2	
	804(5).2	24
803(23)	803(5).2	
	803(5).2	50
803(24)	804(2).2	18
	804(5).1	
	804(5).2	
	804(5).2	10
	804(5).2	12
	804(5).2	26
804	803.1	
	803.1	1
	803(1).2	
	804(1).2	
	806.1	
804(a)	804.1	
804(b)(1)	802.3	4
	804(1).1	
	804(1).2	
	804(1).2	9
804(b)(2)	804(2).2	
804(b)(3)	802.1	
	802.3	77
	804(3).2	
	804(3).2	10
	804(3).2	20
804(b)(4)	804(4).1	
	804(4).2	
804(b)(5)	803(1).2	
	804(1).2	
	804(1).2	10
	804(1).2	28
	804(5).1	
	804(5).2	
805	805.2	
	805.2	3
806	804(1).2	11
	806.1	
	806.1	4

FEDERAL RULES OF EVIDENCE

Rule	This Work Sec.	Note
806 (Cont'd)	806.1	11
	806.1	17
	806.1	18
	806.1	19
	900.1	10
901	900.1	
901(a)	104.2	
	900.1	
	1100.1	8
901(b)	901.1	
	901.7	
901(b)(1)	901.1	
901(b)(2)	901.2	
901(b)(3)	901.3	
901(b)(5)	901.5	
901(b)(6)	901.6	
901(b)(8)	901.8	
901(b)(9)	901.9	
901(b)(10)	901.10	
902	901.10	
	902.1	
902(1)	902.1	
902(1)—(5)	901.7	
902(2)	902.1	
902(3)	902.1	
902(4)	803(5).2	
	803(5).2	1
	902.1	
902(5)	902.1	18
902(8)	902.1	
902(9)	902.1	
902(b)(4)	901.4	
903	903.1	
Art. 10	1001.1	
1001	1001.1	
1001(3)	1001.1	35
	1002.1	
	1002.1	8
1001(4)	1003.1	
1002	1002.1	
1003	1002.1	
	1003.1	
	1004.1	
1004	1004.1	
	1005.1	
	1007.1	4
1005	1005.1	
	1007.1	4
1006	1006.1	
	1006.1	23
	1006.1	26
	1103.2	1
1007	1007.1	
1008	1008.1	
1008(a)	1008.1	10
1008(b)	1008.1	10

UNIFORM RULES OF EVIDENCE

Rule	This Work Sec.	Note
401	607.1	8

903

TABLE OF CASES

A

Aalholm v. People, 211 N.Y. 406, 105 N.E. 647 (N.Y.1914)—§ **803(7).1, n. 1**; § **804(4).1, n. 1, 5, 13, 16, 20.**

A and M, Application of, 61 A.D.2d 426, 403 N.Y.S.2d 375 (N.Y.A.D. 4 Dept.1978)—§ **503.4**; § **503.4, n. 1.**

Abbe by Abbe v. Board of Educ., 186 A.D.2d 102, 587 N.Y.S.2d 707 (N.Y.A.D. 2 Dept. 1992)—§ **803(3).1, n. 27.**

Abbondola v. Church of St. Vincent De Paul, 205 Misc. 353, 123 N.Y.S.2d 32 (N.Y.Sup.1953)—§ **803(5).1, n. 53.**

Abbott v. Doughan, 204 N.Y. 223, 97 N.E. 599 (N.Y.1912)—§ **601.2, n. 21, 23.**

Abel, United States v., 469 U.S. 45, 105 S.Ct. 465, 83 L.Ed.2d 450 (1984)— § **607.2, n. 15**; § **607.6**; § **607.6, n. 30, 34, 36, 37**; § **610.1, n. 8**; § **610.2, n. 4.**

Able Cycle Engines, Inc. v. Allstate Ins. Co., 84 A.D.2d 140, 445 N.Y.S.2d 469 (N.Y.A.D. 2 Dept.1981)—§ **609.1, n. 10.**

Abrams v. Ocean Club, Inc., 602 F.Supp. 489 (D.C.N.Y.1984)—§ **803(7).2, n. 8.**

Abrevaya v. Palace Theatre & Realty Co., 25 Misc.2d 600, 197 N.Y.S.2d 27 (N.Y.Sup.1960)—§ **201.1, n. 28, 44.**

A.C. v. B.C., 12 Misc.2d 1, 176 N.Y.S.2d 794 (N.Y.Sup.1958)—§ **503.2, n. 10.**

Accardi v. City of New York, 121 A.D.2d 489, 503 N.Y.S.2d 818 (N.Y.A.D. 2 Dept. 1986)—§ **607.3, n. 1.**

Accent Designs, Inc. v. Jan Jewelry Designs, Inc., 827 F.Supp. 957 (S.D.N.Y. 1993)—§ **1006.1, n. 26.**

Acebedo, People v., 156 A.D.2d 369, 548 N.Y.S.2d 324 (N.Y.A.D. 2 Dept.1989)— § **901.7, n. 7.**

Acevedo, People v., 515 N.Y.S.2d 753, 508 N.E.2d 665 (N.Y.1987)—§ **404.1**; § **404.1, n. 77.**

Acevedo, People v., 389 N.Y.S.2d 811, 358 N.E.2d 495 (N.Y.1976)—§ **1100.1, n. 5**; § **1102.1, n. 23**; § **1105.1, n. 11, 13, 14.**

Ackerson, People v., 149 Misc.2d 882, 566 N.Y.S.2d 833 (Monroe Co.Ct.1991)— § **502.1, n. 12.**

Acklin, People v., 102 Misc.2d 596, 424 N.Y.S.2d 633 (N.Y.Sup.1980)—§ **702.1**; § **702.1, n. 67.**

Acomb, People v., 87 A.D.2d 1, 450 N.Y.S.2d 632 (N.Y.A.D. 4 Dept.1982)— § **104.1, n. 15**; § **607.6, n. 18**; § **611.3, n. 9.**

ACS Hosp. Systems, Inc. v. Montefiore Hosp., 732 F.2d 1572 (Fed.Cir.1984)— § **301.8, n. 8.**

Adams v. Greenwich Ins. Co., 70 N.Y. 166 (1877)—§ **607.5, n. 23.**

Adcor Realty Corp. v. Srogi, 54 A.D.2d 1096, 388 N.Y.S.2d 962 (N.Y.A.D. 4 Dept.1976)—§ **803(6).1, n. 4.**

Addington v. Texas, 441 U.S. 418, 99 S.Ct. 1804, 60 L.Ed.2d 323 (1979)—§ **300.4, n. 19, 31**; § **509.1**; § **509.1, n. 24.**

Admiral Ins. Co. v. United States Dist. Court for Dist. of Arizona, 881 F.2d 1486 (9th Cir.1989)—§ **501.2, n. 28.**

Adoption of Baby Boy L., Matter of, 157 Misc.2d 353, 596 N.Y.S.2d 997 (N.Y.Fam.Ct.1993)—§ **702.1, n. 47.**

Adorno, People v., 128 Misc.2d 389, 489 N.Y.S.2d 441 (N.Y.City Crim.Ct.1984)— § **701.1, n. 4.**

A–85–04–38, Matter of, 138 Misc.2d 786, 525 N.Y.S.2d 479 (N.Y.Sup.1988)— § **502.1, n. 74.**

Aetna Cas. and Sur. Co. v. Brice, 72 A.D.2d 927, 422 N.Y.S.2d 203 (N.Y.A.D. 4 Dept. 1979)—§ **301.5, n. 35.**

Aetna Cas. & Sur. Co. v. Santos, 175 A.D.2d 91, 573 N.Y.S.2d 695 (N.Y.A.D. 2 Dept. 1991)—§ **301.5, n. 35.**

Afarian, People v., 202 Misc. 199, 108 N.Y.S.2d 533 (Broome Ct.1951)— § **514.1, n. 5.**

Affleck, United States v., 776 F.2d 1451 (10th Cir.1985)—§ **703.2, n. 11.**

A.F.L. Falck, S.p.A. v. E.A. Karay Co., Inc., 722 F.Supp. 12 (S.D.N.Y.1989)— § **1004.1, n. 14.**

Agajanian, United States v., 852 F.2d 56 (2nd Cir.1988)—§ **607.8, n. 44**; § **614.2, n. 2.**

Agent Orange Product Liability Litigation, In re, 611 F.Supp. 1223 (S.D.N.Y. 1985)—§ **401.2**; § **401.2, n. 2, 4, 16**; § **703.2**; § **703.2, n. 4**; § **803(5).2, n. 23.**

Agluzzi v. Aluzzo, 286 A.D. 399, 143 N.Y.S.2d 51 (N.Y.A.D. 4 Dept.1955)— § **601.2, n. 33, 34.**

Agosto, In re, 553 F.Supp. 1298 (D.C.Nev. 1983)—§ **503.5, n. 22.**

Agosto, People v., 540 N.Y.S.2d 988, 538 N.E.2d 340 (N.Y.1989)—§ **607.6, n. 8, 9.**

Agueci, United States v., 310 F.2d 817 (2nd Cir.1962)—§ **300.3, n. 51.**

Aguilar v. State, 279 A.D. 103, 108 N.Y.S.2d 456 (N.Y.A.D.1951)—§ **601.1, n. 11, 46, 49**; § **804(1).1, n. 24.**

905

TABLE OF CASES

Aguirre–Parra, United States v., 763 F.Supp. 1208 (S.D.N.Y.1991)—§ **104.2, n. 9.**

Agustino–Hernandez, United States v., 14 F.3d 42 (11th Cir.1994)—§ **803(5).2, n. 9.**

Aharonowicz, People v., 529 N.Y.S.2d 736, 525 N.E.2d 458 (N.Y.1988)—§ **402.1, n. 31, 56.**

Aievoli's Will, In re, 272 A.D. 544, 74 N.Y.S.2d 29 (N.Y.A.D. 2 Dept.1947)—§ **601.2; § 601.2, n. 10, 27.**

Air Crash Disaster at John F. Kennedy Intern. Airport on June 24, 1975., In re, 635 F.2d 67 (2nd Cir.1980)—§ **106.2, n. 1; § 406.2, n. 16; § 1103.2, n. 5, 6.**

Air Disaster at Lockerbie Scotland on Dec. 21, 1988, In re, 37 F.3d 804 (2nd Cir. 1994)—§ **702.2, n. 13; § 704.2, n. 4.**

Air Et Chaleur, S.A. v. Janeway, 757 F.2d 489 (2nd Cir.1985)—§ **608.2, n. 52; § 611.5, n. 4.**

Ajmal, United States v., 67 F.3d 12 (2nd Cir.1995)—§ **614.2, n. 10.**

Alaire, People v., 148 A.D.2d 731, 539 N.Y.S.2d 468 (N.Y.A.D. 2 Dept.1989)—§ **505.1, n. 7.**

Alamo, People v., 298 N.Y.S.2d 681, 246 N.E.2d 496 (N.Y.1969)—§ **402.1, n. 48.**

Albergo, United States v., 539 F.2d 860 (2nd Cir.1976)—§ **901.5, n. 21.**

Alberti v. New York, L. E. & W. R. Co., 118 N.Y. 77, 23 N.E. 35 (N.Y.1889)—§ **1104.1, n. 2.**

Alessi, United States v., 638 F.2d 466 (2nd Cir.1980)—§ **404.2; § 404.2, n. 27; § 901.6, n. 9.**

Alex, People v., 260 N.Y. 425, 183 N.E. 906 (N.Y.1933)—§ **607.5, n. 6.**

Alexander v. Kramer Bros. Freight Lines, Inc., 273 F.2d 373 (2nd Cir.1959)—§ **801(1).3, n. 18.**

Alexander, People v., 371 N.Y.S.2d 876, 333 N.E.2d 157 (N.Y.1975)—§ **401.1, n. 16.**

Alford v. Sventek, 439 N.Y.S.2d 339, 421 N.E.2d 831 (N.Y.1981)—§ **606.1, n. 3, 14; § 1107.1, n. 16.**

Alicea, People v., 306 N.Y.S.2d 686, 254 N.E.2d 915 (N.Y.1969)—§ **201.1, n. 10, 28, 45.**

Al–Kanani, Abdul Karim, People v., 351 N.Y.S.2d 969, 307 N.E.2d 43 (N.Y. 1973)—§ **502.1, n. 58.**

Allan v. Keystone Nineties, Inc., 74 A.D.2d 992, 427 N.Y.S.2d 107 (N.Y.A.D. 4 Dept. 1980)—§ **701.1, n. 8.**

Alldread v. City of Grenada, 988 F.2d 1425 (5th Cir.1993)—§ **501.2, n. 48.**

Allen, People v., 140 A.D.2d 229, 528 N.Y.S.2d 380 (N.Y.A.D. 1 Dept.1988)—§ **1102.1, n. 4, 6.**

Allen, People v., 104 Misc.2d 136, 427 N.Y.S.2d 698 (N.Y.Sup.1980)—§ **501.3, n. 32.**

Allen, People v., 67 A.D.2d 558, 416 N.Y.S.2d 49 (N.Y.A.D. 2 Dept.1979)—§ **608.2, n. 24; § 609.1, n. 48, 51.**

Allen, People v., 300 N.Y. 222, 90 N.E.2d 48 (N.Y.1949)—§ **804(2).1; § 804(2).1, n. 16.**

Allen v. Seacoast Products, Inc., 623 F.2d 355 (5th Cir.1980)—§ **1102.2, n. 9.**

Allen v. Stokes, 260 A.D. 600, 23 N.Y.S.2d 443 (N.Y.A.D. 1 Dept.1940)—§ **401.1, n. 48; § 1102.1, n. 2, 15.**

Allen v. West Point–Pepperell Inc., 848 F.Supp. 423 (S.D.N.Y.1994)—§ **500.2, n. 5.**

Allery, United States v., 526 F.2d 1362 (8th Cir.1975)—§ **503.5, n. 13.**

Allied Corp. v. Town of Camillus, 590 N.Y.S.2d 417, 604 N.E.2d 1348 (N.Y. 1992)—§ **405.1, n. 35.**

Allied Stevedoring Corp., United States v., 241 F.2d 925 (2nd Cir.1957)—§ **803(2).2, n. 3.**

Alling, People v., 511 N.Y.S.2d 225, 503 N.E.2d 690 (N.Y.1986)—§ **404.1; § 404.1, n. 31, 41.**

Alling, People v., 118 A.D.2d 960, 500 N.Y.S.2d 186 (N.Y.A.D. 3 Dept.1986)—§ **404.1, n. 41.**

Allman, People v., 41 A.D.2d 325, 342 N.Y.S.2d 896 (N.Y.A.D. 2 Dept.1973)—§ **503.3, n. 30.**

Allweiss, People v., 421 N.Y.S.2d 341, 396 N.E.2d 735 (N.Y.1979)—§ **404.1; § 404.1, n. 55.**

Almestica, People v., 397 N.Y.S.2d 709, 366 N.E.2d 799 (N.Y.1977)—§ **803(2).1, n. 14.**

Almonte, United States v., 956 F.2d 27 (2nd Cir.1992)—§ **607.8, n. 46; § 901.1; § 901.1, n. 11.**

Alpex Computer Corp. v. Nintendo Co., Ltd., 770 F.Supp. 161 (S.D.N.Y.1991)—§ **408.2, n. 6, 7.**

Alpine Forwarding Co. v. Pennsylvania R. Co., 60 F.2d 734 (2nd Cir.1932)—§ **301.8, n. 5.**

Al–Rowaishan Establishment Universal Trading & Agencies, Ltd. v. Beatrice Foods Co., 92 F.R.D. 779 (D.C.N.Y. 1982)—§ **501.3, n. 40, 55.**

Altobello v. Borden Confectionary Products, Inc., 872 F.2d 215 (7th Cir.1989)—§ **609.2, n. 12, 17.**

Altruda, United States v., 224 F.2d 935 (2nd Cir.1955)—§ **1103.2, n. 3.**

Alvarez, United States v., 833 F.2d 724 (7th Cir.1987)—§ **611.5, n. 16.**

Alvino, People v., 525 N.Y.S.2d 7, 519 N.E.2d 808 (N.Y.1987)—§ **404.1; § 404.1, n. 32, 40; § 611.1, n. 9.**

Alwadish, People v., 502 N.Y.S.2d 989, 494 N.E.2d 94 (N.Y.1986)—§ **802.2, n. 94.**

Amaro v. City of New York, 386 N.Y.S.2d 19, 351 N.E.2d 665 (N.Y.1976)—§ **1101.1, n. 18, 20, 24.**

TABLE OF CASES

Amato, United States v., 15 F.3d 230 (2nd Cir.1994)—§ **802.3, n. 62.**

AMBAC Indem. Corp. v. Bankers Trust Co., 151 Misc.2d 334, 573 N.Y.S.2d 204 (N.Y.Sup.1991)—§ **501.1, n. 73, 80, 83.**

Amendolare v. Schenkers Intern. Forwarders, Inc., 747 F.Supp. 162 (E.D.N.Y. 1990)—§ **404.2, n. 22.**

American Broadcasting Companies, Inc. v. Wolf, 76 A.D.2d 162, 430 N.Y.S.2d 275 (N.Y.A.D. 1 Dept.1980)—§ **201.1, n. 9, 41.**

American Cas. Co. of Reading, Pennsylvania v. Nordic Leasing, Inc., 42 F.3d 725 (2nd Cir.1994)—§ **301.8, n. 13.**

American Cyanamid Co., United States v., 427 F.Supp. 859 (D.C.N.Y.1977)— § **804(5).2, n. 1.**

American Export Lines, Inc., Complaint of, 73 F.R.D. 454 (S.D.N.Y.1977)— § **803(5).2; § 803(5).2, n. 18.**

American Ins. Co. v. North American Co. for Property and Cas. Inc., 697 F.2d 79 (2nd Cir.1982)—§ **408.2, n. 4.**

American Lithographing Co. v. Dorrance–Sullivan & Co., 241 N.Y. 306, 150 N.E. 125 (N.Y.1925)—§ **802.2, n. 34.**

American Oil Co. v. Pennsylvania Petroleum Products Co., 23 F.R.D. 680 (D.C.R.I.1959)—§ **513.2, n. 7.**

American Seal–Kap Corp. v. Smith Lee Co., 154 Misc. 176, 277 N.Y.S. 549 (N.Y.Sup. 1935)—§ **513.1, n. 6.**

American Standard Inc. v. Pfizer Inc., 828 F.2d 734 (Fed.Cir.1987)—§ **501.2, n. 11.**

American Tel. and Tel. Co., United States v., 524 F.Supp. 1381 (D.C.D.C.1981)— § **511.2, n. 7.**

American Tel. and Tel. Co., United States v., 642 F.2d 1285, 206 U.S.App.D.C. 317 (D.C.Cir.1980)—§ **501.3, n. 53.**

American Tel. & Tel. Co., United States v., 498 F.Supp. 353 (D.C.D.C.1980)— § **802.3, n. 28.**

American Union Line v. Oriental Nav. Corporation, 199 A.D. 513, 192 N.Y.S. 154 (N.Y.A.D. 1 Dept.1922)—§ **611.1, n. 1.**

Amerine Nat. Corp. v. Denver Feed Co., 493 F.2d 1275 (10th Cir.1974)—§ **405.2, n. 14.**

AMFAC Distribution Corp. v. Harrelson, 842 F.2d 304 (11th Cir.1988)—§ **902.1, n. 30.**

Amoco Production Co. v. United States, 619 F.2d 1383 (10th Cir.1980)—§ **1005.1; § 1005.1, n. 8.**

Amuso, United States v., 21 F.3d 1251 (2nd Cir.1994)—§ **401.2; § 401.2, n. 17; § 702.2, n. 12.**

Amway Corp. v. Shapiro Exp. Co., Inc., 102 F.R.D. 564 (D.C.N.Y.1984)—§ **401.2, n. 3.**

Anderson v. City of New York, 657 F.Supp. 1571 (S.D.N.Y.1987)—§ **803(5).2, n. 20, 22.**

Anderson v. Commercial Travelers Mut. Acc. Ass'n, 73 A.D.2d 769, 423 N.Y.S.2d 542 (N.Y.A.D. 3 Dept.1979)—§ **803(5).1, n. 29.**

Anderson v. Donis, D.P.M.P.C., 150 A.D.2d 414, 541 N.Y.S.2d 25 (N.Y.A.D. 2 Dept. 1989)—§ **702.1, n. 24, 80.**

Anderson, People v., 184 A.D.2d 922, 584 N.Y.S.2d 946 (N.Y.A.D. 3 Dept.1992)— § **412.1, n. 17.**

Anderson, People v., 184 A.D.2d 1005, 584 N.Y.S.2d 349 (N.Y.A.D. 4 Dept.1992)— § **611.4, n. 3.**

Ando v. Woodberry, 203 N.Y.S.2d 74, 168 N.E.2d 520 (N.Y.1960)—§ **401.1, n. 53; § 802.1, n. 18; § 802.2, n. 22.**

Andre, People v., 185 A.D.2d 276, 585 N.Y.S.2d 792 (N.Y.A.D. 2 Dept.1992)— § **607.4, n. 37.**

Andresen v. Maryland, 427 U.S. 463, 96 S.Ct. 2737, 49 L.Ed.2d 627 (1976)— § **509.1, n. 70.**

Andrew Crispo Gallery, Inc. v. C.I.R., 16 F.3d 1336 (2nd Cir.1994)—§ **1001.1, n. 27.**

Andrews v. Metro North Commuter R. Co., 882 F.2d 705 (2nd Cir.1989)—§ **702.2, n. 2; § 704.2, n. 10.**

Angel F., Matter of, 166 A.D.2d 890, 560 N.Y.S.2d 549 (N.Y.A.D. 4 Dept.1990)— § **607.5, n. 5.**

Angelilli, United States v., 660 F.2d 23 (2nd Cir.1981)—§ **406.2; § 406.2, n. 7; § 702.2, n. 4.**

Anglin, People v., 136 Misc.2d 987, 519 N.Y.S.2d 586 (N.Y.Sup.1987)—§ **802.2; § 802.2, n. 14.**

Anheuser–Busch Brewing Co. v. Hutmacher, 127 Ill. 652, 21 N.E. 626 (Ill.1889)— § **1002.1, n. 14.**

Ankersmit v. Tuch, 114 N.Y. 51, 20 N.E. 819 (N.Y.1889)—§ **611.1, n. 4, 7.**

Annunziato, United States v., 293 F.2d 373 (2nd Cir.1961)—§ **803(1).2, n. 40.**

Anonymous v. Mellon, 91 Misc.2d 375, 398 N.Y.S.2d 99 (N.Y.Sup.1977)— § **803(5).1, n. 28.**

Anonymous, People ex rel. v. Saribeyoglu, 131 Misc.2d 647, 501 N.Y.S.2d 286 (N.Y.Sup.1986)—§ **509.1; § 509.1, n. 23.**

Anonymous Attorneys v. Bar Ass'n of Erie County, 393 N.Y.S.2d 961, 362 N.E.2d 592 (N.Y.1977)—§ **514.1, n. 10.**

Antommarchi, People v., 590 N.Y.S.2d 33, 604 N.E.2d 95 (N.Y.1992)—§ **300.4, n. 41, 43, 44.**

Apicella v. McNeil Laboratories, Inc., 66 F.R.D. 78 (D.C.N.Y.1975)—§ **405.2; § 405.2, n. 7; § 803(6).2, n. 5.**

Aponte, United States v., 31 F.3d 86 (2nd Cir.1994)—§ **608.2, n. 49.**

Appeal of (see name of party)
Application of (see name of party)

Application to Take Testimony in Criminal Case Outside Dist., In re, 102 F.R.D. 521 (D.C.N.Y.1984)—§ **1107.2, n. 6.**

TABLE OF CASES

Apter v. Home Life Ins. Co. of New York, 266 N.Y. 333, 194 N.E. 846 (N.Y.1935)—**§ 502.1, n. 52, 60.**

Arabadjis, People v., 78 A.D.2d 614, 432 N.Y.S.2d 391 (N.Y.A.D. 1 Dept.1980)—**§ 614.1, n. 17.**

Arango–Correa, United States v., 851 F.2d 54 (2nd Cir.1988)—**§ 404.2, n. 16; § 1101.2, n. 2, 10; § 1104.2, n. 12.**

Arce, People v., 397 N.Y.S.2d 619, 366 N.E.2d 279 (N.Y.1977)—**§ 100.2, n. 6.**

Archer v. New York, N. H. & H. R. Co., 106 N.Y. 589, 13 N.E. 318 (N.Y.1887)—**§ 611.3, n. 34; § 901.1, n. 8; § 1103.1, n. 1, 9; § 1104.1, n. 2.**

Arhin, People v., 203 A.D.2d 62, 609 N.Y.S.2d 604 (N.Y.A.D. 1 Dept.1994)—**§ 611.2, n. 18.**

Armedo–Sarmiento, United States v., 545 F.2d 785 (2nd Cir.1976)—**§ 103.2, n. 5.**

Arnold v. Owens, 78 F.2d 495 (4th Cir. 1935)—**§ 409.2, n. 2.**

Arnold, People v., 354 N.Y.S.2d 106, 309 N.E.2d 875 (N.Y.1974)—**§ 804(2).1; § 804(2).1, n. 21; § 804(5).1, n. 8.**

Arnott, United States v., 704 F.2d 322 (6th Cir.1983)—**§ 611.5, n. 15.**

Aronoff, United States v., 466 F.Supp. 855 (D.C.N.Y.1979)—**§ 501.2, n. 53.**

Arrasmith, United States v., 557 F.2d 1093 (5th Cir.1977)—**§ 701.2, n. 6; § 702.1, n. 3.**

Arrington, United States v., 867 F.2d 122 (2nd Cir.1989)—**§ 802.3, n. 72.**

Arroyo v. City of New York, 171 A.D.2d 541, 567 N.Y.S.2d 257 (N.Y.A.D. 1 Dept. 1991)—**§ 401.1, n. 45.**

Arroyo, People v., 446 N.Y.S.2d 910, 431 N.E.2d 271 (N.Y.1982)—**§ 804(1).1; § 804(1).1, n. 26, 35.**

Arroyo–Angulo, United States v., 580 F.2d 1137 (2nd Cir.1978)—**§ 410.2, n. 7.**

Arthur, People v., 99 A.D.2d 595, 471 N.Y.S.2d 412 (N.Y.A.D. 3 Dept.1984)—**§ 1101.1, n. 24.**

Arvelo v. Multi Trucking, Inc., 194 A.D.2d 758, 599 N.Y.S.2d 301 (N.Y.A.D. 2 Dept. 1993)—**§ 802.2, n. 73.**

Ashe v. Swenson, 397 U.S. 436, 90 S.Ct. 1189, 25 L.Ed.2d 469 (1970)—**§ 404.2, n. 11.**

Ashner, People v., 190 A.D.2d 238, 597 N.Y.S.2d 975 (N.Y.A.D. 2 Dept.1993)—**§ 607.6, n. 27; § 611.3, n. 32.**

Associated General Contractors of America, New York State Chapter, Inc. v. Lapardo Bros. Excavating Contractors, Inc., 43 Misc.2d 825, 252 N.Y.S.2d 486 (N.Y.Sup. 1964)—**§ 201.1, n. 52.**

Associated Press v. Walken, 388 U.S. 130 (1967)—**§ 402.2, n. 6.**

Association Against Discrimination in Employment, Inc. v. City of Bridgeport, 647 F.2d 256 (2nd Cir.1981)—**§ 201.2, n. 4.**

Atherton, United States v., 936 F.2d 728 (2nd Cir.1991)—**§ 607.6, n. 37.**

Atkins, People v., 630 N.Y.S.2d 965, 654 N.E.2d 1213 (N.Y.1995)—**§ 702.1, n. 43; § 901.9, n. 6.**

Atkinson, Matter of Estate of, 117 A.D.2d 843, 498 N.Y.S.2d 543 (N.Y.A.D. 3 Dept. 1986)—**§ 614.1, n. 3.**

Atlantic Financial Management Securities Litigation, In re, 121 F.R.D. 141 (D.Mass.1988)—**§ 612.2, n. 19.**

Attridge v. Cencorp Div. of Dover Technologies Intern., Inc., 836 F.2d 113 (2nd Cir.1987)—**§ 606.2, n. 2.**

Augustine v. Village of Interlaken, 68 A.D.2d 705, 418 N.Y.S.2d 683 (N.Y.A.D. 4 Dept.1979)—**§ 802.2; § 802.2, n. 22.**

Auld v. Estridge, 86 Misc.2d 895, 382 N.Y.S.2d 897 (N.Y.Sup.1976)—**§ 803(6).1, n. 1.**

Ault v. International Harvester Co., 117 Cal.Rptr. 812, 528 P.2d 1148 (Cal. 1974)—**§ 407.1, n. 22; § 407.2, n. 4.**

Ausch v. St. Paul Fire & Marine Ins. Co., 125 A.D.2d 43, 511 N.Y.S.2d 919 (N.Y.A.D. 2 Dept.1987)—**§ 300.4, n. 18, 22, 33.**

Austin by Austin v. Bascaran, 185 A.D.2d 474, 585 N.Y.S.2d 859 (N.Y.A.D. 3 Dept. 1992)—**§ 1104.1, n. 41, 50; § 1105.1, n. 11.**

Auto Owners Ins. Co. v. Bass, 684 F.2d 764 (11th Cir.1982)—**§ 1107.2, n. 2, 4.**

Avena v. Clauss & Co., 504 F.2d 469 (2nd Cir.1974)—**§ 406.2, n. 17.**

Avery v. Lee, 117 A.D. 244, 102 N.Y.S. 12 (N.Y.A.D. 1 Dept.1907)—**§ 501.1, n. 40.**

Awkard, United States v., 597 F.2d 667 (9th Cir.1979)—**§ 601.3, n. 19.**

Axelrod v. Rosenbaum, 205 A.D.2d 722, 613 N.Y.S.2d 707 (N.Y.A.D. 2 Dept.1994)—**§ 1102.1, n. 14.**

Ayala, People v., 194 A.D.2d 547, 598 N.Y.S.2d 318 (N.Y.A.D. 2 Dept.1993)—**§ 611.3, n. 21.**

Ayala, People v., 554 N.Y.S.2d 412, 553 N.E.2d 960 (N.Y.1990)—**§ 103.1, n. 49; § 804(1).1, n. 32, 38, 41.**

B

B., In re, 30 A.D.2d 442, 293 N.Y.S.2d 946 (N.Y.A.D. 1 Dept.1968)—**§ 601.1, n. 37.**

Babbitt, United States v., 683 F.2d 21 (1st Cir.1982)—**§ 607.3, n. 23.**

Baby Boy B., Matter of, 163 A.D.2d 673, 558 N.Y.S.2d 281 (N.Y.A.D. 3 Dept. 1990)—**§ 612.1, n. 7.**

Baccio v. People, 41 N.Y. 265 (N.Y.1869)—**§ 607.5, n. 5; § 702.1, n. 59.**

Bach's Estate, In re, 81 Misc.2d 479, 365 N.Y.S.2d 454 (N.Y.Sur.1975)—**§ 201.1, n. 36.**

Bacic, People v., 202 A.D.2d 234, 608 N.Y.S.2d 452 (N.Y.A.D. 1 Dept.1994)—**§ 614.1, n. 22, 24.**

TABLE OF CASES

Bacon v. Frisbie, 80 N.Y. 401 (1880)—§ **501.1, n. 5, 8, 13, 15, 38.**

Bac Tran, People v., 589 N.Y.S.2d 845, 603 N.E.2d 950 (N.Y.1992)—§ **802.2, n. 86, 94.**

Badger v. Badger, 88 N.Y. 546 (1882)—§ **803(7).1, n. 20.**

Badr v. Hogan, 555 N.Y.S.2d 249, 554 N.E.2d 890 (N.Y.1990)—§ **103.1, n. 50;** § **607.2, n. 21;** § **608.2, n. 4, 5, 13, 14, 16, 17.**

Baecher v. Baecher, 58 A.D.2d 821, 396 N.Y.S.2d 447 (N.Y.A.D. 2 Dept.1977)—§ **502.1, n. 82.**

Bagaric, United States v., 706 F.2d 42 (2nd Cir.1983)—§ **608.2, n. 39;** § **901.4, n. 14.**

Bagby, People v., 492 N.Y.S.2d 562, 482 N.E.2d 41 (N.Y.1985)—§ **509.1, n. 45, 51.**

Bahadar, United States v., 954 F.2d 821 (2nd Cir.1992)—§ **804(3).2, n. 18.**

Bailey v. Baker's Air Force Gas Corp., 50 A.D.2d 129, 376 N.Y.S.2d 212 (N.Y.A.D. 3 Dept.1975)—§ **406.1, n. 38.**

Bailey v. Meister Brau, Inc., 57 F.R.D. 11 (D.C.Ill.1972)—§ **501.2, n. 49;** § **612.2, n. 17.**

Bairnco Corp. Securities Litigation, In re, 148 F.R.D. 91 (S.D.N.Y.1993)—§ **501.2, n. 37.**

Baker, Matter of Estate of, 139 Misc.2d 573, 528 N.Y.S.2d 470 (N.Y.Sur.1988)—§ **501.1, n. 74, 75.**

Baker, People v., 296 N.Y.S.2d 745, 244 N.E.2d 232 (N.Y.1968)—§ **106.1, n. 6, 8;** § **607.5, n. 20, 39, 44.**

Baker, United States v., 926 F.2d 179 (2nd Cir.1991)—§ **408.2, n. 15.**

Baker v. United States, 401 F.2d 958, 131 U.S.App.D.C. 7 (D.C.Cir.1968)—§ **404.1, n. 71.**

Bakhtiar, United States v., 994 F.2d 970 (2nd Cir.1993)—§ **804(3).2, n. 17.**

Balazinski v. Lebid, 65 N.J.Super. 483, 168 A.2d 209 (N.J.Super.A.D.1961)—§ **803(5).2.**

Baldwin v. New York Cent. & H. R. R. Co., 2 N.Y.S. 481 (N.Y. Super.1888)—§ **409.1, n. 8.**

Balfany, United States v., 965 F.2d 575 (8th Cir.1992)—§ **803(1).2, n. 52.**

Ball, United States v., 988 F.2d 7 (5th Cir. 1993)—§ **604.2, n. 4.**

Ballay, In re, 482 F.2d 648, 157 U.S.App. D.C. 59 (D.C.Cir.1973)—§ **300.4, n. 1, 38.**

Ballott, People v., 286 N.Y.S.2d 1, 233 N.E.2d 103 (N.Y.1967)—§ **509.1, n. 31.**

Baltimore City Dept. of Social Services v. Bouknight, 493 U.S. 549, 110 S.Ct. 900, 107 L.Ed.2d 992 (1990)—§ **509.1, n. 70.**

B. Altman & Co. v. City of White Plains, 456 N.Y.S.2d 755, 442 N.E.2d 1266 (N.Y. 1982)—§ **803(6).1, n. 4.**

Balzano, United States v., 687 F.2d 6 (1st Cir.1982)—§ **1003.1, n. 5.**

Bankers Trust Co. v. Publicker Industries, Inc., 641 F.2d 1361 (2nd Cir.1981)—§ **612.2, n. 4, 12.**

Bank of Buffalo v. Skinitis, 36 A.D.2d 891, 320 N.Y.S.2d 304 (N.Y.A.D. 4 Dept. 1971)—§ **509.1, n. 71.**

Bank of New York v. United States, 174 F.Supp. 911 (D.C.N.Y.1957)—§ **804(4).2;** § **804(4).2, n. 5.**

Banks, People v., 552 N.Y.S.2d 883, 552 N.E.2d 131 (N.Y.1990)—§ **702.1;** § **702.1, n. 61, 62.**

Banks, People v., 439 N.Y.S.2d 916, 422 N.E.2d 576 (N.Y.1981)—§ **103.1, n. 6.**

Bannister v. Town of Noble, Okl., 812 F.2d 1265 (10th Cir.1987)—§ **1104.1, n. 49.**

Barash, United States v., 365 F.2d 395 (2nd Cir.1966)—§ **103.2, n. 16.**

Baratta, United States v., 397 F.2d 215 (2nd Cir.1968)—§ **612.2, n. 5.**

Barbagallo v. Americana Corp., 306 N.Y.S.2d 466, 254 N.E.2d 768 (N.Y. 1969)—§ **103.1, n. 50.**

Barbati, United States v., 284 F.Supp. 409 (D.C.N.Y.1968)—§ **801(2).2, n. 2;** § **804(5).2;** § **804(5).2, n. 2.**

Barber v. Page, 390 U.S. 719, 88 S.Ct. 1318, 20 L.Ed.2d 255 (1968)—§ **801(1).3, n. 3;** § **804.1;** § **804.1, n. 9;** § **804(1).2;** § **804(1).2, n. 14.**

Barber, People v., 186 A.D.2d 483, 589 N.Y.S.2d 409 (N.Y.A.D. 1 Dept.1992)—§ **607.4, n. 37;** § **803(2).1, n. 2, 10.**

Barber, People v., 543 N.Y.S.2d 365, 541 N.E.2d 394 (N.Y.1989)—§ **402.1;** § **402.1, n. 36, 39;** § **608.1, n. 7.**

Barber v. Town of Northumberland, 88 A.D.2d 712, 451 N.Y.S.2d 291 (N.Y.A.D. 3 Dept.1982)—§ **501.3, n. 14.**

Barbieri, People v., 207 A.D.2d 554, 616 N.Y.S.2d 80 (N.Y.A.D. 2 Dept.1994)—§ **804(3).1, n. 38.**

Bari, United States v., 750 F.2d 1169 (2nd Cir.1984)—§ **607.7, n. 21.**

Barker, People v., 153 N.Y. 111, 47 N.E. 31 (N.Y.1897)—§ **300.4, n. 43.**

Barker, United States v., 735 F.2d 1280 (11th Cir.1984)—§ **701.2, n. 5;** § **901.2, n. 15.**

Barker v. Washburn, 200 N.Y. 280, 93 N.E. 958 (N.Y.1911)—§ **601.1, n. 7, 46.**

Barlow, United States v., 693 F.2d 954 (6th Cir.1982)—§ **804(5).2, n. 15.**

Barnes v. Maguire, 62 A.D.2d 1076, 403 N.Y.S.2d 797 (N.Y.A.D. 3 Dept.1978)—§ **408.1, n. 9.**

Barnes, People v., 175 A.D.2d 695, 572 N.Y.S.2d 686 (N.Y.A.D. 1 Dept.1991)—§ **1105.1, n. 5.**

Barnes, People v., 429 N.Y.S.2d 178, 406 N.E.2d 1071 (N.Y.1980)—§ **300.4, n. 46.**

Barnes v. United States, 412 U.S. 837, 93 S.Ct. 2357, 37 L.Ed.2d 380 (1973)—§ **302.1, n. 12, 28;** § **302.2, n. 2, 6.**

TABLE OF CASES

Barnes, United States v., 464 F.2d 828, 150 U.S.App.D.C. 319 (D.C.Cir.1972)—§ **804(2).2, n. 10.**

Barnes' Estate, In re, 37 Misc.2d 833, 237 N.Y.S.2d 183 (N.Y.Sur.1962)—§ **802.2, n. 35.**

Barney's Will, In re, 185 A.D. 782, 174 N.Y.S. 242 (N.Y.A.D. 1 Dept.1919)—§ **803(7).1, n. 6; § 901.8, n. 5.**

Barnhart, People v., 66 Cal.App.2d 714, 153 P.2d 214 (Cal.App. 2 Dist.1944)—§ **801.1, n. 23.**

Barrett v. United States, 651 F.Supp. 606 (S.D.N.Y.1986)—§ **804(1).2, n. 28.**

Barr Marine Products, Co., Inc. v. Borg-Warner Corp., 84 F.R.D. 631 (D.C.Pa. 1979)—§ **501.2, n. 10.**

Barr Rubber Products Co. v. Sun Rubber Co., 425 F.2d 1114 (2nd Cir.1970)—§ **300.4, n. 37.**

Barry v. Manglass, 55 A.D.2d 1, 389 N.Y.S.2d 870 (N.Y.A.D. 2 Dept.1976)—§ **407.1, n. 22.**

Barsky v. United States, 339 F.2d 180 (9th Cir.1964)—§ **503.5, n. 10.**

Bartelini, People v., 285 N.Y. 433, 35 N.E.2d 29 (N.Y.1941)—§ **804(2).1, n. 2, 9.**

Bartkowiak v. St. Adalbert's Roman Catholic Church Soc., 40 A.D.2d 306, 340 N.Y.S.2d 137 (N.Y.A.D. 4 Dept.1973)—§ **300.3, n. 35.**

Bartlett, United States v., 794 F.2d 1285 (8th Cir.1986)—§ **412.2, n. 10.**

Bartlett, by Bartlett v. General Elec. Co., 90 A.D.2d 183, 457 N.Y.S.2d 628 (N.Y.A.D. 3 Dept.1982)—§ **407.1, n. 18.**

Barton v. Diesel Const. Co., Inc., 47 A.D.2d 729, 365 N.Y.S.2d 197 (N.Y.A.D. 1 Dept. 1975)—§ **501.3, n. 14.**

Barzaghi v. Maislin Transport, 115 A.D.2d 679, 497 N.Y.S.2d 131 (N.Y.A.D. 2 Dept. 1985)—§ **803(3).1, n. 65.**

Baskerville, People v., 469 N.Y.S.2d 646, 457 N.E.2d 752 (N.Y.1983)—§ **302.1, n. 18, 28.**

Bass, People v., 140 Misc.2d 57, 529 N.Y.S.2d 961 (N.Y.Sup.1988)—§ **502.1, n. 66; § 505.1, n. 11, 15.**

Batease v. Dion, 275 A.D. 451, 90 N.Y.S.2d 851 (N.Y.A.D. 3 Dept.1949)—§ **608.2, n. 10; § 609.1, n. 9, 13.**

Batista, People v., 113 A.D.2d 890, 493 N.Y.S.2d 608 (N.Y.A.D. 2 Dept.1985)—§ **608.2, n. 10.**

Battease, People v., 124 A.D.2d 807, 509 N.Y.S.2d 39 (N.Y.A.D. 2 Dept.1986)—§ **702.1, n. 80.**

Battles, People v., 83 A.D.2d 164, 443 N.Y.S.2d 932 (N.Y.A.D. 4 Dept.1981)—§ **404.1, n. 57.**

Bauernfeind v. Albany Medical Center Hosp., 195 A.D.2d 819, 600 N.Y.S.2d 516 (N.Y.A.D. 3 Dept.1993)—§ **103.1, n. 47.**

Baumann v. Steingester, 213 N.Y. 328, 107 N.E. 578 (N.Y.1915)—§ **501.1, n. 45.**

Bautista, United States v., 23 F.3d 726 (2nd Cir.1994)—§ **615.2, n. 8.**

Baxter v. Palmigiano, 425 U.S. 308, 96 S.Ct. 1551, 47 L.Ed.2d 810 (1976)—§ **514.2; § 514.2, n. 7.**

Bay, United States v., 748 F.2d 1344 (9th Cir.1984)—§ **1102.2, n. 5.**

Bayne, People v., 601 N.Y.S.2d 464, 619 N.E.2d 401 (N.Y.1993)—§ **404.1; § 404.1, n. 30.**

Bayron, People v., 495 N.Y.S.2d 24, 485 N.E.2d 231 (N.Y.1985)—§ **801(2).1, n. 8, 9.**

Bazelais, People v., 98 A.D.2d 802, 470 N.Y.S.2d 25 (N.Y.A.D. 2 Dept.1983)—§ **1104.1, n. 38, 45.**

Bazza v. Banscher, 143 A.D.2d 715, 533 N.Y.S.2d 285 (N.Y.A.D. 2 Dept.1988)—§ **802.2, n. 7.**

B.D. Intern. Discount Corp., In re, 701 F.2d 1071 (2nd Cir.1983)—§ **408.2, n. 5.**

Beach v. Richtmyer, 275 A.D. 466, 90 N.Y.S.2d 332 (N.Y.A.D. 3 Dept.1949)—§ **402.1, n. 25.**

Beach v. Shanley, 476 N.Y.S.2d 765, 465 N.E.2d 304 (N.Y.1984)—§ **508.1; § 508.1, n. 10.**

Beach, United States v., 296 F.2d 153 (4th Cir.1961)—§ **1108.2; § 1108.2, n. 8.**

Beakes v. Da Cunha, 126 N.Y. 293, 27 N.E. 251 (N.Y.1891)—§ **406.1, n. 2, 9.**

Beale, People v., 73 A.D.2d 547, 423 N.Y.S.2d 6 (N.Y.A.D. 1 Dept.1979)—§ **609.1, n. 4.**

Beam, People v., 455 N.Y.S.2d 575, 441 N.E.2d 1093 (N.Y.1982)—§ **404.1, n. 57.**

Bean, People v., 284 A.D. 922, 134 N.Y.S.2d 483 (N.Y.A.D. 3 Dept.1954)—§ **406.1, n. 14.**

Beard v. Ames, 96 A.D.2d 119, 468 N.Y.S.2d 253 (N.Y.A.D. 4 Dept.1983)—§ **501.1, n. 60, 74.**

Beard v. Mitchell, 604 F.2d 485 (7th Cir. 1979)—§ **607.5, n. 59.**

Beard, People v., 74 A.D.2d 926, 426 N.Y.S.2d 90 (N.Y.A.D. 2 Dept.1980)—§ **201.1, n. 43.**

Bearss v. Westbury Hotel, Inc., 33 A.D.2d 47, 304 N.Y.S.2d 894 (N.Y.A.D. 1 Dept. 1969)—§ **704.1, n. 5.**

Bear Stops, United States v., 997 F.2d 451 (8th Cir.1993)—§ **412.2, n. 8.**

Beasock v. Dioguardi Enterprises, Inc., 117 A.D.2d 1016, 499 N.Y.S.2d 560 (N.Y.A.D. 4 Dept.1986)—§ **501.3, n. 12.**

Beaulieu, People v., 40 A.D.2d 942, 339 N.Y.S.2d 234 (N.Y.A.D. 4 Dept.1972)—§ **402.1, n. 33.**

Beavers, People v., 127 A.D.2d 138, 514 N.Y.S.2d 235 (N.Y.A.D. 1 Dept.1987)—§ **607.8; § 607.8, n. 41, 42.**

Bechard v. Eisinger, 105 A.D.2d 939, 481 N.Y.S.2d 906 (N.Y.A.D. 3 Dept.1984)—§ **601.2, n. 25.**

Beck v. Dye, 200 Wash. 1, 92 P.2d 1113 (Wash.1939)—§ **803(1).2, n. 4.**

TABLE OF CASES

Becker v. American Airlines, Inc., 200 F.Supp. 243 (D.C.N.Y.1961)—§ **405.2**; § 405.2, n. 9.

Becker v. Koch, 104 N.Y. 394, 10 N.E. 701 (N.Y.1887)—§ **607.4, n. 17, 18, 19, 20**; § 611.2, n. 18.

Becker, People v., 215 N.Y. 126, 109 N.E. 127 (N.Y.1915)—§ **804(2).1**; § **804(2).1, n. 7**.

Beckles, People v., 128 A.D.2d 435, 512 N.Y.S.2d 826 (N.Y.A.D. 1 Dept.1987)—§ 404.1, n. 29.

Bedonie, United States v., 913 F.2d 782 (10th Cir.1990)—§ **601.3, n. 15**; § 608.1, n. 19.

Beech Aircraft Corp. v. Rainey, 488 U.S. 153, 109 S.Ct. 439, 102 L.Ed.2d 445 (1988)—§ **106.2, n. 5**; § **702.2, n. 19**; § **803(5).2**; § 803(5).2, n. 5, 17.

Beecher, People v., 122 A.D.2d 407, 505 N.Y.S.2d 222 (N.Y.A.D. 3 Dept.1986)—§ 611.1, n. 12.

Beech-Nut Nutrition Corp., United States v., 871 F.2d 1181 (2nd Cir.1989)—§ 802.3, n. 62.

Beechum, United States v., 582 F.2d 898 (5th Cir.1978)—§ 404.1, n. 17; § 404.2, n. 6.

Begay, United States v., 937 F.2d 515 (10th Cir.1991)—§ 412.2, n. 8.

Begley v. Prudential Ins. Co. of America, 154 N.Y.S.2d 866, 136 N.E.2d 839 (N.Y. 1956)—§ 301.5, n. 27.

Beisheim v. People, 26 Misc.2d 684, 39 N.Y.S.2d 333 (N.Y.Sup.1942)—§ **901.8, n. 5**.

Bekins Record Storage Co., Inc., Matter of, 476 N.Y.S.2d 806, 465 N.E.2d 345 (N.Y. 1984)—§ **501.1, n. 22, 37, 39, 40**.

Bekins Storage Co., Matter of, 118 Misc.2d 173, 460 N.Y.S.2d 684 (N.Y.Sup.1983)—§ 501.3, n. 9.

Belge, People v., 59 A.D.2d 307, 399 N.Y.S.2d 539 (N.Y.A.D. 4 Dept.1977)—§ **501.1, n. 3, 12, 13, 31**.

Belge, People v., 83 Misc.2d 186, 372 N.Y.S.2d 798 (Onondago Co.Ct.1975)—§ 501.1, n. 25.

Bell, People v., 481 N.Y.S.2d 324, 471 N.E.2d 137 (N.Y.1984)—§ 401.1, n. 49.

Bell, People v., 425 N.Y.S.2d 52, 401 N.E.2d 175 (N.Y.1979)—§ 802.2, n. 92.

Bellamy, People v., 97 A.D.2d 654, 469 N.Y.S.2d 181 (N.Y.A.D. 3 Dept.1983)—§ 607.7, n. 16.

Bellinzoni v. Seland, 128 A.D.2d 580, 512 N.Y.S.2d 846 (N.Y.A.D. 2 Dept.1987)—§ 702.1, n. 80.

Belmar v. City of Syracuse, 100 A.D.2d 745, 473 N.Y.S.2d 624 (N.Y.A.D. 4 Dept. 1984)—§ 103.1, n. 42.

Bendectin Litigation, In re, 857 F.2d 290 (6th Cir.1988)—§ 615.2, n. 2.

Benedetto, United States v., 571 F.2d 1246 (2nd Cir.1978)—§ 402.2, n. 3, 11.

Benitez, United States v., 920 F.2d 1080 (2nd Cir.1990)—§ **103.2, n. 10**; § **105.2, n. 11**.

Benjamin v. Benjamin, 106 A.D.2d 599, 483 N.Y.S.2d 418 (N.Y.A.D. 2 Dept.1984)—§ 301.4, n. 4.

Benjamin, United States v., 328 F.2d 854 (2nd Cir.1964)—§ 901.6, n. 8.

Bennett v. Crescent Athletic–Hamilton Club, 270 N.Y. 456, 1 N.E.2d 963 (N.Y. 1936)—§ **607.4, n. 16**; § **611.3, n. 22**.

Bennett, People v., 583 N.Y.S.2d 825, 593 N.E.2d 279 (N.Y.1992)—§ **401.1**; § 401.1, n. 9, 19; § 608.2, n. 31.

Bennett, People v., 169 A.D.2d 369, 573 N.Y.S.2d 322 (N.Y.A.D. 3 Dept.1991)—§ 509.1, n. 40.

Bennett v. Saeger Hotels, Inc., 209 A.D.2d 946, 619 N.Y.S.2d 424 (N.Y.A.D. 4 Dept. 1994)—§ **103.1, n. 45**; § **601.1, n. 62**.

Bennett, United States v., 848 F.2d 1134 (11th Cir.1988)—§ 604.2, n. 6.

Bennette, People v., 451 N.Y.S.2d 647, 436 N.E.2d 1249 (N.Y.1982)—§ **609.1**; § **609.1, n. 5, 37**; § **614.1, n. 13**.

Beno, United States v., 324 F.2d 582 (2nd Cir.1963)—§ 607.3, n. 23.

Benoit, People v., 8 A.D.2d 626, 185 N.Y.S.2d 622 (N.Y.A.D. 2 Dept.1959)—§ **1101.1, n. 2, 8**; § **1105.1, n. 14**.

Benson, People v., 206 A.D.2d 674, 614 N.Y.S.2d 808 (N.Y.A.D. 3 Dept.1994)—§ 607.7, n. 13.

Bent, People v., 160 A.D.2d 1176, 555 N.Y.S.2d 454 (N.Y.A.D. 3 Dept.1990)—§ **801.1**; § **801.1, n. 49**.

Benzinger, People v., 364 N.Y.S.2d 855, 324 N.E.2d 334 (N.Y.1974)—§ **300.3, n. 30**; § **300.4, n. 47, 48**.

Berg, People v., 464 N.Y.S.2d 703, 451 N.E.2d 450 (N.Y.1983)—§ 105.1, n. 11.

Berge, People v., 103 A.D.2d 1041, 478 N.Y.S.2d 433 (N.Y.A.D. 4 Dept.1984)—§ 402.1, n. 35.

Berger v. City of New York, 157 Misc.2d 521, 597 N.Y.S.2d 555 (N.Y.Sup.1993)—§ 803(1).1, n. 20.

Bergeron, People v., 125 A.D.2d 927, 510 N.Y.S.2d 323 (N.Y.A.D. 4 Dept.1986)—§ 412.1, n. 23.

Bergstein v. Board of Ed., Union Free School Dist. No. 1 of Towns of Ossining, Et Al., 357 N.Y.S.2d 465, 313 N.E.2d 767 (N.Y.1974)—§ 801.1, n. 39.

Berkey Photo, Inc. v. Eastman Kodak Co., 74 F.R.D. 613 (D.C.N.Y.1977)—§ **501.3, n. 55**; § **612.2, n. 20**.

Berkley, People v., 157 A.D.2d 463, 549 N.Y.S.2d 392 (N.Y.A.D. 1 Dept.1990)—§ 505.1, n. 9.

Berkovich v. Hicks, 922 F.2d 1018 (2nd Cir.1991)—§ **401.2, n. 4**; § **404.2, n. 19, 21**; § **612.2, n. 3**; § **614.2, n. 5, 6**.

Berkowitz, People v., 428 N.Y.S.2d 927, 406 N.E.2d 783 (N.Y.1980)—§ 802.2, n. 94.

TABLE OF CASES

Berkowitz v. Simone, 96 R.I. 11, 188 A.2d 665 (R.I.1963)—§ **802.2, n. 49.**

Berkowsky v. New York City Ry. Co., 127 A.D. 544, 111 N.Y.S. 989 (N.Y.A.D. 1 Dept.1908)—§ **612.1, n. 8.**

Bernal, People v., 162 A.D.2d 362, 557 N.Y.S.2d 319 (N.Y.A.D. 1 Dept.1990)—§ **607.8, n. 29; § 801(1).2, n. 13.**

Bernal, United States v., 719 F.2d 1475 (9th Cir.1983)—§ **806.1, n. 20.**

Bernard, People v., 625 N.Y.S.2d 67 (N.Y.A.D. 2 Dept.1995)—§ **1104.1, n. 43.**

Bernstein v. Bodean, 443 N.Y.S.2d 49, 426 N.E.2d 741 (N.Y.1981)—§ **611.2, n. 1; § 611.3, n. 30.**

Bernstein v. Holtz, 34 Misc. 795, 69 N.Y.S. 892 (N.Y.Sup.1901)—§ **803(4).1, n. 1.**

Bernstein v. New York, 517 N.Y.S.2d 908, 511 N.E.2d 52 (N.Y.1987)—§ **300.3, n. 16, 17, 18.**

Bernstein v. Tisch, 102 A.D.2d 778, 477 N.Y.S.2d 149 (N.Y.A.D. 1 Dept.1984)—§ **802.2, n. 34.**

Berroyer v. Hertz, 672 F.2d 334 (3rd Cir. 1982)—§ **611.5, n. 6.**

Berthoumieux v. We Try Harder, Inc., 170 A.D.2d 248, 566 N.Y.S.2d 240 (N.Y.A.D. 1 Dept.1991)—§ **604.1, n. 3.**

Bertolotti, United States v., 529 F.2d 149 (2nd Cir.1975)—§ **1108.2, n. 4.**

Bethune, People v., 105 A.D.2d 262, 484 N.Y.S.2d 577 (N.Y.A.D. 2 Dept.1984)—§ **611.4, n. 1; § 705.1, n. 13; § 1105.1, n. 11.**

Betts, People v., 520 N.Y.S.2d 370, 514 N.E.2d 865 (N.Y.1987)—§ **509.1; § 509.1, n. 39; § 608.2, n. 23, 31.**

Betts, People v., 272 A.D. 737, 74 N.Y.S.2d 791 (N.Y.A.D. 1 Dept.1947)—§ **1004.1, n. 6.**

Beverly Hills Fire Litigation, In re, 695 F.2d 207 (6th Cir.1982)—§ **606.2, n. 6.**

Bevilacqua v. Gilbert, 143 A.D.2d 213, 532 N.Y.S.2d 15 (N.Y.A.D. 2 Dept.1988)—§ **408.1, n. 9.**

Bevill, Bresler & Schulman Asset Management Corp., Matter of, 805 F.2d 120 (3rd Cir.1986)—§ **501.2, n. 39, 43.**

Bhatt, People v., 160 Misc.2d 973, 611 N.Y.S.2d 447 (N.Y.Sup.1994)—§ **502.1, n. 72.**

Bibbins v. Dalsheim, 21 F.3d 13 (2nd Cir. 1994)—§ **606.2, n. 6.**

Bibbs, United States v., 564 F.2d 1165 (5th Cir.1977)—§ **607.8, n. 51.**

Bieter Co., In re, 16 F.3d 929 (8th Cir. 1994)—§ **500.2, n. 8; § 501.2, n. 2, 34.**

Bigelow-Sanford, Inc. v. Specialized Commercial Floors of Rochester, Inc., 77 A.D.2d 464, 433 N.Y.S.2d 931 (N.Y.A.D. 4 Dept.1980)—§ **408.1, n. 1, 6, 9; § 802.2, n. 19.**

Bilkovie v. Loeb, 156 A.D. 719, 141 N.Y.S. 279 (N.Y.A.D. 1 Dept.1913)—§ **1102.1, n. 10.**

Billups, People v., 526 N.Y.S.2d 939, 521 N.E.2d 1082 (N.Y.1988)—§ **607.7, n. 13.**

Billups, People v., 132 A.D.2d 612, 518 N.Y.S.2d 9 (N.Y.A.D. 2 Dept.1987)—§ **103.1, n. 27; § 607.7, n. 13.**

Bilzerian, United States v., 926 F.2d 1285 (2nd Cir.1991)—§ **501.2, n. 4, 47.**

Birbal, United States v., 62 F.3d 456 (2nd Cir.1995)—§ **103.2, n. 24.**

Birch v. Carroll, 210 A.D.2d 119, 620 N.Y.S.2d 56 (N.Y.A.D. 1 Dept.1994)—§ **614.1, n. 7.**

Birnbaum, United States v., 337 F.2d 490 (2nd Cir.1964)—§ **802.3, n. 62; § 1104.2, n. 19, 20.**

Birney, United States v., 686 F.2d 102 (2nd Cir.1982)—§ **404.2, n. 19.**

Birsten, Estate of, 104 Misc.2d 345, 428 N.Y.S.2d 392 (N.Y.Sur.1980)—§ **901.7, n. 10.**

Bishin v. New York Cent. R. Co., 20 A.D.2d 921, 249 N.Y.S.2d 778 (N.Y.A.D. 2 Dept. 1964)—§ **803(3).1, n. 35, 36.**

Bishop, People v., 206 A.D.2d 884, 615 N.Y.S.2d 163 (N.Y.A.D. 4 Dept.1994)—§ **607.8, n. 21.**

Bisno v. United States, 299 F.2d 711 (9th Cir.1961)—§ **514.2, n. 4.**

Bizzard, United States v., 674 F.2d 1382 (11th Cir.1982)—§ **500.2, n. 8.**

Black, People v., 180 A.D.2d 806, 580 N.Y.S.2d 444 (N.Y.A.D. 2 Dept.1992)—§ **801.1, n. 39.**

Blackwood v. Chemical Corn Exchange Bank, 4 A.D.2d 656, 168 N.Y.S.2d 335 (N.Y.A.D. 1 Dept.1957)—§ **607.8, n. 32.**

Blackwood, United States v., 47 F.2d 849 (1st Cir.1931)—§ **902.1, n. 25.**

Blake v. People, 73 N.Y. 586 (1878)—§ **701.1, n. 8.**

Blanche, People v., 152 A.D.2d 770, 543 N.Y.S.2d 548 (N.Y.A.D. 3 Dept.1989)—§ **607.7, n. 11.**

Blanding v. Cohen, 101 A.D. 442, 92 N.Y.S. 93 (N.Y.A.D. 1 Dept.1905)—§ **902.1, n. 4.**

Blankenship, United States v., 923 F.2d 1110 (5th Cir.1991)—§ **601.3, n. 4.**

Blas, United States v., 947 F.2d 1320 (7th Cir.1991)—§ **612.2, n. 15.**

Bledsoe v. Salt River Valley Water Users' Ass'n, 179 Ariz. 469, 880 P.2d 689 (Ariz. App. Div. 2 1994)—§ **1106.1, n. 5.**

Bliss, United States v., 642 F.2d 390 (10th Cir.1981)—§ **201.2, n. 22.**

Blitz, United States v., 533 F.2d 1329 (2nd Cir.1976)—§ **801(1).3, n. 8, 13.**

Bloodgood v. Lynch, 293 N.Y. 308, 56 N.E.2d 718 (N.Y.1944)—§ **103.1, n. 18, 22, 23.**

Bloom, People v., 193 N.Y. 1, 85 N.E. 824 (N.Y.1908)—§ **502.1, n. 45.**

Bloom, United States v., 237 F.2d 158 (2nd Cir.1956)—§ **405.2, n. 16.**

TABLE OF CASES

Bloss v. Ford Motor Co., 126 A.D.2d 804, 510 N.Y.S.2d 304 (N.Y.A.D. 3 Dept. 1987)—§ **501.3, n. 10.**

Blum v. Fresh Grown Preserve Corporation, 292 N.Y. 241, 54 N.E.2d 809 (N.Y. 1944)—§ **300.3; § 300.3, n. 22.**

Blum v. Schlegel, 150 F.R.D. 42 (W.D.N.Y. 1993)—§ **508.1; § 508.1, n. 13; § 508.2; § 508.2, n. 8.**

Blyden, People v., 142 A.D.2d 959, 531 N.Y.S.2d 72 (N.Y.A.D. 4 Dept.1988)—§ **803(2).1, n. 6.**

B'Nai Jonah v. Kuriansky, 172 A.D.2d 35, 576 N.Y.S.2d 934 (N.Y.A.D. 3 Dept. 1991)—§ **504.1; § 504.1, n. 4.**

Bodensteiner v. Vannais, 167 A.D.2d 954, 561 N.Y.S.2d 1017 (N.Y.A.D. 4 Dept. 1990)—§ **401.1, n. 23, 46.**

Boesenberg's Estate, In re, 265 A.D. 484, 39 N.Y.S.2d 418 (N.Y.A.D. 1 Dept.1943)—§ **601.2, n. 79.**

Boice, People v., 89 A.D.2d 33, 455 N.Y.S.2d 859 (N.Y.A.D. 3 Dept.1982)—§ **612.1, n. 12.**

Bolden, People v., 459 N.Y.S.2d 22, 445 N.E.2d 198 (N.Y.1982)—§ **801(2).1, n. 5.**

Bolick, United States v., 917 F.2d 135 (4th Cir.1990)—§ **607.5, n. 49.**

Bolm v. Triumph Corp., 71 A.D.2d 429, 422 N.Y.S.2d 969 (N.Y.A.D. 4 Dept.1979)—§ **405.1, n. 14; § 407.1, n. 17.**

Bolm v. Triumph Corp., 350 N.Y.S.2d 644, 305 N.E.2d 769 (N.Y.1973)—§ **407.1, n. 12.**

Bombard v. Albany County, 94 A.D.2d 910, 463 N.Y.S.2d 633 (N.Y.A.D. 3 Dept. 1983)—§ **501.3, n. 27.**

Bombard, People v., 5 A.D.2d 923, 172 N.Y.S.2d 1 (N.Y.A.D. 3 Dept.1958)—§ **406.1, n. 14.**

Bonanno, United States v., 487 F.2d 654 (2nd Cir.1973)—§ **901.5, n. 19.**

Bonilla, People v., 102 A.D.2d 739, 476 N.Y.S.2d 573 (N.Y.A.D. 1 Dept.1984)—§ **607.6, n. 7.**

Bonner's Will, In re, 266 N.Y.S.2d 971, 214 N.E.2d 154 (N.Y.1966)—§ **803(1).1, n. 46.**

Boor v. Moschell, 8 N.Y.S. 583 (N.Y.Sup. 1889)—§ **803(4).1, n. 1.**

Bopple v. Supreme Tent of Knights of Maccabees of the World, 18 A.D. 488, 45 N.Y.S. 1096 (N.Y.A.D. 4 Dept.1897)—§ **601.1, n. 12.**

Borawick v. Shay, 68 F.3d 597 (2nd Cir. 1995)—§ **601.3, n. 19.**

Borden v. Brady, 92 A.D.2d 983, 461 N.Y.S.2d 497 (N.Y.A.D. 3 Dept.1983)—§ **703.1; § 703.1, n. 7, 13, 14, 15; § 705.1, n. 8.**

Bornholdt, People v., 350 N.Y.S.2d 369, 305 N.E.2d 461 (N.Y.1973)—§ **607.8, n. 21.**

Bornhurst v. Massachusetts Bonding & Ins. Co., 289 N.Y.S.2d 937, 237 N.E.2d 201 (N.Y.1968)—§ **301.5; § 301.5, n. 36.**

Borrero, People v., 311 N.Y.S.2d 475, 259 N.E.2d 902 (N.Y.1970)—§ **300.4, n. 49.**

Botsch, United States v., 364 F.2d 542 (2nd Cir.1966)—§ **300.3, n. 52; § 300.4, n. 73.**

Boulahanis, United States v., 677 F.2d 586 (7th Cir.1982)—§ **804.1, n. 31; § 804(5).2, n. 15.**

Bourjaily v. United States, 483 U.S. 171, 107 S.Ct. 2775, 97 L.Ed.2d 144 (1987)—§ **802.2, n. 87; § 802.3; § 802.3, n. 36, 37, 41; § 803(1).1, n. 16; § 804(3).1; § 804(3).1, n. 49; § 804(3).2, n. 12; § 804(5).2, n. 35.**

Bouton, People v., 428 N.Y.S.2d 218, 405 N.E.2d 699 (N.Y.1980)—§ **402.1, n. 37, 58; § 608.1, n. 6, 15; § 803(7).1, n. 23; § 1108.1, n. 2.**

Bowen, People v., 431 N.Y.S.2d 449, 409 N.E.2d 924 (N.Y.1980)—§ **103.1, n. 3.**

Bowen, People v., 65 A.D.2d 364, 411 N.Y.S.2d 573 (N.Y.A.D. 1 Dept.1978)—§ **509.1, n. 81; § 802.2, n. 32.**

Bowen v. Preferred Acc. Ins. Co. of New York, 68 A.D. 342, 74 N.Y.S. 101 (N.Y.A.D. 2 Dept.1902)—§ **804(4).1, n. 3.**

Bower v. Weisman, 674 F.Supp. 113 (S.D.N.Y.1987)—§ **401.1, n. 47.**

Bowers, United States v., 660 F.2d 527 (5th Cir.1981)—§ **201.2, n. 20.**

Bowley, People v., 59 Cal.2d 855, 31 Cal. Rptr. 471, 382 P.2d 591 (Cal.1963)—§ **1104.1, n. 7.**

Bowne of New York City, Inc. v. AmBase Corp., 150 F.R.D. 465 (S.D.N.Y.1993)—§ **501.2, n. 2.**

Boyarsky v. G.A. Zimmerman Corp., 240 A.D. 361, 270 N.Y.S. 134 (N.Y.A.D. 1 Dept.1934)—§ **1102.1, n. 27; § 1104.1, n. 32, 42, 47, 48, 51.**

Boyce, United States v., 849 F.2d 833 (3rd Cir.1988)—§ **804(3).2, n. 11.**

Boyd v. Boyd, 164 N.Y. 234, 58 N.E. 118 (N.Y.1900)—§ **601.2, n. 50.**

Boyd, People v., 189 A.D.2d 433, 596 N.Y.S.2d 760 (N.Y.A.D. 1 Dept.1993)—§ **801(2).1, n. 20.**

Boyd, People v., 462 N.Y.S.2d 435, 448 N.E.2d 1346 (N.Y.1983)—§ **607.5, n. 35.**

Boyd v. United States, 116 U.S. 616, 6 S.Ct. 524, 29 L.Ed. 746 (1886)—§ **509.1; § 509.1, n. 66.**

Boylhart v. Di Marco & Reimann, 270 N.Y. 217, 200 N.E. 793 (N.Y.1936)—§ **201.1, n. 43.**

Boyling, People v., 84 A.D.2d 892, 444 N.Y.S.2d 760 (N.Y.A.D. 3 Dept.1981)—§ **801.1, n. 38; § 803(1).1, n. 41.**

Bracco v. Mabstoa, 117 A.D.2d 273, 502 N.Y.S.2d 158 (N.Y.A.D. 1 Dept.1986)—§ **803(3).1, n. 27.**

Brackeen, United States v., 969 F.2d 827 (9th Cir.1992)—§ **609.2, n. 14.**

Brady v. Chemical Const. Corp., 740 F.2d 195 (2nd Cir.1984)—§ **701.2, n. 11.**

TABLE OF CASES

Braidlow, United States v., 806 F.2d 781 (8th Cir.1986)—§ **611.5, n. 21, 22.**

Branch v. Ogilvy & Mather, Inc., 765 F.Supp. 819 (S.D.N.Y.1990)—§ **801.1, n. 25; § 804(5).2, n. 12.**

Branch, People v., 161 A.D.2d 776, 556 N.Y.S.2d 122 (N.Y.A.D. 2 Dept.1990)—§ **900.1, n. 15; § 1101.1, n. 14.**

Brand v. Brand, 811 F.2d 74 (2nd Cir. 1987)—§ **601.3, n. 2.**

Brandon v. Caterpillar Tractor Corp., 125 A.D.2d 625, 510 N.Y.S.2d 165 (N.Y.A.D. 2 Dept.1986)—§ **105.1, n. 3; § 407.1, n. 21.**

Brandon v. Collins, 267 F.2d 731 (2nd Cir. 1959)—§ **901.3, n. 25.**

Brandon's Estate, Matter of, 448 N.Y.S.2d 436, 433 N.E.2d 501 (N.Y.1982)—§ **404.1; § 404.1, n. 51, 88.**

Branzburg v. Hayes, 408 U.S. 665, 92 S.Ct. 2646, 33 L.Ed.2d 626 (1972)—§ **508.2; § 508.2, n. 1, 10.**

Bras v. Atlas Const. Corp., 153 A.D.2d 914, 545 N.Y.S.2d 723 (N.Y.A.D. 2 Dept. 1989)—§ **501.3, n. 34.**

Braswell v. United States, 487 U.S. 99, 108 S.Ct. 2284, 101 L.Ed.2d 98 (1988)—§ **509.1, n. 65.**

Braun v. Ahmed, 127 A.D.2d 418, 515 N.Y.S.2d 473 (N.Y.A.D. 2 Dept.1987)—§ **300.2, n. 4.**

Breed v. United States Dist. Court for Northern Dist. of California, 542 F.2d 1114 (9th Cir.1976)—§ **500.2, n. 6.**

Brennan v. Commonwealth Bank & Trust Co., 65 A.D.2d 636, 409 N.Y.S.2d 266 (N.Y.A.D. 3 Dept.1978)—§ **402.1, n. 11.**

Brennan v. Hall, 131 N.Y. 160, 29 N.E. 1009 (N.Y.1892)—§ **804(3).1, n. 26.**

Brennan, United States v., 798 F.2d 581 (2nd Cir.1986)—§ **404.2, n. 20; § 607.5, n. 66, 67; § 801(1).3, n. 23, 24.**

Brensic, People v., 517 N.Y.S.2d 120, 509 N.E.2d 1226 (N.Y.1987)—§ **804(3).1, n. 43, 46.**

Bretagna, People v., 298 N.Y. 323, 83 N.E.2d 537 (N.Y.1949)—§ **300.3, n. 1, 11.**

Brezinski v. Brezinski, 94 A.D.2d 969, 463 N.Y.S.2d 975 (N.Y.A.D. 4 Dept.1983)—§ **301.7, n. 4.**

Brezinski v. Brezinski, 84 A.D.2d 464, 446 N.Y.S.2d 833 (N.Y.A.D. 4 Dept.1982)—§ **601.2, n. 29, 53.**

Briar Hill Apartments Co. v. Teperman, 165 A.D.2d 519, 568 N.Y.S.2d 50 (N.Y.A.D. 1 Dept.1991)—§ **803(3).1, n. 14; § 1001.1, n. 29; § 1002.1, n. 11; § 1006.1; § 1006.1, n. 8.**

Brice v. Bauer, 108 N.Y. 428, 15 N.E. 695 (N.Y.1888)—§ **409.1; § 409.1, n. 5.**

Bridges, People v., 142 Misc.2d 789, 538 N.Y.S.2d 701 (Monroe Co.Ct.1989)—§ **505.1, n. 6; § 506.1, n. 2.**

Briggs, People v., 190 A.D.2d 995, 593 N.Y.S.2d 622 (N.Y.A.D. 4 Dept.1993)—§ **803(2).1, n. 8.**

Briggs v. Waldron, 83 N.Y. 582 (1881)—§ **803(4).1, n. 11; § 803(5).1, n. 38.**

Brill v. Brill, 222 N.Y.S.2d 321, 178 N.E.2d 720 (N.Y.1961)—§ **803(4).1, n. 14; § 803(5).1, n. 40; § 901.7, n. 12.**

Brink v. Stratton, 176 N.Y. 150, 68 N.E. 148 (N.Y.1903)—§ **607.6, n. 7, 24, 29; § 610.1, n. 6.**

Brink's Inc. v. City of New York, 717 F.2d 700 (2nd Cir.1983)—§ **514.2; § 514.2, n. 6.**

Brisbane, People v., 203 A.D.2d 89, 610 N.Y.S.2d 223 (N.Y.A.D. 1 Dept.1994)—§ **607.4, n. 43.**

Brooks, People v., 131 N.Y. 321, 30 N.E. 189 (N.Y.1892)—§ **607.6, n. 7, 25, 29.**

Brooks v. Rochester Ry. Co., 156 N.Y. 244, 50 N.E. 945 (N.Y.1898)—§ **607.8, n. 18.**

Brooks, United States v., 536 F.2d 1137 (6th Cir.1976)—§ **410.2, n. 5.**

Broun v. Equitable Life Assur. Soc. of United States, 512 N.Y.S.2d 12, 504 N.E.2d 379 (N.Y.1986)—§ **704.1, n. 5, 12.**

Brown v. Board of Ed. of Topeka, Shawnee County, Kan., 347 U.S. 483, 74 S.Ct. 686, 98 L.Ed. 873 (1954)—§ **202.1; § 202.1, n. 18.**

Brown v. Brown, 51 Misc.2d 839, 274 N.Y.S.2d 484 (N.Y.Fam.Ct.1966)—§ **301.4, n. 20.**

Brown v. Coca-Cola Bottling, Inc., 54 Wash.2d 665, 344 P.2d 207 (Wash. 1959)—§ **801.1, n. 5.**

Brown v. Lynaugh, 843 F.2d 849 (5th Cir. 1988)—§ **605.2, n. 1.**

Brown, People v., 610 N.Y.S.2d 956, 632 N.E.2d 1279 (N.Y.1994)—§ **404.1; § 404.1, n. 69.**

Brown, People v., 594 N.Y.S.2d 696, 610 N.E.2d 369 (N.Y.1993)—§ **802.2, n. 90; § 803(1).1; § 803(1).1, n. 5, 6; § 803(1).2, n. 1, 11; § 900.1, n. 6.**

Brown, People v., 179 A.D.2d 485, 579 N.Y.S.2d 15 (N.Y.A.D. 1 Dept.1992)—§ **803(1).1, n. 14.**

Brown, People v., 522 N.Y.S.2d 837, 517 N.E.2d 515 (N.Y.1987)—§ **803(1).1; § 803(1).1, n. 31; § 804(2).1, n. 33.**

Brown, People v., 126 A.D.2d 657, 511 N.Y.S.2d 86 (N.Y.A.D. 2 Dept.1987)—§ **611.1, n. 4.**

Brown, People v., 128 Misc.2d 149, 488 N.Y.S.2d 559 (Madison Co.Ct.1985)—§ **902.1, n. 14.**

Brown, People v., 423 N.Y.S.2d 461, 399 N.E.2d 51 (N.Y.1979)—§ **606.1, n. 16, 18; § 1107.1, n. 14, 15; § 1108.1; § 1108.1, n. 11, 19.**

Brown, People v., 308 N.Y.S.2d 825, 257 N.E.2d 16 (N.Y.1970)—§ **804.1; § 804.1, n. 5; § 804(3).1; § 804(3).1, n. 2, 29; § 804(5).1; § 804(5).1, n. 7.**

TABLE OF CASES

Brown v. Piper, 91 U.S. 37, 1 Otto 37, 23 L.Ed. 200 (1875)—§ **201.1, n. 20;** § **201.2, n. 1.**

Brown v. Ristich, 366 N.Y.S.2d 116, 325 N.E.2d 533 (N.Y.1975)—§ **601.1, n. 10;** § **603.1, n. 8.**

Brown, United States v., 43 F.3d 618 (11th Cir.1995)—§ **300.4, n. 74.**

Brown, United States v., 9 F.3d 907 (11th Cir.1993)—§ **803(5).2, n. 4.**

Brown, United States v., 547 F.2d 438 (8th Cir.1977)—§ **607.5, n. 55.**

Brown v. United States, 356 U.S. 148, 78 S.Ct. 622, 2 L.Ed.2d 589 (1958)—§ **509.1;** § **509.1, n. 12, 38, 48.**

Brown v. Walter, 62 F.2d 798 (2nd Cir. 1933)—§ **411.2, n. 1.**

Brown v. Western Union Tel. Co., 26 A.D.2d 316, 274 N.Y.S.2d 52 (N.Y.A.D. 4 Dept.1966)—§ **607.8, n. 26;** § **612.1, n. 9, 10, 12, 14;** § **803(2).1, n. 7.**

Browne v. City of New York, 213 A.D. 206, 211 N.Y.S. 306 (N.Y.A.D. 1 Dept.1925)—§ **201.1, n. 35.**

Browne, United States v., 313 F.2d 197 (2nd Cir.1963)—§ **614.2, n. 1.**

Brown for Brown v. Bowen, 668 F.Supp. 146 (E.D.N.Y.1987)—§ **804(4).2;** § **804(4).2, n. 2.**

Browning–Ferris Industries of South Jersey, Inc. v. Muszynski, 899 F.2d 151 (2nd Cir.1990)—§ **201.2, n. 10.**

Brownko Intern., Inc. v. Ogden Steel Co., 585 F.Supp. 1432 (D.C.N.Y.1983)—§ **802.3, n. 14.**

Brown's Estate, Matter of, 390 N.Y.S.2d 59, 358 N.E.2d 883 (N.Y.1976)—§ **803(4).1, n. 8;** § **803(5).1, n. 37.**

Bruce v. Christian, 113 F.R.D. 554 (S.D.N.Y.1986)—§ **501.2, n. 34.**

Brundige v. Bradley, 294 N.Y. 345, 62 N.E.2d 385 (N.Y.1945)—§ **601.2;** § **601.2, n. 37.**

Brunson, People v., 151 A.D.2d 303, 542 N.Y.S.2d 571 (N.Y.A.D. 1 Dept.1989)—§ **804(5).1, n. 19.**

Brush v. Olivo, 81 A.D.2d 852, 438 N.Y.S.2d 857 (N.Y.A.D. 2 Dept.1981)—§ **300.2, n. 23.**

Bruton v. United States, 391 U.S. 123, 88 S.Ct. 1620, 20 L.Ed.2d 476 (1968)—§ **105.1;** § **105.1, n. 14;** § **105.2, n. 10;** § **106.2, n. 11;** § **802.2, n. 87;** § **802.3, n. 48;** § **804(1).2, n. 9;** § **804(3).1;** § **804(3).1, n. 53.**

Bryant, United States v., 480 F.2d 785 (2nd Cir.1976)—§ **1104.2, n. 9, 12, 14.**

Buchalter, People v., 289 N.Y. 181, 45 N.E.2d 225 (N.Y.1942)—§ **607.5, n. 19.**

Buchanan, People v., 145 N.Y. 1, 39 N.E. 846 (N.Y.1895)—§ **607.5, n. 18;** § **611.4, n. 1, 3.**

Buchanan, United States v., 985 F.2d 1372 (8th Cir.1993)—§ **1104.2, n. 6.**

Buchanan, United States v., 787 F.2d 477 (10th Cir.1986)—§ **615.2, n. 9, 10, 11.**

Buck v. Hunter (In re Fay), 404 N.Y.S.2d 554, 375 N.E.2d 735 (N.Y.1978)—§ **301.4, n. 7.**

Buck Const. Corp. v. 200 Genesee Street Corp., 109 A.D.2d 1056, 487 N.Y.S.2d 198 (N.Y.A.D. 4 Dept.1985)—§ **705.1, n. 8.**

Buckingham Mfg. Co., Inc. v. Frank J. Koch, Inc., 194 A.D.2d 886, 599 N.Y.S.2d 155 (N.Y.A.D. 3 Dept.1993)—§ **802.2, n. 73.**

Buddenseick, People v., 103 N.Y. 487, 9 N.E. 44 (N.Y.1886)—§ **1104.1, n. 14.**

Bueno–Risquet, United States v., 799 F.2d 804 (2nd Cir.1986)—§ **1004.1, n. 2.**

Buffalo, City of v. J. W. Clement Co., Inc., 45 A.D.2d 620, 360 N.Y.S.2d 362 (N.Y.A.D. 4 Dept.1974)—§ **804(1).1, n. 22.**

Buffalo Structural Steel Co. v. Dickinson, 98 A.D. 355, 90 N.Y.S. 268 (N.Y.A.D. 4 Dept.1904)—§ **1107.1, n. 2.**

Buggs, People v., 109 A.D.2d 1052, 487 N.Y.S.2d 202 (N.Y.A.D. 4 Dept.1985)—§ **608.2, n. 10.**

Buie, People v., 201 A.D.2d 156, 615 N.Y.S.2d 794 (N.Y.A.D. 4 Dept.1994)—§ **803(1).1, n. 17.**

Bulaich v. AT & T Information Systems, 113 Wash.2d 254, 778 P.2d 1031 (Wash. 1989)—§ **408.2, n. 3.**

Bulger, People v., 52 A.D.2d 682, 382 N.Y.S.2d 133 (N.Y.A.D. 3 Dept.1976)—§ **401.1, n. 49.**

Bullard v. Pearsall, 53 N.Y. 230 (1873)—§ **607.4, n. 23, 24.**

Bulova Watch Co., Inc. v. K. Hattori & Co., Ltd., 508 F.Supp. 1322 (D.C.N.Y.1981)—§ **202.1, n. 4, 5, 12.**

Burack, Matter of Estate of, 201 A.D.2d 561, 607 N.Y.S.2d 711 (N.Y.A.D. 2 Dept. 1994)—§ **1102.1, n. 1;** § **1104.1, n. 35, 49.**

Burdick v. Shearson American Exp., Inc., 160 A.D.2d 642, 559 N.Y.S.2d 506 (N.Y.A.D. 1 Dept.1990)—§ **402.1, n. 11.**

Burke v. Tower East Restaurant, 37 A.D.2d 836, 326 N.Y.S.2d 32 (N.Y.A.D. 2 Dept. 1971)—§ **701.1, n. 8.**

Burket, United States v., 480 F.2d 568 (2nd Cir.1973)—§ **1108.2, n. 3.**

Burkey v. Ellis, 483 F.Supp. 897 (D.C.Ala. 1979)—§ **802.3, n. 28.**

Burse, United States v., 531 F.2d 1151 (2nd Cir.1976)—§ **300.4, n. 74.**

Burtis v. Dalsheim, 536 F.Supp. 805 (D.C.N.Y.1982)—§ **901.5, n. 20.**

Burtrum, United States v., 17 F.3d 1299 (10th Cir.1994)—§ **502.2, n. 3.**

Bush, United States v., 47 F.3d 511 (2nd Cir.1995)—§ **614.2;** § **614.2, n. 9, 11.**

Busshart v. Park, 112 A.D.2d 787, 492 N.Y.S.2d 284 (N.Y.A.D. 4 Dept.1985)—§ **509.1, n. 4.**

TABLE OF CASES

Butez v. Fonda, J. & G. R. Co., 20 Misc. 123, 45 N.Y.S. 808 (N.Y.Sup.1897)—§ 1102.1, n. 12, 15.

Butler v. Mail & Express Pub. Co., 171 N.Y. 208, 63 N.E. 951 (N.Y.1902)—§ **1001.1**, n. 28.

Butler v. Mutual Life Ins. Co. of New York, 225 N.Y. 197, 121 N.E. 758 (N.Y.1919)—§ **301.4**; § 301.4, n. 10.

Butler, People ex rel. v. McNeill, 30 Misc.2d 722, 219 N.Y.S.2d 722 (N.Y.Sup.1961)—§ 201.1, n. 26.

Butt, United States v., 955 F.2d 77 (1st Cir.1992)—§ **607.7, n. 20.**

Butterly, People v., 303 N.Y.S.2d 57, 250 N.E.2d 340 (N.Y.1969)—§ **401.1, n. 16.**

Butts v. Secretary of Health and Human Services, 706 F.2d 107 (2nd Cir.1983)—§ 301.8, n. 8.

Buzzi, People v., 238 N.Y. 390, 144 N.E. 653 (N.Y.1924)—§ **802.2**; § 802.2, n. **63, 65, 66.**

Byrd, People v., 187 A.D.2d 724, 590 N.Y.S.2d 511 (N.Y.A.D. 2 Dept.1992)—§ **801(2).1, n. 31.**

Byrd, United States v., 750 F.2d 585 (7th Cir.1984)—§ **503.5, n. 11.**

Byrnes, People v., 352 N.Y.S.2d 913, 308 N.E.2d 435 (N.Y.1974)—§ **1001.1, n. 35;** § 1002.1, n. 15; § 1104.1; § 1104.1, n. 3, 6, 7, 13.

C

Caccese, People v., 211 A.D.2d 976, 621 N.Y.S.2d 735 (N.Y.A.D. 3 Dept.1995)—§ 803(1).1, n. 62, 74.

Cade, People v., 539 N.Y.S.2d 287, 536 N.E.2d 616 (N.Y.1989)—§ **607.8, n. 40, 43.**

Cadillac Motor Car Co. v. Johnson, 221 F. 801 (2nd Cir.1915)—§ **406.2, n. 19.**

Caha v. United States, 152 U.S. 211, 14 S.Ct. 513, 38 L.Ed. 415 (1894)—§ **203.2, n. 3.**

Cain v. George, 411 F.2d 572 (5th Cir. 1969)—§ **801.1, n. 18.**

Calandra v. Norwood, 81 A.D.2d 650, 438 N.Y.S.2d 381 (N.Y.A.D. 2 Dept.1981)—§ 803(2).1, n. 11.

Calbas, United States v., 821 F.2d 887 (2nd Cir.1987)—§ **901.4, n. 13.**

California v. Byers, 402 U.S. 424, 91 S.Ct. 1535, 29 L.Ed.2d 9 (1971)—§ **509.1, n. 72.**

California v. Green, 399 U.S. 149, 90 S.Ct. 1930, 26 L.Ed.2d 489 (1970)—§ 801(1).2, n. 2; § 801(1).3; § 801(1).3, n. 1; § 801(2).2, n. 8; § 804(1).2; § 804(1).2, n. 3, 19; § 804(3).2, n. 12.

California Ass'n of Bioanalysts v. Rank, 577 F.Supp. 1342 (C.D.Cal.1983)—§ **902.1, n. 19.**

Calizaire, People v., 190 A.D.2d 857, 593 N.Y.S.2d 879 (N.Y.A.D. 2 Dept.1993)—§ **604.1, n. 7.**

Callahan, United States v., 588 F.2d 1078 (5th Cir.1979)—§ **614.2, n. 10.**

Callister's Estate, In re, 153 N.Y. 294, 47 N.E. 268 (N.Y.1897)—§ **601.2, n. 68, 79.**

Calvano, People v., 331 N.Y.S.2d 430, 282 N.E.2d 322 (N.Y.1972)—§ **402.1**; § 402.1, n. 13, 20, 49; § 404.1, n. 38.

Cambindo Valencia, United States v., 609 F.2d 603 (2nd Cir.1979)—§ **803(2).2, n. 2;** § 901.5, n. 12.

Cameron, United States v., 814 F.2d 403 (7th Cir.1987)—§ **607.7, n. 25;** § **609.2, n. 13.**

Campanile, United States v., 516 F.2d 288 (2nd Cir.1975)—§ **401.2, n. 11.**

Campbell v. Board of Ed., 310 F.Supp. 94 (D.C.N.Y.1970)—§ **901.9, n. 14.**

Campbell v. City of Elmira, 198 A.D.2d 736, 604 N.Y.S.2d 609 (N.Y.A.D. 3 Dept. 1993)—§ **607.8, n. 5;** § 801(1).2, n. 7.

Campbell v. Greer, 831 F.2d 700 (7th Cir. 1987)—§ **609.2, n. 2, 3.**

Campbell v. Pure Oil Co., 92 Ga.App. 523, 88 S.E.2d 630 (Ga.App.1955)—§ **1002.1, n. 5.**

Camperlengo v. Blum, 451 N.Y.S.2d 697, 436 N.E.2d 1299 (N.Y.1982)—§ **502.1**; § 502.1, n. 4, 69, 70.

Camporeale, United States v., 515 F.2d 184 (2nd Cir.1975)—§ **1108.2, n. 3.**

Canady, People v., 186 A.D.2d 749, 589 N.Y.S.2d 184 (N.Y.A.D. 2 Dept.1992)—§ 806.1, n. 13.

Cann v. Ford Motor Co., 658 F.2d 54 (2nd Cir.1981)—§ **407.2**; § 407.2, n. 5.

Canonico, People v., 187 A.D.2d 267, 589 N.Y.S.2d 868 (N.Y.A.D. 1 Dept.1992)—§ 611.1, n. 12.

Caperna v. Williams–Bauer Corp., 184 Misc. 192, 53 N.Y.S.2d 295 (N.Y.A.D. 1 Dept. 1945)—§ **607.1, n. 6.**

Capers, People v., 105 A.D.2d 842, 482 N.Y.S.2d 37 (N.Y.A.D. 2 Dept.1984)—§ 901.1, n. 16; § 1101.1, n. 15.

Capitol Cab Corporation v. Anderson, 194 Misc. 21, 85 N.Y.S.2d 767 (N.Y.Mun.Ct. 1949)—§ **615.1, n. 7.**

Cappetta v. Santucci, 399 N.Y.S.2d 638, 369 N.E.2d 1172 (N.Y.1977)—§ **509.1, n. 74.**

Capra v. Lumbermens Mut. Cas. Co., 43 A.D.2d 986, 352 N.Y.S.2d 58 (N.Y.A.D. 3 Dept.1974)—§ **301.3, n. 7.**

Capra, People v., 269 N.Y.S.2d 451, 216 N.E.2d 610 (N.Y.1966)—§ **502.1, n. 19.**

Caprara v. Chrysler Corp., 436 N.Y.S.2d 251, 417 N.E.2d 545 (N.Y.1981)—§ **407.1**; § 407.1, n. 2, 9, 11, 22, 31; § 702.1; § 702.1, n. 79.

Caprara v. Chrysler Corp., 71 A.D.2d 515, 423 N.Y.S.2d 694 (N.Y.A.D. 3 Dept. 1979)—§ **1102.1, n. 26;** § 1104.1, n. 42, 49, 51.

TABLE OF CASES

Caprio, People v., 25 A.D.2d 145, 268 N.Y.S.2d 70 (N.Y.A.D. 2 Dept.1966)—**§ 803(2).1, n. 12.**

Capron v. Douglass, 193 N.Y. 11, 85 N.E. 827 (N.Y.1908)—**§ 502.1, n. 44.**

Capuano, People v., 15 A.D.2d 400, 225 N.Y.S.2d 252 (N.Y.A.D. 4 Dept.1962)—**§ 607.6, n. 12.**

Caputo v. Joseph J. Sarcona Trucking Co., Inc., 204 A.D.2d 507, 611 N.Y.S.2d 655 (N.Y.A.D. 2 Dept.1994)—**§ 615.1, n. 12.**

Cardascia, United States v., 951 F.2d 474 (2nd Cir.1991)—**§ 801.1, n. 25; § 803(1).2, n. 30; § 804(5).2, n. 12, 37.**

Carden v. Allstate Ins. Co., 105 A.D.2d 1048, 483 N.Y.S.2d 486 (N.Y.A.D. 3 Dept.1984)—**§ 501.3, n. 16.**

Cardillo, United States v., 316 F.2d 606 (2nd Cir.1963)—**§ 611.5, n. 18.**

Cardinal, United States v., 782 F.2d 34 (6th Cir.1986)—**§ 412.2, n. 10.**

Carey Resources, Inc., State v., 97 A.D.2d 508, 467 N.Y.S.2d 876 (N.Y.A.D. 2 Dept. 1983)—**§ 509.1; § 509.1, n. 9, 53, 56, 71.**

Carlisle v. County of Nassau, 64 A.D.2d 15, 408 N.Y.S.2d 114 (N.Y.A.D. 2 Dept. 1978)—**§ 615.1, n. 9.**

Carlisle v. Norris, 215 N.Y. 400, 109 N.E. 564 (N.Y.1915)—**§ 607.4, n. 3, 7, 18.**

Carlo v. Queens Transit Corp., 76 A.D.2d 824, 428 N.Y.S.2d 298 (N.Y.A.D. 2 Dept. 1980)—**§ 501.3, n. 17.**

Carlson, United States v., 547 F.2d 1346 (8th Cir.1976)—**§ 804(5).2, n. 15.**

Carl Wagner and Sons v. Appendagez, Inc., 485 F.Supp. 762 (D.C.N.Y.1980)—**§ 802.3, n. 21.**

Carmack, People v., 405 N.Y.S.2d 446, 376 N.E.2d 919 (N.Y.1978)—**§ 609.1, n. 33.**

Carmona, People v., 606 N.Y.S.2d 879, 627 N.E.2d 959 (N.Y.1993)—**§ 504.1; § 504.1, n. 7.**

Carpenter v. Romer & Tremper Steamboat Co., 48 A.D. 363, 63 N.Y.S. 274 (N.Y.A.D. 3 Dept.1900)—**§ 601.2, n. 8, 38.**

Carpus, People v., 2 A.D.2d 653, 152 N.Y.S.2d 27 (N.Y.A.D. 4 Dept.1956)—**§ 605.1, n. 3.**

Carr, United States v., 584 F.2d 612 (2nd Cir.1978)—**§ 607.8, n. 45.**

Carracedo, People v., 147 Misc.2d 1093, 559 N.Y.S.2d 784 (N.Y.Sup.1990)—**§ 804(1).1, n. 45.**

Carrasco, People v., 125 A.D.2d 695, 509 N.Y.S.2d 879 (N.Y.A.D. 2 Dept.1986)—**§ 1104.1, n. 26, 27.**

Carrasquillo, People v., 204 A.D.2d 735, 612 N.Y.S.2d 424 (N.Y.A.D. 2 Dept.1994)—**§ 609.1, n. 40.**

Carriage House Motor Inn, Inc. (Motel Property) v. City of Watertown, 136 A.D.2d 895, 524 N.Y.S.2d 930 (N.Y.A.D. 4 Dept.1988)—**§ 607.8, n. 9, 18.**

Carringi v. International Paper Co., 184 A.D.2d 137, 591 N.Y.S.2d 600 (N.Y.A.D. 3 Dept.1992)—**§ 705.1, n. 9.**

Carroll v. Gammerman, 193 A.D.2d 202, 602 N.Y.S.2d 841 (N.Y.A.D. 1 Dept. 1993)—**§ 614.1, n. 5.**

Carroll v. Gimbel Bros. New York, 195 A.D. 444, 186 N.Y.S. 737 (N.Y.A.D. 1 Dept. 1921)—**§ 1001.1, n. 26.**

Carroll, People v., 117 A.D.2d 815, 499 N.Y.S.2d 135 (N.Y.A.D. 2 Dept.1986)—**§ 412.1, n. 11.**

Carroll v. Roman Catholic Diocese of Rockville Centre, New York, 26 A.D.2d 552, 271 N.Y.S.2d 7 (N.Y.A.D. 2 Dept.1966)—**§ 1103.1, n. 6.**

Carroll, United States v., 510 F.2d 507 (2nd Cir.1975)—**§ 404.2, n. 20.**

Carroll's Estate, In re, 153 Misc. 649, 275 N.Y.S. 911 (N.Y.Sur.1934)—**§ 601.2, n. 42.**

Carson, United States v., 702 F.2d 351 (2nd Cir.1983)—**§ 105.2, n. 1.**

Carson, United States v., 464 F.2d 424 (2nd Cir.1972)—**§ 1104.2, n. 14, 15; § 1108.2, n. 2.**

Carte Blanche (Singapore) PTE., Ltd. v. Diners Club Intern., Inc., 130 F.R.D. 28 (S.D.N.Y.1990)—**§ 501.2, n. 7.**

Carter, Matter of, 102 Misc.2d 867, 424 N.Y.S.2d 833 (N.Y.Sup.1980)—**§ 300.4, n. 16.**

Carter, People v., 564 N.Y.S.2d 992, 566 N.E.2d 119 (N.Y.1990)—**§ 404.1, n. 62.**

Carter, People v., 389 N.Y.S.2d 835, 358 N.E.2d 517 (N.Y.1976)—**§ 614.1, n. 17.**

Carter, People v., 371 N.Y.S.2d 905, 333 N.E.2d 177 (N.Y.1975)—**§ 607.1, n. 3.**

Carter-Wallace, Inc. v. Otte, 474 F.2d 529 (2nd Cir.1972)—**§ 804(1).2; § 804(1).2, n. 24.**

Carvalho, United States v., 742 F.2d 146 (4th Cir.1984)—**§ 804(4).2, n. 6.**

Carvel Corp. v. Lefkowitz, 106 Misc.2d 284, 431 N.Y.S.2d 609 (N.Y.Sup.1979)—**§ 513.1, n. 8.**

Carver v. United States, 164 U.S. 694, 17 S.Ct. 228, 41 L.Ed. 602 (1897)—**§ 806.1, n. 11.**

Casamento, United States v., 887 F.2d 1141 (2nd Cir 1989)—**§ 802.3, n. 70; § 804(3).2, n. 17.**

Cascone, People v., 185 N.Y. 317, 78 N.E. 287 (N.Y.1906)—**§ 402.1, n. 45; § 608.2, n. 19.**

Caserta, People v., 277 N.Y.S.2d 647, 224 N.E.2d 82 (N.Y.1966)—**§ 607.5, n. 31, 44.**

Casey, People v., 72 N.Y. 393 (1878)—**§ 608.2, n. 23.**

Casey v. Tierno, 127 A.D.2d 727, 512 N.Y.S.2d 123 (N.Y.A.D. 2 Dept.1987)—**§ 803(3).1, n. 27.**

Cassas, People v., 622 N.Y.S.2d 228, 646 N.E.2d 449 (N.Y.1995)—**§ 501.1;**

TABLE OF CASES

§ 501.1, n. 89; § 607.8, n. 9; § 802.2, n. 70.

Cassidy, People v., 213 N.Y. 388, 107 N.E. 713 (N.Y.1915)—**§ 509.1, n. 49.**

Castillo, People v., 592 N.Y.S.2d 945, 607 N.E.2d 1050 (N.Y.1992)—**§ 510.1; § 510.1, n. 2, 7, 13.**

Castillo, People v., 417 N.Y.S.2d 915, 391 N.E.2d 997 (N.Y.1979)—**§ 300.3, n. 18.**

Castillo, United States v., 14 F.3d 802 (2nd Cir.1994)—**§ 607.5, n. 66, 67; § 801(1).3, n. 23, 24.**

Castillo, United States v., 924 F.2d 1227 (2nd Cir.1991)—**§ 702.2, n. 13.**

Castleberry v. Hudson Valley Asphalt Corp., 60 A.D.2d 878, 401 N.Y.S.2d 278 (N.Y.A.D. 2 Dept.1978)—**§ 405.1, n. 9.**

Castro, People v., 144 Misc.2d 956, 545 N.Y.S.2d 985 (N.Y.Sup.1989)—**§ 702.1, n. 58; § 803(3).1, n. 71; § 901.9, n. 8.**

Castro, People v., 101 A.D.2d 392, 475 N.Y.S.2d 840 (N.Y.A.D. 1 Dept.1984)—**§ 404.1, n. 62; § 607.3, n. 19, 21.**

Castro, United States v., 813 F.2d 571 (2nd Cir.1987)—**§ 106.2; § 106.2, n. 3, 7, 13.**

Castro-Ayon, United States v., 537 F.2d 1055 (9th Cir.1976)—**§ 801(1).3, n. 14.**

Castro-Romero, United States v., 964 F.2d 942 (9th Cir.1992)—**§ 611.5, n. 11.**

Catalfamo v. Boucher, 33 A.D.2d 1081, 307 N.Y.S.2d 678 (N.Y.A.D. 3 Dept.1970)—**§ 408.1, n. 11.**

Caten v. Salt City Movers & Storage Co., 149 F.2d 428 (2nd Cir.1945)—**§ 803(6).2, n. 9.**

Catholic Guardian Soc. of Diocese of Brooklyn, Inc. on Behalf of Ricardo V. v. Elba V., 628 N.Y.S.2d 796 (N.Y.A.D. 2 Dept 1995)—**§ 604.1, n. 7.**

Caton v. Doug Urban Const. Co., 493 N.Y.S.2d 453, 483 N.E.2d 128 (N.Y. 1985)—**§ 705.1; § 705.1, n. 3.**

Catron, People v., 143 A.D.2d 468, 532 N.Y.S.2d 589 (N.Y.A.D. 3 Dept.1988)—**§ 604.1, n. 8.**

Caudle, United States v., 606 F.2d 451 (4th Cir.1979)—**§ 611.5, n. 21, 22.**

Caulfield v. Board of Ed. of City of New York, 486 F.Supp. 862 (D.C.N.Y.1979)—**§ 201.2, n. 7.**

Caupain v. Johnson, 20 A.D.2d 712, 247 N.Y.S.2d 345 (N.Y.A.D. 2 Dept.1964)—**§ 612.1, n. 18.**

Causey, United States v., 834 F.2d 1277 (6th Cir.1987)—**§ 607.8, n. 44, 45.**

Caviness, People v., 379 N.Y.S.2d 695, 342 N.E.2d 496 (N.Y.1975)—**§ 607.2, n. 9; § 607.5, n. 2; § 609.1, n. 31; § 801(1).2, n. 20; § 803(1).1; § 803(1).1, n. 15, 22.**

Cefaro, People v., 296 N.Y.S.2d 345, 244 N.E.2d 42 (N.Y.1968)—**§ 104.1, n. 33.**

Central of Georgia Ry. Co. v. Reeves, 288 Ala. 121, 257 So.2d 839 (Ala.1972)—**§ 801.1, n. 12.**

Central Petroleum Corp. v. Kyriakoudes, 121 A.D.2d 165, 502 N.Y.S.2d 1017 (N.Y.A.D. 1 Dept.1986)—**§ 408.1, n. 5, 6.**

Central R. Co. of N. J. v. Jules S. Sottnek Co., 258 F.2d 85 (2nd Cir.1958)—**§ 803(3).2, n. 22.**

Cereste v. New York, New Haven & Hartford R. Co., 231 F.2d 50 (2nd Cir. 1956)—**§ 405.2, n. 1.**

Certain Complaints Under Investigation by an Investigating Committee of Judicial Council of Eleventh Circuit, Matter of, 783 F.2d 1488 (11th Cir.1986)—**§ 511.2, n. 6.**

Certain Real Property and Premises, Known as 890 Noyac Rd., Noyac, N.Y., United States v., 945 F.2d 1252 (2nd Cir.1991)—**§ 402.1, n. 17.**

Chabica v. Schneider, 213 A.D.2d 579, 624 N.Y.S.2d 271 (N.Y.A.D. 2 Dept.1995)—**§ 612.1, n. 21.**

Chadwick v. Fonner, 69 N.Y. 404 (1877)—**§ 802.2, n. 37.**

Chaika v. Vandenberg, 252 N.Y. 101, 169 N.E. 103 (N.Y.1929)—**§ 301.5, n. 31.**

Chamberlain, People v., 38 A.D.2d 306, 329 N.Y.S.2d 61 (N.Y.A.D. 4 Dept.1972)—**§ 404.1, n. 31.**

Chambers v. Mississippi, 410 U.S. 284, 93 S.Ct. 1038, 35 L.Ed.2d 297 (1973)—**§ 607.4, n. 44, 45; § 804(5).1, n. 14.**

Chambers, People v., 125 A.D.2d 88, 512 N.Y.S.2d 89 (N.Y.A.D. 1 Dept.1987)—**§ 803(1).1; § 803(1).1, n. 52.**

Champagne v. Shop Rite Supermarkets, 203 A.D.2d 410, 610 N.Y.S.2d 559 (N.Y.A.D. 2 Dept.1994)—**§ 607.8, n. 16.**

Champeau v. Fruehauf Corp., 814 F.2d 1271 (8th Cir.1987)—**§ 1105.2, n. 1.**

Chan, People v., 110 A.D.2d 158, 493 N.Y.S.2d 778 (N.Y.A.D. 2 Dept.1985)—**§ 601.1, n. 46; § 611.3, n. 8.**

Chandler v. Roudebush, 425 U.S. 840, 96 S.Ct. 1949, 48 L.Ed.2d 416 (1976)—**§ 803(5).2, n. 23.**

Chanler v. Manocherian, 151 A.D.2d 432, 543 N.Y.S.2d 671 (N.Y.A.D. 1 Dept. 1989)—**§ 1005.1, n. 2.**

Chapman v. California, 386 U.S. 18, 87 S.Ct. 824, 17 L.Ed.2d 705 (1967)—**§ 103.2, n. 28.**

Charkow, People v., 142 A.D.2d 734, 531 N.Y.S.2d 120 (N.Y.A.D. 2 Dept.1988)—**§ 608.2, n. 10.**

Charles, People v., 137 Misc.2d 111, 519 N.Y.S.2d 921 (N.Y.Sup.1987)—**§ 801.1, n. 23.**

Charles RR, Matter of, 166 A.D.2d 763, 563 N.Y.S.2d 123 (N.Y.A.D. 3 Dept.1990)—**§ 502.1, n. 78.**

Charlton, People v., 192 A.D.2d 757, 596 N.Y.S.2d 210 (N.Y.A.D. 3 Dept.1993)—**§ 412.1, n. 11.**

Charter v. Chleborad, 551 F.2d 246 (8th Cir.1977)—**§ 411.2, n. 4.**

Chasalow v. Board of Assessors of County of Nassau, 176 A.D.2d 800, 575 N.Y.S.2d

TABLE OF CASES

129 (N.Y.A.D. 2 Dept.1991)—§ **201.1, n. 51.**

Chase Manhattan Bank, Application of, 191 F.Supp. 206 (D.C.N.Y.1961)—§ **203.2, n. 9.**

Chavez, United States v., 979 F.2d 1350 (9th Cir.1992)—§ **607.8, n. 46.**

Check, United States v., 582 F.2d 668 (2nd Cir.1978)—§ **103.2, n. 4, 7; § 801.1, n. 44.**

Cheeney v. Arnold, 18 Barb. (N.Y.) 434 (1854)—§ **611.2, n. 16, 17.**

Chemical Leaman Tank Lines, Inc. v. Stevens, 21 A.D.2d 556, 251 N.Y.S.2d 240 (N.Y.A.D. 3 Dept.1964)—§ **803(3).1, n. 27; § 805.1, n. 1; § 805.2, n. 2.**

Chenango Bridge Co. v. Paige, 83 N.Y. 178 (1880)—§ **804(3).1, n. 12.**

Chesapeake & Delaware Canal Co. v. United States, 250 U.S. 123, 39 S.Ct. 407, 63 L.Ed. 889 (1919)—§ **803(4).1, n. 12; § 803(5).1, n. 4; § 803(5).2, n. 3.**

Chevron Corp. v. Pennzoil Co., 974 F.2d 1156 (9th Cir.1992)—§ **501.2, n. 47.**

Childs, People v., 161 Misc.2d 749, 615 N.Y.S.2d 232 (N.Y.Sup.1994)—§ **412.1, n. 26.**

Chin, People v., 499 N.Y.S.2d 638, 490 N.E.2d 505 (N.Y.1986)—§ **607.6, n. 13, 24; § 611.3; § 611.3, n. 1, 4, 10.**

Chirse, People v., 132 A.D.2d 615, 517 N.Y.S.2d 772 (N.Y.A.D. 2 Dept.1987)—§ **503.3, n. 19.**

Chnapkova v. Koh, 985 F.2d 79 (2nd Cir. 1993)—§ **607.7, n. 22; § 608.2; § 608.2, n. 44; § 803(3).2, n. 28.**

Christian, United States v., 786 F.2d 203 (6th Cir.1986)—§ **611.5, n. 19.**

Christina F., Matter of, 549 N.Y.S.2d 643, 548 N.E.2d 1294 (N.Y.1989)—§ **804(5).1; § 804(5).1, n. 27.**

Christopher B., Matter of, 192 A.D.2d 180, 600 N.Y.S.2d 531 (N.Y.A.D. 4 Dept. 1993)—§ **803(3).1, n. 25.**

Cibro Petroleum Products, Inc. v. Sohio Alaska Petroleum Co., 602 F.Supp. 1520 (D.C.N.Y.1985)—§ **405.1, n. 21; § 405.2, n. 12; § 406.2, n. 23.**

Cicale, United States v., 691 F.2d 95 (2nd Cir.1982)—§ **803(1).2, n. 43.**

Ciervo, People v., 178 A.D.2d 486, 577 N.Y.S.2d 140 (N.Y.A.D. 2 Dept.1991)—§ **702.1, n. 80.**

Cintron, People v., 552 N.Y.S.2d 68, 551 N.E.2d 561 (N.Y.1990)—§ **601.1, n. 45.**

Cioffi, People v., 150 N.Y.S.2d 192, 133 N.E.2d 703 (N.Y.1956)—§ **801(2).1, n. 14.**

Cirale v. 80 Pine St. Corp., 359 N.Y.S.2d 1, 316 N.E.2d 301 (N.Y.1974)—§ **511.1; § 511.1, n. 1; § 511.2, n. 3.**

Cirillo, United States v., 425 F.Supp. 1254 (D.C.N.Y.1977)—§ **406.2, n. 2.**

Citron, United States v., 783 F.2d 307 (2nd Cir.1986)—§ **1103.2, n. 6, 8, 9.**

City of (see name of city)

Claar v. Burlington Northern R. Co., 29 F.3d 499 (9th Cir.1994)—§ **702.2, n. 30.**

Clapp v. Wilson, 5 Denio (N.Y.) 286 (1848)—§ **697.5, n. 18.**

Clark v. Brooklyn Heights R. Co., 177 N.Y. 359, 69 N.E. 647 (N.Y.1904)—§ **1102.1, n. 24.**

Clark v. Dada, 183 A.D. 253, 171 N.Y.S. 205 (N.Y.A.D. 4 Dept.1918)—§ **601.2, n. 31.**

Clark v. Douglass, 5 A.D. 547, 40 N.Y.S. 769 (N.Y.A.D. 3 Dept.1896)—§ **702.1, n. 33; § 900.1, n. 17; § 901.3, n. 11.**

Clark v. National Shoe & Leather Bank of City of New York, 164 N.Y. 498, 58 N.E. 659 (N.Y.1900)—§ **803(2).1, n. 13.**

Clark, People v., 203 A.D.2d 935, 611 N.Y.S.2d 387 (N.Y.A.D. 4 Dept.1994)—§ **801.1, n. 23.**

Clark, People v., 178 A.D.2d 258, 577 N.Y.S.2d 790 (N.Y.A.D. 1 Dept.1991)—§ **804(5).1, n. 18.**

Clark, People v., 122 A.D.2d 389, 504 N.Y.S.2d 799 (N.Y.A.D. 3 Dept.1986)—§ **701.1, n. 8; § 901.2, n. 4.**

Clark, United States v., 613 F.2d 391 (2nd Cir.1979)—§ **611.5, n. 9.**

Clarke v. New York City Transit Authority, 174 A.D.2d 268, 580 N.Y.S.2d 221 (N.Y.A.D. 1 Dept.1992)—§ **803(3).1, n. 5, 27.**

Clark-Fitzpatrick, Inc. v. Long Island R. Co., 162 A.D.2d 577, 556 N.Y.S.2d 763 (N.Y.A.D. 2 Dept.1990)—§ **501.1, n. 85.**

Claxton v. Thackston, 201 Ill.App.3d 232, 147 Ill.Dec. 82, 559 N.E.2d 82 (Ill.App. 1 Dist.1990)—§ **501.1, n. 66.**

Cleague, People v., 292 N.Y.S.2d 861, 239 N.E.2d 617 (N.Y.1968)—§ **300.4, n. 49; § 401.1, n. 7.**

Clear, In re, 58 Misc.2d 699, 296 N.Y.S.2d 184 (N.Y.Fam.Ct.1969)—§ **505.1, n. 19.**

Clemente v. Carnicon-Puerto Rico Management Associates, L.C., 52 F.3d 383 (1st Cir.1995)—§ **1107.2, n. 2, 7.**

Clemente, United States v., 640 F.2d 1069 (2nd Cir.1981)—§ **608.2, n. 40.**

Clift v. Moses, 112 N.Y. 426, 20 N.E. 392 (N.Y.1889)—§ **601.2; § 601.2, n. 34, 51.**

Cobb v. County of Monroe, 7 Misc.2d 141, 165 N.Y.S.2d 583 (N.Y.Sup.1957)—§ **901.8, n. 5.**

Cociancich v. Vazzoler, 48 A.D. 462, 62 N.Y.S. 893 (N.Y.A.D. 2 Dept.1900)—§ **1007.1, n. 4.**

Coffey, People v., 227 N.Y.S.2d 412, 182 N.E.2d 92 (N.Y.1962)—§ **607.5, n. 35; § 801(2).1, n. 15.**

Cohen v. I. Goodman & Son, 205 A.D. 312, 199 N.Y.S. 497 (N.Y.A.D. 1 Dept.1923)—§ **509.1, n. 4.**

Cohen v. Kindlon, 366 F.2d 762 (2nd Cir. 1966)—§ **1103.2, n. 1, 2.**

Cohen, People v., 431 N.Y.S.2d 446, 409 N.E.2d 921 (N.Y.1980)—§ **1105.1, n. 7.**

Cohen v. Uniroyal, Inc., 80 F.R.D. 480 (D.C.Pa.1978)—§ **501.2, n. 37.**

919

TABLE OF CASES

Cohen, United States v., 888 F.2d 770 (11th Cir.1989)—§ **607.5, n. 53.**

Cohen, United States v., 384 F.2d 699 (2nd Cir.1967)—§ **803(3).2, n. 19.**

Cohn v. United States, 258 F. 355 (2nd Cir.1919)—§ **1005.1, n. 12.**

Colas, People v., 206 A.D.2d 183, 619 N.Y.S.2d 702 (N.Y.A.D. 1 Dept.1994)—§ **404.1, n. 15.**

Cole v. Canno, 168 A.D. 178, 153 N.Y.S. 957 (N.Y.A.D. 3 Dept.1915)—§ **1004.1, n. 2.**

Cole Fischer Rogow, Inc. v. Carl Ally, Inc., 29 A.D.2d 423, 288 N.Y.S.2d 556 (N.Y.A.D. 1 Dept.1968)—§ **201.1, n. 47.**

Coleman v. Alabama, 399 U.S. 1, 90 S.Ct. 1999, 26 L.Ed.2d 387 (1970)—§ **801(2).2, n. 4.**

Coleman v. Bruch, 132 A.D. 716, 117 N.Y.S. 582 (N.Y.A.D. 1 Dept.1909)—§ **901.8, n. 5.**

Coleman v. New York City Transit Authority, 371 N.Y.S.2d 663, 332 N.E.2d 850 (N.Y.1975)—§ **601.1, n. 14, 18; § 607.6, n. 3, 4, 8, 10.**

Coleman, People v., 451 N.Y.S.2d 705, 436 N.E.2d 1307 (N.Y.1982)—§ **607.2, n. 9, 11; § 608.2, n. 6, 8.**

Coleman's Will, In re, 111 N.Y. 220, 19 N.E. 71 (N.Y.1888)—§ **701.1, n. 8.**

Cole, People v., 43 N.Y. 508 (1871)—§ **611.3, n. 5.**

Colletti, United States v., 984 F.2d 1339 (3rd Cir.1992)—§ **609.2, n. 19.**

Colletti, United States v., 245 F.2d 781 (2nd Cir.1957)—§ **607.3, n. 23.**

Collins v. Caldor of Kingston, Inc., 73 A.D.2d 708, 422 N.Y.S.2d 524 (N.Y.A.D. 3 Dept.1979)—§ **802.1, n. 8.**

Collins v. Wyman, 38 A.D.2d 600, 328 N.Y.S.2d 725 (N.Y.A.D. 2 Dept.1971)—§ **701.1, n. 8; § 901.2, n. 8.**

Colocotronis Tanker Securities Litigation, In re, 449 F.Supp. 828 (S.D.N.Y.1978)—§ **501.2, n. 38.**

Colon, People v., 281 A.D. 354, 119 N.Y.S.2d 503 (N.Y.A.D. 1 Dept.1953)—§ **1001.1, n. 11, 31.**

Colon, United States v., 880 F.2d 650 (2nd Cir.1989)—§ **404.2, n. 31.**

Colton v. United States, 306 F.2d 633 (2nd Cir.1962)—§ **501.2, n. 2, 6, 10, 12, 22.**

Columbia Pictures Industries, Inc. v. Stein for Senator Committee, 77 A.D.2d 836, 431 N.Y.S.2d 23 (N.Y.A.D. 1 Dept. 1980)—§ **802.2, n. 1.**

Columbia & P. S. R. Co. v. Hawthorne, 144 U.S. 202, 12 S.Ct. 591, 36 L.Ed. 405 (1892)—§ **407.2; § 407.2, n. 1.**

Comer v. Pennsylvania R. Co., 323 F.2d 863 (2nd Cir.1963)—§ **607.6, n. 39.**

Comer, People v., 146 A.D.2d 794, 537 N.Y.S.2d 272 (N.Y.A.D. 2 Dept.1989)—§ **607.4, n. 37.**

Comfort, People v., 151 A.D.2d 1019, 542 N.Y.S.2d 84 (N.Y.A.D. 4 Dept.1989)—§ **804.1, n. 28.**

Commercial Trading Co., Inc. v. Tucker, 80 A.D.2d 779, 437 N.Y.S.2d 86 (N.Y.A.D. 1 Dept.1981)—§ **802.2, n. 47.**

Commercial Union Ins. Co. v. Boston Edison Co., 412 Mass. 545, 591 N.E.2d 165 (Mass.1992)—§ **1106.1, n. 8, 9.**

Commissioner of Social Services v. Philip De G., 463 N.Y.S.2d 761, 450 N.E.2d 681 (N.Y.1983)—§ **301.7; § 301.7, n. 5; § 514.1; § 514.1, n. 12; § 803(3).1, n. 73.**

Commodity Futures Trading Com'n v. Weintraub, 471 U.S. 343, 105 S.Ct. 1986, 85 L.Ed.2d 372 (1985)—§ **501.2; § 501.2, n. 28, 41.**

Commonwealth v. ____ (see opposing party)

Community Service Soc. v. Welfare Inspector General, 91 Misc.2d 383, 398 N.Y.S.2d 92 (N.Y.Sup.1977)—§ **505.1, n. 1.**

Complaint of (see name of party)

Compton v. Davis Oil Co., 607 F.Supp. 1221 (D.C.Wyo.1985)—§ **803(7).2, n. 6.**

Computer Associates Intern., Inc. v. Altai, Inc., 982 F.2d 693 (2nd Cir.1992)—§ **706.2, n. 6.**

Conboy, McKay, Bachman & Kendall v. Armstrong, 110 A.D.2d 1042, 488 N.Y.S.2d 901 (N.Y.A.D. 4 Dept.1985)—§ **300.2, n. 15.**

Concepcion, United States v., 983 F.2d 369 (2nd Cir.1992)—§ **404.2, n. 20.**

Conde, People v., 16 A.D.2d 327, 228 N.Y.S.2d 69 (N.Y.A.D. 3 Dept.1962)—§ **806.1, n. 12.**

Condon, People v., 309 N.Y.S.2d 152, 257 N.E.2d 615 (N.Y.1970)—§ **404.1; § 404.1, n. 54.**

Conklin, People v., 102 A.D.2d 829, 476 N.Y.S.2d 602 (N.Y.A.D. 2 Dept.1984)—§ **1001.1, n. 32.**

Conklin, People v., 175 N.Y. 333, 67 N.E. 624 (N.Y.1903)—§ **803(1).1, n. 56.**

Conkling v. Weatherwax, 181 N.Y. 258, 73 N.E. 1028 (N.Y.1905)—§ **300.2, n. 7.**

Conley v. Meeker, 85 N.Y. 618 (1881)—§ **607.5, n. 21, 25.**

Conlin, United States v., 551 F.2d 534 (2nd Cir.1977)—§ **1006.1, n. 12, 24; § 1103.2, n. 8.**

Connecticut Light & Power Co. v. Federal Power Com'n, 557 F.2d 349 (2nd Cir. 1977)—§ **803(5).2, n. 3; § 803(7).2, n. 7.**

Connelly, People v., 359 N.Y.S.2d 266, 316 N.E.2d 706 (N.Y.1974)—§ **1101.1, n. 17, 20.**

Connor v. New York Life Ins. Co., 179 A.D. 596, 166 N.Y.S. 985 (N.Y.A.D. 2 Dept. 1917)—§ **803(5).1, n. 27.**

Consolazio, People v., 387 N.Y.S.2d 62, 354 N.E.2d 801 (N.Y.1976)—§ **501.3, n. 32.**

Consolidated Laundries Corp., United States v., 291 F.2d 563 (2nd Cir.1961)—§ **405.2, n. 6.**

TABLE OF CASES

Consolidated Midland Corp. v. Columbia Pharmaceutical Corp., 42 A.D.2d 601, 345 N.Y.S.2d 105 (N.Y.A.D. 2 Dept. 1973)—§ **803(5).1, n. 1, 3.**

Constable v. Matie, 199 A.D.2d 1004, 608 N.Y.S.2d 10 (N.Y.A.D. 4 Dept.1993)— § **411.1, n. 9.**

Contemporary Mission, Inc. v. Bonded Mailings, Inc., 671 F.2d 81 (2nd Cir.1982)— § **401.2, n. 4.**

Contes, People v., 467 N.Y.S.2d 349, 454 N.E.2d 932 (N.Y.1983)—§ **300.3, n. 27.**

Contini v. Hyundai Motor Co., 840 F.Supp. 22 (S.D.N.Y.1993)—§ **803(5).2, n. 33.**

Conyers, People v., 438 N.Y.S.2d 741, 420 N.E.2d 933 (N.Y.1981)—§ **401.1, n. 45;** § **509.1, n. 83;** § **607.8, n. 24;** § **802.2, n. 30, 33.**

Conyers, People v., 424 N.Y.S.2d 402, 400 N.E.2d 342 (N.Y.1980)—§ **509.1, n. 82.**

Cook v. Cook, 8 A.D.2d 964, 190 N.Y.S.2d 955 (N.Y.A.D. 2 Dept.1959)—§ **502.1, n. 39.**

Cook, People v., 159 Misc.2d 430, 603 N.Y.S.2d 979 (N.Y.Sup.1993)—§ **802.2, n. 90;** § **803(1).1, n. 16, 20.**

Cooke, People v., 292 N.Y. 185, 54 N.E.2d 357 (N.Y.1944)—§ **615.1, n. 3, 4.**

Cooper v. Asplundh Tree Expert Co., 836 F.2d 1544 (10th Cir.1988)—§ **608.1, n. 19.**

Cooper, People v., 307 N.Y. 253, 120 N.E.2d 813 (N.Y.1954)—§ **501.1, n. 47.**

Cooper-Rutter Associates, Inc. v. Anchor Nat. Life Ins. Co., 168 A.D.2d 663, 563 N.Y.S.2d 491 (N.Y.A.D. 2 Dept.1990)— § **501.1, n. 62.**

Cope v. Sibley, 12 Barb. (N.Y.) 521 (1850)— § **611.2, n. 15;** § **611.3, n. 21.**

Corallo, United States v., 413 F.2d 1306 (2nd Cir.1969)—§ **300.3, n. 51.**

Corcoran v. Peat, Marwick, Mitchell and Co., 151 A.D.2d 443, 542 N.Y.S.2d 642 (N.Y.A.D. 1 Dept.1989)—§ **501.3, n. 9, 11.**

Corcoran v. Village of Peekskill, 108 N.Y. 151, 15 N.E. 309 (N.Y.1888)—§ **407.1, n. 4.**

Corey, People v., 148 N.Y. 476, 42 N.E. 1066 (N.Y.1896)—§ **701.1, n. 8;** § **900.1, n. 1;** § **901.2, n. 6.**

Cornier v. Spagna, 101 A.D.2d 141, 475 N.Y.S.2d 7 (N.Y.A.D. 1 Dept.1984)— § **803(3).1, n. 27.**

Corning v. Walker, 100 N.Y. 547, 3 N.E. 290 (N.Y.1885)—§ **601.2, n. 69.**

Cornwell v. Cleveland, 44 A.D.2d 891, 355 N.Y.S.2d 679 (N.Y.A.D. 4 Dept.1974)— § **611.2, n. 19.**

Corona, United States v., 849 F.2d 562 (11th Cir.1988)—§ **502.2, n. 3.**

Cosentino, United States v., 844 F.2d 30 (2nd Cir.1988)—§ **607.5, n. 49, 50, 52, 53;** § **607.6, n. 34.**

Costanzo, United States v., 581 F.2d 28 (2nd Cir.1978)—§ **802.3, n. 14.**

Cota, United States v., 953 F.2d 753 (2nd Cir.1992)—§ **802.3, n. 55.**

Cote v. Gentile, 257 F.Supp. 603 (D.C.Conn. 1966)—§ **411.2, n. 7.**

Cotter, United States v., 60 F.2d 689 (2nd Cir.1932)—§ **514.2, n. 4.**

Couch v. United States, 409 U.S. 322, 93 S.Ct. 611, 34 L.Ed.2d 548 (1973)— § **500.2, n. 4.**

Counihan v. J.H. Werbelovsky's Sons, Inc., 5 A.D.2d 80, 168 N.Y.S.2d 829 (N.Y.A.D. 1 Dept.1957)—§ **702.1, n. 81.**

County Court of Ulster County, N. Y. v. Allen, 442 U.S. 140, 99 S.Ct. 2213, 60 L.Ed.2d 777 (1979)—§ **302.1, n. 7, 8, 10, 11.**

Court of Oyer and Terminer of the County of New York, People ex rel. Phelps v., 83 N.Y. 436 (1881)—§ **611.3, n. 23.**

Courtney v. United States, 390 F.2d 521 (9th Cir.1968)—§ **514.2, n. 4.**

Cousins v. Instrument Flyers, Inc., 405 N.Y.S.2d 441, 376 N.E.2d 914 (N.Y. 1978)—§ **203.1, n. 11.**

Cover v. Cohen, 473 N.Y.S.2d 378, 461 N.E.2d 864 (N.Y.1984)—§ **407.1;** § **407.1, n. 20, 23, 26;** § **407.2, n. 3;** § **803(3).1;** § **803(3).1, n. 23;** § **805.1;** § **805.1, n. 4.**

Cox v. Administrator United States Steel & Carnegie, 17 F.3d 1386 (11th Cir. 1994)—§ **501.2, n. 47, 53.**

Cox v. State, 171 N.Y.S.2d 818, 148 N.E.2d 879 (N.Y.1958)—§ **802.2;** § **802.2, n. 50;** § **803(3).1;** § **803(3).1, n. 26.**

Craft, People v., 321 N.Y.S.2d 566, 270 N.E.2d 297 (N.Y.1971)—§ **702.1, n. 40.**

Cramer v. Kuhns, 213 A.D.2d 131, 630 N.Y.S.2d 128 (N.Y.A.D. 3 Dept.1995)— § **406.1;** § **406.1, n. 40;** § **802.1, n. 11;** § **803(5).1, n. 15.**

Crampton, People v., 107 A.D.2d 998, 484 N.Y.S.2d 721 (N.Y.A.D. 3 Dept.1985)— § **804.1, n. 29.**

Crandall, People v., 500 N.Y.S.2d 635, 491 N.E.2d 1092 (N.Y.1986)—§ **404.1;** § **404.1, n. 34, 65.**

Crater Club, Inc. v. Adirondack Park Agency, 86 A.D.2d 714, 446 N.Y.S.2d 565 (N.Y.A.D. 3 Dept.1982)—§ **201.1, n. 9.**

Cratsley, People v., 629 N.Y.S.2d 992, 653 N.E.2d 1162 (N.Y.1995)—§ **803(3).1, n. 12.**

Crawford v. Nilan, 289 N.Y. 444, 46 N.E.2d 512 (N.Y.1943)—§ **607.5, n. 29, 31, 32;** § **801(1).2, n. 16;** § **803(1).1, n. 56.**

Crawford v. Nilan, 264 A.D. 46, 35 N.Y.S.2d 33 (N.Y.A.D. 3 Dept.1942)—§ **611.3, n. 19, 20.**

Crawford, People v., 143 A.D.2d 141, 531 N.Y.S.2d 598 (N.Y.A.D. 2 Dept.1988)— § **412.1, n. 23.**

Creaghe v. Iowa Home Mut. Cas. Co., 323 F.2d 981 (10th Cir.1963)—§ **801.1, n. 21.**

TABLE OF CASES

Creasy, People v., 236 N.Y. 205, 140 N.E. 563 (N.Y.1923)—§ **704.1, n. 5.**
Cree v. Hatcher, 969 F.2d 34 (3rd Cir. 1992)—§ **609.2, n. 14, 17.**
Creedon, In re, 264 N.Y. 40, 189 N.E. 773 (N.Y.1934)—§ **512.1, n. 4.**
Crespo, United States v., 422 F.2d 718 (2nd Cir.1970)—§ **302.2, n. 5.**
Criden, United States v., 633 F.2d 346 (3rd Cir.1980)—§ **508.2, n. 2.**
Crimmins, People v., 367 N.Y.S.2d 213, 326 N.E.2d 787 (N.Y.1975)—§ **509.1, n. 37.**
Crimmins, People v., 310 N.Y.S.2d 300, 258 N.E.2d 708 (N.Y.1970)—§ **1107.1, n. 15.**
Crisafi, United States v., 304 F.2d 803 (2nd Cir.1962)—§ **607.5, n. 55.**
Cronin, People v., 470 N.Y.S.2d 110, 458 N.E.2d 351 (N.Y.1983)—§ **702.1, n. 9, 71;** § **704.1;** § **704.1, n. 5, 8, 19.**
Cross v. Cross, 108 N.Y. 628, 15 N.E. 333 (N.Y.1888)—§ **607.4, n. 11.**
Crossman v. Crossman, 95 N.Y. 145, 30 Hun. 385 (1884)—§ **1003.1, n. 9.**
Croton–on–Hudson, Village of v. State, 48 Misc.2d 1092, 266 N.Y.S.2d 567 (N.Y.Ct.Cl.1966)—§ **103.1, n. 36.**
Crow–Crimmins–Wolff & Munier v. County of Westchester, 126 A.D.2d 696, 511 N.Y.S.2d 117 (N.Y.A.D. 2 Dept.1987)—§ **408.1, n. 4.**
Cruden v. Bank of New York, 957 F.2d 961 (2nd Cir.1992)—§ **501.2, n. 47.**
Cruz v. New York, 481 U.S. 186, 107 S.Ct. 1714, 95 L.Ed.2d 162 (1987)—§ **105.1, n. 16.**
Cruz v. New York City Transit Authority, 136 A.D.2d 196, 526 N.Y.S.2d 827 (N.Y.A.D. 2 Dept.1988)—§ **406.1;** § **406.1, n. 36, 39.**
Cruz, United States v., 981 F.2d 659 (2nd Cir.1992)—§ **702.2, n. 10.**
Cruz, United States v., 894 F.2d 41 (2nd Cir.1990)—§ **805.2, n. 4.**
Cruz, United States v., 797 F.2d 90 (2nd Cir.1986)—§ **103.2, n. 13;** § **804(3).2, n. 17.**
Culhane, People v., 408 N.Y.S.2d 489, 380 N.E.2d 315 (N.Y.1978)—§ **406.1, n. 7.**
Cullen v. Margiotta, 811 F.2d 698 (2nd Cir. 1987)—§ **404.2;** § **404.2, n. 21, 39.**
Cullinan v. Horan, 116 A.D. 711, 102 N.Y.S. 132 (N.Y.A.D. 2 Dept.1907)—§ **1001.1, n. 13, 14.**
Culpepper, United States v., 834 F.2d 879 (10th Cir.1987)—§ **1107.2, n. 3.**
Culver, People v., 192 A.D.2d 10, 598 N.Y.S.2d 832 (N.Y.A.D. 3 Dept.1993)—§ **412.1, n. 25.**
Cummins v. County of Onondaga, 618 N.Y.S.2d 615, 642 N.E.2d 1071 (N.Y. 1994)—§ **301.4, n. 3.**
Cummiskey v. Chandris, S.A., 719 F.Supp. 1183 (S.D.N.Y.1989)—§ **803(1).2;** § **803(1).2, n. 15.**

Cunningham v. Housing Authority of City of Opelousas, 764 F.2d 1097 (5th Cir. 1985)—§ **614.1, n. 5;** § **614.2, n. 2.**
Cunningham, United States v., 723 F.2d 217 (2nd Cir.1983)—§ **410.2, n. 8.**
Cunningham, United States v., 672 F.2d 1064 (2nd Cir.1982)—§ **501.2, n. 5.**
Cuno, Inc. v. Pall Corp., 121 F.R.D. 198 (E.D.N.Y.1988)—§ **501.2, n. 34.**
Curcio v. United States, 354 U.S. 118, 77 S.Ct. 1145, 1 L.Ed.2d 1225 (1957)—§ **509.1;** § **509.1, n. 58.**
Curdgel, People v., 611 N.Y.S.2d 827, 634 N.E.2d 199 (N.Y.1994)—§ **410.1;** § **410.1, n. 5, 9, 11.**
Curdgel, People v., 191 A.D.2d 743, 594 N.Y.S.2d 410 (N.Y.A.D. 3 Dept.1993)—§ **410.1, n. 13.**
Curley v. United States, 160 F.2d 229, 81 U.S.App.D.C. 389 (D.C.Cir.1947)—§ **300.3;** § **300.3, n. 35, 54.**
Curro, United States v., 847 F.2d 325 (6th Cir.1988)—§ **804(5).2, n. 15.**
Curry, People v., 157 A.D.2d 623, 550 N.Y.S.2d 641 (N.Y.A.D. 1 Dept.1990)—§ **702.1, n. 80.**
Curtis Pub. Co. v. Butts, 388 U.S. 130, 87 S.Ct. 1975, 18 L.Ed.2d 1094 (1967)—§ **402.2, n. 6.**
Cuthell, Matter of, 193 Misc. 226, 83 N.Y.S.2d 902 (N.Y.Sup.1948)—§ **803(5).1, n. 26, 27.**
Cynthia B. v. New Rochelle Hosp. Medical Center, 470 N.Y.S.2d 122, 458 N.E.2d 363 (N.Y.1983)—§ **502.1, n. 53.**
Czajka v. Hickman, 703 F.2d 317 (8th Cir. 1983)—§ **609.2, n. 13.**

D

Dachille, People v., 14 A.D.2d 554, 218 N.Y.S.2d 156 (N.Y.A.D. 2 Dept.1961)—§ **607.8, n. 29;** § **801(1).2, n. 13.**
Dadanian, United States v., 818 F.2d 1443 (9th Cir.1987)—§ **607.5, n. 53.**
Daghita, People v., 299 N.Y. 194, 86 N.E.2d 172 (N.Y.1949)—§ **503.1, n. 1;** § **503.3;** § **503.3, n. 1, 7.**
D'Agostino, People v., 120 Misc.2d 437, 465 N.Y.S.2d 834 (Monroe Co.Ct.1983)—§ **803(5).1, n. 7.**
D'Agostino, United States v., 338 F.2d 490 (2nd Cir.1964)—§ **1005.1, n. 11.**
D'Alessio v. Gilberg, 205 A.D.2d 8, 617 N.Y.S.2d 484 (N.Y.A.D. 2 Dept.1994)—§ **501.1, n. 34.**
Daliendo v. Johnson, 147 A.D.2d 312, 543 N.Y.S.2d 987 (N.Y.A.D. 2 Dept.1989)—§ **803(1).1;** § **803(1).1, n. 67.**
Dallago v. United States, 427 F.2d 546, 138 U.S.App.D.C. 276 (D.C.Cir.1969)—§ **1108.2, n. 1, 3.**
Dallas County v. Commercial Union Assur. Co., 286 F.2d 388 (5th Cir.1961)—

TABLE OF CASES

§ 804(5).2; § 804(5).2, n. 4; § 902.1, n. 3.

Dalrymple v. Williams, 63 N.Y. 361 (1875)—§ **606.1, n. 10.**

D'Amato, People v., 105 Misc.2d 1048, 430 N.Y.S.2d 521 (N.Y.Sup.1980)—§ **503.3, n. 18.**

Dananel, People v., 183 A.D.2d 778, 584 N.Y.S.2d 485 (N.Y.A.D. 2 Dept.1992)—§ **1102.1, n. 17.**

Dance v. Town of Southampton, 95 A.D.2d 442, 467 N.Y.S.2d 203 (N.Y.A.D. 2 Dept. 1983)—§ **402.1, n. 45;** § **608.2, n. 19;** § **609.1, n. 5.**

Danehy, United States v., 680 F.2d 1311 (11th Cir.1982)—§ **607.5, n. 60.**

D'Angelo v. Columbia Fire Ins Co of Ohio, 118 F.Supp. 474 (D.C.N.Y.1954)—§ **803(2).2, n. 4.**

Daniels v. Patterson, 3 N.Y. 47 (1849)—§ **103.1, n. 32.**

Daniels, People v., 102 Misc.2d 540, 422 N.Y.S.2d 832 (N.Y.Sup.1979)—§ **702.1, n. 48.**

Daniels, People v., 376 N.Y.S.2d 436, 339 N.E.2d 139 (N.Y.1975)—§ **300.3, n. 8.**

Daniels v. Smith, 130 N.Y. 696, 29 N.E. 1098 (N.Y.1892)—§ **1004.1, n. 21.**

Darden, People v., 356 N.Y.S.2d 582, 313 N.E.2d 49 (N.Y.1974)—§ **510.1;** § **510.1, n. 1, 2, 7;** § **510.2, n. 4.**

Dart Associates v. Rosal Meat Market, Inc., 39 A.D.2d 564, 331 N.Y.S.2d 853 (N.Y.A.D. 2 Dept.1972)—§ **902.1, n. 10.**

Dartmouth Plan, Inc. v. Valle, 117 Misc.2d 534, 458 N.Y.S.2d 848 (N.Y.Sup.1983)—§ **803(4).1, n. 10;** § **803(5).1, n. 37.**

Dashnau, People v., 187 A.D.2d 966, 591 N.Y.S.2d 124 (N.Y.A.D. 4 Dept.1992)—§ **606.1, n. 15.**

Da Silva, United States v., 725 F.2d 828 (2nd Cir.1983)—§ **802.3, n. 32.**

Datskow v. Teledyne Continental Motors Aircraft Products, a Div. of Teledyne Industries, Inc., 826 F.Supp. 677 (W.D.N.Y.1993)—§ **1106.1, n. 3.**

Dattner v. Pokoik, 81 A.D.2d 572, 437 N.Y.S.2d 425 (N.Y.A.D. 2 Dept.1981)—§ **802.2, n. 1.**

Daubert v. Merrell Dow Pharmaceuticals, Inc., 43 F.3d 1311 (9th Cir.1995)—§ **702.2, n. 26.**

Daubert v. Merrell Dow Pharmaceuticals, Inc., ___ U.S. ___, 113 S.Ct. 2786, 125 L.Ed.2d 469 (1993)—§ **702.2;** § **702.2, n. 17;** § **901.9;** § **901.9, n. 10.**

Daughtry, People v., 202 A.D.2d 686, 610 N.Y.S.2d 54 (N.Y.A.D. 2 Dept.1994)—§ **1102.1, n. 20.**

Dave Levine & Co. v. Wolf's Package Depot, 29 Misc.2d 1085, 138 N.Y.S.2d 427 (N.Y.Sup.1955)—§ **901.4, n. 5.**

Davenport v. Ourisman–Mandell Chevrolet, Inc., 195 A.2d 743 (D.C.App.1963)—§ **1001.1, n. 25.**

Davidson v. Cornell, 132 N.Y. 228, 30 N.E. 573 (N.Y.1892)—§ **703.1, n. 17;** § **803(1).1;** § **803(1).1, n. 61, 64, 76.**

David T., Matter of, 102 Misc.2d 956, 424 N.Y.S.2d 842 (N.Y.City Fam.Ct.1980)—§ **201.1, n. 41.**

Davis v. Alaska, 415 U.S. 308, 94 S.Ct. 1105, 39 L.Ed.2d 347 (1974)—§ **505.1, n. 15;** § **607.2, n. 19;** § **607.6, n. 1, 27, 32;** § **611.3, n. 2, 4, 31.**

Davis v. Blum, 70 A.D.2d 583, 416 N.Y.S.2d 57 (N.Y.A.D. 2 Dept.1979)—§ **402.1, n. 28;** § **406.1, n. 28.**

Davis, People v., 405 N.Y.S.2d 428, 376 N.E.2d 901 (N.Y.1978)—§ **607.5, n. 29, 33, 36, 43.**

Davis, People v., 400 N.Y.S.2d 735, 371 N.E.2d 456 (N.Y.1977)—§ **401.1;** § **401.1, n. 37, 51;** § **607.1, n. 8;** § **802.2, n. 9.**

Davis, People v., 21 Wend. (N.Y.) 309 (1839)—§ **607.5, n. 23.**

Davis v. Solondz, 122 A.D.2d 401, 504 N.Y.S.2d 804 (N.Y.A.D. 3 Dept.1986)—§ **404.1;** § **404.1, n. 94, 95.**

Davis, United States v., 787 F.2d 1501 (11th Cir.1986)—§ **608.1, n. 21.**

Davis, United States v., 766 F.2d 1452 (10th Cir.1985)—§ **607.5, n. 51.**

Davis, United States v., 617 F.2d 677, 199 U.S.App.D.C. 95 (D.C.Cir.1979)—§ **410.2, n. 7.**

Dawson, People v., 428 N.Y.S.2d 914, 406 N.E.2d 771 (N.Y.1980)—§ **607.5, n. 19;** § **607.8, n. 8, 22, 23.**

Day, United States ex rel. Fong on v., 54 F.2d 990 (2nd Cir.1932)—§ **1102.2, n. 2.**

Dayanim v. Unis, 171 A.D.2d 579, 567 N.Y.S.2d 673 (N.Y.A.D. 1 Dept.1991)—§ **803(3).1, n. 68.**

Dean v. Trans World Airlines, Inc., 924 F.2d 805 (9th Cir.1991)—§ **609.2, n. 14.**

De Baillet–Latour v. De Baillet–Latour, 301 N.Y. 428, 94 N.E.2d 715 (N.Y.1950)—§ **300.3, n. 14;** § **1102.1, n. 6.**

DeBenedetto by DeBenedetto v. Goodyear Tire & Rubber Co., 754 F.2d 512 (4th Cir.1985)—§ **614.2, n. 10.**

De Cabia, People v., 10 Misc.2d 923, 172 N.Y.S.2d 1004 (Nassau Co.Ct.1958)—§ **802.2, n. 104.**

Decina, People v., 157 N.Y.S.2d 558, 138 N.E.2d 799 (N.Y.1956)—§ **502.1;** § **502.1, n. 13, 23, 28, 32.**

Deckard, United States v., 816 F.2d 426 (8th Cir.1987)—§ **201.2, n. 16.**

Defares, People v., 209 A.D.2d 875, 619 N.Y.S.2d 375 (N.Y.A.D. 3 Dept.1994)—§ **804(3).1, n. 38.**

De Feo v. Merchant, 115 Misc.2d 286, 454 N.Y.S.2d 576 (N.Y.City Ct.1982)—§ **301.5, n. 41.**

DeFillipo, United States v., 590 F.2d 1228 (2nd Cir.1979)—§ **302.1, n. 13;** § **302.2, n. 6.**

TABLE OF CASES

DeGeorge, People v., 543 N.Y.S.2d 11, 541 N.E.2d 11 (N.Y.1989)—§ **607.8, n. 24.**

Deister, People ex rel. v. Wintermute, 194 N.Y. 99, 86 N.E. 818 (N.Y.1909)—§ **512.1, n. 4.**

Deitsch, People v., 237 N.Y. 300, 142 N.E. 670 (N.Y.1923)—§ **607.5, n. 9.**

DeJesus v. City of New York, 199 A.D.2d 139, 605 N.Y.S.2d 253 (N.Y.A.D. 1 Dept. 1993)—§ **803(3).1, n. 63.**

De Jesus, People v., 514 N.Y.S.2d 708, 507 N.E.2d 301 (N.Y.1987)—§ **505.1, n. 9.**

DeJesus, People v., 101 A.D.2d 111, 475 N.Y.S.2d 19 (N.Y.A.D. 1 Dept.1984)—§ **607.4, n. 37, 38, 40.**

De Jesus, People v., 399 N.Y.S.2d 196, 369 N.E.2d 752 (N.Y.1977)—§ **614.1, n. 12, 16, 18.**

De Laurent v. Townsend, 243 N.Y. 130, 152 N.E. 699 (N.Y.1926)—§ **601.2, n. 30, 83.**

Delaware v. Fensterer, 474 U.S. 15, 106 S.Ct. 292, 88 L.Ed.2d 15 (1985)—§ **705.2; § 705.2, n. 3.**

Delaware v. Van Arsdall, 475 U.S. 673, 106 S.Ct. 1431, 89 L.Ed.2d 674 (1986)—§ **607.6, n. 32.**

Delehanty, Matter of, 202 Misc. 40, 115 N.Y.S.2d 610 (N.Y.Sup.1952)—§ **509.1, n. 4.**

DeLillo, United States v., 620 F.2d 939 (2nd Cir.1980)—§ **607.4, n. 48.**

De Lillo, United States v., 448 F.Supp. 840 (D.C.N.Y.1978)—§ **501.2, n. 42.**

Dellarocco, People v., 115 A.D.2d 904, 496 N.Y.S.2d 801 (N.Y.A.D. 3 Dept.1985)—§ **608.2, n. 12.**

De Long v. County of Erie, 469 N.Y.S.2d 611, 457 N.E.2d 717 (N.Y.1983)—§ **702.1; § 702.1, n. 6; § 704.1; § 704.1, n. 6.**

DeLong, People v., 206 A.D.2d 914, 615 N.Y.S.2d 168 (N.Y.A.D. 4 Dept.1994)—§ **612.1, n. 4.**

Del Toro Soto, United States v., 676 F.2d 13 (1st Cir.1982)—§ **609.2, n. 14.**

De Luca v. Kameros, 130 A.D.2d 705, 515 N.Y.S.2d 819 (N.Y.A.D. 2 Dept.1987)—§ **702.1, n. 25; § 803(1).1, n. 66.**

DeLuca v. Ricci, 194 A.D.2d 457, 599 N.Y.S.2d 267 (N.Y.A.D. 1 Dept.1993)—§ **801.1, n. 23.**

De Lucia, People v., 282 N.Y.S.2d 526, 229 N.E.2d 211 (N.Y.1967)—§ **606.1, n. 3, 5, 11, 12, 14; § 1107.1, n. 15.**

DeLuna, United States v., 763 F.2d 897 (8th Cir.1985)—§ **611.5, n. 6.**

Del Vermo, People v., 192 N.Y. 470, 85 N.E. 690 (N.Y.1908)—§ **803(1).1; § 803(1).1, n. 25; § 1103.1, n. 1, 10.**

Dembeck, People v., 145 Misc.2d 442, 546 N.Y.S.2d 936 (Suffolk Dist.Ct.1989)—§ **702.1, n. 44; § 901.9, n. 6.**

Demerritt, People v., 113 A.D.2d 898, 493 N.Y.S.2d 626 (N.Y.A.D. 2 Dept.1985)—§ **412.1, n. 11.**

Demery, People v., 60 A.D.2d 606, 400 N.Y.S.2d 135 (N.Y.A.D. 2 Dept.1977)—§ **601.1, n. 19; § 607.6, n. 8.**

Denaro v. Prudential Ins. Co. of America, 139 N.Y.S. 758 (N.Y.A.D. 2 Dept.1913)—§ **502.1, n. 28.**

Dennis, United States v., 843 F.2d 652 (2nd Cir.1988)—§ **103.2, n. 17; § 501.2, n. 8.**

Dennis, United States v., 625 F.2d 782 (8th Cir.1980)—§ **607.8, n. 44, 45.**

Dentes v. Zimmerman, 159 Misc.2d 415, 605 N.Y.S.2d 188 (N.Y.Sup.1993)—§ **614.1, n. 10.**

Department of Public Welfare of City of New York v. Hamilton, 282 A.D. 1025, 126 N.Y.S.2d 240 (N.Y.A.D. 1 Dept. 1953)—§ **1102.1, n. 10.**

Department of Social Services on Behalf of R. Children v. Waleska M., 195 A.D.2d 507, 600 N.Y.S.2d 464 (N.Y.A.D. 2 Dept. 1993)—§ **803(3).1, n. 25.**

Derderian v. Polaroid Corp., 121 F.R.D. 13 (D.Mass.1988)—§ **501.2, n. 49; § 612.2, n. 17.**

Dermatossian v. New York City Transit Authority, 501 N.Y.S.2d 784, 492 N.E.2d 1200 (N.Y.1986)—§ **301.6, n. 1, 2; § 401.1, n. 53; § 408.1, n. 1.**

Derrick v. Wallace, 217 N.Y. 520, 112 N.E. 440 (N.Y.1916)—§ **402.1, n. 68; § 607.5, n. 24, 25, 26; § 609.1, n. 1.**

De Salvo v. Stanley–Mark–Strand Corporation, 281 N.Y. 333, 23 N.E.2d 457 (N.Y. 1939)—§ **405.1; § 405.1, n. 17.**

Deshong v. City of New York, 176 N.Y. 475, 68 N.E. 880 (N.Y.1903)—§ **301.4, n. 6; § 803(4).1, n. 9.**

DeSilva v. Rosenberg, 129 A.D.2d 609, 514 N.Y.S.2d 104 (N.Y.A.D. 2 Dept.1987)—§ **502.1, n. 43.**

De Sisto, United States v., 329 F.2d 929 (2nd Cir.1964)—§ **801(1).3; § 801(1).3, n. 9; § 801(2).2, n. 12.**

Detrich, United States v., 865 F.2d 17 (2nd Cir.1988)—§ **801.1, n. 9.**

Detweiler, Matter of Estate of, 121 Misc.2d 453, 467 N.Y.S.2d 766 (N.Y.Sur.1983)—§ **601.2, n. 82.**

Deutsch, United States v., 987 F.2d 878 (2nd Cir.1993)—§ **509.1, n. 47.**

Deutschmann v. Third Ave. R. Co., 87 A.D. 503, 84 N.Y.S. 887 (N.Y.A.D. 1 Dept. 1903)—§ **514.1, n. 1.**

DeVaul v. Carvigo Inc., 138 A.D.2d 669, 526 N.Y.S.2d 483 (N.Y.A.D. 2 Dept.1988)—§ **201.1, n. 44.**

DeVillio, United States v., 983 F.2d 1185 (2nd Cir.1993)—§ **404.2, n. 21; § 802.3, n. 56; § 804(3).2, n. 18.**

Devin, United States v., 918 F.2d 280 (1st Cir.1990)—§ **601.3, n. 9.**

De Waay v. Dominick, 174 F.2d 204 (2nd Cir.1949)—§ **411.2, n. 5.**

DeWeerth v. Baldinger, 658 F.Supp. 688 (S.D.N.Y.1987)—§ **803(7).2, n. 4.**

TABLE OF CASES

De Yong v. De Yong, 263 A.D. 291, 32 N.Y.S.2d 505 (N.Y.A.D. 1 Dept.1942)—§ **803(5).1, n. 23.**

Dianda, People v., 524 N.Y.S.2d 381, 519 N.E.2d 292 (N.Y.1987)—§ **401.1, n. 30.**

Diaz, People v., 111 Misc.2d 1083, 445 N.Y.S.2d 888 (N.Y.Sup.1981)—§ **1102.1, n. 5.**

Diaz, People v., 433 N.Y.S.2d 751, 413 N.E.2d 1166 (N.Y.1980)—§ **702.1, n. 77.**

Diaz v. United States, 223 U.S. 442, 32 S.Ct. 250, 56 L.Ed. 500 (1912)—§ **807.1, n. 10.**

Diaz–Albertini's Estate, In re, 153 N.Y.S.2d 261 (N.Y.Sur.1956)—§ **601.1, n. 24.**

Dibble v. Dimick, 143 N.Y. 549, 38 N.E. 724 (N.Y.1894)—§ **100.2, n. 4.**

DiBlasio v. Keane, 932 F.2d 1038 (2nd Cir. 1991)—§ **510.2**; § **510.2, n. 5.**

Dickerson, People v., 70 A.D.2d 623, 416 N.Y.S.2d 622 (N.Y.A.D. 2 Dept.1979)—§ **607.8, n. 9.**

Dickman, People v., 397 N.Y.S.2d 754, 366 N.E.2d 843 (N.Y.1977)—§ **609.1**; § **609.1, n. 32.**

DiDomenico, United States v., 985 F.2d 1159 (2nd Cir.1993)—§ **702.2, n. 12**; § **704.2**; § **704.2, n. 12.**

Di Giovanni, United States v., 544 F.2d 642 (2nd Cir.1976)—§ **802.3, n. 14.**

Dill, Commonwealth v., 156 Mass. 226, 30 N.E. 1016 (Mass.1892)—§ **1001.1, n. 13.**

Dillenbeck v. Hess, 539 N.Y.S.2d 707, 536 N.E.2d 1126 (N.Y.1989)—§ **502.1, n. 2, 5, 18, 39, 55.**

Di Loretto, People v., 150 A.D.2d 920, 541 N.Y.S.2d 260 (N.Y.A.D. 3 Dept.1989)—§ **602.1, n. 1**; § **612.1, n. 4, 14.**

DiLuca, People v., 85 A.D.2d 439, 448 N.Y.S.2d 730 (N.Y.A.D. 2 Dept.1982)—§ **1108.1, n. 7.**

DiMaria, United States v., 727 F.2d 265 (2nd Cir.1984)—§ **803(1).2**; § **803(1).2, n. 33, 48.**

DiMichel v. South Buffalo Ry. Co., 590 N.Y.S.2d 1, 604 N.E.2d 63 (N.Y.1992)—§ **501.3, n. 23**; § **1104.1, n. 34.**

Dinan, People v., 15 A.D.2d 786, 224 N.Y.S.2d 624 (N.Y.A.D. 2 Dept.1962)—§ **901.5, n. 4.**

DiNapoli, United States v., 8 F.3d 909 (2nd Cir.1993)—§ **804(1).2**; § **804(1).2, n. 4.**

Dinnan, In re, 661 F.2d 426 (5th Cir. 1981)—§ **512.2, n. 2.**

Diocese of Buffalo, N.Y. v. McCarthy, 91 A.D.2d 213, 91 A.D.2d 1210, 458 N.Y.S.2d 764 (N.Y.A.D. 4 Dept.1983)—§ **611.3, n. 6.**

Dior, United States v., 671 F.2d 351 (9th Cir.1982)—§ **201.2, n. 22.**

DiPaolo v. Somma, 111 A.D.2d 899, 490 N.Y.S.2d 803 (N.Y.A.D. 2 Dept.1985)—§ **407.1, n. 7.**

DiPaolo, United States v., 804 F.2d 225 (2nd Cir.1986)—§ **607.7, n. 24, 25.**

DiPiazza, R., People v., 300 N.Y.S.2d 545, 248 N.E.2d 412 (N.Y.1969)—§ **703.1**; § **703.1, n. 3.**

DiRose v. PK Management Corp., 691 F.2d 628 (2nd Cir.1982)—§ **703.2, n. 1**; § **705.2, n. 6.**

District of Columbia v. Arms (United States Reports Title: District of Columbia v. Armes), 107 U.S. 519, 17 Otto 519, 2 S.Ct. 840, 27 L.Ed. 618 (1883)—§ **405.2, n. 3.**

DiTommaso, United States v., 817 F.2d 201 (2nd Cir.1987)—§ **614.2, n. 6.**

Diversified Industries, Inc. v. Meredith, 572 F.2d 596 (8th Cir.1977)—§ **501.1, n. 64**; § **501.2, n. 34, 50.**

Dixon, People v., 138 A.D.2d 929, 526 N.Y.S.2d 269 (N.Y.A.D. 4 Dept.1988)—§ **803(1).1, n. 59.**

D.K.G. Appaloosas, Inc., United States v., 630 F.Supp. 1540 (E.D.Tex.1986)—§ **802.3, n. 28.**

Dlugash, People v., 395 N.Y.S.2d 419, 363 N.E.2d 1155 (N.Y.1977)—§ **106.1, n. 7.**

Dlugosz v. New York Cent. Mut. Fire Ins. Co., 132 A.D.2d 903, 518 N.Y.S.2d 237 (N.Y.A.D. 3 Dept.1987)—§ **404.1, n. 93.**

Doane, People v., 208 A.D.2d 971, 617 N.Y.S.2d 232 (N.Y.A.D. 3 Dept.1994)—§ **609.1, n. 7.**

Dodge v. Gallatin, 130 N.Y. 117, 29 N.E. 107 (N.Y.1891)—§ **901.8, n. 5.**

Doe, In re, 964 F.2d 1325 (2nd Cir.1992)—§ **502.2**; § **502.2, n. 5.**

Doe, Matter of, 101 Misc.2d 388, 420 N.Y.S.2d 996 (N.Y.Sup.1979)—§ **501.1, n. 71.**

Doe v. Hynes, 104 Misc.2d 398, 428 N.Y.S.2d 810 (N.Y.Sup.1980)—§ **502.1, n. 87.**

Doe v. New York University, 511 F.Supp. 606 (D.C.N.Y.1981)—§ **803(5).2, n. 23.**

Doe, People v., 158 Misc.2d 863, 602 N.Y.S.2d 507 (N.Y.City Crim.Ct.1993)—§ **604.1, n. 6.**

Doe, People v., 463 N.Y.S.2d 405, 450 N.E.2d 211 (N.Y.1983)—§ **509.1, n. 74.**

Doe v. Poe, 189 A.D.2d 132, 595 N.Y.S.2d 503 (N.Y.A.D. 2 Dept.1993)—§ **501.1, n. 15, 68.**

Doe v. United States, 487 U.S. 201, 108 S.Ct. 2341, 101 L.Ed.2d 184 (1988)—§ **509.1, n. 55.**

Doe, United States v., 465 U.S. 605, 104 S.Ct. 1237, 79 L.Ed.2d 552 (1984)—§ **509.1**; § **509.1, n. 62, 64, 70.**

Doe v. United States, 666 F.2d 43 (4th Cir.1981)—§ **412.2, n. 6, 8.**

Doggett, People v., 83 Cal.App.2d 405, 188 P.2d 792 (Cal.App.1948)—§ **1104.1, n. 7.**

Dohring, People v., 59 N.Y. 374 (1874)—§ **605.1, n. 1**: § **606.1, n. 1.**

Dokes, People v., 584 N.Y.S.2d 761, 595 N.E.2d 836 (N.Y.1992)—§ **615.1, n. 8.**

TABLE OF CASES

Dolan, People v., 172 A.D.2d 68, 576 N.Y.S.2d 901 (N.Y.A.D. 3 Dept.1991)—§ **611.3, n. 26.**

Dolan, People v., 186 N.Y. 4, 78 N.E. 569 (N.Y.1906)—§ **1001.1, n. 4.**

Dolan v. United Cas. Co., 259 A.D. 784, 18 N.Y.S.2d 387 (N.Y.A.D. 4 Dept.1940)—§ **801.1, n. 7.**

Dole v. Local 1942, Intern. Broth. of Elec. Workers, AFL–CIO, 870 F.2d 368 (7th Cir.1989)—§ **510.2, n. 10.**

Dolitsky v. Bay Isle Oil Co., Inc., 111 A.D.2d 366, 489 N.Y.S.2d 580 (N.Y.A.D. 2 Dept.1985)—§ **300.3, n. 35.**

Donahue v. Meagley, 220 A.D. 469, 221 N.Y.S. 707 (N.Y.A.D. 4 Dept.1927)—§ **701.1, n. 8.**

Donaldson, People v., 107 A.D.2d 758, 484 N.Y.S.2d 123 (N.Y.A.D. 2 Dept.1985)—§ **702.1, n. 80.**

Donaldson, People v., 36 A.D.2d 37, 319 N.Y.S.2d 172 (N.Y.A.D. 4 Dept.1971)—§ **702.1, n. 39.**

Donaldson, United States v., 978 F.2d 381 (7th Cir.1992)—§ **804.1, n. 35.**

Donohoe v. Consolidated Operating & Production Corp., 736 F.Supp. 845 (N.D.Ill. 1990)—§ **601.3, n. 3.**

Donohue v. Losito, 141 A.D.2d 691, 529 N.Y.S.2d 813 (N.Y.A.D. 2 Dept.1988)—§ **803(3).1, n. 27.**

Donovan v. Crisostomo, 689 F.2d 869 (9th Cir.1982)—§ **804(3).2; § 804(3).2, n. 3.**

Donovan v. Moore–McCormack Lines, 266 A.D. 406, 42 N.Y.S.2d 441 (N.Y.A.D. 1 Dept.1943)—§ **607.5, n. 48.**

Dooley v. Boyle, 140 Misc.2d 177, 531 N.Y.S.2d 161 (N.Y.Sup.1988)—§ **501.1, n. 69.**

Doreen J. v. Thomas John F., 101 A.D.2d 862, 476 N.Y.S.2d 10 (N.Y.A.D. 2 Dept. 1984)—§ **801.1, n. 39.**

Dorthy, People v., 156 N.Y. 237, 50 N.E. 800 (N.Y.1898)—§ **608.2, n. 10.**

Dotson, United States v., 799 F.2d 189 (5th Cir.1986)—§ **608.1, n. 23.**

Dougherty v. Milliken, 163 N.Y. 527, 57 N.E. 757 (N.Y.1900)—§ **702.1, n. 8; § 704.1, n. 9.**

Dougherty, United States v., 895 F.2d 399 (7th Cir.1990)—§ **103.2, n. 19.**

Doukas v. America on Wheels, Levittown, New York, Inc., 154 A.D.2d 426, 545 N.Y.S.2d 928 (N.Y.A.D. 2 Dept.1989)—§ **704.1, n. 5.**

Dowling v. American Hawaii Cruises, Inc., 971 F.2d 423 (9th Cir.1992)—§ **500.2, n. 4.**

Dowling v. Jones, 67 F.2d 537 (2nd Cir. 1933)—§ **901.7, n. 21.**

Dowling v. United States, 493 U.S. 342, 110 S.Ct. 668, 107 L.Ed.2d 708 (1990)—§ **404.1, n. 79; § 404.2; § 404.2, n. 10; § 608.2, n. 48.**

Downey v. Owen, 98 A.D. 411, 90 N.Y.S. 280 (N.Y.A.D. 4 Dept.1904)—§ **501.1, n. 6.**

Downing, United States v., 753 F.2d 1224 (3rd Cir.1985)—§ **702.2, n. 16.**

Downs v. N.Y. Central R.R. Co., 47 N.Y. 83 (1871)—§ **611.2, n. 10, 21.**

Doxtator v. Swarthout, 38 A.D.2d 782, 328 N.Y.S.2d 150 (N.Y.A.D. 4 Dept.1972)—§ **501.3, n. 35, 36; § 612.1, n. 21, 28, 30.**

Doyle v. Hofstader, 257 N.Y. 244, 177 N.E. 489 (N.Y.1931)—§ **509.1, n. 7.**

Doyle v. Ohio, 426 U.S. 610, 96 S.Ct. 2240, 49 L.Ed.2d 91 (1976)—§ **509.1; § 509.1; § 509.1, n. 80, 84; § 607.8, n. 45; § 802.2, n. 31.**

Doyon v. Bascom, 38 A.D.2d 645, 326 N.Y.S.2d 896 (N.Y.A.D. 3 Dept.1971)—§ **300.2, n. 23.**

Drake, In re, 786 F.Supp. 229 (E.D.N.Y. 1992)—§ **804(5).2, n. 21.**

Drake v. Herrman, 261 N.Y. 414, 185 N.E. 685 (N.Y.1933)—§ **513.1, n. 1, 3.**

Drelich, People v., 123 A.D.2d 441, 506 N.Y.S.2d 746 (N.Y.A.D. 2 Dept.1986)—§ **504.1; § 504.1, n. 5.**

Drews, United States v., 877 F.2d 10 (8th Cir.1989)—§ **607.5, n. 53.**

Dring, United States v., 930 F.2d 687 (9th Cir.1991)—§ **607.5, n. 60.**

Drinon v. Wilson, 113 F.2d 654 (2nd Cir. 1940)—§ **1102.2, n. 6.**

Droz, People v., 384 N.Y.S.2d 404, 348 N.E.2d 880 (N.Y.1976)—§ **410.1, n. 3.**

Duchowney, People v., 166 A.D.2d 769, 563 N.Y.S.2d 524 (N.Y.A.D. 3 Dept.1990)—§ **702.1, n. 80.**

Dudley v. County of Saratoga, 145 A.D.2d 689, 535 N.Y.S.2d 231 (N.Y.A.D. 3 Dept. 1988)—§ **405.1, n. 12.**

Dudley, People v., 167 A.D.2d 317, 562 N.Y.S.2d 66 (N.Y.A.D. 1 Dept.1990)—§ **607.7, n. 8.**

Dudley, People v., 301 N.Y.S.2d 9, 248 N.E.2d 860 (N.Y.1969)—§ **503.3; § 503.3, n. 14.**

Dufel v. Green, 622 N.Y.S.2d 900, 647 N.E.2d 105 (N.Y.1995)—§ **704.1; § 704.1, n. 14.**

Duffy v. The People, 26 N.Y. 588 (1863)—§ **801.1; § 801.1, n. 45.**

Duffy, People v., 367 N.Y.S.2d 236, 326 N.E.2d 804 (N.Y.1975)—§ **608.2, n. 6, 10; § 609.1, n. 6.**

Duffy, United States v., 454 F.2d 809 (5th Cir.1972)—§ **1001.1, n. 25.**

Dufresne v. Duemler, 108 A.D.2d 1102, 485 N.Y.S.2d 879 (N.Y.A.D. 3 Dept.1985)—§ **401.1, n. 47.**

Duke, People v., 147 A.D.2d 989, 147 A.D.2d 990, 538 N.Y.S.2d 886 (N.Y.A.D. 1 Dept.1989)—§ **803(1).1, n. 10.**

Dukes v. Rotem, 191 A.D.2d 35, 599 N.Y.S.2d 915 (N.Y.A.D. 1 Dept.1993)—§ **401.1, n. 33.**

TABLE OF CASES

Dukett, People v., 110 A.D.2d 940, 487 N.Y.S.2d 875 (N.Y.A.D. 3 Dept.1985)—§ **608.2, n. 10.**

Dulin v. Maher, 200 A.D.2d 707, 607 N.Y.S.2d 67 (N.Y.A.D. 2 Dept.1994)—§ **703.1, n. 1.**

Dunbar, Estate of, 139 Misc.2d 955, 529 N.Y.S.2d 452 (N.Y.Sur.1988)—§ **601.2, n. 73.**

Dunbar Contracting Co., People v., 215 N.Y. 416, 109 N.E. 554 (N.Y.1915)—§ **901.5;** § **901.5, n. 1, 2;** § **901.6, n. 1.**

Duncan v. Clarke, 308 N.Y. 282, 125 N.E.2d 569 (N.Y.1955)—§ **601.2;** § **601.2, n. 17, 22.**

Duncan, People v., 412 N.Y.S.2d 833, 385 N.E.2d 572 (N.Y.1978)—§ **607.8, n. 28, 29, 34;** § **801(1).2, n. 13.**

Dunloy, United States v., 584 F.2d 6 (2nd Cir.1978)—§ **801.1, n. 42.**

Dunn, People v., 204 A.D.2d 919, 612 N.Y.S.2d 266 (N.Y.A.D. 3 Dept.1994)—§ **103.1, n. 1.**

Duplan Corp. v. Deering Milliken, Inc., 397 F.Supp. 1146 (D.C.S.C.1974)—§ **501.3, n. 43.**

Duplan Corp. v. Moulinage et Retorderie de Chavanoz, 509 F.2d 730 (4th Cir.1974)—§ **501.3, n. 44.**

Dupree, People v., 88 Misc.2d 791, 388 N.Y.S.2d 1000 (N.Y.Sup.1976)—§ **508.1, n. 16.**

Durrani, United States v., 835 F.2d 410 (2nd Cir.1987)—§ **300.4, n. 75;** § **803(5).2, n. 20.**

Durrani, United States v., 659 F.Supp. 1183 (D.Conn.1987)—§ **802.3, n. 26.**

Dutton v. Evans, 400 U.S. 74, 91 S.Ct. 210, 27 L.Ed.2d 213 (1970)—§ **802.2, n. 87;** § **802.3;** § **802.3, n. 48, 68;** § **804(3).2, n. 12.**

Duysburgh, Matter of Will of, 154 Misc.2d 82, 584 N.Y.S.2d 516 (N.Y.Sur.1992)—§ **203.1, n. 10.**

Dyla, People v., 169 A.D.2d 777, 565 N.Y.S.2d 143 (N.Y.A.D. 2 Dept.1991)—§ **1104.1, n. 35.**

E

Earl, People v., 632 N.Y.S.2d 689 (N.Y.A.D. 3 Dept.1995)—§ **607.7, n. 9.**

Easley v. City of New York, 189 A.D.2d 599, 592 N.Y.S.2d 690 (N.Y.A.D. 1 Dept.1993)—§ **705.1, n. 8.**

East Egg Associates v. Diraffaele, 158 Misc.2d 364, 600 N.Y.S.2d 999 (N.Y.City Civ.Ct.1993)—§ **802.1, n. 9.**

Easter, People v., 90 Misc.2d 748, 395 N.Y.S.2d 926 (Albany Co.Ct.1977)—§ **505.1, n. 19.**

East Kentucky Rural Elec. Co-op. Corp. v. Phelps, 275 S.W.2d 592 (Ky.1955)—§ **802.1, n. 1.**

Eastland v. United States Servicemen's Fund, 421 U.S. 491, 95 S.Ct. 1813, 44 L.Ed.2d 324 (1975)—§ **511.2, n. 5.**

East Tennessee, V. & G. Ry. Co. v. Daniel, 91 Ga. 768, 18 S.E. 22 (Ga.1893)—§ **607.3, n. 17.**

Ebramha, People v., 157 Misc.2d 217, 157 Misc.2d 222, 596 N.Y.S.2d 295 (N.Y.City Crim.Ct.1992)—§ **803(4).1, n. 13;** § **803(5).1, n. 39.**

Ecco High Frequency Corp. v. Amtorg Trading Corp., 81 N.Y.S.2d 610 (N.Y.Sup.1948)—§ **201.1, n. 9, 28, 41.**

Eckhaus v. Alfa–Laval, Inc., 764 F.Supp. 34 (S.D.N.Y.1991)—§ **501.2, n. 19.**

Eden Toys, Inc. v. Marshall Field & Co., 675 F.2d 498 (2nd Cir.1982)—§ **201.2, n. 8.**

Ed Guth Realty, Inc. v. Gingold, 358 N.Y.S.2d 367, 315 N.E.2d 441 (N.Y.1974)—§ **803(3).1, n. 13;** § **1001.1, n. 6, 29;** § **1002.1, n. 11;** § **1006.1;** § **1006.1, n. 4.**

Edington v. Mutual Life Insurance Co., 67 N.Y. 185 (1876)—§ **502.1, n. 17, 29.**

Edmonds v. United States, 273 F.2d 108, 106 U.S.App.D.C. 373 (D.C.Cir.1959)—§ **802.3, n. 4.**

Edmonson, People v., 555 N.Y.S.2d 666, 554 N.E.2d 1254 (N.Y.1990)—§ **801(2).1, n. 12, 13.**

Edney, People v., 385 N.Y.S.2d 23, 350 N.E.2d 400 (N.Y.1976)—§ **501.1, n. 54;** § **501.3, n. 29;** § **502.1, n. 81.**

EDP Medical Computer Systems, Inc. v. Sears, Roebuck and Co., 193 A.D.2d 645, 597 N.Y.S.2d 461 (N.Y.A.D. 2 Dept.1993)—§ **509.1, n. 57.**

Edwards, People v., 419 N.Y.S.2d 45, 392 N.E.2d 1229 (N.Y.1979)—§ **803(1).1, n. 34.**

Egan, People v., 78 A.D.2d 34, 434 N.Y.S.2d 55 (N.Y.A.D. 4 Dept.1980)—§ **804(3).1, n. 56.**

Eggers, Matter of Will of, 122 Misc.2d 793, 471 N.Y.S.2d 570 (N.Y.Sur.1984)—§ **901.7, n. 10.**

Ehrlich v. American Moninger Greenhouse Mfg. Corp., 309 N.Y.S.2d 341, 257 N.E.2d 890 (N.Y.1970)—§ **601.2, n. 33.**

Ehrlich v. Howe, 848 F.Supp. 482 (S.D.N.Y.1994)—§ **501.3, n. 41, 55;** § **612.2, n. 18, 19.**

Eichner v. Dillon, 73 A.D.2d 431, 426 N.Y.S.2d 517 (N.Y.A.D. 2 Dept.1980)—§ **300.4, n. 33.**

8.41 Acres of Land, More or Less, Situated in Orange County, State of Tex., United States v., 680 F.2d 388 (5th Cir.1982)—§ **405.2, n. 15.**

Eighth Judicial Dist. Asbestos Litigation, In re, 152 Misc.2d 338, 576 N.Y.S.2d 757 (N.Y.Sup.1991)—§ **803(5).1, n. 10.**

860 Fifth Ave. Corp. v. Tax Commission of City of New York, 200 N.Y.S.2d 817, 167 N.E.2d 455 (N.Y.1960)—§ **405.1, n. 26.**

TABLE OF CASES

Elkaim v. Elkaim, 176 A.D.2d 116, 574 N.Y.S.2d 2 (N.Y.A.D. 1 Dept.1991)—§ 201.1, n. 45; § 803(3).1, n. 6; § 803(4).1, n. 4; § 803(5).1, n. 8.

Ellarson v. Ellarson, 198 A.D. 103, 190 N.Y.S. 6 (N.Y.A.D. 3 Dept.1921)—§ 607.7; § 607.7, n. 2, 3, 4.

Ellenbogen, United States v., 365 F.2d 982 (2nd Cir.1966)—§ 1103.2, n. 3, 5, 7.

Ellis v. International Playtex, Inc., 745 F.2d 292 (4th Cir.1984)—§ 803(6).2, n. 12.

Ellis, People v., 94 A.D.2d 652, 462 N.Y.S.2d 212 (N.Y.A.D. 1 Dept.1983)—§ 611.2, n. 4.

Elmendorf v. Ross, 221 A.D. 376, 222 N.Y.S. 737 (N.Y.A.D. 3 Dept.1927)—§ 608.1, n. 8.

Elsenlord v. Clum, 126 N.Y. 552, 27 N.E. 1024 (N.Y.1891)—§ 804(4).1, n. 6, 20.

Elwell, People v., 428 N.Y.S.2d 655, 406 N.E.2d 471 (N.Y.1980)—§ 510.1, n. 5.

Elwood v. City of New York, 450 F.Supp. 846 (D.C.N.Y.1978)—§ 803(5).2, n. 23.

Ely, People v., 164 A.D.2d 442, 563 N.Y.S.2d 890 (N.Y.A.D. 3 Dept.1990)—§ 804.1, n. 30; § 804(1).1, n. 44.

Ely, People v., 510 N.Y.S.2d 532, 503 N.E.2d 88 (N.Y.1986)—§ 401.1, n. 50; § 404.1; § 404.1, n. 27; § 900.1, n. 3, 15; § 901.5; § 901.5, n. 9; § 1104.1; § 1104.1, n. 11, 20, 23, 36.

Ely, People v., 115 A.D.2d 171, 495 N.Y.S.2d 240 (N.Y.A.D. 3 Dept.1985)—§ 607.7, n. 7.

Emens v. Lehigh Val. R. Co., 223 Fed. 810 (D.C.N.Y.1915)—§ 803(1).2, n. 1.

Emery v. Litchard, 137 Misc. 885, 245 N.Y.S. 209 (N.Y.Sup.1930)—§ 409.1, n. 8.

Endervelt v. Slade, 625 N.Y.S.2d 210 (N.Y.A.D. 1 Dept.1995)—§ 103.1, n. 43.

Endervelt v. Slade, 162 Misc.2d 975, 618 N.Y.S.2d 520 (N.Y.Sup.1994)—§ 601.2, n. 50.

Eng v. Scully, 146 F.R.D. 74 (S.D.N.Y. 1993)—§ 401.2, n. 2, 3; § 404.2, n. 38.

Engebretsen v. Fairchild Aircraft Corp., 21 F.3d 721 (6th Cir.1994)—§ 703.2, n. 11.

Engel v. Lichterman, 95 A.D.2d 536, 467 N.Y.S.2d 642 (N.Y.A.D. 2 Dept.1983)—§ 301.2, n. 3; § 301.5, n. 41.

Engel by Engel v. Lichterman, 479 N.Y.S.2d 188, 468 N.E.2d 26 (N.Y.1984)—§ 301.3, n. 8.

Enrique, People v., 587 N.Y.S.2d 598, 600 N.E.2d 229 (N.Y.1992)—§ 615.1, n. 8.

Environmental Protection Agency v. Mink, 410 U.S. 73, 93 S.Ct. 827, 35 L.Ed.2d 119 (1973)—§ 511.2, n. 15.

Eppendorf v. Brooklyn City & Newtown R.R. Co., 69 N.Y. 195—§ 406.1, n. 24.

Epps, People v., 21 A.D.2d 650, 249 N.Y.S.2d 639 (N.Y.A.D. 1 Dept.1964)—§ 1108.1, n. 5.

E. R. Carpenter Co. v. ABC Carpet Co., Inc., 98 Misc.2d 1091, 415 N.Y.S.2d 351 (N.Y.City Civ.Ct.1979)—§ 501.1, n. 87; § 612.1, n. 27.

Erie County Bd. of Social Welfare on Complaint of McCarter v. Holiday, 14 A.D.2d 832, 220 N.Y.S.2d 679 (N.Y.A.D. 4 Dept. 1961)—§ 201.1, n. 43.

Erie R. Co. v. Tompkins, 304 U.S. 64, 58 S.Ct. 817, 82 L.Ed. 1188, 11 O.O. 246 (1938)—§ 301.8, n. 10.

Erskine Edward Rudolph F., Matter of, 100 A.D.2d 878, 474 N.Y.S.2d 137 (N.Y.A.D. 2 Dept.1984)—§ 301.5, n. 29.

Esdaille, United States v., 769 F.2d 104 (2nd Cir.1985)—§ 1102.2, n. 7.

Esmond v. Thomas Lyons Bar and Grill, 26 A.D.2d 884, 274 N.Y.S.2d 225 (N.Y.A.D. 3 Dept.1966)—§ 301.4, n. 8; § 301.5, n. 29.

Espinosa v. A & S Welding & Boiler Repair, Inc., 120 A.D.2d 435, 502 N.Y.S.2d 451 (N.Y.A.D. 1 Dept.1986)—§ 705.1, n. 9.

Espinoza, United States v., 406 F.2d 733 (2nd Cir.1969)—§ 103.2, n. 16.

Esquilin, People v., 207 A.D.2d 686, 616 N.Y.S.2d 364 (N.Y.A.D. 1 Dept.1994)—§ 1105.1, n. 12.

Esser v. Brophey, 212 Minn. 194, 3 N.W.2d 3 (Minn.1942)—§ 408.1, n. 2.

Estate of (see name of party)

Estes, United States v., 793 F.2d 465 (2nd Cir.1986)—§ 503.5, n. 17; § 801(1).3, n. 18.

Esteves, People v., 152 A.D.2d 406, 549 N.Y.S.2d 30 (N.Y.A.D. 2 Dept.1989)—§ 802.2, n. 77; § 804(5).1, n. 18.

Esther T., Will of, 86 Misc.2d 452, 382 N.Y.S.2d 916 (N.Y.Sur.1976)—§ 804(4).1, n. 9.

Etheridge, People v., 71 A.D.2d 861, 419 N.Y.S.2d 188 (N.Y.A.D. 2 Dept.1979)—§ 801.1, n. 39.

Etheridge, United States v., 424 F.2d 951 (6th Cir.1970)—§ 804(2).2; § 804(2).2, n. 7.

Euge, United States v., 444 U.S. 707, 100 S.Ct. 874, 63 L.Ed.2d 141 (1980)—§ 509.1, n. 31.

Eureka Inv. Corp., N.V. v. Chicago Title Ins. Co., 743 F.2d 932, 240 U.S.App.D.C. 88 (D.C.Cir.1984)—§ 501.2, n. 26.

Eutectic Corp. v. Metco, Inc., 61 F.R.D. 35 (D.C.N.Y.1973)—§ 501.2, n. 10.

Evans, People v., 202 A.D.2d 377, 610 N.Y.S.2d 192 (N.Y.A.D. 1 Dept.1994)—§ 609.1, n. 44.

Evans, People v., 457 N.Y.S.2d 757, 444 N.E.2d 7 (N.Y.1982)—§ 410.1; § 410.1, n. 6.

Evans, United States v., 796 F.2d 264 (9th Cir.1986)—§ 501.2, n. 38.

Evans, United States v., 484 F.2d 1178 (2nd Cir.1973)—§ 602.2, n. 2.

Evans v. Willson, 133 Misc.2d 1079, 509 N.Y.S.2d 296 (N.Y.City Civ.Ct.1986)—§ 609.1, n. 12.

TABLE OF CASES

Ewings, United States v., 936 F.2d 903 (7th Cir.1991)—§ **607.5, n. 50.**

F

F.A.A. v. Landy, 705 F.2d 624 (2nd Cir. 1983)—§ **803(5).2, n. 23.**

Fabric Garment Co., United States v., 366 F.2d 530 (2nd Cir.1966)—§ **803(5).2, n. 44.**

Fagan v. Newark, 78 N.J.Super. 294, 188 A.2d 427 (N.J.Super.A.D.1963)— § **803(3).1, n. 32.**

Fagin v. Fagin, 88 Misc. 304, 151 N.Y.S. 809 (N.Y.Sup.1914)—§ **301.4, n. 17, 20.**

Fagiola v. National Gypsum Co. AC & S., Inc., 906 F.2d 53 (2nd Cir.1990)— § **901.3, n. 21; § 1006.1; § 1006.1, n. 14.**

Fahey v. South Nassau Communities Hospital, 197 Misc. 490, 95 N.Y.S.2d 842 (N.Y.Sup.1950)—§ **606.1, n. 4.**

Fairchild v. Union Ferry Co. of New York & Brooklyn, 121 Misc. 513, 201 N.Y.S. 295 (N.Y.Sup.1923)—§ **803(7).1, n. 9; § 901.8, n. 5.**

Faison, United States v., 679 F.2d 292 (3rd Cir.1982)—§ **804.1, n. 35.**

Falk v. Kalt, 44 Misc.2d 172, 253 N.Y.S.2d 188 (N.Y.Sup.1964)—§ **501.1, n. 87; § 612.1, n. 25.**

Fall Brook Coal Co. v. Hewson, 158 N.Y. 150, 52 N.E. 1095 (N.Y.1899)—§ **607.4, n. 12.**

Falletto, People v., 202 N.Y. 494, 96 N.E. 355 (N.Y.1911)—§ **804(2).1, n. 4, 13.**

Fanelli v. di Lorenzo, 187 A.D.2d 1004, 591 N.Y.S.2d 658 (N.Y.A.D. 4 Dept.1992)— § **402.1; § 402.1, n. 18, 21; § 803(3).1, n. 68.**

Fappiano, People v., 134 Misc.2d 693, 512 N.Y.S.2d 301 (N.Y.Sup.1987)—§ **607.7, n. 17.**

Fardan, People v., 607 N.Y.S.2d 220, 628 N.E.2d 41 (N.Y.1993)—§ **607.3, n. 19; § 609.1; § 609.1, n. 43, 45.**

Farley, United States v., 992 F.2d 1122 (10th Cir.1993)—§ **803(1).2, n. 52.**

Farmers' Loan & Trust Co. v. Siefke, 144 N.Y. 354, 39 N.E. 358 (N.Y.1895)— § **300.2, n. 2.**

Farmers' Loan & Trust Co. v. Wagstaff, 194 A.D. 757, 185 N.Y.S. 812 (N.Y.A.D. 2 Dept.1921)—§ **601.2, n. 76, 79; § 804(4).1, n. 21.**

Farner v. Paccar, Inc., 562 F.2d 518 (8th Cir.1977)—§ **407.2, n. 4.**

Farnham, United States v., 791 F.2d 331 (4th Cir.1986)—§ **615.2, n. 6.**

Farrell, People v., 458 N.Y.S.2d 514, 444 N.E.2d 978 (N.Y.1982)—§ **803(3).1; § 803(3).1, n. 38.**

Farris, Commonwealth v., 251 Pa.Super. 277, 380 A.2d 486 (Pa.Super.1977)— § **801.1; § 801.1, n. 47.**

Farrow v. Allen, 194 A.D.2d 40, 608 N.Y.S.2d 1 (N.Y.A.D. 1 Dept.1993)— § **502.1, n. 27, 40, 59, 61, 62.**

Farrow, People v., 176 A.D.2d 130, 574 N.Y.S.2d 17 (N.Y.A.D. 1 Dept.1991)— § **611.1, n. 10.**

Fatico, United States v., 458 F.Supp. 388 (D.C.N.Y.1978)—§ **300.4; § 300.4, n. 35, 36.**

Fausek v. White, 965 F.2d 126 (6th Cir. 1992)—§ **501.2, n. 37.**

Favala v. Cumberland Engineering Co., a Div. of John Brown Inc., 17 F.3d 987 (7th Cir.1994)—§ **501.2, n. 31.**

Fayerweather v. Ritch, 195 U.S. 276, 25 S.Ct. 58, 49 L.Ed. 193 (1904)—§ **605.2, n. 5.**

F. Children, In re, 199 A.D.2d 81, 604 N.Y.S.2d 956 (N.Y.A.D. 1 Dept.1993)— § **803(3).1, n. 25.**

Feaster v. New York City Transit Authority, 172 A.D.2d 284, 568 N.Y.S.2d 380 (N.Y.A.D. 1 Dept.1991)—§ **405.1, n. 3; § 1106.1, n. 2.**

Feblot v. New York Times Co., 346 N.Y.S.2d 256, 299 N.E.2d 672 (N.Y. 1973)—§ **106.1, n. 8.**

Federal Chandros, Inc. v. Silverite Const. Co., Inc., 167 A.D.2d 315, 562 N.Y.S.2d 64 (N.Y.A.D. 1 Dept.1990)—§ **509.1, n. 11.**

Federal Exp. Corp. v. Pan American World Airways, Inc., 623 F.2d 1297 (8th Cir. 1980)—§ **405.2, n. 14.**

Fediuk, People v., 498 N.Y.S.2d 763, 489 N.E.2d 732 (N.Y.1985)—§ **503.3; § 503.3, n. 17.**

Fein v. Weir, 129 A.D. 299, 114 N.Y.S. 426 (N.Y.A.D. 1 Dept.1908)—§ **103.1, n. 16.**

Feinerman, Matter of, 97 A.D.2d 920, 470 N.Y.S.2d 762 (N.Y.A.D. 3 Dept.1983)— § **301.3, n. 7.**

Feinstein v. Goebel, 144 Misc.2d 462, 544 N.Y.S.2d 968 (N.Y.Sup.1989)—§ **805.1, n. 3.**

Feld, People v., 305 N.Y. 322, 113 N.E.2d 440 (N.Y.1953)—§ **607.5, n. 39; § 1103.1, n. 5; § 1104.1, n. 31.**

Felder, People v., 375 N.Y.S.2d 98, 337 N.E.2d 606 (N.Y.1975)—§ **801.1, n. 39; § 803(1).1, n. 42.**

Felder, People v., 39 A.D.2d 373, 334 N.Y.S.2d 992 (N.Y.A.D. 2 Dept.1972)— § **615.1, n. 1, 5.**

Feldman, People v., 299 N.Y. 153, 85 N.E.2d 913 (N.Y.1949)—§ **104.1, n. 20.**

Feldman, People v., 296 N.Y. 127, 71 N.E.2d 433 (N.Y.1947)—§ **300.4, n. 45.**

Feldsberg v. Nitschke, 427 N.Y.S.2d 751, 404 N.E.2d 1293 (N.Y.1980)—§ **607.3, n. 5; § 611.1, n. 8, 10, 12; § 611.2, n. 6.**

Felice v. Long Island R. Co., 426 F.2d 192 (2nd Cir.1970)—§ **801(1).3, n. 18; § 803(3).2, n. 29; § 805.2, n. 3.**

TABLE OF CASES

Felix, United States v., 503 U.S. 378, 112 S.Ct. 1377, 118 L.Ed.2d 25 (1992)—§ **404.2**; § **404.2, n. 14.**

Felt v. Olson, 435 N.Y.S.2d 708, 416 N.E.2d 1043 (N.Y.1980)—§ **702.1**; § **702.1, n. 38.**

Ferguson v. Commissioner, 921 F.2d 588 (5th Cir.1991)—§ **603.2, n. 1.**

Ferguson, People v., 606 N.Y.S.2d 145, 626 N.E.2d 930 (N.Y.1993)—§ **1102.1, n. 4.**

Fernandez, People v., 35 N.Y. 49 (1866)—§ **701.1, n. 5.**

Fernandez, United States v., 480 F.2d 726 (2nd Cir.1973)—§ **614.2, n. 4.**

Ferrara v. Galluchio, 176 N.Y.S.2d 996, 152 N.E.2d 249 (N.Y.1958)—§ **801.1, n. 6, 31.**

Ferrara v. Poranski, 88 A.D.2d 904, 450 N.Y.S.2d 596 (N.Y.A.D. 2 Dept.1982)—§ **803(3).1, n. 22.**

Ferraro, People v., 293 N.Y. 51, 55 N.E.2d 861 (N.Y.1944)—§ **612.1, n. 4, 5, 12;** § **804(1).1, n. 42.**

Ferrer v. Harris, 449 N.Y.S.2d 162, 434 N.E.2d 231 (N.Y.1982)—§ **406.1;** § **406.1, n. 29.**

Ferris v. Sterling, 214 N.Y. 249, 108 N.E. 406 (N.Y.1915)—§ **411.1, n. 6;** § **607.5, n. 29, 35.**

F.H. Krear & Co. v. Nineteen Named Trustees, 810 F.2d 1250 (2nd Cir.1987)—§ **611.5, n. 21, 22;** § **702.2, n. 7, 13.**

Fiacco v. City of Rensselaer, N.Y., 783 F.2d 319 (2nd Cir.1986)—§ **401.2, n. 2.**

Fiataruolo v. United States, 8 F.3d 930 (2nd Cir.1993)—§ **702.2, n. 12;** § **704.2, n. 8.**

Fibron Products, Inc. v. Hooker Chemical Corp., 26 Misc.2d 779, 206 N.Y.S.2d 659 (N.Y.Sup.1960)—§ **513.1, n. 3.**

Fields, People v., 151 A.D.2d 598, 542 N.Y.S.2d 356 (N.Y.A.D. 2 Dept.1989)—§ **803(2).1, n. 9.**

Fields, People v., 38 A.D.2d 231, 328 N.Y.S.2d 542 (N.Y.A.D. 1 Dept.1972)—§ **503.3;** § **503.3, n. 16.**

Figueroa, People v., 173 A.D.2d 156, 568 N.Y.S.2d 957 (N.Y.A.D. 1 Dept.1991)—§ **502.1, n. 67.**

Figueroa, People v., 153 A.D.2d 576, 544 N.Y.S.2d 618 (N.Y.A.D. 2 Dept.1989)—§ **607.4, n. 17.**

Figueroa, United States v., 618 F.2d 934 (2nd Cir.1980)—§ **404.2;** § **404.2, n. 25.**

Filesi v. United States, 352 F.2d 339 (4th Cir.1965)—§ **804(3).2, n. 7.**

Findlay, In re, 253 N.Y. 1, 170 N.E. 471 (N.Y.1930)—§ **103.1, n. 2;** § **804(4).1, n. 15, 24.**

Finger Lakes Plumbing & Heating, Inc. v. O'Dell, 101 A.D.2d 1008, 476 N.Y.S.2d 670 (N.Y.A.D. 4 Dept.1984)—§ **501.1, n. 72.**

Finkielstain, United States v., 718 F.Supp. 1187 (S.D.N.Y.1989)—§ **612.2, n. 15.**

Finn v. Morgan, 46 A.D.2d 229, 362 N.Y.S.2d 292 (N.Y.A.D. 4 Dept.1974)—§ **501.1, n. 50, 57;** § **611.3, n. 34.**

Fiore, People v., 356 N.Y.S.2d 38, 312 N.E.2d 174 (N.Y.1974)—§ **404.1;** § **404.1, n. 47.**

Fire Ass'n of Philadephia v. Oneida County Macaroni Co, 294 F. 633 (2nd Cir. 1923)—§ **611.5, n. 2.**

First Federal Sav. & Loan Ass'n of Pittsburgh v. Oppenheim, Appel, Dixon & Co., 110 F.R.D. 557 (S.D.N.Y.1986)—§ **501.2, n. 19.**

First Southwest Lloyds Ins. Co. v. MacDowell, 769 S.W.2d 954 (Tex.App.-Texarkana 1989)—§ **703.2, n. 11.**

Fischer v. Citizens Committee, 72 Misc.2d 595, 339 N.Y.S.2d 853 (N.Y.Sup.1973)—§ **511.1, n. 9.**

Fischer v. I.R.S., 621 F.Supp. 835 (N.D.N.Y. 1985)—§ **511.2, n. 15.**

Fish v. Georgia–Pacific Corp., 779 F.2d 836 (2nd Cir.1985)—§ **407.2;** § **407.2, n. 10.**

Fisher v. State, 7 Ark.App. 1, 643 S.W.2d 571 (Ark.App.1982)—§ **1104.1, n. 12.**

Fisher v. United States, 425 U.S. 391, 96 S.Ct. 1569, 48 L.Ed.2d 39 (1976)—§ **501.1, n. 24;** § **501.2, n. 3, 6;** § **509.1, n. 70.**

Fisher, United States v., 518 F.2d 836 (2nd Cir.1975)—§ **503.5, n. 10.**

Fisher, United States v., 455 F.2d 1101 (2nd Cir.1972)—§ **1101.2, n. 5.**

Fishman v. Scheuer, 384 N.Y.S.2d 716, 349 N.E.2d 815 (N.Y.1976)—§ **103.1, n. 50;** § **801(1).2, n. 16.**

Fitzgerald, People v., 156 N.Y. 253, 50 N.E. 846 (N.Y.1898)—§ **509.1, n. 35.**

Fitzgerald, People v., 101 Misc.2d 712, 422 N.Y.S.2d 309 (Westchester Co.Ct. 1979)—§ **503.4;** § **503.4, n. 3.**

Fitzgibbons Boiler Co. v. National City Bank of New York, 287 N.Y. 326, 39 N.E.2d 897 (N.Y.1942)—§ **607.8, n. 4.**

Fitzpatrick, People v., 386 N.Y.S.2d 28, 351 N.E.2d 675 (N.Y.1976)—§ **607.4;** § **607.4, n. 1, 26, 34;** § **607.8, n. 26;** § **801(1).2, n. 10.**

Flah's, Inc. v. Richard Rosette Elec., Inc., 155 A.D.2d 772, 547 N.Y.S.2d 935 (N.Y.A.D. 3 Dept.1989)—§ **1103.1, n. 2, 9.**

Flanigan, People v., 174 N.Y. 356, 66 N.E. 988 (N.Y.1903)—§ **901.4, n. 3;** § **1101.1;** § **1101.1, n. 13, 16.**

Florida, State of v. Axelson, 80 Misc.2d 419, 363 N.Y.S.2d 200 (N.Y.Sup.1974)—§ **502.1, n. 82.**

Fleming v. Ponziani, 299 N.Y.S.2d 134, 247 N.E.2d 114 (N.Y.1969)—§ **300.2, n. 14;** § **301.5;** § **301.5, n. 7, 16, 20, 38.**

Fletcher v. Weir, 455 U.S. 603, 102 S.Ct. 1309, 71 L.Ed.2d 490 (1982)—§ **607.8, n. 45.**

Fleury v. Edwards, 251 N.Y.S.2d 647, 200 N.E.2d 550 (N.Y.1964)—§ **601.2, n. 58;**

TABLE OF CASES

§ 804(1).1; § 804(1).1, n. 4, 7, 28; § 804(5).1; § 804(5).1, n. 2.

Flores, People v., 138 A.D.2d 512, 526 N.Y.S.2d 125 (N.Y.A.D. 2 Dept.1988)—§ **1002.1, n. 10.**

Floyd, United States v., 555 F.2d 45 (2nd Cir.1977)—§ **802.3, n. 76.**

Flushing Nat. Bank v. Transamerica Ins. Co., 135 A.D.2d 486, 521 N.Y.S.2d 727 (N.Y.A.D. 2 Dept.1987)—§ **509.1, n. 8.**

Flynn v. Manhattan and Bronx Surface Transit Operating Authority, 473 N.Y.S.2d 154, 461 N.E.2d 291 (N.Y. 1984)—§ **802.2, n. 52; § 805.1; § 805.1, n. 6.**

Flynn v. Manhattan and Bronx Surface Transit Operating Authority, 94 A.D.2d 617, 462 N.Y.S.2d 17 (N.Y.A.D. 1 Dept. 1983)—§ **803(1).1, n. 38.**

Fogel v. Chestnutt, 668 F.2d 100 (2nd Cir. 1981)—§ **705.2, n. 6.**

Folio Impressions, Inc. v. Byer California, 937 F.2d 759 (2nd Cir.1991)—§ **602.2, n. 4, 7, 8.**

Fondal, People v., 154 A.D.2d 476, 546 N.Y.S.2d 26 (N.Y.A.D. 2 Dept.1989)—§ **1104.1, n. 36, 44.**

Fonfrias, People v., 204 A.D.2d 736, 612 N.Y.S.2d 421 (N.Y.A.D. 2 Dept.1994)—§ **804(3).1, n. 37, 38.**

Fong on, United States ex rel. v. Day, 54 F.2d 990 (2nd Cir.1932)—§ **1102.2, n. 2.**

Fontenot, United States v., 14 F.3d 1364 (9th Cir.1994)—§ **803(1).2, n. 19, 29.**

Food Pageant, Inc. v. Consolidated Edison Co., Inc., 445 N.Y.S.2d 60, 429 N.E.2d 738 (N.Y.1981)—§ **702.1, n. 22.**

Foot v. Bentley, 44 N.Y. 166 (1870)—§ **1001.1, n. 3; § 1002.1, n. 4, 13.**

Forchalle, People v., 88 A.D.2d 645, 450 N.Y.S.2d 220 (N.Y.A.D. 2 Dept.1982)—§ **610.1, n. 3.**

Forcione, People v., 156 A.D.2d 952, 549 N.Y.S.2d 248 (N.Y.A.D. 4 Dept.1989)—§ **704.1, n. 17.**

Ford, People v., 497 N.Y.S.2d 637, 488 N.E.2d 458 (N.Y.1985)—§ **300.4, n. 46, 49.**

Ford v. Snook, 205 A.D. 194, 199 N.Y.S. 630 (N.Y.A.D. 4 Dept.1923)—§ **103.1, n. 2.**

Ford, United States v., 771 F.2d 60 (2nd Cir.1985)—§ **804(3).2, n. 18.**

Forrester, United States v., 60 F.3d 52 (2nd Cir.1995)—§ **701.2, n. 12.**

Forsythe, State v., 243 La. 460, 144 So.2d 536 (La.1962)—§ **801.1, n. 22.**

Fortunato v. Ford Motor Co., 464 F.2d 962 (2nd Cir.1972)—§ **103.2, n. 15; § 405.2; § 405.2, n. 2; § 1105.2, n. 4.**

Foster v. California, 394 U.S. 440, 89 S.Ct. 1127, 22 L.Ed.2d 402 (1969)—§ **801(2).2, n. 4.**

Foster, People v., 490 N.Y.S.2d 726, 480 N.E.2d 340 (N.Y.1985)—§ **300.3, n. 27.**

Foster, People v., 313 N.Y.S.2d 384, 261 N.E.2d 389 (N.Y.1970)—§ **803(3).1; § 803(3).1, n. 33, 37.**

Foster, United States v., 9 F.R.D. 367 (D.C.N.Y.1949)—§ **607.1, n. 4.**

Foster–Holcomb Inv. Co. v. Little Rock Pub. Co., 151 Ark. 449, 236 S.W. 597 (Ark.1922)—§ **1004.1, n. 22.**

Four Corners Helicopters, Inc. v. Turbomeca, S.A., 979 F.2d 1434 (10th Cir.1992)—§ **1105.2, n. 2.**

Fowler, People v., 46 A.D.2d 838, 361 N.Y.S.2d 408 (N.Y.A.D. 3 Dept.1974)—§ **611.3, n. 25.**

Fox v. Reil, 3 Johns 477 (1808)—§ **903.1, n. 1.**

Fox, United States v., 721 F.2d 32 (2nd Cir.1983)—§ **509.1, n. 63, 64.**

Francis v. Franklin, 471 U.S. 307, 105 S.Ct. 1965, 85 L.Ed.2d 344 (1985)—§ **302.1, n. 2, 4, 5, 6, 7, 9; § 302.2, n. 4.**

Franck by Franck v. Minisink Valley School District, 136 A.D.2d 588, 523 N.Y.S.2d 573 (N.Y.A.D. 2 Dept.1988)—§ **702.1, n. 9.**

Frank, United States v., 494 F.2d 145 (2nd Cir.1974)—§ **604.2, n. 4.**

Frankenthal, United States v., 582 F.2d 1102 (7th Cir.1978)—§ **605.2, n. 5; § 607.6, n. 36.**

Franklin Washington Trust Co., Matter of, 1 Misc.2d 697, 148 N.Y.S.2d 731 (N.Y.Sup.1956)—§ **501.1, n. 71.**

Frase v. Henry, 444 F.2d 1228 (10th Cir. 1971)—§ **406.2, n. 14.**

Frederick R.C. v. Helene C., 153 Misc.2d 660, 582 N.Y.S.2d 926 (N.Y.Sup.1992)—§ **502.1, n. 73, 77.**

Freeland, People v., 506 N.Y.S.2d 306, 497 N.E.2d 673 (N.Y.1986)—§ **702.1, n. 44; § 901.9, n. 6.**

Freeland, People v., 369 N.Y.S.2d 649, 330 N.E.2d 611 (N.Y.1975)—§ **601.1, n. 57, 59; § 607.7; § 607.7, n. 3, 14.**

Freeman v. Johnston, 614 N.Y.S.2d 377, 637 N.E.2d 268 (N.Y.1994)—§ **300.2, n. 22.**

Freeman, People v., 217 N.Y.S.2d 5, 176 N.E.2d 39 (N.Y.1961)—§ **801(1).2, n. 11.**

Freeman, United States v., 619 F.2d 1112 (5th Cir.1980)—§ **701.2, n. 10.**

Freeman, United States v., 302 F.2d 347 (2nd Cir.1962)—§ **607.4, n. 45; § 607.5, n. 51.**

Freidin, United States v., 849 F.2d 716 (2nd Cir.1988)—§ **803(3).2; § 803(3).2, n. 10.**

Freitas v. Geddes Sav. and Loan Ass'n, 481 N.Y.S.2d 665, 471 N.E.2d 437 (N.Y. 1984)—§ **300.4, n. 21.**

Frey v. Department of Health and Human Services, 106 F.R.D. 32 (D.C.N.Y. 1985)—§ **802.3, n. 29.**

TABLE OF CASES

Friedel v. Board of Regents of University of New York, 296 N.Y. 347, 73 N.E.2d 545 (N.Y.1947)—§ **611.3, n. 3, 29, 30.**

Friedman, United States v., 854 F.2d 535 (2nd Cir.1988)—§ **615.2, n. 9, 11, 12; § 806.1, n. 19.**

Friedrich v. Martin, 294 N.Y. 588, 63 N.E.2d 586 (N.Y.1945)—§ **601.2; § 601.2, n. 13, 24.**

Friend, Application of, 411 F.Supp. 776 (D.C.N.Y.1975)—§ **501.2, n. 19.**

Frieson, People v., 103 A.D.2d 1009, 478 N.Y.S.2d 213 (N.Y.A.D. 4 Dept.1984)—§ **611.1, n. 12.**

Frost v. McCarger, 29 Barb. (N.Y.) 617 (1859)—§ **607.5, n. 27.**

Fruin-Colnon Corp., Traylor Bros., Inc. and Onyx Const. & Equipment, Inc. v. Niagara Frontier Transp. Authority, 180 A.D.2d 222, 585 N.Y.S.2d 248 (N.Y.A.D. 4 Dept.1992)—§ **802.2, n. 75.**

Frye v. United States, 293 F. 1013 (D.C.Cir. 1923)—§ **702.1; § 702.1, n. 14; § 702.2, n. 14; § 901.9, n. 4.**

Frymire-Brinati v. KPMG Peat Marwick, 2 F.3d 183 (7th Cir.1993)—§ **702.2, n. 33.**

Fuentes, United States v., 563 F.2d 527 (2nd Cir.1977)—§ **900.1, n. 3, 14; § 1104.2; § 1104.2, n. 7.**

Fuhrer, Matter of, 100 Misc.2d 315, 419 N.Y.S.2d 426 (N.Y.Sup.1979)—§ **504.1, n. 8.**

Fulkerson v. Holmes, 117 U.S. 389, 6 S.Ct. 780, 29 L.Ed. 915 (1886)—§ **804(4).2; § 804(4).2, n. 7.**

Fuller, People v., 431 N.Y.S.2d 357, 409 N.E.2d 834 (N.Y.1980)—§ **300.3, n. 13; § 601.1, n. 30; § 607.4, n. 33.**

Fuller, People v., 300 N.Y.S.2d 102, 248 N.E.2d 17 (N.Y.1969)—§ **509.1; § 509.1, n. 26, 28.**

Fullerton v. City of Schenectady, 285 A.D. 545, 138 N.Y.S.2d 916 (N.Y.A.D. 3 Dept. 1955)—§ **300.2, n. 9.**

Furia v. Mellucci, 143 Misc.2d 596, 541 N.Y.S.2d 727 (N.Y.Sup.1989)—§ **411.1, n. 8, 11.**

Furst, United States v., 886 F.2d 558 (3rd Cir.1989)—§ **804(5).2, n. 10.**

Fury Imports, Inc. v. Shakespeare Co., 554 F.2d 1376 (5th Cir.1977)—§ **803(4).2, n. 2.**

Fusco v. General Motors Corp., 11 F.3d 259 (1st Cir.1993)—§ **1105.2, n. 2.**

G

Gaccione v. State, 173 Misc. 367, 18 N.Y.S.2d 161 (N.Y.Ct.Cl.1940)—§ **201.1, n. 44.**

GAF Corp., United States v., 928 F.2d 1253 (2nd Cir.1991)—§ **802.1, n. 13; § 802.3, n. 1, 3.**

Gaglia v. Wells, 112 A.D.2d 138, 490 N.Y.S.2d 829 (N.Y.A.D. 2 Dept.1985)—§ **501.3, n. 14.**

Gaimari, People v., 176 N.Y. 84, 68 N.E. 112 (N.Y.1903)—§ **607.1, n. 3.**

Gaind, United States v., 31 F.3d 73 (2nd Cir.1994)—§ **607.1, n. 4; § 607.5, n. 53.**

Gaines v. United States, 349 F.2d 190, 121 U.S.App.D.C. 213 (D.C.Cir.1965)—§ **612.2, n. 7.**

Galanek v. New York City Transit Authority, 53 A.D.2d 586, 385 N.Y.S.2d 62 (N.Y.A.D. 1 Dept.1976)—§ **803(3).1, n. 35.**

Gall v. Gall, 114 N.Y. 109, 21 N.E. 106 (N.Y.1889)—§ **100.2, n. 6; § 301.4, n. 8.**

Gallagher v. City of New York, 30 A.D.2d 688, 292 N.Y.S.2d 139 (N.Y.A.D. 2 Dept. 1968)—§ **405.1, n. 8.**

Gallo, People v., 234 N.Y.S.2d 193, 186 N.E.2d 399 (N.Y.1962)—§ **106.1, n. 5, 7.**

Gallo v. Supermarkets General Corp., 112 A.D.2d 345, 491 N.Y.S.2d 796 (N.Y.A.D. 2 Dept.1985)—§ **1102.1, n. 14.**

Galuska v. Arbaiza, 106 A.D.2d 543, 482 N.Y.S.2d 846 (N.Y.A.D. 2 Dept.1984)—§ **1104.1, n. 21.**

Garces v. Hip Hosp., Inc., 201 A.D.2d 615, 608 N.Y.S.2d 237 (N.Y.A.D. 2 Dept. 1994)—§ **607.8, n. 18; § 702.1, n. 82.**

Garcia v. City of New York, 23 A.D.2d 734, 258 N.Y.S.2d 213 (N.Y.A.D. 1 Dept. 1965)—§ **1102.1, n. 16.**

Garcia, People v., 196 A.D.2d 433, 601 N.Y.S.2d 482 (N.Y.A.D. 1 Dept.1993)—§ **702.1, n. 9.**

Garcia, United States v., 900 F.2d 571 (2nd Cir.1990)—§ **607.3, n. 23.**

Garcia, United States v., 848 F.2d 1324 (2nd Cir.1988)—§ **105.2, n. 7.**

Garcia-Duarte, United States v., 718 F.2d 42 (2nd Cir.1983)—§ **801.1, n. 25; § 803(3).2, n. 19.**

Gardner, People v., 163 A.D.2d 892, 559 N.Y.S.2d 63 (N.Y.A.D. 4 Dept.1990)—§ **302.1, n. 23.**

Garelli v. Sterling-Alaska Fur & Game Farms, Inc., 25 Misc.2d 1032, 206 N.Y.S.2d 130 (N.Y.Sup.1960)—§ **201.1, n. 44.**

Garneau, People v., 120 A.D.2d 112, 507 N.Y.S.2d 931 (N.Y.A.D. 4 Dept.1986)—§ **803(5).1, n. 6.**

Garner v. Wolfinbarger, 430 F.2d 1093 (5th Cir.1970)—§ **501.2; § 501.2, n. 35.**

Garnsey v. Rhodes, 138 N.Y. 461, 34 N.E. 199 (N.Y.1893)—§ **607.6, n. 7.**

Garraway, People v., 187 A.D.2d 761, 589 N.Y.S.2d 942 (N.Y.A.D. 3 Dept.1992)—§ **1104.1, n. 40.**

Garrett v. Howden, 73 N.M. 307, 387 P.2d 874 (N.M.1963)—§ **803(1).2, n. 4.**

Garris, United States v., 616 F.2d 626 (2nd Cir.1980)—§ **804.1; § 804.1, n. 32.**

TABLE OF CASES

Garsten v. MacMurray, 133 A.D.2d 442, 519 N.Y.S.2d 563 (N.Y.A.D. 2 Dept.1987)—§ **801.1**; § **801.1, n. 33.**

Garthe v. Ruppert, 264 N.Y. 290, 190 N.E. 643 (N.Y.1934)—§ **406.1, n. 41.**

Gault, Application of, 387 U.S. 1, 87 S.Ct. 1428, 18 L.Ed.2d 527 (1967)—§ **509.1**; § **509.1, n. 21.**

Gavigan v. Otis Elevator Co., 117 A.D.2d 941, 499 N.Y.S.2d 253 (N.Y.A.D. 3 Dept. 1986)—§ **501.3, n. 22.**

Gay, People v., 7 N.Y. 378 (1852)—§ **607.5, n. 3.**

Geaney, United States v., 417 F.2d 1116 (2nd Cir.1969)—§ **104.2, n. 9**; § **802.3**; § **802.3, n. 50.**

Gearhart, People v., 148 Misc.2d 249, 560 N.Y.S.2d 247 (Nassau Co.Ct.1990)—§ **502.1, n. 66**; § **505.1, n. 11.**

Geders v. United States, 425 U.S. 80, 96 S.Ct. 1330, 47 L.Ed.2d 592 (1976)—§ **615.1, n. 8**; § **615.2, n. 8.**

Gedrin by Gedrin v. Long Island Jewish-Hillside Medical Center, 119 A.D.2d 799, 501 N.Y.S.2d 426 (N.Y.A.D. 2 Dept. 1986)—§ **402.1, n. 45**; § **608.2, n. 20.**

Geffers v. Canisteo Cent. School Dist. No. 463201, 105 A.D.2d 1062, 482 N.Y.S.2d 635 (N.Y.A.D. 4 Dept.1984)—§ **501.1, n. 87**; § **501.3, n. 35**; § **612.1, n. 28.**

Gelikkaya, People v., 618 N.Y.S.2d 895, 643 N.E.2d 517 (N.Y.1994)—§ **607.8, n. 11.**

Gellman, United States v., 677 F.2d 65 (11th Cir.1982)—§ **609.2, n. 14.**

Gelzer, United States v., 50 F.3d 1133 (2nd Cir.1995)—§ **900.1, n. 10**; § **901.1, n. 15**; § **1101.2, n. 14, 15.**

General Acc. Fire & Life Assur. Corp., Ltd. v. Krieghbaum, 46 A.D.2d 713, 360 N.Y.S.2d 310 (N.Y.A.D. 3 Dept.1974)—§ **704.1, n. 5.**

General Elec. Co., State v., 201 A.D.2d 802, 607 N.Y.S.2d 181 (N.Y.A.D. 3 Dept. 1994)—§ **502.1, n. 9, 27.**

General Foods Corp., United States v., 446 F.Supp. 740 (D.C.N.Y.1978)—§ **406.2, n. 1.**

Genn, People v., 144 Misc.2d 596, 545 N.Y.S.2d 478 (N.Y.Sup.1989)—§ **201.1, n. 8.**

Gentile v. County of Suffolk, 926 F.2d 142 (2nd Cir.1991)—§ **803(5).2**; § **803(5).2, n. 29, 36.**

Gentile v. County of Suffolk, 129 F.R.D. 435 (E.D.N.Y.1990)—§ **803(5).2, n. 31.**

Gentry, United States v., 925 F.2d 186 (7th Cir.1991)—§ **803(4).2, n. 1.**

Geo. C. Christopher & Son, Inc. v. Kansas Paint & Color Co., Inc., 215 Kan. 185, 523 P.2d 709 (Kan.1974)—§ **1108.1, n. 14.**

Geoghegan, People v., 431 N.Y.S.2d 502, 409 N.E.2d 975 (N.Y.1980)—§ **804(3).1**; § **804(3).1, n. 44.**

George v. Celotex Corp., 914 F.2d 26 (2nd Cir.1990)—§ **803(7).2, n. 2, 5**; § **901.8, n. 11.**

George v. State, 134 A.D.2d 847, 521 N.Y.S.2d 593 (N.Y.A.D. 4 Dept.1987)—§ **802.2, n. 35.**

George Backer Management Corp. v. Acme Quilting Co., Inc., 413 N.Y.S.2d 135, 385 N.E.2d 1062 (N.Y.1978)—§ **300.4, n. 17, 25.**

George Foltis, Inc. v. City of New York, 287 N.Y. 108, 38 N.E.2d 455 (N.Y.1941)—§ **300.3, n. 37**; § **301.2, n. 6**; § **301.6**; § **301.6, n. 1, 3, 4.**

Georges v. American Export Lines, Inc., 77 A.D.2d 26, 432 N.Y.S.2d 165 (N.Y.A.D. 1 Dept.1980)—§ **402.1**; § **402.1, n. 14.**

Geraci, People v., 625 N.Y.S.2d 469, 649 N.E.2d 817 (N.Y.1995)—§ **300.4, n. 4, 19**; § **802.2**; § **802.2, n. 15**; § **804(1).1**; § **804(1).1, n. 48**; § **804(5).1**; § **804(5).1, n. 10**; § **807.1**; § **807.1, n. 1.**

Gerdvine, People v., 210 N.Y. 184, 104 N.E. 129 (N.Y.1914)—§ **607.6, n. 8.**

Gerhart, United States v., 538 F.2d 807 (8th Cir.1976)—§ **1002.1, n. 2**; § **1008.1, n. 4, 10.**

Gestetner Holdings, PLC v. Nashua Corp., 784 F.Supp. 78 (S.D.N.Y.1992)—§ **408.2, n. 9.**

Getch, People v., 429 N.Y.S.2d 579, 407 N.E.2d 425 (N.Y.1980)—§ **302.1, n. 25, 27.**

Getty v. Town of Hamlin, 127 N.Y. 636, 27 N.E. 399 (N.Y.1891)—§ **407.1, n. 5.**

Gezzo, People v., 307 N.Y. 385, 121 N.E.2d 380 (N.Y.1954)—§ **501.1, n. 86**; § **612.1, n. 15.**

Ghaloub, United States v., 385 F.2d 567 (2nd Cir.1966)—§ **1005.1, n. 10.**

Gibson v. Casein Mfg. Co., 141 N.Y.S. 887 (N.Y.A.D. 3 Dept.1913)—§ **406.1, n. 34.**

Gibson, People v., 218 N.Y. 70, 112 N.E. 730 (N.Y.1916)—§ **1004.1, n. 17.**

Gibson, United States v., 675 F.2d 825 (6th Cir.1982)—§ **615.2, n. 12.**

Gibson v. Von Glahn Hotel Co., 185 N.Y.S. 154 (N.Y.Sup.1920)—§ **201.1, n. 31.**

Gichner v. Antonio Troiano Tile & Marble Co., 410 F.2d 238, 133 U.S.App.D.C. 250 (D.C.Cir.1969)—§ **804(3).2**; § **804(3).2, n. 1.**

Gifford, People v., 2 A.D.2d 634, 151 N.Y.S.2d 980 (N.Y.A.D. 3 Dept.1956)—§ **615.1, n. 14, 15.**

Gilan, United States v., 967 F.2d 776 (2nd Cir.1992)—§ **404.2**; § **404.2, n. 7.**

Gilberg v. Barbieri, 441 N.Y.S.2d 49, 423 N.E.2d 807 (N.Y.1981)—§ **803(5).1, n. 49.**

Gilbert v. California, 388 U.S. 263, 87 S.Ct. 1951, 18 L.Ed.2d 1178 (1967)—§ **801(2).2, n. 2, 3.**

Gilbert v. Cosco Inc., 989 F.2d 399 (10th Cir.1993)—§ **1105.2, n. 3.**

TABLE OF CASES

Gilbert, United States v., 668 F.2d 94 (2nd Cir.1981)—§ **609.2, n. 21.**

Gilleo v. Elizabeth A. Horton Memorial Hosp., 196 A.D.2d 569, 601 N.Y.S.2d 332 (N.Y.A.D. 2 Dept.1993)—§ **607.6, n. 6.**

Gilliam v. Lee, 32 A.D.2d 1058, 303 N.Y.S.2d 966 (N.Y.A.D. 2 Dept.1969)—§ **408.1;** § **408.1, n. 8.**

Gilliard v. Long Island R. Co., 413 N.Y.S.2d 116, 385 N.E.2d 1044 (N.Y.1978)—§ **405.1, n. 10.**

Giraldo, United States v., 822 F.2d 205 (2nd Cir.1987)—§ **801.1, n. 28.**

Giro, People v., 197 N.Y. 152, 90 N.E. 432 (N.Y.1910)—§ **1001.1, n. 12.**

Gissendanner, People v., 423 N.Y.S.2d 893, 399 N.E.2d 924 (N.Y.1979)—§ **505.1, n. 15;** § **506.1, n. 4.**

Glasser, United States v., 443 F.2d 994 (2nd Cir.1971)—§ **801.1, n. 27.**

Glasser v. United States, 315 U.S. 60, 62 S.Ct. 457, 86 L.Ed. 680 (1942)—§ **802.3, n. 43.**

Gleason, People v., 285 A.D. 278, 136 N.Y.S.2d 220 (N.Y.A.D. 1 Dept.1954)—§ **404.1;** § **404.1, n. 60.**

Glenn, United States v., 667 F.2d 1269 (9th Cir.1982)—§ **609.2, n. 17.**

Glennon, People v., 175 N.Y. 45, 67 N.E. 125 (N.Y.1903)—§ **607.6, n. 14.**

Glines v. Baird's Estate, 16 A.D.2d 743, 227 N.Y.S.2d 71 (N.Y.A.D. 4 Dept.1962)—§ **501.1, n. 72.**

Glusaskas v. John E. Hutchinson, III, M.D., P.C., 148 A.D.2d 203, 544 N.Y.S.2d 323 (N.Y.A.D. 1 Dept.1989)—§ **406.1, n. 21;** § **1104.1, n. 50;** § **1105.1, n. 5.**

Goddard, People v., 153 A.D.2d 758, 545 N.Y.S.2d 42 (N.Y.A.D. 2 Dept.1989)—§ **601.1, n. 59.**

Goetz, People v., 135 Misc.2d 888, 516 N.Y.S.2d 1007 (N.Y.Sup.1987)—§ **804.1, n. 27.**

Goggins, People v., 356 N.Y.S.2d 571, 313 N.E.2d 41 (N.Y.1974)—§ **510.1, n. 2, 5, 9;** § **510.2, n. 3.**

Goings v. United States, 377 F.2d 753 (8th Cir.1967)—§ **612.2, n. 7, 9, 10, 11.**

Goldberg, In re, 91 F.2d 996 (2nd Cir. 1937)—§ **901.3, n. 26.**

Goldberg, Matter of Will of, 153 Misc.2d 560, 582 N.Y.S.2d 617 (N.Y.Sur.1992)—§ **804(1).1, n. 16.**

Goldberg v. National Life Ins. Co. of Vermont, 774 F.2d 559 (2nd Cir.1985)—§ **401.2, n. 4.**

Goldberg, United States v., 401 F.2d 644 (2nd Cir.1968)—§ **1103.2, n. 1, 7.**

Goldberger & Dubin, P.C., United States v., 935 F.2d 501 (2nd Cir.1991)—§ **501.2, n. 3, 12.**

Golden v. Horn & Hardart Co., 244 A.D. 92, 278 N.Y.S. 385 (N.Y.A.D. 1 Dept.1935)—§ **802.2, n. 76.**

Goldfarb, Matter of, 160 Misc.2d 1036, 612 N.Y.S.2d 788 (N.Y.Sup.1994)—§ **502.1, n. 63.**

Goldfeld, People v., 60 A.D.2d 1, 400 N.Y.S.2d 229 (N.Y.A.D. 4 Dept.1977)—§ **612.1, n. 4, 14.**

Goldman v. County of Nassau, 170 A.D.2d 648, 567 N.Y.S.2d 360 (N.Y.A.D. 2 Dept. 1991)—§ **702.1, n. 80.**

Gold–Mark 35 Associates v. State, 210 A.D.2d 377, 620 N.Y.S.2d 110 (N.Y.A.D. 2 Dept.1994)—§ **405.1, n. 36.**

Goldner v. Kemper Ins. Co., 152 A.D.2d 936, 544 N.Y.S.2d 396 (N.Y.A.D. 4 Dept. 1989)—§ **1105.1, n. 3, 13.**

Goldstein v. New York Daily News, 106 A.D.2d 323, 482 N.Y.S.2d 768 (N.Y.A.D. 1 Dept.1984)—§ **501.3, n. 22.**

Gomboy v. Mitchell, 57 A.D.2d 916, 395 N.Y.S.2d 55 (N.Y.A.D. 2 Dept.1977)—§ **701.1, n. 8.**

Gomez v. Great Lakes Steel Div., Nat. Steel Corp., 803 F.2d 250 (6th Cir.1986)—§ **1006.1;** § **1006.1, n. 16.**

Gomez, United States v., 921 F.2d 378 (1st Cir.1990)—§ **103.2, n. 5.**

Gomez–Norena, United States v., 908 F.2d 497 (9th Cir.1990)—§ **103.2, n. 8.**

Gonzalez v. Medina, 69 A.D.2d 14, 417 N.Y.S.2d 953 (N.Y.A.D. 1 Dept.1979)—§ **607.4, n. 18.**

Gonzalez v. New York State Liquor Authority, 331 N.Y.S.2d 6, 282 N.E.2d 101 (N.Y.1972)—§ **103.1, n. 19, 25.**

Gonzalez, People v., 509 N.Y.S.2d 796, 502 N.E.2d 583 (N.Y.1986)—§ **401.1;** § **401.1, n. 25, 28, 36.**

Gonzalez, People v., 100 A.D.2d 852, 474 N.Y.S.2d 97 (N.Y.A.D. 2 Dept.1984)—§ **406.1, n. 14.**

Gonzalez, People v., 64 A.D.2d 534, 406 N.Y.S.2d 488 (N.Y.A.D. 1 Dept.1978)—§ **901.7, n. 7.**

Gonzalez, United States v., 922 F.2d 1044 (2nd Cir.1991)—§ **1101.2, n. 1, 4, 6.**

Gonzalez, United States v., 748 F.2d 74 (2nd Cir.1984)—§ **408.2, n. 15.**

Gonzalez' Estate, In re, 6 Misc.2d 118, 156 N.Y.S.2d 28 (N.Y.Sur.1956)—§ **901.10, n. 1.**

Goodfriend, People v., 106 Misc.2d 989, 436 N.Y.S.2d 826 (N.Y.Sup.1981)—§ **702.1, n. 23.**

Goodman, People v., 511 N.Y.S.2d 565, 503 N.E.2d 996 (N.Y.1986)—§ **404.1;** § **404.1, n. 76.**

Goodman's Will, In re, 2 A.D.2d 558, 157 N.Y.S.2d 109 (N.Y.A.D. 1 Dept.1956)—§ **902.1, n. 9.**

Goodright v. Moss, 2 Cowp. 591, 98 Eng. Rep. 1257 (1777)—§ **601.1, n. 23.**

Goodwin, People v., 179 A.D.2d 1046, 579 N.Y.S.2d 805 (N.Y.A.D. 4 Dept.1992)—§ **412.1, n. 17.**

TABLE OF CASES

Gordillo, People v., 191 A.D.2d 455, 594 N.Y.S.2d 60 (N.Y.A.D. 2 Dept.1993)— § **801(2).1, n. 33.**

Gordon, People v., 202 A.D.2d 166, 608 N.Y.S.2d 192 (N.Y.A.D. 1 Dept.1994)— § **609.1, n. 44;** § **702.1, n. 75.**

Gordon, People v., 40 A.D.2d 835, 337 N.Y.S.2d 331 (N.Y.A.D. 2 Dept.1972)— § **402.1, n. 56.**

Gordon v. State of Idaho, 778 F.2d 1397 (9th Cir.1985)—§ **603.2, n. 1.**

Gordon, United States v., 655 F.2d 478 (2nd Cir.1981)—§ **504.2, n. 2.**

Gordon v. United States, 383 F.2d 936, 127 U.S.App.D.C. 343 (D.C.Cir.1967)— § **609.2, n. 7.**

Gotti, People v., 146 Misc.2d 793, 552 N.Y.S.2d 485 (N.Y.Sup.1990)— § **802.2, n. 105;** § **804(3).1, n. 52.**

Gotti, United States v., 644 F.Supp. 370 (E.D.N.Y.1986)—§ **805.2, n. 8.**

Gotti, United States v., 641 F.Supp. 283 (E.D.N.Y.1986)—§ **803(5).2, n. 14, 49;** § **804(5).2;** § **804(5).2, n. 22.**

Gould, People v., 54 Cal.2d 621, 7 Cal.Rptr. 273, 354 P.2d 865 (Cal.1960)— § **801(2).2, n. 2.**

Gould, United States v., 536 F.2d 216 (8th Cir.1976)—§ **201.2, n. 21.**

Government of Virgin Islands v. Carino, 631 F.2d 226 (3rd Cir.1980)—§ **402.2, n. 5.**

Government of Virgin Islands v. Grant, 775 F.2d 508 (3rd Cir.1985)—§ **607.5, n. 49.**

Government of Virgin Islands v. Jacobs, 634 F.Supp. 933 (D.Virgin Islands 1986)— § **412.2;** § **412.2, n. 5.**

Government of Virgin Islands v. Joseph, 765 F.2d 394 (3rd Cir.1985)— § **803(7).2, n. 9.**

Government of Virgin Islands v. Nicholas, 759 F.2d 1073 (3rd Cir.1985)—§ **606.2, n. 9.**

Government of Virgin Islands v. Petersen, 553 F.2d 324 (3rd Cir.1977)—§ **610.2, n. 1.**

Gower, People v., 397 N.Y.S.2d 368, 366 N.E.2d 69 (N.Y.1977)—§ **803(3).1, n. 39, 59;** § **803(5).1, n. 6.**

Grady v. Corbin, 495 U.S. 508, 110 S.Ct. 2084, 109 L.Ed.2d 548 (1990)—§ **404.2, n. 15.**

Grady, United States v., 544 F.2d 598 (2nd Cir.1976)—§ **803(5).2;** § **803(5).2, n. 8.**

Graf v. Aldrich, 94 A.D.2d 823, 463 N.Y.S.2d 124 (N.Y.A.D. 3 Dept.1983)— § **501.3, n. 17.**

Graham, People v., 57 A.D.2d 478, 394 N.Y.S.2d 982 (N.Y.A.D. 4 Dept.1977)— § **1001.1, n. 6, 34;** § **1002.1, n. 18.**

Graham by Graham v. Murphy, 135 A.D.2d 326, 525 N.Y.S.2d 414 (N.Y.A.D. 3 Dept. 1988)—§ **103.1, n. 7.**

Grainger, People v., 114 A.D.2d 285, 498 N.Y.S.2d 940 (N.Y.A.D. 4 Dept.1986)— § **105.1, n. 5;** § **607.8, n. 10.**

Grand Jury Investigation, In re, 599 F.2d 1224 (3rd Cir.1979)—§ **501.3, n. 41, 43.**

Grand Jury Investigation of Onondaga County, Matter of, 463 N.Y.S.2d 758, 450 N.E.2d 678 (N.Y.1983)—§ **502.1, n. 22, 35, 65, 68.**

Grand Jury Proceeding, Cherney, Matter of, 898 F.2d 565 (7th Cir.1990)—§ **501.2, n. 14.**

Grand Jury Proceedings, In re, 867 F.2d 562 (9th Cir.1989)—§ **502.2, n. 3.**

Grand Jury Proceedings Auclair, In re, 961 F.2d 65 (5th Cir.1992)—§ **501.2, n. 25.**

Grand Jury Proceedings, Detroit, Mich., Aug. 1977., In re, 434 F.Supp. 648 (D.C.Mich.1977)—§ **501.2, n. 40, 43.**

Grand Jury Proceedings (Doe), 452 N.Y.S.2d 361, 437 N.E.2d 1118 (N.Y. 1982)—§ **500.1, n. 1;** § **501.3, n. 29;** § **502.1, n. 37;** § **505.1, n. 1.**

Grand Jury Proceedings Under Seal v. United States, 947 F.2d 1188 (4th Cir. 1991)—§ **501.2, n. 24.**

Grand Jury Subpoena Dtd. January 4, 1984, In re, 750 F.2d 223 (2nd Cir. 1984)—§ **500.2, n. 4.**

Grand Jury Subpoena Duces Tecum Dated Dec. 14, 1984, Y., M.D., P.C. v. Kuriansky, 513 N.Y.S.2d 359, 505 N.E.2d 925 (N.Y.1987)—§ **502.1, n. 68, 71;** § **509.1, n. 74.**

Grand Jury Subpoena Duces Tecum Dated November 16, 1974, Matter of, 406 F.Supp. 381 (D.C.N.Y.1975)—§ **501.2, n. 21, 25, 26.**

Grand Jury Subpoena Duces Tecum Dated Oct. 29, 1992, In re, 1 F.3d 87 (2nd Cir.1993)—§ **509.1, n. 63, 64, 67.**

Grand Jury Subpoena Duces Tecum Dated Sept. 15, 1983, In re, 731 F.2d 1032 (2nd Cir.1984)—§ **501.2, n. 10, 15, 16, 22.**

Grand Jury Subpoena for Attorney Representing Criminal Defendant Reyes-Requena, In re, 926 F.2d 1423 (5th Cir. 1991)—§ **501.2, n. 14.**

Grand Jury Subpoenas Dated Oct. 22, 1991, and Nov. 1, 1991, Matter of, 959 F.2d 1158 (2nd Cir.1992)—§ **501.3, n. 37, 40;** § **509.1, n. 60.**

Grand Jury Subpoenas Duces Tecum, In re, 798 F.2d 32 (2nd Cir.1986)—§ **501.2, n. 39.**

Grand Jury Subpoenas Issued to Thirteen Corporations, In re, 775 F.2d 43 (2nd Cir.1985)—§ **509.1;** § **509.1, n. 61.**

Grand Jury Subpoena United States, In re, 755 F.2d 1022 (2nd Cir.1985)—§ **503.5, n. 14.**

Grandmont, United States v., 680 F.2d 867 (1st Cir.1982)—§ **609.2, n. 14, 17.**

Grant, People v., 210 A.D.2d 166, 620 N.Y.S.2d 358 (N.Y.A.D. 1 Dept.1994)— § **100.2, n. 8;** § **608.2, n. 16.**

Grant, United States v., 967 F.2d 81 (2nd Cir.1992)—§ **900.1, n. 10;** § **1101.2, n. 13, 14, 16.**

TABLE OF CASES

Grattan v. Metropolitan Life Insurance Co., 92 N.Y. 274 (1883)—§ **106.1;** § **106.1, n. 2, 3, 6, 7.**

Grattan v. People, 491 N.Y.S.2d 125, 480 N.E.2d 714 (N.Y.1985)—§ **505.1, n. 15.**

Gratton v. Dido Realty Co., Inc., 89 Misc.2d 401, 391 N.Y.S.2d 954 (N.Y.Sup.1977)—§ **300.2, n. 19.**

Gravel Products Division of Buffalo Crushed Stone Corp. v. Sunnydale Acres, Inc., 10 Misc.2d 323, 171 N.Y.S.2d 519 (N.Y.Sup.1958)—§ **803(4).1, n. 1.**

Gravely, United States v., 840 F.2d 1156 (4th Cir.1988)—§ **607.8, n. 44, 45.**

Gray v. Brooklyn Heights R. Co., 175 N.Y. 448, 67 N.E. 899 (N.Y.1903)—§ **611.2, n. 5.**

Gray v. Busch Entertainment Corp., 886 F.2d 14 (2nd Cir.1989)—§ **105.2, n. 2, 4.**

Gray v. Kaufman Dairy & Ice-Cream Co., 162 N.Y. 388, 56 N.E. 903 (N.Y.1900)—§ **802.2, n. 35.**

Gray v. Metropolitan St. Ry. Co., 165 N.Y. 457, 59 N.E. 262 (N.Y.1901)—§ **607.5, n. 18.**

Gray, People v., 622 N.Y.S.2d 223, 646 N.E.2d 444 (N.Y.1995)—§ **609.1, n. 6.**

Gray, People v., 41 A.D.2d 125, 341 N.Y.S.2d 485 (N.Y.A.D. 3 Dept.1973)—§ **609.1, n. 13.**

Gray v. State, 181 Md. 439, 30 A.2d 744 (Md.1943)—§ **1001.1, n. 12.**

Grcic v. City of New York, 139 A.D.2d 621, 527 N.Y.S.2d 263 (N.Y.A.D. 2 Dept. 1988)—§ **611.3, n. 17.**

Green, People v., 576 N.Y.S.2d 75, 581 N.E.2d 1330 (N.Y.1991)—§ **804(1).1, n. 39.**

Green, People v., 121 A.D.2d 739, 504 N.Y.S.2d 460 (N.Y.A.D. 2 Dept.1986)—§ **1102.1, n. 3, 4.**

Green, People v., 430 N.Y.S.2d 267, 408 N.E.2d 675 (N.Y.1980)—§ **302.1, n. 27.**

Green, United States v., 561 F.2d 423 (2nd Cir.1977)—§ **401.2;** § **401.2, n. 13.**

Greenberg v. Manlon Realty, Inc., 43 A.D.2d 968, 352 N.Y.S.2d 494 (N.Y.A.D. 2 Dept.1974)—§ **803(5).1, n. 18.**

Greene v. New England Mut. Life Ins. Co., 108 Misc.2d 540, 437 N.Y.S.2d 844 (N.Y.Sup.1981)—§ **502.1, n. 38, 42.**

Greene, People v., 153 A.D.2d 439, 552 N.Y.S.2d 640 (N.Y.A.D. 2 Dept.1990)—§ **702.1, n. 80.**

Greener v. General Electric Co., 209 N.Y. 135, 102 N.E. 527 (N.Y.1913)—§ **803(1).1;** § **803(1).1, n. 26.**

Greenhagen, People v., 78 A.D.2d 964, 433 N.Y.S.2d 683 (N.Y.A.D. 4 Dept.1980)—§ **611.2, n. 17.**

Greenwood, United States v., 796 F.2d 49 (4th Cir.1986)—§ **607.6, n. 34, 35.**

Greer, People v., 397 N.Y.S.2d 613, 366 N.E.2d 273 (N.Y.1977)—§ **609.1, n. 7.**

Greer, United States v., 643 F.2d 280 (5th Cir.1981)—§ **608.1, n. 18.**

Gregg, People v., 203 A.D.2d 188, 611 N.Y.S.2d 151 (N.Y.A.D. 1 Dept.1994)—§ **1105.1, n. 11.**

Gregory M., Matter of, 184 A.D.2d 252, 585 N.Y.S.2d 193 (N.Y.A.D. 1 Dept.1992)—§ **803(3).1, n. 51.**

Grey v. Grey, 47 N.Y. 552 (1872)—§ **601.2, n. 50.**

Grey Bear, United States v., 883 F.2d 1382 (8th Cir.1989)—§ **611.5, n. 13.**

Grieco v. Cunningham, 128 A.D.2d 502, 512 N.Y.S.2d 432 (N.Y.A.D. 2 Dept.1987)—§ **501.3, n. 35.**

Grier, People v., 162 A.D.2d 416, 557 N.Y.S.2d 68 (N.Y.A.D. 1 Dept.1990)—§ **608.2, n. 10.**

Griffin, People v., 138 Misc.2d 279, 524 N.Y.S.2d 153 (N.Y.Sup.1988)—§ **607.7, n. 9, 10, 11.**

Griffin, People v., 323 N.Y.S.2d 964, 272 N.E.2d 477 (N.Y.1971)—§ **801(2).1, n. 15.**

Griffin v. California, 380 U.S. 609, 5 Ohio Misc. 127, 85 S.Ct. 1229, 14 L.Ed.2d 106 (1965)—§ **509.1, n. 34;** § **514.2, n. 2.**

Griffin Mfg. Co. v. Gold Dust Corp., 245 A.D. 385, 282 N.Y.S. 931 (N.Y.A.D. 2 Dept.1935)—§ **513.1, n. 1.**

Griffiths v. Metropolitan St. Ry. Co., 171 N.Y. 106, 63 N.E. 808 (N.Y.1902)—§ **502.1, n. 24.**

Griggs v. Children's Hosp. of Buffalo, Inc., 193 A.D.2d 1060, 599 N.Y.S.2d 197 (N.Y.A.D. 4 Dept.1993)—§ **803(1).1, n. 20.**

Griswold v. Hart, 205 N.Y. 384, 98 N.E. 918 (N.Y.1912)—§ **601.2;** § **601.2, n. 48.**

Grobin v. Grobin, 184 Misc. 996, 55 N.Y.S.2d 32 (N.Y.Sup.1945)—§ **503.2, n. 6.**

Groff, People v., 524 N.Y.S.2d 13, 518 N.E.2d 908 (N.Y.1987)—§ **601.1, n. 43.**

Grogan v. Dooley, 211 N.Y. 30, 105 N.E. 135 (N.Y.1914)—§ **409.1;** § **409.1, n. 1.**

Grooms, United States v., 978 F.2d 425 (8th Cir.1992)—§ **607.8, n. 47.**

Gross v. Greer, 773 F.2d 116 (7th Cir. 1985)—§ **803(1).2, n. 14.**

Gross v. Sormani, 50 A.D. 531, 64 N.Y.S. 300 (N.Y.A.D. 2 Dept.1900)—§ **901.2, n. 1.**

Gross v. United States Fire Ins. Co., 71 Misc.2d 815, 337 N.Y.S.2d 221 (N.Y.Sup. 1972)—§ **509.1, n. 11.**

Grosso v. United States, 390 U.S. 62, 88 S.Ct. 709, 19 L.Ed.2d 906 (1968)—§ **509.1, n. 73.**

Grow Tunneling Corp. v. Consolidated Edison Co. of New York, Inc., 195 A.D.2d 325, 600 N.Y.S.2d 30 (N.Y.A.D. 1 Dept. 1993)—§ **612.1, n. 7.**

Grun v. Sportsman, Inc., 58 A.D.2d 802, 396 N.Y.S.2d 250 (N.Y.A.D. 2 Dept. 1977)—§ **401.1, n. 33.**

TABLE OF CASES

Grunewald v. United States, 353 U.S. 391, 77 S.Ct. 963, 1 L.Ed.2d 931 (1957)—§ **802.2, n. 104;** § **802.3, n. 64.**

Grutz, People v., 212 N.Y. 72, 105 N.E. 843 (N.Y.1914)—§ **404.1;** § **404.1, n. 49, 50;** § **704.1, n. 2.**

Guarino v. Woodworth, 204 A.D.2d 391, 611 N.Y.S.2d 638 (N.Y.A.D. 2 Dept.1994)—§ **802.2, n. 27.**

Guarisco v. E. J. Milk Farms, 90 Misc.2d 81, 393 N.Y.S.2d 883 (N.Y.City Civ.Ct. 1977)—§ **609.1, n. 11.**

Guccione v. Hustler Magazine, Inc., 632 F.Supp. 313 (S.D.N.Y.1986)—§ **802.3, n. 21.**

Guidice, People v., 612 N.Y.S.2d 350, 634 N.E.2d 951 (N.Y.1994)—§ **803(3).1;** § **803(3).1, n. 48.**

Guinan, United States v., 836 F.2d 350 (7th Cir.1988)—§ **804(5).2, n. 15.**

Gulf Oil Corp., United States v., 760 F.2d 292 (Temp.Emer1985)—§ **501.3, n. 53.**

Gullo v. Califano, 609 F.2d 649 (2nd Cir. 1979)—§ **803(3).2, n. 31.**

Gurney, Becker & Bourne, Inc. v. Benderson Development Co., Inc., 420 N.Y.S.2d 212, 394 N.E.2d 282 (N.Y.1979)—§ **802.2, n. 34.**

Gurski v. Sapowitch, 276 A.D. 821, 93 N.Y.S.2d 159 (N.Y.A.D.1949)—§ **601.2, n. 54.**

Gutierrez v. City of New York, 205 A.D.2d 425, 613 N.Y.S.2d 627 (N.Y.A.D. 1 Dept. 1994)—§ **611.3, n. 30.**

Gutierrez v. Iulo, 156 Misc.2d 79, 591 N.Y.S.2d 711 (N.Y.Sup.1992)—§ **103.1, n. 46;** § **702.1, n. 80.**

Gutierrez, United States v., 576 F.2d 269 (10th Cir.1978)—§ **901.4, n. 15.**

Gutman, United States v., 725 F.2d 417 (7th Cir.1984)—§ **601.3, n. 13;** § **607.7, n. 23.**

H

H., In re, 41 A.D.2d 817, 342 N.Y.S.2d 696 (N.Y.A.D. 1 Dept.1973)—§ **601.1, n. 37.**

Hadden, People v., 95 A.D.2d 725, 464 N.Y.S.2d 134 (N.Y.A.D. 1 Dept.1983)—§ **611.3, n. 18, 25.**

Haddock, United States v., 956 F.2d 1534 (10th Cir.1992)—§ **1003.1, n. 5.**

Hadley v. Clabeau, 140 Misc.2d 994, 532 N.Y.S.2d 221 (N.Y.Sup.1988)—§ **601.2, n. 4, 47.**

Hagedorny, People v., 272 A.D. 830, 70 N.Y.S.2d 511 (N.Y.A.D. 2 Dept.1947)—§ **801(2).1, n. 14.**

Hageman v. Jacobson, 202 A.D.2d 160, 608 N.Y.S.2d 180 (N.Y.A.D. 1 Dept.1994)—§ **607.8, n. 9.**

Haley v. Hockey, 199 Misc. 512, 103 N.Y.S.2d 717 (N.Y.Sup.1950)—§ **1102.1, n. 27;** § **1103.1, n. 6;** § **1104.1, n. 47.**

Hall v. Allemannia Fire Ins. Co. of Pittsburgh, 175 A.D. 289, 161 N.Y.S. 1091 (N.Y.A.D. 4 Dept.1916)—§ **611.3, n. 17.**

Hall v. American Bakeries Co., 873 F.2d 1133 (8th Cir.1989)—§ **612.2, n. 9.**

Hall v. General Motors Corp., 647 F.2d 175, 207 U.S.App.D.C. 350 (D.C.Cir.1980)—§ **1105.2, n. 4.**

Hall, United States v., 739 F.2d 96 (2nd Cir.1984)—§ **801(1).3, n. 18.**

Hallenbeck v. Vogt, 9 A.D.2d 836, 192 N.Y.S.2d 945 (N.Y.A.D. 3 Dept.1959)—§ **602.1, n. 5.**

Hallock v. State, 485 N.Y.S.2d 510, 474 N.E.2d 1178 (N.Y.1984)—§ **802.2, n. 72.**

Halloran v. Virginia Chemicals Inc., 393 N.Y.S.2d 341, 361 N.E.2d 991 (N.Y. 1977)—§ **406.1;** § **406.1, n. 5, 15;** § **607.3, n. 19, 20;** § **611.3, n. 34.**

Hamar v. Isachsen, 58 A.D.2d 988, 397 N.Y.S.2d 485 (N.Y.A.D. 4 Dept.1977)—§ **601.2, n. 19.**

Hambrick, People v., 122 A.D.2d 163, 504 N.Y.S.2d 540 (N.Y.A.D. 2 Dept.1986)—§ **610.1, n. 7.**

Hambsch v. New York City Transit Authority, 480 N.Y.S.2d 195, 469 N.E.2d 516 (N.Y.1984)—§ **703.1, n. 11, 13;** § **1004.1;** § **1004.1, n. 8.**

Hamburg, In re Estate of, 151 Misc.2d 1034, 574 N.Y.S.2d 914 (N.Y.Sur. 1991)—§ **601.2, n. 4, 30.**

Hamby v. Bonventre, 36 A.D.2d 648, 318 N.Y.S.2d 178 (N.Y.A.D. 3 Dept.1971)—§ **608.2, n. 10.**

Hamel, People v., 96 A.D.2d 644, 466 N.Y.S.2d 748 (N.Y.A.D. 3 Dept.1983)—§ **1107.1, n. 4, 6.**

Hamilton, People v., 526 N.Y.S.2d 421, 521 N.E.2d 428 (N.Y.1988)—§ **807.1, n. 7.**

Hammond v. Varian, 54 N.Y. 398 (1873)—§ **901.2, n. 2, 5.**

Hampton, People v., 38 A.D.2d 772, 327 N.Y.S.2d 961 (N.Y.A.D. 3 Dept.1972)—§ **803(3).1, n. 45.**

Hancock v. Dodson, 958 F.2d 1367 (6th Cir.1992)—§ **502.2, n. 1.**

Handicapped Child, Matter of, 118 Misc.2d 137, 460 N.Y.S.2d 256 (N.Y.Sup.1983)—§ **502.1, n. 74.**

Haney v. Mizell Memorial Hosp., 744 F.2d 1467 (11th Cir.1984)—§ **611.5, n. 14.**

Hanf, People v., 159 Misc.2d 748, 611 N.Y.S.2d 85 (Monroe Co.Ct.1994)—§ **502.1, n. 12, 29.**

Hanley v. Donoghue, 116 U.S. 1, 6 S.Ct. 242, 29 L.Ed. 535 (1885)—§ **203.2, n. 2.**

Hanlon v. Ehrich, 178 N.Y. 474, 71 N.E. 12 (N.Y.1904)—§ **607.8, n. 7, 31, 32.**

Hannah v. Baylon Holding Corp., 320 N.Y.S.2d 35, 268 N.E.2d 775 (N.Y. 1971)—§ **803(7).1, n. 16.**

Hanrahan v. New York Edison Co., 238 N.Y. 194, 144 N.E. 499 (N.Y.1924)—§ **607.4, n. 8, 15.**

TABLE OF CASES

Haran by Haran v. Union Carbide Corp., 506 N.Y.S.2d 311, 497 N.E.2d 678 (N.Y. 1986)—§ **407.1**; § **407.1, n. 19, 28.**

Harding v. Conlon, 159 A.D. 441, 144 N.Y.S. 663 (N.Y.A.D. 1 Dept.1913)—§ **607.8, n. 36.**

Harding, People v., 371 N.Y.S.2d 493, 332 N.E.2d 354 (N.Y.1975)—§ **804(1).1, n. 31, 33, 40.**

Harding v. State, 5 Md.App. 230, 246 A.2d 302 (Md.App.1968)—§ **601.1, n. 61.**

Hardy v. Johns–Manville Sales Corp., 681 F.2d 334 (5th Cir.1982)—§ **201.2, n. 15.**

Harkavy's Estate, In re, 184 Misc. 742, 56 N.Y.S.2d 700 (N.Y.Sur.1945)—§ **601.2, n. 32.**

Harper & Row Publishers, Inc. v. Decker, 423 F.2d 487 (7th Cir.1970)—§ **501.1, n. 64.**

Harrell, People v., 187 A.D.2d 453, 589 N.Y.S.2d 531 (N.Y.A.D. 2 Dept.1992)—§ **1104.1, n. 38, 44.**

Harrell, People v., 87 A.D.2d 21, 450 N.Y.S.2d 501 (N.Y.A.D. 2 Dept.1982)—§ **503.4, n. 4.**

Harrigan v. New England Mut. Life Ins. Co., 693 F.Supp. 1531 (S.D.N.Y.1988)—§ **803(1).2, n. 25.**

Harrington v. Schiller, 231 N.Y. 278, 132 N.E. 89 (N.Y.1921)—§ **601.2, n. 28.**

Harrington v. Sharff, 305 F.2d 333 (2nd Cir.1962)—§ **802.3, n. 13.**

Harris v. New York, 401 U.S. 222, 91 S.Ct. 643, 28 L.Ed.2d 1 (1971)—§ **104.2**; § **104.2, n. 14**; § **607.8, n. 10.**

Harris, People v., 199 A.D.2d 636, 604 N.Y.S.2d 1005 (N.Y.A.D. 3 Dept.1993)—§ **1104.1, n. 26, 28.**

Harris, People v., 151 A.D.2d 981, 542 N.Y.S.2d 71 (N.Y.A.D. 4 Dept.1989)—§ **412.1, n. 21**; § **608.2, n. 10, 11.**

Harris, People v., 132 A.D.2d 940, 518 N.Y.S.2d 269 (N.Y.A.D. 4 Dept.1987)—§ **412.1**; § **412.1, n. 20, 21.**

Harris, People v., 456 N.Y.S.2d 694, 442 N.E.2d 1205 (N.Y.1982)—§ **501.1**; § **501.1, n. 44, 46, 78**; § **611.1, n. 4, 7, 9.**

Harris, People v., 84 A.D.2d 63, 445 N.Y.S.2d 520 (N.Y.A.D. 2 Dept.1981)—§ **1108.1, n. 19.**

Harris, People v., 303 N.Y.S.2d 71, 250 N.E.2d 349 (N.Y.1969)—§ **509.1, n. 75.**

Harris, People v., 209 N.Y. 70, 102 N.E. 546 (N.Y.1913)—§ **801.1**; § **801.1, n. 36**; § **803(1).1, n. 39.**

Harris, United States v., 995 F.2d 532 (4th Cir.1993)—§ **702.2, n. 11.**

Harris, United States v., 733 F.2d 994 (2nd Cir.1984)—§ **103.2, n. 27**; § **801.1, n. 43**; § **803(1).2, n. 24.**

Harris v. United States, 371 F.2d 365 (9th Cir.1967)—§ **510.1, n. 4.**

Harris v. Village of East Hills, 50 A.D.2d 921, 377 N.Y.S.2d 619 (N.Y.A.D. 2 Dept. 1975)—§ **105.1, n. 3, 6.**

Harris v. Wilson, 7 Wend. 57 (1832)—§ **104.1, n. 17.**

Harrison, Matter of Estate of, 184 A.D.2d 42, 590 N.Y.S.2d 318 (N.Y.A.D. 3 Dept. 1992)—§ **301.7, n. 4.**

Harrison, People v., 628 N.Y.S.2d 939, 652 N.E.2d 638 (N.Y.1995)—§ **301.4, n. 6.**

Harrison v. United States, 392 U.S. 219, 88 S.Ct. 2008, 20 L.Ed.2d 1047 (1968)—§ **802.1, n. 13.**

Hart v. Community School Bd. of Brooklyn, New York School Dist. No. 21, 383 F.Supp. 699 (D.C.N.Y.1974)—§ **706.2, n. 9.**

Hart v. Lancashire & Yorkshire Railway, 21 Law Times (U.S.) 261—§ **407.2, n. 2.**

Hartford v. Palmer, 16 Johns. (N.Y.) 142 (Sup.Ct.1819)—§ **601.1, n. 56.**

Hartford v. Regal Shoe Store No. 162, Inc., 20 Misc.2d 1055, 192 N.Y.S.2d 167 (N.Y.Mun.Ct.1959)—§ **201.1, n. 39.**

Hartford Fire Ins. Co. v. M/V Savannah, 756 F.Supp. 825 (S.D.N.Y.1991)—§ **802.3, n. 21.**

Hartley v. Szadkowski, 32 A.D.2d 550, 300 N.Y.S.2d 82 (N.Y.A.D. 2 Dept.1969)—§ **406.1**; § **406.1, n. 4, 25**; § **406.2, n. 13**; § **701.1, n. 10.**

Hartshorn v. Metropolitan Life Ins. Co., 55 A.D. 471, 67 N.Y.S. 13 (N.Y.A.D. 4 Dept. 1900)—§ **701.1, n. 8.**

Hartzell v. United States, 72 F.2d 569 (8th Cir.1934)—§ **1002.1, n. 14.**

Harvey v. Mazal American Partners, 581 N.Y.S.2d 639, 590 N.E.2d 224 (N.Y. 1992)—§ **1102.1, n. 23, 25.**

Harvey, United States v., 588 F.2d 1201 (8th Cir.1978)—§ **609.2, n. 13.**

Harvey, United States v., 547 F.2d 720 (2nd Cir.1976)—§ **607.6, n. 38.**

Harwood, United States v., 998 F.2d 91 (2nd Cir.1993)—§ **801.1, n. 25**; § **803(1).2, n. 28**; § **804(3).2, n. 20.**

Hastings v. Chrysler Corp., 273 A.D. 292, 77 N.Y.S.2d 524 (N.Y.A.D. 1 Dept. 1948)—§ **702.1, n. 86.**

Hatch v. Elkins, 65 N.Y. 489 (1875)—§ **801(1).2, n. 5**; § **802.2, n. 42.**

Hauver, People v., 129 A.D.2d 889, 514 N.Y.S.2d 814 (N.Y.A.D. 3 Dept.1987)—§ **412.1**; § **412.1, n. 12.**

Havens, United States v., 446 U.S. 620, 100 S.Ct. 1912, 64 L.Ed.2d 559 (1980)—§ **607.3**; § **607.3, n. 13.**

Hawkins, People v., 109 N.Y. 408, 17 N.E. 371 (N.Y.1888)—§ **803(1).1, n. 72.**

Hawkins v. United States, 358 U.S. 74, 79 S.Ct. 136, 3 L.Ed.2d 125 (1958)—§ **503.5**; § **503.5, n. 4.**

Hawley, United States v., 554 F.2d 50 (2nd Cir.1977)—§ **609.2, n. 2, 7.**

Hawthorne v. Eckerson Co., 77 F.2d 844 (2nd Cir.1935)—§ **408.2, n. 6.**

Hayden's Estate, In re, 176 Misc. 1078, 29 N.Y.S.2d 852 (N.Y.Sur.1941)—§ **804(4).1, n. 22.**

TABLE OF CASES

Hayes v. Claessens, 234 N.Y. 230, 137 N.E. 313 (N.Y.1922)—§ **802.2, n. 36.**

Hayes v. Henault, 131 A.D.2d 930, 516 N.Y.S.2d 798 (N.Y.A.D. 3 Dept.1987)— § **612.1, n. 15.**

Hayes v. State, 50 A.D.2d 693, 376 N.Y.S.2d 647 (N.Y.A.D. 3 Dept.1975)—§ **803(3).1, n. 27; § 805.1, n. 2.**

Hayes, United States v., 553 F.2d 824 (2nd Cir.1977)—§ **609.2, n. 4, 7, 11, 12, 15, 16.**

Haymes v. Haymes, 157 A.D.2d 506, 549 N.Y.S.2d 698 (N.Y.A.D. 1 Dept.1990)— § **706.1, n. 6.**

Haynes v. United States, 390 U.S. 85, 88 S.Ct. 722, 19 L.Ed.2d 923 (1968)— § **509.1, n. 73.**

Hazelwood School Dist. v. United States, 433 U.S. 299, 97 S.Ct. 2736, 53 L.Ed.2d 768 (1977)—§ **404.2, n. 34.**

Headley v. Tilghman, 53 F.3d 472 (2nd Cir.1995)—§ **801.1, n. 19.**

Healy v. Rennert, 213 N.Y.S.2d 44, 173 N.E.2d 777 (N.Y.1961)—§ **803(1).1, n. 56; § 804.1, n. 24; § 804(1).1; § 804(1).1, n. 6, 11.**

Hedges, People v., 98 A.D.2d 950, 470 N.Y.S.2d 61 (N.Y.A.D. 4 Dept.1983)— § **502.1, n. 19.**

Hedman, United States v., 630 F.2d 1184 (7th Cir.1980)—§ **607.4, n. 46.**

Heffron, People v., 59 A.D.2d 263, 399 N.Y.S.2d 501 (N.Y.A.D. 4 Dept.1977)— § **410.1, n. 10.**

Hefte v. Bellin, 137 A.D.2d 406, 524 N.Y.S.2d 42 (N.Y.A.D. 1 Dept.1988)— § **803(3).1, n. 4.**

Heilbronn v. Herzog, 165 N.Y. 98, 58 N.E. 759 (N.Y.1900)—§ **611.1, n. 1.**

Heitner, United States v., 149 F.2d 105 (2nd Cir.1945)—§ **802.1, n. 7; § 802.3, n. 13.**

Helgesen, United States v., 513 F.Supp. 209 (D.C.N.Y.1981)—§ **201.2, n. 7.**

Hellenic Lines Limited v. Gulf Oil Corp., 340 F.2d 398 (2nd Cir.1965)—§ **802.3, n. 13.**

Heller v. Murray, 112 Misc.2d 745, 447 N.Y.S.2d 348 (N.Y.City Civ.Ct.1981)— § **702.1, n. 34; § 901.3, n. 12.**

Helminski v. Ayerst Laboratories, a Div. of American Home Products Corp., 766 F.2d 208 (6th Cir.1985)—§ **615.2, n. 2.**

Helmken v. City of New York, 90 A.D. 135, 85 N.Y.S. 1048 (N.Y.A.D. 1 Dept.1904)— § **611.2, n. 8.**

Helt v. Metropolitan Dist. Com'n, 113 F.R.D. 7 (D.Conn.1986)—§ **501.2, n. 38.**

Hendricks, People v., 114 A.D.2d 510, 494 N.Y.S.2d 729 (N.Y.A.D. 2 Dept.1985)— § **611.1, n. 10.**

Henry v. Gutenplan, 197 A.D.2d 608, 604 N.Y.S.2d 757 (N.Y.A.D. 2 Dept.1993)— § **802.2, n. 73.**

Henry v. Lewis, 102 A.D.2d 430, 478 N.Y.S.2d 263 (N.Y.A.D. 1 Dept.1984)— § **502.1, n. 40, 72.**

Henry v. Speckard, 22 F.3d 1209 (2nd Cir. 1994)—§ **607.6, n. 32.**

Henry, United States v., 47 F.3d 17 (2nd Cir.1995)—§ **611.5, n. 21.**

Henson, People v., 349 N.Y.S.2d 657, 304 N.E.2d 358 (N.Y.1973)—§ **404.1; § 404.1, n. 42.**

Herman, United States v., 544 F.2d 791 (5th Cir.1977)—§ **410.2, n. 5.**

Hernandez–Fundora, United States v., 58 F.3d 802 (2nd Cir.1995)—§ **201.2, n. 5, 19, 23.**

Herr, People v., 203 A.D.2d 927, 611 N.Y.S.2d 389 (N.Y.A.D. 4 Dept.1994)— § **1102.1, n. 4.**

Herring v. Hayes, 135 A.D.2d 684, 522 N.Y.S.2d 583 (N.Y.A.D. 2 Dept.1987)— § **702.1, n. 82.**

Herring, People v., 135 Misc.2d 487, 515 N.Y.S.2d 954 (N.Y.Sup.1987)—§ **1103.1, n. 4.**

Herring, United States v., 602 F.2d 1220 (5th Cir.1979)—§ **614.2, n. 2.**

Herrmann v. General Tire and Rubber Co., Inc., 79 A.D.2d 955, 435 N.Y.S.2d 14 (N.Y.A.D. 1 Dept.1981)—§ **501.1, n. 87; § 501.3, n. 35; § 612.1, n. 21, 28.**

Herzig v. Swift & Co., 146 F.2d 444 (2nd Cir.1945)—§ **1001.1, n. 2.**

Hesdra's Will, In re, 119 N.Y. 615, 23 N.E. 555 (N.Y.1890)—§ **806.1; § 806.1, n. 5.**

Hethier v. Johns, 233 N.Y. 370, 135 N.E. 603 (N.Y.1922)—§ **502.1, n. 43.**

Hickey, United States v., 917 F.2d 901 (6th Cir.1990)—§ **601.3, n. 11.**

Hickman v. Taylor, 329 U.S. 495, 67 S.Ct. 385, 91 L.Ed. 451 (1947)—§ **501.2, n. 7; § 501.3; § 501.3, n. 1, 8.**

Hickman, United States v., 592 F.2d 931 (6th Cir.1979)—§ **614.2, n. 6.**

Hicks, United States v., 748 F.2d 854 (4th Cir.1984)—§ **607.5, n. 49.**

Hill, People v., 195 N.Y. 16, 87 N.E. 813 (N.Y.1909)—§ **803(1).1, n. 72.**

Hillman, People v., 246 N.Y. 467, 159 N.E. 400 (N.Y.1927)—§ **201.1, n. 39.**

Hills, People v., 140 A.D.2d 71, 532 N.Y.S.2d 269 (N.Y.A.D. 2 Dept.1988)— § **401.1, n. 49; § 404.1, n. 39.**

Hinds v. John Hancock Mut. Life Ins. Co., 155 Me. 349, 155 A.2d 721 (Me.1959)— § **301.5, n. 12, 15, 33, 50.**

Hine v. New York El. R. Co., 149 N.Y. 154, 43 N.E. 414 (N.Y.1896)—§ **803(1).1, n. 42.**

Hines, People v., 102 A.D.2d 713, 476 N.Y.S.2d 851 (N.Y.A.D. 1 Dept.1984)— § **201.1, n. 41.**

Hines, People v., 90 A.D.2d 621, 456 N.Y.S.2d 235 (N.Y.A.D. 3 Dept.1982)— § **901.7, n. 7.**

TABLE OF CASES

Hines, People v., 284 N.Y. 93, 29 N.E.2d 483 (N.Y.1940)—§ **607.8, n. 36**; § **806.1**; § **806.1, n. 9.**

Hines, People v., 168 Misc. 453, 6 N.Y.S.2d 2 (N.Y.Sup.1938)—§ **802.2, n. 104.**

Hing Shair Chan, United States v., 680 F.Supp. 521 (E.D.N.Y.1988)—§ **201.2, n. 7**; § **803(3).2, n. 20**; § **902.1**; § **902.1, n. 21.**

Hinkley, People v., 178 A.D.2d 800, 581 N.Y.S.2d 253 (N.Y.A.D. 3 Dept.1991)—§ **611.1, n. 10.**

Hinksman, People v., 192 N.Y. 421, 85 N.E. 676 (N.Y.1908)—§ **608.1, n. 1, 5.**

Hinshaw v. Keith, 645 F.Supp. 180 (D.Me. 1986)—§ **803(5).2, n. 49.**

Hippocrates Mertsaris v. 73rd Corp., 105 A.D.2d 67, 482 N.Y.S.2d 792 (N.Y.A.D. 2 Dept.1984)—§ **100.2, n. 7.**

Hiss, United States v., 88 F.Supp. 559 (D.C.N.Y.1950)—§ **607.7, n. 20.**

Hitsman, United States v., 604 F.2d 443 (5th Cir.1979)—§ **902.1, n. 30.**

Hoag v. Wright, 174 N.Y. 36, 66 N.E. 579 (N.Y.1903)—§ **601.1, n. 1, 12**; § **607.6, n. 19.**

Hoagland v. Kamp, 155 A.D.2d 148, 552 N.Y.S.2d 978 (N.Y.A.D. 3 Dept.1990)—§ **702.1, n. 24.**

Hoats, People v., 102 Misc.2d 1004, 425 N.Y.S.2d 497 (Monroe Co.Ct.1980)—§ **803(5).1, n. 4.**

Hoberman v. Lane, 85 A.D.2d 595, 444 N.Y.S.2d 704 (N.Y.A.D. 2 Dept.1981)—§ **607.8, n. 21.**

Hoenig v. Westphal, 439 N.Y.S.2d 831, 422 N.E.2d 491 (N.Y.1981)—§ **501.3, n. 16**; § **502.1, n. 53.**

Hoff v. State Farm Ins. Co., 48 A.D.2d 1001, 369 N.Y.S.2d 256 (N.Y.A.D. 4 Dept.1975)—§ **411.1, n. 5.**

Hoffman v. City of New York, 141 Misc.2d 893, 535 N.Y.S.2d 342 (N.Y.Sup.1988)—§ **803(3).1**; § **803(3).1, n. 77**; § **1104.1, n. 20.**

Hoffman v. Ro–San Manor, 73 A.D.2d 207, 425 N.Y.S.2d 619 (N.Y.A.D. 1 Dept. 1980)—§ **501.3, n. 10, 27.**

Hogan v. O'Brien, 212 A.D. 193, 208 N.Y.S. 477 (N.Y.A.D. 3 Dept.1925)—§ **301.4, n. 12**; § **301.5, n. 4.**

Hogan, United States v., 763 F.2d 697 (5th Cir.1985)—§ **607.4, n. 48.**

Holbrook v. New Jersey Zinc Co., 57 N.Y. 616 (1874)—§ **902.1, n. 11.**

Holcomb v. Holcomb, 95 N.Y. 316 (1884)—§ **601.2**; § **601.2, n. 45.**

Holland, United States v., 526 F.2d 284 (5th Cir.1976)—§ **607.5, n. 55.**

Holland v. United States, 348 U.S. 121, 75 S.Ct. 127, 99 L.Ed. 150 (1954)—§ **300.4**; § **300.4, n. 68, 73.**

Hollaway, People v., 132 A.D.2d 940, 518 N.Y.S.2d 487 (N.Y.A.D. 4 Dept.1987)—§ **607.5, n. 8.**

Hollien v. Kaye, 194 Misc. 821, 87 N.Y.S.2d 782 (N.Y.Sup.1949)—§ **501.1, n. 52**; § **505.1, n. 4.**

Holmgren v. State Farm Mut. Auto. Ins. Co., 976 F.2d 573 (9th Cir.1992)—§ **501.3, n. 43.**

Holshek v. Stokes, 122 A.D.2d 777, 505 N.Y.S.2d 664 (N.Y.A.D. 2 Dept.1986)—§ **703.1, n. 10, 11.**

Holtzman v. Hellenbrand, 92 A.D.2d 405, 460 N.Y.S.2d 591 (N.Y.A.D. 2 Dept. 1983)—§ **802.2, n. 17**; § **804(1).1, n. 50**; § **807.1, n. 8.**

Hon, United States v., 904 F.2d 803 (2nd Cir.1990)—§ **900.1, n. 10**; § **1101.2, n. 14.**

Honigman's Will, In re, 203 N.Y.S.2d 859, 168 N.E.2d 676 (N.Y.1960)—§ **601.2, n. 63.**

Hoopes v. Carota, 544 N.Y.S.2d 808, 543 N.E.2d 73 (N.Y.1989)—§ **501.1, n. 29, 30, 31, 73, 74.**

Hoover v. Durkee, 212 A.D.2d 839, 622 N.Y.S.2d 348 (N.Y.A.D. 3 Dept.1995)—§ **1105.1, n. 7, 11.**

Hopkins v. Dow Corning Corp., 33 F.3d 1116 (9th Cir.1994)—§ **702.2, n. 29.**

Hoppe v. G.D. Searle & Co., 779 F.Supp. 1413 (S.D.N.Y.1991)—§ **401.2, n. 3**; § **804(1).2**; § **804(1).2, n. 26.**

Horowitz, In re, 482 F.2d 72 (2nd Cir. 1973)—§ **501.2, n. 2, 46.**

Horton v. Smith, 433 N.Y.S.2d 92, 412 N.E.2d 1318 (N.Y.1980)—§ **103.1, n. 1.**

Houston Oxygen Co. v. Davis, 139 Tex. 1, 161 S.W.2d 474 (Tex.Com.App.1942)—§ **803(1).2, n. 1.**

Howard v. McDonough, 77 N.Y. 592 (1879)—§ **612.1, n. 6, 7.**

Howard, United States v., 774 F.2d 838 (7th Cir.1985)—§ **1006.1, n. 23**; § **1103.2, n. 1.**

Howard–Arias, United States v., 679 F.2d 363 (4th Cir.1982)—§ **1101.2, n. 16.**

Hoya Saxa, Inc. v. Gowan, 149 Misc.2d 191, 571 N.Y.S.2d 179 (N.Y.Sup.1991)—§ **201.1, n. 47.**

Hubbard v. Briggs, 31 N.Y. 517 (1865)—§ **806.1, n. 11.**

Huddleston v. United States, 485 U.S. 681, 108 S.Ct. 1496, 99 L.Ed.2d 771 (1988)—§ **104.2**; § **104.2, n. 2, 3**; § **404.1**; § **404.1, n. 19**; § **404.2**; § **404.2, n. 1**; § **900.1, n. 10.**

Hudson, United States v., 970 F.2d 948 (1st Cir.1992)—§ **607.8, n. 53, 55.**

Hudson v. Varney, 196 A.D.2d 856, 602 N.Y.S.2d 176 (N.Y.A.D. 2 Dept.1993)—§ **803(5).1, n. 42.**

Hudy, People v., 538 N.Y.S.2d 197, 535 N.E.2d 250 (N.Y.1988)—§ **404.1**; § **404.1, n. 11, 83, 85**; § **607.2, n. 9**; § **607.6, n. 16, 27**; § **611.3, n. 31.**

TABLE OF CASES

Huertas, People v., 554 N.Y.S.2d 444, 553 N.E.2d 992 (N.Y.1990)—§ **607.5;** § **607.5, n. 12, 13;** § **801.1;** § **801.1, n. 8;** § **801(2).1;** § **801(2).1, n. 23.**

Huff v. Bennett, 6 N.Y. 337 (1852)—§ **612.1, n. 2;** § **901.2, n. 4.**

Huggins v. Castle Estates, Inc., 369 N.Y.S.2d 80, 330 N.E.2d 48 (N.Y.1975)—§ **300.4, n. 28.**

Hughes v. Kackas, 3 A.D.2d 402, 161 N.Y.S.2d 541 (N.Y.A.D. 3 Dept.1957)—§ **502.1, n. 46.**

Hughes, People v., 466 N.Y.S.2d 255, 453 N.E.2d 484 (N.Y.1983)—§ **601.1;** § **601.1, n. 4, 60;** § **702.1;** § **702.1, n. 53.**

Hughson v. St. Francis Hosp. of Port Jervis, 93 A.D.2d 491, 463 N.Y.S.2d 224 (N.Y.A.D. 2 Dept.1983)—§ **500.1, n. 8;** § **502.1, n. 22, 43.**

Hull v. Littauer, 162 N.Y. 569, 57 N.E. 102 (N.Y.1900)—§ **300.3, n. 38;** § **607.1, n. 6.**

Hults, People v., 557 N.Y.S.2d 270, 556 N.E.2d 1077 (N.Y.1990)—§ **601.1, n. 64, 69;** § **607.8, n. 12.**

Humphrey v. Norden, 79 Misc.2d 192, 359 N.Y.S.2d 733 (N.Y.City Fam.Ct.1974)—§ **505.1, n. 7, 19.**

Hunt v. Liberty Lobby, 720 F.2d 631 (11th Cir.1983)—§ **803(4).2, n. 1.**

Hunter v. Derby Foods, 110 F.2d 970, 17 O.O. 384 (2nd Cir.1940)—§ **803(5).2, n. 41.**

Hunter v. New York, O. & W. Ry. Co., 116 N.Y. 615, 23 N.E. 9 (N.Y.1889)—§ **201.1;** § **201.1, n. 7, 9, 11, 17, 42, 43, 47, 53.**

Hunter, People v., 131 A.D.2d 877, 517 N.Y.S.2d 234 (N.Y.A.D. 2 Dept.1987)—§ **1102.1, n. 17.**

Hunter, People v., 358 N.Y.S.2d 360, 315 N.E.2d 436 (N.Y.1974)—§ **702.1, n. 30;** § **901.3, n. 4.**

Huntley, People v., 87 A.D.2d 488, 452 N.Y.S.2d 952 (N.Y.A.D. 4 Dept.1982)—§ **1107.1, n. 14.**

Huntley, People v., 255 N.Y.S.2d 838, 204 N.E.2d 179 (N.Y.1965)—§ **104.1, n. 33.**

Hurd, State v., 86 N.J. 525, 432 A.2d 86 (N.J.1981)—§ **601.1, n. 64.**

Hurlburt v. Hurlburt, 128 N.Y. 420, 28 N.E. 651 (N.Y.1891)—§ **501.1, n. 57.**

Hussain, People v., 165 A.D.2d 538, 568 N.Y.S.2d 966 (N.Y.A.D. 2 Dept.1991)—§ **105.1, n. 18.**

Hutcher, United States v., 622 F.2d 1083 (2nd Cir.1980)—§ **103.2, n. 2.**

Hutchinson v. Groskin, 927 F.2d 722 (2nd Cir.1991)—§ **103.2, n. 4, 6;** § **703.2, n. 10.**

Hutchinson v. Shaheen, 55 A.D.2d 833, 390 N.Y.S.2d 317 (N.Y.A.D. 4 Dept.1976)—§ **611.1, n. 5.**

Hutson, United States v., 821 F.2d 1015 (5th Cir.1987)—§ **803(4).2, n. 3.**

Hyatt, United States v., 565 F.2d 229 (2nd Cir.1977)—§ **901.5, n. 15.**

Hyde v. County of Rensselaer, 434 N.Y.S.2d 984, 415 N.E.2d 972 (N.Y.1980)—§ **105.1, n. 9;** § **405.1;** § **405.1, n. 4, 11.**

Hydrolevel Corp. v. American Soc. of Mechanical Engineers, Inc., 635 F.2d 118 (2nd Cir.1980)—§ **803(1).2, n. 23.**

Hygh v. Jacobs, 961 F.2d 359 (2nd Cir. 1992)—§ **704.2;** § **704.2, n. 6.**

Hyman, People v., 284 A.D. 347, 131 N.Y.S.2d 691 (N.Y.A.D. 1 Dept.1954)—§ **608.2, n. 10.**

Hyman v. Revlon Products Corp., 277 A.D. 1118, 100 N.Y.S.2d 937 (N.Y.A.D. 2 Dept.1950)—§ **513.1, n. 4.**

Hymes v. McDermott, 82 N.Y. 41 (1880)—§ **901.2, n. 3, 5, 7.**

Hyson, United States v., 721 F.2d 856 (1st Cir.1983)—§ **601.3, n. 11.**

I

Iacobelli Const., Inc. v. County of Monroe, 32 F.3d 19 (2nd Cir.1994)—§ **702.2, n. 33.**

Iaconetti, United States v., 540 F.2d 574 (2nd Cir.1976)—§ **804(5).2;** § **804(5).2, n. 6, 11, 26.**

Iaconetti, United States v., 406 F.Supp. 554 (D.C.N.Y.1976)—§ **802.3;** § **802.3, n. 31.**

Iannelli v. Powers, 114 A.D.2d 157, 498 N.Y.S.2d 377 (N.Y.A.D. 2 Dept.1986)—§ **702.1, n. 22.**

Iannucci v. Board of Sup'rs of Washington County, 282 N.Y.S.2d 502, 229 N.E.2d 195 (N.Y.1967)—§ **901.9, n. 14.**

Ibanez v. Pfeiffer, 76 Misc.2d 363, 350 N.Y.S.2d 964 (N.Y.City Civ.Ct.1973)—§ **702.1, n. 31;** § **901.3, n. 5.**

Iberian Tankers Co. v. Gates Const. Corp., 388 F.Supp. 1190 (D.C.N.Y.1975)—§ **408.2, n. 12.**

I.C.C. Metals, Inc. v. Municipal Warehouse Co., 431 N.Y.S.2d 372, 409 N.E.2d 849 (N.Y.1980)—§ **301.4, n. 13;** § **301.5, n. 23.**

Idaho v. Wright, 497 U.S. 805, 110 S.Ct. 3139, 111 L.Ed.2d 638 (1990)—§ **804(5).1;** § **804(5).1, n. 21;** § **804(5).2;** § **804(5).2, n. 16, 28.**

Impagliazzo v. Nassau County, 123 N.Y.S.2d 819 (N.Y.Sup.1953)—§ **201.1, n. 39.**

Imperial Meat Co. v. United States, 316 F.2d 435 (10th Cir.1963)—§ **1108.2, n. 7.**

Inadi, United States v., 475 U.S. 387, 106 S.Ct. 1121, 89 L.Ed.2d 390 (1986)—§ **802.2, n. 87;** § **802.3;** § **802.3, n. 38;** § **803(1).1, n. 16, 20;** § **804(3).1;** § **804(3).2, n. 12;** § **804(5).2, n. 35.**

Index Fund, Inc. v. Hagopian, 677 F.Supp. 710 (S.D.N.Y.1987)—§ **803(5).2, n. 47.**

TABLE OF CASES

Ingram, People v., 527 N.Y.S.2d 363, 522 N.E.2d 439 (N.Y.1988)—§ **404.1, n. 37.**
In Interest of Goodwin, 366 N.W.2d 809 (N.D.1985)—§ **509.1, n. 27.**
Inniss, People v., 612 N.Y.S.2d 360, 634 N.E.2d 961 (N.Y.1994)—§ **607.6, n. 13, 25.**
In re (see name of party)
Insana, United States v., 423 F.2d 1165 (2nd Cir.1970)—§ **607.8, n. 44, 45; § 801(1).3, n. 7.**
Inserra, United States v., 34 F.3d 83 (2nd Cir.1994)—§ **900.1, n. 10; § 901.1, n. 17.**
International Adhesive Coating Co., Inc. v. Bolton Emerson Intern., Inc., 851 F.2d 540 (1st Cir.1988)—§ **703.2, n. 2; § 705.2, n. 2.**
International Business Machines Corp., United States v., 90 F.R.D. 377 (D.C.N.Y.1981)—§ **804(1).2, n. 13.**
International Paper Co. v. Federal Power Commission, 438 F.2d 1349 (2nd Cir. 1971)—§ **511.2, n. 8, 11.**
Interstate Cigar Co., Inc. v. I. B. I. Sec. Service, Inc., 105 Misc.2d 179, 431 N.Y.S.2d 1016 (N.Y.Sup.1980)—§ **513.1, n. 7.**
Investigation Into a Certain Weapon, People v., 113 Misc.2d 348, 448 N.Y.S.2d 950 (N.Y.Sup.1982)—§ **501.1, n. 17, 26.**
Investors Funding Corp. of New York Securities Litigation, In re, 635 F.Supp. 1262 (S.D.N.Y.1986)—§ **401.2, n. 2, 4.**
Iron Shell, United States v., 633 F.2d 77 (8th Cir.1980)—§ **607.5, n. 54; § 803(1).2, n. 52.**
Isaacs, Estate of, 86 Misc.2d 954, 383 N.Y.S.2d 976 (N.Y.Sur.1976)—§ **601.2, n. 2, 6, 22.**
Iseman v. Delmar Medical–Dental Bldg., Inc., 113 A.D.2d 276, 495 N.Y.S.2d 747 (N.Y.A.D. 3 Dept.1985)—§ **502.1, n. 54.**
Isidron, People v., 209 A.D.2d 718, 619 N.Y.S.2d 329 (N.Y.A.D. 2 Dept.1994)—§ **607.6, n. 8.**
Ismail v. Cohen, 706 F.Supp. 243 (S.D.N.Y. 1989)—§ **404.2, n. 37.**
Ivic, United States v., 700 F.2d 51 (2nd Cir.1983)—§ **300.4; § 300.4, n. 70.**

J

Jackson v. Denno, 378 U.S. 368, 84 S.Ct. 1774, 12 L.Ed.2d 908 (1964)—§ **104.1, n. 33.**
Jackson, People v., 545 N.Y.S.2d 95, 543 N.E.2d 738 (N.Y.1989)—§ **607.6, n. 13.**
Jackson, People v., 491 N.Y.S.2d 138, 480 N.E.2d 727 (N.Y.1985)—§ **300.3, n. 28, 35.**
Jackson, People v., 382 N.Y.S.2d 736, 346 N.E.2d 537 (N.Y.1976)—§ **404.1; § 404.1, n. 61.**
Jackson, United States v., 60 F.3d 128 (2nd Cir.1995)—§ **615.2, n. 5, 6, 7.**
Jackson, United States v., 726 F.2d 1466 (9th Cir.1984)—§ **300.4, n. 74.**
Jackson, United States v., 588 F.2d 1046 (5th Cir.1979)—§ **607.5, n. 60.**
Jackson, United States v., 576 F.2d 46 (5th Cir.1978)—§ **607.7, n. 25.**
Jackson v. Virginia, 443 U.S. 307, 99 S.Ct. 2781, 61 L.Ed.2d 560 (1979)—§ **300.3, n. 27, 55.**
Jacobi v. Order of Germania, 26 N.Y.S. 318 (N.Y.Sup.1893)—§ **901.10, n. 2.**
Jacobowitz, United States v., 877 F.2d 162 (2nd Cir.1989)—§ **801(2).2; § 801(2).2, n. 9.**
Jacobs, United States v., 475 F.2d 270 (2nd Cir.1973)—§ **1004.1, n. 2; § 1008.1, n. 9.**
Jacqueline F., Matter of, 417 N.Y.S.2d 884, 391 N.E.2d 967 (N.Y.1979)—§ **501.1; § 501.1, n. 32, 35, 36, 76.**
Jakobleff v. Cerrato, Sweeney and Cohn, 97 A.D.2d 834, 468 N.Y.S.2d 895 (N.Y.A.D. 2 Dept.1983)—§ **501.1, n. 72.**
James v. Metro North Commuter R.R., 166 A.D.2d 266, 560 N.Y.S.2d 459 (N.Y.A.D. 1 Dept.1990)—§ **501.3, n. 19, 22.**
James v. River Parishes Co., Inc., 686 F.2d 1129 (5th Cir.1982)—§ **301.8, n. 8.**
James, United States v., 609 F.2d 36 (2nd Cir.1979)—§ **801(1).3, n. 18.**
James K. Thomson Co. v. International Compositions Co., 191 A.D. 553, 181 N.Y.S. 637 (N.Y.A.D. 1 Dept.1920)—§ **801.1, n. 16.**
Jamison, People v., 419 N.Y.S.2d 472, 393 N.E.2d 467 (N.Y.1979)—§ **614.1, n. 13, 14.**
Jamison v. Walker, 48 A.D.2d 320, 369 N.Y.S.2d 469 (N.Y.A.D. 2 Dept.1975)—§ **804(3).1; § 804(3).1, n. 3, 20, 31.**
Janetka v. Dabe, 892 F.2d 187 (2nd Cir. 1989)—§ **803(5).2, n. 31.**
Japanese Electronic Products Antitrust Litigation, In re, 723 F.2d 238 (3rd Cir. 1983)—§ **103.2, n. 22; § 703.2, n. 8; § 804(5).2, n. 10.**
Jarrett v. Madifari, 67 A.D.2d 396, 415 N.Y.S.2d 644 (N.Y.A.D. 1 Dept.1979)—§ **300.4, n. 6; § 401.1, n. 33, 34.**
Jarvis v. Metropolitan St. Ry. Co., 65 A.D. 490, 72 N.Y.S. 829 (N.Y.A.D. 2 Dept. 1901)—§ **103.1, n. 15, 36.**
Jasinski v. New York Cent. R.R., 21 A.D.2d 456, 250 N.Y.S.2d 942 (N.Y.A.D. 4 Dept. 1964)—§ **405.1, n. 8.**
J. Baranello and Sons v. Chase Manhattan Bank, N.A., 119 A.D.2d 550, 500 N.Y.S.2d 727 (N.Y.A.D. 2 Dept.1986)—§ **300.4, n. 5.**
Jeanneret v. Vichey, 693 F.2d 259 (2nd Cir.1982)—§ **803(7).2, n. 3.**
Jeanne TT, Matter of, 184 A.D.2d 895, 585 N.Y.S.2d 552 (N.Y.A.D. 3 Dept.1992)—§ **505.1, n. 6.**

TABLE OF CASES

Jean P. v. Roger Warren J., 184 A.D.2d 1072, 584 N.Y.S.2d 256 (N.Y.A.D. 4 Dept.1992)—§ **301.5, n. 29.**

Jeffries v. Nix, 912 F.2d 982 (8th Cir. 1990)—§ **412.2, n. 5.**

Jenkins v. Anderson, 447 U.S. 231, 100 S.Ct. 2124, 65 L.Ed.2d 86 (1980)— § **509.1; § 509.1, n. 86; § 607.8, n. 45; § 802.2, n. 31.**

Jenkins, People v., 392 N.Y.S.2d 587, 360 N.E.2d 1288 (N.Y.1977)—§ **510.1; § 510.1, n. 12.**

Jenkins v. 313–321 W. 37th Street Corporation, 284 N.Y. 397, 31 N.E.2d 503 (N.Y. 1940)—§ **607.4, n. 31.**

Jenkins, United States v., 496 F.2d 57 (2nd Cir.1974)—§ **801(2).2, n. 12.**

Jensen v. Shady Pines Inc., 32 A.D.2d 648, 300 N.Y.S.2d 746 (N.Y.A.D. 2 Dept. 1969)—§ **601.1, n. 29, 33.**

Jessica G, Matter of, 200 A.D.2d 906, 607 N.Y.S.2d 156 (N.Y.A.D. 3 Dept.1994)— § **804(5).1, n. 29.**

Jeter, People v., 587 N.Y.S.2d 583, 600 N.E.2d 214 (N.Y.1992)—§ **702.1, n. 20, 51; § 901.3, n. 6.**

Jewell v. Irvmac Shoe Shops, Inc., 19 Misc.2d 815, 187 N.Y.S.2d 412 (N.Y.Sup. 1959)—§ **601.2, n. 14.**

Jezowski v. Beach, 59 Misc.2d 224, 298 N.Y.S.2d 360 (N.Y.Sup.1968)—§ **901.1, n. 10.**

Jiminez, People v., 100 A.D.2d 629, 473 N.Y.S.2d 593 (N.Y.A.D. 2 Dept.1984)— § **1101.1, n. 24.**

J. K. Lasser & Co., In re, 448 F.Supp. 103 (D.C.N.Y.1978)—§ **501.2, n. 24.**

J.M. Rodriguez & Co., Inc. v. Moore–McCormack Lines, Inc., 345 N.Y.S.2d 993, 299 N.E.2d 243 (N.Y.1973)— § **300.2, n. 17.**

Johantgen v. Hobart Mfg. Co., 64 A.D.2d 858, 407 N.Y.S.2d 355 (N.Y.A.D. 4 Dept. 1978)—§ **1007.1, n. 5.**

John Blair Communications, Inc. v. Reliance Capital Group, L.P., 182 A.D.2d 578, 582 N.Y.S.2d 720 (N.Y.A.D. 1 Dept. 1992)—§ **501.1, n. 85; § 501.3, n. 34.**

John Doe Corp., In re, 675 F.2d 482 (2nd Cir.1982)—§ **501.2, n. 9, 15, 17, 46; § 501.3, n. 56.**

John Doe, Inc., In re, 13 F.3d 633 (2nd Cir.1994)—§ **501.2, n. 18.**

John Doe, Inc., Application of, 120 Misc.2d 508, 466 N.Y.S.2d 202 (N.Y.Sup.1983)— § **502.1, n. 11.**

Johnny P., People v., 112 Misc.2d 647, 445 N.Y.S.2d 1007 (N.Y.City Crim.Ct. 1981)—§ **604.1, n. 3.**

Johnpoll, United States v., 739 F.2d 702 (2nd Cir.1984)—§ **302.1, n. 13; § 302.2, n. 6.**

Johnson v. Ashby, 808 F.2d 676 (8th Cir. 1987)—§ **611.5, n. 7.**

Johnson v. Celotex Corp., 899 F.2d 1281 (2nd Cir.1990)—§ **614.2, n. 6.**

Johnson v. Johnson, 47 Misc.2d 805, 263 N.Y.S.2d 404 (N.Y.Sup.1965)—§ **503.2, n. 9.**

Johnson v. Lutz, 253 N.Y. 124, 170 N.E. 517 (N.Y.1930)—§ **803(3).1; § 803(3).1, n. 1, 15; § 803(3).2; § 803(3).2, n. 3; § 805.1, n. 1, 2; § 805.2, n. 2.**

Johnson, People v., 620 N.Y.S.2d 822, 644 N.E.2d 1378 (N.Y.1994)—§ **503.4, n. 4.**

Johnson, People v., 163 Misc.2d 256, 620 N.Y.S.2d 200 (N.Y.Sup.1994)— § **804(2).1, n. 5.**

Johnson, People v., 190 A.D.2d 910, 593 N.Y.S.2d 589 (N.Y.A.D. 3 Dept.1993)— § **406.1, n. 11.**

Johnson, People v., 173 A.D.2d 734, 570 N.Y.S.2d 616 (N.Y.A.D. 2 Dept.1991)— § **801(2).1, n. 17.**

Johnson, People v., 172 A.D.2d 329, 568 N.Y.S.2d 611 (N.Y.A.D. 1 Dept.1991)— § **611.2, n. 6.**

Johnson, People v., 457 N.Y.S.2d 230, 443 N.E.2d 478 (N.Y.1982)—§ **801(2).1, n. 33.**

Johnson, People v., 345 N.Y.S.2d 1011, 299 N.E.2d 256 (N.Y.1973)—§ **801(2).1, n. 33.**

Johnson, People v., 185 N.Y. 219, 77 N.E. 1164 (N.Y.1906)—§ **601.1, n. 34.**

Johnson, United States v., 594 F.2d 1253 (9th Cir.1979)—§ **1006.1, n. 13.**

Johnson, United States v., 382 F.2d 280 (2nd Cir.1967)—§ **404.2, n. 16.**

Johnston, People v., 228 N.Y. 332, 127 N.E. 186 (N.Y.1920)—§ **608.2, n. 21, 30.**

Johnston, United States v., 578 F.2d 1352 (10th Cir.1978)—§ **615.2, n. 9.**

Joint Eastern and Southern Dist. Asbestos Litigation, In re, 119 F.R.D. 4 (E. & S.D.N.Y.1988)—§ **501.3, n. 55; § 612.2, n. 19.**

Joint Eastern and Southern Districts Asbestos Litigation, In re, 830 F.Supp. 686 (E. & S.D.N.Y.1993)—§ **706.2, n. 8.**

Joint Eastern and Southern Districts Asbestos Litigation, In re, 798 F.Supp. 925 (E. & S.D.N.Y.1992)—§ **401.1, n. 47.**

Joint Eastern Dist. and Southern Dist. Asbestos Litigation, In re, 995 F.2d 343 (2nd Cir.1993)—§ **407.1, n. 25; § 407.2; § 407.2, n. 8.**

Joint Eastern & Southern Dist. Asbestos Litigation, In re, 52 F.3d 1124 (2nd Cir. 1995)—§ **300.3, n. 48; § 702.2, n. 31, 32.**

Joint Eastern & Southern Dist. Asbestos Litigation, In re, 964 F.2d 92 (2nd Cir. 1992)—§ **705.2; § 705.2, n. 4.**

Jonathan Woodner, Co. v. Higgins, 179 A.D.2d 444, 578 N.Y.S.2d 561 (N.Y.A.D. 1 Dept.1992)—§ **301.5, n. 41.**

Jones v. Benefit Trust Life Ins. Co., 800 F.2d 1397 (5th Cir.1986)—§ **605.2, n. 4.**

Jones v. Maloney, 277 N.Y. 437, 14 N.E.2d 782 (N.Y.1938)—§ **601.2, n. 40.**

TABLE OF CASES

Jones v. Morgan, 90 N.Y. 4 (1882)—§ **405.1, n. 34.**

Jones, People v., 193 A.D.2d 696, 598 N.Y.S.2d 40 (N.Y.A.D. 2 Dept.1993)—§ **608.2, n. 10.**

Jones, People v., 190 A.D.2d 31, 596 N.Y.S.2d 811 (N.Y.A.D. 1 Dept.1993)—§ **607.8, n. 9, 39.**

Jones, People v., 541 N.Y.S.2d 340, 539 N.E.2d 96 (N.Y.1989)—§ **201.1, n. 11, 19, 55;** § **703.1, n. 17;** § **705.1;** § **705.1, n. 5.**

Jones, People v., 136 A.D.2d 740, 524 N.Y.S.2d 79 (N.Y.A.D. 2 Dept.1988)—§ **607.8, n. 21;** § **608.2, n. 10.**

Jones, People v., 135 A.D.2d 652, 522 N.Y.S.2d 228 (N.Y.A.D. 2 Dept.1987)—§ **801.1, n. 15.**

Jones, People v., 118 Misc.2d 687, 461 N.Y.S.2d 962 (Albany Co.Ct.1983)—§ **702.1, n. 39.**

Jones, People v., 316 N.Y.S.2d 617, 265 N.E.2d 446 (N.Y.1970)—§ **300.4, n. 43.**

Jones v. Reilly, 174 N.Y. 97, 66 N.E. 649 (N.Y.1903)—§ **501.1, n. 23.**

Jones v. Southern Pacific R.R., 962 F.2d 447 (5th Cir.1992)—§ **406.2;** § **406.2, n. 11.**

Jones v. State, 93 Misc.2d 916, 403 N.Y.S.2d 691 (N.Y.Ct.Cl.1978)—§ **607.4, n. 7.**

Jones, United States v., 29 F.3d 1549 (11th Cir.1994)—§ **201.2, n. 4.**

Jones, United States v., 24 F.3d 1177 (9th Cir.1994)—§ **702.2, n. 30.**

Jones, United States v., 958 F.2d 520 (2nd Cir.1992)—§ **1001.1, n. 14.**

Jones, United States v., 900 F.2d 512 (2nd Cir.1990)—§ **608.2, n. 38.**

Jones, United States v., 580 F.2d 219 (6th Cir.1978)—§ **201.2, n. 22.**

Jones, United States v., 402 F.2d 851 (2nd Cir.1968)—§ **804(1).2, n. 9.**

Jordan v. Parrinello, 144 A.D.2d 540, 534 N.Y.S.2d 686 (N.Y.A.D. 2 Dept.1988)—§ **607.4, n. 11, 21;** § **611.2, n. 19.**

Jordan, People v., 59 A.D.2d 746, 398 N.Y.S.2d 556 (N.Y.A.D. 2 Dept.1977)—§ **607.4, n. 31.**

Joseph v. Krull Wholesale Drug Co., 147 F.Supp. 250 (D.C.Pa.1956)—§ **405.2, n. 14.**

Joseph, People v., 622 N.Y.S.2d 505, 646 N.E.2d 807 (N.Y.1994)—§ **615.1, n. 8.**

Joyce v. Kowalcewski, 80 A.D.2d 27, 437 N.Y.S.2d 809 (N.Y.A.D. 4 Dept.1981)—§ **803(3).1, n. 62.**

J.R. Stevenson Corp. v. Dormitory Authority of State of N.Y., 112 A.D.2d 113, 492 N.Y.S.2d 385 (N.Y.A.D. 1 Dept.1985)—§ **501.3, n. 16.**

Judson v. Fielding, 227 A.D. 430, 237 N.Y.S. 348 (N.Y.A.D. 3 Dept.1929)—§ **607.8, n. 19.**

Judson, People ex rel. v. Thacher, 55 N.Y. 525 (1874)—§ **512.1, n. 3.**

Julian, People v., 392 N.Y.S.2d 610, 360 N.E.2d 1310 (N.Y.1977)—§ **901.1, n. 2, 4;** § **1101.1;** § **1101.1, n. 2, 19.**

Jung Hing, People v., 212 N.Y. 393, 106 N.E. 105 (N.Y.1914)—§ **607.5, n. 2.**

Jung Yen Loy v. Cahill, 81 F.2d 809 (9th Cir.1936)—§ **803(5).2, n. 50.**

Justice, People v., 172 A.D.2d 851, 569 N.Y.S.2d 456 (N.Y.A.D. 2 Dept.1991)—§ **607.6, n. 24.**

Justin EE, Matter of, 153 A.D.2d 772, 544 N.Y.S.2d 892 (N.Y.A.D. 3 Dept.1989)—§ **201.1, n. 36, 51.**

K

Kaczmarek v. Allied Chemical Corp., 836 F.2d 1055 (7th Cir.1987)—§ **602.2, n. 9.**

Kahan, United States v., 572 F.2d 923 (2nd Cir.1978)—§ **802.3, n. 75.**

Kahane, United States v., 396 F.Supp. 687 (D.C.N.Y.1975)—§ **201.2, n. 8.**

Kalaydjian, United States v., 784 F.2d 53 (2nd Cir.1986)—§ **603.2, n. 1, 5;** § **610.2, n. 1.**

Kampiles, United States v., 609 F.2d 1233 (7th Cir.1979)—§ **802.3, n. 27.**

Kampshoff, People v., 53 A.D.2d 325, 385 N.Y.S.2d 672 (N.Y.A.D. 4 Dept.1976)—§ **607.7, n. 8, 18.**

Kandel v. Tocher, 22 A.D.2d 513, 256 N.Y.S.2d 898 (N.Y.A.D. 1 Dept.1965)—§ **501.3, n. 19.**

Kanovsky, United States v., 618 F.2d 229 (2nd Cir.1980)—§ **801.1, n. 42.**

Kanston, People v., 192 A.D.2d 721, 597 N.Y.S.2d 152 (N.Y.A.D. 2 Dept.1993)—§ **801(2).1, n. 31.**

Kapinos by Kapinos v. Alvarado, 143 A.D.2d 332, 532 N.Y.S.2d 416 (N.Y.A.D. 2 Dept 1988)—§ **611.1, n. 5.**

Kaplan, In re, 203 N.Y.S.2d 836, 168 N.E.2d 660 (N.Y.1960)—§ **501.1;** § **501.1, n. 32, 33.**

Kaplan v. City of New York, 10 A.D.2d 319, 200 N.Y.S.2d 261 (N.Y.A.D. 1 Dept. 1960)—§ **405.1, n. 7;** § **405.2, n. 3.**

Kaplowitz by Katz v. Borden, Inc., 189 A.D.2d 90, 594 N.Y.S.2d 744 (N.Y.A.D. 1 Dept.1993)—§ **706.1, n. 5.**

Kapuscinski v. Kapuscinski, 75 A.D.2d 576, 426 N.Y.S.2d 582 (N.Y.A.D. 2 Dept. 1980)—§ **601.1, n. 31.**

Karashik v. Brenner, 111 A.D.2d 150, 489 N.Y.S.2d 9 (N.Y.A.D. 2 Dept.1985)—§ **705.1, n. 8.**

Karnes, United States v., 531 F.2d 214 (4th Cir.1976)—§ **614.1, n. 11;** § **614.2, n. 2.**

Karns v. Emerson Elec. Co., 817 F.2d 1452 (10th Cir.1987)—§ **704.2, n. 1.**

Kasper v. Buffalo Bills of Western New York, 42 A.D.2d 87, 345 N.Y.S.2d 244 (N.Y.A.D. 4 Dept.1973)—§ **802.2, n. 76.**

TABLE OF CASES

Kass, People v., 302 N.Y.S.2d 807, 250 N.E.2d 219 (N.Y.1969)—§ **402.1, n. 33;** § **608.2, n. 12.**

Kates, People v., 444 N.Y.S.2d 446, 428 N.E.2d 852 (N.Y.1981)—§ **702.1, n. 42.**

Katsougrakis, United States v., 715 F.2d 769 (2nd Cir.1983)—§ **804(3).1;** § **804(3).1, n. 50;** § **804(3).2;** § **804(3).2, n. 13;** § **806.1, n. 19.**

Katz v. Assessor and Bd. of Assessment Review of Village/Town of Mount Kisco, 82 A.D.2d 654, 442 N.Y.S.2d 795 (N.Y.A.D. 2 Dept.1981)—§ **405.1, n. 28.**

Katz, People v., 209 N.Y. 311, 103 N.E. 305 (N.Y.1913)—§ **607.5, n. 29, 31, 39.**

Katz, United States v., 425 F.2d 928 (2nd Cir.1970)—§ **801.1, n. 24.**

Katz v. United States, 389 U.S. 347, 88 S.Ct. 507, 19 L.Ed.2d 576 (1967)— § **401.1, n. 54.**

Kaufman v. Eli Lilly and Co., 492 N.Y.S.2d 584, 482 N.E.2d 63 (N.Y.1985)—§ **606.1, n. 4.**

Kaufman v. Rosenshine, 97 A.D. 514, 90 N.Y.S. 205 (N.Y.A.D. 1 Dept.1904)— § **501.1, n. 79.**

Kay v. Metropolitan St. Ry. Co., 163 N.Y. 447, 57 N.E. 751 (N.Y.1900)—§ **607.4, n. 16.**

Kearney v. The Mayor, Aldermen and Commonality of the City of New York, 92 N.Y. 617 (1883)—§ **1004.1, n. 4;** § **1008.1, n. 2.**

Keating, People v., 286 A.D. 150, 141 N.Y.S.2d 562 (N.Y.A.D. 1 Dept.1955)— § **511.1, n. 9.**

Keegan v. Green Giant Co., 150 Me. 283, 110 A.2d 599 (Me.1954)—§ **902.1;** § **902.1, n. 23.**

Keen v. Overseas Tankship Corp., 194 F.2d 515 (2nd Cir.1952)—§ **103.2, n. 8.**

Keenan v. Gigante, 417 N.Y.S.2d 226, 390 N.E.2d 1151 (N.Y.1979)—§ **504.1;** § **504.1, n. 2, 3.**

Keenan's Estate, In re, 302 N.Y. 417, 99 N.E.2d 219 (N.Y.1951)—§ **803(6).1, n. 2.**

Keet v. Murrin, 260 N.Y. 586, 184 N.E. 104 (N.Y.1932)—§ **408.1;** § **408.1, n. 10.**

Kehn, People v., 109 A.D.2d 912, 486 N.Y.S.2d 380 (N.Y.A.D. 3 Dept.1985)— § **702.1, n. 78.**

Keindl, People v., 509 N.Y.S.2d 790, 502 N.E.2d 577 (N.Y.1986)—§ **702.1, n. 61;** § **704.1, n. 5, 12.**

Kelleher v. F.M.E. Auto Leasing Corp., 192 A.D.2d 581, 596 N.Y.S.2d 136 (N.Y.A.D. 2 Dept.1993)—§ **802.2, n. 75, 76;** § **804(3).1, n. 55.**

Kellerman, United States v., 431 F.2d 319 (2nd Cir.1970)—§ **100.2, n. 6;** § **103.2, n. 18, 20.**

Kellum, Matter of, 52 N.Y. 517 (1873)— § **406.1, n. 10, 14.**

Kellogg, People v., 210 A.D.2d 912, 621 N.Y.S.2d 418 (N.Y.A.D. 4 Dept.1994)— § **612.1, n. 8.**

Kelly v. Diesel Const. Division of Carl A. Morse, Inc., 358 N.Y.S.2d 685, 315 N.E.2d 751 (N.Y.1974)—§ **803(3).1, n. 25.**

Kelly, People v., 124 A.D.2d 825, 509 N.Y.S.2d 44 (N.Y.A.D. 2 Dept.1986)— § **608.2, n. 10.**

Kelly, United States v., 349 F.2d 720 (2nd Cir.1965)—§ **803(2).2;** § **803(2).2, n. 5.**

Kelly v. Wasserman, 185 N.Y.S.2d 538, 158 N.E.2d 241 (N.Y.1959)—§ **803(3).1;** § **803(3).1, n. 21;** § **805.1, n. 1;** § **805.2, n. 2.**

Kelly v. Watson Elevator Co., 309 N.Y. 49, 127 N.E.2d 802 (N.Y.1955)—§ **607.1, n. 4.**

Keltner v. Ford Motor Co., 748 F.2d 1265 (8th Cir.1984)—§ **406.2, n. 12.**

Kemp, People v., 59 A.D.2d 414, 399 N.Y.S.2d 879 (N.Y.A.D. 1 Dept.1977)— § **503.3, n. 13.**

Kenford Co., Inc. v. County of Erie, 55 A.D.2d 466, 390 N.Y.S.2d 715 (N.Y.A.D. 4 Dept.1977)—§ **501.1, n. 21.**

Kennedy v. Great Atlantic & Pacific Tea Co., Inc., 551 F.2d 593 (5th Cir.1977)— § **605.2, n. 3.**

Kennedy, People v., 510 N.Y.S.2d 853, 503 N.E.2d 501 (N.Y.1986)— § **803(3).1;** § **803(3).1, n. 2, 6, 7;** § **803(5).1, n. 8.**

Kennedy, People v., 70 A.D.2d 181, 420 N.Y.S.2d 23 (N.Y.A.D. 2 Dept.1979)— § **611.3, n. 24.**

Kennedy, People v., 417 N.Y.S.2d 452, 391 N.E.2d 288 (N.Y.1979)—§ **300.3, n. 15, 35;** § **300.4, n. 47;** § **608.2, n. 28.**

Kennedy, People v., 313 N.Y.S.2d 123, 261 N.E.2d 264 (N.Y.1970)—§ **404.1;** § **404.1, n. 52.**

Kennedy's Will, In re, 167 N.Y. 163, 60 N.E. 442 (N.Y.1901)—§ **803(1).1, n. 46.**

Kenneth M., Matter of, 130 Misc.2d 217, 495 N.Y.S.2d 131 (N.Y.Sup.1985)— § **509.1;** § **509.1, n. 19.**

Kenny, People v., 331 N.Y.S.2d 392, 282 N.E.2d 295 (N.Y.1972)—§ **701.1, n. 8;** § **702.1;** § **702.1, n. 1.**

Kent's Will, In re, 169 A.D. 388, 155 N.Y.S. 894 (N.Y.A.D. 4 Dept.1915)—§ **803(1).1, n. 46.**

Kentucky v. Stincer, 482 U.S. 730, 107 S.Ct. 2658, 96 L.Ed.2d 631 (1987)—§ **611.3, n. 4, 31.**

Keohane v. New York Cent. R. Co., 418 F.2d 478 (2nd Cir.1969)—§ **405.2, n. 6.**

Keough, People v., 276 N.Y. 141, 11 N.E.2d 570 (N.Y.1937)—§ **602.1, n. 8;** § **703.1;** § **703.1, n. 2;** § **803(1).1;** § **803(1).1, n. 69.**

Keplinger, United States v., 776 F.2d 678 (7th Cir.1985)—§ **501.2, n. 39.**

Kercheval v. United States, 274 U.S. 220, 47 S.Ct. 582, 71 L.Ed. 1009 (1927)—

TABLE OF CASES

§ 410.1; § 410.1, n. 4; § 410.2; § 410.2, n. 1; § 802.1; § 802.1, n. 17; § 802.3, n. 5.

Kerr v. United States Dist. Court for Northern Dist. of California, 511 F.2d 192 (9th Cir.1975)—§ **500.2, n. 6.**

Kerwood v. Hall, 201 A.D. 89, 193 N.Y.S. 811 (N.Y.A.D. 3 Dept.1922)—§ **601.2, n. 8.**

Kesseler v. Kesseler, 225 N.Y.S.2d 1, 180 N.E.2d 402 (N.Y.1962)—§ **706.1, n. 1, 2.**

Khadaidi, People v., 201 A.D.2d 585, 608 N.Y.S.2d 471 (N.Y.A.D. 2 Dept.1994)—§ **803(3).1, n. 61.**

Khan, People v., 200 A.D.2d 129, 613 N.Y.S.2d 198 (N.Y.A.D. 2 Dept.1994)—§ **105.1, n. 18.**

Khan, United States v., 821 F.2d 90 (2nd Cir.1987)—§ **607.5, n. 66, 67;** § **801(1).3, n. 18, 23, 24.**

Killip v. Rochester General Hospital, 1 Misc.2d 349, 146 N.Y.S.2d 164 (N.Y.Sup. 1955)—§ **502.1, n. 49.**

Kimberlin, United States v., 805 F.2d 210 (7th Cir.1986)—§ **601.3, n. 19.**

Kindberg's Will, In re, 207 N.Y. 220, 100 N.E. 789 (N.Y.1912)—§ **300.2, n. 21.**

Kinder, People v., 126 A.D.2d 60, 512 N.Y.S.2d 597 (N.Y.A.D. 4 Dept.1987)—§ **501.1, n. 18.**

King v. Ashley, 179 N.Y. 281, 72 N.E. 106 (N.Y.1904)—§ **501.1, n. 21.**

King v. Burkowski, 155 A.D.2d 285, 547 N.Y.S.2d 48 (N.Y.A.D. 1 Dept.1989)—§ **611.1, n. 10.**

King v. Conde, 121 F.R.D. 180 (E.D.N.Y. 1988)—§ **500.2, n. 7.**

King v. New York Central & Hudson River R.R. Co., 72 N.Y. 607 (1878)—§ **1100.1, n. 6, 12.**

King v. United States, 576 F.2d 432 (2nd Cir.1978)—§ **606.2, n. 10.**

King, United States v., 560 F.2d 122 (2nd Cir.1977)—§ **607.8, n. 55.**

Kinne, People v., 527 N.Y.S.2d 754, 522 N.E.2d 1052 (N.Y.1988)—§ **803(3).1, n. 61.**

Kinslow, United States v., 860 F.2d 963 (9th Cir.1988)—§ **609.2, n. 14.**

Kirkby's Estate, In re, 57 Misc.2d 982, 293 N.Y.S.2d 1008 (N.Y.Sur.1968)—§ **803(5).1, n. 33.**

Kiser v. Bailey, 92 Misc.2d 435, 400 N.Y.S.2d 312 (N.Y.City Civ.Ct.1977)—§ **601.2, n. 5.**

Kish v. Board of Educ. of City of New York, 559 N.Y.S.2d 687, 558 N.E.2d 1159 (N.Y. 1990)—§ **105.1, n. 7, 12;** § **401.1, n. 45.**

Kissinger v. State, 126 A.D.2d 139, 513 N.Y.S.2d 275 (N.Y.A.D. 3 Dept.1987)—§ **201.1, n. 35.**

Kitching, People v., 577 N.Y.S.2d 231, 583 N.E.2d 944 (N.Y.1991)—§ **401.1, n. 30.**

Kittredge v. Grannis, 244 N.Y. 168, 155 N.E. 88 (N.Y.1926)—§ **804(3).1, n. 11.**

Kizer, United States v., 569 F.2d 504 (9th Cir.1978)—§ **607.7, n. 25.**

Klatz v. Armor Elevator Co., Inc., 93 A.D.2d 633, 462 N.Y.S.2d 677 (N.Y.A.D. 2 Dept. 1983)—§ **405.1, n. 13, 14.**

Klein v. Harris, 667 F.2d 274 (2nd Cir. 1981)—§ **509.1, n. 18, 50.**

Klein, People v., 266 N.Y. 188, 194 N.E. 402 (N.Y.1935)—§ **601.1, n. 39.**

Klein v. Prudential Ins. Co. of America, 221 N.Y. 449, 117 N.E. 942 (N.Y.1917)—§ **502.1, n. 22.**

Klein, United States v., 488 F.2d 481 (2nd Cir.1973)—§ **103.2, n. 9, 10;** § **801(1).3, n. 8.**

Klug, In re, 32 A.D.2d 915, 302 N.Y.S.2d 418 (N.Y.A.D. 1 Dept.1969)—§ **505.1, n. 19.**

Knapp, People v., 139 A.D.2d 931, 527 N.Y.S.2d 914 (N.Y.A.D. 4 Dept.1988)—§ **803(1).1, n. 38.**

Knapper, People v., 168 A.D.2d 234, 562 N.Y.S.2d 475 (N.Y.A.D. 1 Dept.1990)—§ **1103.1, n. 9.**

Knapper, People v., 230 A.D. 487, 245 N.Y.S. 245 (N.Y.A.D. 1 Dept.1930)—§ **614.1, n. 22, 23.**

Knatz, People v., 76 A.D.2d 889, 428 N.Y.S.2d 709 (N.Y.A.D. 2 Dept.1980)—§ **607.7, n. 12.**

Knight, People v., 587 N.Y.S.2d 588, 600 N.E.2d 219 (N.Y.1992)—§ **607.8, n. 23, 40, 43.**

Knight, People v., 534 N.Y.S.2d 353, 530 N.E.2d 1273 (N.Y.1988)—§ **201.1, n. 46.**

Knight–Ridder Broadcasting, Inc. v. Greenberg, 518 N.Y.S.2d 595, 511 N.E.2d 1116 (N.Y.1987)—§ **508.1;** § **508.1, n. 7.**

Knorr v. Pearson, 671 F.2d 1368 (Cust. & Pat.App.1982)—§ **801.1, n. 24.**

Knowell, People v., 127 A.D.2d 794, 512 N.Y.S.2d 190 (N.Y.A.D. 2 Dept.1987)—§ **607.7, n. 6.**

Knuckles, United States v., 581 F.2d 305 (2nd Cir.1978)—§ **802.3, n. 75.**

Koerner, People v., 154 N.Y. 355, 48 N.E. 730 (N.Y.1897)—§ **502.1, n. 15.**

Koester v. Rochester Candy Works, 194 N.Y. 92, 87 N.E. 77 (N.Y.1909)—§ **607.4, n. 19, 32;** § **607.8, n. 6;** § **804(4).1, n. 4.**

Kohan, United States v., 806 F.2d 18 (2nd Cir.1986)—§ **801.1, n. 42.**

Kohl, People v., 532 N.Y.S.2d 45, 527 N.E.2d 1182 (N.Y.1988)—§ **300.4; n. 40, 63.**

Kohlmeyer, People v., 284 N.Y. 366, 31 N.E.2d 490 (N.Y.1940)—§ **701.1, n. 8;** § **803(3).1, n. 60.**

Kollmer v. Slater Elec., Inc., 122 A.D.2d 117, 504 N.Y.S.2d 690 (N.Y.A.D. 2 Dept. 1986)—§ **408.1, n. 4.**

Kollore, People v., 151 Misc.2d 384, 573 N.Y.S.2d 357 (N.Y.City Ct.1991)—§ **803(5).1, n. 5.**

TABLE OF CASES

Kolp, People v., 49 A.D.2d 139, 373 N.Y.S.2d 681 (N.Y.A.D. 3 Dept.1975)— § **1002.1, n. 5.**

Koretta W., Matter of, 118 Misc.2d 660, 461 N.Y.S.2d 205 (N.Y.Fam.Ct.1983)— § **505.1; § 505.1, n. 16.**

Korte v. New York, N.H. & H.R. Co., 191 F.2d 86 (2nd Cir.1951)— § **803(3).2, n. 36.**

Kosinski v. Woodside Const. Corp., 77 A.D.2d 674, 429 N.Y.S.2d 783 (N.Y.A.D. 3 Dept.1980)—§ **801.1, n. 20.**

Koska, United States v., 443 F.2d 1167 (2nd Cir.1971)—§ **1104.2, n. 14.**

Koskerides, United States v., 877 F.2d 1129 (2nd Cir.1989)— § **804(3).2, n. 17.**

Kotteakos v. United States, 328 U.S. 750, 66 S.Ct. 1239, 90 L.Ed. 1557 (1946)— § **103.2, n. 28.**

Koump v. Smith, 303 N.Y.S.2d 858, 250 N.E.2d 857 (N.Y.1969)—§ **502.1, n. 50, 51, 81; § 503.3, n. 26; § 505.1, n. 8.**

Kourtalis v. City of New York, 191 A.D.2d 480, 594 N.Y.S.2d 325 (N.Y.A.D. 2 Dept. 1993)—§ **404.1; § 404.1, n. 96, 97; § 405.1, n. 3.**

Kovel, United States v., 296 F.2d 918 (2nd Cir.1961)—§ **501.1, n. 54; § 501.2, n. 24.**

Kozlowski v. City of Amsterdam, 111 A.D.2d 476, 488 N.Y.S.2d 862 (N.Y.A.D. 3 Dept.1985)—§ **803(5).1; § 803(5).1, n. 13.**

Kozman v. Trans World Airlines, 236 F.2d 527 (2nd Cir.1956)—§ **406.2, n. 20.**

Kracker v. Spartan Chemical Co., Inc., 183 A.D.2d 810, 585 N.Y.S.2d 216 (N.Y.A.D. 2 Dept.1992)—§ **703.1, n. 1, 11.**

Kraft, People v., 36 N.Y.S. 1034 (N.Y.Sup. 1895)—§ **104.1, n. 18.**

Kramer v. Haeger Storage Warehouse Co., 123 A.D. 316, 108 N.Y.S. 1 (N.Y.A.D. 1 Dept.1908)—§ **103.1, n. 13.**

Kramer v. Time Warner Inc., 937 F.2d 767 (2nd Cir.1991)—§ **201.2, n. 4.**

Krammer v. Commonwealth, 87 Pa.St. 301 (1878)—§ **404.1, n. 46.**

Kraus v. Brandstetter, 185 A.D.2d 300, 586 N.Y.S.2d 270 (N.Y.A.D. 2 Dept.1992)— § **501.1, n. 43, 61.**

Kravitz v. Long Island Jewish–Hillside Medical Center, 113 A.D.2d 577, 497 N.Y.S.2d 51 (N.Y.A.D. 2 Dept.1985)— § **607.5, n. 3, 23, 27; § 608.1, n. 7.**

Krawitz, People v., 151 A.D.2d 850, 542 N.Y.S.2d 824 (N.Y.A.D. 3 Dept.1989)— § **509.1, n. 43.**

Kress, People v., 284 N.Y. 452, 31 N.E.2d 898 (N.Y.1940)—§ **802.2, n. 68.**

Krinsky v. Krinsky, 208 A.D.2d 599, 618 N.Y.S.2d 36 (N.Y.A.D. 2 Dept.1994)— § **301.7, n. 4.**

Kroh, United States v., 915 F.2d 326 (8th Cir.1990)—§ **607.5, n. 51.**

Kruglikov v. Kruglikov, 29 Misc.2d 17, 217 N.Y.S.2d 845 (N.Y.Sup.1961)—§ **504.1, n. 8.**

Krulewitch v. United States, 336 U.S. 440, 69 S.Ct. 716, 93 L.Ed. 790 (1949)— § **802.3; § 802.3, n. 63.**

Kucel v. Walter E. Heller & Co., 813 F.2d 67 (5th Cir.1987)—§ **203.1, n. 11.**

Kulak v. Nationwide Mut. Ins. Co., 386 N.Y.S.2d 87, 351 N.E.2d 735 (N.Y. 1976)—§ **103.1, n. 9; § 702.1, n. 4; § 704.1, n. 3, 5.**

Kunglig Jarnvagsstyrelsen v. Dexter & Carpenter, 32 F.2d 195 (2nd Cir.1929)— § **802.3, n. 1.**

Kupau, United States v., 781 F.2d 740 (9th Cir.1986)—§ **602.2, n. 8.**

Kuriansky v. Professional Care, Inc., 158 A.D.2d 897, 551 N.Y.S.2d 695 (N.Y.A.D. 3 Dept.1990)—§ **803(5).1, n. 48.**

Kusek, United States v., 844 F.2d 942 (2nd Cir.1988)—§ **612.2, n. 5.**

Kusek, United States v., 647 F.Supp. 1150 (S.D.N.Y.1986)—§ **802.3, n. 73, 77.**

Kushner, United States v., 135 F.2d 668 (2nd Cir.1943)—§ **1001.1, n. 27.**

Kuss, People v., 81 A.D.2d 427, 442 N.Y.S.2d 313 (N.Y.A.D. 4 Dept.1981)— § **1108.1, n. 6.**

Kuss, People v., 345 N.Y.S.2d 1002, 299 N.E.2d 249 (N.Y.1973)—§ **402.1; § 402.1, n. 46; § 608.1, n. 11.**

Kwiatkowski v. John Lowry, Inc., 276 N.Y. 126, 11 N.E.2d 563 (N.Y.1937)— § **804(3).1; § 804(3).1, n. 8.**

Kwoh v. Delum Builders & Suppliers, Inc., 173 A.D.2d 326, 575 N.Y.S.2d 465 (N.Y.A.D. 1 Dept.1991)—§ **601.2, n. 8.**

Kyles, United States v., 40 F.3d 519 (2nd Cir.1994)—§ **105.2, n. 11.**

L

Labate v. Plotkin, 195 A.D.2d 444, 600 N.Y.S.2d 144 (N.Y.A.D. 2 Dept.1993)— § **702.1; § 702.1, n. 83.**

La Beau v. People, 34 N.Y. 222 (1866)— § **608.2, n. 11.**

La Belle, People v., 276 N.Y.S.2d 105, 222 N.E.2d 727 (N.Y.1966)—§ **106.1, n. 7.**

Labenski, People v., 134 A.D.2d 907, 521 N.Y.S.2d 608 (N.Y.A.D. 4 Dept.1987)— § **412.1; § 412.1, n. 18, 19.**

LaChance v. New York State Racing and Wagering Bd., 118 A.D.2d 262, 504 N.Y.S.2d 635 (N.Y.A.D. 1 Dept.1986)— § **509.1, n. 6.**

Lafflin v. Buffalo & S. W. R. Co., 106 N.Y. 136, 12 N.E. 599 (N.Y.1887)—§ **405.1, n. 18.**

Lagana, People v., 365 N.Y.S.2d 147, 324 N.E.2d 534 (N.Y.1975)—§ **801(2).1, n. 7.**

Laidlaw v. Sage, 158 N.Y. 73, 52 N.E. 679 (N.Y.1899)—§ **300.3, n. 6.**

TABLE OF CASES

Laka v. Krystek, 261 N.Y. 126, 184 N.E. 732 (N.Y.1933)—§ **601.2, n. 8, 16.**

Lake Ontario Nat. Bank v. Judson, 122 N.Y. 278, 25 N.E. 367 (N.Y.1890)—**§ 611.1, n. 1.**

Lamar v. Micou, 114 U.S. 218, 5 S.Ct. 857, 29 L.Ed. 94 (1885)—§ **203.2, n. 2.**

Lamberson v. Village of Allegany, 158 A.D.2d 943, 551 N.Y.S.2d 104 (N.Y.A.D. 4 Dept.1990)—§ **501.3, n. 19.**

Lamborn v. Dittmer, 873 F.2d 522 (2nd Cir.1989)—§ **401.2, n. 3.**

Lam Lek Chong, United States v., 544 F.2d 58 (2nd Cir.1976)—§ **802.3, n. 74, 77.**

Lammes, People v., 208 A.D. 533, 203 N.Y.S. 736 (N.Y.A.D. 4 Dept.1924)—§ **804(4).1, n. 3.**

Lamont, United States v., 565 F.2d 212 (2nd Cir.1977)—§ **402.2, n. 12.**

Lance, United States v., 853 F.2d 1177 (5th Cir.1988)—§ **1104.2, n. 10.**

Landmark Ins. Co. v. Beau Rivage Restaurant, Inc., 121 A.D.2d 98, 509 N.Y.S.2d 819 (N.Y.A.D. 2 Dept.1986)—§ **501.3, n. 18.**

Landof, United States v., 591 F.2d 36 (9th Cir.1978)—§ **612.2, n. 3.**

Landon v. Preferred Acc. Ins. Co. of New York, 43 A.D. 487, 60 N.Y.S. 188 (N.Y.A.D. 2 Dept.1899)—§ **803(1).1, n. 56.**

Lane, People v., 451 N.Y.S.2d 6, 436 N.E.2d 456 (N.Y.1982)—§ **404.1; § 404.1, n. 70.**

Lang, United States v., 589 F.2d 92 (2nd Cir.1978)—§ **804.1, n. 26; § 805.2, n. 4, 6.**

Langert, Application of, 5 A.D.2d 586, 173 N.Y.S.2d 665 (N.Y.A.D. 1 Dept.1958)—§ **511.1; § 511.1, n. 4, 9.**

Langford v. Cameron, 73 A.D.2d 1001, 424 N.Y.S.2d 41 (N.Y.A.D. 3 Dept.1980)—§ **902.1, n. 10.**

Langford, United States v., 990 F.2d 65 (2nd Cir.1993)—§ **404.2, n. 20.**

Langley v. Wadsworth, 99 N.Y. 61, 1 N.E. 106 (N.Y.1885)—§ **611.3, n. 17.**

Langlois, People v., 122 Misc.2d 1018, 472 N.Y.S.2d 297 (Suffolk Co.Ct.1984)—§ **201.1, n. 45, 50.**

Lanier, United States v., 578 F.2d 1246 (8th Cir.1978)—§ **803(4).2, n. 1.**

Lanza v. New York State Joint Legislative Committee on Government Operations, 164 N.Y.S.2d 9, 143 N.E.2d 772 (N.Y. 1957)—§ **501.1, n. 48; § 502.1, n. 31.**

Lanza, United States v., 790 F.2d 1015 (2nd Cir.1986)—§ **608.2, n. 43.**

Larkin v. Nassau Elec. R. Co., 205 N.Y. 267, 98 N.E. 465 (N.Y.1912)—§ **607.8; § 607.8, n. 1, 3, 4, 13, 20, 28, 29, 30, 32, 34; § 801(1).2; § 801(1).2, n. 13, 14, 15.**

Larsen v. Vigliarolo Bros., Inc., 77 A.D.2d 562, 429 N.Y.S.2d 273 (N.Y.A.D. 2 Dept. 1980)—§ **701.1; § 701.1, n. 6, 8; § 702.1, n. 5.**

Larson v. Jo Ann Cab Corp., 209 F.2d 929 (2nd Cir.1954)—§ **300.4, n. 5, 35.**

Latzer v. Abrams, 602 F.Supp. 1314 (D.C.N.Y.1985)—§ **412.1, n. 9.**

Laundry, People v., 122 A.D.2d 450, 504 N.Y.S.2d 840 (N.Y.A.D. 3 Dept.1986)—§ **412.1, n. 23.**

Lauro, People v., 91 Misc.2d 706, 398 N.Y.S.2d 503 (N.Y.Sup.1977)—§ **803(1).1, n. 57.**

Lawal, United States v., 736 F.2d 5 (2nd Cir.1984)—§ **803(1).2; § 803(1).2, n. 49.**

Lawrence, Village of v. Greenwood, 300 N.Y. 231, 90 N.E.2d 53 (N.Y.1949)—§ **405.1, n. 25.**

Laws, People v., 203 A.D.2d 34, 610 N.Y.S.2d 196 (N.Y.A.D. 1 Dept.1994)—§ **611.3, n. 34.**

Lawson, United States v., 872 F.2d 179 (6th Cir.1989)—§ **607.5, n. 62; § 801(1).3, n. 19.**

Lawson, United States v., 683 F.2d 688 (2nd Cir.1982)—§ **410.2, n. 4, 9; § 607.8, n. 50.**

Lawson, United States v., 653 F.2d 299 (7th Cir.1981)—§ **701.2, n. 9; § 703.2, n. 10.**

Lay, People v., 254 A.D. 372, 5 N.Y.S.2d 325 (N.Y.A.D. 2 Dept.1938)—§ **502.1, n. 36.**

Lazzaro v. Maugham, 10 Misc. 230, 30 N.Y.S. 1066 (N.Y.City Ct.1894)—§ **1001.1, n. 5.**

Leary v. Albany Brewing Co., 77 A.D. 6, 79 N.Y.S. 130 (N.Y.A.D. 4 Dept.1902)—§ **104.1, n. 30; § 802.2, n. 60.**

Lebrecht v. Bethlehem Steel Corp., 402 F.2d 585 (2nd Cir.1968)—§ **405.2, n. 6.**

Lechoco, United States v., 542 F.2d 84, 177 U.S.App.D.C. 9 (D.C.Cir.1976)—§ **607.5, n. 59.**

Lechuga, United States v., 975 F.2d 397 (7th Cir.1992)—§ **803(5).2, n. 3.**

Lediard, People v., 80 A.D.2d 237, 438 N.Y.S.2d 540 (N.Y.A.D. 1 Dept.1981)—§ **402.1, n. 48, 53.**

Ledwon, People v., 153 N.Y. 10, 46 N.E. 1046 (N.Y.1897)—§ **300.3, n. 6.**

Lee v. City Brewing Corporation, 279 N.Y. 380, 18 N.E.2d 628 (N.Y.1939)—§ **300.3, n. 21.**

Lee v. Decarr, 36 A.D.2d 554, 317 N.Y.S.2d 226 (N.Y.A.D. 3 Dept.1971)—§ **702.1, n. 5; § 803(3).1, n. 17.**

Lee v. Illinois, 476 U.S. 530, 106 S.Ct. 2056, 90 L.Ed.2d 514 (1986)—§ **804(3).2, n. 16.**

Lee v. Lee, 51 A.D.2d 576, 378 N.Y.S.2d 459 (N.Y.A.D. 2 Dept.1976)—§ **503.2, n. 5.**

Lee v. Pennsylvania R. Co., 192 F.2d 226 (2nd Cir.1951)—§ **406.2; § 406.2, n. 21.**

Lee v. Shields, 188 A.D.2d 637, 591 N.Y.S.2d 522 (N.Y.A.D. 2 Dept.1992)—§ **703.1, n. 11.**

Lee, United States v., 800 F.2d 903 (9th Cir.1986)—§ **1102.2, n. 8.**

TABLE OF CASES

Leesona Corp. v. Varta Batteries, Inc., 522 F.Supp. 1304 (D.C.N.Y.1981)—§ **706.2, n. 7.**
LeGrand, People v., 67 A.D.2d 446, 415 N.Y.S.2d 252 (N.Y.A.D. 2 Dept.1979)—**§ 508.1, n. 15.**
Legrande, People v., 176 A.D.2d 351, 574 N.Y.S.2d 780 (N.Y.A.D. 2 Dept.1991)—**§ 804(1).1, n. 52.**
Leland v. Oregon, 343 U.S. 790, 72 S.Ct. 1002, 96 L.Ed. 1302 (1952)—§ **300.4, n. 65.**
Le Long v. Siebrecht, 196 A.D. 74, 187 N.Y.S. 150 (N.Y.A.D. 2 Dept.1921)—**§ 501.1, n. 17, 52; § 505.1, n. 4.**
Lemmons, People v., 387 N.Y.S.2d 97, 354 N.E.2d 836 (N.Y.1976)—§ **302.1, n. 30.**
Lenny McN., Matter of, 183 A.D.2d 627, 584 N.Y.S.2d 17 (N.Y.A.D. 1 Dept. 1992)—**§ 501.3, n. 15, 35; § 612.1; § 612.1, n. 28, 31.**
Lentino v. Rosedale Gardens, Inc., 79 A.D.2d 554, 433 N.Y.S.2d 805 (N.Y.A.D. 1 Dept.1980)—§ **300.4, n. 5.**
Leonard, People v., 201 N.Y.S.2d 509, 167 N.E.2d 842 (N.Y.1960)—§ **701.1, n. 8.**
Leonardi, United States v., 623 F.2d 746 (2nd Cir.1980)—§ **607.8, n. 45.**
Leonardo, People v., 199 N.Y. 432, 92 N.E. 1060 (N.Y.1910)—§ **607.3, n. 22.**
Leone, People v., 307 N.Y.S.2d 430, 255 N.E.2d 696 (N.Y.1969)—§ **702.1, n. 48.**
Leon, Matter of, 421 N.Y.S.2d 863, 397 N.E.2d 374 (N.Y.1979)—§ **803(3).1; § 803(3).1, n. 24.**
Leonti, People v., 262 N.Y. 256, 186 N.E. 693 (N.Y.1933)—§ **606.1, n. 17.**
Leo Spear Const. Co. v. Fidelity & Cas. Co. of New York, 446 F.2d 439 (2nd Cir. 1971)—§ **1107.2, n. 6.**
Leotta v. Plessinger, 209 N.Y.S.2d 304, 171 N.E.2d 454 (N.Y.1960)—§ **301.4, n. 15; § 301.5, n. 31; § 411.1, n. 5, 12.**
Lerner v. Karageorgis Lines, Inc., 497 N.Y.S.2d 894, 488 N.E.2d 824 (N.Y. 1985)—§ **203.1, n. 7.**
Lerner v. Seaboard Coast Line R. Co., 594 F.Supp. 963 (D.C.N.Y.1984)—**§ 803(5).2, n. 21.**
LeRoy v. Sabena Belgian World Airlines, 344 F.2d 266 (2nd Cir.1965)—**§ 803(5).2, n. 3.**
Lessin v. Direct Delivery Service, 10 A.D.2d 624, 196 N.Y.S.2d 751 (N.Y.A.D. 1 Dept. 1960)—§ **803(1).1, n. 66.**
Letendre v. Hartford Acc. & Indem. Co., 289 N.Y.S.2d 183, 236 N.E.2d 467 (N.Y. 1968)—§ **607.8, n. 5; § 801(1).2; § 801(1).2, n. 3; § 802.2; § 802.2, n. 43; § 804(5).1; § 804(5).1, n. 4.**
Leucadia, Inc. v. Reliance Ins. Co., 864 F.2d 964 (2nd Cir.1988)—§ **404.2; § 404.2, n. 36.**
Leucadia, Inc. v. Reliance Ins. Co., 101 F.R.D. 674 (D.C.N.Y.1983)—§ **501.2, n. 49.**

Levan, People v., 295 N.Y. 26, 64 N.E.2d 341 (N.Y.1945)—§ **701.1, n. 9.**
Leven v. Tallis Dept. Store, Inc., 178 A.D.2d 466, 577 N.Y.S.2d 132 (N.Y.A.D. 2 Dept. 1991)—§ **1104.1, n. 14.**
Levine v. Bornstein, 13 Misc.2d 161, 174 N.Y.S.2d 574 (N.Y.Sup.1958)—§ **509.1, n. 11.**
Levine v. Levine, 451 N.Y.S.2d 26, 436 N.E.2d 476 (N.Y.1982)—§ **615.1, n. 6.**
Levinsky's Will, In re, 23 A.D.2d 25, 258 N.Y.S.2d 613 (N.Y.A.D. 2 Dept.1965)—**§ 501.1, n. 40, 70.**
Levy v. Corn, 191 A.D. 56, 180 N.Y.S. 794 (N.Y.A.D. 1 Dept.1920)—§ **1108.1, n. 1.**
Levy, United States v., 578 F.2d 896 (2nd Cir.1978)—§ **410.2, n. 7.**
Lewis v. Baker, 526 F.2d 470 (2nd Cir. 1975)—§ **803(3).2; § 803(3).2, n. 39.**
Lewis v. Lewis, 85 Misc.2d 610, 381 N.Y.S.2d 631 (N.Y.Sup.1976)—**§ 803(5).1, n. 28.**
Lewis v. New York City Housing Authority, 151 A.D.2d 237, 542 N.Y.S.2d 165 (N.Y.A.D. 1 Dept.1989)—§ **504.1, n. 10.**
Lewis, People v., 196 A.D.2d 742, 602 N.Y.S.2d 6 (N.Y.A.D. 1 Dept.1993)—**§ 609.1, n. 40.**
Lewis, People v., 514 N.Y.S.2d 205, 506 N.E.2d 915 (N.Y.1987)—§ **401.1; § 401.1, n. 42; § 404.1; § 404.1, n. 3, 82.**
Lewis, United States v., 626 F.2d 940, 200 U.S.App.D.C. 76 (D.C.Cir.1980)—**§ 609.2, n. 13, 17.**
Lewis, United States v., 565 F.2d 1248 (2nd Cir.1977)—§ **801(2).2, n. 11.**
Lewis v. Velez, 149 F.R.D. 474 (S.D.N.Y. 1993)—§ **803(3).2; § 803(3).2, n. 28, 42; § 803(5).2, n. 30.**
Leyra, People v., 151 N.Y.S.2d 658, 134 N.E.2d 475 (N.Y.1956)—§ **401.1, n. 14.**
Leyva, People v., 379 N.Y.S.2d 30, 341 N.E.2d 546 (N.Y.1975)—§ **302.1, n. 24.**
Liberatore, People v., 581 N.Y.S.2d 634, 590 N.E.2d 219 (N.Y.1992)—§ **510.1, n. 2, 7.**
Liberto v. Worcester Mut. Ins. Co., 87 A.D.2d 477, 452 N.Y.S.2d 74 (N.Y.A.D. 2 Dept.1982)—§ **402.1, n. 27.**
Liberty Mut. Ins. Co. v. Rotches Pork Packers, Inc., 969 F.2d 1384 (2nd Cir.1992)—**§ 201.2, n. 4.**
Licari v. Elliott, 455 N.Y.S.2d 570, 441 N.E.2d 1088 (N.Y.1982)—§ **300.2, n. 4.**
Liccione, People v., 430 N.Y.S.2d 36, 407 N.E.2d 1333 (N.Y.1980)—§ **802.2, n. 98.**
Liccione, People v., 63 A.D.2d 305, 407 N.Y.S.2d 753 (N.Y.A.D. 4 Dept.1978)—**§ 104.1, n. 18; § 802.2; § 802.2, n. 81, 95; § 804(2).1; § 804(2).1, n. 14, 23; § 805.1, n. 7.**
Lichtenstein v. Montefiore Hospital and Medical Center, 56 A.D.2d 281, 392 N.Y.S.2d 18 (N.Y.A.D. 1 Dept.1977)—**§ 505.1, n. 3.**

TABLE OF CASES

Liebman, United States v., 742 F.2d 807 (3rd Cir.1984)—§ **501.2, n. 14.**

Lifrieri, People v., 157 Misc.2d 598, 597 N.Y.S.2d 580 (N.Y.Sup.1993)—§ **503.3, n. 13.**

Lightly, United States v., 677 F.2d 1027 (4th Cir.1982)—§ **601.3, n. 9.**

Lilley, United States v., 581 F.2d 182 (8th Cir.1978)—§ **804.1, n. 8; § 804(3).1, n. 31.**

Lillie v. United States, 953 F.2d 1188 (10th Cir.1992)—§ **1107.2, n. 6.**

Linda O., Matter of, 95 Misc.2d 744, 408 N.Y.S.2d 308 (N.Y.City Fam.Ct.1978)—§ **609.1, n. 11.**

Linda S., Matter of, 148 Misc.2d 169, 560 N.Y.S.2d 181 (N.Y.Fam.Ct.1990)—§ **804(5).1; § 804(5).1, n. 23.**

Lindeman v. Slavin, 184 A.D.2d 910, 585 N.Y.S.2d 568 (N.Y.A.D. 3 Dept.1992)—§ **406.1, n. 13.**

Lindsay v. Academy Broadway Corp., 198 A.D.2d 641, 603 N.Y.S.2d 622 (N.Y.A.D. 3 Dept.1993)—§ **803(3).1, n. 27.**

Lindsay v. Ortho Pharmaceutical Corp., 637 F.2d 87 (2nd Cir.1980)—§ **803(5).2, n. 3.**

Lindstrom, United States v., 698 F.2d 1154 (11th Cir.1983)—§ **607.7, n. 20.**

Lippert, People v., 138 A.D.2d 770, 525 N.Y.S.2d 390 (N.Y.A.D. 3 Dept.1988)—§ **412.1, n. 11.**

Lipsius v. White, 91 A.D.2d 271, 458 N.Y.S.2d 928 (N.Y.A.D. 2 Dept.1983)—§ **300.3, n. 35.**

Lipsky v. Commonwealth United Corp., 551 F.2d 887 (2nd Cir.1976)—§ **410.2, n. 10.**

Lis v. Robert Packer Hospital, 579 F.2d 819 (3rd Cir.1978)—§ **611.5, n. 17.**

Litherland v. Petrolane Offshore Const. Services, Inc., 546 F.2d 129 (5th Cir. 1977)—§ **611.5, n. 11.**

Litton Systems, Inc. v. American Tel. and Tel. Co., 700 F.2d 785 (2nd Cir.1983)—§ **802.3, n. 25; § 803(5).2, n. 23.**

Lium v. Ploski, 87 A.D.2d 860, 449 N.Y.S.2d 297 (N.Y.A.D. 2 Dept.1982)—§ **402.1, n. 26.**

Livant v. Adams, 17 A.D.2d 784, 232 N.Y.S.2d 641 (N.Y.A.D. 1 Dept.1962)—§ **614.1, n. 17.**

Livingston v. Arnoux, 56 N.Y. 507 (1874)—§ **804(3).1; § 804(3).1, n. 13; § 804(3).2, n. 22.**

Livingston, United States v., 816 F.2d 184 (5th Cir.1987)—§ **609.2, n. 19.**

Lloyde, People v., 106 A.D.2d 405, 482 N.Y.S.2d 326 (N.Y.A.D. 2 Dept.1984)—§ **615.1, n. 15.**

Lobel V American Airlines, 205 F.2d 927 (2nd Cir.1953)—§ **1105.2, n. 3.**

Lo Bue, United States v., 180 F.Supp. 955 (D.C.N.Y.1960)—§ **901.4, n. 16.**

Locascio, United States v., 6 F.3d 924 (2nd Cir.1993)—§ **703.2, n. 7.**

Lock v. Fisher, 104 Misc.2d 656, 428 N.Y.S.2d 868 (N.Y.Fam.Ct.1980)—§ **803(5).1, n. 28.**

Loetsch v. New York City Omnibus Corporation, 291 N.Y. 308, 52 N.E.2d 448 (N.Y.1943)—§ **801.1; § 801.1, n. 35, 38; § 803(1).1, n. 41.**

Loinaz v. EG & G, Inc., 910 F.2d 1 (1st Cir.1990)—§ **611.5, n. 6.**

Lois Sportswear, U.S.A., Inc. v. Levi Strauss & Co., 104 F.R.D. 103 (D.C.N.Y. 1985)—§ **501.2, n. 48; § 501.3, n. 54.**

Lollar, United States v., 606 F.2d 587 (5th Cir.1979)—§ **608.1, n. 21, 23.**

Lombardozzi, United States v., 335 F.2d 414 (2nd Cir.1964)—§ **612.2, n. 2.**

Longo v. D'Apice, 154 A.D.2d 726, 546 N.Y.S.2d 907 (N.Y.A.D. 2 Dept.1989)—§ **512.1, n. 4.**

Lopato v. Kinney Rent–A–Car, Inc., 73 A.D.2d 565, 423 N.Y.S.2d 42 (N.Y.A.D. 1 Dept.1979)—§ **103.1, n. 14.**

Lopez, People v., 67 A.D.2d 624, 411 N.Y.S.2d 627 (N.Y.A.D. 1 Dept.1979)—§ **402.1, n. 52.**

Lopez v. Senatore, 494 N.Y.S.2d 101, 484 N.E.2d 130 (N.Y.1985)—§ **704.1, n. 17, 18.**

Lopez, United States v., 937 F.2d 716 (2nd Cir.1991)—§ **802.3, n. 62.**

Lopez, United States v., 611 F.2d 44 (4th Cir.1979)—§ **607.7, n. 21.**

Lopez, United States v., 584 F.2d 1175 (2nd Cir.1978)—§ **802.3, n. 78.**

Lopez, United States v., 328 F.Supp. 1077 (D.C.N.Y.1971)—§ **201.2, n. 6.**

Lord, United States v., 907 F.2d 1028 (10th Cir.1990)—§ **607.5, n. 53.**

Lorde v. Guardian Life Ins. Co. of America, 252 A.D. 646, 300 N.Y.S. 721 (N.Y.A.D. 1 Dept.1937)—§ **502.1, n. 7, 18.**

Lorenz v. Valley Forge Ins. Co., 815 F.2d 1095 (7th Cir.1987)—§ **501.2, n. 47.**

Losada, United States v., 674 F.2d 167 (2nd Cir.1982)—§ **105.2, n. 1; § 804.1, n. 15.**

Loschiavo v. Port Authority of New York, 462 N.Y.S.2d 440, 448 N.E.2d 1351 (N.Y. 1983)—§ **802.2; § 802.2, n. 58.**

Los Robles Motor Lodge, Inc. v. Department of Alcoholic Beverage Control, 246 Cal.App.2d 198, 54 Cal.Rptr. 547 (Cal. App. 3 Dist.1966)—§ **801.1, n. 22.**

Loughan v. Firestone Tire & Rubber Co., 749 F.2d 1519 (11th Cir.1985)—§ **406.2, n. 12.**

Loughlin v. City of New York, 186 A.D.2d 176, 587 N.Y.S.2d 732 (N.Y.A.D. 2 Dept. 1992)—§ **300.3, n. 36; § 607.1, n. 6.**

Loughran v. Markle, 242 A.D. 331, 275 N.Y.S. 721 (N.Y.A.D. 3 Dept.1934)—§ **803(5).1, n. 10.**

Louis Harris and Associates, Inc. v. deLeon, 622 N.Y.S.2d 217, 646 N.E.2d 438 (N.Y. 1994)—§ **300.2, n. 20.**

TABLE OF CASES

Louis Vuitton S.A. v. Spencer Handbags Corp., 765 F.2d 966 (2nd Cir.1985)—§ **1104.2, n. 16.**

Lourido, People v., 522 N.Y.S.2d 98, 516 N.E.2d 1212 (N.Y.1987)—§ **802.2, n. 29.**

Love, Matter of, 413 N.Y.S.2d 919, 386 N.E.2d 830 (N.Y.1978)—§ **300.4, n. 27.**

Lowney, Matter of Estate of, 152 A.D.2d 574, 543 N.Y.S.2d 698 (N.Y.A.D. 2 Dept. 1989)—§ **301.5, n. 29.**

Lowrance v. State, 185 A.D.2d 268, 586 N.Y.S.2d 21 (N.Y.A.D. 2 Dept.1992)—§ **511.1, n. 5.**

Lozado, People v., 210 A.D.2d 83, 620 N.Y.S.2d 32 (N.Y.A.D. 1 Dept.1994)—§ **601.1, n. 65.**

LTV Securities Litigation, In re, 89 F.R.D. 595 (D.C.Tex.1981)—§ **501.2, n. 11, 37.**

Luce v. United States, 469 U.S. 38, 105 S.Ct. 460, 83 L.Ed.2d 443 (1984)—§ **103.2, n. 23; § 609.2; § 609.2, n. 8.**

Luck v. United States, 348 F.2d 763, 121 U.S.App.D.C. 151 (D.C.Cir.1965)—§ **609.2, n. 7.**

Ludkowitz, People v., 266 N.Y. 233, 194 N.E. 688 (N.Y.1935)—§ **804(2).1, n. 5, 12.**

Lugo, People v., 202 A.D.2d 248, 608 N.Y.S.2d 632 (N.Y.A.D. 1 Dept.1994)—§ **608.2, n. 31.**

Luke, People v., 136 Misc.2d 733, 519 N.Y.S.2d 316 (N.Y.Sup.1987)—§ **803(1).1; § 803(1).1, n. 7.**

Lumumba, United States v., 794 F.2d 806 (2nd Cir.1986)—§ **803(5).2, n. 3; § 902.1, n. 16.**

Lundell v. Ford Motor Co., 120 A.D.2d 575, 502 N.Y.S.2d 63 (N.Y.A.D. 2 Dept. 1986)—§ **501.3, n. 26.**

Lundgren v. McColgin, 96 A.D.2d 706, 464 N.Y.S.2d 317 (N.Y.A.D. 4 Dept.1983)—§ **606.1, n. 3.**

Lunney v. Graham, 91 A.D.2d 592, 457 N.Y.S.2d 282 (N.Y.A.D. 1 Dept.1982)—§ **615.1, n. 9, 11.**

Lutwak v. United States, 344 U.S. 604, 73 S.Ct. 481, 97 L.Ed. 593 (1953)—§ **503.5, n. 9; § 802.2, n. 104; § 802.3; § 802.3, n. 66.**

Luz P., Matter of, 189 A.D.2d 274, 595 N.Y.S.2d 541 (N.Y.A.D. 2 Dept.1993)—§ **601.1, n. 12, 55; § 604.1, n. 5; § 702.1; § 702.1, n. 12, 70.**

Lyde, People v., 160 A.D.2d 817, 554 N.Y.S.2d 74 (N.Y.A.D. 2 Dept.1990)—§ **608.1, n. 5.**

Lynch v. Mutual Life Ins. Co. of New York, 55 Misc.2d 179, 284 N.Y.S.2d 768 (N.Y.Sup.1967)—§ **502.1, n. 42.**

Lynch, People v., 296 N.Y.S.2d 327, 244 N.E.2d 29 (N.Y.1968)—§ **501.1, n. 81.**

Lynes, People v., 425 N.Y.S.2d 295, 401 N.E.2d 405 (N.Y.1980)—§ **104.1; § 104.1, n. 25; § 900.1; § 900.1, n. 2, 20; § 901.1, n. 7; § 901.4, n. 4; § 901.5, n. 6; § 901.6; § 901.6, n. 2.**

Lynn v. Lynn, 628 N.Y.S.2d 667 (N.Y.A.D. 1 Dept.1995)—§ **300.4, n. 14.**

Lyon v. Ricker, 141 N.Y. 225, 36 N.E. 189 (N.Y.1894)—§ **804(3).1; § 804(3).1, n. 23.**

Lyons, People v., 593 N.Y.S.2d 776, 609 N.E.2d 129 (N.Y.1992)—§ **401.1, n. 30.**

M

Macana, People v., 615 N.Y.S.2d 656, 639 N.E.2d 13 (N.Y.1994)—§ **401.1, n. 27, 29.**

MacDonald, United States v., 688 F.2d 224 (4th Cir.1982)—§ **803(5).2, n. 20.**

Mackell, People v., 47 A.D.2d 209, 366 N.Y.S.2d 173 (N.Y.A.D. 2 Dept.1975)—§ **611.2, n. 4, 22.**

Mackey, People v., 425 N.Y.S.2d 288, 401 N.E.2d 398 (N.Y.1980)—§ **608.2, n. 27; § 609.1, n. 15, 42.**

Macklowitz, People v., 135 Misc.2d 232, 514 N.Y.S.2d 883 (N.Y.Sup.1987)—§ **803(3).1, n. 10.**

Mackston v. State, 126 A.D.2d 710, 510 N.Y.S.2d 912 (N.Y.A.D. 2 Dept.1987)—§ **201.1, n. 14, 38.**

Maddox, People v., 139 A.D.2d 597, 527 N.Y.S.2d 89 (N.Y.A.D. 2 Dept.1988)—§ **606.1, n. 4.**

Maddox, United States v., 444 F.2d 148 (2nd Cir.1971)—§ **803(3).2, n. 27; § 805.2, n. 3.**

Madeline Marie Nursing Homes, In re, 694 F.2d 433 (6th Cir.1982)—§ **203.2, n. 1, 5.**

Maerling, People v., 485 N.Y.S.2d 23, 474 N.E.2d 231 (N.Y.1984)—§ **607.8, n. 10, 11; § 611.3, n. 26.**

Maerling, People v., 413 N.Y.S.2d 316, 385 N.E.2d 1245 (N.Y.1978)—§ **804(3).1; § 804(3).1, n. 32; § 804(3).2, n. 22.**

Magee, People v., 128 A.D.2d 811, 513 N.Y.S.2d 514 (N.Y.A.D. 2 Dept.1987)—§ **607.4, n. 38, 43.**

Magett, People v., 196 A.D.2d 62, 608 N.Y.S.2d 434 (N.Y.A.D. 1 Dept.1994)—§ **401.1, n. 27.**

Magna, In re, 258 N.Y. 82, 179 N.E. 266 (N.Y.1932)—§ **301.5, n. 22.**

Magri, People v., 170 N.Y.S.2d 335, 147 N.E.2d 728 (N.Y.1958)—§ **201.1, n. 15, 46; § 702.1, n. 50; § 901.9, n. 7.**

Mahaney v. Carr, 175 N.Y. 454, 67 N.E. 903 (N.Y.1903)—§ **1001.1, n. 27.**

Mahlandt v. Wild Canid Survival & Research Center, Inc., 588 F.2d 626 (8th Cir.1978)—§ **802.3; § 802.3, n. 35.**

Mahoney v. New York Central Railroad, 234 F.2d 923 (2nd Cir.1956)—§ **406.2, n. 4.**

Mahoney v. Staffa, 184 A.D.2d 886, 585 N.Y.S.2d 543 (N.Y.A.D. 3 Dept.1992)—§ **501.3, n. 9.**

TABLE OF CASES

Majeed, People v., 204 A.D.2d 986, 613 N.Y.S.2d 69 (N.Y.A.D. 4 Dept.1994)—**§ 608.1, n. 9.**

Malagon, People v., 431 N.Y.S.2d 460, 409 N.E.2d 934 (N.Y.1980)—**§ 802.2, n. 93.**

Maldonado, People v., 199 A.D.2d 563, 606 N.Y.S.2d 258 (N.Y.A.D. 2 Dept.1993)—**§ 601.1, n. 36.**

Maldonado–Rivera, United States v., 922 F.2d 934 (2nd Cir.1990)—**§ 611.5, n. 19, 20; § 802.3; § 802.3, n. 59; § 901.4, n. 11.**

Malek v. Federal Ins. Co., 994 F.2d 49 (2nd Cir.1993)—**§ 610.2, n. 4; § 615.2, n. 4; § 803(3).2, n. 7.**

Malfitano, Appeal of, 633 F.2d 276 (3rd Cir.1980)—**§ 503.5, n. 14.**

Malinsky, People v., 255 N.Y.S.2d 850, 204 N.E.2d 188 (N.Y.1965)—**§ 510.1, n. 2.**

Malizia, People v., 92 A.D.2d 154, 460 N.Y.S.2d 23 (N.Y.A.D. 1 Dept.1983)—**§ 803(1).1; § 803(1).1, n. 50.**

Malloy v. Hogan, 378 U.S. 1, 84 S.Ct. 1489, 12 L.Ed.2d 653 (1964)—**§ 509.1; § 509.1, n. 2.**

Malphurs, People v., 111 A.D.2d 266, 489 N.Y.S.2d 102 (N.Y.A.D. 2 Dept.1985)—**§ 1102.1, n. 5.**

Manarite, United States v., 448 F.2d 583 (2nd Cir.1971)—**§ 302.2, n. 7.**

Mancusi v. Stubbs, 408 U.S. 204, 92 S.Ct. 2308, 33 L.Ed.2d 293 (1972)—**§ 804.1; § 804.1, n. 11; § 804(1).2; § 804(1).2, n. 21.**

Mandel, People v., 61 A.D.2d 563, 403 N.Y.S.2d 63 (N.Y.A.D. 2 Dept.1978)—**§ 412.1, n. 7.**

Mandel, United States v., 591 F.2d 1347 (4th Cir.1979)—**§ 608.1, n. 19.**

Mandeville v. Reynolds, 68 N.Y. 528 (1877)—**§ 803(4).1, n. 7; § 803(5).1, n. 36.**

Mangan, United States v., 575 F.2d 32 (2nd Cir.1978)—**§ 103.2, n. 10; § 803(1).2; § 803(1).2, n. 41; § 803(6).2, n. 3; § 901.3, n. 16, 23; § 901.4, n. 6.**

Mangiaracina v. New York Telephone Co., 105 A.D.2d 695, 481 N.Y.S.2d 134 (N.Y.A.D. 2 Dept.1984)—**§ 404.1, n. 99, 100.**

Manley, United States v., 632 F.2d 978 (2nd Cir.1980)—**§ 510.2; § 510.2, n. 9.**

Mann, People v., 336 N.Y.S.2d 633, 288 N.E.2d 595 (N.Y.1972)—**§ 402.1, n. 20; § 404.1, n. 38.**

Mann v. University of Cincinnati, 824 F.Supp. 1190 (S.D.Ohio 1993)—**§ 502.2, n. 1.**

Mansaw, United States v., 714 F.2d 785 (8th Cir.1983)—**§ 609.2, n. 13.**

Manse v. Hossington, 205 N.Y. 33, 98 N.E. 203 (N.Y.1912)—**§ 103.1, n. 10.**

Mantello, People ex rel. Saafir v., 163 A.D.2d 824, 558 N.Y.S.2d 356 (N.Y.A.D. 4 Dept.1990)—**§ 803(3).1, n. 61.**

Manton, United States v., 107 F.2d 834 (2nd Cir.1939)—**§ 1001.1, n. 27.**

Manufacturers and Traders Trust Co. v. Servotronics, Inc., 132 A.D.2d 392, 522 N.Y.S.2d 999 (N.Y.A.D. 4 Dept.1987)—**§ 501.1, n. 85.**

Manuta v. Lazarus, 104 Misc. 134, 171 N.Y.S. 1076 (N.Y.City Ct.1918)—**§ 1107.1, n. 2, 11.**

Manzanillo, People v., 145 Misc.2d 504, 546 N.Y.S.2d 954 (N.Y.City Crim.Ct.1989)—**§ 502.1, n. 86.**

Marcantoni, United States v., 590 F.2d 1324 (5th Cir.1979)—**§ 1001.1, n. 25.**

Marchand, United States v., 564 F.2d 983 (2nd Cir.1977)—**§ 801(1).3; § 801(1).3, n. 11; § 801(2).2, n. 10.**

Marchetti v. United States, 390 U.S. 39, 88 S.Ct. 697, 19 L.Ed.2d 889 (1968)—**§ 509.1, n. 73.**

Marchini, United States v., 797 F.2d 759 (9th Cir.1986)—**§ 804(5).2, n. 15.**

Marcucci v. Bird, 275 A.D. 127, 88 N.Y.S.2d 333 (N.Y.A.D. 3 Dept.1949)—**§ 701.1, n. 7.**

Marcus, People v., 137 A.D.2d 723, 524 N.Y.S.2d 806 (N.Y.A.D. 2 Dept.1988)—**§ 105.1, n. 18.**

Mariani, United States v., 725 F.2d 862 (2nd Cir.1984)—**§ 300.3, n. 53, 56.**

Marigliano v. City of New York, 196 A.D.2d 533, 601 N.Y.S.2d 161 (N.Y.A.D. 2 Dept. 1993)—**§ 803(3).1, n. 61.**

Marin, People v., 86 A.D.2d 40, 448 N.Y.S.2d 748 (N.Y.A.D. 2 Dept.1982)—**§ 501.3, n. 11, 29.**

Marin, United States v., 669 F.2d 73 (2nd Cir.1982)—**§ 106.2, n. 7.**

Marine Midland Bank v. Russo Produce Co., Inc., 427 N.Y.S.2d 961, 405 N.E.2d 205 (N.Y.1980)—**§ 401.1, n. 34; § 509.1, n. 10; § 514.1; § 514.1, n. 8; § 514.2; § 514.2, n. 5.**

Mariner, People v., 147 A.D.2d 659, 538 N.Y.S.2d 61 (N.Y.A.D. 2 Dept.1989)—**§ 1105.1, n. 4, 7, 8.**

Marion v. B. G. Coon Const. Co., 216 N.Y. 178, 110 N.E. 444 (N.Y.1915)—**§ 1004.1, n. 8; § 1104.1, n. 21.**

Maritime Cinema Service Corp. v. Movies en Route, Inc., 60 F.R.D. 587 (D.C.N.Y. 1973)—**§ 513.2, n. 7.**

Maritime Ventures Intern., Inc. v. Caribbean Trading & Fidelity, Ltd., 722 F.Supp. 1032 (S.D.N.Y.1989)—**§ 802.3, n. 36, 49.**

Mark v. Colgate University, 53 A.D.2d 884, 385 N.Y.S.2d 621 (N.Y.A.D. 2 Dept. 1976)—**§ 702.1, n. 84.**

Markel v. Spencer, 5 A.D.2d 400, 171 N.Y.S.2d 770 (N.Y.A.D. 4 Dept.1958)—**§ 300.3, n. 2.**

Marks v. King, 64 N.Y. 628 (1876)—**§ 103.1, n. 35.**

TABLE OF CASES

Marks, People v., 188 N.Y.S.2d 465, 160 N.E.2d 26 (N.Y.1959)—§ **104.1**; § **104.1, n. 14, 33**; § **803(1).1, n. 34.**

Marks, United States v., 816 F.2d 1207 (7th Cir.1987)—§ **607.8, n. 49.**

Marks' Estate, In re, 33 A.D.2d 1029, 307 N.Y.S.2d 950 (N.Y.A.D. 2 Dept.1970)— § **1001.1, n. 33.**

Maroon v. Immigration and Naturalization Service, 364 F.2d 982 (8th Cir.1966)— § **901.7, n. 19.**

Marrero, People v., 183 A.D.2d 728, 583 N.Y.S.2d 468 (N.Y.A.D. 2 Dept.1992)— § **801(2).1, n. 9, 33.**

Marrone v. United States, 355 F.2d 238 (2nd Cir.1966)—§ **103.2, n. 16.**

Marrow v. Marrow, 124 A.D.2d 1000, 508 N.Y.S.2d 789 (N.Y.A.D. 4 Dept.1986)— § **503.2, n. 3.**

Marshall v. Davies, 78 N.Y. 414 (1877)— § **611.1, n. 4.**

Marshall, People v., 306 N.Y. 223, 117 N.E.2d 265 (N.Y.1954)—§ **105.1, n. 7**; § **802.2, n. 99.**

Martell v. Boardwalk Enterprises, Inc., 748 F.2d 740 (2nd Cir.1984)—§ **702.2, n. 8.**

Martin v. Alabama 84 Truck Rental, Inc., 417 N.Y.S.2d 56, 390 N.E.2d 774 (N.Y. 1979)—§ **608.2, n. 10.**

Martin v. City of Cohoes, 371 N.Y.S.2d 687, 332 N.E.2d 867 (N.Y.1975)—§ **103.1, n. 7.**

Martin v. Hillen, 142 N.Y. 140, 36 N.E. 803 (N.Y.1894)—§ **601.2, n. 71.**

Martin v. Maintenance Co., Inc., 588 F.2d 355 (2nd Cir.1978)—§ **1102.2, n. 8.**

Martin v. Ohio, 480 U.S. 228, 107 S.Ct. 1098, 94 L.Ed.2d 267 (1987)—§ **300.4, n. 66.**

Martin A. v. Gross, 194 A.D.2d 195, 605 N.Y.S.2d 742 (N.Y.A.D. 1 Dept.1993)— § **511.1, n. 5.**

Martinez, People v., 177 A.D.2d 600, 575 N.Y.S.2d 938 (N.Y.A.D. 2 Dept.1991)— § **412.1, n. 17.**

Martinez, United States v., 54 F.3d 1040 (2nd Cir.1995)—§ **300.3, n. 53.**

Martorella v. Prudential Ins. Co. of America, 238 A.D. 532, 264 N.Y.S. 751 (N.Y.A.D. 4 Dept.1933)—§ **804(3).1**; § **804(3).1, n. 17.**

Martyn v. Braun, 270 A.D. 768, 59 N.Y.S.2d 588 (N.Y.A.D. 2 Dept.1946)—§ **411.1, n. 7.**

Marulli v. Pro Sec. Service, Inc., 151 Misc.2d 1077, 583 N.Y.S.2d 870 (N.Y.Sup.1992)—§ **703.1, n. 10.**

Marx & Co., Inc. v. Diners' Club Inc., 550 F.2d 505 (2nd Cir.1977)—§ **702.2, n. 9**; § **704.2**; § **704.2, n. 7.**

Maryland v. Craig, 497 U.S. 836, 110 S.Ct. 3157, 111 L.Ed.2d 666 (1990)— § **804(5).2, n. 35.**

Marzano, United States v., 537 F.2d 257 (7th Cir.1976)—§ **607.6, n. 37, 38.**

Marzano, United States v., 149 F.2d 923 (2nd Cir.1945)—§ **614.2, n. 1, 2, 4.**

Maschi, People v., 426 N.Y.S.2d 727, 403 N.E.2d 449 (N.Y.1980)—§ **103.1, n. 11.**

Masemer v. Delmarva Power & Light Co., 723 F.Supp. 1019 (D.Del.1989)— § **803(5).2, n. 38.**

Mashley v. Kerr, 419 N.Y.S.2d 476, 393 N.E.2d 471 (N.Y.1979)—§ **103.1, n. 3.**

Maslinski v. Brunswick Hosp. Center, Inc., 118 A.D.2d 834, 500 N.Y.S.2d 318 (N.Y.A.D. 2 Dept.1986)—§ **606.1, n. 15.**

Mason, People v., 186 A.D.2d 984, 590 N.Y.S.2d 811 (N.Y.A.D. 4 Dept.1992)— § **103.1, n. 29.**

Massachusetts Mut. Life Ins. Co. v. Brei, 311 F.2d 463 (2nd Cir.1962)—§ **103.2, n. 16**; § **502.1, n. 25, 26.**

Mastan Co., Inc. v. Weil, 84 A.D.2d 657, 444 N.Y.S.2d 315 (N.Y.A.D. 3 Dept.1981)— § **1001.1, n. 27, 30.**

Mastberg, United States v., 503 F.2d 465 (9th Cir.1974)—§ **701.2, n. 7.**

Mastin v. Village of Lima, Livingston County, 86 A.D.2d 777, 448 N.Y.S.2d 274 (N.Y.A.D. 4 Dept.1982)—§ **300.4, n. 29.**

Mastrangelo, United States v., 693 F.2d 269 (2nd Cir.1982)—§ **802.2, n. 16**; § **804(1).1**; § **804(1).1, n. 51**; § **807.1, n. 10.**

Mastrianni's Estate, Matter of, 55 A.D.2d 784, 389 N.Y.S.2d 914 (N.Y.A.D. 3 Dept. 1976)—§ **601.2, n. 62.**

Match v. Match, 146 Misc.2d 986, 553 N.Y.S.2d 626 (N.Y.Sup.1990)—§ **706.1, n. 4.**

Mather, People v., 4 Wend. (N.Y.) 229 (1830)—§ **611.2, n. 5, 9, 10, 13, 15, 20.**

Matlock, United States v., 415 U.S. 164, 94 S.Ct. 988, 39 L.Ed.2d 242 (1974)— § **802.3, n. 7.**

Matott v. Ward, 423 N.Y.S.2d 645, 399 N.E.2d 532 (N.Y.1979)—§ **702.1, n. 26**; § **705.1**; § **705.1, n. 11.**

Matter of (see name of party)

Matthews, In re, 714 F.2d 223 (2nd Cir. 1983)—§ **503.5, n. 23.**

Matthews, United States v., 20 F.3d 538 (2nd Cir.1994)—§ **804.1, n. 25**; § **804(3).2**; § **804(3).2, n. 15.**

Matthews' Estate, In re, 153 N.Y. 443, 47 N.E. 901 (N.Y.1897)—§ **301.4, n. 7.**

Mattiace, People v., 567 N.Y.S.2d 384, 568 N.E.2d 1189 (N.Y.1990)—§ **103.1, n. 39**; § **609.1**; § **609.1, n. 15, 34.**

Mattox v. United States, 156 U.S. 237, 15 S.Ct. 337, 39 L.Ed. 409 (1895)—§ **806.1, n. 11.**

Mattox v. United States, 146 U.S. 140, 13 S.Ct. 50, 36 L.Ed. 917 (1892)—§ **606.2, n. 5**; § **804(2).2, n. 12.**

Matusow, United States v., 244 F.2d 532 (2nd Cir.1957)—§ **901.7, n. 20.**

Mauchlin, United States v., 670 F.2d 746 (7th Cir.1982)—§ **901.3, n. 22.**

TABLE OF CASES

Maxwell, People v., 122 A.D.2d 435, 504 N.Y.S.2d 832 (N.Y.A.D. 3 Dept.1986)—§ **412.1, n. 19.**

Maxwell, United States v., 383 F.2d 437 (2nd Cir.1967)—§ **1004.1, n. 2.**

May, People v., 162 A.D.2d 977, 557 N.Y.S.2d 203 (N.Y.A.D. 4 Dept.1990)—§ **1002.1, n. 10.**

Mayer, United States v., 556 F.2d 245 (5th Cir.1977)—§ **611.5, n. 20.**

Maynard v. Sayles, 817 F.2d 50 (8th Cir. 1987)—§ **406.2, n. 9.**

Mayrant, People v., 401 N.Y.S.2d 165, 372 N.E.2d 1 (N.Y.1977)—§ **609.1, n. 31.**

Mazzilli, United States v., 848 F.2d 384 (2nd Cir.1988)—§ **614.2, n. 6.**

M. B. A. F. B. Federal Credit Union v. Cumis Ins. Soc., Inc., 681 F.2d 930 (4th Cir.1982)—§ **602.2, n. 7.**

MCA, Inc. v. Wilson, 425 F.Supp. 443 (D.C.N.Y.1976)—§ **803(1).2, n. 9.**

McCandless v. Beyer, 835 F.2d 58 (3rd Cir. 1987)—§ **302.1, n. 10, 11.**

McCart, People v., 157 A.D.2d 194, 555 N.Y.S.2d 954 (N.Y.A.D. 4 Dept.1990)—§ **704.1, n. 19.**

McCarthy v. Arndstein, 266 U.S. 34, 45 S.Ct. 16, 69 L.Ed. 158 (1924)—§ **509.1, n. 1.**

McCarthy v. Meaney, 183 N.Y. 190, 76 N.E. 36 (N.Y.1905)—§ **612.1, n. 9.**

McCarthy v. Stanley, 151 A.D. 358, 136 N.Y.S. 386 (N.Y.A.D. 3 Dept.1912)—§ **601.2, n. 55.**

McClanahan v. United States, 230 F.2d 919 (5th Cir.1956)—§ **514.2, n. 4.**

McClard v. United States, 386 F.2d 495 (8th Cir.1967)—§ **611.5, n. 10.**

McClean, People v., 515 N.Y.S.2d 428, 508 N.E.2d 140 (N.Y.1987)—§ **607.5; § 607.5, n. 29, 32, 33, 37, 42, 46.**

McClendon, United States v., 454 F.Supp. 960 (D.C.Pa.1978)—§ **804(3).2, n. 11.**

McCloud v. Marcantonio, 106 A.D.2d 493, 483 N.Y.S.2d 31 (N.Y.A.D. 2 Dept. 1984)—§ **300.3, n. 34.**

McClure by Young v. Baier's Automotive Service Center, Inc., 126 A.D.2d 610, 511 N.Y.S.2d 50 (N.Y.A.D. 2 Dept. 1987)—§ **803(3).1; § 803(3).1, n. 4, 67.**

McCormack, People v., 278 A.D. 191, 104 N.Y.S.2d 139 (N.Y.A.D. 1 Dept.1951)—§ **503.3, n. 25.**

McCormick, People v., 278 A.D. 410, 105 N.Y.S.2d 571 (N.Y.A.D. 1 Dept.1951)—§ **607.4, n. 27.**

McCrary-El v. Shaw, 992 F.2d 809 (8th Cir.1993)—§ **602.2, n. 6.**

McCray v. Illinois, 386 U.S. 300, 87 S.Ct. 1056, 18 L.Ed.2d 62 (1967)—§ **510.2; § 510.2, n. 8.**

McCullock v. H.B. Fuller Co., 61 F.3d 1038 (2nd Cir.1995)—§ **104.2, n. 13; § 702.2, n. 12.**

McCullough, People v., 73 A.D.2d 310, 425 N.Y.S.2d 982 (N.Y.A.D. 1 Dept.1980)—§ **803(1).1, n. 36.**

McCurdy, People v., 86 A.D.2d 493, 450 N.Y.S.2d 507 (N.Y.A.D. 2 Dept.1982)—§ **1107.1, n. 4.**

McDaniel, People v., 595 N.Y.S.2d 364, 611 N.E.2d 265 (N.Y.1993)—§ **607.5; § 607.5, n. 2, 5, 6, 7, 9, 10, 29, 33, 34, 42.**

McDaniel, People v., 165 A.D.2d 817, 560 N.Y.S.2d 160 (N.Y.A.D. 2 Dept.1990)—§ **601.1, n. 36.**

McDermott, Estate of, 112 Misc.2d 308, 447 N.Y.S.2d 107 (N.Y.Sur.1982)—§ **901.7, n. 8, 11.**

McDermott v. Manhattan Eye, Ear and Throat Hospital, 255 N.Y.S.2d 65, 203 N.E.2d 469 (N.Y.1964)—§ **509.1, n. 9; § 601.1, n. 8, 16.**

McDermott, People v., 160 Misc.2d 769, 610 N.Y.S.2d 984 (Nassau Dist.Ct.1994)—§ **901.6, n. 1.**

McDermott, People v., 180 Misc. 247, 40 N.Y.S.2d 456 (N.Y.Sup.1943)—§ **605.1, n. 1.**

McDonald v. McDonald, 196 A.D.2d 7, 608 N.Y.S.2d 477 (N.Y.A.D. 2 Dept.1994)—§ **502.1, n. 52.**

McDonald v. Metropolitan St. Ry. Co., 167 N.Y. 66, 60 N.E. 282 (N.Y.1901)—§ **300.3; § 300.3, n. 24.**

McDonald v. Wesendonck, 30 Misc. 601, 62 N.Y.S. 764 (N.Y.Sup.1900)—§ **804(3).1, n. 16.**

McDonnell v. Nassau County, 129 Misc.2d 228, 492 N.Y.S.2d 699 (N.Y.Sup.1985)—§ **702.1, n. 24.**

McDowell, People v., 210 N.Y.S.2d 514, 172 N.E.2d 279 (N.Y.1961)—§ **607.6, n. 26.**

McFarland v. Gregory, 425 F.2d 443 (2nd Cir.1970)—§ **405.2; § 405.2, n. 5.**

McGee, People v., 508 N.Y.S.2d 927, 501 N.E.2d 576 (N.Y.1986)—§ **608.2, n. 24, 29; § 609.1, n. 49.**

McGee, People v., 424 N.Y.S.2d 157, 399 N.E.2d 1177 (N.Y.1979)—§ **104.1, n. 28; § 900.1; § 900.1, n. 1, 12; § 901.1; § 901.1, n. 1; § 1100.1, n. 3; § 1101.1; § 1101.1, n. 10; § 1104.1, n. 25, 29.**

McGee, People ex rel. v. Walters, 476 N.Y.S.2d 803, 465 N.E.2d 342 (N.Y. 1984)—§ **803(3).1; § 803(3).1, n. 40.**

McGovern v. Oliver, 177 A.D. 167, 163 N.Y.S. 275 (N.Y.A.D. 1 Dept.1917)—§ **411.1, n. 6.**

McGovern, United States v., 499 F.2d 1140 (1st Cir.1974)—§ **611.5, n. 12.**

McGrath, United States v., 613 F.2d 361 (2nd Cir.1979)—§ **803(3).2, n. 18.**

McGrath, United States v., 558 F.2d 1102 (2nd Cir.1977)—§ **801(1).3, n. 18.**

McGraw v. Ranieri, 202 A.D.2d 725, 608 N.Y.S.2d 577 (N.Y.A.D. 3 Dept.1994)—§ **802.2, n. 27.**

TABLE OF CASES

McGregor–Doniger Inc. v. Drizzle Inc., 599 F.2d 1126 (2nd Cir.1979)—§ **702.2, n. 5.**

McGuinness v. De Sapio, 9 A.D.2d 65, 191 N.Y.S.2d 798 (N.Y.A.D. 1 Dept.1959)—§ **512.1, n. 5.**

McHenry v. Chadwick, 896 F.2d 184 (6th Cir.1990)—§ **609.2, n. 14.**

McHugh, People v., 124 Misc.2d 559, 476 N.Y.S.2d 721 (N.Y.Sup.1984)—§ **1106.1, n. 1.**

McKeever, United States v., 169 F.Supp. 426 (D.C.N.Y.1958)—§ **1104.2, n. 6.**

McKenzie, People v., 499 N.Y.S.2d 923, 490 N.E.2d 842 (N.Y.1986)—§ **302.1, n. 20, 22.**

McKeon, United States v., 738 F.2d 26 (2nd Cir.1984)—§ **501.1;** § **501.1, n. 93;** § **802.1, n. 3;** § **802.3;** § **802.3, n. 2, 23, 28.**

McKie v. Taylor, 146 A.D.2d 921, 536 N.Y.S.2d 893 (N.Y.A.D. 3 Dept.1989)—§ **501.3, n. 19.**

McKinney v. Grand Street, P. P. & F. R. Co., 104 N.Y. 352, 10 N.E. 544 (N.Y. 1887)—§ **502.1, n. 45.**

McKinney, People v., 299 N.Y.S.2d 401, 247 N.E.2d 244 (N.Y.1969)—§ **404.1, n. 31.**

McKinnon v. Bliss, 21 N.Y. 206 (1860)—§ **803(7).1;** § **803(7).1, n. 25.**

McKnight By and Through Ludwig v. Johnson Controls, Inc., 36 F.3d 1396 (8th Cir.1994)—§ **1105.2, n. 2, 3.**

McLoghlin v. National Mohawk Val. Bank, 139 N.Y. 514, 34 N.E. 1095 (N.Y.1893)—§ **405.1, n. 24.**

McLucas, People v., 256 N.Y.S.2d 799, 204 N.E.2d 846 (N.Y.1965)—§ **509.1, n. 34.**

McMorrow v. Schweiker, 561 F.Supp. 584 (D.N.J.1982)—§ **803(5).2;** § **803(5).2, n. 56.**

McNaier v. Manhattan Ry. Co., 4 N.Y.S. 310 (N.Y.Sup.1889)—§ **1102.1, n. 16;** § **1103.1, n. 3.**

McNeill, People ex rel. Butler v., 30 Misc.2d 722, 219 N.Y.S.2d 722 (N.Y.Sup.1961)—§ **201.1, n. 26.**

McPartlin, United States v., 595 F.2d 1321 (7th Cir.1979)—§ **500.2, n. 8.**

McRorie v. Monroe, 203 N.Y. 426, 96 N.E. 724 (N.Y.1911)—§ **1001.1, n. 11.**

Mead, Matter of Estate of, 129 A.D.2d 1008, 514 N.Y.S.2d 581 (N.Y.A.D. 4 Dept. 1987)—§ **601.2, n. 59;** § **804(1).1, n. 23.**

Mechanick v. Conradi, 139 A.D.2d 857, 527 N.Y.S.2d 586 (N.Y.A.D. 3 Dept.1988)—§ **1104.1, n. 50;** § **1105.1, n. 11.**

Meckel v. Continental Resources Co., 758 F.2d 811 (2nd Cir.1985)—§ **301.8;** § **301.8, n. 11.**

Medical Therapy Sciences, Inc., United States v., 583 F.2d 36 (2nd Cir.1978)—§ **607.5;** § **607.5, n. 50, 57, 59.**

Medico, United States v., 557 F.2d 309 (2nd Cir.1977)—§ **803(1).2;** § **803(1).2, n. 2;** § **804(5).2;** § **804(5).2, n. 8, 36;** § **1101.2, n. 7, 10.**

Medina, People v., 130 A.D.2d 515, 515 N.Y.S.2d 94 (N.Y.A.D. 2 Dept.1987)—§ **406.1, n. 14.**

Medina–Gasca, United States v., 739 F.2d 1451 (9th Cir.1984)—§ **804(4).2, n. 6.**

Mees, People v., 420 N.Y.S.2d 214, 394 N.E.2d 283 (N.Y.1979)—§ **404.1;** § **404.1, n. 23.**

Mehrmanesh, United States v., 689 F.2d 822 (9th Cir.1982)—§ **609.2, n. 14.**

Meiselman v. Crown Heights Hospital, 285 N.Y. 389, 34 N.E.2d 367 (N.Y.1941)—§ **104.1, n. 2;** § **300.3, n. 34, 44;** § **702.1;** § **702.1, n. 72.**

Mejia-Alarcon, United States v., 995 F.2d 982 (10th Cir.1993)—§ **103.2, n. 25.**

Mejia-Valez, United States v., 855 F.Supp. 607 (E.D.N.Y.1994)—§ **803(1).2;** § **803(1).2, n. 10;** § **806.1, n. 19.**

Melendez v. New York City Transit Authority, 196 A.D.2d 460, 601 N.Y.S.2d 489 (N.Y.A.D. 1 Dept.1993)—§ **901.10, n. 3;** § **1104.1, n. 14.**

Melendez, People v., 449 N.Y.S.2d 946, 434 N.E.2d 1324 (N.Y.1982)—§ **607.5, n. 20;** § **611.4;** § **611.4, n. 3, 4;** § **801.1, n. 40.**

Melia, United States v., 691 F.2d 672 (4th Cir.1982)—§ **607.5, n. 52, 56.**

Melkon v. H. B. Kirk & Co., 220 A.D. 180, 220 N.Y.S. 551 (N.Y.A.D. 1 Dept.1927)—§ **601.2, n. 35.**

Melski, People v., 217 N.Y.S.2d 65, 176 N.E.2d 81 (N.Y.1961)—§ **503.3;** § **503.3, n. 4, 9.**

Mendel, United States v., 746 F.2d 155 (2nd Cir.1984)—§ **803(3).2, n. 16;** § **1101.2, n. 14.**

Mendes, People v., 164 N.Y.S.2d 401, 143 N.E.2d 806 (N.Y.1957)—§ **614.1, n. 13, 15, 17.**

Mendez, People v., 155 Misc.2d 368, 589 N.Y.S.2d 268 (N.Y.Sup.1992)—§ **804(2).1, n. 24, 25, 26.**

Mendez v. United States, 732 F.Supp. 414 (S.D.N.Y.1990)—§ **801.1, n. 42;** § **803(1).2, n. 51.**

Mennuti, United States v., 679 F.2d 1032 (2nd Cir.1982)—§ **103.2, n. 12.**

Mentz, United States v., 840 F.2d 315 (6th Cir.1988)—§ **201.2, n. 16.**

Mercado, People v., 188 A.D.2d 941, 592 N.Y.S.2d 75 (N.Y.A.D. 3 Dept.1992)—§ **610.1, n. 4.**

Mercado, People v., 162 A.D.2d 722, 557 N.Y.S.2d 123 (N.Y.A.D. 2 Dept.1990)—§ **607.4, n. 37.**

Mercado, People v., 157 A.D.2d 457, 549 N.Y.S.2d 383 (N.Y.A.D. 1 Dept.1990)—§ **601.1, n. 36.**

Mercatante v. Hyster Co., 159 A.D.2d 492, 552 N.Y.S.2d 364 (N.Y.A.D. 2 Dept. 1990)—§ **1104.1, n. 50;** § **1105.1, n. 6, 11.**

Merchants Mut. Ins. Co. v. Arzillo, 98 A.D.2d 495, 472 N.Y.S.2d 97 (N.Y.A.D. 2 Dept.1984)—§ **803(5).1, n. 45.**

TABLE OF CASES

Meritor Sav. Bank, FSB v. Vinson, 477 U.S. 57, 106 S.Ct. 2399, 91 L.Ed.2d 49 (1986)—§ **412.2, n. 3.**

Merrick Holding Corp. v. Board of Assessors of Nassau County, 410 N.Y.S.2d 565, 382 N.E.2d 1341 (N.Y.1978)— § **405.1, n. 29.**

Merrill Lynch Realty Commercial Services, Inc. v. Rudin Management Co., Inc., 94 A.D.2d 617, 462 N.Y.S.2d 16 (N.Y.A.D. 1 Dept.1983)—§ **612.1, n. 28, 29.**

Mertz, People v., 506 N.Y.S.2d 290, 497 N.E.2d 657 (N.Y.1986)—§ **301.7; § 301.7, n. 8; § 302.1, n. 23; § 702.1, n. 45; § 803(3).1, n. 39, 59, 61, 73.**

Meschino v. International Tel. and Tel. Corp., 563 F.Supp. 1066 (D.C.N.Y. 1983)—§ **802.3, n. 17.**

Messina, United States v., 507 F.2d 73 (2nd Cir.1974)—§ **1101.2, n. 3.**

Metzger, United States v., 778 F.2d 1195 (6th Cir.1985)—§ **803(5).2, n. 54.**

Metzler v. United States, 64 F.2d 203 (9th Cir.1933)—§ **803(1).2, n. 21.**

Meyer v. Supreme Lodge K. P., 178 N.Y. 63, 70 N.E. 111 (N.Y.1904)—§ **502.1, n. 16.**

Meyer Bros., Inc. v. Higgins, 232 A.D. 783, 249 N.Y.S. 921 (N.Y.A.D. 2 Dept.1931)— § **513.1, n. 6.**

Meyerhofer v. Empire Fire & Marine Ins. Co., 497 F.2d 1190 (2nd Cir.1974)— § **501.2, n. 19.**

Meyers v. United States, 171 F.2d 800, 84 U.S.App.D.C. 101 (D.C.Cir.1948)— § **1001.1, n. 7, 11.**

Meyer's Estate, In re, 206 Misc. 368, 132 N.Y.S.2d 825 (N.Y.Sur.1954)— § **803(5).1, n. 28.**

Mezger's Estate, In re, 154 Misc. 633, 278 N.Y.S. 669 (N.Y.Sur.1935)—§ **611.3, n. 7.**

Mezzanatto, United States v., ___ U.S. ___, 115 S.Ct. 797, 130 L.Ed.2d 697 (1995)— § **410.2, n. 9.**

M. Groh's Sons v. Groh, 177 N.Y. 8, 68 N.E. 992 (N.Y.1903)—§ **103.1, n. 17.**

Michael M., People v., 162 Misc.2d 803, 618 N.Y.S.2d 171 (N.Y.Sup.1994)—§ **601.1, n. 65; § 607.6, n. 16.**

Michaels, People v., 168 A.D. 258, 153 N.Y.S. 796 (N.Y.A.D. 2 Dept.1915)— § **607.5, n. 22.**

Michalow, People v., 229 N.Y. 325, 128 N.E. 228 (N.Y.1920)—§ **607.6, n. 17, 29.**

Michelson v. United States, 335 U.S. 469, 69 S.Ct. 213, 93 L.Ed. 168 (1948)— § **402.1; § 402.1, n. 4, 5, 33, 42; § 402.2; § 402.2, n. 8; § 608.1, n. 11, 19.**

Michigan v. Harvey, 494 U.S. 344, 110 S.Ct. 1176, 108 L.Ed.2d 293 (1990)—§ **607.8, n. 10.**

Michigan v. Lucas, 500 U.S. 145, 111 S.Ct. 1743, 114 L.Ed.2d 205 (1991)—§ **412.1, n. 5.**

Michoud Indus. Facilities, United States v., 322 F.2d 698 (5th Cir.1963)—§ **405.2; § 405.2, n. 17.**

Mid-Continent Petroleum Corp., United States v., 67 F.2d 37 (10th Cir.1933)— § **803(5).2, n. 50.**

Middleton, People v., 444 N.Y.S.2d 581, 429 N.E.2d 100 (N.Y.1981)—§ **702.1, n. 19, 20.**

Mideastern Contracting Corporation v. O'Toole, 55 F.2d 909 (2nd Cir.1932)— § **411.2, n. 6.**

Miklejohn, People v., 184 A.D.2d 735, 585 N.Y.S.2d 454 (N.Y.A.D. 2 Dept.1992)— § **803(1).1, n. 38.**

Mikulec, People v., 207 A.D. 505, 202 N.Y.S. 551 (N.Y.A.D. 3 Dept.1924)—§ **804(2).1, n. 19.**

Mikus v. United States, 433 F.2d 719 (2nd Cir.1970)—§ **1104.2, n. 16, 18, 19, 20.**

Miles, United States v., 413 F.2d 34 (3rd Cir.1969)—§ **607.4, n. 39.**

Milio v. Railway Motor Trucking Co., 257 A.D. 640, 15 N.Y.S.2d 73 (N.Y.A.D. 1 Dept.1939)—§ **401.1, n. 33.**

Miller v. Adkins, 9 Hun. 9 (N.Y.1876)— § **601.2, n. 80.**

Miller v. Alagna, 203 A.D.2d 264, 609 N.Y.S.2d 650 (N.Y.A.D. 2 Dept.1994)— § **803(3).1, n. 27.**

Miller v. Food Fair Stores, Inc., 63 A.D.2d 766, 404 N.Y.S.2d 740 (N.Y.A.D. 3 Dept. 1978)—§ **201.1, n. 45.**

Miller v. Greenwald Petticoat Co., 192 A.D. 559, 183 N.Y.S. 97 (N.Y.A.D. 1 Dept. 1920)—§ **612.1, n. 15.**

Miller v. National Cabinet Co., 204 N.Y.S.2d 129, 168 N.E.2d 811 (N.Y. 1960)—§ **702.1, n. 26.**

Miller v. Nationwide Mut. Fire Ins. Co., 100 A.D.2d 727, 473 N.Y.S.2d 658 (N.Y.A.D. 4 Dept.1984)—§ **802.2, n. 54.**

Miller v. New York Produce Exchange, 550 F.2d 762 (2nd Cir.1977)—§ **803(5).2, n. 23.**

Miller, People v., 199 A.D.2d 692, 605 N.Y.S.2d 160 (N.Y.A.D. 3 Dept.1993)— § **803(3).1, n. 39.**

Miller, People v., 150 A.D.2d 910, 541 N.Y.S.2d 257 (N.Y.A.D. 3 Dept.1989)— § **803(3).1, n. 47.**

Miller, People v., 140 Misc.2d 247, 530 N.Y.S.2d 490 (N.Y.City Ct.1988)— § **601.1, n. 55; § 604.1, n. 5, 8.**

Miller, People v., 384 N.Y.S.2d 741, 349 N.E.2d 841 (N.Y.1976)—§ **402.1; § 402.1, n. 6, 60; § 803(1).1, n. 59.**

Miller, People v., 358 N.Y.S.2d 733, 315 N.E.2d 785 (N.Y.1974)—§ **402.1; § 402.1, n. 35, 55.**

Miller, People ex rel. Wallington Apartments v., 288 N.Y. 31, 41 N.E.2d 445 (N.Y.1942)—§ **301.4, n. 6; § 301.5, n. 22.**

956

TABLE OF CASES

Miller v. Poretsky, 595 F.2d 780, 193 U.S.App.D.C. 395 (D.C.Cir.1978)—§ **404.2, n. 35.**

Miller, United States v., 381 F.2d 529 (2nd Cir.1967)—§ **801(2).2, n. 10.**

Miller v. Universal City Studios, Inc., 650 F.2d 1365 (5th Cir.1981)—§ **615.2, n. 9, 12.**

Millers' Nat. Ins. Co., Chicago, Ill. v. Wichita Flour Mills Co., 257 F.2d 93 (10th Cir.1958)—§ **1105.2, n. 1.**

Millington v. New York City Transit Authority, 44 A.D.2d 542, 353 N.Y.S.2d 469 (N.Y.A.D. 1 Dept.1974)—§ **801(1).2, n. 9.**

Mills v. Davis, 113 N.Y. 243, 21 N.E. 68 (N.Y.1889)—§ **804(3).1, n. 5.**

Mills, United States v., 895 F.2d 897 (2nd Cir.1990)—§ **404.2, n. 18.**

Milone v. General Motors Corp., 84 A.D.2d 921, 446 N.Y.S.2d 650 (N.Y.A.D. 4 Dept. 1981)—§ **501.3, n. 12.**

Mincey v. Arizona, 437 U.S. 385, 98 S.Ct. 2408, 57 L.Ed.2d 290 (1978)—§ **607.8, n. 11.**

Mindlin v. Dorfman, 197 A.D. 770, 189 N.Y.S. 265 (N.Y.A.D. 1 Dept.1921)—§ **607.8, n. 38.**

Minsky., People v., 227 N.Y. 94, 124 N.E. 126 (N.Y.1919)—§ **607.4, n. 5, 8, 19, 21, 25;** § **607.5, n. 4.**

Miranda v. Arizona, 384 U.S. 436, 10 Ohio Misc. 9, 86 S.Ct. 1602, 16 L.Ed.2d 694, 36 O.O.2d 237 (1966)—§ **607.8, n. 10.**

Miranda v. Miranda, 184 A.D.2d 286, 584 N.Y.S.2d 818 (N.Y.A.D. 1 Dept.1992)—§ **501.1, n. 19.**

Mirenda, People v., 297 N.Y.S.2d 532, 245 N.E.2d 194 (N.Y.1969)—§ **509.1, n. 34;** § **607.5, n. 45;** § **901.1, n. 6;** § **901.4, n. 2;** § **1101.1, n. 3, 5, 6;** § **1103.1, n. 10.**

Misek–Falkoff v. International Business Machines Corp., 144 F.R.D. 48 (S.D.N.Y. 1992)—§ **502.2, n. 9.**

Mishlanie, People v., 24 Misc.2d 277, 204 N.Y.S.2d 450 (Oneida Co.Ct.1960)—§ **804(4).1, n. 4.**

Mitchell v. Hoke, 930 F.2d 1 (2nd Cir. 1991)—§ **804(5).2, n. 1, 23.**

Mitchell, People v., 461 N.Y.S.2d 267, 448 N.E.2d 121 (N.Y.1983)—§ **501.1, n. 11, 12, 51;** § **611.3, n. 35.**

Mitchell, People v., 40 A.D.2d 117, 338 N.Y.S.2d 313 (N.Y.A.D. 3 Dept.1972)—§ **404.1, n. 68.**

Mitchell, United States v., 725 F.2d 832 (2nd Cir.1983)—§ **300.4, n. 74, 75.**

Mitchell, United States v., 556 F.2d 371 (6th Cir.1977)—§ **607.5, n. 55.**

Mobil Oil Corp. v. Department of Energy, 520 F.Supp. 414 (D.C.N.Y.1981)—§ **511.2, n. 2.**

Mobley, People v., 450 N.Y.S.2d 302, 435 N.E.2d 672 (N.Y.1982)—§ **801(2).1;** § **801(2).1, n. 4, 33.**

Mobley, United States v., 421 F.2d 345 (5th Cir.1970)—§ **804(2).2, n. 9.**

Mold Maintenance Service v. General Acc. Fire & Life Assur. Corp., Ltd., 56 A.D.2d 134, 392 N.Y.S.2d 104 (N.Y.A.D. 4 Dept. 1977)—§ **501.3, n. 18.**

Molineux, People v., 168 N.Y. 264, 61 N.E. 286 (N.Y.1901)—§ **401.1, n. 44;** § **404.1;** § **404.1, n. 5, 44;** § **405.1, n. 2;** § **702.1, n. 32, 35, 36;** § **900.1, n. 17, 19;** § **901.1, n. 9;** § **901.2, n. 4;** § **901.3, n. 1, 10, 14.**

Monahan v. Monahan, 29 A.D.2d 1046, 289 N.Y.S.2d 812 (N.Y.A.D. 4 Dept.1968)—§ **804(1).1, n. 20.**

Montalvo v. Morales, 18 A.D.2d 20, 239 N.Y.S.2d 72 (N.Y.A.D. 2 Dept.1963)—§ **802.2;** § **802.2, n. 24;** § **803(5).1, n. 50.**

Montalvo, United States v., 271 F.2d 922 (2nd Cir.1959)—§ **1101.2, n. 8, 9.**

Monteleone by Monteleone v. Gestetner Corp., 140 Misc.2d 841, 531 N.Y.S.2d 857 (N.Y.Sup.1988)—§ **615.1, n. 12.**

Montes v. Metropolitan St. Ry. Co., 77 A.D. 493, 78 N.Y.S. 1059 (N.Y.A.D. 2 Dept.1902)—§ **201.1, n. 13, 16, 24.**

Montgomery, People v., 195 A.D.2d 886, 600 N.Y.S.2d 814 (N.Y.A.D. 3 Dept. 1993)—§ **803(3).1, n. 46, 62.**

Montgomery, People v., 103 A.D.2d 622, 481 N.Y.S.2d 532 (N.Y.A.D. 4 Dept. 1984)—§ **607.1, n. 4.**

Moody, People v., 195 A.D.2d 1016, 600 N.Y.S.2d 581 (N.Y.A.D. 4 Dept.1993)—§ **1104.1, n. 5;** § **1108.1, n. 3.**

Mooney, People v., 560 N.Y.S.2d 115, 559 N.E.2d 1274 (N.Y.1990)—§ **702.1;** § **702.1, n. 63.**

Moore v. Leventhal, 303 N.Y. 534, 104 N.E.2d 892 (N.Y.1952)—§ **607.5, n. 29, 35.**

Moore, People v., 499 N.Y.S.2d 393, 489 N.E.2d 1295 (N.Y.1985)—§ **410.1, n. 10.**

Moore, People v., 42 A.D.2d 268, 346 N.Y.S.2d 363 (N.Y.A.D. 2 Dept.1973)—§ **608.2, n. 10.**

Moore v. St. John's Episcopal Hosp., 89 A.D.2d 618, 452 N.Y.S.2d 669 (N.Y.A.D. 2 Dept.1982)—§ **502.1, n. 35.**

Moore, United States v., 970 F.2d 48 (5th Cir.1992)—§ **502.2, n. 1, 3.**

Moore, United States v., 786 F.2d 1308 (5th Cir.1986)—§ **702.2, n. 11.**

Moore, United States v., 571 F.2d 76 (2nd Cir.1978)—§ **302.2, n. 7;** § **803(1).2, n. 39.**

Moorer, People v., 77 A.D.2d 575, 429 N.Y.S.2d 913 (N.Y.A.D. 2 Dept.1980)—§ **105.1, n. 4, 6;** § **609.1, n. 19.**

Morales, People v., 591 N.Y.S.2d 825, 606 N.E.2d 953 (N.Y.1992)—§ **601.1, n. 40.**

Morales, People v., 159 A.D.2d 86, 559 N.Y.S.2d 869 (N.Y.A.D. 1 Dept.1990)—§ **1108.1, n. 7.**

TABLE OF CASES

Morales, People v., 121 A.D.2d 240, 503 N.Y.S.2d 374 (N.Y.A.D. 1 Dept.1986)—**§ 606.1, n. 17.**

Moran, United States v., 194 F.2d 623 (2nd Cir.1952)—**§ 1102.2, n. 4; § 1104.2, n. 19.**

Moret, United States v., 334 F.2d 887 (2nd Cir.1964)—**§ 1103.2, n. 4.**

Morehouse v. Mathews, 2 N.Y. 514 (1849)—**§ 701.1, n. 1.**

Morgan v. Labiak, 368 F.2d 338 (10th Cir. 1966)—**§ 500.2, n. 6.**

Morgan, People v., 175 A.D.2d 930, 573 N.Y.S.2d 765 (N.Y.A.D. 2 Dept.1991)—**§ 1104.1, n. 28.**

Morgan, People v., 171 A.D.2d 698, 567 N.Y.S.2d 166 (N.Y.A.D. 2 Dept.1991)—**§ 609.1, n. 44.**

Morgan, People v., 561 N.Y.S.2d 408, 562 N.E.2d 485 (N.Y.1990)—**§ 804(3).1, n. 46.**

Morgan, People v., 151 A.D.2d 221, 547 N.Y.S.2d 711 (N.Y.A.D. 4 Dept.1989)—**§ 804(1).1, n. 42.**

Morgan Guar. Trust Co. v. Hellenic Lines Ltd., 621 F.Supp. 198 (D.C.N.Y.1985)—**§ 801.1, n. 24.**

Morlang, United States v., 531 F.2d 183 (4th Cir.1975)—**§ 607.4, n. 48; § 612.2, n. 9.**

Moro, People v., 297 N.Y.S.2d 578, 245 N.E.2d 226 (N.Y.1969)—**§ 302.1, n. 28.**

Morrison, People v., 195 N.Y. 116, 88 N.E. 21 (N.Y.1909)—**§ 402.1, n. 45; § 608.2, n. 19.**

Morris' Will, In re, 277 A.D. 211, 98 N.Y.S.2d 997 (N.Y.A.D. 3 Dept.1950)—**§ 804(4).1, n. 17, 20.**

Morss v. Morss, 11 Barb. (N.Y.) 510 (1851)—**§ 605.1, n. 2.**

Mortimer, United States v., 118 F.2d 266 (2nd Cir.1941)—**§ 1006.1, n. 12.**

Morton, People v., 189 A.D.2d 488, 596 N.Y.S.2d 783 (N.Y.A.D. 1 Dept.1993)—**§ 1107.1, n. 9, 11.**

Moses, People v., 482 N.Y.S.2d 228, 472 N.E.2d 4 (N.Y.1984)—**§ 401.1, n. 14; § 802.2, n. 10.**

Moses, United States v., 15 F.3d 774 (8th Cir.1994)—**§ 803(1).2, n. 19.**

Moshier, People v., 181 A.D.2d 800, 581 N.Y.S.2d 369 (N.Y.A.D. 2 Dept.1992)—**§ 607.8, n. 10.**

Moskowitz v. Lopp, 128 F.R.D. 624 (E.D.Pa. 1989)—**§ 501.2, n. 37.**

Moskowitz, United States v., 581 F.2d 14 (2nd Cir.1978)—**§ 801(2).2, n. 10.**

Moss, People v., 587 N.Y.S.2d 593, 600 N.E.2d 224 (N.Y.1992)—**§ 801(2).1, n. 19.**

Moyer, People v., 186 A.D.2d 997, 588 N.Y.S.2d 457 (N.Y.A.D. 4 Dept.1992)—**§ 900.1, n. 15; § 1101.1, n. 24.**

Mravlja v. Hoke, 22 A.D.2d 848, 254 N.Y.S.2d 162 (N.Y.A.D. 3 Dept.1964)—**§ 106.1, n. 13.**

Muccia, People v., 139 A.D.2d 838, 527 N.Y.S.2d 620 (N.Y.A.D. 3 Dept.1988)—**§ 804(1).1, n. 44.**

Mulderig, In re, 196 Misc. 527, 91 N.Y.S.2d 895 (N.Y.Sur.1949)—**§ 601.2, n. 7.**

Mulgrave, People v., 163 A.D.2d 538, 558 N.Y.S.2d 607 (N.Y.A.D. 2 Dept.1990)—**§ 503.3, n. 22.**

Mulhado v. Brooklyn City R.R. Co., 30 N.Y. 370 (1864)—**§ 1102.1, n. 13, 16.**

Mullaney v. Wilbur, 421 U.S. 684, 95 S.Ct. 1881, 44 L.Ed.2d 508 (1975)—**§ 302.1, n. 4.**

Mullin, People v., 393 N.Y.S.2d 938, 362 N.E.2d 571 (N.Y.1977)—**§ 402.1, n. 1.**

Mullings, United States v., 364 F.2d 173 (2nd Cir.1966)—**§ 502.2, n. 1.**

Mullins, People v., 179 A.D.2d 48, 582 N.Y.S.2d 810 (N.Y.A.D. 3 Dept.1992)—**§ 103.1, n. 23.**

Murdock v. Waterman, 145 N.Y. 55, 39 N.E. 829 (N.Y.1895)—**§ 802.2, n. 38.**

Murphy, In re, 560 F.2d 326 (8th Cir. 1977)—**§ 501.3, n. 43.**

Murphy, People v., 128 A.D.2d 177, 515 N.Y.S.2d 895 (N.Y.A.D. 3 Dept.1987)—**§ 802.2, n. 68.**

Murphy v. Waterfront Commission of New York Harbor, 378 U.S. 52, 84 S.Ct. 1594, 12 L.Ed.2d 678 (1964)—**§ 509.1, n. 5.**

Murray v. Narwood, 192 N.Y. 172, 84 N.E. 958 (N.Y.1908)—**§ 300.2, n. 16.**

Murray, People v., 158 Misc.2d 952, 601 N.Y.S.2d 1019 (N.Y.Sup.1993)—**§ 601.1, n. 37, 43.**

Murray, People v., 90 A.D.2d 640, 456 N.Y.S.2d 445 (N.Y.A.D. 3 Dept.1982)—**§ 1001.1, n. 36.**

Murray v. Smith, 155 A.D.2d 963, 547 N.Y.S.2d 774 (N.Y.A.D. 4 Dept.1989)—**§ 601.2, n. 18.**

Musacchia, United States v., 900 F.2d 493 (2nd Cir.1990)—**§ 103.2, n. 11.**

Musczak's Estate, In re, 196 Misc. 364, 92 N.Y.S.2d 97 (N.Y.Sur.1949)—**§ 601.2, n. 32.**

Musmacher, People v., 133 A.D.2d 352, 519 N.Y.S.2d 253 (N.Y.A.D. 2 Dept.1987)—**§ 100.2, n. 7; § 611.1, n. 1.**

Muth v. J & T Metal Products Co., Inc., 74 A.D.2d 898, 425 N.Y.S.2d 858 (N.Y.A.D. 2 Dept.1980)—**§ 803(2).1, n. 6.**

Mutual Life Ins. Co. of New York v. Hillmon, 145 U.S. 285, 12 S.Ct. 909, 36 L.Ed. 706 (1892)—**§ 801.1, n. 32; § 803(1).1; § 803(1).1, n. 47; § 803(1).2; § 803(1).2, n. 36.**

Myerson, United States v., 18 F.3d 153 (2nd Cir.1994)—**§ 401.2; § 401.2, n. 19.**

Myrick v. United States, 332 F.2d 279 (5th Cir.1963)—**§ 1003.1, n. 6.**

N

Nachtsheim v. Beech Aircraft Corp., 847 F.2d 1261 (7th Cir.1988)—**§ 703.2, n. 11.**

TABLE OF CASES

Nakasian v. Incontrade, Inc., 78 F.R.D. 229 (D.C.N.Y.1978)—§ **404.2, n. 33.**

Namet v. United States, 373 U.S. 179, 83 S.Ct. 1151, 10 L.Ed.2d 278 (1963)—§ **509.1, n. 54.**

Nanda v. Ford Motor Co., 509 F.2d 213 (7th Cir.1974)—§ **1105.2, n. 1.**

N and G Children, Matter of, 176 A.D.2d 504, 574 N.Y.S.2d 696 (N.Y.A.D. 1 Dept. 1991)—§ **504.1;** § **504.1, n. 6.**

Napiearlski v. Pickering, 278 A.D. 456, 106 N.Y.S.2d 28 (N.Y.A.D. 4 Dept.1951)—§ **603.1, n. 9.**

Napoletano, People v., 58 A.D.2d 83, 395 N.Y.S.2d 469 (N.Y.A.D. 2 Dept.1977)—§ **404.1;** § **404.1, n. 28.**

Napolitano v. Branks, 141 A.D.2d 705, 529 N.Y.S.2d 824 (N.Y.A.D. 2 Dept.1988)—§ **803(3).1, n. 5.**

Nappi v. Gerdts, 103 A.D.2d 737, 477 N.Y.S.2d 202 (N.Y.A.D. 2 Dept.1984)—§ **612.1, n. 12.**

Naranjo, People v., 194 A.D.2d 747, 600 N.Y.S.2d 81 (N.Y.A.D. 2 Dept.1993)—§ **412.1, n. 11.**

Nash v. United States, 54 F.2d 1006 (2nd Cir.1932)—§ **105.2, n. 9.**

Nassau Ins. Co. v. Murray, 414 N.Y.S.2d 117, 386 N.E.2d 1085 (N.Y.1978)—§ **301.3, n. 8;** § **301.5, n. 41.**

Natale v. Niagara Mohawk Power Corp., 135 A.D.2d 955, 522 N.Y.S.2d 364 (N.Y.A.D. 3 Dept.1987)—§ **703.1, n. 11.**

Natale, United States v., 526 F.2d 1160 (2nd Cir.1975)—§ **901.4, n. 13.**

Nathan, United States v., 536 F.2d 988 (2nd Cir.1976)—§ **1006.1, n. 24.**

National Hotel Management Corp. v. Shelton Towers Associates, 188 A.D.2d 305, 590 N.Y.S.2d 476 (N.Y.A.D. 1 Dept. 1992)—§ **804(1).1, n. 21.**

National States Elec. Corp. v. LFO Const. Corp., 203 A.D.2d 49, 609 N.Y.S.2d 900 (N.Y.A.D. 1 Dept.1994)—§ **803(3).1, n. 36.**

Navarro de Cosme v. Hospital Pavia, 922 F.2d 926 (1st Cir.1991)—§ **803(1).2, n. 52.**

Nay v. Curley, 113 N.Y. 575, 21 N.E. 698 (N.Y.1889)—§ **106.1, n. 2, 5, 15;** § **601.2;** § **601.2, n. 72.**

Naylor, People v., 120 A.D.2d 940, 502 N.Y.S.2d 856 (N.Y.A.D. 4 Dept.1986)—§ **503.3, n. 18.**

Neal, People v., 191 A.D.2d 256, 595 N.Y.S.2d 17 (N.Y.A.D. 1 Dept.1993)—§ **412.1, n. 11.**

Neal, People v., 181 A.D.2d 584, 581 N.Y.S.2d 681 (N.Y.A.D. 1 Dept.1992)—§ **105.1, n. 1.**

Neal, United States v., 36 F.3d 1190 (1st Cir.1994)—§ **900.1, n. 10.**

Nearpass v. Tilman, 104 N.Y. 506, 10 N.E. 894 (N.Y.1887)—§ **601.2, n. 15.**

Neff, In re, 206 F.2d 149 (3rd Cir.1953)—§ **509.1, n. 51.**

Negron, United States ex rel. v. State of N. Y., 434 F.2d 386 (2nd Cir.1970)—§ **604.2, n. 6.**

Neidert v. Austin S. Edgar, Inc., 204 A.D.2d 1030, 612 N.Y.S.2d 529 (N.Y.A.D. 4 Dept.1994)—§ **703.1, n. 1.**

Neil v. Biggers, 409 U.S. 188, 93 S.Ct. 375, 34 L.Ed.2d 401 (1972)—§ **801(2).2, n. 4.**

Nellis v. Air Line Pilots Ass'n, 144 F.R.D. 68 (E.D.Va.1992)—§ **501.2, n. 38.**

Nelson v. Brady, 268 A.D. 226, 50 N.Y.S.2d 582 (N.Y.A.D. 1 Dept.1944)—§ **702.1, n. 37;** § **901.3, n. 15.**

Nelson v. O'Neil, 402 U.S. 622, 91 S.Ct. 1723, 29 L.Ed.2d 222 (1971)—§ **801(1).3;** § **801(1).3, n. 4.**

Nelson v. X–Ray Systems, Inc., 46 A.D.2d 995, 361 N.Y.S.2d 468 (N.Y.A.D. 4 Dept. 1974)—§ **704.1, n. 5, 11.**

Nersesian, United States v., 824 F.2d 1294 (2nd Cir.1987)—§ **803(1).2, n. 46.**

Nettles, People v., 118 A.D.2d 875, 500 N.Y.S.2d 361 (N.Y.A.D. 2 Dept.1986)—§ **804(1).1, n. 46.**

Neu, People v., 126 A.D.2d 223, 513 N.Y.S.2d 531 (N.Y.A.D. 3 Dept.1987)—§ **404.1, n. 57.**

Neufeld, People v., 165 N.Y. 43, 58 N.E. 786 (N.Y.1900)—§ **1101.1, n. 4.**

Nevins v. Great Atlantic and Pacific Tea Co., 164 A.D.2d 807, 559 N.Y.S.2d 539 (N.Y.A.D. 1 Dept.1990)—§ **702.1, n. 9.**

New v. Cortright, 32 A.D.2d 576, 299 N.Y.S.2d 43 (N.Y.A.D. 3 Dept.1969)—§ **1102.1, n. 16.**

New England Mut. Life Ins. Co. v. Anderson, 888 F.2d 646 (10th Cir. 1989)—§ **902.1, n. 20.**

New Jersey v. Portash, 440 U.S. 450, 99 S.Ct. 1292, 59 L.Ed.2d 501 (1979)—§ **104.2, n. 15;** § **509.1;** § **509.1, n. 77;** § **607.8, n. 11.**

Newman v. Clayton F Summy Co, 133 F.2d 465 (2nd Cir.1942)—§ **203.2, n. 2.**

Newman v. Consolidated Edison Co., Inc., 79 Misc.2d 153, 360 N.Y.S.2d 141 (N.Y.Sup.1973)—§ **901.7, n. 6.**

New Mexico Sav. & Loan Ass'n v. United States Fidelity & Guaranty Co., 454 F.2d 328 (10th Cir.1972)—§ **612.2, n. 7.**

New York v. Conyers, 449 U.S. 809, 101 S.Ct. 56, 66 L.Ed.2d 12 (1980)—§ **509.1, n. 85.**

New York, City of v. Pullman Inc., 662 F.2d 910 (2nd Cir.1981)—§ **803(5).2, n. 21.**

New York, City of v. State, 389 N.Y.S.2d 332, 357 N.E.2d 988 (N.Y.1976)—§ **300.2, n. 18.**

New York, City of v. Vanderveer, 91 A.D. 303, 86 N.Y.S. 659 (N.Y.A.D. 1 Dept. 1904)—§ **201.1, n. 37.**

New York, City of v. Wilson & Co., 278 N.Y. 86, 15 N.E.2d 408 (N.Y.1938)—§ **803(5).1, n. 19.**

TABLE OF CASES

New York County DES Litigation, In re, 171 A.D.2d 119, 575 N.Y.S.2d 19 (N.Y.A.D. 1 Dept.1991)—§ **406.1, n. 12.**

New York County DES Litigation, In re, 168 A.D.2d 44, 570 N.Y.S.2d 804 (N.Y.A.D. 1 Dept.1991)—§ **502.1, n. 52.**

New York & Cuba Mail S. S. Co. v. Continental Ins. Co. of City of New York, 117 F.2d 404 (2nd Cir.1941)—§ **803(5).2, n. 44.**

New York Foreign Trade Zone Operators, Inc., United States v., 304 F.2d 792 (2nd Cir.1962)—§ **803(3).2; § 803(3).2, n. 36, 41.**

New York, State of v. Blank, 820 F.Supp. 697 (N.D.N.Y.1993)—§ **1004.1, n. 4.**

New York, State of v. Hendrickson Bros., Inc., 840 F.2d 1065 (2nd Cir.1988)—§ **802.3, n. 36; § 805.2, n. 7.**

New York Water Co. v. Crow, 110 A.D. 32, 96 N.Y.S. 899 (N.Y.A.D. 2 Dept.1905)—§ **804(3).1, n. 25.**

New York, West Park (Manhattan Town) Clearance Project, In re City of, 154 N.Y.S.2d 1, 136 N.E.2d 478 (N.Y.1956)—§ **1107.1, n. 12.**

Niagara Falls Urban Renewal Agency v. 123 Falls Realty, Inc., 66 A.D.2d 1009, 411 N.Y.S.2d 752 (N.Y.A.D. 4 Dept.1978)—§ **405.1, n. 32.**

Niagara Mohawk Power Corp. v. Stone & Webster Engineering Corp., 125 F.R.D. 578 (N.D.N.Y.1989)—§ **501.3, n. 33, 53.**

Niang, People v., 160 Misc.2d 500, 609 N.Y.S.2d 1017 (N.Y.City Crim.Ct. 1994)—§ **803(4).1, n. 13; § 803(5).1, n. 39.**

Nicastro v. Park, 113 A.D.2d 129, 495 N.Y.S.2d 184 (N.Y.A.D. 2 Dept.1985)—§ **300.3, n. 21.**

Nicole V., Matter of, 524 N.Y.S.2d 19, 518 N.E.2d 914 (N.Y.1987)—§ **804(5).1; § 804(5).1, n. 25.**

Nicolo v. Greenfield, 163 A.D.2d 837, 558 N.Y.S.2d 371 (N.Y.A.D. 4 Dept.1990)—§ **501.1, n. 60.**

Niesig v. Team I, 559 N.Y.S.2d 493, 558 N.E.2d 1030 (N.Y.1990)—§ **501.1, n. 67.**

Nieskes & Craig, Inc. v. Schoonerman, 40 A.D.2d 931, 337 N.Y.S.2d 750 (N.Y.A.D. 4 Dept.1972)—§ **300.3, n. 17.**

Nieto, People v., 97 A.D.2d 774, 468 N.Y.S.2d 504 (N.Y.A.D. 2 Dept.1983)—§ **801(1).2, n. 12.**

Nieves v. City of New York, 109 N.Y.S.2d 556 (N.Y.Sup.1951)—§ **802.2, n. 67.**

Nieves, People v., 186 A.D.2d 276, 588 N.Y.S.2d 305 (N.Y.A.D. 2 Dept.1992)—§ **607.7, n. 5.**

Nieves, People v., 501 N.Y.S.2d 1, 492 N.E.2d 109 (N.Y.1986)—§ **801.1, n. 13; § 803(1).1, n. 32; § 804(2).1; § 804(2).1, n. 6, 31; § 804(5).1; § 804(5).1, n. 11.**

Niles v. State, 201 A.D.2d 774, 607 N.Y.S.2d 480 (N.Y.A.D. 3 Dept.1994)—§ **1104.1, n. 14.**

Nisoff, People v., 369 N.Y.S.2d 686, 330 N.E.2d 638 (N.Y.1975)—§ **601.1, n. 30, 35, 39, 42.**

Nisonoff, People v., 293 N.Y. 597, 59 N.E.2d 420 (N.Y.1944)—§ **803(3).1; § 803(3).1, n. 42; § 803(5).1, n. 2.**

Nisonoff, People v., 267 A.D. 356, 45 N.Y.S.2d 854 (N.Y.A.D. 1 Dept.1944)—§ **803(3).1, n. 45.**

Nissen v. Rubin, 121 A.D.2d 320, 504 N.Y.S.2d 106 (N.Y.A.D. 1 Dept.1986)—§ **803(1).1, n. 66.**

Nissho–Iwai Co., Ltd. v. M/T Stolt Lion, 719 F.2d 34 (2nd Cir.1983)—§ **300.4, n. 35.**

Nitzberg, People v., 287 N.Y. 183, 38 N.E.2d 490 (N.Y.1941)—§ **401.1, n. 52.**

Nival, People v., 353 N.Y.S.2d 409, 308 N.E.2d 883 (N.Y.1974)—§ **801(2).1, n. 6, 7.**

Nixon, United States v., 779 F.2d 126 (2nd Cir.1985)—§ **804(5).2, n. 38.**

Nixon, United States v., 418 U.S. 683, 94 S.Ct. 3090, 41 L.Ed.2d 1039 (1974)—§ **511.2, n. 4, 12.**

N. L. R. B. v. Federal Dairy Co., 297 F.2d 487 (1st Cir.1962)—§ **612.2, n. 10, 11.**

Noble v. Marx, 298 N.Y. 106, 81 N.E.2d 40 (N.Y.1948)—§ **607.6, n. 11.**

Noble, United States v., 754 F.2d 1324 (7th Cir.1985)—§ **609.2, n. 11, 12.**

Nobles, United States v., 422 U.S. 225, 95 S.Ct. 2160, 45 L.Ed.2d 141 (1975)—§ **412.1, n. 5; § 501.3; § 501.3, n. 3, 37, 48, 55; § 612.2, n. 17.**

Noce v. Kaufman, 161 N.Y.S.2d 1, 141 N.E.2d 529 (N.Y.1957)—§ **401.1, n. 33.**

Nordhauser v. New York City Health and Hospitals Corp., 176 A.D.2d 787, 575 N.Y.S.2d 117 (N.Y.A.D. 2 Dept.1991)—§ **802.2, n. 75.**

Norfleet v. New York City Transit Authority, 124 A.D.2d 715, 508 N.Y.S.2d 468 (N.Y.A.D. 2 Dept.1986)—§ **1105.1, n. 4, 9, 10.**

Norman, People v., 627 N.Y.S.2d 302, 650 N.E.2d 1303 (N.Y.1995)—§ **300.3, n. 31.**

Northwestern Mut. Life Ins. Co. v. Linard, 359 F.Supp. 1012 (D.C.N.Y.1973)—§ **300.3, n. 46.**

Northwestern Nat. Cas. Co. v. Global Moving & Storage Co., 533 F.2d 320 (6th Cir.1976)—§ **1107.2, n. 2.**

Norton, People v., 164 A.D.2d 343, 563 N.Y.S.2d 802 (N.Y.A.D. 1 Dept.1990)—§ **803(1).1, n. 38.**

Norton, United States v., 867 F.2d 1354 (11th Cir.1989)—§ **606.2, n. 7.**

Noseworthy v. City of New York, 298 N.Y. 76, 80 N.E.2d 744 (N.Y.1948)—§ **300.4, n. 13; § 607.6, n. 8, 11.**

Nowack v. Metropolitan St. Ry. Co., 166 N.Y. 433, 60 N.E. 32 (N.Y.1901)—§ **802.2; § 802.2, n. 64.**

TABLE OF CASES

Nowakowski's Estate, In re, 162 N.Y.S.2d 19, 142 N.E.2d 198 (N.Y.1957)—§ **300.3, n. 37;** § **607.1, n. 5.**

Nucci, People v., 162 A.D.2d 725, 557 N.Y.S.2d 422 (N.Y.A.D. 2 Dept.1990)— § **804(1).1, n. 46.**

Nunez, United States v., 658 F.Supp. 828 (D.Colo.1987)—§ **1006.1, n. 25.**

N. V. Maatschappij Voor Industriele Waarden v. A. O. Smith Corp., 590 F.2d 415 (2nd Cir.1978)—§ **702.2, n. 6.**

O

Oates, United States v., 560 F.2d 45 (2nd Cir.1977)—§ **803(5).2;** § **803(5).2, n. 6;** § **804(5).2, n. 27.**

Oates' Will, In re, 171 A.D. 679, 157 N.Y.S. 646 (N.Y.A.D. 2 Dept.1916)—§ **607.8, n. 18.**

Obayagbona, United States v., 627 F.Supp. 329 (E.D.N.Y.1985)—§ **801(1).3, n. 18, 19;** § **803(1).2;** § **803(1).2, n. 7, 17.**

Obermeier, Matter of Estate of, 150 A.D.2d 863, 540 N.Y.S.2d 613 (N.Y.A.D. 3 Dept. 1989)—§ **301.4, n. 5.**

O'Brien v. Equitable Life Assur. Soc. of United States, 212 F.2d 383 (8th Cir. 1954)—§ **301.5, n. 6.**

O'Bryan, People v., 36 A.D.2d 548, 317 N.Y.S.2d 34 (N.Y.A.D. 3 Dept.1971)— § **1101.1, n. 3.**

Ocampo, United States v., 650 F.2d 421 (2nd Cir.1981)—§ **803(7).2, n. 8.**

Ocasio, People v., 416 N.Y.S.2d 581, 389 N.E.2d 1101 (N.Y.1979)—§ **608.2, n. 25, 29;** § **609.1, n. 48, 51.**

Ochs, People v., 163 N.Y.S.2d 671, 143 N.E.2d 388 (N.Y.1957)—§ **601.1, n. 19.**

O'Connell v. Jacobs, 181 A.D.2d 1064, 583 N.Y.S.2d 61 (N.Y.A.D. 4 Dept.1992)— § **401.1, n. 45;** § **402.1, n. 25.**

O'Connor v. Larson, 74 A.D.2d 734, 425 N.Y.S.2d 702 (N.Y.A.D. 4 Dept.1980)— § **501.3, n. 27.**

O'Connor, People v., 85 A.D.2d 92, 447 N.Y.S.2d 553 (N.Y.A.D. 4 Dept.1982)— § **501.1, n. 9, 15, 39.**

Oddo, United States v., 314 F.2d 115 (2nd Cir.1963)—§ **406.2, n. 3.**

O'Dea v. Amodeo, 118 Conn. 58, 170 A. 486 (Conn.1934)—§ **301.5, n. 43.**

Odom, United States v., 736 F.2d 104 (4th Cir.1984)—§ **601.3, n. 9, 13;** § **603.2, n. 4.**

O'Gee v. Dobbs Houses, Inc., 570 F.2d 1084 (2nd Cir.1978)—§ **703.2, n. 11;** § **803(1).2, n. 51.**

Oglesby, People v., 137 A.D.2d 840, 525 N.Y.S.2d 304 (N.Y.A.D. 2 Dept.1988)— § **609.1, n. 15.**

O'Gorman, People v., 91 Misc.2d 539, 398 N.Y.S.2d 336 (N.Y.Sup.1977)—§ **505.1, n. 10.**

O'Hagan v. Dillon, 76 N.Y. 170 (1879)— § **611.2, n. 16.**

Ohanian v. Avis Rent A Car System, Inc., 779 F.2d 101 (2nd Cir.1985)—§ **606.2, n. 7.**

Ohio v. Roberts, 448 U.S. 56, 100 S.Ct. 2531, 65 L.Ed.2d 597 (1980)—§ **804.1;** § **804.1, n. 13;** § **804(1).2;** § **804(1).2, n. 16;** § **804(3).1;** § **804(3).1, n. 47;** § **804(3).2, n. 12;** § **804(5).2, n. 30.**

Ohio–Sealy Mattress Mfg. Co. v. Kaplan, 90 F.R.D. 21 (D.C.Ill.1980)—§ **501.2, n. 10.**

Okafor, People v., 130 Misc.2d 536, 495 N.Y.S.2d 895 (N.Y.Sup.1985)—§ **807.1, n. 8.**

Olin Corp. v. Insurance Co. of North America, 603 F.Supp. 445 (D.C.N.Y.1985)— § **408.2, n. 4, 8, 10.**

Oliver v. Bereano, 267 A.D. 747, 48 N.Y.S.2d 142 (N.Y.A.D. 1 Dept.1944)— § **201.1, n. 32.**

Oliver, United States v., 626 F.2d 254 (2nd Cir.1980)—§ **804.1, n. 31;** § **804(3).2, n. 10, 11.**

Olsen, People v., 357 N.Y.S.2d 487, 313 N.E.2d 782 (N.Y.1974)—§ **611.1, n. 11.**

Olsen, People v., 292 N.Y.S.2d 420, 239 N.E.2d 354 (N.Y.1968)—§ **701.1, n. 8.**

Olshansky v. Prensky, 185 A.D. 469, 172 N.Y.S. 856 (N.Y.A.D. 2 Dept.1918)— § **601.1, n. 32, 33;** § **603.1, n. 3.**

Oltarsh v. Aetna Ins. Co., 256 N.Y.S.2d 577, 204 N.E.2d 622 (N.Y.1965)—§ **411.1, n. 13.**

Omar B., Matter of, 175 A.D.2d 834, 573 N.Y.S.2d 301 (N.Y.A.D. 2 Dept.1991)— § **703.1, n. 10.**

Omar Intern., Inc. v. ALAF General Organization for Fodder, 817 F.Supp. 394 (S.D.N.Y.1993)—§ **802.3, n. 8.**

O'Neal v. Morgan, 637 F.2d 846 (2nd Cir. 1980)—§ **802.3;** § **802.3, n. 10, 11, 12.**

Oneida Indian Nation of New York v. State of N. Y., 691 F.2d 1070 (2nd Cir.1982)— § **202.1, n. 3.**

Oneida Nat. Bank & Trust Co. of Central New York v. Kranz, 70 Misc.2d 595, 334 N.Y.S.2d 336 (N.Y.Sup.1972)—§ **601.2, n. 25.**

O'Neill v. Oakgrove Const., Inc., 528 N.Y.S.2d 1, 523 N.E.2d 277 (N.Y.1988)— § **508.1;** § **508.1, n. 6, 8;** § **508.2, n. 2.**

O'Neil's Estate, In re, 20 A.D.2d 741, 246 N.Y.S.2d 892 (N.Y.A.D. 3 Dept.1964)— § **601.2, n. 54.**

Opera v. Hyva, Inc., 86 A.D.2d 373, 450 N.Y.S.2d 615 (N.Y.A.D. 4 Dept.1982)— § **407.1, n. 18.**

Opper v. United States, 348 U.S. 84, 75 S.Ct. 158, 99 L.Ed. 101 (1954)—§ **300.3, n. 50.**

O'Rama, People v., 574 N.Y.S.2d 159, 579 N.E.2d 189 (N.Y.1991)—§ **802.2, n. 8.**

Orco Bank, N.V. v. Proteinas Del Pacifico, S.A., 179 A.D.2d 390, 577 N.Y.S.2d 841 (N.Y.A.D. 1 Dept.1992)—§ **501.1, n. 84.**

TABLE OF CASES

Ordway, In re, 196 N.Y. 95, 89 N.E. 474 (N.Y.1909)—§ **201.1, n. 36.**

Oreck Corp. v. Whirlpool Corp., 639 F.2d 75 (2nd Cir.1980)—§ **802.3; § 802.3, n. 33, 49.**

Oregon v. Hass, 420 U.S. 714, 95 S.Ct. 1215, 43 L.Ed.2d 570 (1975)—§ **607.8, n. 10.**

Oregon Steam–Ship Co. v. Otis, 100 N.Y. 446, 3 N.E. 485 (N.Y.1885)—§ **301.4, n. 2; § 1002.1, n. 14.**

Orena, United States v., 32 F.3d 704 (2nd Cir.1994)—§ **901.4, n. 12; § 1101.2, n. 9.**

Oringer v. Rotkin, 162 A.D.2d 113, 556 N.Y.S.2d 67 (N.Y.A.D. 1 Dept.1990)— § **502.1, n. 85.**

Orlick v. Granit Hotel and Country Club, 331 N.Y.S.2d 651, 282 N.E.2d 610 (N.Y. 1972)—§ **405.1; § 405.1, n. 15, 16.**

Ortega, People v., 578 N.Y.S.2d 123, 585 N.E.2d 372 (N.Y.1991)—§ **510.1, n. 2, 5.**

Ortho Pharmaceutical Corp. v. Cosprophar, Inc., 828 F.Supp. 1114 (S.D.N.Y.1993)— § **803(3).2, n. 14.**

Ortiz, People v., 198 A.D.2d 912, 604 N.Y.S.2d 462 (N.Y.A.D. 4 Dept.1993)— § **604.1, n. 7.**

Ortiz, People v., 560 N.Y.S.2d 186, 560 N.E.2d 162 (N.Y.1990)—§ **300.4, n. 55.**

Ortiz, People v., 156 A.D.2d 77, 554 N.Y.S.2d 107 (N.Y.A.D. 1 Dept.1990)— § **404.1, n. 57.**

Ortiz, People v., 141 Misc.2d 747, 534 N.Y.S.2d 316 (N.Y.Sup.1988)—§ **410.1, n. 14; § 802.1, n. 10.**

Ortiz, People v., 135 A.D.2d 743, 522 N.Y.S.2d 647 (N.Y.A.D. 2 Dept.1987)— § **100.2, n. 8.**

Ortiz, People v., 100 A.D.2d 6, 473 N.Y.S.2d 288 (N.Y.A.D. 4 Dept.1984)—§ **802.2, n. 104.**

Ortiz, People v., 119 Misc.2d 572, 463 N.Y.S.2d 713 (N.Y.Sup.1983)— § **804(5).1; § 804(5).1, n. 13.**

Ortiz, United States v., 857 F.2d 900 (2nd Cir.1988)—§ **404.2, n. 32.**

Ortiz, United States v., 553 F.2d 782 (2nd Cir.1977)—§ **609.2, n. 7.**

Oshatz, United States v., 912 F.2d 534 (2nd Cir.1990)—§ **402.1, n. 51; § 402.2, n. 13; § 404.2, n. 16.**

O'Shea v. Sarro, 106 A.D.2d 435, 482 N.Y.S.2d 529 (N.Y.A.D. 2 Dept.1984)— § **703.1, n. 14.**

Osnato v. New York City Transit Authority, 172 A.D.2d 597, 568 N.Y.S.2d 821 (N.Y.A.D. 2 Dept.1991)—§ **607.3, n. 22.**

Osorio, People v., 550 N.Y.S.2d 612, 549 N.E.2d 1183 (N.Y.1989)—§ **501.1, n. 49, 51, 53, 54, 58.**

Osterhoudt, In re, 722 F.2d 591 (9th Cir. 1983)—§ **501.2, n. 14.**

Ostrer, United States v., 422 F.Supp. 93 (D.C.N.Y.1976)—§ **614.2, n. 2.**

O'Sullivan, People v., 104 N.Y. 481, 10 N.E. 880 (N.Y.1887)—§ **607.5, n. 8; § 803(1).1, n. 58.**

Otero v. Jennings, 698 F.Supp. 42 (S.D.N.Y. 1988)—§ **404.2, n. 37.**

Outley v. City of New York, 837 F.2d 587 (2nd Cir.1988)—§ **607.2; § 607.2, n. 16; § 607.6, n. 35.**

Overseas Development Disc Corp. v. Sangamo Const. Co., Inc., 840 F.2d 1319 (7th Cir.1988)—§ **203.2, n. 9.**

Overseas Nat. Airways, Inc. v. General Elec. Co., 119 Misc.2d 72, 462 N.Y.S.2d 984 (N.Y.Sup.1983)—§ **804(1).1, n. 16.**

Overseas Trust Bank Ltd. v. Poon, 181 A.D.2d 762, 581 N.Y.S.2d 92 (N.Y.A.D. 2 Dept.1992)—§ **602.1, n. 5.**

Owens, People v., 203 A.D.2d 106, 610 N.Y.S.2d 485 (N.Y.A.D. 1 Dept.1994)— § **609.1, n. 43.**

Owens, People v., 291 N.Y.S.2d 313, 238 N.E.2d 715 (N.Y.1968)—§ **509.1; § 509.1, n. 44.**

Owens, United States v., 484 U.S. 554, 108 S.Ct. 838, 98 L.Ed.2d 951 (1988)— § **801(2).2; § 801(2).2, n. 5; § 803(2).2; § 803(2).2, n. 8.**

Owens, United States v., 789 F.2d 750 (9th Cir.1986)—§ **801(2).2, n. 6.**

Owens–El, United States v., 889 F.2d 913 (9th Cir.1989)—§ **602.2, n. 4, 5, 12.**

P

Paccione, United States v., 949 F.2d 1183 (2nd Cir.1991)—§ **402.2, n. 13; § 404.2, n. 30.**

Pacelli v. Nassau County Police Dept., 639 F.Supp. 1382 (E.D.N.Y.1986)— § **804(1).2, n. 11.**

Pacelli, United States v., 521 F.2d 135 (2nd Cir.1975)—§ **607.7, n. 23.**

Pacelli, United States v., 470 F.2d 67 (2nd Cir.1972)—§ **801(1).3; § 801(1).3, n. 6.**

Pache v. Boehm, 60 A.D.2d 867, 401 N.Y.S.2d 260 (N.Y.A.D. 2 Dept.1978)— § **606.1, n. 10.**

Pacheco v. United States, 367 F.2d 878 (10th Cir.1966)—§ **1105.2, n. 3.**

Paddack v. Dave Christensen, Inc., 745 F.2d 1254 (9th Cir.1984)—§ **703.2, n. 10.**

Padgett v. Brezner, 359 S.W.2d 416 (Mo. App.1962)—§ **1001.1, n. 7.**

Pageau, United States v., 526 F.Supp. 1221 (D.C.N.Y.1981)—§ **1104.2, n. 3, 18, 20.**

Painton v. Northern Central Ry. Co., 83 N.Y. 7 (1880)—§ **300.3, n. 21.**

Pallma v. Fox, 182 F.2d 895 (2nd Cir. 1950)—§ **1006.1, n. 12.**

Palma S. v. Carmine S., 134 Misc.2d 34, 509 N.Y.S.2d 527 (N.Y.Fam.Ct.1986)— § **804.1, n. 21; § 804(1).1, n. 5, 25.**

Palmer v. Hoffman, 318 U.S. 109, 63 S.Ct. 477, 87 L.Ed. 645 (1943)—§ **803(3).1;**

TABLE OF CASES

§ 803(3).1, n. 30; § 803(3).2; § 803(3).2, n. 33.

Palmer v. Krueger, 897 F.2d 1529 (10th Cir.1990)—§ **411.2, n. 3.**

Palmer v. Palmer, 162 N.Y. 130, 56 N.E. 501 (N.Y.1900)—§ **301.4; § 301.4, n. 18.**

Palumbo, United States v., 639 F.2d 123 (3rd Cir.1981)—§ **804(3).2, n. 10, 11.**

Panter v. Marshall Field & Co., 80 F.R.D. 718 (D.C.Ill.1978)—§ **501.2, n. 37.**

Paoli R.R. Yard PCB Litigation, In re, 35 F.3d 717 (3rd Cir.1994)—§ **702.2, n. 27; § 703.2, n. 9.**

Paone, United States v., 782 F.2d 386 (2nd Cir.1986)—§ **802.3, n. 58.**

Papadakis, United States v., 572 F.Supp. 1518 (D.C.N.Y.1983)—§ **804(5).2, n. 15.**

Pape, United States v., 144 F.2d 778 (2nd Cir.1944)—§ **501.2, n. 14.**

Papo, People v., 80 A.D.2d 623, 436 N.Y.S.2d 65 (N.Y.A.D. 2 Dept.1981)— § **410.1, n. 10.**

Pappalardo, People v., 152 Misc.2d 364, 576 N.Y.S.2d 1001 (N.Y.Sup.1991)— § **804(1).1, n. 49.**

Pappas v. Middle Earth Condominium Ass'n, 963 F.2d 534 (2nd Cir.1992)— § **802.3; § 802.3, n. 18.**

Park v. New York Cent. & H. R. R.R. Co., 155 N.Y. 215, 49 N.E. 674 (N.Y.1898)— § **402.1, n. 16, 20.**

Parker v. Gladden, 385 U.S. 363, 87 S.Ct. 468, 17 L.Ed.2d 420 (1966)—§ **606.1, n. 13; § 606.2, n. 5.**

Parker, United States v., 834 F.2d 408 (4th Cir.1987)—§ **503.5, n. 19.**

Parker, United States v., 491 F.2d 517 (8th Cir.1973)—§ **1108.2, n. 1.**

Parks, People v., 390 N.Y.S.2d 848, 359 N.E.2d 358 (N.Y.1976)—§ **601.1; § 601.1, n. 11, 13, 36, 49, 50, 53; § 603.1, n. 2; § 607.5, n. 3; § 607.7, n. 8; § 611.1, n. 13; § 702.1; § 702.1, n. 66.**

Parsons v. Honeywell, Inc., 929 F.2d 901 (2nd Cir.1991)—§ **804(5).2; § 804(5).2, n. 17; § 805.2, n. 5.**

Parsons v. Syracuse, B. & N. Y. R. Co., 205 N.Y. 226, 98 N.E. 331 (N.Y.1912)— § **406.1, n. 34.**

Partin, United States v., 493 F.2d 750 (5th Cir.1974)—§ **607.7, n. 20.**

Pascal's Will, In re, 15 Misc.2d 767, 182 N.Y.S.2d 927 (N.Y.Sup.1959)—§ **201.1, n. 45.**

Paschall, People v., 91 A.D.2d 645, 456 N.Y.S.2d 828 (N.Y.A.D. 2 Dept.1982)— § **406.1, n. 14.**

Passenger, People v., 175 A.D.2d 944, 572 N.Y.S.2d 972 (N.Y.A.D. 3 Dept.1991)— § **607.7, n. 11.**

Passino v. DeRosa, 199 A.D.2d 1017, 606 N.Y.S.2d 107 (N.Y.A.D. 4 Dept.1993)— § **103.1, n. 44; § 803(3).1, n. 65.**

Passos–Paternina, United States v., 918 F.2d 979 (1st Cir.1990)—§ **1107.2, n. 1, 5.**

Pataki v. Kiseda, 80 A.D.2d 100, 437 N.Y.S.2d 692 (N.Y.A.D. 2 Dept.1981)— § **501.3, n. 22.**

Patrick, People v., 182 N.Y. 131, 74 N.E. 843 (N.Y.1905)—§ **501.1, n. 79.**

Patterson v. New York, 432 U.S. 197, 97 S.Ct. 2319, 53 L.Ed.2d 281 (1977)— § **300.4; § 300.4, n. 59; § 302.1, n. 4.**

Patterson, People v., 165 A.D.2d 886, 560 N.Y.S.2d 357 (N.Y.A.D. 2 Dept.1990)— § **611.3, n. 13.**

Patterson, People v., 48 A.D.2d 933, 369 N.Y.S.2d 534 (N.Y.A.D. 2 Dept.1975)— § **105.1, n. 5.**

Pau v. Yosemite Park and Curry Co., 928 F.2d 880 (9th Cir.1991)—§ **804(2).2; § 804(2).2, n. 17.**

Paulin, People v., 518 N.Y.S.2d 790, 512 N.E.2d 312 (N.Y.1987)—§ **401.1, n. 28.**

Paulino, People v., 187 A.D.2d 736, 590 N.Y.S.2d 532 (N.Y.A.D. 2 Dept.1992)— § **105.1, n. 13.**

Paulsen v. Catherwood, 27 A.D.2d 493, 280 N.Y.S.2d 491 (N.Y.A.D. 3 Dept.1967)— § **802.2, n. 35.**

Pavao, People v., 464 N.Y.S.2d 458, 451 N.E.2d 216 (N.Y.1983)—§ **607.2, n. 8; § 607.3, n. 3; § 607.5, n. 24; § 608.1; § 608.1, n. 2, 5, 10, 13; § 608.2, n. 16; § 609.1, n. 35.**

Payden, United States v., 622 F.Supp. 915 (D.C.N.Y.1985)—§ **801.1, n. 24.**

Paylor, People v., 518 N.Y.S.2d 102, 511 N.E.2d 370 (N.Y.1987)—§ **401.1; § 401.1, n. 31.**

Payne v. New Hyde Park Dodge, 163 A.D.2d 285, 557 N.Y.S.2d 152 (N.Y.A.D. 2 Dept.1990)—§ **802.1, n. 13.**

Pearce v. Stace, 207 N.Y. 506, 101 N.E. 434 (N.Y.1913)—§ **701.1, n. 8.**

Pease, People v., 27 N.Y. 45 (1863)— § **512.1, n. 3.**

Pedroza, United States v., 750 F.2d 187 (2nd Cir.1984)—§ **609.2, n. 7, 10; § 802.3, n. 9.**

Pekarz, People v., 185 N.Y. 470, 78 N.E. 294 (N.Y.1906)—§ **701.1, n. 8.**

Pekelis v. Transcontinental & Western Air, 187 F.2d 122 (2nd Cir.1951)— § **803(3).2; § 803(3).2, n. 35.**

Peninsula Nat. Bank of Cedarhurst v. Hill, 52 Misc.2d 903, 277 N.Y.S.2d 162 (N.Y.A.D. 2 Dept.1966)—§ **406.1, n. 14.**

Penn v. Kirsh, 40 A.D.2d 814, 338 N.Y.S.2d 161 (N.Y.A.D. 1 Dept.1972)—§ **805.1, n. 1.**

Pennick, People v., 204 A.D.2d 988, 612 N.Y.S.2d 723 (N.Y.A.D. 4 Dept.1994)— § **1001.1, n. 31.**

Pennsylvania v. Muniz, 496 U.S. 582, 110 S.Ct. 2638, 110 L.Ed.2d 528 (1990)— § **509.1, n. 31.**

TABLE OF CASES

Pennsylvania v. Ritchie, 480 U.S. 39, 107 S.Ct. 989, 94 L.Ed.2d 40 (1987)—§ **502.1, n. 86;** § **506.1, n. 5.**

Pennsylvania Dental Ass'n v. Medical Service Ass'n of Pennsylvania, 745 F.2d 248 (3rd Cir.1984)—§ **703.2, n. 1.**

Penny "MM" v. Bruce "MM", 118 A.D.2d 979, 500 N.Y.S.2d 199 (N.Y.A.D. 3 Dept. 1986)—§ **301.5, n. 29.**

Penthouse Intern., Ltd. v. Playboy Enterprises, Inc., 663 F.2d 371 (2nd Cir. 1981)—§ **513.2, n. 5.**

People v. _____ (see opposing party)

People by Fischer v. Dan, 41 A.D.2d 687, 342 N.Y.S.2d 731 (N.Y.A.D. 4 Dept. 1973)—§ **508.1, n. 16.**

People ex rel. v. _____ (see opposing party and relator)

People of Territory of Guam v. Ignacio, 10 F.3d 608 (9th Cir.1993)—§ **803(1).2, n. 19.**

Peoples Nat. Bank of Rockland County v. Weiner, 129 A.D.2d 782, 514 N.Y.S.2d 772 (N.Y.A.D. 2 Dept.1987)—§ **301.4, n. 21.**

Perazone v. Sears, Roebuck and Co., 128 A.D.2d 15, 515 N.Y.S.2d 908 (N.Y.A.D. 3 Dept.1987)—§ **407.1, n. 18.**

Pereira v. United States, 347 U.S. 1, 74 S.Ct. 358, 98 L.Ed. 435 (1954)—§ **503.5, n. 18, 19.**

Perez, People v., 198 A.D.2d 446, 604 N.Y.S.2d 152 (N.Y.A.D. 2 Dept.1993)—§ **604.1, n. 7.**

Perez, People v., 193 A.D.2d 630, 597 N.Y.S.2d 445 (N.Y.A.D. 2 Dept.1993)—§ **607.5, n. 36.**

Perez, People v., 118 A.D.2d 431, 499 N.Y.S.2d 716 (N.Y.A.D. 1 Dept.1986)—§ **410.1, n. 10.**

Perez, People v., 300 N.Y. 208, 90 N.E.2d 40 (N.Y.1949)—§ **1102.1, n. 27;** § **1104.1, n. 6.**

Perma Research and Development v. Singer Co., 542 F.2d 111 (2nd Cir.1976)—§ **1106.1, n. 10.**

Permian Corp. v. United States, 665 F.2d 1214, 214 U.S.App.D.C. 396 (D.C.Cir. 1981)—§ **501.2, n. 50.**

Perrin v. Anderson, 784 F.2d 1040 (10th Cir.1986)—§ **406.2, n. 15.**

Perry v. Fiumano, 61 A.D.2d 512, 403 N.Y.S.2d 382 (N.Y.A.D. 4 Dept.1978)—§ **505.1, n. 19.**

Perry v. Leeke, 488 U.S. 272, 109 S.Ct. 594, 102 L.Ed.2d 624 (1989)—§ **615.1, n. 2, 7, 8;** § **615.2, n. 8.**

Perry v. Metropolitan St. Ry. Co., 68 A.D. 351, 74 N.Y.S. 1 (N.Y.A.D. 2 Dept. 1902)—§ **1102.1, n. 13.**

Perry, People v., 473 N.Y.S.2d 966, 462 N.E.2d 143 (N.Y.1984)—§ **300.4, n. 55.**

Perry, United States v., 643 F.2d 38 (2nd Cir.1981)—§ **402.2, n. 10.**

Perryman, People v., 178 A.D.2d 916, 578 N.Y.S.2d 785 (N.Y.A.D. 4 Dept.1991)—§ **412.1, n. 11.**

Persico, People v., 157 A.D.2d 339, 556 N.Y.S.2d 262 (N.Y.A.D. 1 Dept.1990)—§ **802.2;** § **802.2, n. 88, 89.**

Persico, United States v., 832 F.2d 705 (2nd Cir.1987)—§ **802.3;** § **802.3, n. 71.**

Peterson, People v., 42 A.D.2d 937, 348 N.Y.S.2d 137 (N.Y.A.D. 1 Dept.1973)—§ **404.1, n. 75.**

Peyro, United States v., 786 F.2d 826 (8th Cir.1986)—§ **601.3, n. 15.**

Pfeil v. Rogers, 757 F.2d 850 (7th Cir. 1985)—§ **804(2).2;** § **804(2).2, n. 14.**

Phan, People v., 150 Misc.2d 435, 568 N.Y.S.2d 498 (N.Y.Sup.1990)—§ **804(1).1, n. 52.**

Phelps, People ex rel. v. Court of Oyer and Terminer of the County of New York, 83 N.Y. 436 (1881)—§ **611.3. n. 23.**

Phibbs, United States v., 999 F.2d 1053 (6th Cir.1993)—§ **601.3, n. 9, 13, 15;** § **607.7, n. 20.**

Philadelphia, City of v. Westinghouse Elec. Corp., 210 F.Supp. 483 (D.C.Pa.1962)—§ **501.1, n. 63;** § **501.2, n. 30.**

Philip M., Matter of, 604 N.Y.S.2d 40, 624 N.E.2d 168 (N.Y.1993)—§ **300.3, n. 44;** § **804(5).1, n. 24.**

Phillips v. Joseph Kantor & Co., 338 N.Y.S.2d 882, 291 N.E.2d 129 (N.Y. 1972)—§ **601.2, n. 64, 82.**

Philpot v. Fifth Ave. Coach Co., 142 A.D. 811, 128 N.Y.S. 35 (N.Y.A.D. 1 Dept. 1911)—§ **615.1, n. 2, 5.**

Phoenix Associates III v. Stone, 60 F.3d 95 (2nd Cir.1995)—§ **103.2, n. 27;** § **106.2, n. 7, 8.**

Piazza, People v., 422 N.Y.S.2d 9, 397 N.E.2d 700 (N.Y.1979)—§ **607.8, n. 31;** § **804(3).1, n. 51, 52.**

Piccola v. Hibbard, 51 A.D.2d 674, 378 N.Y.S.2d 163 (N.Y.A.D. 4 Dept.1976)—§ **300.4, n. 24.**

Piehnik v. Graff, 158 A.D.2d 863, 551 N.Y.S.2d 656 (N.Y.A.D. 3 Dept.1990)—§ **801.1, n. 39.**

Pierce v. F.R. Tripler & Co., 955 F.2d 820 (2nd Cir.1992)—§ **104.2, n. 10;** § **408.2, n. 1.**

Pierce v. Ramsey Winch Co., 753 F.2d 416 (5th Cir.1985)—§ **1006.1, n. 18.**

Pieropan, People v., 72 Misc.2d 770, 340 N.Y.S.2d 31 (Oneida Co.Ct.1973)—§ **702.1, n. 52.**

Pierre, People v., 157 Misc.2d 812, 599 N.Y.S.2d 412 (N.Y.City Crim.Ct.1993)—§ **803(3).1, n. 49.**

Pierre, People v., 157 A.D.2d 750, 550 N.Y.S.2d 44 (N.Y.A.D. 2 Dept.1990)—§ **803(3).1, n. 11.**

Pierre, United States v., 781 F.2d 329 (2nd Cir.1986)—§ **607.5, n. 66, 67, 68;** § **801(1).3, n. 23, 24, 25.**

TABLE OF CASES

Piggie, United States v., 622 F.2d 486 (10th Cir.1980)—§ **201.2, n. 5.**

Pignataro, People v., 263 N.Y. 229, 188 N.E. 720 (N.Y.1934)—§ **802.2, n. 69.**

Pike, People v., 519 N.Y.S.2d 1052, 513 N.E.2d 1320 (N.Y.1987)—§ **1103.1, n. 10.**

Pike, People v., 131 A.D.2d 890, 517 N.Y.S.2d 246 (N.Y.A.D. 2 Dept.1987)—§ **1103.1, n. 10.**

Pilarinos, United States v., 864 F.2d 253 (2nd Cir.1988)—§ **802.3, n. 20.**

Pina v. Henderson, 752 F.2d 47 (2nd Cir. 1985)—§ **201.2, n. 2.**

Pineda, People v., 160 A.D.2d 649, 559 N.Y.S.2d 266 (N.Y.A.D. 1 Dept.1990)—§ **604.1, n. 7.**

Pinkerton v. United States, 328 U.S. 640, 66 S.Ct. 1180, 90 L.Ed. 1489 (1946)—§ **804(3).2, n. 28.**

Pinkham v. Burgess, 933 F.2d 1066 (1st Cir.1991)—§ **411.2, n. 2.**

Pink Supply Corp. v. Hiebert, Inc., 612 F.Supp. 1334 (D.C.Minn.1985)—§ **804(3).2, n. 6.**

Pinto, United States v., 850 F.2d 927 (2nd Cir.1988)—§ **1006.1; § 1006.1, n. 20.**

Pioneer Hi–Bred Intern. v. Holden Foundation Seeds, Inc., 35 F.3d 1226 (8th Cir. 1994)—§ **702.2, n. 29.**

Pisani, United States v., 773 F.2d 397 (2nd Cir.1985)—§ **614.2, n. 3.**

Pitts, United States v., 569 F.2d 343 (5th Cir.1978)—§ **901.2; § 901.2, n. 19.**

Piwowarski v. Cornwell, 273 N.Y. 226, 7 N.E.2d 111 (N.Y.1937)—§ **301.5, n. 31.**

Plache, United States v., 913 F.2d 1375 (9th Cir.1990)—§ **501.2, n. 45.**

Plante, United States v., 472 F.2d 829 (1st Cir.1973)—§ **607.5, n. 55.**

Platner v. Platner, 78 N.Y. 90 (1879)—§ **103.1, n. 13, 35; § 106.1, n. 12.**

Platt v. Elias, 186 N.Y. 374, 79 N.E. 1 (N.Y.1906)—§ **301.2, n. 1, 4, 5.**

Playboy Enterprises, Inc. v. Chuckleberry Pub., Inc., 486 F.Supp. 414 (D.C.N.Y. 1980)—§ **408.2, n. 6.**

Plaza v. Estate of Wisser, 211 A.D.2d 111, 626 N.Y.S.2d 446 (N.Y.A.D. 1 Dept. 1995)—§ **502.1, n. 64.**

Plaza Hotel Associates v. Wellington Associates, Inc., 372 N.Y.S.2d 35, 333 N.E.2d 346 (N.Y.1975)—§ **405.1, n. 27.**

Plummer, People v., 365 N.Y.S.2d 842, 325 N.E.2d 161 (N.Y.1975)—§ **401.1, n. 15.**

Pobliner, People v., 345 N.Y.S.2d 482, 298 N.E.2d 637 (N.Y.1973)—§ **401.1, n. 49; § 1101.1, n. 1; § 1102.1; § 1102.1, n. 19; § 1104.1; § 1104.1, n. 17, 18.**

Pointer v. Texas, 380 U.S. 400, 85 S.Ct. 1065, 13 L.Ed.2d 923 (1965)—§ **801(1).3, n. 3; § 804(2).2, n. 13.**

Pok Rye Kim v. Mars Cup Co., Inc., 102 A.D.2d 812, 476 N.Y.S.2d 381 (N.Y.A.D. 2 Dept.1984)—§ **802.1, n. 9.**

Pollock, People v., 429 N.Y.S.2d 628, 407 N.E.2d 472 (N.Y.1980)—§ **609.1, n. 30.**

Pollock v. Pollock, 71 N.Y. 137 (1877)—§ **300.3, n. 23; § 607.4, n. 36.**

Pollock v. Rapid Indus. Plastics Co., Inc., 113 A.D.2d 520, 497 N.Y.S.2d 45 (N.Y.A.D. 2 Dept.1985)—§ **301.4, n. 3.**

Polowichak, United States v., 783 F.2d 410 (4th Cir.1986)—§ **1108.2, n. 4.**

Polsky v. Union Mut. Stock Life Ins. Co., 80 A.D.2d 777, 436 N.Y.S.2d 744 (N.Y.A.D. 1 Dept.1981)—§ **502.1, n. 25.**

Polycast Technology Corp. v. Uniroyal, Inc., 125 F.R.D. 47 (S.D.N.Y.1989)—§ **501.2, n. 42.**

Poole v. State, 290 Md. 114, 428 A.2d 434 (Md.1981)—§ **607.4, n. 39.**

Pope v. Allen, 90 N.Y. 298 (1882)—§ **601.2, n. 36.**

Poppe v. Poppe, 165 N.Y.S.2d 99, 144 N.E.2d 72 (N.Y.1957)—§ **503.3; § 503.3, n. 2, 3, 31.**

Population Services Intern. v. Wilson, 398 F.Supp. 321 (D.C.N.Y.1975)—§ **202.1, n. 16.**

Portelli, People v., 257 N.Y.S.2d 931, 205 N.E.2d 857 (N.Y.1965)—§ **607.6, n. 15.**

Porter v. State, 5 Misc.2d 28, 159 N.Y.S.2d 549 (N.Y.Ct.Cl.1957)—§ **901.8, n. 4.**

Porter v. Whitehall Laboratories, Inc., 9 F.3d 607 (7th Cir.1993)—§ **702.2, n. 30.**

Posado, United States v., 57 F.3d 428 (5th Cir.1995)—§ **702.2, n. 29.**

Poslock v. Teachers' Retirement Bd. of Teachers Retirement System, 209 A.D.2d 87, 624 N.Y.S.2d 574 (N.Y.A.D. 1 Dept.1995)—§ **601.2; § 601.2, n. 43.**

Postley, Will of, 125 Misc.2d 416, 479 N.Y.S.2d 464 (N.Y.Sur.1984)—§ **502.1, n. 45, 49.**

Potter v. Browne, 197 N.Y. 288, 90 N.E. 812 (N.Y.1910)—§ **607.6, n. 24; § 608.2, n. 21.**

Potts v. Mayer, 86 N.Y. 302 (1881)—§ **601.2, n. 80.**

Potts v. Pardee, 220 N.Y. 431, 116 N.E. 78 (N.Y.1917)—§ **301.5, n. 31.**

Power v. Crown Equipment Corp., 189 A.D.2d 310, 596 N.Y.S.2d 38 (N.Y.A.D. 1 Dept.1993)—§ **407.1, n. 21.**

Powers v. Powers, 629 N.Y.S.2d 984, 653 N.E.2d 1154 (N.Y.1995)—§ **300.3, n. 43; § 301.7; § 301.7, n. 4, 13; § 803(3).1; § 803(3).1, n. 74.**

Praetorius, United States v., 622 F.2d 1054 (2nd Cir.1979)—§ **607.6, n. 38; § 607.8, n. 53.**

Premises Known as 281 Syosset Woodbury Road, United States v., 862 F.Supp. 847 (E.D.N.Y.1994)—§ **503.5, n. 20; § 514.2, n. 9.**

Presler, People v., 134 A.D.2d 866, 521 N.Y.S.2d 920 (N.Y.A.D. 4 Dept.1987)—§ **804(3).1, n. 54.**

Press, United States v., 336 F.2d 1003 (2nd Cir.1964)—§ **801.1, n. 42.**

TABLE OF CASES

Preston v. State, 152 A.D.2d 943, 543 N.Y.S.2d 823 (N.Y.A.D. 4 Dept.1989)—§ **803(5).1, n. 46.**

Pretino, Matter of Will of, 150 Misc.2d 371, 567 N.Y.S.2d 1009 (N.Y.Sur.1991)—§ **501.1, n. 80;** § **501.3, n. 33.**

Pretto v. Leiwant, 80 A.D.2d 579, 435 N.Y.S.2d 778 (N.Y.A.D. 2 Dept.1981)—§ **607.6, n. 6.**

Price, United States v., 792 F.2d 994 (11th Cir.1986)—§ **806.1, n. 4.**

Price Bros. Co. v. Philadelphia Gear Corp., 629 F.2d 444 (6th Cir.1980)—§ **605.2, n. 3.**

Priest v. Hennessy, 431 N.Y.S.2d 511, 409 N.E.2d 983 (N.Y.1980)—§ **501.1, n. 9, 10, 13, 14, 31, 76.**

Prince, People v., 106 A.D.2d 521, 483 N.Y.S.2d 57 (N.Y.A.D. 2 Dept.1984)—§ **804(1).1, n. 29.**

Prink v. Rockefeller Center, Inc., 422 N.Y.S.2d 911, 398 N.E.2d 517 (N.Y. 1979)—§ **502.1, n. 30, 41, 52, 54;** § **503.3;** § **503.3, n. 12, 24, 32.**

Priolo v. Lefferts General Hospital Inc., 54 Misc.2d 654, 283 N.Y.S.2d 203 (N.Y.Sup. 1967)—§ **407.1, n. 8.**

Pritchard, United States v., 973 F.2d 905 (11th Cir.1992)—§ **609.2, n. 7, 14, 21.**

Pritchett, United States v., 699 F.2d 317 (6th Cir.1983)—§ **605.2, n. 4.**

Provenzo v. Sam, 296 N.Y.S.2d 322, 244 N.E.2d 26 (N.Y.1968)—§ **801.1, n. 39.**

Provost, United States v., 875 F.2d 172 (8th Cir.1989)—§ **412.2, n. 10.**

Pryce, United States v., 938 F.2d 1343, 291 U.S.App.D.C. 84 (D.C.Cir.1991)—§ **607.7, n. 19, 20.**

Pryor, People v., 70 A.D.2d 805, 417 N.Y.S.2d 490 (N.Y.A.D. 1 Dept.1979)—§ **402.1, n. 51.**

Public Operating Corp. v. Weingart, 257 A.D. 379, 13 N.Y.S.2d 182 (N.Y.A.D. 1 Dept.1939)—§ **1006.1, n. 11;** § **1103.1, n. 6.**

Pugliese, United States v., 712 F.2d 1574 (2nd Cir.1983)—§ **103.2, n. 14;** § **104.2, n. 12.**

Pujana–Mena, United States v., 949 F.2d 24 (2nd Cir.1991)—§ **402.2;** § **402.2, n. 7.**

Pulley, United States v., 922 F.2d 1283 (6th Cir.1991)—§ **615.2, n. 6.**

Punis v. Perales, 112 A.D.2d 236, 491 N.Y.S.2d 451 (N.Y.A.D. 2 Dept.1985)—§ **301.7, n. 4.**

Purcell, People v., 103 A.D.2d 938, 479 N.Y.S.2d 768 (N.Y.A.D. 3 Dept.1984)—§ **1107.1, n. 4, 6, 15.**

Purnell v. Lord, 952 F.2d 679 (2nd Cir. 1992)—§ **401.2, n. 3.**

Puzzo, United States v., 928 F.2d 1356 (2nd Cir.1991)—§ **801.1, n. 42.**

Q

Quaglio v. Tomaselli, 99 A.D.2d 487, 470 N.Y.S.2d 427 (N.Y.A.D. 2 Dept.1984)—§ **803(3).1, n. 18.**

Quail Ridge Associates v. Chemical Bank, 174 A.D.2d 959, 571 N.Y.S.2d 648 (N.Y.A.D. 3 Dept.1991)—§ **501.1, n. 62.**

Qualls, People v., 447 N.Y.S.2d 149, 431 N.E.2d 634 (N.Y.1981)—§ **103.1, n. 24.**

Quevas, People v., 595 N.Y.S.2d 721, 611 N.E.2d 760 (N.Y.1993)—§ **607.5, n. 11;** § **801(2).1;** § **801(2).1, n. 10.**

Quin v. Lloyd, 41 N.Y. 349 (1869)—§ **103.1, n. 11, 14.**

Quinn, United States v., 18 F.3d 1461 (9th Cir.1994)—§ **702.2, n. 29.**

Quintel Corp., N.V. v. Citibank, N.A., 567 F.Supp. 1357 (D.C.N.Y.1983)—§ **501.2, n. 38.**

Quinto, United States v., 582 F.2d 224 (2nd Cir.1978)—§ **607.5, n. 62;** § **801(1).3;** § **801(1).3, n. 16.**

R

Rabinowitz, United States v., 578 F.2d 910 (2nd Cir.1978)—§ **608.2, n. 42.**

Radjpaul v. Patton, 145 A.D.2d 494, 535 N.Y.S.2d 743 (N.Y.A.D. 2 Dept.1988)—§ **615.1, n. 9.**

Radosh v. Shipstad, 285 N.Y.S.2d 60, 231 N.E.2d 759 (N.Y.1967)—§ **401.1;** § **401.1, n. 23, 39;** § **1102.1, n. 2.**

Rad Services, Inc. v. Aetna Cas. and Sur. Co., 808 F.2d 271 (3rd Cir.1986)—§ **514.2, n. 8.**

Radtke, People v., 631 N.Y.S.2d 763 (N.Y.A.D. 2 Dept.1995)—§ **501.1, n. 77.**

Radus, Matter of, 140 A.D.2d 348, 527 N.Y.S.2d 840 (N.Y.A.D. 2 Dept.1988)—§ **601.2, n. 74.**

Rahming, People v., 311 N.Y.S.2d 292, 259 N.E.2d 727 (N.Y.1970)—§ **402.1, n. 45;** § **608.2, n. 20.**

Rainbow v. Albert Elia Bldg. Co., Inc., 79 A.D.2d 287, 436 N.Y.S.2d 480 (N.Y.A.D. 4 Dept.1981)—§ **407.1;** § **407.1, n. 16.**

Rainbow Family, United States v., 695 F.Supp. 314 (E.D.Tex.1988)—§ **902.1, n. 18.**

Raizen, People v., 211 A.D. 446, 208 N.Y.S. 185 (N.Y.A.D. 2 Dept.1925)—§ **803(1).1, n. 72.**

Raja, People v., 77 A.D.2d 322, 433 N.Y.S.2d 200 (N.Y.A.D. 2 Dept.1980)—§ **801(1).2, n. 12;** § **803(2).1;** § **803(2).1, n. 1.**

Ramirez, United States v., 910 F.2d 1069 (2nd Cir.1990)—§ **201.2, n. 7.**

Ramirez, United States v., 894 F.2d 565 (2nd Cir.1990)—§ **105.2, n. 3, 6, 9;** § **404.2, n. 4, 17.**

Ramirez, United States v., 871 F.2d 582 (6th Cir.1989)—§ **601.3, n. 14;** § **607.7, n. 25.**

Ramos, People v., 141 Misc.2d 930, 535 N.Y.S.2d 663 (N.Y.Sup.1988)—§ **612.1, n. 11, 16.**

TABLE OF CASES

Ramos, People v., 309 N.Y.S.2d 906, 258 N.E.2d 197 (N.Y.1970)—§ **604.1, n. 4, 7.**

Ramundo v. Guilderland, 142 A.D.2d 50, 534 N.Y.S.2d 543 (N.Y.A.D. 3 Dept. 1988)—§ **407.1, n. 6.**

Randall v. Warnaco, Inc., Hirsch-Weis Div., 677 F.2d 1226 (8th Cir.1982)—§ **1105.2, n. 1.**

Randall Elec., Inc. v. State, 150 A.D.2d 875, 540 N.Y.S.2d 901 (N.Y.A.D. 3 Dept. 1989)—§ **408.1, n. 4.**

Randolph, People v., 40 A.D.2d 806, 338 N.Y.S.2d 229 (N.Y.A.D. 1 Dept.1972)— § **901.1, n. 5, 16; § 901.4, n. 1.**

Randy Intern., Ltd. v. Automatic Compactor Corp., 97 Misc.2d 977, 412 N.Y.S.2d 995 (N.Y.City Civ.Ct.1979)—§ **501.1, n. 5.**

Rangel, United States v., 585 F.2d 344 (8th Cir.1978)—§ **1002.1, n. 1.**

Ranofsky v. Frank, 208 A.D. 213, 203 N.Y.S. 160 (N.Y.A.D. 1 Dept.1924)— § **603.1, n. 9.**

Rao, People v., 107 A.D.2d 720, 484 N.Y.S.2d 76 (N.Y.A.D. 2 Dept.1985)— § **1107.1, n. 4.**

Raphaely Intern., Inc. v. Waterman S.S. Corp., 972 F.2d 498 (2nd Cir.1992)— § **902.1, n. 17.**

Rappy, United States v., 157 F.2d 964 (2nd Cir.1946)—§ **612.2, n. 2.**

Rastelli, People v., 371 N.Y.S.2d 911, 333 N.E.2d 182 (N.Y.1975)—§ **802.2, n. 87.**

Ravich, United States v., 421 F.2d 1196 (2nd Cir.1970)—§ **401.2, n. 11;** § **1101.2, n. 5, 7, 10.**

Rawley v. Brown, 71 N.Y. 85 (1877)— § **301.5, n. 42.**

Raynolds v. Vinier, 125 A.D. 18, 109 N.Y.S. 293 (N.Y.A.D. 4 Dept.1908)—§ **1108.1, n. 1.**

Raysor v. Port Authority of New York and New Jersey, 768 F.2d 34 (2nd Cir. 1985)—§ **607.5, n. 49.**

Razauckas v. New York Dugan Bros., 263 A.D. 1002, 33 N.Y.S.2d 411 (N.Y.A.D. 2 Dept.1942)—§ **603.1, n. 8.**

Re, United States v., 336 F.2d 306 (2nd Cir.1964)—§ **803(3).2, n. 8.**

Rea, United States v., 958 F.2d 1206 (2nd Cir.1992)—§ **801.1, n. 25.**

Rector, People v., 19 Wend. 569 (1838)— § **607.5, n. 27.**

Redd, People v., 164 A.D.2d 34, 561 N.Y.S.2d 439 (N.Y.A.D. 1 Dept.1990)— § **606.1, n. 3, 4, 5.**

Redvanly v. NYNEX Corp., 152 F.R.D. 460 (S.D.N.Y.1993)—§ **501.3, n. 37.**

Reed v. McCord, 160 N.Y. 330, 54 N.E. 737 (N.Y.1899)—§ **802.1;** § **802.1, n. 4;** § **802.2;** § **802.2, n. 4, 51.**

Reed, People v., 386 N.Y.S.2d 371, 352 N.E.2d 558 (N.Y.1976)—§ **300.3, n. 7.**

Reed, United States v., 639 F.2d 896 (2nd Cir.1981)—§ **801.1, n. 42.**

Reese, People v., 258 N.Y. 89, 179 N.E. 305 (N.Y.1932)—§ **201.1, n. 37.**

Regan v. National Postal Transport Ass'n, 53 Misc.2d 901, 280 N.Y.S.2d 319 (N.Y.City Civ.Ct.1967)—§ **803(5).1, n. 29.**

Reger, People v., 13 A.D.2d 63, 213 N.Y.S.2d 298 (N.Y.A.D. 1 Dept.1961)— § **612.1, n. 6, 7, 12, 13, 15, 18.**

Regina, People v., 277 N.Y.S.2d 683, 224 N.E.2d 108 (N.Y.1966)—§ **103.1, n. 24;** § **106.1, n. 8;** § **602.1, n. 7;** § **607.1, n. 4;** § **607.5, n. 19, 41.**

Reid v. Quebec Paper Sales & Transp. Co., 340 F.2d 34 (2nd Cir.1965)—§ **803(1).2, n. 53.**

Reilly v. Barrett, 220 N.Y. 170, 115 N.E. 453 (N.Y.1917)—§ **300.2, n. 15.**

Remmer v. United States, 347 U.S. 227, 74 S.Ct. 450, 98 L.Ed. 654 (1954)—§ **606.2, n. 4.**

Rendo v. Schermerhorn, 24 A.D.2d 773, 263 N.Y.S.2d 743 (N.Y.A.D. 3 Dept.1965)— § **411.1, n. 3.**

Renegotiation Bd. v. Grumman Aircraft Engineering Corp., 421 U.S. 168, 95 S.Ct. 1491, 44 L.Ed.2d 57 (1975)—§ **511.2, n. 15.**

Rengifo, United States v., 789 F.2d 975 (1st Cir.1986)—§ **1104.2, n. 11, 13, 15;** § **1108.2, n. 2.**

Rensing, People v., 250 N.Y.S.2d 401, 199 N.E.2d 489 (N.Y.1964)—§ **601.1, n. 10, 46, 47;** § **607.7, n. 6.**

Republic Gear Co. v. Borg-Warner Corp., 381 F.2d 551 (2nd Cir.1967)—§ **501.3, n. 37.**

Ressler, People v., 269 N.Y.S.2d 414, 216 N.E.2d 582 (N.Y.1966)—§ **503.3, n. 4.**

Revlon, Inc. v. Carson Products Co., 602 F.Supp. 1071 (D.C.N.Y.1985)— § **803(5).2, n. 23.**

Rex Paving Corp. v. White, 139 A.D.2d 176, 531 N.Y.S.2d 831 (N.Y.A.D. 3 Dept. 1988)—§ **201.1, n. 35.**

Reyes v. Missouri Pac. R. Co., 589 F.2d 791 (5th Cir.1979)—§ **406.2, n. 12;** § **609.2, n. 13.**

Reynoso, People v., 537 N.Y.S.2d 113, 534 N.E.2d 30 (N.Y.1988)—§ **803(1).1;** § **803(1).1, n. 44.**

Rheaume v. Patterson, 289 F.2d 611 (2nd Cir.1961)—§ **607.7, n. 24.**

Riccardi, United States v., 174 F.2d 883 (3rd Cir.1949)—§ **612.2, n. 6, 8, 10, 13.**

Ricciuti v. New York City Transit Authority, 754 F.Supp. 980 (S.D.N.Y.1990)— § **803(5).2, n. 31.**

Ricco, People v., 452 N.Y.S.2d 340, 437 N.E.2d 1097 (N.Y.1982)—§ **607.8, n. 10;** § **801.1, n. 37;** § **803(1).1, n. 40.**

Rice, People v., 555 N.Y.S.2d 677, 554 N.E.2d 1265 (N.Y.1990)—§ **607.5, n. 6, 9, 16;** § **801(2).1;** § **801(2).1, n. 21.**

Rich v. Ellerman & Bucknall S.S. Co., 278 F.2d 704 (2nd Cir.1960)—§ **1102.2, n. 8.**

TABLE OF CASES

Rich, United States v., 580 F.2d 929 (9th Cir.1978)—§ **803(4).2, n. 4.**

Richards v. Robin, 178 A.D. 535, 165 N.Y.S. 780 (N.Y.A.D. 1 Dept.1917)—§ **803(5).1, n. 10.**

Richardson v. Marsh, 481 U.S. 200, 107 S.Ct. 1702, 95 L.Ed.2d 176 (1987)—§ **105.1, n. 16, 17.**

Richardson v. Perales, 402 U.S. 389, 91 S.Ct. 1420, 28 L.Ed.2d 842 (1971)—§ **803(3).2, n. 30.**

Richardson-Merrell, Inc. Bendectin Products Liability Litigation, In re, 624 F.Supp. 1212 (S.D.Ohio 1985)—§ **803(6).2, n. 11.**

Richetti, People v., 302 N.Y. 290, 97 N.E.2d 908 (N.Y.1951)—§ **301.5, n. 22.**

Richter, United States v., 826 F.2d 206 (2nd Cir.1987)—§ **607.1, n. 4.**

Ricken, People v., 242 A.D. 106, 273 N.Y.S. 470 (N.Y.A.D. 3 Dept.1934)—§ **806.1; § 806.1, n. 7.**

Riddle v. Memorial Hospital, 43 A.D.2d 750, 349 N.Y.S.2d 855 (N.Y.A.D. 3 Dept. 1973)—§ **1102.1, n. 24.**

Ridings v. Vaccarello, 55 A.D.2d 650, 390 N.Y.S.2d 152 (N.Y.A.D. 2 Dept.1976)—§ **300.3, n. 2.**

Riggs' Estate, In re, 68 Misc.2d 760, 328 N.Y.S.2d 138 (N.Y.Sur.1972)—§ **804(4).1, n. 17, 21.**

Rigie v. Goldman, 148 A.D.2d 23, 543 N.Y.S.2d 983 (N.Y.A.D. 2 Dept.1989)—§ **406.1; § 406.1, n. 14, 19.**

Riley, United States v., 657 F.2d 1377 (8th Cir.1981)—§ **804(3).2, n. 10.**

Riley v. Wieman, 137 A.D.2d 309, 528 N.Y.S.2d 925 (N.Y.A.D. 3 Dept.1988)—§ **702.1, n. 24.**

Rinaldi v. Holt, Rinehart & Winston, Inc., 397 N.Y.S.2d 943, 366 N.E.2d 1299 (N.Y. 1977)—§ **300.4, n. 30.**

Rinaldi & Sons, Inc. v. Wells Fargo Alarm Service, Inc., 383 N.Y.S.2d 256, 347 N.E.2d 618 (N.Y.1976)—§ **300.4, n. 6.**

Rincon, United States v., 28 F.3d 921 (9th Cir.1994)—§ **702.2, n. 11.**

Rinke, United States v., 778 F.2d 581 (10th Cir.1985)—§ **612.2, n. 10.**

Rios, People v., 191 A.D.2d 722, 595 N.Y.S.2d 524 (N.Y.A.D. 2 Dept.1993)—§ **1102.1, n. 2.**

Risikoff v. Metropolitan Life Ins. Co., 188 Misc. 768, 66 N.Y.S.2d 878 (N.Y.Sup. 1946)—§ **803(5).1, n. 25.**

Risoli v. Long Island Lighting Co., 195 A.D.2d 543, 600 N.Y.S.2d 497 (N.Y.A.D. 2 Dept.1993)—§ **802.2, n. 75.**

Rittenhouse v. Town of North Hempstead, 11 A.D.2d 957, 205 N.Y.S.2d 564 (N.Y.A.D. 2 Dept.1960)—§ **601.1, n. 31.**

Rivera v. City of New York, 200 A.D.2d 379, 606 N.Y.S.2d 193 (N.Y.A.D. 1 Dept. 1994)—§ **801.1, n. 39.**

Rivera, People v., 192 A.D.2d 363, 595 N.Y.S.2d 782 (N.Y.A.D. 1 Dept.1993)—§ **802.2, n. 103.**

Rivera, People v., 182 A.D.2d 1092, 583 N.Y.S.2d 78 (N.Y.A.D. 4 Dept.1992)—§ **615.1, n. 13.**

Rivera, People v., 172 A.D.2d 1059, 569 N.Y.S.2d 316 (N.Y.A.D. 4 Dept.1991)—§ **611.2, n. 8.**

Rivera, People v., 158 A.D.2d 723, 552 N.Y.S.2d 171 (N.Y.A.D. 2 Dept.1990)—§ **412.1, n. 19.**

Rivera, People v., 101 A.D.2d 981, 477 N.Y.S.2d 732 (N.Y.A.D. 3 Dept.1984)—§ **608.2, n. 10.**

Rivera, People v., 413 N.Y.S.2d 146, 385 N.E.2d 1073 (N.Y.1978)—§ **802.1, n. 9; § 802.2, n. 3.**

Rivera, People v., 59 A.D.2d 874, 399 N.Y.S.2d 662 (N.Y.A.D. 1 Dept.1977)—§ **901.5, n. 5.**

Rivera, People v., 58 A.D.2d 147, 396 N.Y.S.2d 26 (N.Y.A.D. 1 Dept.1977)—§ **501.1; § 501.1, n. 92; § 607.8, n. 9.**

Rivera, People v., 293 N.Y.S.2d 271, 239 N.E.2d 873 (N.Y.1968)—§ **509.1, n. 31.**

Rivera, United States v., 61 F.3d 131 (2nd Cir.1995)—§ **106.2, n. 7, 8.**

Rivera, United States v., 22 F.3d 430 (2nd Cir.1994)—§ **701.2, n. 1, 11.**

Rivera, United States v., 837 F.Supp. 565 (S.D.N.Y.1993)—§ **501.1, n. 16; § 501.2, n. 8, 22.**

Rivera, United States v., 971 F.2d 876 (2nd Cir.1992)—§ **611.5, n. 5; § 615.2, n. 3, 5.**

Rivera v. W. & R. Service Station, Inc., 34 A.D.2d 115, 309 N.Y.S.2d 274 (N.Y.A.D. 1 Dept.1970)—§ **301.5, n. 32.**

Rivera by Rivera v. City of New York, 160 A.D.2d 985, 554 N.Y.S.2d 706 (N.Y.A.D. 2 Dept.1990)—§ **1102.1, n. 14.**

Rivett v. Rivett, 270 A.D. 878, 61 N.Y.S.2d 7 (N.Y.A.D. 4 Dept.1946)—§ **503.2, n. 4.**

Roach, People v., 215 N.Y. 592, 109 N.E. 618 (N.Y.1915)—§ **901.3, n. 8.**

Roach, United States v., 590 F.2d 181 (5th Cir.1979)—§ **601.3, n. 11, 13; § 607.7, n. 23.**

Roberge v. Bonner, 185 N.Y. 265, 77 N.E. 1023 (N.Y.1906)—§ **300.4, n. 7.**

Roberge v. Winne, 144 N.Y. 709, 39 N.E. 631 (N.Y.1895)—§ **104.1, n. 16.**

Roberts, Commonwealth v., 108 Mass. 296 (1871)—§ **804(2).1, n. 10.**

Robert S., Matter of, 438 N.Y.S.2d 509, 420 N.E.2d 390 (N.Y.1981)—§ **402.1; § 402.1, n. 61.**

Roberts, People v., 178 A.D.2d 622, 577 N.Y.S.2d 672 (N.Y.A.D. 2 Dept.1991)—§ **501.3, n. 32.**

Robillard v. Robbins, 168 A.D.2d 803, 563 N.Y.S.2d 940 (N.Y.A.D. 3 Dept.1990)—§ **704.1, n. 14.**

Robilotto, United States v., 828 F.2d 940 (2nd Cir.1987)—§ **503.5, n. 7.**

TABLE OF CASES

Robinson v. City of Albany, 14 A.D.2d 626, 218 N.Y.S.2d 421 (N.Y.A.D. 3 Dept. 1961)—§ **100.2, n. 6.**

Robinson v. Missouri Pacific R. Co., 16 F.3d 1083 (10th Cir.1994)—§ **1104.2, n. 21.**

Robinson, People v., 200 A.D.2d 693, 606 N.Y.S.2d 908 (N.Y.A.D. 2 Dept.1994)— § **404.1, n. 26.**

Robinson, People v., 158 A.D.2d 628, 551 N.Y.S.2d 599 (N.Y.A.D. 2 Dept.1990)— § **1104.1, n. 31.**

Robinson, People v., 510 N.Y.S.2d 837, 503 N.E.2d 485 (N.Y.1986)—§ **404.1;** § **404.1, n. 16, 57;** § **404.2, n. 5.**

Robinson v. Shapiro, 646 F.2d 734 (2nd Cir.1981)—§ **103.2, n. 25;** § **401.2, n. 2, 4;** § **804(5).2;** § **804(5).2, n. 19.**

Robinson v. Shapiro, 484 F.Supp. 91 (D.C.N.Y.1980)—§ **803(1).2, n. 8.**

Robinson, United States v., 485 U.S. 25, 108 S.Ct. 864, 99 L.Ed.2d 23 (1988)— § **509.1, n. 36.**

Robinson, United States v., 560 F.2d 507 (2nd Cir.1977)—§ **401.2;** § **401.2, n. 5, 6, 7;** § **1101.2, n. 7, 10.**

Robinson, United States v., 544 F.2d 110 (2nd Cir.1976)—§ **607.3, n. 18;** § **803(4).2, n. 2.**

Robinson v. Watts Detective Agency, Inc., 685 F.2d 729 (1st Cir.1982)—§ **607.4, n. 46.**

Robinson's Will, In re, 257 A.D. 405, 13 N.Y.S.2d 324 (N.Y.A.D. 4 Dept.1939)— § **1001.1, n. 3;** § **1003.1, n. 9.**

Robles v. Exxon Corp., 862 F.2d 1201 (5th Cir.1989)—§ **606.2, n. 7.**

Roche v. Brooklyn City & N. R. Co., 105 N.Y. 294, 11 N.E. 630 (N.Y.1887)— § **803(1).1, n. 43.**

Rock v. Arkansas, 483 U.S. 44, 107 S.Ct. 2704, 97 L.Ed.2d 37 (1987)—§ **601.1;** § **601.1, n. 15, 68.**

Rockland County Dept. of Social Services on Behalf of Michael McM. v. Brian McM., 193 A.D.2d 121, 602 N.Y.S.2d 416 (N.Y.A.D. 2 Dept.1993)—§ **502.1, n. 84.**

Rodawald, People v., 177 N.Y. 408, 70 N.E. 1 (N.Y.1904)—§ **402.1;** § **402.1, n. 59;** § **803(1).1, n. 60.**

Rodenhouse v. American Cas. Co. of Pa., 20 A.D.2d 620, 244 N.Y.S.2d 856 (N.Y.A.D. 4 Dept.1963)—§ **601.2;** § **601.2, n. 39.**

Rodolitz v. Boston–Old Colony Ins. Co., 74 A.D.2d 821, 425 N.Y.S.2d 353 (N.Y.A.D. 2 Dept.1980)—§ **703.1, n. 11.**

Rodriguez v. New York City Transit Authority, 151 Misc.2d 1027, 574 N.Y.S.2d 505 (N.Y.Sup.1991)—§ **502.1, n. 14.**

Rodriguez, People v., 563 N.Y.S.2d 48, 564 N.E.2d 658 (N.Y.1990)—§ **300.4, n. 55.**

Rodriguez, People v., 145 Misc.2d 105, 546 N.Y.S.2d 769 (N.Y.Sup.1989)—§ **601.1, n. 55;** § **604.1, n. 8.**

Rodriguez, People v., 143 A.D.2d 854, 533 N.Y.S.2d 331 (N.Y.A.D. 2 Dept.1988)— § **607.6, n. 15.**

Rodriguez, People v., 485 N.Y.S.2d 976, 475 N.E.2d 443 (N.Y.1984)—§ **1102.1, n. 6.**

Rodriguez, People v., 378 N.Y.S.2d 665, 341 N.E.2d 231 (N.Y.1975)—§ **503.3, n. 1;** § **514.1;** § **514.1, n. 3.**

Rodriguez, United States v., 43 F.3d 117 (5th Cir.1995)—§ **611.5, n. 4.**

Rodriguez, United States v., 968 F.2d 130 (2nd Cir.1992)—§ **602.2, n. 7.**

Rodriguez, United States v., 706 F.2d 31 (2nd Cir.1983)—§ **804.1, n. 25.**

Rodriguez, United States v., 424 F.2d 205 (4th Cir.1970)—§ **604.2, n. 5.**

Rodriguez v. Zampella, 42 A.D.2d 805, 346 N.Y.S.2d 558 (N.Y.A.D. 3 Dept.1973)— § **803(3).1, n. 67.**

Roe v. Nichols, 5 A.D. 472, 38 N.Y.S. 1100 (N.Y.A.D. 2 Dept.1896)—§ **803(4).1, n. 1.**

Roemer v. Board of Public Works of Maryland, 426 U.S. 736, 96 S.Ct. 2337, 49 L.Ed.2d 179 (1976)—§ **203.2, n. 4.**

Roge v. Valentine, 280 N.Y. 268, 20 N.E.2d 751 (N.Y.1939)—§ **607.8, n. 4.**

Rogers, People ex rel. Singer v., 254 A.D. 865, 4 N.Y.S.2d 905 (N.Y.A.D. 2 Dept. 1938)—§ **605.1, n. 1.**

Rogers v. Ritter, 79 U.S. 317, 20 L.Ed. 417 (1870)—§ **901.2, n. 11.**

Rogers v. United States, 340 U.S. 367, 71 S.Ct. 438, 95 L.Ed. 344 (1951)—§ **509.1, n. 50.**

Rohner's Estate, In re, 94 Misc.2d 596, 404 N.Y.S.2d 1017 (N.Y.Sur.1978)—§ **901.7, n. 9.**

Rohrmayr v. City of New York, 33 A.D.2d 920, 307 N.Y.S.2d 539 (N.Y.A.D. 2 Dept. 1970)—§ **804(1).1, n. 22.**

Roldan–Zapata, United States v., 916 F.2d 795 (2nd Cir.1990)—§ **802.3, n. 57.**

Roman v. Bronx–Lebanon Hospital Center, 51 A.D.2d 529, 379 N.Y.S.2d 81 (N.Y.A.D. 1 Dept.1976)—§ **300.4, n. 11.**

Roman v. Vargas, 182 A.D.2d 543, 582 N.Y.S.2d 1020 (N.Y.A.D. 1 Dept.1992)— § **704.1, n. 19.**

Romandette, People v., 111 A.D.2d 1040, 490 N.Y.S.2d 347 (N.Y.A.D. 3 Dept. 1985)—§ **607.4, n. 36, 37.**

Romano v. Howarth, 998 F.2d 101 (2nd Cir.1993)—§ **803(3).2, n. 6.**

Romano v. Romano, 280 N.Y.S.2d 570, 227 N.E.2d 389 (N.Y.1967)—§ **300.2, n. 23.**

Romano, United States v., 684 F.2d 1057 (2nd Cir.1982)—§ **801.1;** § **801.1, n. 26.**

Ronny, In re, 40 Misc.2d 194, 242 N.Y.S.2d 844 (N.Y.City Fam.Ct.1963)—§ **201.1, n. 51.**

Root v. Wright, 84 N.Y. 72 (1881)—§ **501.1, n. 38, 56.**

Rosa, United States v., 11 F.3d 315 (2nd Cir.1993)—§ **803(5).2;** § **803(5).2, n. 12.**

Rosado v. Mercedes–Benz of North America, Inc., 90 A.D.2d 515, 454 N.Y.S.2d

TABLE OF CASES

759 (N.Y.A.D. 2 Dept.1982)—§ **501.3, n. 14.**

Rosado, People v., 39 A.D.2d 871, 333 N.Y.S.2d 181 (N.Y.A.D. 1 Dept.1972)—§ **404.1, n. 62.**

Rosado v. Wyman, 322 F.Supp. 1173 (D.C.N.Y.1970)—§ **901.9; § 901.9, n. 13.**

Rosado v. Wyman, 304 F.Supp. 1350 (D.C.N.Y.1969)—§ **901.9, n. 13.**

Rosario v. General Motors Corp., 148 A.D.2d 108, 543 N.Y.S.2d 974 (N.Y.A.D. 1 Dept.1989)—§ **501.3, n. 25.**

Rosario v. Kuhlman, 839 F.2d 918 (2nd Cir.1988)—§ **607.3, n. 18; § 804(1).1, n. 52.**

Rosario v. New York City Transit Authority, 73 A.D.2d 912, 423 N.Y.S.2d 254 (N.Y.A.D. 2 Dept.1980)—§ **802.2, n. 2.**

Rosario, People v., 213 N.Y.S.2d 448, 173 N.E.2d 881 (N.Y.1961)—§ **501.3, n. 30; § 505.1, n. 13; § 612.1, n. 19.**

Rose v. Clark, 478 U.S. 570, 106 S.Ct. 3101, 92 L.Ed.2d 460 (1986)—§ **302.1, n. 6.**

Rose v. Thau, 45 A.D.2d 182, 357 N.Y.S.2d 201 (N.Y.A.D. 3 Dept.1974)—§ **606.1, n. 10.**

Rosenbaum v. Podolsky, 97 Misc. 614, 162 N.Y.S. 227 (N.Y.Sup.1916)—§ **1001.1, n. 5.**

Rosenberg v. Equitable Life Assur. Soc. of United States, 148 A.D.2d 337, 538 N.Y.S.2d 551 (N.Y.A.D. 1 Dept.1989)—§ **801.1, n. 7.**

Rosenberg v. Grace, 158 Misc.2d 32, 600 N.Y.S.2d 425 (N.Y.Sup.1993)—§ **601.2, n. 59; § 804(1).1, n. 23.**

Ross, United States v., 33 F.3d 1507 (11th Cir.1994)—§ **611.5, n. 22.**

Ross, United States v., 321 F.2d 61 (2nd Cir.1963)—§ **801.1, n. 13; § 901.5, n. 17; § 1004.1, n. 4.**

Rossi v. Blue Cross and Blue Shield of Greater New York, 542 N.Y.S.2d 508, 540 N.E.2d 703 (N.Y.1989)—§ **501.1, n. 7, 10, 27, 41, 60, 61, 67, 77.**

Rost v. Brooklyn Heights R. Co., 10 A.D. 477, 41 N.Y.S. 1069 (N.Y.A.D. 2 Dept. 1896)—§ **1102.1, n. 15.**

Rothman v. City of New York, 273 A.D. 780, 75 N.Y.S.2d 151 (N.Y.A.D. 2 Dept. 1947)—§ **804(1).1, n. 18.**

Rothschild, People v., 361 N.Y.S.2d 901, 320 N.E.2d 639 (N.Y.1974)—§ **509.1, n. 79; § 607.8, n. 24; § 802.2, n. 32.**

Rouse v. County of Greene, 115 A.D.2d 162, 495 N.Y.S.2d 496 (N.Y.A.D. 3 Dept. 1985)—§ **501.3, n. 35; § 612.1, n. 21, 28, 29.**

Rouse v. Whited, 25 N.Y. 170 (1862)—§ **106.1, n. 2, 5, 11.**

Rousseau v. Bleau, 131 N.Y. 177, 30 N.E. 52 (N.Y.1892)—§ **501.1, n. 50.**

Rovetuso, United States v., 768 F.2d 809 (7th Cir.1985)—§ **607.3, n. 6.**

Roviaro v. United States, 353 U.S. 53, 77 S.Ct. 623, 1 L.Ed.2d 639 (1957)—§ **510.1, n. 1, 4; § 510.2; § 510.2, n. 1.**

Rowe v. Farmers Ins. Co., Inc., 699 S.W.2d 423 (Mo.1985)—§ **607.4, n. 45.**

Rozanski, People v., 209 A.D.2d 1018, 619 N.Y.S.2d 441 (N.Y.A.D. 4 Dept.1994)—§ **611.2, n. 18.**

Ruberto v. C.I.R., 774 F.2d 61 (2nd Cir. 1985)—§ **803(5).2, n. 55; § 1001.1, n. 27; § 1003.1, n. 6.**

Rubin, Matter of, 100 A.D.2d 850, 474 N.Y.S.2d 94 (N.Y.A.D. 2 Dept.1984)—§ **509.1, n. 57.**

Rubin v. Alamo Rent-A-Car, 190 A.D.2d 661, 593 N.Y.S.2d 284 (N.Y.A.D. 2 Dept. 1993)—§ **502.1, n. 22.**

Rubin, People ex rel. v. Tax Commission, 9 A.D.2d 47, 189 N.Y.S.2d 784 (N.Y.A.D. 3 Dept.1959)—§ **201.1, n. 40.**

Rubin, United States v., 609 F.2d 51 (2nd Cir.1979)—§ **103.2, n. 9, 12; § 607.5, n. 65; § 801(1).3, n. 22.**

Rudd, People v., 196 A.D.2d 666, 601 N.Y.S.2d 933 (N.Y.A.D. 2 Dept.1993)—§ **703.1, n. 18.**

Rudolph v. John Hancock Mut. Life Ins. Co., 251 N.Y. 208, 167 N.E. 223 (N.Y. 1929)—§ **802.2, n. 53.**

Ruff, People v., 185 A.D.2d 454, 586 N.Y.S.2d 327 (N.Y.A.D. 3 Dept.1992)—§ **803(3).1, n. 50.**

Ruff v. St. Paul Mercury Ins. Co., 393 F.2d 500 (2nd Cir.1968)—§ **203.2, n. 8.**

Ruffin, United States v., 575 F.2d 346 (2nd Cir.1978)—§ **103.2, n. 12; § 803(5).2; § 803(5).2, n. 10, 43.**

Rugendorf v. United States, 376 U.S. 528, 84 S.Ct. 825, 11 L.Ed.2d 887 (1964)—§ **510.2; § 510.2, n. 7.**

Ruggiero, United States v., 928 F.2d 1289 (2nd Cir.1991)—§ **900.1, n. 9, 11; § 1104.2, n. 9.**

Ruhala v. Roby, 379 Mich. 102, 150 N.W.2d 146 (Mich.1967)—§ **801(1).2, n. 1.**

Rukaj, People v., 123 A.D.2d 277, 506 N.Y.S.2d 677 (N.Y.A.D. 1 Dept.1986)—§ **606.1, n. 13, 17.**

Russ, People v., 581 N.Y.S.2d 152, 589 N.E.2d 375 (N.Y.1992)—§ **607.4, n. 41.**

Russell v. New York State Elec. & Gas Corp., 276 A.D. 44, 93 N.Y.S.2d 3 (N.Y.A.D. 3 Dept.1949)—§ **901.6; § 901.6, n. 4.**

Russell, People v., 179 A.D.2d 521, 579 N.Y.S.2d 18 (N.Y.A.D. 1 Dept.1992)—§ **607.5, n. 19.**

Russell, People v., 165 A.D.2d 327, 567 N.Y.S.2d 548 (N.Y.A.D. 2 Dept.1991)—§ **801(2).1, n. 16.**

Russell, People v., 530 N.Y.S.2d 101, 525 N.E.2d 747 (N.Y.1988)—§ **103.1, n. 1.**

Rutter, People v., 202 A.D.2d 123, 616 N.Y.S.2d 598 (N.Y.A.D. 1 Dept.1994)—§ **1101.1, n. 24.**

TABLE OF CASES

Ryan v. Dwyer, 33 A.D.2d 878, 307 N.Y.S.2d 565 (N.Y.A.D. 4 Dept.1969)—**§ 408.1, n. 11; § 607.5, n. 18, 19; § 607.6, n. 6.**

Ryan v. The People, 79 N.Y. 593 (1880)—**§ 607.6, n. 12.**

Ryan v. United Parcel Service, 205 F.2d 362 (2nd Cir.1953)—**§ 1102.2; § 1102.2, n. 10.**

Ryder v. Cue Car Rental, Inc., 32 A.D.2d 143, 302 N.Y.S.2d 17 (N.Y.A.D. 4 Dept. 1969)—**§ 301.5, n. 32.**

Ryder's Will, In re, 279 A.D. 1131, 112 N.Y.S.2d 601 (N.Y.A.D. 4 Dept.1952)—**§ 601.2, n. 56.**

S

Saafir, People ex rel. v. Mantello, 163 A.D.2d 824, 558 N.Y.S.2d 356 (N.Y.A.D. 4 Dept.1990)—**§ 803(3).1, n. 61.**

Saaratu, People v., 143 Misc.2d 1075, 541 N.Y.S.2d 889 (N.Y.Sup.1989)—**§ 502.1, n. 19.**

Sabater, United States v., 830 F.2d 7 (2nd Cir.1987)—**§ 901.1; § 901.1, n. 13; § 1101.2, n. 12.**

Sabathie v. Russo, 21 A.D.2d 911, 252 N.Y.S.2d 15 (N.Y.A.D. 2 Dept.1964)—**§ 804(1).1, n. 20.**

Sacasas, United States v., 381 F.2d 451 (2nd Cir.1967)—**§ 804(2).2; § 804(2).2, n. 5.**

Sackett, United States v., 598 F.2d 739 (2nd Cir.1979)—**§ 803(3).2; § 803(3).2, n. 9, 23.**

Sacks v. Town of Thompson, 33 A.D.2d 627, 304 N.Y.S.2d 729 (N.Y.A.D. 3 Dept. 1969)—**§ 203.1, n. 11.**

Sadowski v. Long Island R. Co., 292 N.Y. 448, 55 N.E.2d 497 (N.Y.1944)—**§ 201.1, n. 43.**

Saez, People v., 513 N.Y.S.2d 380, 505 N.E.2d 945 (N.Y.1987)—**§ 607.4, n. 2, 37.**

Safeway Stores, Inc. v. Combs, 273 F.2d 295 (5th Cir.1960)—**§ 801.1, n. 4.**

Saks Intern., Inc. v. M/V Export Champion, 817 F.2d 1011 (2nd Cir.1987)—**§ 803(3).2, n. 15.**

Salerno, United States v., 974 F.2d 231 (2nd Cir.1992)—**§ 804(1).2, n. 5.**

Salerno, United States v., 505 U.S. 317, 112 S.Ct. 2503, 120 L.Ed.2d 255 (1992)—**§ 804(1).2; § 804(1).2, n. 1.**

Salerno, United States v., 937 F.2d 797 (2nd Cir.1991)—**§ 802.3, n. 30; § 804(1).2, n. 2.**

Salim, United States v., 855 F.2d 944 (2nd Cir.1988)—**§ 603.2, n. 2; § 604.2, n. 7.**

Salim, United States v., 664 F.Supp. 682 (E.D.N.Y.1987)—**§ 804.1, n. 18; § 804(1).2, n. 23; § 806.1, n. 18.**

Salko, People v., 417 N.Y.S.2d 894, 391 N.E.2d 976 (N.Y.1979)—**§ 104.1, n. 32; § 801.1; § 801.1, n. 14, 29; § 802.2; § 802.2, n. 78, 79, 82.**

Salko, People v., 60 A.D.2d 307, 401 N.Y.S.2d 494 (N.Y.A.D. 1 Dept.1978)—**§ 802.2, n. 83.**

Salmon v. Sunday, 134 Misc. 475, 235 N.Y.S. 672 (N.Y.Sup.1929)—**§ 601.1, n. 37.**

Salvador, United States v., 820 F.2d 558 (2nd Cir.1987)—**§ 804(3).2, n. 18.**

Sampol, United States v., 636 F.2d 621, 204 U.S.App.D.C. 349 (D.C.Cir.1980)—**§ 607.7, n. 25; § 610.2, n. 1.**

Samuel, People v., 327 N.Y.S.2d 321, 277 N.E.2d 381 (N.Y.1971)—**§ 509.1, n. 74.**

Samuels, People v., 250 Cal.App.2d 501, 58 Cal.Rptr. 439 (Cal.App. 1 Dist.1967)—**§ 1104.1, n. 7.**

Sanchez, People v., 154 A.D.2d 15, 551 N.Y.S.2d 206 (N.Y.A.D. 1 Dept.1990)—**§ 404.1, n. 57.**

Sanchez, People v., 475 N.Y.S.2d 376, 463 N.E.2d 1228 (N.Y.1984)—**§ 300.4, n. 49.**

Sanchez, United States v., 790 F.2d 245 (2nd Cir.1986)—**§ 605.2, n. 4.**

Sanchez, United States v., 603 F.2d 381 (2nd Cir.1979)—**§ 801(2).2, n. 10.**

Sanchez by Sanchez v. City of New York, 201 A.D.2d 325, 607 N.Y.S.2d 321 (N.Y.A.D. 1 Dept.1994)—**§ 511.1, n. 5.**

Sanders, People v., 451 N.Y.S.2d 30, 436 N.E.2d 480 (N.Y.1982)—**§ 802.2, n. 94.**

Sandgren, People v., 302 N.Y. 331, 98 N.E.2d 460 (N.Y.1951)—**§ 300.4, n. 53.**

Sandoval, People v., 357 N.Y.S.2d 849, 314 N.E.2d 413 (N.Y.1974)—**§ 103.1, n. 39; § 402.1; § 402.1, n. 69; § 607.2, n. 11; § 608.2; § 608.2, n. 6, 26; § 609.1; § 609.1, n. 11, 14, 20.**

Sands v. News America Pub. Inc., 161 A.D.2d 30, 560 N.Y.S.2d 416 (N.Y.A.D. 1 Dept.1990)—**§ 501.3, n. 20.**

Sandstrom v. Montana, 442 U.S. 510, 99 S.Ct. 2450, 61 L.Ed.2d 39 (1979)—**§ 201.1, n. 62; § 302.1, n. 2, 4, 6, 14.**

Sansevere v. United Parcel Service, Inc., 181 A.D.2d 521, 581 N.Y.S.2d 315 (N.Y.A.D. 1 Dept.1992)—**§ 806.1; § 806.1, n. 14.**

Santana v. New York City Transit Authority, 132 Misc.2d 777, 505 N.Y.S.2d 775 (N.Y.Sup.1986)—**§ 604.1, n. 8.**

Santana, People v., 159 Misc.2d 301, 604 N.Y.S.2d 1016 (N.Y.Sup.1993)—**§ 601.1, n. 64.**

Santana, People v., 73 A.D.2d 977, 424 N.Y.S.2d 237 (N.Y.A.D. 2 Dept.1980)—**§ 614.1, n. 17.**

Santarelli, People v., 425 N.Y.S.2d 77, 401 N.E.2d 199 (N.Y.1980)—**§ 404.1; § 404.1, n. 86.**

Santariga v. McCann, 161 A.D.2d 320, 555 N.Y.S.2d 309 (N.Y.A.D. 1 Dept.1990)—**§ 501.3, n. 24, 26.**

TABLE OF CASES

Santiago, People v., 197 A.D.2d 756, 602 N.Y.S.2d 732 (N.Y.A.D. 3 Dept.1993)—§ **1107.1, n. 4.**

Santiago, People v., 255 N.Y.S.2d 864, 204 N.E.2d 197 (N.Y.1964)—§ **608.2, n. 22.**

Santos, United States v., 372 F.2d 177 (2nd Cir.1967)—§ **802.3;** § **802.3, n. 26, 28.**

Santosky v. Kramer, 455 U.S. 745, 102 S.Ct. 1388, 71 L.Ed.2d 599 (1982)—§ **300.4, n. 31.**

Sanza, People v., 121 A.D.2d 89, 509 N.Y.S.2d 311 (N.Y.A.D. 1 Dept.1986)—§ **404.1, n. 57.**

Sappe, United States v., 898 F.2d 878 (2nd Cir.1990)—§ **404.2, n. 18.**

Saranac Land & Timber Co. v. Roberts, 208 N.Y. 288, 101 N.E. 898 (N.Y.1913)—§ **803(5).1, n. 2.**

Sarasohn v. Kamaiky, 193 N.Y. 203, 86 N.E. 20 (N.Y.1908)—§ **1001.1, n. 3;** § **1002.1, n. 6.**

Saribeyoglu, People ex rel. Anonymous v., 131 Misc.2d 647, 501 N.Y.S.2d 286 (N.Y.Sup.1986)—§ **509.1;** § **509.1, n. 23.**

Sarmiento-Perez, United States v., 633 F.2d 1092 (5th Cir.1981)—§ **804(3).2, n. 11, 12.**

Sarra, People v., 283 A.D. 876, 129 N.Y.S.2d 201 (N.Y.A.D.1954)—§ **609.1, n. 6.**

Sarzano, People v., 212 N.Y. 231, 106 N.E. 87 (N.Y.1914)—§ **804(2).1, n. 3.**

Sasso, United States v., 59 F.3d 341 (2nd Cir.1995)—§ **607.7, n. 21.**

Saunders v. Champlain Bus Corp., 263 A.D. 683, 34 N.Y.S.2d 447 (N.Y.A.D. 3 Dept. 1942)—§ **610.1, n. 6, 10.**

Saunders, United States v., 736 F.Supp. 698 (E.D.Va.1990)—§ **412.2, n. 8.**

Savage, People v., 431 N.Y.S.2d 382, 409 N.E.2d 858 (N.Y.1980)—§ **509.1, n. 89;** § **607.8, n. 21.**

Sawyer v. Dreis & Krump Mfg. Co., 502 N.Y.S.2d 696, 493 N.E.2d 920 (N.Y. 1986)—§ **300.4, n. 15;** § **702.1, n. 22;** § **703.1, n. 1;** § **705.1, n. 10.**

Sawyer, United States v., 607 F.2d 1190 (7th Cir.1979)—§ **803(5).2, n. 8.**

Scales, United States v., 594 F.2d 558 (6th Cir.1979)—§ **1006.1, n. 23.**

Scalone v. Phelps Memorial Hosp. Center, 184 A.D.2d 65, 591 N.Y.S.2d 419 (N.Y.A.D. 2 Dept.1992)—§ **502.1, n. 52.**

Scarola, People v., 530 N.Y.S.2d 83, 525 N.E.2d 728 (N.Y.1988)—§ **401.1;** § **401.1, n. 1;** § **1102.1, n. 4, 8.**

Scarpa, United States v., 913 F.2d 993 (2nd Cir.1990)—§ **803(1).2;** § **803(1).2, n. 13.**

Schabel v. Onseyga Realty Co., 233 A.D. 208, 251 N.Y.S. 280 (N.Y.A.D. 4 Dept. 1931)—§ **103.1, n. 28.**

Schaeffer v. General Motors Corp., 372 Mass. 171, 360 N.E.2d 1062 (Mass. 1977)—§ **1106.1, n. 8.**

Schaff's Estate, In re, 274 A.D. 1020, 85 N.Y.S.2d 147 (N.Y.A.D. 3 Dept.1948)—§ **601.2, n. 7.**

Schainuck, People v., 286 N.Y. 161, 36 N.E.2d 94 (N.Y.1941)—§ **607.8, n. 25, 31.**

Scharfenberger v. Wingo, 542 F.2d 328 (6th Cir.1976)—§ **901.3, n. 17.**

Scharlack v. Richmond Memorial Hosp., 102 A.D.2d 886, 477 N.Y.S.2d 184 (N.Y.A.D. 2 Dept.1984)—§ **502.1, n. 39.**

Schatzle, United States v., 901 F.2d 252 (2nd Cir.1990)—§ **402.2, n. 5;** § **704.2, n. 10.**

Schechter v. Klanfer, 321 N.Y.S.2d 99, 269 N.E.2d 812 (N.Y.1971)—§ **300.4, n. 14, 15.**

Schechtman v. Lappin, 161 A.D.2d 118, 554 N.Y.S.2d 846 (N.Y.A.D. 1 Dept.1990)—§ **1107.1, n. 5.**

Schelberger v. Eastern Sav. Bank, 470 N.Y.S.2d 548, 458 N.E.2d 1225 (N.Y. 1983)—§ **301.4, n. 9;** § **301.5;** § **301.5, n. 24.**

Schenectady Discount Corp. v. Dziedzic, 31 N.Y.S.2d 636 (N.Y.Co.Ct.1941)—§ **201.1, n. 23.**

Scherback v. Stern, 246 A.D. 746, 283 N.Y.S. 804 (N.Y.A.D. 2 Dept.1935)—§ **603.1, n. 9.**

Schevling v. Johnson, 122 F.Supp. 87 (D.C.Conn.1953)—§ **411.2, n. 7.**

Schindler v. Royal Ins. Co., 258 N.Y. 310, 179 N.E. 711 (N.Y.1932)—§ **803(5).1, n. 42, 51.**

Schlessel, People v., 196 N.Y. 476, 90 N.E. 44 (N.Y.1909)—§ **106.1, n. 10.**

Schmerber v. California, 384 U.S. 757, 86 S.Ct. 1826, 16 L.Ed.2d 908 (1966)—§ **509.1, n. 31, 90.**

Schneider v. Kings Highway Hosp. Center, Inc., 500 N.Y.S.2d 95, 490 N.E.2d 1221 (N.Y.1986)—§ **300.2, n. 5;** § **300.3, n. 16.**

Schneider, People v., 366 N.Y.S.2d 419, 325 N.E.2d 877 (N.Y.1975)—§ **611.3, n. 9.**

Schneider v. Revici, 817 F.2d 987 (2nd Cir. 1987)—§ **401.2, n. 4;** § **803(6).2, n. 4.**

Schneiderman v. United States, 320 U.S. 118, 63 S.Ct. 1333, 87 L.Ed. 1796 (1943)—§ **300.4, n. 31.**

Scholle, United States v., 553 F.2d 1109 (8th Cir.1977)—§ **607.5, n. 59.**

Schonfeld v. United States, 277 F. 934 (2nd Cir.1921)—§ **1107.2, n. 1, 6.**

Schoonmaker v. Wolford, 20 Hun. 166 (N.Y. 1880)—§ **601.2, n. 30.**

Schozer v. William Penn Life Ins. Co. of New York, 620 N.Y.S.2d 797, 644 N.E.2d 1353 (N.Y.1994)—§ **104.1, n. 13, 28;** § **703.1, n. 11;** § **803(3).1, n. 75;** § **1001.1, n. 6, 35;** § **1002.1, n. 16;** § **1004.1;** § **1004.1, n. 3, 4, 7;** § **1008.1, n. 1, 4.**

Schreiner, People v., 570 N.Y.S.2d 464, 573 N.E.2d 552 (N.Y.1991)—§ **601.1, n. 64.**

TABLE OF CASES

Schulman's Estate, In re, 189 Misc. 672, 72 N.Y.S.2d 239 (N.Y.Sur.1947)—§ **601.2, n. 66.**

Schultz v. Tecumseh Products, 310 F.2d 426 (6th Cir.1962)—§ **203.2, n. 2.**

Schultz v. Third Avenue R.R. Co., 89 N.Y. 242 (1882)—§ **607.6, n. 7, 20, 24.**

Schwab, United States v., 886 F.2d 509 (2nd Cir.1989)—§ **608.2;** § **608.2, n. 37, 46, 50.**

Schwartz v. 38 Town Associates, 187 A.D.2d 377, 589 N.Y.S.2d 487 (N.Y.A.D. 1 Dept. 1992)—§ **611.3, n. 7.**

Schwartzman, People v., 299 N.Y.S.2d 817, 247 N.E.2d 642 (N.Y.1969)—§ **402.1, n. 33;** § **404.1;** § **404.1, n. 35;** § **607.3;** § **607.3, n. 2, 8;** § **608.2, n. 9, 16;** § **609.1, n. 50;** § **611.1, n. 8;** § **611.3, n. 29.**

Schwimmer, United States v., 892 F.2d 237 (2nd Cir.1989)—§ **501.2, n. 24, 27.**

Scop, United States v., 846 F.2d 135 (2nd Cir.1988)—§ **701.2, n. 12;** § **703.2, n. 1;** § **704.2;** § **704.2, n. 3.**

Scopo, United States v., 861 F.2d 339 (2nd Cir.1988)—§ **804(3).2, n. 19.**

Scott, People v., 120 Misc.2d 313, 465 N.Y.S.2d 819 (Monroe Co.Ct.1983)—§ **1108.1, n. 2.**

Scott v. Spanjer Bros., Inc., 298 F.2d 928 (2nd Cir.1962)—§ **706.2, n. 4.**

Scrima, United States v., 819 F.2d 996 (11th Cir.1987)—§ **703.2, n. 2.**

Scudero v. Campbell, 288 N.Y. 328, 43 N.E.2d 66 (N.Y.1942)—§ **407.1;** § **407.1, n. 30.**

Scull, People v., 378 N.Y.S.2d 30, 340 N.E.2d 466 (N.Y.1975)—§ **503.3, n. 13.**

Scurti v. City of New York, 387 N.Y.S.2d 55, 354 N.E.2d 794 (N.Y.1976)—§ **202.1, n. 10.**

Sealed Case, In re, 877 F.2d 976, 278 U.S.App.D.C. 188 (D.C.Cir.1989)—§ **501.2, n. 48.**

Sealed Case, In re, 754 F.2d 395, 244 U.S.App.D.C. 11 (D.C.Cir.1985)—§ **501.2, n. 16.**

Sealed Case, In re, 737 F.2d 94, 237 U.S.App.D.C. 312 (D.C.Cir.1984)—§ **501.2, n. 7.**

Sealed Case, In re, 676 F.2d 793, 219 U.S.App.D.C. 195 (D.C.Cir.1982)—§ **501.2, n. 44, 52;** § **501.3, n. 43.**

Seaman v. Fedourich, 262 N.Y.S.2d 444, 209 N.E.2d 778 (N.Y.1965)—§ **803(5).1, n. 31.**

S.E.C. v. Forma, 117 F.R.D. 516 (S.D.N.Y. 1987)—§ **501.2, n. 19, 43.**

S.E.C. v. Musella, 578 F.Supp. 425 (D.C.N.Y.1984)—§ **201.2, n. 7.**

S.E.C. v. Singer, 786 F.Supp. 1158 (S.D.N.Y.1992)—§ **401.2, n. 3;** § **602.2, n. 7.**

Sees v. Massachusetts Bonding & Ins. Co., 243 A.D. 400, 277 N.Y.S. 198 (N.Y.A.D. 1 Dept.1935)—§ **803(1).1, n. 56.**

Segal, United States v., 534 F.2d 578 (3rd Cir.1976)—§ **611.5, n. 15.**

Segal Lock & Hardware Co. v. F.T.C., 143 F.2d 935 (2nd Cir.1944)—§ **513.2, n. 6.**

Seijo, United States v., 595 F.2d 116 (2nd Cir.1979)—§ **804.1, n. 17.**

Seiler v. Lucasfilm, Ltd., 808 F.2d 1316 (9th Cir.1986)—§ **1001.1;** § **1001.1, n. 22;** § **1008.1;** § **1008.1, n. 6.**

Seit, People v., 629 N.Y.S.2d 998, 653 N.E.2d 1168 (N.Y.1995)—§ **607.5, n. 29, 44;** § **801.1, n. 41;** § **801(1).2, n. 17.**

Seligson, Morris & Neuburger v. Fairbanks Whitney Corp., 22 A.D.2d 625, 257 N.Y.S.2d 706 (N.Y.A.D. 1 Dept.1965)—§ **401.1, n. 35.**

Selkowitz v. County of Nassau, 408 N.Y.S.2d 10, 379 N.E.2d 1140 (N.Y. 1978)—§ **702.1, n. 7;** § **704.1;** § **704.1, n. 7.**

Senecal v. Drollette, 304 N.Y. 446, 108 N.E.2d 602 (N.Y.1952)—§ **601.1, n. 10;** § **602.1, n. 6.**

Serna, United States v., 799 F.2d 842 (2nd Cir.1986)—§ **410.2, n. 6;** § **804(1).2, n. 11;** § **806.1, n. 18.**

Serrano, People v., 258 N.Y.S.2d 386, 206 N.E.2d 330 (N.Y.1965)—§ **803(5).1, n. 47.**

Service Fire Ins. Co. of N.Y. v. Lederman, 279 A.D. 319, 109 N.Y.S.2d 812 (N.Y.A.D. 3 Dept.1952)—§ **607.8, n. 8, 9.**

Sessa, United States v., 806 F.Supp. 1063 (E.D.N.Y.1992)—§ **502.1, n. 73;** § **502.2, n. 9.**

Settles, People v., 412 N.Y.S.2d 874, 385 N.E.2d 612 (N.Y.1978)—§ **804(3).1;** § **804(3).1, n. 39.**

716 Third Ave. Holding Corp., In re, 225 F.Supp. 268 (D.C.N.Y.1964)—§ **1004.1, n. 4.**

Sexton, People v., 187 N.Y. 495, 80 N.E. 396 (N.Y.1907)—§ **607.4, n. 3, 21.**

Shannon, People v., 207 A.D.2d 727, 616 N.Y.S.2d 615 (N.Y.A.D. 1 Dept.1994)—§ **804(3).1, n. 46.**

Shapiro, People v., 431 N.Y.S.2d 422, 409 N.E.2d 897 (N.Y.1980)—§ **404.1, n. 72.**

Shapiro, People v., 308 N.Y. 453, 126 N.E.2d 559 (N.Y.1955)—§ **501.1, n. 82;** § **509.1, n. 38, 41.**

Shapiro v. United States, 335 U.S. 1, 68 S.Ct. 1375, 92 L.Ed. 1787 (1948)—§ **509.1, n. 72.**

Shargel, In re, 742 F.2d 61 (2nd Cir.1984)—§ **501.2, n. 9, 12, 13.**

Sharon v. Time, Inc., 103 F.R.D. 86 (D.C.N.Y.1984)—§ **402.2, n. 6, 11;** § **404.2, n. 20.**

Sharrow v. Dick Corp., 629 N.Y.S.2d 980, 653 N.E.2d 1150 (N.Y.1995)—§ **606.1;** § **606.1, n. 6.**

Shatkin v. McDonnell Douglas Corp., 727 F.2d 202 (2nd Cir.1984)—§ **703.2, n. 3.**

973

TABLE OF CASES

Shatkin v. McDonnell Douglas Corp., 565 F.Supp. 93 (D.C.N.Y.1983)—§ **705.2, n. 6.**

Shaughnessy v. Monahan, 79 Misc.2d 648, 361 N.Y.S.2d 101 (N.Y.Sup.1974)— § **512.1, n. 4.**

Shaw v. Scoville, 369 F.2d 909 (2nd Cir. 1966)—§ **103.2, n. 16.**

Shaw v. Tague, 257 N.Y. 193, 177 N.E. 417 (N.Y.1931)—§ **201.1, n. 32.**

Sheedy v. Stall, 255 Or. 594, 468 P.2d 529 (Or.1970)—§ **801.1, n. 20.**

Sheehan's Will, Matter of, 51 A.D.2d 645, 378 N.Y.S.2d 141 (N.Y.A.D. 4 Dept. 1976)—§ **601.2, n. 9.**

Sheen, Estate of, 145 Misc.2d 920, 548 N.Y.S.2d 618 (N.Y.Sur.1989)—§ **605.1; § 605.1, n. 4.**

Shelton v. American Motors Corp., 805 F.2d 1323 (8th Cir.1986)—§ **501.3, n. 40.**

Shepard v. United States, 290 U.S. 96, 54 S.Ct. 22, 78 L.Ed. 196 (1933)— § **803(1).1, n. 48; § 803(1).2; § 803(1).2, n. 31; § 804(2).1; § 804(2).1, n. 9, 28; § 804(2).2; § 804(2).2, n. 2.**

Sher, People v., 301 N.Y.S.2d 46, 248 N.E.2d 887 (N.Y.1969)—§ **1107.1, n. 15.**

Sherman v. Irving Merchandise Corp., 26 N.Y.S.2d 645 (N.Y.Sup.1941)—§ **615.1, n. 10.**

Sherman v. Tamarack Lodge, 146 A.D.2d 767, 537 N.Y.S.2d 249 (N.Y.A.D. 2 Dept. 1989)—§ **802.2, n. 75, 76.**

Sherrell Perfumers, Inc. v. Revlon, Inc., 524 F.Supp. 302 (D.C.N.Y.1980)— § **804(5).2, n. 12.**

Shields, People v., 81 A.D.2d 870, 438 N.Y.S.2d 885 (N.Y.A.D. 2 Dept.1981)— § **1102.1, n. 6.**

Shilitano, People v., 218 N.Y. 161, 112 N.E. 733 (N.Y.1916)—§ **401.1, n. 15.**

Shillcutt v. Gagnon, 827 F.2d 1155 (7th Cir.1987)—§ **606.2, n. 9.**

Shirer v. O. W. S. and Associates, 253 S.C. 232, 169 S.E.2d 621 (S.C.1969)— § **1002.1, n. 5.**

Shirley C., Matter of, 136 Misc.2d 843, 519 N.Y.S.2d 328 (N.Y.Sup.1987)—§ **201.1, n. 43.**

Shirvani v. Capital Investing Corp., Inc., 112 F.R.D. 389 (D.Conn.1986)—§ **501.2, n. 37.**

Shortridge, People v., 491 N.Y.S.2d 298, 480 N.E.2d 1080 (N.Y.1985)—§ **804(3).1; § 804(3).1, n. 6.**

Shulman, United States v., 624 F.2d 384 (2nd Cir.1980)—§ **802.3, n. 14.**

Shultz v. Rice, 809 F.2d 643 (10th Cir. 1986)—§ **611.5, n. 10.**

Shu-Tao Lin v. McDonnell Douglas Corp., 574 F.Supp. 1407 (D.C.N.Y.1983)— § **703.2, n. 5.**

Shutt v. Pooley, 43 A.D.2d 59, 349 N.Y.S.2d 839 (N.Y.A.D. 3 Dept.1973)—§ **411.1, n. 5.**

Sibley by Sibley v. Hayes 73 Corp., 126 A.D.2d 629, 511 N.Y.S.2d 65 (N.Y.A.D. 2 Dept.1987)—§ **502.1, n. 52.**

Siderius v. M.V. Amilla, 880 F.2d 662 (2nd Cir.1989)—§ **201.2, n. 7.**

Siegel v. Crawford, 266 A.D. 878, 42 N.Y.S.2d 837 (N.Y.A.D. 2 Dept.1943)— § **509.1, n. 8.**

Siegel v. Waldbaum, 59 A.D.2d 555, 397 N.Y.S.2d 144 (N.Y.A.D. 2 Dept.1977)— § **601.2; § 601.2, n. 59, 60; § 804(1).1, n. 23.**

Sigman-Weiss Consultants, Inc. v. Raiff, 149 Misc.2d 111, 563 N.Y.S.2d 618 (N.Y.Sup.1990)—§ **804(1).1, n. 19, 23.**

Silver v. New York Cent. R. Co., 329 Mass. 14, 105 N.E.2d 923 (Mass.1952)— § **801.1, n. 17.**

Silver, People v., 354 N.Y.S.2d 915, 310 N.E.2d 520 (N.Y.1974)—§ **302.1, n. 30.**

Simblest v. Maynard, 427 F.2d 1 (2nd Cir. 1970)—§ **300.3, n. 48.**

Simcuski v. Saeli, 406 N.Y.S.2d 259, 377 N.E.2d 713 (N.Y.1978)—§ **300.4, n. 20.**

Simmons, People v., 365 N.Y.S.2d 812, 325 N.E.2d 139 (N.Y.1975)—§ **804(1).1, n. 34.**

Simmons, United States v., 923 F.2d 934 (2nd Cir.1991)—§ **300.3, n. 50; § 802.3, n. 58.**

Simmons v. United States, 390 U.S. 377, 88 S.Ct. 967, 19 L.Ed.2d 1247 (1968)— § **509.1, n. 31; § 801(2).2; § 801(2).2, n. 4.**

Simmons, Inc. v. Pinkerton's, Inc., 762 F.2d 591 (7th Cir.1985)—§ **607.3, n. 6.**

Simon v. G.D. Searle & Co., 816 F.2d 397 (8th Cir.1987)—§ **501.2, n. 10.**

Simpson v. Foundation Co., 201 N.Y. 479, 95 N.E. 10 (N.Y.1911)—§ **103.1, n. 13; § 411.1; § 411.1, n. 1.**

Sims v. Sims, 75 N.Y. 466 (1878)—§ **607.5, n. 22.**

Sinatra v. Heckler, 566 F.Supp. 1354 (E.D.N.Y.1983)—§ **201.2, n. 7.**

Sinatra, People v., 134 A.D.2d 738, 521 N.Y.S.2d 551 (N.Y.A.D. 3 Dept.1987)— § **601.1, n. 36.**

Sindona, United States v., 636 F.2d 792 (2nd Cir.1980)—§ **804.1, n. 16.**

Singer, People v., 300 N.Y. 120, 89 N.E.2d 710 (N.Y.1949)—§ **607.5; § 607.5, n. 29, 39, 40; § 1101.1, n. 7.**

Singer, People ex rel. v. Rogers, 254 A.D. 865, 4 N.Y.S.2d 905 (N.Y.A.D. 2 Dept. 1938)—§ **605.1, n. 1.**

Singer, United States v., 785 F.2d 228 (8th Cir.1986)—§ **509.1, n. 18.**

Singh, United States v., 628 F.2d 758 (2nd Cir.1980)—§ **611.5, n. 20.**

Singletary v. Secretary of Health, Ed. and Welfare, 623 F.2d 217 (2nd Cir.1980)— § **701.2, n. 4.**

Sirico v. Cotto, 67 Misc.2d 636, 324 N.Y.S.2d 483 (N.Y.City Civ.Ct.1971)— § **1001.1, n. 35; § 1002.1, n. 16.**

974

TABLE OF CASES

Sirota v. Solitron Devices, Inc., 673 F.2d 566 (2nd Cir.1982)—§ **300.3, n. 48.**

Sitaras v. Ricciardi & Sons, Inc., 154 A.D.2d 451, 545 N.Y.S.2d 937 (N.Y.A.D. 2 Dept. 1989)—§ **702.1, n. 9;** § **704.1, n. 5, 12.**

Sitrin Bros., Inc. v. Deluxe Lines, Inc., 35 Misc.2d 1041, 231 N.Y.S.2d 943 (Oneida Co.Ct.1962)—§ **614.1, n. 22.**

Siwek v. Mahoney, 383 N.Y.S.2d 238, 347 N.E.2d 599 (N.Y.1976)—§ **201.1, n. 35.**

Six Grand Jury Witnesses, In re, 979 F.2d 939 (2nd Cir.1992)—§ **501.2, n. 5.**

Skelka v. Metropolitan Transit Authority, 76 A.D.2d 492, 430 N.Y.S.2d 840 (N.Y.A.D. 2 Dept.1980)—§ **802.1, n. 13.**

Sklaire v. Estate of Turner, 12 A.D.2d 386, 212 N.Y.S.2d 389 (N.Y.A.D. 3 Dept. 1961)—§ **601.2, n. 46, 69.**

Slater v. Slater, 78 Misc.2d 13, 355 N.Y.S.2d 943 (N.Y.Sup.1974)—§ **509.1, n. 9.**

Slatinsky v. Bailey, 330 F.2d 136 (8th Cir. 1964)—§ **1104.2, n. 6.**

Slatterie v. Pooley, 6 M. & W. 665, 151 Eng.Rep. 579 (Exch.1840)—§ **1007.1, n. 3.**

Slattery v. Marra Bros., 186 F.2d 134 (2nd Cir.1951)—§ **1102.2, n. 8.**

Slaughter, People v., 189 A.D.2d 157, 596 N.Y.S.2d 22 (N.Y.A.D. 1 Dept.1993)—§ **801.1, n. 1;** § **803(1).1, n. 20.**

Sleasman v. Sherwood, 212 A.D.2d 868, 622 N.Y.S.2d 360 (N.Y.A.D. 3 Dept.1995)—§ **201.1, n. 36.**

S. Leo Harmonay, Inc. v. Binks Mfg. Co., 597 F.Supp. 1014 (D.C.N.Y.1984)—§ **408.2, n. 17.**

Sliker, United States v., 751 F.2d 477 (2nd Cir.1984)—§ **104.2;** § **104.2, n. 6;** § **105.2, n. 8;** § **201.2, n. 23;** § **601.1, n. 1;** § **900.1;** § **900.1, n. 1, 2, 8;** § **901.5;** § **901.5, n. 13;** § **1001.1, n. 14.**

Sliney, People v., 137 N.Y. 570, 33 N.E. 150 (N.Y.1893)—§ **502.1, n. 15.**

Sloan v. New York Central R.R. Co., 45 N.Y. 125 (1871)—§ **611.2, n. 15.**

Slocovich v. Orient Mut. Ins. Co., 108 N.Y. 56, 14 N.E. 802 (N.Y.1888)—§ **803(6).1, n. 5.**

Slotnik v. State, 129 Misc.2d 553, 493 N.Y.S.2d 731 (N.Y.Ct.Cl.1985)—§ **612.1, n. 27.**

Slusarczyk v. Slusarczyk, 41 A.D.2d 593, 340 N.Y.S.2d 250 (N.Y.A.D. 4 Dept. 1973)—§ **601.2, n. 20.**

Small, People v., 177 A.D.2d 669, 576 N.Y.S.2d 595 (N.Y.A.D. 2 Dept.1991)—§ **804(1).1, n. 47.**

Smalley v. United States, 798 F.2d 1182 (8th Cir.1986)—§ **607.7, n. 24.**

Smalls, United States v., 438 F.2d 711 (2nd Cir.1971)—§ **803(2).2;** § **803(2).2, n. 6.**

Smith v. Bailey, 14 A.D. 283, 43 N.Y.S. 856 (N.Y.A.D. 1 Dept.1897)—§ **409.1, n. 8.**

Smith, Commonwealth v., 151 Mass. 491, 24 N.E. 677 (Mass.1890)—§ **802.2, n. 101.**

Smith v. Lehigh Valley R. Co., 177 N.Y. 379, 69 N.E. 729 (N.Y.1904)—§ **1102.1, n. 2;** § **1102.2, n. 6.**

Smith, People v., 195 A.D.2d 112, 606 N.Y.S.2d 656 (N.Y.A.D. 1 Dept.1994)—§ **804(3).1, n. 52;** § **1102.1, n. 5.**

Smith, People v., 192 A.D.2d 806, 596 N.Y.S.2d 539 (N.Y.A.D. 3 Dept.1993)—§ **412.1, n. 23.**

Smith, People v., 166 A.D.2d 385, 561 N.Y.S.2d 189 (N.Y.A.D. 1 Dept.1990)—§ **611.1, n. 11.**

Smith, People v., 87 A.D.2d 357, 451 N.Y.S.2d 429 (N.Y.A.D. 1 Dept.1982)—§ **1108.1;** § **1108.1, n. 13, 16.**

Smith, People v., 436 N.Y.S.2d 867, 418 N.E.2d 382 (N.Y.1980)—§ **803(1).1, n. 34.**

Smith, People v., 62 A.D.2d 1043, 404 N.Y.S.2d 48 (N.Y.A.D. 2 Dept.1978)—§ **201.1, n. 55.**

Smith, United States v., 727 F.2d 214 (2nd Cir.1984)—§ **608.2, n. 49, 51.**

Smith, United States v., 551 F.2d 348, 179 U.S.App.D.C. 162 (D.C.Cir.1976)—§ **609.2, n. 14.**

Smith v. United States, 348 U.S. 147, 75 S.Ct. 194, 99 L.Ed. 192 (1954)—§ **300.3, n. 50.**

Snelling's Will, In re, 136 N.Y. 515, 32 N.E. 1006 (N.Y.1893)—§ **607.6, n. 8, 18.**

Snyder v. Massachusetts, 291 U.S. 97, 54 S.Ct. 330, 78 L.Ed. 674 (1934)—§ **807.1, n. 10.**

Socialist Workers Party v. Attorney General of United States, 458 F.Supp. 895 (D.C.N.Y.1978)—§ **511.2, n. 10.**

Society for Good Will for Retarded Children, Inc. v. Cuomo, 718 F.Supp. 139 (E.D.N.Y.1989)—§ **803(5).2, n. 35.**

Soden v. Freightliner Corp., 714 F.2d 498 (5th Cir.1983)—§ **703.2, n. 2.**

Soltis v. State, 188 A.D.2d 201, 594 N.Y.S.2d 433 (N.Y.A.D. 3 Dept.1993)—§ **406.1, n. 8.**

Sommers v. Sommers, 203 A.D.2d 975, 611 N.Y.S.2d 971 (N.Y.A.D. 4 Dept.1994)—§ **201.1, n. 35.**

Sopar v. Storar, 438 N.Y.S.2d 266, 420 N.E.2d 64 (N.Y.1981)—§ **300.4, n. 19, 31.**

Soper, People v., 243 N.Y. 320, 153 N.E. 433 (N.Y.1926)—§ **901.3, n. 7.**

Sorensen By and Through Dunbar v. Shaklee Corp., 31 F.3d 638 (8th Cir.1994)—§ **702.2, n. 30.**

Sorge, People v., 301 N.Y. 198, 93 N.E.2d 637 (N.Y.1950)—§ **607.2, n. 25;** § **608.2;** § **608.2, n. 2, 12, 13, 17, 21, 23;** § **609.1, n. 5.**

Sorrells v. United States, 287 U.S. 435, 53 S.Ct. 210, 77 L.Ed. 413 (1932)—§ **402.1, n. 12.**

Sorrentini, People v., 26 A.D.2d 827, 273 N.Y.S.2d 981 (N.Y.A.D. 2 Dept.1966)—§ **601.1, n. 57.**

TABLE OF CASES

Sostre, People v., 70 A.D.2d 40, 418 N.Y.S.2d 662 (N.Y.A.D. 2 Dept.1979)—§ 803(1).1, n. 36.

Southard v. Curley, 134 N.Y. 148, 31 N.E. 330 (N.Y.1892)—§ 300.4, n. 26.

South Dakota v. Neville, 459 U.S. 553, 103 S.Ct. 916, 74 L.Ed.2d 748 (1983)—§ 509.1, n. 90.

Southern Ry. Co. v. Madden, 235 F.2d 198 (4th Cir.1956)—§ 409.2, n. 2.

Southland Corp., United States v., 760 F.2d 1366 (2nd Cir.1985)—§ 801.1, n. 43; § 803(1).2; § 803(1).2, n. 20.

Sowle, People v., 68 Misc.2d 569, 327 N.Y.S.2d 510 (Fulton Co.Ct.1971)—§ 201.1, n. 5.

Spampinato v. A. B. C. Consol. Corp., 360 N.Y.S.2d 878, 319 N.E.2d 196 (N.Y. 1974)—§ 607.4, n. 2, 18.

Spano, People v., 57 A.D.2d 715, 395 N.Y.S.2d 548 (N.Y.A.D. 4 Dept.1977)—§ 106.1, n. 12.

Special Federal Grand Jury Empanelled Oct. 31, 1985 Impounded, Matter of, 819 F.2d 56 (3rd Cir.1987)—§ 802.3; § 802.3, n. 15.

Special September 1978 Grand Jury (II), In re, 640 F.2d 49 (7th Cir.1980)—§ 501.3, n. 8.

Spectrum Systems Intern. Corp. v. Chemical Bank, 575 N.Y.S.2d 809, 581 N.E.2d 1055 (N.Y.1991)—§ 104.1, n. 35; § 501.1; § 501.1, n. 2, 3, 12, 19, 21, 22, 28, 42, 67, 77.

Speiser v. Randall, 357 U.S. 513, 78 S.Ct. 1332, 2 L.Ed.2d 1460 (1958)—§ 300.4, n. 3.

Sperling, United States v., 726 F.2d 69 (2nd Cir.1984)—§ 608.2, n. 38; § 803(1).2; § 803(1).2, n. 44.

Spett v. President Monroe Bldg. & Mfg. Corp., 278 N.Y.S.2d 826, 225 N.E.2d 527 (N.Y.1967)—§ 802.2; § 802.2, n. 61.

Spier v. Barker, 363 N.Y.S.2d 916, 323 N.E.2d 164 (N.Y.1974)—§ 704.1, n. 5.

Spigarolo v. Meachum, 934 F.2d 19 (2nd Cir.1991)—§ 603.2, n. 3.

Spitaleri, People v., 212 N.Y.S.2d 53, 173 N.E.2d 35 (N.Y.1961)—§ 410.1; § 410.1, n. 2; § 802.1; § 802.1, n. 16.

Splawn v. Lextaj Corp., NV, 197 A.D.2d 479, 603 N.Y.S.2d 41 (N.Y.A.D. 1 Dept. 1993)—§ 801.1, n. 39; § 803(3).1, n. 20; § 805.1, n. 11.

Spondre, In re, 98 Misc. 524, 162 N.Y.S. 943 (N.Y.Sur.1917)—§ 1001.1, n. 13.

Sporck v. Peil, 759 F.2d 312 (3rd Cir. 1985)—§ 501.3, n. 40; § 612.2, n. 20.

Spotford, People v., 627 N.Y.S.2d 295, 650 N.E.2d 1296 (N.Y.1995)—§ 404.1, n. 14.

Spotted War Bonnet, United States v., 882 F.2d 1360 (8th Cir.1989)—§ 601.3, n. 10.

Sprynczynatyk v. General Motors Corp., 771 F.2d 1112 (8th Cir.1985)—§ 601.3, n. 19.

Square Liner 360°, Inc. v. Chisum, 691 F.2d 362 (8th Cir.1982)—§ 1006.1, n. 26.

Squires, People v., 171 A.D.2d 893, 567 N.Y.S.2d 555 (N.Y.A.D. 2 Dept.1991)—§ 608.2, n. 10.

Stacey, People v., 173 A.D.2d 960, 569 N.Y.S.2d 470 (N.Y.A.D. 3 Dept.1991)—§ 801(2).1, n. 18.

Stacy v. Graham, 14 N.Y. 492 (1856)—§ 607.8, n. 36; § 806.1, n. 11.

Stafford v. Mussers Potato Chips, Inc., 39 A.D.2d 831, 333 N.Y.S.2d 139 (N.Y.A.D. 4 Dept.1972)—§ 702.1, n. 5.

Stanard, People v., 396 N.Y.S.2d 825, 365 N.E.2d 857 (N.Y.1977)—§ 611.2, n. 7; § 611.3, n. 32.

Stanard, People v., 344 N.Y.S.2d 331, 297 N.E.2d 77 (N.Y.1973)—§ 404.1; § 404.1, n. 8, 58.

Stanchich, United States v., 550 F.2d 1294 (2nd Cir.1977)—§ 803(1).2, n. 39.

Standard Chartered Bank PLC v. Ayala Intern. Holdings (United States) Inc., 111 F.R.D. 76 (S.D.N.Y.1986)—§ 501.2, n. 48.

Standard Textile Co., Inc. v. National Equipment Rental, Ltd., 80 A.D.2d 911, 437 N.Y.S.2d 398 (N.Y.A.D. 2 Dept. 1981)—§ 803(3).1, n. 11.

St. Andrassy v. Mooney, 262 N.Y. 368, 186 N.E. 867 (N.Y.1933)—§ 301.5, n. 31.

Stanley, People v., 185 A.D.2d 827, 586 N.Y.S.2d 649 (N.Y.A.D. 2 Dept.1992)—§ 801(2).1, n. 32, 33.

Stanley, United States v., 896 F.2d 450 (10th Cir.1990)—§ 701.2, n. 3.

Starr v. Campos, 134 Ariz. 254, 655 P.2d 794 (Ariz.App.1982)—§ 1106.1, n. 8, 9.

State v. _____ (see opposing party)

State of (see name of state)

State of N. Y., United States ex rel. Negron v., 434 F.2d 386 (2nd Cir.1970)—§ 604.2, n. 6.

Stavris, People v., 75 A.D.2d 507, 426 N.Y.S.2d 741 (N.Y.A.D. 1 Dept.1980)—§ 607.8, n. 16.

Stavroula S. v. Guerriera, 193 A.D.2d 796, 598 N.Y.S.2d 300 (N.Y.A.D. 2 Dept. 1993)—§ 803(5).1, n. 46.

Stawski v. John Hancock Mut. Life Ins. Co., 7 Misc.2d 424, 163 N.Y.S.2d 155 (N.Y.Sup.1957)—§ 201.1, n. 26, 40.

Stay v. Horvath, 177 A.D.2d 897, 576 N.Y.S.2d 908 (N.Y.A.D. 3 Dept.1991)—§ 601.2, n. 4, 8, 23.

Steele v. Lord, 70 N.Y. 280 (1877)—§ 1001.1, n. 8; § 1004.1, n. 2.

Steele, People v., 168 A.D.2d 937, 565 N.Y.S.2d 339 (N.Y.A.D. 4 Dept.1990)—§ 608.2, n. 12.

Steele, People v., 311 N.Y.S.2d 889, 260 N.E.2d 527 (N.Y.1970)—§ 300.4, n. 54, 55.

Steele v. Taylor, 684 F.2d 1193 (6th Cir. 1982)—§ 807.1, n. 12.

TABLE OF CASES

Stein v. Lebowitz–Pine View Hotel, Inc., 111 A.D.2d 572, 489 N.Y.S.2d 635 (N.Y.A.D. 3 Dept.1985)—§ **607.8, n. 31.**

Steinberg v. New York Life Ins. Co., 263 N.Y. 45, 188 N.E. 152 (N.Y.1933)—§ **502.1, n. 3, 34, 43.**

Steinberg, People v., 170 A.D.2d 50, 573 N.Y.S.2d 965 (N.Y.A.D. 1 Dept.1991)—§ **404.1, n. 43.**

Steinbrecher v. Wapnick, 300 N.Y.S.2d 555, 248 N.E.2d 419 (N.Y.1969)—§ **509.1;** § **509.1, n. 15, 45.**

Steiner, People v., 148 A.D.2d 980, 539 N.Y.S.2d 217 (N.Y.A.D. 4 Dept.1989)—§ **1101.1, n. 24.**

Steinhardt Partners, L.P., In re, 9 F.3d 230 (2nd Cir.1993)—§ **501.2, n. 50;** § **501.3, n. 52.**

Stemmler v. Mayor of City of New York, 179 N.Y. 473, 72 N.E. 581 (N.Y.1904)—§ **802.1, n. 10.**

Stephens v. People, 19 N.Y. 548 (1859)—§ **607.3, n. 16.**

Sterling Nav. Co., Ltd., Matter of, 444 F.Supp. 1043 (D.C.N.Y.1977)—§ **804(1).2, n. 11.**

Stern v. Aetna Cas. & Sur. Co., 159 A.D.2d 1013, 552 N.Y.S.2d 730 (N.Y.A.D. 4 Dept.1990)—§ **612.1, n. 21, 28, 29.**

Sternberg v. Sternberg, 81 A.D.2d 1010, 440 N.Y.S.2d 96 (N.Y.A.D. 4 Dept. 1981)—§ **601.2, n. 75.**

Steuerwald v. Jackson, 123 A.D. 569, 108 N.Y.S. 41 (N.Y.A.D. 2 Dept.1908)—§ **104.1, n. 30;** § **802.2, n. 60.**

Stevens v. Kirby, 86 A.D.2d 391, 450 N.Y.S.2d 607 (N.Y.A.D. 4 Dept.1982)—§ **803(3).1, n. 26;** § **803(5).1;** § **803(5).1, n. 12.**

Stevens, People v., 560 N.Y.S.2d 119, 559 N.E.2d 1278 (N.Y.1990)—§ **1102.1, n. 20.**

Stevenson, People v., 163 A.D.2d 854, 558 N.Y.S.2d 383 (N.Y.A.D. 4 Dept.1990)—§ **609.1, n. 15.**

Stewart v. Baltimore & O. R. Co., 137 F.2d 527 (2nd Cir.1943)—§ **803(1).2, n. 53.**

Stewart, People v., 188 A.D.2d 626, 591 N.Y.S.2d 483 (N.Y.A.D. 2 Dept.1992)—§ **607.6, n. 20.**

Stewart, People v., 173 A.D.2d 877, 570 N.Y.S.2d 834 (N.Y.A.D. 2 Dept.1991)—§ **802.2, n. 80.**

S. T. Grand, Inc. v. City of New York, 344 N.Y.S.2d 938, 298 N.E.2d 105 (N.Y. 1973)—§ **802.2, n. 26;** § **803(5).1;** § **803(5).1, n. 43, 44;** § **803(5).2, n. 46.**

Stiasny v. Metropolitan St. Ry. Co., 58 A.D. 172, 68 N.Y.S. 694 (N.Y.A.D. 1 Dept. 1901)—§ **1104.1, n. 4.**

Stirling, United States v., 571 F.2d 708 (2nd Cir.1978)—§ **410.2, n. 7.**

Stissi v. Interstate and Ocean Transport Co. of Philadelphia, 765 F.2d 370 (2nd Cir.1985)—§ **702.2, n. 8.**

St. John, People v., 74 A.D.2d 85, 426 N.Y.S.2d 863 (N.Y.A.D. 3 Dept.1980)—§ **503.3, n. 30;** § **803(1).1, n. 58.**

St. Mary's Honor Center v. Hicks, ___ U.S. ___, 113 S.Ct. 2742, 125 L.Ed.2d 407 (1993)—§ **301.8;** § **301.8, n. 1, 3, 4.**

Stock, United States v., 948 F.2d 1299, 292 U.S.App.D.C. 191 (D.C.Cir.1991)—§ **607.8, n. 45.**

Stokes v. Delcambre, 710 F.2d 1120 (5th Cir.1983)—§ **1107.2, n. 5.**

Stokes v. People, 53 N.Y. 164 (1873)—§ **302.1, n. 25.**

Stone, People v., 358 N.Y.S.2d 737, 315 N.E.2d 787 (N.Y.1974)—§ **703.1;** § **703.1, n. 4.**

Stone v. United States, 385 F.2d 713 (10th Cir.1967)—§ **701.1, n. 10.**

Stoppick v. Goldstein, 174 A.D. 306, 160 N.Y.S. 947 (N.Y.A.D. 2 Dept.1916)—§ **601.1, n. 37.**

Storrs, People v., 207 N.Y. 147, 100 N.E. 730 (N.Y.1912)—§ **802.2;** § **802.2, n. 99, 100.**

Stovall v. Denno, 388 U.S. 293, 87 S.Ct. 1967, 18 L.Ed.2d 1199 (1967)—§ **801(2).2, n. 3.**

Strassman, United States v., 241 F.2d 784 (2nd Cir.1957)—§ **1108.2, n. 3.**

Stratton, United States v., 779 F.2d 820 (2nd Cir.1985)—§ **602.2, n. 12;** § **804(3).2, n. 17.**

Strauch v. Hirschman, 40 A.D.2d 711, 336 N.Y.S.2d 678 (N.Y.A.D. 2 Dept.1972)—§ **701.1, n. 10;** § **704.1, n. 5, 11;** § **802.2, n. 76.**

Strauss v. Douglas Aircraft Co., 404 F.2d 1152 (2nd Cir.1968)—§ **404.2, n. 41.**

Strehle v. United States, 860 F.Supp. 136 (S.D.N.Y.1994)—§ **803(5).2, n. 32.**

Streitferdt, People v., 169 A.D.2d 171, 572 N.Y.S.2d 893 (N.Y.A.D. 1 Dept.1991)—§ **404.1;** § **404.1, n. 73;** § **608.1, n. 4, 8, 12.**

Stridiron, People v., 352 N.Y.S.2d 179, 307 N.E.2d 242 (N.Y.1973)—§ **607.6, n. 14.**

Stroh v. General Motors Corp., 213 A.D.2d 267, 623 N.Y.S.2d 873 (N.Y.A.D. 1 Dept. 1995)—§ **501.1, n. 55.**

Stroman, People v., 83 A.D.2d 370, 444 N.Y.S.2d 463 (N.Y.A.D. 1 Dept.1981)—§ **300.3, n. 36;** § **607.1, n. 6.**

Strong, Matter of Estate of, 168 Misc. 716, 6 N.Y.S.2d 300 (N.Y.Sur.1938)—§ **804(4).1, n. 13.**

Strother, United States v., 49 F.3d 869 (2nd Cir.1995)—§ **607.8, n. 45, 46.**

Strozier, People v., 116 Misc.2d 103, 455 N.Y.S.2d 217 (N.Y.Just.Ct.1982)—§ **1104.1, n. 46.**

Stubbs v. Dudley, 849 F.2d 83 (2nd Cir. 1988)—§ **300.3, n. 48.**

Sturgeon v. Delaware & H.R. Corp., 2 A.D.2d 725, 152 N.Y.S.2d 371 (N.Y.A.D. 3 Dept.1956)—§ **611.2, n. 4.**

TABLE OF CASES

Suarez, People v., 148 Misc.2d 95, 560 N.Y.S.2d 68 (N.Y.Sup.1990)—§ **503.3, n. 20, 21.**

Suarez v. United States, 309 F.2d 709 (5th Cir.1962)—§ **604.2, n. 4.**

Suburban Sew 'N Sweep, Inc. v. Swiss-Bernina, Inc., 91 F.R.D. 254 (D.C.Ill. 1981)—§ **501.1, n. 88;** § **501.2, n. 51.**

Sudlow v. Warshing, 108 N.Y. 520, 15 N.E. 532 (N.Y.1888)—§ **1005.1, n. 7.**

Suffolk County Dept. of Social Services on Behalf of Michael V. v. James M., 608 N.Y.S.2d 940, 630 N.E.2d 636 (N.Y. 1994)—§ **803(5).1, n. 42.**

Sugarman v. New England Mut. Life Ins. Co., 201 F.Supp. 759 (D.C.N.Y.1962)—§ **803(3).2, n. 22.**

Sugden, People v., 363 N.Y.S.2d 923, 323 N.E.2d 169 (N.Y.1974)—§ **602.1, n. 8;** § **703.1;** § **703.1, n. 5;** § **803(1).1;** § **803(1).1, n. 70;** § **803(3).1;** § **803(3).1, n. 52.**

Sugrue, People v., 103 A.D.2d 785, 477 N.Y.S.2d 425 (N.Y.A.D. 2 Dept.1984)—§ **1102.1, n. 6;** § **1105.1, n. 11.**

Sullivan, People v., 177 A.D.2d 673, 576 N.Y.S.2d 599 (N.Y.A.D. 2 Dept.1991)—§ **402.1, n. 35.**

Sullivan, People v., 160 A.D.2d 161, 559 N.Y.S.2d 881 (N.Y.A.D. 1 Dept.1990)—§ **100.2, n. 7.**

Sullivan v. Smith, 198 A.D.2d 749, 604 N.Y.S.2d 304 (N.Y.A.D. 3 Dept.1993)—§ **501.3, n. 19.**

Summa, People v., 140 Misc.2d 763, 531 N.Y.S.2d 993 (Suffolk Dist.Ct.1988)—§ **702.1, n. 39.**

Summers, People v., 49 A.D.2d 611, 370 N.Y.S.2d 204 (N.Y.A.D. 2 Dept.1975)—§ **801(1).2, n. 12.**

Sutherland, People v., 252 N.Y. 86, 168 N.E. 838 (N.Y.1929)—§ **302.1, n. 15.**

Sutherland by Sutherland v. County of Nassau, 190 A.D.2d 664, 593 N.Y.S.2d 287 (N.Y.A.D. 2 Dept.1993)—§ **1102.1, n. 24.**

Sutter, People v., 162 A.D.2d 644, 556 N.Y.S.2d 959 (N.Y.A.D. 2 Dept.1990)—§ **105.1, n. 18.**

Sutton, United States v., 41 F.3d 1257 (8th Cir.1994)—§ **607.8, n. 55.**

Sutton, United States v., 801 F.2d 1346, 255 U.S.App.D.C. 307 (D.C.Cir.1986)—§ **106.2;** § **106.2, n. 9.**

Swamp, People v., 622 N.Y.S.2d 472, 646 N.E.2d 774 (N.Y.1995)—§ **100.2, n. 4;** § **300.3, n. 26;** § **601.1, n. 1.**

Swan, United States v., 396 F.2d 883 (2nd Cir.1968)—§ **901.3, n. 24.**

Sweeper, People v., 122 Misc.2d 386, 471 N.Y.S.2d 486 (N.Y.Sup.1984)—§ **807.1, n. 4.**

Swoboda v. We Try Harder, Inc., 128 A.D.2d 862, 513 N.Y.S.2d 781 (N.Y.A.D. 2 Dept.1987)—§ **701.1, n. 8.**

Sydney, People v., 195 A.D.2d 763, 600 N.Y.S.2d 358 (N.Y.A.D. 3 Dept.1993)—§ **801(2).1, n. 29.**

Sylla, People v., 154 Misc.2d 112, 584 N.Y.S.2d 985 (N.Y.City Crim.Ct.1992)—§ **803(3).1, n. 51.**

Sylvania Elec. Products, Inc. v. Flanagan, 352 F.2d 1005 (1st Cir.1965)—§ **1008.1, n. 9.**

Sylvestri, Matter of Estate of, 405 N.Y.S.2d 424, 376 N.E.2d 897 (N.Y.1978)—§ **702.1, n. 34;** § **901.3, n. 12.**

Symbol Technologies, Inc. v. Opticon, Inc., 935 F.2d 1569 (Fed.Cir.1991)—§ **705.2, n. 2.**

Szeliga v. General Motors Corp., 728 F.2d 566 (1st Cir.1984)—§ **1105.2, n. 1.**

T

Taft v. New York City Transit Authority, 193 A.D.2d 503, 597 N.Y.S.2d 374 (N.Y.A.D. 1 Dept.1993)—§ **803(1).1, n. 20;** § **803(3).1;** § **803(3).1, n. 28;** § **805.1;** § **805.1, n. 9.**

Taggart v. Alexander's Inc., 90 A.D.2d 542, 455 N.Y.S.2d 117 (N.Y.A.D. 2 Dept. 1982)—§ **402.1, n. 25.**

Tai, People v., 145 Misc.2d 599, 547 N.Y.S.2d 989 (N.Y.Sup.1989)—§ **611.3, n. 32;** § **806.1, n. 17.**

Tait, People v., 234 A.D. 433, 255 N.Y.S. 455 (N.Y.A.D. 1 Dept.1932)—§ **607.5, n. 21, 22.**

Tallo v. United States, 344 F.2d 467 (1st Cir.1965)—§ **514.2, n. 4.**

Tamarin v. Adam Caterers, Inc., 13 F.3d 51 (2nd Cir.1993)—§ **1006.1, n. 12.**

Tameling v. Commissioner, 43 F.2d 814 (2nd Cir.1930)—§ **901.4, n. 8.**

Tancredi v. Mannino, 75 A.D.2d 579, 426 N.Y.S.2d 577 (N.Y.A.D. 2 Dept.1980)—§ **601.2, n. 82.**

Tankleff, People v., 622 N.Y.S.2d 503, 646 N.E.2d 805 (N.Y.1994)—§ **401.1, n. 35.**

Tanner v. United States, 483 U.S. 107, 107 S.Ct. 2739, 97 L.Ed.2d 90 (1987)—§ **606.2;** § **606.2, n. 3, 8.**

Taormina v. Goodman, 63 A.D.2d 1018, 406 N.Y.S.2d 350 (N.Y.A.D. 2 Dept.1978)—§ **702.1, n. 24.**

Tapia, People v., 114 A.D.2d 983, 495 N.Y.S.2d 93 (N.Y.A.D. 2 Dept.1985)—§ **1104.1, n. 30;** § **1108.1, n. 6.**

Tarlowe v. Metropolitan Ski Slopes, Inc., 322 N.Y.S.2d 665, 271 N.E.2d 515 (N.Y. 1971)—§ **705.1;** § **705.1, n. 2.**

Tarsia, People v., 427 N.Y.S.2d 944, 405 N.E.2d 188 (N.Y.1980)—§ **702.1, n. 49.**

Tart v. McGann, 697 F.2d 75 (2nd Cir. 1982)—§ **803(6).2, n. 4.**

Tax Commission, People ex rel. Rubin v., 9 A.D.2d 47, 189 N.Y.S.2d 784 (N.Y.A.D. 3 Dept.1959)—§ **201.1, n. 40.**

TABLE OF CASES

Taylor v. Baltimore & O. R. Co., 344 F.2d 281 (2nd Cir.1965)—§ **803(3).2, n. 37.**

Taylor v. Commercial Bank, 174 N.Y. 181, 66 N.E. 726 (N.Y.1903)—§ **802.2, n. 55.**

Taylor v. Kentucky, 436 U.S. 478, 98 S.Ct. 1930, 56 L.Ed.2d 468 (1978)—§ **302.1, n. 17.**

Taylor v. New York City Transit Authority, 424 N.Y.S.2d 888, 400 N.E.2d 1340 (N.Y. 1979)—§ **1104.1, n. 6, 14.**

Taylor, People v., 206 A.D.2d 904, 616 N.Y.S.2d 116 (N.Y.A.D. 4 Dept.1994)—§ **1101.1, n. 17.**

Taylor, People v., 197 A.D.2d 841, 602 N.Y.S.2d 255 (N.Y.A.D. 4 Dept.1993)—§ **1103.1, n. 10.**

Taylor, People v., 186 A.D.2d 367, 588 N.Y.S.2d 156 (N.Y.A.D. 1 Dept.1992)—§ **1102.1, n. 8.**

Taylor, People v., 586 N.Y.S.2d 545, 598 N.E.2d 693 (N.Y.1992)—§ **803(2).1; § 803(2).1, n. 5.**

Taylor v. Reo Motors, Inc., 275 F.2d 699 (10th Cir.1960)—§ **1108.2; § 1108.2, n. 5, 6.**

Taylor, United States v., 464 F.2d 240 (2nd Cir.1972)—§ **300.3, n. 52, 56.**

Teeter, People v., 62 A.D.2d 1158, 404 N.Y.S.2d 210 (N.Y.A.D. 4 Dept.1978)—§ **802.2, n. 104.**

Teicher, United States v., 987 F.2d 112 (2nd Cir.1993)—§ **610.2, n. 4.**

Teitler, United States v., 802 F.2d 606 (2nd Cir.1986)—§ **105.2, n. 9; § 802.3, n. 64.**

Telford, People v., 134 A.D.2d 632, 521 N.Y.S.2d 523 (N.Y.A.D. 2 Dept.1987)—§ **404.1, n. 75.**

Tellier, United States v., 255 F.2d 441 (2nd Cir.1958)—§ **501.2, n. 20, 22.**

Tennant v. Dudley, 144 N.Y. 504, 39 N.E. 644 (N.Y.1895)—§ **408.1, n. 2.**

Tepper v. Tannenbaum, 83 A.D.2d 541, 441 N.Y.S.2d 470 (N.Y.A.D. 1 Dept.1981)—§ **601.2, n. 81.**

Tepper v. Tannenbaum, 65 A.D.2d 359, 411 N.Y.S.2d 588 (N.Y.A.D. 1 Dept.1978)—§ **601.2, n. 81.**

Terpstra v. Niagara Fire Ins. Co., 308 N.Y.S.2d 378, 256 N.E.2d 536 (N.Y. 1970)—§ **404.1; § 404.1, n. 24, 91.**

Terrasi v. South Atlantic Lines, 226 F.2d 823 (2nd Cir.1955)—§ **803(3).2, n. 38.**

Terrell, United States v., 390 F.Supp. 371 (D.C.N.Y.1975)—§ **801(1).3, n. 8.**

Terry, People v., 83 A.D.2d 491, 445 N.Y.S.2d 340 (N.Y.A.D. 4 Dept.1981)—§ **401.1, n. 29.**

Terry, United States v., 702 F.2d 299 (2nd Cir.1983)—§ **106.2, n. 6, 8; § 608.2, n. 39; § 803(1).2, n. 22; § 1101.2, n. 8.**

Tevaha, People v., 620 N.Y.S.2d 786, 644 N.E.2d 1342 (N.Y.1994)—§ **103.1, n. 19.**

Texas Dept. of Community Affairs v. Burdine, 450 U.S. 248, 101 S.Ct. 1089, 67 L.Ed.2d 207 (1981)—§ **301.8, n. 1.**

Thacher, People ex rel. Judson, 55 N.Y. 525 (1874)—§ **512.1, n. 3.**

Thai, United States v., 29 F.3d 785 (2nd Cir.1994)—§ **601.3, n. 10; § 603.2, n. 3.**

The Dutchess of Kingston's Trial, 20 How.St.Trials 573 (1776)—§ **502.1, n. 1.**

Theodore Zaleski, General Contractor, Inc., People v., 46 Misc.2d 993, 261 N.Y.S.2d 325 (Schenectady Co.Ct.1965)—§ **603.1, n. 8.**

Thevis, United States v., 665 F.2d 616 (5th Cir.1982)—§ **807.1, n. 12.**

The William J. Riddle, 102 F.Supp. 884 (D.C.N.Y.1952)—§ **607.1, n. 3.**

Thiele v. Hickey, 6 A.D.2d 939, 175 N.Y.S.2d 792 (N.Y.A.D.1958)—§ **411.1, n. 3.**

Thom v. Jaymee Fashions, Inc., 35 A.D.2d 946, 316 N.Y.S.2d 595 (N.Y.A.D. 1 Dept. 1970)—§ **614.1, n. 4.**

Thomas v. Central Greyhound Lines, Inc., 6 A.D.2d 649, 180 N.Y.S.2d 461 (N.Y.A.D. 1 Dept.1958)—§ **1105.1, n. 4, 8, 9.**

Thomas, People v., 213 A.D.2d 73, 628 N.Y.S.2d 707 (N.Y.A.D. 2 Dept.1995)—§ **609.1, n. 15.**

Thomas, People v., 184 A.D.2d 1069, 584 N.Y.S.2d 766 (N.Y.A.D. 4 Dept.1992)—§ **606.1, n. 15.**

Thomas, People v., 523 N.Y.S.2d 437, 517 N.E.2d 1323 (N.Y.1987)—§ **407.1, n. 33.**

Thomas, People v., 507 N.Y.S.2d 973, 500 N.E.2d 293 (N.Y.1986)—§ **804(3).1, n. 46.**

Thomas, People v., 91 A.D.2d 857, 458 N.Y.S.2d 383 (N.Y.A.D. 4 Dept.1982)—§ **610.1, n. 3.**

Thomas, People v., 434 N.Y.S.2d 941, 415 N.E.2d 931 (N.Y.1980)—§ **509.1, n. 6, 46, 52.**

Thomas, People v., 412 N.Y.S.2d 845, 385 N.E.2d 584 (N.Y.1978)—§ **509.1, n. 90; § 607.6; § 607.6, n. 21; § 702.1, n. 41; § 802.1, n. 7; § 802.2; § 802.2, n. 5.**

Thomas v. Resort Health Related Facility, 539 F.Supp. 630 (D.C.N.Y.1982)—§ **408.2, n. 1, 11.**

Thomas, United States v., 768 F.2d 611 (5th Cir.1985)—§ **607.5, n. 60.**

Thomas, United States v., 610 F.2d 1166 (3rd Cir.1979)—§ **201.2, n. 22, 23.**

Thomas, United States v., 521 F.2d 76 (8th Cir.1975)—§ **1108.2, n. 1.**

Thompson v. Manhattan Ry. Co., 11 A.D. 182, 42 N.Y.S. 896 (N.Y.A.D. 2 Dept. 1896)—§ **801.1, n. 12.**

Thompson, People v., 186 A.D.2d 768, 589 N.Y.S.2d 68 (N.Y.A.D. 2 Dept.1992)—§ **801.1, n. 28.**

Thompson, People v., 75 A.D.2d 630, 426 N.Y.S.2d 829 (N.Y.A.D. 2 Dept.1980)—§ **402.1, n. 48.**

Thompson, People v., 34 A.D.2d 561, 309 N.Y.S.2d 861 (N.Y.A.D. 2 Dept.1970)—§ **601.1, n. 55.**

TABLE OF CASES

Thompson, People v., 212 N.Y. 249, 106 N.E. 78 (N.Y.1914)—§ **404.1**; § **404.1, n. 80.**

Thompson, United States v., 708 F.2d 1294 (8th Cir.1983)—§ **701.2, n. 8.**

Thompson v. United States, 342 F.2d 137 (5th Cir.1965)—§ **612.2, n. 9, 12.**

Thorn, People v., 156 N.Y. 286, 50 N.E. 947 (N.Y.1898)—§ **1107.1, n. 12, 15.**

Thrower v. Smith, 62 A.D.2d 907, 406 N.Y.S.2d 513 (N.Y.A.D. 2 Dept.1978)—§ **106.1, n. 13;** § **802.2, n. 2.**

Tibbetts v. Sternberg, 66 Barb. (N.Y.) 201 (1870)—§ **612.1, n. 16.**

Tice, People v., 131 N.Y. 651, 30 N.E. 494 (N.Y.1892)—§ **509.1, n. 40;** § **611.3, n. 27.**

Tillem, United States v., 906 F.2d 814 (2nd Cir.1990)—§ **608.2, n. 35.**

Tillman v. Lincoln Warehouse Corp., 72 A.D.2d 40, 423 N.Y.S.2d 151 (N.Y.A.D. 1 Dept.1979)—§ **803(7).1;** § **803(7).1, n. 7;** § **901.8, n. 1.**

Tinney v. Neilson's Flowers Inc., 61 Misc.2d 717, 305 N.Y.S.2d 713 (N.Y.Sup.1969)—§ **502.1, n. 49.**

Tipton, United States v., 964 F.2d 650 (7th Cir.1992)—§ **901.2;** § **901.2, n. 12.**

Tissois, People v., 531 N.Y.S.2d 228, 526 N.E.2d 1086 (N.Y.1988)—§ **104.1, n. 35;** § **505.1;** § **505.1, n. 12;** § **506.1, n. 4.**

T.J. Gulf, Inc. v. New York State Tax Com'n, 124 A.D.2d 314, 508 N.Y.S.2d 97 (N.Y.A.D. 3 Dept.1986)—§ **301.5, n. 41.**

Toho Bussan Kaisha, Ltd. v. American Pres. Lines, Ltd., 265 F.2d 418 (2nd Cir.1959)—§ **1001.1, n. 3;** § **1002.1, n. 12.**

Toll v. State, 32 A.D.2d 47, 299 N.Y.S.2d 589 (N.Y.A.D. 3 Dept.1969)—§ **803(3).1;** § **803(3).1, n. 19, 22, 35;** § **805.1, n. 2, 11;** § **805.2, n. 2.**

Tomaiolo, United States v., 249 F.2d 683 (2nd Cir.1957)—§ **402.2, n. 14;** § **514.2, n. 4.**

Tomanelli v. Lizda Realty, Ltd., 174 A.D.2d 889, 571 N.Y.S.2d 171 (N.Y.A.D. 3 Dept. 1991)—§ **803(3).1, n. 6.**

Tomaschoff v. Stapleton Drug Co., 263 A.D. 728, 30 N.Y.S.2d 724 (N.Y.A.D. 2 Dept. 1941)—§ **100.2, n. 6.**

Tome v. United States, ___ U.S. ___, 115 S.Ct. 696, 130 L.Ed.2d 574 (1995)—§ **607.5;** § **607.5, n. 63;** § **801(1).3;** § **801(1).3, n. 20.**

Tome, United States v., 3 F.3d 342 (10th Cir.1993)—§ **607.5, n. 63;** § **801(1).3, n. 20.**

Tompkins v. Fonda Glove Lining Co., 188 N.Y. 261, 80 N.E. 933 (N.Y.1907)—§ **804(3).1, n. 28.**

Tompkins v. R. B. D. Land Exchange, Inc., 89 A.D.2d 698, 453 N.Y.S.2d 817 (N.Y.A.D. 3 Dept.1982)—§ **103.1, n. 7.**

Toney, United States v., 615 F.2d 277 (5th Cir.1980)—§ **609.2, n. 11.**

Tooley v. Bacon, 70 N.Y. 34 (1877)—§ **103.1, n. 18.**

Toomey v. Farley, 156 N.Y.S.2d 840, 138 N.E.2d 221 (N.Y.1956)—§ **610.1, n. 5.**

Topel v. Long Island Jewish Medical Center, 446 N.Y.S.2d 932, 431 N.E.2d 293 (N.Y.1981)—§ **702.1, n. 76.**

Torelli v. City of New York, 176 A.D.2d 119, 574 N.Y.S.2d 5 (N.Y.A.D. 1 Dept.1991)—§ **704.1, n. 12.**

Torem v. 564 Cent. Ave. Rest., Inc., 133 A.D.2d 25, 518 N.Y.S.2d 620 (N.Y.A.D. 1 Dept.1987)—§ **300.4, n. 10, 12.**

Torre, People v., 399 N.Y.S.2d 203, 369 N.E.2d 759 (N.Y.1977)—§ **106.1, n. 8.**

Torres, People v., 213 A.D.2d 797, 623 N.Y.S.2d 645 (N.Y.A.D. 3 Dept.1995)—§ **803(3).1, n. 46.**

Torres, People v., 184 A.D.2d 605, 584 N.Y.S.2d 631 (N.Y.A.D. 2 Dept.1992)—§ **801(2).1, n. 11.**

Torres, People v., 175 A.D.2d 635, 572 N.Y.S.2d 269 (N.Y.A.D. 4 Dept.1991)—§ **104.1, n. 15.**

Torres, People v., 118 A.D.2d 821, 500 N.Y.S.2d 178 (N.Y.A.D. 2 Dept.1986)—§ **615.1, n. 6;** § **1001.1, n. 34;** § **1002.1, n. 18.**

Torres, People v., 128 Misc.2d 129, 488 N.Y.S.2d 358 (N.Y.Sup.1985)—§ **702.1, n. 61.**

Torres, People v., 72 A.D.2d 754, 421 N.Y.S.2d 275 (N.Y.A.D. 2 Dept.1979)—§ **610.1, n. 7.**

Torres, United States v., 901 F.2d 205 (2nd Cir.1990)—§ **300.4, n. 71;** § **803(1).2;** § **803(1).2, n. 47.**

Torres, United States v., 845 F.2d 1165 (2nd Cir.1988)—§ **401.2, n. 19.**

Torres, United States v., 519 F.2d 723 (2nd Cir.1975)—§ **802.3, n. 14.**

Tortorice, People v., 142 A.D.2d 916, 531 N.Y.S.2d 414 (N.Y.A.D. 3 Dept.1988)—§ **1104.1, n. 5.**

Tosto v. Marra Bros., 275 A.D. 686, 86 N.Y.S.2d 549 (N.Y.A.D. 2 Dept.1949)—§ **300.3, n. 36.**

Townes, People v., 104 A.D.2d 1057, 480 N.Y.S.2d 962 (N.Y.A.D. 2 Dept.1984)—§ **201.1, n. 55.**

Toys R Us, Inc. v. Canarsie Kiddie Shop, Inc., 559 F.Supp. 1189 (D.C.N.Y.1983)—§ **804(5).2, n. 37.**

Tracy, United States v., 36 F.3d 187 (1st Cir.1994)—§ **609.2, n. 12.**

Tracy, United States v., 12 F.3d 1186 (2nd Cir.1993)—§ **104.2;** § **104.2, n. 8;** § **105.2, n. 3, 5;** § **802.3;** § **802.3, n. 51.**

Trammel v. United States, 445 U.S. 40, 100 S.Ct. 906, 63 L.Ed.2d 186 (1980)—§ **500.1, n. 2;** § **500.2, n. 3;** § **503.5;** § **503.5, n. 1;** § **504.2, n. 2;** § **601.1, n. 20.**

Trebor Sportswear Co., Inc. v. The Limited Stores, Inc., 865 F.2d 506 (2nd Cir. 1989)—§ **408.2;** § **408.2, n. 13.**

TABLE OF CASES

Tremaine, Matter of Estate of, 156 A.D.2d 862, 549 N.Y.S.2d 857 (N.Y.A.D. 3 Dept. 1989)—§ **601.2, n. 29, 53.**

Trimarchi, People v., 231 N.Y. 263, 131 N.E. 910 (N.Y.1921)—§ **402.1;** § **402.1, n. 56.**

Trimarco v. Klein, 451 N.Y.S.2d 52, 436 N.E.2d 502 (N.Y.1982)—§ **406.1;** § **406.1, n. 6, 37.**

Tromblee v. North American Acc. Ins. Co., 173 A.D. 174, 158 N.Y.S. 1014 (N.Y.A.D. 3 Dept.1916)—§ **803(1).1, n. 43.**

Trombley v. Seligman, 191 N.Y. 400, 84 N.E. 280 (N.Y.1908)—§ **1001.1, n. 28.**

Tropea v. Shell Oil Co., 307 F.2d 757 (2nd Cir.1962)—§ **406.2, n. 18.**

Trowbridge, People v., 305 N.Y. 471, 113 N.E.2d 841 (N.Y.1953)—§ **607.5, n. 16;** § **801(2).1;** § **801(2).1, n. 1.**

Trustees of Union College of Town of Schenectady v. City of New York, 65 A.D. 553, 73 N.Y.S. 51 (N.Y.A.D. 2 Dept. 1901)—§ **201.1, n. 38;** § **803(5).1, n. 32.**

Trusts & Guarantee Co. v. Barnhardt, 270 N.Y. 350, 1 N.E.2d 459 (N.Y.1936)—§ **301.7, n. 4.**

Tubular Products, Inc. v. Jacobson, 138 A.D.2d 371, 525 N.Y.S.2d 655 (N.Y.A.D. 2 Dept.1988)—§ **1107.1, n. 11.**

Tucker v. Salomon Elimelech, 184 A.D.2d 636, 584 N.Y.S.2d 895 (N.Y.A.D. 2 Dept. 1992)—§ **703.1, n. 11.**

Tucker, People v., 153 A.D.2d 164, 550 N.Y.S.2d 1 (N.Y.A.D. 1 Dept.1990)—§ **1108.1, n. 7.**

Tucker, United States v., 380 F.2d 206 (2nd Cir.1967)—§ **510.2, n. 2.**

Tumerman, People v., 133 A.D.2d 714, 519 N.Y.S.2d 880 (N.Y.A.D. 2 Dept.1987)—§ **804(1).1, n. 46.**

Tunnell, United States v., 667 F.2d 1182 (5th Cir.1982)—§ **611.5, n. 13.**

Tunstall, People v., 479 N.Y.S.2d 192, 468 N.E.2d 30 (N.Y.1984)—§ **103.1, n. 41;** § **601.1, n. 67.**

Turbide, United States v., 558 F.2d 1053 (2nd Cir.1977)—§ **510.2;** § **510.2, n. 6.**

Turkel v. American Ry. Express Co., 188 N.Y.S. 207 (N.Y.Sup.1921)—§ **602.1, n. 3.**

Turner v. Sunshine Taxi Corp., 269 A.D. 997, 58 N.Y.S.2d 422 (N.Y.A.D.1945)—§ **804(1).1, n. 20.**

Turner Press, Inc. v. Gould, 76 A.D.2d 906, 429 N.Y.S.2d 239 (N.Y.A.D. 2 Dept. 1980)—§ **401.1, n. 34.**

Tutino, United States v., 883 F.2d 1125 (2nd Cir.1989)—§ **105.2, n. 6, 9, 11.**

Tuzzio, People v., 201 A.D.2d 595, 608 N.Y.S.2d 226 (N.Y.A.D. 2 Dept.1994)—§ **804(1).1, n. 47.**

Tveraas v. Coffey, 818 F.Supp. 75 (D.Vt. 1993)—§ **803(5).2, n. 34.**

20th Century Wear, Inc. v. Sanmark–Stardust Inc., 747 F.2d 81 (2nd Cir.1984)—§ **612.2, n. 5, 6, 10, 13.**

Two Stables, Inc. v. Cornelius, 145 A.D.2d 685, 534 N.Y.S.2d 827 (N.Y.A.D. 3 Dept. 1988)—§ **407.1, n. 8.**

2641 Concourse Co. v. City University of New York, 135 Misc.2d 464, 515 N.Y.S.2d 994 (N.Y.Ct.Cl.1987)—§ **804.1, n. 19.**

Tyrrell, People v., 101 A.D.2d 946, 475 N.Y.S.2d 937 (N.Y.A.D. 3 Dept.1984)—§ **611.2, n. 17.**

U

Udeagu, United States v., 110 F.R.D. 172 (E.D.N.Y.1986)—§ **410.2, n. 9.**

Union Bank of Brooklyn v. Deshel, 139 A.D. 217, 123 N.Y.S. 585 (N.Y.A.D. 2 Dept. 1910)—§ **408.1, n. 6.**

Unique Concepts, Inc. v. Brown, 659 F.Supp. 1008 (S.D.N.Y.1987)—§ **706.2, n. 7.**

United Air Lines, Inc. v. Austin Travel Corp., 867 F.2d 737 (2nd Cir.1989)—§ **803(5).2, n. 30.**

United Shoe Machinery Corp., United States v., 89 F.Supp. 357 (D.C.Mass. 1950)—§ **501.1, n. 3;** § **501.2;** § **501.2, n. 1.**

United States v. _____ (see opposing party)

United States, In re, 565 F.2d 19 (2nd Cir. 1977)—§ **510.2, n. 11.**

United States ex rel. v. _____ (see opposing party and relator)

United States Football League v. National Football League, 842 F.2d 1335 (2nd Cir. 1988)—§ **106.2, n. 8;** § **401.2, n. 4;** § **406.2;** § **406.2, n. 5, 6;** § **805.2, n. 4.**

United States Homes, Inc. v. Yates, 174 N.W.2d 402 (Iowa 1970)—§ **1001.1, n. 7.**

United States Vinegar Co. v. Schlegel, 143 N.Y. 537, 38 N.E. 729 (N.Y.1894)—§ **103.1, n. 36.**

Universal Carloading & Distribution Co., Inc. v. Penn Cent. Transp. Co., 101 A.D.2d 61, 474 N.Y.S.2d 502 (N.Y.A.D. 1 Dept.1984)—§ **408.1, n. 1.**

Universal Grain Corp. v. Lamport & Holt Line, 54 N.Y.S.2d 53 (N.Y.Sup.1945)—§ **1001.1, n. 2, 15.**

University of Pennsylvania v. E.E.O.C., 493 U.S. 182, 110 S.Ct. 577, 107 L.Ed.2d 571 (1990)—§ **500.2, n. 4.**

Upjohn Co. v. United States, 449 U.S. 383, 101 S.Ct. 677, 66 L.Ed.2d 584 (1981)—§ **501.1, n. 20, 65;** § **501.2;** § **501.2, n. 4, 5, 11, 29, 31, 32, 34;** § **501.3, n. 42.**

Upshaw, People v., 138 A.D.2d 761, 526 N.Y.S.2d 575 (N.Y.A.D. 2 Dept.1988)—§ **802.2, n. 68.**

Uss v. Town of Oyster Bay, 376 N.Y.S.2d 449, 339 N.E.2d 147 (N.Y.1975)—§ **1101.1, n. 2;** § **1105.1, n. 2, 10, 13, 14;** § **1108.1, n. 1.**

TABLE OF CASES

V

Vadney v. United Traction Co., 193 A.D. 329, 183 N.Y.S. 926 (N.Y.A.D. 3 Dept. 1920)—§ **201.1, n. 25.**

Vagelos v. Robinson, 37 A.D.2d 544, 322 N.Y.S.2d 384 (N.Y.A.D. 1 Dept.1971)— § **203.1, n. 11.**

Vails, People v., 401 N.Y.S.2d 479, 372 N.E.2d 320 (N.Y.1977)—§ **404.1; § 404.1, n. 63.**

Valdes, United States v., 417 F.2d 335 (2nd Cir.1969)—§ **1102.2, n. 3; § 1104.2, n. 1.**

Valdivia, People v., 108 A.D.2d 885, 485 N.Y.S.2d 580 (N.Y.A.D. 2 Dept.1985)— § **610.1, n. 3.**

Valencia, United States v., 826 F.2d 169 (2nd Cir.1987)—§ **103.2, n. 22; § 802.3; § 802.3, n. 22.**

Valente v. Pepsico, Inc., 68 F.R.D. 361 (D.C.Del.1975)—§ **501.2, n. 26, 37.**

Valenti v. Mesinger, 175 A.D. 398, 162 N.Y.S. 30 (N.Y.A.D. 1 Dept.1916)— § **607.4, n. 12.**

Valentine, United States v., 637 F.Supp. 196 (S.D.N.Y.1986)—§ **803(1).2, n. 26.**

Vanderbilt (Rosner-Hickey), Matter of, 453 N.Y.S.2d 662, 439 N.E.2d 378 (N.Y. 1982)—§ **501.1, n. 17, 24, 25, 50, 83; § 503.3; § 503.3, n. 23, 27.**

Vanderbosch, United States v., 610 F.2d 95 (2nd Cir.1979)—§ **609.2, n. 1, 4.**

Vander Wel v. Palazzo, 155 A.D.2d 387, 548 N.Y.S.2d 14 (N.Y.A.D. 1 Dept.1989)— § **1104.1, n. 21.**

Van Gaasbeck, People v., 189 N.Y. 408, 82 N.E. 718 (N.Y.1907)—§ **402.1, n. 41.**

Van Meerbeke, United States v., 548 F.2d 415 (2nd Cir.1976)—§ **601.1, n. 58; § 601.3, n. 16.**

Van Riper v. United States, 13 F.2d 961 (2nd Cir.1926)—§ **901.5, n. 15; § 901.6; § 901.6, n. 7.**

Van Valkenburgh's Will, In re, 164 Misc. 295, 298 N.Y.S. 819 (N.Y.Sur.1937)— § **601.2, n. 12.**

Van Volkenburgh's Adm'x, In re, 254 N.Y. 139, 172 N.E. 269 (N.Y.1930)—§ **601.2, n. 65, 70, 83.**

Vanwort, United States v., 887 F.2d 375 (2nd Cir.1989)—§ **802.3, n. 62.**

Van Wycklyn v. City of Brooklyn (State Report Title: Van Wycklen v. City of Brooklyn), 118 N.Y. 424, 24 N.E. 179 (N.Y.1890)—§ **704.1, n. 5, 10.**

Varcoe v. Lee, 180 Cal. 338, 181 P. 223 (Cal.1919)—§ **201.1, n. 65.**

Varela v. Previti, 64 A.D.2d 560, 406 N.Y.S.2d 830 (N.Y.A.D. 1 Dept.1978)— § **607.8, n. 26, 27.**

Vargas, People v., 630 N.Y.S.2d 973, 654 N.E.2d 1221 (N.Y.1995)—§ **509.1, n. 54.**

Varsos, People v., 182 A.D.2d 508, 582 N.Y.S.2d 193 (N.Y.A.D. 1 Dept.1992)— § **804(1).1, n. 43.**

Veal v. New York City Transit Authority, 148 A.D.2d 443, 538 N.Y.S.2d 594 (N.Y.A.D. 2 Dept.1989)—§ **611.1, n. 10.**

Veal, People v., 158 A.D.2d 633, 551 N.Y.S.2d 602 (N.Y.A.D. 2 Dept.1990)— § **1102.1, n. 8.**

Vega v. Jacobs, 84 A.D.2d 813, 444 N.Y.S.2d 132 (N.Y.A.D. 2 Dept.1981)—§ **405.1, n. 8, 12.**

Vega, United States v., 589 F.2d 1147 (2nd Cir.1978)—§ **614.2, n. 7.**

Vegas, United States v., 27 F.3d 773 (2nd Cir.1994)—§ **806.1, n. 18.**

Veliz v. Crown Lift Trucks, 714 F.Supp. 49 (E.D.N.Y.1989)—§ **1104.2, n. 20; § 1105.1, n. 6; § 1105.2, n. 1, 3.**

Ventimiglia, People v., 438 N.Y.S.2d 261, 420 N.E.2d 59 (N.Y.1981)—§ **103.1, n. 38; § 404.1; § 404.1, n. 10, 67; § 404.2, n. 23.**

Ventura, People v., 360 N.Y.S.2d 419, 318 N.E.2d 609 (N.Y.1974)—§ **611.1, n. 10.**

Ventura v. Ventura, 53 Misc.2d 881, 280 N.Y.S.2d 5 (N.Y.Sup.1967)—§ **301.4, n. 20.**

Veras v. Truth Verification Corp., 87 A.D.2d 381, 451 N.Y.S.2d 761 (N.Y.A.D. 1 Dept.1982)—§ **801.1, n. 39.**

Vereen, People v., 410 N.Y.S.2d 288, 382 N.E.2d 1151 (N.Y.1978)—§ **509.1, n. 35.**

Vermeule v. City of Corning, 186 A.D. 206, 174 N.Y.S. 220 (N.Y.A.D. 4 Dept.1919)— § **802.1, n. 12.**

Vermont Com'r of Banking and Ins. v. Welbilt Corp., 133 A.D.2d 396, 519 N.Y.S.2d 390 (N.Y.A.D. 2 Dept.1987)—§ **803(3).1, n. 4.**

Vernet v. Gilbert, 90 A.D.2d 846, 456 N.Y.S.2d 93 (N.Y.A.D. 2 Dept.1982)— § **501.3, n. 19, 22.**

Vernon v. New York City Health and Hospitals Corp., 167 A.D.2d 252, 561 N.Y.S.2d 751 (N.Y.A.D. 1 Dept.1990)—§ **609.1, n. 10, 11.**

Vest, United States v., 842 F.2d 1319 (1st Cir.1988)—§ **607.5, n. 62; § 801(1).3, n. 19.**

Viacom Intern., Inc. v. Midtown Realty Co., 193 A.D.2d 45, 602 N.Y.S.2d 326 (N.Y.A.D. 1 Dept.1993)—§ **702.1, n. 22.**

Victor, Matter of, 422 F.Supp. 475 (D.C.N.Y.1976)—§ **501.1, n. 88; § 501.2, n. 51.**

Victor, People v., 477 N.Y.S.2d 97, 465 N.E.2d 817 (N.Y.1984)—§ **300.4, n. 51.**

Victoria, United States v., 837 F.2d 50 (2nd Cir.1988)—§ **614.2, n. 3, 6.**

Victor R., People v., 161 Misc.2d 212, 613 N.Y.S.2d 567 (N.Y.Sup.1994)— § **803(1).1, n. 17, 24.**

Vidal, People v., 309 N.Y.S.2d 336, 257 N.E.2d 886 (N.Y.1970)—§ **103.1, n. 20, 21, 25.**

Viemeister v. White, 179 N.Y. 235, 72 N.E. 97 (N.Y.1904)—§ **202.1; § 202.1, n. 4, 13.**

TABLE OF CASES

Vigilant Ins. Co. v. Rippner Elec. Const. Corp., 196 A.D.2d 494, 601 N.Y.S.2d 137 (N.Y.A.D. 2 Dept.1993)—§ **704.1, n. 2.**

Villa v. Vetuskey, 50 A.D.2d 1093, 376 N.Y.S.2d 359 (N.Y.A.D. 4 Dept.1975)— § **106.1, n. 18.**

Village Bd. of Village of Pleasantville v. Rattner, 130 A.D.2d 654, 515 N.Y.S.2d 585 (N.Y.A.D. 2 Dept.1987)—§ **501.1, n. 84.**

Village of (see name of village)

Vincent, People v., 34 A.D.2d 705, 309 N.Y.S.2d 690 (N.Y.A.D. 3 Dept.1970)— § **607.5, n. 8;** § **611.2, n. 8.**

Vincent v. Thompson, 50 A.D.2d 211, 377 N.Y.S.2d 118 (N.Y.A.D. 2 Dept.1975)— § **607.8, n. 5;** § **801(1).2;** § **801(1).2, n. 6.**

Vingelli v. United States, Drug Enforcement Agency, 992 F.2d 449 (2nd Cir. 1993)—§ **501.2, n. 14.**

Vinson, People v., 104 Misc.2d 664, 428 N.Y.S.2d 832 (N.Y.Sup.1980)—§ **702.1, n. 48.**

Viola, United States v., 35 F.3d 37 (2nd Cir.1994)—§ **103.2, n. 4.**

Viserto, United States v., 596 F.2d 531 (2nd Cir.1979)—§ **803(5).2, n. 48.**

Vispetto v. Bassuk, 41 A.D.2d 958, 343 N.Y.S.2d 988 (N.Y.A.D. 2 Dept.1973)— § **704.1, n. 4, 5.**

Vita v. Heller, 97 A.D.2d 464, 467 N.Y.S.2d 652 (N.Y.A.D. 2 Dept.1983)—§ **301.5, n. 41.**

Vivero, United States v., 413 F.2d 971 (2nd Cir.1969)—§ **611.5, n. 3.**

Vogelstein, People ex rel. v. Warden of County Jail of New York County, 150 Misc. 714, 270 N.Y.S. 362 (N.Y.Sup. 1934)—§ **500.1, n. 1;** § **501.1, n. 2, 32, 71.**

von Bulow, In re, 828 F.2d 94 (2nd Cir. 1987)—§ **501.2, n. 44, 46, 53.**

von Bulow by Auersperg v. von Bulow, 811 F.2d 136 (2nd Cir.1987)—§ **508.1;** § **508.1, n. 11;** § **508.2;** § **508.2, n. 3.**

Von Sachs v. Kretz, 72 N.Y. 548, 10 Hun. 95 (1878)—§ **1006.1, n. 3.**

W

Wachowicz, People v., 292 N.Y.S.2d 867, 239 N.E.2d 620 (N.Y.1968)—§ **401.1, n. 8.**

Wachs v. Commercial Travelers Mut. Acc. Ass'n of America, 283 A.D. 29, 125 N.Y.S.2d 857 (N.Y.A.D. 1 Dept.1953)— § **607.8, n. 18, 31.**

Wade, United States v., 388 U.S. 218, 87 S.Ct. 1926, 18 L.Ed.2d 1149 (1967)— § **509.1, n. 31;** § **801(2).2, n. 3.**

Wagner v. Tucker, 517 F.Supp. 1248 (D.C.N.Y.1981)—§ **601.3, n. 2.**

Walder v. United States, 347 U.S. 62, 74 S.Ct. 354, 98 L.Ed. 503 (1954)—§ **607.3, n. 14.**

Wali, United States v., 860 F.2d 588 (3rd Cir.1988)—§ **806.1, n. 18.**

Walker v. North Dakota Eye Clinic, Ltd., 415 F.Supp. 891 (D.C.N.D.1976)— § **803(6).2, n. 4.**

Walker, People v., 611 N.Y.S.2d 118, 633 N.E.2d 472 (N.Y.1994)—§ **607.2;** § **607.2, n. 10;** § **607.5, n. 17;** § **608.2, n. 6, 7, 13;** § **609.1;** § **609.1, n. 31, 39.**

Walker, People v., 116 A.D.2d 948, 498 N.Y.S.2d 521 (N.Y.A.D. 3 Dept.1986)— § **607.7, n. 17.**

Walker, People v., 110 A.D.2d 730, 487 N.Y.S.2d 613 (N.Y.A.D. 2 Dept.1985)— § **607.8, n. 11.**

Walker, People v., 198 N.Y. 329, 91 N.E. 806 (N.Y.1910)—§ **104.1, n. 1;** § **201.1, n. 62;** § **300.3, n. 39.**

Walker, United States v., 613 F.2d 1349 (5th Cir.1980)—§ **611.5, n. 21.**

Wallace v. Wallace, 216 N.Y. 28, 109 N.E. 872 (N.Y.1915)—§ **501.1, n. 57.**

Wallington Apartments, People ex rel. v. Miller, 288 N.Y. 31, 41 N.E.2d 445 (N.Y. 1942)—§ **301.4, n. 6;** § **301.5, n. 22.**

Walsh v. Staten Island Obstetrics & Gynecology Associates, P.C., 193 A.D.2d 672, 598 N.Y.S.2d 17 (N.Y.A.D. 2 Dept. 1993)—§ **702.1, n. 85.**

Walstatter, People v., 440 N.Y.S.2d 615, 423 N.E.2d 38 (N.Y.1981)—§ **1105.1, n. 14.**

Walters, People ex rel. McGee v., 476 N.Y.S.2d 803, 465 N.E.2d 342 (N.Y. 1984)—§ **803(3).1;** § **803(3).1, n. 40.**

Walton v. Stafford, 14 A.D. 310, 43 N.Y.S. 1049 (N.Y.A.D. 1 Dept.1897)—§ **201.1, n. 16, 20, 47, 48, 49.**

Wammock v. Celotex Corp., 793 F.2d 1518 (11th Cir.1986)—§ **607.8, n. 51, 53, 54.**

Wank v. Ambrosino, 307 N.Y. 321, 121 N.E.2d 246 (N.Y.1954)—§ **300.4, n. 14.**

Wanoskia, United States v., 800 F.2d 235 (10th Cir.1986)—§ **1105.2, n. 3.**

Ward v. Kovacs, 55 A.D.2d 391, 390 N.Y.S.2d 931 (N.Y.A.D. 2 Dept.1977)— § **601.2, n. 81.**

Ward v. New York Life Ins. Co., 225 N.Y. 314, 122 N.E. 207 (N.Y.1919)—§ **300.4, n. 6;** § **601.2;** § **601.2, n. 41.**

Ward v. Succession of Freeman, 854 F.2d 780 (5th Cir.1988)—§ **501.2, n. 37, 44.**

Ward, United States v., 173 F.2d 628 (2nd Cir.1949)—§ **901.4, n. 8.**

Warden of County Jail of New York County, People ex rel. Vogelstein v., 150 Misc. 714, 270 N.Y.S. 362 (N.Y.Sup.1934)— § **500.1, n. 1;** § **501.1, n. 2, 32, 71.**

W., Arlene v. Robert D., 36 A.D.2d 455, 324 N.Y.S.2d 333 (N.Y.A.D. 4 Dept.1971)— § **611.2, n. 19.**

Warner Bros., Inc. v. Dae Rim Trading, Inc., 677 F.Supp. 740 (S.D.N.Y.1988)— § **404.2, n. 21, 40.**

TABLE OF CASES

Warren v. Applebaum, 526 F.Supp. 586 (D.C.N.Y.1981)—§ **803(5).2, n. 45.**

Warth v. Kastriner, 114 A.D. 766, 100 N.Y.S. 279 (N.Y.A.D. 2 Dept.1906)—§ **601.2, n. 55.**

Washington v. Armstrong World Industries, Inc., 839 F.2d 1121 (5th Cir.1988)—§ **703.2, n. 3.**

Washington v. Bank for Savings in City of New York, 171 N.Y. 166, 63 N.E. 831 (N.Y.1902)—§ **804(4).1, n. 2, 20.**

Washington v. Long Island R. Co., 13 A.D.2d 710, 214 N.Y.S.2d 115 (N.Y.A.D. 2 Dept.1961)—§ **1105.1, n. 2.**

Washington, People v., 528 N.Y.S.2d 531, 523 N.E.2d 818 (N.Y.1988)—§ **611.1, n. 10.**

Washington, People v., 96 A.D.2d 996, 467 N.Y.S.2d 87 (N.Y.A.D. 3 Dept.1983)—§ **1101.1, n. 14.**

Washington v. Texas, 388 U.S. 14, 87 S.Ct. 1920, 18 L.Ed.2d 1019 (1967)—§ **601.1, n. 14.**

Washington, United States v., 592 F.2d 680 (2nd Cir.1979)—§ **105.2, n. 3.**

Washington–Baltimore Newspaper Guild, Local 35 v. Washington Star Co., 543 F.Supp. 906 (D.C.D.C.1982)—§ **501.2, n. 38.**

Waterman v. Whitney, 11 N.Y. 157 (1854)—§ **803(1).1, n. 46.**

Watford, People v., 146 A.D.2d 590, 536 N.Y.S.2d 835 (N.Y.A.D. 2 Dept.1989)—§ **607.8, n. 29; § 801(1).2, n. 13.**

Watkins, People v., 63 A.D.2d 1033, 406 N.Y.S.2d 343 (N.Y.A.D. 2 Dept.1978)—§ **503.3, n. 11.**

Watkins, People v., 89 Misc.2d 870, 393 N.Y.S.2d 283 (N.Y.Sup.1977)—§ **503.3, n. 29.**

Watson, People v., 100 A.D.2d 452, 474 N.Y.S.2d 978 (N.Y.A.D. 2 Dept.1984)—§ **803(1).1, n. 11.**

Watson, People v., 85 A.D.2d 920, 446 N.Y.S.2d 775 (N.Y.A.D. 4 Dept.1981)—§ **601.1, n. 59; § 607.7, n. 12.**

Watson v. State, 53 A.D.2d 798, 385 N.Y.S.2d 170 (N.Y.A.D. 3 Dept.1976)—§ **611.2, n. 3.**

Watson, United States v., 669 F.2d 1374 (11th Cir.1982)—§ **608.1, n. 19, 20, 22, 23.**

Watts, People v., 456 N.Y.S.2d 677, 442 N.E.2d 1188 (N.Y.1982)—§ **300.4, n. 52, 55.**

Watts v. Swiss Bank Corp., 317 N.Y.S.2d 315, 265 N.E.2d 739 (N.Y.1970)—§ **203.1, n. 7.**

Wausau Sulphate Fibre Co. v. Commissioner of Internal Revenue, 61 F.2d 879 (7th Cir.1932)—§ **901.7, n. 18.**

Way, People v., 465 N.Y.S.2d 853, 452 N.E.2d 1181 (N.Y.1983)—§ **300.3, n. 34.**

Weaver's Estate, In re, 58 Misc.2d 901, 297 N.Y.S.2d 201 (N.Y.Sur.1969)—§ **514.1, n. 1.**

Webb, People v., 195 A.D.2d 614, 601 N.Y.S.2d 127 (N.Y.A.D. 2 Dept.1993)—§ **509.1, n. 47.**

Webb, People v., 157 Misc.2d 474, 597 N.Y.S.2d 565 (St. Lawrence Co.Ct. 1993)—§ **604.1, n. 8.**

Webster, People v., 139 N.Y. 73, 34 N.E. 730 (N.Y.1893)—§ **607.6, n. 3; § 607.7, n. 12; § 608.2, n. 3; § 1102.1, n. 1; § 1104.1, n. 6.**

Webster, United States v., 734 F.2d 1191 (7th Cir.1984)—§ **607.4, n. 47, 48.**

Weichert, United States v., 783 F.2d 23 (2nd Cir.1986)—§ **103.2, n. 23; § 608.2, n. 41.**

Weil v. Investment/Indicators, Research and Management, Inc., 647 F.2d 18 (9th Cir. 1981)—§ **501.2, n. 37.**

Weinberg, Matter of Estate of, 133 Misc.2d 950, 509 N.Y.S.2d 240 (N.Y.Sur.1986)—§ **501.1, n. 6, 52.**

Weinberg, People v., 183 A.D.2d 932, 586 N.Y.S.2d 132 (N.Y.A.D. 2 Dept.1992)—§ **803(3).1, n. 14; § 1006.1; § 1006.1, n. 6.**

Weinberger, People v., 239 N.Y. 307, 146 N.E. 434 (N.Y.1925)—§ **803(2).1; § 803(2).1, n. 3.**

Weiner v. Mager & Throne, 167 Misc. 338, 3 N.Y.S.2d 918 (N.Y.Mun.Ct.1938)—§ **902.1, n. 6.**

Weinstein v. Daman, 132 A.D.2d 547, 517 N.Y.S.2d 278 (N.Y.A.D. 2 Dept.1987)—§ **1105.1, n. 11.**

Weinstein, People v., 156 Misc.2d 34, 591 N.Y.S.2d 715 (N.Y.Sup.1992)—§ **702.1, n. 54.**

Weisman, United States v., 624 F.2d 1118 (2nd Cir.1980)—§ **106.2, n. 8.**

Weiss v. Chrysler Motors Corp., 515 F.2d 449 (2nd Cir.1975)—§ **611.5, n. 3.**

Weiss, People v., 19 A.D.2d 900, 244 N.Y.S.2d 914 (N.Y.A.D. 2 Dept.1963)—§ **201.1, n. 31.**

Weiss, United States v., 930 F.2d 185 (2nd Cir.1991)—§ **103.2, n. 2; § 607.6, n. 36.**

Welch, People v., 16 A.D.2d 554, 229 N.Y.S.2d 909 (N.Y.A.D. 4 Dept.1962)—§ **607.4, n. 26.**

Wellington Associates v. Vandee Enterprises Corp., 75 Misc.2d 330, 347 N.Y.S.2d 788 (N.Y.City Civ.Ct.1973)—§ **1102.1, n. 11.**

Wellisch v. John Hancock Mut. Life Ins. Co., 293 N.Y. 178, 56 N.E.2d 540 (N.Y. 1944)—§ **301.4, n. 9; § 301.5, n. 25, 27.**

Wells, United States v., 446 F.2d 2 (2nd Cir.1971)—§ **504.2, n. 2.**

Wells' Will, In re, 129 Misc. 447, 221 N.Y.S. 714 (N.Y.Sur.1927)—§ **201.1, n. 12.**

Wendel's Estate, In re, 146 Misc. 260, 262 N.Y.S. 41 (N.Y.Sur.1933)—§ **1102.1, n. 10.**

Wepy by Wepy v. Shen, 175 A.D.2d 124, 571 N.Y.S.2d 817 (N.Y.A.D. 2 Dept.1991)—§ **502.1, n. 43.**

TABLE OF CASES

Werlich, In re, 230 N.Y. 516, 130 N.E. 632 (N.Y.1921)—§ **301.4, n. 19.**

Werner v. Sun Oil Co., 493 N.Y.S.2d 125, 482 N.E.2d 921 (N.Y.1985)—§ **702.1, n. 75.**

Wertling v. Manufacturers Hanover Trust Co., 118 Misc.2d 722, 461 N.Y.S.2d 157 (N.Y.City Civ.Ct.1983)—§ **201.1, n. 28, 45.**

Wesley, People v., 611 N.Y.S.2d 97, 633 N.E.2d 451 (N.Y.1994)—§ **103.1, n. 40;** § **702.1;** § **702.1, n. 11, 17, 21, 57;** § **702.2, n. 15;** § **803(3).1;** § **803(3).1, n. 70;** § **901.9;** § **901.9, n. 3.**

West v. New York Cent. & H. R. R. Co., 55 A.D. 464, 67 N.Y.S. 104 (N.Y.A.D. 4 Dept.1900)—§ **1004.1, n. 6.**

Westfall, People v., 95 A.D.2d 581, 469 N.Y.S.2d 162 (N.Y.A.D. 3 Dept.1983)—§ **412.1;** § **412.1, n. 13.**

Westhampton Adult Home, Inc. v. National Union Fire Ins. Co. of Pittsburgh, Pa., 105 A.D.2d 627, 481 N.Y.S.2d 358 (N.Y.A.D. 1 Dept.1984)—§ **501.3, n. 18.**

Westinghouse Elec. Corp. v. City of Burlington, Vt., 351 F.2d 762, 122 U.S.App.D.C. 65 (D.C.Cir.1965)—§ **510.1, n. 4.**

Westinghouse Elec. Corp. v. Republic of Philippines, 951 F.2d 1414 (3rd Cir. 1991)—§ **501.2, n. 50.**

Westmoreland v. CBS Inc., 601 F.Supp. 66 (D.C.N.Y.1984)—§ **802.3, n. 21.**

Wetterer v. Soubirous, 22 Misc. 739, 49 N.Y.S. 1043 (N.Y.Sup.1898)—§ **902.1, n. 11.**

Whalen v. Roe, 429 U.S. 589, 97 S.Ct. 869, 51 L.Ed.2d 64 (1977)—§ **502.2, n. 1.**

Whalen's Estate, In re, 146 Misc. 176, 261 N.Y.S. 761 (N.Y.Sur.1932)—§ **804(4).1;** § **804(4).1, n. 17, 18.**

Wheeler v. United States, 159 U.S. 523, 16 S.Ct. 93, 40 L.Ed. 244 (1895)—§ **601.1, n. 35.**

Whelan v. Lynch, 60 N.Y. 469 (1875)—§ **803(6).1, n. 3.**

Whelan v. Penn Central Co., 503 F.2d 886 (2nd Cir.1974)—§ **1102.2, n. 8.**

Whitaker, Matter of Estate of, 120 Misc.2d 1021, 466 N.Y.S.2d 947 (N.Y.Sur. 1983)—§ **803(5).1, n. 29.**

White v. Illinois, 502 U.S. 346, 112 S.Ct. 736, 116 L.Ed.2d 848 (1992)—§ **802.2, n. 90;** § **803(1).1, n. 20;** § **804(5).2, n. 36.**

White v. Molinari, 160 A.D.2d 302, 553 N.Y.S.2d 396 (N.Y.A.D. 1 Dept.1990)—§ **401.1, n. 6, 24.**

White v. Old Dominion S. S. Co., 102 N.Y. 660, 6 N.E. 289 (N.Y.1886)—§ **408.1;** § **408.1, n. 3;** § **408.2, n. 16;** § **802.2, n. 20.**

White, People v., 211 A.D.2d 982, 621 N.Y.S.2d 728 (N.Y.A.D. 3 Dept.1995)—§ **1101.1, n. 7.**

White, People v., 541 N.Y.S.2d 749, 539 N.E.2d 577 (N.Y.1989)—§ **801(2).1, n. 27.**

White, People v., 439 N.Y.S.2d 333, 421 N.E.2d 825 (N.Y.1981)—§ **1107.1, n. 8.**

White, United States v., 950 F.2d 426 (7th Cir.1991)—§ **501.2, n. 22.**

White, United States v., 545 F.2d 1129 (8th Cir.1976)—§ **503.5, n. 12.**

White, United States v., 223 F.2d 674 (2nd Cir.1955)—§ **1001.1, n. 12.**

White v. Zutell, 263 F.2d 613 (2nd Cir. 1959)—§ **803(3).2, n. 26.**

Whitehead, People v., 142 A.D.2d 745, 531 N.Y.S.2d 48 (N.Y.A.D. 3 Dept.1988)—§ **702.1, n. 71.**

Whitehurst v. Wright, 592 F.2d 834 (5th Cir.1979)—§ **607.4, n. 48.**

White Industries, Inc. v. Cessna Aircraft Co., 611 F.Supp. 1049 (D.C.Mo.1985)—§ **803(6).2;** § **803(6).2, n. 10.**

White's Will, In re, 160 N.Y.S.2d 841, 141 N.E.2d 416 (N.Y.1957)—§ **804(1).1;** § **804(1).1, n. 14.**

Whitman Delicatessen, Inc. v. State Liquor Authority, 83 A.D.2d 963, 443 N.Y.S.2d 14 (N.Y.A.D. 2 Dept.1981)—§ **801(1).2, n. 8.**

Whitmore, People v., 123 A.D.2d 336, 506 N.Y.S.2d 231 (N.Y.A.D. 2 Dept.1986)—§ **607.6, n. 8.**

Whittington, United States v., 783 F.2d 1210 (5th Cir.1986)—§ **901.2, n. 14.**

Wieber, People v., 202 A.D.2d 789, 609 N.Y.S.2d 398 (N.Y.A.D. 3 Dept.1994)—§ **607.4, n. 43.**

Wiener, United States v., 534 F.2d 15 (2nd Cir.1976)—§ **401.2, n. 11;** § **1101.2, n. 8.**

Wiggins, People v., 189 A.D.2d 908, 593 N.Y.S.2d 62 (N.Y.A.D. 2 Dept.1993)—§ **804(1).1, n. 46.**

Wightman v. Campbell, 217 N.Y. 479, 112 N.E. 184 (N.Y.1916)—§ **103.1, n. 12, 19.**

Wilber v. Gillespie, 127 A.D. 604, 112 N.Y.S. 20 (N.Y.A.D. 1 Dept.1908)—§ **601.2, n. 6.**

Wildbur v. ARCO Chemical Co., 974 F.2d 631 (5th Cir.1992)—§ **501.2, n. 38.**

Wilds, People v., 141 A.D.2d 395, 529 N.Y.S.2d 325 (N.Y.A.D. 1 Dept.1988)—§ **300.4, n. 45;** § **614.1, n. 22, 24.**

Wiley, United States v., 846 F.2d 150 (2nd Cir.1988)—§ **611.5, n. 13.**

Wilkes, United States v., 451 F.2d 938 (2nd Cir.1971)—§ **901.5, n. 18.**

Wilkins v. Earle, 44 N.Y. 172 (1870)—§ **301.4, n. 3.**

Wilkins, People v., 490 N.Y.S.2d 759, 480 N.E.2d 373 (N.Y.1985)—§ **500.1, n. 7;** § **502.1;** § **502.1, n. 80;** § **509.1, n. 42.**

Wilkinson, United States v., 754 F.2d 1427 (2nd Cir.1985)—§ **801(1).3, n. 18.**

William Gardam & Son v. Batterson, 198 N.Y. 175, 91 N.E. 371 (N.Y.1910)—§ **1004.1, n. 16.**

TABLE OF CASES

William L. Mantha Co. v. De Graff, 242 A.D. 666, 273 N.Y.S. 384 (N.Y.A.D. 2 Dept.1934)—§ **601.2, n. 7.**

Williams v. Alexander, 309 N.Y. 283, 129 N.E.2d 417 (N.Y.1955)—§ **803(1).1;** § **803(1).1, n. 73;** § **803(3).1;** § **803(3).1, n. 63;** § **803(3).2, n. 22, 24.**

Williams v. Brown, 53 A.D. 486, 65 N.Y.S. 1049 (N.Y.A.D. 2 Dept.1900)—§ **201.1, n. 39.**

Williams v. Lord, 996 F.2d 1481 (2nd Cir. 1993)—§ **402.1, n. 62;** § **402.2, n. 5.**

Williams v. Metropolitan Transp. Authority, 99 A.D.2d 530, 471 N.Y.S.2d 310 (N.Y.A.D. 2 Dept.1984)—§ **501.3, n. 22.**

Williams, People v., 620 N.Y.S.2d 811, 644 N.E.2d 1367 (N.Y.1994)—§ **300.3, n. 31, 33.**

Williams, People v., 206 A.D.2d 917, 614 N.Y.S.2d 842 (N.Y.A.D. 4 Dept.1994)—§ **1104.1, n. 39.**

Williams, People v., 598 N.Y.S.2d 167, 614 N.E.2d 730 (N.Y.1993)—§ **412.1;** § **412.1, n. 3.**

Williams, People v., 142 A.D.2d 310, 536 N.Y.S.2d 814 (N.Y.A.D. 2 Dept.1988)—§ **804(3).1, n. 54.**

Williams, People v., 130 Misc.2d 773, 497 N.Y.S.2d 849 (N.Y.Sup.1986)—§ **1102.1, n. 8.**

Williams, People v., 451 N.Y.S.2d 690, 436 N.E.2d 1292 (N.Y.1982)—§ **609.1, n. 20, 31.**

Williams, People v., 431 N.Y.S.2d 477, 409 N.E.2d 949 (N.Y.1980)—§ **105.1, n. 9.**

Williams, People v., 187 N.Y.S.2d 750, 159 N.E.2d 549 (N.Y.1959)—§ **103.1, n. 27, 32;** § **607.7, n. 3, 13, 18.**

Williams, United States v., 927 F.2d 95 (2nd Cir.1991)—§ **804.1, n. 28;** § **804(3).2, n. 19.**

Williams, United States v., 583 F.2d 1194 (2nd Cir.1978)—§ **901.5, n. 22.**

Williams by Williams v. Roosevelt Hosp., 497 N.Y.S.2d 348, 488 N.E.2d 94 (N.Y. 1985)—§ **502.1, n. 4, 10, 20, 21, 33.**

Williamson v. United States, ___ U.S. ___, 114 S.Ct. 2431, 129 L.Ed.2d 476 (1994)—§ **804(3).1, n. 35;** § **804(3).2;** § **804(3).2, n. 21.**

Willie Buie, People v. (N.Y.1995)—§ **607.5, n. 2.**

Will of (see name of party)

Wilmington Trust Co. v. Manufacturers Life Ins. Co., 749 F.2d 694 (11th Cir. 1985)—§ **607.8, n. 53.**

Wilson, In re Will of, 103 N.Y. 374, 8 N.E. 731 (N.Y.1886)—§ **601.2, n. 11, 26.**

Wilson v. Bodian, 130 A.D.2d 221, 519 N.Y.S.2d 126 (N.Y.A.D. 2 Dept.1987)—§ **803(3).1;** § **803(3).1, n. 35, 66, 68.**

Wilson v. City of Chicago, 6 F.3d 1233 (7th Cir.1993)—§ **608.1, n. 17.**

Wilson, People v., 207 A.D.2d 463, 615 N.Y.S.2d 769 (N.Y.A.D. 2 Dept.1994)—§ **1104.1, n. 29.**

Wilson, People v., 195 A.D.2d 493, 600 N.Y.S.2d 113 (N.Y.A.D. 2 Dept.1993)—§ **801(2).1, n. 20.**

Wilson, People v., 485 N.Y.S.2d 40, 474 N.E.2d 248 (N.Y.1984)—§ **503.3, n. 8.**

Wilson v. Snow, 228 U.S. 217, 33 S.Ct. 487, 57 L.Ed. 807 (1913)—§ **901.8, n. 8.**

Wilson, United States v., 586 F.Supp. 1011 (D.C.N.Y.1983)—§ **402.2, n. 11.**

Wilson v. United States, 116 F. 484 (9th Cir.1902)—§ **1108.2, n. 9.**

Wilson v. Zapata Off-Shore Co., 939 F.2d 260 (5th Cir.1991)—§ **803(1).2, n. 52.**

Winder v. Pollack, 151 N.Y.S. 870 (N.Y.Sup. 1915)—§ **803(4).1, n. 1.**

Wingate, United States v., 520 F.2d 309 (2nd Cir.1975)—§ **804(1).2, n. 12.**

Winship, In re, 397 U.S. 358, 90 S.Ct. 1068, 25 L.Ed.2d 368 (1970)—§ **300.4, n. 3, 39, 67;** § **302.1, n. 3.**

Wintermute, People ex rel. Deister v., 194 N.Y. 99, 86 N.E. 818 (N.Y.1909)—§ **512.1, n. 4.**

Wisan, People v., 132 Misc.2d 691, 505 N.Y.S.2d 361 (N.Y.Sup.1986)—§ **802.2, n. 104.**

Wise, People v., 413 N.Y.S.2d 334, 385 N.E.2d 1262 (N.Y.1978)—§ **509.1, n. 76;** § **607.3, n. 3;** § **607.8;** § **607.8, n. 15, 21, 29, 41;** § **801(1).2, n. 13.**

Wisniewski v. Jem Novelty Corp., 22 A.D.2d 10, 253 N.Y.S.2d 418 (N.Y.A.D. 1 Dept. 1964)—§ **411.1, n. 4.**

Witherel v. Balling Const., Inc., 99 A.D.2d 646, 472 N.Y.S.2d 218 (N.Y.A.D. 4 Dept. 1984)—§ **406.1, n. 4, 28.**

Witness Before Grand Jury, In re, 791 F.2d 234 (2nd Cir.1986)—§ **503.5, n. 15.**

Wolfe v. Madison Ave. Coach Co., 171 Misc. 707, 13 N.Y.S.2d 741 (N.Y.Sup.1939)—§ **105.1, n. 2, 6, 8;** § **607.8, n. 19.**

Wolff, People v., 24 A.D.2d 828, 264 N.Y.S.2d 40 (N.Y.A.D. 4 Dept.1965)—§ **802.2, n. 104.**

Wolfle v. United States, 291 U.S. 7, 54 S.Ct. 279, 78 L.Ed. 617 (1934)—§ **503.5;** § **503.5, n. 6.**

Wolper v. New York Water Service Corp., 276 A.D. 1106, 96 N.Y.S.2d 647 (N.Y.A.D.1950)—§ **1001.1, n. 15;** § **1004.1, n. 23.**

Wong, People v., 601 N.Y.S.2d 440, 619 N.E.2d 377 (N.Y.1993)—§ **300.3, n. 31, 32.**

Wong, People v., 150 Misc.2d 554, 568 N.Y.S.2d 1020 (N.Y.Sup.1991)—§ **702.1, n. 65.**

Wong Sun v. United States, 371 U.S. 471, 83 S.Ct. 407, 9 L.Ed.2d 441 (1963)—§ **801.1, n. 46.**

Wood, Matter of, 430 F.Supp. 41 (D.C.N.Y. 1977)—§ **505.2;** § **505.2, n. 1.**

Wood, People v., 582 N.Y.S.2d 992, 591 N.E.2d 1178 (N.Y.1992)—§ **401.1, n. 49;** § **1102.1, n. 20;** § **1104.1, n. 18.**

TABLE OF CASES

Wood, People v., 126 N.Y. 249, 27 N.E. 362 (N.Y.1891)—§ **503.3, n. 25.**
Wood, People v., 497 N.Y.S.2d 340, 488 N.E.2d 86 (N.Y.1985)—§ **603.1, n. 5, 6;** § **610.1, n. 3.**
Wood, United States v., 943 F.2d 1048 (9th Cir.1991)—§ **1006.1, n. 19.**
Woodby v. Immigration and Naturalization Service, 385 U.S. 276, 87 S.Ct. 483, 17 L.Ed.2d 362 (1966)—§ **300.4, n. 31.**
Wooden, People v., 66 A.D.2d 1004, 411 N.Y.S.2d 759 (N.Y.A.D. 4 Dept.1978)—§ **607.5, n. 6.**
Woodner, United States v., 317 F.2d 649 (2nd Cir.1963)—§ **300.4, n. 73.**
Woods, People v., 202 A.D.2d 1043, 610 N.Y.S.2d 108 (N.Y.A.D. 4 Dept.1994)—§ **103.1, n. 24.**
Wood's Estate, Matter of, 436 N.Y.S.2d 850, 418 N.E.2d 365 (N.Y.1981)—§ **601.2;** § **601.2, n. 1, 4, 67, 68, 73, 75.**
Workman, People v., 308 N.Y. 668, 124 N.E.2d 314 (N.Y.1954)—§ **1103.1, n. 7.**
Workman, People v., 283 A.D. 1066, 131 N.Y.S.2d 100 (N.Y.A.D. 2 Dept.1954)—§ **103.1, n. 10.**
Wortherly, People v., 68 A.D.2d 158, 416 N.Y.S.2d 594 (N.Y.A.D. 1 Dept.1979)—§ **803(1).1, n. 28.**
Wrenn v. Secretary, Dept. of Veterans Affairs, 918 F.2d 1073 (2nd Cir.1990)—§ **408.2, n. 4.**
Wrigglesworth, People v., 204 A.D.2d 758, 611 N.Y.S.2d 678 (N.Y.A.D. 3 Dept. 1994)—§ **607.7, n. 12.**
Wright v. Doe d. Tatham, 7 Ad. and E. 313, 112 Eng.Rep. 488 (Court of Exchequer Chamber, 1837)—§ **801.1;** § **801.1, n. 10.**
Wright v. New York City Housing Authority, 208 A.D.2d 327, 624 N.Y.S.2d 144 (N.Y.A.D. 1 Dept.1995)—§ **300.4, n. 14.**
Wright, People v., 161 A.D.2d 743, 558 N.Y.S.2d 842 (N.Y.A.D. 2 Dept.1990)—§ **702.1, n. 65.**
Wright, People v., 159 A.D.2d 282, 552 N.Y.S.2d 285 (N.Y.A.D. 1 Dept.1990)—§ **611.2, n. 6.**
Wright, People v., 290 N.Y.S.2d 930, 238 N.E.2d 330 (N.Y.1968)—§ **801(2).1, n. 14.**
Wright v. United States, 559 F.Supp. 1139 (D.C.N.Y.1983)—§ **606.2, n. 9.**
Wright, United States v., 542 F.2d 975 (7th Cir.1976)—§ **607.3, n. 23.**
Wright Root Beer Co. of New Orleans v. Dr. Pepper Co., 414 F.2d 887 (5th Cir. 1969)—§ **804(1).2, n. 23.**
Wylie v. Marley Co., 891 F.2d 1463 (10th Cir.1989)—§ **501.2, n. 43.**

Y

Yager Pontiac, Inc. v. Fred A. Danker & Sons, Inc., 69 Misc.2d 546, 330 N.Y.S.2d 409 (N.Y.Sup.1972)—§ **601.2, n. 5.**
Yakobov, United States v., 712 F.2d 20 (2nd Cir.1983)—§ **803(5).2;** § **803(5).2, n. 11, 51.**
Yamin, United States v., 868 F.2d 130 (5th Cir.1989)—§ **1001.1, n. 26.**
Yannon v. RCA Corp., 100 A.D.2d 966, 475 N.Y.S.2d 107 (N.Y.A.D. 2 Dept.1984)—§ **802.2, n. 53.**
Yaron v. Yaron, 83 Misc.2d 276, 372 N.Y.S.2d 518 (N.Y.Sup.1975)—§ **502.1, n. 76;** § **505.1, n. 5, 19.**
Yarusevich, People v., 81 A.D.2d 528, 438 N.Y.S.2d 94 (N.Y.A.D. 1 Dept.1981)—§ **611.2, n. 17.**
Yates v. Bair Transport, Inc., 249 F.Supp. 681 (D.C.N.Y.1965)—§ **803(3).2;** § **803(3).2, n. 4, 32;** § **805.2;** § **805.2, n. 1.**
Yazum, People v., 246 N.Y.S.2d 626, 196 N.E.2d 263 (N.Y.1963)—§ **401.1, n. 11;** § **802.2, n. 13.**
Yeo, United States v., 739 F.2d 385 (8th Cir.1984)—§ **609.2, n. 14, 17.**
Yonkers Contracting Co., Inc., United States v., 701 F.Supp. 431 (S.D.N.Y. 1988)—§ **804(1).2, n. 10;** § **804(5).2;** § **804(5).2, n. 13, 34.**
Yonko, People v., 359 N.Y.S.2d 54, 316 N.E.2d 338 (N.Y.1974)—§ **601.1, n. 36.**
Young v. Abrams, 698 F.2d 131 (2nd Cir. 1983)—§ **302.1, n. 24;** § **302.2, n. 7.**
Young v. Shulenberg, 35 A.D. 79, 54 N.Y.S. 419 (N.Y.A.D. 3 Dept.1898)—§ **804(4).1, n. 21.**
Young v. Shulenberg, 165 N.Y. 385, 59 N.E. 135 (N.Y.1901)—§ **804(4).1;** § **804(4).1, n. 10, 17, 21.**
Young, United States v., 745 F.2d 733 (2nd Cir.1984)—§ **611.5, n. 8;** § **702.2, n. 3.**
Young Ah Chor v. Dulles, 270 F.2d 338 (9th Cir.1959)—§ **804(4).2, n. 9.**
Yu–Leung, United States v., 51 F.3d 1116 (2nd Cir.1995)—§ **103.2, n. 4, 24, 25.**
Yut Wai Tom, People v., 439 N.Y.S.2d 896, 422 N.E.2d 556 (N.Y.1981)—§ **614.1;** § **614.1, n. 13, 18, 19.**

Z

Zabrocky, People v., 311 N.Y.S.2d 892, 260 N.E.2d 529 (N.Y.1970)—§ **608.2, n. 14.**
Zackowitz, People v., 254 N.Y. 192, 172 N.E. 466 (N.Y.1930)—§ **404.1, n. 1, 2.**
Zaken v. Boerer, 964 F.2d 1319 (2nd Cir. 1992)—§ **802.3;** § **802.3, n. 16.**
Zappola, United States v., 646 F.2d 48 (2nd Cir.1981)—§ **804.1, n. 31.**
Zaulich v. Thompkins Square Holding Co., 10 A.D.2d 492, 200 N.Y.S.2d 550 (N.Y.A.D. 1 Dept.1960)—§ **803(3).1, n. 27.**
Zayas, People v., 202 A.D.2d 324, 609 N.Y.S.2d 9 (N.Y.A.D. 1 Dept.1994)—§ **103.1, n. 48.**

TABLE OF CASES

Zeeck v. Melina Taxi Co., 177 A.D.2d 692, 576 N.Y.S.2d 878 (N.Y.A.D. 2 Dept. 1991)—§ **401.1, n. 29.**

Zeidman, United States v., 540 F.2d 314 (7th Cir.1976)—§ **803(4).2, n. 1.**

Zeleznik v. Jewish Chronic Disease Hospital, 47 A.D.2d 199, 366 N.Y.S.2d 163 (N.Y.A.D. 2 Dept.1975)—§ **611.2, n. 5.**

Zenith Radio Corp. v. Matsushita Elec. Indus. Co., Ltd., 505 F.Supp. 1190 (D.C.Pa.1980)—§ **803(3).2, n. 17, 21; § 903.1, n. 3.**

Zenni, United States v., 492 F.Supp. 464 (D.C.Ky.1980)—§ **801.1, n. 19, 23.**

Zerilli v. Smith, 656 F.2d 705, 211 U.S.App. D.C. 116 (D.C.Cir.1981)—§ **508.2, n. 2.**

Zigouras, People v., 163 N.Y. 250, 57 N.E. 465 (N.Y.1900)—§ **611.4, n. 6.**

Zimmer v. Cathedral School of St. Mary and St. Paul, 204 A.D.2d 538, 611 N.Y.S.2d 911 (N.Y.A.D. 2 Dept.1994)—§ **502.1, n. 54.**

Zimmer v. Third Ave. R. Co., 36 A.D. 273, 55 N.Y.S. 314 (N.Y.A.D. 2 Dept.1899)—§ **607.6, n. 5.**

Zimmerman v. Nassau Hospital, 76 A.D.2d 921, 429 N.Y.S.2d 262 (N.Y.A.D. 2 Dept. 1980)—§ **501.3, n. 14.**

Zinman v. Black & Decker (United States), Inc., 983 F.2d 431 (2nd Cir.1993)—§ **607.5, n. 55; § 609.2, n. 19, 20.**

Zippo Mfg. Co. v. Rogers Imports, Inc., 216 F.Supp. 670 (D.C.N.Y.1963)—§ **803(1).2, n. 27; § 803(6).2, n. 9; § 901.9, n. 14.**

Zirinsky v. Zirinsky, 138 A.D.2d 43, 529 N.Y.S.2d 298 (N.Y.A.D. 1 Dept.1988)—§ **706.1, n. 1.**

Zolin, United States v., 491 U.S. 554, 109 S.Ct. 2619, 105 L.Ed.2d 469 (1989)—§ **501.2, n. 18.**

Zucker v. Whitridge, 205 N.Y. 50, 98 N.E. 209 (N.Y.1912)—§ **406.1, n. 24, 27, 34.**

Zuniga, In re, 714 F.2d 632 (6th Cir.1983)—§ **502.2, n. 2.**

INDEX

References are to Sections

ABSENCE
Accident or mistake, uncharged crimes to prove absence of, 404.1(d)
    Civil cases, 404.1(*l*)
Business records, absence of; hearsay, 803(4).1(a)
    Federal rules, 803(4).2
Escape or flight, relevancy considerations, 401.1(a)
Missing witnesses rule, 401.1(a)
    Federal rules, 401.2
Original evidence, absence of. Best Evidence Rule, generally, this index
Public records, absence of; hearsay exception, 803(4).1(b), 803(5).1(n)
    Federal rules, 803(5).2(e)
Unavailability, generally, this index

ACCIDENT OR MISTAKE
Uncharged crimes to prove absence of, 404.1(d)
    Civil cases, 404.1(*l*)

ACCIDENTS
    See also Negligence; Personal Injury Actions, generally, this index
Dead man's statute, facts of accident exception, 601.2(e)
Liability Insurance, generally, this index
Photograph of site, 1104.1(a)
Presumptions, driver presumed to have owner's permission, 301.4
Prior accidents, generally inadmissible, 406.1(d)
Reports,
    Hearsay exception, 803(3).1(a)
        Federal rules, 803(3).2
    No work product immunity, 501.3(b)(1)
Similar occurrences, 405.1(b)
    Federal rules, 405.2(a)
Subsequent Remedial Measures, generally, this index

ACCOMPLICES
Bias and interest of witnesses, 607.6(a)
Corroboration, 300.3(a)(1)

ACCOUNTANTS
Retained to facilitate communication, attorney-client privilege applicable, 501.1(e)
    Federal rules, 501.2

ACQUIRED IMMUNE DEFICIENCY SYNDROME
AIDS, generally, this index

ACQUITTAL
Burden of production,
    Federal rules, 300.3(b)

ADMINISTRATIVE PROCEEDINGS
Medical records, hearsay exception,
    Federal rules, 803(3).2
Self-incrimination, privilege against, 509.1(a)

ADMISSIBILITY. specific index headings

ADMISSIONS
Acts, as, 802.2(a)
    Federal rules, 802.3(b)

INDEX

ADMISSIONS—Continued
Adoptive, 802.2(e)
    Federal rules, 802.3(b)
Against interest, generally. Declarations, this index
Agent's or servant's statements as, 802.2(f)
    Federal rules, 802.3(c)
Best evidence rule satisfied, 1007.1
Coconspirator's statements, 802.2(g)
    Federal rules, 802.3(d)
Completeness doctrine, 106.1
Compromise, admissions made during negotiation, 408.1
Conduct as, 802.2(a)
Confessions, distinguished from, 802.1
Evidentiary admissions, 802.1
Guilty pleas,
    Informal admission in related litigation, as, 802.2(a)
    Withdrawn, 410.1
        Federal rules, 410.2
Inculpatory words used during compromise negotiations, 802.2(a)
Judicial admissions, 802.1
Party-opponent, statements not hearsay, 801(1).1
Payment of medical and similar expenses, 409.1
Pleadings, 802.1
    Federal rules, 802.3(a)
Preliminary rulings, 104.1(b)
Principle and surety, 802.2(b)
Prior inconsistent statements by adverse party, 607.4(b)
Privity, statements of person in, as, 802.2(c)
Representative capacity,
    Federal rules, 802.3(b)
    Statements made in as, 802.2(d)
Silence, as, 802.2(b)
    While in custody, 509.1(c)
Sobriety test, refusal to submit to, 509.1(c)
Speaking agent, 104.1, 802.2(f)
Statements, as, 802.2
    Federal rules, 802.3(b)
Subsequent Remedial Measures, generally, this index

ADULTERY
Husbands and wives, incompetent to testify, 503.2

ADVERSE INFERENCE
Failure to call witness, from, 401.1(a)
Invoking privilege, from, 514.1
Suppression of evidence, from, 401.1(a)

ADVERSE PARTY
Leading questions permissible on direct examination, 611.2(b)
    Federal rules, 611.5(b)
Prior inconsistent statements as admissions, 607.8(a)(3)
Refreshing recollection, right of inspection, 612.1(b)
    Federal rules, 612.2

ADVERSE POSSESSION
Burden of persuasion, clear and convincing evidence, 300.4(b)(2)

AFFIDAVITS
Public officers,
    Facts or acts performed, hearsay exception, 803(5).1(b)
Public records,
    Maps or surveys, hearsay exception, 803(5).1(d)

AFFIRMATIONS
Oaths and Affirmations, generally, this index

AFFIRMATIVE DEFENSES
Burden of proof, 300.2
    Burden of persuasion, 300.3(a)(2)

INDEX

AFFIRMATIVE DEFENSES—Continued
Burden of proof—Continued
  Burden of production, 300.3(a)(2)
    Shifting of burden,
      Constitutionality, 300.4(d)(2)
      Federal rules, 300.4(e)
Reasonable doubt, 300.4(d)(2)

AGE
Competency of witnesses, 601.1(e)
Display of person for determination of, 1102.1
  Federal rules, 1102.2
Lay opinion regarding, 701.1
  Federal rules, 701.2

AGENTS
Attorney-client privilege, 501.1(e)
Dead man's statute,
  Deceased agent, principal not entitled to invoke statute, 601.2(c)
  Transaction between decedent and principal, agent competent to testify, 601.2(b)
  Transaction between decedent's agent and interested witness, 601.2(d)
Emergency medical technicians, privilege only if physician's agent, 502.1(b)
Speaking agent rule, 104.1(b)
Statements made by, as admissions, 802.2(f)
  Federal rules, 802.3(c)

AIDS
Patient-Physician Privilege, 502.1(a)

ALCOHOL
Impeachment based on consumption of, 607.7(a)
  Federal rules, 607.7(b)
Intoxication, generally, this index
Sobriety test,
  Expert testimony regarding, 702.1(c)
  Refusal to submit to as admission, 509.1(c)
Witnesses under influence of, effect on competency, 601.1(g)
  Federal rules, 601.3

ALIASES
Explanation admissible to rehabilitate, 607.5(a)(2)(a)
Impeachment purposes, 607.2
Prior acts of misconduct, admissibility as, 608.2(a)

ALIBI
Burden of production,
  Federal rules, 300.4(e)

AMNESIA
Burden of persuasion, preponderance of evidence, 300.4(b)(1)

ANNULMENT
Corroboration, 300.3(a)(1)

APPEAL
Conviction of crime offered to impeach,
  Effect of pending appeal, 609.2
  Pretrial ruling, 103.2(d)
Harmless error, 103.1(e)
  Federal rules, 103.2(e)
Objections, generally, this index
Offer of proof to preserve error, 103.1(c)
  Federal rules, 103.2(c)
Preserving error for appeal, 103.1(a)
  Federal rules, 103.2(a)

ARRESTS
Bias or interest of witness, 607.6(a)
Character in issue, arrest irrelevant, 608.2(a)
Cross-examination of character witness regarding defendant's prior arrests, 402.1(d)

INDEX

ARRESTS—Continued
Impeachment value, 608.2(a), 609.1(a)
Silence following, 509.1(c)

ARSON
Burden of persuasion, clear and convincing evidence, 300.4(b)(2)

ASSAULT AND BATTERY
Character of defendant in civil case, 402.1(b), 402.1(c)

ATTORNEY-CLIENT PRIVILEGE
Generally, 501.1 et seq.
Accountants retained to facilitate communication, 501.1(e)
    Federal rules, 501.2
Address of client, disclosure, 501.1(c)
Agents of attorney or client, 501.1(e)
    Federal rules, 501.2
Attorney-client relationship,
    Existence, 501.1(b)
    Federal rules, 501.2
Burden of establishing applicability, 501.1(a)
Business communications not privileged, 501.1(d)
Communications, 501.1(c)
Confidentiality, 501.1(e)
Corporate application, 501.1(f)
    Federal rules, 501.2
Death, effect, 501.1(a)
Discovery, documents disclosed during, 501.1(h)
    Federal rules, 501.2
Documents, 501.1(a), 501.1(b), 501.1(c)
    Federal rules, 501.2
    Inadvertent disclosure during discovery, waiver of privilege, 501.1(h)
Eavesdroppers, 501.1(a), 501.1(e)
Employees of corporation, control over disclosure, 501.1(f)
    Federal rules, 501.2
Exceptions, 501.1(g)
    Federal rules, 501.2
Federal rules, 501.2
Fiduciary duty owed by client to party seeking disclosure, exception, 501.1(g)
Fruits or instrumentalities of crime, 501.1(c)
Future crime or fraud, exception to privilege, 501.1(g)
    Federal rules, 501.2
Identity of client, disclosure, 501.1(c)
    Federal rules, 501.2
Invocation of privilege, 501.1(a)
Joint client rule, 501.1(e)
    Federal rules, 501.2
Joint defense doctrine, 501.1(e)
    Federal rules, 501.2
Legal advice, 501.1(d)
    Federal rules, 501.2
Malpractice allegation, exception, 501.1(g)
Personal communications not privileged, 501.1(d)
Proceedings in which privilege may be invoked, 501.1(a)
Proposed New York Evidence Code, 501.1(a)
Public policy exception, 501.1(g)
Refreshing memory of witness with privileged communication, 501.1(h), 612.1(b)
    Federal rules, 501.2, 612.2
Shareholder actions, exception, 501.1(g), 501.2
Tangible objects, 501.1(c)
Waiver, 501.1(a), 501.1(h)
    Document used to refresh memory, 612.1(b)
        Federal rules, 612.2
    Federal rules, 501.2
    Malpractice allegation, exception, 501.1(g)
Who may assert privilege, 501.1(a)

INDEX

ATTORNEY-CLIENT PRIVILEGE—Continued
Will contests,
Disclosure disgracing decedent's memory, 501.1(a), 501.1(g)
Exception to privilege, 501.1(g)

ATTORNEYS
Attorney-Client Privilege, generally, this index
Disbarment, impeachment value, 608.2(b)
Statements and questions by, not evidence, 100.2
Work Product Immunities, generally, this index

AUDIO TAPES
Recordings, generally, this index

AUTHENTICATION AND IDENTIFICATION
See also Real and Demonstrative Evidence, generally, this index
Generally, 900.1 et seq.
Admission to establish authenticity, 900.1
Ancient documents, 901.8(a)
    Federal rules, 901.8(b)
Ballistics, expert comparison and analysis, 901.3(a)
Burden of proof, 900.1
Business records, exception to personal knowledge requirement, 901.1(a)
    Federal rules, 901.1(b)
Certified copies, self-authenticating, 901.7(a)
    Federal rules, 902.1(b)
Chain of custody, 901.1(a), 1101.1
    Federal rules, 901.1(b), 1101.2
Circumstantial evidence of authenticity, 901.4(a)
    Federal rules, 901.4(b)
Commercial paper, self-authenticating, 902.1(b)
Comparisons by trier or expert witness, 901.3(a)
    Federal rules, 901.3(b)
Computer-generated data, 901.9(b)
    Graphics, 1106.1
Conversations. Telephone Conversations, generally, post
Criminal actions, burden of proof, 900.1
Currency, 901.1(b)
Documents, 901.1(a)
    Acknowledged, 902.1(a)
        Federal rules, 902.1(b)
    Ancient, 901.8(a)
        Federal rules, 901.8(b)
    Content identification, 901.4(a)
        Federal rules, 901.4(b)
Drugs, 901.1(a), 1101.1
Expert comparison and analysis, 901.3(a)
    Federal rules, 901.3(b)
Federal rules, 900.1 et seq.
Fingerprints, expert comparison and analysis, 901.3(a)
Foreign records, 901.7(a), 902.1(a)
    Federal rules, 902.1(b)
Handwriting, 702.1(c)
    Expert opinion, 901.3(a)
        Federal rules, 901.3(b)
    Lay opinion, 901.2(a)
        Federal rules, 901.2(b)
Jury determination of authenticity, 900.1
Lay opinion on handwriting, 901.2(a)
    Federal rules, 901.2(b)
Methods provided by statute or rule, 901.10(a)
Motion pictures and videotapes, 1104.1(d)
    Federal rules, 1104.2(d)
Newspapers and periodicals,
    Federal rules, 902.1(b)
Official publications, 902.1(a)
    Federal rules, 902.1(b)

INDEX

AUTHENTICATION AND IDENTIFICATION—Continued
Photographs, 901.1(a), 1104.1(a)
    Federal rules, 1104.2(a)
Place of custody used to authenticate, 901.4(a)
Process or system, 901.9(a)
    Federal rules, 901.9(b)
Proposed New York Evidence Code, 900.1 et seq.
Public records, 901.7(a), 902.1(a)
    Federal rules, 901.7(b), 902.1(b)
Real property,
    Foreign conveyances, 902.1(a)
    Title documents, 901.8(a)
Recordings, 901.1(a), 1104.1(c)
    Criminal cases, burden of proof, 900.1
    Federal rules, 1104.2(c)
    Voice identification, 901.5(a)
Samples, authenticity for comparison, 901.3(a)
    Federal rules, 901.3(b)
Scientific evidence, 901.9(a)
    Federal rules, 901.9(b)
Self-authentication, 902.1(a)
    Certified copies of public records, 901.7(a)
    Federal rules, 902.1(b)
Silent witness theory of authentication, 1104.1(a), 1104.1(b), 1104.1(d)
    Federal rules, 1104.2(a), 1104.2(b), 1104.2(d)
Statutory methods, 901.10(a)
    Federal rules, 901.10(b)
Stipulation to establish authenticity, 900.1
Subscribing witnesses, 903.1
Tangible objects, 1101.1
Tariff or classification, 902.1(a)
    Federal rules, 902.1(b)
Telephone conversations,
    Caller identification, 901.5(a)
        Federal rules, 901.5(b)
    Content identification, 901.4(a)
        Federal rules, 901.4(b)
    Listener identification, 901.6(a)
        Federal rules, 901.6(b)
    Voice identification, 901.1(a)
Testimony of witness with knowledge, 901.1(a)
    Federal rules, 901.1(b)
Trade inscriptions, 902.1(a)
    Federal rules, 902.1(b)
UCC provisions, 902.1(b)
Voice identification, 901.5(a)
    Burden of proof, 900.1
    Conversation participants attesting to accuracy, 901.1(a)
    Federal rules, 901.5(b)
    Voiceprints, expert comparison and analysis, 901.3(a)
Voir dire of witnesses regarding, 611.3(d)
Wiretaps, voice identification, 901.5(a)
    Federal rules, 901.5(b)
X-rays, 901.9(b), 1104.1(b)
    Federal rules, 1104.2(b)

BACKGROUND EVIDENCE
Credibility, 607.5(a)(1)(n.1)
    Federal rules, 607.5(b)(n.49)
Noncollateral, use for impeachment, 607.3
Uncharged crimes, 404.1(g)

BAILMENT
Conversion or loss of property, presumptions, 301.4

BEST EVIDENCE RULE
    Generally, 1001.1 et seq.

INDEX

BEST EVIDENCE RULE—Continued
Admission of party as genuineness of contents, 1007.1
Applicability of rule, 1001.1(a)
Business records,
    Originals, as, 1002.1
    Voluminous records summarized, 1006.1(a)
        Federal rules, 1006.1(b)
Carbon copies accepted as originals, 1002.1
Collateral matters, 1004.1(d)
Computer printouts,
    Originals, as, 1002.1
    Summaries, 1006.1(a)
Confessions, 1001.1(a)
Correspondence, originals, 1002.1
Court and jury, functions of, 1008.1(a)
    Federal rules, 1008.1(b)
Definitions, 1001.1(b)
Duplicates, 1003.1
Federal rules, 1001.1 et seq.
Inscriptions, 1001.1(b)
Judgments, 1001.1(a)
Loss or destruction of evidence, 1004.1(a)
Notice to produce original, 1004.1(c)
Originals, 1002.1
    Excusable loss or destruction of, 1004.1(a)
    Opponent possessing, 1004.1(c)
    Unobtainable, 1004.1(b)
Photographs,
    Originals, 1002.1
Proposed New York Evidence Code, 1001.1 et seq.
Public records, 1005.1(a)
    Federal rules, 1005.1(b)
Real property title documents, 1001.1(a), 1005.1(a)
Receipt for payment of debt, 1001.1(a)
Recordings,
    Originals, 1002.1
Refreshing memory, inapplicable to, 1001.1(b)
Secondary evidence, 1004.1
Summaries, 1006.1(a)
    Federal rules, 1006.1(b)
Transcripts, 1001.1(a)
Voluminous writings summarized, 1006.1(a)
    Federal rules, 1006.1(b)
Will contests, 1003.1
X-rays, 1002.1
    Excusable loss or destruction of, 1004.1(a)

BIAS AND INTEREST OF WITNESS
    Generally, 607.6(a)
Credibility, 607.1 et seq.
Federal rules, 607.6(b)
Group affiliations, 610.1
Own witness, impeachment generally prohibited, 607.4(a)
Religious belief, 610.1
    Federal rules, 610.2

BIGAMY
Spousal privileges, 503.3(c)

BLOOD TESTS
DNA reports, hearsay exception, 803(3).1(c)
Genetic markers, hearsay exception, 803(3).1(c)
Intoxication, to prove,
    Expert testimony regarding, 702.1(c)
    Refusal to submit to as admission, 509.1(c)
Relationship, to prove; expert testimony regarding, 702.1(c)

INDEX

BREATHALYZER TEST
Expert opinion regarding, 702.1(c)

BRIBE
Bias and interest of witness, 607.6(a)

BURDEN OF PERSUASION
Burden of Proof, this index

BURDEN OF PRODUCTION
Burden of Proof, this index

BURDEN OF PROOF
  Generally, 300.1 et seq.
  Affirmative defenses, 300.2
    Burden of persuasion, 300.3(a)(2)
    Burden of production, 300.3(a)(2)
    Criminal proceedings,
      Reasonable doubt, 300.4(d)(2)
  Allocation, factors influencing,
    Access to evidence, 300.2
    Change in status quo, 300.2
    Fairness, 300.2
    Policy, 300.2
    Practicality and convenience, 300.2
    Probabilities, 300.2
  Authentication and identification, 900.1
  Burden of persuasion,
    Affirmative defenses, 300.3(a)(2)
      Duress, 300.4(d)(2)
      Entrapment, 300.4(d)(2)
      Insanity, 300.4(d)(2)
      Reasonable doubt, 300.4(d)(2)
    Civil proceedings,
      Clear and convincing evidence, 300.4(b)(2)
        Federal rules, 300.4(c)
      Preponderance of evidence, 300.4(b)(1)
    Clear and convincing evidence,
      Arson, 300.4(b)(2)
      Civil proceedings, 300.4(b)(2)
      Contracts,
        Mistake, 300.4(b)(2)
        Reformation, 300.4(b)(2)
      Defamation, 300.4(b)(2)
      Federal rules, 300.4(b)(2)
        Moral turpitude, 300.4(b)(2)
      Fraud, 300.4(b)(2)
      Malice, 300.4(b)(2)
      Paternity, 300.4(b)(2)
      Real property,
        Adverse possession, 300.4(b)(2)
        Gifts, decedent's pre-death transfer by, 300.4(b)(2)
        Implied easements, 300.4(b)(2)
      Usury, 300.4(b)(2)
    Criminal proceedings,
      Affirmative defenses,
        Reasonable doubt, 300.4(d)(2)
      Circumstantial evidence, 300.4(d)(1)
        Federal rules, 300.4(e)
      Reasonable doubt, 300.4(d)(1)
    Defined, 300.1
    Jury instructions, 300.4(a)
    Preponderance of evidence,
      Amnesia, 300.4(b)(1)
      Civil proceedings, 300.4(b)(1)
        Federal rules, 300.4(b)(1)
      Wrongful death actions, 300.4(b)(1)
        Noseworthy doctrine, 300.4(b)(1)

INDEX

BURDEN OF PROOF—Continued
Burden of production,
  Affirmative defenses, 300.3(a)(2)
    Shifting of burden,
      Constitutionality, 300.4(d)(2)
      Federal rules, 300.4(e)
  Circumstantial evidence, 300.3(a)(1)
    Federal rules, 300.3(b)
  Corroboration, 300.3(a)(1)
    Accomplice testimony, 300.3(a)(1)
    Annulment, 300.3(a)(1)
    Confessions, 300.3(a)(1)
    Federal rules, 300.3(b)
    Minors, unsworn testimony, 300.3(a)(1)
  Defenses,
    Federal rules, 300.4(e)
  Defined, 300.1
  Direct evidence, 300.3(a)(1)
  Directed verdict motion, 300.3(a)(1)
    Federal rules, 300.3(b)
  Dismissal of actions, 300.3(a)(1)
  Federal rules, 300.3(b)
  Judgment notwithstanding verdict motion, 300.3(a)(1)
  Presumptions, effect,
    "Bursting bubble" rule, 301.5(a)(1), 301.5(b)
    Hybrid approach rule, 301.5(b)
    Morgan rule, 301.5(a)(2), 301.5(b)
    Thayer rule, 301.5(a)(1)
  Prima facie evidence, 301.7
  Rebuttal evidence, 300.3(a)(2)
  Self-defense,
    Federal rules, 300.4(e)
  Shifting of burden, 300.3(a)(2)
    Affirmative defenses, 300.4(d)(2)
      Duress, 300.4(d)(2)
      Entrapment, 300.4(d)(2)
      Insanity, 300.4(d)(2)
  Sufficiency test, 300.3(a)(1)
    Federal rules, 300.3(b)
Contracts, 300.2
Negligence, 300.2
Reasonable doubt,
  Criminal proceedings,
    Burden of persuasion, 300.4(d)(1)
Uncharged crimes, 404.1(a)
  Federal rules, 404.2(a)
Witnesses, incompetency, 601.1(a)

BUSINESS PRACTICE
Habit, 406.1(b)
  Federal rules, 406.2(a)
Similar transactions, 405.1(c)
  Federal rules, 405.2(b)

BUSINESS RECORDS
Absence of, hearsay, 803(4).1(a)
  Federal rules, 803(4).2
Best evidence rule, 1002.1
Dead man's statute, applicability, 601.2(a)
Exception to personal knowledge requirement, 901.1(a)
  Federal rules, 901.1(b)
Hearsay exception, 803(3).1(a)
  Federal rule, 803(3).2
Prior inconsistent statements recorded verbatim, 607.8(b)
Proposed New York Evidence Code, 803(3).1(d)
Self-incrimination, privilege against, 509.1(b)

997

INDEX

CENSUS
Judicial notice,
    Adjudicative facts, 201.1(c)(4)
Population certificates, hearsay exception, 803(5).1(k)

CERTIFICATES
Agricultural inspection, hearsay exception, 803(5).1(j)
Baptismal, hearsay exception,
    Federal rules, 803(5).2(f)
Birth, hearsay exception, 803(5).1(h)
Death, hearsay exception, 803(5).1(h)
Marriage, hearsay exception, 803(5).1(f)
    Federal rules, 803(5).2(f)
Population, hearsay exception, 803(5).1(k)
Public officers,
    Facts or acts performed, hearsay exception, 803(5).1(b)
Surveyor's standard, hearsay exception, 803(5).1(l)

CHAIN OF CUSTODY
Tangible evidence, 901.1(a), 1101.1
    Federal rules, 901.1(b), 1101.2

CHARACTER EVIDENCE
    Generally, 402.1, 402.2
Character in issue, 402.1(b)
Civil cases, proof of conduct, 402.1(c)
Community reputation, defined, 402.1(d)
Credibility of witnesses, character evidence to prove, 608.0 et seq.
Criminal cases, proof of conduct, 402.1(d)
    Federal rules, 402.2, 413.1
Defamation cases, character of victim in issue, 402.1(b)
Effect of, 402.1(e)
    Federal rules, 402.2
Entrapment, evidence to rebut, 402.1(b)
Federal rules, 402.2
Habit, distinguished from, 402.1(c), 406.1(a)
Hearsay exception,
    Federal rules, 803(7).2(c)
Homicide victim, 402.1(f)
    Federal rules, 402.2
Impeachment
        See also Impeachment, generally, this index
    Character witness, 402.1(d)
Jury instructions on, 402.1(e)
    Federal rules, 402.2
Method of proof, 402.1(d)
    Federal rules, 402.2
Proposed New York Evidence Code, 402.1(h)
Rape victim, 412.1
    Federal rules, 412.2
Reputation, 803(7).2(c)
    Hearsay exception, method of proof, 402.1(b)
Truthfulness,
    Bad character for, use to impeach, 608.1(a)
        Federal rules, 608.1(b)
    Evidence of; use to rehabilitate, 607.5(a)(2)(b)
Uncharged Crimes, generally, this index
Victim of homicide, 402.1(f)
    Federal rules, 402.2

CHARTS
Aids distinguished from evidence, 1006.1(b)
Demonstrative evidence, as, 1103.1
    Federal rules, 1103.2

CHILD ABUSE
Child's testimony from separate room, 601.1(e)
Hearsay exception, out-of-court statements made by children, 804(5).1

INDEX

CHILD ABUSE—Continued
Physician-patient privilege inapplicable, 502.1(a), 502.1(d), 502.1(e)
Rape crisis counselor privilege inapplicable, 506.1
Social worker privilege inapplicable, 505.1

CHILDREN
See also Parent and Child, generally, this index
Abuse. Child Abuse, generally, this index
Bias and interest as witness, 607.6(a)
Competency as witness, 601.1(e)
  Federal rules, 601.3
Custody, character of parent in issue, 402.1(b)
Display of child to permit age determination, 1102.1
  Federal rules, 1102.2
Juvenile Delinquency, generally, this index
Leading questions permissible on direct examination, 611.2(b)
  Federal rules, 611.5(b)
Legitimacy, competency of spouse to testify regarding, 601.1(c)
Paternity Proceedings, generally, this index
Privileged communications with parents, 503.4
  Federal rules, 503.5(b)
Sex crime cases, separate testimonial room, 601.1(e)
Support enforcement proceedings, competency of spouse as witness, 601.1(c)
Unsworn testimony, 601.1(e)
  Corroboration, 300.3(a)(1)

CHIROPRACTORS
Privileged communications. Physician-Patient Privilege, generally, this index

CIRCUMSTANTIAL EVIDENCE
Authenticity, of, 901.4(a)
  Federal rules, 901.4(b)
Burden of production, 300.3(a)(1)
  Federal rules, 300.3(b)
Corroboration, 300.3(a)(1)
  Federal rules, 300.3(b)
Defined, 300.3(a)(1)
Jury instructions,
  Reasonable doubt, 300.4(d)(1)
    Federal rules, 300.4(e)
Relevancy considerations, 401.1(a)
Sufficiency test, 300.3(a)(1)
  Federal rules, 300.3(b)

CIVIL PROCEEDINGS
Burden of persuasion,
  Clear and convincing evidence, 300.4(b)(2)
  Preponderance of evidence, 300.4(b)(1)
Commitment proceedings, self-incrimination, privilege against, 509.1(a)

CLERGY
Privileged communications, 504.1
  Federal rules, 504.2

COHABITATION
No spousal privilege, 503.3(c)

COLLATERAL MATTERS
Best evidence rule, 1004.1(d)
Contradiction of witness on, 607.3
Relevancy considerations, 401.1(b)

COMMERCE
Judicial notice, adjudicative facts, 201.1(c)(11)

COMMERCIAL PAPER
Self-authenticating, 902.1(b)

INDEX

COMMERCIAL PUBLICATIONS
Hearsay exception,
    Federal rules, 803(6).2

COMMITMENT PROCEEDINGS
Self-incrimination, privilege against, 509.1(a)

COMMON-LAW MARRIAGE
Spousal privileges, 503.3(c)

COMMON SCHEME OR PLAN
Uncharged crimes to prove, 404.1(e)

COMPETENCY OF EVIDENCE
    Generally, 100.2, 601.1(a)

COMPETENCY OF WITNESSES
    Generally, 601.1 et seq.
Age, 601.1(e)
    Federal rules, 601.3
Alcohol, under influence of, 601.1(g)
Burden of proof, 601.1(a)
Children, 601.1(e)
    Federal rules, 601.3
Communication-impaired persons, 601.1(f)
Convictions, 601.1(d)
Dead Man's Statute, generally, this index
Deaf persons, 601.1(f)
    Interpreters for, 604.1
        Federal rules, 604.2
Discretion of trial judge, 601.1(a)
    Federal rules, 601.3
Drugs, under influence of, 601.1(g)
    Federal rules, 601.3
Expert opinion, 702.1
    Federal rules, 702.2
Federal rules, 601.3
Hypnotically induced memory, 601.1(h)
    Federal rules, 601.3
Interest in outcome, 601.1(b)
Interpreters, 604.1
    Federal rules, 604.2
Intoxication, 601.1(g)
    Jurors, 606.2
Judges as witnesses, 605.1
    Federal rules, 605.2
Jurors as witnesses, 606.1
    Federal rules, 606.2
Lay opinion, 701.1
    Federal rules, 701.2
Memory hypnotically induced, 601.1(h)
    Federal rules, 601.3
Mental capacity, 601.1(f)
    Federal rules, 601.3
Narcotics, under influence of, 601.1(g)
    Federal rules, 601.3
Oaths and Affirmations, generally, this index
Party to action, 601.1(b)
    Spouse of, 601.1(c)
Per se disqualifications, 601.1(a)
Personal knowledge, 602.1
    Federal rules, 602.2
Presumption of competency, 601.1(a)
Religious beliefs, 610.1
    Federal rules, 610.2
Rule of competency, 601.1(a)
Spouse of party, 601.1(c)

INDEX

COMPETENCY OF WITNESSES—Continued
Unsworn evidence,
    Child testifying, 601.1(e)
    Mentally infirm witness, 601.1(f)
Voir dire of witness, 611.3(d)

COMPLETENESS DOCTRINE
    Generally, 106.1
Federal rules, 106.2
Proposed New York Evidence Code, 106.1

COMPROMISES AND OFFERS TO COMPROMISE
    Generally, 408.1, 408.2
Federal rules, 408.2
Inculpatory words used during negotiations as admission, 802.2(a)
Pleas and plea discussions, generally, this index
Proposed New York Evidence Code, 408.1
Settlement agreement with party, bias and interest of witness, 607.6(a)

COMPUTER-GENERATED DATA
Authentication, 901.9(b)
Business records, hearsay exception, 803(3).1(a)
Demonstrative evidence, use as, 1106
Graphics, 1106
Printouts, best evidence rule, 1002.1
Summaries, 1006.1(a)

CONCEALMENT OF EVIDENCE
Generally, 401.1(a)

CONDITIONAL RELEVANCY
    Generally, 104.1(a)
Federal rules, 104.2

CONFESSIONS
Admissions, distinguished from, 802.1
Best evidence rule, 1001.1(a)
Burden of production,
    Corroboration, 300.3(a)(1)
Clergy, privileged communications, 504.1
    Federal rules, 504.2
Limited admissibility, 105.1
    Federal rules, 105.2
Preliminary rulings, 104.1(b)
    Federal rules, 104.2
Suppressed due to Miranda violations, use to impeach, 509.1(c), 607.8(a)(1)

CONFIDENTIAL COMMUNICATIONS
Privileges, generally, this index

CONFRONTATION RIGHT
"Bruton" rule, 105.1, 105.2
Cross-examination, 611.3(a)
    Federal rules, 611.5(c)
Exposure of biased witness, 607.6(a)
    Federal rules, 607.6(b)
Hearsay exceptions, consistency with,
    Coconspirator's statements, 802.2(g), 802.3(d)
    Declaration against interest, 804(3).1(b)
    Dying declaration, 804(2).2
    Former testimony, 804(1).1(b), 804(1).2
    General rule, 804(5).2
    Police records, 803(3).1(b)
    Residual or catchall exception, 804(5).2

CONFUSION
Basis for exclusion of relevant evidence, 401.1(b)

"CONNECTING UP"
Conditional relevance shown later, 103.1(c), 104.1(a)

INDEX

"CONNECTING UP"—Continued
Conditional relevance shown later—Continued
    Federal rules, 103.2(c), 104.2

CONSCIOUSNESS OF GUILT
Relevancy considerations, 401.1(a)

CONSPIRACY
Foundation for admissibility of coconspirator statements, 104.2
Statements made during and in furtherance of as admission, 802.2(g)
    Federal rules, 802.3(d)

CONSTITUTIONAL LAW
Affirmative defenses, shifting burden of production, 300.4(d)(2)
Criminal proceedings, presumptions,
    Constitutional restraints, 302.1(a)
Fifth amendment privilege against self-incrimination, 509.1(a) et seq.
Fourth amendment rights,
    Preliminary rulings, 104.1(b)
    Violations, basis for exclusion of relevant evidence, 401.1(b)
Sixth amendment confrontation right. Confrontation Right, generally, this index
Suppressed confession admissible to impeach, 509.1(c), 607.8(a)(1)

CONTRACTS
Burden of proof, 300.2
Mistake, burden of persuasion,
    Clear and convincing evidence, 300.4(b)(2)
Negotiations, 408.2
Reformation, burden of persuasion,
    Clear and convincing evidence, 300.4(b)(2)
Similar transactions, 405.1(c)
    Federal rules, 405.2(b)
Trade secrets, privilege, 513.1

CONTRADICTION OF WITNESSES
Impeachment, generally, this index
Own witness, 607.4(a)
Prior Inconsistent Statements, generally, this index

CONVERSATIONS
Recordings, generally, this index
Telephone conversations, generally. Authentication and Identification, this index

CONVERSION
Bailment, presumptions, 301.4

CONVICTION OF CRIME
Appeal, effect on offer to impeach, 609.2
Competency of witnesses, 601.1(d)
Criminal judgments of conviction, hearsay exception, 803(5).1(*o*)
Extrinsic evidence admissible to show, 609.1(a)
Impeachment, 601.1(d), 609.1
    Civil cases, 609.1(b)
    Criminal cases, 609.1(c)
    Federal rules, 609.2
    Pretrial ruling on admissibility, 609.1(c)
        Appellate review of, 103.2(d)
Judgment of previous conviction, hearsay exception,
    Federal rules, 803(5).2(d)
Juvenile delinquency adjudications, not admissible as convictions, 609.1(a)
    Federal rules, 609.2
Own witness, prior convictions to soften blow of cross-examination, 607.4(a), 607.5(a)(1)
Proposed New York Evidence Code, 609.1(c)
Relevancy considerations, 609.1(c)
    Federal rules, 609.2

COPIES
Best Evidence Rule, generally, this index

INDEX

CORPORATIONS
Attorney-client privilege, application, 501.1(f)
    Federal rules, 501.2
Corporate employees, generally. Employers and Employees, this index
Self-incrimination, privilege against, 509.1(b)
Shareholders,
    Competency as witnesses, dead man's statute, 601.2(b)

CORROBORATION
Burden of proof, 300.3(a)(1)
    Burden of production,
        Accomplice testimony, 300.3(a)(1)
            Federal rules, 300.3(b)
        Annulment, 300.3(a)(1)
        Confessions, 300.3(a)(1)
        Minors, unsworn testimony, 300.3(a)(1)
    Federal rules, 300.3(b)
Circumstantial evidence, 300.3(a)(1)
    Federal rules, 300.3(b)

CREDIBILITY OF WITNESSES
    Generally, 607.1 et seq.
Attacking and supporting hearsay declarant, 806.1
Character evidence to prove, 608.0 et seq.
Impeachment, generally, this index
Rehabilitation and Support of Credibility, generally, this index

CRIMES AND OFFENSES
    See also Criminal Defendants, generally, this index; Criminal Proceedings, generally, this index
Attorney-client privilege, exception when future fraud contemplated, 501.1(g)
    Federal rules, 501.2
Criminal judgments of conviction, hearsay exception, 803(5).1(o)
Informer privilege, 510.1
    Federal rules, 510.2
Judgment of previous conviction, hearsay exception,
    Federal rules, 803(5).2(d)
Prior Crimes or Misconduct, generally, this index
Social worker privilege, exception for future crimes or harmful acts, 505.1
Uncharged Crimes, generally, this index
Victims of Crime, generally, this index

CRIMINAL CHARGES
Multiple counts, evidence of other counts, 404.1(i)

CRIMINAL DEFENDANTS
Aliases, used to impeach, 607.2
Arrests, generally, this index
Character evidence as proof of conduct, 402.1(d)
    Federal rules, 402.2
Codefendants; self-incrimination, privilege against, 509.1(b)
Confessions, generally, this index
Confrontation Right, generally, this index
Consciousness of guilt evidence, relevancy, 401.1(a)
Conviction of crime offered for impeachment, 609.1(c)
    Federal rules, 609.2
Cross-examination, 509.1(b)
Flight evidence, relevancy, 401.1(a)
    Federal rules, 401.2
Guilty pleas, generally. Pleas and Plea Discussions, this index
Hypnotically induced memory, 601.1(h)
    Federal rules, 601.3
Past recollection recorded, using to identify, 803(2).1
Physical features, injuries as evidence without testifying, 1102.1
Pleas and Plea Discussions, generally, this index
Postcrime conduct, relevancy, 401.1(a)
Prior Crimes or Misconduct, generally, this index
Prior identification by witness, 607.5(a)(1), 801(2).1, 801(2).2

INDEX

CRIMINAL DEFENDANTS—Continued
Privileged communications, joint defense doctrine, 501.1(e)
    Federal rules, 501.2
Real evidence, as, 1102.1
Recalling by court for questioning, 614.1(a)
Self-Defense, generally, this index
Self-incrimination, privilege against, 509.1(b), 509.1(c)
    Prior acts of misconduct used to impeach, 608.2(a)
        Federal rules, 608.2(b)
Sexual history, 413.1
Uncharged Crimes, generally, this index
Unsworn evidence against, 601.1(e), 601.1(f)
Victim's physician-patient privilege, defendant may not assert, 502.1(b)
Voice as real evidence, 1102.1
    Federal rules, 1102.2
Wealth, relevancy, 401.1(b)
Witnesses, as; sequestration, 615.1

CRIMINAL PROCEEDINGS
Affirmative defenses, burden of persuasion,
    Preponderance of evidence, 300.4(d)(2)
Authentication and Identification, generally, this index
Burden of persuasion, reasonable doubt, 300.4(d)(1)
Criminal Defendants, generally, this index
Criminal judgments of conviction, hearsay exception, 803(5).1(*o*)
Defenses, generally, this index
DNA analysis, expert testimony regarding, 702.1(c)
Impeachment of own witness with prior inconsistent statements, 607.4(b)
    Federal rules, 607.4(c)
Insanity as affirmative defense, expert testimony, 703.1
Interpreter, waiver of right to obtain, 604.1
Judicial notice, effect, 201.1(e)
    Federal rules, 201.2
Jury views, 1107.1
    Federal rules, 1107.2
Law enforcement records, hearsay exception, 803(3).1(b)
Motions in limine, 103.1(d)
    Federal rules, 103.2(d)
Pleas and Plea Discussions, generally, this index
Presumptions,
    Constitutional restraints, 302.1(a)
    Federal rules, 302.2
    Motor vehicles, weapons in,
        Presumption of possession, 302.1(b)
    Receiving stolen property, possession, 302.1(b)
Prior inconsistent statements used for impeachment, 801(1).2(a)
Recorded recollection, use, 803(2).2
Rosario rule, 612.1(b)
Secondary evidence of document in defendant's possession, 1004.1(c)

CROSS-EXAMINATION
    Generally, 611.3(a)
Character witnesses, 402.1(d)
    Federal rules, 402.2
Completeness doctrine, 106.1
    Federal rules, 106.2
Confrontation Right, generally, this index
Federal rules, 611.5(c)
Impeachment, generally, this index
Judicial discretion, 611.3(c)
    Federal rules, 611.5(c)
Leading questions, 611.2(b)
    Federal rules, 611.5(b)
Question, Form of, generally, this index
Recross, 611.4
    Federal rules, 611.5(c)
Scope, 611.3(b)

INDEX

CROSS-EXAMINATION—Continued
Scope—Continued
    Federal rules, 611.5(b)
Self-incrimination, privilege against, 611.3(a)
Voir dire of the witness, 611.3(d)
Waiver of right, 611.3(a)
Witness unavailable for, 611.3(a)

CUMULATIVE EVIDENCE
Exclusion, 401.1(b)

CUSTODY OF CHILDREN
Character of parent in issue, 402.1(b)

CUSTOM
Habit and Custom, generally, this index

"DAUBERT" STANDARD
Foundation for expert testimony based on out-of-court material, effect on, 703.2
Scientific evidence, 702.2(b)

DEAD MAN'S STATUTE
    Generally, 601.2
Accident, facts exception, 601.2(e)
Agents,
    Deceased agent, principal not entitled to invoke statute, 601.2(c)
    Transaction between decedent and principal, agent competent to testify, 601.2(b)
    Transaction between decedent's agent and interested witness, 601.2(d)
Business records, 601.2(a)
Communication within statute, 601.2(d)
Corporate shareholders, competency as witnesses, 601.2(b)
Decedent's testimony, introduction of as waiver, 601.2(f)
Definitions,
    Person interested in event, 601.2(b)
Disqualified witnesses, 601.2(b)
Documentary evidence, generally not barred, 601.2(a)
Exceptions, 601.2(e)
Failure to object to competency, 601.2(f)
Federal rules, 601.3
Former testimony exception, 601.2(e)
Indirect proof, rule against, 601.2(d)
Life insurance beneficiaries, standing to invoke statute, 601.2(c)
Negligent operation of vehicle exception, 601.2(e)
Parent and child, 601.2(b)
Parties, incompetent witnesses, 601.2(b)
Pension beneficiaries, standing to invoke statute, 601.2(c)
Person interested in event, defined, 601.2(b)
Predecessors in interest, 601.2(b)
Preliminary hearings, inapplicable to, 601.2(g)
Prohibited subject matter, 601.2(d)
Protected persons, 601.2(c)
    Testimony or examination as waiver, 601.2(f)
Renunciation of interest, 601.2(b)
Spouses, 601.2(b)
    Joint property ownership, survivor competent to testify, 601.2(e)
Standing to invoke, 601.2(c)
Successors in interest, 601.2(c)
Transaction within statute, 601.2(d)
Waiver, 601.2(f)
Will contests, 601.2(b)

DEAF PERSONS
Competency as witnesses, 601.1(f)
Interpreters for, 604.1
    Federal rules, 604.2

DEATH
Attorney-client privilege, effect on, 501.1(a)
Burden of proof, effect on, 300.4(b)(1)

INDEX

DEATH—Continued
Dead Man's Statute, generally, this index
Dying declarations,
    Hearsay exception, 804(2).1
        Federal rules, 804(2).2
Physician-patient privilege, effect on, 502.1(a) et seq.
Spousal privileges, 503.3(e)
Suicide, physician-patient privilege applicable despite lack of consent to treatment, 502.1(b)
Wrongful death actions,
    Burden of persuasion, preponderance of evidence, 300.4(b)(1)
        Noseworthy doctrine, 300.4(b)(1)

DEBTORS AND CREDITORS
Joint debtors,
    Survivor, protected by dead man's statute, 601.2(c)
Receipt for payment, best evidence rule, 1001.1(a)

DECLARATIONS
Against interest, 804(3).1
    Civil cases, 804(3).1(a)
        Federal rules, 804(3).2
    Criminal cases, 804(3).1(b)
        Federal rules, 804(3).2
    Federal rules, 804(3).2
    Hearsay exception, 802.1, 804(3).1
Dying,
    Hearsay exception, 804(2).1
        Federal rules, 804(2).2
Pedigree, hearsay exception, 804(4).1
    Federal rules, 804(4).2

DEFAMATION
Burden of persuasion, clear and convincing evidence, 300.4(b)(2)
Character of victim in issue, 402.1(b)

DEFENDANTS
Criminal Defendants, generally, this index

DEFENSES
Affirmative Defenses, generally, this index
Burden of production,
    Federal rules, 300.4(e)
Reasonable doubt, 300.4(d)(2)

DEFINITIONS
Burden of persuasion, 300.1
Burden of production, 300.1
Circumstantial evidence, 300.3(a)
Community, reputation in, 402.1(d)
Declarant, 801.1(a)
Direct evidence, 300.3(a)
Duplicate, best evidence rule, 1001.1(b)
Evidence, 100.2
Hearsay, 801.1(a)
Judicial notice,
    Adjudicative facts, 200.1
    Legislative facts, 200.1
Judicial notice of law, 200.1
Original, best evidence rule, 1001.1(b)
Person interested in event, dead man's statute, 601.2(b)
Personal knowledge, 602.1
Photographs, best evidence rule, 1001.1(b)
Presumption, 301.2
Real and demonstrative evidence, 1100.1
Recent fabrication, 607.5(a)(2)(c)
Recordings, best evidence rule, 1001.1(b)
Relevancy, 401.1
Statement, 801.1(a)

1006

INDEX

DEFINITIONS—Continued
Unavailability, 804.1
Writings, best evidence rule, 1001.1(b)

DELAY
Basis for exclusion of relevant evidence, 401.1(b)

DEMEANOR EVIDENCE
Effect on credibility, 607.1

DEMONSTRATIVE EVIDENCE
Real and Demonstrative Evidence, generally, this index

DENTISTS
Privileged communications. Physician-Patient Privilege, generally, this index

DEPOSITIONS
Ordered by judge, 614.1(a)
Own witness if deposition introduced as affirmative evidence, 607.4(a)

DIAGRAMS
Demonstrative evidence, as, 1103.1
    Federal rules, 1103.2

DIRECT EVIDENCE
Burden of production, 300.3(a)(1)
Defined, 300.3(a)(1)
Relevancy considerations, 401.1(a)

DIRECT EXAMINATION
Examination, generally, this index

DIRECTED VERDICT
Burden of production, 300.3(a)(1)
    Shifting of burden, 300.3(a)(2)

DISABLED PERSONS
Interpreters for, competency as witnesses, 604.1
    Federal rules, 604.2
Mental or sensory impairment, impeachment value, 607.7(a)

DISCOVERY
Attorney-Client Privilege, generally, this index
Depositions, generally, this index
Documents disclosed, waiver of privilege or immunity, 501.1(h), 501.3(b)(2)
    Federal rules, 501.2, 501.3(c)
Notice to produce not discovery device, 1004.1(c)
Work Product Immunities, generally, this index

DISHONESTY
Character Evidence, generally, this index
Credibility of Witnesses, generally, this index
Crime of, conviction offered to impeach, 609.1
    Federal rules, 609.2
Perjury, generally, this index
Rehabilitation and Support of Credibility, generally, this index
Reputation, use to impeach, 608.1(a)
    Federal rules, 608.1(b)

DISMISSAL OF ACTIONS
Burden of production, 300.3(a)(1)

DIVORCE
Custody of children, character of parent in issue, 402.1(b)

DNA
Analysis, expert testimony regarding, 702.1(c)
Records and reports, hearsay exception, 803(3).1(c)

DOCTORS
Medical Diagnosis and Treatment, generally, this index
Physician-Patient Privilege, generally, this index

INDEX

DOCUMENTS
Acknowledged,
  Self-authenticating, 902.1(a)
    Federal rules, 902.1(b)
Ancient,
  Authentication, 901.8(a)
    Federal rules, 901.8(b)
  Hearsay exception, 803(7).1(b)
    Federal rules, 803(7).2(b)
Attorney-client privilege, 501.1(a), 501.1(c)
  Federal rules, 501.2
Authentication and Identification, generally, this index
Best Evidence Rule, generally, this index
Records and Reports, generally, this index
Refreshing recollection, admissibility, 612.1(a)
Self-incrimination, privilege against, 509.1(b)

DOMESTIC RELATIONS PROCEEDINGS
Court-appointed expert witnesses, 706.1

DRAWINGS
Demonstrative evidence, as, 1103.1
  Federal rules, 1103.2

DRUGS
Authentication and identification, 901.1(a), 1101.1
Impeachment,
  Based on consumption of, 607.7(a)
    Federal rules, 607.7(b)
  Drug use at time of operative event, 601.1(g)
Marijuana,
  Opinion testimony, 702.1(a)
Witnesses under influence of, effect on competency, 601.1(g)
  Federal rules, 601.3

DUE PROCESS
Criminal proceedings,
  Presumptions,
    Constitutional restraints, 302.1(a)
  Statutory permissive inference,
    Rational connection test, 302.1(a)

DUPLICATES
Best Evidence Rule, generally, this index

DURESS
Burden of persuasion, 300.4(d)(2)
Burden of production,
  Federal rules, 300.4(e)

DYING DECLARATIONS
Hearsay exception, 804(2).1
  Federal rules, 804(2).2

EAVESDROPPING
Attorney-client privilege, 501.1(a), 501.1(e)
Physician-patient privilege, 502.1(b)
Spousal privileges; recordings, admissibility, 503.3(a)

ELECTIONS
Voting, secrecy of vote privilege, 512.1
  Federal rules, 512.2

EMERGENCY MEDICAL TECHNICIANS
Physician-patient privilege not applicable unless acting as physician's agent, 502.1(b)

EMINENT DOMAIN
Similar sales, 405.1(d)

INDEX

EMPLOYERS AND EMPLOYEES
Attorney's employees, applicability of attorney-client privilege, 501.1(a), 501.1(e)
    Federal rules, 501.2
Bias and interest of witness, 607.6(a)
Corporate employees,
    Control over corporation's distribution of communication, 501.1(f)
        Federal rules, 501.2
    Witnesses, as; dead man's statute, 501.1(f)
Negligence actions, character of employee in issue, 402.1(b)
Social agency employees, social worker privilege inapplicable, 505.1

ENTRAPMENT
Burden of persuasion, 300.4(d)(2)
Burden of production,
    Federal rules, 300.4(e)
Character of defendant in issue, 402.1(b)

ERROR
Harmless, 103.1(e)
    Federal rules, 103.2(e)
Plain error doctrine, 103.2(a)

ESCAPE
Relevancy considerations, 401.1(a)

EXAMINATION
Cross-Examination, generally, this index
Judicial questioning of witnesses, 614.1(b)
    Federal rules, 614.2
Jurors questioning witnesses, 614.1(c)
    Federal rules, 614.2
Question, Form of, generally, this index
Redirect and recross, 611.4
    Federal rules, 611.5(c)
Testimony, generally, this index
Voir dire of witness, 611.3(d)

EXCEPTIONS TO HEARSAY RULE
Absence as basis for unavailability, 804(1).1(b), 804.1
"Catchall" exceptions, 804(5).1
    Federal rules, 804(5).2
Child abuse, out-of-court statements made by children, 804(5).1
Declarant unavailable, 804.1 et seq.
    Absence as basis for unavailability, 804(1).1(b), 804.1
    Assertion of self-incrimination privilege as basis for unavailability, 804.1
    Death or illness as basis for unavailability, 804.1
    Declarations against interest. Against interest, generally. Declarations, this index
    Dying declarations, 804(2).1
        Federal rules, 804(2).1
    Former testimony, 804(1).1(a)
        Civil cases, 804(1).1(a)
        Criminal cases, 804(1).1(b)
        Federal rules, 804(1).2
    Lack of memory as basis for unavailability, 804.1
    Refusal to testify as basis for unavailability, 804.1
    Threats and intimidation used against witness, 807.1
Declarant's availability immaterial, 803.1 et seq.
    Accident reports, 803(3).1(a)
        Federal rules, 803(3).2
    Admissions, generally, this index
    Agriculture inspection certificates, 803(5).1(j)
    Ancient documents, 803(7).1(b)
        Federal rules, 803(7).2(b)
    Business records, 803(3).1(a)
        Federal rule, 803(3).2
    Character reputation,
        Federal rules, 803(7).2(c)

INDEX

EXCEPTIONS TO HEARSAY RULE—Continued
Declarant's availability immaterial—Continued
  Commercial publications,
    Federal rules, 803(6).2
  Computer information, 803(3).1(a)
  Criminal judgments of conviction, 803(5).1(o)
  DNA reports, 803(3).1(c)
  Excited utterances, 803(1).1(b)
    Federal rules, 803(1).2(b)
  Family records, 803(7).1(a)
    Federal rules, 803(7).2(a)
  Genetic markers, 803(3).1(c)
  Government records, 803(3).1(c)
  Hospital records, 803(3).1(c)
  Intent, expressions of, 803(1).1(c)
    Federal rules, 803(1).2(c)
  Investigatory reports by governmental agencies, 803(5).2(a)
  Judgment of previous conviction,
    Federal rules, 803(5).2(d)
  Justice of the peace proceedings, 803(5).1(m)
  Law enforcement records in criminal cases, 803(3).1(b)
  Learned treatises, 803(6).2
    Federal rules, 803(6).2
  Market reports, 803(6).1
    Federal rules, 803(6).2
  Medical diagnosis or treatment, statements, 803(1).1, 803(1).1(d)
    Federal rules, 803(1).2(d)
  Medical records, 803(3).1(c)
    Federal rules, 803(3).2
  MRIs, 803(3).1(c)
  Past recollection recorded, 803(2).1
    Federal rules, 803(2).2
  Population certificates, 803(5).1(k)
  Present sense impressions, 803(1).1(a)
    Federal rules, 803(1).2(a)
  Proposed New York Evidence Code §803, 801(1).2(b)
  Public Records, generally, this index
  Recorded recollection, 803(2).1
    Federal rules, 803(2).2
  Regularly kept records, 803(3).1(a)
  Religious institution records, 803(5).1(p)
    Federal rules, 803(5).2(f)
  Reputation, 803(7).1(c)
    Federal rules, 803(7).2(c)
  Spontaneous statements, 803(1).1
  State department records, 803(3).1(c)
  State of mind or physical condition, 803(1).1(c)
    Federal rules, 803(1).2(c)
  Surveyor's standard, 803(5).1(*l*)
  Weather records, 803(5).1(i)
  Writings, recorded recollection, 803(2).1
    Federal rules, 803(2).2
  X-rays, 803(3).1(c)
Family history, 804(4).1
  Federal rules, 804(4).2
Notice required for residual exception, 804(5).2
Pedigree, 804(4).1
  Federal rules, 804(4).2
Personal history, 804(4).1
  Federal rules, 804(4).2
Probative value required for residual exception, 804(5).2
Residual exceptions, 804(5).1
  Federal rules, 804(5).2
Unavailability defined, 804.1

EXCITED UTTERANCES
Hearsay exception, 803(1).1(b)

INDEX

EXCITED UTTERANCES—Continued
Hearsay exception—Continued
    Federal rules, 803(1).2(b)

EXCLUSION OF WITNESSES
Exclusion from courtroom, 615.1
    Federal rules, 615.2

EXCLUSIONARY RULES
Evidence admitted for impeachment purposes despite, 607.3
Relevancy considerations, 401.1(b)

EXECUTORS AND ADMINISTRATORS
Dead Man's Statute, generally, this index
Will Contests, generally, this index

EXPERIMENTS AND DEMONSTRATIONS
Effects of human injuries, 1102.1
    Federal rules, 1102.2
Jury experimentation, 1108.1
    Federal rules, 1108.2
Real and demonstrative evidence, as, 1105.1
    Federal rules, 1105.2

EXPERT TESTIMONY
    Generally, 702.1(a)
Basis of testimony, 703.1
    Federal rules, 703.2
Bias and interest of witness, 607.6(a)
Blood tests, 702.1(c)
Comparisons by experts, 901.3(a)
    Federal, 901.3(b)
Computer-generated graphics used in conjunction with, 1106.1
Conclusory opinions, 704.1
Court-appointed experts, 614.1(a), 706.1
    Federal rules, 706.2
"Daubert" standard, scientific evidence, 702.2(b)
Disclosure of facts underlying opinion, 705.1
    Federal rules, 705.2
Eyewitnesses, psychologist testimony to unreliability of, 702.1(c)
Federal rules, 702.2(a)
Foundation for testimony based on out-of-court material, 703.1
    Federal rules, 703.2
"Frye" standard, scientific evidence, 702.1(b)
Hair analysis, 702.1(c)
Handwriting, 702.1(c), 901.3(a)
    Federal rules, 901.3(b)
Hearsay as basis of, 703.1
    Federal rules, 703.2
Hypothetical question to elicit testimony, 705.1
    Federal rules, 705.2
Impeachment of experts, 702.1(f)
    Learned treatises, use, 803(6).1
        Federal rules, 803(6).2
Information compiled by experts, trial preparation immunity, 501.3(b)(1)
    Federal rules, 501.3(c)
Interested observer, 702.1(d)
Interpreters qualified as experts, 604.2
Medical testimony, 702.1(c)
Mental condition of witness, regarding, 607.7(a), 702.1(c)
Personal knowledge, 602.1, 703.1
    Federal rules, 703.2
Physical condition, 702.1(c)
Polygraph, 702.1(b), 702.1(c)
Pretrial discovery concerning experts, 501.3(b)(1)
    Federal rules, 501.3(c)
Prior inconsistent statements, impeachment by, 607.8(a)(2)
Problems of expert testimony, 702.1(c)

INDEX

EXPERT TESTIMONY—Continued
Proposed New York Evidence Code, 702.1(a), 703.1, 706.1
Psychiatrists, professional reliance rule, 703.1
Qualifications, 702.1(e)
    Federal rules, 702.2(a)(n.12)
Radar gun, 702.1(c)
Rape trauma syndrome, 702.1(c)
Sanity, 702.1(c)
Scientific evidence, recurring problems, 702.1(c)
    Standard for novel theories and methods, 702.1(b)
        Federal rules, 702.2(b)
Sobriety tests, 702.1(c)
Stipulation to expert's qualifications, 702.1(e)
Ultimate issues, 704.1
    Federal rules, 704.2
Voir dire of witness, 611.3(d)

EXTRINSIC EVIDENCE
Bias and interest of witness, admissible to show, 607.6(a)
    Federal rules, 607.6(b)
Character for truthfulness, admissible to show, 608.1(a)
    Federal rules, 608.2
Conviction of crime, admissible to show, 609.1(a)
Impeachment purposes, 607.2
    Admissible for noncollateral matters, 607.3
Mental or sensory impairment, admissible to show, 607.7(a)
    Federal rules, 607.7(b)
Prior inconsistent statements, admissibility to prove, 607.8(a)(3)
    Federal rules, 607.8(b)
Prior misconduct to impeach, extrinsic evidence prohibited, 608.2(a)
    Federal rules, 608.2(b)

EYEWITNESSES
Habit evidence, effect of eyewitnesses, 406.1(e)
Psychologist testimony to unreliability, 702.1(c)

FALSE STATEMENT
Dishonesty, generally, this index
Perjury, generally, this index

FAMILY
History, hearsay exception, 804(4).1
    Federal rules, 804(4).2
Records, hearsay exception, 803(7).1(a)
    Federal rules, 803(7).2(a)

FEDERAL RULES
Absence of public records, hearsay exception, 803(5).2(e)
Accident reports, hearsay exception, 803(3).2
Admissions,
    Acts, as, 802.3(b)
    Adoptive, 802.3(b)
    Agent's or servant's statements as, 802.3(c)
    Coconspirator's statements, 802.3(d)
    Pleadings, 802.3(a)
    Statements, as, 802.3(b)
Ancient documents,
    Authentication and identification, 901.8(b)
    Hearsay exception, 803(7).2(b)
Attorney-client privilege, 501.2
Authentication and identification, 900.1 et seq.
    Ancient documents, 901.8(b)
    Circumstantial evidence of authenticity, 901.4(b)
    Comparisons by trier or expert witness, 901.3(b)
    Lay opinion on handwriting, 901.2(b)
    Methods provided by statute or rule, 901.10(b)
    Process or system, 901.9(b)
    Public records, 901.7(b)

INDEX

FEDERAL RULES—Continued
Authentication and identification—Continued
  Self-authentication, 902.1(b)
  Telephone conversations, 901.6(b)
  Testimony of witness with knowledge, 901.1(b)
  Voice identification, 901.5(b)
Baptismal certificates, hearsay exception, 803(5).2(f)
Best evidence rule, 1001.1 et seq.
Bias and interest of witness, 607.6(b)
Burden of proof,
  Burden of persuasion,
    Civil proceedings,
      Clear and convincing evidence, 300.4(c)
    Clear and convincing evidence, 300.4(b)(2)
      Moral turpitude, 300.4(b)(2)
    Preponderance of evidence,
      Civil proceedings, 300.4(b)(1)
  Burden of production,
    Acquittal motion, 300.3(b)
    Affirmative defenses,
      Shifting of burden, 300.4(e)
    Alibi, 300.4(e)
    Circumstantial evidence, 300.4(e)
    Corroboration,
      Accomplice testimony, 300.3(b)
    Defenses, 300.4(e)
    Directed verdict motion, 300.3(b)
    Duress, 300.4(e)
    Entrapment, 300.4(e)
    Insanity, 300.4(e)
    Self-defense, 300.4(e)
    Sufficiency test, 300.3(b)
  Corroboration, 300.3(b)
Business records, hearsay exception, 803(3).2
  Absence of records, 803(4).2
Character evidence, 402.2
  Hearsay exception, 803(7).2(c)
Circumstantial evidence,
  Authenticity, of, 901.4(b)
  Corroboration, 300.3(b)
Clergy, privileged communications, 504.2
Commercial publications, hearsay exception, 803(6).2
Competency of witnesses, 601.3
  Credibility, 607.1 et seq.
    Rehabilitation of, 607.5(b)
  Interpreters, competency as witnesses, 604.2
  Judges as witnesses, 605.2
  Jurors as witnesses, 606.2
  Oaths and affirmations, 603.2
  Personal knowledge, 602.2
Compromises and offers to compromise, 408.2
Conviction of crime offered for impeachment, 609.2
Corroboration,
  Burden of proof, 300.3(b)
  Circumstantial evidence, 300.3(b)
Credibility of witnesses, 607.1 et seq.
  Rehabilitation of, 607.5(b)
Criminal proceedings,
  Presumptions, 302.2
Cross-examination, 611.5(c)
Dead man's statute, 601.3
Declarations against interest, 804(3).2
"Door opening" rationale for introduction of extrinsic evidence of contradiction, 607.3
Dying declarations, hearsay exception, 804(2).2
Excited utterances, hearsay exception, 803(1).2(b)
Expert testimony, 702.2(a), 703.2

INDEX

FEDERAL RULES—Continued
Expert testimony—Continued
    Court-appointed experts, 706.2
Expressions of intent, hearsay exception, 803(1).2(c)
Family history, hearsay exception, 804(4).2
Family records, hearsay exception, 803(7).2(a)
Foreign records, hearsay exception, 803(3).2
Former testimony, hearsay exception, 804(1).2
Government communications, privilege, 511.2
Habit and custom, 406.2
Hearsay, 801.1(a)
Identification testimony not considered hearsay, 801(2).2
Impeachment, 607.1 et seq.
    Bias and interest of witness, 607.6(b)
    Mental or sensory impairment, 607.7(b)
    Own witness, 607.4(c)
    Prior crimes or misconduct, 608.2(b)
    Prior inconsistent statements, 607.8(b)
    Truthfulness, bad reputation for, 608.1(b)
Informer privilege, 510.2
Interpreters, competency as witnesses, 604.2
Investigatory reports by governmental agencies, hearsay exception, 803(5).2(a)
Journalist privilege, 508.2
Judges, competency as witnesses, 605.2
Judgment of previous conviction, hearsay exception, 803(5).2(d)
Judicial notice,
    Adjudicative facts, 201.2
        Commerce and trade matters, 201.2
        Effect, 201.1(e)
        Facts ascertained from reference to reliable sources, 201.1(b)(2)
        Geographical facts, 201.2
        Jury instructions, 201.2
        Post-notice hearing, 201.2
        Procedure, 201.2
        Public records, 201.2
        Scientific and mechanical facts, 201.2
    Judicial notice of law,
        Discretionary, 203.2
        Mandatory, 203.2
        Notice, 203.2
    Legislative facts, 202.1
        Defined, 200.1
Jurors, competency as witnesses, 606.2
Lay opinion, 701.2
    Handwriting, 901.2(b)
Learned treatises, hearsay exception, 803(6).2
Liability insurance, 411.2
Library records, privileged communications, 507.2
Market reports, hearsay exception, 803(6).2
Marriage certificates, hearsay exception, 803(5).2(f)
Medical diagnosis or treatment, statements; hearsay exception, 803(1).2(d)
Medical expenses, payment, 409.2
Medical records, hearsay exception, 803(3).2
Mental or sensory impairment, impeachment by, 607.7(b)
Oaths and affirmations, 603.2
Order of trial, 611.5(a)
Own witness, impeachment of, 607.4(c)
Past recollection recorded, hearsay exception, 803(2).2
Pedigree, hearsay exception, 804(4).2
Personal history, hearsay exception, 804(4).2
Personal knowledge, competency of witnesses, 602.2
Physician-patient privilege not recognized, 502.2
Pleas and plea discussions, 410.2
Political vote, 512.2
Present sense impressions, hearsay exception, 803(1).2(a)
Presumptions, criminal proceedings, 302.2

INDEX

FEDERAL RULES—Continued
Prior consistent statements not hearsay, 801(1).3(b)
Prior crimes or misconduct, impeachment by, 608.2(b)
Prior inconsistent statements,
    Impeachment by, 607.8(b)
    Statements not hearsay, 801(1).3(a)
Privileges, 500.2
Question, form of, 611.5(b)
Rape crisis counselor, privileged communications, 506.1
Real and demonstrative evidence, 1100.1 et seq.
    Drawings, diagrams and models, 1103.2
    Exhibits in jury room, 1108.2
    Experiments and demonstrations, 1105.2
        Jury conducting experiments, 1108.2
    Jury views, 1107.2
    Persons, physical features and injuries, 1102.2
    Photographic and related evidence, 1104.2
    Tangible objects, 1101.2
Real property, documents affecting interest in; hearsay exception, 803(5).2(c)
    Statements contained in, 803(7).2(b)
Recorded recollection, hearsay exception, 803(2).2
Redirect and recross examination, 611.5(c)
Refreshing memory, 612.2
Regularly kept records, hearsay exception, 803(3).2
Rehabilitation of credibility, 607.5(b)
Relevancy, 401.2
Religious belief of witness, 610.2
Religious institution records, hearsay exception, 803(5).2(f)
Reputation, hearsay exception, 803(7).2(c)
Residual hearsay exceptions, 804(5).2
Rulings on evidence, 103.2
Sexual history, 413.1
Shield laws, 412.2
Social worker privilege, 505.2
Spousal privileges, 503.5
State of mind, hearsay exception, 803(1).2(c)
Subsequent remedial measures, 407.2
Trade secrets, 513.2
Treatises, hearsay exception, 803(6).2
Truthfulness, bad reputation for, 608.1(b)
Ultimate issues, opinion testimony, 704.2
Uncharged crimes, 404.2
Vital statistics, hearsay exception, 803(5).2(b)
Witnesses,
    Calling or questioning by court or jury, 614.2
    Exclusion from courtroom, 615.2
Work product immunities, 501.3(c)

FIDUCIARIES
Attorney-client privilege, fiduciary duty owed by client to party seeking disclosure, 501.1(g)

FILMS
Motion Pictures and Videotapes, generally, this index

FINGERPRINTS
Identification, expert comparison and analysis, 901.3(a)

FLIGHT
Relevancy considerations, 401.1(a)
    Federal rules, 401.2

FOREIGN RECORDS
Authentication, 901.7(a), 902.1(a)
    Federal rules, 902.1(b)
Hearsay exception,
    Federal rules, 803(3).2

INDEX

FORMER TESTIMONY
Dead man's statute exception, 601.2(e)
Hearsay exception, 804(1).1(a)
   Civil cases, 804(1).1(a)
   Criminal cases, 804(1).1(b)
   Federal rules, 804(1).2

FOUNDATION QUESTIONS
Authentication and Identification, generally, this index
Business records, hearsay exception, 803(3).1(a)
   Absence of,
      Federal rules, 803(3).2
   Federal rules, 803(3).2
Impeachment by prior inconsistent statements, 607.8(a)(3), 801(1).2(a)
   Federal rules, 607.8(b)
Maps, hearsay exception, 803(5).1(d)
Other accidents, 405.1(b), 405.2(a)
Real and Demonstrative Evidence, generally, this index

FRAUD
Attorney-client privilege, exception when future fraud contemplated, 501.1(g)
   Federal rules, 501.2
Burden of persuasion, clear and convincing evidence, 300.4(b)(2)
Conviction offered to impeach, 609.2
Medicaid practices, exception to physician-patient privilege, 502.1(d)
Prior instances of fraud, 404.1(*l*)
   Impeachment value, 608.2(b)
Social worker privilege, exception for fraud, 505.1
Spousal privileges, exceptions, 503.3(e)
   Federal rules, 503.5(a)
Work product immunities, exception for fraud, 501.3(c)

FREEDOM OF INFORMATION LAW
Privilege for official information, effect, 511.1
   Federal application, 511.2

FREEDOM OF THE PRESS
Journalist privilege, 508.1
   Federal rules, 508.2

"FRYE" STANDARD
Authentication of scientific evidence, 901.9(a)
   Computer-generated graphics, 1106.1
Federal application, 702.2(b)
Scientific theories, novel; expert testimony, 702.1(b)

GENETIC MARKERS
Hearsay exception, 803(3).1(c)

GOVERNMENT COMMUNICATIONS
Investigatory reports, hearsay exception, 803(5).1(c)
Privilege, 511.1
   Federal rules, 511.2
Records, hearsay exception, 803(3).1(c)

GRAND JURIES
Plea bargain, testimony against others induced by; admissibility, 410.1

GUARDIANSHIP PROCEEDINGS
Physician-patient privilege, exception; mentally ill parents, 502.1(d), 502.1(e)

GUILT OR INNOCENCE
Defendant's conduct offered to prove consciousness of guilt, 401.1(a)
Guilty pleas,
   Admission in related litigation, used as, 802.2(a)
   Withdrawn, 410.1, 802.1
      Federal rules, 410.2

HABIT AND CUSTOM
   Generally, 406.1, 406.2

INDEX

HABIT AND CUSTOM—Continued
Business habit, 406.1(b)
    Federal rules, 406.2(a)
Character evidence, distinguished from, 402.1(c), 406.1(a)
Custom and usage as standard of care, 406.1(f)
    Federal rules, 406.2(c)
Eyewitnesses present, 406.1(e)
Federal rules, 406.2
Industry standards, 406.1(f)
    Federal rules, 406.2(c)
Institutional habit, 406.1(b)
    Federal rules, 406.2(a)
Limited to personal conduct, 406.1(d)
Negligence,
    Federal rules, 406.2(b)
    Non-workplace situations, 406.1(d)
    Workplace situations, 406.1(c)
Professional habit, 406.1(b)
    Federal rules, 406.2(a)
Proposed New York Evidence Code, 406.1(d), 406.1(e)
Standard of care, custom and usage, 406.1(f)
    Federal rules, 406.2(c)
Workplace habit, 406.1(c)

HAIR ANALYSIS
Expert testimony regarding, 702.1(c)

HANDWRITING
Expert testimony regarding, 702.1(c), 901.3(a)
    Federal rules, 901.3(b)
Lay opinion regarding, 701.1, 901.2(a)
    Federal rules, 701.2, 901.2(b)
Specimen authenticity, 901.3(a)

HARMLESS ERROR
    Generally, 103.1(e)
Federal rules, 103.2(e)

HEALTH AND HOSPITALIZATION INSURANCE
Physician-Patient Privilege, generally, this index

HEARINGS
Federal rules,
    Judicial notice, adjudicative facts,
        Post-notice hearing, 201.2
Preliminary hearings, dead man's statute inapplicable, 601.2(g)

HEARSAY
    Generally, 801.1 et seq.
Absence as basis for unavailability, exception, 804(1).1(b), 804.1
Absence caused by party as basis for unavailability, 807.1
Accident reports, exception, 803(3).1(a)
    Federal rules, 803(3).2
Admissions, generally, this index
Agriculture inspection certificates, exception, 803(5).1(j)
Ancient documents, exception, 803(7).1(b)
    Federal rules, 803(7).2(b)
Assertions, 801.1(b)
    Self-incrimination privilege as basis for unavailability, exception, 804.1
Business records, exception, 803(3).1(a)
    Federal rule, 803(3).2
"Catchall" exceptions, 804(5).1
Character reputation, exception,
    Federal rules, 803(7).2(c)
Child abuse, out-of-court statements made by children; exception, 804(5).1
Clarifying words accompanying ambiguous acts, 801.1(c)
Commercial publications, exception,
    Federal rules, 803(6).2

1017

INDEX

HEARSAY—Continued
Computer information, exception, 803(3).1(a)
Confrontation Right, generally, this index
Consistent statements, not hearsay, 801(1).2(b)
    Federal rules, 801(1).3(b)
Credibility of declarant, attacking and supporting, 806.1
Criminal judgments of conviction, exception, 803(5).1(o)
Declarant unavailable, generally. Exceptions to Hearsay Rule, this index
Declarant's availability immaterial, generally. Exceptions to Hearsay Rule, this index
Declarations against interest, exception. Against interest, generally. Declarations, this index
Definition, 801.1(a)
DNA reports, exception, 803(3).1(c)
Double hearsay, 805.1
    Federal rules, 805.2
Dying declarations, exception, 804(2).1
    Federal rules, 804(2).2
Exceptions to Hearsay Rule, generally, this index
Excited utterances, exception, 803(1).1(b)
    Federal rules, 803(1).2(b)
Expert testimony, basis of, 703.1
    Federal rules, 703.2
Family history, exception, 804(4).1
    Federal rules, 804(4).2
Family records, exception, 803(7).1(a)
    Federal rules, 803(7).2(a)
Federal rules, 801.1(a)
Former testimony, exception, 804(1).1(a)
    Civil cases, 804(1).1(a)
    Criminal cases, 804(1).1(b)
    Federal rules, 804(1).2
Genetic markers, exception, 803(3).1(c)
Government records, exception, 803(3).1(c)
Guilty pleas, withdrawn, 802.1
Hospital records, exception, 803(3).1(c)
Identification testimony not considered hearsay, 801(2).1
    Federal rule, 801(2).2
Impeachment of hearsay declarants, 806.1(a)
Inconsistent statements, not hearsay,
    Federal rules, 801(1).3(a)
Indirect hearsay, 801.1(e)
Intent, expressions of, 803(1).1(c)
    Federal rules, 803(1).2(c)
Intimidation of witness as admission, 802.2(a)
Investigatory reports by governmental agencies, exception, 803(5).2(a)
Judgment of previous conviction, exception,
    Federal rules, 803(5).2(d)
Justice of the peace proceedings, exception, 803(5).1(m)
Lack of memory as basis for unavailability, exception, 804.1
Law enforcement records in criminal cases, exception, 803(3).1(b)
Learned treatises, exception, 803(6).2
Market reports, exception, 803(6).1
    Federal rules, 803(6).2
Medical diagnosis or treatment, statements; exception, 803(1).1, 803(1).1(d)
    Federal rules, 803(1).2(d)
Medical records, exception, 803(3).1(c)
    Federal rules, 803(3).2
MRIs, exception, 803(3).1(c)
Nonassertive conduct, 801.1(b)
Nonhearsay, 801(1).1
    Distinguished from, 801.1(a)
Notice required for residual exception, 804(5).2
Operative words, 801.1(c)
Past recollection recorded, exception, 803(2).1
    Federal rules, 803(2).2
Pedigree, exception, 804(4).1

1018

INDEX

HEARSAY—Continued
Pedigree, exception—Continued
    Federal rules, 804(4).2
Personal history, exception, 804(4).1
    Federal rules, 804(4).2
Personal knowledge of out-of-court statement, 602.1
    Federal rules, 602.2
Population certificates, exception, 803(5).1(k)
Present sense impressions, exception, 803(1).1(a)
    Federal rules, 803(1).2(a)
Prior statements by witness, not hearsay, 801(1).1
    Consistent statements, 801(1).2(b)
        Federal rules, 801(1).3(b)
    Inconsistent statements, 801(1).2(a)
        Federal rules, 801(1).3(a)
Probative value required for residual exception, 804(5).2
Proposed New York Evidence Code §803, 801(1).2(b)
Public Records, generally, this index
Recorded recollection, exception, 803(2).1
    Federal rules, 803(2).2
Records,
    Absence of, 803(4).1(a)
    Business transactions,
        Absence of, 803(4).1(a)
Refusal to testify as basis for unavailability, exception, 804.1
Regularly kept records, exception, 803(3).1(a)
Religious institution records, exception, 803(5).1(p)
    Federal rules, 803(5).2(f)
Reputation, exception, 803(7).1(c)
    Federal rules, 803(7).2(c)
Residual exceptions, 804(5).1
Spontaneous statements, exception, 803(1).1
State department records, exception, 803(3).1(c)
State of mind,
    Exception, as, 803(1).1(c)
    Federal rules, 803(1).2(c)
    Nonhearsay, as, 801.1(d)
Statements, 801.1(a)
    Against interest, generally. Declarations, this index
Statements not hearsay, 801(1).1
Surveyor's standard, exception, 803(5).1(*l*)
Threats and intimidation used against witness as basis for unavailability, **exception, 807.1**
Verbal acts, 801.1(c)
Weather records, exception, 803(5).1(i)
Within hearsay, 805.1
    Federal rules, 805.2
Writings, recorded recollection; exception, 803(2).1
    Federal rules, 803(2).2
X-rays, exception, 803(3).1(c)

HIV
AIDS, generally, this index

HOSPITALS
Records,
    Hearsay exception, 803(3).1(c)
    Mental impairment of witness, admissibility, 607.7(b)
    Physician-patient privilege, 502.1(b)

HOSTILE WITNESSES
Bias and interest of witness, 607.6(a)
Leading questions permitted, 607.4(a)
    Direct examination, 611.2(b)
        Federal rules, 611.5(b)

HUSBANDS AND WIVES
Marriage, generally, this index
Privileged communications. Spousal Privileges, generally, this index

INDEX

HUSBANDS AND WIVES—Continued
Spouses, generally, this index

HYPNOSIS
Effect on witness competency, 601.1(h)
    Federal rules, 601.3

IDENTIFICATION OF EVIDENCE
Authentication and Identification, generally, this index

IDENTIFICATION OF PERSONS
Criminal defendants,
    Past recollection recorded, using to identify, 803(2).1
Dental records, physician-patient privilege inapplicable, 502.1(a), 502.1(e)
Fingerprints, generally, this index
Handwriting, generally, this index
Intermediate, admissibility, 801(2).1
Lineup identification, admissibility, 607.5(a)(1)
Prior identification under nonsuggestive circumstances, 607.5(a)(1)
Statements not considered hearsay, 801(2).1
    Federal rule, 801(2).2
Voice identification, generally. Authentication and Identification, this index

IDENTITY
Informer, disclosure, 510.1
Uncharged crimes as proof of, 404.1(f)

IMPEACHMENT
    Generally, 607.2 et seq.
Bias and Interest of Witness, generally, this index
Character of witness used to impeach, 402.1(g), 608.0 et seq.
    Bad character for truthfulness, 608.1(a)
        Federal rules, 608.1(b)
Character witnesses, impeachment of, 402.1(d)
Collateral matters, 607.3
Confession suppressed due to Miranda violations, used to impeach, 509.1(c), 607.8(a)(1)
Contradiction, 607.3
    Own witness, contradiction permitted, 607.4(a)
Conviction of Crime, generally, this index
Credibility of witnesses, 607.1 et seq.
    Attacking and supporting, 806.1(a)
    Own witness, impeachment prohibited, 607.4(a)
    Rehabilitation and Support of Credibility, generally, this index
"Door opening" rationale for introduction of extrinsic evidence of contradiction, 607.3
Drug use at time of operative event, 601.1(g)
Experts, of, 702.1(f)
Extrinsic evidence used for, 607.2, 607.3
Hearsay declarants, 806.1(a)
Impairment, mental or sensory; due to, 607.7(a)
    Federal rules, 607.7(b)
Intoxication at time of operative event, 601.1(g)
Learned treatises, use of, 803(6).1
    Federal rules, hearsay exception, 803(6).2
Mental infirmities used for, 601.3, 607.7(a)
    Federal rules, 607.7(b)
Noncollateral matters, 607.3
    Bias and interest of witness, 607.6(a)
    Mental or sensory impairment, 607.7(a)
    Prior inconsistent statements on material issues, 607.8(a)(3)
Own Witness, this index
Prior Crimes or Misconduct, generally, this index
Prior Inconsistent Statements, generally, this index
Rape victim, sexual history to impeach, 412.1
Refreshing memory, document introduced into evidence by adversary, 612.1(b)
    Federal rules, 612.2
Rehabilitation and Support of Credibility, generally, this index
Religious belief of witness, 610.1
    Federal rules, 610.2

INDEX

IMPEACHMENT—Continued
Sensory impairment, 607.7(a)
Silence while in custody, 509.1(c)
Statements made during plea negotiations used to impeach, 410.1
Subsequent remedial measures to impeach witness denying responsibility, 407.1(e)
Truthfulness,
    Bad reputation for; use to impeach, 608.1(a)
        Federal rules, 608.1(b)
    Evidence of; use to rehabilitate, 607.5(a)(2)(b)
        Federal rules, 607.5(b)
Violation of sequestration, 615.1
    Federal rules, 615.2

INCONSISTENT STATEMENTS
Prior Inconsistent Statements, generally, this index

INDUSTRY STANDARDS
Habit and custom evidence, 406.1(f)
    Federal rules, 406.2(c)

"INEXTRICABLY INTERTWINED"
References to uncharged crimes, 404.1(h)

INFORMERS
Privileged communications, 510.1
    Federal rules, 510.2
    Proposed New York Evidence Code, 510.1

INJURIES
Medical Diagnosis and Treatment, generally, this index
Personal Injury Actions, generally, this index
Real and demonstrative evidence of, 1102.1
    Federal rules, 1102.2

INSANITY
Sanity, generally, this index

INSCRIPTIONS
Best evidence rule, 1001.1(b)
Trade inscriptions, self-authenticating, 902.1(a)
    Federal rules, 902.1(b)

INSPECTION RIGHT
Criminal prosecutions, Rosario rule, 612.1(b)
Refreshing memory, adversary's right of inspection, 612.1(b)
    Federal rules, 612.2

INSTRUCTIONS TO JURY
Burden of persuasion, 300.4(a)
Character evidence, 402.1(e)
    Federal rules, 402.2
Circumstantial evidence, reasonable doubt, 300.4(d)(1)
    Federal rules, 300.4(e)
Criminal proceedings, presumption of innocence, 302.1(b)
Judicial notice,
    Adjudicative facts, 201.1(e)
        Federal rules, 201.2
        Proposed New York Evidence Code, 201.1(f)
Limited admissibility, 105.1, 105.2
    Federal rules, 105.2
Missing witnesses, inference from, 401.1(a)
    Federal rules, 401.2
Presumptions,
    Civil proceedings, 301.5
        Federal rules, 301.8
    Criminal proceedings, 302.1
        Federal rules, 302.2
Privileges, inference from, 514.1
Reasonable doubt, 300.4(d)(1)

INDEX

INSTRUCTIONS TO JURY—Continued
Reasonable doubt—Continued
    Circumstantial evidence, 300.4(d)(1)
        Federal rules, 300.4(e)
Self-incrimination, privilege against, 509.1(b)
Stricken evidence, disregard, 100.2, 103.1(a)
Subsequent remedial measures, 407.1(e)

INSURANCE
Claims, social worker privilege, 505.1
Liability Insurance, generally, this index
Life Insurance, generally, this index
Physician-Patient Privilege, generally, this index
Previous claims, 404.1(l)

INTENT
    See also State of Mind, generally, this index
Expressions of intent, hearsay exception, 803(1).1(c)
    Federal rules, 803(1).2(c)
Uncharged crimes to prove, 404.1(c)
    Civil cases, 404.1(l)

INTEREST
Bias and Interest of Witness, generally, this index
Declarations against, 804(3).1
    Civil cases, 804(3).1(a)
        Federal rules, 804(3).2
    Criminal cases, 804(3).1(b)
        Federal rules, 804(3).2
    Federal rules, 804(3).2
    Hearsay exception, 802.1
Interested observer, expert testimony, 702.1(d)
Pecuniary interest,
    Declarations against, 804(3).1(a)
Proprietary interest,
    Statements against, 804(3).1(a)
Witnesses, interest in outcome, 601.1(b), 601.2
    Federal rules, 601.3

INTERPRETERS
Competency as witnesses, 604.1
    Federal rules, 604.2

INTERROGATION
Examination, generally, this index

INTIMIDATION OF WITNESS
Hearsay exception, 807.1

INTOXICATION
Competency of witness, 601.1(g)
    Jurors, 606.2
Expert opinion regarding, 702.1(c)
Impeachment purposes, 607.7(a)
    Federal rules, 607.7(b)
    Noncollateral fact, 607.3
Lay opinion regarding, 701.1
    Federal rules, 701.2

JOURNALISTS
Privileged communications, 508.1
    Federal rules, 508.2

JUDGES
Calling witnesses, 614.1(a)
    Federal rules, 614.2
Competency as witnesses, 605.1
    Federal rules, 605.2
Experts appointed by, 706.1

INDEX

JUDGES—Continued
Experts appointed by—Continued
  Federal rules, 706.2
Judicial Notice, generally, this index
Preliminary rulings, responsibilities, 104.1(a)
  Federal rules, 104.2
Questioning witnesses, 614.1(b)
  Federal rules, 614.2
Secondary evidence, judicial determination of foundation for admissibility, 1008.1(a)
  Federal rules, 1008.1(b)

JUDGMENT AS MATTER OF LAW
Directed Verdict, generally, this index

JUDGMENT NOTWITHSTANDING VERDICT
Burden of production, 300.3(a)(1)

JUDGMENTS
Best evidence rule, 1001.1(a)
Consent judgment between federal agency and private corporation, admissibility, 410.2
Personal family, general history, or boundaries,
  Federal rules, hearsay exception, 803(5).2(d)
Previous convictions, hearsay exception,
  Federal rules, 803(5).2(d)

JUDICIAL NOTICE
Generally, 200.1 et seq.
Adjudicative facts,
  Animal characteristics, 201.1(c)(10)
  Census data, 201.1(c)(4)
  Challenging, 201.1(e)
  Commerce and trade matters, 201.1(c)(11)
    Federal rules, 201.2
  Court records, 201.1(c)(2)
  Court's discretion, 201.1(d)
  Current events, 201.1(c)(7)
  Days and dates, 201.1(c)(8)
  Defined, 200.1, 201.1(a)
  Effect, 201.1(e)
    Federal rules, 201.1(e)
    Proposed New York Evidence Code, 201.1(f)
  Facts ascertained from reference to reliable sources, 201.1(b)(2)
    Federal rules, 201.1(b)(2)
    Proposed New York Evidence Code, 201.1(b)(2)
  Federal rules, 201.2
  Function, 201.1(a)
  Geographical facts, 201.1(c)(5)
    Federal rules, 201.2
  Historical facts, 201.1(c)(6)
  Human characteristics, 201.1(b), 201.1(c)(9)
  Introduction of contradictory evidence, 201.1(e)
  Judge's personal knowledge distinguished, 201.1(b)
  Jury instructions, 201.1(e)
    Federal rules, 201.2
  Jury's general knowledge distinguished, 201.1(b)
  Notorious facts, 201.1(b)(1)
  Post-notice hearing,
    Federal rules, 201.2
  Procedure, 201.1(d)
    Federal rules, 201.2
  Public officials, 201.1(c)(3)
  Public records, 201.1(c)(1)
    Federal rules, 201.2
  Scientific and mechanical facts, 201.1(b), 201.1(c)(12)
    Federal rules, 201.2
  Time of sunset, 201.1(b)
Judicial notice of law,
  Choice of law rules, 203.1

INDEX

JUDICIAL NOTICE—Continued
Judicial notice of law—Continued
  Defined, 200.1
  Discretionary, 203.1
    Federal rules, 203.2
  Foreign law, pleading requirements, 203.1
  Mandatory, 203.1
    Federal rules, 203.2
  Notice, 203.1
    Federal rules, 203.2
Legislative facts, 202.1
  Defined, 200.1
  Federal rules, 202.1

JURISDICTION
Absence from, as basis for unavailability, 804.1

JURORS
Competency as witnesses, 606.1
  Federal rules, 606.2
Questioning witnesses, 614.1(c)
  Federal rules, 614.2

JURY
Authenticity, jury determination of, 900.1
Exhibits in jury room, 1108.1
  Federal rules, 1108.2
Experiments by jury, 1108.1
  Federal rules, 1108.2
Fact-finding based on general knowledge, 201.1(b)
Instructions to Jury, generally, this index
Note-taking by, 1108.1
  Federal rules, 1108.2
Preliminary rulings, responsibilities, 104.1(a)
  Federal rules, 104.2
Secondary evidence, fact-finders as to ultimate issue of accuracy, 1008.1(a)
  Federal rules, 1008.1(b)
Views, 1107.1
  Federal rules, 1107.2

JUSTICE OF THE PEACE
Proceedings,
  Hearsay exception, 803(5).1(m)

JUVENILE DELINQUENCY
Adjudications, not admissible as convictions, 609.1(a)
  Federal rules, 609.2
Social worker privilege, applicability, 505.1

LANGUAGE
Interpreters, competency as witnesses, 604.1
  Federal rules, 604.2

LAW CLERKS
Judicial, competency as witnesses, 605.2

LAWYERS
Attorneys, generally, this index

LAY OPINION
  Generally, 701.1
Federal rules, 701.2
Handwriting, 901.2(a)
  Federal rules, 901.2(b)
Proposed New York Evidence Code, 701.1
Ultimate issues, 704.1
  Federal rules, 704.2

LAYING A FOUNDATION
Foundation Questions, generally, this index

INDEX

LEADING QUESTIONS
Generally, 611.2(b)
Federal rules, 611.5(b)
Hostile witnesses, 607.4(a)
Refreshing memory, 612.1(a)

LEARNED TREATISES
Hearsay exception, 803(6).2
  Federal rules, 803(6).2
Impeachment of expert, for, 702.1(f)

LEGISLATIVE HEARINGS
Self-incrimination, privilege against, 509.1(a)

LIABILITY INSURANCE
Generally, 411.1
Attorney-client privilege, insurer as agent, 501.1(e)
Claims evaluations, work product immunities, 501.3(b)(1)
Federal rules, 411.2

LIBRARY RECORDS
Privileged communications, 507.1
  Federal rules, 507.2

LIE DETECTOR
Scientific evidence, expert testimony, 702.1(b), 702.1(c)

LIFE INSURANCE
Beneficiaries, no standing to invoke dead man's statute, 601.2(c)
Physician-patient privilege, contractual waiver enforceable, 502.1(c)

LIMITED ADMISSIBILITY
Generally, 105.1
Federal rules, 105.2
Proposed New York Evidence Code, 105.1

LIQUOR
Alcohol, generally, this index

MALICE
Burden of persuasion, clear and convincing evidence, 300.4(b)(2)

MALPRACTICE, LEGAL
Allegation waives attorney-client privilege, 501.1(g)

MALPRACTICE, MEDICAL
Character evidence as proof of conduct, 402.1(c)

MAPS
Demonstrative evidence, as, 1103.1
  Federal rules, 1103.2
Public records, hearsay exception, 803(5).1(d)

MARIJUANA
Opinion testimony regarding, 702.1(a)

MARRIAGE
Adultery, husbands and wives incompetent to testify, 503.2
Annulment; burden of production, corroboration, 300.3(a)(1)
Social worker privilege inapplicable to client's spouse, 505.1
Spousal Privileges, generally, this index
Spouses, generally, this index

MATERIALITY OF EVIDENCE
Distinguished from relevancy, 401.1(a)

MEDICAID
Fraud, exception to physician-patient privilege, 502.1(d)

MEDICAL CORPORATIONS
Privileged communications. Physician-Patient Privilege, generally, this index

INDEX

MEDICAL DIAGNOSIS AND TREATMENT
Expert testimony, 702.1(c)
Physician-Patient Privilege, generally, this index
Reports concerning examinations subject to disclosure, 501.3(c)
    Statements, hearsay exception, 803(1).1, 803(1).1(d)
        Federal rules, 803(1).2(d)
Unauthorized practice, proof of negligence, 502.1(a)
Unauthorized treatment, evidence or prior similar acts, 404.1(l)

MEDICAL EXPENSES
Payment, admissibility, 409.1
    Federal rules, 409.2

MEMORY
Credibility of witnesses, 607.1 et seq.
Hypnotically induced, competency of witnesses, 601.1(h)
    Federal rules, 601.3
Impeachment due to impairment of, 607.7(a)
Lack of, basis for declarant unavailability, 804.1
Refreshing Memory, generally, this index

MENTAL CAPACITY
Administrative proceedings,
    Self-incrimination, privilege against, 509.1(a)
Commitment proceedings,
    Self-incrimination, privilege against, 509.1(a)
Credibility of witness, 607.1 et seq.
Dead Man's Statute, generally, this index
Expert testimony, 702.1(c)
Impeachment value, 601.3, 607.7(a)
    Federal rules, 607.7(b)
Interested observer testimony for impaired witnesses, 702.1(d)
Leading questions permissible on direct examination, 611.2(b)
    Federal rules, 611.5(b)
Presumption, 301.4
Psychiatric evaluation of witness, power to order, 607.7(a)
    Federal rules, 607.7(b)
Sanity, generally, this index
Unsworn testimony due to infirmity, 601.1(f)
Witnesses, competency, 601.1(f)
    Federal rules, 601.3

MILITARY SECRETS
Privilege, 511.2

MINISTERS
Privileged communications, 504.1
    Federal rules, 504.2

MINORS
Children, generally, this index
Juvenile Delinquency, generally, this index
Parent and Child, generally, this index

MIRANDA WARNINGS
Violations, suppressed confession used to impeach, 509.1(c), 607.8(a)(1)

MISCONDUCT
Prior Crimes or Misconduct, generally, this index

MISSING WITNESSES RULE
Relevancy considerations, 401.1(a)
    Federal rules, 401.2

MISTAKE
Accident or Mistake, generally, this index

MODELS
Demonstrative evidence, as, 1103.1
    Federal rules, 1103.2

INDEX

MODUS OPERANDI
Uncharged crimes as proof of, 404.1(f)

MOTION PICTURES AND VIDEOTAPES
Person's conduct involved in litigation, no work product immunity, 501.3(b)(1)
Real and demonstrative evidence, as, 1102.1, 1104.1(d)
    Federal rules, 1104.2(d)

MOTIONS
Motions in limine, 103.1(d)
    Federal rules, 103.2(d)
Motions to strike, 103.1(a)
    Failure to "connect up", 103.1(c)
        Federal rules, 103.2(c)
    Federal rules, 103.2(a)
"Sandoval motion", 609.1(c)
"Ventimiglia" motion, 404.1(a)

MOTIVE
Uncharged crime evidence to prove, 404.1(b)

MOTOR VEHICLE ACCIDENTS
Accidents, generally, this index

MOTOR VEHICLES
Negligent operation, exception to dead man's statute, 601.2(e)
Speed, lay opinion regarding, 701.1
    Federal rules, 701.2
Weapons in, presumption of possession, 302.1(b)

MURDER
Affirmative defenses,
    Shifting burden of production, 300.4(d)(2)

NARCOTICS
Drugs, generally, this index

NARRATIVE TESTIMONY
Within court's discretion, 611.2(a)
    Federal rules, 611.5(b)

NEGLIGENCE
    See also Accidents, generally, this index
Burdens of proof, 300.2
Habit and custom,
    Federal rules, 406.2(b)
        Non-workplace situations, 406.1(d)
        Workplace situations, 406.1(c)
Insurance coverage, relevancy, 411.1
Operation or ownership of vehicle,
    Dead man's statute, exception, 601.2(e)
Res ipsa loquitur,
    Inference, 301.6
Standard of care in industry or trade, 406.1(f)
    Federal rules, 406.2(c)
Subsequent remedial measures,
    Federal rules, 407.2
Unauthorized practice of medicine, proof, 502.1(a)

NEGOTIATIONS
Compromises and Offers to Compromise, generally, this index
Pleas and plea discussions, generally, this index

NEWS REPORTERS
Privileged communications, 508.1
    Federal rules, 508.2

NEWSPAPERS AND PERIODICALS
Advertisements, actions for nonpayment; secondary evidence, 1004.1(d)
Self-authenticating, 902.1(a)

INDEX

NEWSPAPERS AND PERIODICALS—Continued
Self-authenticating—Continued
 Federal rules, 902.1(b)

NOLO CONTENDERE
Plea, 410.1

NONCOLLATERAL MATTERS
Bias and interest of witness, 607.6(a)
Contradiction of witness on, 607.3
Mental or sensory impairment of witness, 607.7(a)
Prior inconsistent statements on material issues, 607.8(a)(3)

NOTARY PUBLIC
Acknowledged documents,
 Self-authenticating, 902.1(a)
  Federal rules, 902.1(b)

NOTICE
Opponent, to,
 Production of original evidence, for, 1004.1(c)
Residual hearsay exception, 804(5).2

NURSES
Physician-Patient Privilege, generally, this index

OATHS AND AFFIRMATIONS
Competency of witnesses, 603.1
 Federal rules, 603.2
Unsworn testimony,
 Child testifying, 601.1(e)
  Corroboration, 300.3(a)(1)
 Failure to object to, 603.1
  Federal rules, 603.2
 Mentally infirm witness, 601.1(f)

OBJECTIONS
Continuing objections, 103.1(a)
 Federal rules, 103.2(a)
Form of question, to, 611.2(a)
General objections, 103.1(b)
 Federal rules, 103.2(b)
Judicial questioning, to, 614.1(b)
 Federal rules, 614.2
Lay opinion, 701.1
Rulings on evidence, 103.1(a)
 Federal rules, 103.2(a)
Specific objections, 103.1(b)
 Federal rules, 103.2(b)
Timeliness, 103.1(a)
 Federal rules, 103.2(a)

OFFER OF PROOF
 Generally, 103.1(c)
Federal rules, 103.2(c)

OFFERS TO COMPROMISE
Compromises and Offers to Compromise, generally, this index
Pleas and plea discussions, generally, this index

OFFICIAL INFORMATION
Privilege, 511.1
 Federal rules, 511.1

OFFICIAL PUBLICATIONS
Self-authenticating, 902.1(a)
 Federal rules, 902.1(b)

OPINION TESTIMONY
 Generally, 700.1 et seq.

INDEX

OPINION TESTIMONY—Continued
Bad reputation for truthfulness, 608.1(b)
Character of accused, 402.1(d)
    Federal rules, 402.2
Conclusory opinions, 704.1
Expert Testimony, generally, this index
Interested observer, 702.1(d)
Lay Opinion, generally, this index
Prior inconsistent statements, impeachment by, 607.8(a)(2)
Ultimate issues, 704.1
    Federal rules, 704.2
Voice identification, 901.5(b)

ORDER OF TRIAL
    Generally, 611.1
Federal rules, 611.5

ORIGINAL WRITINGS RULE
Best Evidence Rule, generally, this index

OTHER ACTS
Habit and Custom, generally, this index
Similar Occurrences, generally, this index
Uncharged Crimes, generally, this index

OVERVIEW AND ORGANIZATION OF BOOK
Generally, 100.1

OWN WITNESS
Contradiction of permitted, 607.4(a)
Credibility, attack prohibited, 607.4(a)
Hostile, leading questions permitted, 607.4(a)
Impeachment,
    Federal rules allow, 607.4(c)
    General prohibition, 607.4(a)
        Exception for prior inconsistent statements, 607.4(b)
Refreshing memory, use of prior inconsistent statements for, 607.4(a)

PARENT AND CHILD
Blood tests to prove relationship, expert testimony regarding, 702.1(c)
Character of parent in issue, child custody, 402.1(b)
Competency of witnesses, dead man's statute, 601.2(b)
Family history, hearsay exception, 804(4).1
    Federal rules, 804(4).2
Family records, hearsay exception, 803(7).1(a)
    Federal rules, 803(7).2(a)
Paternity Proceedings, generally, this index
Privileged communications, 503.4
    Federal rules, 503.5(b)

PARTIES
Admissions, generally, this index
Adverse Party, generally, this index
Competency as witnesses, 601.1(b)
    Dead man's statute, 601.2(b)
Interested witnesses, 607.6(a)
Statements given to opponent, no work product immunity, 501.3(b)(1)
Witnesses, as; sequestration, 615.1
    Federal rules, 615.2

PARTNERSHIPS
Surviving member, protected by dead man's statute, 601.2(c)

PAST RECOLLECTION RECORDED
Distinguished from refreshing memory, 612.1(a)
Hearsay exception, 803(2).1
    Federal rules, 803(2).2

PATERNITY PROCEEDINGS
Burden of persuasion, clear and convincing evidence, 300.4(b)(2)

INDEX

PATERNITY PROCEEDINGS—Continued
Witnesses, competency of spouses as, 601.1(c)

PECUNIARY INTEREST
Declarations against, 804(3).1(a)

PEDIGREE
Hearsay exception, 804(4).1
    Federal rules, 804(4).2

PENSIONS
Dead man's statute, standing, 601.2(c)

PERJURY
Conviction of crime offered to impeach, 609.1(c)
    Federal rules, 609.2
Plea bargaining statements, admissible in prosecution for perjury, 410.2
Prior instances of perjury, impeachment value, 608.2(b)

PERSONAL HISTORY
Hearsay exception, 804(4).1
    Federal rules, 804(4).2

PERSONAL INJURY ACTIONS
    See also Accidents, generally, this index
Photographs of injuries, 1102.1
    Federal rules, 1102.2
Physician-patient privilege, 502.1(c)
X-rays, 1104.1(b)
    Federal rules, 1104.2(b)

PERSONAL KNOWLEDGE
Authentication and identification testimony, 901.1(a)
Competency of witnesses, 602.1
    Federal rules, 602.2
Expert testimony, basis of, 703.1
    Federal rules, 703.2
Hearsay, personal knowledge of out-of-court statement, 602.1
    Federal rules, 602.2
Lay opinion, 701.1

PERSONS
Real or demonstrative evidence, as, 1102.1
    Federal rules, 1102.2

PHARMACISTS
Physician-patient privilege not applicable, 502.1(b)

PHOTOGRAPHS
Authentication and identification, 901.1(a), 1104.1(a)
    Federal rules, 1104.2(a)
Best Evidence Rule, generally, this index
Demonstrative evidence, as, 1104.1(a)
    Federal rules, 1104.2(a)
Gruesome photographs, relevancy, 401.1(b), 1102.1
Injuries, of, 1102.1
    Federal rules, 1102.2
Person's conduct involved in litigation, no work product immunity, 501.3(b)(1)
Prior identification, using evidence of, 801(2).1
    Federal rule, 801(2).2

PHYSICAL CONDITION
Expert testimony regarding, 702.1(c)
Hearsay exception, 803(1).1(c)
    Federal rules, 803(1).2(c)
Lay opinion regarding, 701.1
    Federal rules, 701.2
Physician-patient privilege, condition in controversy, 502.1(c)
Real evidence, as, 1102.1
    Federal rules, 1102.2

INDEX

PHYSICAL EVIDENCE
Real and Demonstrative Evidence, generally, this index

PHYSICAL EXAMINATION
Medical Diagnosis and Treatment, generally, this index

PHYSICIAN-PATIENT PRIVILEGE
    Generally, 502.1, 502.2
Addicts, reporting requirement, 502.1(d)
AIDS, 502.1(a), 502.1(d)
Child abuse, disclosure required, 502.1(a), 502.1(d), 502.1(e)
Chiropractors, 502.1(a)
Dangerous client of psychologist, reporting, 502.1(e)
Death, effect, 502.1(a) et seq.
Dental records for identification of persons, privilege inapplicable, 502.1(d)
Dentists, 502.1(a)
Eavesdroppers, 502.1(b)
Elements of the privilege, 502.1(b)
Emergency medical technicians, privilege only if physician's agent, 502.1(b)
Exceptions, 502.1(d)
    Psychologist-patient privilege, 502.1(e)
Factors to sustain claim of, 502.1(b)
Federal law not recognizing, 502.2
Fraudulent Medicaid practices, exception, 502.1(d)
Guardianship and custody, mentally ill parents, 502.1(d), 502.1(e)
Gunshot and knife wounds, reporting requirement, 502.1(d)
Hospital records, 502.1(b)
Incapacitated persons, exception, 502.1(d)
Insanity plea, 502.1(c)
Life insurance, contractual waiver enforceable, 502.1(c)
Nurses, 502.1(a)
Personal injury actions, 502.1(c)
Physical or mental condition in controversy, 502.1(c)
    Psychologist's privilege, 502.1(e)
Podiatrists, 502.1(a)
Proposed New York Evidence Code, 502.1(a), 502.1(e)
Psychologists, 502.1(e)
    Federal cases, 502.2
Psychotherapist-patient privilege, 502.2
Reporting requirements, 502.1(d), 502.1(e)
Scope, 502.1(b)
Suicide, privilege applicable despite lack of consent to treatment, 502.1(b)
Third person present, effect, 502.1(b)
Unauthorized practice of medicine, proof of negligence, 502.1(a)
Victims, privilege may not be asserted by criminal defendant, 502.1(b)
Waiver, 502.1(c)
Will contests, 502.1(a)

PLEADINGS
Admissions, as,
    Federal rules, 802.3(a)

PLEAS AND PLEA DISCUSSIONS
    Generally, 401.2, 410.1
Agreement with government, admissibility to show bias, 607.6(b)
Consent judgment between federal agency and private corporation, admissibility, 410.2
Federal rules, 410.2
Grand jury testimony against others induced by plea bargain, admissibility, 410.1
Guilty pleas,
    Admission in related litigation, used as, 802.2(a)
    Withdrawn, 410.1, 802.1
        Federal rules, 410.2
Nolo contendere, 410.1
    Federal rules, 410.2
Perjury, statements admissible in prosecution for, 410.2
Proposed New York Evidence Code, 410.1, 411.1
Statements made during negotiations used to impeach, 410.1

INDEX

PODIATRISTS
Privileged communications. Physician-Patient Privilege, generally, this index

POLITICAL VOTE
Privileges, 512.1, 512.2

POLYGRAPH
Scientific evidence, expert testimony, 702.1(b), 702.1(c)

POPULATION CERTIFICATES
Hearsay exception, 803(5).1(k)

PREDECESSORS IN INTEREST
Competency as witnesses, dead man's statute, 601.2(b)

PREJUDICE
Relevancy considerations, 401.1(b)
    Character evidence, 402.1(a)
    Conviction of crime offered to impeach, 609.1(c)
        Federal rules, 609.2
    Federal rules, 401.2
    Liability insurance, 411.1, 411.2
    Subsequent remedial measures, 407.1(a)
    Uncharged crimes, 404.1(a)

PRELIMINARY HEARINGS
Dead man's statute inapplicable, 601.2(g)

PRELIMINARY RULINGS
Admissions, 104.1(b)
Conditional relevancy, 104.1(a)
    Federal rules, 104.2
Confessions, 104.1(b)
    Federal rules, 104.2
Conviction of crime, admissibility to impeach, 609.1(c)
Fourth amendment rights, 104.1(b)
Judge, responsibilities, 104.1(a)
    Federal rules, 104.2
Jury, responsibilities, 104.1(a)
    Federal rules, 104.2
Motions in limine, 103.1(d)
    Federal rules, 103.2(d)
Prior crimes or misconduct used in cross-examination of criminal defendant, 608.2(a)
Privileges, 104.1(b)
Uncharged crimes, admissibility determination, 104.2, 404.1(a)

PRESENT SENSE IMPRESSIONS
Hearsay exception, 803(1).1(a)
    Federal rules, 803(1).2(a)

PRESUMPTIONS
    Generally, 301.1 et seq.
Bailment, conversion or loss of property, 301.4
"Bursting bubble" rule, 301.5(a)(1), 301.5(b)
Conclusive, 301.3
Conflict of presumptions, 301.4
Continuation of status or condition, 301.4
Creation, reasons for,
    Access to proof, 301.4
    Probability, 301.4
    Procedural convenience, 301.4
    Social policy, 301.4
Criminal proceedings, 302.1 et seq.
    Constitutional restraints, 302.1(a)
    Federal rules, 302.2
    Motor vehicles, weapons in,
        Presumption of possession, 302.1(b)
    Presumption of innocence, 302.1(b)
    Receiving stolen property, possession, 302.1(b)

INDEX

PRESUMPTIONS—Continued
Criminal proceedings—Continued
    Statutory permissive inference,
        Rational connection test, 302.1(a)
Death, of,
    Absence for more than three years, 301.4
    Simultaneous death in common disaster, 301.4
Defined, 301.2
Federal proceedings,
    Cases governed by federal law, 301.8(a)
    Cases governed by state law, 301.8(b)
Hybrid approach rule, 301.5(b)
Inference distinguished, 301.2
Intent, natural consequences of person's acts, 302.1(a), 302.1(b)
Jury will follow judge's instructions, 105.1
Legitimacy of children, 301.4
Mailing, presumption of receipt, 301.4
Marriage, validity of, 301.4
Mental competency, 301.4
Morgan rule, 301.5(a)(2), 301.5(b)
Motor vehicle accidents,
    Driver presumed to have owner's permission, 301.4
Possessor is owner, 301.4
Presumption of receipt upon proof of mailing, 301.4
Prima facie evidence distinguished, 301.2
Promissory note, signature valid, 301.5(b)
Public officials perform tasks in accordance with lawful procedure, 301.4
Rebuttable, 301.3
Release, due execution, 301.5(b)
Res ipsa loquitur,
    Inference distinguished from presumption, 301.6
Suicide, against, 301.4, 301.5(b)
Thayer rule, 301.5(a)(1), 301.5(b)
Witnesses, incompetency, 601.1(a)

PRIESTS
Privileged communications, 504.1
    Federal rules, 504.2

PRIMA FACIE EVIDENCE
Burden of production, shifting, 301.7

PRIOR CONSISTENT STATEMENTS
Rehabilitation of credibility with, 607.5(a)(1), 607.5(a)(2)(c)
    Federal rules, 607.5(b)
    Statements not hearsay, 801(1).2(b)
        Federal rules, 801(1).3(b)
Statements not considered hearsay, 801(1).2(b)
    Federal rules, 801(1).3(b)
Substantive evidence, as, 607.5(b)

PRIOR CRIMES OR MISCONDUCT
Advance accreditation of witnesses, 607.5(a)(1)
Character evidence,
    Criminal cases, 402.1(d)
    Not admissible to rehabilitate, 607.5(a)(2)(b)
Competency of witnesses, 601.1(d)
Explanation admissible to rehabilitate, 607.5(a)(2)(a)
Impeachment value, 608.2(a)
    Conviction of Crime, generally, this index
    Federal rules, 608.2(b)
Juvenile delinquency adjudications, impeachment value, 609.1(a)
Pretrial ruling as to acts used in cross-examination of criminal defendant, 608.2(a)
Proposed New York Evidence Code, 608.2(a)
Truthfulness,
    Bad character for, use to impeach, 608.1(a)
    Evidence of, use to rehabilitate, 607.5(a)(2)(b)
Uncharged Crimes, generally, this index

INDEX

PRIOR INCONSISTENT STATEMENTS
Adverse party, by, 607.8(a)(1), 607.8(a)(3)
Denial, prior consistent statements to corroborate, 607.5(a)(2)(c)
    Federal rules, 607.5(b)
Explanation admissible to rehabilitate, 607.5(a)(2)(a)
Form of statement, 607.8(a)(1)
Impeachment by, 607.8(a)(1)
    Declarant unavailable, 607.8(a)(3)
    Extrinsic evidence, admissibility to prove, 607.8(a)(3)
        Federal rules, 607.8(b)
    Federal rules, 607.8(b)
    Foundation requirements, 607.8(a)(3)
        Federal rules, 607.8(b)
    Nature of inconsistency, 607.8(a)(2)
    Own witness,
        Federal rules allow impeachment, 607.4(c)
        Impeachment generally prohibited, 607.4(a)
            Exception, 607.4(b)
Omissions in prior statements, 607.8(a)(2)
Refreshing memory, use for, 607.4(a)
Silence as, 607.8(a)(2)
    Federal rules, 607.8(b)
Statements not considered hearsay, 801(1).2(a)
    Federal rules, 801(1).3(a)
Substantive evidence, as,
    Statements by adverse party, 607.8(a)(1)
Truth of matter asserted, not offered to prove, 607.8(a)(1)

PRIVILEGES
    Generally, 500.1 et seq.
Accountants, 500.2(n.4)
Adverse inference from, 514.1
    Federal rules, 514.2
Attorney-Client Privilege, generally, this index
Civil rights cases, 500.2(n.6)
Clergy, 504.1
    Federal rules, 504.2
Comment upon, 514.1
    Federal rules, 514.2
Exclusion of relevant evidence, basis for, 401.1(b)
Federal rules, 500.2
Fifth amendment. Self-Incrimination, Privilege Against, generally, this index
Government communications, 511.1
    Federal rules, 511.2
Incompetency of spouses. Spousal Privileges, generally, this index
Informer privilege, 510.1
    Federal rules, 510.2
Journalist privilege, 508.1
    Federal rules, 508.2
Library records, 507.1
    Federal rules, 507.2
Military secrets, 511.2
Parent-child, 503.4
    Federal rules, 503.5(b)
Physician-Patient Privilege, generally, this index
Political vote, 512.1
    Federal rules, 512.2
Preliminary rulings, 104.1(b)
Psychologist, 502.1(e)
Psychotherapist, 502.2
Rape crisis counselor, 506.1
    Federal rules, 506.2
Scholars, 500.2(n.4)
Self-critical analysis, 500.2(n.4)
Self-Incrimination, Privilege Against, generally, this index
Social worker privilege, 505.1
    Federal rules, 505.2

INDEX

PRIVILEGES—Continued
Spousal Privileges, generally, this index
State secrets, 511.2
Trade secrets, 513.1
    Federal rules, 513.2
Voir dire of witnesses regarding, 611.3(d)
Waiver, document used to refresh memory, 612.1(b)
    Federal rules, 612.2
Work Product Immunities, generally, this index

PRIVITY
Admissions, statements of persons in, as, 802.2(c)

PROBABILITY
Generally, 401.1(a)

PROBATIVE VALUE
    Generally, 401.1(a)
Relevancy considerations,
    Character evidence, 402.1(a)
    Conviction of crime offered to impeach, 609.1(c)
        Federal rules, 609.2
    Federal rules, 401.2
    Hearsay, residual exception, 804(5).2
    Liability insurance, 411.1, 411.2
    Subsequent remedial measures, 407.1(a)
    Uncharged crimes, 404.1(a)
Residual hearsay exception, 804(5).2

PRODUCTS LIABILITY
Court-appointed expert witnesses, 706.1
Experiments and demonstrations, 1105.1
    Federal rules, 1105.2
Feasibility issue, subsequent design change, 407.1(d)
    Federal rules, 407.2
Insurance coverage, relevancy, 411.1
Subsequent remedial measures, 407.1(c)
    Federal rules, 407.2
Warnings, subsequent remedial measures, 407.1(c)

PROFESSIONAL SERVICE CORPORATIONS
Medical practice,
    Privileged communications. Physician-Patient Privilege, generally, this index

PROPERTY
Sales, evidence of similar transactions,
    Federal rules, 405.2(c)

PROPOSED NEW YORK EVIDENCE CODE
Attorney-client privilege, 501.1(a)
Authentication and identification, 900.1 et seq., 901.7(a)
Best evidence rule, 1001.1 et seq.
Business records, 803(3).1(d)
Character evidence, 402.1(h)
Character of homicide victim, 402.1(f)
Clergy, privileged communications, 504.1
Completeness doctrine, 106.1
Compromises and offers to compromise, 408.1
Conviction of crime, offered to impeach, 609.1(c)
Court-appointed expert witnesses, 706.1
Dying declarations, 804(2).1
Expert opinion, 702.1(a)
Government communications, privilege, 511.1
Habit and custom, 406.1(d), 406.1(e)
Hearsay exceptions, declarant's availability immaterial, 801(1).2(c)
Informer privilege, 510.1
Judicial notice,
    Adjudicative facts,
        Effect, 201.1(f)

INDEX

PROPOSED NEW YORK EVIDENCE CODE—Continued
Judicial notice—Continued
  Adjudicative facts—Continued
    Facts ascertained from reference to reliable sources, 201.1(b)(2)
    Jury instructions, 201.1(f)
Lay opinion, 701.1
Limited admissibility, 105.1
Market reports, commercial publications, 803(6).1
Marriage certificates, hearsay exception, 803(5).1(f)
Medical diagnosis or treatment, statements; hearsay exception, 803(1).1(d)
Physician-patient privilege, 502.1(e)
Pleas and plea discussions, 410.1, 411.1
Political vote privilege, 512.1
Prior crimes and misconduct to impeach witness, 608.2(a)
Privileges, comment or inference, 514.1
Public records, 803(5).1(b)
  Absence of, 803(5).1(n)
  Ancient maps and real property records, 803(5).1(d)
Refreshing witness' recollection, adversary's right of inspection, 612.1(b)
Relevancy, 401.1(c)
Spousal privileges, 503.3(e)
Subsequent remedial measures, 407.1(f)
Trade secrets, 513.1
Unavailability, requirements, 804.1
Uncharged crimes, 404.1(a)
Vital statistics, hearsay exception, 803(5).1(h)

PROPRIETARY INTEREST
Statements against, 804(3).1(a)

PSYCHIATRISTS
Expert testimony by,
  Professional reliance rule, 703.1
  Ultimate issues, 704.2
Physician-Patient Privilege, generally, this index

PSYCHOLOGISTS
Privileged communications, 502.1(e)
  Federal cases, 502.2

PUBLIC OFFICIALS
Certificate or affidavit of facts or acts performed, hearsay exception, 803(5).1(b)
Judicial notice,
  Adjudicative facts, 201.1(c)(3)

PUBLIC POLICY CONSIDERATIONS
Compromises and offers to compromise, 408.1, 408.2
Exception to attorney-client privilege, 501.1(g)
Subsequent remedial measures, 407.1(a)

PUBLIC RECORDS
Absence of, hearsay exception, 803(4).1(b), 803(5).1(n)
  Federal rules, 803(5).2(e)
Agriculture inspection certificates, hearsay exception, 803(5).1(j)
Authentication and identification, 901.7(a), 902.1(a)
  Federal rules, 901.7(b), 902.1(b)
Baptismal certificates, hearsay exception,
  Federal rules, 803(5).2(f)
Best evidence rule, 1005.1(a)
  Federal rules, 1005.1(b)
Birth certificates, hearsay exception, 803(5).1(h)
Business records hearsay exception, 803(5).1(a)
Certificate of affidavit of public officer, hearsay exception, 803(5).1(b)
Common law hearsay exception, 803(5).1, 803(5).1(a)
Death certificates, hearsay exception, 803(5).1(h)
Federal rules, hearsay exception, 803(5).2(a)
Investigatory reports by governmental agencies, 803(5).1(c)
  Federal rules, 803(5).2(a)

INDEX

PUBLIC RECORDS—Continued
Investigatory reports by governmental agencies, hearsay exception, 803(5).1(c)
Judgments as to personal family, general history, or boundaries,
    Federal rules, hearsay exception, 803(5).2(d)
Judicial notice,
    Adjudicative facts, 201.1(c)(1)
        Federal rules, 201.2
Maps, ancient, hearsay exception, 803(5).1(d)
Marriage certificates, hearsay exception, 803(5).1(f)
    Federal rules, 803(5).2(f)
Missing persons, hearsay exception, 803(5).1(g)
Population certificates, hearsay exception, 803(5).1(k)
Presumption of death, hearsay exception, 803(5).1(g)
Proposed New York Evidence Code, 803(5).1(b), 803(5).1(d)
Real property, hearsay exception, 803(5).1(d)
    Documents affecting interests in,
        Federal rules, 803(5).2(c)
        Statements contained in,
            Federal rules, 803(7).2(b)
    Out-of-state, 803(5).1(e)
Reports made pursuant to duty, hearsay exception,
    Federal rules, 803(5).2(a)
Vital statistics, hearsay exception,
    Federal rules, 803(5).2(b)
    Proposed New York Evidence Code, 803(5).1(h)

QUESTION, FORM OF
    Generally, 611.2(a)
Argumentative questions, 611.2(a)
    Federal rules, 611.5(b)
Federal rules, 611.5(b)
Harassing questions, 611.2(b)
    Federal rules, 611.5(b)
Leading questions, 611.2(b)
    Federal rules, 611.5(b)
    Hostile witnesses, 607.4(a)
Narrative testimony within court's discretion, 611.2(a)
    Federal rules, 611.5(b)
Repetitive questioning, 611.2(b)
    Federal rules, 611.5(b)

RABBIS
Privileged communications, 504.1
    Federal rules, 504.2

RADAR
Scientific evidence, expert testimony, 702.1(c)

RAPE
Sex offenses, generally, this index

RAPE CRISIS COUNSELORS
Privilege, 506.1, 506.2

REAL AND DEMONSTRATIVE EVIDENCE
    Generally, 1100.1 et seq.
Authentication and Identification, generally, this index
Chain of custody, 901.1(a), 1101.1
    Federal rules, 901.1(b), 1101.2
Charts, 1103.1
    Federal rules, 1103.2
Clothing and jewelry, 1101.2
Computer-generated graphics, 1106.1
Definitions, 1100.1
Diagrams, 1103.1
    Federal rules, 1103.2
Drawings, 1103.1
    Federal rules, 1103.2

INDEX

REAL AND DEMONSTRATIVE EVIDENCE—Continued
Drugs, 1101.1
Exhibits in jury room, 1108.1
    Federal rules, 1108.2
Experiments and demonstrations, 1105.1
    Federal rules, 1105.2
    Jury conducting experiments, 1108.1
        Federal rules, 1108.2
Federal rules, 1100.1 et seq.
Fungible items, 1101.1
Injuries, 1102.1
    Federal rules, 1102.2
Jury,
    Exhibits in jury room, 1108.1
        Federal rules, 1108.2
    Experiments by jury, 1108.1
        Federal rules, 1108.2
    Views, 1107.1
        Federal rules, 1107.2
Maps, 1103.1
    Federal rules, 1103.2
Models, 1103.1
    Federal rules, 1103.2
Motion pictures and videotapes, 1102.1, 1104.1(d)
    Federal rules, 1104.2(d)
Persons, physical features and injuries, 1102.1
    Federal rules, 1102.2
Photographs, 1102.1, 1104.1(a)
    Federal rules, 1102.2, 1104.2(a)
Silent witness theory of authentication, 1104.1(a), 1104.1(b), 1104.1(d)
    Federal rules, 1104.2(a), 1104.2(b), 1104.2(d)
Sound recordings, 1104.1(c)
    Federal rules, 1104.2(c)
Tangible objects, 1101.1
    Federal rules, 1101.2
Transcripts of recordings, 1104.1(c)
    Federal rules, 1104.2(c)
Weapons, 1101.2
X-rays and analogous medical pictorial processes, 1104.1(b)
    Federal rules, 1104.2(b)

REAL PROPERTY
Adverse possession, burden of persuasion,
    Clear and convincing evidence, 300.4(b)(2)
Conveyances of foreign property, self-authenticating, 902.1(a)
Documents affecting interests in, hearsay exception,
    Federal rules, 803(5).2(c)
    Statements contained in,
        Federal rules, 803(7).2(b)
Forfeiture action, character of occupant in issue, 402.1(b)
Gifts, decedent's pre-death transfer by,
    Burden of persuasion, clear and convincing evidence, 300.4(b)(2)
Implied easements, burden of persuasion,
    Clear and convincing evidence, 300.4(b)(2)
Joint ownership, surviving spouse competent to testify, 601.2(e)
Public records, hearsay exception, 803(5).1(d)
    Out-of-state property, 803(5).1(e)
Sales, evidence of similar transactions, 405.1(d)
Title documents,
    Authentication, 901.8(a)
    Best evidence rule, 1001.1(a), 1005.1(a)

REASONABLE DOUBT
Burden of Proof, this index
Character evidence raising, 402.1(e)
    Federal rules, 402.2

INDEX

REBUTTAL
Burden of production, 300.3(a)(2)
Character evidence, prosecution's rebuttal, 402.1(d)
Defendant's evidence of good character,
    Federal rules, 402.2
Order of trial, 611.1
    Federal rules, 611.5(a)
Rape victim's evidence, 412.1
    Federal rules, 412.2
Scope, 611.1
    Federal rules, 611.5(a)
Uncharged crimes, 404.1(k)

RECEIVING STOLEN PROPERTY
Presumptions, possession, 302.1(b)

RECENT FABRICATION
Defined, 607.5(a)(2)(c)
Prior consistent statement to rehabilitate credibility, 607.5(a)(1), 607.5(a)(2)(c)
    Federal rules, 607.5(b)

RECOLLECTION
Memory, generally, this index
Past recollection recorded, hearsay exception, 803(2).1
    Federal rules, 803(2).2
Refreshing Memory, generally, this index

RECORDED RECOLLECTION
Hearsay exception, 803(2).1
    Federal rules, 803(2).2

RECORDINGS
Authentication and Identification, generally, this index
Best Evidence Rule, generally, this index
Composite, 1006.1(b)
Criminal cases, burden of proof of authentication, 900.1
Demonstrative evidence, as, 1104.1(c)
    Federal rules, 1104.2(c)
Distinguished from fungible material, 901.1(a)
Person's conduct involved in litigation, no work product immunity, 501.3(b)(1)

RECORDS AND REPORTS
Absence of, hearsay exception, 803(4).1(b)
Ancient documents, hearsay exception, 803(7).1(b)
    Federal rules, 803(7).2(b)
Business Records, generally, this index
Commercial publications,
    Federal rules, hearsay exception, 803(6).2
Court records,
    Judicial notice, adjudicative facts, 201.1(c)(2)
Dental records, physician-patient privilege inapplicable, 502.1(a), 502.1(e)
Drug dealer's customer book,
    Federal rules, 803(3).2
Family records, hearsay exception, 803(7).1(a)
    Federal rules, 803(7).2(a)
Foreign records, generally, this index
Government records, hearsay exception, 803(3).1(c)
    Investigatory reports, 803(5).1(c)
Hospital records, hearsay exception, 803(3).1(c)
Law enforcement records in criminal cases, hearsay exception, 803(3).1(b)
Library Records, generally, this index
Market reports, hearsay exception, 803(6).1
    Federal rules, 803(6).2
Medical records, hearsay exception, 803(3).1(c)
    Federal rules, 803(3).2
Public Records, generally, this index
Regularly kept records, hearsay exception, 803(3).1(a)
    Accidents, 803(3).1(a)

INDEX

RECORDS AND REPORTS—Continued
Regularly kept records, hearsay exception—Continued
  DNA reports, 803(3).1(c)
  Federal rules, 803(3).2
  Genetic markers, 803(3).1(c)
  Law enforcement records in criminal cases, 803(3).1(b)
  Medical records, 803(3).1(c)
    Federal rules, 803(3).2
  MRIs, 803(3).1(c)
  State department records, 803(3).1(c)
  X-rays, 803(3).1(c)
Religious institutions, hearsay exception, 803(5).1(p)
  Federal rules, 803(5).2(f)
State department records, hearsay exception, 803(3).1(c)
Weather records, hearsay exception, 803(5).1(i)

RECROSS EXAMINATION
  Generally, 611.4
  Federal rules, 611.5(c)

REDIRECT EXAMINATION
  Generally, 611.4
  Federal rules, 611.5(c)

REFRESHING MEMORY
  Generally, 612.1(a)
Adversary's right of inspection, 612.1(b)
Best evidence rule inapplicable, 1001.1(b)
Federal rules, 612.2
Hypnosis, 601.1(h)
  Expert testimony, 702.1(c)
  Federal rules, 601.3
Leading questions permissible to refresh, 611.2(b)
  Federal rules, 611.5(b)
Past recollection recorded distinguished, 612.1(a)
Prior inconsistent statements used for, 607.4(a)
Privileged or immune communications, 501.1(h), 501.3(b)(3), 612.1(b)
  Federal rules, 501.2, 612.2
Proposed New York Evidence Code, 612.1(b)

REHABILITATION AND SUPPORT OF CREDIBILITY
  Generally, 607.1 et seq., 607.5(a)(2)
Advance accreditation, 607.5(a)(1)
  Federal rules, 607.5(b)
Convictions, revelation to soften blow of cross-examination, 607.4(a), 607.5(a)(1)
  Federal rules, 607.5(b)
Explanation of impeaching facts, 607.5(a)(2)(a)
  Federal rules, 607.5(b)
Federal rules, 607.1, 607.5(b)
Prior consistent statements used for, 607.5(a)(1), 607.5(a)(2)(c)
  Federal rules, 607.5(b)
  Statements not considered hearsay, 801(1).2(b)
Prior crimes or misconduct,
  Explanation admissible to rehabilitate, 607.5(a)(2)(a)
Prior identification of persons under nonsuggestive circumstances, 607.5(a)(1)
  Federal rules, 607.5(b)
Prior inconsistent statements,
  Explanation admissible to rehabilitate, 607.5(a)(2)(a)
Recent fabrication, prior consistent statement to rehabilitate, 607.5(a)(2)(c)
  Federal rules, 607.5(b)
Sexual assault cases, prompt complaint doctrine, 607.5(a)(1)
Truthfulness,
  Evidence of good character for, 607.5(a)(2)(b)
    Federal rules, 607.5(b)

RELEVANCY
  Generally, 400.1 et seq.
Authentication and Identification, generally, this index

INDEX

RELEVANCY—Continued
Character Evidence, generally, this index
Circumstantial evidence, 401.1(a)
Collateral matters, 401.1(b)
Compromises and Offers to Compromise, generally, this index
Conditional relevancy, 104.1(a)
    Federal rules, 104.2
Consciousness of guilt evidence, 401.1(a)
Conviction of crime offered to impeach, 609.1(c)
    Federal rules, 609.2
    Habit and Custom, generally, this index
Definition, 401.1
Demonstrative evidence, 1103.1
Direct evidence, 401.1(a)
Discretion of trial court, 401.1(a), 401.1(b)
    Federal rules, 401.2
Exclusionary rules, 401.1(b)
Experiments and demonstrations, 1105.1
    Federal rules, 1105.2
Federal rules, 401.2
Flight evidence, 401.1(a)
    Federal rules, 401.2
Fourth amendment violations, basis for exclusion of relevant evidence, 401.1(b)
Habit and Custom, generally, this index
Impeachment, generally, this index
Insurance coverage, 411.1
Judicial discretion, 401.1(a), 401.1(b)
    Federal rules, 401.2
Liability Insurance, generally, this index
Materiality of ultimate fact, 401.1(a)
Medical expenses, payment of, 409.1
    Federal rules, 409.2
Missing witnesses rule, 401.1(a)
    Compromises and Offers to Compromise, generally, this index
    Federal rules, 401.2
Photographs, 1104.1(a)
    Federal rules, 1104.2(a)
    Gruesome, 401.1(b), 1102.1
Pleas and Plea Discussions, generally, this index
Postcrime conduct, 401.1(a)
Prejudice, generally, this index
Privileges, basis for exclusion, 401.1(b)
Probability, 401.1(a)
Probative Value, generally, this index
Proposed New York Evidence Code, 401.1(c)
Subsequent Remedial Measures, generally, this index
Sexual history, generally. Sex Offenses, this index
Shield Laws, generally, this index
Similar Occurrences, generally, this index
Subsequent Remedial Measures, generally, this index
Sufficiency distinguished, 401.1(a)
Suppression of evidence, 401.1(a)
Tangible objects, 1101.1
    Federal rules, 1101.2
Trustworthiness, lack of; basis for exclusion, 401.1(b)
Ultimate fact, materiality, 401.1(a)
Uncharged Crimes, generally, this index
Wealth, 401.1(b)
Witnesses not called, 401.1(a)

RELIGIOUS BELIEFS
Clergy, privileged communications, 504.1
    Federal rules, 504.2
Competency of witness, 601.1
Witness, effect of on credibility, 610.1
    Federal rules, 610.2

INDEX

RELIGIOUS ORGANIZATIONS
Records, hearsay exception, 803(5).1(p)
    Federal rules, 803(5).2(f)

REMEDIAL MEASURES
Subsequent Remedial Measures, generally, this index

REPAIRS
Subsequent Remedial Measures, generally, this index

REPORTERS
Privileged communications, 508.1
    Federal rules, 508.2

REPRESENTATIVE CAPACITY
Statements made in, as admission, 802.2(d)

REPUTATION
Character Evidence, generally, this index

RES IPSA LOQUITUR
Negligence, inference, 301.6

RETIREMENT DEATH BENEFITS
Dead man's statute, standing, 601.2(c)

RULINGS ON EVIDENCE
    Generally, 103.1 et seq.
Completeness rule, 106.1
    Federal rules, 106.2
"Connecting up," conditional relevance shown later, 103.1(c)
    Federal rules, 103.2(c)
Federal courts, 103.2
Harmless error, 103.1(e)
    Federal rules, 103.2(e)
Limited admissibility, 105.1
    Federal rules, 105.2
Motions, generally, this index
Objections, generally, this index
Offer of proof, 103.1(c)
    Federal rules, 103.2(c)
Preliminary Rulings, generally, this index

SANITY
    See also Mental Capacity, generally, this index
Burden of production,
    Federal rules, 300.4(e)
Insanity as affirmative defense,
    Burden of persuasion, 300.4(d)(2)
    Expert testimony, 703.1
Lay opinion regarding, 701.1
    Federal rules, 701.2
Psychiatric testimony, 702.1(c)

SCIENTIFIC EVIDENCE
Authentication and identification, 901.9(a)
    Computer-generated graphics, 1106.1
    Federal rules, 901.9(b)
Expert testimony, 702.1(c)
    Novel theories and methods, 702.1(b)
        Federal rules, 702.2(b)
Radar gun, 702.1(c)
Reports concerning scientific tests subject to disclosure, 501.3(c)

SECONDARY EVIDENCE
Best Evidence Rule, generally, this index

SELF-DEFENSE
Burden of production, federal rules, 300.4(e)
Character of victim, 402.1(f)

INDEX

SELF-DEFENSE—Continued
Character of victim—Continued
    Federal rules, 402.2

SELF-INCRIMINATION, PRIVILEGE AGAINST
    Generally, 509.1(a) et seq.
Business records, 509.1(b)
Civil cases, 509.1(a)
Codefendants, 509.1(b)
Commitment proceedings, 509.1(a)
Corporations invoking, 509.1(b)
Criminal proceedings, 509.1(b)
Cross-examination, 611.3(a)
Documents, criminal cases, 509.1(b)
Inference from, 514.1
Investigation stage, application during, 509.1(c)
Mental illness, commitment proceedings, 509.1(a)
Prior misconduct used to impeach, 608.2(a)
    Federal rules, 608.2(b)
Testimony, criminal cases, 509.1(b)
Unavailability, self-incrimination privilege as basis, 804.1
Waiver, 509.1(a), 509.1(b)

SENSORY CAPACITY
Impeachment, 607.7(a)
    Federal rules, 607.7(b)

SEQUESTRATION OF WITNESSES
Exclusion from the courtroom, 615.1
    Federal rules, 615.2

SERVANTS
Statements made by, as admissions, 802.2(f)
    Federal rules, 802.3(c)

SETTLEMENTS
Compromises and Offers to Compromise, generally, this index
Pleas and Plea Discussions, generally, this index

SEX OFFENSES
Advance accreditation of victim, prompt complaint doctrine, 607.5(a)(1)
Child Abuse, generally, this index
Child's testimony from separate room, 601.1(e)
Identity of rapist in issue, testimony of prior description admissible, 607.5(a)(1)
Prior sexual encounters with victim, 404.1(j)
Prior sexual misconduct by victim, use to impeach, 608.2(a)
Prompt complaint doctrine, 607.5(a)(1)
Psychiatric evaluation of witness, power to order, 607.7(a)
Rape crisis counselor, privileged communications, 506.1
    Federal rules, 506.2
Rape shield law, 412.1
Rape trauma syndrome, expert testimony regarding, 702.1(c)
Sexual history,
    Defendant's previous relations with rape victim or others, 413.1
    Federal rules, 413.1
    Victim's sexual history and reputation, 412.1, 412.2
Victim's clothing, generally inadmissible, 412.1

SEXUAL HISTORY
Sex Offenses, this index

SHIELD LAWS
Journalist privilege, 508.1
Sex-crime victims, 412.1
    Federal rules, 412.2

SIGNATURE
Handwriting, generally, this index

INDEX

SILENCE
Admission, as, 802.2(b)
Custody, during, 509.1(c)
Hearsay, 801.1(b)
Prior inconsistent statement, as, 607.8(a)(2)
    Federal rules, 607.8(b)
Silent witness theory of authentication, 1104.1(a), 1104.1(b), 1104.1(d)
    Federal rules, 1104.2(a), 1104.2(b), 1104.2(d)

SIMILAR OCCURRENCES
    Generally, 405.1, 405.2
Accidents, 405.1(b)
    Federal rules, 405.2(a)
Business transactions, 405.1(c)
    Federal rules, 405.2(b)
Federal rules, 405.2
Foundation for, 405.1(b)
    Federal rules, 405.2(a)
Judicial discretion, 405.1(d)
    Federal rules, 405.2(c)
Real property sales, 405.1(d)
    Federal rules, 405.2(c)

SOBRIETY TESTS
Expert testimony regarding, 702.1(c)
Refusal to submit to as admission, 509.1(c)

SOCIAL WORKERS
Privileged communications, 505.1

SOUND RECORDINGS
Recordings, generally, this index

SPEED
Lay opinion regarding, 701.1
    Federal rules, 701.2

SPONTANEOUS STATEMENTS
Excited utterances, hearsay exception, 803(1).1(b)
    Federal rules, 803(1).2(b)
Present sense impressions, hearsay exception, 803(1).1(a)
    Federal rules, 803(1).2(a)

SPOUSAL PRIVILEGES
    Generally, 503.1 et seq.
Bigamous relationships, 503.3(c)
Cohabitation, no privilege, 503.3(c)
Common-law marriage, 503.3(c)
Communication made during marriage, 503.3(c)
Confidential communications privilege, 503.3(a) et seq.
    Federal rules, 503.5
Death, 503.3(e)
Eavesdropping, admissibility of recordings, 503.3(a)
Exceptions, 503.3(e)
Federal rules, 503.5
Fraud, exception, 503.3(e)
    Federal rules, 503.5(a)
Incompetency in adultery cases, 503.2
Induced by marital relationship, 503.3(b)
Matrimonial communications privilege, 503.5(b)
Parent-child privilege, 503.4
    Federal rules, 503.5(b)
Proposed New York Evidence Code, 503.3(e)
Testimonial privilege, 503.5(a)
Waiver, 503.3(d)

SPOUSES
Adultery, incompetent to testify, 503.2
Competency as witnesses, 601.1(c)

INDEX

SPOUSES—Continued
Competency as witnesses—Continued
    Dead man's statute, 601.2(b)
        Joint property ownership, survivor competent to testify, 601.2(e)
Social worker privilege inapplicable to client's spouse, 505.1
Spousal Privileges, generally, this index

STATE OF MIND
Hearsay exception, 803(1).1(c)
    Federal rules, 803(1).2(c)
Nonhearsay, 801.1(d)
Victim's state of mind in homicide prosecution, 402.1(f)

STATE SECRETS
Privilege, 511.2

STATEMENTS
Adoptive admissions, 802.2(e)
Against interest, generally. Declarations, this index
Agents making, as admission, 802.2(f)
Coconspirators, as admission, 802.2(g)
    Federal rules, 802.3(d)
Hearsay, 801.1(a)
Party's statements as admission, 802.2
Pedigree, hearsay exception, 804(4).1
    Federal rules, 804(4).2
Prior Consistent Statements, generally, this index
Prior Inconsistent Statements, generally, this index
Representative capacity, statements made in as admission, 802.2(d)

STIPULATIONS
Authenticity, to establish, 900.1
Expert's qualifications, 702.1(e)
Intent, stipulation to preclude evidence of uncharged crimes, 404.1(c)

STRICT LIABILITY
Products Liability, generally, this index

SUBSEQUENT REMEDIAL MEASURES
    Generally, 407.1, 407.2
Control in issue, 407.1(e)
Criminal cases, 407.1(f)
Federal rules, 407.2
Impeachment of witness who denies responsibility, 407.1(e)
Instructions to jury, 407.1(e)
Negligence, 407.1(b)
    Federal rules, 407.2
Ownership in issue, 407.1(e)
Products liability, 407.1(c)
    Feasibility issue, 407.1(c), 407.1(d)
    Federal rules, 407.2
Proposed New York Evidence Code, 407.1(f)
Warnings, 407.1(b) et seq.
    Federal rules, 407.2

SUCCESSORS IN INTEREST
Dead man's statute, protected by, 601.2(c)

SUFFICIENCY OF EVIDENCE
Burden of Proof, generally, this index
Relevancy distinguished, 401.1(a)

SUICIDE
Physician-patient privilege applicable despite lack of consent to treatment, 502.1(b)

SUPPRESSION OF EVIDENCE
Confession suppressed, admissible to impeach, 509.1(c), 607.8(a)(1)
Relevancy considerations, 401.1(a)
Suppression hearings regarding informers, 510.1

INDEX

..BLE EVIDENCE
..al and Demonstrative Evidence, generally, this index

TAPE RECORDINGS
Recordings, generally, this index
Motion Pictures and Videotapes, generally, this index

TARIFF OR CLASSIFICATION
Self-authenticating, 902.1(a)
    Federal rules, 902.1(b)

TAXES
Assessment cases, comparable sales, 405.1(d)
Nonpayment as basis for impeachment, 608.1(a)
    Federal rules, 608.2

TEACHERS
Interested observers, testifying as, 702.1(d)

TELEPHONE CONVERSATIONS
Authentication and Identification, this index
Recordings, generally, this index

TESTIMONY
    See also Witnesses, generally, this index
Cross-Examination, generally, this index
Expert Testimony, generally, this index
Former Testimony, generally, this index
Jury, note-taking during, 1108.1
    Federal rules, 1108.2
Lay Opinion, generally, this index
Narrative testimony within court's discretion, 611.2(a)
    Federal rules, 611.5(b)
Oaths and Affirmations, generally, this index
Opinion Testimony, generally, this index
Order of trial, 611.1
    Federal rules, 611.5(a)
Question, Form of, generally, this index
Rebuttal, scope, 611.1
    Federal rules, 611.5(a)
Recross examination, 611.4
    Federal rules, 611.5(c)
Redirect examination, 611.4
    Federal rules, 611.5(c)
Refreshing Memory, generally, this index
Self-incrimination, privilege against, 509.1(b)
Sequence of testimony at trial, 611.1
    Federal rules, 611.5(a)
Unsworn testimony,
    Child testifying, 601.1(e)
        Burden of production, corroboration, 300.3(a)(1)
    Failure to object to, 603.1
        Federal rules, 603.2
    Mentally infirm witness, 601.1(f)
Witness with knowledge, authentication, 901.1(a)
    Federal rules, 901.1(b)

TRADE
Judicial notice, adjudicative facts, 201.1(c)(11)

TRADE INSCRIPTIONS
Self-authenticating, 902.1(a)
    Federal rules, 902.1(b)

TRADE SECRETS
Privilege, 513.1
    Federal rules, 513.2

TRANSCRIPTS
Best evidence rule, 1001.1(a)

INDEX

TRANSCRIPTS—Continued
Recordings, of; as demonstrative evidence, 1104.1(c)
    Federal rules, 1104.2(c)

TREATISES
Hearsay exception, 803(6).2
    Federal rules, 803(6).2
Impeachment of expert, for, 702.1(f)

TRUSTWORTHINESS
Lack of, basis for exclusion of relevant evidence, 401.1(b)

TRUTHFULNESS
Character Evidence, this index
Credibility of Witnesses, generally, this index
Dishonesty, generally, this index
Impeachment, this index
Prior Crimes or Misconduct, this index
Rehabilitation and Support of Credibility, this index

ULTIMATE FACT
Materiality, relevancy considerations, 401.1(a)

ULTIMATE ISSUES
Opinion testimony, 704.1
    Federal rules, 704.2
    Lay opinion, 701.1

UNAVAILABILITY
Absence caused by party as basis, 807.1
Absence from jurisdiction as basis, 804.1
Death or illness as basis, 804.1
Declarant unavailable
        See also Exceptions to Hearsay Rule, this index
    Impeachment by prior inconsistent statements, 607.8(a)(3)
Defined, 804.1
Documents,
    Best Evidence Rule, generally, this index
Lack of memory as basis, 804.1
Refusal to testify as basis, 804.1
Self-incrimination privilege as basis, 804.1
Threats and intimidation used against witness as basis for unavailability, 807.1
Witness unavailable for cross-examination, 611.3(a)

UNCHARGED CRIMES
    Generally, 404.1, 404.2
Absence of accident or mistake, 404.1(d)
    Civil cases, 404.1(*l*)
Amorous design, 404.1(j)
Background evidence, 404.1(g)
Burden of proof of involvement in, 404.1(a)
    Federal rules, 404.2(a)
Civil cases, 404.1(*l*)
    Federal rules, 404.2(c)
Common scheme or plan, 404.1(e)
Defendant's previous relations with rape victim or others, 413.1
Federal rules, 404.2
Identity of person charged, 404.1(f)
Impeachment value, 607.2, 607.3, 608.2(a)
    Federal rules, 608.2(b)
Inextricably intertwined to crime charged, 404.1(h)
Intent, 404.1(c)
    Civil cases, 404.1(*l*)
Modus operandi, 404.1(f)
"Molineux" exceptions, 404.1(a) et seq.
Motive, uncharged crime evidence to prove, 404.1(b)
Multiple counts, 404.1(i)
Preliminary hearing to determine admissibility, 104.2, 404.1(a)
Pretrial notice, federal cases, 404.1(b)

INDEX

...ED CRIMES—Continued
 ..ural guidelines for federal practice, 404.1(b)
 ..posed New York Evidence Code, 404.1(a)
Rebuttal, 404.1(k)
Relevancy, 400.1, 401.1(b)
Sex cases, 404.1(j)
Stipulations, intent, 404.1(c)

UNCONSCIOUS PERSONS
Consent to sobriety tests, 702.1(c)

UNIFORM COMMERCIAL CODE
Authentication provisions, 902.1(b)

USURY
Burden of persuasion, clear and convincing evidence, 300.4(b)(2)

VERDICT
Juror's competency to testify regarding, 606.1
 Federal rules, 606.2

VICTIMS OF CRIME
Character of, 402.1(f)
 Criminal case,
  Federal rules, 402.2
Homicide victim, character, 402.1(f)
 Federal rules, 402.2
Physician-patient privilege, criminal defendant may not assert victim's privilege, 502.1(b)
Rape victim, character, 412.1
 Federal rules, 412.2
Sex Offenses, generally, this index
Wounds as real evidence, 1102.1
 Federal rules, 1102.2

VIDEOTAPES
Motion Pictures and Videotapes, generally, this index

VOICES
Authentication and Identification, this index
Real and demonstrative evidence, as, 1102.1
 Federal rules, 1102.2

VOIR DIRE
Witnesses, of, 611.3(d)

VOTERS AND VOTING
Secrecy of vote privilege, 512.1
 Federal rules, 512.2

WAIVER
Attorney-client privilege, 501.1(a), 501.1(h)
 Federal rules, 501.2
 Malpractice allegation waives privilege, 501.1(g)
Cross examination right, 611.3(a)
Dead man's statute, 601.2(f)
Interpreter, right to obtain in criminal proceedings, 604.1
Objections, failure to timely object, 103.1(a)
 Federal rules, 103.2(a)
Physician-patient privilege, 502.1(c)
Self-incrimination, privilege against, 509.1(a), 509.1(b)
Spousal privileges, 503.3(d)
Work product immunities, 501.3(b)(3)
 Federal rules, 501.3(c)

WARNINGS
Subsequent remedial measures, 407.1(b) et seq.

WEAPONS
Motor vehicles, in; presumption of possession, 302.1(b)

INDEX

WEATHER
Records, hearsay exception, 803(5).1(i)

WILL CONTESTS
Attorney-client privilege,
    Disclosure disgracing decedent's memory, 501.1(a), 501.1(g)
    Exception to privilege, 501.1(g)
Best evidence rule, 1003.1
Competency of witnesses, dead man's statute, 601.2(b)
Physician-patient privilege, 502.1(a)
Subscribing witnesses, 903.1

WIRETAPS
Voice identification, generally. Authentication and Identification, this index

WITNESSES
Absence of, as basis for unavailability, 804(1).1(b)
Advance accreditation, 607.5(a)(1)
    Federal rules, 607.5(b)
Bias and Interest of Witness, generally, this index
Calling by court, 614.1(a)
    Federal rules, 614.2
Character witnesses, testimony, 402.1(d)
Civil cases, identity discoverable, 501.3(b)(1)
Competency of Witnesses, generally, this index
Confrontation, defendant's right,
    Cross examination, 611.3(a)
        Federal rules, 611.5(c)
    Exposure of biased witness, 607.6(a)
        Federal rules, 607.6(b)
Control of, 401.1(a)
Credibility of Witnesses, generally, this index
Criminal cases, disclosure of statements required, 501.3(b)(2)
Cross-Examination, generally, this index
Dead Man's Statute, generally, this index
Exclusion from courtroom, 615.1
    Federal rules, 615.2
Expert Testimony, generally, this index
Failure to call, 401.1(a)
Foundation,
    Business records, hearsay exception, 803(3).1(a)
    DNA reports, hearsay exception, 803(3).1(b)
    Law enforcement records in criminal cases, hearsay exception, 803(3).1(b)
Impeachment, generally, this index
Informer as, 510.1
Interested witnesses, 607.6(a)
Interpreters, 604.1
    Federal rules, 604.2
Intimidation as admission, 802.2(a)
Judicial questioning of, 614.1(b)
    Federal rules, 614.2
Jurors questioning, 614.1(c)
    Federal rules, 614.2
Lay Opinion, generally, this index
Missing witness rule, 401.1(a)
    Federal rules, 401.2
Oaths and Affirmations, generally, this index
Opinion Testimony, generally, this index
Order of witnesses, 611.1
    Federal rules, 611.5(a)
Own Witness, generally, this index
Personal knowledge, 602.1
    Authentication testimony, 901.1(a)
        Federal rules, 901.1(b)
    Federal rules, 602.2
Prior Consistent Statements, generally, this index
Prior Crimes or Misconduct, generally, this index

INDEX

..ESSES—Continued
..ior Inconsistent Statements, generally, this index
Question, Form of, generally, this index
Recalling to stand, 611.1
Refreshing Memory, generally, this index
Rehabilitation and Support of Credibility, generally, this index
Religious beliefs or opinions, 610.1
    Federal rules, 610.2
Self-incrimination, privilege against, 509.1(b)
Sequestration, 615.1
    Federal rules, 615.2
Subscribing witnesses, 903.1
Testimony, generally, this index
Threats and intimidation used against, hearsay exception, 804(1).1(b)
Unavailability, generally, this index
Voir dire, 611.3(d)

WORDS AND PHRASES
Definitions, generally, this index

WORK PRODUCT IMMUNITIES
    Generally, 501.3
Accident report, no immunity, 501.3(b)(1)
Civil cases, 501.3(b)(1)
Criminal cases, 501.3(b)(2)
    Federal rules, 501.3(c)
Documents inadvertently disclosed, waiver of immunity, 501.3(b)(2)
    Federal rules, 501.3(c)
Exceptions, 501.3(b)(1)
Experts, information concerning, 501.3(b)(1)
    Federal rules, 501.3(c)
Federal rules, 501.3(c)
Films, photographs, audio tapes, video tapes,
    Person's conduct involved in litigation, no immunity, 501.3(b)(1)
Fraud, exception, 501.3(c)
Insurance claims evaluations, 501.3(b)(1)
Opinion work product, 501.3(c)
Ordinary work product, 501.3(c)
Refreshing memory of witness with immune communication, 501.3(b)(3)
Statements given by party to opponent not immune, 501.3(b)(1)
Trial preparation materials, 501.3(b)(1)
Waiver, 501.3(b)(3)
    Federal rules, 501.3(c)
Witnesses,
    Civil cases, identity discoverable, 501.3(b)(1)
    Criminal cases, disclosure of statements required, 501.3(b)(2)
        Federal rules, 501.3(c)

WRITINGS
Authentication and Identification, generally, this index
Best Evidence Rule, generally, this index
Recorded recollection, hearsay exception, 803(2).1
    Federal rules, 803(2).2

WRONGFUL DEATH ACTIONS
Burden of persuasion, preponderance of evidence, 300.4(b)(1)
    Noseworthy doctrine, 300.4(b)(1)

X-RAYS
Authentication, 901.9(b), 1104.1(b)
    Federal rules, 1104.2(b)
Best evidence rule, 1002.1
    Excusable loss or destruction of x-rays, 1004.1(a)
Demonstrative evidence, as, 1104.1(b)
    Federal rules, 1104.2(b)
Hearsay exception, 803(3).1(c)

†